COLLINS
ENCYCLOPAEDIA OF
SCOTLAND

COLLINS ENCYCLOPAEDIA OF SCOTLAND

Edited by John Keay and Julia Keay

HarperCollins*Publishers*

To the memory
of
Dr Ian Grimble

HarperCollins*Publishers*
77−85 Fulham Palace Road,
Hammersmith, London W6 8JB

The HarperCollins website address is:
www.**fire**and**water**.com

First published by HarperCollins*Publishers* 1994

This revised edition published by HarperCollins*Publishers* 2000
1 3 5 7 9 8 6 4 2

Copyright © John Keay and Julia Keay 1994, 2000

A catalogue record for this book is
available from the British Library

ISBN 0 00 710353 0
Set in Linotron Joanna by
Rowland Phototypesetting Ltd,
Bury St Edmunds, Suffolk

Printed and bound in Great Britain by
The Bath Press, Bath

CONTENTS

EDITORS' NOTE AND ACKNOWLEDGEMENTS

Distilling and presenting information in an accessible format has long been a Scottish speciality. The *Statistical Accounts*, for instance, the **Encyclopaedia Britannica** and the *Dictionary of National Biography* were all Scottish initiatives. Inexplicably, though, there has not previously been a comprehensive encyclopaedia of Scotland. We have therefore been obliged to devise our own criteria and would like to emphasise that this book is encyclopaedic only in the sense that it embraces the widest possible range of subjects, not that it treats all or any of them exhaustively.

In respect of places, geographical features, sites and buildings, those included are those located in Scotland plus one, **Berwick-upon-Tweed**, which once was. Animate subjects (including people), their institutions and activities, have been selected on the basis of Scottish provenance or association. Thus, by virtue of their provenance, entries appear for **James Boswell**, **whisky**, **curling** and *Primula scotica* while **Dr Johnson**, **brewing**, **football** and **heather** appear by virtue of their associations. Entries on, for instance, **cricket**, **Chartism**, **temperance** and **juniper** merely betray editorial indulgence.

For any inconsistencies, inaccuracies or omissions we take full responsibility as editors. The presumption underlying a book of this sort remains troubling, and we are all too aware that a work twice as long could scarcely do Scotland justice.

Michael Alcock, then of Aurum Press, originally commissioned the work and his perhaps rash decision to leave its composition entirely in our hands has been appreciated. Subsequently Richard Johnson and Robert Lacey at HarperCollins have grappled with its inexorable expansion and patiently shepherded it through production,

Janice Robertson having undertaken the unenviable task of a mammoth final editing. We are most grateful to all of them.

The project would, of course, have been unthinkable without the enthusiasm and expertise of more than 100 specialist contributors. Their work accounts for over a third of the entire text and it is with pleasure and gratitude that we acknowledge them overleaf. Many wrote just one or two entries but a few contributed more substantially and collaborated in the selection of subject matter. Our special thanks to J Malcolm Allan, Claudia Bolling, Patrick Cadell, Robert Calder, Alastair Campbell of Airds, Marion Campbell, Graeme Cruickshank, Gordon Donaldson, David Finkelstein, Professor R D S Jack, Norman Newton, Robin Nicholson and J R Nicolson.

Yet others have not only contributed and collaborated but have brought to the work that humour or hospitality which turned a daunting task into such a delightful exercise that we now relinquish it with regret. For their kindness, correspondence and encouragement, mere thanks seem quite inadequate. They are Neil Macara Brown, Charles Gore, Dr Ian Grimble, Philip Long, Michael Moss, Alexander Mullay, Dr John Purser, Iain Russell and Professor Derick S Thomson.

Finally a hug and thank you to Alexander, Anna, Nell and Sam, our four no-longer children. For six years they have shared their home and parents with a wordy sibling, never grudging its exorbitant demands while contributing not a little to its relentless upbringing.

John Keay and Julia Keay January 1994

EDITORS' NOTE TO SECOND EDITION

The first edition of this book appeared in 1994. A few minor corrections were incorporated in subsequent reprints, but this new edition provides the first chance for extra entries, substantial updates and a much-needed expansion of the index. We are extremely grateful to the publishers, and to Richard Johnson in particular, for commissioning it.

The following pages include a thousand or more additions to existing entries plus over a hundred completely new entries. Among the additions there is much to celebrate, from the return of the **Stone of Scone** to the opening of the **Museum of Scotland** in Edinburgh and the buy-outs of **Eigg** and **Knoydart**. **Kippen**'s mighty vine receives the attention it deserves, **Skye** gets its bridge and **Inverurie** is back on the railway (from which it had been unaccountably severed in the first edition).

Of the new entries, the longest must be that for the **Scottish Parliament**. At the time of writing, its powers and constitution as laid down by the Scotland Act of 1998 are clear enough, although its procedures and impact have yet to manifest themselves.

Of the other new entries some lament the lately deceased; others merely betray glaring omissions in the first edition. Combined, they exhibit that delicious variety which has made even the revision of this book a delight. Here, amongst many newcomers, now appear **Alexander** ('the Corrector') **Cruden** of the *Biblical Concordance*, **Agnes Murray** of 'the muckle mou'' (from whom **Sir Walter Scott** claimed descent) and wee **David Ritchie** (who scared the wits out of him). In the persons of **Fitzroy Maclean** and **Charles McIntosh** Ian Fleming's 'James Bond' is improbably challenged by Beatrix Potter's 'Mr McGregor'. The castles of **Melville** and **Dalhousie** at last thrust themselves on the editors' attention. And **Bothy Ballads** and **Scottish Ethnology** are no longer ignored.

The local authorities have all been changed (again) and the sports entries have all been updated. From **Billy Bremner** to **Matt Busby** and **Bill Shankly**, the boot is particularly well represented; so, too, the pen, with **Norman MacCaig**, **Sorley MacLean** and **George Mackay Brown**. Both the new Smiths are from Argyll – **John** who would have been Prime Minister and **Iain Crichton** of *Consider the Lilies*; the 'M's include two formidable crusaders, 'Mad Mitch' (**Colin Mitchell**) who 'saved the Argylls' and the enigmatic **St Moluag** who converted **Lismore**; from opposite corners of the political arena come **Jo Grimond**, **Mick McGahey** and **Sir Alec Douglas-Home;** and **Dolly the Sheep**, with her own far from woolly entry, upstages **Greyfriars Bobby** (see **Edinburgh**) and even 'the Turra Coo' (see **Turriff**).

Our greatest debt is, as before, to our contributors and, for this edition, especially to Neil Macara Brown whose versatility and wit are matched only by a genius for compression. The list of contributors includes a few new names but rather more old ones, some sadly no more. Amongst the deceased is **Ian Grimble**. He more than anyone gave of that encouragement, scholarship and cheer which made this book what it is. We miss him much and now dedicate the book to his memory.

John and Julia Keay 2000

CONTRIBUTORS

Marquess of Ailsa
Shiona Airlie
J Malcolm Allan
Jane Anderson
John F Anderson
Bernard Balfour
William Baxter
Frank Beattie
Barbara Bell
John Blaxter
Alan Bold
Claudia Bolling
Iain G Brown
Jonathan Brown
Neil Macara Brown
Adam Bruce
Charles Burnett
Patrick Cadell
James B Caird
Robert Calder
Donald Cameron yr of Lochiel
Joy Cameron
Alastair Campbell of Airds
Marion Campbell
Michael Clancy
Ray Collier
Graeme Cruickshank
Ian Cunningham
Bess Cuthbert
Tess Darwin
Marysa Demoor
Dougal Dixon
Gordon Donaldson
Islay Donaldson
Gavin Douglas
Horst Drescher
Callan Duck
Baron Duckham
Alastair Durie
Ronald Eden
Ian Edwards
David Finkelstein
Archie L Foley
Kathy Fraser

Lucy Gordon
Charles Gore
John Greig
Ian Grimble
Jean Hadfield
Stephen Hall
Duff Hart-Davis
Elizabeth Havern
Joy Hendry
David Hewitt
Andrew Hill
Julian Hill
Bevis Hillier
Lord Home of the Hirsel
Gillian Hughes
Irene Hughson
Robert Hughson
Gordon Irving
R D S Jack
Anna Keay
John Keay
Julia Keay
Sam Keay
Rudolph Kenna
Mary Kennaway
Alison Kinnaird
Elizabeth Layhe
Maurice Lindsay
Philip Long
Donald Low
E Mairi MacArthur
Neil MacCormick
Norman A M MacDonald
Norman H MacDonald
Mary McGrigor
Ian MacIntyre
Iain Maciver
Susanah Mackay-James
Alan McKinlay
Lachlan Mackintosh of Mackintosh
Charles MacLean
Charles McMaster
George McMurdo
Ian Macneil of Barra

Sir William Macpherson of Cluny
Ernest Mehew
Michael Moss
Alexander Mullay
Charles Munn
Thom Nairn
Norman Newton
Robin Nicholson
J R Nicolson
S J Noble
Ian A Olson
Isabelle Paterson
Mairi Paterson
Peter Payne
R V Pringle
John Purser
Geoffrey Reynolds
Trevor Royle
Sally Joyce Rush
Iain Russell
Lady Saltoun
Eric Simpson
Kranti Singh
Ian R Smith
Sir David Steel
A M Stevenson
Catriona Stewart
Kirsteen Stewart
Ralph Stewart-Wilson
Lord Strathspey
Virginia Sumsion
Ian Sutherland
Philip Taylor
William Taylor
Derick S Thomson
A E Truckell
Judy Urquhart
Harry Watson
William Waugh
J Lockhart Whiteford
Tim Williams
Robert Wolrige Gordon
M Yaseen
William Zachs

ix

READER'S GUIDE

All entries are arranged alphabetically, but frustration may be avoided by bearing in mind the following points:

Biographical Entries

Since celebrity may be transitory, only the dead qualify for entries of their own and there may be a slight prejudice against the recently deceased. They and the living may nevertheless feature in the text. Having established that a subject does not have its own entry, the reader is urged to consult the index where page references will be found for every topic not accorded an individual entry.

With the exception of saints, kings and queens (who appear under their regnant titles – **Robert I**, **James VI**, etc) and some pseudonyms, all biographical entries are located under the surname of the subject. This rule has been applied even to titled persons, so that **James Graham, Marquis of Montrose**, appears under 'G' not 'M'. Many titles, eg **ARGYLL, Earldom, Marquisate and Dukedom of**, have their own entries, where the reader should quickly discover that an Earl of Argyll is likely to be found under **Campbell**. Where the title does not have its own entry there may be a cross-referring entry; failing that, the reader should again consult the index.

It will be noted that popularised, very often anglicised, sobriquets such as 'Mary Queen of Scots', 'Bonnie Prince Charlie', 'Robert the Bruce' have mostly been discarded as inappropriate.

Topographical Entries

Although the Scottish counties were abolished in 1975, their replacements (Regions and Districts – both abolished in 1995 – and currently Council Areas) have proved either too vast, too transitory or too confusing to be much use for locational purposes. Topographical entries are therefore generally credited to the counties in which they lay prior to 1975 and which are still used as the basis of Land Registration in Scotland. (See also maps p.xiv and xv). It should, though, be borne in mind that the county boundaries have themselves been subject to occasional adjustment and may be adjusted again.

Sub-Entries

Because they tend to confuse the alphabetical arrangement, sub-entries have been kept to a minimum. They are nevertheless unavoidable and feature prominently in the longest entries – **Edinburgh**, **Glasgow**, etc. Thus the entry on, for instance, the **Scott Monument**, lies not amongst the entries beginning with 'S' but amongst the Edinburgh sub-entries beginning with 'S'. Other major entries are treated in the same way. Thus **shipbuilding** is broken into sub-headed sections with sub-entries for individual shipbuilding yards.

Cross-References

Throughout the text cross-references are indicated by **bold** characters where they first occur within an entry. To avoid repetition and save space, information contained in a cross-referenced entry is not normally regurgitated in the parent entry. The reader is therefore urged to follow up cross-references whenever in doubt.

Bibliographical References

The inclusion of a general bibliography, whether by way of acknowledging sources or suggesting further reading, has been deemed impracticable. It would simply be too long to be of much value. Some bibliographical references are however included in individual entries.

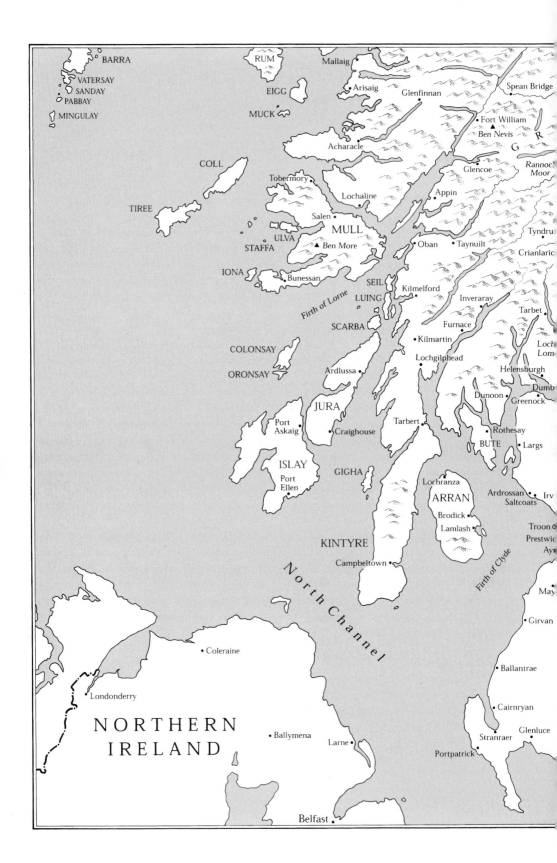

NORTH
SEA

ENGLAND

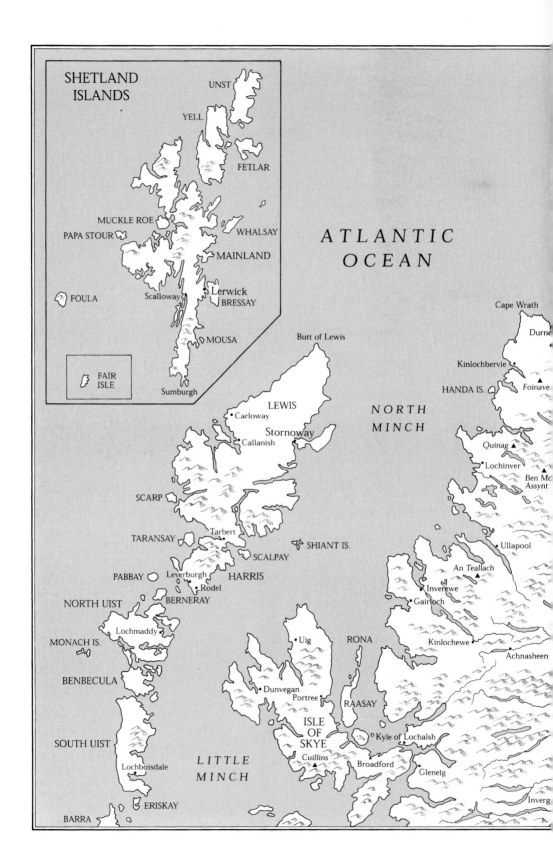

SHETLAND
ISLANDS

UNST

YELL

FETLAR

MUCKLE ROE

PAPA STOUR

WHALSAY

MAINLAND

FOULA

Scalloway

Lerwick
BRESSAY

MOUSA

FAIR
ISLE

Sumburgh

ATLANTIC
OCEAN

Cape Wrath

Durne

Kinlochbervie

HANDA IS.

Foinave

Butt of Lewis

LEWIS

Carloway

Stornoway

Callanish

NORTH

MINCH

Quinag

Lochinver

Ben Mc
Assynt

SCARP

TARANSAY

Tarbert

SHIANT IS.

SCALPAY

Ullapool

PABBAY

Leverburgh

HARRIS

Rodel

An Teallach

NORTH UIST

BERNERAY

Inverewe

Gairloch

Lochmaddy

MONACH IS.

Uig

RONA

Kinlochewe

Achnasheen

BENBECULA

Dunvegan

Portree

RAASAY

ISLE
OF
SKYE

Kyle of Lochalsh

SOUTH UIST

Lochboisdale

LITTLE

MINCH

Cuillins

Broadford

Glenelg

Inverg

ERISKAY

BARRA

xiv

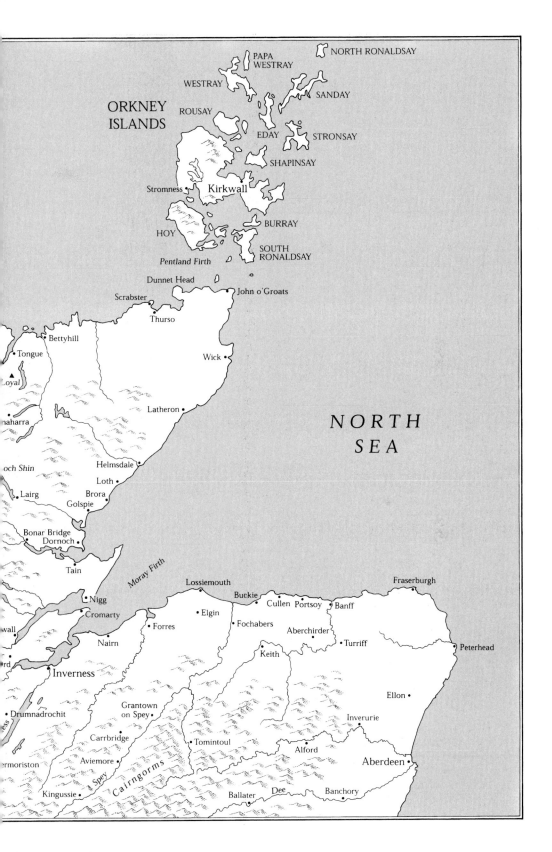

NORTH RONALDSAY

PAPA
WESTRAY

WESTRAY

SANDAY

ORKNEY
ISLANDS

ROUSAY

EDAY   STRONSAY

SHAPINSAY

Stromness   Kirkwall

BURRAY

HOY

SOUTH
RONALDSAY

Pentland Firth

Dunnet Head

John o'Groats

Scrabster

Thurso

Bettyhill

Tongue

Loyal

Wick

naharra

Latheron

NORTH
SEA

och Shin

Helmsdale

Loth

Lairg

Brora

Golspie

Bonar Bridge
Dornoch

Tain

Moray Firth

Lossiemouth

Fraserburgh

Nigg

Buckie

Cullen Portsoy   Banff

Cromarty

Elgin

Fochabers

Forres

Aberchirder

Nairn

Keith

Turriff

Peterhead

wall

Inverness

Ellon

rd

Drumnadrochit

Grantown
on Spey

Inverurie

Carrbridge

Tomintoul

Alford

ess

Aviemore

Cairngorms

Aberdeen

rmoriston

Spey

Kingussie

Ballater   Dee   Banchory

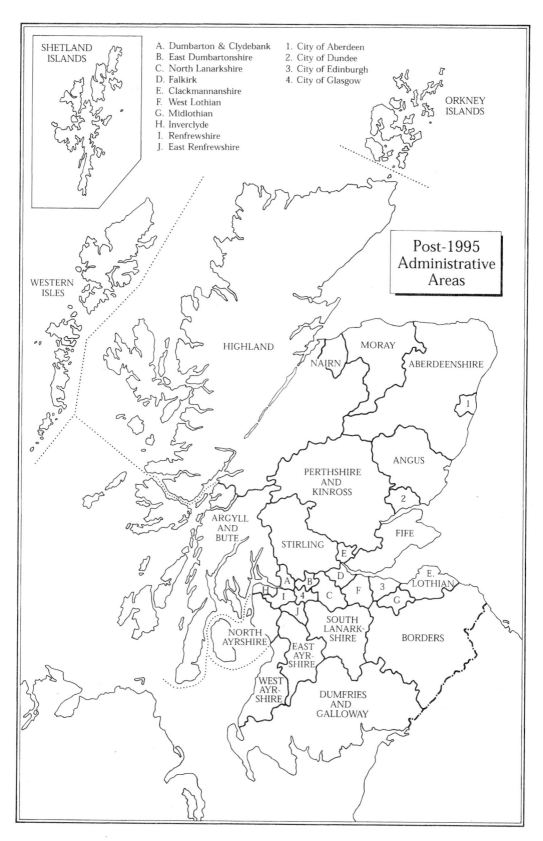

SHETLAND
ISLANDS

A. Dumbarton & Clydebank
B. East Dumbartonshire
C. North Lanarkshire
D. Falkirk
E. Clackmannanshire
F. West Lothian
G. Midlothian
H. Inverclyde
I. Renfrewshire
J. East Renfrewshire

1. City of Aberdeen
2. City of Dundee
3. City of Edinburgh
4. City of Glasgow

ORKNEY
ISLANDS

Post-1995
Administrative
Areas

WESTERN
ISLES

HIGHLAND

NAIRN

MORAY

ABERDEENSHIRE

1

ANGUS

2

PERTHSHIRE
AND
KINROSS

FIFE

ARGYLL
AND
BUTE

STIRLING

E

E.
LOTHIAN

A B
H I 4 C
J

D
F 3
G

SOUTH
LANARK-
SHIRE

BORDERS

NORTH
AYRSHIRE

EAST
AYR-
SHIRE

WEST
AYR-
SHIRE

DUMFRIES
AND
GALLOWAY

AARON SCOTUS (d.1052) Music Theorist

Aaron was a Scottish Benedictine who became abbot of St Martin's, Cologne, as well as abbot of St Pantaleon. Three treatises ascribed to him were known to 17th and 18th century bibliographers – *De Utilitate Cantus Vocalis, De Modo Cantandi et Psallendi,* and *De Regulis Tonorum et Symphoniarum.* All are lost. He is said to have introduced a new office of St Gregory the Great.

ABBEY CRAIG, Nr Stirling

Although the name derives from **Cambuskenneth Abbey** at its base, this isolated and wooded outcrop of rock commands attention as the plinth for the Wallace Monument. It stands immediately opposite **Stirling Castle** with the river Forth and **Stirling Bridge**, scene of **William Wallace**'s most famous battle, between and below. The Craig, site of a hill fort evidenced by ramparts and vitrified remains, is 360ft (110m) high to which the monument adds a further 220ft (67m). The latter was erected by public subscription at the instigation of the Rev Dr Charles Rogers in 1859–69. **J T**

J T Rochead's Wallace Monument atop Abbey Craig (SP)

Rochead's design, comprising a tower rising from a courtyard and topped by a tiered stone crown, has been much criticised for its fanciful combination of secular and ecclesiastical elements. A spiral stair gives access to a vaulted chamber in each storey and to the parapet above from which the view cannot be faulted. Above the main entrance is a bronze of Wallace while his sword forms part of the visitor display.

ABBOTSFORD, Roxburghshire

Walter Scott bought the farm of Cartleyhole on the southern bank of the river **Tweed** just west of **Melrose** in 1811. He renamed it Abbotsford after the river crossing used centuries before by the abbots of **Melrose**; he rendered it habitable, and a year later he moved with his family from their rented home at Ashiestiel near **Clovenfords**. Over the next 12 years he extended the policies from 100 to 1000 acres (40 to 400ha), planted thousands of trees, and converted the farmhouse into what he himself described as a 'conundrum castle'. Abbotsford has been called 'Walter Scott's greatest historical novel', 'an architectural monstrosity' and 'a fantasy'. Edward Blore and William Patterson were responsible for designing the neo-Baronial mansion, but Scott was involved in every step of the process, building Scotland's history into the house just as he did into his books; the main entrance based on the porch to **Linlithgow Palace**, the library ceiling a copy of that at **Roslin Chapel**; a cloister arch from Melrose here, oak panels from **Dunfermline** Kirk there and the door of **Edinburgh**'s **Tolbooth** elsewhere, while built into the very fabric of the house are stones salvaged from historical sites all over the Borders. He spent a fortune on Abbotsford, but the period of its building was also the period of his greatest literary output; he wrote most of his 'Waverley' novels here and the fruits of his talent paid for the construction of his passion.

Only two years after the completion of Abbotsford, however, he was overtaken by the disastrous bankruptcy of his publishers **Archibald Constable** & Co, and of his printers **James Ballantyne** & Co, with combined debts of over £120,000. As a partner in Constables, Scott could have chosen to become bankrupt, but instead he pledged his future literary earnings to a trust which gradually repaid his creditors. The extraordinary effort

Sir Walter Scott and his Friends at Abbotsford, *by Thomas Faed; Scott on the right, reading (SNPG)*

wore him out and he died at Abbotsford on 21 September 1832. The house and its contents remain intact, including Scott's own collection of treasures – **Rob Roy**'s sword and sporran, **Queen Mary**'s crucifix, **Claverhouse**'s pistols, **Prince Charles Edward Stewart**'s hunting knife, a purse made by **Flora MacDonald**, **Montrose**'s sword, the keys of **Loch Leven Castle** and other historical relics, together with his library of 20,000 volumes. The most stirring survival, though, and the most popular with the thousands of visitors to Abbotsford, is the small study with its desk and leather-covered chair where he created so many of his masterpieces.

ABBOTT, John Sutherland (1900–79) Shoe Manufacturer

Jack Abbott was intimately associated with the **Kilmarnock**-based company of Saxone which still maintains a familiar retail presence. Born in Northampton, he was educated at **Ayr** Academy after his family moved to Scotland. His father George and his uncle Frank, along with **George Clark**, founded the Saxone shoe company in the early years of the century. After attending Cambridge University the young Abbott joined them in 1920. Two years in the United States revolutionised his ideas on marketing and promotional style. After World War II, now in charge of the company, he developed a distinctive chain of retail shops where his creative approach to the selling of both high fashion and traditional shoes met the growing demand of the 1950s. In 1962 he launched the famous 'Hush Puppies'.

ABDIE, Fife

A parish south-east of **Newburgh**, Abdie is notable for its parish church on the edge of Lindores Loch. It was consecrated by David de Bernham, Bishop of **St Andrews**, in 1242 and, with the addition of a north transept in the 17th century, remained in use till 1827. 19th century restorations pre-empt analysis but the lancet windows are certainly original. It has been adopted as the burial place of the Balfour family whose ruinous Denmylne Castle (16th century) stands near Newburgh. Abdie's now parish church is by **William Burn** (1827). In the churchyard a symbol stone with particularly elaborate crescent and V-rod symbol has at some time been adapted for use as a sundial. Overlooking **Lindores Abbey**, Clatchard Craig (300ft/91m) is the site of a pre-**Roman** hill fort 'remarkable for the extent and complicated character of its defences'. Comparisons with that on Norman's Law (936ft/285m) to the east have revealed little convergence of design although the two are thought to have been in contemporaneous occupation.

ABELL, John (1650–1724) Male Soprano and Composer

Abell was born in **Aberdeen** and joined the Chapel Royal in London as singer, violinist and lutenist in the 1680s. **Charles II** sent him to Italy to study and he travelled regularly with **James VII** as well as organising lavish musical entertainments and causing a scandal by marrying into the nobility. After the 1688 Revolution he was dismissed on account of his Roman Catholicism and sought his fortune precariously on the Continent.

The King of Poland threatened him with wild boars to make him sing, on which prompting he claimed he never sang better in all his life. He returned to England in the 1690s. His published compositions include *A Collection of Songs in Several Languages* (1701) exploiting his remarkable voice. The *Third Song* is in fact an obsequious cantata extolling the virtues of King William and his victory over the Roman Catholic **Stewart** cause at the Battle of the Boyne. He also composed a coronation ode for Queen Anne (1702) and a substantial birthday cantata (wrongly ascribed to Eccles and more recently wrongly described as a coronation ode) while employed in Dublin by the Viceroy of Ireland. He died in poverty. See H G Farmer, *A King's Musician for the Lute and Voice* in Hinrichsen's *Music Book* vol vii, London, 1952.

ABERCHIRDER, Banffshire

A tiny burgh, 'one of the least known and visited in mainland Scotland' (**N Tranter**), Aberchirder stands halfway between **Huntly** and **Banff**. It was founded (1764) by Alexander Gordon of Auchintoul (great-nephew of **General Patrick Gordon**) who removed thence the settlement which had grown up around his Kinnairdy Castle. This is an L-plan tower house beside the river **Deveron** at nearby Bridge of Marnoch. The graveyard of the pre-**Reformation** church of St Marnoch (or Marnan), a Celtic saint supposedly buried here in about 650, survives; but the present church dates from 1792. It was the scene of a celebrated 'intrusion' which provoked the 1843 **Disruption**. Aberchirder is also known as Foggieloan – 'mossy field' – doubtless a reflection on its moorland setting.

ABERCORN, West Lothian

According to Bede this peaceful little village on the south shore of the Firth of Forth was the site of an episcopal see in the late 7th century; the Bishop, Trumwin or Trumwine, and his monks being forced to flee their monastery in 685 by rampaging **Picts**, fresh from victory over the Northumbrians at the **Battle of Dunnichen**. Most of the present church at Abercorn dates from the 16th century and later, but it includes a (blocked) 12th century Norman doorway which led into the original two-cell church. Local patrons were responsible for the construction of the three burial aisles which were added to the south side of the church, the Duddingston aisle (1603), the Binns Aisle for the Dalyell family (1618) and the Philipstoun enclosure (1728). Inside the church the elaborate Hopetoun Loft, added in 1708, was designed by **William Bruce** who was still working on nearby **Hopetoun House**.

ABERCROMBY, Sir Ralph (1734–1801) General

Born at **Menstrie**, **Clackmannanshire**, Ralph Abercromby was educated at Rugby and studied law at **Edinburgh University** and in Leipzig before joining the 3rd Dragoon Guards in 1756 and serving in the Seven Years' War. He rose to lieutenant-colonel (1773) before becoming MP for Clackmannanshire (1774–5). Knighted in 1795, he returned to the army with the rank of major-general and distinguished himself in Flanders and the West Indies. After commanding the British troops in Ireland (1797) and Scotland (1798–9), he led the expedition against the French in the Mediterranean where, in 1801, he commanded the successful landing at Aboukir Bay but died shortly afterwards in Alexandria of wounds received in the battle.

His eldest son John (1772–1817) and youngest son Alexander (1784–1853) pursued comparably distinguished military careers, the former rising to lieutenant-general and temporary Governor of Madras (1812) and the latter fighting in the Peninsular and Waterloo campaigns before also becoming MP for Clackmannanshire. His second son James (1776–1858) was called to the English Bar (1801), was MP successively for Midhurst, Calne and **Edinburgh** (1832), became Speaker of the House of Commons (1835–39) and was raised to the peerage as 1st Baron Dunfermline.

Ralph's younger brother Robert (1740–1827) also rose to the rank of general, having served throughout the American War and spent seven years in India as Governor of Bombay and Commander-in-Chief of the Indian forces; knighted (1792), he, too, was MP for Clackmannanshire (1798) and Governor of **Edinburgh Castle** (1801).

ABERDEEN

The city district and **royal burgh** of Aberdeen, Scotland's third largest city, occupies the area between the mouths of the rivers **Don** and **Dee** in **Aberdeenshire**. Ptolemy identified it as 'Devana'. The city's name probably derives from *aber* (the mouth of the river) -*Don*. The area is one of the richest in stone circles, standing stones, and Pictish symbol stones of all classes.

For many centuries Aberdeen was relatively isolated from the rest of Scotland by marked physical features – to the east and north the 'wild and wasteful' North Sea, to the west the **Cairngorms** and the Grampians and to the south a barrier of great historical importance – the Mounth, a chain of hills stretching along the south of 'Royal Deeside' to the coast near Aberdeen. This isolation made the city much more cosmopolitan than might be expected, as it was easier to trade with Europe than with the rest of Britain.

Consequently there are to be found in the local dialect not only native **Pictish** and **Gaelic** words and names but also words brought in by trade with Danes, Norwegians, Swedes, Germans and Dutch. The **auld alliance** also brought in its share of French words. In return Aberdeen exported woollens, fish and men. Most of the last were students from Aberdeen's two universities – **King's** and **Marischal** – for it was once proudly boasted that the city had as many universities as all of England. It was only in 1860 that the two were united into the **University of Aberdeen**. Consequently the list of Aberdonian doctors, missionaries, engineers, soldiers, scholars, merchants, teachers and nurses is an impressive one.

Despite the use of Scandinavian words in the local dialect, there is only one **Viking** name in the surrounding area – St Olaf – the site of a well which is said to commemorate the last battle between the Scots and the Vikings. In 1153 a Viking poet narrates how Eysteinn, son of Harald, 'spread his sails to the South and steering along the Eastern shores of Scotland brought his ships to Aperdion, where he killed many people and wasted the city'. A decade later the situation had altered completely and Svein Asliefsson, one of the last and some

say the greatest of the Vikings, spent a month in 'Aperdion' in consultation with the young King of Scotland, **Malcolm IV** ('the Maiden').

With one of the most complete sets of civic records in Britain, Aberdeen can trace its foundation as a royal burgh to the reign of **David I** (1124–53), as the city's first charter, granted by **William the Lion** about 1171, refers to an agreement between the burgesses and 'the Lion's' grandfather David I. The earliest charters refer to the rights of trade, showing that the city already had markets for wool (stockings were exported to Europe at a very early date), hides, meal and dried salted fish.

William the Lion was a generous benefactor to Aberdeen, for besides its first extant charter he also gave his 'palace' to the Trinity (or Red) Friars about 1211 AD to establish a monastery in the city. A decade later **Alexander II** helped found the Dominican (or Black) Friars in the same area. The Carmelite (or White) Friars did not appear until late in the 15th century. In addition to the religious foundations, the two great military orders – the Knights Templar and Hospitaller – as well as a convent of St Katherine of Sienna were present in Aberdeen. The **Reformation** which swept Scotland in 1560 caused little disruption in the city. The Roman Catholic Bishop, William Gordon, kept his post and welcomed **Queen Mary** to stay in his palace during her visit to the north-east in 1562. The bishop retained control over Church property until his death in 1577, while his canons handed over their revenues to the town in exchange for a life-rent. In turn the city fathers found that the debris from the despoiled monasteries was useful for burgh repairs and construction, and it has been truly said that 'there never was a better bargain driven'.

The two mainstays of any medieval 'toun' were the kirk and the castle. Aberdeen's castle is mentioned as being repaired in 1264. One of the tradesmen who worked on the building was Ricardus Cementarius (Richard the Mason) who is recorded as the first Alderman, or Provost. His name can be seen at the head of the list of provosts (now Lord Provosts) of Aberdeen who can be traced without a break from 1272 to the present.

Robert I and his family found the city of Aberdeen 'trusty and well-beloved'. Tradition has it that the citizens in support of King Robert attacked the English garrison in the castle and put them all to the sword after the Bruce's victory over his local enemies, the **Comyns**, at the **Battle of Inverurie**. The password used on that occasion, 'Bon Accord', was then supposedly conferred on the city as its motto.

Whatever the truth of this story, it is interesting that the burgh's armorial bearings, three silver-coloured towers on a red background, are surrounded by the double tressure of the Royal Arms of Scotland, obviously a mark of royal favour. The animal supporters of the shield have changed over the centuries. In 1430 these were lions, which have become leopards. The use of lions as supporters has led people to suppose that William the Lion had sanctioned them. Others argue that Robert I, because of 'Bon Accord', had given the royal approval. Five Scottish burghs have the royal leopards in their armorial bearings, and so it must be assumed that the armorial grant came from **James I**, as his Privy Seal resembles the city's coat of arms.

If Robert I did not actually grant a coat of arms to the city, he was certainly one of its greatest benefactors. In gratitude to the citizens for their support throughout the **Wars of Independence**, in 1319 he gifted to them his hunting forest of Stocket. Renamed the Freedom Lands, the revenue from the forest was paid into a Common Good Fund – which at present stands in excess of £20 million, making the city one of Scotland's richest.

Another benefaction from the Bruce (whose daughter Matilda married the Town Clerk, Thomas Isaac, and whose sister Christian latterly lived and died in Aberdeen) was the **Brig o' Balgownie**, which was built across the river Don in 1320 on the orders of the King.

Although the King had ordered the Brig o' Balgownie, the funds for the work came from the purse of the then Bishop of Aberdeen, Henry Cheyne of Inverugie. His successors were to complete another task Bishop Cheyne had started. This was the building of a **Cathedral** dedicated to **St Machar**, supposedly one of **St Columba**'s monks who founded a church in the city area late in the 6th century. The building took several centuries to complete, the final touches being put to it in about 1522, shortly before the Reformation. It has been claimed as the largest granite-built cathedral in the British Isles.

A later Bishop, **William Elphinstone**, obtained a Papal Bull in 1495 from Pope Alexander VI to found a college in the Aulton of Aberdeen (or **Old Aberdeen**). At first known as St Mary's, it was later named **King's College** in honour of **James IV**. The Bishop, following the example of his predecessor Bishop Cheyne, caused a bridge to be built over the River Dee to give travellers from the south ease of passage into the city. The **Bridge of Dee**, with its seven semi-circular arches, was completed in 1527 and is still in daily use. Nearly 100 years after the founding of the Catholic King's College, **George Keith**, the Fifth **Earl Marischal** of Scotland, founded a Protestant university, Marischal College, in the centre of the burgh.

Throughout the centuries, Aberdeen has played a notable part in Scottish history. The citizens had aided Bruce in the battles against English domination, culminating at **Bannockburn** in 1314, and nearly a century later were to contest the bid by the Lords of the Isles to block the ambitions of the Stewart Earls of Albany in the northeast. In 1411, under the leadership of their Provost Robert Davidson, Aberdonians were amongst those who met the Highland Host led by **Donald Lord of the Isles** at **Harlaw**, some 15 miles from the city. The ensuing struggle saw Provost Davidson and many of the burgesses being slain. The battle was indecisive, but it was Donald's forces who withdrew, while the Provost was carried home on his shield to be buried in the 'Mither Kirk' of St Nicholas (Aberdeen's patron saint). His sword, and the flag used on that day, are still to be seen in the city.

Highlanders again advanced on Aberdeen in 1644, under the leadership of **James Graham Marquis of Montrose**, during the Civil War, the first shots of which had been fired in the Grampian region at **Turriff** some five years earlier. This time the Highlanders defeated the citizens and in one day, 13 September 1644, more Aberdonians were killed than died in air raids during the whole of World War II. Six years later, in 1650, after the capture and execution of Montrose, his arm was sent to the city where it remained nailed to the Tolbooth door. Montrose's severed limbs were to stay scattered until after the Restoration, when his half-brother Harry Graham received permission to gather the remains together for decent burial.

Between the Restoration in 1660 and the end of **Stewart** hopes at **Culloden** in 1746, Aberdeen continued to be involved in national affairs. After the **Battle of Killiecrankie** (1689) the Highland host again threatened the burgh, but **General Mackay** fortunately got there first, and the remnants of **Dundee**'s army withdrew later to be defeated at the Haughs of Cromdale. In December 1715 **James Francis Edward Stewart**, 'the Old Pretender' stayed in Skipper Scott's house or inn on the **Castlegate**. The strongly **Jacobite** town council greeted him with loyal pleasure, and in return James made Provost Bannerman a knight. But the honour was not to last. Shortly afterwards James returned to the Continent, his cause in ruins. His followers, George Keith 10th Earl Marischal and the **Earl of Errol**, both lost their estates. The sale of the Keith property at Drumlithie, to the south of Aberdeen, forced William Burness, the father of the poet **Robert Burns**, to move eventually to **Alloway** in **Ayrshire**. 'Sir' Patrick Bannerman, although put on trial in England, lived to tell the tale, as did many of the other Jacobite supporters who fled abroad to await another opportunity to support the White Cockade. When **Prince Charles Edward Stewart**, the 'Young Pretender' came to claim the throne for his father, Aberdeen was again involved as the Duke of Cumberland, son of George II, spent six weeks in the city before setting out for Culloden. His troops were billeted in what is now **Robert Gordon's College**, built on part of the ground belonging to the Blackfriars.

Provost James Gordon of Rothiemay had drawn up the first plan of Aberdeen in 1661, for which the town council awarded him 'a silver cup, a silk hat, and a silken gown for his bedfellow'. The map shows a typical Scottish medieval burgh with a castle site, a loch, a kirk and a port. The first two have long since gone but the last two remain, both altered nearly out of recognition. Gordon's map shows two areas – 'New Aberdeen' and 'Old Aberdeen' – which confuse visitors and locals alike. Old Aberdeen was, under the Bishop, a **burgh of barony** in its own right from 1498, whereas Aberdeen was a royal burgh from at least the 12th century [see **Local Government**]. Over the years the name of the burgh of barony around St Machar's Cathedral and King's College has undergone several changes – Kirkton of St Mary's, Kirkton of Aberdon – but was usually known locally as Aulton, from the Scots 'auld' (old) and 'toon' (town or settlement), as opposed to the 'new' town of New Aberdeen. The other Aberdeen was incorrectly named 'New' to differentiate it from 'Old' Aberdeen. In 1891 the two burghs, royal and baronial, became one. The city had expanded to the north; it had also started to move to the west.

It was this expansion to the west, or inland, which shaped Aberdeen into the city recognisable today. New main streets were built to link the city to the south and north main roads. **Union Street**, the major shopping area, is named for the union of Britain and Ireland in 1801. Holburn Street is the link southwards, while **King Street** takes traffic north. Aberdeen was fortunate enough to have two architects of vision during the period when it became 'the Granite City': John ('Tudor Johnnie') Smith, the first City Architect, and **Archibald Simpson**. Not only did they have great skills; they also served the citizens well by working in close harmony with each other. 'Tudor Johnnie's' father, William 'Sink-'em' Smith, had been a mason responsible for early Aberdeen buildings, and John's son, also William, was the architect of many fine buildings including **Balmoral Castle** (aided, of course, by Prince Albert).

The granite industry of Aberdeen and the north-east not only supplied materials for home use, but also exported worldwide. Napoleon III's tomb, **Queen Victoria**'s mausoleum, London's streets, the docks of Rio de Janeiro, all have Aberdeen granite in them. But when a demand for coloured stone arose, and when cremation reduced the demand for gravestones, the industry declined to near oblivion.

As well as its granite, Aberdeen was also known in the 19th century for its **shipbuilding**. Sailing ships such as *Scottish Maid* and *Cairngorm* could beat the Yankees at the tea-carrying trade thanks to their streamlined 'Aberdeen Bow'. But the crowning glory came in 1868 when the **Thermopylae** was launched. Designed by Hercules Linton, who was born near, and trained in, Aberdeen, she was probably the fastest sailing ship of all time. Only the **Clyde**-built *Cutty Sark* was her equal.

Steam led to the demise of the clipper ships. However the new motive power was put to use in steam trawlers – 'Smokey Joes'. Once again fish became a staple industry of Aberdeen. The new **railway** system ensured fresh Aberdeen fish was in London's Billingsgate market for next morning. The wealth produced was equal to that from farming, the granite industry or papermaking. As demand for granite dwindled so also, for various reasons, the supply of fish diminished. Nevertheless Aberdeen continued as a prosperous town, mainly thanks to diversification of its economy through the centuries.

The last 25 years, with the discovery and development of **oil and gas** in the North Sea to the east and north-east of Aberdeen, have witnessed some of the most spectacular changes in the city. The skyline, so long dominated by kirks and colleges, is now dominated by high-rise buildings in modern concrete and glass. National banks, shops and building societies have displaced old-established private Aberdeen firms, and granite buildings, once the hallmark of Aberdeen, are altered into a bland 'could-be-anywhere' format. Despite these obvious changes, the city of Aberdeen – with some 7000 years of history behind it – remains a more compact and attractive metropolis than most others of its size.

Bon Accord Square

Reminiscent of **Edinburgh**'s **New Town**, the dignified terraces of Bon Accord Square and its adjacent Crescent date from the 1830s and are considered to be **Archibald Simpson**'s domestic masterpiece. The architect himself is commemorated with a block of, naturally, granite whereon he is described as 'a pioneer of civic design in this, his native city'. In Bon Accord Terrace, which links the square to **Union Street**, there is an inconspicuous stone with a plaque identifying it as the Crabstone, once the boundary marker of lands held by John Crab or Craib. He, or possibly his son, was the military engineer who devised the fortifications and catapults which enabled the Scots to retain **Berwick** against English attack in 1319. The Crabstone was a noted meeting point for the medieval city and the site of a battle in 1571 between the **Huntly Gordons**, who had lately burnt **Corgarff Castle** and now held Aberdeen on behalf of **Queen Mary**, and the Forbeses who had the support of the Regent **Earl of Mar**. The latter were worsted. It was also hereabouts that on 'Black Friday' (13 September 1644) **Montrose** defeated the **Covenanting** forces at the **Battle of Aberdeen** (or Justice Mills), the prelude to his long-remembered sack of the city.

Bridge of Dee

Built 1520–7 as a link to the south, initiated by **Bishop Elphinstone** and finished by **Bishop Dunbar**, the bridge was considered unique in medieval Scotland with its seven semi-circular granite arches. On the upstream butresses are 28 shields, inscriptions and panels, including those of the founding Bishops, the City of Aberdeen, the **Regent Albany** [see **John Stewart**] and the boy King **James V**.

At one time a port (or gate) was built across the southern end, but it failed to stop the **Marquis of Montrose** when he attacked the city in 1639. The port was removed in 1774 as it was an obstacle to increasing traffic. Some 50 years later the bridge was widened, again to satisfy the needs of traffic.

On the north-west corner of the bridge there stood a chapel dedicated to the Virgin Mary. During the **Reformation** (1560) a mob from the south broke into the chapel and stripped the gold and silver from the statue of Our Lady of Bon Accord. The wooden figure was then thrown in to the River Dee. Legend has it that the remains were picked up at sea by a Flemish ship and taken to the Continent. The statue now stands in the Church of Nôtre Dame de Finisterre, Brussels. A replica of Our Lady of Bon Accord can be seen in St Peter's Chapel, **Castlegate**, Aberdeen.

Bridge of Don

Built in 1831 by John Smith with **Thomas Telford** as consultant, the five-arched Bridge of Don is downstream of the **Brig o' Balgownie** which it was designed to relieve. It was widened in the 1950s. Immediately to the south is the Seaton residential district of **Old Aberdeen**, while the fast-growing suburb to the north is also known as Bridge of Don. Here are the Aberdeen Exhibition and Conference Centre and much industrial development.

Brig o' Balgownie

Tradition has it that bridge-building started as early as 1290 to make a road link to the north over the river **Don**. However, it was not until 1329 that the work was completed on the orders of **Robert I**, a great patron of Aberdeen. The money actually came from Bishop Cheyne, whose see was at the nearby **St Machar's**

Aberdeen's Brig o' Balgownie in the late 19th century (GWWA)

Aberdeen continued

Cathedral. There is an oracular rhyme by **Thomas the Rhymer** (of Ercildoune):

> Brig o' Balgownie, wicht's thy wa'
> Wi' a wife's ae son, an' a Mare's ae foal
> Doon shalt thou fa'.

Lord George Byron, who was educated at Aberdeen Grammar School and was 'a wife's ae son', was terrified as he rode over the bridge in case his horse was 'a mare's ae foal', an incident which he would recall until the end of his life. Thus between Thomas's prophecy and the Bishop's payment, there arose another couplet – 'Built by a Bishop's purse, doomed by the Devil's curse'.

In 1605 Sir Alexander Hay left the modest sum of £2 5s8½d for the upkeep of the bridge. This money was wisely invested and when the new Bridge of Balgownie was built further down the river in 1830 the whole cost, £16,000, was met from Sir Alexander's bequest. The money continues to accumulate and at present stands in excess of £100,000, despite having been used to furnish many other bridges and roads in north-east Scotland. After 700 years the Brig o' Balgownie still stands, but is open only to foot passengers.

Broad Street

Leading north from **Castle Street** to Gallowgate and **Old Aberdeen**, Broad Street has been much developed as a civic focus. St Nicholas House (1962), a tower block devoted to the city's administration, dwarfs **Marischal College** opposite and overwhelms **Provost Skene's House**. The north end of the street is intersected by Upperkirkgate, with some fine 18th and 19th century buildings, which leads west to the **Church of St Nicholas** and Schoolhill (**Robert Gordon's College, Aberdeen Art Gallery**, etc).

Castle Street/Castlegate

This street-cum-square, now a continuation of **Union Street**, was the heart of pre-19th century Aberdeen, its seat of authority and its market place. In medieval times it had also been the gate (or 'gait', approach) to the castle, which was destroyed in the 14th century [see **Castlehill**]. Besides the **Town House** (incorporating the old Tolbooth) and the **Mercat Cross**, and not forgetting the **Salvation Army Citadel**, here too are the Plainstanes, a raised area round the now restored Castlegate Well which served the city's 'peripatetics' as an exchange for both stocks and gossip. Mary Duff, the object of the affections of a precocious eight-year-old Don Juan who later became **Lord Byron**, lived in an adjacent house. **King Street**, with **Archibald Simpson**'s (now) Clydesdale Bank on the corner, heads north; **Marischal Street** with James Burn's (now) Bank of Scotland on the corner leads south. In between is the Justice Port leading east to Gallowhill (for hanging felons) or Heading Hill (for burning witches). At the opposite, west, end, **Broad Street**, Union Street and Shiprow correspond.

Castlehill

Castlegate once gave access at its eastern end to the hill whereon stood the medieval castle. The castle was replaced by a chapel to **St Ninian** in the 14th century, 'hopin by that meins that the hill being converted to a holy use, it would be unlawful to imploy it to a profayne use'. Unfortunately the **Reformation** put paid to such hopes; **General Monk**'s troops refortified it during the Civil War, a barracks was built in the 18th century, and in 1969 this was replaced by two tower blocks which, insists the guide book produced by the Royal Institute of Architects in Scotland, 'do not sit ill on Castlehill'.

Christ's College

Terminating the west end of **Union Street** at Holburn junction, Christ's College (1850) is Tudor Gothic but with a castellated tower with angle turret. It was designed by Thomas Mackenzie as a place of training for ministers of the **Free Church** and complements the castellar style of **Marshall Mackenzie**'s later **Salvation Army Citadel** at the opposite, distant, end of Union Street.

Duthie Park

On a bend in the **Dee** south of Ferryhill, the grounds of Arthurseat were bequeathed to the expanding city as a park by Miss Charlotte Duthie and opened by Princess Beatrice in 1883. An obelisk commemorating **Sir James MacGrigor** of Royal Army Medical Corps fame was removed here from **Marischal College** in 1906; and the Winter Gardens containing tropical birds and plants erected in 1972. From Deeside Drive skirting the park the George VI Bridge (1939) spans the Dee to Kincorth, a 1940s housing development.

Footdee

South-west of **Castle Street** on a narrow tongue of land between the harbour and the sea, Footdee is indeed at the foot of the **Dee** although both this etymology and its spelling seem to be a 19th century gentrification. The original name, the common pronunciation and a still current spelling is Fitty or Futtie. Once a **fishing** village, it was redesigned as three squares of cottages by John Smith in the early 19th century following alterations to **Aberdeen harbour**. It remains distinct and characterful with shipyards on the harbour side and a lifeboat station facing out to sea. The peninsula ends with the long North Pier which marks and protects the entrance to the harbour.

Golden Square

Built 1810–21, Golden Square was part of a grand design, never effectively followed, for the new town that developed west of the Denburn following the creation of **Union Street**. Its terraced houses are typically two-storeyed with a continuous cornice and roof parapet. A feature of the square was once its well, named after the city's guild of Hammermen. Its place has now been taken by a statue of **George Gordon**, 5th **Duke of Gordon** which was once in **Castlegate**. 'A bad statue but still very ornamental,' thought **Henry, Lord Cockburn**, adding that 'So far as I know this is the first granite statue in Scotland.'

The Green

A lively imagination is required to visualise this erstwhile thoroughfare below **Union Street** as the original heart of the city. Here, beside the Denburn, was the early medieval market place, although no vestige of

A Friday rag fair around the Mercat Cross in Castle Street (GWWA)

the timbered township which must have surrounded it remains other than some 12th century monastic graves found to the south near Guild Street. When the market moved east to **Castlegate** in perhaps the 14th century, its main access route over the Denburn by Bow Brig (demolished 1851) passed this way and continued to do so until Union Street provided the 19th century's version of a flyover.

Hazlehead Park

Off Queen's Road in the west end of the city, the expanse of Hazlehead Park (acquired 1920) provides a variety of sports facilities, much woodland, a maze, a rose garden, and other less permanent attractions. Nearby is the **Gordon Highlanders'** Museum and, not far away, the Rubislaw Granite Quarry, a hole 465ft (142m) deep out of which has been cut the raw material for many of London's public buildings, more of Aberdeen's, and for projects worldwide ranging from a Japanese temple to Sebastopol's docks. The quarry was closed in the 1970s.

King Street

Leading north from **Castle Street**, King Street begins in style with the curved Corinthian portico of **Archibald Simpson**'s (now) Clydesdale Bank (1839–42). Above the portico the terracotta sculpture is of Ceres, goddess of abundance, with attendants, by James Giles; there is a gilded plasterwork of the Parthenon frieze within. The street continues its Greek revival theme in Simpson's Medical Hall (1820) and John Smith's North Church (1830), both with Ionic porticos, plus numerous town houses. The exception is Simpson's Gothic **St Andrew's Cathedral**.

King's College, Old Aberdeen

Bishop **William Elphinstone** (1431–1514), wanting greatly to increase the level of education, both lay and clerical, in northern Scotland, requested Pope Alexander VI, better remembered in history as a member of the poisonous Borgia family, to establish a university in the north of Scotland. This was done by Papal Bull in 1495 and the new college, at first called St Mary's after the Virgin, was later named King's in honour of **James IV**.

The building material is not, as one might suppose, granite, but sandstone from Covesea near **Elgin** on the **Moray** coast. The crown which tops the tower has only one equal in Scotland – on **St Giles** in **Edinburgh**. Additions were made alongside the original chapel and library by **Bishop Gavin Dunbar** who built a round tower in 1525, and by Roundhead officers who contributed the Cromwell Tower erected in 1658 during the Protectorate. Both buildings still exist, as does the chapel of 1500 which has no aisle but a fine apse, traceried windows and superb medieval woodwork in the screen, stalls and ribbed ceiling.

In 1932 Elphinstone Hall was built to honour the quincentenary of the good bishop's birth. Since the war the expansion of King's has gone on apace. There is now a five-storey chemistry block, a space-age building for Natural Philosophy and various large modern buildings for other Arts and Sciences.

West front of King's College chapel and tower (RWB)

Although the founder himself was originally buried in front of the altar in the chapel, he is now commemorated by a magnificent tomb and sarcophagus, whereon his effigy lies guarded by the Seven Virtues, on the lawn outside the building – a fitting tribute to a man of many talents.

Links, King's and Queen's

On the strength of its two-mile Beach Esplanade along the sands between the **Don** and the **Dee**, Aberdeen has been billed as 'the largest holiday resort in Scotland'. Since the city wisely turns its back on the North Sea's breezes, this is no Corniche. The northern section comprises the King's Links, the southern leading to **Footdee** the Queen's Links. Here, in defiance of the elements, is Codonna's vast amusement centre, the Beach Ballroom (1926), a children's village and other fairground attractions. **Golf** may be played on either links.

Marischal College

James VI gave a charter for Marischal College to be established in 1593. The original buildings, those of the Franciscan (or Greyfriar) monks who had vacated them in 1560, were gifted to the new university by its founder, **George Keith, 5th Earl Marischal**, who saw it as a Protestant rival to the Catholic **King's College**. When questions were raised as to the sources of his wealth, and to the propriety of using a Catholic establishment for a Protestant university, the Earl replied, 'They haif said. Quhat say they? Lat thame say' – an inscription which is to be found carved into the fabric of the building to this day.

Between 1836–44 parts of the medieval building were replaced by a new quadrangle designed by **Archi-**

The granite façade of Marischal College soon after completion in 1891 (GWWA)

Aberdeen continued

bald Simpson. Further changes were made in 1906 when the monastery church was demolished and a massive 400ft (122m) frontage and 235ft (72m) tower of **Kemnay** granite was built in elaborate perpendicular Gothic – a monument to the architect **A Marshall Mackenzie** and the skills of the nameless granite workers of Aberdeen.

Despite extensive internal conversion, the college has always been cramped by its central city site. Yet it holds a treasured place in the hearts of many Aberdonians who look upon it as 'the second largest granite building in the world' (after the Spanish Escorial) and feel it 'captures the aspiring quality of cloud-capt towers'.

Marischal Street

Laid out in 1767 to provide direct access from **Castle Street** south to the then pier and **harbour**, Marischal Street represents the first phase in Aberdeen's modern expansion. It starts where previously had stood the **Earl Marischal**'s Hall whence **Queen Mary** had been obliged to watch the execution (1562) of Sir John Gordon, third son of the 4th **Earl of Huntly** (who had himself just died after defeat at **Corrichie**). The adjacent building, Pitfodel's Lodging, was replaced (1801) by James Burn's bank, now the Bank of Scotland, an 'early essay in white granite' with a façade incorporating classical pilasters and a deep cornice. Georgian houses line the street in its descent towards the harbour. The irregularity of the ground necessitated the construction of Bannerman's Brig over what became Virginia Street.

Mercat Cross

Reputed to be the finest original burgh cross in Scotland, Aberdeen's Mercat Cross in the **Castlegate** was built by John Montgomery in 1686 in the shape of a hexagon with arches between the angles and a column above with a finial in the shape of a white marble unicorn. Around the parapet are large bas-relief carvings representing the ten **Stewart** monarchs from **James I** to **James VII** plus the Royal Arms and those of the city.

Old Aberdeen

Whilst **King's College** and **St Machar's** still confer an air of scholarship on Old Aberdeen (or Aulton – see main **Aberdeen** entry), this was a separate burgh as late as 1890 and had its own High Street, **railway**, **canal** and public buildings. The Town House (1788) in the cobbled High Street is a Georgian design of three storeys with a short clock tower surmounted by a belfry. Also cobbled and lined with neat 18th and 19th century houses is College Bounds where once stood the parish church of St Mary ad Nives; only its 'Snow Churchyard' remains. **Archibald Simpson**'s St Mary's Free Church survives in the High Street and dates, naturally, from the 1843 **Disruption**. Outside it there is a fragment of the old Mercat Cross. The tree-lined Chanonry, where once the canons of the cathedral lived, leads to St Machar's past the **Cruickshank Botanic Gardens**.

Provost Ross House

Built in 1593, this is thought to be the work of the mason Andrew Jamesone, father of the artist **George Jameson(e)**. Situated in the ancient Shiprow, it passed through various owners until it was acquired in 1702 by the Provost whose name it bears. Ross had trading interests in the Netherlands and it is said that the area of Mastrick in Aberdeen is named after Maastricht in Holland. The Provost himself died in Amsterdam in 1714. The house was restored in 1954 and is now the Maritime Museum.

Provost Skene's House

Situated in the Guestrow, reputed to be the area of the guest-houses for the Greyfriars Monastery, the house dates from 1545. It was acquired by Provost George Skene in 1669. One of its main attractions is the painted ceiling in the long gallery which is unique in Scotland because of its medieval religious themes. The Duke of Cumberland lodged in the house for some six weeks, and was given the Freedom of the City, before his departure for **Culloden** Moor in April 1746. The house is now a period museum and restaurant.

Robert Gordon's College

After Aberdeen Grammar School, the second oldest school in the city. It was built in 1739 to the design of **William Adam**, father of the famous **Adam brothers**. Its founder, **Robert Gordon**, was an Aberdeen merchant who specialised in trade with Eastern Europe. He left money for a 'hospital' or boarding school for the sons of poor burgesses of the city. In 1881 it was renamed 'College' and became a fee-paying school. In 1909 the college established the Robert Gordon Institute of Technology (RGIT) which became the Robert Gordon University in 1992. During the '45 **Jacobite Rising** the Duke of Cumberland's troops were billeted here prior to their departure for **Culloden** Moor.

St Andrew's Cathedral, King Street

Built (1816) by **Archibald Simpson** in the Gothic perpendicular style, St Andrew's is the episcopal cathedral. The chancel was added by G E Street in 1880 and the porch by **Sir Robert Lorimer** in 1911. An ornate interior which led John Betjeman to declare this 'Aberdeen's best modern building' includes ceilings decorated with coats of arms, those in the north transept being of **Aberdeenshire Jacobite** families and those in the south transept of the American states. St Andrew's is considered the mother church of the American **Episcopalian** community since it was in Aberdeen that Samuel Seabury, first US bishop, was consecrated (1784) by three Scottish bishops. Consecration in England was out of the question since Seabury could not and would not swear allegiance to George III. There is a jewelled chalice presented by the diocese of Connecticut and a marble statue of Bishop John Skinner who presided over Seabury's consecration.

St Machar's Cathedral, Old Aberdeen

Legend has it that a church of some kind has existed on this site since the middle of the 6th century. The story further continues that St Machar, a disciple of **St Columba**, was told by God in a dream to go from **Iona** and travel in the lands of the **Picts** until he came to a spot where a river took the shape of a bishop's crook or staff. The saint discovered such a site on the river **Don** near the sea and built a primitive church there.

The twin towers of St Machar's Cathedral in Old Aberdeen (RWB)

The existing granite building dates from the 14th century with additions continuing up to the **Reformation** of 1560. A fine Bishop's Window commemorates the three bishops mainly responsible for the cathedral – Bishop Lichtoun who oversaw the building of the twin towers to the west which so resemble those of a castle; **Bishop Gavin Dunbar** who inspired the unique heraldic ceiling of c1520 which portrays the coats of arms of the monarchs of Europe and the archbishops, bishops, dukes, earls and nobles of Scotland; and **Bishop Elphinstone** who added the third central tower as well as planning a choir and transepts. Unfortunately in the 1650s during Cromwell's Protectorate stones were taken from the buttresses of this tower to build a fort in the city centre; the resulting weakness caused the tower to fall in 1688 taking with it the Bishop's uncompleted choir. The Bishop's Palace next to the cathedral has gone, its stones also used for the Cromwellian fort, but the cathedral graveyard remains.

St Mary's Cathedral, Huntly Street

The Cathedral, Aberdeen's third, of St Mary of the Assumption belongs to the Roman Catholics. Built by Alexander Ellis in 1860, exactly 300 years after the proscription of the Mass, it is a tall building of white granite in the pointed style with a 200ft (61m) spire added in 1877 and one of the highest in the city. The interior is pleasantly austere and airy with fine stained glass and a nave clerestory. Huntly Street is towards the west end of **Union Street**. John Smith had planned it as a square (like **Golden Square**) but realised only the classical Blind Asylum which stands back from the street.

St Nicholas Church

The 'Mither Kirk' of Aberdeen is mentioned in a Papal Bull from Nicholas Breakspear (Adrian IV), the only

English Pope, as existing in the mid-12th century. After 1560 the building was divided into two parish 'kirks' – the East (or New) Church (previously the chancel), and the West (or Town) Church (previously the nave). A disastrous fire in 1874 destroyed much of East St Nicholas which was replaced with a structure 'of inspired meanness' (C Graham). A year later the medieval wooden steeple was rebuilt with a tower and spire of granite and the West Church redesigned by James Gibbs. There is in the tower a carillon of 48 which regularly play. Beneath the East Church has survived St Mary's Chapel which dates from the early 15th century and was known originally as Our Lady of Pity's Vault. The churchyard extends back to **Union Street** from which it is screened by John Smith's Ionic colonnade (1830) resembling that in London's Hyde Park Corner.

Salvation Army Citadel

In **Castlegate** and with a castellate silhouette to rival the nearby **Town House**, this unlikely place of worship was built (1893–6) by James Souttar, a local architect with Scandinavian connections who published a history of English Gothic in Swedish. The Citadel replaced the 18th century Record Office. Its bay windows and great tower with angle turrets, one so tall and topped with crenellation as to suggest a factory chimney, were inspired by **Balmoral Castle**.

Torry

On the south bank of the **Dee**, and so technically in **Kincardineshire**, Torry was once a separate village but since the construction of the **Victoria Bridge** (1881) has become a suburb of the city. Here was based the trawl **fishing** industry which accounted for Aberdeen's turn of the century prosperity and which attracted labour even from England. Tenement blocks and a garden city were laid out on the edge of Tullos Hill where now, between Torry and **Nigg** Bay, are the headquarters of the numerous **oil** companies operating in the North Sea. West of Torry the south bank of the Dee terminates in a **golf course**, the Torry Battery, and **Robert Stevenson**'s Girdleness Lighthouse (1833).

Town House

There has been a Town House (or Tolbooth) in Aberdeen since at least 1191 and one on the present site in the **Castlegate** since 1394. The present Town House was erected in 1870 and is built of **Kemnay** granite. Its soaring clock tower is some 190ft (58m) high and within it is the Charter Room, containing probably the most complete set of civic records in Britain. Behind the Victorian façade of the present Town House and Sheriff Courthouse there still remains part of the previous Tolbooth. This building, with its own tower (1615), belfry (1627) and spire (1726), still contains the cells in which condemned men were kept in chains until their public execution outside in the Castlegate. Equivalent to **Edinburgh**'s 'Heart of Midlothian', the gaol is known as the 'Mids o' **Mar**'; the Old Tolbooth is open to the public.

Triple Kirks

Opposite the City **Art Gallery** the tall brick spire is that of The Triple Kirks (1843), a rare example of ecclesiastical work by **Archibald Simpson** in a material other than granite. The date gives the clue to the building's provenance, 1843 being the year of the **Disruption**. Unable to accept any notion of civil interference in the affairs of the Church, the ministers of the two **St Nicholas** churches, plus he of the Belmont Street South Church (John Smith, 1830, now called West St Nicholas Kirk House), urgently required new premises for their congregations. The Triple Kirks, three in one (and hopefully for the price of one), proved to be the answer. Known as the East, West and South Churches, none is now used for worship.

Union Street

Often compared with **Edinburgh**'s **Princes Street**, this is Aberdeen's main east-west thoroughfare and shopping street. Dead straight, undulating and nearly a mile long, it was laid out in 1801, named after the union of Britain and Ireland, and nearly bankrupted the city before it was completed in mid-century. It nevertheless proved the key to growth. It eliminated the tortuous approach by way of the Denburn and Puttachie defiles (both of which had to be bridged) and so provided a direct and imposing access route from the south and west to the city's hub around **Castle Street** (which became its continuation); in the process it opened up for development the land beyond the Denburn so that it now forms the main link between the later neo-classical town (including **Golden Square**, **Bon Accord Square**, etc) and the older city.

Although never a uniform composition and latterly much pocked with the plate glass and neon insignia of the high street retailers, Union Street retains its architectural coherence thanks to the ubiquitous use of granite and to a continuity of restrained Georgian design with many columned façades and matching cornices. The work of **Archibald Simpson** is in evidence, as in the Union Buildings (1819) and the Assembly Rooms Music Hall (1820). The single-span Union Bridge (1805) over the Denburn was built by Thomas Fletcher with advice from **Telford** and others. It was widened and substantially altered a century later.

Victoria Bridge

Designed in 1881 by Edward Blyth, the five-arched Victoria Bridge was built after a ferry accident in which 32 were killed. It is still the first bridge across the **Dee** (as re-routed in 1868) and led to the south bank development of **Torry** as a port, suburb and now industrial complex. Upriver the bridge was preceded by the Wellington Suspension Bridge (built 1829) and the **Bridge of Dee**; it has since been succeeded by the Queen Elizabeth Bridge (1983) and the George VI Bridge [see **Duthie Park**].

Wallace Tower

Although known as the Wallace Tower, this Z-plan tower house has no connection with **William Wallace**; 'Wallace', in this case, is a corruption of 'Well-House', a reference to a nearby city well. The correct name of the building is Benholm's Tower (or Lodging) after its

Union Street and Bridge, Aberdeen, in the 1880s(GWWA)

Aberdeen continued

owner Sir Robert Keith of Benholm, brother of the 5th **Earl Marischal**. A sculptured figure of a knight in full armour on one of the towers is pointed out by locals as being that of William Wallace, but the armour dates from the period the tower was built, c1600. In 1963 the tower was demolished to make way for a multinational store, and although re-erected at Tillydrone in the area of **St Machar's Cathedral**, it is obviously out of its natural environment as a Scottish laird's town house within the local burgh. The tower is not open to the public.

ABERDEEN, Battle of (1644)

After victory at **Tippermuir**, **James Graham, Marquis of Montrose** led his Royalist troops east and north to appear before **Aberdeen** on 13 September. A demand for its surrender in the King's name was rejected and a drummerboy accompanying Montrose's emissary was shot. Maddened by this wanton act, Montrose prepared his 1500 Irish and Scots followers for battle. As at Tippermuir, the opposition were numerically superior but tactically naïve. Their cavalry swept round Montrose's flanks and found themselves cut off; their infantry fell back before the ferocity of **Alasdair MacDonald**'s Irish contingent. There followed a long remembered sack of Aberdeen in which the Irish distinguished themselves as merciless victors. Lacking the troops to hold the city, Montrose withdrew towards Speyside and, performing a complete circuit through **Rothiemurchus** and **Angus**, repressed the pursuing force under **Argyll** at **Fyvie** before retiring undefeated into the Highlands, there to resume his run of victories at **Inverlochy** in the New Year.

ABERDEEN, Earldom and Marquisate

Among the many who pride themselves that they do not descend from the original Seton of **Huntly**, but are **Gordons** in the male line, are those who became Earls of Aberdeen. The contrast appeared starkly to **Charles I** when John Gordon of **Haddo** gave his life gallantly in the Royalist cause while the 2nd Marquess of Huntly proved, in the King's own words, 'feeble and false'. John of Haddo's son became Lord Chancellor of Scotland in 1682 with the rank of Earl, remained a **non-Juror** throughout William II's reign without mishap, and took no part in the **Union** of 1707. It was the **4th Earl** (1784–1860) who became a pacifist Prime Minister and resigned soon after the outbreak of the Crimean War in 1854 to devote himself to the improvement of the Haddo estate. The **7th Earl** (1847–1934) served as Lord Lieutenant of Ireland and Governor-General of Canada, and was created a Marquess in 1915. With his wife Ishbel he published the eccentric memoirs *We Twa*, 1925 and *More Cracks with We Twa*, 1929. His grandsons the 4th and 5th Marquesses conveyed the house of Haddo to the **National Trust for Scotland**, with the chapel in which the first ecumenical religious services in Scotland had been held.

ABERDEEN ART GALLERY

Aberdeen possesses one of the finest small public collections in the United Kingdom. Particularly strong in the 19th century British School, it also has a significant number of diverse and eclectic items, a tribute to the acumen of a number of local individuals whose generous donations form the basis of the collection.

The gallery, an undistinguished essay in the classical manner, was built in 1885 as an exhibiting space for the Aberdeen Artists' Society, but has since been extended. Although the city owned a number of pictures and sculptures at this stage, it was not until 1900 and the

Alexander MacDonald Bequest that a proper representative collection began to take shape. Not only did MacDonald leave his excellent collection of Victorian paintings to the gallery, including works by Millais and Watts, but, more importantly, a large sum of money to be invested and spent specifically on paintings less than 25 years old. This far-sighted stipulation has enabled the gallery to assemble a first-rate collection of modern British and European art, many pictures bought directly from the artists. Major works by Clausen, **Orchardson**, Leger, Sickert, Pasmore, Spencer, Hitchens and Auerbach have been purchased with funds from the MacDonald Bequest. In 1901 another local collector, Sir James Murray, was appointed Chairman of the Gallery Committee. As well as contributing towards an extension to the gallery, in 1925 he helped purchase a particularly fine Monet. On his death he left much of his own collection to the gallery, including **Sir John Lavery**'s masterpiece The Tennis Party.

A further bequest in 1921 from a local advocate, Alexander Webster, formed the backbone of the gallery's collection of British watercolours. This has since been built upon and is now a notably strong part of the city's holdings. The Webster Bequest also included an important collection of china and a cash donation. The latter has been put towards many significant acquisitions including paintings by the French Barbizon painters and the Scottish Colourists [see **Painting**]. The gallery has kept pace with most of the new movements in 20th century British art and nearly all the major names are well represented. The last two significant bequests concerned the local artist and print-maker James McBey (1883–1959). In 1959 one of his most important patrons, H H Kynett of Philadelphia, gave the Aberdeen gallery a virtually complete collection of the artist's prints. Two years later McBey's widow financed the construction of a Print Room and Library which has been the setting for some of the gallery's most interesting research and exhibitions. Aberdeen Art Gallery continues its policy of exhibiting and acquiring the finest contemporary art. It possesses an almost perfectly proportioned collection of British 18th–20th century art which never fails to delight.

ABERDEEN HARBOUR

Thanks to the service requirements of the North Sea **oil and gas** industry **Aberdeen** remains a busy port. While other port cities have turned away from their docklands or redeveloped them, here the harbour is still a clamorous presence in the heart of the city and at the mouth of the **Dee**. Until the 18th century siltation and off-shore sandbars restricted the draught of vessels able to take advantage of the estuarine shelter. A quay on the north bank and a bulwark on the south helped the river to scour its bed but not till construction (1781) of David Smeaton's North Pier and its subsequent extension by **Telford** was the encroachment of the coastal sandbar contained. Further dredging and quay construction in the 19th century resulted in the cutting of a more southerly channel for the Dee, its previous channels becoming the Victoria Dock (with Upper Dock) and the Albert Basin. These, with the Dee itself, form the three-fingered harbour. It is linked to the sea by a short navigation channel along whose north shore towards **Footdee** the **shipbuilding** industry developed while the south bank (**Torry**) became the main **fishing** port. Passenger traffic, once an important trade, is now represented by the P&O ferry to **Shetland** which sails from Victoria Dock while the Albert Basin is reserved mainly for freight. Research and survey vessels, pipe laying barges, and a variety of supply and support ships, all involved in the oil and gas industry, make up the bulk of traffic. Their

Aberdeen Harbour as photographed by George Washington Wilson (GWWA)

unusual profiles contrast strangely with the city skyline and with the quayside architecture which includes **Marshall Mackenzie**'s neo-classical Harbour Office (1883–5) on Trinity Quay and the Old Customs House (1771) on Regent Quay. Also overlooking the harbour from the north is **Provost Ross House** where the Maritime Museum contains displays of the port's development and of its fishing, whaling, shipping and shipbuilding past.

ABERDEEN UNIVERSITY
Formed in 1860 as the result of the fusion between **King's** and **Marischal**, the University's student population has risen steadily since the end of World War II to a peak of over 11000. The university established the first mixed-sex halls of residence in Britain (Foresterhill in 1939; Crombie Hall in 1960). In the 1900s the trend seemed to be to close King's and concentrate the student population in Marischal, but nowadays the pendulum has swung away from the downtown Marischal and towards the leafy peace of King's. **Henry, Lord Cockburn** had recommended such a move in 1842: 'They should have given up the one in the town [Marischal] and made the old, venerable, well placed, academic looking King's College the single seat of their science.'

ABERDEEN-ANGUS CATTLE
The Angus Doddie and Buchan Humlie gave rise to this breed in the late 18th century, a time when advances in farming and a quickening market for fine beef meant cattle raising became a highly profitable part of Scottish farming. From 1820 Hugh Watson of Keilor, then **William McCombie** of Tillyfour consolidated the new breed.

They developed a very prepotent breed, ie one which reliably passes on its distinctive characteristics to its offspring even when mated to a very different breed. These characteristics included black colour, hornlessness, and an excellent though not particularly lean carcase. Worldwide these bulls have been mated with local breeds to produce fine beef animals.

Today there are 50 million Aberdeen-Angus type cattle. Up to the late 1960s Scots-bred Aberdeen-Angus bulls, famous for their compact form, were sold worldwide, notably from the **Perth** bull sales of MacDonald Fraser & Co, and the world record price for a bull (which still stood in 1990) was set there in 1963 – 60,000 guineas. Lately Aberdeen-Angus cattle have met stiff competition from Continental breeds such as the Charolais and Limousin which produce lean beef, of admittedly lower quality but more economically. Breeders are developing a new, big-bodied Aberdeen-Angus to compete. By 1999 50% of all the cattle in Argentina, one of the great beef-rearing countries of the world, were Aberdeen-Angus and 75% of the country's beef cattle had Angus blood.

ABERDEENSHIRE
Before the **local government** reorganisation of 1975, Aberdeenshire formed the north-eastern 'shoulder' of Scotland. The county comprised 1,246,585 acres (517,255ha), making it the sixth largest of the pre-1975 counties. With 85 miles of coastline, it stretched from

Inverness-shire and **Banff** in the west to **Kincardine**, **Perthshire** and **Angus** in the south. It was described in the *Third Statistical Account* (1960) as 'essentially a glaciated lowland region fronting the Moray Firth and North Sea with an upland or mountainous rim on the south and west . . . drained and dissected by the main streams of the rivers **Dee**, **Don**, **Deveron**, Ugie and Ythan, all flowing eastwards'. The area featured prominently in the 14th century **Wars of Independence**, and later came under the influence of the **Forbes** and **Gordon** families.

The administrative centre was **Aberdeen**, the county's burghs comprising **Ballater**, **Ellon**, **Fraserburgh**, **Huntly**, **Inverurie**, **Kintore**, **Oldmeldrum**, **Peterhead**, **Rosehearty** and **Turriff**. Some rearrangement of parishes took place between Aberdeenshire and Banffshire after the 1889 Local Government (Scotland) Act. Until the arrival of the 1970s oil boom **agriculture**, **forestry** and **fishing** were the county's main occupations, with the papermaking industry second only in importance to Midlothian's at one time. With the local government reorganisation of 1975, Aberdeenshire was wholly absorbed into Grampian Region; since the 1995 reorganisation the Districts of Banff and Buchan, Gordon, and the northern part of Kincardine and Deeside have together comprised the Aberdeenshire Council Area.

ABERDOUR, Fife
Winner of the accolade for the best-kept station in Scotland for 11 successive years, Aberdour stands opposite **Inchcolm** at the mouth (*aber*) of the Dour burn. This once divided it into two burghs, Easter and Wester Aberdour. On the burn's left bank St Fillan's Church retains its original Romanesque chancel (1140); the subsequent additions of porch and aisles are no later than 1608. De-roofed and neglected in the 19th century, this little gem is now restored and back in use. Beside it Aberdour Castle is still the property of the Douglas **Earls of Morton**. It was originally granted by **Robert I** to **Thomas Randolph, Earl of Moray**, whose second son granted it under a charter of barony to **Sir William Douglas**, 'the Knight of Liddesdale' in 1342 (one of whose brother's descendants was created Earl of Morton in 1456). The oldest part of the castle is the 14th century tower, of which only a gable survives above first floor level. An adjoining 16th century block stands to the roofless wall head and, beyond this, a 17th century L-plan mansion, roofed and floored, completes the façade's long advance through history. Beyond the terraced gardens the 16th century **doocot** is shaped like a beehive with accommodation for 600 pigeons. Already in disrepair by 1700, the castle was damaged by fire in 1715 and finally abandoned in 1725 when the Earl moved across the burn to Aberdour House (17th century and later, previously called Cuttlehill).

ABERFELDY, Perthshire
The small town of Aberfeldy is on the right bank of the **Tay** six miles from **Loch Tay**. Its Taybridge (1733–5, on the road to **Tummel Bridge**) may be considered **Wade**'s finest, although it was in fact designed by **William Adam**. Robert Southey, accompanied by **Telford**, later complained that the parapets were too high, the four obelisks inappropriate, and the

foundations of the five arches suspect. Yet it still stands, its humpbacked carriageway carrying a weight of traffic which Wade can scarcely have dreamed of. Nearby on the bank was erected the **Black Watch** monument, an artificial cairn, cemented below, and surmounted by a kilted soldier; another soldier appears to be climbing up the side of it. Gaelic and English inscriptions record the first gathering (1839) and muster (1840) of the regiment. Erected in 1887, the monument was split by lightning and has since been repaired. In the town itself a watermill has been restored and may be seen working. It is fed from the Urlar burn which, descending from the Falls of Moness, flows through the wood known as the Birks of Aberfeldy (though **Robert Burns** may have meant the birks (birches) of Abergeldie). The town's distillery produces John Dewar and may be visited.

ABERFOYLE, Perthshire

The **tourist** centre for the **Trossachs**, Aberfoyle is of no great antiquity. In **Scott**'s *Rob Roy* it was a clachan (hamlet) where the eponymous hero met Bailie Nicol Jarvie. No vestige of the clachan is now visible amid the car parks and holiday emporia. The Queen Elizabeth Forest Park laps around the town and there is a **Forestry Commission** Visitor Centre named after David Marshall, chairman of its benefactory body, the **Carnegie** Trust.

ABERGELDIE CASTLE, Nr Balmoral, Aberdeenshire

A simple rectangular house with a prominent angle turret elaborately corbelled, Abergeldie stands on the south bank of the **Dee**. It was built by John Gordon in the 16th century but its chief claim to fame is that from 1848 it was leased to the royal family as a dower house for **Balmoral**. Amongst those who used it as their Scottish home was the Prince of Wales, the future Edward VII. It is now back in **Gordon** hands and the later adjoining mansion, which provided much of the accommodation, has been demolished. The **Burns** poem 'The Birks of Aberfeldie' should possibly be called 'The Birks of Abergeldie'. According to **Dorothy Wordsworth**, at the time there were birches aplenty by the Dee but none at all beside the **Tay**.

ABERLADY, East Lothian

This village on the south shore of the Firth of Forth takes its name from the Pefferburn, once known as the Leddie. Formerly the port for **Haddington**, the harbour has been allowed to silt up and the shallow sandy sea-flats of Aberlady Bay, a Nature Reserve since 1952, provide excellent wintering for large numbers of waders and seabirds. The 19th century Aberlady Parish Church has a 15th century square tower and a replica of an 8th century fragment of an Anglian cross-shaft (the original is in **Edinburgh**'s **Royal Museum**). A mile to the east Luffness House was originally a late 16th century T-plan tower house but additions by **William Burn** (1822), Thomas Brown (1825) and **David Bryce** (1846 and 1874) have turned it into something much more ornate. A fragment of the 13th century Carmelite Friary remains in the grounds.

Between Aberlady and Longniddry and overlooking the Firth of Forth, Gosford House was built (1790–1800) by **Robert Adam** for the Earl of Wemyss. The dramatic effect of Adam's original façade, with its three great arched windows, was somewhat diminished by the addition (1891) of a rusticated arcade running the length of the front. This and other alterations and extensions, including the rebuilding of Adam's demolished wings and the creation of the magnificent marble hall, were the work of William Young (1843–1900, architect of **Glasgow**'s **City Chambers**). Still the home of the Earl of Wemyss and March, Gosford houses an important collection of paintings.

ABERLEMNO, Angus

Midway between **Forfar** and **Brechin**, Aberlemno is a most important site for the study of **Pictish** art. Two cross-slabs and a symbol stone are located beside the B9134 road, a third cross-slab is in the churchyard, and a fourth, discovered at nearby Woodrae and for some time in the possession of **Sir Walter Scott**, is now in the **Royal Museum** in **Edinburgh**. Of the roadside stones the symbol stone is the earliest (7th century) while the tall (3m) cross-slab is the most elaborately carved. It is also one of rather few such stones known to be in its original position. Less weathered and also elaborately carved is the cross-slab in the churchyard, one side of which depicts a battle with both cavalry and infantry which may be that of Nechtans Mere at **Dunnichen** in 685 (although the stone is a century later).

On Finavon Hill the rampart walls, partly vitrified, of an Iron Age fort have been excavated and carbonised planks dated to the 8th–6th centuries BC. There are

7th century Pictish symbol stone at Aberlemno (HS)

also two stone castles in the vicinity, both ruinous. Flemington is L-plan and 17th century; Melgund, also L-plan but larger and with an extension, is 16th century having been built by **Cardinal David Beaton** and Margaret (or Marion) Ogilvy, his wife or mistress (or both, the relationship losing its legitimacy on his taking holy orders).

ABERLOUR, Banffshire

Properly Charlestown of Aberlour after its founder, Charles Grant of Wester Elchies [see **Archiestown**], Aberlour stands on the right bank of the **Spey** and on the site of a church (little but the graveyard survives) and a well dedicated to **St Drostan**. It consists of a long tree-lined street on the **Grantown-Keith** road and was once best known for its large **Episcopalian** orphanage, more recently for the Aberlour-Glenlivet distillery. Aberlour House, towards **Craigellachie**, is the prep school for **Gordonstoun**. To the north rises Ben Aigan, to the south Ben Rinnes (2755ft/840m).

ABERNETHY, Perthshire

Here in 1072 **Malcolm III 'Canmore'** met and made peace with William the Conqueror who had invaded Scotland to pre-empt the interference in English affairs which Malcolm's marriage to **Margaret**, sister of Edgar Atheling, seemed to presage. According to the chronicler **John of Fordun**, Malcolm 'gave hostages [to William] and was his man', concessions which have been taken to imply homage and feudal submission. The pencil-thin round tower, 74ft/22.5m high, in the centre of the village, may also date from the 11th century; alternatively its round Norman arches may represent alterations to a much earlier tower. The only similar tower in Scotland is that at **Brechin**. With a fine prospect over the mouths of the **Earn** and **Tay**, it served as a look-out and possibly as a place of rather constricted refuge for the clergy of Abernethy's **Culdee** and later Augustinian monastery. At its base there is a broken **Pictish** symbol stone. Abernethy was an important Pictish settlement; at Castle Law to the south-west there are extensive remains of an Iron Age fort and at Carpow to the north-east evidence of a **Roman** fort. The place should not be confused with Abernethy Forest on Speyside, nor has it any connection with the Abernethy biscuit (originally shortbread with caraway seeds) which was concocted by John Abernethy, surgeon (1764–1831).

ABERNETHY, Treaty of (1072)

A treaty forced on **Malcolm III 'Canmore'** by William the Conqueror whereby the Norman King of England agreed to a cessation of hostilities in return for the Scottish King's acknowledgement of William as overlord. To ensure his compliance, William took Malcolm's 12-year-old son Duncan (later and briefly **King Duncan II**) back to his court in England as a hostage.

ABOYNE, Aberdeenshire

North-west of Aboyne, off the road to Tarland, prehistoric remains include the Tomnaverie stone circle and the Balnagowan 'Necropolis' with its Blue Cairn (3rd–4th millennium BC), a 53m long mound of boulders, plus numerous smaller collections of stones cleared

Abernethy's 11th century round tower (HS)

from adjacent fields in the 1st millennium BC. A **Pictish** cross-slab, the Formaston Stone, with symbols and Ogam inscription, now stands in the grounds of Aboyne Castle which itself incorporates part of the 17th century castle. Otherwise Aboyne, originally Charlestown of Aboyne after Charles Gordon, 1st Earl of Aboyne and a son of the 2nd Marquis of **Huntly**, is like so much of Deeside largely a Victorian creation. The Earldom was absorbed by the **Gordons** of Huntly and the village owes its spruce appearance to the beneficence of the millionaire Sir Cunliffe Brooks whose daughter married the 11th Marquis of Huntly. The Aboyne **Highland Games**, held in September on the triangular village green and presided over by the Marquis as chief, date from 1867 and are rated one of the premier gatherings.

ACHAIUS, King?

It has been suggested that the Latinised 'Achaius' could be 'Angus' or more probably 'Eochaid', a **Pictish** name by which one of **Kenneth mac-Alpin**'s grandchildren and successors was known. This is not, though, the Achaius who was the first Bishop of **Glasgow**; nor can it be the Achaius whom legend supposed to have inaugurated the **auld alliance** by assisting the Emperor Charlemagne against the Saxons in the early 9th century.

ACHALLADER, Nr Bridge of Orchy, Argyll

The ruins of this castle, built originally in the 16th century by Angus Mac-an-Leister, first known chief of the Fletchers, stand a mile north-east of Loch Tulla. c1590, Sir Duncan Campbell of Glenorchy, aiming at possession, sent an English soldier to put horses in a cornfield by the castle. The Fletcher laird remonstrated in Gaelic, but was not understood. He shot the soldier and, while he evaded justice, Campbell laid legal claim to his land. The tower built by Sir Duncan in 1600 consisted of three storeys and a garret, with pistol holes in the walls. Burned by **Jacobites** in 1689, it was never restored. In 1691 the Jacobite leaders, including MacIan of **Glencoe**, were summoned by John Campbell Earl of **Breadalbane** to its makeshift accommodation. There they signed the Treaty of Achallader, an armistice in their fight to restore **James VII** to the British throne. Secret dealings were suspected and harsh words were exchanged, but it was finally agreed that the Jacobite chiefs should receive financial compensation and should be given time to obtain James VII's approval. These provisos led to the delays and accusations of ill-faith which prompted the **Glencoe Massacre**.

ACHAMORE GARDENS, Isle of Gigha

The gardens of Achamore House in the sheltered southeastern corner of **Gigha** were planted in the early 1940s by the then owner of the island, Sir James Horlick of bedtime beverage fame. The climate is mild, the site sheltered by the island's hilly spine and the soil a sandy, lime-free loam; fine broad-leafed woodland offers protection to the shrubs and plants which include rare tropical species as well as some of the more exotic rhododendrons and azaleas. Since 1962 the plants have been in the care of the **National Trust for Scotland**, who established a propagation programme to establish some of the Gigha species in other gardens in the west of Scotland, particularly **Brodick**; the gardens are open to the public.

ACHAVANICH, Caithness

A horseshoe setting of 30 **standing stones** (out of what may originally have been a total of 54), Achavanich overlooks Loch Stemster and dates from about 2000 BC. Its significance remains obscure, since it does not appear to be associated with a burial, nor can any astronomical purpose be detected.

ACHNABRECK, Nr Lochgilphead, Argyll

The Bronze Age cup-and-ring markings at Achnabreck are the finest examples of a kind of rock carving which occurs widely in the west and north of Scotland, **Galloway** and the north of England. Usually found on natural outcrops of rock, these decorative carvings take the form of a small incised 'cup' mark with three or more concentric rings. Single cup-marks, pecked grooves and spirals are also found. They are assumed to date from around 1800 BC to no later than 1200 BC.

There are two rock sheets at Achnabreck: the largest one has over 50 cup-and-ring markings, many linked by grooves emanating from the central cup. In one case nine concentric rings occur. The second area of carving is notable for one very large cup-and-ring mark measuring almost 1m in diameter; seven rings surround a central cup from which two grooves also emanate.

The implication of these enigmatic carvings, which also occur on **standing stones**, cists and isolated single boulders, has been the cause of much speculation. Explanations offered include star maps, topographical maps, records of important familial or tribal events, primitive calendars, acts of penance and 'art'. A possible association with areas of metallurgical interest has also been proposed. It remains a tantalising mystery.

ACHNACARRY, Inverness-shire

Between Lochs **Arkaig** and Lochy, Achnacarry has been the home of the **Camerons of Lochiel**, chiefs of the **Clan Cameron**, since the 1660s. The present house, designed by **James Gillespie Graham**, dates from 1802 and combines a baronial flourish (crenellated parapet, corner turrets) with gothick detail (windows etc). It replaced the castle burnt in 1746 by either George Munro of Culcairn or Edward Cornwallis on behalf of the Duke of Cumberland. This was in reprisal for 'the gentle Lochiel's' crucial role in the 1745 **Jacobite Rising**. An incomplete avenue of beeches is said to be that which Lochiel was planting when word of **Prince Charles**'s landing sent him dashing to **Loch nan Uamh**. Another avenue, now more a forest road (leading to Loch Arkaig), is 'The Dark Mile'. Here and in adjacent Glen Cia-aig the Prince hid after **Culloden** and before making his circuitous escape back to Loch nan Uamh. Two centuries later, in the summer of 1928, Achnacarry house and estate were rented by a cosmopolitan party of sportsmen supposedly for the shooting and fishing. In fact the group comprised top executives from the British, European and American oil industries trying to hammer out a formal international treaty for oil producers – a forerunner of OPEC. Their resulting 'Achnacarry' or 'As-Is' Agreement later foundered for lack of support from the United States and the Soviet Union. During World War II Achnacarry was used as a commando training centre, hence the Commando Memorial above **Spean Bridge**.

ACKERGILL CASTLE, Nr Wick, Caithness

This medieval tower on the east coast of **Caithness** passed with an heiress from the Cheyne family to the **Keiths**. They sold their property to the Earl of Caithness (1612) and the tower passed subsequently to the Dunbars of Hempriggs, once one of the two largest landowners in Caithness. In the mid-19th century it was restored by **David Bryce**, but still preserves many of its original features, including the two vaulted halls connected by straight stairs in walls over 9ft (3m) thick and the deep well within the entrance. 18th century **doocots** are preserved nearby.

ADAM, James (1732–94) Architect

Younger brother of **Robert Adam**, James followed his father **William** into the architectural profession, but all his life remained in the shadow of his elder brother. In 1760 he set off on a tour of Italy with the draughtsman George Richardson. The journal of this was published in 1831, wrongly attributed to his brother. In 1763 he returned to London and joined his brother's firm as a junior partner. Although he collaborated with Robert on many buildings, his contribution to the distinct 'Adam' style seems to have been small. In 1769 he succeeded his brother as 'Architect of the King's Works'. After Robert's death he was responsible for the design of **Glasgow**'s Tron Kirk (1794), Barony Church (1798, now dem.) and the Assembly Rooms (1796–8, now dem.) He is thought to have shown an interest in the theory of architecture and to have written the introduction to *The Works in Architecture of Robert and James Adam*, 1773.

Two other brothers, John, the eldest, and William, the youngest, were also involved in the family firm and in the ill-fated Adelphi development off London's Strand. So named because *adelphoi* is the Greek for 'brothers', this vast project was seen not just as an Adam extravaganza but as a Scottish one. The 'Four Scotchmen, by the name of Adams/Who keep their coaches and their madams' incurred the scorn of Horace Walpole who attributed their winning of the riverside development to royal favouritism.

O Scotland, long has it been said
Thy teeth are sharp for English bread
What seize our bread and water too
And use us worse than jailors do;
'Tis true, 'tis hard; 'tis hard; 'tis true.
Ye friends of George and friends of James
Envy us not our river Thames;
The Princess, fond of raw-boned faces,
May give you all our posts and places;
Take all to gratify your pride,
But dip your oatmeal in the Clyde.

ADAM, Robert (1728–92) Architect

Probably the most famous Scottish architect, Robert Adam was born in **Kirkcaldy**, **Fife**, and educated in **Edinburgh**, mixing with people like **Adam Smith** and **David Hume**. In 1745–6 he entered his father, **William Adam**'s, architectural firm. He embarked on the grand tour, together with the Hon Charles Hope (of **Hopetoun House**) in 1754. Most time was spent in Rome where Adam studied the antiquities and became acquainted with Piranesi. In 1757 he visited and drew Diocletian's palace in Split, the drawings being published in 1764. Adam returned to London in 1758 and set up practice. He was already well connected through his Scottish links and those he had forged in Rome. In 1761 he was awarded one of the two newly created posts of 'Architect of the King's Works' and between c1760–80 became the most fashionable architect in England. During that period he revolutionised English domestic design by introducing a new and elegant repertoire of architectural ornament based on a wide variety of classical sources instead of the rigid grammar of the accepted architectural orders. His greatest impact was on interior design; his use of elaborate plasterwork with neo-classical and Renaissance motifs in rooms for which he had designed every little detail influenced designers all over Europe. The output of his London office was immense, mostly concerned with the remodelling of country houses. From 1768 onwards Adam embarked on his most ambitious scheme, the Adelphi, a terrace of 24 grand houses on the north bank of the river Thames. The enterprise turned out to be a financial disaster; in the end the properties had to be disposed of by lottery. This episode did much damage to Adam's reputation. After having worked in England most of his life he spent the last 10 years exclusively in Scotland. From this period date the **Register House**, (1774–92), the elevation designs for **Charlotte Square** (1791),

both in Edinburgh, and **Culzean Castle**, **Ayrshire** (1777–92).

ADAM, William (1684–1748) Architect and Builder

William Adam, father of **Robert** and **James**, was the leading Scottish architect of his time. He was also a building contractor and successful businessman, on good terms with the aristocracy and intellectuals of the **Scottish Enlightenment**. His father had operated a building firm in **Kirkcaldy** which William turned into the largest construction and contracting enterprise in Georgian Scotland. A **Presbyterian Whig**, in 1728 Adam became 'Clerk and Storekeeper of the King's Works in Scotland' and from 1730 onwards 'Mason to the Board of Ordnance in North Britain', a position which brought him large contracts for military fortifications after the '45 **Jacobite Rising** (**Fort George**, 1748–69). Stylistically he was no supporter of the English neo-Palladian school. Instead Adam used a wide variety of sources for his designs, often reminiscent of Continental Baroque, as well as Gibbs and Vanbrugh. From 1727 he planned to publish a book, but his *Vitruvius Scoticus*, featuring most of his buildings, was only published posthumously in 1812 by his grandson. Among his greatest achievements were **Hopetoun House** (begun 1721) and **Duff House** (1735). Disputes with the 1st **Earl of Fife** over the latter threatened his bankruptcy and hastened his death.

ADAMNAN (ADOMNAN), Saint (c625–704)

An Irish monk of royal descent, Adamnan was educated in Donegal and is thought to have reached **Iona** sometime before 673. He became its ninth abbot in 679 and in that capacity twice visited Northumbria (684 and 688). Bede describes him as 'a good man, and wise, and most excellently instructed in knowledge of the scriptures' who tried but failed to bring Iona and the **Celtic Church** in line with Anglian and Roman practice in such matters as the date of Easter. He also revisited Ireland and there at the synod of Birr (697) promulgated the 'Law of the Innocents' (or Adamnan's Law) designed to protect women, children and those in holy orders from violence, especially in time of war. It was apparently signed not only by the Irish kings but also by those of **Dalriada** and of the **Picts**.

Adamnan wrote an account of the Holy Places, derived from information provided by a Gaulish bishop, but is best known for his *Vita Sancti Columbae*, finished some time in the 690s (see *Adomnan's Life of Columba*, edited by A O and M O Anderson, 1991). A true hagiographer, Adamnan baulks at no miracle however improbable so long as it can be credited to **Columba**; and he exaggerates Columba's influence as well as his sanctity. Such licence was expected, as well as being politically expedient. Yet, if one may judge from the spread of ecclesiastical dedications in Scotland and especially east of the Highlands, 'the real apostle to the Picts was not Columba but Adomnan' (M Lynch). By 727 his relics were being treated as those of a saint and, had a successor written a *Vita* of Adamnan, his reputation would no doubt outshine that of Columba. 'Adomnan' seems to have been the original spelling but 'Adamnan', implying 'the little Adam', became common after the 10th century.

ADVOCATES, Faculty of

An advocate is the Scottish equivalent of a barrister (counsel, attorney), with the Lord Advocate being the equivalent of the English Attorney-General. The Faculty of Advocates is simply the collective Bar in Scotland. Its origins are traceable to **James V**'s 1532 foundation of a College of Justice whereby the **Court of Session** was to hear civil and ecclesiastical causes previously handled by the episcopal courts. See also **Legal Professions**.

AE, Dumfriesshire

Short on consonants but long on conifers, the Forest of Ae clothes the hills between Nithsdale and Annandale north of **Dumfries**. The village of the same name was a 1947 creation of the **Forestry Commission** which here undertook experiments in **forestry** practice. In the 18th century Dalswinton to the south-east belonged to Patrick Millar of the **Carron Company** who was **Burns**'s landlord at Ellisland [see **Thornhill**] and a keen improver. On his loch at Dalswinton **William Syming-ton** conducted the first steamboat trials. Burns is said to have been present for the maiden voyage.

AED

The name appears twice in the **Dalriada** king lists and was also that of a son of **Kenneth mac-Alpin** who ruled for a year (878–9) before being killed by Giric, son of Donald. It reappears in the reign of **David I** when an 'Aed' or 'Heth' was **Earl of Moray**. His assumed descendants, the MacHeths, assisted **Somerled** against **Malcolm IV** and were later granted the **Earldom of Ross**, their descendants becoming the **MacKays**. 'Aed' or sometimes 'Aodh' is also assumed to be a variant of 'Hugh'.

AFFLECK CASTLE, Monikie, Nr Dundee

This rectangular tower, with just sufficient in the way of a projecting staircase jamb to qualify as L-plan, was built by the family of Affleck, or Auchinleck, of that Ilk in the late 15th century. Although unoccupied since the 1760s, it is far from ruinous. More keep than castle, it rises through five storeys to a corbelled parapet with two square cap houses commanding extensive views across the **Tay** to **St Andrews**. The third floor solar, or drawing room, with pillared fireplace and adjoining chapel 'has few equals in Scotland'. South, near Craigton, the tall (105ft/32m) tower known as the 'Live and Let Live Monument' was erected by grateful tenants of William Ramsay Maule, 1st Lord Panmure. On the same hill is a **Celtic** cross known as the Camus Stone.

AGRICOLA, Cnaeus (Gnaeus) Julius (37–93 AD) Roman General

Born in Provence, Agricola was elected consul in 77 and sent to Britain as governor. His subjugation of the country culminated with the invasion of Scotland and several campaigns of conquest therein. These began (80–1) with an advance to the Forth-**Clyde** valley and the establishment there of a line of forts whence (83) further lines of advance struck north through **Perthshire** and **Aberdeenshire** to the Moray Firth. Numerous forts and campsites have been identified [**Inchtuthil**, **Ardoch**, **Stracathro**, etc]. No advance was made into the Highlands, but in 84 a final campaign brought the **Caledonii** to battle at the still unidentified **Mons Graupius**. **Galgacus** and the Caledonii were defeated and, after taking hostages from the 'Borestii' (people of **Forres**?), Agricola's forces withdrew. His fleet, which kept the advancing legions supplied, proceeded north to **Orkney** and **Fair Isle** and established that Britain was indeed an island. In 87 Agricola was recalled to Rome by an emperor jealous of his achievements. Tacitus, who had married Agricola's daughter, took it on himself to defend the general's achievements in a panegyric, *Agricola*, to which we owe most of what is known about these first **Roman** campaigns in Scotland.

AGRICULTURE

In pre-modern times every adult Scot would have had personal experience of a time of great shortage, even famine. What determined the well-being of most Lowland Scots and their Highland counterparts was the state of the harvest or the condition of their stock. Except when the climate was exceptionally unkind, as in the 1690s when the harvest failed three years out of four, the old system of communal farming [see **runrig**] coped, inefficient though it was in its use of land and labour. It was a situation of broad equilibrium with landowners creaming off most of any surplus. Rents were paid in a mixture of cash, services and produce, even down to 'one reek hen' demanded by the Lordship of **Huntly** from the tenants of Ruglen's Croft in 1601.

It is against this backdrop that the transformation of Scottish agriculture has to be viewed; from being amongst the most backward in Europe, it had become by the early 19th century generally admired for its efficiency and, except in areas such as the western Highlands, well able to feed reliably and consistently an ever-increasing population while releasing labour to elsewhere in the economy. Of course there had always been exceptions to the general picture of backwardness; commercial farming in the Borders went back to the monastic holdings of abbeys such as **Melrose**; and the Lothians had long had a reputation for the fertility of their soil (did not **Hector Boece** call it 'the most plentuus ground of Scotland'?). But what had been exceptional became the norm as improvement spread in the later 18th century. The processes of change involved many elements: there were new methods of working the land, involving the use of rotations and crops such as the turnip and the potato; drainage and the clearance of stones permitted new technology; Small's plough allowed the horse to replace the ox, and saved on both human and animal labour. New terms of land layout with fields separated by dyke or hedge were also part of the improvement as were new structures of land-holding by which the old joint-tenancies were done away with in favour of single substantial tenants encouraged by long leases.

Improvement has, perhaps, too often been attributed to the activities and example of a few 'names' such as Cockburn of Ormiston and **Grant of Monymusk**. While not wishing to belittle their contribution, more general economic factors appear to have underpinned change. The growth of urban markets and increasingly efficient transport both stimulated improvement and prompted the specialisation of agriculture in Scotland (the south-west in dairying, Tayside in potatoes and fruit, and so on). Sometimes change was rapid in response to new opportunities: the arrival of steamship services in the 1820s allowed the north-east of Scotland to establish a large and profitable trade in meat to London, a development which the **railways** confirmed by allowing the transit of dead meat. But more often change was cautious and gradual. It took time for the right rotational patterns to be worked out or the correct dosage of lime to be found for a particular soil. And there was a wide variety of regional diversity. Mostly, for example, improvement involved the consolidation of holdings into larger units, a process which surprisingly seldom provoked resistance from those displaced or threatened. There are lowland precursors of the protests evoked by Highland **clearances**, but not many; the **Levellers** of **Galloway** in the 1720s are an isolated exception. In the north-east, however, estates wishing to extend their cultivable land hit on the device of the improving **croft**: a holding of marginal land let at minimal charge for the crofter to bring into cultivation. Once the work of reclamation was complete, the crofter usually lost his holding. As one crofter's son, clipper captain Alexander Smith, remarked, 'After I had reached an age to observe how farmers were treated, I resolved that I would go to sea.'

As late as 1881, agriculture still employed over 150,000 workers in Scotland, some as hired labour in the structured hierarchy of the large farm, others as the only labour on a small holding. There was still some use of migrant labour though thanks to the arrival of the reaper large bands of Irish or Highland harvest labour were no longer to be seen; George Hope of Fenton Barns in **East Lothian** needed only 16 additional reapers in 1867 whereas a few years previously he had employed as many as a hundred. If seasonal labour for the grain harvest was less in demand, in 'tattie' and fruit picking its use was to continue much longer. Despite the arrival of grain from overseas, Scottish agriculture held its own in the 19th century, as is evidenced by the substantial steadings, farm houses and cottages to be seen to this day.

The 20th century saw a roller-coaster of experience. During the wars agriculture was encouraged by high prices to produce more; every ton grown at home was one less to import in scarce shipping. And the response in production was remarkable. The acreage under grain in Scotland was pushed up by a fifth between 1916–18, some of it by the conversion of good permanent pasture; yet the reward to agriculture for its efforts was short-lived. The government quickly abandoned protection (was not cheap food the more important consideration?) and prices tumbled; in the early '20s oats fell in price by two-thirds in a mere 12 months, wool by three-quarters. Things then stabilised until the late 1920s when general depression set in. Prices again fell sharply, and farmers everywhere, whether in grain or livestock, suffered. There are sad tales of flocks being driven to **St Boswells** market and taken away again because no bid at all could be obtained. There was some recovery in the later 1930s and during World War II when agriculture once again became a national priority. The stresses of pre-war and post-war life were considerable and, unnoticed by many, a fundamental change – a virtual second Agricultural Revolution – was underway

as mechanisation gathered momentum. The tractor and the combine gained the ascendancy, and with their arrrival went not just the horse (200,000 in 1914, a few hundred by 1963) but a whole way of life in rural Scotland. Who now cared for the horseman's word? Or the world that revolved around the use of the horse? There has been, and continues to be, a steady reduction in the agricultural workforce, down now to perhaps only 25,000. With them went the stooks and stockyards once so familiar.

The problems of present-day agriculture in Scotland stem from shifts in the scale and structure of European Community subsidy; it would seem extraordinary indeed to the improvers of the 18th century that it would pay better through set-aside schemes not to produce than to use the land.

AIDAN (AEDAN) (d.606) King of Dalriada
A descendant of **Fergus Mor** through the house of Gabhran, Aidan was inaugurated King of **Dalriada** at **Dunadd** by **Columba** c574 at possibly the first Christian coronation in Britain. As pugnacious as he was pious, Aidan led his army of Scots in a succession of battles against the **Picts**, winning some and losing some, before finally being soundly defeated by the Angles at 'Degsastan' (somewhere in Northumbria) in 603.

AIDAN, Saint (d.651)
From **Iona** Aidan was summoned by King Oswald to his kingdom of the Angles, Northumbria, stretching from **Edinburgh** to York. As bishop he rechristianised the north-east to the **Celtic Church**. As founding abbot of Lindisfarne he established a community at **Melrose** which trained **St Cuthbert**, later himself prior of Lindisfarne. He died at Edinburgh.

AIKMAN, William (1682–1731) Portrait Painter
Aikman was the most sucessful Scottish portraitist of his generation who without decline enjoyed the patronage and friendship of the leading aristocratic, literary and political figures of the day. Born near **Arbroath** into the landed gentry, his decision to follow an artistic career was not made until after his graduation from **Edinburgh University** in 1701. After studying briefly in **Edinburgh** with the Dutchman Sir John de Medina – the leading portraitist to the Scottish aristocracy – Aikman moved to London and then in 1707 to Italy and Rome where he came under the influence of Carla Maratta. In Florence he was patronised by the Medicis and in 1709 travelled to Constantinople and Smyrna, his return to Edinburgh in 1711 coinciding with Medina's death. Aikman's ability to couple a strong sense of his sitter's presence within a clear and dignified formal design, and his own social positition (he was closely related to the **Clerks of Penicuik** and his friends included **Allan Ramsay** and **Duncan Forbes of Culloden**, the future Lord Advocate) were to prove a highly successful combination and, aided further by the lack of any significant rival, he quickly established his pre-eminence. In 1723 ambition forced his move to London where he was assured the patronage of the Scottish nobility that had settled there after the **Union** of 1707; he received in his first year commissions to paint the

Self portrait by William Aikman (SNPG)

Prime Minister Sir Robert Walpole, the **Duke of Argyll** and Lady Burlington. His prolific output was eventually to dilute the quality of his painting but the financial burden imposed on him by the upkeep of his large studio did not allow him to turn work away. In 1730, at the height of his career, but suffering increasingly from ill health, he undertook a commission to paint the royal family. He died in London shortly after its completion and was buried in Edinburgh.

AILSA CRAIG

Ailsa Craig lies in the **Clyde** estuary 10 miles out to sea from **Girvan**. 'In lonely sublimity, towering above the sea and little ships' (**Wordsworth**), it has been known to generations of Glaswegians as 'Paddy's milestone', due to its position about halfway between **Glasgow** and Belfast. Two miles in circumference, it can be walked round at low tide and is inhabited by about 9500 breeding pairs of gannets – 5% of the global population – in the world's second largest gannetry (after **St Kilda**).

The Craig, 1114ft (339m) high, is of micro-granite, the grey rock speckled with a blue mineral, riebeckite. The distinctive character of the rock has enabled geologists to trace the path of Ice Age glaciers which picked up the micro-granite as they passed over Ailsa Craig. These 'erratics' were taken south to the Isle of Man, Cumbria and as far as Wales. The micro-granite fills the pipe which fed a Tertiary volcano some 60 million years ago. Erosion subsequently removed the volcano down to the pipe. The exposed micro-granite was formerly quarried for **curling** stones; the quarrymen's cottages and a narrow-gauge tramway running from the quarry on the north coast of the island to the lighthouse jetty can still be seen. The rounded, grassy top is surrounded by vertical cliffs up to 500ft (150m) in height, of columnar basalt. At their base are several caves, where

dolerite dykes cut the granitic rock. About 300ft (90m) above the lighthouse are the ruins of a castle tower.

The island forms part of Knockgerran barony in **Dailly** parish, **Ayrshire**; the present proprietor is the Marquess of Ailsa, Earl of Cassilis [**Kennedys**]. There is a spectacular view from the summit stretching from the Isle of Man and Ireland to **Jura**, **Kintyre**, **Arran**, **Cowal** and the **Renfrewshire** hills.

AIRDRIE, Lanarkshire

Airdrie's pedigree closely resembles that of **Coatbridge**, both originally being hamlets in the parish of Monkland, just west of **Glasgow**, which grew phenomenally in the 19th century. But while Coatbridge could be described (1898) as 'a desolate black district of smoke, coal, and ashes, treeless, sunless . . . scarified and loaded with rubbish heaps' (Fullarton's *Gazetteer*), Airdrie's case was less hopeless. Although **coal**-mines and shale oil extraction disfigured the landscape, the infernal element added by **iron** works was here replaced by the regimentation of **cotton** mills. Airdrie boasted some experience in textiles having begun its expansion ahead of the Industrial Revolution with an 18th century boom in handloom weaving. Two roofless weavers' cottages were renovated in the 1980s and now present a period (early 19th century) display, one being a gallery, the other a reconstructed but 'n ben.

AIRDS (AIRS) MOSS, Battle of (1680), Nr Cumnock, Ayrshire

On 22 July, exactly a month after the provocative **Declaration of Sanquhar**, its **Cameronian** authors were tracked down by dragoons sent by **General Tam Dalyell**. The **Covenanters** numbered less than 60 and the action was restricted almost entirely to their 20 horsemen. But if scarcely a battle, it was nevertheless a crushing defeat for the soldiers of King Jesus. Amongst the dead were both Michael and **Richard Cameron**, and amongst the prisoners was **David Hackston of Rathillet**, one of **Archbishop Sharp**'s murderers and the ablest of the Cameronian commanders.

AIRPORTS

Scotland has 52 civil airports or airfields, 32 of them licensed by the Civil Aviation Authority, the remainder being mainly for leisure use by flying and gliding clubs. In addition, there are 14 permanent helipads. These totals do not include military fields, of which more than 120 have been established since World War I. All but six are abandoned or converted to civilian use. The major airports are:

GLASGOW Formerly known as Abbot's Inch, **Glasgow** Airport opened seven miles west of the city centre on 2 May 1966, when nearby Renfrew closed, its main runway being later incorporated into the M8 motorway which gives the newer Glasgow Airport ideal road links. With two runways (2658 x 46m and 1088 x 46m), Glasgow is being rapidly expanded to benefit from the 1990 'open skies' policy which allowed transatlantic airlines to operate. Regular shuttles ply to and from London and there are connections for the Highlands and Islands, air traffic movements totalling c80,000 in 1989.

PRESTWICK Situated two miles north of **Ayr**, **Prestwick** Airport dates back to 1933 and boasts two runways of 2987m and 1829m at approximate right angles. Improving road and rail links, particularly the opening of the M77 from Glasgow, have led to increased services including scheduled flights to London, Dublin, Belfast and Paris, charter flights to holiday destinations and more weekly wide-bodied scheduled freighter services than any other UK airport.

EDINBURGH First used by the Royal Flying Corps in 1915, Turnhouse Airport was transformed into the present-day **Edinburgh** facility with the opening of a new 2560 x 46m east-west runway in 1976, in addition to an older runway of 1829 x 46m, and with new passenger facilities just north of the A8 only seven miles from **Princes Street**. Edinburgh Airport is Scotland's fastest-growing airport, around 80% of its 4.3 million annual passengers travelling on scheduled UK and European services.

ABERDEEN Situated since 1934 at Dyce, five miles northwest of the city, **Aberdeen**'s airport has a main runway of 1829 x 46m. Its traffic figures, considerably swollen by **oil**-related business in recent years, include 39,000 rotary-wing movements each year, making it the world's busiest commercial heliport.

DUNDEE Opened in 1963, **Dundee**'s Riverside Airport is situated 2½ miles west of the city, and has a hard-surfaced runway of 1100 x 30m.

The 27 remaining Scottish airports licensed by the CAA are: **Barra**, **Benbecula**, **Campbeltown**, **Cumbernauld**, **Dounreay (Thurso)**, **Eday**, **Fair Isle**, Flotta, **Glenrothes**, **Inverness**, **Islay**, **Kirkwall**, **Lerwick**, **North Ronaldsay**, **Papa Westray**, **Perth (Scone)**, **Sanday**, Scatsta, **Stornoway**, Stronsay, **Sumburgh**, **Tiree**, **Unst**, **Westray**, **Whalsay**, **Wick**, **Wigtown**.

AIRTH, Stirlingshire

Although much reclaimed land now intervenes between this village and the Forth, it was a port of note until 1745 when, after seizure by the **Jacobites**, government vessels burnt all the Airth shipping. 'The loss was severely felt by the trading-people of Airth and trade has since moved to Carronshore and **Grangemouth**' (*Statistical Account*). Supposedly founded by **William the Lion** but refounded in 1597, Airth retains many 18th century buildings and has been compared with **Culross**. Part of Airth Castle dates from about 1500, the result of compensation paid to Robert Bruce of Airth by **James IV** whose father had destroyed the previous building before the **Battle of Sauchieburn**. Known as Wallace's Tower, it perhaps recalls the sacking of its predecessor by **William Wallace** to rescue his uncle, the priest of Dunipace. The derelict church nearby (rebuilt mid-17th century) has an Airth aisle of c1450 and an Elphinstone aisle of 1593. The latter relates to the Elphinstones who built the early 16th century Tower of Elphinstone in what is now Dunmore Estate to the west. Better known is the Dunmore Pineapple, 'the most bizarre building in Scotland'. Stone-built on a classical base, its first floor incorporated in a prickly and elongated pineapple, this

Airth Castle as drawn by R W Billings c1840 (RWB)

summerhouse was erected in 1761 as the centre of a range of buildings overlooking the estate gardens; it is now let as holiday accommodation after restoration by the **National Trust for Scotland**.

ALAN OF GALLOWAY (d.1234)

The last holder of the former Princedom of **Galloway** (reduced by formation of the Earldom of **Carrick** for kinsmen), Alan was Constable of Scotland; his second wife was the eldest daughter of **David of Huntingdon**, brother of **William the Lion**. Having large estates in England, he was given lands in Ireland for supplying mercenaries, and was present at Runnymede for Magna Carta. His fleet routed a Norwegian expedition (1230).

He was buried in **Dundrennan Abbey**, leaving three daughters [see **Devorguilla Balliol**] and a natural son Thomas for whom Galloway rebelled (1235); Thomas was placed in Balliol custody until 1296 when, very old, he was produced as an English pawn.

ALBA

It was reported in the 6th century BC that people, probably from Brittany, were trading with 'Ierne' and 'Albion'. The early Irish forms were Eriu and Albu, the latter defining the whole of Britain. The Alps have a similar derivation, while the term 'Britannia' was substituted for Albion in **Roman** times. Alba then became the country beyond the Roman wall, and when **Kenneth mac-Alpin** conquered the **Picts** in about 850 and created the kingdom of the Picts and Scots in this region, it was called Alba. The 11th century *Duan Albanach*, Scotland's earliest Gaelic poem, still gives the country this name, and it remains the Gaelic term for Scotland to this day. But the latter (ie 'Scotland') superceded it in the new language of the Lowland administration, while Alba (Albany) was relegated to the title of a royal dukedom in 1398.

ALBANY, Dukedom of

Created in 1398 for **Robert Stewart**, third son of **Robert II**, the Dukedom of Albany passed to his son **Murdoch** but lapsed on his death in 1425. Revived c1458 for Alexander, second son of **James II** and inherited by Alexander's son **John Stewart** (Governor of Scotland 1515–24), who died childless in 1536, the title has since been used only intermittently, most commonly for the second son of a king. **Prince Charles Edward Stewart** styled himself Count of Albany from c1777 and in 1783 legitimised his daughter Charlotte as the Duchess of Albany. **Queen Victoria** made her youngest son Leopold Duke of Albany in 1881 and his son, also Leopold, Duke of Saxe-Coburg, was the last holder of the title which, along with his other British titles, was forfeited in 1917.

ALBANY, Louise, Countess of (1752–1824)

Louise Maximiliana Emmanuela, eldest daughter of Prince and Princess Stolberg-Gedern, married **Prince Charles Edward Stewart** by proxy (she in Brussels, he in Paris) in March 1772; the couple – she 19 years old and he 52 – met for the first time three weeks later in Italy where the marriage was solemnised. Delighted with the idea of being 'Queen of Great Britain', Louise stayed with her morose and increasingly drunken husband for eight years before running away with her lover, the poet Count Vittorio Alfieri, in 1780. She never set foot in Scotland and only once visited England, after Charles's death. She herself died, childless, in Florence in 1824.

ALDER, Ben, Inverness-shire

Rising above the north shore of Loch Ericht on the inaccessible margins of **Rannoch**, **Lochaber** and **Badenoch**, Ben Alder (3800ft/1148m) has nothing to do with alder trees. The name derives from *All Dhobhar*, a rock stream, which descends to the loch near 'Prince Charlie's Cave'. The cave, in fact a shelter, was where **MacPherson of Cluny** hid **Prince Charles Edward Stewart** after **Culloden** and the Prince's flight to the **Hebrides**. It is probably the same as 'Cluny's Cage' which MacPherson himself continued to use as a refuge over the next nine years [see **Newtonmore**].

ALDIE CASTLE, Kinross-shire

In a commanding situation two miles south of Crook of Devon [see **Glen Devon**], restored Aldie was originally a standard rectangular tower (early 16th century) of four storeys with corner turrets and stepped gables but no parapet. To this additions were made in the succeeding century until the buildings formed four sides of a small courtyard. In mid-17th century it belonged to James Mercer of **Perth** but little is known of its earlier history. About a mile to the east Cleish Castle (L-plan 16th century, restored) was where **Queen Mary** was taken after her escape from **Loch Leven Castle**; and about a mile further east Dowhill Castle, now a vestigial ruin, may once have been grander than either, the original tower having apparently been extended 'to form a palace'.

ALDRED, Guy Alfred (1886–1963) Anarchist

Aldred was born in Clerkenwell, London, on Guy Fawkes Day. Known as the 'Knickerbocker Politician' (he habitually wore a Norfolk jacket, knickerbocker trousers, stockings and boots), he frequently stood in general and municipal elections, urging voters not to select him and pledging not to take his seat if elected. Elections, be believed, were of value to working class people only as opportunities to re-affirm socialist and anarchist values.

A journalist by training, Aldred founded the Bakunin Press in London in 1907. This brought his first of many brushes with the law when he took over the printing of an Indian nationalist magazine and received 12 months' imprisonment for seditious libel. After further imprisonment as a conscientious objector in World War I he moved permanently to **Glasgow**, establishing Bakunin House in the city's West End, a publishing and meeting centre for revolutionaries. He became a leading force in the Anti-Parliamentary Communist Federation – popularly known as the 'Anti-Panties', and after a police raid on Bakunin House in 1921 was found guilty of 'conspiracy to excite popular disaffection'. He was later prosecuted for publishing pro-birth control literature.

All his life Aldred defended freedom of speech and during the 1920s and 30s he campaigned vigorously against Glasgow Corporation bans on holding meetings on **Glasgow Green**. As a 'Free Speech Candidate' he once stood for 14 municipal wards simultaneously. By the mid-30s, along with disaffected sections of the **Independent Labour Party** on Clydeside, he formed the United Socialist Movement and worked to expose Communist behaviour during the Spanish Civil War, which, like his dedicated opposition to Stalinist terror, earned him undying hatred from Communist Party activists.

As well as publishing revolutionary newspapers and pamphlets, Aldred set up a free advice service for Glasgow's slum dwellers and rapidly became expert on housing, marriage and consumer law. These activities brought public admiration from Sir Percy Sillito, Glasgow's Chief Constable and a doughty campaigner against municipal corruption. For many years Aldred corresponded with the wealthy peace campaigner Sir Walter Strickland, a legacy from whom allowed him to set up the Strickland Press in 1938. His paper *The Word* advocated democratisation of the armed forces, defended the rights of conscientious objectors and was one of the first papers to denounce the use of atomic weapons against Japan.

In the 1950s Aldred supported anti-nuclear movements and continued to stand in elections, urging voters to take full responsibility for their own lives and to ignore parliamentary activity. Ill and failing, he stood as an independent socialist candidate in the 1962 by-election at Glasgow Woodside. A lifelong teetotaller and non-smoker, he lived in spartan circumstances and died, having previously willed his body to medical research, with two shillings in his pocket.

ALEXANDER I (c1077–1124) King

Fifth son of **Malcolm III 'Canmore'** and **Queen Margaret**, Alexander was born at **Dunfermline** and succeeded his brother **Edgar** in 1107, but only to that part of the kingdom north of the Forth and **Clyde**; **Strathclyde**, Teviotdale and Lothian south of **Lammermuir** had been bequeathed by Edgar to his younger brother David as Earl. A resolute monarch, known as both 'the strong' and 'the fierce', he was also a devout patron of the Church, reviving the see of **Dunkeld**, establishing the Augustinian priory at **Scone** and the abbey on the island of **Inchcolm**, and defending the bishopric of **St Andrews** against English attempts to bring it under the influence of the Archbishop of York.

He married Sybilla, illegitimate daughter of Henry I of England, and had no legitimate children, although descendents of his natural son Malcolm MacHeth would later unsuccessfully lay claim to part of **Caithness**. Alexander died at **Stirling**, was interred in Dunfermline's Abbey Church, and was succeeded by his brother **David I**.

ALEXANDER II (1198–1249) King
Son of **William the Lion** and Ermengarde de Beaumont, Alexander II was born at **Haddington**, and succeeded his father in 1214 at the age of 16. His reputation is that of a wise and well-loved king who could nevertheless be ruthless in the face of rebellion and insurrection. (In c1222 he caused the hands and feet of 80 men to be cut off because they had been present at the murder of his Bishop Adam of **Caithness**). More politician than warrior, he shelved his early claims to Northumberland, Cumberland and Westmorland in a treaty with Henry III of England in 1217 (sealed by his marriage to Henry's sister Princess Joan) and finally renounced them in the **Treaty of York** in 1237. A stout defender of the independence of the Scottish Church, Alexander was responsible for founding **Blackfriars Monastery**, **Perth**, **Balmerino Abbey** and **Pluscarden Abbey** as well as the castles of **Kildrummy** and **Eilean Donan**. Joan's death, childless, in 1238 was followed a year later by his marriage to Marie de Coucy, daughter of a French nobleman, by whom he had his only son, later **Alexander III**. During an expedition to recover by force the **Hebrides** from King Haakon IV of Norway he fell ill and died on the island of **Kerrera** off **Oban** on 8 July 1249. He was buried at **Melrose Abbey**.

ALEXANDER III (1241–86) King
The only son of **Alexander II** and Marie de Coucy, Alexander III was born at **Roxburgh** and inaugurated as king at a ceremony at **Scone** in 1249 when he was eight. He was married two years later to **Princess Margaret**, daughter of Henry III of England, to whom he had been betrothed in infancy. In 1263 he successfully countered an invasion by King Haakon of Norway at the **Battle of Largs**. Although Scotland prospered during his mostly peaceful reign, Alexander himself was less fortunate. In 1275 his wife died; in 1281 his daughter Margaret was married to Haakon's grandson, Eric II of Norway, but in 1283 she died giving birth to a daughter (who would herself briefly become Queen of Scotland as the infant **Margaret**, Maid of Norway); his younger son David died in 1281 and his elder son and heir Alexander in 1284, both childless. So in 1285, in an effort to restore the succession, Alexander married Yolande of Dreux. Less than six months later, on the night of 19 March 1286, while he was riding back from **Edinburgh** to join his wife at **Kinghorn** in **Fife**, his horse stumbled and threw him over a cliff – the body of the last of Scotland's Celtic kings was found on the beach next morning.

ALEXANDER, Sir William, 1st Earl of Stirling (c1567–1640) Poet and Statesman
Born at **Menstrie Castle**, **Clackmannanshire**, he made the Grand Tour of Europe as tutor to **Archibald Campbell, Earl of Argyll** and in c1602 became tutor to **Prince Henry**, son of **James VI**. Moving to London with the court after the **Union of the Crowns** (1603), he was knighted (1609) and on the death of Prince Henry (1612) was attached as courtier to the household of Prince Charles. Among the favours he was granted in this capacity was a charter (1621) for 'Nova Scotia in America' – a vast tract of land in which he endeavoured to establish a Scottish colony to rival those of the English, the French and the Dutch. Although two shiploads of settlers did travel to Nova Scotia, the colony never took root and the territory was finally ceded to the French in 1632 as part of the marriage settlement of **Charles I**.

As Secretary of State for Scotland from 1626 until his death, Alexander's strongly Royalist political views made him widely unpopular. He was created Viscount in 1630 and Earl of **Stirling** in 1633. His poetry included a collection of songs and sonnets published as *Aurora* (1604) and the massive and turgid *Doomsday* (1614), while his tragedies, *Darius* (1603), *Croesus* (1604), *The Alexandrian Tragedy* (1605) and *Julius Caesar* (1607) are acknowledged to have a certain style. He died, bankrupt, in London.

ALEXANDRIA, Dunbartonshire
'We now crossed the water of Leven which, though nothing near so considerable as the **Clyde**, is much more transparent, pastoral and delightful'. This description of the Vale of Leven, in which Alexandria is the largest town, was written by the 18th century novelist **Tobias Smollett**, a native of the area. The qualities of the Leven which he admired made it ideal for the development of bleaching in the 18th century and later dyeing and calico-printing. By the 19th century the Vale of Leven had also become famous for its turkey-red dyeing, and factories lined both sides of the river. Unfortunately the 20th century brought decline and depression as foreign markets for printed cloth were lost.

The town was named after Lieutenant Alexander Smollett of Bonhill, who was killed in the Battle of Alkmaar in 1799. Its most impressive building is the former Argyll Motor Works, an industrial palace with ornamental gates and gilt dome. Opened in 1906, it was the most successful Scottish motor manufacturer of its day, but the firm failed and went into liquidation in 1914. During World War I the building was used as a munitions factory and later became a Royal Naval torpedo factory. Situated opposite the Vale of Leven Hospital, it now forms part of an industrial estate. Bonhill, Alexandria's neighbouring parish, also born of the river, was famous for a halfpenny toll bridge built in 1836, which became known as the 'Bawbee Bridge'.

ALFORD, Aberdeenshire
More a town than a village, Alford (pron. Afford) is the commercial centre for the Howe of Alford, a rich agricultural area on the **Don**. Here was fought the 1645 **Battle of Alford**; **Montrose** spent the previous night at Asloun Castle (now a ruin) to the south-west; to the south-east is **Balfluig Castle** and to the north-west **Terpersie**. Although no longer on the **railway**, Alford has a transport museum and its own narrow-gauge line running to Haughton Country Park. The town was the

birthplace of the poet **Charles Murray**, who derived his inspiration from the surrounding hills and his medium from the local dialect. At Old Keig, two miles north, there is a recumbent stone circle one of whose stones is the largest known. Its weight is estimated at 53 tons and it is thought to have been brought from seven miles away, a task which would have required over 100 labourers.

ALFORD, Battle of (1645)
Continuing his run of victories over the **Covenanting** forces, on 2 July **James Graham Marquis of Montrose** enticed Lieutenant-General Baillie into battle by concealing most of his force behind the Gallows Hill, a strong position south of the river **Don**, some two miles west of the present village of **Alford** in **Aberdeenshire**. Each army numbered about 2000 men. **Alasdair MacDonald** was absent, but Montrose placed his Irish musketeers in support of the **Gordon** cavalry, commanded by the Lords Gordon and Aboyne (**Huntly**'s sons) on the wings. Lord Gordon, supposedly infuriated by the sight of his father's cattle penned behind the enemy's line, precipitately charged Baillie's left wing. Both the Royalist wings closed on Baillie's centre and at the sight of a token reserve, his seasoned troops turned. For Montrose the triumph was marred by the death of Lord Gordon, killed in pursuit of General Baillie. The latter's cousin recorded 'we are amazed that it should be the pleasure of God to make us fall thus the fifth time [**Tippermuir**, **Aberdeen**, **Inverlochy**, **Auldearn**, **Alford**] before a company of the worst men on earth.'

ALIEN ACT (1705)
Part of the acrimonious build-up to the 1707 **Act of Union**, the Alien Act was passed by the English Parliament in response to the Scottish Parliament's **Acts of Security**. It was tantamount to an ultimatum. Unless by September 1705 (the Act was passed in February) either Scotland had accepted the Hanoverian succession or negotiations for Union were underway, the Scots were to incur penalties in England which could make all (except those domiciled there) aliens and which would close England to Scottish exports of cattle, **linen** and **coal**. The last particularly was a formidable threat and though initial Scottish reaction may be judged by the riots in **Edinburgh** and by the 'trial' and execution of **Captain Thomas Green** a few weeks later, saner counsels eventually prevailed and the punitive clauses were held in abeyance.

ALLAN, David (1744–96) Painter
Born in **Alloa**, the son of the shoremaster, Allan studied in **Glasgow** at the **Foulis** Academy (1755–64) and then in Rome where, under the influence of the leading neo-classicist and fellow Scot **Gavin Hamilton**, he aspired towards a career as a history painter. Though his efforts in the discipline (now considered of little merit) met with considerable success, his studies of the Rome Carnival – which would earn him the sobriquet 'the Scottish Hogarth' – indicate the more domestic and original course his art was to follow. Returning to Scotland in 1780 he flourished as a portrait painter and in 1786, his influence widening, he succeeded **Runciman** as Master of **Edinburgh**'s **Trustees' Academy**.

David Allan, a self portrait of 1770 (SNPG; in the Collection of the Royal Scottish Academy)

Regretting local uninterest in heroic or historic subjects, Allan addressed himself increasingly to the commonplace, a genre he pioneered in his homeland and one which was to become a major preoccupation for Scottish artists throughout the 19th century. Whilst his studies of Edinburgh 'Street Cries' or detailed recordings of civic events remain of valuable documentary interest, his portrayal of Scottish customs and traditions, in such works as *The Penny Wedding* (1795, **National Galleries of Scotland**) or in his illustrations to the songs of **Burns**, are the earliest artistic contribution to the wider, particularly literary, late 18th century interest in a distinctly Scottish culture. Though his painting is often characterised by an awkwardness in draughtsmanship, a quality that adds naïve charm to his portraiture, Allan found this ideally suited to his genre work. His illustrations to **Allan Ramsay**'s pastoral *The Gentle Shepherd* are perhaps the finest examples of his work in this vein.

ALLAN, Sir William (1782–1850) Historical Painter
Along with **David Wilkie** and **Robert Scott Lauder**, Allan was one of the most successful practitioners of history painting in early–mid-19th century Scotland. Born in **Edinburgh**, the son of an officer of the **Court of Session**, his early artistic career was conventional – the local Trustees' School, a brief period at the Royal Academy, an attempt to emulate the London success of his friend Wilkie – but took a dramatic turn with his decision to visit Russia in 1805. There his experiences – shipwreck, reception and patronage at the Courts of St Petersburg, visits to the Tartar Cossacks, witnessing the bloody end of Napoleon's invasion – gave him the subject matter and inspiration for a painting career on

Sir William Allan in Circassian dress, by William Nicholson (SNPG)

his return to Edinburgh in 1814. Later his friendship with **Walter Scott** resulted in a number of depictions of Scottish History, the best of which are *The Murder of Rizzio* (1833, **National Gallery of Scotland**) and the unfinished *Battle of Bannockburn*. Such paintings enjoyed more popularity, but his finest works were his intimate interior scenes of Scott's home, **Abbotsford**, and his later masterpiece, *The Slave Market, Constantinople*, painted in 1838 after further Oriental adventures. His vivid sketches from these trips suggest an affinity with the French Romantic masters, especially Delacroix, and are a world away from his rather stiff, contrived Scottish scenes. Allan was a figure of considerable influence in Edinburgh and his numerous accolades included a knighthood, Presidency of the **Royal Scottish Academy**, Limnership to her Majesty and Mastership of the **Trustees' Academy**. His influence as a teacher was not so substantial as Lauder's and in his last years he was more in demand as an administrator than as an artist.

ALLARDICE, Captain Robert Barclay (1779–1854) Walker

Commonly known as 'Captain Barclay', Robert Barclay Allardice inherited the Barclay estates of Urie near **Stonehaven** in 1797. He entered the 23rd Regiment of (appropriately) Foot in 1805, served as aide-de-camp to the **Marquis of Huntly** in the Walcheren expedition of 1809, was a successful cattle-breeder (establishing the first herd of **shorthorn cattle** in Scotland), an unsuccessful claimer of earldoms (**Airth**, **Strathearn** and **Menteith**), and undisputed 'king of the long-distance pedestrians'. His early ambulatory achievements included walking 70 miles in 14 hours at the age of 19, and 90 miles in 21½ hours two years later. The feat for which he is best remembered, however, took

place in 1809 when he was bet 1000 guineas to walk 1000 miles in 1000 hours, and to cover one mile in each and every hour. Setting off on 1 June round a specially prepared course at Newmarket, he walked one mile in every hour of a staggering 42 days, finally winning his bet on 12 July. 'None the worse for this exploit, except for a weight loss of 32 lbs' (M Jebb), he later retired to his estate and lived to the age of 75.

ALLARDYCE, Alexander (1836–96) Author and Editor

Born in Tillyminit, the son of an **Aberdeenshire** farmer, Alexander Allardyce was educated at Rhynie Parish School and **Aberdeen** Grammar School, and attended the **University of Aberdeen** from 1863–7. In 1867 he went to India to work as the assistant editor of *The Friend of India*. He returned to Britain in 1871, but in 1873 went back again as editor of the *Indian Statesman*, leaving in 1875 to edit the *Ceylon Times*. He returned to Britain in 1876 and shortly afterwards joined the editorial staff of **William Blackwood** & Sons. On the death of the head of the firm, John Blackwood, in 1879, Allardyce became chief literary advisor to his successor William Blackwood III, and main editor of **Blackwood's Magazine**. During the next 16 years Allardyce wrote over 70 articles for *Blackwood's Magazine*, and contributed pieces to such journals as *The Cornhill Magazine*, *The Courant* and *The Good Word*. He wrote three novels: *The City of Sunshine* (1877) set in India; *Balmoral: A Romance of the Queen's Country* (1893); and *Earlscourt: A Novel of Provincial Life* (1894). He also edited two works of Scottish interest: *Letters from and to Charles Kirkpatrick Sharpe* (1888) and, under the title of *Scotland and Scotsmen in the Eighteenth Century* (1888), the journals of John Ramsay of Ochtertyre (1736–1814), an agrarian improver and an acute observer of **Edinburgh** society during the **Scottish Enlightenment**.

ALLOA, Clackmannanshire

The county town of **Clackmannanshire** since 1822, Alloa (or Alloway) had grown as an important port 'where the navigation of the Firth of Forth begins' (D Defoe). Defoe compared its trade with that of **Glasgow** and **Leith** and by the 1770s it was exporting a third of Scotland's total **coal** production. **David Allan**, the artist, was the son of the harbour master. But in the 19th century it lost out to siltation and the **railways** and, while the town found ample compensation in manufacturing industry, the port was finally infilled in 1951. Today Alloa is renowned for its yarns (Paton and Baldwin), its beer (Allied Lyons and Maclay's) and its glassmaking (United Glass). The last was introduced in 1750 and now accounts for the largest bottle production in the UK. Its past is preserved in a 19th century glass cone, a brick-built kiln which is the last of its kind in Scotland.

Glass-making was the idea of Lady Frances **Erskine of Mar** whose family looms large in the town's history. Granted lands here in 1363, they built Alloa Tower in the 15th century and added to it as their fortunes prospered. The 3rd Lord Erskine was responsible for the young **James V** after **Flodden**, and the 6th, created **Earl of Mar** by **Queen Mary**, had custody of the young **James VI**. By the 18th century the tower was part of a fine square of buildings, much too grand to be called a castle according to Defoe, and with magnificent gardens. Forfeiture followed the **6th (11th) Earl**'s disastrous conduct of the 1715 **Jacobite Rising**; the estates were later restored only for the house to be burnt down in 1800. The tower alone remains. Semi-derelict, empty and boarded up for nearly two hundred years, it was gifted by the 13th Earl of Mar and Kellie to the Alloa Tower Building Preservation Trust in 1988. Following an eight-year restoration programme, the tower was opened to the public in 1996. Other relics of old Alloa include a mercat cross (1690), the home of its sculptor, Tobias Bauchop (1695), and the tower (like that of the tolbooth in **Clackmannan**) of old St Mungo's parish church (1680). The new St Mungo's (1817) with a 207ft (63m) spire, is by **James Gillespie Graham**.

ALLOWAY, Ayrshire

'To try to imagine Alloway without **Burns** is as difficult as trying to see the Sahara without sands – and quite as futile' (T Lang). The ancient parish of Alloway was united with the parish of **Ayr** towards the end of the 17th century. Since 1935 the former has officially been

The Burns Monument and Brig o' Doon at Alloway, Ayr (GWWA)

a suburb of the latter and would be unremarkable had it not been the birthplace (25 January 1759) of the 'Heaven-taught ploughman'. The Burns Cottage, built in the 1730s by Burns's father and by far the oldest house in Alloway, is a single-storey, two-roomed, thatched but 'n ben, an alehouse for most of the 19th century but acquired by the Burns Monument Trustees in 1880 and since immaculately restored; the remains of the Auld Kirk, dating from 1516 and ruined even in Burns's day, are a high point on the Burns pilgrimage as the scene of the grotesque demon revelry in the tale of *Tam o' Shanter* and as the burial place of Burns's father; the nearby Brig o' Doon, a single arch with cobbled footway thought to date from the 15th century, was Tam's escape route from the witches who dared not cross running water. The Burns Monument, on a promontory on the east bank of the Doon, was built (1820–3) to **Thomas Hamilton**'s competition-winning design of 1818. Consisting of a triangular base supporting nine Corinthian columns surmounted by a cupola terminating in a gilt tripod, 'an elegant and effective essay in Grecian design', it stands over 60ft (18m) high and is set amidst ornamental gardens containing statues of Tam and Souter Johnnie by the **Ayrshire** sculptor James Thom.

ALNESS, Ross & Cromarty

A town and parish but not a burgh, Alness on the Cromarty Firth has grown prodigiously with the industrial development of this corner of Easter **Ross**. It stands at the mouth of the Alness, or Averon, river between **Evanton** and **Invergordon**. The old parish church west of the river is now roofless but was in use until the 1930s. The foundation dates back to at least the early 13th century and the present structure, last rebuilt in 1780, incorporates substantial medieval remains. The graveyard contains many old burial stones, and memorial plaques commemorate the Munro families of nearby Lealty and Teaninich. Still more ruinous is the site of St Ninian's Church in the neighbouring parish of Rosskeen. Hereabouts are several chambered cairns and the remains of Newmore Castle, a Munro property before it passed to the **Mackintoshes**. The Ardross Estate, with a Victorian castle, occupies part of the Alness glen. Close by were found two **Pictish** symbol stones now in the **Inverness** Museum.

ALPIN (d.c840) King of Scots

The 34th King of **Dalriada**, Alpin was supposedly the son of Eochaid, perhaps by a **Pictish** mother. After reigning for perhaps three years, he was killed 'by a single man hiding above a ford' while he was raiding **Galloway**. He is commemorated by a **standing stone** *Lecht-elpin* (now Laight). He was the father of **Kenneth I** and **Donald I**.

ALTNAHARRA, Sutherland

This is probably a corruption of the Gaelic *Allt na h-àiridhe* (Shieling Burn) or possibly *Allt na h-eirbhe* (Fence Burn). The township stands at the west end of Loch Naver on what used to be the frontier between the province of **Strathnaver** and the **Earldom of Sutherland** to its south. Above rears Ben Klibreck (3154ft/961m), a part of the mountain chain known as the *Crioch Ardain* (Frontier Heights). Nearby are the only cross-roads in Strathnaver, bizarrely marked by two huge stone pillars. About 1850 these cost the life of the **Duke of Sutherland**'s ploughman in **Tongue**, whose name was Macpherson. He had been sent to **Caithness** with a cart to collect them, but the Halladale river ferryman refused to entrust their weight to his boat. Macpherson therefore took them south to Kinbrace, where stormy weather compelled him to continue to **Golspie** and round to **Lairg**. Exposed to the elements on this immense journey, he died of pneumonia soon after delivering the pillars to the spot where they now stand.

ALVA, Clackmannanshire

Between **Menstrie** and **Tillicoultry**, Alva is the most central of the Hillfoots (ie on the southern fringe of the **Ochils**) villages. Growing rapidly in the 19th century thanks to its water- and then steam-powered woollen mills, it is now a modest town with Strude (or Boll) Mill (1820) still prominent, six storeys high by 25 windows long with a central pediment. Alva House, now demolished, was once the home of a cadet branch of the **Erskines of Mar** (and **Alloa**), one of whom extracted large quantities of silver from an adjacent glen in the early 18th century. In 1775 the house was acquired and greatly extended by John Johnstone, one of the most notorious Bengal Nabobs who figured prominently in the East India Company's last ditch endeavours to fight off government control. The Johnstone Mausoleum (1790) survives, a classical building by John and **Robert Adam**.

ALVIE, Inverness-shire

South of **Aviemore** near the **Spey**, the parish church of Alvie stands whitewashed and restored (1952 by **Sir Basil Spence**) on a promontory in Loch Alvie. Nearby Kinrara estate was the spot chosen by Jane (or Jean) née Maxwell, Duchess of Gordon, for her Highland home in 1770. Unfortunately tenantry to the number of about 100 had first to be removed from the land. In 1794 the Duchess proved a staunch supporter of her husband's efforts to raise the 100th Regiment (**Gordon Highlanders**); all recruits were promised a kiss from her ladyship's lips. She is buried here and there is a monument to her memory as also one to that of her son, **George Gordon**, 5th Duke of Gordon. Her daughter Georgina, later Duchess of Bedford [see **Kincraig**], stirs less ambivalent memories as 'the steady close friend and protector of all poor people' (C Fraser-Mackintosh). Sir George Henschel, first conductor of the Boston Symphony Orchestra, retired to Alvie and is buried there.

ALYTH, Perthshire

This small burgh on the **Perthshire/Angus** border, once a centre of cloth manufacture, has a mercat cross dated 1670 and a **Pictish** cross-slab in the vestibule of the church (1839). A burn flows through the red sandstone nucleus of the town and there is a folk museum. Higher up the social spectrum the Ramsay family of Bamff House and the Ogilvies of Airlie [see **Kirriemuir**] are commemorated in a monument to 'Three Brave Men' who died in the Boer War. Remains of a church dedicated to **St Moluag** survive as The Arches while Barry Hill, to the north-east, has a large vitrified fort with several ramparts; it is said to be the place where Queen Guinivere, wife of King Arthur, was imprisoned.

AMISFIELD TOWER, Nr Dumfries

'One of the most picturesque of the later tower houses', Amisfield stands five miles north of **Dumfries** off the A701 to **Moffat**. Armorial arms with initials and date identify it as having been built by a member of the Charteris family in 1600. **MacGibbon and Ross** recognised 'a most striking example of adherence to the old keep plan' beneath 'a multiplicity of turrets and ornaments'. With cap house stacked on turret, these add three storeys to the five of the tower and give that familiar impression of the upper works erupting from the tower and trickling down the walls. 'One is filled with wonder that so much could have been erected upon so small a place without looking cheap and over-dressed, which it does not, for the scale is faultless' (S Cruden). As at **Comlongan**, a later mansion adjoins the tower and has ensured its upkeep.

AMPHIBIANS AND REPTILES

The only snake to be found in Scotland is the adder (*Vipera berus*); conspicuous zigzag markings on its back are a ready means of identification. Its other name of

Amisfield Tower from the south-east, by MacGibbon and Ross (MR)

northern viper refers to its habit of producing live young (*vivipera*, L. 'bring forth alive') – sometimes as many as 20 – as opposed to eggs. It is found in a wide range of habitats from moorland to woodland, hedgerow and farmland, and will eat mice, voles, lizards, frogs and toads. It is rare for anyone to be killed by an adder bite – unless the victim is allergic to them – although it can make some people ill. Those bitten are no longer treated with serum as many people reacted more to this than to the original poison; now antibiotics are used. Unfortunately there has been a long history of persecution by man and the senseless killing of adders has had a drastic effect on the population.

Scotland's only other snake-like animal is the slow worm (*Anguis Fragilis*) which is in fact a legless lizard, as opposed to the common lizard (*Lacerta Vivipara*) which is widespread. Changes such as drainage have not affected amphibians in Scotland as much as those elsewhere in Britain, and there are still considerable numbers of frogs and common toads. The natterjack toad (*Bufo Calamita*) can still be found in the south-west. Assessing the distribution of the smooth (*Triturus Vulgaris*) and the palmate newt (*Triturus Helveticus*) has caused problems largely because of the difficulty in distinguishing between the females of the two species. The great crested or warty newt (*Triturus Cristatus*) is much rarer than the palmate but the distribution of all three is confused by introductions and escapes from captivity.

ANCRUM, Roxburghshire

The name of this village, which lies just to the west of the main A68 **Melrose** to **Jedburgh** road, was originally Alncromb or Alnecrumb, signifying a crook or bend on the river Aln or Ale, and describing its position on a sharp curve of the river just above its junction with the Teviot. Sited as it is on the main invaders' route north, Ancrum suffered severely in several border struggles, particularly in 1544 when the villages of Nether and Over Ancrum were burnt by the Earl of Hertford. The latter was never rebuilt [see **Battle of Ancrum Moor**]. On Peniel Heugh just across the A68 are remains of a series of hill-forts dating from early Iron Age and **Roman** times.

ANCRUM MOOR, Battle of (1545)

Before the worst depredations of Henry VIII's **Rough Wooing** of the child **Queen Mary, Archibald Douglas, 6th Earl of Angus**, had been in favour of an Anglo-Scottish marriage alliance. But as English forces under the Earl of Hertford systematically wasted southern Scotland his adherence to this cause wavered. Finally Henry went too far even for Angus. When a 5000-strong English army under Sir Ralph Eure and Sir Brian Layton burned both the town and the abbey of **Melrose** – the heart of Douglas country – Angus gathered an army of his own and went after the villains who had dared to desecrate his family's graves. Joined by Arran, Rothes and Scott of Buccleuch, yet still with a force only half the size of the enemy's, Angus took the over-confident English by surprise at Ancrum Moor on 27 February. In the battle that followed both Eure and Layton were killed. But if the Scottish victory was sweet, it was short-lived; by the autumn southern Scotland was again being trampled under Hertford's vicious boot.

ANDERSON, Arthur (1792–1868) Shipowner and Philanthropist

Born in **Shetland**, Arthur Anderson started life curing fish before volunteering to serve in the Royal Navy during the Napoleonic Wars. Paid off in 1815, he walked from Portsmouth to London where he secured a position as a clerk in the office of Brodie McGhie Willcox, shipbrokers. He soon became a partner and in 1825 the firm began to purchase ships on its own account. Nine years later they formed the Peninsular Steam Navigation Company to operate regular steamer services to Spain and Portugal. By 1840 the new line was so successful that services were extended to Alexandria in Egypt and the name changed to the Peninsular & Oriental Steam Navigation Co (P&O). Within two years P&O had begun sailings to India and the East by way of the Cape of Good Hope. Arthur Anderson was still Chairman at the time of his death aged 76. 'This benign and noble man retained throughout his life a sense of humour undimmed by worldly wisdom or good works; and it is generally agreed that no Shetlander has ever done more for his own people' (**E Linklater**). He founded the islands' first newspaper (1836), set up a fish processing factory on **Vaila** (1837), won the **Orkney** and Shetlands Parliamentary seat (1847) and founded the **Lerwick** Widows' Homes (1865) for the wives of seafarers lost at sea and the Anderson Education Institute (1862), now Anderson High School, the principal educational institution in Shetland. The house where Anderson was born, Bod of Gremista, was restored as a museum by P&O to mark the company's 150th anniversary.

ANDERSON, John (1726–96) Educationalist

Born in **Rosneath, Dunbartonshire**, the son of the minister, Anderson was brought up in **Stirling** and educated at the **University of Glasgow**. He became Professor of Oriental Languages at Glasgow in 1756 and of Natural Philosophy in 1760, earning a reputation as an approachable and enthusiastic teacher, and his *Institutes of Physics* (1786) became a standard work. An active promoter of **education** for the working classes, he established twice-weekly classes in applied science for the working men of **Glasgow**, declaring that he gained as much practical knowledge from his students as they did theoretical knowledge from him. He died leaving a stipulation in his will that his effects should be used to establish an institution in the city for the education of the 'unacademical classes'. 'Anderson's University' (also known as the 'Andersonian Institute') was granted a charter in 1797; by 1831 there were 13 professors, and in 1886 it joined other educational establishments to form the Glasgow and West of Scotland Technical College, later the **University of Strathclyde**, where there is still an Andersonian Library.

ANDERSON, John, 1st Viscount Waverley (1882–1958) Statesman and Administrator

Born at Eskbank, **Midlothian**, and educated at **George Watson's College** and **Edinburgh University**, John Anderson entered the Civil Service in 1905, working successively in the Colonial Office, the National Health Insurance Commission, the Ministry of Shipping and the Local Government Board before becoming Chairman of the Board of Inland Revenue (1919–22). Governor of Bengal from 1932–7, he was elected Independent Nationalist MP for the Scottish Universities (1938–50), rising as swiftly through the political ranks as he had through those of the Civil Service; from Lord Privy Seal in 1938, Home Secretary 1939–40, Lord President of the Council 1940–3 to Chancellor of the Exchequer 1943–5, where he earned an enduring reputation as the man responsible for implementing (although not inventing) the PAYE system of income tax collection. His later positions included Chairman of the Atomic Energy Advisory Committee and the Port of London Authority. Knighted in 1919, he was created a Viscount in 1952 and awarded the Order of Merit in 1958.

ANDERSON, John (1893–1962) Philosopher

The controversial and iconoclastic father of modern Australian philosophy, Anderson was born at Stonehouse, **Lanarkshire**. His father was a fiery socialist headmaster and his older brother William (1889–1955) became from 1921 till his death the first Professor of Philosophy at Auckland, New Zealand. After **Glasgow University** (MA Mathematics 1916, Philosophy 1917), John taught at **Edinburgh** (1920–6) and was then appointed Challis Professor of Philosophy at the University of Sydney 1927–58. *Anderson's Social Thought* (1979) by A J Baker describes a progress from Marxism through radical positions to virulent anti-Communism, with Anderson ever insisting on the need for dissent and the spirit of enquiry as a political force. A keen public disputant, his *Education and Inquiry* (1980, ed D Z Phillips) stresses a central concern. His heroes were Socrates and Herakleitos. Stability is a tension of opposing forces; to maintain disinterestedness, one requires investigation of *what is the case*; education, classicism and art demand the recognition and opposition of forces hostile to them. Rethinking tradition, he opposed fashionable novelty (not least in education) and conservatism alike. As a writer he favoured vivid compression. He published no book but as a teacher left his mark on pupils notable in the **law**, economics and other fields. He died in Sydney. *Studies in Empirical Philosophy* (1962) is Anderson's own selection of his essays. *Australian Realism* (1986), A J Baker, is an excellent account of Anderson's thought.

ANDERSON, Robert Rowand (1834–1921)
Architect

Scotland's leading late Victorian/Edwardian architect is remembered today not only for his buildings but also for his role as an educator and the effective founder of the unified professional representation of architects in Scotland. Born in **Edinburgh**, he initially trained in **law**; but while serving with the Corps of Royal Engineers he studied construction and architectural design. He then worked in England under Sir George Gilbert Scott. He set up practice in Edinburgh around 1885, quickly developing a very successful firm with a considerable output which served as a springboard for many of the architects of the next generation. Rowand Anderson worked in a wide range of styles from Gothic (**Scottish National Portrait Gallery** and **Museum of Antiquities**, Edinburgh, 1885–90) to classical (MacEwan Hall and **Medical School, Edinburgh University**, 1889–97); his practice also undertook many restorations. He was largely responsible for setting up formal architectural education in Scotland, organised the various regional architectural organisations into the Institute of Architects in Scotland, and became its first President. He also originated the National Art Survey. In 1902 he was knighted for his services, and in 1916 received the RIBA Gold Medal.

ANDREW, Saint

Apostle and martyr, fisherman brother of St Peter and Scotland's patron saint (shared with Greece, Russia and Roumania), Andrew was reputedly crucified at Patras on a cross of X shape, now the white cross on blue of the Saltire flag. A **Pictish** King Angus adopted him as patron in the 8th or 9th century when legends say the cross appeared in the sky during a decisive battle. Relics of the saint were brought to **Fife**, either from St Wilfred's Hexham Abbey or by St Regulus, for the church at Kilrymont which became the cathedral of **St Andrews**, replacing **Dunkeld** in importance. St Andrew's Day, 30 November, is not a public holiday but is much celebrated by expatriates.

ANGUS

Before the **local government** reorganisation of 1975, the county of Angus, also known as Forfarshire, comprised 540,352 acres (218,677ha) north of the **Tay** estuary. Its coastline ran from **Dundee** on the Firth of Tay, 37 miles northwards to **Montrose** on the North Sea coast. From the coast inland, Angus comprised a coastal plain up to 8 miles wide in places, fringed by the **Sidlaw Hills**, peaking at 1492ft/455m at Craigowl in the west of the county and diminishing towards the north-east. North of the Sidlaws is **Strathmore**, a 400ft

(120m) high vale 12 miles wide in the **Brechin** area, sweeping down to sea-level near Montrose. The foothills of the **Grampians** rose to 3100ft/945m on the northern fringe of the county, which had no natural frontiers other than the sea. It was bounded by **Perthshire** in the west, **Aberdeenshire** to the north, and **Kincardineshire** to the north-east.

Over the centuries Angus has been invaded and settled by a succession of **Picts, Romans**, Danes, Angles, **Vikings** and English. Its county town was **Forfar**, but Dundee was the largest conurbation. **Arbroath, Brechin, Carnoustie, Kirriemuir, Monifieth** and **Montrose** were the other burghs. **Agriculture** and **fishing** were the principal occupations in the landward county. The 1891 local government reorganisation caused some rearrangement of parishes on the Perthshire boundary; in the 1975 reorganisation Angus was entirely absorbed into Tayside Region, but in 1995 it regained its former status as an individual Council Area.

ANGUS, Earldom of

One of the seven original **Celtic earldoms**, Angus passed in the 13th century through the heiress Matilda to the Anglo-Norman Umfravilles, a line that expired in 1381. In 1389 **Robert II** granted the earldom to George Douglas, whose mother had been the latest heiress of Angus (the Douglas Earls of Angus becoming known as the 'Red' Douglases to distinguish them from the 'Black' Douglas descendants of the **'Good' Sir James Douglas**). The 5th Douglas Earl of Angus was **Archibald 'Bell-the-Cat'** and it was the 6th Earl who married the widowed Queen **Margaret Tudor**, whose daughter was the mother of **Henry Stewart, Lord Darnley**. The 10th Earl gambled without scruple or luck in the religious and political lottery of **James VI**'s reign until he died abroad in 1611. The 11th Earl was created Marquis of Douglas (1633) and his title passed eventually to the **Dukes of Hamilton**.

ANGUS, Marion (1866–1946) Poet

One of Scotland's undervalued women poets, Marion Angus was born in **Aberdeen** and raised in **Arbroath**, the daughter of a minister of the **United Free Church**. She led a secluded life, living mostly in Aberdeen but briefly in **Helensburgh** and **Edinburgh**. She never married or took a recognisable role in public life, apart from being an early and active member of PEN. From her north-east father and her Borders mother she inherited the Scots tradition in its two most vibrant strands, developing a great love for the Scottish **ballads**. **Helen B Cruickshank** remarked that she 'had the tang of the North East in her tongue' and from her pen flowed a Scots that was natural, effortless and strongly redolent of the Scots of the ballad. In fact her poems retained a purer strain of Scots than that of many **'Kailyard'** writers, to the extent that she and **Violet Jacob** were precursors of the Scots renaissance, spearheaded by **Hugh MacDiarmid**.

ANNAN, Dumfriesshire

A **royal burgh** since at least the time of **James V**, a port of some consequence, a centre of handloom weaving and a market town, Annan stands near the mouth of the river Annan between **Dumfries** and **Gretna**. Its motte is associated with the **Bruce** family who may have been based here before removing to **Lochmaben**. The Brus (Bruce) Stone, with an inscription possibly referring to **Robert I**, was removed in the 19th century but rediscovered in Devon and returned in 1925. **Thomas Carlyle** was a pupil, and later taught, at the Annan Academy where he met and was befriended by **Edward Irving**, a native of the town to whom a statue was erected in the old churchyard (1882). Also born in Annan were **Hugh Clapperton**, **Mungo Park**'s successor in West Africa, and Thomas Blacklock, the blind poet whose approval and friendship dissuaded **Robert Burns** from emigration.

ANNAN, Battle of (1332)
On the capture of **Sir Andrew Moray** by **Edward Balliol**'s English supporters, **Sir Archibald Douglas** was chosen to succeed as Guardian for **David II**. He promptly assembled a small army, which included **Robert the Steward** (later Robert II) and **John Randolph, 3rd Earl of Moray**, and launched a dawn attack on Balliol's camp at **Annan** in **Dumfriesshire**. Taken by surprise, the half-dressed Balliol was forced to leap on the nearest horse and make an undignified dash south to safety in Carlisle.

ANNE OF DENMARK (1574–1619)
Younger daughter of Frederick II, Princess Anne of Denmark married **James VI** in Oslo in 1589, and eventually bore him seven children. Their eldest son **Henry**, Duke of Rothesay, Earl of Carrick and Prince of Wales, died of typhoid in 1612 at the age of 18; their second son would become **Charles I**. Her conversion to Catholicism in 1609 incurred the fury of the ultra-Protestants, but her dowry of £150,000 was a welcome boost to the nation's depleted coffers.

ANSTRUTHER, Fife
Post-war house-building at the west end of Anstruther (local pron. 'Enster') has almost succeeded in joining that town to its neighbour **Pittenweem**. Formerly the parish and **royal burgh** of Anstruther Wester extended as far as the bridge over the Dreel Burn, which formed the boundary with Anstruther Easter. Both Anstruthers had a long history as **fishing** and trading ports before achieving royal burgh status in the 1580s [see **Local Government**]. In 1929 they were amalgamated with Kilrenny and Cellardyke to form the United Burghs of Kilrenny, Anstruther Easter and Anstruther Wester – the longest burgh name in Scotland. The main harbour area, in Shore Street, Anstruther Easter, was once the home of sailing ships which plied to the Baltic for timber and iron, and to the Mediterranean ports for wine. In the late 19th century it became the home port for the large Cellardyke fishing fleet, and was the major fishing port in **Fife** until overtaken by Pittenweem in recent years. A former shipchandler's at Harbourhead is now the Scottish Fisheries Museum, and the Waid Academy (1886) is the only secondary school in the **East Neuk**. Famous local men include Captain Sir James Black, who twice nailed his colours to the mast at Trafalgar, **Dr Thomas Chalmers**, Founder of the **Free Church**, and Professor William Tennant, author of *Anster Fair*. The west side of Burnside Terrace is in Anstruther Easter, but the east side leads into the former fishing village of Cellardyke. The old boundary of Caddies Burn now flows under Burnside Terrace to the Forth.

Steam drifters at Anstruther (GWWA)

The Cellardyke fishermen, or 'Dykers', were noted for their prowess at the great-line or 'gartlin' fishing, and James Methuen, prince of 19th century fishcurers, once described Cellardyke as 'the cod emporium of Scotland'. The large **herring** fleet moved to Anstruther's new Union Harbour in the 1860s, although the fishermen continued to live at Cellardyke, many of them in houses erected on land which their ancestors feued from the Beaton lairds at Kilrenny, relatives of **Cardinal David Beaton**. The hamlet of Kilrenny itself, a few hundred yards inland, consists of a few streets of former weavers' and farm labourers' cottages leading to the parish church and graveyard. The original church was dedicated in 1243, but the present structure dates from 1808. Formerly Cellardyke and Kilrenny together made up the parish and burgh of Kilrenny (originally a burgh of regality, but for all practical purposes regarded as a royal burgh like its neighbours).

ANTIQUARIES OF SCOTLAND, Society of

Founded in 1781 by David Stewart Erskine, 11th Earl of **Buchan** (1742–1829), the Society of Antiquaries brought together those interested in the preservation of Scotland's antiquities and the publication of material relevant to them (eg five volumes of *Archaeologica Scotica*). Though financially parlous during its early decades, the Society also accumulated a museum of artefacts including the cannon **Mons Meg** (1820). In 1848 **Daniel Wilson** undertook to organise this collection on the understanding that the government would then take it over. It thus formed the basis of the Scottish Museum of Antiquities now incorporated in the **Royal Museum of Scotland**. Wilson also started (1854) publication of the Society's *Proceedings* which remains the leading archaeological journal in Scotland.

ANTONINE WALL, The

The 37-mile **Roman** wall across the waist of Scotland between the firths of Forth and **Clyde** was built following instructions in c139 AD from the emperor Antoninus Pius to his governor in Britain, Quintus Lollius Urbicus, to subdue the Lowland tribes and establish a new frontier north of Hadrian's Wall. The circumstances surrounding the early supercession of the latter are unknown as are those surrounding the apparent abandonment of the new frontier in c155, although it may have been briefly reoccupied c159–63. Unlike Hadrian's Wall, Antoninus' was of turf, probably with a timber parapet, on a stone base. It stood about 3m high with a broad (12m) ditch on the north side and, some way back, a military road linking its numerous forts. Inscriptions indicate its builders to have been the II, IV and XII Legions. Some 17 forts have been identified, at about two-mile intervals, plus a bridge over the Kelvin at Balmuildy and several fortlets and signal towers. Some of these were evidently built before the wall, others after and to the rear, as at Rough Castle (near **Falkirk**). Further-flung forts, as at **Ardoch**, served as outposts. Built from east to west, the wall ran from Bridgeness (near **Bo'ness**) to Old Kilpatrick (near **Bearsden**). The best remains are in the vicinity of Falkirk (including Rough Castle), where the wall is sometimes known as Graham's or Gavin's Dyke, one Robert Graham being credited with overrunning the wall in c500 AD; other sections are visible at Castlecary, and at **Duntocher** and Bearsden. Subsidiary forts have been identified along the south of the Firth of Clyde and along the supply route from the west end of Hadrian's Wall.

APPIN MURDER

On the afternoon of 14 May 1752 four men were wending their way southward through the wood of Lettermore in **Appin, Argyll**. A shot rang out from the hillside, and Colin Campbell of Glenure, King's Factor for the forfeited **Jacobite Cameron** estates of Callart and Mamore and the estate of Stewart of Ardshiel, fell from his horse, dying, with two musket balls in his back.

The assassination caused immediate reaction from the authorities, anxious to quell any incipient attempt at insurrection in the Highlands and to demonstrate their loyalty to the Hanoverian Crown. A wide-ranging series of inquiries was set up locally; the results – the *Precognitions* of the case – were the basis on which it was decided to prosecute James Stewart – 'James of the Glens' – as being 'art and part of', or an accessory to, the murder. This, it was claimed, had actually been carried out by Alan Breck Stewart. Alan Breck was an Army deserter who had changed sides in the **'45 Jacobite Rising**, after which he had fled to France and joined the French service. He made several clandestine visits to Appin and acted as a contact between Ardsheal, exiled leader of the clan, and his tenants who were still supporting him as well as paying rent to the government. One copy of the *Precognitions* survives in the **National Library of Scotland**, although the authorities had ordered them all to be destroyed.

James Stewart was Ardsheal's half-brother and there is little doubt of his being guilty as charged, ie as an accessory. He was tried at **Inveraray** by a jury not surprisingly made up largely of Campbell lairds and hanged on a gibbet overlooking the straits at **Ballachulish** where his bones, wired together, dangled for many years as a terrible warning.

The case was much used as anti-government propaganda and continues to rouse fierce controversy even today. There has been much writing on the subject which, if anything, has still further confused the issue. Among the culprits is **Robert Louis Stevenson** with *Kidnapped* which has been responsible for the nickname of 'The Red Fox' for Glenure, a sobriquet he never bore in real life.

Alan Breck escaped back to France; he is on record as claiming his innocence of the shooting. Theories abound as to the actual killer; they include various neighbouring Camerons; one of the Maclarens, ancestral allies of the Appin Stewarts, and several among the Appin Stewarts themselves. Certain families in the locality are said to possess the secret which is still passed to the heir on his coming of age.

The actual identity of the murderer is now unlikely to be exposed; it is possible only to speculate. It might be worthwhile wondering who was sufficiently important to James Stewart that he gave his life rather than talk; could it have been a close relative, his son, for instance? Or even Stewart of Appin himself, a weak chief, passed over for command of the clan in battle, who might have sought this occasion of making his mark with his people? We shall probably never know.

The barely visible outline of Rough Castle on the Antonine Wall (HS)

APPLECROSS, Ross & Cromarty

A village, a parish, and a large elevated peninsula, Applecross has nothing to do with apples and only incidentally with crosses. The name derives from the village, originally Aber-Crossan (the Estuary of the Crossan). Here **St Maelrubha** founded a Celtic Christian community in 673 AD. It lasted about two centuries and was then destroyed by **Vikings**, the last cleric being the 'Red Priest of Applecross' who is said to have bequeathed the monastic lands to his daughter. Of this establishment the only surviving relics are a cross-slab by the gate of the churchyard and further fragments, some with elaborate designs, in the church. The remains of a 15th century chapel are also visible in the churchyard but the present building dates from 1817. The Applecross peninsula had neither road nor bridge in the late 18th century and belonged entirely to **Mackenzies**. The first road was that from Kishorn (where industrial detritus testifies to the loch's recent use as an **oil**-platform construction site) to Applecross over the Bealach na Ba (Pass of the Cattle), 2053ft/625m. A further road round the peninsula to Shieldaig followed in 1970 but the area still enjoys a reputation for inaccessibility. Cattle were the traditional support of the scattered communities. In 1792 Applecross supported three blacksmiths who for their services were entitled to the heads of all slaughtered cows – 'a privilege they still claim,' says the *Statistical Account*, 'but it is rarely complied with'.

ARBROATH, Angus

Both as port and resort Arbroath (abbreviation of Aberbrothock) has had a mixed press. In 1655 Thomas Tucker declared it 'a small town without anye trade'. **Dr Johnson** thought better of it, reckoning the sight of 'Aberbrothick' ample compensation for the arduous journey on which he was just embarking. But he was speaking of **Arbroath Abbey**, not the town which a century later *Murray's Guide* would dismiss as 'standing on a height above the sea where a dirty stream pours itself into a harbour of small account'. The abbey and the **Bell Rock Lighthouse** apart, Murray could find nothing worth a mention and so turned to **Scott**, a favourite fall-back; Arbroath was the 'Fairport' of *The Antiquary*.

Burgh status dates from the foundation of the abbey (1178), from which its early history is indistinguishable. So well endowed were both that in 1446 competition for the post of Bailie between the Lindsay and Ogilvy families resulted in the murder of the Lindsay **Earl of Crawford** and the defeat of the Ogilvies in an engagement known as the battle of Arbroath. **Royal burgh** status came courtesy of **James VI** in 1599. The harbour was already in existence and, however minuscule its trade, supported a **fishing** fleet. In the nearby fishermen's cottages haddock were smoked unsplit [see **Findon**] to produce the famous Arbroath Smokies. Connecting the harbour and the abbey is the High Street with a neo-classical Town House (1803) and other municipal buildings. Industrial development is mainly to the west, visitor attractions along the sea-front and

33

culminating to the north in a dramatic cliff walk to Auchmithie, a former fishing village. Of architectural note are the mausoleum (in the Western Cemetery) and the residence-cum-art school (**Hospitalfield**) of Patrick Allan-Fraser, a local artist and educator of eclectic tastes. Both structures defy description but doubtless provided his students with a challenge as to who could identify the most architectural styles. The town is unusually well endowed with sports facilities and has produced Scotland's most distinguished athlete of recent years, Liz McColgan.

ARBROATH, Declaration of (1320)

Sometimes called the Declaration of Independence, the Declaration of **Arbroath** was a letter dated 6 April 1320 to Pope John XXII in the name of the Community of the Realm. It was sealed by eight earls and 31 barons and written in the **Abbey of Arbroath** by its Abbot, **Bernard of Linton**, Chancellor of Scotland. The original is in vigorous Latin.

Former Popes had endorsed Scottish independence; but Pope John accepted English claims, in 1319 summoning four bishops to answer accusations of rebellion. The Declaration attempts to counter this enemy propaganda.

Opening with a narrative of origins (the 'Scottish nation' came from Scythia to find a habitation in the west – curiously previewing recent theories of Celtic migrations) and stressing the patronage of **St Andrew**, St Peter's brother, the letter summarises the evils of Edward I's tyranny and proceeds to the accession of **Robert I** 'who has brought salvation to his people through the safeguarding of our liberties'.

'Yet,' it continues in oft-quoted words, 'even the same Robert, should he turn aside from the task and yield Scotland or us to the English king or people, him we should cast out as the enemy of us all, and choose another king to defend our freedom; for so long as a hundred of us remain alive, we will yield in no least way to English dominion. For we fight, not for glory nor for riches nor for honour, but only and alone for freedom, which no good man surrenders but with his life.'

ARBROATH ABBEY, Arbroath, Angus

The extensive ruins of Arbroath Abbey 'afford ample testimony of its ancient magnificence' according to **Dr Johnson**. Although little remains of the conventual buildings, the church is well represented by portions of the south nave and transept (with fine lancet windows plus the circular aperture known as 'The Round O' which once served ships as a beacon), by part of the presbytery, and by much of the main west front where two towers flanked a deeply recessed entrance with, above it, a delicately pillared gallery, or tribune, open on both sides and an unusual feature in an early Gothic church. Additionally the abbot's house, though much altered to other purposes, survives plus the north gatehouse in the once enclosing wall. All except the last are late 12th/early 13th century, the abbey having been founded by **William the Lion** in 1178. It was dedicated to St Thomas à Becket, a close friend of William and the 'troublesome priest' who was murdered by Henry II of England in 1170. The favoured

Arbroath Abbey; part of the south nave (RWB)

monks were those of the reformed Benedictine order known as Tironensians who were already established at **Kelso**. William's high opinion of St Thomas is evidenced in the generous endowments and privileges (including custody of the **Monymusk Reliquary**) granted to the monastery and in the fact that he himself was buried there, before the high altar.

Amongst its distinguished abbots Arbroath numbers **Bernard of Linton**, Chancellor of Scotland, who probably drafted, and certainly presided over, the gathering of nobles which approved and despatched the **Declaration of Arbroath** on 6 April 1320. Two centuries later **James Beaton**, Archbishop of **St Andrews**, secured the post of abbot for his nephew **David Beaton**, the last abbot to live in the monastery and who as Cardinal transferred (1546) the office to his nephew, **James Beaton**. Lord John Hamilton was **commendator** in the post-**Reformation** period; the lands and revenues of the abbey were later confirmed as Hamilton property while the church and buildings were raided by the burghers of Arbroath as a handy source of fine building stone. Even Dr Johnson's strictures failed to put a stop to this practice; not till 1815 were the first steps taken to preserve the remaining fabric. In 1950 it was in the abbey that the **Stone of Scone** was symbolically deposited by those who had removed it from Westminster Abbey. Hopes that it might be allowed to stay there were dashed when Scotland Yard detectives quickly drove it back to London, although it has since been returned to Scotland and now lies in **Edinburgh Castle**.

ARBUTHNOT, John (1667–1735) Physician, Writer and Literary Humorist

Arbuthnot was born at **Arbuthnott** in **Kincardineshire** into a staunchly **Jacobite** family; his father was an **Episcopalian** priest, one of his brothers fought with **Claverhouse** at **Killiecrankie** and another joined the **Earl of Mar** in the 1715 Jacobite Rebellion. Of a more scholarly bent, John studied at **Aberdeen** and Oxford universities before graduating MD from **St Andrews** in 1696 and moving to London. In 1705 he was appointed physician to Queen Anne, but her death in 1714 had an undeservedly adverse effect on his medical career. Already a close friend of Swift and Pope, and with several published works to his name including *An Examination of Doctor Woodward's Account of the Deluge* (1697), *History of John*

John Arbuthnot, 'the most universal genius', by William Robertson (SNPG)

Bull (1712) and *The Art of Political Lying* (1712), he became a well-known figure on the London literary scene. Described by **Dr Johnson** as 'the most universal genius' and by the *Oxford Companion to English Literature* as 'witty, kind-hearted and absent-minded', Arbuthnot co-wrote the disastrous theatrical comedy *Three Hours After Marriage* with Pope and Gay in 1715, *An Essay Concerning the Nature of Ailments* in 1731, and the *Memoirs of Martinus Scriblerus*, published posthumously with Pope's *Works* in 1741.

ARBUTHNOTT, Kincardineshire

Two miles inland from **Inverbervie**, the house and lands of Arbuthnott have been in the family of that name since the 12th century. The house dates from the 15th but was extensively added to and altered by succeeding generations; the interior panelling and plasterwork, some of the 17th century, is exceptionally fine. Older and recognisably so is the little church of St Ternan. The pointed chancel arch dates from 1242 while the Lady Chapel (or Arbuthnott Aisle), with priest's house above, is a remarkably complete survival from 1500. Flanked by a bell-tower and sturdily buttressed, it was built by Sir Robert Arbuthnott and looks more tower house than church. The rest of the building was heavily restored in the 19th century, notably by **Marshall Mackenzie**. It figures in *Sunset Song* by **Lewis Grassic Gibbon** who is buried in the churchyard.

Nearby Allardyce Castle, 16th century but too altered to betray its original plan, merits attention for its elaborate corbelling, an arrangement whereby the normally regular courses of projecting masonry at the base of the turret are replaced by a fanciful battlemented pattern. The castle passed to the **Barclays of Urie** in the 18th century, the walking wonder **Captain Robert Barclay Allardice** being its last owner of that name.

ARCHERS, ROYAL COMPANY OF, The Queen's Body Guard for Scotland

The Royal Company was organised in 1676 by 'an influential Body of Noblemen and Gentlemen who met for the purpose of encouraging the Noble and Useful Recreation of Archery', its Captain General being the first Marquess of **Atholl**. In 1704 it received a royal charter from Queen Anne in return for a 'Reddendo' or a pair of barbed arrows to be presented when required – a pair in this case meaning three.

During the **Jacobite Risings** its loyalty was somewhat suspect but George IV placed it beyond question in 1822 when he appointed the Royal Company King's Body Guard for Scotland, an honour confirmed at **Queen Victoria**'s first visit in 1842, although a misunderstanding by the Queen's cavalry escort on her arrival left a perspiring Body Guard trotting disconsolately far behind her carriage.

Today the Royal Company of Archers still attends Her Majesty on official occasions in Scotland. The senior officer is the Captain General with, as other officers, four captains, four lieutenants, four ensigns and 13 brigadiers.

The affairs of the Company are controlled by the Council whose President is Silver Stick for Scotland, the appointment of Gold Stick for Scotland being held by the Captain General. Nowadays there are some 400 members with a further number on the non-active list. As always, the ranks of the Body Guard contain many of the most famous names among the nobility and gentry of Scotland together with a strong Service flavour, both serving and retired. Membership has always spread right across Scotland and it is untrue to suggest that the Company was ever primarily a Lowland body. Membership confers no military status as was once claimed, but the Royal Company under arms receives compliments from the armed forces and officers are once again included in the Official Army List.

Although sombre, the Archer in his green field dress laced with black with crimson lights, is a splendid figure, topped by a stiff Kilmarnock bonnet adorned by a rather tactless white cockade and eagle's feathers – one for a member, two for officers and three for the Captain General. Officers wear swords of which Archers carry a shorter version together with the long bow. By tradition, the Secretary sports a prodigious condor's feather.

The Company still engages actively in archery, practising in summer in the gardens of **Holyrood** and in winter in their indoor butts at Archer's Hall for a lengthy list of trophies of which the oldest is the Musselburgh Arrow founded in 1603. The annual Queen's Prize is presented in person by Her Majesty. These trophies together with many portraits adorn the magnificent Archer's Hall in Buccleuch Street, **Edinburgh**, where members meet for social occasions.

Candidates for the Royal Company are put up to the Council and, if accepted, placed on a waiting list for admittance. Membership is eagerly sought after and highly regarded.

ARCHIE'S ROCK, Inshlaggan, Inverness-shire

In the time of **Robert I** Glengarry was held by three brothers belonging to a sept of the **MacDonalds**. Anxious to dispossess them, Duncan MacDonell of **Morar** conspired with **Cameron of Lochiel** and **Fraser of Lovat** each to kill one brother. The eldest brother was killed at a Fraser dinner and the second was waylaid by Lochiel's men. That left the third brother, Archie, for Duncan MacDonell. Out hunting together, the two men came to the steep crag above Inshlaggan where Mac-Donell innocently enquired whether his companion could tell the time by the sun. 'While the latter was gazing up at the sky,' writes Edward Ellice, 'Duncan MacDonell, with a swift stroke of his sword, lopped off Archie's head, and the head, as it rolled down the rocks, groaned out "Two o'clock".' Hence Archie's Rock and hence the long and troublesome **MacDonell** tenure of Glengarry.

ARCHIESTOWN, Moray

So named in honour of its founder, **Sir Archibald Grant** of **Monymusk**, Archiestown is a typical 18th century planned village with a grid street-plan and a spacious shady square (actually rectangular). Grant intended it as a weaving centre but, no distance from the **Spey**, it is now better known for its nearby distilleries of Cardhu, Tamdhu, Knockando and Macallan. Wester Elchies, a **Grant** property near **Aberlour**, is early 17th century, once L-plan but later extended to Z-plan. It was the home of the evangelical Charles Grant, a distinguished servant of the East India Company in Bengal and later its Chairman, who was no doubt responsible for the Indian sculptures in the grounds. As Archibald founded Archiestown, so Charles founded Charlestown (of Aberlour).

ARCHITECTURE

Although **brochs**, **duns** and other structures now considered archaeological evince considerable stone-building skills, the history of Scottish architecture is usually taken to begin in the 12th century. The Canmore dynasty, particularly **David I** (r.1124−53), laid the foundations of medieval Scotland and its architecture. David's attempts to structure Scottish society on the Anglo-Norman model of feudal and ecclesiastical rule gave an impetus to religious and military building, some of which is still standing today.

Stone castles, replacing the wooden motte and bailey (mound and enclosure) constructions, first appeared in the late 12th century and followed the model of the Norman keep (**Castle Sween**). Hardly any of these early structures have survived and many of the motte and bailey sites were rebuilt later in stone (**Urquhart Castle**, **Huntly Castle**). The typical 13th century castle was of the enclosure type, consisting of a high stone curtain wall with the principal buildings built against the enclosure rather than free-standing within it. Prominent examples survive, albeit with later additions and alterations, at **Caerlaverock Castle**, **Kildrummy Castle** and **Rothesay**. These castles, like the early churches and monasteries, largely followed the style and designs used in England at the time.

Romanesque and Gothic forms were introduced with the new monastic foundations and the restructuring of the Scottish dioceses by David I. Large-scale building activity followed during the 12th and 13th centuries. **Dunfermline Abbey** nave, the choirs of **Jedburgh** Abbey and **Glasgow Cathedral**, and **St Magnus Cathedral** in **Kirkwall** conformed to what are generally known as the Romanesque, Transitional and Early English styles. Sometimes, as in the case of Dunfermline and Kirkwall, this was probably because the masons previously worked in England. Although these monastic and cathedral buildings were large and lavish constructions, 12th and 13th century parish churches were very simple − small, aisle-less rectangles of which only the larger examples had apses or chancels.

The 14th century **Wars of Independence** disrupted most building activities and effectively cut many of the architectural ties with England. During the 15th century Scottish architecture took a quite different path. The most significant development saw the evolution of the tower house, a fortified laird's residence and the most distinctive, though not unique, domestic structure in Scottish architecture. Early tower houses were simple rectangles, arranged vertically and usually on three floors with the hall and main entrance on the first floor and a vaulted ground floor for storage (**Threave Castle**, **Neidpath Castle**). Essentially defensive buildings, they often had gun-loops and corbelled and crenellated parapets above walls thick enough to accommodate a newel stair.

Early 15th century ecclesiastical architecture seems to have looked partly to France, with whom Scotland had close ties at the time, for inspiration (**Melrose Abbey**). **Dunkeld** Cathedral, with its cylindrical nave piers, also looked to the Continent and the Low Countries for the latest ideas. But a newly-emerging Scottish independence in design could be felt. This was most apparent in the parish churches and collegiate chapels which were assuming greater prominence. Rather austere, they usually consisted of a rectangular plan, often aisle-less and with a polygonal apse, pointed barrel vaults, a roof of stone flags and windows of curvilinear tracery (St Mary's, **Dunglass**; **St Giles**, **Edinburgh**).

16th Century
The fortified tower house replaced the castle and accounted for the majority of secular buildings during the 16th century. The original simple rectangular plan was extended by adding on further towers to form L-plans or Z-plans; often such additions were tacked on to earlier houses (**Craigmillar Castle**, Edinburgh; **Claypotts Castle**). Tower houses grew taller, establishing a tradition of perpendicularity in marked contrast to the more horizontal profile of England's domestic architecture. As the need for defence diminished during the course of the century thanks to growing political stability, the social standing of the castle or tower house increased. A stone-built house had always been a sign of rank and the elaboration of defensive features for ornamental purposes has to be seen in this context. An abundance of castellated turrets and stair towers, mock crenellations and gunloops began to typify tower house design (**Craigievar Castle**, **Tolquhon Castle**, **Glamis Castle**) and reached its peak in the early 17th century. This concern for appearance was equally reflected in the increased attention to carved detail such as armorial panels and inscriptions. A desire for more prestigious buildings was also demonstrated by the activities of the designers of the Royal Works.

The mid-16th century rebuilding of the royal palaces at **Falkland** and **Stirling**, for example, produced the earliest attempts at coherent Renaissance design. This break with the Gothic traditions of the past was facilitated by the influx of French craftsmen after the renewal of the Franco-Scottish alliance by the marriage of **James V** and **Mary of Guise**. But French Renaissance influence did not spread. Any classical motifs used outside the royal circle were for ornamental purposes only (**Castle Menzies**, Tolquhon).

In ecclesiastical architecture the pre-**Reformation** decades of the 16th century witnessed the construction of collegiate churches and the rebuilding or enlarging of large town churches. Much disillusioned with the monastic orders, lay benefactors preferred to endow colleges of priests maintained by votive masses paid for by the congregation. This development dates from the 14th century but became general, in both rural areas and burghs, during the 15th and 16th centuries (**Seton** Church, **East Lothian**; **Innerpeffray**, **Perthshire**).

The building activity that resulted in churches such as **Holy Rude**, Stirling and St Michael's **Linlithgow** (both begun in the 15th century) was not only a result of the mounting criticism of the Catholic Church but also of the flowering of burgh architecture. The 16th century saw a diversification of trades and crafts and the establishment of new markets and close mercantile ties with the Low Countries. Since David I had issued the first royal charters during the 12th century, **royal** and **baronial burghs** had become a third tier in Scottish society (together with the Church and the nobility). From the mid-16th century onwards a gradual rebuilding of most burghs was under way, replacing many of the medieval wooden houses with stone-built structures. These plain, mostly two-storey, so-called 'bastel houses', often followed the medieval tradition of a vaulted store/cellar on the ground floor with the principal rooms on the first floor, accessible by an outside stair. Such stone houses often had cantilevered timber fronts (**John Knox House**, Edinburgh) or stone fronts (**Gladstone's Land**, Edinburgh; Sailors' Walk, **Kirkcaldy**).

17th Century

The **Reformation** (1560) led to the secularisation of Church wealth. In addition, the nobility benefited from a period of comparative stability. The combination of these factors yielded an upsurge in building work.

The 'baronial' tower house reached its apogee at the beginning of the century with increased emphasis on internal comfort and decoration. Painted ceilings were slowly replaced through the increased use of ornamental plasterwork. The mock defensive character of many 16th century tower houses made way for symmetry and formality in planning and the use of mostly Dutch pseudo-classical decorative motifs, in particular in plaster and woodwork (**Holyroodhouse**). One of the earliest buildings showing the successful fusion of vernacular elements, Dutch pattern books and Italian formal planning was **Heriot's Hospital**, Edinburgh, by the royal master mason, William Wallace. In the second half of the 17th century **Sir William Bruce** and his circle introduced fully-developed classicism. The Res-

toration (1660) brought many ambitious nobles to office and a period of major country house building began. The most important break with traditional Scottish building was the planning of these houses. Unlike tower houses, mansions such as **Leslie** and Balcaskie in **Fife** or Kinross House, **Kinross-shire** were planned on a horizontal axis and consisted of a series of rooms arranged in order of importance and often including state apartments. Externally plain, the design was based on symmetry and dominant gables. The interior was often lavish and extravagant with a wealth of plaster ceilings and carved woodwork.

This domestic building boom was in no way complemented by a period of increased church building. Ecclesiastical building traditions were severely disrupted by the Reformation. On the one hand it coincided with a fundamental change in architectural form and design and, on the other, the new Church was not inclined to sanction large-scale building programmes. Most of the existing churches could be easily adapted to the new forms of worship. Of the few churches that were built, most followed a T-plan with internal galleries. Experiments such as the churches at **Lauder**, **Burntisland** or the **Canongate Church** in Edinburgh were exceptions. The use of Gothic forms still persisted into the 17th century (**Lyne** Church, **Peeblesshire**), presumably because of its conservative connotations.

It was also a time of great burgh expansion and rebuilding. In particular **James VI** encouraged trade and created a string of royal burghs along the coast of Fife to encourage sea and coastal exchange. Many such burghs invested in the rebuilding of their Tolbooth, which was tax office, council chamber, court and prison. Tolbooths were often crowned by steeples and used Dutch architectural elements, the Low Countries being a model of mercantile success. The new Tolbooths (**Crail**, **Musselburgh**, **Tain**) became affirmations and indicators of burghal prestige. Many members of the nobility acknowledged the importance of their burghs by establishing lodgings in the towns. These lairds' or rich merchants' houses often simply retained their tower house style, transplanted into an urban setting, such as the Study, **Culross**, the Chambers Institute, **Peebles** (formerly the lodgings of the **Queensberry** family) or, on a much grander scale, the **Argyll Lodging**, Stirling. Although the burghs have lost most of their early buildings, many retain much or even all of the original street pattern and planning, (Edinburgh, **Jedburgh**, Peebles, **Forres**). This usually follows a system of closes and wynds leading off a wide High Street which doubles as market place. Houses often fronted their wynds, thus presenting gable ends to the High Street.

18th Century

Georgian Scotland witnessed fundamental changes in architecture and planning as well as in political and social structures. The **Act of Union** introduced a period of relative stability, but large-scale building programmes by the nobility did not take place until the second half of the century. In the early 18th century many of Scotland's most talented architects, such as **Colin Campbell** and **James Gibbs**, leading figures of the Palladian revival in Britain, had to look to England for their opportunities. Meanwhile in Scotland the architectural scene was dominated by **William Adam** (**Hopetoun House**; **Duff House**; **Mavisbank House, Midlothian**). He introduced Scotland to the Palladian villa, often in his rather unusual style indebted to Wren and Vanbrugh as well as to contemporary English examples. During the second half of the century, with increasing building activity, William's son **Robert Adam** became the leading exponent of the neo-classical style. His impact on Scotland is seen mainly in castle design (**Culzean**; Seton) and in his public building in Edinburgh (**Register House**; **Old University**).

Church building during the 18th century was on a modest scale. Having finally adopted the classical mode, the majority of rural churches still followed the simple rectangular or T-plan. These were often plain and harled, with ornamental belfries or towers (**Cromarty**; **Gifford**; St Nicholas, **Lanark**).

One of the major contributions to the face of Georgian Scotland was the foundation of new towns and villages all over the country. Many of these were attached to estates, such as **Inveraray** or **Blair Atholl**, or connected to industries such as weaving and, especially, **fishing** (**Thurso**, Gifford, **Grantown-on-Spey**, **New Lanark**). These villages were often not only uniform in purpose but also in design. The formal planning of the 18th century and the gridiron plan has left a distinct mark on many small towns and villages in Scotland. Most famous of all is, of course, Edinburgh where the **New Town** is Britain's largest coherent Georgian development. The foundation and enlargement of settlements was greatly helped by the development of comprehensive road and, later, **canal** systems, and bridges. These made large parts of Scotland accessible for the first time and opened up new routes for industry and commerce.

In the new towns and in the older burghs as well as in the countryside, a distinct type of medium-sized domestic dwelling began to develop shortly after the Act of Union. These were usually two-storey, plain, symmetrically-fronted and planned blocks with a gable roof. Popular not only with the lesser country laird but also with ministers, merchants, rich craftsmen and eventually farmers, they spread throughout Scotland and their variations were commonplace until the early 20th century.

19th Century

Socially, politically and technologically, the 19th century was a time of great change. This was reflected in the diversification of building forms and types. The question of style, leading to High Victorian eclecticism, became an all-encompassing concept in architecture. Rapid urban development caused the municipal authorities and commercial companies to assume an equal if not larger stake in the patronage of architecture than that of the nobility.

The first half of the century was stylistically dominated by the Greek Revival movement led by Edinburgh architects such as **W H Playfair** and **Thomas Hamilton**. The **Royal High School**, the galleries on **The Mound** and the design of the New Town made Edinburgh the centre of the classical revival. Although classicism lost its predominance in the eclectic historicism of the later 19th century, Scotland continued to produce some of

Britain's foremost classical designers, notably Glasgow's **Alexander 'Greek' Thomson**. **William Burn** and above all **David Bryce** led the great surge in country house building. Their clients were first the gentry, dissatisfied with Georgian house planning, and then the wealthy industrialists and Victorian middle classes. At the height of this 'building boom' came the development of the Scottish baronial revival. Inspired by medieval revivalism and a sentimental nationalism and popularised by **Sir Walter Scott** at **Abbotsford** and Prince Albert at **Balmoral**, the baronial and other revival styles extended to the suburban villas of the prosperous middle classes and professionals. The characteristic Scottish tenement of the Victorian period was equally affected. Turrets, gables, dormers, columns, pilasters and pediments adorn the tenements and terraces of Edinburgh, Glasgow and most of Scotland's smaller cities and towns.

Church buildings shared in the general building boom of the 19th century. Scotland's population quadrupled between 1801 and 1901 and the formation of the **Free** and the **United Presbyterian Churches** in the 1840s led eventually to large-scale building programmes in the latter half of the century. The accepted style for ecclesiastical architecture was still Gothic. Particularly notable are **St John Tolbooth** and **St Mary's Cathedral**, Edinburgh, and the churches by **F T Pilkington** (Barclay Church, Edinburgh; St John's, **Kelso**). Many of the later churches tried to emulate traditional Scottish designs, spurred on no doubt by rising antiquarian interest.

As architectural forms and types multiplied, cities, burghs and small towns began to build schools, hospitals, libraries and meeting halls. Urban expansion led to the development of suburbs and new residential areas. Tenements, detached or semi-detached villas, and terraces dominated the fringes of towns. Most of the central areas were rebuilt with larger and more diverse structures suited to the pace of Victorian society. Shops, department stores, banks, hotels and office blocks began to dominate the townscape, while industrial growth led to the development of slums in the cities, particularly Glasgow, and in smaller industrial communities such as mining or steelworking villages.

Increasing industrialisation was evidenced in the construction of large factories, mills, steelworks, workers' housing and in the introduction of new building materials and technologies such as **iron and steel**. These were used not only in the fire-proofing of industrial buildings but also in mainstream architecture – for example in the pioneering Gardner's furniture store in Glasgow. Bridge building was the obvious field for new engineering methods and materials (**North Bridge**, Edinburgh; **Forth Railway Bridge**).

The introduction of **railways** had a further significant impact. Railway stations proliferated and Scotland became a favourite holiday retreat for the English middle and upper classes. This led to the building of many hotels (Atholl Palace Hotel, **Pitlochry**) and a kind of 'resort architecture' full of decorative woodwork and picturesque bays and gables. **Strathpeffer** is the supreme example.

20th Century

Not until World War I can a discernible break with Victorian architectural styles be found. Edwardian architecture followed largely established routes of eclectic design, prominent exponents being **Sir Robert Rowand Anderson** and Sir J J Burnet. The English domestic revival had its equivalent in a Scottish vernacular revival, of which **Sir Robert Lorimer** was the leading exponent, specialising in restoration schemes and the revival of the tower house. Both world wars disrupted building activities and stylistic development. The inter-war period was responsible mainly for the large-scale public housing programmes which have shaped the appearance of most towns and cities. Worth noting was a brief building boom during the 1930s, giving Scotland the typical 30s bungalow and some token Art Deco and modern designs such as Maybury Roadhouse, Ravelston Gardens and **St Andrew's House**, Edinburgh. Modern architecture did not arrive until after World War II and was used for social buildings such as schools and universities (Stirling, Edinburgh) and hospitals, but most of all for housing. Glasgow suffered from 60s redevelopment and demolition, and now sports Britain's largest collection of high-rise housing blocks. But attitudes have changed since the 1960s and clearance and redevelopment have now made way for retention and renewal. In the past few decades much attention has been paid to the conservation and restoration of the fortunately large and varied historic housing stock. At times this has produced mock historical architecture such as the **Crown Plaza Hotel** in Edinburgh. To find a successful solution for the harmonious co-existence of old and new is one of the main challenges facing Scottish architecture today.

ARDCHATTAN PRIORY, Argyll

This ancient house stands on the north shore of **Loch Etive** about four miles east of North **Connel**. The priory was founded in 1230 by Duncan MacDougall, Lord of Lorne, as a house of the **Valliscaulian** order. It, and the church of the same period, were built of local granite, the medieval masonry of large blocks being bounded with slate pinnings. About 1490–1510 a choir and a north sacristy were added and the south range altered to include a refectory, still used as a dining room. In 1309 **Robert I**, after capturing **Dunstaffnage**, summoned the local chiefs to a conference at Ardchattan. In the mid-16th century John Campbell, son of Campbell of **Cawdor**, became Prior. In 1602, following the **Reformation**, his son Alexander acquired the property for himself and it has remained with his descendants. The south range of the house became the family residence. The remaining buildings were used as the parish church until 1731. The house was enlarged and altered on the plans of Charles Wilson, a **Glasgow** architect, between 1847 and 1855. The ruins of the choir and transepts, entrusted to the Department of the Environment in 1954, contain carved tombstones, mostly of the **Loch Awe** and **Iona** schools of the 14th and 15th centuries.

ARDCLACH, Nairnshire

A large parish lining the Findhorn south of **Nairn**, Ardclach is also a small, plain house known as the Bell Tower. It stands in a commanding position some way from its now deserted church and measures 14ft square,

being two storeys beneath a pitched roof with a chimney at one end of the ridge and a belfry at the other. There is a date, 1655, and initials, possibly those of a Brodie of Lethen. Besides summoning the faithful to church, it served as a prison (windowless first floor) and a watch-tower (second floor with tiny windows and shot holes). Detached belfries are not unknown but this is the only one that housed malcontents and look-outs as well as bells. At nearby Ferness there is a **Telford** bridge (1805) and at Dulsie a more spectacular **Wade** bridge (1750), both over the Findhorn.

ARDERSIER, Nr Inverness

On the Moray Firth, Ardersier was once the twin villages of Stewarton (Stuarton), belonging to the **Stewart Earls of Moray**, and Campbelltown belonging to the **Campbells of Cawdor**. It now serves as a dormitory for **Inverness**, 10 miles south-east, and for workers (when required) in a vast construction yard for **oil**-production platforms. 200 years ago it similarly accommodated and victualled those involved in servicing nearby **Fort George**.

ARDGAY, Ross & Cromarty

Just south of **Bonar Bridge** at the head of the **Dornoch Firth**, the village of Ardgay stands near the confluence of the Carron and Shin-Oykell rivers. Strathcarron is infamous as the scene of one of the best documented **clearances** when, in May 1845, 80 people evicted from neighbouring Glen Calvie took refuge in the churchyard of Croick (10 miles west of Ardgay). Their hardships were witnessed by a reporter from *The Times* and their bitterness recorded in messages scratched on a window in the church. Many were later settled in Ardgay and at **Edderton** and Shandwick near **Fearn**. Known as the Kyle of **Sutherland**, the united streams of the Oykell and Shin debouch into a loch north of Ardgay near which is Carbisdale Castle, baronial and now a youth hostel but close to the site of the **Battle of Carbisdale** (1650) where ended the military exploits of **James Graham, Marquis of Montrose**.

ARDNAMURCHAN, Argyll

For a peninsula covering approximately 200,000 acres (81,000ha), Ardnamurchan ('point of the great ocean') features a remarkable variety of scenery. Although the soil is thin, the whole having been scraped by a sheet of ice at the end of the last Ice Age, the landward end is wooded and hilly; along the south coast road steep burns tumble into Loch Sunart where rocky, seaweed-strewn bays shelter seal colonies; halfway along its 17-mile length the trees give way to heath and moorland, providing a windswept platform for views over **Muck**, **Rum** and **Eigg** to the north, **Coll** and **Tiree** to the west and **Mull** to the south – exceptional views even by West Highland standards. Round Ardnamurchan point (the most westerly spot on the UK mainland, crowned by a lighthouse built in 1849) the north-western shore has fine shell-sand beaches and slowly disintegrating **crofting** townships, communities scattered and cottages inexorably being converted into or replaced by holiday homes.

At Ardslignish, at the foot of Ardnamurchan's highest hill Ben Hiant (1729ft/527m), is the *Cladh Chiaran*, or graveyard of St Ciaran (d.548), with a tall pillar of red granite carved with a cross thought to have been dedicated to the Irish saint by **St Columba**. Ruined **Mingary Castle**, parts of which date from the 13th century, was the stronghold of the MacIans of Ardnamurchan, kinsmen to the **MacDonald Lords of the Isles** who held the peninsula for 400 years. From **Kilchoan**, the main 'town' on Ardnamurchan, a car ferry operates to **Tobermory** on Mull.

ARDOCH FORT, Braco, Perthshire

The elaborate rectangle of grassy ditches and ramparts at Ardoch make it 'one of the most impressive forts in the **Roman** Empire'. They enclose an area of about 2ha and date from the Severan (c210 AD) and Antonine (c150 AD) periods, although the outer rampart and the site itself are probably Agricolan (80s AD). The buildings would have been of timber. A tombstone, now in **Glasgow**'s **Hunterian Museum**, indicates that an early garrison included a cohort of 'Hispani'. Aerial photography has revealed the existence of Roman staging posts in the area. From these, from the watchtowers of Fendoch (**Sma' Glen**) and Gask Ridge, and from other fortified settlements (Dalginross near **Comrie**, **Inchtuthil**, etc) a surprisingly detailed picture of Roman occupation north of the Forth-**Clyde** has been reconstructed, although the chronology is open to debate.

ARDRISHAIG, Argyll

On the western shore of Loch Gilp, an arm of Loch Fyne, Ardrishaig's claim to attention is its position at the southern end of the Crinan **Canal** (opened 1801). Passengers on the twice-daily ferry service from **Glasgow** transferred at Ardrishaig to a canal-boat for their onward journey through the canal to Crinan, from where another ferry plied the northern route to **Oban**, **Fort William** and, after the 1822 opening of the Caledonian Canal, **Inverness**. The west coast **fishing** fleet also took advantage of the canal when heading to and from the rich waters of the **Hebrides**, thus avoiding the hazardous 80-mile voyage round the Mull of **Kintyre**. Ardrishaig was active as a fishing port during the 19th century **herring** boom, but with the departure of the shoals and the withdrawal (1972) of the ferry service, now seems sadly dispirited. **The Rt Hon John Smith MP**, leader of the Labour Party, though born in **Dalmally**, was raised in Ardrishaig.

ARDROSSAN, Ayrshire

Seaport and former holiday town on the **Clyde** coast between **Irvine** and **Greenock**, Ardrossan is the ferry point for **Arran** and (commercial traffic only) Ireland.

Prior to 1805, when **Hugh Montgomerie 12th Earl of Eglinton** began to plan a seaport to be connected by **canal** to **Glasgow**, only a few rough cottages existed at Ardrossan. The Earl dreamed of a port 'which would be to Glasgow as Liverpool is to Manchester'. Although the bay was surveyed by **Thomas Telford** and a **rail** link to the city established as early as 1840, Earl Hugh's hopes never materialised. Much of the port's early trade came from the Eglinton family **coal**-mines a few miles inland, but this trade had virtually vanished by the eve of World War II – as had the small **herring** fishing fleet also based at Ardrossan.

Although a number of antiquities (mainly hill forts) can be found in the immediate hinterland, few major historical sites exist in the town. The remains of a (probably) 12th century castle overlook central Ardrossan, and are reputed to have had associations with **William Wallace**. The building is said to have been demolished by Cromwell.

Small-scale **shipbuilding** began in Ardrossan in the mid-19th century and petered out by the early 1970s. A small specialist **oil** refinery remains; but so does unemployment. Exports of **steel** from the Garnock Valley ended with the collapse of that industry in the 1970s. In the mid-1980s the Three Towns Housing Association began extensive rehabilitation work in Ardrossan, but sub-standard housing remains a serious problem.

ARDTORNISH CASTLE, Morvern, Argyll

Overlooking the Sound of **Mull** near **Lochaline**, this ruined hall-house with walls nearly 3m thick was crudely 'restored' in 1873 and 1914. Surviving details indicate 12th–13th century origins. Disappointing at close range, the massive block is still impressive from seaward; there are subsidiary buildings below, and several landing places. In its prime Ardtornish could signal to **Duart** and **Aros**, and its war galleys commanded the seaway. Built by heirs of **Somerled**, it became a principal castle of the **MacDonald Lords of the Isles**. John, 1st Lord, died there in 1387, and his great-grandson the 4th Lord conferred there with Edward IV of England's ambassadors in 1462, signing the Treaty of Ardtornish (or **Westminster-Ardtornish**) which led to the forfeiture of the Lordship in 1493. Thereafter the MacLeans of Kingairloch held the site until the 17th century.

ARDVRECK CASTLE, Nr Inchnadamph, Sutherland

The gaunt ruins of Ardvreck rise to three storeys on a peninsula jutting into Loch Assynt. Built by the **MacLeods** who acquired Assynt in the 13th century, the castle is said to date from 1490, or sometimes 1590. More certainly, in 1650 the laird of Assynt was responsible for capturing **James Graham, Marquis of Montrose**, after the latter's defeat at the **Battle of Carbisdale** which ended his brief second campaign on behalf of the future **Charles II**. Montrose was held at Ardvreck prior to being despatched to **Edinburgh** and the gallows. Not long after the **Mackenzies** established themselves in Assynt and built nearby Calda House. Both Calda and Ardvreck were destroyed by fire in the 18th century. The latter, long inhabited by a wicked old dowager, is said to have been struck by lightning after five years of dismal harvests and fruitless **fishing**. A curse had evidently been put upon the district and few doubted but that the harridan at Ardvreck had a hand in it.

ARGYLL

Second only in area to its northern neighbour **Inverness-shire,** the county of Argyll comprises 1,712,321 acres (692,967ha), or 1,788,834 acres if waters, marsh and foreshore are taken into account. It stretches 115 miles from north to south with a coastline so indented that its total length is some 2290 miles. Bounded by Inverness-shire on the north and **Perthshire** and

Dredging the docks at Ardrossan in the late 19th century (GWWA)

Dunbartonshire to the east, it contains the 3689ft (1124m) peak of Ben **Cruachan**, while its southernmost point, the **Mull of Kintyre**, is further south than the Northumbrian town of Amble. The county contains some 90 islands, the most important being **Mull**, **Iona**, **Tiree**, **Lismore**, **Jura**, **Islay**, **Gigha** and **Colonsay**, and many sea lochs, including Lochs Fyne, Long, **Etive**, Linnhe and Sunart as well as the freshwater **Loch Awe**. Nearly all of the county passed into the Argyll & Bute District of Strathclyde Region in the **local government** reorganisation of 1975, although the **Ardnamurchan** area and electoral divisions of **Ballachulish** and **Kinlochleven** were lost to Highland Region. With the return to unitary authorities in 1995, however, the

Glen Shira, near Inveraray, Argyll, probably by Patrick Nasmyth (NGS)

northern part of Dunbartonshire including the town of **Helensburgh** became part of the Argyll & Bute Council Area. Argyll's county town is **Lochgilphead**; the other important burghs are **Campbeltown, Dunoon, Inveraray, Oban** and **Tobermory**. In 1996 the population of Argyll & Bute was estimated at 89,461 but the shifting of boundaries makes it hard to compare this with previous figures.

ARGYLL, Earldom, Marquisate and Dukedom of

Since their support of **Robert I** (the Bruce) the chiefly line of the **Campbells** of **Loch Awe** had enjoyed the monarch's confidence. On the erection of Parliamentary Peers from the body of landholders, Sir Duncan Campbell of Loch Awe had been named Lord Campbell in 1445. His grandson and successor Colin was promoted to be Earl of **Argyll** in 1457. He held a number of important offices under the Crown and married the joint heiress of the **Stewart** Lords of **Lorne**, adding that dynastically important title to his own as the result of a deal with his wife's uncle. The **8th Earl** was created Marquis of Argyll by **Charles I** in 1641 but lost his head on the scaffold at the Restoration when the Argyll titles were forfeited. His son the **9th Earl** was restored to that title but not to the marquisate which lapsed. He too was to be beheaded but his son, **Archibald the 10th Earl**, was created Duke of Argyll and Marquis of **Kintyre** and Lorne in 1701. The **2nd Duke**, a famous soldier politician, was in 1719 also created Duke of Greenwich but on being succeeded by his brother Archibald who had already been created Earl of **Islay** in his own right, the Greenwich title, which had been granted to the 2nd Duke and his heirs of the body only, came to an end. After the marriage of the Marquis of

Lorne (later 9th Duke of Argyll) to her daughter HRH Princess Louise, **Queen Victoria** wanted to make her son-in-law a duke. His father, however, successfully pleaded against this on the grounds that there was no greater honour in Scotland than the already existing Dukedom of Argyll. But in 1892 the 8th Duke of Argyll was granted this title again as a UK Dukedom as well as a Scottish one. He thus became entitled to a permanent seat in the House of Lords instead of having to undergo periodic election to become one of the few representative Scottish Peers so qualified to attend.

ARGYLL & SUTHERLAND HIGHLANDERS, The (Princess Louise's)

The present regiment dates from 1881 when the 91st Argyllshire Highlanders were amalgamated with the 93rd Sutherland Highlanders. At the same time the Highland Borderers Light Infantry Militia, the Royal Renfrew Militia, and the existing Volunteer Infantry Battalions of the Counties of **Argyll**, **Dumbarton**, **Stirling**, **Clackmannan** and **Kinross** also became part of the new regiment.

The 91st (originally 98th, renumbered 1798) was raised on behalf of the **Duke of Argyll** by Sir Duncan Campbell of Lochnell in 1794. They saw early service at the Cape, fought through the Peninsular Campaign and during the 19th century saw much action in South Africa. In 1809 they were among those regiments who lost the **kilt** and their Highland identity; in 1864 they were clothed once more in **tartan**, this time in trews of the Campbell of Cawdor sett.

The 93rd were raised by General William Wemyss of Wemyss, cousin of the Countess of Sutherland, and were embodied in 1800. They were badly mauled at the Battle of New Orleans in 1812, won imperishable renown in the Crimea as 'The Thin Red Line' at Balaclava, and at the Relief of Lucknow during the Indian Mutiny won six VCs.

In World War I the Argylls raised 27 battalions winning 78 battle honours. In World War II battalions of the Argylls fought in France in 1940, North Africa, Crete, Abyssinia, Malaya, Sicily, Italy and north-west Europe and were awarded 61 battle honours, which the two awarded in Korea brought to a grand total of 161 for the regiment. Since then the 1st Battalion has seen probably more active service than any other infantry unit in the army: Palestine, Korea, Suez, Cyprus, Borneo, Aden and Northern Ireland. In 1971 the 1st Battalion was threatened with disbandment. A massive petition was signed by over a million people and the Argylls survived as a single company and were restored to full battalion strength the following year.

Since 1881 the regimental tartan has been the Government sett worn by the 91st on raising and by the 93rd throughout its service. The regiment marches past in quick and slow time to 'Hielan' Laddie', 'The Campbells are Coming', 'The Skye Boat Song' (pipes) and 'The Thin Red Line' and 'The Garb of Old Gaul' (band). Dress distinctions include the red and white dicing on the glengarry, and the 'swinging six' white tassels of the dress sporran. Her Majesty the Queen has been Colonel-in-Chief of the regiment since 1947.

ARGYLL'S RISING (1685)

Archibald Campbell, 9th Earl of Argyll (son of the 1st Marquis) offered a qualified acceptance of the self-contradictory Second **Test Act** (1681) and was condemned for treason. He escaped to Holland in disguise, where he joined other exiles plotting to secure the **Duke of Monmouth**'s succession to **Charles II** – a plot deeply penetrated by spies, and over-optimistic about likely support at home. In April 1685 Monmouth sailed for Somerset and Argyll for **Kintyre**. The Marquis of **Atholl**, administering Argyll's forfeited estates, already had troops at **Inveraray** and was joined by other clans loyal to **James VII**. After briefly holding **Tarbert** and Eilean Dearg castles, Argyll marched towards **Glasgow** but his forces deserted him; in June he was executed, like his father, at **Edinburgh**. His supporters and many innocent clansmen were severely treated and plundered; damage claims later cost the loyalists dear and weakened **Jacobite** support, Atholl himself eventually turning against King James.

ARISAIG, Inverness-shire.

A village and district in south **Morar**, Arisaig has some of the finest sandy beaches in Britain and is closely associated with the escapades of **Prince Charles Edward Stewart** who landed at **Loch nan Uamh** in July 1745 and eventually escaped back to France from there in September 1746. The village stands at the head of Loch nan Cealt (Ceall, Cilltean), the loch of the churches, and contains besides the tall St Mary's Catholic Church (the population is largely Catholic) the remains of a 16th century church dedicated to the Celtic **St Maelrubha** (from whom **Loch Maree** in **Ross**-shire derives its name). In the churchyard is buried the great Gaelic poet and **Jacobite**, **Alexander MacDonald** (Alasdair mac Mhaigstir Alasdair), who hailed from **Loch Shiel**. Loch nan Cealt witnessed the post-**Culloden** engagement between some English frigates and the two French ships sent to supply the Jacobites. The French escaped after landing their gold which was then carried to Loch Arkaig, hidden and, it is said, never found. In World War II Arisaig House, now a hotel, was the headquarters for the Special Operations Executive (SOE) whose agents trained in the area prior to being dropped in occupied territory.

ARKAIG, Loch and River, Inverness-shire

The loch, of great beauty, is 12 miles long; the river, beside which stands **Achnacarry**, is barely one mile long. Hereabouts, possibly in the loch, a hoard of gold bullion was supposedly buried in 1746. Sent from France to meet **Jacobite** expenses, it arrived too late, **Prince Charles Edward** having already made his escape. Part was nevertheless landed, spirited into the hills, and hidden – the Arkaig, or Jacobite, Treasure. The mystery of its whereabouts remains, in spite of heavy trolling of the loch for its large cannibal trout.

ARKINHOLM, Battle of (1455)

As the last crushing blow in **James II**'s defeat of the Black Douglases, a force of 200 men from the leading Borders families under the Laird of Johnstone overwhelmed the remaining Douglas supporters. **James, 9th Earl of Douglas**, had already fled over the border to

England, but his three brothers, Archibald, Earl of **Moray**, Hugh, Earl of Ormond, and John, Lord Balvenie, made a final stand at Arkinholm on the Esk near Langholm. Their defeat was total; Moray was killed in the battle, Ormond was captured and executed, while Balvenie fled over the border to join his brother.

ARMSTRONG, Johnnie (d.1529) Border Reiver

A particularly dashing scion of the unruly Borders family of Armstrong, Johnnie's main stronghold, of which no trace now remains, was Gilnockie Tower on the river Esk near **Langholm**, although his secondary castle, **Hollows Tower**, is still an impressive ruin. Immortalised as the 'Borders Bandit' by the **ballad** 'Johnnie Armstrong', his exploits made a mockery of the authority of **James V** in the notoriously lawless Debateable Lands. He was finally captured by a ruse devised by the 17-year-old King who invited the Armstrongs to a 'conference' at Caerlanrig Chapel in Teviotdale in 1529. Johnnie arrived with his usual train of 36 followers only to find himself surrounded by the King's far larger army. Despite his offers to make a deal, Johnnie Armstrong and his 36 followers were all hanged as an example to other reivers and freebooters who flouted the King's Law.

ARMSTRONG, William, 'Kinmont Willie' (c1530–post 1597) Border Reiver

One of the most successful of the Border Reivers, at the height of his career 'Kinmont Willie' (so-called after his keep at Kinmont near Canonbie in **Dumfriesshire**) could rally up to 1000 horsemen for his raids into Northumberland and Cumberland, on one occasion driving off an estimated 3000 head of cattle and sheep. Not averse to plundering north of the border too, he joined the **Earls of Bothwell** and **Home** on a raid in 1585 against **James VI** at **Stirling**. His disregard for any authority was so blatant that it became almost a matter of honour with the Wardens on both sides of the border to see who could catch him first. In the event it was the English deputy warden who, by dint of breaching a pre-arranged day of truce with the reivers, captured Willie and marched him off to Carlisle Castle. So incensed were his Scottish counterparts at this treachery that Walter Scott of Buccleuch, Keeper of Liddesdale and a kinsman of Willie's, took matters into his own hands and raided Carlisle.

And have they ta'en him, Kinmont Willie,
Against the truce of Border tide?
And forgotten that the bold Buccleuch
Is Keeper here on the Scottish side?

(from the **ballad** 'Kinmont Willie', retold by **Sir Walter Scott** in *Minstrelsy of the Scottish Border*)

The famous raid on Carlisle Castle became part of Borders folklore, and resulted in a distinct cooling of relations between the Scottish and English Border Wardens. Willie himself, in the best tradition of outlaws, died in his bed, although the exact date and location of his death remain unknown.

ARNISTON HOUSE, Nr Gorebridge, Midlothian

William Adam designed Arniston House for **Robert Dundas** (1685–1753), son of Robert Dundas, Lord Arniston, on the site of an older house on the estate from which the family took their title. Commissioned before the death of Lord Arniston in 1726, the house was incomplete at the time of the architect's (1748), whereupon it was taken over by his son John Adam. The nine-bay balustraded front, connected to twin pavilions on either side of the forecourt, has not benefited from the addition of a Victorian porch; the interiors, completed c1755, have some notable baroque plasterwork by Joseph Enzer.

ARNOT, Hugo (1749–87) Lawyer and Historian

The son of a **Leith** merchant and ship-owner named Pollock (but taking his mother's maiden name on falling heir to Balcormo, **Fife**), Arnot joined the **Faculty of Advocates** in 1872; asthma aggravated by exertion precluded his anticipated rise to stardom at the bar. He, who had in his youth clattered on horseback to the end of Leith Pier in a high sea, became very nervous – a condition attributable to his incredible thinness. That this Falstaff in reverse 'looked like his meat' was the jest of **Henry Erskine** when he spotted him eating dried haddock in **Edinburgh**'s **High Street**. However Arnot's ability, public spirit and extreme eccentricity – combined with his caustic wit – guaranteed popularity among such **Scottish Enlightenment** figures as **Henry Home**. He first published *An Essay on Nothing* in 1776; his wonderful *History of Edinburgh* followed in 1778. In 1785 his *Collection of Celebrated Criminal Trials* consolidated his reputation as a chronicler.

AROS CASTLE, Isle of Mull

A ruined 13th century castle on a rocky promontory, Aros faces **Ardtornish** across the Sound of **Mull**. It was a hall-house within a curtain wall. The ground level is now choked with fallen masonry; the main entrance to the living quarters was probably an external stair, as at **Dunstaffnage**. The first-floor doorway, facing landward, is traceable, and one handsome window looks south. Built by the **MacDougall** heirs of **Somerled**, Aros may be one of four castles whose surrender to Scotland was demanded by **Alexander II** in 1249. It passed to the **MacDonalds** and thence to the **MacLeans**, and in 1608 was the scene of a notorious Court when **James VI**'s Commissioner seized many island chiefs. Last garrisoned in 1690, by **Campbells**, it was 'ruinous and useless' soon after. A dun, Cnoc na Sroine, above Glenaros, sights across Mull to Loch na Keal; it may possibly have been re-used as a signal station or site for warning beacons.

ARRAN, Earls of

The island of **Arran** was bestowed by King **Somerled** on his son Angus and claimed *jure uxoris* in 1255 by Alexander Stewart, co-Regent of Scotland. It passed from Norwegian to Scottish sovereignty in 1266 and was first erected into an earldom in 1467 in favour of Thomas Boyd when he married **James III**'s sister Mary. When the Boyds lost power and were forfeited, Mary was torn from the husband she loved and married instead to the relatively elderly James, Lord Hamilton, in 1474. Their son, also **James Lord Hamilton**, was created Earl of Arran in 1503, and the title remained in Hamilton hands except for the interval in which James Stewart was appointed guardian to the mad Earl in 1580 and was given his title by **James VI** in the following year. After Stewart's downfall in 1586 (his head was placed on the end of a spear, his body consumed by dogs and swine), it was restored to the lunatic Earl. On the latter's death in 1609 it passed to his nephew the 2nd **Marquis of Hamilton**. So the island of Arran remained the property of this great family until its last heiress, the Duchess of Montrose, bequeathed it to the **National Trust for Scotland**. The Irish Earldom of Arran, a creation of 1762, has no connection with this island or its rulers.

ARRAN, Isle of, Firth of Clyde

The island of Arran (Gaelic 'peaked island') lies in the Firth of **Clyde** 14 miles from the mainland coast to the east and four miles from the **Kintyre** peninsula to the west, from which it is separated by Kilbrannan sound. The population of about 3500 trebles in summer. Arran is linked to the Lowlands by the car ferry from Brodick to **Ardrossan** and to the Highlands at Claonaig in Kintyre, reached by car ferry from Lochranza. Arran is 20 miles long and 10 miles wide, encircled by 56 miles of coast road, much of it on the 25ft raised beach. Only two roads cross the island; the 'string road' across the middle from **Brodick** to Blackwaterfoot and another road across the south-eastern corner from Lamlash to Lagg.

Often described as a microcosm of the Scottish landscape, the island is divided in two by the Highland Boundary Fault. The northern half is rough and mountainous. The highest hill is the granitic Goat Fell (2868ft/874m; Norse: *geit-fjall*, 'goat-mountain'), an igneous intrusion into surrounding Devonian sandstones and schists. The rugged peaks of Beinn Bhreac (2332ft/711m) and Beinn Tarsuinn (2706ft/825m) are visible over a wide area of the west of Scotland. From **Islay** and **Jura** they are seen over the top of Kintyre, while they can also be seen from tall buildings in **Glasgow**. The profile of the 'Sleeping Warrior' of Arran as seen from the Clyde coast is unforgettable.

The southern half of the island has a gentler landscape, reflecting the underlying **geology** which is mostly New Red Sandstone, cut by igneous dykes. Glacial erratics brought from the northern mountains during the last Ice Age dot the landscape in the south. Geologically, Arran is of great interest because of its complexity, and is a popular destination for university field trips. **Sir Archibald Geikie** worked out the history of Arran's rocks in the late 19th century, while **James Hutton** had confirmed his theories of igneous geology there 100 years earlier.

Arran has had a long and often turbulent history. In prehistoric times it was settled by Neolithic farmers who have left their traces in the fine chambered **cairns** at Torrylin, Clachaig, East Bennan, Monamore and the Giants' Graves (two together, near Whiting Bay). In the Bronze Age many stone circles and **standing stones** were erected, notably at Machrie Moor. There is another stone circle close to the Brodick-Lamlash road, and other standing stones round Brodick and Dippen. Dun Fionn, on the headland between Brodick and Lamlash, is a fine example of an Iron Age **dun**. There are others at Corriecreavie and on King's Cross Point, at the south end of Lamlash Bay. Larger forts are also present, for example on the high ridge on the north side of North Glen Sannox. There is a 'vitrified' fort, with burnt stone in the rampart, on the north side of Sannox Bay.

Arran was sacked by **Vikings** in 797, and was one of the islands claimed by **Magnus Barelegs**, King of Norway in 1098. It did not become part of the Kingdom of Scotland until the **Treaty of Perth** in 1266. In 1503 it was granted by royal charter to the **Hamiltons**. Successive **Earls of Arran** played major roles on the stage of Scottish politics. During Cromwellian times the island was occupied, though the garrison was attacked and massacred at Corrie. Widespread **clearances** in the 19th century to make way for large-scale, enclosed sheep farms led to the emigration of one-third of the population and effectively killed off Gaelic culture on the island.

The main town and principal ferry terminal is Brodick (pop. 1000; Norse *breidr vik*, 'broad bay'), with many hotels and guest houses, shops, a Tourist Information Centre and an interesting and informative museum. At the north end of Brodick Bay is **Brodick Castle** with its gardens, formerly a residence of the Dukes of Hamilton but now owned by the **National Trust for Scotland**, which also owns the spectacular backdrop of Glen Rosa and Goat Fell. The central round tower dates from the 15th century, but the building has been added to many times over the years, notably in the 1840s. The interior is lavishly furnished and decorated.

The island's other ferry terminal is at the north end, at the village of Lochranza, from where a landing-craft type vessel plies to Claonaig, near Skipness, during the summer season. In the sea loch is a 16th century castle, overlying an earlier fortification which, together with **Skipness Castle**, guarded the approaches to Kilbrannan sound for the **Lords of the Isles**. There are a number of settlements on the west side of Arran, of which the largest is Blackwaterfoot, close to the archaeologically rich area of Machrie Moor. In the Bronze Age, this area was an important ritual centre; some of the stones may have been used as primitive astronomical observatories to track the movements of sun, moon and stars. On the coast nearby is Drumadoon, with interesting geology and a spectacular Iron Age fort.

The Brodick Castle passing Goat Fell, Isle of Arran (BRC)

From the south end of the island there are fine views down the Firth of Clyde over Pladda Island, with a lighthouse, to **Ailsa Craig**, **Galloway**, Kintyre and Northern Ireland. On the east side are the villages of Whiting Bay, a centre for arts and crafts of all kinds, and Lamlash. The sheltered waters of Lamlash Bay have become a centre for water sports; **Holy Island**, a mile offshore, provides the shelter. It was an Early Christian and medieval monastery. The cave of St Molaise, at the base of Mullach Mor (1030ft/314m) has Viking inscriptions. In 1263 King Haakon of Norway anchored his fleet in Lamlash Bay before the **Battle of Largs**.

The main industries are **tourism**, including many small-scale craft shops, farming, a luxury-food processing factory, and a little commercial **fishing**. Outside Brodick, the island is uncrowded and unspoiled and ideal for all manner of outdoor pursuits.

ARROCHAR, Dunbartonshire

At the head of Loch Long, Arrochar has always been a **fishing** and farming area. The *Old Statistical Account* of 1792 reports '**Herring** is to be found in abundance. For these two seasons past, each man employed in herring-fishing has almost cleared £8 on average.' Created from Luss Parish, the area was the setting, in the days of clan feuding, for cattle-stealing. Neighbouring Tarbet was visited in 1263 by **Vikings**, who crossed from Arrochar to Tarbet by pulling their longships over the narrow isthmus between Loch Long and **Loch Lomond**, a remarkable feat that was ill-rewarded by defeat in the **Battle of Largs**. Arrochar is now much frequented by climbers, the proximity of Ben Arthur (usually named the Cobbler because of its profile) and Ben Narnian offering excellent rock-**climbing** within easy reach of central Scotland.

ARROL, Sir William (1839–1913) Civil Engineer

Born in Houston, **Renfrewshire**, Arrol started work aged 9 in a thread factory, then trained as a blacksmith and engineer before starting his own business in 1868. The Dalmarnock Iron Works in the east end of **Glasgow** was completed in 1871 and he then began building bridges. Quickly establishing a reputation for the quality of his **railway** work, he won the contract to build the **Forth Bridge** in 1879, but when the **Tay Bridge** collapsed in December the contract was cancelled. In 1882 he was finally awarded the contract to build both the new Tay and Forth Bridges. These were completed in 1887 and 1890 (when Arrol was knighted) and remain his most enduring monuments in Scotland. He was also responsible for the magnificent Tower Bridge in London and for the construction of numerous **engineering** works.

ARTICLES, Lords of the

For logistical reasons from the late 14th century onwards the conduct of parliamentary business was often left to a delegated commission or committee rather than to the full assembly of the three estates. Initially the work of this commission for 'determining the articles' involved actually enacting legislation; but by the late 15th century its role was closer to that of a parliamentary committee for drafting legislation and presenting it to Parliament for formal approval. Membership of the committee was supposedly representative of that of parliament but in the 17th century **James VI** and **Charles I** secured powers of patronage over it which made the committee an effective means of controlling parliamentary business. Lords of the articles were often also members of the Privy Council and since the committee could also initiate legislation it came to be seen as a tool of royal authority which reduced Parliament to a cipher. It was therefore abolished in 1641 but restored at the Restoration only to be abolished again after the Revolution of 1689.

ATHELSTANEFORD, East Lothian

Three miles north of **Haddington**, the village of Athelstaneford gets its name from a possibly legendary 9th or 10th century battle at which the **Picts** and the Scots combined to defeat the Northumbrian King Athelstane. The legend continues to assert that during the battle a white cross of clouds was seen to float against the blue sky; as a result of the victory **St Andrew**, whose colours these were, was adopted as Scotland's patron saint. A St Andrews flag now flies by a plaque erected in 1965 to commemorate this improbable tale. The playwright **John Home** (1722–1808) was minister of Athelstaneford until the first performance of his play *Douglas* was greeted with rapture by audiences in **Edinburgh** (1756) but by outrage on the part of the Kirk authorities; a year later, when the play was performed at Covent Garden with spectacular success, Home resigned from the ministry.

ATHOLL, Earldom, Marquisate and Dukedom of

This is one of the original **Celtic earldoms**. After the male line expired in 1211 the title passed to David of Strathbogie by female descent. Opposition to **Robert I** resulted in forfeiture, and the earldom remained crown property until 1457. **James I** had returned from his captivity with Joan Beaufort as his bride. After his murder Queen Joan made a second marriage with the Black Knight of **Lorne**, Stewart of Balvenie, and **James II** bestowed the earldom on their son John. In 1629 it passed again through female descent to John Murray of Tullibardine, son of Lady Dorothea Stewart. His heir was created first Marquis of Atholl, and made the Stanley marriage through which his family inherited the sovereign Lordship of Man. By the time they did so, Queen Anne had elevated them to a dukedom. This great property was endangered in the 1745 Rising, when the **Jacobite Lord George Murray** besieged his brother the Duke in **Blair Castle**, the last to undergo a siege. But Lord George's son married the Duke's daughter and heiress and succeeded to the castle his father had battered. The dukes remain the only British subjects permitted to maintain a private army, the **Atholl Highlanders**, to which **Queen Victoria** granted permission to bear firearms.

ATHOLL, Katharine, Duchess of (1874–1960) Politician

Born Katharine Marjory Ramsay on 6 November 1874, the 4th daughter of Sir James Ramsay of Bamff, near **Alyth**, Katharine studied music with the intention of making it her career before marrying the Marquis of Tullibardine, later 8th Duke of Atholl, on 20 July 1899. After settling at **Blair Castle**, she edited *The Military History of Perthshire*, 1908. She sat on a committee investigating medical services to the Highlands and Islands and on the **Perthshire** Education Committee. During World War I she worked providing comforts for the Scottish Horse [see **Yeomanry**], and visited Egypt to entertain them.

Her political involvement started with campaigning for her husband before he assumed the dukedom in 1917. In 1923 she successfully stood as Conservative candidate for West Perthshire (becoming the first Scottish woman MP), and in 1924 she became Minister at the Department of Education (the first Conservative woman minister). She also studied foreign affairs such as the India Bill and the rise of fascism in Germany and Spain. Her outspoken opposition to the latter increasingly brought her into conflict with her party and led to her resigning the whip. The clash with the constituency party came to a head in 1938 when, after being criticised for her opposition to the government's appeasement policy, she decided to resign her seat and fight a by-election. With the whole of the Conservative Party machine against her, and with little encouragement from her supporters in the party, she lost by 1313 votes. The invasion of Poland and the declaration of war proved her views on the desirability of re-armament and her doubts on appeasement to have been correct. After the war she continued her many campaigns and, though widowed in 1942, lived on at Blair Castle until her death.

ATHOLL, Perthshire

The province, Forest and estate (one of the largest in Scotland) of Atholl are bounded to the north by **Badenoch**, east by **Glen Shee** and **Braemar**, west by **Rannoch Moor** and south by Lochs Tummel and Rannoch. Once the **Pictish** province of Athfodla, it commanded the north-south routes across the **Grampians** (eg **Drumochter Pass**) and comprises dramatic mountain scenery throughout. **Blair Atholl** at the junction of Glens Tilt and Errochty has **Blair Castle**, the home of the **Dukes of Atholl**. Most of Atholl's followers were originally of the Clan Donnachaidh (Duncan), adherents of **King Duncan I** who was killed by **MacBeth**. There is a clan museum by the **Falls of Bruar**. Their descendants, often called Robertson after Robert Duncan who was granted the barony of Struan for bringing one of **James I**'s murderers to justice, boast a long tradition of **Stewart** and **Jacobite** loyalty.

ATHOLL HIGHLANDERS, The, Regiment

Descended from a long line of clansmen of the Earls and then **Dukes of Atholl**, and from the 77th Atholl Highlanders raised to fight in the American War of Independence, today's corps is famous as 'the only private army in Britain'. In its present form it can be traced to that Victorian extravaganza, the 'Eglinton Tournament' of 1839 [see **Montgomerie**] when the Duke's heir Lord Glenlyon, fighting as 'The Knight of the Gael', decided to take with him a bodyguard of kilted Highlanders some 60 strong, clad in blue tunics and Murray of Atholl **tartan**.

The strength of the corps was greatly increased for the visit to **Dunkeld** of **Queen Victoria**, when the uniform adopted was more or less identical with that worn today. In 1845 Queen Victoria presented the corps with a pair of colours, thus investing it with a semi-official status, and for a time the officers even appeared on the Army List. At its greatest strength it mustered four companies, each some 40 strong.

Fallen into abeyance for a number of years, the Atholl Highlanders were revived in 1966 by the 10th Duke and numbered some 50 with an artillery detachment which appeared on parade to fire salutes, plus an excellent pipe band. The Duke was colonel and the officers members of his family or local lairds. Many of the members were former servicemen and a retired general was in the ranks as a private.

The uniform consists of a blue tunic with white facings (red for pipers and drummers), blue glengarry worn with a sprig of **juniper** behind the Duke's crest of a savage in chains, and Murray of Atholl **kilt** with white belts. The officers also have an evening Mess Kit which is seen at the **Perth** and Royal Caledonian Balls. The Atholl Highlanders in the main confine their appearances to Atholl itself although from time to time they have paraded at **Edinburgh**.

AUCHANS CASTLE, Nr Troon, Ayrshire

Only a mile from the ruins of **Dundonald Castle**, the L-plan castellated mansion of Auchans was built in 1644 by Sir William Cochrane of Coldoun. Created Earl of Dundonald by **Charles II** in 1669 for his services to the

Auchans Castle, Ayrshire (RWB)

Royalist cause, Cochrane had purchased the Dundonald estate from the Wallace family in 1638 and proceeded to raid the ruins of Dundonald Castle for building materials for Auchans. Described by **MacGibbon and Ross** as 'a characteristic and pleasing example of the Scottish mansion of the 17th century', by 1890 parts of the castle had been converted into workmen's houses and the whole was falling into disrepair. It is now ruinous. In 1726 Auchans passed to the Earls of Eglinton, and the last permanent resident of the vast house was Susannah, Countess of Eglinton, eccentric widow of the 9th Earl and a famous beauty in her youth, who entertained **Johnson** and **Boswell** to dinner in 1773, and was reputed to have tamed rats to keep her company at mealtimes. She died there in 1780 at the age of 91.

AUCHENBLAE, Kincardineshire

This is the main village of Fordoun parish, once a **burgh of barony** and famous as the birthplace of **John of Fordoun** (or Fordun), the 14th century chronicler upon whose *Chronica gentis Scotorum* the 15th century *Scotichronicon* was based. It is not to be confused with the modern village of Fordoun on the A94 two miles away. Auchenblae's church (1892) replaced a ruin in its churchyard which was once the mother kirk of **The Mearns** and the Chapel of St Palladius, an Irish bishop whose bones were allegedly brought here by St Ternan. There is a **Pictish** cross-slab set into one of the walls and a memorial to the martyr **George Wishart** whose family lived nearby. Another famous son was **James Burnett, Lord Monboddo**, 'the magnetism of whose conversation' easily drew even **Dr Johnson** and **James Boswell** out of their way. However 'wretched' Monboddo House, their dinner there was a great success; the travellers rejoined the main road under the expert guidance of one of Monboddo's 'savages', an African who rejoiced in the name of 'Gory'.

AUCHENCRAW, Berwickshire

As 'Edincraw', the village of Auchencraw was long associated with witchcraft: 'In Edencraw, where the witches bide a''. Records show that seven or eight witches were burnt by Home of Renton, Sheriff of **Berwickshire**. Auchencraw's Laird (early 1800s) performed the ceremony of 'scoring above the breath' (a scratch on the forehead) on the last local witch, Margaret Girvan, after a storm ruined his crops.

AUCHENGEICH PIT DISASTER (1959)

Scotland's worst mining accident of the 20th century took place at Auchengeich, Chryston, **Lanarkshire** on 18 September 1959. An electrical fault in equipment 1000ft (305m) below ground caused a fire whose smoke engulfed an underground train carrying 48 miners. Only one managed to escape the choking fumes and make his way to safety. Rescue workers were unable to reach any other victims because of the persistence of the fire, and it proved necessary to flood the mine, closing it permanently.

AUCHINDRAIN, Argyll

This 'Museum of Farming', six miles west of **Inveraray** (open Easter to October) may be unique in mainland Britain. It consists of a group of houses and barns, formerly a multiple-tenancy farm (the typical pre-**crofting** Highland tenure), preserved in *situ* with tools and furnishings. Begun in 1963 on the retirement of the last tenant, the buildings now contain a range of equipment covering the last two centuries. After an introductory display, visitors walk from house to house at will; a full tour takes about one hour.

AUCHINLECK, Ayrshire

Anciently pronounced and sometimes spelled 'Affleck', Auchinleck is Boswell country. The estate was granted to Thomas Boswell (one of **James IV**'s favourite courtiers who died with him at **Flodden**) when he married the Auchinleck heiress in 1504, and was created a **burgh of barony** in 1507. Alexander Boswell (1706–82), father of the biographer, took the title Lord Auchinleck

on his appointment as Lord of Session (1754), and it was he who commissioned the building of Auchinleck House, possibly from one of the **Adam** brothers, in 1760. The result was not to everyone's liking; the Duchess of Northumberland thought it 'but a middling house, the pediments terrible loaded with ornaments of trumpets and maces and the deuce knows what', while **Dr Johnson**, taken to stay there in 1773 by **James Boswell** (who warned the doctor to avoid three topics in conversation with his irascible father: Whiggism, **Presbyterianism** – and Sir John Pringle), 'was less delighted with the elegance of the modern mansion than with the sullen dignity of the [ruined] old castle'. In the churchyard of the Barony Parish Church (1838) in the village of Auchinleck is the Boswell Aisle (1754), added by Lord Auchinleck to the earlier partly pre-**Reformation** church and now serving as a Boswell Museum.

AUCHTERARDER, Perthshire

Although the town's long and unremarkable main street scarcely smacks of religious fervour, Auchterarder's history is rich in theological matter. In 1717 the local presbytery, adopting a purist approach to **Calvinist** predestination, concocted a dangerously worded tenet that to forsake sin was not essential for God's chosen elect – the Auchterarder Creed. In 1834 it was again the presbytery of Auchterarder which rejected Robert Young, a lay presenter, who then appealed against the decision in the **Court of Session** – events which led to the **Disruption**. The town was burnt by **Jacobites** after the **Battle of Sheriffmuir** and again during the '45. Rebuilt, it became a **linen**-weaving centre and latterly switched to woollens. It is a **royal burgh** and, with **Crieff**, one of the main towns in **Strathearn**.

AUCHTERMUCHTY, Fife

The name, beloved of **music hall** comedians, means simply 'the place of the wild boar', whence indeed **Queen Mary** is said to have hunted in the then undrained Howe of **Fife**. A **royal burgh** since 1517 and once a centre of handloom weaving, it has since declined in importance, though not in character, with many 18th century houses including the high-towered Town House. Myres Castle, once Z-plan and dating from 1549, belonged to the Scrymgeour family, John Scrymgeour being Master of Works at **Falkland** and **Holyroodhouse** in the early 16th century. Later (1883) it was the birthplace of **Reginald Fairlie**, the architect. 'The Wife of Auchtermuchty', a poem of popular currency but uncertain provenance, records the disastrous results of role reversal when the 'gudeman' swaps his plough for the household chores and his wife vice versa. Fair sickened by just a day of 'hussyskep' and 'meikle schame', he calls off the deal 'for I and this house will nevir do well'.

AULD ALLIANCE, The

As Scotland's 'auld enemy' is always England, so its 'auld alliance' is always that with France. Although there may have been earlier precedents, the first documentary evidence of an offensive and defensive alliance between the French and Scottish monarchs is the 1295 treaty between **John Balliol** and Philip IV. It was aimed at

Edward I of England and was to have been cemented by a marriage between **Edward Balliol**, John's son, with a niece of Philip. Renewed by **Robert I** (Treaty of Corbeil, 1326), the alliance served Scotland well during the **Wars of Independence** and became the mutually accepted response to English aggression against either party. It was repeatedly renewed during the next two centuries (1371, 1391, 1428, 1448, 1484 and 1492), but when the 1512 renewal resulted in the defeat of **Flodden** its utility was questioned and in Scotland enthusiasm waned. Not so in France, where the success of the English Reformation was seen as the best of reasons for upgrading the Scottish alliance. Dynastic ties were strengthened, with two French brides being provided for **James V** and the Dauphin for his daughter **Mary**. In the aftermath of English attacks during the **Rough Wooing**, the **Treaty of Haddington** (1548), which sealed this last arrangement, made France the guarantor of Scottish liberties and installed French troops in Scotland. The high point of French influence came soon after during the regency of **Mary of Guise**; but already shared hostility towards England was contradicted by supporters of the Scottish **Reformation** who naturally looked to England as their guarantor. Recognition of the claims of Mary or **James VI** to the English throne also necessitated a more amenable attitude towards the Tudors. In **Lord James Stewart** and **Maitland of Lethington** Mary found herself dependent on men wholly committed to the English alliance; the auld alliance may be said to have died with her, although it would resurface briefly during the Cromwellian period and was vicariously revived by the **Jacobites**.

Besides its political and dynastic dimension, the auld alliance implied a degree of social and cultural exchange between France and Scotland. The traffic in brides and embassies encouraged a French appreciation of things Scottish, especially soldiers, and a Scottish appreciation of things French, especially claret; a considerable trade in both resulted. Cooks and chroniclers, musicians and masons attached to royal and ecclesiastical missions brought French tastes to Scotland which are still clearly traceable in Scots **architecture**, vocabulary, **law** and **philosophy**. Long since it has become politically redundant, the term 'auld alliance' continues to enjoy ill-defined currency as an all-purpose antidote to anglicisation; it has also been revived to add substance and credibility to nationalist claims for an independent Scotland within the European Community.

AULDEARN, Nairnshire

Two miles east of **Nairn**, the village and parish of Auldearn are best known for the **Battle of Auldearn** (some of the fallen are buried in the churchyard) and for the Boath **doocot**, a circular late 17th century building with a conical roof, now in the care of the **National Trust for Scotland**. It stands on the site of Old Eren (hence 'Auldearn'), once a royal castle where in 1180 **William the Lion** issued a charter to the burgesses of **Inverness**. Boath House, formerly a property of the **Earls of Dunbar and March**, was redesigned by **Archibald Simpson** in 1825. One of its lairds, Sir Frederick Dunbar, was 'reputed to be the last man in the North to bowl underarm in serious **cricket**' (**N Tranter**).

AULDEARN, Battle of (1645)

The site of the battle lies south of the the A96 road approximately three miles east of **Nairn**. After success at **Inverlochy** and a less successful raid on **Dundee**, **James Graham, Marquis of Montrose**, in command of the Royalist army with about 1750 men including 250 cavalry, was encamped at **Auldearn**. Sir John Hurry (or Urry), marching through the night from **Inverness** with his **Covenanters**, intended surprise but, fearing that heavy rain had dampened the powder, made his men discharge their muskets. The noise alerted Royalist sentries. **Alasdair MacDonald**, commanding his Irish soldiers, charged but, hampered by boggy ground, was only just saved by the **Gordon** cavalry. Montrose, with the main body of infantry, then joined Alasdair. The Covenanters, finding themselves surrounded, were cut down in their ranks. Montrose estimated that Hurry had lost half his army.

AVIATION

Scotland's involvement in aviation may have begun in 1577 when John Damian jumped from **Stirling Castle** with wings strapped to his arms and was lucky to escape with only a broken thigh. Over two centuries later **James 'Balloon' Tytler**, also editor of the *Encyclopaedia Britannica*, made the first successful balloon descent in Britain (1784). By the late 19th century heavier-than-air aircraft were becoming practical. The 8th Duke of Argyll, an enthusiast, was elected first President of the Aeronautical Society of Great Britain in 1866. Percy Pilcher, an assistant to the Professor of Naval Architecture at the **University of Glasgow**, began experimenting with gliders at **Cardross** in 1895 and made successful flights in England from 1896–9 before his death in a flying accident.

After the Wright brothers made their first powered flight in the United States in 1903 there were further experiments in Scotland. Aviation meetings were held in 1910 and 1914, and two flying schools established. In 1913 **William Beardmore** & Co began building Austro-Daimler aero-engines and took out a licence to build Deutsche Flugzeuge Werke aeroplanes. Scottish Aviation was founded at **Prestwick** in 1914 principally to train pilots. During World War I Beardmores and several other **Clyde shipbuilding** and **engineering** firms became involved in aircraft construction, including G & J Weir, whose managing director **William Weir** became the first Air Minister. Beardmores was the only Scottish firm to build airships, including the R34 and the engines for the ill-fated R101. In the interwar

The David and Goliath of Beardsmore Aviation: a Sopwith Camel and a V/1500 at Inchinnan (BRC)

depression Beardmore was forced to abandon building airframes and aero-engines.

With re-armament Scottish Aviation acquired Prestwick aerodrome in 1936 and within three years was operating the largest air training school in Scotland. In 1933 G & J Weir built one of the first auto-giros (the precursor of the helicopter). Rolls-Royce and the Blackburn Aircraft Company (**Dumbarton**) opened factories in the west of Scotland in 1939. During the war the west of Scotland became an important centre of aircraft and aero-engine manufacture, employing over 30,000 people. Only Rolls-Royce and Scottish Aviation survived the war, the latter producing the Jetstream aircraft until the 1990s. A training school for civil pilots from all over the world is based at **Perth**.

AVIEMORE, Inverness-shire

A **railway** station on the main line to **Inverness** (completed 1898), Aviemore began the 20th century without even an inn; the nearest was three miles away at Lynwilg. Things changed in the 1960s when the place was designated as the Highlands' first purpose-built resort. Centres – conference, leisure, visitor, sports, **ski**, health and heritage – have since proliferated along with hotels, hostels, chalets and caravan parks. Tastes not catered for in Aviemore are essentially those which do not lend themselves to mass organisation. A link with the age of steam is maintained in the Strathspey Railway which runs from here to **Boat of Garten**. Behind the station Craigellachie rock marks the beginning of Strathspey proper and of **Grant** (Seafield) territory; it ends 47 miles downstream at the other **Craigellachie** near **Aberlour**. From Aviemore a road and trails lead east up into the heart of the **Cairngorms**, providing access to Glen More Forest Park, **Rothiemurchus Forest** and the ski slopes of Cairngorm itself.

AWE, Loch, Argyll

One of the largest freshwater lochs in Scotland, Loch Awe is 24¼ miles (38.8km) long from Ford at the south-east end to the outflow at the Awe **Hydro-Electric** Barrage. The rivers Orchy and Strae, which converge near **Kilchurn Castle**, are the two main feeders. The loch is dominated to the north by the great mountain of **Cruachan** (3672ft/1119m). To the south the slopes are more gentle.

Loch Awe was undoubtedly settled in Neolithic times, and there are many ancient burial **cairns** near the shore line. A number of **crannogs** (man-made islands) may be seen, dating from 500 BC. Early Christian settlements at Kilmahog (on the north shore) and on the Island of Innishail were established by the 10th century. The castles of Fraoch Eilean, **Innischonnel** and Fincharne, built as a line of defence, date from the 13th century.

Until recent times the loch was the highway for the whole area, roads being virtually non-existent, and there were regular steamer services. The **railway** reached Lochawe village in 1880. A ferry from Portsonachan to Taycreggan ran from 1400–1947, and another from Portinnisherrich to Dalavich from 1571–1902.

Loch Awe is renowned for its brown trout, some of legendary size. Pike, perch and char are also indigenous and there are now two commercial trout farms. Since 1945 the water of Loch Awe has been used in the Pump Storage System of the Cruachan Hydro-Electric Scheme; electricity is also generated at the Awe Barrage and at Inverawe Power Station, near the mouth of the River Awe.

AYR, Ayrshire

Capital of the province of **Kyle**, county town of **Ayrshire**, headquarters of the Kyle & Carrick District of Strathclyde Region and now headquarters of the South Ayrshire Council Area, Ayr has a history dating back to the early 13th century when it was granted a charter by **William the Lion** (c1204). In c1297 it was the scene of one of **William Wallace**'s first confrontations with the occupying English when he set fire to their garrison, and on 26 April 1315 the first meeting of the Scottish Parliament after **Bannockburn** took place in St John's Kirk for the purpose of granting the succession, in the event of the death of **Robert I**, to the King's brother **Edward Bruce**. The area around the church was requisitioned by Cromwell in the 1650s for the construction of a citadel; the church was later demolished although sections of the citadel walls remain, as does the tower of St John's, dating from c1300 but converted into a private house in the 1850s. The Auld Brig of Ayr probably dates back almost as far as St John's although the present four-arched stone bridge is of c1470. It owes its celebrity, and therefore its continued existence, to **Robert Burns**, whose birthplace, **Alloway**, is now a southern suburb of Ayr. His poem 'The Brigs of Ayr' is a sharp exchange of insults between the spirits of the Auld Brig and its new (1787–8) **Robert Adam**-designed neighbour. The New Brig, 'buskit in a braw new coat, that he, at Lon'on, frae ane Adams got', pours scorn on the Auld:

> Will your poor, narrow foot-path of a street,
> Where twa wheel-barrows tremble when they
>   meet,
> Your ruin'd, formless bulk o' stane and lime,
> Compare wi' bonnie brigs o' modern time?
> There's men o' taste wou'd tak the Ducat stream
> Tho' they should cast the very sark and swim,
> E'er they would grate their feelings wi' the view
> O' Sic an ugly, Gothic hulk as you.

The Auld Brig gives as good as he gets:

> Conceited gowk! puff'd up wi' windy pride!
> This mony a year I've stood the flood an' tide;
> And tho' wi' crazy eild I'm sair forfairn,
> I'll be a brig when ye're a shapeless cairn!

Nearly a century later the Auld Brig had the last laugh when the New was indeed reduced to a 'shapeless cairn' by a flood and replaced (1877) by the existing five-arched New Brig.

The Wallace Tower (1833) in the High Street was described in 1898 as being 'one of the most conspicuous, if not the most tasteful, objects in Ayr', while a later observer thought the statue (by James Thom) of the hero in his niche on the tower made him look 'more like an angry schoolmaster than the champion of his race'. The statue of Burns (George Lawson, 1891) in its eponymous Square, however, is considered 'exceptionally well executed' and 'one of the best of the poet'. **Brigadier General James Neill**, 'hero' of Lucknow and a native of Ayr, is commemorated by a Matthew Noble statue in Wellington Square.

When Daniel Defoe visited the town in the early 18th century he found it 'like an old Beauty, shewing the Ruins of a good Face; apparently not only decay'd and declin'd, but decaying and declining every Day, and from being the fifth Town in Scotland, is now like a Place forsaken; the Reason of its Decay is the Decay of its Trade . . . nothing will save it from Death if Trade does not revive.' Ayr not only survived but, in the 19th century, started once more to thrive, both as an administrative centre and as a seaside resort. The former is amply illustrated by **Thomas Hamilton**'s neo-classical Town Buildings (1827–32) with spectacular three-storeyed, many-pillared, 226ft (69m) spire terminating in a slender obelisk. The seaside attraction was responsible for the many Victorian residential villas, the development of the racecourse (which moved in 1907 to today's site from Belleisle, where racing had been enjoyed since 1576 and which is today Scotland's only Group One course and venue for the Scottish Grand National), its three **golf courses**, and the many **tourist** amenities along its miles of golden sands.

AYRSHIRE

Before the **local government** reorganisation of 1975, Ayrshire was a maritime county 78 miles long and up to 28 miles wide, and 'resembles in shape the crescent of the waxing moon' as the *Third Statistical Account* quaintly put it in 1951. With an area of 724,239 acres (293,095ha), this was the seventh largest Scottish county and the largest in southern Scotland. It was divided by the rivers Irvine and Doon into three: Cunninghame in the north, **Kyle** in the middle and **Carrick** in the south. The Ayrshire area is believed to have been inhabited for around 6000 years. Although claimed by the Scottish King **Duncan** in the 11th century, it was nearly invaded by Norwegians in 1263, before they were defeated at **Largs**, and was the base from which both **Wallace** and **Bruce** launched their campaigns.

Ayr was the county town, the burghs comprising **Ardrossan**, Cumnock & Holmhead, Darvel, Galston, **Girvan**, **Irvine**, **Kilmarnock**, **Kilwinning**, **Largs**, **Maybole**, Newmilns & Greenholm, **Prestwick**, **Saltcoats**, **Stevenston**, Stewarton and **Troon**. Occupations included **agriculture** (especially early potatoes), **fishing**, mining and some heavy **engineering** in the Kilmarnock area. **Tourism** has been important since the **railway** age. In 1975 the county was wholly absorbed into **Strathclyde** Region, but since 1995 has been divided into three administrative areas: North Ayrshire (comprising Cunninghame and the Isle of Arran), East Ayrshire (Cumnock & Doon Valley and Kilmarnock & Loudoun) and South Ayrshire (Kyle & Carrick).

AYRSHIRE CATTLE

These red-brown and white, horned dairy cattle have spread far and wide, to the USSR, Canada and Kenya, but especially to Finland which now has the biggest population of the breed, 500,000 cows. The Ayrshire arose from late-18th century matings of Teeswater cattle with the local stock. It was recognised by the Highland and Agricultural Society in 1814 and within 60 years

Ayr in the 1880s: the High Street and Wallace Tower (GWWA)

had been widely exported. Indeed, it was at that time the only firmly established British dairy breed apart from those of the Channel Islands.

It was supreme in Scotland until quite recently, when the Friesian took over. In England, many farmers adopted the Ayrshire especially in the 1920s and 30s when in the eastern counties the tenancies of bankrupt English farmers were bought up by Scots who then brought their families, chattels and Ayrshire cows south by special train. Their success helped to popularise the Ayrshire but, as in Scotland, it has now been all but eclipsed by the Friesian.

Smaller and hardier than the Friesian, Ayrshire cattle have adapted well to tough conditions, giving good yields of milk on relatively poor keep. Though these qualities are no longer particularly advantageous in British dairy farming, the Ayrshire, being a relatively undemanding dairy animal, is an extremely valuable genetic source whose time may well come again.

AYTON, Berwickshire

The village of Ayton, on the river Eye in **Berwickshire**, has recently been bypassed by the A1, thus restoring its peace and quiet. Settlement took place during the reign of **David I** (1124–53) with the founding of a castle by the Anglo-Norman De Vescies. This was destroyed in 1498. In 1851 a castellated mansion (by **James Gillespie Graham**) replaced a second castle which had been destroyed by fire in 1834. It forms a prominent landmark. In 1472 Ayton became the property of the **Homes**. The church was united to **Coldingham** Priory until the **Reformation**. A Gothic-style church replaced the old one in 1865.

AYTOUN, William Edmonstoune (1813–65)
Poet and Humorist

Aytoun was born in **Edinburgh** on 21 June 1813. His father, Roger Aytoun, was a Writer to the Signet and a founder of the **Edinburgh Academy**, and his mother was a friend of **Walter Scott**. He was educated at the Edinburgh Academy and studied law at **Edinburgh University** (1828–33). On graduating he spent a year travelling and studying German literature. In 1835 he also became a Writer to the Signet, but dedicated much time to literary work.

Aytoun's first work, a collection of romantic verse pastiches, *Poland, Homer and Other Poems* (1832), was published while he was still an undergraduate. In 1836 he became a contributor to **Blackwood's Magazine**, a connection that lasted until his death. Between 1836 and 1865 he wrote over 200 poems, reviews, satires and short stories for the journal. In 1844 he became a formal member of the staff of *Blackwood's*, and the following year was appointed Professor of Rhetoric and Belles Lettres at Edinburgh University, a post he filled with much success. In 1849 Aytoun married Jane Emily, the

Professor W E Aytoun, by James Archer, 1855 (SNPG)

daughter of **John Wilson** ('Christopher North'). He continued to practise **law** and to write, and in 1852, as compensation for his services as a political writer, the newly elected Tory Party of Lord Derby apppointed him Sheriff of **Orkney** and **Shetland**. The following year he was awarded an honorary degree from Oxford University.

In conjunction with Theodore Martin, Aytoun had brought out the *Bon Gaultier Ballads* (1845), a series of parodies of contemporary verse, and in 1848 he published *Lays of the Scottish Cavaliers and other Poems*. A group of **ballad** romances that had appeared previously in *Blackwood's*, they were modelled on works of Sir Walter Scott and **Thomas Babington Macaulay**, concerned with Scottish historical subjects and heroes, and proved extremely popular with Victorian audiences. Aytoun also published a mock heroic poem, *Firmilian, or The Student of Badajoz* (1855), after its successful appearance in *Blackwood's* in 1854 under the pseudonym T Percy Jones. The work, a satirical attack on what Aytoun called the Spasmodic School (eg **Alexander Smith**), proved an extremely cutting parody of their turgid styles and extravagant themes and effectively ended their popularity. Other works of Aytoun included *Ballads of Scotland* (1858), *Bothwell* (1856) and an autobiographical novel, *Norman Sinclair* (1861).

B

BADENOCH, Inverness-shire

This ancient province at the geographical heart of the Highlands comprises the upper strath of the river **Spey** roughly from **Laggan** to **Aviemore**. Hemmed in between the **Monadhliath** and the Monadh Ruadh (or **Cairngorms**) it was, and still is, home to members of the ancient Celtic **Clan Chattan** including the **Mac-Phersons** and the **Mackintoshes**. But since the 13th century its overlords have been of Norman descent, first the **Comyns** and then the **Stewarts** (eg **Alexander Stewart**, 'Wolf of Badenoch'), latterly the **Grants** and **Gordons**. Its combination of fine pasture, majestic woodland and bleak hill is unrivalled. The main centre was **Kingussie** but with the area's development as a mountain playground Aviemore now attracts more visitors.

BAGPIPES

HIGHLAND The origins of the Highland bagpipes are obscure, but they were in use as military instruments and for **clan** gatherings and laments by the mid-16th century. They still serve these functions, to which have been added military marches and dance music. The air is supplied by the mouth to a bag operated by the elbow and fed to the chanter and drones, which are two or three in number. Native close-grained woods have been used, but African blackwood is now the favourite. The single reed is enclosed in the conical chanter which uses an open fingering system, ensuring that the sound is continuous. Complex 'grips' or decorations are used to give the impression of repeated notes and variations in volume, as well as to point the rhythm. The nine-note scale is uniquely tuned to achieve three interlocking pentatonic scales of acoustic purity. Powerful and richly toned, the Highland bagpipes, both as solo instruments and in pipe bands, are the most widely played bagpipes in the world. See *Canntaireachd*, **Pipe Bands**, pipers, *Piobaireachd*.

LOWLAND These bellows-blown bagpipes with cylindrical chanter produce a sweet tone similar to the Northumbrian pipes.

BORDER Also bellows-blown pipes with three drones and conical bore chanter, these were used by town pipers for reveilles and curfews, probably from the late 16th century on, frequently accompanied by a drum.

CAULD-WIND Air from a bellows is cold, unlike air from the mouth via a bag. Thus the term 'cold-wind' is applied to a variety of bellows-blown pipes.

PASTORAL These bellows-blown pipes with open chanter use soft reeds, allowing for overblowing and consequent extension of the range to two octaves. A possible ancestor of the Irish *uillean* pipes.

See R D Cannon, *The Highland Bagpipe and its Music*, Edinburgh, 1988 and F G Collinson, *The Bagpipe*, London, 1975.

BAIKIE, William Balfour (1825-64) Explorer

Born at **Kirkwall**, Baikie studied medicine at **Edinburgh University**, subsequently joining the Royal Navy as a surgeon. In 1854, appointed as surgeon/naturalist on the 260-ton schooner *Pleiad* engaged in exploring the river Niger in West Africa, Baikie found himself in charge of the expedition after a dispute with the ship's captain. By pioneering a method of malarial prophylaxis later used by **Livingstone** (and credited to the latter), the young Orcadian succeeded in penetrating 250 miles further inland than any previous explorer, and returning safely to tell the tale. His 1856 book of the voyage is almost a traveller's handbook, detailing local languages and customs and flora and fauna.

On a second voyage on the *Pleiad* in 1857, Baikie met with misfortune, his ship being wrecked. Undaunted, he created a settlement at Lokoja, at the confluence of the Niger and Benue, constructing roads, establishing a market for local goods and produce, and persuading neighbouring rulers to allow free rights of passage to and from it. To this commercial stimulus he added a cultural one, translating parts of the Bible and Prayer Book into Hausa. He wrote 'we have discovered an available highway conducting us into the very heart of a large continent', and his example did much to signpost that highway for others to follow. One of the most systematic and scientific of Scotland's many 19th century explorers, he died when on leave at Freetown in Sierra Leone. He is commemorated by a monument at St Magnus Cathedral, Kirkwall.

BAILLIE, Lady Grizel (1665-1746)
Songwriter

Born on Christmas Day 1665, Grizel (or Grisell) was the eldest of the 12 children of **Sir Patrick Hume of Polwarth**, a close associate of **Fletcher of Saltoun** and **Duncan Forbes of Culloden**. Persecuted for his views, and accused of having sheltered **Robert Baillie of Jerviswood** (who was executed for involvement in the Rye House Plot, 1683), Sir Patrick at one point hid for a month in the family vault at Polwarth Kirk a mile away from home, with Grizel stealing out in the dark to supply him with food; another month was spent under the floorboards of his house before the family were able to escape to Utrecht. Their exile ended with the landing of William of Orange in England. Grizel married George Baillie of Jerviswood, Robert's son, in 1692, and they spent much of their married life in **Edinburgh** and London where he was an MP and Lord of the Treasury. In 1725 they began the building of **Mellerstain House** in **Berwickshire**. Although she is remembered as a songwriter, only two of Grizel's songs remain, the best-known being 'Werena my heart licht I wad die', made even more famous by being quoted by **Robert Burns**.

Lady Grizel Baillie, from an engraving by G J Stodart (SW)

BAILLIE, Dame Isobel (1895–1983) Singer

Born at **Hawick**, **Roxburghshire** but educated at the Manchester High School where her family had moved, Isobel Baillie studied with Guglielmo Somma in Milan and went on to become an outstanding interpreter of oratorio, especially in the *Messiah* and in the taxing soprano solo in the Brahms *Requiem*. In 1933 she became the first British artist to sing at the Hollywood Bowl. The purity and clarity of her singing particularly impressed Toscanini. She made recordings throughout her long career, beginning with the acoustic horn and ending in the age of stereo.

BAILLIE, Joanna (1762–1851) Poet and Dramatist

Born in **Bothwell**, **Lanarkshire**, the daughter of a minister, and cousin to the surgeons **John** and **William Hunter**, Joanna Baillie moved to London in her twenties. Although they received critical acclaim and were admired by **Sir Walter Scott**, neither her poetry – much of it written in Scots – nor her plays – of which she wrote many in the grand tragic style – won much popular success.

BAILLIE, Matthew (1761–1823) Pathologist

Born at **Shotts**, Baillie studied medicine at Oxford and inherited an anatomy school in London from his uncle **William Hunter** at the age of 22. His greatest achievement was the publication in 1795 of *Morbid Anatomy of some of the most Important Parts of the Human Body*, the first book on pathology to appear in the English language, and the first to be arranged in a systematic manner, greatly advancing medical teaching. He died in London and was buried in Westminster Abbey.

BAILLIE, Robert (1602–62) Scholar and Divine

Born and educated in **Glasgow**, Baillie was ordained by the Archbishop to the parish of **Kilwinning**. Originally in favour of episcopacy, he objected strongly to the **1637 Book of Common Prayer**. A member of the 1638 **General Assembly**, he adopted a moderate **Covenanter** line and later joined the **Resolutioners** in opposition to the severity of the **Act of Classes**. From 1642 he was Professor of Divinity at Glasgow, attended the Westminster Assembly from 1643 and in 1649 went to Holland with other divines to persuade **Charles II** to accept the Covenant and the crown. After the Restoration, in 1661 he became principal of **Glasgow University**. His letters and journals are a major source for the period.

BAILLIE, Robert, of Jerviswood (c1634–84) Covenanter

Great-grandson of **John Knox** and son-in-law of **Archibald Johnston of Warriston**, one of the principal framers of the National **Covenant**, Robert Baillie was a linguist, mathematician and scientist. Captured in London in the summer of 1683 and accused of involvement in the Rye House Plot against **Charles II**, Baillie was examined by judges and once by the King himself, but refused either to confess or to implicate any of his fellows. In November he was sent, in company with other Scottish prisoners including **William Carstares** and Mure of Rowallan, to **Edinburgh**, 'where laws were more arbitrary and where torture could be applied to compell confession' (A Smellie). Held in Edinburgh's **Tolbooth** for 10 months, he still refused to speak, but was eventually incriminated by evidence extracted from Carstares under torture with thumbscrews. Tried once for harbouring outlawed preachers and fined £6000, Baillie was tried again in front of 'the Bluidy Advocate', **George Mackenzie** on 23 December 1684 and found guilty; 'his head was to be placed on the **Netherbow**, his limbs scattered throughout Scotland, his possessions forfeit and his blood tainted'. Sentence was carried out the following day.

BAIN, Alexander (1818–1903) Psychologist and Philosopher

An **Aberdeen** weaver's son, Bain won a bursary to **Marischal College** and was its outstanding graduate in 1840. He wrote for the *Westminster Review*, studied anatomy and chemistry, but lost or was denied teaching posts on account of his radical views. In 1842 he met J S Mill and other sympathisers in London. Combining a career of writing and teaching with social work, he settled there (1848). On his marriage he retired to Richmond to complete *The Senses and the Intellect* (1855), and *The Emotions and the Will* (1859). Denied the **St Andrews** Chair in Logic and Rhetoric, he was given the new Aberdeen one (1860–80) by the Crown. He founded and funded the journal *Mind* (1876–92). **James Mill**'s disciple and biographer, Bain was a 'painstaking' and systematic observer of mental phenomena, whose approach to psychology was physiological. His theory was summarised in **Encyclopaedia Britannica**: 'Psychology' (1886). He also wrote at length on physics, **education**, grammar, rhetoric, logic and ethics. *The Autobiography of Alexander Bain* was edited by W L Davidson (1904).

BAIRD, Sir David (1757–1829) Soldier

Born at Newbyth, **East Lothian**, Baird went to India in 1799 as captain in a Highland regiment. In the Second Mysore War he was wounded and captured at the battle of Polilur (1780) near Kanchipuram when a force of 3800 were practically annihilated by Hyder Ali's troops while trying to join up with **Sir Hector Munro**'s army. Taken to Srirangapatnam, Baird was held for 44 months in atrocious conditions. His cave-like cell is still visible, though whether he was tied throughout to a fellow-prisoner (much pitied by Baird's mother as 'the man chained to our Davie') is uncertain. Revenge came in the Fourth (and last) Mysore War when Baird, now Major-General, was given command of the final assault on Srirangapatnam, much to the irritation of Arthur Wellesley, the future Duke of Wellington. 'General Baird and the heroes of Seringapatam' thenceforth became a popular toast. Baird went on to command the first Indian troops to reach the Mediterranean (in the 1801 expedition against the French in Egypt) and the force which wrested the Cape from the Dutch in 1805–6. He was also at the siege of Copenhagen (1807) and at Corunna (1809) where he lost an arm. Four times Parliament passed a vote of thanks to him; he was knighted (1804) and created a baronet.

BAIRD, Edward McEwan (1904–49) Painter

Baird was born in **Montrose** and educated at the Montrose Academy. He enrolled at the **Glasgow School of Art** in 1924 where he graduated with the Newbery Medal for best student. A post-diploma travelling scholarship was spent in Italy where the meticulous and scholarly work of Piero della Francesca significantly affected his art. He returned to Montrose in 1928, working in a seclusion disrupted only by a period teaching (1938–40) at **Dundee** College of Art. Baird was an intellectual whose devotion to ideals and to his own work made him disparaging of concession and half-measure. He followed with interest the latest artistic developments and he found in Surrealism, to which his painting is indebted, an uncompromisingly modern trend of thought portrayed in a virtuoso language that must have recalled for him the achievements of the Italian quattrocento. His own Birth of Venus (1934) is wholly surreal in its ambiguous use of realistic technique to depict unlikely subject matter yet, like his other essays in this style, it remains plausible. Baird's critical temperament would never let him consider a work finished, while persistent ill health reduced his output still further. In the 1940s his condition worsened and his work as a war artist was limited mainly to portraiture. Montrose often appeared as a backdrop in his canvases; his ability to absorb a variety of international influences yet maintain a strong sense of Scottish identity and history distinguishes his work from the more fashionable Frenchified styles adopted by many of his contemporaries.

BAIRD, John Logie (1888–1946) Inventor

Born at **Helensburgh**, John Logie Baird, pioneer of television and radio, was a son of the manse. Educated at **Glasgow** Academy and at the city's Royal Technical College, now the **University of Strathclyde**, Baird emigrated to the West Indies for a while before returning

John Logie Baird, pencil drawing by James Kerr-Lawson (SNPG)

to live in England and launching himself on a career of speculative invention.

Early commercial enterprises such as manufacturing undersocks, soap and jam were followed by technical products and processes which showed a high degree of ingenuity. In 1926 Baird transmitted a crude television picture from one room to another, and the following year succeeded in sending a picture by telephone wire from London to Glasgow, topping this with a transatlantic transmission in 1928. The following year he enabled the BBC to show its first television picture, working up to the transmission of mechanically scanned 240-line pictures by 1936. Unfortunately for Baird, this was no match for EMI's electrically scanned 410-line process, which the BBC considered in parallel with Baird's before plumping for the latter. Nevertheless, Baird did much to popularise and promote the idea of television, and latterly studied such refinements as colour, 3D and large-screen TV.

His other enterprises included fibre-optics and radio direction finding (eg radar), the latter giving rise to the belief among his admirers that his contribution to developing Britain's radar defences during World War II has never been officially acknowledged. It is perhaps unfortunate that Baird did not obtain an academic appointment to offer him a more secure foundation from which his undoubted technical expertise could flourish.

BALCASKIE HOUSE, Pittenweem, Fife

West of **Pittenweem**, Balcaskie was an L-plan tower of c1630 which **Sir William Bruce** bought from the Moncrieffs in 1665 and then transformed into a Renaissance mansion, duplicating the original tower house to achieve a symmetry, adding corner pavilions to both, and further extending them with screen walls linked to extensive flanking service wings. The central section linking the two towers was heightened in the 18th century and embellished by **William Burn** in the 19th. Within, the fine painted and plaster ceilings on the first floor are original 17th century. Between the house and the sea Bruce laid out Scotland's first Italianate terraced garden with balustrades and classical busts facing towards the **Bass Rock**. In the grounds are twin circular **doocots**, impressive approaches, and the less impressive remains of Abercromby Church.

BALFLUIG CASTLE, Alford, Aberdeenshire

The L-plan tower house which once belonged to a branch of the Forbes family was in a ruinous state when in the 1960s it became one of the first to be restored with the aid of the Historic Buildings Council. In support of the grant application, W Douglas Simpson described it as 'a quite exceptional building'; the date on the door, 1556, coincided with a lull in castle building; its plan with two re-entrant angles was unusual; so were some of its architectural details such as a gun-loop which suggested the same mason as at **Abergeldie**; the roof, though not original, was probably that added after its burning in the **Battle of Alford**; and its loss as a prominent landmark in the Howe of Alford 'would be widely regretted'. The restoration fully justified this partisan plea.

BALFOUR, Andrew (1630–94) Physician

Born at Denmiln, **Fife**, Balfour studied medicine at **Edinburgh**, London and Paris. After returning to the Scottish capital he realised the need for a regular supply of medicinal plants and, with **Robert Sibbald**, founded the Physic Garden first near **Holyrood**, then at **Trinity College Kirk**, on the site of the present **Waverley Station**. The collection became the basis for the **Royal Botanic Garden**, and also enhanced Edinburgh's reputation as a medical centre. Balfour became the third President of the **Royal College of Physicians**.

BALFOUR, Arthur James (1848–1930) Politician

The only Scottish Secretary later to become Prime Minister, Arthur Balfour was born on his family's estate of **Whittinghame**, **East Lothian**. Probably thanks to his family's intellectual interests, he showed a considerable philosophical bent, but his connections with the Salisbury family offered him a dazzling political career which he began by entering Parliament as Conservative member for Hertford in 1874. In 1886 he was awarded the post of Secretary for Scotland, enjoying cabinet rank – unusual at that time and probably facilitated by being nephew of Lord Salisbury, the then Prime Minister. Agitation for **crofting** reform was high on the political horizon but, after firmly resisting this, Balfour was moved, after only a few months, to the even stormier waters of the Irish Secretaryship, where he showed little sympathy for the concept of Home Rule.

His later years included a lacklustre three years as Prime Minister from 1902–5, and he was Foreign Secretary when he made his celebrated Balfour Declaration in 1917 in favour of a Jewish homeland in Palestine.

Arthur James Balfour, by Sir James Guthrie (SNPG)

So strongly did he identify himself with this concept, later made possible by Britain adopting a League of Nations mandate to govern Palestine, that his life was regarded as being in some danger when he visited Damascus in 1925. 'He rose by opposing in Ireland the very principle of nationality which he ended by advocating in Palestine' (DNB). An influential statesman, if not an immortal politician, Balfour died on 19 March 1930 and was buried at Whittinghame. The Jewish community is said to have mourned him with honours never before accorded to a Gentile.

BALFOUR, Gilbert (d.1576) Adventurer and Murderer

A member of the house of Mountquhannie in **Fife**, Gilbert was involved with his two brothers, Robert and James (**Sir James Balfour of Pittendreich**), in the murder of **Cardinal Beaton** in 1546 and was then besieged with their accomplice, **John Knox**, in **St Andrews Castle**. On its surrender he joined Knox in the French galleys. Knox did not attribute the support of the Balfour brothers to piety, saying that they had 'neither fear of God nor love of virtue, further than their present commodity persuaded them'. Gilbert survived to marry Margaret Bothwell, sister of **Bishop Adam Bothwell** of **Orkney**, who endowed them with a gift of Church lands in the isle of **Westray** in 1560. Here he built the astonishing castle of **Noltland**, with its circular stone stair second in size only to that of **Fyvie**, and its massive provisions for defence.

His appointment as Master of **Queen Mary**'s Household is a curious example of that monarch's erratic judgement, and it enabled Balfour to play what may have been the decisive part in the murder of her husband King Henry, hitherto **Lord Darnley**. Balfour subsequently retired to Orkney where, in the office of Sheriff, he quarrelled with Bishop Adam and refused admittance to **James Hepburn, Earl of Bothwell**, who had been created Duke of Orkney by Queen Mary at the time of her marriage to him. Yet he espoused the cause of the deposed Queen, for which he was convicted of treason and forfeited by Parliament in August 1571. In the following spring he was among those who captured and briefly held **Blackness Castle** on her behalf. By this time her bastard brother **Robert Stewart** had obtained from Bishop Adam all the temporalities of Balfour's see. When he sought to include the Westray property already alienated to Gilbert Balfour, the Privy Council ordered him to surrender 'the house and fortalice of Westraw' to its legal owner. Whether or not Balfour did so, Noltland, built by the slave labour of wretched Orcadians for a seedy adventurer, was never of any use to him. Compelled to flee abroad, he took service in the army of Sweden, where he was executed in 1576 for his part in a plot to murder the King.

BALFOUR, Isaac Bayley (1853–1922)
Botanist
Son of **John Hutton Balfour**, Regius Keeper of **Edinburgh**'s **Royal Botanic Garden**, Isaac Bayley Balfour was born in Edinburgh and spent much of his spare time at the Garden learning a variety of practical skills. He studied botany at **Edinburgh University**, where he assisted his father, then Professor of Botany, and went on to become a lecturer himself and take the Chair of Botany in **Glasgow** at the age of 26. In 1884 he became Professor of Botany at Oxford, where he greatly improved the Botanic Garden, library and herbarium. Most significantly he introduced new ideas from the Continent that helped to change the whole approach to botany in Britain, moving the emphasis from studying dead specimens to using living material. He was the founder editor of the now world-renowned journal *Annals of Botany*.

In 1889 he returned to become Professor of Botany and Keeper of the Royal Botanic Garden in Edinburgh, following in his father's footsteps to the extent of holding the posts for the same period of 34 years. As well as re-organising and re-equipping the Garden, Bayley Balfour increased public access and instituted lectures on elementary botany and horticulture which retain their popularity over a century later. Meanwhile from 1910–20 he was also busy establishing adjacent to the Garden a new University Department of Botany, where previously the Professor had taught almost singlehanded. Before he died he was created a KBE.

BALFOUR, Sir James, of Pittendreich
(1525–83) Politician and Jurist
As clever as he was corrupt, Balfour achieved Machiavellian distinction as a political opportunist during the turbulent early decades of the **Reformation**. Switching allegiance back and forth between the Catholic **Queen Mary** and the Protestant party, he not only survived but prospered, and this in spite of clear evidence of his involvement (along with brothers **Gilbert** and Robert) in the murder of **Darnley**.

His prominence can be gauged by the offices he held during this troubled time. He was the Official of Lothian, Judge of the Bishop of **St Andrews** from 1554–5; in the post-Reformation period he was appointed as an extraordinary Lord of Session (1561) followed by appointment as a Lord of Session (1563); when the Commissary Court was created in 1563 to replace the Ecclesiastical Courts, he became Commissary, was made Privy Councillor (1565) and Clerk Register (1566). He resigned the Registership to become Lord President in 1567.

His principal contribution to written law was the authorship of *Practicks: or a System of the more Ancient Law of Scotland* (1574), a useful collection of statute law and decided cases which provides much material for legal historical research today. His son Michael was created Lord Balfour of Burleigh (1607).

BALFOUR, John, of Kinloch (fl.1679)
Covenanter
Sometimes called 'Captain Burleigh' or 'Burley', giving rise to confusion with the Balfours of Burleigh, John of Kinloch's 'burly' was in fact a nickname on account of his physical appearance. Also described as being 'squint-eyed and of a very fierce aspect' and 'the Jehu of the **Covenant**', he was the leader of the band of three fanatical **Fife** Covenanters responsible for the murder of **Archbishop Sharp** on Magus Muir (1679). He was also one of the participants in the **Rutherglen Declaration** (1679), fought at the **Battle of Drumclog** (1679) and took part in **Argyll's Rising** (1685), although he may not have survived that as nothing is known of his later life.

BALFOUR, John Hutton (1808–84) Botanist
Born in **Edinburgh**, the son of a surgeon turned publisher, Balfour studied medicine and botany in Edinburgh and Paris, returning to practise in his home town in 1834 and spending his holidays botanising. In 1836 he was one of ten founder members of the Botanical Society of Edinburgh, which began the herbarium collection and library now housed in the **Royal Botanic Garden**.

Balfour gradually moved from medicine to botany and in 1841 he took the Chair of Botany in **Glasgow**, returning to Edinburgh to become the last Professor of Medicine and Botany and to be Keeper of the Royal Botanic Garden, where he increased the area and established a Museum of Economic Botany and the beautiful temperate Palm House that graces the Garden to this day.

At that time Edinburgh had the largest school of botany in Britain, and Balfour was an excellent teacher. As well as lecturing, he used the Garden and glasshouses for demonstration, and introduced practical laboratory work using newly developed microscopy techniques. He inspired such enthusiasm in his students that they willingly arrived at 6 am to help set up demonstrations for 8 o'clock classes. However, it was field work that he really loved, especially in pursuit of alpine plants. On Saturdays and vacations he led excursions throughout Scotland, and he even took his students as far as Switzerland, not just hunting rare species but teaching what is now called ecology.

BALFOUR COMMISSION

The Royal Commission on Scottish Affairs was set up on 25 July 1952 'to review the arrangements for exercising the functions of HM Government in relation to Scotland'. Its remit included administrative, but not political, devolution. Chaired by the 3rd Earl Balfour (1902–68), it reported in July 1954. It suggested that 'Scotland's needs and points of view should be known and brought into account at all times in the formation and execution of policies', but its recommendations were mainly concerned with administrative detail, eg that highways should come under the aegis of the Scottish Office.

BALFRON, Stirlingshire

Just north of the Endrick Water in west **Stirlingshire**, Balfron was founded in 1789 by Robert Dunmore as accommodation for workers in his Ballindalloch **cotton** mill. In the grounds of Ballindalloch House there is a 17th century sundial topped with a small obelisk. **David Bryce** designed Ballinkrain Castle (1868) and **Alexander 'Greek' Thomson**, a native of the place, Balfron Manse. Edinbellie, to the east, is the supposed birthplace of **John Napier**, the inventor of logarithms and, much later, was the home of Jean Key whose abduction proved the undoing of **Robin Oig MacGregor**. The name Balfron or 'town of mourning' is said to refer to an earlier loss when the children of the 'town', now only a village and then scarcely a clachan, were killed by wolves.

BALLACHULISH, Argyll

Straddling the narrows at the mouth of **Loch Leven**, Ballachulish once owed its celebrity to slate **quarrying** and traffic jams. The quarries, dating from the 17th century, closed in the 1950s and have since been partially landscaped; the ferries, cause of the traffic delays, were pensioned off in the 1970s when a new bridge was opened across the narrows. Thus the driver is spared that most delicate of calculations, whether more seconds will be saved by driving the 23 switchback miles round the loch or by sitting tight in the queue for the ferry; and at last the people of South Ballachulish can enjoy normal intercourse with their brethren of North Ballachulish. At the south end of the bridge is a cairn commemorating James Stewart of **Appin Murder** fame, and just off Ballachulish proper lies the island of St Munda, resting place of MacIan of **Glencoe Massacre** fame.

BALLADS

As stories in song, ballads belong to oral tradition and may date back as far as the Middle Ages. Collected, written down, published and popularised by, among others, **Sir Walter Scott** (notably in The Minstrelsy of the Scottish Borders, 1802–3), they form the bulk of Scotland's folk literature, described by an American critic as 'unsurpassed by any in the world' . It was probably Scott who coined the term 'Border Ballads' although the main collections have in fact been made in north-east Scotland, especially **Aberdeenshire**, whence Scott himself seems to have appropriated some material. More recently **Edinburgh University**'s School of Scottish Studies has tapped rich veins in **Angus**, **Perthshire** and amongst the itinerant tinkers. '**Bothy Ballads**', a term originally used of the earthier and often hilarious songs popular among farm labourers in the north-east, is sometimes used to distinguish the north-east tradition from that of the Borders.

Some ballads, like 'Lord Randal', belong to an international repertoire; Scandinavian influences have been detected in others; but most appear to be indigenous. The tunes are wide ranging, often pentatonic, and of hypnotic power, while stanzas are typically of two or four lines. The narratives usually focus on a single event and rely heavily on dramatic dialogue. Most draw on history, some being profoundly tragic such as 'Sir Patrick Spens' or 'The Twa Corbies'; Border Ballads tell of cattle raids and skirmishes ('Kinmont Willie', '**Johnnie Armstrong**'); and there are many dealing with prediction, the supernatural, and the legends of **Thomas the Rhymer**. Didactic and personal asides are rare, the authors being anonymous and composition no doubt cumulative as succeeding exponents added to or extemporised on existing verses.

Scott apart, major collections were made by David Herd (Ancient and Modern Scottish Songs, 1776) and by the American F J Child (English and Scottish Ballads, 1882–98), who draws heavily on the important manuscript collection of Anna Gordon, née Brown, of **Falkland** (1747–1810). A larger collection of some 3000 texts and tunes was made by the **Buchan** schoolmaster **Gavin Greig** and edited by Alexander Keith as Last Leaves of Traditional Ballads and Ballad Airs, 1925. The extent to which some collectors, Scott included, improved, anglicised, or added to authentic material, and the wider question of whether an oral song tradition is enriched or impoverished by being elevated into literature, are hotly debated.

BALLANTRAE, Ayrshire

On the coast equidistant between **Girvan** and **Cairnryan**, the **fishing** village of Ballantrae at the mouth of the river Stinchar should have been, but was not, the scene of **Robert Louis Stevenson**'s Master of Ballantrae; that honour goes to Borgue in **Kirkcudbrightshire**, Stevenson just pinching the 'more musical' name. The ruins of Ardstinchar Castle (c1450) overlook Ballantrae harbour and the church (1819) has a memorial to David MacGibbon (of **MacGibbon and Ross** fame). Its peace now somewhat diminished by the volume of traffic on the coast road, Ballantrae has developed as a retirement and holiday village, a fate that has also befallen Lendalfoot a few miles to the north, another erstwhile fishing village with its own ruined Carleton Castle (15th century). Halfway between the two, Bennane Head is the site of Sawney Bean's cave, home of the notorious and possibly legendary family of cannibals who ambushed, robbed and then devoured passing travellers.

BALLANTYNE, James (1772–1833) and John (1774–1821) Printers and Publishers

Sons of a merchant, the Ballantyne brothers were born in **Kelso** and attended the same school as **Walter Scott**. James went on to **Edinburgh University** (1785–6), where he trained for the **law**. He became a solicitor's apprentice, and in 1795 established his own law office, which he gave up the following year to begin printing and editing the Kelso Mail. In 1802, having previously printed some of Walter Scott's **ballads**, he undertook the printing of the first two volumes of Scott's *The Minstrelsy of the Scottish Borders*. With Scott's encouragement and financial help, he moved his printing works to **Edinburgh**, where he was joined by his younger brother John. John had previously worked in a merchant bank in London before becoming a clerk in his brother's firm.

In 1808 the firm expanded into publishing, printing and bookselling, with John as head of the firm and Walter Scott as a silent half-partner. Their fine printing work was very successful and attracted much custom, yet the firm suffered financial losses throughout its existence. John died on 16 June 1821, and in 1826 the firm was involved in the financial failure of the publisher **Archibald Constable**, following which it was forced to declare bankruptcy. James was kept on as an employee of the creditors' trustees, editing the *Weekly Journal* and managing the printing office. He died on 17 January 1833.

BALLANTYNE, R(obert) M(ichael) (1825–94) Children's Writer

Born in **Edinburgh**, the nephew of **James and John Ballantyne**, printers and publishers to **Sir Walter Scott**, R M Ballantyne was educated at **Edinburgh University**. In 1841 he went to Canada and for six years worked as a clerk for the Hudson's Bay Company, returning to Edinburgh in 1848 to work as a clerk with the North British **Railway** Company. That same year he published his first book, *Hudson's Bay, Everyday Life in the Wilds of North America*. Its success led to his being taken on as a partner in the publishing house of Thomas Constable in 1852 and from then on he wrote copiously, publishing more than 90 titles, mostly adventure stories for children in the *Boy's Own* tradition, the best-known of which was *The Coral Island* (1857). His autobiography, *Personal Reminiscences in Book-making*, was published in 1893. He died in Rome.

BALLATER, Aberdeenshire

This small town between **Aboyne** and **Braemar** epitomises Royal Deeside. It was once the local rail-head, **Queen Victoria** having objected to the continuation of the line past **Balmoral** to **Braemar** as an invasion of privacy. Thus, like **Crathie** Church, Ballater station became hallowed ground for newshounds and loyal subjects anxious to glimpse the royal party as they disembarked for Balmoral – a cachet that has not yet extended to **Aberdeen**'s Dyce Airport, favoured disembarkation point since the closure of the **railway**. The town is neat and comparatively new, having resulted from the determination of Colonel Francis Farquharson and his son to exploit the supposed properties of the nearby spring of Pananich in the 1790s. The 19th century's craze for both spas and royalty assured its success. The Royal Bridge, opened by the Queen in 1885, spans the **Dee**, and the town hall doubles as a memorial to Prince Albert.

Behind the town the rock defile known as the Pass of Ballater runs west from Tullich, a much older village with the remains of a pre-**Reformation** church and a large collection of **Pictish** symbol stones, to Glen Gairn where the church is dedicated to **St Kentigern**. Gairnshiel Bridge, further west, is a fine single span of 1754,

part of the **military road** from **Blairgowrie** to Speyside and **Fort George**. Complementing Glen Gairn but on the south side of the Dee is Glen Muick which flanks the Balmoral estate and contains Knock Castle, a ruined 16th century tower of the **Huntly Gordons**, and Birkhall, a royal dower house where Florence Nightingale once stayed.

BALLINDALLOCH, Banffshire

Where the Avon joins the **Spey**, the township and district of Ballindalloch contains several **Clava cairns** (one with passage) at Lagmore West and Marionburg, St Peter's Church at Inveravon with four incised **Pictish** symbol stones, and Ballindalloch Castle, a much extended 16th century Z-plan fortalice which since the 18th century has been a **Grant** (now MacPherson Grant) property. Near Marypark is the Glenfarclas Distillery and from Dalnashaugh a road leads up Glenavon to more distilleries in **Glenlivet** and **Tomintoul**.

BALLINGALL, Sir George (1780–1855) Military Surgeon

Born at Forglen, **Banff**, and schooled in **Falkland, Fife**, Ballingall went to **St Andrews** and then **Edinburgh University**, where he studied medicine from 1803. Licensed by the Royal College of Surgeons in 1805, he did not graduate MD until 1819, having interrupted his studies to serve as assistant surgeon with the British forces in India, Java and France. In 1822 he gained the Chair of Military Surgery at Edinburgh, then the only one in Britain, holding it until his death. The leading authority on battlefield wounds, he amassed a grisly collection of specimens of broken and battered bones still in the Anatomy Department. His *Outlines of Military Surgery* (1830) was definitive, going into five editions, the last coeval with the Crimean War. In it he describes 'one of the earliest examples of the rehabilitation of severely disfiguring maxillo-facial injuries' (Bell *et al* 1999). Most famously, he restored the features of Alphonse Louis, the 'Gunner with the Silver (articulated) Mask' in 1851.

BALLIOL, Devorguilla (c1209–90)

Her Gaelic name *dearbh-fhorghoill* means 'true judgement'. Youngest daughter of **Alan of Galloway**, she married (1233) John Balliol of Barnard Castle, Co Durham, and had four sons and three daughters. Inheriting much of **Galloway** plus lands in **Aberdeenshire** and **Angus**, and in the Honour of Huntingdon, she transmitted a claim to the throne to her only surviving son, **John Balliol** [see **David of Huntingdon**]. With her husband she was active in Anglo-Scots politics (he was among Henry III's representatives during the minority of **Alexander III**).

When John died (1268) Devorguilla had his embalmed heart encased in an ivory shrine and placed before her at meals, when she gave its share of every dish to the poor. She erected friaries (Dominicans at **Wigtown**, Franciscans at **Dundee** and **Dumfries**), endowed a hostel for poor scholars at Oxford (later Balliol College) and founded **Sweetheart Abbey**. She is also credited with the first stone bridge at Dumfries. She died at Buittle Castle and was buried in her abbey with the casket in her arms.

BALLIOL, Edward (?1283–1364) 'King'

Son of **King John Balliol**, Edward was a prisoner in England after John's abdication, though acknowledged as heir by many Scots. Released to France, he was recalled to England in 1324. In 1332, during an Anglo-Scots peace (**Treaty of Edinburgh**), he led 88 ships from the Humber to **Kinghorn** in **Fife**, overcame a Scots army at **Dupplin** and was crowned at **Scone**. Soon chased out of **Annan**, 'one leg booted and the other bare', he took refuge behind English armies. He survived as a puppet-king during the minority of **David II** until 1356, when Edward III dismissed him with a pension; he died at Bailleul (whence the family's name) in Picardy.

BALLIOL, John (1249–1313) King

Son of **Devorguilla Balliol**, John married Isabella, daughter of the Earl of Surrey (Warenne). Three elder brothers predeceased him, leaving him vast English and Scottish estates. His claim to the throne (1291) was contested by a dozen rivals (the **Competitors**) including **Robert Bruce of Annandale**. Dreading civil war, the Guardians of Scotland invited Edward I of England to conduct an inquiry; he began by demanding allegiance and custody of important castles.

John's claim was the strongest. Enthroned at **Scone** on St Andrew's Day 1292, he soon found Edward's interventions intolerable. When Edward demanded Scots troops for war in France, the Community of the Realm induced John to abrogate his allegiance, and themselves renewed the **auld alliance** with France (1295); Edward invaded Scotland, sacking **Berwick** and routing the feudal army at **Dunbar**.

John fled and sued for peace; he made abject surrender at **Stracathro**, July 1296, and was stripped of the royal insignia (whence his byename 'Toom Tabard' – empty surcoat). Imprisoned in the Tower of London, then released into Papal custody, he was finally given his ancestral home, Bailleul in Picardy, where he died, leaving a son **Edward Balliol**, who renewed the claim to Scotland.

BALLOCH, Dunbartonshire

Boating and pleasure cruises have long attracted **tourists** to Balloch on the southern shore of **Loch Lomond**. The first steamboat *Marion* came to the loch in 1816. Balloch Castle, dating from 1238, was the historic home of the **Earls of Lennox**, but was replaced in the 19th century by the castellated mansion of today.

BALMANNO CASTLE, Nr Bridge of Earn, Perthshire

Built soon after 1570 when the estate passed to the Auchinleck family, this is an L-plan tower house chiefly notable for the much admired restoration carried out by **Sir Robert Lorimer** in 1916. Alterations included heightening the stair turret and adding new wings and courtyard; more typical is Lorimer's attention to the interior details of plasterwork and timber. Not far away on the Glenearn estate Ecclesiamagirdle House, a modest T-plan building of 1648, badly needs a modern Lorimer after being vacant for 20 years. The delightful name (apparently pronounced 'Exmagriddle') derives from the pre-**Reformation** chapel of St Grill or Gillan,

one of **St Columba**'s harpers, the ruins of which stand near the house.

BALMERINO ABBEY, Fife

West of **Newport-on-Tay**, Balmerino was founded in 1226 by Ermengarde, widow of **William the Lion**, and her son **Alexander I**. Like nearby **Lindores** it was an offshoot of a Borders establishment, in this case the Cistercian abbey of **Melrose**; and like Lindores it suffered during the hostilities of the **Rough Wooing**, in this case at the hands of the English who 'burnt the house and everything in it' (1547). 12 years later it was overtaken by the **Reformation**. By 1588 the church had been destroyed and in 1603 it was made into a temporal lordship for the Elphinstone family. James Elphinstone, 1st Lord Balmerino (1553–1612) was an **Octavian** and **Arthur, 6th Lord** (1688–1746), a noted **Jacobite**. Captured at **Culloden** he was executed on Tower Hill but not before making a great impression. 'The most natural brave old man I ever saw' (Horace Walpole), he reaffirmed his allegiance to the cause and then donned a plaid cap, declaring that he would die a Scotsman. The title was forfeited. Of the abbey Defoe found 'nothing worth observation, the very ruins being almost eaten up by time'. The 15th century vaulted chapter house remains notable with surviving piers and fine capitals.

BALMORAL CASTLE, Deeside, Aberdeenshire

The Balmoral estate, halfway between **Ballater** and **Braemar**, is mentioned in the 15th century and passed from the Gordons of **Huntly** to the Farquharsons of Inverey (west of Braemar) in 1662. From them the banking Duffs, **Earls of Fife**, acquired it (1798) in debt settlement and it was their lessee, Sir Robert Gordon (brother of the **4th Earl of Aberdeen**), whose hospitality invited **Queen Victoria**'s attention. While the royal family, accompanied by the royal physician, were not amused by a wet week at Ardverikie on **Loch Laggan**, the latter's son and Sir Edwin Landseer were enjoying fine views and dry going with Gordon. The Queen and Prince Consort went to see for themselves and in 1848, after the death of Gordon, assumed the lease. Much taken with 'this dear paradise', in 1853 they purchased the estate outright for £31,500; it remains the personal property and summer holiday residence of the sovereign.

The castle (1855), designed by William Smith of **Aberdeen** under the supervision of the Prince Consort, replaced the Gordon residence which was demolished. Intended to accommodate guests and entourage in excess of 100 persons, it is of vast proportions, fine materials (especially the pale grey ashlar) and excellent workmanship. Opinions differ as to its architectural merits, vernacular features being much in evidence but the whole being more suggestive of a *schloss* than a tower house. The grounds are splendidly planted and well endowed with cairns, statues and cottages commemorating various members of the royal family.

BALNAKIL (Balnakeil), Durness, Sutherland

'Township of the Church' in English, Balnakil occupies the exceptionally fertile limestone outcrop which extends north to Farout (Faraid) Head in the parish

Balmoral Castle as rebuilt for Queen Victoria and Prince Albert (SP)

of **Durness**. Here the medieval bishops of **Caithness** maintained a farm; but no ecclesiastical remains are to be seen other than the roofless ruins of the church which Donald Mackay, 1st Lord Reay, built here soon after his succession as clan chief in 1614. Near its entrance the great Gaelic **bard Rob Donn** Mackay was buried in 1778. Nearby stands the mansion in which the heirs to the chiefship used to live until their removal to **Tongue** on their accession, administering the granary and **deer forests** of the far west. The 4th Lord Reay continued to live at Balnakil from his succession in 1748 until his death in 1761, and every aspect of the society over which he presided is described in the racy, witty and sometimes vitriolic verses of Rob Donn. His collected poems were not published until 1829, when an imposing monument was raised to his memory in Balnakil cemetery.

BALNAVES, Henry (c1512–79) Reformer, Lord of Session

Born in **Kirkcaldy** and educated at **St Andrews** and Cologne, where he came into contact with Swiss and German reformers, Balnaves was created a Lord of Session by **James V** in 1538 and was briefly Secretary of State (1543) before being imprisoned for six months in **Blackness Castle** for his Protestantism. In 1546 he joined **John Knox** and the murderers of **Cardinal Beaton** in St Andrews Castle; when the castle was captured by the French troops of **Mary of Guise**, he was sent with Knox as a prisoner first to the galleys and then to Rouen, where he wrote his treatise on *Justification by Faith* (published in 1584 as *The Confession of Faith* with notes and introduction by Knox). In 1556 he was allowed to return to Scotland where he was active on behalf of the **Lords of the Congregation**, being reinstated as Lord of Session in 1563.

BALQUHIDDER, Perthshire

The village (or Kirkton) of Balquhidder is at the east end of Loch Voil in the **Trossachs**; the Braes of Balquhidder (celebrated in song by **Robert Tannahill**) extend along the lochside; Balquhidder parish originally embraced a still larger tract from **Loch Lomond** to mid Loch Earn. Once the home of the MacLaren clan, the area is now more commonly associated with the **MacGregors** and especially **Rob Roy**, whose grave and those of his wife and two sons are in the little churchyard. The present church, designed by **David Bryce**, was built by David Carnegie of Stronvar in 1885. It superseded the now roofless ruin (dated 1631) in the churchyard which in turn replaced a 13th century church (foundations only survive) supposedly built over the grave of St Angus. The Celtic saint's gravestone, possibly 9th century, has been removed to the new church along with a bell donated by **Robert Kirk** in 1684 and a curious hollowed-out boulder which serves as a font. Here in 1589 some MacGregors swore over the decapitated head of a royal forester never to reveal the murderer – and then presented the head to the lady of Ardvorlich [see **Lochearnhead**]. The place has since become something of a MacGregor shrine and in 1975 MacGregors from all over the world gathered here to celebrate the bicentenary of the ending of the proscription of the name MacGregor.

BALVENIE CASTLE, Dufftown, Banffshire

Beautifully sited above the junction of Glens Fiddich and Rinnes (and now sandwiched between two distilleries), Balvenie has been identified as the 13th century castle of Mortlach belonging to the (Black) **Comyn Earls of Buchan**. Some earthworks and lower masonry courses are its only vestiges. By the early 15th century the castle, as Balvenie, was in Black **Douglas** hands, whence it passed to John Stewart, 1st Earl of Atholl and his much married wife Margaret, the 'Fair Maid of Galloway' (widow of the **8th Earl of Douglas** and divorced wife of the **9th**). It was their descendant John Stewart 4th Earl of Atholl (1542–79) who transformed Balvenie from a simple quadrangular castle of enclosure with chambers ranged against the walls into a stylish residence. This was achieved by demolishing much of the east wall and rebuilding this end of the castle as a Renaissance palace with a massive round tower at the angle (as at **Huntly**).

The castle changed hands frequently in the 17th century. **Montrose** rested his men there after the inconclusive Battle of **Fyvie** (1644) and here **General Alexander Leslie**'s **Covenanters** routed (1649) a Royalist force, taking 900 prisoners. 'Forth Fortune and Fill thy Coffers', the motto of the Stewart Atholls which appears below their arms on the new building, could have been meant for the upstart **Duffs** of Braco (later **Earls and Dukes of Fife**) who finally acquired the castle, and hopefully some of its historical kudos, as a debt settlement (1687). Cannily negotiating the **Jacobite** troubles

The 16th century east wing of Balvenie Castle as a romantic 19th century ruin (RWB)

while continuing their empire building (**Duff House, Dufftown, MacDuff**, and a new house at Balvenie) the Duffs finally moved out in 1724, watching the place crumble for two centuries until (1929) the trustees of the 6th Earl and 1st Duke entrusted the derelict remains to the nation.

BANAVIE, Fort William, Inverness-shire

Now rather overwhelmed by **Fort William**'s sprawl, Banavie was once the terminus for steamers on the Caledonian **Canal**. The flight of eight locks, which here lower the canal by 64ft (19.5m) (and which **Telford** named 'Neptune's Staircase'), involved too long a delay for impatient Victorian trippers from **Inverness**; they preferred to be shuttled into Fort William by carriage. Two or three hotels sprang up and Banavie briefly enjoyed resort status. Across the Lochy stand the two **Inverlochy Castles** and upstream the remains of the two Tor Castles. One, a 19th century house and later hotel, burnt down in 1950; of the other, an ancient fortress much disputed by **Mackintoshes** and **Camerons** in the 14th–16th centuries, only foundations remain.

BANCHORY, Kincardineshire

Though on the banks of the **Aberdeenshire Dee**, Banchory was part of **Kincardineshire**, a Burnett of Leys having insisted that the lands of his **Crathes Castle** (two miles east) be in the same shire as those of his **Muchalls Castle** (near **Stonehaven**). St Ternan is supposed to have founded a monastery here in the 5th century, but little else is recorded of the place until the 19th century made Deeside fashionable. As a resort (in which Somerset Maugham recovered from TB) and as an overspill

for **Aberdeen**, Banchory quickly became a town. Apart from Crathes, its main attractions are its sheltered situation and the falls on the river Feugh which here joins the **Dee** from the south. Down its defile comes the road from Cairn o' Mount, one of the highest (1475ft/450m) in Scotland; the tower on a hill to the west is a monument to General Sir William Burnett. Also south of the Dee is Tilquhilly Castle, a plain and unsung 16th century Z-plan tower house which may appeal to those who find Crathes, almost opposite, an over-iced confection. North of the town rises the Hill of Fare whereon was fought the **Battle of Corrichie** (1562), a fact memorialised on a plaque erected by the Deeside Field Club.

BANFF, Banffshire

At the mouth of the **Deveron** on the Moray Firth, and spilling down the cliffside in a series of terraces, the small town of Banff possesses a period character in no way equalled by **MacDuff**, its upstart rival across the Deveron. Its charter as a **royal burgh** is said to date from 1163 and to have been confirmed by **Robert Bruce** in 1324. Then a thanedom of the **Comyn Earls of Buchan**, it later passed to the Ogilvies of Deskford (eventually Earls of Findlater), one of whom built the so-called castle (1750) to a **William Adam** design on the site of the Comyn fort. It is not to be compared with **Duff House**, Adam's masterpiece on the outskirts of the town. Near the harbour a burial aisle of more Ogilvies is all that remains of the pre-**Reformation** church. Banff's *grand siècle* was really the late 18th/early 19th century and in buildings like the parish church of St Mary (1790), the portico-ed and cupola-ed Trinity Alva church (1844), the equally neo-classical Banff Academy building (1836), and the Town House (1796) with its tapering clock steeple (1764), a strong Regency flavour remains.

This is echoed in a host of fine town houses in High Shore (No 1 is actually a mini tower house of 1695) and High Street, as well as several warehouses near the now silted-up harbour. From High Street steep lanes descend to Low Street, the main thoroughfare where at a widened intersection, the Plainstones, stand the Town House, the tall 16th century Mercat Cross, and a cannon captured at Sebastopol. It was probably here that the gallows were erected in 1700 or 1701 for James MacPherson, not the translator of Ossian, but a freebooter and fiddler who played the famous rant that bears his name on the way to his execution. He then offered his fiddle to the crowd but, finding no takers, snapped it in two before ascending the scaffold. **Burns**, visiting Banff in 1780, captured the defiant spirit of 'MacPherson's Farewell':

Sae rantingly, sae wantonly, sae dauntingly gaed he;
He played a spring and danced it round beneath the gallows tree.

Sands, **golf courses** and caravan sites fringe the town. A fine seven-arched bridge by John Smeaton (1779) spans the Deveron beside Duff House estate. Three miles inland, but within Banff parish, stands the well restored 16th century Inchdrewer Castle, another property of the Ogilvies whose principal residence was **Boyne Castle**.

BANFFSHIRE

Before the **local government** reorganisation of 1975, Banffshire was an almost wedge-shaped county, 10 miles wide in the south, broadening to 31 miles of Moray Firth coastline in the north. With the 4296ft (1309m) Ben MacDhui in its extreme south-west corner, the county was drained by the rivers Avon, **Deveron**, Isla and **Spey**, the last forming the county's western boundary. Comprising 403,054 acres (163,114ha), Banffshire was entirely absorbed into Grampian Region in 1975, and divided into the Districts of Moray and Banff & Buchan; since 1995 the former has been part of the Moray Council Area and the latter part of Aberdeenshire.

The county was the scene of much religious strife in the 17th and 18th centuries, and its boundaries were not formalised until the Local Government (Scotland) Act of 1889. Its administrative centre was **Banff**, one of two **royal burghs** in the county, the other being **Cullen**, the remaining burghs comprising **Aberchirder, Buckie, Charlestown of Aberlour, Dufftown, Findochty, Keith, MacDuff, Portnockie** and **Portsoy. Agriculture** and **forestry** were matched in importance by **fishing** – 13 ports operated under the twin fishing administration areas centred on MacDuff and Buckie – and there were 25 **whisky** distilleries active in the 1960s.

BANK HOLIDAYS

Bank holidays in Scotland are governed by the Bank Holidays Act 1871, and were originally so called by the parliamentary sponsors of the legislation, as the term 'public holidays' was expected to generate hostility from **temperance** organisations fearing widespread public drunkenness, in addition to a traditionally negative reaction from employers. Closure of the banks, it was believed, would discourage trade on days prescribed as holidays. Currently Scottish bank holidays are held on the following days: 1 and 2 January; Good Friday; May Day; Spring Holiday (last Monday in May); First Monday in August; Christmas Day; Boxing Day.

Not all of the above are Scottish holidays – often shops and local authority services operate as usual on bank holidays. Spring and autumn holidays are held in various towns and cities on varying dates, and the tradition of staggered summer holidays for individual communities still holds good. For example, **Edinburgh**'s Trades Holidays comprise approximately the first fortnight in July, followed by the **Glasgow Fair** traditionally starting on the second Friday of the month. The best guide to the sometimes confusing pattern of Scottish local holidays is the booklet *Scottish Trades and Shop Holidays* published annually by William Culross & Son of **Coupar Angus**.

BANKS AND BANKING

BANK OF SCOTLAND AND ROYAL BANK OF SCOTLAND
A year after the Bank of England was set up, allegedly by **William Paterson**, the Bank of Scotland was founded (1695) in **Edinburgh**. Its monopoly powers were allowed to lapse early in the next century and out of 'the equivalent' (the financial settlement necessitated by the **Act of Union** and the failure of the **Darien scheme**) the Royal Bank of Scotland was founded (1727) also in

Edinburgh. Supported by **John Campbell 2nd Duke of Argyll** and other **Whig** interests, the Royal Bank 'may be seen as part of Walpole's system of political control in Scotland' (S G Checkland). Both banks would remain in different political camps, 'the Bank' Tory and tainted with **Jacobitism**, 'the Royal' Whig and Hanoverian.

Elsewhere in Scotland banking services such as discount and exchange were provided by merchants. But the growing pace of economic development in the 18th century was ill-served by the two Edinburgh banks concentrating most of their credit in Edinburgh; except for the more senior **Tobacco** Lords, **Glasgow**'s merchants were unknown in the capital and so at a disadvantage. To meet this situation small private banks borrowed from the Edinburgh banks and extended credit to Glasgow and elsewhere. The merchants themselves soon followed suit by setting up provincial banks, a freedom not allowed to English merchants. In attempting to quash these rivals, the two Edinburgh banks had some success although the **Dundee** Banking Company, for instance, survived.

BRITISH LINEN BANK On an initiative from the Board of Trustees for Manufactures (set up in the wake of the '45 **Jacobite Rising**), the British Linen Bank was founded in 1746 to develop the Scottish **linen** industry. It had some support from the Royal Bank and through the Linen Company's commercial agents soon developed rudimentary banking services in the provinces. It was thus the pioneer of branch banking although the Bank of Scotland had tried unsuccessfully to develop a branch network in the 1690s and again in the 1730s; it succeeded at a third attempt in the 1770s. The Royal, by contrast, maintained just one branch, that established in Glasgow in 1783; with **David Dale** as one of its two managing agents, this branch nevertheless became one of the busiest bank offices in the UK.

CURRENCY AND CREDIT Nearly all these banks issued their own bank notes and there was a clear danger, in the 1760s, that this would lead to monetary instability. Some modest regulation by statute in 1765 and the opening of the note exchange a few years later regularised matters and the note issue became one of the most popular and successful aspects of the activities of Scottish banking. The existence of a note exchange also brought more mutual respect into inter-bank relations. Although the bulk of lending was by discounting trade bills, the cash credit (forerunner of the modern overdraft) was developed by the Royal Bank early in the century; soon all banks offered advances to their customers by this means. Similarly the acceptance of deposits and the paying of interest was by no means a new idea, but the Scots were the first to develop it as a significant and continuing activity on a large scale. It first developed in Glasgow and Dundee where the pace of economic progress was most rapid and the demand for funds greatest.

UNION AND CLYDESDALE BANK Throughout the Industrial Revolution the banking system grew in a fairly dynamic and, on the whole, relatively stable basis. Branch systems were enlarged and new provincial banking companies continued to be formed. The growth of industry and commerce was such that many of the smaller provincial banking companies and private banks ceased to be able to provide the scale of financial services required by their customers. This was particularly evident in the 1830s with the growth of the **iron** industry and the building of **railways**. A new generation of banks included four major joint-stock ventures in the west of Scotland which were designed to break the ultra-conservatism of Edinburgh's financial tutelage and meet the demands of 'the Empire's second city'. These were the Union Bank of Scotland (1830), the Western Bank of Scotland (1832), the Clydesdale Bank (1838) and the City of Glasgow Bank (1839). The Clydesdale could pass as a sober, liberal, middle-class institution but the Western and City of Glasgow proved much more adventurous. Scornful of large reserve holdings, the Western in particular captured the aggressive spirit of the times and by 1850 had 72 branches, then the largest network in the world.

SAVINGS BANKS Somewhat in the background another trend was developing which was to have a significant impact on Scottish life. The first Savings Bank, accepting deposits and paying interest on small sums, was founded in **Ruthwell** in **Dumfriesshire** in 1810 by the Rev Henry Duncan. From there the movement spread throughout the country and to many other parts of the world. These were not commercial banks for they did not lend money to businesses or issue bank notes. Their deposits were, for the most part, invested with the Commissioners for the National Debt. Nevertheless their contribution to the cult of Scottish thrift was enormous. Moreover, their off-shoots, the penny savings banks, carried the tradition to all levels of Scottish society.

ANGLO-SCOTTISH RIVALRY In 1826, concerned that the note issues of an otherwise undeveloped English banking system had contributed to the financial crisis of that year, the government determined to curb note issues throughout the UK and to outlaw all notes below £5 in value. The outcry in Scotland in defence of, essentially, the £1 note brought Parliamentary enquiries which resulted in the exemption of the Scottish note issuing system. Amongst defenders of the system was **Sir Walter Scott** who, as 'Malachi Malagrowther', championed the Scottish £1 note which thenceforth acquired a national symbolism; the Bank of Scotland's £1 note still carries a portrait of Scott.

A further series of commercial crises in the 1830s and early 1840s resulted in 1845 legislation, despite protests from Scotland, which had the effect of confining the note issue to banks already in existence. Since that time no major commercial banks have been formed. It has sometimes been claimed that this marked the end of Scotland's most dynamic period of banking development, but the number of branches continued to grow as did the volume of lending and deposit-taking.

Between 1845–70 the number of Scottish banks declined from 17 to 10, partly due to amalgamations but also as a result of two sensational crashes amongst Glasgow's joint-stock ventures. In 1857 the Western Bank, which had been in difficulty twice before but now boasted 100 branches and paid-up capital second only to the Royal Bank, closed its doors with liabilities of £9 million; and in 1878 the City of Glasgow Bank went down in even more dramatic circumstances; only 254 of its 1819 shareholders remained solvent while evidence of fraud and incompetence resulted in the trial of its directors, three of whom were imprisoned. Both banks had allowed their major loans to become perilously concentrated in a handful of companies; both crashes had disastrous consequences for their investors although not for the general public; and both were to some extent blamed on the reluctance of the Edinburgh banks to afford rescue facilities.

Meanwhile London was fast developing as an international financial centre and in the 1860s the Scottish banks began to open offices there despite a storm of protest from the English banks. In 1874 the Clydesdale Bank opened three branches in the north of England. This provoked howls of outrage from English bankers and the government appointed a committee of inquiry. Evidence was taken but no report was produced. Nevertheless the Clydesdale, and the other Scottish banks which were about to follow its example, abandoned plans to open English branch networks. There the matter stood for a century. The Scots confined themselves, apart from their London offices, to Scotland and the English banks agreed not to open north of the border.

This was an important decision because at that time banking was underdeveloped in England and it seems that the Scots would have had the strength to stage takeover bids for many of the English banks. Over the next 30 years the English banks, by processes of merger, acquisition and takeover, and also by extensive branch-opening, consolidated their position and the 'Big Five' emerged. The Midland Bank, by 1913, was the largest bank in the world. Towards the end of World War I some of the English banks turned their attention to Scotland and Ireland and began a process of acquisition. Four of Scotland's eight banks were taken over in this way although these takeovers were referred to as 'affiliations' and the Scottish banks retained their identities, note issues and boards of directors. Nor does there appear to have been much direct interference in the activities of these affiliated banks by their English parents.

RECENT DEVELOPMENTS In the inter-war period deposits grew healthily as the savings ratio held up well; the branch system increased by 50%; but lending suffered badly. Banks drew heavily on their reserves and were generally very supportive of their customers. After World War II business remained good but government monetary controls prevented the banks from lending as much as they would have wished. The Radcliffe Committee, reporting in 1959, was quite complimentary about the Scottish banks. A certain amount of merger activity had reduced the number to six, two of them English-owned, while the Royal Bank owned two small English banks.

An easing of government controls in the 1960s led to steadier growth as the banks voluntarily abandoned their cartel and began to compete more actively. The result was a dramatic growth in the number of services including credit cards and cheque guarantee cards; banking was transformed into a more customer-conscious and cost-conscious business. Further merger

activity took place in the late 1960s and early 70s, reducing the number of banks to three. Only the Clydesdale, the smallest of the three, remained under English control.

The Savings Bank movement also underwent change in the 1970s and 80s. The largest UK savings bank was the Savings Bank of Glasgow; others were small, with only a few branches, and local business. Some diversification into current accounts in the 1960s had met with success but there was concern in the industry that many were unprofitable. The Page Report (1973) recommended that the movement be concentrated in regional banks under a holding company and that the resultant organisations should become competitive with the commercial banks. These structural changes were introduced in 1975 and the new business activities followed. It was then announced that the savings banks would be sold to the public. This was a controversial move as until then it had been assumed that the banks were mutual organisations owned by their depositors. Nevertheless privatisation went ahead in 1986 and was accompanied by further restructuring which left Scotland with just one savings bank – TSB Scotland plc.

In the 1970s English banks began to open branches north of the border and the Scots opened branches in England. The English incursion amounted to very little and there was never any attempt to establish extensive branch networks. The Scots incursion was of a more substantial nature and the Royal Bank decided to dispense with the name of its last English subsidiary. This made it the only bank with a branch network throughout the United Kingdom.

Merchant banks such as Edinburgh's Noble, Grossart & Co began to be formed. Traditionally found only in England, these provided specialised services for corporate clients. Bank of Scotland, which had acquired the old British Linen Bank in 1971, relaunched its merchant bank subsidiary using the old name. Overseas banks also began to come to Scotland, mainly to Edinburgh, now financial centre of an **oil**-producing country. Finding itself in some difficulties Midland Bank sold the Clydesdale Bank to National Australia Bank in 1988.

Throughout the 19th and 20th centuries the Scots had exported their banking system and their bankers to all corners of the world. The Scottish banker became a component of the Scottish diaspora every bit as important as the doctor, the engineer and the missionary. The attention paid to education was manifest in the formation of the Institute of Bankers in Scotland in 1875 (since 1993 the Chartered Institute of Bankers in Scotland) – the world's oldest professional body for practising bankers.

See S G Checkland, *Scottish Banking, A History 1695–1973*, 1975.

BANNATYNE MANUSCRIPT

In 1568 George Bannatyne, a young man of 23 from a family of **Edinburgh** lawyers and merchants, had to cease working because of an epidemic of plague. He occupied himself by compiling, from a variety of earlier manuscript and printed sources, what he himself called a book of **ballads**. In doing so he 'saved the literature of a whole nation' (**Sir Walter Scott**), allowing posterity to know much more than would otherwise have been the case of Scottish literature of the 15th and 16th centuries. Many of his sources have not been preserved and his is frequently the only or the best copy of a poem. He includes more than half the accepted corpus of **William Dunbar**. He has 10 of the fables of **Robert Henryson** and the most complete text of his *Orpheus and Eurydice*, as well as several smaller poems. He is a major source for **Alexander Scott** and William Stewart. His is one of only two copies of **Sir David Lindsay**'s *Thrie Estaitis*. Other named authors are **Sir William Alexander** (1st Earl of **Stirling**), John Bellenden, John Heywood, Sir Richard Holland, Walter Kennedy, **Alexander Montgomerie** and **Robert Sempill**. Poems of doubtful or unknown authorship include 'Christis Kirk on the Green', 'Ballad of Kynd Kittock', 'The Freiris of Berwik' and 'Colkelbie Sow'. In all there are over 400 poems, divided by Bannatyne into five sections: ballads of theology, ballads of wisdom and morality, merry ballads, ballads of love, and fables. Bannatyne had probably already collected the love poems in 1565, but in the altered circumstances after the abdication of **Queen Mary** in 1567 he adapted and arranged these and his other sources to a more moralistic and Protestant scheme, presumably in the hope (not achieved) of publication.

The manuscript descended through Bannatyne's daughter's family until 1712, when it was given to William Carmichael; his son, the 4th Earl of Hyndford, gave it to the **Advocates' Library** in 1772 and it passed to the **National Library** in 1925. In the 18th century it was used by **Allan Ramsay** and Thomas Percy; in the 19th century the Bannatyne Club, for the publication of works of Scottish literature and history, was named after the compiler; and in the 20th century the editing of poems from the manuscript culminated in the publication of a full edition by the Scottish Text Society (1928–34) and of a facsimile by the Scolar Press (1980).

BANNERMAN, Helen (1862–1946) Author

Born in **Edinburgh**, daughter of the Reverend Robert Boog Watson, a **Free Church** minister, Helen spent 10 years of her childhood in Madeira during her father's ministry to the Scots Church in Funchal. Thereafter privately educated in Edinburgh, she was awarded an external degree from the **University of St Andrews** (which did not then admit women) in 1887. In 1889 she married Will Bannerman, a brilliant and energetic doctor in the Indian Army Medical Service, and returned with him to India where his work involved pioneering and often hazardous research into plague. Her *Story of Little Black Sambo*, first published in 1899, was originally written in the form of illustrated letters to her two daughters who, following convention, were sent home to be educated in Britain. She never made any money from this very successful first book, having on bad advice sold the copyright for a meagre sum. This error of judgement resulted in unauthorised editions appearing, particularly in America, with different illustrations that introduced an offensive racist slant to the work never in the original. She lived in India until 1918, published nine further children's books, and died in Edinburgh at the age of 84.

BANNERMAN, John MacDonald, Lord Bannerman of Kildonan (1902–69) Gaelic Activist

Bannerman was born in **Glasgow** and first achieved celebrity as a **rugby** player, being capped for Scotland 37 times. He failed to win election to Parliament as a Liberal candidate but was a noted broadcaster and Gaelic enthusiast. President of **An Comunn Gaidhealach**, he both composed and sang Gaelic songs of great popularity. He was created a life peer in 1967.

BANNOCKBURN, Stirlingshire

The large village of Bannockburn is now almost contiguous with St Ninians (with a fine steeple of 1734) and so **Stirling**. It lies south-east of the battlefield, was once famous for its **tartan** weaving, and subsequently became a **coal-mining** village. The old bridge over the Bannock Burn has an inscription dating it to 1516 but with many subsequent repairs. A mile south Bannockburn House is a large symmetrical four-storey block of classical proportions but flanked by projecting wings with crow-stepped gables reminiscent of the tower house. The elaborate internal plasterwork suggests a post-Restoration date of 1670–80 but, empty for some years, its condition in 1990 was unknown, the local council having been unable to gain access. In 1746 it was the property of Sir Hugh Paterson whose **Jacobite** sympathies resulted in its use as a headquarters by **Prince Charles Edward** in January of that year. Here the Prince first met his future mistress Clementina Walkinshaw. To the west, across the motorway, Old Sauchie (a now restored tower house of 1541 with later additions) recalls the adjacent site of the **Battle of Sauchieburn** and the subsequent murder of **James III** at Milton Farm nearby.

BANNOCKBURN, Battle of (1314)

The decisive battle in the **Wars of Independence** resulted from an agreement between Philip de Mowbray (the Scottish knight with whom the English king Edward II had entrusted the custody of **Stirling Castle**) and **Edward Bruce** (with whom his brother **Robert I** had entrusted the siege of the castle) that de Mowbray would surrender if he had not been relieved by midsummer. This forced Edward II to march northward and Robert I to prepare for a set battle – neither willingly.

Edward raised some 16,000 infantry, 2500 mounted knights, and a 20-mile supply train; on 22 June all these marched 22 miles from **Edinburgh** to **Falkirk**. Robert I, with around 6000 spearmen, a few archers and 500 light horse, withdrew from Torwood to a deerpark ('New Park') traversed by a **Roman** road, with farmland to the east, rising moorland to the west, the Bannock Burn running through bog to a gorge on the south, and St Ninians' Kirk to the northward. The farmland ended half a mile from the park in a steep slope down to the peaty Carse of Stirling and tidal Forth.

The battle (23–24 June) is recounted in great detail by chroniclers, although experts still disagree about precise sites. The English cavalry charged to open the road, almost captured Robert, and were driven back with heavy losses; another column was broken by **Thomas Randolph**'s spearmen near St Ninians. After a night of scant rest the cavalry again charged against the Scots who were drawn up in four 'battails' (Randolph, **James Douglas** and **Walter Stewart**, Edward Bruce, and Robert himself) formed into flexible squares of spearmen called 'schiltrons'. The English infantry could not deploy on the narrow front, and all were driven back into the Bannock Burn with terrible results. Edward I and 500 of his knights reached Stirling, but Mowbray refused them admission; surrender was imminent and the English king could not be allowed to fall into Scottish hands. So they rode around the castle and escaped, reaching Winchburgh before resting the horses and continuing to **Dunbar**, shadowed all the way by Douglas. The Earl of Pembroke piloted 2000 Welshmen away on foot to Carlisle; most English leaders were killed or made prisoner. Unhappily, though survivors praised Robert's human courtesy, it was 14 years before Edward's successor offered peace (**Treaty of Edinburgh**).

The site of the battle, or part of it, is now vested in the **National Trust for Scotland** 'on behalf of the Scottish nation'. A rotunda, an equestrian statue of Robert I and the heritage centre stand where the remains of a boarstone mark Robert's probable command post.

BAPTIE, David (1822–1906) Encyclopaedist

Baptie's *Musical Scotland* (Paisley, 1894) is an inaccurate but still much quoted biographical dictionary. Other publications include *A Handbook of Musical Biography* (London, 1883 and 1887), *Musicians of All Times* (London, 1889) and *Sketches of the English Glee Composers* (London, 1895). He was born in **Edinburgh** and died in **Glasgow**.

BARBOUR, John (c1320–95) Poet

Sometimes called the father of Scottish vernacular poetry, Barbour was a member of the royal household, holding financial offices there and being sent on two embassies to France. By 1357 he had become Archdeacon of **Aberdeen**. His claim to poetic fame rests on his lengthy Romance *The Brus* (c1375). Centred on **Robert I** it traces the **Wars of Independence** from their origins, through **Bannockburn**, to the Irish wars and the deaths of Bruce and the **Black Douglas**.

Barbour's strengths lie in his powerful narrative, supported by a clear style and the ability to highlight, rhetorically, any moments of drama. The poem is of some value to the historian, as the archdeacon did use evidence from older contemporaries who had lived under Robert I. But his work is declared to be a Romance and departs from historical accuracy where the conventions of that mode dictate. Thematically, the idea of liberty is retained in its purity by grafting the patriotic deeds of Robert I's grandfather (Bruce the **Competitor**) on to his grandson's later life, so omitting the early period when Robert I served the English. The character so created is compared regularly with the nine worthies and three matters of the Romance genre in an effort to claim a tenth worthy and a fourth matter for Scotland. Politically, the romanticised valour of the past acts as an example for the weaker rulers of Barbour's own day.

BARCALDINE CASTLE, Argyll

Barcaldine is a scattered settlement five miles north of **Connel**. The castle, an L-shaped fortalice 500 metres from the south shore of Loch Creran, was built in 1609 by Sir Duncan Campbell of Glenorchy (Duncan of the Seven Castles) and was known as the Black Castle because of its dark stones. In 1691 MacIan of **Glencoe** [see **Glencoe Massacre**] was detained here by the weather on his way to take the oath of allegiance at **Inveraray**. When Patrick Campbell, father of the Colin Campbell shot in the **Appin Murder**, moved to Innerergan House around 1724, the castle fell into disrepair and was not restored until 1896.

BARCLAY, Andrew (1814–1900) Engineer

Born at Kilbirnie, **Ayrshire**, Andrew Barclay worked with various employers from the age of 11 until he set up his own **engineering** works in **Kilmarnock** in 1840. A keen astronomer, he directed his inventive genius into the building of large telescopes before turning to steam trains. He pioneered the 'fireless steam locomotive' which could work in places where fire was a danger; a working example is preserved at the Scottish Industrial **Railway** Centre. The company he founded became a leader in **locomotive building** and examples of his work are found all over the world.

BARCLAY, David, of Urie (1610–86) Soldier

David, father of **Robert Barclay**, began the family's association with Quakerism when he joined the sect in 1666. He had previously served as an officer in Gustavus Adolphus' army during the Thirty Years' War and then, like his close associate **John Middleton**, in the **Covenanting** army. In 1648 he was amongst the **Engagers** who marched south in support of **Charles I** but later came to terms with Cromwell and sat in the Commonwealth Parliament. After the Restoration he was briefly imprisoned (1665–6). His son, in spite of a Catholic education abroad when his father was in England, also became a Quaker in 1667.

BARCLAY, Robert, of Urie (1648–90) Quaker

Born at **Gordonstoun** and educated at the Scots College in Paris by his Catholic uncle, Robert Barclay joined the Society of Friends in 1667. A persecuted and often imprisoned Quaker scholar (who once startled the residents of **Aberdeen** by walking through the streets clad in sackcloth and ashes), and an associate of Penn and Fox, he became a proprietor and then Governor of East New Jersey Quaker colony, although he never visited it. He preferred his estate of Urie near **Stonehaven** where he became a leading agricultural improver. His collected writings, *Truth Triumphant*, were published posthumously in 1692.

BARDS, Local or 'Village'

Members of a professional order of poets/musicians, bards were inferior only to the *filidh* (a higher rank of poet) in early Celtic society and later incorporated both orders. They sang of the heroic deeds of the **clans**, but also of matters of local interest, commentary in verse on the latter being part of a strong tradition in Gaelic Scotland. It is perhaps related, in terms of ancestral tradition, to similar verse-making in Ireland, and also in Scots-speaking areas of Scotland. There have been opposing tendencies either to disparage such verse as being parochial or to exalt it as 'the true voice of the people'. Neither extreme reaction is justified.

The general purpose of this verse is to provide a local and contemporary commentary on events. This usually features local characters and often has a humorous, comical or satirical tone. A short selection of situations that have produced such songs (taking a 20th century **Lewis** context for illustration) might run as follows: (1) a man who walked from Tarbert to Bayble and complained of having sore feet; (2) a group of young men who go on a drinking spree which ends up in a ditch by the roadside; (3) the introduction of artificial insemination for cattle; (4) the creation of a Western Isles Council; (5) a shoal of whales coming ashore about 1930; (6) the appearance of margarine in the local diet.

That listing perhaps over-emphasises the comical side of the tradition. It is possible to accommodate more serious topics, such as going to war or returning from it, emigrating to Canada, political events, etc. And it may be appropriate to attach to this tradition the very large numbers of songs in praise of localities, and also elegies for prominent people, especially men of religion. The last class certainly has links with more formal elegies, but has been developed in local contexts. The songs in praise of localities enjoyed a huge popularity in the 19th century and the first half of the 20th, the surge in their composition being of course directly related to the Highland diaspora. In due course it became possible to publish collections consisting largely of songs about specific areas or islands, and such songs are still very popular at concerts and *ceilidhs*, whether in **Glasgow** or in the Highlands.

It is difficult to pinpoint the starting-point of these various traditions. Localised verse is probably ancient, but we see it first appearing in manuscript collections only in the 17th century (eg the **Fernaig MS**), and we glimpse the tradition in a few satirical passages in poems by the MacMhuirich bards [see **Gaelic Verse**]. The theme of praise of locality surfaces in Alasdair mac Mhaighstir Alasdair's (**Alexander MacDonald**) '*Smeòrach Chlann Raghnaill*', in praise of Clanranald and **Uist**, and **John MacCodrum**'s '*Smeòrach Chlann Dòmhnaill*' in praise of the **MacDonalds** and **Uist**. There is some dispute as to which of these came first, for both would seem to date from the 1750s or so. The humorous and comical verse of the tradition is prominent in MacCodrum's work and also in **Rob Donn**'s from the north of Scotland. That tradition has probably been developed most vigorously in the islands, with numerous examples from **Skye** and the Western Isles generally; it can provide quite hilarious entertainment.

For some textual examples, see Dòmhnall Ruadh Mac an t-Saoir; Tormod MacLeòid, *Bàrdachd à Leòdhas* ('Poetry from Lewis', 1969) and Eachann Camshron, *Na Bàird Thirisdeach* ('The Three Bards', 1932).

BARR, Archibald (1855–1931) Engineer

Barr was born in Glenfield near **Paisley**, the son of a yarn merchant. After serving his apprenticeship as an engineer, graduating BSc from **Glasgow University** and working as an assistant in the University, he was appointed (1884) Professor of **Engineering** at the Yorkshire College of Science in Leeds. There, in 1888, he and the Professor of Physics, William Stroud, invented an optical range-finder. In 1893 they formed the company which became, in 1913, Barr & Stroud Ltd, to develop, manufacture and market this and other inventions. Barr, a talented mechanical engineer and designer and a shrewd businessman, remained the senior partner in the firm until his death.

He returned to Glasgow University in 1889 as Professor of Civil Engineering and Mechanics. A protégé of **Lord Kelvin**, he actively encouraged closer contacts between local industry and his department. The number of engineering students rose from 39 to over 200 during his tenure of the chair (1889–1913). He helped to set up the Faculty of Science in 1893 and to create the lectureship in Electrical Engineering five years later. In 1901 he raised money from the University, industrialists and charitable trusts to build and equip the famous **James Watt** Engineering Building.

When he retired in 1913, Barr was able to devote his energies to the flourishing business of Barr & Stroud, which had moved in 1904 from cramped premises off **Glasgow**'s Byres Road to a purpose-built factory in Anniesland. Before 1914, Barr & Stroud supplied range-finders to most of the world's leading navies; the Japanese considered the instruments played a major role in their victory over the Russian fleet at the Battle of Tsushima in 1905. In 1917 the company began to manufacture submarine periscopes, and became the sole supplier of these instruments to the Royal Navy. Other Barr & Stroud products included binoculars, gunsights and motorcycle engines.

A member of the Scottish Auto Club, Barr organised the first motor car reliability trials in Scotland in 1901. He was also a member and President of the Scottish Aeronautical Club and he organised the first **aviation** meeting in Scotland (**Lanark**, 1910). He became a Fellow of the Royal Society in 1923.

BARR'S IRN-BRU

In 1901 soft drinks manufacturer Andrew G Barr developed the recipe for a new product made from fruit extract and iron salt; he launched the sweet fizzy drink in the west of Scotland under the name 'Iron Brew'. The trademark, a hairy Highlander, became a well-known advertising symbol, but Iron Brew really captured the imagination of the Scottish public during the 1940s, when the company introduced the cartoon strip series *The Adventures of Ba-Bru*, featuring the eponymous turban-wearing boy and his kilted friend Sandy.

In 1946, after competitors began producing their own 'iron brews', A G Barr & Co renamed their drink 'Irn-Bru'. The company's flair for publicity ensured continued success, despite stiff competition from multi-national companies such as Coca Cola. Popular belief in the powers of Irn-Bru as a hangover 'cure' no doubt helped. During the 1970s Ba-Bru and Sandy were quietly replaced by a variety of characters demonstrating the miraculous powers of 'Your Other National Drink' which, the public was informed in the 1980s, was 'Made in Scotland from Girders'. In response to growing concern about the effects of excessive sugar intake, Barr's introduced a low calorie Irn-Bru in 1985. A sustained campaign to break into the English soft drinks market began in 1990, with a humorous television advertising campaign and public relations blitz. Although A G Barr's factory remains in **Glasgow**, the firm is expanding rapidly south of the border.

Kisimul Castle in Castlebay, Barra (GWWA)

BARRA, Isle of, Outer Hebrides

At the southern end of the Outer **Hebrides**, the island of Barra is separated from **South Uist** by the Sound of Barra and the island of **Eriskay**. Only eight miles from north to south and four–five miles wide, it supports a population of c1300 in its 20 square miles. About 12 miles of road encircle the island, with a northern spur to the airport at Traigh Mhor and the jetty at Eoligarry. The island takes its name from St Barr (Finbarr); the church of Cille Bharra near Northbay dates from the 12th century. There are prehistoric **cairns** and **brochs**.

The main village is Castlebay, linked to **Oban** and Lochboisdale in South Uist by car ferry. It takes its name from the picturesque and much-photographed **Kisimul Castle**, the ancestral stronghold of the **MacNeils** of Barra from 1427 when they received a charter from Alexander, **Lord of the Isles**, confirmed by **James IV** in 1495.

Heavy debts forced them to sell the island to Colonel Gordon of Cluny in 1838 who immediately offered to sell it on to the government for use as a penal colony. The offer was refused. **Clearances** later in the 19th century led to massive emigration.

Gaelic culture is strong and healthy in Barra, sustained by the Church and by a rich store of folklore and song. The island has a reputation as a place which knows how to enjoy itself, and with its Catholic tradition is unhindered by Sabbatarianism. The church in Castlebay, Our Lady, Star of the Sea, was built in 1889. Overlooking the town is the mountain of Heaval (1260ft/384m) with a striking statue of the Virgin and Child, erected in 1954, on its southern slopes.

Castlebay was once the site of a thriving **herring** industry, but now supports only a small-scale commercial fishery catching mainly white fish, prawns and lobsters. Most islanders are **crofter**-fishermen, keeping sheep and cattle and growing a few vegetables, especially potatoes. **Tourism** is increasingly important. There is a daily air service to **Glasgow**; the airstrip is on the beach at Traigh Mhor, the only one in the United Kingdom where schedules are shown as 'subject to tides' (landings are not possible within three hours either side of high tide). The air service was started by Northern & Scottish Airways Ltd in 1936, and since 1975 has been operated by Loganair.

BARRA CASTLE, Oldmeldrum, Aberdeenshire

Built round three sides and lacking either machicolation or corbelled corner turrets, Barra is unusual both in its ground plan and elevation. The simple profile of three circular towers and tall chimneyed gables nevertheless 'gives a remarkably pleasing and picturesque effect' (**MacGibbon and Ross**). It stands on the supposed site of **Robert I**'s defeat of John Comyn, **Earl of Buchan** in 1308 [see **Battle of Inverurie**] and was probably built by George Seton, Chancellor of **Aberdeen University**, soon after 1600. 'Externally it gives a more complete picture of how a great house of the 17th century looked in the mid-18th century than any other' (M Lindsay).

BARRHEAD, Renfrewshire

The small industrial town of Barrhead, situated to the south-west of **Glasgow**, has a short history. It grew out of the merging of several small villages on the banks of the Levern Water, which expanded rapidly at the end of the 18th century because of the growth of the textile industry. The Levern and its tributaries provided water for early bleachfields (1765). They were also a source of water-power and the first **cotton** spinning mill was built in 1780 – one of the earliest in Scotland. **Coal** was mined locally, mostly from short-lived, shallow workings that provided fuel for metal foundries. **Shanks**, the famous firm of sanitary engineers, began as brass founders, producing valves and fittings in 1856. Barrhead's mills and mines have long since ceased to be, and even Armitage Shanks, as it had become, stopped production in 1992, leaving a legacy of industrial dereliction. The problem has been partly overcome by the creation of parkland along the Levern.

BARRIE, Sir J(ames) M(atthew)
(1860–1937) Playwright and Novelist

Barrie was born in **Kirriemuir**, **Angus**, the ninth child of a weaver, and educated at **Glasgow**, **Forfar** and

J M Barrie, Peter Pan's creator, by William Nicholson (SNPG)

Dumfries Academies and **Edinburgh University** from where he graduated in 1882. After a year and a half as a journalist for the *Nottingham Journal*, he returned home to Kirriemuir where he began contributing semi-fictional sketches of Scottish life set in 'Thrums' (a thinly disguised Kirriemuir) to the *St James's Gazette* and the *Cornhill Magazine*. These were later published as *Auld Licht Idylls* (1888), and established him as a leading figure of the **'Kailyard'** school.

In 1885 Barrie moved to London, where he began writing for various magazines and journals, including the *British Weekly*. His first novel, *Better Dead*, was published at his own expense in 1886, and met with limited success. He was more successful with his second novel, *When a Man's Single*, published under the pseudonym 'Gavin Ogilvy' in 1888. This was followed by *Auld Licht Idylls* and a second collection of 'Thrums' sketches, *A Widow in the Thrums* (1889). His most successful novel was *The Little Minister* (1891), a tale of a **Presbyterian** minister and his love for a gypsy girl. First serialised in

Good Words, it was subsequently dramatised for the stage in 1897.

In 1894 Barrie married a young actress, Mary Ansell. The marriage was not a success, and the bitterness and acrimony it engendered were reflected in Barrie's last novels, *Sentimental Tommy* (1896) and *Tommy and Grizel* (1900). The couple divorced in 1909. The death of his mother in 1895 also had a strong effect on Barrie; his idealisation and affection for her is evident in the biographical novel *Margaret Ogilvy*, published in 1896.

It was during this period that Barrie began concentrating on writing plays, and by 1900 he was devoting himself exclusively to producing plays for the British and American markets. It was to be a lucrative field for him. The stage production of *The Little Minister*, for example, earned him almost £90,000 in box-office receipts in Britain and the USA between 1897–8. Other successes included *The Wedding Seat* (1897), *Quality Street* (1901), and *The Admirable Crichton* (1902).

It is, however, as the creator of *Peter Pan, or The Boy Who Wouldn't Grow Up* (1904) that Barrie is remembered. A tale set in a land inhabited by fairies, pirates and an alligator with an eight-day clock inside it, the work was written for the children of the Llewelyn Davies family, whom Barrie had first met in 1896. It was to be his greatest success, and has remained popular ever since.

Barrie continued to explore the idea of intermingling fantasy with reality in subsequent works such as *A Kiss for Cinderella* (1916), *Dear Brutus* (1917), *The Mary Rose* (1920) and *The Boy David* (1936). His later years were marked by various political and academic honours for services to literature. He was awarded honorary degrees by the Universities of **St Andrews** (1898), Edinburgh (1909), Oxford (1926) and Cambridge (1930), and received a baronetcy in 1913 and the Order of Merit in 1922. He was elected Rector of the University of St Andrews in 1922, where he delivered a rectorial address on 'Courage', subsequently published, and from 1930–7 he served as the Rector of the University of Edinburgh. He died on 19 June 1937, and was buried alongside his mother in Kirriemuir.

BARRY, 'James' Miranda Stuart
(c1790–1865) Doctor

In the days when a career in medicine was forbidden to women, Dr Barry worked her way right through to the highest rank in the British Army Medical Service masquerading as a man, successfully concealing her gender from everyone until her death. Little is known of her early life. She graduated MD from **Edinburgh University** in 1812 and the following year joined the Army as a surgeon's mate. Working her way up, she served in the Cape of Good Hope, Mauritius, Jamaica, St Helena and at Corfu where she treated casualties from the Crimean War, her main concerns being the soldiers' diets and living conditions. In 1857 she became Inspector-General of Military Hospitals in Montreal and Quebec. Two years later she retired on half pay, and died in London in 1865.

BARTHOLOMEW, John George
(1860–1920) Cartographer

Three generations of Bartholomews preceded John George as **Edinburgh** cartographers and engravers, the firm of John Bartholomew & Son being founded by his grandfather (1805–61) in the year of John George's birth in Edinburgh. After education at the High School and **University**, John George joined his father in the business and in 1888 took over its management; he immediately formed a partnership with **Thomas Nelson** and restyled the company as 'The Edinburgh Geographical Institute' with imposing premises in Park Road (which he so named). An early cartographical innovation was the 1880 introduction of colour shading to enhance contours. This 'layer-colour' system (light blue shading to darker blues for ocean depths, greens to browns and white for land heights) was adopted in the 1895 *Survey Atlas of Scotland* and soon became standard. In 1899 appeared *The Atlas of Meteorology* and in 1911 *The Atlas of Zoogeography*, two in a series which was never completed but which spawned a host of less ambitious productions where maps were deployed in the service of history, commerce, ethnology, civil **engineering** etc. Massive print runs of **railway** and road maps plus standard works like *The Times Survey Atlas of the World* (1922) brought the firm prosperity and a reputation second to none. John George, its architect, performed a similar service for the **Royal Scottish Geographical Society** (Hon Sec 1884–1920), and in both was succeeded by his son John (1890–1962) and grandson John C, although the firm passed out of family ownership in 1980 and is now part of Harper**Collins**. After a long illness John George died in Portugal. He is credited with having named a continent 'Antarctica' (from two Greek words), also two minute islands – St Winifred's and St Rosalind's in **Loch Lomond** near **Luss**.

BARTON, Andrew (d.1511) and Robert (c1470–1540) Seamen

Sons of John Barton, a seaman from **Leith** who had commanded one of **James III**'s ships, the Barton brothers were merchant seamen and privateers who drew the attention of **James IV** to their successful endeavours by sending him three barrelfuls of Flemish pirates' heads, captured from around the Scottish coasts. So destructive were they of English shipping that Henry VIII sent a punitive expedition against them under Sir Edward Howard. Andrew was fatally wounded in the encounter, while Robert went on to become Comptroller during the Regency of **John Duke of Albany**.

BASS ROCK, East Lothian

Situated in the Firth of Forth three miles north-east of **North Berwick**, this prominent island, one mile in circumference and rising steeply on all sides to a height of 350ft (107m), is a volcanic plug dating back to early Carboniferous times. It was described by **Boece** as 'ane wounderful crag, risand within the sea, with so narrow and strait hals [access] that no schip nor boit may arrive bot allanerlie [alone] at ane part of it'. The Bass has a lighthouse, remains of the 16th century chapel built on the site of the cell of St Baldred, a 7th or 8th century hermit, and the still-imposing ruins of an earlier fortress. Bought by the government from the Lauder family in 1651, the island was used as a prison, particularly for the confinement of **Covenanters**, including **Alexander Peden** imprisoned here from 1673–8 and **John Black-**

Waiting for the 'Homeward Bound'. The Bass Rock, from an engraving (SP)

adder who died here in 1686, and of **Jacobites**, a group of whom captured the Rock in the name of the exiled **James VII** in June 1691 while the members of the garrison were occupied unloading a delivery of coal. Provisioned by the French and by the occasional plunder of passing ships, the Jacobites held out until April 1694 when they were finally granted an amnesty. Now a wildlife sanctuary, the Bass is home to a famous colony of gannets as well as numerous other **seabirds**.

See also **Geology**.

BATHGATE, West Lothian

This industrial town at the eastern end of Scotland's central industrial belt lays claim to considerable antiquity, having been given by **Robert I** as the dowry for his daughter **Marjorie** on her marriage to **Walter the High Steward** in 1316. The centre of a medieval sheriffdom and a staging post on the main **Edinburgh-Glasgow** road, it expanded rapidly in the 18th century as a centre for handloom weaving. A measure of its 18th century growth was the fact, noted in the old *Statistical Account*, that 'about 1750 there were not above 10 families in the parish of Bathgate who used tea, and now [40 years later] there is not above twice that number who do not use it.' **Coal** and shale mining followed, **James 'Paraffin' Young** setting up his first paraffin refinery here in 1850, and in the 20th century Bathgate was home to one of the premier car and truck manufacturing plants in Britain. **Sir James Young Simpson** (1811–70) was a native.

BAXTER, William Alexander (1877–1973) Preserve Manufacturer

Baxter's working life began at the early age of six in his father's grocery shop at **Fochabers**, the village of his birth. Here **whisky** wholesaling had flourished alongside his mother's home-made jelly and jam production. 'WAB', as he was known, extended this sideline by virtue of legendary salesmanship and manufacturing acumen. With the completion of the Speyside factory in 1916 the patronage of local nobility led to the mass production of simple foods of great quality for the upper classes. Orders from Harrods and Fortnum & Mason were followed, thanks to the mediation of the Duke of Gordon, by supplies to Buckingham Palace. The jams, beetroots and soups, especially the Royal Game Soup, became celebrated products at the quality end of the market. WAB remained President of the company until his death at the age of 96, overseeing the enormous expansion of what remained a romantic enterprise.

BBC SCOTTISH SYMPHONY ORCHESTRA
Scotland's first full-time professional orchestra, the BBC Scottish Symphony Orchestra was established in **Edinburgh** in 1935 under the guidance of the BBC's Head of Music, **Ian Whyte**, who succeeded Guy Warrack as its Principal Conductor. Despite three separate attempts to disband it, the orchestra has grown steadily in numbers and reputation under a variety of distinguished conductors including Sir Alexander Gibson, Norman del Mar, James Loughran, Christopher Seaman and Jerzy Maksimiuk. The repertoire has been wide-ranging and includes a substantial number of Scottish works, and the orchestra tours regularly. Its commitment to **broadcasting** is balanced by public appearances, including concert seasons and performances at the **Edinburgh Festival** and the London Proms.

BEARDMORE, William, Lord Invernairn (1856–1936) Industrialist
Born in **Greenock**, Beardmore was educated at **Ayr** Academy, **Glasgow**'s Royal College of Science and Tech-

'A happy group of Beardmore Transport at Dalmuir'. Locomotives for India and Nigeria; motorcycle, car and taxi for the home market (BRC)

nology, and London's Royal School of Mines. He served an apprenticeship at the Parkhurst Forge, founded by **David Napier** but since acquired by Beardmore's father. On the latter's death he became a partner and subsequently founded William Beardmore & Co which, in its early 20th century heyday, became one of the largest **engineering** concerns in Britain. As well as merchant and naval shipping, Beardmore's built cars, **locomotives** and aircraft, including the R34, the first airship to make a double crossing of the Atlantic. Knighted in 1914, he was created Lord Invernairn in 1921 and retired in 1929. Already in trouble, Beardmore's main yard closed a year later. With a big cigar and a masterful way with union bosses like **Davie Kirkwood**, William Beardmore cultivated his autocratic image. Shackleton's naming of the Beardmore Glacier in his honour does not appear to have been intended as other than a compliment.

BEARSDEN, Dunbartonshire
A salubrious residential town six miles north-west of **Glasgow**, Bearsden lies on the line of the **Antonine Wall**. Remains of a **Roman** bath-house were excavated

in 1973. For many Bearsden is synonymous with wealth, but it was not prosperous when, before the 19th century, it was simply 'Kirktoune'. Bearsden became a burgh in 1958.

BEATON, David (c1494–1546) Cardinal
Born at Balfour (**Markinch**), educated for the Church at **St Andrews**, **Glasgow** and Paris, by 1519 Beaton was

Cardinal David Beaton, from an engraving (SW)

Chancellor of **Glasgow Cathedral**. In 1524 he became Abbot of **Arbroath** and was twice ambassador to France through the influence of his uncle, **James Beaton**, whom he succeeded as Archbishop of St Andrews in 1539. Made Bishop of Mirepoix by Francis I of France for his Francophile stance, he was appointed a Cardinal by Clement VII in 1538. As Chancellor in 1543 his pro-French policies resulted in English invasions of Scotland [see **Rough Wooing**]. His persecution of Protestants, including **George Wishart** (burnt in 1546), contributed to his own assassination three months later, leaving several children by a mistress.

BEATON, James (c1480–1539) Archbishop of St Andrews
Probably born at Balfour (**Markinch**), Beaton (or Bethune) rose rapidly in Church and state to be Abbot of **Dunfermline** in 1504 and High Treasurer in 1505. Appointed Bishop of **Galloway** in 1508, he was raised to Archbishop of **Glasgow** before he could be consecrated. As High Chancellor, after crowning **James V** following the battle of **Flodden** in 1513, he was a Regent in the absence of the **Duke of Albany**. His stabilising influence during the minority was rewarded by the Archbishopric of **St Andrews** (1522), where the Lutheran **Patrick Hamilton** was burnt for heresy (1528). In retirement Beaton developed the **University of St Andrews**.

BEATON, James (c1517–1603) Archbishop of Glasgow

A nephew of **Cardinal David Beaton**, and educated by him in Paris, this Beaton was Abbot of **Arbroath** from 1543 until appointed Archbishop of **Glasgow** in 1552. He was consecrated in Rome at the wish of **Queen Mary**. At the **Reformation** in 1560 he removed himself, and the records of the diocese, to France. As a result, most of the latter were lost at the time of the French Revolution. Both Mary and **James VI** appointed him ambassador to France (where he remained for over 40 years), even rehabilitating him and restoring his titles in 1587 and 1598 though he was never a Protestant.

BEATSON, Sir George Thomas (1848–1933) Physician

A medical graduate from Cambridge, George Beatson was appointed physician in charge of **Glasgow**'s first cancer hospital in 1893. He was the first doctor to treat breast cancer by removal of the ovaries and also pioneered the use of radium for cancer treatment and research. A life-long supporter of the Territorial Army (in which he held the rank of lieutenant-colonel), Beatson also founded the Scottish branch of the British Red Cross and played a leading role in providing Scotland with an effective ambulance service. The Glasgow Cancer Hospital was renamed the Royal Beatson Memorial Hospital in 1953 but closed in 1988 and was replaced by the Beatson Oncology Centre at Glasgow's Western Infirmary – the second largest of its kind in Britain. The Beatson Institute at **Maryhill**, funded by **Sir Isaac Wolfson**, is now one of Britain's 'big four' cancer research facilities.

BEATTIE, James (1735–1803) Poet and Moral Philosopher

From **Laurencekirk**, **Kincardineshire**, the son of a shopkeeper and small farmer, Beattie studied classics at **Marischal College**, **Aberdeen** (1749–53). From 1753–8 he was a schoolmaster at Fordoun, near Laurencekirk, where he met and became a close friend of **James Burnett, Lord Monboddo**. During this time he also began contributing poetry to the *Scots Magazine*. In 1758 he became a master at Aberdeen Grammar School, a post he held until suddenly appointed Professor of Moral Philosophy and Logic at Marischal College (1760–1790).

His *Original Poems and Translations* (1761), a collection of pieces contributed to the *Scots Magazine*, attracted favourable notices, but held work of slight consequence. He achieved more notice with the publication of *An Essay on the Nature and Immutability of Truth* (1770) attacking the philosophical ideas of **David Hume** and George Berkeley. As a result of the work's success, Beattie was made an honorary LL.D. by Oxford University in 1773. In the same year he was summoned to meet King George III, who bestowed on him an annual pension of £200. Beattie subsequently wrote several philosophical works exploring the application of religion to philosophy, including *Dissertations Moral and Critical* (1783), *Evidences of the Christian Religion Briefly and Plainly Stated* (1786), and *Elements of Moral Science* (1790–3). A passionate anti-slavery campaigner, he lectured 'On the Awfulness and Expediency of Slavery' (1778) and became a member of William Wilberforce's Committee for the Abolition of Slavery in 1788. He died in Aberdeen.

Today, however, Beattie is best remembered for his long poem *The Minstrel*, published in two parts (1771, 1774). The work, in Spenserian stanzas, foreshadows the Romantic movement in its thematic treatment of nature and beauty. An edition of his poetry, edited by **Alexander Dyce**, was published in 1831, and a biography by Sir William Forbes in 1806.

BEATTIE, William Hamilton (1840–98) Architect

A pupil of **David Bryce**, Beattie is most famous for his hotels. In the centre of **Edinburgh** he designed the Carlton on **North Bridge** (1898), the Clarendon (1875–6) and, most notably, the North British (1895). Part of the redevelopment of North Bridge, this huge hotel, now renamed the **Balmoral**, with its clock tower, remains one of Edinburgh's best-known landmarks. It is said that Beattie won the competition for the hotel through the influence of Charles Jenner, for whom he had designed the Jenners department store in **Princes Street** in 1893. Jenners, at the time the largest store in Britain, still impresses through its complex façade and rich interior. Beattie's hidden Venetian Gothic stationery warehouse in West Register Street (1864) is unusual for Edinburgh, and offers a welcome surprise for anyone venturing into the alleys and lanes next to **Register House**. His buildings were technically advanced, both Jenners and the North British Hotel being largely fireproof through the use of floors made of Stuart's Granolithic; his shop fronts at No 16 **George Street** had iron window mullions and transoms.

BEAULY, Inverness-shire

West of **Inverness** the Beauly Firth, an upper basin of the Moray Firth, receives the Beauly river from **Strathglass** (and Glens Affric and Cannich). The town of Beauly stands near the mouth of the river in rich farming country backed by wooded hills. Hence the descriptive *beau-lieu* – Beauly – and the nearby Beaufort Castle, home of the **Frasers of Lovat**, who evidently cherished their Norman origins. Alternatively the French nomenclature may be traced to the **Valliscaulian** monks, originally from Burgundy, who established Beauly priory in 1230. Its founder was Sir John Bisset of nearby Aird and Lovat; a Bisset heiress subsequently married a Fraser to whom the Lovat lands passed.

Of the priory only the church, and that a roofless ruin, survives. Cruciform without aisles or towers, its glory lies in its 13th century trefoil windows in the south wall of the nave and in the arcaded windows of the chancel. It was considerably altered in the late Middle Ages and again in the 16th century when **Robert Reid**, Abbot of **Kinloss** and Bishop of **Orkney**, was also Prior of Beauly. In 1582 the lead was removed from the roof, by 1633 the church was 'badly decayed', and in the 1650s Cromwellian troops removed some of the stone to build Inverness citadel. The north transept was partly restored in 1901 as a burial aisle for the **Mackenzies of Kintail**, of whose ancestor Sir Kenneth Mackenzie (d.1491) there is a recumbent effigy. Amongst those also commemorated here is the Fraser of Lovat who fell in the **Battle of the Shirts**. There is also a

Pictish symbol stone from Balblair south of the river.

The town was laid out by Thomas Fraser of Strichen, Lord Lovat, in 1840. In the main square stands a monument (1905) commemorating the raising of the **Lovat Scouts** for service in the Boer War. Lovat Castle, near Balblair, has long since disappeared as has Dounie Castle, its successor, destroyed by Cumberland shortly before its proprietor (**Simon Fraser, Lord Lovat**) was executed on Tower Hill. Beaufort Castle, home of the chief of the Lovat Frasers until it was sold in 1995, is Victorian Baronial (rebuilt in 1937). It stands near Kiltarlity, where there are both an old and a new Lovat church. The burial place of the Lovat Frasers is now, however, at the Catholic church in Eskadale (1826) where are also buried the **Sobieski Stewart** brothers who lived at Aigas. Other notable Fraser properties hereabouts include Moniack (with a 17th century L-plan nucleus) and Reelig (with woodland planted by the Himalayan traveller **James Baillie Fraser**), while Wardlaw (Kirkhill) was the home of Rev James Fraser, author of the Fraser chronicles known as the Wardlaw Manuscript.

BEGG, James (1808–83) Churchman and Nationalist

A native of New Monkland, Begg was minister of **Paisley** and Liberton before siding with **Dr Thomas Chalmers** during the **Disruption**. Thereafter, as a **Free Church** leader in **Edinburgh**, he pursued social and political grievances as radical as his religious views. The latter included intense anti-Catholicism and opposition to attempts to reunite the **Presbyterian** Churches; the former led him to inveigh against bad housing and intemperance, prime causes (according to Begg) of illegitimacy, and to advocate extensions of both the franchise and **education**. Poverty, ignorance, crime, sectarianism and most other ills he ascribed, in a pamphlet of 1850, to a national decline which, in a pamphlet of 1871, he traced to 'A violation of the **Treaty of Union**'. Supported by the activities of **William Burns** and **Duncan McLaren**, Begg thus became an early advocate of reinstating a Scottish Secretary of State or, failing that, a Scottish Parliament, views posthumously adopted and republished by the **Scottish Home Rule Association**.

BEITH, John Hay, 'Ian Hay' (1876–1952) Writer

The grandson of John Alexander Beith, a founder of the **Free Church**, John Hay was born in Manchester but educated at **Fettes College, Edinburgh**, to which, after Cambridge, he returned as an enthusiastic teacher and games master, His first novel, Pip (1907), sold well and after two more successes he resigned from teaching to become as 'Ian Hay' the author of some 20 usually humorous and undemanding narratives. Best known was probably The First Hundred Thousand (1915) about conscripts in World War I, Beith himself having joined the **Argyll and Sutherland Highlanders**, won an MC and risen to major. After the war he lived mainly in London, writing also for the theatre (eg Tilly of Bloomsbury, 1919), and collaborating fruitfully with other authors (eg P G Wodehouse, with whom he wrote A Damsel in Distress, 1928, and Leave it to Psmith, 1930). As director of War

Office publicity (1938–41) he enjoyed the rank of major-general and wrote a short history of the army. Other histories included one of the **Royal Company of Archers** (1951) of which he was a member. He died in Petersfield.

BELL, Alexander Graham (1847–1922)
Inventor

Born in **Edinburgh**, Alexander Graham Bell, the son of **Alexander Melville Bell**, rapidly acquired his father's interest in alphabetising a phonetic language, particularly in relation to assisting the deaf to communicate. After a spell teaching in **Elgin**, as well as studying in England, the 23-year-old Bell was persuaded by his parents to move to the USA in the hope of escaping the tuberculosis which claimed both his talented brothers. He reluctantly complied, settling in the Boston area, where he soon became Professor of Vocal Physiology at Boston University, devoting himself to teaching deaf children by day and to experimenting with telecommunications by night.

A semi-scientific education, dogged patience, and an acute sense of hearing stood him in good stead in his twin careers of bringing relief to children who were unable to make themselves understood, and inventing. His advocacy of teaching articulation brought him admiration and affection, but it was his tinkering with electrical apparatus that was to make him a millionaire. Theorising that the human voice could be relayed along a telegraph wire through electrical induction, Bell found commercial backers and worked on a suitable device, as far as his commitments allowed. In June 1875, over a crude telephone-like apparatus, Bell's assistant Thomas Watson heard his mundane but nevertheless classic words 'Come here, Mr Watson, I want to see you,' spoken from a neighbouring room. Considerable development had still to take place, but Bell meanwhile lodged a preliminary patent application – on the same day as a commercial rival.

To make such an application, he had to take American citizenship, which he did at the age of 27, disappointed when the British government offered him no encouragement in his research. Although he exhibited his apparatus successfully at the Centennial Exhibition in Philadelphia in 1876, and so excited the interest and approval of **Lord Kelvin**, commercial exploitation was slow, despite the fact that his telephone required no special training to operate. In an 18-year period Bell's patents, vested from the first in a company with his early backers as partners, were tested in around 600 court cases. Not a single one was lost, and Bell, who by this time had married Mabel Hubbard, the deaf daughter of one of his backers, was able to enjoy the fruits of his invention.

Bell never lost his compassion for the deaf, subscribing generously to their charities; indeed he once wrote to his wife, 'I think I can be of far more use as a teacher of the deaf than I can ever be as an electrician.' In 1878, when well on the way to becoming a millionaire, he arranged on a British visit for a specialist to teach articulation to deaf children in **Greenock**, and when the appointment was delayed, taught at the **Renfrewshire** school himself. He died at his Nova Scotia home and was buried locally. The company he started went on to employ one million people, yet his primary concern had always been to bring the disadvantaged into communication with others.

BELL, Alexander Melville (1819–1905)
Phoneticist

Founder of the science of phonetics, Alexander Melville Bell was born in **Edinburgh**. He became interested in teaching the deaf and speech-impaired, developing a physiological alphabet called the Visible Speech System, to represent visually the articulating workings of the vocal cords. He taught in Edinburgh, London and Ontario before becoming an American citizen in 1897. His son **Alexander Graham Bell** is better remembered, although the father brought the power of communication to numberless handicapped.

BELL, Rev Andrew (1753–1832)
Educationalist

Born in **St Andrews**, the son of a local bailie, Andrew Bell was educated at **St Andrews University** and, after taking **Episcopal** orders, became Chaplain to the East India Company in Madras in 1787. Given charge of the Madras Male Orphan Aslyum, but unable to find sufficient teaching staff, he devised a system of mutual tuition by the pupils which proved both effective and popular. In 1797 he returned to Britain and published details of his 'Madras System' which, by the time of his death, had been adopted in as many as 10,000 British schools, the best-known being Christ's Hospital in London and Madras College in St Andrews; the latter was founded in 1832 with a bequest of £50,000 from Bell himself. Prebendary of Westminster from 1819, he was buried in Westminster Abbey.

BELL, Sir Charles (1774–1842) Surgeon

Born near **Edinburgh**, Charles Bell was apprenticed to his elder brother **John Bell** to be a surgeon, and became a Fellow of the **Royal College of Surgeons** of Edinburgh in 1799. In 1804 he went to London and published *Essays on the Anatomy of Expression in Painting* (1805), which showed his talents as anatomist, sculptor and artist. Six years later he took over the old Hunterian Anatomical School in Windmill Street.

His main area of research, however, was into the functions of the nerves. By this time the structure of the body's nervous system was known; its function was not. Bell worked out that certain nerves have a fixed course from a definite part of the brain to a definite part of the body and that different nerves have different functions. His *New Idea of the Anatomy of the Brain* (1811) first described these discoveries and his *An Exposition of the Natural System of the Nerves of the Human Body*, in which he described the functions of the facial and respiratory nerves, developed them. Here he also identified paralysis of the seventh facial nerve, still called Bell's palsy.

Despite popular belief, Bell was not really a military surgeon. His only military experience was in treating the wounded after the Battle of Waterloo. But his drawings of their wounds form part of his famous collection of paintings, now in the Museum of the Royal College of Surgeons of Edinburgh, to which he also sold his pathological and anatomical specimens. Surgeon to the Middlesex Hospital from 1814, Bell was instrumental in raising funds to start the Middlesex Hospital Medical School, which admitted its first students in 1835. He did not stay there long, returning to Edinburgh in 1836 to be Professor of Surgery.

BELL, George Joseph (1770–1843) Jurist

Brother of **John** and **Charles**, the surgeons, George Joseph preferred to follow in the footsteps of another brother, a Writer to the Signet. Having passed advocate in 1791 he became Professor of Scots Law in the **University of Edinburgh** in 1822. Although a Principal Clerk of Session in 1832, it was in the field of legal writing and **law** reform that Bell shone. He was the author of a number of legal text books, earning him a place among the Scottish Institutional writers, including a *Treatise on the Law of Bankruptcy in Scotland*, 1800 (reissued under the title *Commentaries on the Municipal and Mercantile Law of Scotland*, 1804) and *Principles of the Law of Scotland*, 1829. He also wrote *Illustrations from Adjudged Cases of the Principles of the Law of Scotland*, 1836–8 and other minor works. Modest and honourable, 'there could not possibly be a better man,' declared **Henry Lord Cockburn**, adding 'he is the greatest legal writer in Scotland next to [**James Dalrymple, Viscount**] Stair'.

BELL, Henry (1767–1830) Shipbuilder

Born in **Linlithgow**, he served an apprenticeship as a millwright before moving to London where he studied under **John Rennie**. Returning to Scotland, he continued his studies whilst he worked as a carpenter. In 1800 he submitted plans to the Admiralty for a steam vessel. His greatest achievement was to direct the building of the **Comet**, although he subsequently built and operated other steam boats. He chose the young **John Robertson** to supply the *Comet*'s engine after the two men met when Bell commissioned Robertson to install

Henry Bell, builder of the Comet, by James Tannock (SNPG)

a steam pumping engine in a hotel at **Helensburgh**. He died in Helensburgh.

BELL, John (1763–1820) Surgeon
Born in **Edinburgh** and educated at the city's High School, John Bell was apprenticed to Alexander Wood as a surgeon and became a Member of the Incorporation of Surgeons of Edinburgh in 1786. There, four years later, he set up a school of anatomy and surgery, outside the influence of **Edinburgh University**, in what was later known as Surgeons' Square. This move followed widespread dissatisfaction with **Professor Alexander Monro (Secundus)**, who taught only theoretical surgery as part of the anatomy course, he himself having no practical operating experience. Bell's innovation was to teach practical anatomy from the surgeon's point of view, and to familiarise his pupils with the subject so that they would be able to operate on any part of the human body at a moment's notice. An outstanding teacher, he was the founder of surgical anatomy. He also published extensively on his speciality. From 1793–1802 *Anatomy of the Human Body* appeared. Next came *Engravings of the Bones, Muscles and Joints* which showed their use to an operating surgeon. At the same time he produced *Discourses on the Nature and Cure of Wounds*, and from 1801–8 he published *Principles of Surgery*.

He also had a very large surgical practice, being consulted by patients from all over Scotland. Amongst his apprentices was his brother **Charles Bell**. In 1799 he gave up teaching, having been excluded from the **Royal Infirmary** after professional disagreements with **Dr James Gregory** and others. He left Edinburgh in 1817 in poor health to go on a European tour, and died in Rome.

BELL, Dr Joseph (1837–1911) Surgeon
Born in **Edinburgh**, the great-grandson of Benjamin Bell (1749–1806), the first to make surgery a distinct subject (but no relation to **John** or **Sir Charles Bell**), Joseph Bell went to **Edinburgh Academy** and studied medicine at **Edinburgh University**, graduating in 1859. In 1863 he became a Fellow of the **Royal College of Surgeons** of Edinburgh.

After a few years lecturing to medical students, Bell started formal training for nurses at Edinburgh's **Royal Infirmary**. His course, the first nurses' training scheme in Scotland, included both lectures and practical laboratory work and was adapted from those at the St Thomas training school for nurses in London started by Florence Nightingale in 1860. In 1887 Bell published *Notes on Surgery for Nurses*, which ran to several editions.

In 1878 **Arthur Conan Doyle** enrolled as a second-year student in Dr Bell's Clinical Surgery class at the Royal Infirmary and became first Bell's dresser and then his out-patient clerk. By Doyle's own admission, Joseph Bell's very remarkable powers of observation and deduction were the inspiration behind his creation of Sherlock Holmes. In fact, because of his remarkable powers, Bell worked with **Sir Henry Littlejohn** on court cases, notably the Chantrelle murder case of 1877.

In 1887 Bell resigned from the Royal Infirmary and became surgeon to the newly founded Royal Hospital for Sick Children. There he did much to develop paediatric surgery and in 1892 published *Five Years Surgery in*

the Royal Hospital for Sick Children, probably the first book devoted to surgery on children. From 1873–96 he edited and contributed many papers to the *Edinburgh Medical Journal*. He retired in 1897.

BELL, Patrick (1799–1869) Inventor
Born at Auchterhouse, near **Dundee**, Bell was the son of a farmer. In 1827 he won a prize from the Highland and Agricultural Society for the construction of a mechanical reaping machine. Four examples were exported to the USA where they became the basis for successive designs. By the time his design had become fully appreciated in this country, Bell had entered the ministry. He died at Carmyllie near **Arbroath**.

BELL, Samuel (c1739–1813) Architect
Bell was the first Town Architect of **Dundee** and the first resident architect in the burgh, although it has been said that he was more a builder as his first major building, St Andrews Church (1772), may well have been based on an original drawing by **James Craig**, the designer of **Edinburgh**'s New Town. In the late 18th century neo-classical style Bell embellished Dundee's town centre with the **Trades Hall** (1776), the English Chapel (later the **Union Hall**, 1783–4), and the Steeple Kirk (1787). He also designed Miln's Building, 136 Nethergate and Nethergate House for Provost Riddoch, the Morgan Tower block of flats in 1794, and the Theatre Royal in 1808–9. His last commissions appear to have been St Rule's Parish Church, **Monifieth**, and Kinnettles Church.

BELL ROCK LIGHTHOUSE AND SIGNAL TOWER, Arbroath, Angus
12 miles south-east of **Arbroath**, the Inchcape or Bell Rock, visible only at low tide, long proved a hazard to shipping entering the Firths of **Tay** and Forth. A first attempt to mark its position was made by an Abbot of Arbroath (Aberbrothock), who supposedly installed the bell which inspired Southey's ballad 'The Inchcape Rock':

> When the rock was hid by the surge's swell
> The mariners heard the warning bell;
> And then they knew the perilous rock,
> And blessed the Abbot of Aberbrothock.

A wooden beacon of 1803 disappeared in the first winter storm and it remained for **Robert Stevenson** to construct (1807–11) the great 120ft (36.5m) tower (including accommodation) which is now 'the oldest sea-swept lighthouse in continuous use in the British Isles'. A base of granite was built on the rock and a duplicate in Arbroath on which each course of masonry was assembled and marked before being shipped. Round the rock a fleet of service vessels, and on it cranes, were assembled in an endeavour quite as hazardous as any subsequently undertaken in the North Sea. When the lighthouse was complete, the duplicate base in Arbroath was dismantled and the stone used in the construction of the Signal Tower on the sea front. From here a lookout was kept for pre-arranged signals from the lighthouse. Failure to signal indicated trouble and a tender would put to sea. Carrier pigeons were also used;

with a fair wind they averaged 11 minutes for the 12 miles. The Signal Tower is now a museum with one room dedicated to the construction of the lighthouse and others to various aspects of civic history and industry.

BELLS
Among the oldest surviving hand bells in Europe are those of Scotland, there being two types, both quadrangular. The first, and earliest, are made of sheet iron, folded, lapped and rivetted. They date from the 8th century and are closely associated with the **Iona** missions to the **Picts**. The second type is of cast bronze, dating from around the 9th century. Three of these exhibit a characteristic, unique to their design, of producing three distinct notes of different pitch from three of the four faces. They may well have been used to accompany **Celtic Plainchant** as well as for healing, exorcism, banishing, gathering the faithful and giving warning. Two may have been especially cast for **Malcolm III 'Canmore'** when he brought the relics of **St Columba** to **Dunkeld**.

BEMERSYDE, Nr Dryburgh, Roxburghshire
The ancient prophecy of **Thomas of Ercildoune** ('Tide, tide, whate'er betide/There'll aye be Haigs at Bemersyde') has been true for all but 60 years of its 800-year history. There were Haigs at Bemersyde in the 12th century, although the oldest part of the present house, the tower, dates back only to 1535. Partially destroyed by Hertford in 1544, Bemersyde was rebuilt in 1581 and altered and enlarged during the 17th and 18th centuries, the 1690 restoration using stones from the nearby ruins of **Dryburgh Abbey**. The direct Haig line died out in the 1860s and Bemersyde went to a **Clackmannanshire** branch of the family. After World War I, however, the house was bought by the nation and presented as a tribute to **Field Marshal Earl Haig** and has since remained in the family.

BENBECULA, Isle of, Outer Hebrides
The connecting link between the larger islands of **North Uist** and **South Uist**, Benbecula measures eight windswept miles west-east by five waterlogged miles north-south. The name is an anglicisation of the **Gaelic** *Beinn a'bhfaodhla*, meaning 'mountain of the fords'. But the mountain, Rueval, is only 409ft (125m) high and the fords (to North and South Uist) have been replaced by road causeways. The native population of about 1300 is divided more or less equally between the Protestantism of North Uist and the Roman Catholicism of South Uist. Gaelic survives as the language of everyday life, although a high proportion of the place-names are of Norse origin. An additional 500 Royal Artillery army personnel and dependants are stationed at their base at Balivanich, providing support for the missile range on South Uist. The operation has expanded greatly from its small beginnings in 1959. An RAF radar station was established in 1972; new radars were constructed on Clettraval, South Uist, in 1981, while the control building and associated facilities are at East Camp, Balivanich.

The underlying **geology** is Lewisian gneiss, the coastline indented, and the land surface of the island a maze of tiny lochans. From the summit of Rueval there is a fine view of the whole island, a view which inspired geologist **John McCulloch** to comment, 'the sea here is all islands, and the land all lakes; that which is not rock is sand; and that which is not mud is bog; that which is not bog is lake; that which is not lake is sea.' **Peat** is exposed on the shore at Borve, proof that the Outer Isles are sinking, albeit extremely slowly, into the Atlantic along their western edge.

Benbecula's natural beauty is somewhat marred by the military facilities, but economically the island has benefited. The army's NAAFI supermarket is the only one in Britain open to the general public. The new secondary school and community centre at Liniclate is one of the most impressive in Britain.

There are several sites of archaeological interest in Benbecula's watery landscape. An exceptionally well-preserved chambered long **cairn** and a ruined passage grave lie close together in the centre of the island, half a mile east of the main road. Near the northern causeway are two stone circles at Gramisdale, but most of their stones have fallen. There is a good example of an Iron Age **dun** on an island in Loch Dun Mhurchaidh, near Knoc Rolum township, joined to the shore by a causeway. Superimposed on the ruins of the dun are the ruins of a 17th century township.

In 1746, disguised as Betty Burke, **Prince Charles Edward Stewart** sailed over the sea to **Skye** from here with **Flora MacDonald** after hiding in a cave for two days. He came within an ace of being captured by the forces of General John Campbell of Mamore. The island was held by Clan Ranald, whose ruined 14th century castle, occupied until 1625, is at Borve. Near their 18th century house at Nunton is a 14th century chapel. The **MacDonalds of Clanranald** owned Benbecula until 1839, when it was sold to Colonel Gordon of Cluny, along with **Barra**, South Uist and **Eriskay**. It stayed in the Gordon family until 1942 when the northern part of the island was sold to the Air Ministry and the remainder to a London banker.

BENNACHIE, Aberdeenshire
Although not especially high, the granite massif of Bennachie is visible from most places in **Aberdeenshire** and has thus become a focus of affection and identity for the lowlanders of the north-east, much climbed at weekends and celebrated in verse.

> But Bennachie! Faith yon's the hill
> Tugs at the hairt when ye-re awa'!
> **(Charles Murray)**

Oxen Craig (1733ft/528m) is the highest peak but Mither Tap (1698ft/518m) the most distinctive. The latter is the site of a summit fort of the 1st millennium BC whose walls and traces of a parapet can be seen. North of Bennachie aerial surveys have revealed the existence of a once large **Roman** fort, thus adding substance to the claim that Bennachie may have been Tacitus' **Mons Graupius**. At **Oyne** there is a **Forestry Commission** visitor centre and the usual signposted footpaths.

BENNETT, James Gordon (1795–1872)
Newspaper Proprietor
The founder of the *New York Herald* was born and educated in **Keith**. Of Catholic parentage he first studied for the

priesthood in **Aberdeen** before suddenly emigrating (1819) to Nova Scotia. There he taught and then travelled south, often destitute, to Boston and New York where he found work with a publisher. By 1827 he was an influential correspondent on *The Courier* and became its editor in 1829 but in 1835 fell foul of its political sympathies and started the *Herald*. At first Bennett produced almost the entire paper himself, working long hours from a basement in Wall Street. By the end of 1836 he had achieved a circulation of 40,000, a figure more than doubled by the time of his retirement in 1867; annual profits were then running at $400,000. Politically independent, often outspoken and never one to shun a sensation, Bennett went to great lengths to scoop the news in the pre-telegraph era, even maintaining a fleet of fast boats off the American coast to intercept ships from Europe and rush the latest to his paper's presses. His flair, along with his wealth and his paper, passed to his son, also James Gordon Bennett, who famously commissioned H M Stanley to search for **Dr Livingstone**.

BENRIG, Battle of (1382)
One of many Scottish attempts to oust the English garrison from **Roxburgh** Castle, the Battle of Benrig resulted in the new English commander, the Baron of Greystoke (near Penrith), being prevented by the Earl of **Dunbar** and **March** from taking up his post. Although Greystoke was defeated, the English garrison at Roxburgh remained in situ until 1460.

BEREGONIUM
As prominently featured in many early histories of Scotland, Beregonium was a place-name derived from Ptolemy's *Geography*, which clearly attributed it to Scotland. **Hector Boece** and **George Buchanan** identified it as having been somewhere near **Lochaber**. Dun Mac Uisneachan, the Fort of the Sons of Uisneach [see **Deirdre**], near Benderloch north of **Oban**, was later claimed as an important **Dalriada** site and assumed to be the self-same Beregonium. Paved streets, columns and water pipes were fancifully identified and Thomas Pennant concluded that as a pre-Dalriadic settlement it might have been 'such a city as Caesar found in our island at the time of his invasion . . . an *oppidum*'. Subsequent research established that, however endowed, the Benderloch **dun** could not possibly have been Beregonium. 'There is not a vestige in the language or traditions of the country that this castle ever bore a name that had the slightest resemblance to Beregonium' (**John Jamieson**). Buchanan and Boece had misunderstood both Ptolemy's orthography and his geography. The word was actually 'Rerigonium' and Ptolemy had placed it somewhere in the vicinity of **Galloway**, where its position and significance remain a mystery.

BERNARD OF LINTON (d.1331) Bishop and Chancellor
A priest of Mordington in **Berwick** (1296), Bernard served as chancellor to **Robert I** (the Bruce) from 1308–28. He was also conjoint 'Vicar' of **Glasgow** following the capture of **Robert Wishart**, Abbot of **Arbroath** (1311), and Bishop of Sodor (from the Norse name for the Western Isles) and Man (1328). He was

possibly the author of the declarations made by the clergy and nobility at the **St Andrews** Parliament of 1309 in favour of Robert and was concerned in their re-issue by the provincial clergy at **Dundee** in 1310. More certainly he was the author of the **Declaration of Arbroath** (1320). After a diplomatic mission to Norway, he also negotiated the treaty of **Inverness**, renewing that of **Perth** (1266) in 1312. At **Bannockburn** (1314) he accompanied **St Columba**'s shrine, the Brecbennoch or **Monymusk Reliquary**, and recorded Robert's pre-battle speech to his troops.

BERNERA BARRACKS, Glenelg, Inverness-shire
Like the **Ruthven Barracks** near **Kingussie**, those of Bernera were designed by **James Smith**. Sited beside the Sound of Sleat and the narrowest crossing to **Skye**, they formed the western extremity of the same Hanoverian line of defences (designed to deter **Jacobites** and quell lawlessness). They were completed in 1722 and, 50 years later, had evidently served their purpose, for **Boswell** and **Johnson** found the Highlands to be traversable 'without danger, fear or molestation' and the garrison reduced to 'only a sergeant and a few men'. In the 1790s the barracks were finally deserted and soon became ruinous. They remain so, though not for want of proposals, including their possible use as a College of Piping.

BERNERA RIOT (1872)
Having purchased the island of **Lewis** in 1844, **Sir James Matheson** appointed as his factor Donald Munro, a local solicitor who quickly acquired so many other offices on the island that a contemporary dubbed him 'his polyonymous omnipotence'. He also acquired a well deserved reputation as the scourge of the **crofting** community. Exasperated by his evictions and high-handedness, in 1872 the crofters of Bernera (an island in Loch Roag on the west coast) refused orders to move their stock and were threatened with a visit from **Stornoway**'s Volunteers (of whom Munro, of course, was commanding officer). Instead of Volunteers there came eviction orders. The officers serving them were pelted with sods; the sheriff-officer had his coat torn. In the mêlée three crofters were arrested. Others appealed to the elderly Sir James who disowned his factor's conduct. The prisoners were duly acquitted and Munro fell from favour, being dismissed in 1875. Like other gestures of defiance by the hitherto submissive crofters, the 'riot' assumed its menace in retrospect and as polemic in radical journals, especially during the **Highland Land War** of which it was a harbinger.

BERNERAY, Outer Hebrides
The island of Berneray (Norse: 'Bjorn's isle') lies in the Outer **Hebrides** between **Harris** and **North Uist** to which it is connected by passenger ferry. It is three miles long, 1½ miles wide, with a population of about 135, engaged in **crofting**, lobster fishing and craft knitting. The fertile machair grazes sheep and cattle. There is a **standing stone** near the town of Borve.

Another island of the same name, uninhabited since its lighthouse was automated, is the most southerly in the chain of the Hebrides. Its southern tip, with sea cliffs over 600ft (183m) high, is known as Barra Head.

BERWICK, Treaties of (1357 and 1560)

Taken prisoner at the **Battle of Neville's Cross** (1346), **David II** remained in captivity in England until 1357 when he was liberated under the terms of the Treaty of Berwick which agreed a ransom of 100,000 merks, to be paid in annual instalments.

The second Treaty of Berwick was negotiated between Thomas Howard, 4th Duke of Norfolk, for Elizabeth I and Scottish commissioners representing **James Hamilton, 2nd Earl of Arran** and the **Lords of the Congregation**. It guaranteed the Scottish Protestants English assistance in ridding Scotland of the French forces of **Mary of Guise**.

BERWICK-UPON-TWEED

Just south of the Scottish border, Berwick-upon-Tweed has played an important role in the history of Scotland and England. Well placed at the lowest crossing point of the **Tweed**, it commands a good site on a rocky coastline, so was an important seaport, place of commerce and military town.

Now in Northumberland, the town has an English MP and is governed by English law, but its **football** team plays in the Scottish League and much commerce comes from the Berwickshire hinterland.

In 833 Berwick was a farming settlement founded by the Saxons, but its importance politically was from 1018 when **Malcolm II** of Scotland claimed the Tweed as a Scottish river and Berwick became part of Scotland. In **David I**'s reign Berwick was one of four Scottish **royal burghs**. **Alexander III** introduced Flemings to the town which became famous for its **wool** trade, the revenue of which greatly contributed to the wealth of Scotland.

Between 1147 and 1482 Berwick changed hands no less than 13 times. The most significant dates in the town's history are:

1174	**William I (the Lion)** lost Berwick to Henry II as ransom after capture at Alnwick.
1189	Richard I (the Lionheart) returned Berwick and some other land to William I (the Lion) to raise funds for his crusades.
1216	After an unsuccessful attempt against Alexander III, King John of England set fire to Berwick on his retreat from **Edinburgh**.
1296	Dissatisfied with **John Balliol**, Edward I took Berwick by force and summoned a Parliament to govern the kingdom he had overrun.
1297	**William Wallace** took Berwick, but the castle withstood the siege, being relieved by the English army.
1312	**Robert I** (the Bruce) attempted to take the town but his presence was betrayed by the barking of a dog.
1314	Edward II fled to Berwick after his defeat at **Bannockburn**.
1318	Bruce took Berwick on 28 March. From here he dated many of his charters and assembled many Parliaments.
1333	Edward III retook Berwick after the **Battle of Halidon Hill**.

1338	Berwick ceased to be a royal burgh of Scotland.
1355	The **Earl of Angus** took Berwick by surprise, but the castle withstood the siege.
1356	Edward III attacked the town which then surrendered.
1377	Seven Scots held Berwick for eight days.
1384	The Scots received Berwick through the corruption of the deputy-governor who then retook the town later that year.
1422	The Governor of Scotland made an abortive attempt to take Berwick.
1459	Henry IV delivered the town into Scots hands during the Wars of the Roses.
1480	The English attempted to take Berwick but failed.
1482	24 August, Berwick was finally ceded to England in the reign of Edward IV.
1551	Edward IV and **Queen Mary** made Berwick a free town independent of both 'states'.

The castle, standing outwith the burgh, was strengthened and fortified over the centuries until it was no longer required. In 1611 it was demolished for buildings elsewhere. The remains were bought in 1843 from the Askew family by the North British Railway Company. Part of the west wall is visible from the **railway** platform, originally the Great Hall where Edward I crowned the puppet King John Balliol.

The Elizabethan walls, built 1558–65 in anticipation of a French or Scots invasion, were designed by an Italian (Portinari), planned by Sir Richard Lee, and are recognised today as one of the best early artillery defences in existence.

The Berwick Bounds were established in 1438 between Berwick and the Border. They comprised land granted to the burgesses of Berwick and strengthened by royal charter in 1604. In 1550 'The Riding of the Bounds' first took place by the garrison who patrolled once a year to prevent encroachments by the Scots. From 1609 the Mayor and Corporation rode the Bounds annually. Now, while enthusiastic riders still patrol the Bounds on horseback, the civic party travels by bus. The Mayor and Corporation of Berwick take precedence over those of all English towns except London and York, and the Mayor's robe is the only purple robe in England.

There has always been a strong religious presence in Berwick, which could at one time boast five orders of friars, a nunnery and five medieval churches. The **Presbyterian** and non-conformist influence has predominated, with **Knox** and Wesley preaching there regularly and Knox being appointed chaplain to Berwick Parish Church for three years. **Robert Burns** visited Berwick in 1787 and is said to have so disliked the town and its burgesses that he stayed only a few hours.

BERWICKSHIRE

A Border county occupying the south-east corner of Scotland, Berwickshire was unique in being named after a town in another country – **Berwick-upon-Tweed** has been English since 1482.

To the east was the North Sea, into which drained the river **Tweed**, which formed part of the county's

78

Berwick-upon-Tweed, by Sam Bough (NGS)

southern frontier and which, fed by the Leader, Black-adder and Whiteadder, reached the sea in Northumberland, Berwickshire's southern neighbour. To the north, beyond the **Lammermuir Hills** was **Midlothian**, with **Selkirkshire** and **Roxburghshire** to the west. The fertile Tweed plain, known as the Merse, occupied the area north of the river, and provided the county with one of its principal occupations, **agriculture**, while fisheries were important in the **Eyemouth** area. This was the biggest burgh, although **Duns** was the county town and **Coldstream** the only other burgh. During Saxon times the area was part of Northumbria, being annexed to Scotland after the **Battle of Carham** in 1018.

In 1975 the county passed completely into Borders Region, most of it to the new District of the same name. **Lauder** and a western part of the old Berwickshire were separated into Ettrick & Lauderdale District, and one parish was transferred to Roxburgh District. Since 1995 Berwickshire has been part of the Scottish Borders Council Area.

BETTYHILL, Sutherland

Known as *Am Blàran Odhar* in the language of the country (The Little Dun-coloured Field), its English name may have derived from a woman who lived locally. What is certain is that it could not have been named after the evicting **Elizabeth, Countess of Sutherland**, who is commemorated very differently in Gaelic. Here was the large church of the parish of Farr, one of the most extensive in Scotland and well populated before the **clearances**. Today it houses the Strathnaver Museum. In the graveyard stands a sculptured **Pictish** cross of exceptional interest dating from about 800. At Bettyhill

has been built the excellent new Farr primary and secondary school providing for scholars whose forebears attended schools in surrounding townships such as Kirtomy. The growth of Bettyhill at their expense is characteristic of the progressive nucleation of Highland rural communities. This is one of the mainland schools in which Gaelic is now in the syllabus, with impressive results.

BIBLE, King James Version (1611)

Probably the best-known and most influential book in the English language, the 1611 Bible was 'Newly translated out of the Original Tongues; with the former Translations compared and revised by His Majesties special Commandment'.

James VI noted the idea at the 1601 **General Assembly** at **Burntisland**; as James I of England he promoted the Hampton Court Conference suggestion of revision in 1604; 47 revisers, drawn from the most eminent scholars and divines of the day and divided into groups dealing with different sections of the Bible, commenced work in 1607. Earlier translations of Coverdale, Wycliffe, Tyndale, Luther and Calvin were coordinated with the earliest Hebrew, Greek and Latin texts then known. The resulting 1611 version – also known as the Authorised Version – superseded the 1560 Geneva Bible (first published in Scotland in 1579) and lasted unchallenged in the English-speaking world until the 1881 Revised Version and 1901 American Standard Version incorporated newly discovered texts.

Among many retranslations this century the colloquial Bible of **James Moffat** in 1935 gained popularity over Shakespearean sonorities. In 1946 **Bridge of Allan** parish kirk session requested a contemporary Bible. The General Assembly adopted the project in 1948 in cooperation with other Churches in Britain. The resulting New English Bible of 1970 avoided both archaic and ultra-modern language.

BIGGAR, Lanarkshire

The history of this burgh (1451) between **Lanark** and **Peebles** is well captured in museums which here proliferate as much as shops. Moat Park Heritage Centre, in a disused church, recalls the distant past when the adjacent mound was a motte (moat) and when **William Wallace** and Sir Walter Newbigging are supposed to have defeated an improbably large English army at the Battle of Biggar (1297). Here too are the archives of the Biggar-based Albion Motor Car Company. Greenhill **Covenanters** House, a 17th century farmhouse, contains period displays and Covenanting relics while Gladstone Court Museum (the name recalling that from Biggar came the family of William Gladstone) contains reconstructions of Victorian and Edwardian town life. Biggar Gas Works Museum continues the Victorian theme with the plant (1839) which produced the town's gas lighting now preserved under the care of the **Royal Museum of Scotland**. A further subject for the town's museum mania will doubtless be Brownsbank Cottage near Candy Hill, home for many years of **Hugh MacDiarmid**. As a collegiate church to the Blessed Mary (1545), the parish church is thought to have been the last built before the **Reformation**. Now much altered and restored, it occupies the site of an earlier church dedicated to St Nicholas. Its benefactor was Malcolm, Lord Fleming, one of the Flemings (later Earls of Wigton) of Boghall, Biggar, of which strange address there remains only a bit of one of the castle's towers. In 1651 Boghall held out for the Commonwealth against **General Alexander Leslie** and suffered damage but its present state is the result of subsequent neglect.

BILSLAND, Sir William (1847–1921) Master Baker

Bilsland was born at Ballat, near **Stirling**, and moved to **Glasgow** at the age of 14. After apprenticeship to a grocer he set up in business and soon acquired a number of bakeries. The big breakthrough came with the siting of a factory at Hydepark Street in **Anderston** where modern technology was employed in the mass production of bread. William's main concern was with the marketing of the firm's standard loaves which were distributed across Glasgow and Scotland by a fleet of vans. The biscuit company of Gray Dunn was taken over in 1912 as the company's interests expanded. A noted philanthropist and a paternalistic employer, Bilsland was also a prominent local politician holding many offices including that of Lord Provost of the City of Glasgow (1905–8). He played a significant role in the construction of both the **Kelvingrove** Galleries and the **People's Palace** and was created a baronet in 1907.

BINNS, House of the, Linlithgow, West Lothian

Home of the long-haired Royalist **Sir Thomas Dalyell**, the House of the Binns (ie bens, mountains) assumed architectural status when rebuilt by Sir Tam's father, also Thomas Dalyell, following his purchase of the property in 1612. Externally only the steep roof and five dormer windows remain visible of the 17th century building. Inside, moulded plaster ceilings and cornices, amongst the earliest examples of this work in Scotland, are also notable. Extensive additions were made to the property in the mid-18th century and by the architect **William Burn** in the early 19th century. The latter included crenellated towers which break up the main façade, battlements, machicolations and rectangular mouldings over the enlarged windows, thus giving the house 'the appearance it has today of a country mansion of the Regency period in the Gothick manner'. It was the first property acquired (1944) by the **National Trust for Scotland** whose guide book endearingly concedes that, though an interesting example of changing tastes, the house 'is not one of particular architectural distinction'.

BIRCH

The lovely and widespread birch tree formerly had a valuable place in the Scottish domestic economy. The wood was used for many household utensils, the branches for **shinty** sticks, and the fine spray for brooms, ropes and withies. The leaves and twigs yielded bright yellow dye, while the bark was rolled into candles and beaten into paper. Birch leaf tea was drunk to relieve rheumatism, and fresh birch sap is a pleasant drink, believed by Highlanders to be beneficial for kidneys and bladder; it also makes delicious wine. It was considered unlucky 'to pu' the birks sae green', and seeing green birch in a dream presaged ill. Birch growing with briars on the graves of two lovers indicated that death had not divided them.

BIRD RESERVES

The list of Scottish nature reserves of ornithological importance is formidable, with over 80 reserves throughout the country, managed by the Royal Society for the Protection of Birds (RSPB), the Nature Conservancy Council (NCC) (absorbed into Scottish Natural Heritage), the Scottish Wildlife Trust, the **Forestry Commission** or as Local Nature Reserves. Habitats vary from remnants of the old **Caledonian forest** that support Britain's only endemic species (the Scottish **crossbill**), to the high tops where confiding dotterels breed; from estuaries that support internationally important wintering populations of wildfowl and **waders**, to the globally important **Flow Country** of **Sutherland**, breeding ground for waders, wildfowl and **divers**. There are no less than 28 **seabird** colonies that support more than 10,000 pairs, most important of which is the **St Kilda** island group which has the largest gannetry in the world and more than a million seabirds breeding on its rocks and cliffs each summer.

Many bird reserves have interpretive facilities in their Visitor Centres, whilst others have nature trails or hides; most also have either permanent or summer wardens to provide visitors with information or in some cases actually show them round. Visitors sometimes imagine that everything is known about the wildlife in these reserves, but this is far from the case, and any wildlife observations are worth sending either to the relevant organisation or to the warden of the reserve in question.

Ariundle Oakwood

This 70ha of sessile oakwood is part of the very large area of broadleaved woodland around Loch Sunart, a few miles west of **Fort William**. It is a National Nature Reserve actively managed to create a diversity of habitat for birds and insects, and has a large population of passerine birds for so northerly a site. Breeding birds within the wood include redstart, tree pipit, wood warbler, goldcrest, tawny owl, woodcock, tree creeper, long-tailed tit and great spotted woodpecker. Along the river and burns breeding birds include grey wagtail, common sandpiper and dipper, while on the edge of the woodland are ring ouzel, wheatear, kestrel and raven. **Golden eagles** are frequently recorded in the glen. There are car parking facilities, and a hard track through the wood affords easy access.

Balranald

This 658ha RSPB reserve and Site of Special Scientific Interest lies on the west coast of **North Uist** in the Outer **Hebrides**, and has been managed by the Society since 1966. The area is an outstanding example of **croft** farming forming a rich habitat, particularly for **waders**. On the west side of the reserve a rocky headland is backed by marram-stabilised dunes which shelter the croft land. Behind the dunes lies the machair that is enriched with shell sand to form fertile land sometimes planted with cereals. There is also a large area of marsh with lochans which again afford good nesting cover and feeding areas. The machair throughout the Uists supports outstanding populations of waders, and Balranald is no exception as there are 300 pairs of lapwing, 100 pairs of redshank, 100 pairs of ringed plover, 100 pairs of oyster catcher and over 80 pairs of dunlin. On the reserve overall about 50 species of birds breed regularly, of which pride of place must go to the **corncrake**; several pairs breed annually. The marsh and lochans support good breeding numbers of duck including mallard, teal, tufted duck, wigeon, shoveller and gadwall. On the drier machair both twite and corn bunting can be found breeding and in recent years fulmars have started nesting on top of the walls of old buildings in the area. The headland Aird an Ronair is a famous point for sea watches as it is further west than any other place in the Outer Hebrides. The rarer skuas and shearwaters are often recorded off this point.

Ben Mor Coigach / Inverpolly

These two nature reserves cover a vast wilderness area of 16,856ha on the **Sutherland**/Wester **Ross** coast. Ben Mor Coigach (6000ha) is the largest reserve owned by the Scottish Wildlife Trust, while the Inverpolly National Nature Reserve is the second largest NNR in Britain. The main attraction of this reserve is its wide variety of habitats; there are several hills over 700m, cliffs, open moorland, large island-studded lochs, **birch** woodland and seashore with marine islands.

Breeding birds on the hills and moorland include **ptarmigan**, raven, golden plover, greenshank, ring ouzel, wheatear and stonechat. Black-throated and red-throated **divers** breed on the lochs, as do red-breasted mergansers, goosanders, common gulls and a few pairs of greylag geese. Burns have breeding birds such as dipper, grey wagtail and common sandpiper, while the woods contain lesser redpoll, woodcock, spotted flycatcher, wood warbler, tree pipit and, unusually this far north, great spotted woodpeckers. A prolonged 'sky watch' can turn up **golden eagle**, peregrine, buzzard and sometimes merlin. On the marine islands breeding birds include arctic and common tern, eider, fulmar, shag and black guillemot, and in winter a small flock of barnacle geese that feed on the grassland. There are interpretive facilities on the east end of Inverpolly in the form of a Visitor Centre and two nature trails at Knockan Cliff near Elphin. The only restriction on access is for short periods during the **red deer** stag cull in late summer.

Caerlaverock

This 5510ha NNR runs along two miles of coastline between the estuaries of the River Nith and Lochair Waters two miles south-east of **Dumfries**. The attraction for **waders** and wildfowl is the combination of low-lying coastal habitats that include sandbanks, saltmarsh, creeks and freshwater marsh. The Wildfowl Trust Refuge at Eastpark is made up of 524ha of farmland and saltmarsh with outstanding viewing facilities. These include 20 hides, two observation towers and an observatory, in front of which is a pond on which up to 17 species of wildfowl can be watched at close quarters. Perhaps the main bird attraction is the very large numbers of geese that frequent the area, the most outstanding being the peak of over 10,000 barnacle geese in mid-November – this is the entire breeding population of Spitzbergen. The peak of the pink-footed geese is later in the winter when around 5000 are present. Both these and the smaller flocks of greylag geese feed on farmland that is deliberately managed for the geese by the Wildfowl Trust. Swans are another feature with up to 350 whoopers, 70 mute swans and smaller numbers of Bewick swans. Ducks include wigeon, shelduck (up to 400), teal, mallard and pintail, all of which attract a fair number of hunting hen harriers, sparrow hawks, peregrines and merlins.

Cairngorm

This National Nature Reserve is by far the largest in Britain at 25,949ha, and its massif reaches an altitude of nearly 1311m between the **Spey** and **Dee** valleys. The high summit plateau is the largest area of high ground in Britain and is important for the rare arctic-alpine birds that nest there. The reserve includes high boulder fields running down to cliffs, extensive heather moorland, bog and mire communities on lower ground, and several sizeable areas of native pinewood. Fortunately (some would say unfortunately) for the naturalist, access to some of the high ground is readily available by chairlift.

One of the specialist birds is the **ptarmigan** which can be seen all year round, although it tends to move lower down the hillsides in prolonged bad weather. Rarer is the dotterel which is present during the summer months and can sometimes be seen in autumn as small flocks prepare to move south for the winter. The third rarity (and the least predictable, as in most years only a very small number of pairs breed) is the **snow bunting**. In winter, however, flocks of snow bunting consisting of breeding birds from Greenland, Iceland and

Scandinavia can be found around the car parks and chairlift stations feeding almost like sparrows. **Golden eagle** and peregrine are regularly present but difficult to spot in such a large area. Even rarer but enticing is the occasional late summer record of snowy owls.

Glen Affric

A famous glen in the Highlands about 28 miles south-west of **Inverness**, with a combination of forest, rivers, lochs, moorland and hills, Glen Affric is particularly popular with naturalists and the public because of the extensive facilities provided by the owners, the Forestry Commission. Although there are planned self-guiding walks radiating out from car parks it is still possible to reach quiet, remoter parts of the forest via the extensive network of rides. The Forestry Commission has established a 1265ha Native Woodland reserve in the forest which includes a remnant of the once extensive old Caledonian pine forest. The area is also included in a much larger SSSI.

Small numbers of **capercaillie** and black grouse breed in the pine woods, the presence of the former indicated more often by the goose-size droppings in rides under large pines than by sightings of the bird itself. **Crested tit** and Scottish **crossbill** are common all year round, as are siskin and lesser redpoll. Other breeding birds include summer visitors such as the tree pipit, wood warbler, pied flycatcher and redstart. On the lochs both red-throated and black-throated **divers** breed regularly as do little **grebes**, uncommon in the north of Scotland. Dipper, common sandpiper and grey wagtail frequent the numerous burns. Raptors include **golden eagle**, peregrine, sparrowhawk, merlin and buzzard. There are occasional restrictions on access in the **deer stalking** season.

Loch Fleet

Immediately south of **Golspie** on the east coast of **Sutherland**, this coastal unit includes the 1163ha reserve managed by the Scottish Wildlife Trust and the Mound Alderwood NNR covering 267ha. A diversity of habitats ranges from alder woodland and pinewood to sand dunes, estuary, brackish loch and coastline. The pinewood supports breeding birds such as redstart, coal tit, goldcrest, siskin and Scottish **crossbill**. In contrast, cliffs running inland from the Mound have large numbers of breeding fulmars that, unusually, extend inland for several miles. The coastline between Embo and Golspie is important for wintering sea fowl including red-throated, black-throated and great northern **divers**, and always the possibility of the much rarer white-billed diver. An oustanding winter assemblage comprises not only 2000 eider (that seems every winter to include an adult male king eider) but also the 2000 long-tailed duck that assemble by late May before their departure for their more northerly breeding grounds. Other sea fowl include common scoter, velvet scoter, red-breasted merganser, goldeneye and, more rarely, the surf scoter. Raptors such as peregrine, **golden eagle**, buzzard, merlin, hen harrier and sparrow hawk, as well as short eared owls, hunt over the sand dunes. Sea watches can produce various skuas, gannets and white-winged gulls, and it is well worth looking out

for **waders** on passage on the Mound and along the coast.

Loch Garten

This RSPB reserve covers 1200 hectares and is an SSSI. It lies a few miles north-east of **Aviemore** and contains a range of habitats including **Scots pine** forest, bog, two lochs, heather moorland and some farmland. The site is world famous for its **ospreys**, a species that returned to breed in Speyside in 1954. There are excellent hide facilities with binoculars and telescopes provided for watching the ospreys. Scottish **crossbills**, **crested tit** and **capercaillie** are among the pinewood bird specialities to be seen on the reserve, and woodcock regularly breed here and can be seen in their display flights – called 'roding' – at dawn and dusk. The capercaillie is an elusive bird, best seen in the early morning, but individuals have been spotted on occasion in front of the osprey hide. Goldeneye can be seen on both Loch Garten and Loch Mallachie during the summer, along with red-breasted merganser. Other interesting breeding birds in the forest include siskin, great spotted woodpecker, redstart and sparrow hawk.

Loch Leven

Although almost adjacent to the A9 at **Kinross** between **Perth** and **Edinburgh**, **Loch Leven** is internationally important for both breeding and wintering widlfowl as it is the largest naturally eutrophic (nutrient over-rich) loch in Britain. On the south shore of the loch lies Vane Farm, an RSPB reserve of 121ha which has been designated a Site of Special Scientific Interest (SSSI). A hide overlooks lagoons that have been created as feeding and resting sites for breeding ducks and **waders** in summer and wildfowl in winter. Telescopes and binoculars are available for view over the reserve and Loch Leven.

Loch Leven itself covers 1597ha and is a National Nature Reserve managed by the Nature Conservancy Council. The shallow loch is ideal for breeding and wintering wildfowl and, of the seven islands, the famous St Serf's Island has over 1000 breeding pairs of duck each summer. These include gadwall, wigeon, shelduck and shoveller as well as the more common mallard and tufted duck. The island also contains a black-headed gull colony and a small colony of common tern. The fascination of the area lies in its great diversity of habitat which attracts a wide range of species including pink-footed geese, greylag geese, great crested **grebe**, wood and green sandpipers, Slavonian grebe, ruff, black-tailed godwit, whooper swans, goldeneye and goosander. It is one of the few bird reserves in Scotland where plenty of bird species are to be seen at any time of the year.

Loch Ruthven

This loch is situated east of **Loch Ness** and 14 miles south of **Inverness**. 12 hectares at the north end of the loch form an RSPB reserve, whilst the whole loch is designated an SSSI. A hide has been constructed within the reserve area in the birch woodland that fringes the loch. The speciality of the loch is the breeding Slavonian **grebes** that build their nests in the emergent aquatic plants and sedge beds. The RSPB and NCC have produced a leaflet designed to alert fishermen to the dangers of drifting too close to these very sensitive breeding areas. Red-throated **diver** and **osprey** feed on the loch; breeding birds include tufted duck, teal and coot; and there is a small colony of common gulls on an island (**crannog**) at the south end. The birch woodlands have breeding species such as lesser redpoll, siskin, pied flycatcher, redstart, sedge warbler and reed bunting. Raptors such as hen harrier and peregrine are regular visitors and ravens breed nearby. **Black grouse** are frequently seen in the area. In winter the loch attracts small numbers of pochard and goldeneye and nearly every winter at least one smew is recorded.

St Kilda

An NNR situated 50 miles west of the **Uists** in the Western Isles, **St Kilda** consists of an archipelago of six main islands that are the remnants of a large ring volcano. The whole reserve covers 853ha. Although the islands are almost entirely cliff-bound, the vegetation on the plateaux is surprisingly rich, and the presence of salt-tolerant plantain swards on the cliff tops indicates how salt spray frequently covers even the highest point. The cliffs rise to 425m on the main island of Hirta and support vast colonies of **seabirds** including the largest gannetry in the world (60,000 pairs) as well as fulmars, puffins and unknown numbers of Leach's and storm petrels. In all 16 species of seabird regularly breed on the islands including impressive numbers of guillemot, razorbill, kittiwake and Manx shearwater. 10 other species breed here regularly, including great skua and whimbrel, and the islands have their own sub-species of wren.

BIRGHAM, Treaty of (1290)

At this village near **Coldstream** on 17 March 1290 a parliament of bishops, earls, abbots and barons, representing the Community of the Realm, authorised the elected Guardians to negotiate a marriage between the six-year-old Queen **Margaret, Maid of Norway**, and the five-year-old future Edward II of England. The negotiations led to the Treaty of Birgham, 18 July 1290, whereby Edward I guaranteed the survival of Scotland 'separate, apart and free without subjection to the English nation', though ruled in partnership. The plan, suggested by **Alexander III** in 1284 and prophetic of 1603 [see **James VI**], was invalidated by the Maid's early death.

BIRKMYRE, Henry (1832–1900) Cordage and Sailcloth Manufacturer

Birkmyre was born in **Port Glasgow** and educated locally. He joined his father's firm at the age of 21 and assumed formal control of the **Gourock** Ropework Company in 1880. Expansion followed the purchase of a converted sugar refinery at Port Glasgow which increased the production of ropes, cordage and cloth. The business was intimately connected with the growth of the **Clyde shipbuilding** industry and in particular the boom in the nearby yards at **Greenock** and to the north of the Clyde. He purchased the **New Lanark** Mills, incorporating them into the company, and pursued an active career in local politics, becoming Lord Provost of Port Glasgow.

BIRNIE, Nr Elgin, Moray

The parish church of Birnie is reputedly the oldest in continued use in Scotland. It dates from the early 12th century but is dedicated to St Brendan the Navigator so must be of **Celtic** origin. Before **Spynie** and **Elgin** it was also a seat of the bishops of **Moray**. The Roman arch dividing chancel from nave, the font and the doorways are all original; but the nave was shortened and the windows enlarged in the 18th century. Its treasures include the Hairy Bible (1774, bound in calfskin), the Celtic Ronnel **Bell** and a **Pictish** symbol stone (including an eagle) beside the gate to the manse.

BIRRELL, John Stewart (1863–1938)
Chocolate Manufacturer

Birrell founded one of the best-known confectionery firms in Scotland, although his background was unimpressive. Born in Rattray, **Perthshire**, his father was a farmer. After being apprenticed to a grocer in **Crieff** he moved to **Glasgow** in 1885, becoming the owner of a number of grocery shops. It was only after 1900 that he began to manufacture chocolates. From a small factory in Partick his business expanded rapidly so that new premises were constructed at Anniesland, the 'Milady' factory. This plant was equipped with modern machinery enabling the mass production of high quality sweets and chocolates to meet a growing demand. The other plank in the firm's success was Birrell's ownership of a chain of shops, concentrated mostly in Scotland but including major centres in England, which put a premium on attractive displays.

BIRSAY, Orkney

This parish in the north-west mainland of **Orkney** is of exceptional interest, both archaeologically and historically. Its **Pictish** homesteads and artefacts on the Brough of Birsay (a tidal island of about 50 acres), and on the mainland opposite, were succeeded by **Viking** settlements and monastic buildings from the time when **Earl Thorfinn** made Birsay his seat. According to the *Orkneyinga Saga* he also planted his cathedral of Christ Church here. The controversy which still surrounds the location of both is explored in *Orkney Heritage* Vol 2, Birsay, 1983. During the tyrannous rule of the **Stewart earls** the building of a grandiose new palace was begun in 1569 and completed before **Earl Robert**'s death in 1593. After the execution of his son and grandson in 1615 the structure became gradually more decayed, until by 1760 it was roofless. The episcopal lands of Birsay had been the most valuable of the Orkney Bishopric before the **Reformation**, when they were expropriated by Earl Robert. It was the good fortune of this parish that the polymath George Low, who had already rescued from **Foula** the only ancient Norse ballads to have survived in the Northern Isles, was minister of Birsay when the first *Statistical Account* was in preparation.

BISHOP, Isabella (née Bird) (1832–1904)
Traveller

The 'dumpily-built, earnest, sickly daughter of a clergyman' (P Barr), Isabella Bird was recommended to take a long sea voyage in 1854 for the sake of her health. Her journey to America and Canada wrought a transformation. The spinal complaint from which she had suffered since childhood miraculously disappeared when she left home, only to recur as soon as she returned. The rest of her life was spent alternating between her travels, often on horseback and in the most spartan of conditions – to Australia, Japan, America, India, Tibet, Korea, Persia and Armenia – and bouts of semi-invalidity in the home of her devoted sister in **Edinburgh**. During her time in Edinburgh Isabella wrote articles for worthy periodicals and involved herself in good works, making friends with intellectuals and ecclesiastics like **John Stuart Blackie**, **Dr John Brown**, **Alexander Smith**, **Sir Joseph Noel Paton**, **Thomas Guthrie** and **Robert Candlish**. She attempted to ameliorate the terrible conditions in the **Old Town** – graphically described in her *Notes from Old Edinburgh* (1869) – and, controversially, assisted the passage of crofters from the **Hebrides** to Canada after her tour of the **Western Isles** in 1861. Having returned from an 18-month trip to Australia, New Zealand, Hawaii and the USA, in 1875 she successfully campaigned for a Cabman's Rest in **Princes Street**, and organised the Grand Bazaar in 1878 for the National Livingstone Memorial which established **Cowgate** Medical Missionary School. Her *Lady's Life in the Rocky Mountains* (1879), written in the form of letters home to her sister, finally made her name as a writer and was followed by books on Hawaii, Japan and Korea, and in 1892 she became the first lady Fellow of the Royal Geographical Society. On her sister's death in 1880 Isabella finally married her long-time suitor, Dr John Bishop. But he died six years later and straightaway she was off again, crossing Morocco's Atlas Mountains on horseback at the age of 70 and finally dying in Edinburgh while planning a return visit to China.

BISHOPTON, Renfrewshire

Until the early decades of the 14th century the lands of Bishopton were in the possession of the Bishopric of **Glasgow**, but passed subsequently to the Brisbane family and then, in 1703, to the Lords of Blantyre. The present village lies in the parish of Erskine, south of the river **Clyde** and six miles north-west of **Paisley**. The farmers of this region had an excellent reputation as breeders of horses and cattle and were well known for the high quality of their dairy products, but many farms were acquired by the government in 1937 to make room for the construction of the Royal Ordnance Factory. The munitions industry was not new to the area – in January 1916 the Georgetown Filling Factory commenced operations and by August of the following year employed over 10,000 workers. The Royal Ordnance Factory was taken over by British Aerospace in 1987, but by 1999 it was under threat of closure.

BLACK, Adam (1783–1874) Publisher

Born in **Edinburgh**, Black established himself in the capital's bookselling community before moving into publishing. In 1827 he bought the *Encyclopaedia Britannica* from **Constable** and published an enlarged 7th edition at an estimated cost of £100,000, thereby ensuring its continued success. He was also responsible for the production of an 8th edition, and his family firm (later Adam and Charles Black) produced 9th and 10th editions, the former in particular being highly praised. Black was the definitive publisher of **Scott**'s Waverley

novels after acquiring the copyrights in 1851. He was both Lord Provost of Edinburgh (1843–8) and MP for the city (1856–65). Three years after his death he was commemorated with a bronze statue in the city's **Princes Street Gardens**.

BLACK, Joseph (1728–99) Chemist

One of chemistry's greatest researchers and teachers, Joseph Black was born in Bordeaux to a Scottish mother

Professor Joseph Black, by David Martin, 1787 (SNPG)

and an Irish father. After studying at both **Glasgow** and **Edinburgh** from the age of 16, he wrote a graduation thesis which identified carbon dioxide for the first time. His other major research achievement was his promotion of his ideas on specific and latent heat, greatly advancing the science of thermodynamics. His tenure of posts at the **Universities of Glasgow** and **Edinburgh** enhanced both those establishments, and he encouraged the developing talents of **James Watt**. He died in Edinburgh.

'BLACK DINNER', The (1440)

On the death of **James I** (1437), **Archibald 5th Earl of Douglas** was appointed Regent during the minority of **James II**, and on his own death in 1439 was succeeded to the earldom by his 15-year-old son William. The currently powerful **Sir William Crichton** and **Sir Alexander Livingston**, governors of **Edinburgh Castle** and **Stirling Castle** respectively, were determined to prevent the young earl growing into his father's position of power and influence and, on 28 November 1440, invited him and his younger brother to dine at Edinburgh Castle. At the end of the meal a black bull's head, symbol of impending death, was placed on the table; the two boys were seized and beheaded on **Castlehill**. Suspicion of complicity in this atrocity fell on their great-uncle, **James Douglas 'the Gross'**, since he inherited the earldom but made no attempt at retribution. Livingston, anxious to placate the Douglas faction, later swore on oath that he had played no part in the crime, but the more honest (or less vulnerable) Crichton seemed to think his action required no justification.

BLACK ISLE, The, Ross & Cromarty

Not black and not an island, the Black Isle is the name given to the east coast peninsula between the Beauly Firth to the south, the Moray Firth to the east, and the Cromarty Firth to the north. Several not very satisfactory explanations are offered for the 'black'; the 'isle' makes sense given that the landward link five miles wide contrasts with 45 miles of coastline, and that before the construction of a road round the firths travellers up the coast arrived and left by ferry. Once also known as Ardmeanach and (approximately) Cromartyshire, it was thus an area of considerable trade and traffic, not the dead-end backwater it appears to be on modern maps. Milbuie, a central ridge of moorland now mainly **forestry**, runs its length with the main areas of settlement to the south and east. Here the soil is 'light and early' with little snow (a possible explanation for the 'black') and esteemed arable and pasture to which flocks from the Highlands are still sent for wintering.

Besides the attractions of **Fortrose** and **Cromarty** itself, the area is rich in ancient remains, chambered **cairns, duns**, and **Pictish** symbol stones. In the west Kinkell Castle near Conon Bridge [see **Dingwall**] dates from 1594. It was originally Z-plan, belonged to a branch of the Mackenzies, and has recently been restored. All of which applies equally to Kilcoy Castle at the southern end of the Black Isle's landward link near **Muir of Ord**. Kilcoy, larger with a fine profile of turrets, Gothic-style dormers and crow-stepped gables, dates from the early 17th century, probably soon after the estate's acquisition by Alexander Mackenzie, a son of the 11th Lord **Kintail**. Nearby on the Beauly Firth, Redcastle (not to be confused with that on **Lunan Bay**) is very much older but currently ruinous. As Edradour it was supposedly founded by **David of Huntingdon** in the late 12th century. The core of the surviving structure is an L-plan fortalice of the 16th century with a 17th century tower in the re-entrant angle and some 19th century additions. **Queen Mary** stayed here, the northernmost point of her peregrination of the northeast in 1562. Originally Bisset and then Douglas property, by 1641 it had been snapped up by the area's ubiquitous Mackenzies.

More Mackenzies are commemorated at Avoch (pron 'Och') west of Fortrose. In the graveyard of the parish church (1670 but much altered subsequently) lies the transcontinental explorer **Sir Alexander Mackenzie**, while nearby Rosehaugh was the estate of **Sir George Mackenzie**, 'the bluidy advocate'. There are **bird reserves** at Munlochy and Udale bays. Celtic saints are commemorated in Kessock (once a ferry, now the bridgehead on the road into **Inverness**), which is named after St Kessock; in Killearnan church near Redcastle, which is thought to have been founded by a supposed cousin of **St Columba** named Iernan or Itrunan; and in Eilean Dhubhaich, yet another name for the Black Isle which either indicates some connection

with St Duthac (Bishop of **Ross**, d.1075) or offers a further explanation for the 'black' (ie *dubh*).

BLACK WATCH, The (Royal Highland Regiment)

In 1881 the 42nd Royal Highland Regiment (The Black Watch) amalgamated with the 73rd (Perthshire) Regiment to form today's Black Watch, together with the Royal Perth Militia and the Volunteer Infantry Battalions of **Perthshire**, **Fife** and **Angus**.

The 73rd had in fact commenced life as the 2nd Battalion of the 42nd, becoming a separate regiment in India in 1786, with **Norman MacLeod of MacLeod** as its first Colonel. It lost its Highland identity in 1809 but regained the title of 'Perthshire' in 1862. It served in New South Wales 1809–14 and the 2nd/73rd was at Waterloo. It saw much service in South Africa and took part in the Indian Mutiny campaign.

The 42nd derived from the six Independent Highland Companies of Foot, raised in 1725 and regimented in 1739 under the Colonelcy of the **Earl of Crawford**. The regiment was originally numbered the 43rd, being renumbered the 42nd in 1751 and granted the title of 'Royal' in 1758. It was early known as *Am Freiceadan dubh* – The Black Watch.

It fought a gallant rearguard action at Fontenoy in 1743 where it gained its Gaelic sobriquet translated as 'The Black Watch of the Battles, First to Come and Last to Go'. In North America, at Ticonderoga, it sustained casualties the like of which were not to be seen again until World War I. Its campaigns included those in Egypt, the Peninsula, Waterloo, the Crimea, the Indian Mutiny and Ashanti. The regiment produced 25 battalions in World War I, winning 76 battle honours. In World War II the regiment fought in France in 1940, North Africa, Crete, Sicily, Italy, Burma, north-west Europe and Greece. Its 63 battle honours include that of Chindits 1944, and with two awarded for Korea bring the regimental total to 172. Since 1945 the Black Watch has been on active service in Korea, Kenya, Cyprus (twice) and in Northern Ireland, and in February 1997 became the last UK Infantry Battalion to serve in Hong Kong.

Most famous of its dress distinctions is the Red Hackle, worn in the bonnet since the 18th century. It wears the dark **tartan** associated with the regimental name. Her Majesty Queen Elizabeth the Queen Mother is Colonel-in-Chief.

BLACKADDER, John (1615–86) Covenanter

As **Covenanter** minister of Troqueer near **Dumfries** from 1652 Blackadder opposed Episcopacy and was deposed in 1662. Outlawed as a hedge preacher in 1674, he escaped to Holland. On his return in 1681 he was arrested and died a prisoner on the **Bass Rock**, the fate of several Covenanters.

BLACKADDER, Robert (d.1508) Archbishop of Glasgow

Educated at **St Andrews** c.1461 and Paris, Blackadder (sometimes also Blacader or Blackader) became an emissary of **James III** and **James IV** in England, France, Spain and Rome. As bishop-elect of **Aberdeen** he was translated to **Glasgow** by 1483, which was raised to an

Archbishopric in 1492. He built the choir screen and aisle of **Glasgow Cathedral** and died on pilgrimage to Jerusalem.

BLACKFACE SHEEP
From the early 1700s this breed spread into lowland Scotland from its unknown English place of origin. In 1752 John Campbell took Blackface sheep into **Dunbartonshire** from **Ayrshire** and the sheep invasion of the Highlands had begun. After the **clearances**, a sheep-based economy was imposed based on the **Cheviot** and the Blackface.

The history of sheep farming in the Highlands is one of struggle against the weather and against harsh economic factors, but today the Scottish Blackface, with 2.5 million ewes, is Britain's most numerous breed. At times the Cheviot has been favoured (most notably when wool prices were high); then the Blackface has staged a resurgence, particularly during periods of harsh weather. The breeds have very different ecological requirements. The Cheviot is known as a 'white hill' breed, as it requires a sward composed mainly of grasses (whose seed heads give the white colour), while the Blackface, with its ability to thrive on heather-dominated ground, is a 'black hill' breed.

Like the Cheviot, the Blackface is a foundation stone of the British sheep industry. Old ewes are sent to low-land farms where they are mated with rams of the Border Leicester breed (or its derivative the Bluefaced Leicester). The crossbred progeny, called Greyfaces or Mules respectively, are profitable lowland sheep.

There are today four races of Blackface: the small and lean Lewis, the heavily fleeced Perth and Lanark, and the Newton Stewart which is thought to have been the most improved.

BLACKIE, John Stuart (1809–95) Scholar
Born in **Glasgow**, the son of a banker, and educated at **Aberdeen** Grammar School, **Edinburgh University**, Göttingen and Berlin, Blackie also studied theology at **Marischal College**, Aberdeen and **law** at Edinburgh, being called to the Scottish Bar in 1834, although he never practised either discipline. In 1834 he published a metrical translation of Goethe's *Faust* and for the rest of his life was a regular contributor to *Blackwood's Magazine*. From 1841–52 he was Professor of Humanities (Latin) at Aberdeen and from 1852–82 Professor of Greek at Edinburgh University. A fervent nationalist and promoter of Celtic culture, he also founded and endowed the Chair of Celtic Studies at Edinburgh in 1882.

BLACKNESS CASTLE, West Lothian
Built on a long narrow spit of land sticking out into the Firth of Forth north of **Linlithgow**, Blackness Castle spent most of its useful career as a state **prison** (**Cardinal Beaton** was held here for part of 1543). There had been a port here from ancient times but the earliest part of the castle, a three-storey tower in a courtyard surrounded by a crenellated wall, dates from c1440 and is thought to have been built by Sir George Crichton (brother of **Sir William Crichton**, Chancellor of Scotland), who later gifted it to **James II**. In 1537 the Keeper of Blackness, **Sir James Hamilton of Finnart**, transformed the castle into 'one of the most formidable

strongholds in Scotland, giving it much of the appearance it still has today' (I MacIvor). Beseiged and damaged by Cromwell's army in 1650, it ceased to be a prison after the **Act of Union** and was maintained as a small garrison, until converted c1870 into an ammunition depot. Handed over to the Ministry of Works in 1912, it was reoccupied during World War I and was thereafter restored as an ancient monument.

BLACKWOOD, William (1776–1834)
Bookseller and Publisher
Born in **Edinburgh**, William Blackwood was apprenticed to a bookseller at the age of 14. After a period in London and **Glasgow**, he established himself as a bookseller and publisher in Edinburgh in 1804. His firm grew rapidly in size and reputation, and in 1817 William Blackwood consolidated his firm's position as a major force in British literary publishing by starting *Blackwood's Magazine*. Authors associated with his firm included **John Galt**, **Susan Ferrier**, Thomas de Quincy and **James Hogg**. William Blackwood died in Edinburgh on 16 September 1834.

BLACKWOOD'S MAGAZINE (1817–1980)
Blackwood's Magazine, or 'Maga', was launched in April 1817 as a Tory response to the **Whig** influenced *Edinburgh Review*. A monthly publication, it was initially produced by the **Edinburgh** publisher **William Blackwood** under the title of *The Edinburgh Monthly Magazine*. After an inauspicious start due to the incompetence of its initial editors, James Cleghorn and Thomas Pringle, Blackwood dismissed them and appointed **John Wilson** and **John Gibson Lockhart**. The renamed *Blackwood's Magazine* was launched in October 1817, with 'The Chaldee Manuscript' as its centrepiece. A satirical attack on leading Scottish Whig literary and political figures, the piece provoked an uproar and established the magazine's reputation overnight. Succeeding issues featured similar attacks on John Keats, Leigh Hunt, **William Wordsworth** and Samuel Taylor Coleridge's *Biographia Literaria*. Critical pieces, however, were not the magazine's only distinguishing point. Early issues featured fiction and verse from such distinguished contributors as **James Hogg**, Thomas de Quincy and **John Galt**.

During the mid-19th to early 20th century *Blackwood's Magazine* featured some of the greatest writers of the Victorian and Edwardian eras. It serialised major novels by Bulwer Lytton, George Eliot, **Margaret Oliphant** and Joseph Conrad, published fiction by Thomas Hardy, Anthony Trollope and William Carleton, critical reviews by Alexander Shand, **William Edmonstoune Aytoun** and Samuel Warren, and political pieces by A W Kinglake and **Alexander Allardyce**.

The magazine's great reputation continued to attract writers in the early 20th century, including **John Buchan**, **Neil Munro**, **'Ian Hay'** and the Australian Henry Lawson. However its old fashioned style, and reliance on military tales and memoirs, made it more and more outmoded as the century progressed, until in December 1980 it ceased publication.

BLADNOCH, Wigtownshire
A mile south-west of **Wigtown**, the village of Bladnoch is famous for its malt **whisky** distillery and for the ruins

of Baldoon Castle. Not spectacular in themselves, the ruins recall **Sir Walter Scott**'s *Bride of Lammermoor*, for Baldoon was the home of David Dunbar, heir to Sir David Dunbar of Baldoon and Scott's original for the bridegroom. Janet Dalrymple, daughter of **Sir James Dalrymple**, later **Viscount Stair**, had become secretly engaged to Archibald 3rd Lord Rutherford but, Rutherford being penniless, her parents disapproved and instructed her to marry David Dunbar instead. The wedding took place at the Kirk of Old Luce on 12 August 1669, on 24 August the newly-weds moved into Baldoon, and on 12 September the bride died. The Bladnoch distillery, the smallest and most southerly in Scotland, had operated since 1817 but closed in 1993.

BLAIKIE, Thomas (1750–1838) Gardener and Botanist

Born at Beechwood on **Corstorphine** Hill in **Edinburgh**, Blaikie was sent to Switzerland in 1775 to search for rare Alpine plants on behalf of Drs John Fothergill and William Pitcairn. Fothergill's botanic garden at Upton, Stratford, rivalled that at Kew; it is assumed that Blaikie worked at the former. At Geneva he met the Alpinist Horace Benedict de Saussure who directed him to the Jura and Salève. After many remarkable mountain crossings he arrived at Chamonix where he encountered the young Michel Gabriel Paccard who, with Jacques Balmat, would make the first successful ascent of Mont Blanc in 1786. With Paccard, Blaikie made several ascents of the Mont Blanc massif, crossing the Bossons and Taconnaz Glaciers and making an attempt of sorts on the Aguille de Gôuter, the highest then reached, and the first serious mountaineering in the Chamonix Valley. In 1776 Blaikie entered the service of the cultured but hapless Comte de Lauraguais (Duc de Brancas) who was improving his estates in Normandy. Through him Blaikie went to work in Paris for the architect François Joseph Belanger, employed by the Comte d'Artois at Bagatelle. He remodelled Parc Monceaux for the Duc d'Orléans from 1785, and at the start of the Revolution (which ruined him) supplied the potatoes with which the Tuileries were planted. According to J C Loudon many of the plants mentioned in Fothergill and Pitcairn's *Hortus Kewensis* were sent home by Blaikie. His *Diary of a Scotch Gardener* reveals his 'astonishing Andrew Fairservice character' (Birrel, 1931).

BLAIR, Hugh (1718–1800) Cleric and Critic

Few reputations can have plummeted from such heights as that of Dr Hugh Blair. Born in **Edinburgh** and educated at the High School and **University**, he was ordained in 1742. As minister of **Lady Yester's Church** and then the High Church of **St Giles** (1758–1800), and as Professor of Rhetoric and Belles Lettres at the University (1762), he became the arbiter of taste and refinement, a paragon amongst preachers, 'the literary pope of Scotland'. **Dr Johnson** endorsed his *Sermons* (1777–1801), whose five volumes became the nation's favourite reading; **David Hume** sought his opinion, **Carlyle** his company, **Burns** his approval. Of the luminaries of the **Scottish Enlightenment**, none enjoyed greater renown in the later 18th century. His *Lectures on Rhetoric and Belles Lettres* (1783) vied with his sermons and have lasted better, leading to his occasional resuscitation

as 'Scotland's greatest literary critic' (D Daiches). His endorsement of **James Macpherson**'s Ossianic fragments was deemed decisive even though he was pontificating 'on a language he did not know, of a past he had not studied, of a poem on whose origins he was utterly mistaken' (H G Graham). Others were equally mistaken. It was not Blair's judgement that undid his reputation but his painfully evident vanity, his sententious vacuity, and his lack of either wit or humour. Well-chosen words, elegant expression, and unexceptionable sentiments have limited appeal; it died very soon after he did.

BLAIR, Patrick (c1661–1728) Physician

A doctor who practised in **Dundee**, London and Boston, Lincolnshire, Blair had the distinction of being the first person scientifically to dissect an elephant. The provenance of the pachyderm in question is unknown but, possibly part of a travelling circus, it had died on the road from **Broughty Ferry** to Dundee. Blair's published medical and botanical works included *Osteographica Elephantica*.

BLAIR ATHOLL, Perthshire

At the gates of **Blair Castle**, Blair-in-Atholl (the original name) is the **Atholl** estate village and a popular **tourist** centre for Glen Tilt and the **Drumochter** and **Killiecrankie** passes. **John Graham of Claverhouse** ('Bonnie Dundee'), the victor and victim of the **Battle of Killiecrankie**, is buried in the churchyard of old St Bride's. The village also boasts a restored and working flour mill dating from 1613 and a display of rural activities and social history known not as a 'heritage centre' but as the Atholl Country Collection. Glen Tilt, wooded then precipitous, was once a much used trail to upper Deeside and **Braemar**. That inveterate rambler **Queen Victoria** explored it in October 1861. A cairn commemorates her picnic spot.

BLAIR CASTLE, Blair Atholl, Perthshire

The ancient seat of the **Dukes of Atholl**, Blair has been through several incarnations, like the Atholl title. Much 19th century castellation by **David** and John **Bryce**, plus an overall coat of whitewash, impart an integrity to an otherwise straggling and incongruous accretion of structures. The Bryces also added the **Fyvie**-like entrance, their brief being to convert Atholl House, 'a large plain white building' according to **Queen Victoria**, into a baronial castle. But that, as the earlier Blair Castle, is what it must have been when in the mid-18th century it was shorn of its top storeys and Georgianised. Of this earlier Blair traces remain in parts of Cumming's Tower supposedly built by **John Comyn**, or Cumming, of **Badenoch** in 1267, and in the various additions made during the 15th and 16th centuries including the range with the main hall. Blair was garrisoned by **James Graham, Marquis of Montrose** in 1644 but 'destroyed' by the Cromwellian storming of 1653. Part, though, must either have survived or been rebuilt, for **John Graham of Claverhouse** also garrisoned it and was then brought there after his death at **Killiecrankie** in 1689. It was supposedly dismantled again in 1690 to deny it to other Highland malcontents yet was capable of withstanding another siege in 1746 when **Lord George**

Murray, brother of the Duke, failed to win it for the **Jacobites**. This episode accounts for the claim that it was the last castle in Britain to be besieged. Royal visitors have included Edward III of England, **Queen Mary** (whose visit was celebrated with a hunt that bagged 360 **red deer** and five wolves), **Prince Charles Edward Stewart**, Queen Victoria, and the future Edward VII (for whom 3000 red deer were mustered).

Internally some old vaulting remains and the rococo plasterwork of the Georgian remodelling is exceptionally fine. As with other ducal castles, the contents on display to the public include tapestries, family portraits by **Raeburn**, **Ramsay**, Zoffany, etc, and an impressive collection of arms. Jacobite relics and natural history are also represented.

BLAIRGOWRIE, Perthshire

Like **Kirriemuir** and **Alyth**, Blairgowrie was once described as 'industrious' because of its **jute** and flax spinning. Today it relies on soft fruit, a small red-stone town famous for its large red raspberries. The river Ericht divides Blairgowrie proper on its right bank from Rattray on its left. Each is a separate parish with its own church, neither of which is remarkable. The area is better endowed with castles, Blairgowrie's Newton being Z-plan and early 17th century while Rattray's Craighall, though completely rebuilt in the 19th century, has the more dramatic site, perched precariously on a ledge above the Ericht; its owner is said to have recognised it immediately in **Scott**'s description of Tully-Veolan in *Waverley*. A mile west of the town Ardblair, originally L-plan and 16th century, retains its courtyard and 'gives a more complete picture of 17th century living than most' (M Lindsay). It passed to the Oliphants of Gask in 1792 and houses relics of their **Jacobite** past and of **Lady Carolina Nairne** (née Oliphant), the songwriter. A lady in green is said to haunt both Newton and Ardblair, possibly the same person but not Lady Nairne. More suited to ghosts, Castle of Clunie stands on a minuscule island, perhaps once a **crannog**, in Loch Clunie. L-plan of about 1500 it was the childhood home of **James (The Admirable) Crichton**. It is now roofless but not ruinous. In the same condition is much larger and later (1870) Achalder House.

BLAKE, George (1893–1961) Novelist

Born in **Greenock**, Blake read **law** at **Glasgow University**, joined the army at the start of World War I, was wounded at Gallipoli and invalided out again, and then entered journalism. After a spell working with **Neil Munro** on the *Glasgow Evening News*, he moved to London in 1923 to edit the popular literary weekly *John O'London's* and two years later became editor of *The Strand Magazine*. One of the founders of The Porpoise Press (publishers of **Neil Gunn**'s first novel *The Grey Coast*, 1926), which was taken over by Faber & Faber in 1930, Blake became a director of Fabers and moved back to Scotland in 1932 to run Porpoise. He lived in **Helensburgh** until 1939, moved back to London to work at the Ministry of Information for the duration of World War II, and then returned to **Glasgow** where he lived until his death. Of his many novels set in Glasgow and Greenock, his best-known, *The Shipbuilders* (1935), explored the social

George Blake, flanked by Neil Gunn and Douglas Young; 1957 drawing by Emilio Coia (SNPG)

and psychological impact of industrial decline and depression on both employer and employee, earning him a reputation as 'the only one of the older generation of Scottish Renaissance writers who faced up to the values and dilemmas of industrial society' (M Lindsay).

BLANE, Gilbert (1749–1834) Surgeon

Responsible for ridding the Royal Navy of its centuries-old foe, scurvy, Gilbert Blane was born at Blanefield, **Stirling**, and graduated in medicine after studying in **Edinburgh** and **Glasgow**. While serving as a naval surgeon in the West Indies, Blane applied the ideas of **James Lind** in providing ships' crews with lime juice and citrus fruits as antiscorbutic precautions, greatly reducing shipboard illness. He helped draft the Quarantine Act of 1799, and was appointed medical adviser to both George IV and William IV. He died in London.

BLANTYRE, Lanarkshire

Of the priory established here in the 13th century by Augustinians from **Jedburgh** only vestiges remain. It stood beside the **Clyde** opposite **Bothwell Castle**. As at **New Lanark** the river provided a ready source of power which in 1785 persuaded **David Dale** to erect another **cotton** mill with housing, school, chapel, etc for the weavers. The enterprise was sold in 1792 and it was thus in Henry Monteith's mill that **David Livingstone** was born and brought up in a one-room tenement in Shuttle Row. Although most of the mill has long since been demolished, the tenement and adjacent buildings have been preserved as the Livingstone National Memorial and Museum (1929). Amongst other displays and memorabilia may be seen the missionary-explorer's Bible and his consular peaked cap.

BLANTYRE PIT EXPLOSION (1877)

Scotland's worst mining disaster, and the second worst in British history, occurred at **Blantyre**, **Lanarkshire**, on 22 October 1877. An underground explosion, the result either of naked-flame illumination or unofficial shot-firing in an environment infested with fire-damp, caused the deaths of 207 men.

The galleries at Blantyre High No 1 Pit were worked on a 'stoop and room' (pillar and stall) method down to 900ft (274m), with natural buttresses in the form of **coal** left undug to shore up the seam roofs. It appeared that safety practices required by the Coal Mines Regulation Act of 1872 were not properly enforced, nor did the rescue arrangements offer hope to any miners trapped underground. An MP living nearby, Alexander MacDonald (himself a former miner and highly respected champion of colliers' rights), prevented – on safety grounds – an *en masse* rescue attempt involving the surviving colliery employees, and he later agitated unsuccessfully in Parliament for the mine-owners to be prosecuted. This followed a public inquiry which exposed unsafe working practices and a catalogue of earlier mishaps in what was known locally as the 'Fiery Mine'. A further 28 men died in another major accident at Blantyre within two years.

BLIND HARPER, The (*Clàrsair Dall, An*) (c1656–c1713) Gaelic Poet

Roderick Morrison of Braga, **Lewis**, was a professional harper who also operated as a poet. This was once a not unusual combination, but he seems to be the last of this line in Scotland. John MacLeod of **Dunvegan** became his patron in 1681. Only seven of his songs survive, some of them with their airs but without evidence of the harp accompaniments. *Creach na Ciadaoin* ('Wednesday's Bereavement') is a moving lament for his patron who died in 1693, and his most famous poem is one addressed to John MacLeod's son Roderick: this is notable for its outspoken criticism of the young spendthrift chief. The poems were edited by William Matheson in the book *The Blind Harper* (1970).

BLIND HARRY, see HARRY THE MINSTREL

BLOODY FRIDAY RIOT (31 January 1919)

The end of World War I threatened industrial Clydeside with a flooding of the labour market (as conscripts were demobilised) and a decline in orders, especially for munitions. To meet this crisis the Scottish Trades Union Congress (STUC), the revived **Clyde Workers Committee** (CWC), and other bodies proposed a reduction in the working week to 40 hours or, in the case of the CWC, to 30. This demand was backed by an unofficial and over-hasty call for a general strike to begin on 27 January 1919.

After the 1916 conviction of the CWC's leaders, the industrial climate of Clydeside had mellowed for the duration of the war. Now, with the new strike call and the re-emergence of militants like **Willie Gallacher**, the spectre of a revolutionary **Red Clydeside** again haunted the Whitehall imagination. Although the strike call was largely ignored elsewhere, and even on Clydeside had only limited support, the deployment of flying pickets several thousand strong created an alarmist atmosphere and threatened to bring **Glasgow** to a standstill. One power station was closed down, voltage was reduced throughout the city, and there was talk of halting the tram services. At the request of the strike leaders the Lord Provost communicated to the Cabinet what was in effect an ultimatum.

On Friday 31 January, while the strike leaders were in the **City Chambers** to hear the government's response, a mass gathering of strikers outside in **George Square**

was repeatedly charged by riot police. It was claimed that the strikers were halting the tram services, although whether this was intentional is not clear. The strikers responded with such missiles as were to hand, mostly lemonade bottles. 40 people were injured, many of them innocent onlookers. Gallacher, **Davie Kirkwood**, and later Emmanuel Shinwell were arrested. According to the Scottish Secretary, the strike was now revealed in its true colours as a 'Bolshevist rising'. Troops were rushed to suppress it and by next morning six tanks and 100 army lorries were on the streets of Glasgow.

Thereafter the strike collapsed amidst recriminations amongst the organising bodies. The STUC hastily backed away from militant action, and retrospectively Bloody Friday was seen as having finally discredited the revolutionary tactics of the CWC. Gallacher and Shinwell were convicted of incitement and received short prison sentences.

BLOODY VESPERS, The (1555)

On New Year's Day 1555 a local feud between two **Moray** families, the Dunbars and the Inneses, came to a head in **Elgin Cathedral**. With a view to slaughtering David and Alexander Dunbar, respectively Dean of Moray and Prior of **Pluscarden**, William Innes and over 100 armed followers descended on the church at Vespers only to find 72 armed Dunbars come for a similar 'service', the murder of the Innes laird. Coincidence or not, the resultant fracas was conducted without regard for the presence of the Holy Sacrament; that, rather than the few recorded 'hurtings', constituted the scandal. The feud continued, but in less sacrilegious circumstances.

BLUE BLANKET, The

This was the name given to the fighting flag of the crafts community of Old **Edinburgh**. Its fabled origin goes back to Crusading times, but a more plausible inception dates from 1482, when **James III**, having been imprisoned in **Edinburgh Castle** by vengeful nobles, was rescued by the ordinary craftsmen of the town. In gratitude the King presented them with a flag which they were given authority to raise and to muster under whenever their sovereign, or their own rights, were threatened. Tradition asserts that when it was unfurled, all the craftsmen of the burgh, and indeed throughout Scotland, were required to rally to it, and fight under the leadership of the Convener of the Edinburgh Crafts Incorporations. It conspicuously failed to protect **James IV** at **Flodden**, but provided good service to **James V**, **Queen Mary** and **James VI**. Most of what is supposedly known about the Blue Blanket comes from an account published in 1722, which claims to be based on 'authentic manuscripts', though the earliest known first-hand reference only dates back to the *Basilikon Doron* of 1599, in which James VI refers to it in less than complimentary terms. Two quite different flags are claimed to be the Blue Blanket: a plain rectangle is housed in the **National Museum**, while an inscribed twin gonfalon (a vertically hung flag) resides in the Trades Maiden Hospital. The name is kept alive by a tavern in the **Canongate**, which has a superb mosaic frieze on its exterior depicting five incidents involving the Blue Blanket.

BLYTH, Robert Henderson (1919–70)
Painter

Blyth's death at the age of 51 cut off a career which still had considerable potential. Born in **Glasgow**, he had entered the **School of Art** there at the age of 15 and immediately rejected the teaching methods which encouraged spontaniety of expression at the expense of analysis and formal composition. In 1940 he came under the tutelage of **James Cowie** at **Hospitalfield** and found much to emulate in the older artist's espousal of line and classical formalism. His application of these principles to his war experiences in France, Holland and Belgium while serving in the RAMC resulted in a series of pictures which, while portraying realistically the activities of war, lent the scenes a neo-romantic and, occasionally, surreal sensibility. Reminiscent of Stanley Spencer, they were unlike anything being painted by a Scot at the time. After the war he taught at **Edinburgh** College of Art and the bravado, colour and lyricism of his contemporaries – **Gillies**, **Maxwell**, **Redpath** – influenced his own work. With Gillies he painted the landscape of eastern Scotland, creating rigid, linear compositions in oil, watercolour and ink which are always filled with unease, the brooding forces of nature always bubbling below the surface. Elected to the **Royal Scottish Academy** in 1957, he was appointed Head of Drawing and Painting at Gray's School of Art in **Aberdeen** three years later. His final paintings of the local landscape show him continuing to explore the dichotomies of the man-made and natural landscapes

BOAT OF GARTEN, Inverness-shire

So named because there was once a ferry, Boat of Garten is a village and resort (with **golf course**) on the west bank of the **Spey** between **Aviemore** and **Grantown**. The short Speyside **railway** (steam) to Aviemore begins here. Loch Garten of **osprey** fame is on the other side of the river in Abernethy forest [see **Bird Reserves**]. This is not to be confused with **Abernethy** on the Firth of **Tay**. Nor should the nearby village of Kincardine, with a church wherein the **Grants** incinerated their Cumming (or **Comyn**) rivals in the 16th century, be confused with the several other Kincardines. At Tullochgorum [see **Rothiemurchus**] there is a stone circle marking a chambered burial **cairn**.

BOECE, Hector (c1465–1536) Historian

Boece (Latin 'Boethius') was born in **Dundee** and appointed by **Bishop William Elphinstone** Principal of the newly founded **University of Aberdeen**. As a Latin scholar he was well qualified for such a position, and in 1527 published his *History of Scotland* to the accession of **James III**. This inventive narrative created a fictitious royal Celtic progenitor of the **Stewarts** called Banquo, at a time when they, as well as the **Bruces** through whom they inherited the Crown, were still living in France. For good measure Boece depicted Gruoch, Scotland's earliest historical Queen Regnant and senior dynast of her time, as the mere Lady Macbeth, burning with desire to occupy a throne. Holinshed followed Boece and Shakespeare read Holinshed. Thus the genius of the English dramatist was inspired by that of the Scottish historian.

BOGLE, George (1746–81) Explorer

Born near **Bothwell** in **Lanarkshire**, Bogle found employment with the East India Company and in 1774 was chosen by Warren Hastings to lead a mission to Tibet. Accompanied by Alexander Hamilton, a fellow countryman, he proceeded from Bengal to Bhutan and thence to Tashilunpo in Tibet. They were the first Britons to reach Tibet and indeed the first to cross the Himalayas. Although prevented from proceeding to Lhasa, Bogle formed a close friendship with the Panchen Lama, took a Tibetan wife, and reckoned his six months in the country the happiest of his life. For one sent to open Tibet to commerce, his parting sentiment amounted to a recantation: 'Farewell ye honest and simple people. May ye long enjoy that happiness which is denied to more polished nations.' Hamilton was sent back to Tibet in 1776 and 1777 but failed to get beyond Bhutan. Bogle was appointed to a new Tibetan mission in 1779 but the mission was still stalled at the time of his death. His report on Tibet dealt with every conceivable aspect of Tibetan life, religion and husbandry; it reveals its author as a genial traveller completely seduced by 'The Forbidden Land'.

BOGUE, David (1750–1825) Missionary

A Congregational minister and a tutor to the Congregational ministry, Bogue was born in **Coldingham**, **Berwickshire** and educated in **Edinburgh**. He was a founder of the London Missionary Society, the British and Foreign Bible Society and the Religious Tract Society. With Dr James Bennet he wrote *A History of Dissenters* (1809).

BONAR BRIDGE, Sutherland

An iron bridge, since replaced, was erected in 1813 under the direction of **Thomas Telford** at the inner narrows of the **Dornoch Firth**. The village which consequently grew here has lost much of its traffic since the new bridge was opened in 1991 to carry the A9 north by a more direct route between **Tain** and **Dornoch**. But Bonar Bridge village still serves Assynt and **Strathnaver**, and its inhabitants maintain craft enterprises and a **tourist** trade.

BONAWE, Taynuilt, Argyll

'Bun Atha', although strictly the mouth of the Awe, now describes the surrounding district including the granite quarry on the north side of **Loch Etive**. The ferry here had long been a central point in the cattle **droving** trade when the Lorn Furnace Company was founded in 1753 by Richard Ford of the Newland Company in Lancashire. Taking advantage of the plentiful and cheap supply of charcoal from the surrounding **birch** and oak woods, and importing iron ore by boat, high quality pig iron was produced at Bonawe until 1875, the River Awe providing the force to drive the blast furnace. The ironworks created a small industrial community with new workers' cottages, a school, a laundry and all the ancilliary industries and buildings needed to service the local and immigrant workforce. The furnace and some buildings remain, now in the care of **Historic Scotland**.

Bonawe ironworks, Taynuilt (HS)

BONE, Sir David Muirhead (1876–1953)
Etcher and War Artist

An outstanding draughtsman and printmaker, Muirhead Bone was at the forefront of the early 20th century etching revival, along with fellow Scots James McBey and **D Y Cameron**. Born in **Glasgow** he initially trained as an architect and his facility in this field informed much of his later work. Evening classes at **Glasgow School of Art** under **Francis Newbery** led him to produce his first set of etchings of Glasgow subjects in 1898. Their popular success drew him to London where a series of exhibitions established his reputation. His

Sir D Muirhead Bone, by Francis Dodd, 1907 (SNPG)

remarkable technical skill and minute observation when dealing with architectural subjects, particularly scaffolding and scenes of demolition, led Sir Kenneth Clarke to compare him to the great Italian etcher Piranesi. In 1916 he was appointed the first official war artist and his detailed and dramatic depictions of the Western Front and warships on the **Clyde** (published monthly in *Country Life*) brought widespread acclaim. After the war he travelled extensively with his wife Gertrude; his drawings and prints of Spain are particularly noteworthy. Bone was unaffected by the collapse of the print market in the 1930s, already enjoying the accolades his reputation had brought him: honorary degrees, trusteeships of the National and Tate Galleries and a knighthood. Appointed official war artist again (1939–45), his age necessarily limited the scope of his contribution. A modest man whose exceptional talents were never stretched, he is perhaps best remembered as a consummate craftsman rather than an innovative artist.

BO'NESS, see BORROWSTOUNNESS

'BONNIE DUNDEE', see JOHN GRAHAM OF CLAVERHOUSE

BONNYMUIR, Battle of (1820)

Uncertainty surrounds the so-called 'Radical War' (or 'Scottish Insurrection') of 1820. As in the 20th century, post-war (Napoleonic) depression and unemployment provoked industrial unrest, evidenced by the 1819 demonstrations of mostly weavers in **Paisley** and **Glasgow**; and such economic discontent easily allied itself to calls for political reform (universal suffrage, annual parliaments, etc). But the 1819 Peterloo Massacre in Manchester revealed a government ready to panic. The repressive legislation that followed and the arrest of 27 Glasgow radicals were also provocative. **Cockburn** insisted that **Edinburgh** was 'as quiet as the grave or even **Peebles**', and **Carlyle**, though not **Scott**, thought the alarm wildly exaggerated. If sedition was in the air, it could have been either radicals or government agents who put up the placards calling for a general strike and uprising. These appeared in Glasgow on April Fool's Day 1820. On 5 April troops lined the streets as 300 dazed radicals answered the call, then quickly dispersed. Meanwhile some **Calton weavers** had marched on **Falkirk**, supposedly to commandeer guns from the **Carron Company**. They were met by troops at Bonnymuir and, after a 'battle' in which four were wounded, they fled. Of 47 people arrested during the 'war' most were acquitted; but three, James Wilson, Andrew Hardie and John Baird, were convicted of sedition and executed, martyrs to the reformist and working-class causes of which more would be heard.

See also **Chartism**, **Trade Unionism**, etc.

BOOK OF COMMON PRAYER (Scottish Prayer Book) (1637)

Introduced by **Charles I** in 1637, the Book of Common Prayer was designed to bring the liturgy used by the Church in Scotland more in line with that used in England and favoured by the King. The hostile reception accorded **James VI**'s **Five Articles of Perth** and his subsequent attempt at liturgical reform (1618) had given fair warning of the dangers involved. Charles, who had visited Scotland in 1633, hoped to anticipate opposition by involving the Scottish bishops in the consultative process. It was they who obtained numerous concessions to Scottish practice so that, instead of a copy of the English Book of Common Prayer as urged by Archbishop Laud, there emerged a compromise between it and the existing Book of Common Order, a Genevan model adopted by the **General Assembly** in 1562. But the new Scottish Prayer Book also included the detested Five Articles; it incorporated a few other suspiciously Roman practices, notably permission for the celebrant to turn his back on the congregation when at the communion table; and worst of all, it contained a proclamation enjoining its use by royal command. This insistence on royal prerogative, without mention of approval by either General Assembly or Parliament, rendered the Book objectionable to Scottish opinion whatever its contents. Discontent, already simmering amongst the clergy, the nobility and the burgesses of **Edinburgh**, quickly focused on the Book's perceived threat to Scotland's **Reformation**. Petitions against it were circulated and crowds massed in Edinburgh. On 23 July its attempted introduction in **St Giles** provoked a riot. So did royal proclamations designed to disperse the mob. The bishops, for their part in drafting and authorising the Prayer Book, were discredited as events moved rapidly towards the drawing up of the **Covenant**.

After the Restoration **Charles II**, learning from past mistakes, made no attempt to impose a compulsory liturgy. Some ministers did however use the Prayer Book publicly and more privately. Reprinted and considerably revised in the 18th century, it 'attained a stable form' in 1764 and survived until the issue of a new Scottish Prayer Book in 1929.

BOOTHBY, Robert John Graham, Lord (1900–86) Politician

Born in **Edinburgh** and educated at Eton and Magdalen College, Oxford, Boothby stood unsuccessfully as Conservative candidate for **Orkney** and **Shetland** in 1923 but was elected MP for East **Aberdeenshire** in 1924, a post he held for 35 years. Parliamentary Private Secretary to Winston Churchill at the Treasury (1926–9) and at the Ministry of Food (1940), he resigned following allegations of impropriety concerning Czechoslovak gold reserves later that same year. Outspoken, unconventional and a vociferous critic of the Establishment, he campaigned vigorously for European unity and homosexual law reform and against the Suez expedition. Made an independent life peer as Baron Boothby of Buchan and Rattray Head (1958), he became a well-known lecturer, author and broadcaster on both radio and television.

BORROWSTOUNNESS (BO'NESS), West Lothian

In the 18th century this town on the east coast of the innermost Firth of Forth was famous for the production and export of **coal** and salt. It was described by Daniel Defoe as consisting of 'one straggling street extended along the shore . . . which has been, and still is, a town of the greatest trade to Holland and France of any in Scotland except **Leith**', the men of the town being 'the best seamen in the Firth'. The opening of the **Forth-Clyde Canal** in 1790 and the construction of **Grangemouth** from 1810 led to the complete eclipse of Bo'ness as a port, and its 'safe and commodious harbour' is now completely silted up. The old town survives, although now merging into its neighbours, and is overlooked by Victorian and Edwardian villas built on the ridge above.

BORTHWICK CASTLE, Nr Gorebridge, Midlothian

Described in 1887 by **MacGibbon and Ross** as 'By far the finest of our castles built on the model of the keep, Borthwick together with its courtyard and outworks, are fortunately all in good preservation and have been little added to or altered.' The same holds true today,

Borthwick Castle, Scotland's tallest tower house (RWB)

and Borthwick remains not only the tallest tower house in Scotland but one of the best preserved. Built in 1430 by Sir William Borthwick on a tongue of land between two small rivers, it stands 110ft (33.5m) high from the base of the tower to the top of the flag-stone roof, the walls are 14ft (4.3m) thick at the base tapering to 6ft (2m) near the top, and the main rectangular block has two tower wings both projecting to the west, making the overall shape of a stumpy U. The whole castle is faced in dressed ashlar, and it has been calculated that the total weight of masonry of this 'inspiring pile' would amount to some 30,000 tons. The vaulted great hall on the first floor, 'the grandest medieval hall in Scotland' (C McWilliam), measures 50ft by 23 ft (15 by 7m), and the kitchen, in the northern tower on the same floor, has a massive fireplace that takes up half the room and is lighted by three windows.

Queen Mary and **Bothwell** came to Borthwick after their marriage in June 1567, pursued by the **Lords of the Congregation** who blockaded the castle, forcing the couple to flee separately, 'Her Majesty in men's clothes, booted and spurred', to meet later in **Dunbar**. Perhaps realising that a great deal of time and ammunition would be wasted in trying to reduce such a massive bulk, Oliver Cromwell wrote to John 8th Lord Borthwick from **Edinburgh** on 18 November 1650 inviting him to surrender, warning him that 'If you necessitate me to bend my cannon against you, you must expect what I doubt you will not be pleased with.' After several days' thought, and a blast from the Protector's cannon which knocked off a section of the parapet, Lord Borthwick 'obtained honourable terms of capitulation' which saved everyone a lot of bother and Borthwick from much more serious damage. During World War II the castle was used to store the public records of Scotland, removed here from Edinburgh for the duration.

BOSWELL, James (1740–95) Biographer

Boswell was born in **Edinburgh**, the son of Lord Auchinleck, a prominent advocate. He was privately educated by a tutor until he was 13, after which he reluctantly studied **law** in Edinburgh, **Glasgow** and Utrecht. He was admitted to the Bar in 1766. His real interests,

James Boswell, aged 25, by George Willison (SNPG)

though, lay in literature and politics, and in 1760 he published his first work, a pamphlet entitled 'A View of the Edinburgh Theatre'. In the same year, while studying in Glasgow, Boswell underwent a religious crisis. He fled to London, where he converted to Roman Catholicism, sampled the London nightlife, and sought escape from his law studies by attempting to gain a commission in a guards' regiment. He was eventually persuaded to return to Glasgow to complete his studies.

In 1762 he passed the examination in Civil Law, and proceeded to London with the aim, once more, of entering a guards' regiment. It was in London that he met **Samuel Johnson** for the fist time on 16 May 1763, a meeting vividly described in Boswell's *Journal* and in his biography of Johnson. Boswell subsequently travelled to Holland, where he pursued further studies in law and courted the Dutch-born novelist Zelide, before touring Germany, where he contrived to meet Rousseau and Voltaire. In 1765, armed with an introduction from Rousseau, Boswell travelled to Corsica to meet the Corsican patriot 'General' Pasquale Paoli, with whom he established a long-standing friendship. Boswell's experiences in Corsica, and his sympathy for the Corsican cause, formed the basis for his first book, *An Account of Corsica*, published in 1768, and for a subsequent edited collection of British *Essays in Favour of Corsica* (1768).

In 1769 Boswell married his cousin Margaret Montgomerie, and settled in Edinburgh to pursue a practice in law. However, the pleasures of London life, the pursuit of his strong political ambitions, and more importantly his intimate friendship with Samuel Johnson continually drew Boswell away from Edinburgh. In 1773 Johnson had Boswell elected a member of the famous Literary Club, whose founding members included Joshua Reynolds, Samuel Goldsmith and Edmund Burke. In the same year, Boswell persuaded Johnson to undertake an extensive tour of Scotland and the **Hebrides**. The journey was written up by Johnson in *Journey to the Western Isles of Scotland* (1775). Boswell's own account, *Journal of a Tour to the Hebrides*, was published in an abridged form in 1785, after Johnson's death. It is by far the livelier of the two accounts, full of vivid narrative and detailed descriptions.

Boswell began contributing to the *London Magazine* in 1777, under the pseudonym 'The Hypochondriack', and in six years produced over 40 articles of a highly personal and reflective nature, on such subjects as drinking, marriage, diaries and conscience. During this period he made annual trips to London to visit Johnson.

On his father's death in 1782, Boswell succeeded to the family estate. The last 13 years of his life, however, were marked by much personal difficulty. In 1784 Johnson died. Boswell committed his energies to collecting material for a biography of his friend and mentor, but the writing of it proved a long and difficult process, and the work was not published until 1791. During this period Boswell also sought, with little success, to further his political career. His attempts were continually frustrated. In 1788, with the help of James Lowther, Earl of Lonsdale, an unscrupulous and powerful political figure in northern England, Boswell eventually obtained the ancillary post of Recordership of Carlisle, but his antipathy for his patron ultimately led him to resign the position in 1790. In 1789 Boswell's wife died, and Boswell spent his final years dissipating in London. He died on 19 May 1795.

For many years Boswell's literary reputation rested on his superb accomplishment in recording the life of Johnson. In both his biography and in his record of their Scottish tour, Boswell displayed a powerful sense of narrative that engaged the reader and vividly conveyed Johnson's character and his social surroundings. Boswell, however, seemed destined to exist solely in the shadow of his mentor. The recovery of Boswell's private papers and original manuscripts from Malahide Castle in Ireland in 1926, 1937 and 1948 has shown his talents to extend beyond that of being a mere recorder of Johnson's words and deeds. His journals were published in the 1950s, and include *Boswell's London Journal* (1950), *Boswell in Holland* (1952) and *Boswell on the Grand Tour*

(1955). These works and the unabridged version of the *Tour* and the *Life of Johnson*, published in 1936 and 1934–40 respectively, have provided more evidence of Boswell's originality, wit and literary talent and in modern opinion have elevated him to rank with Samuel Pepys as one of the foremost chroniclers of British culture and society of his time.

BOTANIC GARDENS
Cruickshank Botanic Garden, Aberdeen
Aberdeen's Cruickshank Botanic Garden is less impressive than those in **Glasgow** and **Edinburgh** but it contains an interesting collection of herbaceous species and flowering shrubs. It was established in 1898 by Miss Anne Cruickshank to serve both the **University** and the public. The original plot was extended in 1909 to the north to include an arboretum area. The central feature of the older part is a sunken garden, from which the systematic beds radiate. There is also a double-sided herbaceous border. The arboretum contains some mature trees forming a woodland garden; a rock garden and lawns with island beds. The university greenhouses are not open to the public.

Dundee University Botanic Garden
Although **Dundee University** Botanic Garden is still young (established 1971) and quite small (8.9 ha), it offers a splendid variety of plants from throughout the world, including European natives, tropical species and succulents. An unusual feature is the 'ecological series' in which British plant associations are planted in a natural sequence, with the montane species at the top of the slope and lowland communities at the foot, demonstrating altitudinal zonation of vegetation. The effect is enhanced by a stream running through the series, providing an opportunity to grow aquatic species and giving damp habitats for European ferns. Elsewhere, some fast-growing trees are already reaching maturity, and these will be gradually thinned to provide a sheltered matrix for other slower-growing or tender plantings. A small formal garden contains medicinal and culinary herbs. In the summer the landscaped tropical glasshouse is dominated by giant Victoria water lilies (up to 2m across). The Visitor Centre contains an excellent introduction to the plant kingdom, past and present.

Glasgow
Glasgow Botanic Garden is run by the city, mainly as a public amenity, although it has close links with teaching and research at the **University**. The present Botanic Garden was established beside the River Kelvin in 1841, but before this there was an earlier one on **Sauchiehall Street** from 1817, and prior to that a Physic Garden started in 1705 in the grounds of Old College. In 1871 an extraordinary dome-shaped glasshouse, the Kibble Palace, was moved from the estate of John Kibble at Coulport beside Loch Long, along the **Clyde** by raft to be re-erected in the Botanic Garden. It remains the garden's most impressive feature and one of the finest buildings in Glasgow. In 1887 Glasgow Corporation took over running the Garden from the Royal Botanical Institute of Glasgow.

The modern garden includes a herb garden (laid out as a monastic garden), systematic order beds and a recently developed arboretum, with a collection of trees introduced to Britain by **David Douglas**. The main range of glasshouses includes displays of succulents, and special collections of ferns, begonias, orchids and aquatic plants. As befits a garden maintained principally as an amenity, there is a particularly attractive display of tender flowering hybrids and cultivars, including fuchsias, calceolarias and pelargoniums. Notable plants in the Kibble palace include a collection of tree ferns and many fine forms of *Camellia Japonica*.

Royal Botanic Garden, Edinburgh
The Royal Botanic Garden **Edinburgh** is Scotland's national botanic garden and one of only two financed by grant-in-aid from the British government (the other is Kew). It is the direct descendant of the Physic Garden established near Holyrood Abbey in 1670 by two Edinburgh doctors, **Robert Sibbald** and **Andrew Balfour**. In 1675 a second garden was established at Trinity Hospital (the site of the present **Waverley Station**), and these two gardens were combined by **John Hope** in 1763 at a new site on Leith Walk. The final move to the present site at Inverleith was in 1820 under the direction of Robert Graham, although the area has been enlarged several times since then, eg in 1864 to include the garden of the Royal Caledonian Horticultural Society and in 1879 to add an arboretum and Inverleith House to the west.

The main aims of the present Botanic Garden are research, education, conservation and amenity. The collections include a large herbarium containing about 2 million dried plant specimens and a famous library of over 100,000 volumes on botany and horticulture. Research takes place on the flora of China, the Himalayas, South-East and South-West Asia (including Arabia) and Brazil; and on particular groups of plants, such as the *Ericeae* (heath family), *Zingiberaceae* (gingers), *Gesneriaceae* (African violet family), conifers, lichens and fungi. For many years rhododendrons have been a speciality of the Botanic Garden, which is now regarded as the leading authority on both taxonomy and cultivation of this genus.

The Botanic Garden receives over three-quarters of a million visitors a year, many from overseas, and including a large number of students and schoolchildren. Both formal and informal education are promoted and the Botanic Garden runs a three-year diploma course in amenity and ornamental horticulture.

Main features of the Garden include a Woodland Garden, Arboretum, Demonstration Garden and Peat garden. The extensive Rock Garden has an international reputation and contains approximately 4000 rare and beautiful alpine plants. Rhododendrons occur throughout and altogether there is a total of about 400 species, including tropical species.

Two original Palmhouses, built in 1834 and 1858, have been restored and are still in use today beside the main range of exhibition plant houses, constructed in 1967. The latter are of a unique style, being suspended from above to create a large, clear space inside for landscaping. Altogether there are 10 plant houses, including two newer houses opened to the public in

1978 and the Alpine House. These provide a range of environments from the hot, moist tropical forest to the arid desert, with cacti over 5m tall. There are special collections of ferns, cycads, orchids, aquatic plants, palms, succulents, tropical peat plants and tropical rock plants. Several hundred endangered plants from throughout the world are grown as part of the Botanic Gardens conservation programme.

The Royal Botanic Garden Edinburgh has three Outstations in Scotland:

YOUNGER BOTANIC GARDEN is situated at Benmore in the Eachaig Valley, seven miles north of **Dunoon**. It became an Outstation in 1928, but many of the trees are older than this; the first recorded plantings were in 1820 and there was a particularly important period of conifer afforestation between 1860–80. Some of the older trees are now over 40m tall, making them among the highest in Scotland. Particularly impressive is the avenue of giant redwoods, but there are very fine douglas firs, western hemlock, silver firs and pines. The mild and very wet climate (2280mm per year) also suits Himalayan rhododendrons and Benmore contains one of the largest collections in Britain. Other features include a collection of flowering trees and shrubs, and a formal garden containing dwarf conifers, herbaceous border and heathers. Benmore Lodge is not open to the public but is used by Lothian Council as an outdoor centre.

LOGAN BOTANIC GARDEN is located on the Rhinns of **Galloway** in the extreme south-west of Scotland where it receives the full warming influence of the Gulf Stream. Because of an exceptionally mild climate it is able to specialise in growing warm-temperate species, which cannot normally be grown outdoors in Scotland. A kitchen garden was established on the site over 100 years ago, but the walled garden and surrounding area were taken over by the Royal Botanic Garden Edinburgh in 1968. Exotic species include well-grown specimens of tree ferns, cabbage palms and Chusan palms. There is also a water garden, **peat** walls and a boggy area dominated by Gunnera. Flowering shrubs, especially camellias, are the main attraction in spring and early summer, while many herbaceous species, including unusual plants from southern Africa, flower in late summer.

DAWYCK BOTANIC GARDEN Situated on the river **Tweed** at Stobo, Dawyck only became an Outstation of the Royal Botanic Garden Edinburgh in 1978, but it has a history of tree planting which goes back more than 300 years. A famous European larch tree is said to have been planted by the Swedish naturalist Linnaeus in 1725, but most of the big conifers (some exceeding 45m tall) were planted in the last century by the Nasmyth family, who subscribed to various plant hunting expeditions including those of David Douglas. During this century more conifers, unusual 'fastigiate' trees (eg the Dawyck beech) and rhododendrons were planted by the Balfour family. Since taking over the arboretum the Edinburgh Botanic Garden has also planted a range of Sorbus, Betula and other plants which thrive in the cold winters and warm, relatively dry summers of Dawyck.

St Andrews University Botanic Garden

The present Botanic Garden at the Canongate was started in 1960 and covers 8ha. Before this there was a Botanic Garden from 1889, founded by Dr John Wilson in the walled garden of St Mary's College. The modern garden is protected from the prevailing westerly winds and the cold winter winds from the North Sea by the careful planting of shelter-belts, mainly of conifers. This has been so successful that some tender species such as the Chusan palm (*Trachycarpus fortunei*) and *Agave americana* grow in sheltered positions outdoors. One of the main features of the Botanic Garden is a peat, rock and water complex, which includes areas for growing plants of bog, scree and meadowland, and semi-mature **Scots pine** and oak trees. There is a collection of rhododendrons, including plants from Joseph Rock's last expedition to Yunnan in 1947, and a large number of the dwarf species. Other Himalayan specialities are grown, especially primulas, gentians, meconopsis and lilies. The collection of alpine plants also includes some rare Scottish natives (eg *Dryas octopetala*). The Botanic Garden has an important educational function and the semi-circular order beds are an essential element for teaching systematic botany to the university students. There are a number of glasshouses: a fern house, xerophytic house, temperate house, stove house, orchid house and alpine house.

BOTHWELL, Adam (c1527–93) Bishop of Orkney

The son of a **Lord of Session**, Adam Bothwell succeeded the reforming **Bishop Robert Reid** in the year after his death (1558). His role as the first incumbent after the abolition of the Catholic Church in Scotland is somewhat ambivalent. He was one of the Commissioners appointed to revise the Book of Discipline in 1564 and, although he only visited his diocese twice, he did tour the islands and attempt to supply their parishes. But these were bones of contention among the creatures of the **Stewart earls**, such as the Reverend Harry Colville whom the people of Orphir so excusably murdered. Bishop Adam's task was not easy. On the other hand, he alienated the church property of **Westray** to his brother-in-law **Gilbert Balfour** and other lands to his cousin Sir John Bellenden. He also demonstrated flexibility in celebrating the marriage of **Queen Mary** to the **Earl of Bothwell** with Protestant rites in May 1567, and then crowning and anointing her baby son James in her place the following July. When he alienated the remaining temporalities of his see to **Robert Stewart** (1570) in exchange for those of the **Abbey of Holyrood**, he complained that he had done so under duress. He continued to use the title of Bishop of **Orkney** until his death, while the eldest of his three sons became a Lord of Session with the title Lord Holyroodhouse. Bishop Adam appears to have walked as delicately as King Agag (I Samuel xv), with greater success.

BOTHWELL BRIG, Battle of (1679)

The dissensions which had dogged the **Covenanters** ever since **Resolutioners** opposed **Protesters** in the 1650s resurfaced as the victors of **Drumclog**, their numbers swollen by some 6000 sympathisers, assembled at **Hamilton** in June 1679. Robert Hamilton, **William Cleland** and more radical elements condemned the **Indulgences** and the 'indulged' clergy; most ministers preferred a more conciliatory approach, which would leave such matters to a **General Assembly** and which acknowledged the authority of King, Parliament and magistrates (the Hamilton Declaration). But while the Covenanters quarrelled, the government acted. A force of 10,000, commanded by the **Duke of Monmouth**, with **Graham of Claverhouse** leading the dragoons and the **Earl of Linlithgow** the infantry, converged on the narrow **Clyde** bridge (now replaced by the A74) at **Bothwell** on 22 June. Out-numbered, out-gunned and disorganised, the Covenanters managed little resistance. Casualties in battle were few, though 200 may have been killed subsequently and 1400 surrendered or were captured. Monmouth seems to have favoured clemency and a new Indulgence was issued in September. Two men, John Kid and John King, were tried and hanged; five more were hanged on Magus Moor for refusing to admit that **Archbishop Sharp** had been murdered; 258 were transported in a ship, The Crown of London, which was wrecked off the coast of **Orkney**. The infamous **'Killing Time'** followed not the battle but the removal of the **Duke of Lauderdale**, the King's Commissioner, who was replaced by the Duke of York (later **James VII**) in December.

BOTHWELL CASTLE, Lanarkshire

'Probably the grandest ruin of its kind in Scotland' (**MacGibbon and Ross**) and 'amongst the foremost secular structures of the Middle Ages in Scotland' (D Simpson), Bothwell Castle stands above a bend in the **Clyde** opposite the site of **Blantyre** priory. It consists of a large courtyard within high surrounding walls com-

Bothwell Castle in a reconstruction suggested by MacGibbon and Ross (MR)

manded by corner towers, in other words a classic castle of enceinte or enclosure. The main tower, a massive keep or donjon, with adjacent wall, is the oldest part and was probably built for Walter de Moravia (ie **Moray**, Murray) in the second half of the 13th century. It was evidently meant as part of a much larger enclosure than now exists, the visible foundations of which may be as much as was ever built in stone. The donjon, separated

from the existing enclosure by its own moat, featured prominently in the **Wars of Independence**. Documentary evidence of its numerous surrenders, two sieges and two partial demolitions has provided a challenge to the architectural interpretation of the remains. Repairs to the donjon, but not reconstruction, were undertaken when the present enclosure was walled by **Archibald ('the Grim') 3rd Earl of Douglas** in the 1360s and by **Archibald 4th Earl** and Duke of Touraine in the early 15th century. Their additions included the well preserved south-east tower and the adjacent great hall (rebuilt about 1500) with chapel and cellars. Yet another Archibald Douglas, the 1st Earl of **Forfar**, acquired the castle in 1669 and used some of its stone to build a Palladian mansion, now demolished. In the 19th century the castle passed to the Countess of Home and still belongs to the **Home** family, although now in state care (**Historic Scotland**).

In Bothwell village to the south-east Archibald the Grim also built the church of St Bride. Only the choir (restored by **Rowand Anderson**), with stone slab roof, remains of the original. Also surviving are the capitals from an earlier Norman church, possibly founded by Walter de Moravia whose gravestone is here. Most of the church was rebuilt by **David Hamilton** in the 19th century with a stained-glass window by Burne Jones. Memorials to the earls of Douglas and the 3rd Duke of Hamilton lie within, while the churchyard contains an elaborate monument to **Joanna Baillie**, who was born in the manse, her father being the minister of St Brides.

BOTHY BALLADS (1830s onwards)

The agricultural revolution from the 1780s onwards replaced the democratic but inefficient **runrig** system centred around self-sufficient townships with a system of larger farms or ferm-touns, often engrossed from smaller units, employing mixed farming and crop rotation. Too large for a family to manage, they required additional 'farm servants', especially as ploughmen, who were commonly the offspring of local farmers and crofters themselves. Servants were usually housed in self-catering accommodation of varying degrees of comfort, known as 'bothies', except in the north-east of Scotland where the servants slept in 'chaumers' (often no more than a loft above the stable) and received their food, light and warmth in the farmhouse kitchen – the 'kitchie' system. Female servants were accommodated in the farmhouse. Paradoxically, as Ian Carter has pointed out in Farm Life in Northeast Scotland 1840–1914 (1979, 1997), the largest known group of 'bothy ballads' originated in the north-east, where there were few bothies. Some define 'bothy ballads' as 'songs sung in the bothy' but this would include popular and music-hall songs as well as vigorous Moody and Sankey hymns. Indeed John Ord's Bothy Songs and Ballads (1930) included almost every song type, from popular song to great ballads. **Gavin Greig** defined them as those songs describing the cycle of work on the touns, from six-monthly feeing market to feeing market, as well as the frankly-drawn characters of the farmer and his family, together with the servants, male and female. Although some of the songs describe harsh conditions imposed by slave-driving farmers, they seem to be less 'protest songs' than entertainment (even sung by the farmers themselves) for kitchen or outhouse, often to celebrate the toughness and skills of the horsemen élite. But a series of agricultural depressions led to a flight from the land to the cities and the colonies, and by the 1920s and 30s the old harsh way of life was but a (often rose-tinted) memory for many. A series of concert-hall entertainers such as Will Kemp (c1889–1965) and George Morris (c1876–1958) wrote, performed, broadcast and recorded a repertoire of largely humorous songs (following in the steps of George Bruce Thomson (c1864–1914), who had composed 'McGinty's Meal-an-Ale' etc. at the turn of the 19th century). Only a handful of the older bothy ballads ('Drumdelgie', 'Bogie's Bonnie Belle', etc.), which were those Kemp and Morris had performed, often in sanitised form, survived this onslaught. The concert-hall tradition has thrived, encouraged by radio and television, with lively performers such as John Mearns (1906–91) and Tam Reid (b.1929); its repertoire is constantly being increased by modern composers such as Charlie Allan (b.1939) and the late Ian Middleton (1936–99).

BOUGH, Sam (1822–78) Painter

A native of Carlisle, Bough was one of the most prominent figures in Scottish art during the second half of the 19th century. The son of a shoemaker, he underwent little formal education and began his career as a scene painter in Manchester, moving to **Glasgow** in 1848. Encouraged by Daniel Macnee he turned to landscape painting and, on early sketching trips to Barncleuth and Cadzow Forest near **Hamilton** (where he moved in 1851), benefited considerably from the company of the younger but more experienced Alexander Fraser. Insisting from the first on the importance of painting *en plein air*, an approach that in the latter part of the century would direct developments in Scottish art, his early fascination with Turneresque atmospheric effect had replaced his interest in the value of record; his style loosened, his brushwork becoming broader and more fluid. He settled in **Edinburgh** in 1855. His vivid evocations of the Scottish landscape and his stirring and highly romantic depictions of scenic events, almost without exception portrayed under the most dramatically lit skies, became widely sought-after and would later bring him substantial wealth. Although a skilled oil painter, his real achievement was as a watercolourist and his free and natural handling of the medium, at his finest in his studies of Forth and East **Fife fishing** villages, considerably influenced the development of its style in Scotland. In spite of his success he never lost his taste for a Bohemian lifestyle and he was not honoured with membership of the **Royal Scottish Academy** until 1875. Shortly before his death he was appointed first Vice-President of the Scottish Society of Watercolourists.

BOWLING, Dunbartonshire

The **Forth–Clyde Canal** enters the Clyde at Bowling. Once the canal handled large quantities of freight, and for many winters Bowling Harbour sheltered the North British **Railways** Clyde Steamer Fleet. The 18th century Customs House is today a reminder of the industrial past, as is the Little Mill Distillery which produced malt **whisky** from around 1800.

BOXING

The rules of boxing were first codified by the Scottish aristocrat Sir John Sholto Douglas, 8th Marquis of Queensberry (1844–1900). In 1866 he published a code of 12 rules to administer the 'noble art', the first being that gloves had to be worn. Although subject to some gradual modification, Queensberry rules have become the basis of the modern sport and are internationally recognised.

Amateur boxing in Scotland is administered by the Scottish Amateur Boxing Association, founded in 1909. 84 clubs are directly affiliated and another 46 which include boxing among their other activities are associated. Tournaments are held regularly with the other home nations, there being usually around seven matches annually, and the Commonwealth Games are contested every four years. Teams are entered in European and world tournaments, and Scottish boxers are able to enter the (English) ABA competitions, as well as attempt to qualify for the Olympics. Probably the best Scottish performance was given in 1956 when Dick McTaggart won a gold medal at the Melbourne Olympic Games.

However, the professional rankings have always been a powerful attraction for aspiring boxers, and Scotland has produced six world champions, all at the lighter end of the scale. Four were champions at flyweight (Lynch, Paterson, McGowan, Clinton) and two at lightweight (Buchanan and Watt).

Benny Lynch (1913–46), born in **Glasgow**, quickly climbed to the top of the flyweight division, becoming world champion by beating Jackie Brown in Manchester in September 1935, and defending successfully over a three-year period. Unfortunately, personal and domestic problems fuelled his alcohol abuse, and, lacking proper medical treatment or counselling, Lynch alienated himself from his supporters and died miserably at the age of 33. His was a tragic life, commemorated in a play by Bill Bryden in 1974.

Jackie Paterson (1920–66) was born at Springside, **Ayrshire**. He came to prominence when he won the world flyweight championship by knocking out Peter Kane at **Hampden** in 1943. Health problems developed and he was unable to defend in 1947, enlisting legal means to retain his title, which he lost the following year to Rinty Monaghan. He died violently in South Africa.

Walter McGowan was born in 1942 at Burnbank, near **Hamilton** and won the flyweight championship of the world in June 1966 by defeating Salvator Burruni at Wembley. He had a tendency to cut easily and in 1968, after fighting at bantamweight, lost his flyweight title to Chartchai Chinoi.

The world lightweight championship was won by Kenny Buchanan of **Edinburgh** (b.1945) when he defeated Ismael Laguna in the sweltering heat of San Juan in September 1970. He successfully defended before coming up against the formidable Roberto Duran, who defeated him in New York in June 1972 in controversial circumstances. Buchanan's claims for a rematch were never conceded by Duran, a long-reigning champion who later acknowledged Buchanan as the best boxer he had met. This was a fairly universal opinion – Buchanan won a New York boxing journalists' poll as the best in the world in 1970, relegating Muhammad Ali to third place. While waiting in vain for a second bout with Duran, Buchanan won back the European championship by the not inconsiderable feat of beating a Sicilian in Sicily. His career was somewhat marred by boxing politics, a premature (and temporary) retirement, and later business difficulties, leading him to undertake unlicensed fights towards the end of his career. Ken Buchanan was arguably Scotland's greatest ever exponent of the noble art, particularly considering that his achievements were almost invariably accomplished outside Scotland.

Jim Watt (b.1948) grew up in Moodiesburn, Glasgow, developing a southpaw style which seemed set to provide him with a reasonable, if not spectacular career. However, when his management was taken over by Terry Lawless, Watt's career blossomed and he became world lightweight champion in April 1979 by defeating Alfredo Petalua. He defended successfully four times, fighting all but his last championship match in front of his own fans. Watt was a brave and resourceful fighter, able to overcome a tendency to bleed easily. He lost his crown to Alex Arguello in June 1981, and retired with honour.

BOYD, Robert, 1st Lord (d.c1481)

Created Lord Boyd of **Kilmarnock** in 1454, and a member of the Council of Regency on the death of **James II**, Robert Boyd stepped quickly into the gap left by the deaths in 1463 of the Queen Regent **Mary of Gueldres** and in 1465 of Bishop **James Kennedy**, the statesman-prelate into whose custody **James III** had passed. In collusion with Robert, Lord Fleming, Gilbert, Lord Kennedy and others, Robert Boyd kidnapped the 13-year-old James from **Linlithgow** in July 1466 and carried him off to **Edinburgh Castle** where his brother, Sir Alexander Boyd, was governor. The period of Boyd ascendancy was, however, brief. Robert was made official guardian of the King in October 1466 and Chamberlain in 1467; his son Thomas married James's sister Mary and was made **Earl of Arran** in 1467; and Robert arranged James's marriage to Margaret of Denmark in 1468. But the following year, in the absence of Thomas in Denmark to bring home the royal bride, James reasserted his independence. Robert Boyd was charged with treason and fled to England. Thomas, warned by his wife, jumped ship in **Leith** and returned swiftly to Denmark; Sir Alexander Boyd was beheaded in November 1469 and all the family's titles and possessions were forfeited to the Crown.

BOYNE CASTLE, Nr Portsoy, Banffshire

Little is known of Boyne's history, which no doubt accounts for the 200-year neglect of its substantial ruins. Yet this castle of enclosure with its elaborate jostle of six round towers beside the Burn of Boyne has long intrigued architectural historians. 'It appears to differ essentially in plan from all the other castles of the period in the north of Scotland' (**MacGibbon and Ross**). The period in question was the problem, for although the four-square design with angle towers and curtain walls belongs to the 13th century, all the architectural details clearly declare for a 16th century provenance. The estate passed to Sir George Ogilvie of Dunlugas

Neglected Boyne Castle in the 1890s (GWWA)

in 1575. If the castle was his creation, the suggestion that it was modelled on its predecessor at Craig of Boyne, now merely a mound, seems plausible. The two towers flanking the gateway resemble the arrangement at **Tolquhon**, but whereas the latter's military credentials are hopelessly compromised by its construction and its fanciful pretensions, Boyne appears to have made few concessions either to fashion or to comfort.

BOYS' BRIGADE, The

Some 20 years before Baden Powell started the Boy Scouts, **William Smith** founded (1883) in **Glasgow** the Boys' Brigade. Its stated object was 'the advancement of God's Kingdom among Boys and the promotion of habits of Reverence, Discipline, Self-Respect, and all that tends towards a true Christian Manliness'. Each company was to be affiliated to its local (usually non-Catholic) church and high priority was given to religious instruction. But to outward appearances it was, and is, a paramilitary organisation with uniforms, pipe bands and a strong emphasis on drill. Only boys between 12 and 17 could join; those under age were expelled, as were miscreants; Smith was nothing if not a strict disciplinarian. Urban-based, the organisation found ready recruits amongst boys whose education had usually ended early and whose employment, if any, was arduous and uninspiring. In the Brigade they found a strong sense of identity and comradeship plus leisure opportunities in the Brigade's halls, summer camps and sporting fixtures. From the first Company in Glasgow, the movement spread rapidly to **Edinburgh** and other Scottish cities, then to London, Manchester and the English cities, and finally overseas (especially Canada, the US, Australia, Nigeria, New Zealand and Singapore). Approached by Baden Powell with the idea of diluting its military aspect, the Brigade stood by its (imitation) guns but did introduce 'wayfaring' which bore some similarity to 'scouting'. Before Smith's death in 1914 its numbers had reached 70,000 and would nearly double in the inter-war years. Head office moved to London but it retains a strong Scottish presence with offices in Glasgow's Bath Street.

BRACKEN

Although considered inferior to **heather** for the same purposes, bracken was widely used in Scotland as bedding for both people and livestock and for thatching, using either entire fronds or stripped stalks alone. In **Argyll** it was the commonest roofing material, but not as durable as heather or straw, a bracken-thatched roof lasting only 10 to 15 years.

The roots were boiled to produce yellow dye, and the fronds for lime green. Medicinally the roots made a remedy for intestinal worms and for rickets in children. Ashes from burnt bracken are high in potash, making excellent fertiliser especially for potatoes, and boiled with tallow made soap; the ashes were also used in the Scottish glass-making industry before soda from sea salt became widely available, and in the mid-18th century the Isle of **Mull** had a significant income from exporting bracken ashes. The more uses that could be found for bracken the better, as clearing it improved pasture.

Ferns generally were thought to have magic properties, including keeping witches away, and featured in many **Gaelic** charms. Although botanically speaking ferns have spores not seeds, Scottish folklore has numerous references to the potency of fern seeds (presumably the spore-bearing body or *sorus*), which worked best if gathered on midsummer eve.

BRAEMAR, Aberdeenshire

At the junction of Glen Clunie (whence comes The Cairnwell/**Glenshee** road) with the **Dee**, Braemar stands among magnificent scenery near the head of Royal Deeside and is now an all too popular **tourist** centre. The village was originally two, Auchendryne on one side of the Clunie and Castleton on the other, the latter named for Kindrochit Castle, now a grassy ruin but dating from the 14th century when it was granted to Malcolm of Drummond by **Robert II**. Thence it passed to the **Earls of Mar**. It was a ruin by 1618 and was replaced by **Braemar Castle**.

The site now occupied by the Invercauld Arms is where the **Earl of Mar** raised his standard in support of **James Francis Edward**, the Old Pretender, when he launched the 1715 **Jacobite Rising**. Invercauld itself, the home of the Farquharsons, lies to the east and was where Mar planned his move and where **'Colonel Anne' Mackintosh** (née Farquharson) again called out the clan in 1745. Near the Invercauld Arms is the cottage in which **Robert Louis Stevenson** began *Treasure Island* in 1881.

West of Braemar a minor road continues along the Dee to **Mar** Lodge and Inverey, another Farquharson property and where there is a monument to John Lamont who rose to be Astronomer Royal of Bavaria. The road turns back at Linn of Dee whence walkers may tackle the river to its source betwixt Cairntoul and Ben Macdui in the heart of the **Cairngorms**.

BRAEMAR CASTLE, Braemar, Aberdeenshire

Built by **John Erskine, 2nd Earl of Mar** in 1628 as a replacement for ruined Kindrochit Castle, Braemar with its castellated turrets and star-shaped enclosing wall looks like a fair imitation in stone of an ambitious sandcastle. In fact it is, or was, a conventional L-plan tower house. Burned out in 1689 by John Farquharson of Inverey to deny it to General Mackay, it was taken over and burnt again by the English after the **Jacobite Risings** of 1715 and 1745. After forfeiture by the **6th Earl of Mar** ('Bobbing John') in 1716, it passed to John Farquharson of Invercauld. In 1748 the castle, still roofless, was leased to the government, repaired and used as a garrison-post on the new **military road** to Speyside and **Fort George**. Hence the outer defensive wall as at **Corgarff**, an extra storey and the improbable battlements (the work of John Adam). It is now back in Farquharson hands and is open to the public.

BRAES, Battle of (1882)

In late 1881 the crofters of several townships of Braes (south of **Portree**, Isle of **Skye**) inaugurated a fight for **crofting** rights, sometimes called the **Highland Land War**, by withholding rents until Lord MacDonald or his factor returned to them the grazings on neighbouring Ben Lee. These grazings had been reclaimed by the MacDonald estate some 17 years previously. The Braes men were responding less to the original injustice than to the immediate shortage of pasture, the success of other rent strikes on Skye, and above all to recent legislation which had conceded secure tenure and arbitration of rents to Ireland's tenantry (the Irish Land Act of 1881).

Retaliation against the Braes rent strike came in the form of eviction notices. In attempting to serve them the Portree sheriff-officer was attacked and his summonses burnt. Clearly the men of Braes were well-organised; but somehow their look-outs were taken by surprise when 12 days later at dawn a posse of 50 **Glasgow** policemen, specially drafted in at the request of the sheriff of **Inverness-shire**, descended on the townships. Some arrests were made and a crowd of irate crofters gathered. Outnumbered, the police were attacked with a hail of rocks as they withdrew to Portree. They responded with baton charges, the crofters with sticks. 'Many were struck and a number more or less injured.' But there were no fatalities and the 'battle' is less notable than the publicity which it received. With the policemen from Glasgow had come newspaper correspondents whose reports on crofting conditions did much to rouse the national conscience.

As a result the five Braes men who had been arrested, though convicted, were only lightly fined. The fines plus legal costs were paid by well-wishers. Attention now switched to the plight of the nearby **Glendale Martyrs**. Meanwhile in Braes the grazings on Ben Lee had been quietly resumed by the emboldened crofters, an arrangement with which the MacDonald estate eventually concurred to the extent of charging rent.

'BRAHAN SEER', see COINNEACH ODHAR

BRAID, James (1870–1950) Golfer

Born in the **Earlsferry** side of Elie, **Fife** on 6 February 1870, Braid was the Scot in the 'great triumvirate' which dominated British **golf** for 20 years before World War I (the others were J H Taylor and Harry Vardon). Braid went to London in 1893 to work as a club-maker, and was based in England throughout his professional career. His first Open win was at Muirfield in 1901 aged 31, and by winning at **St Andrews** in 1910 he became the first player to win five Open championships. (His other wins were in 1905, 1906 and 1908, and he was runner-up on three occasions.) The achievement was particularly remarkable for the short time in which it was accomplished. Only Tom Watson's five Opens between 1975 and 1983 can compare. Noted for his power and imperturbability, in the 1908 Open at **Prestwick** he took an 8 at the Cardinal hole, after a brush with the Cardinal bunker and its sleepers, but still went on to win with a record aggregate of 291. Braid also made a major contribution to **golf course** design, and was a founding member of the Professional Golfers Association.

BRAIDWOOD, Thomas (1715–1806)
Teacher

Braidwood's pioneering Academy for the Deaf and Dumb, instructing in the three 'Rs', was at St Leonard's, **Edinburgh**, c1764–84, in an area which consequently became known as the 'Dumbiedykes'; it was the first regularly organised institution of the kind in Great Britain. 'The Dummie Hoose' began with a single pupil, but when Dr **Samuel Johnson** – who observed 'they hear with the eye' – visited in 1773 there were a dozen. Perhaps Braidwood's greatest success was the remarkable deaf and dumb John Philip Wood (1762–1838), later Auditor of Excise in Scotland and author of *The Parish of Cramond* (1794) and *The Peerage of Scotland* (1813). Financial difficulties forced Braidwood to move to London – too late for the £100 bestowed by George III, which was diverted to Edinburgh Riding School instead.

BRANDER, Pass of, Argyll

Along the line of the Pass of Brander a geological fault threw down the rocks on the south-west side about 400 million years ago while the rock on the north-east side is about 600 million years old. The movement of this fault also crushed the rocks so that during the Ice Age (which ended in Britain about 10,000 years ago) ice carved out the Pass, thus making it the outfall for **Loch Awe** which now drains into **Loch Etive** through what is more a gorge for the River Awe than a pass.

In 1309 John MacDougall of **Lorne**, holding the Pass for Edward II, was defeated by **Robert I** [see **Cruachan**]. Piles of stones south-west of the river reputedly mark graves. Circa 1960 a barrage was built across the river to divert water into the Inverawe Power Station. This, by raising the height of the loch, submerged some of the most famous **fishing** pools in the Pass.

BRANXHOLME CASTLE, Nr Hawick, Roxburghshire

On a steep bank overlooking the river Teviot, the ancient seat of the Scotts of Buccleuch shared the fate of many Borders towers, being burned in 1532 by the Earl of Northumberland and almost destroyed in 1570 on the orders of Queen Elizabeth of England, provoked beyond endurance by the support of the then knight of Branxholme for the cause of **Queen Mary**. Most of Branxholme now dates from the subsequent rebuilding (1574). Still owned by the Scotts (now **Dukes) of Buccleuch**, it was used by **Sir Walter Scott** as the principal setting for his *Lay of the Last Minstrel*, in which 'nine-and-

twenty knights of fame', vividly described, 'hung their shields in Branksome Hall'.

BREADALBANE, Perthshire

From 'Braid-alban' (the upper part of **Alba**(n)), this large and scenically rich tract of the central Highlands comprises essentially the upper **Tay** basin and marches with **Atholl, Lochaber, Lorne, Menteith** and **Strathearn**. Although a division of some antiquity it carried no title until in 1681 **John Campbell of Glenorchy** was created Earl of Breadalbane and Holland, he having had to relinquish the **Earldom of Caithness** after restoration of its rightful heir. As the rapacious earls extended their lands, which were rumoured to reach from the east coast to the west, the earldom quickly outgrew the geographical Breadalbane. No less rapidly were the estates broken up and sold in the late 19th and early 20th centuries. **Taymouth Castle**, seat of the Earls (sometimes Marquises), survives although no longer in Breadalbane ownership. So does the title, though little is heard of its holder.

BRECHIN, Angus

Though small for a town, Brechin is not averse to reminding the world that it is in fact a city. It was once a bishopric, has yet a cathedral (though its status is now that of parish church), and doggedly fields a **football** team named Brechin City (or, provocatively, 'Brechin City Nil'). The cathedral stands above the South Esk river flanked by the round tower which could be a minaret but is in fact the only remains of the original **Culdee** foundation of **Kenneth II**. Built about 1000 AD,

Brechin Cathedral and round tower (RWB)

it is older than that at **Abernethy**, the only comparable structure in Scotland, and has a short pointed spire, added later and giving the effect of a sharpened pencil. The total height is 26m with a slight taper, the design following that of similar belfry-cum-watch-towers in Ireland. The Culdee foundation was re-established as a Roman bishopric by **David I** in 1153 but the little cathedral of today dates from the 13th century and its splendid square tower with pointed spire from the 14th. Neglected after the **Reformation**, its transepts were demolished in the 19th century, but have since been rebuilt and restored. Within there are some interesting tombstones, cross slabs from the 8th and 9th centuries and a remarkably well carved 'hogback' tombstone (11th century).

Brechin Castle, home of the Earls of **Dalhousie**, stands nearby, the present building being 18th century. In one of its predecessors Sir Thomas Maule held out against Edward I's army for three weeks in 1303. The city's only other structure of antiquarian interest is a wall with a pointed arch which once belonged to the Maison Dieu almshouse founded in 1256. During his 'restless pilgrimage' of 1618, John Taylor, the Thames waterman and poet, stayed in both castle and almshouse but he fails to identify where in Brechin he experienced such a rotten night. This was caused by the attentions of 'a wench both deaf and dumb' who tried to climb into bed with him. Having just walked from Deeside over Cairn o' Mount he was unable to take advantage of the situation, though her breath was 'sweet as sugar-carrion' and she 'well-shouldered beneath the weaist'. He bundled her out and 'for want of a locke or latch, I staked up my door with a great chaire'.

BREMNER, Billy (1942–97) Footballer

Born in **Stirling** and there raised, perhaps not enough, the diminutive Bremner was rejected as 'too small' by both Arsenal and Chelsea when he journeyed south in search of **football** fame (he stood 5' 5½'' in his stockings). London's loss, however, became Leeds' gain. He joined the club in 1959 and stayed there for 17 years, becoming its most capped player (with 585 League appearances) and its most successful captain (with two League titles, one FA Cup, one League Cup and two European Fairs Cups). A midfielder, tenacious and tough in the tackle but with good passing skills and vision, he was adored by the fans and was voted 'Player of the Year' in 1970.

He first played for Scotland in 1965 and marked Pele in a Brazil game at **Hampden** in that year; he got a black eye from the legend's elbow for his close attentions. He was outstanding in another Brazil game, the 0–0 draw during the 1974 World Cup; but pride of place amongst his 54 caps must surely go to that won at Wembley in 1967 when, as captain, he led the team which humbled the then world champions of England. Although he never played for a Scottish club, his passion typified the Scottish game. It also spilled over into indiscipline. In a 1974 Charity Shield game he was both sent off for a brawl with Kevin Keegan and earned a fine and ban for removing his shirt. Two years later a nightclub fracas in Copenhagen while on Scotland duty brought him a five-year ban from international football. In the same year he left Leeds for Hull City, then Doncaster Rovers,

but returned to manage Leeds from 1985–8 and Doncaster thereafter. He died from a heart attack.

BREMNER, Robert (c1713–89) Music Publisher

Bremner started publishing editions of Scottish music in **Edinburgh** in 1754, but opened his main shop in London in 1762 where he was London agent for the St Cecilia Society. His high-quality publications include *Twelve Scots Tunes* and *Instructions for the Guitar*, both for the English guitar; *The Harpsichord Master: The Rudiments of Music*, and re-issues of works by **McGibbon** and Craig as well as collections of Scots tunes. He became the wealthiest music publisher in Britain. His most important publication was the six overtures by **Kelly**. A number of settings and small items are assumed to be his own compositions.

BRESSAY, Shetland

Opposite the town of **Lerwick** lies the island of Bressay, six miles long and curved parallel to the shore of the **Mainland**, providing a natural breakwater that makes Lerwick Harbour one of the best in northern Europe. Bressay derives a considerable amount of benefit from this situation. For generations the island's crofters have found a ready market for their milk and potatoes, while Bressay's fish meal and oil plant handles surplus fish from vessels that land their catch at Lerwick, as well as catches of industrial species such as blue whiting and sand-eel.

At the south end of the island the lofty sandstone cliffs of Bard Head and the Ord, seen for many miles to seaward, pin-point the entrance to Lerwick Harbour, as does the beam of Bressay lighthouse by night.

Bressay is an attractive island with an area of 11 square miles and a population approaching 400. In 1975 a roll on-roll off car ferry replaced the small motor launches on the route across Lerwick Harbour. The island is part of the Garth Estate, whose proprietor, John Scott, lives at Gardie House, a splendid 18th century mansion.

BREWING AND BREWERIES

Although primarily a distilling nation, Scotland has a brewing tradition which reaches back well beyond that of **whisky** distilling, in fact to earliest recorded times. Yet scant attention has been paid to an industry which has assumed a position of some significance in its own right and in its linkages with other occupations, notably **agriculture**, **coal-mining**, glass-blowing and sugar-boiling.

The art of brewing is reputed to have originated in the Middle East in about 4000 BC, and within a couple of millennia to have spread to Continental Europe and then to these islands. In Scotland it is known that even in pre-**Roman** times the indigenous populations made a crude form of ale from wild barley fermented with **rowan**, spruce, broom, **heather** and suchlike. The **Pict-ish** method of brewing has been lost in the mists of time, but from about the 12th century brewing was reintroduced from the Continent by religious orders and became extensively practised in monastic establishments such as **Holyrood**, **Crossraguel** and **Melrose**. It remained the exclusive preserve of the clergy for several centuries, but by the 15th century secularisation had

'Tom', a George Younger's dray horse, and his draymen, in 1875 (SBA)

taken place, and brewing had become widely adopted as a domestically-based rural activity, seasonal in nature, following on from the harvest cycle, and more often practised in the home by womenfolk. At a time when the water supply was notoriously poor, ale became a staple part of the diet. Most brewers would only produce enough to satisfy their family's needs, but from the late 15th century 'publick' brewers and brewing victuallers began to make an appearance. It is known that **James IV**, whilst returning from his coronation at **Scone Palace** in 1488, stopped at Blackford to purchase a barrel of ale for 12 Scots shillings.

By the 17th century in the larger towns and nascent industrial centres, commercial brewing began to be prevalent, with breweries being established in **Edinburgh**, **Ayr**, **Leith**, **Stirling** and **Bo'ness**. In rural areas and country towns, however, due to ancient guild and craft restrictions, growth was hindered. But over the following century sustained **population** growth, increased urbanisation, and the rise of the wage economy led to an unprecedented level of demand which could only be met by commercial brewing. Some of the most revered names in Scottish brewing history were established at this time, notably Archibald Campbell (Edinburgh, 1710) John Fowler (**Prestonpans**, 1720), Hugh and Robert Tennent (**Glasgow**, 1740), William Younger (Edinburgh, 1749) and George Younger (**Alloa**, 1762). By the early 19th century the old burghal restrictions had crumbled, and public breweries had become established in most towns of any size, except perhaps in the far north-west of the country. By 1850 even fairly modest towns such as **Nairn**, **Peebles** or **Cupar** could boast several breweries apiece, and commercial brewing began to supersede domestic

brewing. This was greatly enhanced by improved roads and the coming of the **railways**.

The number of commercial breweries reached a peak of nearly 300 by the mid-19th century; but from that time came a trend towards rationalisation and concentration into larger units which proved irreversible. This resulted in the industry becoming heavily concentrated in the Central Belt of Scotland, with Edinburgh, Glasgow and Alloa the major centres. Domestic brewing had been virtually eliminated, but Scottish ales and beers achieved a high reputation with 'Scotch Ales' renowned for quality worldwide. Indeed, from the mid-19th century till World War II, Scotland accounted for nearly one-third of all British beer exports, and Scottish brewers were heavily involved in the colonial and military trades, in particular for India Pale Ales (IPA).

This heavy dependence on the export markets caused problems as the 20th century unfolded. Two world wars and the decline of Britain's imperial and military roles led to over-capacity, and the 1960s witnessed a wave of takeovers and closures, with many famous names going to the wall, such as Aitkens, Campbells, and Geo Youngers. Whereas in 1960 Scotland could boast some 27 breweries, today only five remain (Edinburgh 2, Alloa 1, Glasgow 1, **Dunbar** 1); in addition a handful of new small breweries are dedicated to producing traditional cask ales.

Scotland is exceedingly fortunate in having plentiful supplies of those two vital ingredients which have rightly made its whisky so renowned, namely pure sparkling water and good barley. These are also essential for good ales and beer. Traditionally, two main types of ale were produced. Pre-eminent was a strong, dark, heavy, sweetish ale known simply as 'Scotch Ale', the drink of the nobility. The other was a weak, thin, poor by-product of Scotch Ale known variously as 'Tuppenny' (from its price per Scots pint at the time of the **Union** of 1707) or small or table beer. This was the drink of the mass of the population, and is referred to by **Burns** in 'Tam o' Shanter'. From the mid-18th century onwards, Porter (a dark, full bodied, but relatively low gravity drink) also became popular until gradually superseded by Pale Ales in the latter part of the 19th century. It was these Pale Ales which in particular made Scotland's reputation in the export markets. In addition, lager was brewed in Scotland from the 1880s, and became very popular after World War II.

Scottish brewing practice differed from that of England in several important respects. In addition to the Scots innovation of sparging (sprinkling malt with hot water) there was a tendency towards higher temperature mashings and much longer lower temperature fermentations. As a result, even today, Light, Heavy, Wee Heavy and Export have no real English equivalents, being for the most part sweeter, darker and less hoppy. Again, the traditional method of categorising beers in Scotland has been by way of the Shilling System (60s., 70s., 80s. etc), this being the 19th century invoice price per barrel. Although in terms of cost this has long ceased to have any relevance, the terminology has recently been reintroduced to give a rough idea of ascending order of strength for mainly cask 'real ales'.

The major brewing companies in Scotland are:

BELHAVEN BREWERY, Dunbar. Scotland's oldest surviving brewery, it was established in 1719 and is still producing fine traditional Scottish ales.

TENNENT CALEDONIAN, Glasgow. Hugh and Robert Tennent started brewing commercially at Wellpark in 1740, although the family had been involved in domestic brewing for several centuries previously. Tennent's ale was supplied to **Prince Charles Edward Stewart**'s army in 1745. Pioneering lager brewers from the 1880s, Tennents merged with and absorbed many other famous Scottish firms such as Aitkens, Fowlers, Jeffreys, Murrays, and Geo Youngers. The company is now owned by the English brewing giants Bass.

WM YOUNGER. Established in Leith in 1749, the firm moved to Edinburgh in 1778 and merged with Edinburgh rivals Wm McEwan (Estd 1856) in 1931 to form Scottish Brewers Ltd (now Scottish & Newcastle Breweries plc). The last of the famed **Canongate** breweries

closed in 1986, but brewing continues at the Fountain Brewery, Edinburgh.

Other extant brewery companies include Maclay & Co (Estd 1830) in **Clackmannanshire** and Caledonian Brewing Co, Edinburgh (Estd 1868). Traquair House Brewhouse, **Innerleithen**, and Broughton Brewery, **Biggar** (Estd 1979), are typical of the small 'new' breweries in Scotland.

BREWSTER, Sir David (1781–1868) Scientist and Inventor

Born at **Jedburgh**, David Brewster was one of Scotland's most eminent scientists – and one of the most underestimated. After entering **Edinburgh University** at the age of 12 to read for the ministry, he showed a scientific bent and began a lifelong preoccupation with optics. He invented the kaleidoscope, the first means of reproducing motion in two dimensions, and took a close interest in early experiments in photography, introducing **Hill** and Adamson to each other. He claimed to have pioneered research on the improvement of lighthouse operation, and actively worked for the introduction of Fresnel lenses into British lighthouses. Brewster was a prolific scientific journalist, writing some 300 papers and editing three journals as well as a scientific biography of Newton. A Fellow of the **Royal Societies** of **Edinburgh** and London, he was principal of both **St Andrews** and Edinburgh **Universities** in succession and played a major role in setting up the British Association for the Advancement of Science.

BRIDIE, James, see MAVOR, Osborne Henry

BRIDGE OF ALLAN, Stirlingshire

Until the 19th century the bridge over the Allan Water three miles north of **Stirling** had two adjacent villages: Inverallan with a water mill, and Pathfoot (on the Airthrey estate) with a copper mine. The mine closed in 1807 but subsequent analysis of the spring water which filled it revealed the saline qualities so valued by the Victorians for their aperient and anti-scorbutic properties. Pumped from the mine to a well-house and 'drunk warm', these waters were the making of the spa which rapidly developed in mid-century under the direction of Major John Henderson. Villas and hotels continued to proliferate until World War I, since when the town has served as a pleasant residential adjunct of Stirling and, since its 1967 foundation, of **Stirling University**. The latter now occupies much of the Airthrey estate, including Airthrey Castle (1791, **Robert Adam** but with Victorian additions), a castellated contrast to the gleaming horizontal rectangles of the other university buildings. On the Hill of Airthrey, amidst the fairways of the Bridge of Allan **golf course**, the large Bronze Age **cairn** of Fairy Knowe was carefully excavated in 1868 and revealed two burials, one in a stone cist.

BRISBANE, Sir Thomas MacDougall (1773–1860) Governor of New South Wales

Born at Brisbane House near **Largs**, **Ayrshire**, Thomas Brisbane joined the army at the age of 16 and rose from ensign to lieutenant-colonel in the space of 11 years. He fought with Wellington in the Peninsula, was made

Beer in bulk from William Younger & Co in the 1950s (SBA)

The Brisbane family vault in Skelmorlie churchyard, Largs (HS)

major-general (1813), KCB (1814) and appointed Governor of New South Wales in succession to **Lachlan Macquarie** (1821). From an early age his passion was astronomy; he had already built an observatory at Brisbane House and one of his first actions on reaching Australia was to build another at Parramatta near Sydney. There he established the two astronomers he had brought out with him expressly for the purpose of mapping and cataloguing the stars of the Southern Hemisphere. Although suspected of having more interest in his hobby than in the government of New South Wales – 'Perhaps the most important mark Brisbane left on Australia is in the name of the town which is now the capital of Queensland' (A D Gibb) – his burial vault in the Skelmorlie churchyard [see **Largs**] shows his children to have been named Eleanor Australia and Thomas Australius MacDougall Brisbane. Returning to Britain in 1825, he was awarded the Royal Astronomical Society's Gold Medal (1828), built and equipped another observatory at Makerstoun near **Roxburgh** (1841) and was President of the **Royal Society of Edinburgh** (1833–60).

BROADCASTING

Broadcasting in Scotland dates effectively from the opening of radio stations in **Glasgow** and **Aberdeen** in 1923; **Edinburgh** and **Dundee** relay stations followed in 1924. They were operated initially by the British Broadcasting Company, a consortium formed the previous year by the manufacturers of wireless sets who had buried their differences at the behest of the Postmaster General; the government wished to avoid the chaos brought about in the United States by the unfettered play of commercial forces. The Company became a Corporation in 1927 and operated under royal charter. Each station was responsible for generating most of its own programmes, usually a mixture of talks and recitals. Glasgow claimed to be the first BBC station to broadcast an entire play, *Rob Roy*, in August 1923, and this was later repeated as the first simultaneous broadcast throughout the UK from a 'provincial' station.

For the next three decades broadcasting in Scotland meant broadcasting by the BBC, the beneficiary of what **John Reith**, its first and greatest Director-General, described with relish as 'the brute force of monopoly'. That monopoly was broken only in 1956 with the

appearance of Scottish Television, the first commercial company to be set up north of the border under the Television Act of 1954.

Reith was not the only Scot to achieve prominence in the new medium. Recounting in his memoirs how he became General Manager of the infant company, he recalled that applications were to be addressed to a board member called Sir William Noble. Reith posted his in the letter-box of the Cavendish Club, and only then did he do what he should have done before – look up Sir William in *Who's Who*: 'Having retrieved my letter I rewrote it with a reference to my Aberdonian ancestry.'

Sir William made the first speech at the formal opening of 2BD, as the Aberdeen station was called. Lord Aberdeen also spoke. The effect of broadcasting in northern Scotland, he declared, would be 'to impart to country life some of the advantages and attractions of the cities'. The new stations quickly became a focus of civic and regional pride. The BBC had no regional organisation in those pioneering days and the Station Directors were allowed considerable independence. The staple fare of the service was music, and they produced about six hours of their own material daily. Programmes tended to be cheap and cheerful: Edinburgh had a 'Spot the Deliberate Mistake' feature. There were prizes of three, two and one guineas for those spotting the most 'anachronisms, incongruities and factual errors'. *Children's Hour* had its own star, 'Auntie Kathleen', (the much-loved Kathleen Garscadden who was *Children's Hour* organiser from 1940–60), and Scottish sports, particularly **football**, have always been well represented.

The values and attitudes that characterised the output of these essentially local stations in the mid-1920s came under pressure as the BBC moved towards a policy of centralisation. This was dictated partly by a shortage of wavelengths, but it was also, as Asa Briggs has pointed out, because the BBC was following the other mass media of the early 20th century in undermining the 'proud provincialism' of the Victorian age. Reith extolled the diffusion of 'the amenities of metropolitan culture'; the local cultural loss, he wrote soothingly to Regional Directors, 'should be, to a considerable extent, offset by the quality of the London programme'.

For Scotland, the development of the BBC's Regional Scheme meant the opening of a new high-power station at Westerglen (near **Falkirk**) with 500ft (152m) aerial masts in 1932. Aberdeen was then converted into a relay station, and the Edinburgh and Glasgow transmitters were closed, although the studios in both cities were extended and modernised.

Staff in Scotland were restive at the impact of the new policies. 'What centralisation is going to do,' wrote the Regional Director, 'is to wipe out 60% of our programmes.' When Andrew Stewart became Scottish Programme Director in 1935, the weekly programme allowance was £520. He did not aim to fill every minute of the evening with 'home performed entertainment'. 'The Scot is and always has been a good European,' he said in a radio talk; programmes should therefore have regard to this international cultural tradition, 'and not to current metropolitan appeal'. In 1935 the **BBC Scottish Symphony Orchestra** was formed; the following year it was on the air for more than 150 hours. By 1936

40% of Scottish homes were listening in, but criticism of the BBC's contribution to national culture was not slow to develop. The historian Christopher Harvie observed 'The BBC in Scotland became a byword for puritanical parochialism,' and 'could have done so much more to cope with Scotland's social and cultural problems'.

World War II found an unwelcome addition to the airways – Radio Free Caledonia, intended by Germany's Dr Goebbels to inflame what was seen as incipient Scottish nationalism.

Although a company called Television Limited had been formed as early as 1925 (by **John Logie Baird** – like Reith, a son of the manse), no television service was available in Scotland till the opening of the Kirk o' Shotts transmitter in 1952, six years after the resumption of the BBC's skeletal pre-war service. Four years later, the Independent Television franchise for central Scotland was awarded to the Canadian-born Roy Thomson (it was, he said, in a phrase that passed into the language, 'a licence to print money').

Competition, in Scotland as elsewhere, raised standards in some respects and lowered them in others. The arrival of STV undoubtedly put the BBC on its mettle, concentrating the corporate mind on meeting specifically Scottish tastes and interests. It also, however, severely tested its commitment to Reith's unbending insistence on giving the audience 'what one believes they should like *and will come to like*'. Both sides remained heavily dependent on their respective networks for much of their output; there was little sign of public dissatisfaction with this arrangement.

Grampian TV followed in 1962, covering Scotland from **Fife** to **Shetland**, the year after Border TV began transmitting to the Borders and Dumfries & Galloway, as well as north-west England. Both stations have suffered from a comparative lack of advertising revenue because of their scattered populations' corresponding lack of purchasing power and, in Border's case, there have been claims that communities only 30 miles from Edinburgh feel less than pleased at receiving local news from Furness and the Isle of Man. A redrafting of the franchise might not go amiss here – although the BBC is not much better, many communities in the Galloway area having to accept 'local' news from Manchester.

Glasgow's domination of the broadcast media, particularly television, has not gone unremarked in other parts of Scotland. STV at least have attempted to make amends with more programmes from Edinburgh, which must still be one of few capital cities without a national television broadcasting centre.

Gaelic television broadcasting is integrated into normal daily programmes from Scottish and Grampian. This usually takes the form of news and current affairs features, with the BBC offering an excellent language-learning course for non-Gaelic speakers, *Can Seo*, in the 1980s.

The end of the television monopoly was followed by the advent of independent radio. By the middle 1970s, local commercial stations like Radio Clyde and Radio Forth had found substantial audiences and thrown the BBC on the defensive. The Corporation responded by enhancing the identity of Radio Scotland and setting up a string of community stations, from Radio nan Eilean in **Stornoway** to Radio Tweed in **Selkirk** and from Radio Shetland in **Lerwick** to Radio Solway in **Dumfries**.

Like broadcasters elsewhere, BBC Scotland and its commercial rivals saw out the 20th century with some apprehension. Digital, satellite and cable, not to mention the internet, were transforming the industry beyond recognition. Although there was disappointment that the regulation of broadcasting was not one of the subjects devolved to the new **Scottish Parliament**, there were also grounds for wondering whether government regulation would ever again be very effective.

BROADFORD, Skye

Stretched out along the coast road around Broadford Bay overlooking Pabbay ('Priest's Island'), a string of small **crofting** communities have grown together to make Broadford, now **Skye**'s largest crofting township. The main 'town' in south Skye, with shops, hotels and an airstrip with flights to **Glasgow** and **Inverness**, Broadford is a popular centre for walkers and climbers exploring the nearby **Cuillins**. **Johnson** and **Boswell** spent the night of 6 September 1773 a mile from Broadford at the now ruined house that Boswell called 'Corrichatachin' and Johnson 'Coriatachan'. Their host was a Mr Mackinnon, 'by whom we were treated with every liberal hospitality, among a more numerous and elegant company than it could have been supposed easy to collect'.

BROADWOOD, John (1732–1812)
Piano-maker

Broadwood (originally Braidwood) was born in **Cockburnspath**. He went to London where in 1761 he was employed in the firm of Schudi, harpsichord makers. He married his employer's daughter, and became manager of the firm, which, as John Broadwood & Sons, is still run by their descendants. Broadwood constructed his first piano in 1780, and thereafter produced a series of innovations in the manufacture of the instrument, many of which were to become standard throughout the industry. His descendant, Amy Broadwood, was a leading folklorist at the beginning of the 20th century.

BROCHS

Striking, enigmatic, and unique to Scotland, prehistoric brochs are circular dry-stone towers whose concave walls make for a distinctive profile like that of the modern cooling tower. About 500 broch sites have been identified; their distribution – mainly **Hebrides**, west Highlands, **Caithness**, **Orkney** and **Shetland** – suggests that the broch was favoured in areas short of timber but well supplied with suitable stone; and their often coastal locations suggest that they belonged either to a sea-faring poeple or to land-based people who feared attack from the sea. All can be dated to the same brief period, roughly 100 BC–100 AD, and all are remarkably similar in construction, arguing for a common provenance. That on **Mousa**, Shetland, the best preserved of all, still stands to a height of 13m above ground level and may once have been 15m high; others were mostly smaller but still impressive for their date. In all cases the walls are thick but hollow, allowing for galleries

Dun Telve, Glen Beag (Glenelg), showing double skin construction of brochs (HS)

and cells within them plus a spiralling staircase to the wallhead by means of slabs tying the inner and outer skins together. Such walls, well seen at **Glenelg**, occupied much of the internal space; the hearth was centrally located and there may well have been timber galleries supported by posts and cross-beams resting on ledges projecting from the walls. Whether and how brochs were roofed is not known.

Their function is also somewhat mysterious. As fortifications they lack the obvious apertures for arrows and projectiles; as refuges they appear too small and ill-equipped with water to accommodate stock as well as people; and as look-out towers they are not always well-sited and usually made redundant by the finer prospect from adjacent hills. Prestige and fashion provide the most convincing answer and lend credence to the theory that they may have been built by a group of professional and itinerant masons who depended on local patronage. This might also explain the existence of a few broch sites in the lowlands around the Forth and **Tay**. It has been argued that the brochs of the Hebrides and especially **Skye** betray a development from **duns**, like that at Ardtreck, where a wall similarly constructed of two skins is merely a curving curtain wall ('semi-brochs'). If this is correct, the broch-building tradition, or the professional broch-builders, must have taken the design from the Hebrides to Orkney and Shetland where slight variations appear and where some brochs have external defensive arrangements.

BRODICK CASTLE, Isle of Arran

Brodick's ascertainable history begins with **James IV**'s grant of the castle and the Earldom of **Arran** to his cousin, James Lord Hamilton, in 1503. There may once have been a **Viking** fort on the same commanding site and remnants of earlier castles may be incorporated in the present castle. But since the place was demolished in 1455 and again in 1544, the present 'Bruce's Room' is certainly a confection and the link with **Robert I** tenuous.

A narrow structure of reddish sandstone with a long and lofty profile, the castle of today progresses westwards from austere antiquity towards a more fanciful grandeur. Thus the oldest section is the uncompromis-

ing east tower built around 1588 by the **2nd Earl of Arran** who was **Queen Mary**'s guardian and Regent. In the Civil War, following the execution of **1st Duke of Hamilton** (1648) and the death in the battle of the 2nd (1651), Cromwell's troops occupied and fortified the castle, extending it considerably westwards with a further plain tower-house section. The third, and much the largest section, was the work of the architect **James Gillespie Graham** in the mid-19th century at the behest of the 10th Duke. A not untypical mix of Scottish Baronial and Gothic Revival, it advances from simple crenellated parapets abutting the previous structure to the ambitious climax of the south-west tower with its corner turrets and corbelling.

The interior is in the neo-Jacobean style of the 1840s. It houses, beside the sporting prints and sumptuous furniture amassed by the Dukes of Hamilton, all that remains of the collections of William Beckford of Fonthill whose daughter married the 10th Duke. Fortuitously the exotica of the author of *Vathek* thus has a suitably Gothic resting place.

In 1895 the castle passed to the 12th Duke's daughter, the Duchess of Montrose. It is she who is credited with having rescued and replanted the woodland policies and gardens, now among the finest in Scotland and notable, inevitably, for their rhododendrons. The whole property is now in the care of the **National Trust for Scotland** and is open to the public.

BRODIE, William (d.1788) Deacon

Edinburgh town councillor, and deacon (head) of the Incorporation of Wrights and Masons, William Brodie led a remarkable double life as pillar of the community by day and leader of a gang of burglars by night. After breaking into the Excise Office in the city's **Chessel's Court** (total haul £16) one of his accomplices was caught, turned King's Evidence, and fingered Brodie, who fled to Holland. Arrested in Amsterdam, Brodie was brought back to Edinburgh for trial and eventual execution. His story is said to have inspired **Robert Louis Stevenson**'s *The Strange Case of Dr Jekyll and Mr Hyde*.

BRODIE, William (1815–81) Sculptor

Born at **Banff** and apprenticed to a plumber, Brodie's skill at modelling inspired his friends to raise money to send him to study at **Edinburgh**'s **Trustees' Academy**, from where he won a scholarship to continue his studies in Rome (1853). A specialist in portrait busts, his major works include statues of **Sir James Y Simpson** (**Princes Street**), **Francis Jeffrey, Sir David Brewster, Lord Cockburn** (Edinburgh's **Parliament House**) and **Queen Victoria** (Windsor Castle). He was also responsible for some of the statues on the **Scott Monument** and for the life-size bronze of **Greyfriars' Bobby** opposite **Greyfriars' Kirkyard**.

BRODIE CASTLE, Nr Forres, Moray

Until acquired by the **National Trust for Scotland**, Brodie Castle had been in the possession of the same family, the Brodies, since it was first built, perhaps as early as the 12th century. Besides being one of the few families still residing on the ancestral lands whence their name derived, the Brodies have the added distinction, unusual in such an ancient landed family, of having seldom impinged on Scottish history and of having never been ennobled. Possibly the continuity of its ownership is of greater note than the castle itself which has been so rebuilt and extended as almost to obliterate any evidence of its real antiquity. Evidently a Z-plan tower house of the late 16th century, it was damaged by fire in 1645 and again in 1786. The central section (of simple aspect but with an exceptionally fine moulded plaster ceiling within) resulted from the rebuilding after the first conflagration; the massive Gothic-style extension, designed by **William Burn**, from the second.

BRORA, Sutherland

This pleasant resort grew round the harbour at the mouth of the Brora River which rises in the tall pyramid of Ben Klibreck. It lies over 12 miles up the coast from **Sutherland**'s ancient capital of **Dornoch** and contained Sutherland's northernmost **coal**-mine. This was exploited first by Jane, Countess of Sutherland, who had shared with **Queen Mary** the bizarre experience of marriage to the **Earl of Bothwell**. Her short-lived son Earl John emulated Sir George Bruce of **Culross** in developing salt pans close to the shaft he sank on Brora links, and using coal to evaporate sea water. Another now defunct industry grew out of the presence of brick clay in the vicinity. **James VI** erected Brora into a **burgh of barony** in 1601, since when it has added a wool mill and a distillery to its enterprises.

BROSNACHADH

This is a Gaelic poetic incitement to battle, probably sung or intoned. The famous **Harlaw** *brosnachadh* by Lachlan Mor MacMhuirich has been reconstructed and music speculatively attached to it. See Derick Thomson, 'The Harlaw Brosnachadh', in *Celtic Studies: Essays in Honour of Angus Matheson 1912–1962*, ed J Carney & D Greene.

BROUGHAM, Henry, 1st Lord Brougham and Vaux (1778–1868)

Born in **Edinburgh** and educated at the city's High School and **University**, Henry Brougham was called to the Scottish Bar in 1800 and was an early and prolific contributor to the *Edinburgh Review*. In 1805 he moved south and spent the rest of his working life in England as a member of the English Bar (1808), MP (1810) and Lord Chancellor (1830–4). Defence Council for Queen Caroline (1820), he was a vehement anti-slavery campaigner, law reformer and promoter of national education, forming the Society for the Diffusion of Useful Knowledge (1825) and being one of the founders of London University (1828). Elevated to the peerage as Baron Brougham and Vaux (pron 'broom and vawks') in 1830, in old age he retired to Cannes to write his 3-vol *Life and Times*, described by Chambers as 'very untrustworthy' and published posthumously in 1871.

BROUGHTON, Peeblesshire

Birthplace of **Sir John Murray of Broughton** (1715–77), the '**Jacobite** Judas', the village of Broughton is situated on the Biggar Water just above its junction with the **Tweed**. Murray's home was destroyed by fire in

1775, but some of the trees on the estate formed the nucleus of the fine gardens of Broughton Place, which occupies the same site and was built in 1938 by **Sir Basil Spence** in Scottish Baronial style. At Dreva Craig about a mile south-east of Broughton the Stone Age hill fort is remarkable for its *chevaux de frise*, a defensive barrier formed of boulders set in the ground like rows of teeth to obstruct attackers. The ruins of the old Broughton Church include fragments of a cell thought to have been occupied in the 7th century by a missionary from **Whithorn**.

BROUGHTY FERRY, Dundee

Three miles east of **Dundee** city centre, Broughty was once a castle, **fishing** village and ferry terminal. Fishing declined in the 19th century due to the inadequacy of the harbour but handsome compensation arrived in the fanciful shapes of Victorian villas built by the nabobs of Dundee's **jute** trade; for a time it was thought that more wealth was concentrated in Broughty Ferry than in any other comparable area in Scotland. But sub-urbanisation had begun, and was completed when in 1966 the ferry to **Newport** (nine times a day at the turn of the century) deferred to the new **Tay** Road Bridge. Only the castle, still jutting prominently into the estuary, bears testimony to Broughty's independent past.

The castle's original five-storey tower was built soon after 1490 when Lord Gray of **Fowlis (Easter)** secured a charter of the rock and fishings of Broughty. In 1547, during the final phase of the **Rough Wooing**, Patrick Lord Gray won enduring infamy by treacherously delivering it to the English invaders who successfully resisted attempts to dislodge them for two years. It changed hands twice during the **Reformation**, was taken by **General Monk** during the Civil War, and served as a prison for **Alexander Leslie**. A roofless ruin by 1820 it was offered for sale with potential for development as an inn or 'delightful residence'. The only, and belated, taker was the government who acquired it in 1855 and redesigned it as a coastal defence battery (1860) adding a new wing and four 68-pound guns. The work was supervised by **Robert Rowand Anderson**, then a young Royal Engineer but already more sympathetic to architectural considerations than military realities. 'Its total demolition would only afford an enemy an hour's pleasant and agreeable recreation, unharassed by any thoughts of possible danger to themselves,' wrote a critic in 1888. More alterations were made and it remained a battery-cum-barracks until after World War II. It is now a museum of local history and of the Dundee whaling industry.

BROWN, Alexander Crum (1838–1922)
Chemist

One of the leading organic chemists of his time, Alexander Crum Brown was born in **Edinburgh**. Most of his career was spent in the capital, where he was Professor of Chemistry for 39 years from 1869. He produced new graphic formulae for compound structures to facilitate chemical teaching and communication, and a mechanical model of the canals of the human ear, greatly advancing contemporary understanding of balance mechanisms.

Broughty Ferry c1900 cowering beneath the palaces of the jute nabobs (GWWA)

BROWN, George Douglas (1869–1902)
Novelist

Born in Ochiltree, **Ayrshire**, Brown was the illegitimate child of a 36-year-old Irish farm girl and a 56-year-old ne'er-do-well from a prosperous family who had found for their black sheep a farm but discouraged him from marrying below himself. Brought up in hardship by his mother, Brown left school early to help out. A headmaster persuaded him back. He went on to **Glasgow University** in 1887. Befriended by Gilbert Murray, then Professor of Greek at Glasgow, he won the 1891 Snell Exhibition to Oxford but in 1895, having just nursed his mother on her deathbed, he took a poor degree. Based in the Home Counties he went on to do minor literary work; he wrote a potboiler under a *nom de plume*, prepared a Scots glossary for a **John Galt** edition and proposed a social history. *The House With the Green Shutters* appeared in 1901 by 'George Douglas'. In August 1902, after some time trying to shrug off recurring symptoms of stress, Brown saw that he was ill. He made a will and set off for a friend's home in London. The friend was away. Brown found another of his friends, but only hours later died of an unidentified illness, aged 33.

The House With the Green Shutters is, by Brown's account, not the anti-**Kailyard** book it has been taken for. Its point is in a realistic working out of character, as in Greek tragedy, but here in vivid Scottish idiom expressing 'the brains' (Brown's words) of Ayrshire country people. With black wit, it depicts a village milieu in which the Gourlay family's fate unwinds. The tragedy bespeaks a moralist not a bitter man; its accomplishment suggests that Brown could have done much more. See *George Douglas Brown* by James Veitch (London, 1952).

BROWN, George Mackay (1921–96) Poet and Novelist

Born in **Stromness**, Brown spent most of his life in **Orkney** whose past and people ebb and flow through his writings with tidal persistence. A travel award from the Society of Authors in 1968 tempted him no further than the **Hebrides** and, despite an international reputation, he clung crag-like to a language and lifestyle of windswept simplicity. His education was much interrupted by tuberculosis. The son of a postman-cum-tailor, he attended Stromness Academy but not till 1951 did he proceed to **Newbattle Abbey** College, where **Edwin Muir** was a crucial influence, and not until 1960, aged 39, did he graduate from **Edinburgh University**. He returned to Edinburgh to do postgraduate work on Gerald Manley Hopkins, another crucial influence, and became a Catholic. By 1964 he was back in Stromness and rarely left thereafter. Much of his inspiration came from the *Orkneyinga Saga* of the Norse Jarls through 300 years of **Viking** expansion: 'Virtually everything he has written has presented Orkney life, past and present, as archetypal, an elemental expression of the meaning of life itself, conveyed through a consistent and overwhelming symbolism of land and sea, of seasonal change and the rites of passage of birth, fruition and death' (Gifford). His significance also lies in his desire to return to the 'golden age' espoused by some of the inter-war **Scottish Renaissance** – Edwin Muir himself, **Neil Gunn**, **Leslie Mitchell**, **Naomi Mitchison**; opposition to progress runs though the seminal *An Orkney Tapestry* (1969) like a light thread. Although many of his stories look firmly to the past, his first two novels do not shy from 20th century concerns; *Greenvoe* (1972) effectively questions the coming of oil to Orkney, and *Magnus* (1973) shocks by comparing the murder of **St Magnus** with Nazi atrocities.

BROWN, John (1810–1882) Essayist and Physician

Born in **Biggar**, **Lanarkshire**, John Brown was the off-spring of a celebrated dynasty of **Presbyterian Secession** ministers. In 1822 his father, a noted Seceder theologian, moved to **Edinburgh**, where Brown attended school and university and was to spend the remainder of his life. A pupil of the surgeon **James Syme**, he enjoyed a busy and successful general practice, and his medical and religious background is reflected in his essays, notably in the major collection *Horae subsecivae* (1858, 1861, 1882).

However, it is for writings in a lighter vein that Brown was especially popular in his time. An ability to engage and entertain his readers flowed naturally from his powers as a raconteur, and his love of and sympathy for animals, particularly dogs, produced his celebrated essays on *Rab and his Friends* (1859) and *Our Dogs* (1862). His literary and intellectual circle included not only Scottish luminaries like Lords **Cockburn** and **Jeffrey**, and the theologian Thomas Erskine of Linlathen, but also John Ruskin and William Makepeace Thackeray, the latter being the subject of a literary biography by Brown (1877). He also wrote about the child author Marjory Fleming (1803–11), whom he referred to as 'Pet Marjorie'. As an essayist, Brown's fluent conversational style, his insight into human behaviour, and his skill as a storyteller have been compared to those of Charles Lamb. Correspondence and papers of Brown and his family can be found in the **National Library of Scotland**.

BROWN, John (1826–83) Servant

Born at Craithenaird, **Balmoral**, the son of a **crofter**, Brown became Prince Albert's ghillie in 1849 and **Queen Victoria**'s personal servant in 1858. After Albert's death the kilted bachelor was brought to the Isle of Wight as the Queen's groom and soon became her constant companion. The relationship provoked innuendoes and jealousies, but Brown's loyalty and the Queen's devotion were unwavering. His faults, including a weakness for **whisky** and a predilection for bluntness, were minor and easily forgiven when he was always on hand to frustrate an attacker or prevent a carriage accident. To her 'Beloved Friend' the Queen dedicated *More Leaves from a Journal of our Life in the Highlands*, 1884; she was narrowly dissuaded from writing a memoir of Brown; and she went to her own grave with a photograph of Brown on her wrist. His guileless familiarity had provided badly needed reassurance and companionship. 'Wumman,' he was once heard to say, 'can ye no hold yerr head up?' as he pricked her chin in an attempt to fasten her cape. The Queen was not unamused.

BROWN, Robert (1773–1858) Botanist

Considered by his contemporaries to be the foremost botanist in Europe, Robert Brown made a major contribution to early scientific knowledge of plants. Born in **Montrose**, he studied medicine and botany at **Edinburgh University**, qualifying as a surgeon in 1793 and botanising while he practised in Ireland. In 1801 he was offered the post of naturalist on Sir Joseph Banks's great expedition to Australia. In four years on the voyage he collected over 4000 specimens, many previously unrecorded, and returned to become Librarian to the Linnaean Society in London, a post he held until 1822, also acting as Banks's librarian from 1810–20.

Botanical collections from all over the world came to him, and his detailed, accurate studies of plant form, anatomy and distribution led to a new system of classification based on natural affinities rather than the artificial groupings devised by Linnaeus. After Banks died in 1823 Brown inherited his herbarium, which he in turn left to the British Museum. In 1831 he made one of the most important scientific discoveries of the 19th century, of the cell nucleus; the great excitement this caused led to rapid improvements in microscope design and consequently wide-ranging developments in scientific knowledge. He was also the first to observe the irregular oscillatory movement of microscopic particles in fluids, caused by molecular 'bombardment'; this is now known as Brownian Movement.

BROWNIES

Robert Kirk in his *Secret Commonwealth* (1691) identified a class of **fairies** who 'enter houses after all are at rest and set the kitchen in order, clearing all the vessels'. 'Such drags,' he continued, 'goe under the name of Brownies.' Undoubtedly the most welcome of all the fairy folk, a brownie could also be pretty handy about the croft, threshing corn during the night as 'the little old man of the barn', or watching over the cattle as the 'gunna'. The last was a rather pitiful figure as described in anonymous verses:

> He's so hungry, he's so thin,
> If he'd come we'd let him in,
> For a rag of Fox's skin
> Is the only thing he'll wear.
>
> He'll be chittering in the cold
> As he hovers round the fold,
> With his locks of glimmering gold
> Twined about his shoulders bare.

Common or kitchen brownies were of a much more robust character. 'They were of short stature, had wrinkled faces and curly brown hair and wore a brown mantle or hood. Some haunted the ruins of old castles or dwelt in the hollows of trees. They lived to a great age. One was reputed to have dwelt in Leithin Hall in **Dumfriesshire** for three centuries, and when he deserted it 'the owners of the hall met with ruin' (D A Mackenzie, 1935).

BRUAR, Falls of, Nr Blair Atholl, Perthshire

In 1787 the **Duke of Atholl** received a respectful poem from a river. 'The Humble Petition of the Bruar Water' requested His Lordship in eight suitably impetuous verses to observe 'How saucy Phoebus's scorching beams,/In flaming summer-pride,/Dry withering, waste my foamy streams/And drink my crystal tide.' In view of which His Lordship was implored to plant the Bruar's banks 'wi' tow'ring trees', advice which was quickly acted upon. For the plea had been penned at the river's request by **Robert Burns**, who would reckon his few days in the area as the happiest of his life.

Thereafter the celebrity of the Falls of Bruar was guaranteed. Most visitors marvelled at their precipitous descent through three successive falls with a total drop of about 60m; but some objected to the proliferation of summerhouses, follies and 'peep-bo places', and some even to the 'tow'ring trees', they being larch and fir rather than the more appropriate **pine** and **rowan**.

BRUCE, Alexander Hugh, 6th Baron Balfour of Burleigh (1849–1921) Secretary of State

Born at Kennet, **Alloa**, Alexander Bruce conducted his political career from the House of Lords as the 6th Lord

A H Bruce, 6th Lord Balfour of Burleigh, by Charles Martin Hardie (SNPG)

Balfour of Burleigh from 1876. Educated at Loretto, Eton and Oxford, Bruce held the Scottish Secretaryship from 1895–1903, overseeing a number of important legislative measures. These included the Public Health (Scotland) Act of 1897, the establishment of the Congested Districts Board in the following year (designed to administer grants for **agriculture** and fisheries in, and migration from, the Highlands), and an 1899 measure to facilitate the promotion of private legislation by local authorities. He was later Chancellor of **St Andrews University**, chairman of the **Carnegie** Trust for the Universities of Scotland, and a leading light in the affairs of the **Church of Scotland**. He wrote a history of Scottish **Presbyterianism**, published in 1911.

BRUCE, Edward (c1276–1318) King of Ireland

The brother of **Robert I** (next in age; three others were executed 1306–7), Edward was flamboyant, brave, ambitious and irresponsible. He led fearsome raids (1306–14) but never understood Robert's policy of

destroying castles; failing to capture **Stirling** (1313) he agreed a year's grace with Philip de Mowbray, making **Bannockburn** inevitable.

Invited to Ireland (1315) by the King of Tyrone with whom he had grown up, he led an army into a year-long campaign and was crowned King of Ireland. Despite reinforcements led by Robert I, he was killed at Dundalk (1318) with many supporters. His death, according to an Irish chronicler, was 'the best thing for Ireland since the expulsion of the **Formorians**'.

BRUCE, James (1730–94) Explorer

Also astronomer, naturalist and linguist, James Bruce (nicknamed 'The Abyssinian') was born at Kinnaird House in **Stirlingshire**, the eldest son of a wealthy landowner, was educated at Harrow School and studied **law** at **Edinburgh University**. In 1753 he married the daughter of a London wine-merchant and joined her family's business; but nine months later his pregnant wife died of consumption and Bruce launched himself on his travels.

Six foot four inches (1.93m) tall, red-haired and arrogant, but also an excellent horseman and superb shot, he spent several years touring Europe and in 1762 was appointed British Consul in Algiers. In 1768 he set out on his famous journey in search of the source of the Nile, travelling from Cairo across the desert to the Red Sea then striking south from Massawa to Axum and Gondar, the principal city of Abyssinia (Ethiopia). After a year at Gondar, during which he was invited to command a troop of the King's horse and managed to cure the Queen of smallpox, he travelled on to Lake Tana which he mistakenly took to be the Nile's source and where he drank a toast to King George III before returning to Gondar and becoming embroiled in a civil war. Leaving in December 1771 and heading westwards

James Bruce before setting out for Abyssinia, by Pompeo Batoni (SNPG)

across the mountains and deserts of Sudan, it took him two years to complete his journey back to Cairo. He finally returned to Scotland in 1774.

So extraordinary were the tales he had to tell about his adventures, and in particular about the habits and customs of the people of Abyssinia, that he was dismissed by many, including **Dr Johnson**, as a fraud. His *Travels to Discover the Sources of the Nile* were published in five volumes in 1790 but these were also universally disbelieved, although subsequent travellers have confirmed their authenticity. (Bruce's reputation was not helped by having a sequel to *Baron Munchausen* dedicated to him by Rudolph Raspe in 1792, although Bruce was not in fact Raspe's model.) His use of a specially-designed portable camera obscura in North Africa was unique, producing many drawings of **Roman** antiquities now in the Royal Library at Windsor Castle.

He married again in 1776 but his wife, 24 years his junior, died in 1788 at the age of 34. Bruce himself died after falling down the stairs at Kinnaird when he was 64.

BRUCE, James, 8th Earl of Elgin and 12th Earl of Kincardine (1811–63) Diplomat

Son of **Thomas Bruce, 7th Earl of Elgin**, James Bruce was educated at Eton and Oxford. MP for Southampton (1841), he succeeded to the Earldoms later that year and went to Jamaica as Governor in 1842 and to Canada as Governor-General (1847–54). Envoy to China (1857), he negotiated the Treaty of Tientsin (1858) and visited Japan before returning to London to become Postmaster-General (1859). In China again from 1860–1, he became the second Viceroy of India (1861) in succession to Lord Canning, but lasted less than two years, dying suddenly at Dharamsala in the Punjab in November 1863.

BRUCE, Marjorie (d.1316)

The only child of **Robert I**'s first marriage, Marjorie was captured, aged 10–12, at **Tain** along with **Isabella, Countess of Buchan**. Confined in the Tower of London in a 'cage' and forbidden speech except with the Constable, she was later sent to a nunnery. Exchanged for English prisoners after **Bannockburn**, she married **Walter Stewart** (1315), whence the **Stewart** succession. She died giving birth to the future **Robert II** after a riding accident.

Her tomb in **Paisley Abbey** is marked by a memorial provided by **Queen Victoria** (her lineal descendant); a damaged effigy is preserved in a reconstructed niche nearby.

BRUCE, Robert of Annandale (1210–95)

Grandfather of Robert I

The **Bruces**, from Brix in Normandy, were in England before the Conquest, kinsmen of the Dukes of Normandy and heirs of the Kings of Brittany. **David I** established them on the flank of restless **Galloway**.

Robert's mother was the second daughter of **David of Huntingdon**, making him nearest lawful native kin of **Alexander II**. He had large English estates and supported Henry III at Lewes (1264). He first married the Earl of Gloucester's sister; after her death he went on crusade (1270), returning to marry a crusader's widow,

and to find his son **Robert** made **Earl of Carrick** on marrying the widowed Countess.

Robert of Annandale was one of 13 claimants (**Competitors**) to the throne in 1291 (others included **John Comyn (i)** by descent from **Donald Bane**, and **John Balliol**). A year-long inquiry led by Edward I of England preferred Balliol, grandson of the eldest daughter of David of Huntingdon. Robert immediately transferred his claim to his son, ending his days in dignified disapproval of King John's mounting problems. Contemporaries knew him as 'le Noble'; historians as 'The Competitor'.

BRUCE, Robert, Earl of Carrick (1242–1304)

In c1271 Robert de Bruce, son of **Robert of Annandale 'the Competitor'** and heir to the Bruce estates, was kidnapped by the widowed Marjorie, Countess of Carrick, and carried off 'by force and for love' to **Turnberry** Castle where they were secretly married. Although the new Earl of Carrick seems not to have objected to his rough treatment, **Alexander III** was outraged at thus losing estates and titles that would, had Marjorie remained a widow, have reverted to the Crown. He therefore seized the Carrick property and returned it only on payment of a large ransom. In 1278 the Earl represented Alexander in negotiations with Edward I, and in 1296 he himself paid homage to the English king, became Constable of Carlisle Castle, fought for Edward against **John Balliol** and put in his own claim to the throne of Scotland on Balliol's defeat. Although this claim was rejected by Edward, two of Carrick's sons did gain thrones – the eldest becoming **Robert I** of Scotland and the second, **Edward Bruce**, being crowned King of Ireland (1315–18).

BRUCE, Thomas, 7th Earl of Elgin and 11th Earl of Kincardine (1766–1841) Soldier, Diplomat and Art Connoisseur

Educated in England and France, Thomas Bruce succeeded to the Earldoms of **Elgin** and Kincardine in 1771, entered the army in 1785, and was successively envoy to the Holy Roman Empire, to Brussels, to Berlin and to the Ottoman Empire. In this last position (1799–1803) he developed an interest in the antiquities of Athens and arranged for the Parthenon Frieze and other sculptures to be transported to England. Controversy over the ethics of this action led to a government inquiry in which Bruce's argument that he was saving them from decay and destruction was accepted, although the controversy continues. The sculptures, known then and since as the 'Elgin Marbles', were bought by the government for the nation in 1816 and housed in the British Museum, while other items from his collection are housed at Broomhall near **Rosyth**, still the home of the Earls of Elgin and Kincardine.

BRUCE, Victor Alexander, 9th Earl of Elgin, 13th Earl of Kincardine (1849–1917)

Viceroy of India

Son of **James Bruce**, 8th Earl of Elgin, Victor Alexander was born in Canada during his father's Governor-Generalship. Educated at **Glenalmond**, Eton and Oxford, he held minor office in Gladstone's Liberal government of 1866 and in 1893 was persuaded by his friend Lord Rosebery (**Archibald Philip Primrose**) to accept the post of Viceroy of India. Without relevant experience and possessing neither great ability nor obvious social talents, his only qualification was that his father had previously held the same post; although he proved a conscientious administrator he was so lacking in self-confidence that he was said to telegraph to London twice a day for instructions. His term of office was marked by widespread political unrest and in 1899 he was replaced as Viceroy by Lord Curzon, later becoming Colonial-Secretary in **Campbell-Bannerman**'s government of 1905–8.

BRUCE, Sir William (c1630–1710) Architect

Apart from his career as an architect, Bruce was something of a political figure, having been a confidential messenger between the Scottish lords and **Charles II** before the Restoration. He was knighted for his services and made 'Surveyor General and Overseer of the King's Works in Scotland'. This post was specifically created for the remodelling of **Holyroodhouse** (1671–9), in which Bruce was assisted by **Robert Mylne**. Bruce gave the palace its symmetrical front and created a complex thoroughly French in character. As a 'gentleman architect', more often than designing houses himself he would give advice on appropriate designs and architects to his friends and acquaintances of the Scottish nobility. The houses he did design were unfortified houses for Scottish lords who abandoned the medieval tower house. 'The Kit [Christopher] Wren of North Britain' according to Defoe, Bruce can be described as the effective founder of classical architecture in Scotland, the knowledge of which derived from his many travels abroad. He put great emphasis on the formal setting of a house, on the relationship between the garden and the landscape and the house itself (**Kinross House**, 1685–93; **Hopetoun House** 1699–1702). After the death of Charles II his political position became uneasy and in trying to build up his estate in **Kinross**, he ended up in financial difficulties.

BRUCE, Dr William Spiers (1867–1921)
Polar Explorer and Oceanographer

One of Scotland's three great polar explorers (with **Captain John Ross** and **Dr John Rae**), and a staunch nationalist, William Bruce trained in medicine at **Edinburgh University**. He spent one winter with the Jackson/Harmsworth Expedition in Franz Josef Land at 80°N and two summers in Spitzbergen with the Prince of Monaco as an all-round scientist covering oceanography, ornithology, biology, geology and meteorology before applying to join Scott's *Discovery* Expedition to Antarctica in 1899. The London Royal Geographical Society never even acknowledged his application. So in 1902–4 Bruce led his own Scottish National Antarctic Expedition, funded by the **Paisley** thread manufacturer Andrew Coats and comprising only Scottish scientists. 'While "Science" was the talisman of the expedition,' wrote Bruce, ' "Scotland" was emblazoned on its flag; and it may be that in endeavouring to serve humanity by adding another link to the golden chain of science, we have also shown that the nationality of Scotland is a power to be reckoned with.' The expedition was a scientific

success, discovering part of the Antarctic coast (which he named Coats Land), establishing the first ever Antarctic base, charting the Weddell Sea and conducting hundreds of oceanographic surveys from his ship, the *Scotia*. Awarded the **Royal Scottish Geographical Society** Medal in 1904 and an honorary doctorate from **Aberdeen University**, Bruce continued to lead expeditions to Spitzbergen until his death 'from exhaustion' at the age of 54.

BRUCE Family

The Bruces acquired their first land in the British Isles in 1101 when King Henry I of England granted the royal manors of Collingham and Righton in Yorkshire to Robert de Brius. Robert was one of five sons of Adam, Lord of Brius in lower Normandy, who was succeeded by his eldest son Adam II. The ruins of the latter's castle can still be seen at Brius (now Brix) some 30 kilometres south of Cherbourg.

Robert de Brius first met the Scots Prince David in Henry I's company. When David succeeded to the Scots throne in 1124 as **David I** he enfeoffed Robert in the Lordship of Annandale. By the turn of the 14th century the Norman and Yorkshire branches of the family had died out, leaving the Bruces of Annandale as the sole surviving representatives of Adam of Brix. In 1304 Robert, 7th Lord of Annandale (**Robert I**), succeeded his father in the lands of the lordship with its caput at **Lochmaben**. In 1306 he successfully prosecuted the Bruce claim to the Scots throne, first contested by his grandfather in 1286.

King Robert I's brother **Edward** had two sons by Isabel of **Atholl** before he was slain at the Battle of Dundalk in 1318. Thomas, the second son, was granted the lands and barony of **Clackmannan** by his cousin King **David II** before 1348. With the death of the King in 1371 Thomas's son Robert became head of the family.

By 1700 the Clackmannan Bruces had spread along the Forth Valley to **Airth**, **Culross** and **Earlshall**, and north into **Perthshire**, **Aberdeenshire** and **Shetland**. A younger son of the Airth branch returned to France where his descendants survive today as the Comtes de Bruce. William Bruce of Clackmannan was one of several Scots to settle in Russia in the 17th century. His eldest son, James Daniel, was created Count Bruce by Peter the Great and his house outside Moscow has recently been turned into a Bruce family museum. Kinsmen of these Bruces settled in Sweden, Prussia and Poland and by the end of the 17th century the first Bruces had arrived in America and the Caribbean.

A number of Bruces left Scotland to chart previously unexplored parts of the world, whether as explorers like **James Bruce** of Kinnaird and General Charles Bruce, as geologists like Professor Lester Bruce, or as oceanographers like Dr Michael Bruce.

The growth of the British Empire brought new opportunities for the family. Its Chiefs and their kinfolk served the Crown as Viceroys, Secretaries of State and Ambassadors. 15 years after Stanley Bruce was elected Prime Minister of Australia, his kinsman, the 10th Earl of Elgin, presided over the 1938 Empire Exhibition in **Glasgow**.

The death of Colonel Henry Bruce of Clackmannan

in 1772 saw his cousin Charles Bruce, 5th Earl of Elgin and 9th Earl of Kincardine, become head of the family. These comital titles were granted to two great-grandchildren of David Bruce of Clackmannan. Sir Thomas Bruce was created Earl of Elgin in 1633 by **Charles I** and the same monarch created Thomas's cousin, Edward Bruce of Carnock, Earl of Kincardine in 1647. When the 4th Earl of Elgin died in 1747 without male offspring, his Scottish titles passed to Charles Kincardine.

While the Bruce seats at Lochmaben and Clackmannan are now protected monuments, the present family seat is at Broomhall in **Fife**. Built in the 17th century by Robert Bruce, Lord Broomhall, one of four Bruce Senators of the College of Justice, and remodelled by Thomas the 7th Earl in 1790, it is the home of the 11th Earl and his family. Above Broomhall flies the Chief's banner which combines the arms of the Bruces of Brix and those of the Bruces of Annandale.

BRYCE, David (1803–76) Architect
Scotland's leading Victorian architect, Bryce perfected the Scottish Baronial style. Born in **Edinburgh**, a pupil and later partner of **William Burn**, he excelled in his recreations of Scotland's romantic past. He pioneered the development of large and loosely planned country houses, each element carefully designed to serve exact needs. His Baronial designs (Craigends, 1857; Castlemilk, 1863) drew their inspiration from 16th century Scottish architecture while the publication of R W Billings's *Baronial Antiquities of Scotland* (1845–52) provided Bryce with many of his details – crowstepped gables, turrets, carved doorways, etc. Bryce was equally at home designing ecclesiastical and commercial buildings. In his banks (British Linen Bank, **St Andrews Square**, Edinburgh, 1846–51) and public buildings he preferred to use Italianate classical styles, much in the manner of Sir Charles Barry. The design for **Fettes College**, Edinburgh (1863–9) was one of the first to revive the French château style. But Bryce was not only stylistically innovative. In his Edinburgh **Royal Infirmary**, a Scottish Baronial design of 1870–9, he took in all the latest ideas about hospital planning, adopting the 'pavilion model' which had developed following Florence Nightingale's reforms of health care. Bryce's output was huge; during his career he received commissions for well over 230 buildings.

BUCCLEUCH, Earldom and Dukedom of
The Dukes of Buccleuch descend from Sir Richard the Scott (1249–85) and from Sir Walter Scott to whom **James II** granted lands in **Selkirkshire** after the death of the **8th Earl of Douglas** in 1452. The family seat of Bowhill remains there to this day. The Earldom dates from 1619 and the Dukedom from 1663 when Anne, daughter and heiress of the 2nd Earl, married **Charles II**'s bastard son, **James Duke of Monmouth**. The title survived his fall, passing to their grandson Francis, the 2nd Duke. The 3rd Duke not only succeeded to the **Douglas** Dukedom of Queensberry, but also married the daughter and heiress of the Duke of Montagu, thus acquiring a third ducal fortune. Its properties flourish still in the possession of the 9th Duke of Buccleuch and 11th Duke of Queensberry.

BUCHAN, Aberdeenshire
This ancient province comprises the north-east shoulder of the Scottish mainland. Bounded on two sides by the North Sea, on the south by the river Ythan (beyond which lies Formartine, then Garioch) and on the west by the river **Deveron** (beyond which is Strathbogie), it also corresponds to the North-East Neuk. Buchan Ness, the most easterly point in Scotland, is just south of **Peterhead** and has a lighthouse. Notorious for its mists, the coast alternates dramatic rock formations [see **Bullers o' Buchan**] with extensive sands and numerous **fishing** villages. Inland the ground is moderately high and not particularly hilly but with many glacial ridges and hollows (the Howes o' Buchan). Unremitting labour over the past two centuries has reclaimed most of it for pasture and arable of the finest. Trees have been encouraged to soften its bare horizons. Yet experts still detect in the character and dialect of its fishing and farming fraternities a measure of its once uncompromising aspect and harsh history.

BUCHAN, Alexander (1827–1907)
Meteorologist
Born at Kinnesswood, **Kinross**, Buchan began a teaching career after studying arts at **Edinburgh University**. Forced to retire from teaching through a throat complaint, he became Secretary of the Scottish Meteorological Society, and soon distinguished himself in his study of the subject, producing two standard textbooks. His demonstration of 'travelling weather' helped to make forecasting possible, and he worked to help establish a meteorological station atop **Ben Nevis**.

BUCHAN, Earldom of
Buchan and **Mar** together comprised one of the **seven** original **Celtic earldoms**, which had become 13 by the time their incumbents and 24 barons regulated the succession to the Scottish Crown in 1284. At first no Anglo-Norman could become an earl save by marriage with an heiress, and this is how William Comyn became Earl of Buchan in about 1212, after the title had been separated from that of Mar. In the decades 1286–1306 the **Comyns** were the most important single family in Scotland, next in succession to the Crown after **John Balliol** and his descendants. After **Robert Bruce** had murdered his Comyn rival in 1306 and been crowned king, he destroyed the family's power base in the long remembered Herschip (harrowing) of Buchan. The earldom was held subsequently by Royal **Stewarts** until in 1617 it was reunited with that of Mar in the person of James Erskine. Both titles continue in that family to this day.

BUCHAN, Isabella, Countess of (c1286–1312)
Isabella was the daughter of the **Earl of Fife**, whose hereditary office was to enthrone Kings of Scots. Aged 20 in 1306, her younger brother the Earl being a prisoner, she commandeered her husband's best horses and galloped to meet **Robert Bruce** at **Scone**. He was crowned before she arrived, but so important was her role that the ceremony was repeated.

Captured that summer at **Tain** with the Queen and **Marjorie Bruce**, Isabella was imprisoned at **Berwick**

Castle in 'a little timber house, latticed so that all can gaze upon her'; released into a kinsman's custody (1310), she died before **Bannockburn**.

BUCHAN, John, 1st Baron Tweedsmuir (1875–1940) Author and Diplomat

John Buchan was born in **Perth**, the eldest son of a **Free Church** minister. His family moved to **Fife** in 1876, and to **Glasgow** in 1888, where Buchan attended the **Hutcheson's Grammar School**. In 1892 he won a bursary to study at **Glasgow University**, where he was taught by the Classics scholar Gilbert Murray and the philosopher Henry Jones. In 1895 he won a scholarship to Brasenose College, Oxford, where he took a First in Greats in 1899 and won the Newdigate Prize (for poetry) in 1898. During this period he read manuscripts for the publisher John Lane, and participated fully in university activities, becoming President of the Oxford Union in his final year. He also wrote prolifically, publishing his first novel *Sir Quixote of the Moors* in 1895, a collection of essays *Scholar Gypsies* in 1896, and contributing to the *Yellow Book*. Other works of this period included *John Burnet of Barns* (1898), a historical romance portraying the lives of the **Covenanters** in the 17th century, and *A Lost Lady of the Old Years* (1899) a novel set in Scotland in 1745.

After graduating, Buchan read for the Bar and worked as an author and journalist, contributing to **Blackwood's Magazine** and *The Spectator*, before joining the staff of Lord Milner, High Commissioner to South Africa, in 1901. He spent the next two years working on the reconstruction of South Africa following the Boer War. From 1903–6 he worked as a barrister and continued his writing career, publishing many short stories and works of non-fiction. He was made a director of the publishing firm Thomas Nelson & Son, and in 1910 published *Prester John*, an adventure tale set in South Africa. His most famous adventure work, *The Thirty-Nine Steps*, followed in 1915. It introduced the character Richard Hannay, who was to feature in succeeding works such as *Greenmantle* (1916), *Mr Standfast* (1919), *The Three Hostages* (1924) and *The Courts of the Morning* (1929).

In 1915 Buchan was appointed a staff member of *The Times*, and covered activities on the Western Front before joining the Intelligence Corps in France. After World War I he became a director of Reuters, and in 1927 was elected an MP representing the Scottish Universities, a position he held until 1935. His literary career continued to flourish; he wrote a novel a year between 1922–36, producing biographies of **James Graham, Marquis of Montrose** (1928) and **Sir Walter Scott** (1932) and studies of General Gordon (1934) and Oliver Cromwell (1934).

In 1933 he was selected as Lord High Commissioner to the **General Assembly of the Church of Scotland**, a post he held until being appointed Governor-General of Canada in 1935. He remained Governor-General until his death in Ottawa on 12 February 1940. His last novel, *Sick Heart River*, was published posthumously in 1941. In all, Buchan produced over 30 novels, 7 short story collections, and almost 100 assorted works of non-fiction during his lifetime. He received several honours in recognition of his literary and political work, including honorary degrees from the **Universities of Edin-**burgh, Glasgow, **St Andrews**, and Oxford, and he was elected Chancellor of the University of Edinburgh in 1937.

BUCHANAN, Clan and Family

The Buchanan lands lie on the east shore of **Loch Lomond**, opposite the small island of Clarinch. The island, whose name became the **clan**'s warcry, was granted to one Absalon (or Anselan) of Buchanan by the **Earl of Lennox** in a charter of 1225. (From Anselan grew the name Macauslan used by some of his descendants; the name Buchanan comes from the Old Gaelic *buth chanain*, meaning 'House of the Canon'.) In 1282 a later Earl of Lennox confirmed a later Buchanan chief in these lands, which remained the home of the clan until the principal family failed in 1682 and they passed to the Marquis of Montrose. Sir Alexander Buchanan was amongst many of the clan who supported the French Dauphin against Henry V of England, and has gone down in history as the man who killed the Duke of Clarence at the Battle of Baugé (1421). A subsequent Buchanan chief died at **Flodden** (1513), and James Buchanan of the Ulster branch of the family became the 15th President of the USA (1857–61).

BUCHANAN, Dugald (Dùghall Bochanan) (1716–68) Gaelic Poet

Born in **Strathyre**, **Perthshire**, Buchanan is generally regarded as the finest evangelical poet in **Gaelic**. His classical craftsmanship makes an unusual blend with the macabre and the apocalyptic in poems that set out to describe the nature of the Almighty, and to give, as Kenneth MacDonald puts it, 'a dramatic presentation of the cosmic and moral upheaval of the Day of Judgement'. His few surviving poems (eight in all) have clear connections with Gaelic tradition; for example he contributed a poem on 'Winter' to the 18th century sequence of seasonal poems, giving it a religious dimension, and his poem *An Gaisgeach* ('The Warrior') makes ironic use of heroic ideals for religious purposes. But even stronger are the influences of evangelical English writers such as Charles Wesley, Edward Young and Isaac Watts; the Scot Robert Blair also leaves his mark. Watts in particular influenced Buchanan deeply; Donald Meek discusses this in some detail in *Gairm* Nos 147 and 148, 1989. For the poetry, see Donald Maclean, *The Spiritual Songs of Dugald Buchanan*, 1913, and for general commentary John Macinnes, 'Gaelic Spritual Verse' in *Transactions of the Gaelic Society of Inverness*, Vol 46, 1971.

BUCHANAN, Francis Hamilton (1762–1829) Botanist.

From near **Callander**, Buchanan took a medical degree at **Edinburgh University** and served as a naval surgeon before going to Bengal in the East India Company's service. In 1794 he accompanied a mission to the Burmese court of Ava and managed to combine his medical responsibilities with some important antiquarian researches into Buddhism. There followed (1800) his appointment to conduct a route survey of newly conquered Mysore to complement the topographical work of **Colin Mackenzie**. The three massive tomes which resulted represent the most comprehensive description of the society, economy, flora, fauna, agriculture and monuments of what is now Karnataka ever undertaken. Here may be found such fascinating information as the method of husbandry employed by cochineal spider farmers. In 1802 Buchanan accompanied a mission to Nepal, then served as surgeon to Lord Wellesley, the Governor-General, and embarked on what promised to be an even more exhaustive statistical survey of Bengal. It was never published. He was appointed Superintendent of the Calcutta Botanical Garden in 1814 but returned to Scotland the following year, becoming Deputy Lieutenant of **Perthshire** and the recognised Chief of **Clan Buchanan**.

BUCHANAN, George (1506–82) Historian and Scholar

'The finest writer of the tongue of ancient Rome since the age of Augustus', and 'one of the founders of modern constitutional liberty', George Buchanan was born in the village of Moss near **Killearn**, **Stirlingshire**, into a family he himself described as 'more remarkable

George Buchanan, from an engraving (SW)

for its antiquity than its opulence'. Educated at the expense of an uncle in Paris (1520–2), **St Andrews** (1524–5) where he studied philosophy under **John Mair** and Paris again (1526–8), he was tutor to Gilbert Kennedy, **Earl of Cassilis**, in Paris from 1529–34 and to a natural son of **James V** in Scotland from 1536–8.

Ordered by the King to write a satire on the Franciscans (whom James suspected of conspiring against him), Buchanan thereby incurred the wrath of **Cardinal Beaton**, who imprisoned him in **St Andrews Castle**. Escaping to France (1539), he became Professor of Latin at Bordeaux before being summoned by the King of Portugal to teach the principles of Aristotelian philosophy at the University of Coimbra (1547).

Imprisoned (1549) by the Inquisition as a heretic, he spent the two years of his confinement working on a translation into Latin of the Psalms of David, and the next 10 years in France and Italy in the study of the Holy Scriptures 'so he might be able to make a more exact judgement of the controversies in religion which employ the thoughts and time of most of the men of these days'. In 1561 he returned to Scotland, embraced the Reformed religion, and became classical tutor to **Queen Mary**, to whom he was intensely loyal until the murder of **Darnley** whereupon he became one of her most ferocious detractors. After her flight to England his *Ane Detectioun of the doinges of Marie quene of Scottes* (1571) was used by the rebel lords as justification for their insurgence.

Awarded the temporalities of **Crossraguel Abbey** in 1564 and appointed by **Regent Moray** as Principal of St Leonards College, St Andrews in 1566, Buchanan was a member of the **General Assembly of the Church of Scotland** and that body's first (and possibly only) lay **Moderator** in 1567. In 1570 he was made Keeper of the Privy Seal, an office which entitled him to a seat in Parliament. An uncompromising disciplinarian of purely academic interests, and a by now elderly bachelor, he was also appointed tutor (1570) to the four-year-old **James VI**, to whom he gave a 'brilliant but brutal' education which included poisoning the child's mind against his mother.

The last years of his life Buchanan devoted to writing, his chief works being *De Juri Regni apud Scotos* (1579) (another justification of Mary's deposition which promulgated the theory that monarchs only exist by the will and for the good of the people), and a 20-volume *History of Scotland* published just before his death in 1582. This great scholar who 'far excelled Erasmus in the originality and boldness of his thinking and in the depth of his political philosophy' (J A Wylie), died in **Edinburgh** and was buried in **Greyfriars' Churchyard**.

BUCHANAN, Robert William (1841–1901) Writer

Though born in Staffordshire, Buchanan was the son of a socialist publisher in **Glasgow** and was educated at **Glasgow** High School and **University**. With a friend, David Gray, he moved to London in 1860. Gray, a weaver's son from **Kirkintilloch**, died of consumption in the following year when his *The Luggie and Other Poems* was in proof. Buchanan, having written a memorial of him, also produced verse (*London Poems*, 1866) as well as plays and novels. But his modest celebrity was achieved as an acerbic critic. In particular Swinburne, Rossetti and the Pre-Raphaelites, anathema to a puritanical socialist, were savaged as belonging to 'The Fleshly School of Poetry'.

BUCHANITES

A religious sect of the late 18th century, the Buchanites were followers of **Irvine**-born Elizabeth Buchan (1738–91), a **Glasgow** dyer's wife who saw visions, left home and husband, and set up in Closeburn, **Dumfriesshire**. Her credibility was much enhanced when a priest (described as having a weak brain) became one of her disciples and she had soon gathered a substantial following of 'innocent country people'. Her chief tenet was that, on a day that she prophesied, all her followers would go to Heaven without having to die first. The Gallovidian writer **John MacTaggart** recorded how 'at last the glorious day arrived; platforms were erected for them to wait on, and Mrs Buchan's platform was exalted above all the others. The hair of each head was cut short, all but a tuft on the top, for the angels to catch by when drawing them up. The momentous hour came. Every station for ascension was instantly occupied. Thus they stood, expecting to be wafted every moment into the land of bliss, when a gust of wind came; but instead of wafting them upwards, it capsized Mrs Buchan, platform and all.' Not surprisingly, much of her support evaporated after the débâcle, although a hardcore of followers remained faithful till her death. Since another of Mrs Buchan's tenets had been that none of her followers was to marry or have any 'love-dealings' with each other, the sect did not long outlast its leader.

BUCKHAVEN, Fife
A **fishing** village on the Firth of Forth which until the late 19th century served the markets of **Leith** and **Edinburgh**, Buckhaven succumbed to **coal-mining** and is now part of a continuous and unfavoured agglomeration stretching through **Methil** to **Leven**. The population was once 'so very clownish', according to Defoe, 'that to be of "the college of Buckhaven" is become a proverb'. Clowning is now reserved for St Andrew's (1825), a **William Burn** church which in 1869 was dismantled and shipped from the town of **St Andrews** to be re-erected in Buckhaven where it has since become a theatre.

BUCKIE, Banffshire
Mare Mater – the Sea our Mother – is the apt motto of Buckie, now within **Moray** Council Area, but formerly the largest town in the county of **Banffshire**. From small beginnings Buckie grew because of the skills and courage of its fishermen, ranked for hundreds of years as among the most enterprising in the British Isles. The present-day town, which is very much a linear development, is an amalgam of once separate villages. The string of small fisher communities, the earliest going back at least to the 17th century, prospered during the 18th and 19th centuries when the settlements of Nether Buckie (or Buckpool) and Easter Buckie combined to become a **police burgh** (1888). Other villages along the coast to the east were subsequently incorporated – Gordonsburgh and Ianstown in 1901 and Portessie in 1903.

Of crucial importance to their development was the construction by local lairds of good harbours. Buckpool harbour (1857), which is now filled in, raised Buckie to the first rank of **fishing** stations. But it was left behind by the splendid deepwater Cluny harbour (1880) built by Gordon of Cluny. The arrival of the **railway** in the 1880s permitted the swift transportation of fish to southern markets.

Population growth was remarkable, rising from 703 in 1794 to 5849 in 1891. 20 years later it peaked at 8897. These years were the town's 'golden age' when Buckie fishermen who had invested heavily in the new steam drifters pursued the shoals of **herring** round the coast of Britain. Its prosperity was reflected in the many fine new houses that were then erected, with outside stairs round the back giving access to the net lofts. But the post-1918 collapse of the herring trade affected Buckie badly and the inter-war years brought hardship to the fishing community. In the 1950s and 60s the fishermen abandoned the outdated steam drifter and with the help of government grants and loans purchased dual-purpose motor vessels. With most boats owned by the fishermen themselves on the share system, the Buckie men adopted new methods and sought new catches, concentrating on white fish and Norway lobsters (for scampi). With a revival of fish processing in the town, the industry entered into a new period of prosperity. This prosperity aided the town's old-established **shipbuilding** yards, which in difficult years had diversified into the construction of naval minesweepers and yachts and other pleasure craft.

Now, with overfishing and EU-imposed quotas on white fish, the fishing industry faces an uncertain future. But Buckie is a town with a great deal of communal strength, despite most of the fleet having to operate away from home.

For visitors there are the old and attractively painted fishermen's houses, a maritime museum and lots of kirks and religious meeting places (including the striking twin-spired Roman Catholic 'chapel'), two **golf courses** and a distillery at Inchgower. There is also a Fisherman's Memorial Chapel which commemorates local sailors who have lost their lives at sea – a poignant reminder that the sea not only gives but takes away.

BULLERS O' BUCHAN, Nr Peterhead, Aberdeenshire
So called from the French *bouillir*, or more plausibly, according to **James Boswell**, the English 'boiler', the Bullers are a dramatic conformation of sea-cliff where, in rough weather, the water boils as in a cauldron. The centre-piece consists of a large circular 'cave' of pink granite, open to the sky, with 150ft (46m) perpendicular sides and a narrow sea entrance through which the waves rush with great fury. 'No man can see it with indifference who has either sense of danger or delight in rarity,' declared **Dr Johnson** who peered down into the cauldron from above, then teetered round its crater on the dangerously narrow path, and finally procured a boat to sail into it (the entrance being so narrow that the oars had to be shipped as they passed in). His attempt to describe the phenomenon was less successful, although it did permit the introduction of a rare English verb: 'it is a rock perpendicularly tubulated, united on one side with a high shore, and on the other rising steep to a great height, above the main sea.' A **fishing** hamlet of much-renovated cottages nestles in the cliffs nearby, as do a great variety of **seabirds**.

BURGHEAD, Moray
Little now remains of the important promontory fort, 'one of the most magnificent centres of **Pictish** power'. However, plans of the site made by **General William Roy** in the 1740s show that there were three stone ramparts which ran for about 240m across the neck of the promontory to enclose an area some 300m long.

The harbour at Buckie c1880 (GWWA)

Radiocarbon dating of charred wood from the surviving wall suggests the fort was built in the 4th or 5th centuries AD. Stone slabs carved with **Pictish** motifs, including a bull (of which two examples are in the local museum) and the great subterranean well with walkway are so exceptional that they were once taken as evidence of **Roman** occupation.

BURGHS, Police, Royal, of Barony etc, see LOCAL GOVERNMENT and LAW

BURKE, William (1792–1829) and HARE, William (d.c1860) Murderers

Two of the most infamous figures in 19th century Scottish history, Burke and Hare were Ulstermen who came to Scotland to work as labourers on the **Union Canal**. While residing in **Edinburgh**, they became aware of the demand for human bodies for anatomy demonstrations at the city's medical school, and are believed to have murdered 16 people to meet it. Contrary to legend, they do not appear to have been 'resurrectionists' or graverobbers, but perfected a method of suffocation which induced death without leaving obvious traces.

After murdering their 16th victim, Burke and Hare, along with the former's mistress and the latter's wife, were arrested; but the lack of evidence led to the Lord Advocate of the time, Sir William Rae, offering virtual guarantee against prosecution if one of them would turn King's Evidence. This William Hare did, sending his former colleague to the gallows in Edinburgh on 28 January 1829. The charge against Burke's mistress, Helen MacDougal, was found not proven, and the Hares fled Scotland. William Hare is said to have died a pauper in London around 1860. No proceedings appear to have been taken against **Robert Knox**, the anatomy lecturer popularly supposed to have been accepting Burke and Hare's supplies on a 'no questions asked' basis. Knox was later immortalised in **James Bridie**'s play *The Anatomist* (1930).

BURN, William (1789–1870) Architect

Although born in **Edinburgh**, Burn started his career in London at the office of Robert Smirke. After returning to Edinburgh in 1812 he began his practice from the family builders' yard. A year later he was invited to report on the plans for the development of **Calton Hill**. In 1816 he entered the competition for the completion of **Adam**'s **University** Building; **William Playfair**'s preferred design established him as one of Burn's main professional rivals. Most of Burn's early works were public buildings. In 1817–18 he received his first country house commission, a subject which was to become his speciality. His office's output was unrivalled and he was patronised by the Scottish and English aristocracy alike. In 1841 **David Bryce** became his pupil and later partner, and in 1844 Burn moved to London. He continued to hold prestigious posts such as 'Consultant Architect to the Government in Scotland'. In 1865 he was one of the assessors of the competition for the Foreign Office in Whitehall. Early in his career Burn had used mainly the Greek Doric (George Watson's Hospital, 1825–8), then moved on to Jacobethan for manor houses (Riccarton, Edinburgh, 1823–7) and finally arrived at Scottish Baronial, a style which was later perfected by Bryce. His many churches were invariably Gothic (**Dunfermline** New Abbey Church, 1818–21). By 1840 Burn had already designed or altered well over 90 country houses, not to mention 30 churches and nearly as many public buildings.

BURNES, Sir Alexander (1805–41) Political Officer and Explorer

Otherwise 'Bukhara Burnes', Alexander was the son of James Burnes(s), provost of **Montrose** and a first cousin once removed of **Robert Burns**. Through the influence of **Joseph Hume** he secured a cadetship with the East India Company, reaching Bombay in 1821. Mercurial, intensely ambitious and a brilliant linguist, he joined the political department in 1829 and was despatched up the Indus river (1830), ostensibly to convey a carriage and horses to Ranjit Singh, Maharajah of Punjab, in fact to survey the political and navigational possibilities of the river. There followed (1832) his much publicised journey in disguise across Afghanistan to Bukhara with Dr James Gerard, one of three brothers from **Aberdeen** who had specialised in exploring the Himalayas. Burnes gave little credit to Gerard, or anyone else, and implied that he was the first Briton to perform this hazardous journey. He was consequently lionised, receiving medals from both the Royal and Paris Geographical Societies and an audience with the King. In 1836 he was sent back to Kabul, supposedly for commercial reasons; while there **John Wood**, under his command, surveyed the upper Oxus while Burnes unearthed evidence of Russian ambitions in Afghanistan. The resultant First Afghan War, an attempt to replace the existing Amir of Kabul, was contrary to Burnes's advice; and he was undoubtedly right. Though ignored, he declined to compromise his meteoric rise by standing on principle and duly returned to Kabul with the invading army as assistant to the incompetent Sir William MacNaghten. He was knighted in 1840 and was one of the first to be hacked to death when in 1841 the Afghans rose against the occupying force. For the ensuing disaster, the worst suffered by the British in Asia until the fall of Singapore in World War II, Burnes cannot be blamed. With him in Kabul died one of his brothers; another, James, became Physician-General in India and wrote a noted account of Sind (now in Pakistan).

BURNET, Gilbert (1643–1715) Churchman and Historian

Burnet was born in **Edinburgh**, a cadet of the Burnetts of Leys, proprietors of **Crathes Castle** on Deeside. Paradoxically, he combined the convictions of a Protestant **Episcopalian** with those of a **Whig**. Professor of Divinity at **Glasgow** (1666), he became chaplain to **Charles II** in 1674 and, although this cannot have been an onerous duty, he refused to augment it with any of the bishoprics he was offered. He retired abroad after the accession of **James VII** and returned at the revolution of 1688, when he at last accepted the Bishopric of Salisbury. He remained influential throughout the reign of Queen Anne and composed a number of controversial works on the issues of Church and state (including a *History of the Reformation*). But his gossipy *History of my own Time* proved to be his most popular production and an important historical source. The outrageous Countess of Dysart, who married the widowed minister **John Maitland, 1st Duke of Lauderdale**, and looted the Maitland castle of **Thirlestane** to embellish her palace of Ham, provided a particularly apt theme for his venomous pen.

BURNET, Thomas (c1632–c1706) Physician

Believed to have been born in **Edinburgh** in the early 1630s, Thomas was the brother of **Gilbert Burnet**, Bishop of Salisbury. He studied medicine at Montpellier, but practised in **Edinburgh**, publishing an important medical textbook, *Thesaurus Medicinae Practicae*, a compendium of contemporary knowledge of the subject. Physician to **Charles II**, and a founder member of the **Royal College of Physicians** of Edinburgh in 1681, Burnet is believed to have died in February 1706.

BURNETT, Duncan (c1590–1651) Composer and Virginalist

A member of the family of Leys in **Aberdeenshire**, Burnett was appointed Master of the Sang Schule in **Glasgow** in 1638, having previously taught in that city. His music book (in the National Library, MS 9447), compiled between 1630–50, contains almost all the known works of **William Kinloch** and includes his own fine setting of *The Queine of Inglands Lessoune* and his magnificent *Pavan*.

BURNETT, James, Lord Monboddo (1714–99) Philosopher and Judge

Born at Monboddo House near **Auchenblae, Kincardineshire**, Burnett was educated at **King's College, Aberdeen** and then studied **law** at **Edinburgh University** and Groeningen. He became an advocate in 1737, Sheriff of Kincardine (1760) and **Lord of Session** (1767), taking the title of Monboddo. A leading figure in the **Scottish Enlightenment**, he was a member of the Select Society and a close friend of **James Boswell's** father. Boswell's visit to Monboddo House with **Dr Johnson** promised trouble in that Burnett was then in the process of publishing his 6-vol *Of the Origin and Progress of Language*, which advanced a pre-Darwinian theory of evolution tracing the origins of man to the orang-utan and insisting that the Nicobar Islanders still retained tails. Such ideas then occasioned much ridicule, heightened by Burnett's renowned eccentricities. But Dr Johnson found himself charmed by Burnett's good sense and was even tempted to agree that the savage enjoyed a better existence than the shopkeeper. Burnett also published a 6-vol *Antient Metaphysics* commending the harmony of science and philosophy.

BURNS, Sir George (1795–1890) Shipowner

The youngest son of the Reverend Dr John Burns of **Glasgow**, George Burns went into partnership in 1823 with his elder brother James as a general merchant. The following year, together with Hugh Matthie of Liverpool, they established a sailing ship service between the two cities. Making a link with the McIvers in 1830, the partners soon dominated the trade between Liverpool, the north of Ireland and the west of Scotland. While James looked after the merchant side of the business, George concentrated on the shipping. In 1838 he and **Robert Napier** won support in the west of Scotland for Samuel Cunard's new British & North American Steam Packet Co – later Cunard & Co. The Burnses represented the line's interests in Glasgow. As the new line prospered, the Cunard, Burns and McIver families gradually bought out the other shareholders. George Burns retired in 1860 to Castle Wemyss at **Wemyss Bay**, dying in 1890 within a year of being created a baronet.

BURNS, Robert (1759–96) Poet

Robert Burns was the eldest son of a professional gardener and unsuccessful tenant farmer in **Ayrshire**. Growing up to a life of demanding physical work, poverty, and acute awareness of social disadvantage, he began to write poetry in an attempt to find 'some kind of counterpoise' to these adverse circumstances (Preface, *Poems, Chiefly in the Scottish Dialect*). By his mid twenties he was an accomplished poet and songwriter, especially in his native Scots. In the summer of 1786, when he was on the point of abandoning farming in Scotland and emigrating to the West Indies, essentially because of a broken love affair, he published his first collection of poems, in an edition of 612 copies printed in the county town of **Kilmarnock**. *Poems, Chiefly in the Scottish Dialect* met with such acclaim in Ayrshire and among west of Scotland people in **Edinburgh** that he changed all his plans and travelled to the capital, where he was enthusiastically welcomed by a number of leading literary figures, partly because the quality of his work appeared to confirm current primitivist theories of genius. Mrs Alison Cockburn, for 60 years one of the acknowledged 'queens' of Edinburgh society, wrote to a friend on 30 December 1786: 'The town is at present agog with the ploughman poet, who receives adulation with native dignity, and is the very figure of his profession, strong and coarse, but he has a most enthusiastic heart of LOVE.'

Among those who saluted the new arrival was **Henry Mackenzie**, whose sentimental novel *The Man of Feeling* Burns intensely admired. Mackenzie praised the 'power of genius' of 'this Heaven-taught ploughman' in an influential essay in his periodical *The Lounger*, and helped Burns arrange publication of an expanded edition of his poems in the spring of 1787.

When Burns received part of the money which the new edition earned for him, he made a number of tours, to the Borders and, more than once, to the Highlands. Otherwise, the capital remained his base until the spring of 1787, when he returned to Ayrshire, although he was to spend the winter of 1787–8 in Edinburgh also. His principal Highland tour was made in company with Willie Nicol, a crosspatch of an Edinburgh dominie whose lack of consideration towards hosts intent on giving Burns a welcome embarrassed the poet more than once, notably at Gordon Castle. Taking Nicol along, Burns noted, was like 'travelling with a loaded blunderbuss at full cock'. Yet the journey brought its own moments of shared pleasure for the pair, including richly varied scenery and sessions of witty talk over a dram. Artistically, Burns drew inspiration from the beauty of unfamiliar forests, lochs and rivers, from battlefields, such as **Bannockburn** and **Culloden**, with challenging historical associations, and from meetings en route with kindred spirits. Near **Dunkeld**, for instance, there was a never-to-be-forgotten opportunity to enjoy the brilliant fiddling of **Niel Gow**, 'a short, stout-built, honest Highland figure'. It is somehow appropriate that from the time of his Highland journey onwards, Burns was to be more and more the nation's outstanding writer and collector of songs. His travels had given him the right to state:

By Oughtertyre grows the aik,
On Yarrow banks the birken shaw . . .
The Highland hills I've wandered wide
And o'er the Lowlands I have been.

In the course of his travels, he had come across people interested in song tradition in different parts of Scotland, had visited places associated with historic events and **ballads** both north and south of the **Highland line**, and had listened attentively to many Highland and Lowland tunes. He now had unrivalled authority as a songwriter and collector, conferred by his first-hand familiarity with new sources of song, as well as by natural aptitude.

Eventually, Burns returned somewhat reluctantly to tenant farming in south-west Scotland. For a time he combined Excise work with farming, then decided to give up farming completely and became a full-time excise officer in **Dumfries**. His most famous poem, 'Tam o' Shanter', was written in 1790 while he was farming at Ellisland, but for the most part he devoted his leisure hours in his later years to his lifelong passion for writing and collecting Scottish songs. From 1788 until his death he was editor in all but name of the greatest of all Scottish song collections, **James Johnson**'s *Scots Musical Museum* (6 vols, 1787–1803), to which he contributed some 200 songs. He also supplied the words of many songs for **George Thomson**'s *Select Collection of Original Scottish Airs* (5 vols, 1793–1818), which claimed Haydn and Beethoven among its musical contributors.

Work pressure was unremitting. Burns was clearly a competent exciseman, for in 1794 he was appointed Acting Supervisor at Dumfries. His health, however, was soon a cause for concern; he suffered from what modern medical research has identified as a

Robert Burns, by Archibald Skirving 1796/8 (SNPG)

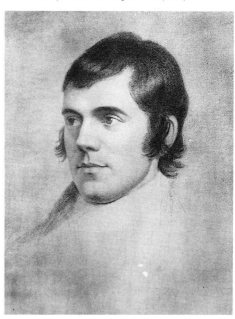

combination of rheumatic endocarditis, a heart condition and brucellosis. In the early summer of 1796 he wrote to his old friend James Johnson, publisher of the *Scots Musical Museum*, 'this protracting, slow consuming illness which hangs over me, will, I doubt much, my ever dear friend, arrest my sun before he has well reached his middle career, & will turn over the Poet to far other & more important concerns than studying the brilliancy of Wit or the pathos of Sentiment.' A young Highlander, James MacDonald, visiting Dumfries in the first week of June, noted in his diary that Burns looked consumptive, adding 'he was in excellent spirits, and displayed as much wit and humour in three hours time as any man I ever knew . . . At parting the poor Poet with tears in his Eyes took an affectionate leave of me. He has vast pathos in his voice, and as he himself says in his Vision, "His eye e'en turned on empty space, beams keen wi' honour".' At the beginning of July, Burns went to Brow Well on the Solway coast in a desperate attempt to improve his health by sea-bathing. On this occasion he greeted Maria Riddell, an acquaintance of many years, with the question, 'Well, madam, have you any commands for the other world?' He died in Dumfries on 21 July.

In common with certain other Scots who have contributed to national myth – **Robert I (the Bruce)**, **Mary Queen of Scots** and **Bonnie Prince Charlie** – Burns has an international reputation. His is an exceptionally personal kind of literary fame. Although celebrated for poetry, which is usually thought of as an intellectual pursuit, he is very often referred to as 'Rabbie Burns'. The familiar form of his name signals affection and acceptance. It is as if Burns is being saluted in a very down-to-earth way, as a creative genius certainly, but also as someone who does not stand on his dignity, a friend to the common man. In keeping with this tradition, people meet at Burns Suppers all over the world each year on and near his birthday, 25 January. The Burns cult is unique, and despite having many detractors, is evidently unstoppable. An American folklorist, Mary Ellen Brown, comments: 'The complete history of the Burns Suppers . . . can certainly never be written, for the custom was a spontaneous growth and its celebrants are now found all over the world.' (*Burns and Tradition*, 1984).

Burns was an outgoing individual, to whom friendship mattered greatly. It is appropriate that his admirers should pay him the compliment of responding with warmth and directness to his personality and achievement, because he cared passionately about democratic social values. The evidence is scattered throughout his work, from the poem which opened his first collection in 1786, 'The Twa Dogs', to a superbly defiant song, 'Is there for honest poverty', written at the height of French Revolutionary fervour in 1793.

Is there for honest Poverty
That hings his head, an' a' that;
The coward slave – we pass him by,
We dare be poor for a' that!
For a' that, an' a' that,
Our toils obscure, an' a' that,
The rank is but the guinea's stamp,
The Man's the gowd for a' that.

What though on hamely fare we dine,
Wear hodding grey, and a' that;
Gie fools their silks, and knaves their wine,
A Man's a Man for a' that;
For a' that, and a' that,
Their tinsel show, and a' that;
The honest man, though e'er sae poor,
Is king of men for a' that.

Ye see yon birkie ca'd a lord,
Wha struts and stares, and a' that;
Though hundreds worship at his word,
He's but a coof for a' that;
For a' that, and a' that,
His riband, star and a' that,
The man of independent mind
He looks an laughs at a' that.

A prince can mak a belted knight,
A marquis, duke, and a' that;
But an honest man's aboon his might,
Gude faith he mauna fa' that!
For a' that, and a' that,
Their dignities, and a' that,
The pith o' sense, and pride o' worth,
Are higher rank than a' that.

Then let us pray that come it may,
(As come it will for a' that),
That Sense and Worth, o'er a' the earth
Shall bear the gree, and a' that.
For a' that and a' that,
It's comin' yet for a' that,
That Man to Man the warld o'er,
Shall brothers be for a' that.

(*hings* hangs, *gowd* gold, *hamely* homely, *hoddin* coarse, homespun, *birkie* conceited fellow, *coof* fool, *aboon* above, *mauna* must not, *fa'* lay claim to, *gree* come off best, *warld* world.)

This is Burns's most famous democratic political song, daring to speak up for the common man, attack social rank, and proclaim the coming of a new age of universal brotherhood. It combines two characteristic features: delight in lyric – associated in the song tradition which Burns inherited with the expression of happiness and positive thoughts – and mastery of a boldly personal kind of satire. A person of very positive outlook, with an exceptional capacity for love and friendship, Burns was also a good hater. Song and satire are complementary in his work, different sides of the same coin. A further characteristic is the ability to put an essential idea in few words. 'It's comin' yet for a' that', he writes. The poet asserts that a shared vision of social unity will prevail – despite every sort of adversity and ideological opposition. Compare his belief in the eventual triumph of human goodness with the message of a 20th century song which has also gone round the world – 'We shall overcome'.

It is Burns's ability to express widely shared feelings simply and memorably which has led to his extraordinary popularity. Another example is 'Auld Lang Syne', which has been adopted by the world as a universally recognised song of parting. A difference between 'Is there for honest poverty' and 'Auld Lang Syne', however, is that the words of the latter song are largely traditional. Although Burns almost certainly gave them their final unity and polish, he claimed only to have collected them. His willingness to give credit to anonymous forerunners whose art inspired his own is a measure of how closely he identified with the rich song tradition of Lowland Scotland, and of the selfless nature of his commitment.

Widespread identification of Burns's name with a habit of falling in love is accounted for partly by the eloquence of 'Ae fond kiss' and 'O my luve is like a red, red rose' – two of the best-known among literally hundreds of love songs – and partly by the fact that he was a highly sexed individual who enjoyed passionate relationships with a number of Scots girls who bore him children. His lovers included Betty Paton, a servant girl on his father's farm, Lochlea; Jean Armour, a stonemason's daughter from Mauchline, whom he eventually married; probably Mary Campbell ('Highland Mary'), around whose name a misleading sentimental myth was to be woven in the 19th century; May Cameron and Jenny Clow, servant girls in Edinburgh; and Anna Park, a barmaid in Dumfries. With regard to his notoriety as a lover of the lassies, it should be borne in mind that Burns belonged to 18th century tenant farming society. Illegitimacy rates were high, both because contraception was unavailable, and because it was sometimes considered a rite of passage in rural Scotland for young men to prove their manhood by seducing girls. The elders of the Kirk, described by Burns as the 'houghmagandie (fornication) pack', strove to deter those in their parish from sexual transgression by making them appear in church on the 'cutty stool' of repentance. So far from producing restraint in the poet, this practice merely fuelled his rebellious spirit. Later, his wife's long-

Mrs Robert Burns (Jean Armour), by J A Gilfillan (SNPG)

suffering tolerance towards her errant husband illustrates another aspect of country living. 'Oor Robin should have had twa wives,' said Jean Armour Burns, and gave a home to Burns's daughter by Anna Park alongside her own offspring.

BURNS, Rev Thomas (1796–1871)

Nephew of the poet **Robert Burns**, Thomas Burns withdrew from the **Church of Scotland** at the 1843 **Disruption** to join the **Free Church** and was appointed the first minister of the proposed Scots colony in New Zealand, a project first planned by **George Rennie** but, post Disruption, taken over by Burns and William Cargill (1784–1860, a veteran of the Peninsular War who claimed descent from the **Covenanter** martyr **Donald Cargill**, although the latter had no recorded legitimate descendants). Leaving the **Clyde** on board the *Philip Laing* on 27 November 1847, Burns and 247 emigrants arrived in Otago Bay on New Zealand's South Island to found the settlement of Dunedin. 20 years later he became the first Chancellor of the town's Otago University.

BURNS, William (c1825–80) Nationalist

A respectable **Glasgow** solicitor who made common cause with **James Grant** and the National Association for the Vindication of Scottish Rights, Burns merits note as the man who first set the world to rights over the use of terms like 'Scotch' and 'English'. In a series of pamphlets ('Scottish Rights and Honour Vindicated', 1854, and '"England" Versus "Great Britain"', 1865) he distinguished the correct term 'Scottish' from the vulgarised 'Scotch' (now reserved solely for whisky and red meat) and railed against the habit of regarding 'English' as synonymous with 'British'. Both errors were common in the 19th century, Scots being nearly as prone to them as Englishmen. Burns considered them clear evidence of an insidious anglicisation of Scottish identity, a view which quickly won support in certain quarters of the Scottish press and was later taken up by the **Scottish Home Rule Association**. He also contributed to nationalist historiography with a 2-vol history of *The Scottish War of Independence: Its Antecedents and Effects* (1874). See H J Hanham, *Scottish Nationalism*, 1969.

'BURNT CANDLEMAS' (1356)

This was the phrase used by Walter Bower, abbot of **Inchcolm**, in the 15th century *Scotichronicon* to evoke the horrors of Edward III's last Scottish campaign which began in early February, possibly on the 2nd, the feast of Candlemas. In January at **Roxburgh**, **Edward Balliol**, having lost what remained of his Scottish patrimony, had resigned his doubtful claim to the Scottish throne to Edward III. With **David II** still in English captivity, such a transfer was seen as an irrelevance in Scotland. Edward therefore marched north to **Haddington** and landed more troops at **Whitekirk** preparatory to a campaign that would not be hindered by anxieties about the effect on Scottish opinion. A trail of smouldering castles, churches and crops marked his progress. Within a year, and following defeat at Poitiers for their French allies, the Scots under Robert the Steward (the future **Robert II**) agreed to treat for peace and the deliverance of David II in return for a heavy indemnity.

121

Coal being loaded at Burntisland docks in the 1880s (GWWA)

BURNTISLAND, Fife

A hill fort on Dunearn Hill to the north-west may have been reoccupied by **Agricola**, Burntisland possessing easy access to **Loch Leven** and central **Fife** as well as 'the best harbour on the Forth'. **Rossend Castle** subsequently guarded the harbour which developed a sizeable trade with the Baltic and France. The town was constituted a **royal burgh** in 1568, wisely capitulated to Cromwell in 1651, but lost most of its overseas trade following the **Act of Union**. Prosperity returned in the 19th century thanks to **coal**, limestone, ferries and a large distillery at Grange, plus some **herring** curing. The 20th century saw an increase in **shipbuilding** and the introduction of aluminium smelting but today the town is projected as a resort. Besides Rossend its chief attraction is the parish church of **St Columba** (1592), 'one of the finest . . . post-**Reformation** churches in Scotland' (G L Pride). Square with angle buttresses and central tower supported internally on piers connected by arches, it is also original, wonderfully simple and highly effective. Here in 1601 the **General Assembly** adopted the proposal for a new translation of the **Bible** which resulted in the Authorised Version of 1611. In Somerville Square is the childhood home of **Mary Somerville**. East, towards Kinghorn, a monument (1887) marks the supposed spot where **Alexander III** fell from his horse to his death in 1286.

BURRA, Shetland

South-west of **Scalloway**, on the west coast of Shetland, lie the twin isles of Burra which are linked together by a bridge. The Norsemen called them *Borgaroy*, the island of the **broch**, a structure which now survives only in the place-name Brough. Papil, at the south end of West Burra, was the site of an early Christian church. Here was found the beautifully sculptured Monks' Stone, an example of early Celtic art which can be seen in Shetland Museum, **Lerwick**.

Traditionally the people of Burra combined **crofting** and **fishing** to make a living, with the latter the more important. Today the islands' fishing fleet consists of 10 white fish vessels between 60 and 90ft (18 and 27m) long and a number of smaller shellfish boats.

The islands' population has risen to almost 900 of whom 400 live in the attractive village of Hamnavoe. Since 1971 the isles of Burra have been linked by bridges to the **Mainland** via the island of Trondra.

BURRELL, Sir William (1861–1958)
Shipowner and Art Collector

Born in **Glasgow**, the son of a shipowner, William Burrell entered the family business aged 15. He and his brother inherited their father's company in 1881 and together introduced a daring policy of ordering ships for low prices during periods of depression, predicting their completion would coincide with economic recovery. Demand in years of growth enabled them to trade at considerable profit and they sold their vessels at the market's height, thus amassing a large fortune. During World War I the remainder of their fleet was bought by the British government and from then until his death William devoted his efforts exclusively to building upon his already substantial collections of paintings, sculpture, ceramics, tapestries and Oriental antiquities.

The quality of his collection demonstrates considerable discernment, though his collecting policy remained unspecific and was guided largely by value for money until the 1930s when he began to ponder the question of its long-term future. Deciding to hand it into public ownership, he increasingly concentrated on enriching particular areas and adding to those more poorly represented. By the time of his death the collection numbered some 8000 items. With the exception of a small group of French paintings presented by Burrell to **Berwick-on-Tweed** (near his home, Hutton Castle), the entire collection was bequeathed to the City of Glasgow in 1944 and placed in store until a suitable site could be found that satisfied his stringent conditions for its display. In 1967 his Trustees agreed to it being housed on the Pollok Estate, itself given to the City by Mrs Maxwell MacDonald with **Pollok House**, and in 1972 the competition to design the gallery was won by Barry Gasson. Finally opened in 1983, the gallery has proved immensely popular and successful in housing Burrell's collection, the size of which means that even now only a quarter may be seen at any one time.

Throughout, Gasson's design is consistently sensitive to the collection's wide variety of needs; the experience of walking through the stone, timber, glass and steel building, incorporating Burrell's important collection of architectural fragments, is delightful. The rich and remarkable range of the collection makes it perhaps the finest to be amassed by any single British individual. Whilst it includes superb objects from antiquity from Iraq, Iran, Egypt, Greece and Italy, Oriental ceramics, jades and bronzes, and 18th and 19th century Japanese prints, the most important part of the collection encompasses Burrell's chief passion, northern European art of the 14th to 17th centuries. The collection of medieval tapestries and stained glass are of particularly outstanding quality. Similarly, early European painting is well represented with good works by Memling, Veneziano, Giovanni Bellini and Cranach, while 19th century French art (Burrell's other great passion) includes works by Géricault, Delacroix, Daubigny, Boudin, Courbet, Daumier, Millet and Degas. Burrell was also the most important patron of the outstanding watercolourist **Joseph Crawhall**, who is represented in the collection by some 140 works.

BURRY MAN, The, Festival

The ceremony of the Burry Man has existed in **South Queensferry** for centuries. Each year a native of the town is elected to the position, and on the second Friday in August he is encased nearly all over in burrs – the spiky seed-cases of the burdock plant. The crown of his head is profusely garlanded with flowers, and he carries two staves likewise decorated, which are also held by two flanking supporters, their assistance being necessary to help him maintain his balance during his awkward, tiring and sometimes painful nine-hour perambulation through the streets of the burgh. He is preceded by a lad ringing a bell, and followed by children chanting a traditional verse. The purpose of the Burry Man Festival is lost in antiquity, though it would seem to relate to a pagan ritual invoking good fortune. His mission may have been to bring good luck to the **herring** fishing (as with similar figures which once existed in **Fraserburgh** and **Buckie**), or it may have represented an appeal for success in the coming harvest. The original reason for holding the ceremony may now be forgotten, but the desire to perpetuate the tradition remains strong. A replica Burry Man may be seen in Queensferry Museum.

BURT, Edmund (d.1755) Author

Although described as an army officer by the editor of Jamieson's 1822 edition of his *Letters from a Gentleman in the North of Scotland*, Edmund (not Edward) Burt was no such thing. He was, in fact, appointed 'under the Privy Seal of Scotland, Receiver General and Collector of the unsold Forfeited Estates in North Britain', among which were the large **Seaforth** estates; and the government enjoined **General Wade** to give him all legal assistance.

In his *Letters* his comments on the Highlands, the scenery and the inhabitants range from whimsical to outrageous, from condescension to acute observation. 'For my part, ever since I have known the Highlands, I have never doubted but the natives had their share of natural understanding with the rest of mankind . . .'

An eye-witness of the building of the **military roads**, Burt's graphic and accurate descriptions are a *sine qua non* for anyone with more than a passing interest in the subject, although his claim that the **Corrieyairack** is 'rendered everywhere more easy for Wheel Carriages than Highgate Hill' is an over-enthusiastic hyperbole.

BUSBY, Sir Matt (1909–94) Football Manager

Son of a Bellshill pit-worker killed at Arras when Matt was only 6, Busby, like his near-contemporary **Bill Shankly**, used his footballing skills to escape a career down the mines. After a trial with Manchester City in 1928 he played as right half-back first for City and then (from 1936) for Liverpool, gaining one full Scotland cap before the start of World War II, and captaining Scotland in unofficial wartime internationals. When he became manager of Manchester United in 1945 he had to start from scratch with a club which, thanks to wartime bombing, did not even have a ground, the team playing instead at City's Maine Road. Under his genial leadership (he was the first manager to pay a full wage to all his squad, regardless of their age) United won the FA cup in 1948 and the League title in 1952 and became the first English club to play in Europe. Seriously injured in the Munich air disaster (6 Feb 1958) which killed 8 of the 'Busby Babes' on their way home from a 3–3 draw with Red Star Belgrade in the European Cup semi-final, Busby recovered but only the support of his wife Jean and his will to honour the dead gave him the strength to continue as United's manager. He built a new team, including George Best and Denis Law as well as survivors like Bobby Charlton, which in 1968 became the first English side to win the European Cup. Awarded the Freedom of Manchester in 1967 and knighted in 1968, Sir Matt Busby stayed with the club as General Manager until 1971 and as a director for the rest of his life. Criticised for being soft on unruly players like Best, his warm bond with both players and media won him widespread respect, and his spirit of supportive management stays with the club.

BUTE, Island of, Firth of Clyde

Nestled between **Arran** and the Cowal district of **Argyll**, the island of Bute is separated from the Scottish mainland by the Kyles of Bute. Along with Arran, the tiny island of Inchmarnock, and the **Cumbraes**, it made up the former county of Bute, after 1975 was been part of the Argyll & Bute District of Strathclyde Region and since 1995 has been part of the Argyll & Bute Council Area.

The island is 15 miles long and three to five miles wide, and its population is concentrated on the main town, **Rothesay**. A frequent vehicle ferry links Rothesay by a one-hour crossing to **Wemyss Bay** on the **Clyde** coast. A **rail** link allows residents to commute to **Glasgow**. A smaller ferry runs from Rhubodach at the north end of Bute to **Colintraive** in Cowal (five-minute crossing). At one time cattle were swum across the narrows.

Geologically, Bute is interesting, as it sits astride the Highland Boundary Fault, marked by Loch Fad, which almost cuts the island in two. To its north are Dalradian schists, to the south Old Red Sandstone and lava flows. Bute is a low-lying island, but its northern end is more hilly, rising to 913ft (278m) on Windy Hill.

There are several important archaeological and historical sites. The chambered **cairn** at Glenvoidean on the north-west coast was excavated during the 1960s; the pottery is in the fine museum in Rothesay. There are several **standing stones** on the island and stone circles at Ettrick Bay and Kingarth. The Iron Age vitrified fort of Dunagoil, on a promontory at the south end of the island, was excavated at the end of the last century and produced many interesting finds. Nearby is St Blane's chapel, dedicated to the early Christian saint and missionary born on Bute in the 6th century. The surviving ruins date from the 12th century.

Rothesay Castle is one of the finest surviving medieval castles in Scotland, dating from the late 12th century, and was formerly the seat of the Marquises of Bute, but **Mount Stuart** on the east coast south of Rothesay is now the family seat. **Kames Castle** is a 16th century tower house built on foundations as old as the 14th century. It housed the Bannatynes of Kames, Chamberlains to the **Stewart** kings when Bute was a royal demesne. The last of the line died in 1780. His nephew was the advocate **Henry Home**, who became Lord Kames in 1799, a founder member of the Bannatyne Club which published a series of books dealing with Scottish history and literature.

BUTTERFLIES

Of the 60 breeding species of butterfly in Britain today, 36 breed north of the border, of which only one species is confined to Scotland. The chequered skipper (*Carterocephalus palaemon*) – a small brown and orange butterfly less than an inch (25mm) across the wings – became extinct in England in 1976 but still occurs in approximately 40 colonies around the **Fort William** area; it is generally found in rides and glades in **birch** and oak woodland on south-facing slopes. It was not found in Scotland until 1942. The preferred food plant of the caterpillars is purple moor grass, although they have been found on slender false broom. The nectar source for the adults covers a range of plants but the main ones are bugle, bluebell and marsh **thistle**. The butterflies are on the wing in May and June and the males often perch on **bracken** or **bog myrtle** from which they hold territory and dart at any other insects that come their way.

Four other species which have most of their population in Scotland are the mountain ringlet (*Erebia epiphron*), the large heath (*Coenonympha tullia*), the northern brown argus (*Aricia artaxerxes*) and the Scotch Argus (*Erebia aethiops*). The last of these is locally common and the rich brown adults can often be seen along roadside verges; unlike most butterflies the weather does not seem to deter them, and they will carry on flying even in slight rain. The butterfly population of Scotland is, however, undergoing changes; drainage is adversely affecting the colonies of the marsh fritillary (*Euphydryas aurinia*) whilst, in contrast, in the 1980s the speckled wood and orange tip saw an expansion of range in the north and west of the Highlands.

BYRON, George Gordon, 6th Baron (1788–1824) Poet

Byron was named after his grandfather, George Gordon of Gight Castle in **Aberdeenshire** (a descendant of **James I**) to whom he was heir through his mother. She, Catherine of Gight, whose father had committed suicide, had fallen victim (1785) to the fortune-hunting rake Captain John Byron. He soon dissipated her fortune (Gight was sold to the nearby Gordons of **Haddo** in 1786) and fled from his creditors to France. It was an inauspicious background for the future poet, especially as his mother seems to have inherited the mental instability of her father. Her child was exposed to alternating explosions of violent temper and affection. To add to the boy's distress, he was born lame. In 1792 his ears were assailed by his mother's yells of grief when the father he did not know died abroad. Worse still, when he was nine years old, living in **Aberdeen**, he fell into the hands of a devout **Calvinist** nurse who sometimes beat him savagely and at others 'used to come to bed with him and play tricks with his person'. This was not an expression of affection, for he was also introduced to the role of voyeur when 'she brought all sorts of Company of the very lowest Description into his apartments' (so his mother's financial adviser Hanson testified.) When he was ten he became heir to the Byron peerage, and exchanged Aberdeen Grammar School for Harrow. But his Scottish background had left an indelible influence on the thoughts and feelings of the poet who was to wage such a relentless war on hypocrisy and cant.

CABER

From the Gaelic word *cabar*, which means 'pole, rafter, antler', etc, the caber in its borrowed form refers specifically to a tree-trunk which is thrown or tossed as a feat of strength. The aim is not to throw it for the maximum distance but to turn it over so that it lies at 12 o'clock from the line of throw; whoever gets closest to it wins. This is perhaps the most spectacular feat to be witnessed at **Highland Games**.

CABRACH, The, Aberdeenshire

This is an upland plateau, mostly barren moor and **heather**, north of the Ladder Hills between **Lumsden** and **Dufftown**. It has been called the 'Siberia of Scotland' and has not changed much since Edward I crossed it heading south for **Kildrummy** when 'there was no more than iii houses in a rowe between two mountaignes'. The houses were probably beside the upper **Deveron** which rises on the Cabrach.

CADELL, Francis Campbell Boileau (1883–1937) Painter

Along with **Fergusson**, **Hunter** and **Peploe**, Cadell is remembered as one of the Scottish Colourists [see **Painting**], a title earned through their shared admiration for French Post-Impressionist painting and their own assimilation of its characteristically fluid style and vivid palette. Born in **Edinburgh**, the son of a doctor, Cadell's talent received early encouragment. Trained initially at the **Trustees' Academy**, he went to Paris in 1899, on the recommendation of Arthur Melville, to study at the Académie Julien. Though he would have seen first-hand the work of Van Gogh and Cézanne and the bold statements of the Fauves, his first exhibition in Edinburgh on his return in 1908 revealed a quieter, impressionistic influence closer in mood to the Harmonies of Whistler. The brilliance of Venice, however, where he spent the summer of 1910, resulted in freely painted studies, accentuated in full reds and greens that dispel the cooler sensibility of his earlier still-lifes and figure studies. A flamboyant character, Cadell was popular in Edinburgh society and his series of fashionable drawing room portraits recall an earlier debt to Manet. The landscapes inspired by his first visit to **Iona** in 1912 achieve an expressive vigour by their use of high keyed colour that would affect all his subsequent output. He saw active service in the war and afterwards embarked on a further series of interiors – where the figure is often eliminated at the expense of the bold, compositional treatment – and dynamic still-lifes that grow progressively more abstract in their concern for the values of colour and shape. The best of these have an intensity which recalls the achievements of Matisse.

CAERLAVEROCK CASTLE, Nr Dumfries

One of the most convincing castles in Britain, Caerlaverock underwent its first siege at the hands of Edward I of England in 1300. Although Edward's triumph proved short-lived – by 1312 the Maxwells of Caerlaverock were back in residence and would remain so, on and off, for the next 400 years – the siege is especially memorable for a description in French left by one of Edward's chroniclers. In shape the castle, then barely completed, 'was like a shield', he writes, 'for it had but three sides round it, with a tower at each corner, but one of them was a double tower, so high, so long and so wide that the gate was underneath it, well made and strong, with a drawbridge and other defences. And I think you will never see a more finely situated castle . . .'

Most of the building in question was demolished a few years later, yet this description remains true of that which replaced it in the mid-14th century and clearly identifies the still impressive ruin of today. The triangular plan is unique in Scotland; one of the single corner towers (named after **Murdoch Stewart, Duke of Albany**, who was incarcerated in it in 1425) remains intact, as do two of the curtain walls plus the massive double tower which constitutes 'the most impressive gatehouse in Scotland' (M Lindsay); the inner moat is still full of water and the remains of three drawbridges have been dredged from its bottom.

Careful attention to the masonry (and the guidebook) reveals further rebuilding in the late 14th century, extensive additions including the distinctive machicolations in the 15th, and more repairs in the 16th. Meanwhile control of the castle passed from Scots to English and back to Scots, with the Maxwells somehow retaining their tenure. Staunch Catholics, they fared better under the united **Stewart** Crown, and created Earls of Nithsdale, embarked on a final building spree in 1634. The date figures on one of the many finely sculpted window heads which adorn the new creation, a nobly proportioned Renaissance house accommodated within the castle courtyard and known rather disparagingly as the 'Nithsdale Apartments'. Two years after this miniature palace was completed, the castle was invested by the **Covenanters**. It capitulated after a 13-week siege. The Nithsdale was gutted and the castle partially demolished and abandoned, in which state it remains, carefully conserved but strangely unfrequented.

CAIRD, Sir James Key (1837–1916) Textile Manufacturer

Born in **Dundee**, Caird entered his father's **jute** and textile business. It remained a modest operation until he inherited control of the Ashton mill in 1870. In the general boom in the **linen** and jute industries Caird proved highly successful on account of his application of modern machinery at both Ashton and Craigie Mills. Profits also flowed from his wide portfolio of overseas and domestic investments. His name is intimately associated with Dundee, two large donations leading to the creation of the public park and the hall which today still bear his name. Created a baronet in 1913, he left an estate worth almost £1.5 million.

Caerlaverock Castle as drawn by R W Billings in the 1840s (RWB)

CAIRD, John (1820–98) Churchman and Academic

A great preacher, born in **Greenock**, he was educated at **Glasgow University** where he was later Professor of Divinity and finally Principal for 25 years. **Queen Victoria** appointed him a chaplain. He did much to raise the standards of the established Church after the low ebb of the 1843 **Disruption**.

CAIRNBULG, Nr Fraserburgh, Aberdeenshire

Amidst the few trees in sight, Cairnbulg Castle was until recently the home of the **Frasers** of Philorth, who founded **Fraserburgh**, two miles to the north. The lower part of the main tower (rectangular with machicolations and battlements) may date from the 13th century when Cairnbulg belonged to the **Comyn Earls of Buchan**. It was acquired by the Frasers in 1375 who rebuilt the tower and in the 16th century added the extensive adjacent structures including a drum tower. The Frasers sold the castle in 1666 and by the 19th century it was a ruin. Restoration was carried out by Sir John Duthie in 1897 from whose son the Frasers repurchased the castle after Philorth was burnt down in 1915.

Huddled on the foreshore nearby, the villages of Cairnbulg, Inverallochy and St Combs owe their existence to the **herring** fishing and, though now dormitories for Fraserburgh, preserve a strong sense of community. At Christmas or New Year each stages a 'Temperance Walk' when fife and drum lead a procession from village to village ending in a grand finale of fraternal feasting and entertainment. Inspired by the **temperance movement** of the 1850s, these 'walks' are no longer patronised solely by total abstainers; they probably never were.

CAIRNDOW, Argyll

Fronting Loch Fyne near the head of the loch, and so a long way indeed from the open sea, Cairndow (pronounced and sometimes spelled 'Cairndhu') thrives on a mix of sheep, salmon and **oyster** farming. The Gothic Revival church (1816) is octagonal like that at **Dalmally** and blends charmingly with the rest of the village. Nearby the woodland garden of Ardkinglas, a magnificent **Lorimer** creation (1907), has a fine collection of rhododendrons and some massive firs, one of which, an *Abies Grandis*, is reputedly the tallest tree in Britain (210ft/67m).

CAIRNESS HOUSE, Crimond, Nr Fraserburgh, Aberdeenshire

Designed by James Playfair, the father of **William Playfair**, for Charles Gordon of Buthlaw, Cairness House (1791–7) is of a plain classical design with carved cornices and a portico of Ionic pillars. This apparent restraint does not bear close inspection, 'Greek, Roman and Egyptian elements being grouped in striking, if not always harmonious apposition' (J G Dunbar); they include rusticated pavilions and Pharaonic tomb motifs.

CAIRNGORMS, The, Aberdeenshire/ Inverness-shire/Banffshire

Although exceeded by **Ben Nevis**, the Cairngorms are the highest mass of mountains in the Grampians and indeed in Britain. Their extent (c300 sq miles) and elevation, the sub-arctic flora and fauna which they support, and the recreational facilities which they afford are distinctly more exciting than their profiles. Even the four summits over 4000ft (Ben Macdui, 4296ft/1310m and second only to Ben Nevis, Braeriach, 4248ft/1295m, Cairntoul, 4241ft/1293m and Cairngorm, 4048ft/1234m) are literary nonentities compared to **Scott**'s **Trossachs**, **Ben Lawers** or **Schiehallion**. Filling the void between Speyside and **Braemar**, but with outlying spurs extending deep into **Aberdeenshire**, they are more correctly the Monadh Ruadh (red hills) as opposed to the **Monadhliath** (grey hills) between Speyside and the **Great Glen**. The north-west corner, rising to Cairngorm and accessible from **Aviemore**, contains the Glen More Forest Park (12,500 acres/5059ha round Loch Morlich) plus the more organised facilities, access directions and **ski** slopes. The southern half, including the **Dee**'s catchment area, comprises the Cairngorm Nature Reserve, the largest in Britain, and is as readily explored from Braemar. **Ptarmigan**, dotterel, **eagles** and **mountain hares** may be seen on the higher ground; the flora includes numerous species found practically nowhere else in Britain. Another rarity is the Cairngorm stone, a smokey yellowish or reddish rock-crystal much favoured for ornamenting dirks, sporrans and brooches.

CAIRNHOLY CHAMBERED CAIRNS, Kirkcudbrightshire

Between **Gatehouse of Fleet** and **Creetown**, a side road leads up the wooded glen of the Kirkdale Burn to the site of these two neolithic **Clyde** or Carlingford chambered **cairns**. The better preserved Cairnholy I (also called 'King Galdus's Tomb') covers an area of about 170 x 50ft (52 x 15m), has a striking crescent-shaped façade of upright slabs with dry-stone walling between and a single chamber; Cairnholy II is smaller, 70 x 40ft (21 x 12m), but with a double chamber. On excavation in 1949 both yielded shards of beaker pottery, fragments of ceremonial weapons and arrowheads.

CAIRNPAPPLE HILL, West Lothian

A mile to the south-east of **Torpichen**, Cairnpapple Hill is one of the most important archaeological sites in Scotland, representing as it does five distinct periods covering as much as 3000 years from c2800 BC. As a central and easily accessible site, it has been thoroughly excavated (particularly by Stuart Piggott in the 1940s) and described (by every writer on Scottish archaeology). The physical evidence, however, would not be easily interpreted by the layman were it not for the provision of a clearly labelled model and accompanying commentary thoughtfully provided by the custodians, **Historic Scotland**. In brief, the five stages are (i) a small cemetery consisting of seven small pits in an arc with an attendant setting of upright stones (sockets only remain); (ii) a henge monument, an 'egg-shaped' stone circle (sockets only) and two small burial pits containing beaker ware; (iii) a large **cairn** some 50ft (15m) in diameter built above two Bronze Age cist burials and using some of the stones from the earlier circle; (iv) an extension of the former cairn to cover two burials in pottery cinerary urns, and (v) four further burials of, as yet, uncertain date. The scattered stones of the cairn have been reassembled into a smaller cairn which provides probably the best point from which to see both the site and the view from Cairnpapple Hill which, on a clear day, can include such far-flung points as Goatfell on **Arran** and **Schiehallion** in the **Trossachs**.

For further reading on the archaeological significance of Cairnpapple Hill see Stuart Piggott's 'The Excavations at Cairnpapple Hill, West Lothian, 1947–8' in *Proceedings of the Society of Antiquaries of Scotland*, Vol 82 and Graham and Anna Ritchie's *Scotland, Archaeology and Early History*, 1981.

CAIRNRYAN, Wigtownshire

Cairnryan, previously called Macherie, on the east shore of Loch Ryan was a tranquil **fishing** village until the start of World War II. In 1941, however, it became the site of a secret military port and naval base for troopships, flying boats, and the construction of components for the 'Mulberry Harbour' used in the 1944 Normandy landings. It later became the European Ferries terminal for the car ferry to Larne in Northern Ireland. Just north of Cairnryan Lochryan House, built in 1701 by Colonel Agnew of Croach, has a high central block with battlemented parapet rising through the hipped roofs of the wings – a most unusual design which 'can be regarded either as a last assertion of the tower-house form or as an anticipation of romanticism' (J G Dunbar).

CAIRNS

Cairns and barrows are found in most parts of Scotland and once served a variety of purposes. Some are simply

Chambered 'Bargrennan' cairn at Cairnholy, Kirkcudbrightshire (HS)

accumulations of stones cleared from adjacent land to make it suitable for arable purposes. Others may represent boundary or route markers; some, in association with recumbent or **standing stones**, timber or earth henge arrangements, may have had some prehistoric astronomical purpose; but the oldest and most interesting are those associated with a funerary function and containing one or more chambers or galleries with or without an access passage. Externally such chambered tombs may appear as long, round, oval, horned or horseshoe cairns. Many appear to have been altered over a long period of use and dating is problematic; they are now thought to span a period from the 4th millennium

BC to the 1st. More depositories than graves, they may contain the bones of numerous burials plus an assortment of grave goods, pottery shards and talismans accumulated over centuries of intermittent use. Based on their design and distribution four main groups may be distinguished: **Clyde** or Carlingford tombs found in **Arran**, **Galloway** and south **Argyll** have usually rectangular chambers composed of massive slabs; Bargrennan tombs, named after that at Bargrennan in **Wigtownshire**, are similar but small and restricted to this part of the country; **Clava** cairns are also restricted to a small area (round **Inverness**) and are circular with passages connecting to a circular chamber; the largest group is that of **Orkney**, **Shetland**, **Cromarty**, **Caithness** and the **Hebrides** where considerable variation is found on the passage-tomb principle, the most notable examples being the massive oval cairn of **Camster** and the elaborate chambered tomb of **Maes Howe**. The chamber-less ring cairns of mainly **Aberdeenshire** and **Kincardineshire** are thought to be developments of the Clava type where ring cairns are found in association with the chambered tombs. Chamber-less round cairns of the Bronze Age, sometimes with kerb stones or standing stones, are widely distributed and often contained burial cists.

CAITHNESS

Caithness forms the extreme north-east of the Scottish mainland, totalling 444,216 acres (179,772ha). The county is fringed by the Pentland Firth to the north, North Sea to the east and Moray Firth to the south-east, with a coastline totalling 105 miles. **Sutherland** forms the county's western border. With its undulating topography, no more than 2313ft (705m) at its highest point (**Morven**), Caithness is closer to **Berwickshire** in physical character than to a 'Highland' county. It was brought under the control of the Scottish Crown in 1196 by **William the Lion**, although enfiefed to the Norse earls of **Orkney** until 1231.

The basic occupations of **agriculture** and **fishing**, along with the nuclear installation built at **Dounreay** in 1955, have not helped stabilise the population. In 1991 this was 26,370, down from 41,111 just over a century previously. **Wick** was the county town, with **Thurso**, marginally larger, the only other burgh. In 1975 Caithness was swallowed up by Highland Region, the Caithness District being centred on Wick – since the 1995 reorganisation of **local government** it has remained part of the Highland Council Area.

CAITHNESS, Earldom of

The mainland pendicle of the Norse Earldom of **Orkney** was erected into a Scottish earldom in the Middle Ages. After the entire property had passed to **Henry Sinclair** in 1379 through an heiress, the King of Denmark-Norway pledged his Crown rights there to **James III** (1468) as security for the dowry of his daughter Margaret. James bought the Sinclairs out of their own rights in Orkney, leaving them Earls of **Caithness**. The **Gordons**, having seized the **Earldom of Sutherland** early in the 16th century, also made a determined attempt to expropriate the Sinclairs. But their tergiversations during the rebellion against **Charles I** helped to deprive them of the prize, and while they were still

under a cloud after the **Restoration**, **John Campbell of Glenorchy** made an attempt to fill the vacuum. He bought up the debts of the 6th Earl of Caithness, on whose death he made 'gross and fraudulent misrepresentations' in 1676, trying to pass himself off as the new earl. He fared no better than the Gordons had done, save that in 1677 he was consoled with the Earldom of **Breadalbane**. The Sinclairs remain earls of Caithness to this day.

CALEDONIA

Tacitus used this term to comprehend all the country north of the Forth-**Clyde** isthmus, while Ptolemy defined the Caledonians as a tribe whose territory extended from **Argyll** to the Moray Firth. They may have been the dominant element in a confederacy. Since the word is apparently pre-Celtic, it suggests that this region was still occupied predominantly by an aboriginal population, among whom the Indo-Aryan **Celts** had been establishing themselves for centuries before Ptolemy's time. In 297 Eumenius first applied the term 'Picti' to these people, and in 310 there is mention of 'Caledonians and other **Picts**'. Professor Kenneth Jackson demonstrated that their languages included an archaic form of the **Celtic** family of **languages** as well as the indecipherable pre-Celtic tongue preserved in the ogam inscriptions. After Caledonia had been transformed into **Alba** by the takeover of **Kenneth mac-Alpin**, a corrupt form of the word survived among the Gaelic speakers, in the mountain name of **Schiehallion** and the place-name **Dunkeld**. In recent times the ancient name of Caledonia has passed into romantic poetry as a synonym for Scotland.

CALEDONIAN FOREST

The old 'wildwood' of Britain once covered much of the landscape and in the north it was dominated by **Scots pine**, the main tree species in the 'Great Wood of Caledon' which covered most of the Highlands. On the warmer south-facing slopes these ancient forests also included oakwoods, **birch**woods, and in the wetter areas, alderwoods. The forest was not continuous as it was interspersed with mosaic patches of river, loch, cliff, hilltop and bog. Now the only fragments of Britain's primeval wilderness live on in northern Scotland where they support a wealth of rare wildlife, such as **crested tit**, **capercaillie**, Scottish **crossbill**, **pine marten** and **wildcat**. The old 'granny' pines are up to 300 years old, and most of the remaining stands are protected either by grant schemes or under legislation which has designated them **National Nature Reserves** or Sites of Special Scientific Interest. The main problem of management is to encourage active regeneration, and often the only way to do this is to exclude stock and fence out or cull **red deer**.

CALLANDER, Perthshire

A thriving little town and one of rather many 'Gateways to the Highlands', Callander owes its existence to the Commissioners for Forfeited [**Jacobite**] Estates who selected this site on the forfeited Drummond lands for 18th century development. Its 19th century popularity came courtesy of **Scott**'s *Lady of the Lake*, the now defunct **railway**, and the Victorian love of spas. Like **Crieff**,

Callander had its hydro and in the 1890s there were six coaches a day plying between the town and the **Trossachs**. Further celebrity came in the 1960s and 70s when the town featured as Tannochbrae in the long-running television series of *Dr Finlay's Casebook*. Within easy walking distance are the Bracklinn and Leny Falls, Ben Ledi and the long embankment of a '**Roman** Camp' supposed to be **Agricola**'s. 'Druidical' practices were reported in Callander parish in the early 19th century. They took place on May Day – Baal-tein (or Beltain) – and All Saints' Eve and involved bonfires, 'a sort of custard', and a drawing of lots. He who drew the blackened oatcake 'was the victim to be sacrificed to Baal'.

CALLANISH, Lewis, Outer Hebrides

The concentration of Bronze Age archaeological remains around the shores of Loch Roag on the west coast of **Lewis** suggests a regional centre of considerable significance in the 2nd millennium BC. More than 20 sites have been recorded, mainly stone circles and **standing stones**. But beyond doubt the finest monument and the centre of this ritual landscape is the site at Callanish (or sometimes 'Calanais') itself, with a circle of 13 standing stones surrounding a tall central monolith 4.75m high. A double line or 'avenue' of stones to the north, and single lines of stones to the east, west and south of the central circle, give the site a cruciform appearance.

The enigmatic stones of Callanish (HS)

Most of the stones are slabs of Lewisian gneiss. The natural grain of this rock gives the stones an ancient and eerie appearance, especially at dusk. The lower parts of the stones are paler because until 1857 they were partially covered by about 5ft (1.5m) of **peat**, which had accumulated since the stones went out of use at the end of the Bronze Age, about 1200 BC.

The interpretation of Callanish is a matter of continuing controversy, centring largely on the possibility of its use as an astronomical 'observatory', marking important events in the movements of the sun, moon and stars. The argument has become largely statistical and is difficult to prove or disprove by excavation. Detailed survey work by local amateurs and by the **Edinburgh University** Archaeological Research Department has laid the groundwork for future studies.

CALTON WEAVERS

The coming of the Industrial Revolution to Scotland intensified conflict between masters and men as social relationships were transformed. The most notable strike and challenge to the authorities was by the Calton Weavers of **Glasgow** in 1787. This suburb of Glasgow was given over mainly to handloom **cotton** weaving and the trouble started when the employers refused to raise workers' wages. On 4 September 1787 the weavers gathered in protest and, joined by their families, went from house to house wrecking looms and throwing the cut webs into the street. The city's Lord Provost, Sheriff and magistrates were called to the scene by the

employers, but were stoned by the crowd, now some 7000 strong, whereupon they in turn summoned the military. When they too were stoned by the rioters, the magistrates read the Riot Act and the soldiers were ordered to fire. Three rioters died immediately, three others died later of their wounds, and many were seriously hurt.

CALVINISM

Scotland has been dubbed a Calvinist country based on its Protestant church-centred image. However for Calvinists the Bible, not the Church, was central to thought and action. As the Word of God it was the sole authority in faith and practice. Calvinism had spread from Switzerland to France and Holland to flourish in Scotland via the reforms of **Knox** and **Melville**. In Germany and England Luther had more influence and lasting effect.

John Calvin was a French biblical scholar and theologian, born in 1509, whose mission was to restore the Church to purity. In Geneva his *Institutes of the Christian Religion* were applied to make the state subject to reformed Church rule in a theocracy dominated by Calvin himself as unopposed dictator. Doctrines of vocation, hard work and moderation developed away from Luther towards predestination and a system of Church courts now identified with **Presbyterians**. Later influences enabled the political principles of democracy, organisation for freedom and the work ethic of capitalism to take root in Europe.

Concentration on The Word in Calvinist worship resulted in their chapels becoming preaching boxes with central pulpits. Metrical psalms, translated by Calvin and others, replaced music, which was proscribed. Congregations of Presbyterians participated in a conservative and severe form of worship without the hymns of Lutherans and Methodists or the chants of Anglicans. Strict moral teaching and a harder theological line, particularly predestination, became ingrown and defensive so that Calvinists were equated with an authoritarian and joyless Christianity in the popular mind.

CAMBUSKENNETH ABBEY, Stirling

About a mile south of **Abbey Craig**, Cambuskenneth may recall a **Kenneth mac-Alpin** victory over the **Picts** (also known as the Battle of Logie). In c1147 **David I** chose the site for an Augustinian abbey whose proximity to **Stirling Castle** ensured both endowments and historical prominence. Edward I visited in 1303–4, **Robert I**'s 1326 Parliament met here to acknowledge **David (II)** as his heir, and in the 15th century **James III** and his Queen, Margaret of Denmark, were buried here. (Coffins disinterred in 1865 were presumed to be theirs and were reburied at **Queen Victoria**'s expense.) At the **Reformation** the lands passed to the Erskine Governor of Stirling Castle, some of the abbey's stone being used in the construction of **John Erskine of Mar's Work** [see **Stirling**] fronting the castle. Today only foundations of the abbey remain plus a gateway and the great campanile, restored 1864 and the only surviving example from medieval Scotland of a free-standing belfry. Its date may be late 13th or early 14th century, the plan square with lofty ground-floor vaulting and pointed double windows at bell-level.

Belfry tower of Cambuskenneth Abbey (RWB)

CAMBUSLANG REVIVAL

This evangelical outburst of tent meetings and outdoor preachings at Cambuslang and **Kilsyth** in 1742 was called 'The Awakening' within the established Church. A predominantly **Lanarkshire** phenomenon under Rev William McCulloch and Rev John Robe, it attracted Wesley's associate George Whitfield to assist; but it was short-lived.

CAMERON, Clan

Whilst numerically not one of the larger **clans**, Clan Cameron has a proud and romantic history and is especially noted for its unwavering loyalty to the **Stewart** kings. With the rallying cry 'Sons of the hounds come hither and get flesh', it is not surprising that General Wolfe, giving an account of the **Battle of Culloden**, states that the Camerons were 'the bravest clan among them'. There are a number of theories as to the origins of the clan, whose first authenticated chief (but styled XI) is Donald Dubh (c1400–60), whose name is the patronymic of Lochiel – MacDomhnuill Dubh (son of dark-haired Donald). Cam-shron, according to Celtic genealogical theory, is a descriptive adjective meaning 'crooked nose', and this description (applicable to one of the early chiefs) was, after the manner of the Gael, passed on to his descendants. It is probable that Donald Dubh was the leader of a confederation of tribes including MacMartins, Macgillonies and MacSorlies, although others suggest that the Camerons were descended from a family which flourished in **Fife** (Sir John de Cambrun signed the Declaration of Independence in 1320) or from a sister of Banquo, or even from the Kings of Denmark.

During the 15th and 16th centuries and without

Crown Charters for their lands, the chiefs of Clan Cameron required all their wits to maintain the clan's autonomy in the face of the expanding power of **Argyll** and **Huntly**. At the same time a vicious feud over land ownership developed with **Clan Chattan**, of whom Mackintosh was chief – it was one of the longest and bloodiest feuds in Highland history, lasting over 300 years.

Clan Cameron was well served by its early chiefs. Donald Dubh's son, Alan nan Creach, was said to have made '32 expeditions into his enemy's country for the 32 years that he lived and 3 more for the three-quarters of a year that he was in his mother's womb'. His son was the first chief to be known as Lochiel. Clan Cameron was now the dominant clan in **Lochaber** and by the early 17th century (and despite the turbulence caused by the power of Huntly and Argyll) maintained its grip on the clan lands which are still today in the hands of the chief.

Sir Ewen Dubh, 18th Chief, born in 1629, was one of the greatest of Highland chiefs. His prime concern throughout his 70 years as chief was to maintain the individuality and independence of his clan. Continuing the tradition of his grandfather, who had risen for **Montrose** and **Charles I**, Ewen supported the Stewart kings. He fought a guerrilla campaign against Cromwell's occupying forces, supported **Charles II** and rallied behind **John Graham of Claverhouse**, 'Bonnie Dundee', at **Killiecrankie**.

With the strong **Jacobite** tradition of the clan, it was natural that **Prince Charles Edward Stewart** expected Lochiel and his clan to support him when he landed in Scotland in 1745. In the 1715 rising, the clan had fought for the Stewart cause under John, the XVIII chief, who having been exiled subsequently made over the estate to his son **Donald**, later the XIX chief and known as 'the Gentle Lochiel'. After his distinguished part in the '45 he escaped to France with Prince Charles, but his brother, Alexander, Jesuit chaplain to the Young Pretender, was captured after Culloden and died in a prison hulk on the Thames. Another brother, Archibald, was a doctor and an ADC to the Prince. He escaped to France but returned to Scotland, was betrayed and executed in 1753, the last man to die for the Jacobite cause.

In 1784 the General Act of Indemnity was passed and the XXII chief was able to buy back his forfeited estates. Clansmen looked forward to his coming and to the return of the old ways, but 40 years had passed and times had changed. The Gentle Lochiel had left Lochaber as the father and protector of his people; his grandson returned as a landlord. Clan Cameron in its old form had ceased to exist and clansfolk were scattered far and wide. However, clan loyalties and traditions were given a new life when the Clan Association was formed in 1889. There are now branches of the Association in nearly all the countries where Camerons are found.

The Camerons have continued to be well served by their chiefs. Donald XXIV was a Member of Parliament and also Lord Lieutenant for **Inverness-shire** and both his son and grandson (the present chief) were created **Knights of the Thistle** and Lord Lieutenants of Inverness-shire.

The clan's armorial bearings are gules (red), three bars or (gold). Until 1745 the crest was an arm holding a sword with the motto *Pro Rege et Patria*. Another crest then emerged, five arrows with the motto *Unite*. The present Lochiel uses both with mottos in the Gaelic form. The plant badge of the Camerons is the oak. There are four **tartans** associated with the clan: Cameron of Lochiel (the personal tartan of the chief and his immediate family), Clan Cameron, Hunting Cameron and Cameron of Erracht. This last was devised for the 79th **Queen's Own Cameron Highlanders**, a regiment which was raised by Alan Cameron of Erracht in 1793.

CAMERON, Sir David Young (1865–1945)
Landscape Painter and Etcher

Best remembered as a landcape painter, D Y Cameron was also a leading figure, along with fellow Scots

Sir David Young Cameron, by A K Lawrence (SNPG)

McBey, **Bone** and Strang, in the early 20th century British etching revival. Born in **Glasgow** into a strongly **Presbyterian** family, it was not until 1884 that he forsook more traditional employment for full-time art studies at the Royal Institution in **Edinburgh**. He took up etching soon after and, influenced by Rembrandt, Whistler and Meryon, produced sets of landscape views at home (**Paisley** 1887, the **Clyde** 1889, London 1899) and abroad (North Holland 1896, Paris 1904, Belgium 1907). His increasingly sophisticated technique (deep burnishings, dramatic highlights) found ready expression in architectural subjects and the landscape of the central Highlands (his home from 1900). Much sought after, his etchings regularly made record prices when sold at auction. In parallel Cameron evolved a distinctive painting technique, rich saturated colours of late afternoon or early morning, applied to enclosed street scenes and, latterly, depopulated, expansive Scottish landscapes. These dominated his work from his period as war artist for the Canadian government in 1917 until his death. He exhibited regularly at the **Royal**

Scottish Academy and the **Royal Glasgow Institute** and his reputation as a painter superseded that as etcher. In his later years he devoted himself to the landscape and to his Church, finding beauty and God in both.

CAMERON, Donald, Younger of Lochiel (1695–1748)

Exiled in France and attainted for his part in the 1715 **Jacobite Rising**, John Cameron of Lochiel, 18th Chief of **Clan Cameron**, subsequently made over his estate to his son Donald, known as 'the Gentle Lochiel'. A farsighted man concerned with the improvement of his land and the welfare of his clan, Donald had no hope that the '45 Rising would succeed and was appalled to hear of **Prince Charles Edward**'s landing with only seven supporters and without French arms or money. Reluctant to commit his clan to war, he nevertheless agreed to meet the Prince and was so captivated by him that he exclaimed 'I shall share the fate of my prince and so shall every man over whom nature or fortune has given me any power.' He fought at the head of his clan throughout, leading the charge on the gates of **Edinburgh** in September 1745, and on their return northwards personally intervening to prevent the Highlanders from sacking **Glasgow** for that city's lack of support for the Prince. He was seriously wounded at **Culloden** and made his way back to **Lochaber** where he saw the Cameron lands laid waste and his house at **Achnacarry** burnt to the ground. In September 1746 he escaped with Prince Charles to France where he died two years later.

CAMERON OF CORRIECHOILLE, John (1780–1856) Drover

Born at **Spean Bridge**, Cameron (or 'Corry') began his **droving** career as a barefoot drover's lad. Saving his wages he bought the odd bullock, rented Corriechoille (**Roy Bridge**) off **Cameron of Lochiel**, and soon became a drover in his own right. He leased more farms and is said to have been able to feed sheep and cattle on his own grazings all the way from **Skye** to **Falkirk**. He thus acquired a virtual monopoly of this important **drove road**. By the 1840s he was reckoned the greatest lease-holder in Scotland and his combined flocks and herds represented the largest holding of livestock in Britain. Numerous anecdotes recall his phenomenal energy, his deceptively scruffy appearance and his canny dealing. One of rather few to acquire a fortune in the Highlands, he eventually joined the massed ranks of the many who have there lost a fortune. No longer a rich man, he died still scouring the country on his wiry little pony at the age of 75. In 50 years he never once missed the three October sales at the Falkirk tryst.

CAMERON, Richard (1648–1680)
Covenanter

Born at **Falkland**, **Fife**, the son of a merchant, Cameron was educated at **St Andrews University** and became precentor and schoolmaster in Falkland under its Episcopal curate. Converted by field preachers, he became one of the most zealous of **Covenanters**, condemning those ministers who accepted the **Indulgences** and being hustled off to Holland in 1678 to learn 'to hold in check the ardencies of his heart and tongue' which threatened

to discredit the Covenanting cause. Ordained in Rotterdam in 1679, he returned to Scotland as inflexible as ever, gathered together an extremist 'army' – the **Cameronians** – and in June 1680 published the **Declaration of Sanquhar**. Fleeing to the hills, he evaded capture for just a month; on 22 July a troop of dragoons under Bruce of Earlshall came across Cameron and his bodyguard of 40 foot and 20 horse at **Airds Moss** (or Ayrsmoss) near **Auchinleck**. After a brave fight, Cameron and his brother Michael, together with nine of their followers, were killed. The head and hands of 'the Lion of the Covenant', were cut off, taken to **Edinburgh** and presented to the Privy Council who ordered them to be displayed at the **Netherbow**.

CAMERONIANS, The (Scottish Rifles)

The regiment derives from the 1881 amalgamation of the 26th (Cameronians) and the 90th (Perthshire Volunteers) Light Infantry which also brought into the regimental ranks the two battalions of the 2nd Royal Lanarkshire Militia and several of the Lanarkshire Volunteer Battalions. The 26th were raised in 1689 by the Earl of Angus from devout **Covenanter** followers of **Richard Cameron**. Still not fully trained, they greatly distinguished themselves by their action at **Dunkeld** against the **Jacobite** victors of **Killiecrankie** in 1689. Subsequent service included the Low Countries, Blenheim, Oudenarde, Ramillies and Malplaquet, the American War of Independence, Corunna and Abyssinia. The 90th were raised in 1794 by **Thomas Graham**, later Lord Lynedoch. They saw service in Minorca, Egypt, the West Indies, the Crimea, the Indian Mutiny and in South Africa, receiving the coveted status of Light Infantry in 1815.

27 battalions of Cameronians served in World War I in Macedonia, Gallipoli, Egypt, Palestine and on the Western Front, winning 63 battle honours. In World War II, the regiment won a further 35 honours, fighting in France in 1940, Sicily, Italy, north-west Europe and Burma where they gained the honour 'Chindits 1944', thus bringing the grand total of battle honours to 113. Post-war active service included Malaya and Aden.

Both the 26th and the 90th had worn ordinary line uniform until 1881 when they were clad in **tartan** trews; originally Government sett, **Douglas** tartan was subsequently adopted. As a Rifle Regiment, black buttons were always worn and the regiment moved at Rifle pace. March past was 'Kenmure's On and Awa'' (pipes) and 'Within a Mile o' Edinburgh Toun' (band). The regiment recruited from **Lanarkshire** and the regimental headquarters were at **Hamilton**. The Cameronians were remarkable for the number of Generals they produced and for the fact that, in memory of their conventicle-protecting days, they were the only regiment permitted to bear arms in church.

In 1959 the regiment chose disbandment rather than amalgamation and a proud saga came to an end. Today the only wearers of the uniform are some members of the 52nd Lowland Volunteers and Army Cadets in Lanarkshire.

CAMPBELL, Angus (Aonghas Caimbeul) (1903–82) Gaelic Writer

Known as *Am Puilean*, Campbell was born in Ness, **Lewis**, and lived for some years in Bernera, **Harris** and **Glas-**

gow. He did his regular army service in India and was a prisoner of war in Poland, returning to Ness after World War II. An interesting and entertaining autobiography *A' Suathadh ri Iomadh Rubha* ('Touching Many Headlands', 1973) brings alive his youthful experiences and his years of captivity. A collection of his poetry, *Moll is Cruithneachd* ('Chaff and Wheat', 1972) is rather more traditional in style, with poems about his Polish prison years providing a vital interlude.

CAMPBELL, Archibald, 5th Earl of Argyll (c1530–73)

Elder son of Archibald, 4th Earl of Argyll by his first wife, Lady Helen Hamilton, daughter of the 1st Earl of Arran, he was sworn a Privy Councillor by **Queen Mary** on her arrival in Scotland in 1561, and although at first opposed to her, became a favourite and supporter of the Queen. He led her army at the **Battle of Langside** in 1568 where unfortunately he fell in a swoon as battle was about to commence. Appointed one of the three Queen's Lieutenants in Scotland in 1570, he was a candidate for the Regency in 1571, which, however, went to the **Earl of Mar**. In 1572 he became Lord High Chancellor of Scotland.

The Earl was married twice, his first wife being the Queen's half-sister Lady Jean Stewart; they were divorced in June 1573 and a few weeks later he married Lady Jane Cunningham, daughter of the 5th Earl of Glencairn. He had no children by either marriage and was succeeded by his brother Colin as 6th Earl.

CAMPBELL, Archibald, 7th Earl of Argyll (1575–1638)

The elder son of Colin, 6th Earl of Argyll, and his second wife Agnes Keith, the 7th Earl succeeded in 1584. Along with his brother Colin, he was the eventual target of the plot led by **Huntly** and Campbell of Glenorchy to assassinate James Stewart, the 'Bonnie Earl of **Moray**', and Campbell of **Cawdor** in 1592. Possibly as a result, he later pursued his foes, notably the **Clans Gregor** and **Donald**, with a ruthless ferocity which earned him the by-name of 'Gillespie Gruamach' – 'Archie the Grim'.

Extensively used to further royal policy, his relationship with **James VI** was equivocal. Failure by the King to prosecute the 1592 plotters allowed them to poison the Earl and his brother who were lucky to survive. On hearing the news of the Earl's defeat by Huntly in 1594 at **Glenlivet**, James is said to have exclaimed 'Fair fa' ye, Geordie Gordon, for sending him back looking sae like a subject!' Campbell is supposed to have engineered the massacre of the Colquhouns at **Glen Fruin** in 1603 to his own ultimate advantage and was granted the rich lands of **Kintyre** in 1607 following their forfeiture by the **MacDonalds** of **Islay** whose later rebellion of 1615 he comprehensively suppressed.

But he fell from grace when, after his conversion to Rome by his second wife, he went to the Low Countries and entered Spanish service. Ordered to return, he failed to do so and was declared traitor in 1618. He finally returned to London and lived out his days in obscurity.

CAMPBELL, Archibald, 8th Earl and Marquis of Argyll (1607–61)

Son of **Archibald, 7th Earl** and of his first wife, Lady Agnes Douglas, daughter of the 8th Earl of Morton,

Archibald Campbell, 8th Earl and only Marquis of Argyll, by David Scougall (SNPG)

Argyll's 8th Earl was educated at **St Andrews**. His first exploit in Crown service led to the dispersal of the MacIans of **Ardnamurchan** in 1625. A Privy Councillor in 1628, he resigned to the King the family's hereditary post of Lord Justice-General the same year, keeping however that of Justiciar of **Argyll** and the Isles. As an Extraordinary Lord of Session in 1638, he signed the **Covenant**. The discovery of a plot to seize his lands of **Kintyre** by the Antrim MacDonells turned him against the King.

Thereafter his loyalties fluctuated as he tried to reconcile his strong religious views with a basic wish to support the monarch. Created Marquis (1641), he raised a regiment for service in Ireland in 1642 and led various forces against the King's adherents, notably those of **Alasdair MacColla (MacDonald)**, **Montrose**'s major-general, who in 1645 brought a motley crew of Irish **MacDonalds** to harry and burn the Campbells in Argyll. A famous countermarch through the mountains brought the Royalist army down on Argyll's troops at **Inverlochy** where **Clan Campbell** sustained the biggest defeat in its history, Argyll fleeing in his galley. His revenge came soon with the defeat and capture of Montrose, and Argyll had the satisfaction of watching his enemy's journey to the scaffold.

He was instrumental in bringing **Charles II** to Scotland in 1650 and placed the crown on the King's head

133

at the coronation ceremony of 1651. Promised a dukedom for his services, only his wife's illness prevented him from taking part in the defeat at Worcester. On Cromwell's take-over of the country he was taken under arrest to **Edinburgh** where he was induced to sign an oath to live peaceably under the new regime, in due course becoming MP for **Aberdeen**.

At the return of the King, Argyll went to London to greet him but was immediately thrown in the Tower. Taken back to Scotland, he was incarcerated in **Edinburgh Castle** when his trial took place. The charges against him were dubious but political considerations won the day and he was condemned to death. He met his fate with a fortitude that negated any previous charge of pusillanimity and was executed at the Cross of Edinburgh on 27 May 1661. His head was displayed on top of the **Tolbooth** where it displaced that of his old enemy Montrose.

CAMPBELL, Archibald, 9th Earl of Argyll (1629–85)

Unlike his father, the **8th Earl and Marquis of Argyll**, the 9th Earl was a consistently loyal supporter of the

Archibald Campbell, 9th Earl of Argyll, possibly by L Schuneman (SNPG)

Royalist cause, fighting as Colonel of the Scots Foot Guards both at **Dunbar** in 1650 and at Worcester in 1651. He joined the Earl of Glencairn's Rising with a Lieutenant-General's commission but later submitted to Cromwell. In favour at the Restoration, his efforts on behalf of his father annoyed the Scots Parliament to the extent that they succeeded in having him imprisoned under sentence of death, which sentence was delayed by royal command. Released in 1663, his lands and title (but not the Marquisate) were restored.

Refusing to sign the **Test Act**, he was condemned to death for treason in 1681 but escaped from **Edinburgh Castle** disguised as his stepdaughter's serving maid and

eventually got away to Holland. In 1685 he returned at the head of an invasion of Scotland designed to restore the Protestant religion; his attempt, like that of the **Duke of Monmouth**'s simultaneous landing in England, failed after an abortive campaign and the Earl was captured and then executed. His courage during his last, short captivity and at his death has long been remembered.

CAMPBELL, Archibald, 10th Earl and 1st Duke of Argyll (c1658–1703)

The eldest son of the **9th Earl** and Lady Mary Stewart, daughter of the 5th Earl of Moray, he did not support his father's rebellion in 1685. One of two Commissioners who offered the Scottish Crown to William and Mary, in 1689 he raised the regiment of the British Army which was employed for the **Massacre of Glencoe**. Appointed a Privy Councillor the same year, he was much trusted by King William who in 1701 conferred on him the Dukedom of Argyll together with a string of subsidiary titles.

He married in 1678 Lady Elizabeth Tollemache from whom he subsequently separated; by her he had two sons who succeeded him as **2nd** and **3rd Dukes** and two daughters. A noted philanderer, he has been credited with the invention of the condom.

CAMPBELL, Archibald, 1st Earl of Islay and 3rd Duke of Argyll (1682–1761) Lawyer and Politician

The second son of **Archibald, 1st Duke of Argyll**, he succeeded his brother **John, 2nd Duke**, in 1743. Originally bred to the **law**, he became a soldier of distinction, serving with gallantry under Marlborough, becoming Colonel of the 36th Foot and Governor of **Dumbarton Castle** before retiring while still in his early twenties. He was a major force in the creation of the **Union** and was awarded with a peerage (1706) as Earl of Islay.

Appointed Lord Justice-General for life in 1710 and to the Privy Council the following year, he became Lord Clerk Register in 1714 and, joining his brother shortly before the **Battle of Sheriffmuir**, was twice wounded. From the mid-1720s, as Walpole's and later Newcastle's ally, he organised and led the Argyll (or 'Argathelian') interest which dominated Scottish politics. 'An amateur inventor of gimcracks in mathematics whose most notable invention was the tight system of management which turned the Scottish electorate into one grand ministerial preserve' (W Ferguson), Campbell and his subordinates (including **Duncan Forbes of Culloden**) dispensed patronage on a grand and unscrupulous scale that effectively muffled all debate.

He also commenced the building of **Inveraray Castle** which was not, however, completed in his lifetime. He died childless and the earlier titles passed to his first cousin Colonel John Campbell of Mamore who became the 4th Duke. His political influence eventually passed to **Henry Dundas**.

CAMPBELL, Clan

If not perhaps the most popular Highland clan, the Campbells are undoubtedly one of the most successful. Even those who do not like them fear, envy and respect them. Possibly they were no worse than their neighbours, only more effective.

The fashion in pedigrees has changed from time to time, and with it origins for the Campbells have been ascribed to Norman, **Dalriadic** and Ancient British roots. The last would seem the correct version although a claimed descent from King Arthur merely betrays the inability of early genealogists to be more specific than indicating that the Campbells originated from the Kingdom of **Strathclyde** and were of high rank. The former name for the Campbells was 'Clann O'Dhuine' from an early ancestor of that name. Duine's son was one Diarmid and from that fact an unjustifiable descent was claimed from the mythical Fingalian hero of the same name [see **Finn mac Cumhal**]. Hence the popular adoption of the style 'Clan Diarmid' for the Campbells, whose surname is a translation of 'crooked mouth', derived from another ancestor marked by that peculiarity.

First of the name on written record is Gillespie who was granted lands in **Menstrie** in 1263. But several generations previously the clan had become established in **Argyll** through marriage with an heiress on Lochaweside, and it was this area that became their base.

Initially the family was subordinate to the great local dynasties of the MacDougall Lords of **Lorne** and the **MacDonald Lords of the Isles**. Sir Colin Campbell was killed in a skirmish with the former in 1294, a cairn still marking the spot where he fell. From him subsequent chiefs of the clan took their chiefly title of *MacCailein Mor* – 'Son of Great Colin' – which is held by the **Duke of Argyll** today.

The family's support for **Robert I** brought them much land and gave them the powerbase on which to grow, initially at the expense of the MacDougalls and then of the MacDonalds whose chiefs, Lords of the Isles, continued to regard themselves as quasi-monarchs independent of the Scottish Crown which in turn used the Campbells to bring this threat under control.

Rewards were substantial and the rise of Campbell power was soon inexorable. A marriage with the heiress of Loudoun brought rich lands in **Ayrshire** and the establishment of a flourishing branch of the clan. The Glenorchy Campbells expanded eastward into **Perthshire** at the expense of all who stood in the way. Another marriage, this time with the heiress of **Cawdor**, established yet another branch of Campbells in the north-east.

In the mid-15th century the Campbell chiefs moved their headquarters from Innischonnell on **Loch Awe** to the salt waters of Loch Fyne at **Inveraray**. In 1470 marriage and a financial deal brought them the prestigious Lordship of **Lorne**. Their territory continued to expand. Acquisition of **Kintyre** from the forfeited MacDonalds in 1607 was followed in 1615 by the purchase of **Islay** by Campbell of Cawdor. MacLean of Duart's debts having been bought out, the Campbell chiefs managed to take over his lands in **Mull** and **Morvern** after a long campaign. The Campbells were uncomfortable neighbours.

The success of the clan is due to a remarkable line of chiefs who combined a Highland powerbase with close contact with the seat of power at Court. Their influence was a major one, firstly in the affairs of Scotland as a whole, and subsequently in those of Great Britain and the Empire. Having espoused the Protestant cause, they pursued an undeviating course despite both the Mar-quis of Argyll** and his son the **9th Earl** losing their heads for their faith.

The 10th Earl was raised to the rank of Duke in 1701. His son, the **2nd Duke of Argyll**, one of the first two Field Marshals ever appointed in the British Army, commanded at **Sheriffmuir** in 1715. The 5th Duke, a noted agricultural improver, also attained Field Marshal's rank; the **8th Duke** was a Cabinet Minister while his heir the Marquis of Lorne, later **9th Duke** and Governor-General of Canada, married **Queen Victoria**'s daughter Princess Louise.

But if the clan could not have achieved its supremacy without this line of chiefs, no more could the chiefs have risen as they did without a remarkable body of clansmen. Renowned for its military prowess, Clan Campbell in the 18th century could put 5000 men into the field, a number unequalled by any other clan. Some dozen regiments of the British Army have been raised by Campbells from the Earl of Argyle's Regiment of 1689 to the 91st, now today's famous **Argyll and Sutherland Highlanders**. A large number of Campbells have attained General or Flag rank; to 50 identifiable Campbells of Cawdor of military age during the two world wars, a total of three VCs, 15 DSOs, three MCs and a DFC were awarded together with a host of lesser decorations. Campbells have attained marked success too in other fields, notably the Church and the **law**. **Sir Henry Campbell-Bannerman** is the only Campbell to have become British Prime Minister.

Most of the old Campbell lands have long since passed into other hands as economic necessity has forced the clan to seek a living elsewhere. But the old roots are still vigorous and Campbells today flourish in all quarters of the globe. Since the war, in Britain, no less than four Campbells have been raised to the peerage, and the banner of MacCailean Mor still flies over the Duke of Argyll's home at **Inveraray Castle**.

CAMPBELL, Colin (1676–1729) Architect

Little is known about Campbell's early career, which he seems to have begun as a lawyer. We know, however, that he studied architecture in Italy. He first made his name as an architect in England in 1715 with the publication of the first volume of the *Vitruvius Britannicus* and his design for Wanstead House (1714–20). The *Vitruvius Britannicus* was a collection of plates of modern English architecture and strongly advocated antique simplicity in favour of the frivolous Baroque current at the time. During his time in Italy Campbell became interested in Palladio and subsequently was the main propagandist of Palladian architecture in Britain. He was probably responsible for the conversion to Palladianism of Lord Burlington, who commissioned Campbell to remodel his house in 1718. In the same year Campbell was made Chief Clerk and Deputy Surveyor of Works in Scotland and one year later he became architect to the Prince of Wales. Apart from Lord Burlington, influential figures such as Robert Walpole were his patrons. Campbell's design for Baldersby Park in Yorkshire (1720–8) laid the foundation for a whole tradition of neo-Palladian villas. Mereworth Castle, Kent (1722–5) was directly based on Palladio's Villa Rotunda. Most of Campbell's designs were for small but immensely elegant and refined country houses.

CAMPBELL, Sir Colin, Lord Clyde (1792–1863) Soldier

Born Colin MacIver, the son of a **Glasgow** carpenter, Campbell owed both his education and his surname to his mother's family, Campbells of **Islay** (although there may be truth in the tale that it was the Duke of York who advised him that Campbell was a good name if he would be a soldier). He served first in the Peninsular War showing, as always, conspicuous bravery and rising from Ensign to Captain. Thereafter promotion, without great social standing, came more slowly. He served in the West Indies in the 1820s but was still only Lieutenant-Colonel in 1841 when he sailed for China and the Opium Wars. Thence he was posted to India (1846) and served with great distinction in the Second Sikh War and on the North-West Frontier. KCB in 1849, he returned home in 1853 and, though aged 60, had yet to conduct his two most distinguished campaigns. The first was in the Crimea where, in command of the Highland Brigade, he won the Battle of Alma and then inspired 'the thin red line' which held the Russian cavalry at Balaclava. There followed almost immediately the outbreak of the Indian Mutiny and a call from Lord Palmerston to take command in India. The relief of Cawnpore (Kanpur) and the second relief of Lucknow in late 1857 confirmed his reputation as perhaps the greatest British soldier of the mid-19th century. An inspirational figure, beloved by his men, he was created Field-Marshal in 1862 and is buried in Westminster Abbey.

CAMPBELL, John (1598–1663) 1st Earl of Loudoun

John Campbell of Lawers was created 1st Earl of Loudoun in 1633 although the patent was witheld by **Charles I** until 1641 when the King created him Chancellor. Initially a leading **Covenanter**, Loudoun briefly joined the **Engagers** in 1650 before siding with **Argyll** in time to avoid disqualification by the **Act of Classes**.

CAMPBELL, John, 1st Earl of Breadalbane (1635–1717)

Notorious scion of the Glenorchy Campbells, John was the great-grandson of Duncan Campbell (c1553–1631, 'Black Duncan of the Castles', 'Black Duncan of the Cows'). Duncan had carved out the Glenorchy domain which 'slippery' John consolidated when created Earl of **Breadalbane** and Holland (1681) after being ordered to relinquish the **Earldom of Caithness** which he had assumed in 1672. Although his loyalties were never steadfast, he had tendered support for William of Orange's succession and now relished a prominent role in the pacification of the Highland **clans** as masterminded by **John Dalrymple of Stair**. The failure of these negotiations [see **Achallader**] led deviously to the **Massacre of Glencoe** which was conducted by a kinsman, Robert Campbell of Glenlyon, and in which John himself was implicated. But 'his evil reputation is not wholly deserved' and his complicity remains 'debatable' (W Ferguson). He was later imprisoned (1695) for **Jacobite** sympathies and opposed the **Union**. But he sat in the Lords as a representative peer and 'repeated his double-dealing in the Fifteen [**Jacobite Rising**]' (Donaldson and Morpeth).

John Campbell, 1st Earl of Breadalbane, by Sir J B de Medina (SNPG)

CAMPBELL, John, 2nd Duke of Argyll (1680–1743)

A soldier of great distinction known in Gaelic as 'Red John of the Battles', the 2nd Duke was already a Privy Councillor when he suceeded (1703). He became a **Knight of the Thistle** in 1704, resigning from the Order on becoming a Knight of the Garter in 1710. Also an Extraordinary Lord of Session and prime mover, with **Queensberry**, of the **Union**, he was encouraged with an English peerage in 1705 as Earl of Greenwich. He held a major command at Oudenarde and was considered unlucky not to have attained the chief command which went to Marlborough. He was, however, promoted to Field Marshal, one of the first two in the British Army, and commanded the government forces at **Sheriffmuir** in 1715, the action which ended the hopes of **James Frances Edward Stewart**. In 1719 he was advanced to the Dukedom of Greenwich and in 1742 became Commander-in-Chief of the Army but died the following year. He was succeeded by his brother in the earlier family titles and outshone by his brother as a political manager.

CAMPBELL, Rev John (1766–1840) Missionary and Explorer

Born in **Edinburgh** and educated at the High School, Campbell trained as a jeweller before becoming a **Presbyterian** minister. He studied in **Glasgow** and became a director of the Edinburgh & Glasgow Missionary Society, organising preaching tours of the Highlands. Since the **Church of Scotland** had not yet started to send missionaries to Africa, Campbell then transferred his attention to foreign missionary work under the auspices of the London Missionary Society. Described as 'a dumpy Scottish minister who traversed the African wastes with a black umbrella to ward off the sun', he left Cape Town in early 1813 and travelled as far north as Bechuanaland to look for possible mission sites, determining the course of the Orange River and discovering the source of the Limpopo River during his 3000-mile journey. He returned to Scotland in 1821.

CAMPBELL, John Francis (1822–85) Gaelic Folklorist

Of the **Campbell** landowners in **Islay**, J F Campbell (known as *Iain Og Ile*) was educated at Eton and **Edinburgh University** and became something of a polymath (inventor, equerry, public servant). In Scotland he is remembered mainly for his pioneering collection of **Gaelic** folklore, especially his *Popular Tales of the West Highlands* (1860–2) and his book of poems about Fionn (**Finn mac Cumhal**) and other heroes, *Leabhar na Fèinne* (1872). Further sections of his huge collections were published in 1940 and 1960, and much remains to be edited from the MSS in the **National Library of Scotland** and the Dewar Manuscripts in **Inveraray Castle**.

CAMPBELL, John Lorne (1906–96) Gaelic Scholar, Folklorist and Farmer

An outstanding **Gaelic** scholar who devoted his life to preserving Celtic tradition in the **Hebrides**, Campbell was born in **Argyll** and educated at Rugby and St John's College Oxford, where he studied rural economy. In 1925, overhearing Gaelic spoken by youths in **Oban**, he began studying the language and exploring the Highlands and Islands, publishing his first book, *Highland Songs of the Forty-Five*, in 1933. A devout Roman Catholic, he believed the purest form of Gaelic tradition was found on Catholic islands such as **Barra** and went to live there, becoming friends with **Compton Mackenzie**. They collaborated on several books and founded the Sea League to protect the rights of local fishermen. In 1935 he married the American photographer and music scholar Margaret Fay Shaw. They worked together recording the oral tradition of the Hebrides on the latest cylinder-and-wire machines at a time when it was possible to be 'in touch with people whose grandfathers' memories reached back to the late 18th century'. In 1938 Campbell borrowed £9000 to buy the long, low, green island of **Canna** where he farmed in the traditional manner, encouraged the Gaelic language and Catholic faith, and collected butterflies. In 1981 he gifted Canna to the **National Trust for Scotland**, who keep his unique collection of 1500 Gaelic songs and 350 folk tales in Canna House.

CAMPBELL, John McLeod, of Rowe (Rhu) (1800–76) Churchman and Reformer

A son of the manse, McLeod Campbell studied at **Glasgow University** before entering the ministry of the **Church of Scotland** at Rhu near **Helensburgh**. Pastoral concern led him to preach sermons (he speaks much of 'joy') which led to his deposition from the ministry in 1831, and the writing of Scotland's great theological/mystical masterpiece *On the Nature of the Atonement* (1868). He had been appalled by the lack of Christian assurance among his flock, the result of the so-called 'Federal Calvinist' doctrine that God loves only the elect. This

seemed not Christian, nor is it what Calvin says. After deposition McLeod Campbell declined to use the devotion of his flock and of his intellectual allies to form a sect. But with help from some he subsisted for 30 years running an open mission to the east end of **Glasgow**. With his old university's award of a doctorate in 1868, 'the heretic had won over the church', and indeed opened it up with real social impact. He wrote a fair amount, but it was in personal contact that he had a huge effect on liberal thinkers across Britain. His co-operative ideal of argument was as mutual enlightenment given the revelation of Common (good) Sense. This very great man is commemorated by a window in **Rosneath** church. See his *Reminiscences and Reflections*, 1873 and *Thoughts on Revelation*, 1862.

CAMPBELL, Sir Malcolm Brown (1848–1935) Greengrocer

Campbell was born in **Kilwinning**, **Ayrshire**. From humble origins as a child labourer and then as an errand boy for a **Glasgow** greengrocer, he rose to become both Chairman and Managing Director of a chain of greengrocers' shops which bore his name. Growth came through his exploitation of the burgeoning customer demand for a wider variety of fresh fruit and vegetables. He achieved fame as the man who introduced the banana to the Scottish palate and as a supplier of exquisite floral decorations. An important feature of his enterprise was the siting of kiosks at **railway** stations across Scotland and into England. In 1922 he was knighted for his services to the fruit trade and to the City of Glasgow.

CAMPBELL, Thomas (1777–1844) Poet

Born in **Glasgow**, the son of a merchant, Thomas Campbell was educated at Glasgow Grammar School and the **University of Glasgow**, where he studied classics. After a period as a tutor in **Mull** he went to **Edinburgh** to study **law**, but soon abandoned this to write poetry. His first work, *The Pleasures of Hope*, was published in 1799. In 1803 he settled in London, but made frequent trips abroad. He was closely associated with establishing the University of London, now University College, London, in the 1820s, and was three times elected Lord Rector of the University of Glasgow between 1827 and 1829.

Campbell published several works of poetry, including *Gertrude of Wyoming* (1809), *O'Connor's Child* (1809), *Theodric* (1824) and *The Pilgrim of Glencoe* (1842). Other works include *Specimens of the British Poets* (1819) and *Life of Petrarch* (1842). He also contributed articles to *The Edinburgh Encyclopaedia*, and from 1820–30 edited *The New Monthly Magazine*. He is chiefly remembered for his **ballad** compositions, which include 'Hohenlinden', 'The Battle of the Baltic', 'Ye Mariners of England' and 'Lord Ullin's Daughter'. He died in Boulogne and was buried in Westminster Abbey.

CAMPBELL, Willielma, Lady Glenorchy (1741–86)

The wife, then young widow, of John Campbell, Viscount Glenorchy (son of the 3rd Earl of Breadalbane), Willielma experienced evangelical conversion. In 1770 she bought a chapel in **Edinburgh** for interdenomi-

Willielma Campbell, Lady Glenorchy, by David Martin (SNPG)

national worship by **Presbyterians** and **Episcopalians** alike to commemorate her husband, and fulfilled what she saw as her mission by making generous endowments to churches in **Breadalbane**.

CAMPBELL-BANNERMAN, Sir Henry (1836–1908) Prime Minister

Born in **Glasgow**, the second son of Sir James Campbell, draper and Lord Provost of Glasgow (1840–3), Henry Campbell added the 'Bannerman' to his name to comply with the terms of the will of a maternal uncle who left him a fortune. Educated at **Glasgow University** and Trinity College, Cambridge, he was a partner in his father's business until 1868 when he became Liberal MP for **Stirling** Burghs, a position he held until his death. Financial Secretary to the War Office (1871–4, 1880–2), Secretary to the Admiralty (1882–4) Chief Secretary for Ireland (1884–5), Secretary for War (1886, 1892–5), he was knighted in 1895, succeeded Sir William Harcourt as leader of the Liberal Party in 1899 and became Prime Minister on **Balfour**'s resignation in 1905. Described as 'a strenuous, uncompromising fighter' and 'a fearless, sagacious and optimistic leader', an advocate of (among other things) self-government for the defeated Boers and women's suffrage, his own administration included Asquith, Lloyd George and Churchill. He resigned on grounds of ill-health in April 1908 and died two weeks later.

CAMPBELTOWN, Kintyre, Argyll

The **royal burgh** of Campbeltown lies at the head of the sheltered waters of Campbeltown Loch. Formerly called *Ceann Loch Cille Chiaran* (Kinlochkilkerran), it was founded in 1607 by the **7th Earl of Argyll** as part of a 'Plantation' policy to import Protestant settlers, mainly from **Ayrshire** and **Renfrewshire**, bringing peace to a turbulent area.

Kilkerran Castle, in ruins, was founded by **James IV** in 1498 as part of his policy for the pacification of the former lands of the **Lords of the Isles**. The Campbeltown Cross, the finest example of a late medieval carved stone cross, dates from 1380 and was brought from Kilkivan near **Machrihanish** to serve as a market cross.

Between 1817–80, 34 **whisky** distilleries were established which, coupled with a large **herring** fishery, brought wealth and prosperity. But in the 1920s many distilleries closed or amalgamated; today only two survive, and the **fishing** fleet is sadly reduced. A small shipyard, seafood processing, clothing factory and creamery provide some employment. Near the recently improved harbour are the Public Library and Museum, housed in a fine sandstone building, a Tourist Information Centre and the oldest surviving cinema in Scotland.

CAMPSIE FELLS, Stirlingshire

As incoming flights descend to **Glasgow** Airport, the Campsie Fells evoke much the same sense of homecoming as the white cliffs of Dover. Strictly speaking the name refers only to the highest, reassuringly wild range between the Endrick and Blane due north of Glasgow. More loosely it is also used to refer to the whole upland area between the **Clyde** at **Dumbarton** and the Forth at **Stirling** which effectively screens central Scotland from **Strathmore** and the Highlands. Also known as the Lennox Hills, this area comprehends the Kilpatrick, Strathblane, **Fintry**, Kilsyth, Gargunnock and Touch Hills. The highest point is Earls Seat, 1494ft (455m), east of **Killearn**; a long escarpment of bare rock follows the northern contours; notable waterfalls include the Loup of Fintry and the Spout of Ballagan near **Lennoxtown**. Between these the highest road across the Fells (B827) is also known as the Crow Road.

CAMSTER, Grey Cairns of, Caithness

This remote moorland site exhibits spectacular Neolithic monuments, including what has been described as the most outstanding long (200ft/61m) horned **cairn** in the country, dated to around 3800 BC. It contains two chambers in beehive structures, both apparently incorporated later in the gigantic elongated mound with horns at either end foreclosing forecourts. Both chambers are entered from passages on the same side. The round cairn nearby is no less remarkable, with a chamber divided into three portions by transverse slabs and its original roof almost intact.

CANALS

Because most centres of population were on the coast or on navigable estuaries, and because the topography of the country was too undulating for easy construction, Scotland has relatively few canals. In 1990 the total mileage administered by British Waterways (who took over responsibility for Scotland's canals on the passing of the Transport Act of 1962) was just over 140. British Waterways' Scottish operations are divided into three areas – the Caledonian and Crinan Areas administering those two canals respectively, and the Lowland Area covering the Forth–Clyde Canal, the Union Canal and the Monklands Canal. Although the Caledonian and Crinan Canals have remained operational since their construction, the Monklands Canal was abandoned in 1950 and by 1965 the other two lowland canals were

The Caledonian Canal at Fort Augustus (BRC)

closed to through traffic. With the launching in 1994 of the Millennium Link Project, however, the Forth–Clyde and Union Canals are set to become fully navigable waterways once again. The aim of the Millennium Project is to restore both these canals and reconnect them at Falkirk, thus re-establishing the waterway connection between the cities of Edinburgh and Glasgow. The centrepiece of the project will be the Millennium Wheel, a 25m-diameter boat-lift which will join the two canals near the Antonine Wall at Falkirk. Funded by, among others, the Millennium Commission, the European Union, Scottish Enterprise and local authorities across lowland Scotland, work started on the £78m Millennium Link in March 1999 and is scheduled to be completed in the spring of 2001.

THE CALEDONIAN CANAL is Scotland's longest, connecting **Corpach** (near **Fort William**) with Clachnaharry (near **Inverness**), although about two-thirds of its 60-mile length comprises existing lochs – Loch Lochy, Loch Oich and **Loch Ness**. Built to allow marine traffic to avoid the Pentland Firth and the attentions of French privateers during the Napoleonic Wars, the canal opened in 1822, its 29 locks allowing passage of vessels of up to 160 x 36ft (49 x 11m). Its principal engineering work, by **Thomas Telford**, is 'Neptune's Staircase', a series of eight locks at **Banavie**, although the entire waterway can be regarded as one of the nation's greatest engineering works from the early 19th century.

THE CRINAN CANAL On the map the obvious place for a canal between Loch Fyne and the Atlantic would be across the mile-wide isthmus at **Tarbert**. But the alternative of a waterway between **Ardrishaig** and Crinan was vigorously canvassed and, though nine miles long, rising to a height of 64ft (19.5m), and involving 15 lochs, the Crinan scheme won. Designed by **John Rennie**, it opened in 1801. The **fishing** fleets of Loch Fyne and the **Clyde** were thus saved the often rough 130-mile passage round the **Kintyre** peninsula. In 1822 the opening of the Caledonian Canal increased this coastal traffic and soon Crinan was being used by daily steamer services between **Glasgow**, **Oban** and Inverness. For the two-hour voyage through the narrow and winding canal passengers were transferrred to a purpose-built steamer 'whose deckhouse when crowded with passengers presented a curious appearance'. In fact many preferred to walk alongside. Nowadays the canal is used almost exclusively by private yachts and motor launches.

THE FORTH–CLYDE CANAL The longest of the lowland canals, and the world's first man-made sea-to-sea ship canal, the Forth–Clyde connected these two estuaries in a 35-mile course from Bowling near Dumbarton to Grangemouth. With 40 locks, five branches (including one into the centre of Glasgow) and connections with two other waterways, it was once the nation's busiest canal. Construction started in 1768 and the canal opened in 1790. Its greatest engineering feature is a 400ft (122m) aqueduct crossing the river Kelvin at a height of 70ft (21m). It came into railway ownership in 1867 but, with falling goods traffic, was formally abandoned in 1962 and breached in a number of places by new road construction. In the 1990s, however, British Waterways are reinventing what was once an industrial and commercial waterway as a leisure and tourism resource; by 2001 the entire length of the Forth–Clyde

Canal should once more be navigable and its link with the Union Canal restored.

THE UNION CANAL Connected with the Forth–Clyde Canal at Port Downie near Camelon (Falkirk) by a flight of 11 locks which dropped its level by 33.5m over a distance of 1.5km, the Union Canal stretched eastwards for 31 miles into central Edinburgh, allowing water-borne transport between the two principal Scottish cities. The original terminus in the capital was Port Hopetoun in Lothian Road, but this was cut back to West Fountainbridge in 1922. Opened in 1822 for coal and passenger traffic, the Union was a contour canal and as such had no locks, but it boasted three aqueducts (over the rivers Almond and Avon and the Water of Leith, the Avon structure being the largest in Scotland at 810ft (247m) long and 86ft (26m) high), and the only canal tunnel in Scotland (640m long at Falkirk). Merged with the Forth–Clyde in 1867 and closed to commercial traffic in 1935, much of the former course of the Union Canal was obliterated by motorways in the Glasgow area. But in 1999 work started on the Millennium Link Project which will replace the 11 linking locks with a 25m diameter boat-lift and restore both the Union Canal and the Forth–Clyde to their former glory.

THE MONKLAND CANAL, still some six miles in length, was opened in 1793 to bring coal into Glasgow. **James Watt** was its surveyor and initial engineer, 18 locks being constructed on its original 12-mile length and an inclined plane opened at Blackhill to gain nearly 100ft (30m) in height by hauling the empty boats up a 1040ft (317m) incline, thus saving time and water supplies passing them through locks. Merged with the Forth–Clyde in 1867, and closed to commercial traffic in 1935, much of its former course is obliterated by motorways in the Glasgow area.

CANALS NO LONGER EXTANT include the Glasgow, Paisley and Johnstone (11 miles, opened 1811, abandoned 1881), the Aberdeenshire (18¼ miles between **Aberdeen** and **Inverurie** with 18 locks, 1796–1854) and 11 minor waterways. Scotland's first ever canal according to the definitive work on the subject, *The Canals of Scotland* by Jean Lindsay, was a ¼-mile waterway that reputedly allowed **Sir Andrew Wood** of **Largo** (**Fife**) to attend the local kirk by boat.

CANDLISH, Robert Smith (1806–73)
Churchman

An **Edinburgh**-born minister of St George's, Edinburgh from 1834, he joined **Thomas Chalmers** at the **Disruption** to organise the **Free Church of Scotland**. Later he became its leader and Principal of its New College in 1862.

CANISBAY, Caithness

Opposite the Isle of Stroma in the Pentland Firth, Canisbay contains a church part of which probably dates back to Catholic times, while its tower of somewhat Danish appearance was built around 1700. It contains a memorial of the family of the 15th century Dutchman Jan de Grot, after whom **John o' Groats** was named. In

1700 the Rev John Brand recorded without enthusiasm that at Candlemas local people went round a chapel on their knees, and baptised themselves with water from the burn. It is less surprising that the last witch trial in **Caithness** was conducted here in 1724, 12 years before such judicial practices were ended by legislation; or that oral tradition preserves the romantic tale of Kirsty Rugg, who eloped with a silkie (**seal**), taking the family's red cow as her dowry.

CANNA, Inner Hebrides

A grassy, basalt-based west-coast island, Canna's pistol shape measures one mile by five and has a resident population of about 16. Its plateau slopes southwards in stepped terraces to the sea and northwards is sliced by steep cliffs swarming with **seabirds**. The off-shore, but footbridge-connected, island of Sanday, or Sand Island, is pitted by volcanic rock to the consistency of plum pudding. The name Canna comes from the Gaelic, either directly from the word *canna*, 'porpoise' or 'young whale', or from the word *kanin* meaning 'rabbit'.

The island was an early Christian settlement and the relics of a nunnery, hard now to distinguish from the natural unevenness of the surrounding rocks, form one of the three oldest **Celtic Church** structures identified in Scotland. Canna formed part of the land attached to the Benedictine monastery on **Iona** and has a weathered cross and a well, attributed with curative powers, connected by a stone watercourse with the sea.

In 1549 Dean Munro described Canna as 'inhabite and manurit with a paroch kirke in it, gude for corn, girsing and **fisching**, with a falcon nest in it'. The island was held by the Clanranalds until, deep in debt in 1820, they sold it to Hector MacNeill. He evicted 200 islanders, in arrears with their rent after the decline of the **kelp** industry, and developed the farming. In 1881 the Thom family, **Glasgow** shipowners, bought the island. Benevolent proprietors, they built the pier and Tighard House. In 1938 the island was acquired by **John Lorne Campbell**, entomologist and, with his wife Margaret Fay Shaw, a scholar of Gaelic literature and culture. He instigated agricultural improvements and planted woodland but, with no heirs, recently gifted the island to the **National Trust for Scotland** who now care for it. A bird sanctuary since 1938, the island is home to 157 different species of bird.

CANNTAIREACHD

Before *piobaireachd* was set down in staff notation, it was communicated from master to pupil by a series of sung musical syllables known as *canntaireachd*, which indicated notes and groups of notes, vowels representing notes and consonants their various embellishments. This was designed for oral use, and is still employed for some teaching purposes, but is not standardised. Imitations of it are known as pseudo-*canntaireachd* which, being unsystematic, is closer to diddling. It was written down for the first time at the end of the 18th century (in the Campbell Canntaireachd, National Library MS).

CAOINE

The *caoine* or keen is the **Gaelic** lament for the dead, originally in three sections, the first a deep murmuring repetition of the name of the dead, the second a dirge (*tuiream*) evoking the dead person's character and virtues, the third a chorus of meaningless syllables (*sesigbhais* and *coronach*). The *caoine* is thought to be pre-Christian in origin and is possibly derived from the call of the redshank.

CAPE WRATH, Sutherland

Wrath represents the Norse *Hav*, meaning ocean, but the peninsula, the north-west extremity of the Scottish mainland, is known as *Am Parbh* in Gaelic. Perhaps this is a corruption of the Isle of **Lewis** term *Am Carbh*, in which case it is still of Norse derivation, as is common among the coastal place-names of these parts. A *Carbh* is a carvel-built boat. Bishop Pococke visited this hilly wilderness in 1760, when the 4th Lord Reay lived in the neighbouring mansion of **Balnakil**. He remarked on the deer hunts that were held there and on the sheep and horses tended by a herdsman. Today the visitor may cross in a ferry from Keoldale to where an intrepid vehicle negotiates the road to the lighthouse on its cliff above the rocks.

Cape Wrath, north-west extremity of the mainland (SP)

CAPERCAILLIE

Big enough to be nicknamed in Gaelic 'the horse of the woods', the capercaillie (*Tetrao urogallus*) has had a chequered history in Scotland. Extensive felling of old pine forest and excessive shooting led to its becoming extinct towards the end of the 18th century, with the last native bird reputed to have been killed in **Aberdeenshire** in 1785. Several attempts to reintroduce it failed, and it was not until 1837, when 50 birds were brought to **Perthshire** from Sweden by the Marquis of **Breadalbane**, that this largest of British game-birds became re-established. Now confined to central and north-east Scotland, numbers in the last two decades have again suffered a dramatic decline, once again through loss of habitat, those surviving fragments of the old **Caledonian pine forest** not being large enough to allow the species to thrive.

It seems regrettable that the bird is so prized by sportsmen; its diet of pine shoots and needles taints the flesh so strongly with resin as to render it quite inedible. Like the **black grouse**, the capercaillie has spectacular displays, and the 'song' of the male has been described as 'beginning with a resonant rattle, continuing with a pop like the withdrawing of a cork, followed by the pouring of liquid out of a narrow-necked bottle and

ending with the sound of knife-grinding'. The male in territory becomes very aggressive and has been known to face up to and attack intruders whether they be other birds, **roe deer**, sheep, dogs or even humans.

CARBERRY HILL, Nr Musselburgh, Midlothian

This was the scene of the encounter (sometimes erroneously called a battle – but there was no fighting) on 15 June 1567 between **Queen Mary** and the **Earl of Bothwell** on the one side and an army of confederate lords led by **James Douglas, Earl of Morton** on the other. The rebel lords declared that they had no quarrel with the Queen, but were adamant that she should leave Bothwell, the man they knew to be guilty of the murder of her second husband, **Lord Darnley**. After prolonged negotiations, which included the suggestion of hand-to-hand combat between a champion from either side, and during which most of the Queen's soldiers drifted away, Mary surrendered to the confederacy of nobles. Bothwell fled to **Orkney** and then **Shetland**, and a few days later the Queen was imprisoned in **Loch Leven Castle** and compelled to abdicate in favour of her son.

CARBISDALE, Battle of (1650)

In a last-ditch attempt to avoid having to sign the **Covenants**, **Charles II** encouraged **Montrose** to return to Scotland to rally Royalists to his cause. Landing in **Orkney** at the beginning of April 1650, Montrose gathered a small force of Orcadians and crossed the Pentland Firth to the mainland. But he was able to attract few followers in the far north and, on 27 April at Carbisdale at the foot of Loch Shin in **Sutherland**, he was met by Colonel Strachan, a doughty **Remonstrant**, at the head of a small, well-organised and passionately committed army. This was Montrose's last battle, and his defeat was swift and complete. Fleeing into the hills, Montrose sought and was granted shelter at the home of MacLeod of Assynt, who promptly turned him over to his enemies for a reward of £25,000. Disowned by his sovereign, who had by this time agreed to sign the Covenants, Montrose was taken to **Edinburgh** and hanged at the **Mercat Cross** on 21 May.

CARDONESS CASTLE, Gatehouse of Fleet, Kirkcudbrightshire

Atop a rocky hillock, Cardoness Castle is a long-derelict tower house of four storeys with a particularly fine hall. Typically supported on a vaulted ground-floor cellar, the hall occupies the whole of the first floor and has an elaborately carved fireplace, mural chambers and window seats. Although there is no evidence of battlements, the stark aspect of the building well conveys the defensive properties of a 15th century tower house. These properties were evidenced in a feasibility study carried out on the castle's strategic potential by English agents for Queen Elizabeth I in the 1560s. 'Yt is nyne foote thick of the wall,' notes the report, and it was out of artillery range from either the sea or the land, the only approach being 'up rockes wheare noo ordnance can be caryed but upoun men's backes'. It belonged to the MacCulloch family whose misdeeds over several generations culminated in the arrest for murder of Godfrey MacCulloch in 1690. He was

executed in **Edinburgh** by 'The Maiden', a Scottish version of the guillotine.

CARDRONA, Peeblesshire

A controversial new village, the first in the **Borders** since the **Duke of Buccleuch** created **Newcastleton** in 1795, Cardrona is situated, rather ominously, on the floodplain of the **River Tweed** between **Peebles** and **Innerleithen**. Comprising 220 houses, a 150-bedroom hotel and a tournament **golf course**, it is the dream of the local farmer whose 11,000 acres provided £5m for its 10-year birth; a Scottish Development Agency study identified tourism as the main local growth industry and predicted the downturn in farming. 'The whole scene hereabouts, from Cardrona to Minchmoor, is beautiful, particularly in the clear and sparkling sunshine of early morning' declares **Robert Chambers** in his *History of Peeblesshire* (1864). May it stay so after the foundation of the village in 1999 with the concomitant rise in levels of noise and pollution – and not render ridiculous the words of the simple 'Morning Serenade' or Tweedside Carol: 'I wish you saw Cardrona Law,/ With furze in all their glory;/Its straggling sheep, its Border keep,/That long will live in story.'

CARDROSS, Dunbartonshire

Situated between **Dumbarton** and **Helensburgh**, and overlooking the river **Clyde**, Cardross has depended on **agriculture** since the mid-17th century. However, in 1822 it was noted that 'some of the toilers of the sea' succeeded in 'turning an honest penny' by gathering whelks. Since then sophisticated farming methods and new housing developments have eroded village life. The site of Cardross Castle lies three miles east of the village near the mouth of the river Leven. Here died **Robert I** in 1329; and hence was taken his heart on its abortive journey to the Holy Land. St Peter's College (1958–66) on the Kilmahew Estate, an A-listed Le Corbusier-like gem, has lain forlorn and empty since the Roman Catholic seminary closed in 1976.

CARFIN, Lanarkshire

Since 1922 this otherwise unremarkable mining village north of **Motherwell** has attracted large numbers of Roman Catholic pilgrims. Returning from a visit to Lourdes, local people, many of Irish and Lithuanian descent, decided to erect a small grotto and well in imitation of those at Lourdes, and to dedicate the shrine to St Thérèse of Lisieux, 'the Little Flower'. The first miraculous cures made the press in 1923 and have continued spasmodically ever since. Voluntary workers and donations have contributed to its growth and vast crowds converge on it on holy days. **Edwin Muir**'s *Scottish Journey* of 1934 includes an interesting account of the shrine.

CARGILL, Donald (1619–81) Covenanter

Born at Rattray, **Perthshire**, son of a notary, and educated at **St Andrews University**, Cargill was ordained minister of the **Barony Church** in **Glasgow** in 1650. Expelled after the Restoration (1662) he became a **Conventicler** and joined **Richard Cameron** in denouncing the **Indulgences**. Wounded at **Bothwell Brig** (1679) he fled to Holland but returned to associate with the

Cameronians. Although not himself present at **Airds Moss** (1680) he preached Cameron's funeral sermon at **Shotts** in **Lanarkshire**. Two months later at Torwood near **Stirling** he preached his most provocative sermon in which he 'excommunicated' the King, the **Dukes of York**, **Monmouth**, **Lauderdale** and **Rothes**, **Sir George Mackenzie** and **General Thomas Dalyell**. For this treason a price of 5000 merks was placed on his head; he was captured at Covington Mill, taken to **Edinburgh** and beheaded at the **Mercat Cross** on 27 July 1681.

CARHAM, Battle of (1018)

A sparsely documented but historically important engagement took place at Carham on the **Tweed** near **Roxburgh** in which the Scots under **Malcolm II**, with the support of **Owen of Strathclyde**, defeated the Northumbrian forces of Earl Uhtred of Bamburgh. As a result of this victory, **Lothian** was restored to Scottish control.

CARLOWAY BROCH, Lewis, Outer Hebrides

The dry-stone **broch** tower of Dun Carloway on the west coast of the **Isle of Lewis** is one of the best-preserved examples of this type of late 1st millennium BC Iron Age homestead. In places the walls survive almost to their original height of 9m, but the main feature of interest is that the collapse of the northern side of the broch has revealed, in section, the way in which the tower was built. Details of the entrance with its guard cell, the hollow-wall construction with

Alexander 'Jupiter' Carlyle, by Sir Henry Raeburn, 1796 (SNPG)

internal staircases, and scarcement ledge supporting a floor, are all clearly visible. The central court is 7.5m in diameter.

CARLUKE, Lanarkshire

A parish and burgh (1662) on the **Clyde** between **Lanark** and **Hamilton**, Carluke (formerly Kirkstyle) is at the heart of Clydesdale's fruit and tomato growing district. The High Mill, once wind-powered, of c1795 is being restored but Maudslie Castle has been demolished and Milton Lockhart House at Miltonhead, the birthplace of **General William Roy**, has been shipped to a theme park in Hokkaido, Japan. It belonged to that cadet branch of the Lockharts of Lee and Carnwath whence came **J G Lockhart**, son-in-law and biographer of **Sir Walter Scott**. Hallbar or Braidwood Tower also passed to the Lockharts (1681) but was once a Douglas property. 'An excellent specimen of the smaller keeps which continued to be erected as late as the 17th century', its date is uncertain. **MacGibbon and Ross** also noticed certain peculiarities, like entrance on the ground floor and battlements on only two sides of the gabled roof, which argued against too early a provenance.

CARLYLE, Alexander (1722–1805) Minister

Nicknamed 'Jupiter' because of his noble profile and bearing, Carlyle entered **Edinburgh University** at an early age and studied at **Glasgow** and Leiden before being ordained in 1745. Minister of **Inveresk** for 57 years (1748–1805), he was leader of the Moderate party of the established Church, moderator of the **General Assembly** (1770) and Dean of the Chapel Royal (1789). The epitome of an **Enlightenment** clergyman, he was friend of **David Hume**, **Adam Smith**, **William Robertson** etc. His *Autobiography*, only published in 1860, gives a flavour of his times.

CARLYLE, Jane Welsh (1801–66) Letter Writer

Jane Baillie Welsh of **Haddington** showed precocious gifts and had private tuition. She and her tutor **Edward Irving** fell in love; but he was promised to another. Of some personal force, and much courted, maybe she needed a stong match for, after some shifts on her part, she married Irving's friend **Thomas Carlyle** in 1826. Financial privations, isolation and loneliness followed, both in **Edinburgh** and on Craigenputtoch farm. A move to London in 1834 began a liberation into society, and friendships; Carlyle's successes improved things. While left much on her own, she supported him with real individual courage, though aware of strains and fluctuations of affection, fed-up, jealous, in love and desperately lonely. She let her moods dominate her when she was expatiating on her circumstances, giving a vivid impression of the discomforts of her life. She had also a sharp wit. Her husband was in Scotland after installation as Lord Rector of **Edinburgh University** when news came of her death. He soon afterwards wrote much of his *Reminiscences* and prepared an edition of her letters, which reveal that her early gifts endured despite her refusal to write in earnest. She is buried at Haddington. See *Letters and Memorials of Jane Welsh Carlyle*, 1883 and J S Collis, *The Carlyles*, 1971.

Mrs Thomas Carlyle (Jane Baillie Welsh), by Kenneth MacLeay
(SNPG)

CARLYLE, Thomas (1795–1881) Writer and Sage

Carlyle rose to colossal literary and moral eminence from very modest beginnings in **Ecclefechan**, **Dumfriesshire**. Educated at **Annan** and at **Edinburgh University**, he showed distinction in mathematics, but a first intention to enter the ministry reached only probation stage. He had lost belief in the biblical foundations of Christianity, though he never lost respect for his parents' practical piety, nor his love and admiration for them. He did whatever was possible to help them and he secured an education and livelihood for his brothers. Rather than the Church he tutored and worked as a mathematics teacher in Annan and elsewhere, before returning to **Edinburgh** in 1819.

A great discovery of his life was German literature – he translated Goethe's *Wilhelm Meister* (1824) and his translations from Hoffmann, Tieck and Jean Paul are masterpieces. Experience of the German language, however, led to his adopting the prose style for which he is famous, or notorious. In it he believed he heard his own voice and something of his father's rather than mere mouthing from books. This prose is realised in *Sartor Resartus* (1835), the eccentric masterpiece (generalised essayistic autobiography) in which he represents the hero's experience of the 'everlasting no' of the vision of the universal machine and the 'everlasting yes' cried out against it by all of his being. Such had been his own experience one day in 1824, when he lived, studied, tutored and agonised in Edinburgh, learning German and translating.

In 1826 he married. **Jane Welsh Carlyle** was from **Haddington**, of strong independent mind and highly precocious intelligence that suggested a literary career

(but she left only bundles of fascinating letters) and did not suggest easy marriage. Both suffered through the later 1820s as Carlyle struggled for a livelihood through editorial and other vicissitudes. Directed always by a moral impulse, not hack or careerist, he lived his belief in the virtue of hard work (and financially had no alternative), producing a mountain of by no means ephemeral articles. Six years lived at Craigenputtoch farmhouse, Dumfriesshire, cannot have rejoiced Jane, but she had married the least complacent of men. She was happier after they moved to Chelsea (1834), and made 5 Cheyne Walk their home for the rest of their lives. She died in 1866, the year of Carlyle's election as Lord Rector of Edinburgh University. All the years in between he had been writing prodigiously, delivering public lectures with success and much personal discomfort; and, till his mother died, returning as often as possible to the parental home.

Huge in his day, Carlyle as a personality is too easy to caricature as a dyspeptic Victorian monster, endlessly grouching. Not a philosopher, poet or novelist, he was something more than a 'critic'; and for all that he wrote *The French Revolution* and *Frederick the Great*, he was not by modern standards either a historian or biographer. He does not fit: amid his many faults his genius is in seeing no reason why he ought to. For all his singularity he was not trying to strike a pose; his intentions were on the whole straightforward, often laudable. At the centre is a resolve to set out his beliefs as he believed and knew them. He is never beguiled by the formulae of 'reasonableness', the trappings of science, or abstract systems. Yet he can lapse into expressing mere prejudice of a none too edifying sort. *The French Revolution*, though not quite a history, tells truths about history; it considers the character of the facts historians deal with. One may also boggle at the work Carlyle had to do after that

Thomas Carlyle, by Alphonse Legros, 1877 (SNPG)

book's manuscript was destroyed in J S Mill's possession (it was supposedly used to light a fire). Mill provided compensation which Carlyle in fact needed to buy the time in which to rewrite. He is a realiser, or an awakener to realisations. His *Reminiscences*, published by his biographer J A Froude, are remarkable as autobiography. Unedited by Carlyle, they express fears he may have had about his life and marriage, thus fostering undue scandal.

No stranger to personal privation, in tackling social issues from the late 1830s (*Past and Present*, 1842) he shows fire, and also a note which led to Herbert Grierson writing the essay 'Carlyle and Hitler'. This defended Carlyle's motives. He was of no party and not a man to be followed; but without knowing what he was arguing against it is easy to misread him. *Heroes and Hero-Worship* may seem to extol the tyrant: really it demonstrates the reality of moral influence, Freud's super-ego, if naïvely. His moral individualism was a huge inspiration to Christian liberal thinkers against the mechanistic radicalism of the Mills. His emphasis on personal character inspired Tennyson and many others unlike him. His idiosyncratic prose broke ground for translation from German; he led an interest in German literature. His eminence as a Victorian was world-wide. Dubbed *par excellence* the Sage, he is a prophet not least in meeting real problems with passion, diagnosis, and answers in metaphor.

The Victorian *Dictionary of National Biography* demonstrates Carlyle's stature in his time with 20 pages and a detailed bibliography. Grierson (*Essays and Addresses*) sums up a century's reverence, matched in books by J A Froude, John Nichol et al. Like Ian Campbell's 1974 biography and A L LeQuesne's little Oxford monograph, many of the books are called simply *Thomas Carlyle*. These two, and perhaps J P Siegel's *Carlyle: The Critical Heritage* (1971), are worth an early glance, for it may not be immediately apparent what Carlyle is about. He wrote nothing designed only for the moment, and no adequate listing of his very voluminous writings can be given in a work of general reference.

CARMICHAEL, Alexander (1832–1912)
Gaelic Editor

Born in **Lismore**, Carmichael worked in the west Highlands as an exciseman, finally settling in **Edinburgh** where his daughter Ella married **W J Watson**. He collaborated with **J F Campbell** in his folklore collection, and made a large collection of his own between 1855–99, consisting mainly of **Gaelic** prayers and invocations, hymns, blessings, charms, but with a significant number of songs. These were collected from mainland and island sources, and the dates of composition probably range over several centuries. His editorial practices arouse a little unease, but there can be no doubting the value of this material. See *Carmina Gadelica*, Vols 1 and 2 (1900), Vols 3 and 4 (ed J C Watson, his grandson, 1940–1), Vols 5 and 6 (ed Angus Matheson, 1954, 1971).

CARNASSERIE CASTLE, Nr Kilmartin, Argyll

A mile to the north of the village of **Kilmartin**, Carnasserie Castle was built in 1565 on the site of an older fortress. Erected by **John Carswell**, minister at the village and Bishop of the Reformed **Presbyterian** Church in **Argyll**, on land granted to him by the **Duke of Argyll**, it dominates the northern access to Crinan Moss and the lands around it. A good, but ruined, example of a 16th century fortified house, with a tower and adjoining contemporary wing, it has been referred to as 'a Renaissance palazzo built by master craftsmen for people of discernment' and is a remarkable example of the mason's craft in a remote area. Revered as Carswell's home when he produced the first Gaelic translation of the Book of Common Order in 1567, the castle was sacked in 1685 by MacLaine of Torloisk when its Campbell owner joined the **9th Earl of Argyll** in the **Monmouth** Rising.

CARNEGIE, Andrew (1835–1919)
Industrialist and Philanthropist

Born in a weaver's cottage in **Dunfermline**, Andrew Carnegie would later proudly proclaim 'I was brought up among **Chartists** and Republicans. Our family life is distinguished for having had an uncle in gaol in Chartist times. My childhood's desire was, to get to be a man and to kill a king.' But the decline of hand-loom weaving forced the family to emigrate to the USA in 1848. Margaret and William Carnegie and their two sons settled in Allegheny, a suburb of Pittsburgh. Starting work as a bobbin boy in a textile mill at the age of 13, Andrew worked long, hard hours in a series of factory jobs until in 1850 he became a telegraphic messenger – his 'first real start in life'. Building on the five years of basic schooling he had enjoyed in Dunfermline, the bright and ambitious messenger was eager to take on extra responsibilities. By 1853 he was personal telegrapher and secretary to one of the superintendents of the Pennsylvania Railroad Company. A tip from his employer set him off on the capitalist path, although his purchase of shares meant he had to borrow funds and also mortgage the family home. When the first dividends were paid, he celebrated 'Eureka! . . . Here's the goose that lays the golden eggs.'

Except for a brief period organising railway operations for the North during the American Civil War, Carnegie stayed with the Pennsylvania Railroad until 1865. While still serving as one of their top executives, he speculated in industries that met the needs of a booming continent. Knowing the railway business, he invested in sleeping cars and involved himself in locomotive construction and bridge building. Having made a great deal of money from a diverse range of investments, he concentrated in later years on his Pittsburgh-based iron and steel business. Carnegie prided himself on his ability to choose his colleagues and subordinates, but in 1892 one of his partners, William C Frick, damaged Carnegie's reputation by using armed **Pinkerton** agents in a disastrous attempt to intimidate striking steelworkers at Carnegie's Homestead Works. Carnegie, who had been holidaying in Scotland at the time, tried unsuccessfully to distance himself from this tragic affair. With the wealth of the USA quadrupling between 1865 and 1900, Carnegie Steel, however, made this 'Star Spangled Scotchman' one of the richest men in the world.

Selling out in 1901 to the newly created United States Steel Corporation, the 'robber baron' turned his attention to shedding his wealth, which he maintained had now to be spent for the betterment of mankind. In various publications, most notably in his *Gospel of Wealth*, he had already evolved philanthropic theories, which were at the same time self-justificatory and socially conscious. Accordingly, Carnegie started to disburse vast sums, largely through trusts and foundations established to assess and meet specific needs. He founded – with his name attached of course – hero funds and educational and cultural trusts and foundations throughout the USA and Britain. Anxious to promote world peace, he paid for the building of a Peace Palace at The Hague and in 1910, convinced that 'the military age is rapidly passing', he gave $10 million for the Carnegie Endowment for International Peace. Back in 1808 his father, Will, had helped to form Dunfermline's Tradesmen's Library, but Andrew went much further by providing 2811 libraries 'for the masses'. His total benefactions have been calculated as in excess of £70,000 000.

Proud of his Scottish origins, Carnegie and his wife Louise holidayed frequently in Scotland, eventually, in 1897, purchasing a Highland estate at Skibo in **Sutherland**. (It says a good deal about his relationship with his mother Margaret that Andrew Carnegie waited until after her death before he married. He was 52 when he finally wed Louise after a long courtship, and their only child, a daughter, died in April 1990 at the age of 93.) Nor did he forget his birthplace. Before his death he bestowed a series of princely gifts on his beloved Dunfermline which he once described as 'the most sacred spot to me on earth'.

CARNOUSTIE, Angus
Here, on the coast between **Dundee** and **Arbroath**, the bucket and spade brigade meet the V-necked knights of the fairway. **Golf** and sandcastles account for the town's popularity, indeed for its very existence. There are no buildings of historic interest but three **golf courses** and many hotels. Inland to the north lies the ancient estate of Panmure which long belonged to the Maule family, Earls of Panmure from 1646 until 1716 when **Jacobite** allegiance brought forfeiture. The Lordship of Panmure was restored in the 19th century and then absorbed into the Earldom of Dalhousie. Panmure House, largely rebuilt by **David Bryce** in 1852, was demolished a century later; its gates, said not to have been opened since the 1716 forfeiture, remain, as does the 'Live and Let Live Monument' [see **Affleck**].

CARNWATH, Lanarkshire
A long street in the midst of moorland, Carnwath's bleak aspect belies its history. In the middle of its **golf course** the Libberton Motte is an impressive relic of the earthworks of a Norman fortification possibly built by William de Sommerville (d.1160) who came hence from Yorkshire in the train of **David I**. The Sommervilles subsequently lived at ruined Couthally (Cowthally, Quodaily) Castle and founded a collegiate church of which the north aisle (15th century) survives next to the later parish church. Here are effigies of its founders and tombs of their successors, the Dalyells (Robert Dalyell was created Earl of Carnwath in 1639) and, in the late 17th century, the Lockharts of Lee. These last have an impressive pedigree, Sir Simon Lockhart having accompanied **Sir James Douglas** on pilgrimage with the heart of **Robert I** in 1329. **Sir Walter Scott**'s tale

of *The Talisman* is based on that of a charm which formed part of the ransom paid to Sir Simon for a Muslim prisoner. Brought back to Scotland, it was known as the 'Lee-penny' and thought to have medicinal properties. A **burgh of barony** since 1451, Carnwath underwent industrial development in the 18th century when two brothers from London called Wilson established an **iron** foundry (1779). **Coal-mining** followed in the 19th century. The market cross dates from 1516 at about which time was run the first Red Hose race, a footrace sometimes claimed as the oldest in Britain, for the prize of a pair of red hose.

CARNYX
A beaten bronze Celtic trumpet, the carnyx was about 6ft (1.8m) in length with a boar's head at the bell end. The only surviving example of the boar's head from a carnyx is **Pictish** in design and dates from around the 1st century BC. It was discovered in **Banffshire**, but the instrument was widely spread throughout Celtic Europe. A replica of this instrument has been made for the **Royal Museum of Scotland** which also holds the original fragment.

CARRBRIDGE, Inverness-shire
This village north of **Aviemore** is the last before the main road to **Inverness** climbs away from Strathspey over the Slochd pass (1332ft/406m). Now bypassed by the A9, it hosts the Landmark Visitor Centre with its ambitious presentation of Highland history and a variety of other family activities. There are numerous hotels and guest houses. The village is named after the single-span bridge (1711) over the Dulnain River which, flowing east to the **Spey**, passes Duthill with its two **Grant** mausolea. Upstream to the west is Inverlaidnan House where **Prince Charles Edward Stewart** paid an unwelcome visit on the eve of the Rout of **Moy**.

CARRICK, Ayrshire
Ayrshire was divided into three ancient regalities, Carrick, **Kyle** and Cunningham, Carrick being part of **Galloway** until c1186 when Duncan was recorded as the first Earl. The southernmost of the three, Carrick is 'bounded on the north by Kyle, on the east by **Dumfriesshire** and the **stewartry** of **Kirkcudbright**, on the south by **Wigton** and on the west by the Atlantic Ocean' (Fullarton's *Gazetteer*). It covers an area of approximately 32 miles by 20, and is for the most part 'a wilderness of remote glens and secluded hills'. The home of the **Bruce family** (who acquired the Earldom of Carrick in c1274 when **Robert de Bruce** married the widowed Marjorie, Countess of Carrick, their son later becoming **Robert I**), Carrick was also the land of the **Kennedys** who were descended through the female line from Duncan, 1st Earl of Carrick. Since 1368 the title has been held by the heir to the throne.

CARRICK CASTLE, Cowal, Argyll
Named for the rock (Gaelic *carraig*) jutting out into Loch Goil on which it stands, Carrick Castle is a three-storey oblong tower house dating from the 15th century. Used as a hunting lodge by **James IV** while in pursuit of wild boar, for which **Cowal** was the last recorded refuge in Britain, Carrick later came into **Campbell** possession

The Edinburgh Castle *calling at Carrick Castle, Loch Goil (BRC)*

and was fortified by **Archibald, 8th Earl of Argyll** in 1651 in preparation for an (unforthcoming) attack by Cromwell's forces. Fired in 1685 following **Argyll's Rising**, it was never restored; although ruined, with roof and internal floors long gone, its walls are still entire.

CARRON COMPANY, Nr Falkirk, Stirlingshire

No single company made a greater contribution to the Industrial Revolution in Scotland than Carron Company. It was founded in 1759 by Samuel Garbett from Birmingham, Dr John Roebuck, an Englishman who had attended **Edinburgh University**, and William Cadell, a merchant from **Prestonpans**. Unlike similar attempts to establish an indigenous **iron** industry (at **Invergarry**, **Bonawe** and **Furnace**), the partners determined on a large-scale enterprise including furnaces, forges and mills; they also decided to use local ore and to smelt it using coke rather than charcoal. Quality ore deposits at **Bo'ness** and **coal** at Kinnaird, the property of the Abyssinian traveller **James Bruce**, suggested the site on Carron Water, whose flow was needed to power the blast furnaces.

The company's first product was cannonballs, but by 1766 **James Watt** was having the cylinder and pistons for his new engine cast at Carron and the furnaces had become a national curiosity 'no less striking than Vesuvius'. **Robert Burns**, calling on a Sunday in 1787, was refused entry and took his revenge with a peevish verse: 'We came na' here to view your warks/In hopes to be mair wise,/But only, lest we gang to hell/It may be nae surprise . . .' A Carron worker penned a rather laboured response which reveals his nationality as English. Evidently much labour came from south of the border.

Early specialities included cylinders, pipes, nails and ornamental grates, the last designed by John Adam who became a partner. First attempts to cast cannon were a failure but, with the development of boring techniques in the 1770s, a shorter and lighter cannon, easy to manoeuvre and with a new type of carriage, was developed. This became known as the carronade. There is some controversy as to its inventor but none as to its sensational success. The Admiralty and the Board of Ordnance endorsed it and it was exported all over the world; throughout the Napoleonic Wars it was the preferred ordnance of Nelson and Wellington.

Buoyed by this success, the company went from strength to strength as heavy industries grew up in central Scotland. **William Symington** was closely involved with Carron, and Henry Shrapnel turned to Carron for the development of his eponymous shot. By 1814 Carron was the largest iron works in Europe with extensive coal interests, its own shipping fleet, and a labour force of over 2000. But in the later 19th century the company encountered intense competition and failed to diversify. It persevered with castings and in the 20th century acquired a near monopoly in telephone kiosks. Divested of its shipping and mining interests, it specialised in domestic products – baths, sinks, cookers – and a few industrial castings until closure in 1982.

CARSE OF GOWRIE, Perthshire

Like **Atholl**, **Breadalbane**, etc, Gowrie was one of the ancient divisions of **Perthshire** and extended on both sides of the **Sidlaw Hills** from the Firth of **Tay** to **Strathmore**. Thus **Blairgowrie** and **Perth** (where the **Earls of Gowrie** resided at Ruthven or **Huntingtower**) were both in Gowrie. But today the term is used almost exclusively for the Carse of Gowrie, an 18-mile strip south of the Sidlaws between Perth and **Dundee** which forms the north shore of the Tay estuary. 'Carse', from a Norse word for marshland, indicates that most of it has been reclaimed. **Pictish** cross-slabs at Benvie, Rossie and St Madoes indicate its early importance while the abundance of castles is testimony to its exceptional fertility as 'the garden of Scotland' and 'an earthly paradise'. Witness **Lady Carolina Nairne**:

> A lassie wi' a brave new gown
> Cam' ower the hills to Gowrie,
> As oh the scene was passing fair
> For what in Scotland can compare
> With the Carse of Gowrie.
> The sun was setting o'er the Tay
> The blue hills melting into grey
> The mavis and the blackbird's lay
> Were sweetly heard in Gowrie.

Its history is a somewhat bewildering story of musical castles as the great landed families progressed from fortalices to mansions. Thus the Hays moved from **Megginch** to Kinfauns, the Grays of **Castle Huntly** succeeded them at Kinfauns, and the Kinnairds of Kinnaird (which was bought by the Threiplands of **Fingask Castle**) progressed to Moncur and Rossie [see **Inchture**]. Although traversed by the main road and **rail** line to Dundee, the Carse, especially along the edge of the Sidlaws, still has great charm and is now an important fruit growing area.

CARSPHAIRN, Kirkcudbrightshire

High on the moors of northern **Kirkcudbrightshire**, but lying just outside the perimeter of the **Galloway** Forest Park, the village of Carsphairn was prominent in **Covenanting** times, being adjacent to the lands of the notorious **Sir Robert Grierson of Lag**. The churchyard was the burial place of the McAdams of nearby Lagwine Hall or Castle which, but for a untimely fire which 'consumed the house', would have been the birthplace of **John Loudoun McAdam** (1756–1836); as it was, his mother was moved to **Ayr** just before the great event. Formerly known for the **iron**, lead, copper, silver and zinc found in the surrounding hills, the scenery around Carsphairn has been dramatically altered by the **forestry** and **hydro-electric** industries, the latter as part of the Galloway power scheme.

CARSTAIRS, Lanarkshire

The Mouse, which traverses Carstairs parish, turns out to be 'a burn with a brief but tortuous course' during which it squeezes through a gorge, the Cartland Crags between Carstairs and **Lanark**, before joining the **Clyde**. The name 'Carstairs' derives from Casteltarras or Castelterres, this being the site of a castle belonging to the bishops of **Glasgow** in the 14th–15th centuries. No vestige remains. In the 19th century Carstairs became a well known **railway** junction where lines to the south from **Edinburgh** and Glasgow converged. The large Carstairs mental hospital is nearby. The village, a mile away, was laid out by Henry Monteith who also built Monteith House (**William Burn**, 1824), now a nursing home. To the south-west the **Roman** fort of Castledykes is still partly visible; from here bronze artefacts found at the nearby Hyndford **crannog** are thought to have come, possibly by trade, possibly by plunder.

CARSTARES, William (1649–1715) Divine

Born at Cathcart, **Glasgow**, the son of a **Presbyterian** minister deprived in 1662, Carstares was educated at **Edinburgh** and Utrecht when his father fled to Holland. In the service of William of Orange he was twice implicated in plots in London against **Charles II**, twice imprisoned and tortured at Edinburgh. In 1684 he returned to Leyden as minister and chaplain to William, whom he accompanied as confidential adviser at the Revolution in 1688. His influence earned him the nickname 'Cardinal Carstares' and his power in ecclesiastical affairs inadvertently founded the **Episcopal Church of Scotland** when he persuaded William towards Presbyterian government for the **Church of Scotland**. He was four times **Moderator** and in 1703 was Principal of **Edinburgh University**. In 1707 he influenced the passing of the **Treaty of Union** and the Hanoverian succession.

CARSWELL, John (c1520–72) Gaelic Translator and Bishop

Rector of his native parish of **Kilmartin** in **Argyll**, chaplain to the Earl of Argyll, and superintendent of the diocese of Argyll and the Isles after the **Reformation** of 1560, Carswell was a graduate of **St Andrews** (1544). In 1567 he produced a **Gaelic** version of the Book of Common Order, first printed in **Edinburgh** in 1564, and referred to as **John Knox**'s Liturgy. This is the earliest printed book in Gaelic, in either Scotland or Ireland. It is written in the classical literary register of the language, and uses much literary elaboration familiar from early Gaelic writing, but has frequent traces of vernacular Scottish Gaelic also. Entitled *Foirm na n-Urrnuidheadh*, it was edited by Robert L Thomson (1970), who gives a detailed account of the text in his introduction. Carswell was buried at **Ardchattan Priory**.

CARVER, Robert (c1484–c1547) Composer

Carver was the outstanding Scottish composer of the 16th century. Little is known about his life, save that he was a canon of the Augustinian abbey of **Scone**, and was almost certainly attached to the **Chapel Royal** in **Stirling** and possibly later to the Stirling Parish **Church of the Holy Rood**. His compositions survive in only one manuscript, partly written in his own hand. They consist of five masses and two motets. His manuscript, known as the *Carver Choirbook* (**National Library**, Adv MS. 5.1.15) is almost the only extant example of pre-**Reformation** Scottish polyphonic music. His 19-part motet *O Bone Jesu* is one of the greatest vocal works of the Renaissance, displaying a command and variety of technique and texture without parallel. It may have been composed at the request of **James IV** as a personal penitential prayer to atone for his involvement in the death of his father, **James III**. The contrast of the vast choral utterances in the name of Jesus with the refined decoration of the more intimate sections is immensely impressive.

Gaude Flore Virginali, on the other hand, is a work of more restrained beauty, though exploring some unusually adventurous harmonies. The text and music depict the seven joys of the Holy Virgin. His 10-part Mass *Dum Sacrum Mysterium* retains medieval traits of symbolism and style; it was used at the coronation of **James V** in 1513, the 10 parts representing the nine orders of angel joined by mankind as the tenth order to complete the heavenly chorus. To achieve this ambitious impression Carver makes use of a uniquely Scottish technique known as *Cant Organe*, formalising a kind of improvised polyphony in which neighbouring chords alternate on a vast and slow-moving timescale, the voices changing places within the overall scheme with a freedom that allows for many dissonances and parallel fifths and octaves.

His *Missa l'Homme Armée*, though closer to the English decorative style, is the only insular Mass to use this tune as its basis, which it does with astonishing virtuosity, incorporating the tune at various speeds and drawing from it to form some of the complex and individual decorative passages. It was perhaps inspired by the example of Dufay whose Mass on the same tune Carver copied into his book. The 5-part Mass *Fere Pessima* demonstrates a command of Continental structural imitation in the service of deep feeling, the closing *Dona Nobis Pacem* being an intense expression of longing and sorrow ending in bleak uncertainty. *Pater Creator Omnium* is a late 4-part Mass, reduced in scale and intent, perhaps under the influence of reformist ideals, or by the restricted forces available in the parish church. It is only recently that Carver's music has become widely available or appreciated for its true worth, the first complete performance being given in a series of concerts in **Glasgow Cathedral** in the summer of 1990. See Isobel Woods, 'Towards a Biography of Carver', in *Music Review*, May 1989 and Richard Turbet's thesis on Carver, in *Brycht Lanternis*, 1989.

CASKET LETTERS

Produced by **James Stewart, Earl of Moray** before Elizabeth I of England in 1568 as proof of **Queen Mary**'s involvement with **Bothwell** in the murder of **Darnley**, the Casket Letters comprised eight letters from Mary to Bothwell, one sonnet written by the Queen and two marriage contracts. Moray claimed that the letters (in a silver casket similar to but not positively identified as the one preserved at **Lennoxlove**) had been handed to the confederate lords by Bothwell's servant at **Edinburgh Castle** in 1567. The debate as to their authenticity has never been resolved. Those who argue that they were genuine claim that they were too elaborate and too convincing to be forgeries; those who argue that they were forgeries point to the fact that had they been genuine Moray would not have allowed 18 months to elapse before presenting them as evidence against Mary. The truth will never be known. The originals disappeared in 1584 when, having passed from Moray to **Morton** to the **Earl of Gowrie**, they returned to the possession of the Crown in the person of **James VI** after Gowrie's forfeiture and execution, the only contemporary copies remaining being those made by the English. Informed opinion seems to have settled for the substance of the letters being genuine although the wording was almost certainly altered.

CASSILLIS (Cassellis), Earldom of

This earldom has been held exclusively by a family generally assumed to be members of the ancient Celtic dynasty of **Carrick** and **Galloway**. John Kennedy of **Dunure**, on the coast of **Ayrshire** north of **Culzean**, received a grant of Cassellis on Doon Water in about 1350. His descendant Sir James Kennedy married Mary, daughter of **Robert III**, and their son was created Lord Kennedy by 1458. The 3rd Baron was raised to the Earldom of Cassillis before he died with his king on the field of **Flodden** in 1513. Gilbert, 3rd Earl (1517–58) was captured at **Solway Moss**; Gilbert, 4th Earl (1541–76) fought for **Queen Mary** at **Langside**; and John, 7th Earl (1646–1701) opposed **Lauderdale** and supported William of Orange. The junior branch of Culzean inherited the earldom in 1762 after defeating a Douglas claim to succession through female descent. It consisted of two bachelor brothers, who transformed the castle and estate of Culzean, employing the services of **Robert Adam**. On the death of the younger in 1794 a cousin succeeded as 11th Earl, whose son formed a friendship with William IV and was created by him Marquess of Ailsa. It was he who introduced yacht building on the **Clyde** and made the final additions to Culzean. The 5th Marquess handed this property to the **National Trust for Scotland** in 1945, and while Dunure has been allowed to become a ruin, his descendants live still in **Cassillis House**.

CASSILLIS HOUSE, Nr Maybole, Ayrshire

The massive 14th century tower of Cassillis standing above the river Doon four miles north-east of **Maybole** was altered in the 17th century when a new square stair tower was added to create an L-plan arrangement. Amongst the surviving original internal features are a vaulted basement and a prison cell built into the 16ft (5m) thick north wall. A further extension of 1830, 'an early example of the Scottish Baronial revival' reminiscent of the work of **William Burn**, has created an impressive mansion, now the home of the Marquess of Ailsa. The **Kennedy** family acquired Cassillis in 1373, when its heiress, Marjory Montgomerie, married Sir John Kennedy, and took their main title from it when David, 3rd Lord Kennedy, was created Earl of Cassillis in 1509.

CASTLE CAMPBELL, Nr Dollar,
Clackmannanshire

Known as Castle Gloom (or Glume) until 1490, this well preserved stronghold high on a rock outcrop between the burns of Care and of Sorrow combines an impressive situation with much historical resonance – plus an inevitable sense of foreboding. **Colin Campbell, 1st Earl of Argyll** evidently felt it, for it was he who, succeeding by marriage plus guile, built the tall rectangular tower, still its nucleus and best-preserved feature, and then petitioned Parliament for the change of name. Thereafter it remained the principal Lowland seat of the mighty **Argyll** family and shared their fortune. A south range of residential buildings with a large first-floor hall was added by the 2nd Earl sometime prior to his death at **Flodden** (1513); it was probably in this building that **John Knox** found shelter and an eager audience as the 4th Earl's protégé in 1556. A further east range plus curtain walls and entrance pend (to complete the courtyard) was added c1600. In 1645 the MacLean contingent in **Montrose**'s army is supposed

'Castle Gloom', otherwise Castle Campbell (RWB)

country, it was described in the *Statistical Account* of 1844 as 'the great mart' which 'in an agricultural point of view, far surpasses any other town in Galloway'; the annual Kelton horse fair was held on Market Hill, the weekly Castle Douglas livestock auctions became the biggest in southern Scotland and its October sale of pedigree **Ayrshires** was said to be the biggest for that breed in the world. In 1961 Carlingwark Loch was the site of a **curling** bonspiel [see **Lake of Menteith**] between **Wigtownshire** and the **Stewartry of Kirkcudbright**.

CASTLE FRASER, Kemnay, Aberdeenshire

Of all the great tower houses of the north-east (**Craigievar**, **Crathes**, **Midmar**), Castle Fraser 'exemp-

'Muchalls-in-Mar', otherwise Castle Fraser (RWB)

to have burnt the castle between the battles of **Inverlochy** and **Kilsyth**, in both of which **Archibald 8th Earl** was defeated. But 'it is more likely that the castle was destroyed nine years later' (S Cruden), when the culprit was that veritable steamroller of strongholds, **General Monk**. The 6th Duke of Argyll sold the castle in the 19th century and it came into state care in 1948. Besides the well preserved tower, unusual features are the gallery/corridor arrangement of the later wings and the little loggia of the east wing.

> O Castell Gloom! on thy fair wa's
> Nae banners now are streamin,
> The houlet [owl] flings amang thy ha's,
> And wild birds there are screamin'.
> (**Lady Carolina Nairne**)

CASTLE DOUGLAS, Kirkcudbrightshire

Unlike many **Kirkcudbrightshire** lochs that have had their levels raised (by damming for **hydro-electricity**), the level of Carlingwark Loch was lowered in 1765 to create easier access to the deposits of marle (a calcareous clay used as manure) on its periphery and in its depths. Land around the lochside hamlet of Causewayend was then feued to workers in the marle-pits and the village was renamed Carlingwark. 30 years later William Douglas, a Penninghame merchant who had made a fortune in the Virginia trade (and had no close connection with the **Douglas** lords of **Galloway**), bought the surrounding land and renamed the village Castle Douglas. He also bought the nearby estate of Gelston and built himself a turreted castle within its policies, although it is uncertain whether this or nearby **Threave** was the eponymous 'Castle'. He laid out his town with elegant streets and houses as a centre of industry and commerce, and it flourished. Well placed in the centre of rich cattle

lifies better than any ... the grandeur of which the native castellated style, without any departure from inherited traditions and techniques, was capable'. This is the verdict of the **National Trust for Scotland**, the castle's present owner. But other authorities detect 'a decidedly French look'. 'Renaissance balustrading in place of battlements and the nicely proportioned cap-house turret all speak of travelled owners' (H Fenwick).

In about 1575, building on to what was probably a simple rectangular tower, Michael Fraser added the square Michael Tower at one angle and began construction of the great round tower (completed in 1630) at the opposite angle, thus achieving the typical Z-plan. Then known as Muchalls-in-Mar, it was renamed Castle Fraser in 1695 and remained in the **Fraser** family until the present century. The cap-house, the round tower's balustrading and an elaborate sculpted coat of arms are distinctive. Inside much has been made of the mural chamber known as the 'Laird's Lug' which supposedly allowed the laird to eavesdrop on conversations in the bedroom above. **Sir Walter Scott** evidently liked the idea and used it in his *Fortunes of Nigel*. More prosaically the orifice has been identified as a strong room.

CASTLE GRANT, Grantown-on-Spey, Moray

The home of the **Grant** family, Castle Grant now stands alone in wooded policies a mile to the north of modern **Grantown** where Sir Ludovic Grant re-established the adjacent village in the 18th century. It was also he who turned the castle back to front by commissioning John Adam to redesign the north aspect with a tall new block of severe façade and to rebuild the east wing. The result reminded **Queen Victoria** of a factory. From behind, the castellar origins of the house are still evident with a four-storey 15th century tower ending in a corbelled parapet from which rises a two-storey watch chamber. Until 1694 it was known as Freuchie Castle, under which name it had been a Grant property since the 14th century, having previously belonged to the **Comyns**. Sir Ludovic married an Ogilvie, heiress to the Seafield earldom, whose descendants, the Ogilvie-Grants, filled the house with fine paintings and furniture. But in the 1950s it was deserted and, after several new owners, was still ranked as one of Scotland's endangered houses in the 1990s. A Category A Listed Building with potential as a Clan Grant centre, its chances of refurbishment look better than most.

CASTLE HUNTLY, Longforgan, Nr Dundee

Not to be confused with **Huntly Castle**, Castle Huntly in the **Carse of Gowrie** is a large L-plan tower house

Castle Huntly in the 1840s (RWB)

built by the 1st Lord Gray of **Fowlis Easter** in 1452. In 1614 it was sold to Patrick Lyon, Lord Glamis and 1st Earl of Kinghorne, who renamed it Castle Lyon. George Patterson, buying it in 1777, restored the old name but continued Lyon's 'improvements', adding false turrets, a crenellated cap-house, and a new entrance. Subsequent use as institutional accommodation has done nothing for its architectural credentials but it remains impressive by virtue of its size (seven storeys, thick walls) and its situation, crowning a rocky bluff.

CASTLE KENNEDY, Nr Stranraer, Wigtownshire

Built in 1607 by John Kennedy, 5th **Earl of Cassillis**, and acquired by **John Dalrymple**, later **1st Earl of Stair**, in 1677, Castle Kennedy comprised a five-storey central block with flanking towers set on a peninsula that had once been an island in Loch Inch, some three miles east of **Stranraer**. Extended and elaborately furnished by the Dalrymples in the late 17th and early 18th centuries, the castle and all its contents (with the exception of three paintings rescued by the servants) were consumed by fire in November 1716. Although the castle was never rebuilt, and remains a stark ruin, the surrounding grounds were transformed into 'one of the loveliest gardens in all of Scotland' by **Field Marshal the 2nd Earl of Stair** (1679–1747), using, one supposes officially, the men of the Enniskillen Fusiliers and **Royal Scots Greys** as labourers. Neglected by successive earls and allowed to become something of a wilderness, the gardens were restored (1841–2) by the 8th Earl, using a copy of the original plan found in one of the gardeners' cottages. The anomaly of 'a garden without a mansion' was rectified in 1867 with the building of Loch Inch Castle in grand Scottish Baronial style north-west of the ruins of Castle Kennedy.

CASTLE MENZIES, Nr Aberfeldy, Perthshire

The Menzies family settled on Tayside from **Dumfriesshire** in the 13th century. Diminutive Comrie Castle, their first base, stands four miles west beside the river Lyon in someone's orchard. It has three low and ruinous storeys. A new house, built near **Weem** in the 15th century, was destroyed by the **Stewarts** of Garth whose Garth Tower, recently restored, stands a few miles north of Castle Menzies. The latter is a large, typical Z-plan tower house with circular turrets, four storeys high in the main block and five in the two square towers. In 1839 Sir Niall Menzies added a west wing and new entrance porch, both by **William Burn**. The castle fell into neglect in the 20th century until taken over by the Clan Menzies Society with help from the state. It is now a **clan** museum and is being restored. The policies – a terraced wall garden greatly overgrown and several fields – may be beyond redemption. The surrounding area, known as the Appin of Dull, is rich in early history [see **Weem**]; villages like Camserney (thatched cottages) and Dull itself seem caught in a time warp.

CASTLE OF MEY, Caithness

This 16th century Z-plan castle overlooking the Pentland Firth was built by the 4th **Earl of Caithness** and passed to his younger son, whose descendant inherited the earldom in 1789. Mey thereafter remained the seat of the earls until 1889 when the 15th Earl died childless. It then became the property of strangers until, in her widowhood, it became the home of the first royal Scottish Consort since medieval times, Queen Elizabeth the Queen Mother.

CASTLE OF PARK, Glenluce, Wigtownshire

An inscription above the doorway of this lofty L-shaped tower house records its completion on 'the first day of March 1590 by Thomas Hay of Park and Ionet Macdovel

[Janet MacDouel] his spous'. Hay's father had been abbot of **Glenluce** (1560) but when Thomas assumed the office of **commendator** he used his authority to begin demolition of the abbey and purloined its masonry for his new castle. The Hays retained Park until the 19th century when it passed to the Cunninghames who installed their farmhands in the then derelict structure. It has since been acquired by the state (**Historic Scotland**) and leased to the Landmark Trust for renovation as holiday accommodation.

CASTLE ROY, Nethy Bridge, Inverness-shire

Poorly documented and visually unimpressive, Castle Roy is undoubtedly old. In **MacGibbon and Ross**'s five volumes on Scotland's several hundred castles (*The Castellated and Domestic Architecture of Scotland*), Castle Roy is the first to be listed (followed by Kinclaven on the **Tay**, now overcome by forestry, and **Lochindorb**). It was probably a stronghold of the Red **Comyns** (*Roy* = red), and is dated to the 13th century. A four-sided enclosure of long ruinous rubble-built walls, it stands on top of a motte. A tower and the doorway and window of dressed stone may have been added later. Originally it was just an enclosure behind high blind walls against which wooden lean-tos would have provided accommodation.

CASTLE STALKER, Appin, Argyll

This ancient tower set on a small rocky island in Loch Linnhe, just off the shore of Appin, is one of the most photographed of Scotland's castles. Standing square, and granite grey, streaked with ochre-coloured lichen, it consists of a three-storey tower house built over a pit prison; the entrance is surmounted by a shield which bore the royal coat of arms.

It is thought to have been built by Duncan Stewart of Appin in c1540 for his kinsman **James IV**, both to maintain **Stewart** interests in the area and as a hunting lodge. The island it stands on is called Rock of the Cormorants, which is the battle cry of the Stewarts of Appin. The castle has passed out of Stewart hands on several occasions in its turbulent history, notably when in the 17th century Duncan Stewart gambled it away to a neighbouring Campbell for an eight-oared galley. Better documented is the period when it was forfeited after the **Battle of Killiecrankie**, Castle Stalker itself surrendering on terms in 1690. It was then garrisoned by Hanoverian troops during the '45 **Jacobite Rising**. It became roofless around 1840, but has now been restored in such a way that it closely resembles the original building.

CASTLE STUART, Nr Dalcross, Inverness-shire

Six miles east of **Inverness**, Castle Stuart (Stewart) is named after the **Stewart Earls of Moray** who acquired the lands of Petty in the 16th century and replaced an old castle with the present tower house in about 1624. Variously described as L-plan and E-plan, it is in fact U-plan, having a central block with two flanking towers on the same side, presumably to combine an aesthetic taste for symmetry with defensive requirements. The towers vary in height from four to six storeys, one with the usual round angle turrets, the other with a later parapet and bartizans, and the main block with unusual

Castle Stuart, in another of R W Billings' engravings (RWB)

square turrets corbelled out diagonally from the angles. Though long empty the castle is now back in use. In the old parish church of Petty are the graves of chiefs of the **Clan Chattan** including some of the **Mackintoshes**.

CASTLE SWEEN, Argyll

On the south shore of Loch Sween, this is probably the oldest castle in the west of Scotland. Named from Suibhne O'Neill [see **Knapdale**], it may be 11th century. It began as a massive wall around a yard and well – a refuge for all within reach. The walls were later raised, a seaward wing, kitchens and 13th century Great Hall, and 15th century 'MacMillan Tower' added, all increasing the menace of the blockhouse viewed from seaward. A slot in the reefs below the walls was a berth for galleys.

In 1260 Red Dugald MacSween held the coast as far as **Skipness**. In 1315 **Robert I (the Bruce)** captured the castle; MacNeills and Macmillans held it for the **Lords of the Isles** to 1493, when it passed to **Campbell** keeping. Sacked in 1646, it had 'great gunnes' in 1652, but was reported 'disarmed and destroyed' after 1685. During the 18th century a dozen families squatted within the walls. It is now an Ancient Monument in the care of **Historic Scotland**.

CASTLECARY, Stirlingshire

Six miles west of **Falkirk** and the victim of a similar congestion of communications (**Antonine Wall**, Forth-**Clyde Canal**, **Glasgow-Edinburgh railway**, Glasgow-Stirling road), Castlecary was the site of an **Agricolan** camp before it became an Antonine fort and may have continued in occupation after the Antonine Wall was abandoned. The castle is of the late 15th century and belonged to the Livingstones of Dunipace before passing to the Baillies and eventually to the Dundas Earls of **Zetland**. To the original tower was added an L-plan east wing in the 16/17th centuries; both are said to incorporate stone removed from the **Roman** site.

CASTLECARY RAIL COLLISION (1937)

35 passengers died and 179 were injured when an **Edinburgh-Glasgow** express travelling at about 70 mph struck the rear of a stationary **Dundee**-Glasgow passenger train near **Castlecary**, six miles west of **Falkirk**, on

10 December 1937. Almost 100 metres of stationary coaches were destroyed in Britain's worst rail accident since **Quintinshill** 22 years earlier. An error of judgement by the Castlecary signalman was responsible, although the express was travelling faster than was safe in the conditions.

CASTLEMILK MOORIT SHEEP
A very rare breed (about 120 ewes in eight flocks in 1988), Castlemilk Moorit sheep developed from **Soay sheep** crossed with other small-bodied breeds by the Buchanan-Jardines near **Lockerbie** up to 1970.

CASTLETON, Caithness
Perhaps named after the **broch**, amongst whose ruins a **Viking** grave was found in 1786 with a pair of tortoise brooches, this hamlet had the good fortune to belong to an improving landlord, James Traill, son of the minister of **Dunnet**. He introduced the first threshing machine to **Caithness**, became Sheriff Depute in 1788, and built the harbours from which local flagstone was exported throughout the 19th century. The village grew into a handsome linear town, suffered a slump when synthetic stone destroyed the trade in flags, and was rescued by the Norfrost factory which produces 6000 refrigerators a week.

CATERANS
From the Gaelic *ceathairn*, a troop (particularly of soldiers), the term 'cateran' was first used in the 16th century to denote Highland reivers or freebooters; more specifically it became the name given to any Highland marauders into the Lowlands. Another possible derivation is from the Welsh *cethern* meaning 'furies' or 'fiends'.

CATERTHUNS, The, Nr Brechin, Angus
'The name is really Caithir or Cader Dun, meaning the Strongpoint of Worship' (**N Tranter**). It is used of two hills north-west of **Brechin** both of which are crowned with Iron Age forts. The Brown Caterthun (285m) has four concentric defensive rings with entrances and some flanking stones embracing an area 330m by 310m. The White Caterthun (302m) has similar defences surrounding a Brobdingnagian stone fort with double walls, the outer 6m thick and up to 3m high. There is a water cistern within and a cup-marked boulder just outside. Both forts are thought to date from about the time of Christ and provide impressive evidence of a pre-**Pictish** society capable of mobilising very considerable manpower.

CATHCART, Charles Murray, 2nd Earl of Cathcart (1783–1859) General
Like his grandfather, his father (**William 1st Earl**) and his brother (**Sir George**) Charles entered the army where, not succeeding to the earldom until he was 60, he was known as Lord Greenock. He served first in Ireland, the Mediterranean and Flanders, then with great distinction in the Peninsular War, with **Thomas Graham** (an uncle by marriage) in Holland, and with his brother at Waterloo, where his horse was shot under him no less than three times. Laden with medals he retired to Scotland where he was Governor of **Edin-**burgh **Castle** (1837–42) and took up scientific pursuits. In 1841 he was credited with the discovery of a new mineral, sulphate of cadmium, which came to light during the excavation of the **Bishopton railway** tunnel on Cathcart land near **Port Glasgow**; still Lord Greenock, the substance was named in his honour 'Greenockite'. He returned to public life as Commander-in-Chief in Canada (1846–9), and like his father and brother eventually achieved the rank of general (1856).

CATHCART, Sir George (1794–1854)
General
A younger son of **William 1st Earl of Cathcart**, Sir George accompanied his father in Russia as ADC (1813–14) and was then ADC (1815–18) to the Duke of Wellington at Quatre Bras and Waterloo. He won few friends in Canada suppressing the 1835–7 rebellion, but wrote an account of the *War in Russia and Germany* in 1812–13 (1850) and achieved major-general in 1851. As Commander-in-Chief South Africa (1852–4) he again crushed unworthy opposition in the Kaffir War; but as a divisional commander in the Crimea he encountered sterner opposition and fell at Inkerman.

CATHCART, William Schaw, 1st Earl of Cathcart (1755–1843) General
The Cathcart family held lands beside the Cart, near **Glasgow**, since the 12th century; the name is supposed to derive from 'Castle Cart' otherwise Cathcart Castle [see **Glasgow: Queens Park**]. William was the son of Charles 9th Baron Cathcart (1721–76), whose mother had been heiress of the Schaws of **Greenock**; hence William's second name and his earliest title, Lord Greenock. His mother was the sister of **Sir William Hamilton** (husband of Nelson's Emma), and his own sister was the much loved but short-lived wife of **Thomas Graham** of Balgowan. William attended **Glasgow University** and qualified as an advocate but, like his father (who had been Cumberland's comrade in arms at **Culloden** and elsewhere), he opted for the army. He first served in America (1777–80) where he commanded the 'Caledonian Volunteers', then Flanders (1793) and Germany (1794–5) by which time he was a major-general. He directed the land forces at Copenhagen in 1807 and was Commander-in-Chief Ireland (1803–5) and Scotland (1812); in the same year he became general. His father had once been ambassador to Russia; in the same capacity (1812–21) General Cathcart completed his career and was created earl (1814).

CATRINE, Ayrshire
A product of the Industrial Revolution, the village on the north bank of the river Ayr was created in 1787 by Claud Alexander of Ballochmyle in association with **David Dale** to house workers in their new Catrine **cotton** mill. By 1836 there were 2645 inhabitants of whom 750 were employed in the spinning works, modelled on Dale's famous **New Lanark** mills and 'one of the best industrial buildings in Scotland' (R Close). Having been in more or less continuous production for nearly 200 years, the Mill was destroyed by fire in 1963, leaving Catrine a community bereft of its *raison d'être*.

CAULFEILD, William (d.1767) Road-builder
Grandson of the first Viscount Charlemont, an Irish peer, William ('Toby') Caulfeild [sic] first came to notice as a subaltern in charge of one of **Wade**'s working parties on the **military roads** in Scotland in 1732. In the same year he was appointed Baggage Master and Inspector of Roads with the rank of major. After Wade's departure in 1740 he remained Inspector of Roads until his death in 1767. During the '45 he was Sir John Cope's Quartermaster. In 1747 he was appointed Deputy Governor of **Inverness** and a Justice of the Peace. Although he was promoted to lieutenant-colonel in 1751, he was always known as 'Major' or 'Governor'.

Between 1740–67 Caulfeild planned and built over 800 miles of roads in Scotland at a building cost of £130,000, making a greater contribution to communications than anyone apart from **Telford**. When not road-making he was a *bon viveur* and entertained lavishly at his house in Cradlehall just outside Inverness. The eponymous 'cradle' was a gadget attached to a block and tackle to hoist to their rooms guests who had succumbed to a surfeit of bumpers of claret.

CAW, Sir James Lewis (1864–1950) Art Historian
Born in **Ayr**, Caw studied at the **Glasgow School of Art**, in **Edinburgh** and on the Continent. He is remembered principally as author of *Scottish Painters, Past and Present* (1908) which, though by no means the first account of Scottish art, remains one of the most comprehensive and widely used works on the subject. In addition he published monographs on the painters **Sir Henry Raeburn**, **Sir James Guthrie** and **William McTaggart**, whose daughter Annie he married. In 1895 he was appointed Curator of the **Scottish National Portrait Gallery** and in 1907 became the first Director of the **National Galleries of Scotland**. He also painted land- and sea-scapes in watercolour, reminiscent of the work of McTaggart, and exhibited regularly at the **Royal Scottish Academy** of which he was elected an Honorary member in 1939. He died at **Lasswade**.

CAWDOR CASTLE, Nairnshire
Though pronounced 'Cawdor' (and so spelled and popularised by Shakespeare), this was originally and more correctly Calder, home of the Thanes of Calder, one of whom (William) erected the massive central tower in 1454. It probably replaced an existing building and has since been partly remodelled, especially at roof level, with unusual angle turrets and guard room. Yet it still dominates the whole complex and gives Cawdor the air of a medieval fortress in good working order. Access was originally to the first-floor hall with the usual vaulted basement below. The latter is still guarded by the iron yett removed from **Lochindorb** at the time of its demolition (1457) and still preserves the remains of a hawthorn or yew where, in fulfilment of the Thane's dream, a donkey came to rest, thus indicating the auspicious site.

The tower was surrounded by a deep ravine and ditch (still crossed by a drawbridge) and probably by a wall of enclosure against which extensive building took place once Cawdor had passed to the **Campbells** of **Argyll** by marriage in 1510. The three-storey west and north

Cawdor Castle, home of the Cawdor Campbells since 1510 (RWB)

ranges (1670s) were linked to the keep by a stair tower and provided the principal accommodation including the Great Hall. Further ranges, giving additional courtyards, were added to the south and east in the 19th century. Gunloops, crowstep gables, dormers and the occasional turret provide both architectural interest and romantic fodder. That 'they represent the traditions rather than the reality of an ancient fortalice' (**MacGibbon and Ross**) scarcely matters. The castle belongs to Campbells, Earls of Cawdor since 1827, and is predicted to remain so for as long as a red-headed maiden is to be found in the vicinity of **Loch Awe**. It is open to the public; the collections of tapestries and portraits are notable as also the gardens. Nearby the church (dating from 1619) of Cawdor, or sometimes 'Campbeltown', and the ruins of that at Barevan, which preceded it, provide a graveyard commentary on the castle as well as being of architectural interest.

CEILIDHS
The **Gaelic** word *cèilidh* means primarily a social visit. Such visits often produced story-telling and singing. In urban colonies of Gaels, any organised gathering (often promoted by a Highland territorial association) acquired the title of *cèilidh*. In turn this has been extended to musical gatherings of an informal nature, whether Gaelic or not. Usually the Gaelic *cèilidh* has a *fear-an-taighe* (literally 'man of the house' but used for 'compere') or in recent times a *bean-an-taighe* ('woman of the house') who keeps the programme moving.

CELTIC ART
This term is used rather generally to refer to a highly decorative, often linear style which appears in a wide range of contexts. This range is wide in terms of loca-

tions, dating and media. The artefacts are ones associated with **Celts** (ie people speaking a **Celtic language**) from southern and south-eastern Europe, through France to Spain, and in the British Isles. They date from the first millennium BC to the present time and include stone carvings, manuscript illuminations, a wide range of jewellery and other decorative objects, including leatherwork, decorated weaponry, household utensils, coins, etc. Additionally the term is sometimes applied to certain modern paintings.

Although Celtic art interacted with the classical art of Greece and Rome, it had its own distinct persona, which it maintained and developed over many centuries. It came to fruition in lands that enjoyed a temperate climate, and had both a stock-raising economy and a strong hunting tradition. Its iconography features intertwining plants and flowers, animals (often very stylised), monsters, heroes and gods and goddesses (for many of its features have pagan references). In some instances, eg in manuscript illumination, the techniques of intertwining tendrils appear, but there is also a highly elaborate linear, part-geometric patterning, and this has become one of the hallmarks of Celtic design, sometimes becoming clichéd. Similar patterns were earlier used as decoration on weapons, torques, brooches, etc, often accompanied by animal motifs.

The relationship between this art and that associated with the **Picts** (symbol stones, etc) is not clear, but there are interactions and connections. Scottish examples of manuscript illumination range from the rather mixed effects of the illustrations in the **Book of Deer** to the microscopic elaboration of the **Book of Kells** illuminations (it is thought that to an important extent this book was created in **Iona**). Elaborate decorative metal-work and jewellery continued to be manufactured until early modern times, and there have been many imitations and developments of such work (especially jewellery) in recent years.

A succession of Scottish painters drew part of their inspiration from Celtic sources, either actual or romantically imagined. **Alexander Runciman** based his series of Ossianic paintings in 1772 on **James Macpherson**'s so-called translations of Ossian, and in this century **John Duncan**'s paintings The Awakening of Cuchulin and Combat of Fionn and Swaran have Celtic inspiration, as has some of **William Johnstone**'s work. Duncan Macmillan sees **William MacTaggart** as a Celtic painter, but this is certainly in a very different sense from that of the ancient formal tradition.

For **Pictish** art, see Isobel Henderson, The Picts, 1967, and 'Pictish Art and the Book of Kells' in R McKitterick et al, Ireland in Early Medieval Europe, 1982. For Scottish illuminated manuscripts, see Ian Fisher in D S Thomson Companion to Gaelic Culture, 1987. For the broad sweep of Celtic art in Europe, see V Kruta et al, The Celts, 1991, a publication coinciding with an elaborate exhibition held at the Palazzo Grassi in Venice in 1991.

CELTIC CHURCH

In Ireland, never colonised by Rome, a form of religious organisation evolved which appears to have been influenced by the practices of the desert fathers of Egypt. These in turn had encountered the austere monasticism of Buddhist monks from India. Irish monasteries belonged to particular tribes, and while there were bishops as well as abbots, the organisation was not a diocesan one. The monks achieved a remarkable degree of cohesion between hitherto combative **Picts**, Gaels and Britons. Patrick, the apostle of the Irish, was possibly a Briton of **Strathclyde**. **Columba** was an Irish prince. His associate Comgall was a Pict, trained in Bangor. These men introduced literacy in the British Isles. The writings of Patrick are the earliest surviving of a native of Scotland. Adomnan (**Adamnan**)'s biography of Columba is by far the country's oldest. At Lindisfarne, where Aidan from **Iona** planted his monastery in 636, the Gaels taught the English to read and write. The ultimate source of their inspiration is attested by the earliest bound book to have survived in these islands, the Gospel of St John buried with **St Cuthbert** at his death in 687. They carried their literacy to Europe, where many of their manuscripts survived after the **Vikings** had destroyed the library of Iona and other religious centres. Celtic monks were also the first to adventure out of sight of land, following the flight of birds to the Faroe islands and Iceland. The Celtic Church discharged the responsibilities of a government at a time when secular leaders had not yet conceived of such obligations. Within their sanctuary sites the Law of Adomnan was enforced. Medical care was provided and monastic husbandry provided for seasons of want. The record is almost unique in Christian history in being without persecution and without martyrs.

CELTIC LANGUAGES

The Celtic family of languages belongs (with Latin, Greek, German, English, French, Russian and many others) to the Western or European section of the Indo-European family. In historical times people speaking a Celtic language have inhabited many different parts of Europe, from the Danube basin and northern Germany to the Atlantic coasts of Portugal, Spain and France. There is no total agreement on the ultimate place of origin of this linguistic group, but there would seem to be a strong case for regarding the regions we now refer to as south-west Germany and Austria as a sphere of strong 'Celtic' influence at an early period, and possibly the area in which the Celts first developed the metal technologies that were to give them a military advantage and thus the ability to dominate all other areas of Europe, for a time.

The Indo-European family as a whole is sometimes said to have its original home in south-eastern Europe, or closer to the Caucasus Mountains, while more recent theories suggest that the European part of the family spread out from a Greek base (in terms, that is, of later geography) which shows earlier Anatolian influences. This spread, it is claimed, took place between 6000 and 2000 BC.

The evidence, however, of the later spread of Celtic peoples in Europe is much less speculative. If we take the time of Alexander the Great (c330 BC) as a vantage point, we can see that at that time the Celts were a powerful people, controlling large areas of Europe, including much of France and Spain, north Italy, south Germany and the valley of the Danube down to the Black Sea. Many ancient place-names in these areas are Celtic, as for instance the names of the Rhine and the

Danube. The Celts had reached Rome by c390 BC, Macedonia about 278 BC, the Atlantic seaboard of Spain before 500 BC and Britain probably as early as 700 BC.

This expansion and rise to power was swift and brief in historical terms, and was followed by a similarly swift decline. The numbers involved were presumably not sufficient to impose their language(s) widely, though they left linguistic traces in other languages and especially in place-names. Although, for example, the Celts had dominated Gaul, the **Romans** conquered it in the 1st century AD and by 500 AD Gaulish was largely extinct, though with some carry-over into Breton. But confirmation of the Celtic occupation remains in archaeological and artistic evidence, as can easily be seen in the rich Celtic holdings of French museums, etc.

From the centuries around the birth of Christ there is evidence of ancient forms of Celtic speech, referred to under such names as Gaulish, Hispano-Celtic, Cisalpine Celtic (in north Italy), Lepontic, etc. When we move, however, to the period of 500 AD onwards, we see a more clearly defined and much more limited area of Celtic speech. This coincides quite closely with what is now regarded as the Celtic territories, or as they are sometimes referred to 'the Celtic Fringe'. It is indeed a fringe when we recall their earlier backcloth.

Celtic speech (as an indigenous rather than an immigrant language) is now confined to western and northern areas of Scotland, parts of Wales, parts of Ireland and parts of Brittany, with the remnant of a once-vigorous colony in Nova Scotia, and with revival movements in the Isle of Man and in Cornwall. In terms of languages, this represents the speech-areas of Scottish Gaelic, Welsh, Irish Gaelic, Breton, Manx and Cornish, and these six make up the Celtic family post-500 AD. In addition a question-mark still hangs over **Pictish**, thought to have much closer affiliations with Gaulish, or with some form of Continental Celtic, than with Gaelic, and possibly to have non-Indo-European ingredients as well, perhaps reflecting on some level(s) of linguistic input from an earlier population in Scotland.

These six Celtic languages (excluding Pictish) fall into two distinct groups: Goedelic and Brythonic. Goedelic includes the three types of Gaelic (Scottish, Irish and Manx), and Brythonic includes Welsh, Cornish and Breton. The Goedelic group is sometimes called Q-Celtic and the Brythonic P-Celtic, labels that refer to merely one difference between the groups, namely their treatment of the Indo-European labio-velar guttural q or k. This sound goes in different directions in these Celtic groups, becoming a c-sound in Goedelic but a p-sound in Brythonic, eg Gaelic *ceithir* (four), Welsh *pedwar* (whereas Latin *quattuor* retains the original sound), or Gaelic *mac* (son), Welsh *map/mab*, and Gaelic *ceann* (head), Welsh *pen(n)*. There are, of course, a good many other standard divergences between Goedelic and Brythonic. Two instances only may be cited here: (1) Indo-European *w* represented in Goedelic by *f*, in Brythonic by *gw*, eg Gaelic *fior* (true), Welsh *gwir*, and (2) initial Indo-European *s* before vowels remaining in Goedelic but lenited in Brythonic, eg Gaelic *sean* (old), Welsh *hen*, or Gaelic *salann* (salt), Welsh *halen*.

Of the six Celtic languages referred to above, only

four survive as indigenous used languages with an unbroken tradition. Welsh is the strongest of these in terms of numbers of native speakers. Scottish Gaelic has a considerably larger corps of native speakers than Irish, but Irish has a larger corps of persons able to use the language. It is hard to get precise numerical information about Breton, but its native base seems to have suffered serious attrition in the last generation. The last native speaker of Manx died in the 1970s and the last native speaker of Cornish in the early 1800s.

It is useful to recall that forms of Celtic were once spoken widely in virtually the whole of the British Isles. The Scottish position is discussed under **Gaelic Language**, but pockets of Celtic speech survived in England until probably the 11th century, with others, eg around Leeds, or in Lincolnshire or Gloucestershire, petering out earlier. The wide spread of Celtic place-names in England reflects the still earlier and wider spread of Celtic languages there.

CELTIC MYTHOLOGY

The beliefs and practices of Celtic mythology are traceable with remarkable uniformity throughout Europe, wherever the Celtic languages were spoken. They can be dated from before 1000 BC, in the time of the Urnfield folk, through the Hallstad and La Tène periods in which Celtic peoples colonised the British Isles, into the Christian era. Their mother goddesses were associated with water and gave their names to the Seine and Marne, the Severn, **Clyde** and **Dee** rivers. Like the Celtic bestiary, which derives from Persian and Scythian art, their female divinities recall Anahita the water goddess who begat Mitra by a virgin birth, as the mediator between Mankind and the cosmic creator Ahura Mazda.

Central to Celtic beliefs was the cult of the head, repository of the soul, and they moved cheerfully between a densely peopled otherworld and one in which humans and divinities could exchange shapes with one another and with animals. The stag god and the divine boar were especially potent mythical beings. As early as the 4th century BC Pythias noted the islands (**Orkney**) named after *Orci*, young pigs, while the outstanding pagan epic, the *Tain Bo Cuálgne*, has as its central theme the rivalry between two divine bulls. The shape changing in both life and death, in which they believed, does not support an assumption that they evolved a doctrine of metempsychosis, and it was certainly an error to suppose that their druids were philosophers comparable to those of the Greeks. The **Roman** authors were partly responsible for these romantic notions, enlarged in the 17th century. In fact the druids were shamans of a people with a predeliction for human and animal sacrifices, who drew no distinction between the natural and the supernatural.

St Brigid of Kildare, commemorated in church dedications and holy wells throughout Britain, patroness of childbirth in the **Hebrides** and revered as the midwife of the Virgin Mary, epitomises the legacy of Celtic mythology. She was the daughter of Dagda, the anthropomorphic father-god who straddled a river to mate with the war-raven goddess Morrigan. Brigid possessed three magic manifestations, the number so dear to the Celtic imagination. They operated in the spheres of fertility, of art and poetry and of healing. The indispensable authority on the subject of Celtic mythology is *Pagan Celtic Britain* (1967) by Anne Ross.

See also **Cú Chulainn, Finn mac Cumhal, Deirdre**.

CELTIC PLAINCHANT

Thought not to exist, Celtic plainchant in fact survives in a 13th century Antiphoner from **Inchcolm**, part of which consists of chants for a service dedicated to **St Columba**. Recent research has shown that some of this material probably came from **Iona** and was composed as early as the 7th century. There are close structural links between the music and the texts, which are typical of early Hiberno-Latin styles. The music is tuneful, makes use of a wide vocal range, and is frequently highly patterned.

See also **Bells**.

CELTIC TWILIGHT

This much-misused phrase has relevance to a literary 'movement', with cross references to associated artistic tendencies, and should be confined to those areas. But such imperatives do not carry weight with politicians and journalists who want to make different points by using the phrase. It seems to have been given its first currency by W B Yeats, who published a collection of stories under that title in 1893. In this he was anxious to use a simple, uncomplicated kind of prose, which he seemed to identify with peasant speech. A little later in the 1890s he wrote to the Scottish writer Fiona MacLeod asking 'her' which of his two styles 'she' preferred, the simple or the ornate, and in another letter of 1901 he advises Fiona MacLeod to seek 'utter simplicity' in writing style (see Richard Ellmann, *Yeats: The Man and the Masks*, esp pp 148–54). Yeats does not seem to have known at this time that Fiona MacLeod was no lady, but in reality **William Sharp**, a writer of fiction, and later of drama, who was drawn to both fantasy and gloom, and a mysterious Celtic past. Although MacLeod and his 'school' were to an extent developing the romanticism of **James 'Ossian' Macpherson** (as was Yeats) and **Sir Walter Scott** in a weak and airy fashion, MacLeod in particular seems to have been influenced by Yeats's early plays, eg *The Land of Heart's Desire*.

The interesting point, which often escapes writers who use the phrase, is that it is extremely hard to find any starting point in Gaelic literature for the ideas of the Celtic Twilight. Simplicity can be found in Gaelic song, but it is not a contrived simplicity, and the kind of romantic mystery and fantasy promoted by the Twilightists seems quite foreign to the native tradition. The Celtic Twilight writers seem to have been seeing something they wanted to see through a mist darkly. The ideas of the Celtic Twilight affected, at least marginally, the work of painters and musicians such as **John Duncan** and **Marjory Kennedy-Fraser**, before the phrase became merely a political pejorative.

CELTS AND GAELS

'Celts' (pronounced 'Kelts') refers to members of the wider groups of people using a **Celtic** (pronounced 'Keltic' except in **football** parlance when it is pronounced 'Seltic') **language** or descended from people who did; 'Gaels' refers to those speaking Gaelic or descended from Gaelic speakers. In origin both terms have a basic language reference and significance, but can be used in transferred senses, as when we speak of **Celtic art**, Celtic archaeology, Celtic law, Gaelic music, Gaelic coffee and so on [see **Celtic Languages**].

CERES, Fife

Ceres (pron. 'series'), not alone in being declared 'the prettiest village in Scotland', has been a **burgh of barony** since 1620. Its history goes back further for the Ceres Games, held in June on the green and renowned for their riotous horse races, are said to commemorate the return of the Ceres men from **Bannockburn**, where they had arrived too late to fight but in time to celebrate. What was once the 17th century court house, tolbooth and weigh-house is now part of the **Fife** Folk Museum where are assembled scenes and implements from the rural past. It overlooks the single-arch Bishop's Bridge, said to be named after **Archbishop Sharp** whose murder in 1679 took place on Magus Muir to the east. There stand two monuments, one commemorating the crime, the other the five **Covenanters** who were wrongfully executed for it. West of Ceres, between **Cupar** and **Ladybank**, Crawford Priory is now a deserted gothick fantasia created by the eccentric Lady Lindsay, a recluse who lived for her menagerie of birds, dogs, a fox and a deer. The smaller ecclesiastical block is by **David Hamilton** (1809) and the larger castellate block by **James Gillespie Graham** (1811).

CHALMERS, George Paul (1833–78) Painter

Along with **William McTaggart**, Chalmers was one of the most successful pupils of **Robert Scott Lauder**. Born in **Montrose** of humble background, his natural artistic talents were apparent from an early age. The early death of his father and straitened family circumstances prevented his removal to **Edinburgh** until after his 20th birthday. There, however, in the hothouse atmosphere

George Paul Chalmers, a self portrait (SNPG)

of Lauder's **Trustees' Academy** he was soon revealed as an exceptionally gifted artist and, along with his contemporaries McTaggart, **Pettie** and **Orchardson**, went on to form something of a golden generation of east-coast Scottish painters. A highly sensitive and intuitive painter, he never found his art easy and his major studio works were usually the result of exceptional struggle. Nonetheless his favoured subjects – portraits, interiors and ethereal landscapes – are mostly executed with exceptional delicacy and fluency of touch; the elusive half-tones are especially well rendered, notably in his masterpiece, The Legend (1864–78, **National Gallery of Scotland**), which, despite 14 years of work, was still unfinished at his death. A popular and sociable figure, Chalmers was elected to the **Royal Scottish Academy** in 1871. It was after an Academy dinner seven years later that he was found, presumed murdered, in a basement area near Edinburgh's **Charlotte Square**.

CHALMERS, James (1782–1853) Inventor

Born in **Arbroath**, Chalmers was a printer and publisher (producing the Dundee Chronicle) who interested himself in postal matters. Believing that a standard postal charge could be introduced nationwide, Chalmers had adhesive postage stamps printed and gummed in 1834 for public exhibition. He appears therefore to have preceded by some six years the more famous introduction of the Penny Post by Rowland Hill, with whom he corresponded.

CHALMERS, Peter MacGregor (1859–1922) Architect

Chalmers was born in **Glasgow**, trained as an architect at **Glasgow School of Art**, and lived and worked in Glasgow all his life. After opening his practice in 1887, he became one of the most prominent church designers of the late 19th and early 20th centuries in Scotland. He was also a scholar and researched and published many studies on the medieval architecture of Scotland. One of his special subjects was **Glasgow Cathedral**, on which he wrote extensively. This knowledge of medieval architecture he used in many restoration projects, including the abbeys of **Melrose** and **Glenluce**, **Iona Cathedral** (restored 1909) and **Paisley Abbey** where he began the restoration of the choir and the cloister in 1912. His main work, however, was the design of churches, chapels and furnishings, principally in the west of Scotland but also in the east and **Edinburgh**. Of his over 50 churches, Cardonald Parish Church (1888), St Kenneth, **Govan** (1898), Scoonie Parish Church, **Leven** (1905) and St Anne, **Corstorphine**, Edinburgh (1912) are notable examples.

CHALMERS, Thomas (1780–1847) Preacher

Born at **Anstruther** in 1780, Chalmers entered **St Andrews University** at the age of 11. He returned there as assistant to the Professor of Mathematics and again, in 1823, as Professor of Moral Philosophy. His main career was as a popular preacher and prolific writer of great social influence, making his name from the pulpits of the Tron Church and the new St John's parish, **Glasgow**.

His development of pastoral care revived the office

Rev Thomas Chalmers and grandson, by D O Hill from an 1844 calotype by Hill and Adamson (SNPG)

of deacon and assigned the elders to social welfare in their districts to relieve the poor. In these new industrial communities popular education, charity and social care were made part of his evangelical Christianity, but firmly within the **Calvinist** ethic of self-help not state aid. For a while, by his own energy, organisation and publicity, the outmoded parish system of care worked in the city only by the subsidy of philanthropy.

He became Professor of Divinity at **Edinburgh University** in 1828 and **Moderator** of the **General Assembly** in 1832 on the back of his Glasgow success. As leader of the Evangelical party of the Church he proposed the Veto Act of 1834, which gave some power to parishes to reject a minister presented by the patron. Eventually his stance against patronage contributed to the **Disruption** of 1843 when he led a third of the ministers out of the established Church to form the **Free Church of Scotland**. He became its first Moderator and died in 1847 as first Principal of its college.

By sheer energy and popular appeal he had stretched the 18th century concepts of his origins to confront 19th century problems; but the strain broke the Church of Scotland for nearly 100 years and left the problems still unsolved.

CHAMBERS, Robert (1802–71) Writer and Bookseller

Born in **Peebles** two years after his brother **William**, Robert Chambers was considered the brains of the family; while William toiled as apprentice to a bookseller, Robert laboured at his studies. Even though he suffered from a painful deformity of the feet, he daily walked the five miles from **Joppa** (where his father was Superintendent of the Salt Pans) to school in **Edinburgh**. But his father having been discharged from his employment over a missing £50, the family was unable to afford to send Robert to study Divinity at **Edinburgh University**. So at the age of 16 he started work as a bookseller with his brother. While William was experimenting with his new hand-press, Robert started to explore Edinburgh's **Old Town**. 'Patiently ranging up one close and down another, ascending stairs and poking into obscure courts, he took note of carvings over doorways, pondered on the structure of gables and . . . extended the scope of his researches until scarcely a bit of the city was left unexplored' (A Turnbull). The result of this industry was the 25-part *Traditions of Edinburgh*, written by Robert, printed, bound and published by William (1824–34), and much admired by, among others, **Walter Scott** who came to the shop to meet the author. In 1832 a similar collaboration produced the first edition of a weekly magazine, *Chambers' Edinburgh Journal*. Robert wrote many other books, including *Vestiges of Creation* (1844), the immediate forerunner of Darwin's *Origin of Species*, the authorship of which he managed to conceal for 10 years, *Biographical Dictionary of Eminent Scotsmen* (1849) and *The Life and Work of Robert Burns* (4 vols, 1851). He became Master of the Merchant Company of Edinburgh and an LL.D of **St Andrews University** just before he died in 1871. After William's death in 1883, Robert's son (also Robert) became head of the firm of W & R Chambers Ltd, and ran the *Journal* until his own death in 1888.

CHAMBERS, Sir William (1723–96)
Architect

Chambers made his name in England as one of the two 'Architects of the King's Works', a post which he shared with another Scotsman, **Robert Adam**. He began his life in Sweden as the son of a Scottish merchant and then travelled widely with the Swedish East India Company. In 1749 he turned to architecture as a profession, went to study in Paris under J-F Blondel and continued his training in Italy until 1755 when he settled in London. His appointment as architectural tutor to the Prince of Wales, the future George III, instantly established him as one of England's leading architects. In 1759 he published his *Treatise on Civil Architecture*, which became a standard work on the orders and their enrichment. Chambers always maintained a high public and professional profile. He was one of the founding members of the Royal Academy where he also exhibited regularly. He was also a member of the French Academy of Arts, a Fellow of the Royal Society and was honoured by the King of Sweden. His most famous work was undoubtedly London's Somerset House (begun 1776), a shining example of contemporary English design, where his interiors rivalled those of Adam. Generally his style fused English Palladianism with the neo-classicism he first became acquainted with in Paris. Many of his designs show great scholarly knowledge, such as the Pagoda, Kew (1757–62). Most of his works are in the south of England, the neo-classical **Duddingston House**, **Edinburgh** (1762–4), 'greatest of all 18th century Edinburgh villas', being a notable exception.

CHAMBERS, William (1800–83) Publisher

Born in **Peebles**, the son of James Chambers [see **Robert Chambers**], William started work at the age of 13 as apprentice to an **Edinburgh** bookseller. He set up on his own at a small shop in Leith Walk in 1819, used his first profits to purchase a hand-press and the following year printed, bound and published 750 copies of his first title, *The Songs of Robert Burns*. Between 1825–30 he wrote the *Book of Scotland*, and in 1832 he printed and published the first edition of *Chambers' Edinburgh Journal*, a weekly magazine costing 1½d with his brother Robert as editor. It was an immediate success and within a few years its circulation had risen to 84,000. Their *Chambers' Encyclopaedia* appeared between 1859–68 in 520 weekly parts again at 1½d each, the work of more than 100 distinguished contributors. In 1859 William presented his native town of Peebles with the Chambers Institution, containing a library of 15,000 books, a natural history museum, art gallery, reading room and lecture hall. As Lord Provost of Edinburgh (1865–9) he concentrated on slum clearance and promoted a scheme for renovating parts of the **Old Town**, including the massive and long-awaited restoration of **St Giles Cathedral**, for which he met the entire cost of £30,000. He died three days before completion of the work, and the first service after the official re-opening was his own funeral.

CHAPEL OF GARIOCH, Nr Inverurie, Aberdeenshire

The Garioch (pron. Geerie) was, like **Buchan** and Formartine, one of the ancient provinces of the north-east, its lordship passing from the Buchan **Comyns** to **Robert I**. Chapel of Garioch, now a village and (with Pitcaple) a parish, stands on the slopes of **Bennachie** and is named after the Chapel of St Mary, confirmed by the abbot of **Lindores** in 1195. A gateway arch with the date 1626 survives beside the parish church (1813). The Leslie stronghold of Balquhain, where **Queen Mary** stayed in 1562, was burnt by Cumberland en route to **Culloden** and remains a ruin. More convincing proof of the region's importance is afforded by the abundance of monoliths. Besides a stone circle at Balquhain, the Maiden Stone of Chapel of Garioch is said to have been named after a daughter of Balquhain who died during her elopement. This is an exceptionally fine cross-slab of pink granite neatly carved in low relief with symbols including the **Pictish** 'elephant'. It is thought to be 'one of the last to be carved in Grampian'. More Pictish slabs are in the grounds of Logie and at Brandsbutt, **Inverurie**. A few miles to the north-east at Daviot the Loanhead stone circle with a giant recumbent and a central ring **cairn** is highly impressive. Pottery finds have led to the conclusion that the circle ceased to be used after about 2000 BC. Two semi-circles of stones beside it have revealed partially burnt human remains and were evidently a Bronze Age cremation ground.

CHARLES I (1600–49) King

The safe delivery of the last king to be born in Scotland occasioned no excitement. **James VI** and Queen Anne already had a most promising heir in **Henry, Prince of Wales**; besides, the new arrival was sickly to the point of being physically retarded. But he had been born in

The Maiden Stone at Chapel of Garioch (HS)

Charles I, by or after Edward Bower (SNPG)

Dunfermline's royal residence and, as **Andrew Carnegie** would put it, 'fortunate indeed [is] the child who first sees the light of day in that romantic city'. Aged three, but still crawling, Charles accompanied his parents south as second in line to the English as well as the Scots throne; aged 12, now walking well, he became heir apparent when his brother died; aged 16, with nothing worse than a stammer, he was created Prince of Wales; and aged 25, a fair marksman and scholar, he was crowned in Westminster Abbey. 'Fortunate indeed' he had been; thereafter, though, he was not.

In 1625, the year of his English coronation, he also married the French princess Henrietta Maria. A happy and fruitful union, it was nonetheless politically ill-fated in that her exaggerated ideas of a sovereign's rights and a subject's obligations accorded disastrously with his own. Once freed of Buckingham's influence (murdered in 1628) Charles received only conjugal encouragement in his resistance to parliamentary accountability and in his insistence on the rights of the Church.

Early fiscal and ecclesiastical differences with both English and Scots Parliaments soon raised constitutional issues. In Scotland his 1625 Act of Revocation threatened not only holders of titles and Crown lands but also those enjoying erstwhile ecclesiastical properties and teinds. Confirmation of such tenures was available but at a cost that few were willing to pay. There was also growing unease over the religious sympathies of a king whose queen attended Mass, whose bishops were to be among the main beneficiaries of the new fiscal pressures, and whose liturgical ideas were decidedly Anglican if not Romish.

The latter became particularly apparent during the King's first visit to Scotland (1633) for a belated coronation at **Holyrood**. The visit – and the building programme entailed in the elevation of **Edinburgh** into a bishopric, a city, and the Scottish capital – bore heavily on burghal pockets. But greater still was the resentment caused by the resuscitation of the **Five Articles of Perth**, the finery displayed at the coronation, and the subsequent reintroduction of the surplice. Failing to halt such measures in Parliament, where the bishops were seen to exercise undue influence, or by personal pleas to the King, the **Presbyterian** opposition (including most of the revocation-threatened nobility) became hopelessly alienated. Influenced by William Laud, Charles now precipitated defiance by the introduction of the 1636 Code of Canons and the 1637 **Book of Common Prayer**. Both were incompatible with **Calvinism** as practised in Scotland for more than a generation and both were imposed by royal prerogative without the consultation of Parliament or **General Assembly**. Petitions against the Prayer Book poured into Edinburgh where the mob readily reinforced them. The petitioners established delegate committees, 'the Tables', which again petitioned the King in vain; frustration led to the drawing up and subscription of the **Covenant** (1638).

With the Covenanters purchasing arms and focusing their ire on the bishops, Charles proffered an olive branch through his commissioner **James Hamilton, 3rd Marquis and 1st Duke**. The Code and the Prayer Book were suspended and a General Assembly called to meet in **Glasgow** (1638). But, as usual with the King's attempts at reconciliation, it was too little too late. The Assembly, packed with Covenanters, proscribed Code and Prayer Book, abolished episcopacy, and defied Hamilton's royal authority by refusing to disband. Charles attempted to reassert himself by force of arms (First Bishops' War) but was frustrated by lack of troops and money, and forestalled by the rapid formation and deployment of the army of the Covenant. Hostilities, never really opened, closed with the Pacification of **Berwick** in June 1639. Both sides were to disarm and consultations were to be opened with a view to finding a settlement. But the Covenanters did not disband and the King, finding his adversaries adamant over the abolition of bishops, sought the support of the English Parliament for a renewal of hostilities. Again he was disappointed in England and again anticipated in Scotland. The army of the Covenant swept south in 1640 (Second Bishops' War) and occupied Newcastle. Peace, as brokered by the Scots commissioners and the English Parliament, left the Scots in occupation of the northern English counties and left Charles obligated to pay their maintenance plus a substantial indemnity before they would withdraw (Treaty of Ripon, 1641).

During his second and last visit to Scotland (1641) the King made further attempts at conciliation but failed to exploit a rift within Covenanting ranks. **James Graham, Marquis of Montrose**'s signature of the Cumbernauld Bond and his overtures to Charles brought only imprisonment, from which the King secured his release. Meanwhile a confused plot to kidnap Hamilton and the **8th Earl of Argyll**, known as 'the Incident', may have been a case of bungled royal intrigue or a cunning ruse by the supposed victims to discredit the King and enhance their own standing.

The common cause established between English parliamentarians and Scots Presbyterians bore further fruit in the 1643 Solemn League and Covenant. During the first phase of the Civil War (1642–6) Scotland was administered by Argyll while Montrose briefly but brilliantly resurrected royal fortunes. When in England the Royalist cause grew hopeless, it was to the Scots army that Charles elected to surrender (1646). But negotiations proved abortive; in return for settlement of the indemnity agreed at Ripon, the King was finally handed over to the English Parliament. Second thoughts were in order when the Presbyterians of the Long Parliament were steadily elbowed aside by the Independents of the New Model Army. Following the King's escape to the Isle of Wight, the **Engagement** at last brought him the support of moderate Covenanters who saw in a cowed but legitimate sovereign a better basis for the long-sought Presbyterian settlement in England than could be hoped for from the turbulent ranks of Cromwell's army. Defeat of the Engagers at Preston (1648) sealed the King's fate. With an obstinacy that suddenly seemed dignified and courageous, Charles was tried by an unrepresentative English Parliament and executed.

CHARLES II (1630–85) King

If **Charles I** was the last king to be born in Scotland, Charles II was the last to be crowned there. The ceremony took place at **Scone** on 1 January 1651, nearly a decade before England restored its monarchy. Technically there was therefore scarcely any interregnum in Scotland. When Charles, after defeat at Worcester, was again forced into Continental exile, Scotland's Royalists could console themselves with the thought that it was not the first time that their **Stewart** monarch had been detained 'over the water'; nor would it be the last. The Stewart succession, sufficiently interrupted in England to make 'the later Stuarts' somehow more expendable, was continuous in Scotland and may help to explain the tenacity of **Jacobite** sentiment after 1688.

Charles had been born in London's St James's Palace, the eldest son of Charles I and Henrietta Maria and the elder brother of James, Duke of York, later **James VII and II**. Both boys were present at the battle of Edgehill and for safety were then sent into exile in France (1645). Amongst those who tutored Charles was Thomas Hobbes and amongst those who charmed him Lucy Walter, who also bore his child, **James** (Scott), later **Duke of Monmouth**. After his father's execution (1649), Charles opened negotiations with both **James Graham, Marquis of Montrose** (who had the formidable support of **Elizabeth of Bohemia**) and commissioners from the **Covenanting** government. But there was no real prospect of these parties uniting and by seeming to support the latter Charles merely undermined the former, who was duly defeated at **Carbisdale** and then hanged. It was therefore under the protection of those who had sold his father to England's parliamentarians, and who were now proudly exhibiting the severed limbs of his best general, that Charles arrived at **Speymouth** in the summer of 1650. Cromwell was still in Ireland and the Covenanters, convinced that righteousness was invincible, were grimly enforcing the **Act of Classes**. Charles was made to sign the Covenant before he could land and thereafter was the reluctant subject of an intensive programme of re-education in the ways of the Lord. He made one attempt to break free, known as 'The Start' [see **Glen Clova**]; but it was only after Cromwell's shattering victory at **Dunbar** and Charles's coronation at Scone that a royal army was at last allowed to take the field. With Cromwell tightening his grip on **Edinburgh** and the Borders, Charles marched south. He found little support in England and was quickly routed at Worcester (1651).

The 1660 Restoration – of the monarchy in England but of the sovereign in Scotland – was demanded 'by English opinion and an English parliament and on promises made to England'. Scotland celebrated with gusto but had made no terms, ventured no opinion, and could scarcely expect its sovereign to have any fond memories of the place. 'The decisive control by English politics over Scottish events had begun, and was to stay' (R Mitchison). Charles never revisited Scotland and was content to leave its management to a privy council run by his commissioners, initially **John Middleton** in Scotland and **Lauderdale** in London. For a country suffering from a decade of over-government this near neglect may be seen as advantageous; the burghs slowly revived and under **Dalrymple** and **Mackenzie** the Scottish **law** underwent an important process of definition.

Religious attitudes were less easily reconciled. Under the Act Recissory all legislation since 1633 was repealed, thus divesting the monarchy of the constitutional fetters imposed in 1640 and the Church of the liberties won in 1638. The consequent restoration of episcopacy and lay patronage was not laced with the obnoxious liturgical trimmings so loved by Charles I and was accepted by **Resolutioners** like **James Sharp** who was appointed Archbishop of **St Andrews** (1661). Nevertheless the settlement obliged new ministers to take the oath of allegiance and existing ministers to be formally presented. Hard-core **Protesters** who declined any such compromise with human authority were deprived of their kirks and parishes but continued preaching in makeshift '**conventicles**'. Attempts at their suppression provoked the **Pentland Rising** and resulted in 20 years of carrot-and-stick repression [see **Indulgences**, **Drumclog**, **Bothwell Brig**, '**Killing Time**'].

Meanwhile Lauderdale had replaced Middleton in Scotland and was himself superseded in the early 1680s by James, Duke of Monmouth and then James, Duke of York. A reign that had begun with the execution of the **8th Earl of Argyll** (for collaboration with Cromwell) ended with the condemnation of the **9th Earl of Argyll** (for refusing to take the **Test Act**, 1681, and involvement in the Rye House Plot, 1683). Never again would Scotland's most powerful family prove other than loyal to the government of the day. A 1669 attempt to unite the Scots and English Parliaments had failed but, by standing aloof, Charles, 'an exact knower of mankind' (Defoe), had done more than anyone to create the conditions and interests favourable to eventual **Union**.

CHARTISM

While in Scotland as elsewhere the Chartist movement (1837–48) achieved little in the way of concrete reform, it did increase awareness of various political and social grievances while furnishing experience in the organisation and management of popular protest. In the wake of the 1832 Reform Act, The People's Charter (adopted 1838) demanded universal male suffrage, annual parliaments, and secret ballots as well as other measures designed to make parliamentary membership more accessible. As in England so in Scotland, Chartist newspapers and associations quickly proliferated and proceded to bombard Parliament with petitions. But these local associations also espoused related causes such as educational reform, Corn Law repeal, **temperance**, **trade unionism**, **co-operative** retailing and religion (a Chartist Church resulted). Heated debate also took place on the proper forms of protest. A mass meeting on **Edinburgh**'s **Calton Hill** rejected the threat of physical violence and insurrection as a legitimate posture and opted for 'moral force'; but more militant Chartists in **Glasgow** and the west of Scotland, most notably **Dr John Taylor**, declined to relinquish this option, although they scarcely used it. After much initial fervour, the movement slumbered but in 1848 briefly revived. Fuelled by unemployment and recession, there was again talk of insurrection and of forming a popular paramilitary force. Lenient sentences handed out to those deemed guilty of incitement deprived the movement of much-needed martyrs and the agitation died down as quickly as it had flared up.

CHASEABOUT RAID (August/September 1565)

This was the name given to the fruitless rebellion, led by **James Stewart, Earl of Moray** with the support of **James Hamilton, Duke of Châtelherault**, against the marriage of **Queen Mary** to **Lord Darnley**. Moray objected to the marriage which, since it was unacceptable to English Elizabeth, wrecked his plans for an Anglo-Scottish alliance. It also threatened considerably to reduce his own influence. However since Darnley could not realistically be opposed on the grounds of his Catholicism (which was so lukewarm as to barely warrant the name), and since Mary had already made reassuring concessions to the reformed Church, few other Protestants could be persuaded to join the rebellion. Refused English support for his rebellion and faced with a spirited campaign led by the Queen herself, Moray was forced to take refuge in England, although he was restored to his half-sister's favour after the murder of **David Rizzio**.

CHATTAN, Clan

The original **clan** was probably descended from Gilliechattan Mor, servant of St Chattan, living at Torcastle in **Lochaber**. In 1291 Angus, Chief of **Mackintosh**, married Eva, the Chattan chief's daughter, and he inherited the chiefship. But Clan Chattan in the 14th and later centuries was not of the same composition or character as the prehistoric clan. It became a confederation of (a) descendants of the original clan (MacPhersons, Cattanachs, Macbeans, Macphails), (b) Mackintoshes and their offshoots (Shaws, Farquharsons, Ritchies, McCombies, MacThomases) and (c) families not originally related by blood (Macgillivrays, Davidsons, Macleans of Dochgarroch, Macqueens of Pollochaig, Macintyres of **Badenoch**, Macandrews).

For over 600 years the Chief of **Clan Mackintosh** was also Chief or Captain of Clan Chattan. In 1938 the chief died without direct male heir and Lord Lyon [see **Heraldry**] held that the chiefship of Clan Chattan had become separate from that of Mackintosh. The present and 33rd Chief is Malcolm Mackintosh of Clan Chattan who resides in Zimbabwe.

CHEPMAN, Walter (c1473–c1528) and MYLLAR, Andrew (fl.1503–08) Printers

Walter Chepman and Androw Myllar are the earliest recorded Scottish printers. Under the terms of a royal patent granted by **James IV** in September 1507, and with the encouragement of **William Elphinstone**, Bishop of **Aberdeen**, they entered into partnership to establish the first national press in the Southgait (now the **Cowgate**) of **Edinburgh** for the purpose of printing lawbooks, Acts of Parliament, chronicles and liturgical works.

Chepman, a wealthy Edinburgh merchant and trusted royal servant, provided the considerable funds necessary for such a pioneering venture, leaving the practical details of the new craft to his partner, the much more obscure Androw Myllar. Myllar had been a bookseller in Edinburgh in 1503 and later went over to France where he gained experience in the art of printing. He is known to have been involved with the production of two books in Rouen in 1505 and 1506, returning shortly afterwards to Scotland and bringing back with him the 'prent . . . and expert men' that give to the first Scottish press the distinctive flavour of the 'auld alliance'.

The success of the Southgait Press was, however, shortlived (1507–10), and of its slender output, only the *Aberdeen Breviary* (1509–10) has survived in more than one copy. To this can be added a few fragments of verse from **Blind Harry**'s patriotic epic *The Wallace* and Sir Richard Holland's allegory the *Buke of the Howlet*, a single leaf of a Donatus grammar printed in Scots and, most precious of all, a unique collection of poetry printed in 1508 and containing verse by two of the major poets of the 'Golden Age', **William Dunbar** and **Robert Henryson**.

Curiously, Myllar's name vanished from imprints after 1508, though it is likely he continued to participate for some time after that. Chepman certainly remained active in both civic affairs and royal service under **James IV** and **V**, though not in printing, with which he seems to have severed his connections after the completion of the *Aberdeen Breviary*. Towards the end of his life he endowed a mortuary chapel in **St Giles Kirk** where he was buried c1528.

CHEVIOT SHEEP

The Cheviot originated from crosses of Borders sheep with the New Leicester from about 1760; the latter, providing the finest meat sheep of its day, had been developed by Robert Bakewell (1725–95) in Leicestershire. In Scotland Cheviots are the dominant breed of the extreme north and of the Borders region. The North Country Cheviot is a thriving breed, relatively large-bodied, with quite good wool. It was introduced to **Caithness** from the Borders by **Sir John Sinclair** in 1792. Merino sheep were crossed with these animals. The Cheviot of the south country is smaller-bodied with erect ears. Its numbers are declining and many Borders flockmasters are using North Country Cheviot rams to breed larger-bodied ewes.

Cheviots have a profound influence throughout the sheep industry because, when five or six years old, ewes are sold from the hill flocks and mated with Border Leicester rams to produce Scotch Halfbred sheep. Male lambs are slaughtered, but the females are valuable breeding stock for lowland farmers, being mated with Suffolks or a similar breed for meat lamb production.

CHIRNSIDE, Berwickshire

Chirnside grew up beside a large **cairn**, probably prehistoric. The village's situation made it vulnerable to invasion from England and active in Border reiving and the **Covenanting** movement. The philosopher and historian **David Hume** was the second son of Joseph Hume of Ninewells, Chirnside. In 1749 he retired to Ninewells where he composed an inquiry *Concerning the Principles of Morals* published in 1751. **Jim Clark**, the World Champion motor racing driver, moved to Edington Mains, Chirnside, from **Fife** in 1942. A clock to his memory stands in Chirnside and his grave is in the village churchyard. The 'Rock House' (probably 19th century) was built into solid rock beside Dexter's mill. It had two rooms each 15ft (4.5m) square but no water, light or sanitation. The roof, now collapsed, was once hidden by a high façade surmounted by stone. In 1917 it suffered a near-miss by a bomb from a passing Zeppelin.

CHISHOLM, Erik (1904–65) Composer and Professor of Music

Chisholm's music blends **Celtic** elements with post-Bartokian influences. His major works include the *Indian* and *Pibroch Piano Concertos* and a ballet for the Celtic Ballet Company, *The Forsaken Mermaid*; but much of his music, including his charming settings of his wife Lillias Scott's poems, is at its most expressive in small lyric and dance forms. He founded the Active Society for the Propagation of Contemporary Music in **Glasgow** in 1929, and was responsible for the first public performances of over 200 new works, including Sorabji's gigantic *Opus Clavicembalisticum*, dedicated to **Hugh MacDiarmid**, and works by Bartok, Hindemith and others, and for mounting the first complete production of Berlioz's *Les Troyens*. After his appointment as Professor of Music at the University of Cape Town (1946) he composed several short operas and, on tour, gave the British premier of Bartok's *Bluebeard's Castle*.

CHRISTISON, Sir Robert (1797–1882) Toxicologist

Born in **Edinburgh**, Christison studied medicine at **Edinburgh University** and in Paris. After returning to Edinburgh he successively held professorships in Medical Jurisprudence and Materia Medica, the latter for 45 years. His main work was on poisons, greatly advancing medical knowledge of their effects on the body as well as forensic studies. He was elected President of the **Royal Society of Edinburgh**.

CHURCH OF SCOTLAND

The concept of a national Church is twofold: either it is universal to a nation or it is recognised as the established, official Church. In the case of Scotland there has been considerable variation between these two.

Tertullian, writing about the year 200, was aware of Christians in parts of Britain 'inaccessible to the

Romans'. This could refer to north of Hadrian's Wall or to Ireland. The first known figure in Scotland is **St Ninian**, a Briton who dedicated a church at **Whithorn** in 397 which is increasingly regarded as the cradle of Scottish Christianity. That he trained in Rome and was there made a bishop presupposes an existing Church requiring his leadership in **Galloway**. The earlier Kirkmadrine stones in **Wigtonshire** bear out this suggestion.

Generally known as the **Celtic Church**, the early Church in Scotland grew to produce the monastic settlements of the **Culdees**, probably from the time of the Irish missionary **St Columba** who was based on **Iona** from 563. Isolated and out of touch, the Church agreed, in a conference at Whitby in 664, to revise its observances in line with the Roman thinking of the Northumbrian Church founded by **St Aidan**. An *Ecclesia Scoticana*, first mentioned in 873 with headquarters then at **Dunkeld**, later took direction from the bishops who claimed for the nation relics of the newly acquired patron saint, **St Andrew**.

Roman organisation and authority came together with **St Margaret** and **Alexander I**. From the 12th to the mid-16th century this **Roman Catholic Church** in Scotland was deeply involved in national affairs but, as in the rest of Europe, subject to the Pope as well as servant to the monarch. Its national independence was affirmed in 1188 by a Papal Bull declaring it a 'special daughter' of Rome, and it played a significant part in defining the nation by the **Declaration of Arbroath** in 1320. But like all large organisations, power and wealth corrupted it; the lives of the related Archbishops of **St Andrews**, James and **David Beaton**, may serve as examples.

Following the introduction of Protestant ideals from the Continent by the **Lollards**, **Hamilton** and **Wishart** were martyred before the **Reformation** proper reached Scotland in 1560. Then, guided by **Knox**, the national Church overthrew Roman decadence to replace it with Calvin's austere teachings. Struggles with the **Stewart** kings increased throughout the 17th century as **Presbyterian** order, taught by **Melville**, alternated with episcopacy. Commitment of the individual and nation to God through the **Covenants** of 1638 and 1643 resulted in religious strife which the saintly **Archbishop Leighton** was unable to prevent. It reached a climax in 1679 with the murder of **Archbishop Sharp** by opportunist Covenanters.

The present Church of Scotland was established as the national Church by law and constitutional change in 1690, but at great cost. In the process episcopal clergy, some 200, were 'rabbled' from western parishes and **Holyrood Abbey** sacked. There was no longer one Church for the nation but a national established Church, the Church of Scotland, and an **Episcopal Church of Scotland**, together with Roman Catholic remnants and Quakers, such as **Barclay**, on opposite extremes of the Christian spectrum.

No sooner had **Carstares** organised Presbyterian government than the 1712 Patronage Act reimposed civil interference in ecclesiastical appointments. The 18th century witnessed a sorry proliferation of splits and factions beginning with the **Secession Church** in 1733. What remained of the established Church of Scotland managed to contain both Moderates, who epitom-

ised the thinking of the **Scottish Enlightenment** and Evangelicals whose influence surfaced in the next century. Outside it were the independent Churches of **Lady Glenorchy** and the **Haldanes**; meanwhile the Episcopalians and **Non-Jurors** suffered for their **Jacobite** sympathies rather than for their beliefs.

The Church of Scotland in all its parishes suffered its greatest division, again over patronage, when in 1843 the **Disruption** detached more than a third of the ministers voluntarily and a similar proportion of the active membership. However, the shock of the rival **Free Church of Scotland**, as well as the other secession Churches and denominations, at last penetrated established complacency. The 19th century was the most active period of church-going, the most supportive of missionaries, the time of theological revision and much parish activity, all of which identified Scotland as a country of the Kirk. By the end of the century reunification had begun, at first outside the main stream. This impetus resulted in the **United Free** and the Established Church of Scotland finally merging in 1929.

Today the Church of Scotland remains the established Church of the nation and through its **General Assembly** attempts to voice the nation's concerns from a perspective that is Christian and Protestant. But unlike the Church of England, it retains no vestige of lay patronage and the sovereign is not its head. Like all denominations it has to contend with a decline of membership in an age of secularisation and varied unbelief. Adapting to change, the form of worship may include more frequent communions, special youth services, and liturgical elements learned from its **Iona Community**, with less emphasis on Old Testament style and the psalms. The preaching of The Word is central still to the purpose and method of the Church and the parish ministry is its strength. Its weakness lies in the burden of too many ageing buildings (the result of past divisions) which are no longer in the best location for **population** changes.

With headquarters and an official residence for the **Moderator** in the **New Town** of **Edinburgh** it has all the bureaucracy and trappings of established Churches elsewhere. As the parent of many other Presbyterian Churches abroad, it commands respect in inter-Church and international bodies. Three centuries after its establishment and four centuries after the Reformation, its heritage, which is not just that of Knox and Calvin but also of Ninian and Columba, retains a life force in the country and further afield. [See chart p. 1041]

CHURCHILL BARRIERS, Orkney

Built after the sinking of HMS *Royal Oak* (14 October 1939) to block the east end of **Scapa Flow** between Mainland, Burray Island and **South Ronaldsay**, they consist of concrete blocks weighing from 5 to 10 tons, over which a road was constructed to link these islands. Italian prisoners of war, captured in North Africa, helped to construct the causeways. They left behind them the superb memento of a Catholic chapel on Lambholm, created out of two Nissen huts joined end to end.

CLACKMANNAN, Clackmannanshire

William Aytoun has one of his characters devoting a vacation to the challenge of discovering Clackmannan

The 14th–15th century Clackmannan Tower (RWB)

since 'no one he had ever encountered had seen it'. East of **Alloa** and only two miles from the Firth of Forth, the one-time county town of **Clackmannanshire** continues to evade celebrity and to render any description open to the imputation of parody. It occupies a ridge with the main street declining, like its history, along the back of the ridge from the 14th–15th century castle past the church to the Tolbooth and Market Place and on down to the art nouveau Town Hall of 1903. The castle, Clackmannan Tower, stands on lands granted to Robert Bruce, an illegitimate grandson of **Robert I**, by **David II** in 1360. Construction of the rectangular tower was followed in the 15th century by the taller square tower to form an L-plan, both towers being crowned with parapeted and machicolated wall-walks. Further additions in the 16th and 17th centuries have been largely demolished except for the fine pedimented entrance. The tower continued in Bruce ownership until 1772, its last resident being Lady Catherine Bruce who was wont to 'knight' favoured guests (including **Robert Burns**) with the double-handed sword of Robert I. Derelict ever since and vulnerable to mining subsidence, the tower remains impressive though 'access is not easy, internal access currently impossible, and the environs a tragic waste of outstanding potential' (A Swan, 1987).

The parish church (1815) is by **James Gillespie Graham** and stands where once stood a chapel to St Serf. Further down, the Market Place contains a 16th century mercat cross with the Bruce arms, a tower with ogee roof (all that remains of the 17th century Tolbooth) and the enigmatic *clach-mannan* or stone of Mannan or Mannau. It rests on top of a monolithic plinth dragged hence from **Abbey Craig** by 16 horses but was previously sited on Lookaboutye Brae, to the south. Though once an object of veneration, its significance is unknown, Mannau being possibly an Iron Age tribe, a local sea-god or the area in which he/they held sway.

CLACKMANNANSHIRE
Scotland's smallest county, comprising 38,700 acres (15,662ha) and with a population of 48,660 (1991), Clackmannanshire lies to the north of the River Forth, with **Stirling** to the west, **Perthshire** to the north, **Fife** to the east and **Falkirk** to the south. Nearly half its area is taken up by the **Ochil Hills**, whose highest point in Clackmannanshire is Ben Cleuch at 2363ft (720m). The southern half of the county comprises the Forth plain, fertile and coal-bearing; agriculture, mining and distilling were traditionally the main occupations. During the **local government** reorganisation of 1975–95, it was converted into Clackmannan District of Central Region, but has since regained its former status as a Council Area. **Alloa** is the county town, the other burghs being **Alva**, **Dollar** and **Tillicoultry**.

CLAIM OF RIGHT, The (1689)
To address the constitutional crisis posed by the flight to France of **James VII** and the arrival of William of Orange, a Convention of Estates was summoned in March 1689. (A Convention was a less formal assembly than a Parliament, though with a similar membership, which could be called at shorter notice, usually for a specific purpose and, crucially in this case, without royal authority.) Letters from William, then James, were read, the former's conciliatory, the latter's minatory. Opinion was already drifting in favour of William when the foremost **Jacobite**, Viscount Dundee (**John Graham of Claverhouse**), absented himself and was then declared a rebel, thus forcing him into armed opposition. It was next resolved that, James having forfeited the throne, it should be offered to William and Mary on terms contained within an accompanying Claim of Right. This elaborated on James's misdemeanours – popery, attempting to overthrow Protestantism, failure to take the coronation oath, and altering the constitution 'from a legal limited monarchy to an arbitrary despotic power' – and then insisted on various constitutional liberties including the exclusion from office of papists and the primacy of the **law** over the royal prerogative. In other words, the Convention in its Claim of Right was changing not only the sovereign but also the nature of his sovereignty. Articles of Grievances elaborated still further and sought to protect parliamentary liberties by condemning the Committee of Articles through which the **Stewarts** had managed Parliament. Thereafter many of William's difficulties with Scotland would hinge on whether or not he had accepted the contractual relationship implied in the Claim of Right before taking the coronation oath.

CLANRANALD, Books of
These are two manuscripts of the late 17th and early 18th centuries, associated with the MacDonalds generally, and more particularly with the Clanranald branch of that clan [see **Clan Donald**]. The Red Book was mainly written by Niall MacMhuirich, **bard** to the Clanranald chiefs. It contains both contemporary and earlier history (seen from a MacDonald perspective), early Irish history and legend, and classical Gaelic poetry by

MacMhuirich and other professional poets. An earlier Red Book may have disappeared; it is rumoured to be somewhere in Australia.

The Black Book seems partly derivative (at least as to its history) from the extant Red Book, but it has a curious mixture of contents, written both in English and Gaelic, touching on topics such as chronology, Irish genealogies, poems about the heraldic symbol of the Red Hand (to which Niall MacMhuirich replies in the Red Book), and Gaelic grammar and prosody. The scribe of this book was Christopher Beaton, one of a learned family of scribes and medics. Both manuscripts were given by the Clanranalds to the National Museum of Antiquities in **Edinburgh** in 1944. They had been edited, but not in detail, by A Cameron in *Reliquiae Celticae* (1892–4).

CLANS

The English word 'clan', denoting a social grouping particularly associated with Scotland, comes from the Gaelic *clann*, for which **Edward Dwelly** gives three meanings: children, descendants, and clan or tribe. The first two give the third its distinctive quality in that most members of a clan share a common descent, however remote, and may thus be regarded as belonging to a single extended family. This relationship may be bolstered by the use of a shared surname, association with a particular territory, wearing of a particular **tartan**, and acknowledgement of a clan chief, coat of arms and clan society. Yet it is incorrect to infer that all who share the same surname belong to the same clan, or that every clan must have a chief, tartan, territory, etc. Such notions owe something to established historical reality but more to 19th century attempts to systematise and romanticise clan society plus 20th century attempts to exploit the 'clan system' commercially.

Three categories of clan may usefully be distinguished. Major power groups such as the **Clan Campbell**, **Clan Donald**, the **Gordons**, and perhaps the **Clan Chattan** and the Mackenzies dominated wide regions, crushing or absorbing minor clans and at times exercising a major influence on national affairs. A second category is typified by the slightly less influential clans: **Frasers**, **Gunns**, **Macphersons**, Maclachlans, Macleans, **MacLeods** etc. Finally the term was also used to designate smaller family groupings in much the same way as it is still used of, for instance, 'the Kennedy clan' (ie members of the late US President's family). Into this last category of clans which in the Scottish context never aspired to any political status fall purely titular entities such as *Clann na H'Oidche* – 'Clan of the Night' (a family of Morrisons on **Mull**); *Clann a Bhreatannaich* – 'Clan of the Britons' (the Galbraith family on **Gigha**); *Clann Mhic Raing* – 'Clan of Raing's children' (the Rankins, pipers to the Macleans) and *Clann Lulich O Thulaich Mhaodain* – 'Clan Lulich of the Hills of Modan' (the MacLulichs).

Origins and Distribution

Clans are generally associated with the Highlands and Islands, and to a lesser extent with other peripheral regions such as **Galloway** and the Borders, because it was in these areas that Scotland's early tribal organisation survived longest. Elsewhere, ie in central Scotland and most of the Lowlands, such kin-based groups were elbowed out by the feudal system which, emanating from the seat of royal authority, spread rapidly wherever bountiful terrain made a relatively small land-holding sufficient for a knight's fief.

It was otherwise in the infertile Highlands, although the division is not a clear one, either geographically or organisationally. Each social system borrowed from the other so that, in Professor T C Smout's definition, Highland society was based on kinship modified by feudalism and Lowland society on feudalism tempered by kinship. The difference is most clearly shown by the feudal insistence on succession by the eldest son as opposed to the ancient **Dalriadic** system of **tanistry**; amongst the clans the latter continued to be invoked long after general acceptance of primogeniture, thus affecting both Highland heraldry and 'official' chiefly pedigrees.

Historians, though, are cautious about juxtaposing a notional 'clan system' with the feudal system since this would suppose an ethnic homogeneity which history emphatically denies. Dalriadic Scots, later Irish, **Picts**, Britons, Norsemen and English all held sway at different times and, along with Normans and Flemings, are represented in the progenitors of the various clans. Thus the **Grants** and the Frasers are among those of Norman origin, while the Sutherlands and the **Murrays** are among those of Flemish origin. Although the arms of the Brodie chief imply a similar origin, this clan has also been credited with a rare Pictish provenance. The Clan Donald are of later (ie post-Dalriadic) Irish descent as are members of the **Argyll** clan confederacy: the MacSweens, **MacNeills**, Lamonts, MacLachlans, MacEwens, MacGilchrists and Highland Livingstones; all trace their descent from the marriage of Anrothan, Prince of the O'Neills, to the dynastic heiress of **Knapdale** and **Cowal**.

Similarly the Gunns and the MacLeods are of **Viking** blood; the Campbells and Galbraiths descend from ancient Britons of the old **Kingdom of Strathclyde**; and Borders familes such as the Swintons are of English stock from the ruling family of Northumberland. The original Dalriadic Kings of Scots are still represented, ultimately by today's British royal family, but also, in their cognisance of the **lion** rampant, by such families as Dunbar, Dundas, Wemyss, Abernethy, Gray and Mac-Duff; though now identified with the eastern Lowlands, all spring in the ultimate male line from the Gaels of Dalriada in Argyll and probably owe their eastward migration to **Kenneth mac-Alpin**'s removal to **Scone** when he combined the crowns of Picts and Scots.

The chiefs of the Moncrieffe Clan take their surname from the Holy Hill of the Picts (Moncrieffe Hill near **Perth**), where ancestors in the female line may have lived for 2000 years; but their armorial bearings display the Dalriadic lion rampant of an incoming Scots ancestor. This migration lends weight to the idea of a supposed massacre of Pictish chiefs by the Scots which would help to explain today's dearth of clans of Pictish origin. Marriage may also have played its part in that royal appointees to a particular territory often sought local legitimacy by marrying a daughter of the old tribal dynasty. Existing inhabitants might then group themselves round the new leader and, as 'Native Men', become part of his clan.

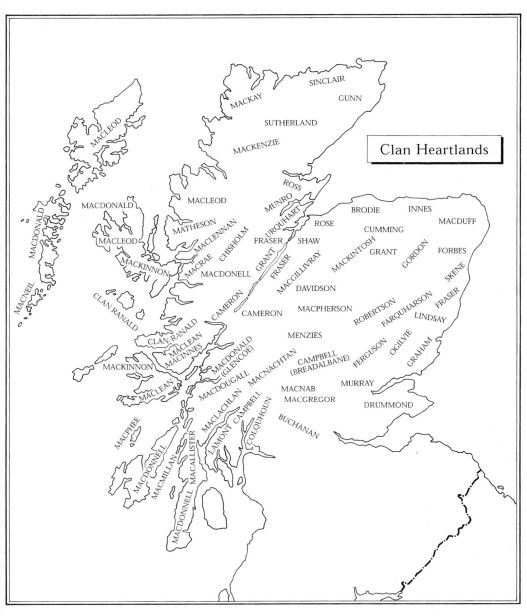

Clan Heartlands

Clans continued

Many of today's clans can be traced back as far as the 13th century, while chiefly pedigrees may be longer (eg descendants of the Irish Prince Anrothan whose lineage extends back to the semi-mythical 5th century Niall of the Nine Hostages).

Over such a long timespan it is unsurprising that clan history exhibits many examples of geographical and social mobility, thus confusing the notion of clan territories and a clan hierarchy. The Frasers, originally from France, settled first in the Borders before moving to **Aberdeenshire**, while the branch known as the **Frasers of Lovat**, thanks to a good marriage, settled on lands at the head of the Beauly Firth. Moving in the opposite

direction, the Macmillans, who are thought to have originated in **Moray**, moved to **Glen Lyon** and then to Argyll where the chief married a MacNeill heiress and settled in Knapdale. Hence the chief's arms display the Dalriadic lion rampant inherited through this marriage, plus the three stars of his ancestral **Moray**.

Sometimes these movements have confusing results; the MacIsaacs were a sept of the **MacDonalds of Clanranald** and MacDonalds by blood. One of the MacIsaac families got into trouble and moved south to Argyll where they took service with the Campbells of Craignish to whom they became armour-bearers. A branch of the Campbells living near **Kilmichael Glassary** likewise got into trouble and had to make a run for it; they settled on the lands of MacDonald of Keppoch in **Lochaber**. They served their new chief loyally for centuries, being known by their by-name of 'Na Glasserich' – the folk from Glassary – and never forgetting their Campbell identity. Thus a branch of the Clan Donald became part of Clan Campbell, and vice versa.

Both Clans Campbell and Donald provide outstanding examples of upward mobility. From Strathclyde, the Campbells married into an early Argyllshire dynasty and by supporting **Robert I** launched themselves on a steady political climb which culminated in their becoming the most powerful clan in the country by the 17th century. This was largely at the expense of Clan Donald. Descended from a grandson of **Somerled**, the Mac-Donald chiefs had ousted more powerful relations to become **Lords of the Isles**. For over 150 years they dominated the west Highlands but, rather than collaborating with the Scottish Crown, preferred to defy it as in the **Treaty of Westminster-Ardtornish** (1462). Discovery of this treaty led to the forfeiture of the lordship and divisions within the clan. One branch, the MacIans of **Ardnamurchan**, were extinguished in the 17th century and another, the MacIans of **Glencoe**, nearly suffered the same fate in the **Glencoe Massacre**.

The Frasers of Lovat were almost wiped out at the Battle of Blar-na-Leine (**Battle of the Shirts**, 1544) against the Clanranald MacDonalds. But perhaps the most unusual story is that of Clan Sween, descendants of that marriage between Prince Anrothan of the O'Neills and the Princess of Cowal. In their day, based on the mighty **Castle Sween**, they were far more powerful than either the MacDonalds or the Campbells of the time. But they played their cards badly both during King Haakon of Norway's invasion of 1263 and during the **Wars of Independence** (when they still boasted a fleet of galleys which they put at the disposal of the English King). Dispossessed of their former position, the MacSween chiefs left Scotland and as a clan went to Ireland, where they became the famous Mac-Sweeney gallowglasses, mercenary soldiers of renown and a rich and successful race once more.

More often hostages to history than masters of their own fate, the clans in general prospered or otherwise depending on the vigour with which the Crown was able to pursue its claim to authority over peripheral regions. Religious divisions in the 16th and 17th centuries, and the subsequent dynastic rivalry between **Jacobites** and Hanoverians, often weakened royal authority to the advantage of the clans. On the other hand a Cromwell or a Cumberland could quickly restore the situation and reinstate the inexorable progress towards national integration. The one exception, the one clan which consistently supported this process, was the Clan Campbell with its loyalty to the **Covenant** and to the Protestant succession. When other clans opposed the Covenant and the Hanoverians they could be seen as expressing resentment of Campbell pre-eminence rather than religious or dynastic conservatism.

Post-1745

There are those who claim that **Culloden** saw the end of the clan system. This is not the case. During the years of conflict there was remarkably little consistency among the majority of Highland clans. The Campbells and the northern clans were largely Hanoverian sup-

porters; a number were staunch in their allegiance to the **Stewarts**, but a larger number still either changed sides, remained neutral or were divided among themelves. Overall, in Scotland as a whole, many more Scots took up arms against **Prince Charles Edward** than for him.

Subsequently the energies of even the most ardent Jacobite clans were diverted into the wholehearted service of the developing British Empire, notably through the services of a series of quite outstanding new Highland Regiments whose qualities were soon a byword. Into their ranks fell the young men of the Highlands, officered by their chiefs and traditional leaders. The part played by the army in perpetuating and indeed creating much of Highland culture cannot be overestimated. For example the **Argyll and Sutherland Highlanders**, raised by Duncan Campbell of Lochnell for the Duke of Argyll as the Argyllshire Highlanders in 1794, carry the boar's head crest and the motto *Ne Obliviscaris* of Mac Cailean Mor on their accoutrements, wear the darker form of the Campbell tartan, march past on parade to 'The Campbells are Coming', and have had many more Campbell officers than any other name, to say nothing of the fact that the last three clan chiefs have themselves held commissions in the regiment.

But for many clansmen enlistment in a Highland Regiment was also an economic necessity. With the arrival of the potato and the eradication of smallpox, the **population** had surged to a level which the land could not support. Helped by the desire of some lairds to clear the ground for the introduction of sheep, and tempted by offers of land grants in the emergent Empire and by employment in the big cities, many thousands of Scots – Lowland as well as Highland – left their ancestral homes. The part played by the traditional clan leaders in this migration can be overstated, with too much made of the brutality shown by the **Countess of Sutherland**'s factor, and too little of the efforts of such as MacLeod of MacLeod who beggared himself to support his people.

Structure

The clan structure was based on the chief, father of his people, leader in war and administrator of the **law**. Around him were grouped his own immediate family and other earlier descendants of the chiefly line who had established themselves as chieftains and lairds in their own right. In the smaller clans this could be a problem. Land had to be recalled in order to supply the needs of newer generations more closely allied to the chief, which meant that families were given land for some three generations, after which it reverted to the chief's gift, leaving only whatever the family had managed to carve out for themselves. Younger sons and their younger sons might hold land temporarily as **tacksmen** or tenants; others might go into trade; social mobility was highly developed.

As we have seen, when surnames came into use, some families found it expedient to take the name of the chief under whose authority they found themselves, while there are those who share descent with the chief but use a different name. In many cases members of septs are the descendants of 'Native Men' or original inhabitants of an area taken over by a strange group. And finally there were the 'Broken Men', out of their own area, frequently on the run. They represented a threat to law and order and the government of the day on several occasions ordered that they should be taken under the proper authority of the nearest chief.

Chiefs

The size and importance of clans varied greatly; during the 17th and 18th centuries – and possibly even before – the most powerful chief of all, Mac Cailean Mor, chief of Clan Campbell, could count on putting some 5000 men into the field; other small clans engaged in Bonds of Manrent with him to gain his protection; his feudal superiority stretched over a large part of the West Highlands and Isles. On the other hand many small clans could field only a few hundred men, and the power of their chiefs in no way matched the strength of such Campbell chieftains as **Breadalbane** and **Cawdor**.

The authority on the status of chiefs and their identity is the Lord Lyon King of Arms [see **Heraldry**], Her Majesty's Supreme Officer of Honour in Scotland. It is he who grants arms to the chief and recognises him in that title. This is the only official recognition a chief receives, since his position confers no rank as such, nor any place in the Official Order of Precedence – although many chiefs also hold peerages or other titles.

The Standing Council of Scottish Chiefs was set up after World War II by the Countess of Erroll, Lord High Constable of Scotland, at the instigation of her husband, Sir Iain Moncrieffe of that Ilk. Most chiefs are members of this body which is, however, self-electing and thus a pressure group rather than a body with any official power. Membership is open to holders of the absolute undifferenced arms of any Scottish stock or stem, provided that such arms were in existence and matriculated in 1672–7 and include hereditary supporters, and also, in exceptional cases, to those whom Lyon has certified to be head of a considerable house or branch, and whom the Committee of the Standing Council agree is suitable. Examples of this latter category are Lord Lovat and MacLeod of the Lewes, neither of whom is chief of his whole name, but who nevertheless are great chiefs in their own right.

There are a number of clans whose chiefs have been swallowed up by the vicissitudes of time and whose identity is unknown. Sometimes this is due to a failure in the blood line when the last chief is left without an heir. If this happens, he or she is able to designate a 'tanister', or heir, even on a temporary basis. This happened in the case of the last Lord Breadalbane, who designated a successor as chieftain of the mighty Campbell branch of Glenorchy 'until such time as the next Earl of Breadalbane shall take his seat in the House of Lords'. It is not possible to pass on a peerage in this way; but the Campbells of Glenorchy will not be left without a leader while the search is on for the earls' successor. Such a search can be difficult; any aspirant must not only prove his own descent but also prove the extinction of any line which may have a superior claim.

Lyon may also entertain a petition to appoint a Commander of a Clan if there is no identifiable chief. The commander will act as and on behalf of the missing chief; he is appointed for a set number of years on the petition of the *Derbhfine* of the clan, which today is taken to be made up of all armigerous persons of the clan and all those possessed of substantial property in Scotland. In this way, recent years have seen the erection of Commanders for the MacGillivrays and the MacPhees, who hold office, subject to the terms of their appointment, until such time – if ever – that the rightful chief is found.

Surnames and Societies

By no means all people of the same name constitute a clan; a vast number of names have never been clans and could never be so in the sense of a shared ancestry. Such worknames as Smith, Taylor, Baxter and the like are to be found throughout the British Isles, as are such descriptive names as Black, Small, Brown, etc. Even patronymics – names beginning in Mac- or ending in -son – are frequently found to descend from totally unrelated sources. But practically every Scottish name has now been assigned as a sept of one or more clans – a pastime assiduously undertaken by the manufacturers and sellers of tartan, so that the thirst of all with a Scottish connection 'to belong to a clan' can be assuaged. Many of the results are optimistic to say the least; while there was a perfectly good family of Camerons who carried on the trade of tailors in Lochaber in times gone by, in no way can this seriously be taken as a good reason for the assignation of all those of the name of Taylor to **Clan Cameron**. Yet such is the case in the make-believe world of clan fantasy.

That there is a problem is undeniable, with several million people overseas desperate to identify with their Scottish origins and unable to find out from where they hail. Given that in the tribal areas at least, 'Broken Men' would attach themselves to the local chief or leader, it seems logical that such people should seek to join a Clan Society, thereby pledging loyalty to its chief. This is the essence of being a clansman – loyalty to a chief – and it is very much what actually happened. Those people who boast of belonging to more than one Clan Society are missing the point. There is also confusion over the status of a Clan Society within a clan. The two are not the same; the Society is but a small part – albeit an important one – of the clan. As such it cannot attempt to speak for the clan as a whole. Anyone of the name is still very much a member of the clan, whether or not they belong to the Society.

In their modern form, the clans are flourishing. Interest in Clan Societies, particularly overseas, is strong and the desire to identify with one's past seems on the increase. There are many more and larger Scottish Gatherings outside Scotland and the number grows every year. Clan chiefs are now domiciled around the world; few indeed are still living on their ancestral lands in Scotland. But they are still recognised and venerated by their clansmen, and many of them travel widely to keep in touch with their people, and to personify as ever that sense of belonging to a family.

CLANS, Battle of the (1396)

This 'fight to the death' was intended to settle once and for all the raging feud between the clans **Chattan** (or **Mackintosh**) and Kay (or **Mackay** or, sometimes, Quhele). On 28 September 1396 30 men from each clan lined up in a purpose-built enclosure on the North Inch at **Perth**. The men of Clan Chattan, finding themselves one short as battle commenced, persuaded 'a gallant saddler of Perth to volunteer his services for half a French gold dollar'. **King Robert III** and several members of his court lined up to watch the slaughter. By the time the King signalled the end of the contest, 29 Kays were dead, the one survivor swimming to safety across the **Tay**, while only 10 of Clan Chattan, and the saddler, lived to fight another day.

CLAPPERTON, Hugh (1788–1827) Explorer

Born at **Annan**, **Dumfriesshire**, the son of a doctor, Hugh Clapperton went to sea at the age of 13, spending some years in the merchant marine before joining the navy. His skills as a navigator led in 1821 to an invitation from the Admiralty to join an African expedition in search of the source of the river Niger, whose upper reaches had been explored and mapped by **Mungo Park** in 1796, but whose source and exact route were still the subject of wild conjecture. With Dr Walter Oudney, an old friend from **Edinburgh**, and Lieutenant Dixon Denham, an able soldier but an unspeakably obnoxious travelling companion, Clapperton set out from Tripoli in early 1822, reaching the shores of Lake Chad 18 months later. Clapperton and Oudney then turned westwards, while Denham set off on a private slaving expedition. In January 1824 Oudney, who was already consumptive, contracted a fever and died. Clapperton, described by a contemporary as 'tall, strong, and possessed of resources of a superior kind', continued alone as far as Sokoto (in the north of what is now Nigeria), where his progress was blocked by an unco-operative Sultan. He returned to England the following year without ever reaching the main river. Although the expedition had failed in its main objective, Clapperton and Oudney had explored Lake Chad and its environs, and 'had filled in some blank spaces on the map, chiefly

Captain Hugh Clapperton, by an unknown artist (SNPG)

owing to the accuracy of Clapperton's surveys'. The results were promising enough for Clapperton to be sent on a similar expedition the following year, this time starting from the Bight of Benin. Once again he reached Sokoto, but this time it was his turn to fall victim to a fatal fever. His travelling companion, Richard Lander, returned to England and in 1830 published *Records of Clapperton's Last Expedition*.

CLAPPERTON, Thomas (1879–1962)
Sculptor

Born and educated in **Galashiels**, and trained there and at **Glasgow** and London art colleges, Thomas Clapperton established his first studio in Paris before settling in London. He is chiefly known for his Great War memorials in several Borders towns, the one at Galashiels – a mounted trooper modelled with great authenticity – arguably being his masterpiece. His most viewed work is the striking statue of **Robert I** at the entrance to **Edinburgh Castle**, while **Selkirk** provides the greatest concentration of his sculptures with five memorials. Other examples may be seen in Glasgow ('Literature' atop the dome of the **Mitchell Library**), London and several other English towns, Cardiff, California and New Zealand. He also executed portrait busts, such as that of **Lord Tweedsmuir** in the **Scottish National Portrait Gallery** [see **Edinburgh**], and nude female statuettes, a selection of which are in Old Gala House.

CLARK, George (1833–1898) Shoe Manufacturer

Clark was born in **Kilmarnock**, the son of a shoe manufacturer who had founded the family business in 1815. He left Kilmarnock in the mid-1850s seeking adventure in Australia but was then ordered by his father to supervise the family's interests in Rio de Janeiro, most of the company's production being destined for Brazil. Five years after returning to Kilmarnock in 1873 he took over as sole partner and proceeded to boost productivity by continual improvement in production methods and machinery. In 1887 both of his sons were taken into partnership. His policy had been to plough profits back into the firm, as a result of which his son inherited a sound enterprise from which he was able to develop the Saxone Shoe Company.

CLARK, Jim (1936–68) Racing Driver

World Champion racing driver Jim Clark was born into a farming family at Kilmany, **Fife**, on 4 March 1936, the family moving to the Borders six years later, where the young Jim Clark grew up at Edington Mains near **Chirnside** in **Berwickshire**. Pursuing a joint career of motoring and farming, it was the former interest which dominated his life, beginning with an appearance as a navigator in the 1955 International Scottish Rally, and driving in local meets. He won his first event driving his own Sunbeam Mk3 saloon at a sprint meeting at Stobs Camp near **Hawick** at the age of 20. Working up through the grades in team racing and rallying, Clark attracted the attention of the Lotus organisation, and embarked on Formula 2 and Grand Prix racing in 1960. Two years later he came close to winning the drivers' championship, achieving this in 1963 with seven Grand Prix victories. He repeated this feat in 1965, including five victories in succession, as well as winning the Indianapolis 500 race. After some technical difficulties in 1966–7 he recovered form and brought his total of Grand Prix victories to 25 – a record at the time. Tragedy struck on 7 April 1968 at Hockenheim in Germany. While practising for a Formula 2 race, his car crashed on a bend at 120 mph, killing him instantly. No definite cause of the accident was ever identified, although a rear tyre puncture was suspected. He had already been described by veteran champion driver Juan Fangio as 'the greatest racing driver in the world'. He was buried in the churchyard at Chirnside and a small museum in the town was dedicated to his memory.

CLARSACH

Clarsach is a **Gaelic** word which originally referred to a wire-strung harp. In the 20th century the name has also been applied to small gut-strung harps. The earliest depictions of triangular-framed harps, ie harps with a fore-pillar, are found on 8th century **Pictish** stones. Pictish harps were probably strung with horse-hair. The instrument apparently spread south to the Anglo-Saxons, who commonly used gut strings, and west to the Gaels of the Highlands and Islands, and to Ireland. The Gaels used wire strings, played with the fingernails, while gut strings are usually played with the pads of the fingers.

The word first appears as *clar shoileach* ('willow board') in a 13th century poem by the Scottish poet Giolla Brighde Albanach. The first player of the harp named in a contemporary source is Adam of Lennox, porter of the **Abbey of Melrose** and subsequently Abbot of **Balmerino** (1252–60).

Both harp and *clarsach* were heard at the courts of the Scottish kings. They were primarily professionals' instruments – harpers were almost always men – but were also played by male and female members of the aristocracy. After 1603 harping died out at court, but the *clarsach* was still part of the households of the Highland chiefs. *Clarsach* players were employed by clans such as the Macleans, **Campbells**, Lamonts and the **MacDonald Lords of the Isles**. The most famous Highland harper was Rory Dall Morison, the **Blind Harper** of **Dunvegan** (c1656–1713).

Perthshire was a particular focus of harping under the patronage of the **Dukes of Atholl** and the Clan Robertson. The MacEwens were harpers to the Robertsons of Lude, in whose family were preserved the Lamont Harp and the **Queen Mary** Harp, both *clarsachs* probably made in **Argyll** in the late 15th century, and both now in the **Museum of Scotland**.

The **Jacobite Rising** of 1745 marked the end of the Highland chiefs' patronage of the *clarsach*, though the instrument and the formal **bardic** poetry which it accompanied had been in decline since the early 17th century. The last *clarsach* player to have links with the old bardic order was William McMurchy who died c1782.

'Port' was the title given to a characteristic group of harp tunes in the mid-16th to mid-17th centuries. These are often found in the lute manuscripts of that period, eg 'Port Ballangowne' and 'Port Robart'. Collectors in the 18th and 19th centuries succeeded in preserving many examples of Scottish harp melodies, some of which show characteristics in common with **piobaireachd**.

Attempts to revive the *clarsach* began in the late 19th century. In 1931 the Clarsach Society was founded. Amongst its growing membership there is a renewed interest particularly in the small, gut-strung harp now commonly referred to as a 'clarsach' but also, recently, in the wire-strung clarsach of the Gaels.

CLASSES, Act of (1649)

With the defeat at **Preston** (1648) of the Scots army marching south to fulfil the **Engagement**, radical **Presbyterians** seized the initiative, marched on **Edinburgh** in the **Whiggamore Raid**, and secured power with the support of Cromwell. Detestation of the Royalist Engagers alone united the Cromwellian and **Whig** interests; it was expressed in the Act of Classes (23 January 1649) which debarred from office prominent Engagers and supporters of **Montrose** (for life), lesser Engagers (for 10 years), sympathisers (for five years) and any officials 'given to uncleanesse, brybery, swearing, drunkenesse' or any other ungodly behaviour including neglect of worship (for one year). This represented a triumph for the fundamentalist clergy who proceeded to abolish clerical patronage and to purge the government, Church and army, with disastrous results at the **Battle of Dunbar** (1650), after which the Act of Classes was rescinded in the summer of 1651.

CLAVA CAIRNS, Inverness

About a mile east of the **Culloden** battlefield, near **Inverness**, this fine group of chambered **cairns** at Balnuaran of Clava are aligned NE-SW, each surrounded by a stone circle. Of the three best-preserved – in fact restored – cairns the one to the south-west is a passage grave bordered by a kerb of massive boulders. The central chamber is oval, measuring 3.5 by 4m. Around the cairn is a circle of 12 stones, of which 10 survive. Excavations in 1828 produced some burnt bone and fragments of two pots, now lost, which appear from contemporary description to have been of late Bronze Age date.

The centre cairn is a ring cairn – that is, it has no passage to the central chamber. Otherwise it is similar to the other two. It is surrounded by a stone circle consisting of nine stones. A strange feature of this cairn is that three of these stones are connected to it by low stony banks. Excavations in 1857 produced only a few flint flakes from the central chamber. The north-east cairn is also a passage grave, and is surrounded by a circle of 11 stones, one of which is decorated with cup-marks and one cup-and-ring mark. The central chamber, 3.8m in diameter, shows signs of corbelling and may once have been completely roofed.

It has been noted that a line through the passages of the two passage graves points exactly to a spot on the horizon corresponding to the midwinter sunset. This is unlikely to be fortuitous, although the significance and meaning of the alignment is a matter of controversy. It also appears that the cairns and their surrounding stone circles are laid out with complex geometrical accuracy, suggesting a knowledge of practical mathematics and astronomy.

Other cairns of this type in the Inverness area suggest a regional Bronze Age culture which built its burial cairns to a slightly different pattern to other regions of

The central Clava cairn and stone circle (HS)

Scotland. The Clava type is very distinctive, although it incorporates the same elements – burial chamber, passages, kerbs – found elsewhere.

CLAYMORE

From the Gaelic *claidheamh mòr* (great/large sword), the claymore is properly the two-handled sword often seen on effigies of Highland warriors on graveslabs. The confusion with the Highland basket-hilted broadsword (which is not specifically Scottish) may stem from the modern practice in Scottish regiments of referring to the latter as a 'claymore' which strictly speaking it is not.

CLAYPOTTS CASTLE, Broughty Ferry, Dundee

Claypotts is not the largest of castles nor the best sited, being now lapped by a housing estate. It is, though, an unusually faithful example of a 16th century Z-plan tower house with a particularly dramatic superstructure. The arms of the Z consist of two round towers which are so plain throughout their lower three storeys that the square gabled garrets above, with their dormers and chimneys, resemble cosy cottages precariously perched on long stone stalks. Turnpike stairs are accommodated in the two angles created by the towers; there are no turrets; a short parapet walk is corbelled out from the main block; all the gabling is crowstepped.

The interior is bare and not particularly remarkable, but safe.

Dates on the towers indicate that construction took place 1569–88, the laird being John Strachan whose arms and initials are also represented. His father had held the estate as tenant of the Abbot of **Lindores** to whom it had originally been granted by **Alexander II** in 1247. The Strachans sold out in 1601 and in 1620 the castle was resold to Sir William Graham of Claverhouse. It is not clear whether the latter's great-grandson, **John Graham** ('Bonnie Dundee'), actually lived here but after **Killiecrankie** (1689) Claypotts was certainly forfeited, passing eventually to James, 2nd **Marquis of Hamilton**. Thus [see **Douglas Cause**] it came into the possession of the **Earls of Home** to whom it still belongs, though managed by the state.

'CLEANSE-THE-CAUSEWAY' (1520)

Sometimes given the grandiose title of 'Battle' and sometimes described as a 'street brawl', this fracas took place in **Edinburgh**'s **High Street** during the absence in France of **John, Duke of Albany** (Regent for **James V**). Involving the **Hamiltons** under the **1st Earl of Arran** and the **Douglases** under **Archibald, 6th Earl of Angus**, it resulted in the former being chased out of Edinburgh and the latter taking control of the city and, eventually, of the King himself. The bemused onlookers were left to 'cleanse the causeway' of the bloody mess they left behind.

CLEARANCES, The

Between 1785 and 1850 the Highlands and Islands witnessed a social and demographic upheaval in which tens of thousands of clansmen were removed from their homes and holdings to make way for large-scale sheep farming. Such agricultural 'improvement', designed to maximise the land's yield and the owner's income, had swept the Lowlands in the 18th century causing some relocation and protest. But 'The Clearances' are usually taken to refer solely to the Highlands and Islands; and because they were conducted in an autocratic and often brutal manner, and because they dissipated and impoverished a population which was also a distinct cultural entity with its own concepts of land tenure and a particularly tenacious attachment to its ancient habitat, the whole subject is fraught with emotive undertones and remains both sensitive and contentious.

Clearance involved two distinct types of removal. On the one hand it was a programme of resettlement within individual estates whereby tenants were evicted from the communal rigs and grazings of their forefathers to more marginal land, usually on the coast. There they were settled on impoverished lots, later known as **crofts**, whose agricultural potential was poor but whose opportunities for **fishing** and **kelping** were supposed to compensate. The second type of removal, though not always forced, was often prompted by the failure of these new lots to provide a living. **Population** pressures, rent increases, downturns in fishing and kelping, and above all the **potato famine** of 1846, resulted in destitution and hence emigration, either to the Lowlands or to the colonies.

Not necessarily corresponding to these two types of removal, two main periods of clearance are discernible; 1785–1820 and 1820–50. The first was characterised by the introduction of *na caoraich mora*, the big sheep (**Cheviot** and **Blackface**). In Easter **Ross, Knoydart**, Glen Garry, the **Uists, Skye, Tiree**, and above all the vast estates of **Elizabeth Countess of Sutherland**, townships were cleared and sometimes burnt, tenants and their livestock evicted, and the land enclosed to create sheep runs. Notorious incidents included the **Kildonan, Strathglass** and **Strathnaver** evictions and notorious evictors **James Loch** and **Patrick Sellar**. Although both before and during this period emigration offered a last-resort solution, it was discouraged by landowners who, mostly **clan** chiefs, still cherished the idea of numerous retainers and needed their labour for kelping; the government endorsed this, needing Highland troops for the Napoleonic wars.

Around 1820 the demand for cattle and kelp declined dramatically. Unable to meet their rents, tenants sank into arrears and apathy. Landlords, faced with a fall in receipts, either resigned themselves to further clearances, like Lord MacDonald who cleared much of Skye and North Uist, or sold out to those who would, as Clanranald of South Uist sold out to the notorious John Gordon of Cluny. Emigration now became a serious alternative, especially on **Lewis**. Although there were further evictions in Easter Ross, the main targets were now the overcrowded and destitute townships of the **Hebrides** and the north-west coast.

The climax came with the potato famine of 1846. Many now saw emigration as the only solution and clearances were therefore justified on humanitarian rather than purely economic grounds. But the famine and the relief measures undertaken to ameliorate it also

David Wilkie's Distraining for Rent; clearances were not restricted to the Highlands (NGS)

brought the plight of the crofters to the attention of a wider audience. Although it would be 30 years before the **Napier Commission** and the **Crofters' Holdings Act** put a stop to clearances – and longer still before they were reversed – post-1855 they showed a marked decline. The ravages of the 1840s had relieved population pressures while an upsurge in fishing and **agriculture** assisted crofting incomes and so landowners' rents.

Whether the evil of the clearances can be attributed largely to the greed of landlords depends partly on one's social perspective and partly on the evidence selected. Estate records often contradict the popular polemics, let alone the later mythology; population figures contradict the notion that clearance boosted emigration. On the other hand there is no question that clansmen felt betrayed by those whom they had once regarded as chiefs and protectors and disgusted by their expensive absentee habits, sentiments which only strengthened when estates passed to non-Highland and non-Gaelic proprietors. Given the widening gulf of class, language and often religion between landlord and tenant, it is hardly surprising that feelings ran high. Add to this two mutually opposed notions of agricultural tenure, hereditary and communal in the case of the oppressed, legalistic and autocratic in the case of the oppressors, and the irreconcilable nature of the evidence may be explained.

CLEGHORN, Hugh (1757–1834) Academic and Empire Builder

Professor of Civil History at **St Andrews University**, Cleghorn appears to have tired of academic life and in 1793 conceived an improbable device for securing the island of Ceylon (Sri Lanka). Sri Lanka had been held by the Dutch since the 17th century, but with Holland now a satellite of revolutionary France, it became fair game in the Anglo-French wars. The Professor's idea was simply to detach its largely mercenary garrison by suborning its commander whose brother he had met in Switzerland. In the spirit of the times, **Dundas** responded favourably and Cleghorn left for India overland together with the Swiss commander. He reached the Malabar coast in 1795 and quickly secured the support of the Madras authorities. They deputed an officer to Sri Lanka who coolly informed the Dutch Governor that unless he handed over his Swiss regiment it would mutiny. He capitulated, and in 1796 Sri Lanka passed to British control where it remained until Independence in 1948. 'The credit for the almost bloodless conquest of Ceylon must go to Professor Cleghorn,' wrote Holden Furber in his biography of Dundas, a verdict supported by Cleghorn's epitaph in Dunino Churchyard, **St Andrews**: 'He was the agent by whose instrumentality the Island of Ceylon was annexed to the British Empire.'

CLELAND, William (1661–89) Covenanter

Born at **Douglas, Lanarkshire**, and educated at **St Andrews University**, Cleland, 'a lad in years but a man in shrewdness and courage', triumphed with the **Covenanters** over **Claverhouse** at **Drumclog** (1679) but fled to Holland after their defeat by **Monmouth** at

Bothwell Brig (1679). He returned to Scotland with **Argyll** in 1685 [see **Argyll's Rising**], fled back to Holland and returned at the Revolution to lead the **Cameronian** Regiment. Although the Cameronians successfully held **Dunkeld** against the **Jacobite** army fresh from its success at **Killiecrankie**, Cleland was killed in the action and buried in Dunkeld Cathedral.

CLERK, Sir John, of Penicuik (1676–1755)
Lawyer, Antiquary, Musician

Clerk was Scotland's leading patron of the arts and arbiter of taste in the first half of the 18th century. He came of a family with strong artistic and scientific leanings. His grandfather had been a merchant and art dealer in Paris in the 1630s and 40s, and became in his own right a leading Scottish collector of pictures and works of art. His father (created a baronet in 1679) was keenly interested in both architecture and mining technology. Upon these inherited tastes and talents Clerk himself was to build a distinguished reputation for learning, love of art, scholarship and enlightened patronage.

Educated at **Glasgow** and Leyden, he made a highly important Grand Tour between 1697–9, visiting the courts of Germany, and then Vienna, Venice, Rome, Naples, Florence and Paris. In Italy the tastes of a lifetime in art and architecture as well as in music were formed. He spent 18 months in Rome and became steeped in the study of classical antiquities and a pupil of the composer and violinist Arcangelo Corelli. Himself an excellent harpsichordist and a capable violinist, Clerk's compositions include five cantatas of outstanding quality.

Although his knowledge of classical architecture and philosophy involved music as a motivating and structural force, he later largely abandoned musical composition (and certainly performance), but his passion for the classical world remained. After his return to Scotland this showed itself in the formation of the leading private collection of **Roman** sculpture, coins, weapons and utensils from Scottish sites. On these subjects Clerk wrote much, though he published relatively little; but a great deal of information is preserved in his extensive correspondence with contemporary antiquaries.

Clerk was called to the Scottish Bar in 1700. A brief political career, culminating in his work as a Commissioner for the **Treaty of Union** in 1707, was followed by the award of the undemanding legal office of a Baron of the Court of Exchequer. This appointment gave Clerk the resources and the leisure to pursue the things that really mattered to him: the improvement of his estates, silviculture, the laying out of his landscape park and a quiet life of cultivated ease. As a literary figure he is of some interest as a historian and poet; and he was an intimate friend of **Allan Ramsay** (1684–1758). As a patron of the arts he is most important as an architectural amateur, and adviser to other owners of country houses; he was an early and influential patron of **William Adam** with whom he co-operated on the design of **Mavisbank**.

Clerk was succeeded by his son James, also an enthusiastic patron of the arts and a competent amateur architect who designed **Penicuik** House. A younger son was the artist and naval tactician John Clerk of Eldin.

CLERK MAXWELL, James, see **MAXWELL**

CLICKIMIN, Shetland

The **broch** of Clickimin, one of **Shetland**'s many archaeological treasures, stands beside the loch of that name between **Lerwick** and its suburb of Sound. While the broch itself is of considerable height, excavations by the Ministry of Public Buildings and Works, 1953–7, established the existence of Iron Age fortifications, from which the brochs developed, and revealed a succession of structures which throw considerable light on the prehistoric peoples of Shetland from the 7th century BC to the 6th century AD.

CLIMATE

Scotland is fortunate in having a temperate climate with only infrequent extremes. In its latitude in the Northern Hemisphere, only the west coast of Canada close to the Alaskan border enjoys a comparable climate, but there low winter temperatures are more severe.

TEMPERATURE The average winter day maximum temperature varies from 6.5–7.5° Centigrade on the west coast to 5.5–6° on the east coast. By night it falls on average to 1.5–2.5° on the west coast and to slightly lower than 0° on low ground in central Scotland. In mid-summer the daily maximum varies on average from 16–17.5° on the west coast to 19° in the east central highlands. The night minimum averages 10–10.5° all over Scotland with the extreme south-west plus the area near **Berwick-on-Tweed**, **Arran**, the south of the **Kintyre** peninsula and the south of **Mull** and **Islay** up to a degree warmer. The highest temperature ever recorded in Scotland is 32.8°C (91°F) observed on several occasions all between 1868 and 1908 at **Selkirk**, **Dumfries**, Swinton (**Berwickshire**) and Stenton near **Dunbar**. Although these readings are not recent, there is no reason to doubt their accuracy. (In those days maximum temperature was measured in degrees Fahrenheit to the nearest whole degree, which accounts for so many occurrences of the same value.)

RAINFALL The annual rainfall varies from more than 4000mm at the western end of **Loch Quoich** to 555mm at Dunbar, the driest place, but much of the low ground east of **Edinburgh** records 650mm or less. By contrast **Glasgow** Airport has an average of 951mm and much of the western Highlands more than 1600mm, with many gauges in mountainous areas recording more than 3000mm in an average year.

238.4mm in a single day was measured at Sloy Dam, west of **Loch Lomond**, on 17 January 1974. This is the highest daily total in Scotland. In a local storm 259mm fell in 22½ hours in December 1954 at Cruadach on **Loch Quoich** while the **hydro-electric** scheme was being built, but this fell over two rainfall days (which run from 9 am GMT to 9 am the next day) so does not count as a record.

Rainfall is probably the most important parameter in Scotland's climate, because of the serious flooding which can result. Probably the most damage in the last 200 years was done by the **Moray** floods of August 1829, when record levels were reached on the rivers Findhorn, **Spey** and Dee. After three days of rain the water in **Loch Ness** rose to record levels in January 1849. On this occasion the run-off was increased because of substantial snowmelt.

In recent years there have been three floods of note. On 16–17 December 1966 250mm of rain was recorded over 16 square miles in **Glen Quoich** and **Glencoe**, 200mm over 526 square miles and 150mm over 1955 square miles. This was not only the worst two-day storm in Britain's meteorological history, but worse than anything that had occurred over any previous six-day period. The record was to last only 15 months for on 26–27 March 1968 a more intense and widespread storm stretched from An Teallach in the north to **Cruachan** in the south and even over to **Mull** and **Skye**, all of which had more than 150mm. Still heavier rain occurred on 5–6 February 1989 in widespread storms from **Loch Shin** to Loch Lomond. 306mm were measured at **Kinlochhourn**, the highest two-day total ever in the United Kingdom; 280mm at Clunes Forest and 260mm at South Laggan, both on **Loch Lochy**, were also recorded. The result, when translated into river run-off, was to cause widespread damage especially in **Inverness** where the **railway** bridge to the north was destroyed. There was other substantial damage to property and stock from **Sutherland** to **Fort William**.

The rainfall of the previous week, or month even, has a great effect on the floods resulting from such heavy rainstorms. In January 1989 more than 700mm was recorded in the higher parts of the Ness catchment. The average fall over the catchment as a whole was probably about 400mm. The ground was therefore saturated, and the rain which fell on 5–6 February ran straight off the hillside.

The conditions necessary for this very high rainfall over periods of a day or more are high humidity in the lowest 1500 metres above the land, and winds greater than 45 mph above the friction layer, say 600m, from a direction at right angles to the mountain barrier – in the Scottish Highlands blowing from approximately west. There must also be pre-existing precipitation at high levels in the atmosphere. This will collect the droplets in the barrier zone as it falls to earth and result in much heavier rainfall inland than on the coast. In the absence of the high-level rain, only a light drizzle will fall on the mountains. This heavy rain will fall in the warm sector of a depression, not, as is usual, before the arrival of the warm front or with the passage of the cold front.

WIND Average wind speed varies considerably over Scotland, from more than 17mph over the Outer **Hebrides** to 10mph in the east central Highlands. It can vary greatly in extreme gales. The highest gust ever recorded on low ground was 142mph at **Fraserburgh** while the **Cairngorm** summit has measured 173mph. The gale of January 1968 caused extensive damage, especially to **forestry** plantations in west central Scotland. The frequency of gales varies across Scotland; Glasgow Airport has only 4.3 in an average year while **Lerwick** has 47.

SUNSHINE June's daily sunshine duration varies from 6.5 hours on the west coast from **South Uist** to

Galloway to less than 5.5 hours in the mountainous inland regions; while the dullest month of the year, December, varies between averages of 1.5 hours on the east coast and extreme south-west coast to less than one hour in the Highlands. Over the year Dunbar is the sunniest place with 1523 hours, while the dullest parts have about two thirds of this total.

SNOW The frequency of snow cover varies considerably from place to place and from year to year. Average days of snow cover vary from 3.5 days on Tiree through 14 days at Edinburgh (though Penicuik only 10 miles away has 30) to Beattock Summit with 38 and Drumochter Pass 70. At greater altitudes the cover is more frequent; sheltered corries in the Cairngorms and on Ben Nevis remain snow-covered through most summers. When considering flooding it is important to remember that if conditions favour snow melt, the run-off caused by the rain could be augmented by the equivalent of 25–30mm of snow melt in a day.

FOG The general visibility over Scotland is very good; inland fogs on calm and cloudless yet humid nights usually clear quickly except possibly in the glens. The fog which drifts in from the North Sea over eastern coastal districts in spring and summer, called 'haar', is often accompanied by beautiful sunlight only a few miles inland. It is caused by warmer air flowing over colder sea and speeding up the evaporation from the sea surface. Moist south-west winds can result in very low cloud, 300m or less above sea level, which can be quite dense and reduce visibility to less than 100m.

CLIMBING AND MOUNTAINEERING

Doughty cragsmen no doubt abounded in clan society; a taste for seabirds and their eggs demanded rock-climbing skills while the reiver's occasional need for sanctuary might necessitate climbing the steepest corrie. But as a recreation, and later a sport, climbing dates only from the 19th century. It began in the Alps and prompted English alpinists to form their own Alpine Club in 1857. Seeking Alpine challenges nearer home they, and their Scottish counterparts, soon turned their attention to the Highlands. There the 'precipitous declivities' so abhorred by Edmund Burt and contemned by Dr Johnson in the 18th century had received a better press by the early 19th. Nature-lovers such as the wandering Wordsworths were charmed by the echoes of the Lake District while geologists like John MacCulloch faithfully related their imposing configuration to Sir Walter Scott – who duly romanticised it. Another scientist, Professor J D Forbes, allowed his interest in glaciation to lure him into the Skye Cuillins in the 1830s. He was followed by Alexander Nicholson who, returning to his native Skye in 1865, began the first serious assault on its peaks. Sgurr Alasdair is named after him.

Word of the stern challenge posed by the Cuillins' rock ridges reached London in the 1880s and the alpinists came north in numbers. Most had previously climbed in the Alps and some as far afield as the Himalayas. They brought basic equipment (Nicholson had had to use his plaid as a rope) and considerable expert-

ise. Charles and Lawrence Pilkington led the charge and were followed by, among others, Norman Collie who paired up with John Mackenzie of Sconser, 'Scotland's first real mountain guide', in a lifetime partnership. All the Skye peaks were conquered and most of the standard rock climbs.

Elsewhere the new craze, facilitated by the opening of railways into the Highlands, had its less illustrious devotees. The Cobbler Club, named for the peak of that name near Arrochar, still a popular destination with Glasgow climbers, had been founded as early as 1866; and in 1887 a group of Aberdeen enthusiasts, returning from lighting a beacon for Queen Victoria's 50th jubilee, paused at the shelter stone of Loch Avon to found the Cairngorm Club. The alpinists responded with the Scottish Mountaineering Club, founded by W W Naismith in Glasgow in 1889; its members included Collie, the Pilkingtons and numerous others from the London Alpine Club and it was immediately recognised as the senior Scottish association. Its journal became the official organ of Scottish mountaineering and in it Sir Hugh Munro published his famous Tables in 1891. Attempts to climb all his 'Munros' effectively claimed the whole of the Highlands for the new climbing fraternity.

During the 1890s the great north-east cliff of Ben Nevis, the Glencoe peaks and those of Arran and Lochnagar were added to the catalogue of classic routes. Ice climbs and winter ascents were pioneered; rock climbs became increasingly difficult. In the early 1900s Harold Raeburn succeeded Collie as the greatest Scottish climber and performed notable feats in the Alps, Caucasus and Norway. The Great War brought this formative period to an abrupt end and it was not until the 1930s that interest and progress revived. A Ladies' Scottish Climbing Club had been founded in 1908 but it was the launch of the Junior Mountaineering Club of Scotland in 1925 and of numerous local clubs, plus the Scottish Mountaineering Club's publication of guides to Ben Nevis, Skye, the Cairngorms etc, which provided the new stimulus. Equipment and clothing improved dramatically largely thanks to the Everest expeditions of the inter-war years. The new generation of climbers included, as well as technical experts such as J H B Bell and Graham MacPhee, a gifted writer and mountain lover in W H Murray (Mountaineering in Scotland, 1947).

Since World War II the popularity of the sport has grown unabated and to some extent its problems are the product of this success. As the explosion in the leisure industry tempted the less experienced into the Highlands, accident rates rose alarmingly. Mountain rescue services, joined by the RAF in 1944, have been kept at full stretch while environmental lobbies have been alerted to the effects of the heavily booted brigades on the often fragile mountain ecology. On the credit side Scottish mountaineers and climbers have won a worldwide reputation through the exploits of Dougal Haston, Hamish MacInnes and others. The purist may still insist that Scotland has only hills and no mountains, but it is now accepted that the only places in the British Isles where mountaineering skills can be learnt and perfected are in the Cuillins, Cairngorms, Ben Nevis or Glencoe in winter. Few British climbers in the Himalayas have not cut their first steps in the Highlands.

Climbing in the southern Grampians: Ben Ledi from Stobinian near Crianlarich (SEA)

CLOVENFORDS, Selkirkshire

In the days when **Walter Scott** was living at **Lasswade** but working (as Sheriff) in **Selkirk**, he would sometimes break his journey to stay at the inn in the hamlet of Clovenfords. Caddenfoots Church a mile to the south has a memorial window to Sir Walter; the village itself has a memorial to the poet and orientalist **John Leyden**, who taught in the Clovenfords school (1792), inscribed by Scott to 'A Lamp too Early Quenched'. The famous **Tweed** vineyards, heated by five miles of cast-iron pipes, were established here in 1868 by William Thomson, gardener to the **Duke of Buccleuch**. Ashiestiel Farmhouse, to which Scott moved in 1804 in order to be closer to his work, 'overhangs the Tweed' within sight of Clovenfords.

CLUNIES-ROSS FAMILY, 'Kings of the Cocos'

The remote Indian Ocean archipelago known as the Cocos and Keeling Islands (after Captain William Keeling who had landed there in the early 17th century) was first settled in 1825 when John Clunies-Ross arrived with his family. The Clunies-Rosses had previously taken refuge in **Shetland** after supporting the 1715 **Jacobite Rising**. John was born (1786) in Shetland and like other Shetlanders chose a life at sea. During the British occupation of Java in the Napoleonic Wars he was serving with the East India Company and married a Malay. His son, John George, and grandson, George (1842–1910), were sent home to Scotland for their education, George studying **engineering** at

Glasgow, before succeeding to the informal supremacy of the islands and also marrying Malays. The islands were declared a British possession in 1857 but without prejudice to the *de facto* chieftainship of the Clunies-Ross family, whose varying fortunes depended entirely on their successful exploitation of coconut oil. In the 20th century the islands came under the control of the Straits Settlements, Singapore, and eventually Australia.

CLUTHAS

Also known as 'penny steamers' (that being the flat-rate charge), the Cluthas (so named from the Gaelic word for the **Clyde**) provided **Glasgow** with a cheap and cheerful means of mass transport at the end of the 19th century. Tall-funelled, **coal**-fired, and screw-driven, they carried up to 360 passengers at a time. The first run, with many intermediary stages, was made between **Victoria Bridge** and Whiteinch (about three miles) on 12 April 1884; the last, along the same route, by Clutha No 11 on 30 November 1903. Competition from the **trams** and **underground** had proved too strong. In their heyday there were 12 Cluthas carrying some 2.5 million passengers a year.

CLYDE, Falls of, Nr Lanark

Prior to 1926 when they were harnessed for **hydro-electricity**, the Falls of Clyde were undoubtedly the most impressive and substantial in Britain. Painted by, amongst many, Joseph Turner and **Jacob More**, they were also enthused over by **Burns**, **Smollett**, Southey, the **Wordsworths** and Thomas Gray. Working downstream, they begin at Bonnington Linn, a wide cascade

Clutha No. 4 passing Glasgow's Broomielaw (LW)

about 10m high whence the river slides into a gorge. A cave here is said to be one of those in which **Wallace** hid from the English, and where the channel is at its narrowest is known as Wallace's Leap. Next comes the celebrated Cora Linn, a succession of falls with a 25m drop. Dorothy Wordsworth was 'much affected' by their majesty; brother William's 'time-cemented tower' above them is ruined Cora Castle. Another gloomy gorge ends at Dundaff Linn, less impressive but notable for the rock known as Wallace's Chair, and for the fact that Dundaff provided the motive power for **New Lanark**. Five kilometres below New Lanark, the last fall is Stonebyres Linn. Although the Falls have been much neglected since the hydro scheme siphoned off most of their water, the Clyde Walkway and the restoration of New Lanark have somewhat revived their popularity and spates are occasionally released as a reminder of their glory.

CLYDE, James Avon, Lord (1863–1944)
Lawyer

Clyde passed advocate in 1887, developed a busy practice, and became a QC in 1901. His political career brought him to hold the two **law** officerships (Solicitor General in 1905 and Lord Advocate from 1916–20) as well as a respectable period as an MP (1905–23). As a member of the **Faculty of Advocates** he was honoured by holding the office of Dean from 1916–20 when he was appointed Lord President. He remained Lord President until 1935 when he retired. He was also an author, contributing to the canon of legal historical texts by his edition of *Hope's Major Practicks* and his translation of *Acta Dominorum Concilli*. His son James L M Clyde was Lord President from 1954–72 and his grandson, Lord Clyde, a Senator of the College of Justice.

CLYDE, River

Scotland's most important river is also its third longest (after the **Tay** and the **Spey**). Allowing for the unreliability of river measurements, a distance of about 100 miles may be suggested for the river above **Glasgow** and about 25 for that below. It rises in **Lanarkshire** and for the most part continues through that county, flowing not west but predominantly north. As so often its exact source is a matter of some dispute but little consequence; for all practical purposes the river may be said to begin where several burns converge at Elvanfoot near **Crawford**. Thence to its semi-circuit of Tinto Hill near **Biggar** the river has the character of a trout (once salmon) stream as it flows briskly through open moorland, often accompanied by the M74 and the main west coast **railway** line to Glasgow; the area is sometimes known as Clydesmuir to distinguish it from succeeding Clydesdale which begins below the **Falls of Clyde**. In between, the river slows and meanders, at one point heading south before receiving from the Douglas Water a sharp reminder of its true course and dutifully heading over the falls near **Lanark**. In the 19th century, before containment for storage and **hydro-electricity**, the river here was at its grandest, the falls along with **New Lanark** rating as one of the major visitor attractions of the British Isles. Between the falls and **Hamilton** the river winds majestically, sometimes steep-sided, through rich agricultural land which has long been highly productive of fruit and vegetables. Strathclyde Country Park between Hamilton and **Motherwell**, followed by **Bothwell Castle** and **Bothwell Bridge**, afford a final respite before the river, now heading west, surrenders to the industrial needs of Glasgow.

Its importance to that city cannot be exaggerated. Glasgow grew up where it is because there the river was first crossable by ford and bridge. But from the 18th century onwards the city prospered by overcoming the handicap of such a shallow-water location, gradually

The Falls of Clyde, by Jacob More (NGS)

scouring and dredging the bed to take ships of ever greater draught. Looking east from the high-level Erskine Bridge, the last on the river, it is well to recall that within recent memory the skyline bristled with the cranes of the largest **shipbuilding** industry in the world, and the river below, now so quiet and puny, was jammed with international shipping. And so it continued down the Firth of Clyde, through **Clydebank** and **Dumbarton** on the north, through **Port Glasgow** and **Greenock** on the south, while ahead, between **Gourock** and **Dunoon**, gaped the gateway to a New World for some, and to a bucket and spade holiday for all, **'doon the watter'**.

CLYDE PORT AUTHORITY

The Clyde Port Authority was established in 1965 as the first estuarial authority in Britain, taking over the functions of the Clyde Navigation Trust, the **Greenock Harbour Trust** and the Clyde Lighthouses Trust. These three bodies had distinguished histories of improving the navigation and harbour facilities which allowed industry to develop. Until the late 18th century the **Clyde** above **Dumbarton** was a narrow winding stream and could only be navigated by small shallow-draught scows (lighters). It was the English engineer James Golborne who began the work of deepening the channel by building a series of breakwaters to speed up the flow of the river which would scour the bottom. This was

successful and by the beginning of the 19th century larger vessels could make their way to the **Broomielaw** Quay in **Glasgow**'s city centre. The Clyde Navigation Trust was established in 1809 and became responsible for the management of the river, including ferries, wharfs, docks and dry docks. Without the efforts of the Trust to deepen the waterway and improve facilities the Clyde **shipbuilding** industry could never have prospered. The Clyde Port Authority still occupies the Trust's handsome offices in Glasgow's Robertson Street, built in 1882–6 and extended in 1905–8. Its frontage has sculpted boats flanking the entrance and a splendid Neptune above. The opulent offices are occasionally open to the public.

CLYDE VALLEY PLAN

Published in 1946, Sir Patrick Abercrombie's Clyde Valley Plan proposed that the answer to **Glasgow**'s problems was 'planned decentralisation of both population and industry'. The Plan, determined to end urban sprawl, recommended that existing towns be constrained by green belts where no development was to be permitted. Within this corset, the only way that Glasgow's population could be reduced was by moving people to new towns outside it. The Labour government readily accepted the proposals, but Glasgow Corporation, threatened with the loss of its ratepayers, resisted by putting forward an alternative of urban renewal. The government won, designating **East Kilbride** as the first new town in 1947, followed by **Cumbernauld** in 1956 and **Irvine** in 1966.

Clyde shipping, both sail and steam, in the 1890s (BRC)

CLYDE WORKERS COMMITTEE, The (1915–19)

The near panic caused by the spectre of **Red Clydeside** stemmed from the fusion of industrial militancy and Marxist ideology which took place within an *ad hoc* body of shop stewards and union leaders known as the Clyde Workers Committee. The CWC had originally been formed to co-ordinate **engineering** workers who struck over a pay award in February 1915. Many of the strikers belonged to small specialised unions with already radical leaderships; others, members of the giant Amalgamated Society of Engineers, were dissatisfied with the compliant policies of their leaders. Hence the formation of a radical Central Labour Withholding Committee which, when the strike was settled, assumed more permanent guise as the CWC. Amongst its office holders were **Willie Gallacher**, John Muir and **Davie Kirkwood**.

During 1915 the CWC supported agitation against rent increases in **Glasgow**. It also organised a protest strike which conveniently coincided with legislation to control rents. This apparent victory reinforced the expectations of revolutionaries like Gallacher and **John MacLean** in the 'political strike'. But the CWC's main battlefield was Clydeside's enormous munitions industry. Here wartime demand, bolstered by statutory regulation, threatened skilled workers with 'dilution' by semi-skilled labourers. A series of protests ensued in which the proletarian and pacifist sympathies of CWC ideologues like Gallacher found common ground with the protectionist craftsmen typified by Kirkwood. When on Christmas Day 1915 Lloyd George attempted to commend dilution to a mass meeting in St Andrew's Hall, he was repeatedly interrupted and drowned out by choruses of 'The Red Flag'. The press was forbidden to report the affair and when **Tom Johnston**'s *Forward* did so, it was duly prosecuted.

The Lloyd George fiasco may not have been the responsibility of the CWC, but it significantly hardened government attitudes in favour of dilution and against CWC intransigence. It was thus no surprise when in February 1916 Gallacher, Muir and Walter Bell were arrested in connection with an article in the CWC's *The Worker* which was deemed seditious. Tried in April, they were sentenced to varying terms of imprisonment. At about the same time MacLean and **James Maxton** were also sentenced on sedition charges. Soon after Kirkwood, who had broken ranks with the CWC over a dilution scheme, also fell foul of the courts and was deported from Clydeside. Thus was the CWC deprived of its leaders and in effect broken.

By way of postscript it was revived by Gallacher and James Messor in late 1917 and, as a Ways and Means Committee, participated in the 1918–19 agitation for a shorter working week. This culminated in the **Bloody Friday** riot in St George's Square (Glasgow) at which Gallacher, Kirkwood et al were re-arrested and militant protest discredited. The banner of Red Clydeside thereafter passed from the revolutionaries of the CWC to the more pragmatic constitutionalists of the **Independent Labour Party** like **John Wheatley**, **Pat Dollan** and James Maxton.

CLYDEBANK, Dunbartonshire

When shipbuilders James and George Thomson moved from **Glasgow** to an area called Barns o' **Clyde** in 1871, they kept the name of their former shipyard 'Clyde Bank'. The company later became **John Brown & Co Ltd**, which built the *Lusitania*, the **Queen Mary** and the *Queen Elizabeth II*. In 1881 the American Singer Manufacuring Company built a sewing-machine factory in the area, and Clydebank grew rapidly. The town faced hardships in the 1930s and 40s when it was badly affected by the Depression and almost destroyed by severe bombing during World War II; only eight houses escaped damage. Rigorous efforts have been made to regenerate Clydebank's economic life since the closure of the Singer factory in 1979, and the drastic contraction of the **ship-building** industry.

COAL-MINING

The principal coalfields in Scotland fall largely within a diagonal tract of land, about 30 miles wide, running roughly south-west from both sides of the Firth of Forth across to the **Ayrshire** coast. This area contains the historical coalfields of **Fife**, **Clackmannan**, **Stirlingshire**, the **Lothians**, **Kirkintilloch**, **Lanarkshire**, **Renfrewshire** and **Ayrshire**. Just outside this belt lie several 'islands' (eg **Sanquhar**), while further afield there have been workings of local significance at such scattered points as **Campbeltown**, **Kintyre** and, much smaller still, in the north of the Isle of **Arran** and at **Brora**, **Sutherland**. The workable seams vary from 34 (total thickness 95ft) in parts of **Midlothian** to two (total thickness 6ft) near Denny. Most coals are of the bituminous kind. The Scottish fields suffer from more difficult geological conditions than most English fields and the intrusion of igneous rock and the steeply inclined edge seams of Midlothian have historically presented mining engineers with many problems.

The eastern fields, especially Fife and Midlothian, were the first to gain importance, and the earliest records, eg those appertaining to **Newbattle Abbey**, show mining on an economic scale from at least the 13th century. **Population** growth and the break-up of ecclesiastical estates at the **Reformation** stimulated both demand and supply. **Edinburgh** ('auld Reekie'), **Leith** and the salt pans of the Forth formed the main markets. Exportation and wider coast-wise sales remained very modest until the 19th century. Mining tended to be extensive rather than intensive, with a scattering of bell pits of small capital input and primitive technology being worked out in succession. **Sir George Bruce**'s colliery at **Culross** was a notable exception. Its fame attracted visits from John Taylor, the 'water poet', and in 1617 from **James VI**. Bruce's mine may well have demonstrated the earliest British example of the Egyptian wheel used for mine drainage. The 17th century brought more persistent endeavours to develop the seams of tidewater in Ayrshire and the **Glasgow** region, but the east easily retained its dominance.

The 18th century witnessed a rising demand for coal by an expanding circle of coal-using industries, such as lime preparation, glass and vitriol making and, most momentous of all after the example of the **Carron Company** in 1760, coke-fired ironworks. The absence of official mineral statistics until 1854 makes estimates mere approximations, but Scottish coal output probably increased from under 400,000 tons in 1700 to around 2 million tons in 1800. By 1806 the **iron** industry alone accounted for 250,000 tons.

Scots coal-mining made many technical advances in the century before Waterloo, though it remained some distance behind Northumberland and Durham. The Newcomen engine was introduced (probably in 1719) but the diminutive scale of the average colliery made its wide adoption uneconomic until industrialisation exerted dramatically new demand patterns. By 1800 the number of such engines approached 80. Surface transport was improved by horse waggonways from 1722 and eventually by **canals**, culminating in the **Forth–Clyde** and Union Canals linking Edinburgh and Glasgow. By 1815 the largest enterprises (admittedly few in number) possessed steam winding and pumping, underground and overground horse railways and, in appropriate cases, longwall extraction instead of the traditional room and stoop. The rapid industrialisation and population growth of the Clyde basin placed a premium on the **Lanarkshire** coalfield (now penetrated by the Monkland Canal), where ironmasters were often in the forefront of colliery development. Many of the earlier coal entrepreneurs had been landed gentlemen such as the **Clerks of Penicuik** and the Cunninghames of Auchenharvie, or aristocrats such as the Earls of **Dundonald**, **Rothes** and **Elgin** or the Marquises of Lothian. But the new iron-making, particularly after the coming of the hot blast furnace from 1828, created capitalist dynasties – notably the Dixons and the Bairds of Gartsherrie – whose empires of coal and iron dwarfed all previous enterprises. Traditional estate mines lost their importance.

An early casualty of the new age was Scotland's unique collier serfdom. Based on a combination of estate customs and Scottish legislation, most notably the Act of 1606, this form of adscription had as its objective the elimination of collier desertion and labour poaching by tying miners (and by implication their offspring) to a specific estate or master for life. Runaways were vigorously pursued and periodic challenges to the system in the **Court of Session** seldom succeeded. After 1760, however, colliery bondage was increasingly perceived by the new coal companies as a major barrier to labour recruitment and its abolition was eventually secured by Acts of 1775 and 1799. Despite high wages the stigma of 'slavery' faded only slowly and it was left to Irish immigration to ease the labour shortage from the 1820s. A further change in labour structure was the proscription of the underground employment of females (chiefly as coal bearers in the stair pits of the Forth basin) under the Mines Act of 1842 (effective 1 March 1843). The 19th century brought many attempts at unionisation by mineworkers, but a truly national union linked to other British regions was not attained until 1894. Miners' leaders who found a wider platform included Alexander McDonald (1821–81) and **James Keir Hardie** (1856–1915). McDonald made greater mining safety one of his concerns, especially after the **Blantyre** disaster had alerted the Scottish conscience to the issue.

With the exception of cyclical downturns, the Scottish coal industry expanded continuously throughout the 19th and early 20th centuries, with Lanarkshire emerging as easily the most productive field followed at a distance by Fife. Output leapt from 15 million tons in 1870 to a summit of 42.5 million tons in 1913 and employment peaked in 1921 at 150,000 mineworkers. Scotland's production failed to reach that of the north of England and was also surpassed by Wales in 1878 and Yorkshire in 1913. With the thicker seams running out after 1900 Scotland sought more cost-effective methods and pioneered machine mining more purposefully than anywhere else in Britain. By 1927 half of Scotland's coal was being mechanically cut, compared with only 23% for the UK as a whole. With demand now dwindling, consequent on the decline of the older 'basic' industries and in the face of alternative energy sources, Scottish experience since 1918 has mirrored that of the other older British coalfields. Production stagnated during the inter-war years and slumped from the 1950s. By this time the state, which had acquired the coalmines on 1 January 1947 under Labour nationalisation policies, had begun a stringent programme of pit closures, particularly serious for the older fields. **Oil** and natural gas monopolised government thinking from the 1970s, though a much leaner coal industry continues to fight for contracts from electricity generating stations.

COATBRIDGE, Lanarkshire

In 1641 the parish of Monkland, so called because it had been granted (1162) to the monks of **Newbattle Abbey**, was divided into New (or East) Monkland and Old (or West) Monkland. Coatbridge, then a village, now occupies most of the latter just as **Airdrie** does of the former. Both grew sensationally during the 19th century thanks to mineral wealth. Black-band ironstone, discovered in the previous century, became commercially exploitable with the 1828 invention of the hot blast furnace while **coal**, ever plentiful, became highly marketable with the opening of the Monkland **Canal** in 1790 and of the Monkland and Kirkintilloch **railway** in 1826. In the first 40 years of the century the population grew sixfold. Fortunes were made, according to a contemporary, 'with a rapidity only equalled by the princely gains of some of the adventurers who accompanied Pizarro to Peru'. Among them were those accumulated by the six sons of Alexander Baird, each of whom is said to have become a millionaire. Gartsherrie Church (1839), built for the family's workers, has outlasted the Gartsherrie Iron Works. In 1934 a mass exodus to Corby in Northamptonshire heralded the end of steel-making and today coal, **iron and steel** have all been consigned to the heritage scrapheap with Summerlee Iron Works ('the noisiest museum in Scotland') hosting a working display of steam-driven machinery and a tramway. Though short on architecture, Coatbridge endorses the idea of leisure-led rejuvenation with the inevitable Country Park (Drumpellier) and the Time Capsule Monklands, described as 'half ice, half water and a whole lot of fun'.

COATS, Thomas (1809–83) Thread Manufacturer

Born in Ferguslie, **Paisley**, Coats joined his brothers' firm of J & P Coats in 1833 as a partner. He took control of the **engineering** side and in 1845, after the death of James, became effective managing partner, overseeing the doubling of production in the 1850s through the expanding markets of the United States. Paisley was the centre for thread manufacture and Coats, along with J & J Clark, also of Paisley, was the largest enterprise in the world. Thomas's control of the company was strengthened after Peter's retirement in 1856. The 1860s and 70s saw expansion both in Paisley and in the firm's US factories. Thomas left over £1.3 million at his death, having played a key role in the huge expansion of the family firm. Unlike his brother Peter, he was never knighted.

COCHRANE, Captain Charles Stuart (b.1796) Troubadour

Cochrane, alias 'Senor Juan de Vega, a Spanish Minstrel', was the second son of Admiral Sir Alexander Cochrane, and was born aboard HMS *Thetis* in which ship were no less than five other Cochranes. Like his cousins, **Thomas Cochrane, 10th Earl of Dundonald** and **John Dundas Cochrane**, he served in the navy during the Napoleonic Wars and then opted for adventure rather than peacetime service. In 1823–4 he travelled up the Magdalena River in Colombia and confidently expected to make a fortune out of copper-mining under the patronage of Simon Bolivar. This venture failed. He returned to Europe and eventually to Britain where he spent 1828–9 travelling the country's byways disguised as a Spanish troubadour complete with guitar. He eventually revealed his true identity in **Edinburgh** and was judged to be 'a little cracked'. This was not in fact the case. Back in France, in 1830 he patented a machine for 'spinning fine Cashmere, the wool of the Thibetan goat'. He set up a mill for the same purpose in **Glasgow** and won an award for his product. It is not known whether the business prospered. He published two books, an account of his Colombian travels and the delightful *Journal of a Tour made by Senor Juan de Vega, a Spanish Minstrel, of 1828–29 through Great Britain and Ireland*.

COCHRANE, Captain John Dundas (1793–1825) Traveller

Known as 'the pedestrian traveller', this Cochrane was the illegitimate son of the awful **Andrew James Cochrane-Johnstone**. He served in the navy during the Napoleonic Wars and then embarked on a series of long walks. Encouraged by his pedestrian prowess, in 1820, on failing to win support for a journey into Africa in the footsteps of **Mungo Park**, he set out to walk round the world. In the process he hoped to establish whether Asia and America were linked by an Arctic land bridge and whether there existed a north-west passage round America. 83 days after leaving Dieppe he reached St Petersburg. Robbed of all he possessed save a couple of waistcoats – one of which he wore as a **kilt** – he entered Moscow after a 32-hour marathon in which he covered 96 miles. Small of stature, his pace was indeed remarkable.

Compromising to the extent of occasionally travelling by boat, horse and sled, he continued across Siberia. A long detour south to the Chinese border was followed by an even longer excursion north to the mouth of the Kolyma River and the Arctic coast. To the discomfort of blisters was added snow blindness and frostbite. For 20 nights he slept in the snow 'without even the comfort of a blanket – a great oversight'. After more scares and still greater hardships he reached the Pacific port of Okhotsk and then Petropavlovsk on the Kamchatka peninsula. There, about half-way round, this most promising attempt to be the first to circumambulate the globe faltered. For while negotiating for permission to cross to Alaska, Cochrane fell hopelessly in love with a 14-year-old Kamchatdale girl. The couple were married soon after and, returning across Russia, took ship from St Petersburg to London in 1823. In 1824 Cochrane visited Colombia in connection with his cousin **Charles Stuart Cochrane**'s mining venture and died there of fever. Mrs Cochrane, 'the first native of Kamchatka that ever visited happy Britain', returned to Russia and 'soon met with many admirers'. Cochrane's narrative of his great journey met with fewer admirers but went through several editions in the 1820s and deserves a wider currency today.

COCHRANE, Sir Robert Thomas (d.1482)
Architect and Courtier

A controversial figure variously described as 'a mason's apprentice' and '**James III**'s prime minister', Cochrane was neither the low-born lackey of his detractors nor the loyal statesman of his admirers. The son of William (de) Cochran(e) (near **Paisley**), he studied architecture in Italy and then found favour with the dilettante James III for whom he is believed to have designed **Stirling Castle**'s Great Hall, 'the first large scale building in the whole of Great Britain to display the influence of the Renaissance' (D McRobert). His personal manner evidently partook of the building's grandiose proportions and, as his influence with the King increased, earned him the jealousy of the nobility. He was held responsible for the imprisonment of James's two brothers, one of whom died in detention; whether the deceased's title, the **Earldom of Mar**, was then conferred on Cochrane is disputed. He was also held responsible for a devaluation of the currency (evidenced in the introduction of lead 'placks') and for the distress this caused. In 1482 concerted action by the nobility led by **Archibald *Bell-the-Cat**' (Archibald being the **Douglas Earl of Angus**, the cat being Cochrane) resulted in the royal favourite being lynched and hanged, along with William Rogers the musician and others, from **Lauder** bridge.

COCHRANE, Thomas, 10th Earl of Dundonald (1775–1860) Admiral

Born at Annfield near **Hamilton**, Cochrane first served under his uncle, later Admiral Sir Alexander Cochrane, in the North Atlantic. Napoleon dubbed him le loup de mer following a series of sensational voyages (1800–10) in the *Speedy*, during which he accounted for more than 50 enemy ships in the Mediterranean, then in the *Pallas*, and eventually in the *Imperieuse*, in which, had she been adequately supported, he might have fired the entire French fleet in an engagement near Rochefort (1809).

Worshipped by his men, Cochrane's success also owed much to his unpredictable tactics, the result of a highly inventive mind, and to his remorseless valour. But such qualities became liabilities in his simultaneous career as a zealous reformer at Westminster. Populist, bellicose and eccentric he antagonised the Admiralty, the courts and the entire Tory establishment, all of whom combined to take their revenge when he became implicated in the stock exchange fraud (1814) engineered by his uncle The Hon **Andrew James Cochrane-**

'The greatest man afloat': Admiral Thomas Cochrane, 10th Earl of Dundonald (SNPG)

Johnstone. Cochrane was almost certainly innocent but in a travesty of a trial he was convicted and sentenced to a fine of £1000 (which he long refused to pay), a spell in the pillory (not carried out), expulsion from the House of Commons (to which he was immediately re-elected), loss of his knighthood (not restored till the 1840s), and prison (not for the first time). He escaped from prison, was rearrested in the House of Commons, and fined a further £100 which was gratefully paid by his Westminster electors, none of whom was allowed to contribute more than one penny each.

Throughout these tribulations he was sustained by the conviction of his innocence plus his enormous popularity and the unswerving support of his child bride. Cochrane is said to have first noticed the 16-year-old Kitty Barnes in a school crocodile. Never averse to prompt action, he immediately eloped with her to Scotland. They were married at the Queensberry Arms Hotel in **Dumfriesshire** (1812), subsequently in an Anglican church in Tunbridge Wells (1818) and finally in the **Church of Scotland** in **Edinburgh** (1825). 'Marry her!' roared Cochrane, 'I would marry her in a hundred churches. I would marry her all over the world . . . I am ready to marry her in every church in London. I would do it a thousand times.' But Kitty thought this was overdoing it. 'There was no end of marrying me . . . I was so tired of being married.'

Possibly with the connivance, and certainly to the relief, of the Admiralty, Cochrane next embarked on a crusade more suited to his fiery temperament and radical sympathies when he sailed to South America as naval Commander-in-Chief of the republican forces in Chile, then engaged in throwing off Spanish colonial rule. In another series of almost incredible exploits (1819–24) he routed the Spanish and then the Portuguese both on sea and on land as Admiral of the Chilean, then the Peruvian, and finally the Brazilian navies. A last assault on the Portuguese squadron 'was, and remains, a feat without parallel in the history of war' (Sir John Fortescue). Although subsequent service as Commander-in-Chief of the Greek Navy (1825–8) was less productive of heroics, he was now acknowledged even by the British Admiral of the Fleet as 'the greatest man afloat'.

In 1831 he succeeded to his father's title as 10th Earl of Dundonald. In London a change of heart and a change of government resulted in the full reinstatement of 'Thomas the Tenth' and to his tally of four admiralships was added a fifth – in the Royal Navy. His exploits provided Captain F Marryat, who had actually served with him, and G A Henty with rich subject matter. He was buried in Westminster Abbey. In South America his name is still revered but in Scotland the country's greatest naval hero is commemorated only by a plaque at **Anstruther** and by HMS *Cochrane*, the name given to the shore base at **Rosyth**.

COCHRANE-JOHNSTONE, Andrew James (b.1767) Fraudster
Every family has its black sheep; the whiter the flock the blacker the renegade. The Hon Andrew James Cochrane (the Johnstone was added when he married Lady Georgiana Johnstone) was one of the many sons of the 8th Earl of Dundonald. One brother became an admiral; so did three of his nephews including the great **Lord Thomas**. Andrew James chose the army and, a colonel at 30, was appointed Governor of St Dominica in the West Indies. 'His rule was marked by tyranny, extortion and vice ... [and] he drove a brisk trade in negroes and kept a harem' (A Cochrane). Court-martialled, he resigned from the army but secured both a seat in Parliament and, through his brother the admiral, further appointments in the West Indies. There he again ran riot, gun-running and swindling on a massive scale. Back in England, in 1814 he exceeded himself by perpetrating a sensational stock exchange fraud. This involved a 'French royalist' coming ashore at Dover with the exciting news that Napoleon was dead. Government stocks immediately rocketed. Cochrane and his associates, having bought heavily in advance, sold out just before the crash that followed news of the disappearance of the 'French royalist'. Investigations eventually led to Cochrane's arrest. He was convicted of conspiracy and, though protesting his innocence, somewhat compromised it by fleeing to the Continent. He never returned. The ignominy was compounded by his refusal to exculpate his nephew, Thomas, whose country thereby lost the services of 'the greatest man afloat'.

COCKBURN, Henry Thomas, Lord Cockburn (1779–1854) Judge and Man of Letters
Born in **Edinburgh** and educated at the city's High School and **University**, Cockburn became an advocate (1800) and was noted for his persuasive pleading in desperate causes; he secured the acquittals of James Steuart (1821) who had killed in a duel Alexander Boswell, son of the biographer, and of Helen MacDougal (1828) common law wife of **William Burke**. In the former he was assisted by **Francis Jeffrey**, a close and lifelong friend. Like Jeffrey, Cockburn underwent a conversion to **Whig** principles, contributed on legal matters to Jeffrey's **Edinburgh Review** and, as Solicitor-General (1830), assisted Jeffrey (then Lord Advocate) with the drafting of the Scottish Reform Bill. When Jeffrey died, Cockburn wrote his *Life of Lord Jeffrey* (1852). This was the only major work published in his lifetime but its vivid character sketches hinted at the wealth that lay in his journals. Published posthumously as *Memorials of His Time* (1856), *The Journal of Henry Cockburn* (1874) and *Circuit Journeys* (1888), Cockburn's journals constitute a remarkable chronicle of a remarkable age and have provided social historians with a wealth of highly quotable material. Besides the famous pen portraits (including one of **Robert MacQueen, Lord Braxfield**, on which **Robert Louis Stevenson** based his Lord Hermiston in *Weir of Hermiston*), Cockburn captures the flavour of turn-of-the-century Edinburgh and the traumas induced by the French Revolution and **Chartism**. Their author had become Lord Rector of **Glasgow University** in 1831 and 1833, a Lord of Session in 1834, and a determined Edinburgh conservationist after whom the city's Cockburn Association is named.

COCKBURNLAW, Berwickshire
Cockburn Law rises to 1066ft (325m), south-east of Abbey St Bathans, surrounded by the Whiteadder stream and crowned by a Bronze Age fort. The ruins on the north-eastern side are variously known as Woden's or Edwin's Hall, or Edinshall Broch, one of 10 Iron Age **brochs** known in Lowland Scotland. The remains are 5ft (1.5m) tall, the walls vary in thickness (around 15ft/4.6m) and measure some 80ft (24m) in diameter. They contain a series of cells and chambers with an additional defence system of earthworks and ditches on the outside.

COCKBURNSPATH, Berwickshire
Mentioned in 1128 as Colbrandspath, Cockburnspath is on the A1 about a mile inland from the **Berwickshire** coast. The Mercat Cross commemorates the marriage of **James IV** to **Margaret Tudor** in 1503 (Cockburnspath was part of her dowry). The village was owned by the Earl of Dunbar and March and then by the Homes until 1443; its final owner was Sir John Hall, Provost of **Edinburgh** (1689), who also owned Aldcambus and Dunglass. Cocksburnspath became a parish in 1609; by 1947 the parish was rejoined with Oldhamstocks; a **United Free Church** existed from 1741 until 1929 when the two churches united, and there has been a school in the village since 1872.

The Dunglass family chapel is known to date from at least 1423, but by 1443 it had become a collegiate church (the first of its kind in Scotland) under the Bishop of **St Andrews**. It fell into disuse in 1689 but still exists with little alteration as a fine example of a medieval church. The early Homes of Wedderburn were buried here, as were the Halls. The Southern Upland Way ends at Cocksburnspath.

Dunglass collegiate church. Cockburnspath (HS)

COCKENZIE AND PORT SETON, East Lothian

On the southern shore of the Firth of Forth and once two separate **fishing** villages, Cockenzie and Port Seton were already combined in the 1794 *Statistical Account* and have since been considered as one, although retaining two harbours, the former improved by **Robert Stevenson** in 1835 and the latter enlarged in 1880. Cockenzie was the destination of the first working **railway** in Scotland constructed in 1722 to transport **coal** from the pits near **Tranent** to the harbour. The unusual Chalmers Memorial Church (1904) with saddleback tower contains some internal features of the 1838 **Free Church** which it replaced. In 1962 Cockenzie acquired the power station which is now 'the chief feature, natural or man-made, of this whole stretch of coast' (C McWilliam). The salt-pans of Port Seton provided alternative employment to its inhabitants from c1630 until the decline of the industry in the mid-19th century. The two-mile stretch of Seton Sands has made the area a popular holiday destination, with **Seton House** and Collegiate Church providing historial and architectural interest.

COCKPEN, Midlothian

An old parish lying between **Lasswade** and **Gorebridge**, Cockpen's romantic, ivy-clad ruin, originally a chapel under **Newbattle Abbey**, resembles 'auld' Alloway Kirk. The only roofed part is the burial aisle of the lairds of nearby **Dalhousie Castle**. From Cockpen William Knox, brother of **John Knox** the **Reformation** minister, tried unsuccessfully to purge nearby **Roslin Chapel** of its 'images and altars'. The old song, 'The Laird o' Cockpen', commemorates Mark Carse of old Cockpen House. Having fled to Holland after the defeat of **Charles II** at Worcester, he found his estate confiscated by Commonwealth adherents on his return after the Restoration. He regained it, however, through playing the king's favourite air, 'Brose and Butter', in the Royal Chapel in London in order to bend the regal ear to his plight.

COINAGE

Although **Roman** coins were used in Scotland, the first coins to be struck in Scotland were the crudely stamped silver pennies, or sterlings, of **David I**'s reign. They closely resemble those of the English King Stephen and so probably date from after 1135, the year of Stephen's accession. David's successors continued to mint their own sterlings, distinguishable by minor changes and by indications of by whom and where they were minted. By 1250 there were at least 16 mints, the largest number ever recorded, scattered about the country from **Inverness** to **Berwick**. Thereafter the number of mints declined as the variety of denominations increased.

185

Early designs and inscriptions continued to resemble English counterparts; halfpennies and farthings were produced by halving and quartering the penny until individual coins appeared about 1280. Large silver groats (initially fourpence) and half-groats (twopence) were added in 1357 when the first gold coin was also struck. This was the noble, worth half a merk or mark; the latter being two thirds of a pound of sterlings, the noble was worth 6s 8d (or 33p in today's terms). The obverse showed **David II** in a ship and holding a shield which for the first time depicted a **lion** rampant. Only two versions of this noble exist and it was probably soon discontinued. It was reintroduced by **Robert III** and then remained a standard issue although its weight decreased in line with reductions in the silver content of the lesser coins. The billon (alloy) penny would eventually be worth only a fraction of a sterling. Debasement also ended parity with the English coinage. Gold crowns and half-crowns, also known as 'lions' and 'demi-lions' or 'demys', appeared during the reign of **James I**, evidently in imitation of the French *ecu*.

Important changes occurred during the reign of **James III**. New gold coins called the 'rider' (because the King was depicted on a galloping horse) of over a pound's value, the 'unicorn' of under a pound and the 'half-unicorn' were minted. So were the first copper coins for the smallest denominations. More notable was the 1485 half-groat which bore the 'first real coin portrait to be seen north of the Alps' (I H Stewart). Instead of the stylised profiles and busts of earlier issues here was a long-nosed James III, crowned and facing half-right. On the obverse the **thistle** made its inconspicuous debut.

The first Scottish coin to bear a date – 1539 – was the gold ducat of **James V** on which the King appears wearing a flat bonnet; hence the ducat, value 40 shillings, was often known as a 'bonnet'. A new and soon popular billon coin, the bawbee, was struck at about the same time with a value of 6 pence. Coins were now invariably dated and, but for an issue of **Stirling** bawbees in the mid-16th century, minted only in **Edinburgh**. New coins – like the post-1553 'testoon' (from *tête* because it bore the monarch's head) and the post-1565 ryal (with an unexplained palm tree perilously ascended by a tortoise on the reverse) – plus frequent new designs, chart the vicissitudes of **Mary**'s reign and the development of **James VI** from beardless youth to beruffed sovereign of both kingdoms. Billon gave way to copper for the smaller denominations, notably the 'turner', worth twopence and named after the French *tournois*. Debasement now meant that the ratio between Scottish and English value denominations was 12:1; thus the large silver Scots 'dollar', a replacement for the ryal, was worth 60 Scots shillings but only 5 English shillings, and the bawbee, value 6 Scots pence, was worth only a halfpenny in English money.

After the **Union of the Crowns** coinage continued to be minted in Scotland but designs and denominations returned to their close affinity with the English coinage. This was partly due to the introduction of minting machinery which replaced the earlier hammered method of production during the reign of **Charles I**. **Charles II** produced an issue of dollars and fractions of a dollar plus a new copper coin, the bodle, worth

twopence. Shilling denominations were favoured by **James VII** and William of Orange, the latter also producing a gold 'pistole' worth one pound English or 12 pounds Scots and said to have been struck from gold imported from Africa by the Scots company best known for its **Darien** débâcle.

An important provision of the 1707 **Act of Union** was the introduction of uniformity in coinage, weights and measures. This applied to the value of coins as well as to their issue and design. The Edinburgh mint was to continue in existence but in fact issued its last coins in 1709; thereafter it remained moribund until abolition in 1817. For the full story see I H Stewart, *The Scottish Coinage*, 1955 and D Bateson, *Scottish Coins*, 1987.

COINNEACH ODHAR, 'The Brahan Seer'

The term 'Brahan Seer', like the Seer's surname of Mackenzie, originates (at least in print) in the best-selling *Prophesies of the Brahan Seer* by Alexander Mackenzie, first published in 1877. In it he introduced him as 'Kenneth Mackenzie, better known as Coinneach Odhar, the Brahan Seer'. The only historical personage behind these designations is the one spelt 'Keanoch Ower' in a Commission of Justice issued in October 1577 at **Holyroodhouse**, authorising the arrest of six men and 26 women on charges of 'diabolical practices of magic, enchantment, murder, homicide and other offences'. The following January their trial was authorised by a second Commission in which the ringleader's name was spelt 'Kennoch Owir'. At least two women were burnt as witches at the Chanonry of **Ross**, though it is not known whether Coinneach Odhar was even caught. His personal name raises no more than a presumption that he was a Mackenzie, and the tradition that he was a native of **Uig** or Ness in **Lewis** does not strengthen it. The **Mackenzies** did not expropriate the **MacLeods** of Lewis until the 17th century. Nor was Brahan Castle in Rossshire, seat of the **Earls of Seaforth**, built in the historical Coinneach Odhar's lifetime. The historical events in which he was implicated are described in Elizabeth Sutherland's centenary edition of Alexander Mackenzie's text. The Gaelic scholar William Matheson investigated 'The Historical Coinneach Odhar and some Prophesies Attributed to Him' in *Transactions of the Gaelic Society of Inverness* (1968). He wrote: 'The name of Coinneach Odhar seems to have acted as a magnet, drawing a host of prophetic utterances to itself.' Some extremely bizarre ones were recorded before they were fulfilled. But the circumstantial story of how the 3rd Countess of Seaforth executed the Brahan Seer during the reign of **Charles II** must be discounted. Quite apart from official records, the Brodies of **Brodie Castle**, father and son, kept diaries in which they would certainly have recorded such a deed, committed by a woman they disliked. So would James Fraser, Minister of the nearby parish of Wardlaw and another diarist.

COLDINGHAM, Berwickshire

The original priory, on the south side of the desolate Coldingham Moor, was built in the 7th century on land granted to Ebba, a Northumbrian princess shipwrecked on the nearby shore, by Oswy. Destroyed by fire c679 and then rebuilt, it was destroyed again in the great

The choir of Coldingham Priory (RWB)

Danish invasion of 866/867 and abandoned for two centuries. In 1098 **King Edgar** granted to the monks at Durham the lands of Coldingham; the monks later built a church but it was 1147 before it again became a priory. In 1509 it was annexed to **Dunfermline** Abbey and was continually occupied until 1560, despite being plundered by King John of England in 1216 and fired by the English under the Earl of Hertford in 1544 (a favourable wind saving it from total destruction). Further damage was inflicted on the hapless priory c1650 by Cromwell. Repaired in 1662, restored in 1854 and renovated in 1954, the north and east walls of the choir of the old monastic church are incorporated in the present parish church. Coldingham Loch, south-west of **St Abbs**, is 274 metres from the shore but 91m above sea level. Triangular in shape and fed by hidden springs, the loch is famous for its very large brown trout.

COLDSTREAM, Berwickshire
From its position on the north bank of the river **Tweed**, Coldstream has always been important as a gateway to England. Although many crossings went unrecorded, it is known that the following crossed by the ancient ford: Edward I in 1296; **Robert I** and **Sir James Douglas** on their way to a peace conference with Edward II; **James IV** with his army on their way to **Flodden** in 1513; and **Montrose** in 1640. By 1766 a seven-arched bridge built by Smeaton (also a designer of lighthouses) had replaced the ford. On the north end stands a red toll, or marriage house, which was second only to **Gretna Green**. Here three Lord Chancellors of England were married (Lords Eldon, Brougham and Erskine). The unofficial 'priests' were local tradesmen.

In 1787 **Robert Burns** crossed the bridge on his first visit to England. On his way back he knelt on the bridge and gave a prayer for his native land which can be found in 'The Cottar's Saturday Night', the first line being 'O Scotia, my dear, my native soil'. The Coldstream Club recorded the event in 1926 by placing a plaque on the bridge. Not far from the bridge is the Charles Marjoribanks monument, a 70ft (21m) obelisk surmounted by stone figures, erected in 1834 to celebrate Marjoribanks's becoming the first elected MP for **Berwickshire** after the passing of the Reform Act of 1832.

The main association of this narrow, clean little town is with the Coldstream Guards – the second oldest known regiment of foot guards. Contrary to popular belief the regiment was not raised in the town but was made up of a unit of Fenwick's and Haselrig's troop raised 10 years previously by **General Monk** to fight Scottish **Presbyterians**. Monk established his headquarters in Coldstream in 1659, but the troops showed more allegiance to their General than to Cromwell, and when he changed sides they went too, so allowing Monk to capture Newcastle on behalf of **Charles II**. Their headquarters were in the Market Square and the guard house is now a museum. 'Coldstream Guards' was just a nickname which stuck; originally they were known as the Second Foot Guards; they received the freedom of the town on 10 August 1968.

During the second week in August the town remembers **Flodden**; banner-carrying horsemen parade through the streets and there are ride-outs to Norham, **Hirsel** and Birgham, Leitholm and, of course, to Flodden field itself. It is thought that the Abbess at Coldstream Priory ordered the bodies of many of the Scots who died in that fateful battle to be buried at the priory in Abbey Road. In the past industry consisted of a **brewery** owned by J & A Davidson, and the first Bible printing factory, owned by Rev Adam Thomson.

COLL, Island of, Inner Hebrides
Measuring 13 miles by four and lying north-west of **Mull**, Coll has a population of about 150. A car ferry from **Oban** calls at the main township, Arinagour, before continuing to the neighbouring island of **Tiree**. The terrain of Coll is generally low-lying but knobbly, due to the underlying Lewisian gneiss, especially in the northern half of the island. The highest hill is Ben Hogh (341ft/104m), on top of which a large glacial erratic is precariously perched.

Coll has a rich archaeological heritage, notably the **cairn** at Arinagour, the **standing stones** at Totronald (mentioned by **Johnson** and **Boswell** who were stormbound here in 1773) and several Iron Age forts; those at Dun an Achaidh and Feall Bay are best preserved. Unusual in the islands, there is a **souterrain** at the Arnabost crossroads.

The medieval church is at Killunaig, on the north-west coast. At the northern tip of the island is the old **crofting** township of Sorisdale, with one thatched house still occupied. At the south end of the island Breachacha Castle has a square keep dating from 1450 and in design is comparable to **Kisimul Castle** in **Barra**. In 1965 it was bought and restored by Major N V MacLean Bristol, a descendant of the Macleans of Coll who owned it from 1631 to 1865. In the surrounding fields many rare breeds of sheep and cattle are kept.

COLLIESTON, Nr Ellon, Aberdeenshire

This **fishing** and smuggling village half-way between **Aberdeen** and **Peterhead** stands on the cliffs and now consists largely of holiday homes. Here was wrecked the St Catherine, a Flemish vessel carrying arms for the Papist Earls **Huntly** and **Errol** in 1594. The Errols' (Old) **Slains Castle** lies just to the north and Forvie Ness, a nature reserve, to the south near the mouth of the Ythan. Forvie's advancing sand-dunes, like those of **Culbin**, once engulfed an entire hamlet, only the ruins of the church being still visible.

COLLINS, William (1789–1853) Publisher

Born in Eastwood, **Renfrewshire**, Collins started professional life as a clerk in a **cotton** mill, running evening classes for the workers in his spare time. In 1813 he opened a school for poor children in **Glasgow**, and the following year became an elder of the **Tron Church**, where he met and made close friends with one of the Tron's regular preachers, **Thomas Chalmers**. In 1819, in partnership with Chalmers's brother Charles, Collins started his own business as a printer, publisher and bookseller. Much of his early success came from the publication of school textbooks, of Thomas Chalmers's works and from his own energetic involvement in the **temperance movement**; in 1839 the Collins press produced an estimated half a million temperance tracts as well as the first edition of The Temperance Society Record, not only printed and published but also written by William Collins. On his death his publishing business was taken over and run by his son, also **William**, and although no longer a family concern and now London-based, as Harper-

Collieston as photographed by George Washington Wilson c1880 (GWWA)

Collins it continues to the present day with an office and printing works in Glasgow.

COLLINS, Sir William (1817–95) Publisher

The son of **William Collins**, founder of Wm Collins, Son & Co Ltd, was born in **Glasgow** and attended Glasgow High School but left aged 12 and soon joined the family business. By 1848 he was a partner. Responding to the demand for Bibles from its **Free Church** connections and to that for school textbooks, the firm expanded rapidly under his control (1853) and employed more than 2000 by the time of his death, with offices in London and elsewhere. Collins also served as councillor, magistrate and Lord Provost of Glasgow (1877–80), for which he was knighted (1881). As 'Water Willie', a zealous teetotaller like his father, he was suitably memorialised in a drinking fountain erected at the entrance to **Glasgow Green**; the 'water' may also have referred to his pioneering exploits as a keen west coast yachtsman.

COLLINSON, Francis (1898–1985)
Musicologist and Composer

Collinson's contribution to Scottish traditional music studies is a major one. His main publications are The Traditional and National Music of Scotland (1966 and 1970); The Bagpipe (1975) and, with J L Campbell, the 3-vol Hebridean Folksongs (1969, 1977, 1981). His compositions consist largely of vocal arrangements of Scots songs.

COLMONELL, Ayrshire

Four miles north-east of **Ballantrae**, the village of Colmonell shares its stretch of the delightful Stinchar glen with no less than five ruined castles; Ardstinchar, Knockdolian, Kirkhill, Craigneil and Pinwherry. The first of these, the ivy-clad remains of a **Kennedy** stronghold at

the mouth of the glen, is said to have played host to **Queen Mary** one night in 1563. Knockdolian, the remains of a 17th century castle built on the site of an older structure, and Kirkhill, again ivy-clad but this time an L-plan turreted house dated 1589, stand near their successors, Knockdolian House (1842) and Kirkhill (1843–5), both thought to be by David Rhind. Craigneil (14th or 15th century) perches precariously on the hillside opposite Colmonell and was comparatively intact until the end of the 19th century when part of it collapsed into a neighbouring **quarry**. Pinwherry Castle to the north, another Kennedy stronghold dating from the 16th century and abandoned before the end of the 18th, is so engulfed in ivy 'it is not easy to say whether this is prising it apart or holding it together' (R Close). Colmonell Church, with some notable modern stained glass, has a memorial to the **Covenanting** martyr Matthew McIlwraith, shot by **Claverhouse**'s dragoons c1679, whose name suggested to **Sir Walter Scott** that of Mucklewrath in *Old Mortality*.

COLONSAY, Island of, Inner Hebrides

12 miles south of the Ross of **Mull** and nine miles west of the island of **Jura**, Colonsay is just over eight miles from north to south, with a maximum breadth of three miles. Aligned NE-SW, it was called descriptively in Gaelic '*Eilean Tarsuing*' – the cross-lying island. Kiloran Bay has one of the finest unspoilt beaches in the **Hebrides**.

The declining population of under 100 live in the three small villages of Scalasaig and Upper and Lower Kilchattan, or scattered around the island in 16 farms and crofts stocked with 500 cattle and 7000 sheep. In 1841 Colonsay and the neighbouring island of **Oronsay** to the south had a population of 979.

Colonsay is rich in archaeological and historical remains, from the **standing stones** at Kilchattan known as 'Fingal's Limpet Hammers' to the deserted township of Riasg Buidhe, abandoned in the 1920s. A kerb **cairn** incorporating a standing stone, behind the hotel at Scalasaig, is a fine example of its kind. Dun Eibhinn, also behind Scalasaig, is an Iron Age fort which in the Middle Ages was occupied by the MacDuffies or MacFies of Colonsay. They were replaced as the ruling family in 1701 by the **MacNeills**.

Colonsay House sits in a pocket of mature woodland in the centre of the island. Built in 1722 by Malcolm MacNeill, it was enlarged in the 19th century. In 1904 the estate was sold to **Donald Smith**, who left the small town of **Forres** on the Moray Firth in 1836 and made his fortune in Canada with the Hudson's Bay and Canadian Pacific Companies. Eventually High Commissioner for Canada in London, he was raised to the peerage in 1897 by **Queen Victoria**, taking the title Lord Strathcona and Mount Royal, from his Scottish estate in **Glencoe** and from Montreal, headquarters of the Hudson's Bay Company.

COLQUHOUN, Robert (1914–62) Painter and Set Designer

Born in **Kilmarnock** and educated at the **Glasgow School of Art** under Ian Fleming, Colquhoun's reputation as one of the most significant of post-war British artists was made entirely outside Scotland. His early portrait drawings are assured and highly articulate and display the talent which won him travelling scholarships to Italy in 1937 and 1939 accompanied by Robert MacBryde, a fellow but less talented student who became his inseparable and lifelong companion. Moving to London in 1941, they shared their first studio with John Minton through whom they met members of the English 'Neo-romantic' group and for a while participated in their lyrical and romantic concern for landscape. In 1943 Jankel Adler encouraged Colquhoun towards the figure and from 1944–7 this subject inspired his finest works. He quickly detached himself from the provincialism of the Neo-romantics and, in a language adopted from Wyndham Lewis and Picasso, painted isolated, solitary figures expressive of a hardship and *angst* that could easily be understood and appreciated in post-war Britain. By 1950 a variety of circumstances – eviction, increasing alcoholism and the commercial failure of his 1950 exhibition – sharply deflated Colquhoun's standing. In 1951 his fortunes temporarily revived with commissions to produce costumes and sets for Massine's *Donald of the Burthens* for Scottish Ballet and again in 1953 for George Devine's *King Lear* at Stratford. In 1958 a retrospective of Colquhoun's work was held at the Whitechapel Gallery, and though well received, the 11 oils he hurriedly prepared are characteristically dull and monochromatic, with a tendency towards the over-monumental.

COLUMBA, Saint (c521–97)

Born at Gartan, Donegal, Columba was neither the first nor the last Irish missionary monk to found monasteries in Scotland. His Latin name, and his Gaelic name 'Columcille', mean 'dove'. However, he was of warring royal lineage, a leader in battle over monastic possessions whose banishment from Ulster in 563 brought him in a curragh to exile in **Iona** with 12 companions.

He had been educated at Derry, where he had built a church, and had founded a monastery at Durrow, where he was a scholar, copying religious texts in the traditional **Celtic art** script and decoration. Through kinsmen, particularly **Aidan** whom he crowned King of **Dalriada**, he was granted Iona. There he founded a monastery from which to evangelise the northern **Picts** under their King Brude at **Inverness**. As abbot of his missionary monks, he was scholar, preacher and diplomat by turns, both autocratic and gentle in dealing with the tribal Scotland of the mainland. The Celtic monasticism he formed was disciplined in prayer and study, a model for those who followed. His biography by **Adamnan** is a main source of information for the period and of the Christianisation of northern Scotland.

Columba's influence also spread from Iona down to western Scotland to link with the earlier Christian foundations derived from **St Ninian** and **Whithorn** two centuries earlier. It continues in his hymns, prayers and example, particularly in the present **Iona Community** with its emphasis on Celtic spirituality in the life of the modern Church. He died at Iona.

COLVILLE, David (1813–98) Iron and Steel Master

The name of Colville is inseparably connected to **iron and steel**-making in Scotland, yet David Colville's early

William McTaggart's The Coming of St Columba (NGS)

career hardly suggested heavy industry. Born in **Campbeltown**, he worked with his father in several local business ventures and then moved to the **Trongate** in **Glasgow** as a provision merchant. Aged 38 he completely changed tack and, in partnership with Thomas Gray, began the production of malleable iron at a plant in Monklands [see **Coatbridge**], the Clifton Iron Works. The partnership was dissolved, despite success, and David decided to strike out on his own. Aged 60 and assisted by his two elder sons, he set up the Dalzell Works near **Motherwell** and close to rich **coal**fields and the **railway** network. Perceiving the threat from steel he then converted his works to the production of mild steel by the Siemens process. The demand from the shipyards ensured rapid expansion during the 1880s. He died, aged 85, three years after the creation of a limited liability company which would tower over the Scottish steel industry for decades to come.

COMET, The

Launched in 1812, this was the first steamboat to ply commercially in Europe. Of wooden construction, she was 42ft long x 11ft beam x 5ft 6in deep (12.8 x 3.3 x 1.6m) and was built by John Wood & Co of **Port Glasgow** for **Henry Bell**. The boiler by **Napier** was set in brick on the starboard side, supplying steam at low pressure to **Robertson**'s engine on the port side. The arrangement necessitated an offset on the funnel which rose from the centre so that it could also serve as a mast carrying a square sail.

The power plant was a modified beam engine fitted with a jet condenser, an air pump and a centrifugal governor. It drove through side rods and levers to a crankshaft beneath the single cylinder. The crankshaft

was originally connected by sprocket drive to two radial paddles on each side and the cylinder of 16in (406mm) stroke and 11½in (290mm) bore developed around 3 hp. On her trials she achieved 5 knots, but was considered underpowered and withdrawn after two months when a larger cylinder of 16in stroke and 12in (300mm) bore was fitted and the paddles changed to one directly driven paddle wheel on each side. These modifications increased her speed to 6.5 knots and she became a popular and economical vessel on the **Clyde**. Still underpowered, she was wrecked in a 6-knot tide in 1820. Robertson's engine was salvaged and gave many years service in a sugar-mill before it was presented to the Science Museum in London in 1862.

COMLONGAN CASTLE, Nr Dumfries

A massive 15th century tower with later adjoining mansion, Comlongan was built by the Murrays of nearby Cockpool, descendants of **Thomas Randolph**, **Robert I**'s Earl of Moray (Murray). The exceptionally thick walls accommodate a maze of mural chambers and flue-like cupboards while the great hall has a notable fireplace and aumbry. **MacGibbon and Ross** found the battlements 'most interesting', part being roofed in to form a long gallery (17th century) while two angles are crowned with gabled cap houses.

COMMENDATORS

Appointed to administer and enjoy the revenues of ecclesiastical benefices, Commendators were originally clerics, but later increasingly laymen who were required to perform no religious duties. In the 16th century the office became in effect a Crown appointment not infrequently deemed an appropriate source of revenue for royal offspring, legitimate and otherwise, as in 1504

The Comet passing Dumbarton Rock (ML)

when **James IV** appointed his 11-year-old bastard son Alexander Stewart to the Commendatorships of the Abbey of **Dunfermline** and the Priory of **Coldingham** as well as to the Archbishopric of **St Andrews**.

COMPETITORS, The

The 13 persons who claimed the throne of Scotland after the death of **Margaret, Maid of Norway** in 1290, were known as the Competitors. They were: **John Balliol**; **Robert Bruce**; **John Comyn (i)**; Patrick, Earl of Dunbar; Patrick Galithly; John Hastings; Florent V, Count of Holland; Roger de Mandeville; Erik, King of Norway; Robert de Pinkeny; William de Ros; Nicholas de Soules and William de Vesci.

Comlongan Castle as drawn by MacGibbon and Ross (MR)

COMRIE, Perthshire

A small town at the junction of Glens Lednock and Artney with Strathearn, Comrie stands astride the **Highland Line** which, besides being a social and geographical frontier, is also a geological fault capable of creating its own disturbances. Local seismologists recorded 7300 tremors in the 1830s, 'sometimes accompanied by a loud report and sulphureous smells'. Damage was negligible. A granite obelisk atop Dunmore hill to the north commemorates **Henry Dundas, 1st Viscount Melville** ('King Harry the Ninth'), whose titles included that of 'Baron Dunira in the County of Perth'. Dunira House, built by **David Bryce** but now a ruin, is three miles west of Comrie and replaced the cottage to which the most powerful man in Scotland (not to mention the Admiralty or the government of India) had retired. The Melville monument is reached via wooded Glen Lednock wherein lie the Falls of Lednock or De'il's Cauldron. The upper part of the glen, once a busy **drove road**, is now a featureless expanse of **hydro-electric** reservoir. The Museum of Scottish Tartans, located for many years in Comrie, has moved to **Stirling**.

COMUNN GAIDHEALACH, An (The Highland Association)

Dedicated to promoting the use and teaching of **Gaelic**, An Comunn Gaidhealach also aims to encourage the study of Highland music, history and literature and, more generally, to further the social and economic betterment of the Highlands and Islands. It was founded in **Oban** (1891) where it staged the first National **Mod** (1892). Mods, both national and provincial, remain high on its list of activities. Its publications have ranged from Gaelic drama to periodicals [see **Gaelic Verse and Prose**] while in the field of education it has lobbied long and with some success to establish Gaelic in school curricula and to ensure a supply of qualified Gaelic teachers. It was once a moving spirit in the Highland Home Industries Association to promote local arts and crafts, in the Comunn na h-Oigridh youth movement, and in efforts to preserve the wearing of Highland dress. Funding comes from public and private sources and from its own fund-raising efforts.

COMYN, John (i) (d.c1303) Guardian and 'Competitor'

Son of John 'the Red' of **Badenoch** and **Tynedale**, this John is sometimes called 'the Black'. As a member of an immensely powerful family, he was one of the six Guardians of the Realm elected on the death of **Alexander III**; he was also a **Competitor** (1291) through his descent from **Donald Bane**. He married **John Balliol**'s sister Eleanor, negotiated the French Treaty (1295), gave John refuge in Badenoch (1296) and was prisoner in England after John's abdication. Released to help his cousin the Earl of Buchan (husband of **Isabella**) suppress unrest in **Moray** (1297) he instead joined **William Wallace**, as did the Earl. He was the father of **John Comyn (ii)**, also 'the Red'.

COMYN, John (ii) (d.1306) Guardian

Son of **John Comyn (i)**, this John was also known as 'the Red Comyn' like his grandfather. Sent to the Tower of London after **John Balliol**'s abdication, he was among those Scots liberated to join Edward I's war in France. With others, he broke away to seek French help for Scotland and made his way homeward to join **William Wallace**.

As a Guardian (1298–1301 and 1302–4) he frequently quarrelled with his colleagues, and at **Peebles** (1299) publicly seized the Earl of **Carrick** (**Robert I**, the Bruce) by the throat. He was active in the war until 1304 when he negotiated good terms and served on Edward's 'Scottish Council' appointed to manage 'the land' (not 'the kingdom').

At a meeting with Robert I in **Devorguilla Balliol**'s **Dumfries** Franciscan priory (10 February 1306) he either refused to support, or threatened to reveal, Robert's plans; he was thereupon stabbed by Robert, his uncle dying with him.

COMYN, Walter, Earl of Menteith (c1190–1258)

The son of William Comyn, 1st **Earl of Buchan** and Justiciar (c1233), and the younger brother of Alexander 2nd Earl (d.1289) and of Richard, Walter supported **Alexander II** and was rewarded with the Lordship of **Badenoch** and probably **Lochaber** (c1229). In c1230 he married Isabella, Countess of **Menteith**, and was soon after confirmed as Earl of Menteith. He founded **Inchmahome Priory** and built a castle at **Ruthven** in Badenoch. In 1235 he assisted in the pacification of **Galloway** and incurred the hostility of Henry III of England for supposedly interfering in Irish affairs. Now immensely powerful, the Comyn family slipped in and out of royal favour with bewildering rapidity but, when in favour, Walter was probably the most powerful figure in the realm. In eclipse at the end of Alexander II's reign, the Comyns returned to power (1249–55) under **Alexander III** but were then in virtual rebellion until securing the King's person and seal in 1257. Walter died childless and was succeeded by his nephew John,

the 'Red' Comyn, son of Richard, and then John's son, **John the 'Black' Comyn (i)** (d.c1303).

CONAN, Saint (7th century)

An Irish missionary priest of the **Celtic Church**, Conan was patron of **Lorne** and reputed tutor of Eugenius (a Latinised version of Ewen), a King of Scots who died in 648. The modern St Conan's Kirk near **Dalmally** on the side of **Loch Awe** in **Argyll** is a remarkable building, worthy of whoever he was.

CONGREGATION, Lords of the

In December 1557, during the regency of **Mary of Guise**, Protestant nobles opposed to the marriage then being negotiated between **Mary**, their future queen, and the Dauphin of France signed a bond to 'maintain . . . and establish the most blessed work of God and his Congregation' against the 'Congregation of Satan', ie Roman Catholicism. It was known as 'the first bond [or band] of the Lords of the Congregation of Christ', the signatories being **Archibald 5th Earl of Argyll**, his son Lord Lorne, Alexander Cunningham 5th Earl of Glencairn, **James Douglas 4th Earl of Morton**, and John Erskine of Dun. Subsequent bonds quickly increased the number and influence of the Lords of the Congregation who, in support of **John Knox** in 1559, opposed Mary of Guise and her French troops with some assistance from Elizabeth of England.

CONNEL, Argyll

The name Connel is derived from the Gaelic *conghail*, meaning 'tumultuous flood', and refers to the Falls of Lora which separate Connel and North Connel as they spill out of **Loch Etive**. The rapids, which are caused by the outflow cascading across a ledge of rock at ebb tide, are named after an early Celtic hero, Laoighre. They are now crossed by the bridge built in 1903 to carry the **railway** across the narrows on the way to **Ballachulish**. Previously a hazardous ferry trip between the two inns was the only way north. Now, with both ferry and railway superannuated, the bridge carries road traffic.

CONSTABLE, Archibald (1774–1827)
Publisher

Born at Carnbee, **Fife**, the son of the factor to the Earl of Kellie, Constable became a bookseller's apprentice to Peter Hill of **Edinburgh**, and in 1795 opened a shop of his own. He began publishing books in 1798, became the owner of the *Scots Magazine* in 1801, and in 1802 began publishing the **Edinburgh Review**. His reputation as a generous and respected publisher attracted many authors to his firm, among them **Walter Scott** who began publishing his work with Constable in 1803. In 1812 Constable purchased the rights to the **Encyclopaedia Britannica** for over £13,000, going on to publish several supplements to it. In 1826 his London agents, Hurst Robinson & Co, collapsed, bringing on the subsequent failure and bankruptcy of Constable's publishing concerns which in turn bankrupted **Ballantyne's** and Scott. Constable struggled on, producing his celebrated *Miscellany*, but the burden of his publishing failure led to an early death.

Archibald Constable, Sir Walter Scott's publisher, by Andrew Geddes (SNPG)

CONSTANTINE I (d.c879) King of Alba

A shadowy figure about whom little is known, Constantine is said to have been a son of **Kenneth mac Alpin**; he was King of **Alba** from c862–79, during which time his kingdom suffered several **Viking** invasions. He had a son Donald (later and briefly **Donald II**), and he was killed in battle possibly against the Danes and was succeeded by his brother **Aed**.

CONSTANTINE II (d.c952) King of Alba (ruled c900–40)

The Anglo-Saxon chronicles record that after one of his unsuccessful attempts to invade Northumbria, Constantine II submitted to the English monarch Edward the Elder, son of Alfred the Great, 'choosing him for his father and lord'. Some historians have interpreted this as granting Edward sovereignty over Scotland; others regard it as being more in the nature of a pact in the face of **Viking** aggression. Whatever the case, Constantine appears to have reneged on his submission, for in 937 he was defeated in battle by Edward's son Athelstan at Brunanburgh on the Solway Firth and forced to submit all over again. He finally renounced his throne in favour of his cousin **Malcolm** and retired to a monastery in **St Andrews**.

CONSTANTINE III (d.997) King of Alba

This Constantine was the grandson of **Constantine II** and son of Culen. King lists and later chronicles are contradictory, but it seems most likely that Constantine III ruled for a mere two years between **Kenneth II** and **Kenneth III**, possibly having killed the former (995) and being killed by the latter (997).

CONVENTICLERS

Covenanting ministers who opposed the reintroduction of episcopacy and of lay patronage under the Restoration settlement, and who resisted subsequent **Indulgences**, were deprived of their parishes. But many parishioners remained loyal to them, especially in the south-west. Hence assembly and worship continued at conventicles, ie unauthorised and outlawed gatherings either in private houses or remote steadings or outdoors. Military defeat [see **Pentland Rising**, **Bothwell Brig**, etc], hefty fines and prosecution [see **Killing Time**] served only to confirm the recalcitrance and extremism [see **Declaration of Sanquhar**] of **Cameronians** and **Gibb**ites, the hard core of the Conventiclers.

CO-OPERATIVE MOVEMENT

Embryo co-operative societies first appeared in Scotland in the late 18th century. The Fenwick Weavers' Society was founded in **Ayrshire** around 1769 and the **Govan** Victualling Society appeared on Clydeside c1800. These indigenous working class institutions pre-dated Robert Owen's more widely known work at **New Lanark**. Few of the early co-operative societies, however, lasted for more than a few years – though the movement re-emerged during **Chartist** agitation in the early 19th century.

Mid-19th century legal changes encouraged co-operation in Scotland. One estimate suggests that the country had perhaps 130 societies – often based on mining and weaving areas – by 1867. The journal *Scottish Co-operator* appeared in 1863, though only isolated issues from this period can be found in modern archives.

Suggestions for a central Scottish wholesale society, similar to the Co-operative Wholesale Society in England, first emerged in 1860. After extended meetings of delegates from local retail societies, the Scottish Co-operative Wholesale Society was formed in **Glasgow** in 1867. Retail societies were largely concentrated on central Scotland's industrial areas – although **Aberdeen**'s Northern Co-operative Society, with an extensive rural network, was also formed in this period and still flourishes. From the outset the SCWS was hampered by a repeated unwillingness by many local societies to deal solely with the movement's own wholesale body. Scottish **banks** also consistently refused loan finance to the SCWS.

From the 1870s, pressure grew to develop aspects of co-operative manufacturing in Scotland. Ventures included a **Clackmannanshire** cloth mill and a co-operative cooperage, and there were short-lived attempts to found co-operative shipyards at **Irvine** and **Dumbarton**. A co-operative **iron**works briefly functioned in Glasgow.

The infant SCWS faced immediate competition from fast-developing private grocery chains – such as **Liptons**, Galbraiths and Templetons. Activists also faced harassment, even dismissal, by their employers. Despite these pressures, strong links were forged with the CWS and the two wholesale groups co-operated in tea-buying and in the formation of the Co-operative Insurance Society.

The SCWS began shirt manufacture in 1880, venturing into footwear, furniture, hosiery and **tobacco** processing before 1900. In 1888 large-scale production for resale to local societies began in the SCWS's Shieldhall works near Glasgow. By 1914 Shieldhall boasted 16 factories with 4000 employees. The site was reputed to contain more industrial processes under one roof than any other production venue in the world. Despite regular boycotts by, among others, Britain's soap manufacturers (causing the SCWS to commence soap production at **Grangemouth**), the SCWS rapidly became Scotland's largest food and clothing wholesaler. Membership of local societies in Scotland rose to 470,000 by the eve of World War I. Scottish co-operators argued for the creation of a Co-operative party as early as 1897. The party was eventually formed on a UK basis in 1907.

The SCWS played a key role in extending shopping facilities at 'city' prices to far-flung parts of the Highlands and Islands of Scotland – where land-owners profited from 'captive' markets. The CWS, SCWS's successor, maintains Highlands and Islands shops today, recognising social need. The SCWS also pioneered mobile shops in rural Scotland.

Scottish co-operators also established one of Britain's first holiday camps – at **Rothesay** – from 1910. The movement was closely associated with the powerful **temperance** lobby. Societies retailing alcohol were banned from SCWS membership until 1958.

Shieldhall and the SCWS continued to dominate Scottish retailing until after World War II, when English-based private supermarket companies increasingly opened outlets in Scotland. Local societies failed to follow populations from traditional city centres to new peripheral housing schemes and many closed or merged. Shieldhall today has little manufacturing function, being mainly a Scottish depot for the Manchester-based CWS.

The SCWS became insolvent in the early 1970s when its banking subsidiary undertook investment activity beyond its financial resources. The functions of the group were taken over by the CWS – which continues to trade extensively north of the border. Scotland still has a number of local retail societies, principally in **Edinburgh** and Aberdeen, with smaller, semi-rural societies still based in **Fife** and on the east coast.

Co-operative ideas remain attractive to many Scots and a number of ventures emerged from the mid-1970s. The *Scottish Daily News* co-operative, formed after Beaverbrook Newspapers closed their Glasgow plant, failed. But a number of other businesses, from specialist retailing to precision **engineering** and advertising, have been more firmly established.

CORGARFF CASTLE, Cockbridge, Aberdeenshire

Oblong, with a four-storey tower and defensive wall all around it, Corgarff's austere architecture is in keeping with its bleak surroundings above the upper **Don** at the start of the **Lecht** pass over to Speyside. It was built, a simple tower, about 1550 but burnt down in 1571 when the laird's wife, Margaret Forbes, her family and servants (24 in all) perished in the flames kindled by Adam Gordon, brother of the 5th **Earl of Huntly**, who claimed it for the deposed **Queen Mary**. It was burnt again in 1689 by the **Jacobites**, served as a recruitment centre for the **Earl of Mar** (1715) in the Jacobite cause, and was destroyed a third time in 1746 when the Jacobites denied it to their enemy. Thereafter it was rebuilt to serve as a Hanoverian barracks and in the 19th century briefly as a post for suppressing the illicit **whisky** trade. It is now in state care and has been restored and whitewashed.

CORNCRAKE

A brown, dumpy, elusive bird that trails its legs in flight, the corncrake (*Crex Crex*) is one of the most threatened breeding birds of Scotland (a 1988 survey located only around 550 calling males). At one time common in hayfields throughout Britain (not cornfields as the name suggests), its territory has shrunk until it is now confined to the west coast of Ireland, isolated spots on the extreme north-western fringes of the Scottish mainland and to the outer isles. The presence of this solitary, crepuscular, skulking bird, sometimes called the landrail, is only betrayed by its strange rasping call which has been likened to the teeth of a comb being drawn repeatedly across a piece of wood, or the ratchet-screech of a snatched-out fishing line.

The reason for its dramatic decline is the change in the method and time of hay-making. In past centuries when hay was cut with the scythe, the remaining grass was still long enough to provide shelter in which the bird could hatch and raise her brood. Once the whole process became mechanised, with grass being cut sometimes as early as May for silage, the corncrake and her nest were at the mercy of the swishing blades of the mechanical reaper which shaves the ground, destroying everything in its path. Once an occasional winter resident, the corncrake is now entirely migratory, spending the winters in southern and eastern Africa and southern Asia.

CORPACH, Fort William, Inverness-shire

The mixed results of **Fort William**'s ambitions as the industrial capital of the Highlands lie scattered to the north round the head of Loch Linnhe and the mouth of Loch Eil. At Corpach in the 1960s £20 million and 80 acres (32ha) were devoted to a pulp and paper mill designed to process the entire sitka spruce product of the Highlands. It was the largest single investment in the area after British Aluminium's nearby plant but by the 1980s it was already proving uneconomical. Previously Corpach was better known as the port at the entrance of the Caledonian **Canal** whose 'Neptune's Staircase' of eight locks conducts hence up to **Banavie**. Kilmallie, once a separate village and the centre of one of the largest parishes in the Highlands, is the burial place of the **Camerons** of Lochiel; there is also a tall obelisk (with epitaph supposedly by **Sir Walter Scott**) to John Cameron of Fassfern who died in action in 1815 just before Waterloo. West, along Loch Eil, Cameron and **Jacobite** associations proliferate at Fassfern House, where **Prince Charles Edward Stewart** spent the night of 21 August 1745, and Kinlocheil where he spent the two previous nights after the gathering at **Glenfinnan** on the 19th.

CORRICHIE, Battle of (1562)

Returning to Scotland in 1561, **Queen Mary** relied on the support and counsel of **William Maitland of Lethington** and **Lord James Stewart** (her illegitimate half-brother), who together represented moderation in religious affairs and amity with England. Lord James was promised, and eventually received, the **Earldoms of Moray** and **Mar**, then being administered by the Catholic **Gordons of Huntly**. The **4th Earl of Huntly** resented the transference of power in the north-east that this represented while Lord James feared the designs of Sir John Gordon (one of Huntly's sons) on the Queen. In August 1562 the Queen toured the north-east visiting **Inverness** and **Aberdeen**. The Gordons held back until Huntly was outlawed for failing to answer a summons from the Privy Council. They then marched on Aberdeen and were defeated by Lord James, now Earl of Moray, on 28 October at Corrichie on the Hill of Fare near **Banchory**. Huntly himself died of apoplexy after capture; Sir John Gordon was executed in Aberdeen. The dual purpose of reducing the might of the Catholic **Gordons** and of appeasing those reformers suspicious of the Queen's pro-Catholic leanings was thus served.

CORRIESHALLOCH GORGE, Braemore, Wester Ross

Perhaps the finest box canyon in Scotland, Corrieshalloch in one of the bleaker parts of the Highlands is 200ft (61m) deep and 50–150ft (15–46m) wide with sides almost sheer. Unlike similar chasms cut in red sandstone by the Beauly and Findhorn, the rock here is a hard schist (or psammitic granulite). Within the gorge's dark, dank depths the flora is of special interest and includes some rare ferns, mosses, grasses and wildflowers which either relish the conditions or have survived thanks to immunity from grazing and muir burn. At the head of the gorge the Falls of Measach, frequently in spate, have a drop of 150ft (46m). They may be viewed from the improbable (and vertiginous) suspension bridge erected in the 19th century by Sir John Fowler (1817–98) who, as joint designer of the **Forth Railway Bridge**, appreciated a handsome span. His house at Braemore, now levelled, was described by *Murray's Guide* as 'a singular creation of art and wealth in this wilderness'; the same may be said of his bridge. The gorge is now the responsibility of the **National Trust for Scotland** and forms part of a **National Nature Reserve**.

CORRIEVRECHAN

A whirlpool and gulf of water running east-west between the islands of **Jura** and Scarba in the Inner **Hebrides** off the mid **Argyll** coast, two miles long and one mile wide, this passage has a reputation of legendary danger. Flood tides, sometimes running 13 miles an hour, meet around a steep pyramidal rock which rises from 110 fathoms to within 15ft of the surface and cause the whirlpool – the noise of the raging waters can be heard over 10 miles away. Locally known as the *Cailleach* or 'hag', the whirlpool itself was called the Cauldron of the Hag with the same reputation as the Lorelei or the Sirens of ancient Greece. Another legend tells of the Prince of Breacon from Norway. Seeking to wed a Princess of the Isles, he was instructed to anchor

for three days and three nights in the strait to win her hand. He chose three cables of hemp, wool and virgin's hair. Each night one cable broke and at last he and his galley were engulfed. His body was dragged ashore by his faithful black dog and carried to a cave on Jura which bears his name, *Uamh Bhreacain* (the cave of Breacon), and thus giving his name to the whirlpool *Coire Bhreacain* (Gaelic).

CORRIEYAIRACK PASS, Inverness-shire

Across this pass over the **Monadhliath** from **Laggan** in **Badenoch** to **Fort Augustus** in the **Great Glen**, **George Wade** constructed his **military road**. It was open by the end of 1731 and, though intended to pre-empt the danger of a second **Jacobite Rising**, was used by **Prince Charles Edward Stewart** in August 1745 as his force marched east from **Glenfinnan**. Carriages were still crossing it in the 19th century and it was much used by **drovers**, but by the 20th century it had degenerated into a footpath only. From the summit the view extends from the **Cuillins** in **Skye** to the Moray Firth. The approach from the east follows the headwaters of the **Spey** which is crossed by Wade's bridge at Garvamore where there was once a barracks, later an inn.

CORROUR, Inverness-shire

Railway ticket offices have been known to deny the existence of this station on the West Highland Line. It stands near the line's highest point (1350ft/411m) in bleak surroundings in the remote north-east corner of **Rannoch Moor**. There is no electricity on the station, no road, and no staff. Sheep appreciate the shelter of the waiting room. A track leads east to Loch Ossian and another may be discerned leading down to the head of Loch Treig.

COTTARS

As labourers and wage-earners who might or might not be sub-tenants, cottars (or cottagers) formed a substratum of agrarian society throughout Scotland from at least the 15th century. The term acquired a slightly more specific meaning in **crofting** areas during the 19th century when the cottar occupied a tenurial limbo between the crofter, who had lands and rights however vulnerable, and the squatter who had none. Typically the cottar occupied a dwelling on a relative's croft of which, through frequent subdivision, he might claim a minimal sub-tenancy or be simply a paid labourer. His chances of being self-supporting were even more hopeless than those of the crofter and his traditional dependence was therefore on casual work with the **fishing** fleets or as a migrant labourer. Numerous wherever the shortage of croft land was most acute, cottars identified closely with crofting grievances in the 1880s and played a prominent role in the agitation which led to the appointment of the **Napier Commission** and to the **Crofters' Holdings Act** of 1886. In the Outer **Hebrides**, particularly **Lewis**, cottars continued to conduct land raids, eg the Park deer raid of 1887, and to agitate for the redistribution of farmland such as that reserved for dairy farming near **Stornoway** by **Lord Leverhulme**. Attempts to assuage this land hunger were not fully met until after World War I when the 1919 Land Settlement (Scotland) Act gave the Board of Agriculture the powers and resources to acquire private land and lease it as crofts.

COTTON

Cotton is a natural fibre grown originally in North America and the West Indies. Its potential as a cheap substitute for **wool** began to be exploited from the mid-18th century in England, particularly in the north Midlands and Lancashire. The spinning and weaving industry in Scotland did not take off until the 1780s, when several large water-powered mills were constructed in the Lowlands, including the **New Lanark** and **Stanley** Mills. With **James Watt**'s improvement of the steam engine, large steam-powered cotton mills and weaving factories were constructed in the bigger towns, particularly **Glasgow** and **Paisley**. The west of Scotland industry soon became renowned for high quality printed fabrics, notably using turkey red dyes. In the first half of the 19th century cotton dominated the west of Scotland economy, helping to stimulate the allied chemical and **engineering** trades. After 1860 cotton lost its position in the face of competition from the north of England and overseas. Many firms closed, a few responded vigorously and imaginatively to the changed economic circumstances, re-equipping and diversifying into specialised products such as **fishing** nets, and seeking new export markets. In Paisley the firms of J & P **Coats** and J & J Clark came to dominate the world market for cotton thread, amalgamating as J & P Coats in 1896. Two years later, the calico printers of the Vale of Leven also combined to form United Red Turkey Company Ltd in a defensive move to protect their markets. In common with the Lancashire industry, Scottish cotton manufacturers were badly hit by the inter-war recession. However, several of the larger firms survived into the post-war years. Some were eclipsed in the 1960s as printed fabric went out of fashion; others like J & P Coats transferred the bulk of production overseas. Even as late as the 1970s, however, Glasgow boasted the largest spinning mill in Britain. Apart from some specialised companies, cotton manufacturing has now ceased in Scotland.

COUPAR ANGUS, Perthshire

So called and spelled to distinguish it from **Cupar** in **Fife**, the small town of Coupar Angus is on the east bank of the river Isla. A stream here joins that river and divides the town, the smaller southern section originally being in the county of **Angus**. Hence the designation although, in the interests of convenience if not logic, the whole town was later incorporated in **Perthshire**. It was once of some importance as the site of a well-endowed Cistercian abbey, founded in the 12th century. Only a gateway remains, much of the old masonry having been used in the fabric of the church (1681 but rebuilt 1857). The town's steeple dates from 1762. A **Roman** camp to the east of the town is distinguishable by its ditches and ramparts.

COURT OF SESSION

The highest civil court in Scotland originated in the 'sessions' of committees set up by Parliament to relieve it of some of the ever-growing burden of appeals and litigation during the reigns of **James I** and **II**. Under **James III** council, or conciliar, sessions – a spin-off of the Privy Council – also shouldered this burden. But it was not until **James IV** established a College of Justice (1532) that suitably paid judges were available to establish some continuity and greater impartiality. A register of the Court of Session's deeds began to appear in 1554. The judges, or Lords of Session, were originally 15 in number, seven of whom plus the Lord President were to be 'spiritual men', ie clerics. This stipulation was overturned at the **Reformation** and constituted a bone of contention between the later **Stewarts** and their subjects. For the later history of the court see **Law**.

COUTTS, John (1699–1751) and Thomas (1735–1822) Bankers

A commission agent and grain dealer who rose to become Lord Provost of **Edinburgh** (1742–4), John Coutts was himself involved in banking, although it was his fourth son Thomas who, in 1788, opened the first branch of Coutts & Company's bank in London.

COVENANTS (1557–1743)

The concept of a special contract, or Covenant, between God and the people is of Old Testament origin. In Scottish Church history it had particular appeal for the **Presbyterians** and followers of **Calvin**'s theory of the elect who were predestined to a personal relationship by a bond with the New Testament Christ, head of the Church. Before the **Reformation** the **Lords of the Congregation** subscribed such a 'band' of intent in 1557 and after it another, the King's Confession of 1581.

Politics and theology combined in opposition to the policies of **Charles I** which were a threat to the freedom of the Church and to Presbyterian principles. When the remote monarch, convinced of his own divine right, unwisely introduced the 1637 **Book of Common Prayer** without involving the **General Assembly**, the objections to anglicising the kingdom and the church came together.

The National Covenant of 1638 renewed and expanded that of 1581 into a public petition which presumed a direct Scottish relationship with God, without the interference of a king and without 'all kinds of Papistry'. In emotive language, citing some 60 Scottish Acts of Parliament and theological statements in plenty, 'Noblemen, Barons, Gentlemen, Burgesses, Ministers & Commons under subscribing' made this relationship plain together with a defence of their rights and beliefs by signing in **Greyfriars' Churchyard**, **Edinburgh**, and at churches throughout the land. Eventually some 300,000 were estimated to have signed copies and become 'covenanted'. It was thought of as a 'glorious marriage of the Kingdom with God'. In addition, but without the text stating it, it provided the excuse for condemning the episcopal system of Church government and reinforced a **Church of Scotland** independent of the king.

When opposition to Charles I deteriorated into civil war the parliamentarians in England sought help from the Scottish standing army. The Scots bargained for a military solution with a religious alliance on their terms. The deal, intending to force England towards reforming the Church of England on a Scottish pattern that was fully Presbyterian, was the Solemn League and Covenant of 1643. Militarily it was successful and was followed by the participation of Scottish divines in the Westminster Assembly. However, Charles's surrender to the Covenanter Army in 1646 served Cromwell's tactical purpose to the extent that the ecclesiastical part of the deal was abandoned as the English Independents grew in influence. The Covenant was anti-Royalist, but the Scots were appalled at the subsequent execution of Charles I in 1649.

In 1650 **Charles II** was compelled to sign the Covenant as a condition of crowning at **Scone** in 1651 before fleeing abroad. Cromwell's subjugation of Scotland after the **Battle of Dunbar** divided the Covenanters whose covenanted King was elsewhere. The most theocratic, and later most rebellious, were from the Lowland west, to which they returned increasingly disaffected during the Commonwealth period.

At the Restoration in 1660 Charles II reneged on the Covenant and restored episcopacy, revoking all acts of the Scottish Parliament from 1640. The Covenanters resisted and then defected from the Church in rebellion. They took to field preaching and worship in **conventicles**, often outdoors. Their strength created *ad hoc* armed groups which were persecuted, both the civil and episcopal powers using military force. The resulting disturbances in the West produced instability from **Glasgow** to the Borders and in Lothian.

Armed skirmishes and battles between Covenanters and government indicate the condition of Scotland after the defeat of the religious revolution by Cromwell and by Charles II. Dissent in religion was harder to put down since, like the **Lollards** of **Kyle** before them, Covenanters of **Ayr** and **Wigton** were well able to debate with curates sent by **Archbishop Leighton** seeking mediation by word not sword. The battles of **Rullion Green**, **Drumclog** and **Bothwell Brig** hardened opposition without changing theology; a military 'solution' was ineffective against fanatics or informed believers. Some 18,000 are estimated to have died in persecutions and encounters between 1661–88, leaving a bitter memory that has tainted and distorted Church and civil history.

The harsh line taken by **Archbishop Sharp** of **St Andrews** led to his murder in 1679 on **Magus Moor** and to the **'Killing Time'** retaliation ruthlessly performed by **John Graham of Claverhouse**, later Viscount Dundee. The violence carried out in the name of religion degenerated into civil disorder creating martyrs of innocent victims and subversive terrorists alike. Emotive elaboration in the fiction of **Scott**, **Galt** and other 19th century romantic writers has clouded the issues into mythology and popular culture.

The Presbyterian settlement in 1690 was not enough to satisfy the extreme Covenanters, such as the followers of **Richard Cameron** who objected to William of Orange as an uncovenanted King. **Cameronians** continued as a sect, though most finally joined the **Free Church** in 1876. The Covenants were invoked and resworn by the **Secession Church** in 1743 and renewed by other dissenters in Scotland, Ireland and the United States. Covenants, political as well as religious, became part of Scottish protest often far removed from their origins in a relationship between God and people.

Presbyterians of the Church of Scotland and their seceders still find it difficult to view the Covenanters dispassionately. The episcopalian image was tarnished by the military coercion employed by the hierarchy. Equally all branches of Christianity have been damaged by the extremists on both sides. However valid in 1581, 1638 or 1643, the Covenants later distracted and detracted from the ethos of the Scottish Church and state.

COWAL, Argyll

The south-eastern extremity of **Argyll** between the sea lochs Long and Fyne comprises the Cowal peninsula. **Dunoon** at its southern tip is the principal town and the site of the annual Cowal games. The name is supposed to derive from 'Comhal', an early **Dalriadic** Scot.

COWDENBEATH, Fife

Industrial optimists billed Cowdenbeath 'The Chicago of **Fife**' as **coal-mining** changed a small rural village into the colliery capital of the Fife coalfield. In the 60 years prior to World War I the population is said to have doubled every decade. Decline has been scarcely less rapid and devastating. A noble attempt at rural rehabilitation can be seen at Lochore Meadows Country Park north of Lochgelly; here pit winding towers vie with the stump of 14th century Lochore Castle as archaeological features in a reconstituted elysium with even a recreated loch.

COWIE, James (1886–1956) Painter

A highly idiosyncratic, yet profoundly influential, figure in 20th century Scottish art, James Cowie represented an

James Cowie, by John Laurie, 1947 (SNPG)

alternative to the typically Scottish **painting** traditions of free handling and bold colouring. Born in **Aberdeen**, he forsook an English Literature degree in favour of teacher-training and studies at **Glasgow School of Art**. Having been a conscientious objector during the war, he resumed teaching at Bellshill Academy, near **Glasgow**, where he stayed until 1935. During this time he perfected his highly academic technique based on meticulous draughtsmanship, elaborate composition and a deep understanding of Renaissance painters and their methods. By the time of his appointment to Gray's School of Art, Aberdeen, in 1935 and to the Wardenship of **Hospitalfield** two years later, his sophisticated and highly finished still-lifes and portrait groups had started to take on increasingly surreal aspects. Inspired by the English Neo-romantic painter Paul Nash, he began to depict unlikely collusions of objects in unsettling and unnatural landscapes. Any danger of surrrealistic *kitsch* is offset by his mastery of technique. Although never enjoying popular acclaim, Cowie was much admired by his fellow artists. As a teacher he had a significant impact on a number of young painters, notably **Henderson Blyth**, **Colquhoun** and **Eardley**. He was elected to the **Royal Scottish Academy** in 1943 and retired from teaching five years later.

COX, James (1809–85) Linen and Jute Manufacturer

Cox was born in Lochee, **Dundee**, and was educated at the city's Academy. Aged 18 he took over the running of his father's **linen** manufacturing business. 13 years later he and his brother Thomas formed a partnership which included their two other brothers. The Cox frères then proceeded to develop the largest **jute** firm in the world. Notwithstanding the vicissitudes of the trade, they were employing some 5000 workers by 1885. Like many of his Dundee contemporaries he developed wide investment interests in shipping, **railways** and in the United States. Wealth brought municipal stature culminating in his tenure of the Provostship of Dundee (1872–5).

COXTON TOWER, Nr Elgin, Moray

'One of the most remarkable buildings of its class in Scotland' declared **MacGibbon and Ross** of this small rectangular tower house. It was remarkable for a number of reasons. The simple plan of four storeys, each with a single room, few windows, angle turrets and a pitched roof with crowstep gables, suggested the 16th century; yet it was dated 1644. Then there was the square parapeted bartizan instead of one of the angle turrets, a feature rare in the area though found at **Claypotts** in abundance. Finally acquired from its Innes builders [see **Speymouth**] by the ubiquitous Duffs of Braco and then neglected for at least a century, it yet remained in surprisingly good condition. This was attributed to the fact that all floors are vaulted, the only timber in the building being that of the door and windows. 'It is built so as to be practically incombustible' and remains so.

CRAIG, James (1744–95) Architect

Born and bred in **Edinburgh**, James Craig is mainly remembered today for his layout of the first Edinburgh

Coxton Tower with square parapeted bartizan (RWB)

New Town. Six plans were received for the competition, held in 1766, to extend Edinburgh on the far side of the **Nor' Loch**. Craig's winning entry consisted of a simple rectilinear plan of three main streets (**Princes Street**, **George Street** and **Queen Street**) which ran parallel, terminated by a square at each end. In 1767 Craig went to London to present his plan to George III. He published a further plan for the layout of roads leading to the **South Bridge** in 1786, which incorporated crescents and octagons, but it was not adopted. Craig's relatively brief career was concentrated entirely on Edinburgh. In 1773 he was the architect and planner of the St James Square development (now demolished). His other works included the Palladian Physicians' Hall in George Street (1775, now dem) and Observatory House on **Calton Hill** (1776–92). Despite his early achievement he was never really successful and ended his career debt-ridden.

CRAIG, Sir John (1874–1957) Steelmaster

Born at New Stevenston, **Lanarkshire**, Craig was educated at Dalziel Public School, **Motherwell**, started as an office boy at **Colville**'s Dalzell Ironworks, and rapidly won notice as a young man of great potential. He took over the running of John Colville's affairs at **Glasgow Royal Exchange** on the latter's election as an MP and in 1910 was invited to become a member of the board. World War I saw both the rapid expansion of Colville's and the sudden deaths of Archibald and David Colville. At the age of 42 John Craig was appointed Chairman of the company. The fact that Colville's survived and continued to grow during the immensely difficult inter-war years was due in large part to his stamina and business acumen. In tandem with **Sir James Lithgow**, Craig set about the rationalisation of the **iron and steel** industry into a modern integrated structure. His final initiative was the siting of a completely integrated steel works near Motherwell, the Ravenscraig project. He was knighted in 1943.

CRAIG, Sir Thomas (1538–1608) Jurist
One of the most influential of early Scots legal writers and recognised as the earliest institutional writer, Craig was admitted advocate in 1563 and the following year was appointed a Justice Depute. Within a decade he was appointed Sheriff of **Edinburgh**. He is renowned as the author of *Jus Feudale* (1655), a textbook of Feudal **Law** which provides much information about the development of Scottish land law and the influence of Civil and Canon Law in that area. He was the principal intellectual support for **James VI** and in that connection, after appointment as a commissioner for a closer union between England and Scotland, he wrote *De Unione Regnorum Britanniae Tractatus* in 1605.

CRAIGELLACHIE, Banffshire
At the junction of the **Spey** and Fiddich, Craigellachie is one of **Banffshire**'s prettiest villages, notable for its distillery, its hotel and its **Telford** bridge. 'The bridge is of iron, beautifully light, in a situation where the utility of lightness is instantly perceived' (Robert Southey, 1819). Possibly the oldest surviving iron bridge in Scotland, it is a single span of nearly 46m springing from stone abutments with round crenellated turrets to cross the Spey in a web of ironwork. It was built 1812–15, the ironwork having been cast in Wales and shipped to the Moray Firth. Craigellachie Rock represents the lower limit of Speyside and, once, of **Grant** territory which upriver ended at another Craigellachie at **Aviemore**. Hence 'Stand Fast, Craigellachie', the Grant motto and, without the 'Craigellachie', the brand name of a Grant **whisky**.

CRAIGIE, Sir William (1867–1957) Linguist and Lexicographer
Born in **Dundee** in a Scots-speaking home, William Craigie learned Gaelic from his grandfather. He read Classics and **Philosophy** at **St Andrews University**, learned French, German and Scandinavian languages in his spare time and became a renowned scholar of Icelandic and Frisian. He achieved Firsts in Mods and Greats at Oxford, and was assistant to the Professor of Humanity at St Andrews from 1893–7 when he joined the *Oxford English Dictionary*, becoming joint-editor of the *New English Dictionary* in 1901. From 1916–25 he was Professor of Anglo-Saxon at Oxford and from 1925–36 Professor of English at Chicago University and editor of the *Dictionary of American English*. The *Dictionary of the Older Scottish Tongue* was Craigie's brainchild, and he continued working on it until his 87th year.

CRAIGIEVAR CASTLE, Nr Alford, Aberdeen
Saddled with superlatives – 'the epitome of the Jacobean renaissance in Scotland', 'the apotheosis of the traditional architectural style', 'the finest tower house of its kind' – Craigievar owes its reputation to a startling perpendicularity, emphasised by the overall pinkish har-

Craigievar Castle, 'the epitome of the Jacobean renaissance' (RWB)

ling, and to a happy neglect which has spared the castle the 19th century extensions lavished on similar buildings. Even the adjacent walls and out-buildings of the traditional barmkin have here been allowed to disappear into oblivion, leaving just the stark thrust of the L-plan tower crowned with its three-storey eruption of turrets, cap-houses, corbels and balustrades.

It was built in 1600–26 as a single entity by William Forbes, the brother of the Bishop of **Aberdeen** and himself a merchant of that city trading to the Baltic; hence his nickname of 'Danzig Willie'. Although the castle is certainly the product of traditional styles and skills, its provenance is not feudal and its context not Highland. More plausibly it has been likened to the prodigy houses of Elizabethan England, a rural celebration of new wealth and eminence but in a vertical format rather than the typically English horizontal. It is said that the staircases are so narrow that though generations of Forbeses might enter by the main door, they all left by a window, there being no possibility of negotiating a coffin down the tower's steps. The property now belongs to the **National Trust for Scotland**.

CRAIGNETHAN CASTLE, Nr Lanark
On a promontory site above the Nethan, a tributary of the **Clyde**, Craignethan Castle was begun about 1530 by **Sir James Hamilton of Finnart**, an illegitimate son of the **1st Earl of Arran**. Familiar with artillery fortifications from his travels in Europe, Sir James appreciated the natural strength of the site with steeply falling ground on three sides, and added to it by constructing a massive rampart, now demolished, across the approach on the fourth, western, side. A ditch fronted the wall and was commanded by a flanking caponier (discovered in 1962). Behind this formidable screen a

rectangular tower house, still reasonably complete, stood within a walled enclosure with square corner towers. A larger walled courtyard was added outside the western rampart sometime before 1579 in which year the **Hamiltons**, after long support of **Queen Mary**, were obliged to surrender both Cadzow [see **Hamilton**] and Craignethan. The latter was then reduced as a place of strength to something close to its modern state. It would appear that Sir James's vaunted artillery defences had in fact never been tested. In 1659 the castle was sold to the **Covenanter** Andrew Hay who built a new house and range in a corner of the outer courtyard. It was bought by the Duke of **Douglas** in the 18th century and thus passed to the **Earls of Home** and eventually, like **Bothwell**, into the guardianship of the state. In spite of denials by **Sir Walter Scott**, who once even considered living in it, Craignethan was almost certainly the model for Tillietudlem Castle in *Old Mortality*.

CRAIGNISH, Argyll

This sea loch and peninsula north of Crinan have attracted settlers from prehistoric times. With relatively sheltered seaways between Ireland and the **Great Glen**, and hill passes to **Loch Awe** and Loch Fyne, the area has been a natural crossroads. Near the tip of the peninsula a stone pier was used by **drovers** shipping cattle from **Jura** [see **Knapdale**], and this is faced across a bay by Craignish Castle (privately owned) which must originally have resembled **Castle Sween** and which required re-roofing in 1414. Near the castle at the roadside is the old parish church of Kilmory ('Kilvaree' locally) containing a number of fine medieval stones.

CRAIGSTON CASTLE, Nr Turriff, Aberdeenshire

Unusually Craigston's ground plan comprises a rectangular block with two parallel gabled wings. This makes it U-plan except that the two wings are linked at their extremities by a fourth-storey arch, as at **Fyvie**, with a most elaborate corbelled and carved balcony, above which there is a balustraded belvedere. More corbelling at the angles of the wings was evidently designed to support turrets which were either never built or speedily demolished. Two-storey wings built in the 18th century flank the tower wings to lend further style to this imposing façade. The main structure was built in 1604–7 by Sir John Urquhart, the so-called Tutor of Cromarty (because he instructed his nephew Thomas Urquhart of Cromarty, who was the father of the better-known polymath and ultra-Royalist, another **Thomas Urquhart**). In the 18th century it was the home of Captain John Urquhart, privateer and pirate, who survived **Sheriffmuir** and then went into exile. It remains in Urquhart possession. The interior includes a noted library and a set of 17th century carved oak panels depicting biblical heroes, Scottish kings, the six Virtues and, improbably, 'Scander Beg, a 15th century Albanian national hero'.

CRAIL, Fife

Four miles east of **Anstruther**, past Caiplie Caves where incised Greek crosses bear witness to early Christian missionary activity, lies the **royal burgh** of Crail. Crail's charter of 1178 makes it one of the oldest royal burghs

in Scotland, and it also has the ruins of a royal castle. Dutch influence is apparent in the 16th century Tolbooth and in the picturesque little harbour, which is reputed to have been built by Dutch women engineers. The town's fortunes were founded on the 'Crail capon', or locally smoked haddock, which was allegedly being traded to Continental Europe as early as the 9th century. The former collegiate church of St Mary, the spacious Marketgate and the many fine old stone buildings testify to the town's former importance. But Crail acquired a deep-sea **fishing** fleet on the lines of those of **Anstruther**, **Pittenweem** and **St Monans**. Like Elie, at the other end of the **East Neuk**, it has preferred to promote itself as a **tourist** centre, and has attracted a large number of retired people from beyond **Fife** as well as 'incomers' who find it a convenient centre for commuting to **St Andrews** or **Dundee**.

CRANNOGS

Dwellings in lochs, rarely in estuaries, crannogs date from prehistoric times. They consist of timber frameworks reinforced with stone, often on a natural-rock core upon which huts were built. Some have shallow underwater causeways to the land; all gave protection from wolves and other raiders. Some bore a single house, others were equivalent to 'moated granges', as when **James VI** demanded the surrender in 1608 of 'the haill houssis strongholdis and crannokis in the Yllis [Isles]'. Many exist in **Lochs Awe**, **Tay** and **Ness**; an early find was at Dumbuck in the **Clyde**. See Ian Morrison, *Landscape with Lake Dwellings*, 1985.

CRARAE, Nr Minard, Argyll

In 1925 Captain (later Sir) George Campbell inherited Cumlodden estate, made Crarae Lodge his home, and began the creation of its woodland gardens. His mother, encouraged by Reginald Farrer, the plant collector, and Sir James Stirling Maxwell of **Pollok** (**Glasgow**), had already begun planting exotic species, but it was Sir George who transformed the small west Highland glen into 'a Himalayan ravine'. Justly famous for its rhododendrons and azaleas, Crarae also boasts a great variety of *eucryphia*, eucalyptus and *nothofagus*, many other exotica, and some noble conifers, all in a magnificent setting overlooking Loch Fyne. The gardens, the property of the Crarae Garden Charitable Trust established in 1978, are open all year round and there is a visitor centre. A Neolithic chambered **cairn**, dating from c2400 BC and once of considerable proportions, was excavated in the 1950s.

CRATHES CASTLE, Banchory, Kincardineshire

Begun in 1553 (although not completed for over a century), Crathes is the earliest of those fairy-tale castles, known as tower houses, whose proliferation in the north-east makes the Grampian region a serious rival to the Loire. Replete with decorative corbelling and a riotous skyline of dormers, turrets round and square, crowsfoot gables, gargoyles and chimney stacks, it lacks both the simple integrity of **Craigievar** and the massive grandeur of **Castle Fraser**. Yet internally it is possibly the most interesting. For where other tower houses rejoice in moulded plaster ceilings, Crathes boasts painted boards and beams depicting heroes of old,

Crathes Castle as drawn by R W Billings in the 1840s (RWB)

musicians, heraldic devices and accompanying texts. Their colour gives the lie to the idea that Jacobean interiors were austere, and the portraits vividly evoke the society of the period.

Until acquired by the **National Trust for Scotland**, the castle had been in the possession of the Burnett family since its construction. As 'Burnard' the family had been granted lands in the **Banchory** area by **Robert I**. An ivory hunting horn, the symbol of tenure, is still preserved in the castle.

To the last residents, Sir James and Lady Burnett, the castle owes its magnificent grounds. Utilising the lofty yew hedges said to have been planted in the 17th century, a series of individual gardens and borders was created, each with its own theme. The ensemble of tower house, timbered and painted interiors and peerless gardens is scarcely rivalled anywhere in the country.

CRATHIE, Deeside, Aberdeenshire

Half a mile from **Balmoral**, Crathie church is where the castle's royal residents attend divine service, an event which attracts other worshippers and onlookers. The church (1895) was designed by **A Marshall Mackenzie** of **Aberdeen** [see **Marischal College**] with a cruciform plan which affords the privacy of a transept for the royal party; numerous busts and memorials commemorate various members of the House of Windsor. It replaced a plainer structure which had itself replaced the old kirk whose ruins are amidst the graveyard beside the **Dee**. Here is buried beneath a lump of granite **John Brown**, **Queen Victoria**'s ghillie and amanuensis. Beyond Easter Balmoral, the estate village, is John Begg's Royal **Lochnagar** Distillery and, to the east, **Abergeldie Castle**.

CRAWFORD, Earldom of

The Lindsays rank with the **Kennedys** among the most impressive of the dynasties of south-west Scotland. Their Lordship of Crawford dates from the 12th century. The 9th Lord Crawford fought at **Otterburn** in 1388 and his adventures earned a place in the pages of Froissart. His cousin, Sir David Lindsay of Glenesk (c1365–1407), married a daughter of **Robert II** and became the 1st Earl. The 4th, Alexander the 'Tiger' Earl (d.1454), was a party to the confederacy with the **8th Earl of Douglas** and the **Lord of the Isles** which provoked **James II** to forfeit Douglas, while Crawford wisely submitted in 1452. The 5th Earl (1440–95) remained loyal to **James III** at **Sauchieburn** in 1488 and his son died with **James IV** at **Flodden**. In the 17th century John Lindsay of another branch of the family was created Earl of Lindsay before he succeeded also as 17th Earl of Crawford. He was a prominent **Covenanter**, kept a prisoner in England during the Protectorate. When the 22nd Earl died in 1808 without offspring the title became dormant until the House of Lords awarded it to James Lindsay, 7th Earl of Balcarres, in 1848. Consequently the present representative of this distinguished family is 29th Earl of Crawford.

CRAWFORD, Lanarkshire

The **Clyde** proper begins at Elvanfoot just south of Crawford village where several burns converge including Clyde's Burn. They rise in a bleak and elevated area of the Lowther Hills, sometimes called the Southern Uplands, which also feed the upper streams of the **Tweed** and, to the south, those of the Nith and Annan. Numerous Iron Age hill forts and settlements testify to the area's strategic importance astride the main north-south axis as represented by the Mennock Pass between **Leadhills** and **Wanlockhead**, the Dalveen Pass on the ancient **Roman** road (now the A707) and Beattock Summit crossed by the M74 and the main **railway** line between **Glasgow** and Carlisle. From Elvanfoot to Crawford and Abington these last follow the line of the Clyde, the area being known as Clydesmuir. Crawford, sometimes known as Crawford-Lindsay or Crawford-Douglas to distinguish it from nearby Crawfordjohn, was held from an early date by the Lindsay family whose scions were ennobled as **Earls of Crawford** in 1399. Their castle of Crawford (or Lindsay) however, passed to the **Douglases** in 1488 and was by them rebuilt in the early 17th century. It is now a ruin and unsafe.

CRAWHALL, Joseph (1861–1913) Painter

Traditionally associated with the **Glasgow** School [see **Painting**], Crawhall was a watercolourist of exceptional ability whose contribution to the art of late 19th century Scotland remains highly individual. Born in Morpeth, Northumberland, the son of a keen amateur artist, Crawhall's talent was apparent from an early age. He began his lifelong relationship with the Glasgow Boys in 1879 when he met E A Walton and with **James Guthrie** they made their first sketching trip together. Like his Glasgow colleagues, Crawhall shared a disregard for the sentimental and historical set-pieces then monopolising the walls of the **Royal Glasgow Institute** and **Royal Scottish Academy**, favouring instead the commonplace subject matter and insistence on first-hand observation practised by the French Realists. In 1882 he visited Paris and enrolled in the atelier of Aimé Morot. Remaining less than two months, this concluded his only formal training.

Crawhall's preferred course of study demanded long and patient observation of his subject from nature which he was then able to recall with a power of memory described as photographic. He is best known for water-colours and gouache studies of animals and birds, the finest of which are often on linen, a technically difficult medium in which he became expert. In 1884 he made the first of many visits to Morocco, where the exotic subject matter and brilliant light inspired some of his most fluid works. From the early 1890s his studies of racecourses, street scenes and hunting meets – subjects chosen where animals predominate – show an increasing gift for design redolent of the sophisticated compositional techniques employed in Oriental art, and an understanding for colour derived from the harmonies of Whistler. Unlike many of the other Glasgow Boys, Crawhall produced until his death works of great flair and originality, often close in subject and method to the scenes of contemporary Parisian life by Degas.

CREETOWN, Kirkcudbrightshire

On the Cree estuary looking across into **Wigton**, Creetown started life as Ferrytown of Cree, being the point at which pilgrims crossed the estuary on their way to and from **Whithorn**. The name was changed when it was raised into a **burgh of barony** for MacCulloch of Barholm (1791). In the 19th century granite quarries opened at Creetown, operated by the Liverpool Dock Trustees who were already **quarrying** at **Dalbeattie**. Creetown as well as Dalbeattie granite was used in the construction of the Thames Embankment and the Mersey Docks. The granite was shipped from Carsluith, four miles south of Creetown, where the ruins of Carsluith Castle perch on a craggy promontory overlooking the bay. Originally a 15th century rectangular tower, it was extended in 1568 when a north wing was added by the Browns (or Brouns) of Carsluith, whose arms are carved over the doorway in the re-entrant angle. Gilbert Broun of Carsluith (d.1612) was the last Abbot of **Sweetheart Abbey**.

Three miles south of Carsluith is another imposing ruin, Barholm Castle, this one a 16th century oblong tower with a small stair tower added in the 17th century. The arched doorway in the re-entrant angle has elaborate moulding decorated with grotesques and ending in two massive carved knots. The MacCullochs of Barholm were enthusiastic supporters of the **Reformation** and entertained **John Knox** in their castle during his 1556 preaching tour of the region. As is often the way with neighbours, the Browns of Carsluith and the MacCullochs of Barholm enjoyed a running feud, based largely on their religious differences, which reached a peak – or maybe a trough – when a MacCulloch was killed by a Brown in 1579.

CRIANLARICH, Perthshire

Boldly signposted as far afield as **Glasgow**, **Perth** and **Fort William**, the village of Crianlarich may come as

a disappointment. The motorist finds a crossroads and a hotel, the **rail** passenger an unmanned station, famed for its tea-room and its **midges**, where the **Oban** and Fort William lines divide. **Ben More** and the **Trossach** peaks provide a fine skyline to the east. West, beside the river Fillan (previously the Cononish and which hereabouts becomes the Dochart) stand the ruins of St Fillan's Priory, a **Celtic** foundation associated with **St Adamnan** to which **Robert I** brought the relic of St Fillan's arm and so founded the Augustinian priory in 1314. The ruin on an island in Loch Dochart east of Crianlarich is that of a castle built by 'Black' Duncan Campbell of Glenorchy in the early 17th century and destroyed soon after by the **Macnabs**. Glen Dochart was the scene of **James Hogg**'s *Spectre of the Glen*.

CRICHTON, James (1560–82) Poet and Scholar

Crichton was born in **Perthshire**, son of Robert Crichton, a Lord Advocate. He was educated at the **University**

'The Admirable' James Crichton, by the 11th Earl of Buchan after an unknown artist (SNPG)

of **St Andrews**, where **George Buchanan** was one of his tutors, and graduated with an MA in 1575. In 1577 he went to France, and in succeeding years lived in various parts of Italy, including Venice, Padua and Mantua. In both countries his intellectual and physical prowess was legendary, and the subject of many tales. While in the service of the Duke of Mantua in 1582 he was killed under mysterious circumstances in a nocturnal brawl. Few of his poetic works survive, and his reputation rests upon the numerous tales surrounding his life, which were collected and recounted in **Sir Thomas Urquhart**'s *Discovery of a Most Exquisite Jewel* (1652). In 1603 he was dubbed 'the Admirable Crichton' in the work *Heroes Scoti* by Johnston.

CRICHTON, Sir William (d.1454) Chancellor

Master of the Household, Keeper of **Edinburgh Castle** and Sheriff of **Edinburgh** under **James I**, William Crichton allied himself with **Sir Alexander Livingston** against the Black **Douglases** during the minority of **James II**. Chancellor of Scotland 1439–44 (and again 1448–53), he was implicated with Livingston in the '**Black Dinner**' in 1440, and is said himself to have placed the symbolic bull's head on the table before the doomed Earl of Douglas. Some even say it was Crichton who murdered the two boys. When **William 8th Earl of Douglas** inherited the earldom from his father **James 'the Gross'** in 1443 and determined to restore his family's fortunes, he contrived a split between the Crichtons and Livingstons and tried to use the latter to depose the former. But Crichton, secure in Edinburgh Castle and impervious to Douglas wrath, aligned himself instead with **Bishop Kennedy** of **St Andrews**. When James II reached his majority he perceived his enemies to be Douglas and Livingston and his friend to be Crichton, who outlived both Livingston and the 8th Earl of Douglas, and remained Chancellor of Scotland until 1453. He was described by **Sir Walter Scott** as 'one of the first laymen in Scotland who attained eminence rather from political than military talents'.

CRICHTON CASTLE, Midlothian

On a hillock on the right bank of the river Tyne not far from **Borthwick**, Crichton Castle appears from the outside massive and forbidding. Yet it has delights within. The oldest part, the keep in the middle of the east side, was built in the late 14th century by John de Crichton who received a charter of barony from **Robert III**. **William Crichton** (d.1454), son of John and Chancellor of Scotland 1439–44 and 1448–53, was in **Edinburgh** when his sworn enemies the **Douglases** besieged and stormed Crichton in 1444; but he thereafter not only rebuilt but extended the castle, and endowed a college close by 'wherein priests were to pray for his salvation and that of his family'. The forfeiture of his grandson William 3rd Lord Crichton in 1483 for conspiracy against **James III** marked the end of Crichton tenure and the start of a century-long game of 'pass the castle'. Awarded by the King in 1484 to Sir John Ramsay of Bothwell, later Lord Bothwell, who fled to England after **Sauchieburn**, Crichton and the Earldom of Bothwell then went to Sir Patrick Hepburn of Dunsyre (1488). **James Hepburn, 4th Earl of Bothwell** (and **Queen Mary**'s third husband) was forfeited in 1567 and Crichton remained untenanted until 1581 when castle and earldom were claimed by **Francis Stewart, 5th Earl of Bothwell**.

Cultured, well educated, much travelled and often in disgrace, it was this strange man who created the delights hidden within. In effect he transformed Crichton Castle into an elaborate Renaissance residence by adding corbelled courses, rooms with handsome fireplaces, panelled ceilings and a scale-and-platt staircase with Renaissance carvings. He also demolished the inner face of the north wing and created the famous courtyard with seven-bay arcade and diamond-faceted stonework elevation, thought to have been inspired by the Palazzo Steripinto at Sciacca in Sicily or the Palazzo dei Diamante at Ferrara. When Stewart fled abroad in disgrace for the

The diamond-faceted stonework of Crichton Castle (RWB)

last time in 1595, the King ordered Crichton to be 'rasit and castin doun'. Fortunately this order was never carried out, but the castle was left instead to crumble. **Sir Walter Scott** celebrated the ruins in *Marmion*:

> Crichton! Though now thy miry court
> But pens the lazy steer and sheep;
> Thy turrets rude, and totter'd keep;
> Have been the minstrel's loved abode
> Oft have I traced within thy fort,
> Of mould'ring shields the mystic sense, –
> Scutcheons of honour, or pretence,
> Quarter'd in old armorial sort
> Remains of rude magnificence.

CRICKET

Cricket in Scotland is played under the aegis of the Scottish Cricket Union. The game has amateur status (unlike in England), although some clubs retain the services of professionals. There is a club structure with a National League, Area Championship and various cups and trophies. The national team participates in the Triple Crown tournament with amateur teams from England, Ireland and Wales, in the European Championship, and by invitation in England's one-day county championships (Benson & Hedges and Natwest). Overseas touring sides regularly play against Scotland and Scottish sides occasionally tour overseas.

Since 1994 Scotland has been an associate member of the International Cricket Council with entry into the ICC Trophy. Third place in the ICC's Kuala Lumpur play-offs in 1997 brought an unexpected appearance in the 1999 World Cup. Not unexpected were the five successive defeats, mostly at the hands of Test-playing nations. But to the extent that Scottish cricket is no longer regarded as a flagrant contradiction in terms, the game's profile was enhanced by this flurry.

HISTORY Cricket was almost certainly introduced into Scotland by government officers during and after the **Jacobite** Rebellions of 1715 and 1745. A match involving English officers is believed to have been played at **Perth** around 1750, although there is a surprising record of Scottish immigrants playing cricket at Savannah, Georgia, in the 1730s, having presumably learned it before emigrating. The first properly recorded match in Scotland took place in September 1785 at Shaw Park, **Alloa**, between the **Duke of Atholl**'s XI and a Colonel Talbot's team. The oldest club is considered to be **Kelso**'s (1821) although **Perthshire** claims the longest continuous existence (from 1826).

The Scottish Cricket Union was set up in 1879, but disbanded in 1883, when Grange Club in **Edinburgh** acted as the Scottish equivalent of the MCC, the SCU re-forming in 1909. The Western Division Union and Border Leagues date from the 1890s, and the county championship from 1902. Scotland's only victory over a Test-playing nation took place on 29 July 1882 when Australia were defeated in a one-day match at Raeburn Place, Edinburgh. Scotland's top scorer that day was Leslie Balfour (later Balfour-Melville), who also represented his country at **rugby** as well as being both lawn tennis and amateur **golf** champion.

PLAYERS Scottish club professionals have been recruited from all over the world. Borderers insist that Wilfred Rhodes learned all he knew when playing for **Galashiels** in 1896–7, and more recently, resident professionals have included the captains of both the Australian and West Indies Test sides (Kim Hughes and Desmond Haynes respectively). Scottish players have appeared frequently in English county teams, but more rarely at Test level.

Douglas Jardine, born in India of Scottish parents, captained England during the infamous 'Bodyline' tour of Australia in 1932–3, and **Inverness**-born J D F Larter played 10 Tests for England in 1962–5 before injury marred his career. More recently Mike Denness, born in Bellshill, **Lanarkshire** – and scorer of 25,886 first-class runs between 1959–80 – captained England in 1973–5. His team returned from the West Indies very creditably with a drawn Test series, but succumbed to the Lillee-and-Thompson-inspired Australian side 'down-under' a year later. Denness was a highly successful captain of Kent CCC, moving in 1977 to the hitherto unsuccessful county of Essex. There, along with fellow-Scot Brian Hardie, he was instrumental in helping Essex win two trophies in a single year (1979). Stenhouse-muir-born Hardie went on to win four Championship medals with his adopted county in a 17-year career in English county cricket.

CRIEFF, Perthshire
Crieff (pop c5600 yet, rather surprisingly, the second largest town in **Perthshire**), spills down a hillside above the river Earn. In the 17th century it was known as

Drummond after its local patrons, the **Drummond Earls of Perth**; but following destruction (1716) by retreating **Jacobites** after **Sheriffmuir**, the name of Crieff (*Crubha Cnoc*, Hill of Trees) was restored. In the 18th century its tryst (October cattle sale) was the largest in Scotland, attracting **droves** from all over the Highlands and Islands and buyers from all over the Lowlands and England. 'At least 30,000 cattle' changed hands in 1722, while hordes of 'Highlandmen' gave the town an unruly reputation and kept **Scott**'s 'kind gallows of Crieff' busy. Decorum was restored with the removal of the tryst to **Falkirk** in the 1770s. In its place came bleaching and tanning under the auspices of the commissioners for the forfeited Drummond estates, and then **education** with, then as now, Crieff's schools attracting pupils and parents from afar. The Victorian mania for **railways** (here now closed) and spas (the Hydro is still the largest hotel) ensured a mushrooming of villas and country houses.

In the High Street are James Square, the artificially levelled town centre with a fountain (1894), the town hall (1842) with jougs (stocks), the cross (1688) of the **burgh of regality** of Drummond, and a 10th century Celtic cross-slab which probably came from elsewhere. Today the town's few industries include **pottery** and glassware.

Drummond Castle (and gardens), home of the Drummond family from 1491, lies three miles south on the **Muthill** road. To the west Tomachastle Hill has a lofty obelisk commemorating **Sir David Baird**, victor of Srirangapatnam, who died in Crieff, while nearby Ochtertyre House was the birthplace of another of Wellington's comrades-in-arms, **Sir George Murray**; the Murray mausoleum stands on the site of the old church of Monzievaird where 'a large number of Murrays with their wives' were burnt by their Drummond and Campbell foes in 1511. North, behind the Knock (cnoc) of Crieff, 911ft (278m), with its **golf course**, Monzie (pron. Monee) Castle was the **Campbell** stronghold. It has a date, 1634, but the castle was incorporated into an **Adam**-style house in about 1795 which was in turn completely refitted by **Sir Robert Lorimer** in the early 20th century.

CROCKETT, Samuel Rutherford (1859–1914) Novelist
Born in Balmaghie, **Kirkcudbrightshire**, of tenant farming stock, Crockett won a bursary to **Edinburgh University**, augmenting it by miscellaneous journalism. After his MA he spent some years as a travelling tutor on the Continent, then entered New College, **Edinburgh**, and in 1886 became **Free Church** minister at **Penicuik**, **Midlothian**, marrying the daughter of a Manchester mill-owner and nonconformist philanthropist. They had four children. His missions for miners and paper-mill workers provided angry insight into poor industrial conditions; he was a leader in relief work after the 1889 **Mauricewood pit disaster**. *The Stickit Minister* (1893), a collection of short stories, many sarcastically exposing humbug in fellow ministers, brought overnight fame. The success in 1894 of *The Raiders* (**Galloway** 18th century adventure) and *The Lilac Sunbonnet* (Galloway love story mocking religious bigotry) led him to resign his ministry for full-time writing.

Often maligned as **'Kailyard'**, he used his knowledge

of Galloway peasants and folklore, railwaymen, history, social injustice and Continental countries for wide-ranging themes and settings: *The Men of the Moss Hags* (**Covenanters**); *The Grey Men* (**Kennedy** feuds in 17th century **Ayrshire**); *Cleg Kelly* (Edinburgh slums); *The Red Axe* (medieval German dukedoms); *The Black Douglas* and *Maid Margaret* (15th century Galloway power struggles and French sorcery); *Kit Kennedy* (Galloway boyhood); *Vida* (**coal-mining**); *Princess Penniless* (feminism and **engineering** works); *The Cherry Riband* (Covenanters in Galloway and Lothian); *The White Plumes of Navarre* (French Huguenots); *The Silver Skull* (Italian banditti), etc.

Growing ill-health necessitated his wintering in France, coming home in summer and autumn. He died suddenly in Tarascon, and was brought back for burial at Balmaghie. Sensational rather than sentimental, his distinctive humour, his ridicule of pretension and his vivid descriptive powers carried him through sometimes wild plots and situations. Posthumous novels include *The Azure Hand* (detective) and *The White Pope* (theological science-fiction), now collectors' pieces.

CROFTERS' COMMISSION, The

The first permanent Crofters' Commission was set up following the **Crofters' Holding Act** of 1886. In 1911 it was superseded by the Land Court and the Board of Agriculture but 40 years later a Commission of Inquiry into **Crofting** Conditions under Sir Thomas Taylor recommended a new permanent Commission which was duly set up in 1955. Charged with directing and developing crofting and with administering grants and loans, it eventually concluded that traditional crofting tenure was obsolete and a barrier to progress given the non-agricultural uses to which crofts could be put. While retaining their preferential status, subsequent legislation has made crofts easier to purchase outright and to transfer.

CROFTERS' HOLDINGS ACT (Crofters' Act) (1886)

Following the report of the **Napier Commission** (but ignoring most of its recommendations), a Crofters' Holdings Bill was drawn up by Gladstone's government to meet the demands of the Highland Land Law Reform Association (**Highland Land League**) and to still the unrest in the **crofting** areas of the Highlands and Islands [see **Battle of Braes, Glendale Martyrs**]. Subject to certain none too stringent conditions, the Bill conferred on crofters security of tenure, a right to compensation for improvements if they removed, a right to bequeath their tenancies, and a right to rent arbitration through the newly created **Crofters' Commission**. It also carefully defined the area to be covered by what was in effect a renunciation of landowners' rights as understood elsewhere in Britain, and a recognition of the distinctive nature of Gaelic land tenure.

Initially the Act, now regarded as 'the Magna Carta of Gaeldom', was opposed by those whom it was supposed to benefit on the grounds that it failed to address the crofters' main grievance, namely the insufficiency of crofting land. The rent strikes and re-occupations associated with the 'Highland Land War' therefore continued. But by 1888 punitive reprisals by the authorities plus news of the highly favourable rent awards

being handed down by the new Crofters' Commission caused the crofters to reconsider their attitude.

CROFTING

The system of small-holding peculiarly associated with the Highlands and Islands, crofting derives from the

George Washington Wilson's 1880s portrait of a Skye crofter (GWWA)

word 'croft' meaning a small farming unit. The word is possibly of Anglo-Saxon origin, but certainly not Gaelic. Indeed it does not appear in Highland records until the 19th century when it quickly acquired its specialised and statutory connotation. In short, the word, like the concept of land tenure which it embodies, is an exotic.

Prior to the 18th century the **clan**-based Gaelic society of the Highlands and Islands acknowledged a system of communal occupancy of the land but not of ownership. Family groups enjoyed grazing and tilling rights in return for rendering military service and/or a share of the crop (typically so much **oatmeal**). The recipient of this tribute was the clan chief or his **tacksman** who acted as protector and arbitrator. With the advent of the cash economy, a process quickened by the early 18th century boom in the export of Highland beef cattle, cash payment readily replaced bolls of oatmeal. Military service and the jurisdictional rights of the chiefs were likewise terminated in mid-century. The pervasive currency of Lowland and English norms, plus the eclipse of the chiefs (who either adopted these norms or sold out to those who did), led to a simple equation of laird with landlord, cash payments with rents, and rent-payers with tenants.

But this landlord-tenant relationship offered the often

205

lease-less tenant little protection at a time when **population** increase and improved farming methods invited a maximisation of rents. The resulting **clearances** saw in many areas and over a long period of time a wholesale removal of tenants to marginal land-holdings. Known as 'lots', or after the 1850s as 'crofts', these units were typically on the coast where the poverty, or absence, of soil might to some extent be offset by the wage-earning possibilities of non-agricultural employment such as **fishing** and **kelp** gathering. Eventually the acute distress, the charitable burden, and the growing resistance (the **Skye Battle of the Braes**, for instance) which resulted from this harsh treatment, played on delicate consciences and alarmist susceptibilities alike. Thus in 1883 the **Napier Commission** was set up by Gladstone to inquire into the condition of 'crofters and **cottars**'.

The Commission's voluminous and detailed report ensured sympathetic legislation which, though it evaded the Commission's proposals, conceded the crofters' demands for fair rents fixed by tribunal, for security of tenure, and for compensation for improvements. This was the **Crofters' Holdings Act** of 1886, 'the Magna Carta of Gaeldom' which elevated the crofter to 'a uniquely privileged position amongst all the tenants in Great Britain' (T C Smout), thus belatedly recognising the distinctive nature of land tenure in the Highlands and Islands.

Subsequent commissions and subsequent legislation have attempted to update the system in line with economic and demographic requirements. A **Crofters' Commission** to administer the scheme and adjudicate on rents disappeared in 1911 and reappeared in 1955, this time to reorganise and reallocate crofts. A Crofting Reform Act of 1976 made it easier for crofters to purchase their crofts. It is now accepted that while some crofts have been amalgamated to form viable agricultural units, many are incapable of providing even a subsistence living. The crofter whose ancestors depended on the supplementary income derived from kelp gathering is now encouraged to diversify into **tourism** (bed and breakfast) and **fish farming**.

In the 1990s present crofting as administered by the Crofters' Commission included some 18,000 crofts of an average of 4 acres (1.6ha) of arable land with access to 30ha common grazing. It is still confined to the seven crofting counties (now Highland Region, the Western Isles, **Orkney** and **Shetland**, and **Argyll**), although two-thirds of crofting land is in the islands. Typically the physical aspect of a crofting township is that of several modern bungalows set well apart from one another, of austere aspect, and each invariably presiding over an unhappy collection of derelict vehicles and rusting machinery. But the crumbling masonry of a previous residence belies the air of ephemeral occupation and the stooked corn, the sleek cattle, the rich sward, and the mountain of **peats** testify to an agricultural tradition which is followed as tenaciously as ever.

CROMARTY, Ross & Cromarty

'A unique example of a small late 18th century burgh which has largely escaped later development' (J Close-Brooks), Cromarty now has the potential of **Culross** as a conservationist's paradise. At the northern tip of the **Black Isle**, west of the south Sutor and so just inside the Cromarty Firth, it was once a **royal burgh** and an important port. The hereditary sheriffdom was held by the Urquhart family, including the unforgettable **Sir Thomas Urquhart**. In the 18th century it became the main town in the 'vagrant and incomprehensible county [of Cromarty]' created out of the scattered estates of the **Mackenzie** Earls of Cromartie. Trade gave way to **fishing** and a new benefactor, Sir Thomas Ross of Pitkerie, built the present harbour and encouraged a host of ancillary industries including rope, **linen** and **iron** works – as well as a **brewery** to wean his Highland labour force off **whisky**. Then, like Culross, Cromarty became a victim of early 19th century technology. The coastal road and **rail** links ignored the Black Isle and Cromarty's ferry across the firth became an irrelevance. Craft industries failed, fishing declined, so did the population. Cromarty became an anachronism which impinged on the outside world only as the birthplace of another maverick, **Hugh Miller**, stonemason, geologist, journalist and preacher.

Miller's cottage, now in the care of the **National Trust for Scotland**, is dated 1711, thatched, harled, crow-stepped and fully equipped with period fittings and memorabilia. Next door the Courthouse (1773–83), also whitewashed, was the work of Sir George Ross and has a copper cupola on the little clock tower and original arrangements in the first-floor courtroom and gaol. These are now an animated museum and a major **tourist** attraction. Ross's Cromarty House (1772) is Georgian and resembles the main block of **Culloden House**. Many other buildings of the Ross period survive including the brewery, harbour, Fishertown, East Kirk and the Gaelic chapel for the Highlanders, where there is a monument to Hugh Miller.

Four miles east of the town Poyntzfield House at Jemimaville dates from 1757 and is a scaled-down version of Foulis Castle near **Evanton**. It was the work of a man named Poyntz whose Dutch wife was called Jemima; hence the odd names. This may have set a precedent for there is a Barbaraville and an Arabella on the other side of the Cromarty Firth. Further east Castlecraig near Culliouden was once a residence of the Bishops of **Ross**. The ruined keep remains, picturesquely sited on a cliff edge.

CROMDALE, Battle of (1690)

Cromdale is a village, parish and range of hills between the **Spey** and Avon (pron A'an) just east of **Grantown** in **Moray**. Hereabouts on 1 May 1690 encamped Major-General Thomas Buchan in command of about 800 Highlanders loyal to **James VII**. Though sorely missing the charismatic **John Graham of Claverhouse, Viscount Dundee**, the victors of **Killiecrankie** suspected no trouble and camped on the open low ground (the Haughs of Cromdale, later the title of a **ballad**). The Williamite troops under Sir Thomas Livingston(e) were equally oblivious of an enemy presence until alerted at **Castle Grant**. Though exhausted by a day's march they agreed that the chance of taking the enemy by surprise was too good to miss. So it proved. In a night assault the **Jacobites**, unprepared, half naked, and hopelessly situated, were routed with the loss of 300. Thus ended the two-year campaign on behalf of James VII and thus began the half century of Jacobite dissent.

CRONIN, A(rchibald) J(oseph) (1896–1981) Novelist

Born in **Cardross, Dunbartonshire**, on 19 July 1896, Cronin was educated at **Dumbarton** Academy and **Glasgow University**, where he studied medicine. He received his MBChB after serving in World War I as a Surgeon Sub-Lieutenant in the Royal Naval Reserve. Following various hospital appointments, he married a fellow doctor, Agnes Mary Gibson, in 1921 and in 1924 became a medical inspector of mines in south Wales. Between 1926–30 he practised in London, but in 1930 ill-health forced him to spend a period recuperating in the west Highlands, during which he wrote his first novel, *Hatter's Castle*, published in 1931. An instant success, it persuaded him to become a full-time writer. During the next 40 years he produced a steady flow of popular works based on his own experiences as a doctor, including *Three Loves* (1932), *Grand Canary* (1933) and two works which were turned into films, *The Keys of the Kingdom* (1942) and *The Green Years* (1945). His best-known work of the prewar period, *The Citadel* (1937), with its controversial attack on the practices of Harley Street doctors, stimulated the political discussions which led to the creation of the National Health Service. Cronin also wrote a play, *Jupiter Laughs* (1940), and an autobiography, *Adventures in Two Worlds* (1952). In the 1960s a popular television and radio series was produced based on Cronin's experiences entitled *Dr Finlay's Casebook*. He died in Switzerland.

CROOKSTON CASTLE, Nr Paisley, Renfrewshire

Expert opinion awards Crookston 'a unique place in Scottish castle-building' in that the main block was once surrounded by four lofty corner towers. Only one of

Crookston Castle near Paisley (ML)

these survives and such is the dilapidated state of the building that its internal arrangements must remain conjectural. It probably dates from the 14th century and was long held by the **Stewarts** of Darnley whose rebellion against **James IV** in 1489 resulted in a damaging siege, and whose number included **Henry Lord Darnley**, husband of **Queen Mary**. In 1757, already a ruin, it passed to the Maxwells of **Pollok** (**Glasgow**) and in 1931 became the first property to be gifted to the **National Trust for Scotland**. It has since been transferred to the care of the Secretary of State.

CROSLAND, T W H, Englishman

Possessed, as he puts it, 'of a large fund of contempt for the Scotch character', Crosland, evidently a journalist, felt compelled to pen a book entitled *The Unspeakable Scot*. It was intended to constitute a devastating attack on Scotland, the Scots and what he calls their 'Doric' pretensions. Published in 1901 when all three political parties were led by Scots – Rosebery (**Archibald Philip Primrose**), **Campbell-Bannerman** and **Balfour** – the book may have been squeezed from English sour grapes, but failed either to cheer its author or to intoxicate its readers. Occasionally it amuses: 'There are only about three decent Scotchmen in England, one of whom is half English, the second half Irish, and the third (week in and week out) half drunk.' Amongst authors who attract Crosland's laboured jibes, **Burns** comes off best, **Barrie** worst. But most of the book is devoted to savaging contemporary London hacks who, though doubtless of Scottish descent, were of little consequence then and none now. The same could be said of their assailant.

CROSSBILL, Scottish

Whether there is a Scottish crossbill (*Loxia scotticus*) is still a matter of conjecture, but if it is a native species rather than a race (and most people now think it is), then it is Scotland's only native species – indeed Britain's sole native species. However, there are still those who believe that it is either a race of the parrot crossbill (*Loxia pityopsittacus*) or even an isolated form of the common crossbill (*Loxia curvirostra*). Whether it is a separate species or not, it is one of the country's earliest-breeding birds; in a good seed year crossbills can be on eggs as early as January. The published estimate of c1000 pairs must be a 'guesstimate' as few surveys have been carried out by even fewer people who can positively identify the bird, although the breeding population in the **Caledonian pine forest** are almost certain to be this species.

The bill of the crossbill is unique – the bills of the young are not crossed, and when crossing does form later the two parts can cross in either direction, some birds having the upper part crossing to the left and some to the right. The dexterity with which the bird deals with pine cones is remarkable (but the strange angle of the points makes it hard for the bird to extract nuts from wire mesh bird-feeders without getting in a most frustrating tangle). Like other birds with red fronts, the swallow and the robin for example, legend would have it that the crossbill got its red feathers when trying to help Christ on the cross. However the crossbill went one further than the others and tried to extract the nails from Christ's hands and feet, and in doing so bent its beak and crossed the two parts.

The gatehouse of Crossraguel Abbey (RWB)

CROSSRAGUEL ABBEY, Nr Maybole, Ayrshire

Founded in the early 13th century by Duncan, Earl of **Carrick**, this small Cluniac monastery was a daughter house of **Paisley Abbey**. The friendship of the Earls of Carrick greatly benefited the monks of Crossraguel (who never numbered more than 10 at any time), for it resulted eventually in the protection of the royal house; **Robert I**, whose father became Earl of Carrick c1274, made generous endowments, as did his son **David II**, and in 1404 **Robert III** granted to the abbey a perpetual free royal charter. In addition to giving the Abbot temporal jurisdiction over Crossraguel lands, the charter brought the monks such privileges as the right to mint their own coins, brew their own ale and fish in the river Girvan. Most of the original stone buildings of the abbey were destroyed during the **Wars of Independence** but, because Crossraguel was remote from centres of population and under powerful protection, their 14th and 15th century replacements suffered neither as the victims of English fury [see **Rough Wooing**], nor as a source of building material for other structures. Occupied until 1592, the ruins are therefore in an excellent state of preservation and comprise church, cloister and inner court dating from the 14th century; there are also choir, chapter house, abbot's house and corrodiars' (pensioners') houses from the 15th century, and four-storey tower-house, turreted gatehouse and dovecote from the 16th. They are in the care of **Historic Scotland** and open to the public.

CROTAL

Crotal (or crottle) was a general Scottish name for more than 40 kinds of lichen used in dyeing, especially of **wool** for tweed, producing a wide range of colours – mainly shades of red to brown – without the need for mordant to fix the dye. Lichens growing on stones were said to yield better dye than those on trees.

Crotal was scraped from rocks using a large spoon, one side filed into a sharp edge with a tip for getting into corners. A sackful of ripe crotal would be collected in a long summer's day (preferably when the moon was waning), then left to soak for about three weeks in a tub of urine. On dyeing day it was layered with two or three washed fleeces in the great three-legged black cauldron that stood by every rural house. A **peat** fire beneath kept the pot simmering for several hours until the wool had absorbed all the lichen's colour, when the fleece would be washed in a stream and laid over a wall to dry. The characteristic smell of **Harris tweed** was a rich combination produced by wool, lichen and urine together, and the use of lichen dyes was said to leave the wool moth-proof.

Fishermen wearing crotal-dyed clothes had also to wear blue as protection from the belief that something plucked from the rocks had to return to the rocks. Powdered crotal worn in the soles of stockings was said to protect the feet from inflammation on long journeys. Lichens are nutritious and have been used as food in lean years; the Arctic explorers John Franklin and **John Richardson** survived 11 days on boiled lichens alone.

CROZIER, William (1897–1930) Painter

A highly gifted and perceptive artist, Crozier was one of the most significant figures, alongside **Gillies**, **Johnstone**, **MacTaggart** and **Maxwell**, to emerge from the **Edinburgh** College of Art in the 1920s. Born in Edinburgh, his first steps towards a business career were confounded by ill-health and he enrolled at the College in 1915. In 1923 he went to Paris and studied under André Lhote whose formal and academic application of Cubist principles, though often giving his own work a distinctively decorative quality, suggested a systematic and intellectual approach to picture-making which greatly appealed to Crozier. From then on his life was spent between Edinburgh, France and Italy, often accompanied on his travels by MacTaggart, with whom he later shared a studio, painting landscapes where colour is kept to low-key greens and browns and detail subordinated in favour of the subject's mass and structure. Crozier's advocation of Lhote's philosophy made a considerable, if short-lived, impression on the young members of the Edinburgh School, most notably on Gillies, who went to study under Lhote in 1924, and MacTaggart, to whom it offered an intellectual approach to painting quite different from the established Scottish traditions of free handling and bold colouring. His own individuality is best seen in his remarkable series of paintings of Edinburgh from **Salisbury Crags** where his applied understanding of formalist principles allowed him to build up a portrait of the city – rendered in earthy solids and planes – which seems highly appropriate to the character of the Scottish capital. A haemophiliac, his death at the age of 33 brought his influence to an early conclusion and the resulting small body of work has regrettably left him the least known of his contemporaries.

CRUACHAN, Argyll

The highest point of the seven peaks of Cruachan is 3689ft (1124m). The mountain is part of one of the newer Caledonian granite masses (the Etive complex) intruded into the surrounding rocks about 400 million years ago. There are conspicuous corries formed during the Ice Age. One corry, facing south-west, was dammed by the North of Scotland **Hydro-electric** Board which opened the **Loch Awe** Scheme in 1965. The power house lies within the mountain below. In 1309 the charge of the Black Douglas from the heights of Cruachan contributed to **Bruce**'s victory over the **Mac-Dougalls** in the **Pass of Brander**. 'Cruachan' remains the rallying cry of **Clan Campbell**.

CRUDEN, Alexander (1701?–70) Author

Born in **Aberdeen**, son of Bailie William Cruden, and educated at the city's grammar school and **Marischal College**, Alexander Cruden's great gift to posterity was his *Biblical Concordance*, a word-reference dictionary to the Bible published in 1737, with new editions in 1761 and 1769 but now sadly long out of print. His career, variously as a tutor, writer, bookseller and editor, was interrupted by bouts of insanity; locked in an asylum in Aberdeen in 1721 'after a disappointment in love of a specially sad nature', he was again confined in a private madhouse in Bethnal Green in 1738 when, 'disappointed in his expectation of a profit' from the *Concordance*, 'his mind became so unhinged that he paid unwelcome addresses to a widow'. He escaped by cutting through the bedstead to which he was chained. Finding employment as corrector of Greek and Latin texts for a London publisher, Cruden's sobriquet of 'Alexander the Corrector' was appropriate also in the role he adopted for the rest of his life – as 'corrector of the morals of the nation'. In this capacity he toured the country lecturing, producing pamphlets and tracts and reproving those who uttered profanities or broke the sabbath. He died suddenly, while still on his knees at prayer in his lodgings in London's Islington, and bequeathed a portion of his savings to found a bursary in his name at Marischal College.

CRUDEN, Harry H (1895–1967)
Housebuilder and Contractor

Born in **Fraserburgh**, Cruden trained as a draughtsman and, after an army career in Kenya, returned to Scotland shortly before World War II. He worked as a timber merchant in a modest-sized firm owned by his wife. In the post-war period his rise was meteoric as he met the massive demand for inexpensive houses with innovative building methods, notably the Cruden House which utilised prefabrication and concrete slabs and tiles. In the quarter century after 1945 more than 25,000 Cruden Houses were built. As demand for this type of housing declined, Cruden diversified into factories, hospitals, churches and schools. After his death the firm continued to shape the physical contours of the Scottish urban environment with projects which included the **Meadowbank** Stadium and several giant shopping centres.

CRUICKSHANK, Helen Burness (1886–1975) Poet

Few would baulk at the description of Helen B Cruickshank as one of the most delightful women of her generation. Born near Hillside in **Angus**, and educated at **Montrose** Academy, she joined the Post Office in London as a civil servant in 1903. There she became involved in the Suffragette movement, and in particular in a Woman Clerks' Association to urge for better pay for women, at whose AGMs luminaries such as George Bernard Shaw harangued the assembled women with saws like 'Gurrls, keep up your combinations.' In 1912 she returned to **Edinburgh** to work in the National Health Insurance Scheme. After World War I she established herself in an artist's eyrie in Shandwick Place, from where she made fruitful contact with the literati of the day, including **Hugh MacDiarmid**, **William Soutar** and many other writers and artists. The death of her father in 1924 forced her to say 'goodbye to my hopes of being able to wed my penniless artist' and 'to bid farewell to my free and easy bohemian life'. She nursed her aged mother for the next 40 years.

Hugh MacDiarmid described her as 'a catalyst' in the Scottish literary renaissance, a compliment borne out by her commitment to the development of Scottish PEN (an international association of Poets, Playwrights, Editors, Essayists and Novelists), of which she was a founder member. Her generous personality encouraged many a talent. What remains of her writings is a body of poems, slight in volume, but redolent of the sights and sounds of Scotland and, more important for succeeding generations, sharp with a political perception of the position of both women and Scotland, always curiously analogous. The quiet but poignant symbolism of such poems as 'The Ponnage Pool' testifies to her fundamentally 20th century understanding of the world. Her keen sense of humour is evident in 'Keepit In' about the wee lass who would rather be 'huntin' tods on Rossie Hill' than imprisoned at a school desk; her acute human perception in poems like 'Beech Leaves', and most poignantly in poems such as 'At the End', where she confronts her ultimate sorrow of lifelong virginity and childlessness. Her *Octobiography*, published posthumously, is inspiring. Although not a great poet, her greatness of spirit more than compensates.

CÚ CHULAINN, Celtic Hero

Cú Chulainn is the hero of a late 1st century immigration into north-east Ireland by the **Celtic** La Tène folk. They came into conflict with other La Tène tribes that had settled in south-west Ireland some two centuries earlier. The epic tales of Cú Chulainn of Ulster's strife with Queen Nedb of Connacht, notable in the *Táin Bó Cúalgne*, are dated to the beginning of the Christian era. They depict an aggressively matriarchal society, in which kings must mate with Nedb as the symbol of their sovereignty: a being very different from Shakespeare's Queen Mab. Cú Chulainn (ie 'the Hound of Culann the smith' because he served in that capacity for a space after killing the smith's dog) did not prevail against Nedb. When, to learn the martial arts, he visited **Skye** (where the **Cuillins** may bear his name), he found two ruling viragoes at each other's throats. His services to one of them were rewarded with favours that resulted in the birth of his son Conlaoch, after his return to Ireland. The tale is interesting as an example of the myths that the Celtic peoples brought with them from the Indo-Aryan lands from which they had migrated. For when Conlaoch returned to Ireland his father did not recognise him before fatally wounding him, as in the story of Sohrab and Rustam. Apart from the polyandrous tale of **Deirdre**, settling beside **Loch Etive** with the three sons of Uisne, these traditions did not find the same favour in Scottish folklore as those of the Ossianic cycle [see **Finn mac Cumhal**] which are set in a slightly later period.

CUDBEAR

A violet powder used to dye silk and **wool**, cudbear derives its improbable name from Dr Cuthbert Gordon who invented the process whereby the dye is extracted from a species of lichen by maceration in ammonia. In 1777 George MacIntosh, the son of a Highland **tacksman**, possibly intrigued by this industrial development of the **crotal** tradition, organised financial backing for the enterprise, then based in **Leith**, and removed it to **Glasgow**. Mainly to guard against industrial espionage he surrounded the factory (including his mansion of Dunchattan) with a 10ft wall and employed almost exclusively Gaelic-speaking Highlanders. For calico printing MacIntosh also produced a Prussian blue dye and started the first factory in Britain for a turkey red known as 'Dale's Red' after the banker and textile magnate **David Dale**. The cudbear business closed down in 1852, probably because of depleted lichen stocks. Thanks to George MacIntosh, his son **Charles MacIntosh** of waterproof fame gained a head start in the application of chemical processes to textiles.

CUILLIN(S), The, Isle of Skye

The name of the hill range which almost bisects the waist of **Skye** is popularly derived from **Cú Chulainn**;

In the Cuillin; Marscow from Sgurr nan Gillean (SP)

other contenders are *cuilionn*, the Gaelic for 'holly', and a Celtic word meaning 'wilderness'. Perhaps more plausibly, given Skye's Norse links, it may derive from *kjollen*, meaning 'keel-shaped ridge' (W H Murray). **Viking** keels were evidently shapely for the Cuillin has long been honoured as presenting the most exciting skyline in Britain, a delight alike to the eye and the boot whenever the cloud cover lifts. Comparison with the adjacent, symmetrically conical Red Hill ('the Red Cuillins') serves only to emphasise the riotous profile of the Cuillin proper ('the Black Cuillins'). The former betray the rounding effects of weathering and erosion which the latter emphatically reject thanks to their composition of gabbro [see **Geology**], the toughest and roughest of magma extrusions 'with a nutmeg grater-like surface in contact with which the human body may almost defy the laws of gravity' (**John Mac Culloch**).

The main ridge, of horseshoe shape, with numerous spurs intersected by deep and often sheer corries includes some 20 **'Munros'** and several striking pinnacles. Although Sghianachs (natives of Skye) have doubtless been scrambling amongst them since time immemorial, MacCulloch failed to scale them, perhaps because he attempted to do so on horseback. But in the mid-19th century it was the charms of Cuillin gabbro which first persuaded alpinists of the climbing potential offered by native hills. All were systematically 'conquered' [see **Climbing and Mountaineering**] by the end of the century. They still attract rock and ice climbers as well as droves of hikers.

Earlier in the 19th century **Scott** (who visited in 1814), MacCulloch and others had alerted the public to the scenic qualities of the Cuillin. They particularly relished the setting of Loch Coruisk, embowered in the

outhern Cuillin and accessible to gentlemen-walkers
only by boat from **Elgol**.

> A scene so rude, so wild as this,
> Yet so sublime in barrenness,
> Ne'er did my wandering footsteps press
> *(Scott, The Lord of the Isles)*

Coruisk, like **Staffa**, became a must for the more adventurous Victorian **tourist** and was duly painted by J M
W Turner and others. Less fanciful visitors have since
feared sunstroke where 'the sun never shone since creation' (MacCulloch) while treading flower-strewn pastures where 'Nor tree, nor shrub, nor plant, nor
flower,/Nor aught of vegetative power,/The weary eye
may ken' (Scott).

CULBIN, Moray/Nairnshire

This large coastal forest between **Nairn** and **Findhorn**
was once prized grazing, then for two centuries desert,
before the persistence of the **Forestry Commission** and
the salt tolerance of Corsican pine reclaimed it. Although
it is likely that sand encroachment took place over several
centuries, the great storms of October 1694 are popularly
credited with having created the desert. Demand for mar-
am grass for thatch had denuded the adjacent dunes
which were swept inland on a westerly gale. The sand-
storm lasted several days, burying fields and livestock,
numerous dwellings, a church and the house of Kinnaird.
A graphic account will be found in David Thomson's
Nairn in Darkness and Light (1987); instances of the church
tower, house chimneys, and fruit trees subsequently
peeking through the sands are also recorded.

CULDEES

In Irish and Scottish Churches of the **Celtic** era appear
communities of Keledei (*Cele dei*): friends of God. These
monastic groups, which existed in isolated pockets as
late as the 14th century around hereditary secular
priests, eventually died out or were absorbed into the
new dioceses.

CULLEN, Banffshire

Historically there are three Cullens. There was the
ancient **royal burgh** which, though dating back to the
late 12th century, was never of any great importance.
While its early site is conjectural, latterly at least it was
situated close to Cullen House, the former residence
of the Earls of Seafield. The late medieval Auld Kirk,
transformed into a collegiate church in 1543, is all that
is left of the now vanished old burgh. In the 1820s the
Earl of Seafield built a handsome new village and erased
the old burgh. New Cullen, with its wide streets centred
on an imposing square, is one of **Moray**'s many attractive planned villages. Separate physically, and formerly
culturally, is the Seatown where the **fishing** community
once lived. With the simple cottage-style houses built
gable end to the Moray Firth, the Seatown skirts the
seashore. The fisherfolk of the Seatown prospered in
the 19th century and by 1881 93 sailing craft were
based in the town. The 20th century brought a severe
decline in the number of both boats and fishermen, as
the fishing industry became centred on **Buckie** and
other large ports.

Even by the early 1900s some of the leading citizens
had seen the writing on the wall and were pushing for
the development of facilities such as a bowling green
and tennis courts to increase the number of visitors to
the town. Today the harbour, which is used mainly for
recreational purposes, and the Links with beach and
golf course, are the focal points for Cullen's summer
visitors. While it sees fewer long-stay visitors than 40
years ago, it still attracts **tourists** and is popular as a
place of abode for commuters and the retired.

Although the coastal **railway** line closed in 1968,
Cullen's stone-built Victorian railway viaducts, the

The shifting sands of Culbin before afforestation (SEA)

longest of eight arches, are now listed structures. They survive as relics of a bygone age, just like the fragments of the Old Town's market cross that were brought c1830 to the New Town square and incorporated in a new Gothic-style frame. Cullen House too, which dates back to the 17th century, passed from the ownership of the Seafields in the 1980s. Although badly damaged in a recent fire, it has been converted into flats.

CULLEN, William (1710–90) Chemist
Born in **Hamilton**, William Cullen studied medicine at **Glasgow** and **Edinburgh** Universities before entering private practice. An interest in chemistry led him to undertake extramural lecturing in the subject at Glasgow, before becoming Glasgow's first Professor of Chemistry in 1747. Both there and at Edinburgh he advanced the industrial and agricultural applications of chemistry and edited the first modern pharmacopoeia in 1776.

CULLODEN, Battle of (1746)
In spite of victory at **Falkirk**, the **Jacobite** host continued its 1746 withdrawal to the comparative safety of the Highlands and, abandoning the siege of **Stirling**, headed for **Inverness**. The Hanoverian army, now under the young and portly Duke of Cumberland, followed up the east coast where ample supplies were received by sea. It was not so with the Jacobites. Their supply arrangements broke down when **John Murray of Broughton** fell ill; much of their artillery had to be abandoned; numbers dwindled as hungry Highlanders foraged wide or drifted home; and distrust worsened between **Lord George Murray** and **Prince Charles Edward Stewart** as the latter relied increasingly on his Irish adviser O'Sullivan. Lord George argued for a dispersal into the hills and guerrilla tactics pending a new campaign in the summer. But, belying appearances, this was still an undefeated army and so long as it remained in the field Charles had high hopes of being reinforced from France. To Murray's consternation it was therefore resolved again to oppose the Hanoverian advance and, to his greater consternation, to do so in pitched battle on an open site totally unsuited to Highland tactics at Drummossie Muir near Culloden. Worse still, as Cumberland approached from **Nairn**, a night attack on his camp proved a dismal muddle. It left the Highlanders sleepless as well as foodless when next day (16 April) the two armies confronted each other.

Cumberland's forces may have numbered about 9000, Charles's about half that. But the latter's were drawn up on a much narrower front between two dykes where crowding exposed them to lethal casualties from the Hanoverians' opening barrage. 20 minutes of this cannonade found the **clan** forces restless for an advance. When the charge was ordered the left declined to obey while the centre veered right to avoid boggy ground. So tightly packed that muskets proved unusable, the right and centre fell upon the Hanoverian left and amidst fearful casualties broke through. But they were then met and repulsed by no less deadly fusillades from the regiment behind. Attempts to disengage persuaded those on the reluctant left that all was lost and Cumberland's cavalry then swung into action to complete the rout. The battle was all over in an hour (1–2pm) but

the slaughter continued until nightfall and resumed again next day; and for weeks thereafter the round-up and the bloody reprisals continued. Hanoverian losses were reckoned at about 300, Jacobite losses, on and off the battlefield, at more like 2000. It was the bloodiest of the Jacobite engagements and the last pitched battle to be fought on British soil.

CULLODEN HOUSE, Nr Inverness
Two miles from the battlefield, the estate of Culloden was acquired by Duncan Forbes, Provost of **Inverness**, in 1621. Here stayed **Prince Charles Edward Stewart** on the eve of the battle, the property then belonging to Lord President **Duncan Forbes**, who tried so valiantly to avert the tragedy. The then house, or castle, was destroyed by fire soon after and replaced in 1772 by the present Georgian mansion consisting of a main block with central pediment and wall-top balustrade plus two smaller flanking blocks. The quality of the interior plaster work suggests that the **Adam** brothers, then working on **Fort George**, may have been involved. The house has recently been used as offices, latterly as a hotel. Outside the gates the octagonal 18th century **doocot** has dormers perforated to appeal to pigeons. The accommodation consists of 640 nest boxes accessible to egg-collectors by a revolving ladder.

CULLODEN MOOR, Nr Inverness
The **Battle of Culloden** (1746) was fought on what was then called Drummossie Muir, a broad ridge of moorland about 500ft (152m) above sea level between the river Nairn and the coastal plain east of **Inverness**. Much of the site has been acquired by the **National Trust for Scotland** whose efforts to restore and preserve it are complemented by displays, signposting and facilities designed to illuminate the action. Near the Visitor Centre (with audio-visual presentations, etc) is the Cumberland Stone from which the Hanoverian commander is supposed to have surveyed the battle site. Old Leanach Cottage, reached through the Visitor Centre, has a **heather**-thatched roof and appears from the outside much as it must have in 1746, although the interior has been changed and then restored. An adjoining barn was burnt down two days after the battle along with the 30 Highlanders who had taken refuge therein. King's Stables Cottage, a similar building, lies further west. Other memorials of the carnage dot the site including the Well of the Dead, the graves of the **clans**, the Irish Memorial of 1963, and the Memorial Cairn of 1881 set up by a descendant of **Duncan Forbes**. Here a commemorative ceremony is held every 16 April. Culloden will ever be more shrine than site for many Highland families; also for those nationalists misled by the cairn's inscription crediting the Highlanders with fighting for Scotland as well as Prince Charlie. In fact more Scots supported, and fought for, Cumberland.

CULROSS, Fife
In 1900 'a decayed **royal burgh** containing many old houses', Culross on the Firth of Forth west of **Dunfermline** could afford to bide its time. Once an important religious centre, then a major port and proto-industrial model, it has since the 1930s been recognised as 'a museum of social history', a 'three dimensional docu-

Culross in its heyday, from John Slezer's Theatrum Scotiae, 1693 (TS)

ment', 'living exemplar of a 16th century Scottish burgh', etc, a worthy subject indeed for meticulous conservation and **tourist** promotion. Tradition has it that St Serf (or Servan) in the 6th century here founded a religious community to which Thenaw (or Thenau, Enoch, etc) repaired for sanctuary after being disowned by her **Pictish** family on her marriage to Owen of **Strathclyde**. On her arrival she is supposed to have given birth to Kentigern (the later **St Mungo**, patron saint of **Glasgow**) at a spot east of the town where still stands the ruin of St Mungo's chapel, built 1503 by **Bishop Robert Blackadder** of Glasgow. St Serf's foundation was succeeded by **Culross Abbey** in the 13th century.

The monks, or more probably their lay brethren, are said to have dug local **coal**. In 1575 this privilege was leased by the post-**Reformation Commendator** of Culross to George Bruce (later Sir George Bruce of Carnock), a local laird probably related to the Bruce Commendator of **Kinloss**. He proceeded to develop commercial 'coal-mines', exporting the product and burning it locally to extract salt. The town was created a royal burgh in 1588 and Bruce's success is reflected in the building of **Culross Palace**. John Taylor, 'the water poet', who was his guest in 1618, has left a detailed description of the main Bruce mine. It reached a mile out into the Firth of Forth, could be entered either from the land or by boat to an off-shore shaft with superstructure above the high-tide mark, and was drained by a continuous conveyor incorporating 36 buckets and worked by horses. Taylor 'did never see, read nor heare of any worke of man that might parallel or bee equivalent with this unfellowed and unmatchable worke'. **James VI** is also supposed to have visited the mine but to have taken fright when ushered out of it

by the off-shore shaft. Unfortunately in 1625, when 'the occasion, inventor and maintainer of it' died, a storm flooded the workings so badly that even the 36 buckets and three horses could not cope.

Coal-mining in Culross never recovered but the burgh continued to enjoy distinction in the manufacture of iron girdles until the **Carron Company** monopolised the trade in the 18th century. Then began that long decay from which the **National Trust for Scotland** rescued the town. The 16th and 17th but mostly 18th century buildings restored by the Trust are numerous, notable being the Town House (1626, rebuilt 1783) and the 'Study' of **Bishop Leighton** of **Dunblane** (1633). The mercat cross has a late 15th century base and the street plan, with narrow wynds, flagged and cobbled, conveys a real if not totally authentic impression of the 17th century burgh lay-out.

CULROSS ABBEY, Culross, Fife

Founded by Earl Malcolm of **Fife** in 1217–18, **Culross** was a small Cistercian monastery under that of **Kinloss** in **Moray**. It just survived till the **Reformation** when (1633) the east choir of the abbey church became the parish church while the west choir and adjoining conventual buildings fell into decay; little more than their foundations survive. The church, with early 16th century tower, was modified in 1824 and restored, including a rebuilding of the south transept, by **Rowand Anderson** in 1905. Since 1624 the north transept has housed the tomb of Sir George Bruce of Carnock (and **Culross Palace**); there is a Renaissance monument and effigies of Sir George, his wife and their eight children. The adjacent manse (1637) was built with material from the ruined west choir, a wing being added in the 19th century. Also sharing the abbey's hill-top site is the once magnificent Abbey House (1608), 'the first Scottish home of any size to show Renaissance influence' (G L Pride). Ruinous in 1800, it was restored in 1830 but redesigned and much reduced in the 1950s.

CULROSS PALACE, Culross, Fife

'Palace' is a mistranslation of the Latin. The *palattium* of **Culross** meant either the principal lodging or great hall, a more apt description of this unpretentious but unique late 16th century laird's town house with its confusing complex of adjacent buildings. The original house, with date 1597 and initials of George Bruce of Carnock, forms the central section of a west range which, running at right angles to it, greatly extended its accommodation in the early 17th century. At about the same time, and as further evidence of Bruce's business success, a substantial but separate house was either built or acquired on the north side of the courtyard. All the principal structures are of three storeys with stepped gables and beautifully carved gablets over the wall-head dormers. Now painted and pantiled, they were originally of bare stone with thatched roofs, less gay but more homely. Their distinction lies, like much else at Culross, in their survival almost unaltered since their construction and in the meticulous restoration and conservation undertaken by the **National Trust for Scotland** and the state. Internally the main features are the great hall, Bruce's strong-room and counting-house, and the magnificent timber painted ceilings and walls. Culross's harbour, or Sandhaven, once adjoined the property offering Bruce an easy overview of his **coal** exports. His successors, created Earls of **Kincardine**, continued in occupation until c1700 when the property was sold to Colonel John Erskine, known as 'the Black Colonel', who seems to have shared it with another Colonel John Erskine, known as 'the White'. Hence it was for long known as 'Colonels' Close'.

CULZEAN CASTLE, Nr Maybole, Ayrshire

As a shelf of rock commanding part of the **Ayrshire** coast and the Firth of **Clyde**, the strategic potential of Culzean (pron. Cul-lane) was recognised by the **Kennedy** family who maintained there a subsidiary castle, later a tower house, from the 12th century. The Kennedys battled hard and married well, becoming **Earls of Cassillis** in 1509. In the 1760s the title passed to Sir Thomas Kennedy of Culzean whose agricultural improvements enabled his brother and successor, David the 10th Earl, to commission a residence worthy of his estate and of the neo-classical age. He turned to **Robert Adam**, then working on designs for a nearby church. As the 18th century drew to a close, the Italianate splendour of Adam's most ambitious Scottish creation took shape.

The great south front, the distinctive drum tower on the cliff side, the kitchen wing, the stabling with its courtyard and clock tower, and of course all the internal features including the gracious oval staircase were the work of Adam. The contrast between dramatic natural setting and refined classical lines has been much remarked. But perhaps it is better stated in terms of the contrast between the wild Atlantic on one side and the elegant palm-shaded terraces, divided by crennellated parapets and pavilions, on the other. The landscape park, created by **Alexander Nasmyth** and two pupils of Capability Brown, covers 565 acres (229ha). It includes a gothick camellia house, aviary and pond plus many exotic trees and shrubs. The whole was made over to the **National Trust for Scotland** (1945) but a flat within the castle was reserved (1946) for the exclusive use of President Dwight D Eisenhower in recognition of his services during World War II.

CUMBRAE ISLANDS, Firth of Clyde

The Great Cumbrae and the Little Cumbrae are two small islands in the Firth of **Clyde** between **Bute** and **Largs**, from where a small car ferry provides a service to Millport, the only village. The main shipping channel into the Clyde passes to the west of the 'Wee Cumbrae', where there was an important lighthouse. The 'Big Cumbrae' reaches a height of 416ft (127m) and is encircled by 12 miles of road. Once a popular resort teeming with day-trippers from **Glasgow** enjoying a day out **'doon the watter'**, it is now a quieter place.

The Episcopal collegiate church at Millport, consecrated in 1876 as the 'Cathedral of the Isles', is the smallest cathedral in Britain. Seating 100 people, it was designed as a theological college by William Butterfield in 1849 in a Victorian Gothic style. Its founder, George Frederick Boyle, later the Earl of Glasgow, had been involved in the Oxford Movement during the late 1840s and the cathedral was his attempt to rejuvenate the **Episcopal Church** in Scotland. The theological college closed in 1885 (its buildings are now used as a retreat and holiday accommodation) but the cathedral still has a small but active congregation. It was in the local parish kirk that, in the early 19th century, the Rev James Adam offered up regular prayers 'for the Great and Little Cumbrae and the adjacent islands of Great Britain and Ireland'.

From 1876 Keppel was the headquarters of the Scottish Marine Biological Association, which moved to **Dunstaffnage**, near **Oban**, in 1970. The buildings are now used by the Universities of **Glasgow** and London. There is an interesting aquarium and museum. Little Cumbrae was maintained as a **deer forest** by **Robert II** and **Robert III**.

CUMBERNAULD, Dunbartonshire

This new town 13 miles from **Glasgow** was developed from 1956 to house some of Glasgow's overspill population. Many have thought Cumbernauld's modern planning and architecture in advance of their time. A new private aerodrome has recently been built. Old Cumbernauld was dependent on the handloom-weaving industry.

CUMNOCK, Ayrshire

A market and **coal-mining** town set in a hollow where the river Glaisnock meets the Lugar Water, Cumnock has 'that particular dour look of a place built to provide – and no more than provide – the houses and streets in which to live and work and observe a **Presbyterian** Sabbath' (T Lang). A **burgh of barony** created for the **Dunbar Earls of March** in 1509, Cumnock holds a proud place in **Covenanting** history; it was to the gallows hill here that the exhumed body of **Alexander Peden** was brought from its resting place at **Auchinleck** to be re-buried at the unconsecrated foot of the gibbet (1686); and it was the citizens of Cumnock who

Culzean Castle from the east (GWWA)

honoured the 'Prophet' by re-siting their cemetery at his side on the 'Hill of Reproach'. The town square, site of the original churchyard, has an unusual square-shafted Mercat Cross (1509, restored 1769) surmounted by a square sundial with ball finial, while the Town Hall is fronted by Benno Schotz's bust of long-time Cumnock resident **Keir Hardie**, organising Secretary of the **Ayrshire** Miners' Association (1879) and a journalist on the *Cumnock News* (1882). The mainstays of the local economy were coal-mining, handloom weaving, **pottery** and the making of snuff-boxes 'the beauty of which rendered the village surpassingly celebrious' (Fullarton's *Gazetteer*). New Cumnock, another mining village six miles to the south on the river Afton (and now also on the A76 **Kilmarnock-Dumfries** road) was developed in the late 17th century to serve the southern end of the widespread parish of Cumnock.

CUNNINGHAM, Sir Alexander (1814–93)
Archaeologist and Soldier

Not just 'the father of Indian archaeology', Cunningham was Indian archaeology for most of his life. The son of the poet **Allan Cunningham**, he attended Christ's Hospital with his elder brother **Joseph**; both were then appointed to Indian cadetships thanks to the influence of **Sir Walter Scott**. Alexander reached India in 1833 as a second-lieutenant and stayed until his retirement as a major-general, having served as ADC to Lord Auckland, as an engineer in both Sikh Wars and in several central Indian states, and as the leader of boundary commissions in Kashmir and Ladakh (1847) and Rajasthan. He was in Burma during the Indian Mutiny.

Throughout this distinguished military progress he sustained an antiquarian curiosity about India's still unravelled ancient history which grew from a hobby into a consuming passion. Within a year of arrival he had contributed a paper on a recently excavated stupa in Punjab and in 1837 was the first to probe the great Buddhist stupa at Sarnath (Benares) where the Buddha preached his first sermon. The Indian origins of Buddhism were still a mystery but in Ladakh and Burma and amongst the ruins of Swat and Sanchi Cunningham's enthusiasm for this forgotten classical age was fired. Aided by the recently translated itineraries of some early Chinese pilgrims to India, he set about identifying the sites and unravelling the chronology of Indian Buddhism. In retirement he was summoned back to India to head the new Archaeological Survey and for a further 15 years tramped the plains of north India, tracking down what Curzon called 'the greatest galaxy of monuments in the world'. In addition to the Survey's annual reports, he wrote on Buddhist history and many individual sites as well as a book on Ladakh which remains the best text on Indian Tibet. He also formed an 'unrivalled' collection of ancient coins, many of which are now in the British Museum.

CUNNINGHAM, Allan (1784–1842) Poet and Man of Letters

Born near Dalswinton, **Dumfriesshire**, Allan Cunningham was apprenticed at the age of 10 to his brother, a stonemason, but spent much of his time reading and

215

remembered for his *Handbook of London* (1849); and Francis (1820–75) edited the works of Ben Jonson, Christopher Marlowe and Philip Massinger.

CUNNINGHAM, Allan (1791–1839) Botanist and Explorer

The sons of a gardener from **Renfrewshire**, Allan Cunningham and his brother Richard (1793–1835) were plant collectors for the Royal Botanic Gardens at Kew. After making an initial collecting trip to South America, Allan arrived in Australia in 1817 and joined several exploratory expeditions in New South Wales before setting out on his own. In 1824 he discovered a pass through the hitherto impenetrable northern Blue Mountains, in 1827 he discovered the great fertile plateau of the Darling Downs and the following year pioneered a new route from the coast to the Darling Downs through a pass that became known as Cunningham's Gap. Richard was appointed Colonial Botanist in 1833, but was drowned (or possibly murdered) on a plant hunting expedition in 1835 whereupon Allan succeeded him in the post, but the rigours of his travels had left him in poor health and he died in Sydney at the age of 48.

CUNNINGHAM, Joseph Davey (1812–51) Historian

Eldest son of the poet **Allan Cunningham**, Joseph was educated at Christ's Hospital in London and was appointed to an Indian cadetship procured for him (as for two of his brothers, **Alexander** and Francis) by **Sir Walter Scott**. Appointed to the staff of the chief engineer in Bengal (1834), he became assistant to the political agent on the Sikh frontier (1837) and for the next eight years held a succession of political appointments on the then north-west frontier. In 1845, promoted to the rank of captain, he became political agent at Bhopal, and five years later produced his definitive *History of the Sikhs* (1849). Greeted with acclaim, described by both British and Sikh historians then and since as 'one of the most valuable books ever published in connection with Indian history', and the making of his reputation as a historian, the book nevertheless was Cunningham's military and political downfall. The official reason for his disgrace was that the book contained confidential information he could only have obtained in his capacity as political agent with the army in the field, but it is significant that some of the allegations it contained shed a harsh light on the activities of his superiors. Whatever the truth of the matter, the publication ended his career as a political agent and he was returned to ordinary regimental duty with the Bengal Engineers. He died suddenly in Ambala at the age of 39.

CUNNINGHAME, John Charles (1851–1917) Iron and Coal Master

The son of Alexander Cunninghame, who along with **James Merry** had created a massive **coal** and **iron** enterprise, John was educated at Harrow and Trinity College, Cambridge. At the age of 25 he joined the business but relied heavily upon Robert Main who was brought from the ironworks at Ardeer as a managing partner. Whilst John probably played a directly interventionist managerial role only from the mid-1870s to the mid-80s,

Allan Cunningham; plaster bust by Sir Francis Legatt Chantrey (SNPG)

writing. As a child he knew **Robert Burns**, a friend and neighbour of his father, and followed at Burns's funeral in 1796; in 1802 he met and became friends with **James Hogg**, and later also gained the friendship of **Walter Scott**. It was around this time that he began writing imitations of Scottish **ballads** which were subsequently collected and published as authentic, traditional pieces in R Cromek's *Remains of Nithsdale and Galloway Song* (1810). Cunningham's authorship of these pieces, although known to many people, was not officially revealed until 1819 in an article by **John Wilson** in *Blackwood's Magazine*.

In 1811 Cunningham moved to London, where he initially worked as a parliamentary reporter, and contributed pieces to *The Literary Gazette*, *The London Magazine* and *Blackwood's*. In 1815 he became the superintendent of works to the sculptor Francis Legatt Chantrey, a position he held until Chantrey's death in 1841. Throughout this period he continued writing prolifically, publishing such works as *Traditional Tales of the English and Scottish Peasantry* (1822), *The Songs of Scotland* (1825), which contains his best poem 'A Wet Sheet and a Flowing Sea', and *Lives of the Most Eminent British Painters, Sculptors and Architects* (1829–33). Cunningham also produced a life of **David Wilkie**, edited an edition of Burns's works in eight volumes, and wrote three undistinguished romances. Of his four sons (three of whom served with distinction in the Indian Army) **Joseph** (1812–51) wrote the definitive *History of the Sikhs*; **Alexander** (1814–93) became the great authority on Indian archaeology; Peter (1816–69) was a prolific author best he nevertheless was Chairman of Merry & Cunninghame for over 40 years. It was during his active stewardship that the partners converted the Glengarnock works (near **Kilbirnie, Ayrshire**) into a technically efficient steel works. He was also drawn into a fundamental reorganisation of the business empire in 1890. His major contribution was as a financier rather than as a businessman; interests in sport, **Freemasonry**, politics and his landed estates occupied the lion's share of his time.

CUNNINGHAME GRAHAM, Robert Bontine (1852–1936) Scholar, Politician and Travel Writer

Born in London, Cunninghame Graham was the eldest son of a Scottish landowner and former major in the **Scots Greys**. His mother was descended from the Spanish aristocracy and he could also claim indirect descent from the **Stewarts**. In later years these connections earned him the nickname 'Don Roberto' and 'El Hidalgo' (the nobleman), and **Andrew Lang** was to call him 'the uncrowned king of Scots'.

His education was diverse. He spent two years at Harrow and several years being privately tutored in England and Belgium. At the age of 17 he went to South America and spent the next seven years travelling, riding with gauchos in Argentina, befriending Buffalo Bill Cody in Mexico and making unsuccessful attempts at cattle ranching. South America left a deep impression on him, and he continually returned there throughout his life.

Graham married Gabriela de la Montiere, the daughter of a Chilean grandee, while on a visit to Paris in 1878. They spent the next two years travelling through the USA and Mexico before returning to settle in Britain. In 1883 Graham's father died, and he succeeded to the family estate in Gartmore, **Perthshire**, which was heavily in debt. Graham was to spend the next decade struggling to maintain the estate in a solvent form.

In 1886 Graham was elected Liberal MP for North-West **Lanarkshire**, a seat he held until 1892. A radical socialist, he was a strong supporter of Parnell and the Irish cause, promoting the rights of miners, and was briefly imprisoned for taking part in the Trafalgar Square riot of 1887. He was also a strong supporter of Scottish Nationalist interests, and on the founding of the Scottish Labour Party in 1888 was elected its first President. Likewise in 1928 he was elected the first President of the newly established **National Party of Scotland**, and in 1934, on its amalgamation with the Scottish Party, became President of the new **Scottish National Party**.

After leaving Parliament, Graham devoted much of his time to travelling and writing. In 1898 he published *Mogreb-el-Acksa*, detailing his travels through Morocco. He followed this with several collections of travel sketches, essays and short stories, including *The Ipane* (1899), *Thirteen Stories* (1900), *Success* (1902) and *Charity* (1912). During World War I he worked to supply the government with horses bought in South America. He died in Argentina.

CUPAR, Fife

Not **St Andrews** but centrally located Cupar was the county town of **Fife**. Anciently the seat of the MacDuff **Earls of Fife** (Castlehill remains but no castle), its earliest charter as a **royal burgh** is 14th century although **Alexander III** may have held an assembly here in 1276. 'Almost all the Jameses, and the unfortunate **Mary**, visited it'; so did **Charles II** in 1650. The tower of the old parish church dates from the 15th century with a 1620 spire, the mercat cross from 1683. Cupar prospered as a market town and a yarn spinning centre, but could never compete with St Andrews as an ecclesiastical centre. Appropriately it saw the first performance (1535) of the anti-clerical *Ane Satire of the Thrie Estatis* by **Sir David Lindsay** of the nearby Mount (on which now stands an obelisk to the 4th Earl of Hopetoun). The play is said to have lasted nine hours.

The town's architecture is mainly Georgian and Victorian with a notable Corn Exchange tower (1861), John Milne's riotous Duncan Institute (with twisted tower, 1870), and a neo-classical prison (**James Gillespie Graham**, 1813), subsequently a seed-merchant's, which was once described as 'totally unfit for the purpose as having more the appearance of a gentleman's seat than a receptacle for persons who have injured society'. 'Gentlemen's seats' abound in this district, including **Scotstarvit Tower** and, hard by, Hill of Tarvit, formerly Wemyss Hall (partly 1696, possibly **Sir William Bruce**), which was redesigned by **Sir Robert Lorimer** in 1905–7 for F B Sharp and the latter's collection of furniture and paintings. Lorimer's subdued creation and Sharp's **Raeburns**, **Ramsays** and Flemish tapestries remain 'a lesson in urbane good manners' according to the **National Trust for Scotland** which now owns the property, part of which has been converted into flats.

CURLING

The sport of curling involves sliding polished circular stones made of granite over a sheet of smooth ice towards a target or 'house' (resembling an archery target) either drawn on the ice (as in outdoor curling) or under the ice (indoor curling), the object being to lay a stone as near the centre as possible. Four players constitute a team, and all four are involved with every stone delivered by their team. The skip (captain), standing behind the 'house', nominates the shot required; once the shot is delivered, the remaining two players accompany the stone up the ice ready to sweep (or stop sweeping) on the instructions of the skip. Sweeping, originally intended to remove twigs, leaves, etc from the path of the stone on outdoor ice, influences the speed at which the stone travels across indoor ice; the friction generated by hard sweeping causing the surface of the ice to melt, creating a thin film of water which allows the stone to aquaplane. Also the atmospheric pressure in front of the stone is reduced and the partial vacuum created draws the stone onwards. Judicious sweeping, and (just as important) lack of sweeping, can significantly affect the resting position of a stone. The name 'curling' comes from the other way of influencing the final position of a stone; by birling (turning) the handle upon release the stone can be made to curl, a clockwise birl making the stone curl to the right, anticlockwise to the left. The distinctive sound of the stone as it travels, particularly across outdoor ice, gave the sport one of its early nicknames, 'the roaring game'.

The origins of the sport are shrouded in the mists of

The Curlers, *by George Harvey (NGS)*

history. Holland can make a claim to be the country where it started, mainly because of background scenes in two mid-16th century paintings by Pieter Breughel the Elder, though the 'stones' are more likely to have been frozen clods. Similarly, other ancient games played in Holland, Switzerland, Germany and Iceland used wooden 'stones'. None of these can truly be said to constitute the game of curling, where the essential implement can only be of stone. On the evidence of surviving relics, most notably old stones, there can be little doubt that Scotland is the home of curling. Certainly it was in Scotland that the sport was nurtured, regulated and became popular, and from where it was exported to many lands, 1804 being a key date, for in that year the clerk of the **Duddingston** Curling Society in **Edinburgh** (founded in 1795, and therefore by no means the oldest) penned the club's rules in the minutes book; these became the basis of the modern game throughout the world.

In the wake of the Duddingston rules being accepted as the basis of the sport, the Royal Caledonian Curling Club (instituted 1838, 'Royal' since 1843), based in Edinburgh, was for long regarded as the ruling authority on the game worldwide. Its first president was arguably curling's greatest innovator, John Cairnie of **Largs**. Curling is now international, being a major sport in most countries of northern Europe and North America. In 1966 the Royal Caledonian Curling Club formed an international committee; known as the International Curling Federation, it became independent in 1973 and nine years later was recognised as the governing body of world curling, with the RCCC acknowledged as the 'mother club'. Since 1991 it has been known as the World Curling Federation, with 30 affiliated nations. The most presitigious tournament is the world championship, dating from 1959, and inevitably dominated by Europe and North America, although the zonal qualifying system ensures one place in the finals for a Pacific nation. The world championship trophy was the Scotch Cup from 1959–67, and the Silver Broom from 1968–85. The women's world championship was first held in 1979. Junior curlers also have world championships, the men since 1975 and the women since 1988. There

have also been European championships for both men and women since 1975. Canada may now claim to be the principal curling nation, but Scotland still holds a strong position: in 1991 Scotland's men were world champions at both senior and junior levels, Scotland's women being world-ranked third at both levels. The only Olympic Gold Medal to be awarded in the sport to date was won by a 'British' team in Chamonix in 1924, all the members of the team being home-based Scots. The Royal Caledonian Curling Club lists 660 clubs with some 22,000 members (with a male:female ratio of 2:1) presently active in Scotland.

There is a wealth of material evidence in Scotland to interest the curling historian – a great variety of venerable stones (some bearing dates and/or initials), equipment such as the now-obsolete 'crampits' and 'trickers' (devices used to give a foothold on the ice), 'cowes' (brooms), medals and trophies, paintings and literature. Indeed, literary references abound with poetry a particularly rich source, and the best of the nation's poets have made worthy contributions – **Robert Burns**, **Allan Ramsay**, **James Hogg** and many more.

Old stones in particular illustrate the various stages of the sport's development. The original stones were 'loofies', palm-sized stones with grooves for finger and thumb, which were thrown in quoit-like fashion. These were replaced by handled stones, many being of enormous size and weight, which meant that strength became the curler's main attribute. The introduction of rounded stones of uniform shape, size and weight placed a premium instead on skill, contact shots being made with the precision of a snooker player. There was a demand for particular types of stones – those quarried from the micro-granite of the volcanic island of **Ailsa Craig** being the most favoured.

Essentially a social game, curling was originally also an exclusively outdoor game – a few days of really hard frost drawing whole communities out onto the ice, work abandoned, as neighbouring parishes played challenge matches. Since the first indoor game (in **Glasgow** in 1907), the outdoor game has almost disappeared. The greatest outdoor curling match of them all, the 'Bonspiel' or 'Grand Match', now only takes place in exceptionally severe winters and has only occurred 33 times in the last 150 years. Held traditionally on the

Lake of Menteith in Perthshire between teams representing the North and the South of Scotland, the Bonspiel is only announced when the ice on the Lake is 10in (253mm) thick. This was increased from the previous limit of 8in (203mm) after the last Bonspiel on 7 February 1979, when the popularity of the sport, the rarity of the occasion, and speedy modern transport brought crowds of upwards of 10,000 players and spectators onto the ice, threatening the safety of all concerned.

CURSE OF SCOTLAND, The

This is usually taken to be the nine of diamonds playing card, though explanations differ. Some hold that Cumberland scribbled the order to give 'no quarter' on such a card at **Culloden**; others that the **Glencoe Massacre** was cryptically authorised using the card, which does indeed bear some resemblance to the arms of **John Dalrymple, 1st Earl of Stair** who may have been responsible. In a very different vein, it has also been suggested that the phrase is an unfortunate misreading of the 'Corse of Scotland', ie the 'Cross', **St Andrew**'s Saltire.

CURSITER, Stanley (1887–1976) Painter and Director of the National Galleries of Scotland

A considerable polymath, Stanley Cursiter is remembered as an eclectic painter, an able administrator and an incisive historian of Scottish art. Born in **Orkney**, he trained at **Edinburgh** College of Art and soon revealed a notable facility for absorbing and reinterpreting the techniques of others. In 1912 he visited the

Chez Nous; self portrait of Stanley Cursiter with his wife and model (SNPG)

avant-garde Futurist exhibition in London and proceded to produce a series of Futurist paintings of Edinburgh scenes – subjects split into conflicting planes in an attempt to represent movement and dynamism – which have since been the object of greater critical attention than they aroused at the time. During the same period, Cursiter was painting elegant interior scenes, fashionable portraits and slick watercolours, suggesting that his talents were more those of a refined and eclectic dilettante than a hardened espouser of the Modern Movement. Cursiter married fellow Orcadian Phyllis Hourston in 1914, and she was the subject of some of his most successful portraits. After an honourable war career he travelled widely with her in Europe painting a large number of bold assured watercolours. In 1925 he was appointed Keeper of the **National Galleries of Scotland** and, five years later, Director. His regime, interrupted by World War II, saw the consolidation of the Scottish collections, but the frustration of his attempts to create a Scottish and modern gallery. Cursiter wrote extensively on Scottish art and through his membership of the **Royal Scottish Academy** and appointment in 1948 as His Majesty's Limner for Scotland was a constant apostle for his national School. He retired to Orkney in the 1960s.

CUTHBERT, Saint (c635–87)

St Cuthbert's early life is closely associated with Lauderdale in **Berwickshire** where he may have been born and where, while shepherding near Oxton, he experienced the vision which persuaded him to become a monk. He entered the monastery of Old **Melrose** and became prior, during which period (670s?), according to Bede, he undertook a voyage to the **Pictish** Niduari or Niuduera who are thought to have been a Christian

219

tribe in **Fife**. He subsequently became Abbot of Lindisfarne, Bishop of Hexham and then Bishop of Lindisfarne. But he continued to hanker after the solitary life of a hermit on Farne Island where he eventually returned and died. The fame of his sanctity spread through the Northumbrian kingdom (including Lothian of which St Cuthbert was the patron).

CUTTY SARK, Sailing Ship

The *Cutty Sark* is perhaps the best-known preserved ship in the world, not least because she has lent her name to a popular brand of Scotch **whisky**. A tea-clipper, she was designed and built by Scott & Linton at **Dumbarton** in 1869. When Scott & Linton went bankrupt the contract was completed by **William Denny & Bros**. She made eight voyages in the tea trade, but failed to beat the record set by earlier vessels. With the coming of the triple expansion engine, clippers could no longer compete in shipping tea and from 1883 the *Cutty Sark* entered the Australian wool trade, making some remarkable passages. In 1895 she was sold to Portuguese owners. Forced to put into Falmouth in a gale in 1922, she was purchased by Captain Wilfred Downman, who restored her. She became a sail training ship in 1936 and, after a public appeal, was preserved at her present location in Greenwich in 1954. She has been open to the public since 1957.

'Craignair was gradually removed and distributed over the world,' the granite being used in the construction of, among other things, Liverpool Docks, the Thames Embankment, the Bank of England, Manchester Town Hall, the Eddystone Lighthouse, the Great and Little Bassas Lighthouses in Ceylon, and the town of Dalbeattie itself. The coming of the **railway** in 1860 encouraged further development and the Dalbeattie merchants 'watched with equanimity the disembowelling of their mountain'. Now the skeleton of Craignair is being picked clean for road chippings.

The town of Dalbeattie has many fine granite buildings but a forlorn air, and the harbour, once alive with ships transporting the granite worldwide, has neither ships nor trade. Just to the south-west of Dalbeattie is the 16th century L-plan tower house of Buittle Place, built from the stones of the ruined Buittle Castle by the site of which it stands. Nothing now remains of the castle, built c1230 by John Balliol, home of his wife **Devorguilla**, birthplace in 1249 of her son **King John Balliol** ('Toom Tabard'), and where she sealed the charter of Oxford's Balliol College in 1282. In **Bruce** hands during the **Wars of Independence**, it was probably dismantled c1313.

DALCROSS, Inverness
North of **Culloden** and **Clava**, Dalcross is part of a parish (combined with Croy in **Nairnshire**), a castle, and a convenient designation for **Inverness**'s overspill including its **airport** and an industrial estate. The castle was built in 1621 by the **Frasers of Lovat** but in c1700 passed to the **Mackintosh** chiefs whose descendants have recently restored it. The design is L-plan but with the two wings offset and linked by a square stair tower. Five storeys high with angle turrets and crow-stepping, it commands fine views over the Moray Firth. Here the Hanoverian troops were marshalled before Culloden. Dalcross airport and industrial estate are in fact in neighbouring Petty parish where **Castle Stuart** is contemporary with Dalcross Castle.

DALE, David (1739–1806) Banker, Industrialist and Philanthropist
The son of a grocer from **Stewarton** in **Ayrshire**, Dale served an apprenticeship as a weaver in **Paisley**, and then spent a year travelling the country buying up and reselling homespun linen yarn before moving to **Glasgow** in 1763 to set up in business as a textile merchant. His disenchantment with the **Church of Scotland** establishment and what he saw as their corrupt system of patronage led him to secede in the 1760s and become a founder member of the 'Old Scotch Independent Church', a strongly missionary sect whose adherents were later absorbed into the United **Presbyterian** Church.

By 1783 he had made a fortune, been appointed the first Glasgow agent for the Royal Bank of Scotland, married a wealthy wife and moved into a mansion in Charlotte Street. His interest in the textile industry continued; he founded a dyeworks at Dalmarnock (with George MacIntosh, father of **Charles**, the inventor of the raincoat) and **cotton** mills at **Catrine** in Ayrshire and **Blantyre** in Lanarkshire as well as at **New Lanark** (with Robert Arkwright), where he was able to put into

DAILLY, Ayrshire
There are two Dailly villages, Old Dailly three miles north-east of **Girvan** and New Dailly three miles north again. The former grew by an ancient ford over the Girvan Water and was superseded by the latter in the middle of the 18th century closer to the **coal**-mines, whose workers it was built to house. Across the ford at Old Dailly is the Baron's Stane, a great granite boulder 12m in circumference and estimated to weigh 37 tons, glacier-borne from the heights above Loch Doon and anciently used as place of assembly and seat of justice.

Of the numerous 'big hooses' on the Girvan Water, Killochan Castle, a striking L-plan tower house of five storeys with a square tower in the re-entrant angle and an unusual round tower at the south-east corner, was built in 1586 for 'Ihone [John] Cathcart of Carltoun'. Bargany dates from 1681 and, despite 18th century, Victorian and modern additions, remains an imposing mansion. Kilkerran was built for Sir James Fergusson c1730 around an older tower and enlarged in c1818. Dalquharran is a dramatic **Robert Adam** castle built in 1785 for Adam's niece and her husband Thomas Kennedy of **Dunure** beside the ruins of Old Dalquharran Castle, a 15th century rectangular fortalice with circular tower; sadly the new(er) Dalquharran is now a roofless shell. Penkill Castle, although dating from the 16th century, is known for its assocation with the Pre-Raphaelite brotherhood. Long a Boyd home, Penkill was restored in 1857–8 by Stephen Boyd and thereafter became a haven and inspiration to his friends **William Bell Scott**, Dante Gabriel and Christina Rossetti and others. Their paintings, drawings and murals together with contemporary furniture and artefacts constituted a remarkable collection, much of which was dispersed in the 1960s, was since restored but dispersed again in the 1990s.

DALBEATTIE, Kirkcudbrightshire
When Robert Heron passed through the 'small village' of Dalbeattie in 1792, it seemed to him 'rather surprising that a situation so favourable has not before this time been occupied by a town or village of considerable magnitude', adding that 'if some suitable manufacture could be established at Dalbeattie, I should expect to see it rise to rival the most considerable towns in this part of **Galloway**'. Less than 10 years later just such a 'manufacture' was established with the opening of the granite **quarry** in Craignair hill just across the river Urr by Andrew Newall in 1800 and later operated by the Liverpool Dock Trustees. During the 19th century

practice some of his progressive ideas on **education** and welfare. His concern at the rate of emigration from the Highlands moved him to establish cotton mills at **Oban** in **Argyll**, **Stanley** in **Perthshire** and Spinningdale in **Sutherland** with the specific intention of creating local employment and prosperity. In later years he was also a director and benefactor of Glasgow's **Royal Infirmary**. In 1800 he sold New Lanark to his son-in-law Robert Owen and retired to his estate near Cambuslang where he died in 1806.

DALHOUSIE CASTLE, Midlothian

An ancient romantic pile overlooking the River South Esk near **Lasswade**, Dalhousie is the oldest inhabited castle in **Midlothian**. The striking L-plan tower of c1450, formed of local hard pink sandstone, stands complete with its curtain wall sheltering most of the later 17–19th century accretions, notably by **William Burn**. A hotel from 1972, the castle was built by the Ramsays of Dalhousie, who owned the barony from 1150; Simon de Ramsay settled in the reign of **David I**. Ramsays long served the Crown; William de Ramsay, signatory of the **Declaration of Arbroath**, backed **Robert Bruce** in the **Wars of Independence** (tradition has **Harry the Minstrel** praising **William Wallace** at Dalhousie during his 15th century peregrinations); Sir Alexander, a 14th century Warden of the Marches and constable of **Roxburgh** Castle, was starved to death in **Hermitage Castle**, and Ramsays fell at **Halidon Hill** and **Flodden**. The 1st Lord Dalhousie was created by **James VI** for services in the **Ruthven Raid**; the 1st Earl of Dalhousie by **Charles II** in 1633; and **James Ramsay** made Marquis. A death in the family is said to be presaged by a branch falling from the Edgewell Oak in the castle grounds; the family seat is now at **Brechin** Castle.

DALKEITH, Midlothian

Six miles south-east of **Edinburgh**, the town of Dalkeith occupies a narrow wedge of land between the rivers North and South Esk. A **burgh of barony** for James Douglas of Dalkeith, later **Earl of Morton**, from 1401, Dalkeith passed to the **Buccleuchs** in the mid-17th century and thereafter grew into a centre for the Lothian **coalfields** and the surrounding agricultural area. The construction of the **railway** between Dalkeith and Edinburgh, commenced in 1827 and opened in 1831, was initially an industrial enterprise 'for the conveyance of coal, and other mineral produce, and manure. Passengers were not thought of in the original estimates of the railway,' which was horse-drawn until mechanisation in 1846, though by 1840 'they had become the chief source of profit' (Fullarton's *Gazetteer*). By that time Dalkeith was rivalling **Haddington** as the country's largest grain-market; the town's Corn Market was built in 1853. The partially ruinous collegiate church of St Nicholas in the High Street dates from the 13th century with alterations, extensions and restoration dating from the 14th, 16th and 19th centuries (the last by **David Bryce** 1851–4). It contains the tomb of and monument to James Douglas (see above) and his wife Joanna. On the other side of the High Street the Tolbooth, dated 1648, has been much altered, its symmetrical front of simple classical form giving it 'a polite look'. The town's situation so close to Edinburgh and on the main A68 Edinburgh road has assured its prosperity as well as its congestion.

Dalkeith House (sometimes 'Palace') at the north end of the town overlooking the river North Esk incorporates parts of 12th/13th century Dalkeith Castle, home of the Earls of Morton, which itself was enlarged in the 15th century. **Cardinal Beaton** was held here in 1543, and in 1547 it gave refuge to the vanquished of the **Battle of Pinkie**, Morton amongst them, until they were forced to surrender to the English. The estate was bought by Francis, 2nd Earl of Buccleuch in 1642 who passed it on to his younger daughter Anne and her husband the **Duke of Monmouth** who were created Duke and Duchess of Buccleuch in 1663. After her husband's execution in 1685 it was Anne who commissioned **James Smith** to restyle (in effect to rebuild) Dalkeith, which he did with great ingenuity, 'masking the older work as best he could on the rear and side elevations, but providing a completely new front of considerable dignity on the east side of the house' (J G Dunbar). The result is the 'grandest of all early classical houses in Lothian', strongly reminiscent of Smith's earlier (and now vanished) **Hamilton** Palace. The interior contains rich oak panelling and some marble fireplaces with carvings by Grinling Gibbons, while the stables and coach house were built c1740 by **William Adam** and the conservatory 1832–4 by **William Burn**. The north drive of Dalkeith House crosses the river by the Montagu Bridge (**Robert Adam**, 1792), originally ornamented by two lifesize statues of stags, 'but they frighted the horses so much that it was found necessary to remove them'. George IV stayed in Dalkeith House on his visit to Scotland in 1822, and **Queen Victoria** spent her first night on Scottish soil here as the guest of the Duke and Duchess of Buccleuch. The main residence in Scotland of the Duke of Buccleuch is Bowhill near **Selkirk**; Dalkeith House is leased to an American university.

DALLAS, Moray

It would be interesting to know who named the Texas oil capital after this very unglamorous village in the middle of **Moray**. Probably deriving from the Gaelic *dail-uisg*, water-meadow, it is low-lying beside the river Lossie. The parish church of St Michael dates from 1794 and was preceded by a **heather**-roofed structure 'without windows save two or three narrow slits which yawned to a very undue width within'. In the churchyard is a 12ft (3.6m) column topped by a fleur-de-lys, the old Mercat Cross. Nearby, Dallas Lodge was built by Sir Robert Gordon of **Gordonstoun** and has a 'Round Square' (actually semi-circular) similar to that at Gordonstoun.

DALMALLY, Argyll

This village lies east of **Kilchurn Castle** at the meeting point of Glens Orchy, Lochy and Strae, where the river Orchy flows into **Loch Awe**. The whitewashed octagonal church of the charming Gothic Revival style also found at **Cairndow** was built in 1811 by the 4th Earl of **Breadalbane**. On the north side of the loch is Lochawe village with St Conan's Kirk dedicated to the Celtic missionary who supposedly lies buried on Innis

Chonain; the church was elaborated over 50 years (1881–1930) by Walter Douglas Campbell and his sister Helen to include three side chapels, a side aisle, a cloister, **standing stones** and numerous other vernacular features all hewn from boulders rolled down from **Ben Cruachan**. A monument to the Gaelic poet **Duncan Bàn Macintyre** looks across the loch from above Dalmally, and another, to **Duncan MacLaren**, from Glen Strae. The village has a livestock mart and holds a noted agricultural show at the end of each summer.

DALMELLINGTON, Ayrshire

The *Old Statistical Account* suggested that the name of this isolated town 15 miles south-east of **Ayr** on the road to **Castle Douglas** was originally 'Dame Helen's Town' 'after a lady of rank and fortune, of the name of Helen, who built a castle near this place'. Chalmers in his *Caledonia*, however, derives the name from the Gaelic *dal*, a valley, and *muilan*, a mill. The peace of the 'neat and compact village' described by an 1843 gazetteer was shattered four years later when the Waterside Ironworks was established with its attendant furnaces, pits and **railway** sidings. A measure of prosperity followed with the entire population seemingly in the employ of the Dalmellington Iron Company by 1898, but it did not last. Heavy industry departed in the 20th century, leaving a town 'with no pretensions to architectural dignity and no evidence of high antiquity'. The Scottish Industrial Railway Centre based at the former Minnivey Colliery now houses an important collection of steam and diesel **locomotives** and rolling stock of different gauges, representing various Scottish industries including **iron and steel**, **coal**, **engineering**, **whisky**, **agriculture** and chemicals. The centre is operated by the **Ayrshire** Railway Preservation Group, a voluntary society of enthusiasts, and is open to the public.

DALMENY HOUSE, West Lothian

The seat of the 7th Earl of Rosebery, Dalmeny House surveys the Firth of Forth between **Cramond** and **South Queensferry**. Designed in 1815 on a plan 'calculated more for comfort and convenience than show' (Macaulay, 1975) by the English architect William Wilkins, it was the first Tudor Gothic Revival house in Scotland. The family acquired the estate in 1662 but clung to Barnbougle Tower by the shore until, tradition says, the 3rd Earl, on rising from dinner, was swamped by a huge wave. In 1774–93 **Robert Adam** planned a 'spectacular triangular castle which . . . would have conjured up an image of the imperial palace of Spalato' (Bolton, 1922), but the present two-storey, seven-bay, L-plan house was created for the 4th Earl; notable are its mullioned Elizabethan windows and the false gables enlivening the composition. The ancient Barnbougle Castle, medieval keep of the Moubrays – Norman knights and crusaders who originally accompanied William the Conqueror to Britain – was rebuilt in 1881 as the private library retreat of the **5th Earl (Archibald Philip Primrose)**, Liberal Party leader and Prime Minister after Gladstone in 1894. In 1878 he married Hannah, heir of Baron Meyer de Rothschild of Mentmore, Buckinghamshire, from where, after its sale in 1977, most of the treasures now displayed at Dalmeny derived; exceptional are the unusually colourful tapestries

designed by Goya for Spanish royal residences, the fine French furniture and Savonnerie carpets of 1680–1780 made for Louis XIV and his successors, and Beauvais tapestries designed from c1740 by François Boucher. The Napoleon Room contains much material associated with the Emperor which was personally collected by the 5th Earl.

DALMENY KIRK, Dalmeny, West Lothian

One of the best-preserved Norman churches in Britain, Dalmeny Kirk, in the planned Rosebery estate village of

South door of Dalmeny Kirk (RWB)

Dalmeny (c1800), crowns the high ground above **South Queensferry**. Dedicated to **St Cuthbert**, the kirk comprises the western tower rebuilt in 1937 – 'It is absolutely much too low' [cf **Kirkliston (Edinburgh)**] (MacWilliam, 1975) – and an oblong nave with a narrower and lower square choir and rounded apse, both of which are exceptionally finely vaulted. Most remarkable is the Romanesque south door (similar to the north door of **Dunfermline Abbey**) which has arch mouldings arranged in receding concentric rings and is elaborately ornamented with intricate 'zodiacal' carvings, possibly derived from the *Bestiary*, a medieval biblical textbook of allegorical horror stories along zoological themes. Inside, a massive carved stone coffin may have been that of a benefactor, or the founder, or one of the wealthy lords of Dalmeny themselves – either Earl Cospatric (d.1138) of **Dunbar**, son of the Earl of Northumberland who fled to Scotland after being forfeited for his rebellion against William the Conqueror – or his son of the same name (d.1166). The Rosebery Aisle, the only addition to the kirk, was built in 1671.

DALRIADA, Kingdom of (c400–800 AD)

Ancient sea-borne links with Ireland produced Gaelic-speaking settlements in **Argyll** before 400. But by 500 Argyll was ruled by **Fergus**, son of Erc, of the Antrim Dal Riata tribe, whose name came to designate his Scottish kingdom. Irish tribal kings were chosen from descendants of any former king down to great-grandsons; they were *Ri* of a *tuath* (community and/or territory, compact enough for all to attend assemblies without becoming 'wayfaring strangers'), under a provincial 'over-king'. Kings were enthroned at sacred centres (eg **Dunadd**). In 572 **St Columba** (whose grandmother was a daughter of Erc) installed his kinsman **Aidan** (Aedan) mac Gabhran with Christian ritual; Aidan was 6th King.

Scots of Dalriada

Dalriadic kings fought **Picts**, Britons, Saxons and each other, the kingship shifting between rival branches. After many setbacks, **Kenneth I**, 36th King of Dalriada, moved his capital to **Scone**, away from **Viking** raids.

According to legend, he also moved the ancestral enthroning-stone, which embodied St Patrick's blessing that wherever it rested the race of Erc should reign. This 'Stone of Destiny' [see **Scone, Stone of**] was used in enthronements until 1249 (**Alexander III**), but it or a substitute was removed to Westminster in 1296, Edward I apparently believing that it gave him the sovereignty of Scotland. From the coronation of **James VI** as James I of England to the present day, descendants of Erc have again been enthroned on it.

DALRY, Ayrshire

Three miles north of **Kilwinning** on the river Garnock, Dalry developed, like **Beith**, **Newmilns** and **Stewarton**, in the 18th century as a weaving centre, and textiles remained its main industry until well into the 20th century. The high clock spire of St Margaret's parish church (David Thomson, 1871–3) is a striking land-

mark. Nearby Blair House is a vast 17th century mansion incorporating the remains of a 14th century tower, while Cleave's Cove in the Duisk glen just to the south is an extensive, stalactite-hung limestone cavern, legendary home of the fairy-folk and a useful refuge for persecuted **Covenanters**.

DALRY (Dalrigh), Battle of (1306)

Fleeing after his defeat by the English under the Earl of Pembroke at **Methven** (19 June 1306), **Robert I** was attacked at Dalry (**Tyndrum**) on 11 August by **John MacDougall of Lorne**, a kinsman of **John Comyn (ii)** whom Bruce had killed in February of that year. Robert's forces were defeated in the battle (during which one of MacDougall's Highlanders ripped the 'Brooch of Lorne' off the Bruce's plaid); his supporters were forced to disperse and Bruce himself fled to **Kintyre** and then to Rathlin.

DALRY, Kirkcudbrightshire

At the top of the main street of Dalry is an ancient chair-shaped rock upon which, according to legend, St John the Baptist once took a breather. The legend probably followed upon the dedication of the church to St John the Baptist, patron saint of the Knights Templar who owned land in the parish.

Anciently called St John's clachan, the village is now also known as St John's Town of Dalry. Noted for the charm and serenity of its surroundings, Dalry has always seemed an unlikely setting for the start of the **Pentland Rising**. Indeed it was merely by chance that four fugitive **Covenanters** were passing through the village on the morning of 13 November 1666 when an old farmer was set upon by a platoon of **James Turner**'s dragoons and threatened with torture for failing to pay government fines. The Covenanters went to his rescue; a fight followed; word reached the congregation of a **conventicle** gathered at nearby Balmaclellan who rushed to join the affray; and the Rising was under way.

DALRYMPLE, Alexander (1737–1808)
Navigator and Hydrographer

Brother of **John**, Lord Provost of **Edinburgh**, and of **Sir David (Lord Hailes)**, Alexander was described by the latter to **Boswell** as 'a more romantic person than our modern world could have produced'. Unfortunately his undoubted idealism was obscured by professional disappointment and extreme irritability. From Madras, where he served in the East India Company (1751–9 and 1775–6), he made two voyages to South-East Asia during which he concluded treaties with the Sultan of Sulu (now Philippines), explored the sea passages between Borneo and New Guinea, and served briefly as Governor of Manila during the British occupation (1762–4). His plan for the establishment of a freeport in the Sulu Sea proved disastrous both for himself (because his insistence on absolute command was rejected) and for those who effected it (they were massacred). But his reasoning and discoveries prompted a revival of British interest in the region which led to the occupation of Penang and Raffles' creation of Singapore.

It was ever Dalrymple's fate to be wrong for the best and most cogent of reasons. Before becoming the Company's first official hydrographer (1779) and then the Navy's (1795) he had been closely involved in the search for the supposed southern continent; he estimated its population at over 50 million and its lateral extent at exactly 5323 miles. He was equally wrong about the North-West Passage. In spite of the backing of both the Royal Society and **Adam Smith**, a close friend, he was passed over as commander of the South Pacific expedition in favour of Captain Cook. Embittered, he nevertheless collaborated on the reports of Cook's voyages and became closely asociated with Sir Joseph Banks, the great impresario of turn-of-the-century travel. Dalrymple published several collections of voyages, numerous reports on obscure geographical locations and several thousand nautical charts. His career, and his life, ended in acrimony; his reputation has suffered accordingly. But his influence was enormous, his honesty unimpeachable and through his hydrographical labours he probably saved more lives than any man of his generation. There is a biography by H T Fry (1970).

DALRYMPLE, Sir David, Lord Hailes
(1726–92) Historian and Judge
Great grandson of **James Dalrymple** (1st Viscount Stair), grandson of Sir David (Lord Advocate 1700–20), and eldest of the 16 children of Sir David of Hailes (1692–1751), David was educated at Eton and Utrecht before being called to the Bar at the Middle Temple. He became advocate (1744) and Lord of Session (1776) as Lord Hailes. A humane and learned judge, he is better known as the patron and friend of **James Boswell** (and hence one of rather few contemporary Scots of whom **Dr Johnson** approved) and as a scholar. His historical interests extended well beyond legal parameters and resulted in the publication of numerous biographical sketches and some seminal source works including the *Annals of Scotland from the Accession of Malcolm III to the Accession of Robert I* (1776) and a further volume continuing the narrative to the accession of the **Stewarts**. Here his vast first-hand knowledge of the unpublished records results in an invaluable record of events which has provided the raw material for many a later historian. He also published an edition of the **Bannatyne Manuscript**, the account of **Charles II**'s vicissitudes after the Battle of Worcester as related to Samuel Pepys, and *The Secret Correspondence Between Sir Robert Cecil and James VI*, etc.

DALRYMPLE, James, 1st Viscount Stair
(1619–95) Jurist
The foremost Scottish jurist of the 17th century, James Dalrymple was influential as a judge, a writer and an administrator. After studying at the **University of Glasgow** he joined those defending the **Covenant** in the Bishops' Wars [see **Charles I**] and then taught at Glasgow as a Regent in the Faculty of Arts (1641–47). He became an advocate in 1648 and, after a successful career including a period as a commissioner for the Administration of Justice under Cromwell and a period out of judicial office due to his refusal to swear not to take arms against the King, he was restored to his post in 1644. He became Lord President in 1671, retired to Holland in 1681 to avoid signing the **Test Act**, but was reappointed in 1688. A strong supporter of the Revolution, he was created Viscount Stair in 1690.

He is best remembered as the author of *Institutions of the Law of Scotland* (1681), the prototype Scottish Institutional text, a fundamental amalgam of the Laws of Scotland written from a natural law standpoint, synthesising the various sources of Scots **law** into a logical and coherent self-supporting system. By writing the *Institutions* Stair not only signalled Scotland's legal links with European jurisprudence, he also preserved Scots law for the future. He also wrote *Modus Litigandi, or Forms of Process delivered before the Lords of Council and Session* (1684) and *Decisions of the Court of Session* (1661). His eldest son, **John**, became **1st Earl of Stair**; and his daughter Janet, who married David Dunbar, was the subject of the tragic events which inspired **Scott**'s *The Bride of Lammermoor* [see **Bladnoch**]. Numerous other children and descendants enjoyed high distinction.

DALRYMPLE, John, 1st Earl of Stair
(1648–1707) Judge
Although his father **James Dalrymple, Viscount Stair**, had resigned as Lord President rather than take the **Test Oath**, John Dalrymple, the Master of Stair, came to terms with **James VII** in 1686 and was appointed Lord Advocate in place of **George 'Bluidy' Mackenzie**. Sent to London by the Convention of Estates to present William of Orange with Scottish conditions for accepting him as king, Dalrymple, like his father able but unscrupulous, was appointed by William to the posts of Lord Advocate (1689) and joint Secretary of State with **Melville** (1691). Responsible in this last capacity for controlling the rebellious Highland **Jacobites**, and lacking the troops to overwhelm them by force, Dalrymple adopted an alternative scheme of negotiation. When after six months this had borne no fruit he lost patience. Sensitive to accusations by Protestants that as a previous supporter of James he still had Catholic leanings, and sharing with many other Lowlanders a fear and loathing of the Highland **clans**, he determined to make an example of one *pour encourager les autres*. In the furore which followed the **Massacre of Glencoe**, for which he was held largely responsible, Dalrymple was forced to resign as Secretary of State (1695). Succeeding as Viscount Stair in 1695, he was made a Privy Councillor (1702), created Earl of Stair (1703) and supported the 1707 **Act of Union**.

DALRYMPLE, John, 2nd Earl of Stair
(1673–1747) Soldier and Diplomat
This Dalrymple's chances of adding another illustrious rung to the Stair dynasty took an early knock when, aged eight, he accidentally shot dead his younger brother. Exiled by his parents, he was educated in Holland and first served under the Prince of Orange before joining the **Scots Guards** (1701). In 1703 he was ADC to Marlborough and served with distinction at Oudenarde and Malplaquet becoming General (1712) and ambassador in Paris (1715). A strong Hanoverian supporter, he there had the satisfaction of frustrating the plans of **James Francis Edward Stewart**, 'the Old Pretender', and securing his expulsion. From 1720 he held the post of Vice-Admiral for Scotland and, falling out with Robert Walpole (1733), looked set for a quiet retirement growing vegetables and living in **Edinburgh**. But aged 70 he was again summoned to diplomatic

duties and made a field marshal; he fought his last battle (Dettingen) and was appointed Commander-in-Chief for the south of Britain (1744) and General of the Marines (1746).

DALWHINNIE, Nr Newtonmore, Inverness-shire

A bleak village on the north side of the **Drumochter Pass** near the head of Loch Ericht, Dalwhinnie has a distillery but otherwise depends on its position astride the road and **railway** to the north. Here early in the last **Jacobite Rising** (August 1745) **Prince Charles Edward Stewart** encamped, having crossed the **Corrieyairack Pass** from the west, and had the satisfaction of seeing General John Cope's force from **Inverness** turning back, thus leaving open the road south that led on to **Prestonpans** and England.

DALYELL, Sir John Graham (1775–1851)
Antiquarian and Musicologist

A graduate of **Edinburgh University** who became a member of the Faculty of Advocates (1796) and Vice-President of the Society of Antiquaries of Scotland (1797), Dalyell was also an amateur musicologist and author of, among other works, *Musical Memoirs of Scotland*, (Edinburgh, 1849) – a book which, though dated, contains a fascinating gathering of information and speculation, much of it still useful. Its interest is focused primarily on the history of instruments used in Scotland, but it ranges far and wide.

DALYELL, General Sir Thomas ('Tam') (c1599–1685)

Member of the well known **West Lothian** family based at **The Binns** near **Linlithgow**, Sir Thomas ('Tam' to

General Thomas 'Tam' Dalyell, by L Schuneman (SNPG)

distinguish him from his father, also Thomas) Dalyell (or Dalziel – both pron. 'dee-ell') took up arms for **Charles I** while in his teens and never swerved in his devotion to the Royalist cause. On hearing of the execution of Charles, Tam swore never to cut his hair or his beard until the monarchy was restored; but he seems to have become attached to his locks, because even after the Restoration he kept them long and flowing. He fought with the Scottish army at Worcester on 3 September 1651 and was taken prisoner, but escaped from the Tower of London and fled to Russia. A spell in the Russian service, during which he achieved high rank under Tsar Mikhailovitch, earned him the nickname 'The Muscovite Devil' (or 'de'il', a pun on his name). Recalled by **Charles II** in 1660, he was Commander-in-Chief in Scotland (1666–85) and in 1681 he raised the **Royal Scots Greys**. 'Bluidy Tam', as he was known for his suppression of the **Pentland Rising** at **Rullion Green**, was buried at **Abercorn** church.

DANCING

The contemporary Scottish repertoire may be divided into three: solo dances, twosomes and set dances (including reels, country dances etc). Their origins are various but thought to be authentically Scottish in the case of reels and some solo dances, although even these have been modified by the vagaries of fashion and the popularity of equivalent forms elsewhere.

The term 'Highland dancing' cuts across these divisions and isolates such indigenous forms. It is closely associated with the Highland regiments as they developed during the 18th and 19th centuries when pipers provided the usual accompaniments. A wider popularity resulted from Victorian patronage of **Highland Games**, of which dancing was always an essential component, and of Highland balls whence the reel acquired fashionable status. The Scottish Official Board of Highland Dancing was founded in 1953 to preserve traditional forms. It also provides guidance and authority, particularly for overseas Caledonian and Highland Societies. Within Scotland the Highland tradition continues to transcend social distinctions. If Jane, Duchess of Gordon (d1812), her daughters and circle danced to the music of **Niel Gow** and **William Marshall** (her sometime butler), so did everyone else, and it has been suggested that many reel forms developed specifically to suit the limitations of the **cottar**'s earthen floor or the **crofter**'s kitchen. Gaelic *puirt a beul* (mouth-music) provided the inspiration for the **Strathspey**; and the Eightsome provides a classic example of a reel which is still as much danced in the village hall as in the ballroom.

Of solo dances the best-known are the Fling and the Sword Dance. The former originally denoted a distinctive step in which the free foot is kicked (or flung) into the air; as such it survives in the setting step of reels and twosomes. The Fling is first noticed as a separate form of dance in 1805 and is now standardised as a virtuoso dance of four to eight steps, each with a distinctive name. The Sword Dance, in which dancers dance over and among grounded swords, dates from at least the 18th century and is a standard item in Highland performances. Other solo dances include **jigs**, hornpipes and the Seann Truibhas.

Twosome or couple dances (eg the 'Gay Gordons') became popular after 1800. The fashion was foreign but the music often used the indigenous patterns of the Strathspey and reel. Hence that form of the polka known as the Schottische, or the Ecossaise. The waltz never became as popular in Scotland as elsewhere but it also forms part of the repertoire now commonly referred to as 'old time dances'.

Set dances, including reels, comprise the major corpus of Scottish dancing and are comprehended by the term 'Scottish Country Dancing'. 'Country' here derives from the French *contre*, ie with two facing lines of dancers; the custom dates back to at least the early 17th century but was probably preceded by the chains and rings and figures-of-eight of Highland reel prototypes. Although the 'country' dancing tradition proved more than a match for the waltz and polka, it found few champions in the dance halls of the conurbations. The Scottish Country Dance Society was formed in 1923 to restore and preserve the tradition.

Of the most-danced reels, the 'Duke of Perth', also known as 'Broun's Reel' or 'Clean Pease Strae' may be named after James Drummond (1713–47), the 3rd **Duke of Perth** who commanded the left wing of the **Jacobite** forces at **Culloden**. The Eightsome, although supposedly composed by the **Duke of Atholl** and friends in the 1870s, contains ancient elements of the Highland reel and is not strictly a 'country' dance since it is based on the circle. The Foursome, or 'Scotch Reel', is also of some antiquity and provides a good example of the change in rhythm (from Strathspey to reel), an unusual feature in social dancing outside of Scotland. 'Strip the Willow', a classic 'country' dance, contains a suggestion of the weaving process with dancers imitating the slalom of the shuttle. The most popular recent introduction to the repertoire must be that devised by men of the **51st Highland Division** while prisoners of war at Laufen during World War II. It was first known as the 'Laufen Reel', then the 'St Valéry Reel' (they had been captured at St Valéry), and finally as the 'Reel of the 51st Division'.

Dance music was first published in the 16th century when such as 'A Hilland Dance' and 'A Scotch Measure' appeared in print in London. Pocket editions of set dances with music and instructions continued to be published until in the 1740s the publishing of dance music in central Scotland began to reach a wide audience. By the 1780s there were at least 100 collections of dance tunes in circulation. A slow decline through the 19th century ended with the founding of the (now) Royal Scottish Country Dance Society, whose publications alone are a testament to the long history of the dancing Scot.

DAPHNE DISASTER (1883)

Shipbuilding's worst accident occurred on 3 July 1883 when 124 men and boys lost their lives. The firm of **Alexander Stephen & Sons** was attempting to complete the coastal steamer *Daphne* before an impending deadline, and launched the vessel in a semi-complete state from their Linthouse yard with 200 men working aboard.

A misunderstanding meant that the designer and the constructors had left vital stability calculations to each other, resulting in the 177ft (54m) craft keeling over to port immediately it entered the **Clyde**. The weight of loose equipment and of the unfortunate workmen increased the listing, allowing water to enter deck spaces left to allow the fitting of boilers. Only about 70 workers managed to scramble to safety before the *Daphne* sank and it proved impossible to rescue any of the remaining 124. The vessel herself was later raised and plied successfully as the *Rose*.

DARIEN VENTURE, The (1698–1700)

As a fit subject for national chagrin the Darien Venture ranks with **Glencoe**, **Culloden** and the **clearances**; its story, like theirs, is easily distorted by mawkish sentiment and recrimination. It began in 1695 when the Scottish Parliament passed an Act, to which the royal assent was duly granted, for the establishment of a 'Company of Scotland Trading to Africa and the Indies'. In that the Company represented the culmination of efforts mostly by **Edinburgh** merchants to find an overseas outlet for Scottish products it became known in Scotland as our 'African' or 'Indian Company'. Later, as the authority for settling a Scottish colony in central America, it was known as the 'Darien Company'. But in London it was ever the 'Scottish East India Company'; and for all the undoubted precedents in Scotland for commercial and colonial enterprise, it was to circumstances in London that the Company was indebted both for its dizzy designs and for their quick disappointment.

The two preceding decades had witnessed sensational growth by the long-established London East India Company. But while EIC stock values had soared, its stockholders had contracted, thus encouraging a host of jealous rivals. Pirates (like **Captain William Kidd**) apart, these interlopers were often men of substance whose city financiers and political sympathisers proceeded to challenge the EIC's monopoly of Eastern trade in the courts and in Parliament. By 1695 this contest was at its height amidst lobbying, bribery and 'dirty tricks' on a massive scale. To legitimise their challenge the interloping interests explored numerous expedients including sailing under foreign flags of convenience. They were well aware of Scottish ambitions and readily championed them.

Thus the very extensive privileges and powers granted to the new Scottish Company were clearly modelled on those of the existing EIC and were probably drafted in London. Half the directors named in the act were London-based; half the capital was to be raised in London; and the Company's affairs, it soon transpired, were to be managed from London. No doubt the Edinburgh contingent appreciated that the commercial and financial experience needed for such a venture could not easily be found in Scotland. But, in the event, there they had to be found. For London's enthusiasm for the Scottish Company, which resulted in the raising of £300,000 in the space of a fortnight, evaporated just as rapidly when the House of Lords protested, King William reneged, and the Commons threatened to impeach the directors. The EIC's monopoly was thus upheld, the interloping interests were given encouragement to bid against the EIC for the monopoly, and the Scots Company was left to languish without official support and with every possible obstacle being placed in its path.

It was a situation guaranteed to provoke Scottish endeavour and to cloud Scottish judgement. The endeavour took the form of a massive fund-raising effort which, by engaging the entire nation, raised a capital of £400,000 – said to have been equivalent to half the total capital at that time available in Scotland. Three ships were ordered from Hamburg and Amsterdam, there being no yards in Scotland capable of building 500-ton Indiamen; stores and trade goods were assembled at the Company's warehouse in **Leith**; an advertisement for 1200 settlers hinted at colonisation rather than trade. But the destination of the armada was kept a secret. It remained so when the fleet, including two smaller vessels, was given a rapturous send-off from Leith on 12 July 1698; not until it called at Madeira were the sealed orders opened. They instructed the expedition to make for the isthmus of Panama and in particular for the Darien coast at its southern extremity (near the present-day Panama's border with Colombia).

The unlikely choice of Darien seems to have come from the fertile brain of **William Paterson**, self-proclaimed founder of the Bank of England, one of the few London-based directors to keep faith with the Company, and now one of the few promoters of the Company to be actually sailing with its first expedition. Paterson had identified the Panama isthmus as ideally sited for engrossing the trade of the Americas and for short-cutting the long sea routes to the East via Capes Horn or Good Hope. The location had been suggested by the travels of William Dampier who had crossed the isthmus in 1679, while the commercial idea had probably come from Paterson's interloping acquaintances, some of whom had controlled a brisk trade across the Malay peninsula between the Indian Ocean and the South China Sea during the 1680s. But Paterson, 'a full convert to his own enthusiasms', had underestimated both the size of the Pacific and, in the absence of a canal, the difficulties of porterage across the isthmus. More crucially he had also underestimated the Spanish who were already established at Cartagena (Colombia) and on the Pacific side of the isthmus.

After a long voyage, on 3 November formal possession was taken of a sheltered harbour at a place called Acla on Spanish maps but immediately renamed Caledonia. A narrow promontory was selected as the site for a fort, Fort St Andrew, and a town, New Edinburgh. Guns and invalids were landed; the construction of a settlement began. The Indian people seemed happy to welcome non-Spanish settlers; treaties were concluded and the canoes of the chiefs flew the Scottish flag. But it was also apparent that the colonists could expect no favours from the English, whose representatives at Jamaica and on the north American seaboard were forbidden by royal proclamation to trade with the Scots, nor from the Spanish who were reportedly mobilising against them. A minor skirmish took place in February 1699 and then one of the Scots ships was taken. A report that reached Edinburgh in March enthused about the new settlement while begging urgently for further supplies. In fact the supply situation was critical, desertions and deaths (from dysentery and fever) were even

more discouraging than the hostility of neighbours, and the settlement was riven by feuds. In June, when the proposal to abandon the colony was discussed by the governing council, only Paterson objected, and he was too sick to be of account.

The return voyage proved even more disastrous than the eight months in Darien. One vessel was unfit to sail, another was abandoned in Jamaica, and a third in New York. Of the 1200 Scots who had set out from Leith in the previous year, only 900 survived the Darien experience and of them 150 died on the voyage north. Fewer still made it back to Scotland aboard the *Caledonia*, the only one of the five original vessels to return.

Although thinking themselves 'starved and abandoned by the world', the first settlers had in fact decamped just as reinforcements were on their way. But the second occupation was also short (November 1699–March 1700) and ignominious, ending with capitulation to the besieging Spaniards. The English, or more correctly Dutch William (for without orders for an embargo the English in the Americas would clearly have welcomed the Scots), were duly blamed for the whole fiasco. But quite apart from the obvious mismanagement of the enterprise, there must be doubt as to whether Darien, previously unoccupied and still surrounded by Spanish settlers, qualified as the virgin territory 'not possest by any European Sovereign' which the Company was alone entitled to settle.

The Company continued for another seven years. Desultory attempts were made to compete in the trade of the East which resulted in the seizure of a Company ship in the Thames and the retaliatory seizure of the *Worcester* at Leith. The *Worcester* belonged not to the old London East India Company but to its new rival, the English East India Company (whose formation had largely contributed to the defection of the Scots Company's London directors). But such niceties were of little account in the acrimonious post-Darien atmosphere. The *Worcester*'s crew was seized, tried for piracy, and convicted, **Captain Thomas Green**, his mate and his gunner being executed. The situation was only defused, and the Company finally wound up, by the **Act of Union** which shrewdly included compensation with interest for all investors. In retrospect the ever plausible Paterson, whose wife had died on the Darien expedition, recalled 'the miscarriage of that design' favourably in that it 'hath contributed to the Union'.

DARLING, Sir Frank Fraser (1903–79)
Ecologist

Although an Englishman by birth, Frank Darling adopted and was adopted by Scotland, a country he described as his 'favourite laboratory' (he also adopted the name 'Fraser', the maiden name of his first wife). A research student at the Institute of Animal Genetics at **Edinburgh University** (1928), he was made Chief Officer of the Imperial Bureau of Animal Genetics in 1930; it was recognition of his abilities as a scientist but not really a post to his liking. Despite his self-confessed 'natural contemplative idleness', he was a prolific, energetic and passionate champion of the 'wholeness and interdependence' of the natural world, who vastly preferred work in the field to work in the office or library. In 1933 he was awarded a **Leverhulme** research fellowship to study **red deer** and, supported by this and subsequent grants from the **Carnegie** and Rockefeller Foundations, he spent the next 15 years studying and writing on deer, sheep, birds, fisheries, **agriculture** and **crofting**. Director of the West Highland Survey from 1944–50 (publishing his definitive *Natural History of the Highlands and Islands* in 1947), he returned to Edinburgh University to become Senior Lecturer in Ecology (1953–8), during which time he advised the Nature Conservancy Council on setting up their red deer research project on the isle of **Rum**. In 1959 he became Vice-President of the World Conservation Foundation based in Washington DC, thereafter travelling 'from Arctic to Tropic', winning international acclaim for his research and for his pioneering work in ecology and conservation. **Reith** Lecturer in 1969, knighted in 1970, he was a Fellow of the **Royal Society of Edinburgh**, a member of the Royal Commission on Environmental Pollution (1970–3) and held honorary degrees from **Glasgow** and **Heriot-Watt Universities**. He died in **Forres**.

DARNAWAY CASTLE, Nr Forres, Moray

Darnaway Forest, once **Comyn** land, was given to **Thomas Randolph** along with the **Earldom of Moray** by **Robert I**. The castle has remained the seat of the Earls of Moray ever since. Rebuilt in 1810, it retains the old banqueting hall with its 15th century open timber roof, 'a specimen almost unique in Scotland' (**MacGibbon and Ross**). Here John Taylor, the 17th century 'water poet' enjoyed four days of 'good cheere in all variety with somewhat more than plentye'. The 'plentye' compared favourably with that at **Castle Grant**, his previous stopover, where dinner had comprised 60 cold platters by way of hors d'oeuvre 'and after that alwayes a banquet'. Darnaway estate has a visitor centre and acres of superb hardwoods. South, where the Findhorn rushes through a gorge, Randolph's Leap commemorates the sort of long-jumping feat usually associated with **Rob Roy MacGregor**. It was probably not attempted by Earl Randolph but by his quarry, Alastair Comyn of nearby Dunphail.

DARNLEY, see STEWART, Henry

DAUNEY, William (1800–43) Lawyer and Musicologist

Dauney was Solicitor General of Guiana (where he died) and author of *Ancient Scottish Melodies* (Edinburgh, 1838). This remarkable book not only contains a transcription of the Skene lute manuscript, well annotated, but a historical introduction which gathers together a vast amount of source material on Scottish music, including many interesting literary references.

DAVACH

This **Gaelic** word meaning a tub or vat was used in **Pictish** (north and east) Scotland to denote a unit of arable land (so comparable to the **ploughgate**). Whether the area thus denoted corresponded to that which a tub of grain would suffice to sow or to that which would yield a tub of grain is uncertain. If, as sometimes inferred, one davach was equivalent to four ploughgates (c400 acres/162ha) it must have meant

the former. On the other hand the overtones of the davach as a form of tribute imply the latter. The davach continued in use as a unit of measurement until the late 18th century in **Invernessshire**.

DAVID I (1084–1153) King

David was the sixth son of **Malcolm III 'Canmore's** second marriage to (**Saint**) **Margaret**, sister of Edgar Atheling. Along with his sister Edith (called Maud, or Matilda, in England) he was sent to England in 1093 and remained for several years at the English court of Henry I. In 1100 Matilda married Henry, and their daughter was the Empress Maud. David's other sister Mary, Countess of Boulogne, was mother of King Stephen's queen (also Maud or Matilda).

On the death of his elder brother **Edgar**, David inherited southern Scotland below the **Forth-Clyde** line, traditionally the portion of the King's heir. However another brother, **Alexander I**, succeeded Edgar and he demurred at this arrangement until David offered to collect his legacy with more knights than Alexander could muster. Henry I had given him the Honour of Huntingdon (manors in 11 counties), married him to the widowed heiress of Northumberland, and made him ruler of Cumbria. Brotherly love rapidly revived.

At Alexander's death in 1124 David needed no borrowed troops (unlike **Duncan II** or Edgar), but brought his own train of knights and clerks to Scotland. He introduced new ideas – trading burghs, silver **coinage**, monasteries of many orders to promote **education** and **agriculture** – but also re-enacted ancient laws and daily gave informal audience to the poor in all the languages of his realm.

He backed his niece, the Empress Maud, against Stephen, and knighted her son at Carlisle. In old age he spent his leisure gardening and grafting apple trees; his was the first garden below **Edinburgh Castle** Rock, and his the **Haddington** orchard that King John (predictably) hacked down in 1215.

He died at Carlisle in May 1153, a year after his son Earl Henry, leaving a peaceful and flourishing country to his eldest grandson **Malcolm IV**.

DAVID II (1324–71) King

David II was the son of **Robert I (the Bruce)** and his queen Elizabeth de Burgh. His marriage to Joan (or Joanna), sister of Edward III of England, took place at **Berwick** on 16 July 1328, when he was four and she seven. Bruce died in 1329 and David was crowned at **Scone** on 24 November 1331, a small sceptre being made for him to hold.

Many whom Bruce had disinherited adhered to **Edward Balliol**, son of the late King **John Balliol**. When Donald **Earl of Mar**, David's guardian, was defeated at **Dupplin Moor**, Balliol was made king. Although defeated at **Annan** by **Sir Archibald Douglas**, Balliol then laid siege to Berwick; Douglas, in trying to relieve the town, was overcome at **Halidon Hill**. David and his queen were kept at **Dumbarton Castle** for safety until arrangements were made for them to go to France. They landed in May 1334, Philip VI receiving them graciously and installing them in Château Gaillard on the Seine.

They returned to Scotland in June 1341 when David

was 17. He adhered to the Franco-Scottish alliance and fought gallantly at the **Battle of Neville's Cross** (1346) until, severely wounded, he was taken prisoner by the English. He remained in captivity in England until 1357 when he was liberated for a ransom of 100,000 merks, to be paid in annual instalments. Some money came from contributions of tax but the greater part was taken from the export duties which trebled in three years.

David ruled with authority and, despite opposition from the nobles, summoned the burgesses to Parliament. Trade increased considerably and Scotland grew in prosperity. The unfavourable opinion of posterity rests largely on his willingness to pursue the idea of a union of the Scottish and English Crowns. It was rejected by the Scottish Parliament and still wins him such pejoratives as 'contemptible' (**Eric Linklater**) and 'deplorable' (**Fitzroy Maclean**). Yet, as noted by Gordon Donaldson, the likelihood of such a union was implicit in his marriage as arranged by his unimpeachable father. Although married a second time (1362) to Margaret Logie née Drummond, he died without a legitimate heir and was succeeded by his nephew, **Robert II the Steward**.

DAVID OF HUNTINGDON (?1144–1219)

The third son of Earl Henry, son of **David I** [see **Malcolm IV**] and the brother of **William the Lion**, David, Earl of Huntingdon and of the Garioch (**Aberdeenshire**), married Maud of Chester, and their (childless) son succeeded to that English earldom. David also left several natural children and three lawful daughters who married **Alan of Galloway**, Robert Bruce and John Hastings, all with descendants who would claim the throne in 1291 [see **The Competitors**].

On William's death, David, a frail old man, supported **Alexander II**'s succession, not appealing to ancient custom which gave him a claim [see **Dalriada**]; some of the 1291 claimants asserted he had thus disqualified his descendants by resigning his own rights.

DAVIDSON, John (1857–1909) Poet

Born at **Barrhead**, **Renfrewshire**, the son of an Evangelical Union minister, Davidson spent some time as a pupil teacher at the Highlanders' Academy in **Greenock**, failed to complete his degree at **Edinburgh University** and taught at schools in **Glasgow**, **Crieff** and **Edinburgh** before moving to London in 1888 to work as a journalist. Having already written four unsuccessful plays and two novels, Davidson had some small success with his collections of poems, In a Music Hall (1891), Fleet Street Eclogues (1893) and Ballads and Songs (1894), but was unable to earn an adequate living, in spite of a grant from the Royal Literary Fund and a Civil List pension. With his wife and two sons he moved out of London in 1897 to live more cheaply first in Sussex and then in Cornwall. Embittered by his lack of success, and mistakenly believing he had cancer, he disappeared in March 1909; six months later his body, with a bullet wound in the skull, was recovered from the sea. A selection of his verse, edited by Maurice Lindsay and with appreciations by T S Eliot and **Hugh MacDiarmid**, was published in London in 1961; another, The Poems of John Davidson, in Edinburgh in 1973 and his biography,

John Davidson: Poet of Armageddon by J Benjamin Townsend in 1961.

DAVIDSON, Randall Thomas (1848–1930)
Archbishop of Canterbury

Edinburgh born, of both **Episcopal** and **Presbyterian** background, Davidson took the Harrow and Oxford route into the Church of England. He progressed from chaplain to his father-in-law **Archbishop Tait**, to Dean of Windsor, via the bishoprics of Rochester and Winchester to be Archbishop of Canterbury from 1903–28. He died as Lord Davidson of Lambeth.

DAVIE, Cedric Thorpe (1913–83) Composer

Born in London, Cedric Thorpe Davie moved to **Glasgow** and studied at the **Royal Scottish Academy**. In 1945 he became Reader and titular Professor of **St Andrews University** Music Department, which he founded and which has since been disbanded. He is best remembered for his music for **Sir David Lindsay**'s Ane Satyre of the Thrie Estaitis (1948) and his arrangements of the music for **Allan Ramsay**'s Gentle Shepherd (1947) and **Burns**'s The Jolly Beggars (1953). These works reflect his abiding interest in the Scottish idiom. He wrote many film scores and incidental music as well as a Symphony in C (1936) and a coronation march 'Royal Mile' (1953).

DEAN CASTLE, Kilmarnock, Ayrshire

Home of the Boyd family from the 14th century until it was seriously damaged by fire in 1735, Dean Castle in **Kilmarnock**'s Dean Park 'was for centuries one of Scotland's most impregnable baronial strongholds' (T Lang). The massive north tower, with vaulted basement, first-floor hall and battlemented parapet walk, was extended in the 15th century by the construction of the detached Palace Range with another great tower and accommodation block, the whole then being surrounded with a courtyard wall. **MacGibbon and Ross** found a strong resemblance between Dean and **Doune Castles**, while the old keep 'strongly recalls that of **Craigmillar**'. The devastating fire of 1735 was followed by the castle's forfeiture to the Crown on the execution of William Boyd, 4th Earl of Kilmarnock in 1746. It stood as an impressive ruin for 150 years until taken over by Lord Howard de Walden in 1905 and substantially restored. It is now open to the public and houses important collections of medieval armour and musical instruments.

DEAN OF LISMORE, Book of the

This is by far the most important manuscript in the history of **Gaelic verse** in Scotland. Without it, we would have lost an illuminating tract of that history. The MS, now in the **National Library of Scotland**, was compiled mainly between 1512–42, by James MacGregor of **Glen Lyon** who held the office of Dean of **Lismore**, but is more intimately associated with **Perthshire**. The collection of verse in the MS has a partial **Campbell** bias, and some input from a prominent **Macnab** gentleman (this being a contiguous Perthshire family), but it also seems to imply a strong connection with the **MacDonalds**, and in particular their professional poets the MacMhuirichs. A possible link here is John MacMhuirich, of that bardic family and himself a poet, since he held ecclesiastical office in the same diocese as MacGregor, and their lives may have overlapped there, at least briefly.

Another interesting overlap can be seen in the MS, which includes some quotations from Scots poetry, various Latin notes, and even a local (**Dunkeld**) shopping list, interspersed with its main business of recording Gaelic poetry. The poetry is written in an orthography that is heavily influenced by the Scots 'notary' style of writing; the conventions of that system are applied, in quasi-phonetic fashion, to Gaelic, although it is quite clear that the Dean and his collaborators were familiar with the orthodox Gaelic conventions. This seems to imply a decision to coalesce conventions (similar to the decision that changed the spelling system of Manx a century later). We see a similar impetus in other documents of the 16th to 18th centuries where, for example, Gaelic personal names and patronymics survive under an orthographic disguise. This orthographic system often makes it difficult to establish an exact Gaelic text, but it also gives valuable clues as to linguistic forms, frequently showing Scottish Gaelic vernacular influence in the literary language of the poetry. **W J Watson** was the first to exploit these opportunities in depth, in his pioneering edition of 1937, *Scottish Verse from the Book of the Dean of Lismore*.

The poetry which is the core of this MS falls into different categories. There is classical verse of Irish provenance (with a good representation of verse by O Dálaigh poets, related to the MacMhuirichs), a significantly early and in some cases distinct corpus of heroic or **ballad** verse on Ossianic and other themes, and, most importantly from a Scottish viewpoint, a selection of Scottish classical Gaelic verse. This last is biased towards Perthshire and **Argyll** verse, with MacGregor poets from Perthshire prominent, and with Campbell and MacDonald professional poets from Argyll. There are occasional outliers eg from **Lewis** and **Badenoch**. In terms of dating, a high proportion of the 88 Scottish poetic items (this total excluding heroic ballads) dates from post-1450, but there are a few earlier items from early in the 15th century, and one from the early years of the 14th.

The collection gives us ample evidence of a network of professional Gaelic poets plying their trade as panegyrists and elegists, with occasional glimpses of them in their admonitory, satirical, and even bawdy roles. We also catch glimpses of amateurs (including women) who had learnt enough of bardic practice to compose poems of courtly love and laments.

For the texts see W J Watson's work referred to above, and Neil Ross's *Heroic Poetry from the Book of the Dean of Lismore* (1939). For further commentary, see W Gillies' 'Courtly and Satiric Poems in the Book of the Dean of Lismore' in *Scottish Studies*, Vol 21 (1977), D S Thomson, *An Introduction to Gaelic Poetry* (1974, 1990) and D S Thomson 'Gaelic Literary Interactions with Scots and English Work: A Survey' in *Scottish Language*, No 5 (Winter 1986).

DEATH

Readers of **Sir Walter Scott**'s novel *The Fair Maid of Perth* will be familiar with his description of the magnificent funeral of a medieval Highland chieftain. Over 300 years later, in the early 18th century, the obsequies of a Highland laird were still extremely impressive. Kinsmen and retainers of the dead chieftain came from near and far to pay their last respects and partake of a feast which went on for several days and nights. Eventually, after copious quantities of **whisky**, claret and other liquors had been consumed, the cortège set out for the kirkyard to the mournful sounds of *piobaireachd* and *coronachs* (dirges).

The Lowland laird was laid to rest with less pomp, but the funeral expenses, which included hefty bills for entertainment, were still formidable, The body was first prepared for burial. This usually entailed half-embalming, after which the corpse was swathed in expensive cere-cloth and placed in the coffin. Until the funeral took place the body was watched over day and night, the watchers being well fortified with food and drink. The actual burial attracted hundreds of beggars and vagrants, clamorous for the alms which were traditionally distributed on these occasions. It was not customary for female mourners to accompany a funeral procession to the graveside; the rules of etiquette also forbade a husband to attend his wife's funeral. One of the strangest Scottish customs relating to funerals of the nobility was the practice of 'tearing' church doors – that is, painting the doors of the local kirk black and decorating them with white or silver tear-shaped drops meant to represent the tears of the mourning family.

At the other end of the social spectrum was the pauper's funeral. The recipient was laid, minus winding sheet, in a makeshift 'kist' (coffin) paid for by the parish, and his mourners – if any – were obliged to perform the obsequies without benefit of cakes and ale. By the late 18th century the undertaker was established as funeral director, and expensive funeral trappings, hitherto the privilege of the rich, were available for hire; coffin palls of various qualities could be obtained on loan from mort-cloth societies. An 18th century hearse, purchased in 1787 by the parish of Bolton near **Haddington**, is preserved in the **Royal Museum** in **Edinburgh**. The wooden body, a 'new fashionable' model, was fitted to a much older undercarriage, and the Bolton hearse may in fact be the oldest surviving road vehicle in Scotland. The undercarriage is fitted with straked iron tyres and the hearse body is embellished with *memento mori* such as death's heads and winged hourglasses.

In Victorian Scotland, funeral practices were generally less ostentatious than those of England – mutes, for example, were regarded as an unnecessary extravagance and were also considered to be in bad taste. Nevertheless many trades and professions became involved in the 'celebration of death' and the mourning department was an integral feature of the great Victorian drapery emporium; of the leading **Glasgow** firm of Copland & Rye, **Sauchiehall Street**, it was observed that 'the imperative necessities imposed by family bereavement are catered for ... with a certainty and expedition beyond all praise.'

In 18th century Scotland only the wealthier classes had been assured of a solemn and dignified burial, but by the second half of the 19th century, by joining a burial society and keeping up payments, a person of relatively modest means could expect to make his last journey in style. He could also expect to end up in one of the new hygienic Victorian cemeteries, park-like creations that were an enormous improvement on the old intramural graveyards. The Glasgow **Necropolis** differed from many other Scottish cemeteries in being established not by a joint-stock company, but by a merchants' incorporation and benevolent association.

Notwithstanding the popularity and success of the Victorian ornamental cemeteries established by private enterprise, many old and grossly congested burial grounds remained in use until the 1860s and beyond. The Burial Grounds (Scotland) Act of 1855 empowered local authorities to acquire land for burial purposes, by compulsory purchase if necessary, to lay out cemeteries, and to purchase existing privately-owned cemeteries if the need arose, while under the provisions of the Nuisance Removal (Scotland) Act of 1856 and the Public Health (Scotland) Act of 1867 town councils were able to take steps to secure the closure of overused burial grounds.

In the palmy days of burial reform, privately-owned cemeteries flourished, but over the years, with most of the lairs disposed of and with expenditure on the laid-out portions of the cemeteries increasing, they gradually ceased to be paying concerns. After World War I many Scottish cemetery companies were operating at a loss, their shares valueless.

Until the end of the 19th century Victorian religious fundamentalism was a formidable obstacle in the path of those pioneers who advocated a revival of the ancient practice of cremation. Glasgow's first crematorium was sponsored by the Scottish Burial Reform and Cremation Society Limited. Designed by James Chalmers, it was erected in the grounds of the city's Western Necropolis at **Maryhill**, and the first cremation took place there on 17 April 1895.

DEE, River, Aberdeenshire/Kincardineshire

Scotland's fifth longest river (85 miles), the Dee has the highest source and straightest course. With few tributaries of note it is comparatively shallow and fast-flowing, invariably rock-strewn, delightful to the eye and exceptionally attractive to salmon and those who fish for them. Add to this the stately policies of **birch** and conifer, the numerous castles and royal connections of Deeside, and it is small wonder that the Dee calls forth the superlatives. 'If a river flows in Paradise,' wrote the angling expert W B Currie, 'it must surely be the Dee.'

It rises at the Wells of Dee (c4000ft/1200m) in the **Cairngorms** between Braeriach, Cairn Toul and Ben Macdui and at first tumbles precipitously south, losing 2000ft (600m) before turning east into the trench, gouged by some Ice Age glacier, that is Glen Dee. At Linn of Dee, more a narrow rock channel than a fall, it is met by the first road, with a bridge opened by **Queen Victoria**. From here to the Muir of **Dinnet**, where the glacier terminated, the river is at its grandest as it races past **Mar** Lodge, Inverey, **Braemar** (where it is joined by the Clunie), under **Caulfeild**'s Invercauld Bridge (1753) and on to **Balmoral**, and **Ballater**'s Royal Bridge (near where the Muick and Gairn join). At the Muir of Dinnet its waters slow and the hills withdraw as the river enters a more lowland and pastoral setting.

To the south, in place of **Lochnagar**, rises the high ground of the Mounth. **Cromar** and **Aboyne**, **Midmar** and **Banchory** give way to **Aberdeen**'s overspill at **Peterculter**. The river enters the sea at Footdee just south of **Aberdeen harbour** from which it was diverted in the 19th century. The last bridge, appropriately for a river that owes so much to her royal patronage, is Victoria Bridge.

DEER, Book of

The 6th century Celtic monastic foundation at **Deer** in **Aberdeenshire** is now remembered for the Book of Deer. The main text of the book is in Latin, and the MS is probably of the 9th century; it has an Old Gaelic colophon, asking for the blessing of those who read it 'on the soul of the poor wretch who has written it'. The MS came into the possession of Cambridge University Library in 1715.

Its importance, however, lies in a set of Gaelic notitiae, written on margins and blank spaces, by five separate hands. It is thought that these were written into the book between 1131 and 1153, but some, especially notes of grants of land, may be copies of earlier grants, or the written forms of orally remembered grants. These notes constitute the earliest surviving examples of continuous Gaelic prose in Scottish manuscripts, and, although the language is basically the literary language common to Scotland and Ireland (a little roughly written, as though by individuals not thoroughly practised in writing), it also shows signs of Scottish vernacular usages already asserting themselves (eg early Scottish-type nasalation).

The notes contain references to various people known from other historical sources, from kings to abbots and more local landowners, such as Mataidín the judge (*brithem*) and Domongart the lector (*fer léginn*) of **Turriff**, the latter reference implying that there was a Celtic monastery at Turriff. These notes also provide useful early evidence of place-names, some including the **Pictish** element *pett*.

For texts and language, see John Fraser, 'The Gaelic Notitiae in the Book of Deer' in *Scottish Gaelic Studies* Vol 5 (1938) and K H Jackson, *The Gaelic Notes in the Book of Deer* (1972).

DEER, Red, Roe and Sika

Red Deer

Although found on open moorland, the indigenous red deer (*Cervus elaphus*) was a woodland animal until the clearance of the forests that once covered most of northern Scotland. Even now, when it can gain access, the red deer will live in woodland – these sylvan dwellers being generally darker and heavier than their moorland counterparts. In summer they often graze or lie upon open hillsides and hill tops where the air is cooler and the insects fewer. In winter they keep to the low ground and at night will graze at the roadsides or on croft land and crops. Deer damage to trees is a major problem and nearly always means extensive and expensive fencing.

Red deer occur throughout Scotland and have been re-introduced to some islands, such as **Rum** and **Raasay**, but the largest numbers are in the Highlands. They will often swim some distance out to freshwater islands where the vegetation – ungrazed by sheep – is lush. Annual census work by the Red Deer Commission had indicated that the country could support 150,000 red deer, but by 1989 the population was over 300,000 with the result that both deer and **agriculture**, including **forestry**, suffered. The reason for the population explosion was a series of mild winters and too few hinds being culled as venison prices fell. Lack of public interest in venison in Britain means that 80% of the meat is exported to Germany.

Stags and hinds live apart for most of the year, with hind herds sometimes numbering several hundred beasts. The rutting season is in September and October; the stags repeatedly wallow in **peat** bogs either to make themselves look more aggressive or to cool them down; and although legend would have stags fighting to the death this rarely happens – most confrontations are settled simply by roaring. The calves are born in the latter half of May and in June with most being born in the second week of June. The stags cast their antlers in March – the larger antlers are cast first – and are regrown again for the rut. The cast antlers are chewed by both stags and hinds to regain some of the lost calcium. Antlers may seem necessary to determine the most successful breeding males, but stags with no antlers – 'hummels' – may win most hinds in the rut because they are generally heavier and in better physical condition.

Roe Deer

Although found in woodland of all types, the indigenous roe deer (*Capreolus capreolus*) prefer dense woodland with grassland nearby for grazing. They are most often seen in the first and last hour of daylight grazing along woodland margins or in rides and glades. Although difficult to census there is some evidence that their numbers are increasing; already present over almost all of the mainland counties of Scotland, their absence from parts of **Sutherland** and **Caithness** is likely to change as the new forestry plantations, mainly of conifers, grow towards the thicket stage. Pressure of numbers in some areas has led to more sightings of these shy creatures on open moorland; one population exists near the top of the **Drumochter Pass** at around 1400ft (427m). Elsewhere they have colonised a marine island three quarters of a mile off-shore near **Lochinver**. Single animals visited the island in the early 1970s and they stayed all year round and bred.

The seasonal behaviour pattern in roe deer is more complicated than with red deer, but at all times there are only likely to be two or three deer together. The rutting season is in late July to mid-August and the buck's antlers are cast in November, to be grown again by March. The antlers are small but sharp and this, combined with the agility of such a small deer, means that roe are seldom kept in deer parks as they can be dangerous. They also have the reputation of being able to get through any fence.

The does are unusual in that delayed implantation takes place: after fertilisation, the blastocyst increases slightly in size but remains free in the uterus from August to late December when implantation occurs; the kids – often twins – are born in May.

Sika Deer

Sometimes called 'Japanese deer', sika deer (*Cervus nippon*) are only slightly larger than roe deer and their reddish-brown coats are spotted during the summer. Almost exclusively woodland animals, but only where there is sufficient cover such as hazel thickets, bramble and **bracken**, they often go unnoticed because of their habit of staying motionless until danger passes. During hours of darkness they will leave the tree cover to feed and browse in glades, rides and open ground. This daily pattern means that they are very difficult to count, and although their distribution is known their numbers have not been estimated.

Stags and hinds are in separate groups in February and March, but then the stags may stay singly until the rut in October and November during which time they wallow in mud and peat bogs in the same way as red deer. During the rut the sika stag's call is a penetrating whistle that is most eerie when coming from dense cover. The calves are born in June and July during which time the stag is growing new antlers.

The feral populations are either from deliberate introductions or escapes from deer parks; since 1970 their numbers have increased and spread mainly due to the increase in forestry plantations. In the mid-1980s a small number of hybrids with red deer were found, and this gave rise to a false assumption that true red deer would be threatened throughout their mainland range.

DEER ABBEY, Aberdeenshire

St Drostan, a **Pict** but a missionary of the **Celtic Church**, is supposed to have reached **Buchan** from **Caithness** c520. Landing in Aberdour (west of **Rosehearty** where there is a St Drostan's Well), he travelled inland to Deer and there founded the monastery in which, c800, the **Book of Deer** was transcribed and illuminated. The exact site of this Celtic foundation was probably other than the sheltered spot chosen for its successor, the Cistercian Abbey of St Mary founded by William Comyn, Earl of Buchan, in 1219. Sadly the remains of the latter are scarcely more informative than its scant documentation. It was evidently a satellite of **Kinloss** Abbey, but in the 16th century its complement of monks seems rarely to have exceeded 12 and it decayed rapidly after the **Reformation**. Not till 1809 was the process temporarily arrested when Sir James Ferguson of Pitfour, a noted patron and improver, took steps to preserve the ruins and landscape the site. 45 years later a descendant, Admiral Ferguson, lit on the idea of converting the place into his personal mausoleum using as building material what remained of the abbey. The Catholic Church regained control in 1930, demolished the mausoleum (only its neo-classical gateway remains) and placed the surviving ruins in state control. Substantial sections of the conventual buildings may be seen, but of the abbey church only its foundations. It was evidently cruciform with a pillared north aisle. The setting, as in a walled garden sloping down to the South Ugie, is particularly charming.

The 1711 'Rabbling of Deer' refers not to monastic depredations but to the climax of a long-running feud between the **Episcopalians** and **Presbyterians** of Old Deer. Encouraged by Episcopalian and **Jacobite** patrons, a mob attacked the presbytery which had assembled for the induction of a new minister. The Presbyterians were routed.

DEER FORESTS

Any sizeable tract of land primarily or partly reserved for **deer stalking** qualifies as a deer forest. But the phrase is misleading in that Highland deer forests have practically no trees – and, in the case of at least one Hebridean deer forest, practically no deer. Others, indeed most, have too many deer. The deer are in fact more plentiful than the trees. Their grazing habits would ensure that things stayed that way were it not for man-made afforestation. Now the **red deer**, having adapted from life in the dappled **Caledonian Forest** to survival on the bare hill, is obligingly readapting to the forest, or rather to the dark canyons of the sitka spruce sierras.

It would be wrong, though, to assume from this that because most Highland deer forests were once forested, the term 'deer forest' originally assumed the presence of trees. Seemingly even in the Middle Ages ' "forest" was a legal and recreational term rather than an ecological one' (A A M Duncan). It denoted marginal land that was grazed little if at all by livestock and could therefore be reserved for hunting, an activity of some economic value, however exclusive. The draconian forest laws typical in England were not replicated in Scotland and perhaps because there was less pressure on land there was less conflict between **agriculture** and sport. This has remained the case. The mid-19th century designation of large tracts of the Highlands as deer forest displaced few tenant farmers (unlike the earlier introduction of sheep ranching) and few sheep. Ironically in most deer forests it is sheep, not deer or trees, that predominate.

DEER STALKING

The practice of stalking **deer** in the Scottish Highlands grew up during the 19th century, when lairds realised how exciting it was to use the primeval skills of covert approach and stealthy movement to come within 100 yards or less of an exceedingly vigilant quarry. Until then deer had been taken by various forms of encirclement, notably the *tinchels*, in which a large number of men formed a ring and drove the deer inwards, either through a pass where riflemen were posted, or into a system of walls and fences which funnelled into a high-sided enclosure known as an *elrig*.

It was not until the early 1800s, however, that stalking began to attract the attention of shooting men south of the border. After pioneer visits from enthusiasts such as the eccentric Yorkshire squire Colonel Thomas Thornton (*A Sporting Tour through the Northern Parts of England and Great Part of the Highlands of Scotland*, 1803) word spread that an outlandish new form of amusement was available in the far north. Highland lairds started to offer their shooting – among them the Duke of Gordon, who first advertised the **Cairngorm** forest of Glenfeshie in 1812 – and a trickle of English riflemen headed for the hills.

Over the next 50 years that trickle became a flood, and the creation of new **deer forests** began in earnest during the 1830s. By then many of the glens had already been emptied by the **clearances**, the people being driven out to make way for sheep; and although some

humans undoubtedly were shifted to clear the ground for deer, it was **agriculture**, rather than sport, that led to most of the evictions.

The southerners poured immense amounts of money into their newly-discovered playground. They built grandiose lodges and smaller bothies, threw bridges over rivers, drove roads deep into the hills, engineered pony-paths and erected march-fences to separate one forest from another, even over the most precipitous slopes, the metal posts often being drilled and leaded into living rock. The result was to freeze a very large area in a state of dereliction – a state which it retains to this day.

The craze for the Highlands grew rapidly, fanned by **Queen Victoria** and Prince Albert, who, after a couple of sighting shots elsewhere, took a long lease on the **Balmoral** estate in 1848 and formed the habit of going there every autumn. Other eager practitioners included the painter Edwin Landseer, who stalked in many forests but in none more keenly than Glenfeshie, whither he pursued his lover Georgiana, Duchess of Bedford. Another influential advocate was William Scrope, who took Bruar Lodge from the **Duke of Atholl**, fell in love with it, stalked there for 10 years, and in 1838 published *The Art of Deer-Stalking* – the first detailed exposition of the subject which has since become a classic. In the same category is *Natural History and Sport in Moray* by Charles St John, the hunter-naturalist whose book describes, among many other adventures, his epic pursuit of the Muckle Hart of Benmore.

As with other species, organised pursuit of the deer paradoxically increased their chances of survival. With much of the human population removed, and poaching for the pot greatly reduced, numbers steadily increased; owners of newly-created forests found that if they left an area quiet, deer would soon colonise it. By the end of the century some 7½ million acres (3 million hectares) were reckoned to be deer ground.

The growth of the new sport produced a fresh breed of hill man – the professional stalker, or gamekeeper, who looked after the forest all year round, and in the autumn led his absentee owner, or his guests, up to the deer. In the early days deerhounds were much used as a back-up to the primitive rifle, which was liable to wound as many beasts as it killed outright: when a stag or hind was hit but not disabled, powerful dogs would be loosed to run it down and bring it to bay. As weapons became more accurate, however, the use of hounds gradually died out. The introduction of telescopic sights, in the 1880s, was at first derided as contemptible and profoundly unsporting; but later common sense prevailed.

In the second half of the 20th century the ponies which traditionally carried dead beasts off the hill gradually gave way to all-terrain vehicles; yet the stalker's ambition remains what it has always been: to approach (if possible) within 100 yards of his quarry and to kill it cleanly with a single shot.

Today the deer face competition from many quarters: hikers, climbers and skiers invade their ground in ever greater numbers, new **forestry** plantations deny them the warmer low ground, and poaching is rife, as is semi-legal shooting by crofters who kill animals who come down to their farms. Nevertheless, deer and deer

A Glen Etive stag brought from the hill by a Highland pony (GWWA)

stalking both flourish. Demand for forests, and for rented stalking, is as keen as ever, both from within Britain and from abroad; and winter counts taken by the Red Deer Commission (founded 1959) show that the total of the Highland herd has risen to its greatest-ever figure of some 300,000.

DEIRDRE OF THE SORROWS (fl.1st century AD?) Legendary Heroine

Though much cherished, the numerous versions of Deirdre's story scarcely agree. Born possibly in Ireland but probably in Scotland (NicCruithnigh, her patronymic, is thought to imply royal **Pictish** descent), she was early betrothed to a King Conchobar of Ulster. During an idyllic childhood in **Argyll** (usually **Loch Etive**, sometimes Glendaruel or Benderloch) she became fast friends with the three sons of Uisneach. One, Naoise, was especially attentive, rendering to her fin, feather and fur in abundance. But the summons to her Ulster nuptials turned joy to sorrow. Although Naoise and his brothers were eventually allowed to acccompany her, the parting from Argyll and childhood prompted the moving verses of 'A Farewell to Alban', in which homesickness was heightened by foreboding. In Ireland, unable to deny her love for Naoise, she alienated her betrothed who then had the sons of Uisneach slain. Deirdre, dying of a broken heart, finally rejoined them in a common grave. Versions of the story, sometimes called the Lay of Deirdre, are found in numerous Gaelic sources including the Book of Leinster, the **Book of the Dean of Lismore**, and the Glenmason MS. It also forms the basis of **James Macpherson**'s 'Darthala'. The genuine Scottish Gaelic tradition was garnered in the **ballads** and published by **J F Campbell** in *Leabhar na Feinne* (1872) and in *Deirdre and the Lay of the Children of Uisne* collected by **Alexander Carmichael** in **Barra** (1904).

DELGATTY (DELGATIE) CASTLE, Nr Turriff, Aberdeenshire

Long and still the home of members of the Hay family (**Earls of Errol**), Delgatty is as interesting inside as out. Painted ceilings and beams have been uncovered and there is some fine ribbed groin-vaulting. Inscriptions of old proverbs evidently come from a book of 1567 and include the fireplace legend 'My hoyp is in ye Lord, 1570'. But

Delgatty Castle from the south-east (MR)

Queen Mary spent three nights here after **Corrichie** (1562), so the building, or parts of it, must be earlier. It is known to have been besieged and burnt by **James VI** in 1594 and to have been rebuilt in 1597. The wing which makes it an L-plan is 17th century. Expert opinion detects many similarities with nearby **Towie Barclay**.

DESKFORD, Banffshire

Inland from **Cullen**, Deskford was once the seat of the Ogilvies of Findlater who became Lords of Deskford (1616), Earls of Findlater (1638) and Earls of Seafield (1701). Their 15th century Deskford Tower, like Findlater Castle on the coast, is worse than ruined but in the shell of Deskford Church an ornate aumbry (recess for holding the sacrament) has been preserved. The inscription dates the work to 'the zeir of God 1551' and identifies its builder as Alexander Ogilvy 'of zat ilk' and his wife Elizabeth Gordon, both of whom are buried in Cullen church. The relief carving of angels holding a monstrance, scroll and vines is exceptionally fine.

DEVERON, River, Banffshire/Aberdeenshire

This is one of Scotland's 10 longest rivers (82 miles); but it is notably shyer than any of the others. No major cities flank its course; no artistocratic mystique clings to its banks; no unmissable visitor attractions crowd its vicinity; and no clichéd verses sing its praises. Its charm is essentially elusive. Rising on the slopes of **The Cabrach** (just in **Banffshire**), the Deveron (*dubh-aran* – 'black water', which is what it is indeed called in its upper reaches) flows alternately north, then east, then north, then east as if undecided whether to disgorge into the North Sea or the Moray Firth. It may once have preferred the latter and have followed the course of the Ythan, but in recorded ages it has always opted for the Firth and an estuary between **Banff** and **MacDuff**. These uncertainties also take it back and forth between Banffshire and **Aberdeenshire**. Its main tributaries are the Bogie at **Huntly**, the Isla from **Keith**, and the Idoch at **Turriff**. In 1924 the Deveron yielded one of the largest salmon landed in Scotland, a fish of 61lbs (27.6kg). The Mrs Morrison who caught it might have quibbled with the Deveron's classification as 'a first-class, second-class salmon river'.

DEVIL'S BEEF TUB, The, Dumfriesshire

This is a deep semi-circular hollow at the head of Annandale north of **Moffat**. The name is said to derive from its immemorial use as a reiver's holding place, the 'beef' being stolen cattle and 'the devil' invariably a Johnstone. A stone commemorates John Hunter, a **Covenanter** shot in 1685; and **Sir Walter Scott**'s *Redgauntlet* retells the story of the **Jacobite** who is said to have eluded capture by leaping into the mist-filled 'blackguard-looking abyss' in 1746. Further up the pass over to Tweeddale a cairn and plaque record the death in 1831 of 'James McGeorge, Guard, and John Goodfellow, Driver' of the **Edinburgh** to **Dumfries** mail coach which was lost in a blizzard.

DEVIL'S ELBOW, The, Perthshire/Aberdeenshire

Between **Glenshee** and **Braemar** the A93 road, roughly following the military road built by **Caulfeild** in the 1750s, climbs to 2199ft (670m), making it the highest trunk road in Britain. A sharp bend on the ascent from Glenshee constituted the 'Devil's Elbow' but this was amputated in the 1960s when the road was realigned and upgraded. The pass is now usually known as Cairnwell after the hill (3090ft/941m) to the west, and the ski slopes, with chair-lift and tows, as Glenshee.

DEVIL'S STAIRCASE, The, Glencoe, Argyll

Not to be confused with the **Devil's Elbow** (**Perthshire**), his **Beef Tub** (**Dumfriesshire**), nor his Cauldrons (**Bute** and Perthshire), the Devil's Staircase is the somewhat zigzag track which climbs from Allt na Feadh near the head of **Glencoe** and then descends to **Kinlochleven**. Once a **drove road**, then a **military road**, it is now part of the West Highland Way.

DEWAR, James (1842–1923) Industrial Chemist

Born at **Kincardine on Forth**, Dewar was successively a student and a lecturer at **Edinburgh University** before heading south and experimenting on the low temperature liquification of gases, including oxygen, nitrogen and hydrogen. In 1872 he produced the forerunner of the thermos flask. Described as 'a superb experimentalist', he developed cordite with Frederick Abel.

DEWAR, John (d.1872) Gaelic Folklorist

Originally a woodman in the employ of the **Duke of Argyll**, Dewar had become interested in collecting and writing down Gaelic folktales, and was in correspondence with **J F Campbell** as early as 1859. Encouraged both by Argyll and by J F Campbell, Dewar made a very large collection of tales. A selection, in English translation, was published in John Mackechnie, *The Dewar MSS* (1964).

DEWAR, John Alexander, Lord Forteviot (1856–1929) Distiller

Dewar was born in **Perth** and educated at the local Academy. With his brother Thomas he succeeded in transforming his father's modest family retail firm into one of the 'big three' of the **whisky** industry with a product which became a household name. John's contribution to financial matters was matched by Tommy's outgoing marketing skills. Merger with Buchanans was followed by the tripartite union which created Distillers Company Ltd in 1925. Both John and Tommy joined the board of the new company. Elected Liberal MP for **Inverness-shire** (1900–16), he was raised to the peerage in 1916 and thus became the first of the 'whisky barons'. His native city benefited from a range of philanthropic endeavours funded out of his huge personal fortune.

DICK, Sir William of Braid (1580–1655) 'The Scots Croesus'

A customs-and-excise farmer who became Lord Provost of **Edinburgh** (1638, 1639), William Dick was reputed to be the city's richest merchant [but see also **George Heriot**]. In 1639 he lent a fortune (variously estimated at £200,000 and £500,000) to the **Covenanting** army to fund **Montrose**'s campaign. The loan was never repaid and Dick died a pauper.

DICKSON, Maggie (fl.1728)
A fishwife hanged in **Edinburgh**'s **Grassmarket** in 1728 for concealing the death of her illegitimate baby, Maggie Dickson's coffin was being transported back for burial in **Musselburgh** when her attendants heard noises from within. The coffin was hastily opened, a stiff dram administered to the supposed corpse, and Maggie revived. Since it was deemed impossible to hang someone who had already been officially pronounced dead, she was allowed to go free. 'Half hangit Maggie', as she was thereafter affectionately known, became the mother of several more children before finally dying in her bed of old age.

DINGWALL, Ross & Cromarty
The county town when there was a county, Dingwall stands where the river Peffer debouches into the Cromarty Firth and near the mouth of the river Conon. **MacBeth** is said to have been born here but the name is Norse *Thing Vollr*, 'the field of the Thing [Parliament]', it replaced the older 'Inverpeffery' or 'Innerfeoran'. The castle, of which nothing remains save the designation of Castle Street, is credited to **William the Lion** and became the hereditary home of the **Earls of Ross** in the 13th and 14th centuries. The once important harbour has also disappeared, choked by mud flats. The Town House and Tolbooth tower date from the early 18th century but include older work; a worn mercat cross stands outside. The parish church of St Clement (1801) is more notable for the **Pictish** symbol stone in the churchyard and the obelisk to **George Mackenzie, 1st Earl of Cromartie**, in the car park. A mightier funerary monument, indeed a lofty tower, is that soaring from the Mitchell Hill cemetery in memory of **General Sir Hector Archibald MacDonald** (1853–1903), 'Fighting Mac' of the Second Afghan War, Mujaba, Omdurman, Kimberley, etc, whose suicide following a scurrilous attack prompted widespread sympathy and the erection of this defiant monument. At Conon Bridge to the south **Telford** built (1809) a five-arched bridge of which the toll house remains. The bridge was replaced by a structure more suited to the traffic of the main A9 to the north, itself (to Dingwall's considerable relief) now redirected across the Cromarty Firth to the east of the town.

DINNET, Aberdeenshire
A Deeside village between **Aboyne** and **Ballater**, Dinnet has a **National Nature Reserve** embracing lochs Kinord and Davan and the Muir of Dinnet. In Kinord is one of the few **crannogs** in Grampian and on another island the remains of a castle supposedly built by **Malcolm III 'Canmore'**, occupied by **James IV** but demolished during the **Covenanting** wars. Nearby Sir Alexander Ogston, physician to **Queen Victoria**, charted two 1st millennium BC agricultural settlements with stone dwellings, stock enclosures and souterrains. A well-preserved cross-slab of the 9th century AD stands near its original position and a granite obelisk of more recent provenance commemorates the Battle of Culblean (1335). On Culblean Hill, north of Cambus o'May village, **Sir Andrew de Moray** [see **Murray**] with the **Earl of March** and **William Douglas** (Knight of Liddesdale) surprised and overran the forces of David of

Strathbogie, Earl of Atholl, who was besieging **Kildrummy** on behalf of Edward III of England and **Edward Balliol**.

DIRLETON CASTLE, Nr North Berwick, East Lothian
Though a medieval castle of enceinte like **Tantallon**, Dirleton could hardly provide a greater contrast. While the former retains its original design and its wild aspect, Dirleton, its **North Berwick** neighbour, has been so often rebuilt that only the stumps of three towers clustered at its south-east extremity give any impression of its 13th century provenance. Standing on a platform of natural rock its once commanding walls are dwarfed by fine trees and mellowed by stylish gardens. Flanking an equally peaceful village green, the whole now provides a suitably hoary centrepiece for what has been called the 'prettiest village in Scotland'. The original castle, including a massive but truncated round tower, was constructed by the de Vaux family, Anglo-Norman favourites of **William the Lion** and **Alexander II**; subsequent additions were the work of the Halyburtons (mid-14th till early 16th centuries), and then the Ruthvens, later **Earls of Gowrie**. Robert Logan of **Restalrig** is said to have demanded Dirleton as his price for joining the **Gowrie Conspiracy** (1600); 50 years later what Logan had described as 'the pleasantest dwelling in Scotland' suffered the same fate as Tantallon when pounded into ruins by **General Monk**'s artillery.

DISARMING ACTS (1716, 1725 and 1747)
Passed by the Westminster government in the aftermath of the 1715 **Jacobite Rising**, the first Disarming Act (1716) imposed fines for possessing arms and invited their surrender. The results were entirely predictable: while the law-abiding **Whig** clans did surrender their weapons, **General Wade** discovered that the Jacobites were importing 'great quantities of broken and useless Arms from Holland and delivering them up to the Persons appointed to receive them'. A second, more effective, Disarming Act was therefore passed in 1725 permitting search and seizure of weapons, while a rigorously enforced third Disarming Act was passed with the **Act of Proscription** in 1747.

DISRUPTION, The (1843)
The national Church in Scotland has at intervals conflicted with authority, both ecclesiastical and political. The authority of Rome was disputed to bring about the **Reformation** of 1560. The authority of the King and of the episcopacy in relation to the **General Assembly** produced **Melville**'s challenge. The ultimate triumph of **Presbyterian** Church government by 1690 divided the Church between the established **Church of Scotland** and a disestablished **Episcopal Church of Scotland**. The 18th century saw **Erskine** dissent resulting in the **Secession Church** and many minor divisions that followed afterwards.

The ultimate split in the established Church itself was as decisive perhaps as the Reformation and as long in coming to a head. The crux of the matter was the establishment which, by the Patronage Act of 1712, gave a local laird the right as patron to appoint the minister of the parish, regardless of the wishes of the congregation,

Dirleton Castle festooned with vegetation in the 1840s (entry p237) (RWB)

which the civil courts could enforce. The Moderates had been content to accept this imposition by the civil power. They were opposed by the rising Evangelical party at the end of the century.

A Ten Years' Conflict resulted in 1843 in the dramatic walk-out of about 190 clergy from the General Assembly of 18 May in **Edinburgh** and a subsequent alternative **Free Church of Scotland**. The same day, its first assembly elected **Thomas Chalmers** as Moderator and those present signed away their parish rights, manses and glebes. Eventually a third of the ministers, 474 out of 1203, set up churches supported by grassroots members able for the first time since a brief period in the 17th century to choose their own clergymen.

Without the financial support of heritors' revenue for a salary and property for worship, the congregations put up a Sustenation Fund, based on a levy of one penny per week from each member, organised by Chalmers. In even small communities it resulted in a second church where one had sufficed, and that peculiarly Scottish proliferation of church buildings.

It had taken the 1832 Reform Act and then the Evangelicals 1834 Veto Act (allowing objection of a patron's choice) to provoke the **Auchterarder** test case of 1838. This was followed by the refusal of Parliament to accept the grievances set out in the **Claim of Right** adopted by the General Assembly of 1842.

A medal of the time refers to 'the Legislature having failed to protect the Church of Scotland in the exercise of her spiritual privileges, essential to a Church of Christ, from the coercive interference of the civil courts'. The essence, however, was ecclesiastical independence and power rather than spiritual belief.

The Church of Scotland was considerably weakened, both materially and intellectually ('The Free Kirk, the wee kirk, the kirk without the steeple; the auld kirk, the cauld kirk, the kirk without the people'). Alienation within communities polarised congregations but the Disruption, coming at the time of industrial expansion in the cities, also awakened the social and theological conscience of Scotland so that the Victorian era was a high point of active membership of churches and their organisations.

Within 50 years a movement for re-unification began. The splits eventually healed in 1929 with the exception of minority Presbyterian dissent.

DIVERS, Black-Throated, Red-Throated and Great Northern

Black-throated divers (*Gavia arctica*) breed on larger lochs, generally on islands where their eggs are laid in a shallow depression close to the water's edge. The birds shuffle rather than walk as their legs are set so far back on their bodies; thus the proximity of the water enables them to seek safety quickly when disturbed. The breeding distribution is in the north and north-west, mainly in the Highlands, and the birds generally feed on large freshwater lochs. There are not more than 100 breeding pairs and these move to the coast for the winter where there is a strong possibility that they are joined in northern waters by black-throated divers from Scandinavia. In the last few decades breeding success has been very

The 1843 Disruption; a key by D O Hill to a painting of the Free Church's first General Assembly which signed the Act of Separation (SNPG)

poor, mainly because dry springs have encouraged the birds to nest low and near the water and the ensuing series of wet early summers have raised the water levels, flooding out and washing away eggs or young chicks. There has been some success with artificial floating islands that rise and fall with the differing water levels. Other problems include the theft of eggs by crows, otters and even **pine marten** – there is one record of an otter attacking an adult black-throated diver on a loch in **Ross**-shire, and although the otter made off on being disturbed, the diver was later found dead on a nearby shore.

Much smaller lochs are used by the red-throated divers (*Gavia stellata*) – and the smaller catchment areas involved suggest that fluctuating water levels are not so critical for this species. The breeding distribution is similar to that of the black-throated diver, but breeding numbers are far greater – probably around 1200 pairs – with the main concentrations in **Shetland** and **Orkney**, where the black-throated diver does not breed. Occasionally red-throated divers have utilised the artificial floating islands, and they have in the past been persecuted for affecting fish-stocks in the small lochs where they breed, although in fact they will usually fly daily to the sea or to larger lochs to feed.

The great northern diver (*Gavia immer*) very rarely breeds in Scotland although for a few years one paired up with a black-throated diver on a loch in Ross-shire and one egg did hatch, but fledging was not successful. About 2000 of these birds over-winter along the Scottish coast, coming from not only the Iceland and Greenland populations but possibly also the North American.

The white-billed diver (*Gavia adamsii*) is a rare winter and spring visitor and difficult to identify from a distance.

All four divers have figured prominently in Scottish folklore, mainly on account of their unearthly and eerie calls; these are made either when the birds are on the water or in flight, and thought to be an indication of impending bad weather. There were myths too, including the belief that at the creation of the world it was

divers that went beneath the waters to bring up the mud to form the basis of the earth. The folk-names for these birds include 'rain goose', 'northern doucker', 'immer goose' (from the Icelandic *himbrini* – great northern diver) and 'loon' (hence 'The Loons' for an area of moorland and loch on Mainland Orkney where red-throated divers breed).

DOGS
12 breeds of dog are recognised by the Kennel Club as Scottish breeds:

BEARDED COLLIE A breed developed over many centuries but known to have been in existence in Scotland since the 16th century, the Bearded Collie is a close relative of the Old English Sheepdog and looks very similar.

CAIRN TERRIER This small, shaggy and very sturdy terrier has been used for centuries in the hunting of foxes, badgers, rabbits, etc. One of Britain's oldest terrier breeds, it was previously called the Short-Haired Skye Terrier, but to avoid confusion with the Skye Terrier (see below) it was officially registered with the Kennel Club in 1910 as the Cairn Terrier, a name indicative of

Bran, a Celebrated Deerhound, by Thomas Duncan (NGS)

its skill in flushing out its prey from amongst the piled-up stones of cairns.

DANDIE DINMONT TERRIER An old breed of terrier with short, strong legs, a 'long, low, weaselly body' (Kennel Club Standard) and a distinctive top-knot, the Dandie Dinmont is thought to have been bred by gypsies from a combination of Scottish and Skye Terriers, with more than a touch of Otterhound and possibly some Bedlington Terrier blood. It acquired its name, and its fame, from **Sir Walter Scott**'s character Dandie Dinmont in *Guy Mannering* who owned several of these 'mustard and pepper' terriers.

DEERHOUND A breed of great antiquity known to have been used as a hunting dog for nearly 1000 years, the Deerhound (previously officially called the Scottish Deerhound) is still used in hare-coursing as well as being a popular show dog. Tall (the breed standard is 30 inches at the shoulder for a dog and 28 for a bitch) and elegant, with an impressive turn of speed, its rough coat usually dark blue-grey in colour but also lighter grey, brindle, yellow or red, the Deerhound has a reputation as a good-natured dog with a tendency to laziness.

GOLDEN RETRIEVER There are uncertainties over the exact origins of this immensely popular breed, as over many others'. Some authorities trace it back to a golden-coated Russian circus dog, possibly the same breed as that crossed with a Tweed Water Spaniel by a nephew of Lord Tweedsmuir in the 1860s. Black Retriever, Irish Setter and Bloodhound strains were then introduced to produce the Golden Retriever. The breed club was founded in 1913.

GORDON SETTER This breed was developed by Alexander, 4th Duke of Gordon (c1745–1827), amongst whose other claims to fame were his role in the raising of the 100th Highlanders (1794), later renumbered 92nd and renamed **Gordon Highlanders**, and his authorship of the song 'There is Cauld Kail in Aberdeen'. Coal black with chestnut red markings, and heavier in build than either the Irish or the English setter, the Gordon (which is also claimed to be the most intelligent of the three) is an excellent retriever and all-purpose gun dog.

ROUGH COLLIE AND SMOOTH COLLIE Two varieties of the same breed that differ, as their names suggest, only in the length of their coats. They are descended from the working collie of the Scottish shepherd and drover. Show breeding, particularly of the Rough Collie, has produced a somewhat romanticised version of the original.

SCOTTISH TERRIER All the wire-haired terrier breeds of the British Isles – Airedale, Cairn, Skye, Yorkshire, etc – are thought to have evolved from a frequently mentioned but ill-defined 'Scotch' Terrier. Variations on the original led to these individual breeds, but the name 'Scottish Terrier' stayed with the small, square and usually black dog now beloved of whisky advertisers. The well-known 'Scottie', formerly variously known as the

Otter Terrier, the Diehard Terrier and the Aberdeen Terrier, has a rather crabbit reputation, but its many admirers laud its affectionate, cheerful nature and its passionate loyalty to its owner.

SHETLAND SHEEPDOG A miniature version of the Rough Collie (13–16 inches at the shoulder to the Collie's 24–26 inches), the Shetland is probably descended from a mainland collie crossed with a smaller and now unknown breed native to the Shetland Islands.

SKYE TERRIER As the Highland pony is said to have developed from crossing stallions from a wrecked ship of the Spanish Armada with native mares on the island of **Rum**, so the Skye Terrier is said to have developed from dogs of a Maltese breed, from another (or maybe the same) Armada shipwreck, mating with indigenous terriers. Its required appearance is 'long, low and profusely coated, twice as long as high' (Kennel Club Standard). Like the Scottish Terrier, the Skye has a reputation for passionate loyalty, a quality amply demonstrated by the most famous member of the breed, **Greyfriars Bobby**.

WEST HIGHLAND WHITE TERRIER 'It so happened,' asserts an Italian writer on dogs, 'that in the middle of the 19th century a breeder of cairns in the county of **Argyll** in England [sic] got some white pups in his litters.' In fact the white colouring was no accident, Colonel Malcolm of Poltalloch in Argyll (in Scotland) having spent some time and effort on developing a strain of white terriers after shooting one of his brown terriers in mistake for a hare. Known successively as the Poltalloch Terrier, the White Scottish Cairn and the Little Skye Terrier, it was eventually recognised in 1904 as the West Highland White Terrier. The 'Westie' is now one of the most popular breeds of dog in the country and makes an ideal family pet.

DOLLAN, Sir Patrick Joseph (1885–1963)
Lord Provost of Glasgow

Born of Irish Catholic parents at Baillieston, **Lanarkshire**, Pat Dollan followed his father into the **coal**-mines while pursuing literary interests of his own. Reading **Thomas Carlyle** contributed to his political awakening; an essay on **Lord Byron** was amongst his first published works and an anthology of **Robert Burns** amongst his last; contributions to the *Glasgow Evening Times* on mining matters brought him to the attention of **John Wheatley**. Through Wheatley he discovered socialism, joined the **Independent Labour Party** (ILP) and moved to **Glasgow** in the employ of *Forward*, the ILP journal. In 1913, having espoused other causes dear to **Red Clydeside**, such as **temperance**, pacifism and secularism, and having married the redoubtable Agnes Moir, socialist and suffragist, he was elected from **Govan** to the Glasgow Town Council.

Although unlike other Red Clydesiders Dollan showed little interest in Parliament, his role in Glasgow's civic politics was to prove crucial. He formed the first Labour group on the council, which in 1920 won 45 seats, thus anticipating the 'wild Clydesiders'' parliamentary triumph of 1922 which Dollan, as Chairman of the Glasgow ILP, largely engineered. Thanks to his expert management, Labour finally won control of the Glasgow Town Council in 1933 and Dollan became Lord Provost from 1938–41.

Naturally 'the most astute politician on Red Clydeside' had to show some flexibility of principle. As a conscientious objector during World War I he forged close links with the leaders of the **Clyde Workers Committee** and shared their aura of martyrdom when he was imprisoned. These links, vital to the success of the ILP, did not however commit him to Marxist ideology. In the late 1920s he was instrumental in defeating **James Maxton**'s attempt to endorse the Communist Party of Great Britain and in the early 1930s he undermined the latter's move to take the ILP out of the Labour Party when he (Dollan) formed the Scottish Labour Party as an ILP breakaway which duly returned to the Labour fold. Pacificism was discarded when as Lord Provost he enthusiastically supported the new war effort. Secularism ended at about the same time when he reconverted to Catholicism. Any residual radicalism went out the window when he accepted a knighthood in 1941.

As propagandist and political manager he had few equals, but no less important were his achievements in local government. The public ownership of transport was one of his priorities and he later became a director of British European Airways, and an authority on civil aviation. Likewise housing; after decades of neglect Glasgow's housing crisis was finally taken in hand after World War II. Dollan favoured the idea of satellite new towns, and it was as Chairman of one of the New Town Development Companies – **East Kilbride** – that he finally retired from Glasgow politics in 1947.

DOLLAR, Clackmannanshire

Though a Hillfoots village like **Alva**, Dollar owes its celebrity not to textiles but to two buildings – **Castle Campbell** and Dollar Academy. The former, up the Dollar glen in the **Ochils**, proved a mixed blessing, its **Argyll** owners attracting the ravages of **Montrose**'s troops in 1645. The village recovered in the late 18th century, as witnessed by the now ruinous Auld Kirk (1775) and Schoolhouse (1780) and the Burnside area where cottages and houses line both sides of an attractive burn. The Dollar Academy was the result of a bequest of £74,000 by John McNabb (1732–1802), a village lad who had borrowed the price of a ticket to **Leith**, sailed to London and there made a fortune as a ship's captain. What he had in mind was 'a charity school for the poor of the parish', but Dollar and its minister had other ideas – plus a better appreciation of what £74,000 could buy. They commissioned a vast neo-classical educational colony centred on a grandly pillared (Doric) and pedimented block (1818–20) by **William Playfair** that would have graced **Edinburgh**'s **New Town**. The poor of the parish were not excluded but the rich of elsewhere, recognising social as well as educational potential in this majestic setting, soon outnumbered them. Co-educational since its founding, the school is now fee-paying and independent.

'DOLLY THE SHEEP'

A revolutionary ruminant, Dolly the Sheep was the first mammal to be cloned, through 'nuclear transfer', from the cultured cells of an adult animal (a mature ewe), at the Roslin Institute, **Midlothian**, in 1997. Two lambs, Megan and Morag, which were genetic copies, or clones, of a nine-day-old embryo, had been carried to term by a surrogate mother two years earlier. These events heralded numerous possible practical benefits in animal husbandry and medical science – growing 'spare parts' and perhaps even human cloning. Dolly's lamb, Molly, was born in 1999. Also at Roslin Biotechnology Centre is PPL Therapeutics, a pioneer in transgenics using dairy cattle genetically engineered to include human genes; these genes programme the production of human-type proteins in milk for later purification and conversion into various forms of drugs and medicines, eg for the treatment of cystic fibrosis. Roslin's Bio-Med company has been sold to Geron, an American firm intending to use the technology to clone patients' cells for transplantation treatments for diseases like Alzheimer's and diabetes. Roslin lies in a cluster of biotechnological competence unique in Europe – 1200 scientists work within a mile's radius – including **Edinburgh University** Technopole and the Moredun Foundation, a world-leading ruminant research facility, based beside the Central Veterinary Laboratory in the International Research Centre, at Pentlands Scientific Park, **Penicuik**. Moredun and Roslin are jointly promoted by Edinburgh BioParks; products like Omniferon, a purified interferon, manufactured by Viragen, a US pharmaceutical firm involved with Scottish Blood Transfusion Services, are being produced for trial treatments of multiple sclerosis, hepatitis C, HIV and herpes.

DON, George (1764–1814) Botanist

One of Scotland's greatest pioneering botanists and gardeners, George Don possessed a broader knowledge of the native flora of his country than any before and most since. Born in **Angus**, the son of a currier, he followed a natural bent towards mechanics by becoming a clockmaker, but spent all his free time exploring the countryside and made his first botanical collections of flowering plants and mosses while still an apprentice in **Dunblane**. He soon gave up clockmaking to become a gardener, initially at Dupplin Gardens and later in England, continuing all the while to search for native plants and finding many previously unrecorded species.

By 1797 he and his wife Caroline Stewart, whom he had met on a botanical expedition, had saved enough money to take a 99-year lease on two acres of land near **Forfar**, where he established a botanical garden which soon acquired a high reputation amongst British botanists. The combination of his skill as a gardener and his unparalleled knowledge of the plants in their natural habitat enabled him to grow a great variety, particularly of aquatics and alpines, ordering the plants according to the Linnaean system. He made a frugal living by selling specimens to botanists, botanical illustrators and gardeners, but still spent as much time as possible plant-hunting in the **Cairngorms**, Grampians and distant **Knoydart**.

His reputation led him to be appointed Superintendent of the **Botanic Garden** in **Edinburgh** in 1802, but he left after only three years, unsuited to city life and the restrictions of working at the garden. He wrote and contributed to several major botanical works, but ran into severe financial difficulty and died in poverty.

DON, River, Aberdeenshire

After the **Tay**, **Spey**, **Clyde** and **Tweed**, the **Dee** and the Don are Scotland's longest rivers. Both rise in the Grampians, flow east across **Aberdeenshire** and reach the sea at **Aberdeen**. Such parallelism has given rise to fierce championship of their respective merits. 'River Dee for fish and tree/But Don for ham and corn' or 'Ae mile o' Don's worth twa o' Dee/Except for salmon, stone and tree'. The Don's stately meadowed progress is compared to the Dee's rocky Highland urgency. The Don is beneficent and amenable, the Dee snobbish and dangerous: 'Bloodthirsty Dee/Each year needs three [victims];/But bonny Don,/She needs none.'

Rising east of the **Lecht** and very near the Avon tributary of the Spey, the Don is Highland enough as it passes **Corgarff** where an evil **kelpie** once held sway. It then winds towards **Glenbuchat** and **Kildrummy** through Strathdon where at Bellabeg the Lonach **Highland Games** are held. In the Howe of **Alford** it slows, then skirts the south side of **Bennachie** in a gorge known as The Lord's Throat. At **Inverurie** it receives the Urie, its largest tributary, and turns south-east towards **Dyce** and Aberdeen with sufficient fall to serve paper mills and other industrial activities. Finally it plunges into another ravine and under the **Brig o' Balgownie** near **St Machar's Cathedral**, then through the arches of **Bridge of Don** and across the sands to a quiet conclusion two miles north of the busy downtown demise of its sister Dee.

DONALD I (d.862) King of Alba

The son of **Alpin** and brother of **Kenneth I**, Donald was variously called 'of ruddy countenance' and 'wanton son of the foreign woman'. During his short reign (858–62) he apparently introduced **Dalriadic** laws into **Pictland**. He died (of illness) near **Scone**, and was succeeded by Kenneth's son **Constantine I**.

DONALD II (d.900) King of Alba

The first to be actually called *Ri Albain*, 'King of Scotland' rather than 'of **Dalriada**' or 'of **Picts**', Donald II was the son of **Constantine I** (son of **Kenneth I**, mac-**Alpin**). He was called *garbh* (rough) or *dasantach* (furious, or cunning). During his reign (c889–900) Norsemen from **Orkney**, led by **Earl Sigurd the Mighty**, held much of northern Scotland down to **Moray**. King Donald was killed 'by men of the **Mearns**, on the path above **Dunnottar**'. He was the father of **Malcolm I**.

DONALD III, Donald Bane, 'the Fair' (c1031–c1100) King

Son of **Duncan I** and younger brother of **Malcolm III** '**Canmore**', Donald Bane lived in peaceful obscurity in the **Hebrides** during the reigns of **MacBeth** and Malcolm, but emerged to claim the throne when Malcolm and his son Edward were killed on the same day in 1093. Described as 'an old Celtic reactionary', 60-year-old Donald Bane's first move was to expel all the English followers who had crowded the court of Malcolm and his English wife **Margaret**. This move delighted those traditionalists who so resented the increasing Anglicisation of Scotland, but enraged the English King William Rufus who placed an army at the disposal of Duncan, Malcolm Canmore's son by his first marriage. Within a

year Duncan had succeeded in ousting Donald Bane and for six months reigned in his stead as **Duncan II** but the 'old Celt' recovered, killed Duncan and resumed the throne. The odds, however, were against Donald Bane – for Malcolm had four more sons, all but one of whom were happy to accept English support, and Donald Bane was finally captured, blinded and imprisoned by the eldest, **Edgar**, in 1097. He died in prison c1100 and was buried on **Iona**.

DONALD, Clan

The Clan Donald, the largest and most powerful **clan** in the Highlands, claim descent from Conn of the Hundred Battles, High King of Ireland c123–73 AD, and from him through Colla Uais, who settled in the **Hebrides** and died c347 AD, to **Somerled**, King of the Isles and Man who was assassinated at **Renfrew** in 1164 at the instigation of **Malcolm IV**, King of Scots. From Somerled's grandson, Donald of Isla, the Clan Donald chiefs took their patronymic *Mac Dhomhnaill*, ie the Son of Donald, from which the modern clan surname Mac-Donald is derived.

Donald's grandson, Angus Og, supported **Robert I (the Bruce)**, and played an important part at **Bannockburn** (1314) when Bruce is said to have addressed him thus: 'My hope is constant in thee,' still repeated as a motto on the arms of **Clanranald**. For his loyal services, Angus Og received from his grateful monarch vast territories in the west Highlands and Islands. They were further augmented by his son and successor 'Good' John of Isla (so called on account of his benevolence to the Church), who declared himself '**Lord of the Isles**'. Clan lands now stretched from the Butt of **Lewis** in the north to **Islay** in the south with the addition of extensive mainland territories including **Kintyre**, **Morvern**, **Glencoe**, **Lochaber**, **Glengarry**, **Knoydart**, **Morar**, **Arisaig**, **Moidart** and others. Many of these territories had been acquired through John's first marriage to his third cousin Amy, heiress of the MacRuaris of Garmoran and the North Isles. The bulk of the MacRuari inheritance was bestowed on Ranald, the eldest surviving son of this marriage, to be held of Donald (the eldest son of John's second marriage with the Princess Margaret, daughter of **Robert II**). Donald thus became 2nd Lord of the Isles in preference to his elder half-brother Ranald.

Donald fought the **Battle of Harlaw** in 1411 against the Scots government to press his wife's claims to the **Earldom of Ross**. But John, 4th Lord of the Isles, lost the Earldom of Ross in 1475 on account of rebellions against the Scottish Crown, and was finally forfeited in 1493.

Several attempts were made by the Islesmen to restore the Lordship and regain the Earldom of Ross, but these attempts effectively ended with the death of Donald Dubh in 1545. Thereafter the various branches of the Clan Donald, viz. Isla, **Sleat**, Clanranald, Glengarry, **Ardnamurchan**, Keppoch, Glencoe and MacAlister of Loup, operated as independent clans under their respective chiefs.

In 1947 the Lord Lyon recognised Alexander Godfrey Macdonald, 7th Lord Macdonald of Slate, as head of the Name and Arms of MacDonald as MacDonald of MacDonald and therefore High Chief of Clan Donald.

His elder son, Godfrey James MacDonald of Mac-Donald, 8th Lord MacDonald, is the present High Chief.

Gaelic Patronymic: *Mac Dhomhnaill* (MacDonald of Mac-Donald)

Emblem: *Fraoch Gorm* (Purple **heather**)

Crest: On a crest coronet or a hand in armour fess proper, holding a cross-crosslet, fitchy, gules

Mottoes: Above escutcheon '*Per Mare Per Terras*' (By Sea and Land); below escutcheon '*Fraoch Eilean*' (The Heathery Isle)

Tartan: MacDonald (Clan Donald)

The Macdonalds of Sleat

The progenitor of this branch of Clan Donald, known also as the MacDonalds of the Isles and Clan Donald North, was Hugh, third son of Alexander, third Lord of the Isles and Earl of **Ross**, from whom the family takes its Gaelic apellation of *Clann Uisdean*. In 1469 John, 4th Lord of the Isles and Earl of Ross, granted to his brother Hugh the lands of Sleat and Castle of Dunscaith in **Skye** and other lands in **Harris** and **Uist**. After the fall of the Lordship of the Isles, Hugh was confirmed in most of the lands he held by the Crown in 1495. Donald Gallach, 3rd Chief, was murdered by his half-brother, Black Archibald, in 1506; Donald Gorm, 5th Chief, was killed while besieging **Eilean Donan Castle** in 1539; and Donald Gorm Og, 8th Chief, was knighted by **James VI** and in 1625 created a baronet of Nova Scotia. Sir James Mor, 2nd Baronet, joined **James Graham, Marquis of Montrose** in support of **Charles I** and in 1661 received a new charter of his lands from Charles II. Sir Donald, 3rd Baronet, joined **John Graham of Claverhouse, Viscount Dundee**, although ill-health prevented him from leading the clan at **Killiecrankie** (1689). Sir Donald, 4th Baronet, supported the **Earl of Mar** in 1715 for which he was attainted. Sir Alexander, 7th Baronet, though a **Jacobite** at heart, decided not to raise his clan for the **Stewarts** in 1745 and risk a second forfeiture of the family estates. Sir James, 8th Baronet, known as 'The Scottish Marcellus', was one of the greatest scholars of his time.

Sir Alexander, 9th Baronet, who raised the 76th (MacDonald's) Highlanders, was raised to the Irish peerage in 1776, with the title of Baron MacDonald of Slate, County Antrim. On account of the matrimonial complications of his second son Godfrey, later 3rd Lord Mac-Donald, Alexander, the eldest son of the latter was served heir to his maternal uncle, William Bosville of Thorpe and Gunthwaite, while his next brother, God-frey, became 4th Lord and succeeded to the MacDonald estates in the Western Isles. This arrangement was confirmed by Act of Parliament in 1847.

In 1910 the grandson of Alexander Bosville, aforementioned, also named Alexander, brought an action in the **Court of Session** and by a decree of that court it was declared that his grandfather had been the eldest legitimate son of the 3rd Lord – which he was under Scots **law** but not under English or Irish law. The younger Alexander Bosville was thereafter declared by Lyon Court [see **Heraldry**] 14th Baronet and (22nd) Chief of the Family of MacDonald of Sleat. His great-grandson, Sir Ian Godfrey MacDonald, of Thorpe and Upper Duntulm, Skye, is the 17th Baronet and 25th Chief of Sleat (*Clann Uisdean*).

Gaelic Patronymic: *MacDhomhnaill nan Eilean* (MacDonald of the Isles)

Emblem: *Fraoch Gorm* (Purple heather)

Crest: A hand in armour in fess proper, holding a cross-crosslet, fitchy, gules

Motto: '*Per Mare Per Terras*' (By Sea and Land)

Tartan: MacDonald of the Isles and Sleat

The Macdonalds of Clanranald

The progenitor of this branch of Clan Donald was Ranald, eldest surviving son of 'Good' John of Isla, 1st Lord of the Isles and High Chief of Clan Donald, by his first wife Amy MacRuari. In 1571 John bestowed on Ranald the bulk of the former MacRuari lands inherited by Amy, which included Moidart, Arisaig, Morar and Knoydart on the mainland, and **Eigg**, **Rum**, the **Uists**, including **Benbecula**, and **Harris** in the North Isles, with other lands. Ranald died at **Castle Tioram**, Moidart, the family seat, in 1386. He was succeeded by his eldest son, Allan, from whom the patronymic *Mac 'ic Ailein* is derived. Allan, 4th Chief, who 'feared neither man nor God' supported his kinsmen Angus Og and Sir Alexander MacDonald of Lochalsh in their efforts to regain the Earldom of Ross for the family. Dougal, 6th Chief, was killed by his own clansmen for his oppressive rule and his sons excluded from the chiefship. The clan chose as Dougal's successor his uncle, Alexander, as 7th Chief. Alexander assumed the style 'Captain of Clanranald'. He was succeeded by his natural son John Moidartach (ie of Moidart), the popular choice of the clan who was, like his grandfather Allan, 4th Chief, renowned as a leader and warrior. He fought and won the Battle of Kinlochlochy (Blar Leine, or the **Battle of the Shirts**) in 1544, against the **Frasers** in support of his cousin Ranald Galla who, with **Lord Lovat** and the Master of Lovat, was killed. Donald, 11th of Clanranald, was knighted by James VI in 1617. Allan, 14th Chief and Captain of Clanranald, led his clan at Killiecrankie in 1689 when only 16 and fell at **Sheriffmuir** in 1715. He was renowned for his chivalry and hospitality. Ranald, 17th Chief was the first to rise for **Prince Charles Edward Stewart** in 1745. Ranald George, 20th Chief, by his extravagance lost the whole family inheritance. He was succeeded by his son Admiral Sir Reginald Mac-Donald KCB, KCSI, RN, as 21st Chief.

The direct line having been terminated by the death of Angus Roderick MacDonald, 23rd of Clanranald in 1944, the chiefship passed to Ranald Alexander Mac-Donald of **Inchkenneth**, now 24th Chief and Captain of Clanranald.

Gaelic patronymic: *Mac Mhic ('ic) Ailein*

Emblem: *Fraoch Gorm* (Purple heather)

Crest: On a castle, triple-towered, a dexter mailed arm embowed holding a sword proper

Mottoes: Above escutcheon 'My Hope is Constant in Thee'; below escutcheon '*Dh' Aindeoin Co Theireadh E*' (Gainsay Who Dare)

Tartan: MacDonald of Clanranald

The MacDonells of Glengarry

This branch of Clan Donald is descended from Donald, second son of Ranald, progenitor of Clan Ranald, and was also known as the Clan Ranald of Knoydart and Glengarry. The original territory of the clan appears to

243

have been North Morar, to which were added Glengarry and **Glen Quoich** by Alexander, 4th Chief, from whom later chiefs took their patronymic of *Mac 'ic Alasdair*. By his marriage with the co-heiress of Sir Donald Mac-Donald of Lochalsh, Alexander, 6th Chief, acquired half of the lands of Lochalsh, Lochcarron and Lochbroom, with the Castle of Strome, which became the principal seat of the family until its 1602 capture and destruction by the **MacKenzies**. Donald MacAngus, 8th Chief, lived to the age of 102. During his time a prolonged feud with the MacKenzies cost him the Ross-shire lands, but this was compensated by the acquisition in 1611 of Knoydart. Angus, 9th Chief, in recognition of his services to the Stewarts, was ennobled by **Charles II** after the Restoration with the title of Lord MacDonell and Aros, 'confined to the heirs male of his body'. Having no sons, the title became extinct on his death. Alasdair Dubh, 11th Chief, ably led the clan at the Battles of Killiecrankie (1689) and Sheriffmuir (1715). The clan was also raised for Prince Charles Edward in 1745 by Donald MacDonell of Lochgarry, the chief's cousin. Glengarry's second son, Angus, was killed at **Falkirk**, and Invergarry Castle was burnt by Cumberland's troops (1746) although the old chief had not taken part in the rising. Alasdair Ranaldson MacDonell, 15th Chief, a colourful and flamboyant character, raised the Glengarry **Fencibles**, of which he became Colonel. A great friend of **Sir Walter Scott**, he was much in evidence during George IV's visit to **Edinburgh** in 1822 and Scott is said to have used the more favourable features of his character on which to model Fergus MacIvor, the hero of *Waverley*. Due to his extravagant life-style, the family estates had to be sold by his trustees.

On the extinction of the direct line with Charles Ran-aldson MacDonell, 18th of Glengarry, in 1868, the chiefship passed to Aeneas Ranald MacDonell of Scotus, great-grandfather of the present and 22nd Chief, Air Commodore A R Donald MacDonell of Glengarry CB, DFC, who distinguished himself as a Spitfire pilot during World War II.

Gaelic Patronymic: *Mac ('ic) Alasdair*

Emblem: *Fraoch Gorm* (Purple heather)

Crest: A raven proper perched on a rock azure

Mottoes: Above escutcheon *'Creagan an Fhithich'* (The Raven's Rock); below escutcheon *'Per Mare Per Terras'* (By Sea and Land)

Tartan: MacDonell of Glengarry

DONALD BREAC (d.642) King of Scots

Invading Ireland for battle at Magh Rath (Moira) in 636, Donald, 10th King of **Dalriada**, activated **St Columba**'s curse on kings who opposed his own O'Neill kinsmen; to this folly the chroniclers attribute other defeats, culminating at Strathcarron against the **Strathclyde** Britons, where Donald was killed and Dalriada was eclipsed for a generation or more.

DONALD DUBH (c1480–1545)

Grandson of John, 4th and last **Lord of the Isles**, Donald Dubh was born at the **Campbell** stronghold of Innis Chonnell on **Loch Awe** after his father Angus's death. After the forfeiture of the Lordship of the Isles (1493) he was held there but rescued by some MacDonalds of **Glencoe** in 1501. Recaptured in 1506, he was imprisoned in **Edinburgh Castle**. He escaped from there in 1544 and was recognised as Lord of the Isles by all the branches of **Clan Donald**, and by many other clan chieftains. At Knockfergus, in Ireland, he assembled a force of 180 galleys and 4000 fighting men, but while organising an invasion of Scotland he died at Drogheda of a sudden fever; the rebellion then collapsed.

DONALDSON, John (c1790–1865) Composer and Professor of Music

The 1822 *Piano Sonata* was the only composition of Donaldson's ever published, but it is an outstanding work, dramatic, deeply felt and structurally interesting. Although Donaldson was trained and practised as an advocate, he became Reid Professor of Music at **Edinburgh University** in 1845 and had to use all his legal skills to force the university authorities properly to enact the will of **General John Reid**. The music lecture room was provided with an organ and acoustical equipment, and Donaldson's choral rehearsals and lectures were well attended. Separate lectures were given for men and women.

DONN, Rob (Robert Mackay) (1714–78) Gaelic Poet

Rob Donn's poems and songs give detailed insights into the **Sutherland** society of the time. They include satirical and admonitory poems about the 'upper' classes as well as a broad range of poems about people he mixed with, in which he underlines their weaknesses and strengths. Born in **Strathmore**, Sutherland, he has sincere elegies for his patron, the **tacksman** Iain Mac Eachainn, for **Murdo MacDonald**, minister of **Durness**, and for the fourth Lord **Reay**; but he has no hesitation in exposing the injustices and hypocrisies he observed. There is much of both quiet and rollicking humour in his work. The poetry and its background have been refreshingly illustrated by **Ian Grimble** in *The World of Rob Donn* (1979). For texts, see Hew Morrison, *Songs and Poems* (1899) and the earliest edition of the poems, entitled *Orain le Rob Donn* (1829). The poems were apparently first written down, from the poet's dictation, by a daughter of John Thomson, also a minister of Durness.

DOOCOTS (DOVECOTES)

The limited assets of a Lowland laird were once listed as 'a pickle land, a muckle debt, a doocot and a law suit'. The remains of these old dovecotes are scattered throughout Scotland in varying states of repair and reveal a former way of life when the meat and eggs from pigeons were a reliable and handy food source throughout the year. Another, less obvious but just as valuable product was the dung from the floor which, as well as being extensively used for manure, was a rich source of potassium nitrate – saltpetre – a vital ingredient of gunpowder. Indeed in 1625 an order went out from **Charles I** that prohibited owners of dovecotes from covering the floors with stone, as this prevented the dung from mixing with the soil which made it more efficient.

Some doocots were built into houses, others set a little apart, such as the one at **Culloden** near **Inverness**. The Culloden dovecote would have supplied the nearby Culloden House and is a fine octagonal building with n impressive 8-sided pyramidal roof which contains he entrances for the pigeons. Inside, the walls are covered with small nesting ledges and there is the remains of a central revolving ladder called a 'potence' which enabled people to climb to the upper nests. In 1990 there were still pigeons nesting in this dovecote, but it seems likely that it went out of serious 'production' after World War II. In contrast the dovecote at Raddery school in **Ross**-shire is over an arch in the farm court entrance and the holes have been blocked off.

The two doocots at **Gordonstoun** are particularly magnificent, with one ('tower type') being a converted windmill and the other ('beehive type') dating back to the 16th century. The entrance to the former is through stone vaults and it has a long ladder inside. Boath dovecote in **Moray** is a landmark in its own right, and the round whitewashed walls stand out conspicuously. There are six dove holes surrounded by a moulded cornice with an oblong window above and a conical slated roof. Phantassie doocot, at **East Linton** near **Edinburgh**, is a massive structure with nesting places for 500 birds. The walls, 4ft (1.2m) thick at the base, project upwards in horseshoe form to enclose a sloping roof, designed to give the 'doos' the benefit of a southern exposure. Both Boath and Phantassie doocots are in the ownership of the **National Trust for Scotland.**

DOON CASTLE, Nr Dalmellington, Ayrshire

Sometimes known as Loch Doon Castle, the ruins of this 14th century castle once stood on an island near the head of Loch Doon on the border between **Ayrshire** and **Kirkcudbrightshire**. During the particularly dry summer of 1826 a fisherman spotted several huge boats

lying on the loch bed near Castle Island. When raised, they were found to be nine ancient canoes, each hollowed out of a single oak tree. Left lying for many years in a shallow pool near the loch, they were eventually moved to **Glasgow**'s **Hunterian Museum**. In the early 1930s the level of Loch Doon was raised by as much as 40 feet as part of the **Galloway hydro-electric** scheme. To save it from inundation, Doon Castle was dismantled and rebuilt on the lochside.

'DOON THE WATTER'

'Doon the water' holidays to **Clyde** coastal resorts were pioneered by wealthy and health-conscious Glaswegians when, in the late 18th century, seabathing became a fashionable medical fad. But the difficulties and expense of travel were potent deterrents until the launch in 1812 of **Henry Bell**'s **Comet**, the Clyde's first steamboat, inaugurated a new era of popular travel.

As the vogue for holidays 'at the coast' spread, existing communities like **Helensburgh**, **Gourock**, **Largs**, Millport, and most of all **Dunoon** and **Rothesay**, were expanded and developed as seaside resorts. Marine villas sprouted in new ribbon developments as, for example, at Inellan and Blairmore near Dunoon, and Kilcreggan and Cove on the Rosneath peninsula. The expanding **railway** network and a competitive fleet of paddle-steamers ensured swift and sure means of travel. Good communications were particularly important for middle-class breadwinners who, while ensuring that their families enjoyed a month or longer at the coast, either commuted to their places of business on a daily basis or visited only at weekends.

Doon Castle as originally sited in Loch Doon (GWWA)

'Doon the watter' aboard the Eagle; a visit to Brodick Fair in the 1880s (BRC)

A moderate rise in the standard of living and more time for leisure also allowed an increasing number of working-class families to savour the delights of a seaside holiday. Although during **Glasgow Fair** boats, trains and resorts were grossly overcrowded, their few days 'doon the watter' afforded a rewarding contrast to the grime and atmospheric pollution of their normal environment. For the many who could not afford even cheap holiday accommodation, a day trip on a paddle-steamer to Rothesay and the Kyles of **Bute** provided excitement enough, especially if Paw, Maw and the weans had embarked on a 'flier' racing rival boats from pier to pier.

Cheaper foreign travel in the 1950s spelt the end of such innocent delights. But the charm and scenic beauty of the Firth of Clyde remain and attract visiting yachtsmen and some **tourists** from airts far beyond the old catchment area of **Glasgow** and the industrial west.

DORES, Nr Inverness

Although the main road through the **Great Glen** now follows the north-west shore of **Loch Ness**, in the 18th century the opposite side was favoured by travellers. Here **General Wade** built his **military road** between **Inverness** and **Fort Augustus** and here in 1773 passed **Dr Johnson** and **James Boswell**. The village of Dores, eight miles from Inverness, was the site of a **kingshouse** (inn) on Wade's road, which continues along the lochside while an alternative but parallel route climbs steeply inland. Nearby the house of Kinchyle was once a MacBain property. The MacBain Memorial Garden, established by the American MacBain of MacBain in 1961,

now serves in its stead. The Kinchyle clava **cairn** was that bypassed by Johnson and Boswell; 'seeing one is quite enough' quoth the Doctor. He was much more intrigued by the chance to explore and disparage the domestic arrangements of a Highland cottage, or 'hut', thought to have been down the loch at An Ihre Mor. Just beyond, Farigaig has an Iron Age fort and **Forestry Commission** visitor facilities. Between here and **Foyers** Aleister Crowley (1875–1947), a 'bad but prolific poet', once made his home at Boleskine. He was better known for his esoteric beliefs and his outrageous but carefully cultivated wickedness. Worshipping the devil and claiming to be the beast from the Book of Revelations, he gave **Loch Ness monsters** a bad name.

DORNIE, Ross & Cromarty

Once **Kintail**'s main **fishing** village, Dornie stands where Lochs Duich and Long open out into Loch Alsh. It is an ancient centre of west Highland Catholicism, a fact recognised by the Duchess of Leeds who here founded a convent and church in the 19th century. The road bridge across Loch Long connects it to Ardelve and forms part of the main road to **Kyle of Lochalsh**. Nearby is **Eilean Donan Castle** and, by way of Killilan and Glen Elchaig, a challenging walk up to the **Falls of Glomach**.

DORNOCH, Sutherland

The capital of the former county of **Sutherland** may have contained a community of the **Celtic Church** long before **David I** referred to its monks in 1140. **St Gilbert of Moray** was elected Bishop of **Caithness** in 1222 and, following the murder of two of his predecessors, had the discretion to move the seat of his diocese out of Caithness to within the sphere of influence of his kinsman, the Earl of Sutherland. He built his cathedral at Dornoch and died in 1245, the last Scotsman to be canonised before the **Reformation**. In 1541 **Robert Stewart**, who never took Holy Orders, became Bishop at the age of 19 and in 1553 bestowed the Church lands of **Strathnaver**, Caithness and Sutherland on his sister's husband, the Earl of Sutherland. This property included the city and palace of Dornoch, the latter a 16th century fortified tower, now the Castle Hotel. While the Bishop departed to exploit the ecclesiastical riches of **St Andrews**, the **Mackays** emulated the piety of their ghostly Father by reducing his cathedral to a ruin in 1570. Daniell's print reveals its condition before **William Burn** undertook its restoration in 1835–7. Since then it has benefited from the philanthropy of **Andrew Carnegie** in nearby Skibo Castle. In 1989 a memorial window was installed in honour of St Gilbert, 750 years after the establishment of his cathedral. It was the medieval monks of St Andrews who discovered the marvellous amenity of Dornoch Links for one of their favourite recreations, and there are many who consider today that this is Scotland's finest **golf course**.

DORNOCH FIRTH, Sutherland/Easter Ross

Also known as the Kyle of **Sutherland**, the firth's waters meet the river Shin as it passes **Carbisdale**, where **James Graham, Marquis of Montrose**, suffered his final defeat in 1650. The actual Narrows (*Caol*, Kyle) occur where the Meikle Ferry crossed from Easter **Ross** to the **Dornoch** peninsula below Skibo Castle. It was the scene of a somewhat inglorious engagement between Hanoverians and **Jacobites** on the eve of **Culloden**, and of a long-remembered tragedy in 1809. Sheriff MacCulloch was returning north from **Tain** with a crowd of people who had attended the market. He used his authority to turn away many from the wherry, but it was still over-crowded when it set out in a dead calm. In mid-channel it capsized in the dark and 70 of its passengers, including the Sheriff, were drowned. In 1991 a bridge across this Kyle was opened by Queen Elizabeth the Queen Mother, greatly shortening the A9 route to **Wick**.

DOTT, Norman (1897–1973) Neurosurgeon

Born in **Colinton**, **Edinburgh**, and based in the capital nearly all his life, Dott was appointed Professor of Surgical Neurology at **Edinburgh University** in 1947, and made a CBE in 1948. His work was characterised by his search for innovative techniques and equipment, the latter often designed by himself. Unusually for a surgeon, he became a popular public figure, much mourned on his death.

DOUGLAS, Lanarkshire

Lands on the Douglas Water are thought to have been granted in the 13th century to a Fleming called either William or Theobald. His descendants adopted the name of **Douglas** for their castle and associated township as well as for themselves, a name which soon became the most powerful in Scotland. **'The Good Sir James'** Douglas, the faithful commander of **Robert I**, laid the foundations of Douglas power but also burnt (1307) Douglas Castle and all within it, including an English garrison. The idea was to deny the place to an advancing English force but the brutality as much as the self-denial

occasioned the sobriquet of the 'Douglas Larder'. Rebuilt, the town and castle remained close to Douglas hearts, many of which were buried, some with their owners, in the then parish church of St Bride. Part of the late-14th century church survives and still contains an effigy reputed to be that of 'The Good Sir James' and others of **Archibald, 5th Earl of Douglas** (d.1439) and of **James, 7th Earl of Douglas** (d.1443), plus his wife. Both earls are styled Dukes of Touraine, a title bestowed on the **4th Earl** by Charles VII of France. The octagonal bell tower of the church was added in the 16th century, the clock supposedly being donated by **Queen Mary**. A further conflagration in the 18th century put paid to Douglas Castle but in c1760 the 1st (and last) Duke of Douglas began erecting a baronial replica. This consisted of only one wing at the time of his death and was never completed. It figured as *Castle Dangerous* in **Sir Walter Scott**'s last novel, published in the year of his death. Later in the 19th century **coal-mining** came to Douglas as to **Hamilton**. Like **Hamilton Palace**, Douglas Castle had to be demolished (1938) because of the consequent subsidence.

DOUGLAS, Archibald (d.1333) Guardian

Youngest brother of **'The Good Sir James'**, Archibald was made Guardian in 1332 in succession to **Donald of Mar** and **Sir Andrew Moray** on behalf of the child King **David II**. Although he succeeded in forcing **Edward Balliol** to flee back to England from **Annan** in December of that year, he was killed at **Halidon Hill** (July 1333) when an English army under Edward III brought Balliol back to claim the Scottish throne.

DOUGLAS, Archibald, 3rd Earl of Douglas (1328-c1400) 'The Grim'

Illegitimate son of **'The Good Sir James'**, Archibald seems, despite his nickname, to have been one of the less belligerent Douglases, acquiring the lordship and castle of **Bothwell** by marriage (to Joanna Moray), the eastern part of **Galloway** as a reward for his loyalty to **David II** and the remainder of Galloway by purchase from the Earl of **Wigtown**. His inheritance of the **Earldom of Douglas** from his cousin James, who died at **Otterburn** (1388), made him unquestionably the most powerful man in the south of Scotland. After the death of David II in 1371, Archibald concentrated on Galloway, building **Threave Castle** and administering imperious but not unjust government to his vast estates. In 1384 his last military action was to secure the surrender of **Lochmaben Castle**, thus removing the only remaining English garrison in Annandale. He died at Threave.

DOUGLAS, Archibald, 4th Earl of Douglas (c1372-1424) 'The Tyneman'

Two years after inheriting the earldom from his father, Archibald 'The Grim', the 4th Earl of Douglas was implicated in the arrest and subsequent death 'in mysterious circumstances' of David, Duke of Rothesay, elder son of **Robert III**, but exonerated – along with the **Duke of Albany** – by royal decree. Married to Robert III's daughter Margaret, Archibald gained his nickname 'The Tyneman' (the Loser) after a series of defeats: first by the English rebel Percy 'Hotspur' at Homildon

(1402) and then, having agreed to pay his ransom by fighting for Hotspur against Henry IV, by the English King at Shrewsbury (1403). Captured by Henry, Archibald was released in an exchange of prisoners in 1407. Mutually suspicious of each other's ambitions, he negotiated a series of deals with Albany (now Regent for James I) which increased both his power and his wealth; but when Albany was succeeded by his son Murdoch – who had other deals in mind, notably with the old Douglas enemy the Earl of March – Archibald saw the advantages of trying to secure the release of James I. In 1424 he led a 10,000 strong army to France to fight for the Dauphin Charles against the English, for which he was rewarded with a lieutenant-generalship of the French army and the Dukedom of Touraine; he met his last defeat and his death at the hands of the English at Verneuil in 1424.

DOUGLAS, Archibald, 5th Earl of Douglas (c1390–1439)

Son of Archibald 'The Tyneman', this Archibald styled himself Earl of Wigtown and, as such, he headed a Scottish force called to France to assist the Dauphin Charles. Victorious at Baugé (1421) but defeated at Crevant (1423), he inherited the Earldom of Douglas on the death of his father at Verneuil (1424). Briefly arrested by James I (1431) in one of his occasional purges of over-powerful nobles but soon restored to favour, he was appointed Lieutenant of Scotland on the succession of the child King James II, and died two years later. The two sons of his marriage to Euphemia Graham (a descendant of Robert II), William, 6th Earl of Douglas, and David were murdered at the 'Black Dinner' in Edinburgh Castle (1440).

DOUGLAS, Archibald, 5th Earl of Angus (c1449–1513) 'Bell-the-Cat'

Leader of the Red Douglases (descendants of George, illegitimate son of the 1st Earl of Douglas (1327–84) and Margaret Stewart, Countess of Angus), Archibald succeeded to the Earldom in 1463 and married Elizabeth, daughter of Lord Boyd, in 1468. History might well have forgotten this 'unreliable lord' were it not for his picturesque sobriquet 'Bell-the-Cat'. This was probably bestowed on him by Robert Lindsay of Pitscottie, who related the story of how a group of disgruntled nobles, including the Earls of Angus, Huntly, Buchan and Lennox, decided in 1482 that they could no longer tolerate the influence on James III of a group of about 20 'low-born familiars' – an influence that was steadily diminishing their own. 'The mice would fain hang a bell around the cat that preyed on them, but which mouse was to bell the cat?' Angus drew the short straw (or possibly volunteered) and, with a kinsman, captured up to seven of the 'familiars' (including Thomas Cochrane, architect of the great hall of Stirling Castle) and hanged them from Lauder Bridge. Angus's other notable achievement was the burning of Bamburgh (1480) in renewed hostilities against Edward IV of England. He fought, with two of his sons, at Flodden and so great was his grief when they were both killed that he retired to Whithorn and there died before the end of the year. Another son was the poet Gavin Douglas.

DOUGLAS, Archibald, 6th Earl of Angus (c1489–1557)

The 6th Earl of Angus succeeded his grandfather 'Bell-the-Cat' (his father having died at Flodden), and in 1514 married Margaret Tudor, widow of James IV and sister of Henry VIII. The marriage, which quickly turned sour and lasted less than five years, disqualified her as Regent for her son James V and the role was assumed by John Stewart, Duke of Albany, thus exchanging a pro-English Regent for a pro-French one. During Albany's frequent and sometimes prolonged visits to France, he left a council of Regency in his place consisting of four Earls – Angus, Arran, Huntly and Argyll. But Angus was too ambitious to accept only a quarter share of power and, now an active agent for English interests, he forced Arran out of Edinburgh [see Cleanse-the-Causeway], established a firm power base in the capital and by 1525 had managed to 'gain control' over the person of James V', holding the 12-year-old King a virtual prisoner in Edinburgh and at Falkland. The next two years saw the power of the Red Douglas at its height, Angus himself becoming Chancellor in 1527 and Douglases installed in every important post in the Household. When, however, James managed to escape in 1528 he rallied the nobles alienated by Angus and hounded his captor over the border, his lands and titles forfeit. Angus remained in England for the rest of James's reign, returning to Scotland in 1543 at the head of a group of pro-English nobles during the minority of Queen Mary. But Henry VIII's heavy-handed treatment of Scotland [see Rough Wooing] was too much even for Angus and in 1545 he led a Scots force to victory at Ancrum Moor and another to defeat at Pinkie (1547).

DOUGLAS, David (1799–1834) Botanist and Plant-hunter

Born at Scone in Perthshire, the son of a stonemason, David Douglas left school at the age of 10 and started work as an apprentice to the head gardener at Scone Palace. In 1820 he was taken on as under-gardener at the Botanic Garden in Glasgow, where his enthusiasm and aptitude caught the attention of the great English botanist William Hooker, who had taken over the Chair of Botany at Glasgow University that same year. On Hooker's recommendation, Douglas was signed up by the Horticultural Society in London to take part in a plant-hunting expedition to China. This expedition was cancelled but Douglas was sent instead to America in 1821. His first trip yielded only some fruit trees, but on two subsequent expeditions to the western US he gathered seed and plants of important garden plants, including annuals (eg Clarkia and Californian poppy), shrubs (eg rose of Sharon and flowering currant), and trees, including his Douglas Fir. He spent most of the next 10 years travelling through the Blue Mountains and Pacific coast of North America collecting plant specimens, keeping voluminous notes, and planning a new venture in which he would walk across Siberia: 'What a glorious prospect!' But in 1834 he stopped off in the Sandwich Islands (Hawaii) on his way home, and on one of his rambles through the hills he fell into a pit dug to catch wild cattle and was gored and trampled to death by a trapped bull. He was buried in Hawaii.

DOUGLAS, Earldom, Marquisate and Dukedom

This ancient Celtic name from the south-west of Scotland first acquired nationwide celebrity through Sir William, who died a prisoner in London as a supporter of the **Wallace** in 1298. His son **'The Good Sir James' Douglas** played a leading part in the triumph of the national cause, and died fighting the Muslims in Spain in 1330 on his way to the Holy Land with the heart of **Robert I**. That heart is borne on the escutcheon of the Douglases to this day. His nephew William became the 1st Earl of Douglas and married the heiress of the **Earl of Mar**, so that his son James inherited both earldoms and was a most eligible husband for **Robert II**'s daughter Isabel. James's death on the field of **Otterburn** in 1388 was celebrated in English and Scottish **ballads**. The death of the young 6th Earl and his even younger brother in 1440 was the subject of another ballad:

> Edinburgh Castle, toune and toure,
> God grant thou sink for sinne,
> An' that even for the **black dinour**
> Earle Douglas gat therein.

They had been invited to dine in the castle with the boy King **James II**, in whose presence they were dragged from the table and despatched. It was a drastic step in the assault on this over-mighty family which culminated at **Stirling** in 1452, when James II murdered **William Douglas, 8th Earl**; the 9th rose in rebellion and was forfeited in 1455. The Douglas Earls of **Angus** were left as the senior branch, of whom the 11th was created Marquis of Douglas by **Charles I**. The 3rd Marquis was created Duke in 1703 but the title then became extinct [see **Douglas Cause**].

Other Douglas titles (besides Douglas and Angus) include (1) the Earldom of **Drumlanrig** and Queensberry, created 1633 for William Douglas, Viscount Drumlanrig. The 3rd Earl was created Marquis (1682) and Duke of Queensberry (1684). On the death of the 4th Duke, the dukedom passed to the **Dukes of Buccleuch** and the marquisate to Charles Douglas of Kelhead. (2) The Earldom of **Selkirk**, created (1646) for William, son of the **1st Marquis of Douglas**. He became Duke of Hamilton by marriage and the title passed to his 3rd son but eventually to the **Dukes of Hamilton**. (3) The **Earldom of Morton**.

DOUGLAS, Gavin (1476–1522) Poet

The lives of most early Scottish poets are clouded in mystery; Gavin Douglas's life is fully charted. This is because he belonged to a noble family, being the son of the **5th Earl of Angus** and Elizabeth, the daughter of Lord Boyd. He chose to make his mark in the Church and had, by 1503, become Provost of **St Giles** in **Edinburgh**. Failure to attain the Archbishopric of **St Andrews** in 1514 was followed by his appointment to the Bishopric of **Dunkeld** the following year. He divided his time between that village and the Bishop's Palace in Edinburgh. But his was not the quiet life that this might suggest, for his birth necessarily involved him in intense political disputes. Later, rivalry with **John Stewart, Duke of Albany** would result in his being accused of high treason and seeking refuge in England.

His last extant letter, written from the 'Inn of Carlyle' on 31 January 1522, speaks eloquently of his isolation and sense of betrayal.

Usually grouped with the other late medieval **makars**, **Henryson** and **Dunbar**, Douglas has several claims for distinctiveness. His major poetic work is the masterly translation of Virgil's *Aeneid*, one of the most popular works in the Middle Ages. Despite this, it had never been fully translated into English and so Douglas's *Eneados* is a pioneering endeavour in itself. But it is much more. From the point of view of authority, of philosophy and content, it is an accurate translation, directly from the Latin, by a scholar. Linguistically, it introduces coinages and so extends the vernacular as a medium, ironically making it a more fitting rival for the Latin from which it is derived. Politically, as Douglas stresses in his first Prologue, it is a work from Scotland, composed 'in the langage of Scottis natioun' (Prol I, 103).

Douglas has a rather diffuse style, deriving in part from his classical training but also, like so many Scots writers, an eye for visual detail and a natural preference for clear, analytical form. These qualities not only serve the *Eneados* (where they are particularly obvious in the introductory Prologues), but also his earlier work *The Palice of Honour*. Here he 'retranslates' the old, expansive Triumph form into a neat, balanced structure. This controlling clarity counterbalances tendencies towards stylistic diffuseness. In both works his comments on other authors and techniques of composition offer a valuable road into literary theory, rhetorically and personally defined.

DOUGLAS, James (c1286–1330) 'The Good Sir James'

The eldest son of William Douglas 'le Hardi' (d.1298 in the Tower of London) and of Isabella Stewart (the aunt of **Walter Stewart** who married **Marjorie Bruce**), James was sent to Paris for safety in 1296 and survived, penniless, until rescued by **Bishop Lamberton** with whom he remained until 1306 when he stole a horse and rode to join **Robert I (the Bruce)**. An outstanding practitioner of guerrilla tactics, in 1307–8 he conducted a brilliant campaign in the south-west, seizing the stores at **Brodick** on **Arran** and retaking his own castle of Douglas after raising local support. In 1309 he joined Robert in **Argyll** and was responsible for outflanking John of Lorne's **Pass of Brander** ambush by scaling the heights of **Ben Cruachan**. He took **Roxburgh** in 1314 and was knighted at **Bannockburn**. During Robert's Irish campaign he acted as Warden of Scotland and raided into England (until 1327), gaining the sobriquet 'the Black Douglas'. It was James who fulfilled Robert's dying wish by carrying his embalmed heart on crusade against the Moors in Spain (Teba des Andales). There he died in battle and is still remembered as *El Gran Duglas*. His natural son, **Archibald 'The Grim'**, succeeded to the **Earldom of Douglas** (created for a nephew of Sir James) as 3rd Earl.

DOUGLAS, James, 2nd Earl of Douglas (d.1388)

Famous for the manner and circumstances of his death, James Douglas, 2nd Earl of Douglas (and also **Earl of Mar**, inherited from his mother), was one of the leaders of the Scottish attack on the Northumberland estates of Henry Percy (Shakespeare's 'Hotspur'). Mortally wounded at the height of the Battle of Otterburn on 5 August 1388, Douglas instructed his lieutenants to hide him in a bush and let no word of his death reach the English.

> My wound is deep; I am fayn to sleep,
> Take thou the vaward of me,
> And hide me by the bracken bush
> Grows on yonder lilye-lee.

The battle raged through the night; Percy saw his case was hopeless and eventually asked one of the Scottish knights to whom he should surrender.

> Thou shalt not yield to lord nor loon,
> Nor yet shalt thou to me,
> But yield thee to the bracken bush
> Grows on yonder lilye-lee.
> ('Ballad of Otterburn', Anon)

The battle (which also became known as the Battle of Chevy Chase) was won, Percy captured, and Douglas's body discovered in the morning; 'thus it was that a dead man won the field'.

DOUGLAS, James, 7th Earl of Douglas (d.1443) 'The Gross'

Second son of **Archibald 'The Grim'**, 3rd Earl of Douglas, James Douglas of **Balvenie** and **Abercorn**, Earl of Avondale, was the great-uncle of William, 6th Earl (murdered with his brother David at the **Black Dinner** (1440) when both were in their teens). Thought to have had more than a little to do with this grisly event, James 'the Gross' thereafter inherited the **Earldom of Douglas** but not all the estates; the lordships of **Bothwell** and **Galloway** went to the sister of the murdered boys, Margaret, Maid of Galloway, and the Lordship of Annandale reverted to the Scottish Crown in the absence of a direct male heir, as did the French titles to the French Crown. Any hopes on the part of the other conspirators to the Black Dinner that this split in the Douglas estates would diminish Douglas power were short-lived; when James 'the Gross' died in 1443, his son **William** inherited as 8th Earl and promptly married his cousin, the Maid of Galloway, thus reuniting the Douglas inheritance.

DOUGLAS, James, 9th Earl of Douglas (1426–88)

Brother of **William, 8th Earl**, James inherited when William was killed by **James II** at **Stirling** (1452). The new Earl raised an army and marched on Stirling, publicly renounced his allegiance to King James and sacked the town. In 1453 he married his brother's widow, the erstwhile Maid of Galloway, and began to foster links with the rising Yorkist party in England. But James won parliamentary exoneration for the murder of the 8th Earl of Douglas, rallied those nobles who shared his fear of Douglas power (and created a few new ones to boost their numbers), and swooped on the Douglas lands. The downfall of the Black Douglases was completed in 1455 when James laid siege to and captured their castle of **Threave**; the 9th Earl fled over the border to England, leaving his three brothers, the Earls of Moray and Ormond and Lord Balvenie, to make a last stand at **Arkinholm** on the Esk near **Langholm**. There they were finally defeated – Moray killed, Ormond captured and later executed and Balvenie fleeing to England to join the 9th Earl, whose estates and titles were now forfeited. An English pensioner for nearly 30 years, he was a signatory to the 1462 **Treaty of Westminster-Ardtornish** and in 1484 made an abortive raid on **Lochmaben** with **Alexander Stewart, Duke of Albany**. Albany escaped but Douglas was captured and sentenced to imprisonment at **Lindores Abbey** where he died, a melancholy recluse, four years later.

DOUGLAS, James, 4th Earl of Morton (c1516–81) Regent

Younger son of Sir George Douglas of Pittendreich (and therefore nephew of **Archibald, 6th Earl of Angus**),

James Douglas, 4th Earl of Morton, c1580; attributed to Arnold Bronckhurst (SNPG)

James became 4th Earl of Morton (1550) by virtue of his marriage to the eldest daughter of the (sonless) **3rd Earl**. A supporter of the English alliance and one of the original **Lords of the Congregation** committed to the **Reformation** and the overthrow of the Catholic Church, Morton was a prime mover in the murder of **David Rizzio** (1566). Dismissed as Chancellor (a position he had held since 1563) he fled to England, but his pardon was engineered by the Queen's new favourite the **Earl of Bothwell**, and by the end of the year he was back in **Edinburgh**. Well aware of plans for the murder (1567) of **Darnley**, Morton was nevertheless careful to distance himself from the event and, on **Mary's** subsequent flight with Bothwell, led the confederacy of rebel lords in pursuit, allowing Bothwell to escape from **Carberry Hill** and accepting Mary's surrender. He led **Regent Moray**'s forces at the **Battle of Langside** (1568), became leader of the King's party after the murder of Moray (1569) and took over the Regency on the death of the **Earl of Mar** in 1572.

His mismanagement of the country's finances was balanced by the firm restraint he imposed on both brawling barons and bellicose Borderers, leading to a period of unaccustomed political stability. But 'his policy of forcing respect for the law was unwelcome to those who had profited by disorder' (G Donaldson), and in 1578 the **Earls of Atholl** and **Argyll** entered an uneasy alliance to oust him from power. Although they did succeed briefly, it was not until the young **James VI** came under the influence of his kinsman **Esmé Stewart**, first cousin of Lord Darnley, that Morton's tenure ended. His opponents flocked to the support of the King's favourite and between them they found it easy to persuade the adolescent King to rebel against a Regent by whom he had been persistently ignored. In December 1580 Morton was arrested. Brought to trial and convicted of 'being council, concealing, and being art and part of the murder' of Lord Darnley, he was beheaded by the 'Maiden' in **Edinburgh**'s **Grassmarket** on 2 June 1581.

DOUGLAS, James, 2nd Duke of Queensberry (1662–1711) 'The Union Duke'

The Queensberry earldom was created (1633) for William Douglas, Viscount **Drumlanrig**, and the marquisate (1682) and dukedom (1684) for the 3rd Earl, also William (1637–95) who, having opposed **James VII**, became President of the Council in 1686. His son, James 2nd Duke, attended **Glasgow University** and served under **John Graham of Claverhouse** in the 1680s before succession to his father's dukedom and his sizeable 'interest' brought him into government as Commissioner for Scotland (1699) with **James Ogilvie, Earl of Seafield**. He weathered the storm over the **Darien** collapse by taking to his bed for much of 1700 and emerged as Secretary of State (1702) under Queen Anne and a key figure in the posturing that led up to the **Union**. Though wrong-footed by the Act of Settlement he secured a vote in favour of selecting commissioners to treat for Union and refused royal assent to the **Act of Security**. In an effort to discredit formidable opposition in Parliament, he then broke news of the **Jacobite** collusion leaked to him by **Simon Fraser of Lovat** ('The Queensberry Plot', 1703). This backfired and **John Hay Earl of Tweeddale**, one of those whom he had attempted to implicate, was appointed Commissioner in his stead. Rehabilitation came in 1706 courtesy of the **Duke of Argyll** (who insisted that Queensberry's support and skills were essential to pushing through the Union, in spite of even Queen Anne's objections to one so 'odious'. In the event Queensberry more than justified Argyll's hopes, both as negotiator with the English Commissioners and as manager of the government interest in Parliament. His rewards, besides the spoils of office, were another dukedom (Dover), another marquisate (Beverley) and another earldom (Ripon).

DOUGLAS, James, Earl of Drumlanrig (1697–1715)

Eldest son of **James Douglas, 2nd Duke of Queensberry**, the Earl of Drumlanrig was a dangerous lunatic who was kept locked up in a wing of **Queensberry House** in **Edinburgh**'s **Canongate**. While 'The Union Duke' and his household were out celebrating the successful conclusion of the Treaty, the Earl broke out of his quarters; the family returned to find that he had come across a young kitchen-boy, the only servant remaining in the house, had spitted and partially roasted him and was in the process of trying to devour him. The scandal was soon out, being widely regarded as 'a judgement upon the Duke for his odious share in the Union'.

DOUGLAS, Katherine (fl.1437)

Sometimes known as Katherine 'Barlass' and presumably one of Joan of Beaufort's ladies-in-waiting, Katherine Douglas is supposed to have barred the door of the royal apartments in **Perth**'s Blackfriars by using her arm as the bolt, or bar, when **James I**'s murderers came to take him (1437). Nothing else is known of her and even this much, written a century after the incident, is uncertain. A surprisingly detailed contemporary account describes the domestic scene on the fateful night; the door would not lock; the King and Queen play chess and then undress for bed; **Robert Graham** and his fellow assailants thunder into the room; the King prises open a manhole and disappears into the sewer; there eventually he is discovered and cut down. As for the Queen's attendants they are portrayed as 'yn a corner of the chamber crying and wepying all destraite' – no mention of anyone sacrificing an arm to make good the missing bolt. Yet there is that detail of the faulty lock, and somehow James found time to get a poker and wrench open the manhole.

DOUGLAS, Thomas, 5th Earl of Selkirk (1771–1820) Emigrationist

The Earldom of Selkirk, created in 1688 for the third son of the 1st **Marquis of Hamilton**, remained with the Douglases until passing to the Dukes of Hamilton in 1855. Thomas Douglas, a seventh son yet the 5th Earl, interested himself, though a Lowlander, in the economic plight of the Highlands. Foreseeing further **clearances**, he fostered emigration schemes to north America. In 1803 he led some 800 emigrants to a successful settlement on Prince Edward Island and in 1804 established a less durable colony at Baldoon on Lake St Clair. These experiments were designed to 'point out the principles on which effective national measures may be grounded'. But the government showed no interest and Selkirk therefore pressed ahead with his own initiatives, purchasing from the Hudson's Bay Company 116,000 square miles of prairie in Upper Canada – the Red River colony of Winnipeg. Hither, during 1812–15, several shiploads of migrants from **Orkney**, **Sutherland** and Ireland trailed west across Canada. In spite of the appalling winters, those who reached Fort Douglas showed a determination to stay. This angered the trapping fraternity of the North West Company who in 1815 and 1816 drove out the colonists. Selkirk marched to their rescue and himself became the object of the Company's hostility. Legal battles in the Canadian courts proved expensive and inconclusive. Though the colony now prospered, Selkirk returned to England to clear his name and died soon after at Pau in the Pyrenees. Among those who acknowledged his integrity and selfless dedication to the dispossessed were William Wilberforce and **Sir Walter Scott** (see J M Gray, *Lord Selkirk of Red River*, 1963).

DOUGLAS, Sir William (c1300–53) 'Knight of Liddesdale'

A Lothian landholder and skilled military tactician, William Douglas was offered the **Earldom of Atholl** in 1341 as a reward for his resolute resistance to **Edward Balliol**. Preferring to strengthen his interests in the Borders, he passed up the Earldom in favour of the Lordship of Liddesdale, reinforcing his position by contriving the death (1342) of Alexander Ramsay, to whom **David II** had given neighbouring **Roxburgh** and Teviotdale. In 1346 Douglas joined David's invasion of England, being captured with the King and several other Scottish knights at **Neville's Cross**. He was eventually murdered by a kinsman in 1353.

DOUGLAS, William, 8th Earl of Douglas (c1425–1452)

Son of **James 'The Gross'**, William succeeded to the earldom in 1443 and married his cousin Margaret, Maid of Galloway, thus reuniting the Douglas estates which had been dispersed on the death of **William 6th Earl** [see **Black Dinner**]. The power of the Douglases was thus restored to levels that seemed once more to threaten the power of the Crown. **James II** perceived an even greater threat when William formed an alliance with the Earl of Crawford and the Earl of **Ross** (also **Lord of the Isles**). He invited Douglas to dine at **Stirling**, apparently to try and dissuade him from this band, but when Douglas refused to oblige the King lost his temper and stabbed him to death, provoking an open feud between Douglas and **Stewart**.

DOUGLAS, William Fettes (1822–91) Painter

Born in **Edinburgh**, Fettes Douglas began his career as a banker, remaining self-taught as an artist. His activities as an antiquarian and collector had a significant effect on his art and the diversity of his interests provided him with an unusual variety of subject matter. In spite of his own academic disposition his early paintings of Scottish history comply with the prevalent mid-century artistic mood, closer to the sincerely felt narratives of Tom Faed than the documentary reconstructions of his fellow antiquarian and painter James Drummond. In 1857 Douglas made his first of many visits to Italy and throughout the 1860s spent lengthy periods in London where he found company amongst the circle of flourishing Scots artists settled there after training in Edinburgh under the distinguished teacher **Robert Scott Lauder**. During these years his themes became increasingly recondite, reflecting his preoccupation with matters scientific and magical. His scenes of alchemists and astrologers overshadowed by books and cryptic apparatus are painted in a harsh, Pre-Raphaelite style, but in *The Spell* (1864, **National Gallery of Scotland**) a reduction in superfluous detail and a progressive awareness of the compositional techniques of **Pettie** and **Orchardson** combined with his ability as a draughtsman mark a forward-looking and sophisticated approach. His considerable breadth of knowledge led to his appointment as Director of the National Gallery of Scotland (1877), a post he held until elected President of the **Royal Scottish Academy** (1882). His acquaintance with Italian art later enriched the colouring of his work and from the 1870s his subjects, favouring artless visual appeal, became more intimate and relaxed. His landscapes in watercolour are amongst the finest of his works and far removed from his otherwise academic reputation.

DOUGLAS CAUSE

The 3rd **Marquis of Douglas** was created **Duke of Douglas** in 1703 and throughout his long life his sister Jane remained his presumptive heir. She made a secret marriage to Sir John Steuart of Grandtully, to whom she bore twin sons in 1748. Jane and one of her sons died in 1753, leaving Alexander Steuart the infant heir to her rights. In 1760 the Duke bequeathed his estates to the boy and died in the following year, when the 7th **Duke of Hamilton** became head of the house of Douglas. He attempted to secure Jane's inheritance by representing that her children were spurious, but the House of Lords found in favour of her son Alexander. In 1790 he was created Baron Douglas of Douglas, and on the extinction of this line his title passed, not to the Douglas Hamiltons, but to the Douglas Homes, **Earls of Home**.

DOUGLAS-HOME, Sir Alec (1903–95) Prime Minister

Described as 'the last gentleman prime minister', Alexander Frederick Douglas-Home was born in London and educated at Eton and Oxford. While he was still at school his father succeeded as 13th **Earl of Home** and Alec Douglas-Home took the courtesy title of Lord Dunglass. A direct man of diffident charm and perfect manners, a good shot, a fine fisherman and an able cricketer who played for the MCC on a tour of Argentina, Home stood unsuccessfully as Conservative candidate for **Coatbridge** in 1928 and was elected MP for South **Lanark** in 1931. Parliamentary Private Secretary to the Minister of Labour from 1935 and to the Chancellor of the Exchequer from 1937, he accompanied Prime Minister Neville Chamberlain to the fateful meeting with Hitler in Munich in 1938, later remarking that 'peace in our time' did allow an essential breathing space. At the start of the Second World War he joined the Lanarkshire **Yeomanry** but was invalided out with tuberculosis of the spine and spent two years on his back in plaster. In 1943 he returned to the House of Commons, attacked the Yalta Agreement and lost his seat at the general election of 1945, regaining it in 1950 only to succeed to the title of 14th Earl of Home on the death of his father in 1951 and move to the House of Lords. Churchill made him the first Minister of State for Scotland, saying, 'All right, have your Home sweet Home. Go and quell those turbulent Scots.' Secretary of State for the Commonwealth Office from 1955 and Lord President of the Council and Leader of the House of Lords from 1957–60, he then became the first member of the House of Lords since before the war to be appointed Foreign Secretary. In charge of Commonwealth Relations during the Suez crisis and of the Foreign Office during the Cuban, when he showed shrewd sense of purpose in dealings with the Soviet Union, Home was chosen by Harold Macmillan in 1963 as his successor. A new Act of Parliament allowed him to renounce his peerage and, as Sir Alec Douglas-Home, he stood once more for Parliament, was elected MP for Kinross & West Perthshire, and became leader of the Conservative Party and Prime Minister. He admitted to having no expertise in economic affairs, once joking that he 'did his sums with matchsticks', was ill at ease on television and pilloried by the new satirical shows like *That Was The Week That Was*; when his government was defeated in the general election of 1964, Home resigned as party leader in favour of Edward Heath and returned to the Foreign Office. A firm believer in the Scots having a greater say in their own affairs, and having previously devised a scheme for a directly elected Scottish assembly with legislative and funding powers, Home supported Labour's **devolution** proposals, but urged a 'No' vote in the 1979 referendum, arguing that the Act was unsatisfactory and voters should wait for 'something better'. When the Conservatives were defeated in the 1974 general election, Alec Douglas-Home, 'that rarest thing in politics – a politician whose word one can trust', returned to the House of Lords as Lord Home of the Hirsel, and to retirement at his home in the **Borders**. His writings include *Border Reflections* (1979) and *Letters to a Grandson* (1983).

DOUNE, Perthshire

Possibly to meet demand from **Doune Castle**, this town was once renowned for its manufacture, begun in 1645 by Thomas Cadell, of firearms ('no pistols made in Britain exceeded them'). In the 19th century two Buchanan brothers established the Deanston **cotton** mill which employed 1000 spinners and weavers, and north of the town there was an important cattle market. Such activities have long since ceased. Even the bridge over the river Teith, built in 1535 by **James IV**'s tailor supposedly to spite the ferryman, has been repaired and widened (slightly) out of recognition. Doune today (pop 4000) has two newer attractions to complement the antiquarian appeal of its castle: Scotland's Safari Park at Blair Drummond and an Antiques Market in the premises of the famed Doune Motor Museum (which closed down in 1998).

DOUNE CASTLE, Doune, Perthshire

Remarkably intact and little modified, Doune Castle is one of the finest surviving castles of enclosure. It stands on a tongue of land at the junction of the rivers Teith and Ardoch and was built in the late 14th century by **Robert Stewart, 1st Duke of Albany** and virtual ruler of Scotland 1388–1420. The lofty parapeted walls and massive gateway tower with steep and vaulted entrance flanked by a guardroom declare its strength. Every turret, machicolation, embrasure and latrine has a defensive function. Steep, easily held staircases twist through

Doune Castle with restorations suggested by MacGibbon and Ross (MR)

the masonry to remote chambers and commanding galleries. But if every inch a fortress, Doune was also a place of stately residence. The gate tower, where the lord resided, contains two splendid halls (one restored in 1883); the north-west tower has a well appointed kitchen; and the connecting range consists largely of the great hall, 72 by 25ft (22 by 7.6m). Further towers with connecting ranges were evidently planned but not constructed.

When **Murdoch, 2nd Duke of Albany**, was executed by **James I** (1425) Doune passed to the Crown and was used as a retreat and dower house by subsequent monarchs. **Queen Margaret** (Tudor) appointed Sir James Stewart as keeper through whose descendants the castle passed to the **Earls of Moray**. In 1745 it fell to the **Jacobites**. Amongst those held prisoner during the rising was the playwright **John Home**, who effected his escape from an upper storey of the north-west tower down the clichéd rope of knotted bed-sheets. After renovation in the 1970s, the castle was given into the care of the state in 1984.

DOUNREAY, Caithness

Britain's first fast-breeder nuclear reactor, built on a wartime airfield on the north coast of **Caithness**, went critical in 1959. Intended to develop fast-breeder and fuel-reprocessing technology to meet the anticipated increase in international demand for nuclear energy and expertise in a period of rapid economic growth, Dounreay grew to represent 20% of Caithness's GDP, **Thurso** to the east quadrupling in size and the workforce rising to 2000. But in the early 1970s the world economy suffered a slowdown, orders for new nuclear power stations slumped, and environmental fears over pollution and the possibility of a Chernobyl-style accident raised doubts over Dounreay's long-term future. The discovery of radioactive particles on the nearby seashore prompted a survey of the site by the Nuclear Installation Inspectorate; this in turn produced the admission that a non-nuclear explosion had taken place in a waste-storage shaft in 1977 and that three employees had received excessive radiation doses in a later accident. These and other safety scares, together with the realisation that Dounreay had become uneconomic, led to the shutdown of the main reactor in 1994. Fuel reprocessing continued, but in May 1998 it was announced that all non-essential work at the plant was to stop and that Dounreay was to be closed down. The process of decommissioning the reactors, retrieving and treating the radioactive waste in the site's storage facilities and decontaminating the area is expected to take 100 years, so the local economy will continue to benefit, and the Dounreay Dome – listed by **Historic Scotland** – will live on as the most famous landmark on Scotland's north coast.

DOW, Alexander (d.1779) Historian and Author

A native of **Crieff**, Dow is said to have fled to the East after killing someone in a duel. He entered the military service of the East India Company in 1763 having already spent some years at the Company's Sumatran outpost of Benkulen, where he seems to have served first as a sailor and then as a secretary (c1760). By 1769

he was a lieutenant-colonel in the Bengal Infantry and a determined author, enjoying the services of that excellent valet **John MacDonald**. Although 'said by those who knew him well to be utterly unqualified for the production of learning or fancy, either in prose or verse', he produced a standard History of Hindustan (1768) several Oriental fantasies and at least two plays. Most of these works were supposedly 'translated from the Persian' although according to Gibbon he had no knowledge of the language. He died at Bhagalpur in Bihar.

DOW, Daniel (1732–1783) Violinist and Composer

Dow's A Collection of Ancient Scots Music of 1776 is a particularly important publication as it contains early printed arrangements of music for violin, harpsichord, piano and flute as well as from the **piobaireachd** and **clarsach** repertoires. He worked mostly in **Edinburgh**, and his **reels** and **Strathspeys** are still popular.

DOWDING, Hugh Caswall Tremenheere, 1st Baron (1882–1970) Air Chief Marshal

Born at **Moffat**, **Lanarkshire**, and educated at Winchester, Dowding joined the Royal Artillery and then the Royal Flying Corps during World War I. Air Commander Trans-Jordan and Palestine (1929) and Air Council Member for Supply and Research (1930–36), he became Commander-in-Chief Fighter Command (1936–40), in which capacity he was the architect of victory in the Battle of Britain. Replaced by William Sholto Douglas at the end of 1940 after what have been described as 'doctrinal battles within the RAF', he retired from active service in 1942 with the rank of Air Chief Marshal.

DOWIE, John Alexander (1847–1907) Preacher

Born in **Edinburgh**, Dowie emigrated to Australia in 1860 and became a Congregational minister in Adelaide (1871). He opened his 'tabernacle for divine healing' at Melbourne in 1882 but eight years later left Australia for America where, as 'Elijah the Restorer', he founded 'Zion's Tabernacle' in Chicago (1893) and 'Zion City', a religious community on Lake Michigan (1900). He enjoyed considerable popular success as a faith healer before being expelled by his Church (1906) and deprived of both funds and property.

DOYLE, Sir Arthur Conan (1859–1930) Author

Doyle was born in **Edinburgh**, one of seven children of a civil servant. Of Irish Catholic descent, he was related to Richard Doyle, popular 19th century illustrator of Punch. He was educated at Stoneyhurst College before matriculating at **Edinburgh University** in 1876, where he studied medicine. His interest in writing was given impetus during this period with the publication of his first story in Chambers' Journal in 1879.

In 1880 Doyle spent seven months as a ship's surgeon on a whaler in the Arctic. The following year he received his medical degree and travelled to Africa as a passenger ship's surgeon. He returned to Britain in 1882 and set up medical practice in Southsea near Portsmouth. He began writing again to supplement his medical income, and in 1887 published the novella *A Study in Scarlet*, which introduced the characters of the detective Sherlock Holmes and his assistant, Dr Watson. Holmes, modelled on one of Doyle's forensic medicine teachers in Edinburgh, **Dr Joseph Bell**, derived his name in part from the American author Oliver Wendell Holmes (1809–94), whom Doyle greatly admired. A second work featuring Holmes, *The Sign of Four*, was published in 1890. Public interest in Holmes grew phenomenally with the publication of a series of Sherlock Holmes tales in the *Strand Magazine* 1891–3. Holmes was killed off in 1893, but due to public demand Doyle was forced to resurrect him in 1902, when he reappeared in the novel *The Hound of the Baskervilles*. The *Strand Magazine* resumed publication of Holmes stories in 1903.

Doyle owed much of his financial success as a writer to Sherlock Holmes, yet set greater store by his other works, which were extremely diverse in nature. He wrote several well received historical romances, including *Micah Clarke* (1889), a tale of the 1685 Rebellion, and *The White Company* (1891), set during the Hundred Years' War with France. He also created a memorable character in Professor Challenger, who was featured in the adventure novels *The Lost World* (1912) and *The Poison Belt* (1913).

During the Boer War of 1899–1902 Doyle served as a medical volunteer and wrote two propagandist works justifying Britain's involvement in South Africa, *The Great Boer War* (1900) and *The War in South Africa* (1902). He was knighted in 1902 for his public services. He was also active as a war correspondent in World War I. In his later years he was to grow extremely interested in spiritualism, publishing several works on the subject, including *The Wanderings of a Spiritualist* (1921) and *The History of Spiritualism* (1926). He died in Sussex.

DRAGONFLIES AND DAMSELFLIES

Because they were believed to sting and were surrounded by an aura of mystery, dragonflies were known as 'Horse-stingers', and damselflies as 'Devil's Darning Needles'. Of the British species of dragonfly, only a few are restricted to Scotland; one such is the Azure Hawker which is fairly widespread but often overlooked because it sometimes feeds a long way from water. Another is the Northern Emerald, although this also occurs in County Kerry in Ireland. Two other species, the Brilliant Emerald and the Downy Emerald, have a southerly distribution but with a few important colonies in northern Scotland. Both were recently discovered in the north after some considerable number of years (1976 and 1978 respectively). The White-faced Darter haunts areas of sphagnum moss with bog pools and is attracted to the white moss when it dries out in summer. Whilst this species does occur in England the main colonies are in Scotland, particularly the north. There is still confusion as to whether the Highland Darter and the Common Darter are different species or two forms of the same species.

The only British damselfly to be confined to Scotland is the very rare Northern Damselfly found only in a few sites in northern Scotland. However in 1981 a new species for Britain was found in open bog conditions in Ireland and proved to be breeding in 1982. This Irish damselfly is a Scandinavian species, leading to speculation that the vast **flow country** of **Caithness** and **Sutherland** might also provide a suitable habitat.

DROVE ROADS

Prior to the construction of **military roads** in the 18th century and **parliamentary roads** in the 19th, transhumance trails and footpaths were the only arteries of trade and communication in inland areas of the Highlands. From **Caithness** and **Kintyre** and from **Skye** and **Aberdeenshire** a host of drove routes converged on **Crieff**, the main tryst in the early 17th century. Since most of these routes crossed the grain of the mountains, they tended to bunch together at obvious passes such as the **Corrieyairack**. But this scarcely justifies the idea of drove 'roads'. Both cattle and drovers had a preference for the open hill and its gratis grazing.

Roads implied constriction. **Wade**, **Telford** and the **Mitchells** (John and **Joseph**) expressed the hope that their new military roads would facilitate cattle **droving**. But landowners saw the provision of these new roads as a chance to contain the drovers and to charge for overnight grazing. The drovers doubtless welcomed the new bridges and the bog causeways, but paved or gritted roads soon took a heavy toll on cloven feet. The art of droving came to depend heavily on pedicure and resulted in the need to shoe cattle. Blacksmiths at **Invergarry**, **Muir of Ord** and **Tyndrum** catered to their requirements at those places on the main drove routes where surfaced road succeeded grassy brae.

An admirable map of drove roads accompanies A R B Haldane's *The Drove Roads of Scotland*, 1952, and innumerable glens boast evidence or traditions of drove roads. In well populated and cultivated areas droving had always to be contained. But in the Highlands and Islands roads remained unpopular with the drovers and, however romantic in their current overgrown state, should not be taken as evidence of organisation or publicspirited endeavour on the part of the drover.

DROVING, Cattle, Sheep, etc

From the 17th to the 19th centuries cattle, and latterly sheep, represented practically the only cash crop produced in the Highlands and Islands. They were also an important feature in the Lowland economy. 'The wealth of the mountains is cattle,' declared **Dr Johnson** in 1773, and it was to realise this wealth that 'the ancient art and science' of droving assumed such importance.

With their abundant summer grazing but negligible winter feed, it was during the autumn that the Highlands and Islands echoed to the drovers' cries. Stock was either bought by the drover at a host of local fairs and markets or, more commonly, collected against a promise of payment less commission from his regular suppliers. The droves thus made up could number many hundreds of beasts and might be on the road for weeks. Between Kylerhea on **Skye** and **Glenelg** on the mainland – a traditional bottleneck since cattle must either swim the narrows or be ferried across – 7000 beasts crossed each year in the 1820s.

From the remoter glens of the north-west, from **Argyll** and **Aberdeen**, a network of **drove roads**, or drove routes, converged on the great trysts, or markets, of **Crieff** and latterly **Falkirk** for the October sales. Here beasts were bought by Lowland and English graziers to

Highland cattle retracing a Wester Ross drove road

be driven to fattening pastures in the Borders, Yorkshire and East Anglia. 30,000 head of cattle changed hands at Crieff in 1723, perhaps 200,000 at Falkirk in the early 19th century. A few drovers, such as **John Cameron** of Corriechoille, acquired considerable fortunes. Many were renowned for their resourcefulness and honesty. All contributed to the integration of remote communities by offering a source of cash and credit and by relaying market information.

In the 17th century droving expertise no doubt owed much to earlier traditions of cattle thieving, once a national pastime in the Highlands. More settled conditions after the **Act of Union** and the suppression of the 1715 and '45 **Jacobite Risings** encouraged peaceful trade; and the Continental wars of 1750–1815 greatly boosted the English demand for beef that could be salted for the troops. Although sheep to some extent replaced cattle in the first half of the 19th century, it was the opening of the Highland **railway** lines (1860–90) that finally put paid to the droving tradition.

DRUM CASTLE, Nr Aberdeen

Like the Burnett family of nearby **Crathes Castle**, the Irvines of Drum received their land charter from **Robert I** and have been there ever since. Originally from **Dumfries**, William de Irwin had been armour-bearer and clerk-register to the King. The single square tower that was then Drum still dominates the property. 70ft (21m)

high and with walls up to 12ft (3.6m) thick, it is a solid and impressive example of an early tower house with rounded angles, corbelled parapet and battlements.

The spelling of the family name changed to Irvine but the custom of the laird's first name always being Alexander lasted for generations. When one Alexander was killed in single combat with a MacLean of **Duart** (who also died) at the **Battle of Harlaw**, his brother Robert changed his name to Alexander rather than break with tradition. The 9th Laird, another Alexander, made a generous endowment to **Aberdeen**'s **Marischal College** and in 1619 added a substantial new house to Drum. This incorporated many features typical of a Jacobean tower house but, unlike **Crathes**, **Craigievar** etc, is less tower and more conventional house. The preference for a horizontal profile is ascribed not, as one might expect, to long experience of the tower's steep staircases, but to the availability of roof timbers thanks to Aberdeen's burgeoning trade with Scandinavia.

In 1871 **David Bryce** redesigned the barmkin courtyard and, soon after, the old tower became a library with the removal of an intermediate floor; a large window was also added. Otherwise the great tower, unharled and unadorned, remains much as it ever was. The property is now in the care of the **National Trust for Scotland**.

DRUMCLOG, Battle of (1679)

John Graham of Claverhouse, hunting down **Covenanters** responsible for the **Rutherglen Declaration**,

The keep of Drum Castle from the north-east (MR)

reached **Strathaven** on 1 June and immediately headed for Drumclog (near Darvel) where an outdoor **conventicle** was said to be in progress. Equipped for war rather than prayer, the Covenanters (including **Sir Robert Hamilton** and **William Cleland**) awaited him. The combatants were few and well-matched, the battle brief. Claverhouse's Highlanders ventured into a bog, were routed by the psalm-singing conventiclers, and forced to flee to the security of **Glasgow**. There they again offered resistance but then withdrew, leaving the burgh to the not-so-tender mercies of the godly. These successes drew many supporters and sympathisers to the insurgents' main camp at **Bothwell Brig**, where Claverhouse would soon enjoy his revenge.

DRUMELZIER, Peeblesshire

Sometimes written Drummelzier (and always pron. Drummelier), this village on the south bank of the river **Tweed** is one of many sites said to be the burial-place of the wizard Merlin. A tumulus near the junction of the Drumelzier Burn (anciently called the Poussil or Powsail Burn) with the Tweed marks the spot, and the legend dates from a prediction made by **Thomas the Rhymer**:

When Tweed and Powsail meet at Merlin's grave
England and Scotland shall one monarch have.

Legend has it that on the day in 1603 that **James VI** was crowned King of England an unprecedented flood raised the waters of the burn so they overflowed into the Tweed just beside the tumulus.

Ruined Tinnies or Thanes Castle by the Tweed was destroyed in 1592 by order of James VI who suspected its owner to have been involved in the **Gowrie Conspiracy**. Three miles east of Drumelzier on the way to Stobo, Dawyck Botanic Garden became an Outstation of the **Royal Botanic Garden**, **Edinburgh** in 1978 but has a history of tree planting which goes back more than 300 years. A famous European larch is said to have been planted by the Swedish naturalist Linnaeus in 1725, but most of the big conifers (some exceeding 45m tall) were planted by the proprietors, the Nasmyth family, who subscribed to various plant-hunting expeditions including those of **David Douglas**.

DRUMLANRIG CASTLE, Nr Thornhill, Dumfriesshire

Completed in 1689 for William Douglas, 1st Duke of Queensberry, Drumlanrig combines both castellar and classical elements in a mansion of palatial dimensions. Indeed Defoe called it 'a palace' and, like Pennant, marvelled at how the orderly symmetry of house and gardens contrasted with its wild and mountainous setting in upper Nithsdale. The design, 'a hollow square' of four equal sides with identical corner towers round a central courtyard, was evidently a compromise and has been criticised. In 1618 a basic lay-out had been proposed probably by William Wallace which closely resembled **Heriot's Hospital** in **Edinburgh**. 60 years later **James Smith**'s design was more influenced by **Holyroodhouse** on which he had worked under **Sir William Bruce**. Corbelled angle turrets and gargoyles recall the older tradition while classical elements include

The north front of Drumlanrig Castle as drawn by MacGibbon and Ross (MR)

the Corinthian pilasters flanking the main entrance and the pedimented windows. The whole is in pink sandstone and may incorporate some walls of the **Douglas** stronghold that preceded it.

The 1st Duke of Queensberry is said to have spent only one night in it and then returned to **Sanquhar** Castle. **Prince Charles Edward Stewart**'s stay in 1745 was also for one night. After the death (1810) of the 4th Duke (the notorious 'Old Q' and **Wordsworth**'s 'Degenerate Douglas' who cut down the surrounding woodlands) it passed to the **Dukes of Buccleuch**. The magnificent collection of furniture and art treasures on display (including Rembrandt's *Old Woman Reading* and works by Holbein, Murillo, etc) are those of the Scotts of Buccleuch.

DRUMLITHIE, Kincardineshire
Upstream from **Inverbervie** and **Arbuthnott**, Drumlithie ('no more than a rickle of houses' according to **Lewis Grassic Gibbon**) is the main village of Glenbervie, an area closely associated with the Burn(e)s family. They are thought to have originated from **Taynuilt** in **Argyll** but farmed here for several generations before William, the father of **Robert Burns**, moved to **Ayrshire**; others stayed in the area including the parents of **Sir Alexander Burnes**. The churchyard has several Burn(e)s tombstones and there is a commemorative cairn by the roadside. The bell tower of Drumlithie, a slender miniature of that in **Brechin**, was erected in 1770 to summon the village's weavers to their looms. 'Folk said for a joke that every time it came on to rain the Drumlithie folk ran out and took in their steeple, that proud they were of the thing' (Lewis Grassic Gibbon). To the east, across the A94, Fiddes Castle was an Arbuthnott stronghold, its two-storey turrets dating it to the end of the 16th century. Basically L-plan, it has an impressive profusion of circular stair towers, one with a parapet, another corbelled out to a square cap house.

DRUMMOND, Annabella or Arabella (c.1350–1401)
Known only for her relationship to others, Annabella Drummond was the daughter of Sir John Drummond of **Stobhall** in **Perthshire**, the wife of **Robert III** (whom she married c1367), and the mother of seven

children including **David, Duke of Rothesay** and **James I**.

DRUMMOND, George (1687–1766) Civic Improver
Six times Lord Provost of **Edinburgh** (1725, 1746, 1750–1, 1754–5, 1758–9 and 1762–3), George Drummond fought against **Mar** at **Sheriffmuir** (1715) and raised the First or College Company (1745) in an unsuccessful attempt to prevent **Prince Charles Edward** and his **Jacobite** army from entering the city. Also a great social improver, he initiated (1725) the raising of funds for the city's first infirmary (chartered in 1736 and later the **Royal Infirmary**), established five medical professorships at **Edinburgh University**, and was the moving spirit behind plans for Edinburgh's **New Town**; his visionary 'Proposals' in 1753 for the bare, wind-swept ridge of the Lang Dykes, north of the **Old Town**, became a reality after the draining of the **Nor'** Loch and the commencement of the **North Bridge**, for which he laid the foundation stone in 1763. He is buried in **Canongate Churchyard**.

DRUMMOND, Henry (1851–97) Populist Theologian and Evangelical
Born in **Stirling**, Drummond studied at **Edinburgh University** without taking a degree, then studied for the ministry of the **Free Presbyterian Church**. Involved with Moody and Sankey evangelism, he became a lecturer at the Free Church College in **Glasgow** and Professor of Natural Science from 1884. As a populist writer on science as well as biology, he researched in the Rockies and wrote on their geology, then in the USA, Central Africa, Japan and Australia; his *Natural Law in the Spanish World*, 1883, dealt with natural selection in evolution. He was also a patron of Scottish literature, in particular of the **Kailyard** novelist **John Watson** ('Ian Maclaren').

DRUMMOND, James (1816–77) History Painter
The son of an **Edinburgh** burgess, Drummond demonstrated an early facility for draughtsmanship, preparing illustrations for the ornithologist Captain Thomas Brown and the surgeon John Lizars before enrolling under **Sir William Allan** at the Trustees' Academy. Like his friend and contemporary **William Fettes Douglas**, he was a scholar whose passion for the history of his country profoundly affected the subject and the style of his art. His paintings were often – in the academic tradition – composed with the aid of costume models placed in a topographical setting and portrayed with a fastidious attention to correct detail that clearly displayed his motivations as more than simply aesthetic. The novels of **Scott** were a frequent source for Drummond's historical reconstructions and in 1855 his reputation was made with the exhibition at the **Royal Scottish Academy** of the *Porteous Mob* (**National Gallery of Scotland**). In spite of the dramatic subject and Drummond's charged lighting, the moment of abduction from *The Heart of Midlothian* is lost to the mid-ground and diminished further by the dominating presence of the old Edinburgh tenements. In 1848 Drummond was elected a fellow of the **Society of Antiquaries** and in 1851 was appointed first curator of the Society's collection (later

to become the basis of the national collection of antiquities). Throughout the mid-century he was engaged in producing studies of the **Old Town** which, if lacking in character, act as a meticulous record of much of the vernacular architecture later lost by demolition. Now primarily of documentary interest, his historical canvases won him widespread renown. As librarian and a master of the Academy Schools he also wielded influence, and was appointed Director of the National Gallery of Scotland in 1868.

DRUMMOND, Margaret (c1472–1502)

Daughter of John, 1st Lord Drummond, Margaret was the mistress from 1496 of **James IV**, to whom some said she was secretly married and by whom she was rumoured to have had a daughter. In 1502 she and her two sisters, Euphemia and Sibilla, were poisoned at **Drummond Castle**, probably by nobles who saw her as an obstacle to the King's marriage to **Margaret Tudor**. The three sisters were buried at **Dunblane Cathedral** where brass plaques in their memory were set into the floor of the choir in 1873 by the Drummond **Earl of Perth**.

DRUMMOND, Thomas (1797–1840)
Inventor

Born in **Edinburgh**, Drummond was educated at the city's **University** before joining the Ordnance Survey in 1820. To assist his surveying work he invented an improved heliostat as well as limelight, achieving an intense white light by burning lime in oxygenated flame. Its principal use was later as stage-lighting in the theatre. Following the 1832 Reform Bill he took charge of the boundary commission for settling parliamentary constituences and in 1835 was appointed Under-Secretary for Ireland. He died of overwork in Dublin, much loved by the Irish and appropriately remembered for the dictum that 'property has its duties as well as its rights'.

DRUMMOND, William, of Hawthornden (1585–1649) Poet

William Drummond was born at **Hawthornden Castle**, the family home perched on a rock above the Lothian river Esk. His father was one of **James VI**'s gentlemen ushers, and his mother a sister of the poet William Fowler. He was educated at **Edinburgh** High School and **University**, studied law at Bourges and Paris, and returned to Scotland when his father died in 1609, to become Laird of Hawthornden. Though associated with James VI's 'Castilean Band' of poets, he was by nature a solitary man, becoming almost a recluse after the death of Euphemia Cunningham of Barns, whom he had intended to marry. Subsequently, however, he took a mistress who bore him three children, and in 1630 he married Elizabeth Logan of **Restalrig**; yet he remained a man out of sympathy with his times. The religious troubles following the National **Covenant** of 1638, which Drummond signed (he also signed the Covenant of 1639, though at heart a Royalist), involved him increasingly in a struggle with poverty and debt litigation. On his death, his large library was left to his old university.

Deeply read in European literature, his involvement

William Drummond of Hawthornden, by an unknown artist (SNPG)

with the Petrarchan tradition ran counter to the metaphysical fashion practised by most of his contemporaries. Although, after the manner of the time, he borrowed heavily from poems by European writers, he always transmuted what he took into his own personal musical style.

His *Teares on the Death of Meliades* commemorated the death of **Prince Henry**, the King's heir. The second, revised edition of Drummond's *Poems, Amorous, Funereall, Divine, Pastoroll in Sonnets, Songs, Sextains, Madrigals* (which first appeared in 1614) came out in 1616, the year King James paid a return visit to Scotland, and two years before Ben Jonson visited Drummond at Hawthornden. *Forth Feasting* followed in 1617, *Flowers of Sion* in 1623, *The Entertainment* in 1633, and posthumously, a somewhat indifferent *History of Scotland* in 1655. His finest prose achievement, *A Cypress Grove*, a meditation upon death (which may have influenced Sir Thomas Browne's *Religio Medici* and *Urn Burial* (1658) written a generation later) appeared with *Flowers of Sion*.

Drummond is perhaps most widely known for his fine sonnet 'For the Baptist', the madrigal beginning 'Like the Idalian queen', and his savage quatrain on the death of the Parliamentarian John Pym. The true depth of his Royalist feelings is revealed in a sonnet, first published in a London selection of his work in 1656, on hearing of the execution of **Charles I**. It begins:

Doth then the World go thus? Doth all thus, move?
Is this the Justice which on earth we find?
Is this the firm decree which all doth bind?
Are these your influences, Powers above?

The best edition of Drummond's complete works is the *Poetical Works*, including *A Cypress Grove*, published by the Scottish Text Society (1913).

Although the major Scottish poet of the later Renaissance, critical doubt surrounds the degree to which Drummond is a 'Scottish' writer. He wrote in English, allied himself with Spenser and Drayton, and the sonnets and madrigals of his *Poems* belong to the tradition of late English Petrarchism. His life, especially in its romanticised form as 'Hermit of Hawthornden', strengthened this sense of apartness from Scottish life and language.

DRUMMOND CASTLE, Nr Crieff, Perthshire

Built by Sir John (later Lord) Drummond in the late 15th century, Drummond Castle replaced **Stobhall** as the seat of the Drummond family until the estate was forfeited following the **1745 Jacobite Rising**. It consists of a single tower and a later lower extension with gateway (1630) by **John Mylne**, both mostly rebuilt since Cromwell's pounding. To them was added a Victorian mansion, occupying the site of an earlier building, which was the home of the Earls of Ancaster, descendants in the female line of the Drummonds and successors to the property after its forfeiture. **James VI** was a frequent visitor while courting **Margaret Drummond** (daughter of Sir John, and later murdered); so was **Queen Mary**. The castle gardens, with elaborate terraced parterres and statuary including Mylne's obelisk-like sundial, are open to the public.

DRUMNADROCHIT, Inverness-shire

This village stands at the head of the largest bay on **Loch Ness** and at the mouth of Glen Urquhart. The southern headland of the bay is occupied by **Urquhart Castle** and further along the main A82 there is a monument to John Cobb who died here in 1952 while attempting the world water-speed record. Drumnadrochit itself offers the Official Loch Ness Monster Centre which attracts many tour parties if few monsters. Up Glen Urquhart a road leads to Glens Cannich and Affric and **Strathglass**. Just short of Cannich the **clava cairn** at Corrimony is exceptionally well preserved. Within a ring of 11 **standing stones** the cairn is penetrated by the usual low passage, here still roofed with its original slabs. The chamber itself is now open but a massive cup-marked stone on top is thought to have been its original capstone.

DRUMOCHTER PASS, Perthshire/
Inverness-shire

Here in bleak surroundings the main road and **rail** links to **Inverness** cross the watershed between the **Tay** and the **Spey**. They roughly follow the line of **Wade**'s military road, commemorated by a stone recording the meeting of the troops working south from Inverness with those working north from **Dunkeld** in 1729. The railway, highest in Britain, rises to 1484ft (452m), the road slightly higher. The pass is flanked by two hogs' backs, the Sow of **Atholl** and the Boar of **Badenoch**, with roadless Loch Ericht reaching south-west to **Ben Alder**, and Gaick forest to the east. **Dalwhinnie** and **Newtonmore** lie along the road and railway down Glen Truim to the north, **Dalnaspidal** and **Blair Atholl** down Glen Garry to the south-east.

DRYBURGH ABBEY, St Boswells,
Roxburghshire

Neither as grand as **Melrose** nor as complete as **Jed-**

burgh, Dryburgh yet has its advocates amongst connoisseurs of Borders abbeys. Set amid trees on the banks of the **Tweed** it has more the romance of a mantled ruin; its conventual buildings (chapter house, vestry, dormitory, etc) are more recognisable; and it boasts two notable graves, those of **Sir Walter Scott** and **Earl Haig**.

The first mention of Dryburgh is in connection with St Modan, a disciple of **St Columba**, who is described as Abbot of Dryburgh in 622. But there is no sign of his abbey. The much rebuilt and oft destroyed ruins of today's Dryburgh date from 1150 when canons of the Premonstratensian order (ie Augustinians from Premonstre in France) settled here under the patronage of Hugh de Moreville, hereditary Constable of Scotland. Although never as generously endowed as Melrose, Dryburgh accumulated sufficient lands and wealth to be a prime target during the turbulent 14th century. Edward II burnt it in 1322 and Richard II in 1385. It was probably never completely rebuilt but there was enough left to attract two further sackings in 1544. By then the last abbot had long since given way to a succession of **commendators** (lay nobles appointed to manage and enjoy ecclesiastical revenues). The Erskine family enjoyed this office 1541–1611. In 1700 Dryburgh, now just the ruin and adjacent fields, passed to Thomas Haliburton, great-grandfather of Sir Walter Scott. The Haliburtons sold out, much to Sir Walter's later chagrin, retaining only 'the right of stretching our bones here'. Hence Scott's privileged resting place.

DRYMEN, Stirlingshire

At the western extremity of **Stirlingshire** where the Endrick approaches **Loch Lomond**, Drymen's history is a tale of three families. Its link with the Drummonds is

Dryburgh Abbey with the tomb of Sir Walter Scott (RWB)

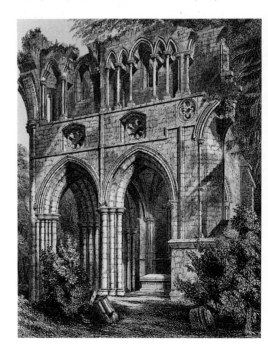

etymological (both from *druimm*, a ridge) and ancient, the family holding lands here of the Celtic **Earls of Lennox** before moving to **Perthshire** [see **Stobhall**]. With the **Buchanans** the link is ubiquitous, the Buchanan estate and parish once covering a vast area of Drymen to Balmaha, the Buchanan Arms being still the most notable hotel, and Buchanan Castle (**William Burn**, 1854) far and away the most spectacular ruin. As for the Grahams the link is conclusive, for the Buchanans, having had the temerity to oppose and then profit from the disgrace of their neighbour **James Graham, Marquis of Montrose**, were eventually forced to sell out to his successors. In the early 18th century the now Dukes of Montrose removed from **Mugdock Castle** to the House of Buchanan and it was they who replaced it with the splendid Buchanan Castle. Only briefly was this aristocratic saga interrupted, notably by the outlawed **MacGregors** who harried the area soon after the arrival of the Grahams. MacGregor chiefs lie buried alongside Buchanans on Inchcailleach, once the site of a Celtic nunnery and one of several islands off the now popular Lomondside sailing resort of Balmaha. By the pass of Balmaha, up which the eastside Loch Lomond road runs to a dead end at Rowardennan beneath Ben Lomond, the MacGregors drove their captured cattle into the safety of the mountains.

DRYSDALE, Learmont (1866–1909)
Composer
Born in **Edinburgh** where he worked as an organist, Drysdale moved to London in 1887, studying at the Royal Academy of Music. He returned to Scotland in 1904 to teach at the then Athenaeum, but gave this up in favour of composition. One of the group of musicians who, along with **Sir Alexander Campbell Mackenzie** and **Hamish McCunn**, tried to give formal composed music a specifically Scottish flavour, Drysdale's concert overture *Tam O' Shanter* blends Wagnerian grandeur with native wit. *The Kelpie*, a dramatic cantata, is a fine example of Drysdale's purposeful and overt compositional style, but the exquisite *Short Trio* shows a refinement and delicacy worthy of the best of Fauré. His comic opera *The Red Spider* received over 100 performances and Farmer speaks in the highest terms of his music for *Hippolytus*.

DUART CASTLE, Isle of Mull
The principal **MacLean** castle, Duart was restored to the clan in 1911, is occupied by the chief, and is usually open to the public. Of all west-coast castles Duart gives the best idea of what they were like in their heyday. It commands the Sound of **Mull**, guards Loch Linnhe and the Firth of Lorn, and sights the castles of **Dunstaffnage**, Dunollie (**Oban**), **Ardtornish** and Achadun in **Lismore**. At first it must have resembled **Castle Sween**, a massive enclosure containing timber buildings and dating from the 12th–13th century, to which has been added a great tower house and later works. Probably begun by **Somerled**'s MacDougall descendants, Duart passed to the **Lords of the Isles** and, by marriage around 1367, to the MacLeans. Besieged by **Campbells** (1645–7), it was garrisoned by Commonwealth forces until the Restoration, restored to the MacLeans, retaken by Campbells and then converted into government barracks from 1741–8.

DUFF, Alexander (1806–78) Missionary
Born in Moulin, **Perthshire** and educated at **St Andrews** (which staid city he stigmatised as a 'mass of moral putrescence' and where he was much influenced by **Thomas Chalmers**, then the **University**'s Professor of Moral Philosophy), Duff graduated in arts and theology in 1828 and immediately accepted an offer from the committee of the General Assembly on Foreign Missions to become their first missionary to India [but see **John Wilson**]. Ordained in 1829, he arrived in Calcutta in 1830 having been shipwrecked twice on the voyage; proof, he thought (if any were needed) that God had some truly important work for him to do in India. Described as 'humourless and austere and endowed with a burning desire to convert the souls of the heathen to Christ' (A D Gibb), in 1830 he opened his first mission school in Calcutta, where teaching was based on his conviction that the English language and Western knowledge were the best weapons with which to undermine the superstitions of Hinduism. His reputation and example decisively influenced British government policy on education in India; in 1835 a minute from the Governor-General, Lord William Bentinck, stated that 'the object of the British government ought to be the promotion of European science and literature amongst the natives of India, and that all the funds appropriated for the purposes of education would be best employed on English education alone'. Instrumental in founding a medical college and later a hospital in Calcutta, as well as the famous Madras Christian College, Duff was also on the committee that drew up the constitution of Calcutta University. Twice Chairman of the **General Assembly** of the **Free Church** (1851 and 1873), he founded the missionary chair at New College, **Edinburgh** and became its first missionary professor.

DUFF, James, 2nd Earl of Fife (1729–1809)
Agricultural Improver
Son of William Duff of Braco, who was created **Earl of Fife** in 1759, James succeeded to the Earldom in 1763. MP for **Banff** (1754, 1761, 1768, 1774 and 1780) and then for **Elgin** (1784), he vastly increased the family estates and was twice awarded the Gold Medal of the Society for the Encouragement of Arts, Manufacture and Commerce for the improvements he wrought in **agriculture**, **forestry** and cattle-breeding. Lord Lieutenant of the county of Banff, he founded the town of **MacDuff** and completed the building of **Duff House** commissioned from **William Adam** by his father in 1735. He was created a British peer by the title of Baron Duff (1790), but since he died childless this title became extinct, the Earldom passing to his brother Alexander.

DUFF, James, 4th Earl of Fife (1776–1857)
Spanish General
Elder son of the Hon Alexander Duff (who became 3rd Earl of Fife in 1809 on the death of his brother **James, 2nd Earl**), James Duff volunteered to fight with the Spanish army against Napoleon in 1808 after the death of his young wife. Instantly made a major-general, he fought with distinction at Talavera (1809) and in the defence of Cadiz (1810), being badly wounded in both engagements and rewarded with a knighthood in the Order of St Ferdinand. He succeeded to the Earldom in

1811 and returned to his Scottish estates to become, like his father and uncle before him, MP for **Banff** and Lord Lieutenant of the county of **Banffshire**.

DUFF, Sir Mountstuart Elphinstone Grant (1829–1906) Administrator and Author

Duff (sometimes Grant Duff) was born at Eden Castle near **Turriff**, the estate of his father, James Grant Duff (1789–1858). The latter had served in Bombay under **Mountstuart Elphinstone** and named his son after him; Resident at Poona and Satara he had also written a standard *History of the Mahrathas*, 1826. Mountstuart inherited his interest in India. After **Edinburgh** and Balliol, Oxford he was called to the English Bar, elected MP for **Elgin** burghs (1857–81) and became Under-Secretary of State for India (1868–74) and the Colonies (1880). In 1881–6 he served as Governor of Madras and, although not a success, did much to beautify the city including the creation of its long Marina, an esplanade named after that in Palermo. On his return he devoted himself to more congenial pursuits as scholar and traveller. He became President of the Royal Geographical Society and the Royal Historical Society, a trustee of the British Museum and rector of **Aberdeen University**. Of his several books, the most enlightening is the 14-volume memoir, *Notes from a Diary*, 1897–1905, a valuable source for social historians of the period.

DUFF HOUSE, Banff

One of **William Adam**'s greatest achievements, Duff House beside the river **Deveron** is a square four-storey baroque mansion incorporating much classical detail, as in the Corinthian pilasters and pediments, with a hint of feudal tradition in the four projecting corner towers. It is said to have been modelled on the Villa Borghese in Rome but a closer relative is Adam's **Hopetoun House**, begun earlier but shorn of many of its baroque features before completion. At Duff, on the other hand, Adam realised his ornate design for the main block but had to abandon the flanking wings with colonnades and pavilions (as at Hopetoun), an omission which largely explains the impression of excessive perpendicularity. The truncated little wing added in the 1870s by a nephew and namesake of **David Bryce** does nothing to redress this.

The house was built for William Duff of Braco, later 1st **Earl of Fife**, a parvenu anxious to proclaim his meteoric rise, who gave Adam a free hand to build (1735–40) the main block but then instituted legal proceedings over the cost. The £2500 for the 36 pilasters, 34 Grecian vases, assorted coats of arms and statuary, all of which were being shipped from the Forth, seems to have been the final straw. What Duff called his 'monstrous house' ground to a standstill and was not completed until his son resumed the work 20 years later.

Although the Prince of Wales was entertained here in 1883, the house was only fitfully occupied and in 1906 was gifted to **Banff** and **MacDuff**. It has subsequently served as a hotel, a nursing home, a prisoner of war camp and a barracks, and is now in the care of the state. The grounds (including several follies and a mausoleum in which the Duffs assembled effigies purloined from elsewhere) are largely occupied by a **golf course.**

William Adam's Duff House at Banff (HS)

DUFFTOWN, Banff

Dufftown in **Moray** District is a thriving centre of the **whisky** industry. As Rome was founded on seven hills, so was Dufftown built amid seven stills, ie the seven distilleries erected in the town between 1823 and 1898. As well as the employment provided by the distilleries themselves, the Glenfiddich Visitor Centre, like others on the Speyside Whisky Trail, is a major **tourist** attraction.

Founded in 1817 by **James Duff, 4th Earl of Fife**, Dufftown was a new planned village set in an area of considerable historic interest. Mortlach Kirk dates back to at least the 13th century, although its legendary associations go back even further. There are a number of ancient carved stones stored in the vestibule of the church, including a **Pictish** 'elephant' stone, and another weathered Pictish so-called 'battle' stone in the kirkyard. On the north side of Dufftown, the medieval **Balvenie Castle** once commanded important passes. A **Comyn** stronghold, this imposing fortress later passed into the hands of the **Earls of Atholl**. In the town itself a notable landmark is the 19th century clock tower, which has served consecutively as local gaol and burgh chambers (Dufftown became a **police burgh** in 1863). It now houses a Tourist information centre for a town where tourism has greatly expanded in recent years. Another, and intriguing, Victorian survival is the custom of holding a Boys' Walk and Ball on New Year's Day.

George Stephen (1829–1921), one of the progenitors of the first cross-Canada railway, was born in Dufftown and is commemorated by a stained-glass window in Mortlach Kirk which includes a representation of a Canadian Pacific Railway locomotive. His many notable benefactions included a cottage hospital.

DUFFUS CASTLE, Nr Elgin, Moray

It has been suggested that the 8 acre (3.2ha) mound on which stand the crumbling remains of Duffus was once an island. This fails to explain the purpose of the surrounding ditch, but certainly it was an extremely strong position and made all the more so by the construction of a steep motte near the centre on which the massive stone keep was built. It was preceded by the timber structure (with bailey) in which **David I** stayed while supervising the foundation of **Kinloss Abbey** and which had been built by Freskin, father of William of Moray, 1st **Earl of Sutherland**, whom David had settled here. The stone castle with its keep and enclosing walls, now much collapsed by subsidence of the mound, probably dates from the early 14th century. **John Graham of Claverhouse, 'Bonnie Dundee'**, stayed here in 1689, by which time the keep had already been abandoned. The nearby old parish church of Duffus is now in state care along with the castle. Roofless and mostly 18th century, it includes a fine vaulted 16th century porch and, in the graveyard, a slender medieval mercat cross dedicated to St Peter.

DUMBARTON, Dunbartonshire

'Dumbarton, it must be owned, presents an irregular and unattractive appearance, little in keeping with its fine surroundings', declared the *Ordnance Gazetteer of Scotland* in 1892. It was created a **royal burgh** in 1222, rivalled **Glasgow** and **Rutherglen** as a market town in the 15th century and subsequently became the county town of **Dunbartonshire**. With its history and aspect both dominated by **Dumbarton Rock**, the town yet boasts another historic site, the collegiate church of St Mary, founded in 1453. The church was built as a semi-monastic establishment for a provost and six priests. It had a brief life, and did not survive the **Reformation** in 1560. A stone arch is all that remains. The growth of **shipbuilding** and **engineering** on the River Leven shaped and developed the town. **Andrew Wood** assembled and perhaps built ships here for his forays up the west coast on behalf of **James IV** and in the 17th century Glasgow's burgesses tried to interest Dumbarton in becoming their deep sea port. Shipbuilding started in the 18th century and by 1853 there were five shipyards. **William Denny** and Brothers, whose workforce built the fastest clipper of all time, the **Cutty Sark**, were the chief employers for over a century. They went into voluntary liquidation in 1963 but their Ship Model Experiment Tank has been retained along with a marine engine designed by **Robert Napier** for the paddle steamer *Leven* in 1824. Near the Leven shipyard Sunderland Flying Boats were produced during World War II. Today **whisky** distilling and warehousing plus light industry have taken the place of the old heavy industries.

DUMBARTON ROCK, Dunbartonshire

As the main stronghold of the **Kingdom of Strathclyde**, the 240ft (73m) rock of basalt known originally as Dun Breatann, the fort of the Britons, has one of the longest histories in the British Isles. Fortified from at least the 5th century, it was 'the rock on the **Clyde**' mentioned by Bede in 730; a royal stronghold in medieval times, subsequently a barracks, and latterly a museum. In 1305 its incumbent, **Sir John Menteith**, held **William Wallace** here prior to his journey to London and execution; and it was the refuge of **Queen Mary** as a child before her flight to France and safety. In 1571 the castle was taken by Thomas Crawford of Jordanhill in an exceptionally daring attack after it had held out for Mary longer than anywhere except **Edinburgh Castle**. The remains of the castle's fortifications sprawl over the rock which terminates in two summits, one of which is known as Wallace's Seat. A steep climb from the 18th century Governor's House gives access to the White Tower whence the view was deemed 'sufficient recompense' for the ascent by a breathless **Dorothy Wordsworth**. Dumbarton's coat of arms, an elephant with a castle for a howdah, illustrates the town's dependence on the Rock.

DUMFRIES

Associated with **Robert I**, **Queen Mary**, **Robert Burns** and **Prince Charles Edward Stewart**, Dumfries has excellent Scottish credentials for a town within sight of England. Its sobriquet 'Queen of the South' (also the name of its main **football** club) was endorsed by English visitors such as Defoe who found 'a prosperous town of merchant adventurers' with the busiest port in southern Scotland. In the 19th century it was 'the metropolis of south west Scotland, a place of elegance, importance and great antiquity' (Fullarton's *Gazetteer*); and so it remains. Gone, though, is the 'very magnificent' castle reported by Defoe but demolished soon after his visit; both its site and its masonry were required for a new church (1727) which was replaced (1867) by that of Greyfriars, fronted by a statue of Burns and prominent at the head of the High Street. It was at an older Greyfriars that in 1306 the future Robert I murdered **John Comyn (ii)**, Roger Kirkpatrick making 'sic-car' (secure, sure) by impaling the dead man on his sword. This establishment is thought to have stood west of the High Street and to be commemorated in 'Friar's Vennel'.

The friary may have been founded by **Devorguilla Balliol** who is also credited with having built the first bridge across the Nith. In the 15th century this 13-arch, probably timber, construction was replaced by the handsome six- (originally nine-) arch bridge, now foot passengers only, which is 'the oldest surviving multiple stone arch bridge in Scotland'. It in turn was superseded upstream in 1794 by the Buccleuch Street Bridge (Thomas Boyd) and downstream in 1927 by St Michael's Bridge. The original burgh, including the castle, lay entirely on the east bank; the west bank, known as Bridgend, later Maxwelltown and now all part of Dumfries, was not even in the same county.

Castle and town changed hands frequently during the **Wars of Independence** and during the subsequent border disturbances. In the 16th century the local Maxwells refortified the castle which submitted to Queen Mary in 1565 but was taken and plundered by the English as late as 1570. **James VI** visited in 1617 and presented a silver gun (now in the museum) as a prize for marksmanship. Self-defence paid off in 1715 when the call to arms, and now the town motto, of 'Alore-burn' (All to the Lower Burn) dissuaded Viscount Kenmure and his **Jacobites** from attack. But in 1745 the town paid dearly for waylaying part of Prince Charles Edward's baggage train, a heavy fine being imposed and the Jacobite army freely plundering.

Although the **Act of Union** had been opposed by 200 **Cameronians** who in 1706 burnt the proposals at the burgh cross, Dumfries benefited more than most from easier access to English and North American ports. From several quays, extending down the Nith from Dockfoot in the town to Glencaple five miles south, the 80 plus vessels owned (1840) by the 'merchant adventurers' passed the Southerness lighthouse (1748 and one of the earliest in England, although subsequently enlarged) en route to Scotland, the United States and the West Indies. There was also a regular steamer service to Whitehaven and Liverpool; but the **railways** as much as the vagaries of the Nith put paid to this traffic in the later 19th century. Dumfries Museum, housed in the Observatory (1835) where there is also a camera obscura, recalls this maritime past plus more distant times with an important archaeological display.

Bridge End or Old Bridge House (c1662 and also a museum) is thought to be the oldest extant house but there are several 18th century buildings, many associated with Robert Burns who came to Dumfries ('Maggie by the banks of the Nith, a dame with pride eneuch') from Ellisland [see **Thornhill**] as an exciseman in 1791 and remained until his death in 1796. His home for most of this period, in what is now Burns Street, has

been restored as a Burns Museum; there are further mementoes of the poet in the Kings Arms and Globe Hotels, the Hole in the Wa' Tavern, and **St Michaels** graveyard. A Burns 'interpretive centre' with exhibition and audio-visual presentation is located in the Old Town Mill; the Gracefield Arts Centre (19th and 20th century Scottish artists including **Hornel** and Blackadder) and the Dumfries Priory Christian Heritage Museum (liturgical vestments and a presentation on the region's religious houses) complete the spectrum of civic displays. The Theatre Royal (1792) is one of the oldest in Scotland and after an uncertain period as a roller-skating rink and cinema is now restored to its original function.

Lincluden Abbey/Church

Reached through a housing estate on the outskirts of the town, Lincluden stands beside a motte near the confluence of the Cluden (**Burns**'s 'Clouden') with the Nith. It was founded in the 12th century as an abbey for Benedictine nuns but this foundation was closed

The choir of Lincluden Abbey, Dumfries, as drawn by R W Billings (RWB)

down in 1389 and replaced by a collegiate church endowed by **Archibald, 3rd Earl of Douglas**. The ruins comprising choir, south transept and a bit of nave are of this early 15th century church; though not large, they possess sculpture and masonry of the highest quality, probably the work of the French master mason John Morow, who worked at **Melrose Abbey**. Outstanding in its heraldic detail and in its architectural elegance is the elaborate arched recess in the choir which houses the tomb and effigy of Margaret, Countess of Douglas, who was the daughter of **Robert III** and the wife of the **4th Earl**, also Duke of Touraine. The rubble remains adjoining the church are those of a 15th century house and tower which continued in use after the **Reformation** but which, like the church, were serving the town's masonry needs by the end of the 17th century. A section of Lincluden's choir stalls found their way to Terregles church, far enough west to be of no interest to either the zealots or the contractors of Dumfries. Indeed the choir of Terregles was built by the Catholic Maxwells as a burial vault in 1583, so *after* the **Reformation**.

Mid Steeple

Designed by John Moffat of Liverpool and built by Tobias Bachup of **Alloa**, the Mid Steeple was erected in 1707 as a gaol, council chamber, courtroom and civic focus, becoming in effect the burgh's tolbooth. It stands in the middle of the High Street, a narrow three-storey block with a pierced parapet at roof level, a first-floor entrance with external forestair at one end, and a prominent clock tower with steeple at the other. The burgh's coat of arms and a statue of its patron, St Michael, flank the entrance. To them was added (1827) a mileage panel giving distances to **Annan**, Carlisle, **Edinburgh**, London, etc, and, more mysteriously, Huntingdon (272 miles); it is assumed that this information was of value to cattle **drovers** heading for the fattening grounds of East Anglia and Lincolnshire. In the courtroom Effie Walker was condemned for child murder, the judgement which inspired her sister **Helen Walker**'s search for clemency and which in turn inspired **Sir Walter Scott**'s *Heart of Midlothian*.

St Michael's Church

The old parish church of St Michael was built in 1745 on the site of its medieval predecessor. A Georgian hall church surmounted by a lofty spire, it was where **Burns** worshipped during his final years and where he was laid to rest. The churchyard contains an impressive array of tombs and mausolea 'rising like mimic temples over the ashes of the gifted and wealthy' according to an 1840 description, 'a forest of obelisks, columns and elevated urns, robed in white painting, and in the dim moonlight like an assembly of spectres'. The plain stone slab under which Burns was buried (1796) made a telling contrast and an apt memorial. But in 1815 it was thought too insignificant for the national bard and, with George IV leading the subscribers, his remains were reburied beneath a Grecian rotunda containing a marble statue representing Burns 'in his rustic dress and employment' being invested with the mantle of 'Coila', said to be either 'the muse of poetry', 'the genius of Scotland', or both. The sculptor was Peter Turnerelli. Nearby a granite obelisk commemorates three **Covenanting** martyrs, two of 1667, one of 1685, and in the church there is a plaque to another poet, **Allan Cunningham**. Here also worshipped the future **Sir J M Barrie**, who was a pupil at the Dumfries Academy, and the future **Sir John Richardson**, the Arctic explorer/naturalist who was the son of a provost of Dumfries.

DUMFRIES HOUSE, Nr Cumnock, Ayrshire

Built (1754–9) for William Dalrymple, 4th Earl of Dumfries and 3rd Earl of Stair, the restrained Palladianism of this fine house is characteristic of John Adam although it is thought to be the work also of his brother **Robert**. The commission was secured for the Adam brothers through the good offices of the Earl of Hopetoun, for whom they had just completed **Hopetoun House**. On the death of the 4th Earl, his title and his house passed to a nephew whose only daughter married the eldest son of the **Marquis of Bute**. On inheriting Dumfries House (c1890) the 3rd Marquis of Bute was unimpressed with this 'homely mansion' and commissioned Robert Weir Schultz to enlarge the two side pavilions; otherwise it is little changed from the original, with lively rococo plasterwork within and elegant policies without.

DUMFRIESSHIRE

Before the **local government** reorganisation of 1975, Dumfriesshire was southern Scotland's second largest county, sharing a 'frontier' with Cumberland, its neighbour to the south-east. Proceeding anti-clockwise, Dumfriesshire shared borders with **Roxburghshire, Selkirkshire, Peeblesshire, Lanarkshire, Ayrshire** and **Kirkcudbrightshire**, with the Solway Firth to the south. The pre-1975 county had an area of 688,067 acres (278,456ha), two-thirds of which was covered by high ground sloping gently from the north, where the highest point was White Coomb at 2695ft (821m), the remainder of the county forming an estuarine plain. The three principal rivers were the Nith, Annan and Esk, all flowing into the Solway, the Esk reaching it nearby in Cumberland.

The population in 1971 was 88,065, mostly engaged in **agriculture, fishing** and light industry with some **coal-mining** in the north-west of the county. **Dumfries** was the largest burgh and county town, the other burghs being **Annan, Langholm, Lockerbie, Moffat, Sanquhar** and **Lochmaben**. In 1975 Dumfriesshire merged with two counties to the west to form Dumfries and Galloway Region, the former county being divided between Nithsdale and Annandale & Eskdale Districts. Since 1995 this same area of Dumfries & Galloway has been a single Administrative Division with a population of c147,000.

DUN, House of, Nr Montrose, Angus

The original designs (1723) of this **William Adam** house for David Erskine (Lord Dun) suggest a much taller and more castellate building. A lofty two-storey entrance arch, reminiscent of those at **Fyvie** and **Craigston** and flanked by Ionic pilasters, survived the scaling down that followed and is the most distinctive feature of the otherwise stern façade. More flamboyant is the ornate plasterwork of the great salon by Joseph Enzer. The house, little altered since Adam built it, has recently been restored by the **National Trust for Scotland** and is now open to the public. A branch of the Erskine family [see **Mar**] had been established at Dun since 1375 and numbered among its scions John Erskine, the scholar [see **Montrose**] and reformer whom even **Queen Mary** found 'a mild and sweet-tempered man and of true honesty and uprightness'.

The nearby Bridge of Dun (1785–7) over the South Esk has three Gothic arches with elaborately pillared piers supporting roadside refuges plus a crenellated parapet, altogether a most ambitious construction for 'a minor road of no importance'.

DUNADD, Nr Lochgilphead, Argyll

The Dark Age fortifications on top of the isolated rocky crag of Dunadd, on the edge of the **Crinan** Moss four miles north of **Lochgilphead**, were probably the 'capital' of the ancient Kingdom of **Dalriada**, established by immigrants from Antrim in Ireland by AD 500. The site consists of a series of defended terraces, surmounted by a summit fort, and has been excavated on three occasions: in 1904, 1929 and 1980–81. Finds from these investigations suggest dates ranging from the 6th to 9th centuries AD, and fine examples of metal-working, including many beautiful brooches, are consistent with its interpretation as royal residence of the kings of Dalriada.

Below the summit fort, on one of the lower terraces, are a rock carving of a boar, an enigmatic description in ogam writing, a rock basin, and the outline of a footprint, all giving rise to speculation that this was the site where the rulers of Dalriada were inaugurated. Echoes of these ceremonies recur later in Highland history with the **Lords of the Isles**, whose inauguration ceremonies at Finlaggan on **Islay** consciously recalled the kings of Dalriada. The carvings are now protected by fibreglass replicas.

The presence of a large number of quern stones, for grinding grain, has suggested the possibility that cereals were brought to the king at Dunadd as tribute. It may be that the kingship was peripatetic, circulating round Dalriada and receiving tribute at other royal forts, notably at Dunollie (**Oban**), **Tarbert** and Dunaverty (**Kintyre**).

DUNBAR, Agnes, Countess of (fl.1338)

Known as 'Black Agnes' because of her dark hair and complexion, she was the daughter of **Thomas Randolph, Earl of Moray**, and the wife of the Earl of March and Dunbar. In 1338, in the absence of her husband, she conducted a resolute and successful defence of Dunbar Castle during a six-month siege by the Earls of Salisbury and Arundel on behalf of the English King Edward III, ostentatiously dusting the debris off the battlements with a kerchief every time a cannon ball scored a hit on the masonry.

DUNBAR, Battle of (i) (1296)

In 1294 Edward I demanded that **John Balliol** supply him with Scots troops to fight in France. The Community of the Realm forced John Balliol to refuse and to renounce his alliance with Edward. The English King's response was to invade Scotland, taking **Berwick** on 30 March 1296. Four weeks later, on 27 April, the English army under the Earl of Surrey overwhelmed the Scots in a pitched battle outside **Dunbar**, many Scottish nobles being taken prisoner and sent south as hostages

DUNBAR, Battle of (ii) (1650)

On the death of **Charles I** (January 1649) the Scots proclaimed **Charles II** King and, ignoring Cromwell's appeal for 'all God's elect to unite with their fellow elect in England', finally confirmed his authority when he signed both **Covenants** (June 1650). Cromwell's response was to invade. In July he crossed the border with 16,000 men and a fleet sailing up the east coast in support, but when he attempted to meet up with his ships at **Leith** he found the Scots army under **David**

Leslie barring his way. A second attempt to make the rendezvous at **Queensferry** met the same obstacle at Corstorphine, and by the end of August Cromwell had to withdraw to **Dunbar**, whither he was pursued by Leslie. The Scots army, initially some 25,000 strong, had been 'purged' of its ungodlier elements – in effect this meant mostly the professional soldiers – by zealous Covenanting ministers determined to enforce the **Act of Classes** to the letter, leaving, according to one disgusted commander, 'an army of clerks and ministers' sons'. Nevertheless Leslie had eventually assembled a force of over 20,000 which, at the beginning of September 1650, massed on Doune Hill overlooking Dunbar. Below, outnumbered and ill-provisioned, Cromwell was trapped between the Scots and the sea, needing 'almost a miracle' to save him. The miracle happened. Despite Leslie's insistence that all they had to do was sit tight and starve Cromwell's troops into surrender, those same zealous ministers were determined to snatch a quick victory and, marshalling the 'clerks and ministers' sons', started to lead them down from the high ground. The more experienced and better disciplined English army was quick to take advantage of this classic military blunder and in the ensuing fighting over 3000 Scots were killed and nearly 10,000 taken prisoner. By December Cromwell was installed in **Edinburgh Castle**.

DUNBAR, East Lothian

A few grizzled fragments on a rocky peninsula at the entrance to Dunbar harbour are all that remain of the castle so dauntlessly defended by **'Black Agnes'**, **Countess of Dunbar** in 1338. Home of the Earls of Dunbar and **March** until their forfeiture to **James I** in 1434, Dunbar had long been, and would remain, an important east coast **fishing** port. A **royal burgh** from 1445, the town was sacked twice (1544 and 1547) by the Earl of Hertford, and the castle twice gave shelter to **Queen Mary**, once in 1566 with **Darnley** after the murder of **Rizzio** and again in 1567 with **Bothwell** after the murder of Darnley. After Bothwell's flight and Mary's surrender at **Carberry** (15 June 1567) the castle, 'so often the asylum of the unfortunate and the guilty' (Fullarton's *Gazetteer*) was ordered to be destroyed. The site of Cromwell's defeat of the **Covenanters** at the **Battle of Dunbar** (1650) lies to the south-east of the town. Cromwell thereafter granted Dunbar the sum of £300 for repairs to its pier.

During the 18th century Dunbar prospered as one of Scotland's major **herring** ports. The Tolbooth in the High Street, of two storeys with a dormered attic and wooden spire, dates from c1650 with later additions, while Lauderdale House at the end of the High Street, 'an impressive mansion which looks slightly out of place in an urban setting' (I & K Whyte) was built c1740 by Captain James Fall MP; his son fell on hard times and sold it to the **Duke of Lauderdale** [see **John Maitland**] who commissioned **Robert Adam** to alter and enlarge it (1788) and it now belongs to the local authority. The parish church (1819–21, **James Gillespie Graham**) incorporates a magnificent monument (originally in an earlier church) complete with a lifesize kneeling statue of its subject, George Home (d.1611), successively High Treasurer of Scotland and Chancellor of the Exchequer in England under **James VI**, who created him Earl of Dunbar in 1605. Now a popular holiday resort, Dunbar claims to be both the driest and the sunniest spot in Scotland.

DUNBAR, Gavin (c1495–1547) Archbishop of Glasgow

Around 1530 the sees of **Aberdeen** and **Glasgow** were both held by Gavin Dunbars. Aberdeen's Bishop Dunbar, Glasgow's uncle, had obtained his see in 1519 and is best remembered for having completed the city's **Bridge of Dee** and much of **St Machar's Cathedral**, including its famous painted ceiling. Glasgow's Dunbar, a product of its **University**, became closely associated with **James V**, acting as his tutor, closest adviser, and Lord Chancellor (1528–39). Archbishop 1525–47, he orchestrated negotiations with the papacy over the diversion of ecclesiastical revenues and appointments to the Scottish sovereign.

DUNBAR, William (1460–c1513) Poet

So little is known about the life of Dunbar that it is safest simply to define him as the 'master-poet' at the court of **James IV**, and the King's most eloquent eulogiser and critic. That role implied that he composed much of his verse at the royal command; some of this was directed at groups in society in order to advise them of regal policy; some was celebratory in nature. Even in the latter category, Dunbar's status as 'master-poet' permitted him to mingle advice with eulogy. So, in The Thrissill and the Rois – a beautifully structured work celebrating James's marriage with **Margaret Tudor** and focused on devices of **heraldry** and hierarchy – the poet can also warn his king against continued philandering now that he is grafted to the Tudor rose.

Hugh MacDiarmid, in urging Scottish poets to return to Dunbar rather than **Burns**, was thinking of medium rather than message. Dunbar's innate conservatism and admiration of English poets and even English cities were anathema to MacDiarmid. His appeal is directed towards Dunbar's linguistic virtuosity. From the lowest of styles, the Flyting ('Mauch muttoun, byt buttoun, peilt gluttoun') to the highest Latinate praise of the Virgin Mary ('Hodiern, modern, sempitern,/Anglicall regyne'), Dunbar pushes the potential of language to its poetic extremes. Even in the least obviously rhetorical of styles – the middle style – he can chill us through repeated refrains and sonorous rhythms. These were written to be read aloud, as Richard Burton noted, in ranking Dunbar's 'Lament for the **Makaris**' among his three favourite lyrics. In one sense it is just a list, a roll-call of dead poets, but the repetitive liturgical tolling of one line from the Office of the Dead – 'Timor Mortis Conturbat Me' – transforms list into personal, penitential appeal. All the spiritual gravity of the Middle Ages is caught up into that one lyric.

As satirist, too, Dunbar has few equals. Whether he is concerned with farcically biting cameos of the courtiers dancing in Ane Dance in the Quenis Chalmer, or appealing to self-interest while condemning it in To the Merchantis of Edinburgh, he is always the master of words, used precisely within a massive vocabulary. Farce can also be the centre for widening circles of satiric seriousness. The personal focus of The Fenzeit Freir of Tungland is the court alchemist and his misguided attempts to fly from the battlements of **Stirling Castle**. No aspect of the farcical moment escapes Dunbar's cruelly vivid imagination, but it is not only Damian who wings his way into a bog, but all false scientists, prelates and doctors at court. The Italian's attempt to rival the birds is then, theologically, converted into pride and he becomes the Antichrist celebrating a parody of the resurrection.

DUNBARTONSHIRE

Before the **local government** reorganisation of 1975, the main body of Dunbartonshire occupied the north bank of the Firth of **Clyde** north-west of **Glasgow**,

Dumbarton Rock and Castle in the 17th century, by John Slezer (TS)

267

stretching from the city's suburbs westwards to **Argyll**. It encompassed some of Scotland's most beautiful scenery around **Loch Lomond**, Loch Long and the Gareloch. Totalling an area of 154,467 acres (62,511ha), the county was fringed by **Perthshire** to the north-east and there reached its highest point at the 3055ft (931m) summit of Ben Vorlich.

Dunbartonshire was unusual for two reasons. It was the last Scottish county to have a 'detached' portion, an 'island' of Dunbartonshire encompassing **Kirkintilloch** and **Cumbernauld** being separated from the rest of the county by six miles of **Stirlingshire** and **Lanarkshire**, surviving even the 1891 Local Government Act intended to remove such anomalies. Another point of interest was the difference in spelling the name of the county town – Dumbarton – while the county was Dunbarton. The latter spelling was etymologically correct, deriving from the Gaelic Dunbritan ('Dun' meaning hill or fort) which was written into the burgh's charter of 1222. 'Dum' is almost certainly a subsequent spelling error in transcription.

Besides Dumbarton, the burghs comprised **Clydebank** (the largest), Cumbernauld, **Bearsden**, Cove & Kilcreggan, **Helensburgh**, **Kirkintilloch** and **Milngavie**. The population in 1971 was 240,050, mostly involved in **agriculture**, manufacturing and industry, including **shipbuilding**. In 1975 the county was swallowed up by Strathclyde Region, most of it into Dumbarton district, along with Clydebank, Bearsden & Milngavie, Strathkelvin and Cumbernauld. In the 1995 reorganisation Helensburgh and its environs became part of Argyll & Bute, Dumbarton & Clydebank became the separate Council Area of West Dunbartonshire, and the remaining parts of Dunbartonshire that of East Dunbartonshire.

DUNBEATH, Caithness

This is one of the east coast ports of **Caithness** which shared in the **herring** boom. An early 19th century fishery store is preserved beside its harbour. By 1840 there were 76 boats operating from here and by 1870 Dunbeath had its stone-built school. In the following decade the father of **Neil M Gunn** built the slate-roofed house on the village terrace in which the novelist was born. This is commemorated by an inscription, and a bronze memorial has been raised to mark the centenary of Gunn's birth. His father was a skipper and his mother the daughter of a seaman, who made every effort to prevent her sons from following such a dangerous calling. Its prosperity had vanished by the time Neil Gunn depicted an upbringing in Dunbeath in his masterpiece *Morning Tide* and the profession of his forebears in *The Silver Darlings*. He also immortalised Dunbeath Water in *Highland River*. On a steep rock south of the harbour stands a castle, of oblong plan with a vaulted ground floor and two spiral staircases leading to the rooms above. This suggests a date very much earlier than 1428, when Dunbeath Castle enters the historical records. It has been occupied without interruption, for the most part by Sinclairs.

DUNBLANE, Perthshire

Named after St Blane, a native of **Bute** who supposedly founded a church beside the Water of Allan in c600, Dunblane still defers to its church, the lavishly restored 13th century **Dunblane Cathedral**. At the end of a twisting High Street, its precincts include the Dean's House, now a museum, ruins of the Bishop's Palace, and the **Leighton** Library. The latter, with crow-step gables and outside stair, was built in the 1680s to house the bishop's book collection and, with 4500 volumes in 32 languages, may be the oldest purpose-built library in Scotland. A lending library in the 18th century, it is now administered by **Stirling University**; the building is maintained by a trust and open to the public. **Prince Charles Edward Stewart** held a ball in Dunblane on his way south in 1745. The town became a spa in Victorian times. On 13 March 1996 Dunblane became the scene of an appalling tragedy when local man Thomas Hamilton burst into Dunblane Primary School and shot dead sixteen five- and six-year-old children and the teacher who was trying to protect them. He then shot himself in the head.

DUNBLANE CATHEDRAL, Dunblane, Perthshire

John Ruskin wrote of the Cathedral of St Blane and St Lawrence, 'I know not anything so perfect in its

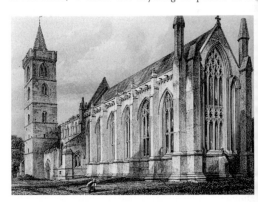

Dunblane Cathedral c1840, before restoration (RWB)

simplicity and so beautiful, as far as it reaches, in all the Gothic.' It reaches, for a cathedral, not far, comprising simply a nave (without transepts), choir and north range (vestry and chapter house). It was laid out by Bishop Clement soon after his election in 1233 although the separate tower (as at **Cambuskenneth**) is earlier, its lower red sandstone storeys dating from c1100. The main building was completed by the end of the 13th century. Its unrestored west façade is particularly fine with deeply recessed portal, three simply traceried lancet windows, and a plain lozenge window above. As at **Dunkeld**, only the choir survived intact the post-**Reformation** neglect; but at Dunblane a series of restorations – re-roofing of the nave and much redesigning of the interior by **Sir Robert Rowand Anderson** and **Sir Robert Lorimer** – revived the building in its modest entirety. Notable features include the carved wooden Chisholm stalls (15th century), Lorimer's choir stalls, Anderson's rood screen and much modern stained glass. Brass plaques on the floor of the choir mark the supposed graves of three Drummond sisters poisoned, it is said, because the liaison of **James IV** with one of them (**Margaret**) jeopardised the expectations of those who urged the King's marriage with **Margaret Tudor**.

DUNCAN I (c1010–40) King

Son of Crinan, Abbot of **Dunkeld**, and Bethoc, daughter of **Malcolm II**, whom he succeeded in 1034, having already succeeded to the **Kingdom of Strathclyde** on the death of his grandfather's old ally **Owen the Bald**, Duncan married a cousin of the Earl of Northumberland and had two sons, **Malcolm III 'Canmore'** and **Donald Bane**. Unlike Shakespeare's portrait which presented him as a wise old man, Duncan was young, rash and not particularly able. He was twice defeated in battle by his cousin **Thorfinn, Earl of Orkney**, incurred heavy losses in a fruitless siege of Durham (1039) and was finally defeated and killed by **MacBeth** near **Forres**.

DUNCAN II (c1060–94) King

The son of **Malcolm III**'s first marriage, Duncan reigned for only a few months in 1094. Taken hostage in 1072, he had grown up in Normandy until freed and knighted by Robert Curthose in 1087. Around 1090 he married Octreda of Northumberland/**Dunbar** (whose father had lost his English earldom for revolt against William the Conqueror and received Dunbar from Malcolm, whose own mother was of the Northumbrian family).

In spring 1094 Duncan led an Anglo-Norman army north and dispossessed his uncle **Donald III** for a few uneasy months. Public resentment of his alien supporters forced him to send them home; left with few followers, he died at Mondynes near **Dunnottar**, fighting his half-brother Edmund (who had backed Donald). Despite his long exile, he was buried in **Iona**. Duncan left a son William, Earl of **Moray**, (d.1151) whose MacWilliam descendants were frequently in revolt until the time of **Alexander II**.

DUNCAN, Adam, 1st Viscount Camperdown (1731–1804) Admiral

'**Dundee**'s second most famous citizen' (after **John Graham of Claverhouse**), Adam Duncan was the second son of Alexander Duncan of Lundie, merchant and Provost of Dundee. He joined the navy in 1746, was present at the blockade of Brest (1759) and commanded the *Valiant* at Havana (1762). Admiral (1795) and Commander-in-Chief in the North Sea (1795–1801), he conducted an effective blockade of Dutch trade routes round the Texel, but his fame stems from his unexpectedly decisive victory over the Dutch fleet under Admiral de Winter at Camperdown off the coast of Holland in 1797. He was awarded a pension of €2000 and created Baron Duncan of Lundie and Viscount Duncan of Camperdown (1797). His son, made Earl of Camperdown in 1831, was responsible for building the splendid mansion in Dundee's **Camperdown Park**.

DUNCAN, Andrew (1744–1828) Physician

Born near **St Andrews**, Duncan studied at **St Andrews University**, going on to **Edinburgh** to follow a medical career. Although not appointed to a professorship until 1790, he is principally remembered for his campaigning after that date for more enlightened treatment for the psychiatrically ill, and for establishing a mental hospital in Edinburgh's **Morningside** in 1813. Although not Scotland's first, this was an important improvement in

Admiral Adam Duncan, 1st Viscount Camperdown, by H-P Dunlaux, 1798 (SNPG)

what was then Scotland's largest city, replacing the horrors of the Bedlam. Duncan was also editor of one of Scotland's earliest scientific journals, the *Medical and Philosophical Commentaries*, from 1773.

DUNCAN, John (1866–1945) Painter

Duncan was the most prominent artist in the Celtic Revival movement that flourished in **Edinburgh** at the end of the 19th century. Born in **Dundee**, he trained as an illustrator before studying art in Antwerp and Dusseldorf where he was deeply influenced by the Belgian and German Symbolist painters. Returning to Edinburgh in the early 1890s he became closely involved with the visionary sociologist **Sir Patrick Geddes** and contributed an impressive series of murals to his **Ramsay Garden** complex on Edinburgh's **High Street**. He also oversaw the artistic element of Geddes' short-lived precious periodical *The Evergreen*, the main mouthpiece of the 'Celtic Renaissance'. From 1901–4 Duncan was Associate Professor of Art in Chicago after which he settled down permanently to a **painting** career in Edinburgh. His method, based on an understanding of Italian Renaissance techniques, applied classical principles to subjects of **Celtic mythology**. This, along with his use of bold colours and close attention to luxuriant detail, places Duncan squarely within the Northern European Symbolist tradition, far divorced from the Art Nouveau ethereality of **Mackintosh** and his followers in **Glasgow**. Between the wars Duncan extended his repertoire to include stained glass and religious subjects. Elected FRSA in 1923 he exerted a considerable influence over many younger artists and his studio was a popular meeting place. In later life he claimed to have seen fairies on **Iona** and his paintings of them are one of the more curious products of 20th century Scottish art.

DUNCAN, Jonathan (1756–1811) Governor of Bombay

Born at Wardhouse, **Angus**, Duncan entered the East India Company as a writer, arriving in Calcutta in 1772. In the same year Warren Hastings began his long tenure of the Governor-Generalship of Bengal. Duncan became one of his protégés, sharing Hastings' love of the country and respect for its peoples and culture. Of blameless character and tireless application, he was appointed Resident at Benares (where he is still remembered as the founder of the first Sanskrit university) in 1788, and in 1795 became Governor of Bombay. His tenure here lasted 16 years, 'the most important perhaps in the whole history of the English [sic] in India' (G Tindall, *City of Gold*). Though opposed to the aggrandising policies of Governor-General Wellesley, he served loyally and deserves to rank with **Thomas Munro** and his successors **Mountstuart Elphinstone** and **John Malcolm** as a paragon amongst administrators and a founding father of British India. He died in Bombay where a monument was erected to his memory at St Thomas Cathedral. It shows Duncan receiving the blessings of Indians for suppressing infanticide and patronising Oriental scholarship.

DUNCANSBY HEAD, Caithness

Situated at the eastern extremity of Scotland's north coast, Duncansby Head corresponds to **Cape Wrath** at its western end. Its rock stacks and geos of wave-torn sandstone are justly famous. There is a lighthouse and the remains of an ancient watchtower.

DUNDAS, Henry, 1st Viscount Melville (1742–1811) Politician

The son of Robert Dundas of Arniston (Lord President of the **Court of Session** 1748–53), Henry attended **Edinburgh** High School and **University**, was admitted a member of the **Faculty of Advocates** (1762), and was Solicitor-General for Scotland at the age of 24. From 1774–90 he was MP for **Midlothian** and from 1790 until his elevation to the peerage (1802) MP for Edinburgh.

In Scotland he held office as Lord Advocate (1775–83), and Keeper of the Signet (1782) and of the Privy Seal (1800) while in effect engrossing and managing the political patronage of the nation for 30 years (1775–1805). From this power base he was able to exercise considerable influence at Westminster and beyond. Chairmanship of a committee on Indian affairs in 1781 made him acknowledged master of a subject which few contemporaries understood. He drafted a Bill to deprive the East India Company of its political responsibilities which, redrafted as Pitt's India Bill of 1784, secured the government of India for Westminster and the patronage of India for Dundas as President of the Board of Control (1793). The increase in the number of Scots who thereafter secured cadetships and writerships in the East India Company was no coincidence; nor, given the calibre of those appointed, was it to the detriment

'*The Uncrowned King of Scotland*'; Henry Dundas, 1st Viscount Melville, by John Rising (SNPG; in the collection of His Grace the Duke of Buccleuch and Queensberry KT)

of India. It was a similar, if less sensational, story in the Navy where Dundas served as Treasurer (1782–3, 1784–1800). He also held the Home and War portfolios at different times.

For the most powerful politician of his day (or since) in Scotland Dundas was well equipped. A stranger to intellectual misgivings, high principles, or even common consistency, he was bluff, plausible and astute. Against his ambiguity on the American War and on the condemnation of Warren Hastings ('the saviour of India' whose removal and eventual impeachment he nevertheless supported) should be set his 1784 Bill for the restoration of forfeited (**Jacobite**) estates and his energetic conduct of the Egyptian campaign. Opposed to reform, not to mention radicalism (he was instrumental in the prosecution of **Thomas Muir**), he was the product of a corrupt system which enabled him to manage and manipulate the restricted electorate with devastating effect, ensuring loyal support for North, Pitt and, briefly, Addington. The same system brought about his downfall when he was impeached (1805) and acquitted for the irregularities of a subordinate. 'Harry the Ninth', 'The Uncrowned King of Scotland' etc, died in Edinburgh having secured the succession of his son, **Robert Dundas**, to much of his 'kingdom'. He is commemorated by a monument outside **Comrie** (where he spent part of his retirement) and another in **St Andrew Square**, Edinburgh (designed by **William Burn**).

DUNDAS, Robert (1685–1753) Judge

The second in a remarkable but confusing succession of eminent jurists, it was this Robert Dundas of Arniston who dented the **Campbell** (**2nd** and **3rd Dukes of**

Argyll) monopoly of Scottish patronage and prepared the way for that of the Dundases (**1st** and **2nd Viscounts Melville**). The son of Robert Dundas, Lord Arniston (d.1726), himself a judge of the **Court of Session**, young Robert replaced the Campbells' **Duncan Forbes** as Lord President (1748–53). His son, yet another Robert Dundas (1713–87), succeeded to the office in 1760, as did his grandson the fourth Robert Dundas (1758–1819). This fourth Robert Dundas married Elisabeth, the daughter of Henry Dundas, 1st Viscount Melville and half-brother of the third Robert. Unlike the meddlesome and dogged Henry (or his son **Robert Saunders Dundas**), all four Roberts Dundas were noted for flair, ingenuity and distinct indifference to hard work. All sat as MPs, either for **Midlothian** or for **Edinburgh**, and formed an important link in the chain of political clientage.

DUNDAS, Robert Saunders, 2nd Viscount Melville (1771–1851) Politician

Following so closely in the footsteps of his father (**Henry Dundas**), Robert Dundas is easily obscured by the latter's long shadow. He too attended **Edinburgh High School**, chose a political career (MP for Hastings, 1794), serving as his father's secretary, becoming a Keeper of the Signet and in 1801 succeeding his father as MP for **Midlothian** (1801) and President of the Board of Control for India. From 1812–27 he was First Lord of the Admiralty, an office also held briefly by his father. The system of political patronage and management of Scotland (and India) perfected by his father was carefully maintained by the son and only fragmented when the Tory Party itself was divided over the leadership of Canning (1827). Melville then served briefly in the Duke of Wellington's ministry before retiring in 1830. 'Though no literary man, he is judicious, clairvoyant, and uncommonly sound-headed, like his father,' wrote Sir Walter Scott.

DUNDAS CASTLE, Queensferry, West Lothian

A plain Tudor-Gothic creation on Dundas Hill above **South Queensferry**, Dundas Castle was designed for James Dundas by **William Burn** in 1818 while **Dalmeny House** was being built on the neighbouring estate. The old Dundas Castle, a 15th century L-plan, four-storeyed, battlemented, corbelled and vaulted keep, was licensed by **Robert Duke of Albany** in 1416 under terms which were renewed by **James I** in 1424 on the understanding that it would belong to the king in time of war. The garden showpiece is the unique Renaissance-style fountain sundial which formerly stood in the enclosed courtyard of the tower which had banqueting houses at each of its angles. The Latin inscription exhorts the visitor 'to observe, read, study and protect the stones through which the spring water is carried; not to destroy, and to quench his thirst in the year 1623 of man's salvation . . . that the fountain is under the protection of the castle . . . and that it is surrounded by guardian spirits to frighten evil-doers'. It was built in 1623 by Sir Walter Dundas when he suffered a fit of pique after being pipped in the purchase of Barnbougle Castle on the Dalmeny estate by the wily 'Tam o' the Cowgate', **Thomas Hamilton, Earl of Haddington**.

DUNDEE

The city of Dundee on the north shore of the Firth of **Tay** has arguably the best site of the four major Scottish cities. The view from the southern landfall of the Tay Road Bridge encompasses the site of an original Mesolithic settlement located on the banks of the estuary, which later expanded up the slope and westwards along the edge of the raised beach, eventually climbing the south slopes of Dundee Law (182m) and the lower slopes of the **Sidlaws** to create modern Dundee. This view also encompasses the suburban settlement of **Broughty Ferry** downstream, and Invergowrie upstream, both 19th century developments. Alternatively from the summit of Dundee Law, to which it is possible to drive, one can see most of the city and its commuter settlements of **Newport** and Wormit on the **Fife** side of the estuary plus the early burgh of **Tayport** from which there was a crossing to Broughty Ferry.

On top of the Law there was an Iron Age fort, Dun Diagh or Diagh's Fort, from which the town may have taken its name. The medieval town was sited on the edge of the estuary where it narrows to less than a mile wide, on the last dry site along its northern shore downstream from **Perth**, and inland from an indented bay between St Nicholas Craig and the Castle Rock, where the second harbour evolved. Up a marked slope from the water's edge, it stood on a level area of sands, gravels and silts interspersed with igneous rock outcrops (almost all removed in the 19th century to provide new north-south streets); at the junction of the igneous and sedimentary rocks, springs and wells furnished a water supply. It was a relatively narrow site backed by marshy ground where the eastward-flowing Scouringburn and a branch of the Dens burn joined before flowing down the slope to a creek near the Mesolithic settlement. Here was probably the earliest harbour, possibly at a crossing point of an early east coast routeway.

The first reference to a more substantial settlement at Dundee is recorded in 1054; in the 12th century it appears to have been a well established town which could provision and accommodate the peripatetic royal court; a charter of burgh status was granted by **William the Lion** c1190. Two parallel streets, the Seagait and Cowgait, developed east of the castle which was sited on the igneous intrusion, some 27m above the river, approximately where the St Paul's Episcopal Cathedral now stands; the castle was built c1290 but probably demolished by 1314.

The High Street developed west of the castle site along with two other streets to the west, the Nethergait nearer the river, and to the north-west the Overgait, now vanished and partly replaced by a shopping precinct in the 1960s. At first **St Mary's Church** lay in the fields beyond the High Street. Thus the medieval layout was of a major street, the High Street, fronted by the town church on the north side with diverging feeder streets at either end, from east, west, north-east and north-west; narrow wynds and entries gave access to the shore; the whole was protected by defences from the end of the 16th century to c1646 with the Cowgait Port, still marked by the Wishart Arch at the eastern limit of the town, and the Murraygait, the principal exit to the north. The West Port, at a bifurcation of the Overgait and the

'Jute-opolis': the city from Dundee Law c1900 (GWWA)

Dundee continued

Hawkhill, and the Cowgait Port marked the former gateways into the town.

The status of Dundee increased with the creation of a sheriffdom in 1359 and the sending of representatives to Parliament; the granting of a charter of feu-ferme a year later demonstrates that the burgesses of Dundee were capable of looking after the financial affairs of the burgh. In the 14th century a wooden tolbooth was erected in the Seagait, and a tron (public weighing beam) was sited just west of the former castle site as the town developed westwards along the High Street and beyond St Clement's (the earliest church, its site now under City Square). The tolbooth was re-sited in a building of over 12m in height near the edge of the present City Square in 1562, and a 'provost' presided over a town council whose officers were appointed by the burgesses.

After the creation of the burgh there is evidence of substantial trading activity, Dundee having been exempted from tolls in all English ports except London. The early burgh traded in goods bought from its agricultural hinterland with **wool**, sheepskins and cattle hides the principal exports; a merchant guild had been established before 1215, one of the earliest in Scotland. Within the burgh the Nine Incorporated Trades (Bakers, Shoemakers, Glovers, Tailors, Bonnetmakers, Fleshers, Hammermen, Weavers and Dyers) indicate the breadth of activity. Trade was established with Flanders and the Baltic and all goods brought to Forfarshire had first to be exposed for sale in Dundee. Dundee ships also carried goods for **Arbroath Abbey** and the Cistercian monastery at **Coupar Angus**. In 1500 the population was c6800; by the 16th century Dundee held second rank in assessment for royal taxation in Scotland and was exporting coarse woollen cloth to the Baltic lands while importing deals, pitch, tar, iron and copper from Sweden; one of the merchant Wedderburns actually resided in Elsinore in Denmark. This period of relative prosperity was cut short by attacks by English armies and particularly by **General Monk**'s destructive sacking of Dundee, by the capture of 60 ships in 1651, and by the consequences of a severe storm which seriously damaged the harbour in 1658, impoverishing Dundee for some 20 years. It is claimed that no town suffered so much during the Civil War except perhaps Drogheda.

After 1690 the dominant basis for Dundee's prosperity was the manufacture and trade in coarse **linen** cloth. The consequent prosperity enabled **William Adam** to be commissioned to design the very fine **Town House** in 1731. Craft suburbs developed, Hawkhill to the west and Hilltown to the north-east of the medieval town, occupied by flax spinners and handloom weavers. By 1735–40 there was a separate community of weavers and bleachers along the Lochee burn. In the suburbs there were also merchants putting out yarn to the weavers and organising the finishing of the cloth.

The relatively broad valley of the Scouringburn and the Lochee, Dens and Dighty burns provided sites for bleaching greens and water for washing cloth; the early flax-spinning mills were often conversions of corn mills.

Dundee continued

small factories where coarse linens were woven on handlooms had been established by 1783 at the West Port and Bonnybank and until the 1820s hand spinners and handloom weavers produced most of the textile output. One of the first signs of the concentration of textiles in Dundee was the establishment of five steam-driven flax mills between 1793–8, all on waterside sites, and in 1806 the erection of the first four-storey mill, the Bell Mill, which had 1200 spindles. By 1822 there were 17 mills, 11 of them built since 1820, and from 1828–36 the foundations of many of the larger mills were laid. This acceleration in textile manufacturing (in 1818 there were 25 manufacturers in the western suburbs; by 1825 there were 45) led to the development of a cloth-finishing area in the Cowgait and on King Street while five bleachfields were located on the Dighty Water within two to five miles of central Dundee. Water supplies for steam raising and wet spinning were often a problem, and maintained the location of the mills along the small burns. Not until 1847 was there a piped water supply from Monikie reservoir. With all this industrial activity locally registered shipping expanded from 8500 tons in the 1790s to 50,000 tons by the 1830s.

A second phase of expansion was based on a new and cheaper fibre, **jute**, which was first experimented with in 1823 and successfully spun on adapted flax-spinning machinery; not until 1848 after power weaving had developed was mill-spun jute yarn used for both warp and weft, but between 1855 and 1857 jute replaced flax as the dominant fibre of the Dundee textile region. From six power-loom factories in 1850, demand for bagging stimulated by the Crimean and American Civil Wars resulted in a further 44 factories being built by 1864 including Cox's Camperdown works in Lochee and others in the original weaving colonies in Hawkhill and Hilltown; jute imports increased from some 30,000 tons in 1858 to over 143,000 tons in 1873. Whaling was another commercial activity, whale oil and water being used to soften the jute fibre before it was spun; the *Terra Nova* was a Dundee-built whaler later used for Polar exploration and the **Discovery** was based on an earlier whaler design.

The concentration of textile operations in Dundee led to rapid population growth. From 1821–31 it grew by some 50% and from 1831–41 by 33%, including 8000 immigrants from Ireland; the foundation of the Dundee Highland Society in 1815 suggests additional long-distance migration into the expanding town. Textile workers were housed in one- and two-roomed flats in tall tenement blocks near the mills. These replaced the irregular and ill-built housing in the older weaving colonies, such as Hilltown, in 1846.

Growth in and around the medieval core, with its elongated east-west axis squeezed between developing industry to the north and the harbour to the south, had hampered movement. But in 1769 Couttie's Wynd

Dundee High Street in 1907 (GWWA)

Dundee's Camperdown Dock c1900 (GWWA)

Dundee continued

between High Street and the harbour was widened to 10 feet to take carts, and from 1783 Crichton Street, the first non-medieval route to the sea, **Castle Street** and Union Street were created to provide better access to the shore while the Nethergait was widened. Dundee almost lacks classical terrace development and compares poorly in this respect with **Aberdeen**; better housing development was rather in detached villas, such as 138 Nethergait, Provost Riddoch's house and now a branch of the Clydesdale Bank. Villa development spread westward north and south of Perth Road, particularly around Magdalen Green.

As a result of the 1825 City Improvement Act, Dock Street was extended westwards and the central area was expanded by draining the Meadows and enlarging the street network. Cowgait and High Street were linked to the Meadowside and Coupar Angus Road with the creation of Panmure Street, Upper Commercial Street and Ward Road; Reform Street and Lindsay Street were created by blasting through the igneous rock outcrops as was the earlier Castle Street. Reform Street, Meadowside, Panmure Street and Ward Road have since become the professional and office area of Dundee, with the Royal Exchange, the **Albert Institute** and the High School of Dundee creating an area distinct from the shopping area to the south. Residential areas developed along the streets leading out of the town. Maryfield and Craigiebank originated in the 1820s, but by 1860 Maryfield had expanded with terrace development. Downfield, originally feued in c1835, grew as a village around Baldovan Station on the Dundee-Newtyle line which opened in 1831. Even before the opening of the

Dundee-**Arbroath** Railway in 1839, villa development had started in Broughty Ferry. The **railway** must have increased the attraction of this, the first of Dundee's residential suburbs for successful entrepreneurs.

The prosperity initiated by the rapid success of jute led to a few public buildings being created in the 1850s (eg the Royal Exchange and Royal Arch), and in the 1860s (two gaols and a courthouse, Morgan Hospital – now Morgan Academy – and the first phase of the Albert Institute), the latter was gifted by the Baxter family and designed by Sir Giles Gilbert Scott, as was St Paul's Episcopal Cathedral. The Baxters made other major benefactions, including the Baxter Park on the northern edge of the industrial and residential area not far from their Dens Mills. They were also instrumental in providing the initial funding for University College, later the **University of Dundee**. The Baxters had taken the gifted and innovative engineer Peter Carmichael into partnership, and he was partly responsible for Dundee's **engineering** tradition, mechanisation and **shipbuilding** being linked to textiles. More numerous were the grand mansions built by the textile magnates in Broughty Ferry, for example Carbet Castle for the Grimonds and Castle Roy for the rival Gilroys, both of which have now been demolished; others were built in the West End. Some of the mills with the most elaborate frontages were also built in the 1860s and 70s, mirroring the success of the manufacturers during this period.

The development of the port of Dundee can also be linked to the prosperous periods of the textile industry. In the early days, the St Nicholas Craig promontory may have acted as a breakwater, but in the 1820s a floating dock and a graving dock were built and an enclosed harbour, the Earl Grey Dock, was completed in 1843; both were eventually infilled to provide a landfall for

he Tay Road Bridge. Further dockland expansion took
lace in the 1860s with the creation of the Camperdown
nd Victoria Docks, where the wooden frigate **Unicorn**,
uilt in 1824, and the *Discovery* are moored. Along the
.orthern bank of the estuary, some 75ha have been
eclaimed, while downstream from the docks is a third
ndustrial area with the former Caledon Shipyard, Briggs
.istillation plants, wood yards and fuel storage tanks.
Jpstream, reclamation was initiated by the railway
ompanies, much of it still occupied by a station and
oods yard; but Tayside House, Tayside Region's headquarters, a leisure centre incorporating swimming
ools, and recently a hotel and an office block have
een built; a supermarket and a second large store
ccupy prime sites along the estuary frontage together
vith recreation ground, Dundee Airport and a modern
extile dyeing factory. There is clearly further scope for
levelopment of this area.

1871 marked the apogee of Dundee textiles, when
axters employed 5000, the Grimonds 3000 and Coxes
.000; Dundee's textile workforce then constituted 10%
f all Scottish textile employees and there were 261
hips registered in Dundee. As early as 1855, machinery
nade in Dundee had been sold to a Calcutta jute mill
nd for about a century Dundonians managed most of
he Indian (and later Bangladeshi) jute mills, but in
871 the Indian mills began to undercut the Dundee
nills. Textiles in Dundee employed a predominantly
emale labour force; of the 34,000 employed in 1912,
ver 60% were female while boys dominated the rest
f the labour force. Before 1914, half of the employed
opulation were in textiles, although after 1911
umbers employed in food, drink and tobacco were
rowing. During World War I, demand for webbing,
acking and tarpaulins was brisk. Jute still employed
1,000 people in 1918, but the world-wide recession
n the inter-war years left over 30% of the labour force
nemployed, and by 1939 the number of textile
vorkers had been reduced to 25,000. With no new
ndustries developing, Dundee had a chronic surplus of
abour.

A fourth industrial area was established after 1946
.long the Kingsway, an outer ring-road to the north of
he city based on the great foresight of **James Thomson**,
he City Architect-Engineer. The first industrial estates
vere laid out by Dundee Town Council; others fol-
owed, developed by the Scottish Industrial Estates Cor-
oration. The employment gaps left by the decline of
he textile industry were filled by the North American
nultinational companies Dayco, Holochrome, National
Cash Register, Timex (closed 1993) and Veeder Root
nd later the French firm Michelin. Clothing, greetings
ards and **whisky** located along the same routeway and
t its eastern end a variety of shopping and leisure out-
ets have developed.

Housing conditions were still poor in 1919, with
53% of the population housed in one or two rooms,
. statistic slightly worse than **Glasgow**'s 62%. From
1919–39, 8177 local authority houses were built,
nainly rehousing families from slum clearance areas
or from overcrowded conditions. The Logie Housing
cheme was the first municipal housing scheme in Scot-
and built under the 1919 Housing Act and incorporat-

ing a central boiler supplying hot water for all the
houses on the estate, one of the first in Europe.
Craigiebank or Craigie Garden Suburb was also planned
by James Thomson and designed by his son for artisans.
In 1936 the Beechwood housing estate was built with
some larger houses (to rehouse larger families) and
praised by the Scottish Office for its layout and design;
one of the serious problems in Dundee was the shortage
of three- to five-roomed houses.

In the post-war period local authority housing
expanded, using cleared areas and empty spaces, and
from 1946 began to be built on the north side of the
Kingsway with five large local authority housing estates
from St Mary's-Ardler in the west to Whitfield in the
east. In the 1960s almost the last vestiges of medieval
Dundee in the Overgait and the Wellgait were demolished and replaced by shopping centres. In other clearance areas, multi-storey tower blocks were erected
replacing the diminishing number of church spires and
factory chimneys as the dominant feature of the skyline.
These shopping centres brought a new dimension to
the development of the core area which had already
been altered in 1930 by the demolition of the Adam
Town House and its replacement by the Caird Hall (the
gift of another textile magnate) fronted by the large
City Square with a new City Chambers which replicated
the pillars and arches of its predecessor. Significant post-
war buildings since the 1960s are the University Tower
Block, Tayside House, Ninewells Teaching Hospital and
the Repertory Theatre. In the 1980s, housing associations and other agencies renovated and upgraded 19th
century tenements and local authority houses while
some of the problem housing estates have also been
restructured and partly rebuilt; the proportion of local
authority houses has fallen dramatically

Much of the wealth generated by textiles was invested
in North America rather than in the fabric of the city,
which may explain the high proportion of local authority houses. The rapid decline in textile employment,
especially jute, prompted the 1982 Dundee Project,
which was envisaged as a major attempt at economic
regeneration, funded by the Scottish Development
Agency, Tayside Region and Dundee District Council
with a £24 million budget. The majority of the investments appear to be associated with six areas in the city
forming Dundee's Enterprise Zone, including a High
Technology Park with serviced sites and financial incentives to private investors; the textile dyeing factory is
one of the first fruits of this initiative.

The face and plan of the city have been altered by
demolition and replacement and by major renovations
of its fabric. With the completion of the last section of
the inner ring-road in 1993 Dundee has most of the
infrastructure required to face the 21st century.

See J M Jackson (ed), 'The City of Dundee', *Third
Statistical Account of Scotland*, Arbroath, 1979; Kay, B (ed),
The Dundee Book, Edinburgh, 1990; C Mckean and D
Walker, *Dundee, An Illustrated Introduction*, RIAS Landmark
Guide, Edinburgh, 1984.

Albert Institute

In 1867 the building which now houses the city's
museums and art galleries (and formerly also housed
the City Library) was built as a memorial to the Prince

Consort through a donation by Sir David Baxter. It was designed by Sir Giles Gilbert Scott, and opened to welcome the British Association to Dundee. In 1887 it was extended to house the Victoria Galleries which would display an annual art exhibition. It has a fine collection of paintings, enhanced in the 1980s by the Orchar Collection formerly housed in the Orchar Gallery in **Broughty Ferry**. Pre-history and archaeology collections are also strong features with a collection of medieval pottery mostly from the Overgait redevelopment site.

Barrack Street Museum

This baroque building with a rotunda on the top floor was designed by **James Thomson** and erected in 1911. It has a permanent, mainly local wildlife exhibition, with other rooms used for short-term specialist exhibitions and houses a Study Collection of plants and animals for use by researchers.

Caird Park and Mains Castle

This park, probably all or part of the original Mains Estate, lies on the central north side of the Kingsway and extends to some 115ha with a **golf course** and sports stadium, which includes an all-weather running track. At its north-east extremity is Mains Castle, a small courtyard castle built by the Grahams of Fintry over a period of 100 years after 1480, with a six-storey, 22m tower, the top of which was rebuilt in 1630. By 1700 it was a good house with enclosed parks, **doocots** and considerable tree planting and about that time the East Range was reconstructed. After c1740 it became dilapidated and was eventually bought by an **Edinburgh** lawyer, who re-roofed the tower and made other repairs. It was bought by Dundee Town Council in 1913 along with nearby land from funds provided by **Sir James Caird**. By the 1960s the condition of the buildings was deteriorating, but in the 1980s Dundee District Council restored the castle, which now houses a restaurant with facilities for functions.

Camperdown Park

On the north-west of the city, this park of c160ha is the former estate of **Admiral Duncan of Camperdown**, whose son commissioned **William Burn** to design a splendid neo-classical mansion in 1824, with fine views of the **Tay** estuary, and laid out the grounds as a grassy parkland with coniferous and deciduous specimen trees. Within the park there is now a Wildlife Centre, adventure play areas, a **golf course** and a riding school. Internal improvements to the house were carried out in 1990–1, funded by the European Regional Development Fund and the City of Dundee District Council.

Castle Street

Created c1796, this street was blasted out of the igneous intrusion on which the castle stood. Captured by the English, then taken by Sir Alexander Scrymgeour who was appointed hereditary Constable by **William Wallace**, the castle was probably retaken by Edward I and finally demolished by **Robert I (the Bruce)**. St Paul's Episcopal Cathedral, built for **Bishop Forbes** in 1853,

now occupies the castle site. Castle Street has several early 19th century buldings, including Samuel Bell's Theatre Royal of 1809, Castle Chambers and, at the foot across Exchange Street, the Exchange Coffee House which also had Assembly Rooms, a Reading Room and a Merchants' Library.

RRS Discovery

Dundee's sea trading and **shipbuilding** experience, particularly in the construction of whaling ships, led in 1899 to the National Antarctic Expedition Committee commissioning Dundee Shipbuilding Company to build Discovery. It was based on the steam-assisted, wood-built whaler design of the 1875 Discovery, lengthened by 10ft (3m) to 226ft (69m) with a displacement of 1620 tons, a double-skinned hull and extra insulation against Polar conditions. Power came from a 450hp engine built by Gourlay Brothers, with sail canvas supplied by Baxter Brothers. The total cost was £51,000 and the ship was launched in March 1901. In the same year she sailed from London under the command of Captain Robert Scott for New Zealand and, fully loaded with stores, left for the Antarctic in December 1901. Survey and scientific work was carried out before wintering in McMurdo Sound. In late 1902 Scott and two companions reached 82°16' South. A second winter was spent in the ice and in January 1904 the Terra Nova and Morning were despatched by the Admiralty to rescue Discovery and its crew. Blasting a channel through the ice they enabled Discovery to escape, arriving back in Britain in September 1904.

Only in 1923–4 was the Discovery again engaged on scientific research, investigating whaling grounds in the South Atlantic and then with Sir Douglas Mawson's Antarctic Research Expedition. After service with Sea Scouts and as a drill ship, she eventually became part of the Maritime Trust Historic Ship Collection in London. Dundee Heritage Trust negotiated her return to Dundee in 1986; restoration work has been carried out and Discovery is open to visitors as a major **tourist** attraction.

Dudhope Castle

Sited on a shelf on the lower slopes of Dundee Law, the first castle was presumably erected by the Scrymgeours of Dudhope, hereditary Constables of Dundee from 1298 who were granted lands on the northern and western sides of the burgh. The original building was replaced by a fortified house c1460 and another c1580. **John Graham of Claverhouse** bought the estate in the 1680s and the building became a **woollen** mill and then a barracks from 1796–1881. Purchased by the town council in 1892, the estate is now a park which includes the house.

Gardyne's House, 70–3 High Street

This town house, whose builders were mariners and shipowners, dates from c1600 but with the interior rebuilt in the early 19th century when tempera ceilings were revealed. It is the city's only surviving house of its period, difficult of access, sited up Gray's Close, hidden behind an 18th century tenement. L-shaped, of five storeys with the exterior built of large hewn stones, it must have been similar to the earlier buildings of the city.

St Mary's Parish Church

Legend has it that **David, Earl of Huntingdon**, brother of **William the Lion**, was beset by a fierce storm on his return journey from the Third Crusade and in thanks for his deliverance built the original church, dedicated c1190. He presented it to the **Abbey of Lindores**, whose Abbot and Convent were given 'liberty to plant schools . . in the said town', and thus the High School of Dundee was established.

Only the Tower of St Mary or the Old Steeple (built c1460) survives of the fabric of the early church. It was evidently one of the largest and finest in Scotland, some 37m long and 53m wide. The site of the early nave is now the Steeple Church; the chancel is now St Mary's. The church was burnt in 1296 by Edward I and again damaged by the English in 1385; the nave was demolished in 1547, and sacked again by the **Marquis of Montrose** in 1644. In 1651 **General Monk**'s cavalry used the north transept as a stable, a desecration repeated by government forces in 1745–6. Later rebuilding provided accommodation for up to four congregations until a fire in 1841 destroyed the eastern section of the church and the library of medieval books and records; but the Old Steeple remained undamaged. St Mary's was rebuilt by **William Burn**; the stained glass of the east window is the work of Sir Edward Burne-Jones and William Morris, and a section of a pre-1722 window depicts emblems of the Incorporated Trades.

The tower of St Mary's parish church c1840 (RWB)

Town House

William Adam had inspected the ruinous 16th century tolbooth in June 1730 and declared it to be in a dangerous condition. In 1731 he designed a replacement which was built in 1732–4 on the site of St Clement's Church and the third tolbooth, 110m broad and 30m wide, rising to a spire of 43m. A ground-level piazza fronted by arcading, which became the meeting place in Dundee, was backed by shops. On the first floor were the Council Chambers, offices and a courtroom; on the second floor an insecure gaol, later moved to the cellars and then to an extension. The stonework proved to be rather soft and the building was later encased in cement. It was demolished when the Caird Hall and the City Chambers were built.

Trades and Union Halls

The Trades Hall, built for the Nine Incorporated Trades in 1776, stood on the site of the 'flesh shambles' immediately west of the present Clydesdale Bank. It was designed by Samuel Bell in an elegant classical style with a room allocated to each trade, altogether a much more comfortable meeting place than the Howff or town graveyard where they had previously met. The Trades Hall faced the Union Hall, originally the English Chapel, at the west end of the High Street, also designed by Samuel Bell in 1783 with a pediment and a gabled façade. When the congregation moved to St Paul's Cathedral, it became the meeting place of a number of literary societies. Both buildings were demolished to enable street widening to take place after 1871.

Unicorn

Berthed in the Victoria Dock opposite **Discovery**, Unicorn, which was laid down at Chatham Dockyard in 1822 as a 150ft (45.7m) long, 46-gun frigate, is now the oldest British ship still afloat. Launched in 1824 in peacetime, roofed over and laid up, she never saw action, but served as a powder hulk from 1857–62 and in 1873 was towed to Dundee to serve as a drill ship for the Royal Naval Reserve; during World Wars I and II she became the Headquarters for the Senior Naval Officer, Dundee. Originally berthed in the Earl Grey Dock, Unicorn was to be scrapped when the **Tay Bridge** was built, but was reprieved, moved to its present berth, and in 1968 the Unicorn Preservation Society was established. The ship is gradually being restored and there are plans to complete the task by providing the rigging.

DUNDEE UNIVERSITY

Founded as an independent academic institution in 1881 through the generosity and foresight of Miss Mary Ann Baxter and Dr John Baxter, University College, like other universities, owes its origin to the desire for liberal **education** and advanced technical instruction in the industrial towns of Britain in the last quarter of the 19th century. Until 1897, when the College became part of **St Andrews University**, its students were prepared for the external examinations of London University. In 1954, Dundee School of Economics was incorporated in University College, which then became known as Queen's College. In 1965 the government took up the Robbins Committee recommendation to found new universities, and Queen's College became the University of Dundee, with Her Majesty Queen Elizabeth the Queen Mother as its first Chancellor.

The nucleus of the original accommodation consisted of four villas in Perth Road built in the late 18th century, and a disused church, but chemistry laboratories were built and in 1902 a medical school. Between 1907–11 engineering laboratories were added as well as physics laboratories, facing the Geddes Quadrangle. The University has since grown along Perth Road and back and across the old Hawkhill Road, with the Faculty of Medicine accommodated at Ninewells Teaching Hospital. Besides Medicine and Dentistry, there are Faculties of Science and Engineering, **Law**, Arts and Social Sciences and Environmental Studies; the latter, founded in 1975, were previously the Departments of Architecture and of Town and Regional Planning in Duncan of Jordanstone College of Art (founded in 1892) within 10 minutes' walk to the west. In 1990 the staff of all other departments of the Jordanstone College became members of the Faculty of Arts and Social Sciences within the University and their students graduate in the University. The University now (1999) has over 11,000 students, including 3000 part-time.

DUNDERAVE CASTLE, Nr Inveraray, Argyll

The *Castle Doom* of **Neil Munro**'s novel, Dunderave stands on a sliver of rock now unhappily sandwiched betweeen the main road round Loch Fyne and the loch itself. It was built as an L-shaped tower house (with a prominent round tower at the angle of the L) by Iain, Chief of the MacNaughtons, in 1596. About 1700 the MacNaughton married a daughter of Campbell of Ardkinglas but then, changing his mind, absconded to Ireland with her sister. The property was thus forfeited to the **Campbells**. By the 1890s it had become a 'ruined tower'. It was rescued and redesigned as a tasteful home by **Sir Robert Lorimer** on behalf of the Noble family whose new Ardkinglas, a magnificent baronial creation across the loch, was also Lorimer's work. His plaster ceilings at Dunderave, based on Jacobean designs, are particularly fine.

DUNDONALD CASTLE, Ayrshire

'A mass of uncouth masonry' on an isolated hill four miles inland from **Troon**, the ruins of Dundonald Castle are largely those of the 14th century tower house built by **Robert II** on his succession to the throne in 1371. Incorporating parts of an earlier castle demolished during the **Wars of Independence** to prevent it falling into English hands, Dundonald became the King's favourite residence and was appropriately grandiose, the main tower measuring some 80ft by 40ft by 70ft high, with vaulted stone ceilings on the first floor and in the Great Hall on the second floor, and a series of shields bearing the **Stewart** arms carved at intervals along the west wall. Robert II died at Dundonald in 1390 as, probably, did his son **Robert III** in 1406; a new wing and barmkin were added in the 15th century and in the 16th the castle passed from royal ownership to the Wallace family. Occupied until the early 17th century it thereafter fell into decay, 'all the wrought stones being taken out from the doorways and windows, and even the corners of the buildings being carried away', some of these depradations dating from 1644 when the new

owner, Sir William Cochrane, was in need of building materials for the construction of nearby **Auchans Castle**. When **James Boswell** visited the 'long unroofed' ruins of Dundonald with **Dr Johnson** in 1773 he found himself unable 'by any power of the imagination, to figure it as having been a suitable habitation for majesty', whereas Johnson 'was very jocular on the homely accommodations of "King Bob" and roared and laughed until the ruins echoed'.

DUNDRENNAN ABBEY, Kirkcudbrightshire

It is generally agreed that the founder of Dundrennan Abbey was **David I**, although some have given the credit to Fergus, Lord of **Galloway**. The date of its foundation (1142) is more certain, as is the fact that its Cistercian monks came from Rievaulx in Yorkshire, and that in its turn Dundrennan was the mother house of **Glenluce** and **Sweetheart Abbeys**. In the absence of any written records, however, little is known of its subsequent history until the **Reformation**. By 1512 the abbey buildings were said to be in a state of collapse; the **commendatorship** passed from **John Maxwell of Terregles, Lord Herries** (c1512–83) to Henry, Bishop of Galloway and then (1541) to Adam Blackadder before returning to Edward Maxwell, son of John, in 1562, ownership finally being secularised when Dundrennan was erected into a lordship for John Murray, later Earl of Annandale, in 1606. It was during Edward Maxwell's tenure that **Queen Mary** came to Dundrennan after her flight from **Langside** and it was from (the later renamed) Port Mary two miles to the south that she set sail the following morning for England, never to return.

Although part of the abbey church was used as the parish church of Dundrennan until the end of the 17th century, the buildings were allowed to fall into ruin

Dunfermline Abbey, by R W Billings (RWB)

Chapter house and transepts of Dundrennan Abbey (HS)

after the closing of the monastery in 1606, many of the stones being removed for the building of houses elsewhere. The depradations continued until **Henry, Lord Cockburn** paid it a visit in 1839: 'Though greatly abridged,' he wrote, 'it is still a beautiful and interesting mass. But every other feeling is superseded by one's horror and indignation at the state in which it is kept. Not a trace of it will be discoverable in 50 years.' Thanks to his outrage, the remains were taken into the care of the Commissioners of Woods and Forests in 1842 and are now in the care of **Historic Scotland**. The north and south transepts and part of the presbytery, with a mixture of pointed Early Gothic and rounded Romanesque arches, are the only sections of the church that survive to their original height, but the façade of the chapter house (rebuilt in the 13th century) is still a delight and together they have a quiet beauty that is reflected in their secluded surroundings.

DUNFERMLINE, Fife

'Fortunate indeed the child who first sees the light of day in that romantic town.' The 'romantic town' so described by **Andrew Carnegie** derived from the physical remnants of Dunfermline's medieval past. Even in today's much expanded burgh, Dunfermline Abbey, the most spectacular of these medieval survivals, is still a dominant feature of the skyline as seen from the south and east. The present abbey, however, is a composite structure with a medieval nave abutting on a 19th century Gothic Revival parish kirk.

The abbey is an ever-present reminder not only of the ecclesiastical importance of this once great Benedictine house, but also of Dunfermline's long history as a place of both royal residence and sepulture. The most visible evidence for this royal connection consists of the words KING ROBERT THE BRUCE cut in stone on the parapet of the tower of the 19th century kirk. The purpose was to mark the dramatic discovery in 1818 of the presumed tomb and remains of **Robert I**. It is thought that the abbey was the chosen burial place of no fewer than seven other kings, four queens, five princes and two princesses. The abbey's association with **Queen Margaret** helps to explain why it was so popular as a royal sepulture; St Margaret's shrine enjoyed considerable prestige and was therefore visited by many pilgrims.

When Margaret married **Malcolm III 'Canmore'** in c1070, Dunfermline was already a place of royal residence. The rather scanty remains of a medieval tower in the burgh's Pittencrieff Park mark the possible site of Malcolm Canmore's tower. While Margaret had founded a Benedictine priory at Dunfermline, it was her third son, **David I**, who raised it to Abbey status in 1128. When the splendid Norman nave was constructed the church of Malcolm and Margaret's time was obliterated except for its foundations which survive under the present floor. With commodious accommodation available at the abbey, Dunfermline continued

279

to be used as a place of royal residence. Local claims that it was the medieval capital of Scotland are quite erroneous, however. In the 16th century the abbey guest house was converted into a royal palace. The last monarch to be born in Scotland, **Charles I**, was born there.

While the **royal burgh** of David I's reign seems to have decayed, a later, more successful abbot's burgh was developed to the north of the abbey precinct. By the late 16th century Dunfermline had acquired *de facto* status as a royal burgh. The **Reformation** brought the closure of the abbey, but the nave survived because it remained in use as a parish kirk. In 1624 a devastating fire destroyed most of the town which at that time had a population of around 1400. The **Union of the Crowns**, which virtually ended the royal connection, also had a detrimental effect on the fortunes of the little burgh.

In the 18th century the town began to prosper, thanks to **coal-mining** and **linen** weaving, and these industries, particularly linen weaving, continued to form the basis for Dunfermline's 19th century expansion. The second half of the 19th century saw the manufacture of fine quality damask linen, a staple product, switch from the handloom to the power-loom, thus ensuring a period of remarkable growth for both the industry and the town. Andrew Carnegie's father had been a victim of the decline of the domestic, handloom form of manufacture, but Andrew made early gifts to his native town, including a public library and baths. His most spectacular benefaction came, however, in 1903 when he gifted the historic Pittencrieff Estate for a public park along with a huge endowment fund to be administered by trustees, 'to bring into the monotonous lives of the toiling masses of Dunfermline more of sweetness and light'. Pittencrieff Glen, though now administered by Dunfermline Council, remains a considerable attraction for residents and **tourists** alike.

In 1903 the decision by the Admiralty to build a naval base at **Rosyth** on the Firth of Forth resulted in a 'garden city' suburb to house dockyard workers. In 1911 the Auld Grey Toun of Dunfermline secured parliamentary approval to extend its boundaries to the sea to incorporate the new community of Rosyth. During the two world wars of the 20th century Rosyth developed into a major base for the British fleet.

The weaving industry collapsed in the 1920s when damask linen fell from favour as a domestic textile. This was a difficult period for Dunfermline as the coal pits in the immediate vicinity of the town were worked out and in 1925 the dockyard had been placed on a 'care and maintenance' basis. Not surprisingly the population fell from c47,000 to c41,000. Some textile manufacturing survived, however, while the introduction of silk manufacture by Swiss firms, and rearmament in the 1930s, helped recovery.

After World War II, although silk manufacture eventually ceased, the development of new industries, including electronics, and most significantly the expansion of the Rosyth dockyard, brought renewed growth and prosperity. As had been the case when the **Forth Railway Bridge** was completed in 1890, the opening in 1964 of the Forth Road Bridge helped spur economic growth and development.

For visitors, apart from Pittencrieff Glen and the abbey and palace (the latter now open to the public), attractions include an updated Andrew Carnegie Birthplace Museum and a major new heritage centre at the late medieval Abbot House, which was one of the key buildings in the former abbey complex.

DUNKELD, Perthshire

After **Killiecrankie** (1689) the victorious Highlanders loyal to **James VII** descended on the **Covenanting Cameronians** who held Dunkeld. Much of the town was burnt in the ensuing battle. Today's Dunkeld, comprising two tightly packed streets beside the river **Tay**, is the result of the rebuilding. The exception is the Gothic cathedral which, mostly ruined and very romantic, rises from shady lawns beside the river. Possibly **St Columba** or **St Adamnan** founded the first monastery at Dunkeld ('the fort of the Celts'). **Kenneth I (mac-Alpin)** adopted the place, along with **Scone**, as his capital and appointed a bishop. The see was revived by **Alexander I** in the early 12th century and the earliest part of the present structure dates from the late 13th century. This is principally the choir which, re-roofed and considerably altered, now serves as the parish kirk. The great nave was the work of Bishops Robert de Cardeny (buried in the south aisle) and Thomas Lauder in the 15th century. The tower was added at the end of the century and on the vaulted ceiling of its ground floor there survive paintings of biblical scenes. These, the fine tracery of the aisle windows, and what must have been more elaborate tracery in the great west window, are the main attractions. In the choir there are two **Pictish** cross-slabs and a recumbent effigy believed to be that of **Alexander Stewart**, the 'Wolf of Badenoch'. Unroofed during or soon after the **Reformation**, the cathedral was further damaged in the aftermath of Killiecrankie.

The charm of today's Dunkeld owes much to the efforts of the **National Trust for Scotland**, under whose auspices most of the terraced houses in Cathedral Street (where **Alexander Mackenzie**, future Prime Minister of Canada, spent his childhood), the Cross and High Street have been restored. The Trust also owns woodlands in the vicinity of the cathedral, and more woodland at The Hermitage, an 18th century folly built by the **Duke of Atholl** beside the river Braan near Inver. The birthplace of **Niel Gow**, Inver lies across the Tay from Dunkeld and was the site of a ferry before **Thomas Telford** built his graceful bridge (1809) downstream. The bridge, with an unusual iron toll-gate, connects with Birnam where a wooded hill (12 miles from **Dunsinane**) is supposed to have been that in Shakespeare's *Macbeth*.

DUNLOP, Ayrshire

The village of Dunlop acquired lasting fame from cheese. The techniques of making the hard cheese from unskimmed milk 'altogether different from the insipid produce of skimmed milk still in use among the peasantry' (Fullarton's *Gazetteer*) were learned in Ireland by Barbara Gilmour, 'a woman whose wits were sharpened and whose range of observation was varied by exile to

John Slezer's Prospect of the Town of Dunkeld, *published in* 1693 (TS)

Ireland' during the persecution of the **Covenanters**. She returned to Scotland, married a Dunlop farmer, and shared her new knowledge with her neighbours. Thanks to its long-keeping qualities and the hard texture which made it easy to transport, the fame of Dunlop cheese spread far and wide, even William Cobbett declaring it 'equal in quality to any cheese from Cheshire, Gloucestershire or Wiltshire'. In the 20th century Dunlop Cheese shared the fate of other excellent individual cheeses (eg the **Gigha**) when the farm-produced version was replaced by a vastly inferior mass-produced commercial creamery product.

DUNLOP, John Boyd (1840–1921) Inventor

Born at Dreghorn, **Ayrshire**, Dunlop was a veterinary surgeon who devised a rubber tyre for his son's tricycle in 1887. This was effectively a reinvention of the design of **Robert W Thomson**, but it benefited Dunlop little. He sold his patent rights early and failed to capitalise on the use of either his name or tyre in modern transport. He died in Dublin.

DUNMORE, Earldom of

Lord Charles Murray, second son of the 1st **Marquess of Atholl** and Lieutenant-Colonel of **Dalyell**'s regiment of horse, was created 1st Earl of Dunmore in 1686. The 4th Earl, John (1732–1809), Governor of New York and Virginia (1770) and of the Bahamas (1787), succeeded to the title in 1756. The 5th Earl bought the Isle of **Harris** in 1834 but died two years later, leaving his son the 6th Earl to handle the island's problems of poverty and overpopulation by offering subsistence **crofters** three years' notice to quit and free passage to Cape Breton. Their resistance to this comparatively

humane attempt at **clearance** resulted in sterner measures being taken for their eviction. Charles Adolphus, 7th Earl (1841–1907), inherited the earldom at the age of three. In 1868 he built Amhuinnsuidhe Castle on Harris and with his wife Catherine Herbert, daughter of the Earl of Pembroke, encouraged the production of **Harris Tweed**. Lord-in-Waiting to **Queen Victoria** (1874–80), he later explored Spitzbergen, Hudson Bay and Arctic Russia before making his famous journey through Kashmir and Tibet in 1892, an account of which he published in *The Pamirs* (1893). He and his cousin the 6th Duke of Atholl are credited (by Sir Iain Moncreiffe) with inventing the eightsome **reel**.

DUNNET HEAD, Caithness

This, not **John o' Groats**, is the northernmost point of the Scottish mainland, a sheer promontory of Upper Old Red Sandstone on which a lighthouse stands 300ft (91m) above the Pentland Firth. The parish of which it forms part is one of those which has preserved a church dating substantially from pre-**Reformation** times. The Reverend Timothy Pont (c1560–c1630), the cartographer, was among its incumbents.

DUNNICHEN (or Nechtansmere), Battle of (685)

For much of the 7th century, before the Scottish nation had been forged, the dominant power in northern Britain was Northumbria. The downfall of Gododdin (a territory based on the **Lothians**) allowed the Northumbrians to enlarge their domain, and their policy of aggressive territorial expansion brought them into direct conflict with the **Picts**. By a combination of dynastic, political and military means, Northumbria came to dominate a large part of southern Pictland. Around 672, following the death of the powerful Northumbrian King Oswin, the Picts attempted to 'throw off the yoke of

281

slavery', but suffered a horrendous defeat at the hands of Oswald's successor Egfrith on the plain of 'Manau' (probably in the area of **Grangemouth**). It was to be a dozen years before they were ready to attempt once more to rid themselves of oppression, under the inspired leadership of their new king, Bruide.

In the spring of 685, Egfrith led a large and powerful Northumbrian force northwards to do battle with the Picts, determined that any rebellious notions which they may have been considering should be crushed by launching a pre-emptive strike against them. It seems that he penetrated into Pictland beyond the extent of Northumbrian control, his most likely route after crossing the **Tay** being up **Strathmore**. Because so little information exists, any account of the battle must be largely speculative, but it seems that Egfrith deviated from his planned course around the **Forfar** region, and headed towards Dunnichen (in the present-day county of **Angus**). Bede explains the reason for this: the Picts feigned flight and lured the Northumbrians into mountainous country. It would appear that Bruide had a plan which involved avoiding the type of ground that had led to the previous defeat, and necessitated enticing the Northumbrian army into his choice of territory. He used the local topography to trap his enemy, with Dunnichen Hill and Nechtan's Mire playing a crucial role. By employing shrewd tactics, the Picts won an overwhelming victory and the majority of the invaders, including Egfrith, were slain.

This outline is based on conjecture, but one fact is known with an astonishing degree of accuracy for a 7th century event: the battle took place at around 3 o'clock in the afternoon of Saturday 20 May 685. It became known to the Irish as Duinn Neachtain (Dun Nechtan – the hill-fort of Nechtan – now corrupted to Dunnichen), to the Britons as Lin Garan (the Pool of the Heron) and to the Angles as Nechtanesmere (the mire of Nechtan). We do not know what the Picts called it, though they have left what may be an even more important record of the battle itself – the highly informative battle-scene on the superb carved stone slab at Kirkton of **Aberlemno**.

The battle had important consequences: it probably ended Northumbrian domination over the Picts (doing likewise for the Scots and Britons also), and permanently checked Northumbrian expansion northward; it may thus have created the circumstances which led to the foundation of Scotland. A cairn was erected at Dunnichen in 1985 to commemorate the 1300th anniversary of this momentous battle.

Dunnottar Castle as the Covenanters' Alcatraz in the 1690s (TS)

The medieval tower of St Serf's, Dunning (HS)

DUNNING, Nr Auchterarder, Perthshire

The church of St Serf in the centre of the village was rebuilt in the 19th century, but its fine early medieval tower remains and has two-light arched Anglo-Saxon windows like those in the towers at Muthill and at St Rule's in **St Andrews**. The medieval village belonged to Lord Rollo of Duncrub whose descendants were still there at the beginning of the 20th century.

DUNNOTTAR CASTLE, Nr Stonehaven, Kincardineshire

More a fortified promontory than a castle, Dunnottar is the most spectacular refuge on the east coast. Encircling cliffs 160ft (50m) high, against which the North Sea pounds relentlessly, raise to the sky a grassy plateau scattered with walls, gables, and a lofty tower, all of reddish sandstone. The only access is by a tongue of land, like a drawbridge, but so much below as to involve a precipitous descent from the mainland and then a long climb through and onto the rock whose crags and fortifications command this perilous approach throughout.

What **Harry the Minstrel** called 'this snuk within the se[a]' supported a **Pictish dun**, a **Celtic** church said to have been founded by **St Ninian**, and a parish church founded by William Wishart of **St Andrews** before **William Wallace** in 1297 and **Andrew de Moray** [see **Murray**] in 1336 attempted to wrest it from the English. From the late 14th century it was in the hands of the **Keith** family who immediately built the keep, an L-plan tower house which is still the most prominent feature and, like most of the later fortifications, commands the landward approach. Further building by the **Earls Marischal** in the 16th and 17th centuries resulted in a quadrangle of well-appointed apartments (the 'Palace'), a hall, a chapel, the so-called Priest's House and the formidable guardhouse arrangements. These proved effective against **Montrose**'s siege in 1645 but not against the Cromwellian artillery in 1651–2; after an eight-month siege Sir George Ogilvy was obliged to surrender this last Royalist redoubt. Happily the Honours of Scotland (the royal **regalia**) and **Charles II**'s private papers, both left here for safe-keeping, were successfully smuggled through the enemy lines. Conflicting stories of how this was managed [see **Kinneff**] may be taken as proof of its success.

Vulnerable to artillery, Dunnottar was relegated to a prison where in 1685 a large body of **Covenanters** was held in appalling conditions (some died and are commemorated in the Covenanters' Stone, itself immortalised in **Scott**'s *Old Mortality*, in Dunnottar churchyard) and where in 1689 several **Aberdeen Jacobites** were held for a year. The 10th Earl Marischal himself joined the 1715 rising and duly forfeited his castle which passed to the **York Buildings Company**. Its lead, the only saleable asset, was stripped and the buildings began their long decay. Their remains, and the mighty plinth on which they stand, now belong to the Cowdray family.

DUNOON, Argyll

Lying at the southern tip of the **Cowal** peninsula, Dunoon overlooks the Firth of **Clyde**, and from **Glasgow** is better served by the **Gourock** ferry than by the long (because of Loch Long) road journey. This, plus, until 1992, the presence of a large US Navy establishment serving the **Holy Loch** submarine base, must account for the town's improbable boast of having more taxis per head of the population than anywhere else in Europe. Its architecture is Seaside Victorian, Seaside Edwardian and Clydeside Resort, the town owing its existence almost entirely to its popularity as a **'doon the watter'** destination.

Its history, though, or that which attaches to the meagre remains of Dunoon Castle, is rich. There was probably a dun or hill-fort on the site from an early period; by the 13th century a stone castle had been built with the rocky hill developed into a 'motte' of the Norman type and the 'bailey' of the castle enclosing the area which is now the Castle Gardens. One of the earliest stone castles in the west of Scotland, probably of the same type as **Castle Sween** in Knapdale, Dunoon Castle was originally held by the Lamonts, an important clan in Cowal who sided with the **Balliols** and Edward I of England against **Bruce** in the **Wars of Independence** and lost much of their power and lands after **Bannockburn**. Taken by Robert Stewart in 1371, the castle became a royal perquisite when Stewart attained the throne as **Robert II**. A century later the then **Earls of Argyll** were appointed hereditary keepers, one condition of their tenure being to supply a red rose as rent on demand.

In the Great Rebellion of 1644–6 the Campbells and the Lamonts were again on opposite sides, the Campbells supporting the **Covenant** while the Lamonts supported **Montrose**. On their way home from Montrose's campaign the Lamonts ravaged Campbell territory, burning Ardkinglas, killing 33 people in Strachur and finally murdering the people of Kilmun who had sought sanctuary in the church. Campbell revenge was swift. The Lamont stronghold, Castle Toward, was besieged and its defenders tricked into surrender by the offer of a safe-conduct which was not honoured. The Lamont men taken prisoner were brought to Dunoon and hanged; in 1906 a Celtic Cross was erected in the town by their descendants. The town's other notable memorial is a statue of **Burns**'s 'Highland Mary' Campbell who hailed from nearby Auchnamore.

In 1822 the Lord Provost of Glasgow, James Ewing MP, bought the land now known as Castle Gardens and constructed a wall around it to ensure the privacy of his holiday home. But the wall also enclosed the ruins of the castle and an area regarded as common ground on which the women of Dunoon had traditionally bleached their linen; each night the women demolished the section of wall that had been built that day until they were eventually arrested and taken to **Inveraray** Jail. A public outcry led Ewing to relent; the women were freed and the Lord Provost confined his wall to the area immediately around his house. All that remains of the original stone castle is the south-west gateway, the remainder having been thoroughly destroyed in 1685 when the **9th Earl of Argyll** was condemned for treason. All that remains of the Lord Provost's wall is a stretch behind the tennis courts.

DUNROBIN CASTLE, Nr Golspie, Sutherland

This stronghold was established on the east coast of **Sutherland** by the descendants of a Fleming who obtained lands here before 1211. His family adopted the name of the Norse south lands (Sutherland) and transformed it into that of a Gaelic clan. Dunrobin was probably named after Robert (Robin), 6th Earl, and is first recorded in 1401. Parts of its original structure are still visible within its enclosed courtyard, encased in later building. This consists principally of the work of Sir Charles Barry, who transformed Dunrobin into a palace resembling a château on the Loire in the mid-19th century. After accidental fire in 1915 its finest rooms were redesigned by **Sir Robert Lorimer**, who also modified Barry's tower. Its owner since 1963 is Elizabeth, Countess of Sutherland, who has opened the castle and its beautiful gardens by the shore to the public.

DUNS

The small Iron Age fort known as the 'dun' (pronounced 'doon') is the commonest type of archaeological monument found in the Highlands and Islands of Scotland, but at the same time one of the least understood. Although there are hundreds of examples, the study of these sites is in its infancy, and only a few have been excavated in modern times.

In general, duns are small, family-size, circular stone forts, of dry-stone wall construction. The walls were never very high but are typically very thick – often 3m or more. The entrances are often fitted with door jambs and bar-holes – features which also occur in **brochs**. The distribution of duns, of which several different types have now been recognised, is primarily along

Dunrobin Castle transformed into a 19th century château (entry p 283) (SP)

the western coastline, particularly in **Argyll** and the **Hebrides**. Typically they are located on rocky knolls and natural crags near the sea, often on raised beaches, but they are also to be found in inland situations. Of the excavated duns, most have been found to have been reoccupied in medieval times. Most were probably built in the first few centuries AD, although some are older, dating from the late 1st millennium BC. They were therefore in use over a considerable period of time.

Of the hundreds of examples, only a few are relatively well preserved. In **Kintyre**, a dun is the latest of three stone forts on Dun Skeig, while the dun at Borgadale, at the south end of the peninsula, is well preserved though not very accessible. In Mid-Argyll, Druim an Duin has two doorways: this feature also occurs at Lecca-more Dun on the island of **Luing**. Dun Aisgain on the island of **Mull**, situated 600m south-west of Burg, is exceptionally well preserved. The walls still stand to a height of nearly 3m, and incorporate a mural gallery, presumably a structural feature to allow greater height to be achieved while still maintaining the stability of the wall. Kildonan galleried dun in Kintyre also has the hollow-walled appearance typical of the later broch, though it is D-shaped in plan. On the Isle of **Skye**, Dun Ringill, on the shores of Loch Slapin, is an impressive site, although very ruinous.

In the Hebrides, duns were often situated on natural or improved islands in inland lochs. This tradition of fortified islands continued into the 16th century. Dun an t-Siamain on **North Uist** is a fine example of this type.

It is thought that most duns were unroofed, containing timber structures, often perhaps leaning against the dry-stone wall. The appearance of these small family-size structures, following on from the massive hill-top forts of the earlier Iron Age, has prompted discussion about the fragmentation of society in the first centuries AD, particularly in the context of the **Roman** occupation of Scotland and the later establishment of the Kingdom of **Dalriada** in Argyll and the southern isles. But not enough is yet known to allow more than speculative ideas about their origins.

DUNS, Berwickshire

The county town of **Berwickshire** jointly with **Greenlaw** from 1853–1903 and then on its own until the 1975 reorganisation of **local government**, Duns was originally built on the eponymous 710ft (216m) dun on the north side of the present-day market town. It was destroyed by the English in the mid-16th century and rebuilt at the foot of the hill. Duns claims to be the birthplace of the medieval philosopher **John Duns Scotus** (c1265–1308), whose statue stands in the public park. Nearby Duns Castle incorporates part of the ancient tower built c1320 by **Randolph Earl of Moray**, to whom the land was granted by his uncle **Robert I** after **Bannockburn**. In 1639 the castle housed **General Leslie**, whose **Covenanting** army camped on nearby Duns Law. Since 1698 the property of the Hay family, Duns Castle is surrounded by an artificial loch and wildlife area run by the **National Trust for Scotland**.

DUNS SCOTUS, John (c1265–1308)
Philosopher

The Subtle Doctor (*Doctor Subtilis*), Duns Scotus was one of the great philosophers; study and use of his works was commended by Pope John XXIII, and he was beatified by Pope John Paul II in 1993.

Although he was certainly from Scotland, the usual attribution of his birthplace to Maxton, **Roxburghshire**, was in 1965 revealed as due to 18th century forgeries by Marianus Brockie in *Monasticum Scoticanum*. His name may derive from the town of **Duns** in **Berwickshire** where there is a statue of him. The first sure record is of his ordination as a priest in Northampton in 1291. He was at Oxford in 1300, perhaps having already studied in Paris, and taught at Cambridge. He was again in Paris by 1302, but between 1303–4 was banished from the city for siding with the papal party in a dispute with the King, Philip the Fair. Back in Paris during 1304, he was created Doctor of Theology in 1305. In 1307 he was sent to Cologne, where he died and was buried in the Franciscan church.

He wrote a great deal, though not all that was attributed to him. A transitional figure, he differentiates between faith and reason, theology and **philosophy**, and between the content of Christian belief and general statements demanding ordinary corroboration. Unlike earlier thinkers, he separates these two sides and attempts their reconciliation. Scotist influence has been pervasive, though the 14th century took it in directions not his own. A potent polemical disputant, he may be read too much as a critic, notably of St Thomas Aquinas, rather than in his own right, although he always bears St Thomas in mind. Manuscript notes of his teaching are widespread across Europe, and because he died before bringing his thoughts together there has been no shortage of problems. **John Mair** was an early editor, who carried over Scotus' influence in ways too little noted. Modern philosophers much indebted to Scotus include C S Peirce and Martin Heidegger. Renaissance scorn of the dry subtleties pursued by his disciples led to coinage of the word 'Duns' or 'dunce' signifying 'a dull, obstinate person impervious to the new learning'.

See F C Coplestone, *A History of Philosophy*, Vol 2, Part II; *Duns Scotus, Philosophical Writings*, ed & trans Allan Wolter, Nelson, 1962; Henry Docherty, 'The Brockie Forgeries', *Innes Review*, 1965.

DUNSINANE HILL, Perthshire

On the edge of the **Sidlaw** Hills eight miles north of **Perth** and 12 miles ESE of Birnam Wood [see **Dunkeld**], from which it is visible, the summit of Dunsinane (or Dunsinann) Hill is ringed by the ramparts of what was probably a timber-laced fort. Excavations in the 1850s discovered a **souterrain** within and evidence of vitrification. It is presumed to be the stronghold in which **MacBeth** awaited his enemies and below which he was defeated, they, according to Shakespeare, advancing with leafy boughs; thus was the prediction fulfilled that MacBeth's immunity would end when 'great Birnam Wood to Dunsinane Hill shall come'. Dramatic licence enabled Shakespeare to leave MacBeth dead on the field of battle; in fact he probably escaped until cornered at **Lumphanan**.

DUNSTAFFNAGE CASTLE, Nr Oban, Argyll

With its landward approach cluttered by **Oban**'s overspill plus a marine laboratory, and with its anchorage busy with charter yachts and **fish farming**, Dunstaffnage has been denied the serene old age that is its due. For around its battered walls, atop a platform of conglomerate, cluster more historical and legendary associations than anywhere else on the west coast. The fort (**dun**) on the promontory (nage, ness) of the Staff must ever have been of vital strategic importance commanding both maritime access to **Loch Etive** and **Lorne** and the most direct route from the Lowlands to the **Hebrides**. According to **Hector Boece** the first fort was founded by a King Ewin either of **Dalriada** or in the 1st century BC. An embassy from the King of the Britons is said to have visited it in search of allies against Julius Caesar. This confuses the tradition of Dunstaffnage having been a seat and burial ground of the Dalriadic kings and the place whence the **Stone of Destiny** was removed to **Scone** by **Kenneth mac-Alpin** in 843.

The ruins of today date from the 13th century and may be attributed to Duncan MacDougall, founder of nearby **Ardchattan Priory**, Lord of Lorne, and a direct descendant of **Somerled**. In 1308 **Robert I** took the castle and garrisoned it against the Lord of Lorne. Sir Arthur Campbell was made Constable for a time, after which the castle and the remaining lands of the Lordship reverted to the **MacDougalls**. In 1470, after a spell with the **Stewarts**, the Lordship and the castle went to Argyll who installed a forerunner of the present Campbell of Dunstaffnage as Captain. True to form, the **Campbells** generally secured Dunstaffnage for the government of the day. In 1554 and again in 1625 military operations against the **MacDonalds** were mounted from Dunstaffnage and in 1674 against the **Macleans** of **Mull**. A **Cameron of Lochiel** was beheaded here in the 16th century; the famous **Colkitto**, father of **Alasdair MacColla**, was hanged nearby in the 17th century; and in the 18th century **Flora MacDonald** was briefly imprisoned in Dunstaffnage.

The last captain to reside in Dunstaffnage moved out in 1810 when the gatehouse was gutted by fire. With its 18th century pedimented dormers peeking over the parapets, this prim gatehouse, since restored, looks distinctly inappropriate beside the rugged and ruinous walls which surround it. Roughly rectangular, the walls include three corner towers, two still standing though the truncated third probably contained the main chambers. The walls incorporate a variety of embrasures, arrow-slits, windows and a fine doorway. For architectural interest the Early Gothic chapel nearby is outstanding, indeed 'worthy in all respects save size', according to the guidebook, 'to take its place alongside the noblest ecclesiastical monuments of contemporary France or the rest of Britain'.

DUNTOCHER, Dunbartonshire

Duntocher ('the causeway fort') was a **Roman** vantage point near the end of the **Antonine Wall**. A bridge across the Duntocher burn was once thought to be of Roman origin and so 'perhaps the most ancient in Scotland'; in 1772 Lord Blantyre put up an inscription crediting it to Quintus Lollius Urbicus. The town became a **cotton** spinning centre in the 19th century, when its population increased as Irish and Highland people came to work in the district's four mills. Nine miles west of **Glasgow**, Duntocher is today a dormitory satellite.

DUNURE, Ayrshire

A small **fishing** village with a sturdy harbour on the coast nine miles south of **Ayr**, Dunure is dominated by the dramatic ruins of mainly 14th century Dunure Castle. The original irregularly shaped keep 'high upon the top of a rock, hanging over the sea' with 15th and 16th century additions was an early stronghold of the **Kennedys** and the scene, in 1570, of the roasting of Allan Stewart, **Commendator** of **Crossraguel Abbey**, by Gilbert Kennedy, 4th **Earl of Cassillis**. The unfortunate Stewart was stripped, bound to a spit, and roasted before the great fire in the 'black vault' of Dunure until he surrendered his lands to the Earl. After such prolonged torture, during which his 'flesch was consumed and brunt to the bones', he signed a paper renouncing the lands of the abbey. The Earl was fined £2000 by the Privy Council for this outrage and thereafter paid his victim a pension, but kept the lands of Crossraguel. The castle and its flanking range of buildings were ruined by 1696 and are now even more so.

DUNVEGAN CASTLE, Isle of Skye

'Dunvegan is a rocky promontory that juts into the bay [Loch Dunvegan] on the west side of **Sky**. The house, which is the principal seat of MacLeod, is partly old and partly modern; it is built upon the rock and looks upon the water.' Thus wrote **Dr Johnson** who spent a wet week here in September 1773. Nothing has changed, least of all the weather. The 'partly old' bits of the castle include remains of a 13th century wall of enclosure, the 14th century keep with dungeon and kitchen and the Fairy Tower (c1500) in which the Doctor slept (as did **Sir Walter Scott** in 1814). The 'partly modern' in 1773 meant the Rory Mor house which connects these two towers, a south wing, and a new front door, the castle being 'accessible only from the water, till the last possessor opened a new entrance by stairs upon the land'. Subsequently the whole structure has been harled, castellated and pepper-potted. If the intention was Baronial, the effect is unhappily reminiscent of an Edwardian seaside folly.

Dunvegan is still 'the seat of **MacLeod**'. It appears to have passed to Leod, the first Chief, when he married the daughter of the Norse Seneschall (Sheriff) of Skye in the 13th century. Today's incumbent, the 29th Chief, flourishes amongst the paraphernalia of what is now one of Skye's major **tourist** attractions, thus justifying the claim that Dunvegan has been continuously occupied by the same family for longer than any other Scottish castle.

Within, the public rooms are richly furnished and well displayed. Clan relics include the Fairy Flag, a much mythologised but sadly threadbare talisman, and Rory Mor's Horn, an ancestral drinking vessel from which the heir to the chiefship must quaff a bottle and a half of claret at one draught ('The present chief performed this feat successfully in 1965; time: 1 min 57 secs' says the guidebook). Other notable *objets* include the

Dunvegan Cup (a chalice of oak with a silver mount and an inscription ascribing its origin to 'Katherine daughter of King Neill, wife of MacGuire Prince of Fermanagh') and a long and decorated lance which once belonged to Tipu Sultan of Mysore (India). It passed to General Norman MacLeod, the 23rd Chief (and the one who had entertained Dr Johnson) during the Third Mysore War. Fine portraits of the General and his second wife by Johann Zoffany hang in the drawing room along with other family portraits by **Allan Ramsay**, **Sir Henry Raeburn**, etc. The castle is screened from its coach park and visitor centre by a picturesque woodland garden.

DUPPLIN, Battle of (1332)

On the death of the Regent **Randolph, Earl of Moray** (July 1332), and the election in his place of the inexperienced Donald **Earl of Mar** (a nephew of **Robert I**), **Edward Balliol** saw his chance to wrest the Scottish throne from the child **David II**. With the tacit support of Edward III of England, he set sail from the Humber at the end of July with 88 ships, landed at **Kinghorn** and marched across **Fife**. He was met by Mar and his army at Dupplin Moor on the river Earn near **Perth** on 12 August. Though the Scots outnumbered the invaders, in the 'confused and disorderly Scottish attack ... the second Scottish battalion trod the first underfoot; more Scots dying by suffocation than by the edge of the sword' (R Nicolson). Among the mass of dead at the end of the day was Donald of Mar. Six weeks later Edward Balliol was crowned at **Scone**.

DURISDEER, Dumfriesshire

Six miles north of **Thornhill**, this village lies beside the Well or Wall Path, once the **Roman** road from Nithsdale over the Dalveen Pass to Elvanfoot on the **Clyde**. The well preserved outline of a small Roman fort of the **Antonine** period is visible about a mile to the north. The village itself is notable for its church (1699) and, in particular, its Queensberry burial vault, designed by **James Smith** the architect of nearby **Drumlanrig** for the 1st Duke of Queensberry and of the elaborate marble monument to the 2nd Duke and his Duchess.

DURNESS, Sutherland

This formerly vast parish extended down the west coast as far as Assynt, and along the north coast to include **Tongue**. In 1638 a separate parish was erected here, for which the 1st Lord Reay built the church with its underground vault. In 1707 the Rev John Mackay, second cousin of the Chief, insisted that Eidrachillis should also be detached from Durness. After the erection of the three separate parishes, Rev Murdo MacDonald arrived (1726) to begin the long ministry which he recorded in a diary, much of which is now lost. He was commemorated by **Rob Donn** Mackay in what many regard as Scotland's finest elegy. Durness had already lost its centre of cultural patronage long before the estate was sold to the house of **Sutherland** in 1829, and today the mansion of **Balnakil** usually stands empty though it is kept in repair. During World War II a radar station was established on Farout (Faraid) Head and its former military buildings have discovered a new use as a crafts centre.

DWELLY, Edward (1864–1939) Gaelic Scholar

An Englishman who was an Army piper and an Ordnance Survey official, Dwelly devoted many years in the late 19th and early 20th centuries to collecting **Gaelic** vocabulary and usage. His large *Illustrated Gaelic to English Dictionary* appeared in parts between 1902 and 1911, and is still widely used in various editions up to 1988. The valuable *Appendix* which he compiled later was published in 1991.

DYCE, Aberdeen

On the **Don** and once a distinct community, Dyce has been largely engulfed by **Aberdeen**'s overspill, and is now administratively part of the city of Aberdeen. The city's **airport**, located here since the 1930s and now much used by helicopters servicing the off-shore **oil** and gas rigs, is one of Scotland's busiest. Oil-related activities dominate the nearby Kirkhill industrial estate. The old parish church, dedicated to St Fergus and now a ruin, dates from before the **Reformation** and there are some **Pictish** symbol stones built into one of the gable walls. On Tyrebagger Hill above the airport the recumbent stone circle has four fine uprights, one of them 11ft (3.3m) tall.

DYCE, Alexander (1798–1869) Scholar and Critic

Alexander Dyce was born in **Edinburgh**, the eldest son of a lieutenant-colonel in the service of the East India Company. He was educated at Edinburgh High School and Exeter College, Oxford. Upon graduation, his father intended him to join the East India Company. Dyce chose instead to become a clergyman, and between 1822–5 served two curacies in Cornwall and Suffolk. In 1825 he left the Church and settled in London to devote himself to literary studies.

Dyce's literary work was mainly editorial in nature. His first major work was *Specimens of British Poetesses* (1825). This was followed by an edition of poems of William Collins (1827) published by William Pickering. Between 1831–5 Dyce continued his association with Pickering, contributing to his 'Aldine' series editions of poems of Alexander Pope (1831), **James Beattie** (1831) and Mark Akenside (1835).

He is best known for his work on texts of 16th and 17th century English authors and dramatists: George Peele (1828–39), John Webster (1830), Robert Greene (1831, 1861), Thomas Middleton (1840), Beaumont and Fletcher (1843–6) and John Ford (1869). He also edited the poems of Sir Henry Wotton (1843) and John Skelton (1843), produced editions of lesser-known Elizabethan and Jacobean works, was the first editor of Sir Thomas More (1844) and edited the works of the classical scholar Richard Bentley (1836–8). His most valuable achievement was the production of a complete edition of Shakespeare's work, published in nine volumes in 1857, which became the classic edition of its time. On his death, Dyce's valuable collection of drawings, prints, manuscripts and books was bequeathed to the Victoria and Albert Museum in London.

DYCE, William (1806–64) Painter and Educationalist

Born in **Aberdeen**, the son of a doctor, Dyce enrolled at the Royal Academy Schools in 1825. Leaving later that same year he made his first visit to Italy where he came into contact with the German Nazarenes and, sharing their disapproval of academic art training, turned to the work of the early Renaissance masters, seeking to retrace their methods, inspiration and purpose. In **Edinburgh** from 1830, he worked as a successful if conventional portraitist, became involved in the **Trustees' Academy** and in 1837, as a result of an essay addressing the issues of contemporary art education, was appointed Superintendent of the new Schools of Design at Somerset House, London. Though the diversity of his interests frequently interrupted his career as a painter (he was active as a scholar and composer of sacred music while his published articles ranged from ecclesiastical architecture to electro-magnetism), he successfully pioneered a revival in fresco painting and was consummate in its techniques. In 1851 he began decorations for the Queen's Robing Room at Westminster Palace, illustrating legends from King Arthur, a project that remained unfinished at his death. Despite his dedication to a renaissance of ennobling and large-scale religious art, his painting in this style remains rather dry and angular. Dyce's finest works, completed in his last 10 years, are his small easel paintings which in their superb draughtsmanship and attention to natural detail are in part indebted to his admiration for the Pre-Raphaelites. Usually landscapes with predominantly religious overtones, they culminated in the extraordinary and haunting *Pegwell Bay* (1858, Tate Gallery), one of the most original British paintings of the mid-century.

DYER, Henry (1848–1918) Pioneer of Japanese Engineering

Henry Dyer was born in **Bothwell, Lanarkshire**. In 1868, after serving his apprenticeship in a **Glasgow engineering** works, he matriculated to study at **Glasgow University** where he became the first Scot ever to win a Whitworth Scholarship. He graduated (1873) with the best academic record of any student to have studied in the **engineering** department. His professor, **Macquorn Rankine**, had no hesitation in recommending him for the post of Principal and Professor of Engineering at the new Imperial College of Engineering in Tokyo.

Dyer carried with him to Japan the crusading zeal of his mentors, Rankine and **William Thomson**, for a course of study in engineering which laid equal emphasis on the theoretical and the practical. The courses he inaugurated in Tokyo required the student to spend two years on general and science subjects, two on technical subjects in the student's chosen field, and two more on purely practical work. To provide a practical training environment for mechanical engineers, he helped set up the Akabane Engineering Works, the largest in Japan, where machinery was manufactured for the country's public works department. Many of the major engineering works carried out in Japan at the end of the 19th century were by his former students, and Dyer sent others to Britain (and particularly to Glasgow) to complete their education and gain first-hand experience of European methods and technology. When he left 'Dyer's College' in 1882, he was made Honorary

Principal and the Emperor awarded him the Third Class of the Order of the Rising Sun, the highest Japanese honour available to foreigners.

After nine years' absence, Dyer was unable to secure a prominent academic post back in Scotland. He became an engineering consultant, but continued to be active in **education**. In 1886 he became a Life Governor of the newly created Glasgow and West of Scotland Technical College, and he was a Governor of the Glasgow and West of Scotland Agricultural College. He became a member of the Glasgow School Board in 1891 and was its President from 1914 until his death.

Dyer published a number of influential papers on the education of engineers, which were often critical of the training made available in Britain and, in 1878, resulted in his being snubbed by the Institute of Civil Engineers. He also published books on the rise of Japan, providing expert comment on the development of a nation which was becoming increasingly powerful in both military and economic terms. There is no doubt that, by establishing a progressive system of education in engineering in Tokyo, Dyer contributed greatly to the progress of Japan as an industrial power. He is today much better known in that country than in his homeland.

EAGLES, GOLDEN

Although *Aquila Chrysaetos* breeds wherever there is suitable upland habitat, it is obviously most numerous in the Highlands and Western Isles. With c450 pairs in territory (1993), Scotland is the breeding ground for almost all the eagles in Britain. But not all will breed, and although some adults stay in territory all year, young birds on attaining independence will often drift south to **grouse** moors where many ringed specimens have been recovered. In the 19th century the bird was threatened with extinction when sheep farmers and grouse-moor owners made it a scapegoat for poor lambings and diminished bags. Its survival, when other large raptors like the **sea eagle**, **osprey** and kite succumbed to such persecution, is as responsible for its celebrity as its size (7ft/2.1m wing span), its majestic flight, and its disdain for civilisation. As a symbol of the untamed Highlands it is eagerly identified – although sometimes mistakenly, as when the amateur ornithologist encounters his first buzzard (or 'tourist's eagle'). Now protected by law and no longer endangered, it yet remains a quarry for egg collectors and the unscrupulous gamekeeper.

From **Roman** times eagles have enjoyed armorial distinction and mythical currency. Legend declares that only the wren flies higher, a feat it achieves by travelling as a passenger to the eagle's maximum altitude and then fluttering a few feet skywards. Allegedly eagles were once eaten, their bone marrow being supposedly efficacious against a variety of ills. In fact eagles' bones, like those of all other birds, are hollow.

EAGLES, SEA or WHITE-TAILED

Slightly larger than the **golden eagle**, *Haliaetus Albicilla* became extinct in Scotland as a result of 19th century persecution. 'By 1879 they were gone from **Mull**, **Jura** and **Eigg**' (**F Fraser Darling**), while the last report of a breeding pair in **Shetland** is from 1911 and in **Skye** from 1916. Unlike the **osprey**, the sea eagle has made no attempt to recolonise, the nearest populations in Iceland and Norway proving too sedentary. However, after two private attempts to reintroduce the bird, the Nature Conservancy Council and the Royal Society for the Protection of Birds undertook a reintroduction programme. During the period 1975–85, 82 young birds were imported under licence from Norway and reared and released on the isle of **Rum**. Not till 1985 was the first chick successfully reared in the wild and although several pairs now attempt to breed every year, they have largely forsaken Rum. Food dumps providing venison and fish failed to detain most; two crossed to Northern Ireland, two were found poisoned and one came to grief on overhead cables. Happily the majority are still alive but it remains to be seen whether the next generation will breed successfully. Fears that the golden eagle may have pre-empted the sea eagle's habitat remain; but the nests of what is probably the rarest breeding bird in Britain are guarded round the clock.

EAGLESHAM, Renfrewshire

Four miles south-west of **East Kilbride**, the village of Eaglesham was founded in 1796 by the 12th Earl of Eglinton to house the workforce of his newly established **cotton** factory. Laid out in an attractive open plan, with two long rows of houses separated by fields and trees, the growth of the village was halted suddenly when the factory burnt down and was never replaced. A monument in the churchyard commemorates two **Covenanters** shot in May 1685 by a party of dragoons who disturbed a **conventicle** on the nearby moors. In 1941 the village hit the headlines when Rudolph Hess made his famous parachute landing nearby, and in 1960 Eaglesham became the first Scottish village to be listed as a place of special historic interest.

EARDLEY, Joan (1921–63) Painter

Despite her English origins, Joan Eardley, in her short career, evolved a far more Scottish idiom to her art than many of her Scots-born contemporaries, whose eyes and hearts were always drawn to France. Born in Sussex, she trained at **Glasgow School of Art** during the war and came briefly under the tutelage of **James Cowie** in the later 1940s. After a period of travel abroad she settled in **Glasgow** and devoted herself to portraying the poor children of the tenements. Sketches from life were worked up into substantial oils, densely and thickly textured. She wrote of the children: 'they are Glasgow . . . this richness', and in her bold, expressive, essentially ugly paintings she evoked both this colour and the drabness of tenement life. In 1956 Eardley moved to the isolated community of Catterline in **Kincardineshire**. The last seven years of her life she devoted entirely to landscape: the dark furious storms of the North Sea, often depicted gathering over luxuriant cornfields, executed in a combination of thick impastos and collage. Her work recalls the German Expressionists and earlier exponents of a northern Romantic landscape tradition and is both unique and inherently suited to the Scottish landscape and psyche. Her premature death from cancer deprived her adopted country of a considerable talent and vision.

EARLSFERRY, Fife

In 1589, when Earlsferry received a new charter to replace one accidentally burnt, the village was described as 'old beyond the memory of man'. The name may derive from a regular ferry crossing in early medieval times to **North Berwick**, although legend records that here MacDuff, **Earl of Fife**, hid from **MacBeth** until friendly fishermen 'ferried' him across the Forth to safety. A cave to the west of the village is still known as 'MacDuff's Cave'.

A street called Liberty joins Earlsferry to its neighbour

'Reddin the lines'; George Washington Wilson's portrait of Elie fishermen (GWWA)

Elie, with which it was amalgamated in 1929. Elie's tidy village green, complete with flagpole, is reminiscent of the English shires rather than the Scottish east coast, and indeed many professional people from England have retired here over the years. Its traditional **fishing** industry was in decline by the late 19th century, but it was to become a popular tourist resort and a mecca for **golfers**. **James Braid**, the famous Open champion, was a local son. In recent years Elie's harbour, dating from 1582, has become a centre for watersports.

EARLSHALL, Leuchars, Fife

Built by Sir William Bruce in 1546 and completed in 1617 by his great-grandson, also Sir William Bruce (but neither of them **Sir William Bruce** the architect), Earlshall is a variation on the conventional L-plan tower house with a stair tower in the re-entrant angle and an additional oval tower on one of the external angles. A further range and wall formed a courtyard with the main block. All, though, was in ruins by 1891 when **Sir Robert Lorimer** embarked on his seven years of much acclaimed restoration. Additions included a gate-house and some topiary chessmen, but his greatest challenge was probably the restoration of the painted ceiling (16th century) in the second-floor Long Gallery, an extraordinarily detailed display of heraldic, historical and zoological subjects painted on the coved ceiling. The name of the property is thought to derive from its once being the residence of the **Earls of Fife**,

whose Leuchars Castle, now vanished, stood nearby. Instead Earlshall now has the RAF as its Leuchars neighbour.

EARLSTON, Berwickshire

On the east bank of the Leader Water, which here forms the boundary between **Berwickshire** and **Roxburghshire**, Earlston was formerly called Ercildoune and is thus famous as the supposed birthplace of 'Thomas the Rhymer', also called **Thomas of Ercildoune** (c1210–c90). A small ruin thought to be the remains of his home was purchased by the **Edinburgh** Borderers' Association in 1895 and marked with a plaque. The fact that the ruin was later declared to be post-13th century has done nothing to dent the legend, and it continues to be called 'The Rhymer's Tower'.

EAS COUL AULIN, Nr Inchnadamph, Sutherland

Sometimes called 'The Maiden's Tresses', Eas Coul Aulin drops 200m in a spectacular cascade which is now regarded as the highest waterfall in the British Isles [see **Falls of Glomach**]. Recognition came late mainly thanks to the fall's remote situation in the Glas Beinn area of **Assynt**. The name, properly Eas a' Chual Aluinn, means 'The Splendid Waterfall of Glencoul'.

EASDALE ISLAND, Argyll

400 yards out from Ellenabeich on **Seil Island**, Easdale was a centre of slate **quarrying** from the 16th century. Operations were first conducted on the shore and above the water level. In the 18th century permanent crews

of quarriers were introduced living in single-storey whitewashed cottages (now mostly converted into holiday homes). In the 19th century a system of outflow channels and sluices allowed the low water level to be worked regardless of tides and the quarries were deepened further as more efficient pumps were invented (both steam engines and windmills being used as motive power); a peak production of 9 million slates was achieved in 1869. The quarries were flooded in November 1881 by a great storm and production was finally halted in 1914.

EAST KILBRIDE, Lanarkshire
Following adoption of the 1946 **Clyde Valley Plan**, East Kilbride became the first of Scotland's new towns. Construction during the 1950s and 60s was no guarantee of architectural distinction but in attracting industry and resolving **Glasgow**'s housing shortage the new town achieved some success. It lies south of the original burgh, once an important source of lime, with Torrance House, previously the home of the Stuarts of Torrance and Castlemilk, providing a headquarters for the new Development Corporation. 'Kilbride' implies that the site was once that of a Celtic foundation dedicated to St Bride, or Bridget. Post-**Reformation** it witnessed the first meeting in Scotland of the Society of Friends (1653), and so enthusiastically did it celebrate the defeat of **John Graham of Claverhouse** at **Killiecrankie** (1689) that the church bell was split. Mains Castle, of 13th century origins, was once held by the **Comyns**, then by the Lindsays of Dunrod. Long Calderwood was the birthplace of **John** and **William Hunter**, the physicians, who are memorialised in the town. A country park with the usual attractions now occupies Calderglen to the south.

EAST LINTON, East Lothian
Described as 'something between a big village and a small town' (I & K Whyte), East Linton owed its 18th and 19th century prosperity to its 16th century bridge where the great mail-road between **Edinburgh** and London crossed the river Tyne. Its current good fortune is to have been bypassed by the main A1. The 18th century Prestonkirk Parish Church on the outskirts of the town includes a magnificent 13th century chancel, by far the most worthwhile piece of 13th century church architecture in **East Lothian**' (C McWilliam). Two miles south-west of the town on a rocky promontory on the south bank of the Tyne are the ruins of **Hailes Castle**, a 13th–14th century castle of enclosure probably built by one of the **Earls of Dunbar**.

EAST LOTHIAN
Before the **local government** reorganisation of 1975, East Lothian, sometimes known as Haddingtonshire, comprised 171,044 acres (69,273ha) stretching from east of **Musselburgh** (then in **Midlothian**) to **Cockburnspath**. The Firth of Forth lay to the north, the North Sea to the east, and **Berwickshire** to the south beyond the **Lammermuir Hills**. The Tyne was the only major river, reaching the sea near **Dunbar**. Because of its location between **Edinburgh** and the English border, the area was frequently razed by invading English troops, and important battles were fought in the county area, at **Dunbar** in 1650 and **Prestonpans** in 1745.

Agriculture was important, along with **fishing** and some **coal-mining** in the west of the county. **Haddington** was the county town, and there were six other small burghs, comprising **Cockenzie** & **Port Seton**, Dunbar, **East Linton**, **North Berwick**, Prestonpans, and **Tranent** (marginally the largest). In 1975 the county passed into East Lothian District, Lothian Region, while 'gaining' the burgh of Musselburgh and the parish of **Inveresk** from Midlothian, and after 1995 this same area once more became a single administrative division.

EAST NEUK OF FIFE
This name is often given to the string of coastal villages on the south-east extremity ('neuk' = promontory) of **Fife** running the 10 miles or so from **Earlsferry** to **Crail**. According to legend, **James II** described the East Neuk as 'the golden fringe on a beggar's mantle', for the **fishing** and Continental trade carried on from these thriving seaports made East Fife one of the few prosperous areas in his poverty-stricken kingdom. Although the East Neuk is often regarded as a historical and cultural unit, and promoted as such for the **tourist** trade, the constituent villages of Elie and **Earlsferry**, **St Monans**, **Pittenweem**, **Anstruther**, Cellardyke (with Kilrenny) and Crail still preserve much of their former individuality.

ECCLEFECHAN, Dumfriesshire
The 'eccle' comes from *eaglais* or *ecclesia*, a church, the 'fechan' denoting either a small church or the Celtic saint to whom it was dedicated. The village so named lies south-west of **Lockerbie** off the M74 and is renowned as the birthplace and burial site of **Thomas Carlyle**. His home, the Arched House, was built by his father and uncle c1791 and is now a museum dedicated to the great man. The family eventually moved to a larger house in the village and in 1828 the newly wed Thomas and **Jane Welsh Carlyle** set up home at Craigenputtock, a still remote farmhouse on the other side of **Dumfries** between Dunscore and St John's Town of **Dalry**. Several **Roman** forts march with the M74 to the east, this being the line of the main north-south Roman road. Burnswark is the more prominent with an earlier hill fort and two Roman camps plus what is taken to be a ballistics practice range. Birrens is 'the most informative of all the Roman sites in south-west Scotland'; from an **Antonine** itinerary it has been identified as Blatobulgium, an outpost of Hadrian's Wall.

ECCLES, Berwickshire
Six miles west of **Coldstream**, the church of Eccles was originally dedicated to **St Cuthbert** and was annexed in 1156 by Gospatrick, **Earl of Dunbar**, to his newly founded convent of Cistercian nuns. Destroyed by Hertford in 1545, little remains of the convent today. **Henry Home** (1696–1782) was born at Kames in the parish of Eccles and took the title Lord Kames on being appointed a judge in 1752. It was to his endeavours as an agricultural improver that the area became renowned for its 'exuberant crops' of wheat, barley and oats.

ECHT, Nr Aberdeen
The **Midmar** villages of Echt and Dunecht (three miles north) flank Barmekin Hill, site of a **Pictish** fort with

five concentric defensive rings, and setting for the conclusion of **Lewis Grassic Gibbon**'s *A Scots Quair*. The area is exceptionally rich in prehistoric remains including the recumbent stone circles at Sunhoney and Midmar Kirk and the **standing stone** circle of Cullerlie. Dunecht Estate and House, a large 19th century confection with prominent turreted gatehouses, belongs to the Cowdray family.

EDAY, Orkney

This is Eidi, Isthmus Island, and it is curious that Gaelic **Lewis** has preserved a truer pronunciation of the Norse word in the Eye peninsula. The Calf of Eday contains one of **Orkney**'s richest archaeological sites, with its tomb of the early Unstan period. Here bronze-users settled later, and iron-workers subsequently built their roundhouses. Eday itself has a scattering of chambered tombs. On one of them, as Gordon Childe observed, 'a spiral pattern has been engraved in the Boyne manner'. The stone bearing this Irish motif, described as a sun symbol, has been taken to the **Royal Museum** in **Edinburgh**. In the 1630s a saltworks was instituted on the island. Its buildings are among the best preserved from the 17th and 18th centuries.

It was on Eday that John Gow, the pirate born in **Stromness**, was captured and carried south to be hanged at Wapping in 1725. He had come to raid the home of the laird, Carrick House, but his ship ran aground and its crew were overpowered. His ship's chest is preserved at Stromness and he is immortalised in **Walter Scott**'s novel *The Pirate*. It was published after the author's visit to the Northern Isles and enabled the Orcadians to identify the writer of the Waverley novels before anyone else in Europe. **St Magnus' Cathedral** in **Kirkwall** was built largely of stone quarried at Fersness on Eday.

EDDERTON, Ross & Cromarty

Near this village on the **Dornoch Firth** an abbey was founded by Farquhar **Earl of Ross** in 1221 (or 1227) but was removed to **Fearn** c1238. In the graveyard of the old parish church stands a **Pictish** cross-slab displaying an equestrian figure on one side and crosses on both but otherwise fairly plain. A mile away in a field the tall fang of stone was probably a Bronze Age **standing stone** which, two millennia later, was incised with the Pictish symbols of fish and double disk with Z rod, now scarcely visible. Opposite is a small stone circle. There are several chambered **cairns** and many hut circles in the area plus Dun Alascaig, the remains of a **broch**.

EDGAR (1074–1107) King

Edgar was the fourth son of **Malcolm III**'s second marriage. Aged 19 at his father's death, he and his younger brothers and sisters took shelter in England with William II (Rufus) who in 1096–7 gave him troops to defeat his uncle **Donald Bane** (and his own elder brother Edmund) and gain the throne. Soon afterwards the King of Norway, **Magnus Barelegs**, brought a formidable fleet into western waters and forced Edgar to cede 'all the isles round which a ship could sail', including **Kintyre** (by drawing his galley overland with sail hoisted at **Tarbert**, Loch Fyne – a familiar device to the Norsemen who traversed Russia to the Volga).

Little else is recorded of Edgar's reign; he was virtually a dependant of William II and Henry I of England (Henry married Edgar's sister Edith or Matilda in 1100). Edgar died unmarried; the kingdom passed peacefully to his next brother **Alexander I**, while the 'king with the Saxon name' was buried in **Dunfermline** with his parents.

EDINBURGH

'A city too well known to admit description' (**Dr Johnson**, 1775), the capital of Scotland enjoys a dramatic hilly site overlooking the Firth of Forth and rising steeply above the Lothian plain. This remarkable landscape results from a succession of **geological** and geomorphological upheavals which occurred over many millennia. About 325 million years ago during Carboniferous times the renowned 'Edinburgh Volcano', which comprised the Castle Rock and **Arthur's Seat**, erupted and poured forth lava flows such as the **Calton Hill** and then became extinct; a rise in sea-level was followed by the gradual formation of sedimentary rocks, with intrusions of igneous material between the strata under the old volcano producing sills like **Salisbury Crags**. During the Ice Age the present profile was carved out by the exceptional west-east (as distinct from the usual south-west to north-east) passage of the ice sheet in the Edinburgh area. In its crucial encounter with the rock of the old volcanic cores, the ice sometimes simply rolled over the obstruction to form gently rounded slopes, such as the **Pentland Hills** on the south-western perimeter of the city; elsewhere, however, it was forced to bifurcate, most notably at the Castle Rock where, with the added pressure, it gouged the deep hollows of the **Grassmarket** and **Cowgate** and **Princes Street Gardens**, formerly the **Nor'** Loch. The characteristic local landform called a 'crag-and-tail' resulted: a rugged cliff of resistant igneous rock situated at the place of impact with the ice to the west protecting a ridge of softer, sedimentary rocks (eg the **Royal Mile**) tapering to nought through the slow passage of the sheet to the east.

CASTLE AND BURGH The basalt plinth of **Edinburgh Castle** provides an ideal site for a fortified settlement which, when man first arrived in the area, could not have been disregarded; its crags on the north, south and west afforded excellent defence and the very steep slope to the north and south of the then narrow ridge of **Castlehill** where it leaves the Rock at the **Esplanade** was also effective; easy access for the inhabitants, however, was given by the gentle eastward slope of the Royal Mile ridge.

For perhaps some 7000 years this commanding location has been continuously inhabited. Although archaeological remains are scant, there is some evidence of communities of hunter-gatherers present along the valley of the **Water of Leith** from at least 5000 BC, farming being introduced c3000 BC and metal-working c2000 BC. Most of the hill-tops in the surrounding area supported fortifications built c1000 BC, the most impressive of which survive on Arthur's Seat in **Holyrood Park**.

The original palisaded enclosure on the Rock formed the nucleus for the later massive medieval structure of the Castle. During **Roman** times the Rock was probably

Edinburgh c1890; looking east from the Castle towards the National Gallery and the Scott Monument (GWWA)

Edinburgh *continued*

occupied by the Votadini, the local tribe whose major fort was at **Traprain Law** in **East Lothian**. In the 2nd century AD the Romans established naval supply bases at **Inveresk** (**Musselburgh**) and **Cramond**, where the rivers Esk and Almond flow into the Firth of Forth on the east and west of the city respectively; they left little other mark on Lothian.

The Castle, in some form, enters recorded history in the early 7th century as Din Eidyn, the stronghold of the Gododdin (the Cumbric name for the Votadini) which the Gaelic-speaking Scots called *Dun Eiden* ('the hill fort of the sloping ridge'). *Eiden* cannot be a corruption of Edwin, King of Northumbria, who died five years before the Rock was captured by the Angles in 638. They eventually abandoned it to the advancing Scots in the middle of the 10th century, but Dun Eiden only ceased to be a frontier stronghold in 1018 when **Malcolm II**, through his victory at **Carham**, secured the Northumbrian province of Lothian for Scotland. Throughout this time there is no indication of any settlement existing separately from the fort.

Until recently, the Castle was the preserve of either the monarchy or the military. The civic settlement which developed into the city of Edinburgh began as a clachan near the top of the Royal Mile ridge on Castlehill, but at some distance from the Castle itself, which main-tained an unbuilt 'military zone' (now represented by the Esplanade) for defensive purposes. From this narrow neck of land the embryo township expanded trumpet-like, eastwards down the slope on to the broader back of the ridge which became the **Lawnmarket** leading to the **High Street** beyond.

Neither the date when the town first became independently established from the Castle nor that of its erection into a burgh is known; the earliest charter has seemingly not survived. Burgh status was achieved certainly no later than the 12th century, however, for a charter of **David I** dating to 1124 which founded **Holyrood Abbey** in what developed into the independent burgh of the **Canongate** refers to Edinburgh as *meum burghum* – 'my burgh' – indicating a royal foundation holding its charter directly from the king. **Royal burghs** alone were permitted to conduct foreign trade; and in 1364 David II granted them a monopoly of such trade within their areas, the source of burghal growth and prosperity. Trade, principally across the North Sea with the Low Countries and the Baltic, was conducted through **Leith**, two miles distant, which assumed such an importance that Edinburgh exerted extreme controls over the port from early times. Merchants using Leith had to reside in Edinburgh and the charter granted by **Robert I** to the city in 1329 included the port, the 'Shore' of which was purchased from Logan of **Restalrig** in 1398 and 1414. This, the oldest extant charter of the burgh which also granted the milling rights on the Water of Leith at the present **Dean Village**, was fortuitously sealed by

293

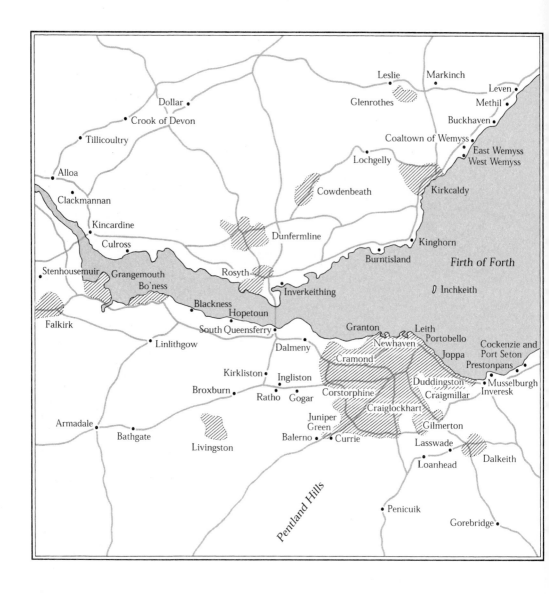

Edinburgh and the Firth of Forth

Edinburgh continued

Robert I at **Cardross** in **Dunbartonshire** only 10 days before his demise; it effectively raised the status of Edinburgh above that of **Berwick**, then the largest and wealthiest burgh in the kingdom although it was perilously placed on the border with, and hence susceptible to seizure by, England.

The early prosperity of Edinburgh, too, was hard won in the face of English incursion although many of its burgesses were in fact the descendants of aliens, including French, Flemish and English craftsmen, planted there when the infant burgh was first nurtured by David I. The developing township was recurrently attacked and occupied by the 'Auld Enemy' during 1335–85 in what was, to all intents and purposes, a continuation of the **Wars of Independence**; most notably in 1385 when Richard II burnt both the High Kirk (**St Giles**

Cathedral), founded by **Alexander II** in c1120, and the adjacent 'praetorium' or town hall, the precursor of the old **Tolbooth** which had been erected near the **Mercat Cross** in c1369.

Despite these punitive blows, Edinburgh had, by the close of the 14th century, grown into the largest and most populous Scots burgh – albeit with perhaps as few as 350 houses sheltering only some 2000 souls; a position which, until the rapid rise of **Glasgow** in the early 19th century, it easily held for the next 400 years.

Medieval commercial pre-eminence was built upon both its merchant trade and its specialised craft industries. The regional capital of a trade zone originally delineated by David I which comprised much of modern Lothian, the city had, through the charter of Robert I, gained direct control over rents, revenues, issues of courts and petty customs all formerly administered by individual royal appointees. ('Great Customs', ie on **wool** and hides, were retained by the Crown.) This early form of self-regulation was the outstanding characteristic of life in Scots royal burghs, and Edinburgh (with, originally, Berwick, **Roxburgh** and **Stirling**) formed one of the Court of Four Burghs which existed in the 13th century.

By the mid-15th century Edinburgh had developed a town council – which secured the right to appoint the Dean of Guild; this exclusive merchant body, which by then included burgesses of the more 'dignified' crafts, had formerly acted as the sole municipal authority. The craft guilds, or 'trades incorporations', which later, in the 17th century, raised convening halls such as the **Tailors' Hall** and the **Magdalen Chapel** (Hammermen) in the Cowgate, originated from this limitation of merchant power. After the merchants themselves, the 14 trades which by 1600 were incorporated by 'seal of cause' under an elected deacon were ranked (according to William Maitland, the first historian of the city, in 1753): 1) Skinner, surgeon, goldsmith, flesher, cordiner (shoemaker), tailor, baxter (baker) and hammerman; 2) Mason or wright; 3) Webster (weaver), waulker (fuller), bonnet-maker and furrier. The most influential and diverse were the hammermen, smiths and metalworkers of all sorts, who maintained their private altar to St Eloi in St Giles. The goldsmiths (including silversmiths) asserted their independence from the hammermen in c1525 and received a royal charter in 1687. Among the 'inferior trades' such as barbers, hatmakers and candlemakers [see **Candlemaker Row**] were also incorporated.

By the early 15th century, 'Royal David's City' had climbed down from the confines of the Royal Mile ridge and spawned its first straggling suburb to the south in the valley of the Cowgate and Grassmarket, beyond the foot of the **West Bow**. Along the opposite, southern slope stretched a consecrated cordon consisting of the Blackfriars' Monastery (1230) to the east, which was later joined by that of the Greyfriars' (1447) in the west, with the **Kirk o' Field** (1275) interceding between. These three great religious houses, which lay outside the early town **walls**, were belatedly enclosed by the **Flodden Wall** after 1513. North of the Royal Mile ridge, by Leith Wynd, lay **Trinity College Kirk** (1462) at the outlet of the Nor' Loch, a 'make-do' defence dammed by **James II** in 1460.

The original Royalty of Edinburgh, determined at 143 acres by David I, has expanded enormously into the 50 square miles of the city as it exists today. For some 250 years, however, until the stranglehold was finally broken by the quantum leap of the 18th century **New Town**, virtually all expansion within the burgh was forced upwards rather than outwards since further lateral growth within the medieval **Old Town** was brought up against the barrier of the Flodden Wall. Thus arose the characteristic 'slit-canyon', clamorous close and court, tenemental architecture of the Old Town which, by all accounts, stunned outsiders by its soaring to impossible heights (in one case to 14 storeys) within the steeply plunging alleys such as **Advocate's Close** which still strike off so suddenly from the sides of the High Street and Lawnmarket.

THE ROYAL CAPITAL At the beginning of the 15th century the Scots Parliament, General Council and Convention of Estates rarely met in Edinburgh, whereas by its close they seldom met elsewhere. The city cannot fully claim to have become the capital, however, until its central administration, with the **Court of Session** under the College of Justice, was finally established there by **James V** in 1532. Although Parliament met regularly in Edinburgh from 1466, both in the Castle and elsewhere, **Parliament Hall** was not built until 1639 – significantly at the demand of the town council which was alarmed at further possible loss of civic status a full generation after the departure of the royal court to London in 1603 on the **Union of the Crowns**.

Always restlessly itinerant, the royal court had, although often based at Holyrood, peregrinated between its palaces at Stirling, **Falkland** and **Linlithgow**. Edinburgh Castle also served as a royal residence from the 11th century, when frequently favoured by **Malcolm III** (his 'capital' was **Dunfermline**). However, **James III** was the first monarch who regularly resided in the city, at either the Royal Apartments (Palace) of the Castle or the guesthouse of Holyrood Abbey. This latter billet touched the heart of his successor, **James IV**, who from 1501 began its elevation into the **Palace of Holyroodhouse**; a long evolutionary process continued by the later **Stewart** monarchs and culminating in the existing showpiece created for **Charles II** in 1671–8.

In 1482 James III granted 'the more principal burgh of our kingdom' its 'Golden Charter' in gratitude for its loyal support and for securing his release from imprisonment in **David's Tower** in the Castle; this invested powers of shrieval jurisdiction in the city magistrates, ie its provost and bailies, giving them virtual control over **local government** administration and the dispensation of justice within the area of their own authority, a privileged measure of independence which they continued to exercise until the Burgh Reform Act of 1833. These rights of sheriffdom were renewed by **James VI** in 1603 on the eve of his departure for England. Earlier, in 1583, James VI had issued the Decreet Arbitral, a court decision which laid down the sett, or constitution, of the burgh (largely unchanged until 1833) after the craftsmen had struggled for a century against the domination of the town council by the merchants. Nonetheless, municipal affairs long remained the preserve of a self-perpetuating oligarchy.

The city burgeoned both physically and intellectually in the 16th century; an indication of its commercial growth being the customs dues of the town, which as a revenue earner for the Crown were £1758 in 1501–2; £2012 in 1550–1 and £8833 in 1597–8. The development of Edinburgh in the post-**Reformation** period is marked by purchases of the superiority of land outside the original royalty of the city, and the construction of large-scale public and private works. In 1617 the High Riggs at **Lauriston** were bought from the Baron of Inverleith; in 1639, the Pleasance and North Leith from the Earl of Roxburghe; in 1648 Inverleith itself; and in 1649 Portsburgh (ie the **West Port** and Potterow at **Bristo**) from the **Earl of Bothwell**. Wester Restalrig, including Calton, was not purchased until 1724. The superiority of the Canongate (with **Broughton**) was obtained in 1636, but the burgh was not incorporated (along with Portsburgh) into the city until 1856.

Portobello was incorporated in 1896 and Leith finally amalgamated with her possessive big sister in 1920 when the villages of **Cramond**, **Newhaven**, **Granton**, **Corstorphine**, **Colinton**, **Liberton** and **Gilmerton** also came within the city. Following the Reformation the comparatively vast grounds of the medieval religious foundations which girdled the southern limits of the Old Town were plundered for sites for new secular institutions.

During the 17th century, the conception of trade as a purely local burgh affair was gradually supplemented by the idea that it was a matter of national concern. As such, Edinburgh had its place in the Scots economy under general laws which applied to the kingdom as a whole and transcended the former code of burgh privileges. That Edinburgh was first in wealth among the other burghs is evident from the large payments of annual land tax, levied at the rate of two to three times the proportion of Glasgow, four to five times that of **Aberdeen** and six times that of **Dundee**. The Edinburgh Company of Merchants emerged and secured a charter in 1681 – in which year the first piped water supply was led to Castlehill from **Comiston** Springs. Local industries included **linen**, woollen and silk manufactories; a foundry (1686); and, in Leith, sailcloth, rope and cordage making, a sawmill and glassworks. The first wholly Scottish-made paper was produced at **Dalry** Mills on the Water of Leith.

The foundation of the Bank of Scotland (1695), followed, after the **Darien Scheme** disaster, by its great rival the Royal Bank of Scotland (1727), gave an early boost to the nascent Scots industrial economy and established the Edinburgh financial and business community whose pumps today prime most profusely between **St Andrew** and **Charlotte Squares**.

The status of Edinburgh increased greatly during the 17th century; it became, albeit briefly, an Episcopal Cathedral See (the diocese being formed from that of St Andrews) and City under Charles I in 1633; and in 1667 the chief magistrate was dignified with the title of 'Lord Provost' even though the abuse of this office had become, like typhus, endemic in Edinburgh during the 17th century. 'High and dirty' (Kirke, 1679), the city was last visited by the 'pest' (Great Plague) in 1645 when Leith was bereaved of 2421 souls, or half its population. By 1694 Edinburgh sheltered c21,000 people, almost three times that recorded (c7500) in the third quarter of the 16th century; by 1750 there were perhaps as many as 60,000 in so small a compass.

During the late 17th and early 18th centuries the anarchical spirit of the Edinburgh 'mob' frequently overflowed onto the city streets. In 1688 the Chapel Royal of Holyrood Abbey was sacked when William of Orange arrived in England; and in 1689 **James VII** was declared forfeit by a Parliamentary Convention of Estates protected by an army of **Covenanters**. For the **Jacobites**, **John Graham of Claverhouse** held his famous postern conference on the Castle Rock with its commander, the Duke of Gordon, who held out for James until 1690 when the cause was dashed by the death of 'Bonnie Dundee' on the Braes of **Killiecrankie**.

The rebellious host – 'Certainly the scots [sic] rabble is the worst of its kind' (Defoe) – its ire quickened by the cruelties of the **Glencoe Massacre** and the Darien disaster, was enraged by the **Act of Union**; in 1706, in a mass insurrection, even before the details of the unpatriotic measure were made plain by Parliament, the mob assailed the pro-Union protagonists, attacked the residence of the Lord Provost and assumed control of the city until quelled by 'the entire army'. The immediate post-Union period found Edinburgh disadvantaged in her trading position under the pressure of English competition within a system of free trade and excise duties strictly exacted on basic industries. The city itself could only thole the grievous loss of the financial and social status formerly afforded by the old Scots Parliament, but in 1736 the mob once again defied the powers of authority by lynching the captain of the town guard in the **Porteous Riot**.

Nevertheless Edinburgh remained loyal to the Hanoverian succession during the 1745 **Rising**. (In the '15 a planned attack on the Castle had been botched by the city Jacobites themselves.) After the defending Dragoons fled from a few Highland flankers in the 'Canter of Coltbrig' at Roseburn near **Murrayfield**, and the crusty Edinburgh Volunteer Force faded away, the magistrates parleyed with **Prince Charles Edward** at Slateford, but **Cameron of Lochiel** opportunely rushed in at the **Netherbow Port**.

THE NEW TOWN In 1752, the Convention of Royal Burghs assented to 'Proposals for Carrying out Certain Public Works in the City of Edinburgh' which resolved: 'let us boldly enlarge Edinburgh to the utmost' – the overture for the creation of the New Town across the Nor' Loch. A separate, at first largely residential development quite divorced in both time and space from the Old, this plan had been adumbrated in various forms since c1700 (after James VII had permitted the possibility of the extension of the ancient royalty in 1688); notably that fleshed out in 1728 by the exiled Jacobite **Earl of Mar**. The town council had met under Lord Provost **George Drummond** 'for the first time after the state of anarchy which had for some time prevailed in the city' during the aftermath of the '45; it expressed concern later reiterated in the 1752 'Proposals' that while Scotland as a whole had prospered since the Union, the capital itself did not reflect this either in its buildings or its transport conveniences. Matters were hastened by the sudden collapse of the side wall of a six-storey tenement 'in which several reputable families lived', and the ensuing structural survey caused houses found 'insufficient' to be pulled down so that 'several of the principal parts were laid in ruins'.

Similar concern over the appearance of the city to 'strangers and others' had been voiced as long ago as the 16th century when Edinburgh assumed full capital status; in 1540 ruinous houses and empty sites in Leith Wynd were denounced as deformities and ordered, under pain of confiscation, to be rebuilt within a year and a day. Stone is recorded in use for domestic building from 1435, but thatch was only forbidden for risk of 'fire and falling' in 1624; and in 1677 fines were imposed on houses not built of stone and covered with slates or tiles. In 1696 arcaded ashlar frontages, like that of **Gladstone's Land**, were standardised by an act of the council in the vain hope that in time the entire High

Street would conform to a single design with, from 1674, regular window lines and, after 1698, not more than five storeys at the front and walls no more than three feet thick.

In 1674 powers of compulsory purchase of derelict property by the town council, hitherto prohibited by the excessive costs of buying densely built-up land, enabled larger new developments to proceed. After the Great Fire of 1676 Robertson's Land, the most splendid residential project prior to the erection of the New Town, rose to 14 storeys between **Parliament Square** and the Cowgate; completed c1684 and destroyed in the fire of 1700, the 'palaces with fronts of marble' of this luckless land were rebuilt to 11 storeys, only to fall again after the Great Fire of 1824 which devastated the south side of the High Street from St Giles to the **Tron**. The 'land' originally incorporated an 'exchange', a mercantile facility superseded in 1760 by the Royal Exchange (**City Chambers**), the only promulgation of the 'Proposals' actually constructed as planned; a cultural counterpart, **St Cecilia's Concert Hall**, has graced the Cowgate since 1763.

Other early attempts were made to rationalise the medieval clutter of the Old Town [see **Mylne's Court**, **James' Court** and **Chessel's Court**], but it was not until **George Square** was laid out in 1766 beyond the royalty that the town council was finally spurred into promoting its bill to extend the royalty, which it had last shelved in 1759 in the face of strong opposition from landowning interests. The council under George Drummond initiated a competition for the design of the 'New Town' on the site of Barefoot's Parks, which had been acquired in 1716 and set for feu in 1763. In 1767 a successful bill for extension was passed, the elegantly simple, classical grid-iron, gold medal winning plan of **James Craig** accepted, and the first house founded at Rose (now Thistle) Court in the same year.

THE LAST 200 YEARS This Augustan or Golden Age of Edinburgh endured until c1830, culminating in the colossal Greek Revival monuments on Calton Hill which earned the city the accolade of 'Athens of the North'. Heralding the advent of the New Town was the accompanying **Scottish Enlightenment**, that remarkable flourishing of the arts and sciences which, for such a small nation, had no parallel in European civilisation. In 1822 **Sir Walter Scott** stage-managed the royal visit of George IV to Scotland, the first by a reigning British monarch since 1641, and one of only two major national events which occurred in the capital during the 19th century. The other was the **Disruption** of the **Church of Scotland** at its **General Assembly** of 1843 from which schism the **Free Church** emerged. The **railways** which arrived in the Haymarket and **Waverley Station** in 1842, crossed and ringed the city by the 1860s, devouring land in Leith, **St Leonards**, **Gorgie** and Dalry. In these ill-planned, populous districts developed the traditional industries of Edinburgh based upon the three 'B's – books, biscuits and beer. Paper, printing, publishing and their allied trades derived their pre-eminence from the city long being a mecca for **education**, **government**, administration and the professions, particularly the Church and the **law**. Brewing built its base on the underground 'lake' of water tapped by deep artesian wells; but of 20 breweries existing before 1940, only two now remain, the Scottish & Newcastle plc conglomerate and the independent Caledonian, which was the last in Britain to use **coal**-fired copper vats. Biscuit-making, developed from flour-milling by the likes of the great Crawfords and McVities, largely departed with them to Manchester, London and elsewhere. A small but technically important **shipbuilding** industry, reflecting the great mercantile past, finished in the 1980s with the closure of Henry Robb & Co of Leith.

The scale of the 19th century Industrial Revolution barely affected Edinburgh when compared to Glasgow or even Dundee. Much of the industry of the city was (and to a lesser extent remains) conducted on a small scale in workshops of skilled craftsmen: notably furniture, ironwork, **pottery** and glass, the latter still produced by Edinburgh Crystal although located at **Penicuik** in **Midlothian**. Both light and electrical **engineering** assumed much importance in the 20th century, with the 'sunrise', or silicon, industries 'locally' based at **Livingston** and elsewhere.

From the mid-19th century Edinburgh embarked upon the reconstruction of much of its developing central business district, found between **Princes Street** and **George Street**, for banks, hotels and offices; her neo-classical monuments were confronted by soaring Victorian Gothic edifices or palatial Italianate stores. Nevertheless the grimy face of the capital still flowered under her cheeky sobriquet 'Auld Reekie', a slur cast upon her smoky aspect from over the Forth in **Fife**, and produced by thousands of unswept 'lums' with constantly lit fires. From 1957 'smokeless zones', planned to embrace the whole city by 1995, were introduced which have caused the 'greening of Edinburgh' (the growth of lichen on its walls) and the cleaning of its sooty stonework on a large scale.

During the 19th century much of the medieval Old Town sunk into a mouldering slum; 'the windes, down which an English eye may look, but into which no English nose would willingly venture, for stinks older than the Union are to be found there' (Southey, 1819). Long overdue civic action was hastened by the fall of the **'Heave Awa' House'** in 1861. The Edinburgh Improvement Act of 1867 which created new streets was the first effort to ameliorate conditions in the Old Town which is today enjoying a renaissance of its social and cultural forms.

The last British bastion of the sedan chair (used until c1850), Edinburgh remains bedevilled by transport problems. Radical 20th century solutions to these were the central plank of the 1948 ('Abercrombie') City Development Plan (approved 1954 and modified 1957). In consequence ruthless redevelopment ruined much of the historic heart of the city during the 1960s and 70s; such horrors as a car park in East Princes Street Gardens next to the **Scott Monument**, although approved by councillors, were prevented by more enlightened groups such as the **Cockburn** Association (The Edinburgh Civic Trust). Amendments in 1965 proposed an Inner Ring Road which would have despoiled the environs of the Water of Leith, **Royal Botanic Gardens**, Holyrood Park and the **Meadows** as well as many

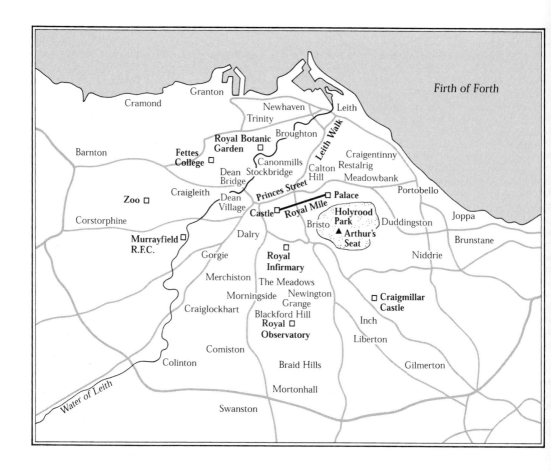

Edinburgh continued

built-up areas. The northern section of this nightmare was scrapped in 1967 but the Buchanan Plan of 1972 – designed for traffic in 1991 – shocked conservationists and citizens alike when, in the hard-fought years until it was abandoned in 1979, the groundwork for these 'Alternatives for Edinburgh' all but destroyed much-loved Tollcross, St Leonards and Greenside. An expanded Outer City Bypass, however, was finally completed in 1990.

In Edinburgh, as elsewhere, there was little statutory protection for buildings of architectural or historical interest before the Town and Country Act of 1969. This, combined with council-blessed pressures for commercial and **University** developments in the low interest rate boom years, caused much of the fine fabric of the city to fall under a seemingly unstoppable siege of its central quarters; particularly on Princes Street and at St James' Square (see **St James' Centre**), but also notably in Nicolson Street and George Square on the **Southside**.

As the City of Edinburgh District (swallowing the western rural communities of **Ratho**, **Kirkliston** and **South Queensferry**) after Scottish local government reorganisation in 1975, Edinburgh survived into the 1980s if no longer centrally intact and somewhat gap-toothed, then at least considerably chastened by her

planning mistakes and by misjudgements of the mood of her people. Edinburgh, restored to single local authority status in 1996, is the second largest financial and administrative centre in the UK after London. Service sector activities – professional, scientific and financial – have always dominated the economy and presently account for four out of every five jobs in the city, which lost more than 17,000 in the manufacturing sector from 1964–75. Edinburgh is a major centre of UK commerce and government and contains the UK headquarters of several major **banks**, insurance companies and other financial institutions. Not surprisingly for a District with 30 designated conservation areas and 2900 listed buildings (Edinburgh has the highest proportion in the UK of its built-up area covered by Conservation Area status), **tourism** has become an all-year-round industry. Both the Old and New Towns enjoy World Heritage status in recognition of their scenic, historic, cultural and architectural importance.

During the early 1990s Edinburgh promoted many development strategies and initiatives, public and private, for the 21st century. The Landscape and Nature Conservation Strategy complemented the wider Green Belt Initiative aiming to maintain and improve the natural buffer with the Lothians. Business and technology parks were constructed in the west of the city, close to the outer bypass and **Edinburgh Airport**; 'Edinburgh Park' was the largest single project completed in the city since the building of the First New Town. South, on the Bush Estate near **Penicuik**, Edinburgh University's 'Technopole', a technological research and development facility modelled on that of the capital's twin town of Nice, operates such biotechnological establishments as the Moredun and Roslin Institutes where '**Dolly the Sheep**' was cloned.

These perimeter developments were balanced by cultural and business projects in the city centre. The **Festival Theatre** (opera house) enlivens otherwise drab Nicolson Street, and the Edinburgh International Conference Centre is the hub of a new business district fronted by the Standard Life Insurance Company headquarters off Lothian Road. Nearby, Saltire Court, a stylish 'European-dimensioned' financial and cultural complex, housing the **Traverse Theatre** and 'facing' both the Castle and the Continent, opened in 1991. This was the largest new building permitted in Edinburgh for many years, and marked a significant sea-change in both the architectural and social face of the city, all too often seen as a stuffy, inward-looking place. That 'frosty' face was also lifted by the Edinburgh Lighting Vision Project which has illuminated landmark buildings at night – no longer can the visitor decry Auld Reekie as 'the darkest and dirtiest city in Europe'.

The regeneration of the south Canongate reaches its apotheosis with the construction of the **Scottish Parliament** building across Holyrood Road from the new *Scotsman* office and the Dynamic Earth attraction. On The Mound, the **Royal Scottish Academy** will be restored and linked by a tunnel in a single complex with the **National Gallery of Scotland**. On **North Bridge**, the old *Scotsman* offices and the former GPO are earmarked for major hotels. Elsewhere, in **Leith** the Ocean Terminal opens around its focus of the restored Royal Yacht *Britannia* in 2001. The wider Waterfront Edinburgh project aims to invest £700m over fifteen years in the transformation of seven miles of the Forth shore, especially **Granton**.

Abbey Strand and Sanctuary

The last gasp on the **Royal Mile** before the gates of the **Palace of Holyroodhouse** are won, Abbey Strand was largely demolished in 1850–60 when **Queen Victoria** was in occasional residence. The Abbey Strand hovels were the haunt of debtors, or 'Abbey lairds', for 300 years after the **Reformation** under a relic of the great medieval right of sanctuary for criminals at **Holyrood Abbey**. These 'Houses of Refuge' were separated from the **Canongate** by a paved 'girth', delineated by the Girth Cross. Latterly, Thomas de Quincey was a frequent 'visitor' (c1835) to the sanctuary which was regulated by a 'Baron Bailie' appointed by the Hereditary Keeper of Holyroodhouse. Although the right of sanctuary has never been repealed, imprisonment for debt practically ceased after 1880 and the Baron Bailie now superintends the 30 High Constables of Holyrood who form a guard of honour there on ceremonial occasions; bi-annually in June they also walk the four- to five-mile boundary of the Sanctuary of Holyrood, which encompasses **Holyrood Park**, pausing halfway for refreshment at **Duddingston**.

Acheson House

Now incorporated with the adjacent **Huntly House** as the **City Museum** in the **Canongate**, Acheson House was built in 1633 for Sir Archibald Acheson, a Secretary of State for Scotland under **Charles I**. The three-storey, rubble-built mansion partly encloses a small screened forecourt forming the original entrance within Bakehouse Close. The pediment of the narrow, heavily moulded main doorway bears the boldly carved and ciphered monogram of Acheson and his wife, Dame Margaret Hamilton; breaking it is their curious crest, a cock crowing over a trumpet and the motto '*Vigilantibus*'. Restored by the **3rd Marquis of Bute** in 1937, it housed the Scottish Craft Centre from 1952–90.

Adam Bothwell's House

A curious barge-shaped building thrusting an unusual semi-hexagonal apse northwards in a bold prow beneath a bartizaned and dormer-pedimented roof, 'Adam Bothwell's House' crouches behind the semi-ruinous anachronism of Byres' Close. Stopped up at its **High Street** entrance, the close 'admirably illustrates the extremely congested conditions that obtained in the 17th and 18th centuries' (RCAHMS, 1950). **Adam Bothwell** (1530–93), Bishop of **Orkney**, Lord of Session and **Commendator** of **Holyrood**, was the great survivor of the internecine politics of 16th century Scotland. In the 17th century the house may have been the warehouse of the wealthy merchant **Sir William Dick of Braid** (1580–1655). He himself dwelt in a first floor house at the close head overlooking the High Street and once supposedly occupied by Oliver Cromwell. Dick died a pauper, but his grandson, Sir James Dick, regained his patrimony and bought **Prestonfield House**. Now reached via **Advocate's Close**, Adam Bothwell's House is, fittingly, offices for the **Faculty of Advocates**. Byres' Close is named from John Byres, a 16th century merchant and 'Old' Provost, 'a truly good and excellent citizen' whose son built Easter Coates House next to where **St Mary's Episcopal Cathedral** now stands.

Advocate's Close

The **Old Town** alley par excellence, (The) Advocate's Close is named after the residence of Sir James Stewart, Lord Advocate of Scotland 1692–1713. At its head, the early 16th century 'Greate Ludging' recorded as 'lying upone ye Kinges Hie Street' opposite the **Luckenbooths** and **St Giles Cathedral**, had both its frontage and interior fashionably remodelled around 1700. This six-storey rubble block, having a corbelled turnpike stair-tower with fortified features to the rear, was restored after 50 years of civic neglect during 1984–5. Within, the tenement completed in 1590 by Clement Cor, merchant, has an adjacent pair of crested and mottoed doorways; BLESSIT BE GOD IN AL HIS GIFTIS and SPES ALTERA VITAE (*Another Hope of Life*); one, leading into the dwelling of Henry Cant with the restored mullioned windows, which contains three vast 'baronial' fireplaces of c1470, is now the offices of the **Old Town** Committee for Conservation and Renewal, and *Old Town and Southside News*. The rest of this 'cliff of masonry' was demolished in civic improvements, 1884–6, when steps were introduced. Previously it had been remarked

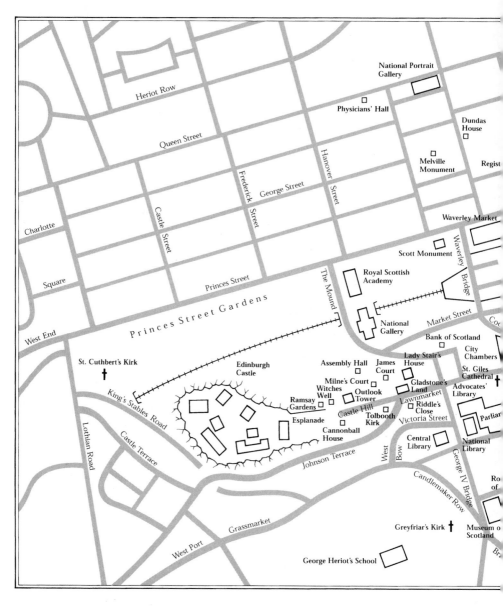

Edinburgh continued

that 'a modern fine lady would be in danger of being seized with a nervous fit at the very prospect of descending the slippery abyss' (Wilson, 1848).

Advocates' Library, George IV Bridge

Founded by the Faculty of Advocates under their Dean, **Sir George ('Bluidy') Mackenzie** of Rosehaugh, in 1682, the Advocates' Library occupies externally undistinguished premises which link with its successor, the **National Library of Scotland**. The Advocates' Library opened in a corner of **Parliament Square** in 1689; Mackenzie insisted that the collection should include History, Criticism and Rhetoric – 'The Handmaidens of Jurisprudence' – as well as legal tomes. Forced into the dingy Laigh Hall of the **Parliament House** by the fire of 1700, from 1815 it occupied the present Upper

Library of the **Signet Library**; the Advocates sold to the Writers in 1826. Their new accommodation, immediately to the south, was begun by **William Playfair** in 1829 and later altered with oriel windows in 1856.

Conceived from the start as far more than a legal library, it early reflected the wide scholarly interests of the lawyers who formed such a vital element in the cultural flowering of Edinburgh in the age of the Enlightenment. Under Keepers like **Thomas Ruddiman** and **David Hume** it acquired a European reputation. **Sir Walter Scott** and **Thomas Carlyle** spoke loudly in praise of its research facilities and its great collections of printed books and manuscripts, unrivalled in Scotland.

The privileges of the Copyright Acts were enjoyed by the Advocates' Library from 1710, but the influx of books put an intolerable burden on the resources of a small private professional body which found itself

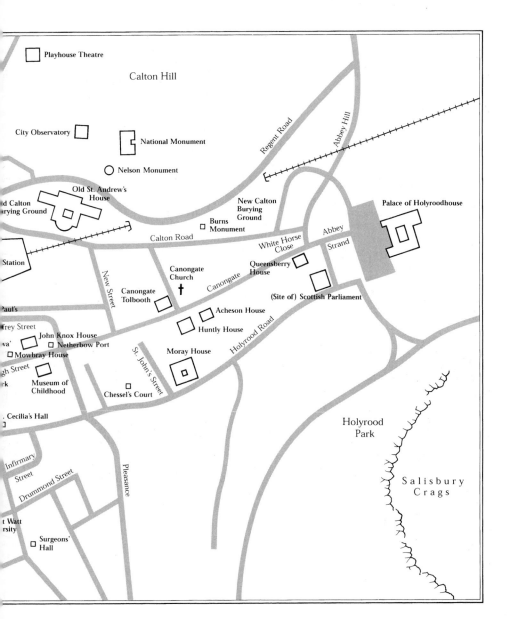

Playhouse Theatre

Calton Hill

City Observatory

National Monument

Nelson Monument

Old St. Andrew's House

ld Calton rying Ground

New Calton Burying Ground

Burns Monument

Palace of Holyroodhouse

Calton Road

White Horse Close

Abbey Strand

Station

New Street

Canongate Church

Canongate

Queensberry House

Canongate Tolbooth

(Site of) Scottish Parliament

Acheson House

'aul's

rey Street

va'   John Knox House
        Netherbow Port
   Mowbray House

Huntly House

gh Street

rk   Museum of Childhood

Moray House

Holyrood Road

St. John's Street

Chessel's Court

. Cecilia's Hall

Holyrood Park

Salisbury Crags

Infirmary Street

Drummond Street

Pleasance

t Watt rsity

Surgeons' Hall

Regent Road

Abbey Hill

Edinburgh continued

running at its own expense a de facto national institution. In 1925 the Faculty gave all but their legal books to the state as the foundation collection of the newly established **National Library** – a total of about 150,000 books and manuscripts. Among the important legal manuscripts retained is the *Regiam Majestatem*, which outlines the Scots and Norman Law conducted in the courts of the early monarchs and underpinning the **Law of Scotland** as later formulated. The Advocates' Library of today serves as the working library of the Scottish Bar.

Anchor Close

A dismal declivity on the down side of the **City Chambers** in the **High Street**, Anchor Close is named after 'The Anchor Tavern', 'noted for suppers of tripe, mince collops, rizzared haddocks, and fragrant hashes that

never cost more than sixpence a head...' (Grant, 1884), of which only an entrance lintel (BE MERCIFUL TO ME) remains. There, c1778–c95, met the most convivial of the Edinburgh literary clubs, the Crochallan Fencibles, so called after the Gaelic lilt (*Crodh Chalein* or 'Colin's Cattle') sung by its worthy host, Dawnay (Daniel) Douglas. The founder and presiding genius of the club, 'blithe **Willie Smellie**' the printer, introduced **Robert Burns** to its luminaries, **Adam Smith**, **Adam Ferguson**, **Henry Mackenzie** and **David Hume**, while preparing the Edinburgh Edition of Burns's poems with William Creech, publisher, at his works in the close in 1787.

Arthur's Seat

Arthur's Seat is a remnant of the 'Edinburgh Volcano' (also including the Castle Rock and **Calton Hill**) which erupted c325 million years ago during early Carboniferous times. This natural sphinx – its craggy profile resembles a lion couchant from the south-west – soars to 823ft (251m) within **Holyrood Park**.

Although much of the old volcano has been eroded or is buried under younger rock formations, enough remains exposed to reveal the stages of the geological succession. The cone erupted, via the Lion's Head (summit) and Lion's Haunch vents, through the existing sediments and lavas of an earlier Castle volcano. The extinct volcanoes became submerged and later buried under thousands of feet of shales. Molten rocks intruded between the horizontal strata under the volcano and formed sills such as **Salisbury Crags**, as well as Samson's Ribs, a c100ft (30m) high 'bending' cliff of columnar basalt similar to formations found at Fingal's Cave on **Staffa**. The rocks around Edinburgh were folded and Arthur's Seat tilted some 25° to the east. Erosion, especially during the Great Ice Age, laid bare the inside of the volcano, notably the two vents forming the twin peaks of Arthur's Seat and the Crow Hill and Calton Hill, both remnants of the cone [see also **Geology**].

Associations with King Arthur probably originated with the Normans. A later explanation considers 'the appellation . . . to be a corruption of the Gaelic *Ard-na-Saighead* (Height of Arrows)' (Maitland, 1753). The summit even holds the scant remains of a 20 acre (8ha) Iron Age fort enclosed by a pair of stone-built defensive ramparts. 'If it was an occupied site, then it must rank as a major *oppidum*, the fourth largest in Scotland' (Feachem, 1977). A Bronze Age weapon hoard of c700 BC, dredged from Duddingston Loch in 1778, indicates the likelihood of 'a settlement with a bronze-smith on the slopes of the hill at about this time' (Ritchie, 1985).

Assembly Closes, Old and New

Two nearby closes on the north side of the **High Street** are both named after 'The Assembly', a private association for dancing which originated in the **West Bow** in 1710. This moved in 1720 to Old Assembly Close where the Musical Society of Edinburgh held concerts in the 'Cross Keys Tavern', prior to their removal to St Mary's Chapel and **St Cecilia's Hall**. Apparently the 'assemblies' were cold occasions, for there was 'no more intercourse between the sexes than between two countries at war' (Goldsmith, 1753).

In 1756, New Assembly Rooms opened in Bell's Wynd. They were long presided over by the redoubtable Miss Nicky Murray, the 'lady directress' from a throne at one end; 'there being but one set allowed to dance at a time, it was seldom that any person was twice on the floor in one night' (Chambers, 1868).

A generation later these premises were eclipsed by the fashionably new suburban venues, firstly (1784) at Buccleuch Place, behind **George Square** on the **Southside**, and soon afterwards (1787) by the very grand suites of the **Assembly Rooms** in **George Street** in the heart of the **New Town**.

Assembly Rooms (& Music Hall)

Opened for the Caledonian Hunt Ball in 1787, the Assembly Rooms in **George Street** were begun (1783) by John Henderson and completed in an unpopular plain classical style. They replaced the **Old Town** venue at **Old** and **New Assembly Closes** where every Thursday gentlemen 'reeled from the tavern, flushed with wine to an assembly of as elegant and beautiful women as any in Europe' (Arnott, 1783). The ballroom measures 92ft by 42ft by 40ft (28 by 13 by 12m) and is 'adorned with crystal lustres'. An attempt to ameliorate the severe frontage was made in 1818 when **William Burn** added the heavy Roman portico. Along with **David Bryce** Burn also added the impressive 108ft by 91ft (33 by 28m) Music Hall in 1843. Since their acquisition by the city after World War II, the Assembly Rooms and Music Hall have played an important role in the **Edinburgh Festival** as a theatre and concert venue. 'No admission without a ticket on any account whatever' (Assembly Rooms Resolutions, 1789).

Balerno

An auld 'ferm toun' located on the highest workable stretch of the **Water of Leith**, Balerno is now a dormitory suburb of Edinburgh. The name is derived from the Gaelic *Baile Airneach*, 'sloe-tree-stead' or *Baile earr-an achaidh*, 'steading at the end of the field'. The Waulk (fulling) Mill of Ballernoch is recorded in 1376 and the Newmills ground corn from 1604–1900. Balerno Paper Mill, which began in 1776, was operated by Nisbet & McNiven, later the famous stationery firm of Waverley Cameron Ltd. Malleny House, a two-storey, seemingly early 17th century, now **National Trust for Scotland** property, incorporates earlier fragments of the house which passed to Sir James Murray of Kilbaberton c1634 and is reputed to have been a hunting lodge of **James VI**. Bavelaw House, a 17th century L-plan tower possibly built for Laurence Scott of Harperrig c1628, was modernised by **Robert Lorimer** c1900; the estate belonged to Fleury de Brade, Sheriff of Edinburgh, in 1230, and was confirmed by **Robert II** to Fairley of Braid in 1381.

Balmoral Hotel

An overblown Edwardian pile dwarfing **Princes Street** at its 'East End', the Balmoral Hotel was opulently refurbished at a cost of £23 million in 1990–1. It began as the North British Railway Hotel in 1902, designed by **W Hamilton Beattie** when the site became available during the reconstruction of the **North Bridge** and **Waverley Station**. Built of about 13,000 tons of Prudham stone and approximately 8 million bricks, it is detailed in a heavy 16th century Franco-German style. Most remarkable is the massive 195ft (59m) high clock-cum-watertower; each clock-face is 13ft (4m) in diameter; each minute-hand measures 6ft 3in (1.9m) and each hour hand 4ft 6in (1.37m); the clock itself keeps two to three minutes fast for those catching trains. Originally the North British had 700 rooms, including 300 bedrooms (the Balmoral has 200); the 'NB' had its own bakery and butchery, and also blended its own **whisky** and bottled its own wine. The central, top-lit Palm Court, redolent of colonial grandeur, remains. 'The architect had specified that the smoking and billiard rooms should be in readily accessible, but retired situations, where they do not interfere with the comfort of the lady guests' (Geddie, 1902).

George Washington Wilson's c1885 panorama of the city from Blackford Hill; Arthur's Seat dominates the skyline (GWWA)

Edinburgh continued

Bank of Scotland, The Mound

A Georgian coffer encased within monumental Roman Baroque in Victorian times, the Bank of Scotland clings to **The Mound**. The original 'strong-box', designed by **Robert Reid** and Richard Crighton and built by William Sibbald in 1802–6, was disparaged for its filing-cabinet aspect northwards to the **New Town**. Accordingly, between 1864–70 the entire structure was recast by **David Bryce** in its present, heavily vermiculated form; the central dome was replaced by an octagonal Renaissance drum with lanterned top crowned by a 2m figure of Fame. Further striking statuary was added in 1878 by Messrs Peddie and Kinnear when they introduced the massive, pilastered retaining wall supporting a terrace with large open-arched pavilions, in place of the original screen wall. The Bank purchased the site in 1800, shortly after the formation of Bank Street as an access in 1798; its previous premises, from c1700–1805, were in the Old Bank Close across the **Lawnmarket** which were demolished for **George IV Bridge** c1827. Before that, premises in **Parliament Square**, burnt down in 1700, had replaced what were supposedly the Bank's earliest premises in Mylne's Square opposite the **Tron**.

Barnton

Perhaps the most prestigious address in west Edinburgh, Barnton lies south of **Cramond** off the Queensferry Road. The suburb's lush villadom developed c1900 after the 'Barnton Express' of the Caledonian **Railway** began rattling through Barnton Park in 1894 (closed 1951). Barnton Park is the 'land of **golf**' (Geddie, 1930) where the exclusive Royal Burgess and Bruntsfield Links Societies established themselves anew from **Musselburgh** [see also **Meadows**] on the 400 acre (161ha) policies of Barnton House. This edifice (c1640–c1900) was castellated by **Robert Adam** c1790 for George Ramsay who had purchased it in 1785. Earlier called Cramond Regis – it was once a royal hunting seat situated on Cramond Muir – it purloined the name of the original Barnton House (rebuilt 1681) to the east, with which estate (Over Barnton) it was joined in 1718.

Bible Land/Shoemakers' Land, Canongate

A five-storey, double fronted and gabled tenement reconstructed in 1954–8, the 'Bible Land' is the easternmost of three lands once owned by the Incorporation of the Cordiners of the **Canongate**. The land is named from the open book, held within a pedimented cartouche containing the emblem of the craft, a currier's knife surmounted by a crown with cherubs' heads, carved in bold relief above the entrance to the central stairwell. The crown, and the rounding or paring knife, are symbolically those of King St Crispin, the patron saint of shoemakers, who was annually crowned by the Cordiners on 25 October, the great holiday event of the Canongate. The westernmost of the Shoemakers' Lands contained the Hall of the Incorporation, built in 1682. A panel is inscribed 'Blessed is he that wisely doth the poor man's case consider'.

303

The Old Town from the New with the Bank of Scotland prominent on the left (GWWA)

Edinburgh continued

Blackford Hill

A rugged outlier of the **Braid Hills** to its south, Blackford Hill forms an urban country park of c100 acres (c40ha) along with the Hermitage of Braid. The 539ft (164m) hill, which is largely composed of volcanic lava and tuffs, was purchased by the city from Lieutenant Colonel Henry Trotter of **Mortonhall**. Soon after, part was relinquished to the government for the **Royal Observatory**; on Observatory Road the red ashlar Harrison Arch by Sidney Mitchell commemorates Lord Provost Sir John Harrison who secured free public access to the hill. On the south side, by the Braid Burn, stands the Agassiz Rock named after Swiss geologist Louis Agassiz who in 1840 pronounced regarding the grooves and striae of this overhanging cliff, 'this is the work of the ice', the first such recognition in Scotland, which stimulated further exploration by Scots glaciologists. Much of the 'tail' of the Blackford Crag towards **Liberton** is occupied by the Kings Buildings, the science campus of the **University of Edinburgh**.

Blackfriars' Street

Anciently Blackfriars' Wynd, Blackfriars' Street was created under the Edinburgh Improvement Act of 1867. The Blackfriars' Monastery, which lay opposite the foot of the wynd, was bequeathed by **Alexander II** to the Dominican Order in 1230, and destroyed by the **Reformation** mob in 1559. The wynd was notorious for the vicious 'tulzie' or street-fight between the warring **Douglas** and **Hamilton** families in April 1520 [see

Cleanse-the-Causeway]. The first printing-press in Scotland was operated at the foot of the wynd in the **Cowgate** by **Chepman and Myllar** in 1506. In 1567 Blackfriars' Wynd was on the return route of **Queen Mary** after her last visit to her sick husband **Lord Darnley** at the **Kirk o' Field**; simultaneously, tradition avers that the henchmen of the Queen's lover, **James Hepburn, Earl of Bothwell**, were spiriting the kegs of gunpowder for the fatal deed down Todrick's Wynd, a lesser alley to the east.

Boswell's Court

An ashlar fronted, five-storey 17th century tenement with mustard-coloured stucco to the rear, Boswell's Court on **Castlehill** is named after Dr John Boswell, the uncle of **James Boswell**. The block was, however, built c1600 for Thomas Lowthian, merchant, whose mark and initials are carved in the stair-tower. At the rear, incorporated in Castlehill School, is an ogival-headed moulded doorway of c1600 with a heraldic tympanum taken from the Duke of Gordon's House (demolished 1890), and closely resembling another at **Morton House**, 'of a type once common in Edinburgh' (McKean, 1985). George, 1st Duke of Gordon (1643–1716) was the captain and constable and keeper of the **Castle** (1686–9) who, while holding it for **James VII**, conferred with **John Graham of Claverhouse, Viscount Dundee**, at the postern gate on the west face of the Castle Rock. From the court, **General Sir David Baird**, the hero of Srirangapatnam, 'as a boy threw cabbage stalks at the chimney vents of the **Grassmarket**' (Keir, 1966).

Braid Hills

Outliers of the **Pentland Hills**, the Braid Hills (max 675ft/205m) stretch across the south of the city from omiston to **Liberton**. The 'furzy hills of Braid' (**Scott**, *Marmion*) comprise a public park of c240 acres (100ha) nking with **Blackford Hill** to the north. The invading rmies of Edward I in 1295 and Oliver Cromwell in 650 both surveyed the city from encampments here. The Hermitage of Braid' by the Braid Burn is a castelated villa built by Robert Burn for Charles Gordon of Cluny in 1785. In the 19th century the Braid Estate was owned by the wealthy merchant and Lord Provost **Sir William Dick**, who also purchased **Prestonfield** and he **Grange**. The Braid Hills were bought by the city of dinburgh in 1889 and the Braids **Golf Course** was hen laid out to silence the golfing lobby who suffered ncreasing restrictions on Bruntsfield Links (see **Meadows**).

Bristo

An early trades suburb of the **Old Town** lying beyond he **Flodden Wall**, Bristo comprised Easter Portsburgh which combined with the **West Port** in the discontiguous **burgh of barony** of Portsburgh. The name may derive from the Society of Brewers, or 'brewsters', settled there in 1598 to draw water from the Burgh Loch (**Meadows**) rather than deplete the town wells. Bristo Street was developed from 1743 by Lady Nicolson who built Nicolson Street and Square, the first planned extensions on the **Southside**. 'Except a mean street called Potterrow and a very short one called Bristo, there were, till within these 12 years, hardly any buildings on the south side of the town' (Arnot, 1779). In Potterrow was the alley named 'General's Entry' possibly after **General Monk** who supposedly lodged here in 650 with **Sir James Dalrymple, 1st Viscount Stair**, but more likely after Dalrymple's grandson, **John, the 2nd Earl**, promoted to lieutenant-general after the Battle of Malplaquet (1709). There, later, lived Mrs MacLerose, the 'Clarinda' of the famous correspondence with **Robert Burns** (as 'Sylvander') while he was convalescent at St James' Square. 'I hope you'll come a-foot, even though you take a chair home. A chair is so uncommon thing in our neighbourhood, it is apt to raise speculation; but they are all asleep by 10.'

Brodie's Close

The stump of an alley which, until 1837, ran down from the **Lawnmarket** to the **Cowgate**, Brodie's Close held the residence of Convener Francis Brodie, wright, glass-grinder and burgess, the father of the notorious **William Brodie**, Deacon of Wrights, who was hanged at the Old **Tolbooth** in 1788. An earlier reincarnation was Little's Close from the mansion built by William Little of **Liberton** and **Craigmillar** in 1570; his brother Clement was the founder of the **University** library in 1580, when he bequeathed 300 books. The 16th/17th century close still comprises two small courts but, though it has been described as the most atmospheric of Edinburgh's closes when seen from the inner court, his itself is destroyed by the omnipresence of the sixties-modern' headquarters of the former Lothian Regional Council. The outer court contains the Roman Eagle Hall with mid-17th century moulded plaster ceilings where Lodge Roman Eagle 160 was established c1780 by the eccentric Dr John Brown (1735–88); he

attacked the traditional medical teachings of Professors **Alexander Monro** and **William Cullen**, publishing his *Elementa Medicinae* in London in 1780. In this scholarly lodge no language was heard except Latin: 'this classical fraternity owed its dissolution to the excesses of its members, wherein they surpassed their brethren in an order not specially noted as patterns of temperance' (Wilson, 1891).

Broughton

A former **burgh of barony**, Broughton began as a possession of **Holyrood Abbey** in the 12th century. Broughton Tolbooth was probably built sometime after the **Reformation** when **Adam Bothwell**, Bishop of **Orkney** was the feudal superior 1568–87. His successor, Sir Lewis Bellenden, a noted trafficker with wizards, launched the village's reputation as a notorious haunt of witches and warlocks, who were often incarcerated in its tolbooth. In 1717 Broughton was the scene of the trial and execution of Robert Irvine who cut the throats of his two young pupils one Sunday morning on Gabriel's Road where **St Andrew Square** now stands. Irvine bore them a grudge for reporting his amorous adventures to their father. Caught red-handed, he tried to cut his own throat and then to drown himself before receiving summary sentence on the following day.

Brunstane House

'A plain edifice in the old Scottish domestic style . . . with few pretensions to ornament or dignity' (Baird, 1898), Brunstane House lies off Milton Road near **Portobello**. Gilbertoun, 'vulgarly called Brunstane', was held 'for service of wood and relief' by the Crichtons in the 15th and 16th centuries. After collusion with the Earl of Hertford in the invasion of 1547, Alexander Crichton was forfeited and Gilbertoun was ordered to 'be cassin doun'. A new L-plan house was probably built c1565 for his son John. By 1639 Brunstane had been remodelled by **John, Lord Maitland**, later 2nd Earl and 1st Duke of Lauderdale. In 1672 he employed **Sir William Bruce**, then working on his ducal seat at **Thirlestane**, to extend his capital 'lodge' as a U-plan. The interior of the villa was transformed in 1733 by **William Adam** for Andrew Fletcher, Lord Milton (nephew of **Fletcher of Saltoun**), who presided at the **Porteous** trial; it still possesses rococo plasterwork by Thomas Clayton and classical landscapes by James Norie.

Burgh Muir

A tract of wooded land formerly occupying the territory to the south of the **Old Town** between the Burgh Loch (now the **Meadows**) and **Blackford Hill**, the Burgh Muir extended for about three miles east to west from **Duddingston** to **Morningside**. It anciently formed the Forest of Drumselch or Drumsheugh ('the ridge of willows'), where **David I**, the founder of the burgh, hunted in 'ane great forest full of hartis, hydis, toddis [foxes] and siclike manner of beistis' (**Holyrood** Charters). He gifted the Burgh Muir to the town in 1128 as common ground for grazing, woodcutting and recreation; it remained open until **James IV** permitted feuing, which began much later, c1586.

The Scots army assembled on the Burgh Muir for the

invasion of England on no less than six occasions, the first time being in 1386; but there is no real evidence for the popular tradition that the standard of **James IV** was raised before the Battle of **Flodden** on the 'Borestane', now built on to the boundary wall of Morningside Parish Kirk.

> Highest and midmost was descried
> The Royal banner, floating wide;
> The staff, a pine tree strong and straight:
>   Pitched deeply in a massive stone
> Which still in memory is shown
> Yet bent beneath the standard's weight.
> <div align="right">(Scott, <i>Marmion</i>)</div>

Burns' Monument

Overlooking the New Calton Burial Ground on the south side of **Calton Hill**, Burns' Monument is one of the ubiquitous variants of the Choragic Monument of Lysicrates at Athens. It was designed by **Thomas Hamilton** in 1830 in a circular style similar to his earlier shrine to **Robert Burns** in **Alloway** Churchyard. The monument arose indirectly from a subscription begun in Bombay in 1812 by one John Forbes Mitchell who was intent on setting up a colossus to Burns in the capital. When finished, a life-size marble statue was executed gratis by John Flaxman, which was later transferred to the **University of Edinburgh** Library Hall, from where it was ejected in 1861 because the 'ploughman poet' could not boast a 'college education'. After a brief sojourn in the **National Gallery of Scotland** from 1861–89, it was moved to the **Scottish National Portrait Gallery**. The monument also formerly housed some interesting relics of the poet which are now displayed with others in **Lady Stair's House** Museum in the **Lawnmarket**.

Calton Hill

The Calton Hill is a remnant of the 'Edinburgh Volcano' [see **Arthur's Seat**]. Composed of terraced lavas, ashes and tuffs, the 355ft (108m) hill is triangular in shape and stretches 1½ miles from its steep, western 'Craigend' near **Princes Street** to the gentler sloping eastern 'Lochend' at **Restalrig**. The upper slopes are preserved as a park containing many of the most remarkable of the city's monuments: the **City Observatory**, **National Monument**, **Nelson Monument**, **Burns' Monument** and the **Dugald Stewart** and **John Playfair** Monuments.

The lower slopes are mainly built upon by the eastern extensions of the **New Town**, including the sweet curve of Royal, Carlton and Regent Terraces, designed by **William Playfair** and built from 1819–60. The dramatic approach to the Old **Royal High School** and Old **St Andrew's House** from the East End along Waterloo Place and Regent Road was cut through the **Old Calton Burying Ground** by Archibald Elliott and **Robert Stevenson** in 1815–19; the ornate Regent Bridge, which vaults Low Calton on a single semi-circular arch of 50ft (15m) span, was opened by Prince Leopold of Belgium in 1819. Crowning Calton Hill is Rock House, the home and studio of the pioneering 19th century photographer **David Octavius Hill**. Below, at

Greenside, the deep hollow served as a medieval tourna ment and pleasure ground where *Ane Satyre of the Thr Estaitis* by **Sir David Lindsay** was played before th Queen Regent **Mary of Guise** in 1544. Greenside part returned to entertainment use in 2000 as an offic cinema and leisure complex incorporating the façade **Lady Glenorchy's** Church.

Cammo House

Cammo forms a decayed 100 acre (40ha) 'wildernes which surrounds the consolidated stump of the on 'commodious mansion' of Cammo House, demolishe in 1980. The lands of Cammo, beyond **Barnton**, passe in the 15th century from the Abbot of **Inchcolm** to th Bishop of **Dunkeld**. Cammo House was built in 169 by Sir John Menzies and owned by **Sir John Clerk** **Penicuik** from 1710–26; under his management th estate was transformed into its present aspect, the land scape garden a 'dummy run' (Tait, 1980) for his late country seat at **Mavisbank**, **Midlothian**. His cousin an successor, John Hog, commissioned **William Adam** t create a **Hopetoun House** at Cammo, but the estate wa sold in 1741 to James Watson of Saughton wh renamed it New Saughton; 'Cammo' was revived b brewer Alexander Campbell in 1873. In 1891 the Mait land-Tennent family took over the estate and house – b then a grim, grey-harled and battlemented four-store block containing 50 rooms. Mrs Margaret Louisa Mait land-Tennent, who lived in seclusion and died in 195 aged 95 (she was buried beneath the lawn), is popularl rumoured only to have ventured forth on nocturna expeditions in dark clothes and in a curtained car drive by her equally reclusive son, Percival Louis. He died a the age of 77 and left the mouldering pile – said b some to have been a model for the House of Shaws i **Robert Louis Stevenson's** *Kidnapped* – to the **Nationa Trust for Scotland**, which handed over managemen to Edinburgh District Council; Percival latterly inhabite a caravan in the grounds while the house literally 'wen to the dogs' – mainly terriers, about 30 all told.

Candlemaker Row

A steep brae which strikes off **George IV Bridge** fo the **Cowgate** and the **Grassmarket**, Candlemaker Row contains the Convening Hall of the Incorporation o Candlemakers, built in 1722. Incorporated before 1517 the noisome craft was settled here on the southern fron tiers of the **Old Town** after a tallow fire in Forrester Wynd, which lay between George IV Bridge an **St Giles Cathedral**; the four-storey rubble tenement ha an obliterated panel which once expounded the mott of the craft: 'Omnia Manifesta Luce' (By light all is revealed) Near the head of 'the Raw' were the 'Harrow' and th 'Selkirk and Peebles' Inns, hearty hostelries enlivene by roistering herdsmen and farmers from the Borders among them **James Hogg**. At the head of Candlemake Row faithfully 'waits' the 'wee dug', **Greyfriars' Bobby**

Cannonball House

'This much altered, early 17th century tenement . . takes its name from an iron shot embedded in its wes gable' (RCAHMS, 1950). In 1630 Alexander Mure, skin ner and burgess, added the rear west crow-steppe gable; the windows have stone ledges with grooves fo

Calton Hill, with the Observatory to the left and Nelson's Monument to the right beside the Parthenon pillars of the National Monument (GWWA)

Edinburgh continued

sliding shutters called 'shots', probably necessitated by the proximity of the **Castle** guns. The eponymous Cannonball was popularly said to have been fired by General Guest during the siege of 1745; more prosaically it was inserted to mark the gravitation height of the first (wooden) piped water supply brought from Comiston to the former **Castlehill** Reservoir opposite in 1681. Incorporated with the adjoining Castlehill School – now the Scotch **Whisky** Heritage Museum – in 1913, the house is now Castlehill Urban Studies Centre for schoolchildren; appropriately the entrance lintel reads Nosce (Teipsum) – 'Know Thyself', an injunction entirely in keeping with the '**Patrick Geddes** Room' inside, which contains some of his stained-glass panels formerly at the **Outlook Tower**.

Canongate

Cosmetically rebuilt and restored from a squalid industrial slum, the Canongate was originally an adjunct of **Holyrood Abbey**, long remaining a separate entity from Edinburgh. The Canongate was founded in 1128 by **David I**, who granted the Augustinian canons of the Castle leave to 'enclose or establish' a burgh on the waste ground lying between **Calton Hill** and **Arthur's Seat** in his hunting forest of Drumselch. From Holyrood, the Canongate crept up the **Royal Mile** ridge until halted at the **Netherbow**; Canongait means the 'way or street of the Canons'. Under the Abbot of Holyrood, the burgesses of the Canongate enjoyed privileges of trade in **royal burghs**; and the **Canongate Tolbooth** existed before 1477.

The star of the Canongate became fully ascendant with the settlement of the **Stewart** court of **James IV** at the **Palace of Holyroodhouse** in the 15th century; it developed as a garden suburb of Edinburgh housing the nobility and justiciary with their retainers. This regal glory departed with **James VI**, and further loss of status was suffered on the **Union of Parliaments** in 1707. 'O Cannigate! Poor elritch hole!/What loss, what crosses does thou thole!/London and Death for thee look drole,/An hing thy head' (**Ramsay**, 1717). Nevertheless, in 1769, before the advent of the **New Town**, the Canongate still boasted among its inhabitants two dukes, 16 earls, two countesses, seven lords, seven Lords of Session, 13 baronets and four commanders-in-chief. Political power hastens to return to the Canongate with the proposed construction of the **Scottish Parliament** opposite the Palace of Holyroodhouse; part of the Canongate Redevelopment Strategy for the old Scottish & Newcastle Breweries site which includes the new Scottish Poetry Library, Scotsman offices and the 'Dynamic Earth' attraction.

307

Canongate Kirk

Lying immediately to the east of the **Canongate Tol-booth**, Canongate Kirk was designed by **James Smith** in 1688 and opened for worship in 1691. The congregation had been displaced from **Holyrood Abbey** Kirk in 1687 by **James VII** who converted the Chapel Royal for the reconstituted **Order of the Knights of the Thistle**. Unique in 17th century Scots church architecture, the plan of the Canongate Kirk is 'a Latin cross with an aisled three-bay nave, transepts, short chancel and apse' (Gifford et al, 1984). A squat Doric portico cowers beneath a lofty curvilinear gable which bears the inescutcheon of Nassau for William of Orange placed in the centre of the royal arms intended for **James VII**. The apex brandishes a set of antlers commemorating the miraculous foundation of Holyrood Abbey by **David I**. The barn-like interior was long unpopular: 'in 1693 complaints are recorded that the echo or "great resonancy" ... hindered hearing' (Selby Wright, 1965). Canongate Manse, built in 1690, stands in Reid's Court to the east.

Canongate Kirkyard

Among others, Canongate Kirkyard contains the remains of **Adam Smith**, who lived and died at **Panmure House** nearby; **George Drummond**, six times Lord Provost and the founding father of the **Royal Infirmary** and orchestrator of the **New Town**; Mrs Agnes MacLehose, otherwise **Robert Burns**'s 'Clarinda'; **Dugald Stewart**, philosopher; **James and John Ballantyne**, the printers of **Scott**'s Waverley Novels; and **Robert Fergusson** under a stone raised by Burns over his unmarked grave: ('No sculptured Marble here nor pompous lay/No storied urn nor animated bust/This simple stone directs Pale Scotia's way/To pour her sorrows o'er her Poet's dust'). Tradition declares that the mutilated body of **David Rizzio** was re-interred here, having been removed from the Chapel Royal.

The Canongate Cross was rebuilt within the kirkyard in 1953; originally it stood nearby, opposite the **Canongate Tolbooth**, until its relocation outside the kirkyard gate in the late 19th century. The octagonal shaft is probably 16th century; the capital, cross head and stepped base (this last made for the re-erection of the **Mercat Cross** in 1866) are of 1888.

Canongate Tolbooth

Straddling Tolbooth Wynd, the Canongate Tolbooth housed the council room and courthouse of the independent **burgh of regality** of the **Canongate**. This mini-bastille or *Hôtel de Ville* was built in 1591 in the contemporary Scoto-French style by Sir Lewis Bellenden of Auchinoul, the superior of the burgh, to replace the 'Auld Tolbuith' noted in 1477. The superiority was bought along with North **Leith** by Edinburgh Town Council who thereafter appointed their 'Baron and Bailie' to govern the Canongate until its incorporation in 1856. A Victorian Gothic restoration of 1879 replaced the carved wooden beams which supported the massive projecting clock (dated 1884 – the successor of a primitive orlech or 'knock') with curved cast-iron brackets. The bells in the steeple tower continue to be rung for the **Canongate Kirk** adjacent. Now part of the **City Museum** based at **Huntly House** opposite, the building houses 'The People's Story', which celebrates the life and work of the ordinary folk of the city.

Canonmills

Like **Stockbridge**, a former milling settlement on the **Water of Leith** on the northern fringe of the **New Town**, Canonmills was, with the **Dean Village**, worked by the Augustinian canons of **Holyrood Abbey** in the 12th century. The Baxters' (bakers') Incorporation of the **Canongate** were long thirled (obliged by law) to grind their corn at Canonmills. Canonmills Haugh, now King George V Memorial Park, held the Royal Patent Gymnasium erected in 1865 by John Cox, a **Gorgie** gelatin manufacturer. Downstream the sadly neglected Warriston Cemetery, laid out in 1842, includes a rare range of catacombs designed by David Cousin; notable monuments include those to **Sir James Young Simpson**, **Adam Black**, **Horatio MacCulloch** and **Robert Scott Lauder** plus a once exquisite arcaded Gothic shrine of white marble and pink glass for the recumbent figure of the 'Red Lady' of Warriston, Mary Ann Manson, who died young at Kasauli in the Himalayas. The laird of Warriston, John Kincaid, was strangled in 1600 by his stable-lad, Robert Weir, who acted on behalf of the wronged mistress of Warriston House (now demolished) and her nurse, Jean Munro. Both women were, like witches, strangled and then burnt on the **Castlehill**; Weir, not caught until 1604, was broken upon the wheel at the **Mercat Cross**. Since 1993 Canonmills has been dominated by the offices of the Standard Life Insurance company, whose vast 5-acre site includes that of Tanfield Hall, the scene of the 1843 **Disruption** of the **Church of Scotland**.

Caroline Park

A pneumatic-looking mansion brazening it out beside **Granton** Gasworks, Caroline Park was created, possibly by **Robert Mylne** and **James Smith**, in 1685–96 for **George Mackenzie**, Viscount Tarbat. Originally Royston House – giving Mackenzie his legal designation of Lord Royston – the house was renamed in 1739 when purchased by **John, 2nd Duke of Argyll** who likely called it after his daughter, the Countess of Dalkeith. Flamboyantly French in aspect, its plain ashlar stonework has bold vernacular gestures in the cyclopean base of rough cut masonry, rusticated pilasters and pronounced quoins. Ogee-roofed pavilions protrude at each corner and the internal accommodation was of the grandest; the ornate plasterwork, woodcarving, wrought iron work and painted panels and ceilings have survived.

Castlehill

A bow-shot from the **Castle**, the narrow winding street of Castlehill was established beyond the Norman military zone, now represented by the **Esplanade**. Castlehill probably developed as a trades suburb of the Castle, possibly predating the foundation of the burgh itself by **David I**. At its head, a barrier blockaded the city from the Castle in turbulent times. Beyond, witches were 'worryit', or burnt, at the stake after being 'drouned' in the **Nor' Loch**; the **Witches' Well** on the wall of the former Castlehill reservoir recalls this wanton slaughter

An early (c1870) photograph of Canongate Tolbooth (with clock) (GWWA)

Edinburgh continued

Castlehill reservoir, reconstructed in 1851, held the original water supply, first brought to the city in wooden pipes from **Comiston** in 1681. Until 1822, at the junction of Castlehill with the **Lawnmarket** and **West Bow**, stood the Weighhouse, or 'Butter Tron', which provided a stage on Corpus Christi Day in 1554 for the Craftsmen's Church Play viewed by **Mary of Guise** from her 'palace' opposite, now the site of **New College** and the **Assembly Hall**.

Central Library

Designed (1887–90) by George Washington Browne in the French Renaissance style, the Central Library reaches upwards through four dismal storeys from the **Cowgate** before breaching the balustrade of **George IV Bridge**; it was first established as the Carnegie Free Library after **Andrew Carnegie** doubled his generous offer of £25,000 for its construction. Edinburgh had earlier rejected the idea of a free library on the grounds that the city was well endowed with private libraries and that such provision would be an unnecessary burden on the rates. The original Reference, Home Reading and Junior sections were expanded after 1930 to include the specialist Fine Art and Music library; the unique Scottish library and the Edinburgh Room were begun in 1932 and expanded in 1961.

Chambers Street

Linking **George IV Bridge** and **South Bridge**, Chambers Street was made in 1871 to provide carriage access to the **Royal Museum of Scotland**. The street, originally paved with 322,000 wooden blocks, was the most commodious of 11 created by the Edinburgh Improvement Act of 1867 under Lord Provost **William Chambers**, whose statue stands in the street centre-stage. During construction, the Architectural Institute suggested that the north side serve as a site for rebuilding deserving examples threatened by the plan to reconstruct the **Old Town**. 'The elevations of the new streets should be plain but of marked character in harmony with those fine specimens of Natural Architecture ... still to be found in great purity in so many of the neglected and overcrowded closes' (1867 Act).

Charlotte Square

The climax of the First **New Town**, Charlotte Square also proved the great climacteric which radically altered the architectural conception of the Second New Town and its successors. It stands at the west end of **George Street** in counterpoint to **St Andrew Square** and is named after Queen Charlotte, wife of George III. The Square was planned by **Robert Adam** in 1791 to present symmetrical north and south sides designed in a uniform Roman temple style of architecture – a revolutionary departure from any street frontage then seen in the city; each 'palace' front veils 11 individual three-storey houses demonstrating, as he put it, 'the rise and fall, the advance and recess and other diversity of forms'. Only the north side was started before Adam died in 1792, but it almost exactly follows his original intentions. On the west side, St George's Church (now West **Register House**) was also designed by Robert Adam, who modelled it on St Paul's Cathedral, and completed in a brutally plain style by **Robert Reid** in 1811; its recessed portico rises squarely to a rotunda, capped by a slim lanterned dome. The importance of Charlotte

Square was recognised in 1930 when the city imposed its first ever preservation order. The entire south side was restored in 1998–9 as the headquarters of the **National Trust for Scotland**; its Georgian House on the north side shows 18th century living and, next door, Bute House is the official residence of the First Minister of the Scottish Parliament.

Chessel's Court

This showpiece combination of rebuilding and restoration in the **Canongate** was undertaken by Robert Hurd & Partners during 1958–67. Colourfully harled Chessel's Court contains Chessel's Buildings, 'the first example of mansion flats in the **Old Town**' (RCAHMS, 1950), built c1745 by Archibald Chessel, wright. 'His widow applied in 1779 for a water-pipe to be led from the fountain well to the Excise Office (then occupying the premises) which was the scene of **Deacon William Brodie**'s last and fatal exploit as a housebreaker' (Boog-Watson, 1975). From 1781–3 the 'cheerful and central' Clark's Hotel, the first in the Old Town 'for the Reception of the Nobility and Gentry' (Stuart, 1952), occupied the east side. Some of the flats in Chessel's Buildings retain stucco work, rococo chimney pieces and painted over-mantels reminiscent of the style of James Norie.

City of Edinburgh Art Centre

A six-storey baroque edifice designed as part of *The Scotsman* office scheme on **North Bridge** in 1899–1902, the City Art Centre was restored and partially converted for exhibition purposes in 1979–80. It was built as a newsprint warehouse and subsequently housed C R McRitchie & Co, a textile manufacturer when, as the city's 'Covent Garden' until the 1970s, Market Street was given over to fruit and vegetable wholesale premises. From the late 1980s the Centre has successfully staged major international attractions: 'The Emperor's Warriors' from Xian, 'The Gold of the Pharaohs' from Egypt, and 'The Sweat of the Sun', more gold from Inca Peru. The top two floors of the building, formerly retained by McRitchies, were refurbished for additional gallery space in 1991–2 to enable, especially, the display of works held in the City Art Collections, notably those purchased from the Jean F Watson Benefaction (1961); and those 300 works collected by the Scottish Modern Arts Association – including paintings by the Scottish Colourists **Peploe**, **Cadell**, **Hunter** and **J P Fergusson** as well as works by **William McTaggart**, **Sir David Young Cameron**, **Stanley Cursiter**, **Joan Eardley**, **W G Gillies** and **Anne Redpath**.

City Chambers, High Street

A palatial, arcaded *Hôtel de Ville* which replaced **Mary King's Close**, amongst others, in 1753–61, the City Chambers were originally designed by John Adam as the Royal Exchange to provide covered accommodation for the business transactions of merchants and lawyers. The exchange was the realised part of a more ambitious scheme which intended housing a City Council Chamber, an **Advocates' Library** and a **Register House** under the same roof. When the Royal Exchange was let in 1761, the Government Customs House, lately of the

Netherbow, was the sole public tenant of the main north office range; the rest was shops, coffee houses and flats. Budging merchants from their time-worn *al fresco* stamping ground at the **Mercat Cross** proved impossible, even after the spiteful removal of this ancient axis for being an 'Incumbrance in the Street' in 1756 – 'Heav'ns earth and seas all in a rage/Like me will perish for exchange' (**James Wilson**, 1756).

In 1762 the town council secured a bolt-hole in the Exchange, later assuming control of the north range or the demolition of their dingy Laigh Council Chamber in the New **Tolbooth**, in 1811; eventually, between 1849–93, they bought the lot. The grand extensions of 1898–9 incorporated and remodelled Writers' Court, in Warriston's Close to the west. The Edwardian baroque north-west wing of 1903–4, which contains the Council Chambers themselves, towers 12 storeys above the sweep of **Cockburn Street** at the rear. The conversation piece in the front courtyard is a rather rampant Bucephalus, greatly restrained by Alexander, the work of **Sir John Steell** brought from **St Andrew Square** in 1916.

City Museum

An enthralling, eclectic collection of artefacts and memorabilia chronicling Edinburgh from earliest times, the City Museum was established at **Huntly House** in the **Canongate** in 1932. The original collection was housed in the **City Chambers** until 1913 when **Lady Stair's House**, which now exhibits the relics of **Robert Burns**, **Sir Walter Scott** and **Robert Louis Stevenson**, was opened off the **Lawnmarket**; the **Canongate Tolbooth** (opposite Huntly House), which now shows 'The People's Story', opened in 1954. Huntly House contains material from **Roman Cramond** and earlier native settlements at **Duddingston** (**Arthur's Seat**) and the Castle Rock; the city's former arts and crafts; its medieval and later merchants' and trades incorporations; its development from **Old** to **New Town**; and the activities of both its kings and commoners in politics, peace and war. Striking individual items include the copy of the National **Covenant** of 1638 signed by **James Graham, Marquis of Montrose**; letters of **Queen Mary, Bothwell**, **Claverhouse** and **William Burke**. Also to be seen are the sword of Captain **Porteous**, the family Bible of the father of **Deacon Brodie**, the collar of **Greyfriars' Bobby**, and the measuring instruments of New Town architect **James Craig**. Reconstructed period interiors include a late 18th century room, a working class kitchen of c1870 and the workshop of a **Leith** clay-pipe manufacturer of the 1920s. Edinburgh silver and glass and Scottish **pottery** are strongly represented. In addition there is a special collection devoted to Field Marshal **Earl Haig**.

City Observatory

Operated by the Astronomical Society of Edinburgh, the City Observatory on **Calton Hill** was founded in 1818 as the New Observatory of the Astronomical Institution of Edinburgh. Based on the Greek Temple of the Winds, its four hexastyle porticoes align with the points of the compass; the dome contains a masonry pillar rising through the first-floor level for holding the astronomical circle. The Playfair Monument was designed in 1825–6 by **William Playfair** in memory of his uncle, John

Playfair, first President of the Institution, who was the prime mover in the foundation of the New Observatory and 'Astronomer Royal' in all but name. The Gothic-style Observatory House was begun in 1776 by Thomas Short, an 'optician astronomer' and the brother of **James Short**, 'Europe's foremost maker of reflecting telescopes' (Bryden, 1968); the design was by **James Craig**, 'hindered' by **Robert Adam** who insisted on a picturesque castellated style. In 1827 Maria Theresa Short, daughter of Thomas Short, set up a wooden observatory behind the unfinished **National Monument**; evicted in 1850, she re-established her 'Popular Observatory' at the **Outlook Tower**. When the New Observatory became the City Observatory in 1896 (on the opening of the Royal Observatory on **Blackford Hill**), a 6-inch (15cm) Cooke photo-visual refractor telescope was installed.

Cockburn Street

A sinuous curve reaching down from the **High Street** to **Waverley Bridge**, Cockburn Street was constructed in 1856 to provide carriage access from the **Old Town** to **Waverley Station**: the first major thoroughfare created wholly therein after the erection of the **Flodden Wall** excepting the **North**, **South** and **George IV Bridges**. Ironically it is named after the preservationist **Henry, Lord Cockburn**. From 1853, the Edinburgh Railway Station Access Company demolished bits of the old closes which lie divided on either side. Cockburn Street achieves a controlled but varied architectural unity through the designs of Messrs Peddie & Kinnear who built most of the existing blocks 1859–64. At the other end of Market Street Jeffrey Street is named after **Francis Jeffrey**, a lifelong friend of Henry Cockburn.

Colinton

Once the Arcadian milling settlement of Hailes, but since renamed and made a suburb (1920), the 'smart little village of Colinton' (Ballantyne, 1844) snuggles in a Red Sandstone gorge carved by the **Water of Leith** at the end of the last Ice Age. It derives from Old Norse 'Kolbeinn's farm', but was earlier called Hailes, Anglian for 'land in the bend of a river'. The mill at Hailes was owned by Thomas of **Restalrig** in 1226, and Hailes Kirk (then on the site of Hailes House, 1761), dedicated to **St Cuthbert** by **Malcolm III 'Canmore'** in c1095, was confirmed to **Dunfermline Abbey** by **Alexander III** in 1250. The present kirk, begun in 1771, replaced that ruined by Cromwell in 1650 which itself likely replaced another destroyed during the invasion of the Earl of Hertford in 1544. Cromwell also burned Colinton Castle before reducing **Redhall**, downstream. In 1666 the **Covenanting** host crossed Colinton Brig before being routed by **General Tam Dalyell** in the **Pentland Hills** at **Rullion Green**; the Covenanters' Monument near Redford House (c1700), consisting of Ionic columns from the Old **Royal Infirmary**, was raised by R A MacFie of Dreghorn Castle (blown up 1955).

Colinton House (**Merchiston Castle** School) was built in 1801–6 by Thomas Harrison for the banker Sir William Forbes of **Pitsligo**, who had purchased Colinton Castle from the Foulis family of goldsmiths in 1800. Spylaw House, deep in Colinton Dell, was converted

from snuff mill into petite Georgian villa for James Gillespie in 1773. Upper Spylaw Mill was one of the earliest paper mills in Scotland, where in 1681 James Lithgow and Nicholas Dechamp were charged with violating the royal monopoly of playing-card manufacturing held by Peter Breusch at **Canonmills** and Restalrig. Derelict Colinton Bank was the summer cottage of **Henry Mackenzie**, 'the Man of Feeling', who first popularised Colinton as a rustic retreat in the 19th century. Permanent residence became practicable after the opening of the Balerno Branch of the Caledonian **Railway** in 1875; villa and 'cottage' developments, notably by **Robert Lorimer** and **R Rowand Anderson**, soon ringed the riverbanks. Earlier, on the Pentland slopes, Bonaly Tower had been started by **William Playfair** for **Henry Cockburn** in 1811. The best literary apostle of Colinton was **Robert Louis Stevenson** who spent his early summers at Colinton Manse. 'That was my Golden Age: *et ego in Arcadia vixi*' (RLS, 1887).

Comiston

A breezy district reaching furth of **Morningside** for the **Pentland Hills**, Comiston was called 'Colmanston' after the Gaelic for Columba. The Caiy or Camus Stane, a 10' (3m) cup-marked, Red Sandstone monolith said to mark an ancient battle, stands near Fairmilehead. Comiston is first recorded as part of the vast Barony of Redhall, near **Colinton**, in the late 13th century. Comiston House, a solid classical villa, now flats, was erected c1815 by Lord Provost Sir James Forrest to replace an earlier mansion of c1610 of which a curious corner turret with gunloops survives. By the road to **Swanston**, at the 'Hunter's Tryst', met the sporting Six Foot High Club founded in 1826 which also admitted 'lesser' literary giants of the stature of **Sir Walter Scott**, **James Hogg** and **John Wilson (Christopher North)** among its fellows. In the Buckstane, an old march stone (now moved) on Braid Road, the royal standard was mounted in the legendary 'Hunt of Pentland' when **Robert I** challenged his knightly entourage to capture an elusive white stag; the beast was brought to bay by 'Help' and 'Hold', the hounds of Sir William Sinclair of **Roslin** and **Penicuik**, who, granted lands at Glencrosse, erected the Chapel of St Katherine-in-the-Hopes there in gratitude. His successors, the Lairds of Penicuik, are, in homage, still bound to attend at the Buckstane should the monarch pass by and give three blasts on the hunting horn. Hence 'Free for a Blast', the motto of **Clerk of Penicuik**.

Corstorphine

An old established village straddling the **Glasgow** road beyond **Murrayfield**, Corstorphine has, since 1920, been swamped by indifferent suburban sprawl. It was founded on a ridge of rock and boulder clay between two former glacial lakes, Corstorphine and Gogar Lochs, both drained by 'the Stank' from the 17th century. The name is from the Gaelic *Crois Torfinn*, 'Torfinn's Crossing', first recorded in the early 12th century. Corstorphine Hill, an eroded volcanic sill rising 530ft (162m) to the north is crowned by Clermiston Tower erected by Robert MacFie of Dreghorn on the centenary of the birth of **Sir Walter Scott** in 1871. Corstorphine Collegiate Kirk, dedicated to St John the Baptist, was founded in the early 15th century by Sir Adam Forrester who purchased Corstorphine in 1736; this votive chapel contains his tomb and effigy. Continued by his son, Sir John, Master of the Household to **James I**, the 'Corstorphine Heirloom' which was grafted on to the earlier, 12th century St Mary's Kirk (demolished 1646) still serves – after many alterations and additions, notably by **William Burn** in 1828 – as the Parish Kirk.

The Forresters' Corstorphine Castle has disappeared but the Dower House (c1660) remains. Their massive, barrel-shaped **doocot**, containing 1060 nests, lies near the magnificent Corstorphine Sycamore, *Acer Pseudoplatanus Corstorphinense* – a botanical sub-species which tradition says came as a sapling from the East in the early 15th century; over 55ft (16m) high and 12½ft (3.8m) in girth, the tree does not produce seed and can only be propagated by cuttings. Under its glorious golden canopy in August 1679 James, Lord Forrester was despatched upon his own sword by his mistress, Christian Nimmo, whose shade, 'the White Lady of Corstorphine', is seen to turn about the tree. In the early 19th century Corstorphine was a spa village known for its Physic and Lady Wells and for its buttermilk, 'Corstorphine Cream'. The Doocot Tapestry Studio (Edinburgh Tapestry Company), founded by the 4th Marquess of Bute, inspired by William Morris and the Arts and Crafts Movement in 1912, accommodates seven weavers.

Cowgate

An infernal bolt-hole for traffic bypassing the **High Street**, the gloom of the Cowgate is deepened by the underbellies of the **South** and **George IV Bridges** which overleap it. Winding some 800 yds (730m) from the **Grassmarket** to the Pleasance, it began as a back lane for driving cattle from plots behind the houses of the High Street to pasture on the **Burgh Muir**. By c1500 the street had become the first fashionable suburb, a *Via Vaccarum* 'where the nobility and chief men of the city reside, and in which are the palaces of the officers of state, and where nothing is mean or tasteless, but all is magnificent' (Alesius, 1529). One courtier, **Thomas Hamilton** of Priestfield (Prestonfield), 1st Earl of **Haddington**, was given the sobriquet 'Tam o' the Cougait' by his royal master **James VI**. A President of the **Court of Session**, he was noted for his 'penetration as a judge, industry as a collector of decisions and talent for amassing wealth'; the King believed him to have discovered the 'Philosopher's Stone' when he had in fact made a lucky strike at his silver mine near **Linlithgow**.

Craigcrook Castle

'The Castle of Indolence' where in 1815 **Francis, Lord Jeffrey** 'set up his rustic household gods' (Cockburn, 1856), Craigcrook Castle lies sheltered on the wooded eastern slope of **Corstorphine** Hill and was likely begun by William Adamson, a merchant burgess who purchased the estate in 1542. Jeffrey took over the lease from **Archibald Constable**, the publisher, and in 1835 engaged **William Playfair** to convert part of the original Z-plan, four-storey tower house and reconstruct its early 17th century extension in baronial style. For 30 years Jeffrey held open house at Craigcrook on Saturdays during the summer court session; legal and literary 'lions'

such as **Henry, Lord Cockburn**, **Henry Mackenzie**, **John Gibson Lockhart** and **Thomas Carlyle** were frequent visitors. 'No other house in Scotland has had a greater influence on literary or political opinion' (Cockburn, 1856). In 1999 the house was the headquarters of a fish-farming company.

Craigentinny

An amorphous municipal and private residential area of 1920s and 30s construction between **Restalrig** and **Portobello**, Craigentinny was farmed in the 19th century as the most extensive sewage-irrigated meadows in Scotland, being amply fed by the city's 'Foul Burn'. The name derives from the Gaelic *creag-an-teine*, 'the rock of (the) fire'. It was detached from the Barony of Restalrig in c1604 when Sir Robert Logan sold the estate to James Nisbet, merchant, who erected Craigentinny House (or 'Castle'). The originally plain, now multi-turreted, four-storey mansion was bought in 1764 by William Miller, a Quaker seedsman and **Jacobite**, who had supplied **Prince Charles Edward Stewart** in 1745 with 50 spades for trenching.

The Craigentinny 'Marbles' contains the remains of William Henry Miller – enclosed in heavy coffins covered with a large flagstone and sunk 20ft (6m) deep (as directed in his will) beneath an astonishing pedimented Roman mausoleum raised by David Rhind in 1848–56. A bibliophile known as 'Measure Miller' from his carrying a footrule to size up a 'tall' copy of a book which he wished to add to his priceless library, Miller was 'at the time of his death . . . currently averred to be a changeling – even to be a woman, a suggestion which his thin figure, weak voice, absence of all beard, and some peculiarity of habit, seemed to corroborate (Grant, 1884). Craigentinny Castle was converted into a Social Centre in 1937, the first in Scotland.

Craigiehall

'A handsome mansion, inviting to peace and retirement by the deep quiet and serenity of its aspect' (Ballingall, 1877), Craigiehall – GHQ Army (Scotland) – has its tranquillity shattered by the Queensferry Road. It was held by John de Craigie in the time of **David I**; the Stewarts of Durrisdeer, **Dumfriesshire** were lairds from 1387–1643 when the estate was sold to John Fairholm, City Treasurer. In 1682 his granddaughter Sophia married the powerful William Johnstone, 3rd Earl (later 1st Marquis) of Annandale, who commissioned **Sir William Bruce**, while working on the neighbouring **Hopetoun House**, to design the present two-storey villa. 'Edinburgh's only example of the comfortable Dutch-classical country house' (Gifford et al, 1984), erected c1695–9. The beautiful parks in the Italian manner were planted by the Hon Charles Hope-Weir, who inherited the estate in 1741.

Craigleith

Edinburgh's original 'hole-in-the-ground', Craigleith **Quarry** was situated off the Queensferry Road about a mile west of the **New Town** which its easily worked but durable sandstone largely created. The very pale orange, fine-grained calciferous sandstone was dumped during the Lower Carboniferous period in the delta of a great river which then covered **Fife** and the **Lothians**;

huge *araucaria* (monkey puzzle or Chilean Pine trees) swept down by the current and buried by the sand were discovered early last century; one of these **fossils**, found in 1830, is in the **Royal Botanic Garden**.

The quarry, which reached 12 acres (4.8ha) and was 200ft (60m) deep by the end of the 19th century, 'a vast hole, the depth of which from its precipitous edges made you dizzy' (Masson, 1894), was at its busiest during the building boom of the 1820s. Worked as early as 1615 when 200 double arch stones were produced for **Edinburgh Castle**, it yielded some huge blocks; in 1791 stones for the six monolithic pillars (22ft x 3ft3in) of the porch of the **University of Edinburgh** required 16 horses each to haul them; and in 1823 one of the largest blocks ever excavated (136ft x 20ft and weighing c1500 tons) went – in smaller pieces – to form the architrave of the **National Monument**. 'Craigleith' gives a fine finish to the **City Chambers**, **Charlotte Square**, **St Andrew's Church**, the Old **Royal High School** and many other buildings. It was last used in a major project at **Leith** Docks from c1895; the quarry ceased working in 1905 but recommenced operations from 1922–41/2 on a reduced scale. Filled in during the 1960s and 70s, only a small sandstone outcrop now shows on the site, which was developed in 1993–4 for a supermarket.

Craiglockhart

A bungaloid suburb between **Colinton** and **Morningside**, Craiglockhart was developed during the 1930s around the Easter and Wester Craiglockhart Hills. 'Craigloch-ard' supposedly derives from their position relative to **Corstorphine** Loch, about two miles to the north, but the land was held by Sir Simon de Loccard, progenitor of the Lockharts of Lee near **Carnwath** in the 12th century. Craiglockhart Tower, a stout little fortalice, is 'without a history' (Grant, 1884). The estate was acquired by the notorious Kincaids in the 15th century; in 1600 John Kincaid seized Isobel Hutcheson from the **Dean Village** but was surprised by **James VI** who was riding nearby. The King threatened to burn Craig House unless she was released, and Kincaid, fined for the outrage, was also ordered to deliver up 'his brown horse' to him.

The present Old Craighouse, begun in 1565 by the Symounes, was altered when the adjoining 'château' of Craighouse (formerly the Thomas Clouston Clinic of the Royal Edinburgh Hospital, now Napier University) was emblazoned across the Easter Hill, above the 'Happy Valley' by Sydney Mitchell in 1889–94. Vast Victorian institutions were foisted upon Craiglockhart: the baronial City Poor House, later Greenlea Old People's Home, in 1867–9; the Craiglockhart Hydropathic Institution, later the Convent of the Sacred Heart, a grand Italianate villa, in 1887–90; and the ruby red 'Japanese' City (Fever) Hospital in 1896–1903 (which includes Milestone House, the first purpose-built AIDS hospice in Britain, 1991). Craiglockhart House, a Tudor Gothic creation near Redhall in Craiglockhart Dell on the **Water of Leith**, was built by Alexander Monro 'Tertius', 'dynastical' Professor of Anatomy at the **University of Edinburgh**, whose grandfather **Alexander Monro 'Primus'** had bought the estate in 1773.

Craigmillar Castle

A largely complete tower house defiantly sited on a low rocky escarpment between **Liberton** and **Duddingston**, Craigmillar Castle is one of Scotland's most impressive

Craigmillar Castle, by R W Billings c1840 (RWB)

medieval remains. Although it is first mentioned in 1212, there is no record of a fortalice until after Sir Simon Preston received charter of the barony from **Robert II** in 1374. The present L-plan tower is not earlier than the mid to late 15th century. The 50–60ft keep, measuring 53ft x 49ft on its longest sides – with walls 9ft thick – stands in a 16th century courtyard enclosed with a strong rectangular curtain wall of c1508. This machicolated defence, a forward fortification still possessing all four bold, round corner towers (30–40ft high), has loops for both guns and cannon. Burnt by the Earl of Hertford in the English invasion of 1544, a further outer wall was later drawn around the castle enclosing an area of 1¼ acres. The original banqueting hall is one of two barrel-vaulted chambers in the tower; adjacent is 'Queen Mary's Room', only 7ft x 5ft (2m x 1.5m), said to have been used by **Mary Stewart** during her frequent sojourns there from 1561. Mary went to Craigmillar – then the residence of former Lord Provost Sir Simon Preston – 'wishing herself dead' after the murder of **David Rizzio** at the **Palace of Holyroodhouse** in 1566. The castle was also the scene, at the end of that fateful year and with or without the Queen's connivance, of the 'Craigmillar Conference' whereby **Bothwell**, **Argyll**, **Huntly** and **Maitland of Lethington** signed the virtual death-warrant of **Henry, Lord Darnley** who was disposed of at the **Kirk o' Field** a few months later. In the civil war following Mary's abdication, Craigmillar was garrisoned against the city by **Regent Mar**, whose ancestor John Stewart, Earl of Mar had been imprisoned by his brother **James III** in the castle and supposedly done to death by being bled in a warm bath. From 1660, when Sir John Gilmour, Lord President of the **Court of Session**, purchased Craigmillar, part was reconstructed for more modern accommodation. Uninhabited since the mid-18th century, Craigmillar became increasingly ruinous, and in 1946 was placed in state care by Sir John Gilmour's descendants.

Cramond

An 18th century industrial village on the Firth of Forth picturesquely restored by the city in the 1960s,

Mills on the Almond below Cramond Bridge in the 1880s (GWWA)

Edinburgh continued

Cramond lies off the Queensferry Road beyond David-son's Mains. 'Cramond' is derived from the Cumbric *Caer Amon*, 'the fort on the (River) Almond', the native name for the **Roman** harbour station which supplied the **Antonine Wall** from 141–61 AD, and was reoccupied by the Emperor Septimius Severus 208–12 AD. The *principia* (headquarters), excavated in 1954–66, lies partly buried beneath Cramond Kirk which possibly originated within the basilica of the fort; well-preserved Roman bath-house remains were unearthed in 1975–8. A remarkable relic of the Roman occupation, a large stone lioness, was recovered from the river mud in 1997 and is now in the **Museum of Scotland**. The present cruciform kirk dates from 1656 when the 'ruin-ouses' of the medieval structure (the 15th century tower survives) were destroyed. Medieval Cramond was under the Bishops of **Dunkeld** who were granted it by **David I** in 1160; their 'summer palace' was Cramond Tower, a small but tall four-storey block of c1580 which, restored c1980, still frowns on the Forth. Cramond House was begun in 1680 by John Inglis, a merchant and **Coven-anter**, who had bought the tower in 1622; enlarged and enclosed by Sir John Inglis in 1771, it was completed by his daughter Lady Anne Torpichen, who demolished half of the village, next to Cramond Inn, in 1826.

In 1751 the Cramond Iron Works were established at Cockle Mill by the Smith & Wrightwork Company of **Leith**, who sold out to the **Carron Company** of **Falkirk** in 1759; from 1770–1860 the Cadell Company employed c100 workers in four mills along the river including Fairafar Forge. The first commercially produced Scottish crude steel came from Cramond. Since 1556 the ferry has plied the river to **Dalmeny** estate which privatised the service in 1622 when old Cramond Brig upstream was rebuilt with stone. There 'Jock' Howieson rescued 'the Gudeman of Ballangeich' (**James V**

in his customary disguise) from thieves and was, in gratitude, granted the adjoining land of Braehead for the service of appearing with a basin of water and a napkin whenever a monarch crosses the brig.

Crown Plaza Hotel, High Street

A mock medieval castle with a bold corner tower dominating the **High Street** between **Niddry** and **Black-friars' Streets**, the former Scandic House Hotel fills the notorious 'Grant's gap-site' which, after hasty demolitions, lay vacant for 25 years. ALL THIS/WARK WAS BEGUN/BE DANCON ON/10.JANUARY.1989/AN ENDIT BE THEM/ON/31.MARCH.1990 reads the bogus jargon on a commemorative panel on this self-styled 'Jewel in the Mile'. The one-acre complex straddles three former closes – Dickson's, Cant's and Strichen's – the latter disingenuously renamed Melrose after the scant remains of the pre-**Reformation** lodging of the Abbot of **Melrose** preserved within; later, in the 18th century, it was the house of **Sir George 'Bluidy' Mackenzie of Rosehaugh**, the founder of the **Advocates' Library**, and afterwards of Alexander Fraser, Lord Strichen, who gave his name to the close.

Currie

A once well-balanced farming and industrial village and the focus on the Lanark Road for **Balerno** and **Juniper Green**, Currie has, since the 1960s, sprawled ceaselessly, becoming a suburb of the city in 1975. It was earlier called Killeith (modern Kinleith) after its chapel or 'cell' dedicated to St Kentigern (**St Mungo**); 'Mungo's Well', covered by the **railway** in 1874, flows near the present Currie Kirk (1784) which shows the foundations of an earlier 14th century church and Templar and Calvary cross-slabs in its graveyard. The kirk, with Lennox (Kil-laird) Tower, a 15th century ruin at Lymphoy House, was a 'special' possession of the Archdeans of Lothian. Kinleith Mill (1618), which produced paper from 1792, early converted to steam power under Henry Bruce after

1844 to become the largest installation on the river, employing 400 persons in 1900. Currie Mill, hard by Currie Brig, ground corn from 1506. The bridge itself, which is declared to be 600 years old, 'needed repair' in 1599; over it in 1666 rode **General Tam Dalyell** on his way to defeat the **Covenanters** at **Rullion Green**.

Dalmahoy House

An austere, rectangular, three-storey and seven-bay 'box' south of **Ratho**, Dalmahoy was designed c1725 by **William Adam** for George Dalrymple, youngest son of the **1st Earl of Stair** who resided at **Newliston** nearby. It was sold c1750 to James Douglas, Earl of Morton. 'Dalmahoy House is finely situated in the middle of the great park containing between 400 and 500 acres [160–200ha], inclosed by one of the best built walls in Scotland … forming altogether a very beautiful and extensive scene' (OSA, 1793). The estate belonged anciently to the Dalmahoys of that Ilk; in 1296 Sir Henry de Dalmahoy submitted to Edward I of England, but may have changed sides during the **Wars of Independence** as the family retained possession until c1710. The house is now the clubhouse of the Dalmahoy **Golf** and Country Club. The 'Dalmahoy Hangings', often termed tapestries but technically otherwise, are said to have been worked by **Queen Mary**'s 'Four Maries' during her imprisonment at **Loch Leven Castle**.

Dalry

'The wretchedly unplanned district of Dalry' (Geddes, 1919), which coalesces with **Gorgie**, developed from c1850 as an industrial suburb south-west of Haymarket on the fringe of the **New Town**. Dalry is Gaelic for the 'King's vale' or 'meadow'; the Dalry Burn drained the Burgh Loch (**Meadows**) from Lochrin to the **Water of Leith** at Roseburn near **Murrayfield**. There Dalry Mills produced the earliest paper manufactured in Scotland c1591. Dalry House was begun as a small three-storey Z-plan villa by John Chiesley in the mid-17th century. Chiesley was a very contentious chap who passed on his hot blood to his daughter, rash Rachel, the unfortunate Lady Grange. At high noon on Easter Sunday 1689 John Chiesley gunned down Lord President **Sir George Lockhart** after the service in **St Giles**. Caught red-handed, he was dragged next day to the **Mercat Cross** where his right hand was chopped off; hanged with the pistol around his neck, his body was exhibited in chains between Edinburgh and **Leith**, and the hand nailed to the **West Port**. Easter Dalry House (18th century) is overshadowed by the disused 5 acre Caledonian Distillery with its great chimney, erected c1850.

Daniel Stewart's Melville College and the Mary Erskine School

A florid, two-storey combination of Elizabethan and Jacobean architectural styles, Daniel Stewart's College (Melville College, formerly the Edinburgh Institution, founded 1832, combined with it in 1972) was designed on its imposing site off Queensferry Road by David Rhind in 1849–55. Originally Daniel Stewart's Hospital, it was founded from the £13,000 residue of the estate of Daniel Stewart (d.1814) of the Scottish Exchequer which had accumulated to £80,000 by 1845. It became an Edinburgh Merchant Company fee-paying day school for boys in 1870. (Stewart also endowed a free school in his native parish of Logierait in **Perthshire**.) The foundation provided for the maintenance of the sons of honest and industrious parents whose circumstances did not enable them adequately to support and educate them at other schools. 'Poor boys of the name of Stewart and Macfarlane, resident within Edinburgh and the suburbs, were always to have a presence' (Grant, 1884). Laid out somewhat like **George Heriot's School**, Stewart's Melville comprises a quadrangle (roofed for the school hall in 1894) enclosed in the U-plan of a now glazed screen and has turreted twin towers.

It enjoys a special relationship with the Mary Erskine School for Girls at nearby Ravelston which was founded as the Merchant Maiden Hospital in 1694 by the Company of Merchants and Mary Erskine (who also founded the Trades Maiden Hospital in 1704). Together the two schools have a jointly managed dual campus of around 1400 pupils which enables co-educational classes in the youngest and oldest grades.

Dean Bridge

The masterful Dean Bridge, designed by **Thomas Telford**, was erected in 1829–32 to span the ravine of the **Water of Leith**, the northern barrier to the expansion of the **New Town** of Edinburgh. Four slender arches of **Craigleith** sandstone, 90ft (27m) in span, carry the carriageway 106ft (32m) above the river, the total length being 447ft (136m). The parapets, raised in 1912 supposedly to deter suicides, were repaired in 1964–5 with stone salvaged from the old Waterloo Bridge in London.

Dean Cemetery

A sepulchred *Who's Who* of the good and great, the Dean Cemetery was laid out on the grounds of the former Dean House above the present **Dean Village** by David Cousin in 1845; the retaining wall above the **Water of Leith** incorporates many of the sculptured stones of the old mansion, erected in 1614. The Edinburgh equivalent of the **Necropolis** in **Glasgow**, it is ironic that its only full-blown architectural monument – a smaller version of that on **Calton Hill** to **Dugald Stewart** – commemorates a Glaswegian, James Buchanan (d.1860). The Dean is, however, better endowed with sculptures, especially bronze reliefs, notably by **William Brodie**, John Hutchinson and John Rhind. The finest group of 19th century architectural monuments to be found in any cemetery in the city lies along the west wall where their designer, **William Playfair**, himself rests among friends, **Henry, Lord Cockburn, Francis, Lord Jeffrey** and Andrew, Lord Rutherford. The northern extension of 1871 includes **Robert Reid** and Thomas Bonnar, architects of the Second **New Town**, artists **Sam Bough** and **David Scott**, the **Nasmyth** family monument, and **David Octavius Hill**.

Dean House was built by William Nisbet who bought the Poultry lands of Dean and the office of Hereditary Poulterer to the King from **John Napier of Merchiston** in 1610; a long gallery contained an arched, painted wooden ceiling, panels from which, largely on religious subjects, are preserved in the **Royal Museum of Scotland**.

Telford's Dean Bridge c1892 (entry p 315) (GWWA)

Edinburgh continued

Dean Orphan Hospital

A conversation piece situated opposite the **Scottish Gallery of Modern Art** on Belford Brae above the **Dean Village**, the Orphan Hospital (now Dean Gallery (Paolozzi Collection)) was designed by **Thomas Hamilton** in 1831–3. 'English Baroque in concept but Neoclassical in detail', it is 'carried out with the utmost precision in **Craigleith** stone' (Gifford et al, 1984). The mixed style of the solid, two-storey H-plan block with its massive Tuscan portico and Vanbrughian toppings is indicative of the restrictions imposed upon Hamilton by the Hospital managers. They did not feel warranted in erecting a building in the expensive Greek or Roman, or even Gothic Elizabethan, style, and decided on a compromise which could, nevertheless, be executed in a substantial manner. More conspicuous are the twin clusters of four openwork chimney towers which also light the stairwells. The two-storey attic crowning the portico carries the clock of the old **Netherbow** which was transferred from the old Orphan Hospital designed by **William Adam** in 1734, which stood below the **North Bridge** on the site of **Waverley Station**; there in 1828 10 children died of cholera, rife because of overcrowding and its lowly situation.

Dean Village

Formerly 'the village of the **Water of Leith**', the Dean Village is a picturesque reminder of medieval mealmilling overshot by the **Dean Bridge** near the west end of Edinburgh. 'The mills at the Dene' were granted by **David I** to the canons of **Holyrood** in 1143. 11 mills

were worked by the town and the Baxters' (bakers') Incorporation during the 17th century. Only the West Mills (rebuilt 1805) remain. Well Court, a romantic vernacular quadrangle comprising workers' houses, a clock tower and a community hall was built in 1884 for **John Ritchie Findlay**, the philanthrophic proprietor of *The Scotsman* **newspaper**.

Donaldson's School for the Deaf

A palatial, Elizabethan-cum-Jacobean masterpiece near **Murrayfield**, the vast Donaldson's Hospital for orphans was designed by **William Playfair** in 1841–51. Early specialising in the education and welfare of deaf children, Donaldson's was founded from the £210,000 fortune left by James Donaldson, a printer and bookseller in the **West Bow**. One of the grandest piles in the city, the almost completed building prompted **Queen Victoria** to remark in 1850 'Your school is finer than any of my Scottish palaces'. The present School for the Deaf emerged in 1938 after amalgamation with the Royal Institute for the Education of the Deaf and Dumb (founded 1810).

The Drum House

So named because of its position on a ridge east of **Gilmerton** on the outer limits of Drumshelch, the old hunting ground of Scots kings, The Drum was erected for James, 13th Lord Somerville by **William Adam** in 1726–34. Originally 'Somerville House', it is a two-storey Palladian mansion with large Venetian windows; only the western of the two planned pavilion wings – incorporating part of the earlier fortified house built by **John Mylne** in 1584 – was completed. The exquisite plasterwork in the hall was created by Samuel Calderwood in 1727 and later continued in the drawing room by Thomas Clayton.

Duddingston

Between **Craigmillar** and **Portobello**, 'Dodynstane' was so named by Dodin, a Norman knight who leased the parish from the Abbot of **Kelso** who had been gifted it by **David I** in the 12th century. The very first inhabitants possibly lived in wooden **crannogs** built on stilts in Duddingston Loch, a glacial lake formerly of much greater extent, now Bawsinch Reserve bird sanctuary. Bronze Age cultivation terraces on **Arthur's Seat** indicate an antiquity perhaps greater than the city itself. Duddingston Kirk, an early 12th century double-cell foundation, is much disguised by 17th and 18th century work; its original entrance has a fine round Norman arch with unusual carvings. The most memorable minister was the artist **Reverend John Thomson**, who named the octagonal Thomson's Tower, his studio on the loch, 'Edinburgh' so that his servant could truthfully say to house callers that he was away in the town. Duddingston was then a community of **coal**-miners and salt-pan workers; a coarse flaxen cloth called 'Duddingston Hardings' was woven in the early 18th century. The 'Sheep's Heid Inn' – named from the homely Scots culinary speciality – claims a long pedigree from at least 1580, when **James VI** is said to have presented the landlord with a silver embellished ram's head; the inn's fine skittle alley is the oldest in Scotland.

Duddingston House

'One of the finest 18th century houses in Britain' (McKean, 1983), Duddingston House was built for the 8th Earl of **Abercorn** by **Sir William Chambers** in 1763. A classical, square-set two-storey block with a grand Corinthian portico with pediment rising full height to a balustrade, the house is linked by a colonnade to the service quadrangle adjacent. The 200 acre (81ha) park (now Duddingston **Golf Course**) was laid out in the flowing landscape style of Capability Brown by James Robertson in 1768; it focused on a domed temple still occupying the highest ground.

Nearby Nairne Lodge, opposite Duddingston Mills, was formerly Caroline Cottage, purchased in 1806 by the **ballad** composer **Carolina, Lady Nairne**. Adjacent stands Cauvin's Hospital, built by Louis Cauvin as 'Louisville'; a French tutor attended by **Robert Burns** in 1787, he left £30,000 for the school opened (1833) for 20 boys, some in 'reduced circumstances'.

Dundas House

The only free-standing mansion erected as an integral part of the **New Town**, Dundas House occupies the centre of the eastern side of **St Andrew Square**. A magnificent three-storey Palladian villa designed by **Sir William Chambers** for Sir Laurence Dundas of Kerse in 1772–4, it was modelled on Marble Hill, Twickenham. Dundas, the son of a bankrupt Edinburgh bailie, rose to become Commissary-General of the Army in Flanders from 1748–59, and was created a baronet in 1762. Prior to the publication of the New Town plan in 1767, Dundas secured a plot of land immediately to the east

of the present Square. Then in 1767 – a mere month and a day after the first feu had been taken up in the New Town – Dundas feued an unspecified area adjoining his existing property (all the other feus are exactly specified). That this site was reserved for **St Andrew's Church** was conveniently overlooked. In 1794 the Excise Office moved into Dundas House, adding the royal arms (which display the pre-1801 version including France) to the pediment. The porch was added in 1828 after acquisition by the Royal Bank of Scotland, the present occupiers, in 1825; the grand, domed banking hall was built in 1857. In the forecourt the Hopetoun Monument commemorates Sir John Hope, 4th Earl of Hopetoun, soldier and eventually Governor of the Royal Bank.

The Edinburgh Academy, Inverleith

Lying long and low like an 18th century garden pavilion, the Edinburgh Academy was designed by **William Burn** from 1823–36 in a Greek Doric style, and resulted from a resolution made 'on top of one of the **Pentlands**' by **Henry Cockburn** and Leonard Horner to establish a new school to arrest the decline of classical education in Scotland. Both themselves products of the High School – 'this hated school', which was 'notorious for its severity and riotousness' (Cockburn, 1856) – they were supported by **Sir Walter Scott** who insisted on English looming large in the curriculum. The Academy was opposed by the town council; its hackles rose at the proposed two-guinea entrance fee which would exclude poor scholars and consign them to the grossly overcrowded High School in a two-tier system, 'thereby destroying one of the proudest characteristics of the Scottish system of education' (Town Council Minute, 1823). The upshot was two new schools: the Academy on a greenfield site north of the **New Town** and the epic **Royal High School** on the **Calton Hill**.

Esplanade

Now the coach park for the **Castle**, where the Military Tattoo is staged during the **Edinburgh Festival**, the Esplanade was originally created as the parade ground for the garrison in 1753. The narrow defensible ridge at the top of **Castlehill**, left as an unbuilt military zone since Norman times, was filled out and levelled with earth dug from the foundations for the **City Chambers**. Between 1625–49, under mandate from **Charles I**, the soil was made that of Nova Scotia so that baronetcies could be more easily enfiefed upon the intending colonists of that distant land. During the 18th century it became a favourite promenade for citizens, even the Lord's Day being 'profaned by people . . . vagueing to fields, gardens, and the Castlehill' (Town Council Minute, 1709). In 1854 the town council asserted its right to ownership of the Esplanade under the terms of their Golden Charter from **James VI**, but the court found in favour of the Crown, whose property it remains. Among the formidable row of military monuments on the north side of the Esplanade is an unadorned block of grey granite commemorating the Ensign Ewart who, as a sergeant in the Royal North British Dragoons, captured the standard of the French 45th Regiment at Waterloo in 1815.

Festival Theatre

A Mecca Bingo Hall from 1964–89, the magnificent old Empire Theatre, opposite Surgeon's Hall in Nicolson Street, was refurbished in 1994 as Edinburgh's long-awaited Opera House. A number of theatres have occupied the site since c1820 – the 'Southminster', 'Queen's Theatre' and, from 1861, 'Dunedin Hall', a wooden building staging circus performances, which became the Empire Palace in 1880. A disastrous fire in May 1911 saw the death on stage of the Great Lafayette, an American illusionist, and members of his company. The present structure (1928) was long a firm favourite for entertainers on the British variety circuit and, in the first 15 years of the **Edinburgh Festival**, was the venue for dance. In the current conversion the plain Art Deco frontage was replaced by a glass façade swept back from the street; the huge domed interior containing c2000 seats (only surpassed in Scotland for capacity by the Playhouse with c3000) will have an extended stage area, 50% greater than that of the Royal Opera House, Covent Garden.

Fettes College

An uncanny combination of solid Scots Baronial and exuberant French Gothic designed by **David Bryce** in 1864–70, the 'Scots Eton' operates along English public school lines. It was endowed by **Sir William Fettes** of nearby Comely Bank, a merchant who was twice Lord Provost of Edinburgh. Beginning with 70 boys, the school proved so successful that after 10 years the roll exceeded 200. (Today there are c500 boarders and day-scholars, both boys and girls.) The foundationers provided for were originally accommodated in spartan conditions in the three-storey, symmetrical H-plan building which is one of the most remarkable edifices in the city. Fettes' most famous former pupil is James Bond; his creator, Ian Fleming, has him fetched up at Fettes after being expelled from Eton.

Flodden Wall

Reluctantly built c1513–60 (after **Flodden**), and dismantled piecemeal from 1787, the Flodden Wall constricted the outward growth of the **Old Town** for 250 years: Edinburgh grew upwards instead, raising tottering tenements up to 14 storeys high. The Flodden Wall was both higher and stronger than its predecessor, the 15th century 'King's Wall' [see **Town Walls**] and measured about 5ft (1.5m) thick and over 25ft (7.6m) high. Its six gates, which included the **West Port** and the **Netherbow Port**, had either bastions or watchtowers strategically placed between. Although untested by siege, major repairs were already required by 1591, when the wall was strengthened by bulwarks and flankers.

It ran for 1 mile 3 furlongs, from the dam and sluice of the **Nor' Loch**, beneath the present **North Bridge**, alongside **Trinity College Kirk** to the foot of Leith Wynd at St Anthony's port. There, and in St Mary's Street, south of the Netherbow, the wall comprised the fronts of the houses themselves. Beyond the **Cowgate** Port, at the foot of the Pleasance, a formidable section of the wall has been preserved and landscaped (1989).

Turning westward into modern Drummond Street, i enclosed the Blackfriars' Monastery. Near **Potterrow** Port on the eastern side of **South Bridge**, the wall bounded the **Kirk o'Field**, now occupied by the **University of Edinburgh** and the **Royal Museum of Scotland**. Beyond **Bristo** Port after enclosing the **Greyfriars** Monastery (now **Kirk**) the wall ran along the Lauriston ridge, a poor defensive position, with the steep drop of the **Grassmarket** behind. In the Vennel, where it plunged northwards to the West Port before ascending the **Castle** Bank, lies the only remaining corner tower.

An extension, the Telfer Wall, which was built by John Tailefer to enclose the suburb of Bristo, 1610–20, was extended as far as the Vennel in 1636 to protect **George Heriot's Hospital** (now **School**). A very well preserved section of this wall, both higher and better built than the Flodden Wall, stands in Heriot Place.

George IV Bridge

Built as a broad elevated street on nine arches (only two are visible), the 275m George IV Bridge vaults the **Cowgate** from the **High Street** to **Bristo** on the **Southside**. Constructed by **Thomas Hamilton** in 1829–32 as the 'New Southern Approach' to the **Old Town**, it complemented his 'New Western Approach' of 1825–36, which linked the **Lawnmarket** with **Lothian Road** at the west end of **Princes Street**. The construction caused the destruction of the picturesque Liberton's Wynd, renowned for the clubbable 'John Dowie's Tavern', where was dispensed the celebrated Younger's 'Edinburgh Ale', 'a potent fluid which almost glued the lips of the drinker together' (Chambers, 1868). Also destroyed was the Old Bank Close, the home of the **Bank of Scotland** for over a century from 1700. At the head of this close, **Sir George Lockhart of Carnwath** was gunned down by 'mad' John Chiesley of **Dalry**. 'I am not one to do things by halves and now I have taught the president how to do justice.'

George Heriot's Hospital/School

'The largest and most perfect early-17th century structure in Scotland' (Rowan, 1975), the great Renaissance palace of George Heriot's School confronts the **Castle** from Lauriston, south of the **Grassmarket**. In 1628 **George Heriot** ('Jingling Geordie'), goldsmith and moneylender to **James VI** and **Anne of Denmark**, bequeathed the residue of his fabulous fortune 'for the maintenance releif bringing up and educatioune of . . . puire fatherles bairnes friemen sones . . . of Edinburgh' in an imitation of Christ's Hospital, London. His 'Wark' was the first completely regular, classically inspired architectural design executed in Scotland; four equal ranges of three storeys, each 164ft (54m) long, are formed round a central half-piazza-ed quadrangle 92ft square; four square bartizaned towers rise one storey higher at each corner. Long erroneously attributed to Inigo Jones, the work was conducted by the masons William Wallace and William Ayton, and latterly **John** and **Robert Mylne**, who crowned the 110ft high clock-tower with its octagonal dome in 1693. In June 1659 30 boys, dressed in regulation 'sad russet' apparel 'with black hattis and stringes' first moved in.

The Hospital was converted into an independent, fee-paying secondary day school in 1886. Now co-

George Heriot's Hospital/School as drawn by R W Billings (RWB)

Edinburgh continued

educational, Heriot's honours the original provision for 'foundations' through the Heriot Trust. On 'June Day' the 'pious and worthie' memory of the founder is celebrated by the 'Buskin' ceremony when the statue of Heriot is garlanded with flowers.

See also **Heriot-Watt University**.

George Square

The earliest and largest of the Georgian squares of Edinburgh, George Square was begun c1766 and completed c1785; it was largely bulldozed under the **University of Edinburgh** Central Redevelopment Plan in the 1960s; only the original west side and a part of the east remains. Constructed outside the **Flodden Wall** by James Brown, who named it after his brother George, the 'Great Square' was complete on the north, east and west sides by 1779. The mason was Michael Nasmyth, father of the artist **Alexander Nasmyth** and grandfather of the inventor **James Nasmyth**. 'The walls are built partly of blue whin, partly of free stone, put alternately in a chequered figure, resembling the stuff that sailors' shirts are made of' (Arnott, 1779). The 'battle' for George Square lasted from 1946, when the University announced its intention to develop it as a student precinct, till 1960 when the conservation lobby was finally crushed at a public inquiry.

George Street

The central east-west axis of the First **New Town**, connecting **St Andrew Square** to **Charlotte Square**, George Street lies along the ridge of the 'Lang Dykes' between and parallel to **Princes Street** and **Queen Street**. Named for George III, it was intended as the main thoroughfare and was accordingly laid out some 20ft (6m) broader than Princes Street. Although conceived as a residential quarter, a hall was constructed at the east end for the **Royal College of Physicians** in 1775. Similarly, **St Andrew's Church** rose opposite in 1785, and the **Assembly Rooms** further west in 1787. As a centre of business and commerce, George Street was until the 1990s given over to the 'white collar' trades of **banking** and insurance, but rationalisations have made many of its bonny banks into bars. Its richly varied architectural parade includes the Italianate achievements of **David Bryce**, the 'builder of banks', who was responsible for the Graeco-Roman Clydesdale Bank (1847), the 'High Renaissance' Bank of Scotland (1874–6) and the **Royal Society of Edinburgh** (1843). The neo-Palladian Life Assurance Office of 1897–1901 re-uses the pediment of the Wise and Foolish Virgins, carved by **Sir John Steell**, which adorned the earlier building designed by David Bryce in 1839.

George Watson's College

The largest co-educational school in Scotland, George Watson's College occupies a mock-classical edifice on a large site off Colinton Road between **Merchiston** and **Morningside**. It was founded (1741) broadly on the lines of **George Heriot's Hospital**. George Watson (d.1723) was a merchant's son who, abandoned at an early age to the care of an aunt, Elizabeth Davidson, became clerk to Sir James Dick of **Prestonfield** and the first accountant of the Bank of Scotland in 1695. He bequeathed £12,000 (which accrued to £20,000 by 1738) to endow a hospital for the maintenance and instruction of sons and grandsons of decayed merchants. (Preference was given to members of the Merchant

Company and those with the name of Watson or David-son.) Watson's originally occupied an imposing **William Adam** building of 1739 which was incorporated as part of the **Royal Infirmary** in 1871; it then, having converted into a fee-paying day school of about 1000 pupils, occupied until 1932 the former Merchant Maiden Hospital (built in 1816 by **William Burn**) at Lauriston. George Watson's Ladies' College, begun in 1871 at **George Square**, amalgamated with the boys' school at Colinton Road in 1974, giving a roll of about 2100 pupils.

Gilmerton

A former **coal** and limestone working village a mile south of **Liberton**, Gilmerton was once a Lothian byword for rough licentious behaviour on account of its annual 'Carter's Play'. First recorded in the mid-12th century, in the early 14th the village was granted to Murdoch Menteith by **Robert I** after forfeiture by Sir William de Soulis, the Hereditary Butler of Scotland and a traitor in English pay. Gilmerton Pit, worked from as early as c1500, closed in 1961; the former limestone **quarries** were declared to be the oldest in Scotland. Gilmerton Cove, a strange series of underground chambers, was supposedly carved from the solid sandstone by the village blacksmith, George Paterson, in 1720–4; including a smithy and forge, top-lit rooms for troglodyte living, bed-recess, stone tables and chairs and a 'drinking-den' with built-in punch bowl, it is said by some to be an enlargement of an earlier, perhaps even prehistoric work. Burdiehouse is said to derive from Bordeaux House, after a colony of weavers who came with **Queen Mary** from France; alternatively it was the somewhat distant residence of her ladies-in-waiting when she occupied **Craigmillar Castle** at the opposite end of Liberton parish.

Gladstone's Land, Lawnmarket

A 17th century merchant's house and booth, Gladstone's Land boldly projects its two tall gablets and steep curving forestair into the **Lawnmarket**; the six-storey ashlar block retains the only surviving original arcaded (or 'piazza') street frontage once declared standard for new buildings in the **Old Town**. The 16th century tenement incorporated at the rear was bought by Thomas Gledstanes, merchant and burgess (an ancestor of W E Gladstone, PM) in 1617. He remodelled and extended this property southwards by encroaching onto the street in two stages – the first probably on timber gable projections, later encased in stone. Gledstanes occupied one floor (possibly the third) and let out the rest to a minister, a knight, a guild officer and another merchant.

Condemned by the city in 1935, the block was presented by its purchaser, Mrs Helen Anderson (a social worker who had ministered to its poor inhabitants), to the **National Trust for Scotland** and leased to the **Saltire Society** until 1977. Restoration by Sir Frank Mears 1935–7 revealed the forgotten arcading behind a contemporary shop façade. Further work in 1980 restored 'leaded lights' together with 'fine internal features such as ceilings and walls painted in tempera with abstract patterns of fruit, flowers, birds and arabesques . . .'

(McKean, 1985). The Land is furnished as a 17th century merchant's house with its ground floor booths restored, and is now open to the public as the National Trust for Scotland's Old Town House; a gilded hawk or 'gled' stooping outside recalls the origin of the name 'Gledstanes'.

Gogar House, Ingliston

An early 17th century, four-storey sentinel hard by Edinburgh Airport, Gogar House ('Castle Gogar') was built for John Couper, merchant, and Harriet Sinclair in 1625; possibly the architect was William Aytoun, one of the master masons responsible for **George Heriot's School**. For its late date, Gogar is curious in containing many discreet stairways and corner cubby-holes.

In 1650 the banks of the Gogar Burn resounded to the 'Gogar Flashes', a brief exchange of artillery fire between Oliver Cromwell and **Sir David Leslie** in which high-calibre field pieces were employed for the first time; the Protector was attempting to go round the marshes, remnants of the old Gogar Loch. The Barony of Gogar belonged to the Forresters of **Corstorphine** in early times, to the Setons in the time of **Robert I**, and later passed to the Logans of **Restalrig**. The disused Gogar Kirk, once the focus for a community of some 300 souls, incorporates in the rebuilding of 1890–1 the 16th century chancel of the old church which went out of use in 1602.

Golfer's Land, Canongate

A demolished 17th century tenement, Golfer's Land is commemorated by a plaque on **Jenny Ha's Changehouse** in the **Canongate**. Traditionally the house was raised by John Paterson, a shoemaker and early leather golf ball manufacturer, with the winnings from a **golf** match in which he partnered the Duke of York (later **James VII**) against two Englishmen of the Court of **Holyrood Palace** over **Leith** Links c1671. 'When Paterson, who, in succession to nine ancestors who had been champions, himself won the championship in the Scots' own game, he began to raise on high from the ground this house, which all alone produced so many champions' (Pitcairne, c1700).

Gorgie

An industrial district blending with neighbouring **Dalry**, Gorgie was a scattered agricultural and milling community on the Calders road until the late 19th century. The name is said to derive from the Old Welsh (British) *gorgyne*, a 'spacious wedge', ie the land lying between the **Craiglockhart** Hills (called the 'Craggis of Gorgie' in 1266) and the **Water of Leith** at Saughton. Gorgie Mills, traceable to 1636, became a prosperous glue and gelatin manufactory in the 19th century (closed 1969) under John Cox. Stenhouse, a three-storey rubble mansion built by Patrick Ellis, merchant, in 1623, incorporates part of the earlier residence of the Stanhope family who were granted the operation of Saughton Mills in 1511; saved by the **National Trust for Scotland** in 1937, it became the Stenhouse Conservation Centre, a working arm of the Ancient Monuments Division of the Scottish Development Department, in 1966. Gorgie's institutions include the large North British Distillery and the former Magdalene

320

nstitution (Springwell House) for fallen females, moved from the Canongate in 1861. Heart of Midothian **Football** Club – 'Hearts', 'the Maroons' or 'the am Tarts' – play at Tynecastle Park.

Grange

A leafy, high-walled Victorian villa suburb, the Grange of **St Giles Cathedral** was farmed on the **Burgh Muir** from c1151. The monks forfeited it in 1355 and Grange House was raised by John Cant in 1592. Demolished in 1936, this 'modest house with a jamb' had been grandly reconstructed by the Dick-Lauder family with **William Playfair** in 1831. In the grounds of the Astley Ainslie Hospital stood the chapel of St Roque, the patron saint of pestilence sufferers, demolished in 1791. Built in 1501–4, it served as the town's first isolation hospital. Nearby, in Sciennes Hill House, home of **Adam Ferguson**, the only meeting between **Walter Scott** and **Robert Burns** took place in the winter of 1786–7.

Granton

A vast Victorian harbour on the Firth of Forth between **Cramond** and **Newhaven**, Granton was begun on Wardie Muir by the **Duke of Buccleuch** in 1835; his 'magnificent enterprise' included the grand hotel and offices built by **William Burn** at Granton Square. Granton Pier was completed in 1845; 'upon the pier are 10 jetties, 2 low water slips, 11 warehouses, and 16 cranes' (*New Statistical Account*, 1845). The stone for construction came from Granton Sea **Quarry**, where large **fossil** *Auracariae*, similar to those found at **Craigleith**, were discovered c1839. By 1855 the west breakwater with steam cranes and patent slip for the repair and construction of vessels up to 12,000 tons was complete, and the east break-

water almost so. The West Harbour was improved and extended for the trawler fleet in 1936. The Granton-Burntisland **Railway** Ferry – the world's first – commenced in 1847 connecting Edinburgh, **Perth** and **Dundee**. This ceased on the opening of the **Forth Railway Bridge**, but car and passenger services continued (as the Forth Ferry from 1919) until 1940. Granton is the focus for 'Waterfront Edinburgh', a 15–year £700m plan to regenerate the Forth shore of the city.

Grassmarket

A broad campus 230 yds long lying below the Castle Rock, the Grassmarket lies on the **Old Town** traffic 'ratrun' between the 'chicanes' of the **Cowgate** and the **West Port**. It was probably the 'newbigging' beneath the **Castle** mentioned in 1363 and long served as the corn and livestock mart of the city. In 1560 the corn market was held at the foot of the **West Bow**, but although it was moved in 1587 behind **St Giles Cathedral**, it returned to the Grassmarket in 1716. A new Corn Exchange was erected on the south side of the street in 1849. Bringing cattle into the burgh had been forbidden by **James III** in 1477; beasts were sold at the west end of the Grassmarket at the West Port for almost four centuries until moved (except for horses) in 1843 to Lauriston nearby. The Grassmarket became the location for the model lodginghouses of the city; the former Castle Trades Hotel, built in 1890, is now modernised as Bowfoot House to accommodate single homeless people. At the Bowfoot, on the site of the common gibbet, is the **Covenanters'** Memorial of 1937 commemorating the many martyrs who 'went to glorify God in the Grassmarket'; their corpses were laid out in the **Magdalen Chapel** nearby.

Edinburgh Castle from the Grassmarket c1868 (GWWA)

Greyfriars' Bobby

Greyfriars' Bobby was a Skye Terrier, long believed to have been the loyal companion of 'Auld Jock' Gray, a **Pentland Hills** farmer who each market day dined at John Traill's Restaurant in Greyfriars' Place in the **Grassmarket**. After Gray's death in 1858 Bobby supposedly continued to turn up for food at John Traill's for 14 years, otherwise lying on or near his master's grave in the kirkyard. This story was concocted by John Traill (who did not operate the restaurant until 1862) and was spiced up by Eleanor Atkinson, an American whose 1912 *Greyfriars' Bobby* still sells. A more plausible and just as agreeable version was uncovered by Forbes MacGregor: Greyfriars' Bobby was a police watchdog owned by John Gray, a market policeman residing in the **Cowgate**, who died of pulmonary tuberculosis in 1858. With 'Bobby', Gray assisted in guarding the animal pens in the Grassmarket on the three nights preceding the Wednesday market and regularly lunched in the Greyfriars restaurant. After his owner's demise, the terrier clung to the kirkyard until his own death in 1872 – but not in all weathers, as he was kept well supplied with creature comforts from houses in **Candlemaker Row**. Greyfriars' Bobby is immortalised in a life-size bronze designed by **William Brodie** which sits upon the granite drinking fountain erected (1872) in memory of Bobby's 'affectionate fidelity' by Baroness Burdett-Coutts at the junction of **George IV Bridge** and Candlemaker Row opposite **Greyfriars' Kirkyard**.

Greyfriars' Kirk

A lengthy 'Dutch barn' which has weathered many strange vicissitudes, the Kirk of the Grey Friars in **Candlemaker Row** occupies the former garden of the Greyfriars' monastery. Colonised from the Netherlands in 1447, the Franciscan friary, which was sacked by the **Reformation** mob in 1558, lay in the **Grassmarket** opposite the **West Bow**. In 1562, **Queen Mary** permitted the grounds to serve as the common burial place instead of the congested 'kirk-heugh' of **St Giles Cathedral**. The kirk was built to relieve the congested **Holyrood Abbey**, **Trinity College**, **St Cuthbert's** and St Giles; opened on Christmas Day 1620, it comprised an aisled nave of six bays abutting a four-storey tower at the west end.

After the reimposition of episcopacy by **Charles I**, the Covenanting minister Andrew Ramsay assisted in framing the National **Covenant** which was first subscribed to by the Scots nobility inside the kirk on 28 February 1638. In 1650 the kirk was wrecked while being used as a barracks during the Cromwellian occupation. Greyfriars', along with Trinity College Kirk, the High School and the College (**University of Edinburgh**), 'war all wasted, thair pulpites, daskis, loftes, saittes, windois, dures, lockes, bandis and all uther thair decormentis war all dung doun by these Inglische sodgeris and brunt to asses' (Nicoll, 1650). Reconstruction was precipitated in 1718 when the tower was destroyed by the explosion of gunpowder stored there since 1706.

Greyfriars' Kirkyard

Greyfriars' bristles with the most remarkable medley of 17th and 18th century monuments in Scotland: the Bannatyne monument, for Thomas Bannatyne (d.1635), has its 'cherubed' aedicule carved with a prospect of the city; the bizarre Bayne of Pitcarley enclosure (1684–5) contains a mausoleum and life-size John Bayne (d.1681); the Martyrs' Monument of 1706 and 1771 commemorates the Covenanters, many of whom were executed in the Grassmarket; the classical mausolea of **William Robertson** (d.1793) and **William Adam** (d.1743), the latter done by his son John Adam in 1753, rival the forbiddingly domed tomb of **Sir George MacKenzie of Rosehaugh** (d.1691), probably designed by **James Smith**. 'Bluidy Mackingie, cam oot if ye daur,/Lift the sneck an' draw the bar' (**George Heriot's Hospital** boys' taunt). The most grisly lies on the east wall of the kirk, where a scything skeleton, brandishing an open Bible, dances a jig on top of a skull: the tomb of James Borthwick, surgeon-apothecary (1615–75). In the part of the kirkyard known as the Covenanters' Prison, 1200 prisoners captured at the **Battle of Bothwell Brig** in **Lanarkshire** by the **Duke of Monmouth** were confined for five months in 1679.

'Heave Awa' House'

This is a squat four-storey block in the **High Street** built in 1862 to replace the tenement which on Sunday 24 November 1861 'ran thegither', killing 35 people. An oriel window, supported by the carved head of a boy on the keystone of the arch of Paisley Close, commemorates the trapped lad, Joseph McIvor, who exhorted his rescuers, 'Heave awa' lads, I'm no deid yet' (falsely rendered as 'chaps' and 'dead' on the scroll). Public outrage at the tragedy caused **Thomas Guthrie** and others to lobby the town council to adopt proper health and safety regulations and led to the appointment of **Dr Henry Duncan Littlejohn** as the first Medical Officer of Health in Scotland in 1862. In 1865 the Littlejohn report entitled *On the Sanitary Condition of the City of Edinburgh* coincided with the election of the philanthropic publisher **William Chambers** as Lord Provost, resulting in the 'Improvement Scheme' of 1866 which swept away the congested slum districts of the **Old Town** and created new streets, among them **Blackfriars' Street** and St Mary's Street, with housing for artisans.

High Street

'The body, as well as the soul, of the Scottish capital' (Geddie, 1913), the High Street falls for a third of a mile as a broad, grey stone tenemental canyon from the **Lawnmarket** to the **Netherbow**. 'The street', as **Allan Ramsay** prosaically called it, has masqueraded under many disguises: 'Via Regia' and 'Vicus Regius' (hence **Royal Mile**); 'the King's Hie Streete or Gait'; and just plain 'Market Street', evincing its original function. It was laid out at a width of 100ft (30m) when the burgh was first established by **David I** c1140. Both sides were bordered by sloping 'tofts' or 'lands' averaging 450ft (137m) long and 25ft (7.6m) wide; each 'closour', or enclosure, comprised a quarter of an acre (1 rood). In time 'closour' came to refer to the then private passage or 'close' alongside the timber-framed dwelling which gave access to the plot behind. (A 'wynd' was a public way.) This medieval garden-city perished in 1544 and 1545 when the burgh was burnt by the Earl of Hertford during the **Rough Wooing**.

After 1600, stone was mainly used for building; in 1677 fines were imposed if other materials were used or if roofs were not slated or tiled. From 1675, arcades, like that of **Gladstone's Land**, were imposed on new frontages to create a covered piazza; the new buildings appeared more vertical with flatter faces of dressed and coursed ashlar, and had regular window-lines. These could only be five storeys high from street level after 1674, but rose to 10 or more storeys on the sharp fall behind.

Holyrood Abbey

Only the gaunt ruin of the late-12th and early-13th century nave, adjoining the **Palace of Holyroodhouse**, remains of the once magnificent, cathedral-sized Abbey of Holyrood. The foundation was made by **David I** in 1128. While riding through Abergare (now the **Canongate**), the King became separated from his companions in the Forest of Drumsheugh and was thrown from his horse and wounded in the thigh by a 'muckle hart' near a spring at the foot of **Salisbury Crags**. In grappling with its antlers, a crucifix came into his hands which put the beast to flight. That night David was supposedly advised in a dream to 'make a house for canons devoted to the Cross' (Holyrood Ordinale, c1450). Accordingly, the Monastery of the Holy Rood (cross), a small, cruciform, Norman style foundation, was completed on a site near the spring of St David's Well (now **St Margaret's**) in 1141 for Augustinian (White) Friars.

The present much larger abbey, in the First Pointed Gothic style, was erected c1195–c1230; 'The façade . . . remains one of the finest early medieval compositions in Britain' (RCAHMS, 1950). The nave, or Abbey Kirk (it served the Canongate Parish from c1450) had to be strengthened by flying buttresses in the late 15th century. It was burnt in 1544 by the English under the Earl of Hertford, and the invaders returned to strip the lead from the roof in 1547. The dangerously weakened choir and transepts were demolished after the **Reformation**, in 1570. The east gable was rebuilt, however, with its 'faire new window' for the coronation of **Charles I**. In 1688 the Edinburgh mob purged the recently refurbished Chapel Royal (as it had become when lavishly fitted out by **James VII** in 1687 for his reconstituted **Order of the Knights of the Thistle**); the Royal Vault itself was desecrated and the remains of **David II**, **James V** and **Henry, Lord Darnley** amongst others 'scattered about like those of sheep and oxen' (Wesley, 1780). Apocalypse came in 1768 when, 10 years after the rotten timbered roof was replaced with heavy stone flags, both the vault and clerestory fell during a storm.

Holyroodhouse, Palace of

Official residence of the British monarch in Scotland, the Palace of Holyroodhouse lies at the tail of the **Royal Mile** between the **Calton Hill** and **Arthur's Seat**. The palace evolved from the old royal guesthouse attached to the adjacent **Holyrood Abbey** and from **James IV**'s transferrence of the royal residence in the city from the **Castle** to a new quadrangular edifice at Holyrood in preparation for his wedding to **Margaret Tudor** in 1503. In 1528–32 his son **James V** added the existing tower containing royal apartments for the king and queen; later, in 1535–6 he reconstructed the west front in early Scots Renaissance style.

Although palace and abbey suffered English attack

The Abbey ruins and the Palace of Holyroodhouse below Arthur's Seat (SP)

during the **Rough Wooing**, the former was restored for **Queen Mary**, who was entertaining **David Rizzio** in one of the two closets off the inner chamber when he was snatched by his assassins. The 'house of kings' (**Robert Louis Stevenson**) ceased to be so with **James VI**'s departure for England (1603), but was restored for **Charles I**'s coronation (1633).

After further destruction by fire in 1650, the present, externally rather plain palace, built around an elegant classical piazza, was designed by **Sir William Bruce** and executed by **Robert Mylne** for **Charles II** in 1671–8; the reconstructed north-west tower was balanced by a similar block at the south-west. It briefly came alive in 1745 when **Prince Charles Edward Stewart** held a levée in the Long Gallery, which contains a curious collection of portraits executed by Jacob de Wit in 1684–6 purporting to represent 111 Scots monarchs dating from Fergus in the 4th century BC. George IV held a similar assembly during his jaunt over the border in 1822; but it was **Victoria** and Albert who, after an enjoyable stay in 1856, began to use Holyrood en route for **Balmoral** and re-established the pattern of royal occupation which continues today.

Holyrood Park

A former royal hunting preserve (part of the Forest of Drumsheugh) which largely comprises **Arthur's Seat**, Holyrood Park (also the 'King's' or 'Queen's' Park) lies east of the **Old Town** and **Southside**. First enclosed by **James V** in c1540, it then formed part of the sanctuary (**Abbey Strand**) of **Holyrood Abbey**. In 1564 **Queen Mary** created an artificial loch in Hunter's Bog as a resort for her courtiers. The first Keeper, Sir James Murray of Arngask, was appointed by the **Regent Moray (Lord James Stewart)** in 1567 and in 1646 **Charles I** created Sir James Hamilton of Priestfield (**Prestonfield**) and his heirs Hereditary Keepers, an office enjoyed until 1845 when it was bought back from Thomas Hamilton, 9th Earl of **Haddington**, to stop him quarrying **Salisbury Crags**. During the 1840s the Queen's Drive and Dunsapie Loch were formed at the instigation of Prince Albert; St Margaret's Loch followed in 1856. On the parade ground along the 'Duke's Wall' (named after the Duke of York, **James VII**) from Holyrood to **Meadowbank**, the Royal Scottish Volunteer Review was held in 1860 before 100,000 spectators; in 1881, at the 'Wet Review', a notably smaller contingent witnessed the 40,000 Scottish Volunteers parade before **Queen Victoria**. At the 'Golden Gates' Muschet's Cairn recalls where Nicol Muschett of Boghall, a surgeon's apprentice, slashed the throat of his wife, Margaret Hall, in 1720.

The Hub

The loftiest building in the city, the 240ft octagonal steeple of the old Highland Tolbooth St John's Kirk, transformed internally into the **Edinburgh Festival Centre** during 1994–9, soars even higher than the summit of **Edinburgh Castle** Rock. 'The Hub', which lies at the junction of **Castlehill** and **Thomas Hamilton**'s 'hideous western approach' (Grant, 1884), forms a striking alignment with **New College and Assembly Hall** when viewed from **The Mound**; in fact it was raised in 1839–44 partly to serve the Tolbooth congregation of **St Giles' Cathedral** and, in its 'Victoria Hall', to house the **General Assembly** of the **Church of Scotland**. The architects were **James Gillespie Graham**, who was responsible for the overall form, and A W N Pugin (of later Houses of Parliament fame), who executed the steeple and the fine Gothic detail. Modern artists have introduced bright colours in the interior, using neon, sculpture and stained glass.

Huntly House

Traditionally but erroneously ascribed to **George Gordon, 1st Marquis of Huntly** who lodged somewhere in the **Canongate**, Huntly House adjoins **Acheson House** opposite the **Canongate Tolbooth**. (The name may originate from a later tenant, the Dowager Duchess of Gordon and subsequently her son, Lord Adam Gordon.) In 1517 three houses stood side by side on the site when it was bought by James Acheson. The three were united in 1570 and extended 10ft into the street, with a uniform corbelled-out rubble and ashlar frontage. The Incorporation of Hammermen purchased and partly converted the property for a convening room in 1647 and sold it in 1762; **Robert Mylne** was consulted in the raising of the front by 'two timber-faced and harled storeys with three broad gables to the street' (Gifford et al, 1985) which remain its most notable feature. This remarkable house was saved by Edinburgh Corporation in 1926 and restored as the **City Museum** in 1932. Formerly dubbed 'The Speaking House' because of the series of Latin mottoes inscribed on the façade, it received an additional one in 1932: *ANTI QUA/TAMEN/JUVEN/ESCO* ('However old, I am getting younger').

The Inch

A rough-cast 17th century pile, The Inch languishes as a rather remote community centre in a large park lying between **Liberton** and **Craigmillar**. It occupies an island (*insch*) site on the former flood plain of the Braid Burn; the original access was by drawbridge across a moat. The three-storey, L-plan house was built for James Winram, Keeper of the Great Seal of Scotland, in 1617 on land granted to **Holyrood Abbey** by **James II**. George Winram, Lord Liberton, a noted **Covenanter**, added a two-storey extension, dated by its dormers to 1634; mortally wounded at the **Battle of Dunbar** against Cromwell in 1650, he possessed the Protector's Sword, a spoil from the Battle of Naseby in 1645. In 1660 the Inch was acquired, together with **Craigmillar Castle**, by Sir John Gilmour, Lord President of the **Court of Session**; the Gilmours probably added the west wing when they transferred their main seat from Craigmillar at the end of the 18th century. A century later Robert Wolrige Gordon Gilmour of Liberton and Craigmillar extensively modernised and extended The Inch; two vaulted chambers and the main hall of the tower, connected by a little stair in the thickness of the wall, survive.

Ingliston

The scene of the Royal Highland Show since 1960, Ingliston near Edinburgh Airport was 'seized' as a permanent site in 1958 by the Royal Highland and Agricultural Society (instituted in 1784). Ingliston House, its 'eccentric baronial' headquarters, was built in 1846 for William Mitchell Innes; the policies became a **golf course** in 1934 when, to make the 12th green, 'Wallace's Switch', a lime tree 23ft (7m) in circumference was felled. The Barony of Ingliston was created for James Inglis in 1631 when the lands of (Kirk)Liston were relinquished by the 4th Lord Torpichen, a descendant of Sir James Sandilands, Preceptor of **Torpichen Priory** and head of the Order of the Knights of St John in Scotland; before 1312 'Temple Liston' had been granted to the Knights Templar by **David I**. 'Ingalstoun' (1406) is thought to be derived from the Scandinavian personal name Ingialdr. The Ingliston Stone, the only **Roman** milestone discovered in Scotland, was found nearby by **Sir Robert Sibbald**; it records road repairs dating to c140 AD and is in the **Royal Museum of Scotland**. The Cat Stane, or 'Battle Stone' by the River Almond marks the burial place of 'Vetta, son of Victor', claimed by **Sir James Young Simpson** to have been the grandfather of Hengist and Horsa, the Jutes who first colonised Kent.

James' Court, Lawnmarket

'A well-known pile of buildings which rises to a vast height at the end of the Earthen **Mound**' (Grant, 1884), James' Court, with its three narrow entrances off the **Lawnmarket**, was speculatively erected (and named) by James Brownhill, wright, during 1723–7. Mimicking **Milne's Court** immediately to the west, it was an early and bold attempt at modernisation in the **Old Town**; the occupants employed their own clerk and scavenger and enjoyed a private lime-tree garden on the north side. Both **David Hume** and **James Boswell** resided

in the massive double north tenement which was destroyed by fire in 1857 and reconstructed 1858–60 by David Cousin in Scots Jacobean style. Of Brownhill's design, only the adjoining eight-storey block, converted to apartments in 1981–2, survives externally intact. In 1895, after a century of neglect, **Patrick Geddes**, who had moved into No 6 James' Court, remodelled the south-east block in Victorian romantic style.

Jenny Ha's Changehouse

The memory of a tavern kept in the 18th century by the hospitable Janet Hall is preserved by the modern public house standing adjacent to **Whitefoord House** in the **Canongate**. Celebrated for its claret drawn straight from the butt, the tavern was a favourite haunt of **Jacobites** who toasted 'the King owre the watter' in 'cappie ale' drunk from wooden 'caups' or **quaichs**, well laced with 'wee thochts' or nips of brandy. Around 1730 it was the sanctum of the English poet John Gay (1685–1732), author of the satirical *Beggar's Opera*, who was often accompanied by **Allan Ramsay**. Gay came to the capital as the private secretary to his crazy patroness, 'Kitty', Duchess of Queensberry ('la Singularité'). The wildest habitué of this howff, however, was the 'Singing Accountant', Jamie Balfour, whose ribaldry is commemorated in wrought-iron on the railings of the veterans' bowling green lying between Whitefoord House and **Whitehorse Close**.

John Knox House, High Street

Buttressing **Moubray House**, the 'improbably picturesque' John Knox House projects its overhanging

John Knox House abutted by Moubray House, or the 'Knox's Temperance Hotel' of George Washington Wilson's day (GWWA)

gables into the **High Street** above the **Netherbow**. An outstanding example of Scots pre-**Reformation** burgh architecture, its tradition as the manse of the great **Presbyterian** reformer is founded only on a reference to its 'tottering bow-window . . . whence **Knox** thundered his addresses to the people' (Murray, 1799). The original two-storey rubble block of c1500 was encased with ashlar in the mid-16th century when an extra storey and attic were added; probably by James Mossman, goldsmith, and his wife Mariot Arres whose armorial bearings are carved on the frontage. Literally a sermon in stone, the house presents a figure of Moses in the shape of a sundial at its corner while a long frieze over the windows of the ground-floor shop has the injunction:

LOVE.GOD.ABVFE.AL.AND.YI.NYCHTBOVR.AS.YI.SELF.

Subdivision occasioned the steep forestair leading to the present entrance, recessed within a rare timbered gallery. Condemned in 1849 as 'an encumbrance to the street', the house was saved by the **Society of Antiquaries of Scotland** and **Henry, Lord Cockburn**, and expensively renovated in 1853. More restorations in 1982 revealed striking painted panels and a fireplace of the 16th century. Operated by the **Church of Scotland** as the John Knox House Museum displaying relics of the reformer, the shop premises are the 'Old Town Enquiry Centre' managed by the adjoining Netherbow Centre, with which it was fully integrated in 1991.

Joppa

'A smokey, malodorous place, consisting of a group of sooty buildings situated on the sea-shore half way between **Portobello** and **Musselburgh**' was how Joppa appeared to **William Chambers** in 1815 when the future publisher and Lord Provost moved there with his brother **Robert**, their father having been appointed manager of the Salt Works. The production of salt by evaporating seawater using **coal** from the shallow local mines had been carried on in Joppa since 1631. More pollution was provided by the brickworks and **quarries**. As the century progressed these industries declined and Joppa assumed a new role as a fashionable watering place for Edinburgh's affluent middle classes. Very soon it became a desirable place to live all the year round, and building development accelerated when the **railway** shortened the journey time to Edinburgh. In the 20th century the villas of earlier years were joined by a few tenements and 1930s bungalows. The salt works closed in 1953 and the site was cleared a few years later. Only a few renovated colliers' and salters' cottages remain as a reminder of its industrial past.

Juniper Green

A former grain, paper and snuff milling settlement which began c1600 by the **Water of Leith** beyond Kingsknowe, Juniper Green is now joined to **Currie** and **Balerno**, its western neighbours, by suburban sprawl. It developed c1800 in a waste of whin and **juniper** and, like **Colinton**, housed the summer villa quarters of Edinburgh citizens; notably Gowanlea, where **Thomas** and **Jane Carlyle** resided for a spell. The earliest and longest-working snuff mills were at Juniper Green; the

East Mill (1749) continued grinding until 1920, while Watt's Snuff Mill (1763) closed c1943. Woodhall Mill (1747) worked lint, then paper and finally cardboard from 1964–84. Curriemuir Mill (1704) is still active as Inglis' Woodhall Grain Mill electrically drying corn; Mossy Mill (1664) also produced paper. Woodhall House (c1630) long housed the **Bannatyne Manuscript** while Baberton House (Kilbaberton), an L-shaped, three-storey turreted affair, was built in 1622–3 by Sir James Murray, the designer of **Parliament House**.

King's Theatre

Long the leading theatre in the city, the King's was built in 1905 and has a great tradition of revue, legitimate theatre and pantomime. It is owned by Edinburgh City Council after many years in the former Howard and Wyndham circuit, and is a touring theatre, used for opera during the **Edinburgh International Festival**. There were originally three balconies, the topmost being removed in 1951.

Kirk o'Field

The collegiate church of St Mary in the Field ('The Kirk o'Field') stood on the site of the **University of Edinburgh** in **South Bridge**. Founded by the Augustinian (White) Friars of **Holyrood Abbey**, it is first recorded in 1275 during the reign of **Alexander III**; it was originally located outside the **Town Wall** – ie 'in the fields' – until enclosed by the **Flodden Wall** after 1513. Granted collegiate status c1500–11, its prebendaries and 'hospital' were burnt by the Earl of Hertford during the English invasion of 1544; the kirk itself was destroyed during the **Reformation** in 1558.

The 'Kirk o'Field' was the scene of the murder in 1567 of **Henry Stewart, Lord Darnley**, consort and 'king' of **Queen Mary**. The Old Provost's House where Darnley lay, confined with either smallpox or syphilis 'in a place of good air where he might best recover his health' (Melvil), was blown up under cover of darkness probably by order of **James Hepburn, 4th Earl of Bothwell**, the lover of the Queen. The unscathed bodies of Darnley and his retainer, clothed in their nightshirts, were found in the fields outside a small postern gate in the Flodden Wall.

Kirkliston

A former farming and milling village above the river Almond in west Edinburgh, Kirkliston is famed for its late-12th century Norman church which, although more altered than nearby **Dalmeny Kirk**, still preserves its tower (somewhat truncated to form a saddle-back roof) with elaborately carved south door. The Newliston aisle of the **Dalrymples of Stair** includes Margaret Ross (d.1692), wife of the notorious **1st Earl of Stair** and the prototype of Lady Ashton in *The Bride of Lammermoor* by **Sir Walter Scott**. The Barony of Liston (from the Gaelic *lios*, garden) was anciently held by the Knights Hospitallers of **Torphichen**; a **burgh of regality** was created in 1621 for the Earl of Winton. Lin's Mill, near the Almond Aqueduct of the **Union Canal**, has a stone commemorating the dust of William Lin (d.1645), locally claimed to have been the last man in Scotland to die of the plague. While Edward I was encamped at Kirkliston before defeating **William Wallace** at **Falkirk** in 1298 his Welshmen mutinied, slaying 18 English ecclesiastics and going over to the Scots' side; 'I care not,' said the 'Hammer of the Scots', 'let my enemies go and join my enemies; I trust that in one day I shall chastise them all.'

Lady Stair's House

A three-storey detached mansion, Lady Stair's House occupies Lady Stair's Close off the **Lawnmarket**. It was built by the wealthy merchant Sir William Gray of Pittendrum in 1622; his eldest daughter disponed to Elizabeth, Dowager Countess of Stair (the widow of **John Dalrymple, 1st Earl of Stair**) in 1719. At the instigation of **Patrick Geddes**, the house was saved from demolition by **Archibald Primrose, 5th Earl of Rosebery**, a collateral descendant of Lady Stair; and during 1895–7 it was re-interpreted in early-17th century style. Gifted to the city in 1907, the mock-medieval interior, now 'The Writers' Museum', displays the City of Edinburgh collection of literary relics of **Robert Burns**, **Walter Scott** and **Robert Louis Stevenson**.

Lady Yester's Kirk

Lying forlornly in Infirmary Street, Lady Yester's Kirk was founded by its 'pious and noble' benefactress, Margaret Ker, daughter of the 1st Earl of Lothian, and wife of James, Lord Hay of Yester, in 1644–7. Lady Hay, as she should be styled, built the original kirk which was at the south-east corner of High School Wynd. In 1650, like **Trinity College** and **Greyfriars'**, it suffered greatly at the hands of Cromwell. In 1803–5 the old kirk was replaced by the present one for 1212 hearers, erected west of the original site on the garden of the **Blackfriars'** Monastery. 'Though tasteless and nondescript in style, it was considered an ornament to that part of the city' (Grant, 1844). The tomb and memorial tablet of its benefactress were both rebuilt into the new church, but it is unlikely that her body was also moved. The tablet reads: 'Pos'd was thy life, prepared thy happy end;/Nothing in either was without commend./Let it be the case of all who live hereafter,/To live and die, like Margaret, Lady Yester./Who died 15th March 1647. Her age 75.'

Lauriston Castle, Cramond

Formerly 'a bare solitary keep . . . staring on the Firth', Lauriston Castle was reborn as a neat Jacobean Revival mansion in 1827. The existing four-storey T-shaped Tower of Lauriston was begun next to the ruin of its predecessor c1590 by Archibald Napier of **Merchiston** after his second marriage to Elizabeth Moubray of Barnbougle [see **Dalmeny House**]; thereby providing Alexander, his eldest son and heir, with an estate. The horoscope or 'celestial theme' of Alexander Napier on the tower front was disarmingly juxtaposed in 1905 with the inscription of Robert Dalgleish, solicitor, who purchased Lauriston in 1656; 'I do not acknowledge the stars as either the rulers of life or the causes of good fortune . . .'. Dalgleish's daughter sold out in 1683 to the wealthy goldsmith William Law, whose brilliant but wayward eldest son **John Law** is synonymous with Lauriston, although he never lived there. The pioneer of paper money, he inherited the family's financial acu-

men and became Comptroller General of the finances of France.

In 1827 Thomas Allan, a banker and noted amateur mineralogist, after whom 'Allanite' is named, employed **William Burn** to extend the tower: 'Mr Burn, architect, would fain have had the old house pulled down, which I wonder at him' (**Scott**, 1827). The present grand Edwardian decorated showpiece was produced during the term of the last private owner, William Robert Reid, the proprietor of a classy cabinet-making firm, son-in-law of William Barton, a sanitary engineer whose company installed the magnificent plumbing, central heating and electric lighting in 1902. A connoisseur of fine English and French 18th century furniture and *objets d'art*, Reid bequeathed the house and contents to the nation in 1926 'with a view to the education of the public taste'. The house is maintained by the City of Edinburgh as a museum, notably displaying a collection of some 100 pieces of Blue John Ware, ornaments made from rare translucent Derbyshire fluorspar often mounted in Sheffield ormulu.

Lawnmarket

The westerly continuation of the **High Street** towards **Castlehill**, the Lawnmarket formed the nucleus of the burgh founded by **David I** in c1140; over 500ft (150m) long and, before encroachments, about 100ft (30m) broad, the cloth market was established there by **James III** in 1477. The original street name was the 'landmarket' where produce from the 'landward' districts was sold. 'On the southern side of the land-market street, corruptly called the lawn-market, on Wednesdays is held a market for **Linnen** and **Woolen** Cloth' (Maitland, 1753). In the 18th century 'The Lawn Mercat' was 'the chief quarter for persons of distinction' (Mackenzie, 1927); the street preserves some of the best continuous groups of close and courtyard architecture surviving in the **Old Town**. Apart from **James'**, **Milne's** and **Riddle's Courts** and **Brodie's Close**, Thomas Fisher's Land is a grand rubble and ashlar double tenement of 1726 and 1752, which was re-built in 1964 partly as the Scottish Central Library of the **Carnegie** Trust. Next to **Gladstone's Land** is the balustraded 'Burns' Land', a curious Scots and Queen Anne confabulation built 1892–3; **Robert Burns** first lodged in the city in 1768 in Baxter's Close near to the entrance to **Lady Stair's House**.

Liberton

A once scattered country village which still largely consists of three Libertons – Nether, Over and Kirk – Liberton lies in the south-eastern suburbs of Edinburgh between **Craigmillar** and **Comiston**. It is erroneously thought to derive from 'leper toun', a hospital for sufferers supposedly having existed nearby, but the family name 'Libertoun' was known 139 years before any outbreak of the disease was recorded near Edinburgh. The 'Chapel of Liberton' with the mill at Nether Liberton, formerly the property of **St Cuthbert's Kirk**, was granted to **Holyrood Abbey** by **David I** in c1143–7 when one Malbet or MacBeth (not the usurper) was Baron of Liberton. The ancient Liberton Kirk, which resembled that of **Corstorphine**, was demolished for the present semi-Gothic creation executed by **James Gillespie Graham** in 1815. Liberton Tower, a gaunt but unusually complete early 16th century tower house of four storeys with slab roof, was built c1500 for Dalmahoy of that Ilk. Liberton House was built c1600 for William Little of Liberton, a merchant who bought the Barony of Over Liberton in 1587. The nearby St Catherine's Balm Well ('the oily well'), recorded in 1526 by **Hector Boece**, is contained in a small vaulted well-house blackened by the bituminous liquid derived from underlying coal deposits; built by order of **James VI** in 1617, it was despoiled by Cromwellian troops but later restored.

Lothian Road

A robust thoroughfare spuriously 'made in a day' in 1785 by **Sir John Clerk of Penicuik**, Lothian Road runs from near Tollcross to the 'West End' of **Princes Street**. The red **Dumfries** sandstone Caledonian Hotel was raised from 1898–1902 on the substructure of the Caledonian Railway Station; the old station yard site is occupied by the Edinburgh Conference and Business Centre. Behind the **Usher Hall** and Royal Lyceum Theatre in Castle Terrace is Saltire House, a cultural and commercial complex, including the Traverse Theatre, which was completed in 1991. Occupying the infamous 'Hole in the Ground' intended for the Edinburgh Opera House which lay vacant for 25 years, this, the most important civic building erected in the city for over 50 years, stands on the site of 'Poole's' Synod Hall, built by James Gowans, until its demolition in 1966. Lothian House stands on the site of Port Hopetoun, a basin at the termination of the **Union Canal**.

Luckenbooths and Krames

A four-storey, timber-fronted pile with 'locked' (ie enclosed) shops, the Luckenbooths encroached into the middle of the **High Street** at **St Giles** until their demolition in 1817. This medieval shopping centre was first (1440) built by the city to raise revenue for the erection of St Giles into a collegiate kirk. Crammed between the kirk buttresses and the Luckenbooth tenement rear were the 'Krames' (German *Kramerai* – 'shopping') – tiny, open wooden stalls first set up by 'shopless traffickers', mainly mercers and clothiers, c1560. 'And merchantis at the stink- and style/Ar hamperit in ane honey came' (**Dunbar**, c1500). The silver (or pewter) 'Luckenbooth Brooch' with its two intertwined hearts design, which is still sometimes given as a token of betrothal, originated here.

Magdalen Chapel

A dusty jewel buried in the **Cowgate** beneath **George IV Bridge**, the Magdalen Chapel was, like the **Tailors' Hall** and **St Giles**, intimately connected with the medieval trades incorporations. The chapel was erected 1541–5 as a bequest of Michael MacQuehen or MacQueen (d.1537) who left £700 Scots towards its building costs which included an almshouse or hospital for seven 'bedemen'; his widow, Janet Rynd, who was later interred within, contributed a further £2000 when other donations were not forthcoming. The confirmation charter of 1547 provided for the patronage of the hospital, dedicated to St Mary Magdalene, to pass to the powerful Incorporation of Hammermen after

the death of the foundress, which occurred in 1553.

During the **Reformation** the chapel's furnishings were destroyed; but in 1578 it hosted what is often erroneously referred to as the first meeting of the **General Assembly of the Church of Scotland** – in effect the birth of **Presbyterianism** under the stewardship of **Andrew Melville**.

The chapel was converted for the Convening Hall of the Hammermen in 1614–15; the steeple tower, with its corbelled bartizan and octagonal lead spire terminating in an ogival head with globe and weather-cock, was added later, 1620–5. The heraldic insignia of the Hammermen over the entrance 'is undoubtedly the most handsome piece of decorative stone-carving to be seen in a similar position in Edinburgh' (RCAHMS, 1950).

Mary King's Close

A steep early-17th century alley in the **High Street** still substantially remaining beneath the **City Chambers** (constructed above it 1753–61), Mary King's Close is likely named after the daughter of a former owner, Alexander King, advocate. 'One of the last strongholds of the plague [1645], the close acquired the reputation of being haunted, and was abandoned about the middle of the 17th century' (RCAHMS, 1950). Some property, however, was occupied prior to a fire at the south end in 1750, for Andrew Bell, the engraver who conceived the *Encyclopaedia Britannica*, then removed from there to nearby **Advocate's Close**; the north end was 'roofless and ruined' in 1845, prior to the construction of **Cockburn Street**.

> Turn, citizens, to God; repent, repent
> And pray your bedlam frenzies may relent;
> Think not rebellion a trifling thing,
> This plague doth fight for Marie and the King.
> (**Drummond of Hawthornden**, 1645)

Meadowbank

The soot-blackened, tenemental canyon on the London Road and **railway** above **Restalrig** is 'broken' by the 15,000 seater Meadowbank Stadium and Sports Centre erected for the Commonwealth Games of 1970. (The Royal Commonwealth Pool cuts a dash on the other side of **Holyrood Park** at **Newington**.) In the 19th century Meadowbank housed the 'Cow Palace', a great dairy guzzling off the **Craigentinny** meadows, where five bumper crops of hay were produced each year through sewage irrigation. Behind the stadium crouches Marionville House, a gloomy mid-18th century mansion raised by the Misses Ramsay with the proceeds of their **High Street** shop selling 'lappet' cloth. Jock's Lodge, where Cromwell was initially repulsed in 1650, 'is said to have derived its name from an eccentric mendicant . . . who built himself a hut there' (Grant, 1884). Piershill was the site of the cavalry barracks, built 1793, until the Scottish Horse 'rode out' to Redford at **Colinton** in 1913.

Meadows and Bruntsfield Links

Formerly the Burgh Loch, lying south of the **Old Town** in the **Burgh Muir**, the Meadows were reclaimed

(1722–40) by Thomas Hope of Rankeillour, President of 'The Honourable Society of Improvers in the Knowledge of Agriculture in Scotland' which met in his house at their east end. Hope had secured a lease on condition that he laid out a ditched walk, enclosed by a hedge, alongside which he planted a row of lime trees. 'Under these poor trees walked and talked and meditated all our literary and scientific and many of our legal worthies' (**Cockburn**, 1856). Opened as a public park in 1860, the Meadows housed the International Exhibition of Industry, Science and Art in 1886.

Bruntsfield links are the last vestige of the Burgh Muir and are renowned for their venerable 36 short-hole **golf course** where the royal game has been played since the 15th century. The Golf Tavern claims a doubtfully long pedigree from 1456.

Frowning over all is the vast 'Transylvanian Gothic' Barclay (Bruntsfield) Kirk. Designed by **Frederick Pilkington** in 1862–4, its 250ft (76m) spire dominates the southern skyline; 'the most disorderly building in the city . . . like a congregation of elephants, rhinoceroses and hippopotamuses with their snouts in a manger and their posteriors turned to the golf players on the links' (Blackie, 1888).

Melville Monument

Modelled on Trajan's Column in Rome, the Melville Monument in the centre of **St Andrew Square** commemorates **Henry Dundas, 1st Viscount Melville**, who 'like a colossus' bestrode late-18th century Scotland. It is a fluted, unornamented Doric column and pedestal, 122ft (37m) high, surmounted by a 14ft (4.2m) statue of Lord Melville. Raised 'by the voluntary contributions of the officers, petty officers, seamen and marines of these united kingdoms', it was designed in 1821 by **William Burn**; he was advised by **Robert Stevenson**, engineer, about the foundation after the residents of the square voiced their fears over its intended height above their houses. The statue, added as an afterthought in 1828, was carved by Robert Forrest from a model made by Sir Francis Chantrey.

Mercat Cross, High Street

Primarily the focus for trade in the medieval burgh, the Mercat Cross also served as a place of execution, a centre of public rejoicing and entertainments, and the locus at which royal proclamations were made. It has probably stood near to its present site just off the **High Street** in **Parliament Square** since the foundation of the burgh by **David I**. In 1503 the 'Cross' basin flowed with wine when **James IV** returned with his bride, **Margaret Tudor**, to celebrate the marriage of 'The Thistle and the Rose'; and in 1513 the '**Blue Blanket**' summoned the citizens to the 'Cross' prior to the fatal march to **Flodden**.

It was rebuilt to widen the street for the royal visit of **James VI** and Queen Anne (1617); a 20ft (6m) shaft, surmounted by the salvaged 15th century capital, was raised on top of a drum-shaped platform. The unpopular demolition of this Cross in 1756 followed the building of the Royal Exchange (now the **City Chambers**) as the bourse for local merchants.

The broken shaft and capital were transferred to '**The Drum**' near **Gilmerton** where a replica still remains. These pieces (the shaft now only 14ft/4.2m) were returned in 1866 and briefly re-erected on a stepped base. The existing Mercat Cross was reconstructed on an octagonal drum, modelled on the likely design of the 1617 restoration, in 1885, largely due to the generosity of W E Gladstone, MP for **Midlothian**. In 1970, however, the eroded shaft and the capital were replaced. The capital, and the eight medallions proclaiming the royal arms of Britain, Scotland, England and Ireland with the arms of Edinburgh, **Leith**, **Canongate** and the **University**, were painted and gilded in 1990.

Merchiston (Castle)

A superior Victorian villa district off Colinton Road near **Morningside**, 'Merchiston' was mentioned as early as 1266 in the Exchequer Rolls. The Tower of Merchiston, since 1964 the stony heart of the 60-times greater Napier University, is a 15th century 4/5 storey L-plan tower house firmly founded upon naked rock. Probably built by Sir Alexander Napier, whose son Sir Archibald erected **Lauriston Castle**, it became the residence of his remarkable grandson **John Napier**, inventor of logarithms. Merchiston Castle School occupied it 1833–1930 before moving to **Colinton** Castle. It contains a highly accomplished painted beamed ceiling of 1591 brought in 1964 from Prestongrange near **Tranent**. In Napier Road nearby stood 'Rockville', popularly styled 'The Pagoda House', built by the architect James Gowans for himself in 1858 and demolished in 1966. Opposite, 'Lammerburn' echoes the technically advanced system of construction employed by Gowans; a standardised 2ft module consisting of a sandstone grid filled with variegated bonded rubble. His 'Waverley' designed in 1884 for the pen-maker Duncan Cameron near **Craiglockhart** has nib-clusters for chimney pots. ('They come as a boon and a blessing to men,/The "Pickwick", the "Owl" and the "Waverley" pen.')

Milne's Court, Lawnmarket

Built in 1690, Milne's Court was the work of **Robert Mylne** in partnership with Andrew Paterson, Deacon of Wrights. The court, situated immediately west of **James' Court** on the north side of the **Lawnmarket**, was the first symmetrically planned development in the **Old Town**. Following his single prototype scheme, 'Milne's Square', opposite the **Tron Kirk**, Mylne built two substantial 5/6-storey blocks, containing 4/5 'fire-rooms', on the north and south of the site cleared of overcrowded closes, while retaining the existing property on the east and west sides. His 'great square building' was for 'the decorment of the good Town' and 'the great convenience and accommodation' of its citizens. Both blocks were restored in 1968–70, incorporating a rebuilt east side, as student residences by the **University of Edinburgh**. The west side was demolished in 1883 for extensions to the adjoining **Assembly Hall**.

Moray House

Built c1625 for Mary Sutton, the Dowager Countess of Home, Moray House fronts the **Canongate** with a lofty gable and tall Tudor chimneys; her daughter, Margaret, Countess of **Moray**, added the east wing c1647. The tall pyramidal capped gate-piers once led to terraced gardens 'of such elegance and cultivated with much care' (Buchanan, 1649), a resort of **Charles I**. Oliver Cromwell occupied the house in 1648, returning in 1650 after the **Battle of Dunbar**. There seems little foundation, however, in the story of the wedding party of **Archibald Campbell, 1st Marquis of Argyll** assailing **James Graham, Marquis of Montrose**, en route to his execution in 1650 from the massively corbelled first-floor balcony. In 1707 the then occupant, **James Ogilvie, Earl of Seafield**, the Lord Chancellor, with his neighbour **James Douglas, Duke of Queensberry**, the Lord High Commissioner, attempted to sign the Articles of the **Treaty of Union** in the still extant garden pavilion, much to the fury of the populace. In 1845 the house became the **United Free Church** Training College from which developed the Moray House Institute of Education campus of today. Inside, both the Cromwell and Balcony Rooms contain exquisite plaster ceilings and richly carved wooden panelling of the 17th century.

Morningside

A populous south-western suburb, butt of countless **music hall** jibes about douce middle-class respectability, Morningside is bordered by the **Grange, Merchiston, Craiglockhart** and **Comiston**. Its portals stand at the Burghmuirhead on 'Holy Corner' by Colinton Road, where four churches shepherd the approaching soul. 'Edinburgh's Bible-belt', however lies at the foot of Morningside Road across the Jordan, a canalised streamlet where lay the land of 'little Egypt', seemingly settled by gypsies in the 16th century; biblical tags such as 'Nile', 'Canaan' and 'Eden' abound on both banks for the names of streets and houses. Little remains of the old village which from c1800 grew into the 'Montpellier of **Midlothian**', a veritable land of milk and honey for villa-quartered valetudinarians. One such, the local laird Francis Garden, Lord Gardenstone, bought Morningside House (c1780–c1895) in 1789, the same year that he built **St Bernard's Well**. East Morningside House (c1726) on Churchhill was the summer residence of the novelist **Susan Ferrier** during the first half of the 19th century.

The older, now vanished, village of Tipperlin nearby was renowned for its damask weaving in the 18th century. Tipperlin Chemical Works was established in 1770 by Dr Thomas Steel, a surgeon who also built a magnesia factory at Canaan in 1797 which supplied the vital ingredient for the pulverised rhubarb and ginger concoction called 'Gregory's Mixture' (**Dr James Gregory** resided at Canaan Lodge). Further industry and ribbon tenement development followed in the late 19th century, but hardly resulted in 'Sodom and Gomorrah' in Morningside; the Volunteer Arms (called 'The Canny Man's' after the proprietor who urged drouthy carters to 'Ca canny man') was the only 'local' for many years. Carter David Loch was robbed in 1814 on Braid Road where the 'Hanging Stanes' mark the place of execution of his assailants Thomas Kelly and Henry O'Neil, the last felons in Scotland despatched on the spot for the crime of highway robbery.

Morocco Land

A reduced 18th century tenement in the **Canongate** replicated in 1957, Morocco Land is named from the enigmatic figure of a Moor adorning its front. Tradition claims that this turbanned and necklaced effigy represents Andrew Grey who, having fled the city to escape arrest for rioting 10 years earlier, returned in 1645 as the captain of a Barbary rover intent on vengeance of Lord Provost John Smith, whose daughter he cured of plague and married instead. A Smith-Gray connection with the property is indeed probable – the 17th century mannikin bears a heraldic device for Smith, and Thomas Gray purchased the original house on that site in 1653; a more prosaic explanation is that the figure is a trades sign, Auld Reekie's equivalent of the cigar-store Indian.

Morton House

Although traditionally the townhouse of the **Regent Morton** who was implicated in the murder of **Lord Darnley**, Morton House in **Blackfriars' Street** probably post-dates him (c1600). Until last century, projecting timber galleries overhung the street; the semi-octagonal stairtower has a late Gothic ogival-headed doorway with a heraldic tympanum similar to one at **Boswell's Court**. Morton (**James Douglas, 4th Earl**) was beheaded in 1581 by the 'Iron Maiden' (now in the **Royal Museum of Scotland** in **Queen Street**), an instrument of execution which he himself had introduced: '. . . a maiden from Halifax. You never saw the like of her, and she'll clasp you round the neck, and your head will remain in her arms' (**Scott**, *The Abbot*).

Mortonhall

An imposing Palladian mansion of three storeys, built for Thomas Trotter in 1769, Mortonhall lies south of the **Braid Hills** between **Comiston** and **Liberton**. Although now divided into luxury apartments, it retains its original interior. In 1765 Trotter, a successful **Cowgate** brewer, demolished the original fortified house purchased in 1635 by John Trotter, 1st Baron of Mortonhall. Family legend declares that their equine name was bestowed by **James III** upon an ancestor who, although his own mount was lame, quickly aided the King in his hour of need; the Trotter arms have a man holding a horse's reins and bear the motto In Promptu. The dower house, Morton House, begun c1705 as a small two-storey Queen Anne period-piece, was given a typically Georgian front c1800; an early 18th century, two-storey belvedere nearby remains 'mightily well situated' (Whyte, 1792).

Moubray House

Abutting **John Knox House** in the **High Street**, Moubray House is the oldest occupied dwelling in Edinburgh, possibly having survived the burning of the city by the Earl of Hertford in 1544. Robert Moubray, a cadet of Barnbougle, built the house as early as 1477, but the present four-storey rubble frontage dates from c1630. The timber-gabled house extends greatly to the rear, supported on massive corbelling in Trunk's Close, where Andrew Moubray, wright, built a 'new' tenement in 1529. Restored by the **Cockburn** Society in 1910, the house was the residence of the artist **George Jamesone** and also has a long literary tradition; in 1710

Daniel Defoe edited the *Edinburgh Courant* from here, and later the shop below was the original premises of **Archibald Constable**.

The Mound

Traditionally begun by an **Old Town** tailor as an improvised causeway – 'Geordie Boyd's Muckle Brig' – in order to reach his **New Town** customers across the partly drained **Nor' Loch** after 1763, The Mound had become a rough ride for carriages by 1784. The 'Earthen Mound' was, on its completion in 1830, calculated to comprise over two million cartloads of 'travelled earth' dug from the foundations of the New Town. 'This is a work unrivalled by any but Alexander the Great's at Tyre' (Creech, 1793). Plans for a proper roadway via Bank Street (built in 1798) to the head of the **Lawnmarket**, first proposed by **Thomas Hamilton** and **William Burn** in 1824, were incorporated in the Improvement Act of 1827; the present scheme was conducted by Hamilton in 1834–5. Nevertheless it is the architect **William Playfair** who is remembered on The Mound: Playfair designed both the **Royal Scottish Academy** in 1822 and the **National Gallery of Scotland** in 1850 which lie at its foot, as well as the **New College and Assembly Hall** (1845–50) at its head.

Murrayfield

The location of the Scottish **Rugby** Union Stadium – inaugurated in 1925 with a 14–11 win over England – Murrayfield lies off **Corstorphine** Road. Murrayfield House was begun by Archibald Murray, advocate, of Cringletie near **Peebles** in 1735; his son Alexander, Lord Henderland, Solicitor General for Scotland, extended it in 1773; his grand-nephew, Sir John Archibald Murray, MP for **Leith** and founder of the *Edinburgh Review*, succeeded **Francis Jeffrey** as Lord Advocate. Murrayfield was developed for villas and terraces from c1860; an industrial wedge intrudes from **Gorgie** at Roseburn.

Roseburn House of three storeys was begun in c1582 by Mungo Russel, merchant burgess who operated **Dalry** Mills, the earliest Scottish paper manufactory. The house was acquired in 1704 by Agnes Campbell, widow of Andrew Anderson, King's Printer, who despite opposition managed to have the appointment bestowed upon herself in 1712. Coltbridge over the **Water of Leith** is 'fancifully derived from the colt which wrought the ferry before the bridge was built' (Boog-Watson, 1920); at the 'Canter of Coltbridge' in 1745 Sir John Cope's cavalry shied off at the sight of only seven struggling Highlanders.

On Corstorphine Hill, Beechwood (Murrayfield Hospital) was built in 1780 for Francis Scott of Harden, and Belmont in 1828 by **William Playfair** for Lord Mackenzie. At Ravelston Dykes, Ravelston House (Mary Erskine School, and model for 'Tully-Veolan' in **Scott**'s *Waverley*) was built for Sir Alexander Keith in c1790; a Palladian pile, it replaced the early-17th century house of George Foulis, goldsmith, of **Colinton**, the tower of which remains. His daughter Marian was abducted in 1654 by a musician, Andrew Hill, who was accused of sorcery; while the judge delayed sentence for 15 days, Hill 'was so eaten and torn by vermin in prison that he died' (Grant, 1884).

Museum of Childhood

The collection of toys, books, games, hobbies and other childhood memorabilia in the Museum of Childhood was pioneered by Joseph Patrick Murray (d.1981), an optician and town councillor who claimed that he did not care for children. As curator, he stated in the first guidebook 'This is not a children's museum, it is a museum about them.' He was moved to found the museum in 1955 when he learned of the plight of two dolls, once owned by **Queen Victoria**, which were destined for London because no place in Scotland would display them. 'A pitiful handful of soldiers, building blocks and railway stuff' of his own was briefly kept in **Lady Stair's House** before removal – with much else – in 1957 to the present **High Street** location in the 18th century 'Hyndford House'. In 1986 the Museum was refurbished and extended into the adjacent South Gray's Close as part of a wider local rebuilding programme. Happily, the area is traditionally recalled as a playful place where romped the three beautiful daughters of Lady Maxwell of Monreith who occupied the second floor c1760; on one occasion Jane, later **Duchess of Gordon**, was seen riding on a sow which a sister thumped 'lustily behind with a stick' (Chambers, 1868).

Museum of Scotland

Like the **Scottish Parliament**, the Museum of Scotland – opened on St Andrew's Day 1998 – was a long time coming. Quite the most exciting Scottish institution built in the 20th century, its design by Benson & Forsyth is a declaration of cultural intent where 'building, display and the history of Scotland become one' (Brown, 1999). A **broch**-like entry, via a confined sloping ramp, slides suddenly into the airy 'castle-yard' of **Hawthornden** Court and on into a plethora of architectural readings. Indeed, the architects have worked a miracle from the cramped **Bristo** Port corner site next to the **Royal Museum of Scotland**, which was cleared as long ago as 1970; the Philp Report in 1952 had recommended a purpose-built facility and the Williams Report in the early 1980s called for a focus of national identity. The quaint, but much loved, National Museum of Antiquities – the basis for the present collection of over 10,000 artefacts – was housed in the **Scottish National Portrait Gallery** from 1890. As the 'Museum of the Society of Antiquaries of Scotland' it had been founded in 1780 by the eccentric 11th Earl of Buchan; the eclectic collection, held in the **Royal Scottish Academy** from 1826, went public in 1859 after being made over to the Government Board of Manufactures in 1851. More selective acquisition of Scottish material from 1870, followed by planned and recorded archaeological excavation, enabled the systematic study and better presentation of Scots history to begin. The rights to Treasure Trove secured many important finds for the nation like the **St Ninian's Isle treasure** unearthed on **Shetland** in 1957.

Operating dramatically on six levels, and incorporating several major artworks by Sir Eduardo Paolozzi and others as integral parts of the design, the new museum – much of which is lit naturally from above – tells a lucid chronological history of the land and people from 3400 million years ago. 'Beginnings' in the basement

The Museum of Scotland, designed by Benson & Forsyth and opened in 1998 (MS)

Edinburgh continued

presents, through rocks and fossils, the foundations of geology, geomorphology and natural history which shaped the landscape before the advent of man; here is found little *Westlothiana* or 'Lizzie', at 338m years old the earliest known fossil reptile in the world. The daily and spiritual lives of the various 'Early People' from c8000 BC and who lived in the period of the **Picts** and **Romans** to 1100 AD are portrayed in over 5000 exhibits, most memorably the symbol stones and the **Hunterston** Brooch. The ground floor tells the stirring tale of 'The Kingdom of the Scots 900–1707', and of its commercial, cultural and religious life – from the early saints of the **Celtic Church** to the **Reformation**; one of the cultural icons on display is the tiny **Mony-musk Reliquary**. 'Scotland Transformed' 1707–1914 on the next level charts the story of Scotland from the **Union of Parliaments**, through the **Jacobite Risings** and the **Scottish Enlightenment**, to the industrialisation which turned a rural economy into a key part of 'the workshop of the world'; the centrepiece is a Newcomen Atmospheric Engine of the type refined by **James Watt**. 'Industry and Empire' continues the theme of the great Scots contribution to the world in engineering, technology and science during the commercial and military expansion of the British Empire and into the 20th century. Tellingly, in the 'Twentieth Century' gallery on the top floor is found, amongst a gallimaufry of everyday objects, a classic television of the 1950s chosen by the son of that medium's pioneer, **John Logie Baird**.

National Gallery of Scotland

A cool, neo-classical temple largely devoted to the easel arts, the National Gallery of Scotland was, like its more showy sister the **Royal Scottish Academy** which also graces the foot of **The Mound**, designed by **William Playfair** for the Board of Manufacturers in 1850–4. The National Gallery presents two quadrastyle Ionic porticos on its north and south fronts and single hexastyle ones on its east and west sides, while the rest of the elevation is formed only by a severely plain, almost flat pilastrade of unfluted orders. A modern subterranean extension was slotted in beneath a raised eastern terrace in 1975–8. Although not large, the collection contains the most important group of Old Masters in Britain outside London, a reputation enhanced since 1946 by the loan of the fine private collection of the Duke of **Sutherland** which includes major paintings by Raphael, Titian and Rembrandt. 30 paintings were also loaned in 1945 from the famous Bridgewater House Collection of the Earl of Ellesmere; two of four by Titian include the large *Diana and Actaeon* and *Diana and Calisto*; the 'Bridgewater' *Madonna* is one of four by Raphael; *The Seven Sacraments* by Nicholas Poussin can be quietly contemplated in an individual, almost religious setting. Early Renaissance works include the delightful *Madonna and Child* of Verrocchio, teacher of Leonardo da Vinci; 16th century Venetian art is represented by Bassano and Tintoretto; 16th century Spanish by El Greco and Velasquez. The 16th and 17th century Flemish schools are well represented by Rubens, van Dyck and the earliest known Vermeer, as well as by works of Rembrandt and Frans Hals. English art of the late 18th and early 19th centuries includes the portraiture of Gainsborough and Reynolds and the landscapes of Constable and Turner; 19th century French art includes Courbet and Corot plus the Impressionism of Renoir, Monet, Degas, Gauguin, Cezanne and Van Gogh. The Scottish Collection is strong with the portraiture of **Allan Ramsay**, **Henry Raeburn** and **David Wilkie** and the highly impressionistic landscapes and seascapes of **William McTaggart**.

National Monument

'Scotland's Pride and Poverty', or 'Edinburgh's disgrace', the unfinished National Monument on **Calton Hill** was intended as a bold memorial to the Scots who died in the Napoleonic Wars. In 1822, the promoters of a project 'to erect a facsimile of the Parthenon' (including **Walter Scott**, **Henry Cockburn** and **Francis Jeffrey**) appealed for £42,000 costs; the architects were C R Cockerell and **William Playfair**. The foundation stone, weighing six tons, was laid on 27 October 1822. Work finally began in 1826, but halted only three years later, by which time only £16,000 had been subscribed; the apotheosis of the 'Modern Athens' was abandoned in 1830. The 12 magnificent Doric columns of the western peristyle are all that was achieved.

National Museum of Antiquities of Scotland, see Museum of Scotland

Nelson Monument

A 'telescopic' tower upended on the rocky apex of **Calton Hill**, the Nelson Monument, designed by **Robert Burn**, was dedicated in 1807, two years after Trafalgar. The 100ft (30m) tower rises to a parapet walk beneath crosstrees supporting a zinc-plated wooden time-ball, 5ft 6in (1.6m) in diameter, which was installed in 1852 to act as a signal whereby ships lying off **Leith** in the Firth of Forth might set their chronometers. From Monday to Saturday the ball was wound to the top of the mast by hand in a physically demanding 10-minute job; the ball was released at 1 pm simultaneously with the time signal from Greenwich and was electrically connected to the '**One o'Clock Gun**' in the **Castle** by a 4000ft (1219m) cable. On 21 October each year, Nelson is remembered by a display of flags on the monument which advise that 'England expects every man to do his duty.'

Netherbow Port

The Netherbow Port was the east gate of the **Old Town** which straddled the junction of the **High Street** with the **Canongate**. A lower bow mentioned in 1369 may have stood where the road narrows outside **John Knox House**. The Netherbow Port was first raised along with the **Flodden Wall** after 1513. Although greatly repaired in 1547 after its reduction by the Earl of Hertford, it was rebuilt in 1571. Finally, in 1606, a new Netherbow Port, modelled on the Porte St Honoré in Paris, was built with a lofty square tower, fine pointed spire and two flanking circular towers. Demolition was decreed by Queen Caroline in 1736 as revenge for the **Porteous Riot**, but it was reprieved on condition that its gates were 'cleekit back'. However they were closed at the time of the 1745 **Jacobite Rising**; the Highlanders, having crossed the **Burgh Muir** by moonlight, were contemplating how to storm the Port when they were surprised to see the gates opening – ironically to admit a civic delegation which had been to plead unsuccessfully

with **Prince Charles Edward**. The Highlanders seized their chance. 'The Temple-Bar of Edinburgh' (**Scott**, *Heart of Midlothian*) succumbed to carriage traffic in 1764 when the magistrates declared it to be 'old rubbish' and 'an encumbrance to the street'. The clock and weathervane were re-erected on the **Dean Orphan Hospital** in 1832.

New College and Assembly Hall

A grimy frown on **The Mound**, New College and Assembly Hall originally comprised the Free High Church and theological college established by the **Free Church of Scotland** after the **Disruption** of 1843. The Tudor-style edifice, which replaced the 'palace' of **Mary of Guise** on **Castlehill**, was designed by **William Playfair** 1845–50. Since 1929, however, when reunion was effected between the **Church of Scotland** and the **United Free Church**, the building has accommodated the **General Assembly of the Church of Scotland** and the Faculty of Divinity of the **University of Edinburgh**. Within the collegiate quadrangle thunders a Bible-brandishing bronze of **John Knox**. The Assembly Hall was adapted to serve as the temporary home of the **Scottish Parliament** in 1999.

Eastwards of New College towers the Jacobean-style Free Church offices of 1851–61, which back onto **James' Court** and contain the Free Church of Scotland College. The Free Church Assembly meets contemporaneously with its bigger sister kirk each May, but separately, in St Columba's Free Kirk (originally St John's), built by **Thomas Hamilton** in Johnston Terrace off the **Lawnmarket** in 1845. At the junction of these two streets with Castlehill stands Tolbooth (St John's, Highland) Kirk of 1839–44, the original venue of the General Assembly of the Church of Scotland. Also in Johnston Terrace is the little St Columba of the Castle Episcopal Church built in 1846–7. Thus were built within three years three churches for three different denominations less than 300m apart.

New Town

The largest Georgian city development in the world, the late-18th and early-19th century New Town covers an area of about one square mile (318ha) and comprises over 11,000 'listed' properties, three-quarters of which are still in residential use. The First New Town was begun in 1767 according to the classic grid-iron plan of 'draughty parallelograms' (**R L Stevenson**) composed by **James Craig**, the winner of the design competition promoted by the city. The orchestrator of this 'symphony in stone' was **George Drummond**, six times Lord Provost (1725–64), whose visionary 'Proposals' for the bare, windswept ridge of the Lang Dykes, north of the **Old Town**, became a reality after the draining of the **Nor' Loch** and the commencement of the **North Bridge**. The symmetrical plan, consisting of three principal, east-west thoroughfares – **George**, **Queen** and **Princes Streets** (with two lesser lanes, Rose and Thistle Streets between) – linking the counterbalanced **St Andrew** and **Charlotte** (originally St George) **Squares**, genuflected to George III and the House of Hanover within a highly stylised political diagram which symbolised the parliamentary **Union** of Scotland and England in 1707. After a mediocre start, the First New Town reached its crescendo in Charlotte Square with the magnificent palace fronts designed by **Robert Adam** in 1791.

The Second New Town was laid out to the north of the First, on the steep slope towards the **Water of Leith**, by **Robert Reid** and William Sibbald in 1802. This scheme focuses on Great King Street, its principal east-west axis which terminates respectively in Drummond Place and the masterful Royal Circus, the latter designed by **William Playfair** in 1822. Westwards, the grand Moray Estate, including the monumental 12-sided Moray Place, was completed on an interlinking, almost cellular system of crescent, oval and octagon plans by **James Gillespie Graham** from 1822–30. Eastern extensions of the First New Town, which were begun by Craig at St James Square in 1791, reached colossal proportions on and around **Calton Hill** after 1815, notably at Royal and Regent Terraces. The great Calton scheme designed by William Playfair after 1819 to link Edinburgh and **Leith** was, apart from London Road, largely stillborn. The West End was first planned by Gillespie Graham in 1813 but the bulk of this area, centring on the octagon of Melville Crescent, was built by Robert Brown and John Lessels 1817–60.

Since 1970 the New Town Conservation Committee has financed restoration schemes in this, the largest and most outstanding urban conservation area in Britain, which is now, with the Old Town, designated a World Heritage Site.

Newhaven

A salty old seaport lying between **Leith** and **Granton**, Newhaven was 'sanitised' by the city in the 1960s and 70s. The 'New' Haven (Blackness, further up the Firth of Forth, was the 'Old') was founded by **James IV** as his royal dockyard in 1504; it was also known as 'Our Lady's Port of Grace' after its chapel dedicated to the Virgin Mary and St James in 1506–8. The warship the **Great Michael**, whose six-year construction 'waisted all the woodis in **Fyfe**' (**Lindsay**, c1530), was launched here in 1511. French, Dutch and Flemish wrights settled by James IV are often claimed to be the ancestors of the traditionally exclusive, still close-knit community. **Oysters** were the economic mainstay in the 16th and 17th centuries. **Herring** followed from 1793, but although Newhaven became the city fishmarket a century later, its **fishing** fleet has departed and little is landed in its Victorian harbour. Yet the 'Bow-Tows', as born-and-bred Newhaveners term themselves, still remain romantically wedded to the sea; the Society of Free Fishermen of Newhaven, under its Boxmaster, was chartered by **James VI** in 1573, and the Newhaven Fishwives Choirs were formerly composed of those colourfully petticoated 'amazons' who traditionally carried the catch, crying 'Caller Ou!' and 'Caller Herrin!' into the capital.

Newington

A southern central district contiguous with the **Southside** on the **Burgh Muir**, Newington is defined on the east and west by **Prestonfield** and the **Grange**. The select Blacket Estate (named after the Bell family seat in **Dumfriesshire**), the first villa development in Scotland, inspired by Regent's Park in London, was begun by **James Gillespie Graham** in 1825 (completed 1860).

Arthur Lodge, an exceptional Grecian villa with incised carving, was probably built by **Thomas Hamilton** in 1827–30; the first resident, David Cunningham, a jeweller and City Treasurer, employed Hamilton on **George IV Bridge** and the **Royal High School**. Mayfield to the south was begun by David Cousin in 1862 and was later home to cartographer Dr **J G Bartholomew** whose business moved into its present premises at the Geographical Institute in nearby Duncan Street in 1911, a Palladian-style piece which reuses the 1815 portico added by Thomas Hamilton to Falcon Hall, the earlier Bartholomew residence in **Morningside**.

Newliston, by Kirkliston

A small austere villa designed in the later plain classical manner by **Robert Adam** in 1789 for Thomas Hog, Newliston lies between **Kirkliston** and **South Queensferry**. The remarkable landscape garden has been laid out by **William Adam** c1730 for **John Dalrymple, 2nd Earl of Stair**, on his retiral to his old tower house at Newliston, which he planned to replace with a magnificent Palladian mansion (100ft x 80ft, 50 x 24m) designed by William Adam, then erecting **Dalmahoy** for his brother George Dalrymple; but of this grandiose scheme only the stable blocks and lodge were completed.

Niddry Street

Formerly the even narrower Niddry Wynd sited further west at the **Tron Kirk**, Niddry Street is reduced to a mean back alley for the **South Bridge**. Here **James VI** and **Anne of Denmark** were put up by Provost Nicol Edward in 1591, while being persecuted by the necromance **Francis Stewart, Earl of Bothwell**. Later, the wynd sheltered the Lodge of Edinburgh, Mary's Chapel No 1, the oldest authenticated **Masonic** lodge in existence. St Mary's Chapel was built by Elizabeth, Countess Ross, widow of John, **Earl of Ross** and **Lord of the Isles**, in 1504. In the early 18th century **James Erskine, Lord Grange**, brother of **John, Earl of Mar**, the ineffectual leader of the 1715 **Jacobite Rising**, lived in the Wynd.

Nisbet of Dirleton's Land

'One of the oldest houses in the burgh', Nisbet of Dirleton's Land in the **Canongate** was reconstructed by the city in 1956. The recessed stairtower and broad crowstepped gable holding an unusual square corbelled projection present strongly fortified features to the street. This frontage, which incorporates original panels inscribed 1619, was remodelled in 1624. Sir John Nisbet, Lord Dirleton (1609–87), was the last Lord Advocate who also sat on the judicial bench; an anti-**Covenanter**, he enjoyed grim reputation second only to his contemporary George **'Bluidy' Mackenzie of Rosehaugh**. He bought **Dirleton Castle** in 1663 and later began Archerfield House nearby. 'A man of great learning . . . of great integrity; only he loved money too much, but he always stood firm to the law' (Burnet, c1700).

Nor' Loch

A noxious lake formerly lying to the north of the **Old Town** on the site of **Princes Street Gardens**, **Waverley Station** and **The Mound**, the Nor' Loch was artificially

Three Generations': G W Wilson's portrait of Newhaven fishwives (GWWA)

Edinburgh continued

created below the Castle Rock in 1460 as the northern defence of the city, the counterpart of the 'King's Wall' [see **Town Walls**] barrier to the south.

The amenity of the Nor' Loch was jealously guarded during the 16th century; eel pie and Nor' Loch trout were delicacies served up in local taverns. But the loch was also used as a corrective for offenders against public morality – mainly women, who were 'dookit twa times frae the pillar and stule be the lochside'. Witches also underwent this ordeal by water, before being 'worryit' (strangled) and burnt on **Castlehill**.

In 1688 parliamentary powers were sought to remove the loch, by then much abused by the citizens and

tanners, but these were not granted until 1723. Only after the projection of the **North Bridge** was the area east of The Mound partly drained by 1763. The remaining western part was finally drained for laying out Princes Street Gardens in 1820.

North Bridge

The North Bridge made real the recurrent dream of extending the city beyond the **Nor' Loch** and building the **New Town**. It was begun in 1765 after partial draining of the Nor' Loch had enabled the laying of the foundation stone in 1763. Dream descended into nightmare in 1769 when the bridge collapsed, taking five lives. The builder **William Mylne** had not founded the south abutment on 'rock or natural earth' as specified. The bridge was finally made passable in 1772. In 1894–5 the original masonry construction was demolished for the present steel-arch extravaganza spanning **Waverley Station**. The A-listed structure consists of three segmental spans of 175ft (53m), comprising deep steel girder arches supported by 18ft (5.5m) thick masonry piers and abutments; designed by Messrs Cunningham, Blythe & Westland, Engineers, it was built by **Sir William Arrol** & Co. 'The Old and New Towns of Edinburgh, although joined by the barely one quarter mile long North Bridge, are separated by a gulf of a thousand years' (Miller, 1864).

Old Calton Burying Ground

This cemetery, on the south-western spur of the **Calton Hill**, was brought into use as an additional town graveyard in 1718. The burying ground on what was called McNeill's Craigs was extended in 1767, and later bisected by Waterloo Place 1815–19. Many of the earlier inhabitants of the **New Town** were interred here, in ground convenient for the developing districts north and north-east of **Princes Street**. Its most famous occupant is **David Hume**, who is commemorated in a fine Roman mausoleum inspired by the tomb of Theodoric at Ravenna and designed by his friend **Robert Adam** (1777). The painter **David Allan** lies nearby. A large obelisk designed by **Thomas Hamilton** honours the political martyrs of the 1793 sedition trials, notably **Thomas Muir of Huntershill**. The Emancipation Monument, hard against the Hume mausoleum and ornamented with statues of Abraham Lincoln and a freed slave, commemorates Scottish-American soldiers of the Civil War. Many other tombs and monuments are noteworthy examples of Scottish funerary art of differing, sometimes traditional, styles.

The New Calton Burying Ground, opened in 1820 in Regent Road to the east, served to re-inter the remains disturbed by the building of Waterloo Place. Noteworthy is the enclosure of the Stevenson family of engineers, whose most famous son, **Robert Louis Stevenson**, lies in Samoa in the South Seas.

Old St Paul's Church, Jeffrey Street

A handsome Episcopal edifice squeezed between North Gray's and Carruber's Closes, Old St Paul's Church (1880–1905) occupies the site of the wool-store in Leith Wynd used by the original disestablished congregation from 1689 after their expulsion from **St Giles**. Unlike the 'qualified' **Episcopalians** who built **St Patrick's Church**, this sect were **Jacobites** disaffected by the Hanoverian dynasty who, until the death of **Prince Charles Edward** in 1788, secretly supported the **Stewart** cause. 'There was hardly a Scottish family of any note adhering to the old loyalties which was not represented among the worshippers of Old St Paul's' (Forbes Gray, 1940). Notable members were Andrew Lumisden, the private secretary to the Prince, one of the first to rally to his standard in 1745 and who later accompanied him into exile in France and Rome; **Thomas Ruddiman**, whose *Caledonian Mercury* was the organ of Jacobitism; Laurence Oliphant of the House of Gask, who first brought to the city the good news of the victory at **Prestonpans**; and his daughter, **Carolina, Lady Nairne**, the **ballad** writer.

Old Town

Comprising the ancient royalty, ie the sanctioned exten of the burgh amounting to 143 acres (58ha) on its foun dation c1140 by **David I**, the medieval Old Town wa confined by the **Flodden Wall** for some 250 years. On of the 'metely good towns' of Scotland remarked upo enviously by Edward I in 1295, the burgh had fewer tha 400 houses, sheltering c2000 souls, even 50 years afte the granting of its royal charter by **Robert I** in 1329 Froissart described it as 'the capital of Scotland where th king chiefly resides when he is in that part of the country' and less than a century later it is stated that 'for a hundre years, the Kings of Scots have had their residence almos constantly in that city' (Major, 1521). Yet Edinburg cannot claim full capital status until 1535, after bot Parliament and the College of Justice finally settled there

As a 'metropolitan city' (1586) rapid developmen forced buildings upwards rather than outwards. Th teeming, tottering tenements maintained a vertical gra dation of society: 'high and dirty' living went 'cheek b jowl' on the common turnpike stair; the upper floor were 'possessed of the genteeler people' (Topham, 1775) In 1760, prior to the **New Town**, Edinburgh was 'a pictur esque, odorous, inconvenient, old-fashioned town o about 70,000 inhabitants' (Chambers, 1868). After th exodus of the rich 'to houses to themselves' c1780, mor robust but less fortunate persons usurped their old resi dences. Much of the medieval Old Town was demolishe under 19th century City Improvement Schemes; of th 200 or so closes existing in 1750, only half remain.

One O'clock Gun

Edinburgh's 'Big Bang', the One O'clock Gun, boom across **Princes Street** from Monday to Saturday. It wa first successfully fired on 7 June 1861 after two failure on the 5th and 6th. The time-gun was installed on Mill' Mount Battery in the **Castle** in the year following th formation of the 1st Edinburgh City Artillery Volunteer in 1860. The idea is supposed to have come from time-gun fired by the concentrated rays of the sun i Paris; but there had been time signals at Greenwich and the time-ball on the **Nelson Monument** on Calto **Hill** had been operational since 1853. The gun was elec tronically synchronised with the time-ball by means of cable originally laid by sailors from **Leith** in just two day The mechanism of the original cannon and electric cloc is in **Huntly House** Museum. Other similar gun formerly existed in **Glasgow**, **Greenock** and Newcastle upon-Tyne but only Edinburgh's piece of field ordnanc still rocks the city, scaring pigeons and terrifying tourist while citizens calmly check their watches.

Outlook Tower

Commanding **Castlehill**, the Outlook Tower an Camera Obscura crown the top of the tenement claime as the townhouse of Ramsay of **Dalhousie**, the cele brated 'Laird o'Cockpen'. To the original four lowe storeys were added two purpose-built upper storey with a rooftop viewing platform c1855, when Maria Theresa Short, daughter of the optician-astronome **Thomas Short**, transferred 'Short's Popular Observa tory' here from the **Calton Hill**. In 1891 the rename 'Outlook Tower' was fitted up by **Patrick Geddes** as a 'index museum to the universe' later described as th

The Old Town from Princes Street Gardens, looking over Waverley Bridge 1890 (GWWA)

Edinburgh continued

first sociological laboratory in the world'. The Camera Obscura focused on the regional 'Prospect' as the starting point for a dizzy descent of the 'Wizard Geddes' tower', through the ever-expanding realms of 'Edinburgh', 'Scotland', 'Language', 'Europe' and 'World' displayed on the successive floors in the Victorian equivalent of the multi-media show, and viewed through the 'Episcope', 'Hollow Globe' and 'Cosmosphere and other appliances'. Stained-glass panels depicting the 'Tree of Life', 'Philosophers' Stone' and 'Valley Section' etc illuminated the connecting stair. The Patrick Geddes Centre for Planning Studies sublets part today.

Panmure House

Brutalised by the adjacent concrete blocks of flats fronting the **Canongate**, Panmure House in Panmure Close was built c1690 as the town residence of the Earls of Panmure in **Angus**. James Maule, 4th Earl, remained faithful to **James VII** after his flight to France in 1687 and proclaimed the 'Old Chevalier' King at the Cross of **Brechin** in 1715. In 1746 therefore, he was attainted and his estates forfeited, the house being later occupied by the Countess of **Aberdeen**. From 1778–90 the two-storey, L-plan rubble-fronted mansion with crowstepped gables and raised courtyard was occupied by **Adam Smith**, the father of political economy and author of The Wealth of

Nations, when appointed Commissioner of Customs. Restored by Edinburgh Corporation in 1957, with a donation from Lord Thomson of Fleet, as the Canongate Boys' Club, the house, now entered via Little Lochend Close, is an intermediate treatment centre for adolescents run by Edinburgh Social Work Department. Dunbar's Close nearby was laid out in the style of a 17th century Edinburgh garden by the Mushroom Trust in 1980.

Parliament House

The redoubt of the independent Scots Parliament from 1639 until the **Treaty of Union** in 1707, Parliament House is a 17th century Scots renaissance masterpiece mockingly masked by early-19th century classical screens. After the permanent establishment of the **Court of Session** and the College of Justice in Edinburgh by **James V** in 1532, the court regularly sat in the Old **Tolbooth** until 1560, when better accommodation was demanded from the town council. Fearful lest the city lose the judicial court as well as that of the monarch who had departed after the **Union of Crowns** in 1603, the town council raised the Parliament House on the site of the manses of the ministers of **St Giles Cathedral**. The design was drawn by Sir James Murray of Kilbaberton, the King's Master of Works, and the work executed under John Ritchie, master-mason. The L-shaped block comprised the Parliament Hall, or 'Outer House' (see below), and the 'Inner House' where the Courts of Session and Exchequer convened. Below in the 'Laigh Hall' were deposited the national records where,

337

gnawed by rats, they gathered dust until transferred to **Register House** in 1789.

Parliament Hall

Unlike that of England, the Scots Parliament, first recorded in 1293, met as a single body in one chamber: no distinction was made among the 'Three Estates' – clergy, nobility and burgesses – which comprised the Parliament and the less formal General Council (later Convention) which developed in the 14th century. Parliament Hall (122ft long and 60ft high), which served the nation from 1639–1707, boasts a 49ft wide hammerbeam or arch-braced roof of dark oak; this carved and gilded 'open' roof was raised c1640 by John Scott, master-wright to the town. The other glory is the great stained-glass south window installed in 1868; by Wilhelm von Kaulbach, it portrays the inauguration of the College of Justice by James V in 1536. Restored by Sir William Nelson, the philanthropic publisher, in 1889–92, Parliament Hall is now a promenade for advocates and their clients.

Parliament Square

A cold, uniformly dull parking precinct lying off the **High Street** behind **St Giles Cathedral**, the Greek colonnades of Parliament Square, 'as foppery calls it' (**Cockburn**, 1856), camouflage a phalanx of buildings associated with the **law** of Scotland. Parliament Square was originally called the Parliament Close or Yard after the **Parliament House** therein. A 'square' was first formed after the Restoration of 1660; the lead eques-

trian statue of **Charles II** in Roman triumphal trapping was erected in 1685. Prior to the building of Parliament House in 1632–9, Parliament Square was the kirk heugh or burial ground of St Giles; a stone inscribed 'I.K.1572' marked the site of the grave of **John Knox** until 1970. Parliament House accommodates the **Court of Session** and the **High Court of Justiciary**, the Supreme Courts of Scotland [see **Law**]; also the 'Law Libraries', ie the **Advocates' Library**, the **Signet Library** and the Solicitors' Library. All the classical frontages of Parliament Square were designed by **Robert Reid** and executed from 1803–30.

Peffermill House, Craigmillar

A kenspeckle, crowstepped mansion surrounded by industry but still surveying **Prestonfield**, **Duddingston** and **Craigmillar**, Peffermill was rescued for an architect's residence in 1981. The three-storey L-plan house was built for Edward Edgar in 1636 – possibly by William Aytoun, master-mason responsible for much of **George Heriot's School**. Peffer (also 'Pepper' or 'Paper') Mill stood north of the house on the Braid Burn. Once condemned as having 'no particular history', it housed, under **Thomas Braidwood** from 1764–83, 'what was probably the first regular organised school in Great Britain for the teaching of the deaf and dumb' (Gray, 1925), an institution which moved even the visiting **Dr Johnson** to extol its successful educational methods. The house was the likely model for the residence of 'the Laird of Dumbiedykes' in *Heart of Midlothian*.

Parliament Hall with 17th century hammerbeam roof (RWB)

enned by **Sir Walter Scott** in the manse garden overlooking Duddingston Loch opposite Peffermill.

Physicians' Hall (Royal College Of Physicians), Queen Street

Chartered by **Charles II** in 1681, the Royal College of Physicians was founded to incorporate and license practitioners in Scotland. Originally the College also controlled apothecaries, but pharmacists have now had their own regulating body for over a century. 'Physicians' Hall' in **Queen Street** was designed by **Thomas Hamilton** in 1845 as a replacement for the earlier edifice, formerly at the east end of **George Street**, which was built by **James Craig** in 1775; a neo-classical triumph of the Greek revival, it 'shows remarkable invention within the confines of a classical terraced frontage' (McKean, 1984). Derived from the Tower of the Winds, the frontage has a Corinthian portico supporting statues of Aesculapius, God of Medicine, and Hippocrates, the 'first' physician, as well as terminating, in the aedicule, in a representation of Hygeia, Goddess of Healing. The College was responsible for establishing the original **Royal Infirmary** in 1729; its great rival, the **Royal College of Surgeons**, however, was responsible for the establishment of the Faculty of Medicine at the **University of Edinburgh** in 1726.

Playhouse Theatre

Built in 1927–9 to designs by John Fairweather of **Glasgow** as a dual-purpose theatre and cinema, the Playhouse at the top of Leith Walk is visually unremarkable but far more spacious than its modest façade would suggest, the auditorium accommodating over 3000. Restored by Lothian Regional Council in 1978–80, further restoration was required after fire caused extensive damage in 1993.

Portobello

Now a suburb of Edinburgh, Portobello reputedly got its name from a house built c1750 on the desolate Figgate Whins, a wild area of the coast between **Leith** and **Musselburgh**. Its owner was a retired naval veteran of the capture of Puerto Bello in Panama in 1739. By the end of the 18th century many fine new houses had been built either as summer residences or permanent homes for members of the Edinburgh middle classes.

Industrial development of the area began in the 1760s when William Jamieson, an Edinburgh architect and builder, opened a brickworks to exploit valuable fireclay deposits under his land. As more clay beds were found, brickworks and **potteries** multiplied and were joined by other types of industry including glass manufacturing and a paper mill. The population grew steadily round these industries and also in the more residential middle-class areas, and in 1833 Portobello acquired burgh status which was given up on amalgamation with Edinburgh in 1896.

Portobello's period as a popular seaside resort dates from the late 19th century and the era of cheap public transport. Trains and **trams** brought thousands to enjoy holidays by the sea. Portobello Pier was unique in Scotland for as well as being a pleasure pier, it was also a port of call for Firth of Forth excursion steamers. Opened in

1871 and demolished in 1917, it was the work of **Thomas Bouch**, designer of the ill-fated **Tay Railway Bridge**.

The popularity of Portobello declined during the inter-war years although day trippers still make the beach busy on fine summer days. Industry has disappeared and little remains to show the variety that once flourished there. However, two bottle kilns have been preserved in Pipe Street to mark the site of the A W Buchan & Co Ltd pottery which was founded in Portobello in 1867 and transferred to **Crieff** in 1972.

Prestonfield House

A superbly situated U-plan mansion of three storeys topped by curvilinear gables, Prestonfield House nestles south of **Arthur's Seat** between **Newington** and **Duddingston**. The present house was built by **Robert Mylne** or **Sir William Bruce** in 1687 to replace the earlier 'Priestfield' which was burnt by students during the 'No Popery' riot of 1681. The then laird, Lord Provost Sir James Dick, was a grandson of the wealthy merchant **Sir William Dick of Braid**, who had bought the estate in 1677. Sir Alexander Dick, who succeeded in 1746, was President of the **Royal College of Physicians** seven years running; probably the first cultivator of rhubarb in Scotland, he received a gold medal for 'the best specimen' from the London Society for Promoting Arts and Commerce in 1774. His bumper crop flourished on ground heavily manured by Sir James – who had cleansed the city streets at his own expense – and went to supply **Dr James Gregory**'s famous 'Mixture'. Now the Prestonfield House Hotel, richly decorated interiors contain Mortlake Tapestries, panels with red leather embossed relief made in Cordova in 1676 (brought from Byres Close) and classical landscapes attributed to James and Robert Norie.

Princes Street

The most scenically picturesque yet architecturally ramshackle main street of any European capital city, Princes Street is renowned for its open aspect southwards to the **Old Town** ridge and the **Castle**. When first named St Giles Street (after the patron saint of the city) on the **New Town** plan of **James Craig**, George III objected: 'his stupidity hindered him from imagining aught beyond a London slum, and he would have none of it' (Boog-Watson, 1920). Accordingly the street name favoured the royal princes the Duke of Rothesay (later George IV) and the Duke of York. The first house was built in 1769 for John Neale, a silk mercer, who availed himself of the offer that it would be rate-free for all time. By 1786 building had proceeded as far as Hanover Street: by 1795 to Frederick Street; and in 1805 all the feus had been taken up. But unlike **George Street** and **Queen Street**, Princes Street did not attract the highest class of resident; commerce invaded from the start, and from 1821 shops and flats were constructed.

From the 1830s Victorian reconstruction transformed the Georgian street; the three best early examples of this phase, however, succumbed in the 1960s: the exuberant Baroque palazzo built in 1855 for the Life Association of Scotland; its more restrained neighbour, the New Club of 1834 and 1859; and the monumental Italian Baroque North British & Mercantile Insurance Company

Princes Street from Waterloo Place c1890 with the Scott Monument but no North British (now Balmoral) Hotel (GWWA)

Edinburgh continued

of 1855–7, an imitation of the 16th century Palazzo Vendramia in Venice. This civic vandalism was condoned by the Princes Street Panel established in 1954 following the recommendations of the Abercrombie Plan of 1948; the street was to have been totally rebuilt to create a continuous covered walkway, cantilevered out at first floor level; the concept was finally abandoned in 1978.

Princes Street Gardens

Previously the site of the **Nor' Loch**, Princes Street Gardens have been a municipal park since 1876. The gardens were first adumbrated on the **New Town** plan in 1766, but the concept of an ornamental terraced canal below the **Castle** was abandoned in 1790 when **The Mound** was formed, dividing the Gardens in two. A culvert cut from **St Cuthbert's Kirk** to the **North Bridge** created a fetid swamp which became 'the receptacle of many sewers and seemingly all the worried cats, drowned dogs and blackguardism of the city' (Cockburn, 1856). The West Gardens (29 acres) were laid out in 1816–20 for the **Princes Street** proprietors west of Hanover Street by James Skene of Rubislaw who lived at No 126. The East Gardens (8½ acres) were created in 1830 but soon altered when the North British **Railway** reached **Waverley Station** in 1845.

Princes Street's panoramas were not preserved without a fight: in 1769–70 development was permitted on the site of the **Balmoral Hotel** (formerly the North British Hotel); further feus were released on the site of the **Waverley Market** on condition that building would not rise above street level. In 1771 arbitration confirmed open garden ground between **Waverley Bridge** and Hanover Street, but feuing was to have been allowed westwards towards **Lothian Road**.

How many statues are there in Princes Street? None, they are all in the Gardens. Apart from that at the **Scott Monument** they include **David Livingstone, John Wilson, Adam Black, Allan Ramsay, Sir James Young Simpson** and **Thomas Guthrie** as well as monuments to **Dean Edward Ramsay**, The **Royal Scots** and **Scots Greys**.

Queen Street

The longest single stretch of Georgian architecture in the **New Town**, Queen Street was named in honour of Charlotte of Mecklenburg Strelitz, wife of George III. It forms a north-facing terrace towards the Firth of Forth, a mirror image of **Princes Street** on the original New Town plan. Building began in 1769 when Robert Orde, Lord Chief Baron of the Scottish Exchequer, engaged **Robert Adam** who completed No 8 for him in 1771. This house stood alone until c1783 when construction commenced at the west corner of North St David Street and gradually extended westwards until completion in c1792; 'the architecture . . . grows progressively less individual and more stereotyped from east to west' (RCAHMS, 1950). At Simpson House (No 52) **Sir James Young Simpson**, Professor of Midwifery, discovered the extended safe use of chloroform during a session of self-experimentation in 1847.

Queensberry House

Belying its strictly utilitarian appearance, Queensberry House in the **Canongate** was remodelled and extended

340

from in 1681 by **James Smith** as a lodging for Charles Maitland, Lord Hatton, who as 3rd Earl and 2nd **Duke of Lauderdale** sold the great mansion to William Douglas, 1st Duke of Queensberry in 1686. It was here that Queensberry's grandson **Lord Drumlanrig** spitted, roasted and partly devoured the kitchen-boy in 1707. After conversion into flats during the 18th century, the house, 'once the brilliant abode of rank and fashion and political intrigue' (**Cockburn**, 1856), was bought by the Board of Ordnance in 1803 and remodelled for barracks by adding an extra storey. Formerly the centre of the F-plan, three-storey building, its advanced wings surmounted with neat ogee roofs, had a "French" (ie mansard) roof with storm windows in the style of the 'Palace of Versailles' (Wilson, 1891). In 1853 the property became a 'House of Refuge for the Destitute', and for fifty years from 1945 was Queensberry House Hospital for the Elderly. A reconstruction of this, the grandest aristocratic townhouse in Scotland in its day – and its lost balustraded tower – is proposed for the **Scottish Parliament** administration.

Ramsay Garden, Castlehill

A fantastical group of flats, Ramsay Garden clings to the steep slope of **Castlehill** and the **Esplanade**. The whole, with its Continental ambience, was both organically and romantically conceived by Professor **Patrick Geddes** as his 'University Hall Extension' to the existing provision in Mound Place. A five-storey co-operative staff block, it was built in Scots Baronial style on the north-west by Henbest Capper in 1892; Geddes himself occupied the 12-roomed third-floor flat. Adjoining 'Ramsay Lodge', with rooms for 45 male students, was built in a more English 'cottage style' by Sydney Mitchell in 1893. This incorporated – and almost engulfed – the 18th century, eccentrically octagonal, so-called 'Goose-pie' House of **Allan Ramsay**, who had retired there c1740 to 'be away from the clatter of the **High Street**'. In 1894 Mitchell also remodelled the adjacent terrace of three garden homes raised in 1768 by **Allan Ramsay**, junior, the royal portrait painter. The old common room of Ramsay Lodge contains five Celtic Revival murals by **John Duncan**.

Ratho

A largely 19th century farming and **quarrying**, now commuter, village on the **Union Canal** in the west of Edinburgh, Ratho became part of the city in 1975. Its name, recorded in the 13th century, may come from the 'raths' or forts found on Kaimes and Dalmahoy Hills to the south. Ratho Kirk, dating from the 12th century, embodies the medieval remains of the ancient St Mary's, a Norman foundation dedicated in 1243 by Bishop de Bernham. Ratho Basin was a staging post on the canal with a Change House for carriage tolls; the double-doored 'Pop Inn' on the towpath allowed thirsty bargees to put away a pint while passing through without losing their horses in the process. George Bryce, son of the owner of the Bridge Inn and known as 'The Ratho Murderer', was the last man publicly hanged in Edinburgh at the **Lawnmarket** in 1864; his victim was Jane Seaton, a local nursemaid. Definitely once a drouthy district with 11 pubs in or near Ratho, Ratho Hall even became a distillery c1845.

Redhall House, Colinton

A commodious Palladian mansion built by James Robertson in 1756–61 for George Inglis, Attorney in Exchequer, Redhall House was constructed with stone from the ruin of Redhall Castle which commanded the **Water of Leith** between **Colinton** and **Slateford**. The medieval Barony of Redhall reached from **Comiston** to **Currie** and included the Commonty of the **Pentland Hills**. Granted to William Cunningham by **Robert III** in 1396, the estate was retained by the family (Lords Kilmaurs and Earls of Glencairn) until 1637. The original hall-house was built in the 13th century. In 1527 the then tower house was bought by Sir Adam Otterburn, later Lord Advocate under **Queen Mary**; he probably commemorated its construction with the carved heraldic panel now on the unusual hexagonal **doocot**, built in 1756. Redhall proved redoubtable in 1650 when 60 men under Sir Andrew Hamilton withstood bombardment by **General Monk** and Cromwell's Ironsides, unaided by the **Covenanter** force of **General Sir David Leslie** encamped nearby.

Register House

'The oldest building in Europe specially designed for the preservation of national archives' (Keir, 1966), Register House is also the finest neo-classical building in Edinburgh. HM General Register House (Old Register House), the headquarters of the Scottish Record Office, which stands at the east end of **Princes Street** opposite **North Bridge**, was designed by **Robert Adam** in 1771. The purpose-built facility was first proposed in 1722, after the **Treaty of Union** guaranteed that the national records would remain in Scotland for all time. The records then mouldered in the Laigh Hall of the **Parliament House** where they had been deposited from 1662; earlier, what had escaped the depredations of Edward I and Oliver Cromwell was kept in the **Castle**. Construction commenced in 1774 with £12,000 funds appropriated by royal warrant from the forfeited **Jacobite** estates after the 1745 **Rising**; the building remained a roofless shell from 1778–85. Nevertheless, by 1789 both the records and their administrative officials had moved in – although, when Adam died in 1792, this accommodation was by no means even externally complete. His design, with internal modifications, was completed in 1822–7 by **Robert Reid**, who also designed St George's Church in **Charlotte Square** which was refurbished for extra accommodation as West Register House in 1971. Old Register House is rectangular in plan, its two storeys enclosing a central dome 70ft (21m) high and 50ft (15m) in diameter which contains the Legal Search Room; the finely decorated ceiling is the work of Robert Adam executed by Thomas Clayton in 1785.

Repository of the main legal and judicial registers and the older historical records, Old Register House holds the Register of Sasines (from 1617), and Deeds (from 1554), registers of the **Court of Session**, High Court of Justiciary, Sheriff, Commissary and other courts; registers of the Great Seal (from 1315) and Privy Seal (from 1488); state papers and administrative records of pre-Union Scotland and records of the post-Union Scottish Exchequer; and many local, church and private archives. New Register House, built 1859–63 behind, is mainly occupied by the General Register Office for Scotland which administers the statutory registration of births, deaths and marriages as well as censuses of **population** (in Scotland); it also holds the parochial registers maintained prior to 1885. Part contains the Court of the Lord Lyon King of Arms [see **Heraldry**]. West Register House holds the records of government departments of Scotland; court processes and warrants of the legal register; maps and plans; and the microfilm collection. A permanent exhibition of the evolution of documents illustrating Scottish history is displayed at West Register House.

Restalrig

An architectural clamjamphray near **Craigentinny**, Restalrig huddles at the foot of the 'Smokey Brae' under the main **railway** at Meadowbank. The Barony of Lestalric, extending from **Leith** to **Portobello**, was owned by the Norman family of de Lestalric in the 12th century. In the 14th century it passed through marriage to the infamous Sir Robert Logan of Restalrig – he who sold the Shore of Leith to Edinburgh. The Logans' power, and tower, were destroyed c1600 after implication in the **Gowrie Conspiracy** against **James VI**; the remains of the tower are attached to Lochend House built c1820 above Lochend Loch where the cylindrical **doocot** was possibly converted into a kiln to burn the clothes of plague victims in 1645. Restalrig Collegiate Kirk, founded by **James III** in 1487, was styled a 'chapel royal' in 1497. The kirk was 'utterlie casten doune' after the **Reformation** in 1560 and destroyed again in 1650 by Cromwell; minimal restoration as a small plain parish kirk was conducted in 1836 by **William Burn**. St Triduana's Aisle ('St Triduana's Well'), the surviving lower storey of a 15th century hexagonal vaulted chapel reconstructed in 1906, is dedicated to the good-looking Greek girl said to have accompanied St Rule when he brought the bones of **St Andrew** to Scotland in the 4th century. Pursued by the **Pictish** King, Nechtan, whose messenger related to her that he desired 'the beauty of her eyes', she accordingly delivered them skewered on a thorn. In medieval times people resorted to 'St Trid Well to mend their ene [eyes]' (**Lindsay**).

Riddle's Court, Lawnmarket

'One of the best preserved examples of old domestic architecture remaining in Edinburgh' (**MacGibbon and Ross**, 1892), Riddle's Court lurks behind the five-storey Riddle's Land fronting the **Lawnmarket**, which was built by George Riddell, burgess and wright, in 1726. Within Riddle's Close, a low barrel-vaulted pend (or passage) with an iron yett leads to an enclosed inner courtyard, 'evidently intended to be capable of defence' (**Chambers**, 1868), and containing the mansion built c1590 by the rich merchant Bailie John McMorran, who was shot dead by a scholar during a barring-out of the **Royal High School** in 1595. In 1598 the town council feasted **James VI** and his bride, **Anne of Denmark**, in the house. 'Macmorran's Ludging' was converted in 1889 as an extension to 'University Hall' residence by **Professor Patrick Geddes** who carved his motto *VIVENDO DISCIMUS* ('By Living we Learn') in the court, and added the wooden 'pentice stair', a curious Victorian

conceit externally connecting first- and second-floor levels. Exceptional interior decorations include a late 16th century painted open-beam ceiling and early-17th century plasterwork within the restored property, now adapted as an Adult Education Centre for the City of Edinburgh Council.

Royal Botanic Garden see BOTANIC GARDENS

(Old) Royal High School, Regent Road

'The noblest monument of the Scottish Greek Revival' (Summerson, 1953), the old Royal High School is dramatically piled up on a sharp bend of Regent Road, on the southern side of **Calton Hill**. Designed by **Thomas Hamilton**, it was built in 1825–9 on 'the only place in the **New Town** now left to which the High School can with any propriety be removed' (Town Council Minutes, 1825). The magnificent Greek Doric composition is based on the Temple of Theseus overlooking the agora in Athens; the central dominating feature is a double hexastyle portico well advanced in relation to its flanking colonnades, which terminate in impressive pilastered pavilions; two small, inwardly facing temples indirectly oppose each other in an off-beat, picturesque manner. Within, the splendid, sunken oval hall has been restored as the debating chamber for the long awaited Scottish Assembly, but the venue was rejected in favour of a new building at Holyrood. Traditionally, the High School dates back to the foundation of **Holyrood Abbey** in c1128; remaining under ecclesiastical tutelage until the **Reformation**, it moved into a new building in the garden of the **Blackfriars'** Monastery in 1577. The successor of this establishment has been in Infirmary Street since 1777. A new co-educational comprehensive establishment opened at **Barnton** in 1969.

Royal Infirmary

Visually marred 'by all manner of additions and makeshift alterations' (Gifford et al, 1984), the Royal Infirmary lies in Lauriston Place. It was built in a French-flavoured Scottish Baronial style by John and **David Bryce** in 1872–9 to replace the congested complex in Infirmary Street in the **Old Town**. The original Infirmary (chartered in 1736) of six beds for the 'sick poor' was in Robertson's Close and was operated by the **Royal College of Physicians** from 1729–38. After a pooling of resources with the **Royal College of Surgeons**, the 'Old' Infirmary, designed by **William Adam**, was opened in 1748 adjacent to the **Old High School**; it housed 228 patients – 'each in a distinct bed' – and was the scene of the pioneering achievements of such as **James Syme, Joseph Lister** and **James Young Simpson** which gave rise to the international reputation still enjoyed by both the 'Royal' and the adjacent Edinburgh Medical School. The plan of the present infirmary, providing 555 beds, was approved by Florence Nightingale before foundation in 1870.

Further expansion saw the 'Diamond Jubilee' Gynaecological Pavilion open in 1900, the Eye and Ear, Nose and Throat Pavilion in 1903, a Skin Pavilion in 1936 and the Simpson Memorial Maternity Pavilion, which replaced an earlier establishment built in 1879.

Prior to the establishment of the Lothian Health Board

n 1974, it was decided to rebuild at **Lauriston** rather han relocate elsewhere; the first phase of a new Royal nfirmary and Medical School was commissioned in 980. The new Royal Infirmary of Edinburgh opens at ittle France, **Liberton**, in 2000.

Royal Mile

Perhaps the largest, longest and finest street for build-ings and number of inhabitants, not in Britain only, out in the world' (Defoe, 1726), the Royal Mile winds downhill from the drawbridge of the **Castle** to the gates of the **Palace of Holyroodhouse**. It comprises success-vely the **Esplanade, Castlehill, Lawnmarket, High Street, Netherbow, Canongate** and **Abbey Strand**. The triking silhouette of the **Old Town** thrusting up from he backbone of 'the Mile', with its multitude of narrow closes, wynds and vennels steeply branching off, has been variously described as 'a rhinoceros skin with many a gnarled embossment', 'an ivory comb whose eeth on both sides are very foul', and 'a guttit haddie [gutted haddock], its myriad bones laid bare'. 'The airest and goodliest street mine eyes ever beheld . . . and many bye-lanes and closes . . . wherein are gentle-nen's houses, much fairer than the buildings of the High Street for in the High Street the merchants and tradesmen do dwell . . . and there is fish, flesh, bread and fruit in such variety' (Taylor, 1618).

Royal Museum of Scotland, Chambers Street

A cast-iron and crystal palace encased within a massive Venetian Renaissance façade, the Royal Museum of Scot-land in **Chambers Street** is the largest museum in Britain outside London. Founded as the Industrial Museum in 1854, it was renamed the Museum of Sci-ence and Art in 1864. The striking design of Captain Francis Fowke of the Royal Engineers was executed in 1861–4, 1870–4 and 1885–8. The Main Hall (270 x 70 x 90ft/82 x 21 x 27m), with its cloistered galleries supported on slender cast-iron columns, has a semi-circular, arched-rib timber and glass roof which permits the maximum use of daylight inside the spectacularly airy construction. In 1904 the institution became the Royal Scottish Museum, a name retained until 1985 when the National Museums of Scotland were adminis-tratively united.

The remarkable Evolution Exhibition was opened in 1975. The Mineral Hall dazzles with the famous collec-tion of Scottish rocks and minerals, crystals and agates; the museum also houses over 30,000 **fossil** fishes, including the collection of **Hugh Miller**. The fine speci-mens in the Mammal Hall are dwarfed by the suspended skeleton of a blue whale stranded at **North Berwick** in 1831. The Main Hall itself contains Asiatic sculpture, while the surrounding galleries show European cer-amics, glass and silver and magnificent Oriental and Islamic decorative art. 'European Art 1200–1800', an outstanding collection of bronzes, maiolica, tapestries, glass, woodwork and metalwork, includes the 17th cen-tury Persian-made silver-gilt **Lennoxlove** Toilet Service. There are 'Western Decorative Art 1850–2000' and 'Art & Industry Since 1850' Galleries. The Power & Progress Gallery displays one of the two oldest surviving steam locomotives, 'Wylam Dilly', built in Scotland with its

twin 'Puffing Billy' in 1813; a rotative beam engine with parts supplied by **James Watt** and Matthew Boulton in 1786; and the pioneering optic of **Inchkeith** lighthouse designed by **Robert Stevenson**. The Egyptian collection has items associated with Akhenaten, Nefertiti and Tut-ankhamun. In 1998 the museum was linked in a single complex with the adjacent new **Museum of Scotland**, which displays the treasures of the nation.

Royal Observatory, Blackford Hill

Transferred from the smoke-stack atmosphere of **Calton Hill** in 1896, the Royal Observatory occupies an impressive 'Graeco-Italian' towered temple – embellished with the signs of the zodiac – on **Blackford Hill**. The resignation of the Astronomer Royal in 1888 had precipitated the suggestion that the underfunded observatory should cease to be a national institution, a move which was forestalled by the 26th Earl of Craw-ford, who offered his collection of astronomical instru-ments and books to the nation on condition that a new Royal Observatory be built to house them. The Observatory still contains 'conventional' telescopes; the 16/24 inch (41/60cm) Schmidt (1951) and the 36 inch (90cm) reflecting telescope, the (equal) largest in Britain. The UK Infrared Telescope (1979) and the **James Clerk Maxwell** Telescope (1987), the largest of a new generation of radio telescopes designed to work at sub-millimetre wavelengths, are located on Mount Kea in Hawaii. The wide-angle UK Schmidt Telescope, also operated by **Edinburgh University** staff, which records the night sky south of the equator, is sited at Sydney Spring Mountain in New South Wales, Australia; this supplies photographic plates, each with the image of about one million stars and galaxies, which are scanned on Blackford Hill by COSMOS (1975), a fast automatic measuring machine which provides infor-mation able to be processed by STARLINK computer into research data used by individual astronomers world-wide. Super COSMOS has been constructed in the Technology and Computing Division, a design pion-eer in the field of infrared equipment. Uniquely, the Observatory is also the University of Edinburgh Depart-ment of Astronomy and Astrophysics, whose Professor doubles as the Astronomer Royal.

Royal Scottish Academy, The Mound

A pure Periclean-Doric style temple originally named the Royal Institution, the Royal Scottish Academy was designed, like the **National Gallery of Scotland**, its more solemn neighbour at the foot of **The Mound**, by **William Playfair**. It was built on 200 piles sunk to stabilise the 'travelled earth' of The Mound in 1822–6, and enlarged by about a third in 1831–6 for the Board of Manufactures and Fisheries. The Scottish Academy, founded in 1826, held its first exhibition in 1827; it received the royal charter in 1837. From 1859–1910 the Academicians occupied half of the National Gallery before the reorganisation of the then Royal Institution. The original sepulchral structure of 1822–6 formed the chrysalis from which the present building emerged; on the sides, 16 fluted Doric columns replaced nine plain; octastyle porticos, composed of the same order, were advanced at both the front and rear; the corner blocks were extended with distyle porticos; an anthemion frieze and other fine ornament was added; and in 1844 the eight sphinxes were discountenanced by the stare of the seated statue of **Queen Victoria** in the guise of Britannia, executed by **Sir John Steell**, which still surmounts the RSA (see also pp 864–5).

St Andrew Square

'The Golden Square', the second richest piece of real estate in Britain, where millions accrue annually to its financial institutions, St Andrew Square is nonetheless poorer in architectural terms than its younger sister, **Charlotte Square**, at the opposite, western end of **George Street**. It dates from the very commencement of the **New Town** in 1767, when Sir Laurence Dundas secured the middle feu of its east side, which was originally earmarked for **St Andrew's Church**. **Dundas House** was designed by the 'Suedo-Scot' **Sir William Chambers** in 1772–4. Earlier, however, Andrew Crosbie, an advocate previously resident in **Advocate's Close** in the **Old Town**, raised No 35, very likely designed by **Robert Adam**, immediately north of the Dundas feu in 1769. No 35 'answers as a wing to Sir Laurence's house. It is to be hoped that, when the magistrates dispose of the correspondent area on the south end they will take care to preserve uniformity by making the house to be raised on it, be built after the design of Mr Crosbie' (Arnott, 1778). This suggestion was in fact adopted by the developer John Young in concert with **James Craig**, the planner of the New Town, so that a harmonious centrepiece to the east side was achieved. In the southwest, at the corner of St David Street – jokingly said to have been named after the great atheist philosopher – **David Hume** lived out his latter days, 'happy with fame and his own cooking' (Keir, 1966).

St Andrew's Church, George Street

Intended as the centrepiece of the east side of **St Andrew Square** (balancing St George's Church in **Charlotte Square** and closing the vista along **George Street**), St Andrew's Church was pre-empted on its supposedly sacrosanct site on the **New Town** plan by **Dundas House** in 1767. St Andrew's therefore was built halfway along the north side of the easternmost section of George Street in 1785. Designed by Andrew Frazer of the Royal Engineers, the church is a plain Pantheon-derived shell fronted by a 40ft (12m) portico of four Corinthian columns. The steeple-tower – also designed by Frazer – was added in 1789 and is made up of ascending rectangular, octagonal and circular storeys; it contains a chime of eight bells 'to be rung in the English manner'. St Andrew's Church was the scene, in May 1843, of the climax of the **Disruption** when 474 of the c1200 ministers present at the **General Assembly of the Church of Scotland** being held therein walked out to found the **Free Church of Scotland**.

(Old) St Andrew's House

Contoured across the southern slopes of the **Calton Hill**, St Andrew's House was built in 1936–9 by Thomas Tait as the principal seat of the Scottish Office. At first the government proposed to foist a bland, low-budget 'box' on the site of the castellated Bridewell and Calton Gaol complex designed respectively by **Robert Adam**

and Archibald Elliott in 1791 and 1815. Concerted opposition by the **Cockburn** Association resulted in a 'climb-down' and an architectural competition was held in 1933. The resulting Cyclopean structure is the finest 1930s building in Scotland, displaying through its symbolic ornament the government's 'determination to demonstrate that a commitment to Scotland as a nation was not solely the prerogative of the Nationalists' (McKean, 1990). Many Scots, however, continued to view its unashamedly authoritarian presence as the mark of a 'colonial power' ruling from outside. The Art Deco influenced structure, opened on the day after war was declared in 1939, consists of a hollow square with two long wings to the east and west; above the massive, thistled portals, half-length 'colossi' represent **Architecture**, Statecraft, Health, **Agriculture**, Fisheries and **Education**. The chambers of the Secretary of State for Scotland within contain walnut panelling from a tree planted at **Balmerino Abbey** by **Queen Mary**. Old and New St Andrew's House, part of the **St James' Centre**, were deserted for the new Scottish Office, opened in **Leith** in 1994.

St Anthony's Chapel

A shattered two-storey ruin on the lower slopes of **Arthur's Seat** in **Holyrood Park**, St Anthony's Chapel was erected c1450 as a beacon for mariners on the Firth of Forth. The chapel may have been connected with St Anthony's Hospital, a preceptory of the Knights Hospitallers in **Leith** founded by **James I** c1430 for sufferers of St Anthony's Fire, or erysipelas (an inflammation of the skin usually affecting the face). The 'Hermitage' near St Anthony's Cave was probably a storehouse for the chapel.

> Now Arthur's Seat shall be my bed,
> The sheet shall ne'er be pressed by me;
> St Anton's Well shall be my drink,
> Since my true love's forsaken me.
>
> (*Trad*)

St Bernard's Well

A mineral spring situated by the **Water of Leith** downstream from the **Dean Village**, St Bernard's Well is covered by an elegant Doric rotunda inspired by the Roman Temple of Vesta at Tivoli. The wellhouse was designed by **Alexander Nasmyth** in 1789 for the eccentric Lord Gardenstone. The pumproom was refurbished in marble and mosaic for William Nelson, the publisher, in 1888 when the statue of Hygieia, Goddess of Health, was also replaced. The sulphurous waters have been likened to 'the washings of a foul gun-barrel'.

St Cecilia's Hall, Niddry Street

A 'surprise' in the **Cowgate**, the scruffy front of St Cecilia's Hall in narrow **Niddry Street** (formerly Wynd) belies the beautiful concert hall behind, which was completed in 1763 by **Robert Mylne** for the Edinburgh Musical Society. The hall is a much reduced model of the Farnese Theatre at Parma. Altered for the 'Freemasons' Hall' of the Grand Lodge of Scotland 1809–44, St Cecilia's Hall suffered much until restored and extended by the **University of Edinburgh**'s Reid

School of Music in 1960 to house the Russell Collection of early keyboard instruments. The acoustics remain excellent, being 'remarkable for the clear and perfect conveyance of sounds without responding echoes' (Chambers, 1868.)

St Cuthbert's Kirk

A shotgun union of a Victorian baroque barn with an elegant Georgian steeple, St Cuthbert's Kirk lies sunk off **Lothian Road** in the hollow of **Princes Street Gardens** behind **St John's Church** in the West End. The kirk traditionally occupies the site of an 8th century **Culdee** foundation dedicated to **St Cuthbert** (c635–87) of the Lothians. However, it is first mentioned as being 'hard by the **Castle**' in the Holyrood Charter (c1140) of **David I**, whose parents, **Malcolm III 'Canmore'** and **Queen Margaret**, possibly founded it. It was rededicated by the Bishop of **St Andrews** in 1242. When the present church was erected between 1892–4, the foundations of at least six earlier churches were found. This basilica-type construction by Hippolyte Blanc replaced the plain box of 1775 (the steeple was added in 1789) which itself had replaced an earlier clutter then in a 'ruinous and irreparable condition'. In the troubled century after the **Reformation**, the 'West Kirk', as it was then known, had suffered greatly from its proximity to the Castle, being used as a battery or redoubt during four sieges: by the **Regent Morton** in 1573, the **Covenanters** in 1640, Cromwell in 1650 and William of Orange in 1689, when the Duke of Gordon, the Castle Governor, long held out for **James VII**. In 1650 the kirk 'was altogider spoyled, nayther pulpit, loft nor seat left therein . . . nayther door, window nor glass' while the roof was riddled with 'shots of canone and muskett' (Nicol, 1650).

Restored in 1990, the kirk interior is remarkable for its lush furnishings, notably those decorating the lofty Renaissance-style apse. There, a tripartite alabaster wall frieze in high relief, divided by pilasters of red Veronese marble and modelled on *The Last Supper* by Leonardo da Vinci, dominates the richly inlaid communion table incorporating the very rare green Aventurine. The font is an adaptation of that in Sienna Cathedral, the statuary on top a copy of that of Michaelangelo in the Church of Our Lady of Bruges. Among the many murals are paintings by **John Duncan** and a fresco of St Cuthbert on Lindisfarne by Gerald Moira. These are outshone by the stained-glass 'David and Goliath' done by Tiffany of New York c1900.

St Cuthbert's Kirkyard

The many venerable monuments in St Cuthbert's Kirkyard are guarded by the restored circular crenellated watchhouse of 1827, a former precautionary measure against bodysnatchers. Here lie Thomas de Quincey, 'the English opium-eater', **Alexander Nasmyth**, artist and architect of **St Bernard's Well**, and **George Meikle Kemp**, the unfortunate designer of the **Scott Monument**.

St Giles Cathedral

A medieval dowager turned drab by the application of a now dark, early 19th century ashlar veneer, St Giles

Lantern tower and spire of St Giles Cathedral (RWB)

Cathedral – 'the High Kirk of Edinburgh' – constricts the **High Street** in front of **Parliament Square**. Although not formally dedicated to St Giles, or Egidius (a Greek hermit who settled in Provence in the 6th century), until 1243, a church seemingly existed in the city from early times. The first primitive foundation recorded in 854 was superseded by a Romanesque construction, 'the palimpsest of the building we know today' (Gordon, 1954). This was probably an unaisled, single cell on the site of the present nave, erected by **Alexander I** c1120; a round-arched, recessed and grotesquely-carved doorway, similar to that at **Dalmeny Kirk**, survived destruction until 1797. The four massive central columns of the crossing which support the 160ft (49m) high lantern tower may be the sole surviving fabric of this Norman foundation. The lantern, or crown of St Giles was raised c1500; the spire is supported by eight pinnacled flying buttresses and surmounted by a golden weathercock positioned in 1567. In 1387 the body of the kirk was broadened by the building of five chapels south of the nave, the beginning of the piecemeal accretions for individuals and incorporations which, from the outset, bedevilled the cruciform design plan as developed c1370–1420. By 1419 the choir, 'the finest piece of late medieval parish church architecture in Scotland' (Gifford et al, 1984) was probably complete; this was remodelled with a central clerestory prior to the elevation of St Giles into a collegiate kirk by **James III** in 1466.

The last Mass was sung in St Giles in March 1560 when the kirk was uneasily tenanted jointly by the Catholic clergy and the Protestant **Lords of the Congregation**; the latter soon 'purged the said kirk of idolatrie' and installed **John Knox** as the city minister. When the Catholic **Mary Stewart** became Queen in August 1561, the kirk became the focus of Knox's great struggle to establish **Presbyterianism**, a torch taken up by later ministers in the 'Tumult of St Giles' when they railed against her son **James VI**. The kirk briefly served as an episcopal cathedral under **Charles I** from 1633–9. In 1637, on the attempted introduction of the English **prayer-book**, a Tron kail-wife, Jenny Geddes, supposedly flung her folding-stool at the Dean, screeching 'Deil colic the wame o' ye!' (May the Devil buckle your belly); the ensuing uproar led to the signing of the National **Covenant** in **Greyfriars' Kirk** in 1638 whereby Episcopacy was abolished.

The quite exquisite 20th century Gothic Revival Thistle Chapel for the Knights of the **Order of the Thistle** was added by **Robert Lorimer** in 1909–11.

St James' Centre

The infamous concrete colossus originally intended to bestride Leith Street by 'the bridge to nowhere', the St James' Centre, built behind **Register House** at the east end of **Princes Street**, was opened in 1970. The Centre's brutally modernist design was conceived in 1964 to relate partly to the 'Wagnerian' Inner Ring Road then planned on its north-eastern flank. In 1965 the coming 'beast' began to devour the split-level Leith Street and the elegantly slummy St James' Square designed in 1773 by **James Craig**, the original planner of the **New Town**. Residents were given only the three weeks over Christmas and New Year in which to object to the compulsory purchase of their property; protests were crushed by a combine consisting of the city council, the private developers and the Scottish Office whose New St Andrew's House towers over the site of the old square. However, the massive public outcry which greeted the sight of the finished construction probably did more to promote conservation in the city than any other *cause célèbre*.

St John Street/Close/Cross

A civic improvement built immediately prior to the **New Town** in 1768, St John Street is still entered from the **Canongate** through a high pend, or vaulted passage, beneath the former townhouse of the Earl of Hopetoun, where **Tobias Smollett** conceived *Humphrey Clinker* in 1766. Strictly private like nearby New Street (built 1760, the abode of **Lords Kames** and **Hailes**), it was guarded by a uniformed steward. Besides many nobility, its single terrace on the east side (demolished c1960) housed **James Ballantyne**, the printer; the eccentric **James Burnett**, **Lord Monboddo**, whose 'learned suppers' were attended by **Robert Burns**; and **Dr John Gregory**, who concocted the rhubarb and ginger panacea 'Gregory's Mixture'.

St John's Close holds Lodge Canongate Kilwinning No 2 (1736), reckoned to be the world's oldest existing **Masonic** premises, where Robert Burns was reputedly installed as its 'Poet Laureate' in 1787. Adjacent lies the Priory of the Most Venerable Order of St John in Scotland on lands owned by the medieval Knights of St John of Jerusalem, who had their preceptory there.

The site of St John's Cross is marked with a Maltese Cross in the Canongate nearby; the apex of a triangle of land with its base on St John's Hill to the south, earlier the property of the Knights Templar. The cross also delineated the extent of the Royalty of Edinburgh on the south side of the Canongate, where proclamations were read as well as at the **Mercat Cross**.

St John's Church, Princes Street

The sole spark of spirituality in **Princes Street**, St John's Episcopal Church stands on the corner of **Lothian Road**, above **St Cuthbert's Kirk**, at the West End. It was designed by **William Burn** in 1815–18 and was extended by the addition of an apse in 1878–82; the church was partly modelled on St George's Chapel, Windsor. The pinnacled tower originally terminated in an open octagonal lantern which crashed through the roof and floor into the vaults beneath during a storm in 1818. 'This was sticking the horns of the mitre into the belly of the church' (**Scott**, 1818). The interior is perhaps the finest achievement of the early Gothic Revival in Scotland; the splendid fan-vaulting of the nave is an interpretation of that at St George's Chapel and the Chapel of Henry VII at Westminster. Behind the high altar, in the apse, is a reredos of Caen stone below the best stained-glass windows, the work of Messrs Clayton & Bell; St John's possesses the finest collection of Victorian stained glass in Scotland.

St Leonards

Site of the hospital and chapel of St Leonard, an appendage of **Holyrood Abbey** built by 1271, the **Southside** 'town' of St Leonards including the Pleasance passed to Edinburgh in 1639; the chapel ruins stood until 1810 on St Leonard's Hill. The villa 'Hermits and Termits' built in 1734 for William Clifton, Solicitor of Excise, was possibly named after two of the crofts of St Leonard's Hospital which may have begun as a hermitage; the house was long the office of the 'Innocent **Railway**', the first city line, which ran from St Leonards to **Dalkeith** (Newtongrange) with branches via **Duddingston** and **Portobello** to Fisherrow (**Musselburgh**) and **Leith**. Commissioned in 1826 to reduce carriage charges from the Lothian **coal**fields, traffic commenced in 1831; passengers were carried from 1834. Operated by horse-traction, with steam engines to haul trains up the inclined plain to St Leonards, the line was 'innocent' because it did not adopt **locomotives** until 1845, rather than for its good safety record.

St Margaret's Well, Holyrood Park

A miniature medieval Gothic masterpiece, St Margaret's Well was re-erected (at the suggestion of **Hugh Miller**) on its present site in **Holyrood Park** hard by the **Palace of Holyroodhouse** in 1860. Its removal was necessitated by the building of the St Margaret's Bogie Works of the North British **Railway** on its original site between

St Margaret's Well before its 1860 removal from Restalrig to Holyrood Park (RWB)

Edinburgh continued

Restalrig and **Meadowbank**, a spot now marked by a rough-hewn boulder.

The architectural arrangements of the well are broadly similar both in period and in style to those of St Triduana's Aisle at Restalrig Kirk; indeed it may earlier have been known as St Triduana's Well. The mid-15th century structure consists of a hexagonal, vaulted stone cell having a cluster of groined sculpturally embossed ribs springing from a central pillar with a grotesque mask from which issues a spring of clear water; the spring previously served St David's Well [see **Holyrood Abbey**].

St Mary's Episcopal Cathedral

The largest and 'the finest church . . . built in Scotland since the Reformation' (Warr, 1960), St Mary's Cathedral in Palmerston Place is the greatest landmark of the West End; it was designed by Sir George Gilbert Scott from 1873–9 in the early Pointed 'Northern English' style, the axis of the 275ft (84m) high central or rood tower coinciding with the centre of Melville Street. The Victorian Gothic creation arose from the legacy left in 1870 by the Misses Walker of Easter Coates, whose quaint little mansion, first built in 1617 and now St Mary's Music School, remains in the shadow of their great bequest; in their memory, the appellation 'Barbara and Mary' is conferred upon the twin western towers, not added until 1915–17. Cruciform in plan and rather eclectically derived from 'everywhere', St Mary's admirably demonstrates the ability of Gilbert Scott to raise massive well-related architectural compositions (as at **Glasgow University**).

St Mary's Metropolitan Cathedral

Brutally oppressed by the **St James' Centre** behind, St Mary's Cathedral seemingly seeks to confirm that 'Ye cannot serve God and Mammon'. St Mary's Chapel, the first Roman Catholic church constructed in the city after the **Reformation**, was designed in 1813 by **James Gillespie Graham**. Only the neo-Perpendicular Gothic front of the original building, which was elevated to cathedral status in 1878, now remains. 'It was the first essay in that peculiar type of Gothic façade which acted as a screen to a simple rectangular auditorium whose bulk was hidden by the flanking houses' (Lindsay, 1948). Following a fire in 1891 St Mary's was rebuilt in rather unusual fashion; the nave spans the width of the original chapel; its combined width, along with the aisles, exceeds their length. St Andrew's Altar, which displays two relics of the national saint, is currently proposed as a focus for the re-establishment of a national shrine of pilgrimage to **St Andrew**.

St Patrick's Church, Cowgate

A plain, two-storey 18th century chapel with a fine octagonal-domed steeple tower, fronted by a 20th century 'triumphal arch', St Patrick's Church holds back from the **Cowgate** within the former grounds of Tweeddale House. The chapel was raised in 1771 for the 'qualified' **Episcopalians** who had met since 1722 in **Blackfriars'** Wynd (**Street**). This sect favoured the 'Glorious Revolution' of 1689, adopting Church of England ritual and praying for King George. In contradistinction were those disaffected by the Hanoverians who, having been expelled from **St Giles** in 1689, continued secretly to support the **Stewart** cause. These **Jacobites** met in Carruber's Close on the site of **Old St Paul's Church**. After the erection of St Paul's (and St George's) Church by Archibald Elliott in York Place in the **New Town** in 1818, the Cowgate chapel was briefly occupied by the **Presbyterian United Secession** congregation until 1856, when it was purchased by the **Roman Catholic Church**. The chapel has thus enjoyed the singular distinction of serving each of the major religious denominations of Scotland. Altered and redesigned in 1890 – 'it is the only Christian church standing south and north we ever saw or heard of!' (Arnot, 1799) – the apse is still adorned with the original mural decorations attributed to **Alexander Runciman**.

St Stephen's Church

A bold exclamation mark terminating the northern vista down Frederick Street, St Stephen's Church was built by **William Playfair** in 1827. The peninsular site called for a 'drastic' design when the original location on the west side of Royal Circus, chosen as the eastern focal terminus along Great King Street, was abandoned. While the exterior is a diagonally-set square, the interior is octagonal. Most impressive is the campanile tower; the bell weighs 18 cwt (16,460kg) and the clock claims to have the longest pendulum (65ft 5in/20m) in Europe. At the arched base of the tower, the main entrance is a yawning maw swallowing the ramp of shallow steps – the passage to the 'Temple of Doom'. There is an unlikely tale that the site was spitefully chosen by the town council to eclipse the **Edinburgh Academy**, built earlier to the north by **William Burn**, the great rival of William Playfair.

Salisbury Crags

A fulmar-infested escarpment bending like a boomerang north-eastwards from **Arthur's Seat**, Salisbury Crags loom large in the Edinburgh landscape. The Crags are possibly the finest example in Scotland of an igneous sill, where a sheet of molten teschenite has been intruded along the horizontally bedded strata of the earlier sandstones. The exposure is sacred to the spirit of the great 'father of modern **geology**', **James Hutton**, who demonstrated in his 'Theory of the Earth' that the Crags were formed by Plutonic forces from the molten magma which had journeyed from the centre of the earth and consolidated with the crust: 'Hutton's Section' shows the junction between the base of the sill and the bedded sediments; 'Hutton's Rock' reveals a band of haematite, vertically locked in a mass of teschenite. Remarkably, these rocks were saved from the wholesale **quarrying** conducted by the Earl of **Haddington**, the Hereditary Keeper of **Holyrood Park**, who was finally halted by the House of Lords in 1831. The 'Radical Road' skirting the base of the Crags was largely due to that good Tory **Sir Walter Scott** who, having immortalised Holyrood Park in *Heart of Midlothian* in 1818, employed a destitute group of radical west of Scotland weavers to break their politics as much as stones:

> Round and round the Radical Road
> The Radical Rascal Ran
>
> *(Local jingle)*

Scott Monument

In **Princes Street Gardens**, the Scott Monument is probably the largest memorial raised to a writer anywhere. Built in 1840–6, it is a soaring Gothic steeple dedicated to the memory of **Sir Walter Scott**. The architect was **George Meikle Kemp**, a joiner and carpenter who taught himself draughtsmanship when his plans to start up his own small business failed; sadly he drowned in the **Union Canal** in 1844, before his master-work was completed. (Architect and author met in 1813 – Kemp had just completed his apprenticeship and was walking

Salisbury Crags and the 'Radical Road' (SEA)

to **Galashiels** to take up his first job when he was given a lift by Scott, then Sheriff of **Selkirkshire**, in his carriage.) Kemp entered the design competition under the pseudonym of 'John Morvo' (or Morrow) , a medieval master-mason of **Melrose** Abbey. Initially placed third, this 'obscure man' elaborated his proposals to win outright in 1838 against strong professional opposition. The builder was David Lind, who had recently constructed the Tolbooth Kirk; the sandstone came from Binny Quarry at Uphall in **West Lothian**. On a stepped base only 55ft (16.7m) square, but resting on foundations 52ft (15.8m) deep, the monument rises to the height of 200½ft (61m). There are 287 steps to the top. Enshrined in the open vault beneath is the seated statue of Scott dressed in a Border plaid and accompanied by his favourite deerhound Maida, carved from a 30-ton block of Carrara Marble (which fell into the harbour at Leghorn in Italy on its way to **Leith**) by **Sir John Steell** 1840–6. 64 niches contain statuettes representing many characters from the works of Scott, mostly added in 1870 and 1881. The structure and its rediscovered vault (intended for Scott's tomb) were restored, but not cleaned, during 1996–8.

Scottish National Gallery of Modern Art, Belford Road

Founded in 1960, the Scottish National Gallery of Modern Art occupies the lengthy, top-heavy Greek Doric Temple of two storeys originally erected as John Watson's Hospital in 1825–8 by **William Burn**. (In 1762 Watson, a Writer to the Signet, had bequeathed £1300 which accrued to £110,000 by 1822; a fee-paying co-educational school from 1934, it was assimilated into **George Watson's College** in 1975.) The Gallery had endured cramped quarters in Inverleith House (1774) at the **Royal Botanic Garden** before moving in 1984 to the spacious grounds at Belford Road near the **Dean Village**. The nucleus of the collection comprises works by pioneer artists of the 20th century, notably the Cubists Braque (*Candlestick*) and Picasso (*La Table de Musicien* and *The Soles*); also an unusually 'dark' study (*La Leçon de Peinture*) by Matisse. French art generally is strong, with some outstanding work by Léger; as are German Expressionism (Feininger, Kirchner, Kokoschka, Dix, Nolde) and Surrealism (Magritte, Miro, Ernst, Dali, Giacometti). During its first decade the Gallery also purchased significant representative works of 20th century British painting and sculpture; most major figures are thus present, including Sickert, Sutherland, Bomberg, Nash and Hockney; also Epstein, Hepworth and Moore, some of whose works, notably *Reclining Figure*, are displayed outside. Contemporary British work includes Freud, Kossoff, Auerbach, Kitaj, Walker, Lebrun, Bellany and the 'younger Scots'. The earlier Scottish Colourists – **Peploe**, **Cadell**, **Hunter** and **Fergusson** – are prominent as are **MacTaggart**, **Cowie**, Colquhoun, MacBryde, **Eardley** and Davie.

Scottish National Portrait Gallery

An 'Italian warehouse' situated at No 1 **Queen Street**, the Scottish National Portrait Gallery was designed in Venetian Gothic style after the Doge's Palace by **R Rowand Anderson** in 1885–90. Until 1998 the long, three-storeyed block of red Dumfries sandstone also accommodated the old National Museum of Antiquities, which collection formed the basis of the new **Museum of Scotland**. The foundation was enabled in 1892 through a donation of £50,000 made by **John Ritchie Findlay**, the proprietor of *The Scotsman*. Outside, historical statuary and symbolic sculpture by W Birnie Rhind weather the east winds; inside the central hall has a star-studded celestial ceiling and colourful historical frieze by W B Hole. The portrait collection is composed of works which were transferred from the **National Gallery of Scotland**, eg *David Hume* by **Allan Ramsay** and *Robert Burns* by **Alexander Nasmyth**; bequests such as *Prince Charles Edward Stuart* by an unknown artist and the gaunt *Robert Louis Stevenson* painted in Samoa by Count Nerli; and purchases such as *Sir Walter Scott* by **Henry Raeburn** and *Mary Queen of Scots* by Peter Oudry. Apart from other royal portraits, there are also many works depicting 'ordinary' Scots notable in **law**, business and the arts, including a number of notable living Scots specially commissioned in recent years.

Scottish Parliament

The devolved Scottish Parliament was officially opened with quiet dignity in its temporary home in the **New College Assembly Hall** on **The Mound** by HM Queen Elizabeth II on 1 July 1999. Members walked up the High Street from the old **Parliament House** in an informal echo of the old 'riding of the Parliament'. This stately procession wound up the **Royal Mile** from the **Palace of Holyroodhouse** to **Parliament Hall**; the **Regalia**, the Cross, Sword of State and Sceptre were borne by the premier earls along with the 'purse and commission' before the Lord High Commissioner, accompanied by Lord Lyon King of Arms, the Heralds Pursuivant and all the officers of state. The 1999 reconvened proceedings began with a 'Fanfare for the Scottish Parliament' conducted by its composer, James Macmillan; also included were 'The Beginning of a New Song' by **Iain Crichton Smith** – an allusion to 'the end o' ane auld sang', the demise of the old Scots Parliament under the **Treaty of Union** in 1707 – and the international democratic anthem, 'For A' That and A' That', by **Robert Burns**. The crown of Scotland from the Regalia, displayed in the old Parliament Hall until 1707, was accompanied from **Edinburgh Castle** by its keeper, the **Duke of Hamilton**, as Scotland's premier nobleman. A new mace of Scottish silver, the symbol of the authority invested in the Parliament, was unveiled by one of the Heralds; its band of gold, panned from Scottish rivers, symbolises the marriage of the Parliament, the land and the people. The head of the mace is engraved 'There shall be a Scottish Parliament', and the words 'Wisdom/Justice/Compassion/Integrity' are woven into the thistle adornments, minding Scots of their aspirations for their elected representatives.

The future, permanent home of the Scottish Parliament occupies part of the site of the former Scottish & Newcastle Breweries complex at the foot of the **Canongate**, opposite the Palace of Holyroodhouse. The modernist design by the Catalan Enric Miralles won a competition which attracted entries from international architects. His controversial 'upturned boats' feature – apparently modelled on craft photographed on Holy Island, Northumberland, which Miralles felt represented Scotland – met with much opposition from those who had long favoured the conversion of the **Old Royal High School** on **Calton Hill**. Described by Donald Dewar as 'a tangible symbol of Scotland's democratic adventure', Miralles' design aims to be a linked group of buildings growing out of the site and complementing the adjoining landscape of Holyrood Park, rather than a single monolithic structure emphasising the importance of the parliament. The main entrance of the six-storey building forms part of a large, pedestrianised public space facing **Arthur's Seat**; MSPs and staff will enter near **Queensberry House**, to be restored as the administration block, and enjoy the tranquillity of a 'secret garden'. The debating chamber, begun as a 'horseshoe' and then bent into a 'banana', has eventually become a semicircular 'elongated chamber' to avoid the confrontational shenanigans which ignite Westminster.

See also **SCOTTISH PARLIAMENT** (pp 895–6).

Signet Library

An exquisite Corinthian-columned cathedral or 'Paradise of Bokes' (Dibdin, 1838), the Signet Library comprises the collection of the Society of Writers to HM Signet in **Parliament Square**. The library was founded in 1722 when the Society (itself formed before 1594) resolved to purchase Scots **law** books and statutes. A general collection, however, was begun in 1778, shortly after which flats were purchased in 'Writers' Court' (now part of the **City Chambers**), convivially close to Cleriheugh's Star and Garter Tavern. The present two-storey premises, designed in 1812–15 by William Stark, have been occupied by the Library since 1815; the Upper Library was the **Advocates' Library** until 1826. This vaulted salon, 132ft (40m) long, 40ft (12m) broad, and running the length of the building, is entered via an imperial stairway added by **William Burn**, and a Corinthian-columned screen beneath a coffered dome, both the work of **William Playfair**, in 1819–20. On the central elliptical dome, painted by Thomas Stotland in 1821, Apollo and the Muses mix with a medley of historical characters.

Slateford and Longstone

At the 19th century 'spaghetti junction' below **Craiglockhart** where the Lanark Road and Caledonian **Railway** cross the **Water of Leith** and **Union Canal**, the former milling and **quarrying** communities of Slateford and Longstone are conjoined by 20th century sprawl. Both the remarkable six-arch 600ft (183m) long and 60ft (18m) high aqueduct built by Hugh Baird in 1818 and the 14-arch railway viaduct of 1847 overshoot Slateford which was torn apart for road working in 1965; only part of the south side, where Slateford House (c1770) and the 18th century Cross Keys Inn front the former Slateford **Secession Church** (1785), remains. Also sadly gone is the 'Slateford Torque', an exceptionally fine gold armlet of c600 BC found during 'railway construction' last century but melted down by an unscrupulous Edinburgh jeweller. In 1745 Gray's Mill at Inglis Green was commandeered by **Prince Charles Edward Stewart** for his headquarters; here he received the magistrates while seeking the surrender of the city. Inglis Green was leased by George Inglis of **Redhall** as a bleaching green to Joseph Reid in 1773; printing and bleaching cloth continued from 1778–1849 when Alexander and John MacNab introduced dyeing, tweed-making and a laundry, a prosperous concern which closed in 1983. Longstone developed last century as 'a bedraggled workers' village' associated with Hailes and Redhall Quarries at Kingsknowe, the former, like **Craigleith**, extensively worked c1800 for building the **New Town**. Slateford Road itself is industrial; the red-brick Caledonian Brewery (1869) is the last in Britain still employing its original **coal**-fired open coppers to boil the malt infusion.

South Bridge

A scruffy 'sortie' connecting the **Old Town** and the **Southside**, the South Bridge was necessitated by the completion of the other half of 'the Bridges', the **North Bridge**, in 1772. The South Brig was designed by Robert Kay as a unified architectural scheme of three-storey buildings and built by Alexander Laing; the foundation stone was laid in August 1785. Consisting of 19 arches (only that over the **Cowgate** is visible), it was opened for carriage traffic by March 1788, 'an operation of astonishing celerity' (Creech, 1793). The profits on the bridge feus were invested to offset the cost of the **University of Edinburgh** which was planned for its southern end at the **Kirk o'Field**. The sudden rise in level at the University is a lasting result of the determined opposition of **Robert Dundas**, Lord President of the **Court of Session**, who resided in nearby Adam Square. Had the bridge maintained an upward or even level course from the **High Street**, his house entrance would have been below the roadway; the bridge commissioners – who included his half-brother, **Henry Dundas, 1st Viscount Melville** – acceded to his single-mindedness.

Southside

Stretching for a mile southwards from the **Old Town** to **Newington**, the Southside is bounded by **Arthur's Seat** and the **Meadows** on its east and west respectively. The area includes **Bristo**, the Pleasance and **St Leonards**. Convivially unplanned, it first grew up beyond the **Flodden Wall** during the hiatus in the building of the **New Town** in the mid-18th century. In 1743 Lady Nicolson permitted the development of Bristo Street, feuing her house grounds for Alison Square in 1749 and for Nicolson Street and Square in 1757. The district first 'took off' in 1766, however, when **George Square** was boldly constructed outside the extended royalty of the city. By 1770 the Southside was popular enough with house-buyers to counteract the successful marketing of the northern extension. But after 1800 the New Town reigned supreme. Nevertheless tenemental development in the Southside reached as far as Clerk Street in 1810, and South Clerk Street followed from 1830. During the 1960s, the Southside suffered from excessive planning blight brought about by the (**North** and **South**) **Bridges** Relief Road proposals and the **University of Edinburgh** Central Redevelopment Plan. Wholesale demolitions for these abortive schemes were wrought at Pleasance, St Leonards and Bristo c1970. The spectre of redevelopment first lifted in 1981 when

the typically mixed range of 18th century vernacular architecture around Haddon's Court and Gibb's Entry was restored and reconstructed for residential purposes by the Crown Estates Commissioners.

Stockbridge

Formerly a milling village on the **Water of Leith**, 'Stock Bridge' acquired its stone bridge in 1786 following the development of the **New Town**. The vicinity was popularised as a rustic retreat for valetudinarians after the discovery of **St Bernard's Well** in 1760. Development began on the St Bernard's estate of the artist **Henry Raeburn**, the son of a local yarn boiler, in 1813 when the Arcadian Anne Street (reputedly named after the artist's wife and likely designed by architect James Milne) was laid out. Milne also built, on a more massive urban scale, the Doric-columned St Bernard's Crescent in 1824. Bohemian Stockbridge was the birthplace of other notable artists: **John Watson Gordon** (1788) and, at nearby Silvermills (supposedly named from the extraction mills erected for **Thomas Hamilton** in 1607), brothers **Robert Scott Lauder** and James Bickford Lauder. **Thomas Carlyle** spent the first 18 months of married life with **Jane Welsh Carlyle** at Comely Bank in their 'trim little cottage, far from all the uproar and putrescences, material and spiritual, of the reeking town' (Carlyle, 1826). The 'Colonies' – 11 rows of terraced housing for artisans – were built at Inverleith by the Edinburgh Co-operative Building Company 1861–1911; plaques depict the tools of the trades involved in their erection – joiner, mason, decorator, plumber and plasterer.

Swanston

An idyllic, once pastoral clachan of early 18th century white-harled and Tay reed thatched cottages – the only such in Lowland Scotland – Swanston braces itself at c600m on the northern slopes of the **Pentland Hills**. The original 10 cottages, forming five blocks picturesquely ranged around the village green, became eight when they were restored for cost-rent housing by the city in 1962–4. The 18th century crowstepped farmhouse and the old schoolhouse (The White House) complete an improbable survivor which was complemented by a square of solid farmworkers' housing in the mid-19th century. At nearby Swanston Cottage, a two-storey villa dating from 1761, **Robert Louis Stevenson** summered with his parents and old nurse, Alison Cunningham, from 1867–80. Built in connection with the tapping of the Swanston Springs to supplement the city's water supply, this 'Municipal Pleasure House' (Stevenson, 1879) was long used by the magistrates for junketing.

Tailors' Hall, Cowgate

Apart from **Magdalen Chapel** and **St Giles Cathedral**, the Tailors' Hall in the **Cowgate** is the most important survivor of the medieval trades incorporations of Edinburgh. Built by 1621, the seat of the Incorporation of Tailors occupies a courtyard fronted until 1940 by a magnificent five-storey tenement of c1650. In 1638 the draft of the National **Covenant** was approved at the hall; it was also used in 1656 by the Scottish Commission of the Protectorate of Oliver Cromwell for the administration of forfeited Royalist estates. The hall was altered in 1757 for the printing works of Provost Alexander Kincaid; and again in 1800 for the Argyle Brewery, latterly Messrs Archibald Campbell, Hope & King until 'rationalisation' in 1971 after takeover by Whitbread in 1967. Restored in 1998 as 'Tailors' Hall Hotel', its 'Three Sisters Bar' claims to be the largest pub in Scotland.

Tolbooth/'Heart of Midlothian'

Demolished in 1811 and 1817, the Tolbooth was the multi-purpose medieval administrative centre for both the city and the state. Situated on the **High Street** at **Parliament Square** in front of **St Giles Cathedral**, this was the booth where tolls and dues were paid, where a bell was rung when goods were to be sold, where civic meetings were convened and where the 10 o'clock curfew was sounded. In 1386 **Robert II** provided a 'bell-house', possibly replacing the former 'praetorium' or town-hall of 1369 which was burnt by Richard II in 1385. The 'Old' Tolbooth was added c1403–30 to accommodate both the local and national legislatures. A separate 'New' Tolbooth was built for the town council at the south-west corner of St Giles after 1562. The 'Old' Tolbooth complex was substantially reconstructed in 1610; this 'bastille' sheltered the Scots Parliament and the College of Justice until the **Parliament Hall** was built in 1639.

After 1640 the Tolbooth was a gaol. Although often decorated with noble heads – **Morton** in 1581, **Montrose** in 1650 and his enemy **Argyll** in 1660 – and presided over by the Town Guard, 'it was a peculiarity of the Tolbooth, that through clanship or some other influence, nearly every criminal of rank confined in it achieved an escape' (Grant, 1884). In 1736 in the **Porteous Riot** Captain-Lieutenant John Porteous, commander of the City Guard, was strung up from a dyer's pole in the **Grassmarket**. On a scaffold designed by himself which stood at the west end of the Tolbooth, **Deacon William Brodie** was hanged for his audacious burglaries in 1788.

The entrance to the Old Tolbooth is marked by variegated granite setts in the shape of the 'Heart of Midlothian' named after the novel of **Sir Walter Scott** which immortalised the old gaol. (The quaint but insanitary custom of spitting on the cente of the heart for good luck supposedly derives from this being the first contemptuous act of prisoners on their release.) Scott himself obtained the Tolbooth door, together with its lock and key, and re-erected it at **Abbotsford**.

Town Walls (King's Wall)

Edinburgh was never encircled by a wall. The **Old Town** was thus protected only on its south side; the **Nor' Loch** made do on the other. (The **Canongate** always lay beyond the pale.) In 1450 **James II** licensed the burgh 'to fosse, bulwark, wall, tower, turret and otherwise strengthen' the King's Wall against 'our enemies of England'. First mentioned in 1472 as forming the boundary of burgess property on the south side of the **High Street**, this forerunner of the **Flodden Wall**

(1513–60) ran for about half a mile east to west, halfway down the slope, from the **Netherbow** to the **West Bow** and the **Grassmarket** where buttressed portions still remain in situ. To hasten the completion of the barrier, **James III** had to impose compulsory levies on the recalcitrant burgesses, who were ordered to fortify their 'heidyaird' dykes meantime.

Considerable portions of the wall were uncovered behind Old **Parliament House** in 1822 and 1845, 'proving it to have been a solid and magnificent piece of masonry, when compared with the hasty erection of 1513' (Grant, 1884).

Trinity

A handsome Georgian and Victorian villa district on the breezy high ground above **Granton** and **Newhaven**, Trinity belonged to the Fraternity of Masters and Mariners of Trinity House, **Leith**, from 1713. The late 18th century development of the farm of Trinity Mains on the fringe of Wardie Muir attracted local merchants and less conventional seekers of summer quarters. Trinity Lodge, the oldest mansion, was built for Robert Johnson, an Edinburgh merchant, in 1774. The later fine little villa of Trinity Grove, built in 1789 for David Hunter of Blackness (**Angus**), whose son Alexander was a partner of **Archibald Constable**, is recalled for its literary connections; sold in 1811 to William Creech, bookseller at the **Luckenbooths** and publisher of the Edinburgh Edition of the poems of **Robert Burns**, it passed in 1815 to John Ballantyne, auctioneer, the brother of **James Ballantyne**, the printer of the Waverley Novels who financially ruined **Sir Walter Scott**. Strathavon Lodge (formerly 'Inverforth'), the summer residence of **Sir James Young Simpson** of Strathavon whose town house was in **Queen Street**, stands on the estate of the demolished Laverockbank House. Challenger Lodge (originally Wardie Lodge and now St Columba's Hospice) a single-storey Grecian villa of c1830 attributed to **William Playfair**, was the residence of the meteorologist and oceanographer **Sir John Murray**.

Trinity College Kirk

A reset, Scots medieval Gothic gem lurking in Chalmers Close off the **High Street**, Trinity College Kirk stood on the site of **Waverley Station** until 1848. The Kirk was founded by **Mary of Gueldres** in 1462 as a memorial to her husband **James II** – with a catch-all dedication to 'The Holy Trinity, The Blessed Virgin, **St Ninian** and All Saints' – and 'finished' (the choir and transepts, but no nave was constructed) in 1531.

The rebuilt fragment consists only of the two-clerestory vaulted choir which has three aisled bays supporting a three-sided apse, the 'glory' of the original foundation – and the earliest in Scotland after **Crossraguel** in Ayrshire. The fine interior is still recognisable as 'the most accomplished building of its time' (Gifford et al, 1984), rivalling contemporary workmanship at **St Giles**. After partial destruction during the **Reformation** the kirk became the property of the Town; in 1638 the National **Covenant** was first read there to the citizenry, two days after the nobility subscribed to

Trinity College Kirk c1840; the site became that of Waverley Station in 1848 (RWB)

it in **Greyfriars'**. It was rebuilt in 1872 as the hall of the New Trinity Church (demolished 1964); the individually numbered stones languished on **Calton Hill** for 30 years during a protracted lawsuit over the proposed site for re-erection. A pair of painted panels, part of the original 15th century 'retable' or altarpiece, and attributed to the Flemish artist Hugo van der Goes, are in the **National Gallery of Scotland**.

Tron Kirk, High Street

The traditional tryst of **Hogmanay** revellers, the disused Tron Kirk ('Christ's Kirk at the tron') languishes in the **High Street** at its junction with the **North** and **South Bridges**. The 'Tron' is named from the salt-tron, a public weighing beam which formerly stood outside. A conglomeration of Gothic and Palladian architecture, it was designed by **John Mylne**, master-mason to both the Town and the Crown under **Charles I**, to house the congregation displaced from **St Giles** when it was elevated into an **episcopal** cathedral. Although begun in 1637 and opened for worship in 1647, the kirk was not completed until 1663. The stylish T-plan was much truncated in 1785–8 for the building of 'the Bridges'. In 1824, the partly melted steeple, 'an old Dutch thing composed of wood, iron and lead' (**Cockburn**, 1856), crashed into the street during the great fire that devastated the south side of the High Street from the Tron to St Giles.

Wanwordy crazy dinsome thing
As e'er was framed to jow or ring
What gar'd them sic a steeple hing
They ken themsel';
But weel I wat, they couldna' bring
Waur sounds frae Hell

(Fergusson, 1779)

Inside, the rare truss-beam timber roof is similar to the hammerbeam one of **Parliament Hall**. The gutted interior preserves the remains of the 16th century Marlin's Wynd, excavated in 1974. The Wynd is named after John Marlin (or Merlioun), the legendary pavior of the High Street in 1532, whom tradition avers to have been buried at its head under six flat stones in the shape of a grave. 'Since Merlin laid Auld Reekie's causey/And made her o' his wark right saucy' (Fergusson,1779).

Tweeddale Court

Situated in the **High Street** near the **Netherbow**, the wrought-iron 'Gothick' gates of Tweeddale Court hold fast Tweeddale House, probably built c1576 by Neil Laing, Keeper of the Signet, but named after **John Hay, 1st Marquis of Tweeddale** who inherited it in 1695 from his grandmother, Margaret Ker, Lady Yester, daughter of Mark Ker, 1st Earl of Lothian. The two-storey house was remodelled by **Sir William Bruce** in 1664 and reconstructed by **John** and **Robert Adam** during 1752–3. From 1791–1808 the house was the British Linen Company Bank; in 1806 a messenger was robbed of £4392 in notes within the close-mouth, in the unsolved 'Begbie Murder'. Messrs Oliver & Boyd, renowned printers and publishers, occupied the premises from 1817–1973. Behind, the 'plantation of lime-trees ... instead of a garden' (Defoe, 1724) was formerly entered by the rebuilt coach-arch from the **Cowgate**. A lean-to shed resting up against a fragment of the **Town Wall** of c1450 within the paved courtyard reputedly housed sedan-chairs. The 18th century tenement on the east side built by **Deacon William Brodie** has housed the Scottish Poetry Library since its inception in 1984.

Usher Hall

Finally found a suitable site off **Lothian Road** in 1910, the Usher Hall was completed under the backdrop of the **Castle** by J Stockdale Harrison in 1914; Andrew Usher, brewer, had given £100,000 for its construction in 1896. The octagonal, copper-domed concert hall, which is boldly executed in fine Darney stone from Northumberland, is adorned with well-endowed muses representing 'Municipal Beneficence', 'The Soul of Music' and other symbolic themes. The auditorium, accommodating 2900, is largely let for various types of concert according to the terms of the original bequest, notably the Royal Scottish Orchestra and the Edinburgh Royal Choral Union; it is also used as a major venue during the **Edinburgh International Festival** and on those rare but glittering occasions when the Freedom of the City is granted to her famous sons and daughters or to other notable persons, most recently to the actor Sean Connery in 1991.

Water of Leith

The Water of Leith flows half to one mile north and west of central Edinburgh. Rising in the **Pentland Hills** above Harperrigg Reservoir, it runs through a string of suburban villages for 20 miles, with a fall of 1250ft (381m) to the Firth of Forth at **Leith**. Once the 'Great Water of Leith', its name derives from the 'water of the hollow' (Geddie, 1896). Indeed at both **Colinton** and **Dean** it has carved out deep post-glacial gorges from the underlying sandstone and shales, but elsewhere it meanders over ancient loch beds. 'Always remarkable for its mills' (OSA 1793), these were established c1200 at Hailes (Colinton), Dean and **Canonmills**. 70–80 mills operated on the lower 10-mile stretch c.1800, making it 'perhaps the most useful river of any ... in all Scotland' (**Chalmers**, *Caledonia*). After 1870, much industry forsook the waterside for steam-driven mills, yet the first Royal Commission on River Pollution found it the most polluted stream in Scotland. Sewerage was completed in 1889, but it is doubtful if the improved water quality equals that of 1617, when an act of the Scots Parliament decreed the standard Stirling Pint Jug contain '3lbs, 7oz. troy of clear running water of the Water of Leith'. The 13-mile Water of Leith Walkway provides public access to this revitalised city amenity, but through rubbish-dumping, **Robert Louis Stevenson**'s epithet 'that dirty Water of Leith' still pertains.

Waverley Bridge

Occupying the site of the 'Little Mound' created at the foot of **Cockburn Street**, Waverley Bridge lies between the **North Bridge** and **The Mound** which both also span the gap between the **Old Town** and **New Town** formerly filled by the **Nor' Loch**. Waverley Bridge was built to enable carriage access from **Princes Street** to the original three termini of the **Waverley Station** after the coming of the **railways** in the 1840s. The first bridge, a triple-arched stone structure, was possibly influenced in its design by **William Playfair**, who designed the tunnel underneath The Mound. This was replaced by an iron skew bridge of three reaches, with a lattice grid construction, in 1870–3; it complemented the major alterations and extensions undertaken at Waverley Station from 1868–74. The present bridge, consisting of heavy plate girders supported on cast-iron columns, was built in 1894–6 by Messrs Cunningham, Blythe & Westland, Engineers. The pierced-iron parapets were replaced by plastic pressings in 1985–6.

Waverley Market

A glaring, Portuguese granite superstructure with triangular fins on its roof deck, suggestive of the prismatic layout within, the Waverley Market (1984) is a speciality shopping mall lying between **Princes Street** and the **Waverley Station**. The original Waverley Market or 'Green Market' was built on the site of the terminus of the Edinburgh, **Perth & Dundee Railway** in 1868; the extensions to the Waverley Station in 1866 displaced the vegetable market which lay in the shadow of the **North Bridge** in Market Street. This first edifice was replaced in 1874–6 by a U-plan hall whose cast-iron columns supported a roof terrace at the level of Princes Street, which was soon encroached upon by street improvements. Multiple usage of the market as a venue for promenade concerts, cattle and flower shows eventually forced much of the fruit and vegetable trade to return reluctantly to Market Street. Before being declared unsafe and demolished in 1974, Waverley Market was the scene of the annual Christmas Carnival, the Ideal Home Exhibition and many memorable **Edinburgh Festival** events.

Waverley Station

Situated below Edinburgh street level, the Waverley Station constitutes a vast area of glass roof stretching from **Waverley Bridge** on the west almost to the **Calton Hill** on the east. Trains have been caught here since June 1846 when the North British **Railway** opened its line eastwards to **Berwick-on-Tweed**, being joined from the west by the Edinburgh & **Glasgow** Railway which horrified **Lord Cockburn** by driving its tracks through Princes Street Gardens, to say nothing of the Haymarket and **Mound** tunnels. The station was then called the General or Joint station, the name 'Waverley' – after **Sir Walter Scott**'s novel – not being used until around 1854. Its construction necessitated the removal of the **Trinity Church** to a new site to the south and the Physic Garden northwards, where eventually it became a constituent part of the **Royal Botanic Garden**.

Canal Street station of the Edinburgh, **Perth & Dundee** Railway occupied a site immediately north-east of Waverley Bridge, offering services to and from **Granton** and **Leith** (the former port providing ferry services by one of the first rail ferries to **Burntisland** and ultimately **Aberdeen**). Departures went by way of a tunnel under **Princes Street**, **St Andrew Square** and Scotland Street.

Taken over by the NBR in 1862, an alternative route via Abbeyhill made the tunnel redundant. It was then used for mushroom growing and car storage, its sealed northern entrance still being visible to passengers on platform 19.

The Waverley itself underwent major rebuildings in 1868–74 and more radically in 1892–7, when it took on its present plan – that of two termini back to front, facing east and west, flanked by an island platform to the south of the main train shed. Boasting 21 platforms totalling 14,000ft (4267m) and an overall area of 23 acres (9.3ha), it was then the largest passenger station in Britain. Its through platforms could accommodate two full-length trains each, and still do. Until the 1930s its signalling arrangements involved four signal boxes, including one of 260 manual levers in a single frame. Since 1991, electric services have reached Waverley from east and west – the only meeting place of the two electrified main-lines between London and Scotland. Suburban services are sparse compared to other cities, perhaps because – as a local newspaper predicted in 1925 – commuters were not prepared to climb the station ramps to Waverley Bridge or the windy Waverley Steps to Princes Street without the help of escalators.

West Bow/Victoria Street

A steep and tortuous, Z-shaped thoroughfare formerly connecting **Castlehill** with the **Grassmarket**, the West Bow (ie arch) was the original processional route into the **Old Town** from the west. The Lower Bow or 'Bowfoot' was joined via Victoria Street to **George IV Bridge** 1835–40 when the Upper Bow or 'Bowhead' was truncated by Victoria Terrace.

During the 17th century the 'sanctified bends of the Bow' housed the pious fraternity of white (ie tin) smiths. At a prayer meeting of these 'Bowhead Saints' in 1670 Major Thomas Weir, Commander of the Town Guard and a strict adherent of the National **Covenant**, made his notoriously frank confessions to the unspeakable crimes of incest, fornication, bestiality and consorting with the Devil. For his pains he was burnt at the Gallowlee between Edinburgh and **Leith**; his crazed sister and accomplice, Grizel, was hanged nearer to home on the common gibbet at the Bowfoot.

A rare group of early 18th century merchants' houses remains at the Bowfoot, notably Thomas Crockett's Land (c1705), the only one not sub-divided into flats. The ornate Bowfoot Well, the grandest of the five (originally 10) surviving Old Town wells, was 'built by **Robert Mylne** under the supervision of **Sir William Bruce**' (Gifford et al, 1984) in 1681.

West Port

A dusty defile curving up from the western end of the **Grassmarket** to the 'Main Point', where three arterial routes branched off for the north, west and south-west corners of the kingdom, the West Port is named from the gate in the **Flodden Wall**. It began as a trades suburb servicing the **Castle** grange farm, which had its stables, orchards and gardens thereabouts. Northwards lay the 'Barasse', the tournament or tilting-ground below the Castle Rock, 'where **James IV** entertained and encountered the errant chivalry of Europe, to the entire dissi-

pation of the treasure of his father's famous "black kist"' (Dunlop, 1889).

The West Port itself was the traitors' gate, where the heads of lesser-ranking criminals were spiked; more pleasantly, the scene of pageantry where **Mary of Guise** was greeted 'with greit triumphe' in 1538, and **James VI** was entertained by *King Solomon* in 1579. The most dramatic episode, however, was the unstaged departure, in 1689, of **John Graham of Claverhouse, Viscount Dundee**; having failed to win over the Lords of the Convention of Estates to the cause of **James VII**, he rode out of the West Port at the head of 60 cavaliers, taking the north road to raise an army in the Highlands.

> Unhook the West Port
> And let us gae free
> For it's up wi' the bonnets
> O' Bonnie Dundee.
>
> (Scott)

Whitefoord House, Canongate

A bland, three-storey block unrelieved by later accretions, Whitefoord House in the **Canongate** was designed by **Robert Mylne** in 1769 for Sir John Whitefoord of Ballochmyle, **Ayrshire**, a patron of **Robert Burns**. Gutted c1850 for industry, the house, with adjoining Callendar House (built for Sir John Callendar of Craigforth), became in 1909 the Scottish Naval, Military and Air Force Veterans' Residence ('The Whitefoord'). The veterans' bowling-green railing celebrates the jaunty 18th century accountant Jamie Balfour, ' a great singer, a great drinker, a great **Jacobite**, and a great golfer' (Stuart, 1952), who frequented the original **Jenny Ha's Changehouse** nearby.

In the 16th century the site was occupied by the townhouse of the Seton Earl of Winton – 'My Lord Seyton's lugeing in the Canongate' (**Scott**, *The Abbot*). **George, 5th Lord Seton** (1530–85), Provost of Edinburgh, welcomed **Queen Mary** and **Lord Darnley** to **Seton** for their honeymoon and, after the murder of **David Rizzio**, accompanied them to **Dunbar**. Robert, 6th Lord Seton, a favourite of **James VI**, was created 1st Earl of Winton in 1600. The lodging fell into disrepair during the attainder of the **Jacobite** 5th Earl, George, from 1715–44, passing to the British Linen Company until demolition in 1766.

Whitehorse Close

A vernacular confection off the **Canongate** at **Holyrood**, Whitehorse Close contains the curious, two-storey former Whitehorse Inn with its twin gables uniformly flanking a central branching forestair. Built for Laurence Ord, merchant burgess, c1683 (the '1623' carved on the central pediment to replace '1523' is too early), who probably also named it. Tradition claims that **Queen Mary** kept her white palfrey here in the Royal Mews which reputedly occupied the site in the 16th century. In 1639 the assembled Lords of the **Covenant** (excepting the **Marquis of Montrose**) were prevented from leaving here to parley with **Charles I** in the 'Stoppit Stravaig'; and in 1745 the Highland officers of the **Jacobite** army lodged here. The first Edinburgh-London stagecoach, the 'Glass Machine', left the inn in 1749, aking 14 days for the journey. The inn was described in 1779 by Arnot as consisting of 'mean buildings; their apartments dingy and dismal; . . . a stranger will perhaps be shocked with the novelty of being shown in by a sunburned wench, without shoes or stockings'. In 1889 the courtyard was remodelled by the Barbour Trust and rented for working-class housing until rebuilt by Edinburgh Corporation during 1961–4 as 15 flats. The adjacent Russell House (named after Sir Robert Russell who was instrumental in its survival) is a tenement of 1697 originally preserved c1900 by **Patrick Geddes** and restored again in 1976.

Witches' Well

A disused bronze Art Nouveau drinking fountain by **John Duncan** erected in 1894 on the west wall of the former **Castlehill** Reservoir facing the **Esplanade**, the Witches' Well marks the execution place of many witches and warlocks from the 16th to the early 18th century. The small relief of witches' heads entwined with a snake is accompanied by an explanatory plaque which reads 'the wicked head and serene head signify that some used their exceptional knowledge for evil purposes while others were misunderstood and wished their kind nothing but good. The serpent has the dual significance of evil and of wisdom. The foxglove sprig further emphasises the dual purpose of many common objects.' The left panel of the basin portrays 'The Evil Eye', while the right holds the 'Hands of Healing'. The last witch was burned in 1722. Fine Celtic Revival mural paintings, also by John Duncan and commissioned by **Patrick Geddes**, are contained in the common room of Ramsay Lodge within the adjacent **Ramsay Garden**.

World's End Close

An insignificant alley in the **High Street** at the **Netherbow**, World's End Close was the 'final frontier' afore the **Town Wall**. Earlier known as Stanfield's Close, it was the residence of Sir James Stanfield of Newmills near **Haddington**, a melancholic English manufacturer who once attempted to throw himself headfirst out of his window. (He was caught by the feet.) When he was found drowned in 1587, his profligate and disinherited son Philip was suspected of having strangled him. While assisting in the re-interment of the corpse after surgical examination, Philip Stanfield was involuntarily subjected to 'Ordeal by Blood': 'In a secret murther if the dead carcasse be at any time thereafter handled by the murtherer, it will gushe out of blood, as if the blood were crying out to heaven for revenge of the murtherer' (**James VI**, *Daemonology*). Ineffectively hanged at the **Mercat Cross**, he was strangled, and his tongue and right hand cut off; his head spiked at Haddington and his body hung in chains between Edinburgh and **Leith**.

EDINBURGH, Treaties of (1328 and 1560)

The first (17 March 1328), between **Robert I** and Edward III, recognised Scotland's independence (ending 30 years of **Wars of Independence**) and arranged the marriage of Robert's son **David II** to Edward's sister Joanna. The treaty was breached in 1332 [see **Edward Balliol**].

The second, also called the Treaty of **Leith** (6 June 1560), was between France and England. It recognised the joint sovereignty of **Mary** and her husband François II and arranged a provisional government, the Regent Queen Mother, **Mary of Guise**, having died during negotiations. France acknowledged Elizabeth as Queen of England; both powers agreed to withdraw troops from Scotland; the reforming Congregation, with English support, enjoyed great influence in the provisional government. 'This marked the joint defeat of France and of Catholicism' (R Mitchison).

EDINBURGH CASTLE

The symbol of Scots sovereignty, the Castle dominates central **Edinburgh** from all quarters. The Castle Rock – a 'Bass Rock upon dry land' (**R L Stevenson**) – which caps the head of the **Royal Mile** is a 437ft (133m) ice-gouged plug of basalt, a remnant of the 'Edinburgh Volcano' [see **Arthur's Seat** and **Calton Hill**].

Legends apart, the Castle was probably first occupied during the Iron Age by the Votadini (Gododdin). In the 6th century, the praises of Din Eidyn (Dunedin – the fortress on the slope) were sung by their **bard** Aneurin in his epic poem Y *Gododdin* when, before their fatal incursion against the Angles of Northumbria at Catraeth (Catterick), the Votadini were customarily feasted with wine and mead from gold cups in the hall of their chieftain, Mynyddog the Wealthy. The 'burg' was captured by the Angles in 638 but they quitted the rock sometime between 954–62 and Lothian was finally secured by the Scots under **Malcolm II** after the **Battle of Carham** in 1018.

The Castle is first recorded as a royal residence in the 11th century when **St Margaret**, the wife of **Malcolm III** (to whom the 12th century **St Margaret's Chapel** is dedicated) died there shortly after learning of her husband's death at Alnwick in 1093. Around her chapel on the highest point of the citadel were likely grouped the earliest medieval buildings; the 12th century St Mary's Kirk, built by her son **David I**, stood on the site of the **Scottish National War Memorial**. David assembled in the Castle the convention of nobles and clergy which developed into the Scots Parliament, first officially convened there in 1215 by **Alexander II**. His son **Alexander III** made the Castle the repository for the national records of Scotland and the **Regalia**. During the disputed succession which followed his reign and began the **Wars of Independence** (1296–1328), Edward I resumed the pattern of alternating occupation of the Castle by the Scots and the English (an English force had held the Rock from 1174–86 after the capture of **William the Lion**) by burning the city and securing the citadel through a three-day siege. In 1313, following its recapture by **Sir Thomas Randolph** and William Francis, when they scaled the Rock at night with 30 men, the Scots themselves razed the defences to deny it again to the 'Auld Enemy'.

Not until the return of **David II** from captivity in England in 1356 did the Castle begin to assume its present form; the royal residence was moved to **David's Tower** which he started to build at the south-eastern extremity of the Rock in 1367. This redoubtable work (which withstood sieges by Henry IV in 1390 and 1400) was completed by his successor **Robert II** in 1377; Robert also added the Constable's Tower which

Alexander Nasmyth's painting of Edinburgh Castle and the Nor' Loch (NGS)

Edinburgh continued

incorporated the gatehouse, at the northern end of the linking cross-wall defence. Sometime during the 1430s **James I** markedly improved the royal lodging in David's Tower by adding a 'Great Chamber', the nucleus of the present Palace developed by his **Stewart** successors. Although **James IV** moved the main royal residence from the Castle to the **Palace of Holyroodhouse** in 1502 for his marriage to Margaret Tudor, he nevertheless initiated a programme of works on the Rock which included the **Great Hall**, its magnificent hammerbeam roof supported on carved stone corbels which possibly represent 'the earliest Renaissance architectural ornament in Britain' (Gifford et al, 1984). The medieval defences, along with David's and the Constable's Towers, were reduced by the **Regent Morton** during the 33-day siege in 1573 when **Sir William Kirkcaldy of Grange** valiantly held the Castle against enormous odds for **Queen Mary**. Thereafter Morton renewed the defences by building the bastion of the Half Moon Battery, adding the Forewall Battery and the Portcullis Gate in place of the Constable's Tower.

During the 17th century the Castle was seriously invested on four occasions in 50 years. In 1639, in the Bishops' Wars, it was seized by the **Covenanters** but returned four months later under the Pacification of **Berwick**. In 1640 **Sir Patrick Ruthven**, who held it for **Charles I**, was forced to surrender by his former Swedish army comrade, **Sir Alexander Leslie**. Following his victory over Leslie at **Dunbar** in 1650, Cromwell took the Castle which was occupied by the English Roundheads until the Restoration. Most memorable, however, is the siege after the Revolution of 1689 when the **Duke of Gordon** unsuccessfully defended the Rock for **James VII**, who had fled to France after William of Orange landed in England; with only 120 men Gordon inflicted some 500 casualties on his opponents before privations finally beat him. During this heroic episode he held his famous final conference with **John Graham of Claverhouse**, at a postern on the western side of the defences after the latter had ridden out of the **West Port** on quitting the Convention of Estates; Claverhouse reputedly urged the Duke to join him on his road north to raise the Highland clans.

The Castle last saw action in the 18th century during the **Jacobite Risings**; some months before the débâcle at **Sheriffmuir**, a ridiculous attempt to scale the Rock by the supporters of the Old Pretender, **James Francis Edward** ended in grand farce; in 1745 the garrison fired on **Prince Charles Edward** at **Holyroodhouse**, the iron shot reaching only just beyond the **Esplanade** where, popular belief has it, it embedded itself in **Cannonball House** on **Castlehill**. Thereafter the Castle became a major military barracks, its noble profile sullied by utilitarian powder magazines and ordnance stores.

After the Napoleonic Wars, when many French and Dutch soldiers were incarcerated in the 'French Prisons' in the vaults below the Great Hall, the Castle was at last appreciated for its historical and romantic associations, notably by **Sir Walter Scott** who was instrumental in the rediscovery of the Regalia and the return of **Mons Meg**. A more enlightened attitude led to much renovation – notably the Great Hall and St Margaret's Chapel during Victorian times.

Now in the care of **Historic Scotland**, which is currently developing its outstanding potential to the full, the Castle of Edinburgh, the most visited attraction in Scotland which, throughout its recorded history, was never stormed, is now daily 'taken' by **tourists** as a matter of course.

David's Tower

The royal redoubt raised by **David II** and **Robert II** in 1367–7, David's Tower (rediscovered in 1891) remains encased within the swelling curve of the Half Moon Battery built by the **Regent Morton** in the 1570s. The tower house, which rose to over 50ft (15m), was the major feature of the medieval Castle until its bombardment by Morton during the siege which ended the three-year occupation by **Sir William Kirkcaldy of Grange**; the collapse of the tower blocked the main well and hastened surrender. The royal apartments were moved from the tower by **James I** in the 1430s when he built the 'Great Chamber' adjacent; this became the nucleus of the present **Palace** in Crown Square, the old 'Castle Yard'. In 1479 **James III** imprisoned his brother **Alexander Duke of Albany** in David's Tower lest he rival his claim to the throne. Albany escaped, however, by making the guards drunk and then stabbing them to death, after which he gratuitously roasted their bodies, clad in full armour, on the fire; 'and there in their armour they broiled and sweltered like tortoises in iron shells' (Grant, 1884).

Great Hall

Built c1500–30 by either **James IV** or **James V**, the Great Hall on the south side of Crown Square was heavily Victorianised by the architect Hippolyte Blanc when commissioned to restore it by the philanthropic publisher William Nelson. The 95ft x 41ft (29 x 12m) Hall had been subdivided as a barracks and hospital from 1650 when Cromwell took the Castle. The fine old open timbered roof of carved chestnut was rediscovered in 1883; its rare hammerbeams are carved with human and animal masks and rest on Renaissance corbels carved with decorated motifs including the royal arms and portraits of James IV and **Margaret Tudor**. Used for ceremonial state occasions and banquets, with the King and courtiers occupying the east end, the Scots Parliament also convened here prior to the erection of **Parliament House** in 1639. The coronation banquet of **Charles I** was held in the Great Hall in 1633, and in 1648 Cromwell was entertained with 'unwonted magnificence' by the **Earl of Argyll**. In an earlier, medieval, hall, was held the **'Black Dinner'** of 1440.

> Edinburgh Castle, toune and toure
> God grant thou sink for sinne,
> An' that even for the black dinour
> Earle Douglas gat therein.
>
> (Trad)

Palace

Forming the east side of Crown Square, the 3–4 storey Palace, containing the old royal apartments and the **Regalia**, occupies the south-east point of the Castle Rock near to the site of **David's Tower**, the earlier royal residence. The southern part of the present Palace probably stands where **James I** built the 'Great Chamber' in the 1430s. In c1500 **James IV** possibly began the Palace along with the adjacent **Great Hall**, works which were likely completed or altered by his son **James V**. Both buildings were modified and sumptuously fitted up for **Queen Mary** and her consort **Lord Darnley**, who frequently stayed there in preference to the less easily defended **Palace of Holyroodhouse**. The northern part was remodelled in 1615–17 in an early, unadorned classical style, as a ceremonial lodging for **James VI** in anticipation of his royal return from London after the **Union of the Crowns** in 1603. Also redecorated at this time was the tiny chamber leading off the Queen's bedchamber in which James VI had been born.

St Margaret's Chapel

The oldest building in **Edinburgh**, St Margaret's Chapel graces the highest point of the Castle Rock. The little rectangular chapel, c30ft x 15ft (9 x 4.6m), is traditionally held to be that used by **Margaret**, the Queen of **Malcolm III**, but was probably erected in the early 12th century by either **Alexander I** or **David I**, her younger sons. After capture of the Castle by Cromwell in 1650 the chapel was put to secular use until 'rediscovered' by the antiquarian **Sir Daniel Wilson** in 1845. Then serving as a powder magazine, it was restored retaining its 18th century roof; the northern entrance doorway was added five years after its rededication in 1934. The plain interior consists of a nave opening through a chancel arch into an apsidal sanctuary which is asymmetrical with the nave. The Norman chancel arch has chevroned carvings similar to the old east processional doorway at **Holyrood Abbey**; the monolithic shafts of its columns were, like the tunnel vault of the nave, replaced in 1851–2. 'From its detail and design this screen cannot be earlier than the first decade of the 12th century and is more likely to date from 1110–20' (RCAHMS, 1950).

Scottish National War Memorial

The National War Memorial on the north side of Crown Square was designed by **Robert Lorimer** in 1924–7 on the site of the 12th century St Mary's Kirk and incorporates the shell of the North Barracks first built in 1755. These were reconstructed as the Hall of Honour containing the memorials of the Scots regiments and other services in which Scots served. The sympathetically subdued exterior presents nevertheless a wealth of figurative sculpture by Pilkington Jackson and others representing Valour, Justice, Peace, Mercy, Knowledge, Freedom and Truth as well as the 'Survival of the Spirit'. In the shrine itself, a polygonal apse projecting on the north side, the names of the slain – some 100,000 – are inscribed on the Rolls of Honour placed in a steel casket. Guarded by bronze angels, the casket rests on a granite altar standing on the naked basalt of the rock which extrudes dramatically through the **Ailsa Craig** granite floor.

Scottish United Services Museum

This was conceived by John, 8th **Duke of Atholl** as an adjunct to the **Scottish National War Memorial** which came into being through his enthusiasm. The War Memorial, in Crown Square, was opened in July 1927. A military museum devoted to the story of Scottish fighting men, their uniforms, equipment, ships and regiments, was a logical extension. In 1930 it became a reality – the first of its kind in the United Kingdom – with the title The Scottish Naval and Military Museum. It was housed in an 18th century building on the west side of Crown Square. The first curator, Major I H Mackay Scobie, quickly commenced the acquisition of material by gift, loan and purchase. Amongst the first exhibits were a commissioned series of 83 carved and painted statuettes depicting the uniforms of the Scottish regiments from 1633 to 1914. These were designed by C D'O Pilkington Jackson and carved by a team of craftsmen.

The museum was closed during World War II and when re-opened in 1949 the name was changed to the Scottish United Services Museum in order to include Royal Air Force material. As the first curator had died in 1947, Major H P E Pereira was appointed in 1948. The Ministry of Works had taken over the financial support of the museum as part of the Edinburgh Castle complex and more space was allotted. The East Museum, on the first floor of the **Palace** block, was opened in 1949 and housed naval, air force and other material. By 1983 the museum had taken over the North Hospital Block situated at the north-west corner of the Castle. Financial management was transferred to the Royal Scottish Museum in 1970 and 15 years later the museum became part of the National Museums of Scotland and was given the internal designation of the Department of Armed Forces History.

The collections are not concerned with battles and the techniques of warfare, but concentrate on dress, equipment and visual references. The uniform holdings are particularly good and include the finest group of Auxiliary Forces material to be found in the UK. Firearms and edged weapons are also extensive, embracing superb examples of presentation swords. The Royal Navy and Royal Air Force sections, though small, are nevertheless interesting and are being developed. Personalia of prominent fighting Scots constitute an important part and include their awards of valour. There are nine Victoria Crosses and a recently acquired very rare New Zealand Cross.

The Fine Art collection consists of oil paintings, watercolours, prints, photographs, silver and glass. There is also an important reference library containing over 10,000 volumes, journals and documents. These are available to students and interested members of the public.

EDINBURGH FESTIVAL

The Edinburgh International Festival of Music and Drama, the first major post-war festival of the arts in Europe, commenced in August 1947; within 10 years it was attracting over 90,000 visitors during its three-week run. Formed under Lord Provost Sir William Falconer, the Festival was seen as a cultural palliative to the depressing problems of post-war reconstruction. The prime mover was H Harvey Wood of the British Council and the first director was Rudolph Bing of the Glyndebourne Festival Opera, who had tried unsuccessfully to stimulate interest in London, Oxford and Cambridge in a 'feast' comparable to those of Salzburg or Bayreuth. His world-wide contacts ensured musical excellence from the outset, securing such as Bruno Walter and the Vienna Philharmonic, Sir John Barbirolli and the Hallé Orchestra, and the Orchestre des Concerts Colonne which played the opening concert.

'Drama has always been the Achilles Heel of the Festival' (Keir, 1966), with concerts, opera and ballet monopolising the main venues of the **Usher Hall**, **King's Theatre** and **Playhouse**; in addition to the Royal Lyceum Theatre, the **Church of Scotland Assembly Hall** has proved a successful substitute for a purpose-built facility, and was transformed in 1948 by the pageantry of The Thrie Estaitis adapted by **Robert Kemp** and directed by Tyrone Guthrie. Art was first fully promoted in 1950 when exhibited in the **Royal Scottish Academy** and the **National Gallery of Scotland**. In 1950 the Edinburgh Military Tattoo was first spectacularly staged on the **Castle Esplanade** before an audience of 5000.

The multi-faceted Fringe and the Film, TV and Book Festivals feed off the publicity generated by the 'official' Festival. The Film Festival has grown from documentaries shown in 1947 to an international festival ranking with those of Cannes and Berlin, while the Fringe, which has been a friendly 'parasite' since the 1948 programme listed 'other attractions' on its 'fringe', has long outgrown the city's capacity. It now accounts for nearly half a million tickets for about 10,000 separate showings performed in over 150 locations before average audiences of 50. New Festival headquarters, dubbed **'The Hub'**, opened in 1999 in the august setting of the former Highland Tolbooth St John's Kirk on **Castlehill**.

EDINBURGH REVIEW

Once the most influential and astringent periodical in Britain, the *Review* was founded in **Edinburgh** in 1802 principally by **Francis Jeffrey**, Francis Horner, **Henry Brougham** and Sydney Smith with **Archibald Constable** as publisher. It had been preceded in 1755 by a publication of the same name which lasted only two issues (one of which contained **Adam Smith**'s first published work) and by the 1773–6 Edinburgh Magazine and Review edited by **Gilbert Stuart**. The failure of both had been ascribed to their over-critical stance but this did not deter Jeffrey, editor 1803–29, from aiming equally high. **Whig** (the magazine's colours were the buff and blue of the party), and catholic in the tradition of the **Scottish Enlightenment**, he encouraged contributions on politics and economics as well as literary matters. The books selected for review were few, the reviews tangential, exhaustive and magisterial. **Carlyle** compared its pronouncements to those of the Delphic oracle; its contributors remained anonymous but its fees were generous and its authority awesome.

Perhaps the greatest tribute paid to the *Review* was the 1809 launch of the no less respected *Quarterly Review*, a

Tory rejoinder to its Whig sympathies, a **John Murray** response to Constable's publishing initiative, and **Walter Scott**'s revenge for a scathing review of *Marmion*. Reform-minded in politics, the *Review* could be less assured when arbitrating literary taste. Jeffrey's 'This will never do!' of Wordsworth's *The Excursion* was typical of the magazine's dismissive attitude towards the Lake poets. Such gaffes, though, failed to diminish an authority which, bolstered by contributions from many of the major literary figures of the 19th century (Carlyle, Hazlitt, **Macaulay**, etc) continued to sustain the magazine until its eventual demise in 1929.

EDINBURGH UNIVERSITY

Although the youngest of the four ancient Scottish universities, the University of Edinburgh – 'The Tounis College' chartered by **James VI** – is the oldest non-ecclesiastical university foundation in Britain; it opened in 1583, when 80 students enrolled under Robert Rollock, the first 'Regent'. The present 'Old College', begun in 1789 on the site of the original clutter of buildings at the **Kirk o'Field**, was designed by **Robert Adam**; his greatest public work, it was originally conceived as the climax of his unsuccessful proposals for **South Bridge** in 1786. Work on the 'Old Quad' ceased in 1793 and was completed in 1818–34 by **William Playfair** who modified the original design. 'Nothing in Scotland is grander than Adam's entrance front' (Gifford et al, 1984): executed in **Craigleith** ashlar, its centre-piece is a Roman triumphal arch which thrusts forward a bold portico of six monolithic columns. The dome, added by **Rowand Anderson** in 1886–8, is surmounted by a gilded figure of youth – 'The Golden Boy' – bearing the torch of learning. The exquisite Greek Revival interiors are all by Playfair: the New Senate Room and the Talbot-Rice Arts Centre above with its lofty Ionic screens are both modelled on the work of Sir John Soane at the Bank of England; the Upper Library Hall is a great neo-classical coffered vault, 138ft (42m) long and 25ft (7.6m) broad, which resonates with 11 galleried bays of bookstacks, now the scene of ceremonial occasions. Today the 'Old Quad' is the administrative centre of the University and the Faculty of Law; the other departments are dispersed near and far, notably in and around **George Square**, at the King's Buildings Science Complex near **Liberton** and at the Agriculture, Forestry and Veterinary outstations at Bush House, **Midlothian**.

Medical School

The largest Victorian development undertaken by the University of Edinburgh, the collegiate Medical School adjacent to the **Royal Infirmary** was designed in early Italian Renaissance style in 1876–86 by **R Rowand Anderson**. During the 18th and 19th centuries Edinburgh was a world centre of medicine. The Faculty of Medicine, third in seniority after Divinity and Law, had been established in 1726 through the efforts of the **Royal College of Surgeons** who then, like the **Royal College of Physicians**, were chartered to teach. The McEwan Hall for general university graduates was added to the Medical School in 1888–97. Behind, preceding both and also in Italianate style, is the **Reid** School of Music designed by David Cousin in 1858.

EDINBURGH ZOO

Covering about 80 acres (30ha) of **Corstorphine** Hill, Edinburgh Zoo – the Scottish National Zoological Park – is the second largest by area in Britain after Whipsnade and has an animal collection second only to London Zoo at Regent's Park. The Royal Zoological Society of Scotland, formed in 1909, acquired Corstorphine Hill House Estate in 1913. The park layout was begun by **Patrick Geddes** and completed in 1927 by his son-in-law Frank Mears; the barless enclosures were inspired by the work of Carl Hagenbeck at Hellingen Zoo near Hamburg, where animals were first displayed in natural settings of grassland, woodland, rock and water. The zoo is especially renowned for its colony of Antarctic penguins, the largest and most successful captive group anywhere, which was started by the first President of the Society, when whaling ships of his firm, **Christian Salvesen** & Co of **Leith**, brought a consignment of the birds from South Georgia in 1919. The first king penguin to be bred in captivity was successfully hatched and reared by its parents in the park; subsequent breeding successes include the birth of a baby white rhinoceros (1990) and two Siberian tiger cubs (1992).

New species are now only acquired through exchange breeding loan programmes with other zoos and not introduced from the wild – red pandas are a recent example. Zoo philosophy has long stressed conservation and education, one of its principal objects being 'to foster and develop among people an interest in and knowledge of animal life'. The Society originated a comprehensive information scheme for each enclosure providing species description and details of distribution, habitat, behaviour etc. It also has an Education Centre especially for schoolchildren.

EDUCATION IN SCOTLAND

Speakers on education in Scotland habitually remind their listeners of the tradition and world-wide reputation of Scottish education. From time to time it may be prudent to investigate the substance of such claims. A group of eminent Scots who embarked upon such an investigation recently had this to say: 'Scottish education can be defined as existing not only for individual advantage and advancement, but for the good of the community as a whole . . . For all its undoubted defects in the past and in the present, Scottish education has been one of the chief underpinnings of Scottish identity' (*Scottish Education: A Declaration of Principles*, 1989).

Current Status

Scotland has about 4000 schools and some fourteen universities. The latter include the four ancient universities (**St Andrews, Aberdeen, Glasgow, Edinburgh**), four mid-20th century foundations (**Stirling**, Glasgow's **Strathclyde**, Edinburgh's Heriot-Watt, and **Dundee**) and six mid-1990s creations (Edinburgh's Napier & Queen Margaret, Glasgow Caledonian, Aberdeen's Robert Gordon, Dundee's Abertay, Paisley, and the Inverness-based University of the Highlands and Islands). Before gaining university status, the last six were numbered amongst the 'Central Institutions' which, together with three Colleges of Education, numerous Colleges of Further Education and a variety of institutions catering for part-time students (from the

Education continued

Open University to community education classes) complete the roll-call of institutions.

Education being one of the subjects devolved to the **Scottish Parliament** under the 1998 Scotland Act, the system is regulated by the Scottish Education and Industry Department headed by its own minister. The Department works with local authorities through a series of Regulations, Circulars and Memoranda. It maintains active and influential contact with educational managers and institutions through a highly professional Inspectorate (HMIS). It deals directly with Central Institutions and Colleges of Education.

Its principal adviser on teacher recruitment, supply and training is the General Teaching Council for Scotland (GTC), which body by an arrangement so far unique to Scotland is also responsible for the registration and conduct of teachers. A Consultative Committee on the Curriculum (CCC) provides practical advice on content and method in schools. The Scottish Qualifications Authority conducts public examinations in Scottish schools and colleges. On all of these bodies, employers, parents, teachers, the churches, universities and the community are represented.

The actual provision of educational facilities, statutorily defined as 'adequate', is the responsibility of the current local authorities, each of which has a Department of Education led by a Director. The councils employ and pay teachers, lecturers and other staff, maintain and equip nursery, primary and secondary schools and further education colleges. Policy is determined by the Education Committee, which normally consists of elected members of the local council supplemented by nominees of special interests such as the Church and teachers; and management of schools is effected in partnership with School Boards, a recent (1989) innovation designed to improve liaison with parents.

Parents have a legal duty to ensure the education of their children between the ages of 5 and 16; and most comply with this duty by making use of the so-called 'state' system. However, about 4% of children in Scotland attend independent schools (both day and boarding), of which there are about 100. Some of these are, or originally were, modelled on English public schools, like Fettes College in Edinburgh; the Edinburgh and Glasgow Academies are day equivalents. All are resourced by fees and endowments and, though not controlled by the state, are subject to inspection.

Public education is financed from two sources – from the central exchequer and from local authority taxes. Local authorities in Scotland receive from the Scottish Department of Education and Industry a grant, based on a somewhat complex formula, to help meet the cost of the services they provide; and this, in the case of City, District and Island Councils, includes education. It is a matter of concern that the proportion of 'central' to 'local' money has been reduced in recent years from roughly two-thirds to just over half of the total expenditure – with no corresponding reduction in 'central' control. The Department also funds the Colleges of Education and Central Institutions directly, and makes other contributions such as those to the Scottish Council for Research in Education (SCRE).

Each university has a considerable degree of autonomy, but they have common interests illustrated by such bodies as the Scottish Universities Council on Entrance (SUCE). While some of their funding arises from endowments, fees and 'marketing', around 80% of their income derives from government through the Universities Funding Council (UFC), a United Kingdom body. Their resources, and thus their policies, are therefore largely dependent on national will as, for example, in 1993, when the central government contribution to the fees of arts students was reduced in an attempt to encourage take-up of places in science subjects.

Teachers' and lecturers' associations (eg AUT(S), EIS, SSTA, PAT, NAS/UWT, HAS) and bodies representing parents (eg NPTC) all and severally influence in varying degrees educational policy in Scotland.

Origins

The origins of the Scottish educational system are to be perceived, albeit dimly, on the shores of **Galloway** or amongst the rocky **Hebrides**. From **St Ninian**'s Candida Casa at **Whithorn** in the late 4th century and from **St Columba**'s monastery at **Iona** in the 6th, monasteries and seminaries were founded widely in Scotland. For the next half-millennium these were centres of teaching and learning. By the very nature of things, what may be called the formal curriculum probably rested on religion and sacred literature, with some attention to ancient languages and astronomy. There would no doubt be, however, for good and practical reasons, instruction in the arts of **agriculture**, building and allied crafts.

The marriage of **Malcolm III 'Canmore'** to the saintly **Margaret** (1069) of England and the accession of their scholarly son **David I** (1084–1153) brought, not for the last time, southern influence to bear on the Scottish educational scene. From the 11th century the **Roman** form of ecclesiastical organisation began to replace the **Celtic** in Scotland; and there was set up the parish system that was long to outlast the **Reformation**. Cathedral and abbey schools appeared in the Scottish burghs, in many cases forming the embryos of the later grammar schools. In addition the Dominican monastic order set up provincial seminaries, providing some kind of model for the later universities.

Those Scots seeking higher learning came in time to seek it on the Continent rather than in southern Britain; and as a result a European rather than an English tradition in education was fostered. The first three Scottish Universities (St Andrews, 1411; Glasgow, 1451; and Aberdeen, 1494) followed the student-led pattern of Bologna rather than the master-dominated pattern of Oxford.

In 1496, an Act of the Scots Parliament was the first in Europe designed to implement a form of compulsory education. It called for the education of the eldest sons of ruling barons, the objective being to provide a class of lawyers to administer justice. Aimed as it was at a limited section of the population, it nevertheless displayed some educational initiative, and it was followed by some effort on the part of the Roman Church to revive and renew its educational activities.

Post-Reformation

By 1560, however, the Reformers had gained the upper hand in Scotland; and amongst their prime objectives was the establishment of a national system of education. The *First Book of Discipline* in 1560 set out a national plan, an ambitious scheme to have elementary schools in every parish, grammar schools in every town, high schools or colleges in every large town and provision for the university study of arts, medicine, **law** and divinity. It was over-ambitious for the turbulence of the times, for the concurrence of Parliament and for the pockets of the heritors; but the next three centuries saw an attempt to turn the ideals of the Reformers into reality.

It is worth noting that the scheme was conceived as contributing to the moral worth of the individual and thereby to the good of the community; that it made no distinction between rich and poor; and that advancement from one stage to the next was to depend on ability – factors that lay at the root of the Scottish tradition of 'democratic meritocracy'.

During the 17th and 18th centuries there was a moderate but steady expansion of both parish and burgh schools. Legislation in respect of the former, notably an Act of 1696, continued to put pressure on the heritors to provide schools and schoolmasters; while the Reformed Kirk through its presbyteries in rural areas and its influence on (and rivalries with) guilds and town councils in the burghs established the 'three Rs' as the fundamentals of Scottish teaching. The Kirk, too, insisted on its right to oversee the appointment of teachers, a concern over the quality of pedagogy which remains to this day – as does a zeal to ensure that they are not spoiled by over-gracious living.

On the negative side there was a fairly determined assault on **Gaelic** culture. Indeed, the Scottish Society for the Propagation of Christian Knowledge (SSPCK), which from 1700 onwards did much valuable work in filling gaps in school provision, was largely moved by a concern to stamp out what its proprietors saw as ignorance and superstition in the Highlands.

By the end of the 18th century, then, Scotland had an imperfect but well established pattern of parish and burgh schools, mostly providing basic literacy and numeracy and a knowledge of the Shorter Catechism. There were four universities (**Edinburgh** had been added in 1586), more widely accessible to young men of talent than was generally the case elsewhere, and offering a breadth of curricular studies, rather than the specialist approach favoured in the south. The Scots, however, took a rather grim pride in their achievements, such as they were; education was seen as a joyless necessity rather than an exciting adventure, and there was even a sense, notably with regard to the Scots **languages**, in which education was seen as the medium for exorcising 'Scottishness'. It was in this mood that Scotland entered the 19th century, awakening to the realisation that the education system was unlikely to be equal to the growing demands of a new industrial age.

State Control

There was still widespread respect for education in Scotland; it was noted in 1796 that 'even day-labourers give their children a good education . . . an important advantage which the Scots as a nation enjoy over the natives of other countries'. But it was also validly observed that 'the want of proper schoolmasters' accounted for much of the ignorance and bigotry which was alleged to prevail in many parts of the country. The cause of this want was the continued failure of the heritors and others to provide the necessary funds to attract educated men into teaching, and so fulfil the aspirations of the authors of the *First Book of Discipline*.

An Act of 1803 was designed to improve matters by laying down improved standards of salary and housing for schoolmasters, imposing more stringent obligations upon heritors to make provision for them, and assigning new powers to the presbyteries to examine and approve the qualities of the dominie. The Act may be seen as the beginning of state control of education in Scotland. It was to usher in some 70 years of growing tension between Church and state over the matter; for the heritors were being called upon to pay the piper, and they were not over-disposed to dance entirely to the Kirk's tune.

Increased (though inadequately) in number by the 1803 Act, parish schools continued as before. They provided an elementary education for those they managed to reach. The dominie would give additional instruction to the 'lad o' pairts', notably in north-east Scotland where the Dick Bequest financed local schoolmasters to upgrade their qualifications. During the first half of the 19th century, the population of the central belt increased from around 85,000 to about half a million. Provision of schools never kept pace, and schooling was only available to a fraction of children in central Scotland. In the Glasgow area, an influx of Irish Roman Catholics fleeing from famine in their native land made a demand for separate school provision.

In the Highlands there was difficulty in providing for the sparse, scattered population, partly due to lack of drive from the centre, partly due to reluctance to cater for Gaelic. SSPCK began to run down its activities in the 1860s. A number of church schools were founded, partly for the same reason that the SSPCK had been founded, partly in an attempt by the Church to counteract growing state control. 'Assembly' schools were set up in the Highlands, 'sessional' schools in the burghs. The Roman Catholic Church and the Scottish **Episcopal Church** also founded schools, as did the **Free Church of Scotland** after 1843. Private 'adventure' schools (many poor and of short duration) abounded; and there were some endowed foundations, a few of which were to survive and prosper.

There were bright spots. Infant school voluntary societies appeared. Industrialists such as Robert Owen at **New Lanark** recognised the value of educating the children of their employees, and their work supplemented the efforts of the parish schools. The classical emphasis and rigid discipline of the burgh schools was modified to some extent by the existence of 'academies' which gave increasing attention to scientific, commercial and practical studies. When, as happened before the end of the century, burgh school and academy combined, they pointed the way to the wide base of academic secondary schooling that characterised the 'senior secondaries' of the 20th century.

David Stow of the Glasgow Education Society was a pioneer in teacher training – a practical concept in which Scotland still excels. The first teachers' training college in Britain, at Dundas Vale in Glasgow (**Cow-caddens**), was based on his work. Various denominational colleges followed, eventually ousting the pupil-teacher system which existed from 1846 until 1906. Even so, by 1872 only one-third of teachers were certificated.

Universities played no part in teacher training as such. However, they produced more graduates than law, medicine and the ministry could absorb – and thus provided a good supply of 'second-choice' teachers. As for the institutions themselves, an Act of 1858 gave control of a university to its Senate and created a Court and General Council. The office of Rector was retained, as a safeguard of student interests. There was still no insistence on minimal entrance standards; and there was a normal pattern of three-year degrees with four-year Honours courses. By 1872 the essentials of the modern Scottish university were recognisable.

Meanwhile the influence of the state in education continued to grow. Grants were made for education in 1833, and an Act of 1838 founded 'parliamentary schools' to plug holes in the existing system. A schools inspectorate was established in 1840. In 1861 power of examination of teachers was removed from the presbyteries and put in the hands of four university boards of professors (arts and divinity) with help from HMIS. The teachers' 'oath of affirmation' was now reduced to promising not to teach against the faith, and Church participation was confined to the right of complaint.

Secular control was becoming firmly established. A 'Revised Code' in 1862 introduced a system of 'payment by results' which had the effect of restricting curricular growth in schools. The essence of the system lay in giving grants to individual schools on the basis of good attendance and subject proficiency. The result did mean greater attention to individual attainment but also led to concentration on 'bread-and-butter' teaching and a meaningless mechanical grind of preparation for assessment rather than for learning. There was some advance in adult education through the Mechanics' Institutes from 1820 onwards – a movement that led in time to technical colleges, central institutions, and even universities.

Despite all this it was evident that schooling was still grossly inadequate and too poorly organised to serve the needs of an industrial and commercial society. To examine the problem, the government in 1864 established a Royal Commission to investigate the system of education in Scotland, and to make recommendations. During the next three years it issued a series of reports, which led to the Education Act of 1872. The Argyll Commission (1864–7) found much that was wrong with education in Scotland – high absenteeism; widely varying standards, especially between rural and urban areas; a shortage of finance; and a general lack of systematic control. Its reports resulted, after much prevarication and furious debate in Parliament, in an Act (1872) 'to amend and extend the law of Scotland on the subject of education in such a manner that the means of procuring efficient education for their children may be furnished and made available to the whole people of Scotland'.

In acknowledging state responsibility for the provision of education, the Act laid down the foundations for today's education system in Scotland, and demonstrated significant differences between Scotland and England (which had had its own major Education Act just two years previously). The Scottish Act established the framework of a graded public system; the English Act merely sought to fill the gaps in a voluntary system. Scottish education was made universal and compulsory; in England much was left to the discretion of local boards. The Scottish unlike the English system demanded certificates of competency and professional training for its teachers. In Scotland there was some provision for secondary education – there was none in the English Act. In Scotland opportunity was given – and eventually taken – to absorb denominational schools within the state system, while religious education was safeguarded by a 'conscience clause'.

The Act provided for the setting up of a 'Scotch' Education Department (in London!); it became the Scottish Education Department in 1918 and moved to Edinburgh in 1939, when it came under the control of the Secretary of State for Scotland (an office dating from 1926, itself developed from the Secretary for Scotland first appointed in 1885). Finance was rationalised in 1908 – when the SED took control of all parliamentary money for Scottish education. In 1958 a government/local authority partnership on finance was established, albeit sometimes an uneasy one.

From 1872 a system of school boards was to supervise all facets of schooling, including the appointment of teachers and the control of finances which came from government grant, local rates and fees. In 1918 these boards were replaced by 38 county and city education authorities; and these in turn gave way in 1929 to general purpose authorities (county and town councils) acting through 'education committees'. In 1974, education passed to the control of the newly-established Regional and Islands Councils.

Elementary education was set on a fairly satisfactory course by the 1872 Act; secondary not to the same degree. In 1882 inspection was imposed on 'higher class' schools; and in 1888 the Higher Leaving Certificate began its long and influential reign over the Scottish secondary school curriculum. Wars and economic crises played their part in the development of secondary schooling; an Act of 1918 re-shaped 'the whole fabric of the Scottish educational system'; and one of 1945 determined that education should be provided 'according to age, aptitude and ability'. The division into 'junior' and 'senior' secondary schools (made in 1936) came to an end in the years after 1964 which saw the introduction of the 'comprehensive' secondary school, now the established pattern in Scotland. Substantial changes in curriculum, examinations and discipline followed a series of major reports in the 1970s.

Further education was rationalised under the SED in 1897, and categorised in 1901 as continued elementary, elementary technical, 3- or 4-year technical and non-vocational. Thus encouraged, there developed from the early Mechanics' Institutes and the like such bodies as the Royal College of Science and Technology and Edinburgh's **Heriot-Watt** College – both now universities.

In 1889 a Universities Act began the process of change whereby the long-standing dominance of the arts faculty in Scotland yielded room for science, and

pecialism began to find parity (at least) with gen-
ralism. There was a wider range of Honours degrees;
ourses became open to women; and chairs in education
made their appearance, although, with one recent
xception, they played no part in initial teacher training,
which remains the responsibility of the Colleges of Edu-
ation. From 1919 university extra-mural departments
elped the growing interest in adult education, crystal-
sed in the Alexander Report (1970). The Robbins
Report of 1963 signalled the establishment of four new
universities in Scotland.

Scottish education has not in its long history been
ree from controversy; but none has been more fierce
han that of the last decade. Recent proposals for change
n curriculum and management are in a centralist direc-
ion (and that, to Scots, means control from London)
nd appear at best to be a desire for administrative
uniformity and at worst the imposition in Scotland of
nglish solutions to English problems. They represent,
t seems, an unwarranted assault on the Scottish edu-
ational tradition. How defensible some of that tradition
s may be debated. The academic bias, the authori-
arianism, the primacy of the teacher, the innate con-
ervatism – all have their supporters. What cannot be
lenied is the Scottish belief, implicit throughout 15
enturies, in the importance of education to the Scottish
ommunity; in the right of every Scottish child to receive
s much education as he can absorb with profit; and in
he justice of the Scottish claim that Scots not only
an but should determine for themselves the kind of
*ducation they need and want.

EDWARD, Robert (c1616–96) Minister and Musician

*dward was born in **Dundee**, graduated at **St Andrews**
n 1632, and was minister of Kirkmichael from 1637
nd of Murroes from 1648. He was ousted at the 1689
Revolution, and died in **Edinburgh**. His so-called commonplace book (National Library MS 9450) contains
over 150 Scottish tunes and songs, in some cases with
heir words. It is the principal source of Scottish 16th
nd 17th century melody, and is to music what the
Bannatyne Manuscript is to literature.

EDZELL, Nr Brechin, Angus

This village and estate passed (1357) from the Stirlings
of Glenesk to the Lindsay **Earls of Crawford** who built
he red sandstone L-plan castle of Edzell in the early
16th century. It was soon extended into a courtyard
rrangement with the addition of a service range,
ntrance and house with round tower. All is now fairly
uinous although the parapet corbelling of the original
ower is still notable. Much more impressive is the
walled pleasure garden with summer-house added in
1604 and undoubtedly an exceptional example of the
Renaissance genius for combining architecture, sculp-
ure and horticulture in a formal pleasance. The enclos-
ng walls of the garden are divided into compartments
by pilasters (now gone) between which a heraldic
device of chequered flower recesses alternates with a
magnificent series of carved bas-relief panels representing the planets, the arts and the virtues. They were
vidently derived from engravings by one of Albrecht

Walls and summer-house of Edzell Castle gardens (RWB)

Dürer's pupils, Sir David Lindsay having travelled extensively on the Continent before bankrupting himself in
the beautification of Edzell. The arrangement and planting of the garden's parterres is elaborate and, though
laid out in the 1930s employing plants unknown to Sir
David, it is hard to imagine him taking exception to a
stiff symmetry which so accurately reflects their setting.

Queen Mary had held a privy council in the castle
in 1562 and **James VI** visited in 1580. It was bought
by the Earl of Panmure in 1715 but forfeited for his part
in the '45 **Jacobite Rising**, passing to the asset-stripping
York Buildings Company who sold off all moveables
including the timbers. It now belongs to the Earls of
Dalhousie and is in state care.

Nearby the Lindsay Aisle of the old church of Edzell
is all that remains of a pre-**Reformation** chapel. North
from Edzell the road to **Fettercairn** crosses the Esk by
Gannochy Bridge (1732) whence a minor road follows
the Esk to Loch Lee, 14 miles into the hills, passing
en route the Colmealie stone circle, the Glenesk Folk
Museum, and the shell of Invermark Castle, a rectangular keep which also belonged to the Lindsays.

EGILSAY, Orkney

Like **Wyre**, Egilsay is a small satellite island of **Rousay**;
all three share the same Community Council. Its name
means 'Church Island' and on its summit stands a 12th
century church with the only surviving round tower in
the Northern Isles, the most conspicuous beacon from
the sea in all **Orkney**. This is almost certainly not the
church in which **Earl Magnus** prayed before his martyrdom, but one built in his memory and dedicated to
him, perhaps on the same site. It is of fine proportions,
with crow-stepped gables and a square-ended chancel
beyond its rectangular nave. It was still in use in the
19th century, when a picture reveals that it possessed

a gabled roof of stone slabs. Its tower was probably taller than it is today and had a conical slab roof. A farmer of Egilsay reduced this beautiful monument to a ruin in order to provide the roofing material for his steading.

EGLINTON TOURNAMENT, see KILWINNING and MONTGOMERIE, Hugh

EIGG, Island of, Inner Hebrides
'If I have to choose among the **Hebrides** . . . I choose Eigg,' wrote **Hugh MacDiarmid**. This dramatically beautiful island measures five miles by seven and lies another seven off the west coast of **Inverness-shire**. Its name, subject to numerous puns, has no connection with eggs, but means 'the notch' in Gaelic and describes the deep divide separating the massive Scurr rock from the rest of the island. This 'most memorable landmark in the Hebridean seas' is a geologically unique mass of pitchstone porphyry 1289ft (393m) high and the prow of the mile-long Scurr ridge. Its black basalt sides are denuded into a jumbled line of ribbed laval columns and its protecting curtain wall creates a micro-climate making Eigg unusually fertile and allowing rare ferns and palm trees to flourish.

Settled since prehistoric times, the island's remains include crude Iron Age forts, a 6th century Christian church, **Viking** burial mounds and many myths. Eigg provided a base from which the **Lords of the Isles** rose to power and their inheritors, the **Clanranalds**, conducted piratical wars. In reduced circumstances after the suppression of the **Jacobite Risings**, the Clanranalds sold Eigg in 1828. A succession of more or less eccentric and unsatisfactory owners followed, one of whom created an Italianate lodge and garden. In 1991, after relations between islanders and the then owner, ex-Olympic oarsman Keith Schellenberg, came under severe strain, a public campaign resulted in the creation of the Isle of Eigg Trust. With funding from a wide variety of sources ranging from private donations to grants from the European Community, the Trust purchased the island. Eigg is now owned and run by a partnership of trustees who include resident islanders and representatives of the Scottish Wildlife Trust and the Highland Council; their stated intention is to 'realise the vision of an island community securing a viable future livelihood whilst sustaining its unique environmental and cultural heritage'. Eigg continues to support a population of around 60 who supplement **crofting** enterprises with other trades.

EILDON HILLS, Roxburghshire
Just south of **Melrose**, the Eildon Hills can either be described as 'a brief mountain range of three conical summits' or as 'one triple-crested height', the highest point of which, the central summit, rises to 1385ft (422m). Their isolated prominence has long made them a place of mystery. According to one legend retold by **Sir Walter Scott**, the Eildons were formerly a single peak which was split into three on the orders of **Michael Scott** 'the Wizard' by a devil whose idle hands threatened greater destruction elsewhere. Another legend has King Arthur and his knights lying asleep beneath the Eildons waiting for the day on which they will rise and

ride again. On the north summit (c1010ft/308m) are the remains of a fortified town later developed by the **Romans** as one of several forts in a network centred on **Newstead** beside Melrose.

EILEAN DONAN CASTLE, Nr Dornie, Wester Ross
The most over-exposed castle in the Highlands, that of Eilean Donan owes much of its celebrity to Kodak. But credit should also be given to George Mackie Watson whose 20th century 'restoration' ensured its calendar credentials, to Colonel Macrae-Gilstrap who commissioned this 'restoration', and to whoever redirected the main road to **Skye** past it. For a 13th century castle of enclosure Eilean Donan, a just-island in the entrance to Loch Duich, provided the perfect site. Built by **Alexander II** to repel **Vikings**, the castle was gifted by **Alexander III** to the Irish Earl of Desmond and subsequently became a stronghold of the **Mackenzies** of **Kintail**, later **Earls of Seaforth**, who installed MacRaes as hereditary keepers. A rectangular keep was added in the 14th century but was taken by the **Earl of Huntly** in 1504. The 5th Earl of Seaforth garrisoned it with Spanish troops during the abortive **Jacobite Rising** of 1719; three English warships were sent to engage them and the castle was blasted to ruins. It remained in this state for more than 200 years. The 'restoration' of the 1930s entailed a complete rebuilding.

ELCHO CASTLE, Rhynd, Perthshire
A large and unusually complex structure, Elcho stands boldly on the banks of the **Tay** three miles below **Perth** where the estuary starts to open out. The central block has four towers (two round, two square), three of them on the north side, thus confounding the usual L-plan/Z-plan classification. Spacious rooms and interior details suggest the late 16th century although the crow-stepped south-east tower may be earlier. It was certainly built for a member of the Wemyss family and remains the property of the Earl of Wemyss and March although, falling into disrepair in the 18th century and being reroofed in 1830, it has been in state care since 1929. A ruinous round tower in the gardens was once part of an outer defensive wall.

ELDER, Alexander (1834–1915) Shipowner
Elder was born in **Glasgow** into a family whose maritime connections were powerful; his father had been manager of **Robert Napier** & Sons, the engine and **shipbuilders**. After education at Glasgow High School Alexander served his time as an apprentice engineer and worked at sea as a maritime engineer. Having moved to Liverpool to take a post as marine superintendent with the African Steam Ship Company he then served on the Board of Trade for two years. With this background and experience he established the British & African Steam Ship Company with the aim of building direct trading links between Glasgow and Africa. In partnership with John Dempster he also formed Elder, Dempster & Company. Although both Elder and Dempster were bought out of their named company in 1884, their continued interest in British & African ensured a lucrative income. Elder continued to live in Southport although he was eventually buried at Glasgow's **Necropolis**.

Many-towered Elcho Castle near Perth (RWB)

ELGIN, Moray

Elgin has been a significant administrative centre since the early Middle Ages. Built on a low ridge of land running from east to west, the early 12th century **royal burgh** was protected by natural barriers – a moss to the north and the winding river Lossie on the other sides. The river too powered the town's mills. In its heyday the royal castle, which stood on the Lady Hill (now dominated by the 1839 monument to the 5th Duke of Gordon) to the west of the medieval burgh, saw many royal visitors, but had been demolished by the 16th century. Elgin gained in importance when the **cathedral** of the Bishop of **Moray** was transferred here in 1224. The cathedral was burnt along with the town by **Alexander Stewart**, the 'Wolf of Badenoch' in 1390 and, though reconstructed, fell out of use after the **Reformation**. Nevertheless, the ruins of the erstwhile 'lantern of the north' are still impressive.

The development around 1700 of **Lossiemouth** as the burgh's port gave a boost to the local economy. But 100 years later the town was in a state of decay. The 19th century, by and large, was a boom period for Elgin and this was reflected in the number and quality of buildings that were erected. Its nodal position as a **railway** centre was a major factor. Starting with a short line to Lossiemouth in 1852, Elgin was linked with **Inverness** and **Aberdeen** in 1858, with Speyside in 1861 and the **Banffshire** coast in 1886. Today only the Inverness to Aberdeen line remains.

Recent decades have brought further growth, with administrative and commercial centralisation, and the establishment of military airbases at **Kinloss** and Lossiemouth. Elgin has long been a favourite place of residence for military personnel, both serving and retired.

While the recent commercial buildings and other developments, including an obtrusive town centre bypass, have been ill conceived, Elgin still possesses many fine buildings. Although parts have been erased, the outlines of the medieval town can still be traced. Some attractive narrow lanes and wynds lead off from the High Street. At the Plainstones the High Street widens; this was where markets were held. Public buildings were built there too, including the burgh (or muckle) cross (1630 but restored in 1888) and the medieval parish kirk which was demolished and replaced in 1828 by **Archibald Simpson**'s St Giles Kirk, an outstanding example of Greek Revival with heavy Doric columns and pediment plus a tall classical tower. Also restored, and now functioning as a Convent of Mercy, is the former church of the Greyfriars, or Franciscans; as with **Pluscarden**, the moving spirit was the **3rd Marquis of Bute**.

Among Elgin's rich architectural heritage are some fine examples of vernacular town houses including, at the east end of the High Street, arcaded dwellings. A good example of the latter is the late 17th century Braco's Banking House where the Duffs of Braco accumulated the fortune that eventually bought them the **Dukedom of Fife**. It is located in an interesting corner, facing yet another cross, the 18th century Little Cross, and close to Elgin Museum (1842, Italianate). Recently reopened after restoration, the museum, which

365

is volunteer-run, houses one of the oldest collections in Britain. Among other fine buildings at the other side of the town, the west end, stands Thunderston(e) House. Built on the site of the former 'Great Lodging' of the Scottish Kings, this 17th century dwelling with elaborately carved dormers is now a hotel.

To the north of the Little Cross, and adjacent to the cathedral, is one of the town's major assets – the Cooper Park. Spacious and conveniently situated, it contains a fine boating pond, a variety of sporting facilities and Great Lodge (dating from 1750), once a property of the Earls of Seafield and latterly the Elgin Library. To the west is Borough Briggs **football** ground, home of the third division team Elgin City.

ELGIN CATHEDRAL

Once probably the most splendid of Scotland's cathedrals and second in size only to **St Andrews**, Elgin was consecrated in 1224 to replace **Spynie** as the cathedral of the see of **Moray**. Generously endowed by **Alexander II**, it was built just outside the burgh of Elgin and adjoined by its own walled township, the chanonry, where dwelt the cathedral's dignitaries. The Bishop's Palace (1406), North College or Deanery (1520) and South College remain, though none of them in their original form, having been despoiled by, amongst others, Alexander **Lord of the Isles** in 1402. It was a similar story with the church. Damaged by fire in the 13th century, it was then savaged by **Alexander Stewart**, the 'Wolf of Badenoch' in 1390 when conflagration of the timbers brought down substantial sections of the structure. Rebuilt in the 15th century it fell a victim to post-**Reformation** neglect and vandalism which culminated in the collapse of the central tower in 1711.

The bishop at the time of the Wolf's raid sadly

Elgin Cathedral by R W Billings c1840 (RWB)

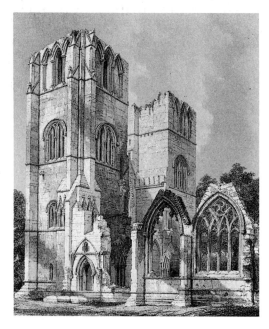

recalled that his church had been 'the ornament of the realm, the glory of the kingdom, the delight of foreigners and stranger guests'. Happily sufficient remains to substantiate the claim. The unusual west front with two towers flanking a deeply recessed portal is of the First Pointed style with a great tracerie window (broken) and double-doored portal screen dating from the 15th century reconstruction. The nave with double aisle is no more, but the windows of two side chapels remain plus substantial sections of the transepts. Most impressive of all are the choir and presbytery, with adjacent aisles, and the great east gable with its many windows (both lancet and rose). Adjoining one of the aisles the octagonal chapter house was given a most elaborate vaulted ceiling of rib and panel construction in the late 15th century and has been carefully restored in recent years. The property is now in the care of **Historic Scotland**; numerous effigies, carved bosses and a **Pictish** cross-slab have also been preserved.

ELGOL, Skye

The **crofting** village of Elgol at the tip of the Strathaird peninsula between Lochs Slapin and Scavaig in southern **Skye** has two famous caves. One, Suidhe Biorach just south of the village, is reputed to have sheltered **Prince Charles Edward Stewart** before his final departure from Skye in 1746. The second, Spar Cave, lies a mile and a half to the east of Elgol on the shore of Loch Slapin, 'its entrance looks like an ordinary fissure, yet conducts to scenes which mock the most elaborate efforts of the arts'. The inner cave was described by **Sir Walter Scott** in a note in his *Lord of the Isles*: 'the cave opens into a splendid gallery, adorned with the most dazzling crystallisations, and finally descends to the brink of a pool of the most limpid water ... surrounded by the most fanciful mouldings in a substance resembling white marble, and distinguished by the depth and purity of its waters ... [it] might have been the bathing grotto of a Naiad.' As early as the 1830s 'serious depredations had been made on the cave's spectacular stalactites 'by that class of virtuosi who ... would no doubt delight to pocket the nose of the Venus de Medici; but they have prompted the proprietor to protect the cave by a gate and padlock, and are in the course of being repaired by the silent and wondrous chemistry of Nature' (Fullarton's *Gazetteer*, 1843). Elgol offers a dramatic view of the **Cuillins**.

ELIZABETH (1596–1662) 'The Winter Queen' of Bohemia

The eldest daughter of **James VI** and **Anne of Denmark** was born at **Falkland Palace** and brought up at **Linlithgow** and, after her father's succession to the English throne, at Coombe Park, Rutland, the home of Lord Har(r)ington. Her passable looks and lively disposition were feted in London and later won her the sobriquet 'Queen of Hearts'; projected suitors included Gustavus Adolphus and Philip of Spain. In 1613 her beloved brother **Henry Prince of Wales** died, his last words being 'Where is my dear sister?' She had been prevented from seeing him for the last five days of his life and immediately after was married, for dynastic reasons, to Frederick V, Elector Palatine.

As the Thirty Years' War began, Frederick was chosen

Elizabeth of Bohemia, 'the Winter Queen', from the studio of Michiel van Mierveld (SNPG)

...nd crowned King of Bohemia (1619); but in Prague 'he combination of his **Calvinism** and Elizabeth's inborn levity' won few friends and after a winter's reign the pair were sent packing by the Catholic League. In greatly reduced circumstances they found sanctuary In Brandenburg, the Palatinate and Holland. Deprived of subjects, they produced children, 13 by the time of Frederick's death in 1631. Survivors included Charles Louis, to whom the Palatinate was restored after the 1648 Peace of Westphalia; Rupert, later the hero of the Royalist cause in the English Civil War; and Sophia who, married to the Elector of Hanover, was the mother of George I. A martyr to the Protestant cause and, incidentally, progenitor of the Hanoverian succession, Elizabeth and her numerous children attracted much sympathy from Protestant England; but she remained dependent on Dutch charity until the Restoration. Parliament then settled her debts and she was allowed to come to London where she died and was buried in Westminster Abbey.

ELLIOT, Sir Gilbert, 1st Earl of Minto (1751–1814) Governor-General of India

The descendant of several Sir Gilbert Elliots, this one's father (1722–77) was also a statesman, Keeper of the Signet, friend of **David Hume**, and a songwriter. The son was born in **Edinburgh** and educated abroad, in Edinburgh and at Oxford. He was called to the English Bar (1774) and elected MP for an English constituency but later for **Berwick**. In the 1780s he interested himself in Indian affairs and played a prominent part in the censure of Sir Elijah Impey and the impeachment of Warren Hastings.

After a brief spell in the 1790s as Viceroy of Corsica he returned to Indian affairs as President of the Board of Control (1806), the government body which had assumed the political functions of the East India Company. Later in the same year he was appointed Governor-General and sailed for India. His policies there, compared to those of his immediate predecessors, were cautious − he annexed only Haryana − and farsighted − he showed clemency in suppressing the Vellore Mutiny and courage in blunting missionary zeal.

But outside India he was far more adventurous, sending missions under **Sir John Malcolm** to Persia and under **Mountstuart Elphinstone** to Afghanistan, and depriving the French of Mauritius and their Dutch allies of the Spice Islands and even Java (1811). He was relieved of office in 1813, principally to make way for a successor to whom favours were owed. The earldom (1813) was his only thanks for he died within weeks of reaching England.

ELLIOT, Gilbert John, 4th Earl of Minto (1847–1914) Governor-General of Canada and Viceroy of India

Born in **Edinburgh** and educated at Eton and Trinity College, Cambridge, Minto joined the army (1867) and served in numerous campaigns including under Lord Roberts in Afghanistan. He was also a noted sportsman and rode four times in the Grand National, coming fourth in 1874, and in the same year winning the French Grand National. In 1883 he served as Military Secretary to the Governor-General of Canada and was himself appointed to that office 1898–1904, presiding over a period of great prosperity and winning considerable popularity.

In 1905 he followed a well-worn path from Canada to India as Viceroy in succession to Lord Curzon, a hard act to follow. But like his great-grandfather **Sir Gilbert Elliot, 1st Earl of Minto**, one of the more successful governors-general, he showed great common sense and is chiefly remembered for the Morley-Minto reforms which gave Indians a say in government for the first time. A criticism was, and remains, that the reforms assumed separate Hindu and Muslim electorates, thus creating a distrust between them which led to Partition in 1947. Minto could hardly have anticipated this; at the time the reforms were well received and, having also found great favour with India's princes, Minto left India (1910) as popular as he had returned from Canada.

ELLIOT, Jean (1727–1805) Poet

Daughter of the second Sir Gilbert Elliot of Minto, Jean Elliot is said to have written 'The Flowers of the Forest' as the result of a wager made by her brother. The poem was written and published, but Miss Elliot herself never acknowledged its authorship, though it was eventually elucidated by both **Burns** and **Scott**. She was said to be the last person in **Edinburgh** to have her own sedan chair.

ELLIOT, Walter (1888–1958) Politician

One of the most highly regarded of Scottish Secretaries of State, Walter Elliot was born at **Lanark** and educated at **Glasgow Academy** and **Glasgow University**, graduating in both science and medicine. After a distinguished war career in World War I, Elliot received a cable inviting him to stand for Parliament, to which he is reported to have replied 'Yes, which side?' As Conservative MP for Lanark, and later **Glasgow** (Kelvinside) and the Scottish Universities, he shone as outstanding ministerial potential, spending a total of some five years in junior posts in the Scottish Office before being appointed Minister of Agriculture in 1932. Here he promoted the seminal ideas of agricultural marketing boards, moving on to become Secretary of State for Scotland in 1936. His tenure included overseeing much of the move of the Scottish Office to **Edinburgh** but he himself moved on to the Health Ministry in 1938.

There are those who consider Elliott's greatest service to have been the saving of the hammer-beam roof of Westminster Hall when the Houses of Parliament were bombed and set ablaze on the night of 10–11 May 1941. Since there were not enough fire hoses, pumps or water to save both Commons Chamber and Hall, Elliot personally broke open the locked north door of the mighty Hall with an axe and persuaded the chief fire officer to deflect the hoses from the Commons Chamber, which was consequently reduced to ashes instead. It took a swift and unerring judgement to prefer the masterpiece of Minister of Works Chaucer to that of Sir Charles Barry.

Elliot's career is considered to have been wrecked by his being identified, rightly or wrongly, with Chamberlain's appeasement policy, and there was no seat for him in Churchill's wartime cabinet. He continued in public life as a freelance journalist and broadcaster, showing a particular interest in the development of the nations of West Africa. Rector of both **Aberdeen** and Glasgow Universities, he received honorary degrees from all four Scottish seats of learning, and was twice appointed Lord High Commissioner to the **General Assembly** of the **Church of Scotland**. He died at his home near Bonchester Bridge, **Hawick**, on 8 January 1958.

ELLON, Aberdeenshire

Once the ancient capital of **Buchan**, Ellon has been deferring to **Aberdeen** ever since the 14th century and now serves as a dormitory for that city's commuters. The **Comyn** Earls of Buchan here commanded a crossing of the river Ythan from their now invisible motte. Ardgith Tower served the same function and was largely rebuilt as Ellon Castle at about the same time (1782) as a stone bridge, still standing, was thrown across the river. George, 'the Wicked' 3rd Earl of Aberdeen, acquired the much extended castle as a convenient (to **Haddo**) home for Penelope Dering from Sussex, one of his three brown-eyed mistresses. At Esslemont, two miles west, are the remains of a medieval tower; at Arnage, four miles north-west, a restored Z-plan tower house; and further north-west is the also restored 16th century L-plan House of Schivas.

ELPHINSTONE, Arthur, 6th Lord Balmerino (1688–1746) Jacobite

Having joined the 1715 **Jacobite Rising** after the **Battle of Sheriffmuir**, Lord Balermino fled to the Continent, was pardoned in 1733, but joined **Prince Charles Edward Stewart** in **Edinburgh** after the **Battle of Prestonpans**. In command of a troop of Life Guards, he fought with the Jacobite army at the **Battle of Falkirk**,

eventually surrendering after **Culloden**. Held prison in the Tower of London until his trial on 28 July 174 he was beheaded on Tower Hill on 18 August, showing no fear at all. 'Indeed the way in which his aged victi walked about the scaffold and examined the axe unnerved the executioner that in the end it took hi three blows to cut off his head' (**Fitzroy MacLean**).

ELPHINSTONE, George, Viscount Keith (1746–1823) Admiral

Born in **Stirling**, son of the 10th Lord Elphinston George Elphinstone entered the navy at the age of 1 and enjoyed a distinguished career which included se vice in America, India, Ceylon and the Mediterranea Rear-admiral (1794) and created Baron Keith in 179 he was commander of the fleet which landed **Aber cromby**'s army in Aboukir Bay (1801). Admir (1801), he was created Viscount Keith (1814) and w involved in the arrangements for Bonaparte's banish ment to St Helena (1815).

ELPHINSTONE, The Hon Mountstuart (1779–1859) Governor of Bombay

Son of the 11th Lord Elphinstone, the youn Mountstuart was brought up in **Cumbernauld** an **Edinburgh** where his father was Governor of **Edin burgh Castle**. He reached Calcutta in the civil emplo of the East India Company aged 16 and there, like man contemporaries, completed his education, acquiring taste for hunting and for classical literature, both Indo Muslim and Graeco-Roman. In 1801 he was appointe assistant to the British agent at Poona and served on th staff of the future Duke of Wellington during the Secon Maratha War. The Duke's high opinion of him may b gauged from his remark that Elphinstone 'should hav been a soldier'.

There followed four years as Resident at Nagpu before he was chosen to lead a mission to Kabul. Th Afghans declined to let it advance beyond Peshawar b Elphinstone came away an early authority on the vexe question of India's north-western frontier. As Reside at Poona (1810–19) he enjoyed his finest hour durin the Third Maratha and Pindari Wars, dealing firmly wit the Peshwa, philosophically with his supersession b **John Malcolm**, and decisively with the Maratha attac (1817) on the Residency and the post-war settlemen He was rewarded with the Governorship of Bomba (1819–27) where he established a lasting system o public education and justice; Elphinstone College wa endowed in his name.

In retirement he travelled extensively in the Mediter ranean and, preferring study (see his standard History India) and solitude, declined a parliamentary seat, a baron etcy and repeated offers of the governor-generalship o India. He died in Surrey. Compared to his illustriou compatriots in India – John Malcolm and **Sir Thoma Munro** – he was less approachable and inclined to snob bery. But such reserve was offset by a modesty an unselfishness rare indeed in the Indian context.

ELPHINSTONE, William (1431–1514)
Bishop of Aberdeen

Although not an Aberdonian by birth (he was bor in **Glasgow**), William Elphinstone, Privy Councillo

Chancellor of Scotland and Bishop of **Aberdeen**, did as much if not more for the city than any native son. After studying law in Paris and Orléans he undertook diplomatic missions on behalf of **James III** to England and the Continent, was ambassador to France under **James IV**, appointed Bishop of Aberdeen in 1483 and Keeper of the Privy Seal from 1492. During his tenure of the see he founded **King's College** in 1495 (the third university in Scotland, first in the north), made additions to **St Machar's Cathedral** and planned the building of the **Bridge of Dee** (completed by **Gavin Dunbar**). Through his influence Scotland's first printing press was established by **Chepman and Myllar**, and his *Brevarium Aberdonense* was printed in 1510. In 1514 he was offered the Archbishopric of **St Andrews**, but before he could take up the post he died in **Edinburgh** in his 84th year. His tomb can be seen outside the chapel of King's College.

ENCYCLOPAEDIA BRITANNICA

The first edition of the *Britannica* was published in instalments in **Edinburgh** in 1768, from a printshop in Anchor Close, sited next to the present **City Chambers**. One of many such compendia of knowledge appearing at that time, the new work was produced not by the 'Society of Gentlemen' described on its title-page, but as a commercial enterprise by printer Colin Macfarquhar and engraver Andrew Bell. The editor of the first edition was **William Smellie** (pronounced 'Smiley') who completed the 3-volume work by 1771.

The second edition (1777–84) was edited by **James Tytler**, a talented but penniless polymath who wrote much of the work himself in expanding it from three to ten volumes; this edition served as the basis for the financially successful third edition, edited by Macfarquhar and George Gleig in 1788–97. A fourth edition followed in 20 volumes around 1810, edited by James Millar, while the fifth and sixth editions were published by the Edinburgh publishing house of **Constable**, the former being edited by Bonar and Millar, the latter by Charles McLaren. A rival house, owned by **Adam Black**, bought the reference work in 1827, spending an estimated £100,000 on a seventh edition edited by McVey Napier in 21 volumes, including the work's first index, and an eighth edition was edited by T S Traill in 1851–60. The ninth (or 'Scholar's') edition (written by 1100 contributors and edited by T S Baynes and **W R Smith**) appears to have been the last produced in Scotland before A & C Black moved to London, the tenth (largely re-issued) edition bearing an Edinburgh imprint in name only. Owned by American interests from around the start of the 20th century, the *Britannica* has been published in the USA since 1921.

ENGAGEMENT, The (1647)

In December 1647 three Scottish commissioners (Loudoun, **Lauderdale** and Lanark) secretly engaged to support **Charles I**, then a prisoner of the Cromwellian army on the Isle of Wight. In return for giving **Presbyterianism** a three-year trial in England and for granting to his Scots subjects the same commercial privileges as were enjoyed by his English subjects, Charles was to be assisted to return to London and to his throne.

Promoted by **James Hamilton** (3rd Marquis, 1st Duke) who had failed to prevent the surrender of the King to the English a year earlier, and supported by a majority which had previously embraced the **Covenant** with enthusiasm, 'the Engagement represents the biggest turn-over of opinion in the century' (G Donaldson) and 'shattered the unity of the Covenanting movement' (I B Cowan). Although the 'Engagers' would be heavily defeated at **Preston** (1648), their mix of Royalist sympathies and national grievances with adherence to the Covenant and moderate Presbyterianism appealed to a broad spectrum of Scottish opinion and anticipated later settlements.

ENGINEERING

Scotland's international reputation for producing engineers and feats of engineering dates from the first stages of the Industrial Revolution in the later 18th century. The large Scottish textiles industry led the way. Scots were trained in the care and maintenance of mill machinery, and some of the more inventive mechanics were able to make modest improvements to the machines. But it was by applying scientific principles to the practical problems of mechanical invention that Scotland won its reputation. The first of the great Scottish engineers was **James Watt** who patented the separate condenser in 1769 and revolutionised the performance and the potential applications of the steam engine. His associate **William Murdock** pioneered gas lighting and also made the world's first model steam carriage. Soon after, **William Symington** and **Henry Bell** made significant contributions to the development of marine steam technology.

Industrialisation also requires the development of improved means of transport, to permit the free movement of raw materials and finished products. **John Rennie**, **John MacAdam**, **Thomas Telford** and **Robert Stevenson** rose to prominence in civil engineering endeavour, planning and overseeing the construction of new roads, bridges, **canals**, harbours and lighthouses all over the British Isles. Like the mechanical engineers, they succeeded because of their ability to apply a theoretical knowledge of industrial processes and of materials to the engineering tasks they undertook.

The emergence of such talent was due in large measure to the nature of the country's **education** system. The parish schools were remarkably successful in educating a large proportion of the population in reading, writing and arithmetic, all basic to a grasp of the latest developments in subjects relating to engineering. At the universities, and at Anderson's College in **Glasgow** (where popular lectures were delivered on science subjects), a spirit of rational scientific enquiry was encouraged, as was the practical application of scientific knowledge to industrial purposes. Scottish artisans and students were educated in a way and in a cultural climate which enabled and encouraged them to take advantage of the innumerable opportunities which opened up during the Industrial Revolution.

In the 19th century, the ready availability of **coal** and blackband ironstone in central Scotland (both of which became ideal for the manufacture of **iron** after James **Neilson** invented the hot blast furnace in 1828), as well as the existence there of a pool of cheap skilled labour, attracted massive investment in the establish-

The engine shop of shipbuilders Alexander Stephen & Sons at Linthouse (BRC)

ment of heavy engineering industries. Scotland became best known for **shipbuilding** and marine engineering, but was also famous for products as diverse as railway **locomotives**, sugar refining machinery and machine tools. Tens of thousands of highly skilled engineering workers were soon employed in the country's workshops and yards.

Civil engineers were also in great demand in the construction of Scotland's extensive **railway** network, and for supplying the growing industrial towns and cities with new roads, sewers, gasworks and waterworks. Structural engineers such as **Sir William Arrol** & Co, who erected the **Tay** and **Forth Railway Bridges** and London's Tower Bridge, were employed on massive railway and construction projects all over the world. Others who left their homeland during the 19th century to pursue their profession were **William Fairbairn**, the London-based industrialist and experimental engineer, **James Nasmyth**, who pioneered the assembly line at his machine-tool factory in Manchester and invented the steam hammer, and **Henry Dyer**, who was the first Principal of the Imperial College of Engineering in Tokyo and is remembered as one of the fathers of the Japanese engineering industry.

The first Scottish institution to offer a systematic course of instruction in engineering science was **Glasgow University**, where the Regius Chair in Civil

Engineering was erected in 1840. The department famous 'sandwich courses' required students to gai practical experience in local engineering workshop during the university holidays. A good balance betwee the practical and the theoretical training of students wa also sought at **Edinburgh University**, where a chair i engineering was erected in 1868. The greatest figure i engineering education during the mid-Victorian perio was undoubtedly **Macquorn Rankine**, Professor o Engineering at Glasgow University 1856–72. Rankin wrote a wide range of textbooks for engineering stu dents, as well as important papers on engineerin theory. He succeeded in persuading the University auth orities to introduce a Certificate in Engineering Scienc in 1862, and his labours to make engineering a degre subject bore fruit after his death when a BSc in subject including engineering was introduced. Rankine mad Glasgow University one of the world's most famou schools of engineering, a feat accomplished with th assistance of **William Thomson, Lord Kelvin**, the Pro fessor of Natural Philosophy.

The Institute of Civil Engineers in Scotland, founde in 1857, and the Scottish Shipbuilders' Association founded three years later, amalgamated in 1866 to form the Institution of Engineers and Shipbuilders in Scot land. This influential body became increasingly con cerned during the 1880s about the availability an quality of theoretical education for budding engineer and engineering workers, and campaigned for a improvement in standards and facilities. In 1886 th lasgow and West of Scotland Technical College was ounded, with the amalgamation of Anderson's College, he Mechanics' Institute, **Allan Glen's** and other technial training institutions, to provide better facilities for hose seeking to follow an industrial profession or trade. The College later became first the Royal Technical Colge (1912), then the Royal College of Science and echnology (1956) and finally the **University of trathclyde**, 1963.) Also in 1886, **Heriot-Watt** College n **Edinburgh** was rebuilt and re-equipped with modern echnical training apparatus. Glasgow University opened he prestigious James Watt Engineering Laboratory in 901, when the art and technical colleges of **Aberdeen, undee**, Edinburgh and Glasgow were constituted as Central Institutions' and granted extra funding to evelop curriculae in science and other subjects. These nd subsequent improvements to the system of technical ducation, with the rigorous apprenticeship training ffered in industry, ensured further generations of ngineers and engineering workers.

Heavy engineering made a magnificent contribution o the British war effort, but the 20th century also vitnessed its gradual decline. Fierce foreign competetion, poor labour relations and the failure to invest in ew technology were all factors in the sad demise of hipbuilding, locomotive, and other engineering firms n the 1960s and 70s. Their closures threw thousands f skilled men out of work. The picture was not entirely leak, however. American and later Japanese light ngineering companies were attracted to Scotland by he reservoir of skilled engineering labour. The estabishment of a Ferranti factory in Edinburgh in 1942 rought electronic engineering to Scotland, and the lectronics industry now employs around 47,000 eople. The retention of the Rolls-Royce aero engine actory at Hillington after the war provided the country vith a large new technologically advanced industry; and he siting of the National Engineering Laboratory at ast Kilbride in 1947 introduced advanced facilities or applied research in mechanical engineering. The niversities, too, have become important centres for ngineering research, working particularly closely with ompanies active in the spheres of aero, optical, offhore and electronic engineering.

With so many, largely **Clyde**-built, ships and locomoives going for export, maintenance requirements had nce established 'the Scots engineer' as an international tereotype – like 'the Irish labourer' and 'the Italian ce-cream salesman'. Times have changed but engineerng remains a favoured vocation in Scotland with many n astro-suited 'Scottie' ready 'to boldly go where no nan has gone before'.

EPISCOPAL CHURCH OF SCOTLAND

A non-established independent Scottish Church since 690, the Scottish Episcopal Church (its correct title) s part of the world-wide Anglican Communion. Its origins are seen to date from the first bishop **St Ninian** n 397 and the missions of **St Columba** which formed he **Celtic Church** that became *Ecclesia Scoticana* from 878. Always an independent Church in **Roman Catholic** nedieval Europe, the Scottish Church was organised nto 13 sees by **Alexander I** and **David I** with archbishprics at **St Andrews** and **Glasgow**.

At the **Reformation** of 1560 the bishops were relieved of their power and the now Protestant Church of Scotland was reorganised on the Genevan pattern by **Knox** with a superintendent in each diocese to coordinate ecclesiastical order. **James VI** twice restored episcopal jurisdiction in order to retain power over the Scottish Church, attempting a Church of England pattern. This led to conflict with **Andrew Melville** from 1572 and the end of Protestant episcopacy in 1592 when **Presbyterians** overthrew the King's 'tulchan bishops' whose function appeared to be to provide revenue for the nobility. Episcopacy was restored in 1610 by consecration of three bishops in London.

When **Charles I** introduced a Scottish Prayer Book in 1637 (provoking a riot in **St Giles, Edinburgh**), the Presbyterian majority responded by condemning episcopacy at the 1638 **General Assembly** after signing of a National **Covenant** in Edinburgh. At the Restoration **Charles II** reintroduced episcopacy. But only one bishop remained from 1638 so four new bishops were consecrated in London in 1661, among whom were the moderate **Leighton** and the extreme **Sharp**, who became Archbishop of St Andrews.

The insurrections of the Covenanters, resulting from conflict between episcopacy and Presbyterian order, were countered by vicious civil force and the unhappiest period of the Scottish Church during which Leighton resigned and Sharp was murdered. Although some two-thirds of the kingdom had accepted episcopacy by the time of the 1688 Revolution, the outcome, politically engineered by **Carstares**, was an established **Church of Scotland** of Presbyterian order, without bishops, in 1690.

The existing bishops, having given their oath of allegiance to **James VII**, felt unable to swear again to William III while the previous monarch still lived. Their scruples brought about their deposition and the division of the heritage of St Ninian. The Scottish Episcopal Church so formed was termed **Jacobite** because of its allegiance to James VII. Covenanters immediately retaliated with the 'rabbling of the curates' when 200 clergy in the west were put out of their parishes without means of support. Other episcopal clergy were gradually replaced by Presbyterians, often against the wishes of the parishioners; some resisted until 1730.

Episcopal clergy and their bishops suffered particular persecution during the Jacobite rebellions in which some were indeed involved. By the 1712 Act of Toleration Episcopalians were permitted to worship using the Church of England Prayer Book and released from a limiting act of the pre-**Union** Scottish Parliament. However, some **Non-Jurors** refused to compromise, retained use of the Scottish Prayer Book of 1637 and refused to pray for the King by name. After the 1715 rebellion strict limitations were empowered by an Act of 1719 whereby no more than nine persons could worship with a family under penalty of imprisonment and closing of the meeting house.

The last pre-Revolution bishop died in 1720, the last archbishop having died in 1704. Bishops and clergy had no jurisdiction over cathedrals, dioceses or parishes. They ministered to a scattered flock travelling from wherever they were able to live. The bishops became an Episcopal College functioning corporately with one elected to preside as *Primus inter pares*. Though few committed themselves to the 1745 Jacobite Rising, two clergy were hung and many meeting houses burnt down. By an Act of 1746, worship was limited to five persons and in 1748 all unqualified clergy (those who had not taken the oath) were barred from acting. Penal laws were not repealed until 1792, following the death of **Prince Charles Edward Stewart** in 1788.

At its lowest ebb the Church had only four bishops and 50 clergy, yet it revised its Scottish liturgy and administration and retained a distinct spirituality. Some pre-Revolution congregations even had continuous existence. These, with the qualified and Non-juring meeting houses, began to be reformed into a Church with seven bishops, by combining the titles of the medieval sees, headed by a Primus, which is the present structure. It even consecrated the first bishop for the United States of America in 1784, thus founding the present worldwide Anglican Communion in the midst of penal disabilities.

Influenced by the Oxford Movement after 1830, new churches were built and Scottish Episcopalianism has grown to a distinctive liturgically based movement of influence despite its numerical size. The first complete cathedral in Britain since the Middle Ages was built at **Perth** by 1851 and dedicated to St Ninian. Cathedrals in the other sees, once more territorially aligned, replaced the medieval ones now in ruins or Presbyterian use.

The Church remains disestablished and independent, likewise independent of the Church of England but in communion with it, as the reformed *Ecclesia Scoticana* of episcopal tradition.

ERIBOLL, Loch, Sutherland

This great sea loch facing the North Atlantic extends for some 10 miles south to the wilderness of the **Reay deer forest**. Its comparatively barren western shore forms a striking contrast to the limestone outcrop on its eastern side where Eriboll farm gives an impression of the Lothians. In earlier times people would cross from Port Chamil to Badilhavish on the east side, rather than make the weary journey over rough ground where there was no road. In 1737 **Murdo MacDonald**, minister of **Durness**, described just such a crossing, impeded by an unfavourable wind, when he observed 'coming into Loch Eriboll two ships which were directed from their easterly course by the same cross wind'. They were far from the only ones to find such shelter in the days of sail. In 1772 the *Adventure* entered the loch to embark 200 passengers bound for South Carolina, but today this deepwater anchorage remains unused by any of the undertakings that have resulted from the extraction of **oil** from the neighbouring sea-beds.

ERISKAY, Island of, Outer Hebrides

The Island of Eriskay (Norse: Eiriks-ey, Eric's Island) lies in the Outer **Hebrides** between **South Uist** and **Barra**. Only 2½ by 1½ miles in size, it is the most densely populated Hebridean island with a population of about 200. The economy of the mainly Roman Catholic community is based on an enterprising **fishing industry**, supplemented by **crofting** and hand-knitted woolly jumpers. There are ferry connections to South Uist and Barra.

Ben Scrien (610ft/186m) is the highest hill, over looking the township of Balla, with a shop, school, pos office and church. St Michael's church was built in 190? by Father Allen MacDonald; the altar is supported on the bow of a lifeboat.

Prince Charles Edward Stewart first landed on Scot tish soil at Eriskay in 1745. The 'Eriskay Love Lilt' is a famous Gaelic folk song. In 1941 the merchant ship *Politician*, carrying 20,000 cases of whisky, foundered off the island. 5000 cases were salvaged locally and unofficially, the basis of **Sir Compton Mackenzie**' novel *Whisky Galore!*; an Ealing comedy film was made on Barra in 1948.

Eriskay ponies are the last survivors of the native Scot tish pony, and are the subject of a conservation breeding scheme. They stand 12–13 hands tall, with small ears and are still used to carry **peat** and **seaweed**.

ERROL, Earldom of

The Lord High Constable ranks after the Blood Roya as the senior subject of Scotland. The office, involving custody of the King's stables [see also **Marischal**], was bestowed on the Norman family of Hay, who settled in Scotland in about 1160. Two decades later a charter for the property of Errol was granted to William Hay, married to the Celtic heiress of Pitmilly. His successor commanded the bodyguard of **Robert I** as Constable and was rewarded with the hereditary office in 1314. In 1429 the family were raised to be Lords of Parliament, and in 1452 the 2nd Lord Hay was created Earl of Errol. Francis Hay, 9th Earl (1564–1631), was associated with the Earl of Huntly and the pro-Spanish faction opposed to **James VI**. He fought at **Glenlivet**, went into exile, returned, but declared himself a Catholic in his will. The 11th Earl acquired dubious fame in a **ballad** in which his Countess accused him of being impotent, which he was able to prove that he was not. Perhaps it was she who was barren, since the pair produced no children. However, the Hays managed without them, to the extent that the 24th Earl of Errol is today the 28th Lord High Constable.

ERSKINE, David Stewart 11th Earl of Buchan (1742–1829)

Remembered as the founder of the **Society of Antiquaries of Scotland** (1780), Buchan was also a zealous parliamentary reformer. In 1768 he drew attention to the fact that the election of the 16 Scottish representative peers to Westminster, previously chosen by Scottish peers themselves from amongst their own number, had become 'a mere ministerial nomination'. His agitation led to the restoration of this right, which had been enshrined in the 1707 **Treaty of Union**.

ERSKINE, Ebenezer (1680–1754) Minister

The father of the **Secession Church**, and of 15 children, Erskine was born at **Dryburgh**, educated at **Edinburgh University** and became chaplain to the **Earl of Rothes** before ordination to Portmoak, **Kinross-shire**, in 1703. An evangelical opposed to the Patronage Act of 1712, he transferred to **Stirling** in 1731. Suspended for his views in 1733, he was allowed to preach until deposed in 1740 when his Associate Presbytery was founded. In 1747 these seceders split over the Burgess oath into urger and Anti-Burger Churches. The secession and ↵rther splits damaged the **Church of Scotland**, eventu-↵ly leading to the major **Disruption** of 1843, again over ↵atronage rather than personality. [See chart p. 995]

RSKINE, Henry (1746–1817) Jurist and ↵olitician

ounger brother of **David Erskine, 11th Earl of uchan**, Henry studied **law** at Edinburgh and **Glasgow** ↵d was admitted to the **Faculty of Advocates** in 1768. ↵n aristocrat with reforming zeal' and a leading **Whig**, ↵e was a founder member of the committee formed in ↵dinburgh in 1783 to press for reform of parliamentary ↵epresentation in Scotland. Later in the same year he ↵eplaced that arch opponent of reform, **Henry Dundas**, ↵. Lord Advocate and in 1785 became Dean of the Faculty ↵f Advocates, a post from which he was eventually ↵emoved by Dundas in 1795. A moderate with little time ↵or militants, Erskine nevertheless offered to defend ↵**homas Muir of Huntershill** at his 1793 trial for ↵edition on condition that he have complete charge of ↵ne defence, an offer refused by the fiery Muir, who was ↵ubsequently found guilty and transported to Botany Bay. ↵1P for **Haddington** Burghs and **Dumfries** burghs ↵(1806), Erskine was again Lord Advocate 1806–7.

The youngest of the three Erskine brothers, Thomas ↵(1750–1823), made a brilliant name for himself at the ↵nglish Bar after an early career in the navy, became ↵ord Chancellor (1806–7) and was created Baron ↵rskine in 1806.

RSKINE, James (1679–1754) Lord Grange

rother of **John, 6th (11th) Earl of Mar**, the ineffectual ↵eader of the 1715 **Jacobite Rising**, James Erskine was ↵. member of the **Faculty of Advocates** from 1705 and

ady Grange (Rachel Chiesley), the ill-fated wife of James Erskine, Lord ↵Grange, attributed to Sir J B de Medina (SNPG)

became Lord Justice Clerk with the title Lord Grange in 1710. In 1732 he conspired, with **Simon Fraser of Lovat**, to get rid of his estranged wife, Rachel Chiesley, who had threatened to denounce him as a Jacobite. She was spirited out of the city in a sedan chair at night and, after being kept in solitary confinement for six months, secretly conveyed into the west Highlands. After surviving two years on Heisker (the **Monach Isles**), she was dumped on St Kilda – 'a vile, neasty, stinking poor isle' she called it – from where, seven years later, she was sent to **Skye** where she died demented in 1745. Meanwhile her husband had publicly celebrated her funeral in **Edinburgh**, become MP for **Stirlingshire** (1734), and secretary to Frederick, Prince of Wales.

ERSKINE, John, of Carnock (1695–1768) Jurist

One of the earliest academic Scots lawyers of the modern epoch, John Erskine was admitted advocate in 1719. He practised at the Bar until appointed Professor of Scots **Law** in the **University of Edinburgh** in 1737. Whilst teaching he wrote a *Principles of the Law of Scotland* (1754). From 1765–8 he concentrated on *The Institutes of the Law of Scotland* (1773). Acknowledged as an institutional writing and used through many editions during the late 18th and 19th centuries, it was largely superseded by **Sir George Mackenzie**'s *Institutions* but is still often referred to in court.

See also **Law**.

ERSKINE, John, 1st Earl of Mar (c1510–72) Regent

Also confusingly referred to as the 6th Earl of Mar on account of his descent from the earlier line [see **Earldoms of Mar**], John 6th Lord Erskine was **Commendator** of **Dryburgh**, **Inchmahome** and **Cambuskenneth** and Keeper of **Edinburgh Castle**. Uncle of **Lord James Stewart**, Earl of Moray (whose mother Margaret Erskine Douglas was his sister), John Erskine was confirmed in the Earldom of Mar after the title was adopted and then relinquished by his nephew (1565). A moderate Protestant, he remained neutral throughout the regency of **Mary of Guise** although wooed energetically by both Protestant and Catholic, but eventually turned against **Queen Mary** after the murder of **Darnley**. Removed from his post as Keeper of Edinburgh Castle by **Bothwell** (1567) but granted the hereditary captaincy of **Stirling Castle** in exchange, he was custodian of the child Prince **James** (VI) and succeeded as Regent on the death of **Lennox** (1571), but held the post for only a year before his own death.

ERSKINE, John, 2nd (or 7th) Earl of Mar (1562–1634)

Son of **John Erskine, 1st** (or 6th) **Earl of Mar**, custodian of and then Regent for **James VI**, this John Erskine was brought up and educated in the company of the young Prince, who nicknamed him 'Jockie o' the Sclates'. He succeeded to the **Earldom of Mar** on the death of his father (1572), became involved in the **Ruthven Raid** (1582), was exiled (1583–5) but later restored to favour and appointed Treasurer in Scotland (1616) after the **Union of the Crowns** (1603) took James south to London.

ERSKINE, John 6th (or 11th) Earl of Mar (1675–1732)

Known as 'Bobbing John' for the frequency and fervour with which he changed sides, John Erskine 6th Earl

John Erskine, 6th Earl of Mar and leader of the 1715 Jacobite Rising, with his son, by Sir G Kneller, 1715 (SNPG)

of Mar was less widely known as an industrial and agricultural improver, developing and exploiting the family estates in **Clackmannanshire** and promoting the development of nearby **Alloa** as a **coal-mining** centre. He served as Secretary of State for Scotland under Queen Anne and, with **James Douglas 2nd Duke of Queensberry**, was one of the main architects of the 1707 **Act of Union**. Unequalled in his 'grovelling sycophancy towards George I' (B Lenman), he reacted to a blatant snub from the Hanoverian by rushing north to raise the **Jacobite** standard for **James Francis Edward Stewart** on the Braes of Mar (1715). Singularly inept as a leader, he failed to defeat **John, 2nd Duke of Argyll** at **Sheriffmuir** despite his vastly superior numbers. He retreated and sailed for France in early 1716, his estates and title forfeited. He later abandoned the Jacobite cause but died in exile at Aix-la-Chapelle.

ERSKINE, Robert (1677–1718) Physician

Sixth son of Sir Charles Erskine of **Alva**, Robert wa apprenticed to an **Edinburgh** surgeon-apothecary at th age of 15, studied anatomy, surgery, chemistry an botany in Paris and graduated MD at Utrecht in 1700 Elected to the Royal Society in 1703, he went to Moscow the following year as physician to Prince Menshiko and in 1705 became doctor to Peter the Grea Appointed Chief Physician to the Tsar and President of the Apothecaries' Chancery (1706), Erskine was in over all charge of the country's medical services, foundee the first Physic Garden at St Petersburg (1714) an encouraged many other Scots physicians and scientist to make their careers in the service of the Tsar. H died on St Andrew's Day 1718 at the age of 41. Hi magnificent library, together with that of his fellow physician **Archibald Pitcairne** which Erskine had pur chased for the Tsar in 1713, became the nucleus of th library of the Russian Academy of Sciences.

ERSKINE, Thomas Alexander, 6th Earl of Kellie (or Kelly) (1732–81) Composer

Initially known on his own estates as 'fiddler Tam Thomas Erskine was one of the most significan musicians in Britain. When his father was imprisonee for supporting the **Jacobites**, Thomas left for Mannhein to study with the elder Stamitz, returning in 1756 as a accomplished violinist and composer. His 10 survivin, symphonies were published by **Robert Bremner** i 1761–7. The best are both lively and refined and mak good use of Mannheim mannerisms such as crescendo and varied dynamics and a new freedom in the use o wind instruments.

The recently discovered **Kilravock** Partbooks (con taining nine quartets, nine trio sonatas and a duo sonat for two violins) reveal a considerable range and variet of style, at times deeply expressive. He arranged an composed a suite of minuets for Lord Stanley's *fête cham pêtre* at the Oaks at Epsom in 1774 – the first ever hel in Britain. His concert aria 'Death is Now My Onl Treasure' may reflect masonic principles – Kelly wa simultaneously Grand Master of both the English an the Scottish **Freemasons**. A number of Kelly works wer written impromptu, particularly for his favourite wine instruments, the parts being produced on the spot with out full scores and then dispersed among the players As a consequence they are all lost.

Kelly was well known as a bon viveur. It was sai that his nose was so red it would ripen cucumbers. He founded the Capillaire Club – an Edinburgh drinkin club which met on Sundays – for which he compose a minuet, and of which Alison Cockburn wrote to **Davi Hume** 'bring you vices we shall find objects for them As for the godly, there is not one here.'

A full evaluation of Kelly's music must wait until th publication of the Kilravock works, but the evidenc already suggests that, for a composer born in the sam year as Haydn, his precocious talents should gain hin a place in the proper study of the early evolution o classical style in Europe.

ERSKINE HOSPITAL, Erskine, Renfrewshire

Erskine House (1828–45, Sir Robert Smirke) was originally the home of the Lords of **Blantyre**. In 1916 i became known as the Princess Louise Hospital for Limbless Sailors and Soldiers and functions today as the Erskine Hospital for disabled ex-servicemen and women – the largest ex-service hospital in the UK with 290 beds. The majority of patients are permanent residents. It operates outwith the National Health Service, and annual running costs exceed £4 million. Within the hospital grounds there is a small housing estate comprising 53 four-apartment cottages for long-term residents. Sheltered workshops provide facilities for bootmaking, furniture repairs, joinery, printing, basketry, etc; there are also six acres of gardens and greenhouses. Products are sold at the hospital and at a shop in **Glasgow**.

ERSKINE OF MAR, Stuart Ruaraidh (1869–1960) Gaelic Nationalist and Writer
Erskine was born in Sussex but came of an old Scottish family. He learned **Gaelic** from his **Harris** nursemaid, and became an enthusiastic Scottish nationalist and founding father of the **National Party of Scotland**. To foster the Gaelic consciousness he founded a number of periodicals, from Am Bàrd (1901–2) to An Ròsarnach (1917–30), but his main periodical was Guth na Bliadhna (1904–25), which was concerned with extending the range of Gaelic writing (to journalism, politics, history, astronomy, art, etc).

ESDAILE, James (1808–59) Hypnotist
Born at **Montrose**, James Esdaile studied medicine at **Edinburgh** before embarking on a 21-year tour of duty in Indian hospitals. Here he became interested in the use of hypnotism as an anaesthetic, personally conducting 100 operations in his first year, including amputations. His methods were physically tiring to implement, and encountered varying patient response. Retired in England, Esdaile died in London.

ESKDALEMUIR, Dumfriesshire
Eskdale's muir is now largely forest. The parish covers most of the White Esk valley above the lower end of which Castle O'er (Over, Overbie) a hill fort of the 1st millennium BC, is now less prominent and accessible than of old. It was once thought to be **Roman**, a provenance now reserved for Raeburnfoot, an **Antonine** fort and staging post nearer Eskdale Church. North of the church the Samye Ling monastery, a Tibetan (Mahayana) Buddhist establishment, is one of the largest Buddhist temples outside Asia, with a resident community of more than 100, accommodation for up to 100 guests, and its own farm, college, library and museum. Such renown as this otherwise bleak district does not owe to the monastery derives from the Observatory further north. Established in 1908 to record terrestrial magnetism and subsequently part of the Meteorological Office, it rivals **Tummel Bridge** for reporting unseasonably low temperatures and **Glen Quoich** for exceptionally high rainfall.

Gazetteers and guidebooks perpetuate the memory of the Handfasting Fair, once held annually near the church, and notorious for a custom whereby unmarried persons of either sex might choose a partner for the coming year on approval, the marriage being solemnised at the next fair if both partners agreed. The pact, somewhat open to abuse, was signified by 'handfasting' or placing the hand of the potential bride round the fist of the potential groom. The custom is said to have lasted until after the **Reformation** and to have attracted some noble patrons including James 6th Earl of **Moray**.

ETHNOLOGY, Scottish
Ethnology encompasses the extensive collection, systematic description, analysis and scholarly interpretation of traditional cultures, explaining their underlying values, their making or meaning, and the way in which they shape national and regional identities. It includes the examination, comparative study and contextualisation of material culture and of narratives, linguistic geography and names, music and song, custom and belief, together with their interrelationships. Although widely established academically in Europe and North America (where it is commonly known as Folklore), it lacked full academic recognition in the United Kingdom until two chairs were created recently in Scotland: Alexander Fenton (b.1929), from the **National Museums of Scotland**, was appointed in 1990 to a new Chair of Scottish Ethnology within the School of Scottish Studies, **Edinburgh**, and David Buchan (1939–94), the ballad scholar, to the Chair of Scottish Ethnology at **Aberdeen University** (est. 1993). Prior to this the School of Scottish Studies (founded 1951) was offering honours courses in Scottish ethnology from 1987. From 1959 material culture studies were being fostered by the Country Life (later the Working Life) Section of the former National Museum of Antiquities of Scotland in 1959, including the establishment of the Scottish Life Archive. Early pioneers included the Reverend Walter Gregor of Pitsligo (1825–97), a founder member of the Folklore Society (1878) who became internationally famous for his prolific ethnological publications in three languages; Sir Arthur Mitchell, whose Rhind lectures on material culture were published as The Past in the Present (1880); and **Gavin Greig** (1856–1914) and James Duncan (1848–1917) of New Deer in traditional music and song. Highland traditional culture was studied by the likes of **John Francis Campbell** of Islay (1822–55) and **Alexander Carmichael** (1832–1912). See Alexander Fenton, 'Scottish Ethnology: Crossing the Rubicon', Scottish Studies, 31 (1993), 1–8.

ETIVE, Loch, Argyll
From the Falls of Lora at **Connel** to the twin peaks of Buachaille Etive at the head of the glen, Etive-side is one of Scotland's prime wildernesses, remote and magnificent. Home of the legendary **Deirdre** and Naoise, it was immortalised in her farewell to the glen: 'Beauteous glen in early morning, Flocks of sunbeams crowd thy fold'. In winter, etymology provides a better clue to the loch's aspect, 'Etive' being the Gaelic for 'raging'.

ETTRICK FOREST, Selkirkshire
The historic name for most of **Selkirkshire**, Ettrick Forest was indeed once heavily forested with a true Caledonian mix of pine, oak, **birch** and hazel. Its wild and trackless terrain sheltered generations of rievers and outlaws, fugitives from justice, or family feud, or battle. Both **Wallace** and **Bruce** used the forest as a guerrilla base during the **Wars of Independence**; as did the

Borders freebooters – Armstrongs, Scotts, Elliots, **Douglases** and others – in their forays against each other and across the border into England. Granted to the Douglases by **Robert I**, it was forfeited by them to the Crown in 1455 whereupon their great rivals the Scotts of Buccleuch 'rose upon their ruins' to hold large areas of Ettrick Forest – as indeed they still do, the Duke of Buccleuch's home being at Bowhill just west of **Selkirk**.

The large herds of **deer** and quantities of wild boar that shared the forest with the fugitives made it a favourite royal hunting ground – **James V** in particular enjoying the chase of both human and animal. The rapid deforestation of much of Ettrick is thought to date from the mid-16th century when, having had his sport, James turned 10,000 sheep out to graze among the trees in 1528; a 19th century gazetteer described Ettrick as 'all one mighty sheepwalk with wave upon wave of long, green rounded hills whose rich grass feeds enormous flocks of **Cheviots**'. The tiny hamlet of Ettrick was both birth and burial place of **James Hogg**, 'the Ettrick Shepherd', who spent his youth as a shepherd on the hills of Ettrick.

EVANTON, Ross & Cromarty

Lacking historical interest or architectural merit, Evanton straggles along the main A9 north of **Dingwall** in Easter **Ross**. It was named after Evan Fraser of Balconie in the early 19th century and now comprises 20th century housing schemes and industrial enterprises. Ben Wyvis (1048m) rises to the west as does the river Glass which approaches Evanton through a two-mile long ravine, more than 100ft (30m) deep and extremely narrow. The ravine is named after its prominent Black Rock of Novar near which is the so-called Fyrish Monument or Temple, in fact a folly which may represent the gates of Negapatnam in south India. It was erected as a job-creation scheme at a time of famine by **Sir Hector Munro** of Novar whose exploits in India culminated in the capture of Negapatnam, then a Dutch port, in 1781.

Besides the Munro estates of Fyrish and Novar, Foulis Castle to the south-west of Evanton is the home of the clan chief. The original castle, granted to the Munros in the mid-14th century, was burnt down by the **Mackenzies** during the '45 **Jacobite Rising**. Its replacement incorporates some of the ruins and comprises a semi-octagonal tower (1762) and a formal E-plan range (1777) with central pediment and first-floor entrance with double staircase, all in the style of John Adam. Foulis Rent House, on the coast south of Evanton, dates from 1740 and was used as a storehouse for rents paid in kind (usually meal) which were then distributed to Munro dependents or shipped to the garrison at **Fort George**.

EWING, James (1855–1935) Physicist

Born in **Dundee**, Ewing studied at **Edinburgh** before being appointed Professor of Mechanical **Engineering** at Tokyo University, where he established a seismological observatory and began important research on magnetism in metals. Appointed Director of Naval Education back in Britain, he showed a genius for cryptography and set up 'Room 40' at the Admiralty to break German wartime signals. He was Principal of **Edinburgh University** 1916–29.

EYEMOUTH, Berwickshire

Originally the port for **Coldingham** Priory, Eyemouth is today the only major sea-port in **Berwickshire**. A holiday resort with the largest population in the district, it is a thriving community with a museum, history trail, **golf course** and swimming pool. The remains of a fort erected by the Duke of Somerset in 1547, can be seen above the bay. It was demolished in 1550, rebuilt by **Mary of Guise** in 1557 and destroyed again in 1560. Two cannon placed there in the 1850s still look out to sea. Created a **burgh of barony** by **James VI** in 1566 with the status of a free port, Eyemouth was soon well known as a centre of the contraband trade; caves in the neighbouring cliffs providing refuge for the smugglers. Subsequently a major **herring** port with a sizeable **fishing** fleet, Eyemouth's harbour was built originally in 1768, but has since been greatly modified. The 1881 **fishing disaster** overcame the town at its most successful. The present fleet consists of about 55 boats of mixed sizes, the 70ft (21m) vessels working from Eyemouth on a five-day basis, but never on a Friday. An annual Herring Queen Ceremony in July celebrates the town's fishing tradition.

EYEMOUTH FISHING DISASTER (1881)

A violent storm on 14 October 1881 blighted the whole east coast of Scotland, but reserved its most deadly effect for the **Berwickshire fishing** village of **Eyemouth**. Between 40 and 45 boats (sources differ) had already put to sea in good weather on that autumn day, although with the barometer dropping. Even this failed to warn the fleet of what was to come, with a hurricane suddenly springing up and the sky turning black. Eyemouth's men faced the unenviable choice of turning into the wind and braving the conditions, or running for shore with the attendant danger of shipwreck. Only 26 of Eyemouth's boats returned, the death-toll finally reaching 129 men and boys, or one in three of the town's fishermen.

'Disaster Day', as it was known locally, is commemorated by a simple monument in a park in the town. A museum was opened in Eyemouth in the incident's centenary year. Its centrepiece is a locally-woven tapestry depicting the horrors of that October day.

FAIR ISLE, Shetland

A natural haven in a waste of seas 25 miles south of Sumburgh Head, Fair Isle is the most southerly of the Shetland Islands. In spite of its small size – less than four square miles – it maintains a population of around 70, dependent mainly on **crofting**. It lies on the shipping routes for vessels passing between Scandinavia and the north of Scotland and, before the two lighthouses were built in 1891, shipwrecks were frequent. The island is also on the route for migrant birds, hence the world-famous Fair Isles bird observatory, established in 1948 by ornithologist George Waterston, which attracts visitors and boosts the islanders' income. Acquired by the **National Trust for Scotland** from Waterston in 1954, Fair Isle is served by a twice-weekly mailboat from Grutness on the Shetland **Mainland**, and there is also an inter-island air service.

Fair Isle is famous for its knitwear. Legends attribute the origins of the unique patterns to Spanish seamen, shipwrecked after the defeat of the Spanish Armada in 1588. The wreck of *El Gran Grifon* has been located and history records the hardship faced by the island's 17 families as they had to share their provisions with 300 shipwrecked seamen for almost two months; but the connection with knitting is disputed by experts, who point out that the Fair Isle patterns are basically Scandinavian.

FAIRBAIRN, Sir William (1789–1874)
Engineer

Fairbairn was born in **Kelso**, the son of a farmer. In 1804 he moved to North Shields and became an apprentice millwright, befriending the young George Stephenson. In 1816 he set up in business in Manchester, initially in partnership with James Lillie, to manufacture and repair textile machinery.

In 1831 Fairbairn conducted the first of many experiments in the design of steam vessels, and four years later he opened a shipyard at Millwall in London, where he built over 100 iron steamships. It was at Millwall that he completed with Eaton Hopkinson his most celebrated series of experiments, testing iron tube sections for **Robert Stevenson**'s revolutionary new **railway** bridges at Conway and the Menai Straits in north Wales.

From 1832 Fairbairn's Manchester works built engines and boilers as well as over 600 **locomotives**. He introduced the double-flued Lancashire boiler, the most popular type ever devised, and published over 80 scientific papers plus several books on **engineering** subjects. In recognition of his immense contribution to engineering practice and theory he was elected a Fellow of the Royal Society (1850), President of the Institution of Mechanical Engineers (1854) and of the British Association (1861). He was created a baronet in 1869.

FAIRIES

Scotland's fairy lore, though incorporating elves, fauns, trolls and the invariably female fairies of Anglo-Saxon tradition, remains essentially **Celtic**. Investigated by such 17th century observers as **Robert Kirk** and **Martin Martin**, it was even then strongest in the Gaelic Highlands and Islands and was closely associated with **second sight**. Kirk's title *The Secret Commonwealth* hints at two essential differences from English lore: Celtic fairy folk (*sith*, *side*) are both male and female, and they are essentially republicans, having no kings or queens such as Oberon, Mab, Titania. Compared to the 'coarser . . . more malignant elves' of Teutonic tradition, **Sir Walter Scott** detected a Celtic 'superiority of taste and fancy which, with the love of music and poetry, has been generally ascribed to their race'. Moreover, according to the Rev Gregorson Campbell of **Tiree**, fairies 'always come from the west', travelling on whirlwinds (and occasionally transporting any humans they encounter on the way). They also ride small horses whose hoofs 'would not dash the dew from the cup of a harebell'.

They live mostly in cavities just under the ground and often in knolls, entering this realm through crannies and fissures in the rock. Kirk says they are divided into tribes and orders (one being **Brownies**) and that they have children, nurses, marriages, deaths and burials 'even as we do (unless they do so for a mock-show or to prognosticate some such things among us)'. They have their own cats, dogs (very big), sheep and cattle but are not above raiding human kitchens and granaries or surreptitiously milking the odd dairy cow. The nastiest sort steal babies and substitute a changeling, a 'peevish old fairy in child form' (D A Mackenzie). Kirk describes their 'astral' bodies as 'so spungious, thin and defecat that they are fed by only sucking into some fine spiritous liquors that pierce like pure air and oil'. Yet they wear the garments of those above ground, mostly 'plaids and variegated garments in the Highlands'.

FAIRLIE, Nr Largs, Ayrshire

Fairlie is now largely a retirement and commuting village. Kelburn Castle nearby is the family seat of the Earls of Glasgow. Racing and cruising yachts were built at Fyfe's yard in Fairlie from the late 18th century until the 1950s. Fyfe yachts were owned by crowned heads and business leaders; **Sir Thomas Lipton** had two of his *Shamrock* Americas Cup challengers built here, and surviving specimens are now highly prized on the international boat market. Originally an important centre for **Clyde** steamer sailings, Fairlie's pier closed in the 1970s.

FAIRLIE, Sir Reginald (1883–1952) Architect

A pupil of **Sir Robert Lorimer**, Fairlie was mainly known for his scholarly domestic and, in particular, ecclesiastical designs. He set up practice in **Edinburgh** in 1909 but interrupted his career to serve in the war. In 1919 he returned to Edinburgh and became one of Scotland's leading architects. He designed, altered and restored well over 60 churches, his most famous work being at **Fort Augustus** Abbey and **St Andrews University** Chapel. He also designed a large number of small parish churches, among them **Methil** Parish Church (1924) and the Catholic Church of St Andrew in **Rothesay** (1923). He altered a large number of houses such as **Floors Castle** (1929) and Melville Castle, **Fife** (1939). Stylistically Fairlie was a traditionalist. This is best illustrated by the modern classicism he displayed in his design for the **National Library of Scotland** in Edinburgh (1934–6). He was a prolific designer of war memorials and responsible for those at **Moffat** (1920), **North Berwick** (1920) and the American-Scottish War Memorial in **Princes Street Gardens**, Edinburgh (1928).

FALAISE, Treaty of (1174)

In an effort to win back the northern English counties ceded to **David I** (1149) but reclaimed from **Malcolm IV** by Henry II of England (1157), **William I** invaded Northumberland in 1174 but was captured after laying siege to Alnwick. Taken as Henry's prisoner first to Northampton and then in his train to Normandy, he was forced to sign the Treaty of Falaise (or Valognes) on 8 December 1174, accepting English overlordship not only of himself, his kingdom and his barons but also of the Scottish Church. The Scottish bishops managed to negate this latter provision by appealing to Pope Clementine to support the independence of the *Ecclesia Scotiae* under the direct jurisdiction of Rome, which appeal was finally granted in 1192. The other conditions of the Treaty, which included surrendering the castles of **Edinburgh**, **Stirling**, **Roxburgh**, **Jedburgh** and **Berwick** to English occupation, remained in force until Henry's death in 1189, when William was able to cancel them in the Treaty (or 'Quitclaim') of Canterbury in return for money needed by Richard I (the Lionheart) for his crusades.

FALCONER, Dr Hugh (1808–65) Botanist

Hugh Falconer was born in **Forres** and educated at **Aberdeen** and **Edinburgh** where he graduated an MD in 1829. He spent some time assisting Dr Wallich with his Indian herbarium before being sent to Landour in the Himalayas to take charge of the sanatorium. In 1831 he became Superintendent of the Saharanpore Botanic Garden where he pursued both botanical and palaeontological research. He is especially known for his discovery of **fossil** mammals in the Siwalik Hills and for the early cultivation of tea in this area. In 1848 he succeeded Dr Wallich as head of the Calcutta Botanic Garden where he introduced chinchona (quinine) and recommended commercial cultivation (it later became an important economic crop). In 1855 he left India to continue his fossil studies in Britain. He died in London.

FALKIRK, Battle of (i) (1298)

In retaliation for a series of ferocious Scottish raids led by **William Wallace** into the northern counties of England, Edward I assembled a powerful army at Newcastle in June 1298. An advance party under the Earl of Surrey, 'his courage somewhat restored after the disaster of **Stirling Bridge**', regained **Roxburgh** Castle, and met up with Edward and the main body of his troops (which included a large number of archers and nearly 3000

cavalry) at **Linlithgow** in July. The Scottish army, half the size, and consisting mostly of spearmen with a small cavalry back-up, was assembled at **Falkirk**. The Scottish defeat that followed on 22 July was as comprehensive as had been their victory at Stirling Bridge 10 months previously. The spearmen grouped in their schiltron were slaughtered, while the cavalry (mostly nobles who still had reservations about Wallace as a leader) quietly withdrew. Wallace escaped with his life intact but his credibility in tatters. He resigned the post of Guardian forthwith and soon afterwards went to France.

FALKIRK, Battle of (ii) (1746)

On his retreat northwards from Derby pursued by Cumberland, **Prince Charles Edward**'s army was reinforced by new musters of **Jacobites** when he crossed the border back into Scotland (December 1745). Now numbering about 8000 men and with the Prince and **Lord George Murray** at its head, it besieged **Stirling Castle**, garrisoned by government troops. A relieving force also numbering about 8000 was despatched from Newcastle under General Henry Hawley. Not anticipating an encounter with the Jacobites until he reached Stirling, Hawley established himself at Callendar House to the south-east of **Falkirk** on the night of 16 January 1746. The following morning his scouts brought word that the Jacobites were massing on the high ground just behind the house. A frantic scramble in heavy rain up the hill to meet the enemy on the plateau was followed by a chaotic battle in mud and mist. The action lasted 'fully 20 minutes' (**Fitzroy MacLean**); government losses numbered some hundreds while the Jacobites, to their surprise, found their casualties numbered less than 50. Hawley retreated to **Linlithgow** and the Jacobites returned to the siege of Stirling, from where, on news of Cumberland's approach in early February, they continued their retreat northwards.

FALKIRK, Stirlingshire

Possessing 'no buildings of . . . any architectural merit erected before the last quarter of the 18th century' (**N Tranter**), Falkirk yet has history, most of it the product of the town's pivotal location in the central belt between Forth and **Clyde**, **Edinburgh** and **Stirling**. Substantial remains of the **Antonine Wall** and its military road survive to the east in the grounds of **Kinneil House** (fortlet) and near Callendar House (400m of wall) and to the west at Watling Lodge (300m of wall) and Tentfield (wall and beacon stances), both near Bonnybridge. Adjoining the last is Rough Castle, the most complete of the surviving forts although evidently one of the smallest. It was excavated in 1904; finds are now in the Edinburgh **Royal Museum of Scotland**.

Where the **Roman** road and wall ran, the Forth-Clyde **Canal**, the Edinburgh-**Glasgow railway**, the north Edinburgh-Glasgow road, and the Edinburgh-Stirling motorway would follow. Industry and most notably the giant **Carron Company**'s foundries would further distort the natural geography of what was once carseland broken by wooded hills and ridges. On Callendar ridge was fought the **first Battle of Falkirk** (1298) while the **second** (1746) took place to the west near Bantaskine where there is a monument.

Most of the land over which Falkirk now sprawls was

once the estate of Callendar or Callenter. The subject of a grant by **Alexander II**, it passed in 1345 to Sir William Livingstone, whose descendants became Earls of Callendar and **Linlithgow** before forfeiture in 1716. Callendar House incorporates part of a 14th century tower house beneath many extensions and remodellings which culminated in an 1870s conversion into one of the largest and most lavish châteaux in Scotland. Now in council care, the building is subject to plans for a museum and 'educational facilities'.

Even in the 1840s Falkirk attracted censure for its chaotic and ugly ribbon developments. These now submerge the once separate villages to the north and west of Carron, Larbert and Stenhousemuir. The latter, even when the Carron Company was in full production, accounted for Falkirk's principal claim to fame, being the final site of the largest livestock tryst (or market) in Scotland and probably Britain. At its height in the mid-19th century 300,000 head of cattle and a similar number of sheep, driven hence from the remotest glens and islands, were sold at the three great fairs in August, September and October. Cattle jams six miles long might clog the approach roads and half a million pounds change hands in the sales.

Nearby Kinnaird Estate was the home of **James Bruce**, the Abyssinian explorer. **Coal** from Kinnaird was decisive in the siting of the Carron foundry and Bruce, its provider, is buried along with other Carron pioneers including William Cadell in the Larbert churchyard. Falkirk's parish church (1811) contains monuments to some of the more notable participants in the two Falkirk battles. There is also a museum specialising in Antonine remains and other subjects of local interest.

Although traditionally in **Stirlingshire**, Falkirk became the centre of the eponymous District of Central Region in the 1975 reorganisation of local government and since the 1995 reorganisation has become the autonomous Falkirk Council Area, which also includes Bonnybridge, Bo'ness, Denny, **Grangemouth**, Larbert, Slamannan and Stenhousemuir.

FALKLAND, Fife

Granted to the MacDuff **Earls of Fife** in 1160, Falkland was already the site of their castle (its outline indicated in the palace grounds) when it passed to **Robert Stewart**, later **Duke of Albany**, in 1371. Herein **David, Duke of Rothesay** and eldest son of **Robert III**, was supposedly starved to death by his uncle Albany (1402). In 1424 the lands reverted to the Crown and the castle became a favourite hunting seat of **James I, II** (who created Falkland a **royal burgh** in 1458) and **III**. **James IV** here entertained Perkin Warbeck, the English pretender, in 1495, and in 1500 began construction of **Falkland Palace**. **James V, Mary** and **James VI** continued to patronise it. The burgh served the palace and thereafter shared its neglect in the late 17th and 18th centuries. Cromwell felled what remained of Falkland forest for timber to build his **Dundee** citadel and in 1648 **Richard Cameron** was born in Cameron House, the son of a local merchant. He taught here briefly before joining the **Covenanters**.

In the 18th century handloom weaving and in the 19th power-loom weaving brought modest prosperity but little development, thus preserving the ancient layout and close harmony of the burgh. In the High Street Moncrieff House (1610) retains its thatched roof and the Hunting Lodge Hotel (1607) its original window mouldings. Numerous other 17th and 18th century houses have been preserved and restored by the combined efforts of the Crichton Stuarts, hereditary keepers of the palace since 1887, and the **National Trust for Scotland**. In 1970 Falkland became the first Conservation Area in Scotland.

The Lomond Hills to the west are of prehistoric note with a commanding hill fort on East Lomond, where a later **Pictish** slab incised with a bull was found, and Maiden Castle, another hill fort, near which were found the cup-and-ring marked stones now in the palace museum.

FALKLAND PALACE, Falkland, Fife

Begun by **James IV** 1500–13 and completed by **James V** 1537–41, the royal hunting lodge of Falkland Palace consisted of ranges of buildings round three sides of an informal quadrangle. Of the north range, which caught fire during Cromwell's occupation, only the foundations survive. The east range (1510) containing the royal lodgings is now represented by its inner (courtyard) wall, which resembles that of the south range, and by Croce House (1529–32), originally a projection and not a separate building, wherein the royal bedchamber has been restored. The great south range (1511–13) with its three-storey twin-towered gatehouse (1539–41) remains intact and alone gives some impression of the palace's former charm. This owes much to the confusing mixture of styles with the street frontage and gatehouse combining vernacular and Gothic while the courtyard façade has Corinthian columns, French medallion busts and Palladian proportions to make it 'the earliest essay in full Renaissance architecture in Britain'. Within, most of this range is still occupied by the royal chapel with an oak screen and painted ceiling surviving from the 16th century. The gardens have recently been revived with great success but no pretence of authenticity. Beyond them the royal tennis court (1539) is one of only two (the other is at Hampton Court) to survive from the 16th century when the game, as copied from the French, was apparently played without rackets. 'It is one of the most difficult ball games and has been likened to chess in its subtleties and complexities' (B Walker and G Ritchie). Like their predecessors, **Mary** and **James VI** continued to patronise Falkland but after the **Union of the Crowns** the only recorded royal visits are those by **Charles I** in 1633 and **Charles II** in 1650–1.

FARMER, Henry George (1882–1965)
Musicologist and Orientalist

One of the leading musicologists and Arabic scholars of his day, Farmer was the author of the first comprehensive history of Scottish music – *A History of Music in Scotland* (1947). The breadth of scholarship in the book is impressive though it is marred by the lack of adequate references and index.

FARNELL, Nr Brechin, Angus

Four miles south of **Brechin**, little Farnell Castle was once the country retreat of the bishops of Brechin.

Courtyard façade of the south range of Falkland Palace, 'the earliest essay in full Renaissance architecture in Britain' (entry p 379) (RWB)

Originally a simple rectangular tower, the circular staircase and additional wing were added after the **Reformation** when the building passed into secular ownership. It has now been restored by the Carnegies of Southesk whose nearby Kinnaird Castle, rebuilt by John Bryce in the 1850s, is everything that Farnell is not – a vast (façade 206ft long), elaborate (towers, balconies, etc) château. David Carnegie (c1535–98) was one of **James VI**'s Privy Councillors; his first son was created Earl of Southesk, 1633 (and his second Earl of Northesk, 1666). The 5th Earl of Southesk forfeited lands and title for his part in the 1715 **Jacobite Rising**, but both were eventually restored [see also **Earldom and Dukedom of Fife**].

FASQUE HOUSE, Nr Fettercairn, Kincardineshire

This castellated mansion of red sandstone dates from 1809 as does its most famous resident, William Ewart Gladstone. His father purchased the property in 1829 and from then until his death in 1851 it was the future Prime Minister's favourite haunt and home. Now open to the public, the house attempts to convey the flavour of life in a Victorian mansion. Gladstone memorabilia have been assembled in the great man's bedroom. The curved cantilever staircase in the entrance hall has been billed as the largest such in the world.

FAST CASTLE, Nr St Abb's Head, Berwickshire

The position of Fast Castle on the rugged coast between **Cockburnspath** and **St Abb's Head** is impressive even today, although time and the elements have reduced the once formidable stronghold to fragmented ruins. Possibly built as a government fortress in the 14th century, it occupies a triangular plateau roughly 700m^2 atop a 48m high crag jutting from the North Sea and separated from the adjacent mainland clifftop by a steep ravine, once crossed by a drawbridge but now by a vertiginous footpath not much more than 1m wide. First mentioned in official records in 1404 when the English king Henry IV appointed his son John of Lancaster, already Governor of **Berwick** and Warden of the East Marches, Keeper of Fast Castle, it was later held by the **Dunbar Earls of March** and may have spent more

time in English hands before passing to the Lumsdens, the **Homes** and, as part of the dowry of Elizabeth Home, eldest daughter of Cuthbert Home (killed at **Flodden**) to Sir Robert Logan, 5th Baron Logan of Restalrig, i 1532. Forfeited by the 7th Baron Logan of Restalri (also Sir Robert) for his part in the **Gowrie Conspirac** (1600), it was abandoned by 1700. Persistent rumour of a treasure buried at Fast Castle date from 1429 whe a Scots ambassador to England, accompanied by 'si trusty men of the realm', passed nearby and was relieve of two thousand merks 'by several men on stout horse who inflicted on the bearers many wounds and carrie off the bags which obtained the treasure to a stron citadel called Fastcastle'. The castle is the 'Wolf's Crag of **Sir Walter Scott**'s *Bride of Lammermuir.*

FAULDS, Henry (1843–1930) Medical Missionary and Pioneer of Fingerprints

The first person to recognise the uniqueness of finger prints and their potential application for forensic sci ence, Henry Faulds was born at Beith, **Ayrshire**. Hi parents' market warehouse business declining, he wen to **Glasgow** at the age of 12 to work as a clerk. At 2 he entered **Glasgow University** to study mathematics logic and classics; four years later he studied medicin at Anderson College (now **Strathclyde University**). H became a **Church of Scotland** medical missionary t India, and in 1874 the first medical missionary of th **United Free Presbyterian Church** to Japan. There h established Tsukiji hospital in Tokyo in 1875, late rejecting the offer of the post of Imperial Physician a it would have ended his work with the poor. At thi time he developed a system of raised script for the blin to read, a precursor of Braille. But a fingerprint foun while studying ancient pottery made him experimen on himself by removing his own prints with chemicals he observed that they grew back in the same distinctiv ridge pattern. Soon after this Faulds assisted the Tokyc police in the correct identification of a burglar, becom ing the first to establish the innocence of a suspect an the guilt of a felon on the basis of their fingerprints. I publishing his research in *Nature* in 1880, he correctl predicted that fingerprints would be transmitted by 'photo-telegraphy'. When Faulds appealed to the elderl Charles Darwin, however, for help to promote research Darwin passed the findings over to his nephew, th scientist Sir Francis Galton. Galton, along with his col league William Henry, later claimed them as their own while Faulds, who is still revered in Japan, died i obscurity in 1930, an embittered man.

FAWSIDE (or FALSIDE) CASTLE, East Lothian

Dramatically sited on a ridge two miles south of **Tranent**, the original Fawside Castle was a four-storey rectangular tower that **MacGibbon and Ross** 'could no ascribe to an earlier date than the latter half of the 14th or the 15th century' although the family name o Fauside was connected with the area as early as the 12th century. The **Battle of Pinkie** (1547) was fough beneath its walls and it must have been about that time that the castle was extended by the addition of a new L-plan tower, larger but less massive, which, by incorporating the keep and later domestic buildings, rendered the whole into one solid block. Ruined by the early 19th century, it was on the verge of demolition in the 1970s but rescued in the nick of time and since fully and sympathetically restored.

FEARN, Ross & Cromarty

Midway between **Nigg** and **Tarbat Ness**, the village of Fearn (or Hill of Fearn) lies in rich farming country at the centre of the peninsula formed by the **Dornoch** and Cromarty Firths. Here was built (from c1288), in succession to that near **Edderton**, a Premonstratensian abbey of which **Patrick Hamilton**, the first **Reformation** martyr, was titular abbot in the early 16th century. The chapel of the old abbey is incorporated in the parish church though much altered following a disaster in 1742 when the vaulted roof collapsed on the parishioners, killing 44. One end of the chancel is a burial place of the Ross family and there is a recumbent effigy in the ruins of one of the transepts.

Pictish cross-slab from Hilton of Cadboll near Fearn (HS)

Peter Fraser, Prime Minister of New Zealand, was born in Fearn but **Sir George ('Bluidy') Mackenzie**, supposedly from nearby Lochslin Castle (now a ruin), was actually a native of **Dundee**. On the coast east of Fearn **Pictish** cross-slabs stood at Shandwick and Hilton of Cadboll. The latter's was removed and is now in the **Museum of Scotland** in **Edinburgh**, but the former's, 'one of the most impressive of all Pictish monuments', still stands above its **fishing** village. Together with that in the Nigg church, these three cross-slabs were once thought to mark the graves of three Norse princes who drowned while pursuing an **Earl of Ross** who had mistreated his countess, their sister.

FENCIBLES, The, Regiments

The term 'Fencible', used on occasion to denote all men liable to or capable of military service, was applied to a number of full-time regiments raised for the British Army for Home Service in time of war. There were three periods in which such regiments were raised in Scotland. During the Seven Years' War an **Argyll** and a **Sutherland** Regiment were raised (1759–63). Both wore Highland Dress. During the American War of Independence there were four Scottish regiments (1778–83); The Argyll or Western, The South, The Duke of Gordon's North Fencibles and the Sutherland Regiment. All except the South Regiment wore Highland dress.

But it was during the Napoleonic period from 1794 onwards that no less than 37 regiments were raised in Scotland. Some 27 of these were Highland and raised very much on a **clan** basis. Several regiments volunteered to extend their services to Ireland where they saw much Active Service and the 3rd Argyllshire Regiment served in garrison in Gibraltar. Some were distinguished by romantic titles, among them The Royal Clan Alpine Regiment, The Regiment of the Isles, Princess Charlotte of Wales's Loyal MacLeod Fencibles, The **Ross and Cromarty** Rangers and The **Caithness** Legion. All were disbanded by 1803.

FERGUS MOR (d.c501)

Son of Erc (thus sometimes Fergus mac Erc), Fergus Mor was the ruler of **Dalriada** or Dal Riata in Ireland, who led a group of his people, the 'Scoti', from Antrim to settle in **Kintyre** and mid **Argyll** in c500 AD. Credited with introducing the **Gaelic language** to Scotland, as well as the term 'Scot' from which the country would take its name, Fergus is also considered the founding father of the royal house of Scotland which would continue (albeit somewhat tortuously and, in the early generations, unverifiably) for nearly 800 years.

FERGUSON, Adam (1723–1816) Philosopher and Historian

The so-called 'father of sociology', Ferguson was born at Logierait, **Perthshire** and attended **Perth** Grammar School and **St Andrews University**. After his MA in 1742 he attended divinity hall for half the normal period and, as a **Gaelic** speaker, was ordained in 1745 chaplain to the (42nd) **Black Watch**. At the Battle of Fontenoy that year, he was pulled back after leading an attack, broadsword in hand. In 1754 he left the army for a literary career in **Edinburgh**. Although becoming **Hume**'s successor at the **Advocates' Library**, then Professor of Natural Philosophy (1759) and Moral Philosophy (1764–85), he was not always at the University; in 1774–5, as young Lord Chesterfield's tutor, he was in Geneva and in 1778 he was appointed commissioner to the American colonies, then engaged in the War of Independence about which he had written a pamphlet. Prematurely aged by a stroke in 1780 he became a vegetarian. He published his History of the Roman Republic in 1783, retired from teaching (1785) and travelled Europe, visiting Rome in 1793. He later lived at **Neidpath Castle**, near **Peebles**, and at **St Andrews** where he died aged 93. His able other work matters far less than the social treatise A History of Civil Society (1767), in

Adam Ferguson, by an unknown artist after Sir Henry Raeburn (SNPG)

which a theme later dubbed 'alienation' was prominent. A German translation influenced Schiller and Hegel, sparked a huge revival of interest in ancient Greece, and was known to Marx. Travellers' reports had shown Ferguson that there were features common to American Indian, ancient Greek and traditional Gaelic society. What if the polished society so dear in his day should weaken passion and humanity, and fragment civil society into cliques without mutual communication? See *An Essay in the History of Civil Society*, introduction by Duncan Forbes (Edinburgh UP, 1966); W C Lehmann, *Adam Ferguson and the Beginnings of Modern Sociology* (1930); David Kettler, *The Social and Political Thought of Adam Ferguson* (1965); N Waszek, *Man's Social Nature* (1988).

FERGUSON, James (1710–76) Instrument Maker

Although a leading astronomical instrument maker, James Ferguson, born at Rothiemay, **Banffshire**, reputedly received only three months' formal education as a child. Educating himself in surveying and associated subjects, he moved to London where he established a reputation for manufacturing the most accurate clocks and astronomical models of his time. Author of popular books on science, and a favourite of George III, Ferguson nevertheless died in unhappy domestic surroundings.

FERGUSON, Patrick (1744–80) Inventor

Born at Pitfours, **Aberdeenshire**, Ferguson was a professional soldier from the age of 15. In 1776 he devised and patented a rifle which could be loaded quickly from the breech, instead of the muzzle, but its success did not impress the conservative military establishment and Ferguson's invention was not generally adopted until some 90 years after his death. This came about in 1780

at the Battle of King's Mountain in the American War of Independence, when Ferguson's corps of Sharpshooters were defeated by a force four times as numerous.

FERGUSON, Robert (c1637–1714) 'The Plotter'

Although a native of **Aberdeenshire**, Robert Ferguson' career and reputation as 'the plotter to end all plotters' (W Ferguson) were made in England. Expediency and a penchant for conspiracy rather than any great political or religious conviction seem to have dictated his involvement in both the Rye House Plot to murder **Charles II** (1683) and Sir George Barclay's plot to assassinate William of Orange (1696), after the failure of each of which he was forced to flee the country. His most successful involvement in a plot was, ironically, the foiling of one; what has been called 'Queensberry's plot' was hatched by **Simon Fraser, 11th Lord Lovat** and condoned by **James Douglas, 2nd Duke of Queensberry** in 1703 with the intention of discrediting their mutual enemy **John Murray, 1st Duke of Atholl**. Ferguson alerted Atholl and it was Fraser and Queensberry who were discredited. Presumably because he had conspired for both Hanoverians and **Jacobites** in his convoluted career, Ferguson was never convicted of any crime, although he was charged with treason in 1704 and held in Newgate before being released without coming to trial.

FERGUSSON, James (1808–86) Architectural Historian

Fergusson was the first to attempt a classification of India's architectural heritage and to relate this vast subject to the architectural traditions of Europe and elsewhere. He was born in **Ayr**, the son of a distinguished army surgeon, and after **Edinburgh** High School joined a family firm in Calcutta. He soon started his own indigo factory and 10 years later had made sufficient money to withdraw from business and devote himself to a study of India's monuments. In 1835 he had built himself a house in London's Langham Place and, somewhat perversely, it was from there that he conducted his study, making frequent tours to India (1835–45) for sketching and measuring monuments, and thereafter relying heavily on the new science of photography. His first interest was in the archaeological remains of Buddhist India, a highly fashionable subject in 1830s India [see **Alexander Cunningham**], but this soon led to a grand classification of Hindu temple styles and Muslim architecture which still has remarkable currency. He also wrote on the Holy Land and on methods of fortification. His only financially rewarding work, the synoptic *A History of Architecture in All Countries from the Earliest Times to the Present Day* (1865–7), was just that, an extraordinary *tour de force* incorporating many of his earlier writings. It was to Fergusson that Schliemann dedicated his great work on Tiryns.

FERGUSSON, John Duncan (1874–1961) Painter

With **Cadell**, **Hunter** and **Peploe**, J D Fergusson was the most forward-looking of the loosely associated group known as the Scottish Colourists [see **Painting**]. Born in **Leith**, he forsook a medical career to train as a painter

Self portrait by John Duncan Fergusson, c1902 (SNPG, reproduced by permission of Perth and Kinross District Council)

and enrolled at the **Trustees' Academy** in **Edinburgh**. Dissatisfied with the teaching there he left after a short period and remained largely self-taught. Inspired by the Glasgow Boys he made regular visits to France from 1895 and in Paris attended the life classes at the Académie Colarossi. His admiration for Whistler influenced the impressionistic handling and muted tonal harmonies of his early still-lifes, landscapes and portraits; but the startling colour in the painting of the Fauves seen in Paris, where he settled in 1907, profoundly altered his style. Adopting their vibrant palette and bold outlining he became one of the foremost of their British exponents and the leading member of a circle of American, English and Scottish painters based in Paris. He exhibited regularly at the Salon D'Automne and the Salon des Indépendants and was made a Sociétaire of both.

The powerful series of female nudes (1910–14) are the most original of all his and the Colourists' works. Inspired by contemporary dance, Fergusson sought to imbue in these highly patterned, statuesque figures something of the vitality of the productions of Diaghilev's Ballet Russe which had taken Paris by storm. Fergusson moved to London in 1914 and as an official war artist produced a memorable series of paintings of Portsmouth Docks, applying to naval subjects a rationalised version, reminiscent of the work of Wyndham Lewis and the Vorticists, of the rhythmic patterning of his earlier style. In 1940 he settled in **Glasgow** where, together with his wife the dancer Margaret Morris, he founded the New Art Club from which emerged the New Scottish Group of Painters.

FERGUSSON, Robert (1750–74) Poet

Born in **Edinburgh**, Fergusson was educated at the Edinburgh High School and in 1762 received a bursary to study at **Dundee** High School. At the **University of St Andrews** (1764–7) he began writing poetry. After the death of his father in 1767, Fergusson was forced to leave **St Andrews** to support his mother and sister. He worked in Edinburgh as a clerk in the Commissary Office, but found time to continue his writing. His first poems, imitations of English pastoral verses, were published in **Ruddiman**'s *Weekly Magazine* in 1771. Fergusson soon turned to writing in Scots, and in 1772 Ruddiman published his first Scots poem, 'The Daft Days'. This was followed by a succession of highly praised works, which were collected and reprinted in 1773, and gained him a reputation in Edinburgh as the poetic successor to **Allan Ramsay**. He continued publishing poetry in the *Weekly Magazine* throughout 1773, and his long poem *Auld Reekie* was published independently in the same year. *Auld Reekie*, perhaps Fergusson's best-known work, is a witty and strong evocation of Edinburgh city life and inhabitants, as well as being a satirical attack on **Dr Johnson**. Fergusson's last poem, 'Codicil to Rob Fergusson's Last Will', was published in December 1773, during a period of ill health. Suffering from bouts of manic depression, he left his job at the Commissary Office in the same month. In July 1774 he suffered a drastic deterioration in his mental and physical state after falling down a flight of stairs. He was locked up in the local Bedlam, where he languished until his death on 17 October 1774. He was subsequently buried in **Canongate Churchyard**.

Fergusson produced over 80 poems, some 33 of which were written in Scots. Although little known outside Edinburgh during his lifetime, his reputation as an original and talented Scots poet grew after his death, and his work had a considerable influence on subsequent Scots poets, most notably **Robert Burns**, who acknowledged his debt to Fergusson by raising a gravestone to him in 1789, inscribed to 'my elder brother in misfortune, but far my elder brother in muse'. Fergusson made particular use of the Standard Habbie, a verse form popular among 18th century Scottish poets. Normally used for satirical purposes, Fergusson extended its range to cover more serious subjects, as evinced in 'The Hallow Fair' and 'Address to the Tron Kirk Bell'. His poetry is noted for its humour, genuineness and vivid evocation of Edinburgh.

FERINTOSH, Ross & Cromarty

This place on the **Black Isle** opposite **Dingwall** now scarcely exists but was once nationally famous for its quantities of fine **whisky** and its anomalous allocation to the county of **Nairn**, from which it was separated by five miles of rough riding plus the Moray Firth. Both distinctions arose from the favours showered on its laird, the father of **Sir Duncan Forbes of Culloden**. By way of compensation and reward for his loyalty to King William in 1689 he was granted duty-free distilling rights in Ferintosh and the title to its barony. The whisky bonanza lasted until 1786, when it was rescinded for a one-off payment of £20,000; the county boundary was rationalised in 1889.

FERNAIG MANUSCRIPT

This is a late 17th century **Gaelic** manuscript, consisting of two notebooks, compiled by Duncan Macrae of Inverinate in Wester **Ross**. It was at one time in the

383

possession of a Matheson, who lived at Fernaig, but is now in **Glasgow University** Library (Gen 85).

The compilation carries strong marks of the collector's predilections. Duncan Macrae (known as *Donnchadh nam Pìos*, ie 'Duncan of the Goblets') had apparently collected poems by like-minded Gaelic country gentlemen with strong interests in Church and politics, and some nostalgia for times past. Among the poets represented by several poems are the two **Mackenzie Chiefs of Achilty**, Donnchadh MacRaoiridh, of the bardic family that served the chiefs of the **MacDonalds of Sleat**, and Mac-Culloch of Park (near **Strathpeffer**), who was in fact the great-grandfather of Duncan Macrae. The Fernaig MS has six of his religious poems, and two by John Stewart of Appin, both of these authors composing in the late 16th century. The political poems in the collection are centred on the events of 1688–9, taking a **Jacobite** stance. More political pamphleteering than poetry, some are in the mode of 'village' poetry.

The antiquarian bent of the compiler is illustrated by the fact that fully half of the poems are in syllabic metres, and a number of them use word-forms and syntax that are characteristic of the classical or 'bardic' verse rather than the Scottish Gaelic vernacular that had largely taken over by Macrae's time [see **Gaelic Verse**]. Macrae used a form of spelling that is based as much on Scots as on Gaelic. This has made for problems of interpretation, but has also provided much evidence of language usage at this time and place. The full value of this evidence has not yet been exploited, but much useful work was done by John Fraser (see *Trans. Gael. Soc. Inverness*, Vol 28, 1914 and *Scottish Gaelic Studies*, Vol 1, 1926. Calum MacPhàrlain's edition of 1923 (*Làmh-sgrìobhainn Mhic Rath*) has a reliable transcription of the MS, but a sometimes eccentric transliteration. (See also Kenneth MacDonald's article in D S Thomson, *Companion to Gaelic Culture*, 1987).

FERNIEHURST CASTLE, Nr Jedburgh, Roxburghshire

On the east bank of the Jed Water about two miles above the town of **Jedburgh**, Ferniehurst Castle was rebuilt in 1598 from the ruins of its predecessor which, like so many Border towers, had a turbulent history. Ancient stronghold of the Kerr family, it was captured by the Earl of Surrey in 1523, retaken by Sir John Kerr in 1549 with the aid of French auxiliaries stationed in the burgh, sheltered the Earl of Westmorland from the wrath of Queen Elizabeth in 1569 and was demolished by the Earl of Sussex in 1570. Its replacement is a handsome L-plan tower house with an unusually large main block, a circular stair-tower, magnificent first-floor great hall and barrel-vaulted kitchen. Still in the Kerr family, it was in use as a youth hostel before being restored and modernised by the Marquis of Lothian.

FERRIER, David (1843–1928) Neurologist

Born in **Aberdeen**, Ferrier converted from studying **philosophy** to **psychology** at the city's **University**, becoming interested in cerebral localisation and succeeding in mapping motor nerves' centres. Appplied in reverse, his research aided discovery of the location of brain tumours, although his experiments on primates were challenged as cruel.

FERRIER, James Frederick (1808–64)
Philosopher

Born in the **New Town** of **Edinburgh**, J F Ferrier was nephew both to the novelist **Susan Ferrier** and on his mother's side to **John Wilson** (Christopher North). After **Edinburgh University** (1825–7) and Oxford (BA 1831), where he worked on a short-lived literary journal and proved a more than competent poet, he wrote for **Blackwood's** and studied for the Scottish Bar. By 1842 he was Professor of Civil History at Edinburgh. He produced an analysis of the **Disruption** dispute that was brilliant and ignored. From 1845 till his death he was Professor of Moral Philosophy and Political Economy at **St Andrews**. He applied twice for **philosophy** lectureships at Edinburgh (1852 and 1856) but the patronage system passed him over for party reasons. His pamphlet *Scottish Philosophy Old and New* contributed to the reform of this scandalous regimen.

The first Briton properly to appropriate German thought, he set great store by his lively *Institutes of Metaphysics* (1854); admirers stress his long essays reprinted in *Lectures and Philosophical Remains* (1866), including the pioneering 'Lectures on Greek Philosophy'. He discusses the basis of perception in interaction between the different senses, and insists that bound up in one's knowledge of anything there must be knowledge of oneself. He pioneered a challenge to the ruling Scots philosophy of his day, relished all intellectual challenge, and showed a rare gift for bringing out the abiding relevance of ancient Greek thought. Involved in translating Goethe, he was notorious for identifying Coleridge's borrowings from Schelling in *Biographia Literaria*. See *Ferrier of St Andrews* (Scottish Academic Press, 1985); 'J F Ferrier' in *Philosophy* (1964); MSS in the **National Library of Scotland**, Arthur Thomson. Ferrier's unpublished 1849–50 lectures are in Edinburgh University Library.

FERRIER, Susan (1782–1854) Novelist

Susan Ferrier was the youngest of 10 children of Helen Coutts and James Ferrier, a prominent **Edinburgh** lawyer. She grew up in Edinburgh, and after a brief spell in London between 1800–4 returned to settle in **Morningside**. Through her close friendship with **Sir Walter Scott** and her family ties to other prominent Edinburgh publishing and literary figures, Ferrier was encouraged to write. Her first novel, *Marriage*, appeared anonymously in **Blackwood's Magazine** in 1818. A second novel, *Inheritance*, also appeared in serial form in *Blackwood's* in 1824. Her last work, *Destiny*, was published in 1831. Her novels, didactic in nature, are notable for their humour and keen observations of Scottish contemporary society and manners.

FETLAR, Shetland

The smallest of the three North Isles of **Shetland**, Fetlar, with an area of 15 square miles, is known as 'The Garden of Scotland' for its fertile soil and the wide expanse of good grazing. On the other hand it lacks a safe anchorage so that **fishing** is limited to boats small enough to be hauled ashore. In 1841 Fetlar had a population of over 700; then came the **clearances**, when whole townships were removed by the laird to make room for sheep. In the early 1980s it seemed that the population had stabilised at around 100, but a depression in **crofting** caused a further decline and the island's viability seemed in doubt. In 1991 a vigorous campaign started to attract incomers to the isle, and by the end of the 1990s the population had again risen to around 100. Fetlar has much to offer, with beautiful scenery and a rich wildlife – the RSPB reserve on Fetlar boasts, among a wealth of other birds, 90% of the British breeding population of red-necked phalaropes. There is no resident landowner, and Brough Lodge, built in the early 19th century for Sir Arthur Nicholson, is now a sprawling ruin. The other 'big house', at Leagarth, was built in 1900 for Sir William Watson Cheyne.

FETTERCAIRN, Kincardineshire

From the village of Fettercairn on the edge of the Howe of the **Mearns** starts the Cairn o' Mount road over to **Banchory** and Deeside. This was the route, notable for its long **cairn** at the summit and for the early single-span Bridge of Dye (1680), by which in 1861 **Queen Victoria** and Prince Albert returned to **Balmoral** after having daringly spent the night at Fettercairn's Ramsay Arms. The royal visit, supposedly incognito, remained no secret; Fettercairn promptly erected a turreted sandstone arch, still standing, to memorialise it. North of the village is **Fasque** and east Fettercairn House, begun by **John 1st Earl of Middleton** in the 1660s, but mostly of later date and uncastellated. Balbegno Castle to the west, also once the property of the Earl, is a more typical L-plan tower house of the 16th century but with enough distinctive features to rank it as 'an important and interesting example'. **MacGibbon and Ross** were particularly impressed by the ribbed and groined vaulting of the main hall and by the carved relief figures, as at **Tolquhon**, on the exterior.

Beyond Fasque the overgrown outlines of far older fortifications testify to the strategic importance of Fettercairn, guarding the Cairn o' Mount pass. These are the **Pictish** Green Castle (Dunfothir or Fotherdun) and its successor, the once mighty Kincardine Castle. In one of them **Kenneth II** was murdered, a victim according to **John of Fordun** of an extraordinarily elaborate booby trap devised by his hostess Finella, daughter of the **Mormaer** of **Angus**. She is commemorated in nearby Strathfinella while her castle, used as late as the 1560s by **Queen Mary** but now scarcely visible, has given its name to the district and county which it once dominated. The mercat cross of **Kincardine** now stands in Fettercairn to which it was removed in 1730.

FETTERNEAR BANNER

Dating from the early 16th century, the Fetternear Banner is, as far as is known, 'the sole specimen of an ecclesiastical banner surviving from pre-**Reformation** times in the whole of Great Britain and one of the very few specimens extant in northern Europe' (McRoberts). The banner is made of a single piece of linen (59 x 31ins approx) upon which is embroidered a typical late medieval passion subject, the Image of Pity; a full-length figure of Christ, covered with wounds from which drops of blood exude, is set within a design consisting of red and gold beaded columns bordered by green foliaceous scrollwork in silk and depicting the various instruments and symbols of the Passion. Part of the ornamentation of the border is composed of a combi-nation of scallop shells from the Graham arms and the heart from the **Douglas** arms. This has led to the conclusion that the banner was intended for processional use by the Holy Blood Confraternity of **St Giles'** in **Edinburgh**, when the brotherhood assumed their new altar in 1518, as one Alexander Graham was 'kirkmaister' of the 'confrary' under the provostship of **Gavin Douglas**. The banner – now in the **Museum of Scotland** – was long preserved by the Leslies of Balquain in **Aberdeenshire**, who in 1859 luckily entrusted this survivor of the Reformation to the church at Fetternear – thus escaping the fire which destroyed nearby Fetternear House.

FETTES, Sir William (1750–1836) Merchant

A successful merchant and underwriter of Comely Bank (near **Stockbridge**), twice Lord Provost of **Edinburgh** (1800 and 1805), and a baronet from 1804, William Fettes left £166,000 for the endowment of a school for orphaned or needy children. The funds accumulated and **Fettes College** (a baronial marvel designed by **David Bryce** from 1864–70) admitted its first 50 pupils in 1870.

FIDDLE, Traditional Scottish Music and The

Stringed instruments played with a bow go back a long way in the musical history of Scotland. The 'Fedyl' and the Rebec are mentioned by **Thomas of Ercildoune** ('The Rhymer') in the 13th century. The **Shetland** 'Gue', the Celtic 'Crwyth' and the Viol preceded the modern violin (Gaelic *Fidheall*, from 'viol'), which arrived in the 16th century. The appearance of an increasing volume of traditional and contemporary music in published form in the latter part of the 17th century clearly reflects its popularity with society as a whole, at the same time indicating something of its significance in the town houses and mansions of the better-off, who readily gave their names as patrons and their cash as sponsors. Unlike its equivalents in other parts of Britain and Europe, the repertoire survives in the most pure form and much of the music is still in print in 19th century editions. Having reached a peak around 1800, the 'craze' passed, leaving the legacy of the **reel**, the Scots Measure, the **jig**, and Scotland's unique contribution to the dance, the **Strathspey**, to say nothing of the vocal repertoire, both Gaelic and Lowland. Where violins are played, violin-making is apt to follow, both as a cottage craft (which still survives) and in the work of professional makers, of whom the Hardies, notably Matthew (1755–1826), are among the most celebrated.

The authors of this musical heritage number perhaps 200 and are sometimes referred to as the Fiddler/Composers, although this does not differentiate between the one and the other, nor identify those many who were simply publishers. **Robert Bremner, James Oswald** and **William McGibbon** had one foot firmly in the world of 'serious' composition. They, with David Young and Adam Craig, were early in the field (1720–50), song melodies predominating. The tidal wave of dance music that follows includes the names of **Daniel Dow**, Neil Stewart, MacGlashan, Ross, Cumming, Riddell, **William Marshall** and the **Gows**, 'Red Rob' Mackintosh, Petrie, Bowie and MacDonald, Joshua and

William Campbell, to mention only a few. William Marshall brought elegance to composition in some contrast to the output of the acknowledged master of all time, **Niel Gow**, whose fire and style colours all work thereafter. Marshall was steward to the **Duke of Gordon**, Gow was under the patronage of the **Duke of Atholl**, and there were many other noble patróns and even some players and composers.

20 years into the 19th century the quadrille and the German waltz take the stage at fashionable assemblies, the polka and the two-step replace the Strathspey and reel. But there then follows, from mid-century, a flurry of re-publishing and the arrival on the stage of **James Scott Skinner**, a second 'master' very different from the first who, with Peter Milne (1824–1908), dominated the scene and extended the traditional period some way into the 20th century. A 'new era' of interest in the fiddle is now manifesting itself, with the added spice of overtones from such widely different sources as Shetland, Ireland and the younger traditions of North America, notably of Cape Breton.

A comprehensive index to the traditional music of Scotland, *The Scottish Fiddle Music Index* (ed Charles Gore) was published in Edinburgh in 1993 listing tune titles and sources from the collections published between c1700 and c1900 and including a theme code index.

FIFE

Before the **local government** reorganisation of 1975, Fife was a peninsular county, and is still often known as the 'wee kingdom' because of its almost self-contained nature (it was never a true kingdom). Bounded by the Firths of **Tay** and Forth to north and south respectively, and by the North Sea to the east, the pre-1975 county had a coastline of 115 miles. It measured 41 miles at its longest point and was 21 miles at its widest extent. **Kinross-shire**, **Clackmannanshire** and **Perthshire** were its western neighbours. Occupying 322,878 acres (130,667ha), the county's highest point was 1713ft (522m) in the Lomond Hills, the principal rivers being the Eden and Leven, both flowing eastwards.

An area prominent in the history of pre-industrial Scotland, the county contained three of the nation's most important towns in **Stewart** times, **Dunfermline**, **Falkland** and **St Andrews**, the last being the site of Scotland's first university, founded in 1411. The Fifers' principal occupations are **agriculture**, **fishing**, formerly **coal-mining**, and some **engineering** and manufacturing. The county town was **Cupar**, somewhat dwarfed by the county's two large burghs, Dunfermline and **Kirkcaldy**, while there were 23 small burghs, plus the new town of **Glenrothes**. In 1975, after considerable public opposition to a proposal to split up the county during local government reorganisation, Fife was transferred intact into Fife Region, subdivided into the Districts of Dunfermline, Kirkcaldy and North-East Fife, and in the 1995 reorganisation retained its status as a single administrative division.

FIFE, Earldom and Dukedom

An Earldom of Fife is first recorded in 1139 in favour of Duncan, who died in 1154. The second Duncan died in 1204 and it fell to the third to be, with **Buchan**, one of the two earls among the Guardians for **Margaret,**

Maid of Norway. He died in 1288, described by the Lannercost Chronicle as 'cruel and greedy beyond average' (however that might be assessed). The fourth and last Earl Duncan was a minor in England when his 19-year-old sister **Isabella** exercised her family's right to crown **Robert I** at **Scone** in 1306. The Countess of Fife resigned her title in 1372, which thereupon passed to **Robert Stewart, Duke of Albany**. With the forfeiture of his son in 1425 it became vested in the Crown.

The Duffs of Braco in **Banffshire**, who acquired the title of Earl of Fife in the peerage of Ireland in 1759, have no traceable connection with the medieval earls. The 5th Earl was created Duke of Fife on his marriage to the Princess Royal in 1889. Their daughter, Princess Maud, married the 11th Earl of Southesk and the title has now passed to the Carnegies of Southesk. Shakespeare's 'MacDuff, Thane of Fife' is a fictional creation although the name MacDuff was associated with the early Earls Duncan, a connection which the Duffs of Braco assiduously fostered so that the eldest son of a Duke of Fife is now Earl of MacDuff.

FIFE, Gentleman Adventurers of

In an attempt to end the bitter rivalry between **MacLeods** and **Mackenzies** over the ownership of the island of **Lewis**, **James VI** decided that since 'the Highlanders that dwelleth in the Isles are all utterly barbarous' the best thing to do was replace them with Lowlanders. In 1598 an act was passed stating that all who claimed to own land in the Highlands and Islands should produce their deeds before the Scottish Privy Council. The MacLeods were unable to comply since their titles had all been stolen by the Mackenzies. Their property thus passed to the Crown, the King handed it on to a group of 12 merchants from **Fife** and told them to settle the island. The 'Gentleman Adventurers' sailed for **Stornoway** with a small army, captured Stornoway Castle and prepared to turn Lewis into a civilised outpost of the Lowlands. But the Mackenzies had a plan; they released the young MacLeod chief from their dungeons, his clansmen rallied to his call, and the Gentlemen were seized, imprisoned and not released until they had sworn to leave Lewis for ever. Once the abashed Gentlemen had gone, the erstwhile rivals took up where they had left off, with the Mackenzies eventually managing to wrest the island from the MacLeods.

FILLAN, Saint (d.777)

One of several Irish clergy of the name, this abbot may have lived near Loch Dochart, **Perthshire**. Of five relics kept by hereditary 'deor' or Dewars (stewards), two now remain in the **Royal Museum of Scotland**: his crozier head, the Quigrich, in a 14th century filigree case returned from Canada, and his bronze bell, retrieved from St Fillan's churchyard [see **Killin** and **Crianlarich**].

FINDHORN, Moray

Once the sizeable port of **Forres**, Findhorn occupies a vulnerable promontory between **Burghead** and Findhorn Bays. It originally stood well to the west, the restless **Culbin** sands burying one Findhorn in 1694 and the Findhorn river consigning another to the bottom of the sea in 1701. Today's village, with some houses

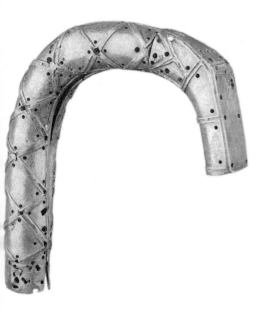

St Fillan's crozier head (© the Trustees of the National Museums of Scotland 1994)

dating from the consequent rebuilding, caters for two distinct groups, the RAF at **Kinloss** and the Findhorn community of enthusiasts in search of a sustainable alternative lifestyle. The latter, founded by an ex-RAF caterer, has attracted many adherents from throughout the UK and abroad. Its experiments in architecture, horticulture and alternative belief systems provoke endless publicity.

FINDLAY, John Ritchie (1824–98)
Newspaper Proprietor

Born in **Arbroath**, the grand-nephew of John Ritchie, one of the founders of The Scotsman (1817), John Ritchie Findlay was educated at **Edinburgh University** and started working for The Scotsman in 1842, becoming its assistant editor and then its proprietor (1870). Secretary of the **Society of Antiquaries** of Scotland for six years, he was also a great benefactor of the arts, donating £50,000 for the creation of the **Scottish National Portrait Gallery** and National Museum of Antiquities of Scotland in 1889 and receiving the Freedom of **Edinburgh** in 1896.

FINDOCHTY, Banffshire

This erstwhile **fishing** port east of **Buckie** was founded in 1716 by Thomas Ord of now ruined Findochty Castle and peopled with fishermen from **Fraserburgh**. The fishermen now work from Buckie leaving Findochty (pron. Finechty) a place of little activity but much charm. Inland, on the Muir of Findochty, was fought the Battle of the Bauds when King Indulph's Scots defeated the Danes under Eric of the Bloody Axe (961).

FINDON, Kincardineshire

Although both the Oxford English Dictionary and Mrs Beeton insist (and who are we to differ?) that **Findhorn** in **Morayshire** gave its name to the finnan haddock, a consensus of Scottish works awards this honour unequivocally to Findon, one of several **fishing** hamlets (Portlethen, Downies) among the cliffs south of **Aberdeen**. Finnan haddock is cured and coloured with peat smoke having first been split open, like a kipper and unlike an **Arbroath** smokie.

FINGASK CASTLE, Nr Perth

In the **Carse of Gowrie** near Rait, Fingask is L-plan of reddish stone, mostly 17th century. The Threipland family, once of **Peebles-shire**, have held it for over 300 years with brief intermissions of forfeiture following the 1715 and 1745 **Jacobite Risings**. The 'Old Pretender' himself, **James Francis Stewart**, is said to have stayed there twice (but probably not 'in February and again in March 1716', since he sailed from **Montrose** for France on 4 February).

FINLAY, Robert Bannatyne, 1st Viscount Finlay (1842–1929) Lord Chancellor

Born in **Edinburgh**, Robert Finlay studied medicine at **Edinburgh University** and qualified as a doctor before being called to the English Bar (Middle Temple) in 1867. Although he practised English law, he represented Scottish constituences in Parliament, being MP for **Inverness** Burghs 1885–92 and 1895–1906 and for Edinburgh and **St Andrews** Universities 1910–16. Knighted on his appointment as Solicitor-General in 1895, he became Attorney-General (1900–06) and a baron on his appointment as Lord Chancellor, a post he held from 1916–18. Created 1st Viscount Finlay in 1919, he then moved into international law as a judge at the Permanent Court of International Justice in The Hague from 1921–8.

FINN MAC CUMHAL (FIONN MAC CUMHAIL, FINGAL, etc) Celtic Hero

While the death of Finn mac Cumhal (pron. 'MacCoul') is recorded in the Annals of the Four Masters under the date 283, and his pedigree given in the Book of Leinster, the supernatural events of his life in the oldest sources are plainly those of **Celtic myth**. The heroic deeds of his warrior band, although originally set in Ireland, became popular themes of medieval **ballads** that circulated throughout Gaelic Scotland. Thus, the scree on the north face of Ben Loyal in **Sutherland** became known in Gaelic as Scree of the Boar, in the belief that this was where Finn's nephew Diarmad had slain the magic boar and dragged it down the slope. A version of the ballad of the death of Diarmad was written down locally in the 1730s. Its circumstances have significant Homeric overtones. Diarmad had eloped with the wife of Finn, like Paris with the wife of Menelaus. He died after a poisonous bristle of the boar entered the only vulnerable part of him, his Achilles heel. Finn's son Ossian is supposed to have outlived the Feinne (or Fingalians, as they became known as a result of **James Macpherson**'s bogus epic).

The **Book of the Dean of Lismore** contains a ballad in which Ossian discusses pagan and Christian values with St Patrick, at the expense of the latter. This theme has an exact parallel in Friesland, where King Radbod refuses baptism from Bishop Wolfran after learning from him that the King's forebears were not in the Christian heaven but among the pagans in hell. With folklore's contempt for chronology the Feinne reappear during the **Viking** age in Scottish ballads. One of them elopes with a Norwegian king's wife, and scatters his fleet when he pursues her. **John Francis Campbell** published his impressive *Leabhar na Feinne* in 1872, but today its themes, after enjoying such a long run of popularity, have largely removed from the fireside to the scholar's study, with Finn mac Cumhal himself.

FINNISTON, Sir Harold Montague
(1912–91) Engineer and Executive

Born in **Glasgow**, Monty Finniston produced a PhD thesis on coke burning at the Glasgow College of Science and Technology (now the **University of Strathclyde**), then worked in the steel industry and, after World War II, as a metallurgist at the Harwell atomic energy research establishment. In 1967 he was appointed to the Board of the British Steel Corporation as technical member, succeeding to the Chairmanship in 1973. The radical reorganisation of the nationalised steel industry into commercial product divisions was largely his work, but he encountered stiff opposition from the Labour government over the closing of unprofitable plants, while the oil price hike of 1973–5 prejudiced his investment plans. When his appointment was not renewed in 1976 he diversified his activities in the business and academic worlds, becoming Chancellor of **Stirling University** and chairing the 1979 government inquiry into **engineering** which resulted in the 'Finniston Report' and the setting up of the Engineering Council. A Fellow of both the Royal Society and the **Royal Society of Edinburgh**, he was knighted in 1973.

FINTRY, Stirlingshire

Like **Balfron**, Fintry higher up the Endrick Water was also founded c1789 to serve a **cotton** mill, the brainchild of Peter Spiers, owner of Culcreuch Castle. This well-preserved 15th/16th century keep with later additions once belonged to the Galbraith descendants of the Celtic **Earls of Lennox**. East of Fintry, beyond the Loup of Endrick (where the river drops 94ft (29m) into a ravine) and overlooking the Carron Reservoir, the motte of Sir John de Graham is a medieval rarity in that it is square rather than round. It is supposed to have been the residence of the Graham who was killed at the first **Battle of Falkirk** (1298) and who is commemorated in **Falkirk** churchyard but may previously have been the principal stronghold of the barony of Dundaff. South-east from Fintry the Crow road climbs over the **Campsie Fells** at 1064ft (324m) to **Lennoxtown** and **Glasgow**.

FISH FARMING

Having about 16,000km of indented coastline with many sheltered bays and fjordal sea lochs, Scotland is well suited to farming of both fin fish and shellfish. Although any management of wild stocks by fishery regulations might be considered as farming, the term is here used to cover the manipulation of stocks in which some of the life history is spent in captivity.

In the earliest form of farming, wild stocks of brown trout and salmon were enhanced by planting out their eggs (stripped from spawning adults) into the head waters of streams to augment the natural production.

As an extension of this the fry were released after raising in a hatchery, in order to circumvent the period of high vulnerability of the very young stages. One of the first hatcheries was at Howieton near **Stirling** which started its operations in 1873 and is still functioning. Rainbow trout (which were not native to Scotland) were introduced later into many lochs and rivers. Stocking of lochs and rivers with a number of species still continues.

A neat extension of these practices is salmon ranching, still in an early stage of development in Scotland but established in Iceland. Salmon are raised in shore-based hatcheries until they reach the sea-going smolt stage. At this point they become naturally 'imprinted' with various characteristics of the home area – a little-understood type of learning that is retained when the smolts go to sea. It enables some to return as mature fish after one or more years of growth in the sea close to the point at which they were released. The advantage of ranching is that the fish must seek out their own food. It is a technique that is best suited to homing species but the disadvantage lies in the high losses experienced during the sea-going phase.

Augmentation of wild stocks by the release of young that have been reared and protected in the vulnerable early life stages is also feasible in shellfish such as lobster that do not stray too far from the point of release. At present shellfish farming is confined to sedentary bivalve molluscs – mussels, **oysters** and scallops. These species filter small particles from the sea and thrive in sites with suitable water quality. Mussel spat settles naturally and grows well on vertical ropes suspended from rafts or buoyed longlines at the surface. Scallop spat is collected in the wild and grown for two years in nets suspended from long-lines. At this stage, the spat is either transferred to suspended lantern baskets or placed in cleaned plots on the seabed. Oyster spat is reared in hatcheries and then grown on in mesh bags, which are held on trestles on the seabed in shallow water. Harvesting is heavy work but relatively simple and independent of the weather in sheltered sites. In 1997 there were 265 sites around the Scottish coast. Production for the table was 1307 tonnes of mussels (estimated site value £1.3 million), 2.8 million shells of Pacific oysters (£0.52 million), 11,000 shells of native oysters (£5500), 223,000 of king scallops (£111,500) and 1.2 million queen scallops (£600,000).

The most dramatic advance in fish farming in recent years involves fish from the salmon family. As a result of pioneer work in Norway it was found that rainbow trout, a normally freshwater species, could be established in sea water. There the higher winter temperatures gave year-round growth and (at first) disease was less of a problem. From the early 1970s rainbow trout were reared in sea cages holding 3–5 tonnes of fish, the original sites being in the **Holy Loch**, Loch Melfort and Lochailort on the west coast. Bigger cages are now used holding 15–20 tonnes. In 1997 4913 tonnes of rainbow trout were produced mostly at freshwater sites, the total value at site being £7.4 million.

As the fish farming industry grew in the 1970s most farmers turned to Atlantic salmon, a higher value fish, and sites were occupied in many parts of the west coast and islands. Like rainbow trout, salmon can be reared in freshwater hatcheries, transferred to seawater cages at the smolt stage and held there until ready to harvest, one to two years later. The fish must be intensively fed, usually on fish-based pelleted diets. The rationale is to turn cheap protein (from industrial offshore fisheries for species like sandeel, capelin and blue whiting) into expensive protein, hence the constraint in all fish farming to produce species for the 'luxury' or high-value market. Salmon were first marketed in substantial quantities in the early 1980s, production rising to an apparent peak of about 40,000 tonnes (value at site £120 million) in 1991. Following a fall in price in the later 1980s as a result of over-production on a worldwide scale (but specially in Norway) it seemed likely that a plateau for production had been reached of under 40,000 tonnes. Thus in 1992 36,000 tonnes were produced with a site value of £108 million. However, in 1998 no less than 110,000 tonnes (value £187 million) were harvested. At present there are about 340 sites on the west coast, the Inner and Outer **Hebrides**, **Orkney** and **Shetland**, employing over 1300 fish farm workers and about twice that number indirectly.

Large numbers of salmon smolts are produced in Scotland for ongrowing (20.8 million in 1992). The smolts are transferred from freshwater hatcheries to the cages of the sea farm sites by road, well-boat or helicopter. The cages are of various designs, the smallest holding a final weight of about 6 tonnes, the largest 60 tonnes, the usual weight being 10–30 tonnes. Many of the best sites have been taken and resistance to further expansion has come from yachtsmen and **tourist** interests, hence the quest for off-shore sites. So-called 'ocean' cages, holding 70–90 tonnes, have been tested; they may be robust enough to withstand winter weather on semi-exposed coasts, but have not yet been adopted. At present huge tensioned nets, made of bulletproof-vest material and anchored to the sea bed, are under trial.

Farming is a high-risk venture for salmon, less so for shellfish whose main predator is the eider duck. Apart from poachers, predators like otters and **seals**, cormorants and herons must be kept at bay from salmon cages. Diseases of the skin, muscle (furunculosis), kidney and pancreas are a scourge in crowded conditions but oral vaccines are being developed. In 1998–9 infectious salmon anaemia caused the temporary closure of many sites and slaughter of the fish. Treatment is also required for parasites such as sea lice (which normally fall off wild salmon as they move into fresh water but remain on those held in sea cages). Earlier treatment by highly toxic chemicals is being superseded by the use of less toxic drugs and by wrasse as cleaner fish in the cages. They pick sea lice off the skin of the salmon in a symbiotic relationship. Fish farming is not for the faint-hearted, as shown by the wreck of the *Braer* off Shetland in early 1993 when over 80,000 tonnes of oil were deposited near an important salmon farming area, tainting the salmon flesh and making it unpalatable.

The farming of truly marine fish has far to go. Again, only a high-value product makes financial sense – the rearing of the young stages is especially difficult and costly. The eggs of marine fish are very small and the newly hatched larvae require the special production of minute living planktonic animals in extremely large numbers. Later the larvae must be weaned as juveniles onto expensive pelleted food. To date only turbot have been marketed, although sole, halibut and even cod are strong possibilites for the future. The best growth is obtained at high temperature and the earlier production of turbot in the 1980s was in tanks fed by the warm effluent of the **Hunterston** Power Station (Firth of **Clyde**). At present only turbot larvae are produced there and all on-growing of juveniles is carried out in Spain. In 1998 6 tonnes of reared halibut were produced in Scotland with a projection for 100 tonnes in 2001, all to be grown in sea cages.

Although Scotland has an ideal coast for so many types of fish farming, the relatively low sea temperatures preclude the use of more exotic species like bass and bream. Diversification may be possible to include more northerly forms like the charr, lumpsucker (for 'caviare') and wolf-fish, but it is likely that the industry will settle near its present level unless new markets can be found. One of these might be for cod. Following heavy overfishing of the high-seas stocks in the North Atlantic, quotas have been drastically reduced. Cage culture of cod on a large scale (even 30,000 tonnes has been suggested) seems to be a likely future development unless there is a dramatic upturn in the fishery.

Employing 2000 site workers and two to three times that number indirectly, and with a site production value approaching £200 million, aquaculture is one of Scotland's major industries.

FISHING (Angling)

The rivers and lochs of Scotland provide some of the finest salmon, sea trout and brown trout fishing in Europe if not the world. In England and Wales coarse fishermen and sea anglers greatly outnumber game fishers. Conversely in Scotland, because of the considerable extent of unpolluted salmon and trout water available at low or reasonable cost, the game fishers are easily in the majority. Angling in Scotland implies fishing for salmon and trout.

The protection of salmon was the subject of legislation probably before the 11th century and was first recorded by the **Scottish Parliament** in 1318. Enormous importance attached to the industry and cured salmon had become one of Scotland's major exports by the 14th and 15th centuries. The fish were netted, taken in traps and cruives, or impaled by leisters (spears) or cleiks (gaffs); but the formal laws of protection ensured they were not hunted to extinction. In the Highlands cured salmon was a vital winter food. Neither there nor elsewhere was 'sport' a relevant consideration.

Salmon (*Salmo salar*) and sea trout (*Salmo trutta*) are anadromous, ie they spend part of their life and make most of their growth in the sea, but run into river systems to spawn. The fry and fingerlings live and grow there before migrating down to the sea as smolts. Brown trout are the same species (*Salmo trutta*) as sea trout but have not migrated to the sea. The west Highland salmon rivers are numerous, short and fast-flowing, typically spate rivers draining rapidly off high hills down the glens to the many sea lochs. Rivers on the east coast are fewer, much larger and of more even flow. They run through gentler straths before joining the sea. These are the more valuable fishings. The burns and freshwater lochs and lochans which hold brown trout are too numerous even to count. Rainbow trout (*Salmo gardineri*) are not indigenous to Scotland and do not breed naturally here. A number of lochs and lakes are artificially stocked for angling purposes.

The west coast rivers mainly have summer runs of grilse (salmon out in the sea for one summer). The east coast rivers have a spring run and have many more large salmon which have been at sea for two years or more. The runs however in these rivers are getting later and later. Salmon can seldom be caught by rod and line in salt water when they are running through to spawn.

Not surprisingly the largest authenticated salmon ever caught by rod and line in Scotland came from Scotland's largest salmon river. In 1922 Miss G W Ballantine landed a 64lb (29.03kg) fish on the **Tay**. The sea trout record is more recent; in 1989 Mr S Burgoyne caught a 22lb 8oz (10.2kg) sea trout on the river Leven which flows out of **Loch Lomond**. The largest brown trout was caught on **Loch Quoich, Inverness-shire**, by Mr J A F Jackson in 1978. Huge brown trout are usually cannibalistic.

In 1862 Scotland was divided into 101 salmon fishery districts, each with the catchment area of a river or group of rivers. The owners of the salmon rivers may set up a District Salmon Fishery Board. These boards can appoint water bailiffs with powers to enforce the law. Each board has the power to raise money by levying a fishing rate on the owners of salmon fisheries in its district. In such instances, since 1989, no local government rates are paid. Almost all river fishings are in private ownership and the fishing policy is dictated by the owner.

The differing seasons for salmon and sea trout fishing were defined by the various districts in 1862. However in practice the season lasts as long as there are salmon in good condition in the river, ie up to some time before spawning. In west coast rivers this roughly means May to mid-October, but on the Tay and **Tweed**, for example, only in December is there no fishing at all.

Fishing as a sport or pastime may be dated to the early 17th century by when, if not before, fly fishing was well established. Fly fishing is the technique of casting with a rod across the water so that the floating fly just below the surface is carried round by the stream in a sweep over the fish lying in the pool. Arthur Johnstone, born in 1587 in **Aberdeenshire**, celebrated the art in Latin verse in his *Apologia Piscatoris*: 'When the nets are idle we hunt the fish with rods. If bait is not to be got . . . the hooks are usually hidden in a many-coloured little feather.' Richard Franck's *Northern Memoirs* (1658) also touches on fly fishing: 'The brighter the day is the obscurer your fly, suppose the day be gloomy you must consult a brighter fly' was his advice to the beginner.

No doubt there was rod fishing in the Highlands much earlier, but most of the **clan** chiefs and **tacksmen** would have had ghillies to provide them with fish (and game generally); few of the salmon and trout would have been rod caught. By the second half of the 18th century, however, the **Duke of Gordon** was letting salmon fishing on the **Spey** for sport. In the post-1745 Highlands communications improved with new roads and bridges. The coming of the **railways** completed the transformation of the area into a playground for the wealthy.

Sportsmen such as Colonel Thornton explored the hills and rivers for sport of all kinds in the early 19th century and duly wrote about the experience. The ken-speckle Colonel's hearty enthusiasm knew no bounds. He was gently lampooned by his contemporary Christopher North [**John Wilson**] in *Noctes Ambrosianae*. Here he is described slowly walking into **Loch Awe** – over the waist, over the chest, over the chin – until the astonished spectators on **Ben Cruachan** could only see the top of his tall hat and an arm holding a rod still flailing the water. The Colonel made it difficult for any fishing disciples to follow in his footsteps. Like many a bluff military man since, he had very little sympathy for foreign place-names. He praises the pike fishing in 'Loch Neiland' (Loch an Eilean) and describes the delights of the smoked salmon he found at the 'Cree in La Roche' inn (**Crianlarich**) when fishing the river Dochart.

A Highland sporting estate became a *sine qua non* for a member of the moneyed classes. Lodges and 'castles' were built everywhere. Here family and friends were entertained for long holidays. *Autumns in Argyllshire with Rod and Gun* by Gathorne Hardy is a period title of the 1880s, typical of numerous such sporting recollections.

In the Lowlands the Tweed was already well developed as fly fishing water when **Sir Walter Scott** wrote in 1820, perhaps not in his best style:

Along the silver streams of Tweed
Tis blithe the mimic fly to lead
When to hook the salmon springs
And the line whistles through the rings.

The influential sporting writer William Scrope, who also popularised the sport of **deer stalking** with a book on the subject, helped to increase the interest in the older sport of fly fishing in his *Days and Nights of Salmon Fishing in the Tweed*. The 'nights', however, were not recondite expeditions after sea trout (which take the fly in the dark) but occasions for 'burning the water' with leisters, ie, spearing salmon having attracted them with a flaming torch. Scrope was writing in a transitional period when the ancient 'primitive' methods were giving way to refined 'field sport' codes of practice.

These latter concepts established fly fishing as the classic rod and line method, superior to bait fishing or spinning. Indeed the 18th century fly patterns Scrope describes were much like our own. Mallard, teal and black game provided feathers as did the barnyard rooster, while black bullocks' hair, hares' fur and spun wool furnished the body of the various flies. The names are now forgotten. 'Toppy', 'Meg in her Braws', 'Lady of Mertoun' have long since given way to the 'Hairy Mary', 'Blue Charm', 'Garry Dog' and 'Shrimp Fly'; but the ingredients are much the same. Exactly which hair or feather excites the fish, and of what hue, remains a permanent fisherman's conundrum.

The Victorians fished with monster 18ft (5.5m) rods of split cane and green heart wood imported from the colonies. Their complex flies – the 'Jock Scott', 'Silver Doctor' and 'Mar Lodge' – sported a multitude of feathers plucked from the gaudiest birds of the Empire. Gut casts had to be soaked before fishing; silk lines carefully dried after use. The modern angler has the advantage of almost trouble-free man-made fibres,

Fishing party near Pitlochry in the 1880s (GWWA)

nylon lines and carbon fibre rods. Tackle is light and strong; flies once more utilitarian. Science and technology play their part as the modern books on the subject confirm.

Salmon and trout fishing in Scotland has never been more popular. It can be enjoyed by all ages and demands no great physical fitness. The great houses and 'castles' of the Victorian era are now in many instances hotels, while self-catering cottages and chalets proliferate to accommodate visiting fishers. Prices of quality salmon fishing to rent or purchase were at an all-time high in the late 1980s. It is very difficult to get onto top beats on such rivers as the Spey, Helmsdale, **Dee**, **Don**, Tay and Tweed. Time-share fishing developed in the 1980s. In 1989, for example, the Beauly, a noted Inverness-shire river, was sold to time-share operators by the **Fraser** family who had owned it for 400 years. Yet because there is such a variety of salmon and trout fishing in Scotland it is still possible to find fishing at reasonable prices for other than the best quality beats. In addition numerous anglers' associations provide fishing to their members at very low cost.

These are, however, anxious times for those concerned about the future of Scottish salmon and sea trout fishing. After a poor season in 1990, down by some 30% on the previous year (itself at a low level), the 1991 season was the worst since records began. The reasons are widely debated. Are the causes man-made or climatic? Is it part of a natural cycle? There is no consensus among experts.

A sporting industry worth over £140 million per year is at risk, but apart from the financial loss, it would be a great national loss if the numbers of salmon and sea trout seriously declined in the rivers to which they have returned since time immemorial. These fish are part of Scottish history. A salmon features in **Glasgow**'s ancient coat of arms. In Gaelic legend it is referred to as 'a mystical fish'. **Martin Martin** writing about **Lewis** in 1703 described how each May Day a man was sent to cross the Barras River at dawn since it was believed that if a woman crossed first no salmon would run up that year.

FISHING INDUSTRY

Sea fishing has long been important in Scotland, both for home consumption and for export. In the Highlands and Islands **crofting** and fishing were combined to produce a living, while in villages which sprang up around sheltered harbours such as those in the **East Neuk of Fife**, fishing became a full-time occupation.

Nowhere in the world is there a greater variety of fish or better fishing grounds than in the North Sea, around the Northern Isles, in the **Minch** and down the west coast. On the seabed, species such as haddock, cod and whiting are fast-swimming above the more sedentary skate, plaice and halibut. Nearer the surface swim the pelagic species, **herring** and mackerel, which congregate in vast shoals at certain times of the year. Nearer the shore crab and lobster can be caught, while along the edge of the shore species such as winkles, cockles and mussels are exposed at low tide.

Originally the bottom-dwelling fish were caught by lines – either the hand line, with one or more hooks attached, or the long-lines with baited hooks at intervals of a few feet which, when joined together and laid on the seabed, might stretch for several miles. In the case of the haddock line fishery the lines were baited at home by women and children while the men snatched a few hours' sleep before the next trip. The baited hooks were arranged carefully in a wooden container so that

Barrels of herring at a fishing station at Skibbadock, Lerwick c1890 (GWWA)

they did not foul each other when the lines were being shot.

In the early days boats were small, undecked and propelled by oars and sail. Nevertheless in some places the scale of fishery was considerable. In **Shetland**, for example, the 'haaf' (or distant-water) fishery employed thousands of men from May to the middle of August each year. Boats known as 'sixerns' (because they had six oars) fished up to 40 miles from land for ling, cod and tusk. Inevitably many boats were lost, the greatest disaster occurring on 16 July 1832, when 105 men were drowned.

Along the east coast in small man-made harbours, heavier-decked boats were in use — the straight-stemmed 'Fifies' of the south-east and the 'scaffies' of the Moray Firth with their raking stems and sterns. They were safer than the open boats of the Islesmen but still many men were lost. Unsurprisingly, most fishermen of the last century were deeply religious; luck, omens, taboo words and other superstitions played an important part in all aspects of fishing. (See Peter F Anson, *Fishermen and Fishing Ways*.)

Changing Techniques

Baited lines were selective in that only large fish were caught while the immature fish were left to grow and replenish the stocks; but when trawls were developed the fish had little chance of escape. In theory the meshes of the trawl were large enough to let the immature fish swim through; in practice large numbers of immature fish were caught and thrown back into the sea dead. The earliest trawls, towed by sailing smacks, were inefficient, but when trawls were towed by a

steam-driven vessel the problem became more serious.

In the 1880s steam trawling became a major industry on the east coast of Scotland, particularly at **Aberdeen**. As the fleet of powerful steam trawlers extended their area of operation, they caused great hardship to line fishermen. Scores of small communities were affected and thousands of fishermen forced to seek other employment or swallow their pride and serve as deckhands on trawlers. When the inshore stocks of haddock became depleted the trawler owners invested in larger vessels, capable of fishing as far away as Faroe and even Iceland.

Salvation for the inshore fishermen came with the introduction of paraffin-burning engines, which gave their boats a wider range; between the wars the seine net (a type of trawl) began to replace haddock lines and brought increased catches and earnings.

Rapid changes have taken place since the end of World War II. Loans and grants were made available by the government and a huge building programme started, resulting in a large fleet of diesel-engined craft, generally 65–75ft (19–23m) long, capable of fishing with drift-nets for herring in summer and reverting to seine net fishing during the remainder of the year. They were fitted with simple echo-sounders to indicate the type of seabed and to locate fish below the boat. In turn these boats were replaced by larger vessels with bigger engines; and seine nets gave way to heavy trawls. Enormous improvements were made in electronic aids to navigation and fish finding, with the result that catches increased still further. **Peterhead** became the major white fish port in the UK, overtaking Aberdeen. The latter lost its trawling fleet in the 1970s when Faroe and Iceland, alarmed at declining fish stocks, extended their fisheries limits out to 200 miles.

During the 1980s over-fishing became a reality in

scottish waters too. The problem was handled by politicians in Brussels after Britain joined the Common Market. Scottish fishermen have to share their fishing grounds with fleets from other EC countries and fishing is now regulated by total allowable catches and national quotas for each species. These are often exceeded, thus hastening the depletion of fish stocks. As the North Sea has declined in importance, greater effort has been placed on west coast grounds; hence the phenomenal rise of ports such as **Kinlochbervie** and **Lochinver**.

Once again the smaller boats have suffered most from over-fishing. Many have switched to other forms of fishing, such as trawling for prawns and fishing with dredges for scallops. Bigger vessels have moved to the edge of the continental shelf, where they catch deep-water species such as grenadiers and rabbit fish, which may become more common in fish shops in years to come.

New ideas are required to save the white fish industry and at last fishermen, politicians and gear manufacturers have come to realise that the answer lies in bigger mesh sizes and in fitting special panels to the roof of the trawl to allow young fish to escape. There is also renewed interest in selective types of fishing, such as lining. The development of automatic baiting and hauling systems has made this old technique an attractive alternative.

Fish Processing

While those people living near the sea may enjoy the luxury of fresh fish, for those living inland fish must be preserved in some way. In the past salt was the great preservative, which allowed an international trade to develop in salt herring and salted and dried cod and ling. It was also found that smoking over a fire of wood chips both retarded decay and gave the fish a pleasant taste.

A layer of ice in a box or basket of fish lowered the temperature and extended the range of fresh fish. As rail and sea links improved in the late 19th century, ice enabled customers in England to eat fresh fish which had been landed as far away as **Mallaig** or Aberdeen. In the case of shellfish it was important to bring catches to the markets alive and again this was only possible with good transport links.

Canning has been carried out on a small scale in Scotland since 1822, when John Moir introduced the new technique at Aberdeen. It remains important at a few places, such as **Fraserburgh** and the Shetland island of **Yell**. A further breakthrough in fish processing was the development between the wars of quick freezing. In the 1950s **Torry** Research Station at Aberdeen helped produce suitable equipment for both freezer trawlers and shore-based processing plants.

As the catch of white fish increased in the 1960s, fresh fish markets became over-supplied; the obvious solution was to build more processing plants, where fish such as haddock and whiting were filleted by hand or machine and then frozen into blocks for export in refrigerated cargo vessels to places as far away as Australia and America. Offal from these plants was converted into high-grade fish meal. Because of the extra cost involved, quick freezing is only viable when fish are plentiful and cheap. As white fish has become scarcer, the fresh fish market is again the more important and many freezing plants have closed down.

FLANDERS MOSS, Perthshire/Stirlingshire

West of **Stirling** as far as the **Lake of Menteith** stretches some of the flattest land in Scotland. Excavated whale-bones indicate that it was once an extension of the Firth of Forth and bog oaks that in **Roman** times it was wooded. But felling and climatic change allowed a massive build-up of **peat** so that by the 18th century the moss of Flanders (including Blair Drummond) covered 10,000 acres (4000ha). The peat, 6–12ft (2–4m) deep, overlaid rich alluvial soil and was deemed suitable for improvement. In the 1770s **Henry Home, Lord Kames** of Blair Drummond and then his son initiated a scheme whereby cultivators, mostly from the Highlands, were given a spade and 19 years' rent-free occupation of as much land as they could clear up to 10 acres (4ha). Canals were dug and sluices designed to wash the dislodged peat into the Forth – where it caused havoc to the **oyster** beds. By 1811 1400 acres (566ha) had been thus reclaimed and now comprise the rich farming of the Carse of Stirling. What remained of the Moss posed a challenge similar to **Rannoch Moor** when a **railway** line was 'floated' across it to **Aberfoyle** in 1882. The **Forestry Commission** has since planted some of it, but several thousand hectares remain, jealously guarded by conservationists.

FLANNAN ISLES, Outer Hebrides

The uninhabited Flannan Isles, or Seven Hunters, lie 23 miles north-west of **Lewis**. On Eilean Mor is the chapel of St Flannan (d.680) and a lighthouse, now automatic, the scene of a famous mystery when the three keepers disappeared without trace in December 1900, probably washed away by a freak wave. This episode is the subject of a poem by Wilfred Gibson and a modern opera by Peter Maxwell Davies. **Martin Martin** (1695) describes how the people of Bernera in Lewis went to the Flannans annually in search of 'fowls, eggs, down, feathers and quills', and **Neil M Gunn**'s Silver Darlings contains a harrowing description of the hazards involved in such an endeavour.

FLEMING, Sir Alexander (1881–1955)
Discoverer of Penicillin

After a rural childhood at Lochfield Farm, near Darvel in **Ayrshire**, Alexander Fleming moved with his brothers to London where he worked for five years as a **shipping** clerk before entering medical school at the age of 20. Qualifying both as a physician and a surgeon, Fleming showed a facility for research work, particularly the devising of innovative laboratory working methods, that led to his being offered a place on the research staff of Sir Almroth Wright at St Mary's Hospital in Paddington. He was to serve in this department for all of his professional life, eventually succeeding Wright as its head.

Service in a military hospital in France during World War I gave Fleming personal experience of the failure of contemporary antiseptics to prevent the contamination of wounds, and it was his subsequent search for a natural agent to solve the problem that was to dominate his work at St Mary's. The first to use antityphoid vaccines on human beings and pioneering the use of salvarsan against syphilis, in 1921 he discovered lysozyme, a natural substance which had a limited usefulness in food preservation, but it was his discovery of the powers of the natural antibiotic *penicillium notatum* which was to make him one of medicine's greatest names.

One summer day in 1928 a glass plate left unwashed in Fleming's laboratory sink, and bearing a sample of septicaemia germs, appeared to have been colonised and cleared by a mould seeded by an airborne spore. Fleming was alert enough to investigate this phenomenon and discovered that this spore, one of countless millions in the atmosphere, had the ability to destroy or inhibit a number of virulent germ samples in the laboratory, including those of streptococcus, staphylococcus, pneumococcus, gonococcus, meningococcus and the diphtheria bacillus. A mycologist colleague, who had apparently been working on the *penicillium* in a different experiment in the same building, identified the strain for Fleming, who then subjected it to laboratory tests.

Unfortunately early indications suggested that the derived substance, which Fleming named penicillin, was unlikely to perform equally well in a clinical environment and was particularly difficult to produce in large quantities, and in a pure form. It has to be said that Fleming appears to have lost faith in his discovery, partly for these reasons and partly because he had other research commitments of economic importance to St Mary's. It is also possible that Fleming was disappointed by penicillin's inability to attack influenza, a disease whose effects he had seen at first hand as it ravaged war-weakened populations across Europe. Indeed, Fleming's historic paper announcing his discovery, in the *British Journal of Experimental Pathology* (Vol 10, 1929) suggests penicillin as a potential laboratory tool for isolating influenza in order to facilitate its study.

Penicillin remained nothing more than a laboratory curiosity until a sample of it was tried out in simple tests on laboratory mice by two Oxford biochemists, Howard Florey and Ernst Chain, searching for likely natural antibiotics at the beginning of World War II. Injecting mice with penicillin (originally supplied by Fleming himself) showed that the substance, even in crude form and in small quantities, could knock out many lethal organisms *in vivo*. By quickly devising methods of purifying penicillin, Florey and Chain gave an amazing healing agent to the world, and it was soon mass-produced in the USA.

Elected FRS in 1943 and knighted in 1944, Fleming, along with Florey and Chain, deservedly won the Nobel Prize for Medicine in 1945. Considerable professional jealousy seems to have been generated by Fleming's acceptance of such honours, his critics arguing that he had failed to develop the world's greatest natural antibiotic, but even his fiercest detractors must concede that he discovered and identified the organism, communicated this (millions-to-one-against) discovery to the medical profession, and provided cultures to any researcher who requested one. Fleming's only fault was, perhaps, that he was too mortal to realise that he had made an immortal discovery.

Also in 1945 he refused a personal gift of $100,000 from the American pharmaceutical industry, instead donating the money to medical research – at a time

when he was reportedly earning only £1000 a year. As a natural substance, penicillin could not be patented under UK legislation although its method of mass-production was patented (by others) in the USA, and Fleming benefited not one penny from his discovery.

He died on 11 March 1955 and his cremated remains were buried in St Paul's Cathedral. For a critical but balanced biography, see *Alexander Fleming* by Gwyn Macfarlane, 1984.

FLEMING, Robert (1845–1933) Financier

Fleming was born and educated in **Dundee**. After a brief clerical career he launched the Scottish American Investment Trust as a way for local people to invest in high-return overseas securities. Hugely sucessful, he established two other local trusts and became involved in other similar Scottish ventures. By the turn of the century he had opened an office in London where he set up Robert Fleming & Company, a merchant bank. It has been estimated that by the 1920s he influenced trusts totalling in excess of £100 million, including considerable interests in the USA. When he died his estate was valued at £2.2 million. He maintained close ties with his native city, becoming a freeman in 1928 and making charitable donations to various civic trusts. Amongst his grandchildren were the writers Peter and Ian ('James Bond') Fleming.

FLEMING, Williamina Paton (1857–1911) Astronomer

Born in **Dundee** as Williamina Stevens, she emigrated to the USA in 1878, settling in Boston. When her marriage failed she took a menial job as a domestic maid with the director of Harvard College Observatory, who fortunately perceived that she had the potential for scientific work and offered her employment at the observatory. Showing a flair for analysing photographic plates of the skies, Fleming discovered over 200 variable stars, 10 novae and in 1890 published a classified catalogue of 10,351 astral bodies. She became only the fifth woman member of the Royal Astronomical Society.

FLETCHER, Andrew, of Saltoun (1653–1716) Patriot

As MP for Haddingtonshire (**East Lothian**) from 1678, Andrew Fletcher opposed **Lauderdale** and the Duke of York (later **James VII**), refused to take the 1681 **Test Oath** and fled to England. In 1685 he joined Monmouth's unsuccessful rebellion and this time fled to Holland, returning at the Revolution. A dogged champion of social and political reform, and convinced that these could only be achieved in a Scotland free from English domination, he was the much-respected leader of the anti-**Union** Country Party in the last Scottish Parliament. His famous 'Limitations' (1705) proposed severe curtailment of royal authority and of the powers and privileges of the nobility. Having campaigned tirelessly in speech and pamphlet against the ultimately inevitable, he retired from political life after the 1707 Union to concentrate on agrarian reform.

FLODDEN, Battle of (1513)

All agree that Flodden was a catastrophic defeat for Scottish pride. For once there were no excuses. 'With

Andrew Fletcher of Saltoun, after William Aikman (SNPG)

every nerve taut to deploy men and guns, an able Scottish king was defeated, his army wiped out, his own life expended, in a struggle with the second string of the English' (R Mitchison). Moreover **James IV** had the wholehearted support of his people; even Highlanders were present and as for the Lowlanders, 'the slaughter struck at every farm and household throughout lowland Scotland'. Worse still, the battle was fought on English soil as a result of Scottish aggression in what now seems an unworthy cause.

Though married to Henry VIII's sister and bound to him by a perpetual treaty of friendship, James IV declared war on England the moment Henry VIII invaded France. The English advance was part of an international offensive organised and sanctioned by the papacy. Scotland had nothing to gain from joining in on either side and, having just renewed the **auld alliance** with France, had contractual relations with both that cancelled each other out. But, anxious to play an international role and incensed by a recent English attack on Scottish shipping, James elected to throw his weight behind France. Thence his fleet, with his best gunners aboard, was despatched while a force about 20,000 strong moved into Northumberland to draw off English troops. They took Norham Castle and other strongpoints before encountering the Earl of Surrey and his son with a force numerically slightly smaller but well equipped with artillery. On high ground west of the river Till, a tributary of the **Tweed**, near Branxton, the Scots took up a tactically advantageous position on 9 September. The English to some extent countered this by moving unopposed round to the west and then commenced a well-directed bombardment. The Scottish response was less accurate and in mid-afternoon James abandoned his position and ordered a full-scale attack. It had some initial effect but in hand-to-hand conflict the Scots found themselves disadvantaged, English halberds proving deadlier than Scottish spears.

There is no Scottish account of the battle but it would seem that James himself prepared to lead by example rather than to command; his fate was unknown until his corpse was found among the slain. With him fell an archbishop (his natural son), abbots, earls (at least 10), and countless lords and lairds. The English figure of 10,000 dead Scots may be only a doubling of the real figure, and English losses were also heavy. The victors did not press their advantage by invading Scotland and the vanquished found no opportunity to avenge their defeat.

FLOORS CASTLE, Kelso, Roxburghshire
Although the original Floors (anciently Fleurs) Castle, built on the banks of the river **Tweed** at **Kelso** for the 1st Duke of Roxburghe from 1718, is widely credited to Sir John Vanbrugh, it is thought that **William Adam** was very much involved in its design. He was certainly superintending building operations there in 1723 and took the credit for the castle in his *Vitruvius Scoticus*. Neither, however, would have recognised their creation once **William Playfair** had completed his 1838–49 remodelling for the 6th Duke. To the original oblong four-storey block with square angle towers, much admired by **Sir Walter Scott** for 'combining the ideas of ancient grandeur with those of modern taste', Playfair added pavilions and stables, courtyard and porte-cochère, corbelling and castellations and pepper-pot turrets beyond counting. The resulting magnificent pile has been described as 'the largest inhabited mansion in Britain' and is still the home of the Duke of Roxburghe.

FLOW COUNTRY, The, Caithness and Sutherland
The term was once reserved for the flat and watery **peat** bogs of west **Caithness** and east **Sutherland** but is now used to designate all the peatlands of these two counties. In area it covers about 400,000ha, or just over half their total area, and consists mainly of 'blanket bog', a distinctive form of peatland incorporating more **heather** and bearberry than is found, for instance, in west coast bogs. This results in a richer and more varied ecology and has made the Flow Country a focus of conservationists' concern and a noted battleground between environmentalists (notably the Nature Conservancy Council) and afforestation interests. The latter, who have already 'reclaimed' 16% of the Flow Country, emphasise its dreary aspect and unproductive nature, the former its unique appeal as the largest blanket bog in Europe and one of the oldest and least disturbed in the world. Its depth (up to 6m) and antiquity contain important data for meteorological historians while its habitat supports numerous rare plants, insects and, most notably, water birds; 66% of Europe's greenshanks are said to breed here, 35% of its dunlin and 17% of its golden plovers.

'FLOWER OF SCOTLAND'
Written in the 1960s by Roy Williamson of The Corries folk-singing duo, 'Flower of Scotland' has become Scotland's unofficial anthem, sung at such sporting occasions as **rugby union** internationals, the **football**

World Cup etc. The first and third verses are most commonly sung. The complete words are as follows:

Oh Flower of Scotland, when will we see your like again
That fought and died for your wee bit hill and glen
And stood against him, proud Edward's army,
And sent him homeward tae think again.

The hills are bare now, and autumn leaves lie thick and still,
O'er land that is lost now, which those so dearly held
That stood against him, proud Edward's army
And sent him homeward tae think again.

Those days are past now, and in the past they must remain,
But we can still rise now and be the nation again
That stood against him, proud Edward's army,
And sent him homeward, tae think again.

Oh Flower of Scotland, when will we see your like again
That fought and died for your wee bit hill and glen
And stood against him, proud Edward's army
And sent him homeward, tae think again.

© The Corries (Music) Ltd

FOCHABERS, Moray

A late 18th century visitor to **Moray** described Fochabers as 'a populous but beggarly village'. This, however, was the old Fochabers which stood close to Gordon Castle, a property of the **Gordons** of **Huntly** from the late 15th century, and was replaced, starting in 1776, by an elegant planned village. With the old village too close to the castle and grounds that he was intent on improving, the 4th Duke of Gordon bought out the holdings of old Fochabers and induced the reluctant inhabitants to move to their new village. While the old village was being obliterated, the John Baxter-designed new Fochabers began to take shape. With its regular street pattern and elegant square, Fochabers is an exceedingly pleasant place. Its strategic situation where the main road from **Elgin** divides – one road going towards **Banff**, the other to **Keith** and **Aberdeen** – and proximity to a major crossing point on the river **Spey**, brings a lot of traffic through the village. Visitor attractions include a small private folk museum (specialising in horse-drawn vehicles), several antique shops, a notable garden centre and nursery, and on the western side of the river, a world-famous food processing factory – **Baxters** of Speyside. Baxters, with its Visitor Centre including a reconstruction of an old grocery shop, draws in many tourists and is a major employer for the area. Although the now greatly diminished Gordon Castle (once 568ft (173m) long) is not open to the public, there are attractive walks in the area; the long-distance footpath, the Speyside Way, passes through the village.

FOOTBALL

Association football, also known as 'soccer' (but not in Scotland where it is more commonly known as 'fitba'),

is administered by a number of organisations, supreme among which is the Scottish Football Association at Park Gardens, **Glasgow**. An associated body, the Scottish Football League, is responsible for the running of the league competitions for the 38 senior teams, while junior football (for adults both professional and amateur) is administered by the Scottish Junior Football Association. A total of 77 clubs are currently affiliated to the SFA, including the senior teams and some playing in a number of linked regional associations, such as the North of Scotland Football Association, which administers the Highland League. Women's football is administered by the Scottish Women's Football Association, founded in 1972.

Football shares its early history with **rugby**. Both games undoubtedly found a common origin in early ball games dating back to **Roman** times, but by the 15th and 16th centuries 'football' was so popular as to be banned by royal edict, on the grounds of interfering with archery practice. Despite this **Queen Mary** is recorded as being an enthusiastic spectator, although she had been dead for some years when the first recorded match was arranged between teams representing Scotland and England in 1599. The venue was Bewcastle in Cumbria, the result being a number of Englishmen taken prisoner and one man disembowelled (the records, incredibly, show that he was 'sewn' back up again). And modern football is often recorded as being too rough . . .

By the second half of the 19th century, the concentration of the population in cities, and the gradual institution of Saturday afternoons free from work, created a demand for public entertainment on a large scale. With most of Scotland's population centred on one massive conurbation and three smaller cities, this demand became particularly acute, and the records show that the burgeoning number of football clubs existing in isolation found difficulty in arranging fixtures with other clubs, and were frequently discomfited to find, when a fixture had been arranged, that the opposition might well be used to playing to a different set of rules. The answer obviously lay in following the English example of setting up cup and league competitions and in attempting to codify the rules.

Compared to England, Scotland was somewhat slow to resolve these dual requirements, the Scottish Football Association being formed at a meeting in Glasgow on 13 March 1873, nearly 10 years after the English organisaton. Interestingly, the formation of the SFA took place only 10 days after the setting up of the Scottish Rugby Union – a sign of the need to impose some kind of order on the differing codes of ball game.

The first members of the SFA were Queen's Park, Clydesdale, Vale of Leven, Dumbreck, Third Lanark Rifle Volunteer Reserves, Eastern, Granville and Rovers. At the same meeting a cup competition was begun which became the Scottish FA Cup, its first winners being Queen's Park, the Glasgow club formed in 1867 which went on to dominate Scottish football until the club's amateur status (which it still retains) led to its eclipse in the inevitable trend towards professionalism. In its heyday Queen's Park represented Scotland in the earliest internationals with England, played twice in the final of the (English) FA Cup in 1884 and 1885 and did not

The Scottish team for the football international against England in 1906 (SEA)

Football continued

concede a goal in six years of domestic competitive football. It was also during a Queen's Park cup tie with Preston North End in 1886 that a foul on the Queen's Park centre forward led to the offender, also a Scot, having to be escorted from the ground. This incident produced the rift between the English and Scots FAs which resulted in the latter banning Scottish clubs from the English competition, 'a declaration of independence which profoundly affected Scottish nationalism' (C Harvie). Thereafter Queen's Park gradually began to lose its pre-eminence in Scottish football, possibly because of its somewhat elitist membership, its popularity being eclipsed by the more down-to-earth Rangers and, later, Celtic. Nevertheless it was Queen's Park's ground of **Hampden Park** which became after 1903 the nation's principal football ground, superior in spectator capacity to Wembley until recent safety legislation was enacted.

Because of the huge earning power of football as spectator entertainment, and the predation by English clubs of Scottish talent, clubs north of the border found it necessary to compensate their players for lost earnings – but often covertly paid even more than that. Professionalism became official in 1893, finally sealing the break from Rugby Union which remained firmly amateur. 'Fitba' became the people's game, more dependent on skill than brawn – making it popular with urban dwellers and miners often rendered diminutive by generations of malnutrition and poor environmental conditions – while requiring no more equipment than a ball and four jackets to act as goalposts. Working-class players good enough to attract the attention of the clubs would not hesitate to turn professional.

The need to grade entrants into the Scottish Cup inevitably led to the setting up of a league system in 1891,

again this coming two years after the English model. Queen's Park refused to join until 1900 because of covert professionalism in the new Scottish League, and entry into the First Division was by invitation only until 1922.

If the Scots lagged behind their southern neighbours in organising the framework of the game, the opposite could be said about different types of play. It is the Scots who were credited with pioneering the modern passing game with each player patrolling a fixed area – previously all players except the goalkeeper appear to have chased the ball wherever it was on the field of play.

As in many small nations, Scotland's football has traditionally been dominated by a very small number of clubs – in Scotland's case, two Glasgow clubs, Rangers and Celtic. Rangers FC are the older, formed in 1873, and playing their earliest games at **Glasgow Green**, before moving to their present venue of Ibrox Park. Celtic were formed in the east end of the city in 1888, being made up of footballers mainly of Irish origin, and largely, although not exclusively, Catholic. With the worsening of British-Irish relations during World War I, it was inevitable that there would be a polarisation of religious fervour around prominent sporting clubs – where one of them had strong Irish origins – and Rangers rapidly took on a mantle of Protestantism, often of the most extreme kind. Until the signing of Maurice Johnston in 1989, it was believed that the club had never signed a Catholic player.

The two clubs, collectively known as the 'Old Firm', have hitherto always been associated with religious sectarianism, frequently creating an ugly atmosphere before, during and after matches between the clubs. Sociologists may ponder the absence of religiously-motivated bloodshed on the Glasgow streets in the style of Belfast – possibly football acts as a vicarious substitute for such violence. There are echoes of this sectarianism in **Edinburgh**, where Hibernian are often thought to represent Catholic interests and Heart of Midlothian the Protestant, although only the most religiously blinkered could discern such associations, and the Old Firm draw much of their support from furth of Glasgow anyway.

The immediate post-World War I years saw huge crowds attracted to football matches. With no television as a counter-attraction, football fans were in the habit of working their Saturday morning shift, and attending the afternoon's match with their haversack containing the remains of their 'piece' (snack), possibly after a quick visit to the pub. A British record crowd of 149,415 watched an England-Scotland international and 147,365 a Celtic-Aberdeen Cup Final within eight days in 1937; immediate post-World War II crowds were often of much the same order. All Scottish grounds then set attendance records which are now unattainable because of long-overdue safety regulations, creating a false yardstick for gauging popularity.

Whilst some fans lament a loss of atmosphere in today's all-seater stadia, it is impossible to deny the progress that has been made in recent years in terms of comfort and safety. Throughout the divisions there are signs of this improvement, from the Caledonian Stadium in **Inverness** through to the three 50,000+ capacity super-stadiums in Glasgow (Ibrox, Celtic Park and Hampden), ensuring Scottish football currently provides the facilities and accessibility to keep pace with the rest of Europe.

Rangers and Celtic have inevitably dominated the post-war years. Rangers were the more successful of the two in the early 1950s, thanks to their 'Iron Curtain' defence deployed around Willie Woodburn, but producing a famous attacking team in the following decade. Wing-half Jim Baxter fed inch-perfect passes to a talented forward line led by Jimmy Millar and with wing wizardry represented by Alex Scott, Willie Henderson and Davie Wilson.

Since 1986 Rangers have imported a number of talented players from England and abroad, achieving considerable success at domestic, if not European, level. Under the management of first Graeme Souness and then Walter Smith the club equalled Celtic's coveted 'nine-in-a-row' record of League championship wins between the years of 1989 and 1997, much to the delight of their supporters. The club's sole honour in European competition came in 1972, when it lifted the European Cup Winners' Cup in Barcelona after beating Moscow Dynamo 3–2. Rangers – or rather their supporters – were the victims of Scotland's worst sporting disaster when, on 2 January 1971, 66 spectators were killed during a crushing incident on Stairway 13 at Ibrox during and after an 'Old Firm' derby [see **Ibrox Disaster**].

Meanwhile Celtic enjoyed success more spasmodically until 1965 when **Jock Stein**, a former centre-half with the club, took over as manager following considerable success with Dunfermline Athletic and a brief spell with Hibs. It took Stein only a few months to secure a Cup Final victory, over his old team Dunfermline, before launching Celtic on a record-breaking spell of nine successive League championships.

As at Dunfermline, Stein's 1960s team contained few players of international standard – they rarely reproduced club form when wearing a Scotland jersey – confirming that Stein's genius lay in super motivating players of no more than average ability and persuading them to give everything in a collective team effort. (Even Kenny Dalglish, an exceptional talent, took some time to reproduce his club form for his country.) Nor was Stein's sucess purely domestic, the 'Bhoys' becoming the first British club to win the European Cup after a famous 2–1 win over Inter Milan in Lisbon in 1967. Stein nearly repeated this with another European triumph three years later, his team narrowly losing a second final in Milan to Feyenoord of the Netherlands.

Hibs, Hearts, Dundee United and Aberdeen have periodically provided opposition to the 'Old Firm' of Celtic and Rangers in the postwar years, but with no regularity. Hibs produced a unique brand of attacking football built around their 'Famous Five' forwards – Smith, Johnstone, Reilly, Turnbull and Ormond – taking the League championship to Easter Road three times in five years in the early 1950s and being denied a fourth championship by the narrowest of margins. In 1955–6 Hibs were the first British team to compete in the European Cup, beating German and Swedish opposition before falling in the semi-final. Hearts had their own 'Terrible Trio' of Conn, Bauld and Wardhaugh, and enjoyed Cup success in 1956 and two League championships not long after.

In the 1980s and early 1990s Aberdeen were on the verge of creating a dominating presence in Scottish football, particularly so when managed by Alex Ferguson in the years 1978–86. Along with three League and four Cup successes, Ferguson masterminded a series of excellent performances in Europe, culminating in winning the European Cup Winners' Cup in Gothenberg in 1983, beating Real Madrid 2–1 after extra time.

Aberdeen became known as one half of the 'New Firm', along with Dundee United. Originally overshadowed by Dundee FC (who enjoyed an excellent League championship win in 1961–2 and a subsequent good run in the European Cup), United were very much newcomers to the winner's podium. They owed their emergence to Jerry Kerr who laid the foundations for an even more successful manager, Jim McLean. McLean is now chairman of the club he took to a League championship in 1983, two League Cup triumphs, an appearance in the final of the UEFA Cup and in the semi-final of the European Cup. Even with the efforts of the 'New Firm', Scottish club football is still heavily dominated by the Old Firm. The Premier Division has only been won four times in 24 years by teams from outside Glasgow.

Present League Arrangement

Since 1994 the 40 senior clubs in Scotland have been arranged into four divisions – Premier, First, Second and Third. Between 1975 and 1994 there had always been just three divisions and it needed the intake of two Highland league teams, **Inverness** Caledonian Thistle and Ross County, before a four-division structure could be sustained. Again the arrangement was disrupted in September 1997 when the ten leading clubs in Scotland announced their intention to resign from he league in search of a more suitable (and profitable) olution. With lucrative television and sponsorship deals n the offing to keep the club chairmen happy, the SPL Scottish Premier League) came to life, up and running n time for the new season of August 1998. With the evel of commercial interest in Scotland's football élite till spiralling it is anyone's guess as to how long the maller clubs will survive the financial strain of the modern game. Still very much in its infancy, the SPL onsists of ten clubs, but just as in 1986, 1988, 1991 nd 1994 the number is on the verge of change. Plans or a 12-team division should become a reality in the 2000/2001 season. Unlike in England, there is no auto-matic relegation for the bottom team in the League into he non-League divisions.

The Scottish Cup is the oldest competition in the ountry for football teams, and is open to all teams ssociated to the SFA, including non-senior sides. The inal is played each May at Hampden Park, home of the Cup's first holder, Queen's Park. It was this competition hat produced what is still regarded as the football vorld's highest score, the 36−0 victory of Arbroath over Bon Accord of **Aberdeen** in the first round in 1885. What is not generally known is that Bon Accord vere in fact a cricket club mistakenly sent an invitation o play in the Cup. The cricket-score result still stands s a record.

The other major competition is the League Cup. This s open only to senior sides and also has its final at Hamp-len, usually in November. At one time played in sections producing quarter-finalists, the competition later became home-and-away competition in its early rounds, but it s now run strictly on cup lines for League clubs only.

Junior football is administered by the Scottish Junior Football Association, founded in Glasgow in 1886. Despite its title, junior football is a game for adults, ome of them professional. A cup competition began n 1887, and is still competed for, the final being held at a senior ground annually in May. At the time of he Association's centenary 168 clubs were members, frequently acting as 'nurseries' for the senior sides (although less often than in previous years) and some-imes as a refuge for those players who have failed to establish a professional career with a senior club.

Women's football is administered by the Scottish Women's Football Association, founded in 1972, super-vising football for women of 14 years and over in both 11- and 5-a-side teams. There are currently (1999) 30 clubs spread over the one senior and three divisional leagues.

International Football

As in rugby, Scotland's first international opponents were England, the 0−0 draw between the two sides at the West of Scotland cricket ground at Partick on St Andrew's Day 1872 constituting the first international football match in history. (Earlier meetings between 'England' and 'Scotland' sides in London are not regarded by historians as truly representative.) With Wales and Northern Ireland, a Home Championship was contested by the two countries until falling gate receipts brought about its demise in 1983−4. However, the England-Scotland match continued annually, tra-ditionally held turn-about in each country until com-plaints about Scottish supporters' alleged vandalism in London led to the 1985 match being switched to Glas-gow. The games were then held sequentially, but were missed out altogether in 1990, due to congested fixture lists before the World Cup, and have since been abandoned.

Scotland gave as good as it received in this fixture over the years, although the English have never appar-ently taken the game as seriously as the Scots, for whom victory over the 'Auld Enemy' is seen as some kind of revenge for English slights real or imagined. Fans who were not alive at the time like to recall the 5−1 drubbing which Scotland's 'Wembley Wizards' handed out to the English in 1928, while doing their best to forget the humiliations of 1955 (2−7) and 1961 (3−9), also at Wembley. In recent years the fixture has produced little in the way of good football, suggesting that the English policy of downgrading it to the status of just another international was rather more realistic than the tra-ditional Scottish policy of seeing it as some kind of 'once-and-for-all' shoot-out to avenge **Flodden**.

World Cup

To date, Scotland has reached the World Cup final stages on eight occasions, in 1954, 1958, 1974, 1978, 1982, 1986, 1990 and 1998. The five consecutive appearances from 1974 are commonly claimed as constituting a record for a team qualifying in competition rather than by right (ie as host or holder); in fact both Mexico and Italy have so qualified six times in succession. After 1954, each tournament involved playing three games, in which a total of only four victories have been achieved. Scotland has never progressed beyond the first stage of the competition's finals, and in 1950, 1962, 1966, 1970 and 1994 failed to reach even that stage.

Like England, Scotland did not participate in the World Cup before World War II, and agreed to attend the first postwar event, held in Brazil in 1950, only if the team was the winner of the British Championship. A 0−1 defeat by England at Hampden put paid to such ambition, although Scotland could still have accepted a place in Brazil. It was not until 1954 that Scotland appeared in the World Cup finals.

1954 SWITZERLAND Scotland's first appearance in the finals scarcely got off to a good start with manager Andy Beattie announcing his resignation before a ball was kicked. The team appeared to play in a style much in keeping with this negative launch, losing 0−1 to Austria and then 0−7 to Uruguay, a team which ever after became something of a *bête noire* to the Scots. It seems strange in retrospect that such a successful and entertain-ing domestic footballing industry − as Scotland's was at that time − should travel so badly.

1958 SWEDEN This second appearance in the finals began more encouragingly with a creditable 1−1 draw with Yugoslavia, but selection errors put paid to future progress, defeats resulting from Paraguay (2−3) and France (1−2). It was to be 16 years before the World Cup finals again counted a Scottish presence, during which interval they had failed to overcome Czechoslo-vakia to qualify for the 1962 tournament, or the Italians

Billy Bremner, Scotland's captain in the 1970s (SEA)

Football continued
or West Germans for the 1966 and 1970 tournaments respectively.

1974 WEST GERMANY Managed by the much-underrated Willie Ormond, and captained by the tactically astute **Billy Bremner**, Scotland made a brave showing in a group which included cupholders Brazil, Yugoslavia and Zaire. The opening match was against the African newcomers of Zaire who shocked the Scots with their excellent ball-control, and Scotland settled too readily for a 2–0 victory, following first-half goals from the Leeds United pair of Lorimer and Jordan, when more goals were vitally needed. Yugoslavia and Brazil, having drawn with each other, put nine and three goals respectively past the Africans without reply, while the Scots could only manage draws with Brazil (0–0) and Yugoslavia (1–1). Eliminated on goal difference, Scotland became one of the first teams to be dismissed from the finals without losing a match, and the team was deservedly fêted on its return.

1978 ARGENTINA Precariously buoyed up by the self-belief of its ebullient manager Ally MacLeod, Scotland experienced a disastrous competition. Not only had MacLeod underrated his first opponents, Peru, but had failed to freshen the midfield he inherited from Ormond, fatally delaying the introduction of Graeme Souness. After a good start against Peru, the Scots missed a penalty and the superior pace of the South Americans, playing in familiar conditions, told in a 1–3 defeat. Matters grew worse when it was learned that winger

Willie Johnston had played after consuming a banned substance, probably for quite innocent reasons. An embarrassing 1–1 draw with Iran followed, the Scots' score coming courtesy of an own goal. Only with the overdue selection of Souness were the Scots able to salvage some pride by beating the ultimate runners-up, the Netherlands, by 3 goals to 2, a goal by Archie Gemmell later being adjudged the best of the tournament. It was the barest of consolations.

1982 SPAIN Jock Stein was Scotland's manager by this time, but not even his most ardent admirers expected much progress in a group with Brazil, the USSR and New Zealand. Playing the last-named first, Scotland scored no fewer than five times, although two vital goals were conceded. In the next match, and despite an excellent early goal by David Narey, the Scots were outclassed by the best Brazilian side since the 1970 competition, eventually losing 1–4. Even a spirited 2–2 draw against the USSR could not take Scotland through to the next stage, and so Jock Stein's only appearance at the World Cup finals ended in disappointment, eliminated once again on goal difference.

1986 MEXICO Having missed the Mexico finals in 1970, Scotland attempted to make amends under the caretaker management of Alex Ferguson 16 years later. Not for the first or the last time, the sectional draw had been unkind to the Scots, placing them in the 'group of death' with Denmark, West Germany and Uruguay. Even with three of these four teams allowed to progress to the next stage, Scotland failed to manage even one win, losing 0–1 to the Danes and 1–2 to the Germans, and then drawing ridiculously with a Uruguayan side reduced to 10 men from the first minute of the match after a foul on Gordon Strachan, the side's only score in the finals. Scotland's lack of striking power was painful to watch and the team returned unfêted.

1990 ITALY Again Brazil were drawn in the same section as Scotland, along with Sweden and Costa Rica. Playing the Central Americans first, Scotland, managed now by Andy Roxburgh, lost 0–1 despite doing most of the attacking, but then beat the Swedes 2–1 in an emotionally-charged match. Unfortunately this charge ran out of current for the crucial game against Brazil, the Scots losing 0–1.

1998 FRANCE Craig Brown was given the dubious privilege of taking his Scotland side into the showpiece opening match of the tournament in Paris's Stade de France against, you guessed it, Brazil. However the Scots, undaunted by the occasion, put in a strong, fighting performance. Going down to an early Brazil goal, they equalised with a John Collins penalty shortly before half-time; only after the self-inflicted agony of a Scottish own goal did the South Americans secure a 2–1 victory. Against Norway, a Craig Burley equaliser won Scotland their solitary point of the tournament in a game where they really should have taken three. The most painful blow was yet to be struck as once more the group's unknown quantity, Morocco, proved to be Scotland's Achilles' heel. They laid bare the national team's frailties with a 3–0 rout in St Etienne.

SCOTTISH SENIOR FOOTBALL CLUBS

Table of Honours to 1999

Club	Founded	Ground	Prem Div	1st Div	2nd Div	3rd Div	Scottish Cup	League Cup	Europe
Aberdeen	1903	Pittodrie	3	1	–	–	7	5	1
Airdrieonians	1878	Broomfield	–	–	3	–	1	–	–
Albion Rovers	1881	Cliftonhill (Coatbridge)	–	–	2	–	–	–	–
Alloa Athletic	1883	Recreation Park	–	–	1	1	–	–	–
Arbroath	1878	Gayfield	–	–	–	–	–	–	–
Ayr United	1910	Somerset Park	–	–	8	–	–	–	–
Berwick Rangers	1881	Shielfield Park	–	–	1	–	–	–	–
Brechin City	1906	Glebe Park	–	–	2	–	–	–	–
Celtic	1888	Celtic Park (Parkhead)	6	29	–	–	31	11	1
Clyde	1878	Broadwood (Glasgow)	–	–	9	–	3	–	–
Clydebank	1965	Kilbowie Park	–	–	1	–	–	–	–
Cowdenbeath	1881	Central Park	–	–	3	–	–	–	–
Dumbarton	1893	Boghead	–	2	3	–	1	–	–
Dundee	1893	Dens Park	–	4	1	–	1	3	–
Dundee United	1910	Tannadice	1	–	2	–	1	2	–
Dunfermline Athletic	1885	East End Park	–	2	2	–	2	–	–
East Fife	1903	Bayview (Methill)	–	–	1	–	1	3	–
East Stirlingshire	1881	Firs Park (Falkirk)	–	–	1	–	–	–	–
Falkirk	1876	Brockville	–	2	4	–	2	–	–
Forfar Athletic	1885	Station Park	–	–	1	1	–	–	–
Hamilton Academicals	1875	Douglas Park	–	2	1	–	–	–	–
Heart of Midlothian	1874	Tynecastle (Edinburgh)	–	5	–	–	6	4	–
Hibernian	1875	Easter Road (Edinburgh)	–	6	3	–	2	2	–
Inverness Caledonian Thistle	1994	Caledonian Stadium	–	–	–	1	–	–	–
Kilmarnock	1869	Rugby Park	–	1	2	–	3	–	–
Livingston	1995	Almondvale	–	–	1	1	–	–	–
Meadowbank Thistle	1974	Meadowbank	–	–	1	–	–	–	–
Montrose	1879	Links Park	–	–	1	–	–	–	–
Morton	1874	Cappielow (Greenock)	–	3	4	–	1	–	–
Motherwell	1886	Fir Park	–	3	2	–	2	1	–

Club	Founded	Ground	Prem Div	1st Div	2nd Div	3rd Div	Scottish Cup	League Cup	Europe
Partick Thistle	1876	Firhill (Glasgow)	–	1	3	–	1	1	–
Queen of the South	1919	Palmerston (Dumfries)	–	–	1	–	–	–	–
Queen's Park	1867	Hampden (Glasgow)	–	–	3	1	10	–	–
Raith Rovers	1883	Stark's Park	–	2	4	–	–	1	–
Rangers	1883	Ibrox (Glasgow)	14	35	–	–	29	21	1
Ross County	1929	Victoria Park	–	–	–	1	–	–	–
St Johnstone	1884	McDiarmid Park (Perth)	–	3	3	–	–	–	–
St Mirren	1877	Love St (Paisley)	–	2	1	–	3	–	–
Stenhousemuir	1884	Ochilview Park	–	–	–	–	–	–	–
Stirling Albion	1945	Annfield Park	–	–	7	–	–	–	–
Stranraer	1870	Stair Park	–	–	2	–	–	–	–

Pre 1976 the winners of the First Division were League Champions.
After 1976 this accolade went to winners of the Premier Division.

LEAGUE CHAMPIONS AND CUP WINNERS (1873–1999)

Season	Scottish League	Scottish Cup
1873–74		Queen's Park
1874–75		Queen's Park
1875–76		Queen's Park
1876–77		Vale of Leven
1877–78		Vale of Leven
1878–79		Vale of Leven
1879–80		Queen's Park
1880–81		Queen's Park
1881–82		Queen's Park
1882–83		Dumbarton
1883–84		Queen's Park
1884–85		Renton
1885–86		Queen's Park
1886–87		Hibernian
1887–88		Renton
1888–89		Third Lanark
1889–90		Queen's Park
1890–91	Dumbarton/Rangers (shared)	Hearts
1891–92	Dumbarton	Celtic
1892–93	Celtic	Queen's Park

	Premier Div	1st Div	2nd Div	3rd Div	Scottish Cup	League Cup
893–94		Celtic	Hibernian		Rangers	
894–95		Hearts	Hibernian		St Bernard's	
895–96		Celtic	Abercorn		Hearts	
896–97		Hearts	Partick Thistle		Rangers	
897–98		Celtic	Kilmarnock		Rangers	
898–99		Rangers	Kilmarnock		Celtic	
899–00		Rangers	Partick Thistle		Celtic	
900–00		Rangers	St Bernard's		Hearts	
901–02		Rangers	Port Glasgow		Hibernian	
902–03		Hibernian	Airdrie		Rangers	
903–04		Third Lanark	Hamilton		Celtic	
904–05		Celtic	Clyde		Third Lanark	
905–06		Celtic	Leith A		Hearts	
906–07		Celtic	St Bernard's		Celtic	
907–08		Celtic	Raith Rovers		Celtic	
908–09		Celtic	Abercorn		(Withheld)	
909–10		Celtic	Leith/Raith		Dundee	
910–11		Rangers	Dumbarton		Celtic	
911–12		Rangers	Ayr Utd		Celtic	
912–13		Rangers	Ayr Utd		Falkirk	
913–14		Celtic	Cowdenbeath		Celtic	
914–15		Celtic	Cowdenbeath			
915–16		Celtic				
916–17		Celtic				
917–18		Rangers				
918–19		Celtic				
919–20		Rangers			Kilmarnock	
920–21		Rangers			Partick Thistle	
921–22		Celtic	Alloa Athletic		Morton	
922–23		Rangers	Queen's Park		Celtic	
923–24		Rangers	St Johnstone		Airdrie	
924–25		Rangers	Dundee Utd		Celtic	
925–26		Celtic	Dunfermline		St Mirren	
926–27		Rangers	Bo'ness		Celtic	
927–28		Rangers	Ayr Utd		Rangers	
928–29		Rangers	Dundee Utd		Kilmarnock	
929–00		Rangers	Leith A		Rangers	
930–31		Rangers	Third Lanark		Celtic	
931–32		Motherwell	East Stirling		Rangers	
932–33		Rangers	Hibernian		Celtic	
933–34		Rangers	Albion Rovers		Rangers	
934–35		Rangers	Third Lanark		Rangers	
935–36		Celtic	Falkirk		Rangers	
936–37		Rangers	Ayr Utd		Celtic	
937–38		Celtic	Raith Rovers		East Fife	
938–39		Rangers	Cowdenbeath		Clyde	
946–47		Rangers	Dundee		Aberdeen	Rangers
947–48		Hibernian	East Fife		Rangers	East Fife
948–49		Rangers	Raith Rovers		Rangers	Rangers
949–50		Rangers	Morton		Rangers	East Fife
950–51		Hibernian	QoS		Celtic	Motherwell

	Premier Div	1st Div	2nd Div	3rd Div	Scottish Cup	League Cup
1951–52		Hibernian	Clyde		Motherwell	Dundee
1952–53		Rangers	Stirling Albion		Rangers	Dundee
1953–54		Celtic	Motherwell		Celtic	East Fife
1954–55		Aberdeen	Airdrie		Clyde	Hearts
1955–56		Rangers	Queen's Park		Hearts	Aberdeen
1956–57		Rangers	Clyde		Falkirk	Celtic
1957–58		Hearts	Stirling Albion		Clyde	Celtic
1958–59		Rangers	Ayr Utd		St Mirren	Hearts
1959–60		Hearts	St Johnstone		Rangers	Hearts
1960–61		Rangers	Stirling Albion		Dunfermline	Rangers
1961–62		Dundee	Clyde		Rangers	Rangers
1962–63		Rangers	St Johnstone		Rangers	Hearts
1963–64		Rangers	Morton		Rangers	Rangers
1964–65		Kilmarnock	Stirling Albion		Celtic	Rangers
1965–66		Celtic	Ayr Utd		Rangers	Celtic
1966–67		Celtic	Morton		Celtic	Celtic
1967–68		Celtic	St Mirren		Dunfermline	Celtic
1968–69		Celtic	Motherwell		Celtic	Celtic
1969–70		Celtic	Falkirk		Aberdeen	Celtic
1970–71		Celtic	Partick Thistle		Celtic	Rangers
1971–72		Celtic	Dumbarton		Celtic	Partick Thistle
1972–73		Celtic	Clyde		Rangers	Hibernian
1973–74		Celtic	Airdrie		Celtic	Dundee
1974–75		Rangers	Falkirk		Celtic	Celtic
1975–76	Rangers	Partick Thistle	Clydebank		Rangers	Rangers
1976–77	Celtic	St Mirren	Stirling Albion		Celtic	Aberdeen
1977–78	Rangers	Morton	Clyde		Rangers	Rangers
1978–79	Celtic	Dundee	Berwick R		Rangers	Rangers
1979–80	Aberdeen	Hearts	Falkirk		Celtic	Dundee Utd
1980–81	Celtic	Hibernian	Queen's Park		Rangers	Dundee Utd
1981–82	Celtic	Motherwell	Clyde		Aberdeen	Rangers
1982–83	Dundee Utd	St Johnstone	Brechin		Aberdeen	Celtic
1983–84	Aberdeen	Morton	Forfar A		Aberdeen	Rangers
1984–85	Aberdeen	Motherwell	Montrose		Celtic	Rangers
1985–86	Celtic	Hamilton	Dunfermline		Aberdeen	Aberdeen
1986–87	Rangers	Morton	Meadowbank		St Mirren	Rangers
1987–88	Celtic	Hamilton	Ayr Utd		Celtic	Rangers
1988–89	Rangers	Dunfermline	Albion Rovers		Celtic	Rangers
1989–90	Rangers	St Johnstone	Brechin		Aberdeen	Aberdeen
1990–91	Rangers	Falkirk	Stirling Albion		Motherwell	Rangers
1991–92	Rangers	Dundee	Dumbarton		Rangers	Hibernian
1992–93	Rangers	Raith Rovers	Clyde		Rangers	Rangers
1993–94	Rangers	Falkirk	Stranraer		Dundee Utd	Rangers
1994–95	Rangers	Raith Rovers	Morton	Forfar	Celtic	Raith Rovers
1995–96	Rangers	Dunfermline A	Stirling Albion	Livingston	Rangers	Aberdeen
1996–97	Rangers	St Johnstone	Ayr Utd	Inverness CT	Kilmarnock	Rangers
1997–98	Celtic	Dundee	Stranraer	Alloa	Hearts	Celtic
1998–99	Rangers	Hibs	Livingston	Ross County	Rangers	Rangers
1999–2000	Rangers	St Mirren	Clyde	Queen's Park	Rangers	Celtic

FORBES, Alexander Penrose (1817–75)
Bishop

After education at Oxford, Forbes became an **Episcopalian** priest influenced by Pusey and the Oxford Movement. As Bishop of **Brechin** from 1848 he built St Paul's Church, **Dundee**, enlarged as his cathedral in 1865. Censured by fellow bishops in a heresy trial in 1860, he nevertheless wrote works of scholarship, editing The Arbuthnot Missal and Kalendars of Scottish Saints.

FORBES, Duncan, of Culloden (1685–1747)
Lord Advocate

Born at Bunchrew, near **Inverness**, educated at **Edinburgh** and Leyden, admitted advocate, and appointed Sheriff of **Midlothian** (1709), Duncan Forbes became one of Scotland's best loved and most trusted judges. A staunch **Whig**, he supported the government in the 1715 **Jacobite Rising** but advocated leniency for the rebels thereafter, protesting against their trial in England and opposing forfeiture of their estates. He succeeded **Robert Dundas** as Lord Advocate (1725) and promptly incurred public censure for ordering **General Wade** to restore order after the **Shawfield Riots** (1725), but earned public gratitude for managing to limit the punishment meted out to the city of Edinburgh after the **Porteous Riots** (1736).

President of the **Court of Session** (1737), he was commissioned by his patron, **John Campbell 2nd Duke of Argyll**, to inquire into conditions on Campbell estates on the islands of **Mull** and **Tiree**; his cogent report, accepted and acted upon by the Duke, recommended the abolition of **tacksmen** who 'exercised a pernicious influence, oppressing the sub-tenants with onerous duties and resisting all attempts at improvement' (W Ferguson). Laird of the Culloden estate near Inverness from the death of his brother (c1735), and thus on intimate terms with most of the chiefs of the Highland **clans**, whether Whig or Jacobite, Forbes's canny diplomatic skills dissuaded many north-eastern Jacobites from joining **Prince Charles Edward Stewart** in the '45, but his pleas for leniency for the Jacobites in the immediate aftermath of **Culloden** were ignored by the vindictive Duke of Cumberland.

FORBES, James David (1809–68) Physicist

Born in **Edinburgh**, J D Forbes became Professor of Natural Philosophy at **Edinburgh University** at the age of 24, specialising in research on the polarisation of radiant heat and contributing to the concept of a continuous radiation spectrum. He also studied glacier composition in Norway and the Alps, while at home he helped reform Scotland's universities by instituting examinations for degrees. In **Skye** he made the first recorded ascents of several peaks in the **Cuillins**, thus pioneering Scottish **climbing**. He was also the first Honorary President of the Alpine Club, founded in London in 1857.

FORBES, William (c1671–1745) Professor of Law

Not much is known of Forbes's early life. His father was Public Professor of Medicine at the University of **Pisa**. The family had **Aberdeen** connections and William may have taken his degree at **Aberdeen University**.

He was admitted advocate in 1696. In 1702 he became Clerk of the Faculty, which involved him in the education and guidance of young advocates. In 1705 he was approved by the Faculty as the Collector of Court Decisions. He continued this task for a number of years and the decisions were published in 1714 as the Journal of the Session containing decisions from June 1705 until November 1713.

In 1714 he was appointed the first Regius Professor of **Law** in the **University of Glasgow** – a considerable achievement and one which enhanced the University's standing and revived law teaching there. His academic position enabled him to produce a number of modern style texts including 'On Elections' (1700), 'The Duty and Powers of Justices of the Peace in this part of Great Britain called Scotland' and a methodical treatise concerning 'Bills of Exchange According to the Analogy of the Law of Scotland' (both 1703) and a 'Treatise on Church Lands and Tithes' (1705). His later book the Institutes of the Law of Scotland was a student textbook published in 1722. Unfortunately his magnum opus, the Great Body of the Law of Scotland, was not published, possibly because it was too great; a manuscript version occupies much space in Glasgow University Library.

FORDELL CASTLE, Fife

Between **Dunfermline** and **Aberdour**, Fordell is a restored Z-plan tower house, four storeys high and dating from the 16th century. The ground floor is vaulted, the coat of arms over the doorway that of the Henderson family who were granted Fordell's lands in 1511. **Queen Mary**'s Room records the Queen's visit for the marriage of one of her maids of honour with a Henderson in 1580. Externally two angle turrets, a caphouse on one tower and a parapet on the other, with dormers and a notable gargoyle, make for a dramatic skyline.

FORDUN (or Fordoun), John of (c1320–c1387) Chronicler

Little is known of the early life and career of this 14th century chronicler save that he might have been a minor priest in **Aberdeen**. He was certainly a Latin scholar of some distinction, and his Chronica gentis Scotorum formed the basis of Walter Bower's 15th century Scotichronicon, the most important source book of Scottish medieval history. Fordun's work has been described as 'an apologia for Scottish independence' full of 'argumentative patriotism' (R Nicholson); it covers the period up to 1383.

FORDYCE, Banffshire

Three miles inland from **Portsoy**, this unspoilt village has Fordyce Castle as a feature of its main street. The L-plan tower house dates from 1592 and was built by Thomas Menzies, an **Aberdeen** merchant; besides the usual crow-stepped gables and angle turrets, the corbelling is especially notable. The ruins of an old church dedicated to St Tarquin (Tarkin, Talacritan) lie to the north. Here too is a burial aisle of the Abercrombys of Glasshaugh whose no longer stately home lies on the road to Sandend, itself an erstwhile **fishing** village. The Ogilvie stronghold of Findlater Castle grew from the cliffs between Sandend and **Cullen**; but little now remains of what must once have been a grimly romantic fortalice.

FORESTRY

Once covered mainly by forest, Scotland now appears to be covered mainly by forestry. With over a million hectares of 'productive woodland' the country has as much forestry as England and Wales combined. But whereas in England and Wales half the afforested area is broad-leaved woodland, in Scotland less than 10% falls in this category; the rest, over 90%, is a dense coniferous monoculture of mainly non-native species, either sitka spruce, Japanese larch or lodgepole pine. Planted in serried ranks over vast areas of the Highlands and south-west during the last 40 years, this afforestation has wrought a visual and social change comparable with that of the **clearances**. It has also boosted the output of timber so that about 14% of the UK's timber requirement is now met from UK forests. This figure is expected to continue to rise slightly ahead of the general increase in consumption.

About half of Scotland's forestry is owned by the state and managed as a public sector enterprise by the **Forestry Commission**. The other half, in private ownership, owes much to Forestry Commission grants and expertise and to government fiscal incentives. Forestry employs directly and on contract about 12,000 people plus another 3000 in the wood processing industry, making it third only to **agriculture** and **tourism** as a rural job-provider.

The planned management of woodland began in the 18th century when agricultural improvers such as **Archibald Grant of Monymusk** and **Robert Barclay of Urie** planted trees for their shelter and amenity value as much as for timber production. In the north-east Grant is said to have planted 5 million trees while, in the 19th century, **George Gordon 4th Earl of Aberdeen** planted 14 million. Victorian landowners like Gordon planted their policies with mixed species, many of them exotica. Woodland management was in the interests of sport and scenic effect, priorities which came in for weighty criticism in the 1917 Acland Report which led to the setting up of the Forestry Commission. Ironically the same priorities, rephrased in terms agreeable to the environmental and tourism lobbies, now feature prominently in the Commission's own manifestos. 'Sustainable' and 'multi-purpose' management, rather than timber production, is emphasised; the stress is on the recreational and conservationist credentials of what is less a 'forestry industry' and more a 'woodland enterprise'.

The Commission's conversion from amenity poacher to keeper of the natural heritage is belated but praiseworthy. Attempts to promote the same awareness amongst private forest owners and management groups have yet to produce comparable results. It thus remains to be seen whether either continued government encouragement of private sector forestry, or indeed the privatisation of government forestry, will represent an acceptable development.

FORESTRY COMMISSION, The

The Commission is a UK government department which manages state-owned forests and is responsible for their production and amenities while also acting as an advisory and implementing body for government **forestry** policy towards both the public and the private sectors. In recognition of the fact that half this forestry is in Scotland, the Commission is based in **Edinburgh** with regional offices throughout the UK.

It was founded in 1919 by Lloyd George's coalition government following a report from a committee under Sir Richard Acland set up by the Asquith government in 1916. World War I, and particularly the demands of trench warfare, highlighted the nation's dependence on timber imports. Acland believed that native forest resources, decimated by the demands of the Industrial Revolution and neglected by the changing pattern of land ownership, could be restored by a state organisation co-ordinating reafforestation through the acquisition and management of land for forestry, through the encouragement and establishment of forest industries, and through research and promotion. The remit given to Lord Lovat, the Commission's first Chairman, was to establish by the end of the century a state forest resource of 715,000ha (in 1992 the total had actually reached 855,000ha), and to encourage private owners to repair wartime ravages and maintain productively 1.2 million hectares (in 1992 1.3 million) of their own woodland as insurance against future emergencies and wars.

Steady progress towards these targets was made during the inter-war years and although World War II did not pose the same timber demands as World War I, consumption continued to escalate. Industry was particularly voracious with wooden pit props being essential to **coal-mining** well into the 1960s. After the war afforestation was therefore accelerated, most notably under the Labour governments of 1964–71. Socialists welcomed the prospect of more land being brought into public ownership and there was an increasing awareness of the recreational importance of forests. Countryside Acts granted the Commission powers to provide facilities for the public; forest trails, parks and lodges began to proliferate. A 1972 review of forestry policy highlighted the Commission's responsibilities as a rural employer and environmental guardian and in 1985 the Wildlife and Countryside (Amendment) Act formalised the Commission's management policy as 'multi-purpose' with commercial timber production being balanced against concern for the environment, species conservation, public recreation and the aesthetics of the landscape. Since then the balance has, if anything, tilted further towards these latter concerns.

In 1992 the Commission was itself reorganised into two units roughly corresponding to its original dual role. Thus Forest Enterprise is now responsible for the management of state-owned forests while the Forest Authority administers government policy to privately-owned woodland and is responsible for research. The analogous division of other state-owned industries prior to their privatisation has been noted.

FORFAR, Angus

A **royal burgh** of some importance, Forfar was described by Edward I as 'a gude town'. Latterly, as the county town of **Angus**, it found less favour. Thomas Morer in 1689 judged it 'a place of no great noise' and *Murray's Guide* of 1898 a 'by no means attractive town'.

the chimney stacks, evidence of Forfar's thriving textile mills, which so upset Murray's contributor, are now gone; Forfar today keeps a low profile.

Situated at the north-east end of the Howe of Angus, the site is said to have witnessed one of the last battles between the **Picts** and the Scots in 845. The burgh was founded in the reign of **David I** whose father, **Malcolm II 'Canmore'**, is said to have held a parliament here in 1057 at which he conferred surnames and titles on the Scottish nobility. The site of his castle is now marked by an octagonal turret which, though formerly the town's cross, was probably not the cross against which a small girl's brains were dashed out in 1230; her only crime was that of being a MacWilliam at a time when MacWilliams were in revolt against **Alexander II**.

In the 17th century Forfar witnessed further sanguinary repression when numerous witches were convicted and burnt. The town's museum contains the notorious 'witch's bridle', an iron gag which was clamped round the victim's head with two spikes that fitted inside the mouth. Witches were not necessarily female. One of the last Forfar convictions for sorcery was of a man. After various methods of torture had been tried to make him confess, without effect, he was at last suspended by the genitals, which produced a confession' (D Webster).

Forfar Town Hall dates from 1788 and the County Buildings from 1873. On the edge of town are the ruins of **Restenneth Priory**.

FORMORIANS

From the early Irish *fomor* and the Gaelic *famhair*, Formorians were giants. In Ireland they may have been giant pirates but in Scotland they mostly dwelt in mountains and were once very numerous. They were usually found in pairs, any free-standing boulders in their vicinity being the result of bombardment, a favourite pastime, in which one Formorian attempted to dislodge another. Some flung battle-axes or quoits; **Hugh Miller** heard of two Formorian cobblers on the opposing headlands of the Cromarty Firth who, having only one set of tools, habitually hurled them back and forth. Another story relates that in a contest between all the Scottish Formorians it was he of Ben Ledi near **Callander** who won; a large rock on the eastern slope of the hill was long known as 'Samson's putting stone'. Evidently Formorian tradition was highly eclectic and readily assimilated biblical figures (such as Samson) and Arthurian heroes (hence **Arthur's Seat** in **Edinburgh**). The same gigantising process was extended to St Patrick (Craig Phadraig near **Inverness**), the Fingalian heroes, **Thomas the Rhymer**, **William Wallace** and **Alexander Stewart** (the 'Wolf of **Badenoch**'). See D A Mackenzie, *Scottish Folklore and Folk Life*, 1935.

FORRES, Moray

A town of great antiquity, Forres was well chosen by Shakespeare, if not by history, as the main setting of *Macbeth* and the place of Banquo's murder. The 'blasted heath' where the two first encountered the witches is supposedly at the Knock of Alves to the east or on 'MacBeth's Hillock' to the west. The 'Palace of Forres' would have been the now vanished castle on Castlehill; there stands in its stead a granite obelisk commemorating James Thomson, a hero of the Crimean War. King

Sueno's Stone, Forres, the tallest and most intricately carved Pictish cross-slab (HS)

Dubh (or Duffus) is said to have been murdered here in 967.

Though the identification of Forres with Ptolemy's 'Varris' is uncertain, there can be no doubt about the antiquity of the so-called Sueno's Stone. It has nothing to do with Shakespeare's Sueno, otherwise Swein Forkbeard, King of Denmark (d1014), but it may well commemorate an earlier battle between native **Picts** and invading Scots. 9th or 10th century and over 6.5m high, it may also be the latest and is certainly the tallest and most elaborately sculpted of all the surviving Pictish cross-slabs. The face without a cross is divided into five crowded panels which, like a strip cartoon, may be read as the narrative of an extremely gory battle and provide an unusually detailed insight into Pictish militaria. 'This is war reporting on a monumentally self-confident scale' (I A G Shepherd). The Witches' Stone, also east of the town centre, is neither Pictish nor Shakespearian but marks the spot where real witches were burnt after having been rolled down Cluny Hill in barrels. The last such bonfire was 200 years ago.

Little of this antiquity is evident in the town's architecture. St Lawrence's parish church and the Town House are both variants of 19th century Gothic. The mercat cross dates from 1844 and the Falconer Museum, neo-classical, from 1870. Founded by **Hugh Falconer** and his brother, it reflects the former's interests – **geology**, botany and India. The 70ft (21m) octagonal tower on Cluny Hill commemorates Lord Nelson and affords fine views. So does Blervie Castle, four miles south, which like its nearby twin, Burgie Castle, is a tower of about 1600. Both were once parts of Z-plan fortalices belonging to the Dunbar family.

FORREST, George (1873–1932) Botanist and Plant-hunter

Born in **Falkirk**, George Forrest went to Australia in his twenties to seek his fortune; unsuccessful, he returned to Scotland and worked for two years in the herbarium of the **Royal Botanic Garden, Edinburgh**. In 1904 he was sent by the **cotton**-broker Arthur Bulley to collect plants in the Yunnan province of western China, the first of seven expeditions to a region of immense botanical and horticultural interest. During 17 years of active plant-hunting he gathered over 30,000 herbarium species, many thousands of packets of seeds and a superb collection of photographs. His important introductions to British gardens included lilies, primulas, gentians, conifers and especially rhododendrons, over 300 of which were described as new species. *Rhododendron forrestii* (named in his honour) is a dwarf species with deep crimson flowers. Forrest proved popular with the native Chinese who assisted in collecting seeds, but had some alarming adventures during border clashes with the Tibetans. He died in China in 1932 of a heart attack while shooting game.

FORSYTH, Alexander (1768–1843) Inventor

Born at Belhelvie, **Aberdeenshire**, Forsyth appears to have graduated at **Aberdeen** at the age of 17 and became a minister. An accomplished shot, he invented a percussion lock to improve contemporary firearms by detonating gunpowder by hammer rather than by a spark. Forsyth's invention eventually entered army use without his knowledge, a government pension being belatedly allocated to him; its first instalment arrived on the day of his death.

FORT AUGUSTUS, Inverness-shire

Before it became the hub of **General Wade**'s network of **military roads** (Inverness-Fort William, Corrie-yairack-Glenelg), Fort Augustus at the head of **Loch Ness** consisted of the hamlet of Kilchumein (named after the Celtic St Chumein) and a barracks established after the 1715 **Jacobite Rising** (of which a vestige remains in the grounds of the Lovat Arms Hotel). In 1730 Wade replaced the latter with his four-bastioned fort and named it with uncanny prescience after the nine-year-old William Augustus, Duke of Cumberland. 16 years later, after a few months in Jacobite hands, the fort became the residence of the Duke who used it as a hunting lodge whence to flush out and butcher the fugitives from **Culloden**. Trophies included the head of Roderick Mackenzie which so resembled that of **Prince Charles Edward** [see **Invermoriston**]. **Dr Johnson** reckoned he had his best night's sleep ever in the fort and **Boswell** noted that, in addition to a fine garden, the garrison could rely on provisions being supplied by a sloop which plied to Inverness.

The fort was still garrisoned when the Caledonian **Canal** opened (1822, with an impressive sequence of locks climbing from Loch Ness) but was sold off in 1867 for £5000 to, ironically, Lord Lovat, descendant of an executed Jacobite. He presented it to the Benedictine order (1867) whose monastery became a school in

1878 and an abbey in 1882, the first monks having come from Ratisbon (Regensburg) which had itself been founded by St Marianus from **Dunkeld** in the 11th century. The school closed for lack of pupils in 1993 and the abbey for lack of monks in 1998. Much of the ground floor of Wade's fort is incorporated into the abbey's buildings which include a cloister (1893) by the younger Pugin and church (1914) by **Reginald Fairlie**. Fort Augustus also has a **Great Glen** Heritage Centre and **Forestry Commission** attractions.

FORT GEORGE, Nr Ardersier, Inverness-shire

Dr Johnson declared Fort George 'the most regular fortification in the island [of Great Britain]'; so it remains. Built (1747–70) in response to the 1745 **Jacobite Rising**, and completed three years before Johnson and **Boswell**'s visit, its defences have never been tested and retain their complex design in pristine condition. The fort stands on 42 acres (17ha) of a sandy promontory that juts out into the Moray Firth 9 miles east of **Inverness**. With sea on three sides its polygonal ramparts have four bastions commanding the seaward approaches but reserve the full Vaubanesque vocabulary of ravelins, lunettes, etc for the landward approach to the east.

Curiously Johnson and Boswell were here entertained by Sir Eyre Coote, the East India Company veteran whose last posting had been as Commander-in-Chief at Fort St George (Madras), a complex closely resembling its near-namesake. Like his counterparts in India, William Skinner, Fort George's designer, had evidently studied his Vauban. Coote was in command of the Fort's garrison which consisted of two regiments. With their stores, powder, ordnance, etc, they were housed in the splendid buildings and terraces grouped round the central parade ground. These were designed and built by **William** and John **Adam** (assisted by **Robert** and **James**) and are still in use as barracks. Parts of the Fort have now been laid out for visitor appeal whilst elsewhere are housed the **Queen's Own Highlanders'** museum and the Seafield collection of militaria, previously kept in **Castle Grant**.

FORT WILLIAM, Inverness-shire

At the head of Loch Linnhe and the entrance to the **Great Glen**, with intersecting routes to **Badenoch** and **Skye**, Fort William's position and strategic importance mirror those of **Inverness**. Devoid of character and deluged by double the latter's rainfall, the town compensates with the proximity of **Ben Nevis** and a spectacular variety of scenery ranging from the Elysian to the Siberian. **General Monk** built the first fort at the mouth of the river Ness in 1654 and named it **Inverlochy** after that which it replaced a mile to the north at the mouth of the Lochy. The adjacent village, dependent on the **herring** fishery and occupying what is now the centre of the town, was known as Gordonsburgh after its Gordon proprietors. In 1690 the fort was greatly enlarged by **General Hugh Mackay of Scourie** and renamed Fort William while Gordonsburgh became Maryburgh (after the joint sovereigns). The fort held out against the **Jacobites** in both 1715 and, after further work by **General Wade**, in 1745. Maryburgh, briefly reverting to Gordonsburgh and then to Duncansburgh, lost its iden-

ity in the 19th century at about the same time as the fort was demolished to make way for the **railway** station (itself now moved to make way for the lochside bypass and a supermarket). The only building of merit is the adjacent St Andrew's Episcopal Church, with spire, of 1880.

In the 19th century the railway, the Caledonian **Canal**, and the west coast steamers transformed the place into a busy **tourist** centre. It remains so with ribbon developments of hotels and guest houses at Achintore along the shore of Loch Linnhe to the south and much activity on the approach roads to the Aonach More **ski** centre to the north-west. Aluminium and wood processing were supposed to elevate the town to industrial prominence in the 20th century. They have left their mark at Caol, Inverlochy and **Corpach** round the head of the loch. The town centre consists of a long High Street off which Cameron Square accommodates the West Highland Museum's collection of local history from Neolithic to Jacobite times. They include the helmet worn by **James Graham, Marquis of Montrose** and victor at the **Battle of Inverlochy**.

FORTH RAILWAY BRIDGE

Situated at the **Queensferry** Narrows, spanning the Firth of Forth about nine miles west of **Edinburgh**, the Forth Railway Bridge has become, like the Eiffel Tower for France or the Taj Mahal for India, the one immediately and internationally recognised Scottish landmark, the construction of which was the greatest single achievement by Britain's 19th century engineers.

Ferries had plied across this narrow part of the Forth estuary for centuries, but the spread of the **railway**

system made improved communications across the Firth imperative, and in 1873 the Forth Bridge Railway Company was set up. The bridge would have to be enormous, to allow 150ft (46m) headroom for ships, yet capable of carrying heavy loads over a 1½ mile distance. Thomas Bouch was appointed designer, but no sooner had he begun preparations for his grandiose suspension bridge, with a central tower 550ft (168m) high, than his **Tay Bridge** collapsed with heavy loss of life; the Forth project was cancelled. Pressure from English railway interests led to it being resurrected, and Sir John Fowler and Benjamin Baker were appointed engineers, with **William Arrol** as principal contractor. This proved to be a winning combination, Fowler and Baker choosing a cantilever principle with three diamond-shaped steel towers 340ft (104m) high carrying a double rail-line 150ft (46m) above high water, and with massive stone approach viaducts to north and south.

Seven years' labour, in which 57 men lost their lives, saw the structure completed. 55,000 tons of steel, 640,000 cu ft (18,122 cu m) of Aberdeen granite, 62,000 cu ft (1755 cu m) of masonry, and 8 million rivets were used in the construction. The last rivet was ceremoniously driven home by the Prince of Wales (later Edward VII) on 4 March 1890, after which the bridge became a vital link for rail services between London, Edinburgh, **Dundee** and **Aberdeen**. Its owning company, the Forth Bridge Railway, was nationalised on 1 January 1948, along with the railway it carries.

Less well known than the Forth Rail Bridge at Queensferry was the 21-arch rail bridge opened in 1885 across the river Forth near Throsk on the line between Larbert and **Alloa**. Complete with steam-powered opening arch, the 492m-long structure carried passenger trains until 1968.

Forth Railway Bridge under construction; one of a series of photographs by George Washington Wilson (entry p. 409) (GWWA)

FORTINGALL, Perthshire

At the entrance to **Glen Lyon**, Fortingall abounds in evidence of its antiquity, including three stone circle arrangements, a Neolithic **cairn**, a **standing stone**, a cup-marked stone, and a medieval homestead once thought to have been **Roman**. The Roman connection persists in the oft-repeated tradition that Pontius Pilate was born in Fortingall, the child of a Roman emissary and a local girl. A rather dishevelled yew tree, supposedly 2–3000 years old and which had a girth of 56½ feet (17m) when measured by Pennant in 1769, still stands (with support) in the churchyard. In the church are a font and 7th century bell said to have been used by **St Adamnan**. James MacGregor (d1551), previously **Dean of Lismore** and compiler of the eponymous Gaelic manuscript, was minister here. The village's neat cottages and the buildings of Glen Lyon Estate are largely 19th century neo-vernacular creations designed by J M MacLaren for Sir Donald Currie.

FORTROSE, Ross & Cromarty

Fortrose and adjacent Rosemarkie stand either side of a long promontory that points from the **Black Isle** into the Moray Firth towards **Fort George**; a ferry once plied across the intervening water (less than a mile). From this promontory, or ross, derives the 'ross' or 'rose' in both Fort-rose and Rose-markie as well as in the Bishopric, **Earldom** and **county** of **Ross**. The promontory is now called Chanonry point and has a **golf course** at the landward end and a lighthouse at its tip. There is a cairn and plaque identifying the site where **Coinneach**

Odhar, 'the Brahan seer', is supposed to have been burnt; the century, let alone the year, is uncertain but the location seems probable, there being a pillar on the ross where witches were burnt. It is claimed that the last witch so to suffer in Scotland died here; but last witches were burnt, as last wolves were shot, in altogether too many places.

Rosemarkie was the site of the first church, possibly established by **St Moluag** in the 6th century or by St Curitan in the 8th. Presumably the Bishops of Ross were based here in the 12th century but in the 13th Bishop Robert (1214–49) commenced building a new cathedral at Fortrose. It was completed in the 15th century, unroofed in the 16th and raided for masonry to build **Inverness** citadel in the 17th. The ground-plan has been unearthed but the only standing structures are two disjointed sections that were originally appendages to the church. The smaller is a rectangular building that adjoined the north wall of the choir; it includes a ground-floor chamber with stone vaulting (13th century) which may have served as the chapter house. The larger section is the roofless shell of the south aisle (14th–15th centuries) which adjoined the nave. It is supposed to have been the work of **Euphemia, Countess of Ross**, who numbered amongst her husbands **Alexander Stewart**, the 'Wolf of **Badenoch**', destroyer of **Elgin Cathedral**. One of three surviving tombs is thought to be hers. The north range served as a tolbooth and gaol in the 18th century which no doubt explains why the little bell tower on the outside wall of the south aisle now has a pointed roof, weathervane and clock.

FORTUNE, Robert (1812–80) Plant Collector

Born at Edrom in the Borders, Robert Fortune worked

at both the **Royal Botanic Garden, Edinburgh** and the Horticultural Society's garden at Chiswick in London. His first plant collecting expedition to China was in 1843 and lasted for three years. His horticulturally valuable collections included chrysanthemums, camellias and azaleas. To avoid recognition as a foreigner he adopted Chinese dress. On his return to Britain he spent a short time as curator of Chelsea Physic Garden before embarking for the Far East again to research the cultivation of tea and collect tea cultivars for growing in India. He retired in 1862.

FOSSILS

Scotland's oldest fossils occur in the Torridonian Sandstone of the north-western Highlands, where microfossils of algal spores have been found, perhaps 1000 million years old. Fossil evidence from the Scottish Highlands is not common, however, because most rocks were metamorphosed during successive mountainbuilding episodes which converted sedimentary rocks – together with their fossils – into schists, gneisses and slates which form the bulk of the mountains. Fossils cannot occur in any rocks derived from magma, such as lava, gabbro and granite.

Fossils from late Pre-Cambrian (Dalradian) rocks have been found in a few localities. Fossilised algae – stromatolites – are preserved in **Islay** and the **Garvellach Islands** dating back 650 million years. More certain Cambrian age fossils have been recognised from the youngest Dalradian rocks near **Callander**, which yielded trilobites, a marine arthropod typical of Lower Palaeozoic times (Cambrian to Silurian). In north-western Scotland the narrow outcrop of Cambrian-Ordovician limestones and quartzites are well known for their marine faunas, particularly the spectacular 'Pipe Rock' seen around **Assynt**. The pipes are burrows of segmented worms, only the burrow is preserved, the soft-bodied worms disintegrating after death. Other creatures around at this time were trilobites, brachiopods and early molluscs, all of which had developed hard parts which survived the process of fossilisation.

The Southern Upland Ordovician and Silurian rocks were not as thoroughly deformed as those in the **Grampians** and have thus preserved a better fossil record. Charles Lapworth's studies of graptolite faunas around **Moffat** in the 1870s were a classic model of how fossils could be used to correlate and date rocks. Graptolites were a common marine organism in Lower Palaeozoic times, floating colonies of polyps whose branching and pendulous forms were preserved in the black Moffat shales as films of carbon and silica. Within the Midland Valley are Ordovician and Silurian 'inliers', older rocks surrounded by younger ones. Some have exquisitely preserved fossils, especially early fish and arthropods. Best known are the superb Silurian 'eurypterids' of **Lesmahagow**, ferocious marine scorpions which grew to two metres in length. Excellent examples can be seen in the **Royal Museum, Edinburgh**.

The Old Red Sandstone outcrops of the Midland Valley and **Caithness/Orkney** have long been famous for fossil fish, collections of which were first made by Robert Dick of **Thurso** in the 1840s and by **Hugh Miller**, the celebrated **Cromarty** stonemason. Early jawless, armoured fish characterise the lower sandstones in the eastern Midland Valley, but the most famous fish beds come from the Middle Old Red Sandstone of Caithness. Here flagstones were deposited in the Orcadian Lake which periodically dried up, killing large numbers of fish such as the scaly Osteolepis and the lung-fish Dipterus. Some of the most spectacular fish beds came from the Upper Old Red Sandstone at Dura Den, **Fife**.

The Old Red Sandstone is also notable for its plant fossils, the most important being from the Rhynie Chert of **Aberdeenshire**. This ancient **peat** deposit was flooded by silica-rich volcanic water, which effectively preserved the tender stems of some of the earliest known plants on earth.

The Carboniferous is perhaps the richest geological period for fossils. Outcrops are confined to the Midland Valley, Borders and **Dumfries** where most fossils are preserved in sequences of limestone, shale, **coal** and sandstone – typical deposits of lagoonal, lacustrine and marine conditions. Land floras are best appreciated at **Glasgow**'s Victoria Park Fossil Grove [see **Geology**]. Limestone preserves rich shelly faunas of brachiopods, corals, crinoids and bivalves many of which lived and died around the Midland Valley's coral reefs at this time. The recent and spectacular discoveries of early fish, shark (the world's oldest), amphibians, spiders and reptiles all come from the rich Carboniferous rocks of central Scotland.

During the succeeding Permian and Triassic periods Scotland became dry and windswept: faunas from these periods are thus sparse. Reptilian footprints were found in the 19th century sandstone quarries of Dumfries and more important skeletal fossils of mammal-like reptiles came from Triassic rocks of **Elgin** and **Lossiemouth**.

In Jurassic and Cretaceous times Scotland was once again invaded by seas creating ideal environments for shelly faunas of ammonite, belemnite and brachiopod. However, much has been lost by erosion and rocks of these periods are confined to the **Hebrides** and Moray Firth shores. The largest outcrops are on **Skye** and **Raasay**. Trotternish rocks yielded Scotland's first dinosaur footprint, now in the **Hunterian Museum**, Glasgow. In **Sutherland** a narrow outcrop of quite fossiliferous Jurassic rocks stretches from **Golspie** to **Helmsdale**, including the **Brora** coal.

Tertiary times were dominated by extensive vulcanicity, but evidence of warm temperate climate and vegetation can be found in the remarkable MacCulloch's Tree [see **Geology**] and the Ardtun leaf beds of **Mull**.

Most recent fossils date from the last Ice Age. Before the build-up of ice, reindeer, mammoth and woolly rhinoceros roamed the Midland Valley, judging from their meagre remains found at Bishopbriggs, Glasgow and in **Ayrshire**. As ice melted sea levels rose and flooded central Scotland's firths, laying down the **Clyde** and Errol Shell Beds, layers of Arctic shells no longer found around Scottish coasts.

See also *Westlothiana* and **Geology**.

FOULA, Shetland

The loneliest inhabited island in the British Isles, Foula lies 27 miles west of **Scalloway**. It is also one of Britain's loveliest islands with sheer cliffs up to 1220ft (372m) high. Predictions that the island would, like **St Kilda**, become depopulated have proved wrong and its now stable population of around 40 depend on **crofting**, **fishing** for lobsters and, since the introduction of an air service, small-scale **tourism**.

As if to recognise the island's refusal to die, **Shetland** Islands Council has spent large sums of money in the construction of a new school, a revolutionary electricity supply (from a combination of wind generator and water turbine) and a new harbour. Nevertheless the island's small cargo vessel still has to be lifted ashore after each trip to the **Mainland** terminal at Walls. Because of its abundant birdlife – the Norsemen called it *Fugloy*, 'the island of birds' – the island is designated a Site of Special Scientific Interest.

Old ways survive longest in Foula. It was one of the last strongholds of the old **Norn** language and it is still one of the last places in Europe to observe Christmas on 6 January according to the old Julian calendar.

FOULIS, David (1710–73) Physician and Composer
Born at Woodhall near **Edinburgh**, Foulis studied medicine in Edinburgh, Leyden (where he may well have pursued his musical interests) and Rheims. In 1737 he became a Fellow of the **Royal College of Physicians** and a committee member of the Edinburgh Musical Society. His only known works are *Six Solos for the Violin*, published in the 1770s but composed over a number of years. They exhibit a lively variety of forms as well as a melodic gift and a skill in writing for the violin that make them a charming set of sonatas.

FOULIS, Robert (1707–76) Printer
Initially apprenticed to a barber, but subsequently studying **philosophy** at **Glasgow University**, Robert Foulis visited Oxford and France with his brother Andrew (1712–75) collecting rare books. On their return to **Glasgow** they set up as booksellers and printers, producing editions of Latin and Greek classics, including a 4-vol edition of Homer (1765–8). Official printers to Glasgow University from 1741, they gained a reputation for immaculate and beautiful printing; **James Boswell**, who met them in 1773, described them as 'the Elzevirs of Glasgow' (Isaak Elzevir having been the official printer to the University of Leyden in the 17th century and internationally renowned publisher of the *Duodecimo* classics).

In 1752 the brothers established an Academy for the encouragement of the fine arts but subsequently ruined themselves in collecting paintings, and both the Academy and the printing business declined. Andrew died in 1775 and Robert took their collection of pictures – which included a remarkable number of Old Masters – to London hoping to raise enough money to revive his business. But the sale realised far less than he had anticipated and he died in poverty.

FOWLIS EASTER, Nr Dundee, Angus
So called to spare the postman confusion with the **Perthshire Fowlis Wester**, Fowlis Easter also has a pre-**Reformation** church. It was built by 'Andrew Lord Gray and his devout wife' in 1453 on the site of an earlier church dedicated to St Marnoch or Marnan. Quite large with traceried windows and a fine entrance, it contains part of the original rood screen and four large pre-Reformation paintings on wood depicting the Crucifixion, Virgin, John the Baptist and St Catherine. The Gray family, responsible for the nearby Broughty Castle and Castle of Huntly (to distinguish it from **Huntly Castle**) at Longforgan, also built Fowlis Castle, once a massive establishment but now represented only by its 17th century Lady's Tower.

FOWLIS WESTER, Nr Crieff, Perthshire
This village is notable for its 13th century church, much restored but little out of character, and for its two **Pictish** cross-slabs. One, built into the interior of the church, has exceptionally fine carving with detail depicting Jonah and the whale and two seated clerics. The other, of reddish sandstone, stands on a plinth on the little village green. Its carving has suffered from exposure, but an unusual procession of a cowherd and cow followed by bearded men is discernible. It is also the only cross-slab in Scotland with protruding arms, a feature more typical of Irish slabs. On the moor north of the village is a collection of **standing stones** and stone circles excavated in 1939.

FOYERS, Falls of, Loch Ness, Inverness-shire
Thanks to the proximity of **Wade**'s military road and then of the Caledonian **Canal**, the Falls of Foyers on the south side of **Loch Ness** enjoyed great celebrity in the 18th and 19th centuries. **Dr Johnson** grumbled at the dangers of approaching their 'dreadful depth'. **Burns** essayed some couplets on their 'mossy floods'. Southey congratulated Wade on having conducted his road so close to them, and **Joseph Mitchell**, who constructed a path to the best vantage point, congratulated 'Dame Nature' on having contrived such a sylvan setting. The most fulsome description is that of Christopher North (**John Wilson**) who reckoned the Falls 'the most magnificent cataract . . . in Britain' and 'worth walking a thousand miles to behold'. The upper falls consist of three leaps while the lower and more impressive cascade descends into an amphitheatre of rock after a fall of about 30m. Sadly the sight is not now as impressive as it once was. The river's catchment area was tapped by Scotland's first commercial **hydro-electric** scheme, opened in 1896 to provide power for aluminium extraction. **William Thomson, Lord Kelvin** was electrical consultant to the project whose stone castellate buildings still stand and whose turbines are the oldest of their kind in Britain. British Aluminium closed the plant in 1967 but a modern power station continues to make heavy demands on the Foyers.

FRASER, Clan
The Frasers probably came from Anjou in France, and the name may derive from either Fredarius or from Fresel or Freseau. Some have suggested that they descend from the tribe called Friselli in **Roman** Gaul, whose badge was a strawberry plant. They first appear in Scotland around 1160 when Simon Fraser held lands in **East Lothian**. Sir Simon Fraser was captured fighting for **Robert I**, and executed with great cruelty by Edward I in 1306. Simon's cousin, Sir Alexander Fraser, Bruce's Chamberlain, was the elder brother of Sir Simon Fraser from whom the **Frasers of Lovat** descend. Alexander married Bruce's sister Mary, previously wife of Sir Neil

Campbell of Lochow. She had been imprisoned in a cage in public by the English. His grandson, Sir Alexander Fraser of Cowie and Durris acquired the Castle (now called **Cairnbulg**) and lands of Philorth in **Aberdeenshire** by marriage with Joanna, younger daughter and co-heiress of the **Earl of Ross** in 1375.

Eight generations later in 1592, Sir Alexander Fraser, 8th Laird of Philorth, received charters from **King James VI** creating the **fishing** village of Faithlie, which he had transformed into a fine town, and the harbour, which he had much improved, into a **burgh of regality** and a Free Port. It was called Fraser's Burgh, and Sir Alexander was authorised to found a university, which was short-lived. He also built **Fraserburgh** Castle, until recently the Kinnaird Head Lighthouse. His son, the 9th Laird, married the heiress of the Abernethies, Lords Saltoun. Their son became the 10th Lord Saltoun who was left for dead after the Battle of Worcester (1651); he survived thanks to his servant James Cardno who rescued him from the battlefield, hid him and nursed him home to Philorth. The family took no part in the **Jacobite rebellions**.

The 16th Lord Saltoun commanded the Light Companies of the First Guards in the orchard outside Hougoumont at the Battle of Waterloo and it was he who first noticed the Imperial Guard emerge from the hollow where they had been hiding all day and drew the Duke of Wellington's attention to them. The 19th Lord Saltoun was a prisoner of war in Germany for most of World War I, was a member of the House of Lords from 1936, and latterly devoted himself to working for the Royal National Lifeboat Institution. He died in 1979 aged 93, and was succeeded by his daughter, Flora Fraser, 20th Lady Saltoun.

Although a Lowland family, the Frasers of Philorth, Lords Saltoun, being the senior line, are Chiefs of the name of Fraser. Lord Lovat is the chief of the very numerous Highland **clan** Fraser of Lovat, based in **Inverness-shire**.

Many distinguished soldiers, sailors and airmen have been Frasers, and many settled in the United States and Canada after the war against the French in Quebec. Others have emigrated to those countries and to Australia and there are now Frasers all over the world.

Chief of the Name: The Lady Saltoun

Arms: On a lozenge-shaped shield, azure, 3 fraises (cinquefoils) argent

Supporters: 2 angels proper with wings expanded and vested in long garments

Crest: 'On a mount in a flourish of strawberries, leaved and fructed proper' – in other words, 'a strawberry plant growing out of a dung-heap'

Motto: '*All my hope is in God*'

Tartan: Fraser.

FRASER, George Sutherland (1915–80) Poet and Critic

Fraser was born in **Glasgow**, and educated at Glasgow, **Aberdeen** (where his father became Town Clerk) and **St Andrews University**. After war service in the Middle East, an experience which inspired some of his best poems, he worked briefly as a critic and journalist before becoming a lecturer at the University of Leicester.

His gently elegiac poetry speaks of regret: regret for being 'always the unlucky one' in his youthful affairs with girls; for being exiled from Scotland; and for the loss of youth and the relentless onward passage of experience. His best-known poem 'The Traveller Has Regrets' (1948) contains the lines:

> The blue lights on the hill,
> The white lights in the bay
> Told us the meal was laid
> And that the bed was made
> And that we could not stay.

This, and the contents of his other books, are gathered together in *Collected Poems* (1981). He also wrote a number of critical studies, including *The Modern Writer and his World*, 1953; *W B Yeats*, 1952; *Vision and Rhetoric*, 1959; *Ezra Pound*, 1966; *Essays on Twentieth-Century Poets*, 1977 and *Alexander Pope*, 1978.

FRASER, House of

The House of Fraser, the largest department store group in the United Kingdom, began in **Glasgow** in 1849 when the first Hugh Fraser opened a cash-only warehouse in **Buchanan Street**. The shop prospered as Glasgow's trade and industry flourished. Following a fire, a lavish new warehouse was constructed by his son Hugh Fraser II in 1889. This was the age of the great Glasgow stores – Wylie & Lochhead, Stewart & MacDonald, and Pettigrew & Stephens. Frasers remained in the second rank until Hugh Fraser III joined the business in 1919. He immediately began to modernise and promote the shop. His father died in 1927 and nine years later he made his first acquisition, buying two warehouses in **Argyle Street** in Glasgow. Other purchases soon followed in the city, elsewhere in Scotland and, after World War II, in England. By the time of his death in 1966 he had won control of a number of famous stores, including Barkers of Kensington and Harrods in Knightsbridge, and had himself been raised to the peerage. Under the control of his son, Sir Hugh Fraser, the House of Fraser took over more stores making it a truly national group. Until 1993 it was controlled from London by the Fayed brothers, who retained Harrods when that year they put most of the other outlets up for sale.

FRASER, James Baillie (1783–1856) Explorer and Artist

Like his brother **William**, Fraser's ambition was to rescue his father's Highland estate of Easter Moniack (now Reelig) near Kirkhill in **Inverness-shire**. Reaching India (1813) and soon abandoning merchant life in 'detestable Calcutta' (1815), he went to join William who was on the move in the Nepal War. Eventually reunited after 16 years apart, the brothers undertook an expedition through the lower Himalayas. Meanwhile 'the Devil of Drawing' had seized James; he journeyed to the sources of both Jumna and Ganges sketching continually 'the stern and rugged majesty of the stupendous Himala'. His *Journal*, recording the history, agriculture, flora, fauna, geology, ethnology, commerce, manufactures and mineralogy of a remote region, and his *Views in the Himala Mountains* were published in 1820.

Back in the Plains he commissioned, with William, a unique collection of Company Drawings of Indians from diverse regions and, now himself an accomplished artist, enlivened Calcutta office life by making drawings of the city which were to become some of the finest Indian aquatints produced in England. He travelled home overland, exploring Persia in native disguise (1820) and subsequently produced several books on Persia. His last work (1851) was a translation from the Persian of the autobiography of James Skinner, founder of Skinner's Horse. At home Fraser concentrated on improving his estate with occasional forays into Persian affairs.

FRASER, Peter (1884–1950) Prime Minister of New Zealand

Born in **Fearn**, **Ross**-shire, Fraser joined the **Independent Labour Party** in London in 1908 and emigrated to New Zealand two years later. Gaoled for his protest against the conscription of men but not the conscription of wealth during World War I, he became Minister of Education when the Labour Party came to power in 1935. At the outbreak of World War II the Prime Minister Michael Savage was terminally ill; Fraser was Acting Prime Minister and took over when Savage died in April 1940. An influential participant in the San Francisco Conference of 1945 which founded the United Nations, Fraser earned a reputation for statesmanship and sound judgement.

FRASER, Simon, 11th Lord Lovat (c1667–1747)

Born at Tomich in **Ross**-shire, son of Thomas Fraser of Beaufort, and educated at **Aberdeen University**, Simon Fraser 'did not have the kind of nature that is attracted by honest labour'. However he had a seemingly limitless capacity for dishonest labour in pursuit of his ambitions – the acquisition of the titles, estates and influence of **Fraser of Lovat**. By means unknown he persuaded his cousin Hugh, 9th Lord Lovat, to nominate his own father Thomas as his heir. Hugh duly died (1696), Thomas inherited, Simon styled himself the Master of Lovat and, on the belt and braces principle, endeavoured to wed the 9th Lord's daughter, whose relatives were preparing to challenge the succession. This scheme foundering, he kidnapped and forcibly married her mother, for which crime he was outlawed.

His father Thomas, 10th Lord, died in 1699 and Simon achieved his first ambition by becoming 11th Lord. Still outlawed and therefore estate-less, he visited the exiled **James VII** in France and swore loyalty to the **Jacobite** cause and support for an invasion of Scotland by Louis XIV. He returned as a Jacobite spy (1703) but promptly revealed their plans to **James Douglas, 2nd Duke of Queensberry** in order to ingratiate himself with the powerful 'Union Duke'. This treachery was revealed with the collapse of the so-called Queensberry Plot [see **Robert Ferguson**]. Lovat fled back to France but was promptly arrested. Imprisoned for the best part of 10 years before staging a dramatic escape, he returned to lead his **clan** for the government against the '15 **Jacobite Rising**, for which service he obtained a full pardon and possession, at last, of the Lovat estates (1716). In 1724, 'sitting in Castle Dounie [or Downie]

near **Inverness** brooding over how to make the Highlands a more profitable place for Simon Fraser of Lovat' (B Lenman), he advocated the revival of the system of **Highland Independent Companies** to subdue the Jacobite clans, one of which companies he would, naturally, command himself. The suggestion led to the arrival in Scotland of **General Wade** to report on conditions in the Highlands but only briefly to Lovat's command of a company – he was removed by Wade on suspicion of pocketing his clansmen's pay.

By the outbreak of the '45 **Jacobite Rising** the 'slippery but ingenious rogue' was 78 years old, thrice married (having quickly tired of the 9th Lord's widow, been widowed himself by the death of his second wife, a Grant, and abandoned by his third, a Campbell), and still hedging his bets. Not until the Jacobite victory at **Prestonpans** did he declare himself for **Prince Charles Edward**, sending his son to arms in the Jacobite cause – a decision he was profoundly to regret after **Culloden**. Taking to the hills, he was captured near Loch Morar and taken to London where he conducted his own eloquent defence at his subsequent trial for treason, and met his death on the block with exemplary dignity.

FRASER, Simon Christopher John, 17th Lord Lovat (1911–95) Soldier and Agriculturalist

Born to the rolling acres of the Lovats' Beaufort Estate, Fraser was educated at Ampleforth College, York and Magdalen College, Oxford, where he reputedly shot a deer in the college deerpark. This prank is supposed to explain Magdalen's reluctance to accept any more Amplefordians for an entire generation. His marksmanship was put to better use in the **Scots Guards** and then the **Lovat Scouts**. After Dunkirk he was involved in the formation of the Special Services Brigade which later became the Commandos. Raids into France and Norway culminated in the disastrous Dieppe raid of 1942 in which he won a DSO. By 1943 he was a brigadier, but in 1944 was seriously wounded during the D-Day landings. Churchill then sent him as his emissary to the Kremlin with an introduction to Stalin which, quoting Lord Byron, called him 'the mildest manner'd man that ever scuttled ship or cut a throat'. A perfectionist of great charm and sensational looks, in 1945 he declined a political career to concentrate on his estates and clan. He became an authority on **shorthorn cattle**, introduced ranching methods and served on **Inverness** County Council for a record 42 years. Tragedy struck late. His youngest son was killed by a buffalo in Tanzania in 1994 and his eldest son died of a heart attack ten days later. An 18-year old grandson succeeded, but Beaufort had to be sold and passed to a scion of newer wealth in the person of Mrs Anne Gloag, the millionaire-proprietress of Stagecoach buses.

FRASER, William (1784–1835) Indian Administrator

A Scots eccentric in India, William, son of Edward Satchwell Fraser, joined the East India Company's Civil Service to seek a fortune to rescue his father's tottering estate of Easter Moniack (now Reelig) near Kirkhill in **Inverness-shire**. Graduating from Fort William College, Calcutta, he started his career as Assistant to the Resident at Delhi (1806). Fraser's immersion in Indian life, his linguistic talents, strong physique and great courage fitted him for work in unsettled areas and subsequently for the position of Political Agent in the Nepal War, during which he was seriously wounded at Kalunga. His contempt for his ineffectual Divisional Commander led him to obtain authority to recruit irregular troops, some of whom formed the 2nd Gurkha Rifles (1815). He regarded an active political and military life as 'the strongest stimulus to existence'.

As Commissioner for the Affairs of Garwhal he toured the Himalayan foothills with his brother **James Baillie Fraser**. He was granted a commission in Skinner's Horse and, resuming his civil duties, became Resident for Delhi (1830). Numerous visitors marvelled at both his accomplishments and his lifestyle. 'Half Asiatick in his habits but in other respects a Scotch Highlander', he was one of the last British to live as a Mughal Nawab in speech, dress and habits, fathering from his harem 'as many children as the King of Persia'. He held Mughal culture in high regard, befriended Ghalib, the greatest Urdu poet, and, with his brother James commissioned a unique set of Company portraits. Ironically, while Commissioner for Delhi, he was assassinated, for which crime a local Nawab was executed. The rancour this occasioned may be judged from the desecration of William's grave at St James', Delhi during the Indian Mutiny.

FRASER, Sir William (1816–98) Historian

An **Edinburgh** solicitor, Fraser was Assistant Keeper of Sasines (1852–80) and of Records (1880–92). He also published more than 40 sumptuous histories of Scotland's aristocratic families based largely on their private archives. Realising their importance to Scottish history, he left a bequest for the endowment of the first ever Chair of Scottish History at **Edinburgh University**. Peter Hume Brown was its first occupant and his 3-vol *History of Scotland* would remain the standard work for the next half century of woeful neglect. Fraser also endowed the Fraser homes at **Colinton**. He served on the Royal Commission on Historical Manuscripts and was made KCB (1887).

FRASER OF LOVAT, Clan

The Frasers of Lovat descend from Sir Simon Fraser (killed at **Halidon**, 1333), brother of Sir Alexander Fraser, Chamberlain of Scotland 1319–26. Simon's grandson, Hugh (fl.1367–c1410), acquired the Bisset lands in **Inverness-shire**, including Lovat, by marriage with an heiress of Lovat. The family thereafter multiplied rapidly and established many cadet branches. Hugh, the 9th Lord Lovat, died in 1696 without male issue but leaving four daughters, between the eldest of whom, Amelia, and Thomas Fraser of Beaufort (fourth son of Hugh, 7th Lord) and his son Simon, the succession was long in dispute. It was eventually decided in favour of **Simon**, later **11th Lord Lovat**. The 'old fox' of the '45 **Rising**, the 11th Lord plotted with both government and **Jacobite** forces, his support being given where he thought it most to his advantage. He was executed for treason (1747) and the title and estates forfeited, but his son Simon, Master of Lovat (1726–82), was pardoned and raised two regiments: in 1757 the 78th Fraser Highlanders who fought with Wolfe at Quebec and with the British armies in the American Revolution; and in 1774 the 71st Fraser Highlanders to serve in North America. His brother Archibald (1736–1815) raised the 'Fraser **Fencibles**' during the Napoleonic Wars. The brothers left no legitimate heirs. In 1837 the peerage, which had been attainted, was restored to their distant cousin Thomas Fraser of Strichen, who was descended from the 4th Lord Lovat. The 16th Lord (1871–1933) raised the **Lovat Scouts** in 1899 to fight in the Boer War and was the first Chairman of the **Forestry Commission** (1919–27). On the death of the **17th Lord Lovat** in 1995 at the age of 83, both his sons having died the previous year, his grandson Simon Fraser (b.1977) became the 18th Lord Lovat and 25th 'MacShimi' (son of Simon), Chief of Clan Fraser of Lovat. The clan crest is 'A buck's head erased proper'; its motto *Je Suis Prest* ('I am Ready'); and its Slogans (ancient) *A Mhor fhaiche* and (modern) *Caisteal Dhuni* (Castle Downie).

FRASERBURGH, Aberdeenshire

Now dwarfed by **Peterhead** and **Aberdeen**, Fraserburgh, on the north-east corner of the **Buchan** coast, remains an important **fishing** port. It is known locally as 'the Broch'; hence, presumably, 'Brochers', the term used throughout Scottish waters to denote east coast fishing crews. Town and harbour radiate from Kinnaird Head, a rocky promontory crowned with a lighthouse that was once a castle. The latter was built about 1574 by Sir Alexander Fraser of Philorth whose grandfather in 1546 had obtained a charter to develop the existing village of Faithlie into a port (known after 1600 as Fraserburgh) [see **Fraser, Clan**].

The castle consists of a four-storey keep, whitewashed, with parapet and bartizans. A fifth storey was removed to make way for the lighthouse (1787); additional windows and the adjacent single-storey stone houses were also added. The site may have been fortified since **Viking** times but the only earlier building is a modest little tower, also on Kinnaird Head but beyond the castle/lighthouse on the edge of the cliff. Why it is called the 'Wine Tower' is not known. It contains three vaulted rooms, one above the other and all small, the topmost of which has finely carved stone pediments. A date in the second quarter of the 16th century has been deduced.

Sir Alexander Fraser's new creation must have been an instant success since in 1595 a university was founded here by **George Keith, 5th Earl Marischal** (and also founder of Aberdeen's **Marischal College**). But Fraserburgh University was short-lived, closing down in 1605 when its principal fell foul of **James VI** by attending the **General Assembly**.

More lasting growth came courtesy of the 19th century **herring** boom. By 1897 Fraserburgh had a fleet of 680 boats, slightly more than **Stornoway**, and so the largest in Scotland. Today fish processing and machine tools buttress the declining fishery. The town retains the compact air of a fishing community while adjacent villages, **Rosehearty**, Inverallochy (with a ruined castle) and St Combs cater for its overspill. The latter two, as well as **Cairnbulg** (to which the Frasers removed from Kinnaird Head and Philorth), lie south amidst wind-swept dunes and gale-stroked scrub. To this bleak landscape refers

Herring boats in Fraserburgh harbour c1900 (GWWA)

J C Milne's dialect verse on the sparse charms of Faithlie/Fraserburgh:

> O Tam, gie me auld Faithlie toon
> Whaur trees are scrunts for miles aroon
> And nae a burn would slake nor droon
> A drunken miller;
> But sands and bents that wear a croon
> O' gowd and siller.

FRAZER, Sir James George (1854–1941)
Anthropologist

Born in **Glasgow**, the son of a chemist, James Frazer was educated at Springfield Academy and Larchfield Academy, **Helensburgh** before graduating from the **University of Glasgow** with an MA in 1874. He went on to study classics at Trinity College, Cambridge, and in 1879 was elected a Fellow of the college. He subsequently undertook studies in **law**, and was called to the English Bar in 1882, but never practised, having begun what would be a lifelong involvement in anthropological studies. His work did much to advance the study of differing cultures and beliefs, and his studies on the evolution of religious belief and ritual culminated in a 12-vol work, *The Golden Bough* (1890–1915). A vast and systematic study of the religious beliefs of the world, it traced what Frazer saw as a linear progression in social evolution from magical through religious to scientific thoughts and beliefs. While Frazer's arguments have been discarded by modern anthropologists, they were a strong influence on the works of writers such as D H Lawrence, T S Eliot and Ezra Pound. *The Golden Bough* subsequently appeared in abridged form in 1920,

and a supplement, *Aftermath*, was published in 1936.

Frazer's other works include *Totemism and Exogamy* (1910), *Folklore in the Old Testament* (1918), *Fear of the Dead* (1933–6) and *Magic and Religion* (published posthumously in 1944). He also made translations with commentary of classics by Pausanius and Ovid. He became Professor of Anthropology at the University of Liverpool in 1907, was knighted in 1914, and awarded the Order of Merit in 1925. He died in Cambridge.

FREE CHURCH OF SCOTLAND

The 1843 **Disruption**, the most devastating split in the **Church of Scotland**, was both inevitable and well planned. Disputes over patronage in the established Church had produced a Veto Act in 1833 that put the Church constitution in conflict with civil government. This led to a Claim of Right which coincided with **Queen Victoria**'s progress through the country in 1842. Then in the spring of 1843 the Chapel Act of the 1834 **General Assembly**, which was to reshape parishes, was declared illegal by the **Court of Session** at the same time as the House of Lords and House of Commons rejected the grievances of the Claim.

The populace anticipated the confrontation at the General Assembly on 18 May 1843. The evangelical clergy party held meetings in the days before and **Dr David Welsh**, the retiring **Moderator** who by custom preached the Assembly sermon, chose the text 'Let every man be persuaded in his own mind'. Instead of convening the Assembly next day, he read a protest and led out, arm in arm, nearly 200 ministers to the Tanfield Hall a mile away through cheering crowds waiting for the moment.

The Free Church thus formed immediately convened its own assembly and **Thomas Chalmers**, leading evangelical and populist theologian, was elected Moderator.

A Free Church minister conducting an open-air service, Skye (SP)

An expert organiser, he had 474 ministers already at hand to sign the Act of Separation and Deed of Demission. This coup eventually included all missionaries in the field and clergy from every presbytery except one. The ablest theologians were amongst them and support was especially strong in the Highlands.

At issue was spiritual independence from civil interference. The need was for churches, manses and financial support to replace those just signed away. Within two years 500 churches were built (including a floating one at **Strontian**); schools were also provided, since schoolmasters, hitherto appointees of the established Church, were driven out; similarly theological colleges. Finance was organised by Chalmers as a levy of one penny per week minimum from every member.

The theological basis of the Free Church was the same as that of the established Church, namely the Westminster Confession which celebrated its bicentenary that year [see **Covenants**]. The only exception lay in the binding principle of 'the freedom and spirituality of the Church of Christ and her subjection to Him as her only Head' in the heritage of **Knox** and **Melville**. There was no change in creed, government or form of worship.

The new Church was, however, open to liberal development, active in social concerns and youth work, and responsive to the environmental challenges of the Victorian era. When patronage, the old sticking point, was nationally removed in 1874 reunification came under early consideration. **Secession Churches** had begun to come together soon after the Disruption to form the **United Presbyterian Church**. By 1900 the Free Church, once it had been released from tight adherence to the Westminster Confession by the 1892 Declaratory Acts, was ready to join with them as the **United Free Church of Scotland**. Unfortunately a minor secession from the Free Church had resulted in the **Free Presbyterian Church** which remained independent along with a rump of the Free Church. [See chart p. 995]

During its existence the Free Church proper was a vital and bold expression of **Presbyterians** in the midst of a rapidly changing society. It took up the cause of disestablishment briefly until the Church of Scotland caught up with its thinking and the Secession Churches provided the example of healing divisions. Reunion left inevitable remnants in each case, but the impact of standing by principles and against interference by civil powers left an affection for it in the history of the Church.

FREE PRESBYTERIAN CHURCH and FREE CHURCH OF SCOTLAND (1900)

These minority **Presbyterian** denominations devolved as remnants from the **Free Church of Scotland**, the Free Presbyterian Church from 1893 and the Free Church from 1900. Both retain their secession on **Calvinist** doctrinal grounds adhering to the Westminster Confession of 1647, metrical psalms and no instrumental music in church.

Both emphasise Sabbatarianism and despise indulgence to the point of being anti-Catholic. Strongest in the Highlands and Gaelic regions, they are still prone to splits, but have influence over the minutiae of observance in public and private life, such as Sunday ferries and licensing. Similarly, in the Lowlands, a Reformed Presbyterian Church upholds and claims **Covenanter** origins. [See chart p. 995]

FREEMASONRY

Freemasonry originated from the Guilds of Operative Masons who built the royal castles, important bridges and great churches. These groups of masons were organised into lodges with a hierarchy which would be recognisable by today's Freemasons.

Such masons were employed by the king and remained in the towns and cities after the specific buildings they had come to work on were finished; the Guild members were the builders who built the cities. As with all guilds, no one could practise unless he was member of a lodge and possessed 'the Mason's Word'. This was obtained at a ceremony at which a form of catechism was rehearsed and which concluded with some mild horseplay. The apprentice then continued working until he was sufficiently skilled to pass another ceremony, after which he became a craftsman. It was not until the mid-18th century that the degree of Master Mason was introduced. It is thought that this was due to a misunderstanding by English Freemasons; for the sake of uniformity it was adopted by the Scots.

Early in the 17th century men of learning and wealth began to join these lodges, and became known as Free or Speculative Masons to distinguish them from the Operative Masons (who worked at the trade). The Free or Speculative Masons were drawn by the philosophy of the Masons and the pursuit of knowledge. The lodges were glad to receive them because they brought patronage, money and enhanced social standing at a time when the amount of building had declined and the lodges needed money to carry on their charitable work. This stemmed from their corporate responsibility for the well-being of sick and elderly Masons and their wives. Collections were taken up and money disbursed for these aims, much as they are today.

The number of Speculative Masons increased throughout the 17th century. One of the most important was William Schaw, the King's Master of Work, who laid down statutes to govern Masonry. Another distinguished Mason was Sir Robert Moray who was initiated into the Lodge of **Edinburgh** in 1641 while engaged as the Quarter-Master General of a Scottish army besieging Newcastle. He was a man of great culture and learning and was deeply interested in the symbolic teachings of the craft. Many men of similar tastes followed him and by the end of the 17th century the lodges were mainly composed of Speculative or Free Masons. New lodges were also being erected, having been chartered by some of the older lodges, such as **Kilwinning**, Edinburgh, **Aberdeen** and **Melrose**.

In the early 18th century the Earl of St Clair, who included Patron of the King's Mason among his titles, became a Freemason. At about the same time four lodges wrote together to all then existing lodges to propose the formation of a Scottish Grand Lodge. England had formed a Grand Lodge in 1718, Ireland in 1725; Scotland formed hers in 1736.

Lord St Clair resigned his hereditary office and was elected the first Grand Master. Grand Lodge had its ups and downs. One of the Founding Lodges left in 1737; another left in 1750 and did not rejoin until 1807 although it continued to charter new lodges. Seven Grand Master Masons went on to become Grand Masters of England, an office that has twice been held by the sovereign.

In 1738 a Provincial Grand Master was appointed to look after those lodges too far from Grand Lodge to be visited by the Grand Master Mason; there are now 32 Provincial Grand Lodges in Scotland. Scottish Freemasonry travelled abroad, and there are 23 District Grand Lodges under District Grand Masters appointed by Grand Lodge. Scottish lodges are working in many African countries, the Caribbean, South America, Western Australia, India, New Zealand, Singapore and Malaysia, Hong Kong and Japan, while isolated lodges may be found in places as diverse as Belgium, Togo, Fiji, Manila and Sri Lanka.

There are other Masonic Orders to which only Master Masons may be admitted. They are the 33rd and Last Degree of the Ancient and Accepted Scottish Rite, the Royal Order of Scotland, the Supreme Grand Royal Arch Chapter of Scotland, the Great Priory of the Temple and Malta in Scotland and the Grand Imperial Council of Scotland. The first two and the last concentrate on Christian teaching. They are of varying antiquity and mainly originated in France in the late 18th century – all except the Royal Order, which uses the oldest Scottish Ritual. It is the only Masonic Order with its headquarters in Scotland which has no equal or similar body in the world.

Candidates for Scottish Freemasonry must believe in a Supreme Being, be of high moral character and be respected members of their community, who abide by the laws of whatever country they happen to be in. Politics and religion may not be discussed in lodge, but colour and creed are no bar to membership.

See also **Edinburgh: Niddry Street** and **St John Street**.

FRESWICK, Caithness

It was in this sandy bay south of **Duncansby Head** that the first **Viking** settlement in **Caithness** was uncovered. Excavation suggests a 13th century date. That is considerably later than the fort built here by Sweyn of Gairsay, 'The Ultimate Viking' of **Eric Linklater**'s story, who met the end he deserved in Dublin in 1171. It was called Lambaborg, but the Aberdonian name Buchollie replaced it when **Robert I** bestowed this property on the Mowats. They sold it to the Sinclairs of Rattar in 1661. The ruins of Buchollie Castle, rebuilt in the 15th century, stand on a rock outcrop whose neck of land has been incised by a ditch.

FURNACE, Argyll

South of **Inveraray** where the Leacann Water enters Loch Fyne, this village, originally Inverleacann, became Furnace in the late 18th century when **iron** smelting was introduced. As at **Invergarry** and **Bonawe**, the industry sought to exploit the local abundance of oak which, as charcoal, fired the furnaces; the ore was imported. Production had ceased by 1843 but one of the furnaces remains near the lochside road which runs north to a large **quarry** and then on to Pennymore Point. South of the village another quarry supplied most of the paving setts for **Glasgow**. Nearby Cumlodden contains the parish church (1841) and the estate office for **Crarae**.

R W Billings' drawing of Fyvie Castle in the 1840s (RWB)

FYFE, David Patrick Maxwell, Lord Kilmuir (1900–67) Lord Chancellor

The son of an **Edinburgh** schools inspector, Fyfe was educated at **George Watson's College** and then Balliol College, Oxford. There he encountered future members of the Conservative Party's inner establishment which, according to the DNB, 'it was his life's ambition to enter'. Called to the English Bar, he became (1934) the youngest KC since the reign of **Charles II** and, with a safe Liverpool seat in the Commons, rose steadily as Solicitor General (1942), Attorney General (1945), Home Secretary (1951) and Lord Chancellor (1954). He won international recognition as Deputy Chief Prosecutor at the Nuremberg trials and was an early Tory convert to the idea of European integration; he also refused, as Home Secretary, a reprieve for Derek Bentley, the last man to be judicially hanged in Britain. Kilmuir's career ended abruptly; in 1962 he was one of those summarily dismissed from the Macmillan cabinet in 'the night of the long knives'. He took no further part in public affairs but was appointed Chairman of Plesseys.

FYFFE, Will (1885–1947) Entertainer

Born in **Dundee**, Will Fyffe started out with his parents in touring shows, travelling the length and breadth of Scotland, and as a boy acted parts like Little Willie in *East Lynne* and Little Eva in *Uncle Tom's Cabin*. He featured as a character comedian on **music hall** bills throughout Britain, and his **Glasgow** 'drunk', singing 'I belong to Glasgow' was a gem, putting the city well and truly on everyone's lips. When he appeared at the London Palladium, so good was his acting that some members of the audience swore he was truly drunk on stage and that it was not just a characterisation. 'Mr Fyffe was not so much a sober man trying to appear drunk as a drunk man trying to appear sober' (James Agate). He was good as 'Daft Sandy', amusing as the guard on a Highland **railway** line, and had another winner in 'Sailing up the **Clyde**'. He had success in appearances in the USA, acted in films like *Owd Bob* and *The Brothers*, and died on 14 December 1947 from injuries received when he fell from the window of a hotel in **St Andrews**.

FYVIE CASTLE, Fyvie, Aberdeenshire

With its six towers, four of them linked to form the grand façade (147ft/45m long), Fyvie in both scale and aspect is more palace than castle. But its main interest lies in its antiquity, for belying the impression of a Victorian Baronial extravaganza, it is in fact a rather successful instance of a genuine tower house being ordered and aggrandised to palatial effect.

Originally a keep, Fyvie belonged to the Crown and was occupied by various sovereigns including Edward I of England and **Robert I** before being granted to Sir Henry Preston (1398) in recognition of his valour at the **Battle of Otterburn**. It subsequently passed to the Meldrum family (1433), the Setons (1596) and then the Gordons of **Haddo** (1733). Each added to it; hence the Meldrum tower of Sir Alexander Meldrum, the two round Seton towers of **Sir Alexander Seton** (later Lord Fyvie, 1st Earl of Dunfermline), and the Gordon tower of The Hon General Gordon, son of the 2nd Earl of Aberdeen. It was probably the Setons who first recognised the building's potential for an integrated palace. The arched entrance, three storeys high, between the twin Seton towers is the most impressive external feature whilst the grand staircase is 'amongst the finest in Scotland' (M Lindsay).

Fyvie was sold again in 1889, this time to **Alexander Leith** (later Forbes-Leith, eventually Lord Fyvie) whose mother claimed descent from Sir Henry Preston. Leith was also of local descent but the fortune he now lavished on Fyvie derived, like that of **Andrew Carnegie**, from American steel production. The results are visible in the Leith tower (designed by John Bryce), in the high standard of upkeep, fittings, etc, in the tapestries and above all in the remarkable collection of paintings which includes many works by **Sir Henry Raeburn** and others by Lely, Reynolds, Gainsborough, etc. The property and most of its contents were sold to the **National Trust for Scotland** in 1984 by Sir Andrew Forbes-Leith whose father had led the consortium which presented **Craigievar** to the Trust.

GAELIC BOOKS COUNCIL

Set up in 1968 with support from the Scottish Education Department, the Council gives financial support and other kinds of impetus to the publication of Gaelic books. Funding was subsequently made the responsibility of the Scottish Arts Council.

The Council is housed in **Glasgow University**, and the Professor of Celtic there is its Chairman. Its remit is to encourage the production of Gaelic books of all kinds, to publicise such books and to help distribute them. This work takes various forms, such as direct grant-aid to publishers for approved titles, encouragement to authors by commissioning, editorial help to authors, commissioning of editorial work, publicity related to new publications, a catalogue of Gaelic books in print, book exhibitions and literary events, and sales trips to all parts of the Gaelic area.

This general encouragement of Gaelic publication has resulted in a marked increase in the number, range and quality of books published. There are two medium-ized publishers involved in this work, Gairm Publications, which spearheaded new developments from the early 1960s onwards, and Acair, a company formed in the mid-1970s. Several other publishers issue occasional Gaelic titles.

GAELIC LANGUAGE

History

Gaelic is the language in longest continuous use in Scotland. Although settlement of Gaelic-speaking people on a significant scale probably first took place in the 5th century AD, there seem to have been sporadic raids and small settlements in the two preceding centuries. The main early settlement, however, was in the west, and the territory was named **Dál Riada** after its Irish original. It is located in **Argyll**. It was to this established 'colony' that **Columba** came in 563, thereafter spreading his missionary activities to other parts of Scotland.

Gaelic spread to these other parts by infiltration of settlers, accompanied in various instances by political domination, military victory or religious conversion. In these ways an ultimate political union was formed between the **Picts** and the Scots, and Scottish (or Scottic) dominance was achieved over the Welsh-speaking kingdoms of central and southern Scotland. This spread of Gaelic settlers is most clearly demonstrated by the coverage of Gaelic place-names, from **Galloway** to **Caithness**, and although their incidence varies widely in intensity (with only slight influence in the south-east and parts

of Caithness) it is only in **Orkney** and **Shetland** that this Gaelic influence is minimal. It is, however, true that Gaelic was not spoken over the whole area of Scotland at any one point in time.

In a political sense, Gaelic seems to have reached its strongest position in the centuries from the 9th to the 12th, having by then won the 'battle' with Pictish and Welsh, and having not yet begun the 'retreat' in the face of the Teutonic 'advance'. We may feel some scepticism over these military terms, as there is not much evidence of linguistic militancy in early times. The main ebb and flow between Gaelic and Norse also falls within the centuries from 800 to 1300 AD.

The influence of the Church in spreading Gaelic is shown in the high incidence of Gaelic place-names with ecclesiastical content: the numerous Kil-names (from *cill* – church, cell), usually combined with saints' names, eg the Kilbrides, Kildonans, etc; names containing elements such as *eaglais* (church) or *annaid* (patron saint's church) etc; or the names of Church officials. Evidence of Gaelic social organisations also shows up in place-names, eg those including the elements *bàrd* (poet), *breitheamh* (judge) or *clàrsair* (harpist).

At the time of its maximum usage Gaelic was the language of the royal court and of courts of **law**, and there existed a fairly wide range of Gaelic 'professionals' such as lawyers, doctors, scribes, historians and poets. Gradually, with the increase of English influence at court, and English and Flemish influence on commerce, Gaelic lost ground in affairs of state, though retaining its dominance in the court and the business of specific chiefs such as those of the **MacDonalds** and **Campbells**. That dominance lasted, almost as an anachronism, in the case of the MacDonalds until the 17th century.

By the Middle Ages we can see evidence of Gaelic 'survival' rather than dominance, in such areas as the eastern seaboard from the Firth of Forth to **Aberdeen**, and in almost all cases any towns of scale are non-Gaelic-speaking. Gaelic lingered in rural areas, surviving for example, in Galloway and parts of **Ayrshire** until the 17th century, in **Angus** rather later, and in a few areas in **Aberdeenshire** (Strathdon and Deeside) into the 20th century. It petered out in parts of west **Perthshire** (eg **Aberfoyle**, Port of **Menteith**) in the early 19th century, but still survives minimally in east Perthshire.

Due to the repulsion of greedy landlords and the attraction of work in the rapidly expanding central (especially **Clyde**) area, there was significant depopulation of Gaelic-speaking areas in the Highlands, and a considerable build-up of Gaelic colonies in the cities and throughout Scotland generally. These city colonies were to become influential in promoting Gaelic in terms of publishing and entertainment, and also in promoting Gaelic educational developments (eg the Gaelic Schools movement of the 19th century). Similar initiatives continue to the present (eg the work of Gairm Publications, STV and the BBC, mainly in **Glasgow**). At the present time, approximately half the number of Gaelic speakers in Scotland live outwith the Gaelic area. The 1991 figure for Gaelic speakers was approximately 65,000.

Forms and Structure

Brought to Scotland by early colonists from Ireland, the language is one and the same, in origin, as Irish Gaelic.

Both should be referred to as Gaelic, and their various period layers as Old Gaelic, Middle Gaelic, Modern Gaelic; though it is desirable to distinguish the modern languages as Modern Irish Gaelic and Modern Scottish Gaelic. Documentary evidence is much more voluminous for the various stages of the language in Ireland, with early glosses on Latin manuscript texts giving evidence of the language in the 8th and 9th centuries. Many of the manuscripts containing these glosses are in Continental libraries, eg in Würzburg, Milan, Turin and Karlsruhe, for the writers of the glosses were apparently monks and missionaries. There are some still earlier sources, often in later manuscripts which have undergone modernisation, and these probably give evidence of Gaelic language as early as the 6th and 7th centuries AD, while Ogam inscriptions may take us back to the 4th century.

The early documentary sources show a highly inflected, highly complex language, with a plethora of verbal forms, an intricate system of infixed and affixed pronouns, and elaborate patterns of word-composition. The early Gaelic language of Scotland must have shared these features, but both Eastern and Western Gaelic were radically simplified in their transition from the Archaic to the Old and Middle periods, just as Anglo-Saxon sires the much less complicated languages of Middle and Modern English.

There are only modest traces of many of these developments in extant Scottish sources. There are indeed Ogam inscriptions in Scotland, but these are mainly in spheres of Pictish influence, though they include Gaelic names. As to early documents, or documents containing early Gaelic material, these are very scarce, the more important being the Senchas Fer nAlban ('History of the Men of Scotland'), perhaps dating from the mid-7th century in its original form (see J W M Bannerman, Studies in the History of Dalriada, 1974), and the **Book of Deer**, a Latin manuscript from Aberdeenshire which contains Gaelic notes dating from c1131–50. From the scanty available evidence there is no clear proof of separate Scottish Gaelic developments in language before the 10th century AD, though it is of course inevitable that some five centuries of Scottish existence had left marks. There is in fact some evidence in the Book of Deer of, for example, the retention of ancient hiatus where it had been lost in Irish Gaelic, and the growth of a different variety of nasalisation.

The situation is complicated by the existence of a literary Gaelic which was, by and large, common to both Scotland and Ireland, and used by the professional classes. Sometimes traces of vernacular usage show through, as in the cases of the Book of Deer and the **Book of the Dean of Lismore**, but there is not a great deal of concentrated evidence of Scottish Gaelic vernacular until we come to relatively modern times, especially the 17th century, though these sources may point us back for generations.

The Gaelic languages of Scotland and Ireland are mutually understandable to some degree, with Donegal Irish Gaelic distinctly closer to Scottish Gaelic. A little study shows the huge overlap clearly. Scottish Gaelic itself has many distinct dialects, the southern ones, eg **Islay** or **Kintyre**, showing stronger affinities with Irish Gaelic, and many differences of accent, intonation and vocabulary between the Gaelic of eg **Perthshire**, **Sutherland**, **Lewis** and **Barra** (although these would seldom seriously hinder communication).

Modern Gaelic is an inflected language, with for example four singular case forms for certain nouns (Nominative, Vocative, Genitive, Dative), separate plural forms (sometimes Nom, Voc, Gen, Dat) and occasionally dual forms. So we use forms such as balach (boy), a bhalaich (O boy), ceann a' bhalaich (the head of the boy), nighean (girl), leis an nighinn (belonging to the girl – ie dative), làmh (hand), dà làimh (two hands), balaich (boys), a bhalachaibh (O boys), cinn nam balach (the heads of the boys), etc. This system of case-inflection has been gradually breaking down (as similar systems did many centuries ago in English and Welsh), and in particular dative and dual forms are in decay, while even the genitive is weakly. The verb has in the main undergone more radical simplification, losing the enormous complexity of its earlier system for the main range of verbs, but retaining some in the case of 11 irregular verbs. In the case of all the verbs, separate forms for the separate persons have largely disappeared, the distinction now depending on the use of the appropriate pronoun: so chuir mi (I put), chuir thu (you put), chuir i (she put), etc. There are still separate active and passive/impersonal forms, distinctions between dependent and independent usage, between indicative and subjunctive, etc.

For many adult learners of Gaelic, one of the most unfamiliar features is initial mutation. The initial consonants or vowels of words can be affected by lenition/aspiration or nasalisation, eg cù (dog), mo chù (my dog); taigh (a house), do thaigh (your house); feadag (a whistle), m'fheadag (my whistle) – in this case the aspiration of f – produces a nil, and the pronunciation is m'eadag; gàrradh (a garden), 'nan gàrradh fhèin (in their own garden) – here the combination of the elements n and g can produce a composite ng sound, strongly nasalised; aodann (a face), nar n-aodann (in our face), a h-aodann (her face). Most of the consonants are affected in this way but, rather awkwardly, the convention is not to show the difference between unlenited and lenited l, n and r.

Gaelic is a strongly idiomatic language, making use, for example, of many combinations of verbs and prepositions to express many nuances.

Gaelic also has a very extensive range of sounds: it is one of the most complex of European languages in this sense, and this has implications for the full mastery of its system in speech, and notable advantages in the range and intricacy of its sound correspondences and contrasts (harmonies and dissonances) in song or poetry.

This necessarily brief summary can be supplemented by reference to D S Thomson, The Companion to Gaelic Scotland, 1987; R Thurneysen, A Grammar of Old Irish, 1946; George Calder, A Gaelic Grammar, 1980; Douglas Clyne, Gaelic Verbs and their Prepositions, 1984; Elmar Ternes, The Phonemic Analysis of Scottish Gaelic, 1973.

GAELIC ORGANISATIONS

A number of new Gaelic organisations were set up in the 1980s in response to the increased level of interest in Gaelic which showed up in Scotland during the 1960s and 1970s. Prominent among these were Comann an Luchd-ionnsachaidh (CLI), whose main concern is to provide language-learning opportunities for adults, and Comhairle nan Sgoiltean Araich (CNSA), whose concern is to establish pre-school Gaelic playgroups. In a growing number of localities, children from such playgroups can proceed to either Gaelic-medium or bilingual Primary schools and so continue with Gaelic-based education through Primary school. Much larger funding was secured for other organisations, such as Comann na Gaidhlig (CNAG), whose role is more difficult to define, but which issues confident press releases regularly, and the Gaelic Arts Project, which encourages Gaelic drama and other Gaelic arts, especially through local festivals (fèisean). Pressure, especially from CNAG, led to the establishing of a Gaelic Television Fund in 1991, and a much increased quota of Gaelic TV programmes came on stream in 1993. There have been spasmodic student Gaelic pressure-groups, such as COGA and DUISG, which have raised Gaelic's profile, eg in University Students' Representative Councils.

See also **An Comunn Gaidhealach**.

GAELIC PSALM SINGING

A specific kind of singing in the Gaelic Church in which the psalm tune is 'lined-out' by a precentor, Gaelic psalm singing is performed slowly in unison or octaves by the congregation with much decoration and with no attempt to produce a uniform choral result. The tunes are post-**Reformation**, but the style, which transforms the melody, shows local variants and is generally agreed to reflect much older vocal practices; known as 'free heterophony', it finds its nearest parallels among the Copts in the Middle East.

GAELIC VERSE AND PROSE

Classical ('bardic') Poetry

From at least as early as the 12th century AD there is evidence of a class of professional Gaelic poets who taught in bardic schools. This evidence refers to Irish instances, and Ireland is of course much richer in ancient evidence of poetic activity than Scotland. Nevertheless hints exist of similar activity in Scotland, as for example in a fragment of Gaelic verse ascribed to Adomnán (**Adamnan**) referring to the death of Brude son of Bile in 685 AD.

By the early 13th century the Irish and the Scottish poetic traditions can be seen in specific contact. About 1215 AD a famous Irish poet Muireadhach O Dálaigh is said to have fled to Scotland; poems of his survive, two of them addressed to early **Earls of Lennox**. He became known as Muireadhach Albanach (Scottish Muireadhach), and a lengthy succession of poets is descended from him, taking the surname of MacMhuirich, this being a later form of Mac Mhuireadhaich (son or descendant of Muireadhach). This line of hereditary poets seems to have had a unbroken succession from the first half of the 13th century until the middle of the 18th. In 1800, one Lachlann MacMhuirich of **South Uist** claimed to be eighteenth in descent from Muireadhach. Only about half of the pedigree is known in any detail, but a succession of MacMhuirich poets over this long period is attested.

For example, a Lachlann MacMhuirich composed a battle-incitement before the **Battle of Harlaw** (1411), and it was probably his grandson, another Lachlann,

who is referred to in a charter of 1485 as archipoeta, ie chief poet, in this instance to the Chief of the MacDonalds of **Kintyre** and **Islay**. It was probably his son, Giolla Coluim mac an Ollaimh (Malcolm son of the learned poet), who wrote several poems in the 1490s, commenting on the downfall of that MacDonald family. Two poets called John are attested in the 16th century, one of them as a cleric in the **Lismore** diocese and the other as the holder of hereditary bardic lands in Kintyre. The bardic family seems to have transferred its services to the Chief of the **Clanranald MacDonalds** in the later 16th century, and a poet called Niall Mór MacMhuirich recalls in verse the celebrations at the wedding of the Clanranald heir to a daughter of MacLeod of **Dunvegan** in 1613.

The two MacMhuirich poets who are most liberally attested are 17th century ones, Cathal and Niall (a younger Neil). Cathal was composing poems about historical characters from c1615–c60, and also reflecting in a sombre, disillusioned way on the decline of bardic patronage, and the thinning in the ranks of trained poets. Despite this pessimism, his successor Niall was still composing heartily in 1715, and perhaps as late as 1719, and his successor Dòmhnall has a few rather clumsy poems which may date as late as the 1740s.

The 500-year dynasty was coming to an end. In terms of the practice of verse using the classical literary language and the range of syllabic metres that were its stock-in-trade, Niall was the last confident practitioner. Various branches of the family, however, sustained an interest in genealogy and poetic lore, and some continued to compose poetry, but in vernacular rather than classical style. A branch in **Cowal** was doing so in the late 18th and 19th centuries, and the tradition continued elsewhere, eg in South Uist and in Nova Scotia, until the 20th century.

For more detailed discussion of this family, see D S Thomson 'The MacMhuirich Bardic Family' in Transactions of the Gaelic Society of Inverness Vol 43, 1963; 'Gaelic Learned Orders and Literati' in Scottish Studies 12, 1968; 'The Poetry of Niall MacMhuirich' in TGSI 46, 1970; 'Niall Mór MacMhuirich' in TGSI 49, 1977; 'Three Seventeenth-Century Bardic Poets' in A J Aitken et al, Bards and Makars, 1977; and R I Black, 'The Genius of Cathal MacMhuirich', in TGSI 50, 1979. For examples of the verse of the Cowal branch, see Gairm Nos 155, 156, 1991.

The MacMhuirichs are the best attested of the professional bardic families in Scotland, but there were other similar families, for example one called MacEwen who acted as **bards** to the **MacDougalls** of **Lorne**, and later to the **Campbells** of **Argyll**. Members of this family are attested from c1400 to the mid-17th century, and a late representative Neil was probably the translator into Gaelic of Calvin's Catechism (1631) (see R L Thomson, Adtimchiol an Chreidimh, 1962). The MacEwens were closely associated with the Earls of Argyll and also with the Campbells of Glenorchy, so it is not too surprising to find one of the latter composing poems in the literary language and metres; these are preserved in the **Book of the Dean of Lismore**.

The Dean's Book also provides evidence of a succession of family bards serving the **MacGregor** Chiefs, and we have evidence of another family called

O Muirgheasáin, who served **Maclean** Chiefs in **Mull**, and later MacLeod of Dunvegan. Eoin Og O Muirgheasáin made an elegy for Sir Roderick MacLeod who died in 1626 (see J MacDonald in *Scottish Gaelic Studies* 8, 1955). It is likely that there were other bardic families wherever powerful Gaelic Chiefs were settled.

There are also instances of the classical language, style and metres of the professional bards being used by amateurs who seem usually to belong to the privileged chiefly classes; presumably this gave them some access to this form of composition.

Poetry and Song in the 16th and 17th Centuries

Alongside the tradition of classical (bardic) poetry there were others; a clearly widespread tradition of song-making [see **Waulking Songs**] which must be ancient but comes more clearly into view from the 16th century, and various traditions of vernacular song and poetry. Some of the poetry can be seen to be related to the classical Gaelic verse in its use of language, motifs and metres. Surviving examples of religious verse from about 1600 show these influences, as does the verse of the **Mackenzies** of Achilty; and many of the functions of the old praise-poets were continued by the vernacular 'clan' poets who succeeded them [see eg **Iain Lom** and An Clàrsair Dall, **the Blind Harper**].

The new class of praise-poets may have links with a particular category of earlier bards whose special function was praise-verse. At any rate, we find links between the bards and the 17th century poets known as *aos-dàna*. It is not clear whether these also represent hereditary lines, but the possibility is strong. Very gradually this tradition of praise-poetry weakens, and begins to merge with the tradition of local or 'village' poetry. The 17th century can be seen as an age of transition reflecting the social changes that attended the gradual Anglicising of some of the main leaders in the old society, or their loss of power in a Scotland steadily succumbing to central government authority.

Only occasionally do these 'foreign' influences intrude in 17th century Gaelic verse, as when *An Clàrsair Dall* castigates the young MacLeod chief for his spendthrift life in the South. Often the picture that emerges is of a still 'heroic' society, occupied with war and hunting, festivity, music, dancing, drinking. Màiri Nighean Alasdair Ruaidh (**Mary MacLeod**) is more concerned with such activities, and with recalling the MacLeods' ancestry, than she is with the ordinary people; even with poets of greater range, like Iain Lom, the official **clan** links remain very strong. We get vivid pictures of battles in his work, yet the driving force behind the poems is often the clan's participation. Other interests occasionally assert themselves, as in *Cumha Choire an Easain* ('The Waterfall Corrie's Lament') by John Mackay, known as *Am Pìobaire Dall* (the Blind Piper). He was piper to Mackenzie of **Gairloch**, but this poem laments the death of Lord Reay, the **Mackay** clan chief. Far from confining himself to Reay's qualities, the poet gives us a series of reminiscences about old times and acquaintances, cast in the form of a dialogue between himself and the corrie he is traversing. They include a detailed and sensuous description of the corrie itself, all the more remarkable as coming from a blind man.

Instances of conventional praise-poetry survive long beyond the 17th century. John MacLean (1787–1848) was still composing elegies for the Laird of Coll in the early 19th century, before he emigrated to Nova Scotia, and there are elegies and eulogies of clerics, both Protestant and Catholic, in modern times.

Evidence of how the less privileged lived and felt is found mainly in anonymous songs of the 16th and 17th centuries. These are a rich source, although very few exist in the original; they were mostly collected and recollected at later periods. Fortunately considerable collections were made in the 18th century, eg James McLagan's collection (in **Glasgow University** Library), collections by Donald MacNicol, Alexander Irvine and others (in the **National Library of Scotland**) and Ewen MacDiarmid's collection (in the Department of Celtic, University of Glasgow). Some appeared in 18th century books, eg John Gillies' anthology of 1786 *Sean Dàin agus Orain Ghaidhealach*. There has been substantial modern publication of such songs, sometimes from the early sources and sometimes from much later oral tradition.

These songs give us a lively and authentic insight into their authors' minds and experiences. For example, they show us members of the persecuted **Clan Gregor** on the run in **Perthshire** and Argyll in the years around 1600, or comment on feuds between MacLeods and MacDonalds in Uist and Skye at that time; others express a woman's admiration for the mid-17th century warrior **Alasdair MacColla (MacDonald)**, or tell of the emptiness and sense of loss an author feels after the loss of a sweetheart, or the death of brothers or a son. Sometimes they give realistic everyday detail of people's lives; their furnishings, work-processes, food or clothes. With their unsentimental detail, they are an invaluable source of information about the lives and circumstances of contemporary Gaels and should be used by any respectable Scottish historian.

Another genre that emerges in the 17th century, and is continued in the 18th, is that of the formal and 'literary' love-song, usually composed by middle-class Gaels perhaps more as a literary exercise than a *cri de coeur*. They may owe something to the *dánta grádha* or courtly love-poems which were practised by both professional and amateur poets earlier, but can have a stylish elegance of their own. Some identify the authors as sons of ministers or tacksmen, while others tell of army experience in Europe. (There was a formidable influx of Highland 'gentlemen' into the army in the 17th and 18th centuries.)

Meantime the old traditions of heroic balladry continued – **ballads** dealing with legendary exploits of Fionn (**Finn mac Cumhal**) and Oscar and **Deirdre** and **Cù Chulainn**. Probably there was not much fresh composition of such verse in the 16th and 17th centuries, but the tradition was kept very much alive, until major collections were made from oral sources in the 18th century.

For texts and discussion see J L Campbell & F Collinson, *Hebridean Folksongs*, Vols 1–3 (1969, 1977, 1981); and D S Thomson, *Introduction to Gaelic Poetry* (1990) and *The MacDiarmid Manuscript Anthology* (1992).

Poetry in the 18th and 19th Centuries.

The classical (bardic) tradition finally petered out in the first half of the 18th century, but praise-poetry was till prominent, as in Donnchadh Bàn's (**Duncan Bàn Macintyre**'s) earlier verse; other examples exist in most of the prominent 18th century poets (**Rob Donn, John MacCodrum, William Ross**, etc). This tradition continued into the 19th century, but with a diminishing emphasis on clan. Apart from brief poems in praise of **Prince Charles Edward Stewart** and a somewhat off-hand praise of **Simon Fraser, 11th Lord Lovat**, Alasdair Mac Mhaighstir Alasdair (**Alexander Mac-Donald**) seems to have had little interest in the praise-poem, though clan poetry is forcefully represented in his *Oran nam Fineachan Gaidhealach* ('Song of the Highland Clans', an incitement composed before the '45 campaign had started). Dùghall Bochanan (**Dugald Buchanan**) chooses an evangelical warrior for his praises.

It is as though the changing ethos of society had freed the poets to look around them in a more open, less blinkered way. Donnchadh Bàn turns to praising a mountain, John MacCodrum gives rein to fun and satire, Rob Donn gives his main attention to a wide range of contemporaries with a mixture of classes, and William Ross can find room for his personal emotional life to enter his poetry. **Jacobitism** had failed, and we see the status quo of the **Union**, and later the Empire, being accepted, with poems at the end of the century about *blàr na h-Olaind* (the Battle of Holland) and later about the Napoleonic Wars, the Crimean War and so on.

But before that decline in Scottish consciousness there was a period of renewed Gaelic awareness, accompanied by a distinct and innovative thrust. Mac Mhaighstir Alasdair was at the forefront of this movement; he was the **Hugh MacDiarmid** of his time. His innovations were built on Gaelic poetic traditions, which he knew well, but took fresh fire from his experience of other literatures. He was innovative also in respect of metrical usage and overall poem-construction, and his model in *Moladh Mòraig* inspired Donnchadh Bàn's use of ceòl-mór [see **Piobaireachd**] metre in his praise of Ben Doran. A long succession of poets followed his lead with poems on the seasons. No one quite matched the vituperation and malice of some of his satirical poems with their frequent political barbs. Yet all of these 18th century poets bring individual insights and techniques into play.

Some had their works published in their own lifetimes, while others, such as Rob Donn, had at least recited them for transcription before they died. Mac Mhaighstir Alasdair published some of his poems in 1751, and others survive in contemporary manuscripts, though it is likely that many were lost. Donnchadh Bàn's first appeared in 1768, and there were later editions in 1790 and 1804, as well as publications of individual poems between 1781–88. In this second half of the 18th century individual collections of Gaelic poetry were first published, and this was also a time of great activity in collecting poems and songs. Again Mac Mhaighstir Alasdair's example was important, though **James Macpherson**'s 'Ossianic' activities probably gave added stimulus.

The 19th century sees a continuation of these trends, but it was also the main century of **clearance** and dispersal. The failure of the kelp industry, the introduction of sheep farming, and the creation of private **deer forests**, led to a huge dispersal of native Highlanders

to the Scottish Lowlands and overseas. These changes are reflected in Gaelic poetry and song. There are protest songs and poems, mainly late in the century, as part of the counter-attack associated with the Land Reform movements of the 1870s–80s when one of the most prominent figures is **Mary Macpherson**. Important predecessors included **William Livingston** of Islay, and on a smaller scale Ewen Robertson of **Tongue**, author of the song *Mo mhollachd aig na caoraich mhòr* ('My Curse on the Big Sheep'): see I Grimble, *The Trial of Patrick Sellar* (1963). More ubiquitous, however, were the nostalgic songs of place, as people in **Glasgow**, **Paisley** or Canada remembered the homes and communities they had left. In course of time these took on some of the characteristics (metrical, etc) of evangelical hymns or the popular **music hall** while a still more ersatz variety of song came to be composed in English (about Bonny Bays and lovely Stornoways). In this welter of activity there were of course some moving and artistic songs, eg by John MacLachlan of Rahoy, Neil MacLeod of Skye, and Murchadh a' Cheisdeir (Murdo MacLeod) of **Lewis**, author of *Eilean an Fhraoich* ('The Isle of Heather').

For further details see D S Thomson, *An Introduction to Gaelic Poetry* (1990) and *Companion to Gaelic Culture* (1983); and Donald Meek, 'Gaelic poets of the Land Agitation' in TGSI 49, 1977.

Earlier Gaelic Prose

Gaelic prose, like Gaelic poetry, has both classical and modern dimensions. The old literary language was used for a wide variety of purposes (history, genealogy, medical writings, religious discourse, philosophy, geography, astrology, etc) and also for fiction and legend, as in the wide range of sagas that has survived. Most of this writing was in manuscript form, and did not appear in print until the 19th and 20th centuries. Although predominantly Irish in provenance, about 30 Gaelic medical manuscripts survive in Scotland, plus a scatter of saga, history and genealogical manuscripts.

A significant proportion of this literature found its way into the oral tradition. No doubt some of the stories had originally come from that tradition and had been re-cast in written form, but it is clear that the process also worked in the opposite direction. Fragments of medical lore survived in oral tradition, and much history, legend and genealogy; but probably the most significant body of prose was oral tales. Some were very lengthy. In 1949 Aonghas Barrach (Angus Macmillan) of **Benbecula** advised the writer that some of his stories would take all night to tell (and he meant seven or eight hours). The fidelity of such versions may be judged from a performance by Duncan MacDonald, the great **South Uist** tradition-bearer, who told a story to an international audience in 1953, unaware that a newly printed version of a previous narration was in his audience's hands. He survived the test brilliantly.

Much of this rich harvest of oral saga was recorded in the later 19th century (by **J F** Campbell, **John Dewar**, etc) and in the 20th century (by collectors like Callum Maclean and Donald Archie MacDonald).

The earliest printed book in Gaelic was **John Carswell**'s of 1567, and the few Gaelic publications between then and 1741 were all of a religious nature such as catechisms. The New Testament first appeared in Gaelic in 1767 (translated by James Stewart of **Killin**) and the Old Testament had all appeared in translation by 1801. This gave a great stimulus to printed prose, especially sermons and religious biography. Secular printed prose made little headway until the foundation of several Gaelic periodicals from 1829 onwards [see **Rev Norman MacLeod (i)**] and, in the later 19th century, the publication of stories strongly influenced by the folk-tale tradition. Demand stemmed from the Gaelic schools, and the response of mainly city-based Gaels to that demand, as well as from the interest created in these Lowland Gaelic communities.

An Comunn Gaidhealach, founded in 1891, gave a further stimulus, and the succession of periodicals continued with those founded by **Ruaraidh Erskine of Mar** and by An Comunn. In the early years of the 20th century the essay became a popular form (Donald Mackinnon, Donald Mackechnie, Neil MacLeod, Donald Lamont and Kenneth MacLeod) while the short story and the novel made some early progress (John MacFadyen, John MacCormick, Angus Robertson and others). In journalism there was a significant output from Angus Henderson of **Ardnamurchan** who wrote frequently in the periodical *Guth na Bliadhna*. It was part of Erskine of Mar's deliberate policy to extend the range of topics discussed in Gaelic, and this aim was shared by An Comunn Gaidhealach which devised a Gaelic vocabulary for the conduct of public meetings, minute-taking, etc.

Gaelic Prose and Drama in the 20th Century

The literary activity encouraged by Erskine of Mar's periodicals in the early part of the century subsided when they ceased publication. *Guth na Bliadhna* came to a stop in 1925, and there was only one subsequent issue of *An Rosarnach* (in 1930). An Comunn Gaidhealach's periodical *An Gaidheal* continued to appear but, as a bilingual magazine involved in reporting An Comunn's business, it did not have much space for creative prose work. The newly created Gaelic radio service gave some encouragement to the short story, still with a folk-tale bias, and the collection *Am Measg nam Bodach* (1938) reflects this.

After World War II it was clear that some fresh impetus was needed. Hoping to provide such stimulus, An Comunn launched the periodical *Alba* in 1948 (ed Malcolm MacLean and T M Murchison) but it was allowed to lapse after the first issue. In 1951 the all-Gaelic periodical *Gairm* was advertised, and began to appear in 1952. It has survived as a quarterly ever since, and has had a crucial influence on Gaelic writing over the last 40 years. *Gairm*'s policy has been to encourage Gaelic writing across a wide spectrum, giving space to items of folk literature, but positively encouraging writing on untraditional topics and the linguistic innovation this has demanded. So, for example, articles appeared on Japanese art, rheumatism, nuclear physics and aspects of biology, as well as on a range of current affairs topics. From the late 1950s a series of books began to appear from Gairm Publications, including school books for various stages, poetry and short stories, discussion of current Gaelic matters (eg *Gaelic in Scotland*, 1976), and a *Gaelic Biology* textbook. This series con-

tinues. The range of children's books, and books in general, has been further increased since the mid-1970s through the publications of a Stornoway publisher, Acair, supported by local authorities. All these publishing activities were greatly stimulated by the support of the **Gaelic Books Council**, founded in 1968.

Probably the genre to benefit most from these opportunities was fiction. From its earliest issues *Gairm* featured short stories. Close on 500 have appeared and there have been many separate collections (eg *Eadar Peann is Paipear/Pen and Paper*, ed 1985 by D I MacIomhair). Both of the early *Gairm* editors, Fionlagh Iain MacDhòmhnaill and Ruaraidh MacThòmais, contributed and Iain Mac a' Ghobhainn (**Iain Crichton Smith**) also appeared at an early stage, as did Hector Maciver. It was Smith who made the greatest contribution, extending the range of stories and using a wide variety of techniques. His earliest collection, set in an island location, *Bùrn is Aran* (Bread and Water, 1960), is something of a classic. Later collections range more widely, (eg *An Dubh is an Gorm/The Black and the Blue*, 1963 and *Na Guthan/The Voices*, 1991). Among other short story writers are Colin Mackenzie, with tales of the supernatural, as in *Oirthir Tìm* (The Edge of Time, 1969); Eilidh Watt, who also dabbles in the supernatural (*Gun Fhois/Without Respite*, 1987); John Murray, whose innovative *An Aghaidh Choimheach* (The Mask, 1973) is mostly set in the cities; Dòmhnall Iain MacIomhair, whose characters often show para-normal characteristics but can be hilarious (*Grian is Uisge/Sun and Rain*, 1991); and Dòmhnall Alasdair (Donald A Macdonald), whose series *Seanchasan à Stobarrag* (Stories from Stobarrag) in *Gairm* gives a humorous picture of village life in Lewis over several decades.

Full-length novels only began to appear from the 1960s onwards. The size of the Gaelic reading public hardly encourages the novelist, especially if he has to make a living from writing. This has not prevented Iain Crichton Smith from producing novels, among them the very successful *An t-Aonaran* (The Loner, 1976). Tormod Caimbeul's *Deireadh an Fhoghair* (End of Autumn, 1979) is also highly regarded. A recent series of short novels for school reading includes Calum MacMillan's *Na Fògaraich* (The Exiles, 1991). Other innovative novels for teenagers have been written by Maoilios Caimbeul (a futuristic fantasy *Talfasg*, 1990) and by Iain MacLeòid, *Spuirean na h-Iolaire* (The Eagle's Claws, 1989) and *An Sgàile Dhorcha* (The Dark Shadow, 1992).

The history of Gaelic drama is even more patchy. In the early 20th century Hector MacDougall and Donald Sinclair wrote dialogues and short plays and An Comunn published an extended series of one-act plays, many of them translations. In the late 1970s there was a short-lived professional company, Fir Chlis; otherwise dramatists have little hope of seeing their work produced, even on radio, let alone television (apart from STV's soap *Machair*). Among the more innovative dramatists are Norman G MacDonald, Finlay MacLeod (an early Pinter fan, as in his *Shoni*) and the late Paul Macinnes. An amateur dramatic festival produces occasional one-acters of quality.

Modern Poetry

By the second half of the 20th century almost no one spoke only Gaelic. Two world wars with general concription, plus the search for employment, destroyed any idea of a Gaelic conservation area; the territory was subsequently blanketed by English language radio and television. Gaelic could not cut clear of English influence, and only extremists still cherish such a dream. A more positive reaction was to enjoy the benefits of an alternative experience while still retaining the Gaelic one, with the further option of extending such experience over European and other frontiers. Educational opportunities threw open the door as never before. One result was the publication of an extensive anthology, *European Poetry in Gaelic*, in 1990. Much traditional verse continued to be written and collected (eg Hector Cameron's, Angus Campbell's and Calum MacNeacail's Skye poetry), while some poets seemed to belong to both the old and the new, more innovative traditions (eg Angus Campbell, James Thomson, Angus Robertson and Roderick MacDonald). MacDonald has translated copiously from Burns; another large work of translation this century was John Maclean's *Odusseia Homair* (1976). Also involved in translation, but writing in Gaelic, Scots and English, is William Neill (b.1922).

The first signs of an expansion of frontiers appeared at the time of World War I, especially in the work of two young Lewis poets who had been students at **Aberdeen University**. One of these, John Munro, was killed in 1918. Only a tiny number of his poems survive, but one in particular, *Ar Tìr 's ar Gaisgich a thuit sa' Bhlàr* ('Our Land and our Heroes who fell in Battle'), shows him in transition from a traditional style of verse to a modern and innovative one. The first part of the poem is in regularly-spaced lines, using traditional symbols of homeland verse, and the second part moves to a fluid, rhythmically varied style as he describes battlefield scenes and explores the Highland soldiers' reactions. This is probably the earliest example we have of a highly sensitive sort of free verse. It was to surface again some 30 to 40 years later. A close friend of Munro's was Murdo Murray, who wrote a few innovative poems during the Great War and was later, to write about Munro (see M Moireach, *Luach na Saorsa*/*The Value of Freedom*, 1970). Their work was first brought to a wider Gaelic audience in James Thomson's 1932 anthology *An Dìleab* (*The Legacy*).

There are hints of contemporary English poetry in Munro's work, and this was to continue in the work of Gaelic poets in the 1930s and later, who were often professionally involved in literary studies or in the teaching of literature. The experience of living with the poetry of Shakespeare, Wordsworth, Eliot or Yeats could hardly fail to leave some mark; and in the specifically Scottish dimension there was also Hugh MacDiarmid.

The oldest member of this new wave, **Sorley Maclean** (b.1911), was strongly influenced by MacDiarmid. He shared his Communist and Nationalist leanings, and was probably influenced by MacDiarmid's long sequence *A Drunk Man Looks at the Thistle* when, in the late 1930s, he put together his sequence *Dàin do Eimhir* (*Poems to Eimhir*, 1943). This has remained Maclean's major achievement. Later collections of his poetry have re-ordered the sequence in curious ways and added sections of another long work also dating from the late 1930s (*The Coolins*) plus occasional poems from the 1950s and later. The

Eimhir sequence combines the themes of love and (leftist) politics in a way that many readers have found interesting and the myth of the poet's decision not to fight in Spain because of his love for Eimhir has lodged itself in critical commentary.

A near contemporary, **George Campbell Hay**, was heavily involved in World War II (as was Maclean), and his poetry was greatly enriched by his experiences, especially in North Africa and Italy. Ruaraidh MacThòmais (b.1921) was the next in this group. In poems dating from the late 1930s and the 1940s, he began to develop a style of free verse that in course of time was to become the norm rather than the exception (see *Creachadh na Clàrsaich*/*Plundering the Harp*, 1982). There followed Iain Mac a' Ghobhainn (b.1928), widely known by his English name Iain Crichton Smith, with poems dating from the early 1950s (eg in the verse and prose collection *Bùrn is Aran*/*Bread and Water*, 1960). The youngest of the group was Dòmhnall MacAmhlaigh (Donald MacAulay, b.1930) who showed a strong preference for free verse and Poundian techniques (see *Seòbhrach às a' Chlaich*/*Primrose Growing out of Stone*, 1967).

The work of these five poets may be said to have transformed the Gaelic poetic tradition. It was a cumulative achievement, gathering strength, subtlety and range from each of the group, and in each decade. It carried sufficient weight to convince most people that the Gaelic poet was living in a new world, and could no longer behave as if that world had not arrived. It also provoked those who found they could no longer automatically sing the new poems, and who missed the familiar beat of the old metrics while failing to hear the subtleties of the new. The magazine *Gairm*, though it continued to feature poetry in the older style, gave much prominence to the new, and attracted some angry criticism thereby. But the tide had turned, and few new writers in Gaelic now use the older styles. This may suggest that the revolution went too far.

Important though style and metrics may be, it was more important that the new poetry was exploring a fresh range of topics and reactions. There was nothing new in reporting on war and battles, but Hay's depiction of an oppressed North African Arab broke new ground, as did his sympathetic exploration of the Arab world generally. Maclean's thoughts on the Spanish Civil War chime with those of English poets of the thirties. The theme of the clearances is tackled in new and exciting ways; Iain Mac a' Ghobhainn sets Lewis against the background of Hiroshima while Dòmhnall MacAmhlaigh, in his Edinburgh back garden, reflects on Maxim Gorky and his attitude to the downtrodden of his own country, or compares the poor in Turkey with the people from his native Bernera (Lewis). Two of these poets have sequences on the people of Glasgow: Mac a' Ghobhainn's *Eadar Fealla-dhà is Glaschu* (*Fun and Glasgow*, 1974) and MacThòmais's 'Air Stràidean Ghlaschu' in his *Smeur an Dòchais* (*Bramble of Hope*, 1992).

The structure of many of the new poems showed a different emphasis on metaphor and symbol, and sometimes a tight organic organisation of the whole, in contrast to the more impressionistic or linear styles of earlier traditions (see D S Thomson, *The New Verse in Scottish Gaelic: A Structural Analysis*, 1974, and *Nua Bhàrdachd*

Ghàidhlig, *Modern Scottish Gaelic Poems*, edited by Donald Macaulay).

Latterly this new tradition has continued to develop, and expand, with a succession of new writers from each decade. The earlier, Aonghas MacNeacail (b.1942), Maoilios Caimbeul (b.1944), Catrìona NicGumaraid (b.1947) and Fearghas MacFhionnlaigh (b.1948), all published collections in the 1970s and 1980s and are still writing strongly, widening poetic horizons with explorations that take them to Japan and native America and into the realms of music, philosophy and evangelical religion. A still younger group includes such poets as Mary Montgomery, Meg Bateman, Anne Frater and Christopher Whyte. Whyte edited an anthology of these eight poets entitled *An Aghaidh na Sìorraidheachd/In the Face of Eternity*, 1991.

GAIRDNER, Charles (1824–99) Banker

Born in **Ayr**, Gairdner began his career in accountancy and quickly gained experience in the fields of stockbroking and insurance. Peter White, a founder member of the **Glasgow** Stock Exchange, offered him a partnership in 1845. Gairdner helped found the Institute of Accountants and Actuaries and, having gained further experience as a liquidator, was appointed General Manager of the Union Bank of Scotland. The bank was heavily involved in financing both the decline of the **cotton** industry and the rise of the metalworking industries to which processes Gairdner brought a highly personalised tight control. He also founded the Adam Smith Club in Glasgow.

GAIRLOCH, Ross & Cromarty

Slight (*gair* = short) by west coast standards, Gair Loch is the first coastal indentation north of Loch Torridon. The large village and **fishing** port of the same name once boasted the most expensive hotel in the north west and has long been a popular centre (now with the inevitable Heritage Museum) for exploring **Loch Maree**, the Torridon/Ben Eighe area, and the splendid coastline. Just south of the village on the An Ard promontory a dun, once nigh impregnable, may still be detected. The region was traditionally **MacLeod** territory until in 1494 the **Mackenzies** secured Gairloch. In the 18th century they built Flowerdale House, or An Tigh Dige, with fine wooded policies, and in the 19th century encouraged the fishing industry. Care should be taken to distinguish this Gairloch, with no naval associations, from the Gareloch in **Dunbartonshire**.

GAL, Hans (1890–1987) Composer and Musicologist

A native of Austria, Gal fled to Britain where he joined the staff of **Edinburgh University** music department when Tovey was professor. Gal is remembered both for his sensitive and scholarly books on Schubert, Brahms and other composers and for his subtle and genial music which includes compositions for a huge variety of genres. As a lecturer, pianist and teacher, his influence on music-making in Scotland was one of enduring inspiration.

GALASHIELS, Selkirkshire

A small, straggling industrial town on the Gala Wate Galashiels 'partakes not a jot of the dinginess, and con fusion, and the concentration of character upon me labour and gain, which so generally belong to places its class; but is lively and mirthful in its appearance, hee ful of the adornings of taste and beauty, seems to recipr cate smiles of gladness with the charming scenery am which it is embosomed, and has the dress and habits f more of rural than of city life' (Fullarton's *Gazetteer*, 1843

Originally a settlement of huts, or 'shiels' by the Ga for the use of pilgrims on their way to **Melrose**, Gal shiels owed its prominence in tweed and **woolle** manufacture to the proximity and strength of curre in the Gala Water, although the latter sometimes threa ened to overwhelm the town which only avoided con plete inundation in the famous floods of 1829 by th prompt felling into the torrent of a whole stand of tre by the bank, thus diverting the worst of the flow. B the middle of the 19th century Galashiels was th premier tweed producing town in Scotland; steam wa supplementing water to power the mills; the populatio rose from 2209 in 1831 to 15,330 by 1881 and i 1909 the Scottish College of Textiles was establishe here to crown its reputation. Its dearth of antiquities although it does have a mercat cross dating from 169 – is compensated for by its possession of 'the mo perfect town memorial in the British Isles' (H Morton); a massive **Robert Lorimer** clock tow fronted by an equestrian statue of a mosstrooper 'Border Reiver' by **Thomas Clapperton**.

GALGACUS or CALGACUS (fl.84/85 AD) Caledonian Chief

All that is known of Galgacus derives from the **Roma** historian Tacitus whose funeral panegyric about **Cnaeu Julius Agricola** tells of the Battle of **Mons Graupiu** Galgacus (possibly from *calgach*, a sword) is identifie as a chief of the defeated *Caledonii* and thus becomes th first Scot to be mentioned by name in a written histor For his own purposes Tacitus portrayed him as a stoc reactionary who perversely valued the independence c his people, 'the most distant inhabitants on earth', abov the benefits of the *pax Romana* which, according to Ga gacus, 'creates a desert and calls it peace'.

GALLACHER, William (1881–1965) Communist MP

Though constrained by his allegiance to Leninist an then Stalinist orthodoxy, for half a century Willie Ga lacher epitomised left-wing militancy as an effectiv champion of industrial unrest, as a model constituenc MP, and as a persuasive purveyor of the **Red Clydesid** image.

He was born of Highland-Irish parentage in **Paisle** His father died when he was seven and, like **John Mac lean**, he took part-time jobs to support his famil through his schooling. Like Maclean he also abjure alcohol, **temperance** providing both men with a cree and a cause until, partly under Maclean's influence it was superseded by socialism. He joined the Soci Democratic Federation and, though no theorist, wa active in its conversion into the British Socialist Part In 1914, after various jobs (and trips to the USA an reland) he established a power base as shop steward at the Albion Motor Works (Scotstoun) and then as chairman of the **Clyde Workers Committee**. Prominent in the CWC protests against the provisions of the Munitions Act he was arrested in 1916 and imprisoned for a year. Further imprisonment followed the **Bloody Friday** demonstration of 1919.

In 1920, invited to attend the Second Congress of the Communist International, he stowed away aboard a Norwegian vessel and eventually turned up in Moscow. There his revolutionary ideas underwent a sea change as Lenin prevailed on him to direct Scottish militancy into parliamentary channels. In this he succeeded to the extent of taking most members of the Scottish BSP into the Communist Party of Great Britain (though not Maclean); but he failed to secure a lasting alliance between the CPGB and the Labour Party.

Arrested for sedition in 1921 and for incitement in 1925 he endured further prison sentences in spite of an offer from George Bernard Shaw to stand bail. He was active amongst the striking Durham miners and in the Unemployed Workers Movement but in the 1930s re-endorsed political action and in 1935 won the West **Fife** constituency as a Communist. He held the seat for the next 15 years, more by assiduously pursuing better social conditions for his constituents than by persuasive ideology. His changing attitudes to the war effort – outright opposition, then wholehearted support – were dictated by the vagaries of Soviet policy. Slavish adulation of Stalin probably lost him his seat in the 1951 election (it went to the Labour party in the shape of the anti-Monarchist Willie Hamilton). An equally uncritical support of national liberation movements found him endorsing Irish reunification, home rule for Scotland and Zionism.

President of the CPGB 1956–63, he remained active in the Amalgamated Engineering Union and the **Co-operative Movement**. He also produced a steady stream of pamphlets and books including *Revolt on the Clyde*, 1936, which may overstate his influence amongst the Red Clydesiders. Honours came to him from the Communist capitals of Eastern Europe but he remained in his council flat in Paisley, dying there in August 1965. 'He left little rancour behind him' (*The Times*) and much genuine affection. 40,000 mourners lined the streets as his coffin, draped in the Red Flag and bedecked with floral tributes from the Soviet bloc, was taken to Woodside Crematorium.

GALLOWAY

The province of Galloway in the south-western corner of Scotland used to include **Carrick** (the southern division of **Ayrshire**) and parts of **Dumfriesshire** but since 1186 has comprised the area from the 'Brae o' Glenapp' in the west to the 'Brig End o' Dumfries' in the east, ie the county of **Wigtownshire** plus the **Stewarty of Kirkcudbright**. The name is a combination of *Gall*, a stranger, and *gaidhel*, or Gael, 'the land of the stranger Gaels', Gaelic-speaking colonists from Ireland settled this, the nearest corner of Scotland to their own shores, in the 8th–10th centuries, overwhelming the resident motley of local tribes, Anglo-Saxon invaders and Norse settlers. Since these early times Gallovidians have considered themselves something of a race apart (as exem-

plified by **John MacTaggart**'s *Gallovidian Encyclopaedia*), fiercely independent and willing to lay down their lives for their freedom (as in the **Wars of Independence**) or their religion, Galloway being described as 'the very forge of the **Covenanters**' battle'.

GALLOWAY CATTLE

A black-polled breed like the **Aberdeen-Angus**, the Galloway is in fact the product of a completely different type of husbandry. Able to cope with cold and wet conditions beyond the tolerance of practically all other cattle breeds, the Galloway is a beast of marginal and hill land while the Aberdeen-Angus is best suited to more gentle conditions.

Galloways were a mainstay of the **droving** trade, being sent south in large numbers from about 1750 to the end of the trade in about 1840. Soon a more complex livestock trade developed. Galloway cows were mated with white **Shorthorn** bulls to produce crossbred cows called Blue-Greys which still today command a high price because their mothers' hardiness is combined with the milking ability of the Shorthorn breed. Blue-Greys are popular suckler cows, ie they are mated with beef bulls such as the Limousin, Charolais or Romagnola to produce calves for sale. Like Galloways, Blue-Greys can winter outside though today most are housed.

Belted, Dun, Red and White Galloways are all variants of the main breed. There is a very strong demand now from Germany for these cattle, and for Blue-Greys, which are popular for grazing lowland heaths, and big prices are paid at the **Castle Douglas** sales. Galloways are also found in the USSR, North America and elsewhere.

GALSTON, Ayrshire

Two dramatically contrasting buildings stand out in the otherwise prosaic mining and **cotton**-weaving town of Galston. Barr Castle is an austere rectangular 15th century tower, practically but not aesthetically improved in 1899 by the addition of an incongruous lid-like roof, and now in use as a masonic hall. At the opposite end of the architectural spectrum is St Sophia's Roman Catholic Church (**Rowand Anderson**, 1885–6), commissioned by the Marquess of Bute in memory of his mother Sophia, freely based on the Hagia Sophia in Istanbul and constructed of most un-Byzantine red-brick.

About a mile to the north of the town Loudoun Castle was one of the grandest houses in Ayrshire before a fire in 1941 left it a gutted shell. Built (1804–11) by Archibald Elliott for 1st Marquis of Hastings, who married a daughter of Campbell of Loudoun, this magnificent castellated mansion, incorporating the 16th century tower of the Campbells of Loudoun which had been besieged and partially destroyed by **General Monk**, and set in a stately park laid out by **Alexander Nasmyth**, earned the sobriquet 'Windsor of the North'.

GALT, John (1779–1839) Novelist

Born in **Irvine**, **Ayrshire**, Galt was the son of a sea captain. His family moved to **Greenock** when he was ten, and he completed his education at the local grammar school. After this he was taken on as an apprentice at the Greenock Custom House, but moved on in 1796 to become a junior clerk in the mercantile offices of James Miller & Co. At the same time he began contribu-

John Galt, by Charles Grey, 1835 (SNPG)

ting essays, verse and stories to local newspapers and journals. In 1804 he moved to London to work in business, but his lack of success led him to study law at Lincoln's Inn. He soon forsook this, and from 1809–11 embarked on extensive travels through Europe, during which he met and befriended **Lord Byron**. On his return he published an account of his travels, followed this with a series of tragedies, and in 1812 published *The Life and Administration of Cardinal Wolsey*.

In 1815 he married Elizabeth Tilloch and shortly afterwards, following another series of failed ventures, began applying himself seriously to the business of writing. He began contributing to the *Monthly Magazine*, and published several textbooks under the pseudonym 'Reverend T Clark'.

In 1820 **Blackwood's Magazine** published *The Ayrshire Legatees*. In 1821 Galt published his best known work, *The Annals of the Parish*. With its simple style and evocative descriptions of events in the life of a parish minister in an imaginary Ayrshire town, *The Annals* established Galt as an important chronicler of contemporary social history in west Scotland. Five other works in the next two years explored similar themes: *The Steam Boat* (1821), *Sir Andrew Wylie* (1822), *The Provost* (1822), *The Entail* (1823) and *Ringan Gilhaize* (1823).

In 1824 Galt became secretary to the Canada Company, a group founded to encourage emigration to the underdeveloped parts of that country. Between 1825 and 1829 he visited Canada as a member of a government commission investigating the issue of emigration, and in 1826 founded the town of Guelph in Ontario. In 1829 he returned to Britain facing massive debt, and spent several months in a debtors' prison. On his release he settled in Greenock to write, and produced several

novels over the next five years, including *Lawrie Tod* (1830), *Bogle Corbet or The Emigrants* (1831) and *Eben Erskine* (1833). Other works published include *The Life of Lord Byron* (1831), his *Autobiography* in 1833 and a series of sketches from his life, *Literary Life and Miscellanies* (1834). He died in Greenock.

GARDEN, Mary (1874–1967) Opera Singer

Born in **Aberdeen**, Mary Garden was taken to America at the age of six by her father who developed the Pierce Arrow Car Co, becoming a millionaire in the process. In 1900 Mary made her debut at the Opéra-Comique in Paris. She had love affairs during this time with the composer Claude Debussy, the conductor André Messager and the director Albert Carré. By Royal Command she appeared at Windsor Castle with Dame Nellie Melba in 1907.

Mary Garden was then invited by Oscar Hammerstein to perform at the newly opened Manhattan Opera House in New York. The Russians Rimsky-Korsakov and Chaliapin were present and reported to be most impressed. She is particularly remembered for creating the role of Mélisande in Debussy's opera *Pélleas et Mélisande* – a role in which the composer regarded her as unsurpassed. She was also principal soprano and, briefly, director of the Chicago Grand Opera during which spell she gave Prokofiev's *The Love of Three Oranges* its premiere.

Although at one time engaged to Harold McCormick, head of International Harvesters and later manager of the Chicago Opera House, Mary Garden never married. In the 1930s she worked for MGM in Hollywood, but just before the outbreak of war returned to Paris. The German invasion saw her back in her native Aberdeen where she had always returned for holidays and which she regarded as home. America called again after the war and in the 1950s she gave a series of lecture tours. Adlai Stevenson, then Mayor of Chicago, declared a

Mary Garden, chalk drawing by Mark Tobey, 1918 (SNPG)

Mary Garden Day' and 'Gardenia' perfume is also named after her.

She died in Aberdeen and is buried there.

GARDENSTOWN, Banffshire

Steeply terraced into the cliffs above Gamrie Bay, Gardenstown has little space for gardens, its name in fact deriving from its 1720 founder, Alexander Garden (or possibly Gordon) of Troup, who ordained it a **fishing** port rather than a horticultural extravaganza. Crovie, another fishing village to the east, is even more cliff-cramped and picturesque; beyond it rears Troup Head, the boundary with **Aberdeenshire**. To the west are the remains of the pre-**Reformation** church of St John, said to have been first built in the 11th century by way of thanksgiving for a defeat of **Viking** raiders.

GARDINER, Sir Frederick C (1855–1937)
Company Chairman

Born in **Kincardine**, Gardiner spent the major part of his career in shipowning and shipbroking, establishing the partnership of James Gardiner & Co with his brother in 1880. He was awarded the KBE in 1921 and elected President of Glasgow's Chamber of Commerce 1919–21. Having withdrawn from shipping, and at a comparatively late stage in his life, he became involved in the electrical industry, succeeding **Bonar Law** as Chairman of the Clyde Valley Power Company. Under his chairmanship Clyde Valley extended its capacity at both its main generating stations, Yoker and Clydesmill, and increasingly became connected to the developing national grid. He left an estate of over half a million pounds.

GARELOCHHEAD, Dunbartonshire

The scene of an 1853 skirmish known as the 'Battle of Garelochhead' which pitted Sir James Colquhoun of Luss plus retainers against a boatload of sabbath-breaking trippers, Garelochhead became a fashionable residential area in the 19th century. Unsurprisingly situated at the head of the Gare Loch, its quietness was further shattered during World War II by the opening of a dock at Faslane, now the Clyde Submarine Base.

GARLIESTON, Wigtownshire

Halfway down the west coast of Wigtown Bay between **Wigtown** and the **Isle of Whithorn**, Garlieston was built as a planned village in the 1760s by Lord Garlies, later 7th Earl of Galloway, and subsequently developed as a centre of **shipbuilding**, **fishing**, and rope and sail making. Garlieston House about a mile to the south was built by his father, the 6th Earl, in 1740 and surrounded by superb trees. The 1844 *Statistical Account* was particularly impressed by a later earl's kitchen garden in which one vine 'produces about 346 bunches [of grapes] a year, each averaging one and a quarter pounds and some of the individual berries are three and a quarter inches in circumference'. Further south still, the ruins of Cruggleton Castle perch 'like a seabird's nest' on high cliffs. Most of the visible remains date from the 15th and 16th centuries but cover remains of an earlier castle on the same site that was occupied in the 13th century by **John Comyn (ii), Earl of Buchan**.

GARTOCHARN, Dunbartonshire

Gartocharn is a quiet rural village a mile from the southern shore of **Loch Lomond** and Ross Priory, where **Sir Walter Scott** once stayed. The former mansion house occupies an early monastic site, and was owned by the Buchanans, an influential local family, until 1925. Gartocharn's most notable landmark is Duncryne Hill, known locally as 'the Dumpling'.

GARVALD, East Lothian

A convent of Cistercian nuns, established at **Haddington** during the reign of **Malcolm IV**, formed a 'branch community' for which they built the village and convent of Nunraw, or 'nun's row' at Garvald, four miles north-east of **Gifford**. It was for the protection of the community against possible English attack that Nunraw Castle, a Z-plan fortalice dating from the mid-16th century, was built nearby. The original castle was incorporated into a baronial mansion by the Dalrymples in 1860 and later belonged to the Hay family before being purchased once again by the Cistercians in 1946; six years later the foundations were laid for their new Abbey of Sancta Maria. Although painstakingly constructed of stone from the quaintly named Rattlebags quarry near **Dirleton**, the new abbey buildings are not immediately recognisable as ecclesiastical, being 'not at pains to be different from a factory or a disciplinary institution' (C McWilliam), but are said to possess an atmosphere of great tranquillity. Nothing now remains of the original medieval village of Nunraw.

GARVELLACH ISLANDS, Argyll

The Garvellachs (Gaelic *Garbh Eileach* – 'rough islands') or Isles of the Sea, lie off the coast of **Argyll** three miles west of Cullipool on the island of **Luing**. Aligned NE–SW, the most northerly of the chain is Dun Chonuill, on which is a 13th century castle. Next is Garbh Eilach, with interesting geological formations, followed by A'Chula, associated with St Brendan, and Eilach an Naoimh ('the saint's island'), where there are Early Christian beehive cells and a medieval monastery, overlooking which is a grave marked by simple cross-marked stones, reputedly of Eithne, the mother of **St Columba** of **Iona**.

GASK, Perthshire

Comprising the villages of Findo Gask and Trinity Gask, this area of **Strathearn** just west of **Perth** is notable for the **Roman** road along the Gask ridge. Its series of nine timbered watchtowers, now barely detectable, 'should be seen as a sort of linear frontier, an early precursor of more complex barriers such as the **Antonine Wall**' (B Walker and G Ritchie). Gask House, an Oliphant property, was visited by **Prince Charles Edward Stewart** in September 1745 and was the birthplace of Carolina Oliphant, later **Lady Nairne**, the song-writer.

GATEHOUSE OF FLEET, Kirkcudbrightshire

Of the many travellers who passed this way and committed their thoughts to paper, all have extolled the beauties of the scenery around Gatehouse of Fleet: 'magnificent', 'opulent', 'glorious', 'exceptionally fine', 'a pleasing vision'. Their comments on the town itself have not been so unanimous. In 1655 Thomas Tucker could be excused for saying it was 'not worth the nameing', for only one house stood at this point on the road where the Fleet river enters Fleet Bay. The same house – from which the town took its name, 'gait' meaning road – was still a solitary dwelling when **General William Roy** drew up his map in 1759. Yet within 40 years there were 'three factories, a brass-foundry, a tannery, a considerable number of hand-looms and a population of 1200', and by 1840 a passing writer was declaring that 'Gatehouse, as to the aspect of its streets and the neatness and beauty of its buildings, is decidedly the most handsome town or village in Galloway, and is equalled by very few in Scotland' (Fullarton's *Gazetteer*).

The transformation had been wrought by James Murray of Broughton (1727–99), a 'benevolent capitalist' with vast estates in Galloway, who laid out the town from 1763 as a centre for **cotton** manufacture and commissioned **Robert Mylne** to design him a suitably aristocratic residence, Cally House, overlooking his creation. The juxtaposition, thought **Lord Cockburn** in 1839, made Gatehouse 'too visibly the village at the Great Man's gate'.

For over a century the town and its industries, which later included three more cotton mills, a **shipbuilding** yard and a **brewery**, thrived. But decline set in during the 19th century and by the end of World War I Gatehouse was being described as 'of a deplorable dullness; the main street full of houses of an almost uniform plainness . . . the secondary streets plainer still and dingy besides' (C H Dick). By 1981 it was once more 'a small place at the head of the estuary'. But the scenery is still unsurpassed.

GEDDES, Andrew (1783–1844) Painter and Etcher

Although Geddes was born and educated in **Edinburgh**, he lived and worked mainly in London and in Italy. Associate of the Royal Academy (1831), he painted mostly portraits, and was an outstanding etcher of portraits, landscapes and copies of old masters. His *Summer* hangs in the **National Gallery of Scotland** in Edinburgh while other works are exhibited in the **Scottish National Portrait Gallery** and in the **Kirkcaldy** Museum of Art.

GEDDES, Patrick (1854–1932) Town Planner and Botanist

The youngest son of an army officer, Patrick Geddes was born at **Ballater**, **Aberdeenshire** but spent his childhood from 1857 in **Perth**, where he was educated at the Academy. In 1871 he joined the local branch of the National Bank of Scotland, but his early passion for natural history, especially botany, drew him in 1874 to the **University of Edinburgh** where, unable to thole formal study indoors, he left after only one week. Nevertheless he was attracted to the 'living laboratory' of the pioneering biologist and thinker T H Huxley at the Royal School of Mines in London's Kensington, which he attended from 1874–6.

While conducting research on flatworms at the Sorbonne marine station at Roscoff, Brittany, in 1879 he discovered chlorophyll, the basic plant substance, present in some low forms of animal life; published by the Royal Society of London, this discovery made

Sir Patrick Geddes, bronze head by Charles James Pibworth, 1907 (SNPG)

Geddes' name familiar to the world of biology. Hope of a 'Scottish Darwin' were confounded, though, when prolonged observation by microscope became impossible after Geddes' sight was damaged by strong sunlight during an expedition to Mexico. While convalescing he began systematising his knowledge via the first of his 'thinking machines'; these were pieces of paper folded according to the relationships of the Positivist philosopher August Comte's four hierarchies of the Sciences and the triad of Place, Work and Folk derived from the socio-biological teachings of Frédéric le Play; they demonstrated that scientific method could be applied to the natural social organism through statistical survey.

Returning to **Edinburgh** in 1880 the unorthodox Geddes failed to secure a senior academic appointment until 1888 when he was appointed Professor of Botany at University College, **Dundee**, a half-yearly post which he held for the next 30 years. After marriage in 1886 Geddes moved from Edinburgh's **Princes Street** to **James Court** where, founding the Edinburgh Social Union, he embarked upon an ambitious renewal programme in the **Old Town**. Changing tack in 1887, he established 'University Hall' on **The Mound**, the first udent residence in Scotland. His vision for 'Town and own' was extended in the **Lawnmarket** and on **Castle-ill** during the next decade, notably in **Riddle's Court** ad at **Ramsay Garden**. From 1887 he initiated the first immer Schools ever held in Europe, a forerunner of ae University Extension Movement.

From his 'sociological laboratory' in the **Outlook ower** he interpreted his socio-geographical 'Valley ection' concept which envisaged the traditional, pre-dustrial occupations as still fundamentally influencing ae development of the 'conurbation' (one of Geddes' eologisms). His sometimes obscure theories were later arified by Lewis Mumford, his 'disciple' in the USA, ad informed the regional planning of Roosevelt's New eal, notably the Tennessee Valley Authority.

Following his plans for **Dunfermline** (1904) and the ivic Survey of Edinburgh (1910), Geddes developed is eclectic Cities Exhibition which he restlessly pro-oted from 1911; his *Cities in Evolution* (1915) endures s the most accessible of his rhetorical writings.

From 1915 Geddes spent most of his time abroad mbroiled in a plethora of projects − many regrettably ither over-ambitious or stillborn. The decade to 1924 *as mainly devoted to planning problems in India but e also prepared a monumental scheme for the new *niversity of Jerusalem in Palestine, where the library lone was built to the designs of his son-in-law Frank *lears. In 1924 a complete breakdown of his health orced him into a Swiss sanatorium. The last blast from ae old 'volcano' was the creation of the Scots College t Montpelier. Knighted in 1931, he died by the Medi-erranean the following year. 'Geddes was on the side f life,' wrote Lewis Mumford in 1944. 'He challenged very success that was bought at the expense of further rowth, further self-renewal.'

¡EIKIE, Archibald (1835−1924) Geologist
orn in **Edinburgh**, Geikie was educated at Edinburgh *Iigh School and studied classics at the **University** but ecame committed to **geology** through his friendship /ith **Hugh Miller**. Asked to join the newly established *ieological Survey in 1855, he went on to become its .rst Scottish Director in 1867. By 1875 all central and *outh Scotland had been mapped under his direction, nd during the 1880s the Survey began mapping the *Iighlands, where progress was slow because of the omplex structures. One of the finest of the Survey's chievements was the discovery of the principle of *hrusting, which placed older rocks above younger *nes. Geikie sent his most able field geologists − Peach nd Horne − to solve the problem, which they did n 1884, the memoir being published by Geikie in 907.

In 1882 Geikie was appointed Director-General of the *ritish Survey, a post he held until 1901. During this ime he was the leading figure in British geology and he most honoured − knighted in 1891, President of *oth the British Association and the Royal Society and .warded the Order of Merit in 1913. He was author f a substantial number of publications and memoirs, ncluding *Textbook of Geology* (1882) and the best known *ancient Volcanoes of Britain* (1897). His brother James Geikie '1839−1915) was also an eminent geologist and Pro-essor of Geology at Edinburgh from 1882−1914.

GENERAL ASSEMBLY OF THE CHURCH OF SCOTLAND

For a week in May this supreme court, legislative body and debating chamber of the **Church of Scotland** meets annually in **Edinburgh**. It attends to all matters spiritual and ecclesiastical of the Church, and comments, often pungently, on important affairs of the state and nation. By law it is the top tier of government and authority of the established church. Items of business are referred up to it from synods, presbyteries, committees and indi-viduals according to **Presbyterian** rule. The monarch may attend, and has, but is usually represented by a Lord High Commissioner with full ceremonial at the opening occasions. The proceedings are published annually as a record of the acts and mind of the church and, to some extent, of the nation.

Some 1200 members, elders and clergy in equal number (called commissioners), are chosen to represent their presbyteries. About one third of the clergy attend each year, in addition to office bearers of the Assembly's committees which report and are listed in the Church of Scotland Year Book. Each session is chaired by the **Moderator** assisted by the Principal Clerk, attended by a Procurator, Solicitor, Chaplains and a Precentor to conduct the metrical psalms of the unaccompanied wor-ship which precedes business.

The first General Assembly of some 40 members met in December 1560, following the **Reformation** led by **Knox**, before **Queen Mary** returned from France. It met irregularly, often in conflict with the **Stewart** monarchs, as when **James VI** reintroduced episcopacy and in 1638 when **Charles I**'s Lord High Commissioner unsuccess-fully attempted to close the session at Glasgow; it con-tinued to meet and banned bishops. (No assembly is ever likely to be as spectacular as that of 1843, at the **Disruption**, when the **Free Church of Scotland** left to hold its own assembly in a nearby hall.) The final settlement of Presbyterian government, steered by **Car-stares** in 1690, set the pattern for all other Presbyterian churches and was enshrined in the 1707 **Union**. Not until 1928 was it settled that only the various churches had the right to call an Assembly. Changes in the consti-tution of the church are referred to the presbyteries under the Barrier Act of 1697 and subsequent legisla-tion. Lesser Presbyterian Churches often still hold their own assemblies around the same date.

The General Assembly is also a social occasion, and an annual garden party is held at **Holyrood Palace** by the monarch or Lord High Commissioner in residence. Both ceremonial and debates are reported in the Scottish press and media in detail and also elsewhere if contro-versial.

GEOLOGY

The word 'geology' was first coined in 1778 by a Swiss scientist but it was in Scotland that much of the pion-eering was accomplished. For its size Scotland has remarkable geological diversity reflecting a long and eventful history of rock formation. This complex geol-ogy was gradually untangled in the 18th and 19th cen-turies by a long line of distinguished geologists beginning with the greatest pioneer, **James Hutton**, and continued by **John Playfair**, **Charles Lyell**, **Roderick Murchison**, **Hugh Miller** and into this century by

Geology continued

Archibald Geikie. The work was continued with the advent of modern technology in geophysical surveying, radiometric dating, seismology and microscopy.

Geological History

In a description of Scottish geological history two basic points need to be remembered. The first is the immense length of geological time: the earth is reckoned to be 4600 million years old; Scotland's oldest rocks are about 3000 million years old, but most of them are less than 1000 million years old; since the Ice Age man has lived in Scotland for about 8000 years. The second is that the component rocks which make up Scotland have formed not only very slowly but in different parts of the earth's surface from where they are now.

The theory of Plate Tectonics describes how the earth's crust is divided into huge plates – or rafts – which 'float' on dense mantle rocks below. Plate movement is slow – usually a few centimetres a year – driven by convection currents in the mantle arising from the earth's hot core. 600 million years ago Scotland was placed 30° *south* of the equator and has moved into its present position 55–60° north of the equator in that time. Scotland has also moved through the earth's climatic belts and Scottish rock formations thus show evidence of tropical, desert and glacial conditions. Volcanic activity, earthquakes and mountain formation are common in our geological record because at various times Scotland was placed on the edges of the earth's component plates where magma activity, rock folding and mountain building were concentrated.

BASEMENT, MOINIAN AND DALRADIAN ROCKS The oldest British rocks outcrop in north-western Scotland and in the Western Isles and are called Lewisian gneiss. The rocks are about 3000 million years old and have been intensely deformed and recrystallised from their original volcanic origins. For 1500 million years the rocks were deeply buried and 'cooked' at high temperatures at the base of the crust; by 1000 million years ago they had been uplifted into a mountain range now represented by the rocks of Greenland, Canada and north-west Scotland, which were linked before the Atlantic Ocean opened to separate them. Overlying the Lewisian in north-west Scotland is Torridonian Sandstone, the oldest sedimentary rock in Britain. Rivers draining the ancient basement rocks of Greenland brought great quantities of sand and pebbles into north-west Scotland 900 million years ago. The sands were deposited in vast deltas burying the gneiss by thicknesses up to 7km (4.3 miles). All that is left now are isolated hills notably in the **Torridon** Forest and Assynt.

To the south and east of the Torridonian are large outcrops of Moinian and Dalradian metamorphic rocks occupying the bulk of the Scottish Highlands. This area, 800 million years ago, was an ocean trough into which river deposits were poured continuously for 500 million years. Consequently a pile of sediments 25km (15 miles) thick accumulated on the subsiding ocean floor. The older Moinian rocks are largely grey, flaggy schists, whereas the younger and more varied Dalradian consists of schists, phyllites, slates, limestones and volcanic rocks, with a remarkable fossil bed exposed in **Islay** –

evidence of great ice sheets covering Scotland 670 million years ago 30° south of the Equator.

CALEDONIAN MOUNTAIN BUILDING Around 500 million years ago the building of the Caledonian mountains began as two crustal plates – America and Europe – converged to close the ocean that separated them. The Moinian and Dalradian sediments which had accumulated in the ocean were intensely folded and crystallised a process called metamorphism, which converted the sedimentary rocks, mainly shales and sandstones, into the hard, brittle schists and slates we see today. The pile of rock was so thick that metamorphism occurred 16km (10 miles) down in the crust, the fact that the metamorphic rocks are now at the surface is testimony to the substantial erosion of the Caledonian mountains since their formation.

The process of crustal collision was so intense that the Dalradian rocks in the Grampians were arched up and over-folded, producing a huge recumbent fold – nappe – stretching from Ireland to **Aberdeen**. A similar nappe in the northern Grampians involved both Moinian and Dalradian, the two nappes being separated by a large thrust called a slide, along which enormous layers of rock were bodily transported. The elucidation of the complex structure of the Grampians owed much to Bailey, Clough, Shackleton and Barrow in this century. In north-west Scotland a telescoping effect occurred with the formation of the Moine Thrust representing a crustal shortening of many miles as the mobile nappes met the resistant gneiss basement. Whole masses of rock were thus lifted bodily and thrust forwards placing older rocks above younger ones, the Lewisian on Cambrian at the remarkable thrust line at Loch Glencoul. Such a reversal of the basic law of geology – which states that if one set of strata rests upon another then the upper one must be younger – was a major discovery by Geikie, Peach and Horne in the late 19th century. Their observations led to worldwide recognition of the phenomenon of thrusting.

As the plates converged the old ocean floor collapsed and dived beneath the advancing Scottish foreland in a process called subduction. The sediments which had accumulated over southern Scotland were lifted and crumpled to form the Southern Uplands. Between **Girvan** and **Ballantrae** is unmistakable evidence of the break-up of the ocean floor with marine sedimentary rocks and pillow lavas which had erupted underwater. Many of the rocks here contain fossils which have provided critical dating for these events. Elsewhere in the Grampians the rocks have undergone too much deformation for most fossil evidence to survive. Right across the Caledonian mountain pile great masses of molten rock rose through the crust to cool into granite. Now these masses are exposed as the familiar and diverse Scottish granites from Aberdeen and **Peterhead** through the **Cairngorms** to **Rannoch Moor**, Etive, **Strontian** and the Ross of **Mull**.

OLD RED SANDSTONE AND CARBONIFEROUS The storms of crustal collision were spent 400 million years ago and Scotland now formed a mountainous tract in a vast supercontinent of Europe and America. Scotland lay 20° south of the equator in a hot, semi-arid climate. The

ld Red Sandstone formed in mountain-girt basins and
ae Midland Valley. As part of the crustal collision great
acks – faults – developed in Scotland, notably the
reat Glen, Highland Boundary and Southern Upland
aults, the last two being the bounding faults of a large
ft valley which formed in Central Scotland. The rift
egan to fill with Old Red Sandstone, mainly river-
orne debris and scree from the newly risen Caledonian
iountains. The total accumulation eventually amounted
o some 10km (6.1 miles) over a period of 50 million
ears. In the Moray Firth, **Caithness** and **Orkney** areas
ae deposits formed in the large Orcadian lake basin,
s flagstones.

The lake spawned a fish fauna, which Hugh Miller
iscovered and described. Plants colonised the land for
ie first time and Scotland is fortunate to have a remark-
ole fossil peat deposit preserved as the famous **Rhynie**
hert in Aberdeenshire. The Old Red Sandstone was
lso a time of extensive volcanic activity – notably in
ne Midland Valley (eg **Ochil** and **Pentland Hills**) and
i the **Glencoe/Oban** area, where there are extensive
va flows. In a few fortuitously preserved places the
ld Red Sandstone can be seen to rest unconformably
1 older schists, a phenomenon discovered by James
utton in **Arran** and at Siccar Point, **Berwickshire**.

The Old Red Sandstone was followed by the Carbonif-
rous, deposits of which are almost all confined to the
lidland Valley. Most of the rocks formed in tropical
onditions when Scotland lay at the Equator, 345–300
iillion years ago. There was substantial volcanic activity
i the Midland Valley early on in the period from **Edin-
urgh** to **Kintyre**. Following the cessation of activity
arm seawater flooded across the valley bringing lime-
ones with superb coral reefs and a host of **fossil** organ-
ms. Indeed spectacular discoveries have been made
icently by Stanley Wood of early sharks, amphibians
nd fish in excellent state of preservation right across
ie Midland Valley. The most impressive evidence of
ie floras of the period can be found at **Glasgow**'s
ictoria Park Fossil Grove. The tropical swamps eventu-
ly turned to coal under great thicknesses of sandstone
nd shale. At one time most of the Midland Valley would
ave been a large **coal** deposit, but at the end of the
arboniferous more mountain building pressures
ilded the Scottish coals into the separate basins we see
day.

EW RED SANDSTONE TO TERTIARY Scotland continued
i drift north, crossing the equator into dry, arid belts.
he rocks of these times – Permian and Triassic – are
alled New Red Sandstone to distinguish them from the
ld and are in part dune-bedded wind-blown sand-
ones. Although well exposed on Arran, most are
ndersea in the **Clyde** estuary, around the coasts of west
:otland and beneath the North Sea. Clearly these areas,
ow occupied by sea, formed as basins of accumulation
ir the New Red Sandstone 300–200 million years ago.
ideed, from Permian to Tertiary times the succession
1 the North Sea is complete and provides the geological
tructure for North Sea **oil** reserves.

In Skye, **Raasay** and Mull, sedimentary strata from
irassic and Cretaceous times occur, showing evidence
f warm, shallow waters lapping around these early

Scottish coastlines. Life in and around the seas was rich
and varied, even large reptiles were present judging
from one surviving dinosaur footprint found in Skye.

During Jurassic times the great American/European
continent began to break apart and new plate movements shifted Scotland further north. About 60 million
years ago Scotland lay close to the cracks forming the
North Alantic Ocean and this resulted in major volcanic
activity. Many igneous centres developed from St Kilda
through Skye, **Ardnamurchan**, **Rum**, Mull and Arran
along a NW–SE axis. Great columns of basalt lava poured
out from the centres, best seen in the 'trap' landscapes
of Skye and Mull. Large volcanic cones and calderas
developed; the Mull volcano had a vent two miles
across. The Ardnamurchan complex formed three successive centres with ring dykes and cone sheets punched
into overlying rocks as the magma chambers filled and
emptied. Groups of dykes emanated from the complexes
– the Arran dykes are so numerous along the Kildonan
shore as to be classified as a 'swarm'.

THE SCOTTISH ICE AGE After the volcanoes became
extinct Scotland slowly assumed its present shape and
form over a period of 50 million years. Erosion cut into
the volcanic centres, the country acquired an easterly
tilt and sediments accumulated in the North Sea. However, the most significant events came within the past
two million years with the onset of the Quaternary Ice
Age.

For reasons still unclear world climate deteriorated
and ice caps developed at the poles in late-Tertiary times.
This deterioration led to the build-up of massive land
ice-sheets; Scotland's ice cap became centred in the
western Grampians and the larger Scandinavian ice cap
was able to push south-west to link up with the Scottish
one for a time. Dating of early ice advances and
recessions is still very sketchy, but Britain has undergone
at least three major glacial phases involving many ice
advances and retreats. The glacial advances, lasting thousands of years, were separated by warmer inter-glacials
when climates were probably warmer than today. The
last main ice advance – the Devensian – peaked about
20–18,000 years ago and has left the most evidence in
the form of moraines and meltwater deposits. During
the earlier phases – like the Anglian – ice spread as far
south as London and was probably 1000–1500 metres
thick in west Scotland. Sea levels fell by as much as
100m during glacial advances, enabling Scandinavian
ice to cross a North Sea emptied of water.

The main effect of glaciation was erosion, especially
in the Scottish mountains where the ice was thickest.
Large valleys were excavated and corries opened up in
the high mountains. New valleys – like the trench in
which **Loch Lomond** sites – were carved by powerful
ice flows utilising massive amounts of boulders, gravel
and debris to erode even the toughest rocks. Many over-
deepened valleys were flooded by the returning sea
levels, thus creating the west Scottish lochs. Huge rock
basins were cut in weaker sedimentary strata especially
in the Firths of Clyde and Lorne. Water depths are an
indication of the magnitude of glacial erosion – the
Firth of Lorne and the Sound of Raasay are over 900ft
(300m) deep in places.

Lowland areas of Scotland were masked by thick layers

of glacial till, pushed by advancing glaciers to form features like the 'drumlin' on which Glasgow is built. During retreat stages, meltwater deposits of sand and gravel formed distinct landforms such as kames and sinuous esker ridges, best seen in Speyside, at **Carstairs** and at **Peebles**.

About 14,000 years ago the Devensian ice melted, sea levels stood high – up to 40m above present levels because central Scotland was still depressed by the weight of the ice burden. Gradually sea levels fell in response to isostatic conditions and a sequence of 'raised beaches' developed. The climate, however, deteriorated again 11,000 years ago and the Scottish mountains experienced another ice advance called the Loch Lomond Stadial from one of its terminus sites. This little ice age lasted barely 1000 years and Scotland became ice free 10,000 years ago. More meltwater features formed, these being especially good at **Connel** and **Ballachulish**.

During post-glacial times Scotland was gradually colonised by forests of **birch**, pine and oak and a fauna of **red deer**, giant fallow deer, great elk, great ox, beaver, wild boar, wolf, brown bear and lynx. The large mammals from early Devensian times – the Woolly Mammoth and Woolly Rhinoceros – did not return. The greatest change, however, came with the arrival of man perhaps 8000 years ago; forest clearance and the extinction of many animal species soon followed. Sea levels continued to fluctuate; some 8000–6000 years ago occurred the Flandrian transgression with the melting of the great North American and Scandinavian ice caps. Seas stood some 15m above present levels forming the post glacial raised beach, now high and dry with further uplifts of land.

Geology and Scenery

Few countries exhibit a more extraordinary variety of geology and scenery than Scotland. Grand rugged mountains, rocky islands, fjord-like lochs, heather-clad moorlands, broad firths and straths are inexorably tied to their underlying bedrocks, to the character of the rocks themselves, their soils, the structure of local and regional geology, and their geological history. What is visible today is a remarkably varied and complex landscape in which the geological framework has been gradually modified by weather, erosion and in most recent times by the work of ice and man.

The further back in geological time the greater are the changes in Scotland's scenery. A few thousand years ago the changes are superficial – different floras, faunas and sea levels. Tens of thousands of years back there were significant climate changes relating to Ice Age waxing and waning. A few million years ago Scotland would look quite different, though the country's main structural frame and its uplands and lowlands had already formed. Sixty million years ago, in early Tertiary times, the last volcanic activity to affect Scotland would have drastically altered the landscape, at least in the west. The earliest evidence of Scotland's modern landscapes, then, dates back perhaps ten million years, to the late-Tertiary.

The fundamental processes of weathering and erosion thus slowly modified the earth's surface. These processes have always operated in the geological past and over a

long period of time their cumulative effect is conside able. To this can be added the formation of new roc both at the surface of the earth – from the breakdow of existing rock – and within the crust from igneo activity such as volcanoes. Then there emerges a cy of rock formation and destruction, a veritable renew of the earth's surface over a long period of time. 2C years ago James Hutton was the first to recognise th cycle – in his most telling phrase 'we find no vestig of a beginning, no prospect of an end . . .'

Scotland is part of Highland Britain – 65% lies abo 400ft (120m), but only 6% is above 2000ft (600m Although not of great altitude Scotland's rugged chara ter is based on the close juxtaposition of high and lo land. A backbone of deeply dissected mountains ru down west Scotland from **Cape Wrath** to the Clyd Valley formation is considerable because of the wett climate, steeper gradients and more intense glaciatio than in any other part of Scotland. East of the mounta mass and in the Southern Uplands are extensive rollin plateaux, often at high elevations like the Cairngorm Coastal lowlands are more extensive in eastern an north-eastern Scotland, but the Central Lowlan between **Fife** and **Ayrshire** are less obviously 'low' lan

Scotland's original drainage pattern may hav developed in response to an easterly tilt, imparted i Tertiary times. These early rivers could have draine into the North Sea from the West Highlands and wei superimposed on an existing geological structur Today's longest Scottish rivers still drain into the Nort Sea – **Tweed**, **Tay**, Forth, **Dee**, **Don** and **Spey**. Whethe this is an inherited pattern from so long ago remai very much disputed by geomorphologists.

The geological map of Scotland exhibits distin trends in the rock structure. The most important is th NE–SW alignment, the Caledonian grain, produced b the building of the Scottish mountains 500 million yea ago. Today the alignment forms a prominent feature c the north-west Highlands, the Grampian mountains an the Southern Uplands. The peninsulas and islands of th west Scottish coast noticeably follow the Caledonia grain.

THE GRAMPIANS The rocks of the grandest Scottis mountains are predominantly hard and crystalline schists, granites and lavas exposed over large parts c the Grampians and Cairngorms. Indeed, they make u Britain's highest mountain **Ben Nevis** (4406ft/1343m the bulk of the Ben is granite, but the uppermost crag and corries are made of tough lava. To the south i Glencoe and the impressive mass of the Etive peaks, **Be Cruachan** (3689ft/1125m) and Ben Starav (3451ft 1052m). All three areas – Nevis, Glencoe and Etive have had a complex geological history of undergroun magma intrusion, caldera formation and exposure c granite bathyliths bringing together quite hard rock over a large area. However, the Cairngorms surpass a of these in sheer bulk, forming the most extensive are above 3000ft (914m) in Britain and the largest outcro of granite covering 160 square miles (410 sq km). Nc surprisingly because of its unique landforms, flora an fauna, Cairngorm is Britain's largest **National Natur Reserve**. Granite reaches its zenith in Aberdeen, a cit built from the rock and most of it wrought from th deep Rubislaw Quarry nearby [see **Quarrying and Extraction**].

The southern Grampians present more diverse relief than those in the north because of the basic differences in geology. The North Grampians – like the **Monadhliath Mountains** – are built of monotonous Moine Schists and many of them are featureless wildernesses of peat moorland. Further south individual monoliths dominate the landscape. **Schiehallion** (3547ft/1081m) is a shapely cone of tough quartzite. **Ben Lawers** (3984ft/1215m) is renowned for a rich arctic-alpine flora, the nutrients for which are derived from the lime schists and basic volcanic rocks building the mountain. The ruggedness of the **Trossachs**, so admired by **Sir Walter Scott**, is caused by steeply inclined schists and grits presenting an attractive combination of crag, loch and forest. Other monoliths surround Loch Lomond – Ben Lomond (3192ft/974m) is a massive schist mountain, like its neighbours Ben More (3843ft/1174m), Ben Vorlich (3088ft/943m), Ben Ime (3319ft/1012m) and Ben Lui (3708ft/1130m).

The western and southern Grampians illustrate perfectly the effects of intense glacial erosion. Superb valleys are cut into the mountains exhibiting broad 'U' shapes – such as Glen Croe; while many are now filled with water – such as Loch Lomond and Loch Long. Around the **Moor of Rannoch** is a pattern of radiating valleys, utilised by glaciers streaming out from the main Scottish ice cap centred in the western Grampians. On the southern side such glacial erosion was facilitated by the arched structures in the schists, allowing glacial penetration in otherwise tough rocks. This feature is particularly well illustrated in the deeply indented glens and lochs around **Cowal** – like Loch Fyne, Loch Striven and Loch Goil.

THE NORTH-WEST The Grampians are clearly limited by two large faults – the geo-fractures of the Great Glen and the Highland Boundary Faults, both active during the later stages of the formation of the Caledonian mountains. Beyond the enormous trench of the glaciated Great Glen lie the western and northern Highlands stretching from **Morvern** to Assynt. Large outcrops of Moine Schist and intruding granites give rise to rugged mountains and a deeply fragmented fjord coastline. Today the peninsulas of **Knoydart**, **Morar**, **Moidart** and Ardnamurchan are some of the remotest in Britain.

North of **Kyle of Lochalsh** the geology changes abruptly at the Moine Thrust, a large dislocation which separates the displaced Caledonian rocks from the ancient basement (or foreland) to the north-west. From Kyle to **Durness** is some of the most distinctive and dramatic scenery in Scotland – bare rocky knolls with peaty lochans on Lewisian gneiss and relict Torridonian Mountains of brown sandstone. Around the type area – Loch Torridon – the sandstone forms majestic mountains like Liathach (3436ft/1054m), Beinn Alligin (3232ft/985m) and Beinn Eighe (3309ft/1009m), the latter capped by white quartzite. To the north is the impressive bulk of An Teallach (3484ft/1062m) and alongside Loch Maree the junction of the Torridonian with the Lewisian is well seen on the lower slopes of Slioch (3217ft/981m), the Torridonian filling an old valley carved in the Lewisian gneiss. This duality in the landscape is best appreciated at Assynt where the Torridonian hills – Suilven (2399ft/731m), Canisp (2779ft/847m) and Quinag (2653ft/809m) – rise abruptly from the ice scoured knob and lochan terrain which so typifies the Lewisian gneiss. Running through Assynt is a swathe of Cambrian limestone, most noticeable at Inchnadamph, giving rise to a landscape of verdant pastures, caves and potholes. The Moine Thrust is also well exposed in Assynt; the effects of the thrusting were to pile up in confusing array layer upon layer of basement and cover rocks, such as Ben More Assynt (3273ft/998m).

THE WESTERN ISLES In the Western Isles the Lewisian gneiss predominates from **Lewis** to **Barra**, but most impressively in the hills of **Harris**; Clisham is the highest at 2622ft (779m). Hereabouts the gneiss forms a bizarre landscape of rocky knolls separated by hollows, sometimes filled by lochans. These glacially scoured bedrocks – bare in Harris, peat covered in Lewis – were the source for the remarkable **Callanish stone circle**. The **Uists** and Barra are best remembered for their machair landscapes and white sands, the sand derived from glacial deposits at the end of the Ice Age. The gneiss is ubiquitous, though, reaching heights like Heaval (1260ft/384m) and Hecla (1988ft/606m). In the case of **Benbecula** post-glacial drowning has led to innumerable marine inlets, which bewildered the pioneer geologist **MacCulloch** when he visited the Western Isles in 1824.

THE NORTH-EAST AND THE NORTHERN ISLES Around the Moray Firth geology and scenery are related to patterns of outcrop of Old Red Sandstone and younger strata giving rise to flatter and more fertile ground. The outcrop of these sandstones widens to include Caithness and the Orkney Islands, with their familiar 'flagstone' landscapes and majestic stratified cliffs. The Old Man of **Hoy**, one of Scotland's best known landforms, owes its preservation as a sea stack to a hard band of lava at the base of the cliff. In west Caithness and east **Sutherland** the limits of the Old Red Sandstone basin are attained and the Moine Schist of the Northern Highlands reappears forming a wide outcrop between Melvich and Loch Eriboll. In fact the Moinian was named from the district of A'Mhoine near Kyle of Tongue, *moine* in Gaelic meaning 'peat'. The Moinian underlies the great and controversial **Flow Country** and the granites, which were intruded into the Moinian outcrop, led to gold mineralisation which gave the **Strath of Kildonan** its Victorian gold rush.

The Moray Firth is aligned in part along an undersea extension of the Great Glen fault which goes on to **Shetland** as the Walls Boundary Fault. The geology of rocky Shetland is quite different from that of Orkney, with extensive outcrops of Dalradian schists more reminiscent of the Grampians. Like the Western Isles, the Shetland islands give the impression of recent drowning with a multitude of peninsulas, skerries, bays and voes. Being so far from the central Scottish ice cap has meant that the post-glacial sea level rise has been critical – the Shetland islands have had no compensatory uplift.

SKYE AND MULL Off the fjord coastline of west Scotland is a motley of islands in the Inner Hebrides. Many of them, notably Skye and Mull, are volcanic in origin and their landscapes display typical 'trap' topography of basalt lava flows. Ben More on Mull (3169ft/966m) is the highest peak on the island and lava from top to bottom. Skye's Trotternish peninsula is a classic Hebridean landscape of massive lava flows, which have tumbled into a bizarre landslip at the Storr and Quirang. Perhaps best known of all is the exquisite island of **Staffa** where the lava cooled into majestic columns, attracting visitors since the eminent naturalist Sir Joseph Banks ventured there in 1772.

This volcanic activity is relatively recent geologically, a mere 60 million years ago – so its landscapes are fresh. Some of the roots of these volcanoes have been exposed by erosion; the **Cuillins** in Skye are a good example where the gabbro magma chamber now provides some of Scotland's best climbing pinnacles; Sgurr Alasdair (3309ft/1009m) is only one of twenty '**Munros**' (peaks over 3000ft/914m) in the dramatic Cuillins ridge. Skye boasts considerable geological diversity with basement Lewisian and Torridonian rocks in the southern Sleat peninsula, fossil-rich Jurassic strata around **Broadford**, the granite Red Hills attaining 2537ft (773m) at Glamaig – part of the Skye igneous centre – and the extensive northern basalt plateau culminating in the strangely weathered 'MacLeod's Tables'.

THE SMALL ISLES Rum, **Eigg**, **Muck**, and **Canna** are, like Skye, products of Tertiary volcanic activity. The Sgur of Eigg (1292ft/394m) is a magnificent pitchstone lava ridge visible from miles around. Geikie believed that the lava represents an infilling of an old valley, the sides of which have been removed by erosion. Rum has the best geology, though, for there is a remarkable variety of igneous rocks from yet another Tertiary centre, well exposed in the pyramidal peaks of Allival (2365ft/721m) and Askival (2659ft/811m).

THE INNER HEBRIDES The remaining Hebridean islands provide equally varied and dramatic scenery. Off Lorne are the Slate Islands – **Easdale**, **Seil** and **Luing** – much quarried in the 19th century, and the more distant **Garvellach Isles** built from upturned glacial deposits, which formed during an Ice Age 670 million years ago. **Scarba** and **Jura** present a more massive appearance, thanks to tough Dalradian quartzite, culminating in the lovely Paps of Jura (2571ft/784m), and crowned by white screes, notoriously difficult for climbers. On Jura's remote west coast are Britain's highest and most magnificent raised beaches. **Islay** presents more contrasts with swathes of Dalradian limestone supporting verdant pastures amidst infertile schists and slates. The limestone belt runs undersea to re-appear on **Lismore** (Gaelic – meaning the 'great garden'). Distant **Coll** and **Tiree** are sufficiently west to form part of the Lewisian basement with a repeat of the Western Isles landforms of rocky knolls, machair and blown sand. Magical Iona, so near to Mull but with very different landscapes, forms another tiny fragment of ancient basement rock. Veins of the famed 'Iona marble' occur within the gneiss and

were extracted on Iona quite close to where **St Columb** came ashore.

ARGYLL The long peninsula of Mid-**Argyll** and Kintyre perfectly exemplifies the direction of the Caledonian grain in west Scotland. This is the heartland of the ancient kingdom of **Dalriada** and the type area for the Dalradian – schists, limestones and slates with intruded igneous rocks. **Knapdale** well illustrates the typical land forms of Mid-Argyll; rocky knolls carved from rough grits and sills are separated by deep marine inlets glacially eroded from softer slates and phyllites. Kintyre however, is less rocky and more fertile, with limestone and mineral-rich volcanics yielding a better soil. The geology changes along the line of the Laggan fault and around **Campbeltown** are reminders of Central Lowlands rocks – Carboniferous coal, limestone and lava flows underlaid by Old Red Sandstone. The Highland Boundary Fault is, however, not present in Kintyre although the rocks indicate that the line of the fault – which normally separates Lowlands and Highlands – should be hereabouts.

ARRAN AND BUTE A similar situation prevails on Arran which has a wide range of rock types and ages – indeed Arran is often thought a microcosm of Scottish scenery rugged mountains in the north and broader, lower ground in the south. The northern granite was intruded into the zone of the Highland Boundary Fault thus confusing the picture, but the rest of the island has a straightforward run of excellent geology from Dalradian schists, through Old Red Sandstone, Carboniferous and Permo-Triassic to the Tertiary igneous centre dominated by the granite mountains round Goat Fell (2868ft/874m). The island has thus great appeal for students of geology; not surprisingly its earliest was James Hutton in 1787.

Bute, too, is bisected by the Highland Boundary Fault which makes a clear trench through the island along Loch Fad. The fault has the effect of bringing weaker (and more fertile) Old Red Sandstone against the harder, acid schists of the Highlands. The contrast in terms of scenery, vegetation and land use is most marked.

THE CENTRAL LOWLANDS Both Bute and Arran belong in part to the Central Lowlands – or Midland Valley as it is often termed. However, through most of their length the Central Lowlands are neither lowland nor valley. Indeed substantial volcanic hills dominate – the Ochils (2362ft/720m), **Sidlaws** (1492ft/455m) and Pentlands (1636ft/499m) in the east and the **Campsie Fells** (1897ft/578m) and Renfrew Heights (1713ft/522m) in the west. In Edinburgh **Arthur's Seat** (833ft/251m) is Scotland's best preserved extinct volcano, complete with lavas, cones, ash bed and the superb scarp face of **Salisbury Crags** sill. Other volcanic pipes form very distinct features in the Central Lowlands – **Dumbarton Rock**, **Bass Rock** and Edinburgh's **Castlehill** are perhaps the best known.

Much of the volcanic activity was related to Old Red Sandstone and Carboniferous times when the Central Lowlands was an active rift valley between the bounding faults – Highland to the north and Southern Upland to the south. Part of the infilling of the rift valley is the ld Red Sandstone, exposed from Strathmore to the lyde. More importantly, the rift allowed the formation f Scotland's Carboniferous **coal**, ironstone, limestone nd **oil** shales, the 19th century exploitation of which as left its impact from Fife to Campbeltown. The oil-hale industry, fathered by **James Young**, has now van-shed from **West Lothian**, other than a few remaining ings' of red shale.

HE SOUTHERN UPLANDS The Southern Uplands Fault orms a tectonic termination to the Central Lowlands nost impressively as the line of the **Lammermuir** and Moorfoot Hills. The fault juxtaposes resistant Ordovician atey rocks against the weaker Carboniferous sand-tones of the Lowlands. The Uplands cross southern cotland in a continuous, though narrow, belt of folded nd steeply inclined slates, flagstones and shales escribed by Geikie as 'crumpled like a pile of carpets'. hese rolling moorlands attain heights over 2500ft 750m) in the Tweedsmuir and Lowther Hills near Moffat. Further south-west, in **Galloway**, the Uplands ave been bolstered by substantial granitic intrusion, nuch like those in the Grampians. The highest ground is in the Rhinns of Kells and Merrick (2764ft/843m) nd at Cairnsmore of Fleet (2331ft/711m). Ironically he Rhinns and Merrick mountains have been carved ot in the granite but from the cooked and hardened country rock' into which the granite was intruded. lsewhere in the Borders igneous rocks have played heir part in forming some of the highest and most listinct scenery – the **Eildon Hills** near **Melrose** are uilt from Carboniferous magmas which have invaded he overlying Old Red Sandstone. The hills are best ppreciated from 'Scott's View' near **Dryburgh**.

To the south the Southern Uplands give way to broad mbayments of flatter ground – the Merse and Tweed owlands form one of these basins in the Carboniferous ocks, another based on Permo-Triassic sandstone is fol-owed by the river Nith into **Dumfries** and the wide iolway plain. The Nith and the Annan have excavated ong valleys through the south flank of the Uplands, aking advantage of younger and weaker strata which nad formed in similar valleys in past geological time. The **Devil's Beef Tub** is one of those hollows exhumed y recent glacial and river activity. The line of the border between Scotland and England crosses the inhospitable Cheviot Hills (2676ft/815m). Although somewhat fea-ureless, these hills are nonetheless formed of yet more gneous rocks – lavas and granite, further testimony to he long and complex volcanic history of the Scottish nountains.

Geological Curiosities

THE ARDNAMURCHAN peninsula ends in the most west-erly point on the British mainland. The peninsula con-ains a remarkable example of 60-million-year-old volcanic activity. Three separate igneous centres were active, each producing their own dykes, vents, lavas and cone sheets. Erosion has reduced the centres to their roots, exposing the concentric arrangement of dykes nd sheets clearly visible on satellite imagery.

ARTHUR'S SEAT AND SALISBURY CRAGS in central Edin-burgh mark the site of a large Carboniferous volcano, active 340 million years ago. The structure is the best preserved volcano in Britain. Originally a volcanic island, Arthur's Seat volcano was subsequently buried beneath thousands of metres of Carboniferous sedimen-tary rock. Magmatic activity led to the injection of the massive Salisbury Crags sill and later crustal movements tilted the whole structure 25° eastwards. Erosion of the overlying rock sequence has now exposed the volcano revealing remarkable detail of the original feature – five cones, including Arthur's Seat, thirteen lava flows and superb columnar structures such as Samson's Ribs, together with a host of sedimentary and igneous fea-tures. The site has consequently been of seminal impor-tance to geological research. Charles Darwin attended lectures here and, more significantly, James Hutton, whose house overlooked Salisbury Crags, found crucial evidence to support his theory of magmatic intrusion. Hutton's famous rock section on the Crags is one of the site's principal attractions.

BALLANTRAE PILLOW LAVAS On the south Ayrshire coast at Downan Point near **Ballantrae** is an excellent occur-rence of unusual pillow lavas. Pillow lavas erupt under water and supply evidence for submarine crustal move-ments. 500 million years ago this part of Scotland lay above the collision zone of the European and American crustal plates. As the plates converged they broke up and undersea eruptions of pillow lavas resulted. Indeed, the whole coastal section from **Girvan** to Ballantrae admirably displays a complex of igneous and sedimen-tary rocks thought to represent fragments of ocean crust thrust against the continental margin of the old Ameri-can plate.

BASS ROCK Situated in the Firth of Forth three miles north-east of **North Berwick**, this prominent island is a volcanic plug, dating back to early Carboniferous times. Like its neighbour North Berwick Law, Bass Rock consists of an infilled volcanic pipe, subsequently eroded to form a stump-like feature. The pale colour of the Bass Rock is not geological; the rock hosts an important gannet colony and its guano.

BEN NEVIS Britain's highest mountain at 4406ft (1343m), and best viewed from the north-west, Ben Nevis was formed by cauldron subsidence 400 million years ago. During the volcanic activity the old Dalradian rocks foundered into the magma chamber, granite then intruded into the void created by the subsidence and eventually the surface lavas sank into the granite. Some 400 million years of erosion and Ice Age attack exposed the old cauldron. Today's mountain consists of a granite base and flanks with upper slopes and summit carved from the lavas.

THE FALLS OF LORA at Connel mark the entrance to **Loch Etive** in north Argyll. During the Ice Age glacial erosion carved a deep valley in what is now upper Loch Etive, but on lower ground to the west glaciers expanded laterally and erosion was reduced leaving a rock barrier at the mouth of the present loch. Post-glacial sea levels rose and flooded the whole valley creat-ing Loch Etive, but the rock barrier was only partially submerged. Thus on an ebb tide Loch Etive drains out into Loch Linnhe in a series of cataracts, and as the tide returns a reverse waterfall occurs, called the Falls of Lora.

GLENCOE has a great appeal to climbers, historians and tourists, but it also has a lot to offer the geologist, for Glencoe's geological history has been as tortuous and violent as its infamous **massacre**. The rocks surrounding the glen on three sides are folded and thrust Dalradian schists, slates, limestones and quartzites. Slate was once extensively quarried nearby at **Ballachulish**. Within the Glen, however, is evidence of violent volcanic activity 400 million years ago. Prolonged vulcanism led to the build-up of a pile of andesite and rhyolite lavas 1500m thick, with 'glowing cloud' eruptions of the type which engulfed Pompeii in AD 79 and Martinique in 1902. Eventually the lavas collapsed into cauldron subsidence along a well-marked ring fault, seen today in Clachaig Gully. Granite welled up into the fracture as part of a massive intrusion which now occupies the Moor of Rannoch and Glen Etive. Ice Age erosion created the modern glen, removing so much rock that its towering pinnacles such as the Three Sisters, Bidean nam Bian and Buachaille Etive Mor reveal the full depth of lavas which had foundered into the Glen cauldron.

KNOCKAN CLIFF, SUTHERLAND Set in the Inverpolly National Nature Reserve north of **Ullapool**, Knockan Rock is a geological site of great importance. The section exposes a succession of younger Cambrian rocks overlain by older Moine Schist, a reversal of the normal geological order, whereby young rocks overlie older ones. Separating the Cambrian from the Moinian is the Moine Thrust, a great horizontal displacement of rocks, brought about by the Caledonian Mountain Building which shortened the earth's crust in Scotland. Metamorphosed Moine rocks were pushed west over Cambrian sedimentary limestones providing a unique puzzle for Scotland's 19th century pioneer geologists. The unravelling of the tangled geology of Assynt led to recognition of the principle of thrust faulting.

MACCULLOCH'S TREE, MULL In the remote Ardmeanach peninsula of western Mull is another remarkable geological phenomenon of the Tertiary Volcanic Province. Sixty million years ago, between sporadic outbursts of lava and in a warm, humid climate, soils developed and supported a substantial flora of oak, hazel, maidenhair and magnolia trees. In 1819 the naturalist **John MacCulloch** toured the Hebrides and found near Burg in Ardmeanach one of these trees which had been overwhelmed by columnar lava. MacCulloch's Tree is most remarkably still vertical, 12m high and 2m wide, exposed by coastal erosion. Much of the trunk was replaced by lava and the feature is really a cast of the original, although generations of fossil collectors have destroyed what little remained of the actual tree. The site is now the property of the **National Trust for Scotland**. MacCulloch's Tree is not unique; there are other examples fossilised in lava on Mull clearly related to the Tertiary 'Leaf Beds' of nearby Ardtun described by the Duke of Argyll in 1851.

OLD MAN OF HOY, ORKNEY One of Scotland's mo[st] familiar landforms, the Old Man of Hoy is situated o[n] the west coast of the Orkney island of Hoy. A tall se[a] stack, 137m high, the result of active marine erosion the stack forms part of impressive 300m cliffs, some o[f] the highest sea cliffs in Britain. The Old Man is forme[d] from Old Red Sandstone, but it rests on a pedestal o[f] resistant Hoy Lava, which has prevented the stack fro[m] falling.

PARALLEL ROADS OF GLEN ROY Glen Roy is a Nation[al] Nature Reserve on the north side of Glen Spean, 3 mile[s] east of **Spean Bridge**. The glen runs north-east fro[m] Roybridge for 7½ miles. The main features are th[e] remarkable series of horizontal terraces or 'roads' alon[g] the sides of Glen Roy, Glen Gloy and Glen Spean. Durin[g] the 19th century the 'roads' were the subject of muc[h] geological research by many famous scientists includin[g] MacCulloch, Murchison, Charles Darwin and the Swis[s] oceanographer Louis Agassiz. In 1840 Agassiz explaine[d] the roads as the shorelines of glacially-dammed lake[s], a view which is now accepted.

In the Loch Lomond Glacial Advance, 11,000 t[o] 10,000 years ago, ice blocked Glen Roy and neighbour[-] ing glens damming large lakes – that in Glen Roy ha[s] been estimated at 16km in length and 200m in depth Shorelines developed at the edges of the lakes, whic[h] in Glen Roy was then 350m in depth. As ice retreate[d] the lake level fell to 320m when a new shore forme[d] Further lowering to 260m occurred when water over flowed into neighbouring glens. So three parallel shore lines can be found in Glen Roy.

The final draining of the lake, according to Professo[r] Sissons, occurred when ice in Glen Spean retreated, an[d] lake waters emptied 'catastrophically' in a phenomeno[n] known as *Jokulhlaup*, an ice-water burst. This great rus[h] of water carved a deep gorge at Spean Bridge escapin[g] into the Great Glen.

SCOTTISH GEMSTONES By definition a gemstone is [a] polished mineral used mainly for jewellery, such as [a] diamond. Although most Scottish minerals do not qual ify as either 'gemstones' or semi-precious stones, Scot land has become known for high quality minerals suc[h] as agates, smoky quartz, rock crystal, serpentine an[d] marble. Perhaps Scottish agate has been the most sough[t] after, and superb collections grace Scotland's nationa[l] and local museums. Agates – or 'Scotch Pebbles' – occu[r] in Old Red Sandstone volcanic suites especially aroun[d] **Perth**, **Montrose**, Fife and the Ayrshire coast. Agat[e] formed from volcanic liquids rich in silica whic[h] became trapped in gas cavities in lava. The process o[f] concentrating the silica led to colour banding which s[o] typifies many agates. The greatest collector of agate[s] was Professor Forster Heddle of **St Andrews Universit[y]** in the late 19th century.

Another popular mineral much used for Victoria[n] jewellery was smoky quartz or 'Cairngorm' whic[h] occurs in cavities and veins in granite, once ver[y] common in the Cairngorms. Other granite outcrop[s] have yielded semi-precious stones such as beryl an[d] topaz, but only in small quantities. Serpentine an[d] marble have been extensively quarried for decorativ[e] purposes – the ever popular 'Iona Pebbles' are marbl[e] streaked with green serpentine, and there are other outcrops at Portsoy, on Shetland and in south Skye.

STAFFA Geologically Staffa is a fragment of the 60-million-year-old Tertiary Volcanic Province. The island's columns are the result of cooling of one lava flow into an extraordinary display of vertical, radiating and converging columns. As the lava cooled, contractional joints developed at right angles to the upper and lower surfaces of the flow; if the surfaces undulated then columns curved accordingly. Staffa's main cave – Fingal's – has been eroded by the sea into the 15m columns in the middle part of the flow; the base of the cliffs has more massive columns overlying a red ash, whilst the uppermost zone is a slaggy crust which cooled the fastest of all.

UNCONFORMITIES The geological phenomenon 'unconformity' is well represented in Scotland. An unconformity is defined as an erosion surface separating groups of rocks of differing ages – older ones below the unconformity are often folded and eroded before younger strata form above them. Unconformities thus represent time intervals and are crucial pieces of evidence in the unravelling of geological history. James Hutton in the 1780s was the first to identify unconformities as he searched for evidence to support his theory of a continually changing earth's surface, in which weathering, erosion, rock formation, folding and uplift are represented. He found three important unconformities in Scotland – one at Siccar Point on the Berwick coast where Old Red Sandstone rests on the upturned edges of Silurian strata, another at **Jedburgh**, and the third at Newton Point in North Arran, where Old Red Sandstone unconformably overlies Dalradian schist. The time interval in the Arran example is of the order of 150 million years.

VICTORIA PARK FOSSIL GROVE, GLASGOW During the building of the park in the 1880s workmen disclosed the stumps of eleven fossilised trees in a former whinstone quarry. The tree stumps and roots had been fortuitously preserved in their original site since the trees died 340 million years ago. After death the stumps were buried by sedimentary shales and sandstones and then covered by a dolerite sill, which acted as a protective cap during long periods of erosion. The stumps are sandstone casts of the original trees, species of *Lepidodendron*, a common Carboniferous Lycopod or Scale Tree. Having uncovered the grove, the local authority had the foresight to erect a glass-roofed shelter around the trees, thus ensuring the survival of an unusual group of fossils.

GIB(B), John (fl.1680) Fanatical Covenanter
A shipmaster from **Bo'ness**, 'Muckle' John Gib had a following of four men and 26 women who called themselves the 'Gibbites' or 'Sweet Singers'. Dismissed by even such resolute **Covenanters** as Donald **Cargill** as 'fanatics with demented enthusiastical delusions', the Gibbites renounced the 'bloody city of **Edinburgh**' and took to the **Pentland Hills** where they fasted and chanted 'penitential and dirge-like psalms', resolving to remain in the wilderness until the city was devoured by the flames of its own evil. Arrested as illegal **Conventiclers**, they were eventually released as harmless lunatics, all except Gib and three others who were transported to America.

GIBB, Andrew Dewar, QC (1888–1974)
Scottish Nationalist
Gibb passed Advocate in 1914 and then saw service in World War I with the **Royal Scots Fusiliers**, acting for a time as adjutant to Winston Churchill. He entered academic law in 1919 in Cambridge, where he taught Scots as well as English law, until promoted to the post of Regius Professor of Law at the **University of Glasgow** (1934–58). His writings ranged over private international law, Scots private law and its history, the international law of war crimes, and imperial and Scottish history. His *Law from Over the Border* is a patriotic Scots lawyer's protest against the anglicisation of Scots **law** by Parliament and the House of Lords in its judicial capacity. Unashamedly a man of the right in politics, he represented a distinctively Scots conservatism which saw its necessary fulfilment in Scottish self-government. In 1930 he was a founder of the 'Scottish Party' which united with the **National Party of Scotland** in 1932 to form the SNP. After the war he was active in the **Scottish Convention** from 1947, and thereafter in the **Covenant** Association.

GIBBON, Lewis Grassic, see MITCHELL, Leslie

GIBBS, James (1682–1754) Architect
Born in **Aberdeen** into a strongly Catholic family, Gibbs was sent to Rome in 1703 to study for the priesthood, but soon turned to **architecture**. He trained under the leading Italian architect Carlo Fontana and made many useful contacts with the English nobility while working in Rome. He moved to London in 1709 where he became one of the most influential church architects of the early 18th century. Closely connected with Wren, he succeeded Dickinson in 1713 as surveyor to the 'Commissioners for building fifty new churches in London'. His italianate designs of St Mary-le-Strand (1714–17) and St Martin-in-the-Fields (1722–6) were widely imitated. His style remained indebted to Wren and his Italian training. He never converted to Palladianism although he later absorbed some of its features. Being a Scot and a Tory, after the death of Queen Anne in 1715 he concentrated much more on private commissions (St Bartholomew's Hospital, London, 1730 onwards; Radcliffe Camera, Oxford, 1737–48). Only very few of his works were in Scotland (**St Nicholas Church** west, Aberdeen, 1751–5; Quarell, **Stirlingshire**, enlarged 1735–6, now demolished.) The so-called 'Gibbs surround', a door or window frame consisting of alternating large and small blocks of stone, is named after him. His 1728 treatise *A Book on Architecture* became an established architectural source book.

GIBSON, Walter (fl.1687) Provost of Glasgow
Described as 'the father of all the trade of all the west coast', Gibson was a prominent **Glasgow** merchant and provost (1687–8) whose mansion of Gibson's Land,

built after the 1677 fire and designed by **Sir William Bruce**, was generally reckoned the finest in the city. It stood 'upon eighteen stately pillars' and furnished **Tobias Smollett** with the setting for *Roderick Random*. Gibson is also remembered as the inventor, or introducer, of 'red **herrings**', sometimes known as 'Glasgow Magistrates' and later as kippers. Organised by Gibson, the salting and smoking of herring at **Gourock**, 'the first place in Britain where red herring were prepared', became an important cottage industry which spread round the Firth of **Clyde** and, most notably, up Loch Fyne.

GIFFORD, East Lothian

This village four miles south of **Haddington** derives its name from the Gifford family whose ancestors came from England and obtained extensive estates in the Lothians during the reign of **David I**. Hugh de Gifford rose to prominence under **William the Lion** and was rewarded by him with the lands of Yester; a later Hugh or Hugo de Gifford (d.1267), built Yester Castle, now in ruins but for the magnificent underground vault or 'Goblin Ha'' which featured in **Sir Walter Scott**'s *Marmion*. In the 15th century the male Gifford line failed and their property passed by the marriage of a daughter to the Hays of Borthwick who were raised via the earldom (1646) to the Marquisate of Tweeddale (1694); **John Hay, 2nd Marquis of Tweeddale**, built Yester House (**James Smith** and Alexander MacGill, 1699–1728) in the grounds of the tower, a 'large austere box of a house' which was almost immediately improved by **William Adam** (1729) and the interior completely and spectacularly remodelled by John and **Robert Adam** (1789). The village of Gifford, which grew up by the gates of Yester House, has a memorial in its early 18th century church to **John Witherspoon**, signatory to the American Declaration of Independence, who was born in Gifford (1723).

GIGHA, Island of, Argyll

The island of Gigha (Norse: *gja-ey* = 'cleft island') lies three miles west of the **Kintyre** peninsula (ferry from Tayinloan). Only 6½ miles long and under two miles wide, it is fertile and productive, supporting a population of about 180, many of whom speak Gaelic. The only village, with the pier, post office and island shop, is Ardminish. The medieval parish church is at Kilchattan; in the burial ground are intricately carved late medieval grave-slabs. Nearby is the 'ogham stone', with an indecipherable inscription in a script brought from Ireland in pre-Christian times.

South of Kilchattan is Achamore House, in private ownership, with surrounding gardens in the care of the **National Trust for Scotland**. The gardens and adjoining woodland, with many exotic azalea and rhododendron species, were developed by Sir James Horlick who bought the island in 1944. The whole island, including a fish farm developed in the 1980s, was sold in 1989 and again in 1992 amid some controversy and local apprehension. The Achamore creamery, which produced a particularly fine cheese, closed for a time in the 1980s and the milk produced by the island's dairy herds was transported daily to **Campbeltown**, but the industry has latterly been revived. The estate, fish-farm

and small-scale commercial **fishing** provide a little employment.

Despite its small size, there are many archaeological sites: **cairns**, **standing stones**, forts and **duns**. A Viking grave found by chance in 1849 at East Tarbert Bay produced an ornate portable balance, with decorative pans and weights. The Norse King Haakon held court in Gigha in 1263, on his way to the **Battle of Largs**.

GILBERT, Saint (d.1245)

For many years Archdeacon of **Moray**, Gilbert was made Bishop of **Caithness** in 1223 with his cathedral at **Dornoch** under both Norse and Scottish influence. He is one of the few Scots (and was possibly the last) to be canonised before the **Reformation**.

GILCHRIST, Sir Andrew (1910–93)
Diplomat

Not an obvious Foreign Office type, Gilchrist was bearded with the stocky build of a front-row forward and a reputation for erudition, independent thinking and attracting trouble. He wrote a trenchant critique of British deployment in the defence of Malaya and demurred over Irish policy; in Rejkjavik his residence was stormed; in Jakarta his embassy was burnt; and in Dublin it was firebombed. Born near **Lesmahagow** and educated at **Edinburgh** Academy and Exeter College, Oxford, he had joined the Colonial Office and first served in Bangkok. After internment by the Japanese in 1941 he was repatriated and served with the Special Operations Executive in Malaya and the Far East. Transferred to the Foreign Office, he was ambassador in Iceland during the Cod War and in Indonesia during the 'Konfrontasi' over Borneo. **Bagpipe** music, played very loudly on his gramophone, is said to have provoked the Icelandic mob; in Jakarta during Sukarno's 'Year of Living Dangerously', he had his own piper who blew defiance from behind the Embassy railings. By contrast the bombing of the British Embassy in Dublin, to which he had removed in 1966, was unannounced and unprovoked. Retiring in 1970, Gilchrist was appointed Chairman of the Highlands and Islands Development Board (1970–6). He wrote poems, novels and translations, loved music and fishing, and was a devoted family man.

GILLESPIE, Robert (1897–1945) Psychiatrist

Gillespie studied medicine at **Glasgow University** before specialising in psychiatry, originally at the city's Gartnavel mental hospital. His principal work was done at Guy's Hospital in London where he specialised in the study of neuroses and devised clinical treatment for the psychiatrically ill as an alternative to incarceration in hospital. During World War II he carried out important research on the psychological effects of warfare, dying shortly after the end of hostilities in October 1945.

GILLIES, William George (1898–1973)
Painter

A prolific painter in oils and watercolours, Gillies is best remembered for his still lifes and landscapes. Born in **Haddington**, **East Lothian**, he commenced his studies at the **Edinburgh College of Art** in 1916, graduating (after a two-year break for military duties) in 1922. He was awarded a travelling scholarship the following year

Self portrait by Sir William George Gillies, 1940 (SNPG)

and, like so many Scottish artists, benefited considerably from the experience. He studied under the French Cubist painter André Lhote in Paris and visited Florence and Venice.

In 1926 he joined the staff of Edinburgh College of Art where he was to remain until 1966. In the inter-war years he was part of a group of highly influential teachers at the College, including **William Crozier**, **William Johnstone**, **John Maxwell**, **William MacTaggart**, and **Anne Redpath**, since loosely grouped together as the 'Edinburgh School'. After World War II as Head of Painting and later Head of the College, Gillies oversaw the injection of new blood from England into the teaching staff, as well as the appointment of his old contemporary, **Robert Henderson Blyth**.

Gillies' own painting style had evolved from a loose interpretation of the Cubist idiom into a broader, more naturalistic framework. Although his oils, particularly his still lifes, never lost all their compositional formality, his watercolours (a medium of which he was a notable master) are free vivid evocations of light, line and colour. For most of his life he lived in the village of Temple in **Midlothian** and views of the surrounding countryside or the neighbouring rooftops provided him with endless subject matter. Although widely honoured (Royal Scottish Academician 1947, CBE 1957, knighthood 1970, Royal Academician 1971) Gillies' reputation, like that of so many of his countrymen, remains essentially local.

GIRNIGOE CASTLE, Nr Wick, Caithness

There can be few castles more deserving of conservation than Girnigoe on its precipitous promontory north of **Wick**. It was built by William Sinclair, 2nd **Earl of Caithness**, after he had surrendered his earldom of **Orkney** to the Crown in 1472. It contains a courtyard behind a tower originally four storeys high and the outlook from all its walls is a dizzy one. Behind its great

ditches the castle was virtually impregnable. In 1606 the 5th Earl built Castle Sinclair, somewhat resembling a renaissance palace, immediately opposite the entrance to Girnigoe. This may have contributed to his insolvency, but in any case he was no match for Sir Robert Gordon, the Tutor of Sutherland, who, as a younger son, was in search of an earldom of his own. He never obtained one, but he did gain possession of Girnigoe for long enough in 1622 to destroy the entire muniments of **Caithness**, as now appears almost certain. Girnigoe itself was much damaged by a bombardment during the usurpation of **John Campbell** of Glenorchy, the future **Earl of Breadalbane**, in 1690. But far less remains of Castle Sinclair.

GIRVAN, Ayrshire

Erected into a **burgh of barony** for Boyd of Penkill [see **Dailly**] in 1686, and overlooked by Knockcushan Hill from where **Robert I** is said to have dispensed justice, the small town of Girvan on the Ayrshire coast has nevertheless suffered a dismal press over the centuries. Dismissed by one traveller in 1655 as possessing 'some five or sixe fisher-boates and not many more houses', in 1793 it was in so miserable a plight that another 'was obliged to move onward to **Kirkoswald** to find a night's lodging', and even by 1843 it was considered 'utterly unworthy of its splendid setting . . . far inferior in neatness and dignity to many Scottish towns of its size'.

The arrival of the **railway** in 1860 marked a turning point. Crouched round its sheltered harbour on the coast between the hills and the sea, with sandy beaches facing out to the dramatic bulk of **Ailsa Craig**, Girvan became a popular holiday resort for **Glasgow** and the industrialised west of Scotland. Its population trebled in summer; boarding houses and hotels were built to accommodate the hordes, boating ponds, bowling greens, golf courses and donkey rides were provided for their entertainment, and hospitals, churches, banks and shops developed to cater for their needs. Where previously the population had been employed either in **herring fishing** or hand-loom weaving, now they diversified into servicing this seasonal invasion and while the fishing fleet continued, steamer services now ran day trips to Ailsa Craig. In 1946 Alexander Noble & Sons Boatbuilding yard was established, but **tourism** continued as the town's mainstay, leading inevitably to the recent decline of both.

GLAMIS, Jane(t) Douglas, Lady (d.1537)

In **James V**'s vicious purge of **Douglases** following his imprisonment (1525–8) by **Archibald, 6th Earl of Angus**, few of that name escaped persecution. As Angus's sister, Jane (or Janet), wife of 6th Lord Glamis, was doomed. Accused (1532) of poisoning her husband, she was burnt to death in 1537 on a charge of plotting to kill the King.

GLAMIS CASTLE, Nr Forfar, Angus

'Rising proudly out of what seems a great and thick wood of trees, with a cluster of hanging towers at the top', Glamis appeared to the poet Thomas Gray 'like nothing I ever saw'. Romance as well as trees shrouded his vision. In the castle's Duncan's Hall, **MacBeth**, the Thane of Glamis, had supposedly entertained his

Glamis Castle as drawn by R W Billings c1840 (RWB)

intended victim; in King Malcolm's Room the blood-stain on the floor was surely that of **Malcolm II**. More in the way of pointed turrets no fairy-tale princess could ask for; and more in the way of living royalty no castle could hope for, this being the childhood home of the Queen Mother and the birthplace of Princess Margaret.

Yet, despite this mix of **Balmoral** and Disneyland, Glamis has a reassuringly respectable pedigree dating from the 15th century when it was a large but simple L-plan tower house incorporating an earlier structure. MacBeth was indeed Thane of Glamis (though not this castle) and Malcolm II was murdered hereabouts. In the 14th century the estate was given to Sir John Lyon by his father-in-law **Robert II**. Lyon's son became Lord Glamis (1445) and probably built the tower house. His descendants were created Earls of Kinghorne (1606) and of Strathmore (1677); the 9th Earl became a Bowes Lyon on marrying a Yorkshire heiress called Bowes. As the family's standing grew so did their castle, pro-digiously. In the 17th century Patrick the 1st Earl, John the 2nd, and Patrick the 3rd added three storeys to the tower house and two substantial wings, subsequently trimmed to L-shapes and culminating in round towers to give an imposing stepped façade. Within, the ceilings were embellished with plasterwork and the walls with paintings while without the policies were graced with statuary; an elaborate sundial and two lead figures of **James VI** and **Charles I** survive. The walls and gateways comprising the outer defences were removed by Capability Brown whose efforts 'to render this splendid old

mansion more parkish, as he was pleased to call it . . . and to bring his mean and paltry gravel walk up to the very door' so enraged **Sir Walter Scott**.

Now a major visitor attraction, the opulence of Glamis may be conveniently contrasted with the simplicity of rural life as displayed in the nearby Angus Folk Museum. This is a row of cottages in Glamis village, restored and furnished to early 19th century standards and giving a detailed insight into the domestic and agricultural life of those who did not live in castles. It is in the care of the **National Trust for Scotland**. In the garden of the village manse stands the King Malcolm stone, a **Pictish** cross-slab that probably never served as Malcolm II's tombstone.

GLAS, John (1695–1775) Minister

Born at **Auchtermuchty** and minister of Tealing near **Dundee** from 1719, Glas's disaffection turned to primitive Christianity, regarding churches and ministry as unscriptural. His sect, the Glassites (later called Sandemanians from his son-in-law Robert Sandeman 1717–71), spread to London and America as independent congregations with elders and no professional ministry.

GLASGOW

The etymology of the name of Scotland's largest city is warmly disputed. Its derivation is surely Celtic and probably **Gaelic**; but with anglicised spellings varying widely from *glas-chu* to *glas-cun*, the component words are uncertain, let alone their precise meaning. In the heyday of 19th century industrialisation *glas* was taken to mean 'grey', leading to such seemingly appropriate

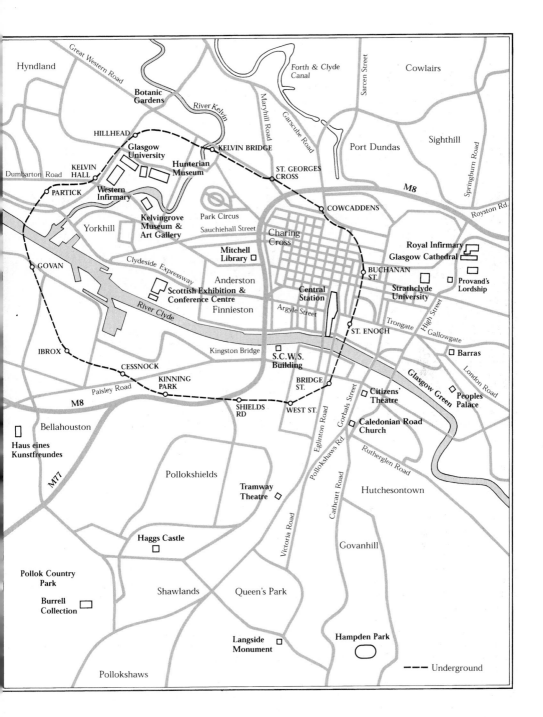

Hyndland

Great Western Road

Forth & Clyde Canal

Cowlairs

Botanic Gardens

River Kelvin

Maryhill Road

Garscube Road

Sarcen Street

Port Dundas

Sighthill

HILLHEAD

Glasgow University

KELVIN BRIDGE

ST. GEORGES CROSS

M8

Springburn Road

Hunterian Museum

Royston Rd.

KELVIN HALL

Dumbarton Road

PARTICK

Western Infirmary

COWCADDENS

Royal Infirmary
Glasgow Cathedral

Provand's Lordship

Kelvingrove Museum & Art Gallery

Park Circus

Sauchiehall Street

Charing Cross

BUCHANAN ST.

Strathclyde University

Yorkhill

Mitchell Library

Anderston

GOVAN

Clydeside Expressway

Scottish Exhibition & Conference Centre

Central Station

River Clyde

Finnieston

Argyle Street

ST. ENOCH

Trongate

High Street

Gallowgate

Barras

London Road

IBROX

Kingston Bridge

S.C.W.S. Building

Glasgow Green

Peoples Palace

CESSNOCK

KINNING PARK

BRIDGE ST.

Citizens' Theatre

Paisley Road

M8

SHIELDS RD

WEST ST.

Eglinton Road

Gorbals Street

Pollokshaws Rd

Caledonian Road Church

Bellahouston

Haus eines Kunstfreundes

M77

Pollokshields

Tramway Theatre

Victoria Road

Cathcart Road

Rutherglen Road

Hutchesontown

Haggs Castle

Govanhill

Pollok Country Park

Burrell Collection

Shawlands

Queen's Park

Langside Monument

Hampden Park

Pollokshaws

– – – Underground

Glasgow and Environs

445

Civitatis GLASGOW ab Oriente Estevo. The Prospect of ye Town of GLASGOW from ye North Ea

The Prospect of ye Town of Glasgow from ye North East
by John Slezer, 1693 (TS)

Glasgow continued

translations as 'the grey blacksmith' ('gow' suggesting *gobha*, a smith) or 'the grey hound ferry' (*cu*, a dog). Currently the favoured derivations are more pastoral and cultural with *glas* taken to indicate 'green' or a 'church'. Hence the popular 'dear green place', 'green hollow', 'dear stream', 'green cloister', 'dear cloister', 'church within the enclosed space', 'church of Cun(tigernus) [Kentigern]', etc.

A gift to the image-makers, such uncertainty also accords well with the city's occasional need to reinvent itself. Those who have hailed, often with disbelief, Glasgow's late-20th century revival as a cultural capital and 'the first successful post-industrial city' would do well to recall that for most of its history a cultural capital with no more in the way of industry and commerce than any other market town was precisely what it was. To its two centuries as 'the workshop of the world' and 'the second city of Europe', or its three as 'the manufacturing and commercial metropolis of Scotland', Glasgow has enjoyed six centuries as a city of scholastic and ecclesiastical eminence. Parallels with **St Andrews** or Oxford may be more apposite than those with Birmingham or Liverpool.

Foundation

Also denied to the pre-industrial burgh on the north bank of the **Clyde** was any political or strategic significance. Geography offered no safe retreat to a rock-girt fortress as at **Stirling** or **Edinburgh**. Their equivalent on the Clyde was downriver at **Dumbarton** where the kings of **Strathclyde** held sway throughout the Dark Ages. Although it would be surprising if somewhere within the now extensive city limits the **Romans** had not earlier established a staging post or fortlet, their **Antonine Wall** passed well to the north to meet the Clyde at New Kilpatrick where remains have been uncovered [see also **Bearsden**]. Not the shallow Clyde at Glasgow but the rock of Dumbarton, the deep water at its base, and a series of forts in **Renfrewshire** covered the wall's western flank.

Like Stirling and **Perth**, Glasgow did command a useful ford. The city would grow up at the lowest point on the undredged Clyde where, just below the tidal reach, the river could usually be crossed on a horse and sometimes on foot. But unlike the Forth and **Tay**, the Clyde scarcely constituted a barrier to either traffic or authority; if anything its mainly north-south axis provided a conduit (followed by the Roman road to Cumbria and by every main west-coast route to the south ever since). The ford was locally useful but not nationally critical. It is significant that the city, far from starting as a riparian entrepôt, began as a green and sylvan shrine a good mile from the river.

Tradition asserts that **St Ninian**, whose **Whithorn** foundation brought Christianity to Strathclyde, established a burial place here beside the little **Molendinar** burn c400 AD. To it, miraculously, came Kentigern (or **Mungo**) some time in the 6th century and here under the patronage of King Rhydderch of Strathclyde he built a church on the site of what is now the **Cathedral** and was consecrated bishop (or whatever the then equivalent was). Nothing survives of his church but St Mungo remains the patron saint of Glasgow. His mother (St Thenew, Thenau, Thennach or Enoch) is remembered in **St Enoch's Square**, the site of one of the city's medieval gates, and his miracles account for

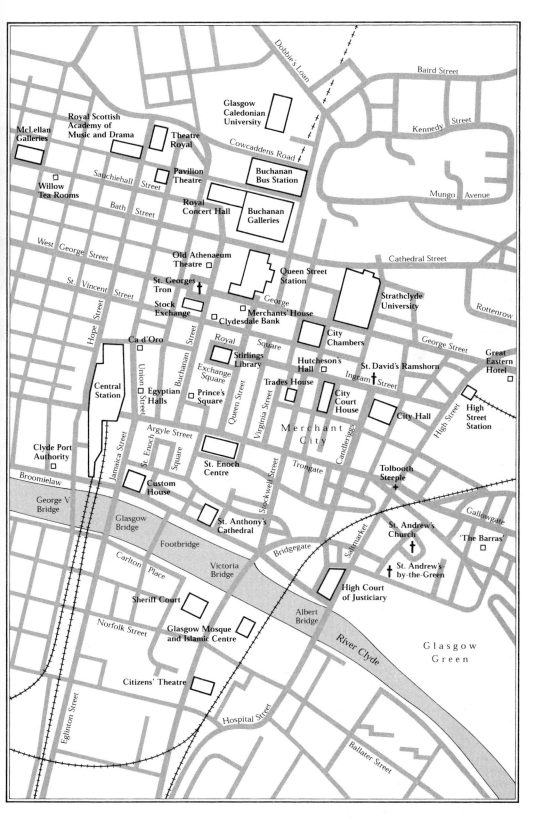

Glasgow City Centre

the curious assortment of objects incorporated in Glasgow's coat of arms (redesigned 1866 by Andrew MacGeorge). A bird, a tree, a fish, a ring, a bell, each represents some item in the Mungo hagiography.

Having given Glasgow a head start on most other Scottish cities, tradition retains an exhausted silence on the next 600 years. It is probable that the see of Glasgow was vacant for much of the 11th century but in 1124 **David I** revived it and installed his chaplain, John Achaius, as bishop. Bishop John is credited with building the first cathedral, on the site of St Mungo's church, in 1136; David I marked the occasion by granting to the bishopric the lands of **Partick**. In 1174 Bishop Jocelyn either rebuilt or completed the cathedral which was consecrated in 1197. At the time Glasgow seems to have been the only bishopric in Scotland with an organised chapter of dean and canons plus the endowments to support them. Jocelyn also secured from **William the Lion** burghal privileges (c1190) including the right to hold a fair. Only fragments of Jocelyn's cathedral remain but **Glasgow Fair** survives as a cherished, if changed, institution.

Scholars and Clerics

Bishop William de Bondington (1233–58) continued the building work of Jocelyn and much of the surviving eastern end of the church is his work. The nave was completed in the following century, making Glasgow Cathedral the second (to St Andrews) largest in Scotland and the only medieval cathedral (excluding **Kirkwall**) to survive more or less intact to the present day.

Although in the 13th century the adjacent 'sleepy cathedral and market town' was of no great importance, it would provide **Harry the Minstrel** with a backdrop against which to set some of **William Wallace**'s less verifiable exploits. **Rutherglen**, a separate burgh with a royal castle and ford just upriver, seems to have been more important and it was there that a parliament was held in 1300 and that Wallace's betrayal was organised in 1305. Glasgow's role in the **Wars of Independence** was not as a political asset but as the see and seat of **Bishop Robert Wishart**.

Evidence of civic ambitions may be traced to the mid-14th century when Bishop Rae sanctioned the first stone bridge across the Clyde (1345) [see **Victoria Bridge**]. But this was still separated from the cathedral town at the top of the hill above the river by open land. A century later, possibly in imitation of the rival see at St Andrews, Bishop Turnbull received papal authority to found a **university** (1451). It first assembled in Blackfriars (founded in the 13th century) and then moved even closer to the Cathedral in **Rottenrow**, before colonising new land (1461) along the line of the **High Street**. This soon developed as the medieval town's main axis.

A charter of 1491 conferred a further privilege on the bishops of Glasgow, that of operating an approved public tron, or weighing scales. Although frequently disputed by Rutherglen and Dumbarton, Glasgow's evident success as a market town occasioned continued expansion. Slowly the town's focus shifted south from the old cross(roads), where Rottenrow/Drygate crossed the High Street near the Cathedral, to a new cross (**Glas-**

gow Cross) where **Gallowgate** and **Trongate** met the **High Street** at its southern extremity. Excluding the Cathedral, the **Bishop's Palace** and adjacent prebendary residences like **Provand's Lordship** (and perhaps Blackfriars and the University) buildings were mainly of timber; **Glasgow Green** was still the Bishop's forest, **Sauchiehall Street** no more than a boggy track through a thicket of willows, and the river was still too shallow for even a medieval port. It was still a cathedral town and, on the wrong side of Scotland for Continental trade, could scarcely compete even with the minor commercial centres dotted along the east coast. It could, though, compete as a cultural and ecclesiastical centre. In 1492, again only a few years behind St Andrews, its see was raised to the status of an archbishopric. Coincidentally in the same year a Genoese mariner was laying the real foundations of Glasgow's future wealth and expansion by discovering that there lay to the west of the Clyde another continent, and one in respect of whose trade Glasgow was better sited.

Reformation

To a town enlivened by the theological debates of its university students and dependent on the wealth and authority of its archbishop, the advent of reformist and anti-clerical ideas occasioned some upheaval but rather less violence than might have been expected. Jeremiah Russell, a Glasgow greyfriar, and John Kennedy, 'a youth from Ayr' were tried and burnt for heresy (1538) beside the Cathedral in spite of **Archbishop Gavin Dunbar**'s disapproval and regardless of the popular outrage. In 1551 **James Beaton**, nephew of **David Beaton** the Archbishop of St Andrews, succeeded Dunbar but was unable to stem the growing tide of reform. In 1560 he fled to France, taking with him the relics, plate and archives of the see and some of those of the University in barrels. His successors, though they included men of learning and probity, were 'tulchan' incumbents who though enjoying the authority of office could lay no claim to its patronage and endowments.

These had passed to secular hands. Describing themselves as 'native born servants of St Mungo and to that kirk [ie Glasgow Cathedral]', the **Earls of Lennox** had been granted the hereditary bailieship of the burgh and during the intrigues of **Queen Mary**'s minority came to consider Glasgow as their fief. In 1543 the forces of **Matthew Stewart, 4th Earl of Lennox**, were besieged in Glasgow 'Castle' (probably the Bishop's Palace), obliged to surrender and then were massacred by those of **James Hamilton, 2nd Earl of Arran**, the then governor of the realm. Lennox sought revenge but his forces were again defeated in 1544 at the Battle of the Butts, after which Arran's troopers plundered the town. Beaton's departure in 1560 provoked further plunder as, with Hamilton's encouragement, the Cathedral was ransacked. Five years later **Henry, Lord Darnley**, the son of the 4th Earl of Lennox, married **Queen Mary** and soon regretted it. After the murder of **Rizzio** he retired to Glasgow and in 1567 was living in a house in Drygate when the Queen coaxed him to Edinburgh and his death at **Kirk o'Fields**. A year later, after her imprisonment at **Loch Leven**, the Queen returned to the Clyde, there to witness the defeat of her forces at **Langside**.

The rivalry for control of Glasgow between the Lennox and Hamilton earls rumbled on; there was another siege in 1570 but in 1578 Robert Stewart, 5th Earl (briefly) of Lennox, was chosen as Lord Provost. Another wave of reformist zeal, fanned by **Andrew Melville**, then Principal of the University, swept the town in 1579; it was said that the Cathedral was only saved from demolition by the intercession of the city's craftsmen who allowed their civic pride in the building to overcome their religious scruples about its Romish associations.

The final break with its ecclesiastical past came when Glasgow hosted the **General Assembly** of 1638. Following the launch of the **National Covenant** in Edinburgh earlier in the same year, the assembled peers, professors, presbyters and elders proceeded to reject Laud's Prayer Book, outlaw episcopacy, excommunicate existing bishops, and further defy royal authority by refusing to disband. The Assembly appears to have enjoyed the whole-hearted support of the burgh and Glasgow thus became firmly identified with the **Covenanting** cause in the ensuing Bishops' Wars.

Trades and Merchants

So protracted was the religious crisis of the 16th and 17th centuries that Glasgow, though losing its ecclesiastical *raison d'être*, for once had ample time to reinvent itself. It did so as a thrusting mercantile city. There is some evidence of commercial activity in medieval times but not until the early 16th century did tradesmen organise themselves into crafts and not till 1605 did merchants organise themselves into a guild. The crafts had meanwhile formed an umbrella organisation of trades under a Convenor. Both trades and merchants established institutions to manage their affairs and care for members who fell on hard times; these were the **Merchants' House** and the **Trades House**, institutions destined to play an important part in the physical development of the city. But as tradesmen and merchants acquired growing power over the regulation of their activities, the administration of the burgh and of justice remained in the hands of the ecclesiastical establishment and its secular supporters.

The burgesses' right to elect their own magistrates, or bailies, was assumed after the 1560 **Reformation** but quashed by **James VI**'s charter of 1611, which made the city a **royal burgh** (as opposed to a burgh of regality under the archbishop), and by that of **Charles I** in 1636. It was reclaimed after the 1638 Assembly, quashed again in 1652, restored by Cromwell in 1655, and quashed yet again after the Restoration. Such vacillation served only to encourage the assertiveness of the burgesses who consistently exploited the vacuum left by the abolition of archiepiscopal patronage and by the secular rivalries which it spawned. Come the 1689 Revolution, William and Mary's grant of free elections 'to continue in all time coming' was something of a formality.

Civil war had wrongfooted the city, support of **Montrose** resulting in exactions and executions from the Covenanting army under **Leslie**. There was little enthusiasm for the forces offered to Charles I under the Solemn League and **Covenant** and reservations about the support offered to **Charles II**. During two brief visits, Cromwell heard a lot of sermons, enjoyed some theological debate, and proved a generous benefactor to both the town and the University. The Restoration of the monarchy, which also meant the restoration of an archbishop, wrung from the town council a weary compliance but did not spare those ministers who continued to avow the Covenant. To flush out such '**Conventiclers**' the forces of **Lauderdale** and **Claverhouse** came and went with occasional skirmishes in the town. More lethal, though, were those 17th century scourges of plague (1646) and fire (especially in 1652 and 1677). The 1652 fire is said to have consumed a third of the city.

Yet three years later Thomas Tucker still found it 'one of the most considerablest burghs of Scotland, as well for the structure of it as for the trade'. An earlier visitor (1636) had guessed the population at 20,000, probably more than double the real figure; but from being eleventh amongst Scotland's burghs in terms of assessed revenue in the 1530s Glasgow had steadily climbed to second (behind Edinburgh) by the 1670s. Another visitor (1662) compared the lay-out with Oxford and joined in the chorus of admiration for the lofty **Tolbooth** erected in 1636 at the focal cross of High Street and Trongate. Tucker was more interested in the city's trade, noting exports of **coal** to Ireland, salt **herring** and coal to France, and imports of timber from Norway as well as extensive links with the Highlands and Islands. Significantly, 'here hath likewise been some who have ventured as farre as the Barbadoes'. He characterised the population as 'traders and dealers', possessed of a mercantile genius and handicapped only by the shallowness of their river 'soe that noe vessells of any burden can come neerer up than within fourteene miles'.

In 1662 a quay for lighters was constructed on the **Broomielaw** and, soon after, negotiations began for a suitable site downriver for a deep sea port. Tucker had noted several possibilities including Newark and it was there in the 1690s that New-Port-Glasgow (later **Port Glasgow**) was laid out. Meanwhile in 1674 the first cargo of Virginia **tobacco** reached the city. More consignments followed before the end of the century as Scottish manufactures, mainly **linen**, began to find their way to the American colonists. England's Navigation Acts outlawed such trade to the Scots but it is clear that well before the **Act of Union**, and in spite of heavy losses over the **Darien Scheme**, Glasgow's merchants were already deeply involved in the American trade.

Tobacco and Sugar

Unrestricted access to the colonies for Glasgow's merchants and compensation for their Darien losses would result from the 1707 Act of Union. Nowhere in Scotland would benefit more. Yet nowhere were the proposals for union more vigorously opposed. In 1706 a patriotic mob wanting nothing to do with England stormed the council chambers, put the provost to flight, and were about to march on Edinburgh when news of approaching dragoons dispersed them. The mob's worst fears of Westminster interference were confirmed in 1725 when England's malt tax, which would significantly increase the price of ale, was extended to Scotland. Again the mob took to the streets and this time vented their rage

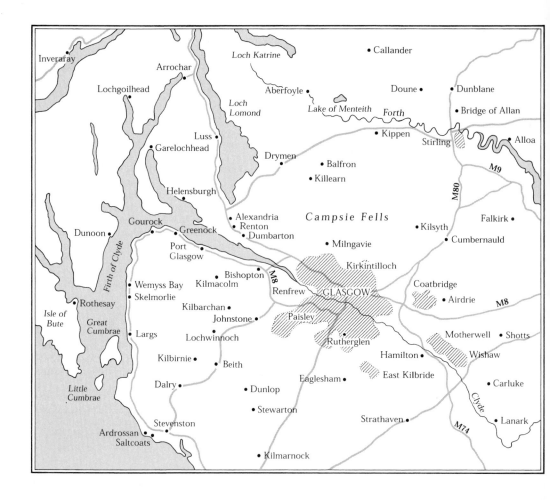

Glasgow and the Firth of Clyde

Glasgow continued

on Shawfield Mansion, the home of the local MP who had actually supported the bill. The **Shawfield Riot**, and the blatantly discriminatory punishments meted out to those involved, lingered long in popular memory; its telling equation of social grievance with nationalist sentiment would not be forgotten.

Two years after the riot Daniel Defoe was penning his much quoted lines about Glasgow: 'a very fine city ... the cleanest and beautifullest and best built city in Britain, London excepted' (the last two words are commonly omitted). His enthusiasm stemmed from an appreciation that here the Union for which he had worked was proving truly beneficial. He admired the width of the streets, the noble Tolbooth, and the arcaded shops behind rows of 'vast square Dorick columns' with houses above. Above all he marvelled at the increase in trade. 'Near fifty sail of ships' were now crossing the Atlantic to Virginia, New England, and the West Indies 'and every year increasing'. By the 1770s the number of vessels engaged in the American trade had risen sensationally to between three and four hundred.

Imports included sugar, either loaded in the West Indies or transhipped in one of the North American ports. The city's earliest attempts at refining date from 1667 and Defoe notes the use of molasses for producing a local spirit. Thereafter molasses and sweets came to represent an important Clydeside industry. To it the manufacture of sugar-processing machinery was added in the 18th century and as late as the 1950s Glasgow was still the world's leader in this specialised field.

But far and away the largest import item was tobacco. Initially Glasgow's merchants were content to freight cargoes. Soon they were operating their own ships and establishing purchasing agencies in the colonies. Thanks to a shorter sailing time and tight profit margins, by the 1770s they controlled a larger share of the American tobacco trade than all the other ports of the UK combined. Most of the product was then re-exported to the European mainland, especially France. Credit requirements generated a sophisticated network of financial services; dockside and storage accommodation at the Lower Clyde ports of Dumbarton, **Greenock** and Port Glasgow grew apace. The trade was of enormous importance in developing a commercial ethos. But it was essentially manipulative commodity dealing involving a number of family-based syndicates. The Tobacco Lords posturing on the plainstanes of Trongate and conspicuously flaunting the city's Calvinist reputation were not major employers and when the trade plummeted as a result of the American War of Independence, there is little evidence of widespread distress. Indeed, it has been shown that even the Tobacco Lords weathered the storm surprisingly well.

Defoe had emphasised that not only was Glasgow well able to maximise its American imports but also to 'sort' cargoes for export to the American colonists 'even without sending to England for them'. He cited linens, muslins, plaids and stockings; also 'servants'. To these were soon added a whole range of manufactured goods suitable for a pioneering economy – farm implements, saddlery and shoes, furniture and ironware, **pottery**, glass, rope. The development of a manufacturing economy in Glasgow stemmed from the boost given to existing crafts/trades by tobacco-generated capital plus the steady demand of a large export market.

By the time this demand faltered due to the American War of Independence, the domestic economy could to some extent replace it. Glasgow had shown no enthusiasm for the **Jacobite** cause but had twice been milked by **Prince Charles Edward Stewart** who exacted cash on his march south and much needed boots and uniforms on his return journey. The city hailed his defeat at **Culloden** with delirious rejoicing. More useful was the social upheaval which followed when improving lairds created a demand for just those agricultural and domestic manufactures developed for the American colonists.

Cotton
By the 1780s the city's population had climbed to 48,000 and its street grid had begun its inexorable march westward. **St Enoch's** and **George Squares**, **Buchanan**, **Jamaica** and **Virginia Streets** were all laid out in 1770–90. North of Trongate the development was known as the New Town or, because of its popularity with the mercantile aristocracy, as The **Merchant City**. But its residential appeal would be short-lived. Between 1780 and 1830 the population would increase four-fold to around 200,000. The Merchant City was promptly gobbled up by the manufacturing metropolis and its commercial services.

For **cotton**, which now replaced both tobacco as the principal American import and linen as the principal textile industry, devoured both labour and land on an unprecedented scale. The technology for mechanised spinning already existed thanks to the likes of **David Dale** and Glasgow's James Monteith. But, waterpowered, the mills must be located by a river with a steady stream and, when steam-powered, water was still essential to mills for bleaching, dyeing and printing. Within 20 miles of the city every river acquired its mills and the adjacent land was turned into printfields and bleachfields. Glasgow was colonising its hinterland with cotton – and then populating it with weavers. Unlike spinning, weaving largely remained a home-based handicraft till the second decade of the 19th century. A vast army of handloom weavers was recruited from the impoverished Irish and Highland immigrants who now came up the Clyde on every tide. For miles around erstwhile crofts became weaving townships; almost without exception Glasgow's modern suburbs first became integrated into the metropolitan economy as weaving villages.

Within the city the growth of a vast industrial proletariat living at or below subsistence level led to a riot of **Calton weavers** in 1787, bread riots in 1800, and the near-uprising of 1819–20 ('The Radical War') which ended at the **Battle of Bonnymuir**. The first resulted from employers refusing to grant the weavers a wage increase, the last from wage reductions as hand-loom weavers faced unemployment when the first power-loom mills came on stream. Their plight worsened in the 1830s and 40s. The cotton industry remained a major employer well into the 20th century but by the 1860s other industries had already begun to supplant it.

Meanwhile the city had spread south of the river, where development of **Gorbals** took place around the turn of the century, and had continued its westward march with the development of Blythswood Estate and **Anderston** where James Monteith had established his first spinning mill. The city's merchant princes were inching towards the navigable section of the Clyde just as the ships themselves were at last bearing down on the city. Although Port Glasgow had been a success, there was still a crying need for a harbour for ocean-going ships adjacent to the city. Reports were commissioned and a plan to dredge the river and confine its flow with jetties was adopted. The scouring effect produced a channel 14ft (4.2m) deep by 1781. Further constriction of the river and reclamation along its banks steadily increased the depth, and so the draught and number of vessels reaching the Broomielaw. The city had at last made good its greatest commercial deficiency and in the process had reclaimed a large area of river frontage well suited for docklands and shipyards.

Coal and Iron
To complete the city's metamorphosis into an industrial power-house, it remained only to exploit its mineral resources. Coal had been locally dug since at least the 16th century; but production increased dramatically with the development of the Monklands coal field in the 1780s and the construction of the Monklands **Canal**; **Govan**'s collieries were probably the most productive of those in the immediate vicinity. Coal-fired steam engines for pumps and traction helped to develop the mining industry and, along with the **railway** boom of the mid-19th century, accounted for much of the demand. The other major coal user was the **iron** industry. David Mushet's discovery of the value of the local black-band ironstone in 1801 'marked the beginning of the modern Scottish iron industry' and **J B Neilson**'s development of the hot-blast furnace in 1828 'made possible its exploitation'.

Iron, and towards the end of the 19th century steel, plus the head start in steam power afforded by the cotton and mining industries, formed the basis of **shipbuilding** and heavy **engineering**. The Clyde's annual shipbuilding output rose sensationally from 20,000 tons in 1850 to nearly 500,000 by 1900 and peaked at nearly 800,000 tons just before World War I. Like no other industry – and few were not represented in Glasgow by 1900 – shipbuilding epitomised Clydeside's industrial might. The castings that emerged from the city's forges, the strip and plate from its furnaces, the ores from its mines, the evil-smelling products of its chemical works,

Glasgow in 1798 from the south end of Bishop Rae's bridge or Glasgow Bridge (ML)

Glasgow continued

and the smoke from its chimneys were mysterious and unlovely. But the ships that reared above the skyline of terraces and tenements were a matter of pride and glory. Fitting out these floating palaces and hotels, or equipping their military and mercantile counterparts, involved every imaginable trade; it is estimated that well over 100,000 workers were dependent on the industry. As another white *Empress* or another red-funnelled Cunarder squeezed downriver on the brimming tide, she carried with her the self-respect of a whole city.

Decline and Renaissance

Glasgow reached its zenith in the Edwardian summer on the eve of World War I when her industry and trade broke all records. Never before had so many ships been built or so much coal mined. With more money in their pockets, Glaswegians flocked to the **music halls** and the **football**. In 1912 as an expression of this achievement the city's boundaries were extended to cover much of what had become Greater Glasgow. Few other cities in the United Kingdom contributed so much to the war effort, few reaped such bitter rewards from victory. Out of war emerged **Red Clydeside**, with a brand of Labour politicians more concerned to preserve skilled jobs than with the general welfare of their supporters. In the immediate aftermath of peace there was an expectation that industry would experience unparalleled prosperity, paving the way for better homes for the heroes. Boom quickly gave way to a recession that was to last for over a decade. Throughout the city life was soon reduced to 'the weary round of seeking work which now seemed to belong to a bygone age'. Many families with skills chose a new life in America or the British Dominions and Colonies. More people emigrated from Glasgow in the 1920s than ever before. For those who stayed conditions grew steadily worse, earning Glasgow a reputation for urban and sectarian violence and squalor, characterised in **A McArthur** and H Kingsley Smith's bestselling novel *No Mean City*, 1935. The Corporation tried to respond to the crisis by building housing schemes on the periphery of the city, such as Riddrie and Knightswood, but nothing could prevent recession turning to slump in the early 1930s.

The symbol of the slump in Glasgow was the looming hull of Ship No 534, the giant Cunarder, standing abandoned on the ways at **Clydebank** after work stopped in 1932. **George Blake**, in his poignant novel *The Shipbuilders*, described the sight as if shipbuilding man had done too much – 'a tragedy beyond economics'. In the depth of the slump the Corporation had started to demolish the worst of the slums in central Glasgow, moving families to new homes in the schemes. When work restarted on Ship No 534 – the *Queen Mary* – in 1934 it was as if a beacon of hope had been lighted. Work flowed in as the country re-armed to fight Hitler's Germany. The war brought relief but also suffering in the blitzes of 1941. With most of the world's heavy industries destroyed, peace in 1945 heralded a false dawn of prosperity that lasted a decade. In this period of misplaced optimism Sir Patrick Abercrombie produced his *Clyde Valley Plan* which proposed the decentralisation of population and industry to new towns in rural settings like **East Kilbride**, set up in 1947. The Corporation for its part embarked on ambitious schemes for new housing to solve the problems of overcrowding once and for all. These were accelerated in the late 1950s with the policy of Comprehensive Development by which whole swathes of Victorian housing were demolished to make way for New Jerusalems. Such an approach was not without its critics who believed one of the world's great Victorian cities was being needlessly destroyed.

By the time work began on the new concrete Glasgow, the revival of foreign competitors was threatening the whole fabric of the city's economy. From the mid-1960s shipyard after shipyard and engineering works after engineering works closed. Within ten years the river was an industrial wasteland and all attempts at reviving the city's traditional industries seemed doomed. The character of the city was changing. Now with two universities, Glasgow was rediscovering its past as a cultural and intellectual centre, challenging the philosophy that had ripped apart Britain's finest Victorian city. Out of this vision emerged a new Glasgow in the 1980s, proud of its past and its own distinct identity – summed up in the upbeat slogan 'Glasgow's Miles Better'. The efforts to preserve and restore were rewarded in the success of the Glasgow Garden Festival in 1988, the European City of Culture in 1990 and City of Architecture and Design in 1999. There are still problems. Glasgow remains a city of multiple deprivation with chronic health and social problems. But

Ceremonial arch and reception at Jamaica Bridge for Queen Victoria's 1849 visit (ML)

Glasgow continued

renewed confidence in the city's future has brought a flowering of literature for the first time since the 18th century with writers like James Kelman, Alasdair Gray and Liz Lochhead. New theatres have opened and the Glasgow **Royal Concert Hall** has been built. By rediscovering a past, Glasgow may have found a future.

Alhambra Theatre

Opened in December 1910 as a once-nightly **music hall**, but without much success, the Alhambra closed down for a short time before re-opening in 1911 on a twice-a-night basis, and featured performers like Grock the Swiss clown, Eugene Stratton, G H Elliot, Scottish comic Neil Kenyon, **Harry Lauder**, Vesta Tilley, Gertie Gitana, Tommy Handley, Stanley Holloway, Will Hay, Jack Hylton and his Band and Gracie Fields. Its first pantomime was in 1917. By 1926 the policy changed to musical comedies, revues and plays. The Wilson Barrett Repertory Company had regular seasons in the 1940s. Howard and Wyndham bought the theatre in 1954 and it became famous for pantomime and lavish 'Five-Past-Eight' revues. Its closure in the summer of 1969, due to rising costs and the increasing popularity of television, marked the end of an era in Scottish theatre.

Allan Glen's School

Allan Glen, a wright and property owner in Glasgow, died in 1850 and left the bulk of his substantial fortune to establish a school 'to give a good practical education to, and preparing for trades or business, from forty to fifty boys'. The school opened in 1853, but it was not until 1876 that the foundations were laid for the school's reputation as a centre for technical training. From 1882 it was affiliated to the Glasgow and West of Scotland Technical College – now the **University of Strathclyde** – but its distinctive tradition of technical and scientific training came to an end in the 1970s with the coming of comprehensive education.

Anderston

Anderston, to the west of 18th century Glasgow, was established as a new weaving village by James Anderston, the owner of nearby Stobcross, in the 1720s. It had an inauspicious start, attracting few settlers. The village was re-established in 1735 by the new owner of Stobcross, John Orr of Barrowfield, and rapidly became an important centre of calico printing, with several large concerns including J & J McIlwham and Grant & Fraser (whose partners provided Charles Dickens with the model for the brothers Cheeryble in *Nicholas Nickleby*). Despite setbacks Anderston prospered and in 1824 became a burgh in its own right. By the 1840s the town had grown so large that it was essentially part of Glasgow and in 1849 it was formally annexed, along with the burghs of **Calton** and **Gorbals**. Thereafter Anderston declined as business moved away from old restricted sites in the city centre, and the area became notorious for its poor housing. The problem had become so intractible by the late 1950s that Anderston was designated a Comprehensive Development Area. Most of the buildings were demolished to make way for concrete high-rise developments dominated by the Anderston Cross centre, designed by R Seifert & Co and constructed in 1973. The shopping area and bus station at its foot are testimony to a hesitant and confused vision of the future.

Argyle Street

One of Glasgow's principal shopping thoroughfares, with a pedestrianised section, Argyle Street runs west from **Glasgow Cross** joining Dumbarton Road at **Kelvingrove Park**. It was originally named St Thenew's (St Enoch's) Gait after the mother of St Kentigern [see **Mungo**]. Until the middle of the 18th century there was little between the High Street and the city's western gate, situated more or less on the site of the **St Enoch** Underground Station. The gate was removed in 1751 and the street renamed after the **Duke of Argyll**, one of the principal supporters of the Hanoverian cause in Scotland. From then on prosperous Glasgow merchants began to build mansions to the west of the old city. But a century later, as more and more people chose to live in the fast developing suburbs, shops and offices came to dominate Argyle Street. The street still contains some magnificent examples of 19th century shopping architecture, including the Argyle Arcade modelled on Continental designs of 1828 and Campbell Stewart and MacDonald's imposing warehouse (department store) on the corner of Buchanan Street (1900-3). The city centre part of the street finishes with the bridge that carries the **railway** from **Central Station** to London.

The Athenaeum

Inaugurated in 1847 at a banquet presided over by Charles Dickens, the Athenaeum was modelled on its namesake in Manchester, but with wider educational objectives, being intended 'to form a literary and scientific institution adapted to the wants of the commercial classes of Glasgow'. Its first home was in Ingram Street, in the **Adam** building of 1796 previously occupied by the Assembly Rooms. The Athenaeum provided subscribers with reading and news rooms, a large library and other facilities for recreation and study. Popular lectures were given under its auspices by guest speakers including Ralph Waldo Emerson and William Makepeace Thackeray. Early morning and evening classes were provided by a department which in 1888 became the Commercial College; a number of clubs, such as the Dramatic Club, met there; and the Athenaeum Schools of Music (1890) and of Art (1891) were formed as a consequence of the popularity of courses in these subjects.

In 1888 the Athenaeum moved to St George's (now Nelson Mandela) Place to a magnificent Beaux Arts building by J J Burnet. In 1890-93 a new building was erected in Buchanan Street, with a rear connection to the St George's Place premises. The extension housed a restaurant, gymnasium, theatre and concert hall. The building on the corner between them, the Liberal Club of 1907-8, was purchased in 1928 by the new Scottish National Academy of Music (SNAM), which was formed round the nucleus of the Athenaeum School of Music and acquired the buildings and funds of the Glasgow Athenaeum Ltd. The West of Scotland Commercial College departed from St George's Place in 1935 to new premises off Pitt Street.

The SNAM became the Royal Scottish Academy of Music in 1944, and the School of Drama was founded six years later. The Royal Scottish Academy of Music and Drama moved in 1987 to purpose built premises in Renfield Street. The Athenaeum building in Nelson Mandela Square was converted to offices, the old Liberal Club reopened as a hotel, and the Buchanan Street Building became the home of the Scottish Youth Theatre.

Barony Church

Glasgow in the 19th century was famous for its churches and its preachers. The Barony Church was perhaps one of the best known, with legendary ministers like **Dr Norman Macleod**. It takes its name from the Barony parish which, with the castle at its centre, encircled the east end of the medieval city. The present building, which replaced a late-18th century church, was designed by Sir J J Burnet and John A Campbell and completed in 1890. Although rugged in its exterior, it is spacious and lofty inside, an excellent example of Scottish Gothic Revival. With the decline of the population in the east end the church closed, but has found a new use as the ceremonial hall of the **University of Strathclyde**.

'The Barras'

There were hawkers trading from barrows in the **Gallowgate** and surrounding streets near **Glasgow Cross** in the 19th century, but it was not until the 1920s that 'The Barras' found a permanent site. A street trader, Margaret McIver, acquired some land on the south side of the Gallowgate, near the site of the old city gate (also known as the 'Barras Yett', ie 'Barrier's Gate'). There she let out stalls, and in 1926 erected a roof over the market. The Barrowland Ballroom, which was built (1934) above it, was severely damaged by fire in 1958, but rebuilt two years later. It became one of the city's top rock concert venues during the 1970s.

'The Barras' grew rapidly after 1926, spilling over from the original site on the Gallowgate to nearby buildings and street pavements, and today it covers most of the ground lying between the Gallowgate and London Road, from Ross Street to Bain Street. Inspired by the **GEAR** project for the regeneration of the east end, the Barrows Enterprise Trust was set up in 1982 to coordinate plans to develop the market. Archways were erected over the entrance streets and facilities such as parking and a crèche were provided. The Barras has become Scotland's biggest covered market place, with ten markets, around 1000 stalls and 100 shops.

Bellahouston Park

South of **Govan**, the **Paisley** road and the M8, Bellahouston Park's 175 acres (71ha) extend almost to

Pollok Country Park. The site was chosen for the 1938 Empire Exhibition dominated by Thomas S Tait's 300ft (91m) steel tower. The tower was supposed to be retained as a permanent reminder of the occasion but was soon demolished lest it serve as a navigational aid to incoming German bombers. The Exhibition, though marred by atrocious weather, attracted 13.5 million visitors, about four times the number who attended Glasgow's 1988 International Garden Festival. A concert hall, a complete Highland village, and one of the first Indian restaurants in Scotland were all upstaged by the giant funfair which included a wall-of-death train ride. The park has subsequently been used for other mass events, including the 1982 visit of Pope John Paul II. In 1990 **Charles Rennie Mackintosh**'s *Haus Eines Kunstfreundes* (House of an Art Lover) was at last realised on the north side of the park.

Blythswood Square

In 1804 William Harley, a successful Glasgow textile merchant, purchased part of Blythswood Estate to the west of Glasgow as a family residence. He soon began to develop the estate as a **tourist** attraction, building a 30ft (9m) tower on top of Blythswoodshill – nicknamed 'Harley's Folly'. Between 1808–16 houses in new streets were laid out between the city and Blythswoodhill, but the depression that followed the end of the Napoleonic Wars undermined Harley's business and he went bankrupt in 1822. William Garden took over Harley's property and with the help of the Glasgow architect John Brash began building the imposing square on top of Blythswoodhill (1823). Garden himself went bankrupt and the development was completed by his trustees. The fine classical houses, originally designed as family homes, have now all been converted into offices and clubs. The whole east side of the square is occupied by the Royal Scottish Automobile Club, reconstructed by the architect James Miller in 1923.

The Bridgegate

The 'Briggait' ('gait' meaning 'the way to') led down from the **Saltmarket** to **Glasgow Bridge** and the Brig Port. It lay at the heart of the 17th century merchants' quarter and boasted great mansions such as the home of Campbell of Blythswood, and the **Merchants' House** (1659) which was one of the city's main social and commercial meeting places. Like most of its neighbours, however, the Merchants' House departed in the early 19th century when the street and surrounding area became an Irish slum; its steeple alone remains, square, 164ft (50m) high, with three balconies, and topped by a sailing ship.

Nearly all the buildings in the Bridgegate were swept away during the 1860s and 70s by the City of Glasgow Union **Railway**, carrying its lines through to **St Enoch's Square** and **High Street**. The construction of the wholesale fish market, baroque outside, cast-iron inside, in 1872–5 (extended 1886 and 1903) brought a solid commercial core back to a street which had become dominated by a barrow trade in secondhand clothes (spilling over from **Paddy's Market**). The fish market

moved to Blochairn in 1977, and an attempt to convert the old building to a Covent Garden style retail market (the Briggait Centre) failed in 1986.

The Broomielaw

Stretching from **Glasgow Bridge** to **Anderston** Quay, the Broomielaw takes its name from the 'Brumelaw Croft', a piece of land which stretched along the **Clyde** from the Old Green to Parson's Haugh, and north as far as the road which became **Argyle Street**. The croft was given up to building during the 18th century. The waterfront of the Broomielaw was the main landing point for goods and victuals brought upriver to the city and a small quay was built there in 1601. It was rebuilt and improved on several occasions during the 17th and 18th centuries, but it was not until the Clyde was deepened, beginning in the 1770s, that the quay was able to receive other than small coastal trading vessels. It was extended in 1792, a new quay was added in 1809, and thereafter the Broomielaw regained from **Port Dundas** the position of Glasgow's main port. Further development of Glasgow Harbour, however, led to a greater specialisation in facilities at the city's riverside quays, and in 1823 the Broomielaw was remodelled by **Thomas Telford** as a steamboat quay. The Broomielaw became the main point of entry of tens of thousands of Irish immigrants after the inauguration of passenger steamboat services from Ireland in 1818, and the departure point for generations of Glaswegian holiday-makers sailing **'doon the watter'** aboard paddle steamers, bound for **Rothesay** and the other Clyde resorts. The quay was closed in 1947.

Famous buildings erected on the Broomielaw Street include the Seaman's Institute and the magnificent **Clyde Port Authority** building on the corner of Robertson Street. The Broomielaw was comprehensively redeveloped during the 1990s, with the Atlantic Quay buildings providing the modernist cornerstone, and the Riverboat Casino a brightly-lit night-time beacon. The Broomielaw Quay is now a stretch of the Clyde Walkway.

Buchanan Street

Named for Andrew Buchanan, a maltster who became one of Glasgow's greatest **Tobacco** Lords, Buchanan Street first appears in the records in 1777. It became one of Glasgow's most fashionable shopping streets, strategically linking **Sauchiehall Street** with **Argyle Street** and possessing popular department stores such as Frasers and Wyllie & Lochhead, as well as the famous Argyll Arcade (1827) at its foot.

Buchanan Street was pedestrianised in 1978, but seemed to lose its popularity with shoppers. However, with the opening in 1987 of the trendy indoor shopping centre, Princes Square, its fashionable status revived. The opening of the **Royal Concert Hall** (1990) at its head, and the vast St Enoch shopping centre (1989) just beyond its southern end, confirmed its position as the stylish spine of the city. Its growing status was reinforced by the opening of another shopping centre, the Buchanan Galleries, in 1999. North of this development, the Buchanan Bus Station is the largest, indeed the 'busiest', in Scotland.

Embarking at the Broomielaw in the 1880s (ML)

Glasgow continued

Ca' D'Oro, Gordon and Union Streets

With Venice's Golden House (hence the name) as his inspiration, John Honeyman (1831–1914) used cast iron and much glass to produce this unique frontage. At street level slender Doric pilasters supporting high round masonry arches frame the window bays. Above, even slimmer Corinthian pilasters act as astragals, with more glass in the form of circular windows completing the filigree effect beneath the crowning cornice. Altogether too light and fanciful a building for its original function as a warehouse, it was converted into a restaurant and, restored in 1988–90 after a fire, into airy retail premises.

Caledonia Road Church, Gorbals

'One of the most remarkable churches in the city' (D Daiches) now stands gutted and forlorn, its best chance of survival lying with the growing clamour to elevate **Alexander 'Greek' Thomson** to the pinnacle currently occupied by **Charles Rennie Mackintosh**. It was Thomson's first church (1856–7), the raised Ionic colonnade being unmistakable and the tall square tower typically eclectic. An adjacent tenement, 37–9 Cathcart Road, was also by Thomson. The church caught fire in 1965 and, threatened by a proposed motorway, has been left as a ruin.

Candleriggs

After the great fire of 1652, Glasgow's candle factories were removed from the old city centre to fields known as the Cornriggs to the west. A path led down from the new industrial area to the **Trongate**, and the Candleriggs Street was formally laid out and built during the 1720s,

with the Ramshorn Kirk (**St David's**) closing the vista to the north. The city's guard house was located at the foot of Candleriggs until 1795, and in 1755 the green (vegetable) market moved there from the Trongate. The green and cheese markets were relocated in a new bazaar (on the site of a bowling green laid out in the 1690s) in 1817, where they remained until the opening of the fruit market at Blochairn in 1969. Glasgow's first street pavement was built in Candleriggs in 1777, from Trongate to Bell Street.

In 1841 the Italianate City Hall (James Cleland) was built through the middle of the bazaar with entrances on Candleriggs and Albion Street. The building has five halls, with the great hall raised on columns between the north and south markets. It became the city's premier venue for large indoor meetings (including 'concerts for the working classes' and the first **General Assembly** of the **Free Church** in 1843) and political rallies.

The Candleriggs entrance to the City Hall was remodelled 1882–6 (John Carrick) when the bazaar was rebuilt. The City Hall then lost favour, due to its crowded position in an area dominated by wholesale warehouses, and after the Corporation acquired the St Andrew's Halls in 1890. When the new halls burned down in 1962, the City Hall became once again a major venue, and continues to host prestigious concerts and events. Since the 1980s work has proceeded on the renovation of Candleriggs warehouses as blocks of flats. The former Fruitmarket has now been redeveloped as a leisure complex, with bars, restaurants and cafés around a central courtyard. There are plans to open a nightclub in the basement.

Carlton Place and Bridge

A miniature version of London's Hammersmith Bridge, the Carlton suspension bridge was built in 1851–3 but, like Hammersmith, required extensive rebuilding 20 years later. For a footbridge it appears unusually elaborate although not out of keeping with the expectations of the merchants John (or James) and David Laurie who had acquired extensive lands south of the river in 1794. Purchased from **Hutcheson's** and Trades Hospital (hence Hutchesontown and Tradeston), this ground was to be laid out as up-market housing. Wide streets with names like Cumberland, Cavendish and Portland recall Mayfair, but within a century the classical tenements had been crowded out by **railways**, industries and indiscriminate development; Mayfair became 'an annexe of the **Gorbals**'. In Carlton Place, facing the river, the Lauries built their own Laurieston House, a large classical terrace with rather shallow external detail but rich interiors said to have been designed by 'Italian artists' who had been decorating Windsor Castle for George IV. Much ingenuity was expended on recessed bookcases and cupboards and, for reasons unexplained, the drawing room floor was 'hung on chains or rods in such a way as to make the tension adjustable' (J Cowan). The house was selected as suitable accommodation for George IV in 1822 but his visit was cancelled.

The Cathedral

The growth of Glasgow during the 19th century into one of the world's principal industrial cities resulted in the destruction of most of her existing buildings. Fortunately the Cathedral, having weathered the **Reformation** and the wars of the 17th century, escaped almost unscathed. Built according to tradition on the site of **St Kentigern**'s cell, the Cathedral was the hub of the medieval city. Not a large building by English or even Scottish standards, it is nevertheless imposing given the impoverished state of the west of Scotland in the Middle Ages. The present building was started by Bishop Jocelyn in the late 12th century and largely completed by the end of the 13th, although the nave seems to include 14th century features. It stood in the shadow of Bishop's Castle, part of whose massive 18th century walls have recently been excavated. Major repairs to the Cathedral were undertaken in the 15th century, including the reconstruction of the central tower and the chapter house, plus the addition of the incomplete **Blackadder** aisles. In 1492 the see of Glasgow was elevated to an archbishopric.

After the Reformation the church was divided between three congregations, an arrangement made possible by dividing the choir from the nave and by the existence of a lower church, beneath the choir, originally designed to hold the relics of St Kentigern. By the 1830s there was concern among Glasgow antiquarians about the state of the building. Following intense lobbying, work began to restore the Cathedral to its original state. Unfortunately the two western towers were swept away (1846) before it was discovered that there was money to replace them. Since then the minister of the Cathedral has been regarded more or less as Glasgow's minister. There have been some well known incumbents including Dr Lang, father of **Cosmo Gordon Lang**, an Archbishop of Canterbury. Recently improvements have been made to the sur-

Glasgow Cathedral c1840, before demolition of its remaining western tower (RWB)

roundings of the building, including the construction of a processional way at the west end and a visitors' centre (now a museum of religion) designed by Ian Begg.

Central Mosque and Islamic Centre

Situated on the banks of the **Clyde** at **Gorbals** Cross, the Mosque is built on a 4 acre (1.2ha) site purchased from Glasgow District Council at a cost of £90,000 in 1970. The total cost on completion was £3 million. Building work started in July 1979 and the site was officially opened on Friday, 18 May 1984 (17 Shaban 1404). It is controlled and managed by the Jamiat Itti-had-Ul-Muslimin (Muslim Mission), a democratic and charitable religious body established in 1944, the earliest and largest Muslim organisation in Glasgow.

The building reflects a blend of modern design and materials with traditional Islamic features such as the minaret, dome, crescent, arches, muqarnas and courtyard. The Mosque faces the Ka'aba (House of God) in Mecca in Saudi Arabia. The architects were the Glasgow-based Coleman/Ballantine partnership. An extension on the adjacent vacant site is intended for the construction of community and social facilities, offices and business development.

This institution serves as the central focal point for 25,000 Muslims in Glasgow and Strathclyde – and as Scotland's first purpose-built Mosque complex, it acts as the symbol of Islam in Scotland. While the majority of Scotland's Muslims are of Pakistani origin, there are also many of Arab, Turkish, African, Malaysian, Bangladeshi and Indian extraction.

Central Station

Glasgow Central Station was opened by the Caledonian **Railway** Company in 1879 as a terminus for southbound passenger services. The eight platforms (a ninth was added in 1889) soon proved inadequate for the growing volume of traffic and the station was greatly extended and remodelled in 1901–5, when four more platforms were added and a second viaduct was built across the **Clyde**, alongside the first, to carry the new approach lines. The original viaduct was removed in 1967 leaving only the granite piers standing.

In 1885 the Central Station Hotel was opened on the corner of Gordon and Hope Streets; with nearly 400 bedrooms it easily surpassed the rival establishment at **St Enoch's** Station. The following year Central Low Level Station was opened on the Glasgow Central Railway. This station closed in 1964, but reopened on the modernised Argyll Line in 1979.

Some of Glasgow's most celebrated landmarks are associated with Central Station. 'The Shell', a World War I naval projectile converted into a charity collecting box, was one of Glasgow's favourite rendezvous. It was moved to a quiet spot near the left luggage office in 1966, but restored to a prominent position in the centre of the concourse in 1988. Another well known meeting place was beneath the bridge carrying the railway over **Argyle Street**; it became known as the 'Hielanders' Umbrella' as it was particularly favoured by visitors from the Highlands and Islands. Of equal sentimental value to generations of Glaswegians was the station's

great train indicator screen, on the upper floor of the pear-shaped 'Torpedo Building' next to the hotel. Built in 1905, its 13 indicator boards visible from every part of the great concourse, the building was converted to a bar restaurant complex in 1987, and the indicator boards replaced with electronic information screens at the platforms.

Despite extensive renovation work during the 1980s, the much admired layout of the Edwardian station has been retained, and few stations in the country can match Central's grandeur.

Chamber of Commerce

The Glasgow Chamber of Commerce, founded and incorporated by royal charter in 1783, is the oldest in the United Kingdom. It was established to represent the interests of Glasgow's commercial and manufacturing community in the wake of the American War of Independence, which undermined the city's valuable trade with Virginia. Prime movers were the Lord Provost and the Chamber's first chairman, Patrick Colquhoun (1745–1820). The Chamber's directors met at least once a month to discuss important matters of trade and industry. Initially they met in the Tontine Tavern in **Trongate**, then in premises in **Virginia Street**, in the Royal Exchange, the **Merchants' House** building in Glassford Street, and in Virginia Street once more, before finding their present home in the Merchants' House Building in **George Square** in 1877.

Charing Cross

Charing Cross was named after its London namesake during the 1850s when **Sauchiehall Street** was extended as a main thoroughfare to what is now **Kelvingrove Park**. By the 1890s it had become the hub of Glasgow's west end, located at the point where the fashionable residential area of Woodlands and Garnethill met industrial **Anderston** and the western edge of the city's commercial district. It was distinguished by several fine buildings including the Charing Cross Hotel (later renamed the Grand, opened in 1878 and closed 1968), the sweeping and very French Charing Cross Mansions (by J J Burnet, 1889–91) and the St George's Mansions on the corner of Woodlands and St George's Roads (1900–1). Its importance was further enhanced in 1877 by the opening of the St Andrew's Halls in nearby Granville Street, and of the **Mitchell Library** in 1911.

Decline came in the late 1960s when the M8 was pushed through the middle, albeit in a cutting, on its way to the **Kingston Bridge**. In an attempt to preserve the continuity of Sauchiehall Street, a raised concrete deck was built to span the motorway on which it was proposed to build shops. The shops, however, were never begun, and the apparently useless 'Bridge to Nowhere' became the subject of numerous jokes aimed at the city's planners.

The Charing Cross Complex (1971–5) is not actually at the Cross but nearby on the south side of Bath Street. It is a concrete wilderness of office blocks and draughty passageways, with Charing Cross Station hidden away inside. Fountain House (1981) is at the Cross on the site of the Grand Hotel, but is no more inspiring and has been likened to 'an incomplete Rubik's Cube'. The building overlooks the Cameron Memorial Fountain of 1896, once a popular meeting place.

In 1991, the 'Bridge to Nowhere' became an annexe of the monolithic pink office development which dominates the south-eastern corner of Charing Cross. Scarred by the motorway, abandoned by its once-famous shops, and literally overshadowed by the new development, Charing Cross appears to have a future only as a nine-to-five office ghetto and a congested traffic junction.

Citizens' Theatre, see Princess's Theatre and THEATRE IN SCOTLAND

City and County Buildings, Wilson Street

In 1835 the Glasgow Court House Commissioners were instructed to arrange for the erection of a new building to accommodate Glasgow's municipal offices, the county offices, and the Sheriff and JP courts. The City and County Buildings, designed by Clarke & Bell in the same Greek Revival style adopted for the adjoining **Merchants' House** building, opened on Wilson Street in 1844. In 1869 the Commissioners acquired the Merchants' House premises to provide additional accommodation. An extension was built facing Ingram Street in 1870–4, but the pressure for space continued to grow with the functions of the Corporation, and in 1890 the city fathers and most of their officials departed for the new **City Chambers** in **George Square**. The great complex they left behind, the three sections forming one great block bounded by Wilson, Hutcheson, Ingram and Brunswick Streets, was devoted entirely to court work.

In 1986 a new Sheriff Court of Glasgow and Strathkelvin opened in Gorbals Street. The old City and County Buildings, in dire need of renovation, await development.

City Chambers, George Square

Occupying the whole of the east side of **George Square** and extending back along George Street, the City Chambers succeeded the **City and County Buildings** in Wilson Street as the headquarters of the city council and, by virtue of their size, magnificence and position, became Glasgow's civic focus. The foundation stone was laid with great ceremony in 1883 and the building opened by **Queen Victoria**, with yet greater ceremony, on 22 August 1888. The competition-winning design by William Young (1843–1900) for an extravagant Italian Renaissance palace coincided precisely with the city fathers' pride in what was then unquestionably the second city of the British Empire. On the central pediment above the façade's three tiers of paired columns a bas relief portrays the enthroned Queen with figures representing England, Scotland, Ireland and Wales flanked by further figures representing the countries of the Empire. Cupolas and statuary flank the pediment, adorn the corner towers, and crown the great central tower. Within, the theme of triumphalist imperialism defers to a hushed basilican opulence. The mosaic ceiling of the loggia is said to comprise 1.5 million pieces;

The City Chambers in George Square (ML)

marble staircases ascend through what Young described as 'tier upon tier of pillars, arches and cornices', also in marble and polished granite. The high standard of craftsmanship is continued throughout, most notably in the woodwork of the Council Chamber and in the arched ceiling of the Banqueting Hall. The latter, with proportions (110 by 48ft/33.5m by 14.6m) worthy of an auditorium, contains murals by Alexander Roche (illustrating the legend of **St Mungo**'s miracle involving the discovery of a ring in the mouth of a salmon), by **Sir John Lavery** (of the **Clyde** in the 19th century) and by Edward Walton (of **Glasgow Green** during the **Glasgow Fair** c1500). The City Chambers extension in George Street by Watson, Salmond and Grey in 1913 is more restrained but no less classical. Ionic arches link it to the main block across John Street.

Clyde Tunnel

Proposals for a road tunnel under the **Clyde** from Whiteinch to Linthouse were first put forward in 1947, but post-war building restrictions and scarcity of building materials delayed the start of construction until 1964. There are in fact twin tunnels, one carrying road traffic south, with a cycle and pedestrian path beneath the roadway, and an adjacent and identical tunnel for northbound traffic. Each tunnel is 2250ft (686m) long and provides a dual carriageway 44ft (13m) wide. They are connected by ramps and cuttings with various access roads and the Clydeside Expressway.

Clydesdale Bank

The Clydesdale Bank building, designed by John Burnet in 1871, dominates **St Vincent Place** in the heart of the city. The Bank is the last surviving Glasgow bank. It was founded in 1838 by James Lumsden and a group of Glasgow merchants to meet their needs for financial services. Under their guidance and that of their successors it prospered and flourished, catering for the increasingly large-scale funding required by the west of Scotland's heavy industries. It became part of the Midland Bank Group in 1920 and merged with the North of Scotland bank in 1950. In 1987 it became the first British bank to be owned by a bank with an overseas head office, the National Bank of Australia. Its offices have grown to include adjoining buildings and a new block originally shared with the Bank of England facing West George Street, constructed in 1979–80 by G D Lodge & Partners.

Cowcaddens

'Formerly common grazing ground for the citizens' cattle' (*Third Statistical Account*), Cowcaddens was heavily developed in the early 19th century as a dormitory area for the adjacent industrial complex around **Port Dundas** [see also **Dobbie's Loan**]. It rapidly acquired an unsavoury reputation for its mix of slum tenements and factories, remaining one of the most densely populated and ill-favoured districts until after World War II. Subsequently cleared, and bisected by the M8 and its feeder roads, the district has yet to discover an alternative identity. Amidst car parks, the Buchanan Bus Station, structures like STV's headquarters, the Royal Scottish Academy of Music and Drama's new Opera School and

Glasgow Caledonian University, a few older buildings survive including the refurbished Piping College and **David Hamilton**'s Dundas Vale Teachers' Centre. It was founded as The Normal School for the Training of Teachers (1836–7), 'the first college of its kind', by David Stow (1793–1864) who, fired by the educational ideas of **Dr Thomas Chalmers** and Samuel Wilderspin, had evolved an enlightened or 'normal' teaching regime which outlawed corporal punishment as well as prizes and emphasised 'Physical and Moral Training', the title of Stow's 1832 manual. **Thomas Carlyle** was one of the unsuccessful candidates for the new college's rectorship. After the **Disruption**, Stow founded a **Free Church** Normal School nearby but now demolished. His name is commemorated in the red brick Stow College (1935).

Custom House

The elegant stone Custom House in Clyde Street was built in 1840 by John Taylor to deal with Glasgow's expanding trade. It has Doric columns and a fine coat of arms. Originally Glasgow's Custom House had been a sub-office of **Port Glasgow** and did not achieve independence until 1780. The Custom Officials collected duty on imports and exports and also maintained registers of ships owned by Glasgow merchants. With the decline in Glasgow's upriver trade the Custom House now serves as the Office of the Procurator Fiscal.

Dennistoun

Considered by Jack House in 1958 as 'the most individual district in the whole of Glasgow', Dennistoun, east of the **Necropolis**, epitomised the independent spirit once found throughout the city's suburbs and especially in such East End districts as Shettleston, Bridgeton, Dalmarnock and Parkhead. Here the blight of industrialisation was at its worst with factories and forges deafening and asphyxiating the inmates of the densely packed and overcrowded tenements. Traditions of 18th century militancy amongst the weavers of adjacent **Calton** resurfaced in the socialist rhetoric of the **ILP**; from Shettleston alone came **Davie Kirkwood**, **John Wheatley** and John McGovern. Post-war programmes of slum clearance, the closure of engineering works and environmental prettification [see **GEAR**] removed most of the worst manifestations of hardship; they also removed most of the people. No longer can 1700 dancers be seen taking the floor simultaneously at the Dennistoun Palais; and the Bridgeton Burns Club must long since have been overtaken as 'the largest in the world'.

Dobbie's Loan

Named after local landowner John Dobbie in the 16th century, Dobbie's Loan is believed to have been a part of the **Roman** road from Glasgow to **Dumbarton**. Stretching from the Bishop's Garden at the **Cathedral** through the common pastures of **Cowcaddens** to Garscube, the pathway was used for generations by drovers bringing their cattle to market at **Glasgow Green**. Because of its popularity as a rural promenade for courting couples, it was also sometimes known as Love Loan.

With the development of **Port Dundas**, Cowcaddens became a major industrial quarter, and the western end of Dobbie's Loan was lined with foundries, workshops

nd warehouses. In 1814 the Glasgow Asylum for Luna-
ics opened on the corner of Dobbie's Loan and Parliamentary Road near the **Royal Infirmary**. The city
poorhouse was built on the site in 1842, when the
asylum was transferred to Gartnavel.

Dobbie's Loan remained a popular business location
even after the decline of the Forth & **Clyde [Union]
Canal**. The redevelopment of the city in the 1960s,
however, resulted in the removal of the eastern end of
the street to make way for a new housing scheme, and
the demolition of most of its industrial and commercial
buildings. It is now primarily used as a feeder route to
the M8 motorway.

Easterhouse

Although ignored by the city's image-makers, Easterhouse on the eastern outskirts beside the M8 remains
a grim reminder of Glasgow's reputation for disastrous
planning, mass unemployment, high crime rates and
grinding poverty. One of many post-war housing
schemes (Drumchapel, Castlemilk, etc), it has come to
epitomise their soulless mix of high density housing
and low level amenities thanks to Billy Connolly's apt
description, 'a desert wi' windaes' – he may have been
referring to Drumchapel – and thanks to television's
taste for documentaries about social deprivation. As first
laid out, Easterhouse had no pubs, no shops, no schools,
no entertainment, no transport, and no jobs. Social
awareness and numerous community schemes have
remedied many of these deficiencies, but not the last.

Egyptian Halls, 84–100 Union Street

Facing the side of **Central Station** and easily missed
amidst the high street mêlée of Union Street, the Egyptian Halls have been described as 'the building in which
[**Alexander**] **Thomson** gathered all his previous motifs
into a single stupendous penultimate composition'
McKean, Walker and Walker). On a cast-iron frame
the façade of four diminishing storeys comprises stacked
banks of uniform columns and pilasters with a band of
decorative detail between each. Those of the first floor
are slender triple stems, of the second sturdier coupled
doubles, and of the third thick stubby singles 'Indian
in proportion but Egyptian in detail' and resembling
the corresponding storey of Thomson's **Grecian Chambers** in **Sauchiehall Street**. A heavy rooftop cornice
lends logic to the load-bearing properties of these last.
The building was originally used for public meetings
but has long been subservient to the retail activities at
street level.

Empire Theatre

At the corner of **Sauchiehall Street** and West Nile
Street, the Empire opened as the Gaiety in March 1874.
A larger theatre, the Empire Palace, was built on the
site in 1897 and became a leading British **music hall**,
featuring British, American and European artistes. It was
rebuilt and enlarged once more in 1931. From the mid-
1930s it acquired, unjustly, the nickname of 'The Graveyard of English Comedians' because of the silent
reception given to London comics. In the 1950s it head-
lined a continuing line of American performers, among
them Laurel and Hardy, Danny Kaye, Liberace and

Sophie Tucker, but had finally to give way to the television age when Moss Empires sold the building for
property development. The final week in March 1963
featured the Red Army Ensemble.

Empress Theatre

Opened on 4 August 1913 at St George's Cross as The
West End Playhouse, renamed the Empress Variety and
Picture Playhouse in March 1914, it became the New
Empress in 1933 when it was taken over by city
businessman George Urie Scott who ran it as a Cine-
Variety Theatre until it, like so many other Glasgow
Theatres, was damaged by fire in 1956. Theatre promoter Alex Frutin bought it in 1962 after his own
Metropole Theatre was also burnt down, and the
Empress became the New Metropole. The Logan family
(including Jack Short and his son Jimmy Logan) ran it
successfully for some years, but the nearby city population found new homes in the suburbs and it stood
empty for several years before being demolished to
make way for new housing.

'Finnieston' Crane

The **Clyde** Navigation Trust's 130-ton crane at Finnieston was removed after the Corporation announced
plans (later shelved) to build a bridge over the Clyde
on its site. To replace it, in 1928 the Trustees ordered
a new cantilever crane to be erected on Stobcross Quay,
500yds (457m) to the west. The 'Finnieston' Crane is
thus properly the 'Stobcross' Crane. Electrically
powered, Crane No 7 (*not* No 5) is 195ft (59m) high,
with a 152ft (46m) hammerhead jib, and cost over
£70,000. It was built by Cowans Sheldon & Co of Carlisle and went into service in 1932. Capable of lifting
loads heavier than the 175 tons safety limit imposed,
it was used to transfer boilers and engines into vessels
being fitted out at Stobcross, and to load heavy machinery such as **locomotives** on to freighters.

Crane No 7 is still used occasionally in cargo loading
on the Clyde, but has also become a symbol of the city's
past prowess in heavy **engineering**. Dominating the
riverside skyline, it has been the centrepiece of several
festival events (including the 1989 Glasgow Garden Festival) and is sometimes described as Glasgow's Eiffel
Tower.

The Forge

The rooftops of Parkhead are interrupted by the curious
pyramidal shapes of the Forge Shopping Centre,
designed by Scott Brownrigg & Turner in 1986–8 as a
deliberate departure from the steelworks and forge of
William Beardmore & Co that previously occupied the
site. The Forge is a vast glass-covered all-weather centre
with most of the leading stores represented. Nothing
remains on the site of the old Beardmore works except
the name.

The Gallowgate

One of Glasgow's oldest thoroughfares, the Gallowgate
was originally a narrow lane leading from **Glasgow
Cross** to the village of Camlachie, three miles to the
east. It is said that it is so called because it was the route
from the **Tolbooth** to a place of public execution on
the Gallowmuir.

Most of the earliest buildings on the Gallowgate were built close to the Cross within the Gallowgate Port (which was demolished in 1849). In 1500, however, Little St Mungo's Church was built just beyond the city gate. It was used for a time after the **Reformation** as a hospital for lepers and plague victims, before falling into disrepair. The famous Saracen's Head Inn was built on the site of the churchyard in 1754, and many famous visitors to Glasgow, including **Burns**, **Boswell** and **Dr Johnson**, stayed there. The inn was converted into dwellings and shops in 1792 and was demolished in 1905.

The Butts, a military training ground, also lay on the north side of the road, to the east of the kirkyard. Two battles were fought there, the first in 1544 when the forces of the Regent **Earl of Arran** defeated those of the Earl of Glencairn and then sacked the city, and the second in 1679, when **John Graham of Claverhouse** repulsed an attack by a party of **Covenanters** and then massacred Glaswegians suspected of sympathising with his enemies. Infantry barracks were built on the Butts in 1795, where they remained until new barracks were completed in **Maryhill** in 1876.

The Gallowgate became notorious for its slums and drinking dens and The City Improvement Trust swept away many of the old vennels and overcrowded back-land tenements during the late 19th century. The street remained unfashionable nonetheless, and a subsequent generation of derelict industrial premises and decayed tenements was removed during the 1970s and 80s as part of the urban renewal programme of the **GEAR** project. The oldest surviving brick dwelling in Glasgow is believed to be the tenement at 394 Gallowgate, built 1771 and restored 1981–3. Despite wholesale demolition and regeneration work the Gallowgate retained much of its distinctive earthy character, and the popularity of the Barrowland Ballroom and the **Barras** market near Glasgow Cross is undiminished.

GEAR

The Glasgow Eastern Area Renewal Project was launched in 1976 as a major initiative to arrest and reverse the process of urban decay. The project was coordinated by the Scottish Development Agency, working with Strathclyde Regional Council, Glasgow District Council, and other bodies interested in 'the comprehensive environmental, social and economic regeneration of the East End'. By 1987, £500 million (including £300 million from the public purse) had been invested in the refurbishment of tenements and building of new homes, the environmental improvement of industrial wasteland, and the construction of over 300 factory units and three health centres.

GEAR had many successes. By 1987 two-thirds of the population lived in new or refurbished homes, and the landscaping of large open sites removed many of the city's worst eyesores. The scheme was criticised, however, for failing to attract businesses offering long-term employment opportunities for local people.

George Square

Front garden of the **City Chambers** and one of the largest open spaces in the city centre, George Square has become a civic focus, doubling as both a setting for ceremony and statuary and as a venue for protest and revelry; in effect it thus combines the functions of London's Trafalgar and Parliament Squares. It was named in honour of George III and laid out in the 1780s in the lands of Deanston as an expensive residential development on the then western fringe of the city. In 1790 the city's first sewer, from the square to **St Enoch's**, testified to its salubrious credentials and in 1792 **Robert** and **James Adam** prepared plans for a large Nash-like terrace on the south side. But this was never built and by the mid-19th century early opulence as represented by residents like the thread-making **Coats** brothers of **Paisley** had moved out; the square's private gardens were being used as a public thoroughfare and the surrounding buildings had largely become hotels. Decline was probably the result of the opening of **Queen Street Station** (1842) on the northern threshold of the square where the adjacent Copthorne Hotel (1807) still betrays its Georgian character despite the addition of a plantless conservatory fronting the square.

Statues had begun to grace the gardens as early as 1810 when local hero **Sir John Moore** of Corunna was so honoured. **James Watt** was erected in 1832, and atop David Rhind's tall Doric column Scotland's first statue of **Sir Walter Scott** took its pride of place in 1838. Thereafter the selection of candidates for petrified commemoration became more arbitrary. 11 in all, they are, in addition to the forementioned, **Colin Campbell (Lord Clyde)**, Robert Peel, William Gladstone, **Thomas Graham**, **Thomas Campbell**, **Queen Victoria** and Prince Albert, **Robert Burns**, and a sometime MP, James Oswald (see M Lindsay's *Portrait of Glasgow* for full detail of each).

The square meanwhile was beginning to assume its institutional character as the new **Merchants' House** (1874–7, John Burnet) reached down the west side from George Street to meet the new Bank of Scotland (1869–74, **J T Rochead**) pushing up from **St Vincent's Place**. Simultaneously the Italianate General Post Office (1875–6, Robert Mathieson) was going up on the south side. In 1883–8 the renaissance of the square was completed as the palatial façade and cupola-ed towers of the **City Chambers** rose along the east side to formalise and focus the whole composition.

With the gardens now gone and the statues adrift in a sea of paving, the square became a forum, with the City Chambers serving as an occasional place of retreat from revellers as on Armistice and VE Days, rioters as on **Bloody Friday** 1919, and fans as in the aftermath of several rock concerts. German bombs, presumably aimed at Queen Street Station, fell on the square on the night of 18 September 1941 but did no great damage and the city's lion-flanked cenotaph continues defiantly to commemorate the dead of both World Wars.

George V Bridge

Until the 1960s construction of the high-level **Kingston** (M8) and **Erskine** Bridges, this was the last **Clyde** bridge both in point of time and in terms of geography; below it the necessity of shipping access to **Anderston** Quay and the **Broomielaw** meant that the river could be crossed only by ferry or tunnel [see **Harbour** and **Clyde Tunnels**]. The bridge was built in 1924–8 (Thomas omers) and the memorial stone laid by George V in 927. The three low spans of reinforced concrete measure 110, 146 and 110ft (33.5, 44.5 and 33.4m). although the balustraded parapets were modelled on hose of **Glasgow (Jamaica) Bridge**, the squat design ttracted much criticism. It was, however, conceded hat it greatly relieved congestion on Glasgow Bridge rom which it is separated only by the **railway** viaduct nto **Central Station**.

;lasgow (Jamaica) Bridge

inking **Jamaica Street** north of the **Clyde** with Bridge nd Eglinton Streets on the south, this was Glasgow's econd stone bridge and its main north-south axis during the city's 19th century heyday. It was first built to design by **Robert** and **William Mylne** in 1767–72 nd was then known as **Broomielaw** Bridge, not succeeding to the title of Glasgow Bridge until the old ilasgow Bridge upstream was demolished (1840s) and eplaced by **Victoria Bridge** (1856). Meanwhile the Iylnes' design had been superseded by the lower profile of **Telford**'s 1833 bridge, itself remodelled and videned in 1894–9 though retaining Telford's granite balustrades.

;lasgow Cross

;lasgow Cross was erected at the foot of the **High Street** ome time after 1170, when **William the Lion** granted he burgh the right to hold a market each Thursday. he Cross stood at the centre of the town where goods vere sold, labour hired, proclamations read and justice lispensed. The **Tolbooth** was built there, where the own council and burgh courts met.

When the city guard house was demolished in 1659 he adjoining Mercat Cross was damaged and removed. he junction of High Street, **Saltmarket**, **Trongate** and he **Gallowgate**, however, continued to be known as

Glasgow Cross, and remained an important gathering place. In 1706 the **Treaty of Union** was burnt at the Cross, and an angry mob stormed the Tolbooth. Public hangings were carried out there from 1788 until 1814, when a new gaol was completed at the foot of Saltmarket.

The Cross and surrounding area were devastated in the great fires of 1652 and 1677. The new stone buildings erected subsequently degenerated into slum dwellings during the 19th century, and most were replaced by the City Improvement Trust after 1866. The construction in 1895 of Glasgow Cross Station, with an octagonal street-level building by J J Burnet (demolished 1923), and a triangular ventilation shaft cut into the middle of the busy Trongate, did nothing to ease traffic congestion at the Cross.

Honeyman & Keppie's grand design of 1914 for the Cross was never fully realised, with only the concave quadrant of offices at the north-west corner and the imposing Mercat Building (for many years occupied by the brash 'Krazy House' store) completed during the 1920s. The Tolbooth Steeple, which had stood alone in High Street since the demolition of the Tolbooth in 1911, remained there after popular resistance to a plan to move it to the centre of the Cross. In 1930 a new Mercat Cross was erected to provide an alternative focal point, but it remains overshadowed by the Mercat Building. The Cross has huge potential as a city centre attraction, but retains its incomplete appearance and serves as little more than a busy crossroads for vehicular traffic.

Glasgow Green

Glasgow's old green stretched from Stockwell Street to St Thenew's (**St Enoch's**) Burn. The land was sold in

Glasgow Bridge, previously Broomielaw or Jamaica Bridge, in the 1880s (GWWA)

parcels for building during the 18th century, but not before the council had begun to re-acquire other parts of the burgh's ancient common lands to form a new green. During the 1660s the Linningshaugh at the foot of the **Saltmarket** had been purchased, and adjacent lands to the east were added. The final purchase was made in 1792, when Provost's (or Fleshers) Haugh, the grazing land upon which the **Jacobite** host paraded in 1746, was added to the New Green.

Between 1815–26 the Green was laid out as a park in the modern sense. The Low Green was raised and the **Molendinar** and Camlachie Burns were culverted to prevent flooding; marshy areas were drained; the ground was levelled; and a carriageway was built for promenaders. When the Cattle Market was opened in Graham Square in 1818, the Skinners' Green at the foot of Saltmarket was also reclaimed and the foul remains of animals which had passed through the hands of the knackers, glue makers, tanners and tripe manufacturers were finally cleaned up.

The Green had been used by generations of Glaswegians as a place for washing and drying clothes and for bleaching; it also provided grazing for the burgh's cattle and sheep. But with the rapid industrialisation of the surrounding area, it came into its own as a leisure amenity. The Glasgow **Golf** Club played there from the 1780s until c1832, as did Glasgow Rangers FC from 1873–75, and many other sporting events were held on the Green. There too, in 1765, while taking a Sunday stroll near the old washing house, **James Watt** hit upon the idea of the separate condenser which was to revolutionise the performance of the steam engine. From the end of the 18th century until 1871 the **Glasgow Fair** spilled onto the western side of the Green from the foot of Saltmarket. The great open spaces also attracted generations of orators, and provided the location for some of the city's largest mass meetings, from the protest demonstrations of the **Calton weavers** in 1787 to the rallies of the **Red Clydesiders** in the 20th century.

Many of Glasgow's most famous landmarks are situated on the Green, including the Nelson Monument (erected 1806), the Doulton Fountain (originally built for the International Exhibition of 1888 in **Kelvingrove Park**), the McLennan Arch at the western entrance (rescued from the façade of the old Assembly Rooms/**Athenaeum** building in Ingram Street) and the **People's Palace**. Generations of amateur **football** players skinned their knees on the blaes football pitches on Fleshers' Haugh, a part of the Green threatened by the District Council in 1990 with private redevelopment as a leisure complex.

The future of the Green as a public park has been threatened on many occasions, most notably in 1828, when there were proposals (frequently revived) to mine the large deposits of **coal** which lie beneath it; in 1847, when the Glasgow Monkland and Airdrie **Railway** Co sought powers to build a viaduct over it; and from the 1960s, when plans were drawn up to build a motorway through it. This latter scheme was subsequently shelved, but not, it is feared, forgotten by a planning authority with a long record of putting the needs of the motorist before those of Glasgow's other residents.

Gorbals

Comprising the central section of the city south of the **Clyde**, Gorbals was originally a village in the parish of **Govan** from which it was disjoined in 1771. However proximity to Glasgow had ever been more decisive, the village anciently serving as an isolation colony for lepers and the superiority of its **burgh of barony** being invariably invested either in Glasgow's archbishop or its magistrates. Growth commenced in the 1730s when a colony of weavers and brewers was established in what Glaswegians then called Bridgend (ie the south end of what is now **Victoria Bridge**). By 1792 Gorbals population had grown to 5000 and the turn of the century saw attempts at formal development as a wealthy suburb [see **Carlton Place**]. This was frustrated by indiscriminate feuing for residential and industrial development in neighbouring Hutchesontown and Tradeston during the mid-19th century.

Formal annexation to the city came in 1846 and for the next century the tenements of Gorbals came to epitomise Glasgow's reputation for abysmal housing and rampant alcoholism, crime, squalor and poverty. As late as the 1950s Gorbals (with Hutchesontown) had the highest population density in the city, its 'socially incompetent families' (terminology used by the 1958 Statistical Report) exposed in such works as Robert McLeish's *The Gorbals Story* and **A Macarthur**'s 1935 *No Mean City* as denizens of 'the most notorious slum in Europe'. Others, notably Lewis Grassic Gibbon (**Leslie Mitchell**), found it 'incredibly un-Scottish' and noted the large immigrant population, including many Jews from central Europe which had settled here in the inter-war years. Designated a Comprehensive Development Area in the late 1950s, the tenements were largely demolished in the 1970s, the population density cut by 75%, and the 'socially incompetent' rehoused in tower blocks or relocated in dispiriting peripheral developments like **Easterhouse**.

Govan

When in 1912, against strong local opposition, Govan was incorporated in Glasgow it was the fifth largest burgh in Scotland – and this in spite of its extensive **Gorbals** district having been detached in the 18th century. The parish originally also included **Partick** on the north bank of the **Clyde**. Govan village, on the south bank, was of great antiquity, the old parish church supposedly occupying the site of a Celtic foundation. This is borne out by the largest collection of early Christian stones in Scotland, once in the churchyard but now in the church. They include a richly carved sarcophagus which is said to have contained the relics of St Constantine and is dated to the 10–11th centuries, five rare hogback tombstones of the 10th century, four crosses (or parts thereof) and numerous recumbent grave slabs, all of a similar date. The parish belonged to the archbishopric of Glasgow and after the **Reformation** passed to **Glasgow University** whose rector, **Andrew Melville**, was also the first minister of Govan.

In addition to **agriculture**, the **Clyde** salmon fishings contributed a substantial revenue and as late as 1830 Govan was considered an idyllic resort on Glasgow's doorstep. All this changed with the opening of the upper Clyde for shipping (1.8m of water in 1770 admitted vessels of no more than 30 tons but by 1840

Glasgow from Glasgow Green, by John Knox (ML)

Glasgow continued

the depth was 5m and the maximum burthen 600 tons) and with the extraction of **coal**. The Govan collieries proved to be the most productive in the Glasgow area, filling 300 ships a year by the 1820s. Coal also attracted industry; in 1841 **Robert Napier**, in 1851 J & G Thomson, and in 1860 **Randolph Elder & Co** established shipyards. Govan became heavily dependent on this one industry and with the introduction of steel fabrication in the 1870s its population grew prodigiously. The price has been paid in the 20th century, Govan's decline being that of **shipbuilding** itself. Its waterfront now comprises largely derelict yards like that of Harland & Wolff, unemployment is amongst the highest in Scotland, and the physical and social fabric of the area is wasting away.

Grand Theatre

Opened on 3 August 1867 as the Prince of Wales Theatre in the **Cowcaddens** district of Glasgow, and damaged by fire two years later, it re-opened on 30 September 1869, closed in March 1881 and re-opened, this time as the Grand Theatre, on 19 September 1881. It managed to stay open for all but three months of World War I (during which pause it changed from **music hall** to cine-variety) but was finally destroyed by fire on 5 September 1918.

Great Eastern Hotel

R F & J Alexander & Co opened their Italianate **cotton** works in Duke Street, opposite the North Prison, in

1849. In 1907–9 the building was converted to serve as a working men's hostel and a sixth floor (containing a roller-skating rink) was added. The privately owned Great Eastern Hotel could accommodate 400 men and was considered to be one of the finest hostels in the city. With the decline in the patronage of itinerant workmen, however, it became better known after 1945 as a 'doss house' for the homeless unemployed. Stories (perhaps apocryphal) abound of bewildered English tourists arriving at its doors having assumed from its grandiose name that it was one of Glasgow's better hotels. The austere beauty of the building's frontage, and its proximity to the expanding Merchant City have inspired rumours that the Great Eastern may be redeveloped as a block of luxury flats.

Great Western Road

The present Great Western Road which links Glasgow with the west Highlands and Islands was authorised as a turnpike road in 1836. Its construction immediately attracted the attention of developers who planted ambitious terraces along its route through **Hillhead** and Kirklee. The first to be constructed was the magnificent Kirklee Terrace, originally Windsor Terrace, designed in 1845 by Charles Wilson in the manner of an Italianate mansion. Others soon followed including Kew Terrace (1849), Grosvenor Terrace by **J T Rochead** in the Venetian style (1855) and the spectacular Great Western Terrace by **Alexander 'Greek' Thomson** (1869). Great Western Road's straight alignment flanked with avenues of trees makes for splendid vistas. The view from Hillhead in the morning looking towards the city and into the sun is one of the best in Glasgow, with the slender

'Drawing salmon nets at Govan' on the undredged Clyde (ML)

Glasgow continued

spires of Landsdowne Parish Church (by John Honeyman, 1862) and St Mary's Episcopal Cathedral (by John Oldrid Scott, 1891) vying for attention.

Grecian Chambers

Alexander 'Greek' Thomson's three-storey Grecian Building was erected in **Sauchiehall Street** in 1865. Despite its name, the architectural detail owes as much to Egyptian as to Greek influences, and its stubby columns, forming an eaves-level gallery, in fact closely resemble those of Thomson's **Egyptian Halls** in Union Street. The shop fronts on the ground floor were restored 1988–9 with uniform plate glass windows in timber frames. The Third Eye Centre, one of Scotland's leading venues for the visual and performing arts since 1975, is the building's most celebrated tenant.

Greenbank Gardens

Greenbank House and gardens on the south side of the city are a remarkable survival – the only complete example of an 18th century mansion of a well-to-do Glasgow merchant. The house was built by Robert Allanson as a country home in 1763 and was purchased by John Hamilton of Rogerton in 1797. It remained in the Hamilton family for almost 150 years until it was acquired by Mr & Mrs William Blyth who were keenly interested in horticulture. They restored and enlarged the garden, making it one of the finest in the city. In 1976 they gifted the house and garden to the **National Trust for Scotland**, which organised a successful appeal to establish a garden advice centre. The rich variety of trees, shrubs and plants is designed to encourage local gardeners to be adventurous in their planting. The house is not open to the public.

Greens' Playhouse

George Green and his sons opened their cinema at the corner of Renfield and Renfrew Streets in 1925, modelling it on the great American movie palaces of the day. Greens' Playhouse was the largest in Europe, with seats for 4400 people, and the famous golden divans in the balcony were immensely popular with courting couples. The ballroom above the cinema had a sprung floor and became one of Glasgow's premier nightspots. It was sold during the 1960s and reopened as a discotheque. Greens' also found difficulty in filling their huge cinema, although it was turned to profitable use occasionally as a concert venue. The Playhouse was sold in 1973 to the owners of the disco, who planned to turn the building into a modern leisure and conference centre. As the Apollo it survived for many years as Scotland's leading rock concert venue, but much-needed investment in building repairs and new facilities was not forthcoming. The Apollo closed its doors and was demolished in 1984.

Haggs Castle, St Andrews Drive, Pollokshaws

Now amid housing but near to the grounds of **Pollok House** and the **Burrell** Collection, Haggs is a tower house bearing the arms and initials of Sir John Maxwell of Pollok and the date 1585. L-plan but much restored, its architectural distinction lies in the mouldings of its string course, wallhead and dormers. It now serves as a museum, principally for children, offering a chance to experience the past by participating in candle-making, weaving, etc.

Hampden Park

Queens Park, Scotland's oldest **football** club, played from 1867 until 1873 at **Queens Park** Recreation Ground. The club then moved to a new pitch in the park, opposite Hampden Terrace on Prospecthill Road, and the small stadium which was built there was named Hampden Park. In 1884 the club built a second Hampden Park on the eastern side of Cathcart Road. When Queens Park moved on once more in 1903, the ground was acquired by Third Lanark FC, who rechristened it New Cathkin Park.

The third Hampden Park was built in a natural hollow to the south of Somerville Drive in Mount Florida, on land purchased by Queens Park in 1900. It was laid out by the influential stadium architect Archibald Leitch, and became the established venue for international and important Scottish Cup matches. The capacity was increased from 44,530 to 125,000 by 1910; and Hampden could claim the distinction of being the world's largest football stadium until the opening of the Maracana in Brazil in 1950. In 1937, when the North Stand was built, Hampden accommodated over 149,000 spectators for a Scotland v England game, the highest attendance ever at a football match in Britain. That year, over 143,000 spectators watched the Aberdeen v Celtic Scottish Cup Final, setting the British record for a club game. A third crowd record, for the largest attendance at a European club competition match, was set in 1970, when 136,000 saw Celtic defeat Leeds United in the semi-final of the European Cup.

Hampden's decline began after World War II with a failure to invest in even the most basic facilities for spectators or to maintain the fabric of the stadium. Although floodlights were erected in 1961 and the West Terracing was finally covered six years later, Hampden remained a dank and unpleasant place on big match days. In 1980 the government reneged on a commitment to assist in the refurbishment of the stadium, and the SFA and Queens Park made a desperate appeal to the public for funds. The decrepit North Stand was demolished, the wood-and-cinder terracings concreted, and other improvements made; the latest in a long line of reductions in the ground's capacity (which was 54,000 in 1991) was also imposed. Its future as Scotland's national football stadium was, after some years of doubt, assured by a redevelopment programme begun in 1993 and completed in 2000.

Harbour Tunnel, Finnieston

Opened on 15 July 1895, the Harbour Tunnel under the **Clyde** comprised, like the later **Clyde Tunnel**, two tunnels, one for southbound traffic and one for north, plus a third for pedestrians. The tunnels were cast-iron tubes and were said to have leaked from the day they were laid; stalactites grew to over 12in (300mm) long. Access was by lift for vehicles and by stairs (138) for pedestrians, the entrance on each side being a handsome rotunda. The tunnel was closed to vehicles in 1943 and to pedestrians in 1980. The two rotunda live on, that on the north bank as a restaurant and that on the south as the 'Dome of Discovery', a science display for children.

Haus eines Kunstfreundes (House of an Art Lover)

This is a recent (1990) realisation in **Bellahouston Park** of an academic design by **Charles Rennie Mackintosh**. Although unbuilt, it was Mackintosh's best-known design on the Continent and, in its austere relationship between form and function, the most influential. In 1901 the German *Zeitschrift fur Innendekoration* held a competition for the design of a 'modern' house for the art lover. Mackintosh's entry was disqualified, not being completed in time, but otherwise would no doubt have won the withheld first prize. In the event he was awarded a special prize and the design was published in portfolio form and widely circulated. The portfolio's preface by Hermann Muthesius explained why: 'The exterior character of the building exhibits an absolutely original character, unlike anything else known. In it we shall not find a trace of the conventional forms of architecture, to which the artist, as far as his present intentions were concerned, was quite indifferent.'

High Street

One of Glasgow's oldest thoroughfares, High Street was originally the track running down from the **Cathedral** to **Glasgow Cross**. The Mercat Cross may have been erected at the top of the street, at the junction of the **Rottenrow** and the Drygate, for a time in the Middle Ages, although no direct evidence survives. As the spine of early Glasgow, many of the city's important buildings and institutions were built on High Street. The Dominicans established their monastery on the east side in 1246 (hence the existence of Blackfriars' Street) and the **University** moved to the first of its new buildings nearby during the 1460s.

In the 19th century most of High Street degenerated into slum housing and the University moved away to Gilmorehill in 1870. Its fine buildings were demolished and the site, with the famous University Gardens, was redeveloped by the **railway** companies as College and High Street Goods Stations. The rest of the street, from the Cross to George Street, was rebuilt under the direction of the City Improvement Trust, which also eased traffic flow by widening the southern end (leaving the **Tolbooth** Steeple to stand isolated) and reducing the steep slope at the Bell o' the Brae near the Cathedral. The remaining Victorian buildings were renovated during the 1980s, as private art galleries and antique shops began to open on what had been as late as the 1970s one of Glasgow's meanest streets.

Hillhead

A mid-19th century suburban development near the **University**, Hillhead was originally part of the Blythswood Estate. It was sold in 1702, along with the Byres of **Partick**, to Andrew Gibson, whose family owned it until 1855. By that time housing development had begun following the construction of the first high-level bridge across the river Kelvin in 1840. Development was mixed and haphazard with villas, terraced houses and blocks of tenements. In 1869 Hillhead, with a population of over 3500, became a burgh in its own right. The burgh was annexed to Glasgow in 1891. Several fine buildings survive in the area including Wellington Church (1882–4), Lilybank House (c1850) with additions by **Alexander 'Greek' Thomson** (1863–5) and North Park House – now the home of BBC (Scotland) (1869). The entrance hall of the BBC has a display of the work of the Bell Brothers, **pottery** owners, who commissioned the building.

Hippodrome

Erected in a startlingly short nine weeks in New City Road under the supervision of E H Bostock, the proprietor of the adjoining zoo, the Hippodrome was managed by Messrs Bostock and Barrassford, with twice-nightly performances. It later became an exhibition hall and then a garage.

The Horse Shoe

John Young opened The Horse Shoe in Drury Street in 1872, reputedly on the site of a public house built in the 1840s. The premises were acquired in 1884 by Captain John Scoullar, who extended and renovated the bar, and is credited with starting a craze in the city for large mahogany-topped island bars, and the pub's design was imitated all over Scotland. Scoullar remodelled the pub in 1901, when the two sitting rooms on either side of the bar were removed.

The Horse Shoe is the last relatively unspoilt example of Glasgow's great Victorian drinking palaces. The centrepiece, the island bar, is described in the *Guinness Book of Records* as the longest pub bar in the world, at just over 104ft (31.7m). The horseshoe motif is everywhere, as are the initials JYW (John Y Whyte was the proprietor from 1923–30). The stock platform in the centre of the bar area still features an old barrel which once contained The Horse Shoe's famous proprietary whisky, 'Lachie'.

Tennent Caledonian acquired The Horse Shoe in 1969, but limited their modernisation to the upstairs dining room, which was altered to serve as a lounge bar.

Hunterian Art Gallery

This new gallery was opened bravely by the **University** in the midst of a serious financial crisis in 1981 to designs by William Whitfield. It houses a wonderful collection of paintings started by **Dr William Hunter** including works by Rembrandt, Stubbs and Chardin. It was not added to significantly until the 1930s when the first of a series of gifts was received from the American artist MacNeill Whistler. These were followed by donations from W A Cargill, Dr Charles Hepburn, and the Macfie brothers whose collection of 20th century Scottish artists (including **MacTaggart**, **Peploe** and **Eardley**) is one of the glories of the gallery. The gallery also contains the **Mackintosh House**.

Hunterian Museum, University of Glasgow

The Hunterian Museum is named after **Dr William Hunter** (1718–83) a graduate of **Glasgow University**, who bequeathed to the University his collection of books, manuscripts, coins, pictures, anatomical and geological specimens, shells and other objects. It took several years for the collection to arrive in Glasgow and for a purpose-built museum to be constructed to designs by William Stark. When the University moved to Gilmorehill a museum was included in the new building.

Over the last two centuries the collections have been expanded with important donations of **Roman** antiquities from the west of Scotland, geological specimens, ethnographical objects particularly from the Pacific, and paintings. The museum itself contains a permanent exhibition of the history of the University. The manuscripts and books are now housed in the University Library, while the pictures are displayed in the **Hunterian Art Gallery**.

Hutcheson's Hall, Hospital and School

By the beginning of the 17th century Glasgow boasted a prosperous merchant and professional community. The brothers George and Thomas Hutcheson, both lawyers, determined to give something back to the city in which they had made their fortunes. Thus when George died in 1639 he endowed a hospital to maintain 12 'decrepit' men. Thomas added to the endowment in 1641 with maintenance for 11 orphans; other endowments followed. In 1790 the Hospital became the owner of St Ninian's Croft on the south side of the river in **Gorbals** parish. The land was at once feued out for new housing and given the name Hutchesontoun. The proceeds were used in 1802–5 to build a handsome new building in Ingram Street to designs by **David Hamilton**, with on the front wall statues of the two brothers carved for the first Hospital in 1655. The building provided a schoolroom on the top floor, a hall to house **Stirling's Library** on the first floor and offices on the ground. The interior was remodelled by John Baird II in 1876, long after the school and library had moved to separate premises. Baird created a spacious hall with ornate plasterwork and heavy panelling, listing the name of Preces and benefactors. The **National Trust for Scotland** raised money as part of its Golden Jubilee Appeal to buy the property in 1982. It was subsequently refurbished in a Regency style by Jack Notman. The Hall, one of the glories of the Merchant City, serves as the Trust's west of Scotland headquarters and is used for public functions. As Glasgow's second oldest school, Hutchesons Grammar School moved to new premises in Crown Street. Amongst its distinguished pupils were **John Buchan** and **James Maxton**.

Jamaica Street

Then on the outskirts of the rapidly developing city, Jamaica Street was laid out in 1761–3 for the homes of the wealthy well away from the smells and hubbub of the **High Street**. The deepening of the **Clyde** and consequent development of the **Broomielaw** Quay at the foot of the street quickly changed its character. Houses were converted into shipping offices and were replaced by large warehouses and business premises. On the west side of the street there is an impressive range of cast-iron fronted warehouses, including the splendid warehouse of the cabinet-makers A Gardner & Sons built in 1855–6 by John Baird I. It has been described as 'one of the great landmarks of Western architecture' in that it represented a highly successful adaptation to the urban scene of the pre-fabricated iron technology used at Crystal Palace. Still sometimes known as Gardner's Building, it was possibly preceded by another iron construction at No 72 (1854) and followed by No 66 (1856–7). Beside Gardner's, Nos 30–4

1864) were built as the headquarters of **G & J Burns**, the shipping partnership that spawned the Cunard Line.

Justiciary Courts

William Stark's Justiciary Courts building, originally accommodating the court house, municipal offices and gaol, was built at the foot of **Saltmarket** 1810–14 to replace the ageing **Tolbooth**. The raising of the roadway leading to the new Hutcheson Bridge in 1829 (to protect it from flooding) did much to spoil the effect of Stark's Greek Revival design, as the plinth on which the building stood disappeared beneath the street level. The dignity of the building was also undermined by the establishment in Jail Square, during the 1820s, of **Paddy's Market** and by the ramshackle theatre buildings erected opposite on the edge of **Glasgow Green**, which during the 1840s were allowed to remain standing long after the end of the annual **Glasgow Fair**.

An old Glasgow insult, 'You'll die facing the monument', refers to the view obtained by condemned men standing on the gallows in Jail Square – that of the Nelson Monument on Glasgow Green. The last man to hang there was the notorious poisoner Dr Pritchard in 1865.

In 1844 the municipal offices were removed to the new **City and County Buildings** in Wilson Street, and the Justiciary Courts building was remodelled with the addition of two minor court halls and waiting rooms. Further extensive alterations to the interior and exterior were carried out in 1910–13, when a second court room was added.

Kelvin Hall

The first Kelvin Hall was built in 1917, but was destroyed by fire in 1925. A much larger and improved building of red sandstone opened on the site in 1927, with the claim that it offered the best exhibition and conference facilities in the UK. The Kelvin Hall was Scotland's leading venue for large events such as the Motor and Ideal Homes Shows, and for boxing. At some time most Glaswegians visited the circus and carnival held there each winter. During World War II it was converted into the country's main factory for barrage balloons.

With the completion of the **Scottish Exhibition and Conference Centre** at nearby Finnieston in 1985, the Kelvin Hall was adapted to new purposes. The Glasgow Transport Museum left its original home in Albert Drive and opened at the rear of the building in 1988. The remaining area was remodelled to accommodate Scotland's largest indoor sports centre, with an international standard running track and spectator facilities.

Kelvin Walkway

It takes imagination and courage to convert a polluted industrial river into an attractive open space where in the late summer and autumn salmon and sea trout can be seen leaping the disused mill weirs. The water power of the river Kelvin, which enters the **Clyde** at Meadowside, was harnessed from medieval times to drive mills that ground corn, ground flint for glassmaking and powered paper factories. The river also exposed **coal** seams, worked from the 17th century. In the 19th century its banks provided a convenient route for **railways**. By the 1970s much of this industrial development was derelict and Glasgow Corporation decided to convert the length of the river between Dawsholm Park and the Clyde into a walkway. It is now a spectacular thoroughfare passing through the length of the west end from post-war council housing to the splendours of Victorian terraces. It passes underneath fine bridges that tower above the river and, towards the north, the monumental aqueduct that carries the Forth & Clyde **Canal**, built in 1787–90.

Kelvingrove Park

Until the council purchased this 66 acre (27ha) site in 1852, **Glasgow Green** was the only public park in the city. The new acquisition, sometimes known as West End Park but previously the policies of Kelvingrove and Kelvingrove House, the property of Provost Patrick Colquhoun, lay along the river Kelvin between the then developing Woodlands Hill [see **Park Conservation Area**] and Gilmorehill (where the **University** would be relocated in the 1870s). In 1888 Glasgow's first International Exhibition was mounted in the park. The theme was oriental as befitted a visit by **Queen Victoria**, recently styled Empress of India, although inside the domed and minar-ed halls the exhibits were of **shipbuilding** and other local industries. Nearly six million visitors attended and the handsome profit which resulted was used to finance the construction of the **Glasgow Art Gallery and Museum** on the south-west edge of the park. Further exhibitions were held in 1901, partly to celebrate the opening of the Museum/Art Gallery, and 1911. The park's monuments are largely leftovers of these exhibitions, exceptions being the Stewart Memorial Fountain (1872, James Sellars) commemorating the provost responsible for Glasgow's **Loch Katrine** water supply, and the 1913 monument to **William Thomson, Lord Kelvin**.

King's Theatre

A classic example of Matcham's design, the King's Theatre in Bath Street was built in 1904 at a cost of £50,000, and has a particularly fine auditorium. It has featured leading British and American actors including Katharine Hepburn and the late Tyrone Power, and launched the popular summer-time entertainments known as 'Half Past Eight' with comedians like **Dave Willis**. Today the home of an annual Christmas pantomime, a lavish production featuring Scottish entertainers from theatre and television, it is owned by Glasgow City Council.

Kingston Bridge

Opened in 1970, the Kingston Bridge carries the M8 across the **Clyde** between **Anderston** and Kingston on two parallel concrete structures, each carrying five lanes of traffic. The central span of the bridge is 470ft (143m) long. Three miles of concrete flyovers and ramps carry the approach roads, offering motorists spectacular views of the city and riverside, but leaving a dark and gaunt landscape for the pedestrians below. By the 1980s the bridge had become a bottle-neck at rush hours as the volume of traffic soared beyond the carriageways' capacity. Plans were revived for another motorway crossing of the Clyde at **Glasgow Green**, probably by tunnel. In 1991 it was found that the bridge required extensive repairs. Lane closures and worse chaos followed.

In 1999, as part of the repair programme, the whole central span was successfully raised by a few millimetres.

The Lighthouse

In Mitchell Street (off **Argyle Street**) the Glasgow *Herald* Building (1893), on which **Charles Rennie Mackintosh** worked as a draughtsman, reopened in 1999 as The Lighthouse, a centre commissioned at a cost of £12m as part of the programme associated with the city's Year of Architecture and Design. The Lighthouse features four exhibition galleries, lecture and education facilities, and a dramatic viewing platform in the tower high above the surrounding rooftops.

Mackintosh House

The approach to the **Hunterian Art Gallery** is interrupted by a door halfway up the wall on which some students once wrote with typical Glasgow humour 'Pity the Postie'. This is the original entrance to **Charles Rennie Mackintosh**'s house, demolished in the 1960s to make way for a new **University** refectory. The University has more than made up for this sacrilege by reconstructing the house within the Hunterian Art Gallery. The result is impressive with original Mackintosh furnishings brought from other houses plus some faithful reproductions. The Studio Drawing Room is perhaps the most typical with its clinical lines. The gallery also houses the Mackintosh Archive including many of his architectural and furniture drawings, and his charming flower paintings.

McLellan Galleries, Sauchiehall Street

Designed by James Smith, this long classical three-storey block was built in 1855 for Bailie Archibald McLellan, a successful coachbuilder with a penchant for collecting 16th and 17th century paintings. Both house and collection were bequeathed to the city fathers who sold some pictures and incorporated the rest in the **Glasgow Art Galleries** collection. A dome was added to the building in 1904 but it collapsed in 1989 when the building was partially destroyed by fire. The galleries, incorporating shops and offices, have since been stylishly restored.

Martyr's Public School, Parson Street

No longer a school, this building (reached from the **Royal Infirmary**) was designed between 1895–8 by **Charles Rennie Mackintosh** when a draughtsman for Honeyman & Keppie. The control of the latter accounts for the traditional Scottish Renaissance style. However, Mackintosh was allowed to experiment with ideas later developed in his first autonomous project, the **Glasgow School of Art**, which established his identity as an architect. Distinctly Mackintosh is the restrained and structurally integrated, rather than applied, decoration. Ventilation shafts disguised as octagonal turrets with bellcast roofs break the roofline. The uniform fenestration lifts at the stair blocks, vertical walls of glass abruptly hitting deep eaves. Inside, Mackintosh sculpts

the open timber trusses over the stairs and gallery into Art Nouveau pendants and tulips, repeating the stone mouldings of the stair entrances. Triangular brackets supporting the iron balusters are leaf shaped. The banding of the tiled dado for the stairs arches over the doorways binding the elements together into a single flowing space.

Maryhill

In 1854 Maryhill was still a pleasant village, with an industrious population of largely Irish extraction, in the parish of East Kilpatrick to the north-west of Glasgow. The name is said to derive from Mary Hill, a mother rather than a mountain, whose daughter Lilias Graham took the pledge in 1829 and so inaugurated the Maryhill **Temperance** Society, the first in Britain. A further claim to attention lay in the Forth & **Clyde Canal** which here sends a spur south to **Port Dundas** and then enters a series of locks (sometimes called Botany Locks) before being carried over the deep vale of the Kelvin in an aqueduct. The locks are currently being restored. The length (350ft/107m), height (70ft/21m) and width (57ft/17m) of the aqueduct (Robert Whitworth, 1787–90) made it one of the wonders of 18th century Scotland. It remains an impressive feature of the **Kelvin Walkway**. A century later Maryhill was annexed (1891) by Glasgow and aggressively developed for residential and industrial purposes. In the process it acquired two notable buildings by **Charles Rennie Mackintosh**, **Queen's Cross Church** and the church hall (1898) beside the Ruchill parish church at the city end of Maryhill.

Merchants' House

When Glasgow began to emerge as a commercial centre her merchants, like those in other towns, had to defend their rights and privileges. The Merchants' House was established towards the close of the 16th century for this purpose and its position confirmed by statute in 1672. A guildhall was built in 1659 in the **Bridgegate**, of which only the spire (1665) survives adjacent to the old fishmarket. The members, presided over by the Lord Dean of Guild, were divided between foreign and home trades. Every merchant who transacted business in the city was required to register as a burgess with the Lord Dean of Guild. Burgesses were permitted to become Members of the Merchants' House and as a result to vote for and be elected to the town council. Apart from its administrative role, the Merchants' House also acted as a charity, maintaining the sick and the poor. In 1874, after a period in temporary premises, the Merchants' House moved into the imposing new range of buildings on the west side of **George Square**. Features from the old hall were incorporated by the architect John Burnet, who included a steeple at the north end of the range to make the merchants feel at home. The symmetry of the range was destroyed by his son who added another storey to the Merchants' House in 1907–9. The Merchants' House now acts entirely as a charitable and ceremonial body. Its Hall is used for functions and meetings.

Mitchell Library

Following **Stephen Mitchell**'s 1874 bequest for a library in his name, the Mitchell opened in Ingram Street

1877. In 1889 it moved to a building in Miller Street, subsequently occupied by the Stirling Library [see **Royal Exchange Square**], and to its present purpose-built premises in 1911. The building by W B Whitie received its familiar green copper dome later and in the 1970s was substantially enlarged. Grazed by the new M8, its walls were clad in ashlar at the same time. Mitchell's beneficence had encouraged numerous other donors, among them **Andrew Carnegie** who laid the foundation stone of the present building. The library remains the largest in Glasgow and, although copyright libraries like the British Library and the **National Library of Scotland** hold more books, the Mitchell is the largest library in Scotland and perhaps Britain offering ticketless access to the general public. Its collection of works by and on **Robert Burns** is exceptional as is its collection of archive material relating to Glasgow and the west of Scotland.

Molendinar Burn

The Molendinar Burn flows down from Hagganfield Loch to the **Clyde**, and it was on the banks of the burn that the earliest settlements in what became Glasgow were built. **St Mungo** established his monastery on the right bank of the Molendinar, and is said to have bathed regularly in its waters while reciting the Psalms. Tradition also has it that it was by the burn, near the point at which it crosses the **Gallowgate**, that he met **St Columba** c582 AD.

The town hall was erected on the Molendinar, at Garngadhill to the north-east of the **Cathedral** during the 1440s. Further south, water from the burn was used in public washing greens and bleaching works, until it became polluted by effluent from the surrounding houses and new industries at the beginning of the 19th century.

In 1883–4 the 'Bridge of Sighs' was built across the Molendinar Ravine to connect the Cathedral with the **Necropolis**; this stretch of the burn was culverted to a depth of 20ft (6m) in 1877 and Wishart Street was later formed along it from Alexandra Parade to John Knox Street. The burn had been culverted in 1817 on its course through **Glasgow Green**, and by 1945 only short stretches remained above ground. Periodic campaigns to persuade the city authorities to clean up the burn and restore it as a public amenity have met with little success.

Necropolis

Scotland's most spectacular Victorian cemetery was established by the **Merchants' House** of Glasgow. The decision to convert the Merchants' Park, a rocky outcrop lying to the east of **Glasgow Cathedral**, into an ornamental cemetery on the lines of Père Lachaise in Paris, was taken in 1829. In 1831 four local architects judged 16 competition entries and awarded the top premiums to David and John Bryce of **Edinburgh**. George Mylne, an experienced landscape gardener, was then invited to lay out the cemetery grounds, using the leading competition entries as a guideline.

James Hamilton produced a design for a bridge across the valley of the **Molendinar**, and the foundation stone was laid in October 1833. In 1838 ornate cast-iron gates, designed by **David Hamilton**, were erected at the entrance to the Necropolis, and in 1839–40 a gatekeeper's lodge was built to a design by the same architect. In the years that followed further improvements were made; retaining walls were provided, additional walks laid out, a superintendent's lodge erected (1848–9) and the Molendinar Burn, which had become heavily polluted, culverted over.

In the early days of the Necropolis lairs were usually only purchased as the need arose. Burial vaults had to be cut out of solid rock, excavation work was carried

The Necropolis c1880 (GWWA)

out not only by day but also at night by torchlight. In 1835 the Merchants' House provided six mausolea for pre-need sales; they were located in a picturesque Jacobean-style edifice designed by John Bryce and situated at the east end of the bridge. Failing to find purchasers, they ended up as store-rooms for the gardeners' tools, and in 1837 Bryce designed the Egyptian Vaults to serve as a temporary resting place for the dead while their tombs were being constructed.

A number of the larger monuments in the Necropolis were raised by public subscription, including the memorials to poets Dugald Moore and William Motherwell. The monument to actor-manager John Henry Alexander of the Theatre Royal, designed by James Hamilton with sculpture by Alexander Handyside Ritchie, is a truly remarkable example of early Victorian mortuary art (1852–3). It depicts a proscenium stage, complete with footlights and curtain, with figures symbolic of Comedy and Tragedy occupying the proscenium niches. Among the other notable monuments are the neo-Romanesque tomb (1842–3) of Major Archibald Monteath, **J T Rochead**'s neoclassical Houldsworth mausoleum (1845), **Alexander Thomson**'s Graeco-Egyptian monument (1858) to the Reverend A O Beattie, and the Art Nouveau tomb of W W Blackie, designed by Talwyn Morris.

With their rich sculpture and florid ironwork, the mausolea on the upper terraces are as powerful an evocation of Victorian Glasgow as the ornate warehouses of the Merchant City. Monuments in memory of scientist **Lord Kelvin**, industrialist **Charles Tennant**, shipbuilder **John Elder**, engineer Henry Dubs, ironfounder Walter MacFarlane, poet William Miller, dramatist Sheridan Knowles, and Corlinda Lee, Queen of the Gypsies, testify to the astonishing diversity of the Necropolis, Valhalla of the Glasgow merchants.

New Metropole Theatre, see Empress Theatre

Paddy's Market

Set up beside the **Justiciary Buildings** in Jail Square in 1824, Paddy's Market was run by Irish second-hand clothes dealers, selling to their immigrant countrymen settled in the area, and for export to Ireland. The rag trade was not confined to the 40 or so stalls in the market proper; it also colonised the edge of **Glasgow Green** and the pavements of the **Saltmarket** and **Bridgegate**. After complaints from local residents that the hawkers were a public nuisance, the council provided accommodation (1844) for a city clothes market in Scanlan's Close, off the Bridgegate.

This officially sanctioned 'Paddy's Market' was demolished in 1866 to make way for the new **railway** approach lines to **St Enoch's** Station. A covered Corporation Clothes Market was subsequently opened in Greendyke Street in 1875, but the 'respectable' rag trade declined and the market was demolished in 1922. The more prosperous traders were able to take stalls at the **Barras** while many hawkers returned to Jail Square, to the Bird and Dog Market building which was vacated after World War I, and to the surrounding streets. After the construction of the city mortuary in Jail Square in 1935, and under increasing pressure from the police to stay off the streets, the hawkers re-established 'Paddy' Market' under and in front of the railway arches in Shipbank Lane. The supposedly colourful character of the market, if it ever existed, had disappeared by the 1970s as 'Paddy's Market' became one of the most bleak and depressing of Glasgow's landmarks. In the late 1990s it remained a flea market patronised by the near destitute, and trendy youngsters courting acquaintance with poverty and city low life.

Palace Theatre

Prior to 1904 the Palace Theatre in Gorbals Street was part of the Grand National Halls where the Saturday afternoon 'bursts' or concerts were held. At these a paper bag with an apple and an orange was given to each patron (mostly children), and at a given time during the show all the empty bags were blown up and, at a word of command, simultaneously burst. In 1904 the hall was taken over by Rich Waldon and named the Palace running as a variety theatre until 1914. Many popular **music hall** performers appeared on its stage, including Neil Kenyon, Marie Kendall, Dr Walford Bodie and Ella Retford.

Palace (Queen's) Theatre

Opened in Watson Street by Mr D S Mackay of Dundee in the 1870s as the Star Music Hall, renamed the Palace in the 1880s and eventually ending up as the Queen's Theatre, this ill-starred venue was finally destroyed by fire in 1952. It became the home of a legendary homespun pantomime each Christmas starring Doris Droy, popular, raucous-voiced comedienne teamed with little comic Sammy Murray.

Park Conservation Area

Developed as a stylish residential area in the mid-19th century, the enclave of Woodlands Hill and adjacent Woodside (between **Sauchiehall Street** and **Great Western Road**) was spared the ravages that overtook nearby **Charing Cross** and now, as the Park Conservation Area, constitutes the city's most satisfying example of Victorian planning and architecture. Long contoured terraces of usually honey-coloured sandstone rise from the simplicity of George Smith's 1830s Woodside developments to the curved splendour of Park (Circus, Place, Terrace, Quadrant), mostly the 1850s creation of Charles Wilson. Here the terraces have a French aspect with château roofs and much decorative detail; a belvedere with a fine statue of Field Marshal Lord Roberts commands access to **Kelvingrove Park**. The skyline of Park is all the more distinctive for its four towers, one definitely a campanile, which invariably trigger memories of San Gimignano. Three belong to Wilson's Trinity College (1856–61), a **Free Church** establishment now converted to flats, and the fourth to Park parish church, now offices. Conversion to offices and **University** accommodation is characteristic of the area but Wilson's Queen's Rooms (1857–8) in La Belle Place, Italianate in spite of the name, though built as a community and concert hall, now serve as a Christian Science church.

Partick

Although on the north bank of the **Clyde** just west of the Kelvin, Partick was once part of **Govan** parish and like Govan was not annexed to Glasgow until 1912. By then it had a proud population of 67,000 who saw no need for the change. 'Partickonians' recalled a distant past when 'Pertick' or 'Pertmet' had been a favourite haunt of the **Strathclyde** kings at **Dumbarton**, indeed 'the Balmoral of the Strathclydian royalty', or when it had been granted to the see of Glasgow by **David I** in 1124. More recent celebrity was also invoked: the Partick Police Force had just won the world tug-o-war championships. As the town council met for the last time to the strains of 'Lochaber No More', the Provost removed his chain and robe declaring 'There they lie, the abandoned habits of the Provost of Partick, taken from him by Act of Parliament.' **Cotton** printing and bleaching in the early 19th century, followed by **ship-building**, had transformed the district into a Clyde clone.

Pavilion Theatre

Described as 'one of the handsomest buildings of its kind in Scotland', the Pavilion in Renfield Street first opened its doors on 29 February 1904. The owners also boasted that 'the decoration is executed in pure Louis XV'. The domed ceiling had a sliding roof 'worked by electricity from the stage, thus ensuring coolness in the hottest weather'. All the **music hall** greats, from Vesta Victoria to Florrie Forde, Gertie Gitana and Marie Lloyd, played the Pavilion, and in the 1940s and 50s its stars were comedians like **Tommy Morgan**, Jack Anthony and **Lex McLean**. Charlie Chaplin appeared as a member of Fred Karno's Army. Although variety seasons no longer feature on the bill, the theatre stays open as a Christmas pantomime house and as a Glasgow base for dozens of one- and two-night shows.

People's Palace

The People's Palace was built on the northern edge of **Glasgow Green** to provide a branch gallery and museum, and reading and recreation rooms for residents of the city's east end. The great steel- and glass-roofed Winter Garden, erected at the rear of the red sandstone building, was built not only as a conservatory, but as a venue for concerts and other social functions.

From the outset, the People's Palace collected artefacts relating to the city's past, but it was not until 1940 that the Glasgow Room at the Kelvingrove **Glasgow Art Gallery and Museum** was closed, and its contents transferred to the branch museum. Subsequently, the People's Palace was recognised as the museum of Glasgow's social and industrial history. Exhibits include trade union banners, recreations of a 'single end', an old newspaper kiosk and a model lodging house cubicle, and hundreds of photographs and paintings of Glasgow and Glaswegians through the ages. The museum also possesses an important women's history collection.

Starved of funding after World War II, the fabric of both the museum building and Winter Garden deteriorated, and there were fears in the 1970s that both, already threatened by proposals for a new motorway, might be demolished. They were saved by the fund-raising activities and lobbying of the Friends of the People's Palace, although the Winter Gardens had to close for a number of years while vital repair work was carried out.

The lavish investment of public funds in building and maintaining the **Burrell** Collection gallery during the early 1980s, and in the disastrous 'Glasgow's Glasgow' exhibition in 1990, provoked criticism from those who sought a greater emphasis in the 'City of Culture' on the history and culture of ordinary Glaswegians. In 1990 the place of the People's Palace in Glasgow's hierarchy of museums and galleries became a highly controversial issue in this debate.

Pollok Country Park

The parklands and gardens of **Pollok House** survive in the midst of Glasgow's urban sprawl due to the foresight of Sir John Stirling Maxwell who made a conservation agreement with the newly formed **National Trust for Scotland** in the 1930s. It was Sir John who had created the park, planting the lime avenue to mark his coming of age in 1888. From then on he made further plantings of trees and shrubs, laying out rhododendron and azalea walks. The gardens in the front of the house were treated more formally, with terracing and a parterre in the 17th century style. The lions on the front terrace were carved by Hew Lorimer in the 1940s. The old kitchen garden to the east of the house is laid out as a demonstration garden for the city's allotment holders. The park houses the **Burrell** Collection museum, which was designed to blend with its wooded surroundings, and a celebrated fold of **Highland cattle**.

Pollok House

Pollok House on the south side of the city is set amongst the magnificent scenery of **Pollok Country Park** and was once the home of one of Glasgow's leading families – the Maxwells of Pollok, patrons of art and learning. The austere classical house, conceived in 1737 for Sir John Maxwell, is the only building within the city's confines that was designed by **William Adam**. Construction began in 1747 and was completed by William's son John in 1752. Two pavilions were added in 1892 by **Sir Robert Rowand Anderson** to house a picture gallery and an elaborate 'modern' kitchen range – now converted into a tea room. The house and park were gifted to the City of Glasgow by the Maxwell family in 1966. The house is open to the public and contains a fine collection of paintings, including works by El Greco, Goya and Blake. It was here in 1931 that a small group of men and women from the Association for the Preservation of Rural Scotland, led by Sir John Stirling-Maxwell, conceived the idea of the **National Trust for Scotland**, and in 1997 Glasgow City Council invited the NTS to take over the management of Pollok House.

Pollokshaws

'The people of Pollokshaws are most anxious not to be confused with the people of Pollokshields' (Jack House in the 1958 *Statistical Account*). The feeling was evidently mutual, inhabitants of the former being known as 'the queer folk o' the Shaws' after an 1850 song of that name. Disparagement may go back further, for when in the 1820s the municipal council petitioned Parliament against the Corn Laws, the Earl of Lauderdale stoutly contended that there was no such place as Pollokshaws. This was considered 'inexcusable ignorance'. It was pointed out to his lordship that the village of Pollokshaws (shaw = grove) in Nether Pollok had made its cartographical debut in 1654 and had been a **burgh of barony** since 1813. In 1742 it had also been the site chosen for the first **linen** print works in the Glasgow area. Further bleach fields and a substantial handloom weaving industry followed but in 1801 John Monteith set up a 200-power-loom mill. Underemployed and underpaid handloom weavers thereafter gained the district a reputation for militancy and here, appropriately, was born **James Maxton** (1885). Pollokshaws was incorporated in Glasgow in 1912.

Port Dundas

The Glasgow branch of the Forth & **Clyde Canal** was extended in 1786–90 from Hamiltonhill to a new basin on eight acres (3.2ha) of land at One Hundred Acre Hill, to the north of the city. The new port and industrial village which was established by the basin was named Port Dundas in honour of Sir Lawrence Dundas, Governor of the Forth & Clyde Navigation Company. The Forth & Clyde was connected with the Monkland Canal in 1790 by a cutting from Port Dundas, which then became Glasgow's premier port until the further deepening of the Clyde and the development of improved harbour facilities on the riverside during the 1820s. In 1843 the then village of Port Dundas was brought within the city boundary and it became the home of distilleries, **engineering** works, grain mills and other industrial buildings, which continued in use long after the decline in the fortunes of the canal. During the early 1990s, warehouse buildings were converted into blocks of flats.

Princes Square

Princes Square was originally an undistinguished square of offices built in 1842 off the east side of **Buchanan Street**. By the mid-1980s many of the tenants had moved out and a plan was conceived to cover over the square and create an up-market shopping complex. Work was started in 1986 to designs by Hugh Martin & Partners. They were careful to preserve the impression of a square with a large circulating area, suitable for concerts and other events. Although criticised by architectural purists, the Square has proved immensely popular with shoppers.

The Princess's Theatre/Citizens' Theatre

Known as the 'Royal Princess's', The Princess's Theatre opened in Gorbals Street in 1878 as Her Majesty's Theatre. The lessee was H Cecil Beryl, and it presented shows from musical comedy through variety to Shakespeare. Harry McKelvie, a legendary Glasgow showman, ran it from the 1920s. A special pantomime favourite was Tommy Lorne, sometimes dubbed the funniest of all Scottish comics. His pantomime titles all had 13 letters. In 1945 McKelvie gave generous terms of lease to the Citizens' Theatre Company who moved over the **Clyde** from the Athenaeum Theatre in Buchanan Street. So the Royal Princess's building, home of much of Scot-

land's best old-time **music hall**, became known as the Glasgow Citizens' Theatre. Today it has been extensively modernised and offers plays of European and international importance as well as an annual pantomime.

Provan Hall

In the unlikely surrounds of **Easterhouse**, Glasgow's most notorious post-war housing scheme, stands one of the two surviving medieval domestic buildings in the city – Provan Hall. This was the country home of the Prebendary of Balernock, a member of the **Cathedral** staff, whose town house was **Provand's Lordship** (the other surviving medieval house). It was built in the late 16th century as a hunting lodge around a central courtyard, and was inherited after the **Reformation** by Sir Robert Hamilton of Goslington. The Glasgow Town Council acquired it in 1667, and after restoration it passed to Dr John Buchanan, a well-known Glasgow antiquarian. By the 1930s it was almost derelict but was then acquired and restored by a group of private individuals who gifted it to the **National Trust for Scotland**. It is leased to Glasgow City Council and used occasionally as a local community centre. It is not open to the public.

Provand's Lordship

The oldest surviving dwelling in Glasgow, Provand's Lordship was built by Bishop Andrew Muirhead in 1471 as the Preceptor's House of the Hospital of St Nicholas, which he founded c1460. The house became the town manse of the Prebendary of Balernock (who was also Lord of Provand [Provan]) and was one of 32 prebendal manses situated in the vicinity of the **Cathedral**. Like many other Glasgow buildings, Provand's Lordship is reputed to have provided accommodation for **Queen Mary** on a visit to the city.

The three storey building was adapted to other uses after the **Reformation**, and was extended in 1670 by its tailor occupier. In 1716 it was placed in the care of the city magistrates. They erected a single-storey lean-to on the south wall as a house for the hangman, who carried out his business in the yard of the Archbishop's Palace from 1784–7. Provand's Lordship continued to be let for commercial purposes, providing premises for 19th century businesses as diverse as an alehouse, a greengrocery and a barber's shop. Falling into disrepair and threatened with demolition, it was leased in 1906 by the Provand's Lordship Society, which restored it as a museum, aided by **Sir William Burrell**, who donated historic furnishings from his collection. In 1970 the city's Department of Museums and Art Galleries assumed responsibility for the museum. It has since become one of the leading attractions of the Cathedral Square tourist and leisure development.

Queen Street Station

Queen Street (originally Dundas Street) Station opened in 1842 as the western terminus of the Edinburgh & Glasgow Railway (which amalgamated with the North British in 1865 [see **railways**]). It was built on the site of the Crawford Mansion and grounds, and is the oldest surviving station in the city. An unusual feature of the track approach to Queen Street is the Cowlairs Incline, a steep gradient nearly 2km in length, hewn through a deep rock cutting and tunnel. Trains were hauled up the incline from the station by a cable worked by a steam winding engine located at the top. The system remained in use until 1907, when powerful locomotives were introduced to assist trains with the ascent.

The station was rebuilt in 1878–80, when its magnificent iron and glass arched roof was erected, and the Low Level Station on the Glasgow City and District Line opened in 1886. The goods station closed in 1964, the site being used instead as a taxi rank and car park; new, unattractive office buildings were subsequently built on **George Square** and Dundas Street. The North British Hotel was opened in 1905, in an early 19th century terrace which was for many years the privately-owned Queen's Hotel, and to which an extra storey and an attic were added. It was refurbished during the 1970s and sold by BR in the 1980s, when it became the Copthorne and acquired its jarring observatory front on George Square.

Queen's Cross Church, Maryhill

The church, at Garscube/Maryhill Road, was designed by **Charles Rennie Mackintosh** when a draughtsman for Honeyman & Keppie between 1896 and 1899. This and the competition drawings for Liverpool Anglican Cathedral, 1903, were his only religious projects. Perhaps at the insistence of Honeyman, the exterior is disappointingly conservative in its use of English Perpendicular Gothic, but introduces Art Nouveau fluidity with details such as the heart-shaped window tracery. The south-west tower copies that of Merriot Church, Somerset, sketched by Mackintosh in 1895. However, the construction and detailing of the interior are powerful and mystical. The broad rectangular nave is spanned by a single wooden barrel vault rising directly from the walls with the necessary 15m steel tie beams left exposed. Plain, square piers and round arches in the south aisle and symbolic motifs in stone and wood recall the ancient Celtic origins of the Scottish church. The abstract stained glass in the east window is an early example of its kind.

Queens Park

The oldest park on the south side of the **Clyde** was laid out by Sir Joseph Paxton, the designer of London's Crystal Palace, after the purchase by the city council of what had been Pathhead Farm in 1857. It covers about 146 acres (60ha) and features an artificial mound with granite staircase from which there is an extensive view of the city. The name derives from its proximity to the supposed site of the **Battle of Langside** in which **Queen Mary**'s forces were disastrously routed by those of Regent **Moray** in 1568. A column flanked by eagles and topped by the lion rampant (Alexander Skirving, 1887) just outside the park commemorates the battle; and in Linn Park some two miles to the south a plaque marks the spot from which the Queen is supposed to have witnessed it; nearby are the vestigial ruins of 15th century Cathcart Castle. Adjacent to the boating lake in Queens Park, Camphill House (1815) houses a Museum of Costume while beside it the imposing Renaissance building which now serves as Langside Hall was once the National Bank in Queen Street, removed and re-erected here in the early 20th century. To the north-east of the park, Pollokshields, one of the more desirable residential areas on the Southside, was annexed by Glasgow in 1891. South-west rise the terraces of **Hampden Park**, the national **football** stadium and also the home ground of Queens Park FC, the oldest club in Scotland. The first recognisable match took place in Queens Park in 1868 when Queens Park FC were challenged by 'Thistle' to a two-hour game 'with twenty players on each side'. 'Would you also be good enough to bring your ball with you in case of any breakdown?' asked the Queens Park secretary.

Glasgow in 1890 from the flagstaff in South Side Park (now Queens Park) (GWWA)

Red Road Flats, Balernock

Built (1964–71) by Glasgow Corporation's Building Department to designs by Sam Bunton & Associates, the two 31-storey tower blocks, and four 31-storey point blocks at Red Road are the tallest residential buildings in Europe. Two 26–28 storey triple slab blocks complete a development which provided 1350 flats of up to five apartments. The scheme was initially popular with residents, many of whom moved there from run-down tenement accommodation. It was not long, however, before the Red Road flats began to acquire an unenviable reputation. Economies had been made in the construction of the buildings, resulting in an underprovision of lifts and, as so often in Glasgow's post-war housing developments, of amenities. The towering grey concrete bleakness of the buildings became oppressive. As established tenants clamoured to be rehoused, a disproportionately high percentage of homeless persons and young single tenants moved in. During the 1970s and 80s, incidences of vandalism, crime and other forms of anti-social behaviour soared.

In a desperate attempt to find a solution to the city's acute high-rise living problem, the council permitted the introduction during the 1980s of radical initiatives to ameliorate conditions. In 1981 one of the tower blocks was renovated and converted to student and executive flats; another was transferred to the YMCA. From 1987 improved security and better refuse and litter collection were introduced, with new letting policies designed to maintain an element of control over the social mix in each building. Concierges were employed to monitor security and maintenance arrangements. The new 'holistic' approach to solving the problems experienced by high-rise tenants showed encouraging signs of success. By 1991 there had been a dramatic reduction in vandalism, lift breakdowns, and the number of vacant flats. The Red Road flats were no longer the city's most notorious tower blocks.

Robroyston

If Langside (see **Queens Park**) in the south-west of the city represents **Queen Mary**'s Waterloo, then Robroyston on the north-east perimeter witnessed that of **William Wallace**. Here in 1305 he was finally betrayed and captured by **Sir John Menteith** on behalf of the English. As for the Queen, capture presaged a journey to London and execution. A 20 foot (6m) granite cross marks the spot. From such an historic past the area could, perhaps, have expected better than to become just another of Glasgow's housing schemes.

Rottenrow

Now a minor street in the much reworked area of the **Cathedral**, Rottenrow or 'Rat Street' was once an important thoroughfare and a fashionable promenade for the canons and clergy. Thomas de Quincey, the author, rented a garret at No 112 (1846–7) and both **Dr David Livingstone** and **Dr Thomas Chalmers** were also one-time residents. For a decade before removing to **High Street** in 1460, **Glasgow University** occupied a building known as the 'Old Pedagogy' on the south side opposite Weaver Street. Ironically the area is now heavily colonised by its would-be rival, **Strathclyde University**.

Royal Concert Hall

The Glasgow Royal Concert Hall was opened on the corner of **Sauchiehall** and **Buchanan Streets** in October 1990, providing the city with a major multi-purpose entertainment venue in time for the final months of Glasgow's year as European City of Culture. A controversial building, the exterior of which has been criticised for its stark severity, it has a main auditorium seating nearly 2500 and has been praised for the quality of facilities provided for audiences and performers. It was popularly christened the 'Lally Palais' in recognition of the close identification with the project of Pat Lally, the Convener of Glasgow District Council. The building is now the focal point of the Buchanan Galleries shopping complex.

Royal Exchange Square and Stirling Library

Filling Royal Exchange Square, the Exchange was the commercial hub of Glasgow for much of the 19th century. Here bargains were struck and members of the notorious Iron Ring met to agree the price of **iron** in the British market. Originally a grand home built in 1788/9 for William Cunninghame of Lainshaw, the building was acquired by the Royal Bank of Scotland in 1817. Ten years later a banking hall was constructed at the back facing on to Buchanan Street, and the house remodelled as an exchange by **David Hamilton** who added a double classical portico to the front. It now houses the Stirling Library, founded by a bequest of Walter Stirling, hunchback and merchant, in 1791 and claimed to be Scotland's first free public library. The main hall of the Exchange is strikingly unaltered from Hamilton's original concept – glowing testimony to the rapid recovery of Glasgow as a commercial centre after the set-back of the American War of Independence.

In 1996 the library reopened as the city's controversial Gallery of Modern Art. It provides a showcase for the talents of local artists such as Peter Howson, Adrian Wiszniewski and Stephen Campbell, as well as a home for an eclectic range of sculptures, installations, paintings and photographs from around the world.

Outside there is an equestrian statue of the Duke of Wellington (1844), often to be seen wearing a traffic cone as a hat, the square being popular with late-night revellers. The neo-classical façades that surround the Exchange were built (1830–9) under the supervision of the Royal Bank of Scotland. In the north-east corner is the Western Club, sole survivor of the city's once numerous gentlemen's clubs.

Royal Faculty of Procurators

The Faculty of Procurators in Glasgow was established in 1796 to regulate legal practice in the city. Before admission a member had to serve an apprenticeship of at least five years with a practising lawyer and one year as a clerk. He also had to have attended law classes at one of the Scottish universities. From 1817 lectures were given in association with the **University** of Glasgow. The handsome Faculty Hall in St George's Place was built to Italian designs by Charles Wilson in 1854–6. The large open hall on the ground floor was originally intended for law classes, but is now used for offices. On the upper floor is a splendidly ornate reading room and the Orr Library designed in 1938–9 by T Harold Hughes. Apart from legal works the library contains an important collection of manuscripts relating to Glasgow.

Royal Infirmary

In 1791 a number of Glasgow's leading citizens petitioned for a Royal Charter to establish a new infirmary where the poor could be treated and medical students given clinical training. The new Infirmary to designs by **Robert** and **James Adam** was opened at Christmas 1794; additional accommodation was provided shortly after the Napoleonic Wars. The Infirmary quickly secured the **University**'s recognition as a leading medical school and clinical professors held Infirmary appointments to allow them to conduct their teaching. After the University moved to Gilmorehill in 1870 the professors transferred to the new Western Infirmary. New chairs were subsequently endowed at the Royal. By the end of the century the original buildings were much too small and they were replaced by the present massive building designed by James Miller, incorporating some of the Adams' design features. This building itself had become inadequate by the 1970s when a new construction programme was initiated with Phase 1 – the Queen Elizabeth Building by **Sir Basil Spence**, Glover & Ferguson – completed in 1982. The Royal Infirmary remains one of Scotland's leading hospitals and centres of medical education.

St Andrew's Cathedral

After the **Reformation**, Glasgow's small **Roman Catholic** community were able to worship only clandestinely. From 1776, however, mass was celebrated in a run-down tenement in Blackstock's Land at the foot of **Saltmarket**, and from 1792 at a tennis court in Mitchell Street. In 1797 a small chapel was built in Marshall's Lane, opposite the Barracks, with accommodation for up to 600 worshippers.

The influx of Irish immigrants to Glasgow after 1800 added greatly to the city's Catholic population, and in 1814 work began on a new chapel in Clyde Street on a prominent riverside site. The work was completed in 1817, despite the hostility of anti-Catholic agitators.

A spiky Gothic caricature of St George's Chapel in Windsor Castle with octagonal towers incorporated in the south façade, the chapel was designed by **James Gillespie Graham**, cost £14,000, and could hold over 2000 people. It was the focal point for Roman Catholic worship in the west of Scotland and became a cathedral in 1889. Much of the interior was renovated after 1889 by Pugin & Pugin.

St Andrew's Church

The scale of the portico of this impressive mid-18th century church so frightened Mungo Naismith, its mason, that he spent the night after the scaffolding had been taken down anxiously watching for signs of subsidence. Modelled on St Martin in the Fields in London, it stands in St Andrews Square off the **Saltmarket** and was built (1732–57) to designs by Allan

Dreghorn with the clear intention of emphasising Glasgow's growing prosperity. The magnificent rococo plasterwork in the interior was by Thomas Clayton. In 1807 the minister, Dr William Ritchie, had the temerity to install an organ; it was immediately removed by order of the Provost. The 19th century exodus of the well-to-do from the **High Street** to the new developments west of the city left the church marooned in an area of growing deprivation.

St Andrew's-by-the-Green

The **Episcopal Church of Scotland** suffered after the **Jacobite** rebellions in which many of its members were implicated. Episcopal chapels were closed and adherents persecuted. Against this background the construction of an Episcopal church – St Andrew's-by-the-Green – in central Glasgow in 1750 seems remarkable. However by that time there were English merchants in the city and the **University** was gaining a reputation for religious tolerance. The classical design, more reminiscent of a meeting house than an English church, was by William Paull and Andrew Hunter. It was comfortably fitted, heated by stoves in winter, and contained an organ, earning it the nickname of the 'Whistling Kirkie', or 'Kirk o'Whistles'. In 1988 the then disused church was saved from demolition and converted into offices.

St David's (Ramshorn) Church

The North West Church was built 1718–24 at the top of the **Candleriggs**, on the lands of Ramshorn, and it soon became known popularly as the Ramshorn Kirk. Architecturally unremarkable, it fell into disrepair and was replaced in 1824 by a T-plan building in the 'florid perpendicular Gothic' style (Groome, 1886), designed by the English architect David Rickman with the assistance of the Superintendent of Public Works, James Cleland. As it no longer lay in the north-west of the expanding city, it was renamed St David's.

The remains of many of Glasgow's most notable citizens, such as **David Dale** and **John Anderson**, were interred in the graveyard. In 1813 the anatomist Granville Sharp Pattison, another lecturer and two students from the College Street Medical School were indicted on charges of removing the body of a less celebrated Glaswegian from its last resting place there.

The church was purchased by **Strathclyde University** in 1982, and reopened in 1991 as a theatre.

St Enoch's Square

The name St Enoch is a corruption of St Thenew, the mother of Glasgow's patron saint, **Mungo**. St Enoch's Church was built on ground at the foot of Buchanan Street in 1780–2 on the site of an earlier chapel dedicated to St Thenew. A square was laid out in front of the church from 1782. The Surgeons' Hall, the Custom House and the homes of some of Glasgow's leading merchants were also located there, but were replaced during the 19th century with shops, warehouses and office buildings.

The character of the square was further altered in 1876 with the opening of the City of Glasgow Union Railway's (later amalgamated with the Glasgow & South Western) St Enoch's Station, the first of the city's great

railway termini. The station's magnificent Gothic St Enoch's Hotel, opened in 1879, was then Scotland's largest, dominating the eastern side of the square and towering over the mock baronial subway station, erected in the middle of 1896. The church, which was rebuilt in 1827, was demolished in 1925.

In its new guise as a travel centre, the subway station survived the modernisation of the **underground** during the late 1970s, but the railway station was closed in 1966 and the hotel in 1974. In 1989 the controversial glass and steel St Enoch's Centre, a massive shopping mall, was opened on the site of the old terminus and hotel.

St George's in the Fields

Another of Glasgow's neoclassical churches, St George's in the Fields (off St George's Road) was built to designs by H & D Barclay in 1885–6. The tympanum over the Ionic portico, depicting Christ distributing the loaves and fishes, is by William Birnie Rhind. It was the last church in Glasgow to be built on the model of a classical temple. The church was closed in 1980 and subsequently converted into offices.

St George's Tron

The Wynd Church, or St George's Tron, designed by William Stark in 1807, stands in the middle of West George Street – a symbol of the opulence and classical elegance of the new town of Blythswood. Stark was heavily influenced in planning the baroque exterior by a recent visit to St Petersburg. The external grandeur, including a tower and obelisk, is not repeated inside the building, which is severe in its simplicity. In 1940 the church amalgamated with the Tron Church where **Dr Thomas Chalmers**, the social reformer and architect of the **Disruption**, had been the minister from 1815–19.

St Rollox Chemical Works, Springburn

In the 1830s and 40s St Rollox was supposedly the largest chemical works in the world, a boast cheerfully proclaimed by the construction of a 455ft (139m) chimney stack, briefly the tallest in Europe, which 'mammoth stalk' continually poured 'its sooty treasures into the region of the clouds'. The chimney, demolished in 1922, was known as 'Tennant's Stalk' after **Sir Charles Tennant**, founder of St Rollox, who had patented a process (invented by his patron **Charles Macintosh**) for producing a dry bleaching powder. By the 1850s St Rollox was churning out 60 tons of soap a week plus various industrical alkalis. 'The most extraordinary part of the work,' according to J D Burn in 1858, 'is that in which the sulphuric acid is made . . . we pass between two mountains of sulphur, each of 5000 tons. We then enter a devil's den with an immense row of glowing furnaces . . . half roasted and our lungs struggling with the atmosphere, loaded with sulphuric gas . . . utterly impossible to describe the scene . . . 58 lead chambers for receiving the sulphuric gas . . . each holds 21,000 cubic feet . . . approached by many miles of wooden stages . . . men moving about like spirits in the fitful glare of the fiery furnace.' The main complex was demolished in 1964–5.

St Vincent Place

When the horse tramway system was laid out in Glasgow in the mid-19th century, the terminus was in St Vincent Place, opening off **George Square**. It was a natural choice at the fast developing commercial centre of the city. The old buildings were soon pulled down to make way for magnificent palaces of commerce. On the north corner with George Square is the old head office of the Bank of Scotland designed by **J T Rochead** and built between 1867–70. The entrance is guarded by two huge statues of Atlantes and the domed banking hall is a delight. Further along the north side is the ornate **Clydesdale Bank** building, designed by John Burnet in 1871. Its offices have since grown to include adjoining buildings and a new block, originally shared with the Bank of England facing West George Street, was constructed in 1979–80 by G D Lodge & Partners. On the south side are two bold insurance company offices – the Scottish Provident building and the Scottish Amicable building (1870–3). Despite heavy traffic, the mass of the offices still conveys the robust determination of Glasgow in the late 19th century.

St Vincent Street Church

On steeply rising ground **Alexander Thomson** created a massive plinth on which to construct his **United Free Church** (1858–9). The plinth is of Pharaonic solidity, the church a classical temple with Ionic colonnade, and the tower an amalgam of Egyptian, Greek and Roman motifs with more than a hint of the Hindu curvilinear. Within, the rich colours and delicate anthemion frieze make an unusual and almost pagan setting for the rigidities of Calvinism. Thomson is said to have been thinking of the temple of Solomon at the time.

Saltmarket

The street leading south from **Glasgow Cross** to the Linninghaugh was originally known as the Waulkers' or the Fullers' Gait, as it led to a *waulk* or fulling mill established on the haugh (riverside) prior to 1422. It became popularly known as the Saltmarket Street some time during the 15th century when, the mill closed, salt sellers conducted their trade there. The Saltmarket originally stopped short of the **Clyde**, although there was access to **Glasgow Bridge** by way of the **Bridgegate**. During the 1790s however, the street was extended to the Clyde, and the first Hutchesontown Bridge was built (1795) linking Saltmarket with the new residential village of that name.

In the 18th century the Saltmarket was one of Glasgow's most fashionable streets. It was lined with piazzas and the mansions of leading merchants; the city's first bank, the Ship Bank, was established on the corner of the Bridgegate in 1749. Its importance was increased by the erection of the **Justiciary Court** building opposite the western entrance to **Glasgow Green** in 1814. But by then the Saltmarket was beginning to degenerate into a slum as the middle classes moved west and poor Irish immigrants moved in. Shebeens, distilling and dispensing illicit liquor, proliferated; so did hotels.

Until 1805, when the slaughter house was relocated north of Clyde Street, the lower Saltmarket was further polluted with dung and putrid remains discarded by the glue renderers, tripe makers and skinners working in the vicinity of the Skinners' Haugh. The **Glasgow Fair** was held at the foot of the Saltmarket from the end of the 18th century until 1871. It attracted the rougher element of the populace, and one of their more disagreeable pastimes was the sport of 'Hunt the Barney', played by mobs of locals rampaging through the Irish quarter. The Irish were the founders of the famous **Paddy's Market**, the old clothes market which began in Jail Square in the 1820s and flourished in and around the Saltmarket until the end of the century.

The Saltmarket was almost completely rebuilt by the City Improvement Trust and the City of Glasgow Union **Railway** Co after 1866. Sandblasting during the 1980s restored the Victorian buildings to their handsome former condition.

Sauchiehall Street

This best-known of Glasgow's streets takes its name from Sauchie Haugh, meaning low-lying ground covered with willow trees. Until the end of the 18th century it remained wet and boggy with nothing much more than a winding track, part of the extensive Blythswood Estate. When development began on Blythswood Hill it soon extended down to Sauchiehall Street with the construction in the early 19th century of classical terraces and villas. The well-proportioned drawing room of one of the terrace houses survives as the dining room of the **Royal Highland Fusiliers** in the Headquarters beside **Charing Cross**. Little else remains of the first houses, which were demolished to make way for commercial developments, like the great warehouses of Pettigrew & Stephen and Copland & Lye – themselves replaced in the early 1970s by the tasteless Sauchiehall Centre.

The street does retain some fine façades from its Victorian heyday as one of Glasgow's premier shopping thoroughfares, notably the recently restored **McLellan Galleries** (built in 1855 to house a bequest of paintings to the city by Archibald McLellan) and the Grecian Mansion designed by **Alexander 'Greek' Thomson** in 1865. At the west end stands the exuberant Charing Cross Mansion in the French style by Burnet Son & Campbell, 1889–91. A first-floor window, bowed with emphatic verticals, just west of the Sauchiehall Centre, is unmistakably **Mackintosh**, in fact the **Willow Tea Rooms**. This section of the street near the city centre has been laid out as a pedestrian shopping area.

Scotland Street School

The school, at 225 Scotland Street, Kingston, was designed between 1904–6 by **Charles Rennie Mackintosh** as a partner of Honeyman, Keppie & Mackintosh and is now a museum. The design, restricted by the stipulations of the parsimonious Govan School Board, is a conventional range of classrooms along an axial corridor with stairs and cloakrooms at either end. Mackintosh corrected the inevitably flat and horizontal pattern of the windows on the north elevation by adding a dramatic re-interpretation of the traditional Scottish stair tower at either end. The towers are, in effect, two glittering, small-paned glass cylinders which anticipate the glass-walled staircases of Walter Gropius. At the base of each are separate entrances for boys and girls;

climbing the floodlighted stairs must have been a magical experience for children from the **Govan** tenements. The budget did not allow for interior decoration (Mackintosh intended full height railings and a black tiled dado on the stairs), but the exterior has some fine Art Nouveau detailing.

SCWS Building

The Scottish Co-operative Wholesale Society was founded in 1868 [see **Co-operative Movement**] and in 1872 began building a series of vast warehouses and workshops in Kingston. The most spectacular, sometimes likened to a French Renaissance palace, is the Society's headquarters, opened on the corner of Paisley Road and Morison Street, on the site of an old shooting gallery, in 1897. The design was rumoured to be a reworked version of one submitted for the competition for the City Chambers, but this was denied by the architects, Bruce & Hay. The SCWS retains a significant presence in the city. Its headquarters are particularly impressive when viewed from the southbound lanes of the **Kingston Bridge**.

Scottish Exhibition and Conference Centre

Queen's Dock, built at Stobcross 1872–80, was closed in 1969. The site was infilled, and the Scottish Exhibition and Conference Centre opened there in 1985. The Clyde Auditorium was added to the complex in 1997. The conference centre is covered by a roof of eight overlapping shiny metal shells, giving rise to its nickname, The Armadillo. It seats over 3000 people, and has proved to be a major asset in Glasgow's drive to capture a large share of the international conference-going business.

The exhibition centre offers a pleasant riverside venue for large shows, exhibitions and displays, but the building itself, surrounded by a vast car park, is uninspiring in appearance and often compared to an oversized aircraft hangar. The Forum Hotel, opened in 1989, provides 284 bedrooms and 14 suites for conference delegates and other visitors. Despite the use of acres of mirror glass in the treatment of the exterior, the building has failed to impress Glaswegians, who have seen their skyline cluttered by a succession of multi-storey slabs since the 1960s. The only building preserved on the old dock site, the Italianate hydraulic pumping station of 1877, was restored as a restaurant complex in 1988. Here is sited the Clyde Maritime Centre and its main exhibit, the 1896 **Clyde**-built sailing ship *Glenlee*.

Springburn

This district to the north-east was absorbed by Glasgow in 1905, at which time its speciality of **locomotive** building was already well established. Railway engines have been described as Glasgow's second heavy industry (**shipbuilding** being the first), and it was concentrated almost entirely at the Hyde Park and Atlas works in Springburn. An amalgamation in 1903 produced the North British Locomotive Company which was the largest in Europe with sixty acres (24ha) of workshops and over 8000 employees. Most production was for export, India taking over 11,000 steam and diesel engines, many of which have outlasted the works that produced them.

The Clyde Auditorium at the Scottish Exhibition and Conference Centre in Glasgow (NK)

Glasgow continued

Stock Exchange

Apart from the **University** and the Stock Exchange, Glasgow has few Gothic Revival buildings. The latter, on the corner of St George's (Nelson Mandela) Place and Buchanan Street, was designed by John Burnet in 1875–6 and is reminiscent of the Law Courts in London's Strand. The Exchange as an institution dates back to 1844, when it operated from rooms in **Royal Exchange Square** and subsequently in Queen Street. Reflecting Glasgow's growing wealth, the number of members grew from 49 in 1845 to 178 by 1899. The volume of transactions had grown so much that a large extension facing into St George's Place was added in the same style between 1902–6. During World War I, when the Exchange was closed, no less than 547 members, clerks and officials joined the services, of whom 120 gave their lives. With the closure of the dealing floor in recent times, the building has been converted into offices.

Templeton's Carpet Factory

On acquiring a site facing **Glasgow Green**, the directors of J & J Templeton, carpet manufacturers, were repeatedly frustrated by the town council's rejection of designs for their proposed new factory. Close to despair they turned to the respected William Leiper (1836–1916) and invited him to propose a building of unimpeachable architectural pedigree. Leiper thought of the Doge's Palace in Venice and duly replicated it in polychromatic brick (1889). On account of some dispute between the

architect and the builder, the façade was untied to the rest of the structure and collapsed during construction, killing 29 weavers. It was rebuilt, substantially extended in the 1930s, and more recently converted into a business centre.

The Tenement House, 45 Buccleuch Street, Garnethill

Typical of thousands throughout the city, this unremarkable four-storey tenement of red standstone contains the flat of a Miss Toward, spinster and also unremarkable, who lived here with her widowed mother (1911–39) and on her own (1939–65). She died in 1975 when the property was bought by Anna Davidson who sold it to the **National Trust for Scotland** in 1982. It is now open to the public. Its interest lies entirely in its fittings and contents. Averse to home improvements, unable to discard anything, and a stickler for 'the old ways', Miss Toward had unwittingly preserved a complete Edwardian interior and filled it with a random archive of her lower-middle-class life in Glasgow throughout the first half of the 20th century. It complements the innumerable cottages and croft houses preserved, or more often restored, elsewhere in Scotland and because of its uncontrived provenance affords an insight into the life of a very ordinary individual. Heritage is triumphantly repulsed by the peccadilloes of a real person.

The Tolbooth

The earliest reference to the Tolbooth (originally 'The Praetorium') at **Glasgow Cross** is from 1454. The old building was demolished in 1626 and a new one erected (1636) on the site at the corner of **High Street** and **Trongate**. It was four storeys high, with a seven-storey,

The SV Glenlee, part of the Clyde Maritime Centre adjacent to the Scottish Exhibition and Conference Centre (NK)

Glasgow continued

126ft (38m) high tower on the eastern side. The building housed the council chambers, municipal offices, archives, court rooms, Dean of Guild Hall and gaol. The tower was adorned with a brass clock and a bell, and a chime of bells was installed in 1665, replaced in 1736 and again in 1881. A town hall, to rehouse the council chambers, offices and assembly rooms, was added to the west side of the Tolbooth in two stages (1736–40 and 1758–60). From 1788 until 1813, public executions were carried out on a special gallows platform attached to the Tolbooth steeple.

In 1812 the old Tolbooth building was sold, and a new warehouse building, in a similar style, erected in its place. The Tolbooth Steeple, however, was preserved by popular demand. When repaired in 1842, it was opened at ground level to enable the pavement on High Street to pass through. Plans put forward in 1914 to relocate it more centrally at Glasgow Cross were not executed, and the Tolbooth Steeple remained on its little traffic island in the widened High Street.

Trades House

Tucked away in Glassford Street in the heart of the Merchant City is the Trades House, one of Glasgow's architectural gems. It was built in 1791–4 to designs by **Robert Adam** and features pillars and pediment on the first floor, balustrade and cupola on the roof. Unfortunately the interior has been much altered and little of Adam's work survives. The Trades House traces its history back to the late 16th century when it was formed to represent the fourteen incorporated trades in the city

– hammermen, tailors, cordiners, maltmen, weavers, bakers, skinners, wrights, coopers, fleshers, masons, gardeners, barbers and dyers. The Trades House is presided over by the Deacon Convenor, elected by representatives of the Incorporations. The members of the Trades House were entitled to vote for, and be elected to, the town council. The Trades House is now largely a charitable institution.

Tramway Theatre

The Tramway Theatre is located in the old Glasgow Corporation Tram Depot in Albert Drive which was built in 1894 and extended 1899–1922. In 1964, one year after the trams disappeared from Glasgow's streets, the depot was occupied by the Glasgow Transport Museum, which remained there until more spacious accommodation became available at the **Kelvin Hall**. The old depot was partly demolished and the remainder was converted into a theatre to stage Peter Brook's production of *The Mahabharata* in 1989. The venue was highly praised, and many of the most prestigious events of the City of Culture programme in 1990 were staged there.

Trongate

The road leading from **Glasgow Cross** to the West Port at the top of Stockwell Street was known in the Middle Ages as St Thenew's Gate, as it formed part of the route to St Thenew's Kirkyard (on the site of which **St Enoch's Square** was later built). In 1491, however, the Bishop of Glasgow was granted the right to set up a public tron, or weigh-bridge, which was erected near the Cross; the road subsequently became known as the Trongate.

The Trongate contained many of Glasgow's finest buildings and some of its smarter shops were set back

The Trongate c1870, by George Washington Wilson (GWWA)

Glasgow continued

from the street behind elegant piazzas. The **Tolbooth** was on the corner of **High Street**, and the Tontine Hotel and coffee house, built in 1781 and occupying part of the adjacent town hall building, became the favourite meeting place for the city's famous **Tobacco** Lords. These wealthy merchants also congregated at the foot of the equestrian statue of King William III, erected outside the town hall in 1734, and they were notoriously unwilling to permit ordinary Glaswegians to share the 'plainstanes' (the wide pavement laid out at the eastern end of the Trongate).

In 1485 the Collegiate Church of St Mary and St Ann was built on the south side of the street. It fell into disrepair after the **Reformation**, and a grass market was established in the burial ground. The church was rebuilt in 1586, and its steeple, modelled on **Glasgow Cathedral**'s, was added in 1631. In 1793 the church was burnt to the ground, reputedly by a gang of well-to-do tearaways known as the Hellfire Club. It was rebuilt once again, to one of **James Adam**'s less inspired designs; and in 1855 the old steeple, which had survived the fire, was opened by arches to permit the pavement to pass through. The church was converted in the late 1970s to become the Tron Theatre, an early contributor to Glasgow's renaissance as a centre for the performing arts.

The original **Hutcheson's Hospital** was built on Trongate 1641–50, but demolished in 1795 to permit the formation of Hutcheson Street. Other important buildings on the street included the guard house, the Shawfield Mansion (damaged in the **Shawfield Riots** in 1725, and later demolished to permit the formation of Glassford Street), the notorious City of Glasgow Bank (whose failure, with debts of over £6 million, in 1878 paralysed the city's commerce) and the famous Panopticon (later the Britannia) **Music Hall**. **Sir John Moore** of Corunna fame was born (1761) in a house in Tron-

gate and **James Watt** had a workshop here in 'Buchanan's Land'.

The West Port was demolished in 1749, its removal improving traffic flow along one of Glasgow's busiest streets. In c1870 the Tontine Hotel (then occupying most of the old town hall) was demolished, and a drapery warehouse built in its place. The famous 'Tontine Faces', which formed the keystones in each of the ten arches of the building's piazza, were saved but dispersed to various parts of the city. In 1895 Glasgow Cross Station was opened on the Trongate. The statue of William III was relocated there, facing westward down the middle of the street, until it was removed again, to Cathedral Square, in 1923. Glasgow Cross Station closed in 1965, leaving only the ventilation shaft, now covered over, as an island in the middle of the street.

Although the Trongate declined in importance at the beginning of the 19th century as the town council moved to the **Justiciary Buildings**, and the merchants moved to new homes and offices further west, it has remained a popular shopping street.

Victoria (Stockwell) Bridge

The somewhat confusing story of Glasgow's bridges begins here, on the site occupied by the Victoria Bridge connecting Stockwell Street with Gorbals Street. Bishop Rae, with the financial backing of Lady Lochow, is thought to have built the first stone bridge in the 14th century, replacing a wooden structure which may well have been in existence intermittently since the time of **William Wallace**. The stone bridge was known as the Glasgow Bridge and had no rival for four centuries until the 1772 opening of the Broomielaw Bridge [see **Glasgow Bridge**]. Periodic spates, however, necessitated rebuilding; it was also widened in 1776 and widened again and strengthened in 1819 by **Thomas Telford**. These improvements were evidently inadequate and the old bridge was demolished to be replaced by the present structure by James Walker. It took three years to build and was opened on 2 January 1854 with great ceremony in spite of the cold; at the time the river was in fact frozen over. Granite-built with five arches, the Victoria was widely regarded as the finest bridge of its day and remains the most handsome in Glasgow. Upstream the Hutchesontown Bridge of 1833 by **Robert Stevenson**, replacing a wooden footbridge, was itself replaced in 1870 by a three-span cast-iron bridge and renamed after Victoria's consort – the Albert Bridge.

Virginia Street

Closely associated with Glasgow's 18th century **Tobacco** Lords, this street in the Merchant City is named after Virginia Mansion, the home of Alexander Speirs whose family were pre-eminent in the trade. Nearby was the tobacco exchange, now Virginia Galleries (No 33), whose Corinthian pilasters may be compared with the Ionic entrance pilasters of No 53 (Virginia Buildings, 1817). In the same street the City of Glasgow Bank had its headquarters. Founded in 1838, it collapsed 40 years later with sensational effect; the financial repercussions throughout Scotland have been compared to those resulting from the failure of the **Darien Scheme**.

Willow Tea Rooms

The Willow Tea Rooms (1903–4) at 217 **Sauchiehall Street** was **Charles Rennie Mackintosh**'s most comprehensive scheme for Catherine Cranston; it ranged from the remodelling of the structure itself, formerly a warehouse, to designing the cutlery. Miss Cranston, owner of four Glasgow tea rooms, recognised the importance of novelty to commercial success and was a liberal client.

The plain white front with a chequered border set the building apart from other commercial premises in the street. Domestic-style, leaded windows advertised the intimacy of the interior, which was to suggest a willow grove: the meaning of 'Sauchiehall'. Spaces were patterns of receding, thin vertical lines using metal screens, wooden panels and the famous tall, ladderback chairs. In the Room de Luxe a semi-abstract tree and leaf motif in coloured glass and lead was repeated across an eye-level frieze of angled mirrors, the door and window. This room has been restored to its original state and use.

GLASGOW ACADEMY

Glasgow Academy was founded in 1846 by a group of **Glasgow** businessmen led by William Campbell of Tullichewen. A magnificent building to designs by Charles Wilson was erected between Elmbank Street and Holland Street. The Academy quickly won a reputation for academic attainment. Following the passing of the 1870 Education (Scotland) Act the Academy was wound up and the property sold to the Glasgow School Board as a home for the High School. Several of the shareholders and old members believed that the school should continue, purchasing ground for a new and equally splendid building designed by H & D Barclay in Colebrook Street off **Great Western Road**. The school remained one of the city's leading independent boys' schools until 1991 when it amalgamated with Westbourne School for Girls, the occupiers of the imposing Kelvinside House in Beaconsfield Road.

GLASGOW ART GALLERY AND MUSEUM

Glasgow Art Gallery and Museum, situated in **Kelvingrove Park**, is the headquarters of **Glasgow**'s Department of Museums and Art Galleries responsible for the municipal collections of Natural History, Archaeology, Ethnography, History and Fine and Decorative Arts. The Department is made up of a further nine branch museums: the **Burrell** Collection, the Museum of Transport, **Pollok House**, **Haggs Castle**, Camphill House, **Provand's Lordship**, the St Mungo Museum of Religious Life and Art, the Fossil Grove [see **Geology**] and the **Rutherglen** Museum.

The nucleus of the city's collection was the bequest in 1854 of Archibald McLellan, a Glasgow coachbuilder, town councillor and magistrate. His insolvency on his death meant the Corporation was eventually forced to purchase his important collection of mainly Dutch, Italian and Flemish paintings, together with the galleries he had built to house them on **Sauchiehall Street**. Further generous donations quickly built upon McLellan's legacy and in the 1870s important bequests of over 100 pictures from William Euing and 70 from Mrs John Graham-Gilbert dramatically increased the size and scope of the collection. Further bequests this century and a series of inspired acquisitions, including the famous purchase of Dali's *Christ of St John on the Cross*, have contributed to what many consider the finest civic collection of art in the United Kingdom.

In 1888 a great International Exhibition was held in Kelvingrove Park to fund the building of a new museum to bring together the city's paintings (rapidly outgrowing the space available in **McLellan's Galleries**) and its collection of historical and scientific objects, which since 1870 had been kept in Kelvingrove House. The richly ornamented, palatial red sandstone building to the design of the English architects J W Simpson and E J Allen, chosen in competition from over 60 entries, was opened in 1901, celebrated by a further International Exhibition, and the city's collections were transferred there in 1902. The simple plan of the building consists of a massive three-storeyed central hall, flanked on the east and west sides by smaller halls surrounded on two floors by exhibition galleries where displays from the permanent collection are augmented by a wide and varied programme of temporary exhibitions. A new acquisition fund has recently been established for the purchase of examples of international contemporary art. These are housed in the new Gallery of Modern Art located in the Stirling Library in **Royal Exchange Square**.

GLASGOW FAIR

In or about 1190, **King William I** granted to the Bishop of **Glasgow** the right to hold an annual fair, for the eight days of the octave of St Peter and St Paul (ie from 7 July). During the 19th century most industries closed for the trade holiday at the time of the Fair, and the Fair Week (which for many became the Fair Fortnight after World War II) began on the second Friday of July.

The Fair was originally held at the junction of **High Street** and the **Rottenrow**, and then on the Old Green at the foot of Stockwell Street. It moved again to the foot of the **Saltmarket**, around Jail Square, at the end of the 18th century. The development of the retail and wholesale trades in Glasgow led to its decline as a market fair, and it was given over almost entirely to refreshment stalls, circuses, freak shows, 'penny geggies' (theatrical shows) and other popular entertainments. The Fair attracted many of the city's roughnecks in search of mischief. It is unclear when the statute compelling every booth-holder to keep a halbert, jack and steel bonnet to hand to assist in quelling outbreaks of disorder was allowed to lapse.

From the 1840s the spilling-over of the Fair booths and stalls onto **Glasgow Green**, and their increasing tendency to linger on after the end of the Fair, provoked protests from local people. In 1871 the Corporation bowed to popular pressure and a new Fair site was established at Vinegar Hill near Camlachie. The new site served only for a short period, however, and the Fair returned to the Green, to Fleshers' Haugh, in the 20th century. 'The Shows' remained hugely popular, but came to consist of the standard rides and other attractions found in fairgrounds all over the country. The revival of more traditional Fair entertainments, such as juggling, dancing, musical and theatrical shows, was

Glasgow Fair in 1825; looking up Saltmarket from the roof of the Court House (ML)

promoted by the city council on a site next to the **People's Palace** in 1990. The Glasgow Fair seems set to continue as an annual festival of entertainment.

GLASGOW SCHOOL OF ART

The school, at 167 Renfrew Street, was begun in 1897 following a competition won by Honeyman & Keppie, architects, with a design by **Charles Rennie Mackintosh**, their senior assistant. The building is celebrated for the way in which it experiments with construction, detailing and site, being at once functional and dramatic. In this sense it is a 'modern' building while being traditionally Scottish in character.

Limited funds would only allow 'a plain building', while the visionary director (1885–1917), **Francis Newbery**, wanted generous studios with large windows. In the event the building had to be completed in two phases; the eastern wing was opened in 1899 and the west wing and attic in 1909. The site is unfavourably long, narrow and steeply sloping. Accordingly, Mackintosh designed a linear sequence of north-facing studios. Steel beams replace supporting walls and sliding partitions connect the studios. Deep, well lit basement studios were won from the site by setting the building back from the street.

Unprecedentedly, the north elevation is a plain wall of glass, abruptly hitting the unusual deep eaves above. Important to the effect, very large window panes are set flush with their frames. The vertical play of the west elevation, exaggerated by the falling ground, is one of Mackintosh's most dramatic translations of traditional Scottish architecture.

This is Mackintosh's first 'through designed' building and the interior is complete with repeating, integrated detail, such as door panels of coloured and leaded glass, and furnishing. Most noteworthy is the Library with its inventive Japanese gallery creating a labyrinthine space within a small room.

GLASGOW UNDERGROUND

Constructed as a 6½-mile circle route in 1896 by the Glasgow District Subway Company, the **Glasgow Underground**'s trains were originally powered by cable, operating on a highly unusual gauge of 4 ft (1220mm), 8½ inches narrower than British Rail. The tunnels vary in depth from 2 to 33.5m below street level. Taken into municipal control in 1923, the line was electrified at 600 volts DC 12 years later, using a third rail, and the system operated comparatively unchanged until 1977.

By that year the underground system, or 'Subway' as it is known to Glaswegians, had been taken over by the **Strathclyde** Passenger Transport Executive, its present owners (1999), who closed the system for modernisation in May 1977. This cost more than anticipated – around £60 million – but the line reopened in April 1980 with new orange-liveried rolling-stock from Metro-Cammell of Birmingham which rapidly earned the system the sobriquet of 'Clockwork Orange'. Automatic ticketing and escalators were also installed. The new service, stopping at 15 stations, provides a peak-time service frequency of a train every four minutes, and every eight minutes off-peak. Up to 90 passsengers can be carried in each of the 33 cars, usually configured in two-coach trains and averaging a speed, including stops, of around 16mph; it takes 24 mins to complete the circle in either direction. In 1999 this enviably cheap public transport service carried nearly 15 million passengers.

GLASGOW UNIVERSITY

The massive neo-Gothic university, built to designs by George Gilbert Scott in 1870 and completed by his son

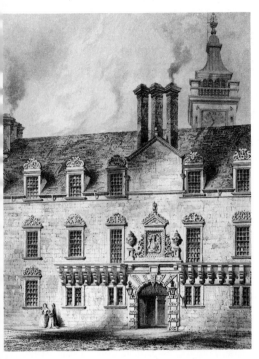

The old University buildings in High Street before demolition in the 1870s (ML)

Oldrid Scott in 1887–91, dominates the skyline of the west end of the city. The University was founded in 1451 by Bishop William Turnbull. After an uncertain start it was re-established in 1577. Despite the political disturbances of the 17th century the University flourished and a magnificent building was constructed in the **High Street**. **Glasgow** became an important seat of learning, attracting and nurturing teachers with an international reputation such as **Francis Hutcheson**, the philosopher (1694–1746), **Joseph Black**, the chemist (1728–1799) and **Adam Smith**, the founder of modern economics (1723–1790). By the end of the 18th century there were nearly 2000 students, making the University of equivalent size to Oxford or Cambridge. It has kept pace with these universities ever since, winning in the 19th century a reputation for the quality of its scientific and medical training and research, with professors like **Lord Kelvin** and **Lord Lister**.

The old University buildings – considered by many to be the finest example of Scottish vernacular architecture – were demolished in the 1870s to make way for a **railway** goods station and the University moved to its present site on Gilmorehill. Since then it has expanded dramatically with many new buildings, some of architec-

tural distinction – notably the Reading Room by T Harold Hughes & D S R Waugh 1939–40, and the **Hunterian Art Gallery** by William Whitfield 1971–81. The University is now one of the largest in the United Kingdom attracting students from many countries and with an international reputation for the quality of its research.

GLEN ALMOND, Perthshire

The river Almond rises within three miles of **Loch Tay** but only joins that river at **Perth**. The intervening glen divides into an upper, Highland, section including the **Sma' Glen** and a lower pastoral section also known as Logiealmond. Logie House stood on the north bank of the river but is now demolished. So is Lynedoch House, the home of **General Thomas Graham** who was created Lord Lynedoch and who developed nearby Pitcairngreen as a bleaching village which was predicted one day to rival Manchester. It failed miserably. South of the river near Perth stands **Huntingtower** and, further up, Glenalmond or Trinity College, an **Episcopalian** public school founded in 1847.

GLEN CINEMA FIRE, Paisley (1929)

Scotland's worst accident in the entertainment industry happened at the Glen Cinema, **Paisley**, on 31 December 1929. It is believed that highly flammable nitrate filmstock caught fire in the overheated conditions of a cramped projection booth behind the auditorium. Being physically separated from the audience, as required by the 1909 Cinematograph Act, the fire should not have threatened the auditorium. Unfortunately a shout of 'Fire' from the audience caused blind panic which ended with 72 children being suffocated as they piled up against a fire exit which had been locked to prevent illicit entry.

GLEN CLOVA, Angus

East of **Glen Isla** two more long glens finger their way into the Grampians. The smaller, Glen Prosen, joins the larger, Glen Clova, near Cortachy [see **Kirriemuir**]. Nearby there is an obelisk commemorating an Earl of Airlie who was killed in the Boer War, also a fountain commemorating Captain R F Scott and Edward Wilson who stayed there while planning their disastrous expedition to the South Pole (1912). Up Glen Clova in 1650 rode the young **Charles II** hopeful of a meeting with his Highland followers ('The Start'); but they failed to materialise and he returned to **Perth**. Clova Castle is thought to have been destroyed by Cromwellian forces at about this time. At Braedownie, where the road ends, Glen Doll opens to the west and a track leads over the Capel Mount to Deeside. Clova is celebrated in an eccentric verse epic called *Willie Wabster's Wooing and Wedding on the Grampian Mountains* by Dorothea Maria Ogilvy (d.1895), a niece of the Earl of Airlie. Extracts quoted by **Nigel Tranter** in *The Eastern Counties* (1972) may encourage further reading:

> Oh barony of Clova, green and grand, strinkled wi'
>   spairgen strype and brattlen green,
> The sweetest strath in a' my fatherland;
> Yet wi' the warld I whammle whan-a-bee,
>   remfeezled runt, I hirple owre the haugh;
> Nae worth for beef or broth or milk o' whey, a
>   rail-e'ed rousy, girnigow-gibbie.

GLEN DEVON, Perthshire and Kinross-shire

The grassy pass through the **Ochil Hills** formed by **Gleneagles** and Glen Devon (and now threaded by the A823) was once popular with cattle drovers. From the watershed the Devon falls steeply, until dammed for a reservoir, as it heads east to Yetts of Muckhart (ie Gates of the Swineherd, where there was once a drovers' toll). Nearby is the village of Pool of Muckhart, once the principal place in 'Muckhartshire'. Beyond, at Crook o'Devon, the river bends back on itself to head south-west for the Forth at **Alloa**, first passing through a deep gorge beneath Rumbling Bridge, so called because of the noise made not by the bridge but by rocks being churned up in the abyss below. Apart from its odd placenames the glen is noteworthy for its scenery and for Glendevon Castle, Z-plan and 17th century with a 15th century nucleus, which belonged to **William, 8th Earl of Douglas** who was murdered by **James II**.

GLEN FAMILY (19th/20th century) Music Publishers

Thomas Glen (1804–73), a **bagpipe** maker and instrument dealer, was suceeded by his sons John (1833–1904) and Robert (1835–1911). John Glen's Early Scottish Melodies (1900) remains a most useful piece of research and the Glen Account Books are a fascinating record of the firm's dealings in the mid-19th century. Alexander (1801–73), brother to Thomas and also a bagpipe maker and music publisher, was succeeded by his son David (b.1850) who published a major collection of bagpipe music over several years. The two firms amalgamated in 1949.

GLEN FRUIN, Battle of (1603)

Following a raid on his property in 1602, Alexander Colquhoun of Luss was granted a lieutenancy by **James VI** to pursue **Clan Gregor**. The following February, when warned of the MacGregors' approach, Colquhoun tried to reach the head of Glen Fruin before confronting them. But Alasdair MacGregor of Glenstrae forestalled him by leading his men from Loch Long over the watershed into the head of the glen, where he divided his forces. He himself took his stance in a narrow defile while his brother remained concealed near the farm of Strone in order to cut off Colquhoun's retreat. The battle took place at Strone. The Colquhouns were surrounded on boggy ground which rendered their horses useless and their foot soldiers, charged by MacGregors, broke ranks and fled. 120 people were killed, amongst them prisoners. Government reprisals included the proscription of Clan Gregor.

GLEN ISLA, Angus

The most westerly of the **Angus** glens (Glens **Clova**, Prosen and Esk), Glen Isla runs parallel to **Glenshee** to which it is connected by road. At its head a track, once a drove road, leads to Deeside over the Monega Pass. Below the pass the Caenlochan Nature Reserve has a flora similar to that of **Ben Lawers**. Further down Forter Castle, an Ogilvy stronghold [see **Kirriemuir**] was sacked by the **Earl of Argyll**'s **Covenanters** in 1640 but has since been renovated, L-plan and five storeys high. After the Isla emerges from the hills north of **Alyth** it passes under Bridge of Craigisla and through

a gorge to drop 80ft (24m) at Reekie Linn. The spray provides the reekie (ie smokey) effect.

GLEN LYON, Perthshire

Possibly the longest (33 miles) glen in Scotland and certainly one of the prettiest, Glen Lyon runs west-east, from **Rannoch Moor** to the meadows of Tayside, and was an important corridor of communication between the Highlands and Lowlands. Ring forts, possibly once **brochs** (eg at Cashlie) are supposedly the 12 castles built by **Fingal** in the glen; it may also have been a **Pictish** stronghold; and there are numerous associations and relics of **St Adamnan** (at Innerwick, Milton Eonan, **Fortingall**, Dull and **Weem**). In the 16th century **Campbells** and **MacGregors** pursued their feud here. MacGregor's leap, in the gorge above Fortingall, is where **Gregor MacGregor** leapt the Lyon to escape his pursuers; Carnbane Castle, further up and now a ruin, is where once he lived. The Campbell stronghold was on the site of **Meggernie Castle**, which passed to the Menzies family after the Campbells of Glen Lyon were discredited by the **Glencoe Massacre**.

Magnificent beech woods above Fortingall give way to larch, spruce and pine above Bridge of Balgie (whence leads a road to **Ben Lawers** and **Loch Tay**) and then to open hill. The glen terminates abruptly in a massive wall of concrete. This hydro dam so raised the water level of Loch Lyon as to make a two-mile lochan into a six-mile reservoir. The lodge and inn of Inverme(a)ran, celebrated in the Gaelic lament Crodh Chailean ('Colin's Cattle') and once an important staging post for droves, were inundated.

GLENBUCHAT CASTLE, Nr Alford, Aberdeenshire

Sometimes spelled 'Glenbucket', this Z-plan tower house, now roofless but far from ruinous, stands on rising ground above the river **Don**. It was built in 1590 by John Gordon and Helen Carnegie whose fate-challenging motto inscribed above the lintel – 'No thing on Earth remanis bot faime' – is now, suitably, illegible. Both square and round turrets protrude from the corners; the stair turrets in the re-entrant angles are supported on arches, or 'squinches', an unusual and attractive arrangement. **Jacobites** to the last, the Gordons joined both the 1715 Rising (proximity to **Kildrummy** may have given them little choice) and the 1745, forfeiting their lands after **Culloden**. Though now in the care of the State, neither the castle nor its wild surroundings betray evidence of zealous conservation and are the better for it.

GLENCOE, Argyll

The area thus designated is usually taken to include not just Glen Coe itself but the whole mountain complex between **Rannoch Moor** and **Loch Leven**. It divides into three. South of Glen Etive (1) the main massif is that of Clachlet with Meall a'Bhuiridh (3636ft/1108m) the highest summit, whose slopes comprise the White Corries (or Glencoe) ski centre (chair lifts, etc). Between Glen Etive and Glen Coe (2) the mountains of Buachaille Etive Mor (3245ft/989m) and Beag, Stob Coire (3657ft/1115m) and Bidean nam Bian (3276ft/995m) crowd upon one another to create a spectacular skyline

and the most popular rock and ice climbing in Scotland. Between Glen Coe and Loch Leven (3) rises the serrated ridge of Aonach Eagach (up to 3173ft/967m), its eastern shoulder crossed by the **Devil's Staircase**. Most of 2 and 3 are owned by the **National Trust for Scotland** which acquired Glen Coe itself in 1935 and the Dalness Estate (Glen Etive) in 1937. It also operates the Glencoe visitor centre at Clachaig and there is a mountain rescue centre nearby.

'All other glens seem tame by comparison' (W H Murray), and just to drive down the main road on a dreich November day can be disconcerting. But tempting as it is to associate this forbidding aspect with historical events, it is clear that the **Glencoe Massacre** occurred in the pastoral lower strath near Glencoe village and not in the defile itself. Likewise neither the rock platform at the head of the glen known as The Study (properly 'stiddie', anvil) nor the Signal Rock at Clachaig served any purpose in the affray. Driving down the pass, the three rocky buttresses of Bidean nam Bian on the left are known as The Three Sisters, and the slit high on the third (Aonach Dubh) above Loch Achtriochan, is Ossian's Cave [see **James Macpherson**], accessible by a rock climb known as Ossian's ladder. The whole area is exceedingly popular with outdoor enthusiasts and tourists.

GLENCOE, Massacre of (1692)

Some three years after the Revolution the government of William and Mary still found itself with the major problem of reconciling the **Jacobite clans** of the western Highlands. Two strategies were contemplated:

the bribing of those concerned, or their removal by government force. The two options were in fact combined with the requirement that all those chiefs concerned should sign an oath of loyalty by 1 January 1692. After much hesitation and after awaiting the agreement of the exiled **James VII**, nearly all did so.

Among those required to take the oath was the aged MacIan of Glencoe, Chief of a small branch of the mighty **Clan Donald**. MacIan left his move too late. When he eventually did set out, he went in the wrong direction, to his old acquaintance Colonel Hill, Governor of the garrison at **Inverlochy**, who was not empowered to administer the oath. By the time he realised his mistake it was too late to reach his correct

destination in **Inveraray** in time. After a horrific journey through the depths of winter he arrived at Inveraray to find the Sherriff, Campbell of Ardkinglas, still absent on holiday following the New Year celebrations. Ardkinglas did in fact accept MacIan's oath, but when the news of his late arrival reached **Edinburgh**, it was seen as providing a pretext for government intervention.

The **MacDonalds** in **Glencoe** were in many ways ideally suited as a target; geographically they were concentrated in an area from which there was no easy escape; politically they were regarded as extreme supporters of the former Catholic regime (although it would appear that they were in fact **Episcopalians**), and they had a shocking record of lawlessness that had made them execrated by their unfortunate neighbours.

Affairs were set in motion by **John Dalrymple, Master of Stair** and Secretary of State for Scotland and orders were passed to the Commander-in-Chief in Scotland, General Sir Thomas Livingston. Before they passed down the military chain of command they were still further backed by the signature of King William himself. Orders to Colonel Hill at **Fort William** were clear. No mercy was to be shown.

To carry out the task, Hill chose his best unit, the Campbell Earl of Argyle's Regiment. On 1 February 1692, two companies were moved into the glen and quartered on the inhabitants who, not having paid their taxes, were liable for the imposed billeting of troops. The inhabitants, initially scared by the arrival of the military, settled down to normal life with the visitors.

Argyle's was one of several regiments raised by the new regime at this period; they included the forerunners of such well known names as the **King's Own Scottish Borderers**, the **Royal Highland Fusiliers** and the **Cameronians**. The only Highland regiment of the period to survive for more than a few months, the regiment was later to serve with great distinction in the Low Countries before being disbanded in 1697.

The commander of the party was Captain Robert Campbell of Glenlyon, a 60-year-old alcoholic, forced to the profession of arms by his disastrous financial affairs to which the depredations of the Glencoe MacDonalds had contributed. His orders when they arrived the night before the massacre were menacingly clear. Two companies were to march over the hills from **Kinlochleven** to bottle up the head of the Glen at first light. More troops would join him from **Ballachulish**. Meanwhile, the orders continued, 'You are hereby ordered to fall upon the rebels the MacDonalds of Glencoe and put all to the sword under seventy . . . See that this be put in execution without fear or favour, or you may expect to be dealt with as not one true to King or Government, nor a man fit to carry a commission in the King's service. Expecting you will not fail in the fulfilling hereof as you love yourself . . .'

So it was that on the morning of 6 February the Massacre began. MacIan, his wife, two of his sons and a number of his clan to the total of 38 in all were killed by the soldiers. The operation, militarily speaking, was a botched one – in some areas deliberately it would appear. The cut-off party failed to arrive in time and many of the MacIans escaped from the Glen only to die as they struggled through the snow-filled passes.

But if the immediate aim was achieved, its repercussions were overwhelmingly negative. Unintentionally the government had handed a golden propaganda opportunity to its enemies. A storm of execration arose directed against all concerned, from the troops on the ground right up to the King.

The task of attributing blame in such circumstances is a recurring problem which has never been satisfactorily achieved. It has not been made any easier by the misconstructions deliberately imposed by political distortion which have largely survived into the popular myths of today. These present the Massacre as an inter-clan act of vengeance, the **Campbells** versus the MacDonalds. This it emphatically was not. Argyle's was a regular red-coat unit of the British standing army acting under orders. Nor was it the cause of the longstanding enmity between the two clans, which was much older and rooted in different foundations.

There have been bloodier and more treacherous massacres in Highland history. But even allowing for the propaganda which Glencoe offered, it is the horrific aspect of a government deliberately attempting genocide which has made the name of Glencoe one of infamy through the ages. The blame probably lies least of all with the perpetrators, regular soldiers carrying out their orders; it would have taken a bigger man than Glenlyon to disobey. The main weight must lie higher up. Several names are mentioned, but it may be no accident that ever since that time the nine of diamonds has been called '**The Curse of Scotland**' – a reference to the nine lozenges displayed on the coat of arms of the Dalrymples of Stair.

GLENDALE MARTYRS

In 1882 the **crofting** communities of Glendale and Husabost (near **Dunvegan** on **Skye**) took a stand against the oppression of their respective landlords in an early phase of the so-called **Highland Land War**. Following the example set by the townships of Braes, they withheld rents, forcibly evicted sheriff-officers, and routed more than one detachment of police. This open defiance, so untypical of the downtrodden crofters but so ominous in the light of events in Ireland, drew a predictable response from the landowners and authorities. Realising that the **Battle of Braes** was not an isolated incident and that a potentially revolutionary situation was developing amongst the Skye crofters, they applied to the government for troops.

The request was eventually (January 1883) granted. But first an official intermediary, backed by the threat of force, was sent to Glendale to reason with the crofters. Arriving by gunboat he succeeded in persuading five of the Glendale men to surrender themselves in order to spare the rest. These, the 'Glendale Martyrs', were tried in Edinburgh and sentenced to two months' imprisonment, whence they returned to Skye as heroes. Meanwhile the publicity given to their case and to that of Braes, plus the activities of the Highland Land Law Reform Association, had led to parliamentary action. Even as the Glendale martyrs served their sentences, the **Napier Commission** began its devastating investigation of crofting conditions. Glendale would continue to make the running in the Highland Land War and one of the 'martyrs', John MacPherson, became a leading activist in the Highland Land Law Reform Association (later the **Highland Land League**).

GLENEAGLES, Perthshire

The name of this north–south glen, which with **Glen Devon** forms a pass through the **Ochils**, has nothing to do with eagles. It is a corruption of *eaglais* or *ecclesia*, a church, in this case the chapel and well of **St Mungo**. The chapel was restored as a Haldane memorial, Gleneagles House (17th century but built from the stones of an older castle) being the home of this distinguished family. Vast Gleneagles Hotel lies well to the west of the glen in spacious surroundings with two celebrated **golf courses**.

GLENELG, Inverness-shire

The only seven-letter palindrome in Highland topography, Glenelg is also exceptionally scenic and, for a piece of mainland, distinctly remote. Bounded on three sides by sea (Loch Duich, Sound of Sleat and Loch Hourn), its only access road is that over the **Mam Ratagan**. This descends into Glen More at the bottom of which is Glenelg village. On the shoreline to the north stand the stark ruins of **Bernera Barracks** with, beyond and precariously sited above the tidal race, the Ferry House, once an inn notorious (thanks to **Boswell** and **Johnson**) for its lack of the most basic amenities. A seasonal ferry shuttles across the 500m of treacherous seaway to the almost deserted township of Kylerhea on **Skye**. This was once the main crossing point for **cattle droves** from the islands. Amidst scenes of activity now unimaginable, thousands of beasts swam, were towed or were ferried through the swirling waters. The slipways they used and the drovers' shielings are still visible.

In Glen Beag, three miles south, are two well preserved Iron Age **brochs**. One mile up the glen Dun Telve broch, partly ruinous, survives to a height of over 10m. The distinctive 'bell' shape and hollow-walled construction technique allowed a great height to be achieved by dry-stone building with the two walls bound together by lintels and wall galleries. A little further up Glen Beag is Dun Troddan, not so well preserved, but still showing clearly the construction technique. When excavated in 1920 few finds were recovered, but a ring of post holes was found at ground level, which presumably supported a raised wooden floor resting on a scarcement ledge.

Further south the road passes above Sandaig, once the home of **Gavin Maxwell** and the setting for his *Ring of Bright Water*. The author's house was burnt down but his ashes are buried here as are some of his otters. The road then passes through Arnisdale to end at the crofting township of Corran on Loch Hourn. The views across to **Knoydart** and Skye are amongst the loveliest on the west coast.

GLENFINNAN, Inverness-shire

At the head of **Loch Shiel** in **Moidart** stands the Glenfinnan Monument marking the spot where on 19 August 1745 **Prince Charles Edward Stewart** raised his standard at the beginning of the last **Jacobite** campaign. He had landed at **Loch nan Uamh** in **Arisaig** on 25 July with a mere handful of supporters. **Cameron of Lochiel**

and others had tried to dissuade him from action. A summons was nevertheless issued. The response was uncertain and on the appointed day the Prince and his companions waited disconsolately in the rain. First to appear were the **Clanranald MacDonalds**. But not till mid-afternoon was the issue decided when over the hills came 700 of Cameron's men. The standard was raised by **William Murray, Marquis of Tullibardine** (and rightful Duke of Atholl), the Prince's father was proclaimed king, and the die was cast. Sublime adventure or mischievous folly, 'those who fought and bled in that arduous and unfortunate enterprise' (as the plaque has it) won posterity's lasting respect. The monument, a slim tower topped with battlements on which stands a kilted soldier (by John Greenshields of Carluke) was erected in 1815 by Alexander MacDonald of Glenaladale, grandson of the Prince's host the night before. It is now in the care of the **National Trust for Scotland** who have erected a visitor centre describing the subsequent campaign. Nearby is held the annual Glenfinnan Gathering and Games.

GLENLIVET, Banffshire

A tributary of the Avon, which itself soon joins the **Spey**, the Water of Livet rises in the Ladder Hills and descends through country sufficiently remote in the 18th century to have sheltered a Catholic seminary and numerous whisky stills. The seminary at Chapeltown, a redoubt of indigenous Catholicism under the protection of the Catholic **Dukes of Gordon**, produced the remarkable Abbé Paul MacPherson (1756–1846) who was engaged, along with the Royal Navy, in an attempt to rescue Pope Paul VI from Napoleon's clutches. It failed, but MacPherson went on to re-establish the Scots College in Rome and to return to Glenlivet. The seminary removed to **Aberdeenshire** soon after and is now Blairs College, **Aberdeen**.

Glenlivet's stills also prospered thanks to a remarkable product. There were allegedly 200 in 1824 when the Distillery Act outlawed them in favour of five authorised establishments, one of which, founded by George Smith in the same year, produced The Glenlivet, most esteemed of the Speyside malts. Near the distillery is the ruined tower of Blairfindy where the 2nd **Marquis of Huntly** was held after capture (1648) by the **Covenanters** and before execution (1649) in **Edinburgh**. Even more ruinous is Drumin Castle, a 14th century stronghold of **Alexander Stewart**, the 'Wolf of Badenoch', above the junction of the Livet and Avon. The **Battle of Glenlivet** (1594) was not fought in the glen but four miles to the north-east off what is now the **Dufftown** road.

GLENLIVET, Battle of (1594)

On the discovery that certain of the Catholic lords of the north-east were in surreptitious and potentially treasonable correspondence with Spain, **James VI** marched north to restore his authority. He sent an advance force under the teenage **7th Earl of Argyll** to meet the rebel army led by **George Gordon, 6th Earl of Huntly** and Francis Hay, 9th Earl of Errol. On 3 October 1594 Huntly and Errol had the better of the engagement (just to the north-east of **Glenlivet**) but fled before the following forces of the King.

Glenluce Abbey, showing the Chapter House windows (HS)

GLENLUCE ABBEY, Wigtownshire

Founded c1190 by Roland of **Galloway** as a Cistercian monastery and daughter house of **Dundrennan Abbey**, Glenluce Abbey is situated on the east bank of the Water of Luce two miles north of Glenluce village. Laid out to the same plan as Dundrennan although on a slightly smaller scale, Glenluce is more ruinous than its mother house, the abbey church, except for the gable of the south transept, being reduced to little more than foundations. The Chapter House however was rebuilt in the early 16th century and is very fine, with Gothic windows, a central shafted pillar from which spring vaulting ribs, and some excellent carving. Little enough is known of the history of the abbey; it was visited once by **Robert I** in 1329 and more than once by **James IV** on pilgrimages to **Whithorn**. In c1565 Gilbert Kennedy, 4th **Earl of Cassillis** is said to have secured the lands of Glenluce by infamy comparable to that which he used to obtain the lands of **Crossraguel** [see **Dunure**]. On this occasion he persuaded a monk to forge the signature of the Abbot (possibly Thomas Hay) on a lease of the abbey; he then hired an assassin to murder the monk and had the assassin hanged for the murder. Hay's son, also Thomas, later assumed the office of **commendator** and used his authority to begin demolition of the abbey and purloined its masonry to build nearby **Castle of Park**. Of the many legends surrounding **Michael Scott 'the Wizard'** (d.c1235), one relates how he lured the spirit of the plague to Glenluce during an epidemic and imprisoned it in one of the abbey vaults.

GLENROTHES, Fife

Established in 1949, this was the second of Scotland's post-war new towns (**East Kilbride** was the first). Unlike others it was not grafted onto or near an existing conurbation but located in central **Fife** to accommodate the mining community anticipated by the opening of a new **coal** seam. This never materialised. Great uncertainty resulted in the 1950s and expectations of a population of 70–95,000 by the end of the century can safely be halved. But attempts to attract other, mainly light, industries have succeeded and thanks to its low-rise and often spacious lay-outs, it compares favourably with other new towns. The architecture, mostly 1960s, includes two notable churches (St Columba's and St Paul's) and the Kingdom shopping centre, said to be one of the country's largest. Modern sculpture is also well represented, from Benno Schotz's socially responsible *Ex Terra*, to Stanley Bonnar's playground hippos. To the south-west Glenrothes has its own airfield and to the north-east it encroaches on **Markinch**.

GLENSHEE, Perthshire

Best known for its winter sports, Glenshee is a long north–south glen up which the A93 from **Blairgowrie** climbs towards the **Devil's Elbow** and Cairnwell Pass heading for Deeside. Technically the ski slopes are in Glen Beag which only becomes Glenshee at Spittal of Glenshee. This village is thought to be named after a hospice (or hospital) which here offered shelter to benighted travellers. To the east is a tumulus and stone circle known as Diarmid's Tomb, the said Diarmid being either the Fingalian hero or the supposed (wrongly) **Campbell** antecedent (but probably not both). 19th century Dalnaglar Castle is prominent below Spittal of

Glenshee; the glen ends at Bridge of Cally. **Wade** built his Blairgowrie-**Fort George** road through the glen but took visits by **Queen Victoria** and Prince Albert to popularise the route.

GLENSHIEL, Battle of (1719)

The only engagement of the 'little' **Jacobite Rising** of 1719, the Battle of Glenshiel was fought between a Jacobite force led by the 10th **Earl Marischal** and a government army under General Wightman. The Jacobite army included some 300 Spaniards sent by Cardinal Alberoni, First Minister of Philip V of Spain, ostensibly to help the Jacobite cause but in reality to divert English attention from his own designs on Italy. The Spanish contingent, originally some 5000 strong but much depleted by storms at sea, arrived in its two remaining frigates in Loch Alsh in April, where they joined the force assembled by **Cameron of Lochiel**, the **Earl of Seaforth** and **Lord George Murray**.

Their hopes of a widespread rising of Jacobites were disappointed, for news of the meagre Spanish presence had spread quickly, but they had mustered almost 1000 men. Seaforth garrisoned **Eilean Donan Castle** as a supply base and installed 50 Spaniards to guard the ammunition while the Jacobite army headed for Glenshiel on its way to the **Great Glen** and, ultimately, **Inverness**. But the government was well informed; at the beginning of June a Royal Navy squadron of three warships blasted Eilean Donan Castle to ruins from the west and General Wightman led his army from Inverness into Glenshiel from the east. The two sides were well matched for size and strength, and the fighting (10 June) lasted some hours with casualties also being about even. But lack of support from Lowland Jacobites had so depressed the morale of the Highlanders that the force was ordered to disband. The Spaniards, most of whom seem to have survived the fighting, surrendered on Marischal's advice, were held as prisoners of war and eventually repatriated.

GLENTROOL, Kirkcudbrightshire

Glentrool lies at the very heart of what was originally (1922) the **Forestry Commission**'s Glentrool Forest Park, since renamed the Galloway Forest Park, some parts of which remain 'the finest and most delectable country in the south of Scotland', while others have been remorselessly forested (7 million trees a year being planted in the 1960s); the whole is sprinkled with picnic sites, viewpoints and forest walkways. Glentrool itself was the scene of **Robert I**'s victory in April 1307 over the English under Aymer de Valence [see **Battle of Glentrool**]. Nearly 400 years later it was also the scene of the slaughter by one Captain Urquhart of Orchar of six **Covenanters**, 'surprised at their prayers and martyred on the spot' in January 1685. Their original memorial stone, thought to be the first erected by **Robert Paterson**, **Scott**'s *Old Mortality*, has been removed to **Newton Stewart** Museum and replaced by a replica.

GLENTROOL, Battle of (1307)

After a year as a fugitive from the wrath of English Edward I and those Scottish nobles who did not support his kingship, **Robert I** went to ground in **Glen Trool** (some eight miles north of present-day **Newton Stewart**). Edward sent a force under Aymer de Valence, Earl of Pembroke (who had worsted Bruce at **Methven** in June 1306), to smoke him out; but Bruce had word of their approach and ordered his men to assemble 'an armoury of boulders' on the crest of precipitous Mulldonach overlooking the glen. The rough terrain forced de Valence's men to abandon their horses and scramble on foot towards 'Bruce's lair'; three blasts from the King's bugle gave the signal, the boulders were sent hurtling down from the tops, and the invaders were swept from the steep hillside. Robert would win an even more important victory over de Valence at **Loudon Hill** a month later before heading north towards **Inverness**.

GLOMACH, Falls of, Kintail, Wester Ross

Although long regarded as the highest waterfall in Britain, the Glomach Falls are in fact exceeded by **Eas Coul Aulin** in **Sutherland**. But connoisseurs still concede that these 'Gloomy Falls' constitute 'Scotland's premier waterfall' (Louis Stott, *The Waterfalls of Scotland*); they have a greater volume, thunder into an awesome gorge, and support a suitably spine-chilling mythology. Fed by three lochans, the Allt a' Ghlomaich (Chasm River) falls about 144m before joining the river Elchaig. The main falls account for about 90m of this drop, but their cascade is broken and dramatised by a projecting buttress in mid leap. Now part of the **National Trust for Scotland**'s **Kintail** property, in wet conditions (not unusual) they remain somewhat difficult to reach and dangerous to inspect – all of which enhances their considerable reputation.

GOATS, Wild

Tribes of goats normally live on cliff faces and scree slopes though they will wander from these to feed. Their origin is obscure, but Stone Age farmers may well have brought them to Britain and there have been tribes in the hills for well over 1000 years, augmented no doubt by beasts turned loose in the 18th century by dispossessed tenant farmers. 200 years ago goats were commoner than sheep in many places and as they were kept for meat, wool and milk they were known in Scotland as the 'poor man's cow'. Unlike the cattle that had to be driven to market before the onset of winter, the goat survived on grazing and browsing. Goats browse on shrubs such as gorse and heather and will also eat leaves and shoots from trees, often standing up on their hind legs to reach a branch.

The rutting season starts in mid August with the billies rising up and crashing long swept-back horns in combat. The kids in most tribes are born in January, which can be, or can herald, the worst of the winter weather, and many die of exposure. These days the breeding tribes are isolated and there is rarely any interchange or interbreeding; this isolation tends to make the tribes vary in colour and horn shape in different areas. G Kenneth Whitehead in his book *The Wild Goats of Great Britain and Ireland* (1972) gives a gazetteer of wild goats to be found in Scotland, and lists no less than 141 sites. These range from north **Sutherland** down to the Borders, with at the top of the listings 38 sites in **Argyll**, down to one site in such places as **Nairn** and **Angus**. These lists are the only ones even to try to estimate the

Scottish population and some of the tribes have become extinct since the book was written. But if we estimate that the average tribe could be 30 individuals (some are much smaller while others number over 100) then the total population could be over 4000.

GOLF

Golf is credited by most of its devotees as a Scottish game. There is evidence that the Scots may once have had golf from the Dutch, but Scotland certainly kept the traditions and practice of the game alive and gave it to the rest of the world, including Holland, if only by re-introduction. There is also some dispute about the derivation of the name, but the most likely candidate is the Scots verb 'to gowff' meaning to cuff or strike hard. This Old Scots word may indeed have derived from the game itself.

The earliest reference to golf is probably **James II**'s decree of March 1457 that 'the futeball and golfe be utterly cryed downe and not to be used'. This and subsequent enactments banning golf were imposed to encourage archery practice and other pursuits more relevant to the national interest. It was not until 1502 that the marriage treaty of **James IV** and **Margaret Tudor** set Scots free to indulge in their national pastime. During **Stewart** times the links of **Leith** and **St Andrews** were the chief golfing centres, with the greatest activity at Leith, due to proximity to **Edinburgh**, the seat of government. The Stewart monarchs themselves, from James IV onwards, were noted as keen golfers, and when **James VI** went south to assume the English throne, he also introduced golf to England.

In times when archery was still important in war and hunting, bowmakers were also suppliers to other sports. When James IV began playing golf at **Perth** after 1502 it was to the local bowmaker that he sent orders for clubs and balls, and 100 years later in April 1603 James VI appointed the Edinburgh bowmaker William Mayne as royal club-maker for his lifetime. Although today's professional golfer has an exalted status, early professionals coached, maintained the links, carried clubs, and were also club- and ball-makers. In the middle of the 19th century Allan Robertson, the first golfer to be

'A Bad Bunker' on North Berwick Links (GWWA)

widely accepted as the best of his time, had a workshop at St Andrews where he and apprentices turned out 'feathery' balls and clubs. Whereas the development of golf-clubs has been gradual and systematic (from assorted wooden-shafted, wooden and iron-headed implements with descriptive names to present-day matched, steel-shafted, numbered sets), the design of balls has undergone distinct changes. The earliest balls were wooden and these were still widely used after 'feathery' balls were available; the latter were much more expensive, though the former split easily. The feathery ball had a three-part stitched leather skin densely packed with feathers. Making one was a skilled time-consuming and, in its latter stages, highly strenuous task when the ball-maker used a packing-ram pressed against his chest. The best ball-makers could produce only a handful a day.

In 1848 the solid gutta-percha ball was introduced. Although the 'guttie', as it was known, was cheaper, more durable and remouldable, it did not immediately replace the feathery. Allan Robertson and other club- and ball-makers were initially hostile to them, as they were to the concurrent change from golf-club shafts made of brittle woods to tougher hickory shafts, fearing loss of trade. Robertson at one stage tried to buy up all the gutta-percha balls to protect his trade. However, it transpired that the loss of revenue from feathery ball-making was more than made up by the increase in the number of players taking up the game due to the reduction in costs. Present-day balls are either of the 'wound' type invented in the US at the start of this century (incorporating a core of tensioned rubber thread), which quickly displaced the guttie as completely as it had supplanted the feathery, or else the newer solid-core type.

The modern history of golf begins with the formation of clubs in the 18th century and the presentation of a trophy for competition. The oldest golf club is the Honourable Company of Edinburgh Golfers, which played its first competition for a Silver Cup on the Links of Leith on 7 March 1744. On 14 May 1754 the example of the Leith golfers was followed by the men of St Andrews, 22 of whom met to subscribe for a Silver Club. The winner of such a trophy would become club captain for the following year, and attach a silver ball to it bearing his name and the date. The next two oldest clubs are the Edinburgh Burgess Golfing Society and the Bruntsfield Links Golf Club. The former claims to have existed since 1735, but has evidence only since 1773; it became 'royal' in 1929, and has been located at **Barnton** since 1895. The latter dates from 1761, and subsequently moved to its present location at Davidson's Mains. Both originally played over the then five or six holes of the Bruntsfield Links, and both moved to **Musselburgh** after the decline of these links. The existing Bruntsfield Links in front of the Golf Tavern has a claim to be the oldest course over which golf is still played, as locals still pitch and putt on the western end of the Edinburgh **Meadows** in front of the tavern which was used as a club house.

The foremost competition in golf is the Open Championship. The first Open Championship was held on Wednesday 17 October 1860. The death of the invincible Allan Robertson of St Andrews the previous year ad left the golf world with no recognised leading layer. Strictly speaking the very first championship was ot 'open', and the eight players who competed were ll professionals. However, on the eve of the second ontest the organisers declared that it would henceorth 'be open to all the world', and in principle this emains the case. All British Opens are played on courses nown as 'links', originally seaside common land whose urf is considered the most favourable for golf. Opens ave been played on 14 British courses. The present ota of seven venues includes the Scottish links at t Andrews, **Carnoustie** and Muirfield on the east oast, and **Troon** and **Turnberry** on the west. The two revious Scottish venues have been **Prestwick** and Musselburgh.

GOLF COURSES

THE PRESTWICK CLUB was founded in 1851 and later nitiated the Open Championship. The first 12 Open championships were played there over three rounds of he 12-hole links from 1860 until 1872. The vast Cardial Bunker at the par 5 3rd hole is faced with railway leepers, which are a distinctive feature of the Old restwick course. The competition was initially for a hallenge Belt, of red morocco, ornamented with silver lates, to become the property of any player winning three years in succession. The first Open was won by Villie Park senior, of the famous **Musselburgh** golfing amily, with 174 for 36 holes. Runner-up to Park was he local favourite, 'Old Tom' Morris from **St Andrews** who was at that time retained as professional by the restwick club. In 1870 his son 'Young **Tom**' Morris von the Belt for his third consecutive year at the age f 19 and so retained it. There was no championship 1 1871. Then the Royal and Ancient Club of St Andrews nd the Honourable Company of Edinburgh Golfers ined with Prestwick in subscribing the Silver Claret ug which became the permanent cup trophy of the pen Championship, to be played in rotation over restwick, St Andrews and Musselburgh links. Young om was the first winner of the Cup in 1872. The 24th nd last Open at Prestwick was played in 1925 when he R&A removed Prestwick, the original sponsor and enue, from the Open rota after the crowd engulfed the cottish-American MacDonald Smith, one of the Smith

brothers originally from **Carnoustie**. He had been leading and would have earned a play-off with the Cornish-American Jim Barnes with a 79, a score bettered by every other player in the final top dozen; but he had a nightmare final round of 82. Spectators were charged gate money at the 1926 Open, and as the popularity of the Open Championships has grown, the ability to accommodate spectators, both on and off the links, has increasingly influenced selection of venues.

ST ANDREWS is universally regarded as the home of golf and the game has probably been played on its links since the 12th century. The club was formed there in 1754. In 1834, while the older **Edinburgh** club was in a period of eclipse due to the decline of the **Leith** Links, the St Andrews club successfully petitioned **King William IV** to designate it 'Royal and Ancient'. The petitioners observed both that the King was also a Duke of St Andrews, and that they predated the first club to be named 'royal' in 1833 – the **Perth** Golfing Society, which had been formed in 1824. From 1897 the R&A was recognised as the rule-giving authority in all countries except the US and Mexico, where the US Golf Association controls the game. In 1919 the R&A took over responsibility for organising the Open.

The St Andrews links was originally 22 holes, 11 out and in. Of the present 18 holes, only 1, 9, 17 and 18 have their own greens. St Andrews' seven shared greens recall golf's origins as a game of outward and inward halves in which the same holes were played in each, but in different directions. The first and last holes are encompassed by the largest single expanse of fairway in golf, crossed by the Swilcan Burn, which guards the first green. The Open was first played for here in 1873 by 26 contestants, and won by the local Tom Kidd with the notably high score of 179 for the 36 holes, due to surface water on the greens. The 461 yard par 4 17th, called the Road Hole, with its green guarded by the Road Hole bunker at the front and by the road itself at the back, is usually a deciding factor. The American Tom Watson lost the 1984 Open there to Severiano Ballesteros of Spain, despite a brilliant bogey 5 recovery

'Old Tom' Morris teeing off in front of the Royal and Ancient clubhouse, St Andrews (GWWA)

after he had put his approach shot over the road up against the stone wall. Perhaps the most enduring Open golf image of St Andrews is the American Doug Sanders' missed 3ft downhill putt at the 18th in 1970, necessitating a play-off which he lost to compatriot Jack Nicklaus. As all the St Andrews courses are municipal, the R&A does not own its own course. The holding of the 119th Open there in 1990 brought St Andrews' total of Opens to 24, equalling that of Prestwick, the original venue.

THE MUSSELBURGH golf club came into being in 1774 with the presentation of a Cup for competition, although golf may have been played on the little links for two or three hundred years. In the mid-19th century Musselburgh was the focus of Scottish golf, being simultaneously the base for the Honourable Company of Edinburgh Golfers, the Royal Burgess Club, the Bruntsfield Links club, and the Royal Musselburgh club. The town was the centre of golf-ball and club manufacturing, and it was there that a tool to cut the standard 4¼ hole was introduced in 1829. An Open was first played there in 1874 and won by Mungo Park (no relation to the explorer). Musselburgh hosted the Open six times, until in 1891 the Honourable Company moved to Muirfield and took the competition with them. The 'Honest Toun', as Musselburgh is called, was both slighted and commercially threatened by the removal of the Open to Muirfield in 1892, when it should have rotated to Musselburgh. Local professional Willie Park junior, who had won the last Open held at Musselburgh in 1889, and in 1887 at Prestwick, stirred up the citizens to promote a championship of their own and collected £100 in prize money. The total prize money at the 1891 Open had been less than £30 and the championship was not so firmly established as to be proof against any such competition. So the Honourable Company raised the Open prize money to £110, and the Musselburgh faction delayed its tournament until after the Muirfield Open. The Open never returned to Musselburgh, but the contest to host the 1892 Open was a milestone in increasing the amount of prize money competed for by professional golfers. The original Musselburgh course was, and still is, only nine holes, and should be more revered, considering its historical significance. One of its opening holes is called the Graves, because the dead Scottish soldiers from the **Battle of Pinkie** of 1547 were buried there. The Musselburgh club was accorded royal status in 1876 and now has its own 18-hole course at Prestongrange, laid out by **James Braid** and opened in 1926.

MUIRFIELD is the present home of the Honourable Company of Edinburgh Golfers, the world's oldest golf club, which originally played over Leith Links, then Musselburgh from 1836–91, and which devised the first set of rules in 1744 for the competition for its Silver Club. Although the R&A presently has the function of lawgiver in golf, originally the St Andrews club simply adopted the Edinburgh club's rules. The parchment on which these original 'thirteen rules of golf' were drafted is in the Honourable Company's archives, with a copy hanging in the Muirfield clubhouse. The Honourable Company has traditionally never employed the service of a club professional. The course has a modern layout as two concentric loops of nine holes, making it an ideally accessible course for the spectator. Muirfield has been the venue for 11 Open championships, the first in 1892, the first time the championship was played over 72 holes; it was won by the great Liverpool amateur Harold Hilton. In 1896 Harry Vardon won the first of his record six Open titles after a play-off with J H Taylor. Here too James Braid won his first Open in 1901, and his third in 1906. The American Walter Hagen won his third Open in 1929, driving far out to the right at the 8th for a short cut to the green. Afterwards trees were planted to close that route. The Englishman Henry Cotton won his third Open in 1948 after King George VI wished him luck on the first tee. The South African Gary Player and Jack Nicklaus won their first British Opens in 1959 and 1966 and in the 1972 Open the American Lee Trevino demoralised English Tony Jacklin by holing a series of chips to regain the title, notably at the long 17th where he holed from the back of the green as Jacklin three-putted. Nick Faldo of England won his first Open here in 1987. Muirfield again hosted the Open in 1992.

TROON More golf is probably played in Troon than in any other town in Scotland. Of its five adjoining courses three are public. The original course was laid out in 1878 with five holes, then extended to 12 holes in 1883, and by 1886 to its 18-hole, counter-clockwise layout. The championship course is known as Old Troon, and virtually adjoins the original Old Prestwick venue. Indeed socialising members used to play a morning round outward for nine holes on one of the courses and an inward nine on the other, have lunch at the destination clubhouse, then travel back with an afternoon round. The Open was first played there in 1923, while Muirfield was undergoing reconstruction work. Englishman Arthur Havers holed a bunker shot at the last hole to win from American Walter Hagen, the holder and subsequent year's winner. Ironically the American found the same bunker with his second shot but narrowly missed his own bunker shot to tie. Old Troon has both the longest and the shortest holes of the Open rota. The 6th is 577yds long and is where in 1982 American Bobby Clampett came to grief, carding an 8, having been leading by five strokes after 36 holes, leaving Tom Watson to claim the title. The notoriously difficult 126yd 8th hole, called the Postage Stamp, is where the 71-year-old American Gene Sarazen holed in one in the 1973 Open, having been an Open winner in 1932. Bobby Locke of South Africa won Troon's second Open in 1950. American Arnold Palmer won his second consecutive Open there in 1962. In the same year, Jack Nicklaus played his first Open and carded a 10 at the difficult 11th hole which runs alongside the railway line, to start with a round of 80. The Troon club became the Royal Troon in the centenary year of 1978, the most recent of the Royal clubs and the only one to have been so honoured by Queen Elizabeth II. The motto of the club – '*Tam Arte Quam Marte*' (more by skill than effort) – concisely sums up sound golfing technique.

CARNOUSTIE The first record of golf at Carnoustie dates to 1650. The first club was formed there in 1842. The course was originally of 10 holes, laid out by Allan Robertson, extended to 18 by 'Old Tom' Morris, and improved by James Braid in 1926 with some new greens, tees and bunkers, and has remained basically unchanged since. Carnoustie was the major contributor to an exodus of notable Scottish players who emigrated to the US to capitalise on the early American golfing boom and found success as professionals, coaches and course designers, most prominently the Smith brothers, Alex, Willie and Macdonald. The first Open to be played here was in 1931; it was won by Edinburgh-born Tommy Armour, who had emigrated to the US in the early 1920s. The Barry Burn winds its way across the fairways, making for a particularly challenging finish, and giving the difficult 432yd 17th its name of Island.

Carnoustie was the scene of the great Ben Hogan's only attempt on the British Open in 1953, the year he also won the US Open and the US Masters. Miraculously restored to fitness after a road accident which was generally thought to have ended his playing career, the serious-minded, unemotional Texan was dubbed the 'wee ice mon' by the Scottish gallery as he methodically assembled a course record 282 (73, 71, 70, 68) to win his Open by four strokes, having improved his score in each successive round. His victory gripped the public imagination, and when the Hogan story was later immortalised in the full-length film Follow the Sun, an important milestone had been marked in the popularisation of the game which was shortly to be accelerated by his compatriot Arnold Palmer. In 1999 Carnoustie staged the Open (won by Scotsman Paul Lawrie) for the first time since 1975, when the American Tom Watson took the first of his five Championship titles. The remaining two of Carnoustie's six Opens were in 1937 (won by Henry Cotton) and 1968 (won by Gary Player).

TURNBERRY was the first purpose-built golf resort, constructed by the Glasgow and South-Western Railway, including a first-class hotel and rail links south to Girvan and north to Ayr and Glasgow. The Turnberry club was founded in 1902. The original course was designed by Willie Fernie, winner of the 1883 Open at Musselburgh, where he edged local Bob Ferguson out of a fourth consecutive win, holing for an eagle 2 on the final hole of a play-off. His scorecard included a 10, the only time an Open winner has been in double figures. Fernie was St Andrews born, but most closely associated with the west coast club at Troon where he was professional for nearly 37 years from 1887 to 1924. By 1907 it was a recognised golfing centre. The two Turnberry courses are named Ailsa and Arran, after Ailsa Craig and the island of Arran. There is a local saying that if you can see Ailsa Craig it's about to rain, and if you can't it's raining.

Turnberry was requisitioned during both world wars. The first occasion had little impact on the courses, but after the construction of an aerodrome in World War II most of the Ailsa course was returfed. Turnberry is the only one of the Open links where the sea actually comes into play, at the par 4 9th with its tee beside the ruins of Bruce's Castle and a lighthouse. The first Open played there was in 1977 on the Ailsa course, replacing Carnoustie on the rota, and witnessing the remarkable duel betweeen Jack Nicklaus and Tom Watson, won by the latter by a stroke. Runner-up Nicklaus had matched Watson for each of the first three rounds, and his final score was 10 strokes better than the third-placed golfer. In Turnberry's second Open in 1986, Greg Norman's winning total of 280 in wind and rain was 12 strokes worse than Watson's 1977 score, despite including a round of 63.

GOLSPIE, Sutherland

This village on the east-coast road, about midway between Inverness and Wick, was endowed in 1808 with the first coaching inn in Sutherland, now the Sutherland Arms Hotel. It also owed its growth to the proximity of Dunrobin Castle. Here the Duchess Millicent, wife of the 4th Duke, established the technical college which John Mackay, the civil engineer from Strathnaver, endowed with a bursary.

GORDON, Alexander, 3rd Earl of Huntly (d.1524)

It was during the reign of James IV that the power of the Gordons of Huntly grew and spread in the north. Unable to supply sufficient royal troops to restore and maintain order in the Highlands and Islands, James was forced to rely on local magnates, in particular Colin Campbell, 1st Earl of Argyll and Alexander Gordon, 3rd Earl of Huntly, to do so on his behalf. Rewarded for his efforts with the governorship of Inverness Castle (1509), Huntly was thus in a position to feather the Gordon nest (seizing among other things the Earldom of Sutherland for his brother Adam Gordon) in the name of the stability of the nation. In joint command with Lord Home of the Scots vanguard at Flodden (1513), he survived the battle, supported the appointment of John Stewart, 4th Duke of Albany as Governor in the minority of James V and was a member of the commission of regency during Albany's absence in France (1517).

GORDON, Elizabeth, Countess of Sutherland (1766–1839)

Countess in her own right [see Earldom of Sutherland], Elizabeth Gordon was already a very rich heiress when she married (1785) George Leveson-Gower, Marquess of Stafford. His vast English estates joined to her vast Scottish holdings made them the largest landowners in Britain. In 1807 they embarked on a policy of agricultural improvement in Sutherland which, planned by James Loch and implemented by Patrick Sellar, resulted in the dreadful Sutherland clearances. 'Between five and ten thousand people' (T C Smout) were evicted, some forcibly, between 1807–21. The estate was notorious for the poverty of its tenants before they started and the Staffords spent lavishly on roads, bridges, harbours and even poor relief. But it was the horrors of eviction that remained in folk memory and which scandalised even the likes of David Stewart of Garth. Stafford was created Duke of Sutherland in 1833, the year of his death.

GORDON, George, 4th Earl of Huntly (1514–62)

Childhood companion of **James V**, George Gordon inherited the earldom and vast estates of his grandfather, **3rd Earl**, in 1524. As commander of James's army he defeated the English at the **Battle of Hadden Rig** (1542), was a member of the council of Regency under **Arran** and **Beaton** and succeeded as Chancellor on the murder of Beaton (1546). Captured at **Pinkie** (1547) he escaped and later accompanied **Mary of Guise** to France (1550) but unlike others was not wooed into supporting the French cause. After some hesitation he joined the **Lords of the Congregation** (1560) and was prepared to accept **Queen Mary** until she transferred the **Earldom of Moray**, which had been given to Huntly in 1549, to her half-brother **Lord James Stewart** (1562), whereupon Huntly withdrew in a rage to his estates. Distrustful of Gordon power, the Queen toured the north-east in August 1562. The Gordon captain of **Inverness** Castle refused her entry without Huntly's permission; Mary's forces captured the castle, hanged the captain and made for **Aberdeen** where the Queen issued a summons to Huntly. When he refused to answer it he was outlawed, which enraged him further; he marched on Aberdeen but was defeated by Lord James Stewart at **Corrichie** (October 1562). Huntly himself died of apoplexy after capture; his son Sir John was executed in Aberdeen, and Huntly was posthumously forfeited by parliament in May 1563.

GORDON, George, 5th Earl of Huntly (d.1576)

Second son of **George Gordon, 4th Earl**, and Sheriff of **Inverness** from 1556–62, George, 5th Earl was imprisoned at **Dunbar** after the battle of **Corrichie**, but was released and restored to the Huntly title and estates by **Queen Mary** on her marriage to **Darnley** and fought at her side in the **Chaseabout Raid** against **James Stewart, Earl of Moray**. He joined Mary at Dunbar after the murder of **Rizzio** and, on her return to **Edinburgh**, became a member of her council and (1566–7) Chancellor. He was a party to, but did not actually take part in, Darnley's murder and, despite the fact that **Bothwell**'s first wife was his sister Jean, he favoured Mary's marriage to Bothwell. He continued to support the Queen's party after her flight to England, but eventually yielded to the *force majeure* and came to terms with Moray (1569).

GORDON, George, 6th Earl & 1st Marquis of Huntly (1562–1636)

Son of **George, 5th Earl of Huntly**, and leader of the northern Catholics, George, 6th Earl was fortunate in his relations with **James VI**. Early favoured by the King for his 'courtlyness', and further advancing his cause by marrying (1588) the daughter of James's favourite **Esmé Stewart**, Huntly benefited from the King's reluctance to antagonise his Catholic subjects. In 1589 Huntly was implicated in a conspiracy with Spanish Catholics; James merely dismissed him as captain of the guard and imprisoned him briefly in **Edinburgh Castle**. The same year he raised a rebellion with the Earl of Crawford; James seemed content with an apology; and in 1592 forgave him after his savage murder of the 'Bonny Earl'

of Moray. Not until Huntly and Errol raised a rebellio in 1594 [see **Battle of Glenlivet**] was James moved a strong response; he bombarded **Huntly Castle** an Huntly fled abroad. He returned, apparently chastene in 1596, submitted to the King and offered to prov his loyalty by 'extirpating the barbarous peoples of th Isles'; though he failed to achieve this, the appreciativ King created him Marquis (1599).

GORDON, George, 2nd Marquis & 7th Earl of Huntly (1592–1649) Royalist

In the Civil War period 'if the house of **Hamilton** wa indecisive, the house of Huntly was wayward' (R Mitch ison). The 2nd Marquis, although suspected of the Cath olic sympathies shown by his parents, adhered to th **Episcopalian** cause during the first Bishops' War [se **Charles I**], and collaborated with Charles I and **Jame 1st Duke of Hamilton** in attempting to drive the **Cov enanters** from the north of Scotland. **Montrose** persuaded him to sign a modified form of the **Covenan** Subsequently he and his son, granted a safe conduct t **Edinburgh**, were imprisoned in the **Castle**, a betray for which Huntly never forgave Montrose.

In March 1644, incited by Sir John Gordon of **Hadd** Huntly rose for the Royalists but was defeated by hi brother-in-law the **8th Earl** (later Marquis) **of Argyl** In the same year he was given the Lieutenancy of th North and excommunicated by the Edinburgh Kirk.

Huntly's sons, though influenced by Argyll to be Cov enanters, fought in the Royalist army of Montrose a the **Battle of Alford** in July 1645. Huntly thereafte refused to co-operate with Montrose but was nonethe less attainted as a Royalist and executed.

GORDON, George Hamilton, 4th Earl of Aberdeen (1784–1860) Prime Minister

Orphaned by the death of his father, Lord Haddo, i 1791 and of his mother, a sister of **General Davi Baird**, in 1795, Gordon attended Harrow and Cam bridge with William Pitt and **Henry Dundas** as his guar dians. In 1801 he succeeded his grandfather as Earl o **Aberdeen** and, after a spell in Greece, 'the travell' thane, Athenian Aberdeen' (**Byron**) was elected a Sco representative peer in the Lords. On diplomatic assign ments leading to the 1815 Treaty of Paris he showe negotiating skills and commendable judgement, bu then returned to his Haddo estate where improvement included his planting of 14 million trees. He was Presi dent of the **Society of Antiquaries** from 1812–46 an tried unsuccessfully to avert the 1843 **Disruption** i the **Church of Scotland**.

Meanwhile he had returned to Westminster politic as Foreign Secretary (1828–30) under the Duke o Wellington and Secretary for War and the Colonie (1834–5) under Robert Peel. He served again unde Peel as Foreign Secretary (1841–6) and won a repu tation for conciliation and non-interference. Thoug described as grave, fastidious, and an uninspirin speaker, in 1853 he was a popular choice as the hea of a coalition ministry which included Gladstone an Palmerston. But the drift towards war in the Crimea and its subsequent conduct, exposed his pacifist repu tation and in 1857 he resigned. He had assumed th name of Hamilton out of respect for the father o

George Hamilton Gordon, 4th Earl of Aberdeen, by Sir Martin Archer Shee, c1838 (SNPG)

his first wife, John Hamilton, Marquis of Abercorn, and his surname thus sometimes appears as the hyphenated Hamilton-Gordon. The 5th Earl of Aberdeen, though one of his sons by his second wife, followed suit.

GORDON, Harry (1893–1954) Entertainer
Renowned for his couthy north-east Scottish humour and quickfire gags, Harry Alexander Ross Gordon from **Aberdeen** was billed as 'The Laird o' Inversnecky'. He produced the Harry Gordon Entertainers at Aberdeen Beach Pavilion from 1924–40, a record, and had a consecutive run of 11 years in pantomime at the **Alhambra**, **Glasgow**, seven of them starring with **Will Fyffe**, where his speciality was playing the pantomime 'dame'. His wife Jose was also an entertainer and played the Principal Boy in pantomime. He had great success as a radio broadcaster in Scotland, and was preparing yet another pantomime at the **Theatre Royal**, Glasgow when he died at the age of 61.

GORDON, John Campbell, 7th Earl of Aberdeen, 1st Marquis of Aberdeen and Temair (1847–1934)
The youngest son of the 5th Earl of Aberdeen, and so grandson of **George Gordon, 4th Earl**, attended **St Andrews** and Oxford universities. He unexpectedly succeeded to the title when his father died and was quickly followed by both his elder brothers; one fell in a shooting accident and the other was presumed lost overboard when serving incognito in the American merchant navy. With strong religious views and an active social conscience, both more than matched by those of his formidable wife (Ishbel Maria Marjoribanks, m.1877), the Earl espoused Liberalism and together 'We Twa' (as they cloyingly dubbed themselves in two

volumes of memoirs) embarked on a bustling career of high office and good deeds.

In 1893 the Earl was appointed Governor-General of Canada where Lady Aberdeen founded the Victorian Order of Nurses and laboured for the Red Cross and the National Council of Women. Briefly Lord Lieutenant of Ireland in 1886, Aberdeen returned to that post in 1906 and remained there for an unprecedented nine years, winning widespread affection while his wife fostered cottage industries and campaigned against tuberculosis. Their combined energies were also lavished on **Haddo** where the house was extended and filled with their memorabilia and the grounds graced with a Canadian log cabin. Here and at House of Cromar, His Lordship's Deeside estate, he built over 500 houses for his tenantry while Her Ladyship founded the Onward and Upward Association for their educational improvement. Both paragons were showered with honours including the Earl's promotion to Marquis on his return from Ireland.

GORDON, Sir John Watson (1788–1864)
Painter
A fashionable **Edinburgh** portraitist, Watson Gordon was the follower and pupil of **Raeburn**, although he never possessed the flair and brio of his master. Born in Edinburgh, the son of a Royal Navy captain, he initially trained as an engineer, but forsook this after meeting **Wilkie** at drawing classes at Edinburgh's **Trustees' Academy**. Unlike many Scottish artists he was not discouraged in his choice of career by his family, indeed his uncle, a painter of slight talent, took pains to introduce him to Raeburn, then at the height of his career.

Watson Gordon flirted briefly with history painting (then deemed the noblest branch of art) but soon devoted himself entirely to the more lucrative field of portraiture, encouraged by Raeburn's success and reputation. After the latter's death in 1823 he became the pre-eminent Scottish portraitist. His brushwork was far tighter than Raeburn's although he shared some of the bravado technique of his English counterpart, Sir Thomas Lawrence, whom he greatly admired. Gordon, too, favoured attention to crisp details, enlivened with silvery highlights, a legacy of his admiration for Velasquez. He enjoyed a wide patronage and as well as painting many of the Scottish aristocracy, had many sitters from the literary world, including **Sir Walter Scott** and **James Hogg**. He had a considerable patronage in London and was elected to the Royal Academy in 1851. He was President of the **Royal Scottish Academy** from 1850 and appointed Her Majesty's Limner for Scotland the same year.

GORDON, Patrick (1635–99) Soldier
Born near **Ellon** in **Aberdeenshire** into a Catholic family, Patrick was sent to the Jesuit college at Braunsberg at the age of 16 but ran away to become a mercenary soldier. He fought on alternate sides in the Swedish war against the Poles (1653–61), being repeatedly captured and fighting for his captors until he was recaptured by the other side. In 1661 he joined the Russian army, rose to the rank of lieutenant-general and became Governor of Kiev and a personal friend of Tsar Peter the Great. He died and was buried in Moscow.

His diary, published by the Spalding Club, **Aberdeen** (1859), is an important source for Scottish mercenaries in the Russian service.

GORDON, Robert, of Straloch (1580–1661)
Cartographer

Born at Straloch near **Inverurie, Aberdeenshire**, Robert Gordon had the distinction of being the first graduate of **Aberdeen**'s **Marischal College** but is chiefly remembered for having rescued Thomas Pont's original maps (1640) and completing them for the Scottish section of Blaeu's *Atlas*. His son John (c1615–86), minister of Rothiemay, published surveys and maps of **Edinburgh** and Aberdeen and wrote a *History of Scots Affairs*. His grandson, also Robert Gordon (1665–1732) made a fortune as a Danzig merchant and was the founder of Aberdeen's **Robert Gordon's College**.

GORDON, Seton Paul (1886–1977)
Naturalist and Writer

Seton Gordon's father was town clerk of **Aberdeen**, but it was at the family's holiday home in **Aboyne** that he was largely brought up. An only child, he scoured the hills and was already a knowledgeable ornithologist and the author of *Birds of the Loch and Mountain* (1907) when he attended **Aberdeen University** (briefly) and then Oxford (1908) to read Natural Sciences. There his unusual accomplishments (including playing **golf** for the University) and influential friendships, eg with the Prince of Wales, were no less noted than his **kilted** appearance; he is said to have worn 'the kilt and only the kilt' from childhood. An exception was made when he donned the uniform of the RNVR (after two more books and a course in **forestry**) for wartime service as organiser of coastal surveillance in the west Highlands. In 1915 he married Aubrey Pease, also a naturalist. Moving from **Oban** to **Aviemore** and the **Hebrides** they eventually settled at Kilmuir on **Skye**'s Trotternish peninsula. Field trips alternated with lecture tours; regular attendance at the several **Highland Games** punctuated the summer; the passing of the years was marked by the accumulation of big-name friendships (Grey of Falloden, **Ramsay MacDonald** and the future George VI) and a succession of successful books (eg *Wanderings of a Naturalist*, 1921, *The Immortal Isle*, 1926, *Days with the Golden Eagle*, 1927). With strong views on **piobaireachd** and **Jacobite** history, Seton Gordon became the epitome of the Highland gentleman as well as the unquestioned authority on Highland wildlife and topography (eg *Highways and Byways in the West Highlands*, 1935). Eight years watching a single eyrie produced *The Golden Eagle, King of Birds*, 1956. The compliment was returned when Raymond Eagle, an Anglo-Canadian, published a Gordon biography, *The Life and Times of a Highland Gentleman*, 1991.

GORDON FAMILY

Gordons have been involved in Scottish history for so long that they are now perceived as a Highland clan; but it is believed that the first Gordons came from Gourdon, in Quercy, France. Earliest records indicate that they settled in **Berwickshire** in the 11th century, where the lands of Gordon near the lower **Tweed** were granted to Adam, 1st of that Ilk, for his support of **Malcolm**

Canmore. Together with French, Norman and English knights, Adam defeated **MacBeth** at **Lumphanan, Aberdeenshire**, in 1057. He later accompanied Malcolm (1093) on his unsuccessful invasion of England when both died. Scotland's struggle for independence caused the Lords of Strathbogie to forfeit their lands two centuries later and the lands of the north-east were given to Sir Adam Gordon 8th who settled at the Bog of Gight, now **Gordon Castle, Fochabers**.

In 1405 a fortunate marriage between Elizabeth Gordon and Alexander Seton brought the lands of Strathbogie together with the Seton's Berwickshire domain as well as **Aboyne**, Glenmuick and Glentanar from a Cluny connection. Elizabeth's uncle 'Old Sir John' was the first Gordon to control Strathbogie from **Huntly**, and his sons, Jock of Scurdargue and Tam of **Ruthven**, were progenitors of all the other Gordon families in the north-east whose descent is traceable from that time. Galloway Gordons descended from Adam 8th Chief.

Throughout the 15th and 16th centuries the Gordons hold on power increased dramatically and the Chief, the Marquis of Huntly, became known as the 'Cock o' the North'. For three centuries they retained their authority north of the **Tay** and were largely unaffected by political and religious strife. The Forbes family provided the main threat to their local supremacy, and a strategic struggle between the two families lasted 200 years, giving rise to the phrase 'Gey Gordons' – which means 'overwhelming' with a sense of hostility.

Gordons were ruthless and uncompromising opponents, but intensely loyal to their supporters. Among the notable characters in history is **George** 'Young Lochinvar', a Galloway Gordon and the **4th Earl** whose historic refusal to leave the stricken field of **Corrichie** gave rise to the Chief's family motto: 'Bydand' (biding, staying on). Loyalty to **Charles I** caused both the **2nd Marquis of Huntly** and Sir John Gordon of **Haddo** to be beheaded and later the **Jacobites** had a firm supporter in Gordon of **Glenbuchat**, a mercenary soldier of genius who remains a neglected hero. In the 18th century Alexander, 4th Duke, and his Duchess, the incomparable Jane Maxwell, 'Flower of Galloway', enlivened contemporary political and military circles and were closely associated with the raising of the **Gordon Highlanders Regiment**. The Haddo branch produced a Prime Minister (1852–5) in **George Hamilton Gordon, 4th Earl of Aberdeen**, and from Gight came the poet George Gordon, **Lord Byron**. Two major military heroes were **General Patrick Gordon of Auchleuchries**, Commander of the Armies of Peter the Great of Russia, and General Charles George Gordon of Khartoum.

The rapid expansion of the Gordons in Scotland differs from that of clans which remained in their original Highland homelands, and explains why the Gordons belong to a house rather than a **clan**.

GORDON HIGHLANDERS, The, Regiment

The regiment dates from the 1881 amalgamation of the 75th Stirlingshire Regiment and the 92nd Gordon Highlanders. The 75th Highlanders were raised in 1787 by Colonel Robert Abercromby of Tullibody for service in India, where they early saw much action; they went on to serve in South Africa, the Indian Mutiny, Egypt

d on the North-West Frontier. In 1809 they lost the
ilt and their Highland identity but the title 'Stir-
ngshire' was introduced in 1862. The 92nd were
ised as the 100th Highlanders by the Duke of Gordon
i 1794, being renumbered 92nd in 1798. Their early
rvice included the Low Countries and Egypt, followed
y Corunna, the Peninsula, Waterloo, Afghanistan and
uth Africa.

The Gordons raised 21 battalions in World War I,
rving on the Western Front and in Italy and winning
5 battle honours. A further 27 were added in World
Var II when the battalion served in France in 1940, in
Ialaya, North Africa, Sicily, Italy and north-west
rope. This brought the total of battle honours to 111.
nce the end of the war the Gordons have seen active
rvice in Malaya and Northern Ireland.

The original **tartan** of the 75th is not certain but it
ay have been akin to what is now known as 'Campbell
f Breadalbane'. The 92nd has always worn the famous
overnment Sett with a yellow stripe, known as the
Jordon' and worn as a **clan** tartan by those of that
ame. On amalgamation the 75th adopted the uniform
f the 92nd and in it stormed the Heights of Dargai. A
lack worm is worn in the gold lace and the spat buttons
re black in memory of **General Sir Ralph Abercromby**
vho fell at Alexandria in 1801. The regiment marches
ast to 'Cock o' the North' in quick time (pipes and
and) and to 'St Andrew's Cross' (pipes) and 'The Garb
f Old Gaul' (band) in slow time. The regiment recruits
om **Aberdeenshire** and the Regimental Headquarters
re in **Aberdeen**. HRH The Prince of Wales is Colonel-
-Chief.

In 1994 the Regiment was amalgamated with the
ueen's Own Highlanders to form The Highlanders
Seaforth Gordon & Cameron).

iORDON-CUMMING, Constance
1837–1924) Travel Writer

orn into a wealthy family at Altyre, **Moray**, Constance
avelled to India at the age of 31 to visit her sister –
n invitation she nearly turned down on the grounds
at surely no one went to India unless they had to. In
e event she had the time of her life and the book she
rote about her two-year stay was a runaway success.
ncouraged to produce more of the same, she sub-
equently travelled, in some style, to Ceylon, China,
apan, Fiji, Tahiti and America, writing a gossipy, enter-
aining book on each country. Her elder brother Roua-
eyn (1820–66) started out as a soldier but became
nown as 'the British lion hunter' from his book *Five
ears of a Hunter's Life in the Far Interior of South Africa* (1850).

iORDONSTOUN, Nr Elgin, Moray

ive miles north of **Elgin** and a mile from **Duffus Castle**,
Jordonstoun House was built (1616) and so named
ollowing the acquisition by the **Gordon Marquis of
Iuntly** of Bog of Plewlands (an Ogstoun then Innes
roperty, most unsuitably named for a Marquis, let
lone a royally patronised boarding school). It com-
rised a central tower flanked by three-storey wings,
ach with angle turrets and hipped roof (instead of the
sual gables). The wings remain but the tower was
eplaced by an oblong block with balustraded roof in
he 18th century. Further additions were made by vari-

ous Sir Robert Gordons, one of whom (d.1709)
exhibited the eccentricities of an inventor and was
dubbed 'The Warlock' or wizard, another of whom
('the Bad Sir Robert') dabbled in smuggling and has a
cave near Covesea named after him. On the latter's death
the house passed to the Gordon-Cummings and in 1934
was acquired as premises for a fee-paying school to
be run in accordance with the community-serving and
character-building principles enunciated by Dr Kurt
Hahn. Royal patronage (ex-pupils include Prince Philip,
the Prince of Wales, Princes Andrew and Edward)
assured its success and there are now extensive ancilliary
buildings.

GOUROCK, Renfrewshire

Although **Port Glasgow**, **Greenock** and Gourock form
a continuous ribbon development along the south bank
of the **Clyde**, there is a marked change of character just
west of Greenock. Quite suddenly the deadly combination of high density housing and industrial wasteland
gives way to seaside bungalows and guest houses.
Instead of derelict shipyards, Gourock has jaunty
marinas and a busy pier whence ferries sail to **Dunoon**
and other points north. The Gourock ropeworks once
provided serious employment but moved to Port Glasgow in the 19th century. Instead the town grew on its
reputation for bracing sea-bathing and other marine
activities. Here **Walter Gibson** pioneered the curing of
'red herrings', later known as kippers, and here, where
the Firth of Clyde opens out with a great bend to the
south, shipping was at its greatest risk. In 1822 the
Catherine of Iona collided with a steamer and sank, 42 out
of 44 being drowned, and in 1825 the *Comet* (not **Henry
Bell**'s vessel) went down after a similar collision; about
60 drowned. The (Granny) Kempock stone, a much
worn monolith of unknown origin, was reputed to offer
some protection against such accidents, various pro-
pitiatory rites being practised by those, like fishermen
and newlyweds, embarking on a high-risk venture. For
having, amongst other enormities, made a pact with
the devil to cast a stone into the sea, Mary Lamont was
burnt for witchcraft in 1662 along with other 'Inverkip
witches'.

West, towards Inverkip, the Cloch Lighthouse with
keepers' cottages (1795–7, Thomas Smith and **Robert
Stevenson**) has also witnessed numerous maritime col-
lisions. Ardgowan House (c1800), a classical mansion
with bowed west front, has been called 'the finest
country house in **Renfrewshire**', while Castle Levan,
inland, is L-plan, one wing late 14th/early 15th century.
It was once a **Morton** stronghold but later passed to
the Shaw-Stewarts who built Ardgowan.

GOVERNMENT AND ADMINISTRATION

The government of Scotland underwent more radical
change in the last 27 years of the 20th century than it
had in the previous 270 years. Two major reorganisations (1975, 1995) of **local government**, UK
membership (1973) of what became the European
Union, and the re-establishment (1998) of a **Scottish
Parliament** with its own executive transformed the
structures of government and resulted in a significant
shuffling of responsibilities. The genesis, composition
and role of the **Parliament** are described under that

heading, while its inauguration and location are noted in the sub-entry 'Scottish Parliament' in the Edinburgh entry. Local government is also the subject of a separate entry.

Notwithstanding all these changes, Scotland remains an integral part of the United Kingdom whose sovereignty is invested in Her Majesty's Government at Westminster. Until 1603, Scotland was a sovereign state with both monarch and Parliament, but in that year the Scottish King, **James VI**, acceded to the throne of England (as James I), creating a **Union of the Crowns**. In 1707 the two countries were joined more closely by the decision of the Scots Parliament to join with its larger English counterpart in forming a new British Parliament, thus creating a long-standing unitary government system. At first, Scotland was allowed 45 representatives in the new House of Commons (to 513 English members), and this subsequently rose to 72, an over-representation compared to England which is likely to be eroded under the terms of the Scotland Act of 1998 which set up the Scottish Parliament.

Under the **1707 Act of Union**, Scotland continued to operate its own recognised Church and **legal system**, while provision was made for the continuation of the office of Secretary of State for Scotland and the Scottish Privy Council. However, both these Scottish institutions soon became moribund, victims of party manoeuvrings at Westminster and the rise to power of the **Dukes of Argyll** before the middle of the 18th century and the **Dundas** family at its end. In the first 40 years after Union, the post of Scottish Secretary was held successively by four incumbents – the **Duke of Queensberry**, the·**Earl of Mar**, the **Duke of Roxburghe** and the **Marquis of Tweeddale**, with the post vacant for a total of 17 of those years. With the Secretaryship moribund, **Henry Dundas** (1742–1811) – Scotland's 'uncrowned king' – became William Pitt's principal ministerial colleague at the time of the Napoleonic Wars, being succeeded by his son, the **2nd Viscount Melville**.

In the 19th century it became increasingly obvious that more Scottish scrutiny of such matters as poor relief, **prisons**, public health and the **fishing industry**, was required, and a framework of Boards gradually grew up under the aegis of the Home Secretary, advised by Scotland's then principal minister, the Lord Advocate [see **Legal Terms**]. A major development occurred in 1872 when a Scottish **Education** Department was set up to supervise the nation's schools, hitherto the responsibility of the **Church of Scotland** (and regarded as being well in advance of England's). This new department originally came under an English Minister, but the trend was inevitably towards the setting up of a co-ordinating post to bring these Scottish threads of government together, and in 1885 the position of Secretary for Scotland was revived. Those holding the post over the next 115 years, including incumbents after 1926 when the office was upgraded to Secretary of State, are listed below.

1885	Duke of Richmond
1886	G O Trevelyan
1886	**Earl of Dalhousie**
1886	**Arthur J Balfour**
1887	Marquis of Lothian
1892	Sir G O Trevelyan
1895	**Alexander Bruce** (Lord Balfour of Burleigh
1903	**Andrew Murray**
1905	**Marquis of Linlithgow**
1905	John Sinclair (Baron Pentland)
1912	T P Mackinnon Wood
1916	Harold John Tennant
1916	Robert Munro (Lord Alness)
1922	Viscount Novar
1924	William Adamson
1924	Sir John Gilmour
1929	William Adamson
1931	Sir Archibald Sinclair
1932	Sir Godfrey Collins
1936	**Walter Elliot**
1938	D J Colville
1940	Ernest Brown
1941	**Thomas Johnston**
1945	Earl of Rosebery
1945	Joseph Westwood
1947	Arthur Woodburn
1950	Hector MacNeil
1951	James Stuart
1957	John S Maclay
1962	Michael Noble
1964	William Ross
1970	Gordon Campbell
1974	William Ross
1976	Bruce Millan
1979	George Younger
1986	Malcolm Rifkind
1990	Ian Lang
1995	Michael Forsythe
1997	Donald Dewar
1999	Helen Liddell (acting)
1999	John Reid (Scottish Secretary)

Six Scottish Secretaries have held their position for a exceptional period. First of these was the Marquis o Lothian who was in office from 1887–92, at a tim when the 1889 Local Government (Scotland) Act for mally set up county councils and when Scotland's uni versities were reformed. John Sinclair (Baron Pentland was a Liberal politician who held the secretaryship fo seven years from 1905 after an army career. Rober Munro (Lord Alness) was Secretary from 1916–22, late being appointed Lord President.

In more recent times Thomas Johnston is agreed t have been one of the most successful incumbents. Hav ing been appointed a Regional Commissioner at th outset of World War II, he became Secretary of Stat in 1941, showing considerable expertise in working i cross-party partnerships to achieve results, including th setting up of the North of Scotland **Hydro-Electri** Board, whose first head he later became. Willie Ros (later Lord Marnock) was well capable of fighting Scot land's corner in Cabinet, and held the post for tw separate periods under Harold Wilson, who named hi the 'Basso Profondo' of Scottish politics.

George Younger presided at St Andrew's House fo nearly seven years, protecting Scotland from some o the more extreme effects of monetarist ideology, an progressing in 1986 to what was seen as a more impor tant Cabinet post (Defence). Usually the position o secretary of State for Scotland is regarded, in Westminster at least, as a political graveyard.

As in England and Wales, the democratisation of Scottish politics proceeded with the five Reform Acts of 1832, 1867, 1884–5, 1918 and 1928, bringing universal suffrage to Scotland with the same exceptions as south of the border. One of the provisions of the first three of these Acts was the increase in the number of Scotland's parliamentary seats at Westminster, gradually growing to the present 72 (although it reached 74 for a time after the 1928 Act).

Eight Scottish Members are additionally returned to the European Parliament in Strasbourg. The constituencies are **Glasgow**, **Strathclyde** (East) and Strathclyde (West), **Lothians**, Mid Scotland and **Fife**, South of Scotland, Highlands and Islands, and North-East. Elections are held every five years.

After 1967 when the **Scottish National Party** unexpectedly captured the safe Labour seat of **Hamilton**, and particularly so after 1974 when the SNP won 11 seats, all UK parties embraced the task of blunting the Nationalist challenge and assuaging moderate Scottish opinion. Labour offered the 1979 referendum (but prejudiced its majority endorsement of devolution by insisting on approval by 40% of the entire electorate); Conservatives emphasised the Cabinet rank of the Secretary of State for Scotland and the wide responsibilities of the Edinburgh-based Scottish Office.

The Scottish Office

Prior to the resounding vote for a Scottish Parliament in the referendum of 1998, the Scottish Office comprehended a variety of devolved administrative functions. Accumulated in the 19th century, when they were overseen by Boards, these functions had in 1939 been organised into departments under the Scottish Secretary and settled in a Scottish Office in Edinburgh. By the 1980s, much augmented, they included **agriculture** and fisheries in Scotland, industry (economic planning and tourism), environment (roads, town and country planning etc.), **education** (including the National Museums, Galleries and Library), and home and health (including police, prison and fire services).

Most of these responsibilities now come within the remit of the Scottish Parliament and its executive. The authority of the Secretary of State for Scotland and of his Scottish Office has thereby been diminished, becoming principally that of representing Scottish interests in areas of UK policy-making which remain reserved to the Westminster government and of acting as liaison between the Edinburgh and London governments. Meanwhile attention and expectation are focused on the structures and departments required for the functioning of the new Scottish administration.

See also **Local Government**.

GOW, Nathaniel (1763–1831) Fiddler

Nathaniel was the most famous of the sons of **Niel Gow**, and though a performer of distinction, is best remembered for his composition of a fine series of dance and song tunes. He was taught by the fiddlers Robert MacIntosh and Alexander McGlashan, as well as by his father, and more unusually received lessons in composition from Joseph Reinagle. In 1791 he became

leader of the orchestra of the **Edinburgh** Assembly, and he reached the peak of his fortunes with the visit of George IV to Scotland in 1822. He continued to publish his father's works along with his own, and indeed was, along with a number of partners, one of the most prolific music publishers of his time.

GOW, Niel (1727–1807) Fiddler

Gow was the first of an extraordinary family of fiddlers and composers, whose melodies are in the heads and

Niel Gow, by Sir Henry Raeburn, 1787 (SNPG)

feet of anyone who has ever danced in Scotland. Niel (sic) was born in Strathbran in **Ross & Cromarty**, and intended for the trade of a plaid weaver, but he early showed an interest in the **fiddle**, and patronage by Stewart of **Grandtully**, and the **Duke of Atholl** launched him on a successful performing career in London and **Edinburgh**. Though his fame was as a performer, his tunes began to appear in print from 1784, and although some were arrangements of older tunes, and others were plagiarised, the majority (and some of the best) were his own. **Raeburn**'s portrait of him in **tartan** breeches and holding his fiddle in the old-fashioned way is well known from a number of copies, notably that at **Blair Castle**.

GOWRIE CONSPIRACY (1600)

Explanations for this affair remain unsatisfactory. **James VI**'s own story was that as he was leaving **Falkland** on 5 August 1600, Alexander Ruthven, younger brother of **John Ruthven, 3rd Earl of Gowrie**, informed him that he had found a man about to bury gold in a field near **Perth**. James rode with Alexander to Gowrie's house in Perth where, as Alexander led him upstairs supposedly to meet with the owner of the treasure, Gowrie locked him in. James managed to shout from a turret window to his courtiers who, breaking into the house, found him grappling with Gowrie. One of them, **John Ramsay**, stabbed Gowrie in the neck and both Gowrie and his brother were killed in the affray. The bodies were taken to **Edinburgh** where, in a macabre sitting of Parliament, both corpses were convicted of treason. The titles, honours and lands of the family were forfeited and the name of Ruthven proscribed by an act of Parliament of 15 November 1600.

Opinions differ as to whether the affair was simply a failed attempt by Gowrie to achieve a Protestant coup by seizing the King's person, or whether James himself, warned of Gowrie's intentions, exploited the situation to achieve the ruin of his enemies. James had cause for hatred. Gowrie was the grandson of Lord Ruthven, ringleader of **Rizzio**'s murderers. His father, **William Ruthven, 1st Earl of Gowrie**, had organised the 'Ruthven Raid' and, when Treasurer, had advanced £80,000 to the King, a debt still owed to his son. The penalties inflicted upon the Ruthvens emphasise the King's animosity.

GRAHAM, James, 5th Earl and 1st Marquis of Montrose (1612–50)

Brought up at **Kincardine** Castle and educated at **St Andrews University**, the young Montrose was one of the four noblemen who drew up the **National Covenant** at **Greyfriars' Kirkyard** in **Edinburgh** in 1638. He fought for the Covenant in the Bishops' Wars [see **Charles I**], but began to find sympathy with the King at a time of civil turmoil and distanced himself from what he saw as the more extreme aspects of **Presbyterianism** in the Cumbernauld Bond (1640). After his refusal to support the Scottish Parliament's union

'Scotland's glory, Britain's pride'; James Graham, 1st Marquis of Montrose, attributed to William Dobson (SNPG)

with the English Roundheads, effectively set up by th〈 Solemn League and Covenant of 1643, he wa〈 imprisoned for five months in **Edinburgh Castle**.

In the following year Montrose was appointed King〈 Lieutenant in Scotland. With an undisciplined Scottish〈 Irish force, he won six battles in a year, at **Tippermui〈 Aberdeen**, **Inverlochy**, **Auldearn**, **Alford** and **Kilsyth〈** showing consummate tactical skill and remarkab〈 leadership. But in attempting to translate his succe〈 into effective control of the lowlands, he allowed h〈 forces to disperse and with his depleted army he wa〈 defeated by **David Leslie** at **Philiphaugh** near **Selkir〈** (1645).

Ordered to disband by the captured King, he escape〈 to Norway, where he was shocked to learn of Charle〈 I's execution, which he determined to avenge. Hi〈 return to Scotland was ill-starred. After losing all bu〈 200 men by shipwreck in **Orkney**, his small force wa〈 defeated at **Carbisdale** on 27 April 1650; Montros〈 himself was soon betrayed by MacLeod of **Assynt** fo〈 the huge sum of £25,000. Taken to Edinburgh he wa〈 sentenced to death by the Scottish Parliament withou〈 trial, hanged and disembowelled on 21 May. Hi〈 remains were given a proper tomb and monument i〈 **St Giles** Edinburgh in 1888.

> Scotland's glory, Britain's pride,
> As brave a subject as ere for monarch dy'd
> Kingdoms in Ruins often lye
> But great Montrose's Acts will never dye.

The verses below William Faithorne's engraving rin〈 true. 'He presents a standard of honesty, generosity an〈 decent dealing which is conspicuously absent in 17t〈 century Scottish politics' (R Mitchison). Companion〈 fought and died for him and enemies marvelled at th〈 courage with which he met his execution.

His talents as a poet have been recognised in recen〈 years with the publication of his collected works i〈 1990 (Mandeville). Biography by C V Wedgwood.

GRAHAM, James (1745–94) Medical Practitioner

Described by the *Dictionary of National Biography* as 'a quac〈 and possibly a madman', James Graham was born i〈 **Edinburgh**'s **Cowgate**. Despite studying medicine a〈 Edinburgh, it is unclear whether he graduated, but h〈 proceeded to sell patent medicines and ingenious cure〈 throughout Britain and America, claiming members o〈 the aristocracy – and even minor royalty – among hi〈 clients. An energetic and successful self-publicist wh〈 was imprisoned several times for fraud, he champione〈 vegetarianism but died comparatively young.

GRAHAM, James Gillespie (1776–1855) Architect

Born in **Dunblane**, **Perthshire** as plain James Gillespie〈 Graham started life as a joiner and mason and sub〈 sequently Clerk of Works on **Skye**. One of his firs〈 commissions as an architect on the mainland was th〈 design of the County Buildings in **Cupar**, **Fife**, in 1810〈 On marrying his second wife, the heiress Margaret Gra〈 ham, he added her name to his own. After that Gillespi〈 Graham built up an extensive practice specialising i〈

astellated country houses (**Taymouth Castle**, Perth-hire, 1838–9) and Gothic churches. The Gothic interiors of his country houses were commended for their detail, an excellent example being the now sadly ruinous Crawford Priory, Fife, which he enlarged in 1811–13. His church designs include St John's Tolbooth, **Edinburgh** (1841–4) and **St Mary's Church** (now Cathedral), Broughton Street, Edinburgh (1813–4). A W N Pugin, a friend of Graham's, often lent a helping hand with his Gothic designs. He is reputed to have done so in the case of St John's Tolbooth and for the design of the romanesque chapel for St Margaret's Convent, Edinburgh (1835).

Graham was also a competent classical designer and planner. He designed the layout and elevations for the Moray estate scheme in Edinburgh's **New Town**. Here he cleverly exploited the terrain with its steep fall towards the Dean valley, and his grand design for the polygonal Moray Place made this development one of the most exclusive addresses in Edinburgh.

GRAHAM, John, of Claverhouse, Viscount Dundee (1648–89) Jacobite Commander

The elder son of Royalists, descended from **Robert III**, and a distant kinsman of **Montrose**, Claverhouse spent

'Bluidy Clavers' or 'Bonnie Dundee'; John Graham of Claverhouse, Viscount Dundee, from a drawing by David Paton (SNPG)

his childhood in Glen Ogilvy near **Dundee**, attended **St Andrews University** and then went to France as a volunteer serving Louis XIV (under the **Duke of Monmouth** and with **Mackay of Scourie**). He joined William of Orange (1674), reputedly saved his life in battle, and was recommended to James, Duke of York at William's marriage to Mary (1677). Returning to Scotland, he commanded an Independent Troop of Horse raised

to suppress seditious **conventicles** in **Dumfries** and **Galloway**, and was given additional powers as **Charles II**'s absolutism increased.

He was later blamed for every atrocity of a savage period ('The Bluidy Clavers'), but in fact urged moderation 'lest severity alienate the hearts of the whole people'. In the 1679 **Covenanters'** rebellion he was defeated at **Drumclog**, helped defend **Glasgow**, and fought at **Bothwell Brig**. His 1674 marriage to Jean Cochrane of a notoriously Covenanting family had briefly damaged his career, but while in England with the Scots Army in 1688 **James VII** made him Viscount Dundee, though ignoring his advice to stand firm.

During the post-Revolution Convention of Estates at **Edinburgh**, March 1689, his life was threatened and he left, first climbing the **Castle Rock** to confer with the **Duke of Gordon** who held the castle for James. Learning of Lochiel's Highland confederacy, and declared a rebel by the Convention, he raised the Standard on Dundee Law, left his wife and new-born son in Glen Ogilvy, and rode north-east to rally support for the **Jacobite** cause. So began four months and 800 miles of rapid marching (from **Inverness** on 8 May, he crossed **Corrieyairack** and **Drumochter** Passes to raid **Perth** on the 10th). With the veteran Lochiel he used Highland skills and shared the clans' hardships, always hoping that James would cross from Ireland with troops. He fell at **Killiecrankie**, his greatest victory. His alternative nickname, 'Bonnie Dundee', was probably conferred by **Sir Walter Scott**.

GRAHAM, Murray Andrew, Viscount Dunedin (1849–1942) Judge and Politician

Dunedin has been called 'the greatest Scottish judge of the century'. Undoubtedly his reputation established by 43 years' service in every judicial capacity was well founded. He was particularly well known and respected for his ability in the area of heritable property, especially the law relating to the conveyancing of land.

Admitted advocate in 1874, he became advocate depute or prosecutor in 1888. His judicial career began with an appointment as Sheriff in 1889. He gave up the Shrieval bench to run for Parliament and was elected MP in 1891 and served until 1905. He was appointed Solicitor General and held the office twice, 1891–2 and 1895–6. Made Lord Advocate, he remained at the post from 1896 to 1903 when he became Secretary of State for Scotland. In 1905 he ascended the **Court of Session** bench as Lord President where he remained until 1913 when he moved to the House of Lords as a Lord of Appeal.

GRAHAM, Sir Robert (d.1437) Regicide

'A man of grete wit and eloquence, wunder suttilye wittyd and expert yn the lawe' ('James I, Life and Death', 15th century, anon), Sir Robert Graham was arrested and expelled from Scotland in 1424 during **James I**'s purge of over-powerful nobles. He joined Atholl's conspiracy against James and was leader of the group that burst into the royal lodging in **Perth**'s **Blackfriars** on the night of 21 February 1437 and murdered the King. He fled into the Highlands but was soon captured and executed at **Stirling**.

GRAHAM, Thomas, Lord Lynedoch (1748–1843) General

Graham was born and educated at the family home of Balgowan near **Methven**; **James 'Ossian' Macpherson** was among his tutors. He went to Oxford, travelled on the Continent, and married a daughter of the 9th Lord Cathcart. In 1785 he played in Scotland's first recorded **cricket** match and three years later bought Lynedoch estate in **Glen Almond**. The country idyll ended abruptly when his wife died (1791). Grief-stricken, he wandered abroad and then returned to raise the Perthshire **Volunteers**, one of the first light infantry regiments, and to represent **Perthshire** as MP (1794–1807). He was not often at Westminster. From 1796–9 he served with his regiment in the Mediterranean (Gibraltar, Minorca, Messina and Malta, which succumbed after a two-year siege), then Ireland (1804–5), then Spain, the Netherlands and Spain again (1808–12). With **Sir John Moore** he underwent the calvary to Corunna and was one of the few who witnessed Moore's death and burial. In the Netherlands he was at last rewarded with the permanent rank (as opposed to volunteer status) of major-general. His finest hour came with the Peninsular War where he won the battle of Barossa (1811) and as lieutenant-general was second only to Wellesley (Wellington). At Ciudad Rodrigo, Badajos, Vittoria and San Sebastian Graham held important commands. He was knighted (1812) but then invalided home with eye trouble brought on by too much peering through a telescope in full sun. In 1814 he commanded the British troops in Holland and was created Lord Lynedoch. He refused a pension but retired to develop his estate, breed stock, race horses, and found the United Services Club. He died aged 95 in London and was buried in Methven beneath an 'overpoweringly ugly tomb' (**N Tranter**).

General Thomas Graham, Lord Lynedoch, by Sir George Hayter, 1822 (SNPG)

GRAHAM, Thomas (1805–69) Chemist and Physicist

Born in **Glasgow** and educated at the city's **University** from the age of 14 to 21, Graham showed a flair for original experimentation, beginning with research on phosphates and arsenates. He was appointed Professor of Chemistry at Glasgow and then University College, London, later becoming Master of the Mint. Graham has been credited with laying the foundations of colloid chemistry, and formulated the law of gas diffusion. He died in London and is commemorated by a statue in Glasgow's **George Square**.

GRAHAME, Kenneth (1859–1932) Author

Born in **Edinburgh**, Grahame was the son of an advocate and a descendant of **Robert I**. Educated at St Edward's School, Oxford, he spent two years working in Westminster for his uncle before beginning as a clerk in the Bank of England in 1879. Around 1886 he began writing essays and short stories, becoming a contributor to W E Henley's *National Observer*. He also contributed to the *Yellow Book*, and in 1893 published a collection of essays, *Pagan Papers*. This was followed by a second collection in 1895, *The Golden Age*, which proved extremely popular and led to the equally successful *Dream Days* (1898). In 1898 Grahame became Secretary of the Bank of England, a position he held until his retirement due to ill-health in 1908. He married in 1899, and in 1908 published the work for which he is best known, the children's classic *The Wind in the Willows*. Written for his son Alisdair, it was subsequently turned into a popular play, *Toad of Toad Hall*, by A A Milne.

GRANDTULLY, Nr Aberfeldy, Perthshire

On the south bank of the river **Tay**, Grandtully (pron 'Grantly') Castle is mainly 16th century with 17th cen-

Grandtully Castle from the south-west, by MacGibbon and Ross c1880 (MR)

tury dormers and turrets. It was built by the Stewarts of Grandtully and may be the original of 'Tully-Veolan' in **Scott**'s *Waverley* (but there are other contenders). Nearby the little white-washed church of St Mary at Pitcairn looks like one of the window-less steadings amidst which it stands. The interior, though, is a revelation, nearly half the vaulted timber ceiling being covered with 17th century Renaissance-style painting

epicting scriptural scenes and armorial panels. A central
panel depicts a vivid death-bed scene. Unusually most
of the angels appear to be pregnant. A mile west of
the castle the **standing stones** of Lundin mark a 2nd
millennium BC burial site which was excavated in 1963.

GRANGEMOUTH, Stirlingshire

In 1843 'of a decidedly pleasing appearance, with some
neat and good houses . . . in a beautiful framework of
rich circumjacent scenery', Grangemouth is now less
appealing, its skyline of docks, refineries and chemical
cracker plants set in a framework of housing estates.
Yet appearances could be misleading even in 1843, for
by then this port where the Grange joins the Carron
and the Forth already epitomised the industrial revolution and 'engrossed the trade of **Stirlingshire**'.
Founded in 1777 by Sir Lawrence Dundas as the Forth
terminal of his Forth-**Clyde Canal**, it benefited even
more from being the natural port for **Carron Company**'s ironworks. To Grangemouth came the ore and
coal and from Grangemouth went the cannon and castings for which Carron became world famous. **Shipbuilding** followed in the second half of the 19th
century, refineries, chemicals and pipelines in the
second half of the 20th. As well as a major industrial
complex it is probably now the busiest port in Scotland.
The town's museum has displays on its canal origins
and on the *Charlotte Dundas*, **William Symington**'s first
canal steamer.

GRANT, Sir Alexander (1864–1937) Biscuit Manufacturer

Grant was born and educated in **Forres** in humble circumstances; his father was a railway guard. After a brief
period working in an office he was apprenticed to a
local baker and then moved to **Edinburgh** where he
gained employment with Robert McVitie. His rise in
the firm was rapid, becoming manager of the new factory built at Gorgie Road and helping establish another
plant in London. Following the retiral of McVitie's partner, Price, and the death of McVitie himself in 1910,
Grant acquired a controlling interest in the company.
Under his leadership it grew to meet the massive urban
demand with a wide and innovative range of bread,
cakes and biscuits. With Grant as chairman and managing director, McVitie & Price became one of the most
famous baking concerns in Britain if not the world.
Grant's philanthropic donations included a sum of
£100,000 which helped found the **National Library of
Scotland**. His baronetcy was awarded (1924) under
controversial circumstances, **Ramsay MacDonald** being
a close friend to whom securities and an expensive car
had been lent. The company's association with literature
was renewed in the 1980s with the establishment of
Scotland's premier literary award, the McVitie Prize for
the Scottish Writer of the Year.

GRANT, Anne, of Laggan (1755–1838) Poet and Essayist

Born in **Glasgow**, the daughter of Duncan MacVicar,
an army officer, Anne spent much of her childhood in
America but returned to Scotland in 1773 when her
father was posted to **Fort Augustus**. Married in 1779
to Rev James Grant, minister of nearby Laggan, she did

Mrs James Grant (*Anne MacVicar*) of Laggan, as drawn by William
Bewick, 1824 (SNPG)

not turn to writing until his death in 1801 left her
with eight children to support. She published a book
of poems in 1802, *Letters from the Mountains* (the work for
which she is best remembered) in 1803, and *Memoirs of
an American Lady* in 1808. In 1810 she moved to **Edinburgh**, being sponsored into literary society by **Walter
Scott** and publishing *Essays on the Superstitions of the Highlands*
(1811).

GRANT, Sir Archibald, of Monymusk (1696–1778) Agriculturalist

Son of Lord Cullen, a Lord of Session, Sir Archibald had
three careers: as a Member of Parliament (from which
he was expelled for fraud); as a leaseholder and manipu-
lator of the dubious **York Buildings Company**; and as
a progressive landowner. His celebrity stems exclusively
from the last. Taking over his father's estate of **Monymusk** in 1716, he took up permanent residence there
in 1734 and began an ambitious programme of
improvement and experiment designed to pay off his
debts and set an example to other lairds. He succeeded
in both and is now acknowledged as a patron saint of
Scottish agriculture.

His improvements included land clearance and
enclosure (ie ridding the fields of rocks which were
then used to construct dry-stone dykes), the planting
of fodder crops like turnips and clover, the introduction
of crop rotation, and a massive afforestation programme. He is said to have planted 5 million trees.
Some of these improvements had been tried elsewhere
in Scotland (eg **Dumfriesshire** enclosures), and all were

modelled on English practice. They met with fierce opposition from tenants and Grant was never averse to invoking coercive powers, likening himself to Peter the Great who 'had more trouble to conquer the barbarous habits of his subjects than in all the other great improvements that he made'. But improved yields and greater security of tenure seem eventually to have reconciled his tenants, while proximity to the markets and shipping of **Aberdeen** provided a ready output for their produce.

The Monymusk papers for 1717–55 have been edited by H Hamilton (Scottish History Society Vol 39, 1945).

GRANT, Clan

Some claim that because of the three ancient crowns in their arms the Grants originated in Scandinavia, others that they were Normans, and hence the names Granchester, Grantham, etc through which the Normans advanced in England. Certainly the earliest recorded Grants (or Le Graunts as then spelt) came to Scotland at the time of Kings **William the Lion** and **Alexander II**. There is very little authentic information about these early Grants, but the present Chief, Lord Strathspey, is recorded as the 32nd.

The principal clan areas are **Aviemore** eastwards, north and south of the river **Spey** to around **Rothes**, with a further area west of **Loch Ness** comprising Glens Urquart and Moriston. The principal seats were **Castle Grant** at **Grantown-on-Spey**, and Balmacaan (demolished post war) at **Drumnadrochit**, sometimes known as Lewistown, after the eldest son of Sir James Grant. Sir James had previously founded and laid out Grantown-on-Spey. The **Cullen** area from about **Buckie** to **Portsoy** was acquired in 1750 by Sir Ludovic Grant through his marriage to the eldest daughter of the Earl of Seafield. The family name was then changed to Ogilvie Grant, and the superb residence of Cullen House became a principal seat of the Grants (now sold and converted into a number of private residences). Typically the chiefs, generally followed by their clansfolk, supported the ruling monarch through the centuries whether of **Stewart** or Hanoverian origin. During Cromwell's rule they kept a low profile and managed to avoid conflict with him.

Septs, or Cadets, of the clan were numerous and some were founded by the chief handing over estates to his younger sons. Examples of these are Glenmoriston, **Rothiemurchus**, Elchies, Kinchurdy, Ballindalloch and **Monymusk**. The Ballindalloch and Monymusk houses are magnificent old Scottish tower houses whereas Castle Grant is rather plain and forbidding in appearance. The Doune at Rothiemurchus, long uninhabitable, has now been restored by Grant of Rothiemurchus. Grant Lodge in **Elgin**, now the Public Library, was the Town House of the chiefs and still contains much material about the clan. It is of particular interest because it was at the centre of the last clan raid by a large party of Grants in 1820.

Apart from the Ogilvie titles of the Earl of Seafield and the Grant titles of Lord Strathspey, there is the Nova Scotia Baronetcy of Dalvey dating from 1688, the Monymusk Baronetcy (NS) dating from 1705, and the Ballindalloch Baronetcy (UK) which was held by Macpherson Grant and dates from 1838. The Chief's Baronetcy of Nova Scotia was of Luss; it was transferred to

the then chief by Queen Anne and dates from 1625.

The motto of the clan is 'Stand Fast Craigellachie' This rallied the clan when a bonfire or fiery beacon had been lit on top of Mount **Craigellachie** signifying danger. The emblem is a sprig of **Scots Pine** (Pinu Silvestris). The correct clan **tartan** is known as the Red Grant but there is also the right to use the Government tartan or **Black Watch**. It is thought to have been earned by virtue of the numerous regiments of **Fencibles** raised by the clan, some of which were embodied in the Black Watch.

See the Chief's book *A History of Clan Grant*, 1983.

GRANT, Elizabeth, of Rothiemurchus (1797–1885) Diarist

Born in **Charlotte Square**, **Edinburgh**, the eldest child of a 'not very remote descendant of the Chief of **Clan Grant**', Elizabeth Grant is remembered for *Memoirs of a Highland Lady*, her lively, detailed reminiscences of family life in Edinburgh and Speyside, written in diary form and published posthumously in 1898. A not very successful lawyer and latterly Member of Parliament, her father's mismanaged financial affairs brought the family to the verge of bankruptcy; her brother William was at one point imprisoned for debt; the household was reduced from 14 indoor servants to two and Elizabeth and her sister Mary paid their wages and the grocery bills by writing short stories for a publication called *The Inspector*. Complete ruin was only averted by the timely appointment of her father to an Indian judgeship in 1827. In India the family's fortunes were restored; Elizabeth met and married Colonel Hay Smith in 1830, and after their return they settled on his estates in Ireland which she managed 'with thrift and patience' until her death at the age of 89.

GRANT, James (1822–87) Author and Nationalist

A distant relation of **Sir Walter Scott**, Grant was born in **Edinburgh** but spent most of his childhood abroad. After a spell in the army (1840–3) he returned to Edinburgh as an architect's draughtsman and then prolific author. His books, some 90 titles in all, include novels dealing largely with historical figures – **Montrose**, **Bothwell**, **Kirkcaldy**, **Rob Roy**, etc – and military histories – a 6-vol history of the Sudan War, three volumes on the history of India, and three on British battles. His *Old and New Edinburgh* (1880), also in three volumes, is considered something of a classic.

In 1852 he published a series of letters and articles on 'Justice for Scotland' which argued that England had repeatedly infringed the **Treaty of Union**. Grievances included the diversion of investment, talent and executive power from Scotland to London; the solution was to restore the Scottish **Secretary of State** and Privy Council and to reinstate the machinery of Scottish **government**. Publicity for this programme was achieved when, with his brother John, James Grant appealed to the Lord Lyon King of Arms to take action against various **heraldic** inconsistencies such as the Royal Navy's continued use of flags showing the cross of St George instead of the Union design, and the improper quartering of the royal arms on the new florin coin. This 'heraldic grievance' would resurface repeatedly in

Nationalist politics. In the 1850s its main product was the shortlived (1853–6) National Association for the Vindication of Scottish Rights (or Scottish Rights Society) founded by Grant and others, which 'restored the idea of nationalism' (William Ferguson) and anticipated nearly all the positions subsequently taken up by the Nationalist movement.

GRANT, James Augustus (1827–92) Explorer

Born in **Nairn**, James Grant was educated at **Marischal College, Aberdeen** before joining the Indian Army in 1846. Decorated for his part in the battle of Gujrat and in the Indian Mutiny, Grant is best remembered for assisting Speke on his expedition to find the source of the Nile in 1860–3. Speke was successful in identifying the source of the White Nile at the northern end of Lake Victoria, although this discovery was disputed by other explorers and Grant was separated from him at the time of Speke's discovery. Grant hurriedly published his own account of the expedition shortly after Speke's sudden death in 1864, taking as his title *A Walk Across Africa*, after Lord Palmerston had jested that Grant seemed to have faced a long walk across the continent. Grant, as brave a soldier as he was enterprising an explorer, later won more battle honours for his part in the Abyssinian campaign of 1868. He died in Nairn.

GRANT, Sir James Hope (1808–75) General

One of rather many Scots heroes of the Indian Mutiny, Grant was born at Kilgraston House, Bridge of Earn, **Perthshire**. After **Edinburgh High School** and a spell in Switzerland he joined the 9th Lancers and served in the Opium War in China (1841–4) under the Waterloo veteran General Alexander Fraser, Lord Saltoun (1785–1853); it was said that Saltoun chose him because he played the violin so well. During the Sikh War of 1844–9 he became lieutenant-colonel and was given command of the regiment. The Mutiny (1857) found him at Ambala where he participated in the famous march to Delhi. After withstanding a long siege there he was also present at both reliefs of Lucknow and that of Kanpur. He emerged with a KCB and the rank of major-general. There followed further service in China, where he commanded the Anglo-French expedition of 1860, and in India where he was commander-in-chief Madras (1862–3). He returned to the UK in 1865 and was Quartermaster-General at the Horse Guards.

GRANTOWN-ON-SPEY, Moray

Built by the laird of Grant on a 'barren heath moor', 221m above sea level and close to the river **Spey**, Grantown was a typical 18th century inland planned village intended as a focal point for new industry. Started in 1766, this neat and pleasantly located village had close on 1000 inhabitants by 1841. Although manufacturing did not develop to any marked extent, Grantown's success as a service centre provided the springboard for its subsequent transformation into a holiday-cum-health resort. The arrival of the **railway** in 1863, allied to enthusiasm for Highland scenery and 'wild sports' and also medical recommendations as to the quality of Strathspey's dry, bracing climate, brought increasing numbers of well-to-do holiday-makers. **Queen Victoria** had made a short visit in 1860, incognito but subsequently well publicised. The town, which became a **police burgh** in 1898, developed into a select inland resort. The provision by local enterprise of facilities for the Victorian vogue sports of **golf**, tennis and bowls helped to maintain its popularity.

Post World War II Grantown has, however, had to absorb many changes. The railway has gone, closed in 1965. Villas that were previously let to long-stay summer residents were converted into boarding-houses and hotels to cater for the new class of short-stay visitor who, touring by car and bus, preferred to move from place to place. To broaden Grantown's appeal, pony trekking and winter sports packages were introduced by some of the local hotels. Although the growth in **skiing** has helped to extend the **tourist** season, the main benefits from the post-1960 development of skiing facilities at **Cairngorm** have gone to **Aviemore** rather than Grantown. Indeed the Aviemore boom, and the consequent focus of attention and publicity given to the Aviemore–Cairngorm 'corridor' has led to much local heart-searching. In recent years more emphasis has been given to the provision of self-catering accommodation in the form of caravans and flats. While Grantown at present lacks the kind of large-scale visitor attraction that draws tourists into Aviemore and **Carrbridge**, it is still a good centre for the more traditional outdoor pursuits of golf, tennis, bowls, **fishing** and gentle walking.

GRAY, Sir Alexander (1882–1968) Poet

Born and educated in **Dundee**, Alexander Gray graduated with first class degrees in mathematics (1902) and economic science (1905) from **Edinburgh University** before continuing his studies at Göttingen and Paris. After 15 years in various departments of the Civil Service, he returned to academic life as Jeffrey Professor of Political Economy at **Aberdeen University** (1921–35) and Professor of Political Economy and Mercantile Law at Edinburgh University (1935–56). He published several academic works, including *Development of Economic Doctrine* (1931) and *Socialist Tradition, Moses to Lenin* (1946), and produced several volumes of songs and ballads translated from Dutch, German and Danish, as well as original poems in English and Scots, including *Any Man's Life* (1924), *Selected Poems* (1948) and *Sir Halewyn* (1949). Knighted in 1947, he served on numerous government commissions and his brilliant academic career was acknowledged in honorary degrees from Edinburgh, Aberdeen and **St Andrews Universities**.

GREAT GLEN, The

Also Glenmore Albin (*Gleann mor na-h Albin* – the great glen of Scotland), the Great Glen is a glaciated trench running for 60 miles from Loch Linnhe at **Fort William** to the Moray Firth at **Inverness** [see also **geology**]. In 1822 the Caledonian **Canal** was cut through the glen linking Lochs Oich, Lochy and **Ness**, in order that 'markets of reciprocal benefit may be opened on both shores and give employment to all those who prefer industry to indigence and idleness, of which there are many thousands in this remote district' (Webster, 1819).

GREAT MICHAEL, The, Warship

In the summer of 1506 James Wilson of Dieppe began constructing a great ship of war for **James IV**'s new navy at **Newhaven** in **Midlothian**. She was launched five years later in October 1511 and not finally completed until early the following year at a total cost of £30,000 Scots, a colossal sum. Although later described as 'the greattest scheip . . . that ever saillit in Ingland or France' it is difficult to be certain of her exact dimensions – probably about 150ft (46m) in length displacing some 1000 tons and with a crew of 295 men. After James IV's death at **Flodden** in 1513, the *Great Michael* was sold to the French for just £18,000. She ended her days as a rotting hulk at Dieppe.

GREBES

Only a handful of the rare black-necked grebe (*Podiceps nigricollis*) and red-necked grebe (*Podiceps griseigena*) nest in Scotland each year, and the Slavonian grebe (*Podiceps auritus*) is one of the rarest and most localised breeding birds in the country – with around 75 breeding pairs much rarer than the golden eagle. The breeding pairs are mainly found round the **Great Glen** in **Inverness-shire**, where they build their floating nests in shallow hill lochs, and it was here that the first pair was found as recently as 1908. Today very few pairs each year successfully bring their young up to the adult stage; the main problems being disturbance from anglers who fish the margins of sedge beds, dislodging the adult grebes and leaving the eggs and the young birds vulnerable to the depradations of hooded crows, otters, mink and even **pine marten**.

Conservationists have long worried about the future of the Slavonian grebe, and the setting up of an RSPB reserve at Loch Ruthven with the willing co-operation of local anglers was heralded as a major step forward. Anglers were given a Code of Conduct asking them to avoid the sedge beds where the grebes were nesting, and the RSPB erected a hide so that members of the public could view the birds without causing any disturbance.

GREEN, Thomas (d.1705) 'Pirate'

Nothing is known of Green other than that, as Captain of the *Worcester*, an English merchantman, he was made a national scapegoat and hanged for piracy on **Leith** sands. The *Worcester* had been forced into the Forth by bad weather. With anti-English sentiment running high in the aftermath of the **Darien Venture** and the first moves towards parliamentary **Union**, she was seized by aggrieved investors of the Scottish African Company and her crew indicted for piracy, robbery and murder. The evidence was exceedingly flimsy. There had been a firing of guns off the Malabar coast of India and talk of prize-taking; it could have been piracy; the victim might have been Scottish. For those who had lost relatives, friends and capital in the Scottish Company, imputation was enough. According to a contemporary ballad:

Of all the pirates I've heard or seen
The basest and bloodiest is Captain Green.

With the **Edinburgh** mob baying for blood, Green, his mate and his gunner were found guilty and hanged. Later evidence suggested that, though he had never encountered a Scottish vessel, Green may indeed have

had dealings with pirates. At the time his only crime was that of being an Englishman in Scotland during the ferment over the Act of Union.

GREENKNOWE TOWER, Gordon, Berwickshire

Although now a roofless shell, Greenknowe well illustrates the transition of the Scottish tower house from fortified dwelling to fashionable residence. The basic arrangement of rooms, one above the other connected by a spiral staircase, corresponds to that of other Border towers like **Newark** and **Smailholm**. But, built much later (1581), Greenknowe hints at gracious living and more fanciful ideas. The main staircase, wider than normal, required an extension of the groundplan into an L-shape. A further stair winds up a turret incorporated in the angle of the L. Windows are far larger than defensive concerns would permit and the circular angle-turrets at the wall heads can never have been other than decorative on a building sited with little regard for natural strength. It was built by James Seton of Touch, passed to the Pringles of Stichel in the 17th century and is now in the care of the Secretary of State (**Historic Scotland**).

GREENLAW, Berwickshire

In 1697 the 'mere village' of Greenlaw became the county town of **Berwickshire**, 'in spite of the superior intrinsic greatness of **Duns**'; an anomaly created by **Sir Patrick Hume of Polwarth** (1641–1724). Having served as adviser to William of Orange in Holland (1683–8), Hume returned to his forfeited estates near Greenlaw after the Revolution, was created Lord Polwarth in 1690, Lord Chancellor of Scotland in 1696, Earl of Marchmont the following year and moved quickly to anchor the seat of local government on his doorstep. As a result the 'mere village' grew into a small town with all the accoutrements of authority: mercat cross, sheriff court, county buildings and gaol. From 1853 Greenlaw was forced to share its county town status with Duns, and in 1903 the honour was awarded entirely to Duns.

Marchmont House between Greenlaw and Polwarth was built c1754 for the 2nd Earl by John and **Robert Adam** to designs by their father **William**. The picturesque Polwarth Church where Sir Patrick was forced to hide (1683) and which he restored in 1703, stands in the grounds of Marchmont. Three miles to the south of Greenlaw the ruins of **Hume Castle**, 'follified' by the 3rd Earl of Marchmont in 1786, enjoy wonderful views over the Berwickshire countryside.

GREENOCK, Renfrewshire

Once the largest of the **Clyde** ports with a **shipbuilding** industry second only to **Glasgow**'s, Greenock has been spared none of Clydeside's decline and is now mocked by its 19th century legacy of too many churches, grandiose banks and extravagant public buildings (including **William Burn**'s 1818 classical Custom House and the 250ft (76m) Victoria Tower which, with its Municipal Buildings, cost over £100,000 in 1886). Notwithstanding Inverclyde development incentives and a large investment by IBM, **Wordsworth**'s prophecy that Greenock's 'scene of refinement not surpassed, and of industry unexampled, in Scotland' could prove transitory now rings sadly true.

> Alas! too busy rival of old Tyre,
> Whose merchants princes were, whose decks were
>   thrones;
> Soon may the punctual sea in vain respire
> To serve thy need.

In the early 17th century there existed only a small fishing village. Under the guardianship of the Shaw (Schaw) family, the village became a **burgh of barony** in 1635 and, thanks to the **herring** boom, 900 boats were operating by the 1670s. In 1707–10, with the American market opened by the **Act of Union**, a harbour was built from a tax on brewers' malt, 'liquidation' of the expense being credited to 'the extreme thirstiness of the inhabitants'. They included many of Highland and Irish descent, Greenock becoming the embarkation point for coastal packets to and from Ireland and the west Highlands as well as America. Phenomenal growth and extensive port development in the late 18th and early 19th centuries made Greenock the principal port in Scotland by 1840. It was also the sixth largest population centre with the largest sugar refining industry, the second largest shipbuilding industry and important sidelines in **pottery** and straw hats.

To meet the challenge of rapid expansion a town plan based on a grid system, much admired at the time and still in evidence, was drawn up in 1818 and a novel water supply devised in the 1820s. This involved creating a reservoir in the high ground to the south (Loch Thom, named after Robert Thom who devised the system) plus an aqueduct (the Cut, 6 miles long and now part of the Clyde-Muirshiel Regional Park) and a further holding reservoir whence the water was conducted in two cascading races to power numerous mills. The collapse of one of the dams involved in this scheme produced catastrophic flooding in the east end of Greenock in November 1835; about 40 people were drowned.

William Kidd is thought to have been born in Greenock, but **James Watt** has no rival as the town's favourite son, his achievements being acknowledged in the James Watt Dock, the Watt Memorial School plus a plaque on his birthplace, the Watt cairn in the cemetery, James Watt College, and the Watt Museum and Library (now incorporating the MacLean Museum and Art Gallery) with a statue by Chantrey. Dying in Greenock, **Burns**'s 'Highland Mary' Campbell has a monument in the cemetery off Inverkip Road while **John Galt** is buried in that off Inverkip Street.

In World War II the docks were badly bombed and the town served as the naval headquarters of the Free French, commemorated by a large Cross of Lorraine in granite above the town.

GREENWICH, Treaty of (1543)

A treaty concluded on 1 July 1543 between Henry VIII of England and **James Hamilton, 2nd Earl of Arran**, Regent of Scotland, agreeing the betrothal of **Mary**, later **Queen of Scots** (then aged six months) to Edward, Prince of Wales (aged six years), and specifying that the marriage be conducted by proxy before Mary

reached the age of ten. Ratified by Arran at **Holyrood** on 25 August, the Treaty was nevertheless repudiated by the Scottish Parliament in December; Henry responded to this snub by despatching (1544) forces under the Earl of Hertford which captured **Leith** and ravaged the Borders [see **Rough Wooing**].

GREGOR, Clan

Traditionally the clan is descended from Griogar, third son of **Alpin**, Celtic King of Scotland c787. Hence the clan motto 'Srioghail mo dhream' (Royal is My Race). The MacGregors held the three glens of the Orchy, the Strae and the Lochy in **Argyll**. Sir John MacGregor, Lord of Glenorchy in the late 12th century, married a beautiful English lady who came to Scotland with **Queen Margaret**. Their son 'Malcolm of the Castles' built many fortalices and reputedly saved a Scottish king from a wild boar by fending it off with a tree until he could kill it; an oak or a fir appear in the armorial bearings.

John of Glenorchy, taken prisoner by Edward I at **Dunbar**, later died in France. His daughter and heiress married John, son of Sir Neil Campbell of **Loch Awe**, but the barony reverted to the MacGregors. Malcolm MacGregor, acting as chief, fought consistently for **Robert I**. John Dhu, who died in 1415, left sons from whom the MacGregors of Roro and Glengyle in **Perthshire**, and Brackly in Argyll, are descended.

In the mid-15th century Duncan, Lord Campbell, acquired the superiority of the MacGregor land. He gave Glenorchy to his son Colin (founder of the House of **Breadalbane**) but retained Glenstrae where the MacGregors remained as vassals of the senior Campbells. In 1519 the heir was disinherited and John MacGregor of Brackly enfeoffed as chief by Argyll.

John, who married Helen, daughter of Sir Colin Campbell of Glenorchy, became hereditary custodian of **Kilchurn Castle**. Unfortunately he died young and his heir, Allaster, influenced by his cousin and tutor Duncan Ladasach (the Lordly) took to crime. Thus, when in 1556 Sir Colin Campbell of Glenorchy, bought the superiority of Glenstrae from the **4th Earl of Argyll** he refused to enfeoff Allaster.

The MacGregors, made landless, retaliated. In 1566 **Queen Mary**, having granted them her peace, asked the Laird of Weem to rent them ground. But in 1569 Glenorchy obtained legal authority to arrest insurgents. **Gregor Roy** of Glenstrae eluded pursuit for a year but was taken by Glenorchy's men and beheaded at **Taymouth** in April 1570. His son Allaster, outlawed for attacking the Colquhouns in **Glen Fruin**, was executed in 1604 and the name MacGregor was proscribed. Further penalties were imposed and in 1633 it became legal to kill MacGregors and to hunt them with bloodhounds.

The clan responded by taking pseudonyms. The MacGregors of Glenstrae, descended from Duncan Ladasach, became Murrays and later **Rob Roy MacGregor** called himself Campbell. c1624 about 300 MacGregors were taken by the **Earl of Moray** from **Menteith** to oppose the MacIntoshes and many settled in **Aberdeenshire**. **Charles II** repealed the Act of 1633, but when the MacGregors supported the **Jacobites** (a MacGregor Regiment fought at **Prestonpans**) the act was renewed by William of Orange. The penal statutes against the clan were finally repealed in 1774 and in 1795 Sir John Murray was confirmed as MacGregor of MacGregor.

GREGORY, David (i) (1627–1720) Physician

Born at Drumoak, **Aberdeenshire**, and brother of **James Gregory (i)**, David was a doctor and landowner who dabbled in scientific experiments. His invention of a military cannon superior to contemporary artillery won him much admiration, but the model appears to have been destroyed at the request of Isaac Newton, who was horrified by its potential. He was father to no fewer than 32 children, including **David Gregory (ii)**.

GREGORY, David (ii) (1659–1708) Mathematician

Born in **Edinburgh** and educated at both **Aberdeen** and Edinburgh, David Gregory (ii) took over the chair of mathematics at **Edinburgh University** (previously held by his uncle **James Gregory (i)**) before taking his MA. He later taught at Oxford and travelled widely to broaden his scientific horizons, but his mathematical theories are not now regarded as original. He was involved in arranging the **Act of Union**, and died the following year.

GREGORY, Duncan (1813–44) Algebraist

Great-great-grandson of **James Gregory (i)**, Duncan Gregory lectured at Cambridge for most of his short life, establishing the *Cambridge Mathematical Journal* and publishing important papers on calculus, geometrical analysis and algebra; this last work was cut short by his early death.

GREGORY or GREGORIE, James (i) (1638–75) Mathematician

Born at Drumoak, near **Aberdeen**, younger brother of **David Gregory (i)**, James Gregory was educated in Aberdeen and Padua and became a professor in both **St Andrews** and **Edinburgh**. His talents were wide-ranging; he created series expressions for trigonometrical functions, produced the first proof of the fundamental theory of calculus and would probably have invented the first reflecting telescope had the technology of his day been equal to his theories. Although believed to have greatly influenced Isaac Newton, Gregory died young and relatively unsung.

GREGORY, James (ii) (1753–1821) Professor of Medicine

Born in **Aberdeen**, Gregory studied medicine at **Edinburgh**, Aberdeen and Oxford, succeeding his father **John Gregory** as professor in medicine at Edinburgh after 1776. Regarded as a good lecturer, he appears to have become embroiled in contemporary controversies, being fined for beating a fellow doctor with a stick, and being suspended by the **Royal College of Physicians**. He was responsible for 'Gregory's Mixture', a well-known laxative.

GREGORY, John (1724–73) Professor of Medicine

Grandson of **James Gregory (i)**, John was born in **Aberdeen** and studied medicine at **Edinburgh** and Leyden. He became professor of medicine at Edinburgh

in 1766 and was Physician to the King in Scotland, but is perhaps one of the less distinguished members of the remarkable Gregory family.

GREGORY, William (1803–58) Chemist

Born in **Edinburgh** on Christmas Day 1803, the son of **James Gregory (ii)**, William studied medicine at the city's university but showed early enthusiasm for chemistry, studying with Justus Leibig at Giessen, later translating much of his teacher's work. Professor of chemistry at **Glasgow**, **Aberdeen** and Edinburgh, Gregory prepared morphine and codeine from opium and isoprene from rubber. Later he encountered hostility for his promotion of occult ideas.

GREIG, Gavin (1856–1914) Folksong Collector

Greig's employment as a schoolmaster did not prevent him from becoming one of the greatest folksong collectors of any age, having gathered 3500 songs in **Aberdeenshire** alone. His scholarly scrupulousness coupled with the desire of his collaborator, Rev Duncan, to complete the collection before publishing any of it, led to a delay in bringing the work to public attention that is only being made good a century later. Vols 1–7 of the **Greig–Duncan Folk Song Collection**, one of the largest and most important in the world, are now (1999) published – Vol 8 is imminent. See Olson, Ian A, 'The Greig-Duncan Folk Song Collection: Last Leaves of a Local Culture?' in *Review of Scottish Culture* 5, 1989.

GREIG, Samuel (1735–88) Admiral of Russian Navy

Born in **Inverkeithing**, Greig joined the British navy and served with distinction in engagements including Quiberon Bay (1759) and the reduction of Havana (1762). Despite his excellent record, his career did not thrive; a recruitment drive by Catherine the Great for British officers to join the Russian navy suggested a move. Master's mate in the British navy (1763), he joined the Russian navy as Captain 1st Rank (1764) and rose through Brigadier (c1767), Rear-Admiral (1770), Vice-Admiral (1775) to full Admiral (1782).

Although Peter the Great (1672–1725) had created an efficient Russian navy, this had deteriorated so badly under his successors that Catherine complained she was inheriting a herring fishing fleet; Greig became her most accomplished and devoted ally in achieving its transformation back into a modern and effective fighting force, recruiting many Scottish officers to assist in the task. Commander of a division under Count Orlov in the battle of Chesme against the Turks in the Mediterranean (1770), he was rewarded with promotion and knighthoods in the orders of St George and St Anna. Further successes during the Mediterranean campaign led to his appointment as governor of the naval port of Kronstadt, whose docks and facilities he extensively reconstructed. His international reputation spread; during a brief visit to Scotland in 1777 he was awarded the Freedom of **Edinburgh** and in 1781 he was elected a Fellow of the Royal Society. In 1788 he commanded the Russian naval fleet in the war against Sweden, blockading the Swedish fleet at Sveaborg and capturing their flagship at the battle of Hogland (July 1788), whereupon Catherine honoured her Scottish champion with further knighthoods, this time of the Orders of St Vladimir and St Andrew. When he died of a fever three months later on board his own flagship at Revel (now Tallinn) in Estonia, the desolate Tsarina ordered a state funeral for him at the Lutheran cathedral and a gold medal to be struck in his honour.

THE GREIG–DUNCAN FOLK SONG COLLECTION

This famous collection of over 3000 folk songs was amassed in the north-east of Scotland by a rural schoolmaster and a **United Presbyterian** minister, in the decade before the Great War. In 1903, **Gavin Greig** (1856–1914), the headmaster of New Deer Public School, was invited by the historical publishing society the New Spalding Club to examine the feasibility of a volume of what remained of traditional music and song in the north-east. An established musical authority who had written and published secular and religious songs, musical plays and operas, and who had edited **Scott Skinner**'s fiddle compendium (as well as publishing poetry, prose and novels), Greig was very doubtful if much of value remained. But within months of collecting from local people of all walks of life, he realised that his region was in fact the centre of a thriving musical and song tradition which would require many years of research if it were to be published to the exacting modern standards being laid down by the Folk Song Society (est. 1899). He obtained the first of many large research grants from the Carnegie Trust for the Universities of Scotland and persuaded his old friend the Reverend James Bruce Duncan of New Deer (1848–1917), then at Lynturk on Donside, to join him in the search. Duncan came from a singing family and brought with him their considerable repertoire. As the years passed, the collection never ceased growing; the inflow was increased by a weekly folk song column Greig ran in the *Buchan Observer* from 1907–11 and by contributions from outwith the region, from such as John Ord of **Glasgow** (1861–1928). Greig's health deteriorated, Duncan's church duties increased, and by their deaths in 1914 and 1917 respectively, little of their findings was ready for a type of publication which the war was jeopardising anyway. Their collection was preserved by the **University of Aberdeen** and by Duncan's daughter Katharine until in the 1960s the University of Aberdeen and the School of Scottish Studies, **Edinburgh**, embarked on joint publication with a distinguished editor, Pat Shuldham-Shaw (1917–77) from the English Folk Dance and Society. Important for its sheer size and the quality of both words and tunes, it was also scrupulously compiled ('Give exactly what you get') by two natives of the region, familiar with its language and culture. They rapidly realised not only that their findings transcended local, regional, national and international boundaries, but also that their informers sang nothing of what passes for the 'Scottish National Song' as composed by **Burns**, **Hogg**, **Lady Nairne** and the like. *The Greig–Duncan Folk Song Collection* is edited by P Shuldham-Shaw and Emily B Lyle et al, (AUP and Mercat Press: 1981 onwards). See Olson, I A, 'The Greig–Duncan Folk Song Collection: Last Leaves of a Local Culture' in *Review of Scottish Culture* 5, 1989.

GRESLEY, Nigel (1876–1941) Engineer

Designer of the world's fastest steam **locomotive**, Herbert Nigel Gresley was born in **Edinburgh** but spent his entire working career in England, being appointed Mechanical Engineer to the Great Northern Railway from 1911 to 1923 and to its successor, the London North Eastern Railway from 1923 until his death. His most famous engines were *Flying Scotsman* and *Mallard*, the latter reaching a record speed for steam traction of 126 mph on 3 July 1938.

GRETNA, Dumfriesshire

The low-lying ground ('gretna' from *gretan-how*, 'large hollow') at the head of the Solway Firth was long classified as 'debatable land', the Anglo-Scottish border being sometimes interpreted as following the Esk, sometimes the Sark, both of which here enter the Firth. Officially the frontier became a border in 1552 when the Sark, the more northerly, was accepted by both parties. But it was not until the **1707 Act of Union** that the 'debatable land' ceased to provide a haven for outlaws and smugglers. Smuggling, especially of **whisky** (which carried a higher duty in England), continued well into the 19th century and tarnished the reputation of the adjacent villages of Springfield, Gretna and Gretna Green. The celebrity, in English eyes, of the last dates from 1754 when a tightening of the marriage laws in England enticed eloping couples to Scotland where marriages before two witnesses without clerical involvement were still legal. Subsequent changes in the law north and south of the border resulted in a convergence of attitudes to civil marriage but still left Scotland offering those under age the possibility of marriage without parental consent. The belief that such marriages were invariably performed by the village blacksmith (the smithy is now a museum) may stem from the near monopoly of presiding over such ceremonies enjoyed from 1791–1814 by one Joseph Paisley. Once a tobacconist, Paisley's prodigious size was matched by a singular capacity for alcohol, 'stentorian lungs' and enormous strength which 'frequently enabled him to straighten horseshoes in their cold state'.

Nearby was fought the **Battle of Solway Moss** and south-west of Gretna, above the Sark, stands the Clochmaben Stone. A boulder, 7ft (2.1m) high, it is said once to have formed part of a stone circle; more certainly it was used as a boundary marker, and a place of exchange and judgement in later **Roman** times. The **Battle of Sark** is said to have been fought in its shadow.

See also **Quintinshill Rail Crash**.

GREY MARE'S TAIL, Nr Moffat, Dumfriesshire

One of several waterfalls known as the Grey Mare's Tail or the Grey Mare's Falls [see **Kinlochleven**], that on the Tail burn between **Moffat** and **Selkirk** is the highest in the Borders with a three-part drop of about 60m. In *Marmion* **Sir Walter Scott** describes how the burn 'White as the snowy charger's tail/Drives down the pass of Moffatdale'. The area, once closely associated with the **Covenanters** who sought refuge in its trackless wilds, is now owned by the **National Trust for Scotland**. A herd of wild **goats**, rare in the Lowlands, is said to frequent the property. The Trust lays great emphasis on the need for extreme caution when negotiating the grassy slopes beside the falls.

GRIERSON, Sir Robert, of Lag(g) (c1655–1733) Anti-Covenanter

The laird of the estate of Lag(g) in **Dumfriesshire**, inherited from his cousin in 1667, Robert Grierson was Steward of **Kirkcudbright** and, as a JP, was responsible for the prosecution of **Conventiclers** and presided over the trial and execution of the **Wigtown Martyrs**. Known to the **Covenanters** as 'the worst villain Scotland ever gave birth to', he became their favourite demon, tales being told of how 'when he was dying he made a wish to have his feet bathed in cold water, but the moment they were immersed, they made it *fizz and boil wi' hellish heat*' (a story that grew from the fact that he suffered from gout), and of how on his death his soul was accompanied to Hell by 'a chariot drawn by six horses and driven by three drivers, all of the Pandemonium stamp, plunging and snorting over the wild waves, attended by black clouds that vomited forth thunder and lightning'. Created a Nova Scotia baronet in 1685, Grierson was fined and imprisoned as a **Jacobite** after the Revolution. He was the original of Sir Robert Redgauntlet of 'Wandering Willie's Tale' in **Walter Scott**'s *Redgauntlet*.

GRIEVE, C M see MACDIARMID, Hugh

GRIMBLE, Ian Naughton (1921–95) Writer and Broadcaster

Grimble's fourteen books, mostly on aspects of Scottish history, included classics like *The Trial of Patrick Sellar* (1962) and *The World of Rob Donn* (1979). A **Gaelic** scholar with a PhD from **Aberdeen University**, he also contributed to *Gairm* and other Gaelic periodicals. His broadcasting was more varied. Between a 1952 programme on 'Stone Age Life in New Guinea' and a 1981 series on Scottish Castles, he addressed the nation on everything from the bagpipes to the Iranian revolution and on everyone from Euripides to Oliver Cromwell. 'Grimble on Genius', on 'Kings, Lords and Commoners', on Islands, on Solitude, on The Horse, on The King of Siam – by radio and television the programmes kept coming. He was an inspired communicator and a much loved presenter, but even this output did scant justice to the catholicity of his scholarship.

Born of Scots parents in Hong Kong, he was schooled in England. His Oxford career as an exhibitioner at Balliol was interrupted by the war during which he learned Japanese, served in India and endorsed the teachings of the Buddha. Returned, he won the high jump at Oxford, swam for Britain and promoted the modern pentathlon. Before joining the BBC he worked as a researcher/librarian in the House of Commons. At the height of his fame as a TV presenter he took a teaching job in Teheran. Despite the considerable risk which attended so conspicuous a figure (he was at least 6'3"), he stayed on to witness the beginnings of the Khomeini revolution and wrote an intriguing but unpublished account of his experiences. Somewhere in between he became an authority on the last Romanovs, the **clan Mackay**, Denmark, the Kurds, heraldry, Joan of Arc, the Icelandic sagas and much else. To an encyclopaedia like this, he was a godsend.

Home was in his beloved **Bettyhill**, in a small house within sound of the **Pentland Firth** but with absolutely no view. His possessions were few – books, biscuits, papers, an old typewriter and a small radio. He watched no television and rarely read a newspaper; but he corresponded prolifically and delightfully. Near and far, many wept at his parting. A portrait hangs in the little Strathnaver Museum which he helped to set up at Farr, Bettyhill.

GRIMOND, Joseph (Jo), (1913–93) Liberal Politician

'A handsome man whose intellect was as clear-cut as his profile', Grimond was the son of a **Dundee** jute manufacturer, educated at Eton and Balliol College, Oxford, and called to the English (Middle Temple) Bar in 1937. In 1938 he married Laura Bonham-Carter, granddaughter of the prime minister Herbert Henry Asquith. After World War II, during which he served with the **Fife & Forfar Yeomanry**, he worked for the **National Trust for Scotland** and stood, unsuccessfully, as Liberal candidate for **Orkney** & **Shetland** in the 1945 general election. He won the seat in 1950 and remained the constituency's Member of Parliament for 33 years. Immensely cultivated, he was known for his charm, self-deprecating wit and intolerance of pomposity and bureaucracy. In 1956 this 'lion in the liberal cause' was made leader of a depleted Liberal Party, now reduced to six MPs. His zeal brought his cause back from the edge of extinction and his ideas, published in *The Liberal Thinker* (1959) and *The Liberal Challenge* (1963), inspired a new generation of Liberal activists. But the Labour victory of 1964 was a blow to his ambitions. Seeing no strategic or tactical role for the Liberals, and tired out by the effort of running a small but national party almost single-handed, he stood down as leader in favour of Jeremy Thorpe in 1967, but remained an MP until 1983 when he was 'relegated to the old folk's home that is the House of Lords'. A Scottish radical at heart, Grimond was inspired by the ruggedly independent communities of Orkney and Shetland which instilled a strong belief in the importance of community and the devolution of power. He campaigned vigorously for economic and social development in the Highlands and Islands and was instrumental in the passing of the **Zetland** and Orkney Council Bills which gave them unique powers over the newly established **oil industry**. Prompted by his belief that 'tolerance, respect, care for other things than power, all that goes to make civilisation, are under attack', he published *A Personal Manifesto* in 1983, and devoted his remaining years to literature, art and gardening at the Old Manse of Firth on Orkney.

GROUSE, Black

The increase in numbers of black grouse (*Lyrurus tetrix*) during the 1960s and 70s brought about by the widespread planting of conifer forests has been reversed in the 1980s and 1990s as the close-packed and fast-growing plantations now blanket vast areas of their preferred habitat. Although for the most part blackgame do nest in conifer woods, they need undisturbed open spaces for their famous 'leks' or mating rituals – among the most spectacular avian sights in Scotland. The males (known as black cocks) display to each other and to the females (greyhens) by trailing their wings, spreading out their glossy black and white lyre-shaped tails and strutting through the grass, darting at each other and uttering their distinctive loud bubbling cries. Most of the display is ritualistic, but occasionally males will actually do battle for the privilege of mating with the rather drab-looking hens who crouch in the grass apparently unimpressed by the proceedings. These 'leks' take place in the early mornings in March and April, and the same 'lekking ground' can be used year after year.

GROUSE, Red

Although not confined to Scotland, the Red Grouse (*Lagopus scoticus*) has come to epitomise the Scottish moors, and large tracts of the uplands are managed for this prized game bird [see **grouse shooting**]. Closely related to the Willow Grouse (*Lagopus Lagopus*) of Norway, red grouse live on well-heathered moorland, relying for food almost entirely on the shoots and fruits of ling **heather** and cranberry. They nest in scrapes in the ground lined with grass or tufts of heather, and lay batches of up to nine eggs which are 'peculiarly beautiful and game-like, of a rich brown colour, spotted closely with black'. Naturalist Charles St John, writing in the early 19th century, remarked even then on 'the immense numbers killed by gun, net and snare, not to mention those which fall a prey to crows, hawks, foxes and other vermin', and attributed the survival of such a persecuted species 'to the preservation carried on by those who rent the shootings'. Such preservation consists mainly of 'muirburn' − the burning of old heather to encourage the new shoots on which the young must feed, while leaving enough long heather nearby to provide cover from predators. Ironically for such a valuable game bird the red grouse, unlike the pheasant, cannot be reared in captivity.

GROUSE SHOOTING

As with other forms of shooting flying, **grouse** shooting was only a minor sport prior to the 19th century. Landowners employed gamekeepers to kill game, and field sports were commonly disregarded as being beneath the dignity of a gentleman. A change in attitude occurred at the end of the Napoleonic Wars, when an increased desire for leisure pursuits coincided with improvements to shotguns, hitherto unwieldy and unsafe, to the extent that they became of similar size and weight to those in use today.

Shooting became generally popular, but intensification of agriculture in England with the invention of the threshing machine meant that wild sport south of the border grew scarce. More demand led to interest in the potential of Scotland and the north of England, increasingly accessible as roads were improved and, later, **railways** built. By 1820 to shoot grouse was to be in the height of fashion. While the English moors have always yielded consistently larger bags than the Scottish, England has never been able to compete with Scotland in the variety of sport its countryside can offer. An autumn holiday in Scotland, centred on grouse shooting, became part of the social scene, the seal on its popularity being set by the purchase of **Balmoral** by **Queen Victoria** in 1852.

The popularity of grouse shooting has remained consistent, with an increasing number of sportsmen coming from overseas. While excellent bags are still achieved in prime years, it is hard to foresee some of the earlier records being surpassed. Notable were Maharaja Duleep Singh's 220 brace over dogs to one gun on 12 August 1871 at **Grandtully** in **Perthshire**. In the south of Scotland the **Buccleuch** estates, on eight recorded days between 1911−15, averaged 733 brace a day.

The best moors in Britain in terms of grouse population are in northern England, and generally the further north one goes from there the less good the quality. It is impossible to categorise exactly the variables that are responsible for this, but rainfall and snowfall, altitude, fertility of the ground as it relates to **heather** quality, and moor management are of prime relevance. The last factor is of crucial importance, especially in relation to predator control, and in particular predation from foxes. Keepering on large moors of poor quality in the north of Scotland is less intense than on relatively small but good moors in the Borders. Hence the northern keepers are hard pressed to effect proper predator control and also to concentrate on habitat management, notably a proper rotation of heather burning.

The practice of grouse shooting comprises three methods, namely driving, walking up, and over pointers or setters. The last, and the most attractive, has become less common due to the cost of keeping dogs for only a short working season, and it is now practised mostly in the far north where dogs lend themselves to finding birds on a large but sparsely populated area. Walking up is also practised where the grouse population is not sufficient to warrant driving. Driven grouse shooting tends to take place on the most productive moors, where it is necessary to make a high annual cull to prevent disease arising. Teams of guns, usually eight in number, are placed in a line of butts, and the birds are driven to them by a line of beaters. The grouse can thus be concentrated over the waiting guns from large areas of ground.

Decline in numbers of **red grouse**, along with **black grouse** or blackgame, has been a feature of recent decades. The record bag of blackgame in Scotland was achieved in 1869, when 247 were killed in a day at Glenwharrie in **Dumfriesshire**. As red grouse have suffered from blanket afforestation of heather moorland, so blackgame have declined through disappearance of scrub **birch** and pine moorland on moorland fringes.

The present outlook is nevertheless encouraging for both species of grouse. The Game Conservancy has launched a project to help interested parties improve the habitat for blackgame, and this project coincides with the government's announcement of new conservation grants for heather improvement and woodland regeneration. Additionally the Game Conservancy has proved that grit, traditionally placed artificially on moorland in winter to aid the digestion of the coarse winter diet can, when treated with an anthelmintic, have a dramatically beneficial effect in combating the crucial problem affecting the health of red grouse, namely the parasitic nematode commonly referred to as the strongyle worm.

These measures, coupled with public recognition that heather moorland must be conserved for its unique animal, bird and plant life, together with the sustained demand for grouse shooting, should ensure the future of grouse.

GRUINARD ISLAND, Ross & Cromarty

It was on this small island in Gruinard Bay between Loch Ewe and Little Loch Broom that the eyes of the Ministry of Defence lighted in the autumn of 1942. They had been looking for some time for a site on which to continue their experiments into the suitabilty of *Bacillus Anthracis* as an agent of biological warfare. A team of scientists from a MOD laboratory at Porton Down in Wiltshire landed on the island in the winter of that year, detonated six small anthrax 'bombs' and withdrew to await the consequences on the flock of sheep placed on Gruinard as 'guinea pigs'. Not surprisingly the sheep all died within a matter of days. For more than 40 years thereafter the island was forbidden territory, bristling with MOD warnings that it was CONTAMINATED and DANGEROUS. Not until 1986–7 was a second team of scientists sent in to clean up the mess made by the first; although the island was thoroughly disinfected and pronounced clear of anthrax contamination, the taint of the experiment has not so easily been eradicated from public perception.

GULLANE, East Lothian

Between **Aberlady** and **Dirleton** on the south shore of the Firth of Forth, Gullane has had cause both to curse and bless its extensive sands. The 12th century church dedicated to St Andrew, of which only the shell remains, was abandoned and its congregation moved to Dirleton in the early 17th century after a series of severe storms buried both church and churchyard under blown sand. Noted in the 19th century as a centre for racehorse training, Gullane and its sands came into their own with the rising popularity of **golf**. Just to the east is the famous Muirfield Course, regularly (and most recently in 1992) home to the British Open Championship, and there are three other 18-hole courses in the immediate vicinity. Gullane is now a desirable residential and commuter town for **Edinburgh**, with many fine 19th and early 20th century villas, as well as a popular destination for sea bathers and a paradise for golfers.

GUNN, Clan

Descended from Gunni, a Norse Orcadian whose wife inherited great estates in **Caithness** and **Sutherland** towards the end of the 12th century, the Gunns occupied the highland districts of Caithness before finally settling in the Sutherland parish of **Kildonan**. The Gunns first rose to historical prominence in 1464 when George Gunn became hereditary 'Crowner' or warden of Caithness. It was George's son James who founded the line of chiefs of Clan Gunn known from him as *Mac Sheumais*; from his other sons descended the 'Robson' Gunns of Braemore, the 'Bregaul' Gunns of Dale, and the Caithness Hendersons and Williamsons. Noted by an early chronicler as 'verie courageous, rather desperat than valiant', the Gunn family trees are thick with lusty fighters, successive clansmen going into battle against the **Keiths**, the Sinclair **Earls of Caithness** and the Aberach Mackays. Sir Iain Moncrieffe of that Ilk relates an anecdote of 1736 in which 'George Gunn, brother of the 7th *Mac Sheumais*, was in danger of his life from a

charge of claiming payment on a forged bill, whereupon the chief attended the Sutherland Regality Court at **Dornoch**, asked to see the bill and then fought off the whole court with a chair while he swallowed the dangerous document.'

Alexander Gunn, the 7th *Mac Sheumais*, supported the Government in the '45 **Jacobite Rising**, and led 120 Gunns into battle alongside the Campbell Earl of Loudoun; his son William, the 8th *Mac Sheumais*, died in India at the Battle of Polilur against Hyder Ali in 1780 [see **General Sir Hector Munro**]. With the death in 1821 of George Gunn, the 10th *Mac Sheumais*, the direct line died out. But the Clan Gunn Society is working hard to maintain links between Gunn clansmen, now (and particularly since the **clearances**) scattered throughout the world.

GUNN, Neil Miller (1891–1973) Novelist

A writer who saw his work in relation to an ancient continuity, Neil Gunn was born in **Dunbeath** (Caithness) but from his early teens lived with an older sister and her husband in **St John's Town of Dalry**, Kirkcudbright-shire. There he received private tuition from both a local headmaster and a minor poet. Civil Service entrance exams took him to London (1907–9) and Senior Civil Service exams to **Edinburgh** (1909–11). Appointed Excise Officer in the Highlands (1911–21) he began a friendship with an Irish colleague, Maurice Walsh, who was also a novelist (Gunn features in Walsh's *The Key Above the Door*), and met Jessie Dallas Frew, 'Daisy'. They were married during Gunn's posting to Wigan in Lancashire (1921–2) and then moved to **Lybster**, Caithness, where he began to write in earnest. In **Inverness** (1923–37) he came into contact with **Hugh MacDiarmid**, Wendy Wood, et al and was covertly (as a Civil Servant) involved in Nationalist efforts. Alleged sometime the best poacher in Caithness, Gunn seems to have taken the same delight in political subterfuge. With the success of *Highland River* (1937) he quit the Civil Service to write full time. After a symbolic but inexpert sail up the west coast (see *Off in a Boat*, 1938) the Gunns settled in Braefarm House, **Dingwall**, moving to Glen Cannich (1950) and finally the **Black Isle** (1959). There were no children of the marriage.

Gunn wrote much occasional prose, some as 'Dane McNeil' in *Scots Magazine*, and also *Whisky and Scotland* (1935) on **whisky**'s mystical and ceremonial significance and fragrance. Wide and deep knowledge of Highland history and folklore he shared with friends active politically. His Zen and other mystical reading informed his later novels, *An Atom of Delight* (1956) being no less a Zen treatise than an eccentric 'autobiography'.

His first novel, *The Grey Coast* (1926), set in his native airt, shows the makings of both economic and domestic tragedy, avoided not least by finding a pot of gold. (Why not?) *Morning Tide* (1931) is a masterpiece, Gunn at his best judged simply as a prose-writer. It depicts a boy's growing experience of reality in a village dominated by the sea – all key themes. *Highland River* (1937) celebrates a boy's awareness, something Gunn ever strove to maintain, and the capacity for surprise and a deepening of insight. A young boy is seen in relation to a wise old man in *Young Art and Old Hector* (1942), a marvel of a book. The sequel to *Young Art*, *The Green Isle* of *Great Deep* (1944), though rooted in folklore, was prompted by the wartime situation and a sense of the inhumanity of fashionable leftisms. Its lively fantasy is a major picture of totalitarianism and machine-mindedness, the culmination of his 'boy' theme.

He also explored his native airt in an historical context. In *Sun Circle* (1933) 9th century conflicts of **Viking** with **Pict**, and of old paganism with Christianity, imply that many meanings live on in a land whose sometime people are also celebrated in *Butcher's Broom* (1934), an even-handed novel of the Highland **clearances**. The major integrative *The Silver Darlings* (1941) is set in Caithness's early 19th century heyday of **fishing**.

'Not a literary man', Gunn sought knowledge and wisdom, and their apt expression as if by a sage or guru. Received categories (as in some literary reference books) do him few favours and at times no justice. Though a man of great friendships (**Edwin Muir**, Grassic Gibbon [**Leslie Mitchell**], James Bridie [**O H Mavor**]), he was essentially involved with the matter of his books. Dark images stir in *The Serpent* (1943), set round the central and very male Tom the Philosopher. The land speaks of peace, which in the early books is contrasted with the wild hazardous sea and in later ones with something in the soul. Whether or not the dark note drew on something in Gunn's private life, it is explored as a new theme in, for instance, *The Key of the Chest* (1945). In *The Drinking Well* (1947) and the psychological *The Shadow* (1948), as in *The Serpent*, the impact of the world outside is felt in his native airt. *The Silver Bough* (1948), with much archetypal lore, *The Well at the World's End* (1951) and his last novel *The Other Landscape* (1954) may be of more specialised appeal. Not so *Bloodhunt* (1952), with Old Sandy's rich down-to-earth wisdom reconciling much and suggesting how closely Gunn's work and life were integrated.

Daisy's death in 1963 brought the additional trial of loneliness to a man in uncertain health. The prospect of *Neil M Gunn: The Man and the Writer* (ed Gifford and Scott, 1973) so delighted him that it is plain how he felt the injustice of being much out of print for years. He died on 15 January 1973. See *Neil M Gunn: A Highland Life*, F R Hart and J B Pick (1981); *Selected Letters*, ed Pick, 1987, Polygon, who with Richard Drew, Canongate and Souvenir Press have reissued most of Gunn's books. There is a bibliography by C J L Stokoe; new selections of minor works and studies are still appearing.

GUTHRIE, James (c1617–61) Martyr

A **Presbyterian** and **Covenanter** minister educated in **St Andrews**, Guthrie moved from **Lauder** to **Stirling** in 1649. Called by Cromwell 'That short man who will not bow', he was leader of the **Protesters** to the **Perth** articles in 1650. Tried for treason for disowning the King's authority, he was hanged at **Edinburgh**'s **Mercat Cross** and his head fixed on the **Netherbow** (drops of his blood, it is said, falling from the arch onto the coach of the **Earl of Middleton** as it passed underneath – 'which all the nobleman's acids could not wash away').

GUTHRIE, James (1859–1930) Painter

One of the most progressive spirits in late 19th century Scottish painting, Guthrie's early commitment to an art based on the direct observation of unpretentious subject

Sir James Guthrie, a self portrait (SNPG)

matter made him a protagonist in the movement known as the Glasgow Boys [see **Painting**]. Born in **Greenock**, Guthrie was intended for a legal career but left **Glasgow University** without completing his degree. He studied only briefly in London under fellow Scot John Pettie whose anecdotal approach he quickly discarded. In 1881 he joined E A Walton and **Joseph Crawhall** at Brig O'Turk where he found his subjects amongst the everyday life of the local community, culminating in his first and ambitious masterpiece *A Highland Funeral* (1881–2, **Glasgow Art Galleries**), a sombre and fittingly low-key work that demonstrates his regard for the painters of the Hague School.

The paintings of rustic life by Jules Bastien-Lepage were to have a profound effect on Guthrie and the other Boys. In 1883, in emulation of Lepage at Damvillers, Guthrie settled in **Cockburnspath** in **Berwickshire** and, adopting the Frenchman's painterly and compositional techniques, produced his finest and most influential works. *To Pastures New* (1882–3, **Aberdeen Art Gallery**), completed before his move, already shows an innovative approach towards design that dispenses with sentimentality, and a final rejection of incident; both characteristics of *The Hind's Daughter* (1883, **National Gallery of Scotland**) or any other of his several major works from this period that, with W Y McGregor's *Vegetable Stall* (1883–4, National Gallery of Scotland), represents the high-point of the group's artistic achievement.

Guthrie did not find these peasant subjects easy and with his rapid acceptance into the academic establishment – he was the first of the Boys to be elected an Associate of the **Royal Scottish Academy** (1888, becoming its President in 1902) – he seemed content to forsake his progressive stance. In the early 1890s he completed a fine series of pastels, the closest he came to Impressionism, but the production of these was short-lived and he is remembered latterly for his stylish, if eventually routine, portraiture.

GUTHRIE, Thomas (1803–73) Minister

Brechin born and **Edinburgh** and Paris educated, Guthrie became minister of Arbirlot in **Angus** and was one of the founders, with **Chalmers**, **Candlish** et al, of the **Free Church**. In 11 months he raised £116,000 towards the building of new manses. A founder also of Ragged Schools from 1847, and industrial schools (later Approved Schools), he was also a **temperance** orator.

HACKSTON, David, of Rathillet (d.1680)
Covenanter
Although present at Magus Moor in 1679, Hackston refused to lead the group in the murder of **Archbishop Sharp** for fear that a private dispute between himself and the Archbishop be thought the motive for the deed. The role of leader was therefore assumed by **John Balfour of Kinloch**. Little is known of Hackston's life prior to this date, save that he came from Rathillet near **Cupar** in **Fife** and that, once converted to the Cause, he became 'the strictest of the strict' in its defence. One of those responsible for posting the **Declaration of Rutherglen**, he commanded **Covenanter** forces at **Drumclog** and fought at **Bothwell Brig**, after which a price of 10,000 merks was put on his head. He joined the **Cameronians**, was captured at **Airds Moss** (22 July 1680) and taken to **Edinburgh** where he was most gruesomely executed, his hands being chopped off before he was hanged, disembowelled and dismembered, his head placed on the **Netherbow** and various limbs being sent to **St Andrews**, **Glasgow**, **Leith** and **Burntisland** for public display.

HADDEN RIG, Battle of (1542)
When **James V** was forced by his clergy to renege on an agreed meeting in York with Henry VII in 1541, the English king was so enraged that he sent a punitive force across the border in August 1542. It was met at Hadden Rig near **Berwick** by a Scots army under the **Earl of Huntly**; in the ensuing battle the English commander Sir Robert Bowes and 600 of his men were taken prisoner. Three months later, however, the English got ample revenge at the **Battle of Solway Moss**.

HADDINGTON, East Lothian
Haddington attracts superlatives. Every complimentary adjective in the thesaurus has at one time been used about the town, its situation, its churches, its streets, the monuments in its graveyards or the character of its residents; it was even described in an 1840 Gazetteer not as the 'county town' but as the 'metropolis' of **East Lothian**. Misfortunes it had aplenty – faults, apparently none. A **royal burgh** from the time of **David I**, it was granted to Ada de Warenne on her marriage to his son Earl Henry in 1139. The birthplace of their grandson **Alexander II** (1198), Haddington was reduced to ashes (literally, since the buildings were all of wood) by the English three times in the 13th century and again in 1356 when Edward III took his revenge for the Scots seizure of **Berwick**, an episode that came to be called

Burnt Candlemas. In 1548–9 it was the scene of a gruelling 16-month siege of the English garrison within by a combined Scots-French force without; on the arrival of a relieving force the English finally withdrew to Berwick leaving the town once more in ruins. Yet the worthy burgesses of the 'Lamp of the Lothians', as the town was called (a name originally given to the Franciscan friar's church destroyed in 1356), pulled themselves and their wrecked town together and started rebuilding; by the end of the 17th century a centre of woollen and broadcloth manufacture, Haddington reached true prosperity in the 18th and early 19th centuries as the most important grain market in Scotland and a staging post on the main **Edinburgh**-Newcastle road.

The parish church of St Mary the Virgin, one of the largest and most impressive of Scotland's late medieval churches, vying with **St Giles** in Edinburgh as the biggest in Lothian, stands away from the town centre on the site of an earlier church overlooking the river. Dating from 1462, St Mary's was severely damaged in the siege of 1548 and although the nave was repaired after the Restoration, the transepts and choir remained in ruins until they were restored in the early 1970s. The medieval sacristy was converted in 1595 into the burial aisle of the Maitlands of Lethington and contains a remarkable marble monument to **John Maitland of Thirlestane**.

Possibly the birthplace of **John Knox** (an honour sometimes awarded to **Gifford**), Haddington was also the birthplace (1801) of **Jane Welsh Carlyle** and (1812) of **Samuel Smiles**, the 'great Victorian exponent of self-help' by whose example the residents of Haddington have continued to be inspired, both in the restoration and conservation of the town's considerable architectural integrity and in the way they adapted to post-war urban pressures. In the 1950s they anticipated the development of Scotland's New Towns by taking in considerable numbers of **Glasgow**'s overspill population and integrating the newcomers into 'small town' life with sympathy and imagination.

HADDINGTON, Treaty of (1548)
Signed between the French and the Scots on 7 July at **Haddington**, **East Lothian**, where their joint forces were laying siege to the English garrison [see **Rough Wooing**], the treaty confirmed the betrothal of **Queen Mary** to the Dauphin of France and promised French assistance in driving the English out of Scotland. Mary arrived at the French court in August 1548, but the English did not withdraw from Haddington until September 1549, or leave Scotland entirely until the signing of the Treaty of Boulogne (March 1550).

HADDO HOUSE, Nr Tarves, Aberdeenshire
More typical of the Borders, the trim Palladian formality of a **William Adam** house replete with sumptuous furnishings, terraced gardens and pheasant-honking policies belies the idea of Grampian as all stern landscape and castellar architecture. Haddo had been **Gordon** territory since the 15th century, but not until 1682 was Sir George Gordon, Lord High Chancellor of Scotland, made Earl of Aberdeen. His son William, 2nd Earl, 'ambitious, financially accumulative [ie rapacious] and

Parish church of St Mary the Virgin, Haddington (entry p 517) (RWB)

a thumping snob' according to a descendant, demonstrated all these traits in consulting **Sir John Clerk of Penicuik** about a house to replace Kellie Tower, exploiting his tenants and marriages to pay for it, then commissioning William Adam to design it and John Baxter to build it. Work began in 1731 and was complete by 1735, though not without alterations to Adam's plans. Further additions, mostly to the flanking wings, were made by **George Gordon, 4th Earl of Aberdeen** (and Prime Minister), while the front entrance was redesigned by **John Campbell Gordon**, 7th Earl and 1st Marquess (also Governor-General of Canada, Ireland, etc) in 1880. The latter was also responsible for two less congruous structures, the non-denominational Gothic Revival chapel by G E Street with stained glass by Sir Edward Burne-Jones, and the timbered Canadian-style community hall, now home of the Haddo House Choral Society.

The original entrance hall or ante-room on the first floor retains its 18th century panelling but is dominated by a marble bust of **Queen Victoria** whose bedroom and dressing room remain much as they were during her visit of 1857. The drawing room contains two Van Dycks, a Domenichino and charming views of Castle of Gight by James Giles. Elsewhere, especially in the dining room, the pictures are mostly family portraits. Connected to the main block by curving quadrants, the south wing is reserved for members of the family and the north wing largely filled by the vast cedar-panelled, ebony inlaid and leather-spined library. Collections of Canadian china, stuffed birds, family memorabilia and castle watercolours fill the intervening rooms. Now

belonging to the **National Trust for Scotland**, the house is open to the public, and the policies constitute Grampian Regional Council's Country Park.

HAGGIS

Known throughout the world as Scotland's national dish (although the Oxford English Dictionary describes it as 'a popular English dish until the 18th century'), haggis is a fine example of the Scots housewife's skill in creating a gourmet dish from the humblest of ingredients. The traditional recipe for haggis lists these as:

> the large stomach bag [of a sheep]
> the small, or knight's hood, bag
> the pluck (including lights, liver and heart)
> beef suet, oatmeal, onions, pepper and salt.

It instructs the cook to put bag and pluck on to boil covered with cold water, 'leaving the windpipe hanging over the edge of the pan to let out any impurities' (F Marian McNeill). (Recipes for more fastidious modern tastes make no mention of 'stomach bag', 'pluck', 'lights' (lungs), 'windpipe' or 'impurities'; instead the 'paunch' is filled with the 'liver, heart and tongue' mixed with onion, oatmeal and seasoning.)

The origin of the word 'haggis' is uncertain. Sometimes given as deriving from the French *hachis* (mince), it more likely comes from the Scots word *hag*, to chop or hack.

In his 'Address to a Haggis', **Burns** attributes the Scottish soldier's fearsome reputation to this 'Great chieftain o' the pudding-race':

But mark the Rustic, haggis-fed,
The trembling earth resounds his tread.
Lap in his walie nieve[1] a blade,
He'll mak it whissle;
An' legs an' arms, an' heads will sned
Like taps o' thrissle.[2]

[1] Slap into his burly fist
[2] Will be lopped off like thistle tops

HAIG, Douglas, 1st Earl Haig of Bemersyde (1861–1928) Soldier

Douglas Haig was born in **Edinburgh** and educated there, at Clifton and then at Oxford. After Sandhurst he first saw action as a cavalry officer in the Sudan (Omdurman) and then the Boer War, where he was credited with having planned the victory at Elandslaagte. In 1903 Kitchener chose him as inspector-general of cavalry in India and, after assisting with **R B Haldane**'s military reforms (1906), he returned to India as chief of staff (1909–13). When World War I broke out he was back at Aldershot, a KCB and a lieutenant-general in command of the 1st Army Corps, which was immediately ordered to France. He succeeded as Commander-in-Chief of the British forces in December 1915 having become a national hero for his calm defiance at Mons and Ypres. On the Somme in 1916, though unpleasing to a horse fancier, cavalry officer and polo player, tanks were first used to effect; nonetheless in the space of four months 90,000 of his men were killed and over half a million wounded. More heavy losses followed during the German offensives of 1917–18. Though Haig deserved every credit for the armistice that followed his final assault (and was duly honoured with KT 1919 and earldom 1921), he was also one of those who regarded the human cost as exorbitant; he devoted the rest of his life to caring for the wounded and bereaved. He created the British Legion (1921) and was its first President as well as Chairman of the United Services Fund. The former Haig family home of **Bemersyde** was bought for him by a grateful nation and **St Andrews University** elected him Rector and then Chancellor. At his own request he was buried at **Dryburgh Abbey**. The suitably equestrian statue of him on Edinburgh's Castle **Esplanade** is by George Wade (1923) and was gifted by a Bombay parsee, Sir Dhumjibhoy Bomanzi.

HAILES CASTLE, East Linton, East Lothian

Two miles south west of **East Linton** on a rocky promontory on the south bank of the Tyne are the ruins of Hailes Castle, a 13th–14th century castle of enclosure probably built by one of the **Earls of Dunbar**. Later a Gourlay stronghold, Hailes then passed to the Hepburns who extended the curtain wall and added a square tower; **James Hepburn, Earl of Bothwell** brought **Queen Mary** here on their flight from **Borthwick** in 1567. Forfeited by the Hepburns and granted by **James VI** to Hercules Stewart, a natural son of Lord John Stewart (himself a natural son of **James V**), Hailes belonged to the Seton family for most of the 17th century and was damaged by Cromwell's troops in 1650. In c1700 it was sold by the Setons to **David Dalrymple**, later Lord Hailes, and in 1926 was given into state care

by its then owner, the Earl of Balfour (the former Prime Minister, **A J Balfour**). Hailes Castle is overlooked by **Traprain Law**, the site of the 1919 discovery of a hoard of 4th century **Roman** silver.

HALDANE, John Scott (1860–1936) Physiologist

Born in **Edinburgh**, Haldane studied medicine at Edinburgh and carried out postgraduate research at **Dundee**, before moving to England in 1887. He specialised in respiratory problems in extreme conditions, studying gassing accidents in mines and how to alleviate the 'bends', an operational hazard facing deep-sea divers. His 1935 monograph *Respiration* is regarded as a masterpiece of its kind. The father of the geneticist J B S Haldane (who later became an Indian citizen) and of the writer **Naomi Mitchison**, Haldane died at Oxford.

HALDANE, Richard Burdon, Viscount Haldane of Cloan (1856–1928) Philosopher and Lawyer

A grandson of **James Haldane**, R B Haldane was the elder brother of **John Scott Haldane** and of Elizabeth Sanderson Haldane (1862–1937), Scotland's first woman JP and a pioneer in nursing and education.

Richard Burdon was born in **Edinburgh** and educated there and in Göttingen. His first love was philosophy. He translated Schopenhauer, read Hegel for relaxation, contributed to *Essays in Philosophical Criticism*, 1883, delivered the 1902–3 Gifford lectures at **St Andrews**, and wrote on relativity. But after Edinburgh he read for the English bar and, law becoming his second love, practised in London and was made QC (1890). Not far behind came politics. Elected for **East Lothian** in 1885, he held the seat until going to the Lords in 1911. His first office was as Secretary of State for War (1905–12) in **Campbell-Bannerman**'s government, where his task was to bring a formidable intelligence and radical thinking to the reorganisation of the military establishment. With relations that included not only divines but also **Sir Ralph Abercromby** of Aboukir and **Adam Duncan** of **Camperdown**, this was not an improbable challenge. The results, including creation of the Imperial General Staff, were appreciated as soon as war broke out.

Created Viscount Haldane of Cloan (near **Auchterarder**), he was next appointed Lord Chancellor (1912) but three years later was relieved of office after a press outcry over his pre-war contacts with Germany. This enabled him to pursue another interest – making higher education available to a wider public. In 1895 he had been one of the founders of the London School of Economics, later helped to set up the University Grants Committee and now became president of Birkbeck College (1919–28). The Liberal Party's indifference to this crusade led him to espouse Labour and he was briefly Lord Chancellor once again in the 1924 Labour government. He is buried at **Gleneagles**.

HALDANE, Robert (1764–1842) and James Alexander (1768–1851)

Brothers and both naval officers of the **Gleneagles** Haldane family, Robert sold his estate at Airthrey to build churches while James toured Scotland from 1797 becoming a peripatetic evangelist. The Tabernacle, built in **Edinburgh**, and other independent Churches, evolved into Congregational or Baptist Churches in the new wave of evangelical foundations.

HALIDON HILL, Battle of (1333)

Having been chased ignominiously out of Scotland by **Sir Archibald Douglas** (Guardian for **David II**) in December 1332, **Edward Balliol** rode back over the border at the head of an English army in March 1333 and laid siege to **Berwick**. He was joined by Edward III in May. Douglas, who had been raiding in Northumberland, marched to the relief of the town and its garrison. But the English were waiting for him in an impregnable position on Halidon Hill commanding all approaches to the town. On 19 July wave after wave of Scots squelched through the bog at the foot of the hill and started to scramble up to attack. It was devastatingly easy for the English archers. Wave after wave of arrows mowed the Scots down as they climbed; six Scottish Earls (**Ross, Lennox, Atholl, Carrick**, Sutherland and Strathearn) died in the carnage, as did Archibald Douglas, '70 barons, 500 knights and spearmen uncountable'. English losses were estimated at 14 men. Berwick surrendered and Edward Balliol was restored.

HALKIRK, Caithness

It must have been close to Braal Castle beside the Thurso river that the earliest episcopal premises of **Caithness** were located. But no trace of them remains today except the Norse name *Ha Kirkja*, High Church. The bishopric of Caithness, separated from that of **Orkney**, was set up by **David I** (1124–53), the premier Baron of England before his succession; and it was understandably regarded as an instrument of his Normanising policies. Andrew, the first Bishop, seems never to have visited his diocese. The successors who did were given short shrift by the rulers of Orkney. It was Bishop Adam who was murdered in Halkirk. **Gilbert of Moray**, who followed him, moved his headquarters to **Dornoch**, behind the strongholds of his **Sutherland** kinsfolk. But Braal Castle continued to be a centre of the secular administration, and was occupied by the Earls of Caithness until the Campbell of Glenorchy usurpation of 1676. Today the substantial ruin of this rectangular keep belongs to Viscount Thurso, of the Ulbster branch which descends from an illegitimate son of the 4th Earl. It was his ancestor, agricultural improver **Sir John Sinclair**, who planned the new town of Halkirk in 1803, with its grid plan and broad streets.

HALL, Sir James (1761–1832) Geologist and Chemist

Born at Dunglass, near **Dunbar**, Hall inherited the family estate at the age of 15, enabling him to travel widely after studying at **Edinburgh** and Cambridge. Although not a professional academic, Hall championed the chemical theories of Lavoisier and showed considerable empirical talents in devising high temperature experiments to prove **James Hutton**'s theories of the volcanic nature of rocks. These did much to secure Hutton's posthumous reputation as the 'father of **geology**' and greatly advanced the experimental aspects of the science. Hall died in Edinburgh.

HAMILTON, Lanarkshire

Amidst extinct **coal** workings, and now badly grazed by the M74 motorway (here with service area and major intersection), Hamilton nevertheless aspires to rehabilitate itself as a resort and leisure centre if not as the genteel ducal appendage of former times. The district was originally called Cadzow, a name retained by the perilous 16th century ruins of Cadzow Castle of which **Sir Walter Scott** wrote a **ballad**. It stands above the Avon, which here joins the **Clyde**, in what is now Châtelherault Country Park. Charters issued from 'Cadihou' by **Alexander II** and **III** show it to have once belonged to the Crown. **Robert I** appears to have granted it to Walter de Homildon and **James II** to have authorised the change of the barony's name (to Hamilton) in a charter of 1445 in favour of the 1st Lord Hamilton who here founded a collegiate church. After her escape from **Loch Leven Castle**, **Queen Mary** was sheltered in Hamilton by Lord John Hamilton, commendator of **Arbroath** and later 1st Marquis of Hamilton.

The original Cadzow Castle probably stood on the Mote Hill, near the M74 and adjacent to the old township of Netherton, whose Celtic cross is now located beside **William Adam**'s Old Parish Church (1772). The churchyard also contains the Heads Memorial commemorating **Covenanters** executed after the 1666 **Pentland Rising**. Hamilton became something of a Covenanters' rallying point. After the **Battle of Bothwell Brig**, **Anne, Duchess of Hamilton**, provided a much-needed sanctuary for some of the vanquished by persuading the Duke of Monmouth to restrain his troops from disturbing her new plantations. There is a Covenanters' Trail and, in the former riding school of the Hamilton dukes, a museum of the **Cameronian** regiment. It stands behind the District Museum, itself an old coaching inn and later assembly hall, which specialises in local displays on coal-mining, transport, weaving (important in the early 19th century) and **Harry Lauder** (buried locally).

Châtelherault

South of the town, the High Parks area of the Hamilton estate around the river Avon is now the publicly owned Châtelherault Country Park (while the Low Parks area round the **Clyde** is Strathclyde Country Park which reaches to **Motherwell**). The gorges of the Avon are particularly dramatic and, besides Châtelherault itself, the park includes Cadzow Castle [see **Hamilton**], privately owned Barncluth (an early 17th century tower house with gardens), plus oaks of perhaps similar age amongst which graze a herd of the original **White Park cattle**.

Though not built until 1732–44, the 'palace' of Châtelherault is named after the French dukedom conferred on **James Hamilton, 2nd Earl of Arran** in 1550. **William Adam**, its architect, referred to his creation as the 'dogg kennels at Hamilton' and part was indeed used as kennels, stables and estate buildings. Other sections served as a hunting lodge and banqueting pavilion, but essentially the whole structure was intended as a landscape folly designed to complete the view from Hamilton Palace. The accommodation is in two buildings at either end of what is otherwise a wall, the total façade thus created being 280ft long and lavishly endowed with the urns and finial balls beloved of the Adams. Behind is a courtyard and gardens. Derelict by 1977, some of the external fabric and most of the internal plasterwork is the result of recent restoration. There is a visitor centre with facilities and displays.

Palace and Mausoleum

Of Hamilton Palace (mainly **David Hamilton**, 1828, with 260ft classical façade), the sumptuous home of the Dukes and of one of the finest art collections in Britain, nothing now remains; the whole was demolished in the 1920s when subsidence, the **coal**-miners' revenge, rendered it unsafe. It stood just to the south of a domed structure familiar to users of the M74 and looking like a cross between a Buddhist stupa and a municipal pumping station. It is in fact the mausoleum (**David Bryce**, 1840) of the 10th Duke and contains vaults and an octagonal chapel with noted echo. Two large stone lions guard it, but the Egyptian sarcophagus wherein lies the Duke has been reburied elsewhere. The cost, £130,000, may prove no guarantee of immortality, the building having already sunk courtesy of the coal extractors.

It stands on the edge of Strathclyde Country Park, most of which is on the **Motherwell** side of the M74. Châtelherault Country Park, also part of the Palace grounds and containing the ducal pavilion and kennels of **Châtelherault**, lies to the south and more properly pertains to Hamilton. Both present environmental reclamation on a grand scale but with an eye to their **tourist** potential rather than their aristocratic heritage.

HAMILTON, Captain Alexander (d.1732) Seaman and Author

Little is known of Captain Hamilton other than what he divulges in his one book, *A New Account of the East Indies* (1727). The book is dedicated to the 5th Duke of Hamilton and the Captain himself was clearly a Scot, one of very few in the East before the mid-18th century. During 35 years of merchant trading and adventure, he seems to have visited every port in the Indian Ocean and South China Sea. His opinions of them, and of the East India Company's employees, are often perceptive (a century before Raffles he identified Singapore as a promising site for an entrepôt), invariably candid, and sometimes scurrilous. The result is a work of enormous historical value that is also highly diverting. Much reprinted, it has been described as the nearest thing to Herodotus' *History*.

HAMILTON, Anne, Duchess of (1632–1716)

Only child of **James, 1st Duke of Hamilton**, Anne became Duchess in her own right on the death after the Battle of Worcester (1651) of her father's brother William, 2nd Duke. She married William Douglas, Earl of Selkirk (1635–94), who was created 3rd Duke of Hamilton on her petition, the **Hamilton** titles thus passing to the **Douglases**. A remarkable lady whose efficiency and determination are in vivid contrast to the instability of most of her male relatives, she administered the Hamilton estates, including the isle of **Arran**, through the perils of the Interregnum, the Restoration, the Revolution of 1688, the **Union** of 1707 and the **Jacobite** uprising of 1715. She passed the title (but not her strength of character) to her eldest son, **James, 4th Duke**, in 1698.

HAMILTON, David (1768–1843) Architect

Although one of **Glasgow**'s leading architects for about 30 years, with a large output, relatively little is known about Hamilton. He started his career as a mason, being admitted to the Incorporation of Masons in 1800. His early designs followed the Greek Revival (Glasgow **Royal Exchange**, 1829–30). He then experimented with Jacobean, Norman and Italianate forms before returning to the classical mode. In 1836 he was one of the four winners in the competition for the Houses of Parliament with a Scottish Jacobean design. His work ranged from country houses (Kincaid House, c1812) to public (Town Buildings, **Port Glasgow**, 1815–16) and commercial buildings (Glasgow Western Bank, Miller Street, 1840). Apart from his design for Donaldson's Hospital in **Edinburgh** (1838, not executed) he confined his practice to Glasgow and the south-west of Scotland.

HAMILTON, Gavin (1723–98) Historical Painter

Probably the most successful Scottish artist of the 18th century, Hamilton enjoyed a remarkable international reputation as an early exponent of the neo-classical revival. Born in **Lanark**, he was educated at **Glasgow University**, and the intellectual understanding of the classics he gained there was put to great use in later days. In 1745 he travelled to Rome and trained under the Italian portraitist Agostino Masucci. He established a portrait practice in London in the 1750s and his refined Italianate style attracted many patrons including the Duchess of **Hamilton**. He successfully adapted his skills to the art of historical painting a few years later (the reverse of the usual practice). Deeply affected by the revival of interest in the classical world and the excavations at Herculaneum and Pompeii, he returned to Rome, in many ways his spiritual home. The large, austere dramatic works that date from this period are the archetype of neo-classical history painting and brought Hamilton considerable wealth and celebrity. A particularly fine example is *Achilles Lamenting the Death of Patroclus* (1763, **National Gallery of Scotland**). Hamilton was highly esteemed as an antiquarian and dealer in Old Master paintings. His patrons included the Prince Borghese, Earl Spencer and the Duc de Rochefoucauld and he was in turn patron to younger artists including fellow Scot **David Allan** and the sculptor Antonio Canova. Although universally praised at the time, Hamilton's work no longer attracts much public acclaim, considered (as is much of the early neo-classicists) both histrionic and unmoving.

HAMILTON, Sir Ian Standish Monteith (1855–1947) General

Though born in Corfu, Hamilton was brought up at the family home in **Argyll**. After Wellington and Sandhurst he joined the 92nd Highlanders and was posted to India, then Natal where he was wounded at Majuba Hill (1881). He returned to South Africa for the Boer War. Showing conspicuous bravery at Elandslaagte and

Ladysmith, he commanded the mounted infantry during the advance on Pretoria and was made Kitchener's chief of staff and KCB. A general (1907), he held various staff appointments before World War I brought him command of the Central Force (1914–15) and then of the disastrous Gallipoli campaign (1915). He published a *Gallipoli Diary* in 1920 and was rector of **Edinburgh University** (1932–5).

HAMILTON, James, 2nd Lord Hamilton, 1st Earl of Arran (c1477–1529)

Son of Sir James Hamilton of Cadzow, 1st Baron Hamilton (d.1479), and of Princess Mary, sister of **James III**, James Hamilton was a privy councillor under **James IV** and was created 1st **Earl of Arran** in 1503 (a title previously held by his mother's first husband, Thomas Boyd, who had forfeited both it and his estates in 1469 on his father's conviction for treason against James III). A member of the Regency Council (1517–20) during the absence in France of **John Stewart, Duke of Albany** (Regent for **James V**), Arran led the Hamiltons in their bitter running feud with the **Douglases** under **Archibald, 6th Earl of Angus**, by whom he was forced to flee **Edinburgh** in 1520 [see **Cleanse-the-Causeway**]. Restored to the Regency Council (1522), he supported the investiture in 1524 of the 12-year-old James V as King. Arran finally had his revenge on Angus, who had held the King captive for three years, by helping the King chase his captor from Scotland, for which aid Arran received Angus's forfeited estates of **Bothwell** as a reward.

HAMILTON, James, 2nd Earl of Arran, Duke of Châtelherault (c1516–75) Regent of Scotland

James Hamilton succeeded his father, **James, 1st Earl of Arran**, in 1529 and, following the death of **James V** in 1542, became Regent during the minority of **Queen Mary**. As great-grandson of **James II** he was also heir-presumptive to the throne. Chronically indecisive, he initially took a pro-English stance, agreeing to the **Treaty of Greenwich** (1543) by which the six-month-old Queen was betrothed to the six-year-old Edward, Prince of Wales; he changed his mind within a year, causing Henry VIII to launch his campaign against the Borders [see **Rough Wooing**]. Arran's Achilles heel was the doubt over the legitimacy of his father's second marriage (of which he was a product) and thus over his own legitimacy. Since jurisdiction over matrimonial affairs lay with the Church, Arran was easily persuaded to support the plans of **Cardinal Beaton** and the Queen Mother **Mary of Guise** for Mary to be betrothed to the French Dauphin. His reward was the French Dukedom of Châtelherault (1549).

In 1554 he agreed to let the Regency pass to Mary of Guise in exchange for her assurances that, should Mary die childless, his claim to the throne would be upheld. However Mary's marriage to the Dauphin in 1558 and her secret agreement on the 'Crown Matrimonial', whereby her husband became King of Scotland, dealt a severe blow to Châtelherault's chances of the succession. So when the **Lords of the Congregation** asked him to act as their candidate should they succeed in deposing the Catholic Queen, he prevaricated only

as long as his even more unstable son, **James, 3rd Earl of Arran**, was held prisoner in France. On Arran's escape in 1559 Châtelherault blithely changed sides again. But not for long. The death of Francis II in 1560 revived his hopes of securing a marriage between the newly widowed Mary and his son, first promoted in 1544. But by 1562 young Arran's instability had teetered into madness; he was locked away and remained so until his death in 1609.

Yet Châtelherault still could not decide on which side of the fence to settle. He opposed Mary's marriage to **Darnley** (whose family stood next in line to the succession after the Hamiltons), raising a rebellion against it with the **Earl of Moray**, was defeated [see **Chaseabout Raid**] (1565) and retired to his estates in France. He emerged to support Mary after her exile, only to be imprisoned by Moray (1569) and finally induced by the English to sign the Pacification of **Perth** (1572) acknowledging **James VI** as her successor.

HAMILTON, James, 3rd Earl of Arran (c1537–1609)

Doomed to spend most of his life as a political pawn, which may or may not have contributed to his mental instability, James, 3rd Earl of Arran was the eldest son of **James, 2nd Earl of Arran**, Duke of Châtelherault and Regent of Scotland. Nominated (1543) as a future husband for the English Princess Elizabeth at the suggestion of Henry VIII, who was angling for an Anglo-Scottish alliance, and then (1544) for **Queen Mary** at the suggestion of his father, who was desperately trying to secure a **Hamilton** succession, the young Arran was held hostage first in **St Andrews** (1543) and then in France (1548–59) to ensure his father's compliance with a Franco-Scottish alliance. On his escape he returned to Scotland where in 1560 his father renewed his efforts to marry him to the now widowed Mary. But by 1562 Arran's instability had crumbled into insanity; he was locked away and remained so until his death in 1609.

HAMILTON, James, 3rd Marquis and 1st Duke (1606–49) Royalist

Born in England, the son of the 2nd Marquis, James succeeded to the title in 1625, became a Privy Councillor in 1628 and served the Protestant cause during the Thirty Years' War before being sent by **Charles I** to deal with Scottish taxation in 1633. In May 1638 he became Commissioner to the Scottish Assembly and in November attended the post-**Covenant General Assembly** in **Glasgow** from which he walked out in anger when his protest against the deposition of bishops was ignored. During the ensuing Bishops' War, he commanded the fleet but failed to give effectual assistance to **Huntly** by landing reinforcements. Having resigned as Commissioner, he returned to Scotland in 1642 to try to dissuade the Covenant leaders from supporting the English Parliamentarians. The King, in gratitude, awarded him the dukedom (April 1643) but his subsequent support of the Solemn League and Covenant resulted in his imprisonment. Released in 1646, he commanded the Royalist army in support of the **Engagement** which was defeated at **Preston** in 1648.

James Hamilton, 1st Duke of Hamilton, by Daniel Mytens, 1629 (SNPG)

He was executed in London on 9 March 1649, having 'shown throughout his life a magic touch that turned all to mud, a gift of invariable failure at the crucial instance' (R Mitchison).

HAMILTON, James, 4th Duke of Hamilton (1658–1712)

Eldest son of **Anne, Duchess of Hamilton** and William Douglas (later 3rd Duke), James inherited more of his grandfather, the **1st Duke**'s, talent for 'invariable failure at the crucial instance' than of his mother's resolute common sense. He spent much of his youth abroad, where he earned a lasting reputation for extravagance and irresponsibility. A supporter of the **Jacobite** cause at the Revolution (1688), he became leader of the anti-Unionist Country Party (1702–7), but his inability to reconcile the interests of his country with those of his personal estates and fortune ('he offered all things to all men' (W Ferguson)) rendered him, and the anti-Unionist cause, ineffectual. The Country Party ceased to exist after the 1707 **Union**, and the Jacobites no longer trusted him; so he offered his support instead to the English Tories under the Earl of Oxford in exchange for the promise of an English dukedom. He was indeed created Duke of Brandon in 1711, but the opposition denied him the right to an hereditary seat in the House of Lords under this title; further, they decided that as Duke of Hamilton he could no longer vote in the election of the 16 elected Scottish peers, a decision in what was regarded as a test case that roused the ire of Scots of all parties and for a while threatened the very fabric of the Union. The following year he experienced his ultimate failure when he fought a duel with Lord Mohun in which both men were killed.

HAMILTON, Sir James, of Finnart (d.1540)
Architect

Natural son of **James, 1st Earl of Arran** (and known to contemporaries and posterity alike as 'the Bastard of Arran', although he was not the only one), James Hamilton spent much of his youth abroad, and took enthusiastic part in his father's feuds with both the **Douglases** and the **Lennoxes** when he returned to Scotland. Described by a descendant as 'a fiery but talented nobleman' (the 'fiery' presumably relates to his cold-blooded murder of his cousin John Stewart, Earl of Lennox in 1526 and the 'talented' to his considerable skill as an architect), he was a close friend of **James V**, became the King's Master of Works and was responsible for the design and construction of **Craignethan Castle**, the fortification of **Blackness Castle**, and the restoration of **Linlithgow** and **Falkland Palaces**. In 1540 allegations were made that he had been involved in a plot against the King. Although no evidence has been found to support the charge, the 'Bastard of Arran' was convicted of treason and beheaded, his considerable fortune then being appropriated by his 'most acquisitive' King.

HAMILTON, John (c1512–71) Archbishop of St Andrews

Natural son of the **1st Earl of Arran** (and therefore half-brother to the **2nd Earl**, Duke of Châtelherault, and to **Sir James Hamilton** of Finnart), John Hamilton, who has been described as 'the brains of the house [of Hamilton]', was an ambitious but moderate churchman, successively **Commendator** of **Paisley** (1525), Bishop of **Dunkeld** (1546) and, after the assassination of **David Beaton**, Archbishop of **St Andrews** (1547). He made genuine, if unsuccessful, attempts to reform Church discipline, summoning a series of councils in 1549, 1552 and 1559, producing the Hamilton Catechism which required improvements in the standard of education of the clergy, and endowing St Mary's College at St Andrews to this end.

A most assiduous promoter of Hamilton interests, he opposed the **Treaty of Greenwich**, whereby **Queen Mary** would have married Prince Edward of England, because he wanted her to marry his nephew **James** (later 3rd Earl of Arran), yet despite being imprisoned (1563–5) by Mary for saying Mass, agreed to annul **Bothwell**'s marriage to Lady Jane Gordon (1567) so Bothwell could marry the Queen. After Mary's deposition he became a committed Marian knowing that, should the succession remain with her son **James**, it would have moved away from the Hamiltons to within reach of his old enemies, the Lennoxes. When **Matthew 4th Earl of Lennox** became Regent for James (July 1570), intent on exacting revenge for the murder of his son **Lord Darnley**, Archbishop Hamilton was captured at **Dumbarton Castle** and hanged for being an accessory to that murder and for complicity in the assassination of Regent **Moray**.

HAMILTON, John, 2nd Lord Belhaven (1656–1708) Anti-Unionist

Belhaven's is a revered name amongst Scottish nationalists because of his much quoted speech of 1706 against the **Union**. An eccentric and controversial figure, he had, like **Fletcher of Saltoun**, opposed **James VII** (and been imprisoned for it), welcomed William of Orange, and espoused agricultural improvement (The Countreyman's Rudiments, 1699) as the answer to Scotland's economic ills. He had also invested £1000 in the **Darien Company** and thus stood to gain from the compensatory offer which would result from Union. Though frequently dismissed as a disappointed place-seeker, he opposed the Union out of a conviction which neither his shaky syntax nor his histrionics could wholly obscure. Visionary outbursts such as 'I think I see our ancient mother Caledonia, like Caesar, sitting in the midst of our senate . . . attending the final blow,' prompted Defoe to lampoon him in The Vision. Belhaven responded in kind and Defoe hit back again, ridiculing his protagonist as 'Supream in Thought, to Grammar unconfin'd'. But the two subsequently became friends and in his History of the Union Defoe memorialised Belhaven as 'a person of extraordinary parts and capacity'.

HAMILTON, Marquisate & Dukedom

This family, which for so long provided the heirs presumptive to the Scottish crown, descended from Walter Fitz Gilbert of Hameldone, on record in 1294. James, created a Lord of Parliament in 1445, married **James III**'s sister Mary and the family's royal descent, rather than any conspicuous merit, led to their elevation to the rank of Marquis in 1599 and Duke in 1643. On the death of the 2nd Duke in 1651 his property, including the island of **Arran**, was administered by the redoubtable **Duchess Anne**, his only child. She guided its fortunes, with a skill more remarkable than that of any of her male forebears, through the perils of the Interregnum, the Restoration, the Revolution of 1688, the **Union** of 1707 and the **Jacobite** uprising of 1715. She married William Douglas, Earl of Selkirk, and their son the **4th Duke of Hamilton** returned to more traditional practices when he fought a duel with Lord Mohun in which both men were killed. It earned him a place in Thackeray's Esmond. From the **2nd Earl of Arran** descend Hamiltons in the male line whose senior representative is the Duke of **Abercorn**. While **Hamilton Palace** in Lanarkshire was dismantled in 1920, the castle of **Brodick** on Arran remains safely in the hands of the **National Trust for Scotland**.

HAMILTON, Patrick (c1498–1528) Protestant Martyr

The proto-martyr of the **Reformation**, descended from an illegitimate granddaughter of **James II**, Patrick Hamilton was educated at Paris and Louvain where Lutheran influences reformed theology. Forced to leave **St Andrews** for Marburg in 1527, he returned, married, was arrested for heresy and burned by **Archbishop Beaton**, a torch which ignited the Reformation.

John Hamilton, 2nd Lord Belhaven, by an unknown artist after Sir G Kneller (SNPG)

HAMILTON, Sir Robert, of Preston (1650–1701) Covenanter

Leader of the group of armed **Covenanters** who read the **Declaration of Rutherglen** (1679), Sir Robert Hamilton was also the leader of the Covenanting forces at **Drumclog** three days later. Described as an 'unbending purist' who believed that 'it is not the endurance but the infliction of pain that makes a true soldier of Christ', he is reputed to have fled the field at **Bothwell Brig** as soon as defeat became inevitable and escaped to Holland.

HAMILTON, Thomas (1563–1637) Advocate

Holder of a confusing series of titles – Lord Drumcairn (1592), Lord Binning (1613), Earl of Melrose (1619), Earl of Haddington (1627) – but best remembered as 'Tam o' the **Cowgate**' (a soubriquet bestowed on him by **James VI** in reference to the location of his **Edinburgh** home), Thomas Hamilton was educated in Paris and followed his father, the judge Lord Priestfield, into the legal profession. Admitted advocate in 1587, he himself became a judge (1592), and four years later was appointed Lord Advocate, a post he held until 1612 when he became Secretary of State. President of the **Court of Session** (1616–27) and Lord Privy Seal (1626), he left a large fortune and an important collection of legal manuscripts.

HAMILTON, Thomas (1784–1858) Architect

Hamilton was a major figure in the Greek Revival style in **Edinburgh** during the early 19th century. His father was a builder and Hamilton began his career as an architect around 1815. In 1816 he entered the competition for the completion of **Adam**'s Old College, **Edinburgh University**. His best-known work is the Royal High School, Edinburgh (1825–9), a dramatic composition on the steep slope of **Calton Hill**. Although most of his works were in the Greek style, he designed a number of churches in the Gothic and Norman manner. A town planner of distinction and an influential figure in the development of Edinburgh, he prepared proposals for the development of the south and west of the Old Town. These were realised by the Edinburgh Improvement Commission in 1827. As architect to the Commission, Hamilton was responsible for the building of **George IV Bridge** (1829–34) and King's Bridge (1829–32). He was also involved in the development of **The Mound** and its galleries, about which he wrote a report in 1830. In 1834 he resigned from his position with the Commission and concentrated on individual projects. Working mostly in Edinburgh, he designed buildings such as the **Royal College of Physicians** (1844–6) and the **Burns Monument** on Calton Hill.

HAMILTON, William, of Bangour (1704–54) Poet

Hamilton's father died in 1705, and in 1711, when Hamilton was still a boy, his mother married **Lord President Dalrymple**, of a highly cultivated but staunchly Whig family. From 1716–20 Hamilton attended **Edinburgh University**, and in the 1720s, perhaps in reaction to his step-family, he joined the **Jacobite** Rankin Club presided over by **Thomas Ruddiman**. Hamilton's first poetry appeared in the 1723 edition of **Allan Ramsay**'s *Teatable Miscellany*, and more in subsequent editions, his most famous poem, *The Braes of Yarrow*, being printed for the first time in 1730. In 1739 he went abroad for his health, meeting **Prince Charles Edward Stewart** in Rome. By 1741 he was back in Edinburgh, and in 1743 he married Katherine Hall of the Dunglass family.

In 1745 he joined the Prince at **Holyrood**, and seems to have become, as it were, publicity officer for the Jacobite cause. His 'Gladsmuir Ode' on the **Battle of Prestonpans** was set to music by **William McGibbon**. His wife died just as the Jacobite forces were about to leave Edinburgh, and he was probably not at Derby. But he was present at both **Falkirk** and **Culloden**.

By the summer of 1746 he had found his way to Sweden, and thence to Paris, settling in Rouen the following year. He returned to Edinburgh in 1750 looking for material for a history of the rising. His health took him back to France in 1753, and he died there in March 1754. He was buried at Holyrood. Described as 'agreeable, learn'd and elegant', and much loved by all who knew him, his talent was essentially lightweight and social, but his poems had great popularity in their day. The first full edition of his work, *Poems on Several Occasions*, was edited by **Adam Smith**, and published by the **Foulis** Press in 1748.

HAMILTON, Sir William (1730–1803) Diplomat and Archaeologist

British ambassador at Naples (1764–1800) and an archaeologist with a passion for volcanoes and earthquakes (but best remembered as the husband of Emma), William Hamilton was the grandson of William Douglas, 3rd **Duke of Hamilton**. Fellow of the Royal Society (1766) and knighted in 1772, he took part in the excavations of Herculaneum and Pompeii and made 22 ascents of Vesuvius (DNB). He married the beautiful but already disreputable Emma Lyon when he was 61 (her senior by 25 years) and seems not to have resented her relationship with Nelson. He left his considerable collection of archaeological specimens to the British Museum.

HARDIE, James Keir (1856–1915) Founder of Labour Party

Like **James Ramsay MacDonald**, his successor in Labour politics, Keir Hardie was born out of wedlock into grinding poverty. His mother, Mary Keir, was a maid near Holytown, a mining village between **Airdrie** and **Motherwell**. There he was born and received the surname Hardie when his mother married David Hardie, a carpenter. His step-father found occasional work in the **Clyde** shipyards; the family moved to **Glasgow** and aged seven Hardie started work as an errand boy. Three years later, the step-father having gone to sea, they moved to Newarthill near Motherwell and Hardie went down the pits. He also began to read ('I owe more to Burns than to any man living or dead'); he attended evening classes and later took an active part in the **temperance movement** and in agitation for better working conditions. Black-listed by the mine-owners, in 1878 he opened a newsagents and tobacconists in Low Waters, **Hamilton**, and began writing for the radical press. As organising secretary of the local miners, he sought common ground with other miners' leaders and set up an embryonic county organisation for **Lanarkshire** and then for **Ayrshire**. By 1886 he was secretary of the umbrella Scottish Miners' Federation.

James Keir Hardie, by H J Dobson, 1893 (SNPG)

He had married a collier's daughter in 1879 and they were now settled in **Cumnock**, which would remain the family home thereafter. He continued to rely largely on earnings from journalism but during the late 1880s became increasingly disillusioned with Liberal politics and favoured the formation of a party specifically representing labour. He stood as a Labour candidate in the 1888 Mid Lanark by-election and in the same year founded the Scottish Labour Party, the first of its kind in Britain and later incorporated in the **Independent Labour Party** (ILP). He also started The Miner (1887) and the Labour Leader (1889) which circulated widely in England. East London militancy during the 1889 dock strike and Hardie's subsequent selection and victory in the West Ham seat in 1892 projected him into the mainstream of UK radical politics. He became founder and chairman of the new ILP (1893–1900) and in parliament as 'the member for the unemployed' caused a sensation by wearing cloth cap and tweeds.

Losing West Ham in 1895 he returned as member for Merthyr Tydfil in 1900 and played the lead role in the establishment of the Labour Representative Committee which became the Labour Party. In 1906 he led the parliamentary party but resigned owing to ill health in the following year; dedicated campaigning up and down the country was taking its toll. He again chaired the ILP in 1913 and the International Socialist Bureau in 1914 but when both trade unionism and proletariat solidarity proved powerless to prevent war, like other radical socialists he was bitterly disappointed. He died of pneumonia aggravated by exhaustion and despair.

HARLAW, Battle of (1411)

One of the bloodiest (hence 'Red Harlaw') engagements fought in Scotland, Harlaw produced no clear victor yet proved decisive for the future of the country. While the young **James I** was a prisoner in England, **Donald Lord of the Isles** led a force of Highlanders and Islanders east, seized **Inverness** and crossed the **Spey**. He was avowedly securing the estates of the **Earldom of Ross** in an attempt to pre-empt the **Stewarts**, and especially the Governor of Scotland, **Albany**. Thus there was an element of Highland backlash against Stewart and Lowland acquisitiveness. But he may also have had encouragement from Henry IV of England who had no love for Albany's pretensions to sovereignty; and he was probably as keen to sack and plunder **Aberdeen** as to secure the Ross lands.

At Harlaw, 2 miles north-west of **Inverurie**, he was opposed by the fighting men of the north-east – Irvines, Leslies, Keiths and Forbeses – plus some Aberdeen burgesses, all under the command of the **Earl of Mar**. The fight raged throughout 24 July and ended with the withdrawal of the invaders. According to **Boece** both sides thought they had lost, according to their descendants both thought they had won. **Sir Walter Scott** and others saw it as a straight Highlanders versus Lowlanders encounter which confirmed their mutual antagonism and the dual nature of Scottish identity. It has also been seen as signalling the failure of Gaeldom to expand its cultural sway outside the Highlands and thus prefigured its eventual marginalisation. A monument was erected on the site of the battle in 1911.

HARRIS, Isle of, Outer Hebrides

The island of Harris (Gaelic Na Hearadh) is not an island at all: together with **Lewis** it forms the largest and most northerly of the Western Isles, Harris taking up the southern third. The long sea lochs of Loch Seaforth and Loch Resort divide the two districts. With a land area of 90 square miles (23,310ha) and a population of c2000 (1999), Harris has a landscape which in places is quite mountainous – very different from the flat peaty lands of Lewis. Clisham (2622ft/799m) is the highest hill in the Outer **Hebrides**. Around it is some of the finest unspoilt wilderness to be found anywhere in Scotland. Archaeological monuments and Norse place-names dot the landscape.

The largest town and ferry terminal is at **Tarbert**, which is connected by Caledonian **MacBrayne's** ferries to **Lochmaddy** on **North Uist** and to **Uig** on the **Isle of Skye**. A passenger ferry plies from **Leverburgh** in Harris to Newtonferry on North Uist. Another ferry serves the off-shore island of **Scalpay**.

One of Scotland's archaeological gems is St Clement's Church at Rodel, on the south-east corner of Harris. Although it has been restored on several occasions, most recently in 1873, most of the walls and the greater part of the tower are medieval, dating from the early 16th century. The windows are square-headed except for the east window, which has a pointed arch with three trefoil panels, above which is a wheel window with six spokes. St Clement's is the finest pre-**Reformation** church in the Western Isles and is memorable also for two magnificent medieval tombs built into its south wall. Rodel was the burial place for many of the **MacLeods of Dunvegan**.

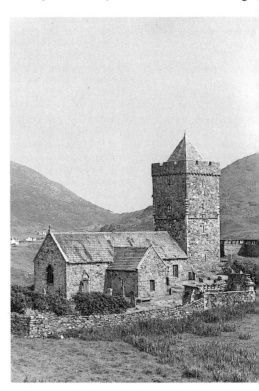

The pre-Reformation church of St Clement at Rodel, Isle of Harris (HS)

nd Harris, and the tomb of Alexander MacLeod of
)unvegan (also known as Alasdair Crotach) is an out-
:anding example of medieval stone carving. It was built
1 1528, although curiously Alexander did not die for
mother 20 years. His tomb consists of a stone effigy in
:hain mail and plate armour, lying with his head on a
:one pillow. Behind the stone figure is a recessed arch
ecorated with panels illustrating a variety of scenes,
ncluding ecclesiastical and biblical figures, a castle, a
alley under sail, and a hunting scene with men holding
iogs observing a group of **deer**. Because this tomb was
uilt into the fabric of the church in the Middle Ages,
nd has never been subject to the ravages of the Heb-
idean weather, the carvings have a freshness and detail
arely seen.

There are many other interesting architectural details
n St Clement's Church, incuding a carving of St Clement
imself with a bull's head beneath his feet, and a *sheila-
a-gig*, a nude female figure, with a child, in a crouched
ttitude, blatantly displaying her vagina. It is thought
hat the purpose of such figures was to attract the atten-
ion of the satanic spirits, representing the evils and
emptations of life, who would follow worshippers into
he building.

The recent history of Harris is closely bound up with
hat of Lewis; both now form part of the all-purpose
ocal authority administered from **Stornoway** by
Comhairle nan Eilean, the Islands' Council. Many
present-day attitudes towards **local government** and
dministration are conditioned by the era of **Lord
.everhulme**, the soap magnate, who bought Lewis and
Harris in 1918–19 and proceeded to introduce ideas
of social engineering which unfortunately met with
a mixed reception and came to an abrupt end with
us death in 1925. His 'Lewis and Harris Welfare and
)evelopment Company Ltd' was an early version of
he local Enterprise Trusts which are now in fashion
again. The economy of Harris is based on **crofting** and
ishing, supplemented by income from **tourism**
and from the district's most famous export, **Harris
weed**.

Just offshore on the west coast of North Harris, oppo-
ite the township of Hushinish, is the small rocky island
of Scarp, rising on its north side to a height of 1011ft
(308m). First settled in 1810, it was abandoned in
1971. In 1884 the population was estimated at around
200. As late as the 1940s it was over 100; now the
:rofters' cottages are used as holiday homes and there
are periodic threats to develop the island as a luxury
ioliday resort. Scarp was the scene of a strange experi-
nent in 1934, when the German rocket scientist Ger-
iardt Zucher tried to persuade the British government
:hat rockets could be used to transport mail and emergency medicines to remote islands. Amid much pub-
icity, 30,000 letters were launched into the Hebridean
air. But the rocket blew up, and this attempt to use
modern technology to solve the perennial problem of
communication with remote communities was not
repeated.

Until recently the most remote community in Harris
was Rhenigdale, accessible only by sea or by a rough
hill track. But after lengthy representations a road was
built, probably just in time to save this community from
abandonment.

HARRIS TWEED

To qualify as Harris tweed, cloth must bear the orb
trademark of the Harris Tweed Association, founded in
1909, and be made in the Outer Hebrides from virgin
Scottish wool, woven on handlooms in the weavers'
own homes.

Tweed is hard-wearing, warm, water-resistant – and
fashionable. The cloth is produced in rolls of 38
weaver's yards (each of 72 inches), 28½ inches wide.
About 650 weavers produce 4.5 million yards of cloth
annually. Originally a domestic activity carried on
mainly by women, the weaving of tweed became a
full-time specialist male occupation, partly because
the flying shuttle in 'modern' looms made the work
heavier. Attempts to rationalise the industry by concentrating production in a factory in **Stornoway** met with
almost total opposition from the weavers. But since
1934 the wool has been dyed, carded and spun in
Stornoway.

Although **Lewis** is now the centre of the tweed industry, it had its origins in **Harris**, where the Earl of Dunmore at Amhuinnsuidhe Castle asked the local weavers
to copy some Murray tartan for his army's kilts. The
pioneers were Marion and Christina MacLeod of Strond,
originally from the island of Pabbay. They were known
as the 'Paisley sisters' as they had been sent there for
training by the Dowager Countess of Dunmore, Catherine Herbert, daughter of the Earl of Pembroke.

Today the industry is subject to the vagaries of the
fashion industry, but in general clothes made from
Harris tweed are highly regarded and priced appropriately. In recent years the amount produced has contracted, as market forces dictate that what was once a
common and serviceable cloth is now a luxury item,
but the islanders have proved adaptable in meeting this
crisis. Some even produce tweed in the old way, hand-
dyeing and carding, spinning on the wheel, hand-
weaving and finishing, producing high quality cloth
selling for up to three times the price of ordinary tweed.
The history of the Harris tweed industry is displayed at
An Clachan, Leverburgh and is described in detail in
Francis Thompson's *Harris Tweed: The Story of a Hebridean
Industry*, 1969.

HARRY THE MINSTREL (fl.1470–92) Poet

It seems unlikely that Harry the Minstrel is to be identified, as was earlier believed, with the 'Blind Harry' of
Dunbar's 'Lament for the **Makaris**'. He flourished in
the late 15th century, was well educated, widely read
and is frequently recorded as having attended **James IV**
when the monarch was in the **Linlithgow** area. His
12-book romance, *The Wallace*, is in the same tradition
as **John Barbour**'s *The Brus*, but it was Harry's poem
which caught the popular imagination and was to
influence (often in prose 'translations') later generations. Both **Burns** and **Scott** pay tribute to it and admit
its power to please. *The Wallace*, while never sentimental,
does play on the emotions. The hero's personal tragedy
is viewed from many dramatic viewpoints while being
balanced against major triumphs, among which the
winning of **Bruce** on to the side of independence is
highlighted. Harry's ability to recreate scenes of battle
and of grief account for the work's hold over the
memory of so many.

HARVEY, Sir George (1806–76) Genre Painter

Harvey, who was born in **Perthshire**, studied in **Edinburgh** under **Sir William Allan** at the **Trustees' Academy**. Although latterly, like Allan, he turned to the historical set-piece, his best work was painted in his early years when he concentrated on depicting local events and people. Such genre painting had been the forte of the young **David Wilkie** and Harvey selected similar low-life subjects – **curling**, schoolchildren, village celebrations – treating them with bravado and fluent brushwork. As with many mid-19th century artists he also aspired to 'serious' subject matter and produced several large canvases of scenes from the history of the **Covenanters** and other Scottish Protestant histories. Although bringing contemporary renown, these are no longer so highly respected. Harvey typifies the Victorian Edinburgh artist whose 'worthy' oils, widely distributed as engravings, are now deemed contrived and stagey without any of the technical élan that typified the work of the English Pre-Raphaelites and their followers. He was closely involved in the founding of the **Royal Scottish Academy** and the Royal Association for the Fine Arts in Scotland and was President of the former institution from 1864 until his death. His popularity encouraged younger artists, such as the Faed brothers, although they sought the greater wealth and celebrity to be found in London.

HAWICK, Roxburghshire

The largest of the Borders towns, Hawick was granted to Douglas of **Drumlanrig** by **James I**, passed to the Scotts of Buccleuch in the early 16th century and suffered the same devastation as its neighbours at the hands of the English during the **Rough Wooing**, few of its buildings surviving the conflagration. Most of the present town dates from the 19th century when increased mechanisation led to a rapid expansion of Hawick's traditional hosiery and knitwear industry; the continuing success of this industry through the 20th century has won the town an international reputation as the home of fine woollens. Hawick's Common Riding Festival, held annually in June, commemorates a band of local youths or 'callants' who in 1514 waylaid a troop of English soldiers from Hexham camped at nearby Hornshole and captured and triumphantly carried home their banner, the 'Hexham Pennant'. Scenes almost as extraordinary brought the town unwelcome publicity when in the 1990s lady riders asserted their right to ride with the gentlemen. The town was bitterly divided over the issue as the rest of Scotland looked askance. Excavations at Hawick Motte, a large flat-topped tumulus near the town centre, dated the site to the 12th century and suggested the possibility that this is all that remains of Hawick Castle which was granted by **William the Lion** to an Englishman by the name of Lovel.

HAWTHORNDEN CASTLE, Midlothian

Between **Roslin** and **Lasswade**, Hawthornden Castle (or House) is a three-storey 17th century mansion grafted onto a ruined 15th century tower house wonderfully sited on the edge of a deep gorge of the river North Esk. Famous as the home of the poet **William Drummond of Hawthornden**, who was responsible for the restoration and rebuilding (a Latin inscription dates the work to 1638), Hawthornden is also renowned for its surrounding woods and gardens; the sycamore under which Drummond is said to have greeted his guest Ben Jonson, who arrived on foot from London in 1618, was an evocative landmark on **Johnson** and **Boswell**'s 1773 tour, the latter determined to see 'Sam Johnson at the very spot where Ben Jonson visited the learned and poetical Drummond, and pleased to think that the place was now visited by another celebrated wit of England'. The rock face below the castle contains a series of artificial caves linked by passages reputed to have been used as a refuge by early **Picts** and to have sheltered **Robert the Bruce** during the **Wars of Independence**. Appropriately, the castle is now a writers' retreat.

HAY, George Campbell (Deòrsa Caimbeul Hay) (1915–84) Gaelic Poet

Son of **John MacDougall Hay**, author of the novel *Gillespie*, Hay learned **Gaelic** in his teens, and came to regard it as his main language for creative work although he also wrote in Scots and English. He is one of the outstanding Gaelic poets of the 20th century.

Most of his Gaelic poetry had been written by the time he was in his early thirties; the latter half of his life was much dislocated by psychiatric troubles. His first Gaelic collection, *Fuaran Slèibh* ('Upland Spring' 1947) shows him in a traditional mould, with delicate poems of nature description, centred on his beloved **Kintyre**, love-poems clearly inspired by the earlier Gaelic *dànta gràdha* or courtly-love poems (and using their metrical models with great skill) and poems with a political and philosophical thrust. This last was to be accentuated in his next collection, *O na Ceithir Airdean* ('From the Four Airts', 1952) which includes a number of powerful political poems such as *Truaighe na h-Eòrp* ('Europe's Piteous Plight') and *Ar Blàr Catha* ('Our Battleground') and philosophical poems, often with a war background, eg *Meftah Babkum Es-sabar?* (a line from an Arabic poem, 'Patience the key to your door?') and *Atman*. This collection also included one of his finest poems, *Bisearta*. Both books contain poems translated from a wide range of languages: Italian, Greek, Arabic, Croatian, French.

His *Wind on Loch Fyne* comes from the same period (1948) and consists of poems in Scots and English with a number of translations from Irish, Gaelic, Welsh, Croatian, etc, and some original poems of his own in French and Norwegian.

Hay's last major publication was the long poem *Mochtàr is Dùghall* ('Mokhtar and Dougall') published in 1982 but apparently written in the mid- to late-1940s. This was intended to be a detailed comparison of Arab and Gaelic lifestyles/philosophies, but the Gaelic section was little more than begun. The Arab section contains some of Hay's most sustained and powerful writing, with brilliantly realised pictures of an Arab family and their desert life.

Hay continued to write spasmodically in his later years, contributing some rather brash nationalistic poems to the *Scots Independent*; his nationalism was always an extremely powerful driving force, and in his finer poems makes a strong contribution to the overall effect

He also contributed a series of poems to *Gairm*, the Gaelic quarterly, in which he reconstructed, with the most delicate skill, fragments of Gaelic folksong.

HAY, John, 2nd Earl and 1st Marquis of Tweeddale (1626–97) and John, 2nd Marquis of Tweeddale (1645–1713)

The Earldom of Tweeddale was created (1646) for John, Lord Hay of Yester (c1593–1654), a Royalist. His son, the 2nd Earl, had nonetheless supported the Solemn League and **Covenant** and opposed **Charles I** at Marston Moor; but he then supported the **Engagement** and fought for Charles at Preston. In this he was not untypical and may be considered something of a barometer of moderate Scottish opinion. At the Restoration he incurred censure and imprisonment for remonstrating against the execution of the **Protester James Guthrie** but by 1663, as president of the council, he was active in moderating persecution of the **Covenanters** and sponsoring the **Indulgences**. He was dismissed by **Lauderdale** in 1674 but readmitted to the privy council in the early 1680s when the administration again required a more conciliatory face. After the accession of William, which he supported, he was appointed Lord Chancellor (1692), created Marquis (1694) and conducted the inquiries into the **Glencoe Massacre**. Partly to take the heat out of this affair William authorised the creation of a Scottish trading company. Tweeddale therefore presided over the soaring expectations and disastrous collapse associated with the **Darien Scheme** and was duly made a scapegoat for it when dismissed from office in 1696.

His son, John 2nd Marquis, played an important and no less creditable role as a leading member of the opposition 'Country' party in negotiations over the Hanoverian succession in the run-up to **Union**. Succeeding **James Douglas, 2nd Duke of Queensberry** as commissioner for Scotland he never enjoyed sufficient support but was widely respected for his honesty and even offered to resign, 'an unprecedented event' (W Ferguson). His reluctant acceptance of the **Act of Security** (1704) invited the English retaliation of the **Alien Act** which further undermined his authority. As his father was brought down by the Darien Scheme, so the son was finally overthrown by its aftermath when, bowing to popular pressure, he failed to prevent the lynching of **Captain Thomas Green** and the appropriation of his vessel. He was dismissed from office but later lent his support to the Union.

HAY, John MacDougall (1881–1919)
Novelist

From **Tarbert** in **Argyll**, Hay attended **Glasgow University** and then taught in **Stornoway** and **Ullapool**. Becoming ill, he returned to Glasgow to read divinity and be ordained. He supplemented his income by freelance journalism and as minister at **Govan**, then Elderslie, wrote his first and most admired novel. This was *Gillespie*, 1914, a tale of ruthless ambition in a small town which has often been compared with **George Douglas Brown**'s *The House with the Green Shutters*. Both take a **Kailyard** setting but, by revealing its dependence on a vile but wholly convincing character, satisfactorily subvert the genre. Hay wrote two other novels but, like

Brown, died prematurely. He was the father of **George Campbell Hay**.

HEATHER

Heather or ling (*Calluna vulgaris*) is a widespread plant, occurring right across northern Europe, but heather-dominated heaths and bogs are nowhere more abundant than in the eastern and central Highlands of Scotland. Most of these heathlands are kept in an open condition with young, vigorously growing heather, by regular burning. This is because young heather shoots are the preferred food of the **red grouse**, an important game bird. The tiny purple flowers are so numerous they can colour a whole hillside in late summer. Heather flowers are an important source of nectar for bees and, in former times, for flavouring heather ale. Among the various traditional uses to which heather has been put are thatch, rope, bedding, brushes and dye. Many unusual forms (eg white or double flowered varieties) have been discovered and are cultivated in gardens. Heather was introduced to North America by Scottish settlers in the 18th century and it now grows wild in some places. There are also three native species of heath in Scotland: the cross-leaved heath (*Erica tetralix*) of wet areas; the bell heath or heather (*Erica cinerea*) of drier heathland; and the rare blue heath (*Phyllodoce coerulea*) found on rocky mountains in central Scotland.

HEBRIDEAN SHEEP

Sometimes wrongly called '**St Kilda** Sheep', these are black coloured, often multi-horned sheep descended from native sheep brought from the Outer Isles to Lowland England and Scotland to form ornamental flocks, mostly in the 19th century. Today they are a rare breed, though increasing in popularity.

HEBRIDES, The

The supreme achievement of the Hebrideans is to have preserved a language of which Stuart Piggott wrote that 'In 250 BC an imaginary aircraft following this route [from Asia Minor to Britain] could have flown over Celtic-speaking peoples from end to end of its course.' The Western Isles of Scotland were called 'Hebudes' by Pliny the Elder in 77 AD. He was followed by Ptolemy who termed them 'Ebudae' in Greek. The present spelling is thought to have originated in a misprint. The Outer Hebrides consist of a chain of islands extending 130 miles from the Butt of **Lewis** in the north to **Barra** Head in the south. The Inner Hebrides east of the **Minch** include the second and third largest islands, **Skye** and **Mull**.

It is among the latter that the earliest human traces have been discovered, Neolithic stone rings and microliths on **Jura** that have been dated to around 6000 BC and artefacts of a slightly later date on the isle of **Oronsay**. The Neolithic people adventured across the Minch with spectacular results. Around 3000 BC they began erecting the sequence of megaliths at **Callanish** on Lewis, of which the most impressive complex answers the description of Diodorous Siculus, visiting in 55 BC. He stated that a round temple stood on an island called Hyperborea where the moon could be seen skimming the horizon every 19 years. It is the most remarkable of many monuments erected throughout the Hebrides during this age.

Increasing settlement by metal-using Beaker folk preceded the deterioration in weather conditions that laid much of the land under **peat**. In the period of instability which these engendered, there arrived the first colonists who introduced dialects of the **Celtic** family of **languages**. The islands are filled with their **duns** and **brochs**. By 297 AD Eumenius was describing certain mainland tribes as Picti, evidently a term defining a mixture of Celtic-speaking and aboriginal folk such as also inhabited the Western Isles. But the symbol stones which mark the frontiers of Pictland are found only in the Inner Hebrides.

So are most of the monastic sites of the **Celtic Church** introduced by the Gaels from Ireland. These had been settling in western Scotland from about 300 AD. In addition to **Iona** itself, there were establishments on Eileach as Naoimh in the **Garvellach** group north of Jura, on Eilean Mor east of Jura and the nunnery on **Canna. St Columba** conversed with **Picts** on Skye through an interpreter according to **Adamnan**, but did not cross the Minch. However, one of the earliest structures of the Celtic Church survives on North Rona, beyond the Butt of Lewis.

The **Viking** colonisation which gathered momentum from the end of the 8th century left Lewis with four out of five place-names of Norse origin. Gaelic could not have taken deep root before the Viking age, yet unlike Pictish **Orkney** or **Shetland**, Lewis witnessed the rout of the Scandinavian tongue. However, 'Lewis intonation bears a striking resemblance to the tonal pattern of my own south-western Norwegian' (Prof Magne Oftedal).

Not so that of **Islay**, which preserves the closest links with the Gaelic of Ireland. Here, when all the Hebrides were ruled by the royal house of Man under the paramount sovereignty of the Norwegian Crown, King Godred died in about 1095. His son Olaf the Black gave his daughter in marriage to **Somerled** of the ancient Gaelic kindreds of **Dalriada**. By the time of his death in 1164 Somerled had restored Mull, Islay and many of the Inner Hebrides to Gaelic control and begun the rebuilding of Iona in stone. From him descended the **MacDonald Lords of the Isles**, who continued to enjoy semi-autonomous rule after the Hebrides had been ceded by Norway to the Scottish Crown in 1266.

There followed an era in which Finlaggan on Islay became the administrative seat of the lordship, where MacDuffies of **Colonsay** were archivists, Morisons from Lewis provided the brieves, while standards of scientific medicine hardly to be found elsewhere in Scotland were upheld by the Beatons, and classical **bardic** poetry was maintained by the MacMhuirich family of hereditary shenachies [see **Gaelic Verse and Prose**]. The source of patronage, as well as of authority, was destroyed when the lordship was forfeited in 1493. Some of the finest masons then moved to Oronsay, whose priory contains their late masterpieces, before the **Reformation** put an end to their activities. Men of poetry and learning found an asylum in **Dunvegan** on Skye until the **MacLeod** Chief became a spendthrift absentee.

During the ensuing breakdown of law and order **James VI** planned to exterminate the Hebrides. In 1607 he wrote to **Lord Huntly** ordering 'the extirpation of the barbarous people in those bounds' and the planting of the isles with 'civil' people. The Hebrideans were barbarous in the Greek sense of the word; that is, they spoke a language not understood by their (English-speaking) neighbours. James had recently become King of England, and 'his passion to show the English that in language, geography and manners the two nations could be one, allowed of no tolerance for the part of the kingdom that could not be squeezed into his model' (J Wormold, *Scotland 1470–1625*).

Although the royal policy of genocide was not immediately successful, Hebrideans bore the brunt of the 19th century **clearances**, while the Act introducing compulsory **education** in 1872 did not recognise the existence of their language. Their local affairs continued to be mismanaged by a variety of mainland authorities until the belated creation of Comhairle nan Eilean (the Council of the Isles) in 1975. They are still bedevilled by absentee landlordism, but at least the Hebrideans are now permitted to administer education in their own tongue, as well as much else. The oldest literary language in Europe after Greek and Latin continues to flourish with a vigour out of all proportion to the number of people who use it.

HELENSBURGH, Argyll & Bute

When the pioneer of steam navigation, **Henry Bell** came to live in Helensburgh in the early 1800s he found it an agreeable residential seaside town popular with **Glasgow** merchants. Bell's move to Helensburgh encouraged him in the project of designing a steamship. He launched the **Comet** on the **Clyde** in 1812, the first practical passenger steamship in Europe. Bell became Helensburgh's first Provost. Named after the wife of Sir James Colquhoun of Luss, who laid out the older part of the town in 1777, Helensburgh remained a place of little consequence until the railway came in 1857, after which it expanded rapidly. It was the birthplace of television pioneer **John Logie Baird**, and is the site of the famous **Hill House** designed by **Charles Rennie Mackintosh** for the publisher W W Blackie. Blackie admired the simplicity of Mackintosh's 'Glasgow Style' and left the design of furniture and colour scheme entirely in his hands. He paid £5000 for the house, a considerable sum in 1904.

Beyond Helensburgh lies **Glen Fruin**, the 'Glen of Sorrow' where there was a brief and bloody battle between the Colquhouns and the **MacGregors** in 1603. Over 140 Colquhouns died but only two MacGregors. As a consequence, the MacGregors were outlawed and their name proscribed, thus providing **Sir Walter Scott** with the mythology for *Rob Roy*. Before the 1975 reorganisation of **local government**, Helensburgh was in **Dunbartonshire**, but when Strathclyde Region was abolished in 1995 the residents of Helensburgh chose to become part of **Argyll** & Bute Council Area.

HELMSDALE, Sutherland

At the northern end of the fertile coastal strip of eastern **Sutherland**, the Helmsdale river pours out of the **Strath of Kildonan**, beneath the **Ord of Caithness**. Here the **parliamentary road** (now the A9) crossed a stone bridge completed in 1811. A substantial harbour was built in 1818, which helped to create a fluctuating **fish-**

ng industry during the 19th century. Since its decline
fish processing factory has been established in the
ormer drill hall and a lobster factory has been set up
beside the harbour.

HENDERSON, Alexander (1583–1646)
Covenanter

Foremost and most statesmanlike of the **Presbyterian**
clergy of the day, Alexander Henderson was born at
Creich, **Fife**, and taught philosophy at the **University
of St Andrews** before being ordained minister of
Leuchars in 1612. A theologian and scholar drawn from
the obscurity of his country parish by the urgency of
the national crisis, his wisdom and moderation counterbalanced the fanaticism of many **Covenanters**. One of
the authors of the **National Covenant** (1638), he was
Moderator of the **General Assembly** (1638), Dean of
the Chapel Royal (1641), Commissioner to the Westminster Assembly (1643) and drew up the Solemn
League and **Covenant** (1643). He spent several months
at Newcastle after the surrender of **Charles I** (1646)
trying unsuccessfully to persuade the King to accept the
Covenant, and died at **Leith** on his return to Scotland.

HENDERSON, Arthur (1863–1935) Politician
and Nobel Peace Prize Winner

Although he was born in **Glasgow**, Arthur Henderson's
family moved to Newcastle-upon-Tyne when he was
nine, and his biographies show that he returned to
full-time education at that age, having already left
school in Scotland. After being active in trade union
and local government circles, Henderson became Secretary of the Labour Party in 1911, a post he held for 23
years, and entered Parliament. He held three ministerial
posts during World War I and was his party's Chief
Whip for three different periods. High office came
his way briefly in 1924 (Home Secretary) and from
1929–31 (Foreign Secretary), at which latter date he led
opposition in the Labour Party to **Ramsay MacDonald**'s
National Government, but lost his parliamentary seat.
Becoming increasingly concerned with international
affairs, Henderson was President of the World Disarmament Conference 1932–4, for which service he received
the Nobel Peace Prize in 1934. His considerable affection for his adopted Tyneside city somewhat dilutes his
qualification as a Scot. He was once recorded as saying
apologetically, 'I was not born a Novocastrian; it was
no fault of mine.'

HENDERSON, Sir David K (1884–1965)
Physician

Born in **Dumfries**, youngest son of a solicitor, David
Henderson was educated at Dumfries Academy and the
Royal High School, **Edinburgh**, and studied medicine
at **Edinburgh University**, graduating in 1907. As a
junior medical officer at the Royal Edinburgh Hospital
he came under the influence of Sir Thomas Clouston
who directed him to a pathological laboratory in
London and the Royal Psychiatric Clinic in Munich.

After some years in America, where he was resident
psychiatrist at a clinic attached to Johns Hopkins Hospital and assistant physician in the Psychiatric Institute of
Manhattan State Hospital, he joined the Royal Army
Medical Corps at the start of World War I and carried

out important research work on psychological disorders
of warfare. During World War II he was a member
of a government committee on nervous and mental
disorders in the armed forces.

In 1920 he was appointed Physician Superintendent
of Glasgow's Gartnavel Hospital, and spent 12 years as
lecturer on Mental Diseases at **Glasgow University**. In
1932 he was elected to the Chair of Psychiatry at Edinburgh University and Physician Superintendent to the
Royal Edinburgh Hospital. Along with Dr R D Gillespie,
he produced *A Textbook of Psychiatry for Students and Practitioners*, a work that won an international reputation. He
was knighted in 1947 and became President of the
Royal College of Physicians in 1949.

HENDERSON, Thomas (1798–1844)
Astronomer

Scotland's first Astronomer Royal, Henderson was born
in **Dundee** and educated locally. Although articled as a
legal secretary, he showed an overwhelming interest in
astronomy, succeeding in being appointed Director of
the Observatory of the Cape of Good Hope. There,
despite ill-health and poor eyesight, he began his most
important achievement, the computation of the parallax
of the nearest star, Alpha Centauri, continuing his
studies on returning to Scotland. Unfortunately a delay
in publishing his results detracted from his reputation.
He died in **Edinburgh**.

HENRY, George (1858–1943) Painter

Born in **Irvine**, **Ayrshire**, Henry trained in **Glasgow** at
the School of Art and at the life classes of William York
MacGregor. His association with the Glasgow School,
of which he is considered a central figure, began in
1881 when he joined **James Guthrie**, E A Walton and
Joseph Crawhall to paint *en plein air* at Brig o' Turk in

George Henry, by T C Dugdale (SNPG)

the **Trossachs**. Influenced by Guthrie's Hague School naturalism, Henry adopted the realist ethos, low-key colouring and square brushwork that characterises the early work of the **Glasgow Boys**, but he soon demonstrated a flair for design that progressively set his own compositions apart.

In 1885 Henry met **E A Hornel** and the artistic productivity of their ensuing friendship gave the impetus for a second phase in the development of the School. Working alongside each other, particularly in the **Galloway** countryside around Hornel's **Kirkcudbrightshire** home, their work assumed an increasingly decorative quality and stylistically grew close, their expressive brushwork creating a richly coloured impasto within which figures merge into landscape in submission to overall design and pattern. Henry's anti-naturalist stance culminated in 1889 with the remarkable *Galloway Landscape* (Glasgow Art Gallery), which in its flattened perspective and symbolist colour and line anticipates the modernism of Gauguin and the Pont Aven School.

Acknowledged by 1890 as the most innovative of the Boys, the novel development of Henry and Hornel's work had been strongly influenced by their enthusiasm for the art of Japan, and in 1893 they left for a 19-month visit there. Sadly many of Henry's oils stuck together on the return journey, though the compositional strengths of his watercolours of geisha girls, street scenes and domestic interiors make them amongst the finest of the many works by British artists who visited or joined in the late-19th century vogue for the Far East.

Henry continued to work on Japanese subjects but increasingly followed a career as a highly successful, though conventional, portraitist. He settled in London in 1906.

HENRY, Prince of Wales (1594–1612)

The eldest son of **James VI** and **Anne of Denmark**, Henry was the first undisputed heir to the thrones of Scotland and England and represents one of history's notable 'might-have-beens'. His birth ended a period of uncertainty and occasioned grand rejoicing; a grand christening at **Stirling Castle**, and a heavy tax to pay for it, failed to staunch the relief of a people 'daft with mirth'. Already Duke of Rothesay and Earl of Carrick, the young Henry accompanied his father to England in 1603 and was created Prince of Wales in 1610. He formed a close friendship, commemorated in a moving correspondence, with the young Lord Harington, and seems to have shunned the sycophants who surrounded his father. He must have proved an abler monarch than his younger brother. But in 1612 both he and Harington succumbed to an epidemic, probably typhoid, which cleared the succession for the future **Charles I**.

HENRYSON, Robert (c1420–c1490) Poet

Records prove little about this major poet of the late medieval period. He was a schoolmaster, probably headmaster of the important abbey school in **Dunfermline** for a period during the 1470s, when he also held the post of notary public. If he can be identified with the Robert Henryson who gained membership of **Glasgow University** in 1462, then he possessed the degrees of Master of Arts and Bachelor of Canon Law, which

Dunbar's poetic reference to 'Maister Robert Henrisoun', and the legal expertise revealed in his verse make plausible. He was dead before 1505, being listed in Dunbar's poetic lament for the past poets of Scotland and England.

Henryson is primarily remembered for his group of *Morall Fabillis*. In fact the grouping idea is a dangerous one as they share only the vividness of amusing tales centred on animals. The sources vary – some are based on the Aesopic tradition and Gualterus Anglicus particularly; others stem from the 'beast epic' popularised in the *Roman de Renart*. Instead of adopting the easy transition from moral to fable in which a truth is first enacted and then explained, Henryson warns us in his Prologue that he will test his readers by greater concealment often shocking us by the conclusions he draws. With the ingenuity and spiritual confidence of the commentator aware that Divine benevolence guarantees any well-intended interpretation, Henryson may draw the well-known stories of Lion and Mouse, Fox and Wolf, Sheep and Dog away from the obvious into the recondite sounding lessons of political or social relevance; of moral or spiritual encouragement; of Christian joy or penitential warning. The reader's intellect must be actively involved and he cannot complain, for at the start he had himself been cautioned to apply 'grit diligence' to 'the subtell dyte of poetry'.

His longer poems (*Orpheus and Eurydice* and *The Testament of Cresseid*) are both clearly structured, primarily intellectual, reactions in neoplatonic spirit to well-known classical tales. The former is one of the very few English or Scottish spiritual journeys of this time, which follow Dante in drawing their hero through Heaven and Hell. Orpheus fails to learn and is damned, where Dante understood and was saved. *The Testament* is at once a reaction (not wholly favourable) to Chaucer's *Troilus and Criseyde* and the provision of a different type of spiritual pilgrimage for her. The judgement of the Parliament of Pagan Gods (she is made a leper) sets up a test in deprivation. Cresseid progresses towards true understanding of charity, limited only by her pagan nature but set against the tragedy of lost potential in worldly terms.

HEPBURN, James, 4th Earl of Bothwell (c1535–78)

Best remembered as the third husband of **Queen Mary**, Bothwell was a powerful influence in southern Scotland during the tempestuous mid-16th century. After succeeding his father to the earldom at the age of 21, he embraced Protestantism while taking a strong anti-English line, and supporting **Mary of Guise** before the return of her daughter Mary Stewart from France, after which he appears to have lost influence at court. Following a period of imprisonment and exile, he gained in stature when Mary ran into difficulties with her nobles, and after 1566 she came greatly to rely on Bothwell, possibly as much for political as romantic reasons. Bothwell almost certainly had a part in the murder of Mary's first Scottish husband, **Darnley**, and after abducting the Queen, divorced his own wife before becoming the Queen's second Scottish husband on 15 May 1567. Within a month, Mary surrendered to the nobles at **Carberry**, near **Musselburgh**, whence

James Hepburn, 4th Earl of Bothwell and third husband of Queen Mary, in 1566 (SNPG)

Bothwell fled to **Orkney** and then Norway, where he was imprisoned. Some 11 years later he died in captivity, and his embalmed body was gruesomely exhibited in a church at Faarevejle in modern-day Denmark. Bothwell's family home, **Crichton Castle**, still stands near Pathhead in **Midlothian**.

HEPBURN, Sir John (c1589–1636) Marshal of France

From **Athelstaneford** in **East Lothian**, Hepburn, though said to have been a Catholic, enlisted with other Scots in the sevice of Frederick, the Elector Palatine, after the latter's marriage to **Elizabeth** ('the Winter Queen'), daughter of **James VI**. He then transferred to Gustavus Adolphus' Scottish regiment, becoming colonel (1625) and commander (1631). In the Thirty Years' War he fought with great distinction and was prominent at the Battle of Breitenfeld and at the capures of Lansberg and Donauworth. Returning to Scotland (1632) he raised a new force of 2000 men (including the future **Earl of Middleton**) for service in France. This Scots Brigade, augmented by old comrades-in-arms from the Swedish regiment, became known as the *Régiment d'Hebron* (ie 'd'Hepburn') or 'Pontius Pilate's Bodyguards' and, returning to Scotland after the Restoration, as the **Royal Scots**. As its *Maréchal de Camp* Hepburn took part in the conquest of Lorraine (1634–5) but was killed during the siege of Saverne in 1636. His memorial in Toul, near Nancy, was destroyed during the French Revolution.

HERALDRY IN SCOTLAND

As a separate nation, Scotland enjoys a system of heraldry recognised as being the purest and best regulated in existence. Responsibility for matters armorial lies with the Lord Lyon King of Arms, Her Majesty's Supreme Officer of Honour in Scotland. Although frequently compared with the English Garter King of Arms, Lyon's position is different and his status is in fact greater since, unlike Garter who reports to the Earl Marshal of England, Lyon has had all heraldic responsibility

in Scotland delegated to him by Act of Parliament on behalf of the Crown.

The origin of his office is lost in the mists of time. It descends from the ancient position of *Sennachie* to the ancient Celtic Kings of Scots long before the dawn of heraldry; much later (but as early as 1318) a Lyon was inaugurated with the rank of Knight at **Arbroath Abbey**. Prior to the **Union**, Lyon was a Great Officer of State and a member of the Scottish Privy Council, from which, today, he is still addressed with the prefix 'The Right Honourable'. He is in fact a judge; his court is one of the oldest judicatures in the land and enjoys considerable powers; these are enforced where necessary, and while fines levied may be light in the first instance, repeated offences may lead to a charge of Contempt of Court with its attendant extremely heavy penalty. Lord Lyon has his office in **New Register House, Edinburgh**, where he is assisted by Lyon Clerk who is also Keeper of the Records. Together with his two secretaries, they comprise the fully paid permanent members of the organisation.

Lyon is however aided by a number of other people. There is an establishment for six other Scottish officers of Arms, three Heralds and three Pursuivants who are at the same time Members of the Royal Household, Members of the Court of the Lord Lyon and Officers of the **Order of the Thistle** of which Order Lyon is Secretary and King of Arms. Originally there were six Heralds and six Pursuivants who, together with Lyon, made up the normal, sacred figure of thirteen members for the Court; by an Act of 1867 the figure was reduced to today's level. The old titles still remain however and are used in turn by newly appointed officers.

The Heralds were Albany, Islay, Marchmont, Ross, Rothesay and Snowdon; the Pursuivants Bute, Carrick, Dingwall, Kintyre, Ormonde and Unicorn. There are also two titles for Pursuivants Extraordinary – temporary officers who may be called into service for specific occasions by Lord Lyon. Carrick is first mentioned in 1368, Albany is on record by 1401, and Unicorn by 1425, while the remainder are all in existence by 1500. While titles such as Lyon and Unicorn have obviously always been in royal service, it would appear that others originated from private Officers of Arms of great magnates. Ross and Dingwall were originally in the service of the **Earls of Ross**; Islay and Kintyre in that of the **Lords of the Isles** and Bute and Carrick of the **Stewart** family before these titles were taken over by the Crown. So today, there are still a number of these private officers; the Earl of Erroll having his Slains Pursuivant, the Earl of Mar Garioch Pursuivant and the Earl of Crawford Lindsay and Endure Pursuivants.

The Officers of Arms assist Lyon on certain state occasions; these include attendance on the Knights of the Thistle; Her Majesty's Representative the Lord High Commissioner to the **General Assembly** of the **Church of Scotland**; the installation of the Governor of **Edinburgh Castle**; royal proclamations on such occasions as the breaking up of Parliament; state visits to Scotland and at national state occasions such as the Coronation.

Royal Officers wear tabards, differing slightly according to rank, which display the quartered Royal Arms of Scotland, worn over a gold laced red and blue uniform of the Royal Household. They wear Tudor bonnets

533

ensigned with an embroidered crowned thistle and carry brass-tipped ebony batons of office.

Heralds and Pursuivants are paid a fee for their services which was fixed in the 17th century; originally intended as a living wage, it has not reflected inflation and is now hardly sufficient for a decent lunch. However Heralds and Pursuivants all practise as heraldic advisers and professional consultants for which they do charge fees; they have a wide-ranging knowledge, and access to Lyon, and their services are constantly in demand.

Lyon Court also includes a Procurator Fiscal, a qualified lawyer who handles legal matters on behalf of Lyon and the Treasury.

Lyon stands in matters heraldic in place of the Queen; it has been said that no other herald in Europe has exercised such powers of jurisdiction or been vested with such dignity and rank. He is responsible for such matters as representation of ancient titles and position, change of name, recording of pedigrees and birth-briefs, the organising and conduct of public ceremony in Scotland, the observation of precedence and all baronetcy claims on which he passes his decision to the Home Secretary.

Peerage claims and claims for the chiefship of clans and families also come to him in the first instance, since the award of the undifferenced arms is in question, together with the grant of the Chiefship of the Name by which chiefship is conferred; in the case of a peerage, it is his matriculation of arms with the additaments appropriate to the holder of a peerage which is taken into account by the Lord Chancellor, who in effect follows Lyon's decision. Appeal against this decision may be made firstly to the Court of Session and then to the House of Lords.

In 1672 it was decreed that all who used arms in Scotland should submit them to Lyon for ratification and recording. Thus began the magnificent series of leather-bound volumes which comprise the Public Register of All Arms and Bearings in Scotland, now nearly 70 in number. Heraldry has always enjoyed high popularity in Scotland and the last 25 years have seen as many grants of matriculations of arms as have the preceding centuries.

It is a remarkably democratic process; Lyon will grant arms to all 'virtuous and well-deserving' Scots who approach him and are willing to pay the necessary fees, which, apart from the Herald Painter's fee, go to the Treasury. In the case of someone descended in the male line from the possessor of arms, a duly differenced form of his ancestor's coat is given, the process in this case being known as 'Matriculation'. Both the Grant and the Matriculation of Arms confer recognition on the recipient as a Noble in the Noblesse of Scotland.

The Granting of Arms to indigenous Scots has been swelled in recent years by grants to many corporate bodies and to those of Scottish descent overseas. In Australia and New Zealand the grant may be direct; in Canada, which now has its own Heraldic Authority, and in the USA the grant is usually to those who can prove descent in the male line from an ancestor born in Scotland; a retrospective grant is made to him and the petitioner will then matriculate a duly differenced form of his ancestor's arms. Grants are also made in the same way in the USA to those who descend from Scots living in America before the Revolution or from Scots in Canada. In exceptional cases Lyon may also entertain petition from those who have been personally appointed by their chief to act as an officer of his clan in a country outwith Scotland who do not otherwise qualify.

Advice on the necessary procedure can be obtained direct from Lyon Clerk, or the services of an Officer of Arms may be employed. As well as having his or her arms recorded in the Public Register, the recipient also receives a magnificent vellum sheet containing the actual grant and an illustration of the arms in question carried out by the Herald Painters attached to the Court.

In Scotland, arms are granted to one person alone who will bear them in their lifetime. They pass on death as an incorporeal fief to the former owner's heir and continue to be borne without further formality although it is recommended that they should be matriculated or 'made up' every three generations or so, or when they have passed through the female line when the recipient is required to take the surname of the original grantee.

The Scottish system of differencing is adhered to strongly; it is based on a set system of different borders which produces a readily recognisable way by which the holder's relationship to the owner of the original arms is deduced. During their minority children are tacitly allowed to use their father's arms with a minor record of difference (crescent for a second son, mullet or star for a third, and so on), but on attaining their majority younger sons must, if they wish to use arms, petition for their own. During his father's lifetime the eldest son may make full use of his father's arms with the addition of a label of three points; his son and heir adding a label of five points and his son and heir (in unusual but not unknown circumstances) displaying a label of no less than seven points. Once understood the whole system is very clear.

Even with new grants, all those of a particular name are expected to show a recognisable reference to it in their arms as if all came from the same family. While this is manifestly unlikely in some cases it is a useful convention and means that very many Scottish shields are immediately identifiable. A Campbell, for instance, will always display the Gyronny of Eight while a Hay will always have a reference to the three escutcheons of the Earl of Erroll, the Chief.

A full grant to an ordinary recipient will consist of a shield, surmounted by the helmet of his rank on which is placed the crest, with above it (not below as in English practice) the motto. To these basic arms, certain additaments can be made; supporters can be granted to Peers of the Realm, to Knights of the Thistle, to Clan Chiefs, to Knights Grand Cross of the various orders and to feudal barons whose tenure predates 1587.

Helmets vary in rank and peers usually display their coronets, also according to rank, while feudal barons may have the display of the baronial chapeau incorporated in their achievement if authorised by Lyon: a red chapeau for a baron in possession of his ancestral fief, a blue chapeau for a family formerly but no longer in possession, both trimmed with ermine in the case of a royal barony or erminois in the case of a baron of Argyll and the Isles. Other barons deriving not from royal authority but from local potentates are reckoned to green chapeaux but the usage is hardly known.

Standards and badges may also be granted by Lyon but, unlike English practice where anyone who wishes and is prepared to pay extra for it will be granted both a badge and a standard, the usage in Scotland is usually limited to those with a need for them, ie those with a following (men who would follow them into war). Here, too, there is a special system according to rank. Standards or headquarters flags are granted to peers (12 yards in length) and to ordinary chiefs (4 yards in length) while in special cases a 4-foot pennon may be granted to those of non-baronial rank on the basis, usually, of their historic position.

Badges may also be granted to corporate bodies although standards are only now given to bodies who are granted supporters. These last are most unlikely to be granted to commercial concerns but may on occasion be granted to bodies which represent Scotland in their particular role.

A chief also has the use of a pinsel, a triangular flag on which are displayed his crest within a buckled strap on which is displayed his motto, inside a circle with his title on it together with his plant badge. This flag may be given temporarily by the chief to one specific person who is to represent him on a specific occasion.

All armigers (owners of coats of arms) may display their arms on a rectangular banner. The sizes laid down by Lyon as appropriate for carrying on public occasions are as follows:

Peers — 48 inches wide by 60 inches high
Feudal Barons — 36 inches wide by 45 inches high
Other Chiefs — 33 inches wide by 42 inches high
Chieftains — 30 inches wide by 36 inches high

There is no officially stated size for the banner of an armiger who is not of chieftainly rank but it should clearly be of a somewhat smaller size.

The owner of arms may display them in the form of a Pipe Banner, a practice still in use today by company commanders in Scottish regiments who possess the right to arms and whose company piper may display them in this form.

It is sadly necessary to stress again that arms in Scotland are personal; there is no such thing as a 'Clan MacX coat of arms'; these arms belong to the chief alone who may not delegate their use to anyone else. His followers may however display their adherence by wearing his crest in a buckled strap with his motto on it; the actual owner of the arms can display his crest on its own without the buckled strap or within a plain circle with his motto on it, while armigers may, if they wish, add one feather, chieftains two feathers and chiefs three to the crest badge in their bonnets. If not actual eagle's feathers, these may be small silver representations added to the badge.

Much mystique is currently attached to this system, particularly overseas where the use of feathers has been allowed in certain circumstances to officials of a local Clan Society; the practice is unlikely ever to have been given as much significance in ancient times as now, while the use of a cap badge in the bonnet would have been well beyond the capacity of most Scots' sporrans.

Use of the clan plant badge is thought to go back centuries and to be a primitive survival, but the most likely form of identification is exemplified by the prosaic but pragmatic use in the '45 **Jacobite Rising** of the White and the Black or Red Cockade or bunch of ribbons in the head-dress.

It appears that, as with the rest of Europe, heraldry came to Scotland around the second quarter of the 12th century; its spread and adoption was rapid, due to the number of European incomers to Scotland at the period and to the clear need for a system that would serve both as a means of battlefield identification and on legal documents in the form of personal seals at a time when writing was not widespread.

However heraldry not only serves as a means of identification but often gives valuable clues as to a person's origin. While not conclusive evidence, it at least provides a clear indication as to who they think they are or would like to be. In this connection a number of great themes run through Scottish heraldry whose origins predate the arrival of the system itself. The lion rampant, which in a form differenced by the double tressure florey counter-florey provides the arms of the King of Scots, traces back to the line of **Kenneth mac-Alpin** in 843; the triple stars of **Moray**, which in all probability denote the rival line of the northern as opposed to the southern **Picts**, combined with the Dalriadic princely line of Loarn, and the boars' heads of the English Princely House of the Earls of Northumbria.

The West Highlands and Islands were late in adopting European heraldry and have never been all that good at conforming to rules laid down in Edinburgh. Heraldry in this area makes much use of symbols which denote a general rather than a specific ancestry from one person; hence as well as the Dalriadic royal lion, frequent use is made of the galley (descent from **Somerled** and the early rulers of the Isles), the Red Hand of Ulster, very often holding a form of cross (for a connection with the O'Neill kindred of **St Columba**) and the mysterious salmon, still a royal fish and of mystic significance among the early Gaels.

With the many incomers to Scotland, both direct from Europe and from south of the border, the wide spread of Scottish heraldry is a fascinating field in which to discern the rich mixture and the links with a distant past that make up the history of a nation to which heraldry bears colourful witness still.

HERIOT, George (1563–1624) Goldsmith

Known as 'Jingling Geordie' and so featured in **Sir Walter Scott**'s The Fortunes of Nigel, 1822, Heriot succeeded his father as an **Edinburgh** goldsmith and became reputedly the richest burgess in the city. In an age when plate and jewellery represented the Crown's most readily transferable asset he held the important post of goldsmith to **Anne of Denmark** (1597) and then her husband **James VI** (1601), being in effect their banker. With James he moved to London in 1603 where he amassed further wealth and was rewarded with an imposition on sugar imports. On his death he bequeathed £23,625 for the foundation of **George Heriot's Hospital/School** (Edinburgh) for educating the sons of impoverished burgesses. **Heriot-Watt University** also perpetuates his name.

HERIOT-WATT UNIVERSITY, Edinburgh

Begun as 'The School of Arts', an evening institution for the instruction of mechanics, in 1821, the Heriot-Watt University has developed its suburban campus at Riccarton Estate near **Currie** since 1974. 'If not the first, it was certainly the second establishment of its kind in Britain' (Cockburn, 1856). The founder, Leonard Horner, a merchant, conceived the idea when he learned from a watchmaker that his apprentices invariably lacked any mathematical education. Established in a house in Adam Square on the corner of **Edinburgh**'s **South Bridge**, 'The Watt Institute and School of Arts', as it was renamed in memory of the inventor **James Watt** in 1841, moved into new buildings designed by David Rhind in **Chambers Street** in 1871. These were expanded in 1886–8, when the institution became the Heriot-Watt College after amalgamation with part of **George Heriot's Hospital** and Trust as a 'people's college' in 1879. The 'Watt', which became a central institution in 1902 and achieved university status in 1966, finally vacated this 'shambling public building' in 1989. The early School of Arts curriculum strictly adhered to Chemistry, Natural Philosophy and Mathematics, but expanded widely from 1832 when English Language and Literature were introduced. The Day Technical College, begun in 1885, appointed professors of Mechanical Engineering, Chemistry, Physics and Electrical Engineering; the Department of Mining was established in 1913. Technical Mycology started in 1905 and developed into the Department of **Brewing**, the only one in a British university today.

HERMITAGE CASTLE, Roxburghshire

Overlooking Hermitage Water in Liddesdale about five miles north-east of **Newcastleton**, the 'dark and venerable tower' of Hermitage is the most imposing as well as the most perfect (thanks to 19th century restoration) of the medieval Border castles. **John of Fordun** suggested that the building of Hermitage so close to the border was one of the causes of a dispute that nearly led to war between Scotland and England in 1243. Certainly there was a castle on this bleak and lonely site at the end of the 13th century, probably built by the de Soulis family, the remains of which form the foundations of the rectangular tower erected by **William Douglas, Knight of Liddesdale** in the middle of the 14th century. Ownership of the castle passed from de Soulis to Douglas to Dacre and back to Douglas hands before being given on the orders of **James IV** by **Archibald Douglas, 5th Earl of Angus** to Patrick Hepburn, 1st Earl of Bothwell in 1492.

It was during the period of Douglas ownership that the main transformation of the castle was effected by the addition of three massive towers, with a fourth even larger tower completing the present structure c1400. The protruding towers on the east and west sides were then joined by linking walls with the great pointed arches which are such a distinctive feature of Hermitage and which, unexpectedly, do not form the main entrances into the castle. The linking walls made it possible to construct a projecting wooden gallery for use in times of siege – the corbels which supported the gallery and the doorways that gave access to it are another striking feature of the ruin.

'Dark and venerable' Hermitage Castle, by MacGibbon and Ross (MR)

Hermitage remained in Bothwell hands for just over a century (the wounded **4th Earl of Bothwell** received a flying visit here from **Queen Mary** on 15 October 1566) until Francis, 5th Earl was attainted in 1594, whereupon it reverted to the Crown before passing to the Scotts of **Buccleuch** and later falling into ruins. Extensively restored during the 19th century by the **Duke of Buccleuch**, it was placed in State care in 1930.

HERRING

Of all the fish in the sea none has meant more to Scotland than the herring. It is a beautiful silvery fish, appearing in enormous shoals at set times of the year in predictable areas, where whole communities were thrown into a frenzy of activity as they sought to reap the benefit of the 'silver harvest' before the shoals dispersed. More than any other fish the herring has attracted the attention of novelists, poets and song writers.

There are several races of herring in the waters around Scotland. The North Sea herring spend much of their time feeding off the shores of Scandinavia, then in summer start their great migration to spawn off the north-east coast of Scotland and around the Northern Isles. They are slightly different anatomically from the herring that come in from the west to spawn in the **Minch** and in the estuary of the **Clyde**.

It was the Dutch who first learnt to benefit from the herring, discovering the art of preserving herring with salt so that they remained edible throughout the winter and into the following year. When economists began to study the problems of the Highlands they saw in herring fishing an answer to unemployment and depopulation. The British Fisheries Society was established in 1788 and began building the town of **Ullapool** on Loch Broom. About the same time the herring fishing was showing signs of promise in **Caithness**, and in 1808 the Society, with **Thomas Telford** as engineer, began to build the village of Pulteneytown on the south side of **Wick**. Before long every little harbour in Scotland had its herring fleet and began exporting barrels of salt herring to Ireland and the West Indies. The boats were under 30ft (9m) long, undecked, and offered little shelter for the crews who shot their fleets of hempen drift-nets and hauled them again by hand. The early days of the industry are vividly described by **Neil Gunn** in The Silver Darlings.

Herring boats entering Aberdeen Harbour, by George Washington Wilson c1880 (GWWA)

By the end of the century the north-east and **Shetland** had begun to dominate the industry after new markets had been found in Germany and Russia. There was also a good demand for fresh herring and for kippers – herring smoked over a fire of wood chips. For Germany herring were preserved in boxes with a mixture of salt and ice and rushed by fast steamships to Hamburg. This practice started about the same time (1890s) as the gold rush in the Klondike area of Canada, hence the name 'klondyking' applied to this trade. When all these markets were satisfied surplus herring were sold cheaply for conversion to guano.

By this time the herring boats were bigger and fitted with steam capstans to take much of the hard work out of hauling the nets. But they were still driven by sail. The introduction of the steam drifter marked a new era; the old-fashioned sailboats were unable to compete and small ports were phased out as the industry became centralised at places like **Lerwick**, Wick, **Peterhead**, **Fraserburgh** and **Stornoway**.

World War I destroyed markets in Europe; they revived only partially when peace was restored. Then in the 1920s the industry was faced with low prices and dear **coal**. In 1935 the Herring Industry Board was set up to try to save the industry, but the great days of the fishery were gone even before World War II disrupted the markets that remained. Herring fishing continued on a much reduced scale in the 1950s and 60s. Motor-boats, although they incorporated electronic aids to navigation and fish finding, still used the old-fashioned drift-net. Elsewhere, developments included the use of sonar to detect shoals and the massive purse seine to trap them. In 1965 200 large Norwegian purse seiners descended on the herring shoals east of Shetland and taught Scottish fishermen a lesson they would never forget; only those who were willing to invest in purse seiners were able to stay in business, with the result that the Scottish herring fleet now totals only 40 vessels, each with the catching power of 10 steam drifters. Not surprisingly they are restricted by quotas.

Predictably the herring came near to extinction in the early 1970s through over-fishing; it was saved only by the imposition of a six-year ban on fishing from 1977–83. The purse seiners survived by starting a new fishery for mackerel, while the markets for fresh and processed herring were lost through lack of continuity. Their recovery is painfully slow. Today the main customers for both herring and mackerel are the East European factory ships (or klondykers) which anchor each summer at Lerwick, Ullapool, Peterhead and Fraserburgh and buy most of the Scottish catch at a fraction of its potential value.

See also **Fishing Industry**.

HIGHLAND CATTLE

This is Britain's most distinctive breed, little changed in historic times, though Victorian owners did improve and develop the breed. Red is the colour most commonly seen today though black (much more common 100 years ago than today), yellow, brindle, white and silver are also known. The Highlander, with the **Galloway**, was a mainstay of the **droving** trade in the late 18th and early 19th centuries. Today it is still greatly valued as a beef cow. Many of the 179 British herds (or more correctly 'folds') are in the lowlands of Scotland and of England and the breed is also well known in the USA (particularly Wyoming) and in Germany. From 1949, the Cadzow brothers of the island of **Luing** developed a new beef breed by crossing Highland cows with Beef **Shorthorn** bulls. The Luing breed is hardy with sufficient milk to rear beef calves economically.

HIGHLAND GAMES

These Games incorporate feats of strength and agility that were practised in the Highlands, no doubt from

Braemar Gathering: Highland Games in the 1880s (GWWA)

very early times, but their formal organisation and annual occurrence in many places in Scotland (and a number elsewhere in the world) seems to have begun about 1820, as part of the romantic revival of Highlandism and tartanry encouraged by **Sir Walter Scott** and King George IV.

One of the earliest descriptions is that of the **Invergarry** games attended by **Joseph Mitchell** in the 1820s. The events included 'dancing, piping, lifting a heavy stone, throwing the hammer, running from the island to Invergarry and back, 6 miles' and 'twisting the four legs from a cow, for which a fat sheep was offered as a prize'. This latter feat proved extremely difficult. 'At last one man succeeded. After struggling for about an hour, he managed to twist off the four legs and as a reward received his sheep with a eulogistic speech from the Chief.'

The association of royalty with Highland Games dates from **Queen Victoria**'s attendance at the **Braemar** Gathering in 1848. The more civilised repertoire of events includes running and jumping, special classes of throwing stones and hammers, and tossing the **caber**, and a wide range of piping and dancing competitions, featuring **dances** such as the Sword Dance and the Seann Triubhas. There is an extensive series of these Games in different locations (eg **Aboyne**, **Luss**, **Crieff**, **Oban** etc) over the months of July to September each year.

HIGHLAND INDEPENDENT COMPANIES, The

In 1666 the **Earl of Argyll** was given leave by **Charles II** to raise a company or 'watch' of 60 men for one year in order to guard the bounds of his territory. The following year the King issued a warrant to the **Earl of Atholl** to raise a force of Highlanders to secure the peace of the Highlands and 'keep watch upon the braes'. During the next 70 years, a number of Highland Independent Companies were raised and disbanded as the political and military situation demanded. The force was part of the British Army but the troops served much as local levies were later to be used around the Empire to act in close support of the regular troops of the garrison, to whom they were frequently attached. With all their local knowledge of the language and the terrain they rendered vital help.

The officers were Highland Lairds, many of them from **Clan Campbell**. Initially the men were probably clothed in their own gear, but it would seem likely that later some attempt was made to dress them in a uniform **tartan**. The only known portrait of an officer of a Highland Company, that of Campbell of Skipness possibly as early as 1715, shows him wearing the long-skirted red coat and breeches of the normal dress for any Army officer of the period.

The final raising of companies took place jn 1725 when six were raised for service. Three of them were Campbell companies, the others being **Grant**, **Munro** and **Fraser**. In 1739 at **Aberfeldy** they were regimented into what was to become that most famous regiment, **The Black Watch**.

HIGHLAND LAND LEAGUE

Founded in London in early 1883, the Highland Land Law Reform Association (after 1886 the Highland Land League) brought together scholars and political reformers sympathetic to the struggle of the **crofting** community. Its luminaries included Charles Fraser-Mackintosh, MP for **Inverness** and a member of the

Napier Commission, Dr Roderick MacDonald of London's Gaelic Society, Alexander MacKenzie, editor of *The Celtic Magazine*, and G B Clark, a radical land reformer. Its first chairman was D H MacFarlane MP who though of Highland birth sat as an Irish nationalist. Indeed the HLLRA took its cue from events in Ireland and it was another Irish nationalist of Highland birth, John Murdoch, who through his editorship of *The Highlander* had done most to articulate crofting grievances and to align the London reformers behind them.

During 1883–4 branches of the HLLRA were formed throughout the crofting counties as men like John MacPherson, one of the **Glendale Martyrs**, hoisted its standard. Its first conference at **Dingwall** in September 1884 rejected the proposals of the Napier Commission, adopted a radical programme of land redistribution, and enjoined its members to support only those Parliamentary candidates who endorsed this programme. When the Third Reform Act enfranchised crofters, four out of the five crofting constituencies returned HLLRA supporters (1886), henceforth known as the 'Crofters' Party'. Although the **Crofters' Holdings Act** of 1886 owed much to the HLLRA's advocacy, the Association opposed it on the grounds that it failed to address the problem of insufficient crofting land. Urging compulsory purchase of lands lost to crofters during the **clearances**, a cause particularly dear to the landless **cottars**, it changed its name to the Highland Land League and both encouraged land raids, especially on **Lewis**, and condemned the reprisals which followed during this final phase of the **Highland Land War** (1886–8).

In the 1890s the League's leaders supported proposals by the Liberal government to investigate the possibility of making more land available for crofting. But when legislation to that effect was not forthcoming both the League and its Liberal allies were discredited. The election of 1897 saw both obliterated by a Conservative/Unionist revival which promised state intervention to purchase and redistribute land for crofting through the Highland Congested Districts Board. The League had lost its mass support in the crofting areas but lingered on as a haven for 'an exotic amalgam of socialists, Gaelic revivalists and Scottish nationalists' (James Hunter).

HIGHLAND LAND WAR (1883–8)

Also known as the 'Crofters' War', the Highland Land War comprehends the numerous acts of civil disobedience by which the **crofting** community of the Highlands and Islands made known its grievances and won recognition of its claims to a unique agrarian status. On occasion the crofters took up arms and on occasion the authorities called in troops. It was also a war in the sense that agitation (rent strikes, repossession of grazings, assaults on the police) was not restricted to the few set pieces like the **Battle of Braes** or **Glendale** but was widespread and continuous throughout the **Hebrides** and much of the Highlands.

There is, however, no record of any lives being lost – other than those of sheep and deer slaughtered as a protest against their occupation of what was once common grazing or to sustain hungry land squatters a long way from home. The guns carried by **Lewis** crofters during a land raid on Park deer forest (1886) seem to have been used solely for this purpose; otherwise the crofters contented themselves with wielding farm implements and sticks and throwing sods and stones. The government was equally reluctant to escalate the struggle. Although gun-boats put in several appearances and troops were stationed in both **Skye** and Lewis, their services were only available as protection for the police. Bayonets were occasionally drawn but no shots were fired. The crofters took matters as far as was necessary for maximum publicity and the authorities no further than was necessary for containment.

The earlier phase of the war (1883–6) centred on Skye and crofters' grievances. These were encouraged by the **Napier Commission** and to some extent met by the working of the **Crofters' Holdings Act**. But the plight of the landless **cottars** remained unaddressed. Thus during its latter phase (1886–8) the war centred on cottars' grievances and on the Isle of Lewis (where cottars were more numerous). After a series of exceptionally rough encounters an upsurge in the **fishing** industry heralded an improvement in cottars' earnings and by the autumn of 1888 troops were withdrawn from Lewis.

HIGHLAND LIGHT INFANTRY, The (City of Glasgow Regiment)

The HLI, as the regiment was popularly known, stemmed from the 1881 amalgamation of the 71st Highland Light Infantry and the 74th Highlanders who were joined by the two battalions of the 1st Royal Lanarkshire Militia and several volunteer battalions of infantry from the same county. The subtitle 'Glasgow' which had been applied to the 71st from 1808–10 was again used in the form above from 1923.

The 71st were raised as the 73rd in 1777 by John Mackenzie, Lord MacLeod, son and heir to the Earl of Cromarty, being renumbered 71st in 1786. After early service in India and at the Cape, they were captured in the abortive Buenos Aires expedition. Distinguished service in the Peninsula followed where the regiment gained the sobriquet 'The Heroes of Vittoria' and in 1810 they were given the coveted status of Light Infantry, exchanging their kilts for the then unique uniform of tartan trews. They fought at Waterloo and saw service in the Crimea and the Indian Mutiny.

The 74th were raised in 1787 for service in India with Major-General Sir Archibald Campbell of Inverneil as their Colonel. At the battle of Assaye in 1803 they were awarded a special third colour. Thereafter they fought in the Peninsula and in South Africa. They lost their Highland identity in 1809 but had it restored to them along with tartan trews in 1845.

The HLI produced 26 battalions for World War I and were awarded 75 Battle Honours, fighting in Gallipoli, Egypt, Palestine, Mesopotamia, on the Western Front and in Russia in 1919. In World War II the HLI fought in France in 1940, Abyssinia, North Africa, Sicily, Italy, Greece and in north-west Europe, winning a further 50 Battle Honours which brought the regimental total to 155. After the war the 1st Battalion saw active service in Palestine and Cyprus. In 1959 they were amalgamated with the Royal Scots Fusiliers. There was much opposition to the marriage, but it went ahead and the very fine result is the **Royal Highland Fusiliers**, a perhaps surprising title for a regiment in the Lowland Brigade.

The 71st wore the Government tartan with a red and white stripe added which became known as 'Mackenzie'; this tartan being worn by the HLI after 1881. The 74th wore Government tartan on raising and 'Lamont' (Government with a white stripe) 1845–81. The regiment succeeded in having the kilt restored at last in 1947. They wore a red and white hackle in the Tam O'Shanter bonnet.

The Regimental Marches were 'Blue Bonnets O'er the Border' (pipes) and 'Whistle O'er the Lave O't' (band). The last Colonel-in-Chief of the HLI was HRH Princess Margaret who was appointed in 1947.

HIGHLAND LINE, The

An imaginary divide between the Highlands and the rest of Scotland (Lowlands), the Highland Line has been variously located. It certainly runs more north-south than east-west and is generally drawn between some point on the Moray Firth and some point on the **Clyde** estuary. All that lies west and north of such a line is taken to be the Highlands although it can be argued that including therein the fertile lowlands of **Caithness** and excluding the uplands of the **Aberdeenshire** Mounth is illogical. Much depends on whether a geographical or a social definition of the Highlands is sought. Typical of such delineations is that given in Fullarton's *Gazetteer of Scotland*: 'The line commences at the mouth of the river Nairn; it then, with the exception of a slight north-eastward or outward curve, the central point of which is on the river **Spey**, runs due south-east until it strikes the river **Dee** at Tullach, nearly on the third degree of longitude west of Greenwich; it then runs generally south until it falls upon the West-water, or the southern large head-water of the North Esk; it thence, over a long stretch, runs almost due south-west, and with scarcely a deviation, till it falls upon the Clyde at Ardmore in the parish of Cardross; and now onward to the Atlantic Ocean, it moves along the frith [firth] of Clyde, keeping near to the continent, and excluding none of the Clyde islands except the comparatively unimportant **Cumbraes**.'

HILL, David Octavius (1801–70) and ADAMSON, Robert (1821–48) Photographers

Hailed as two of the finest proponents of the portrait photograph, Hill and Adamson began their famous collaboration in **Edinburgh** in 1843. Previously, Adamson had produced photographs in **St Andrews** using Fox Talbot's Calotype method, which was not patented in Scotland, while Hill was an established artist and Secretary to the **Royal Scottish Academy**. While working on a composite painting of the dissenting ministers who formed the **Free Church** 'split' from the **Church of Scotland** in 1843, Hill decided to photograph the sitters as an aid to painting them. His partnership with Adamson facilitated this, but was soon extended to include other stylish portraits ranging from individual figures in the photographers' studio on Edinburgh's **Calton Hill** to groups of **Newhaven** fishermen and soldiers in the **Castle**, in all producing 1800 pictures in 4½ years.

Adamson died young in 1848, and although his partner continued photographing (as well as painting – the Free Church picture was not finished until 1866), his work never quite recaptured a quality which was obvi-ously the product of a good working partnership. The bulk of their work can be seen at the **Scottish National Portrait Gallery** in Edinburgh. 'Hill and Adamson are universally accorded first place in the annals of photography ... it is indeed astonishing that in its very first years the new art should have reached its highest peak in the magnificent achievements of these two Scottish photographers' (Helmut Gernsheim).

HILL HOUSE, Helensburgh

Designed between 1902–3 by **Charles Rennie Mackintosh** for the enlightened **Glasgow** publisher W W Blackie, the Hill House is an essay in Mackintosh's ideas for a through designed 'modern' house. A stark and simple translation of the supremely functional traditional Scottish house, it leaves behind the English Arts and Crafts 'White House' by Baillie Scott nearby. The 'L' plan allowed a dramatic roofscape of long, unbroken ridges and gable ends. This is emphasised by the smooth, harled walls rising clean from the horizontal terraces of the formal garden. Windows are small and placed as required rather than for external effect. Inside, typically dark intimate spaces alternate with light and are threaded with repeating patterns of colour and detail. Furnishing and decoration are integrated into the design. Ample cupboards and seats are fitted into the walls maximising the use of the small spaces, and, together with fireplaces and lights, introduce restrained decoration into each room. The Hill House is now in the care of the **National Trust for Scotland**, and is open to the public.

HIRSEL, The, Coldstream, Berwickshire

Family home of **Alec Douglas-Home** (14th Earl of Home before renouncing the title to become Prime Minister in 1963 and created a Life Peer in 1974 as Baron Home of the Hirsel), The Hirsel has been the seat of the **Earls of Home** since 1611. There is documentary evidence of a house 'at the dwelling place of Hirsel or Spylaw (a ridge on the estate overlooking the horizontal with England) in 1589 and again in 1611, when the Home family bought 'the lands of Hirsel with the tower'. There is no definite evidence of a house on the present site until **Robert Gordon of Straloch**'s map of 1640. By 1760 the original U-plan house had had two wings added to the north. It was altered again in 1813–18 by Atkinson and **William Burn**, in 1858 by **David Bryce** and James Campbell Walker, and in the 1890s George Henderson added a music room and chapel. In 1958–9 it was returned to the plan of the 1850s by Ian Lindsay.

The word Hirsel as an agricultural term denotes an area of land carrying sheep. Archaeological investigations have revealed settlements in the surrounding fields dating back to Neolithic times. The early 18th century landscape designers started the layout of the grounds that is little changed today though enlarged – particularly with the addition of the Lake, excavated from a 'moss' in the 1780s, and the Rhododendron Wood, Dundock, planted in the 1880s. Since 1960 the walled garden, which alone employed about 12 men in the early years of the century, has declined and the grounds immediately round the house have been planted with shrub and rose beds, borders and thousands of bulbs. There are many old deciduous trees, the oldest a sycamore near the walled garden said to have been planted to commemorate the **Battle of Flodden** in 1513, and the whole estate is host to over 160 species of birds during a year. The grounds are permanently open to the public and there is a museum and craft centre.

HISLOP, Joseph John (1887–1977) Opera Singer

Although initially trained in **Edinburgh** (his birthplace) and Gothenburg as a photo-process engraver, and with ambitions to be a portrait painter, Hislop was to become one of the world's leading tenors, sharing roles with Gigli and appearing with Galli-Curci, Chaliapin, Melba and Tetrazzini. Chaliapin said of him 'tonight I sang with a real tenor, not a painted doll'. He toured the world, being particularly successful in Los Angeles and San Francisco, but returning to Sweden (where his vocal training had begun) in 1936 to teach. His pupils included Birgit Nilsson and Jussi Björling. See Michael Turnbull's 'Joseph Hislop' in Stretto Vol 7, No 2, 1987.

HISTORIC SCOTLAND

Since 1991 Historic Scotland has been an executive agency looking after some 300 historic properties – ranging from **Edinburgh Castle** to a disused railway viaduct near **Montrose**. Formerly known as the Historic Buildings and Monuments section of the Scottish Development Department, and answerable to the Secretary of State for Scotland, Historic Scotland has a current budget of £31 million and a staff of over 600. Its other tasks include listing buildings and monuments worthy of conservation, excavating historic sites and providing grant aid for the repair and preservation of appropriately historic buildings.

The Royal Commission on Ancient and Historical Monuments of Scotland is a separate agency staffed by Crown servants but is sponsored by Historic Scotland and is concerned with the recording and studying of Scotland's buildings' heritage. It has an extensive publishing programme detailing descriptions of monuments and buildings, and maintains the National Monuments Board of Scotland in the form of library and illustration collections, including aerial photographs.

HODDAM CASTLE, Nr Ecclefechan, Dumfriesshire

Standing beside the Annan River and below **Repentance Tower**, Hoddam dates from about 1550 and was built by John Maxwell, Lord Herries. Originally an L-plan tower house, it was swallowed up within successive extensions, the most notable of which were by **William Burn** in the 1820s. These have since been demolished as have some of the considerable additions made in the 1870s. **Sir Walter Scott** is said to have been a frequent visitor when the castle was owned by the Sharpe family and to have hereabouts found many of the settings for Guy Mannering and Redgauntlet. He would not be amused by the castle's 20th century fate. A youth hostel in 1935, requisitioned by the War Office during World War II, it was being used as an administrative building for the surrounding caravan park in 1998.

HOGG, James (1770–1835) Poet and Novelist

One of the most important Scottish writers of the 19th century, James Hogg is also known as 'the Ettrick Shepherd', a literary personality devised by himself to emphasise his unusual cultural experience. He was born at Ettrick in the Scottish Borders, probably towards the end of November 1770, his father being an impoverished (and later failed) tenant farmer and his mother one of a notable peasant family named Laidlaw. A compelling story-teller with a fine ear, he died a nationally recognised poet and song-writer, his work having been promoted by **Scott** and appreciated by **Byron**. Hogg's Memoir of the Author's Life and his letters give a humorous yet moving outline of the career of a unique and complex personality, full of vanities and vagaries yet impressively shrewd and tenacious.

His youth was spent as a shepherd, but like his father he had a leaning towards unsuccessful farming speculations. His first substantial literary earnings were lost in this way, and he subsequently found that 'having appeared as a poet, and a speculative farmer besides, no one would now employ me as a shepherd'. It was thus 'in utter desperation' that in 1810 he set off for **Edinburgh** to become a literary man. In 1815 the now famous poet was generously granted by the **Duke of Buccleuch** the little farm of Altrive rent free, a longed-for home in his own native district. Many of his later stories are dated from Altrive, and it was there he brought his bride in 1820. Financial problems, exacerbated by the leasing of a second farm (Mount Benger), were ever-present, but he nevertheless wrote that 'so uniformly happy has my married life been, that on a retrospect I cannot distinguish one part from another, save by some remarkably good days of **fishing**, shooting and **curling** on the ice.'

James Hogg, 'the Ettrick Shepherd', by William Bewick, 1824 (SNPG)

He achieved recognition from the essentially urban community based in Edinburgh by acute manipulation of his rural upbringing. Firstly, his direct experience of Scottish peasant society gave him an authority no middle-class collector could claim. Following his meeting with the **ballad**-collecting Scott in 1802 he published a volume of his own ballad imitations, *The Mountain Bard* (1807), while his important series of tales *The Shepherd's Calendar* (1829) recorded for the readership of **Blackwood's Magazine** the lifestyle and beliefs of the traditional farming community into which he had been born. The stories of *The Brownies of Bodsbeck* (1818) and *Winter Evening Tales* (1820), besides many of his numerous songs and magazine tales, fascinate as works of a highly individual genius which are yet representative of a particular society. Secondly, Hogg presented himself as the successor to the mantle of **Robert Burns**, divinely inspired if largely uneducated. *The Queen's Wake* (1813), which made Hogg famous, relates a poetic contest at the court of **Queen Mary**, exploring the theme of national poetry, art and inspiration. Hogg himself adopted the Bard of Ettrick's motto *Naturae Donum* (Nature's Gift) on his seal, and Nicholson painting his portrait in 1815 saw not the working-man of over 40 but an innocent youth with fervid eyes. In his *Noctes Ambrosianae* **John Wilson** ludicrously combined these two aspects of the Ettrick Shepherd, who then became a good-hearted, vain, ignorant old buffoon with an incongruous streak of noble lyricism and patriotic feeling. Hogg himself may have been greatly amused, but his loyal friends and the young wife he married in 1820 were indignant at the travesty.

Many of Hogg's most significant works, however, seem hardly consonant with this image in that they display wide if desultory reading, an intimate acquaintance with contemporary literature, and an experimental and highly idiosyncratic use of accepted literary forms. This is evident in *The Spy* of 1810–11, his experiment with the by then somewhat moribund form of the essay-periodical. The accomplished literary parodies of *The Poetic Mirror* (1816) may be instanced here, fantastic romances such as *The Surpassing Adventures of Allan Gordon* or *The Three Perils of Man* (1822), and various analyses of past and present Scottish character and society in *Tales of the Wars of Montrose* (1835) or *The Three Perils of Woman* (1823). The work judged as his masterpiece today, *The Private Memoirs and Confessions of a Justified Sinner* (1824), is also in this category, with its linguistic brilliance, its double narrative, and its inward exploration of the national and individual psychology. This haunting account of a tormented soul may be considered the most significant Scottish novel of the 19th century, and it is moreover the creative origin of several recent works of fiction.

Intriguingly described by the scholar Thomas Crawford as 'a Blake with a comic vision', Hogg as a man and as a writer had an ebullience and energy all his own, and remains an instantly recognisable, immediate and distinctive Scottish voice.

HOGMANAY

The name given to 31 December (or to gifts given and received on New Year's Eve) is generally agreed to come from the Old French *aguillanneuf*, 'last day of the year',

via the northern French dialect version of the same word, *hoguinané*. **John MacTaggart**, however, gives a more appealing derivation in his *Gallovidian Encyclopaedia*:

> I think *hog-ma-nay* means *hug-me-now*. Kissing, long ago, was a thing much more common than at present [1824]. People in the days gone by saluted others in churches with *holy kisses*; and this *smacking* system was only laid aside when priests began to see that it was not *holiness* alone prompted their congregations to hold up their *gabs* to one another like *Amous dishes*, as **Burns** says. At weddings too what a kissing there was; and even to this day, at these occasions much of it goes on; and on the happy nights of *hog-ma-nay* the kissing trade is extremely brisk, particularly in *Auld Reekie*; then the lasses must kiss with all the stranger lads they meet, while phrases not unlike to 'John, come kiss me now' or 'John, come *hug* me now' are frequently heard. From such causes, methinks, *hog-ma-nay* has started. The hugging day, the time to *hug-me-now*.

HOLLOWS TOWER, Canonbie, Dumfriesshire

Two miles north of Canonbie, Hollows Tower stands above the Esk and is associated with **Johnnie Armstrong** whose nearby Gilnockie Tower now exists only as foundations. Hollows, or Holehouse, is 16th century and oblong in plan with four storeys, corbelled parapet, and crow-stepped garret. An Augustinian priory at Canonbie is thought to have been destroyed by the English in 1542 after the **Battle of Solway Moss**. In the 19th century **coal** was worked in the district, the last pits closing in 1922.

HOLY ISLAND, Lamlash Bay, Arran

A mile off the south-east coast of **Arran** in the Firth of **Clyde** and providing shelter for Lamlash Bay, Holy Island owes its name to the 6th century **St Molaise** who went into retreat in a cave on the western shore at the base of Mullach Mor (1030ft/314m). **Viking** inscriptions in the cave possibly date from the 13th century when Haakon of Norway sheltered his fleet in Lamlash Bay on his way to defeat at the **Battle of Largs**. The remains of a 14th century monastery and chapel testify to the island's continued sanctity, although the legend of the Holy Island farmer who murdered his wife after she had presented him with his 15th daughter momentarily dims the aura. In private hands for many years, Holy Island was sold in 1992 to the monks of the Samye Ling Buddhist monastery at **Eskdalemuir** who have established it as a retreat for people of all faiths as well as their own monks and nuns.

HOLY LOCH, Argyll

Reaching two miles into the **Cowal** peninsula from the Firth of **Clyde** just north of **Dunoon**, Holy Loch has none of the tranquillity its name might evoke. Until 1992 the deep-water anchorage and service depot for the United States submarine base, with attendant pontoons and gantries, its shores are fringed with holiday villas, retirement homes and their attendant facilities. Tradition has it that the loch received its name when, in the 12th century, a ship carrying a load of earth from the Holy Land to place beneath the foundations of **Glasgow Cathedral** foundered in its waters while sheltering from a gale. More probably the 'Holy' refers to the church in the village of Kilmun on the loch's northern shore. Of the original collegiate church, founded by Sir Duncan Campbell of Lochow in 1442 and dedicated to St Mundus or Munna, a 7th century **Culdee** who was one of the most eminent disciples of **St Columba**, only the tower survives; its replacement dates from 1841. The vault was the traditional burial place of the Argyll family and contains the remains of, among others, the **8th Earl and 1st Marquis of Argyll**, executed in 1661. Kilmun now has an arboretum and visitor centre run by the **Forestry Commission** for those wishing to explore the Argyll Forest Park.

HOME, Henry, Lord Kames (1696–1782)
Judge, Philosopher, Improver

The son of George Home of Kames near **Eccles** in **Berwickshire**, Henry was called to the Bar in 1723 and defended Captain Porteous in 1736, the latter's subsequent pardon provoking the **Porteous Riot**. In 1752 he was appointed judge with the title Lord Kames. A distinguished judicial career followed. He also served on the board managing those estates forfeited after the '45 **Jacobite Rising** and on the Board of Trustees for the Encouragement of the Fisheries, Arts and Manufactures of Scotland which took up the idea of a Forth-**Clyde canal**. At Kames and more notably at Blair Drummond, which belonged to his wife's family, he pioneered agricultural improvements which included the partial reclamation and settlement of **Flanders Moss**.

But all this was overshadowed by the ideas and influence which emanated from his pen. Home was a pivotal figure in the **Scottish Enlightenment**, co-founding the **Edinburgh** Philosophical Society and publishing works on **philosophy**, natural law, literary criticism and historical enquiry as well as on jurisprudence and **agriculture**. **David Hume**, **James Boswell** and **Adam Smith** were his protégés; **Thomas Reid**, Benjamin Franklin and **James Burnett** (Lord Monboddo) his close friends. *Essays on the Principles of Morality and Natural Religion* (1751) suggested that moral laws were founded not just on David Hume's mix of childhood influences but were rooted in the human constitution, and as immutable as the laws of nature. Thomas Reid developed this idea in his common-sense philosophy while the **General Assembly** debated its heretical potential. Home's legal works were less controversial and included comparative studies of the English and Scottish law and investigations of legal history as well as standard collections of decisions of the **Court of Session**. There are biographies by W C Lehmann (1971) and I S Ross (1972).

HOME, John (1722–1808) Minister, Historian and Playwright

Born in **Leith**, the son of the town clerk, and educated at the **University of Edinburgh**, Home was licensed a probationer of the kirk by the presbytery of Edinburgh in 1745, the year of the last **Jacobite** Rebellion. He enlisted on the Hanoverian side, was taken prisoner after the **Battle of Falkirk** and held at **Doune Castle**. On his release he became Minister of **Athelstaneford** in **East Lothian**, a post he held until 1757. His first verse tragedy, *Agis*, was rejected by David Garrick in

London, as was his second, *Douglas*, but this was produced in Edinburgh in 1756 where it had a long and successful run. The kirk authorities were outraged by the impropriety of a **Presbyterian** minister excelling in a field of which they so strongly disapproved and proceedings were initiated against him; but a year later *Douglas* was performed at Covent Garden with spectacular success and Home resigned from the ministry.

Douglas was heralded as the beginning of a Scottish national drama, but following his appointment as private secretary to the **Earl of Bute** in London in 1757, Home chose rather to write for the London stage. Later he became tutor to the Prince of Wales, and in this influential position was able to secure London productions for all his plays. However, none of his work was nearly as successful as *Douglas*, which on the night of its first performance elicited the cry 'Whaur's yer Wully Shakespeare noo?'

HOME, Lordship and Earldom of

The uncertainty of spelling (and pronunciation) of the name Home dates from some of the earliest charters at the beginning of the 12th century. Even father and son sometimes used different forms. The first direct ancestor of the present family to assume the surname of Home was William, nephew of Waldeve 4th Earl of Dunbar, descendant of the great Gospatrick, Earl of Northumberland. William inherited the lands of Home through his father, Patrick of **Greenlaw**, who was the younger son of Gospatrick. The first Lordship was conferred on Sir Alexander Home when he was made a Lord of Parliament by **James III** in 1473 having been Ambassador Extraordinary to England. This branch of the family continued in direct succession until the 2nd Earl, dying

Sir Alec Douglas-Home, Lord Home of the Hirsel, by Avidor Arikha, 1988 (SNPG)

without an heir, was succeeded by Alexander's brother John's great-great-great-grandson.

The earldom was conferred on the 6th Lord Home, the fifth Alexander to hold the title, by **James VI** by whom he was also made a Privy Councillor and held in high favour. Not all Homes were so treated, sometimes deservedly, and over the centuries the family fortunes waxed and waned. The 3rd Earl held the vanguard at the **Battle of Flodden**. Although he routed the division which opposed him, he then decided that he could do no more and took his men home. They were almost the only 'Flowers of the Forest' to survive, and there was a very considerable stigma on the family for very many years. He later stood against Regent **Albany**, was tried for treason, and executed with his brother.

Other Homes have played other parts. Among them have been two Great Chamberlains of Scotland, a Keeper of the Great Seal of Scotland, a General of the Mint, a Governor of Gibraltar, an Ambassador to France and a Prioress of the Abbey of St Bothans in the **Lammermuirs**, Wardens of the East and Middle Marches and, in this century, Foreign Secretary and Prime Minister.

In 1832 the family name became Douglas-Home on the marriage of the future 11th Earl to the sister and co-heiress of Lord Douglas. The Earl was created Baron Douglas on the death of his brother-in-law in 1875.

The 14th Earl disclaimed the title for life on becoming Prime Minister in 1963 as **Sir Alec Douglas-Home** and was created a Life Peer as Baron Home of the **Hirsel** in 1974. On his death in 1995 his son David succeeded as 15th Earl.

HOOD, James Archibald (1859–1941) Coal Master

Hood came of a family steeped in **coal-mining**, his father Archibald having acquired a number of pits. Born in **Lasswade**, **Midlothian**, he was educated in Swansea, to where his father had temporarily moved, and later at Clifton College, Bristol. When Archibald achieved the amalgamation of his Whitehill Colliery with the neighbouring Newbattle Collieries, James became general manager of the newly formed Lothian Coal Company Ltd, and then chairman (1911), a position he held until his death. Under his direction the company progressed technically as electrical power was applied underground and as steel props replaced wooden. Owning several pits in Lothian he employed over 2000 men. He also followed his father's lead in sponsoring model housing for miners, most notably in the company village of Newtongrange, and in supporting social institutions, such as libraries and **football** clubs.

HOODED CROW

The two forms of European crow – the black carrion crow (*Corvus corone corone*) and the grey and black hooded crow (*Corvus corone cornix*) – are classed as a single species because, where their ranges overlap, they interbreed readily. The hooded crow and the hybrids in Britain are confined to Scotland, with the narrow hybrid zone running north-east from **Arran** up to **Inverness** and then along the east coast of the Highlands into **Caithness**. The two forms are believed to have evolved during the last Ice Age when the European crow was separated into isolated populations.

The hooded crow is a powerful, active and voracious bird, feeding on almost anything, but preferring carrion. It raids the nests of other birds, stealing and eating both eggs and chicks; the nestlings of the **red grouse** are a particular favourite. It preys on small mammals too, and will even kill newborn lambs, making the 'hoodie' one of the worst enemies of both farmer and gamekeeper. 'If there is one bird which we would wish to see reduced in numbers,' wrote **Frank Fraser Darling** in 1969, 'it is the hoodie crow; but there is little likelihood that the species will become conveniently rare.'

HOPE, Dr John (1725–86) Botanist

Born in **Edinburgh**, John Hope studied botany in Paris under Bernard de Jussieu and graduated in medicine at **Glasgow University**. In 1750 he became a member of the **Royal College of Physicians** in Edinburgh (he was elected Fellow in 1762 and President in 1764) and began to practise medicine. From 1761 he took on the joint appointments of Professor of Botany and *materia medica* at **Edinburgh University** and King's Botanist and Superintendent of the **Royal Botanic Garden Edinburgh**. He created a new Botanic Garden on **Leith** Walk, combining the collections of two former gardens at **Trinity Hospital** and **Holyrood Abbey**. Among the plants he introduced to Scotland was rhubarb. He was distinguished in both experimental and field botany and one of the earliest advocates of the Linnaean system of classification. He was also respected as a teacher; and his students included **William Roxburgh** and **Archibald Menzies**. Hope died in 1786, and Roxburgh later named the important tree genus *Hopea* in his honour.

HOPE, John Adrian Louis, 7th Earl of Hopetoun and 1st Marquis of Linlithgow (1860–1908) Governor-General of Australia

One of many earldoms created to smooth the passage of the **Act of Union**, that of Hopetoun was conferred (1703) on Charles Hope, great-grandson of **Sir Thomas Hope**. Fighting descendants included John 4th Earl who served in the **Black Watch**, took command at Corunna after the death of **Sir John Moore** (1808) and succeeded **Thomas Graham** of Balgowan in the Peninsular War (1813). His grandson, the 7th Earl, was born at Hopetoun, educated at Eton and succeeded to the title in 1873. Lord-in-Waiting to **Queen Victoria**, a Deputy Lieutenant for **Linlithgow**, etc, and high commissioner to the **General Assembly** (all in the 1880s), he was sent overseas in 1889 as Governor of Victoria in Australia. He returned in 1895 and served as Paymaster General in Salisbury's last ministry before being appointed Lord President and President of the Institute of Naval Architects; ships and horses were his main interests. The creation of the Commonwealth of Australia in 1900 saw him appointed the first Governor-General but he resigned after less than two years complaining that the remuneration was insufficient. He was created Marquis on his return and soon after sold to the government for £122,500 what then became the **Rosyth** naval dockyard. His last public office was as Secretary of State for Scotland in the **Balfour** administration (1905). He died at Pau in the Pyrenees and was succeeded by his son, **Victor Alexander John Hope**, future Viceroy of India.

HOPE, Sir Thomas, of Craighall
(c1580–c1646) Lord Advocate

An **Edinburgh** advocate of merchant stock, Hope was first prominent conducting the defence (1606) of John Forbes (minister of **Alford**, d.1634) and other ministers who had held a **General Assembly** in **Aberdeen** (1605) contrary to the prorogation of **James VI**. In 1625 he prepared a deed revoking James's grants of church property; but, upholding the royal prerogative while defending the Scottish church, he was made Lord Advocate (1626) and in 1634 secured the conviction for treason of James Elphinstone, Lord Balmerino (d.1649) who had petitioned an increasingly arbitrary **Charles I**. In 1638 Hope reasserted the Assembly's independence by declining to declare the **Covenant** illegal and ruling against episcopacy. He compiled two collections of *Practicks* which supplemented the work of **Sir James Balfour** and produced three sons all of whom became Lords of Session and one, also Sir Thomas (1606–43), Lord Justice General. Descendants became Earls of Hopetoun as a reward for supporting the **Union** and later Marquises of **Linlithgow**.

HOPE, Victor Alexander John, 2nd Marquis of Linlithgow (1887–1952) Viceroy of India

India being the only colonial appointment above that of Canada or Australia, when the 2nd Marquis of Linlithgow was appointed Viceroy in 1936 it was as if his career had taken over where the **1st Marquis**'s left off. Like his father, he had been born at Hopetoun, educated at Eton, succeeded to the title in his twentieth year, and sided with the Unionists in politics. He was Civil Lord of the Admiralty (1922–4) and, though he declined the governorship of Madras (1924), clearly had his sights set on India as early as 1926. A member of the joint Committee on Indian Constitutional Reform (1933–4), Baldwin selected him for the viceroyalty as a safe pair of hands for implementing the Committee's proposals. He was also 'devoid of charm and . . . with a marked tendency to create unnecessary work and probe into matters best left to others'. This was the verdict of Penderel Moon, an ICS man, but it was echoed by Nehru's 'heavy of body and slow of mind, solid as a rock and with almost a rock's lack of awareness'. He also laboured under the delusion that British rule would last for another 50 years. On the other hand he conscientiously introduced provincial autonomy and expanded the executive council to include an Indian majority. His rock-like qualities kept him in office for the longest stint since **Dalhousie** and proved invaluable during the war, while his diligence ensured the availability of India's vast manpower. But in the process he alienated the Congress Party, encouraged the sectarian polarisation of politics which eventually led to the demand for Pakistan becoming irresistible, and ignored the signs of impending famine in Bengal. Relieved by Wavell in 1943, he became chairman of the Midland Bank and chancellor of **Edinburgh University** (1944), a post which he held until his death.

HOPEMAN, Moray

Between **Lossiemouth** and **Burghead**, Hopeman is a typical Moray Firth **fishing** port, unnoticed until far away a trawler is lost and suddenly the world hears of another 'tight-knit community united in grief'. It was founded in 1805 by William Young of Inverugie, later notorious for his part in the **Sutherland clearances**. The harbour was added 30 years later by Admiral Archibald Duff. Hopeman stone is much quarried, and from the village a clifftop walk leads to the caves, one with **Pictish** carving, of Covesea (pron 'Causie').

HOPETOUN HOUSE, West Lothian

The lands of Hopetoun were bought by Sir John Hope (third son of **Sir Thomas Hope of Craighall**) from Sir William Seton in 1678. Sir John, who at about the same time was made sheriff of 'Linlithgowshire' (**West Lothian**), died in a shipwreck in 1682, leaving his estates to his infant son Charles (b.1681). In 1698, when the boy was 16, his mother commissioned **Sir William Bruce** to design Hopetoun House. Bruce's plan, published in *Vitruvius Britannicus*, shows a square three-storey central main block crowned by a cupola and linked to angle pavilions by convex colonnades, and the house he built (1699–1702) was generally agreed to be one of the grandest of his great country mansions. However in 1703 Sir Charles Hope was created Earl of Hopetoun in anticipation of his continuing support for the **Union**, and before long Bruce's mansion was found wanting. In 1721 **William Adam** was commissioned to turn Hopetoun House into something more akin to a palace, a task which, with the later assistance of his sons John and **Robert**, he successfully accomplished. Bruce's central block (which never received its cupola) was retained, although its east front was rebuilt with a new attic floor and balustrade; his pavilions were replaced with new flanking blocks (with cupolas) and his convex colonnades (which may never have been built) replaced with new concave colonnades. The final house equated neither with Bruce's plan nor with Adam's own first design, and the overall impression is inevitably of a compromise. But palatial it certainly is, and as stately a stately home as any earl could have desired. In 1902 the 7th Earl of Hopetoun was created Marquis of Linlithgow, and Hopetoun House is still the home of his descendants.

HORNEL, Edward Atkinson (1864–1933) Painter

Hornel was one of the most significant contributors to the **Glasgow** School of **painting**. Although born in Australia, he was brought to **Kirkcudbright** when only one year old. After an unremarkable training in the **Edinburgh Trustees' Academy** from 1880–3 he went to Antwerp where he studied under Verlat. On his return to Scotland in 1885 he responded immediately to the Hague School-influenced rustic naturalism in the work of **James Guthrie** and his fellows and, joining with them, Hornel adopted the distinctive attributes of the Glasgow Boys' style.

Of all the associations between the Boys, the friendship Hornel developed with **George Henry** was to prove the most artistically innovative. Influenced by the paintings of Monticelli and by the adventurous compositions and technique of Arthur Melville, both progressively discarded the realist ethos that had characterised the earlier work of the School in favour of a decorative and increasingly symbolic approach to their subject matter. Whilst

Hornel's motifs during this period – often goat- or sheep-herds within a landscape setting – suggest a continued interest in the pastoral, the broad handling, diminished perspective and frieze-like arrangement of his compositions point to an allegorical intention fitting with his interest in **Galloway** folklore and **Celtic mythology**. These developments climaxed in Hornel and Henry's collaborative work *The Druids: Bringing in the Mistletoe* (1890, **Glasgow Art Galleries**), a masterpiece of the Glasgow School that links artistic activity in the west of Scotland with wider burgeoning claims for the socialistic possibilities in decorative art, then finding particular expression in Edinburgh under the efforts of **Patrick Geddes**.

Hornel's friendship with Henry culminated in 1893 with their visit to Japan, and the exotically coloured and patterned works he exhibited on his return met with critical success. He settled in Kirkcudbright but in his subsequent paintings was unable to recapture the vitality of his Japanese paintings and his work became increasingly formulaic and mannered. In spite of this his popularity continued and it is for the highly decorative scenes of girls at play which he produced in endless variation for the remainder of his career that he is principally remembered.

HORNPIPE

The hornpipe is a dance form similar to the **jig** but with a different metre for the music, sometimes with three, sometimes two beats to the bar. Mattheson writing in the 18th century is probably right in declaring it to be Scottish in origin, and it may be identified with the Scotch Measure.

HORSES AND PONIES

HIGHLAND PONY Often called the Garron (although strictly speaking this Gaelic word should only be used for a gelding), the Highland pony is characterised by a deep chest and powerful frame. Now a great favourite in trekking centres because of its reliability and sure-footedness, the Highland pony has had a long and important history, having been used as a draught animal for pulling carts and as a beast of burden for carrying **peats** from the cuttings, **grouse** off the Victorian moors and the carcases of **deer** off the hill – indeed many are still used for this last purpose today. The Highland pony averages between 13.2 and 14 hands in height and its colour varies greatly; it can be dun, black, brown, grey or chestnut, and has a distinctive eel stripe along its back. Several viable studs exist, including one on the island of **Rum** in the **Hebrides** that is reputed to have improved the quality of its strain by using stallions from the wrecked Spanish Armada. There are two theories about these so-called Spanish stallions: one is that they were deliberately released from the galleons as the ships tried to escape from the British fleet and those that swam ashore on Rum brought in fresh blood to the ponies already on the island. The other is that both stallions and mares reached the island from the galleons and were the original stock for the breed. Both are questionable; although all livestock was ordered off the galleons by the Admiral of the Spanish Fleet, it happened off the east coast of Scotland and most of the pack animals were mules.

SHETLAND PONY One of the smallest breeds of pony in the world, generally measuring no more than 1m at the shoulders, the Shetland Pony is stockily built and very strong and hardy. The origins of the 'Sheltie' are uncertain, although records of its presence in the **Shetland Islands** dating back to the **Viking** era suggest a possible Norse introduction. Its hardiness, and the thickness of its shaggy winter coat, made it the ideal **crofter's** pony as it seemed to thrive if left to run wild and forage for itself during the bleak winter months when fodder was scarce. Used primarily as a pack pony to carry peats and **seaweed** on Shetland crofts, a grimmer task lay in store for the Shetland pony in the industrial 19th century when its tiny size ideally suited it for working in **coal-mines**. Today, far from its native shores, it is doomed to be the pampered pet of generations of infant equestrians – its bad-tempered reputation apparently the result of too many titbits and not enough discipline.

CLYDESDALE Industry in Lowland Scotland in the 18th and early 19th centuries needed industrial horses, so breeders in **Lanarkshire**'s **Clydesdale** (regarded as the country's best horse-breeding area) turned to Flanders for new strains to increase the size, weight and strength of the native horses. The first truly 'native' Clydesdale sire – a stallion called 'Glancer' – is recorded in 1810; the family tree of the Clydesdale can be traced back to 1840 and the Clydesdale Horse Society and Stud Book were started in 1877. At an average of 17 hands, the Clydesdale is not quite as large as either the Shire or the Suffolk Punch (the other two native British heavy breeds), but its long stride and sound feet made it ideal for hauling heavy loads along urban streets.

HOSPITALFIELD, Arbroath

The house of 19th century artist and collector Patrick Allan-Fraser (1813–90), Hosptitalfield House, near **Arbroath**, was transformed in the 20th century into an influential art school which nurtured some of the most talented artists of the period. Originally built as part of a medieval monastery, the house came into the hands of Patrick Allan upon his marriage to Elizabeth Fraser in 1843. He had trained as an artist in **Edinburgh** alongside **Robert Scott Lauder** and like him had travelled to Italy where he had specialised in picturesque landscape views. Allan came from a wealthy middle-class Arbroath family and his return to Scotland and marriage to Elizabeth was a timely union for the Frasers whose estates had fallen into disrepair. Adding the Fraser name to his own, Allan proceeded to revive the family fortunes and by 1849 was in a sufficiently strong financial position to rebuild Hospitalfield. Taking his inspiration from **Walter Scott** and the author's improvements to **Abbotsford**, Allan-Fraser constructed a remarkable essay in the Scots baronial manner, working solely with the estate craftsmen, attempting consistently to homogenise the building with local materials and natural forms. He also began to collect contemporary art, particularly painting and sculpture by the colleagues had known in Edinburgh and London. Allan-Fraser became an influential and revered patron in the Scottish art world and was elected an honorary member of the **Royal Scottish Academy**.

Patrick and Elizabeth Allan-Fraser died childless and

in their will endowed the house, its contents and the estates as a foundation for the promotion of art in Scotland. Under the terms of the Patrick Allan-Fraser Trust Hospitalfield became a residential art school offering scholarships for both teachers and students. It was not until the 1930s, however, that it began to play an important role in the art-teaching world. By that stage the four Scottish art schools were well established and Hospitalfield became an important secondary base for the more enthusiastic teachers and students, particularly in the summer months. A number of inspiring resident wardens, notably **James Cowie**, were to attract many of the most promising Scottish artists who later recalled their time at Hospitalfield as seminal to their development. These included **Robert Henderson Blyth**, **Joan Eardley**, **Robert Colquhoun** and James McIntosh. Patrick Allan-Fraser would doubtless be pleased to learn that the bucolic setting and whimsical architecture of his former home has done so much to foster the work of Scottish artists in the 20th century.

HOWDEN, James (1832–1913) Engineer
Born in the east of Scotland, Howden served an apprenticeship with a **Glasgow engineering** firm before setting up in business on his own in 1862 to build marine engines and boilers. His firm prospered particularly after his invention of the forced draught system in the mid-1880s. This used waste gases, previously exhausted up the funnel, to heat the air used in the combustion chamber for a more efficient use of fuel. Later he diversified into land-based engineering installations. His firm survives and has supplied boring equipment for the Channel Tunnel.

HOY, Orkney
Named 'Haey' (Norse for 'High Island'), this is the second largest and most mountainous of the **Orkney** islands. It contains the only rock-cut tomb in the British Isles, known as the Dwarfie Stone. A chamber, with cells on either side, has been hewn out of a free-standing block of red sandstone, and beside its entrance lies another block which used to seal the entrance. In 1850 Major William Mouncey, a former spy in Iran, took up a brief residence in the stone and commemorated his visit with Persian graffiti, a bizarre alternative to those

The Old Man of Hoy, Orkney (SEA)

of the **Vikings**. Hoy is equally celebrated for its natural features. St John's Head, over 1000ft (300m) high, was first climbed in 1970; the Old Man of Hoy, a 450ft (137m) free-standing stack, in 1966 [see also **Geology**]. Long before, **Celtic** monks had built their hermitages in these dramatic settings. Seeking a more delicious solitude, the composer Sir Peter Maxwell Davies has for many years made his home in Rackwick, the only township facing the Pentland Firth. The local folk museum expounds the history and botany of this beautiful valley. At Lyness the naval base is closed, but the naval cemetery remains in which casualties of the Battle of Jutland were interred in 1916 and victims of the sinking of HMS *Hampshire* in the same year. An interpretation centre preserves the history of Lyness, while beyond its wharves **oil** tankers lie beside the terminal in the neighbouring isle of Flotta.

HUMBIE, East Lothian
Itself barely a village, Humbie was notable for its 'Children's Village', a charitable foundation of 1886 run as a holiday centre for disabled children from **Edinburgh**. Later (1968) the Algrade Charitable Trust Residential School for children with mental disabilities run by evangelical Christians, it was closed down in 1995 amid allegations of abuse, and the residents moved to **Musselburgh**. There are several large houses in the vicinity: Johnstounburn, a 19th century 'tower house' built onto its 17th century predecessor, with an unusual two-chambered **doocot** with nests for 2000 birds; Keith Marischal, built c1589 in the form of a hollow square using timbers that were a present from the King of Denmark in appreciation of the services of **George Keith, 5th (4th) Earl Marischal** in negotiations for the marriage of the Princess **Anne of Denmark** to **James VI**; later neglected, the house was restored in the 18th and 19th centuries; Oxenfoord Castle, built (1780) for the Dalrymples (later **Earls of Stair**), incorporating an earlier tower, and modernised in 1840 by **William Burn**, was later an exclusive girls' boarding school.

HUME, Allan Octavian (1829–1912)
Founder of India's Congress Party
The son of **Joseph Hume** (1777–1855) of **Montrose**, who after service with the East India Company sat as a radical MP for 36 years, Allan Octavian was born in London and, though keen to join the navy, was sent to Haileybury. After completing the East India Company course there, he studied medicine and surgery at University College Hospital, and while at UCH found time to delve into botany and ornithology. He left for India in 1849 to join the Bengal Civil Service and was District Officer of Etawah in the United Provinces. While District Officer he founded 181 free schools for Indians as well as arranging scholarships for higher studies.

Hume was not only interested in social change. He wanted educated Indians to take part in the running of the government, to strengthen the hand of the British. With his intimate knowledge and the trust Indians placed in him, he played a very important part in controlling the Mutiny of 1857, and for this he was made CB. He was also fearless and, with little respect for higher authority if he thought it misguided, criticised Lord Lytton for wasting 'millions and millions of Indian money'. For this criticism he was removed from the post of Secretary for Agriculture. In 1822 he retired from the service and settled in Simla, devoting most of his time to Indian ornithology and to the social and political uplift of Indians. In both he was a pioneer. His bird books are much sought-after today and his Indian National Union, formed following an appeal to Calcutta University graduates for 50 volunteers who would 'scorn personal ease . . . to secure greater freedom', was a participant in the first Indian National Congress in 1885.

Hume himself is often credited with founding the party which emerged from these annual Congresses. With more time and resources than most of the participants, he served the organisation as its secretary and helped to transform it from what the Viceroy Lord Dufferin called 'a microscopic minority' into a representative body attracting support from all over India.

Hume left India for England and with the help of Lord Ripon, R T Reed and others organised for Indian news to be published in a number of newpapers, such as the *Leeds Mercury, Manchester Guardian, Scotsman* and *Glasgow Daily Mail*. By 1887 he was able to establish a Congress organisation in Britain and devoted all his time to this till his death in 1912.

In the same year at the Bankipore Session of the Congress it was unanimously passed that Allan Octavian Hume be acknowledged as the father and the founder of the Indian National Congress. 35 years later the Congress under Jawarhalal Nehru assumed its almost continuous supremacy of independent India's political life.

HUME, David (1711–76) Philosopher

One of the greatest of all philosophers, David Hume was born in **Edinburgh**, the second son of a **Berwickshire** laird. He attended **Edinburgh University** as a **law**

David Hume, by Allan Ramsay, 1766 (SNPG)

student but notoriously devoted more time to Latin literature than to his textbooks. After two years he quit official study for a business career in Bristol, leaving that after two years to live frugally in France, and write.

Confusion persists from a statement he made about his desire for literary fame, as if that meant just a reputation or *succès de scandale*. There is much more to his books than that could ever allow. He sought fame by exercising his great literary gifts and intelligence in the effort to bring a new genre into being. *A Treatise of Human Nature* (1739) had as its substance an account of man's nature which advanced **Hutcheson**'s writings by applying the observational methods which Hume's Edinburgh teachers had commended in the science of Boyle and Newton. Hume fancied readers would share his interest, understand and debate his book, but it 'fell dead-born from the press'. Subsequent history shows that Hume did not simply misjudge the work's prospects but failed to appreciate the extent of his own philosophical penetration. To say that a breakthrough in understanding of the *Treatise* came 200 years later with N Kemp Smith's classic *The Philosophy of David Hume* (1941) stresses how radical Hume's masterpiece was.

Recovery from disappointment did not take long, says Hume. Certainly he was averse to the sort of feeling failure might well have caused; for he advocated calm passions as opposed to 'enthusiasm', the fanatical or ill-tempered characteristic of confused religionists from which he had recoiled. Indeed since his work emphasises that the interests or passions of people are products of nurture or experience, the author of *A Treatise of Human Nature* had come near to predicting its lack of success. Back on the family estate (1739) Hume worked at readying his *Essays, Moral and Political*, whose success in 1741 doubtless helped to mitigate any residual disappointment. Hardly so his unhappy attempt to become Professor of Moral Philosophy at Edinburgh (1744), where not only his reputed irreligion but friends' doubts as to his suitability went against him.

He left Berwickshire as companion to the mad Marquis of Annandale in 1745 and went to France as secretary to General St Clair in 1746. Returning home, he worked on the revised and cut adaptation of the *Treatise*, later called *An Enquiry Concerning Human Understanding*, which was published without success in 1748. Hume was again pursuing a diplomatic career with St Clair in the embassies of Vienna and Turin at the time. He came back to disappointment but with £2000. In 1751 he moved to Edinburgh, his hardly sanguine feelings about the state of his literary fame being eased that year when his *Political Discourses* were well received. Their influence on **Adam Smith** was great; 'the main errors of *The Wealth of Nations*,' wrote Robert Adamson, 'are to be found in the deviations from the principles of the *Political Discourses*.' Also extant then, the *Dialogues Concerning Natural Religion* seemed too hot to publish. As it was, Hume was refused the chair of Logic in **Glasgow** (1751); but when appointed librarian of the **Advocates' Library**, his prospects seemed better.

In 1753 there began a new departure, his *History of England*, the final part of which was published in 1761. His biggest literary success, the *History* was weak on early periods and, where better informed, rather a tract. But it gave a backbone for later historians to work on, and has pages important yet for general political theory. The period also saw publication of *Four Dissertations* (1757), including 'On the Passions' and 'The Natural History of Religion'. The latter, an account of the development of religious ideas, includes passages deemed highly sensitive at the time but which in fact embody with incredible subtlety his near extravagant sense of humour. In spite of setbacks and a not immodest realisation of the limits of human intelligence, Hume displayed good nature informed by an entirely unmalicious sense of the ridiculous. Accusations of notoriety-seeking fed on this; so too did J G Hamann, the great precursor of European romanticism and a crucial religious thinker.

As Secretary to the British Embassy in Paris (1763–6) *le bon David* loved and was loved by French society, his ideas on religion being no handicap. He left Edinburgh again (1767) as General Conway's secretary in London, and tried to help Rousseau, who was then dodging the disfavour created by *Emile*. Hume provided him with a sanctuary in England. In 1769, back in Edinburgh for good, Hume moved to a new home in St David Street, enjoying friendship with **William Robertson**, Adam Smith, *et al*, while filling his idle hours and capacious frame with his last great passion, cookery. An intestinal disorder showed in 1775. In 1776, after some relief at Bath, he was ill before he reached home. 'I am, or rather was . . . a man of mild dispositions,' began a serene valedictory note. He died on 25 August of that year. *The Dialogues Concerning Natural Religion* were eventually published in 1779.

The upshot of Hume's work is not the scepticism projected on it by taking some of his statements out of context. We have no knowledge of causation, he argued, apart from our being somehow constrained to believe in it; we cannot and do not form that belief in it which is in us already by reasoning from any principles. Not all beliefs are knowledge; some are, of course, false. But Hume allows no knowledge of matters of fact which is not belief – no utter certainty, no valid 'reason' issuing independent edicts and verbal formulae. But equally such beneficial determining passions and propensities need no more be resented than the likewise unwilled beating of one's heart.

Morality, according to Hume, forms in the early years of life, within the family. Sociability, sympathy, affection and concern for both self and others are the springs of moral life. Although saying that reason is and should be slave to the passions, he does not advocate emotionalism but points to how beliefs come into being through forces tending to their rightness, including reasonable persuasion. Insisting that legitimate human pretensions can only be modest and limited, he is sceptical as to what can be known. Mind is a diverse unity hanging together, shaped and changed by tacit believing, by nurture, experience and habit. To fancy one's mind immutable is, after all, to stifle habits of doubt and of trying to learn. Men *are* creatures of habit, bad and good.

Hume's *Treatise* and *Enquiry* are in various editions, as are his essays, and there are sundry compilations. See *The Philosophy of David Hume* by N K Smith (1941); *Hume's*

Philosophical Development by J Noxon (1973); *Hume's Intentions*, J Passmore (rev ed 1968); *Hume's Philosophical Politics*, Duncan Forbes (1975); *The Life of David Hume*, E C Mossner (1954); *The Letters of David Hume*, ed J Y T Greig, 1932.

HUME, Joseph (1777–1855) Radical Politician

Born in **Montrose**, where his widowed mother sold crockery in the market to support his education, Hume took up medicine, became a fellow of the **Edinburgh Royal College of Surgeons**, and in 1797 secured a posting in the East India Company. Ten years in India

Joseph Hume, by John Graham Gilbert (SNPG)

brought him distinction as a speaker of Hindustani and Persian, plus a considerable fortune. On his return he travelled extensively through Britain and the Mediterranean, produced an English version of Dante's *Inferno* in blank verse, and entered both Parliament and the councils of the East India Company. During a long association with both he specialised in exposing abuses and championing the oppressed. The Reform Bill, the repeal of the Corn Laws, the abolition of flogging in the army and impressment in the navy, Catholic emancipation, financial reform – all were grist to this fine example of the **Scottish Enlightenment** who led the radical party for 30 years. He served on a record number of Parliamentary committees and in the chamber 'spoke longer and oftener and probably worse than any other member' (DNB) – yet seldom to no effect. Twice Rector of **Aberdeen University**, during his more than 40 years as an MP he also represented Aberdeen burghs (not to mention Weymouth, the Border burghs, Middlesex and finally Montrose). Of his six children it was surely **Allan Octavian Hume**, founder of the Indian Congress Party, who most took after his father.

HUME, Sir Patrick, of Polwarth (1641–1724)

A committed **Presbyterian** who was twice imprisoned (1674 and 1678) for 'remonstrating against the tyranny of the **Duke of Lauderdale**'s administration', Patrick Hume was then accused of having sheltered his friend **Robert Baillie of Jerviswood**, at that moment imprisoned and later executed for involvement in the Rye House Plot (1683). Hume went into hiding, spending a month in the family vault at Polwarth Kirk (with his daughter **Grizel (Baillie)** stealing out in the dark to supply him with food), and another month under the floorboards of his house, before escaping to Utrecht. His estates were forfeited and his wife and 12 children joined him in Holland where he became an adviser to William of Orange. Emerging only briefly in 1685 to join **Argyll's rising**, he remained in Holland until 1688 when he accompanied William of Orange to England. On the success of the Revolution, the Polwarth estates were restored and thereafter Sir Patrick's years 'were passed in honour and affluence'; created Lord Polwarth in 1690, he became Lord Chancellor of Scotland in 1696 and was made Earl of Marchmont the following year.

HUME, Tobias (c1569–1645) Composer and Mercenary Soldier

Little is known of Hume's life save through his two London publications of 1605 and 1607; but his name and former profession as a mercenary soldier in Sweden, Russia and Poland make it almost certain that he was Scottish. His compositions are largely for viola da gamba, in which he was a pioneer, and they were seen as rivals by Dowland, who favoured the lute. Hume's ensemble pieces and songs are also very fine and his music ranges from entertaining imitations of warfare and hunting to deeply-felt Pavans which exhibit a combination of adventurousness and refinement of technique. He died in abject poverty, after unsuccessfully petitioning the House of Lords for assistance.

HUME CASTLE, Berwickshire

From the 12th century Hume Castle has shared the surveillance of the eastern Borders with Wark Castle on the banks of the river **Tweed** in Northumberland. It witnessed many stirring deeds on both the local and national scene, suffered many sieges and changes of ownership, and was host to many personages from Kings and Queens to bloody heads hung in triumph from its battlements during the stormy earlier centuries.

It was the headquarters of the **Home** family from c1214 when, with all its lands, it was granted to William of Home by **William the Lion**, until c1611 when the Homes bought the **Hirsel**. In 1650 it was demolished by Cromwell's troops under the command of Colonel Fenwick, despite Governor Cockburn's defiant message:

I Willie Wastle
Stand firm in my Castle
And a' the dugs o' your toun
Will no' bring Willie Wastle doun.

['Willie Wastle' (or Wastell) was the subject of a contemporary children's rhyme, like 'Wee Willie Winkie']

In 1786 a crenellated wall was built by the 3rd Earl of Marchmont to **William Adam**'s design. This really turned the castle into an oversize folly, but restored its dominance and it can still be seen from, and provides a view of, a wide area. It has recently been renovated by the **Berwickshire** Civic Society.

HUNTER, George Leslie (1879–1931) Painter

Born in **Rothesay**, Hunter's family emigrated to California in 1892 where he first worked as an illustrator. In c1904 a visit to Paris encouraged him to paint and upon his return to San Francisco he began preparing for his first exhibition, but all his work was destroyed on the eve of its opening by the earthquake of 1906. He returned to Scotland and resumed his career as an illustrator, moving between **Glasgow**, London and France. He worked throughout the war years of 1914–18 as a farm-labourer in **Lanarkshire**, though continuing to paint.

The dark and restrained tones and finish of Hunter's earliest surviving still-lifes suggest that, like **Peploe**, he was initially inspired by 17th century Dutch painting and by the work of Manet. Though he knew and admired the work of Van Gogh, Cézanne and the other Post-Impressionists, Hunter, unlike his fellow Scottish Colourists **Cadell**, **Fergusson** and Peploe, found much at fault in modern French painting and the interest he developed in colour, light and form, the common ground of all their work, was to grow more slowly and intuitively. The paintings of Matisse provided the greatest influence on his development and in 1922 he saw a major exhibition devoted to the artist. That same year he also visited Venice where the brilliantly coloured oil-studies he painted en plein air encouraged him towards an increasingly free and spontaneous handling of paint. In contrast, the works he painted in Scotland – in **Fife** and at **Loch Lomond** – are naturally more subdued and cooler in tone.

From 1927 he lived in the south of France where his erratic temperament and lifestyle contributed further to his already poor health and in 1929 he was forced to return to Glasgow. In the years before his death he produced some of his most controlled and balanced compositions, characteristics often missing from his work which in general is uneven in quality. The originality and progression demonstrated in his late works distinguish him from his fellow Colourists, whose paintings towards the end of their careers tend towards repetition [see **Painting in Scotland**].

HUNTER, John (1728–93) Surgeon

Born in Long Calderwood near **East Kilbride**, John Hunter went to London in 1748 to join his brother, **William Hunter**, the obstetrician. There he studied anatomy under William Cheselden and surgery under Percival Pott, becoming house surgeon at St George's Hospital, 1756.

As an army surgeon at Belleisle and in Portugal during the Seven Years' War he gained practical experience in dealing with gunshot wounds, of which he wrote the first scientific account (The Blood, Inflammation and Gunshot Wounds, 1794). It was during this spell in the army (1761–3) that he started his famous collection of animal and human anatomical specimens which, by the time of his death, would number over 13,000 items. In 1767 he became a Fellow of the Royal Society and in 1768 a Member of the Surgeons' Incorporation and surgeon at St George's Hospital.

An avid educator, recognised as the father of comparative anatomy, Hunter founded the *Lyceum Medicum Londinense* and the Society for the Improvement of Medical Knowledge, and in 1785 built a museum to house his collection of anatomical specimens where he encouraged his students to study the development and structure of both humans and animals. His own anatomical and physiological research produced the revolutionary *Treatise on Human Teeth* in 1770 and *Observations on certain parts of the Animal Oeconomy* in 1786.

Appointed Assistant Surgeon-General to the Army in 1786 and Surgeon-General four years later, he was Inspector General of the Regimental Hospitals, and introduced a proper career structure for young army surgeons. The government eventually bought his museum and handed it over to the Royal College of Surgeons of England in 1800. Although both the College and Museum were badly damaged in an air raid during World War II, more than 3500 of John Hunter's original specimens survived and, together with additional physiological specimens, can still be viewed today.

HUNTER, William (1718–83) Surgeon

Born at Long Calderwood, **East Kilbride**, the elder brother of **John Hunter**, William studied for the Church at **Glasgow University** for five years before changing course in 1737 to study medicine at **Edinburgh**. In 1741 he moved to London to continue his training, concentrating on obstetrics, and in 1764 was appointed Physician to Queen Charlotte. He founded his own school of anatomy in 1771, improved the teaching of surgical techniques and published the first textbook properly illustrating the human uterus, thus greatly advancing the science of gynaecology. He died in 1783, bequeathing his school of anatomy to his nephew **Matthew Baillie** and his science collections to the **Glasgow University** museum which now bears his name.

HUNTERSTON, Ayrshire

Until 1957 Hunterston Castle (16th century) and Hunterston House (1799) – renovated in 1913 and 1920 respectively by **Robert Lorimer** – were the only buildings of any size in Hunterston. Then in 1964 Queen Elizabeth the Queen Mother officially opened the first Hunterston Nuclear Generating Station (Hunterston A) for the South of Scotland Electricity Board. Seven years in the making, it was hailed as the most powerful nuclear generating station in the world. Three years later the neighbouring Hunterston B became operational, this one nine years in the making, and in 1979 they were joined by the British Steel Corporation's vast deep-water iron ore terminal with attendant infrastructure. Although careful landscaping minimised the visual impact of this multipartite industrial monster on the previously unspoilt countryside, it has never been possible to ignore its rather lowering presence.

The famous Hunterston Brooch (now in the **Museum of Scotland** in **Edinburgh**) was found on a hillside by a shepherd on the Hunterston House estate in 1830. Dating from c700 AD, cast from silver and richly decor-

Silver and gilt Hiberno-Saxon annular brooch found at Hunterston in 1830 (© the Trustees of the National Museums of Scotland 1994)

ated with gold, silver and amber insets, the brooch is thought to be the work of an Anglo-Saxon craftsman, probably working in Ireland or western Scotland and much infuenced by Celtic designs.

HUNTINGTOWER, Nr Perth

Built by the **Ruthven** family in the 15th and early 16th centuries, Huntingtower was the scene of the infamous **Ruthven Raid** in 1582. The raiders included several Protestant nobles, including Lord Ruthven, recently made Earl of Gowrie; their prey was the 15-year-old **James VI** who was forcibly detained for ten months in what was then called 'House of Ruthven' (or 'Ruthven Castle'). Although the King exacted ample revenge when in 1584 Gowrie was executed, the vendetta apparently continued. Both the new Earl and his brother were murdered as a result of the so-called **Gowrie Conspiracy** of 1600 and, as if to make doubly sure, James then proscribed even the name of 'Ruthven'. Thus was the House of Ruthven 'in all time coming' to be known only as 'Huntingtour'.

Then as now the house was two houses, an earlier rectangular tower house separated by about 10ft (3m) from a newer nearly-L-shaped tower house. In the 17th century the gap between them was filled with a plain three-storey addition. But the legend of how the athletic Dorothea, daughter of the 'Raider', leapt this gap in her nightgown to avoid being detected in her lover's bed persisted and was recorded by the traveller Thomas Pennant in the late 18th century. If, as related, the maiden and her swain next day eloped, the feat seems singularly pointless as well as improbable.

In 1670 the house passed to the Earl of Atholl whose grandson, **Lord George Murray**, the future **Jacobite** commander, was born at Huntingtower in 1694. By 1900 the place was in a ruinous condition whence it was rescued by the state. The exceptionally fine painting, both abstract and representational, on the plaster-

Huntingtower (Ruthven Castle) as drawn by R W Billings (RWB)

work and timbered ceiling of the hall of the eastern tower dates from about 1540 and is some of the earliest still in existence.

HUNTLY, Aberdeenshire

Where the river Bogie joins the **Deveron**, in a level plain surrounded by hills, the trim little burgh of Huntly is the principal town in the district of Strathbogie and was once the home of the senior branch of the great **Gordon family** [see also **Huntly Castle**]. The town was laid out on a grid pattern in the 18th century by which time the castle was already abandoned and the Dukes of Gordon (previously **Earls and Marquises of Huntly**) had removed to **Fochabers**. It is basically two straight streets converging in a spacious square wherein are two **standing stones** and a Victorian town hall. From the square a tree-lined avenue leads north to the castle after passing under the clocktower and archway of Huntly Academy, previously the Gordon Schools (founded in 1839 by the widow of the 5th Duke).

HUNTLY, Earldom and Marquisate

Gordon and Huntly are both placenames originating in the Scottish **Border** country. **Robert I** rewarded a Gordon for his belated support with the lands of Strathbogie (in Aberdeenshire) which passed through an heiress to Sir Alexander Seton in 1445. He was created Earl of Huntly and his son married a daughter of **James I**. The 3rd Earl survived **Flodden** in 1513 with his brother Adam, whom he had assisted to seize the **Earldom of Sutherland** during the royal minority. Thus the family which was to be the scourge of Gaelic Scotland gradually consolidated its power in the north. It was invested with vice-regal powers against which even the Lords of the Privy Council protested in 1605: 'Anent the Lieutenancy, they think it likewise unreasonable that the King's power should be put in the hands of a subject to conquer lands himself.' But the 6th Earl of Huntly had promised **James VI** the 'extirpation of the barbarous peoples of the Isles', and though he failed to achieve this, his attitude was sound in the eyes of the King, who created him a Marquis (1599). Since the Dukedom of Gordon created (1684) by **Charles II** became extinct in 1836, this remains the rank borne by the Chief today.

See also **Corrichie, Battle of**.

HUNTLY (STRATHBOGIE) CASTLE, Huntly, Aberdeenshire

A drawing of 1799 by John Claude Nattes shows Huntly Castle in its short-lived château splendour. Above the plain stonework of the three lower storeys the building erupted with a fairytale skyline of projecting dormers, oriels and belvederes ideally suited to pining princesses. During his exile in France (1594–7) the 6th Earl of

Huntly (Strathbogie) Castle; George Gordon 1st Marquis of Huntly and his wife proclaim their new creation (RWB)

Huntly had clearly explored the Loire and been impressed by Blois.

What remains today is but a sad and truncated shell. The château, sometimes called a palace, was the third castle to occupy the site. The first, a motte (still visible) and bailey arrangement of earth and timber, belonged to the Celtic **Earls of Fife** and was built in the 12th century. The second, built about 1400 after **Robert I** had conferred Strathbogie on the **Gordons** of **Huntly**, was an L-plan tower house, the remains of which lie north of the château which itself stands on the lower storeys of the third, an oblong keep with a circular south-west tower begun about 1450. The new structure coincided with the pre-eminence of the **Gordon Earls of Huntly**; **James IV** was here to celebrate the marriage of Perkin Warbeck with Lady Catherine Gordon in 1496 and **Mary of Guise** stayed in 1556. But the 'Cock o' the North' failed to adjust his faith to the **Reformation**; his castle was pillaged after the Battle of Corrichie (1562) and bombarded again in 1594. Restored as 1st Marquis of Huntly in 1597, George Gordon commenced the elaborate upper storeys across which his name is writ large (upon the south front); there is also a relief portrait of him on one of the elaborate stone fireplaces, while his arms feature prominently in what is 'probably the most splendid heraldic doorway in the British Isles' at the base of the north-east tower.

Wrong-footed by the Reformation, the Huntly Gordons also misread the Civil War. In 1640 the **Covenanting** Army occupied Huntly. **Montrose** held it briefly in 1644 but **General Leslie** starved out and then slaughtered its garrison; Royalist to the last, the 2nd Marquis of Huntly was duly executed in **Edinburgh** (1649). Thereafter the building suffered from neglect and then depredation. The roof was still largely intact when Nattes visited in 1799, but had long since disappeared when the building passed into the care of the state in 1923.

HUTCHESON, Francis (1694–1746)
Philosopher

'The never to be forgotten Hutcheson', as his pupil **Adam Smith** called him, was born in County Down, Ireland, the son and grandson of Irish dissenting clergy of **Ayrshire** stock. At **Glasgow University** (1710–16) he was a pupil of Gershom Carmichael whose chair in Moral Philosophy he filled in 1729. In between he ran a **Presbyterian** academy in Dublin where he wrote several books, including his most noted, *An Inquiry into the Original of Our Ideas of Beauty and Virtue* (1725 et seq). Personal qualities obvious in Dublin fitted him as professor at Glasgow. He pioneered lectures in English rather than Latin and though he taught rather in the manner of a preacher, the matter was intellectually solid. His writings influenced his age and country, and reached such admiring readers as Thomas Jefferson and other American founding fathers. His pupils were important in early American colleges.

Hutcheson rejects the Hobbes/Mandeville view of morality as based in calculation of selfish interest. Drawing on Shaftesbury, he more systematically argues that intuition of virtue, as of beauty, is basic to moral decisions. With this Moral-Sense theory of ethics he sees Sympathy taking the part of self-love (there is *no sole source* of morality) and 'sociability'. A long entry in the **Encyclopaedia Britannica** 9th edition reflects abiding interest (1881). His death in Dublin was not the end of an era. Smith responded to his ideas on economic topics, **Hume** to his Moral-Sense theories. He was thus a profound influence on the **Scottish Enlightenment** and is also considered one of the originators of utilitarianism. See W R Scott's *Francis Hutcheson* (1902); 'Francis Hutcheson' by T D Campbell in *The Origins and Nature of the Scottish Enlightenment* (ed Campbell and Skinner 1983).

HUTCHISON, Isobel Wylie (1889–1982)
Traveller

Born at Carlowrie near Kirkliston, Hutchison attended Studley Horticultural College (1917–19), and studied religion and philosophy at King's College London (1920) and languages in France and Italy before starting her travels in earnest in 1923 when she visited Egypt and Palestine. However, cold northern frosts rather than burning Biblical suns called her and in 1925 she walked 260 miles across Iceland from north to south in 14 days. In 1927 she became the first European woman to land in east Greenland, where she botanised; she returned in 1928 and, during a year living in the west coast village of Umanuk, climbed one of the highest peaks in north-west Greenland. In 1933 she made a daunting first visit to Alaska to collect specimens for the Royal Herbarium at Kew and the Museum of Ethnology at Cambridge; three years later she visited the Aleutian Islands, returning via Japan and Siberia. Awarded the **Mungo Park** medal by the **Royal Scottish Geographical Society**, her travel books – *On Greenland's Closed Shore* (1930), *North to the Rime-Ringed Sun* (1934), *Stepping Stones from Alaska to Asia* (1937) – are illustrated with her own watercolours.

HUTTON, James (1726–97) Geologist
James Hutton was born in **Edinburgh** and educated at the **University** where he studied first chemistry and later medicine. He completed his studies at Leyden, where he graduated as a doctor in 1749. He never practised medicine, going instead to farm in Norfolk in the 1750s, and it was here he first developed an awareness of **geology**. He returned to Scotland in 1754 to farm estates in **Berwickshire** and later went into partnership with a friend in an Edinburgh chemical factory producing salammoniac from **coal** soot. The venture succeeded, providing Hutton with considerable income to pursue his geological research.

He returned to Edinburgh for good in 1767, living at St John's Hill overlooking **Salisbury Crags**. He developed friendships with leading figures in the Scottish Enlightenment, notably **Adam Smith** and **Joseph Black**. Another friend was the landscape artist John Clerk of Eldin, a keen geologist who accompanied Hutton on his field excursions. Clerk's sketches are among the earliest geological records and stand testimony to his skill and Hutton's eye for detailed observations.

Hutton's interests in geology took over his life; he wrote scientific papers for the newly established **Royal Society of Edinburgh** and in 1788 put together his ideas about the formation of rocks into a *Theory of the Earth*. Contrary to contemporary opinion, which was split between 'Vulcanists', followers of Continental explorers like Desmerest and De Saussere, who favoured the molten theory, and 'Neptunists', supporters of the German Professor Werner who thought that all rocks formed under water, Hutton propounded the idea of a rock cycle in which old rocks are destroyed by weathering and new ones form from their sediments.

Hutton and Clerk undertook crucial field excursions in the years 1785–8 looking for evidence to back up his Theory. He found unconformities on **Arran**, at **Jedburgh** and at Siccar Point in Berwickshire. In Glen Tilt in 1785 he discovered granite veins cutting across schists – a sight that 'filled him with delight', similar ones being found in **Galloway** and Arran.

Concerted attacks goaded the ageing Hutton into expanding his 1788 Theory, incorporating the new field evidence in 1795, but illness overtook him and he died in 1797, being buried in Edinburgh's **Greyfriars' Churchyard**. His Theory eventually had a tremendous impact on 19th century thought, but in the immediate years after his death his ideas were rejected by the academic establishment. Part of the problem lay in his obscure style of writing, but here **John Playfair** came to his aid by publishing *Illustrations of the Huttonian Theory* in 1802.

HYDRO-ELECTRIC POWER
Scotland, with its heavy rainfall and extensive mountainous areas, is ideally suited to hydro-electric power production. The total annual production of approximately 3,735,000 MW hours is, however, only 13.5% of the total Scottish output, the bulk being derived from **oil**, **coal** and nuclear power. This figure excludes private industrial power production. While remote areas may be totally dependent on hydro-electricity, its contribution to the power requirements of Scotland as a whole lies in the fact that hydro power can be switched on and off easily in response to the highly variable electricity demand over the course of a day.

A conventional hydro-electric installation consists, essentially, of a reservoir, pipelines linking the reservoir to the generating station, and a tailrace discharging water from the turbines back into a loch or river. The major installations, listed below, consist of a linked series of reservoirs and generating stations, designed to optimise water use. Many schemes include catchwater intakes connected to aqueducts which cross watersheds and increase the catchment area of the reservoir. Some water from the **Spey** Valley, for instance, ends up in the river Tummel at **Pitlochry**. In addition to these schemes operated by the electricity boards and supplying the National Grid, there were extensive industrial works in the **Fort William** and **Kinlochleven** areas which generated power for aluminium smelting.

The operational flexibility of hydro-electricity compared to thermal and nuclear power, combined with the fluctuating daily demand, means that it is economic to operate pumped storage schemes. These put the conventional layout into reverse, ie, during the night power is used to pump water into the upper reservoir so that the daytime peak output can be increased. The hydro-electric installation becomes a giant, rechargeable battery. There are two such schemes in Scotland – **Cruachan** which discharges into **Loch Awe**, and Foyers which discharges into **Loch Ness**. The quoted output for these stations refers to the amount generated. As much, if not more electricity, is consumed in pumping.

The earliest installations were those built to provide power for aluminium smelting, the pumped storage scheme at Foyers replacing the earliest of these which was built before the turn of the century. The original turbine and the control gear, acknowledging **William Thomson**, later Lord Kelvin, as consultant, can be seen in the entrance hall of the modern plant. A number of early private works were also constructed, such as that supplying the castle on the Isle of **Rum**. Some developments, including part of the present Tummel scheme as well as that in **Galloway**, were completed between the two World Wars, but the bulk of construction occurred after World War II. Following completion of the conventional power schemes by the mid-1950s, increased technological sophistication led to the development of the pumped storage schemes, Cruachan being completed first in 1965. Recent work by the North of Scotland Hydro-Electric Board and then Scottish Hydro-Electric has been consolidation – small-scale plants and distribution schemes (including submarine cables) to ensure that electric power is available to all.

To many, hydro-electricity is the ideal power source – no waste products to be disposed of and no atmospheric pollution. But it too has environmental costs. Although many reservoirs are natural lochs whose level has been raised and controlled, land and the communities that lived nearby have been lost by inundation. The drawing down of reservoir levels (inevitable if they are to fulfil their storage function) leads to barren, unsightly shorelines, often in areas of great natural beauty. Rivers, too, are affected. Abstraction can lead to dry river beds, most noticeably in the river Garry beside the A9. At other times, accusations of flooding as a result of power station operation have been made. All these changes have considerable impact on migratory salmon and sea trout but, although many dams have fish passes which permit the movement of fish over them, the consequences of hydro-electric operations are difficult to assess. The visual impact of the dams themselves, apart from the shoreline problem referred to earlier, is a matter of taste. To some they are intrusions in the landscape; to others they are symbols of a natural resource being wisely used. Long lines of pylons are ugly unless you have tried to read by the light of an oil-lamp.

AFFRIC-BEAULY HYDRO-ELECTRIC SCHEME This involves six power stations on the Beauly River and its tributaries. The four stations on the upper tributaries receive water through supply aqueducts from large reservoirs. Monar Dam, at the head of Strathfarrar, is one of the few arch dams in Britain. The lower two power stations, on the Beauly River itself, have little associated storage and utilise the natural fall of the river.

AWE HYDRO-ELECTRIC SCHEME The hydro-electric works on Loch Awe involve both conventional power generation and a major pumped storage development. Water from the pumped storage scheme discharges into the north end of the loch, beside the **Dalmally-Oban** road although the power station itself is a considerable distance inside the shoulder of Ben Cruachan. At times of high power demand, water from the reservoir is used to generate electricity. The turbines can be reversed and operated as pumps so that, at off-peak times, power from elsewhere can be used to fill Cruachan Reservoir. Besides being a major technical development in helping to cope with fluctuating power demands, the Cruachan Scheme is also a major **tourist** attraction. The hills to the west of Loch Awe form the catchment for a small conventional power scheme; the level of the loch has been raised by a dam and much of its natural outflow is diverted through an aqueduct to a power station near the tidal limit of **Loch Etive**.

BREADALBANE HYDRO-ELECTRIC SCHEME This involves two, physically separate, schemes which are controlled and operated as one. The first utilises water from **Glen Lyon** and the river Lochay. After a circuitous passage through a series of aqueducts and reservoirs, the outflow is finally discharged into **Loch Tay** near **Killin**. The second component catches some of the water draining into Loch Tay through a series of aqueducts but the bulk comes from the headwaters of the river Earn and its tributaries. Its main power station is at **St Fillans** at the east end of Loch Earn.

CONON HYDRO-ELECTRIC SCHEME The river Conon enters the **Cromarty Firth** at **Dingwall** and there are six power stations within its catchment. The lowest of these, the dam and power station at Torr Achilty near **Strathpeffer**, regulates the flow in the lower river, The other stations exploit the upper reaches of the Conon and its tributaries, the Orrin and the Black Water.

CLYDE HYDRO-ELECTRIC SCHEME The hydro-electric works on the river **Clyde** are one of the two small schemes in southern Scotland which supply the National Grid. This small scheme utilises the potential of the Falls of Clyde, immediately upstream from the restored industrial village of **New Lanark**. Power generation does reduce the grandeur of the falls and, on occasions, generation is stopped so that the full flow of the river can be seen.

FOYERS HYDRO-ELECTRIC SCHEME This is a pumped storage development on the eastern side of Loch Ness. It is operated in a similar way to that at Awe, although the power station is at the loch side. The upper reservoir is Loch Mohr, adjacent to the **Fort Augustus**-Strathnairn road. The pumped storage works replace a much earlier conventional scheme which was used for smelting aluminium ore. Nearby is a small conventional installation on the Foyers River.

GALLOWAY HYDRO-ELECTRIC SCHEME The Galloway is the larger of the two hydro-electric installations in southern Scotland supplying the National Grid, but its output is small compared to that of the larger Highland schemes. It comprises four small power stations north of **New Galloway**. Water from these is discharged through Loch Ken and the river Dee, finally entering the Solway Firth at **Kirkcudbright**.

GARRY-MORISTON HYDRO-ELECTRIC SCHEME The Rivers Garry and Moriston drain the mountains to the west of the **Great Glen**, the outflow from the Garry discharging into Loch Oich and that from the Moriston into Loch Ness. The upper Garry catchment is one of the wettest areas in Britain [see **Loch Quoich**]. The layout of the Garry scheme is simple – two large reservoirs with associated power stations. The Moriston works involve a number of aqueducts which alter the natural drainage.

SHIN HYDRO-ELECTRIC SCHEME This is the most northern hydro-electric scheme in Scotland. It is centred on Loch Shin whose level has been raised by the construction of a dam at **Lairg** which has a small power station built into it. At the upper end of the loch a power station utilises water diverted from the river Cassley.

Part of the outflow from Loch Shin is carried through an aqueduct to a third power station at Invershin.

SLOY-SHIRA HYDRO-ELECTRIC SCHEME This exploits the power resources of the mountains to the north-west of **Loch Lomond**. Water from it is discharged into the upper end of Loch Lomond and into the head of Loch Fyne. A complex system of tunnels and aqueducts means that the natural drainage of the area is considerably changed. The initial development, centred on Sloy Power Station on Loch Lomond, was the first major scheme completed by the North of Scotland Hydro-Electric Board following its formation during World War II. Subsequent development on the Loch Fyne side involved the construction of the first large pre-stressed concrete dam in western Europe at Allt-na-Lairig.

TUMMEL HYDRO-ELECTRIC SCHEME This scheme comprises a chain of nine reservoirs and power stations extending west from Pitlochry towards **Rannoch Moor** and north towards **Dalwhinnie**. To the east of Dalwhinnie, water from the river Spey is diverted through a series of aqueducts. The lowest dam at Pitlochry regulates the flow of water into the river Tummel. The adjacent fish-ladder, installed to permit the passage of migratory salmon, is a popular tourist attraction.

the latter, including cloister, chapter house (octagonal, vaulted and very fine) and refectory, were used as a private residence after the **Reformation** by a James Stewart whose heirs received the title Lord St Colme in 1611. Thanks to their island situation, the monastic buildings remain in surprisingly good order. They were placed in state care in 1924 by the **Earl of Moray**, one of whose ancestors had succeeded to the Lordship of St Colme.

IBROX DISASTER (1971)

For many years Britain's worst sporting disaster was the Ibrox accident in **Glasgow**, in which 66 people died. On 2 January 1971, at the end of the traditional New Year **football** match between the 'Old Firm' of Rangers and Celtic, some spectators lost their footing on Stairway 13 when exiting from the stadium. A human avalanche developed, with many people trapped under those from behind in a pile of bodies 2m high, while the luckier spectators were trapped from the waist down. Many of the casualties were caused by asphyxiation and multiple injuries. The resulting inquiry failed to establish the precise cause of the tragedy, but sheer weight of numbers was undoubtedly a factor.

INCHCOLM, Firth of Forth

'St Colme's Inch' (inch = isle), as it is called in *Macbeth*, lies three quarters of a mile from the **Fife** coast and can today be reached either by scheduled service from **South Queensferry** or, nearer, from **Aberdour**. Apart from **Inchcolm Abbey**, its only attractions are much verdure and some military debris. Like other islands in the Firth it was incorporated into the defences designed to protect **Rosyth** naval base and **Edinburgh** during the two world wars. Gun and searchlight emplacements survive as do concrete shelters and a brick-built NAAFI. Aesthetic comparisons with the remains of the abbey are best not drawn.

INCHCOLM ABBEY, Inchcolm, Firth of Forth

Legend identifies St Colm with **St Columba**, making Inchcolm 'the **Iona** of the east coast'. According to **Hector Boece**, it was hallowed ground in the 11th century when the Danes paid large sums to have their dead buried there (hence William Shakespeare's mention of the island in *Macbeth*); and there is textual evidence of hermits on the island in the early 12th century. One of these is supposed to have fed and sheltered **Alexander I** when he was marooned on the island by the weather (1123). In gratitude the King determined to build a priory and chose Augustinian canons to found it. The earliest extant charter dates from 1162 when the canons were already in residence. The foundation attracted numerous endowments on the mainland and was raised to the status of abbey in 1235.

During the 14th century the abbey was often attacked and plundered by English vessels. More peacable times in the 15th century saw a redesigning of the abbey church and extensive additions to the conventual buildings. Save for the tower, the former is no more; but

INCHKEITH, Firth of Forth

Midway between **Leith** and the **Fife** coast, this uninhabited island is about half a mile long and derives its name from its medieval proprietors, the **Keith** family, hereditary **Earls Marischal**. In 1497 **Edinburgh**'s plague victims were ordered to assemble at Leith for shipment to the island, 'there to remain till God provide for their health'. He probably didn't, for a decade later **James IV**, intent on a bizarre experiment in linguistics, marooned two babies and a dumb wet nurse on the again deserted island. That they survived is cause for wonder, that they also evolved a language recognised as 'guid Ebrew' beggars belief. In 1549 the English under the Duke of Somerset garrisoned the island but were ejected by the French and the island fortified. Although this fort was demolished in 1567, a stone bearing the initials MR (Maria Regina) and date 1556 is said to survive. The first lighthouse was built in 1803. Gun emplacements and wireless facilities followed.

INCHKENNETH, Isle of, Nr Mull, Argyll

'A glittering pastoral isle' off the west coast of **Mull** at the mouth of Loch na Keal, Inchkenneth was named after one of **St Columba**'s followers, Cainneach, and served **Iona** both as a granary, when the island became too populous, and as a burial ground for Highland chiefs when the sea was too wild for crossing to Iona. Around the ruined chapel lie a number of sculptured slabs and Celtic crosses. **Boswell** and **Johnson** stayed here in 1773 as guests of Sir Alan MacLean of **Duart**, whose house impressed them with its 'unexpected neatness and convenience'.

INCHMAHOME PRIORY, Lake of Menteith, Perthshire

Founded in 1238 by **Walter Comyn, Earl of Menteith**, this Augustinian priory on an island in the **Lake of Menteith** comprises a substantial ruin in a highly attractive setting. A Celtic monastery dedicated to an Irish St Colman or Macholmoc may have preceded it. The remains of the 13th century church, with elegant choir and much altered nave, are sufficient to give a good idea of the original. The domestic buildings, ranged round the cloister, are more fragmentary, although calefactory and chapter house remain complete. In the latter are kept a fine double effigy of a 13th century Earl and Countess of Menteith along with other statuary. The choir of the church contains several Graham graves, including that of **Robert Bontine Cunninghame Graham** and his Spanish wife.

Inchmahome was visited by both **Robert I** and **II**. In the 16th century the Erskine family acquired the **commendatorship**. After the Battle of **Pinkie** (1547) **Lord John Erskine**, guardian to **Mary**, sent the young

Inchmahome Priory on the Lake of Menteith (HS)

Queen to Inchmahome for her safety. Then aged four, and during a stay of barely three weeks, she probably skimped on the scholastic and horticultural feats subsequently ascribed to her island sojourn. Both island and priory passed to the **Dukes of Montrose** in the later 17th century and to the crown in 1926. They are now in the care of **Historic Scotland** and may be visited by ferry (seven minutes) during the summer.

INCHTURE, Perthshire

A parish and a village nearer **Dundee** than **Perth**, Inchture must once have been an island (*insch*) when the **Carse of Gowrie** was a watery marsh. To the south Kinnaird Castle, a lofty tower now restored, may date from the 14th century, its lands having supposedly been granted to Randolph Rufus in 1170. Rufus' descendants adopted the name of Kinnaird but sold the property to the Threiplands of **Fingask Castle** in 1674. It was possibly then that they moved to Moncur Castle, nearer Inchture and now a ruin. Created Lords of Kinnaird in 1682, they then moved to Drimmie House and finally to Rossie Priory, to the north. Here the ancient abbey had been in the care of **St Andrews** until the **Reformation** when it passed to the **Duke of Lennox**. Kinnaird completely demolished whatever building

remained, removed even the village, and built a new mansion (1807). By the turn of the century it housed one of the finest art collections in the country which is said to have included a Leonardo, a Veronese, a Tintoretto, what was thought to be a Michelangelo *Crucifixion*, a Rubens, a van Dyck, a Gainsborough, etc.

INCHTUTHIL FORT, Nr Murthly, Perthshire

Situated on a bend in the river **Tay**, the **Roman** fort at Inchtuthil is less impressive than **Ardoch** but has yielded more in the way of archaeological information. Workshops, granaries, officers' quarters, headquarters and even a hospital with 'operating theatre' have been identified. The most surprising find (1961) was a cache of ironware including 9 tyres and 875,428 nails. Coins dating from 85 AD attest its **Agricolan** origin but it was evidently incomplete when abandoned and systematically dismantled in 87 AD. The outer stone wall, 1.8km long, was demolished; glass and pottery smashed; nails removed and hidden – a fine example of site reclamation presumably designed to deny the locals the advantages of Roman technology. Apparently the fort's ovens had never been used and the bath house was still awaiting its hot water supply.

INDEPENDENT LABOUR PARTY, The

The Independent Labour Party was founded in Bradford

n 1893 with **James Keir Hardie** as its undisputed leader; its aim was to gain representation, independent of the Liberals, in the House of Commons. It affiliated to the Labour Representation Committee in 1900 and thus to the Labour Party in 1906. From its inception and throughout its existence, Scotland proved to be the party's most fruitful territory. Recent study has demonstrated that the ILP established important active networks of members in working-class communities, particularly in the west of Scotland, in the period prior to World War I when the housing question and the issue of rents were acute.

Apart from Hardie and **James Ramsay MacDonald**, notable figures included **John Wheatley**, **James Maxton**, **Patrick Dollan** and **Tom Johnston**. The latter, who edited the ILP's paper *Forward*, was a polemicist against the fundamentalist Marxism of **John McLean**. These individuals formed the core of the generation of so-called **'Red Clydesiders'** returned to Parliament in 1922.

But there was at the heart of the ILP a contradiction between their electoralism plus support for the Labour Party and their increasing alienation from the moderation and later bankruptcy of the Labour leadership's policies as exemplified by MacDonald. The crisis came to a head in the minority government of 1929–31 when MacDonald abandoned Labour and formed a national government which the ILP Conference in 1932 voted to quit; the majority of its MPs left to stay with the Labour Party.

From then on its influence declined despite its commitment to the anti-fascist struggle at home and in Spain. In 1940 Maxton and Campbell Stephen opposed a vote of confidence in the new coalition government. The ILP's contribution can perhaps best be summarised as having provided the conscience of the Labour Party. It had supplied a generation of talented 'left reformist' activists and intellectuals to the Labour cause.

INDULGENCE, Declarations of (1669, 1672, 1679, 1687)

In the carrot-and-stick treatment of the **Covenanters** by the later **Stewarts**, the stick took the form of ruthless repression (**Pentland Rising**, **Bothwell Brig**, **Killing Time**) and the carrot that of Declarations of Indulgence designed to conciliate moderate resistance and isolate traitorous 'phanaticks'. The First Indulgence (1669) resulted in 43 deprived ministers being restored to their parishes and the Second (1672) in about 90 more being accommodated. But the fact that 'indulged' ministers remained staunch **Presbyterians** invited hostility from the established church (as evidenced by **Archbishop Burnet**'s Glasgow Remonstrance, 1669), while the fact of their having implicitly accepted state sanction brought accusations of erastian compromise from their **Cameronian** colleagues [see **Richard Cameron**]. Meanwhile repression of those who refused indulged status intensified. After Bothwell Brig, and largely on **Monmouth**'s initiative, the Third Indulgence (1679) would have authorised indoor conventicles but was largely negated by a decree of the bishops (1680) including Burnet now of **St Andrews**. The Fourth Indulgence (1687), actually two, arose less from reaction to the Killing Time than from **James VII**'s anxiety to extend relief to his Catholic co-religionists. In granting to all subjects the right 'to meet and serve God in their own way, be it in chapels, private houses or places purposely hired or built for that purpose', he opened the way to a restoration of Presbyterianism and so 'transformed the ecclesiastical situation' (G Donaldson).

INGLIS, Dr Elsie Maud (1864–1917)
Surgeon and Suffragette

Born in India, Elsie Maud Inglis came to Scotland in 1886 to attend the **Edinburgh** School of Medicine for Women, which had just been set up by Dr **Sophia Jex-Blake**. Three years later she went to study in **Glasgow** with **Sir William McEwen**, who aroused her interest in surgery. In 1892 she qualified as a Licentiate of all three Scottish Medical Schools. Her first post was in what later became the Elizabeth Garrett Anderson Hospital for Women in London, but was then a general hospital. Horrified by the appalling facilities and lack of specialised treatment for female patients, she became firmly convinced that conditions would only improve if women ran their own affairs. She therefore dedicated herself to the suffrage cause.

In 1894 she returned to Edinburgh to set up a practice with another woman doctor, and in 1904 opened her own small maternity hospital, completely staffed by women and specifically for the poor, in Edinburgh's **High Street**. Later the Elsie Maud Inglis Memorial Hospital, this was amalgamated with the Bruntsfield Hospital in 1911. In 1906 she founded the Scottish Women's Suffragette Federation (SWSF).

At the outset of World War I she offered her services to the Royal Army Medical Corps and to the Red Cross, but was rejected by both. Undaunted, and with the help of the SWSF, she raised enough money to equip and staff two ambulance units staffed by women and sent them to France and Serbia in 1915. She herself went to Serbia with one of the units and set up three more hospitals, known as the Scottish Women's Hospitals, where her efforts at improving hygiene eliminated rampant typhus and greatly reduced other epidemics. Taken prisoner by the Austrians, she was repatriated early in 1916 and immediately started raising funds for another hospital in Russia, where she went later that same year. Forced to retreat by the invading German armies, she worked tirelessly on behalf of Serbian troops throughout the summer of 1917, finally returning home in October, a sick woman. She died in November 1917 of cancer in Newcastle-upon-Tyne.

INGLIS, John, Lord Glencorse (1810–91)
Judge

Inglis was the younger son of a minister, also John, of Tibbermore (**Tippermuir**) and **Greyfriars'**, **Edinburgh** who became Moderator of the **General Assembly** and initiated a scheme for evangelisation in India. The son was born in Edinburgh, educated at **Edinburgh High School**, **Glasgow University** and Balliol College, Oxford. Admitted to the **Faculty of Advocates** in 1835, he became Solicitor-General in 1852 and won lasting fame when he secured a 'Not Proven' verdict for **Madeleine Smith**. He was briefly MP for Stamford (1858) and in the same year made Lord Advocate, taking the title of Glencorse. From 1861 until his death he served as Lord Justice General and Lord President of the **Court of Session**. His *Historical Study of Law*, 1863, and other works made him the outstanding jurist of his day. He was also active in encouraging historical research and higher education (Rector of Glasgow and **St Andrews**, Chancellor of Edinburgh).

INNERLEITHEN, Peeblesshire

Tradition states that the church of Innerleithen was granted by **Malcolm IV** to the monks of **Kelso** in 1159, and endowed by him with the right of sanctuary in memory of his natural son who was drowned in the river Leithen, his body lying in the church for a night before removal for burial. Since Malcolm himself would have been only 18 in 1159, and was nicknamed 'the Maiden' since he never even looked like getting married, the son must have been a well-kept secret and not much more than a baby.

The town of Innerleithen and its near neighbour Walkerburn were tweed-milling communities. Walkerburn now houses the Scottish Museum of Wool Textiles. Pioneered in Scotland at places like **Galashiels**, wool-milling was brought here by Alexander Brodie, an enterprising blacksmith from **Traquair** who went to London to seek his fortune and, having made it, returned home and used it to found a **woollen** mill in 1790. The mineral spring at Dow or Doo's (Dove's) Well just above Innerleithen was the town's other source of wealth and fame. From the beginning of the 19th century the restorative powers of the waters, said to be similar to those of Harrogate, turned the town into 'a choice retreat for invalids, the medical properties of its well being expressly framed to bear salutiferously upon visitors' (Fullarton's *Gazetteer*, 1843). The popularity of the spa was vastly increased by the publication in 1824 of **Sir Walter Scott**'s novel *St Ronan's Well*, said to be based on Doo's Well (which was promptly renamed St Ronan's). Robert Smail's Printing Works in Innerleithen High Street, now run by the **National Trust for Scotland**, were founded in 1837. The printing press, which dates from 1887, was originally driven by water-wheels lowered through the floor of the building into a lake fed by the river Leithen.

INNERPEFFRAY LIBRARY, Nr Crieff, Perthshire

In 1610 James Drummond, 1st Lord Madderty, built Innerpeffray Castle as the family home. Some 50 years later his grandson, David 3rd Lord Madderty, established a library in St Mary's Chapel, burial place of the Drummonds, some 800m from the castle. In a will drawn up in 1680 he states that he has erected a library in the east end of the churchyard and a school to the east of that. A later will of 1691 endows 5000 Scots merks (approximately £270) for the upkeep of the library and school, requires a trust to be set up to administer the endowment, and states that the library and school are for the education of the people, particularly young students of the area.

Lord Madderty's sons having predeceased him, the title went to his brother William, 1st Lord Strathallan, who put the will into effect. The trust was set up in 1694 and still runs the affairs of the school and Scotland's oldest lending library. The present library build-ing was erected adjacent to the chapel in 1751 by Rober Hay Drummond, a descendant of the 1st Viscoun Strathallan, when he was Bishop of Sarum. He late became Archbishop of York. On his death many of hi books were added to the library. The last borrowing from the library were in 1968, since which time th books have been available for reference only, and a museum pieces. Some 3000 pre-1800 volumes are housed there, the earliest dating from 1502; among th rarest are **Hector Boece**'s *Hystory and Croniklis of Scotlan* (1540), perhaps the finest example of 16th centur Scottish printing; and the first translation into Scots, o English, of any great classical poet, Virgil's *Aeneid o* **Bishop Gavin Douglas**, printed in London in 1550; th fine collection of bibles includes one which belonge to **James Graham, Marquis of Montrose**.

INNISCHONNEL CASTLE, Loch Awe, Argyll

Innischonnel stands magnificently on an island close t the south shore of **Loch Awe**, about 8½ miles (14km north-east of Ford. Its origins are obscure, but the south east tower is as early as the 13th century. The south-wes tower and west range, containing vaulted cellars an the dining hall, were rebuilt during the 15th century by Sir Duncan Campbell of Lochawe. An ante-roon gives access to a bottle-necked dungeon. Innischonne is first recorded in 1308 as held by John MacDouga of **Lorne** for Edward II of England. But following hi defeat, the barony of Loch Awe reverted to Sir Coli Campbell by a charter of **Robert I** of 1315. Whe the **1st Earl of Argyll** (1433–93) made **Inveraray** hi headquarters, Innischonnel, under hereditary captains was used mainly as a prison. The castle remained inhabited until the early 18th century, and is now a picturesque ruin.

INSCH, Aberdeenshire

This large village/small town midway between **Inveru-rie** and **Huntly** lies just to the west of Dunnideer Hil (876ft/267m), a notable landmark crowned with a ta stack of masonry which is in fact a gable wall pierce by an arched window. It is all that remains of one of Scotland's earliest (c1260) stone castles, once the property of Sir Jocelyn Balliol, brother-in-law of **Devor-guilla Balliol**. Its stonework was largely provided by a prehistoric hill fort, rectangular in shape and vitrified with three outer walls/ridges ringing the hill and the castle. Amongst several monoliths in the area, the Picardy stone is especially interesting as still being ir its original situation; it is of rough hewn whinstone incised with the usual **Pictish** symbols. Three mile south-west of Insch is **Leslie Castle** and, at nearby Auch-leven, Lickleyhead Castle, a substantial L-plan towe house with prominent two-storey angle turrets and a heavily corbelled four-storey staircase turret. It was buil in 1629, probably by the Forbeses of Leslie, possibly incorporating an earlier tower.

INVERARAY, Argyll

Once the county town of **Argyll**, Inveraray gaily front Loch Fyne, its whitewashed terraces reflecting in the water an elegant 18th century 'new town' become a modest 20th century tourist attraction. The **castle**, o similar provenance and appeal, stands half a mile to the orth near the mouth of the river Aray. Prior to the 740s, the town itself occupied this site along with the hen castle. When burnt by **Montrose** in 1644 this town vas little more than a fishing village. It had, however, ts own sheriff and court by virtue of the Argyll family's resence and it was thanks to them that in 1648 it ecame the first **royal burgh** in Argyll.

The 'new town' was occasioned by the demolition f the old when the **3rd Duke of Argyll** decided that is new castle required greater seclusion. Work began n both in 1744 to designs by Roger Morris with **William Adam** as clerk of works. In time Morris and Adam vere succeeded by **Robert Mylne** and John Adam. It s not certain to whom individual buildings should be scribed, but the frontage of the Great Inn (previously he Argyll Head, then the Argyll Arms) seems to have een John Adam's. Amongst its early guests were **oswell** and **Johnson**; the latter found it 'not only ommodious but magnificent' and marked the occasion y an improvised 'Meditation on a Pudding'.

From the inn the north frontage continues with a eries of Mylne arches through which a fine avenue of eech trees, very much a feature of the new policies nd recently replanted, leads towards the later **Episcopal** hurch (1866) with detached tower (1914) and notable ells. The main street, also at right angles to the north rontage, encircles a two-part parish church (1798), ne side being for Gaelic services and the other for nglish; the steeple was removed in 1941 and the Gaelic ection has since been changed into the church hall. eyond are the 18th century 'lands', tall tenement-like uildings, one of which was the birthplace of **Neil Munro**, and which have since been pleasantly restored. The 19th century courthouse and gaol, after long lan-uishing in dereliction, have now been opened as a tourist experience'.

Herrings, a feature of the town's arms, its motto 'May there always be a herring in your net') and once ts economic mainstay, no longer throng the loch, but n Dewar's Boot Store (where else?) Loch Fyne's famed ippers can yet be purchased. Gone too are the pleasure teamers whose presence at the pier added so much to he town's aspect and to its shops' takings. The tour uses which in summer clog the waterfront are a poor ubstitute.

A mercat cross, with late medieval tracery and poss-bly from **Kintyre** or **Iona**, fronts the main street and monument to Neil Munro stands atop Cladich Hill on he road to **Dalmally**. It overlooks a deserted township, now deep in forestry, of which Munro wrote in Nettles':

> O sad for me Glen Aora [Aray]
> Where I have friends no more,
> For lowly lie the rafters
> And the lintels of the door.
>   The friends are all departed,
> The hearthstones black and cold,
> And sturdy grow the nettles
> On the place beloved of old.

INVERARAY CASTLE, Inveraray, Argyll

Nothing remains of the great tower house that was home for the Earls (later **Dukes**) **of Argyll** from the 15th century when they moved thither from **Innischonnel**. It was evidently impressive, its present 18th century replacement being deemed 'inferior' and 'neither attractive nor imposing' by Victorian guidebooks. To meet such criticisms, conical pepper pots were hastily added to the corner towers and the roof was raised to accommodate rows of dormers (1877–8). Happily further plans to baronialise the formal four-square 18th century mansion were abandoned.

Sir John Vanbrugh is credited with its original inspiration but, as with **Inveraray** town, the castle's design is largely the work of Roger Morris, **Robert Mylne** and **William** and John **Adam**. With several design changes including the introduction of gothick features, the work progressed fitfully from 1744 till the 1780s when decorative French interiors were much in vogue. Hence the embossed and delicately painted plasterwork of the state dining and drawing rooms (by Girard and Guinand), possibly the finest neo-classical decoration in Britain. Period furniture and Beauvais tapestries, a fine collection of porcelain, and **Campbell** portraits by all the major Scots and English portraitists, are also on display. More to Victorian taste would have been the main hall, which soars to the full height of the house and is decorated with weaponry arranged in fans, roundels and florets. Display cases contain more weapons and ceremonial robes plus the distinctly pitiful sporran and dirk handle of **Rob Roy MacGregor**.

Outside, the four symmetrical façades of greenish stone rise from a sunken and waterless moat. The fiction of a defence capability is continued in the watch-tower (18th century) atop Duniquaich Hill. But the Aray Bridge, the estate buildings and the avenues of lime and cherry bespeak the formality of the Augustan age. Now a major tourist attraction, especially for Campbells, the castle remains the home of the 12th Duke of Argyll and his family.

INVERBERVIE, Kincardineshire

Of the two towns of Inverbervie and Gourdon (between **Montrose** and **Stonehaven**) the former is the older, having been granted **royal burgh** status in 1341 when the young **David I**, returning from refuge in France, made a storm-affected landfall here. Craig David, the alternative name for the headland of Bervie Brow, commemorates the event. The little town grew on **linen** production in the 18th century and is said to have had the first spinning machine for linen yarn in Scotland. Gourdon, its port to the south, throve on fishing and as late as the 1960s was the most prosperous hand-line fishing port in Scotland. Between the two towns stands Hallgreen Castle, 16th century and originally L-plan; inland towards **Arbuthnott** is Allardyce Castle; and down the coast beyond Gourdon is Benholm Tower, a 15th century keep with parapets, bartizans and a later cap-house, once the property of the Keith family, **Earls Marischal**.

INVERESK, Midlothian

The name is correctly that of the parish which includes **Musselburgh**, but is now more commonly applied to the village once immediately south of Musselburgh but now a suburb. In 1840 it consisted 'chiefly of cottages ornees, villas and neat houses concatenated on both sides of a round along Inveresk Hill . . . the tout ensemble presenting the aspect of a pleasing series of rural and gardened dwellings' (Fullarton's *Gazetteer*). Most of the 'gardened dwellings' were built by professional men or wealthy merchants from **Edinburgh** in the early 18th century, and their charm – and the integrity of the village – survive thanks to the efforts of the Inveresk Preservation Society and the **National Trust for Scotland**. St Michael's parish church at the west end of the village was built in 1805 on the site of its predecessor which, according to the **Rev Alexander 'Jupiter' Carlyle**, minister of Inveresk for 57 years, had been constructed on the site soon after the introduction of Christianity out of the ruins of the **Roman** fort, 'the site of whose praetorium it usurped'.

INVEREWE, Wester Ross

When **Osgood MacKenzie** took over Inverewe in 1862, Am Ploc Ard, the promontory in Loch Ewe which he selected as the site for his garden, was mainly bare rock and peat hags; its only trees were two scrub willows barely a metre high; Atlantic gales deluged it in salt spray; the rainfall was 60 inches (1.5m) per annum; and the latitude was the same as that of parts of Greenland. Yet with the help of shelter belts, fences, much inspired experimentation, endless patience and a goodly gang of estate workers who had to manhandle the soil and seaweed in creels, Inverewe was eventually transformed into one of the most exotic woodland and garden preserves in Europe. The 2500 species which now flourish in its 50 acres (20ha) include magnificent rhododendrons and magnolias, Chilean Flame Flowers, Chatham Island Forget-me-nots, South African agapanthus, American lilies and Japanese hydrangeas. On MacKenzie's death in 1922 his daughter, Mrs Mairi Sawyer, continued the work until in 1952 she presented the garden plus an endowment for its maintenance to the **National Trust for Scotland**. Now equipped with a visitor centre, it continues to be one of the main tourist attractions in this remote part of the Highlands and 'a unique national asset' (W H Murray).

INVERGARRY, Inverness

Where the river Garry enters Loch Oich stands the Raven's Rock of Invergarry, battle-cry, crest, gathering ground and castle of the **MacDonells** of Glen Garry, a branch of the **Clan Donald**. Reflecting the turbulent fortunes of its inmates, the castle was repeatedly attacked, often deserted and frequently razed, notably in 1654 by General **George Monk**, in 1716 by its then English garrison, and in 1746 by the Duke of Cumberland. After the last it was never rebuilt and remains a ruin; it had evidently been an L-shaped tower house of five or six storeys. Staunch adherence to the **Jacobite** cause and a refusal to come to terms with the cash economy so impoverished the MacDonells that in 1860 Glen Garry was sold to the Rt Hon Edward Ellice MP who had already acquired **Glen Quoich** in 1838. Invergarry House, near the castle, was built by the Ellice family in 1869, the work of **David Bryce**.

As inveterate Jacobites, Catholics, mighty hunters and unashamedly feudal chiefs, the MacDonells invited a romantic image in keeping with their surroundings.

On **Alasdair MacDonell** 15th of Glengarry **Sir Walter Scott** based the character of Fergus MacIvor in *Waverley*. But belying this reactionary impression, Alasdair's father entered into an agreement in 1727 with Thomas Rawlinson, an Englishman, for the conduct of the 'Trade, Mystery and Business of making Pig Iron'. The Invergarry foundry, using locally produced charcoal to smelt English ore, was one of the first in the Highlands and over the next decade some 2500 tons were produced.

INVERGORDON, Ross & Cromarty

On the north shore of the Cromarty Firth and commanding the narrows between its outer (**Nigg**) and inner sections, Invergordon was once the small port and castle of Inverbreakie with a ferry to the **Black Isle**. It acquired its new name when purchased and replanned by Sir William Gordon of Embo in the 18th century. A new harbour was built in 1828 and subsequently extended. 'The finest deep water anchorage in Europe' has since been exploited by the Royal Navy, which maintained a dockyard and refuelling base here until 1956, by the RAF which operated flying boats during World War II, by the British Aluminium Company whose massive smelter and jetties succeeded the Navy and latterly by **oil**-rig construction and maintenance facilities. Further industries, including a large grain distillery, have relocated in the town.

INVERKEITHING, Fife

Near the north end of the Forth Road Bridge, Inverkeithing has been a **royal burgh** since 1165. As a port and strategic ferry point, well endowed with customs rights, it was of considerable importance long before its late prominence thanks to **coal-mining**, ship-breaking and paper-making. A plaque in the high street recalls the birthplace of **Sir Samuel Greig** whose achievements are recorded in the museum in Inverkeithing Priory (14th century but remodelled as a 17th century tenement). Also 14th century is the short tower of St Peter's parish church, the nave and aisles being Gothic Revival by **James Gillespie Graham**. The font, rediscovered after being hidden during the Reformation, bears the arms of **Annabella Drummond**, wife of **Robert III** and possibly once resident here. Other notable buildings include Fordell's Lodging (c1670), the town house of the Hendersons of **Fordell Castle**, and the Tolbooth (18th century). The mercat cross has an octagonal shaft which may date from 1398 topped by a unicorn of 1688. East at Dalgety Bay, a dormitory new town, stand the ruins of St Bridget's church, consecrated in 1244 but mostly later and unusual in that a laird's house was built against its west gable in 1610. The surroundings once belonged to Donibristle Castle/House, the home of the **Earls of Moray** in the 17th–19th centuries but thrice burnt down. Service wings, stables and chapel survive to give some idea of its massive scale.

INVERKEITHING, Battle of (1651)

On 20 July 1651 a brief encounter at **Inverkeithing** on the north shore of the Firth of Forth saw a Royalist force supporting **Charles II** intercept but fail to halt the northward progress of the Cromwellian army, which then went on to occupy **Perth**.

INVERLOCHY, Battle of (1645)

The third of **Montrose**'s great victories followed a Christmas raid on **Inveraray**, stronghold of his **Covenanting Campbell** adversaries, and a long march back up the coast to the **Great Glen**. There, at Kilchumein (**Fort Augustus**), he learned that **Argyll** (**Archibald, 8th Earl and 1st Marquis**) was behind him at Inverlochy (near **Fort William**) with 3000 men. In a famous counter-march he led his force back through the mountains to a position above **Inverlochy Castle**, from where, at first light on 2 February, he descended upon the Covenanters.

Alasdair MacDonald and Manus O'Cahan, commanding the Irish Division, were positioned in the wings of the army, while the centre was divided into three lines. The Irish charged first, routing the Lowland infantry. Montrose then ordered the centre to advance, the Covenanters' ranks were broken and the castle surrendered. Argyll, with a dislocated shoulder, watched from a galley. 1300 of his men were massacred as they fled. Their commander, General Campbell of Auchinbreck, was beheaded by Alasdair MacDonald. 'Through God's blessing,' wrote Montrose to **Charles I**, 'I am in the fairest hopes of rendering this kingdom to your Majesty's obedience . . . and shall be able to come to your Majesty's assistance with a brave army.'

INVERLOCHY CASTLE, Fort William, Inverness

There are two Inverlochy Castles. The one not at the mouth of the Lochy was known as Torlundy and is a Victorian mansion built for Lord Abinger, subsequently the home of Joseph Hobbs [see **Spean Bridge**], and currently a very expensive hotel. The other, a mile to the south-west and once with a moat that was filled from the river, is a crumbling fort of great but uncertain antiquity. The rectangle of curtain walling with four round towers at the corners suggests the 13th century and it is thought that it may have been the creation of **Sir John Comyn (i)** of Badenoch (d.1303). It subsequently passed to the Bruces and then the **Huntly Gordons**. Nearby was fought the **Battle of Inverlochy** (1645). A still earlier structure on the same strategic site seems probable (there are some connections with Banquo, Thane of Lochaber) and according to **Boece** there was once a rich and cosmopolitan city here. **King Achaius** is supposed to have signed a treaty with Charlemagne in it in 790, after which it was destroyed by the **Vikings**. If there is any truth in this, they did a very thorough job.

INVERMORISTON, Inverness-shire

This village stands on the north-west shore of **Loch Ness**, between **Fort Augustus** and **Drumnadrochit**, and at the mouth of Glenmoriston up which **Dr Johnson** and **James Boswell** rode en route to **Glenelg** and **Skye**. The road was then (1773) under construction. They spent an anxious night at Anoch, near Torgyle (with a fine bridge built by **Wade**, rebuilt by **Joseph Mitchell**), trying to decide whether or not to undress. The innkeeper, 'a sensible fellow', was about to emigrate, his rent having been quadrupled. When he talked of the '45 **Jacobite Rising** Boswell 'could not refrain from tears'. No doubt he told of the Seven Men of Moriston (three Chisholms, a MacDonald, a Campbell, a Grant and a MacGregor) who hid **Prince Charles Edward Stewart** during his post-**Culloden** flight and safely delivered him to the **Camerons**; perhaps also of Roderick Mackenzie, a lookalike of the Prince, who was cornered by Cumberland's men in Glenmoriston and, pretending that he was indeed the Prince, was shot for refusing capture, thus buying precious time for the real fugitive. His sacrifice is remembered in the Mackenzie Monument, a cairn with a plaque, near the head of the glen.

Inverlochy Castle, by Horatio McCulloch (NGS)

INVERNESS

At the north-western extremity of the **Great Glen**, **Dr Johnson**'s 'capital of the Highlands' might also be described as their hinge. The cleft of the Great Glen, with formidable hills on either side and the great stretch of **Loch Ness** through its midst, practically severs the north of Scotland from the rest of the country. Only between Loch Ness and the Beauly Firth is there ready access across a fertile coastal plain. Here the short and fast-flowing river Ness bars the way, an asset as much as an obstacle; its ferries or bridges represented a source of income and a strategic prize well worth defending. Inverness grew as a port, mart and administrative centre, but it began as a fort.

Defence remained its priority well into the 18th century because, as well as being pivotal to Scotland's north–south axis, it also commanded the east–west corridor from the Great Glen to the Laigh of **Moray**. Through this gap Highland free-booters, ambitious clan chiefs, and latterly disaffected **Jacobites** habitually descended on the rich pastures not just of Moray but of **Aberdeen** and **The Mearns**. In the opposite direction government troops and road engineers marched into the Gaelic Highlands. They were followed by Victorian tourists; by 1900 three steamer loads a day sailed from Inverness down the Caledonian **Canal** heading for **Fort Augustus**, **Banavie** (**Fort William**) and **Oban**. The city, brisk and bright, is not of the Highlands but it remains the key to them. Its modest size belies its importance just as its jaunty aspect belies its antiquity.

Evidence of early occupation survives in the remains of a **Clava** ring **cairn** in the Raigmore housing estate (Clava itself is only five miles to the east), in the hill fort of **Craig Phadraig**, and in the late-7th century Knocknagel symbol stone (with a finely inscribed boar). **Adamnan** records that **St Columba** here met Brude or Bridei (c555–84), king of the northern and still unchristianised **Picts**, in his hill-fort (possibly Craig Phadraig). The 11th century castle which features so much in Shakespeare's *Macbeth* (but where **Duncan I** was probably not murdered) is thought to have been somewhat east of the present castle. A timber construction, it was replaced by a stone-built fortress on Castle Hill which was probably in existence when Inverness became a **royal burgh** during the reign of **David I** and was fortified with a ditch by **William the Lion**.

Although partly destroyed by **Robert I**, the castle was rebuilt in the early 15th century and continued to serve as royal power base in the keepership of the **Mackintosh** chiefs. It was sacked by both **Alexander** and **John, Lords of the Isles**, and visited by **James I**, **III** and **IV**. The latter appointed the Gordon **Earls of Huntly** its keepers. **Mary of Guise** held a convention of estates here in 1555 but when **Queen Mary** sought admittance in 1562 she was rebuffed by Alexander Gordon who was eventually ejected and hanged for his insolence; his patron, **George Gordon 4th Earl of Huntly**, received his desserts soon after at **Corrichie**. In 1645 it held out against **Montrose**, was repaired in 1718 and extended by **George Wade** in 1725 who renamed it Fort George. In 1745 it was held by Cope and **Loudoun** but in 1746 was taken and systematically blown up by **Prince Charles Edward Stewart**. The demolition expert, a Frenchman, is said to have blown himself up, and his

dog, in the process; the latter survived minus a tail. A a barracks the castle's role was assumed by the new **Fort George** at **Ardersier** and as a landmark by the castellated gothick 'castle' designed in part by **William Burn** in the 1830s which now serves as a court house

The town, also on the right (east) bank of the river developed to the north of the castle in what is now the heart of the city between the main bridge and the East gate. The first recorded bridge, 'the famousest and finest off Oak in Brittain' was destroyed by Donald, another Lord of the Isles, in 1411. A replacement, also of wood was condemned by Richard Franck, the Cromwellian trooper and angler, as 'the weakest that ever straddled over so strong a stream'. It duly collapsed in 1664 and was replaced in the 1680s by a fine stone structure of seven arches. This was swept away in 1849 by the swollen river which still menaces its several replacements (road, rail and foot) whenever spate condition and flood tides combine.

North of the bridge and of the castle the town extended along Castle Wynd and **Church Street**, where are located the few ancient structures which destruction and development have spared, towards the port area As with other east-coast ports, trade was mainly with England and the Baltic; the abundance of fine timber in **Strathglass** also encouraged **shipbuilding**. Hereabout Cromwell built a great star-shaped citadel of his own using the local timber plus stone from Blackfriars and other religious establishments as far away as **Fortrose Kinloss** and Beauly. It stood three storeys high and could accommodate 1000 men but was demolished after the Restoration, only an ogee-roofed clock tower and a bit of rampart remaining. Defoe maintained that so many of Cromwell's troops eventually settled in the area that the local cuisine, agriculture and speech all took on a markedly English character. Dr Johnson also remarked on this, Hanoverian troops having further diluted the population.

Although the lay-out of the old city is still recognisable and although there are a few 18th century buildings even on the west bank, the architecture is overwhelmingly post 1800. Like the castle, the Town House and the **Cathedral** (also on the west bank) are Victorian The advent of the **railway** (from **Nairn** in 1854 and from the south direct via **Aviemore** in 1898) and the opening of the Caledonian Canal (1822) assured the city's future as an administrative centre for the Highlands and as their principal resort. Here today are located the headquarters of the Highland Region, Highland Radio, Highlands and Islands Enterprise, **Crofters' Commission**, **An Comunn Gaidhealach**, Red Deer Commission, etc. The excellent Eden Court Theatre, hospitals and educational establishments (including the Inverness College of Further Education, now part of the University of the Highlands and Islands) serve a vast area; so does the airport at **Dalcross**. Housing estates have sprung up to match industrial estates. Yet thanks to its long river frontages, the distant hills and the quality of the light, the city retains its peculiar character, not Highland but decidedly north of Scotland.

Bridge Street

From the Ness Bridge to the High Street, Bridge Street is short and busy. On the south side a modern building

Inverness in the late 17th century; drawing by John Slezer (TS)

houses the Art Gallery and Museum while the gothick Town House (1882) is where Lloyd George held a cabinet meeting in 1921; the signatures of those present, including Winston Churchill, are displayed plus several portraits. Outside stands a mercat cross and beside it the Clach-na-Cudainn, or stone of the tubs, on which the townswomen once rested their containers when carrying water and washing from the river bank. Victorian guidebooks call it the town's 'palladium', a reference to some prophecy that so long as the stone remains undisturbed the city will prosper. Opposite, where Church Street runs north, the old Court House and gaol (1789) occupy the site of the Tolbooth and have a fine steeple (1791). The multi-storey block facing the river on the corner of Bank Street (Bridge House, home of the Highlands and Islands Enterprise Board) contains the reconstructed vaults of the 16th century house in which **Queen Mary** stayed in 1562.

Church Street

Inverness was slow to embrace **Presbyterianism**. A writer in the 1840s was embarrassed to report that 'seventy years ago only three ladies with straw bonnets were to be seen in the High Church'. This was the old parish church, rebuilt in 1772, located on St Michael's mount and after which Church Street is named. 'High', of course, refers to its elevation, including a tower (partly 16th century) and spire (17th century), not to its doctrines. The mausoleum and enclosure of the Robertsons of Inshes (1660) is elaborately decorated and pillared. Other religious establishments hereabouts include Greyfriars Free church, once the Gaelic church, and the small graveyard of Blackfriars (Dominican) monastery founded in 1233 but demolished to build Cromwell's citadel. Here is the supposed grave and

effigy of Alexander Stewart, Earl of Mar, the son of the **'Wolf of Badenoch'** and the 'victor' of **Harlaw**. Abertarff House (1590s), with a projecting stair turret topped by a square crow-stepped watch-room, is the oldest building in the city and has been neatly restored by the **National Trust for Scotland**, which now occupies it. Opposite, Dunbar's Hospital (1669) has also been restored. It was gifted to the burgh by Provost Dunbar and has variously served as a library, school, fire station, old people's home, possibly even as a hospital.

Craig Phadraig

On a wooded hill west of the river Ness, this vitrified fort was in occupation from around 500 BC and again in the 6th and 7th centuries AD. There are, though, doubts about the state of its fortifications in 565 and therefore whether it can have been the headquarters of King Brude. Above the recent forestry its concentric ramparts surround the summit in a rough rectangle and were evidently of timber-laced stonework. Finds here included a clay mould for casting a metal hanging-bowl. The original is in the **Royal Museum of Scotland**, a copy is in the Inverness Museum.

St Andrew's Cathedral

South of the Ness Bridge the west bank of Inverness exhibits a leafy and spacious decorum. The Eden Court Theatre, hotels and villas are dominated by St Andrew's Cathedral, the principal church of the ecclesiastical see of **Moray**, **Ross** and **Caithness**. Consecrated in 1869, it was the first cathedral to be built in Britain since the **Reformation**. The design, cruciform and Gothic, is the work of the prolific local architect Sir Alexander Ross. He intended the massive twin towers to be topped by spires but these were never built. Five gold ikons were presented by the Tsar of Russia and the font is modelled on that by Thorwalden in Copenhagen.

565

INVERNESS-SHIRE

Scotland's largest county, Inverness-shire has an area of over 4000 square miles stretching from the Moray Firth on the east, down the **Great Glen** to **Fort William** then north-westwards to include the **Isle of Skye**. Before the **local government** reorganisation of 1975 the county also included the islands of **Barra**, **Harris**, **North Uist**, **South Uist** and **St Kilda**, but since 1975 these have officially been designated part of the Western Isles. Inverness-shire contains Britain's highest mountain, **Ben Nevis** (4406ft/1343m) and such major lochs as Ness, Oich, **Laggan**, Erricht, Lochy and **Shiel**. Its western seaboard is heavily indented by sea lochs. The **Spey**, Ness and Beauly are the main rivers. The area encompasses many of the events of Scotland's past, culminating in **Culloden**, the last battle fought on British soil, in 1746. The population of Inverness-shire has been estimated (1996) at 106,230, occupied in sheep farming, forestry, **fish farming**, and some aluminium smelting and pulp milling, with tourism becoming increasingly important. **Inverness** is the county town and the only large burgh, with Fort William and **Kingussie** as the only small burghs. Divided into four Districts of Highland Region – Inverness, **Badenoch** & Strathspey (with part of **Moray**), **Lochaber** (with three areas from **Argyll**) and Skye & Lochalsh – in the local government reorganisation of 1975, Inverness-shire remained part of the Highland Council Area in the changes of 1995.

INVERSNAID, Falls of, Loch Lomond, Stirlingshire

Near enough to the Inversnaid Hotel for the American writer Nathaniel Hawthorne to hear them from his bed, the Falls of Inversnaid were also evoked by William Wordsworth in 'The Highland Girl'. More unexpectedly, they were later celebrated by Gerard Manley Hopkins whose 'Inversnaid' concludes with a verse that must appeal to all who know the west Highlands:

> What would the world do, once bereft
> Of wet and wilderness? Let them be left,
> O let them be left, wildness and wet;
> Long live the weeds and the wilderness yet.

Residents may find it significant that Hopkins' sentiments resulted from a visit of just a couple of days. Like so many other once mighty waterfalls, Inversnaid has been sorely depleted by a **hydro-electric** scheme and by a rearrangement of its catchment for reservoir purposes.

INVERURIE, Aberdeenshire

Where the river Urie meets the **Don** the granite town of Inverurie was once the principal centre of the **Garioch** but is now in Gordon district. The town hall, of Grecian aspect, dates from 1863 and St Andrew's parish church, of Gothic aspect, from 1840. But the town has been a **royal burgh** since at least the time of **Queen Mary** and a place of strategic and agricultural importance since much earlier. Hereabouts were fought the **Battles of Inverurie** (1307) and **Harlaw** (1411); few districts have a greater abundance of **standing** and symbol stones; there is also a historical museum.

The best stone circle, with recumbent, is at Easter Aquhorthies. It is now in state care as is the Brandsbu symbol stone with an ogam inscription. At Broomen of Crichie, near Port Elphinstone across the Don, a circl henge with two standing stones and another **Pictis** symbol stone is all that remains of a 'late neolith ceremonial complex of considerable importance' (I (Shepherd). More symbol stones, one incised with trotting horse, are in the old graveyard beside the Bass a grassy mound that was once the motte of **David c Huntingdon**, great-great-grandfather of **Robert I**.

Inverurie has produced two very different poets Arthur Johnston (1587–1641) who compiled a anthology of Scottish poems in Latin and wrote verse on Donside which earned him the unlikely sobrique of 'the Scottish Ovid', and William Thom, the 'weaver poet' (1798–1848) whose passionate invectives agains industrial exploitation are to be preferred to his mor sentimental rhymes.

Although its days as a centre of **locomotive** production are long gone, Inverurie remains proud of it **railway** station which, when built in 1902, was th largest on the **Aberdeen–Elgin** line. Many of its origina trimmings fell victim to the Beeching cuts of the 1960s but 1991 refurbishments have restored much of its Vic torian splendour. Opposite the Broomend paperwork is Kinkell church, a ruin but 16th century and with grave slab depicting an armoured knight identified a Gilbert de Greenlaw who was killed at Harlaw.

INVERURIE, Battle of (1308)

The date and place of this decisive confrontatio between **Robert I** (the Bruce) and John Comyn, Ear of Buchan, are debated. *The Edinburgh History of Scotland* (B Nicholson, 1989) argues for 23 May 1308; others hav suggested January 1308 or even Christmas 1307. Th site may have been where **Barra Castle** now stands, i which case those who call it the Battle of Barra Hill ar right. What is certain is that Bruce rose from his sick-be to lead his troops and roundly defeated the partly Eng lish troops of John Comyn (son of Alexander, Earl o Buchan and husband of **Isabella, Countess of Buchan** and not to be confused with **John, 'the Black Comyn** or **John, 'the Red Comyn'**, both of whom were dead) There followed the 'herschip' or harrying of **Bucha** when Bruce's troops ravaged the whole earldom.

IONA (ICOLMKILL), Island of, Nr Mull, Inner Hebrides

A kilometre off the south-west tip of **Mull**, Iona i 5.5km long by 2km wide. Its 880ha are approximatel one-third arable and two-thirds rough pasture. Mostl Lewisian gneiss with Torridonian sediments along th eastern coast, the earliest permanent habitation of th island is unknown. There are traces of Stone Age culti vation, and an Iron Age fort occupied cBC 110–AD 200 It is not clear whether there was a resident populatior on the island when **St Columba** landed in 563 AD, no when a population outside of the monastery became established. The medieval parish church of St Ronar indicates a secular population by that period. A clea picture of the tenantry emerges in the 18th century, by which time the island had passed from Maclean of **Duar** into the Argyll Estate. The first full list of inhabitants totalling 249, was drawn up in 1779 for the 5th Duke of Argyll. Contemporary efforts to expand the economy through flax-spinning, commercial **fishing** and marble **quarrying** had limited success, and in 1802, as part of the 5th Duke's agricultural reforms, Iona was divided into individual crofts thus ending the **runrig**, or communal, system of working the land. Houses were built on these holdings and a new village street erected in its present location.

Many travellers commented on the fertility of the island and the quality of its crops and livestock. Exporting of cattle and surplus grain, plus earnings from seasonal work in the Lowlands and from **kelp** harvesting, enabled the **crofters** to meet both their rents and their own needs, despite rapid population growth. This reached a peak of over 520 by the late 1830s. The **potato failure** of 1846 and succeeding years brought severe destitution and subsequent emigration led to a sharp fall in numbers to 263 inhabitants by 1861. Three farms eventually formed from the combining of vacated crofts. The resident population today is around 90, their livelihoods deriving largely from farming, crofting, fishing and **tourism**.

Since the late 18th century the island has seen a steady stream of visitors. A summer steamship service was sailing three times a week from the **Clyde** by the 1830s and daily from **Oban** by the end of the century. Now the island is linked all year round by car ferry via Mull to Oban. The two present-day hotels were opened 1867–8.

In 1828 the parish church and manse were built under the Parliamentary Scheme supervised by **Thomas Telford**. Prior to that, the minister for Kilfinichen and Kilviceuen parish crossed from Mull several times a year. At the **Disruption** of 1843 the Iona minister, and around half the congregation, joined the **Free Church**.

Two years later the Duke of Argyll allowed them a site for a church. In 1900 this became the **United Free Church**, joining the **Church of Scotland** in 1929. The school dates from 1774, established initially by the Scottish Society for the Propagation of Christian Knowledge (SSPCK). A library building opened in 1904 thanks to a donation from **Andrew Carnegie**. Collections of books had been gifted from as early as 1820 by visitors including Rev Legh Richmond and tour operator Thomas Cook. Islanders raised funds in the 1920s for a village hall for recreational and community use.

In 1979 the island, excluding the **cathedral** and other ecclesiastical buildings, was sold by the Duke of Argyll to the Sir Hugh Fraser Foundation in memory of the late Lord Fraser of Allander, and gifted to the **National Trust for Scotland**.

IONA CATHEDRAL (ST MARY'S ABBEY) AND COMMUNITY

The earliest buildings of the religious establishment founded by **St Columba** after his arrival on the island in 563 were probably in the vicinity of the present abbey church. According to **Adamnan** they consisted of a church, a cell for the abbot, huts for the brethren, a refectory and a guest house, all enclosed by a rampart, remains of which are still visible. In the centuries after Columba's death on **Iona** in 597 his foundation and the island itself were frequently invaded and pillaged by Norsemen, and the monastery was several times destroyed and rebuilt. That the spritual strength of the community survived these depradations is evidenced by remains of the four great crosses, St Oran's, St John's, St Matthew's and St Martin's (the most complete), all

Iona Cathedral before restoration, by R W Billings (RWB)

of which date from the 8th and 9th centuries. Through this period too, the devotion of the monks and the sanctity of Columba's memory confirmed Iona as an unrivalled place of pilgrimage and a burial place for kings: '48 Scottish, 8 Norwegian and 4 Irish kings' being the traditional total of interred monarchs. The earliest of the existing ecclesiastical buildings on the island, St Oran's Chapel, dates from the 12th century and was built as a mortuary chapel by the predecessors of the MacDonald **Lords of the Isles**.

In c1200 Reginald, Lord of the Isles and son of **Somerled**, established a Benedictine community on Iona; a nunnery was added a few years later and the abbey church, dedicated to the Virgin Mary, was extended over the following centuries to become the cathedral for the bishopric of the Isles from 1499 until 1660 when the bishopric was moved to **Rothesay**. Although the monastery was then repressed, the cathedral church suffered more from disuse and decay following the seizure of the island by the MacLeans of **Duart** and its subsequent possession by the **Campbells** of **Argyll**. It was during this period of delapidation that **Boswell** and **Johnson** visited Iona in 1773, an experience that prompted the latter to the 'sublime passage': 'The man is little to be envied, whose patriotism would not gain force upon the plain of Marathon, or whose piety would not grow warmer among the ruins of Iona.'

In 1899 the ruins were presented by the 8th Duke of Argyll to the **Church of Scotland** in order that they might be restored and brought back into use as a place of worship; his wishes were respected and the first service took place in the repaired abbey in July 1905. In 1938 the Iona Cathedral Trust (the Trustees being *ex-officio* office-bearers of the Church of Scotland and Scottish Universities) handed over the remaining restoration of the monastic buildings to the Iona Community, founded by **Rev George MacLeod (Lord MacLeod of Fuinary)**; maintenance and repair by the Iona Cathedral Trust is ongoing, and the Community operates as a centre of pilgrimage and retreat for Christians of all denominations from all over the world.

IRON AND STEEL

Several primitive bloomeries and forgeries operated in Scotland in the late medieval period and a number of charcoal-burning furnaces were built in the early 18th century (**Invergarry, Furnace, Bonawe**, etc), but it was not until 1759, when the **Carron Company** pioneered the process of smelting with coke, that it was recognised that Scotland's geological resources were capable of sustaining a substantial iron industry. Even then progress was slow. Despite the establishment of several iron works, including those at Wilsonstown, Muirkirk, Omoa, Calder and Shotts, it was still possible in 1814 for **Sir John Sinclair** to class the iron industry among 'the secondary or less important Manufactures of Scotland'.

Yet within a few years pig iron production was to enjoy a remarkable expansion. In 1830, 27 furnaces had produced about 38,000 tonnes or about 5% of British output; by 1860 133 furnaces were in blast, producing about one million tonnes, or about a quarter of the total British make. The transformation was a consequence of the introduction of the hot-blast in 1828. **J B Neilson**'s discovery that raising the temperature of the blast of air through the furnace reduced the amount of fuel used in the smelting process not only resulted in greatly diminished costs of production but made possible the exploitation of Scotland's unique blackband ironstone. Within a decade the costs of iron production in Scotland were lower than those of any other region in Great Britain.

The industry was dominated by a small group of men who became wealthy by seeking a modest unit return on a huge turnover, the bulk of which was despatched to markets outside Scotland. The dependence of the industry on the vagaries of the export trade might have been lessened had the great ironmasters processed more of their pig iron themselves, but after a number of abortive attempts to do so, they abandoned their interest in puddling, whereby pig iron is converted into the much tougher and resilient malleable or wrought iron, apparently convinced that their profits would be maximised by concentrating on smelting and by investing heavily in **coal-mining**. By this policy the ironmasters opened the way for newcomers to venture into the malleable iron trade, and in the 1850s numerous small enterprises were promoted, many of them on or near the banks of the Monkland **Canal**. For a time there were handsome profits to be made from supplying the **railways, shipbuilders** and heavy **engineers**, but then came cheap steel, which threatened to destroy their prosperity.

Bessemer's process of converting pig iron into steel, devised in 1856, was immediately taken up by many Scottish ironmakers, but when William Dixon's early trials failed, the wisdom of the great Scottish ironmasters' concentration on pig iron production seemed to be confirmed. Once again it was left to others to process their pig. The first firm effectively to do so was the newly created Steel Company of Scotland in 1872, a firm that employed Siemens' open hearth process. When it became obvious that steel would eventually replace malleable iron in the heavy and light engineering industries, the wrought ironmakers realised that they either became steelmakers or went out of business. Many chose steel – among them were **David Colville** & Sons and **William Beardmore** & Co – and by 1885, when total production approached a quarter of a million tonnes, over 40% of the British make of Siemens steel was being produced by ten Scottish firms, the majority of whom *purchased* rather than made their principal raw material.

The result was an almost total lack of integration. The Scottish steelmakers did not make iron, and few ironmasters made steel, or if they did, conducted the sequential processes in different locations. Such conditions made the lowest possible costs of production by hot metal working unattainable. This was a major structural weakness. Even more alarming was the industry's increasing dependence upon the notoriously fluctuating shipbuilding industry; over 60% of Scotland's output of steel, 1.5 million tonnes in 1913, was destined for the shipbuilding yards of the **Clyde**, Belfast and the north-east of England.

The policies adopted to meet the demands of World War I and the post-war boom intensified these funda-

Glengarnock ironworks in the 1870s (GWWA)

mental problems. The immediate effect of the war was to increase Scotland's steelmaking capacity and to concentrate control of the industry. The Ministry of Munitions induced David Colville & Sons – by 1904 the largest firm in the industry – to increase their output of steel by taking over the Clydebridge Steel Company and the Glengarnock Iron & Steel Company and by putting down new plant. But while Scotland's steelmaking capacity was substantially enlarged, not a single new blast furnace was built, and the industry emerged from the war with the imbalance between its iron and steel sections exacerbated and the lack of integration between them reinforced. Furthermore, believing that the end of hostilities would be followed by a massive shipbuilding programme, the shipbuilders sought to safeguard their steel supplies by a frantic scramble to acquire control of the Scottish steelmakers. By the end of 1920 almost the entire steelmaking capacity of Scotland was in their hands. For example, Harland & Wolff, themselves part of Lord Pirrie's Royal Mail group of shipping lines, had purchased Colville's; the Steel Company of Scotland had been purchased by a consortium of Clydeside shipbuilders headed by Stephens of Linthouse; and the Clyde Iron Works and Calderbank Steel Works had been purchased by **Lithgows** of Port Glasgow.

To the extent that the Scottish steel industry had become dependent upon shipbuilding for its market, its relative stagnation during the period 1921–38 was beyond its control, but the shipbuilders' ownership of the industry undoubtedly reduced its ability to make the required response. By the late 1920s it had become clear that nothing less than the creation of a fully integrated iron and steelmaking complex on a tidewater site would ensure the long-term survival of the industry. That this radical solution was not adopted was largely due to the depressed state of the industry, which made the raising of capital impossible. Ownership by the

financially embarrassed shipbuilders presented an additional obstacle to thorough rationalisation. Merger, followed by the concentration of output in the most modern existing plant was an obvious alternative, yet even this more modest objective was not easily attained because of the multi-layered ownership of the industry. The steel companies were owned by the shipbuilders, who themselves had become heavily indebted to the banks (including the Bank of England), and, because of loans made under the Trade Facilities Act, to the Treasury. In seeking to protect their own interests, these creditors pursued policies which rarely, if ever, were congruent with vigorous restructuring, a situation compounded by conflicts of interest between shipbuilders, family groups and customers within individual firms. The result was almost complete paralysis.

Not until 1931, when **John Craig** of Colvilles and Sir James Lithgow combined their iron and steel interests in Colvilles Ltd, was any progress made. Within five years, having bought the Steel Company of Scotland and the Lanarkshire Steel Co, Colvilles Ltd controlled over 80% of Scottish steel production. A modernisation programme begun in 1936 culminated in the linkage of new blast furnaces at Clyde Iron Works with refurbished steel melting furnaces at Clydebridge Steel Works. For the first time, hot metal working on a large scale was possible in Scotland. But although the relative inefficiency of the Scottish iron and steel industry had been greatly reduced by 1939, there still seemed a need for a tidewater works on a deep-water location.

An opportunity to make good this deficiency arose in the immediate aftermath of World War II when Colvilles were pressed to undertake such a scheme. But their careful estimates of future demand, the current availability of coking coal, pig iron and scrap, and their deep sense of social responsibility towards those whose livelihoods depended on existing works, made Colvilles persevere with a more 'practical' programme of modernisation, the centrepiece of which was the creation of the Ravenscraig complex at **Motherwell** in the late 1950s. This decision made the decline of the Scottish steel industry inevitable, for long-term success (even survival) now demands fully integrated works on tidewater sites. What made things worse was the government's insistence that Colvilles erect a strip mill at Ravenscraig, the capital cost of which combined with severe undercapacity working meant that when the Colville group passed into public hands in 1967, it was technically bankrupt.

Disaggregated figures – were they available – would probably reveal that the Scottish iron and steel industry worked at a loss ever after. It would appear that the losses per ton of finished steel production in Scotland were far higher than those of any other steelmaking area in Great Britain, reflecting the relatively smaller scale, the lower proportion of capacity-utilisation, and the higher cost of fuel in Scotland. When to these losses are added the higher freight charges per unit of delivered output of Scottish steel products, the pressures upon the British Steel Corporation to close down what was left of Colvilles' heritage were understandable. Only the political power of the Scottish lobby prevented Ian MacGregor from doing so in the early 1980s. And if the fortunes of BSC were subsequently transformed by ruthless economies, its Scottish component, despite a marked increase in productivity and efficiency, continued to be regarded as the weakest geographical division. Thus, when privatisation took place in December 1988, the Scottish steel industry was doomed, for the Scottish lobby had little influence over British Steel. In April 1991, the hot strip mill at Ravenscraig ceased production; and in September 1992 Ravenscraig closed down completely. Weakened by the exhaustion of indigenous raw materials and emasculated by the collapse of shipbuilding, the Scottish steel industry had been condemned to a lingering death by what can now be seen as past errors of judgement.

IRVINE, Ayrshire

At the heart of the modern industrial New Town of Irvine lies a very ancient burgh, Irvine having been granted a charter in 1308 by **Robert I** in recognition of the services of its inhabitants in the **Wars of Independence**, an earlier charter probably having been awarded in c1240 by **Alexander II**. Ruined Seagate Castle, dating from the 14th century and once the town house of the Montgomerie Earls of Eglinton, stood originally by the sea, but the shifting sands that proved such a bane to navigation have left it stranded in the middle of the town. There are claims that Seagate, like many another **Ayrshire** castle, was visited by **Queen Mary** in her 1563 peregrination of the county. Certainly **Robert Burns** stayed in Irvine for two years from 1781 while he learnt the flax-dressing trade; a plaque marks his cottage in Glasgow Vennel, and the Irvine Burns' Club claims to be the oldest in the world, with an unbroken record of Burns' Night observance dating from 1827. The town was also the birthplace of the novelist **John Galt** (1779–1839), the poet James Montgomery (1771–1854) and Elizabeth Buchan (1738–1791), founder of the fanatical **Buchanite** sect.

At one time rivalling **Ayr** as the principal town in Ayrshire, Irvine was the main seaport for trade from **Glasgow** to Ireland and beyond from the 16th century until the development of **Port Glasgow** in the early 18th century and thereafter still prospered as the main port serving the **Kilmarnock coal**fields. c1720 Defoe found 'more trade at Irwin by a great deal than at Air, nay, than in all the ports between it and **Dumfries**'. 20th century industrial decline was anticipated and largely diverted by Irvine's selection in the early 1970s as the site for a New Town, with the town's long sandy beaches encouraging the subsequent development of its leisure facilities, including the Magnum Centre, Scotland's largest indoor and outdoor sports and recreational complex, and Sea World.

IRVING, Edward (1792–1834) Preacher

This **Annan**-born assistant to **Thomas Chalmers** became a successful preacher at London's Caledonian Church in 1822. Convicted of heresy and deposed on announcing the Second Coming in 1833, he developed as a mystic the Irvingite Church with speaking in tongues. Later forms were the Catholic Apostolic and Pentecostal Churches.

ISLAY, Island of, Inner Hebrides

The island of Islay (pron. 'eye-la' and sometimes spelled 'Isla' or 'Ilay') lies 15 miles off the west coast of **Argyll** and only 23 miles north of Northern Ireland across the North Channel. It is the most southerly of the Inner **Hebrides** and, with a land area of 246 square miles (63,714ha), one of the largest Scottish islands, covering 25 miles from north to south and 19 miles from west to east.

Islay's **geology** is complex, and includes the most southerly outcropping of Lewisian gneiss, in the southern half of the Rinns peninsula. The Port Askaig boulder bed supplies evidence of an ice age in late Pre-Cambrian times, while the broad bands of Islay limestone make the pastures of the central corridor of the island green and fertile. In the south-east bands of epidiorite provided the raw material for the finely carved late-medieval grave-slabs which grace the island's churches.

The natural environment is very varied, with a wide range of habitats from mountainous moorland to the sheltered woodland round the head of Lochindaal. Ornithologists find Islay especially appealing; the rare native chough breeds there, while from early October to the end of April it plays host to large populations of migrating geese. The wintering population of barnacle geese, which come to Islay from breeding grounds in the east of Greenland, is now aproaching 25,000, while up to 4000 white-fronted geese are also present. About 110 species of bird breed on Islay, and even on a short visit it should be possible to see over 100 species.

Islay's strategic location and agricultural fertility combined to give it a rich cultural heritage. Archaeological riches range from **standing stones** and stone circles, as at Ballinaby and Cultoon, to chambered **cairns**, forts, **duns** and, unusually, a **broch** at Dun Bhoraraig, near Port Askaig. The quaintly named Dun Nosebridge is exceptionally well preserved; its Norse name (*knaus-borg* – the fort on the crag) is one of many place-names which derive from the **Viking** conquest and settlement of Islay from AD 800–1156. The medieval chapel and Early

Bunnahabhainn distillery and village, Islay (BRC)

Christian cross at Kilnave, the **Iona**-style wheelcross at **Kildalton** and the intricate abstract carving of the 14th century cross at Kilchoman are noteworthy.

Historically, Islay's main importance was as the administrative capital of the **Lords of the Isles**, the ancestors of **Clan Donald**. From **Somerled**'s victories in the 12th century until the forfeiture of the Lordship in 1493, the military and naval base at Dunivaig on the south coast and the civil headquarters on two small islands on the inland Loch Finlaggan were the centres of power for an administration which at its maximum extent in the early 15th century ruled all of the islands off the west coast of Scotland and almost the whole of the western seaboard from **Cape Wrath** to the Mull of **Kintyre**. Technically under the sovereignty of Norway until the **Treaty of Perth** in 1266, the subduing of Clan Donald and the eventual integration of its vast territories into the Kingdom of Scotland was a process which was not finally completed until after the final defeat at **Culloden** in 1746.

The population of Islay has steadied at just under 4000, having declined from a maximum of 15,000 in 1831. The largest town is Port Ellen, with a ferry terminal, while the administrative capital of the island is Bowmore. These centres of population, and the villages of Port Charlotte, Portnahaven and Port Wemyss, were established by Campbell of Shawfield lairds in the 18th and 19th centuries. Other settlements include the distillery villages of Caol Ila and Bunnahabhainn in the north, Bruichladdich in the Rinns, and Laphroaig, Lagavulin and Ardbeg in the south-east; their names are a catalogue of some of the finest malt **whiskies** in Scotland, which constitute Islay's best-known and most lucrative export. Keills and Ballygrant are small villages based

originally on weaving and **quarrying**. Port Askaig, with a tiny resident population, is one of the busiest places on the island with ferries connecting with both the mainland at Kennacraig and with Feolin on **Jura**. The airport at Glenegedale has a twice-daily link with **Glasgow** Airport; an emergency air ambulance operates as required.

Islay's main industry is **agriculture**, with beef cattle and sheep predominating. Dairy herds sustain a creamery at Port Charlotte which makes and exports a fine cheese. **Fishing**, once the mainstay of the island's economy along with farming, is carried on in a small way, mainly for the export market. **Tourism** is a growth industry; 45,000 summer visitors come by the Caledonian **MacBrayne** ferries and an additional 11,000 arrive by air.

ISLES, LORDS OF THE

From the time of **Somerled** in the middle of the 12th century until their final forfeiture in 1493, the Lords of the Isles controlled large parts of the Western Isles [see **Hebrides**] and western seaboard of Scotland. Their influence within their own territories was enormous, and hopes for a resurgence of their power were not finally abandoned by the island clans until the final defeat at **Culloden** in 1746.

Somerled claimed descent through his father Gillebride from the kings of **Dalriada**, and styled himself Ri *Innse Gall is Cind tire* – Ruler of the Islands of the Strangers (Hebrides) and **Kintyre**. In Latin he was called *Rex Insularum* – King of the Isles. He had a son Reginald (Rognvaldr), whose son Donald gave his name to the **Clan Donald**.

Donald's son Angus Mor died around 1292; during his rule the territorial sovereignty of the area changed from Norway to Scotland under the **Treaty of Perth**

(1266), but his son **Angus Og** advanced the cause of the lineage by backing **Robert I** at **Bannockburn** in 1314, leading men from Kintyre and **Islay**. He became a close friend and confidant of the King, and died at Finlaggan, on Islay, in 1328.

John of Islay, son of Angus Og, was the first to use the title *Dominus Insularum*, 'Lord of the Isles' (rather than *Rex Insularum*), probably out of deference to his father-in-law, who was the heir of the **Stewart** kings of Scotland. For this reason he is sometimes reckoned as the first Lord of the Isles. His first marriage was to Amie MacRuari, and his second was to Margaret Stewart, daughter of Robert Stewart who became **King Robert II** of Scotland, thus uniting the lineages of Somerled's descendants. He died in 1387.

He was succeeded by his son, Donald of **Harlaw**, named after the battle of 1411 which was one of the great but inconclusive confrontations between Highland and Lowland Scotland. Donald married Mary Leslie, heiress to the **Earldom of Ross**, as a result of which the Lords of the Isles claimed all the islands off the west coast of Scotland and all the western coast from **Cape Wrath** to the Mull of Kintyre as well as Easter **Ross** and possessions in **Moray** and **Buchan**. Donald's son Alexander succeeded in 1423, and after many adventures made peace with the King and was appointed Royal Justiciar for Scotland north of the river Forth. He died at **Dingwall** in 1449 and was buried at the cathedral at **Fortrose** to reinforce his family's claim to the Earldom of Ross.

His son John, the last Lord of the Isles, quarrelled continually with his wife, with his son, and with the King. His downfall was caused by the discovery in 1475 that he had negotiated a treaty with Edward IV of England in 1462 – the **Treaty of Westminster-Ardtornish**. His lands were forfeited, but his island possessions restored following promises of good behaviour. His son and heir Angus was murdered at **Inverness** in 1490, apparently while planning to regain control of Ross. In 1491 his nephew Alexander of Lochalsh took over the struggle but was killed. In 1493 **James IV** lost patience, and again all the lands of the Lordship were forfeited, this time for ever. The last Lord of the Isles, John, died either at **Dundee** or **Paisley** in 1503. The title survives and is held by the Prince of Wales.

John's grandson **Donald Dubh** was born at the **Campbell** stronghold of **Innischonnel** on **Loch Awe**

after his father's death. After the forfeiture of 1493 he was held there but rescued by some **MacDonalds of Glencoe** in 1501. After three campaigns by government forces he was recaptured in 1506 and imprisoned in **Edinburgh Castle**. He escaped from there in 1544 and was recognised as Lord of the Isles by all the branches of Clan Donald, and by many other clan chieftains. At Knockfergus in Ireland he assembled a force of 180 galleys and 4000 fighting men, but while organising an invasion of Scotland he died at Drogheda of a sudden fever at the end of 1545; the rebellion then collapsed.

The administrative capital of the Lordship was at Finlaggan on Islay. Dean Donald Munro, writing in 1549, describes how the 14 members of the Council of the Isles, which met on the small Eilean na Comhairle ('council isle') at Finlaggan, 'decernit, decreitit and gave suits furth upon all debaitable matters according to the Laws made by Renald McSomharkle [Reginald, son of Somerled] callit in his time King of the Occident Isles ... In thair time thair was great peace and welth in the Iles throw the ministration of Justice.'

On Eilean Mor, at Finlaggan, which is linked to the Council Isle by a causeway, there are the remains of a chapel and over 20 buildings, many of which date from the time of the Lords of the Isles. Archaeological excavations sponsored by the **National Museums of Scotland** are currently under way.

The Clan Donald historian Hugh MacDonald, writing in about 1625, gives details of the inauguration ceremonies of the Lords of the Isles, which include the tradition of a footprint stone, now lost, to show that he promised 'to walk in the footsteps of his predecessors, and that he was installed by right in his possessions'. He carried a white rod, to symbolise his power to rule, his forefathers' sword, to signify his duty to defend and protect his people, and wore a white tunic to show his 'innocence and integrity of heart'. After the ceremonies, which were carried out by a bishop and seven priests, the company feasted and celebrated for a week.

It is more than likely that these traditions preserve elements going back as far as the 5th century rulers from Dalriada, from whom Somerled and the Lords of the Isles claimed descent. The military headquarters of the Lordship, probably from the time of Somerled, were at Dunivaig on the south-east coast of Islay.

J

JACOB, Violet (1863–1946) Poet

Born into a proud aristocratic family, the Kennedy-Erskines of the **House of Dun** near **Montrose**, Protestant reformers who trace their lineage back to the time of **John Knox** and beyond, Violet Jacob belongs to a tradition of aristocratic Scottish songstresses like **Lady Nairn** and **Grizel Baillie** who have done much to preserve the Scots **language** in pure strain. While the language of her home was unmistakably Scots, her real grip of the language came about because, as **Helen B Cruickshank** relates, 'as a bairn she was aye in and oot amo' the ploomen's feet at the Mains o' Dun.' She married an army officer, Arthur Otway Jacob, and spent many years of married life in India, Egypt and England. Her only child, Harry, was killed at the Battle of the Somme.

In her lifetime her poetry was highly successful, especially 'Tam i' the Kirk', which became one of Scotland's favourite recital pieces. She had the genuine voice of the folk in her blood, and the feel of the braes and straths of **Angus** and Strathtay which she never ceased to love though far removed. The song-like quality of her poems is reflected in the fact that many of them have been set to a melody in the folk style. She also wrote four novels, *The Sheepstealers*, *The History of Aythan Waring*, *The Interloper* and *Flemington*, the latter described by **John Buchan** as the best Scots novel to appear since **Stevenson**'s *Master of Ballantrae*. Her novels are all out of print, but her Diaries and Letters from India (ed Carol Anderson, Canongate) were published in 1990.

JACOBITE RISINGS (1689–1746)

After the accession of William and Mary in 1688–9 those who continued to support **James VII** and then his son **James Francis Edward Stewart** ('the Old Pretender') as the legitimate kings of Scotland were known as Jacobites. The word comes from the Latin for James (ie *Jacobus*) but also carried pejorative undertones, the biblical Jacob having deceived his father Isaac into giving him the blessing intended for his brother Esau; the reference here was to the **Whig** fabrication that James Francis Edward was not actually the son of James VII and Mary of Modena but a 'suppositious child' adopted to provide a continued focus for **Stewart** loyalty.

Jacobite sentiment was not restricted to Scotland and there is ample evidence to show that James VII, his son, and his grandson (**Charles Edward Stewart** – 'the Young Pretender') were as anxious to regain the English throne as the Scottish, seeing the latter largely as a platform from which to secure the former. But in Scot-

Mrs Arthur Jacob (Violet Kennedy-Erskine), chalk drawing by an unknown artist (SNPG)

land residual loyalties to the house of Stewart, and in particular to a Stewart king who was outlawed by the English, found much historical sanction; conversely a Stewart queen called Mary who, married to a foreign prince (William of Orange), showed no interest in Scotland roused little sympathy. Additionally the Williamite recognition of the Scottish Church predisposed Scottish Episcopalians in favour of the Jacobites and, more crucially, the unpopularity of the **1707 Union** and then the Hanoverian succession, plus the cynical management of Scottish affairs from London both before and after the Union, would give Jacobite claims an often undeserved nationalist appeal.

From the Jacobite court in France, and then Italy, contacts were maintained with Scotland throughout the period 1689–1745 and were readily reciprocated, especially in parts of the Highlands and north-east. Military insurrection broke out, or nearly did, on five occasions:

DUNDEE'S REVOLT, 1689 Outlawed by the 1689 Convention of Estates [see **Claim of Right**], **John Graham of Claverhouse**, once detested as 'Bluidy Claver'se' the persecutor of the **Covenanters** and now reincarnated as the heroic Viscount ('Bonnie') Dundee, rallied Jacobite support mainly amongst the Highlanders and inflicted a crushing defeat on the Williamite forces under **Hugh MacKay of Scourie** at Killiecrankie. Sadly for his cause, he was killed in the process and his forces were later routed at the Haughs of **Cromdale** (1690). The revolt enjoyed little influential support and had depended heavily on Dundee's personal qualities.

THE FRANCO-JACOBITE INVASION, 1708 James VII had died in 1701, William in 1702. In Scotland the **Darien** disaster and the Act of Union played into Jacobite hands while in Europe the War of Spanish Succession found Louis XIV, opposed by Queen Anne's government, happy to support the Jacobite cause; the French King had already recognised James Francis Edward Stewart as King of England, Ireland and Scotland. With the Pretender aboard, a small fleet sailed from Dunkirk to the Forth with plans to land at **Burntisland** and make for **Stirling**. There was every evidence that resistance would be minimal and support widespread. But the French commander was easily cowed by the arrival of English ships under Admiral Byng and, despite James's pleas to be landed, sailed up the **Fife** coast and then back to France.

MAR'S REBELLION (THE 'FIFTEEN'), 1715–16 Queen Anne died in 1714 and to continued resentment against the Union and its unpopular manifestations (in a malt tax and the Toleration and Patronage acts which alienated ecclesiastical opinion) was added that against the Hanoverian succession. Amongst those disappointed of office under the new king was **John Erskine, 11th Earl of Mar**, not previously a noted Jacobite but now sufficiently disaffected to raise the standard of revolt in the north-east and proclaim James king. The **Duke of Argyll (John Campbell, 2nd Duke)**, who now rallied the government forces to oppose Mar, reckoned that nine out of ten Scots would support the uprising, though not because they were all Jacobites. In England there was also widespread disenchantment with the Whig domination of office under the first Hanoverian and some sympathy for the Jacobite cause which led to a revolt in the north-east. The situation could hardly have been more favourable; nor could it have been worse managed. Though supported by the most influential nobles in the north-east (the **Earl Marischal, Huntly**) and the most powerful clans in the north-west (**MacDonalds, Camerons, Mackintoshes**), Mar delayed too long and then, though outnumbering the enemy by four to one, was checked by Argyll in the indecisive **Battle of Sheriffmuir**. An attempt to link up with other Jacobites in the Borders and **Edinburgh** was frustrated and **Inverness** was retaken for the government by **Simon Fraser of Lovat**. By the time 'James VIII' landed at **Peterhead** to claim his patrimony, it had already been lost. He stayed in Scotland over Christmas 1715 but sailed back to France in February, the leaders of the rising either accompanying or following him.

THE HISPANO-SCOTTISH INVASION, 1719 Following the 1713 Treaty of Utrecht, James removed his court to Italy and in a changed European order found new support from the Spanish government of Philip V. Anglo-Spanish hostilities in 1719 persuaded the Spanish foreign minister, Cardinal Alberoni, of the desirability of an invasion of south-west England accompanied by a diversionary landing in north-west Scotland. The former, which James was to accompany, had to be aborted after a storm but the diversionary expedition

went ahead regardless. Several hundred Spanish soldiers and a few Jacobites under the Earl Marischal, the **Marquis of Tullibardine**, and the **Mackenzie** chief the **Earl of Seaforth** landed in **Kintail** in Inverness-shire and took **Eilean Donan Castle**. In June they were defeated at the **Battle of Glenshiel** by a government force from Inverness under General Joseph Wightman. Eilean Donan was retaken by a naval landing party and the Spanish sailed for home leaving the Jacobite leaders to find their own way through the Highlands.

THE FORTY-FIVE, 1745–6 Nearly a generation later most Scots had become resigned to the Union whose benefits were becoming increasingly apparent. Support for the Jacobite cause lingered on only in the Highlands and even there the roads and garrisons established by **General Wade** and others looked capable of containing dissent. Another rising should never have been considered and should certainly never have so nearly succeeded. Once again, though, it had French encouragement if not much actual support; and more important, it had in Prince Charles Edward Stewart, 'the Young Pretender', a young and charismatic figurehead whose energy and valour still outshone his numerous shortcomings. With considerably less support than Tullibardine and company in 1719, Charles and the **Seven Men of Moidart** reached the Scottish mainland at **Loch nan Uamh** in **Arisaig** and raised the Jacobite standard at **Glenfinnan** in August 1745. Six weeks later, with his forces growing by the day, he had swept through the Highlands, defeated the government forces under General Cope at **Prestonpans**, and overrun Scotland.

By December he had reached Derby, still undefeated; but, finding practically no support in either the Lowlands or England, the Highland troops were looking increasingly like demonstrators who had assembled on the wrong day. A withdrawal that could easily have become a rout was skilfully managed and at **Falkirk** in January 1746 the Jacobite army again inflicted defeat on government forces under General Hawley. Hawley was replaced by William Augustus, Duke of Cumberland who followed the retreating and now diminishing Jacobite host north towards Inverness. **Lord George Murray** and other Jacobite commanders favoured a withdrawal in to the hills and a guerrilla campaign. Charles and his closest Irish advisers insisted on a final battle and chose the disastrous moorland site of **Culloden**.

In the last pitched battle on British soil the exhausted and depleted Jacobites were routed (16 April 1746). Charles evaded capture and for five months was concealed by loyal adherents who smuggled him out to **South Uist** and then back across the Highlands before he took ship to France. Others fared less well as Cumberland exhibited a taste for reprisals which earned him the sobriquet of 'butcher'. Equally draconian legislation followed with a disarming act, forfeiture of estates, proscription of Highland dress, and abolition of heritable jurisdictions. The military, economic and customary structure of the **clan** system was thus destroyed and with it all prospects of further Jacobite resistance.

JAMES I (1394–1437) King

Born in **Dunfermline** Monastery on St James Day, 25 July 1394, James was the second son of **Robert III** and his Queen **Annabella**. After their eldest son, **David Duke of Rothesay**, was murdered, Robert III, alarmed for James's safety, sent him to France in 1406. But the ship was taken by pirates off Flamborough Head and the 12-year-old prince was handed over as a prisoner to Henry IV of England. Robert died suddenly soon afterwards and his brother, the **Duke of Albany**, became Regent of Scotland.

James was held prisoner for 18 years, mostly in the Tower of London. Receiving a sound education, he became both scholar and musician. In 1419 Albany sent a Scottish contingent to France to fight for the Dauphin against Henry V. Henry summoned James to his camp to order his countrymen to surrender, but, on James's refusal, he did not retaliate. James remained with Henry throughout the ensuing campaign and accompanied his funeral cortège from France in 1422.

The Duke of Albany had died in 1420 and the incompetence of **Murdoch**, the son who succeeded him as Regent, drove Scotsmen to demand their King's return. The terms agreed for his release in 1423 [see **Treaty of London**] included the provision of 21 hostages to stand security for his £40,000 ransom.

In February 1424 James married Lady Joan Beaufort, daughter of the Earl of Somerset (the collection of poems *The Kingis Quair*, attributed to James, has passages traditionally praising her beauty), and in April of that year crossed the border back into Scotland to be crowned at **Scone**. His priority on regaining his kingdom was to curb the power of the nobles. In 1425 he ordered the arrest of his cousin Murdoch of Albany, two of his sons and his father-in-law the Earl of Lennox, who were tried for lawlessness and beheaded at **Stirling**. In August 1428 he summoned the Highland chiefs to **Inverness** where Alexander **Lord of the Isles** was taken into temporary custody. He then appointed **John Cameron**, Bishop of **Glasgow**, as his Chancellor and with him reorganised the country's economy and administration and introduced the principal of representation to Parliament. He also renewed the 'auld alliance' with France in 1428 and in 1436 his daughter Margaret married the Dauphin of France.

In 1437 a conspiracy headed by the **Earl of Atholl** resulted in James's murder by **Sir Robert Graham** in the royal lodging of the Blackfriars in **Perth**. The conspiracy was partly dynastic in that Atholl was the only surviving son of **Robert II** by his second marriage, and partly political in that James's rapacious ways and well meant but obsessive law-making had produced 'a sort of medieval totalitarianism' (R Nicholson).

JAMES II (1430–60) King

The only survivor of twin sons born to **James I** and his Queen Joan at **Holyrood** on 16 October 1430, James succeeded in 1437 after his father's murder. During his minority the most powerful families in Scotland were the Crichtons and the Livingstons, the latter allied to the Douglases. James was present at the 'Black Dinner' in **Edinburgh Castle** when his cousins, the young Earl of Douglas and his brother, were murdered on the orders of the governor **Sir William Crichton**.

In 1449 James married **Mary of Gueldres**, a princess noted for her piety, whose dowry included cannons superior to any cast in Scotland. Advised by **James Ken-**

James II, by an unknown artist (SNPG)

nedy, Bishop of **St Andrews**, to deal separately with his enemies, James arrested and imprisoned the Livingstons when the 8th Earl of Douglas was in Rome. Later he summoned Douglas himself to **Stirling Castle** under a safe conduct to ask him to forgo his liaison with the **Earl of Ross** and the **Lord of the Isles**. Douglas refused and James, losing his temper, stabbed him before his bodyguard killed him.

The civil war which ensued between Douglas and **Stewart** supporters resulted in victory for James, whose cannons reduced rebel strongholds. Subsequently the Parliament of 1455 enacted the forfeiture of the Douglas estates and strengthened the King's position by vesting key fortresses and customs in the Crown.

James was then predominant to the point where the Lord of the Isles was amongst the host which he led against **Roxburgh** Castle in 1460. But there, during an inspection, one of the cannons exploded and James was killed outright.

JAMES III (1452–88) King

The eldest surviving son of **James II** and **Mary of Gueldres**, James was nine when hastily crowned at **Kelso** following his father's death at **Roxburgh** (1460). Like other **Stewarts** his reign therefore began with a minority during which domestic affairs were dominated by the struggle for guardianship of his person and foreign affairs by the possibilities of his marriage. A governing council presided over by his mother and **Bishop James Kennedy** exploited the civil war in England to obtain the cession of **Berwick** but in doing so alienated the Yorkists; Edward IV posted notice of his displeasure by signing the **Treaty of Westminster-Ardtornish** (1462) with John **Lord of the Isles** and **Earl of Ross**. Following Mary's death (1463) and then

Kennedy's (1465), the King was abducted by the brothers **Robert Lord Boyd** and Sir Alexander Boyd, the latter Keeper of **Edinburgh Castle** and instructor to the boy King in chivalric pursuits. The Boyds took in hand the King's marriage (1469) to Margaret, daughter of Christian I of Denmark and Norway. Favourable terms included the pledge of **Orkney** and then **Shetland** as security for part payment of her dowry. When this failed to materialise the overlordship of both finally passed to the Scottish Crown; in the meantime the **Sinclair Earl of Orkney** was persuaded to swap his earldom for **Ravenscraig** (Mary of Gueldres' castle and lands in **Fife**) thus, in respect of Orkney, transferring the property as well as the title to the King.

The marriage marked the end of Boyd supervision (one was executed, another exiled) and the beginning of James's personal reign. Tradition dismisses him as 'inopportune', 'irrelevant', 'inactive', 'unstable' and 'avaricious'. His inglorious demise may account for some of these pejoratives but the evidence from a reign lasting for 20 years is otherwise inconclusive. Having two adult brothers to whom dissidents would inevitably turn was a handicap faced by practically none of the other kings James. Of one brother, John **Earl of Mar**, little is known except that in 1479 he died while in the bath. At the time he was in James's custody on the grounds of having truck with witches and warlocks; but he was in the bath to be bled, presumably because he was ill; it could have been murder, natural causes or medical negligence. The other brother, Alexander **Duke of Albany**, was also imprisoned on a similar pretext but fled to France. At about the same time relations between James and Edward IV, correct since James had secured the submission of John of the Isles, broke down in recriminations about recent border raids. An English fleet created some havoc in the Firth of Forth and burnt **Blackness** (1480); there was more fighting in 1481; and in 1482 an English army, supporting the returned Albany as 'Alexander IV' of Scotland, crossed the border.

James seemed well prepared to meet it but at this critical juncture he was betrayed by his own nobility. Their discontent may have stemmed from the King's misuse of demissions (pardons in return for payments) or from a debasement of the currency, but it focused on the low-born favourites and courtiers with whom he habitually consorted, especially **Robert Cochrane**. In the well known lynching at **Lauder** Bridge, **Archibald 'Bell the Cat' Douglas** and his confrères hanged Cochrane and others, sent the King prisoner to **Edinburgh**, and left the country undefended. Albany and the English advanced to Edinburgh; tortuous negotiations followed (1482). The English won back Berwick, the king his freedom, and Albany his lands and titles plus that of 'lieutenant-general of the realm'. But his triumph was short-lived as James adroitly out-manoeuvred him and forced him back into exile.

The turmoil in Scotland had been as nothing compared to that in England but in 1485 Henry VII emerged triumphant and James was at last able to restore good relations with his southern neighbour. Anglo-Scottish amity was always bad news for the freebooters of the Borders and it was from there that James was threatened in 1487. Lord **Home** took strong exception to the King's

obtaining a grant of **Coldingham Priory**. Supported by the Hepburn family, the Homes refused a summons to court and managed, in the absence of the legitimacy that might have been obtained from Albany, to secure the person of the heir apparent, James **Duke of Rothesay**. With war imminent the King fled across the Forth in one of **Andrew Wood**'s ships; negotiations took place at Blackness but hostilities soon resumed and in June he led his forces, mainly from the north, against those of the Border lairds under the command of his 15-year-old son. They met at **Sauchieburn** near **Bannockburn**. Both armies flew the royal standard but it was James IV who won. His father escaped from the battlefield but 'fell into the hands of vile persons and was slain'. A prophecy that he would be betrayed by his nearest of kin is supposed to have been responsible for the imprisonment of his brothers in 1479; it was fulfilled by his son in 1488.

JAMES IV (1473–1513) King

Fifteen when he overthrew his father at **Sauchieburn**, James IV was judged old enough not to need a regent. He was also old enough to feel remorse; he wore an iron chain by way of penance and made pilgrimages to **Tain** (St Duthac) and **Whithorn** (St Ninian). History, though, has been more indulgent, preferring to exonerate the son and condemn the father, usually for faults – like dalliance with musicians, poets and architects, misplaced clemency towards enemies, hot-headedness in battle – which in the son become shining virtues. Thus **James III** is an 'Irrelevance on the Throne' while James IV is 'The Glittering and Tragic King' (E Linklater). But 'the creditable figure which James IV cuts is partly an illusion arising from the dearth of evidence about earlier monarchs' (G Donaldson). Treasury accounts are uniquely complete for the new reign, and for the new King there are testimonials from international figures like Pedro de Ayala (the honey-tongued Spanish Ambassador) and Erasmus (who never met the King). Were such materials available for his father's reign it is likely that the full treasury, the impressive navy, the Renaissance court, etc with which James IV is associated should be credited to James III.

Doubts about the circumstances of James IV's succession may explain his being crowned (1488) at **Scone** (stone-less yet the touchstone of Scottish sovereignty). The Border lairds who had won Sauchieburn reaped their rewards while those who tried to avenge defeat were deprived of their castles. Otherwise conciliation prevailed at home while the **auld alliance** was confirmed abroad and skirmishes with the English kept to a minimum. This left James free to adopt a more assertive policy in the north-west where the **Lord of the Isles** was again suspected of treasonable dealings along the lines of the 1462 **Treaty of Westminster-Ardtornish**. Four times between 1493–8 expeditions, both naval and military, set off for **Kintyre**, **Oban** and the sound of **Mull**; they returned successful, the Lordship of the Isles was forfeited, and James is widely credited with having at last extended royal authority into the Gaelic west. But neither the soft glove epitomised in the 1493 pacification of **Dunstaffnage** nor the strong arm suggested by the 1494 hanging of John of **Islay** had any lasting effect. In the end (1498) James virtually resigned the task to the **Campbells** in the south and the **Gordons** in the north.

Meanwhile relations with England had deteriorated when the Yorkist pretender, Perkin Warbeck, was given a warm Scottish welcome (1495), a wife and, in return for the promise of **Berwick**, an army. But Perkin showed no enthusiasm for the subsequent invasion of Northumberland and his dismissal in 1497 at last opened the way for a renewal of Anglo-Scottish marriage proposals which, like so much else, dated back to James III's reign. Female companions, most notably **Margaret Drummond** to whom he wrote poems and may have been secretly married (she was mysteriously but most conveniently poisoned in 1501), had not been lacking in the King's life and he had at least three illegitimate children. But the offer of **Margaret Tudor**, daughter of Henry VII, promised to neutralise English hostility and to give the **Stewarts** an interest in the English succession. After waiting for Margaret to achieve a respectable age (14), they were married in 1503; exactly 100 years later that interest in the English succession bore fruit.

The 1497 treaty of perpetual amity between Scotland and England lasted 15 years. It was broken in complex international circumstances which found unlikely bedfellows such as the Pope and Henry VIII jointly engaged in a 'crusade' against the 'heretical' Louis XII of France. James could have stood aloof but was at the time infatuated with the idea of leading a crusade against the Turks. Ships like the **Great Michael** and campaigns such as those in the Western Isles had convinced him of Scotland's naval might, and his admirals, **Andrew Wood** and the **Bartons**, had already been in action on Denmark's behalf. But the Pope treated his offer to sail against the Turk with contempt while Louis, urging a renewal of the Auld Alliance, promised support. When English ships molested Scottish shipping in the Pope's name James renewed the French alliance (1511), and when Henry VIII invaded France James deemed it safe to cause a diversion by crossing the border (1513).

He had miscalculated. Although the fleet had some success in Ireland and the army took Norham and a couple of other castles in Northumberland, it was overtaken at **Flodden** by the old Earl of Surrey and his son with a force only slightly inferior in numbers and better equipped. James could still have withdrawn; he had siphoned off a large English force and so discharged his duty to Louis. But he did not, and in the ensuing battle his misplaced bravery was equalled only by tactical naivety. Excommunicated for having broken the treaty of perpetual amity, he fell in a cause that was not obviously Scotland's and in a battle that should never have been fought.

With him he took the flower of the Scottish nobility who had adorned what is generally conceded to have been a glittering court. Thanks to those copious sources, James is revealed as the patron of poets like **Gavin Douglas** and **William Dunbar**, the builder of stately palaces at **Holyrood**, **Falkland**, **Linlithgow** and **Stirling**, a pioneer of compulsory education for the landed classes, the founder of **Aberdeen**'s **King's College** with its first medical faculty, and a standardiser of administration and justice. Renaissance values had reached Scotland and the trappings of a centralised state had begun

to emerge. But in risking his life when his successor was only a year old, James jeopardised all.

JAMES V (1512–42) King

Elder and only surviving son of **James IV** and **Margaret Tudor**, James V succeeded his father when he was only 17 months old, and spent the first 15 years of his life being 'coupit from hand to hand' while first his mother, then **John, 4th Duke of Albany** and finally an assortment of Scotland's nobles governed on his behalf. For two years from 1526 he was held a virtual prisoner by his erstwhile stepfather, **Archibald Douglas, 6th Earl of Angus**, who quickly filled every important administrative and ecclesiastical post with his own relations. When James escaped in 1528 he took his revenge: Douglases were outlawed, their lands forfeit and their power destroyed. His consuming hatred for the Douglases, and through them for the English, left him also with a deep distrust of the nobility, and it was this as much as any notion of equality that moved him to replace them in positions of power with lesser men. It was to the slighted nobles that James became 'the Ill-Beloved'.

James V, from one of the Stirling Heads (carved wood medallions from Stirling Castle) (© the Trustees of the National Museums of Scotland 1994)

Careless, and sometimes downright corrupt, management during his minority had left Scotland all but bankrupt; an intolerable situation to a most acquisitive king. Fortunately James was able to exploit the Pope's fears about the spread across Europe of the **Reformation**, and his anxiety lest Scotland follow the lead of England and make the King the head of the Church; in return for James's renewed commitment to the Catholic Church and Papal authority, the Pope sanctioned the introduction of a perpetual tax of £10,000 a year from the Scottish prelacies, and a temporary tax amounting to one-tenth of all Scottish ecclesiastical revenues. The King also extracted from the anxious Pope the right to nominate bishops, later using this power to elevate several of his illegitimate sons to high ecclesiastical office.

Tutored during his childhood first by **Sir David Lindsay of the Mount** and then by **Gavin Dunbar**, James's cultural education had not been neglected (he completed the building of **Falkland Palace** and made improvements at **Stirling** and **Linlithgow** as well as refurbishing the **Regalia**). His moral education, however, certainly had been neglected; his much vaunted sympathy with the 'common people' (amongst whom he chose to wander disguised as 'the Gudeman of Ballangeich') has been re-interpreted as 'a taste for low company' acquired as a result of Angus 'encouraging him in a precocious career of vice' from an early age. By the age of 21 he acknowledged three illegitimate children and was later recorded as having sired at least seven, all by different mothers.

Obsessed by now with the accumulation of wealth, and having pondered but rejected the idea of marrying one of his mistresses, James decided to acquire a wife with a large dowry. Various possibilities were considered, the final choice coming down to either Marie de Vendôme or the Princess Madeleine, daughter of Francis I. Upon the former being revealed as a 'misshapen hunchback', James settled for the frail Madeleine; they were married on 1 January 1537, but by July Madeleine was dead. A year later he was married again (thus acquiring a second dowry), this time to **Mary of Guise**.

Divisions between Crown and nobles were widened by the King's attempts to bring much-needed law and order to the outlying corners of his kingdom, notably the Highlands and the Borders, by appointing his own agents to govern in the place of local barons. The Borders families of Armstrong, Hepburn, Home, Maxwell and Scott were particular targets and his punitive action against them included the infamous hanging of **Johnnie Armstrong**. Not surprisingly the Borders families would not rush to his support in times of imminent conflict.

Increasingly alarmed by the threat of attack from the Continent, Henry VIII arranged a meeting with James in York in an effort to wean his Scottish nephew from French and Catholic influence. The Scottish clergy refused to let James attend; the English King took umbrage; and by 1542 the two countries were at war. A reluctant Scots army managed to hold off the English invasion at the **Battle of Hadden Rig** in August, but, falling into confusion and disarray, were overwhelmed at the **Battle of Solway Moss** in November. James retired to Linlithgow and then to Falkland Palace in a state of depression and collapse. His wife had borne him one son in 1540 and another in 1541, but by the end of that year both had died. On 14 December 1542, six days after the birth of his daughter, **Mary**, James died at the age of 30.

JAMES VI (1566–1625) King

The son of **Queen Mary** and **Lord Darnley**, James is widely regarded as Scotland's most successful sovereign, yet he could hardly have had a more inauspicious background. His mother had been terrorised into abdicating soon after his birth by her bastard half-brother (**Lord James Stewart**) whom she had favoured with the earldom of **Moray** and much besides. Moray became Regent in the name of a child who, only 13 months old, sat

James VI, aged 39, from a panel dated 1595 and attributed to Adrian Vanson (SNPG)

listening to an interminable sermon from **Knox** at his coronation. His senior tutor, before he was four years old, was **George Buchanan**. The captive Queen was appalled when she heard of Buchanan's appointment, but even the toys she sent him were withheld, while the boy was treated instead to grotesque libels on her character from the prime source of their invention.

He grew up in **Stirling Castle**, the favourite place of his forebears, in the custody of the Countess of Mar, who treated him with unloving severity. Here he learned of the murder of his first Regent in 1570, and actually saw his grandfather **Lennox**, the second Regent, being carried dying into the castle in the following year. In 1578 the first palace coup occurred, in which the Earls of Argyll and Atholl attempted to supplant the fourth Regent, **Morton**, and the King's 'acceptance of government' was proclaimed in **Edinburgh**. It was the first of a series of attempts to sieze power by taking possesssion of the boy King; from these he was to emerge nine years later 'un vieux jeune homme' as a Frenchman observed.

When James was 13 years old his handsome young Catholic cousin **Esmé Stewart** paid a visit from France. In his infatuation James created him Duke of Lennox and his companion Earl of Arran. They secured the execution of Regent Morton in 1581 on a charge of complicity in the murder of the King's father. Calderwood wrote that they 'foully misused his tender age', mistaking the guilty party in the seduction. The Ruthvens, leaders of the extreme Protestant party, found revenge in the **Ruthven Raid** whereby James was kidnapped and Lennox compelled to return to France, where he died in 1583. James escaped and had **Gowrie** executed, while he mourned the loss of Lennox in passionate poems. It was not until 1600 that he completed his revenge on the Ruthven family in the mysterious episode known as the **Gowrie Conspiracy**.

By this time he had also clipped the wings of the Calvinist divines who asserted that his kingdom belonged to Jesus Christ (in other words, themselves), while he was merely 'God's sillie vassal'. The alliance of nobles and clergy was epitomised by Robert Bruce (c1544–1631), son of the bold bad baron of **Airth** Castle, who followed John Knox in the pulpit of **St Giles**. James drove him into exile, while gaining control of the **General Assemblies** by manipulating the times and places of their meetings.

His treatment of his Gaelic subjects was less excusable and strongly influenced by racial prejudice. 'As for Highlanders,' he wrote, 'I shortly comprehend them all in two sorts of people: the one that dwelleth on the mainland that are barbarous, and yet mixed with some show of civility; the other that dwelleth in the Isles and are all utterly barbarous.' He instructed his son to think of them merely as wolves or wild boars. His solution was to order their total extermination, and the settlement of their islands with English-speaking lowlanders. Ultimately this policy was implemented, not in Scotland but in Northern Ireland, where the consequences of what James liked to call his kingcraft are still to be seen. His racial arrogance was perhaps demonstrated most clearly when he ordered the aesthetically pleasing spectacle of Negroes dancing naked in the snow in the presence of his brother-in-law the King of Denmark. This caused their deaths, as James must have known it would.

That he was also something of a misogynist was probably due to the malign influence of Buchanan, though he did resist his tutor's insistence that his mother was an adulteress and a murderess. He supervised personally the torture of women accused of witchcraft; though for the satisfaction of this taste men would do. His detailed instructions for the torture of Guy Fawkes reveal his expertise. A warlock who influenced the fears and prejudices of the King was Stewart of Bothwell, one of the pestilential brood of bastards produced by **James V**. His coven played their part (allegedly) in raising the storm which delayed the return of James with his bride **Anne of Denmark** in 1590. The King's book on demonology, published in 1597, provided useful material for Shakespeare's *Macbeth*, and proves the King's belief in the efficacy of witchcraft.

Such was the character of the erudite and crafty monarch who used all his skill to secure the goal of his ambitions, the throne of England. He had curbed his unruly nobility, frustrated the pretentions of his clergy, allowed the English Queen to murder his mother with scarcely a protest, and promoted a new order of servants, 'such as he might convict and were hangable' (eg **Maitland of Thirlestane**, James Elphinstone, **Thomas Hamilton**, Alexander Seton). He had failed to place the Crown finances on a sound footing, but that was not uncommon in his time. An English diplomat described him in 1601: 'He is of medium stature and of robust constitution; his shoulders are broad but the rest of his person from the shoulders down is rather slender . . . He is patient in the work of government, makes no decision without obtaining good counsel, and is said to be one of the most secret princes in the world.'

In 1603, at the age of 37, he succeeded to the throne of England and embarked upon what Professor Gordon Donaldson has described as the *damnosa hereditas* of the Virgin Queen; most historians have judged that he did little, if anything, to improve it. He dreamed of creating a united kingdom of Great Britain, but he arrived with a retinue of ravenous favourites who alienated English public opinion. The most flagrant was Robert Carr, one of the Kerrs of Ferniehurst. The King 'leaneth upon his arm, pinches his cheek, smooths his ruffled garment, and, when he looketh at Carr, directeth discourse to divers others'. So Lord Thomas Howard told Sir John Harington, adding, 'he was with him a boy in Scotland and knoweth his taste and what pleaseth'. Since Carr possessed nothing save stunning good looks and insolence, few could fail to guess what that was. Carr became the first Scot to sit in the House of Lords, as Earl of Somerset. After his fall from favour the English youth George Villiers took his place, whom King James would address: 'Sweetheart, blessing blessing blessing on my sweet Tom' (though 'Steenie' was to become his favourite pet name). Villiers soon became Duke of Buckingham and the most powerful man in the land, his only credentials the face and legs immortalised in London's National Portrait Gallery.

The catastrophe was the death of James's elder son, **Henry Prince of Wales**, in 1612. Prince Charles (later **Charles I**) became the heir and had already fallen completely under the pernicious influence of Buckingham by the time his father died. The best influence that James bequeathed to him was his pacific policy during the carnage of the Thirty Years' War. Yet paradoxically it was precisely this that prevented Charles from raising an army (for which Parliament would not have refused supplies) before he faced what has been aptly described as the country's last baronial war, the Great Rebellion.

JAMES VII (1633–1701) King

James, Duke of York, second son of **Charles I**, was the most anomalous of men. During the Civil War he was made a prisoner of Parliament but escaped abroad in 1648. The most eligible Princess of France, La Grande Mademoiselle, described him as 'very pretty, with a good face and a fine figure'. To this he added a reputation for courage, loyalty and good sense when he served under Turenne and earned the rank of lieutenant-general. He had just been appointed High Admiral of Spain when the restoration of his brother **Charles II** placed him in command of the English fleet instead. His only act of folly had been to sign a promise of marriage to the commoner Anne Hyde, which King Charles ordered him to honour. They were married a month before their first child was born; but soon James was outstripping the King himself in the range of his infidelities. However, he took his duties at the Admiralty seriously, as Pepys recorded. In 1664 Charles bestowed on him the American provinces previously controlled by the Dutch, now re-named in his honour New York. There, while still a Protestant, James introduced the principle of religious tolerance that has endured to this day in the USA.

It was in 1668 that James embraced Catholicism with the extremism and fervour of the convert. Two years later he was a party to the secret treaty of Dover in which Charles II gave furtive notice of his own conversion, and undertook to restore Catholicism in his kingdoms in exchange for French gold. His Declaration of Indulgence in 1672 caused such uproar that it was withdrawn, and Parliament passed the Test Act which denied office to any but Anglicans. James, now a widower without a son, was still heir presumptive. In 1673 he married the devout Catholic Mary of Modena. There followed the Popish Plot and the Earl of Shaftesbury's attempt to bar the throne to a Catholic by his Exclusion Bill. The wily Charles outwitted him, sending his brother to rule Scotland, where the record of his regime is a creditable one.

When James succeeded to the Crown (1685) at the age of 51 he promised 'to defend and support' the Church of England, and he was known to be a man of his word, unlike his brother. Parliament voted him the most generous funding ever bestowed on a Stuart monarch. Charles II's bastard son the **Duke of Monmouth** took the field as a Protestant champion in 1685, assisted by the **Earl of Argyll** in Scotland, and was defeated and executed. When James suspended nearly all the religious penal laws in 1687 he earned the gratitude of the Quakers. He still enjoyed much goodwill when, in April 1688, the seven bishops refused to read his Declaration of Indulgence from their pulpits, were brought to trial and acquitted by the jury.

James VII as Duke of York, by Sir Peter Lely (SNPG)

In June Queen Mary gave birth to a son (**James Francis Edward Stewart**, 'the Old Pretender') after six pregnancies which had produced no living heir. While the child's paternity was being questioned, the King's nephew William of Orange landed in October with an army of which the Scots Brigade under **General Hugh Mackay** was the most effective weapon. Compounding his earlier mistakes, James took not a single step that displayed either good sense or even the old courage. There have always been those who have supposed that his breakdown was caused by syphilis, to which his extraordinary promiscuity lends some credence. But as an observer at the French court remarked before his

death in exile, 'our good King James was a brave and honest man, but the silliest I have ever seen in my life'. William II/III, who dethroned him, was his antithesis, a Calvinist, odious but not silly, and with a penchant for choirboys which protected his person from syphilis and his country from a Dutch heir.

JAMESON (or JAMESONE), George (1589/90–1644) Painter

The first outstanding figure to emerge in Scottish **painting**, Jameson dominated the earliest years of a native tradition in portraiture that would culminate in the achievements of **Allan Ramsay** and **Sir Henry Raeburn**. He began his apprenticeship in 1612 under the craftsman-painter and fellow Aberdonian John Anderson and may have completed his studies outside Scotland. Jameson's first known commissions indicate he was working in **Aberdeen** from 1620. The prominence of his clients and his reputation expanded rapidly and by 1628 his only real competition, the Scots born but Dutch trained Adam de Colone, had either died or left the country. Such was Jameson's consequent pre-eminence that for the period remaining until his death, no other artist in Scotland, other than his pupil **Michael Wright**, remains recorded by name.

In 1633 the demand for his talents – which would lead to overproduction – brought him to **Edinburgh** where he was commissioned to prepare celebratory decorations for the arrival of **Charles II**. Achieving national renown in his own day, the finest of his portraits, such as that of Mary Erskine, Countess Marischal (1626, Scottish National Portrait Gallery) are characterised by a sensitive and domestic approach, private rather than stately. In his last years he completed a number of self-portraits, the most significant (Scottish National Portrait Gallery) clearly indicating his profession and a portent of the artist's newfound status in Scotland after the iconoclasm of the **Reformation**.

JAMESON, Sir Leander Starr (1853–1917) Pioneer and Statesman

After studying medicine in **Edinburgh**, his birthplace, and London, Jameson emigrated to southern Africa and in 1878 joined a practice at Kimberley. There he became one of Cecil Rhodes's closest friends and ablest disciples. In 1889 he went north at Rhodes's request to sweet-talk the Matabele chief with whom **Robert Moffat**'s son had concluded a treaty. Next year he began settling pioneers in Mashonaland (Zimbabwe), and in 1891 he was in charge of the British South Africa Company's new Rhodesian settlement. Dashing and energetic, he improvised freely, winning the affection of the settlers and the distrust of the Matabele who had eventually to be defeated. In 1895 he was chosen by Rhodes to lead the support force being offered to the disgruntled, unenfranchised and largely English element in the Boer Transvaal who were known as *Uitlanders*. But when the *Uitlanders* shied away from open revolt, the support force invaded regardless. This was the infamous and ill-fated Jameson Raid. Rhodes was chiefly responsible, but the blame fell largely on the impetuous Jameson. Routed, captured, extradited and convicted, he received a short prison sentence but, like his mentor, was soon back in favour. In 1900 he was elected to the Cape Assembly and became Premier of the Cape Colony 1904–8. A baronetcy in 1911 completed his rehabilitation and in 1913 he became President of the British South Africa Company.

JAMESON, Robert (1774–1854) Mineralogist

Born at **Leith**, Jameson held the post of Professor of Natural History at **Edinburgh University** for 50 years, where he earned a reputation as a teacher of 'rare sympathy and understanding' and where his students included Charles Darwin. Although he promoted the Wernerian Theory of geology, in mistaken opposition to the volcanic theories of the city's own **James Hutton**, Jameson's main contribution to science was his collection of over 70,000 natural history specimens, which formed the basis of the **Royal Museum of Scotland**'s collection.

JAMIESON, Rev John (1759–1838)

Lexicographer

Born in **Glasgow**, Jamieson studied theology and in 1797 became a Minister of the **Secession Church**. He lived for many years in **Forfar** where he met the great Icelandic antiquarian Grim Thorkelin. Thorkelin encouraged him to note down 'the remarkable and uncouth words of the district', and over 20 years later Jamieson's notebooks were published as *An Etymological Dictionary of the Scottish Language*. Many distinguished people, including **Sir Walter Scott**, helped by contributing excerpts from literary texts and examples of oral usage. Jamieson's was the first dictionary in Britain to back up its definitions with accurate references to written texts, and to place quotations in chronological order, thereby illustrating the historical development of the language.

JARDINE MATHESON & CO

A major trading and financial conglomerate employing, through affiliated companies, some 76,000 people, Jardine Matheson was founded by two Scots in the late 1820s. James Matheson (1796–1898) from **Lairg**, had gone to India as a 'country trader', ie someone engaged in the inter-port trade of the East. Moving to Canton in his early 20s, he prospered with a number of companies before joining William Jardine (1784–1843). The latter, from near **Lochmaben**, had been a surgeon in the East India Company before taking shares in a ship-owning venture and then joining Cox & Beale, an established Canton house which he and Matheson took over.

Like other merchant houses in the East, the new partnership prospered courtesy of the East India Company. The EIC produced and marketed opium in India but could not export it to China, where lay the main demand, for fear of contravening Peking's ban on the substance and so inviting a retaliatory stoppage of its access to China's valuable tea. Yet tea purchases, if they were not to be a colossal drain on the EIC's bullion, had somehow to be financed by supplying China with the only crop which was in demand there. The answer was to let unofficial 'country traders' handle the opium and smuggle it into China. They did so with such success that the India-China opium trade became the largest commerce of the time in any commodity and accounted for most of Jardine Matheson's turnover. A decade later,

in 1833, the EIC was deprived of its monopoly of the China-UK tea trade and this too soon yielded handsome profits to Jardine Matheson. But without the 'front' provided by the EIC, the partners found themselves exposed to official Chinese hostility. They were obliged to trade from hulks moored off-shore and then from islands in the mouth of the Pearl River. One of these, favoured by the partners, was Hong Kong. In defence of the interests of companies like Jardine Matheson, the British government engaged in the Opium Wars of the 1840s and emerged with the possession of Hong Kong Island.

Jardine had returned to London in 1839, there to advise Lord Palmerston during the first Opium War. As *taipan* Matheson stayed on till 1842 and then returned to Scotland, and specifically to the **Isle of Lewis**, which he bought in 1844. Money made in opium was sunk into **oatmeal** and seed potatoes as he endeavoured to protect his tenantry from the ravages of the **potato famine**; hundreds of miles of road were built as also his **Stornoway** Castle. Further jobs were provided by an ambitious scheme to remove the island's blanket of **peat**, reclaiming land for **agriculture** and using the peat to produce a tar. But this scheme eventually failed and even Matheson's fortune afforded the island little more than a brief taste of sufficiency. The origins of this fortune are celebrated at Ardross Castle, near **Alness** (built between 1845–50 by Matheson's nephew Alexander); the gateposts leading to the castle are decorated with griffins holding opium poppy heads.

Meanwhile the Jardine Matheson Company continued to flourish. Its tea-clippers were replaced by steam-ships after the opening of the Suez Canal and in 1876 it introduced the steam locomotive to China. With a trading network covering the whole of the East, it was on one of Jardine Matheson's ships that Prince Ito of Japan escaped to the West to learn about modern technology. The Chinese Communists eventually nationalised the company's mainland interests, and its shipping was sold off in the 1980s.

JARLSHOF, Shetland

Within sight and sound of the bustling modern airport of **Sumburgh**, at the southern tip of the **Mainland** of **Shetland**, lies one of the world's greatest archaeological treasures, discovered in the 1890s when a winter storm peeled back the covering of sand to reveal a cross-section of Shetland's history from Neolithic times to the **Viking** era.

Above a Stone Age settlement stand the remains of a **broch** and modifying this structure are the wheel-houses for which this site is so well known. Next came the Norse farmhouse, followed by a medieval farmhouse and, lastly, the mansion house built by **Robert Stewart** in the 16th century – the building to which **Sir Walter Scott** in *The Pirate* gave the name Jarlshof.

JEDBURGH, Roxburghshire

The tranquil charm of Jedburgh, once the county town of **Roxburghshire**, belies its tempestuous history. Its name (or some of the alleged 84 variations thereon) is perpetuated in such sanguinary souvenirs of this history as 'Jedhart justice', the practice of hanging a man first and trying him later; the 'Jeddart staff', an eight-foot pole surmounted by a vicious hook or axe-head (local

Wheel-houses at Jarlshof, Shetland (entry p 581) (HS)

expertise with this weapon had the Earl of Surrey exclaiming that the men of Jedburgh were 'the boldest men and the hottest that ever I saw in any nation'); or 'Jethart Hand-ba', a ballgame said to have originated in Jedburgh men playing with the heads of slain Englishmen.

The growth of the town round its medieval **Abbey** in the direct line of the main route north from England guaranteed Jedburgh a high historical profile. Its ancient castle was one of five fortresses ceded to England under the **Treaty of Falaise** (1174) to provide security for the ransom of **William the Lion**. Previously a royal residence (**Malcolm IV** died there in 1165), it later resumed that function; one of the short-lived sons of **Alexander III** was born there in 1263 and in 1285 it was the scene of the wedding feast after Alexander's second marriage, to Yolande of Dreux, which had been consecrated in the Abbey. Such an irresistible attraction did it become to the English, however, and so frequently was it attacked, occupied, recaptured and attacked again, that the castle was finally demolished in 1409 on the orders of the Scottish parliament. Its place is now occupied by the county gaol, built in 1832. None of the six smaller towers built thereafter for the protection of the

town survived the attacks of 1523 by the Earl of Surrey and 1544–5 by the Earl of Hertford which destroyed the Abbey. The sturdy little mansion-house of the Lord Compositor, however, does survive although it is better known as '**Queen Mary**'s House', having been the monarch's lodging for a month in October 1566, during which she made her famous flying visit to the **Earl of Bothwell** lying wounded in **Hermitage Castle**. Purchased for the town in 1928, and re-roofed but otherwise unaltered since the 16th century, it is now a museum. The town was the birthplace in 1780 of the mathematician **Mary Somerville**, and a year later of the scientist **David Brewster**.

JEDBURGH ABBEY, Jedburgh, Roxburghshire

Standing on a terraced slope above the Jed Water, the abbey church forms **Jedburgh**'s centrepiece, imparting a venerable air to the whole town. Though smaller than its **Melrose** and **Kelso** equivalents, it is more nearly complete and decidedly impressive. Founded under **David I**'s patronage as a priory for Augustinian canons from Beauvais in France, it was promoted to abbey status in about 1154. In 1285 **Alexander III**'s marriage to Yolande de Dreux was consecrated here but in 1297 the Abbey was ransacked in the war between **John Balliol** and Edward I. It witnessed further assaults

West front of Jedburgh Abbey (RWB)

Francis, Lord Jeffrey, chalk drawing by William Bewick (SNPG)

during the wars of the 15th century and worse in the 16th century, being bombarded and burnt in 1523 by the Earl of Surrey and in 1544–5 by the Earl of Hertford. By then there were only eight canons left who were presumably dispersed during the **Reformation**.

In spite of these attacks, the only obvious deficiency in the abbey church of today is a roof. Built during the 12th–15th centuries, it is a fine example of the Transitional (from Romanesque to Gothic) style. This is typified in the great west façade with its round-arched doorway of six carved and recessed 'orders' with, high above, a 15th century rose window like that at **Dryburgh**. The nave, with gallery above it and clerestory above that, has more arches than an aqueduct, some pointed, some round; the gallery triforium consists of pointed arches within rounded ones. An unusual feature of the presbytery is the way the main piers actually envelop these gallery arches. Below the church the terraced cloister, chapter house and cellars are currently being excavated. Some interesting finds are displayed in the museum.

JEFFREY, Francis, Lord Jeffrey (1773–1850)
Judge and Man of Letters

Like his friend and biographer **Henry Cockburn**, Jeffrey was born and educated in **Edinburgh** before reading Greek and philosophy at **Glasgow University**, then law and history at **Edinburgh University**. By the time he became an advocate (1794) he was already a committed **Whig** and, finding this no professional advantage, turned to political debate and literary criticism. In 1802, together with Sydney Smith, Francis Horner and **Henry Brougham**, he founded the *Edinburgh Review* (1802) and became its paid editor (1803–29). Controversial and increasingly dedicated to Whig reform, the *Review* pro-

spered in spite of **Sir Walter Scott** withdrawing as a contributor, in spite of Thomas Moore challenging Jeffrey to a duel (both men were arrested), and in spite of Jeffrey's misguided 'This will never do' of Wordsworth's *The Excursion*. He was perhaps a better judge of contributors than of poets, affording encouragement to both **Thomas Carlyle** and **Thomas Babington Macaulay**. With Whig fortunes improving Jeffrey's career revived. He was made Dean of the Faculty of Advocates (1829), Lord Advocate (1830–4), elected MP (1831) and appointed judge of the **Court of Session** (1834–50). He was responsible with Cockburn for the drafting of the Scottish Reform Bill and for a decision in favour of the **Free Church** at the **Disruption**. Meanwhile at his Edinburgh home of **Craigcrook** he continued to pronounce on literary matters as an 'official observer' and to offer encouragement to the likes of Charles Dickens.

JEX-BLAKE, Sophia (1840–1912) Pioneer of Medical Education for Women

Born in Hastings, Sussex, and educated at Queen's College for Women, London, Sophia Jex-Blake studied medicine in New York 1865–7. Barred, as a woman, from continuing medical studies in England, she approached the Faculty of Medicine at **Edinburgh University** (1869) and, together with five other women, persuaded the authorities – against mass opposition from the male students – to give her permission to attend lectures. In 1874 Dr Jex-Blake opened the London School of Medicine for Women, and in 1878 the first dispensary for women and children in Edinburgh, where she worked for 21 years. In 1886 she became Dean of the Edinburgh Women's Medical College and helped found the Edinburgh Hospital for Women and Children (the Bruntsfield).

JIG

A lively dance form, the jig is high-stepping and usually with six quavers and two beats to the bar. The word as applied to dance makes its first appearance in Scottish literature in the 16th century. It also applies to a satirical type of song which may have involved dance or action also with strong Scottish associations in its early history. It is now accepted that the French *Gigue* is derived from the Jig.

'JOCK TAMSON'S BAIRNS'

An endearing epithet for all Scots worldwide – almost a generic term for the nation itself – this supposedly derives from a habitual reference by the illustrious **Rev John Thomson of Duddingston** to his flock of parishioners as his own, or 'Jock Tamson's, bairns'.

JOHN O' GROATS, Caithness

It was first told in **Sir John Sinclair**'s *Statistical Account* in the 1790s how the Dutchman Jan de Grot and his two brothers came here in the reign of **James IV**. John is said to have instituted the ferry which still makes the 6½-mile journey to **South Ronaldsay** (**Orkney**), and to have built an octagonal house giving each of his eight sons a separate entrance. It even possessed an octagonal table if this tradition is to be believed. The term 'from Land's End to John o' Groats' (c870 miles) has helped to maintain this unexciting resort as a tourist trap.

JOHNSON, James (c1753–1811) Music Publisher

Johnson initiated *The Scots Musical Museum*, a major collection of Scottish song to which **Robert Burns** was to become the chief contributor and editor. It was issued in six volumes between 1787 and 1803, the tunes being provided with figured basses, a fact which militated against the popularity of the series. However, it is still one of the most important collections of Scottish song, especially in later editions with notes added by Stenhouse and Sharp.

JOHNSON, Dr Samuel (1709–84) Lexicographer

Born in Lichfield, the son of a bookseller, Johnson received his early education locally and from his father's stock, before going to Oxford in 1727, though he did not graduate. On the failure of his own school at Edial in 1737, he moved to London, supporting himself by journalism, particularly by contributions to the recently founded *Gentleman's Magazine*, in which he published imaginative accounts of Parliamentary debates.

In 1747 he set out his plans for his *Dictionary*, and having received an advance for the work, employed six assistants, five of whom are said to have been Scotsmen. The *Dictionary* appeared in 1755 to great acclaim, and remains a remarkable work of scholarship. From 1750–62 Johnson edited *The Rambler*, and in 1759 he published *Rasselas*, in his lifetime his most popular work.

His claim to lasting fame, however, is as the subject of one of the greatest biographies in the English language. On the advice of Lord Hailes [see **Dalrymple**], **James Boswell** sought Johnson out as a literary figure of some interest, and first made his acquaintance in May 1763. They remained friends until Johnson's death, and

without the other, neither would be remembered today.

In 1773, after much persuasion, Johnson agreed to tour the Highlands in Boswell's company, and the resulting account in *A Journey to the Western Islands of Scotland*, which appeared in 1775, is of some social as well as literary interest. It is also one of his last works.

Cantankerous, reactionary, opinionated and bullying Johnson undoubtedly was, but his sharply expressed views on men and things, as reported by Boswell, have conferred a posthumous celebrity on one whose literary reputation might otherwise have died with him.

JOHNSTON, Alexander Keith (i) (1804–71) and (ii) (1846–79) Cartographers

The elder Johnston, born near Gorebridge, **Midlothian**, attended **Edinburgh High School** and **University** and, after being apprenticed to James Kirkwood, engraver, set up in business with his brother William as a mapmaker in 1826. They produced atlases of exceptional quality plus the first physical globe for which Keith received a medal at the 1851 Great Exhibition. In 1871 he was awarded the Royal Geographical Society's Patron's Gold Medal for services to geography. His son, the younger A K Johnston, trained as a draughtsman in the business, and from 1869 ran its London branch. He served on a mapmaking commission in Paraguay (1873) and wrote an account of it before being invited by the RGS to lead its 1879 expedition to Lake Nyasa. Dysentery struck as soon as he reached East Africa. He staggered on and was carried for a great distance, but eventually died about 120 miles inland from Dar-es-Salaam. Leadership of the expedition devolved onto **Joseph Thomson**.

JOHNSTON, Archibald, of Warriston (1611–63) Covenanter

Born in **Edinburgh**, Archibald Johnston was the legal brain behind the drawing up of the National **Covenant** (1638). Qualified as an advocate (1633), he framed the enactments of the **General Assembly** (1638), became a Lord of Session (1641), one of the commissioners to the Westminster Assembly (1643), Lord Advocate (1646) and Lord Clerk Register (1649 and again 1657 for Cromwell). Described as a 'canny, lynx-eyed lawyer' (**Thomas Carlyle**), 'a man walking on the dizzy verge of madness' (C V Wedgwood) 'with one foot in fanaticism' (R Mitchison), Johnston became a leading **Remonstrant** opposing the **Engagement** and refusing to accept **Charles II** as King, and was one of three Scottish judges appointed by Cromwell to superintend the administration of the law in Scotland. On the Restoration (1660) a warrant was issued for his arrest but he fled to Germany and then France where he was eventually captured at Rouen in 1663. He spent six months in the Tower of London before being moved to Edinburgh's **Tolbooth**. Tried and condemned to death for co-operation with the Cromwellian regime, he was beheaded at the **Mercat Cross** on 22 July 1663.

JOHNSTON, Sir Reginald Fleming (1874–1938) Sinologist

Born in **Edinburgh**, Johnston studied history at **Edinburgh University** and Magdalen College, Oxford. He was appointed a Hong Kong Cadet in 1898 and went

Archibald Johnston, Lord Warriston, by George Jamesone (SNPG)

on to become District Officer in Weihaiwei, Shandong Province from 1906–19 and Commissioner, Weihaiwei from 1927–30. Employed as tutor to the last Emperor of China from 1919–25, he travelled extensively throughout the Chinese Empire and was greatly influenced by Chinese Buddhism. His publications include travel books, *Buddhist China* (1913) and *Twilight in the Forbidden City* (1926) about his imperial tutoring. He was the only European ever to have been appointed a mandarin of the first rank. A close friend of **James Stewart Lockhart**, he shared his belief in the importance of maintaining Chinese identity and institutions in British colonies there.

JOHNSTON, Robert (c1500–c1560)
Composer and Priest
Johnston came from **Duns** in **Berwickshire** but fled to England accused of heresy in the 1530s. His style reflects the developments in church music at the time of the **Reformation**, moving towards a greater simplicity and use of the vernacular. The early *Ave Dei Patris* gives each invocation of the Virgin a different vocal scoring, blending free and imitative counterpoint. The skill of his part-writing is particularly evident in the two-part *Dicant Nunc Judei*, and *Benedicam Domino* (which uses both Latin and English) is bright and straightforward, occasionally making use of close imitation: it was originally in honour of Queen Elizabeth. *Defiled Is My Name* sets a poem said to have been written by Anne Boleyn on the eve of her execution. Johnston's music is rarely dramatic, but its elegance, sophistication and refinement make for many works of intelligence and beauty.

JOHNSTON, Thomas (1881–1965) Author and Politician
One of Scotland's best-known Secretaries of State, Tom Johnston was born at **Kirkintilloch** on 2 November 1881. After journalistic experience on local newspapers owned by a relative, Johnston became editor of the **ILP** newspaper *Forward* which he went on to edit for 27 years. At **Glasgow University** he impressed contemporaries as campaign manager for **Keir Hardie**, who was bidding unsuccessfully for the rectorship, and it was not long before Johnston himself entered politics, winning the West Stirlingshire seat in 1922 at the second attempt. By this time he had published his impassioned *History of the Working Classes in Scotland*, as well as texts on women's emancipation and an attack on the aristocracy – the latter apparently such causing Johnston much embarrassment in later years as his career progressed.

Losing his seat in 1924, he returned to Parliament the following year after a by-election victory in **Dundee**, but succeeded in recapturing his West Stirlingshire constituency in 1929. After junior ministerial experience at the Scottish Office and a Cabinet seat as Lord Privy Seal, he found himself out of Parliament again in 1931–5, before regaining his seat once more. A firm opponent of appeasement towards Hitler, Johnston was selected to become Regional Commissioner for Scotland at the outbreak of war, with Lords Airlie and Rosebery as his assistants. The evacuation of children from Scotland's cities was one of their principal tasks, and Johnston impressed political friends and foes alike with his ability to work with people from widely disparate backgrounds.

This talent showed to best advantage when, requested by Churchill in 1941 to become Secretary of State for Scotland, Johnston insisted on working alongside a Scottish Council of State comprising all previous incumbents of the post still living. With such cross-party support, he rendered memorable service to his country, setting up a Scottish Council on Industry and culminating in the setting up of the North of Scotland **Hydro-Electric** Board. In this innovative enterprise, considerable reassurance had to be given to a rural population concerned about the future of the Scottish landscape, and Johnston handled such opposition intelligently, becoming the Board's first head when he left politics in 1945. He refused a peerage and continued as head of the board until 1959.

JOHNSTONE, James 'Chevalier de' (1719–c1800) Soldier
A much quoted authority on the 1745 **Jacobite Rising**, Johnstone was the son of an **Edinburgh** merchant who joined **Prince Charles Edward Stewart** in exile and served as ADC to **Lord George Murray** and the Prince, 1745–6. After **Culloden** he escaped to France and served with distinction in the French forces in America, earning the Cross of St Louis and a pension. His *History of the Rebellion of 1745* (1820) was first published in France.

JOHNSTONE, Renfrewshire
From a population of 10 in 1781 (Brig o') Johnstone had grown to 7000 by 1841, a rapid growth 'not exceeded in Scottish statistics'. **Cotton** spinning, then **coal** and **engineering**, provided the dynamic and, although this phenomenal growth conformed rigidly to the grid street plan commissioned by George Houston, the local laird and developer, it was no guarantee of distinguished architecture. Demolition (1950) of the

Houstons' Johnstone Castle, with castellation possibly by **James Gillespie Graham**, fell short of sacrilege. (A fragment of its earlier nucleus was retained.) Here, briefly and unhappily in 1848, stayed Frederick Chopin, the guest of Ludovic Houston 'whose daughter was studying music'. Also gone is Cochrane Castle, the home of the illustrious Cochranes, earls of Dundonald, who preceded the Houstons; its site is marked by a tower (1896) erected to commemorate the Cochrane link.

JOHNSTONE, William (1897–1981) Painter

Born in Denholm, **Roxburghshire**, the son of a farmer, Johnstone studied at the **Edinburgh** College of Art from 1919–23. He had little respect for the teaching methods there and with the composer **F G Scott** (a cousin) and the writer C M Grieve (**Hugh MacDiarmid**) formed a triumvirate that Scott considered would be at the core of a renaissance in the Scottish arts. In 1925 a travelling scholarship took Johnstone to Paris where he studied under André Lhote and made friends with, among others, Chagall, Zadkine, Giacometti and Severini. Whilst there he found in Surrealism a depth and freedom of expression which he felt related closely to the symbolic art of his own Celtic background. Returning to **Selkirk** in 1927 he began to incorporate Surrealistic elements into his pictures of the Borders countryside and, in his desire to evoke something of the primeval spirit of his surroundings, quickly evolved his own artistic idiom.

His work over the next decade remains amongst the most original for that period in British art and culminated in the highly complex *A Point in Time* (1929/37, **Scottish National Gallery of Modern Art**), a landscape of metamorphising, bio-morphic forms that had found its starting point in his 'horror in the disease of war'. Economic circumstances meant Johnstone worked as a teacher for most of his career and, while this interfered considerably with his own painting, he was largely responsible as Principal of Camberwell School of Arts and Crafts (1938–46) and of the Central School, London (1947–60) for the foundation of modern art education principles in Britain. On his retiral in 1960 he returned to the Borders, dedicating himself to farming though he continued to paint until his death.

JONES, John Paul (1747–92) Seaman

Born John Paul, the son of a gardener at Arbigland near **Kirkbean** (**Kirkcudbrightshire**), the future 'founder of the American navy' went to sea at the age of 12. For ten years he served on ships involved in the slave trade, acquiring great skills in seamanship but displaying what **John MacTaggart** calls 'a quick, fiery temper and a mad, ambitious, aspiring nature'. The latter won him few friends and even American biographers find it hard to explain away the mutiny and two charges of manslaughter which resulted from his disciplinary excesses. Become thus a fugitive from British justice, in 1774 he settled in Virginia, changed his name to Paul Jones, and espoused the cause of the American Revolution. In 1775 he hoisted the Continental flag aboard the *Alfred*, the first naval vessel procured by Congress, and in 1776 began that series of dazzling exploits on which rests his reputation as, in British eyes, a notorious pirate and, in American eyes, a doughty patriot.

Early successes in the Americas were followed by a posting to friendly France whence in the *Ranger* he entered the Irish Sea, attacked Whitehaven in Cumbria, and then sailed into familiar waters at the mouth of the Kirkcudbrightshire Dee. A plan to abduct the Earl of Selkirk, who had once vowed to bring him to justice, failed because the Earl was not at home. Jones contented himself with removing the family silver and, after acquiring more substantial prizes such as the sloop *Drake*, retired to Brest. In 1779, commanding the *Bonhomme Richard*, he again entered Scottish waters and threatened to fire **Leith** before falling in with a convoy of 41 ships off Flamborough Head. In the ensuing engagement, reckoned 'one of the most desperate and sanguinary in naval history', Jones's courage was matched by great ingenuity.

He returned to France and a hero's welcome which included plaudits from Congress, honours from Louis XVI, and overtures from Paris's *femmes du monde*. He responded to all with enthusiasm. Back in Philadelphia in 1781 he was given command of the *America*, the largest ship in the navy; but he never sailed in her. Seemingly his excessive vanity plus what even the *Dictionary of American Biography* calls 'defects of taste and character [arising] from his indifferent breeding and education' handicapped his career. He was sent back to Europe as a prize agent in 1783 and, after a short and unhappy interlude in command of a Black Sea squadron in the service of Catherine the Great, he died in Paris. Shortly before his death Thomas Jefferson had conferred on him the only gold medal of Congress ever struck for an officer of the Continental navy. In 1905 at the Annapolis Naval Academy, remains that were probably not Jones's were laid to rest by President Roosevelt and subsequently accorded one of the most elaborate pieces of monumental sculpture in the US. There is also a national monument to Jones in Washington DC; and in the church of **Kirkbean**, **Kirkcudbrightshire** there is a memorial font donated by the US Navy in 1945.

JUNIPER

Juniper (*Juniperus communis*) and **Scots Pine** are Scotland's only native conifers. Two forms of juniper occur in the Highlands, a low creeping form and a taller columnar type. The needles are short, sharp and usually in whorls of three. The cones are berry-like, blue when ripe, with a glaucous sheen. In former times these were collected in the Highlands for their medicinal value (particularly for stomach ailments and fevers), and large quantities were exported to Holland for flavouring gin. The wood was traditionally used for making handles for dirks (small daggers worn in the sock) and the roots woven into baskets.

JURA, Island of, Inner Hebrides

The island of Jura (Norse *dyr-ey*, deer-island) lies to the east and north of its more fertile neighbour, **Islay**. It is 27 miles (43km) from north to south and 5–6 miles (8–10km) wide, tapering towards its nothern end which approaches to within 4 miles (2.5km) of the Scottish mainland. One of the last great wildernesses in the British Isles, it is almost cut in two by Loch Tarbert. Its southern half is dominated by three rounded, conical peaks, known as the 'Paps of Jura' since at least the end

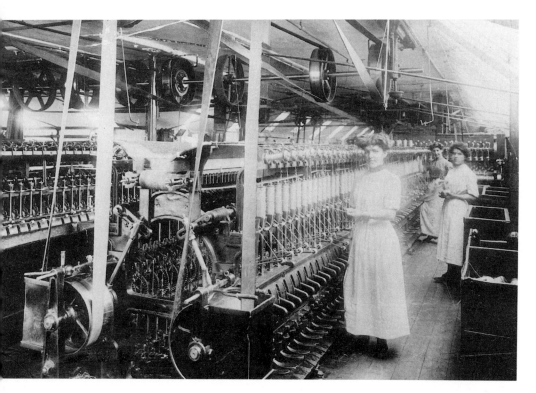

Cop winder in a Dundee jute mill c1910 (SAU)

of the 16th century. Formed of quartzite, they owe their distinctive form to frost shattering at the end of the last Ice Age which has left spectacular scree slopes on their higher levels. These mountains dominate not only their immediate environment but also form part of the seascape for many miles around. From **Kintyre, Colonsay, Coll, Tiree and Mull**, and from the high tops on the western seaboard of Scotland from **Skye** to **Arran** and even from the Isle of Man and Ben **Lomond**, they form part of the distant horizon. The other important topographical feature associated with Jura is the renowned whirlpool of **Corrievreckan** – *Corrie-Bhreacan*, the cauldron of Breckan.

Scattered archaeological remains show that Jura was inhabited in prehistoric times, starting with mesolithic sites around 7000 BC. There is a single Neolithic burial **cairn** south of Strone farm, while seven sites with **standing stones** attest to a Bronze Age population in the south-east of the island. There are several iron age forts and **duns**, of which the most spectacular is An Dunan on Lowlandman's Bay, to the south-east of Ardmenish.

The population of Jura has dwindled over the last 150 years from around 1000 to just over 200 today. On the other hand, the island's 5000 **red deer** are the main attraction for the sporting estates which attract wealthy visitors. With only one hotel and limited bed and breakfast accommodation, tourism, apart from day visitors from Islay, is a very small-scale industry. Most of the inhabitants work in **agriculture**, **forestry**, or as estate workers. A distillery in Craighouse provides employment and produces a fine, peaty malt **whisky**.

George Orwell wrote his novel 1984 at Barnhill at the northern end of Jura during the summer months from 1946–9. Every summer brings its quota of literary pilgrims, who would all agree with Orwell's description of his cottage: 'it's in an extremely un-getatable place.' He almost drowned in the Corrievreckan, along with his son and two friends, exploring the whirlpool in a small boat.

JUTE

A vegetable fibre obtained from plants of the genus *corchorus*, jute is grown mostly in the Indian subcontinent. British textile manufacturers began to experiment with it in the 1820s, but it was in the 1830s that its full potential as a material for cheap cloth was realised when industrialists in **Dundee** discovered a method of preparing the brittle fibre for spinning and weaving by saturating it in animal oil (initially whale oil) and water. During the Crimean War (1852–4) Britain's supply of Baltic hemp and flax were cut off just when huge quantities of sacking, horseblankets and other canvas goods were required for the military. Dundee ('Juteopolis') met the demand by increasing production and with this stimulus the city's jute industry became the world's largest. By 1880 the Camperdown Works in Lochee employed 5000 people. Ten years later 40,000 Scots (75% of them women) were employed in the industry.

Calcutta's first jute mill opened in 1854, and Indian competition, especially at the cheap end of the market, had become intense by the end of the 19th century. Dundee's jute industry survived partly on the strength of heavy demand during times of war in Europe and the USA and partly by supplying jute canvas to the carpet and linoleum industries. Despite rationalisation and the creation of the Jute Industries Ltd conglomerate in 1920, the industry stagnated during the inter-war years. After World War II jute import controls were lifted, bulk-handling techniques were introduced in the grain industry, and cheap synthetic materials suitable for sacking were developed. The 19,000 Scots employed in the jute industry in 1950 had become less than 1000 by 1988. Ironically some manufacturers survived by switching to the manufacture of products made from polypropylene, the synthetic jute substitute.

K

'KAILYARD' SCHOOL

Kailyards are Scottish cabbage patches, 'kail' being kale, a humble and disparaged brassica but palatable if not overcooked. Much the same goes for those late 19th century writers derogated as the 'Kailyard' school of Scottish fiction by the Edinburgh academic J H Millar in 1895. His targets were **S R Crockett**, **John Watson** and particulary **James Barrie**, with the latter's *Window in Thrums* typifying the genre. 'Kailyard' stories are usually set in a fictitious village or country town in some pre-industrial utopian era. Their characters, probably a minister, a schoolmaster, a tenant farmer and his 'gudewife', are solid, hard-working, decent types for whom things usually turn out well in the end; prodigals return, virtue is rewarded, religion upheld. They are no more ashamed of sentiment than their creators are of sentimentality. Scots idiom and words are used to establish a strong Scottish identity but not in such profusion as to discourage an English reader. This was important, for 'Kailyard' stories enjoyed great popularity in England and America as well as in Scotland, outlasting even the works of **George Douglas Brown** and **John MacDougall Hay** which, as it were, rotavated the 'Kailyard' and revealed its seamier reality.

Barrie and the rest were fine writers and by no means all their works qualify as 'Kailyard'. Nor did the term become redundant after them. Applied disparagingly to any literary or media production giving a sentimental or nostalgic gloss to Scotland's rural past, it is probably as current today as it ever was; give or take a century, **A J Cronin**'s Tannochbrae could be over the hill from Thrums. The roots of the genre have been convincingly traced back through **Henry Mackenzie**'s fiction to the Common Sense philosophy of the **Scottish Enlightenment**. With edifying tales so long established in popular favour, it is unsurprising that 'kail' in various forms continues to appeal to the Scottish palate.

KAMES CASTLE, Isle of Bute

Near Port Bannatyne, Kames is a 16th century tower, possibly with 14th century foundations, to which a house was added in 1799. In his biography of John Stirling, the Irish writer who was born here, **Thomas Carlyle** called it 'delapidated'; soon after, it was restored by **David Bryce**. Long the home of the Bannatyne family, it had passed to a nephew, the future Lord Kames (**Henry Home**), in 1780 and later to the Earls of **Bute**.

KATRINE, Loch, Trossachs, Perthshire

'The scenery of Loch Katrine,' according to an 1840s gazetteer, 'was comparatively speaking but little known, notwithstanding its magnificence, till the publication of *The Lady of the Lake*; but the splendid descriptions of that fine poem soon spread its fame as far as the English language is understood, and it is now visited by almost every stranger who makes the tour of Scotland.' In a note to his 'fine poem', **Sir Walter Scott** derived the name from the '**caterans**' or free-booters who frequented its vicinity in olden times; this word in itself possibly derives from the Welsh *cethern*, 'furies', the old name for the loch, according to Professor **W J Watson**, being Loch Ceiteirein, the Loch of the Furies or Fiends.

Eight miles long by an average of one mile wide, flanked by 'lofty mountains and a receptacle for the hundreds of streams which, after rain, foam down their rugged sides', Loch Katrine was **MacGregor** country long before Scott 'discovered' it. Accessible then only by way of a precipitous track through the narrow defile from Loch Achray (now the route taken by the main road from **Aberfoyle**), this 'inland sea' was refuge and lair for the outlawed clan and its most famous son **Rob Roy**, born at Glengyle at the west end of the loch. Until the 1850s the loch drained eastwards through the narrow defile into Lochs Achray and Venachar to the river Teith and ultimately the Forth. In 1859, the opening of J F Bateman's Glasgow Waterworks, a masterpiece of aqueducts and tunnels running a distance of 34 miles and carrying the 'pure soft water of Katrine' to **Glasgow**, diverted the flow and raised the level of the loch by some 17ft (5m). The steamer *Sir Walter Scott* now makes three tours of the loch each day throughout the summer, **tourist** guides still pointing out the scenery of Scott's poem to visitors 'as if it had formed one of the ancient traditions of their fatherland'.

KAY, John (1742–1826) Barber and Artist

Born in **Dalkeith**, the son of a mason, and apprenticed to a local barber at the age of 13, John Kay set up his own barber shop in **Edinburgh**'s **Parliament Square** in 1771. His spare time was devoted to drawing portraits and caricatures of the city's celebrities, many of whom he numbered among his customers. Described by the publisher **Robert Chambers** as 'the most exact and faithful likenesses that could have been represented by any mode of art', Kay's portraits were so successful that in 1785 he gave up barbering and concentrated on drawing, turning his premises into a studio and print shop. In all he etched the plates of about 900 portraits, his subjects ranging from **Adam Smith** and Lord Kames (**Henry Home**) to street-traders and fishwives, 361 of which were published posthumously in 1837–8 and in two volumes as *Original Portraits and Caricature Etchings* with text by James Paterson and James Maidment in 1877, a unique and invaluable record of 'the public characters of every grade and kind' of Edinburgh during the **Enlightenment**. Kay died at the age of 84 and was buried in **Greyfriars' Churchyard**.

KEILLER, John Mitchell (1851–99) Preserve Manufacturer

Keiller was born in **Dundee** and educated at Dundee High School and **Edinburgh University**. He then

589

entered the long-established family firm of James Keiller & Co where his great-aunt Margaret had first made the marmalade for which the company became famous. John displayed his business acumen through his wide portfolio of investments. He supervised the expansion of the company and ensured that *Keiller's Dundee Orange Marmalade* became one of the first trade marks registered following the 1876 legislation. A year later he assumed control of the firm and reconstructed the Dundee factory to produce a variety of sweets. In 1893 Keiller's became a limited company, although John's active participation declined due to ill health. He died on a cruise bound for the West Indies.

KEITH, Banffshire

An agricultural, distilling and former woollens centre, Keith stands beside the Isla and is the second largest town in **Banffshire**. Belying appearances, it is of considerable antiquity, the name supposedly deriving from *cet*, *ceto* or *coet*, an old Celtic for a 'wood', or *ket* or *kett*, an old Scots word for a 'peat moss' or 'moor'. The **Keith** family, **Earls Marischal**, derived their name not from here but from the Keith in **East Lothian**. Antiquities include the Auld Brig across the Isla (a humped-back single span of 1609) and a remnant of Milton Castle, an Ogilvie stronghold. **St John Ogilvie** (1579–1615), Scotland's only post-**Reformation** saint, is said to have been born at Drumnakeith near the town, and is commemorated by a statue at St Thomas's Catholic Church built (1831) with financial assistance from Charles X of France who briefly sought sanctuary in Scotland. Its copper dome dominates New Keith, the upper section of the town laid out by the Earl of Findlater in the 18th century. A third section, on the other side of the Isla, is the 1817 creation of the **Earl of Fife**, descendant of another of Keith's famous sons, William Duff of Braco (a nearby farm). The upstart Duffs habitually named their foundations after themselves (**Dufftown**, **MacDuff**), but in this case happily avoided 'Duff Keith' in favour of Fife Keith. The town has numerous distilleries, a mart and a major agricultural show, but its once important textile industry was finally wiped out with the closure in the mid-1990s of Kynoch's Isla Bank Mills. The parish church of St Rufus (1816–19) with lofty clock tower is 'one of the finest examples of Perpendicular Gothic in Northern Scotland' (**N Tranter**). Keith folk are sometimes known as 'Cairds', not because a caird is a tinker but because the hill south of the town is Caird's Hill.

KEITH, George 5th (4th) Earl Marischal (c1553–1623)

The founder of **Aberdeen**'s second university (**Marischal College**) was educated at its first (**King's College**) and then in Calvinist Geneva. After succeeding his grandfather as **Earl Marischal** (1581) he stood by **James VI** after the **Ruthven Raid** and in 1585 was involved in the defence of **Stirling Castle** against those nobles sympathetic to the Raiders and lately returned from exile. In 1589 he was chosen as the royal emissary to arrange the marriage with **Anne of Denmark** and to fetch the bride. Bad weather, for which Keith was subsequently exonerated, forced the returning party to seek shelter in Norway. The impatient James sailed from Scotland to meet his bride and the wedding took place in Oslo. Keith was subsequently a privy councillor and much concerned in the congenial (for a strict Calvinist) task of hunting down and prosecuting his northern rival, the Catholic **Earl of Huntly**. The **Reformation** may also have triggered his foundation of Marischal College in 1593. **Andrew Melville** and the **General Assembly** had drawn up plans for a restructuring of the universities whereby specialised teaching would replace the old system of a 'regent' who taught everything. 'But the plan seems to have encountered opposition and this was one reason why the Earl Marischal founded his new college' (G Donaldson); another may have been that in Aberdeen's numerous and well-endowed friaries he had a ready source of finance for the new institution. He died at **Dunnottar**.

KEITH, James Francis Edward (1696–1758)
Prussian Field Marshal

Keith was born at Inverugie (**Peterhead**), the son of the 9th (sometimes 8th) **Lord Marischal** and the brother of George (c1693–1778) the 10th (or 9th, but definitely the last). Educated in **Aberdeen** (under **Robert Keith**) and **Edinburgh**, he was heading south (1715) to take up a commission in the army when in York he met his brother George heading north to join the **Earl of Mar's Jacobite Rising**. James went with him and thereafter the brothers were nigh inseparable. Together they proclaimed James VIII ('The Old Pretender') at the mercat cross in **Aberdeen**'s **Castlegate**, fought at **Sheriffmuir**, welcomed James at Fetteresso (their **Kincardineshire** home), and escaped to France in 1716. Three years later both returned to Scotland for the next abortive Jacobite landing, fought at **Glenshiel**, and again escaped. Neither took part in the '45.

After nine years in the Spanish service, James joined

Field Marshal James Francis Edward Keith, by Antoine Pesne (SNPG)

he Russian army (1730) and was appointed to command the Empress Anna's bodyguard. As major-general he served in the Polish War of Succession (1733–5) and in the war with Turkey where he was badly wounded in the knee at Otchakoff. Brother George sped to his aid from Spain and whisked him off to Paris for medical attention and then to London (1740) where he had an audience with George II. Peace was later made with both the brothers but their forfeited estates and title were not returned. James went back to Russia as governor of Ukraine and commanded the Russian forces in the war with Sweden; there he adopted a bewitching young orphan as his mistress. Resigning, he was immediately (1747) recruited by Frederick the Great as field marshal and was soon joined in the Prussian service by brother George as one of Frederick's chief ambassadors. James was made Governor of Berlin (1749) and with Frederick won most of the early battles of the Seven Years' War but received a mortal wound at Hochkirch. Several memorials were erected in his honour in Germany and there are as many books about him in German as English. He was unquestionably the most successful of all the Scots who fought under foreign colours.

KEITH, Robert (1681–1756) Bishop

From **Aberdeen**'s **Marischal College**, Keith became a leading light in the **Episcopal Church** as coadjutant Bishop of **Edinburgh** (1727–33), Bishop of **Fife** (1733–43) and primus as Bishop of **Orkney** and **Caithness**. He was also a historian, compiling a *Catalogue of Scottish Bishops*, 1755, and writing a *History of the Affairs of Church and State in Scotland*, 1734. The latter deals mainly with the reign of **Queen Mary** and, though in narrative form, was the product of extensive archival research.

KELLIE CASTLE, Pittenweem, Fife

Abandoned for 50 years, Kellie was practically a ruin when Sir James Lorimer leased it in 1878. Recognising the place as an exceptionally elegant Jacobean residence 'of special interest for the fact that no external alterations appear to have been made on it later than 1606', he and his son, **Sir Robert Lorimer**, undertook a painstakingly faithful restoration of this 'masterpiece of Scottish baronial'.

Originally comprising a single keep, Kellie had been greatly extended by the Oliphant family in the late 16th and early 17th centuries. The tower had been raised, two additional towers constructed, and a connecting section incorporating a great hall added to complete a T shape. These additions included the corbelled angle turrets and corner turrets typical of a Jacobean tower house. The plaster work and panelling of the interior were not installed until the Restoration. Miraculously surviving the years of neglect, the moulded 'vine ceiling' compares with similar work at **Holyroodhouse** and **Thirlestane**.

Sir Robert Lorimer took the gardens in hand and Kellie became both inspiration and showplace for his own architectural ideas and designs. One of the tower rooms is now devoted to an exhibition of his work including furniture designs. After prolonged uncertainty, the property was purchased by his son, the sculptor Hew Lorimer, and is now managed by the **National Trust for Scotland**.

KELLS, Book of

When **Iona** came under repeated attack by the **Vikings** around 800 AD the relics of **St Columba** were removed to the new monastery of Kells in County Meath, Ireland. It seems almost certain that the most famous Celtic illustrated manuscript, the Book of Kells, now in the library of Trinity College Dublin, was transferred at about the same time. It may not have been finished at the time of its removal and, although the probability is that it was mainly produced in Iona, it has also been suggested that on stylistic grounds it should be credited to a *scriptorium* in eastern (**Pictish**) Scotland, possibly **St Andrews**. 'The supreme artistic achievement of **Celtic Christianity**', it was one of many gospel-books produced by monastic *scriptoria* in Ireland, Scotland and Northumbria. Figurative and abstract similarities with both the designs on early Pictish stones and those on the Iona stone crosses are striking.

KELP

The use of ashes from burnt seaweed – mainly *Fucus* species – to make a kind of salt was well established in Scotland several hundred years ago, and by the 1800s was valued at £80,000 a year – equivalent to the rent from 150,000 acres (60,750ha) of **Hebridean** arable land. One objective of the Highland **clearances** was to provide landowners with large supplies of cheap labour for the heavy and unpleasant work of kelp making. The average family of working men, women and children earned £6 to £10 a year kelping.

Most seaweed collection was done in the summer months at low tide, cutting weed with a reaping hook or sickle then dragging it in with a heather rope on the incoming tide. Creels full of weed were then carried ashore and spread out to dry, being turned occasionally to prevent fermentation. When enough weed was dried to make about a ton of kelp, it was forked into a trench – the kiln – 12 to 24ft long by 2 or 3ft wide, and 2ft deep, with stone walls and a turf bottom.

There the weed was kept burning with straw or heather for four to eight hours. It was a skilled job (often done by women) keeping the flames steady without letting in air, and the heat was intense. Once all the weed was alight, two or three men would rake and pound the mass together using long-handled iron clubs. The kiln was then covered with seaweed and stones to keep the contents dry. Next day it was cool enough to be broken into lumps and loaded onto ships for export, to be used as the raw material for a variety of chemical processes, especially in the manufacture of soap and glass. In the 1820s, however, the kelp industry declined due to cheap foreign imports of similar products.

KELPIES

'Evil disposed beings of the supernatural stamp', according to **John MacTaggart**, kelpies were 'thought by the superstitious to haunt fords and be the cause of people getting themselves drowned in crossing such places'. One such resided in the deep pools of the upper river Garry near Garrygoualach. As depicted by the designer of the first cover of *Punch* it had the front end of a pop-eyed cow and the rear end of a scaly mermaid. 'One Sunday, a long time ago' this apparition surprised eight children playing on one of the river's islands.

Incautiously they climbed on its back, to which they immediately adhered and were then drowned as the monster retired to its watery lair. But one, wiser than the rest, merely touched the beast and was able to escape by quickly severing his finger. The island is still called Eilean na Cloinne, the children's island.

Such is the species referred to by **Burns** in his *Address to the Deil*. Others, usually *each oisge* (water horses), live in lochs, pools and along the coast. Lochs Achtriachtan (**Glencoe**), **Ness**, Rannoch, **Awe** and Coruisk are all said to support a kelpie, but the most formidable breed is that found in Loch Treig (near **Corrour**). Several attempts to capture one are on record, including a hook-and-line approach related by **Sir Walter Scott** when the hooks, actually anchors, were baited with dog carcases. A cannier way to tackle the water horse is to remove his bit, without which the creature is said to be powerless and surprisingly docile.

KELSO, Roxburghshire

Although nearby Old **Roxburgh** with its ancient castle was the **royal burgh**, the town of Kelso grew to prominence by virtue of its medieval abbey and its ford over the river **Tweed**. The strategic importance of its situation at the confluence of the Tweed with the Teviot and within so short a distance of the border guaranteed the town a turbulent history; it was burned in 1523 by Lord Dacre, in 1542 by Norfolk and in 1545, spectacularly, by the Earl of Hertford. Although **Kelso Abbey** never recovered from Hertford's savagery, the town itself was rebuilt and by the end of the 16th century was once more being described as a 'pretty market-town'. The young **Walter Scott** attended Kelso grammar school for six months while he was convalescing locally with his aunt; two of his classmates were the brothers **James and John Ballantyne**, later his printers and publishers. John Ballantyne started work on the *Kelso Mail* in 1796 and six years later used the paper's presses to print the first two volumes of Scott's *Minstrelsy of the Scottish Borders*. 20th century visitors arriving in Kelso's elegant cobbled square with 'tall, demure, many-storeyed houses' (H V Morton) have remarked how much more it resembles a French town than a Scottish one, an impression no doubt enhanced by the stately presence of **Floors Castle** on the town's north-western extremity.

KELSO ABBEY, Kelso, Roxburghshire

All that survives of Kelso Abbey is officially described as a 'stump', albeit a big and exceptionally interesting stump. The first of **David I**'s several foundations, it dates from 1128 when Tironensian monks (an ascetic Cistercian order based at Tiron in France) began building what was probably the largest of the Border abbeys in the 12th century. From a description written in 1517 we know that, unusually, it had transepts at both ends, thus giving a groundplan somewhat like the cross of Lorraine. The scale is apparent from what remains, notably much of the transepts and porch at the west end. Turrets and apertures give a strong impression of castellated solidity while the façade of the north transept is rated the most spectacular piece of Romanesque architecture in Scotland.

After the death of **James II** at the siege of **Roxburgh** (1460) **James III** was crowned in Kelso Abbey. There-

West front of Kelso Abbey as drawn by Billings c1840 (RWB)

after its history is simply that of oft repeated devastation, most notably by the Earl of Hertford in 1545 when the Abbey stoutly resisted, the defenders retreating into one of the towers eventually to be massacred to a man. By 1587 there were no monks and little abbey left. Nevertheless, **Covenanters** used the ruins as a barracks, part was adapted as a kirk and part as a gaol. Further destruction in the 18th century resulted in the 'stump' of today which was placed in state care in 1919.

KEMNAY, Aberdeenshire

South-west of **Inverurie** on the flanks of **Bennachie**, the large village of Kemnay is still best known for its granite. This 'magnificent silver-grey stone has a light tinge of brown caused by the tints of felspar and contains both black and white mica' (Cuthbert Graham). In the 19th century the quarrying on Paradise Hill increased the population of the village from 600 to over 3000 – more than twice what it is today. Kemnay granite is said to have been used in at least seven of the bridges over the Thames and in numerous other buildings; as the industry declined, Kemnay masons took their skills to places as distant as New York and Odessa. The main quarry closed in 1960.

KEMP, Andrew (fl.1570) Musician

One of the contributors to the 1566 Scottish Psalter, Kemp was an able musician, holding the post of Master of the Sang School in **Aberdeen** from 1570–3, having previously been employed at the sang schools in **Dundee** and **St Andrews**.

KEMP, George Meikle (1795–1844)
Draughtsman

The designer of one of **Edinburgh**'s most famous landmarks, the **Scott Monument**, Kemp was born near **Biggar**, the son of a shepherd. He trained as a carpenter from 1809–13 and worked mainly in Edinburgh, **Glasgow**, **Lanarkshire** and the Borders. The Border abbeys first acquainted him with Gothic architecture and by drawing the ruins he laid the foundations of his knowledge of Gothic forms. He was able to broaden this knowledge by visiting the great cathedrals while working in England and France in the 1820s. Back home in Scotland he became draughtsman and modelmaker to **William Burn**. In 1834 the credit for his drawings for the **Glasgow Cathedral** restoration was taken by **James Gillespie Graham**, but the project eventually came to nothing. Kemp's triumph came in 1836 with the competition for the Scott Monument. He won third prize in the first competition after Thomas Rickman and Charles Fowler, but the committee decided to hold a second, which Kemp won. The monument was built between 1840–6. Kemp never saw the finished work; he accidentally drowned in the **Union Canal** in 1844.

KEMP, Robert (1908–67) Dramatist

The son of a minister, Kemp was born on **Hoy** in **Orkney** and attended **Aberdeen University**. He then worked for the *Manchester Guardian* before joining the BBC (1937) as a producer. Having successfully pioneered radio drama in Scots (Lallans) [see **Language**] he began writing his own plays (*Whuppity Scoorie*, *The Other Dear Charmer*) and in 1948 ambitiously adapted **Sir David Lindsay**'s *Ane Pleasant Satyre of the Thrie Estaitis* for the Tyrone Guthrie production at the **Edinburgh Festival**. Now resident in Edinburgh, he left the BBC (1948) and helped found the Edinburgh Gateway Theatre (1953). He also wrote novels and journalism but is best remembered for having reinstated the Scots (Lallans) **theatre**.

KENMORE, Perthshire

Between the east end of **Loch Tay** and the main gates of **Taymouth Castle**, the little village of Kenmore owes its form, charm and much of its architecture to the Campbells of **Breadalbane**, Taymouth's once mighty lairds. The parish church, facing the gates, and the adjacent hotel where **Robert Burns** wrote some lines over the fireplace, date from 1760, the Tay bridge from 1774. Two miles east off the **Aberfeldy** road, the Croft Moraig stone circle is one of Perthshire's most complex. Excavated in 1965, the site was found to include timber and stone arrangements from three distinct periods.

KENNAWAY, James (1928–68) Novelist

From **Auchterarder** (**Perthshire**), Kennaway was educated at Glenalmond and then, after National Service, at Trinity College, Oxford. His first novel *Tunes of Glory* (for which he also wrote the screenplay for the 1960 film) was published in 1956; it draws on his army experience. *Household Ghosts*, set in Scotland, followed. As *Country Dance*, it too became a film as well as a stage play. Four further novels and some short stories appeared in the 1960s. Aged 40, Kennaway was killed in a motoring accident. There is a biography (1981) by Trevor Royle.

KENNEDY Family

The origins of the Kennedy family are thought to be from the Cuneada, a tribe that dominated the south-west of Scotland in the 5th century, spreading down the west of England, occupying Cumbria and Gwynedd in Wales. The Cuneada also spread to southern Ireland. Kennedys became involved in the affairs of **Carrick** and Henry Kennedy is on record as being killed in 1185 whilst fighting against Roland, the cousin of Duncan, Earl of Carrick. Other Kennedys appear during the reign of **Alexander III** and in 1372 **Robert II** confirmed to John Kennedy of Dunure the grant by Neil, 2nd Earl of Carrick to Roland de Carrick and his heirs of the office of Chief or 'Kenkynol' of the Clan, with that of Bailie of Carrick and the right of leading the men of Carrick in battle. This implies that John Kennedy was descended through the female line from Duncan, 1st Earl of Carrick; the arms borne by John Kennedy, 'a chevron between three cross-crosslets', are very similar to those borne by the ancient Earls of Carrick.

It is from John Kennedy of Dunure, who acquired the lands of Cassillis in 1361, that the present Chief (the Marquess of Ailsa) and many other families in Carrick are descended. Hence the old rhyme:

> Twixt Wigton and the town of Ayr,
> Portpatrick and the Cruives of Cree,
> No man needs think for to bide there,
> Unless he court with Kennedie.

John Kennedy's grandson Gilbert Kennedy was created Lord Kennedy in 1458; David Kennedy, 3rd Lord, was created Earl of Cassillis by **James IV** in 1509 and was killed along with his monarch at **Flodden** in 1513. William IV raised Archibald Kennedy 12th Earl of Cassillis to the dignity of Marquess of Ailsa in 1831.

James Kennedy, a grandson of Sir Gilbert Kennedy of Dunure, was consecrated Bishop of Dunkeld in 1438, and was translated to the Bishopric of **St Andrews**, where he founded and liberally endowed St Salvator's College. Walter Kennedy of Glentig was amongst other things a poet, and is referred to by **Gavin Douglas** in his *Palace of Honour* written in 1505 as 'Greite Kennedie'. Heavily involved on both sides in the religious troubles that beset Scotland during the time of **Charles I** and **II**, many Kennedys emigrated to Northern Ireland, America and other parts of the world.

Little is known of Kennedy activities at **Largs** or **Bannockburn**, but the family was certainly represented at both. Later Hugh Kennedy of Ardstynchar, a younger son of Sir Gilbert Kennedy, commanded the Scots contingent under Joan of Arc at the raising of the seige of Orléans in 1429, and there were many Kennedys among the numerous Ayrshiremen who died at Flodden and at **Pinkie**. The name is not absent from the recorded casualty list of any other famous fight, whether in Scotland's wars, internal or external, or in Great Britain's.

As improvers and builders, Thomas and David, the 9th and 10th **Earls of Cassillis**, rebuilt **Culzean** to the designs of **Robert Adam**, and introduced modern methods of agriculture into Carrick. Kennedys have also played their part in public life as Members of Parliament and Provosts of **Edinburgh** and **Ayr**. There have been Kennedys in the Church, at the Bar, in the Army and the Navy, in the Universities, and active in the professions, arts, science and commerce, as they still are today.

KENNEDY, David (1825–86) Singer

Perhaps the first Scottish singer after **John Abell** and **John Wilson** to make an international reputation, David Kennedy made several world tours accompanied by his family, including his daughter **Marjory Kennedy-Fraser**, who sang with and accompanied him. Like Wilson, he specialised in Scots song, though he included music from oratorio and other sources.

KENNEDY, James (c1406–65) Bishop of St Andrews

Grandson of **Robert III** and nephew of **James I**, this Catholic churchman was created Bishop of **Dunkeld** in 1437 and Bishop of **St Andrews** in 1440, while adviser to **James II**. A leader of the 'old lords' in the minority of **James III**, he founded **St Salvator's College** of the **University of St Andrews**, and is buried there.

KENNEDY-FRASER, Marjory (1857–1930) Musician

The daughter of **David Kennedy**, Marjory Kennedy-Fraser was herself a singer, pianist, folk-song collector and arranger. She is chiefly remembered for her series of publications *The Songs of the Hebrides* which achieved a huge success and are still sung by Gaels and Sassenachs

Marjory Kennedy-Fraser (nee Kennedy), by John Duncan, 1931 (SNPG)

alike. Kennedy-Fraser was well aware that in bringing to the concert hall the material she collected (chiefly in the Western Isles) she was losing something of the originals. She maintained that sensitive accompaniment was necessary to make up for the loss. Her success or otherwise is still much disputed. If her work is assessed as original folk-influenced art music then some of it stands up very well indeed. As a folklorist, however,

she is untrustworthy, though much of the blame should also fall on her Gaelic-speaking collaborator, Rev Kenneth MacLeod, minister of **Gigha** for many years.

KENNETH I (MAC-ALPIN) (d.858) King of Alba

The 36th King of **Dalriada** (c840) and King of **Picts** (843), Kenneth I died of illness at Forteviot. He established his rule probably by a blend of hereditary claim and conquest, moving his centre eastwards under **Viking** pressure on the coasts and either founding or enlarging **Dunkeld** to hold the relics of **St Columba**. By 858 he 'ruled the **Tweed**'. A daughter married Run, King of **Strathclyde**, and their son Eochaid followed Kenneth's brother **Donald I** and Kenneth's cousins **Constantine** and **Aed** to the throne, thus strengthening the union of the kingdoms.

KENNETH II (d.995) King of Alba

A son of **Malcolm I**, Kenneth II reigned from 971–95, succeeding Culen, another great-great-grandson of **Kenneth I**. He was patron of the church of **Brechin** and was killed at **Fettercairn** 'by treachery' (later chronicles report the daughter of the Thane of Angus arranging a lethal booby-trap in revenge for the death of her only son). Kenneth tried to change the laws of succession [see **Dalriada**] in his own son's favour, perhaps provoking hostility; he was succeeded by Culen's son **Constantine III** (995–97) and **Kenneth III**, before **Malcolm II**, his own son, gained the throne.

KENNETH III (d.1005) King of Alba

The son of Dubh (reigned 962–6, son of **Malcolm I**), Kenneth III reigned from 997–1005; he was called Donn (brown-haired). Defeated and killed by **Malcolm II**, son of **Kenneth II**, he left sons who did not gain the throne; one was probably father of Gruoch [see **MacBeth**].

KENTIGERN, Saint, see MUNGO

KER, William Paton (1855–1923) Philologist

W P Ker, born in **Glasgow**, studied first at **Glasgow University**, then Oxford. His philosophical background was crucial, leading him to think much about the place, purpose and focus of literary studies. Fellow of All Souls, Oxford, and assistant in Latin at **Edinburgh**, 1879, he became Professor of English Literature and History at Cardiff (1883–9), then of English Language and Literature at London. As Professor of Poetry at Oxford from 1920, his list of scholarly prizes grew. Yet he was not deskbound, and died in a climbing accident soon after retirement.

This premature end meant that he could not work up the extensive notes of his long career. Their range is vast and beyond his still classic studies of earlier periods (*Epic and Romance*, 1896, *The Dark Ages*, 1904); far from all have since been edited and published. What he wrote of, he read in the original: Old Norse, Greek, dialects of Latin, medieval French, etc. A very great historian, slow to judge, he had a unique appreciation of different cultures and eras; identifying the strengths and weaknesses of an approach, he moderates claims, attends to detail, never bandies generalities such as 'modernism' as become; yet his exposé of literary fashion has been ignored. In his honour a W P Ker Memorial Lecture was established at Glasgow University. Other works include: *Medieval English Literature*, 1912; *The Art of Poetry*, 1923; *Collected Essays*, 1925; *Form and Style in Poetry*, 1928; *On Modern Literature*, 1955. B Ifor Evans' *Tradition and Romanticism*, 1940, exemplifies Ker's method.

KERRERA, Isle of, Argyll
Sheltering **Oban** Bay, this four-mile-long island shows an unusual diversity of geological features for its size. The **Vikings** held sway here as long ago as the 8th century and **Alexander II** died in Horseshoe Bay in 1249 while leading his fleet against the Norsemen. Its position between **Mull** and the mainland meant that it was long used as a droving station; cattle were ferried to Barr-nam-Boc and then driven to the north of the island before being forced to swim across to the mainland. Gylen Castle at the southern end of the island was the **MacDougalls**' second stronghold (after Dunollie). Built in 1582 beside a spring, it was called 'the castle of fountains'. It was besieged and burnt by **General Leslie** and the **Covenanters** in 1647 when the famous **Brooch** of **Lorne**, seized from **Robert I** in 1306, was lost to the clan for 200 years. At the other end of the island stands a monument to David Hutcheson, the predecessor of **MacBrayne's**, who first organised regular ferry services between Oban and the **Hebrides**.

KIDD, William (c1645–1701) Pirate
Captain Kidd's origins are obscure. He was certainly Scottish and probably the son of a **Greenock** minister. He first surfaces in 1689 as a hardy and experienced buccaneer in the Caribbean. By 1691 he was settled in New York, then a fort and pirate haven. He married there and engaged in the young colony's vicious squabbles before sailing to London in 1695 where he secured a royal commission to operate as a privateer against the pirates then plaguing the East India trade from their bases in Madagascar. By way of New York Kidd reached Madagascar and, far from suppressing the pirates, joined them. Whether he did so by design or under pressure from his mutinous crew is still debated. An attack on the richly laden *Quedah Merchant* secured both his fortune and his fate. Returning to the Americas he was arrested, sent to England for trial, and hanged. C N Dalton's *The Real Captain Kidd* (1911) attempts a rehabilitation; R C Ritchie's *Captain Kidd and the War against the Pirates* (1986) enlarges on the political background.

KILBARCHAN, Nr Paisley, Renfrewshire
Previously known as Kylberhan or Kilberchan, meaning the 'church, cell or retreat of Barchan', after a 7th century saint who spent part of his life in a cell on the site of the present Kilbarchan West Parish Church, this small town was a prominent centre of the handloom weaving industry in the mid-18th century. In 1791 there were 383 looms in the village and by 1836 this number had risen to 800, but with the advent of the power-loom in the 1880s the prosperity of the village declined dramatically. A typical weaver's cottage by Kilbarchan Cross was acquired by the **National Trust for Scotland** in 1954 and restored as a weaving museum. The Kilbarchan Steeple was erected in 1755 and includes a niche containing a bronze statue of Robert 'Habbie' Simpson (1550–1620 – the nickname denoting a native of Kilbarchan), a renowned piper.

KILBIRNIE, Ayrshire
The Barony Parish Church of Kilbirnie is a well-kept secret. Dating from 1470 (nave) and 1490 (tower), with aisles added in 1597 for the Cunninghames of Glengarnock and 1642 for Sir John Crawford, the centrepiece of the interior is the carved oak Crawford Loft or Gallery. Supported by elegant Corinthian pillars and intricately carved with 'flowing vine patterns, wreathed foliage, thistles, rosettes and other emblems, several cherubs which could by no means be described as cherubic and a St Andrew who is downright villainous' (T Lang), the gallery was commissioned in c1705 by the 1st Viscount Garnock and completed by a row of carved coats of arms along the front.

KILBRANDON REPORT
The Kilbrandon Report was the short title given to the report of the Royal Commission on the Constitution, set up in 1969. This followed the sensational capture of the previously safe Labour seat of **Hamilton** by the **Scottish National Party** and was a sign of Labour's concern for its heartland. The Commission's Chairman was Lord Crowther until his sudden death in February 1972, when he was succeeded by one of the Commission's members, Lord Kilbrandon (1906–89), who led it to its reporting stage in October 1973. Assemblies were recommended for Scotland and Wales ('devolution would do a great deal to meet complaints which are essentially regional in character') with finance on a block-grant principle from Westminster, and a transferable voting system. With Labour no longer in power, there was no rush to implement the report's suggestions, which were themselves somewhat compromised by a minority dissenting report from two of the commissioners.

KILCHURN CASTLE, Nr Dalmally, Argyll
Kilchurn was part of the Lordship of Glenorchy granted by Sir Duncan Campbell of Lochow to his son Colin (ancestor of the Earls of **Breadalbane**) in 1492. Sited on a peninsula at the north-east end of **Loch Awe** to guard Glen Orchy and Glen Strae, the five-storey tower house was built c1440. The ground floor gives access to a courtyard containing buildings of originally the same date. But the castle was damaged by **MacGregors**, and Sir Duncan Campbell of Glenorchy, having suppressed them, rebuilt the south-west and south-east ranges between 1614–19. Beginning in 1690, **John, 1st Earl of Breadalbane** added two ranges of four-storeyed barracks on the north-west side. The initials above the entrance are those of himself and his wife. The castle, garrisoned during the 1745 **Jacobite Rising**, was unroofed in 1775. It was taken over by the Department of the Environment in 1953.

KILDALTON CROSS, Islay
The Early Christian wheel cross beside the chapel of Kildalton, on the south-east coast of **Islay**, is the finest example of its kind outside **Iona**. Carved from a single block of locally quarried epidiorite 2.6m high, its vivid

Kilchurn Castle at the head of Loch Awe; Dalmally and Ben Lui beyond (entry p 595) (SP).

depictions of biblical scenes and its large projecting bosses make it an impressive memorial to the vitality of the early **Celtic Church**.

The 9th century Kildalton Cross (HS)

The front of the cross has scenes illustrating the story of Abraham and Isaac, David confronting a lion and, on the lower arm, the Virgin and Child guarded by two angels. One of the raised bosses on the rear of the cross is a typical 'bird's nest' with three eggs, thought to symbolise the Trinity.

The Kildalton cross dates stylistically to the beginning of the 9th century – just before the **Viking** raids which devastated the Celtic church in the Western Isles. In the 1890s, the remains of a victim of the Viking ritual killing of spreadeagling, in which the 'blood eagle' of the lungs was removed and held aloft, were found underneath the cross.

No trace now remains of the Early Christian chapel and monastery at Kildalton. The surviving remains date from the revival of chapel-building under the **Lords of the Isles** in the 14th century. Within the walls of the well-preserved but roofless medieval chapel are displayed some of the late medieval carved grave-slabs of the period 1350–1500, commonly found in chapels and burial grounds in the West Highlands.

KILDONAN, Strath of, Sutherland

The valley through which the salmon-rich **Helmsdale** river runs for upwards of 20 miles is named after a saint, possibly of **Pictish** origin, who was trained at **Whithorn** and murdered on the Isle of **Eigg** in 617. This is the ancient territory of **Clan Gunn**, although belonging to the feudal superiority of **Sutherland**. Its population in 1811 was 1574. By 1831 the number had been reduced to 257. The means by which this was achieved are recorded in the *Memorabilia Domestica* of **Donald Sage**, then living in the manse of his father, the minister of Kildonan. Any defence of the **Countess of Sutherland** who was responsible for the **clearance**

596

undermined by her own letters, in which she threatned that the families of young men who failed to enlist in her regiment would be replaced by sheep. The amilies of those who preferred other regiments were victed at the next term on her orders, while even those who had shown total subservience were later to receive the same treatment in the name of Improvement. Gold as been found in burns that feed the Helmsdale river, causing periodical bursts of mini-Klondike activity.

KILDRUMMY CASTLE, Nr Alford, Aberdeenshire

Boldly sited and commanding the main route from the Don to Moray, Kildrummy is probably the oldest surviving stone castle in **Aberdeenshire** and, though a shattered ruin, one of the largest in Scotland. It was supposedly built by one of the Celtic **Earls of Mar** on instructions from **Alexander II** in about 1230. Soon after was added the lancet-windowed chapel whose strictly east-west orientation means that it protrudes from the curtain wall at an odd angle. By the end of the century the four round angle towers and the double towers of the gateway had been erected and, but for the addition of a barbican and of the 16th century Elphinstone tower house, the giant pentagonal structure was complete.

Similarities with **Bothwell Castle** and, in respect of the gatehouse, with Harlech and Caernarvon in Wales, have been noted; the latter is not improbable since Edward I twice visited and took an interest in the construction. In 1306 the defences were first tested when Sir Neil (or Nigel) Bruce, brother of **Robert I**, was eventually forced to surrender to the English after a prolonged siege. **David II** visited as a guest in 1341 and as a requisitioner in 1362; the Earls of Mar lost and

Kildrummy Castle as drawn by David MacGibbon c1880 (MR)

regained the stronghold many times until, in 1435, **James I** acquired both the earldom and the castle. Burnt by John Strachan of Linturk in 1530, it was captured by Cromwell in 1654, burnt again by **John Graham of Claverhouse** in 1690, and took its final curtain call when **John Erskine, 11th Earl of Mar** ('Bobbing John') here planned the 1715 **Jacobite Rising**.

KILLEARN, Stirlingshire

The birthplace of **George Buchanan** and site of a large obelisk commemorating the event, Killearn lies at the western extremity of the **Campsie Fells**. Its old parish church (1734) is a ruin, its new parish church (1826 and 'not unnecessarily ugly' according to C MacKean) is now the parish hall, and its actual parish church a fine cruciform building of 1800 by **John Bryce**. **Charles Rennie Mackintosh** had a hand in Auchinibert House and in Moss House which replaced that in which Buchanan was born. West, at Gartness on the Endrick Water, **John Napier of Merchiston** lived, undisturbed by the churning of its pot (or falls) but so easily distracted from his logarithms by the distant clattering of a mill that he was obliged to tell the miller to stop production. So deep was his concentration that he frequently wandered about in his nightclothes 'earning the reputation amongst the papisticated hobnails in his vicinity of being a warlock'. Near Killearn is the Glengoyne Malt Distillery.

KILLIECRANKIE, Battle of (1689)

The high point in the first **Jacobite** rebellion occurred in the Pass of Killiecrankie, near **Pitlochry** in **Perthshire**, on 27 July 1689. Viscount Dundee (**John Graham of Claverhouse**) learnt that **General Hugh MacKay** intended to march from **Stirling** to recover **Blair Castle** and garrison **Inverlochy**. Dundee therefore moved from **Glen Roy** over the **Drumochter Pass** and

encamped on the 26th with 2500 Jacobite Highlanders near Blair. MacKay reached **Dunkeld** that night. With 4000 foot, two cavalry troops, three small cannon of Commonwealth vintage, and 1200 packhorses, he spurned reports of Dundee's approach.

The track through the gorge ran near the river, wide enough for three men or one laden horse. A lone sniper, Farquhar MacRae, hindered the advance while Dundee's army raced uphill above Lude towards Orchil. Mackay's advance-guard reported movements ahead; the Williamite army deployed uphill through woods to a crest overlooked by another already held by the clans. To cover them MacKay stretched his line to three ranks deep.

For two hours they eyed each other, Mackay 'annoying' Dundee with cannon shots (until the limbers collapsed), Dundee waiting for westering sun. At 7 pm the clans stood up and charged, yelling and firing one close-range volley before drawing broadswords. MacKay's men were swept away, leaving only the outside flankers; the rout overwhelmed the baggage-train and choked the pass.

Dundee had led the charge, but fell dying; MacKay's younger brother was killed (occasioning reports of the General's death); casualties were immense on both sides, but amply replaced, on the Jacobite side, by hitherto cautious adherents. MacKay rallied 400 men and led them south-westward to **Weem**; by 10 August he was at **Aberdeen** with a new army (but nobody remembers that).

Today the Pass of Killiecrankie belongs to the **National Trust for Scotland** who run an informative visitor centre, but the actual battleground is in private ownership.

In 1915 a Scots soldier on the Somme wrote, paraphrasing Wordsworth's 'In the Pass of Killykranky', 'O for an hour of Dundee!'

KILLIN, Perthshire

At the head of **Loch Tay**, beneath the slopes of **Ben Lawers**, and beside the Falls of Dochart ('possibly more painted by artists than any other in Scotland' according to a 19th century guidebook), Killin is a sizeable but pretty village closely associated with the **Macnab** family. The Macnab residence was Kinnell, where there is a circle of **standing stones**; the clan's burial place is on an island amidst the lower falls. Waterfalls evidently appealed to the Macnabs for Sir Allan, a 19th century head of the clan, was responsible for avenging an American raid into Canadian territory by 'sending the rebel steamer *Caroline* in flames over the Falls of Niagara'. Under **Breadalbane** pressure many Macnabs emigrated. The power of the Breadalbanes, then mere Campbells of Glenorchy, is represented by Finlarig Castle, unsafe, overgrown and spooky, but L-plan, 16th century, and still substantial. Nearby is an execution pit where the gentry were beheaded in private while commoners were strung up from an adjacent gallows. The eight healing stones of **St Fillan**, an 8th century Irish missionary [see **Crianlarich**] stand near the Bridge of Dochart; each supposedly corresponds to that part of the body for which it may be efficacious.

KILLING TIME, The

This much, but loosely, used phrase refers to the period of acute **Presbyterian** persecution during the ascendancy in Scotland of **James**, Duke of York and then **VII** in the 1680s. Suggested dates vary from 1680-5 to 1684-8. 'The notion that a British sovereign might have a Presbyterian conscience in Scotland and an episcopalian conscience in England had not yet emerged' (G Donaldson). Adherence to the **Covenant** was seen as treason and, backed by the **Test Act**, the heavy-handed justice designed to root out **Conventiclers** was applied even to moderate Presbyterians. Principal villains included **Graham of Claverhouse**, **Grierson of Lagg** and Bruce of Earlshall; their victims, many nameless, included John Brown of Priesthill and the **Wigtown Martyrs**. In the south-west especially, the innocent and defenceless suffered atrocities; and the conditions of detention under which prisoners were held at, for instance, **Dunnottar Castle**, were appalling. Yet there were probably no more than 100 summary killings. The **Cameronians** could be just as brutal to their enemies as the Royalists. They declared themselves in rebellion against the state and cannot have been surprised to be treated accordingly.

KILMACOLM, Renfrewshire

Between **Paisley** and **Port Glasgow** the Gryfe Water and its tributaries supported several weaving communities of which **Kilbarchan**, Bridge of Weir and Kilmacolm (pron. Kilma-coom) attracted respectable residential development in the 19th and 20th centuries. At Bridge of Weir the up-market **railway** suburb of Ranfurly recalls the ancient and now insignificant ruins of Ranfurly Castle, home of the Knoxes who were **John Knox**'s antecedents. Kilmacolm is more notable for its **Charles Rennie Mackintosh** associations, including Windyhill (1899), Auchenbothie Lodge (1901) and Cloak. Nearby Duchal, once the site of a castle belonging to the Lords Lyle, is now represented by a modest Palladian mansion of 1768. 'Quarrier Homes', adjacent to it, were founded by William Quarrier (1829-1903), a self-made **Greenock** businessman, as a home for orphans (1871) and later epileptics. With their own church, school, bakery and fire service, the 'Homes' became a self-contained village.

KILMARNOCK, Ayrshire

Legend suggests that Kilmarnock owes its origin to an Irish missionary called Mernoc or Marnoc who settled in Scotland in the 7th century and established a church and community here. Little is known of the town from that time until about the 14th century, which saw the beginning of a long association with the Boyd family. Given lands around Kilmarnock for their part in the **Battle of Bannockburn**, the Boyds soon became suzerains of Kilmarnock. Their ancestral home, **Dean Castle**, stands at the northern end of the town.

Built at the crossroads of the western end of the **Irvine** valley and the route from **Ayr** to **Glasgow**, Kilmarnock was a flourishing trading centre before it became a **burgh of barony** in 1591. Industries such as tanning, carpet weaving and the making of bonnets, hose and shoes became established and Kilmarnock began to rival the ancient **royal burghs** of Ayr and Irvine in trade with home and foreign markets.

The 17th century **Covenanting** times were anxious

The Cross, Kilmarnock, from a photograph by George Washington Wilson (GWWA)

days for Kilmarnock folk and several atrocities were committed. The following century saw the town caught up in the **Jacobite Risings** of 1715 and 1745 (Lord Kilmarnock was executed in 1746 for his part in the '45), but by the time **Robert Burns** came to Kilmarnock to have the first edition of his works printed in 1786 by John Wilson, there was enough prosperity to ensure a healthy list of patrons.

As this prosperity increased the town grew ambitious. The first two decades of the 19th century brought exciting ventures, notably the **Kilmarnock & Troon Railway**, the first constructed in Scotland under an Act of Parliament. The railway served the **coal**-mines which fuelled the industrial revolution. The 19th century saw the industrialisation of the town and several notable companies were founded in the 19th and early 20th centuries. The most important of these were **Johnnie Walker** (**whisky**), Glenfield and Kennedy (hydraulic engineers), **Andrew Barclay** & Co (**locomotive** builders), Saxone (shoes) and BMK (carpets). All these firms flourished, but the decline of industry in the 1970s took a heavy toll and Kilmarnock suffered serious unemployment.

John Finnie Street is hailed as an outstanding example of planned Victorian architecture. The Dick Institute, now a museum and art gallery in the care of the East Ayrshire Council, was built at the turn of the century

with money provided by James Dick and named in honour of his brother Robert. James Dick made his fortune from gutta-percha. He had an upholstery business in Glasgow, but when gutta-percha came on the market he decided that this was an ideal material for shoes. Even today Glasgow folk describe a particular type of footwear as 'gutties'. Other buildings of note in Kilmarnock are the Laigh Park, part of which dates to 1410; the Burns Monument in the Kay Park, opened in 1879 and recently refurbished; the Palace Theatre and the Dean Castle, which although seriously damaged by fire in 1735, was restored in the first half of the 20th century. It is now open to the public and houses important collections of medieval armour and musical instruments.

Some new light engineering and other industries were created in the town during the 1980s, but it still has not recovered from the loss or decline of traditional heavy industries, and although efforts to attract investment are being made, particularly through the Kilmarnock Venture, the town remains economically depressed.

KILMARNOCK & TROON RAILWAY

Towards the end of the 18th century **coal** was being extracted in increasing quantities around **Kilmarnock**. Transport to the coast was difficult and proposals to build a **canal** the nine miles to **Troon** fell through. A more ambitious plan to build a plateway of 4ft (1.2m) gauge received Parliamentary approval in 1808. Work started immediately and took four years to complete. It was the first **railway** in Scotland built under Parliamentary authority; it carried passengers from June 1812 and Scotland's first steam locomotive was tried on the line around 1817. In 1847 the original gauge was replaced by a standard (1.44m) edge rail. Various alterations have been made to the line, although much of it still follows the original 1812 route. Along the original route is the world's oldest railway viaduct.

KILMARTIN, Argyll

Five miles north of the mid-Argyll town of **Lochgilphead** is the Kilmartin valley, containing one of Scotland's most interesting landscapes of archaeological monuments: a linear cemetery of five Neolithic and Bronze Age **cairns** unique in Scotland, Temple Wood stone circle, the X-shaped setting of the Nether Largie **standing stones**, a henge and standing stones at Ballymeanoch, and several cup-and-ring rock carvings.

The oldest monument in the group is the Neolithic burial cairn at Nether Largie South, which yielded Early Neolithic pottery when explored by Canon Greenwell

10th century stone cross at Kilmartin with rare crucifixion figure (HS)

in 1864. Several secondary cists inserted into the body of the cairn show that it was in use as a burial place well into the Bronze Age.

Nether Largie Mid is an Early Bronze Age cairn, excavated in 1929, 32m in diameter, with traces of a boulder kerb surviving. The side slabs of one of its cists are carefully grooved to take the end slabs – a technique borrowed from carpentry. Nether Largie North is of the same period, 21m in diameter, still standing 2.7m high. The underside of the capstone (excavated in 1930) is decorated with cup marks and axe carvings. At the north end of the linear cemetery is the Glebe cairn near Kilmartin church (with a fine collection of medieval carved stone grave-slabs). Excavations at the Glebe cairn in 1864 revealed a central cist covered by an enormous capstone. The finds included Bronze Age pottery and a crescentic necklace.

The larger of the two stone circles at Temple Wood, near the Nether Largie South cairn, originally had 22 stones, of which 13 survive. The diameter was just over 12m. One of the stones has a pecked double-spiral design, spread across two faces of the stone, the full extent of which was revealed in recent excavations (1974–9). Here, ritual activity began before 3000 BC, with the setting up and dismantling of an arrangement of timber posts and the subsequent construction of the smaller circle to the north-east. The main circle was built in several phases, beginning before 2500 BC. It would be reasonable to regard this site as the centrepiece of the Kilmartin ritual landscape.

The Ballymeanoch henge monument is unusual in Argyll, but fits well with the rest of the Bronze Age monuments at Kilmartin. Now much denuded, it originally consisted of a bank and ditch encircling a cairn 21m in diameter in which were two burial cists, one with an Early Bronze Age beaker. It has been suggested that the stone settings at Ballymeanoch and Nether Largie South may have been used in the Bronze Age as a lunar observatory, for plotting the complexities of the moon's orbit. If so, eclipse prediction would have been theoretically possible and could have been an impressive means of social control by a religious élite. In any event, the archaeological monuments of the Kilmartin valley, and the rock carvings at Cairnbaan and **Achnabreck** near Lochgilphead, show this to have been an area of major importance in the Bronze Age.

The present-day village and church of Kilmartin date from the mid-19th century. The excellent Kilmartin House Museum of Ancient Culture won the Scottish Museum of the Year Award in 1998.

KILMAURS, Ayrshire

A former weaving village two miles north-west of **Kilmarnock**, Kilmaurs was created a **burgh of barony** in 1527 by the Earl of Glencairn. At its heart is the miniature tolbooth known as the 'jougs' from the iron neck-ring still attached to one wall. Home to a variety of industries including **coal-mining**, millinery and hosiery, Kilmaurs was particularly renowned for its cutlery: 'the breakfast knives of the Kilmaurs cutlers were alleged to be superior to the produce of even Sheffield or Birmingham' (Fullarton). The parish church (1888, Robert Ingram) includes the Glencairn Aisle (1600), which contains among other Cunningham of Glencairn graves the monument to the 8th Earl complete with weeping figures of his children.

Nearby Rowallan Castle dating from 1562 is L-plan with courtyard, but has an unusually imposing grey stone façade with twin circular towers flanking the first-floor entrance. The home of the Mures of Rowallan (Elizabeth Mure was the first wife of **Robert II** and mother of **Robert III**), the castle came into the ownership of the Corbett family (Barons Rowallan from 1911) in the early 20th century, Thomas Godfrey Polson Corbett (1895–1977) 2nd Baron Rowallan, being Chief Scout 1945–59.

KILMICHAEL GLASSARY, Nr Dunadd, Argyll

The prominent 19th century church stands on an older site (carved stones in graveyard). The fields below, towards the inn and beyond the 18th century bridge, were the site of the greatest midsummer market in the west, where **Islay**, **Jura** and **Kintyre cattle** were traded [see **Knapdale**] for onward droving to **Crieff** or **Falkirk** and into England. The Marquis of Atholl's army encamped here during the **Argyll's Rising** in 1685. A large rock-sheet carved with prehistoric cup-and-ring marks lies beside the branch road opposite the church.

KILMORY KNAP, Knapdale, Argyll

2½ miles beyond **Castle Sween**, Kilmory's 13th century church houses fine 8th–16th century carvings. A good range of designs, the oldest on the left of the door, includes armed men, ships, tools; the High Cross commemorating a MacMillan castle-keeper has been moved indoors for protection from weathering. Here the castle garrison worshipped. The fine-grained local stone was shipped as far as **Iona**; other accessible displays may be seen at Keills across the loch, and at **Kilmartin**, **Craignish**, Kilberry and **Saddell**. After the **Reformation** only 'Emblems of Mortality' were allowed (skull, crossed bones, hourglasses, cherubs, open book) and the old skills were lost.

KILRAVOCK CASTLE, Nairnshire

Two miles from the **Campbells' Cawdor** and rather overshadowed by it, Kilravock (pron. 'Kilrock') belongs to **Nairnshire**'s other great family, the Roses (or sometimes Rosses, possibly descendants of the Celtic **Earls of Ross**). The family has been here since the 13th century and in 1460 was authorised by the **Lord of the Isles** to 'upmak a tour' (build a tower). A massive square keep of five storeys plus a gabled garret with wall-top walk and bartisans was the result. It stands above a steep drop to the river Nairn. In the 17th century it was extended with the addition of an adjacent mansion linked to the tower by a square stair tower. The mansion has four storeys, a steeply pitched roof with dormers, and two stair turrets. Further additions were made in the 18th century and much of the interior remodelled. It was in the original keep that **Queen Mary** was entertained in 1562; and in the mansion that **Prince Charles Edward Stewart** was so charmed by Sir Hugh Rose's violin rendition of an Italian minuet. On the same day **Cumberland** was residing in Rose's house in **Nairn**. Next day, his birthday, Cumberland called at Kilravock

Kilravock Castle, by R W Billings (RWB)

and drily remarked 'You had my cousin here yesterday.' On the third day the cousins' paths finally crossed – at **Culloden**.

KILSYTH, Battle of (1645)

Almost a year to the day since commencing his remarkable campaign, **James Graham, Marquis of Montrose** won his sixth and last great battle at Kilsyth. Knowing that Lieutenant-General Baillie was pursuing him, he had encamped in a hollow above the Colzium burn, a tributary of the Kelvin, about a mile east of Kilsyth (Stirlingshire). 16 August was very hot, and the Highlanders in Montrose's army discarded their plaids and tied their long shirts between their knees to prepare for action. Baillie, approaching from the west, attempted to outflank the Royalists. **Alasdair MacDonald**, discovering his intention, launched a precipitate charge which overcame the **Covenanters'** centre. The van, after crossing the burn, was defeated largely by the **Gordons** and **Ogilvies**. Covenanting losses were heavy. Montrose now had all Scotland at his mercy. **Edinburgh** released its Royalist prisoners and sent money, **Glasgow** feasted and feted him. Montrose became the King's Lieutenant Governor of Scotland and a new Parliament was summoned. It never met. Within a month the victor of Kilsyth had become the vanquished of **Philiphaugh**.

KILT

The word is not Scots or Gaelic; neither, arguably, is the pleated, knee-length garment to which it refers, in spite of this having become the *sine qua non* of Highland and formal Scottish dress. Like the **tartan** patterns of the tweed from which most kilts are made (although worsted is now common), the subject is contentious. The word is English and was first used in the 18th century; it possibly derives from 'quilt' because the padding of the kilt's pleats gives a quilted effect, or because the kilt in its earlier form of a plaid or blanket served as a bed covering. More probably it derives from an earlier word of Scandinavian origin, 'to kilt' in Middle English meaning to hitch up or tuck up the skirt with a string.

The Gaelic word is *fealeadh*, *fealeadh mor* designating an untailored plaid which, somewhat like a sari, is folded, draped, belted and pinned about the person, while *fealeadh beg*, anglicised as 'filibeg' or 'philibeg', denotes the 'tucked' and tailored version covering only from the waist to the knee which is now called the kilt. How and when this last developed is warmly disputed. Some argue for an ancient derivation from the **Roman** tunic by way of the Celtic *leine* or long shirt; others point to an article in the **Edinburgh Magazine** of March 1785 which maintained that it had been invented by Thomas Rawlinson, an Englishman in charge of smelting at **Invergarry** and **Tyndrum** in the 1730s who persuaded his workforce to dispense with the upper part of their *fealeadh beg* as an unnecessary encumbrance to manual labour. Portraits of Highlanders from the 17th and 18th centuries show various ways of wearing the *fealeadh mor* including as a *fealeadh beg* (ie with no part of it draped over the upper body); the English contribution probably lay simply in the tailoring.

Equally contentious is the issue of whether the kilt

MacDonnell of Glengarry; Sir Henry Raeburn's portrait embodies Walter Scott's romantic ideal of the kilted Highland chief (NGS)

or trews has the longer pedigree. The latter developed from hose, typically tartan from early times, and were confidently adopted by **Sir John Sinclair** for his regiment of **Caithness Fencibles** raised in the late 18th century. The importance of kilt, plaid, trews and tartan as symbols of Highland and **clan** identity is clearly shown in the 1747 **Jacobite** reprisal **Act of Proscription** which specifically mentions all four, along with shoulder belts and anything else pertaining to 'Highland Garb', as forbidden. By thus defining and clarifying the Highlanders' wardrobe, the Act probably did more than anything else to associate kilt etc with martial endeavour and Scottish identity. Its survival was guaranteed with its adoption by Highland regiments and its promotion by **Sir Walter Scott** for the 1822 visit of George IV. The same factors gave enormous impetus to the developing argument over the authenticity of particular tartans and provoked largely spurious claims about the rights and wrongs of almost every item of Highland dress.

KILWINNING, Ayrshire

The Abbey of Kilwinning was founded c1150 for a colony of Tironensian monks from **Kelso** and dedicated, like the church it replaced, to the now elusive St Wynnin (Winnin or Winning), a Scottish (or Irish) saint from the 6th (or 8th) century. Kilwinning's fame as the Mother Lodge of Scottish **freemasonry** dates from the abbey's building; the first Free Masons being itinerant bands of skilled European artisans and craftsmen who worked on religious establishments, those at Kilwinning 'communicated their secret to some of the more respectable natives and thus formed the earliest lodge of Scottish free-masons' (Fullarton). The buildings of the abbey, when complete, covered several acres and were stately and magnificent. Largely destroyed at the **Reformation**, even the scant remains are impressive, the 13th century church's south gable being nearly entire. One of the two original towers survived the Reformation only to be struck by lightning in 1814; a replacement, not attached to the remaining ruins, was designed by **David Hamilton** (1815) as much, it is thought, to provide a continuing venue for the annual archery contest or 'papingo shoot' as to cater for the town's spiritual needs. Documented since 1488, the contest originally involved tethering a live parrot (popinjay, or papingo) to the top of a pole to be shot at by Kilwinning's company of archers. A wooden model stuck with brightly coloured feathers later took the place of the live bird, the target then being suspended from a horizontal pole projecting from the abbey tower. The Kilwinning Popinjay Festival, although transposed to 'the Upper Ward of Clydesdale', was the setting of the opening scenes of **Sir Walter Scott**'s *Old Mortality*.

In the grounds of his magnificent Eglinton Castle (John Paterson, 1796–1802) set in parkland to the south-east of Kilwinning, **Hugh Montgomerie**, 13th Earl of Eglinton staged the immensely elaborate Eglinton Tournament in 1839, with all the medieval splendour of jousting and swordplay. A crowd estimated at 80,000 gathered to watch the spectacle, which was promptly swamped by three consecutive days of heavy rain. The cost of the tournament, combined with the cost of construction of the **Ardrossan Canal**, spelled financial disaster for the Eglinton family. Their huge castle was

Ruins of Kilwinning Abbey, Ayrshire (RWB)

unroofed and abandoned in 1925, badly battered by Commando training in World War II, and finally demolished in 1973.

KINCARDINE ON FORTH, Fife

Once a detached bit of **Perthshire**, and not to be confused with numerous other Kincardines, Kincardine on Forth is the one with the bridge, which from 1936 (its opening) till 1964 (the opening of the Forth Road Bridge at **South Queensferry**) was the last, most easterly, bridge between **Edinburgh** and **Fife**. It was once a place of salt pans, then in the 18th–19th centuries an important Forth port and **shipbuilding** centre, second only to **Leith**. Now it is flanked by power stations, Longannet on one side and Kincardine on the other. Apart from a few 18th century houses the only architectural attraction is **Tulliallan Castle**. A nearby building (1820) of the same name but no distinction is part of a police college.

KINCARDINESHIRE

Before the **local government** reorganisation of 1975, Kincardineshire was an east-coast county bounded by the North Sea to the east, **Aberdeenshire** to the north and north-west, and **Angus** to the south and south-west. It included part of the city of **Aberdeen** in its most north-easterly parish. Overall, the county's area was 244,428 acres (98,993ha). Topographically it had four main areas – the **Grampians** to the west, Deeside to the north-west, the coastal area, and the **Howe o' Mearns**, a continuation of the fertile valley of **Strathmore**. The county was often known as the Mearns, and as such

was immortalised in **Lewis Grassic Gibbon**'s novel *Sunset Song*.

The county town was **Stonehaven**, the other small burghs being **Banchory**, **Inverbervie** and **Laurencekirk**. Population in 1971 was 26,059, occupied in **agriculture** and **fishing**, although some **oil**-related activities grew in importance towards the end of the county's official existence. This came in 1975 when, along with some areas of Aberdeenshire, Kincardineshire was transformed into Kincardine & Deeside District of Grampian Region, with the parish of Nigg being transferred to the City of Aberdeen District. In the second reorganisation in 1995, Kincardine & Deeside District became part of the Aberdeenshire Council Area.

Kincardineshire took its name from a former royal palace and town [see **Fettercairn**] in Fourdoun parish which fell into decline around 1600, when Stonehaven became the county capital.

KINCRAIG, Inverness-shire

Between **Kingussie** and **Aviemore**, Kincraig is a village of several parts near Loch Insch, through which flows the **Spey**. The loch was named after the mound, once an island (*innis*), known as Tom Eunan whereon stands a church (1792) of ancient pedigree. Here **St Adamnan** (Eunan) is supposed to have founded what is sometimes claimed as 'the earliest ecclesiastical site on the mainland of Scotland' (M McLaren). In the vicinity is Dunachton estate, now a Highland Wildlife Park, Invereshie, once a MacPherson (later MacPherson-Grant) property, and Glen Feshie, in which the Duchess of Bedford, daughter of Lady Jane Gordon [see **Alvie**] built a 'rustic colony of wood huts' wherein Edwin Landseer stayed and painted. The Feshie rises close to the source of the Aberdeenshire **Dee**; from the glen there is access to Lin of Dee, above **Braemar**, and to the peaks of the southern **Cairngorms**.

KING EDWARD, Nr Turriff, Aberdeenshire

The name of this parish has nothing to do with the victor of **Berwick**, the vanquished of **Bannockburn**, nor any other English monarch; rather it is an 18th century anglicisation of Kineddar, a castle of which name, once a stronghold of the **Comyn Earls of Buchan**, is still visible. More plausible is the linkage between the parish and the pink-skinned and immensely popular strain of potato of the same name. **Craigston Castle** stands within the parish; the only sizeable village is Newbyth.

KING'S OWN SCOTTISH BORDERERS, The

The KOSB were raised in **Edinburgh** in 1689 by the Earl of Leven; it is said that two hours sufficed for the ranks to be filled. In 1751 it became the 25th (Edinburgh) Regiment and in 1782 the 25th (Sussex) Regiment, since its Colonel, Lord George Lennox, had his main estates in that county. In 1805 it became the 25th, The King's Own Borderers; in 1881 The King's Own Borderers, and in 1887 it acquired its present title. In 1881 it was joined by Volunteers from the Border Counties and in 1886 by the Militia Battalion from the same area.

It saw early service in Ireland and the Low Countries, served at Namur in 1695 and fought at both

Sheriffmuir and **Culloden** against the **Jacobites**. It later served in the West Indies and on the North-West Frontier. Twelve KOSB battalions were raised in World War I, serving in Italy, Gallipoli, Egypt, Palestine and on the Western Front, winning 75 battle honours. In World War II the regiment fought in France in 1940, Burma and in north-west Europe, winning a further 43 honours. Since the end of the war the KOSB have seen service in Palestine, Korea, Malaya, Aden, Borneo, Northern Ireland and in the Gulf. The 3 battle honours for Korea brought the regimental total to 130.

The regiment assumed **tartan** trews in 1881; originally of Government tartan, they were changed to Leslie in 1900. The KOSB march past to 'Blue Bonnets over the Border' and 'The Garb of Old Gaul' in quick and slow time respectively to both pipes and band. Regimental Headquarters are in England, in **Berwick-upon-Tweed**. The Colonel-in-Chief of the Regiment is HRH Princess Alice, Duchess of Gloucester.

As one of the 25 senior infantry regiments, the KOSB escaped amalgamation in 1881 and again in 1993, when plans to link the regiment with **The Royal Scots** were shelved.

KINGSHOUSES

Kingshouses were inns set up in the 18th century with the cooperation of the government and local landowners on the **military roads**, usually on the site of former construction camps, and so-called because they were on the newly-made 'King's Highways'. (The innkeeper usually had a parcel of land to help him eke out a reasonable living.) In their early days refreshment and accommodation often tended to be basic. Quite a number are still identifiable, if only by site. Some, such as Old Blair, Dalnacardoch and Pitmain, lost their identity and purpose when **railway** became the popular means of travel in the 19th century; others, such as Garbhamor and **Tummel Bridge**, when the military roads were superseded or fell out of use. The Kingshouses in **Strathyre** and **Glencoe** retain both their name and function. Among those still operating under other names are the Ericht Hotel at **Dalwhinnie** and the hotels at Amulree, **Weem** and White Bridge.

KINGUSSIE, Inverness-shire

On the upper **Spey**, Kingussie (pron. Kin-youssie) is an important **tourist** centre with **golf course**, **skiing** (**Aviemore**), wildlife park (**Kincraig**) and a host of other outdoor activities. It was founded by the Duke of **Gordon** in the late 18th century, but was preceded by nearby Ruthven (just across the Spey) where the **Comyn** lairds of **Badenoch** once had a castle and where now stand the remains of **Ruthven Barracks**. James ('**Ossian**') **Macpherson** was born, and once taught, in Ruthven. He later built nearby Balavil (or Belville) on the site of Raits Castle, scene of a massacre of Comyns by the **Mackintoshes**; he is commemorated in Lynchat graveyard, though buried in Westminster Abbey. Kingussie is supposed to have been founded by **St Columba** to whom was dedicated a church to the west of the town beside the river Gynack; only the remains of its graveyard survive. The later parish church of St Columba (rebuilt 1926) contains a memorial to Peter Mackenzie of Tarlogie, Count of Serra Largo (1856–1931). The

town stretches along its High Street, once the busy A9 but now mercifully bypassed. Here are the Court House (1806) and the main shops. In parallel Spey Street the Highland (**Am Fasgadh**) Folk Museum comprises a reconstruction of 18th century domestic and agricultural life founded by Dr I F Grant in 1935. Exhibits include furniture, weapons, tools and the last stage coach to operate in Britain (from Kingussie to **Fort William** in 1914).

KINLOCH, George (1775–1833) Radical

Inheriting the Kinloch estate near **Meigle** in 1796, George Kinloch first betrayed his radical sympathies, the result of education in revolutionary France, when he resigned his commission in the local **militia** on the grounds that a standing army was unnecessary in time of peace. The 1819 Peterloo massacre in Manchester brought a stronger protest when he presided at a **Dundee** meeting which condemned the official action and called for universal suffrage. A warrant was issued for his arrest but he jumped bail and fled back to France. He returned after three years and lived under cover in London until a pardon enabled him to resume his lairdly duties in **Perthshire**. After the 1832 Reform Bill he was elected as the first MP for Dundee but died soon after. A statue (1872) commemorates him in Dundee's Albert Square. See C Tennant, *The Radical Laird* (1970).

KINLOCH, William (fl.1580) Composer

All of Kinloch's surviving compositions are for virginals. They display a brilliance of technique and a command of keyboard texture, although there is little in the way of contrapuntal device. A command of large-scale forms is found in his *Ground* and *Battel of Pavie* – the latter a fascinating and particularly successful essay in the popular genre of battle music. A sportive *Fantasie* and a formally innovative *Galliard of the Lang Pavan* are also distinguished. His music can be sombre but it is rarely sorrowful, vivacity and tunefulness being its chief characteristics. It is possible that he is the Kinloch referred to by James Lauder in a letter implying that Kinloch was a secret agent to the imprisoned **Queen Mary**.

KINLOCH RANNOCH, Perthshire

At the east end of Loch Rannoch (although the name suggests the head of the loch at the west end), this village commands access to an area of great scenic note. The loch itself is 10 miles long, the north side affording views to **Schiehallion** and west to the hills above **Glencoe** while the south side is clothed by Rannoch Forest and the Black Wood of Rannoch, a remnant of the old **Caledonian Forest**. Here, at Dall, is Rannoch School (run on similar lines to **Gordonstoun**) and at Camghouran a burial place of the **Camerons**. From Bridge of Gaur at the head of the loch the road continues west to a dead end at Rannoch Station on the edge of **Rannoch Moor**. An obelisk in Kinloch Rannoch commemorates **Dugald Buchanan**, the Gaelic poet who was once the local schoolmaster. To the east Dunalastair is the name of the **hydro-electric** reservoir between Lochs Rannoch and Tummel, of the one-time seat of the **Struan** Robertsons, and of a wildly extravagant baronial mansion, also known as Mount Alexander, which was built in 1852. 100 years later it was abandoned and is now a sorry ruin.

KINLOCHBERVIE, Sutherland

Writing for the new *Statistical Account of Scotland* in 1840, the minister of Edderachillis stated that Kinlochbervie contained one of the two churches in his parish. He also remarked on the excellent harbours of its indented coastline facing the North Minch. 'They are sufficient to afford safe anchorage to the whole naval and mercantile shipping of Great Britain,' he boasted. Kinlochbervie is today a busy **fishing** port, and its prosperity might have been greater if the waters of the **Minch** had been closed earlier to foreign trawlers. This was provided for by the Sea Fisheries Regulation (Scotland) Act of 1895, but it lay dead on the statute book until 1964, doubtless through the influence of distant powerful lobbies.

KINLOCHHOURN, Inverness-shire

Such is the tilt of the Highlands that Kinlochhourn on the west coast is barely a mile from the east-west watershed (Lochs Garry and **Quoich**, beside which the single track road to Kinlochhourn winds gently uphill, drain into Lochs Oich and **Ness** and so to the Moray Firth). The final descent to Kinlochhourn was rated by Sir J Lubbock 'one of the most striking examples of desolate and savage scenery in Scotland' and a fine example of 'ice action'. Kinlochhourn itself consists of little more than a dead end, a shooting lodge, and some fields and foreshore. That it once supported a considerable population was largely thanks to the **herring** which invaded Loch Hourn in such shoals that boats became stuck in them and buckets of fish could be obtained by the scoopful. There is a graphic description in Pennant. From Kinlochhourn tracks lead to Barrisdale and Inverie in road-less **Knoydart** and to Corran, Arnisdale and Glen Beag in **Glenelg**.

KINLOCHLEVEN, Argyll

At the head of Loch Leven and bisected by the river Leven, which is also the **Argyll**/Inverness boundary, Kinlochleven is actually in two counties. The **Inverness-shire** bit is properly Kinlochmore and boasts a waterfall known, like many others, as the Grey Mare's Fall. It is rated 'one of the best half-dozen great falls in Scotland' (Louis Stott). Descending past spectacularly sited Mamore Lodge, the burn responsible launches itself from the top of a cliff face to drop 60m into a hidden gorge. Kinlochleven, hemmed in by hills, bypassed by the **Ballachulish** Bridge, and starved of sun if not rain, owes its dour aspect and its very existence to the British Aluminium Company whose smelter was opened in 1908. The Blackwater reservoir and the company's hydro scheme were created by damming the Leven whose considerable catchment area south of **Ben Nevis** is also owned by the company. Happily a suggestion that the town be renamed Aluminiumville was not adopted. By 1999 the British Aluminium (renamed Alcan) workforce, which at its peak had stood at over 200, was down to 60 workers, and the company announced plans to close the smelter completely in the year 2000.

KINLOSS, Moray

Abbeys and airfields typify the Laigh of **Moray**; Kinloss has both. Compared to the RAF station, the Cistercian abbey is an insignificant ruin, its most prominent feature the gable of a 16th century tower house itself constructed out of the ruins of the abbot's house. But once Kinloss was a most important monastery, founded by **David I** in 1151, generously endowed, and the parent house of **Deer** and **Culross**. Edwards I and III both stayed here. Its abbots were entitled to a seat in Parliament and included **Robert Reid**, later Bishop of **Orkney**, President of the Court of Session and 'founder' of **Edinburgh University**. At the **Reformation** it was seized by Edward Bruce, who became **Commendator** and Baron Kinloss; his son Thomas was created **Earl of Elgin** by **Charles I**. Soon after, Cromwellian forces removed much of the Abbey's masonry to construct a fort in **Inverness**. Latterly the graveyard, like so much else in the vicinity, has accommodated more airmen than abbots.

KINNEFF, Nr Inverbervie, Kincardineshire

During the Cromwellian siege (1651–2) of **Dunnottar** it was to Kinneff Church that the Honours of Scotland (crown, sceptre and sword [see **Regalia**]) were smuggled for safety. One version of the much-told story awards the credit to Christian Grainger, wife of the incumbent Rev James Grainger, who on a visit to the castle hid the regalia about her person and boldly walked out through the enemy lines; the Cromwellian commander is said to have helped her to mount her horse. More plausibly another version says that it was the Graingers' servant who, making a practice of gathering seaweed at the base of Dunnottar's cliffs, there retrieved the regalia when they were lowered to her and conveyed them to her master in a creel of dulse. Grainger then concealed them beneath his pulpit where they remained, except for monthly airings, until the Restoration. A plaque recalls the bravery of the Graingers and a monument that of Sir George Ogilvy, commander of Dunnottar. But the church itself is an 18th century replacement, albeit 'an excellent example of a substantial T-plan Scottish kirk'. Three miles north and part of the same parish is the cliff-top **fishing** village of Catterline, latterly much patronised by artists including **Joan Eardley**.

KINNEIL HOUSE, Bo'ness, West Lothian

Kinneil House was built in the 1540s-50s for **James Hamilton, 2nd Earl of Arran** and **Duke of Châtelherault**, on lands given to the Hamilton family by **Robert I**. The house consists of two distinct sections, a fortified tower house dating from 1546 and an adjacent (and later connected) three-storeyed 'palace' added from 1553. The tower house was ruined during Châtelherault's exile in France after the abortive **Chaseabout Raid** (1565) and remained so until 1677 when **Anne, Duchess of Hamilton** rebuilt and extended it by the addition of two square towers linking the house with the palace. From c1760–75 Kinneil was leased to Dr John Roebuck, one of the founders of the **Carron Company**. During Roebuck's tenure and with his encouragement, **James Watt** built the first full-scale steam engine in one of the estate cottages which was converted into his workshop. The educationalist, writer and philosopher **Dugald Stewart** lived at Kinneil from 1809 until his death in 1828, but thereafter the house fell into disrepair. It was scheduled for demolition in 1936, a process averted by the discovery of remarkable 16th and 17th century tempera wall and ceiling paintings hidden behind later panelling. Restoration work followed and in 1975 the house was taken into state care. The easternmost section of the **Antonine Wall**, which ended at **Bo'ness**, passed between Kinneil House and Watt's workshop, and although no trace is visible here, the remains of an Antonine fortlet lie about half a mile to the west, finds from which are on display in the small museum.

KINROSS, Kinross-shire
Though on the western shore of **Loch Leven** and astride the main road north to **Perth**, Kinross was 'a sleepy little town' in 1898; now bypassed by the M90 it is scarcely any livelier. The Tolbooth (17th century) was restored and redecorated by **Robert Adam** whose father **William** lived at Blairadam, four miles south. North, Burleigh Castle near Milnathort, ancestral home of the **Balfours of Burleigh**, has an early 16th century tower, square and now roofless, to which was added in 1582 an adjoining range terminating in an end tower. Still intact, this distinctive tower has a rounded base which is corbelled out to a square and gabled attic room. Nearby in the vicinity of the two **standing stones** of Orwell several Bronze Age cists and burials have been excavated. Adjacent to Kinross itself and facing **Loch Leven Castle** with 'one of the most perfect landscape gardens in Scotland' running down to the loch, Kinross House is the renowned creation of **Sir William Bruce**, previously of **Balcaskie** (Fife). Bruce acquired the Kinross estate in either 1675 or 1681 and seems to have planned a residence for the Duke of York (**James VII**) but to have proceeded with it for himself. Construction began about 1685, towards the end of his career, and the result is the most dignified and best preserved of his Palladian mansions. Defoe's verdict, 'the most beautiful and regular piece of architecture in all Scotland, perhaps in all Britain', has been echoed by succeeding generations. The one-word motto above Sir William's arms on an internal pediment is 'IRREVO-CABILE'.

KINROSS-SHIRE
Scotland's second smallest county before the local government reorganisation of 1975, Kinross-shire comprised 52,025 acres (21,070ha) situated in central Scotland to the south-east of **Perthshire** and west and north-west of Fife. The largest natural feature was **Loch Leven** (14 sq.m/3626ha) with the **Ochil Hills** to the north, Lomond Hills to the east and Benarty and Cleish hills to the south. The main occupations were **agriculture** and textiles. There was only one burgh – **Kinross** itself. With such a small population – 6347 in 1971 – the county was paired with Perthshire for administrative purposes under the Local Government (Scotland) Act of 1929. Kinross-shire had 15 representatives on a joint county council of 100, the county town having only a county clerk's office administering pre-1975 responsibilities, such as housing. In the 1975 reorganisation, Kinross-shire was entirely absorbed into Perth & Kinross District of Tayside Region, and with the abolition of the regions in 1995 the county became known as Perthshire & Kinross.

KINTAIL, Ross & Cromarty
This district in Wester **Ross**, scenically one of the finest, comprises a triangle of shoreline, hill and glen between Lochs Duich and Long (the two arms of Loch Alsh) and extending inland to the watershed and the heads of Glens Affric and Cannich. Much of it, including Ben Flada (or Attow), the **Falls of Glomach**, and the row of peaks above Glen Shiel known as The Five Sisters, belongs to the **National Trust for Scotland** whose visitor centre is at Morvich. Historically Kintail is associated with the **Mackenzies**, who were Lords of Kintail before they became **Earls of Seaforth**, and with the Macraes whose loyalty to the Mackenzies as their hereditary keepers of **Eilean Donan Castle** won them the sobriquet of 'Mackenzie's shirt of mail'. In 1719 the **5th Earl of Seaforth** and his companions chose Eilean Donan and Kintail as their mainland base when endeavouring to raise the **Jacobite** clans. The expedition ended disastrously at the **Battle of Glenshiel**, an event recalled by **Dr Johnson** and **James Boswell** as they passed the site in 1773. In no mood for Boswell's platitudes, Johnson pounced on his companion's description of one of The Five Sisters as 'immense'; it was just 'a considerable protruberance'. But when confronted by a crowd of Macraes who had never tasted bread and spoke not a word of English, the Doctor, sensing novelty at last, noticeably mellowed.

KINTORE, Nr Inverurie, Aberdeenshire
This village-size burgh, ribboning the A96, is blessed with a stately town house of the 1740s plus a clock tower of 1772. Nearby is the ruined tower of Hallforest Castle, a lairdship granted to Sir Robert Keith, **Robert I**'s Knight **Marischal**. Two miles north-east across the **Don**, Balbithan Castle/House is an L-plan tower house in which the wing (1630) is unusually the same length as the main block. It was radically altered in the 19th century but retains its charm.

KINTYRE, Argyll
The peninsula of Kintyre (Gaelic *ceann-tire*, 'land's end') is a 40-mile long finger of land, averaging 8 miles in width, pointing to the coastline of Antrim, the ancestral home of the Scots who settled **Argyll** before AD 500. Only the 12 miles of the North Channel separate the Mull (head or tip) of Kintyre from Ireland, with which there were close links, notably when under the control of the MacDonalds of Dunivaig and the Glens.

The main town is **Campbeltown**, a **royal burgh** founded in 1607 as a 'plantation' of Lowland settlers intended to bring peace to a turbulent area. Its wealth was based on **whisky** distilling and **fishing** – both industries now sadly in decline. A small shipyard, seafood processing, a clothing factory, some light industry and **tourism** provide employment. Sheep, beef **cattle**, dairy farming and **forestry** are the basis of the rural economy of Kintyre.

The underlying **geology** of the peninsula consists mainly of mica schists, with outcrops of epidiorite and economically important areas of Old Red Sandstone and Carboniferous deposits. The sandstone was used to build the tenements of Campbeltown, while **coal** measures were exploited from the time of **James IV** until 1967, when the post-war Argyll Colliery at Machrihanish was closed. The mining village of Drumlemble was connected to Campbeltown first by a coal **canal** (1794) and then by a **railway** (1877–1931). From 1901 until its closure the Campbeltown and Machrihanish Light Railway – always known as 'the wee train' – carried passengers to the hotels and championship golf course at Machrihanish.

Kintyre has a rich archaeological heritage. In the **Campbeltown** Museum are Mesolithic flints, Neolithic pottery from chambered **cairns**, and finds from Bronze Age cists, including a jet necklace. **Standing stones** dot the landscape, and many hills are topped by Iron Age forts and **duns**, as at Dun Skeig, Bealloch Hill and Kildonan.

At the north end of the peninsula a narrow neck of land joins Kintyre to the rest of Argyll at **Tarbert**, a small fishing port and yachting centre overlooked by the ruins of a medieval royal castle. Here **Magnus Barelegs** had himself pulled across the isthmus in a skiff in 1098 to claim Kintyre for the Norse. On West Loch Tarbert is the ferry terminal of Kennacraig, linking Kintyre with **Islay**, **Jura** and **Colonsay**. The main road to Campbeltown runs down the west side of the peninsula with fine sea views, through the villages of Whitehouse, Clachan, Tayinloan (ferry to **Gigha**), Muasdale, Glenbarr, Bellochantuy and Kilkenzie.

On the east coat of Kintyre the main villages are **Skipness** (13th century castle), Claonaig (linked by ferry to Lochranza in **Arran**), Carradale, **Saddell** (ruined Cistercian abbey and castle) and Peninver.

At the bottom of the peninsula is the village of Southend, site of a massacre following the surrender of Dunaverty Castle in 1647. A winding, single track road continues to the Mull of Kintyre, famous for its lighthouse (1820) and as the subject of a popular song by Paul McCartney. On 2 June 1994 the Mull of Kintyre was the scene of the RAF's worst peacetime accident when an RAF Chinook helicopter on a flight from Belfast to Inverness crashed into the hillside, killing all 29 people on board – 4 crew and 25 of Northern Ireland's most senior police and intelligence experts.

KIPPEN, Stirlingshire

A village of some character with 18th century inn and smithy, Kippen faces across **Flanders Moss** to the **Trossachs**, backing onto and up the Fintry Hills. 'Oot o' this world and intae Kippen' doubtless refers to this commanding situation or perhaps to the villagers' reputation as rigid **Conventiclers**. In the 1691 'Hership of Kippen' **Rob Roy MacGregor** harried the neighbourhood, made off with all its cattle, and defeated a detachment of dragoons sent to intercept him. Jean Key, for whose abduction his son (**Robin Oig MacGregor**) would be hanged, lies buried in the churchyard. **Sir David Young Cameron** once stayed in the village and here painted some of his finest landscapes.

In 1890 Duncan Buchanan, a gardener from **Culzean Castle**, set up a market garden in the village of Kippen specialising in vines. He planted several, one of which, of the Gros Colman variety, was to flourish in an extraordinary way over the next 70 years. A huge glasshouse was built, 200 yards long, with hot-water pipes heated by an anthracite boiler; by 1900 the vine was bearing 600 bunches of grapes, a yield that increased to an annual average of 2000 bunches with a record 3249 in 1963 – individual bunches weighing as much as 8 or 10 lbs; by 1960 the vine covered an area of 5000 sq ft, its main stem measuring 55 inches in diameter. In 1922 the Kippen Vine was recognised as the largest indoor vine in the world (later recorded in *The Guinness Book of Records*), the glasshouse was opened to the public for an entry charge of sixpence and grapes from the Kippen Vine were sold in the best stores of **Edinburgh**, **Glasgow** and London. But as imported grapes became plentiful and cheap, and labour and heating costs increased, the vine ceased to be profitable and it was put up for sale. When no buyer materialised Selby Buchanan, son of Duncan and cultivator of the vine since 1933, himself sawed through the main trunk in early 1964. Today a housing estate stands where the vine grew.

KIRK, Sir John (1832–1922) Consul-General

Born in Barry, near **Dundee**, the son of a minister, John Kirk studied medicine at **Edinburgh University** and, after a short period at the Royal Infirmary, went to the Crimea as a medical officer. His first botanical collections were in the Mediterranean, including Mount Olympus and Mount Ida. He then joined **David Livingstone** on his second Zambesi expedition (1858–63) as naturalist and physician. Their explorations took them to the Shire valley and highlands in the south of present-day Malawi (the highlands in particular Kirk thought well suited to European settlement). He made the first botanical collections from the region, including the arrow poison plant and important heart drug *Strophanthus kombe*.

So highly was Kirk regarded as an explorer that **Sir Roderick Murchison** of the Royal Geographical Society suggested he might lead the 1866 expedition to Lake Victoria. (But would Stanley have bothered to go looking for Kirk?) Instead he was appointed HM Vice-Consul and surgeon in Zanzibar (where he established a fine botanical garden) and assisted Livingstone, who had taken the leadership himself, to launch the expedition and then acted as its agent and conduit with the world. Stanley criticised him for not keeping the expedition adequately supplied, but relations were later patched up and at Livingstone's funeral in London Kirk was a pall-bearer along with Stanley and **James Grant**.

He returned to Zanzibar as Consul-General (1873) and then political agent (1880), cultivating a relationship with the Sultan on which were laid 'the foundations of British power in East and Central Africa' (A Moorehead). This began with what amounted to a deal whereby the Sultan would close his slave market in return for continued British support of his sovereignty. German ambitions in the area were resolutely met but the eventual Anglo-German carve-up (1886) abruptly reversed this policy and Kirk returned to London. He played an active part in winning concessions for **William MacKinnon**'s British East Africa Company (1887) and was knighted in 1881. He retired to Sevenoaks in Kent and died at the age of 90.

KIRK, Robert (c1641–92) Minister

Episcopal priest, later **Presbyterian** minister of **Aberfoyle**, Kirk supervised the production in London of a

Gaelic Bible and himself translated the metrical psalms into Gaelic. Now he is a recognised authority for folklore students as author of *The Secret Commonwealth of Elves, Fauns and Fairies* (1691) who reputedly spirited him away.

KIRKBEAN, Kirkcudbrightshire

12 miles south of **Dumfries** by the **Solway Firth** coast road, and a little way inland, the village of Kirkbean is proud of its claim to have been at the forefront of the 18th century agricultural revolution. The claim rests on the reputation of pioneer improver William Craik of nearby Arbigland. Kirkbean is also more proud than it used to be of its other famous son, **John Paul Jones** (1747–92), whose father was the gardener at Arbigland. Branded during his lifetime, and for many years thereafter, as a 'notorious pirate', he is now acknowledged to have been the founder of the American navy. The font in Kirkbean's church (1776) was presented in his memory to the 'officers and men of the United States Navy who served in Britain under the command of Admiral Harold R Stark' in July 1945.

The 'rude harbour' at Carsethorn on the coast a mile to the east of Kirkbean was once a staging point for the Liverpool steam-packet, which called twice a week in summer and once a week in winter to take local livestock to the lucrative markets of England. At Preston, two miles to the south, the 6-foot-high unadorned freestone market cross is thought to be all that remains of a medieval village: it was unearthed in the middle of the 18th century and re-erected on a granite base. The picturesque lighthouse on Southerness Point (1748) is the oldest in **Galloway**.

KIRKCALDY, Fife

Long known as 'the lang toun', Kirkcaldy embraces a number of once-distinct communities, the two constituent parts with the longest history being Kirkcaldy itself and the once independent burgh of Dysart. The first reference to Kirkcaldy as such was in 1128 when **David I** confirmed a grant of the shire (or estate) of Kircalethin to **Dunfermline Abbey**. By the 14th century Kirkcaldy had emerged as one of the subordinate burghs of Dunfermline Abbey. In 1451 the Abbey relinquished most of its rights over the town to the bailies and community. A few years later **James II** started to construct a coastal fortress for his French Queen **Mary of Gueldres** at Ravenscraig just to the east of Kirkcaldy. After her death **Ravenscraig Castle** became a Sinclair possession. Occupying a dramatic and strategic position on a craggy headland, Ravenscraig is a fine example of an early artillery fortification.

Further east by Dysart harbour is another late medieval ruin – the grim-looking St Serf's church tower. Resembling a laird's tower house, this tower is attached to the former St Serf's parish kirk whose documented history goes back to the 13th century. The tower served as a good navigational landmark for the sailors of Dysart and would have been a welcome refuge in times of trouble. Thanks to the growth of their trade and commerce, both towns prospered and by the 16th century were represented in the Convention of Royal Burghs. This gave them *de facto* status as **royal burghs**, although Kirkcaldy gained statutory recognition in 1644.

The basis for their prosperity was **coal**, worked in

R W Billings' drawing of Dysart, Kirkcaldy (RWB)

the area at least as early as the 15th century. As well as being a valuable export, coal provided the fuel for the manufacture of salt, another commodity which made an important contribution to the local economy. The 'Saut Toun' and 'Little Holland', descriptive names applied to Dysart, are indicative of the specialised nature of the industry of that community and also of its commercial links. Fine vernacular buildings near the harbour at the Pan Ha' (the haugh where salt pans once stood) are physical reminders of the prosperity engendered in the heyday of the 'Saut Toun'. Kirkcaldy, too, has an interesting survival at the Sailors' Walk – two 17th century houses now fused into one. The Sailors' Walk houses, like many of their Dysart equivalents, were restored by the **National Trust for Scotland**.

In both communities the seamen's guilds gained power and influence. Sailors and traders using Kirkcaldy's harbour paid a levy which went into a strong box, the Prime Gilt Box. The funds so raised helped to provide for indigent members or their dependents. The Kirkcaldy Prime Gilt Box, with its three separate locks, can be seen in the town's remarkably fine museum and art gallery.

The civil wars and the Dutch and French wars of the 17th century cost the burghs dear both in terms of ships lost and lives sacrificed. By the early 18th century Dysart was in decay, being, according to Daniel Defoe, 'a most lamentable object of a miserable dying corporation'. While Kirkcaldy too had suffered setbacks, Defoe found it to be a very well built town with clean and well paved streets. There was a shipyard for building and repairing ships and, as well as coal and salt, corn and **linen** were exported in considerable quantities. While the **Union** with England in 1707 had a detrimental effect on their trade, the growth of the linen trade and an expanded demand for coal brought about a revival in both burghs by the end of the 18th century.

Both Kirkcaldy and Dysart faced competition from new settlements founded by neighbouring lairds. It was the ensuing linear development, to the south and north-east of Kirkcaldy, that led to it being labelled 'The Lang Toun'. To the south the Linktown of Abbotshall (so named because it was located on seaside lands that had once belonged to Dunfermline Abbey) was a 17th century creation. It was the annual fair of the Linktown (created a **burgh of barony** in 1672) that survives as the famous Kirkcaldy Links Market which lays claim to being the longest street fair in Europe. Pathhead, which became notable as a centre for weaving and nail manufacture, was developed by the lairds of Dunnikier on the other side of Kirkcaldy at the top of the steep path that led to Dysart. In the 18th century the villages of Sinclairtown and Gallatown were built on the main road that led to Cupar.

The Linktown was the birthplace of **William Adam** and his even more famous son **Robert**. William, son of a Linktown stonemason, was an entrepreneur as well as the founder of a dynasty of architects. He commenced his business career in the Linktown, establishing a brick and tile works with his future father-in-law.

Another notable resident of 18th century Kirkcaldy was **Adam Smith**, who was not only brought up in the town but also wrote his great work *The Wealth of Nations* there. According to tradition it was his observation of the work of the Pathhead nailers that brought home to this pioneer of economics the advantages of division of labour. **Thomas Carlyle** was another literary figure who had a Kirkcaldy association: he taught at the Burgh School from 1816–18.

Textile manufacture, including spinning and weaving coarse linen and canvas, became a boom industry in 19th century Kirkcaldy and Dysart. Some canvas was used for backing in floorcloth manufacture, which started in Kirkcaldy in 1847 with the erection by **Michael Nairn** of a large factory in Pathhead. The invention of linoleum gave this industry a tremendous boost. The factory, opened in 1847, had been given a contemptuous nickname by local doubters. But by the end of the 19th century 'Nairn's Folly' and the other huge factories erected by local entrepreneurs were a source of considerable pride, the manufacture of linoleum having grown to be, in both financial and olfactory terms, the most noted of all Kirkcaldy's industries.

There were, however, other forms of employment, including engineering works and four potteries. The latter included Robert Heron's Gallatown Pottery, which made the now highly valued and eminently collectable Wemyss Ware [see **Pottery**]. Gallatown, along with the other industrial suburbs of Sinclairtown, Pathhead and Linktown, was incorporated into Kirkcaldy in 1876. Dysart, on the other hand, maintained its separate status until 1930.

The 1920s and 30s saw a falling away of significant industries like coal and textiles, and the complete demise of pottery manufacture. In the 1940s, however, there were spectacular new sinkings at Frances and Seafield collieries, with the exploitation of seams that extended under the Forth. But geological difficulties and fire damage caused pit closures and the 1980s saw the end of deep mining in the Kirkcaldy area. Fortunately the effect has not been too catastrophic

as Kirkcaldy has long had the benefit of a good mix of industries. The growth of electronics in particular has helped to compensate for the loss of coal and for the very considerable decline in linoleum manufacture. Floor-coverings, now mostly made of vinyl, are still a Kirkcaldy speciality. Even linoleum has been making a comeback; visitors to 'The Lang Toun' may occasionally detect that distinctive, but not unpleasant, 'queer-like smell' that emanates from what was once Kirkcaldy's best-known product:

> For I ken masel' by the queer-like smell
> That the next stop's Kirkcaldy.
> (from 'The Boy in the Train', Mary Campbell Smith, 1913)

KIRKCALDY, Sir William, of Grange (c1520–73)

Eldest son of Sir James Kirkcaldy of Grange, **James V**'s Treasurer, William shared his father's opposition to **Cardinal Beaton** and supported Henry VIII's plan to marry the infant **Queen Mary** to Edward, Prince of Wales. One of a group of Protestant **Fife** lairds involved in the murder of Beaton (May 1546), he was sent to France, where he earned a reputation as 'a valiant soldier'. Allowed to return to Scotland in 1556 under Mary's policy of conciliation between Protestant and Catholic, he opposed her marriages to **Darnley** and **Bothwell** because they did not further the pro-English cause. He was involved in the **Chaseabout Raid** (1565) and pursued **Bothwell** to **Shetland** after the Battle of **Carberry** (1567), hoping to bring him to justice for the murder of Darnley and thus rid the Queen of another disastrous husband. But he also opposed Mary's deposition and, after the murder of **Regent Moray** (1570), became one of the leaders of the Queen's Party, holding **Edinburgh Castle** for her (1571–3) until its dramatic bombardment and capture by the English-supported King's Party, whereupon he was executed.

KIRKCUDBRIGHT, Kirkcudbrightshire

Although the burgh status of Kirkcudbright (pron. Kirk-coo-bry) can only be confirmed from 1330, there was a community here in the 13th century when the ancient fortress of Castlemains or Castledykes (of which only some fragmentary foundations now remain) came into the hands of **John Balliol** as successor to the Lords of Galloway. Edward I of England is thought to have stayed here in 1300. It was a **Douglas** stronghold while they held the lordship, became Crown property [see **Stewartry**] when their power was crushed by **James II** in 1455, and was gifted with some attached land by charter of **James IV** in 1508 to the burgesses 'for the common good of the inhabitants', by which time the original castle had been partly destroyed by a Manx fleet under Thomas, Earl of Derby. In 1582 Sir Thomas MacLellan of Bombie, a kinsman of the unfortunate McLellan hanged at **Threave** by **William, 8th Earl of Douglas** in 1452, built his new **MacLellan's Castle**, the ruins of which still dominate the town.

The 17th and 18th centuries saw hard times in Kirkcudbright: Thomas Tucker commented in 1655 that although 'it is a pretty and one of the best ports on this side of Scotland . . . there are a few, and these very poore, merchants, or pedlars rather, tradeing for Ireland', a situation that did not seem to have improved by the time of Daniel Defoe's visit in the 1720s. 'Here is a pleasant Situation, and yet nothing pleasant to be seen. Here is a Harbour without Ships, a Port without Trade, a Fishery without Nets, a People without Business; and, that which is worse than all, they do not seem to desire Business, much less do they understand it.' He put this apathy down to poverty and laid the blame on the gentry: 'they will not turn their hands to business or improvement . . . for those things are not (forsooth) fit for Gentlemen.'

Yet things did improve, for by 1844 **Lord Cockburn** was full of praise: 'I doubt if there be a more picturesque country town in Scotland. Small, clean, silent and respectable, it seems (subject, however, to one enormous deduction) the type of a place to which decent characters and moderate purses would retire for quiet comfort.' The 'enormous deduction' concerned the 'dismal swamps of deep sleechy mud' exposed in the heart of the town by the ebbing tide. He would be pleased to know that the tidal marshland has since been drained for development, but maybe less delighted to find that the old harbour is now buried under a car park.

In the late 19th century the town was colonised by artists. Broughton House in the High Street, once the home of the Murrays of Broughton [see **Gatehouse of Fleet**], was later the home of **E A Hornel**, an early luminary of the Kirkcudbright artists' colony, who left his house, pictures, furnishings and extensive library to the town on his death in 1933. Also in the High Street is the 16th century Tolbooth, repaired and extended in the 17th century when the Mercat Cross (1610) was placed at the head of its outside stone stair. The north-west wall still boasts the town 'jougs', iron manacles by which malefactors were tethered in public punishment.

The 'kirk' of St Cuthbert (Cudberct, Cudbright), dedicated possibly as early as the 8th century but more likely in the 12th century and from which the parish took its name, stood a little way above and to the north-east of the town. The churchyard has memorials to several **Covenanters** as well as one to 'William Marshall, Tinker, who died 28th Nov'r. 1792 at the advanced age of 120 years'.

KIRKCUDBRIGHTSHIRE

Before the **local government** reorganisation of 1975, this county in south-west Scotland was also known as the **Stewartry** of Kirkcudbright, as for centuries before the democratisation of local government it came under the jurisdiction of a royal steward appointed by the **Balliol** family in the 14th century. Its area of 574,024 acres (232,479ha) was bordered by **Wigtownshire** to the west, **Ayrshire** to the north and **Dumfriesshire** to the east, with 50 miles of irregularly indented coastline on the Solway Firth. The northern half of the county was hilly, its highest point being Merrick at 2764ft/842m. The principal rivers were the **Dee**, Ken, Cree and Ure. **Agriculture** was the principal occupation for the somewhat sparse population of 27,375 (1971) as well as aggregate workings. Along with neighbouring Wigtownshire, this was one of only two mainland counties in Scotland whose boundaries

did not require redesignation under the Local Government (Scotland) Act of 1889.

Kirkcudbright was the county town, although **Castle Douglas** and **Dalbeattie** were slightly more populous, the other small burghs comprising **Gatehouse** and **New Galloway**. In the 1975 local government reorganisation most of the county was transformed into the Stewartry District of Dumfries and Galloway Region, and in the 1995 reorganisation, together with Wigtownshire, became part of the Dumfries and Galloway Council Area.

KIRKINTILLOCH, Dunbartonshire

The oldest burgh in Dunbartonshire, Kirkintilloch can also claim to have produced the oldest **railway** (1826) and the oldest motor-bus (1912) in the county. The Kirkintilloch-Monkland Railway was opened to carry **coal** from the Monklands area to the Forth & **Clyde Canal**. Coal-mining was one of the main local industries in the 1830s and beyond. However handloom-weaving was, for a long time, the main preoccupation for local people. West of **Cumbernauld** and sheltered by the Campsie Hills, Kirkintilloch boasts a former Secretary of State for Scotland, **Thomas Johnston**, who was in office during most of World War II.

KIRKOSWALD, Ayrshire

Four miles south-west of **Maybole** on the main A77 **Ayr-Stranraer** road, the village of Kirkoswald is another compulsory stop on the **Burns** Trail. In 1775, at the age of 16, the future poet was sent to stay with his maternal uncle at nearby Ballochneil farm in order to study mathematics and land-surveying under Hugh Rodger, the Kirkoswald dominie. The church attended by Burns, now ruined but with a fine collection of 18th century tombstones, was replaced in 1777 by the present parish kirk designed by **Robert Adam** (currently working on **Culzean**) at the expense of David, Earl of Cassillis. The most famous house in Kirkoswald, however, is Johnnie Souter's Cottage. Built in 1785–6 by John Davidson, the village souter (cobbler) and the 'ancient, trusty, drouthy cronie' of *Tam o' Shanter*, the charming, single-storey thatched cottage with flag floors and box beds has been restored by the **National Trust for Scotland** and is open as a museum.

KIRKWALL, Orkney

The name Kirkjuvagr, Church Bay, appears first in the *Orkneyinga Saga* under the date 1046, nearly a century before the building of its Cathedral of St Magnus begun. The saga describes in graphic detail how **Earl Magnus** was murdered by his cousin Earl Haakon on **Egilsay** and buried in **Birsay**, where miracles attributed to his sanctity led to his canonisation in 1135. The sister of Magnus was married to a Norwegian named Kol, who persuaded his cousin **Rognvald** to swear that he would build a minster in honour of his uncle if he should gain the earldom. Both came to pass. Work was started on the Cathedral in 1137, and in 1965 a chapel of St Rognvald was designated within it. Here may be seen carved figures of Kol, St Rognvald and Orkney's first Bishop William, designed by **Stanley Cursiter** and carved by Reynold Eunson, both Orcadians.

The earliest work was executed by masons of the

Cathedral of St Magnus, Kirkwall (RWB)

Durham school, and as it continued into the 13th century there is evidence to suggest that a French architect and masons were engaged. The warm red stone was quarried nearby, but the yellow sandstone with which it alternates so effectively is thought to have been brought from the isle of **Eday**. The Cathedral of St Magnus in Kirkwall and that of **St Mungo** in **Glasgow** are the only pre-**Reformation** cathedrals in Scotland that remain structurally complete.

A Bishop's Palace was built beside the church at the same time, and in it Haakon IV of Norway died on his way home in 1263, after his unsuccessful attempt to assert his sovereignty over his Hebridean possessions. Before the end of the 13th century **Margaret of Norway**, infant heir to the Scottish throne, died on the sea voyage to her kingdom. Her body lay in the Cathedral until it could follow that of the great King Haakon back to Norway. **Bishop Robert Reid**, founder of **Edinburgh University**, added the round tower of the palace which remains the best-preserved feature of the ruin today.

When **James III** acquired Orkney he bestowed the Cathedral on the provost, bailies, council and community by the same charter of 1486 in which he erected Kirkwall into a **royal burgh**. John Mooney's *The Cathedral and Royal Burgh of Kirkwall* (1943) offers a perspicacious explanation for this eccentric grant.

Opposite the Cathedral entrance stood premises in which members of the clergy were housed, and here Archdeacon Gilbert Foulzie, the first Protestant minister of Kirkwall, established himself. It was he who added the arched gateway that guards the courtyard in 1574. Early in the 17th century a tight-fisted Baikie of

Tankerness acquired it as his town house and added the west wing. Now this mansion, which would do credit to a far larger metropolis, houses Orkney's outstanding museum.

But the most impressive secular building in a conservation area packed with architectural treasures is the Renaissance Earl's Palace which the odious **Earl Patrick Stewart** started to build in 1600, beside the Cathedral and the Bishop's Palace. He was executed in 1615 before it was completed, and after its slates were removed and sold, it became increasingly ruinous. It is the Cathedral which remains intact, and which, in **Eric Linklater**'s words, 'dominates with the negligence of eight hundred years' authority the small, self-satisfied, and thriving town of Kirkwall'.

KIRKWOOD, David (1872–1955) Labour Politician

Treasurer of the **Clyde Workers Committee** in 1916 and the most outspoken of the Labour candidates who triumphantly swept the polls in 1922, Davie Kirkwood had the full-blooded pedigree of a **Red Clydesider**. Yet, no revolutionary, he eventually went to the House of Lords. Some historians infer that Kirkwood was never that principled, others that Clydeside was never that red.

Born in the Parkhead district of **Glasgow**, he left school at 12 and became an apprentice engineer at the Parkhead Forge of **William Beardmore** & Co Ltd, munitions manufacturers. By 1914 he was chief shop steward and, though on excellent terms with Beardmore, a member of the radical **Independent Labour Party**. He endorsed the Clyde Workers Committee's defence of the status of skilled engineers against 'dilution' by semi-skilled workers (1915–16), but only to the extent of demanding that such 'dilution' be supervised by the skilled. A compromise along these lines, drawn up by his mentor and impresario **John Wheatley**, split the CWC. When Parkhead came out on strike over its implementation, the CWC withheld support; Kirkwood was amongst those arrested and deported (but only as far as **Edinburgh**). A martyr but in the cause of demarcation rather than socialism or pacifism, Kirkwood won support from the Labour Party and then from Winston Churchill, the new Minister for Munitions. On the latter's intervention he was reinstated at Beardmore's and then eagerly collaborated in boosting production. Although involved in the **George Square** riot of **Bloody Friday** 1919, he was not convicted. In the same year he was elected to Glasgow Town Council and in 1922 won the **Dumbarton** Burghs Parliamentary seat for the ILP.

Though twice suspended and invariably outspoken, Kirkwood cheerfully embraced the bonhomie of Westminster. In 1932 he switched from the ILP to the Labour Party. He continued to espouse the cause of the unemployed and homeless and is best remembered for his 1933 campaign to have work restarted on the *Queen Mary* in the aftermath of the Great Depression. During World War II he served on various committees and was ennobled as Baron Kirkwood of Bearsden in 1947. Glorying in Britain's imperial heritage while romanticising about Scottish Home Rule, the firebrand of Parkhead emitted only a cosy Bearsden glow in his final years. A fine orator and a valued friend, he shared with fellow Clydesiders like **William Gallacher** and **John MacLean** strong religious and temperance principles. Kirkwood's autobiography, *My Life of Revolt* (1935), has an introduction by Winston Churchill.

KIRRIEMUIR, Angus

A small and close-knit town of red sandstone, Kirriemuir was once a centre of hand-loom weaving and then of **jute** processing. Edwardian society knew it as the birthplace and inspiration of **J M Barrie**, whose home at 9 Brechin Road was supposedly in danger of being removed by *Peter Pan* fans to the United States until it came into the possession of the **National Trust for Scotland** and was converted into a Barrie shrine. Here is the little wash house which inspired Pan's Wendy House and, amongst the memorabilia, a letter from Captain Scott in the Antarctic to Barrie, his godfather. Kirriemuir itself provided the model for 'Thrums', setting of several Barrie sketches now largely (and perhaps best) forgotten.

West and north of the town the uplands are Ogilvy country. Sir Walter Ogilvy of Lintrathen (whose loch now supplies **Dundee**'s water) was authorised to build Airlie Castle by **James I** in 1432. A descendant was made Earl of Airlie in 1639 but in 1640 'the bonnie hoose o' Airlie' was taken and destroyed by the **Covenanting Earl of Argyll**. All that remains is part of a tower and some enclosing wall behind which stands its Georgian replacement. The Ogilvies were never without alternative accommodation. North of Kirriemuir, Cortachy Castle, a 16th century Z-plan with an additional tower in one of the angles, also fell to Argyll (1641), but was restored, then burnt by Cromwellian forces,

restored again and subsequently extended. It remains with the Earls of Airlie, the brother of the present Earl being the Hon Angus Ogilvy, husband of Princess Alexandra. Also in Ogilvy hands was nearby Inverquharity Castle (originally L-plan and 16th century). It belonged to the senior branch of the family who acquired the Nova Scotia barony of Inverquharity in 1626. Staunch Royalists, one Ogilvy was captured at **Philiphaugh** and executed in **Glasgow** (1646) while another fought at the Battle of the Boyne and composed the song 'It was a' for our Rightful King'.

By way of contrast on the other (south-east) side of the town ruined Ballinshoe (pron. Benshee) Tower exemplifies the mini tower house – two storeys and an attic, one turret, one turnpike staircase. The area is rich in **standing stones**, symbol stones and cross slabs, an excellent example being that at Cossans near **Glamis Castle**.

KISIMUL CASTLE, Isle of, Barra

Kisimul Castle gives its name to the village of Castlebay on the isle of **Barra**. Dating from the 11th century, it consists of a square keep within a curtain wall, which is shaped to fit the contours of the islet on which it stands. The ancestral stronghold of the **MacNeils** of Barra from 1427, it is similar in design to other early castles in the west of Scotland, such as **Dunstaffnage**, **Tioram**, **Mingarry** and Breachacha (**Coll**). It was bought in 1937, along with 12,000 acres of land, by the 45th MacNeil of Barra, an American architect who restored it to its present state before his death in 1970. According to clan tradition, a retainer used to announce daily from the castle walls: 'MacNeil has dined. The Kings, Princes and others of the earth may now dine.'

KNAPDALE, Argyll

Deeply indented by Lochs Coulisport and Sween [see **Castle Sween**], the district of Knapdale extends from **Tarbert** to the Crinan **Canal**. From early times settlement was mainly coastal, relying on boats; the east coast road was not made until 1790. Around 1050 the area was possessed by an Irish prince of the O'Neills, but it throve under the **Lords of the Isles** when **James IV** granted it to the **Earl of Argyll**. He imported **Campbell** kinsmen but left some older families in place – **MacNeils** and MacMillans and, at Kilberry, MacMurachies to c1600 (their Kilberry Castle is now buried within Victorian additions and privately occupied.)

Knapdale had its share of wars, but by 1700 enjoyed a flourishing **cattle** trade and had over 3000 inhabitants. Cattle from **Kintyre** passed through Tarbert and westward through the hills, on tracks traceable on aerial photographs, returning to **Loch Fyne** near Inverneill. At Keills a massive quay is where **Islay** and **Jura** stock was landed, and driven along trails marked by prehistoric **standing stones** to cross the Add at Crinan Ferry. Both routes converged on the great annual market of **Kilmichael Glassary**, where drovers assembled drafts for **Crieff** and **Falkirk**. The trade collapsed with the ending of the Napoleonic Wars, but livestock rearing remains a major industry in Knapdale.

KNOX, Andrew (1559–1633) Bishop

'The man who did most to extend crown authority in the [western] isles' (G Donaldson), Knox studied for the priesthood at **Glasgow University** and was appointed minister of **Paisley**. He helped frustrate the 1592 Spanish 'conspiracy' by **George 1st Marquis of Huntly** and other Catholic sympathisers and was appointed Bishop of the Isles (c1600). In 1608 with Lord Ochiltree he invited the principal chiefs to attend a sermon aboard a ship in the Sound of Mull and there held them prisoner. But this may have been a separate incident to that in 1609 when much the same group attended a conference at **Iona** and pledged themselves to observe Knox's Statutes of Icolmkill (ie Iona). The statutes constituted an important attempt to pacify the region on a basis other than settlement by Lowlanders, as attempted in **Kintyre** and **Lewis**, or the support and elevation of an amenable clan, typically the **Campbells**. Besides providing for the acceptance of the reformed church and its ministers, the statutes sought to make each chief responsible for the good behaviour of his clansmen by standing bond for them and regularly attending a council for the Isles. Additionally inns were to be established, **bards** and other trouble-makers suppressed, fire-arms restricted and heirs sent to the Lowlands for education. The last provision was reinforced by a ruling (1616) that only those who spoke English could inherit property. In 1611 Knox was also appointed to the see of Raphoe in Donegal and it was there that he died.

KNOX, John (c1513–72) Reformer

All his life just a priest or minister, Knox wielded such influence as a preacher that he became, and remains, the key figure of the Scottish **Reformation**. He dominates church history, larger than life, like his statues at **Glasgow Necropolis** and the **General Assembly** Building in **Edinburgh**.

Parts of his colourful life are obscured in myth including the date of his birth at **Haddington**, **East Lothian** and his university education (Glasgow or, more likely,

John Knox, from a popular engraving (SW)

St Andrews). Although ordained as a priest in the Roman church, he never had a parish appointment. Instead he studied **law**, becoming notary in c1540 then tutor to the sons of local lairds by 1544. When these gentry gave asylum to **George Wishart**, the Lutheran-influenced reformer, Knox accompanied him as protector during preaching tours of Lothian.

Wishart sent Knox away just before he was arrested and subsequently burnt at St Andrews in March 1546; Knox joined the Reformers who had retaliated by murdering **Cardinal Beaton** in May. Already an informed dissident, he was called to preach to the Reformers during their occupation of St Andrews Castle. This start to his ministry was brief. French troops of Regent **Mary of Guise** captured both the castle and Knox who spent the 19 months from July 1547 a prisoner rowing the galleys.

He seems to have had an affinity with English reformers and supported alliance with the English to counter French domination in Scotland. In February 1549 English influence aided his release. He came to the safe court of Edward VI where his denunciation of the Mass and doctrine was acceptable. Sent to the parish of **Berwick** to preach, in 1550 he moved to St Nicholas Church, Newcastle. By now he was well known for his writing as well as his preaching. He participated in the revision of the second English Prayer Book of 1552. He declined the bishopric of Rochester and a London parish in 1553 when his views became more radical. On the death of Edward he returned to Newcastle and then fled to France to avoid the persecutions of **Mary Tudor**.

He accepted a call to the English congregation in Frankfurt, but was soon in dispute over ceremonies and prayer book usage. In 1554 he went to Geneva where, under the influence of Calvin, he studied and wrote. He accepted the tenets of predestination and the Elect, both of which became part of Scottish **Presbyterian** thinking. In ten years he had moved from Wishart's Lutheran reformed faith in Scotland, through Protestant Anglican observance, to the **Calvinist** position and the disciplined structure of presbyters. Each step was further away from, and more opposed to, his Roman Catholic origins.

Visiting Scotland in 1555 and 1556 he found rapid progress in reformed influence among the aristocracy. He was able to preach and dispute in **Kyle (Ayrshire)**, Edinburgh and **Castle Campbell** before returning to a congregation in Geneva, where he stayed for two years.

His tract *The First Blast of the Trumpet Against the Monstrous Regiment of Women* (1558) aimed against Marian persecutions in England unfortunately appeared after Elizabeth I, a Protestant, had succeeded. He lost support in England and was refused a permit to visit the country although he had married an English wife in 1553. The tract was also aimed at Mary of Guise, Regent for **Queen Mary**, who married the French heir that year.

Knox ended 12 years' exile by returning to Edinburgh in May 1559 when Scottish Protestants, the **Lords of the Congregation** who had signed a 'Band' or covenant to reform the Scottish church in 1557, were in armed revolt. His sermon on 11 May at **Perth**, 'vehement against idolatry', ended in a mob riot which then despoiled churches and monasteries. But there could be no real headway until the fortuitous death of the Regent in 1560. Knox preached in **St Giles**, but had to flee Edinburgh briefly; then preached at **Stirling** where he emphasised trust in God not military might. English help in the form of a fleet and army was not refused as temporary support.

From 1559, as ordained minister of St Giles', Knox became chief inspiration and influence of the Scottish **Reformation**. Parliament abolished Papal authority, the Mass was forbidden and a Confession of Faith approved, establishing Protestantism. Knox, with five other ministers, wrote the *First Book of Discipline* to regulate parish revenue, education and provision for the poor. Church organisation was based on the Genevan pattern with elders, Kirk sessions and a General Assembly in ecclesiastical parallel to the Three Estates of parliament.

Queen Mary returned home to Scotland a young widow in 1561. She allowed the continuation of reform in return for having her own Mass undisturbed. This compromise brought a clash with Knox's principles. His condemnation of her Mass and of dancing at court resulted in the famous spirited debates between the Queen and Knox, the spokesman of the Church.

Knox refused all office, though not the salary equivalent of Superintendent. His own uncompromising views alienated some of his own supporters. In 1564, aged 50, he remarried to a 17-year-old daughter of Lord Ochiltree, a Stewart collateral. Knox approved of the murder of **Rizzio**, as he had that of Cardinal Beaton, but he had no known part in the plots or the enforced abdication of the Queen in favour of the infant **James VI** in 1567.

During such violent changes he usually made a tactical withdrawal, in this last case to Ayrshire to write and revise his *History of the Reformation in Scotland*, or to England to arrange the Anglican education of his sons by his first marriage. In his later years he was infirm from the effects of a stroke, but still able to preach in the full vehement style he learned from Wishart. His last sermon was on 9 November 1572 in St Giles'. He died on 24 November leaving a void in the leadership of the Reformation that was later filled by **Andrew Melville**.

KNOX, Robert (1791−1862) Surgeon

Born in **Edinburgh** and educated at the Royal High School, Knox graduated from **Edinburgh University** with an MD in 1814. He became an assistant surgeon in the army, was sent to Brussels in 1815 to treat the casualties from the Battle of Waterloo and to the Cape of Good Hope in 1817. Whilst there, he did research in ethnology and zoology, collecting many Bantu skulls and artefacts. He left the army in 1820 and after studying for a while in Paris, was elected a Fellow of the **Royal Society of Edinburgh** for his research on the anatomy of the eye. He became a Fellow of the **Royal College of Surgeons of Edinburgh** in 1825.

Taking over John Barclay's anatomy classes in Surgeon's Square in 1824, Knox quickly gained a reputation as an outstanding anatomist, but one indelibly tarnished by his association with Messrs **Burke and Hare**, from whom he obtained cadavers for dissection. After Burke was hanged in 1828 a committee was set up to examine Knox's role in the affair. It concluded that he was innocent of any involvement in the murders, but that he should have found out where the cadavers

came from. As a result of this notorious case, the Anatomy Act, regulating the supply of bodies to anatomy departments, was passed in 1832 and is still in force today.

In 1831 Knox resigned as Conservator of the College's museum and in 1844 he went first to **Glasgow** and then to London. In 1846 he gave popular but anti-semitic lectures on the 'Races of Man' in Manchester and Newcastle, which he published in 1850. In 1856 he became pathological anatomist to the Cancer Hospital, Brompton. He died in London and was buried in Woking in an unmarked grave. In 1966 the Royal College of Surgeons of Edinburgh laid a granite plaque on it. Knox is the subject of **James Bridie**'s play *The Anatomist* (1931).

KNOYDART, Inverness-shire

Also known as the 'Rough Bounds', the west-coast peninsula of Knoydart lies between Lochs Nevis ('Heaven') and Hourn ('Hell'), a mountainous limbo almost severed even from **Glen Garry** inland by the much raised waters of **Loch Quoich**. No road enters Knoydart, the nearest being at **Kinlochhourn** or **Mallaig**, whence there is a boat. The only village is Inverie on Loch Nevis with a track which bisects the peninsula to Barrisdale, passing between Meall Buidhe (3107ft/ 947m) and Ladhar Beinn (3343ft/1019m, the most westerly **Munro** on the mainland).

Knoydart's wondrous isolation and exceptionally wild character contrast with its unhappy history. Once belonging to the **MacDonells of Glengarry**, it eventually shared the fate of Glens Quoich and Garry. Promised land in Australia, the not inconsiderable population was cleared in 1853 by Josephine MacDonell and shipped off to Nova Scotia. The estate was then sold and sold again, repeatedly. In 1948 land raiders calling themselves the Seven Men of Knoydart staked a claim and were promptly taken to court by the then owner and dispossessed. Enthusiasm for self-sufficiency and isolation has latterly attracted many eager pioneers from outside the Highlands; in the 1990s several changes of ownership culminated in 1999 when a buy-out, generously funded by several public bodies, was completed and the estate, though reduced by earlier parcel sales, finally passed into the ownership of the resident community.

KYLE, Ayrshire

Ayrshire was divided into three ancient regalities or 'bailiewicks': **Carrick**, Kyle and Cunningham. Kyle, the middle one, covers an area of some 380 square miles extending from the river Irvine in the north to the river Doon in the south, and is crossed from east to west by the river Ayr which divided the district into Kyle Stewart to the north and King's Kyle to the south. Its name, unlike the Kyles in the north (**Kyle of Lochalsh, Kyleakin**, etc, which come from the Gaelic *caol* − a strait), is thought to have derived from the Gaelic *coill* or *coille*, signifying 'wood' after the extensive forests which once covered the area.

KYLE OF LOCHALSH, Ross & Cromarty

The **railway**, extended with great difficulty the ten miles from Stromeferry in 1897, was the making of Kyle of

Kyle of Lochalsh station c1900 (GWWA)

Lochalsh which then replaced both **Glenelg** as the main ferry point for **Skye** and Plockton as the main port on the Lochalsh peninsula. In October 1995, almost exactly a century later, the ferry was replaced by the Skye Bridge and, deprived of its status as a terminus, Kyle's future is uncertain. Much of the peninsula, formed by Lochs Carron and Alsh, comprises the Balmacara estate of the **National Trust for Scotland**. It includes Lochalsh woodland garden, the late 18th century planned port village of Plock (now the resort village of Plockton), the crofting township of Drumbuie (to protect which the Trust claims to have fought 'the most stubborn and expensive amenity battle in history') and the ruins of Strome Castle (on the north shore of Loch Carron), once a stronghold of the **MacDonells of Glengarry** but captured in 1609 (or 1603) by Kenneth Mackenzie 1st Lord of **Kintail** and blown up. Nearby Stromeferry, on

the south side of Loch Carron, was once a place of some importance, its ferry being the only means of proceeding up the west coast and its station being the end of the line. The extension of the railway and, more recently, a new road round the loch put paid to its pretensions. There could be a lesson here for Kyle of Lochalsh.

KYLEAKIN, Skye

The nearest point on **Skye** to the Scottish mainland, the village of Kyleakin is named for the strait, or 'kyle', through which the Norwegian King Haakon IV (thus 'akin') sailed in 1263 on his way to defeat at the **Battle of Largs**. For long the Skye terminus for the ferry from **Kyle of Lochalsh**, Kyleakin is now bypassed by traffic using the Skye Bridge, constructed at a cost of over £22m under the government's Private Finance Initiative and opened in October 1995. The remains of Castle Maol (or Moil), a 14th century keep, overlook the village.

LADYBANK, Fife

The Howe of Fife, once marsh from which the monks of **Lindores** extracted **peat**, was drained in the 19th century and then crossed by the Forth–**Tay railway**. Where this joined the line from **Perth** became Ladybank Junction around which grew up the **linen** manufacturing town of the same name. The station, dating from 1847, is one of the oldest in Scotland basically unaltered. At Monimail to the north stands **Melville House** with Fernie Castle (16th–19th centuries) to the east of it. West, near Collessie, are numerous prehistoric sites including the forts of Maiden and Agabatha Castles, several tumuli and barrows, the Newton (9ft/2.7m high and once sculpted) and the Collessie **cairns** (excavated in 1876–7 when over 2000 cartloads of stones were removed to get at the few relics).

LADYKIRK, Berwickshire

On the north bank of the river **Tweed** looking across into England, Ladykirk marks the site of an ancient ford which, before the building of a bridge in 1839, 'often gave passage to armies of invasion and other travellers' (Fullarton's *Gazetteer*). One of those travellers in 1499 was **James IV** who was nearly swept away by a sudden spate. In gratitude for his deliverance from drowning he ordered the building of a church dedicated to 'Our Lady'. 'The erection which sprang up in fulfilment of his vow was called Ladykirk and imposed its name on the parish.' Said to be one of the last churches built in Scotland before the **Reformation**, the Ladykirk has a stone-slabbed roof supported by massive external buttresses and a square three-storeyed tower surmounted by a later belfry which may be by **William Adam**.

LAGGAN, Loch, Inverness-shire

Like other lochs, Laggan at the headwaters of the river Spean is four miles longer and several feet deeper thanks to a **hydro-electric** dam. Its chief ornament, on the south shore, is Ardverickie, a 19th century Disneyland castle of turrets and towers which greatly took **Queen Victoria**'s fancy. Her visit, however, coincided with a period of torrential rain. She decided not to buy it and chose **Balmoral** instead. It was built (1840) by the Marquess of Abercorn and is still privately owned.

LAING, Alexander Gordon (1793–1826) Explorer

One in a long line of Scottish venturers into the African interior (**Park**, **Bruce**, **Campbell**, **Clapperton**, **Grant**, **Livingstone**), Alexander Gordon Laing was the son of an **Edinburgh** schoolmaster. As an officer in the Royal African Colonial Corps, he made three sorties into West Africa from Sierra Leone before arriving in Tripoli in 1825 with a commission from the Colonial Office to cross the Sahara to Timbuctu and the mysterious river Niger. While waiting for the necessary permissions he fell in love with the daughter of the British Consul and, four days before his departure for the interior, he persuaded her father to marry them. This he did reluctantly and on the condition that the couple did not cohabit 'until the marriage can be confirmed by a clergyman of the Established Church' on Laing's return. He never did return.

Although there were recognised caravan routes to Timbuctu, the desert was controlled by raiding tribes who lived almost entirely on the plunder of passing caravans. Laing and his party, which included two English boatbuilders whose skills he intended to use on the Niger, travelled safely for five months before being attacked by Tuareg tribesmen who raided their possessions and left them for dead. His manservant, his guide and the two boatbuilders were indeed dead; Laing was not, in spite (as he wrote to his patient wife in Tripoli) of 'twelve sabre cuts to the head, from which much bone has come away, a divided ear, three severed fingers, one shattered wrist, a badly gashed leg and a musket ball through hip and back'. Two months recuperating in the tent of one of his camelherds set him back on the road, and on 13 August 1826 he stumbled into Timbuctu, the first Christian ever to reach the fabled city. He stayed only long enough to take a tour of the town and despatch the letter to his wife before leaving by the most direct route to the west coast. Then, like so many others, he disappeared into the void of Africa.

Two years later the story filtered back to Tripoli; just outside Timbuctu Laing and his remaining servant had been attacked again; both men were killed, Laing decapitated and his volumes of painstaking notes, maps and observations scattered to the desert winds.

LAING, David (1793–1878) Antiquary

A prolific editor of Scottish texts, Laing was born to books, his father William being a highly successful bookseller and antiquarian book dealer with premises in **Edinburgh**'s **Canongate**. David's education was curtailed in favour of an apprenticeship under his father during which he toured the Continent as a discriminate buyer. A partner in 1821, he was already editing collections of **ballads** when in 1823 he became secretary and mainstay of the Bannatyne Club (for which he edited 39 editions) and in 1826 a Fellow of the **Society of Antiquaries** (to whose *Transactions* he invariably contributed). The Librarianship of the **Signet Library** followed in 1837. 'No wise man will undertake a literary work on Scotland without taking counsel with Mr Laing' (Cosmo Innes). Amongst the literary giants whose texts he edited were **William Dunbar**, **Sir David Lindsay** and **Robert Henryson**; historical texts included the journals and letters of **Robert Baillie** (for 1637–62) and John Colville (for 1582–1603); best-known is his 6-vol *Works of John Knox* (1849–64). He died unmarried but the possessor of a magnificent library which took over a month to auction.

LAING, Ronald David (1927–89)
Psycho-analyst

Glasgow-born, Laing graduated from the university's Medical School and practised as a psychiatrist before moving to London in 1956 to train in psycho-analysis. At the Tavistock Clinic he specialised in schizophrenia and in the 1960s wrote a succession of books, including *The Divided Self* and *The Self and Others*, which popularised the idea that insanity was largely induced and that schizophrenia was a strategy adopted by the sufferer 'in order to live in an unliveable situation'. His rapport with the insane and his efforts to provide them with a more compassionate environment won wide acclaim. He became something of a cult figure in the late 1960s, experimenting with psychedelic drugs and spending a year (1971–2) practising meditation under Buddhist tutelage in Sri Lanka. A brilliant communicator with a striking presence and much charm, he wrote poetry and was an accomplished pianist. His later works contain much speculation and suggest a retreat from earlier certainties. Fittingly he died in the '60s sunset-retreat of St Tropez.

LAIRG, Sutherland
This is the only entirely land-locked parish in **Sutherland**. Compensation is provided by Loch Shin, the largest freshwater loch in the county, 24 miles long and an average of one mile in width. At its south-east end, where there is a **hydro-electric** dam, stands the township of Lairg. The parish also contains in Ben Clibreck one of the county's highest hills, beside which the pass ran north from the Sutherland earldom into the **Mackay** province of **Strathnaver**. In addition to the cattle sales, every August Lairg holds the largest one-day sheep sale in the United Kingdom.

LAMBERTON, Berwickshire
Three miles from **Berwick**, Lamberton belonged to the monks of **Coldingham** until the **Reformation**. Here on 1 August 1503 **Margaret Tudor** was given into the safe-keeping of **James IV**'s Commissioners on her way to **Edinburgh** to marry the Scottish King. She returned to the church in June 1517 as a widow. It is now a ruin.

LAMBERTON, William (d.1328) Churchman
Bishop of **St Andrews** from 1298, Lamberton became a Guardian of the Kingdom and assisted at the coronation of **Robert I** in 1306 at **Scone**. Captured at the Battle of **Methven** and imprisoned in England by Edward II, after **Bannockburn** he returned to complete building his cathedral in 1318.

LAME HECTOR (Eachann Bacach) (c1600–post1650) Gaelic Poet
Hector Maclean was probably in some sense an official poet in the family of the **Macleans** of **Duart** in **Mull**. He is given the title *aos-dàna*, which is applied to several 17th century poets who are not professionals in the classical-**Gaelic** sense. Six or seven of his poems survive, the most remarkable being *A' Chnò Shamhna* ('The Hallowe'en Nut'), an elegy for Sir Lachlan Maclean of Duart. This is the earliest instance we have of the extended strophic paragraph metre, and the poem is rich in language and imagery. For Eachann Bacach's works, see Colm O Baoill, *Bàrdachd Chloinn Ghill-Eathain*, 1979.

LAMMERMUIR HILLS, East Lothian/ Berwickshire
These high rolling uplands comprise the southern third of **East Lothian** and the northern half of **Berwickshire**, run from **St Abb's Head** on the east coast to the Gala Water in the west, and form the eastern extremity of the Southern Uplands. Named after Lammer Law, one of the highest points at 1733ft/582m, they are for the most part 'an extensive curvature of wild, cheerless heights, nowhere bold and imposing in aspect, and often subsiding into low rolling table-lands of bleak moor'; appropriately gloomy as a setting for **Walter Scott**'s *Bride of Lammermoor*, although the drama on which the novel was based was in fact played out in **Wigtownshire** [see Bladnoch].

LAMOND, Frederic (1868–1948) Pianist and Composer
Though chiefly remembered for the power and depth of his Beethoven playing, Lamond was a pupil and renowned interpreter of Liszt. His compositions include a *Symphony in A*, a *Cello Sonata*, an orchestral overture *Aus Dem Schottischen Hochlande* in the Scottish-Germanic vein, an energetic *Piano Trio* and a set of *Clavierstucke, Opus I*, which are subtle and beautiful studies in keyboard writing. He spent most of his life in Germany but returned to Britain with the rise of Hitler and died in **Stirling**.

LAMONT, Donald (Dòmhnall MacLaomainn) (1874–1958) Gaelic Writer
Lamont came from **Tiree** and spent the years from 1908–46 as minister of **Blair Atholl**. He edited the **Gaelic** supplement of *Life and Work* from 1907–50, contributing a long series of essays on a wide range of subjects: nature, current affairs, literature: etc. But his most individual essays are in the form of a sustained, humorous but critical commentary on an imaginary parish which he calls Cille-Sgumain. His writing was an important influence in the growth of fluid, relatively uncomplicated Gaelic prose. A selection from his huge output was edited in Thomas M Murchison, *Prose Writings of Donald Lamont*, 1960.

LANARK, Lanarkshire
For a **royal burgh** and once county town of considerable repute and undoubted antiquity, Lanark is poorly endowed with tangible remains. The castle where **William the Lion** granted a charter to **Ayr** c1197 and which subsequently featured in the **Wars of Independence** exists only as a mound and in the name of Castlegate. Of the medieval parish church dedicated to **St Kentigern** only some pointed arches of the north aisle (15th century) survive plus the bell, often recast and now located in 'the ungainly parish church of St Nicholas' (1777). Here too is a huge statue of **William Wallace** who may once have lived in Castlegate. Legend (mostly Blind **Harry**'s) has it that, to avenge the killing of his wife, Wallace and his supporters raised the standard of revolt in 1297 by attacking Lanark's English garrison and killing its commander.

As if to compensate for the lack of architectural antiquities, the burgh clings to its social heritage. Lanimers, celebrated in early June, recalls the ancient Riding of the Marches, a civic procession to inspect the burgh's boundaries which once had a religious dimension and is still celebrated with great gusto. Less well known, Whippity Scourie 'takes place at 6 pm on the 1st March and is essentially an exorcism ceremony' (I MacLeod and M Gilroy).

As a **Covenanting** centre in the 17th century, Lanark was one of the towns in which parts of the body of **Robert Baillie of Jerviswood** were exhibited after he was hung, drawn and quartered in 1684. Jerviswood House, his home and that of his daughter-in-law **Lady Grizel Baillie**, still stands, an L-plan tower with extensions but without castellations. Smyllum Park (c1740 but refronted in 1800) more than compensates with square towers, round towers and a great central drum tower. It was built for William Smellie, the gynaecologist, but is now a 'forlorn wreck' and the subject of conservationist ire. Other noted sons of Lanark include **Robert MacQueen** (Lord Braxfield) and **'Lugless Will' Lithgow**. 19th century travellers patronised Lanark as a centre from which to visit the Falls of Clyde, **New Lanark**, Cartland Bridge (**Telford**, 1822–3) and Cartland Crags. To these attractions may now be added **Craignethan Castle** and the inevitable country park, here that of Lanark Moor. The surrounding district is still a major producer of fruit and now salad crops, mostly under glass.

LANARKSHIRE

Before the **local government** reorganisation of 1975, Lanarkshire was one of Scotland's most important counties, occupying the **Clyde** basin from the Lowther hills north-westwards all the way to the suburbs of **Glasgow**. As the relevant volume of the *Third Statistical Account* observed in 1960, 'at one extreme the pastoral parish of Dunsyre has 8 persons to the square mile, while at the other, the industrial parish of **Rutherglen** has 11,130.' The county was fringed by **Stirlingshire**, **Dunbartonshire** (detached area), **West Lothian, Midlothian, Peeblesshire, Dumfriesshire, Ayrshire, Renfrew** and the city of Glasgow, there being no fewer than 10 points on the county boundary where three counties met. The Clyde was obviously the most important river, fed by the Douglas, Avon, Nethan and Calder. The northern area was heavily industrialised, with steelmaking a major occupation, and there is an extensive belt of fruit-growing under glass in mid-Clydesdale, with agriculture the main land-use south-eastwards down the Clyde valley, which is followed by road and rail links to England. The county's highest point, 2403ft/732m, was located in the Lowther Hills, and the overall area was 535,605 acres/216,920ha (in 1961).

Hamilton was the county town, with other large burghs comprising **Airdrie, Coatbridge, East Kilbride** (a New Town), Glasgow, **Motherwell** & Wishaw, and Rutherglen, the smaller burghs being **Biggar, Bishopbriggs** and **Lanark**. In 1975 the whole county was swallowed by Strathclyde Region, but divided into seven district councils – Glasgow, Strathkelvin, Monklands, Motherwell, Hamilton, East Kilbride and Clydesdale. In the 1995 reorganisation of local government the City of Glasgow was granted its own unitary authority; Clydesdale, East Kilbride and Hamilton formed the South Lanarkshire Council Area and the remaining districts that of North Lanarkshire.

LANG, Andrew (1844–1912) Journalist

A native of **Selkirk**, Andrew Lang spent two years at **St Andrews University** and one at **Glasgow University** before winning a Snell Exhibition to Balliol College, Oxford. He was to stay at Oxford, first as a student, later as a Fellow of Merton College, until 1875. That year he married, moved to London and launched himself on a highly profitable journalistic career.

Andrew Lang first made his mark on the literary scene as a poet. Together with Austin Dobson and Edmund Gosse he formed the core of what came to be known as the 'English Parnassians'. As he grew older, however, the poetic muse left him and he turned his attention to more 'serious' matters.

With *Custom and Myth* (1884), *Myth, Ritual and Religion* (1887) and *The Making of Religion* (1898) he became one of the most authoritative voices on anthropology. His classical studies at Oxford led him first to collaborate on the translation of the *Odyssey* (1879) with S H Butcher, and the *Iliad* (1883) with Walter Leaf and Ernest Myers, and later to defend the genius of Homer in *Homer and the Epic* (1893), *Homer and His Age* (1906) and *The World of Homer* (1910).

It was in his capacity as a folklorist, however, that he started to edit his well-known 'coloured' fairy books. *The Blue Fairy Book* (first published in 1889) was followed by 11 companion volumes which were to cater to the young reading public's taste for generations to come.

Lang's biographical monographs showed a marked preference for the scapegoat. He enthusiastically took

Andrew Lang, by Sir William Blake Richmond (SNPG)

up the cudgels for such different historical characters as Joan of Arc, **Prince Charles Edward Stewart** and **Queen Mary**. Lang always aimed at a truthful reflection of his investigations even though the external evidence at times proved his original convictions wrong. His study of Scottish historical characters and mysteries reached its acme with the publication of the 4-vol *History of Scotland* (1900, 1902, 1904, 1907).

But Andrew Lang was first and foremost a journalist. He was one of the most prolific, most influential and best-paid writers of his day. Budding authors knew their career was made if their work caught Lang's favourable attention. He supported such writers as Rudyard Kipling, Henry Rider Haggard and **Robert Louis Stevenson**. Some of his articles in the *Daily News*, the *St James Gazette*, the *Sun* or the *Independent* were reprinted; many others, equally important, such as his monthly 'causerie' 'At the Sign of the Ship' (*Longman's Magazine*), were left to disintegrate on the library shelves.

Towards the end of his life lengthy retreats to Scotland grew more and more frequent. He died at Tor-na-Choille, **Banchory**.

After his death his name disappeared into obscurity. He was reproached for not having recognised the genius of great authors such as Thomas Hardy and Henry James. Instead he had championed the romance, the adventure story, or what he would call 'a good yarn'. Only recently with the re-evaluation of writers like Haggard and Stevenson has his criticism been viewed from a different, more appreciative angle. See: Marysa Demoor (ed) *Friends Over the Ocean: Letters from Andrew Lang to his American Correspondents*, Ghent, 1989; Marysa Demoor, *Dear Stevenson: Letters from Andrew Lang to Robert Louis Stevenson with five letters from Stevenson to Lang*, Louvain, 1990; Roger Lancelyn Green, *Andrew Lang: A Critical Biography*, Leicester, 1946; and Eleanora De Selms Langstaff, *Andrew Lang*, Boston, 1978.

LANG, Cosmo Gordon (1864–1945)
Archbishop of Canterbury
Born at **Fyvie**, Lang was a Church of England curate at Leeds in 1890. As Dean of Oxford he became Bishop of Stepney before being created Archbishop of York in 1908. From 1928–42 he was Archbishop of Canterbury, and on his retiral he was made Baron Lang of Lambeth.

LANG, John Dunmore (1799–1878)
Australian Minister
Born in **Greenock**, the son of a smallholder and carpenter, Lang attended **Largs** school and **Glasgow University** before being ordained and then following his brother to Australia in 1823. A rigid **Presbyterian**, he founded Sydney's first **Church of Scotland** church, numerous schools and the Presbyterian Australian College. During a long and colourful career as an outspoken patriot, a formidable propagandist and a contentious churchman, he pleaded against the use of the colony as a penal dumping ground and shuttled back and forth to Britain urging and often financing a series of emigration schemes to what he called 'the Promised Land'. Highland emigration to Australia in the 1830s and after the **potato famine** of the 1840s–50s can largely be credited to Lang's initiatives. He is also credited with

having anticipated the 1843 **Disruption** when in 1842 he was excommunicated by the established church after one of many ructions. From 1843 he served on the New South Wales legislature but continued to respond violently to criticism and was frequently penalised, sometimes gaoled. He wrote extensively on emigration and compiled *An Historical and Statistical Account of New South Wales*, 1834, modelled on **Sir John Sinclair**'s Scottish series and designed to promote Scottish emigration. He died and is buried in Sydney.

LANGBANK, Renfrewshire
On the southern shore of the river **Clyde** opposite the town of **Dumbarton**, Langbank owed its existence as a village to the opening of the **Glasgow** to **Greenock** railway in 1841 – prior to that it was a scattered community of farms. The St Vincent's Conference Centre and Holiday Home was previously known as 'The Hollies' and until 1980 functioned as a Roman Catholic boarding school for boys. There are many fine Victorian villas in the village, and Finlaystone Castle (architect Sir John Burnet) was built in the early 19th century on the site of an ancient castle of the same name. While in the ownership of James Cunningham, 14th (and last) Earl of Glencairn, Finlaystone was visited by his friend **Robert Burns**, whose initials are scratched on a window; it is now the home of the chief of Clan MacMillan. A **crannog** was excavated at Langbank in 1902.

LANGHOLM, Dumfriesshire
Eight miles from England and much engaged in the cross-border trade of reivers and drovers, Langholm became a modest industrial centre in the 19th century with **cotton** and tweed mills. Its other product was men. The Library Buildings, appropriately, were the birthplace of C M Grieve (**Hugh MacDiarmid**), whose poem on Langholm's Common Riding captures the excitement of 'the muckle toon's' July fair. In the market place the statue is of a son of the local minister, Admiral Sir Pulteney Malcolm (1768–1838) who served under Nelson in the Mediterranean, became Commander-in-Chief there in 1828, and in between commanded St Helena and its celebrated captive, Napoleon Bonaparte. His even more famous brother, **Sir John Malcolm**, is commemorated in the giant obelisk on a hill to the east. Two other brothers (out of ten) were also knighted. A place of many roads and bridges (here the Wauchope and Ewes join the Esk), Langholm also claims **Thomas Telford**, born near Westerkirk (where there is a memorial). He served his apprenticeship as a mason in the town working on the three-arched bridge over the Esk. The Duchess Bridge, a footbridge serving the **Duke of Buccleuch**'s former Langholm Lodge, is claimed as the oldest (1813) surviving cast-iron bridge in Scotland. It was designed not by Telford, but by William Keir; whether it predates Telford's better-known **Craigellachie** Bridge is debatable. Nearby **Arkinholm** was the site of the battle sometimes called the Battle of Langholm.

LANGSIDE, Battle of (1568)
On 2 May 1568 **Queen Mary** escaped from **Loch Leven Castle**, made for **Hamilton** and within a week had gathered an army of some 6000 supporters. Reluctant

to place herself completely in Hamilton hands, she resolved to make for the one important stronghold still in Marian hands – **Dumbarton Castle**, held for her by Lord Fleming. But her half-brother, **Lord James Stewart** (Regent Moray), knew the danger of allowing her to reach such an impregnable refuge. Camped at **Glasgow**, he moved to intercept her with a smaller but better-organised force under **Kirkcaldy of Grange**. The armies met at the village of Langside (now a suburb of **Glasgow**, see **Queens Park**), where the fighting lasted barely 45 minutes. Casualties were slight thanks to Moray's orders that 'prisoners were to be brought in rather than corpses', but Mary's army scattered and she herself fled first to **Dundrennan** and then across the **Solway** to England.

LANGUAGE, SCOTS

For such a small country, Scotland has a remarkably varied linguistic history. Place-name scholars have put forward various hypotheses concerning the language(s) spoken north of the Cheviots before the arrival of the **Romans**, but all we can say with certainty is that by the time of the Romans' departure in the 5th century AD, a northern form of British P-Celtic, sometimes known as Brythonic or Cumbric, was spoken in the area between the present Scottish-English border and the Forth-**Clyde** line, while a related language seems to have been the main vernacular of the **Picts** further north. These languages can best be described as an early form of Welsh.

The 5th and 6th centuries saw the arrival in southern Britain of the North Germanic Angles and Saxons, Jutes and Frisians, and the migration into western Scotland of the Gaelic (Q-Celtic) speaking Scots of north-east Ulster. In the following centuries the advancing Angles extended their new kingdom of Northumbria from the Humber estuary to the Firth of Forth, and their Germanic dialect gradually ousted the native Celtic of the **Lothians**, Borders and **Strathclyde**. Place-names such as **Leith**, **Linlithgow**, **Glasgow**, **Tranent**, **Penicuik** and **Peebles** bear witness to the ancient Gaelic inhabitants of the area, while Germanic -*ham* and -*ton* names like Whittinghame, Coldingham, Tyningham, Haddington and Mordington date from the later Anglian settlements. The vernacular of these northern Angles was one of the ancestors, if not perhaps *the* ancestor, of the Scots language.

While the Angles were establishing themselves in south-east Scotland, the Scots were sweeping east and north into the heart of Pictland. In 843 **Kenneth mac-Alpin** became King of both Scots and **Picts**, and the subsequent disappearance of the Pictish nation and its language is one of the great mysteries of Scottish history. Only the enigmatic symbol-stones of Pictland and a number of distinctive place-names survive as reminders of a once great and powerful people.

The obliteration of Pictish identity may have been hastened by the arrival in the 9th century of Scandinavian invaders who settled in large numbers in **Orkney**, **Shetland** and **Caithness**, as well as in the south-west of Scotland. The Scandinavian 'Norn' dialect of Orkney and Shetland survived well into the 18th century.

By the 10th and 11th centuries Gaelic must have been in use to some extent all over Scotland, but in the 12th century it began to lose ground to Northern English. The Normanised Kings of Scotland, particularly **David I** (1124–53), were impressed by the social and cultural innovations of Anglo-Norman England, and many Anglo-Norman and Flemish landowners were given grants of land north of the border. English and French monks were introduced in the native religious houses, and English-speaking burgesses flocked to the newly-founded **royal burghs** and **burghs of barony**. Although the upper classes spoke Norman French, the native language of most of these new immigrants was a type of Northern English heavily influenced by the Scandinavian tongue of the former **Viking** settlements of northern England. This Scandinavianised Northern English of the early burghs was to develop into the later Scots tongue, aided no doubt by the presence in the south-east of a long-established Old English dialect.

THE CHRONOLOGY OF SCOTS The language of Lowland Scotland is conventionally described as 'Older Scots' until about 1700 and 'Modern Scots' thereafter. 'Older Scots' itself can be further subdivided into 'Pre-literary Scots', 'Early Scots' and 'Middle Scots' as follows:

PRE-LITERARY SCOTS (−C1375) Until the late 14th century the nature of the spoken language must be inferred from occasional Scots words, place-names and personal names in the large corpus of Latin charters and similar documents.

EARLY SCOTS (C1375−1450) Imaginative literature in Scots commences in 1375 with the epic poem *The Brus* by **John Barbour**, Archdeacon of **Aberdeen**. Almost contemporary with this is the metrical *Legends of the Saints*, a vernacular translation of the Latin *Legenda Aurea*. From 1424 the Acts of the Scottish Parliament were written in Scots, indicating that the language was judged fit for the full range of stylistic uses or 'registers'. No doubt the earlier **Wars of Independence** had an influence on the linguistic as well as the political independence of Scotland. In England, the growing dominance of London English relegated the vernacular of northern England to the status of a provincial dialect, while the originally identical dialect north of the Cheviots became the standard language of the nation-state of Scotland, at least as far as the **Highland Line**, beyond which Gaelic still held sway.

MIDDLE SCOTS (1450−1700) The late 15th and early 16th centuries gave rise to a new flowering of Scots literature in the shape of the poets **Robert Henryson**, **William Dunbar** and **Gavin Douglas**. But to most Scots their language was still 'Inglis' (the term 'Scots' is first recorded in 1494), and the writings of Chaucer and his successors were widely admired and imitated.

This impulse towards Anglicisation grew apace at the **Reformation**, when the English Geneva Bible and an English Psalter were adopted by Scots who had no equivalent of their own. **John Knox** himself sedulously anglicised the language he employed in his writings, to the undisguised scorn of his Catholic opponent **Ninian Winzet**, who once rebuked Knox for employing 'Southeron' (ie Southern English) instead of the 'auld plane Scottis' he had learned at his mother's knee. But Winzet was making a political rather than a linguistic point, and most of his contemporaries would have found this distinction rather exaggerated.

Much of what *was* distinctive about Scots derived from foreign borrowings. From Norman and early Central French came many words originally shared with English, but which have survived only in Scots, and the Franco-Scottish or **auld alliance** of 1296–1560 undoubtedly added many more. Such words as *ashet, eal, coup, tassie, disjune* and *fash* may seem rather antiquated now, but *vennel, Hogmanay, douce* and *stovies* are not yet out of fashion.

Between the 12th and 18th centuries contacts with the Low Countries were frequent and close, and indeed many Flemish craftsmen settled in Scotland, while Scottish traders had their staple ports in the Netherlands. Dutch and German steamers were still plying to and from some east coast ports until the outbreak of World War II. To these influences we owe such Scots expressions as *craig* (neck), *coft* (bought), *dub, howf, pinkie* and even the name of that most Scottish of sports, *golf*.

MODERN SCOTS (1700–   ) The **Union of the Crowns** in 1603, and the subsequent departure of the Scottish court to London, was the beginning of the end of Scots as a full national language fit for all spheres of activity. Scottish writers began to cast their thoughts in an English mould, and **James VI** himself, on becoming James of England, set about revising his earlier Scots writings for southern readers. The **Union** of the Parliaments in 1707 accelerated the demise of the standard language of Stewart Scotland, and although the native intelligentsia were to enjoy a new Golden Age at the **Scottish Enlightenment**, they had by then reached such a stage of linguistic schizophrenia that they succumbed to the new vogue for printed lists of 'Scotticisms' to be avoided in refined speech. The philosopher **David Hume** himself compiled such a list. Meanwhile, the Scots tongue continued an underground existence as the daily vernacular of the people, and the language of popular **ballads**, proverbs and the like. As fewer and fewer of the educated classes used Scots on a regular basis, so the fallacious notion came about that Scots was no more than a debased form of 'proper' (ie Southern) English.

The '**Kailyard**' writers of Victorian times complacently went with the tide, and used Scots mainly for comic or sentimental effect. In the 20th century more committed writers such as Christopher Grieve (**Hugh MacDiarmid**) have felt obliged to ransack the Older Scots tongue in order to reinvigorate the tired modern literary language. Their linguistic experiments in the resulting 'Synthetic Scots' or 'Lallans' (=Lowlands) compel respect and admiration, but remain far from the daily speech of the average Scot. For better or worse, Scots-speakers remain wedded to their local dialects, and show little enthusiasm for an artificially revived standard Scots on the model of the Norwegian 'Nynorsk'. Even the spelling system for Lallans remains a controversial and hotly-debated issue.

This entry is headed 'Scots Language', but to what extent can Scots truly be called a language? In its literary Golden Age in the 15th and 16th centuries it may have differed as much from English as Spanish from Portuguese, or Swedish from Danish. Indeed the Scandinavian parallel is a good one, for while a linguist might describe the mutually comprehensible tongues of Denmark, Norway and Sweden as dialects of Scandinavian, the politician is forced to concede that these are the national languages of three independent sovereign states. There is some truth in the old adage that 'a language is a dialect with an army and a navy'.

LARGO, Fife

This large parish between **Leven** and **Earlsferry** on Largo Bay in the Firth of Forth was the home of two notable sea-dogs: **Sir Andrew Wood** ('the Scottish Nelson') and **Alexander Selkirk** ('Robinson Crusoe'). The latter is celebrated with a statue in the main street of Lower Largo and the Crusoe Hotel; the former in ruined Largo Tower (17th century) which stands on the site of Wood's fortalice near Largo House, and in the outline of a **canal** on which Wood could be rowed to church. The church (of Upper Largo) has a tower of 1628 and chancel of 1623 incorporated in a 19th century Gothic cruciform design. In the churchyard is a reassembled **Pictish** cross-slab, part of which once served as a drain cover. 'Almost in the same league as **Mavisbank**' (M Dean and M Miers), Largo House (1750 and at least partly John Adam) is an even more tragic case. Like other redundant mansions it was made available to Polish refugees during World War II. Considered beyond redemption after their occupancy, it was de-roofed and remains so.

North of Upper Largo, Norrie's Law is the site of a much-worked **cairn** which in 1819–22 yielded a hoard of silverware. Part of the find is thought to have been sold privately and melted down but pins, plaques and bracelets, many bearing Pictish symbols, eventually found their way into the national collection and compare in importance with the **St Ninian's Treasure**. To the west, on the Lundin Links Ladies Golf Course, three massive **standing stones** were doubtless once part of a circular setting. East, Balcarres, a tower house of 1595 submerged in baronial additions by **William Burn** and **David Bryce**, was the home of Colin Lindsay, 3rd Earl of Balcarres and a loyal supporter of the **Stewarts**, who, becoming reconciled to their exile, himself returned to settle his redundant soldiery in the specially designated village of Colinsburgh (1705).

LARGS, Ayrshire

The town's original name of Leargs is said to derive from the Gaelic term for a 'plain with a slope', and indeed the town does lie on a narrow plain between the sea and a 1500ft/457m escarpment to the east, on the **Ayrshire** coast 13 miles south of **Greenock**. The first historical reference to Largs came with suggestions of a Christian church being established there in 711. In 1263 a Norse army under King Haakon was defeated at Largs by a Scots force under **Alexander III**. The battle is commemorated by 'The Pencil' monument, 1 mile south of the town.

Until Largs became a popular summer resort in the mid-19th century, its main trades were weaving and **fishing**, with smuggling an occasionally lucrative sideline. With the arrival of the **railway** line from **Glasgow** in 1885 Largs became a favourite destination for

holidaymakers, especially during the **Glasgow Fair** when the population trebled to perhaps 30,000 people. The holiday trade declined dramatically after World War II.

Largs contains a number of important historical relics, principally the Skelmorlie Aisle, erected by Sir Robert Montgomerie in 1636. The chapel boasts a magnificent 17th century painted ceiling and an 18ft (5.4m) high monument sculpted in Dutch style with figures, fruits, instruments and weapons. A reputed medieval gallows mound stands near the Skelmorlie Aisle and there is a neolithic chambered tomb in Douglas Park. In the Skelmorlie churchyard the burial vault of **Sir Thomas MacDougall Brisbane** (sixth Governor of New South Wales) has plaques commemorating his children, Eleanor Australia and Thomas Australius MacDougall Brisbane. The local museum has some work by Victorian society photographer John Fergus.

Until recently architectural enthusiasts visited Largs to see the work of Art Deco café and cinema architect James Houston. With the demolition of Houston's outstanding Moorings café/ballroom (built 1936) little of his work now remains. Only Nardini's café/restaurant on the town's promenade survives as a reminder of the Golden Age of Scotland's seaside 1930s.

LARGS, Battle of (1263)

More a skirmish, Largs (30 September–4 October 1263) decided the future of the **Hebrides**. In 1098 **Edgar** had ceded the Hebrides to Norway, whose kings rarely exercised control over them. **Alexander III** offered to buy them back; Haakon IV indignantly refused and, learning of Scots raids on **Skye**, assembled a fleet which sailed via **Shetland**, **Orkney**, **Stornoway**, **Kyleakin** (perhaps 'Haakon's narrows') and **Oban**, gathering reinforcements including Manx ships. Rounding **Kintyre** he gave protection to **Saddell Abbey**, captured Dunaverty, and led 200 ships to Lamlash on **Arran**.

Alexander, at **Ayr**, exchanged embassies, led by Eoghann MacDougall (King of the Southern Isles, Lord of Argyll, he achieved neutrality). Many Norse crews grew impatient for loot; Haakon sent detachments to **Bute** and **Loch Lomond** (50 galleys hauled overland at **Tarbet**), and paraded the main fleet past Ayr to anchor off **Largs**. An equinoctial gale wrecked some ships and dismasted others; for four stormy days confused fighting raged along the shore, neither side able to deploy fully. On 5 October good weather enabled Haakon to withdraw; the Scots expected other landings, but the fleet broke up. Haakon died in Orkney in December. His son Magnus V accepted Alexander's offer (**Treaty of Perth**, 1266) and the King of Man submitted to Scotland at **Dumfries**.

LASSWADE, Midlothian

The section of the river North Esk between **Roslin** and Lasswade was sufficiently fast-flowing to power the paper-mills for which Lasswade was famous in the 18th and 19th centuries. Here also were **oatmeal** and barley mills, a distillery, a candle factory, an **iron** and brass foundry, a gunpowder factory and a celebrated carpet factory. Lasswade was joined with Bonnyrigg in 1929 and the gaps left by the passing of its traditional industries have been partially filled with the creation of an industrial estate. The medieval parish church (abandoned in 1793 and in ruins since the mid-19th century) was the burial place of **William Drummond of Hawthornden** (1585–1649), and Lasswade's literary fame was guaranteed when **Sir Walter Scott** spent the first six years of his married life at Lasswade Cottage where he was visited by the **Wordsworths** and **James Hogg**

LATHERON, Caithness

Situated at the junction of the A9, which runs up the coast to **Wick**, and the road across the Causeway Mire to **Thurso**, Latheron owed its growth to the 19th century **herring** boom. But it possesses a past, attested by **Pictish** symbol stones, by the tradition of a medieval monastery, and by fragments of a castle. Its 18th century church has been transformed into the **Clan Gunn** centre.

LAUDER, Berwickshire

The only **royal burgh** in **Berwickshire**, with a charter dating from 1502, Lauder over the centuries has not enjoyed a good press; remembered mainly for the 1482 hanging from its bridge (long gone) of the low-born favourites of **James III** by **Archibald 'Bell-the-Cat' Douglas, 5th Earl of Angus**, it was later described as 'plain and irregular in its houses, desolate and chilly in the aspects of its streets . . . and just as dull a place as well can be conceived' (Fullarton's *Gazetteer*, 1843). However Lauder does boast an imposing 18th century town hall and an interesting church, built in 1673 by **Sir William Bruce** for the **Duke of Lauderdale**, centrally planned in the shape of a Greek cross (ie with all four arms the same length) and with the pulpit in the middle under the octagonal tower. The **Covenanting** martyr **James Guthrie** (1617–61) was minister of Lauder from 1642–9. Just to the north-east of the town, **Thirlestane Castle** is the dominant feature of the burgh just as its owners, the Maitlands, were the dominant family in the area and, for a time, in Scottish history.

LAUDER, Sir Harry (1870–1950) Entertainer

Even at the height of his fame as an international **music hall** star, Harry Lauder remained proud of his humble beginnings. Born in a cottage at **Portobello**, the son of a potter, he spent his boyhood working 12-hour shifts in an **Arbroath** flax-mill and his teens as pitboy in a **coal**-mine at **Hamilton**. A visit to a travelling circus in Arbroath gave him his first glimpse of showbusiness and first prize in a singing contest set him firmly on the boards. After early success in Scotland and then in England he was booked on a US tour, the first of 22 American triumphs during which he would eventually earn $5000 a week and play **golf** with Presidents.

His love for his wife Nancy inspired two of his most

Sir Harry Lauder; 1915 caricature by H M Bateman (SNPG)

successful songs, 'I Love a Lassie' and 'Roamin' in the Gloamin''. The song 'Keep Right on to the End of the Road' was written after his son John was killed in action in World War I. The writer H V Morton, who met him in an **Aberdeen** hotel in 1928, described him as 'small, sturdy and smooth of face. He wore hexagonal glasses and smoked a six-inch briar pipe. His glengarry was worn at a jaunty angle and, as he walked, the almost ankle-length Inverness cape which he wore exposed a bit of a MacLeod **kilt**. The superior person will perhaps sniff if I suggest that no man since **Sir Walter Scott** has warmed the world's heart to Scotland more surely than Sir Harry Lauder. His genius is a thing apart.'

Many in Scotland today do indeed deprecate Lauder for creating a false image of a kilted, ultra-thrifty Scot, but the greatest tribute to his memory is the fact that his songs are sung nearly every day somewhere in the world. His philosophy was simple: 'Aye, I'm tellin' ye . . . happiness is one of the few things in this world that doubles every time you share it with someone else.'

LAUDER, Robert Scott (1803–69) History Painter and Teacher

Although one of the most influential mid-19th century Scottish painters, Lauder never achieved the fame to which he seemed destined. Born in **Edinburgh** he studied at the **Trustees' Academy** under the landscape painter Andrew Wilson. Like many of his contemporaries he spent a few years in London, returning to Edinburgh in 1826. He befriended the popular landscape painter, the **Rev John Thomson** of Duddingston, who abetted Lauder's election to full membership of the **Royal Scottish Academy** at the unusually early age of 27. Lauder married Thomson's daughter Isabella and together they travelled to Italy, where they stayed until 1838.

Lauder then settled in London and, influenced by the Italian masters, devoted himself to historical painting, emulating their concern with 'finish' and sophisticated painterly technique. He unsuccessfully entered the 1847 competition for murals for the recently rebuilt Houses of Parliament and it is possible that this failure (of what he saw as the potential culmination of his career) affected his decision to return to Edinburgh in 1852 to take up the mastership of the Trustees' Academy, the most influential art school in Scotland at the time. It was in this new role, however, that he found his forte. He imposed Italian teaching methods which emphasised the importance of composition, and encouraged pupils to paint (rather than just draw) at the earliest opportunity. His appreciation of the Venetian painters interested Lauder in the use of colour and his bold experimentation in this area had a marked impact on a rising generation of artists – notably **Chalmers**, **Orchardson**, MacWhirter and **McTaggart** – who were later to recall the debt they owed to their inspiring teacher.

As a consequence of his return to Edinburgh and his concentration on his teaching duties, commercial success always eluded Lauder. A paralysing stroke ended his career in 1861 and it is a sad irony that although he lived to see his teaching methods replaced by less imaginative, conservative approaches, he died before witnessing the remarkable artistic flowering of the generation of painters he had taught [see **Painting in Scotland**].

LAUDER, Sir Thomas Dick (1784–1848)
Author

'A very accomplished gentleman' (**Lord Cockburn**), Lauder 'could make his way in the world as a player, or a **ballad** singer, or a street fiddler, or a geologist, or a civil engineer, or a surveyor, as easily and eminently as an artist or a layer out of ground'. He dabbled in all but he excelled as a congenial companion and author. The descendant of Sir John Lauder (1647–1722), advocate and diarist of Fountainhall, **East Lothian**, he served briefly in the **Cameron Highlanders** before retiring to the estate of his wife at Relugas near **Elgin**, there no doubt 'laying out ground'. He also wrote, first a notable paper showing that the Parallel Roads of Glen Roy [see **Geology**] were not artificial but the result of lacustrine action, then contributions to **Blackwood's** and two romances (*Lochindhu*, 1825 and *The Wolf of Badenoch*, 1827, both widely read and translated). He also witnessed, sketched and wrote an *Account of the Great Moray Floods of 1829*, which became a classic, and then moved (1831) to The Grange, **Edinburgh**, in which city he cut a kenspeckle figure, as renowned for his company as for his appearance ('a profusion of grey grizzly hair tossed over head, face and neck . . . a tall gentleman-like Quixotic figure').

Appointment (1839) as Secretary of the Board of Manufactures and Fisheries provided scope for his **engineering** expertise and opportunity to travel. Topographical works included *Highland Rambles and Legends to Shorten the Way* (3 vols, 1837) and, his final flourish dictated while on his deathbed, *Scottish Rivers* (1847). This deals with the Jordan, the **Tweed** and the Tyne and is not such an eccentric collection as it sounds. The Jordan turns out to be a burn, rich in Edinburgh history, which flows past The Grange, and the Tyne is that of East Lothian rather than Newcastle. He left two sons and 10 daughters.

LAUDERDALE, Earldom and Dukedom
The Maitlands descended from Normans who crossed the Channel with William the Conqueror and spread north after **David I** had inherited the crown of the Scots in 1124. Sir Richard Maitland married Avicia, the heiress of **Thirlestane**, where the family have maintained themselves ever since in the pass of Lauderdale. Sir William died at **Flodden** in 1513 and his son Sir Richard became a distinguished historian, lawyer and poet, whose priceless collection of the **Makars** was later purchased by Samuel Pepys and is preserved in Magdalene College, Cambridge. Richard's two remarkable sons served both **Queen Mary** and **James VI**, and the family was rewarded in 1616 with the Earldom of Lauderdale.

The 2nd Earl was probably the ablest of them. He became known as 'King of Scotland', and was raised to a dukedom (1672) by **Charles II** when he married the Countess of Dysart. She, according to **Bishop Burnet**, conducted herself 'with a haughtiness that would have been shocking in a queen', and seriously damaged his reputation. In 1680 he was dismissed and his dukedom died with him two years later. Since then the family has produced members of varied distinction, including the naval captain to whom Napoleon surrendered in 1815. The present 17th Earl does not, however, possess Thirlestane Castle, which passed through the daughter of the 15th Earl's heir to the Maitland-Carews.

LAURENCEKIRK, Kincardineshire
The **Mearns** village of Conveth was developed as Laurencekirk when in the 1760s Francis Garden, Lord Gardenston of Troup [see **Gardenstown**] purchased the local estate of Johnston. 'He has encouraged the building of a manufacturing village of which he is exceedingly fond, and has written a pamphlet upon it, as if he had founded Thebes,' noted **James Boswell** without approval. Boswell's father had given Gardenston 5 guineas towards a monument for **Thomas Ruddiman**, once the local schoolmaster; 'but the monument, it i believed, has not been erected'.

The Johnston tower to the south-east is a 19th century folly and has no connection with Ruddiman or Gardenston. It stands on Garvock Hill, where occurred the gruesome murder of John Melville, Sheriff of Kincardine, in 1420. When **James I** expressed a wish to see Melville 'sodden and supped in broo', a party of local lairds took him at his royal word and slayed, boiled and seasoned the mortal remains of Melville before supping on their broth. West, towards **Fettercairn**, the small L-plan Thornton Castle may date from 1531 but has been extended.

LAURIE, Anna ('Annie') (1682–1764)
The subject of a song made famous by Alicia Anne Spottiswoode [**Lady John Scott**] was born in Maxwelton House near **Moniaive** which had been built by her grandfather. The earliest version of 'Annie Laurie' is thought to have been written by her ardent admirer William Douglas of Fingland, a young **Jacobite** officer. His (or her) ardour evidently cooled, for the man who wrote 'But for Annie Laurie I'd lay me doon and dee' did no such thing, marrying a Miss Clerk of Glenboig in 1706. Anna herself married (1710) Alexander Ferguson of nearby Craigdarroch. The popular version of 'Annie Laurie' was largely revised and set to music in 1835, Spottiswoode supposedly conserving the first verse, changing the second and adding the third.

LAVERY, Sir John (1856–1941) Painter
A leading member of the late-19th century **Glasgow** School [see **Painting in Scotland**], Lavery went on to enjoy an international reputation as one of the most successful and honoured portraitists of his age. Born in Belfast and orphaned while young, he was raised in Ulster and then **Ayrshire**. He moved to Glasgow in 1873 and, while working as a photographer's assistant, studied at the Haldane Academy of Art. In 1881 he went to Paris and enrolled at the fashionable Académie Julien, coming under the influence of the French Realist painters and in particular the rustic naturalism of Jules Bastien-Lepage. Adopting Lepage's artistic language – low-key, level-toned colouring, attention to foreground detail, emphasis on the composition's horizontal planes – Lavery's gentle evocations of French rural life, painted mostly at the idyllic Grez-sur-Loing, the artists' colony he first visited in 1883, are amongst the finest of the many French-inspired *plein-air* paintings produced by British artists during this period.

Lavery's family circumstances meant he was dependent entirely on sales for his living and his cautious response to the socially aware subjects of Realism, seen at best in *The Tennis Party* (1885, Aberdeen Art Gallery),

stylish and highly original portrayal of the middle
asses at play, resulted in works combining widespread
ublic appeal with the innovations but without the
Kailyard' themes of the Glasgow School. Lavery's activ-
y recording the spectacle of the 1888 Glasgow Inter-
ational Exhibition led to his commission to record the
ate visit of **Queen Victoria**, assuring his future as a
ortrait painter. In 1896 he moved to London where
is services became widely in demand. International
access largely extinguished his ability as an innovative
tist and he is remembered latterly as the archetypal
ecorder of Edwardian society, producing works of con-
derable flair, though little insight, indebted stylistically
o Whistler. Appointed an official war artist in 1916,
is numerous accolades included membership of the
oyal Scottish Academy and Royal Academy, Presi-
ency of the Royal Portrait Society and a knighthood
n 1918.

AW

cots Law was expressly preserved by the **Treaty of
Union** with England in 1707. Its retention, and that of
ne **Church of Scotland** and the Scottish **educational**
ystem, can be seen in retrospect as a means of conserv-
ng Scottish culture for posterity. Additionally Scots Law
olds a special place amongst the world's legal systems.
s nature could be characterised as one of selective
orrowing from Roman or Civil Law, Canon Law, Eng-
sh Law and other miscellaneous systems (such as the
aw Merchant, Mosaic, French and Feudal Law). Some
f these influences have been consistently strong, such
s Romano Canonical Law, stretching from Scotland's
nclusion in Christendom through to the present time,
r English Law, particularly from 1707. The ability of
cottish parliamentarians and jurists of all epochs to
veave from the various contributing sources a coherent
ystem has been marked.

Most modern legal systems are derived either from
oman Law or English Common Law. Roman or Civil
aw is the principal foundation in most European states,
Hispanic America, Quebec, Louisiana, South Africa and
cotland. English Common Law holds sway in the USA
nd most Commonwealth countries (except where
slamic or native legal systems have competence). The
osition of Quebec, Louisiana, South Africa and Scot-
and is perhaps most particular in as much as all have
Roman Law conceptual foundation to which English
Common Law methods are applied. Thus Scots Law has
special place in the family of the world's legal systems,
nd makes a particular contribution to the preservation
f Scottish identity.

General History

re-Norman Times
The law and legal systems which prevailed in Scotland
rior to the Feudal Period (post-1000 AD) are
unknown. There is some evidence that, as in Ireland,
he Brehons formed a legal caste in Celtic Scotland. The
Brehon had the duty to declare the Celtic customs in
ccordance with the 'Old Law', which was always cus-
omary. There is only scanty written evidence of Brehon
aw in Scotland (eg in the **Book of Deer**). The system
f **Tanistry**, whereby the Celtic kings were elected along

with the heir apparent, led to intertribal rivalry and
murder. Accordingly primogeniture as a means of succession to chieftainship and subsequently kingship was
a natural and necessary development.

The Feudal Period
There was no Norman conquest of Scotland. However
after William I established his rule in England in 1066
Norman influence spread into Scottish Lowland society.
The feudal system was its prime characteristic. This had
its origin in the political and military necessities of
medieval society. But it was more than a military system:
it was also a political, social and economic one within
the framework of a system of law.

The principal relationship in the feudal system was
that between superior (or lord) and vassal (or tenant).
The land was granted by the superior to the vassal in
knight fief, to be held so that one or more knights could
be provided for the lord. The vassal owed a duty of
homage and fealty. A vassal could also hold his land
from the superior in return for certain services, some
of which were purely ceremonial (eg being a standard
bearer), and some of more practical application (eg
supplying bread or flour). The superior in exchange
granted protection to the vassal. A grant or disposition
of land was confirmed by a charter in writing specifying
the rights and duties of both parties.

Feudal Land Law
The vassal held the land from the superior with a life
interest only. It was in the interest of the superior that
the land was held by loyal and capable men, so that
where the duty in the tenure was military, known as
ward holding (ie the provision of a knight), the crown
had the right to repossess the land if the heir in possession was a child or a female. Despite emphasis on
the military nature of feudalism, an heir could negotiate
with the superior to avoid the rigours of tenure by
paying a relief or money equivalent.

The interest of the Crown remained however in the
land. When knights became redundant due to the longbow and the development of artillery, new forms of
tenure emerged, particularly blench tenure (where no
feuduty passed) and feu farm tenure (Socage).

Besides regulating land tenure, the feudal system was
also a decentralised form of government. The grant of
local power and responsibilities, plus deficiencies in
royal power, led Scotland to be divided into separate
principalities called 'regalities'. Thus the old Celtic
system changed in time from a customary one to a
strictly organised and regulated Norman French Society.

Feudal Theory and Administration
The change in tenure and government brought about
by feudal theory assumed that the King was the universal
landowner and fountain of justice. But whilst in England
the superiority of the Crown ensured that feudal theory
was matched by historical fact, in Scotland this was
never the case.

From the middle of the 11th century onwards there
was, though, a growing influence from Norman settlers
at the court of **Malcolm III 'Canmore'**. After 1124 the
process of Anglo-Normanisation gained momentum,
and **David I** professed himself openly in favour of the

introduction of the feudal system. Many Scots were educated at the English Court; David himself spent time at the court of William Rufus. In 1107 he became Prince of Cumbria, married Matilda grand-niece of William, and became Earl of Huntingdon. As such he was a direct vassal of William II of England.

Many famous families came to Scotland at this time, including the Huntingdons, the Lindsays, the Somervilles and the **Bruces**. The process of Normanisation proceeded when David reorganised the government and judicial system, the Church and the burghs.

THE GOVERNMENT AND JUDICIAL SYSTEM With the construction of a centralised system of government based on Anglo-Norman barons holding sway over large areas of the country, the king was able to create a bureaucracy. He started by establishing the great offices of state:

The Chancellor – was the principal officer of state, the administrative nerve centre of the new system of government and law, around which the judicial system revolved.

The Chamberlain – was the main officer of state dealing with financial matters. He also supervised the **royal burghs** and the raising of dues and customs.

The Constable – was responsible for the King's peace, an important concept in feudal theory because a crime was an even greater evil if committed in the King's presence. As the 'King's peace' gradually extended to include all the King's subjects, so too did royal justice.

The Justiciar – was delegated to deal both with general administration and specifically the administration of justice. He held both civil and criminal jurisdiction on four circuits, or 'ayres', twice each year. Originally there were two justiciars, one for the north and one for the south, but by the time of **Robert I** the number had risen to five. Their jurisdiction included the pleas of the Crown dealing with arson, robbery, murder and rape, and extended to perambulation and measurement of land, and the supervision of sheriffs.

The King's Council – comprising magnates or tenants-in-chief and other important figures which advised the King, the Council would eventually divide to perform certain specialised functions. Thus by the end of the 13th century the 'parliament' emerged as the sitting of the Council in its guise as the supreme court which set out the law and allowed for its alteration. The general Council, in so far as it deliberated matters of state, evolved into the 'Convention of Estates'.

Court of Barony – The King promoted local control through the emergence of barony and regality courts. Barons were the 'Great Men' who held lands direct of the King by a grant in *liberam baroniam*. Barony tenure established an administrative unit, and baronial rights included a responsibility for keeping ordinary public justice within the confines of the barony. To assist in this endeavour the baron had the rights of *fossa and furca*,

the ditch and the gallows, interpreted as the pow of life and death over those living in his barony. development of baronial holding was 'holding i regality' which occurred where the King gave so gre a right to a baron that it excluded the rights of th King's officers (with the exception of the right to tr treason). Baronies of regality were in effect litt kingdoms.

Sheriffs – Probably building on an Anglo-Saxon mode David I also established the office of sheriff in Scotland The function of both shrieval and baronial jurisdictio was to hold down the country. The sheriff administere an area in the immediate neighbourhood of his castle He was the representative of royal judicial power in th environs, but had other functions, military, financi and administrative. An act of the Scottish Parliament i 1305 stipulated that sheriffs should serve for life, an gradually the office became hereditary. The sheriff cou administered both civil and criminal jurisdictions wit the exception of pleas of the Crown. The jurisdictio could be narrowed by the extent of the royal grant. Th sheriff could hear appeals from the baronial court, b was not capable of dealing with questions relating t the four pleas of the Crown, nor had he jurisdictio within regalities or burghs.

THE CHURCH David I favoured the growth of the Churc and many religious orders established monasteries an communities throughout Scotland. These ecclesiastic foundations brought with them their own law an judicial structure in terms of the Canon Law and churc courts. The tribunals of Papal judges-delegate an legates as well as the courts of the diocesan officials an commissaries were important in the development c Scots Law in that Canon Law provided a route for th reception of Roman Law when aspects of canonical pro cedure were adopted by secular courts.

THE BURGHS Another feature of the reign of David was the grant of charters establishing burghs whic were towns or settlements in the neighbourhood c castles. Burghs were centres of administration and wer granted trade privileges such as a market or fair. Burg courts soon emerged dealing with civil and petty crimi nal matters, and the Dean of Guild court also develope with peculiar jurisdiction over building and publi safety. The *curia quatour burgorum*, or court of four burghs began meeting from 1292 to deal with appeals fron burgh courts. In time the *leges quatour burgorum*, a collec tion of laws based on an English model, became recog nised as the authoritative statement of burgh law.

See also **Local Government**.

From the 12th Century to the Reformation

It has been said that a person crossing the **Twee** between 1200 and 1328 would not have been awar that he had crossed the border from England to Scotland But in legal terms it was quite clear that Scoto-Norma law differed, though not greatly, from Anglo-Norma law. As time passed the differences between the tw systems became more marked. For example there wa less reliance on technicalities and legal fictions in Scot land. But in addition to borrowings from Romano 'anonical Law, there is also evidence of widespread borrowing from the law of England; this can be seen n the emergence of brieves and of charter registers, nd the existence of the *Regiam Majestatem* and the *Leges Quatour Burgorum*. Brieves, a specific form of writ obtainable from the Chancery, are instructions from the King o a local official to put certain questions to a jury in order to ascertain the truth. The Scottish brieves mirrored the English writs, including the brieve of right, the brieve of mort d'ancestor, and the brieve of nul dissasine. Similarly the *Regiam Majestatem* is a law book which follows closely the English text *De Legibus et Consuetudinibus Anglicae*, describing the law and customs of England (written by Glanvill).

It was compiled, along with the *Quoniam Attachiamenta*, during the reigns of **David II** and **Robert II.** These comprised the great books of 'Old Law' which in the 5th century were subject to law reform provisions. Commissions were established to 'see and examine' the books of Old Law and to 'mend the laws that needed amendment'. The Leases Act of 1449 indicated a turning point in the feudal system, and Acts relating to Prescription, ie time bar, were enacted.

This legislative activity emanated from the increasingly influential Convention of Estates. Parliament was a unicameral body, the High Court of Parliament, which incorporated the General Council or 'Three Estatis' – ecclesiastics, Nobles and Burgesses. The Estates met infrequently throughout the 15th and 16th centuries. Much of the legislative and judicial work of Parliament was undertaken by committees. Judicial matters from the mid-14th century were delegated to a committee of Parliament comprised of auditors, whereas legislative matters were passed to the Lords of Articles (articles = bills, or proposals for legislation). The Lords of Articles were abolished in 1690.

Real progress in judicial matters only began with the reign of **James I**. In 1426 an Act was passed prescribing that the chancellor and discreet persons from the Estates should hear 'causes and complaints'. This court sat until 1470. Judicial matters were dealt with after 1478 by direct approach to the council dealing with civil causes. In 1491 the Chancellor began sitting with Lords of Session (or Council) three times a year and the 16th century brought a new proposal from the Privy Council for a body to hear civil cases – later known as the Session'.

However, the principal development of the early 16th century was the foundation of the College of Justice in 1532. After an expensive war (**Flodden** was fought in 1513) **James V** needed to replenish his coffers. Pope Paul III needed loyalty and such was the statecraft of the times that James approached the Pope for funds. The Pope granted a tithe on the Church in Scotland in 1531, one of the conditions of which was that the King would establish a College of Justice. In 1535 the Bull was granted establishing the court (which had been set up in 1532), and in 1541 Parliament ratified the Papal Declaration.

By 1560 (a mere 28 years after the College of Justice's institution) the **Reformation** in Scotland was in full swing. Papal jurisdiction was abolished in that year, but the Canon Law, except in so far as expressly departed

from, remained in force. Furthermore, the local courts of the diocesan officials and commissaries were not abolished, and limped on in face of growing opposition, anti-Catholic sentiment, and the emergent judicial structure of the **Church of Scotland**.

The Church of Scotland established courts of kirk sessions, presbyteries, synods, and the **General Assembly**. The **Court of Session** and the new ecclesiastical courts operated the old ecclesiastical jurisdiction until the establishment of the (secular) Commissary Court in 1563. The central commissary court in **Edinburgh** took on the newly created jurisdiction over divorce (reformed theology, as distinct from the Catholic regime, permitted divorce at Common Law for adultery and, by an Act of Parliament in 1573, for desertion), marriage and legitimacy. The inferior commissaries at local level assumed the jurisdiction for the confirmation of testaments.

The College of Justice in its early days had dealt with a body of underdeveloped civil and criminal law. There was little legal literature. Scots Acts and the books of the Old Law were about all to which the litigant could refer. It was only with the establishment of the court that this situation improved, with judges (eg **Balfour** and **Spottiswoode**) noting their decisions in books of practick.

The Union of the Crowns to the Union of the Parliaments

After the **Union of the Crowns** in 1603 attempts were made to re-establish the Justice Ayres by which **royal burghs** were governed and, following the English model, Justices of the Peace were enhanced in their powers. But religious questions dominated the politics of the day and the policy pursued by **Charles I** led to a growing opposition to the royal authority. Civil unrest festered and in 1638 the National **Covenant** was signed in **Greyfriars' Churchyard**.

With the establishment of the Commonwealth, Scotland, Ireland and England became united for the first time (1654). Cromwell had already appointed seven commissioners to dispense justice in 1650 following the dissolution of the Scots Parliament and the Court of Session. A decade later the Restoration saw the Privy Council emerge as the instrument of royal authority and the Court of Session re-established. A major development was the 1672 establishment of the High Court of Justiciary as the supreme criminal court in Scotland. It comprised a Justice General, Justice Clerk and five commissioners of justiciary (ipso facto judges of the Court of Session by the Criminal Procedure Act of 1887). The court not only sat in Edinburgh but single judges also moved round the country on circuit, recalling the ayres from which the court was derived.

The Lord Justice Generalship was a powerful office developing from the medieval justiciar. During the 16th century the office became hereditary in the **Argyll** (Campbell) family, but reverted to the Crown in the early 17th century.

From the early 15th century Scotland had aspired to register all deeds transferring title to land. The Registration Act 1617 had provided for the recording of all instruments of sasine (infeftment) within 60 days of the sasine, and also established particular shrieval registers. Now the Registration Act (1681) brought burghal tenure into the scheme of recording by the establishment of Burgh Registers and, in **Paisley**, the Register of Booking. There is therefore an unbroken history of land transactions in Scotland stretching back to the early part of the 17th century.

In tandem with the emergence of the High Court of Justiciary and the Register of Sasines, Parliament also passed statutes on a range of topics relating to civil law. These included the Courts Act 1672, an Act against unlawful dispositions and alienations by bankrupts (the Bankruptcy Act 1621), statutes on prescription (time bar) in 1617 and 1619, and acts establishing entail or tailzie (1685). Later in the century a welter of legislation covered guarantees (1693), tutors and curators (1696), blank bonds and trusts (1696), and the Criminal Procedure Act (1701) which prevents wrongful imprisonment and delays in trials.

The Union of Scotland and England

Although the kingdoms had shared a monarch since 1603 their political, legal and social systems remained distinct if converging. Attempts to negotiate a union met with no success until the passing of the **Aliens Act** 1705 concentrated the minds of Scots Parliamentarians. The Parliaments appointed Commissioners and in 1706 negotiations took place in London leading to agreement on free trade, complete union, the succession to the throne, taxation, the judicial system and Parliamentary representation. The Articles of Union were ratified by both the Scots and English Parliaments in early 1707 and became operative on 1 May 1707. In October 1707 the first Parliament of Great Britain convened at Westminster.

The Treaty of **Union** made specific provision for the preservation of the Scottish Legal System. Article XIX provides 'that the Court of Session or College of Justice do after the Union and notwithstanding thereof remain in all time coming within Scotland, and that the Court of Justiciary do also after the Union . . . remain in all time coming.'

Provision was also made for the preservation of subordinate jurisdictions (Art XIX) and heritable jurisdictions (Art XX). The articles provided that no cause in Scotland should 'be cognisible by the Courts of Chancery, Queen's Bench, Common Pleas or any other Court in Westminster Hall'. Appeals were however taken to the House of Lords because it did not sit in Westminster Hall. Article XVIII provided for the preservation of Scots Law 'and that all other laws in use within the Kingdom of Scotland do . . . remain in the same force as before'.

These however could be altered by the Parliament of Great Britain in an unrestrained manner where the laws concerned 'public right, policy and civil government', but where private right was concerned only alterations for the 'evident utility of the subjects within Scotland' were permitted. The 'evident utility' provision has since been hotly debated.

The Post-Union Period

The immediate post-Union period was not a particularly happy one. In 1707 the Scottish Privy Council, despite protest, was abolished and in 1708 the English law of torture was imported into Scotland.

In 1707–8 the Earl of Rosebery took an appeal to the House of Lords; this was followed by the appeal of James Greenshields, an Anglican priest who was imprisoned for using the Anglican liturgy, but was liberated upon appealing the decision of the Court of Session to the House of Lords. It was a decision of fundamental importance to the development of law in the United Kingdom from 1711 to the present day. The fact that the House of Lords decision could rule in matters of Scots civil law meant that a court most of whose members had no experience of Scots Law could affect or change the law as applied in Scotland. Much which was not law in Scotland but which had effect in England was imported into the Scots system, such as the doctrine of common employment (ie an employer was not liable for injuries caused to one employee by another by virtue of their common employment). This doctrine, brought into the Scots Law of delict in 1858 had to be removed by statute 90 years later in the Law Reform (Personal Injuries) Act 1948.

The great 19th century reorganisation of the English court system, the Juridicature Act 1873, included a provision for the removal of the Scots appellate jurisdiction; this provision was however not implemented and the Appellate Jurisdictions Act 1876 allowed for the appointment of Scottish Lords of Appeal in Ordinary. Accordingly since then there has always been at least one Scottish Lord of Appeal in Ordinary.

The **Jacobite Risings** brought much havoc in their wake and provided justification for retributive justice. After the '15 a Forfeited Estates Commission was established to administer the estates of those found to have committed treason by following the Pretender. A commission of Oyer and Terminer was established in Scotland to apply the English laws of treason, and after the '45 even harsher methods of control were adopted. With only insignificant exceptions, the Heritable Jurisdictions Act 1747 abolished the heritable jurisdictions of Feudal Lords in Scotland. This Act breached the Treaty of Union which expressly preserved the feudal right to hold court, but otherwise might be thought to have improved the provision of justice. Military tenures were also abolished, and as part of the demilitarisation of Highland life **clan** badges and **tartans** were abolished.

The Heritable Jurisdictions Act 1747 left a judicial vacuum and, as so often happened in Scots legal history, an institution already established evolved to fill the space – the sheriff. Many sheriffs held their office on an hereditary basis with a qualified depute actually holding court. Upon the hereditary office ceasing, the sheriff depute filled the role of sheriff. The sheriff depute (from 1828, the sheriff) appointed sheriffs substitute who held office under him. In 1787 sheriffs substitute became salaried and in 1877 the sheriff substitute became a Crown appointee.

The Court of Session was relatively unchanged by the upsets of the 18th century. However the 19th century saw great change. In 1808 the Inner House split into two divisions, the First Division presided over by the Lord President and the Second Division by the Lord Justice Clerk. Numerous other changes occurred throughout the early years of the century. The numbers of judges changed from 8 Inner House judges and 5 Outer House judges in 1830 to 15 judges with the passage of the Administration of Justice (Sc) Act 1848.

The Court of Session Act 1850 allowed substantial procedural or adjective change. Shorthand writers' notes were allowed by the Conjugal Rights Act 1861. Rules of Court were, and still are, made by Act of Sederunt and an early 20th century consolidation was revised into the Rules of Court 1936.

Throughout the 19th century the Court of Session absorbed the jurisdictions of many courts, including the civil jurisdiction of the Court of Admiralty in 1830. In contravention of the Treaty of Union, the court's prize jurisdiction had been given over to the English Court of Admiralty in 1825. The Commissary Court jurisdiction in status cases was transferred in 1836, the inferior commissary jurisdiction (succession cases) having been given to the Sheriff Court in 1823, and the Teind Court (dealing with tithes and stipends) was established in 1708 and formalised in 1839.

Law and the Universities

The development of Scots Law in the post-Union period was the outstanding achievement of Scottish jurists and judges. It coincided in great measure with that flowering of arts, literature and philosophy which constituted the **Scottish Enlightenment** – an epoch of intellectual activity on a grand scale embracing almost every field of human endeavour and contributing in no small way to the concept of modern civilisation. This climate allowed the emergence of Scots Law as a university-taught discipline, the flourishing of academic and practical writers, and the appointment of some startling talents to the bench.

Although Scotland had boasted three medieval universities, **St Andrews** (1413), **Glasgow** (1451) and **Aberdeen** (1496), the teaching of law before the 18th century did not have a very distinguished history. Before the 15th century Scots who wanted to study Civil or Canon Law went to universities in Italy, France, Germany or the Low Countries. The English universities in Oxford and Cambridge (which taught civil law) were closed to Scots. St Andrews had the teaching of Civil and Canon Law as one of its objects but not much seems to have been achieved there; indeed it appears no law teaching occurred there at all. Glasgow University, founded in 1451 by Pope Nicholas V as a *Studium Generale* for the study of arts and Canon and Civil Laws, was active in the early years with a number of distinguished students in law; but law teaching failed during the early 16th century. Stair later taught at Glasgow and was Regent there, but in Arts, not Law. In Aberdeen law teaching was advanced as the lectures of William Hay show, but after the Reformation Canon Law studies failed here also.

Despite plans in the *First Book of Discipline*, effective law teaching was not commenced in the Scottish universities after the Reformation and students continued to go abroad, particularly to Leyden or Utrecht in Holland or to the Protestant German universities. However, in 1714 the teaching of Scots Law was recommenced at Glasgow with the appointment of **William Forbes** as first Regius Professor of Law. Forbes taught from 1714–45 and was followed by Sheriff William Crosse (1745–50) who probably did not teach. Hercules Lindsay succeeded

Crosse, having already taught at Glasgow as assistant to Forbes. After Lindsay, **John Millar**, the doyen of the Scottish Enlightenment, assumed the chair. He lectured from 1761–1801 and built a considerable international reputation.

In Edinburgh law teaching had originally been undertaken by way of private tuition by advocates (there was talk of an 'Inn of Court' in 16th century Edinburgh). The university began teaching law only in the first decade of the 18th century. Three chairs were established: in 1707 the Chair of Public Law and the Law of Nations, in 1709 Civil Law and in 1722 Scots Law. The first Professor of Scots Law was Alexander Bayne of Rires (1722–37), who was followed by **John Erskine** of Carnock (1737–65).

The Scottish tradition of writing learned treatises was firmly established by the 18th century. Prior to then, **James Dalrymple**, 1st Viscount Stair, had set the mould in his *Institutions of the Law of Scotland* (1681). In writing this seminal work Stair managed both to follow the European tradition and yet still contribute to the preservation of Scots Law. He drew on the scanty written resources, including the Black Acts, a collection of Scots Statutes, the writings of Skene, the Practicks of Balfour and Spottiswoode, the *jus feudale* of **Craig**, and wove these national sources with those of the civilians and canonists of the Continent – particularly the Dutch jurists of the Natural Law School. However the achievement of Stair was undoubtedly the creation of considered systematic and logical presentation of the principles of Scots municipal law.

In addition to signifying the establishment of the Scots legal system as a self-contained body of law, Stair provided a model for other writers. **Mackenzie of Rosehaugh** produced his *Institutions of the Law of Scotland* in 1684. This shorter work was a well respected student text. The 18th century saw further writing on the institutional model. Forbes wrote his *Institutes* in 1722, Bankton produced *An Institute of the Laws of Scotland* in 1751–3. John Erskine of Carnock, the second Professor of Scots Law at the University of Edinburgh, also produced institutional writings in the *Principles of the Law of Scotland*, an elementary text designed to update Mackenzie, and *An Institute of the Law of Scotland*, an altogether more extensive text. This work appeared posthumously in 1773 but swiftly gained acceptance and a high measure of respect from the juristic community.

The judiciary of the 18th century included the notable **Duncan Forbes of Culloden** (1685–1747), a former Lord Advocate and industrial magnate who was appointed Lord President in 1737. During the ten years of his tenure he increased the business carried on by the court. Another outstanding appointment to the bench was **Henry Home, Lord Kames**. Appointed in 1755 he was prodigious in literary output including matters of law, philosophy and history.

The 19th Century

The 19th century saw great efforts to establish democracy in the United Kingdom and reform in the law. Reform came via an increase in the number of statutory provisions and heightened English influence from the House of Lords.

The 1884 Reform Act increased Scots representation

in Parliament to 72 (its current number) and presaged the creation of an individual Secretary of State for Scotland in 1885. The Burgh Police (Sc) Acts 1892 and 1903 and the Town Councils (Sc) Act 1900 empowered local burghs and councils to provide for good order and public health.

Legal and juristic writers during the 19th century responded to the reforms promulgated by Parliament and interpreted by the courts. David Hume, Professor of Scots Law at Edinburgh (1786–1822), produced his *Commentaries on the Law of Scotland Respecting Crimes*, an influential work on criminal law, and a highly prized volume of *Decisions*. **George Joseph Bell**, Professor of Scots Law at Edinburgh (1822–43), wrote the *Commentaries on the Law of Scotland and on the Principles of Mercantile Jurisprudence* and *Principles of the Law of Scotland*; both works are highly respected and hold institutional status.

The contributions of **Lord Cockburn** and **Walter Scott** are not best known in legal circles, but, like Thomas Thomson and Cosmo Innes, they did much to promote interest in and knowledge of Scottish history and the history of Scots Law.

During the second half of the 19th century **Lord President Inglis** distinguished himself with fine judgements while his fellow judges produced standard texts which were in use until very recently, including Lord McLaren's works on *Wills and Succession* and *Court of Session Practice*, and Lord Fraser's trilogy on domestic relationships, *Husband and Wife*, *Parent and Child* and *Master and Servant*.

The talents of the bench, the bar and the academics were tested by the welter of statutory amendment during the 19th century. In the true Victorian tradition, commerce and industry benefited from regulation including the Limited Liability Act 1855 (which with the Joint Stock Companies Act 1856 and Companies Act 1862 established the basis for Company Law and limited liability) and the Mercantile Law Amendment (Sc) Act 1856 (which brought together certain aspects of the contract laws of Scotland and England and laid the way for the Sale of Goods Act 1893).

The Partnership Acts 1865 and 1890 provided the statutory framework for the pursuit of commercial activities outwith the concept of limited liability. The Bills of Exchange Act 1882 permitted the widespread use of bills or cheques which assisted commercial development, and the Merchant Shipping Acts 1862 and 1894 reflected the UK's premier position in the 19th century trading system.

The position of employers and employees was regulated by the early Truck Act 1831 followed by the Trade Union Act 1871 amended in 1876, the Employers and Workmen Act 1875, and the Employers' Liability Act 1880. Later the Truck Act 1896 and the Workmen's Compensation 1897 presaged further legislation in the field.

Other areas of law affected by this legislative activity included bankruptcy with the Bankruptcy Act 1856; the law of husband and wife with the Conjugal Rights (Sc) Amendment Act 1861; the Married Women's Policies of Assurance (Sc) Act 1880 and the Married Woman's Property (Sc) Act 1881; crofting law with the **Crofters' Holdings (Sc) Act** 1886, and conveyancing with the

Conveyancing (Sc) Act 1874; and the Heritable Securities (Sc) Act 1894. Criminal procedure was reviewed by the Criminal Procedure Act 1887.

The 20th Century

The development of the law of Scotland during the 20th century followed the pattern of the 19th and the changes wrought by judiciary and legislature were extensive and far reaching. Notable in their contributions from the Bench were Lord Dunedin, Lord Cooper of Culross, Lord MacMillan and Lord Reid. The most important decision in the development of the law of delict or tort arose from the Scottish case of Donaghue vs Stevenson decided in 1932 in the House of Lords. This famous 'snail in the ginger beer bottle' case arose from Mr Donaghue consuming ginger beer which allegedly contained a decomposed snail. As a result of this polluted drink Mrs Donaghue became unwell and sued the manufacturers. The court held that the manufacturer of food or drink owed a duty of care to the ultimate consumer where there was no opportunity for intermediate inspection. The decision in this case – which happened in **Paisley** – has been adopted throughout the common law world as a clear and intelligible statement of principle from which most English-speaking jurisdictions can derive applicable or persuasive law.

Academic writers of the 20th century included Professor Rankine of Edinburgh University, author of *Leases* and *Land Ownership*, Professor Gloag of Glasgow University, author of a standard text on *Contract*, Professor T B Smith of the University of Edinburgh, author of *A Short Commentary on the Law of Scotland* and editor of *The Stair Encyclopaedia of the Laws of Scotland* and Professor John Halliday of the University of Glasgow, law reformer and author of *Conveyancing and Law Practice*.

Legislative reforms of the 20th century changed the statute book beyond all recognition, especially after World War II. The pre-war period witnessed some fundamental changes, notably the Conveyancing (Sc) Act 1924 which modernised much conveyancing law and practice, and the Marriage (Sc) Act 1939 which abandoned the old Canon Law forms of marriage by (1) de presenti consent and (2) promittio subsequente copula. These forms of marriage had been made illegal by the Catholic Church at the Council of Trent in 1563. The effect of the 1939 legislation was to require marriage to be regular, ie before a clergyman or registrar.

The post-war period saw more change and at a faster rate assisted by the Law Reform Committee for Scotland and, since 1965, by the Scottish Law Commission, a statutory body established to review and propose systematic development and reform.

Notable post-war legislation includes the Succession (Sc) Act 1964 which abandoned the feudal/Norman scheme of male-dominated primogeniture in succession to heritable property in favour of a more humane and socially acceptable system; the Social Work (Sc) Act 1968 which established Children's Panels in Scotland as an alternative method of dealing with questions of care and supervision; and, in the area of Family Law, the Divorce (Sc) Act 1976, the Matrimonial Homes (Family Protection) (Sc) Act 1989, the Family Law (Sc) Act 1985 and the Law Reform (Parent and Child) (Sc) Act 1986, all of which modernised the law relating o family affairs making it fairer and more responsive to changing social conditions.

In the field of contract, the Consumer Credit Act 1974 is the most significant statute of the modern era, having altered the Scots Common Law in many fields. The Prescription (Sc) Act 1973 dealing with time bar and its operation in various circumstances repealed many medieval statutes. The Consumer Protection (Sc) Act 1987 not only introduces new elements into Scots Law but is a clear example of the implementation of a European Community Directive.

The principal codification of Company Law was promulgated in 1948 and, after many years of piecemeal amendment partly in response to the directives from the European Community, was reconsolidated in the Companies Act 1985.

Conveyancing was reformed by three major statutes in the 1970s. The Conveyancing and Feudal Reform (Sc) Act 1970 introduced a new form of security and created new methods of altering real burdens or conditions. The Land Tenure Reform (Sc) Act 1974 allowed for the redemption of feu duty and other forms of periodic payment related to tenure, and finally the Land Registration (Sc) Act 1979 provides for a new form of Land Register where titles to land are the subject of a government-backed indemnity.

In 1949 a considerable reform of the system of Legal Aid was undertaken. The Legal Aid and Solicitors (Sc) Act 1949 updated the scheme for assistance for those not wealthy enough to undertake litigation privately (which had existed since 1424) and also established the Law Society of Scotland. The Legal Aid legislation was overhauled in 1986 and an independent administrative body – the Scottish Legal Aid Board – was established.

The Branches of Scots Law

The principal division in Scots Law is that between public law, where the state in some manifestation is involved, and private law where only private persons are involved.

Public Law

In the public law the major topics are constitutional law, administrative law and criminal law and procedure. Constitutional law concerns those matters which relate to the unwritten constitution of the UK, including the position of the Queen in Parliament, Parliamentary law and procedure, constitutional conventions, the nature of cabinet government under the law, and the organisation and regulation of executive functions and local authorities. Administrative law deals with questions of public administration by the executive and administrative branches of government.

Almost all prosecution of criminal offences in Scotland is undertaken at the instance of the Crown in the person of the Lord Advocate or the Procurator Fiscal. Accordingly criminal law and procedure falls into the public law category. Private prosecution, though rare, is possible. The criminal law is still in great measure a customary law, statute intruding only in certain respects eg road traffic legislation.

Private Law

Scots private law is the system of law regulating the affairs of private individuals based on statutory provisions, judicial precedent, custom and institutional writings. The private law has been affected in many respects by the reception of English Law, but still closely resembles the civilian legal origins of Scots Law. The principal topics in private law are Persons, Obligations, Property, Trusts, Succession, Bankruptcy and Private International Law.

THE LAW OF PERSONS regulates those aspects of the personality, capacity or status of individuals and incorporations and provides the baseline for the superstructure of all other branches of Scots Private Law. 'Persons' are recognised as Pupils (boys aged 14 and under and girls aged 12 and under), Minors (either sex from pupillarity to 18) and Adults (persons older than 18). Pupils have no legal personality but are represented by their Tutors (ie parent or other guardian); a Minor has greater but not complete capacity in law and acts with the consent of the Curator [see **Legal Terms**] where applicable. The principal relationships in the law of persons are Parent and Child, Husband and Wife, Guardian and Ward.

Parent and Child – There was formerly a division of the status of children into legitimate or illegitimate. The illegitimate child was subject to many legal disabilities or restrictions and was regarded as filius nullius, no one's child. Most of these restrictions have been removed through statutory intervention and illegitimacy now no longer represents as serious a legal disability as it once did. Adoption is possible, having been introduced by statute in 1924. Parents are subject to alimentary obligations in respect of their children which can be enforced by court action.

Husband and Wife – A marriage may be regular, ie by a clergyman or a registrar, or irregular, ie by cohabitation with habit and repute. In respect of relations within marriage Scots Law provides for presumptions as to the ownership of property. All the former disabilities which attached to women in marriage have been removed by statute; the wife no longer submerges her legal personality in that of her husband. Scottish women almost invariably assume their husband's name on marriage, but this is merely a matter of custom and is by way of an alternative name.

Either party to a marriage may sue or be sued; no liability attaches to a spouse by the mere fact of marriage. Being a spouse accords no special protection in the criminal law – a husband can be tried for the rape of his wife. There are mutual obligations of aliment and adherence between a husband and wife. The only grounds for nullity of marriage are lack of consent or impotence. Divorce is also competent on the grounds of irretrievable breakdown of marriage. Irretrievable breakdown of marriage may be established by evidence of: adultery, unreasonable behaviour, desertion for 2 years, separation for 2 years with consent to divorce or separation for 5 years without consent. In connection with a decree of divorce the court may make ancillary orders regulating custody of or access to children, capital payments, periodical allowance, aliment and division of property.

Guardian and Ward – In addition to the pupil/minor, tutor/curator relationships, other forms of wardship exist including guardians appointed for court purposes ie tutors or curators *ad litem*, and guardians appointed in cases of mental incapacity.

Other Persons in Scots Law – are partnerships (a partnership is a separate legal person from the individuals which form the partnership) and limited companies.

THE LAW OF OBLIGATIONS

Contract Law – This branch of the law of obligations permits the formulation of contracts by unilateral promise or bilateral agreement. There is no law of consideration in Scotland.

There are rules for the constitution and proof of contracts. Some contracts can only be constituted in writing – so called *obligations literis* – the principal ones being contracts for sale or purchase of heritable property (essentially land and buildings), contracts to pay money and contracts of employment. Others may only be proved by writ or oath, ie obligations for payment of more than £100 Scots (£8.33). Contracts may be set aside for invalidity, error, fraud, force and fear, facility and circumvention or undue influence.

Where a breach of contract occurs the remedies at the hand of the injured party include retention of title or price, court action for price, rescission, court action for damages for loss and specific implementation. However the old Roman classification of contracts into real, verbal, literal and consensual no longer has the validity it once had and attempts to maintain that order appear increasingly sterile and may mislead.

Specific contracts recognised in Scots Law include: loan, deposit and pledge (governed by the Consumer Credit Act 1974), sale (governed by the Sale of Goods Act 1979), mandate, agency, and employment (now governed in many respects by statute).

There is also a body of quasi contractual law based on civil law remedies such as the *conditio indebiti* and the *conditio causa data, cause non secuta* and remedies for recompense.

Delict – This branch of the law of obligations relates to those obligations which arise from the operation of law emanating from a general principle of liability, to the effect that a person is liable for loss caused to another by a failure in the duty of care, which may be either intentional or negligent. The law of delict is analogous to the English Law of Tort, but does not slavishly follow the system of denominated torts. There are delicts known by particular names, eg assault, defamation or negligence, but these do not have the technical meaning which the English system attaches.

THE LAW OF PROPERTY The principal distinction in the Scots law of property is between heritage, especially land and buildings, and movables, things physically movable and movable rights.

Heritable Property – – The feudal system applies in Scotland and all land in Scotland (except **Udal** land in **Orkney** and **Shetland** and Allodial Land owned by the Prince of Wales) is owned by the Crown who has granted rights in land to tenants in chief, who in turn have created subtenants, and so on to those who enjoy actual possession of the land. That person who holds land has the *dominium utiel* or useful ownership and holds his estate or land as a vassal from a superior who in turn holds his estate from his superior and so forth to the Crown. Each person holding an interest has his title circumscribed by the conditions in the title or grant under which the land is held. Real rights to estates in land are constituted by recording the deed in the General Register of Sasines or the Land Register of Scotland.

Jura in re aliena, rights in another's property, eg servitudes, life rents, and other feudal rights, are permitted in Scots Law. Leasehold, where a tenant acquires an interest in property for a limited period of time in exchange for a periodical payment known as rent, is also permitted.

Movable Property – may be things (objects which are physically movable) or incorporeal rights. In respect of movable items, rights of title or ownership pass only with delivery, subject to statutory exceptions such as sale of goods and hire purchase. Incorporeal movables (where the movable property is not a physical item) include rights in patents, trade marks, copyrights designs and other forms of intellectual property. Rights in incorporeal movables are transferred by way of assignation.

TRUSTS Trusts in Scotland have quite a different place in the law from their English counterparts. A trust arises where property is transferred from one person (the truster) to another (the trustee) to be held for the benefit of the truster or some third party. Property so transferred becomes the absolute property of the trustee subject to the conditions or purposes of trust and the trustee's fiduciary duty. There are many types of trusts and the fiduciary relationship appears in partnerships, curatories, executries and bankruptcy as well as in the so-called public trusts where the purposes are for the common good such as charitable works or educational pursuits.

SUCCESSION The Law of Succession deals with the transfer of property upon the death of the owner. A cardinal feature of the Scots Law of Succession is that of the legal rights of the surviving spouse or children. These rights to shares of movable estate, ie the movable property of the deceased, are indefeasible debts owed by the deceased and exist in both testate and intestate estates. A surviving spouse is entitled to half of the movable estate if there are no children and to one third if there are children. Similarly surviving children are entitled to half of the movable estate if the deceased's spouse is also dead and to one third if the spouse survives.

Succession may be testate or intestate. Testate succession arises where the deceased left a will, which may appoint executors and make specific bequests. Intestate succession is where no will has been left, in which case the law provides a framework of prior rights in favour of spouse and legal rights in an effort to supply the lack of expressed wishes.

BANKRUPTCY The law of bankruptcy regulates the situation where a debtor is unable to meet his debts through insolvency. In such circumstances the debtor's property is taken over through the court procedure of sequestration and given to a trustee who proceeds to administer the property for the behoof of the bankrupt's creditors. This could involve selling the assets and distributing a dividend.

PRIVATE INTERNATIONAL LAW Scots law has an important body of private international law which provides rules for the resolution of international problems including choice of law and jurisdiction and the recognition of non-Scottish judgements.

LAW, James (c1560–1632) Bishop of Orkney

The son of a **Fife** laird, Law shares with **John Spottiswoode** the distinction of having been reprimanded by their Synod, while serving as **Presbyterian** ministers, for playing **football** on the Sabbath. Both men were eventually elevated to the office of Archbishop, not because **James VI** had learned of their profane enthusiasm for football, but because they were supporters of his ecclesiastical policies. Law also possessed the erudition to recommend him to the royal pedant, as did Spottiswoode. King James had appointed Law to the See of **Orkney** in 1605, whose assets **Earl Patrick Stewart** had been exploiting so ruthlessly. In 1608 the Bishop wrote to James: 'Alas, dear and dread Sovereign, truly it is to be pitied that so many of your Majesty's subjects are so manifoldly and grievously oppressed; some by ejection and banishment from their homes and native soil, others by contorting the laws and extorting their goods, the most part being so impoverished that some of them neither dare nor may complain, but in silent and forced patience groan under their grievance.' It is agreeable to record that Law became Archbishop of **Glasgow** in the year (1615) after that in which Earl Patrick was executed. He married three times and left three sons.

LAW, John (1671–1729) Financier

From **Lauriston** in **Edinburgh**, John Law was the son of a wealthy goldsmith. He attended Edinburgh High School and then turned his considerable facility with numbers to financial deals and gambling systems, so acquiring the name of 'Beau Law'. Removed to London he fought a duel with Edward 'Beau' Wilson over a lady of their acquaintance and killed him. He was imprisoned but eventually escaped to Holland, then France and Italy where he studied banking methods, made money, and eloped with someone's wife. In 1705 he was briefly in Scotland; he submitted proposals for reforming the economy, including the issue of bank notes, and petitioned for an indemnity in England. Both were rejected. Back on the Continent he made similar proposals for the management of the French and Genoese economies – and more money. In 1716 his proposal for a joint stock bank in France was at last accepted, the Banque Générale becoming France's first bank. Law

became a French citizen and (1718) a Catholic. It was also on his initiative that a company was set up to exploit the French possessions in what is now the USA and to found the township of New Orleans. Shares in the company brought him untold wealth; he was elected a member of the Académie Française and in 1820 appointed Controller-General of the nation's finances. In the same year the company collapsed, the currency was devalued, and Law fled. He retired to Venice and there died. His son, Jean, had meanwhile achieved some celebrity in India as one of the main French protagonists opposed to Clive's takeover of Bengal.

LAWERS, Ben, Nr Killin, Perthshire

At 3984ft/1214m Ben Lawers is the highest hill in **Perthshire**. It rises in grassy slopes from the north bank of **Loch Tay** and, along with neighbouring peaks (including Ben Ghlas, 3668ft/1118m) forms one of Scotland's most important nature reserves. By a geological freak of folding strata and erosion, calcareous schists of great age form the higher parts of the hill. The consequent lime outcrop is ideal for a unique arctic-alpine flora including saxifrages, snow gentian, alpine lady's mantle and alpine forget-me-not. Protection from sheep and plant hunters has long been a priority (protection from walkers and amateur botanists is rapidly becoming another). The **National Trust for Scotland** acquired about 8000 acres (3240ha) in 1950 to which the Nature Conservancy Council added 11,000 (4455) to form the national nature reserve in 1975. An information and visitor centre is sited on the Bridge of Balgie road, whence trails lead to the tops.

LAZYBEDS

Desperate attempts to cultivate hill or moorland that had never been regarded as arable, lazybeds (Gaelic *feannagan*) were **crofting**'s 19th century response to the impoverishment and acute shortage of cultivable land. They were created by digging drainage trenches with a *cas chrom* (foot plough, spade) and piling the extracted sods soil-up on a central strip. Manured, this ridge was then usually planted with potatoes. Considering the labour involved, only a seriously warped sense of humour can account for their being called 'lazybeds'. Although long since abandoned, the forlorn ridges straggling up remote hillsides through the sourest of soils can still be discerned in many parts of the Highlands and Islands.

LEADHILLS, Lanarkshire

Though far from the Highlands, Leadhills and **Wanlockhead** are traditionally regarded as the highest villages in Scotland (c1350ft/411m). The watershed between the **Clyde** and Annan divides them (Wanlockhead thus being in **Dumfriesshire**) while a common heritage of lead-mining in bleak and remote surroundings unites them. It is supposed that the **Romans** exploited this mineral although its rediscovery is credited to Matthew Templeton c1517. At their height in 1810 the Leadhills mines produced 1400 tons annually with a then value of £45,000. Falling returns led to their closure in 1928. Silver was also mined; and the streams panned for gold which attracted the attentions of Elizabeth I of England and has been incorporated in the regalia of other English and Scots sovereigns. Leadhills was the birthplace of **William Symington** and of **Allan Ramsay**, the latter the son of the superintendent of the mines. His name is given to the village library, founded 1741 and sometimes wrongly described as the oldest subscription library in Britain.

LECHT, The, Banffshire/Aberdeenshire
At about 2100ft/640m above sea level, the Lecht road is the second highest in the British Isles. (**The Devil's Elbow**, now Cairnwell Pass, exceeds it.) Bleak and subject to snow closure any time from November to April, it connects Strathdon and Deeside with Strathavon and Speyside, following the line of the **military road** of 1754 from Cockbridge to **Tomintoul**. 'Lecht' (or 'laight') denotes a flat stone used for a grave or, as in this case, for a marker, this being the watershed of the Grampians and the boundary between **Aberdeenshire** and **Banffshire**. **Corgarff Castle** guards the pass two miles to the south.

LEE, Baroness Jennie (1904—88) Socialist
The wife of Aneurin Bevan (1867—1960, shadow Foreign Secretary) and the creator of the Open University was born in Lochgelly, the daughter of a **Fife** miner who was a member of the **Independent Labour Party** (ILP). She went to school in **Cowdenbeath** and then to **Edinburgh University** where the fiery activism of a committed socialist first surfaced. After a couple of years' teaching she pulled off a major coup when she won (1929) North Lanark for the ILP with a 6000 majority. The advent of a 24-year-old female socialist provoked amazement at Westminster, but it was short-lived: she lost the seat in 1931. Three years later she married Nye Bevan, also from a mining and ILP background. Her career took second place to his, but she lectured and wrote, notably the autobiographical *Tomorrow is Another Day*, 1939, and *Our Ally, Russia*, 1941; she also did a stint as lobby correspondent for the *Daily Mirror*. The ILP's wartime pacifism drove her into the Labour Party for which she was elected in 1945. With a 20,000 majority at Cannock (in the Midlands) she espoused left-wing causes and after the death of Nye in 1960 was a jealous guardian of his reputation and ideals. Harold Wilson's appointment of her to a new post with responsibility for the arts (1965) enabled her to set up the Open University, a fitting complement to Nye's 1948 creation of the National Health Service. She became Chairman of the Labour Party (1967) but lost her seat in 1970 and was created a life peer. *My Life with Nye* appeared in 1980.

LEGAL PROFESSIONS
The Scottish legal professions are, like their English counterparts, divided into advocates (analogous to English barristers) and solicitors.

THE FACULTY OF ADVOCATES The Scottish Bar is constituted by the Faculty of Advocates, as part of the College of Justice. It is led by the Dean of Faculty, an elected officer who exercises administrative and disciplinary power over the Faculty members. Advocates have universal rights of audience before courts and tribunals unless excluded by statute. The Faculty maintains the distinction between senior and junior members of the Bar. Since 1897 a roll of Queen's Counsel 'learned in the law' has existed in Scotland, to which advocates so qualified may aspire. Until recently they had exclusive rights of audience before the House of Lords, the Judicial Committee of the Privy Council, the **Court of Session** and the High Court of Justiciary.

SOLICITORS constitute the larger of the two professions. Solicitors are 'men of business' for their clients, dealing with all manner of legal affairs including litigation, conveyancing, executory and trust work and general advising. The profession is regulated by statute and is governed by the Council of the Law Society of Scotland, which deals with the admission, professional regulation and discipline of solicitors. Professional discipline is maintained through a Law Society Client Relations and Complaints Office which investigates complaints of professional misconduct and inadequate professional services. The Law Society may prosecute solicitors before the independent Scottish Solicitors Discipline Tribunal. The Scottish Legal Services Ombudsman, an independent lay appointee, may investigate complaints regarding the Law Society's handling of a complaint.

The Law Society maintains an unlimited guarantee fund to indemnify clients in the event of dishonesty by solicitors and a compulsory insurance scheme to compensate in cases of professional negligence. The Law Society cannot deal with complaints of negligence.

There are other non-statutory groups, societies or faculties of solicitors, some of great antiquity including the Society of Writers to HM Signet, a part of the College of Justice, the Royal Faculty of Procurators in **Glasgow** and the Society of Advocates in **Aberdeen**. Admission as a solicitor is a prerequisite to admission as a notary public. The Scottish notary is a member of a separate profession, as is his Continental counterpart.

See also **Law**, **Legal System**, **Legal Terms**.

LEGAL SYSTEM
The sources of Scots Law are Legislation, Precedent, Institutional Texts and Custom.

Legislation
EUROPEAN COMMUNITIES LEGISLATION As a constituent legal system of a Community member state, European Community law forms a source of law for Scotland. All Community treaties (eg the Coal and Steel Treaty, the Economic Community Treaty, the Euratom Treaty and the Single European Act) apply, as do the regulations, directives and decisions of the Council of Ministers, the Commission and the European Court of Justice.

PARLIAMENTARY LEGISLATION The Statutes or Acts of the Parliament of Scotland to 1707 (in so far as not abrogated by desuetude), the Parliament of Great Britain (1707—1800) and of the United Kingdom (1801—present) as applicable, and the new **Scottish Parliament**, apply in Scotland. In addition to which primary legislation, there is also subordinate or delegated legislation formed by Orders of Council Ministerial Rules, Orders and Instruments and local authority bylaws. Acts of Sederunt and Acts of Adjournal which regulate court procedure are similarly a source of adjective or procedural law.

Precedent

Judicial precedent is a court decision comprising a principle or rule which can be applied in subsequent cases. Decisions of judges may contain statements of principle or of the rules of law which assume the status of a source of law second only to Acts of Parliament. In the absence of relevant statutory provision, judicial precedent prevails as a source of law.

The doctrine of precedent operates within the hierarchy of the courts and the following general principles apply:

1 Decisions made by the House of Lords in Scottish appeals bind the House itself, subject to limited exceptions, and all lower Scottish courts.
2 Decisions made by either division of the Inner House of the Court of Session bind each division and all lower courts.
3 Decisions of single judges, sheriffs principal and sheriffs are not binding.

Institutional Texts

Certain highly respected authors of law texts written principally in the 17th, 18th and 19th centuries are accorded a special place as a source of law. The institutional writers are: Craig, *Jus Feudale* (1655); Stair, *The Institutions of the Law of Scotland* (1681); Erskine, *Institute of the Law of Scotland* (1773); Bell, *Commentaries on the Law of Scotland* (1800) and *Principles of the Law of Scotland* (1829); **Mackenzie**, *Laws and Customs of Scotland in Matters Criminal* (1678); Hume, *Commentaries on the Law of Scotland Respecting Crimes* (1797); and Alison, *Principles* (1832) and *Practice of the Criminal Law of Scotland* (1833).

Custom

Custom or long-observed practice may be looked to as a source of law in default of any other source.

Equity

The principles of natural justice and fairness have always formed a source of Scots Law and have been applied by the courts without distinction from the law. Therefore Scots Law has avoided the highly complex juristic construct of Equity which applies in England.

See also **Law**, **Legal Professions**, **Legal Terms**.

The Courts

Civil and Criminal Jurisdictions

The highest civil appellate court is the House of Lords which sits in Westminster. The judges who sit in the House are the Lord Chancellor, the Lords of Appeal in Ordinary, and those peers who hold or have held high judicial office. The House of Lords has an appellate jurisdiction from Scottish courts in civil matters only; it has no Scottish criminal jurisdiction.

The superior court in Scotland is the Court of Session formed by the Inner House (comprising the first and second divisions) and the Outer House (where only single judges or Lords of Session also styled Senators of the College of Justice sit). The principal judge is the Lord President, who leads the first division, whereas the Lord Justice Clerk leads the second division. The court sits only at Parliament House in **Edinburgh**.

The superior criminal court in Scotland is the High Court of Justiciary, formed by the Lord Justice General (who is *ipso facto* Lord President), the Lord Justice Clerk and the Lords Commissioners of Justiciary. There is a court of Criminal Appeal. The High Court sits both in Edinburgh and on circuit.

The lower court in Scotland is the Sheriff Court. Each Sheriffdom (of which there are six) has a Sheriff Principal with Sheriffs sitting in each main town. This court has both civil and criminal jurisdictions. The civil jurisdiction, though inferior, is extensive and the majority of civil cases raised in Scotland are taken in the Sheriff Court. There is appeal from Sheriff to Sheriff Principal and thence to the Inner House of the Court of Session. An appeal may be taken to the Inner House directly. From the Inner House further appeal may be taken to the House of Lords. In criminal matters the Sheriff also has a wide jurisdiction in relation to most crimes; only those of greatest gravity lie outwith the Sheriff's jurisdiction. There is no appeal from Sheriff to Sheriff Principal in criminal cases, the appeal lies to the court of criminal appeal.

The court dealing with petty criminal matters is the District Court. Each local authority district has a Magistrate's Court. The magistrate may be a lay justice sitting with an assessor or a stipendiary magistrate who is legally qualified.

Other Courts

1 The court of the Lord Lyon – dealing with matters of **heraldry**.
2 The Scottish Land Court – dealing with disputes between landlord and tenant, especially in the **crofting** counties.
3 The Teind Court – dealing with disputes in respect of teinds or tithes.
4 Church Courts of the **Church of Scotland**, including the **General Assembly**, the Synods, presbyteries and Kirk Sessions.

Tribunals

Many administrative tribunals sit in Scotland, including:

1 The Employment Appeals Tribunal which hears appeals from Industrial Tribunals also sitting in Scotland.
2 The Immigration Appeals Tribunal which deals with appeals from Immigration Tribunals.
3 The Lands Tribunal for Scotland which deals with the discharge or variation of land obligations and questions of compensation for compulsory purchase.

LEGAL TERMS, Glossary of

Absolvitor – A type of decree in civil actions. The court granting such a judgement decides in favour of the defender by absolving him from the pursuer's claims.

Action – The term used for civil court proceedings whereby the pursuer asks the court for a remedy against his opponent, the defender. In the **Court of Session** actions will begin by the lodging of the writ known as a summons. A Sheriff Court action commences when an initial writ is lodged.

Acts of Adjournal – Rules made by the High Court of Justiciary for regulating procedure in criminal cases.

Acts of Sederunt – Rules made by the Court of Session for regulating procedure in civil cases.

Adjudication – A method of attaching land in security of sums owed.

Admonition – The most lenient form of punishment in criminal cases. An admonition is a warning by the judge to a person convicted of a crime about his future behaviour.

Advocate – A member of the **Faculty of Advocates** or Scottish Bar, sometimes referred to as counsel.

Aliment – A payment of money made under a duty to maintain a relative, either at law or enforced by the court. The duty to aliment subsists generally in the domestic relationships of husband and wife, parent and child, and guardian and ward.

Allenarly – An old Scottish word meaning 'only'.

Allodial – Allodial land is land owned outright and absolutely, and is not held of the Crown. It is a feature of the feudal system and occurs only in land held by the Crown, the Prince of Wales and High Steward of Scotland, and by the Church.

Art and Part – A term of criminal law meaning an accessory.

Assoilzie – To decide in favour of a defender.

Avizandum – A medieval Latin word meaning to reserve a case for further consideration.

Books of Council and Session – The register of documents held by the keeper of the registers, in which a variety of deeds are registered for preservation and execution.

Candlemas – Scots quarter day, 28 February.

Caution – A form of guarantee or security, used particularly to ensure that estates controlled by appointed persons, ie, executors dative, are indemnified against loss.

Confirmation – A decree of court conferring upon an executor the administrative title to possess, ingather and distribute a deceased person's estate.

Curator – A form of guardian arising naturally in the relationship of minor children to their parents. The concept has been extended to (1) persons of unsound mind to whom a *curator bonis* may be appointed, who looks after the ward's affairs; and (2) the *curator ad litem*, a person appointed to act on behalf of a minor in court proceedings.

Dead's Part – That portion of a person's estate over which he has the power to dispose by will in any way he desires. It is that part of the movable estate not subject to either Prior or Legal Rights.

Debate – An argument as to the law made in the context of a civil court action.

Decree – A final judgement of a court in a civil action.

Defender – The person against whom a civil action is raised (in English Law the 'defendant')

Delict – A civil wrong or action committed in breach of the legal duty of care in respect of which there is an obligation to make reparation.

Diligence – The term denoting the legal procedure by which a creditor enforces a decree of the court against a debtor.

Excambion – A contract of exchange whereby one area of ground is swapped for another.

Executor – The representative of a deceased person, but with his liability limited to the extent of the estate under his care. The executor's function is to ingather and distribute the deceased's estate acting under the authority granted by the decree of confirmation.

Feu – An area of land held by a vassal from a superior in return for periodical services or payment. The majority of land in Scotland is held by feudal tenure.

Fiar – A person having right in land which is subject to a life rent in favour of another person. The fiar has rights of actual possession, use and enjoyment which revert to him upon expiry of liferent.

Forisfamiliation – The act of a minor or pupil child leaving the family home and setting up on his or her own.

Furthcoming – A type of court action whereby a claimant to monies held by a third party may establish his right to them.

Grassum – A single or lump sum payment made in addition to rent in respect of the acquisition of leased property.

Ground Annual – A payment made annually and the implementation of a contract of ground annual registered against a property. Since 1970 it has been illegal to create ground annual.

Haver – A person possessing documents or other items which may be needed in evidence in a court case.

Heritable Property – All immovable things. For example, land and buildings or items attached to land in an immovable way, such as trees or certain crops.

Holograph – A deed written by a grantor in his own hand. Holograph writings do not require to be witnessed if signed. A document which is not holograph may be 'adopted as holograph' by the signatory writing the words 'adopted as holograph' above his signature, thereby importing that the deed is as if written in his own handwriting. Such a document does not require witnesses.

Homologation – A form of personal bar whereby effect can be given to a contract even though it has been informally constituted. Homologation is an act which confirms or adopts the imperfect contract as binding.

Hypothec – Right in security over movables without possession. Hypothecs derive by law or by contract. Those usually encountered are the landlord's hypothec and the solicitor's hypothec.

Induciae – A period during which a person must take some specific action in response to a duly notified legal document, ie the 14-day period from service of a writ in which a defender must intimate to the court his intention to defend.

Infeftment – The act of completing title formally indicated by a symbolic gesture of taking possession of land or buildings. Now achieved by the recording in the appropriate division of the General Register of Sasines or in the Land Register of Scotland of the deed transferring title.

Inhibition – A personal diligence which prohibits the person inhibited from dealing with or alienating his heritable property to his inhibiting creditor's prejudice.

Initial Writ – The court document used in Sheriff Court procedure for initiating ordinary actions.

Interdict – A court decree ordering the defender to desist from some activity which is causing harm, injury or alarm to the pursuer.

Interlocutor – An interim decision of a court, generally, but not exclusively, dealing with procedural matters.

Jus Quaesitum Tertio – The right of a third party bestowed upon him by a contract between two other persons and to which he is not a party.

Justice of the Peace – Magistrates appointed in terms of the District Court (Scotland) Act 1975. The justice

administers summary criminal justice in the district court.

Lammas – A Scottish quarter day, 28 August.

Lawburrows – A form of action whereby a defender is obliged to find caution not to molest the pursuer.

Legal Rights – Rights to property in a deceased person's estate to which certain specified persons are entitled. These rights are satisfied from movable property only. The legal rights recognised in Scotland are (1) the *jus relictae*, the right of a widow to share in her deceased husband's movables, which extends to one third of the estate if children (or their issue) survive, and to one half if there are no children; (2) the *jus relicti*, the right of a widower to his wife's movable estate in the same proportions as the *jus relictae*; and (3) the *legitim*, the right of a child (or issue) to a share in the deceased parent's movable estate, extending to one third if one of the parents survives and to one half if both parents are deceased.

Lien – A right in security with possession in favour of a creditor. The usual liens encountered are the solicitor's liens over a client's documents and papers for unpaid fees, the accountant's lien over a client's documents and papers for unpaid fees and the unpaid seller's lien.

Liferent – A right to hold and enjoy heritable property during the holder's lifetime on the understanding that the property will be returned to the fiar without its substance being wasted.

Locus Poenitentiae – The opportunity to think again whereby a person is able to withdraw from a contract which is not binding because it is informally constituted. *Locus poenitentiae* may be defeated by the operation of the doctrine of personal bar.

Lord Advocate – The chief law officer of the Crown in Scotland. The Lord Advocate, originally King's Advocate, has full discretion over criminal prosecution and advises the government on Scottish legal affairs. The office dates from 1478, and in the 17th and 18th centuries its incumbent effectively headed the Scottish administration. Under the Scotland Act of 1998 the Lord Advocate becomes an essential member of the Scottish Executive, although the holder of the office need not be a Member of the Scottish Parliament.

Lord President – The presiding and principal judge of the Court of Session since its foundation as the College of Justice in 1532. Since 1837 the office has included that of Lord Justice General [see **Legal System** – The Courts].

Lords of Session – The judges of the Court of Session. Originally 15, of whom 7 were to be clerics, the Lords of Session were invariably laymen after 1640, their number being reduced to 13 in the 19th century. It has since been increased to 21.

Majority – The status of adulthood with full legal

capacity. Formerly reached at 21, since 1970 the age of majority is 18.

Mandate – A contract of agency whereby one person instructs another to act on his behalf; generally the service is provided gratuitously.

Martinmas – A term day in Scotland, 28 November.

Messenger-at-Arms – An officer of the court empowered to perform acts of diligence for the enforcement of court orders.

Minor – A person in minority, ie a girl aged between 12 and 18 or a boy aged between 14 and 18. A minor has limited legal capacity and may enter contracts with the consent of the curator. A minor who has no curator has the same contractual capacity as a person in majority. Contracts entered into by a minor are voidable to 22 years of age, upon the minor showing that there is *enorm lesion* or that the consideration involved in the contract was grossly disproportionate to that which might have been obtained.

Novodamus – A form of feudal charter whereby a grant of land is made in new terms. This enables the real burdens or conditions attaching to land to be changed.

Obiter Dictum (Plural: Obiter Dicta) – An expression of opinion by a judge which is peripheral or non-essential to the decision of a case.

Obligatio Literis – One of that category of contracts which must be constituted in writing. The writing must be formal (performed before witnesses) or holograph or adopted as holograph.

Panel – The accused in a criminal case.

Pari Passu – A phrase meaning on an equal footing, often used when referring to the sharing of assets in an insolvent case.

Personal Bar – A legal doctrine whereby the person is inhibited from enforcing his legal rights due to his own actions, which have prejudiced his position.

Poinding – A form of diligence whereby a court decree is enforced. Where a charge has been raised on a debtor and has not been paid the creditor may instruct a sheriff officer to poind the movable property of the debtor. The sheriff officer inventorises the debtor's property and such goods are rendered litigious. The next stage in enforcement is warrant sale.

Power of Attorney – A deed granted by one person constituting another the grantor's factor with power to act on the grantor's behalf in relation to all or specifically stated aspects of the grantor's affairs.

Prescription – The effect of the passage of time on a person's rights or obligations. Periods of time differ as per the rights or obligations affected. The principal prescriptive periods are:

1 Positive prescription – 10 years, relating to defective titles to land.
2 The long negative prescription – 20 years, extinguishing the obligations of any kind in property.
3 Five years prescriptive period, extinguishing obligations in respect of contract or delict.
4 The triennium – three years, extinguishing the right to action for personal injury or death.

Prior Rights – Rights of a surviving spouse in the deceased intestate's estate which take precedence over legal rights and dead's part. The rights include rights to a specified value of heritable property. The surviving spouse is also entitled to the furniture and plenishings, and lastly is also entitled to a sum of money. All the levels of financial value of the constituent elements of the prior rights are specified in an order by the Secretary of State.

Probative – A probative document is one which complies with specified formalities and is therefore deemed to prove its content and date. Probative documents used in judicial proceedings create a presumption of genuineness because they have been signed in accordance with the statutory formality.

Procurator Fiscal – A public officer (usually a civil servant) appointed by the Lord Advocate to prosecute offences in the Sheriff Court and the District Court.

Proof – The trial of the facts in civil actions.

Queen's and Lord Treasurer's Remembrancer – An officer of the royal household whose functions relate to the collection of the expenses of the Lord Advocate's Department and the collection of monies due to the Crown, for example when the Crown is the *ultimus haeres* in the estate of a person who died without any known successors.

Ratio Decidendi – The rule or principle of law which is fundamental to a judge's decision.

Record – A document used in court processes which is a cumulative formulation in a logical and cohesive manner of the statements in fact of a pursuer in a case (the condescendence) with the defendant's defences to the action to which the pleas in law (basis of law) of both pursuer and defender are added.

Reddendo – The duty paid by a vassal to his superior in the context of the feudal system.

Regalia – Divided into the *regalia majora* and the *regalia minora*, these are rights in and to the land and other property which belong to the Crown. *Regalia majora*, eg the sea within territorial limits and navigable rivers, cannot be alienated by the Crown, whereas *regalia minora*, eg rights to the seashore and to certain fish and animals, may be disposed of to the public.

Register of Sasines – The principal register in Scotland for the recording of deeds transferring the burdening or in some other way affecting title to land. The Register is being replaced by the Land Register of Scotland.

Rei Interitus – Physical destruction of property which is the subject of a contract, causing the discharge of that contract.

Rei Interventus – Another aspect of personal bar.

Relict – An old Scottish word for the surviving spouse, either widow or widower.

Res Ipsa Loquitur – A doctrine applicable in the law of delict whereby a presumption of fact is taken as accepted and shifts the onus of proof from the pursuer to the defender.

Res Judicata – The concept that the courts can reach final decisions arising from certain proven fact situations which preclude further action on the same grounds.

Sasine – The act of taking possession of property. Originally sasine was transferred by a symbolic ceremony on the ground, but is now completed by registration of the appropriate deed in the Register of Sasines or the Land Register of Scotland.

Search for Incumbrances – A record of entries in the public registers, eg the register of sasines or the register of inhibitions and adjudications.

Sequestration – A court supervised process whereby a bankrupt's property is made over to a trustee who then ingathers and distributes for the benefit of the bankrupt's creditors.

Servitude – A benefit attaching to one plot of ground which burdens another plot of ground owned by another party. Servitudes customarily encompass rights of access or rights of way and wayleaves for public utilities.

Sheriff Officer – An officer of the Sheriff Court empowered by his commission to do diligence in the enforcement of court decrees.

Signet – The seal of the Court of Session which is adhibited to writs and summonses issued through the court in Edinburgh.

Sist – An aspect of court procedure where a particular action is suspended for procedural purposes.

Solatium – An alternative term for a head of loss detailed as pain and suffering, loss of faculties and amenities and loss of expectation of life.

Solemn Procedure – A procedure used in criminal prosecutions on indictment. Solemn procedure consists of a trial before a judge and jury of 15 persons. It is to be contrasted with summary procedure where a judge or sheriff sits alone.

Solicitor – A legal practitioner admitted to the practice of law, by the Court of Session, and governed by the practice, rules and regulations of the Law Society of Scotland, a statutory body established under the Solicitors (Scotland) Act 1980. A solicitor is a 'man of business' and undertakes a great variety of work for his client including, but not exclusively, conveyancing, executory work, court practice, company work, taxation and a whole range of legal questions in respect of which a client may need advice.

Solicitor General – The Crown's agent in civil actions. The office dates from 1587 and complements that of Lord Advocate, making the Solicitor General the second law officer of the Crown in Scotland. Under the Scotland Act of 1998 the Solicitor General becomes an essential member of the Scottish Executive, although the holder of the office need not be a Member of the Scottish Parliament.

Tacit Relocation – A procedure whereby a contract of a specified duration (typically a lease) has expired without either party giving notice of intent to terminate and which is deemed to continue for one further year.

Teind – One tenth of the produce of land originally donated to the church.

Tenendas – A clause in feu deeds defining the tenure by which land is held.

Tholing an Assize – A defence to a criminal accusation that the matter has already been decided by a court of competent jurisdiction.

Tutor – The person who has the capacity and power to control a pupil child.

Uberrimae Fidei – A Latin phrase meaning 'the utmost good faith'. The concept is of particular application to contracts of insurance where there is an obligation on parties to disclose all material facts.

Udal Land – A form of tenure of land in **Orkney** and **Shetland**. Udal land is distinct from feudal land and udalers acknowledge feudal duty but possess their land absolutely.

Ultimus Haeres – The doctrine of the law of succession whereby the Crown takes as the ultimate of the beneficiary where a deceased person dies leaving no heirs.

Ultra Vires – The doctrine of *ultra vires* dictates the competence, powers and capacities of certain bodies and persons to act. The doctrine applies in company law and administrative law and circumscribes the activities of corporate bodies.

Verdict – The judgement of a criminal court. In Scotland there are three verdicts which a court may make:

1 Guilty, where the accused has been found to have committed the crime with which he has been charged.
2 Not Guilty, whereby the Crown has not proved its case and the accused is discharged as innocent.
3 Not Proven, where the judge or jury is not satisfied that the Crown has proven its case against the accused. Where a 'not proven' verdict is returned the accused is discharged on the basis that he is innocent.

Vexatious Litigant – A person who takes court action without foundation or from malice or in breach of an agreement not to take such action. If a court declares a person to be vexatious he may not take court action without the permission of the court being specifically obtained beforehand.

Volenti non Fit Injuria – The application of the doctrine of consent to the Scots law of delict. If a person has knowingly or willingly exposed himself to injury he may not be able to succeed to a claim for that injury. Therefore sportsmen and persons who have undergone medical operations may have claims defeated which derive from activities to which they have consented.

Whitsunday – A term day in Scotland – 28 May.

See also **Law**, **Legal Professions**, **Legal System**.

LEIGHTON, Robert (1611–84) Archbishop of Glasgow

The son of a **Presbyterian** minister, Robert Leighton studied at **Edinburgh University** and at Douai before being appointed minister of **Newbattle** in 1641. A prodigious scholar, he became Principal of Edinburgh University in 1653 and held the post until created Bishop of **Dunblane** by **Charles II** in 1661. Leighton advocated compromise or 'comprehension' as a way of healing the rift between Presbyterian and **Episcopalian**. In 1670 he succeeded **Burnet** as Archbishop of **Glasgow** but the policy of **Indulgences**, implying toleration rather than comprehension, satisfied neither Leighton nor the radical **Covenanters**. He resigned in 1674, retired to Sussex, and died in London. His mild nature, piety and scholarship (the Leighton Library in Dunblane testifies) were notable in an age of bigotry.

LEISHMAN, Sir William (1865–1926) Bacteriologist

Born in **Glasgow**, Leishman pursued medicine through a military career, rising to be Director General of Army Medical Services by the time of his death. He was instrumental in introducing typhoid vaccinations for troops as well as carrying out research on Dumdum fever, and perfecting a staining technique to detect malaria in blood. He died in London.

LEITH, Alexander, Baron Leith of Fyvie (b.1847) Steel Magnate

The son of Admiral John Leith and Margaret Forbes, Alexander set himself the challenge of emulating an ancestor, Sir Henry Preston of Fyvie, by establishing his heirs as lairds of **Fyvie Castle** and worthy members of the landed aristocracy. He achieved this by marrying (1871) Marie Louise January, the daughter of a director of the Joliot Steel Company of Illinois, by eventually becoming that company's president and principal shareholder, and by then forming the Illinois Steel Company, said to have been the largest in the world. In 1889, now calling himself Forbes-Leith, he duly purchased Fyvie for £175,000 and began lavishing his large fortune and considerable taste on refurbishing and adding to the castle and on filling it with *objets d'art* and paintings. Begun in great style, the enterprise was sadly halted when his only son was killed in the Boer War. In 1905 Alexander was created 1st – and only – Baron Leith of Fyvie. His daughter inherited the property; her grandson sold it to the **National Trust for Scotland**.

LEITH, Edinburgh

The first settlement at the mouth of the **Water of Leith** [see **Edinburgh**] was probably prehistoric, although the earliest written reference dates from 1143. The port expanded under successive monarchs, trading with France and the Low Countries and later with the Baltic and the Americas. Leith was Scotland's principal port until the mid-19th century, dealing in grain, flax, sugar, timber, **iron**, paper and **whisky**. The profits of this commerce went into the Edinburgh coffers from 1329 onwards when Leith became the official port of the burgh of Edinburgh.

In the following centuries the development of the port was interrupted by a succession of disasters; it was attacked and nearly flattened by the English in 1544 and 1547; **Mary of Guise** moved the seat of government to Leith in 1548 and built fortifications around the heart of the town only for an army of Protestant reformers to lay siege in 1560 and demolish the walls. In 1561 **Queen Mary** arrived in Leith to a ceremonial welcome on her return from France; and in 1645 a plague killed almost two thirds of the population.

The 17th century saw the emergence of **shipbuilding** as the main employer. In 1698 the **Darien Expedition** set sail from Leith; Scotland's first dry docks were built here in 1720; and, during the second half of the 18th century, the town began to acquire a fashionable gloss as holiday villas sprouted on the outskirts and the Honourable Company of Edinburgh Golfers developed Leith Links as their home course with a smart new clubhouse.

Leith became an independent burgh in 1833 when the cost of the upkeep of Leith docks bankrupted Edinburgh. In 1920, despite the burgh's progressive record and in the face of fierce local opposition, Leith was amalgamated with Edinburgh. Economic decline threatened with the end of shipbuilding in 1984, but much of Leith has been transformed in recent years into a fashionable residence and workplace. In 1995 the Scottish Office was relocated at Victoria Dock, and in May 1998, after decommissioning by the Queen (and in the face of fierce competition from **Glasgow** and Manchester to offer the ship a long-term home), the Royal Yacht *Britannia* arrived at the port of Leith. After refitting and refurbishment, *Britannia* was opened to the public in October of that year. The Royal Family are still able

On the Quay at Leith, *by David Octavius Hill (NGS)*

to use the yacht as a residence if they visit Edinburgh, in which case the public will be excluded.

LEITH HALL, Kennethmont, Nr Huntly, Aberdeenshire

The **National Trust for Scotland**, which owns Leith Hall, admits it is 'not particularly distinguished architecturally'. Built round a quadrangle, the north side consists of a modest 1650s tower, the south of a late 18th century house of neo-classical pretensions, and the east and west of linking blocks liberally supplied with Victorian baronial pepperpots. Harled and slated, it all hangs together surprisingly well. For three centuries the property belonged to the Leith, then Leith-Hay, family whose improving fortunes and widening interests are all faithfully reflected in the furnishings, *objets* and paintings. The gardens, also pleasing rather than impressive, have two **Pictish** symbol stones.

LENNOX, Earldom and Dukedom

The Celtic earldom or mormaerdom of Lennox comprised **Dunbartonshire**, a large part of **Stirlingshire**, and parts of **Perthshire** and **Renfrewshire**. Earl Malcolm of Lennox supported **Robert I**, fought at **Bannockburn** and was killed at **Halidon**; Earl Duncan was

beheaded at **Stirling Castle** (1425) alongside his son-in-law **Murdoch Duke of Albany**. Sir John Stewart, Lord Darnley, was recognised as Earl of Lennox in 1473, had his title revoked in 1476, restored again in 1488, revoked in 1489 for rebelling against **James IV** but restored for a third time later that year – he died in 1495; his son Matthew, the 2nd Stewart Earl of Lennox, was killed at **Flodden**; John, 3rd Stewart Earl, died at **Linlithgow** (1526) in an attempt to free **James V** from his captivity by the **Earl of Angus**. His son, Matthew, 4th Stewart Earl, married Margaret, the daughter of Angus and **Margaret Tudor**; their elder son **Henry Stewart, Lord Darnley**, married **Queen Mary**. The title passed to Robert Stewart, Bishop of **Caithness**, son of the 3rd Earl, who resigned it in 1580, whereupon **James VI** (son of Mary and Darnley), awarded it to his cousin **Esmé Stewart** whom he created Duke of Lennox in 1581. On the death of the 6th Duke without surviving heirs (1672) the title reverted to **Charles II** who gave it to one of his natural sons, already Duke of Richmond. The 6th Duke of Richmond and Lennox was created **Duke of Gordon** in 1876.

LENNOXLOVE, East Lothian

The Maitlands bought the estate of Lethington near **Haddington** from the Giffords in 1385 and built the massive three storey L-plan tower house in the 15th century. The home in the 16th century of **William Maitland**, **Queen Mary**'s 'Secretary Lethington', the tower was extended in 1626 with the addition of the long east wing, a two-storey cap-house on the original parapet walk and various internal improvements, and in 1644 with a further tower to the south-east. With the failure of the Maitland line on the death of **John Maitland, 1st Duke of Lauderdale** in 1682, Lethington was sold to Charles Stewart, Duke of Richmond and Lennox, whose wife **Frances** '*la belle Stuart*', was the favourite, and possibly mistress, of **Charles II**; when she died in 1702 her will decreed that Lethington be henceforth known as Lennoxlove. After further extensions and alterations in the 19th and 20th centuries, including those undertaken for the Baird owner by **Robert Lorimer** in 1912, the house was purchased by the Duke of Hamilton in 1947. Amongst the many treasures it contains are the death mask of Queen Mary, a silver casket similar to, or perhaps even the very one, that contained the notorious **Casket Letters**, and a rich collection of furnishings, paintings and porcelain, including many pieces from the demolished Hamilton Palace.

LENNOXTOWN, Stirlingshire

Although 'Lennox' derives from Levenach (ie the vale of the Leven, in **Dunbartonshire**), the **Earldom of Lennox**, like the Lennox Hills (see **Campsie Fells**) came to comprehend a wide swathe of country north of **Glasgow** stretching from **Dumbarton** to **Stirling**. Lennoxtown, north of **Kirkintilloch**, was founded in the late 18th century as a calico and colliery town, usurping its older neighbours of Clachan of Campsie and Milton of Campsie. Also a usurper, Lennox Castle is a baronial pile once reckoned one of the most spacious and superb mansions in Scotland, of c1840 by **David Hamilton** for John Kincaid-Lennox whose claim to the earldom of Lennox was rejected. To the west, at the base of the Campsie Fells between Lennoxtown and Strathblane, Craigend was the birthplace of **Sir Thomas Mitchell**, the Australian explorer, while the Ballogan Burn has a noted waterfall.

LERWICK, Shetland

Lerwick, the only town on Shetland, owes its origin to trade with Dutch **herring** fishermen in the early 17th century. For hundreds of years the Dutch had regarded **Bressay** Sound (now Lerwick Harbour) as a safe haven for their large fleet of sailing vessels, whose crews went ashore for recreation and to trade with the local people. The site of the early market, mid-way between Lerwick and **Scalloway**, is still known as the Hollanders Knowe.

From 1615 onwards Lerwick grew as a line of shops and houses along the shore. When more space was required, a parallel row of buildings was erected on land reclaimed from the sea. Between these two runs Commercial Street, paved with slate and as crooked as the old shoreline it once followed. It is still the commercial heart of the town, with shops, banks and offices serving an island population of 23,000, plus the seamen from a dozen different nationalities who call at this crossroads of the North Sea.

Since 1900 Lerwick has been a major herring port. In the peak years of the fishery over a thousand vessels assembled here each summer. The town's population trebled as fishermen were joined by the fish workers who gutted the herring and packed them in barrels with salt. Lerwick is still the main herring and mackerel port in Britain and a fleet of 40 purse seiners land as much fish as did 400 steam drifters between the wars. The curing yards that fringed the shores of Lerwick's North Harbour have been replaced by the East European klondykers, which anchor in the harbour and process the fish. Their crews spend their leisure time in shopping and sightseeing – just as the Dutchmen did until the early part of this century.

Since the early 1970s Lerwick has been an important supply base for North Sea **oil**. The industry has brought prosperity to Lerwick Harbour Trust who have invested their profits in industrial sites, better facilities for the **fishing** industry, and the 64-bedroom Shetland Hotel at Holmsgarth, opposite the large ferry terminal where the P&O vessels disembark passengers and unload their cargo.

The town has several distinctive buildings including the Town Hall, built in 1882, the Anderson High School, the oldest part of which dates from 1862, and Fort Charlotte, the first permanent building in Lerwick, constructed in the 1660s to defend Lerwick from its friends, the Dutch, at a time when England was at war with Holland.

Lerwick is famous for the **Viking** festival of Up-Helly-Aa, held on the last Tuesday of January each year. A replica Viking longship is burnt as the spectacular climax to a procession when upwards of a thousand guisers carry lighted torches through the darkened streets of the town.

LESLIE, Sir Alexander, 1st Earl of Leven (c1582–1661)

Alexander Leslie was probably the son of George Leslie of Balgonie, who commanded the garrison of the Castle of **Blair** in the reign of **James V**. He began his military

General Alexander Leslie, 1st Earl of Leven, attributed to George Jamesone (SNPG)

career in Holland before going to Sweden where he rose to the rank of Field Marshal. In 1638, aged 56, 'the little old crooked soldier' took command of the Scottish Army of the **Covenant** during the Bishops' Wars [see **Charles I**] and in 1640 he advanced into England, defeating the Royalists at Newburn and holding Newcastle for the Parliamentarians. Charles I, trying to conciliate his enemies, created him Earl of Leven (1641), but in 1644 he and **David Leslie** contributed to the defeat at Marston Moor of the Royalist army. He opposed the **Engagement** but after Charles I's execution, firmly gave allegiance to **Charles II**. He fought against Cromwell at **Dunbar** and was afterwards imprisoned in the Tower of London. Freed on the intercession of the Queen of Sweden, he died at an advanced age at Balgonie in **Fife** [see **Markinch**].

LESLIE, David, Lord Newark (d.1682)

The grandson of the 5th Earl of **Rothes**, Leslie fought for Gustavus Adolphus of Sweden during the Thirty Years' War, before returning to Scotland to join the army of the **Covenant** in which he became a lieutenant-general. He commanded the cavalry at the Battle of Marston Moor in 1644. In 1645 he surprised and defeated **Montrose** at **Philiphaugh** and was blamed for the subsequent massacre of soldiers and camp followers. In 1647 he commanded the army which drove **Alasdair MacDonald** and his Irish force from **Kintyre** and again he allowed the slaughter of men who had refused to make unconditional surrender when the fortress of Dunaverty was taken. In 1650, while commanding the Covenant army, he was defeated by Cromwell at **Dunbar** and, in the following year, when fighting for **Charles II**, was defeated at Worcester and imprisoned in the Tower of London. Released at the Restoration, he was granted the Lordship of **Newark** by **Charles II** in 1661.

LESLIE, Fife

'A prosperous and busy place' at the turn of the century, the flax and bleaching burgh of Leslie, unlike many of its neighbours, missed out on the **coal** age. On the Green is the Bull Stone, a deeply grooved block of granite to which cattle were tied for the jolly village sport of bull-baiting. Dogs (bull terriers?) endeavoured to fasten on to the victim's nose, 'the only protection offered the bull being a hole in the ground into which the bull might thrust this vulnerable part' (B Walker, G Ritchie). It was outlawed in 1835. Besides **Leslie House**, notable buildings include the late 16th century Strathendry Castle, where the young **Adam Smith** is said to have been briefly kidnapped by gypsies, and adjacent Strathendry House (**William Burn**, 1824).

LESLIE, John, 6th Earl of Rothes (c1600–41)

George 4th Earl (d.1558), a Lord of Session, and Andrew 5th Earl (d.1611) had invariably aligned with the Protestant nobility although the former was acquitted of the murder of **Cardinal Beaton** and the latter, like other reformist nobles, sided with **Queen Mary** after her escape from **Loch Leven** in 1568. John 6th Earl, a grandson of the 5th, betrayed stronger religious sentiments. Succeeding to the earldom in 1621, he opposed **James VI**'s Romish concessions embodied in the **Five Articles of Perth** and then **Charles I**'s reintroduction of church vestments and the Prayer Book. In 1638 he helped draft the **Covenant** and at the **Glasgow** Assembly later in the same year played a leading role. By 1640 suspicion of **Argyll** was dividing the ranks of the Covenanters and Rothes seemed amenable to approaches from the King but died the following year.

LESLIE, John, 7th Earl and 1st Duke of Rothes (1630–81)

The eldest son of **John 6th Earl** 'inherited his father's licentiousness without his gift of commending himself to the godly' (G Donaldson). He also inherited his father's improved relations with the Royalists and, joining the army, fought for **Charles II** at Worcester (1651) where he was captured. Seven years' detention under the Protectorate made him a leading contender for office after the Restoration; he was duly appointed Lord of Session and President of the Council with responsibility for the Treasury under **John Earl of Middleton** as Commissioner (1661). In spite of his father's role in drawing up the **Covenant**, he now became the scourge of its adherents, aligning himself with **Archbishop James Sharp** and outlawing **Conventiclers**. Such loyalty brought him the senior post of Commissioner in Scotland in succession to Middleton in 1663. He presided over **James Turner**'s oppression of Conventiclers, over the suppression of the **Pentland Rising**, and over the brutal repression which followed. But in 1667 he was made Lord Chancellor, in effect a side-lining, as **John Maitland 2nd Earl of Lauderdale** came north to take over the reins of government and introduce more conciliatory policies. Rothes joined the opposition to Lauderdale and was created 1st Duke of Rothes in 1680. He having no male heir, the dukedom lapsed but the earldom descended through the female line.

LESLIE CASTLE, Nr Insch, Aberdeenshire

'One of the most advanced specimens in its class of the mansions of **Aberdeenshire**' (**MacGibbon and Ross**), Leslie was built by William Forbes in 1661 and may be the latest of the fortified tower houses. Large and L-shaped, it has a square and spacious stair tower in the re-entrant angle plus gun loops and angle turrets. But crow-stepping had gone out of favour and the chimneys take the form of individual shafts set diagonally in the English Jacobean fashion. The building has recently been restored.

LESLIE HOUSE, Leslie, Fife

The former seat of the Earls of Rothes and 'the glory of **Fife**' (Defoe), Leslie House (1667–74) was, before the disastrous fire of 1763, a quadrangular, three-storeyed 'palace' in the style of **Holyroodhouse**. This is hardly surprising as **Sir William Bruce**, **Robert Mylne** and **William Adam** were all concerned in its construction.

Meticulously detailed domestic and estate records give a vivid picture of gracious living 17th and 18th century style. In the Gallery, which was 3ft (1 metre) longer than that of Holyroodhouse, a Rembrandt hung amongst portraits of the family, the Scottish nobility and royalty. The Library, regarded as one of the finest in Scotland, catered for all tastes, from Locke's *Human Understanding* to Farquhar's *Beaux' Stratagem*; from Molière's plays to logarithmic tables. Among the 60 rooms, all sumptuously furnished, were, inevitably, a King's Room, a billiard room and, surprisingly, a bathroom. There was also a complete range of 'offices', gyle-house (brewhouse), bakehouse, slaughterhouse, salthouse, washhouse, dairy and armoury. In the walled garden the earls, who were all keen agriculturalists and horticulturalists, grew figs, apricots, peaches, nectarines, cantaloupe melons, garlic, scorzonera, fennel, asparagus and artichokes, in addition to the full range of trees and more common flowers, fruits and vegetables.

Garden produce naturally featured prominently on the menus. Beef, mutton, veal, poultry, eggs and game were all produced on the estate, as were trout, sea trout, perch and eels. With the Firth of Forth only a few miles away the normal North Sea fish were in abundance, with the frequent addition of **oysters** and lobster (cheaper than cod). Full use was made of offal in the form of **haggis**, tripe, ox and pigs' feet, black and white puddings and 'sheep's heid' broth. There were occasional purchases of caviar, truffles, morilles, vermicelli, olives and mangoes. Among the wines listed are sherry, port, malaga, champagne and burgundy, all in the bottle, but the earls shipped claret by the hogshead and bottled it themselves. Brandy featured prominently, with to a lesser degree rum and, more unusually, arrack. They brewed their own ale, and at one hay harvest 429 pints (244 litres) were consumed.

The fire, on Christmas Day 1763, destroyed three of the wings and most of the furnishings. The surviving wing was reconstructed as the new Leslie House which continued as a private home until 1953 and is now a Church of Scotland eventide home.

LESMAHAGOW, Lanarkshire

The name of this village west of **Lanark** derives from 'Les', a green or enclosure (or possibly from the French *église*, church), and 'mahago', a Celtic saint latinised as 'Machutus' and to whom a priory was dedicated in 1144 by **David I**. The monks, originally from **Kelso**, are said to have pioneered Clydesdale's fruit growing industry. Excavations in the 1970s revealed part of the priory's foundations. Like other **Lanarkshire** villages, Lesmahagow's subsequent history includes 17th century **Covenanting** and 19th/20th century **coal-mining**. Nearby Black Hill (**National Trust for Scotland** and a noted viewpoint) is topped by an Iron Age fort and settlement surrounding a Bronze Age **cairn**.

LEUCHARS, Fife

A parish lying to the north of the river Eden, and its main village, Leuchars is renowned for its RAF station and its parish church. The latter, on a hillock, retains its 12th century chancel and apse, sometimes described as the finest examples of Norman architecture in Scotland. Both have two tiers of blind arcading, the arches, capitals and pilasters displaying much detail. They were restored by **Reginald Fairlie** in 1914. Although the octagonal bell tower dates from about 1700 and the Victorian romanesque nave (John Milne) from 1857, the ensemble is not disastrous. First mention of the church comes from 1187 when it belonged to

Apse and chancel of Leuchars parish church (RWB)

St Andrews priory whose Bishop Bernham dedicated it in 1244. The district also boasts two fine bridges across the Eden: Guard Bridge (15th century) has six arches and bears the initials and arms of **James Beaton**, Archbishop of **St Andrews**, while Dairsie Bridge (c1530) has three arches and just the Archbishop's initials. Near the latter are Dairsie church, 'a peculiar hybrid of Gothic and Renaissance' dating from 1621, and Dairsie Castle, the shell of a 16th century tower house.

LEVELLERS' REVOLT, The (1724)

'The first instance in Scottish history of a popular revolt with the character of class war' (T C Smout), this protest movement was restricted to small tenant farmers and agricultural workers in **Dumfriesshire** and **Galloway**. It arose from the policy of enclosures and evictions pursued by local landowners who were among the first to benefit from the greatly increased cattle trade with England following the **Union** of 1707. Resistance was slow to materialise and many had emigrated before two Galloway victims of eviction refused the summons to remove and, joined by other sympathisers, formed themselves into organised bands who roamed the countryside throwing down enclosing dykes ('levellers') and killing numbers of cattle, most notably in the estate of Baldoon. The unrest lasted about six months but was eventually put down by the army; many Levellers were arrested, some deported. The movement is clear evidence that resistance to agricultural improvement and enclosure was not restricted to the 19th century Highlands. But though anticipating the **clearances**, the Levellers Revolt is more redolent of radical dissent in the south-west during the 17th century. Like the **Conventiclers** and the **Cameronians**, the Levellers drew up their own covenant, enjoyed the encouragement of radical ministers, and even pinned their manifesto to the church at **Sanquhar** in imitation of the **Sanquhar Declarations**.

LEVEN, Fife

From **Loch Leven** the river Leven flows east to reach the Firth of Forth in the parish of Scoonie. A fragment of the old parish church survives as does a **Pictish** cross-slab found in the churchyard and now in the **Royal Scottish Museum, Edinburgh**. At the mouth of the river, once noted for its 'pure and limpid waters', the village of Leven was a **linen** weaving centre. Development of the **Fife coalfields** in the late 19th century changed the character of both village and river. Leven became the eastern extremity of Fife's industrialised coastline and is still paying the price.

LEVEN, Loch, Kinross-shire

This shallow freshwater loch, pear-shaped and eight miles in circumference, was once larger and deeper. It was partially drained in the 17th century by **Sir William Bruce** to create a foreshore garden for **Kinross House** and again in the 19th century. As a result its two principal islands were enlarged and others added. On the largest, St Serf's, are located the scant remains of a priory founded on a site previously occupied by a **Culdee** foundation and, before that, supposedly given to St Serf (Servan, Servatius) by the **Pictish** King Brude. Andrew Wyntoun, the chronicler, was prior 1395–1413. The other island is that of **Loch Leven Castle, Queen Mary**'s prison. The loch's warm water and weedy bottom encourage aquatic life. Loch Leven trout, once thought to be a distinct species, are silvery, without the red spots of most brown trout, and pink-fleshed. Also large, plentiful and active, they make the loch an angler's paradise with a record catch in 1960 of 80,000 fish. Equally important as a freshwater wintering station for geese, swans and ducks, Loch Leven is a National Nature Reserve with, at Vane Farm, 'the first nature centre in Britain' where the RSPB has hides and a display on the local geology, flora and fauna. However, severe pollution in the form of toxic algae has threatened the future of both the loch's wildlife and its famous **fishing**.

LEVER, William Hesketh, Lord Leverhulme (1851–1925) Industrialist and Philanthropist

The son of a Bolton soapmaker, Leverhulme founded Port Sunlight in 1888 and Lever Brothers in 1890. His international business empire, Unilever, brought him fame and fortune. In 1918 he bought the islands of **Lewis** and **Harris** in the Outer **Hebrides** and in the next five years spent £875,000, intending to redeem the islands from poverty and create wealth for the islanders through enterprise and the exploitation of the natural resources of the sea. He bought **fishing** boats, and built a cannery, ice-factory, roads and bridges, and a light **railway**. He planned to use spotter planes to locate **herring** shoals, and created MacFisheries, his own chain of retail fish shops. A full account of his activities can be found in Nigel Nicolson's *Lord of the Isles*. In 1923 he was forced to abandon his plans for Lewis, and gifted 64,000 acres (25,920ha) of **Stornoway** Parish to the

people, to be administered by the elected Stornoway Trust. His withdrawal from Lewis caused an economic slump, leading to the emigration of over a thousand able-bodied men to North America. After the collapse of his schemes for Lewis, Leverhulme turned his attention to Harris, where the peaceful little village of Obbe was renamed Leverburgh and transformed into a bustling harbour town with all kinds of public works projects. But in May 1925 Leverhulme died, and all developments stopped. Instead of becoming a town with a projected population of 10,000, Leverburgh reverted to a sleepy village.

LEWIS, Outer Hebrides

The 'island' of Lewis (Gaelic *Leodhas* – 'marshy') makes up the northern two thirds of the largest and most northerly island in the Outer **Hebrides**; the southern third being the less populous but scenically more dramatic **Harris**. Lewis has a land area of 600 square miles and a population of just over 20,000.

Stornoway is the largest town in the Hebrides, and the administrative capital of the Western Isles, which today are run by Comhairle nan Eilean, the Islands' Council. Stornoway has a fine natural deep-water harbour, a ferry service connects with **Ullapool** on the Scottish mainland, and its airport is linked by scheduled services with **Benbecula**, **Barra** and **Glasgow**. Stornoway has some interesting buildings, notably Lews Castle, built with money made from opium and tea by Sir James Matheson (founder with another Scot of **Jardine Matheson & Co**), who owned the island from 1844 until his death in 1878.

Geologically, Lewis is the most interesting of the Outer Hebrides. The underlying rock is the eponymous Lewisian gneiss, the oldest rock in Europe and at 2900 million years over half the age of the earth itself. Around Barvas on the west side of Lewis is a large exposure of granite, while around Stornoway is Torridonian sandstone. There is evidence in glacial striations on rocky outcrops of at least two ice ages, while the most recent geological deposit is the blanket **peat** which covers much of today's landscape but started to form only 5000 years ago.

Lewis is well known for its spectacular archaeological monuments, notably the Bronze Age **standing stones** at **Callanish**. The true dimensions of the 47 surviving stones, which date from around 1800 BC, were not appreciated until 1857 when 5ft (1.5m) of peat which had accumulated since the end of the Bronze Age was removed. There are many other stone circles and single standing stones from the same period. At Ballantrushal, on the west coast of Lewis just north of Barvas, the tallest standing stone in the Hebrides (19ft/5.8m high) overlooks the sea.

At **Carloway**, the well-preserved **broch** tower testifies to the engineering skills of house builders in the late Iron Age. West of **Callanish** is the township of **Uig**, where a magnificent Norse **chess set** of walrus ivory, dating from the 12th century, was found in the sand dunes in 1831. Much reproduced, the original pieces are divided between the British Museum in London and the **Museum of Scotland** in **Edinburgh**. The Outer Hebrides were first raided by **Vikings** in the 9th century and then settled extensively by Norse colonists. Many place-names of Norse origin testify to 350 years of Norse rule. Legally, the Western Isles were under Norse sovereignty until 1266.

Not far from Stornoway, the medieval chapel on the Eye peninsula dedicated to **St Columba** is an important ecclesiastical site; the Butt of Lewis, the northern tip of the island, is crowned by a lighthouse, and the nearby township of Europie has the restored 12th century chapel of St Moluag (Teampull Mholuidh). To the west of Barvas is the township of Arnol where there is a small folk museum in a black house (tigh dubh), last occupied in 1964. The walls are nearly 2m thick, and the roof was thatch over turf. There was no chimney, but smoke from a peat fire in the middle of the floor escaped through the roof. This architecture, apparently primitive, was in fact better adapted to Hebridean wind and rain than the modern bungalows now seen throughout the islands.

On the road to Point, just to the east of Stornoway, stands a monument to the saddest disaster ever to befall the Hebrides, where the ebb and flow of history has witnessed many tragic scenes. On New Year's Eve 1918 the Admiralty yacht Iolaire left **Kyle of Lochalsh** carrying 260 naval ratings home from the Great War to their villages on Lewis. A gale blew up from the south; in the early hours of New Year's Day the Iolaire struck a rock at the entrance to Stornoway harbour and foundered. 208 men, who had come through four years of war, died within a mile of their home. Every village in the island, indeed almost every home, was affected. Combined with the death toll of the war, and the emigrations which followed it, the Iolaire disaster affected succeeding generations profoundly and its influence can still be traced.

The economy of Lewis is still based on the traditional industries of **crofting** and **fishing**, and tweed, despite various attempts to broaden the industrial base, notably by **Lord Leverhulme** who bought the island in 1918 and gave much of it back to its people in 1923. The Highlands and Islands Development Board has done much to encourage the island's economy, despite some spectacular failures. The growth of cooperatives and craft associations are evidence of the realisation that in a fragile community cooperation is essential. Unemployment figures are well above the national average, and the emigration of young people to the mainland and beyond is a perennial problem. Since the **1843 Disruption** the vast majority of the people of Lewis have belonged to the **Free Church**, which still wields considerable influence.

Lewis is the most powerful surviving bastion of Gaelic life and culture, in which the promotion of the Gaelic language through broadcasting and publishing is all important. Radio nan Eilean, the Gaelic local radio station run by the BBC, Gaelic television programmes, constantly expanding, and the Stornoway publisher Acair are all important influences in island culture, as is Comhairle nan Eilean's bilingual policy. One of the finest evocations of island life is Devil in the Wind by Charles MacLeod. The foremost Celtic scholar of the present generation, Professor Derick Thomson, is a Lewisman, while the Gaelic (and English) poet and novelist **Iain Crichton Smith** has a deservedly international reputation.

LEXICOGRAPHY

The science of lexicography, or dictionary-making, has been practised by the Scots since the 16th century. In 1597 Sir John Skene (c1543–1617), then Lord Clerk Register, published his Verborum Significatione in which he explained in his native Scots some of the technical terms, both Latin and Scots, employed in the 'Auld Laws' of Scotland. Brief definitions and speculative etymologies were followed by detailed explanations of the legal technicalities involved. Skene's work is still of value to modern lexicographers of Scots.

The next important figure in Scotland's lexicographical history also had a legal background. **Thomas Ruddiman** (1674–1757), a native of **Banffshire**, was Under-Keeper of the **Advocates' Library** in **Edinburgh** when, in 1710, he wrote his A Glossary or Alphabetical Explanation of the Hard and Difficult words in Gavin Douglas's Translation of Virgil's Aeneid, published as an appendix to his own edition of **Douglas**'s translation of 1513. Ruddiman had a sound knowledge of vernacular Scots, and there is some justification for his publisher's claim that the glossary 'may serve for a Dictionary of the Old Scottish Language'.

Ruddiman's contemporary and fellow-lexicographer, **Samuel Johnson**, published his A Dictionary of the English Language in 1755. Considering his alleged Scotophobia, it is remarkable that Johnson's six amanuenses included no fewer than five Scots. Of Mr Maitland we know little beyond his surname. The Macbean brothers were Gaels, one of whom later became librarian to the **Duke of Argyll**. Francis Stewart was the son of an Edinburgh bookseller, and Robert Shiels was a literary hack who wrote at least part of Cibber's The Lives of the Poets. Johnson was fond of all his 'painful labourers', as **Boswell** called them, and did what he could in later years to further their careers and assist them financially.

The opening years of the 19th century saw the publication of the **Rev John Jamieson**'s An Etymological Dictionary of the Scottish Language (1808), the first true historical dictionary in these islands. Although its faults are many, particularly on the etymological side (Jamieson was misled into thinking that Scots was a Scandinavian tongue), it remains a major authority on the Scots language.

Jamieson's lexicographical contemporaries included John Boag, a **West Lothian** schoolmaster whose Imperial Lexicon appeared in 1847–8, and John Ogilvie, a Banffshire ploughman turned mathematics teacher, who brought out his Imperial Dictionary in 1850. Victorian Britain put a high premium on intellectual self-improvement, and the growing demand for dictionaries and encyclopaedias was met in large part by the Scottish publishing houses of **Collins** and **Chambers**, founded in 1819 and 1820 in **Glasgow** and Edinburgh respectively.

But the achievements of earlier lexicographers pale in comparison with those of **Roxburghshire**-born **James Murray** (1837–1915), editor of the Oxford English Dictionary (OED) and arguably the greatest lexicographer of all time. Murray's life and achievements are detailed elsewhere in this volume, as are those of his colleague and eventual successor **William Craigie** (1867–1957), the son of a jobbing gardener in **Dundee**. Craigie was the inspiration behind both the Scottish National Dictionary (SND) and the Dictionary of the Older Scottish Tongue (DOST), the former of which deals with the modern Scots of the post-**Union** period, while DOST charts the Older Scots of medieval and early modern Scotland.

The year 1985 saw the publication of the *Concise Scots Dictionary* (CSD), a one-volume distillation of SND and DOST which has quickly established itself as a worthy successor to Alexander Warrack's *A Scots Dialect Dictionary*, published by Chambers in 1911. Further lexicographical projects are planned by the Scottish National Dictionary Association. Meanwhile, the runaway success of CSD and such regional glossaries as Michael Munro's *The Patter* (Glasgow dialect) testify to the continuing strength and popularity of the Scottish lexicographical tradition, a tradition which has grown from a variety of roots: the **Calvinist** work ethic; the high moral seriousness which has typified Scottish education from the time of **John Knox**; and, perhaps, an ingrained conviction that knowledge of languages was a sure means of advancement in the world. The **Galloway** shepherd's son and poet **Alexander Murray** is said to have mastered French, German, Latin, Greek, Hebrew, Arabic, Abyssinian, Anglo-Saxon and Welsh by the age of 18; and similar achievements are recorded of **John Leyden**, William Tennant, the OED's James Murray, William Craigie and many another 'lad o' pairts'.

LEYDEN, John (1775–1811) Poet and Orientalist

Of wild appearance and wondrous learning, Leyden might better be described simply as a genius. When he died aged 35 he had already mastered 30 languages, qualified as a cleric and surgeon, and achieved distinction as a poet, folklorist and philologist. Amongst his admirers were such assorted luminaries as **Sir Walter Scott**, **James Hogg**, **Sir John Malcolm**, Sir Stamford Raffles and **Henry Lord Cockburn**. The last could think of 'no walk in life, depending on ability, where Leyden could not have shone'. Son of a shepherd in **Roxburghshire**, he matriculated from **Edinburgh University** aged 15, then worked as a tutor and qualified as a preacher. His first published work was a history of African discoveries (1799). There followed poems, **ballads** and the journal of a Highland tour (in search of Ossian) plus research and contributions for Scott's *Border Minstrelsy*. By 1803 he was of a mind to follow **Mungo Park**'s trail into Africa but was persuaded instead to go to Madras as assistant surgeon. He acquired an MD at **St Andrews** inside six months and headed east, never to return. In 1804 he supplemented the work of **Francis Buchanan** in Mysore and in 1805 reached the Malabar coast whence he sailed for Penang, there to acquire a closer knowledge of the South East Asian languages than any contemporary. Back in Calcutta he was appointed by **Lord Minto** Professor of Hindustani, a judge, and eventually assay-master of the mint, while continuing his linguistic researches and his translations. In 1811 the Java Expedition took him to Batavia (Jakarta) where he died of fever contracted while poring over native manuscripts. Where, had he lived, his errant genius might next have led is an intriguing question.

LIDDELL, Eric (1902–45) Athlete

Regarded by many as the greatest athlete Scotland has ever produced, Eric Henry Liddell was born to Scottish parents at Tientsin, China. After attending school in England, Liddell showed a facility for short-distance running at **Edinburgh University**. Coached by Tom Mackerchar, and despite an unorthodox – indeed almost ungainly – head-back running style, Liddell won an award as Scotland's outstanding athlete five years in succession. He showed an almost equal prowess on the **rugby** field, being capped for Scotland seven times. But it was the 1924 Olympic Games in Paris which crowned his short career as a runner. A deeply religious man, he refused to run in the 100 metres heats because they were scheduled for a Sunday, and instead triumphed against the world's best in the 400 metres to win Olympic gold. He claimed that the secret of his success was 'that I run the first 200 metres as fast as I can. Then, for the second 200 metres, with God's help, I run harder.'

Despite his triumph, he decided after graduating from Edinburgh (where the university Principal insisted on crowning him with oleastor, as a substitute for olive leaves, such was his eminence in his adopted city) to dedicate his life to spreading Christianity in China. It was there, in a Japanese internment camp at Weifeng, that he died of a brain tumour on 21 February 1945, towards the end of World War II.

In 1991 a monument was unveiled to Liddell's memory at Weifeng in Shandong province and a community centre dedicated to him at Holy Corner, Edinburgh. His athletic career was featured in the film *Chariots of Fire*, interwoven with that of Harold Abrahams. Liddell was played by the tragically short-lived Scottish actor Ian Charleson, and much of the shooting was done in Scotland. The film won four Oscars, including 'Best Film', in 1982.

LIND, James (1716–94) Physician

Born in **Edinburgh**, Lind served as surgeon in the Royal Navy before qualifying as MD at **Edinburgh University**. During his naval service he demonstrated that fresh fruit and lemon juice were important antiscorbutics, capable of eliminating the sailor's oldest seaboard enemy, scurvy. He published *A Treatise of the Scurvy* – a 'classic of medical literature' – in 1753. The Admiralty failed to implement Lind's findings until much later, when these were championed by **Gilbert Blane**. Lind also researched tropical diseases and the distillation of fresh water, but his discovery of scurvy prevention was still unimplemented when he died at Portsmouth in 1794.

LINDORES ABBEY, Newburgh, Fife

Founded probably as a priory by **David Earl of Huntingdon** in 1178 and as an abbey in 1191, Lindores was an off-shoot of the Tironensian (Benedictine) abbey of **Kelso** whence came Guido, first abbot, who 'built the place from the foundations'. With a complement of 20–30 monks it became an important **Fife** monastery but was sacked by locals about 1543, according to **Sir Ralph Sadler**, and then 'reformed' during a visit by **John Knox** in 1559. It has since been raided as a source of good building stone convenient to **Newburgh**. The usual ground plan of church, chapter house and cloister is discernible but only a gateway and a section of tower still stand.

LINDSAY, Alexander Dunlop, Lord Lindsay of Birker (1879–1952) Philosopher and Educationalist

Born in **Glasgow**, Lindsay was the son of the **Free Church** College Principal T M Lindsay (1843–1914), author of a great *History of the Reformation*. After **Glasgow University**, an Oxford scholarship and lectureships, he became a fellow of Balliol College, Oxford (1906), where he produced a standard translation of Plato's *Republic* plus prefaces for Everyman's Library philosophy texts. He also wrote much on morals and politics, essays and popular books, eg *The Two Moralities* (1942). From 1922–4 he was Professor of Moral Philosophy and a Workers' Education Association (WEA) pioneer at Glasgow. He became Master of Balliol in 1924 and as a social campaigner and **Independent Labour Party** supporter, was a force in founding the Modern Greats school and, as Vice Chancellor of Oxford, the Cavendish Laboratory. In the 1938 Oxford by-election he ran Quintin Hogg a good second as an anti-appeasement candidate and he broadcast on democracy through the 1930s and the war. *The Modern Democratic State* (1943), an outstanding but direly neglected work, ought to be known in 1990s Eastern Europe. In it he argues that there is no democracy save in the operative ideal called the Modern Democratic State whose religious and moral roots he traces. An eschewal of formality should not disguise his depth; his is a delightfully blunt wit. On a post-war commission to reform German universities he was made a peer (1946), and in Staffordshire, scene of his early WEA work, he was founding father and till his death first Principal of Keele University. (See *Lindsay and Keele*, W B Gallie, 1960 and *A School of Thinking*, R R Calder, Polygon, 1991. *A D Lindsay* by Drusilla Scott, Lindsay's daughter, is definitive.)

LINDSAY, Sir David (c1486–1555) Poet

Lindsay (or Lyndesay) belonged to a prominent family of 'The Mount' near **Cupar** and was a 'familiar' at the court in his youth under **James IV**. He rose to higher rank in the days of **James V**, first as herald and then as knight and Lord Lyon, King of Arms. Active in the political events of the day, he was sent on embassies to France and there gained the knowledge of that country's literature and culture which would enrich his poetry and drama.

Lindsay is the first major poet whose voice is clearly that of the Renaissance and (at least as precursor) the **Reformation**. He retains certainty in the overall pattern of divine benevolence, but it moves into the background in forceful satirical and political verse directed against the abuses of Church and State in the Scotland of his day. There is a consistence of vision which impresses and underlies poetry as diverse as *The Testament of the Papyngo* and *Kitteis Confessioun*. It allows one character, John the Commonweill, to exit from an early poem (*The Dreme*) vowing to return only when Scotland is well governed. Duly, he does return – about 25 years later – at the very stage in *Ane Satyre of the Thrie Estaitis* when that demand has been satisfied. This ambitious morality play, *Ane Satyre*, remains Lindsay's greatest achievement. Skilfully mingling English with French conventions, farce with homily, and cameo with pageant on a gigantic scale of time and space, he brings first ruler and then ruled from guilty chaos into moral order.

LINDSAY, James Bowman (1799–1862) Wireless and Electrical Pioneer

Unaware of the work of Samuel Morse or Heinrich Hertz, Lindsay took out a patent in 1854 for a method of transmitting messages by using water as the conductor, and actually sent signals two miles across the River **Tay** at **Dundee**. Two pairs of huge copper plates on opposite sides of the channel were connected by wires to a primitive wet cell battery as generator; breaking the contacts of each pair of plates caused the weak flickering of a needle on a crude coil. Although he replicated his apparatus for sending communications over the Solent after underwater cables parted, Lindsay refused a post at the British Museum which would have allowed further development of his ideas. Instead, he spent his last eight years compiling a dictionary containing 53 languages which remained unfinished on his death. A native of Carmyllie, **Angus**, and a graduate in arts and divinity at **St Andrews University** who went on to lecture at the Watt Institute in Dundee, Lindsay also experimented with electric light production; he was among the first – in 1834 – to light his own house with electricity. Marconi, who grasped the possibilities of wireless transmission through the air, said that Lindsay 'must go down in posterity as the first man who thoroughly believed in the possibility and utility of long distance wireless telegraphy'.

LINDSAY, Robert, of Pitscottie (c1500–65) Historian

Born at Pitscottie, near **Cupar** in **Fife**, Lindsay is known for writing *The Historie and Cronicles of Scotland* covering the years 1435 to 1565. Written in Scots, it was meant as a continuation of **Hector Boece**'s *Scotorum Historiae*, and was one of **Sir Walter Scott**'s main historical sources for his novels on the period. Although the work has been found to be inaccurate in detail, Lindsay's style is vivid, graphic and entertaining. The work was first published in 1728 and subsequently edited in three volumes by A J G Mackay between 1899 and 1911.

LINEN

Spinning and weaving linen from flax was a staple industry of Scotland from medieval times. Linen production was conducted at first on a small scale for domestic purposes, but by the end of the 17th century Scottish linens were being exported to London. Many of the well-known Gaelic **waulking songs** have their origins in the process of waulking, or fulling, linen cloth by hand. After the **Union** and the **Jacobite Risings** linen manufacture was encouraged by the Board of Trustees for Manufactures, partly to stimulate employment in the Highlands, thus reducing the danger of revolution. Output quadrupled in the 30 years after 1740 to reach 13 million yards. Linen was used to make tablecloths, shirts, underwear, sailcloth, socks, bags and ropes. Spinning began to be mechanised in the 1780s with the construction of mills in **Angus** and **Aberdeenshire**. There was a boom in power spinning and weaving in the 1820s, with the east coast towns of **Arbroath** and **Dundee** emerging as centres of the industry.

Linen remained an important part of Scotland's textile trade until the mid-19th century when, like **cotton**, it encountered difficulties, particularly in the substitution of **jute** for flax. The capacity of the industry was halved between 1850 and 1900 with Angus and **Fife** bearing the brunt of the contraction. A few firms maintained their business by concentrating on specialist parts of the market, particularly the weaving of fine linen and lawns in **Dunfermline**.

At the end of the century the largest spinners of linen thread in the west of Scotland and Ulster merged to form the Linen Thread Company. After doing well supplying canvas to the Royal Navy during World War I, the large Dundee firms amalgamated as the Low & Bonar Group in 1924. In recent times both the Linen Thread Company (later Lindustries) and Low & Bonar diversified away from linen manufacture. Growing flax and making linen, once commonplace throughout Scotland, has now almost totally disappeared. However, flax is making a comeback with the discovery of chemical means of retting.

LINKLATER, Eric Robert (1899–1974)
Novelist

The son of a master mariner from Dounby in **Orkney**, his mother the daughter of a Swedish ship's captain, Linklater chanced to be born in South Wales. This he forgot so thoroughly that even *The Times* obituary stated he had been born in Dounby. He was sent first to the grammar school and then to the **University of Aberdeen**, whence he absconded to serve, under-age, as a private in the **Black Watch** during World War I. A severe head wound drove him back to continue his medical studies, until he abandoned these to graduate in English literature.

He had determined to be a writer, for which he prepared himself next by joining the staff of *The Times of India* in Bombay in 1925. But the land of his forebears was central to his inspiration, as he demonstrated in one book after another: *White-Maa's Saga* (1929), *The Men of Ness* (1932), *The Ultimate Viking* (1955) and many short stories. These reveal another gift which found hilarious expression in the satirical novel *Juan in America* (1931). Its publication brought him international fame. He had perfected the 'classically elegant comic style' which Goethe had praised in the *Don Juan* of Lord Byron, and he used it for the same purpose, to depict the human scene in all its variety with tolerance, candour and a humour that never lacked compassion. His Rabelaisian wit was not unconsciously influenced by **Sir Thomas Urquhart** of **Cromarty**, in sight of which he spent some of the most productive years of his life before **Nigg Bay** was abandoned to the needs of the **oil** industry.

Loving courage as Byron had done, he enjoyed the society of soldiers and sailors. Loving beauty and talent, he married Marjorie MacIntyre, one of the most beautiful and accomplished women of his time. In his autobiography *The Man on My Back* (1941) he wrote that 'few authors can spare for their own lives much of the colour, the adventuring and vivacity of their work'. Linklater possessed more than enough exuberance and generosity for both.

LINLITHGOW, West Lothian
An ancient **royal burgh** pleasantly situated along the south side of the eponymous loch, Linlithgow originally consisted of a single street running east to west with a number of very brief lanes and narrow alleys running off each side. Many of the houses were built by the Knights of St John whose preceptory was at **Torpichen** just to the south, while others were the property of 'grandees who nestled under the warm wing of the royal court' (Fullarton's *Gazetteer*) at **Linlithgow Palace**. **Ninian Winzet**, 'the elected champion of popery in logical tiltings with **John Knox**', was rector of Linlithgow School from c1551 until his banishment in 1562. Nos 44–48 High Street are probably the oldest remaining buildings in the town, dating from the late 16th or early 17th century. They were restored by the **National Trust for Scotland** in 1958 but are leased to private occupiers and not open to the public.

St Michael's Parish Church near the Palace is considered one of the finest medieval churches in Scotland. Dating from the 15th century when it replaced a previous church destroyed by fire, it underwent major restoration in the 19th century, the original medieval crown steeple being removed in 1820 for fear its weight would damage the structure beneath, not to be replaced until 1964 when the controversial new steeple 'resembling a wigwam without its cover' (C McWilliam) was funded by public subscription.

LINLITHGOW PALACE, West Lothian
One of the most magnificent and visible of Scotland's ancient monuments, Linlithgow Palace stands on a promontory jutting into Linlithgow Loch hard by the M9 **Stirling-Edinburgh** motorway. There was a royal manor house on the site from the time of **David I**, converted (1301–2) by Edward I of England into a base for his siege of Stirling. The English garrison was captured (1313) by a mere handful of Scottish soldiers smuggled inside the walls in a hay-cart and the manor house was rebuilt during the reign of **David II** (1329–71) but destroyed by fire in 1424. It was **James I** who initiated the building of the present palace in 1425, **James III** and **James IV** in turn made alterations and additions, the latter adding the south face and thus completing the quadrangle, and **James V**, born in the Palace in 1512, strengthened the fortifications, moved the entrance and built the magnificent King's Fountain in the courtyard.

In 1542 **Queen Mary** was born in the Queen's Suite in the north range, a section of the Palace later found to be dangerously insecure; in 1607 the Earl of Linlithgow approached **James VI** with the news that 'the north quarter of your Majesties' Palice of Linlythgw is fallin, rufe and all, within the wallis, to the ground.' The collapsed section was not repaired until 1617–19, but by then James VI and his court had moved to London and the Palace's glory days were over. **Charles I** was the last monarch to stay here, which he did briefly in 1633; Oliver Cromwell spent the winter of 1650–1 at Linlithgow and **Prince Charles Edward Stewart** rested in the by now decaying Palace for a night on his way to Edinburgh in 1745. The following year during Cumberland's pursuit of the **Jacobites** on their flight northward, the Duke and his army spent the night of 31 January in the Palace and, whether by accident or design, set fire to their quarters before leaving. 'Before the danger was discovered, the roof was mantled in flame; and being covered with lead, it sent down such a shower of melted metal as entirely precluded any attempt to arrest the

Linlithgow Palace in the late 17th century, by John Slezer (TS)

conflagration' (Fullarton's *Gazetteer*). A century later the ruins were taken over by the Ministry of Works and made safe and are now in state care.

LION, Scottish

The lion is regarded as the king of the beasts and thus a fitting symbol of kings and kingdoms. Since the 12th century the lion has been used as a heraldic device by many kings and ancient families in northern Europe and was possibly adopted by **William I** of Scotland (1165–1214). This is suggested by his sobriquet, 'The Lion'. **Alexander II** (1214–49) certainly employed a rampant lion on his Great Seal. On the royal shield the Scottish lion has always been rampant, ie shown standing erect on hind legs with head in profile and forelegs extended. By the reign of **Alexander III** (1249–86) the lion was surrounded by a double tressure flory counter flory. As well as the rampant lion, a seated lion holding a sword was chosen for the royal crest during the lifetime of **David II** (1329–71). Around 1542 this seated lion was given a sceptre to hold as well as the sword. Standing lions were employed as heraldic supporters on the Privy Seals of Scottish kings from 1372 until 1603.

The King of Arms, the Lord Lyon [see **Heraldry**], takes his title from the royal beast, and certain gold coins from the reign of **Robert III** (1390–1406) and **James II** (1437–60) were called 'lions' because they bore that device on one side. There is a suggestion that Scottish monarchs kept a real lion when in residence at **Stirling** and **Edinburgh Castles**, as each building has an area within the walls called 'the Lion's Den'.

LIPTON, Sir Thomas (1850–1931) Retailer

Tommy Lipton was born in a **Gorbals** tenement, the son of Irish parents. He left school at ten, and five years later emigrated to America where he found work in a grocer's. Aged 20 he returned to **Glasgow** and opened his first ham and egg shop in Stobcross Street. The shop rapidly became a UK chain which made Lipton 'the largest retail provision dealer in the world'. His success stemmed partly from tireless labour, partly from a flair for advertising; the latter was typified by his gigantic cheeses which made their shop window appearance in the run-up to Christmas and, like Christmas pudding, were wont to include silver coins. Near riots ensued when they were finally cut and sold. Lipton acquired tea estates in Sri Lanka and meat processing facilities in America. He was a millionaire by the age of 30, but spent much of his fortune challenging for the Americas Cup with a succession of yachts called *Shamrock*. He never won, but gained a reputation as the world's best loser.

LISMORE, Island of, Argyll

Lying in the southern end of Loch Linnhe between **Morvern** and the north end of mainland **Argyll**, the island of Lismore is a 10-mile-long by 1½-mile-wide limestone upthrust, and its commanding position and fertility have given it a distinctive history. The Royal Commission on Ancient and Historical Monuments (1974) describes 32 sites, including a reasonably preserved **broch**. There are island place-names linking with Fingalian tradition, though the actual naming of the island – *lios mor* meaning 'great garden' or 'enclosure' – is attributed to **St Moluag** (d.592), who legendarily beat his rival **St Columba** to land by cutting off his little finger and hurling it ashore. His *Bachull Mor* or 'great staff' is still with its hereditary keepers, the Livingstone family. The island is rich in Christian tradition, and when the Church of Rome superseded the **Celtic Church** c1200 it became the centre of a bishopric; the parish church contains the remains of the cathedral, and at Achadun are the ruins of the castle residence. The important **Book of the Dean of Lismore**, a 16th century collection of **Gaelic poetry**, is in the **National Library of Scotland** in **Edinburgh**.

Although for long joined with the parish of **Appin** (Stewart country), since the 16th century land ownership has been dominated by **Campbells**. Lady's Rock at the entrance to the Sound of Mull just off **Stevenson**'s 1833 lighthouse was in 1527 the scene of the infamous marooning of the Earl of Argyll's daughter, rescued by Lismore men to the eventual discomfiture of her Mac-Lean of **Duart** husband. Two Stewarts are buried on Lismore, however: the legendary 16th century 'Donald of the Hammers', who grew up to avenge the slaughter of his family by Campbells, and Duncan Stewart, murdered at Duart in 1519, whose tombstone can be seen in the church. Munro (1594) reports an island rich in cattle, horses, 'cornes' (ie barley for **whisky**) and oaks. But most of the hardwoods have long gone to burn the lime so valuable to the surrounding mainland, and there are traces of the industry everywhere. There is a little arable still, but it is sheep pasture that gives the island its special lush texture. 293 plant species have recently been recorded, and 129 bird species.

In 1775 there was a 'rage for emigration' (to North Carolina) and in 1831 the population was 1497. By 1885 it had dropped to 600 in 150 dwellings, and by 1946 to 206. It now stands at about 140, with the scatter of ruined crofts a reminder of how many had to find subsistence from limeworks, land and small **fishing** boats. The Statistical Account of 1845 records Gaelic giving way to English, 3 schools and few illiterates under 40; there was 'an unnecessary number of dram shops', and for fuel **peat** had to be imported and laboriously 'tramped by the men and formed by the women's hands'. Although a steamer service was just coming on the scene, the islanders, then as now, were hit by carriage costs.

Achnacroish is seven miles by ferry from **Oban**, but the usual route for visitors is from Port Appin (less than a mile). An excellent way of appreciating the island is by bicycle; a local car may also be hired. There is one shop, and a guesthouse in the former manse. The most sheltered anchorage lies in the complex of islets off Port Ramsay.

LISTER, Joseph, Lord (1827–1912) Surgeon

English by birth, Joseph Lister married a Scot, spent most of his professional life in Scotland, and did almost all his pioneering research in Scottish hospitals. Born in Essex, he qualified as a doctor at University College Hospital, London in 1852 and became FRCS in the same year. In 1853 he came to **Edinburgh** to gain further practical experience of surgery under Professor **James Syme**. Crucially for him a young surgeon, R J Mac-Kenzie, was killed in the Crimea in 1854, leaving vacancies both in the **Royal Infirmary**, Edinburgh and in teaching at the **Royal College of Surgeons** of Edinburgh. Lister was elected to both, becoming FRCSE in 1855. In 1856 he married Syme's daughter Agnes, became Professor of Surgery at the **University of Glasgow** (1860) and surgeon at the Royal Infirmary (1861).

One of the fundamental surgical problems of the time was the appalling death rate from infections such as tetanus, blood poisoning and gangrene. Louis Pasteur was engaged in research on the fermentation of wine, which he found was caused by minute living organisms in the air. Lister took Pasteur's results a stage further, realising that, whilst some of these organisms could be beneficial, others could be harmful, causing postoperative wound infections. He began experimenting with carbolic acid, by soaking lint or calico in the new substance and applying it to the wound. This was effective up to a point, but did not solve the problem of infection around stitching, since silk, the most commonly used ligature, did not absorb the carbolic acid well. Lister then experimented with catgut obtained from sheep. This was found to absorb the carbolic acid much more effectively.

In 1869 Lister returned to Edinburgh as Regius Professor of Surgery, and continued his experiments with the introduction of gauze swabs, also soaked in carbolic acid, and later developed a spray for disinfecting operating theatres. Although effective, the device was unwieldy and was soon superseded. One of these sprays can still be seen at the Museum of the Royal College of Surgeons of Edinburgh. In 1877 Lister became Professor of Surgery at King's College Hospital in London.

LISTON, Robert (1794–1847) Surgeon

Born at Ecclesmachan, near **Linlithgow**, Liston studied medicine at **Edinburgh** and London, being appointed a surgeon at Edinburgh's **Royal Infirmary** in 1827. Failing to obtain a professorial appointment, he continued his career in London. Credited with conducting the first public operation using anaesthetic, Liston was one of the most distinguished surgeons even before the time of anaesthetics, noted for his speed and strength.

LITHGOW, Sir James (1883–1952) Shipbuilder

Lithgow was apprenticed to his father's shipyard in **Port Glasgow**. When his father died prematurely in 1908 he and his brother Henry took over the business and soon expanded it. He was recalled from the Front in 1917 to help build standard ships to defeat the German U-Boat campaign. During and after the war the business was further extended, but with the downturn in **shipbuilding** in the 1920s he became a spokesman for the whole industry. He was the natural choice to head National Shipbuilders Security Ltd formed to rationalise the trade in 1930. Successful in winning the confidence of shipbuilders, government and the banks, he sought to foster new industries through his own business and the Scottish National Development Council. A committed Christian, he gave of his wealth to establish the **Church of Scotland**'s fund for retiring ministers and to the **Iona Community**.

LITHGOW, William (c1582–1650) Traveller

Born in **Lanark**, Lithgow there seduced a girl of good family and was obliged to absent himself. He travelled to **Orkney** and **Shetland**, then in England, Germany, the Netherlands, Spain, North Africa and the Middle East, claiming to have covered 36,000 miles, much of it on foot. In Spain he fell foul of the Inquisition and had his ears chopped off. Back in Scotland as 'Lugless Will' he wrote an account of his wanderings, or rather a *Totall Discourse of the Rare Adventures and Painfull Peregrinations of Long Nineteen Yeares*, 1623. Like most such travelogues, it was thought somewhat fabulous (and possibly was), but was nevertheless read. Lithgow took to the road again but returned to Lanark to die. He also wrote religious propaganda, reportage and verse, notably 'The Pilgrim's Farewell to his Native Country', 1618.

LITTLEJOHN, Sir Henry Duncan
(1826–1914) Medical Officer of Health
Born in **Edinburgh** and graduating MD from **Edinburgh University** in 1847, Littlejohn became a Fellow of the **Royal College of Surgeons** of Edinburgh in 1854. There he lectured on medical jurisprudence at the Extra Mural Medical School (a separate medical school owned by the two Royal Medical Colleges in Edinburgh) from 1855–97.

Although forensic medicine was not yet a science in its own right, he was often called to give evidence before the courts. His greatest achievement, however, lay in the field of public health. He was appointed the first Medical Health Officer for Edinburgh in 1862 and three years later published a report on the sanitary state of the city, which firmly established his reputation. He oversaw the sanitary arrangements in new developments, educated people on the importance of cleanliness and good sanitation, and urged the town council to obtain an Act of Parliament compelling doctors to notify the Public Health Department of every case of certain infectious diseases. This Act was passed in 1879 making Edinburgh the first city in Britain to have such legislation. As a result of his endeavours, typhus and smallpox were virtually eradicated from the city.

In 1897 Littlejohn was appointed Professor of Medical Jurisprudence at Edinburgh University, a post which he held until 1906. During that time he advised the town council on the building of what is now the City Hospital, which opened in 1903 as a fever hospital. He died in Edinburgh.

LIVERPOOL SCOTTISH, The, Regiment
Patriotic enthusiasm during the Boer War led to the raising of a Scottish Regiment of Volunteers in Liverpool. The regiment was embodied in 1900 under the title of the 8th (Scottish) Volunteer Battalion, the King's Liverpool Regiment. In 1908 the title was changed to the 10th (Scottish) Battalion, the King's (Liverpool) Regiment while in 1937 the unit became the Liverpool Scottish, the **Queen's Own Cameron Highlanders**.

The unit sent a service section to the **Gordon Highlanders** in South Africa during the Boer War and became entitled to that battle honour. Three battalions were raised in World War I, seeing action on the Western Front where they won 12 battle honours. The Medical Officer of the 1st Battalion, Captain Noel Chavasse, RAMC, won the Victoria Cross and bar, one of only three men ever to have achieved this extraordinary distinction. The regiment raised two battalions in World War II, but neither went overseas although one company served in Norway. In 1967 the regiment was reduced, one company becoming part of the 51st Highland Volunteers.

The original uniform was drab tunic with red facings while the **kilt** was of Forbes **tartan** in deference to the first Commanding Officer. The Regimental March is 'The Glendaruel Highlanders'.

LIVESTOCK FARMING
Before the industrial revolution Scottish farming, particularly in the Highlands, was a self-sufficiency system. Cattle and sheep were far too valuable for slaughter, being used respectively for work and for milk, and for wool and milk. Calf and lamb competed with the family for the meagre milk output. **Goats** were of great value to the people, though **pigs** were relatively unimportant.

Lowland farming was more productive but, as was also the case in the Highlands, the main source of cash was the sale of cattle to dealers who made up drove herds which walked to the markets at **Crieff** and **Falkirk** for the journey south. Such cattle were pastured on unimproved and unfertilised ground and typically took four or five years to reach sale weight of 150kg (3 cwt). Often they were fitted with shoes for part of the journey south, which they covered at the rate of about ten miles per day. The **drovers** were a major means of communication around Britain at the time, also they handled large sums of money and several of the Scottish **banks** trace their origin to the activities of these traders. Cattle destined for London were fattened on the marsh pastures outside Norwich to a weight of 250kg (5 cwt). Drove cattle were one of Scotland's major exports in pre-industrial times.

The change from a simple subsistence economy to a complex market economy followed the availability of cheap fertilisers such as nitrates from Chile and elsewhere, basic slag from the **iron** industry and town sewage brought by the new **canal** and **railway** systems. Most important, industrial prosperity eventually led to landlords investing in drainage, fencing, the rationalisation of holdings through enclosure, and the provision of winter housing for cattle. The results were better crop yields and the availability of high-quality feeds for cattle, with consequently the development of new breeds of beef cattle and the growth of commercial pig and chicken farming.

Another source of cash was the **horse and pony** trade. These were used by farmers, though in a self-sufficient system they were less appropriate a use of resources than were oxen. Horses need oats and good grass while oxen could subsist on crop residues. However oxen were not popular for road or town use and of course could not be ridden or used in **coal**-mines, and this lack of a market led to their replacement on farms by horses and ponies.

Dairy produce was mostly butter and cheese though town dairies did produce milk for the growing industrial communities. Many such dairies were scandalously unhygienic, but the 'Willowbank Dairy' of John Harley in **Glasgow** was one of the wonders of the age with its hygienic, spa-like conditions and visitor's gallery. Sadly this enterprise only lasted from 1809–16, but it helped to show the way. After about 1875, when Empire and American meat out-competed home produce, British cattle farmers switched to milk production, superseding the town dairies, and the liquid milk market became the basis of the livestock industry.

The hill sheep industry has shown much less dramatic

structural changes than the rest of Scottish livestock farming. This is partly because of conservatism, partly because the forces of nature bear heavily and uncontrollably on hill flocks. Without government subsidies the industry would evaporate because profit margins are so low. This would lead to unpredictable changes because the hill flocks are the very basis of the British sheep industry.

The great contributions of Scotland to the world's livestock farming have been the developments in agricultural and veterinary science made and propagated in Scottish universities and colleges and transmitted across the world, like so many technical advances, by emigrant Scots. Also enormously important have been the **Aberdeen-Angus** and Beef **Shorthorn** cattle breeds, whose descendants populate the plains and pampas of North and South America.

LIVINGSTON, Sir Alexander of Callendar (d.1450) Keeper of Stirling Castle

Head of the baronial family of Livingston, Sir Alexander was prominent amongst those jostling for control of the government during the minority of **James II**, his main rivals being the Crichtons and the **Douglases**. After the death (1439) of the Regent, **Archibald 5th Earl of Douglas**, Livingston manoeuvred the young King into his clutches at **Stirling Castle** and then managed to imprison James's mother Queen Joan and her new husband also in Stirling, releasing them only when he had been granted official custody of the King until he came of age. Both he and **William Crichton**, Governor of **Edinburgh Castle**, were implicated in the murder (1440) of the young Earl of Douglas and his brother [see **'Black Dinner'**], but Livingston vehemently denied any involvement. The remaining years of James's minority saw a continuous succession of quarrels and shifting alliances between the Livingstons, Crichtons and Douglases and, not surprisingly, one of James's first acts on reaching his majority was to arrest and imprison Livingston for 'crymes committit agaynis the king'. His lands were forfeited and he died the following year.

LIVINGSTON, West Lothian

The parish of Livingston is thought to have been named after one Leving, possibly a merchant from Flanders, who settled here c1120 and whose son 'Thurstanus filius Levingi' witnessed a charter confirming a grant of the church by **David I** to the monks of **Holyrood**. Early a 'fructiferous' agricultural area, it became increasingly industrialised with the development of **coal-mining** and the extraction of shale-oil. Livingston's position on the main **Edinburgh-Glasgow** road and **railway**, and the steady decline of its scattered industrial communities, made it an obvious choice for both geographical and social reasons for the site of the fourth (after **East Kilbride**, **Glenrothes** and **Cumbernauld**) of Scotland's New Towns (1962). The initial target population of 70,000 now looks unrealistic. By 1995 it stood at 44,000. But the four industrial estates and Science Park successfully attracted manufacturing and high-technology industries, increasingly well-serviced by the growing motorway network. Livingston is now the largest town in the **Lothians** after Edinburgh.

LIVINGSTON, William (Uilleam MacDhunleibhe) (1808–70) Gaelic Poet

Born in Kilarrow, **Islay**, Livingston lived in **Comrie**, **Greenock** and **Glasgow**. Having taught himself Greek, Latin and Scottish history, he wrote **Gaelic verse** on historical and legendary themes, including several long battle-poems such as *Cath Monadh Braco* ('Battle of Braco Moor') and *Na Lochlannaich an Ile* ('The Norsemen in Islay'). These tend to be diffuse, though they have very vivid passages. In *Fios thun a' Bhàird* ('A Message to the Poet') he focuses much more sharply on the devastating effect of the Islay **clearances**. For texts, see *Duain agus Orain le Uilleam MacDhunlèibhe*, 1882.

LIVINGSTONE, Dr David (1813–73) Missionary and Explorer

One of the world's greatest explorers, David Livingstone was born in a Clydeside tenement at **Blantyre**, eight miles from **Glasgow**, on 19 March 1813. Although his childhood education ended at the age of ten, young Livingstone showed an amazing mental facility for studying while working at his loom in the local **cotton** mill, where he walked 20 miles during the course of every 14-hour day. He may have read the accounts of such fellow-Scots as **Park** and **Clapperton**, but appears to have been inspired by the works of Karl Gutzläff (1803–51), the German missionary who believed that missionaries to unexplored lands should have a medical education. After first studying medicine at Glasgow, and as a trainee missionary with the London Missionary Society, Livingstone set foot in Africa at Cape Town in March 1841.

Livingstone's explorations can be divided into three great journeys, in which he covered an astonishing 30,000 miles of the Dark Continent. After finding difficulties in settling in southern Africa, although he there married Mary Moffat, the daughter of the distinguished missionary **Robert Moffat**, Livingstone managed to

Dr David Livingstone; drawing by Edward Grimston, 1857 (SNPG)

travel north through the Kalahari desert and discover Lake Ngami with William Oswell. He then crossed the 'T' of his northward trek by first travelling west through the heart of the continent to the Atlantic at Luanda, and then retracing his steps eastwards, mostly along the Zambesi, to Quelimane on the Indian Ocean. During the second half of this journey he saw Victoria Falls for the first time, and made a successful if hazardous descent to the sea. Unfortunately an instrument fault, coupled with an uncharacteristic error of observation, made him conclude that the Zambesi was navigable right into central Africa, and he communicated this misconception to the Foreign Office during his triumphant return to Britain in 1856.

Returning to the area in 1858 as the head of an expensively-equipped expedition, complete with a dismantled steam launch, Livingstone realised that he had failed to observe the insurmountable Kebra Basa rapids on the Zambesi, and instead turned northwards to explore the Shire valley, discovering Lake Nyasa. In so doing, he inadvertently opened the area to slave procurement, and suffered a personal tragedy when his wife Mary, determined to join him in Africa, succumbed to illness and died at Shupanga in 1862. With the expedition's original purpose unfulfilled, it was recalled soon after, although Livingstone then showed his navigational skill by sailing the expedition's small launch to Bombay using sails to supplement the 8 days' fuel load on the 45-day voyage.

In 1866 he returned to Africa for the last time, hoping to collect data on the river systems in East Central Africa, but this expedition found him failing in health and indecisive in leadership, while navigational problems minimised the scientific value of his carefully-noted observations. When seriously ill at Ujiji on Lake Tanganyika in 1871, he was visited by Henry Morton Stanley, a Welsh-born American journalist, who greeted him with the immortal phrase 'Doctor Livingstone, I presume?' Stanley's was one of four expeditions seeking information on Livingstone's whereabouts and welfare, and his writings put the seal on the Scottish explorer's fame.

Livingstone was anguished by the slave trade (he had previously released over 150 slaves by holding their captors at gunpoint), and could not be persuaded to leave Africa. Ironically, he was frequently reduced to accepting assistance from Arab slave-traders as his final trek, in the area of Lake Chaya, turned into a nightmare of bad weather and increasing ill-health. He died on his knees in an attitude of prayer on 1 May 1873 at Chitambo (now in Zambia). His faithful followers buried his heart locally and then embalmed his body before carrying it 1500 miles to the coast, a journey of mortal danger for them in such a superstitious environment. Their beloved master's remains were buried with full honours in Westminster Abbey in 1874.

Livingstone has had his critics; he appears to have been an ineffective missionary, but there is no minimising his contribution to the science of exploration. He showed that it was possible for a white man to settle in the interior of Africa, and even more importantly to coexist with the indigenous populations. His journeys succeeded in catching the imagination of his generation, greatly focusing attention on the need to explore the Dark Continent, and to stop the still-prevalent slave trade. Prompted to action, the British government ensured that no more slaves could be sold openly at Zanzibar in 1873, the year of Livingstone's death, although the trade continued illicitly for some years. For a clinical evaluation of Livingstone's achievements despite his ill-health, see Dr Oliver Ransford's *David Livingstone: The Dark Interior* (Murray, 1978).

LOCAL GOVERNMENT

BURGHS Until 1975 the burgh lay at the heart of local government administration in Scotland. First established by **David I** in the first half of the 12th century, they numbered no fewer than 300 by the beginning of the 18th century, not all of them surviving. Different varieties of burghs existed – royal burghs were the most powerful, being represented in the pre-1707 Scots Parliament. Free burghs held Crown-granted trading privileges, and were sometimes called 'burghs of barony'. From 1560, some kirk sessions in these burgh communities were invested with educational and poor relief responsibilities, the cost being met by local landowners in a forerunner to the rating system.

By the 19th century, particularly after the Reform Act of 1832, royal and some barony burghs became subject to popular election, while a number of new Parliamentary burghs were created by the Act. In the smaller burghs, popularly elected commissioners were appointed alongside the old undemocratic councils to provide certain public services. From 1833–92 it was possible for a burgh to have either of two systems of organisation – either governed by a provost, bailies and councillors, or by police commissioners and magistrates – authorities with the latter system being known as police burghs. Burghs of barony tended to disappear at around this time, with the passing of the 1892 Burgh Police (Scotland) Act. The Town Councils (Scotland) Act passed eight years later standardised burgh councils uniformly under a provost, bailies and councillors.

While far short of the democratically answerable councils of our own time, the burgh system did offer a stable form of local government for its time. By 1914 Scottish local government was fully democratised and in 1929 legislation created three different categories of burgh – cities (four in number), large burghs (19) and small (178). These, along with the counties mentioned below, were swept away by reorganisation in the 1970s.

The county system evolved equally slowly, with justices of the peace being made responsible for public order and highways, and county councils being gradually established around what were formerly medieval sheriffdoms, the new councils being developments of landowners' committees which took on public duties from the 17th century. County councils were formalised by the 1889 Local Government (Scotland) Act, and lasted until reorganisation in 1975.

Counties and County Towns Prior to 1975 Reorganisation (see map on page xvi)

County	County Town
Aberdeen	Aberdeen
Angus	Forfar
Argyll	Inveraray (Lochgilphead)

Ayrshire	Ayr
Banff	Banff
Berwick	Greenlaw (Duns)
Bute	Rothesay
Caithness	Wick
Clackmannan	Alloa
Dumfries	Dumfries
Dunbarton	Dumbarton
Fife	Cupar
Inverness	Inverness
Kincardine	Stonehaven
Kinross	Kinross
Kirkcudbright	Kirkcudbright
Lanark	Lanark (Hamilton)
East Lothian	Haddington
Midlothian	Edinburgh
West Lothian	Linlithgow
Moray	Elgin
Nairn	Nairn
Peebles	Peebles
Perth	Perth
Renfrew	Renfrew (Paisley)
Ross & Cromarty	Dingwall
Roxburgh	Jedburgh (Newtown St Boswells)
Selkirk	Selkirk
Stirling	Stirling
Sutherland	Dornoch (Golspie)
Wigtown	Wigtown (Stranraer)
Orkney	Kirkwall
Shetland (Zetland)	Lerwick

(Names in brackets indicate either that the county town changed at some time between 1894–1975, or that the County Headquarters were located in other than the county town, or, in the case of Shetland, that the name of the county changed.)

LOCAL GOVERNMENT SINCE 1975 The Local Government (Scotland) Act passed by the Labour government in 1973 and operative from 1975 ordained a two-tier system of nine regional councils under which there were 53 district councils (plus three island councils performing the functions of both region and district). But this system, and especially the vast Labour-dominated Strathclyde Region, which embraced half of Scotland's total population, did not find favour with Conservative governments anxious to curtail council spending. It was accordingly abolished by the Local Government (Scotland) Act of 1994 which reinstated a single-tier system comprising 29 unitary authorities (plus three island authorities). Occasion was also taken to transfer some responsibilities from local government to other authorities (eg water and sewerage to three Water Authorities) or the Scottish Office (eg all roads except local ones). Additionally, in view of the small size of some of the new authorities, some other responsibilities (eg police and fire services) were retained on a regional basis and handled by joint boards (representing, for instance, 12 councils in the case of Strathclyde Police). The aim of reducing district–region friction and duplication was worthy but the result was some fragmentation and much inconsistency in the portfolios of individual councils. All these unitary councils and joint boards remained in operation at the time when the new **Scottish Parliament** came into existence. The Councils are set out in the following table along with their regional and district equivalents as per the previous (1975) system.

Under the Scotland Act of 1998 none of the responsibilities (structural, financial, supervisory etc) in respect of local government in Scotland which had previously belonged to the Westminster Parliament were reserved to it. They therefore devolved to the Scottish Parliament; and a commission chaired by Neil McIntosh was set up to consider relations between the Scottish Executive and local government. But how in practice the new parliament will reconcile brave words about increasing local government discretion and accountability with the responsibilities of funding and supervising it (and the consequent temptation to intervene and suborn) remains to be seen.

See also **Government and Administration**.

Composition of new council areas in terms of old Regions/Island Areas/Districts

New Council Area	Region/Islands Area	District	Population	Area (Ha)
Aberdeen, City of	Grampian (part)		**218,220**	**18,581**
		Aberdeen City	218,220	18,581
Aberdeenshire	Grampian (part)		**223,630**	**631,787**
		Banff & Buchan	88,020	153,214
		Gordon	79,650	222,126
		Kincardine & Deeside	55,960	256,447
Angus	Tayside (part)		**111,020**	**218,148**
		Angus	97,420	204,172
		Dundee City (part)	13,600	13,976
Argyll & Bute	Strathclyde (part)		**90,550**	**692,967**
		Argyll & Bute	63,260	657,856
		Dumbarton (part)	27,290	35,111

Composition of new council areas in terms of old Regions/Island Areas/Districts continued

New Council Area	Region/Islands Area	District	Population	Area (Ha)
Borders, The	Borders		**105,300**	**473,379**
		Berwickshire	19,350	91,421
		Ettrick & Lauderdale	35,040	137,150
		Roxburgh	35,350	154,554
		Tweeddale	15,560	90,254
Clackmannan	Central (part)		**48,660**	**15,662**
		Clackmannan	48,660	15,662
Dumbarton & Clydebank	Strathclyde (part)		**97,790**	**16,223**
		Clydebank	46,580	3,651
		Dumbarton (part)	51,210	12,572
Dumfries & Galloway	Dumfries & Galloway		**147,900**	**643,903**
		Annandale & Eskdale	37,130	155,929
		Nithsdale	57,220	143,479
		Stewartry	23,690	168,631
		Wigtown	29,860	175,864
Dundee, City of	Tayside (part)		**153,710**	**6,515**
		Dundee City (part)	153,710	6,515
East Ayrshire	Strathclyde (part)		**123,820**	**125,199**
		Cumnock & Doon Valley	42,840	87,700
		Kilmarnock & Loudoun	80,980	37,499
East Dunbarton-shire	Strathclyde (part)		**110,220**	**17,182**
		Bearsden & Milngavie	41,050	3,737
		Strathkelvin (part)	69,170	13,445
East Lothian	Lothian (part)		**85,640**	**67,772**
		East Lothian	85,640	67,772
East Renfrewshire	Strathclyde (part)		**86,780**	**17,269**
		Eastwood	62,600	11,994
		Renfrew (part)	24,180	5,275
Edinburgh, City of	Lothian (part)		**441,620**	**26,228**
		Edinburgh City	441,620	26,228
Falkirk	Central (part)		**142,610**	**29,924**
		Falkirk	142,610	29,924
Fife	Fife		**351,200**	**132,256**
		Dunfermline	130,150	30,806
		Kirkcaldy	148,630	24,484
		North East Fife	72,420	76,966
Glasgow, City of	Strathclyde (part)		**623,850**	**17,504**
		Glasgow City (part)	623,850	17,504
Highland	Highland		**206,900**	**2,578,379**
		Badenoch & Strathspey	11,100	234,892
		Caithness	26,370	179,772
		Inverness	63,850	286,691

New Council Area	Region/Islands Area	District	Population	Area (Ha)
		Lochaber	19,410	455,031
		Nairn	10,850	42,394
		Ross & Cromarty	50,260	506,545
		Skye & Lochalsh	11,870	272,145
		Sutherland	13,190	600,909
Inverclyde	Strathclyde (part)		**89,990**	**16,179**
		Inverclyde	89,990	16,179
Midlothian	Lothian (part)		**79,910**	**35,587**
		Midlothian	79,910	35,587
Moray	Grampian (part)		**86,250**	**223,823**
		Moray	86,250	223,823
North Ayrshire	Strathclyde (part)		**139,020**	**88,387**
		Cunninghame	139,020	88,387
North Lanarkshire	Strathclyde (part)		**326,750**	**47,358**
		Cumbernauld & Kilsyth	63,930	10,409
		Monklands	102,590	16,667
		Motherwell	143,730	17,175
		Strathkelvin (part)	16,500	3,107
Orkney Islands	Orkney		**19,760**	**99,165**
Perthshire & Kinross	Tayside (part)		**130,470**	**531,146**
		Dundee City (part)	2,810	3,110
		Perth & Kinross	127,660	528,036
Renfrewshire	Strathclyde (part)		**176,970**	**26,139**
		Renfrew (part)	176,970	26,139
Shetland Islands	Shetland		**22,830**	**143,808**
South Ayrshire	Strathclyde (part)		**113,960**	**120,223**
		Kyle & Carrick	113,960	120,223
South Lanarkshire	Strathclyde (part)		**307,100**	**177,116**
		Clydesdale	58,290	132,916
		East Kilbride	83,690	28,474
		Glasgow City (part)	57,620	2,502
		Hamilton	107,500	13,224
Stirling	Central (part)		**81,630**	**219,588**
		Stirling	81,630	219,588
West Lothian	Lothian (part)		**146,730**	**42,504**
		West Lothian	146,730	42,504
Western Isles	Western Isles		**29,410**	**313,353**
SCOTLAND			**5,120,200**	**7,813,254**

Population figures are provisional 1993 estimates based on the 1991 Census.

LOCH, James (1780–1855) Agricultural Improver

Born and brought up at Drylaw House in **Edinburgh**, Loch was called to the English Bar (1801) and specialised in conveyancing before being attracted to estate management and the economic potential of rationalised land use. A chance meeting with the Marquess of Stafford, husband of **Elizabeth Gordon Countess of Sutherland**, led to his appointment (1813) as commissioner for the vast **Sutherland** estates. He was MP for **Wick** and the Northern Burghs from 1830–55 but is remembered as the moving spirit behind the notorious Sutherland **clearances**. Living mostly in Edinburgh and London and with little experience of conditions in the Highlands, he nevertheless formed high expectations of their agricultural potential and a rather low opinion of their inhabitants; though condemning some of the more extreme methods of **Patrick Sellar**, he advocated forcible removal where necessary. Prebble (*The Highland Clearances*, 1963) calls him 'the creator of the policy of improvement'; he did not originate improvement but in his *Account of the Improvements on the Estates of Sutherland*, 1820, he offered a well-argued accountant's justification. Tenantry were not to be removed simply to free land for sheep but so that, otherwise employed in **fishing**, etc, they might increase their economic potential, thus enabling them to pay higher rents for their holdings.

LOCHABER, Inverness-shire

Now centred on **Fort William**, the ancient lordship of Lochaber extends north from **Loch Leven** to Glen Garry and west from **Badenoch** to **Moidart**. A mid-19th century gazetteer describes it as 'one of the most dreary, mountainous and barren districts in Scotland' where, suitably, the country's last wolf may have been shot (by Sir Ewen Cameron in 1680). This distinction is claimed by several other localities while few modern writers would describe as 'dreary' such beauty spots as Glens Nevis and Roy or Lochs Arkaig and Garry. **Ben Nevis** and the Nevis range dominate the skyline much as **Camerons of Lochiel** and **MacDonalds** (**MacDonells**) of Keppoch (near Roy Bridge) have long dominated its society. Bestriding the western entrance to the **Great Glen**, in earlier times Lochaber was repeatedly contested between the **Campbells of Argyll** and the MacDonalds of the Isles with occasional incursions from the **Stewarts** of Badenoch and the **Huntly Gordons**. Later it became a hotbed of **Jacobite** dissent.

LOCHALINE, Morvern, Argyll

On the Sound of **Mull**, Lochaline has a car ferry to Fishnish (**Mull**) and a fine view down the sound to **Ardtornish** and **Duart** Castles. Inland the ruined Kinlochaline Castle, a 15th century keep built by either the MacInneses or the MacLeans, contains above the main fireplace a stone panel depicting, unusually, a naked lady. **Morvern** sand, with a high silica content that makes it ideal for optical glass manufacture, has been extensively excavated since 1939.

LOCHEARNHEAD, Perthshire

Lochearnhead lost its **railway** station to Dr Beeching in the 1950s and its main hotel to fire in the 1970s. But the suitability of Loch Earn (seven miles long) for watersports has been some compensation. This village lies at the western end, corresponding to **St Fillan's** at the eastern end. Edinample Castle, a Z-plan tower house two miles east, was built by 'Black' **Duncan Campbell of Glenorchy** in the early 17th century although it may incorporate an earlier **MacGregor** stronghold. Further along the south side of the loch, Ardvorlich House has been the home of the **Stewarts** of Ardvorlich since at least 1589 when the decapitated head of the King's forester, with a crust in his bloodless lips, was presented to the lady of Ardvorlich, who was also the deceased's sister. This was by way of a poacher's revenge on the part of some MacGregors who had fallen foul of the forester. The distraught lady, who happened to be pregnant, took to the hills and there gave birth to James Stewart, also known as the 'Mad Major'. He served under **Montrose** and provided **Sir Walter Scott** with the model for Allan Macaulay in *A Legend of Montrose*. A nearby tombstone commemorating seven marauding **MacDonalds of Glencoe** 'killed when attempting to harry Ardvorlich' (1620) seems an almost superfluous reminder of the lawlessness that characterised the Highland marches.

LOCHGILPHEAD, Argyll

Unsurprisingly, Lochgilphead lies at the head of Loch Gilp, a short and shallow arm of **Loch Fyne** which at low tide is mostly mud flats. Until the 19th century it was a small **fishing** village. Two events account for its subsequent elevation. In 1801 the opening of the Crinan **Canal**, which starts at nearby **Ardrishaig**, made it a popular watering place. Loch-front villas sprang up, plus a large poorhouse and a lunatic asylum. The latter is now represented by the Argyll and Bute Hospital. The 1975 reorganisation of **local government**, which constituted an Argyll and Bute District within Strathclyde Region, provided the second boost. Lochgilphead succeeded **Inveraray**, the county town of **Argyll**, as the new district headquarters (a role it retained with the 1995 abolition of the Regions and the creation of the Argyll and Bute Council Area); nearby Kilmory Castle was purchased at considerable expense as the district council offices; further administrative buildings were soon found essential; and Lochgilphead basked in a new era of expansion and investment.

LOCHINDORB CASTLE, Nr Grantown-on-Spey, Moray

In bleak surroundings between **Grantown** and **Forres**, the ruined walls of Lochindorb Castle occupy an island, partly man-made, in the loch of the same name. It means 'loch of trouble' and so it proved when in 1372 **Robert II** granted the stronghold to his third son, **Alexander Stewart, Earl of Buchan** and 'Wolf of Badenoch'. Originally the property of the **Comyns** of Badenoch, it had been captured by Edward I in 1303 and had provided a refuge for Katherine Beaumont, Countess of Atholl, who fled there from **Kildrummy** in 1335. Besieged by the Regent **Sir Andrew Moray**, she and 'othir ladys that ware luvely' were rescued by Edward III in 1336. It was then used as a prison before becoming the Wolf's lair. **James II** eventually ordered its destruction (1458) by **Campbell** of **Cawdor** but as late as the 18th century the four corner towers of its enclosing walls

Lochindorb Castle, the Wolf of Badenoch's stronghold (MR)

were still standing. Now only one remains, trees benefit from the shelter of the walls, and of the Lochindorb kail, 'a mixture of red cabbage and common turnip', there is no trace. With turnip-shaped roots weighing up to a pound, it was possibly akin to kohl rabi.

LOCHINVER, Sutherland
In 1840 Lochinver was described as 'the only place deserving the name of a village' in Assynt. It did not even possess a minister, although a pier had been built recently to serve its natural harbour. Today it ranks with **Kinlochbervie** as one of the two busiest **fishing** stations on this coast. It lies in particularly dramatic surroundings, its hinterland of gneiss dotted with innumerable lochans and behind these the separate natural sculptures of Canisp and **Suilven**, Quinag and Ben More Assynt.

LOCH LEVEN CASTLE, Kinross-shire
On an island near the western edge of the loch, **Loch Leven** Castle is first mentioned as having been besieged by the English in 1301. **Robert I** twice visited but, contrary to his normal custom, did not destroy it. In 1335 it was one of five strongholds which held out for **David II** and as such withstood a siege which is said to have included an attempt to flush out the garrison by raising the level of the loch. In 1390 it was granted to Sir Henry Douglas and was still in Douglas hands when in 1567 **Queen Mary** was incarcerated here following her surrender at **Carberry Hill**. Her plight was immediately heightened by the double blow of forced abdication and a spontaneous miscarriage (possibly of twins, presumably **Darnley**'s). Escape after nearly a year

Loch Leven Castle, where Queen Mary was imprisoned (MR)

was arranged by William Douglas, the keeper of the castle's boats and an admirer; within weeks Mary had a new gaoler in the person of Elizabeth of England. The Douglases of Loch Leven succeeded to the **Earldom of Morton** whose 9th Earl sold the castle and lands to **Sir William Bruce**, builder of **Kinross House**. By the mid-18th century the castle was roofless and ruinous but the square keep (15th century) remains structurally complete, with three corner turrets though without its gabled roof and cap-house. Unusually, the main entrance is to the second floor. Of the adjoining barmkin (courtyard) little more than the outer wall and part of a corner tower remain. Originally these buildings included kitchens and a great hall.

LOCHMABEN, Dumfriesshire
The 14th tee on Lochmaben **golf course** has been described as 'one of the great shrines of Scottish history'; artefacts found here (excluding discarded tees) are now in the **Dumfries** Museum. For it once served an even nobler purpose as the motte and earliest castle of the **Bruce** family. The site and the lordship of Annandale were conferred on Robert de Brus by **David I** in c1124 and hereabouts the future **Robert I** spent much of his childhood, although the motte was superseded, probably in his lifetime, by a stone castle, the remains of which stand on a promontory at the southern end of Castle Loch. Adjacent to it is a peel built by Edward I in 1298 and, although Robert I conferred Lochmaben on **Thomas Randolph**, the castle was probably built by the English and certainly held for them for most of the 14th century. It was regained in 1384 by the **Douglases** and in 1455 became a Crown property, much favoured by **James IV** and visited by **Queen Mary** and Lord Darnley in 1565. The hereditary keepership was held by the Maxwells until 1609, then by the Murrays, created Earls of Annandale in 1624, then by the Johnstones of Hartfell to whom the earldom passed in 1661. By then the castle was already crumbling. It evidently covered a large area and was ingeniously defended by walls and moats including a 6m wide canal in front of the southern curtain wall.

Under royal patronage the burgh (possibly since the time of Robert I, whose statue here was erected in 1879) profited from tolls on the cross-border cattle trade and from customary exactions on local agriculturalists. Several lochs dot its immediate neighbourhood and were once renowned as the only Scottish haunt of the *Coregonus Vandesius (Willoughbii)*, otherwise the vendace, a small fish with a heart-shaped mark between the eyes, said to have been introduced by Queen Mary and to be delicate eating. Indifferent to all known baits, it is caught only by net and that seldom. A Vendace Club met here annually for the purpose in the 19th century but by 1972 the fish was reported (T Weir) extinct in all the lochs except the Mill Loch.

Rammerscales, a Georgian manor house to the south of the town, was built in 1760 for Dr James Mounsey, physician to Tsarina Elizabeth of Russia. To the north Elsieshields, a late 16th/early 17th century tower closely resembling **Amisfield**, was more recently the home of Sir Stephen Runciman, the historian.

LOCHMADDY, North Uist
Named for the two projecting basalt crags, *Madadh Mor*

and *Madadh Grisionn* (**Gaelic** *Madadh*, a dog; *grisionn*, brindled), that flank the entrance to its sheltered and island-studded harbour, Lochmaddy is the principal village of **North Uist**. The waters of the eponymous loch cover an area of nine square miles, but 'so remarkable are its projections and sinuosities that its coast line has been found to measure 200 miles' (Fullarton's *Gazetteer*). In the 18th and early 19th centuries these waters yielded a copious harvest of *fucus*, the bladder-wrack seaweed used in the **kelp** industry. Lochmaddy is the port of call for ferries from **Tarbert**, **Harris** and Uig, **Skye**.

LOCHNAGAR, Aberdeenshire

South of **Balmoral** in a triangle formed by the **Dee** and Glens Muick and Callater, Lochnagar is a small loch (*loch-nan-gabhar*, loch of the goat) and a large hill, an outlier of the **Cairngorms** once known as the White Mounth but now named as per the loch. It has several

Lochnagar, from an engraving (SP)

summits, the highest some 3786ft (1154m), some fine corries and, where the granite has been exposed to weathering, some distinctly architectural forms. The view if clear extends to Ben Lomond, **Ben Nevis** and beyond. Apart from its overview of Balmoral, royal connections include an attempted ascent by **Queen Victoria** in 1861 and a children's book by Prince Charles in the 1980s. **Byron** had already ensured its place in English verse:

England! thy beauties are tame and domestic
To one who has roved o'er the mountains afar:

Oh, for the crags that are wild and majestic!
The steep frowning glories of dark Lochnagar.

or:

The infant rapture still survived the boy,
And Lochnagar with Ida looked o'er Troy.

LOCHWINNOCH, Renfrewshire

Beside a loch, once of the same name but now Castle Semple Loch, Lochwinnoch village retains only the gable and belfry of St Winnoc's Church, also known as 'Auld Simon'. An erstwhile weaving and bleaching centre where the Calder River enters the loch, the place is now mainly residential but with facilities for the vast Clyde-Muirshiel Regional Park which embraces Lochwinnoch Nature Reserve (including RSPB centre), Castle Semple Country Park and much of the intervening ground between here and **Greenock**. Barr Castle, an early 16th century square tower, remains complete to the wall-head but of Castle Semple nothing remains, and of Castle Semple House, its 18th century successor, only incidental items such as the west gate and a hectagonal folly known as The Temple (1770). Semples held lands at nearby Elliston (or Elziotstoun), with ruins of a 15th century castle, as early as the 13th century and also built the Peel (c1550), a low tower on what was then an island, plus the well preserved ruin that was once a Collegiate Church. Built in 1504, it was extended soon after with an apse in which was placed the elaborate funerary monument to the Lord Sempill (Semple) killed at **Flodden**. In 1727 the Semples sold out to the MacDowalls of Garthland who planned the village, built the house, and are responsible for whatever else is not of Semple provenance. The vast hill fort on Walls Hill near Howwood (the rare double 'w' resulting from elision of 'Hollow-wood') is of course an exception. It has been conjectured that this was a Celtic 'oppidum' and possibly the capital of the Damnonii in **Roman** times.

LOCKERBIE, Dumfriesshire

Until 21 December 1988 [see **Lockerbie Air Crash**] this small red-stone market town in Annandale was best known for its August lamb sale, the successor of the great livestock tryst, 'last and largest in Scotland', which grew up on Lamb Hill to meet English demand following the **Act of Union**. Two families dominate the town's history, the Johnstones and the Jardines. To the former belonged the Old Tower of Lockerbie, a small fortalice which subsequently served as the town gaol. The main Johnstone stronghold was Lochwood Castle, some way north off the road to Beattock. The ruins of the L-plan tower house date from the 15th century; there is an adjacent motte which preceded it. Lochwood was occupied by the English in 1547–50 and burnt by the Maxwells in 1585 and/or 1592. The Johnstones took revenge in the last of the Border feuds by massacring (1593) a Maxwell contingent at Dryfe Sands, two miles west of the town. The 'Lockerbie Lick', here inflicted, refers to the Johnstone practice of slashing the faces of their defeated foes so as to leave a recognisable scar. Near Lochwood's once 'lofty towers where dwelt the Lord of Annandale' is Spedlins Tower (15th and 17th century), once a Jardine home and in the 19th century part of the Jardinehall estate of the Jardines of Apple-garth. These and the Jardines of Castlemilk (south of Lockerbie and where **Castlemilk sheep** originated) were beneficiaries of the family's involvement in the tea-and-opium China trade begun by William Jardine of Lochmaben, a surgeon and merchant who formed the famous **Jardine Matheson** partnership.

LOCKERBIE AIR CRASH (1988)

On the evening of 21 December 1988 a Pan Am Boeing 747, registration N739PA, crashed in a fireball on the town of **Lockerbie, Dumfriesshire**, in Britain's biggest aeronautical disaster. All 243 passengers and 16 crew were killed on board flight 103 en route from London Heathrow to New York, as well as 11 Lockerbie residents. There was no Mayday call from the stricken airliner and radar returns indicated that the plane had broken into five sections almost instantaneously, indicating the presence of a bomb on board.

Wreckage scattered over a huge area, some items being found up to 80 miles from Lockerbie. Four houses in the Sherwood Crescent area of the town were obliterated and a further 16 rendered uninhabitable as the plane's ground impact registered 1.6 on the Richter scale. Bodies literally rained from the sky, 60 of them landing on the local golf course; others fell on inhabited areas. Emergency services raced into action from all over southern Scotland and parts of northern England, but no one could have survived an explosion and fall from 31,000ft (9449m), nor could there be any survivors from the four houses struck by the aircraft's flaming left wing and undercarriage.

A memorial service was held at Dryfesdale Parish Church on 4 January 1989 and a memorial to the dead is sited there. The Fatal Accident Inquiry into the Lockerbie Disaster opened at **Dumfries** in October 1990, chaired by Sheriff John Mowat. The separate Aircraft Accident Report concluded that the incident had been caused by 'the detonation of an improvised explosive device' concealed inside a transistor radio stowed in the forward luggage hold.

Considerable controversy was caused by the revelation that US diplomatic personnel had been warned in December 1988 of a likely terrorist attack on an American airliner flying westward from Europe, and there were allegations that details of the bomb had been circulated to airport security staff, but ignored. At the time of writing the perpetrators of this tragedy had not been brought to justice, although a trial was underway.

LOCKHART, Sir George, of Carnwath (c1630–89) Advocate and Judge

The son of Sir James Lockhart of Lee (d.1674), a judge and Royalist who was knighted by **Charles I** and imprisoned by Cromwell, George was the younger brother of **Sir William** (1621–75) who married Cromwell's niece and represented the Commonwealth in France. Admitted as an advocate in 1656, becoming the equivalent of Lord Advocate under Cromwell and, after the Restoration, Dean of the Court of Advocates and Lord President of the Court of Session (1685), Sir George neatly bridged the family's divided loyalties. He was also MP for **Lanarkshire** in both the English (1658–9) and Scottish (1681–2) Parliaments. His knighthood was conferred in 1663 and the **Carnwath** estate acquired by purchase. Notable actions in which he was involved included the unsuccessful defence of both James Mitchell and **Archibald Campbell 9th Earl of Argyll**, plus a 1689 alimony judgement against John Chiesley of Dalry and in favour of Mrs Chiesley. Chiesley retaliated, shooting Carnwath dead outside his house off **Edinburgh**'s **High Street**.

LOCKHART, George, of Carnwath (1673–1731) Jacobite

As MP (1702–15) for **Edinburgh** and then **Wigton**, Lockhart was a vocal critic of **Union** with England and a covert supporter of the **Jacobite** cause. Although he always insisted that Union would be 'Scotland's ruin', he was chosen as one of the commissioners appointed in 1706 to negotiate the nature and terms of the treaty. His opposition proved ineffectual and served only to strengthen his attachment to **James Francis Edward Stewart** 'the Old Pretender', whom he saw as representing Scotland's best chance of undoing the Union. In 1715 he was arrested for supporting **Mar**'s rebellion but subsequently freed without a trial. He remained in Scotland and acted as one of the Jacobites' most respected advisors from 1718–27 when he was obliged to flee to Holland. He returned the following year but, like his father **Sir George Lockhart**, died a violent death when killed in a duel. His *Memoir of the Affairs of Scotland from Queen Anne's Succession to the Commencement of the Union* (1714) is a valuable source for the Union, as are his *Papers on the Affairs of Scotland* for the Jacobite cause.

LOCKHART, Sir James Haldane Stewart (1858–1937) Sinologist

Born on the family estate of Ardsheal, **Argyll**, Dux of **George Watson's College, Edinburgh**, and Greek gold medallist at **Edinburgh University**, James Lockhart was appointed a Hong Kong Cadet in 1878. He supervised Britain's acquisition of the New Territories in 1898 and was the first Special Commissioner of them. He was also Hong Kong's most senior permanent official in the 1890s. As Commissioner for Weihaiwei, Shandong Province, from 1902–21 he was responsible for preserving the Chinese identity of Hong Kong and Weihaiwei. A Confucian, he was fluent in several Chinese dialects and an expert numismatist. His publications included *Manual of Chinese Quotations* (1893) and *Currency of the Farther East* (1895–8). He died in London in 1937, leaving his considerable collection of Chinese art and papers to his former school.

LOCKHART, John Gibson (1794–1854) Biographer and Critic

Born at Cambusnethan, **Lanarkshire**, the son of a **Church of Scotland** minister, Lockhart grew up in **Glasgow**, where he attended primary and high school before entering the **University of Glasgow** in 1805. In 1808 he won a Snell Exhibition scholarship to Balliol College, Oxford. He graduated with a First in Classics in 1813 and returned to Scotland to take up law in **Edinburgh**, being called to the Bar in 1816. Lockhart's interests, however, lay more in literary work, and in 1816 he travelled to Germany with the financial backing of the publisher **William Blackwood**, and subsequently translated Schlegel's *Lectures on the History of Literature*.

In 1817 Lockhart became a contributing editor to **Blackwood's Magazine**. Together with **John Wilson** and **James Hogg**, he published the Chaldee Manuscripts in October 1817, a bitter satire of Edinburgh society that established the reputation of the newly founded magazine overnight. Lockhart's penchant for caustic wit manifested itself in the subsequent attacks on Leigh Hunt and the 'Cockney School' of poetry, John Keats's *Endymion*, and Samuel Taylor Coleridge's *Biographia Literaria*.

In 1818 Lockhart met and formed a warm friendship with **Sir Walter Scott**. He married Scott's daughter Sophia in 1820, and began concentrating on other areas of literary work. In 1819 he had published *Peter's Letters to his Kinsfolk*, a clever portrait of Edinburgh society. He followed this with a series of successful novels, *Valerius* (1821), *Adam Blair* (1822), *Reginald Dalton* (1823) and *Matthew Wald* (1824). In 1825 he moved to London to become editor of **John Murray**'s *Quarterly Review*. During this period he also began writing a series of biographies, publishing *A Life of Burns* in 1828, and a *Life of Napoleon Buonaparte* in 1829. His best-known work, *Memoirs of the Life of Scott*, was published in seven volumes between 1837 and 1838 and was for many years the standard work on Scott's life.

Lockhart's later years were clouded by illness and family problems. In 1831 one of his sons died, followed in 1837 by Sophia, and he grew estranged from his other son, Walter, who entered the army in 1846 and died in 1853. That same year Lockhart relinquished the editorship of the *Quarterly Review*. He died at **Abbotsford** on 25 November 1853 and was buried at **Dryburgh Abbey** at Walter Scott's feet. A two-volume biography of Lockhart by **Andrew Lang** was published in 1896.

LOCKHART, Sir Robert Hamilton Bruce (1887–1970) Diplomat and Writer

It was Lockhart's boast, not the only one, that he had 'not a drop of English blood'. He was born in **Anstruther**, the son of a local schoolmaster, and educated at **Fettes** (**Edinburgh**) and in Berlin. A spell on a family rubber plantation (1908–10), later recalled in *Return to Malaya*, 1938, preceded entry to the Foreign Office. Sent to Moscow as Vice-Consul (1911), he played an important liaison role during the war but was recalled after a minor sex scandal and then reinstalled as an unofficial agent in 1918. In this doubtful capacity he was arrested as a spy by the Soviet authorities and condemned to death for a supposed plot against the life of Lenin. His freedom was obtained thanks to a swap with Litvinoff, a Russian agent, and in 1920 he was sent to Prague as commercial secretary. The Russian experience provided the material for *Memoirs of a Secret Agent*, 1932, reprinted 18 times, and the Czech experience for *Retreat from Glory*, 1934. He had become a Catholic and in 1928 had resigned from the Foreign Office to work for Beaverbrook's *Evening Standard* where he edited the 'Londoner's Diary'. During World War II he liaised with Jan Masaryck and the Czech government in exile, and directed the British propaganda effort, receiving a KCMG in 1943. More books followed after the war, including one on **fishing**, a favourite hobby. None gave him immunity from financial embarrassment; living beyond his means, like adventure, he relished as an occupational hazard.

LOCKHART, Sir William, of Lee (1621–75)
Soldier and Diplomat

Son of Sir James Lockhart of Lee and brother of **Sir George of Carnwath**, William served in the French army and was knighted (1646) by **Charles I** after first serving against him in the Bishops' Wars. He supported the **Engagement**, fought at the battles of Preston and Worcester, but in 1652 defected to the Commonwealth and was appointed a commissioner for Scotland with a seat in the Protectorate Parliament. He also married Cromwell's niece. As a now trusted emissary he represented the Protectorate in France and commanded the English troops at the siege of Dunkirk. He fell from grace at the Restoration but served again as ambassador to France in 1674.

LOCOMOTIVE BUILDING

One of the nation's most important industries between the 1830s and the 1960s, Scottish locomotive building was contemporaneous with the reign of steam power on the world's **railways** and in industry. With **coal** being mined in Scotland from the Middle Ages, steam power was introduced into the coalfields for pumping purposes as early as the 18th century and later for transport. The *Perseverance*, built by Timothy Burstall at **Leith** Mills in 1829, is generally believed to be the first steam locomotive constructed in Scotland. It was intended for competition at the Rainhill Trials won by Stephenson's *Rocket*. An accident on the way to the event prevented Burstall's engine from arriving in time, but this 57cwt (2900kg) vertical-boiled machine, with no separate condenser, would have been an unlikely winner, unable to exceed 4mph. Four years later Carmichaels of **Dundee** built two locomotives, the *Earl of Airlie* and the *Lord Wharncliffe*, for the 4½ft (1.37m) gauge Dundee & Newtyle Railway and these appear to have given some 20 years' service.

Soon Scotland's locomotive industry took two quite separate forms: railway workshops connected to the nation's five principal railways, and commercial firms supplying railways and industrial companies throughout the world.

Until 1923, when Scottish railways were grouped with English concerns in two large super-companies (the London North Eastern and London Midland & Scottish railways), each of the five principal companies had workshops capable of building locomotives. The largest, the North British Railway (not to be confused with the North British Locomotive Company – see below), built 33 engines at its St Margaret's Works in **Edinburgh** until construction and major repairs were moved to Cowlairs in **Springburn** around 1865. Here 900 engines were constructed before 1924, not far from the Caledonian Railway's works at **St Rollox** where 3000 men were employed in building up to a thousand locomotives over a 70-year period. The Glasgow South Western Railway had its works at **Kilmarnock**, building 392 engines between 1857 and 1921, but the remaining two lines bought most of their engines from commercial firms, although the Highland built 41 at Lochgorm (**Inverness**) and the Great North of Scotland built 12 at Kittybrewster (**Aberdeen**) and **Inverurie**.

Loading a Glasgow-built locomotive for the Spanish National Railways (ML)

Dundee and Leith were two early commercial loco-building towns, while Kilmarnock had a number of engine-making works, one successfully adapting to later forms of power. But it was **Glasgow** which soon became the leading loco-producing centre in Scotland, indeed in Europe, with, apart from the NBR and CR works in the Springburn area, such firms as **Beardmore**, Neilson, Dübs and Sharp Stewart, the last three of these combining in 1903 to make up the North British Locomotive Company.

This became Britain's greatest locomotive builder, producing 26,755 units (including those from its constituent companies) – four times as many as its nearest British rival. Scarcely any part of the British Empire did not see NBL engines at work, as well as South America, Russia and China. Nor was the domestic market ignored, with locos delivered to all of the four grouped railways between 1923–48, including Southern Railway 'King Arthur' 4–6-0s, **Gresley**-designed A1 Pacifics for the LNER, and 'Royal Scot' 4–6-0s for the rival LMS. Huge orders were placed for heavy freight engines during World War II, and some 700 were produced.

British orders ceased not long after nationalisation of Britain's railways in 1948. New standard steam types were built exclusively in BR workshops, while NBL was so wedded to the steam engine that it had difficulty adapting to new forms of power, and chose to specialise in diesel-hydraulic (rather than diesel-electric) transmission systems. Its later diesel deliveries were not particularly successful and the firm closed in 1962.

LOLLARDS

Followers of John Wycliffe, translator of the Bible into English, in the late 14th century, Lollards were preachers to the people against corruption in Church and State. In Scotland John Resby, an English priest, was martyred at **Perth** in 1407. Thirty 'Lollards' from **Kyle** in **Ayrshire** were arraigned by **Archbishop Blackadder** in 1494 but dismissed without penalty.

LOM, Iain (John MacDonald) (c1625–post 1707) Gaelic Poet

Iain Lom's poems provide a commentary on a series of events, military and political, from the mid-1640s to the **Union of Parliaments** in 1707. His stance is, on a local level, that of a bard to the **MacDonalds** of Keppoch (who were his kinsmen), and of a champion of the MacDonalds in general, and on a more national level, of a Catholic with strong **Jacobite** sympathies and a fiercely independent attitude. There is a tradition that he was intended for the priesthood. Perhaps his subtle handling of argument mirrors some such training, and his ribald satire may suggest a personality that led him away from such a calling.

His earliest known poem is probably that on the **Battle of Inverlochy** (1645), a vivid, concise account leading to a bitter condemnation of the **Campbells**, who lost the battle. Probably from 1646, we have his lament for the young Angus of Keppoch, killed in a skirmish near **Killin**:

> I'm a goose that is plucked
> without feather or brood,
> or like Ossian condemned by St Patrick.

663

The Prince Consort on Loch Lomond in 1863; photograph by George Washington Wilson (BRC)

Before the end of the 1640s he had shown his strong anti-English bias, urging **Charles II** to stand by his Scottish supporters. He has a poem on Charles's coronation in 1660. In the later 1670s and the 1680s he takes the Marquis of **Atholl**'s side against the Campbells, recounting their skirmishes. Late poems are centred on the **Battle of Killiecrankie** (1689), the **Massacre of Glencoe** (1692), the accession of William and Mary to the throne, and finally the Union of Parliaments, which he sees as the result of bribery. Other poems celebrate chiefs or, in the case of a series from the early 1660s, call for revenge on their murderers.

The matter of this poetry is in the main clan business and politics with a strong national dimension. It might seem of more interest to the historian than to the poet, but Iain Lom's fresh and individual use of language, his ready resource of imagery, and his colourful and sinuous style of argument, give interest and distinction to his poetry.

For the texts, and their historical background, see Annie M Mackenzie *Orain Iain Luim, Songs of John MacDonald, Bard of Keppoch*, 1964, and for additional literary commentary, D Thomson *An Introduction to Gaelic Poetry* 1974, 1990.

LOMOND, Loch, Dunbartonshire/Stirlingshire

The third longest loch in Scotland (after Lochs **Awe** and **Ness**), Loch Lomond is also the third deepest (after Lochs **Morar** and Ness). 22.6 miles (36.2km) from **Ardlui** in the north to **Balloch** in the south and 5 miles (8km) across at its widest point, its surface area of 27.45 sq.m. (7110ha) makes it the largest expanse of fresh water in Britain.

Described by geologist **John MacCulloch** as 'unques-tionably the pride of all our lakes – incomparable in its beauty as in its dimensions, exceeding all others in variety as it does in extent and splendour', Loch Lomond owes its celebrity in part to the fact that it lies so close to **Glasgow**, and in part to the song 'The Bonnie Banks o' Loch Lomond', written in 1746 by a homesick **Jacobite** languishing in a Carlisle gaol. Shaped like an elongated spanner, the northern end of the loch – the handle – has been described as a 'mountain-cleaving ravine', while the broader southern end has 'an outline soft and low, and the aspect of nature fertile in the highest degree' (Fullarton's *Gazetteer*). Ben Lomond, at 3192ft (973m) the most southerly '**Munro**' in Scotland, lies midway down the loch on the eastern shore.

The 30 islands in Loch Lomond vary in size from the merest rocky knoll to Inch Murrin which measures 2 miles by 1 mile. The loch also boasts more varieties of fish than any other in Scotland, including salmon, sea-trout, brown trout, record-breaking pike, and the powan or 'fresh-water **herring**' thought to be descended from salt-water herring marooned in the loch after the last Ice Age and found only here and in Loch Eck.

Fed by the rivers Endrick, Uglas, Luss, Fruin, Falloch and countless smaller streams, and draining via the river Leven into the **Clyde** at **Dumbarton**, Loch Lomond is a popular centre for all kinds of watersports, but it is more than a workers' playground; it provides the water supply for much of Scotland's central industrial belt, while many of its erstwhile feeder streams have been diverted to the Sloy-Shira **Hydro-electric** scheme to provide power for Glasgow.

LONDON, Treaty of (1423)

The terms agreed in London on 4 December 1423 for the release of **James I** from his 18-year captivity in England included the provision of 21 hostages to stand security for his £40,000 ransom, payable in six annual instalments, and an undertaking that the Scots would give no further assistance to the French until James's obligations were met in full.

LONDON SCOTTISH, The, Regiment

The renewed threat of French invasion in 1859 led to the raising of the Volunteer Force throughout the country for home defence. Following on the earlier Scottish Corps raised in London in Napoleonic times, a Scottish Regiment was again raised from Scotsmen in London. The first Colonel was Lord Elcho, later Earl of Wemyss; there were six companies. All wore uniforms of hodden grey, the colour adopted by many Volunteer Corps of the period, while only one of the six companies was kilted. This number was gradually increased until in 1872 the whole regiment appeared in the **kilt**.

The regiment was originally the 15th Middlesex Rifle Volunteers, becoming the 7th Middlesex in 1880 and the 14th Battalion The London Regiment on the formation of the Territorial Forces in 1908. In 1935 it became a battalion of the **Gordon Highlanders** under its present title.

The regiment was awarded the battle honour 'South Africa 1900–02' in honour of the many members it sent to the Boer War. In 1914 the 1st Battalion was the first Territorial Battalion into action in a particularly hard-fought action at Massines. Three battalions served throughout the war on the Western Front, in Macedonia and in Palestine, winning 41 battle honours. The regiment also produced three battalions in World War II in which the 1st Battalion served in Italy winning 18 battle honours. The 3rd Battalion became a unit of heavy anti-aircraft gunners and served in North-West Europe while the 2nd Battalion served at home. The total of battle honours is therefore 60. In both World Wars the regiment produced a notable number of officers for other – particularly Scottish – regiments.

The regiment was reduced in 1967 to a company of the 51st Highland Volunteers. The hodden grey kilt is still worn. The Regimental March is 'Hielan Laddie'. HM Queen Elizabeth the Queen Mother is Honorary Colonel.

LORIMER, Sir Robert (1864–1929) Architect

Born in **Edinburgh**, the son of a law professor, Lorimer was educated at **Edinburgh University**. The move of his family to **Kellie Castle in Fife**, which his father restored, laid the foundations of his future career. In 1885 he was apprenticed to **Sir Robert Rowand Anderson** and four years later he went to London to complete his education under G F Bodley and James MacLaren. Lorimer returned to Edinburgh to set up practice in 1893 and one of his first commissions was the restoration of **Earlshall** in Fife (1895). Following his teacher Anderson, he developed an interest in Scottish Vernacular architecture. As a member of the Arts and Crafts Movement, he was also influenced by R N Shaw and eventually became the leading exponent of the Scottish Vernacular Revival. Most of his work was domestic and included much restoration and alteration work (**Dunrobin Castle**, 1914–19; **Leslie House**, 1906–7; **Balmanno Castle**, 1916–21). He also altered and remodelled a number of small suburban villas in Edin-

Sir Robert Lorimer, by John Henry Lorimer, 1886 (SNPG)

burgh (St Leonards and Westerlea, Murrayfield, 1912 and 1913). Other restoration schemes included national monuments such as **Paisley Abbey** (1923–8) and **Dunblane Cathedral** (1912–14). Knighted in 1911, he was given prestigious public commissions such as the Chapel of the **Knights of the Thistle** in **St Giles' Cathedral** (1909) and, above all, the **Scottish National War Memorial** Chapel in **Edinburgh Castle** (1924). Lorimer's son, Hew, was the sculptor responsible, among other things, for the statue of Our Lady of the Isles at Rueval on **South Uist** (1957).

LORNE, Argyll

The coast and fertile inland areas between Loch Leven in the north and Lochs **Awe**, Avich and Melfort in the south comprise the ancient district of Lorne, which further divides into Appin in the north and Netherlorn in the south. The name may derive from Loarn, son of Fergus and grandson of Erc, who settled in Argyll in about 500 AD. The Lordship of Lorne was long held by the MacDougalls of **Dunstaffnage** until their defeat by **Robert I**. The modern Marquisate of Lorne is a title usually held by the eldest son of the **Duke of Argyll**. Benderloch hosts the annual Lorne Show; nearby the Lynn of Lorne is the strait between **Lismore** and the mainland, while the Firth of Lorne denotes the sea approaches to Loch Linnhe.

LORNE, Tommy (1895–1935) Comedian

Real name Hugh Corcoran, Tommy Lorne was a lanky, lugubrious **Glasgow** comedian with a wide mouth and a high-pitched cracked voice. He starred at the **King's**, **Edinburgh**, and the **Theatre Royal**, Glasgow after serving in India in World War I. He became a pantomime 'hero' in Glasgow and Edinburgh. His popular catchphrases were 'In the name o' the wee man!' and 'Ah'll get ye! An' if Ah don't get ye, the coos'll get ye!' He died of pneumonia at the age of 40.

LOSSIEMOUTH, Moray

The birthplace of **James Ramsay MacDonald** and a still-important **fishing** port, Lossiemouth is five miles north of **Elgin** on a promontory which is the most northerly point on the south shore of the Moray Firth. It was developed as Elgin's port after the silting up of nearby Loch Spynie and the river Lossie in the 17th century. When the Seatown of Lossiemouth itself was threatened by sand, a Colonel Brander of Pitgaveny House near Spynie built (1839) and considerably developed (1893) the new harbour and planned village of Branderburgh, now fully integrated into the town. Ramsay MacDonald's birthplace was in the Seatown at 1 Gregory Place where there is a plaque; his study has been recreated in the museum in Pitgaveny Street; his grave is in Spynie churchyard. Residents declare Lossiemouth to have the lowest rainfall in the British Isles. To the dry fog-free skies of the **Moray** coast it owes its popularity with fishing fleets, tourists and pilots, there being large RAF establishments at both Lossiemouth and Kinloss. East to **Speymouth** stretch miles of sand, west to Covesea (with an **Alan Stevenson** lighthouse of 1844) **golf** links, cliff walks and more beaches. **Duffus Castle**, **Coxton Tower**, **Spynie Palace** and **Gordonstoun** all lie inland.

LOST CLAN, The

In 1445, if not earlier, Charles VII of France formed the *Garde Ecossais*, an élite corps of 100 Scots guardsmen and 200 Scots archers which was to remain the senior contingent in the French monarchy's household corps until the French Revolution. Following defeat at Pavia in 1525 the remnants of Francis I's *garde* were retreating through the Alps when they were stopped by blizzards near the Simplon Pass. They decided to settle there and their descendants, known as 'the Lost Clan', are reputedly still in the area.

LOTH, Sutherland

This coastal parish extends for about 11 miles along the eastern coast of **Sutherland**, from Kintradwell in the south to the **Ord of Caithness**. Its greatest breadth is five miles and it contains only the villages of **Helmsdale** and Port Gower. The latter was planted as a settlement for people evicted from the inland straths, although it contains no adequate harbour. It was named after the English family of Leveson-Gower into which the **Countess of Sutherland** had married. The last wolf to be killed in Sutherland (c1700) is commemorated by a stone in Glen Loth and there are several **brochs** in the vicinity including Cinn Tolle.

LOUDON, John Claudius (1783–1843)
Landscape designer

Born at Cambuslang, **Lanarkshire**, the son of a farmer, Loudon was sent at the age of 12 to work for John Mawer, a pioneering nurseryman and hothouse expert at Easter **Dalry**. In 1798, while studying botany, chemistry and agriculture at **Edinburgh University**, he assisted Messrs Dickson and Shade in **Leith** Walk. His interest in landscape was primed by Professor Andrew Coventry who lectured on the aesthetics of Sir Uvedale Price, derived from such artists as Claude Lorraine and Nicholas Poussin, which saw the landscape in terms of a unified composition. In 1803 Loudon went to London where he was befriended by Sir Joseph Banks and the philosopher Jeremy Bentham, whose philanthropic ideas affected him deeply. He made the first of four continental journeys – to Scandinavia, Poland and Russia – in 1813. In 1816 he devised the wrought-iron sash bar which allowed the construction of dome-shaped glasshouses for plants. His first book, the massive *Encyclopaedia of Gardening*, was published in 1822; he began the *Gardeners' Magazine* (1826–34) and the *Magazine of Natural History* (1828–36). From the 1820s he became concerned about the diffusion of education and knowledge, and was a pioneer in the field of environmental education and planning – in many ways a forerunner of **Patrick Geddes**. However, he is remembered for his major design projects – Derby Arboretum (the first public park in Britain) and Birmingham Botanic Gardens. 'His works are his best monument', declares his simple gravestone at Kensal Green, raised in the same year as his *On the Laying Out, Planting and Management of Cemeteries* first appeared.

LOUDOUN HILL, Battle of (1307)

Robert I followed up his April victory at **Glentrool** over Aymer de Valence, Earl of Pembroke, with another, even more comprehensive victory over de Valence's English forces at Loudoun Hill on 10 May 1307. The battle (fought near Darvel in **Ayrshire** on almost the same site as the 1679 **Battle of Drumclog**) gave new impetus to Bruce's campaign for Scottish freedom from English interference and attracted many more Scots to his side.

LOVAT SCOUTS

A special unit was raised by Lord Lovat in early 1900 for service in the Boer War in South Africa. Its establishment was some 250 strong, split into a mounted and a foot company, and the 1500 men from across the Highlands who applied to join were largely keepers, stalkers and ghillies whose powers of observation and knowledge of fieldcraft were outstanding. In 1901 a second contingent replaced the first; both gave excellent service in this specialised role of Scouts which in many ways resembled that of today's SAS.

After the war, Lord Lovat was authorised to expand his force into two Regiments of Yeomanry, the 1st and 2nd Lovat Scouts, recruited from the Northern Highlands and the Outer Isles. They mobilised in 1914 as part of the Highland Mounted Brigade and in September 1915 embarked for Gallipoli. Service in Egypt followed and in September 1916 the two regiments were combined as the 10th Battalion (Lovat Scouts) Queen's Own Cameron Highlanders, serving as such in Macedonia as an infantry battalion.

In 1939 they went to war once more, initially as part of the 9th Scottish Division. In May 1940 they were dismounted and sent to garrison the Faroe Islands where they spent the next two years. In 1944 they went to Canada where they trained as a mountain regiment in the Rockies after which they went to war in Italy, fighting through until the end of the war in Europe which found them in Austria. Their final service was over a year spent in Greece.

The Lovat Scouts were raised once more in 1947, initially as a squadron of the Scottish Horse. In 1949 they became a unit of the Royal Artillery, initially as 677 Mountain Regiment Royal Artillery (Lovat Scouts) TA, with subsequent changes to 540 Light Anti Aircraft Regiment in 1950, 532 LAA Regiment in the same year, and reverting once more to 540 Light Anti Aircraft Regiment Royal Artillery (Lovat Scouts) TA in 1954. On the reorganisation of the TA in 1967 they were reduced to one battery in **Orkney** and **Shetland**, which in 1971 changed role yet again to become an infantry company of the 51st Highland Volunteers. Finally the Orkney and Shetland components were split into parts of separate companies of the same battalion.

Throughout, they have maintained their proud identity with 'Lovat Scouts' as part of their title and today still wear the Scout bonnet with blue and white dicing and Lord Lovat's crest as badge. For the first time in their history, however, all ranks of the Lovat Scouts are now kilted in Fraser **tartan**.

LOW, William (1858–1936) Provision Merchant

Born in **Kirriemuir**, Low went to work at an early age in his brother's grocery shop in **Dundee** and by the age of 21 was effectively running the business. His brother James concentrated on wholesaling and with this support William was soon able to open a string of retail outlets in Dundee. Expansion continued when a partnership was formed with his brother-in-law to create Messrs William Low & Company, which became a limited company in 1917. By this time a nationwide chain of branches had been established throughout Scotland; supermarkets followed and in the 1990s the company was taken over by Tesco. Low himself played a prominent role in **education**, holding the position of Rector's Assessor at **St Andrews University** for almost 20 years. He lived as a landed gentleman on his estate at Belbo whilst maintaining not only the thriving grocery business but a wide range of financial interests, particularly in insurance companies.

LOWE, Peter (c1550–c1612) Surgeon

Believed to have been born in Errol, **Perthshire**, Lowe graduated in surgery in Paris, spending 22 years on the Continent before settling in **Glasgow**. Here he held a town council contract to treat the poor, and founded the Faculty of Physicians and Surgeons in Glasgow in 1599. Despite his appointment as surgeon to **James VI**, he was twice pilloried for religious offences.

LUING, Isle of, Argyll

One of the 'slate islands', Luing's (pron. 'Ling') history of quarrying started at Cullipool and Toberonachy in 1749 and continued until 1965. The island is now better known for the cattle that bear its name, a breed developed in the 1960s by the Cadzow brothers. They were not the first to make use of its five miles of low-lying fertile gound; the Marquis of **Breadalbane** had previously developed an experimental dairy farm from which 90 gallons of milk were exported daily to **Oban**. Like many of the inner islands, Luing's remains bear witness to a prosperous past, whether it be the two great Iron Age fortresses, the water mill at Achafolla, the church at Kilchattan or the quarriers' houses. More recently there was a vast lobster storage pond at Cullipool.

LULACH (d.1058) King

Son of Gruoch – wife of **MacBeth**, King of Scotland, **mormaer** of **Moray** – by her first husband (and therefore more easily identified as the stepson of MacBeth), and known as 'The Simpleton' or 'The Fool', Lulach was placed on the throne on the death of his stepfather in December 1057, but lasted only four months as king, being defeated and killed by his successor **Malcolm III** at **Strathbogie** in March 1058. He had one son, Malsnechtai (d.1085), whose descendents, among them the Earls Angus and Malcolm of Moray, would briefly and unsuccessfully press their claims to the throne by challenging the rule of both **Malcolm Canmore** and **David I**.

LUMPHANAN, Nr Aboyne, Aberdeenshire

Here, not at **Dunsinane**, died **MacBeth**, King of Scotland. Fleeing towards **Moray** he was allegedly cut off and killed in single combat by the Earl MacDuff in 1057. The well from which he last drank, the stone where he fell, and the cairn beneath which he was buried (before being disinterred for reburial in **Iona**) are all duly commemorated. About 200 years later the Durward family held sway from a motte known as the Peel of Lumphanan. This is a flat-topped oval mound, with a moat, which would have been crowned with a timber castle. It is of considerable size and stands 9m above the moat. The mound's enclosing wall and some stone foundations within are later.

LUMSDEN, Aberdeenshire

This sizable village on high ground fronts the main road through a gap between the **Cabrach** plateau and the Correen hills leading from Donside to **Moray**. It was developed in the 19th century by the Lumsden family of nearby Clova where there was once a monastery founded by **St Moluag**. A few miles south stand the ruins of **Kildrummy Castle** and north the still-occupied Craig Castle, an early 16th century L-plan tower house of the Gordons of Auchindoir with fine rib vaulting and an enclosed parapet/gallery. Hereabouts stood the motte of Auchindoir, a **Comyn** fort, and St Mary's Church, Auchindoir. Built in the 13th century, remodelled in the 16th and now a ruin, this simple stone church has a south doorway with double arch and contrasting mouldings of excellent craftsmanship.

LUNAN BAY, Angus

This fine stretch of sand between **Montrose** and **Arbroath** terminates to the south in the 250ft (76m) headland of Red Head. Halfway along, where the Lunan Water reaches the sea, stands Red Castle, supposedly built by **William the Lion** but now comprising a ruined keep with dungeon pit dating from the 15th century. It passed to **Cardinal David Beaton** in the 16th century

as did Ethie Castle to the south of Red Head. This latter, greatly extended subsequently by the Carnegie Earls of Northesk, was the home of Beaton and Marion Ogilvy [see **Aberlemno**] from 1538 until his murder in 1546. For a while thereafter, it is said, the Cardinal continued to frequent the house, 'unexplained footsteps on otherwise silent nights' being presumed his.

LUNNA, Shetland

Once an important **fishing** station and the centre of a powerful estate, Lunna on the north-east corner of **Shetland**'s **Mainland** was chosen in 1941 as a secret base for Norwegian freedom fighters (including the legendary Leif Larsen), who supplied the underground movement in their German-occupied homeland and returned with refugees. Although **Scalloway** became the main base in 1942, Lunna was retained for special operations. Lunna House, now a seasonal hotel, dates from the 17th century, while Lunna Kirk, built in 1735, is one of the oldest still in use in Shetland.

LUSS, Dunbartonshire

On the banks of **Loch Lomond**, Luss is often described as one of Scotland's most beautiful villages and is much patronised by television crews. It has been connected with the Celtic missionary Kessog, who brought Christianity to the area at the beginning of the 6th century. He had a monastic retreat on the island of Inchtavannach

Drochil Castle, near Lyne, by R W Billings (RWB)

opposite the village. St Kessog was martyred at Bandry, 1½ miles south of Luss, in 520 AD where a cairn supporting his effigy stood until the 18th century. It was moved to the parish church in Luss where it remains today. The population of the village has declined steadily since the early 19th century.

LYBSTER, Caithness

A carved cross on a stone found beside the harbour, and the fact that the Norsemen called this place Haligoe, suggest that there may have been a Christian **Pictish** community here in pre-**Viking** times. A Norse *skali* (hall) is commemorated only by the name Skaill. The creation of Lybster as a village was largely the achievement of General Patrick Sinclair, a cousin of agricultural **Sir John**. In 1810 he built the first pier, at the outset of the **herring** boom. It was about this time that **Thomas Telford** constructed what is now the A9 which runs through Lybster making possible the coach service from **Inverness** to **Wick** which commenced in 1819. On a slope at Mid Clyth, not far from Lybster and the A9, about 200 **standing stones** radiate in two separate fans. They are assessed in Alexander Thom's *Megalithic Lunar Observatories*, 1971.

LYELL, Sir Charles (1797–1875) Geologist

Born at Kinnordy, **Angus**, Lyell received all his education in England, graduating in classics from Oxford University in 1819. His interest in **geology** was fired by attending Dr Buckland's lectures at Oxford and from reading William Smith's research into fossils. Lyell travelled extensively in Europe, widening his knowledge and gathering information for his famous *Principles of Geology* published in 1830. This work and the later *Elements of Geology* became standard texts in the 19th century, enshrining many of **James Hutton**'s ideas. Lyell was appointed to the chair of Geology at London University in 1831, he was a Fellow of the Royal Society and was knighted in 1848.

LYNE, Peeblesshire

Three miles west of **Peebles**, the small village of Lyne stands on a tributary of the river **Tweed** and is generously endowed with sites of archaeological and historical interest. The **Roman** camp on a level plateau immediately east of the bridge dates from the **Antonine** period (cAD 158) and has remarkably well-preserved ramparts enclosing the 6-acre fort. To the east of the fort Lyne Church, 'one of the smallest in Scotland', was built (1640–5) by John Hay of Yester, later 1st Earl of Tweeddale, and has a rare contemporary oak pulpit and two panelled and canopied oak pews inscribed with the initials of John Hay and his second wife, Margaret, daughter of the 6th Earl of Haddington.

On the south bank of the river opposite Lyne the ivy-covered ruin of Barns Tower dates from 1489, while three miles upstream are the imposing and slightly sinister remains of Drochil Castle. Construction of this massive edifice, described by Daniel Defoe as one of the two monuments in this part of Scotland to 'the Vanity of Worldly Glory' (the other was **Traquair**), was started in 1578 by the **Regent Morton**, who is thought to have intended it as a palace rather than a castle, a theory borne out by the disproportionately small towers. Unique amongst 16th century castles (or palaces) in that it was designed as a double tenement divided by a gallery or corridor running the length of each floor and off which the various apartments opened, Drochil was never completed, Morton being executed in 1581 for complicity in the murder of **Darnley**.

LYON KING OF ARMS, see **HERALDRY**

MCADAM, John (1806–83) Radical Propagandist

Born at **Port Dundas** in **Glasgow**, McAdam's initiation into radical activism began in 1820 when with his father, a farmer turned carter, he attended the execution of James Wilson [see **Battle of Bonnymuir**]. He was involved in agitation for the 1832 Reform Bill but then emigrated to Canada (1833–5) and the United States (1835–47) where he worked mostly as a shoemaker while imbibing republican sympathies. On returning to Glasgow he joined his brother in the highly successful Hyde Park Pottery. Yet affluence failed to staunch his passionate advocacy of reformist causes. He was active in the **Chartist** movement and in the 1850s supported John Bright, though preferring universal to mere household suffrage. He also organised support for nationalist and republican movements in Europe, becoming a close associate of Lajos Kossuth, the Hungarian nationalist, the Italians Giuseppe Mazzini and Garibaldi, and the French socialist Louis Blanc: 'it is something to have the confidence and be called friend by such men'. This was no idle boast; he urged Mazzini and Kossuth to cooperate, visited Italy, and if Mazzini's hero-worship of McAdam did not quite rival McAdam's of Mazzini, he was at least held in regard. Garibaldi's proposed visit to Glasgow in 1864 saw McAdam's 'Glasgow's Working Men for Garibaldi' and his 'Ladies Garibaldi Benevolent Association' at loggerheads. Yet as propagandist and fund-raiser, McAdam's tireless advocacy raised popular consciousness and anticipated the internationalism of later radicals such as **John MacLean** and **William Gallagher**. His autobiography has been published by the Scottish Historical Society, 1980.

MCADAM, John Loudon (1756–1836) Inventor

Born in **Ayr**, the son of a landowner, McAdam amassed a fortune as a merchant and prize agent in New York during the American Revolution, returning to **Ayrshire** in 1783 to purchase the estate of Sauchrie. Among several official posts he held that of turnpike road trustee. British roads were notoriously bad at this time; dirt tracks became impassable in wet weather and those paved with stones fell quickly into disrepair, damaging stage coaches and other wheeled vehicles. In an attempt to improve the condition of Ayrshire's roads, McAdam embarked on a series of experiments to find a more suitable road surface.

He acquired control of the British Tar Company in 1790, but the business was initially unprofitable and five years later he was forced to sell Sauchrie to settle pressing debts. He moved to the south coast of England, working on various enterprises while retaining control of his company in Scotland. He also continued his research in road management and maintenance, and in 1815 was given the opportunity to put his ideas into practice when he was appointed Surveyor to the Bristol Roads.

McAdam was interested primarily in the introduction of a sound system of professional road management to ensure that the nation's highways were properly maintained. His ideas on road administration were eagerly taken up by the more progressive turnpike trusts. He also had strong views on construction and surfacing, believing that a road could be supported directly on the subsoil so long as the latter was levelled and well drained. His preferred road surface consisted of a 10in (250mm) cambered layer of broken and graded stone chips, which were compacted by traffic to interlock and form an impervious, hard-wearing and easily-maintained paving. McAdam's road surfaces were cheaper than those of **Thomas Telford** because they did not require heavy and expensive foundations.

McAdam became surveyor to 18 of Britain's turnpike trusts, and he acted as consultant to many more. He wrote several influential books and his sons William, (Sir) James and Loudon, and his grandsons William and Christopher also became road surveyors and consultants, introducing and popularising his methods of road management and surfacing all over Britain. 'Macadamised' road surfaces were adopted throughout Europe and the USA, permitting a revolution in the speed and reliability of road transport. They proved durable and capable of carrying all modes of wheeled transport until the advent of the pneumatic tyre and the motor car.

MACALISTER, Clan

A branch of **Clan Donald**, the MacAlisters are descended from Alexander (Alasdair), son of Donald of Islay, **Lord of the Isles** and great-grandson of the mighty **Somerled**. Their lands were in **Kintyre**, the chief of the family holding the estate of Loup on West Loch Tarbert; when **James III** was sharing out some of the confiscated lands after the submission of the Lords of the Isles in 1475, Charles MacAlister was made Steward of Kintyre. The MacAlisters of **Tarbert** were constables of Tarbert Castle on Loch Fyne. Alexander of Loup fought with **Claverhouse** at **Killiecrankie** (1689), survived that battle and escaped to Ireland where he then fought for **James VII** at the Battle of the Boyne (1690). Early in the 19th century the chief of the MacAlisters of Loup moved to the Lowlands after inheriting an estate in **Ayrshire**. Today there are as many of the name in the south-west of Scotland as in Kintyre. The badge of the MacAlisters is the heath, the motto *Per Mare Per Terras* (By Sea and Land) and the crest a dexter hand holding a dirk in pale, both proper.

MCALPINE, Sir Robert (1847–1934) Builder and Public Works Contractor

Born at Newarthill, **Lanarkshire**, Robert McAlpine began working down the mines at the age of eight, and when he was 22 started his own building business which became highly successful. Through his sons, McAlpine's company became one of Britain's best-known public contractors, internationally famous as the builders of Wembley Stadium. However, Sir Robert's best-loved Scottish memorials are his concrete bridges for the **Mallaig** extension of the West Highland **Railway**. Constructed 1897–1901, these include the 21-arch **Glenfinnan** viaduct, 1248ft/380m long and up to 100ft/30m high, as well as Borrodale Viaduct with its unprecedented 127½ft/38.86m span, 86ft/26m high. Their innovative construction in concrete was necessitated by unsuitable local stone and the need for economy, earning their builder the nickname 'Concrete Bob'. He was knighted in 1918.

MACARTHUR, Alexander (1901–47)
Novelist

A sometime **Glasgow** baker, often unemployed, who died a destitute on the banks of the **Clyde** after swallowing a lethal dose of disinfectant, MacArthur sounds like a character out of one of his own books. He was also amongst the most influential Glaswegians of the 20th century. His **Gorbals** novel *No Mean City* (1935) is said never to have been out of print and to have sold more than a million copies worldwide. But this success came too late to save its author and has scarcely endeared his memory to fellow Glaswegians. *No Mean City* is 'a terrible story of drink, poverty, moral corruption and brutality' which reinforced the mid-century perception of Glasgow as an urban jungle terrorised by razor-slashing gangs and drunks. Co-authored by a London publisher's editor, who no doubt tinkered with its syntax but did nothing to moderate its tone, it invited the city fathers' censure and is still faulted on points of detail rather than celebrated as history. In 1969 a second MacArthur novel, *No Bad Money*, about a Gorbals brothel, appeared; his executor claims there are more.

MACASKILL, Angus (1825–63) Giant
Born on the island of **Berneray** in the Sound of **Harris**, Angus Macaskill finds a place in the *Guinness Book of Records* as 'the tallest Scotsman and the tallest recorded "true" (non-pathological) giant'. He stood 7ft 9in (2.36m) tall and was commensurately strong, reputedly able to lift a hundredweight (50kg) with two fingers and hold it at arm's length for ten minutes. He died on Cape Breton Island, Nova Scotia, and is commemorated by a cairn on his native island.

MACAULAY, Clan
There are two separate clans of this name, the **Lewis** branch – the Macaulays of Uig – being of Norse or **Viking** origin and taking their name from 'Olaf', while the Lowland branch – the Macaulays of Ardencaple – take their name from Amalghaidh (pron. 'Auleth'), one of the sons of a 13th century **Earl of Lennox**. Many of the Lewis Macaulays settled on the mainland in **Sutherland** and **Ross**, and it is from this branch that the historian **Thomas Babington Macaulay** is descended. As one-time allies of the **MacGregors**, the Macaulays of Ardencaple in **Dunbartonshire** fell foul of the **Campbells**, but retained their lands and Ardencaple Castle until 1767 when the chief was obliged to sell it for debt. It was bought by the Campbells but later fell into ruin. The badge of the Macaulays is the pine and cranberry, the motto *Dulce Periculum* ('Sweet is Danger'),

and the crest is an antique boot couped at the ankle with a spur thereon, proper.

MACAULAY, Thomas Babington, Lord (1800–59) Writer and Politician
Grandson of the **Inveraray** minister who had befriended **Johnson** and **Boswell**, Macaulay was born in Leicestershire. Immensely precocious, he studied and won a Fellowship at Trinity College, Cambridge. His 1825 *Edinburgh Review* essay on Milton gave entrée into London society, and he was feted as a talker. Though in financial straits, his 1829 *Edinburgh Review* essay on **James Mill** (which shook J S Mill's faith) won him a 'rotten borough' Parliamentary seat. Eloquence on behalf of the 1832 Reform Act won more admirers. He became a commissioner on the Board of Control for India. Still writing for the *Edinburgh Review*, his Parliamentary career (distinguished in ethics and rhetoric) paused in 1834. Need of funds sent him to Calcutta, a seat on the Indian Supreme Council and a huge salary. In Bengal he exerted an ill-received liberalising influence, drafted a penal code and deepened his studies. MP for Edinburgh (1838–47, senior government posts 1839–41, 1846–7), he began work on his *History of England* and was still writing it when he lost his seat. In 1848 the first two volumes came out to acclaim. Edinburgh re-elected him in 1852; then his health broke. Volumes three and four (1855) had a vast international sale. Elected Rector of **Glasgow University** (1849) and created Baron Macaulay of Rothley (1857), only his heart disease curtailed his *History*. He never spoke in the House of Lords. Dubious of generality but sharp on particulars, his is the honest art of the advocate – widely learned, brilliantly illustrative, contemptuous of dissent. That rather than profundity marks out the *Essays*, and the vivid but sometimes injudicious *History*.

MACBETH (c1005–57) King
MacBeth (*mac-Bethad* 'Son of Life') was the son of a ruler of **Moray** and of a daughter of either **Kenneth II** or **III** (or possibly **Malcolm II**). He killed and succeeded (1040) **Duncan I** to become a powerful and prosperous king; on pilgrimage to Rome in 1050 he 'scattered alms like seed-corn'. His queen was Gruoch, granddaughter of Kenneth II with a son by her first husband (another ruler of Moray). In 1054 **Malcolm III 'Canmore'** invaded with an English army and defeated MacBeth at **Dunsinane**; in 1057 a second invasion caused MacBeth's death at **Lumphanan**.

He was succeeded by his stepson **Lulach**, called 'The Simpleton' or 'The Fool' (*fatuus*), for a few months until he too was killed at Essie in Strathbogie, leaving descendants to contest the throne against Canmore for a century. The chroniclers say nothing more about Queen Gruoch, Shakespeare's 'Lady Macbeth'.

It is noteworthy that however bitter the feuding between rival claimants, from **Aidan mac Gabhran** to Lulach, defeated kings were given burial in **Iona**. The tradition ended with **Duncan II** and **Donald III (Bane)**, although the island was then within the Kingdom of the Isles.

MACBRAYNE, David (1818–1907) Shipowner
The name MacBrayne is synonymous with sea connections to the Western Isles and Highlands and survives

in the merged form of Caledonian MacBrayne. David MacBrayne was born in **Glasgow** into a family steeped in shipping connections. He joined a shipping office, apparently that of David and Alexander Hutcheson, to train as a clerk. When his uncles, James and **George Burns**, the founders of the steamship company of the same name, shifted their main area of interest to the Atlantic trade, the Hutchesons and David MacBrayne inherited their company which had operated on the west coast. They made the most of the opportunity, capitalising on the heavy west-coast passenger and agricultural traffic and exploiting the growing Victorian **tourist** trade. In 1878 David became sole proprietor after the retiral of the two Hutcheson brothers and proceeded to construct a larger fleet. He bequeathed to his two sons a shipping company which had won a virtual monopoly of traffic to the Western Isles.

MACCAIG, Norman (1910–97) Poet and Teacher

Although born in **Edinburgh** – he stayed there all his life – MacCaig's Highland ancestry pervades much of his landscape; **Sutherland** especially is identified as 'MacCaig country'. Educated at the **Royal High School**, he gained Honours in Classics at **Edinburgh University** (1928–32). A conscientious objector in World War II, he held posts at Edinburgh and **Stirling** Universities (1967–78) and was awarded the Queen's Poetry Medal. His early work in the 1940s was part of the New Apocalypse movement, but in 1955 he swerved away from surreal obscurantism with the publication of *Riding Lights*. His *oeuvre*, exclusively in English, is large – he seized the moment of inspiration, claiming he rarely revised – and one of metaphysical reflection. He explores the relationship between himself as observer, and the world as observed, with wonderful wit, often coming like Donne, through his syllogistic skill, to surprising but logical conclusions. One of the great Scots poets in English of the 20th century, he was a friend of **Hugh MacDiarmid**, **Sidney Goodsir Smith** and **Sorley MacLean**. His *Collected Poems* first appeared in 1985; read 'Double Life' for starters.

MCCANCE, Sir Andrew (1889–1983) Metallurgist

McCance was born at Cadder, near **Glasgow**, and was educated at **Crieff**, **Alan Glen's School**, Glasgow and the Royal School of Mines in London. Later, in 1916, he gained a BSc from London University. At **Beardmore's** Parkhead Forge he became assistant manager, leaving in 1918 to set up as a manufacturer of alloy and special steels with the Clyde Alloy Steel Company. When **Colville's** was formed he took a place on the board and was instrumental, as general manager and director, in implementing the rationalisation which led to the formation of the Colville Group in 1936. Knighted in 1947, he produced a post-war plan for the steel industry which led to the creation of the new complex at Ravenscraig. He retired in 1965 having established a reputation as a distinguished metallurgist. He also supervised the establishment of the Royal College of Science and Technology in Glasgow which in 1964 became **Strathclyde University** where today there stands a building named after him.

MCCANCE, William (1894–1970) Painter

Best remembered for his part in the **Scottish Renaissance**, McCance was born in **Cambuslang**, near **Glasgow**, the son of a miner. He studied at the **Glasgow School of Art** from 1911–15 and in 1918 married Agnes Miller Parker, later to become one of Britain's foremost printmakers. Moving to London in 1920 McCance worked as an illustrator, lecturer and critic (he was the art correspondent for the *Spectator* 1923–6), which brought him into contact with an English art world heated over the issues and implications of Post-Impressionism. Abandoning his own earlier tempered, representational style, he began to make paintings synthesising the angular expressiveness of Vorticism with the cooler, reasoned Cubism of Léger that, particularly in his semi-abstract renderings of natural forms, are amongst the most independent British works of the period. McCance attributed his ability to reconcile so successfully in his own art such progressive but differing tendencies as something peculiar to his nationality, later writing that the Scots, with their 'natural gift for construction, combined with a racial aptitude for metaphysical thought and a deep emotional nature', were perfectly suited to play a central part in the advancement of European painting. His appointment as controller of the private Greynog Press in Wales (1930–3), where he oversaw the production of many of its finest publications, largely curtailed his activities as a painter and the remainder of his career was spent in teaching and writing.

MACCODRUM, John (Iain MacCodrum) (c1693–1779) Gaelic Poet

A native of **North Uist**, MacCodrum's songs date from his middle age and after. He was appointed family **bard** by Sir James MacDonald of Sleat in 1763 (this being a conscious revival of an old office). His work is an amalgam of localised ('village') poetry, official praise poetry and satire, with entertaining descriptions of old age, suffering from fever, and the merits and demerits of **whisky**, plus panegyrics and elegies for notables of his time. See William Matheson, *The Songs of John MacCodrum*, 1938 and D Thomson, *An Introduction to Gaelic Poetry*, 1974, 1990.

MCCOMBIE, William (1805–80) Cattle Breeder

Known as the 'grazier king', McCombie was born at Tillyfour in the Howe of **Alford** where his father was a tenant farmer and cattle dealer. Although he attended university in **Aberdeen** he soon returned to Tillyfour and to farming, having sensed the potential for meat exports offered by the **railways**. He began breeding **Aberdeen-Angus cattle** in 1840 and over the next 40 years won almost every prize on offer. He was the first Scot to exhibit fatstock at Birmingham and won awards at the Paris exhibition of 1878. When **Queen Victoria** visited Tillyfour in 1867 he was able to assemble 400 head. In the same year he published his standard *Cattle and Cattle Breeders* and in 1868 was elected MP for West Aberdeenshire; this is said to have made him the first tenant farmer in Scotland to sit in the House of Commons. Seven years later he was able to purchase Tillyfour.

MACCORMICK, John MacDonald (1904–61)
Scottish Nationalist

MacCormick was a **Glasgow** lawyer and the leading figure in Scottish nationalism in the mid-20th century. In 1928 as a student he took the lead in founding the **National Party of Scotland**, and in 1932 brought about union with the Scottish Party to form the **Scottish National Party**. He was National Secretary to both NPS and then SNP until 1942 when, after controversy over policy as regards the war, MacCormick resigned. Together with colleagues he then formed the **Scottish Convention** as an all-party pressure group. After the war, it convened the series of Scottish National Assemblies which in due course launched for signature the **Scottish Covenant**, calling for a Scottish Parliament for Scottish affairs. The Covenant gained two million signatures and contributed greatly to an enhanced Scottish political consciousness, subsequently evidenced in SNP successes. MacCormick's own party involvement after the war was as a Liberal, and he fought the general elections of 1945 and 1959 as well as a by-election in **Paisley** in 1947.

Of Highland parentage on both sides, he had a deep appreciation of Scottish poetry and culture, and a strong sense of attachment to the Scottish countryside, particularly the Ross of **Mull** (his ancestral home), **Knapdale**, Edinbane (**Skye**) and Glenurquhart. He married a fellow nationalist, Margaret Miller, in 1938. They had two daughters and two sons, the eldest of whom, Iain, won **Argyll** for the SNP in the two elections of 1974. In 1950 John was elected Rector of **Glasgow University**, serving until 1953 with pleasure and distinction. His role in the **Stone of Destiny** affair of 1950–51 is vividly recounted in his autobiographical *The Flag in the Wind*, 1955. He left a mark on constitutional law in the case of MacCormick v Lord Advocate (1953 SC) which unsuccessfully challenged the Queen's title as 'Elizabeth the *Second*', but succeeded in redefining attitudes to the 1707 **Treaty of Union** in constitutional law. He had poor health owing to stones in the kidneys, and died at the age of 57.

MACCRIMMON FAMILY, Pipers

The MacCrimmons, hereditary pipers to **MacLeod of Dunvegan**, were leading pipers and pipe teachers through the 17th and 18th centuries. The first of whom we know with certainty was Donald Mór, born about 1570. On his death in 1640, he was succeeded as hereditary piper by his son Padruig Mór, and then by his grandson Padruig Og who died after 1730. The family continued to serve as pipers at **Dunvegan** for two further generations, but after 1746 the position was nominal. Padruig Og seems to have been responsible for founding the MacCrimmon piping school at Boreraig, which finally closed around 1770. The MacCrimmon tradition was handed down through Padruig Og's pupil John Dall Mackay of **Gairloch** and John Mackay of **Raasay**, to **Angus Mackay**, whose publication of the *piobaireachd* transmitted to him by his father is regarded as being of the highest authority.

MCCULLOCH, Horatio (1805–67) Landscape Painter

The quintessential Scottish Victorian painter, McCulloch is best known for his dramatic Highland landscapes. He was born in **Glasgow** and managed, despite there being no official art schools or exhibiting institutions, to secure an early training under the local exponent of the **Nasmyth** tradition of landscape painting, John Knox. But **Edinburgh** beckoned and in 1825 he moved there, making a living as a copyist of watercolours and hand-tinter of engravings for the firm W H Lizars. McCulloch was greatly impressed by the work of Nasmyth which he saw in Edinburgh, as well as the sublime and dramatic effect used by the talented amateur **Thomson of Duddingston**. He returned to Glasgow in 1828 and for the next ten years established his reputation as an accomplished landscape painter. It was only, however, after he returned for good to Edinburgh in 1838 and began to travel further afield for his subject matter that he achieved more enduring celebrity. His depictions of the remote northern landscape, executed on a large scale with broad effects and exaggerated perspectives, appealed to Victorian taste. His technical skill and masterly sense of composition ensured considerable popularity and his works were engraved and distributed widely. His paintings epitomise the romanticised mid-19th century view of Scotland and it was against the rather contrived melodrama of such work that the later avant-garde Glasgow Boys [see **Painting**] reacted. As with many popular Victorian artists, McCulloch's reputation waned remarkably in the early 20th century. Ironically his over-fondness for bitumen (supposed to give paintings an aged patina, but which eventually discolours and cracks) has meant that some of his finest paintings have fared little better.

MACCULLOCH, John (1773–1835) Geologist

Famous for his 4-volume account of *The Highlands and Western Islands of Scotland* (1824) in letters addressed to **Sir Walter Scott**, with whom he had travelled, John MacCulloch was born in Guernsey. He later studied medicine at **Edinburgh**, and 'the boyish wanderings of his college days' were extended with a series of annual journeys between 1811–21. First an army surgeon, then a chemist to the Board of Ordnance and lecturer at RMA Woolwich, his main reputation was as a geologist ('As an original observer he yields to no other geologist of our time'), and he produced the first Geological Map of Scotland (1836). His 79 papers cover topics in physics, maths, mechanics, architecture, zoology and botany as well as **geology**; he was a musician and artist too, regretting that he could not publish his drawings with his 1824 book. His tireless attachment to the Highlands was shot through by a sceptical pursuit of the truth and a passionate, often humorous concern for 'the people as they now are' that offended some of his contemporaries. While travelling with his new (1835) bride he was thrown from his coach and died from the resultant leg amputation.

MACCUNN, Hamish (1868–1916) Composer

At the age of 15 and with the help of a scholarship, MacCunn, son of a **Greenock** shipowner, became the youngest student and one of the first at the newly formed College of Music in London. He had already started composing at the age of five, abandoned an oratorio at the age of 12, and composed his best-known work, the concert overture *Land of the Mountain and the*

Flood, at 17. This precocious start was followed by his greatest achievement, the opera *Jeanie Deans* based on **Scott**'s *Heart of Midlothian* and first performed in **Edinburgh** in 1894. This is the finest British opera of its day and reflects MacCunn's great sympathy for the human voice, also expressed in a number of dramatic cantatas (of which 'The Lay of the Last Minstrel' is the best-known), in the opera *Diarmid* and in over 150 songs, many of great beauty.

MacCunn burnt himself out, undertaking heavy conducting tours with the Carl Rosa opera company and having been one of the prime movers in support of British opera as well as encouraging productions of operas by Wagner and others in English. His style was overtly Scottish (though clearly well aware of Wagnerian precedents), his orchestration masterly and his melodic gift outstanding. In a fascinating interview with George Bernard Shaw, MacCunn made it clear that he was less interested in abstract music than in music which told some kind of a story; hence the absence of chamber music from his oeuvre. He married the daughter of the painter John Pettie, but died of throat cancer at the age of 48, leaving one son.

See also **Charles O'Brien**.

MACDIARMID, Hugh (C M Grieve) (1892–1978) Poet

Widely acknowledged as Scotland's greatest 20th century poet and polemicist, 'Hugh MacDiarmid' was born Christopher Murray Grieve in the **Dumfriesshire** mill town of **Langholm** on 11 August 1892. The son of a rural postman, MacDiarmid was brought up in a strongly religious household and one of his earliest influences was the local minister, T S Cairncross, a pub-

Christopher Murray Grieve ('Hugh MacDiarmid'), by R H Westwater, 1962 (SNPG)

lished poet who preached in Langholm South United Free Church from 1901–7. Another potent influence was the composer **F G Scott**, MacDiarmid's English teacher at Langholm Academy from 1905–8 and the man to whom the poet dedicated his masterpiece, *A Drunk Man Looks at the Thistle*.

Leaving Langholm in 1908, MacDiarmid went to **Edinburgh** to train as a teacher at Broughton Junior Student Centre where a third influence entered his life. George Ogilvie, Principal Teacher of English at Broughton, was both Christian socialist and enthusiastic reader of the Nietzschean *New Age* magazine. Already in revolt against the **Presbyterianism** of his youth, MacDiarmid became a disciple of Nietzsche; aspiring to be a superman beyond good and evil, he was involved in the petty theft of books from Broughton and asked to leave, eight days before the death of his father on 3 February 1911. Thanks to Ogilvie, MacDiarmid got a journalistic job with the *Edinburgh Evening Dispatch* but was sacked for selling review copies of books.

After working as a journalist in Wales and Scotland, MacDiarmid enlisted in 1915 and was sent, the following year, to Salonika as a Sergeant with the RAMC. In Salonika he began to write long letters to Ogilvie (the correspondence continued until 1930), outlining his plans to return to Scotland as a nationalist poet. However, the verse and prose he composed during World War I (some of it collected in *Annals of the Five Senses*, 1923) were in English and in the Georgian mode.

MacDiarmid married Peggy Skinner in 1918 and, 3 years later, settled down with his wife in **Montrose** where he worked as a reporter on the *Montrose Review* until 1929. In this period he served as a town councillor, parish councillor and justice of the peace; fathered two children; founded and edited the *Scottish Chapbook*, the *Scottish Nation* and the *Northern Review*; founded the Scottish centre of PEN (the international association of Poets, Playwrights, Editors, Essayists and Novelists); and helped found the **National Party of Scotland** in 1928. It was in Montrose, too, that Christopher Murray Grieve adopted the MacDiarmid pseudonym for his work in Scots: *The Watergaw*, one of his most enduringly popular lyrics, appeared in the *Scottish Chapbook* of October 1922.

Writing in **Scots** [see **Language**] rather than English, MacDiarmid found his distinctive voice, his argumentative eloquence. As a child in Langholm he had absorbed the rhythms of spoken Scots; now he extended the range of the language by adding to it a rich vocabulary derived from etymological dictionaries, thus creating what he called 'Synthetic Scots', a demanding literary idiom rejecting regionalism and the platitudes of the post-**Burns**ian tradition. MacDiarmid's Synthetic Scots was self-consciously modernist in intention, owing more to the spirit of Joyce's *Ulysses* than to contemporary vernacular verse.

His two volumes of Scots lyrics, *Sangschaw* (1925) and *Penny Wheep* (1926), were followed by a Scots meditative monologue in 2685 lines, *A Drunk Man Looks at the Thistle*, arguably the greatest long poem ever produced in Scotland. In this MacDiarmid offered a Scottish answer to Joyce: *Ulysses* unfolds during a single day, *A Drunk Man* in a single night. The eponymous drunk, initially a fallen man incapacitated by spirits, rises to a spiritual resurrection as he contemplates the human, political and metaphysical nature of Scotland: 'He canna Scotland see what yet/Canna see the Infinite,/and Scotland on true scale to it.' MacDiarmid presented the Drunk Man as a Scottish saviour, 'A greater Christ, a greater Burns', a deliberately blasphemous and provocative notion.

Having risen 'To heichts whereo' the fules ha'e never recked' in *A Drunk Man*, MacDiarmid soon collapsed in his private life. He went to London in 1929 to work on **Compton Mackenzie**'s magazine *Vox*, which folded after a few months; he fell from an open-top double-decker bus, sustaining severe concussion; he lost his wife to a millionaire **coal**-merchant, Peggy divorcing him in 1932; he was unable to shape his second long poem *To Circumjack Cencrastus* (1930) into a worthy successor to *A Drunk Man*. MacDiarmid might never have survived the disasters he endured in England had he not met Valda Trevlyn, the pugnacious Cornish woman he married in 1934.

MacDiarmid, Valda and their son Michael lived on the **Shetland** island of **Whalsay** from 1933–42, a time of considerable poverty as described in MacDiarmid's autobiography *Lucky Poet* (1943). Though he suffered a serious breakdown in 1935, MacDiarmid wrote some of his finest poems in Whalsay, erudite English poems including *On a Raised Beach* and the unfinished epic *Cornish Heroic Song for Valda Trevlyn*. He was also active as an idiosyncratic Communist, joining the Party in 1934 and irritating it until his expulsion in 1939.

In World War II, MacDiarmid worked in an engineering firm in **Glasgow**, then settled, from 1951 to the end of his life, in a hillside cottage near **Biggar**, **Lanarkshire**. Never willing to become an establishment figure, he rejoined the Communist Party in 1957 and in 1964 stood unsuccessfully as a Communist candidate in the Kinross and West Perthshire constituency of the Prime Minister, **Sir Alec Douglas-Home**, a man he dismissed as 'a zombie'. MacDiarmid died of cancer in Edinburgh on 9 September 1978, a controversial figure to the last.

See *The Complete Poems of Hugh MacDiarmid* ed Michael Grieve and W R Aitken (2 vols, Penguin, 1985); *The Letters of Hugh MacDiarmid* ed Alan Bold (Hamish Hamilton, 1984). The standard biography is *MacDiarmid* by Alan Bold (John Murray, 1988, rev Paladin, 1990).

MACDONALD, Alasdair MacColla (c1605–47) Royalist

Alasdair, 3rd son of **Coll Ciotach MacDonald** of Colonsay and ambidextrous like his father, grew 6ft 6in (1.98m) tall and prodigiously strong. As a Catholic, Coll Ciotach forfeited his lands for refusing to sign the **Covenant** in 1639 and the family moved to Antrim where Alasdair fought against the English with great distinction. In 1644 he was commissioned by the Earl of Antrim to invade the west coast of Scotland in support of the Royalist cause. During the following year he collaborated with **Montrose** in a spectacularly successful campaign, but in September 1645 withdrew to make an invasion of **Argyll**. He caused enormous devastation until, in May 1647, **David Leslie** defeated him in **Kintyre**. Escaping to Ireland, he opposed the English at Knocknannus, was taken prisoner and executed, without trial, in November 1647.

MACDONALD, Alexander (Alasdair mac Mhaighstir Alasdair) (c1695–c1770) Gaelic Poet

From **Moidart**, with parental connections with **Benbecula** and **Morvern**, and ancestral links with the Clanranald and MacDonald of **Islay** chiefs and with the royal family (**Robert II**), MacDonald is usually regarded as the outstanding Gaelic poet of the 18th century. The details of his early career are conjectural. It is clear that he was well read in **Gaelic poetry** and Scottish history, and familiar with Classical and Scots and English literature, or parts of these. He could write the Old Gaelic script, and had studied classical Gaelic versification. He is thought to have studied at **Glasgow University**; he was perhaps intended for a legal career, but spent his early and middle years as a teacher with the Society for the Propagation of Christian Knowledge. Abandoning this work, he transferred to the Catholic Church as preparations for the '45 **Jacobite Rising** were intensifying. He fought in that campaign, and has left an account of it in English (in the Lockhart Papers). He was, briefly, bailie of **Canna** around 1750, and spent his later years in **Morar** and **Arisaig**. There is evidence of a tempestuous life, both in documents and in the poetry.

His poetry has a wide range. A high proportion is on public/political topics, but this bias may be imposed by the surviving sources. There are apparently early poems of a consciously 'literary' sort: an address to the Muses, an elegy for a pet dove. The sensuous *Moladh Mòraig* ('Praise of Morag') and its lurid counterpart, the 'Dispraise of Morag', probably date from the 1730s. A group of nature poems suggest deep familiarity with Gaelic nature verse and some specific impetus from James Thomson's *Seasons*, probably in the expanded 1738 edition. Two seasonal poems, on Winter and Summer, survive, giving detailed description and showing careful overall design.

His poetry on political topics seems to span the quarter century from 1724 to 1749 (see D S Thomson, *The Political Poetry of Mac Mhaighstir Alasdair*, 1991), with exhortatory poems before the '45 Rising, a few campaign poems, a number commenting on the Disarming and Disclothing Acts and the hopes of a fresh rising. Some have an extraordinary blend of exuberance and contemplation. He sees the action against a historical and partly philosophical background, and very occasionally we catch a glimpse of his personal emotional response, as when his anger readily turns to satire in a poem dating from 1746. Here he discusses attitudes to **Charles I** and then George I.

> There is no true excuse,
> but weak prevarication,
> injustice that is patent
> even to one born blind;
> if it were simply creed
> because he was not nurtured
> in the faith as Luther taught,
> O if that were the case
> why with ill-will did you condemn
> his ancestor to death?
>   The boar who's called King George,
> son of the German sow,

his friendship and his love
is the raven's for the bone;
he pulled us from our pelt;
the traitor caught and plundered us
and then killed us outright.
    We're not his people anyway
and so he doesn't care
if we beat each other up.

Mac Mhaighstir Alasdair's bent for satire surfaced in both local and national contexts, and can move towards extreme ribaldry and vituperation. Some of his later editors felt constrained to suppress some of his work. The political satire in particular has more general interest.

His longest poem, and one of the most skilfully constructed, is his *Birlinn Chlann Raghnaill* 'Clanranald's Galley', dating from c1750. **Hugh MacDiarmid** produced a lively version of this, on the basis of a prose translation. A small group of poems from MacDonald's Morar and Arisaig days shows the old blend of satire and serene nature description. Not surprisingly, it is said that his ghost has been seen in Uist even in the present century.

The best text of the political poems is in J L Campbell's *Highland Songs of the Forty-Five*, 1933, 1984. A & A Mac-Donald's text of the poems, 1924, is the most complete, but it is not reliable.

MACDONALD, Coll Ciotach (Colkitto) (c1570–1647)

Coll Ciotach ('left-handed Coll' due to his being ambidextrous) was born in Antrim and spent most of his childhood on **Colonsay**, ancestral home of his family. He won renown in Ireland, fighting for the Catholics, before becoming involved in the rising of his cousin, Sir James MacDonald, in 1614–15. Freed after an amnesty, he held Colonsay from the Crown until, having refused to sign the **Covenant** in 1639, he was taken prisoner by **Argyll** and held in **Dunstaffnage Castle**. Released in 1645 he then supported the campaign of his son **Alasdair MacColla MacDonald** (also Colkitto), until taken prisoner in **Islay** in 1647. He was hanged near Dunstaffnage and is supposedly buried beneath the steps of the chapel.

MACDONALD FAMILIES, see CLAN DONALD

MACDONALD, Flora (1722–90) Jacobite

'A woman of middle stature, soft features, gentle manners and elegant presence' thought **Dr Johnson** when he met Flora on **Skye** in 1773. **Boswell** agreed but thought her short; numerous other descriptions testify to her fine appearance and innocent gentility. She was the daughter of a tacksman in **South Uist** but he died soon after her birth and her mother remarried, perhaps involuntarily, a **MacDonald** of **Armadale**. She was brought up by the Clanranald family and then by Lady Margaret MacDonald of Skye who completed her schooling in **Edinburgh**. Returned to Skye, she was visiting her brother in South Uist in 1746 when approached about what she thought a 'fantastical' scheme to smuggle **Prince Charles Edward Stewart** from the Outer **Hebrides**, now over-run with government soldiers seeking the Prince, to Skye. Persuaded

Flora MacDonald at the time of her release, by Richard Wilson, 1747 (SNPG)

perhaps by Clanranald, perhaps by the Prince, she agreed. The Prince joined her boat to Skye late on 27 June in **Benbecula**; he was dressed in a blue and white frock as 'Betty Burke, an Irish girl'. Next morning they were almost taken by troops as they approached Waternish but in the afternoon reached the safety of Kilbride adjacent to the home of Lady MacDonald. With her help, Flora and 'Betty' crossed the island to **Portree** whence the latter proceeded to **Raasay** after presenting Flora with a gold locket containing his portrait.

When the escape became known, Flora was arrested and sent to London. She spent a short time in the Tower and, released by the 1747 Act of Indemnity, returned to Skye where she married (1750) Allan MacDonald of Kingsburgh. It was there that Johnson and Boswell sought her out. They learnt of the MacDonalds' plan to emigrate to America (1751) where Allan served in the army until captured during the War of Independence. Flora returned to South Uist in 1779 and lived with her brother until Allan's release. They then re-established themselves at Kingsburgh where she died in the bed that had been occupied by the Prince on his way to Portree and by Dr Johnson on his way to **Dunvegan**.

MACDONALD, George (1824–1905)

Clergyman, Novelist and Poet

Born at **Huntly**, **Aberdeenshire**, Macdonald was the son of a farmer. He won a bursary in 1840 to **King's College**, **Aberdeen**, where he graduated with a science degree in 1845. He subsequently moved to London where he tutored and undertook theological studies at Highbury Technical College (1848–50). He became a Congregational minister in 1850 but, after several ministries, resigned in 1855 to dedicate himself to writing.

In 1855 he published his first work, *Within and Without*, followed by an allegorical romance, *Phantastes: A Faery Romance for Men and Women* (1858). Macdonald became a lecturer at Bedford College, London in 1859, and continued writing works of diverse nature, including fantasies (*The Portent*, 1895), Scottish-based novels (*Alec Forbes*, 1868, and *Malcolm*, 1875), historical novels (*St George and St Michaels Wind*, 1871) and children's fairy tales (*At the Back of the North Wind*, 1871 and *The Princess and Curdie*, 1888). Macdonald's reputation today rests on his works of fantasy and fairy tale which influenced 20th century writers such as J R R Tolkien and C S Lewis. In 1877 Macdonald was awarded a Civil List Pension of £100. From 1881 ill health forced him to spend much of his time in drier climates, and he died in Bordigherra, Italy.

MACDONALD, Sir Hector Archibald (1853–1903) Soldier

MacDonald, the son of a **Dingwall** crofter, enjoys the distinction, almost unique in the 19th century, of having risen from the ranks to Major-General. After working in a Dingwall draper's shop, he joined the 92nd **Gordon Highlanders** and during the Second Afghan War acquired a formidable reputation as 'Fighting Mac', the hero of many engagements including Lord Roberts' famous march from Kabul to Kandahar. It was Roberts who promoted him to 2nd Lieutenant. He fought at Majuba on the way home from India and again covered himself with glory. From 1883–99 he served in Egypt and Sudan, becoming a popular hero after playing a decisive role at Omdurman, and then in India. In 1900 he succeeded **General Andrew Wauchope** in command of the Highland Brigade in the Boer War as a Major-General. He was made a KCB in the same year and in 1902 was commanding the British troops in Ceylon when 'an opprobrious accusation' was lodged against him with the Governor-General. He was granted home leave; some weeks later he shot himself in a Paris hotel room. This tragic end to a dazzling career greatly upset his home town of Dingwall where a massive tower was defiantly erected in his memory.

MACDONALD, James (1906–91) Sound Effects Artist

It is not generally known that after 1947 Mickey Mouse, the world's best-loved cartoon character, was a Scot. James MacDonald, born in **Dundee** but educated in Philadelphia, had found his way to the Walt Disney studios as a dance band drummer. Switching to sound effects, he remained with Disney for 40 years, creating such aural cameos as the rippling waterfalls in *Snow White and the Seven Dwarfs* (1937), a gurgling whale for *Pinocchio* (1940) and the tinkling shimmer of a bedewed cobweb in *Alice in Wonderland* (1951). His first voice effect was as chief yodeller and stand-in sneezer for Snow White's seven dwarfs. Then came the big break. Disney's bronchial baritone could no longer be made to match the squeaky utterances of his most famous creation. MacDonald, who had already provided the speeded-up voice track for other rodents (notably the Chipmunks), took over as Mickey Mouse. He subsequently produced many other noises for Disney's *True Life Adventures* and died in Glendale, California.

MACDONALD, James Ramsay (1866–1937) Prime Minister

MacDonald was born in his grandmother's two-roomed 'but and ben' in **Lossiemouth**, the illegitimate child of Mary Ramsay and a ploughman from the **Black Isle** called MacDonald. Similarities with the origins of **James Keir Hardie** have been noted; but being one of the underprivileged in rural Lossiemouth was much preferable to being down and out in the **Lanarkshire coal** fields. MacDonald attended a board school at Drainie, had the time to read voraciously, and aged 16 was taken on as a pupil-teacher in the school. After an abortive foray to Bristol, where he came into contact with radical socialism for the first time, he moved to London, joined the Fabian Society, and eked out a precarious living as a clerk before being taken on as secretary to a prospective Parliamentary candidate. He also took up journalism and was now involved with the Social Democratic Federation. In 1894 he wrote personally to Keir Hardie to seek admission to the **Independent Labour Party** (ILP) and stood as its candidate in Southampton (1895).

The next year he married Margaret Ethel Gladstone, the great-niece of **Lord Kelvin** and daughter of Dr John Gladstone, a professor of chemistry and co-founder of the YMCA. Although she died in 1911, she compensated for his lack of social graces, provided him with financial independence, and bore him six children. Dextrously combining working-class credentials with middle-class security, and still with one foot in the radical ILP and the other in the Fabian think-tank, he became secretary of the Labour Representative Committee (which soon became the Labour Party) and a member of London County Council (1901). In 1906 he was returned as MP for Leicester and soon emerged as the Parliamentary Labour Party's ablest speaker, theorist and organiser. He

James Ramsay MacDonald, by Ambrose McEvoy, 1926 (SNPG)

was its leader from 1911–14 but, in accordance with the ILP's pacifist stance, resigned over the Great War although, having opposed it, he then accepted defeat and argued for the war effort. This was misunderstood by ILP colleagues who thought he had betrayed his party, and by the general public who thought he had betrayed his country. He lost his seat in 1918 but in 1922 was returned for Aberavon and with the support of **Red Clydeside**'s influx of new MPs was re-elected leader of the party.

He led the first (minority) Labour administration in 1923–4 and the second in 1929–31, but a third (1931–5) in coalition with the Tories badly discredited him in Labour eyes. He had broken with and marginalised **James Maxton** and the Clydeside contingent, plus the ILP, and now seemed to be taking moderation and gradualism to new and unacceptable extremes in the name of political responsibility. In 1935 he lost his seat to Emmanuel Shinwell and died two years later while aboard ship crossing the Atlantic. He was buried in the churchyard of **Spynie**.

MACDONALD, John (1741–?) Valet and Footman

MacDonald's *Travels*, the well attested source for a remarkable life story, began early. Their author, born near **Inverness**, was orphaned when his mother died in childbirth and his father disappeared with the **Jacobite** army. In search of the latter, his sister, aged 14, took the road south with her brothers 'Daniel, seven; I, four and a half; and Alexander, two and a half'. Arousing some sympathy and more curiosity, the little vagabonds eventually begged their way to **Edinburgh** where, after anxious months on the streets, they found employment. John worked his way up from diminutive postillion to strapping groom, mainly in the service of Lady Anne Hamilton of Bargany near **Ayr**. Ever appreciative of his situations, in 1760 he found even more congenial employment as valet and personal servant to a succession of gentlemen, 27 in all, including **Colonel Alexander Dow**, James ('Ossian') **Macpherson** and the brothers of Campbell of Shawfield [see **Shawfield Riots**] and of **Adam Ferguson**. With them he saw the world, travelling through England, Ireland, the Continent and India where his highly readable *Travels* provide a unique view of personalities and places as seen not by a servant of the East India Company but by a servant's servant. He has two other claims to fame: by an odd coincidence he was the only man to witness the death of Laurence Sterne (*Tristram Shandy*, etc); and he was widely credited with having introduced to Britain the idea of carrying umbrellas instead of the then conventional sword. This social development, notes MacDonald's editor, may have saved as many lives by disarming the gentry as it did by warding off shower-induced chills. MacDonald's travels apparently ended when in 1779 he finally married Malilia, a Spanish girl 20 years his junior with whom he had already had one child. They settled in Toledo where MacDonald wrote his travelogue and where he presumably lived happily ever after.

MACDONALD, Sir John Alexander (1815–91) Premier of Canada

MacDonald was born in George Street, **Glasgow** but his father, an evicted **Dornoch** crofter, emigrated to Canada with his family in 1820.

MacDonald was therefore educated in Kingston, Ontario and had no further connection with Scotland. He was, though, surrounded by Scots, both adversaries and colleagues, throughout his long political career. Having studied law he entered politics as a Conservative Member of the Provincial Assembly and, following a difficult relationship with its leader, Sir Allan MacNab, succeeded him in 1844. He retained the leadership throughout most of the next 45 years. His first ministry was formed in 1857 but it was his championship of the British North America Act (1867), welding the deeply divided colonies of what is now Canada into a federal dominion, that won him fame as the dominion's founding father. In the same year he was created KCB and became the first Premier of the new dominion. He was defeated (1873) over scandals relating to the Canadian Pacific Railway by the Liberals under **Alexander Mackenzie** (aided by the Conservative traitor **Donald Smith**); but he returned to power in 1878 and by privatising its construction made possible **George Stephen**'s completion of the Canadian Pacific, a project which did much to make his federal dominion a practical reality.

MACDONALD, Sir John Hay Athole, Lord Kingsburgh (1836–1919)

Born in **Edinburgh** and educated at the **Edinburgh Academy** and Edinburgh and Basle Universities, John MacDonald became an Advocate in 1859. He was Solicitor-General from 1876–80, Lord Advocate and MP for the Universities of Edinburgh and **St Andrews** 1885–8, and Lord Justice Clerk 1888–1915. From 1888–1901 he was also Brigadier-General of the Forth Brigade of Volunteers. A pioneer of motoring and of the uses of electricity, his exertions led to the introduction of postcards in Britain. The first President of the RSAC, he was captain of the Royal & Ancient **Golf** Club (1887) and Archangel of the Catholic Apostolic Church. His publications include *Treatise on Criminal Law of Scotland*; *Our Trip to Blunderland* (Ill. Charles Doyle); *50 Years of It, or The Experiences and Struggles of a Volunteer of 1859*; *Life and Jottings of an Old Edinburgh Citizen*. He died in Edinburgh.

MACDONALD, Rev Murdo (1696–1763)

Minister of **Durness** from 1726 until his death, MacDonald kept a voluminous diary, now lost. The considerable portions that have been transcribed and published (eg in *The World of Rob Donn*, **Ian Grimble**, 1979) attest its value. **Rob Donn** Mackay commemorated his minister in what many consider to have been his finest elegy. Macdonald's son Joseph wrote *A Treatise on the Theory of the Scots Highland Bagpipe* and made a *Collection of Highland Vocal Airs*, both pioneer achievements. They were published after his death in India in 1763.

MACDONALD, Sir Peter (1898–1983) Biscuit Manufacturer

The son of the head gamekeeper to the **Earl of Moray**, MacDonald was born in **Darnaway** in **Moray**. After serving with the **Black Watch** in World War I he embarked on a career as a solicitor. As a close associate of **Sir Alexander Grant**, he became legal adviser to

McVitie & Price during the 1930s. After the death of Sir Alexander in 1937 and of his son Sir Robert a decade later, MacDonald came to head the firm and was specifically responsible for seeking a merger with another biscuit firm, Macfarlane Lang. This was achieved in 1948 with the creation of United Biscuits of which MacDonald became chairman. In the post-war period automation in the production of reduced product lines brought enlarged turnover and profits. Knighted in 1963, MacDonald guided United Biscuits to a series of mergers before retiring in 1964, to be replaced by Hector Laing. His extensive business interests, his holding of public offices in **Edinburgh** and his devotion to the **Church of Scotland** occupied the time spent apart from United Biscuits.

MACDONALD, Thomas Douglas (1906–75)
Novelist

From **Montrose**, MacDonald trained as a teacher in **Aberdeen** and spent most of his life as a schoolmaster in the Highlands and Western Isles. He learned Gaelic and under the pseudonym of 'Fionn MacColla' published several novels, some historical like *Ane Tryall of Hereticks*, 1962, and several highly critical of the morality and influence wielded by **Presbyterian** ministers within their Highland congregations (*And the Cock Crew*, 1945, *The Ministers*, 1979). He also wrote an autobiography, *Too Long in this Condition*, 1975.

MACDONALDS OF CLANRANALD and MACDONALDS OF SLEAT, see CLAN DONALD

MACDONELL, Alasdair Ruadh (c1725–61)
13th Chief of Glengarry

The eldest son and heir of John MacDonell, 12th of Glengarry, he was a serving officer in the *Ecossais Royales* or French Royal Scots at the outbreak of the '45 **Jacobite Rising**. Along with other officers, Alasdair Ruadh was given permission to return to Scotland to lead out the Glengarry Clan for **Prince Charles Edward Stewart**, but the ship on which he was travelling was intercepted by a British Man o' War and he was taken prisoner and lodged in the Tower of London until after the Rising. After his release and subsequent return to his impoverished estates in the Highlands, he became involved in the **Jacobite** plotting for another rising which took him back and forth between the UK and France. Unsuccessful in obtaining the command of a French regiment through the influence of the exiled **Stewarts** (it was given instead to the son of **Cameron of Lochiel**), he was reputed to have become a British government spy, informing its ministers under the pseudonym of 'Pickle' of the various plots being hatched by the Jacobites abroad. The case against him has never been proved, but even if it was true he does not seem to have profited by it, as when he died unmarried in 1761 his estate was in a very poor financial state. A slightly shady character, and by no means one of the most outstanding Glengarry chiefs, Alasdair Ruadh was succeeded by his nephew Duncan, son of his younger brother Angus, who led the Glengarry clan for Prince Charles Edward and was accidently shot in the streets of **Falkirk** by one of **Clanranald**'s men who fired off a musket – his share

in the spoils from the recent **Battle of Falkirk** – to clear the barrel. To prevent a feud between the men of Glengarry and Clanranald and the likelihood of the former leaving the Prince's army, the Clanranald man responsible had to be put to death.

MACDONELL, Archibald Gordon (1895–1941) Writer

MacDonell is famous for one book, *England, Their England* (1933), especially Chapter VII. Repeatedly anthologised as 'The Village Cricket Match', it is a hilarious account of a 'Coarse Cricket' encounter between a very mixed team from the London publishing world and a Kentish village side (Fordenden). Born in **Aberdeen**, but educated at Winchester, MacDonell served on the Western Front with the Royal Field Artillery in the **51st Highland Division** 1916–18 before becoming a writer and journalist. *England, Their England*, a picaresque account of a young Scotsman's attempt to survive the Great War and later to understand the English and their way of life between the wars, is a literary and historical treasurehouse. It contains a rich description of the London publishing scene and places such as the Western Front and the infamous Craiglockhart Hospital. It is also a rewarding hunting ground for thinly-disguised characters of the time such as 'Alexander Ogilvy', the editor of the *Illustrated Planet* obsessed with Scottish genealogy (ie John Malcolm Bulloch of *The Sphere*). Although only the cricket account is well known, MacDonell's perceptive and gently ironic humour, a sort of combination of Mark Twain and Stephen Leacock, pervades the entire book; the depiction of scenes such as the country-house weekend or the English presence at the League of Nations are comic masterpieces. The conclusion of the book – that the English are at heart a race of (gentle and kindly) warrior-poets – is perhaps the only part that appears dated.

MACDONELLS OF GLENGARRY, see CLAN DONALD

MACDONNEL OF KEPPOCH, Sìleas (Sìleas na Ceapaich) (c1660–c1729) Gaelic Poet

MacDonnel has 23 poems ascribed to her, on political, **clan**, moral and religious topics. She criticises the **Jacobite** clans for their lack of forceful action after **Sheriffmuir** (1715), laments the death of the Glengarry chief in the early 1720s, makes a song criticising sexual licence, composes several hymns, and a simple but moving lament for the harper Lachlan Mackinnon. See Colm O Baoill, *Bàrdachd Shilis na Ceapaich* 1972 and D Thomson, *An Introduction to Gaelic Poetry*, 1974, 1990.

MACDOUGALL, Clan

Though now small, the MacDougall clan is one of the oldest in Scotland, and at one time held great power in **Argyll** and the islands. It takes its name from Dugall, a son of **Somerled**. After the death of Somerled in battle in 1164 Dugall was styled King of the South Isles and Lord of **Lorn**. He held most of Argyll and the islands of **Mull, Lismore, Kerrera, Scarba, Jura, Tiree, Coll** and the smaller islands near them. To defend their dominions Dugall's son and grandson, Duncan and Ewen, built castles such as **Dunstaffnage**, Dunollie and

Duntrune on the mainland and Aros, Cairnburgh, Dunchonnel and Coeffin on the islands. Sea power was important to them and they owned a large fleet of swift galleys. Duncan also founded the **Priory of Ardchattan** in 1230.

Ewen was in a difficult position when Scotland and Norway were at war for he held his mainland possessions from Scotland and the island ones from Norway. He tried to remain loyal to both sides but finally decided to support **Alexander III** and gave back the islands to Norway. When the islands were ceded to Scotland in 1266 his family reclaimed them.

The fourth chief, Alexander, married a Comyn whose nephew, **John 'the Red' Comyn**, was murdered by **Robert I** in **Dumfries**. This started a blood feud with **Bruce**. The MacDougalls were victorious at the Battle of **Dalrigh** but were later defeated at the **Pass of Brander**, and so lost their castles and their lands. Dunollie and most of the mainland possessions were later returned but, with the exception of Kerrera, the islands were not. The seventh chief, Ewen, married a granddaughter of Robert I but the marriage produced no sons so a cousin succeeded in 1375. The Lordship of Lorn, however, passed through the marriage of Ewen's daughter to the **Stewarts** and then to the **Campbells**, later the **Dukes of Argyll**.

The MacDougalls fought on the Royalist side during the **Covenanting** Wars. Many were massacred at the siege of Dunaverty after surrendering through lack of water; Gylen Castle on Kerrera was taken and burnt. Dunollie managed to hold out only to be taken a few years afterwards and garrisoned by Cromwellian troops until the restoration of the monarchy.

In 1715 the MacDougalls fought on the **Jacobite** side and were present with their chief, Iain Cair, at **Sheriffmuir**. When the rising collapsed the chief went into exile in France and was later a fugitive in Scotland until pardoned in 1727 and allowed to return to Dunollie. His lands were restored (1745) to his son, Alexander, who did not join in the '45 **Rising** though his brother and other clansmen fought at **Culloden**.

The clan motto is *Buaidh no Bas*, 'Conquer or Die', and their badge is bell **heather**. The present chief (31st) is Morag MacDougall. The **tartan** is a red one of five colours, including the blue stripe denoting descent from royalty.

MACDUFF, Banffshire

Previously the village of Doune or Down, MacDuff was founded in 1783 by Lord Duff, 2nd **Earl of Fife**, who also completed **Duff House** on the **Banff** side of the river **Deveron**. Geographically this river is all that divides the two townships although in terms of history and economic profile they could hardly be more different. Where Banff is sedate and charming, MacDuff is almost busy and brash. The former's harbour is now a silted irrelevance while the latter's (1763 but much extended 1966) is home to a large **fishing** fleet. Banff has town houses; MacDuff just housing. The waterfront is nevertheless attractive and ends in an open-air swimming pool, more like a rock pool, at Tarlair, once celebrated for its spring water and now for its **golf course**. A tall Italianate church with clock tower presides over the burgh. The suggestion that MacDuff is to Banff as

Glasgow is to **Edinburgh** may prove as unacceptable to the folk of MacDuff as it would be meaningless to Glaswegians.

MCEWAN, William (1827–1913) Brewer

Born in **Alloa**, McEwan worked in his uncle's Heriot Brewery before himself brewing at the Fountain Brewery in **Edinburgh** in 1856. The expanding markets in the west of Scotland proved most profitable as did trade with the Empire. During the 1880s his enterprise grew rapidly and on the basis of this secure industrial achievement he entered politics as a Liberal, holding an Edinburgh seat until 1900. At this point he delegated the running of the company to his nephew, George Younger. A large part of his considerable personal fortune, enhanced by many **railway** investments, was donated to projects in his adopted city, eg the McEwan Hall at the **University of Edinburgh**.

MACEWEN, Sir Alexander (1875–1941)
Gaelic Nationalist

The son of a Recorder of Rangoon and grandson through his mother of a Sheriff-Substitute, MacEwen qualified in law at **Edinburgh University** and practised in **Inverness**. From 1925 until 1931 he served as Provost, and also acted as Chairman of the Islands Committee of the County Council, aided by his knowledge of Gaelic. He was active as a member of the Education Committee and became Chairman of the Directors of the Royal Northern Infirmary. A Liberal, he was Chairman of the Scottish Self-Government Party before being elected President of the **Scottish National Party**. He stood as SNP candidate for the Western Isles in 1935 and in 1939 he joined with **Dr John Lorne Campbell** in proposing the creation of a Highlands Development Board with adequate Gaelic representation on it. His opinions are preserved in *The Thistle and the Rose*, 1932 and *Towards Freedom*, 1938.

MCEWEN, John (1887–1992) Forester

Born at **Fortingall**, **Perthshire**, but moving to **Argyll** at the age of 7, John McEwen was the son of an estate worker whose treatment at the hands of his landowning employers formed his son into a lifelong radical socialist. Eschewing such private employment, McEwen went to work for the **Royal Botanic Gardens** in **Edinburgh** (1908) and for the newly formed **Forestry Commission** (1920). Two years later he organised the Commission's foresters-in-charge into the Workers' Trade Union (now incorporated in the TGWU) and was a founder member of the Society of Foresters of Great Britain. In 1947–8 he took part in the Census of Woodlands, and was inspired by its findings to produce the first of his two revelatory publications on landownership in Scotland, *The Acreocracy of Perthshire – Who Owns Our Land?* published by the Perthshire Fabian Society in 1971 and revealing that nearly half the total acreage of the county was owned by a mere 31 individuals. Six years later, together with his second wife Margaret whom he had married in 1967 when he was 80, he produced *Who Owns Scotland?*, a work he described as being 'devoted to exposing the irresponsible and damaging attitude of landlords . . . and pointing the way to . . . the nationalisation of all our land'. OBE for his services to forestry (1963) and Fellow of the **Royal Scottish Geographical Society** (1980), McEwen died in September 1992, two days short of his 105th birthday.

MCEWEN, Sir John Blackwood (1868–1948)
Composer

The influence of his native Border Country (he was born in **Hawick**) was to remain a powerful force in McEwen's distinguished but neglected output as a composer. Works such as *Grey Galloway* (1909, the third of his symphonic poems) and the *Solway Symphony* (1922) bring impressionistic techniques to Scottish idioms. An early admirer of the work of Debussy, his own response to France finds delightful expression in the *Three Songs* of 1905, the stylistically adventurous *Vignettes* for piano (1913) and the quartet *Biscay* (1913) with its poetic images of lighthouse, sand-dunes and cheerful cockle-gatherers. These last two were composed while on leave from teaching at the Royal Academy of Music. McEwen had been suffering from insomnia, partly brought on by a typical selflessness in his work to set up the Society of British Composers. The *Three Preludes* for piano of 1920 show an increasing freedom in the use of dissonance and reflect McEwen's open-minded approach which he encouraged in his students.

The undemonstrative but profoundly intelligent refinement of much of McEwen's music requires a quality of attention too rarely accorded it. The gentle humour and subtle grades of colour and texture in the wind quintet *Under Northern Skies* and the bitter rhetoric contrasted with deliberately false innocence of the *Fantasy Trio* (1943), composed in the dark days of the war, are unseductive but deeply rewarding.

McEwen studied first at **Glasgow**, briefly at the Royal Academy of Music in London, and then taught in the **Glasgow Athenaeum** before returning to London where, in 1924, he succeeded **MacKenzie** as Principal of the Royal Academy of Music. He retired in 1936 and left the bulk of his estate to promote Scottish chamber music at his old university.

MACEWEN, Sir William (1848–1924)
Surgeon

Born in **Rothesay** and qualifying in medicine at **Glasgow University**, MacEwen distinguished himself in the antiseptic surgery pioneered by **Lister**. He removed the first brain tumour in 1879, and produced a surgical cure for the locally endemic disease of rickets.

McGAHEY, Michael (1925–99) Trade Unionist

Born in **Shotts**, **Lanarkshire**, to a Catholic mother and a father who was a founder member of the Communist Party of Great Britain, McGahey followed his father into the mining industry at the age of 14, supplementing his truncated formal education by studying politics and literature at classes organised by the Communist Party and the local area NUM. An impassioned speech against an unofficial miners' strike in 1948, which he feared would threaten the future of the newly-nationalised industry, brought him to the attention of miners' union leaders and he made steady progress through the union hierarchy, becoming President of the Scottish Area of the National Union of Mineworkers in 1967 and Vice President of the National Union of Mineworkers in 1973, a post he held until his retirement in 1986. A fiery orator and uncompromising champion of workers' rights, McGahey spearheaded the miners' strikes of 1972–4 which led to the defeat of Edward Heath's Conservative government, and had to endure a prolonged and vicious media campaign which vilified him as 'Mick the Red'. He was also a great believer in Scottish home rule and in another typically eloquent speech in 1968 managed to swing the weight of the Scottish Trades Union Congress behind the campaign for a **Scottish parliament**.

MACGIBBON, David (1831–1902) and ROSS, Thomas (1839–1930) Architectural Historians

MacGibbon and Ross were responsible for the first systematic classification of Scottish architecture. Their five volumes on *The Castellated and Domestic Architecture of Scotland* (1887–92), followed by three on *The Ecclesiastical Architecture of Scotland* (1896–7), contain their own drawings and descriptions of nearly every castle, tower house, mansion and noteworthy church, plus the history of each and a chronological classification of the whole. Most of the research was done in the field, by train, bicycle and on foot; the materials for such a comprehensive survey simply did not exist in print. The result, much raided but little revised by subsequent writers, was 'a corpus of national architecture which will probably never be equalled' (S Cruden). Yet the real achievement was that this immense undertaking represented only a spare-time activity for two architects with a busy practice to maintain. MacGibbon, from **Edinburgh**, had taken Ross, from Errol then **Glasgow**, into his family practice in 1862. They specialised in High Street banks, hotels, theatres and housing terraces, mostly in Edinburgh and usually of baronial character, although MacGibbon's tastes in French architecture (he also wrote on the architecture of Provence) and Ross's for American styles are also evident.

MCGIBBON, William (d.1756) Violinist and Composer

Son of a professional oboist, McGibbon was **Edinburgh** born, studied in London and returned to his native city where he remained until his death. His three sets of Scots folk-tunes blended Italian and Scottish styles, but his earlier works are thoroughly Italianate, some being avowedly composed 'in imitation of Corelli'. Between 1720 and 1745 he published four sets of trio sonatas (24 in all), besides six sonatas for flute or violin and continuo (1740) and six for two flutes and continuo (1748). He was employed by the Edinburgh Musical Society (formed in 1728) as leading violinist, and some of his works require a standard of technique unmatched elsewhere in the British Isles. His style is fluent rather than characteristic, but elegant and spacious.

MCGILL, James (1744–1813) Canadian Merchant and Benefactor

The founder of Montreal's great university was born in **Glasgow**, the son of a merchant whose antecedents had been hammermen. He attended **Glasgow University** and emigrated to Canada about 1765. First he engaged in the fur trade, then invested heavily in the North West Company, and finally in land, becoming 'the richest man in Montreal'. He also held public office as a Member of the House of Assembly and Colonel of the 1st Battalion of the Montreal Militia. He died suddenly but fortunately had made a will in which one of his estates, Burnside, plus £10,000, were left for the endowment of a college or university that would bear his name. A charter for McGill University was obtained in 1821 thanks to the good offices of **John Strachan** and teaching commenced in 1829.

MACGILLIVRAY, William (1796–1852)
Naturalist
MacGillivray spent most of his childhood in **Harris** although born in **Aberdeen** and returning there for an MA from **King's College** (1815). He then contemplated medicine but preferred natural science. Vacations spent tramping the hills, on one occasion walking to London to visit the British Museum, combined ornithological, botanical and zoological research. He served as assistant to **Robert Jameson**, Professor of Natural History at **Edinburgh University**, and as conservator for the museum of the **Royal College of Surgeons** (1831–41) before becoming Professor of Natural History at **Marischal College**, Aberdeen (1841). Books and papers on every branch of natural history from shells to mammals won him recognition as an outstanding all-round naturalist; but he is commonly remembered as the father of British ornithology, a status that rests on his 5 volume *A History of British Birds*, 1837–52; even Audubon acknowledged it as the best of its kind. His son John (1822–67) followed his example and was naturalist on several voyages in the southern hemisphere before electing to settle there.

MCGONAGALL, William (1825/30–1902)
Poet
McGonagall was born in **Edinburgh** either in 1825 or 1830, the son of an Irish **cotton** weaver. He grew up in **Orkney** and **Dundee**, where he learned the weaving trade, and in 1846 married Jean King. From an early age McGonagall was interested in the theatre and in Shakespeare, whose works he would often recite in public houses. He became an amateur Shakespearian actor, and performed with various groups at the Dundee Theatre Royal. He soon branched out into poetry and published his first book of verse, containing the popular 'Railway Bridge of the Silvery Tay', in late 1877. He became a well-known figure throughout central Scotland, giving public readings and selling broadsheets of his poetry. He visited London in 1886, and in 1887 travelled to New York, seeking to extend his reputation abroad. Disappointed in his quest, he returned penniless and on a ticket purchased through the generosity of a Dundee patron. A selection of his poetry was published as *Poetic Gems* in 1890 and a further undiscovered collection in 1962. Their inimitable combination of bathos, perversity, irrelevance, wayward rhymes, and confused scansion have earnt him the title of 'the world's worst poet', a hard won and wholly deserved accolade quite compatible with the affection in which he is held and the frequency with which he is quoted [see **Nairn**].

MACGREGOR, Alasdair (1587–1604) Last Chief of Glenstrae
Alasdair Roy MacGregor was the heir of **Gregor Roy MacGregor** (executed 1570) and, like him, never enfeoffed. Illiterate, but skilled in the use of weaponry and a superb athlete, he grew up in Glen Strae (**Dalmally**). In 1590 he was attainted (when his clansmen murdered a Drummond), but **James VI** pardoned him in 1596. In 1603 the MacGregors defeated the Colquhouns in **Glenfruin** and for this the clan was proscribed. Alasdair was seized at Ardkinglas (**Cairndow**), but while crossing **Loch Fyne** to **Inveraray** he jumped overboard and escaped. He surrendered to **Argyll** who, having promised him amnesty, had him conveyed to England and then promptly re-arrested and hanged.

MACGREGOR, Gregor Roy, of Glenstrae (c1540–1570) Clan Chief
Gregor Roy, second son of Allaster MacGregor of Glenstrae, succeeded as chief of the **Clan Gregor** on the death of his elder brother. In 1560 when he came of age, Sir Colin Campbell of Glenorchy, superior of his land, refused to enfeoff him and in 1563 Glenorchy secured a government grant of all MacGregor's family property. Two years later the sons of the Dean of **Lismore** were murdered and Gregor received a warrant from **Queen Mary** to kill the assassins. But in 1569 a contract was signed by the **Earl of Atholl**, Glenorchy and others to suppress Clan Gregor. Gregor and his wife Marion, daughter of Campbell of Glenlyon, were hiding in a cave above **Loch Tay** when he was seized by Glenorchy's men. He was executed at the Castle of Balloch (later called **Taymouth Castle**) on 7 April 1570.

MACGREGOR, James Mor (1689–1754)
Jacobite Exile
James Mor was the eldest son of **Rob Roy MacGregor** but, the name MacGregor then being proscribed, he took the surname of Drummond. A tall, handsome man, he was a skilled horseman and a piper. In 1736 he was implicated when his brother **Robin Oig MacGregor** murdered a MacLaren. Brought to trial, he was also accused of cattle stealing and of breaking out of prison. But so skilfully was his defense conducted that the charges were found not proven.

In 1745, while fighting for the **Jacobite** cause with his cousin MacGregor of Glengyle, he captured and destroyed the fort of **Inversnaid**. Later, as a captain in the MacGregor Regiment, he was wounded in the thigh at the **Battle of Prestonpans**.

In 1752 he and his brother were again tried, this time in the High Court of Justiciary in **Edinburgh**, for the abduction of a woman named Jean Key. Convicted, James Mor was imprisoned in **Edinburgh Castle**, but escaped, thanks to the connivance of his daughter, disguised as a cobbler. Reaching Paris, he appealed unsuccessfully to **Prince Charles Edward Stewart** for financial assistance. Letters reveal that he then tried to sieze Alan Breck Stewart [see **Appin Murder**] to exchange with the British Parliament for a pardon. But the attempt failed and James Mor died in Paris in great poverty. In Scotland he left a widow and 14 children.

MACGREGOR, John (1825–92) Author and Canoeist

Although born in Kent and never resident in Scotland, John MacGregor took his Scottish descent so seriously that, as with his other enthusiasms – travel, philanthropy, evangelism and canoeing – it became part of his unusual personality. He was invariably known as 'Rob Roy'; so, confusingly, were his successive canoes and also his dog. As a part-time soldier he organised and commanded the only company of London Volunteers to wear the **kilt**. Called to the Bar in 1851, he practised little. In 1849 he had toured the eastern Mediterranean, shot a Nile crocodile, timed a tortoise across the field of Marathon and written a work on Arab music. There followed further tours in Europe, where he became the 33rd climber to reach the top of Mont Blanc ('drank a bottle of good champagne there and had breakfast'), North America, Russia, Lapland and north Africa. In between he preached 'the good old Bible' as one of the much ridiculed soap-box orators of the 'Open Air Mission', worked for London's underprivileged in the Ragged Schools Union, and promoted a number of bizarre job-creation schemes including his Shoeblack Brigade which positioned uniformed boot-blacks on every street corner in the metropolis. He also sponsored swimming proficiency tests and lifeboats, equating buoyancy and life-saving with the Christian's need for resilience against life's temptations.

To such a muscular evangelist, the canoe came as a revelation of amphibious self-sufficiency. MacGregor introduced canoeing, practically unknown outside North America, to Britain, where he founded the Canoe Club (with the Prince of Wales as President), to Europe (*A Thousand Miles in the Rob Roy Canoe, The Rob Roy in the Baltic*) and to the Middle East (*The Rob Roy on the Jordan*). The last voyage included a passage through the as yet uncompleted Suez Canal which enabled MacGregor to claim that he was the first to take a boat from the Mediterranean to the Red Sea. His books, richly deserving of reprints, were as popular as his lectures; the royalties from both went to deserving causes. In 1873 the end of his travels came not from death or ill health but marriage. The eccentric firebrand became a much loved father wont to take his family holidays in **Argyll**.

MACGREGOR, Rob Roy (1671–1734) Outlaw

Rob Roy MacGregor, named for his red hair (roy, *ruadh* = red), was born at the head of **Loch Katrine** in the **Trossachs**, the third son of Lieutenant-Colonel Donald MacGregor of Glengyle (of Glenorchy stock) and his wife Margaret Campbell. They and their clan were Protestant. Gifted with strength and exceptionally long arms, MacGregor was renowned for his skill with the broadsword. Aged 18 he fought under **Viscount Dundee** at **Killiecrankie** in 1689, and later joined the Lennox Watch, a body of Highlanders who gave protection in the Lowlands in return for payment termed 'blackmail'. He married Mary Campbell of the Comer, on the east side of Ben Lomond, in 1693.

In 1694, when proscription on the name **MacGregor** was renewed, he took the surname of Campbell. In 1701 he acquired the lands of Craigroyston and later those of **Inversnaid** on the east shore of **Loch Lomond**. He also rented grazing at **Balquhidder** in Perthshire. In 1708 he became a cattle dealer and, prospering, bought further property. In 1711 he raised £1000 sterling from the Duke of Montrose and others to buy and collect herds. But his chief drover, a MacDonald, absconded with the letters of credit. Accused of embezzlement, Rob Roy was gazetted in the *Edinburgh Evening Courant* and all magistrates and officers of HM Forces were entreated to sieze him. On 3 October 1712 a warrant for his arrest was issued by the Lord Advocate on Montrose's instigation. On failing to answer the summons MacGregor was outlawed forthwith. His wife and family were evicted from Craigroyston by Montrose's factor, Graham of Killearn.

MacGregor then leased Auchinchisallen in Glen Dochart from the **Earl of Breadalbane**, a political enemy of Montrose. Unable to pursue his trade, he relied on sheep and cattle lifting and on the receipt of blackmail. From the Trossachs he raided the Lowlands, particularly the lands of Montrose.

He mobilised **Clan Gregor** for the **Jacobite** cause in 1715. The MacGregors raided the Lennox, seized the boats of the Colquhouns on Loch Lomond and, in the **Callander** area, captured 22 government guns. After the **Battle of Sheriffmuir**, in which he remained inactive, he was attainted of High Treason and Auchinchisallen was burnt by government mercenaries. In 1716 **John, Duke of Argyll** allowed him to build a house in Glen Shira, but his wife remained at Loch Katrine.

Rob Roy's exploits became legendary. He twice escaped from imprisonment and when captured near **Stirling** he was mounted on a horse tied behind one of his captors; but while crossing the river Forth at the Fords of Frew he cut the belt that held him and, plunging into the river, managed to regain his freedom.

In 1725 he submitted to **General Wade** and received the King's pardon. Having been converted to Catholicism, he died on 31 January 1734 at Inverlochlarig Beag at the head of the Glen of Balquhidder.

MACGREGOR, Robin Oig (1715–54) Outlaw

Robin Oig, the fifth and youngest son of **Rob Roy MacGregor**, was reputedly small in stature and impetuous. In 1736, after Rob Roy's death, a quarrel arose with a MacLaren who was claiming land already rented by the MacGregors. Robin, supposedly encouraged by his brothers, shot MacLaren in the back when he was ploughing and, failing to stand trial, was outlawed. He fled to France and enlisted with General Campbell. Wounded at the Battle of Fontenoy and taken prisoner by the French, he returned home in 1746 and decided to seek his fortune by marrying Jean Key, a well endowed widow of 18. In 1750, with the help of his brothers **James Mor** and Ronald, he carried her off from the farm of Edinbellie, near **Balfron**. They were married at Rowardennan but she died the following year.

Robin Oig was seized and brought before the High Court of Justiciary in **Edinburgh** accused of abduction and forcible marriage. The defense of **Henry Home** (later Lord Kames) that the marriage had been solemnised with the lady's free will was dismissed. Robin was found guilty and executed.

MACGREGOR, Sir William (1846–1919)
Colonial Administrator

The son of a Towie (**Aberdeenshire**) farmer, Mac-Gregor attended **Aberdeen** Grammar School and **University** before qualifying as a doctor (1874) and embarking on one of the more agreeable colonial careers. His first posting was as surgeon in the Seychelles, followed by Mauritius then Fiji. Already something of a fixture in the South Seas, in 1888 he was appointed the first British administrator and, 1895, the first Lieutenant-Governor of New Guinea. Here during ten years he successfully combined organisation, pacification and exploration (for which he received the Royal Geographical Society's Founder's Medal in 1896). His next posting was as Governor of Lagos, where he assisted Ronald Ross's anti-malarial campaign, and then of Newfoundland, whence he conducted a survey of Labrador. In 1909, no doubt with a shiver of relief, he returned to the Pacific as Governor of Queensland where he is remembered as founding father and first Chancellor of Queensland University. He retired in 1914 and, already KCMG and GCMG, was made a Privy Councillor. He is buried in Towie churchyard.

MCGRIGOR, Sir James (1771–1858) Military Surgeon

Born in Cromdale, **Banffshire**, McGrigor was educated at **Aberdeen** Grammar School and **Marischal College**, Aberdeen. He completed his medical studies in **Edinburgh** and entered the Medical Department of the army in 1793 as Surgeon 88th Connaught Rangers. He served in Europe, Egypt, the East and West Indies and India, becoming Inspector General of Hospitals in 1809 and Chief of the Medical Staff of Wellington's army in the Peninsula in 1811. He defied Wellington's orders by loading ammunition wagons with wounded, but the Duke, after a reprimand, asked him to dine the same night. McGrigor was director of the Army Medical Department from 1815–51, knighted in 1814 and created a baronet in 1831. He is commonly regarded as the father of the Royal Army Medical Corps and his portrait by **Sir David Wilkie** hangs in the RAMC's London headquarters.

MACINTOSH (MACKINTOSH), Charles (1766–1834) Chemist

Born in **Glasgow**, the son of a factory owner producing chemical dyes, MacIntosh attended **Joseph Black**'s chemistry classes, making two important discoveries of his own. He invented a process for producing bleaching powder (chloride of lime), subsequently patented by **Charles Tennant** for his **St Rollox** works. He then devised a waterproof material by combining wool fibre with indiarubber, creating the garment which still bears his name.

MCINTOSH, Charles (1839–1922) Postman and Naturalist

The original who likely inspired the character of Mr McGregor in Beatrix Potter's *Tale of Peter Rabbit*, Charlie was born at Inver, **Dunkeld**; his father was a handloom weaver, fiddler and music teacher. After a broken education in Birnam and at the Royal Grammar School in Dunkeld, in 1857 he lost all the fingers and the thumb of his left hand while working with a circular saw. A rural postman for the next 32 years, he also enjoyed a wide reputation as 'The Perthshire Naturalist'. His special study was mycology; he discovered 13 species new to Britain and 4 to science. Mutual love of fungi brought him together with the 26-year-old Beatrix, who holidayed locally, when she plucked up the courage to show him her drawings in 1892; 'I have been trying all summer to speak with that learned but extremely shy man . . .'. In September 1893 she wrote the charming picture letter which prompted her stories.

MACINTYRE, Duncan Bàn (Donnchadh Bàn Mac an t-Saoir) (1724–1812) Gaelic Poet

Donnchadh Bàn was born in Glenorchy, and worked mainly as a forester or gamekeeper in **Perthshire** and **Argyll** until 1767 when he moved to **Edinburgh** and to service in the City Guard. In Perthshire his employer was the **Earl of Breadalbane**, and another patron was John Campbell of Killin, principal cashier of the Royal Bank of Scotland; he also knew the Rev James Stewart of Killin, translator of the New Testament into Gaelic, and his son John who in fact saw Donnchadh Bàn's poems through the press in 1768.

Some of his early poems are traditional praise-poems to his local patrons; there are also one recording his undistinguished army service at the **Battle of Falkirk** (1746), poems about hunting and drinking and a song to his bride, Màiri Bhàn Og; this is somewhat formal in the main, with a nod towards Cupid, but it comes alive where he uses metaphors from nature to describe Màiri ('a tree in blossom', 'a sea-trout newly landed', 'a swan on the sea'). In Edinburgh he was to write rather repetitive poems about the **bagpipes**, and light verse about many experiences. He continued composing songs until late in life, his *Cead deireannach nam beann* ('Final Farewell to the Hills') being made in 1802.

His finest and most individual poetry is centred on the countryside he knew in his youth and early manhood, and on the hunting of the deer, subjects which bring his poetry to a rich and exotic life. It is likely that he was influenced by the nature poetry of Alasdair Mac Mhaighstir Alasdair (**Alexander MacDonald**), and this shows both in his song about summer and in his choice of an elaborate metre in his greatest poem *Moladh Beinn Dòbhrain* ('Praise of Ben Doran', a hill above Bridge of Orchy). This is a metre based on ceòl mòr, the classical music of the bagpipes, echoing in part that structure, with changes of rhythm, rhyming trisyllables, etc. But whatever the influences, he makes the theme his own, especially in the Ben Doran poem, with its torrent of detailed but affectionate description, of flora and fauna, fish and bird-life, but above all the many varieties of deer, young and old, male and female, in their lovingly observed moods. It has been suggested that in this poem we find the praise-poem coming to its ultimate perfection, surprisingly without reference to chiefs or warriors.

The poems have most recently been edited in Angus MacLeod's *The Songs of Duncan Bàn Macintyre*, 1952. **Iain Crichton Smith** has published an English verse translation, *Ben Dorain*, 1969.

MACKAY, Alexander Murdoch (1849–90)
Missionary

Born at **Rhynie, Aberdeenshire**, the son of the **Free**

Church minister, Mackay was educated at **Aberdeen** Grammar School and studied engineering at **Edinburgh University**. In 1873 he went to work as a draughtsman at an engineering works in Berlin where he became deeply involved with the Lutherans. With their encouragement he joined the Church Missionary Society and in 1876 joined their mission to Uganda. The natives of the East African kingdom benefited rather more from his engineering skills – which taught them to make and repair their own tools (and, inadvertently, their own firearms) – than from his bigoted religious zeal, which led him into bitter conflict with Muslim, Catholic and what he called 'naked savage' alike. When interdenominational feuding turned into civil war in Uganda in 1887, Mackay withdrew to Tanganyika where he turned his attention to politics, arguing strongly for British intervention in and eventual colonial control over Uganda. He caught malaria and died at Usambiro on the edge of Lake Victoria in 1890.

MACKAY, Angus (1813–59) Piper

Mackay was not only a great piper, son of a great teacher, John MacKay of **Raasay** whose piping was derived directly from the **MacCrimmons**, but was determined that his father's *canntaireachd* should be preserved. In 1838 he published 61 *piobaireachd* learnt from his father, and at his death left manuscript volumes containing another 183, besides small music. His link with the MacCrimmons, and the accuracy of his transcriptions have given his work an authority which is still acknowledged today. He was piper to **Queen Victoria**.

MACKAY, Clan

This clan has preserved the oldest of clan banners, known as the *Bratach Bhàn*. It depicts a lion rampant within the tressure flory counter-flory which denotes royal descent. Of comparable antiquity are the arms of Mackay of **Strathnaver**, in 1503 preserved in the Balfour MS and shown as the three stars of the royal house of **Moray**, with a hand in chief attesting true descent. This heraldic evidence fortified the late Sir Iain Moncrieffe's conclusion that the original Aodh [see **Aed**] was the eldest son of **Malcolm III 'Canmore'** and **Queen Margaret** to whom they gave the Saxon name of Aethelred. As Abbot of Dunkeld he was debarred from the succession, but he married the senior dynast of the royal house, granddaughter of Queen Gruoch (defamed as Lady Macbeth). Their son Angus son of Aethelred, gaelicised to Aodh, became King of Moray on the death of his uncle Maelsnechtai without an heir in 1095.

But the Mackays also had a claim to the Crown of the Scots senior to that of the Margaretsons. Allying themselves with the house of **King Somerled**, they asserted their title until, in the reign of **Malcolm IV**, they were expelled from Moray '*extra montanas Scoticae*'. Beyond those mountains to the north lay the province of Strathnaver, where Angus Mac Aoidh (or Aed) was described in 1427 as the leader of 4000 Strathnaver men. He was already married to the sister of **Donald of the Isles**.

In the following century the **Gordons**, having acquired the earldom of **Sutherland** by force and fraud, set out to expropriate the Mackays of Strathnaver. By 1554 they had destroyed the Mackay Chief's stronghold, Castle Borve; in 1570 he was reduced to the status of a vassal of the Gordons. His successor **Donald** raised the Mackay regiment in 1626 which fought with such distinction in the Thirty Years' War; he was created Lord Reay. But regrettably he then abandoned his claim to the stars of Moray in favour of a variant of the heraldry of Forbes, another clan harrassed by the Gordons. It consists of three muzzled bears' heads and a chevron containing a roebuck's head between two hands holding daggers towards it. The crest, which forms the clan badge, is an arm grasping a dagger with the motto '*Manu Forte*'. This proved an empty boast when the degenerate 7th Lord Reay sold his entire estate to the house of Sutherland in 1829, despite the evictions which **Elizabeth Countess of Sutherland** had carried out in the Naver valley during the previous decade.

Meanwhile in the Netherlands Barthold Mackay, junior descendant of an earlier Lord Reay, had been created Baron in 1822. His son Aeneas, Lord Mackay of Ophemert, succeeded as the 10th Lord Reay on the extinction of the senior branch. The 13th resumed British citizenship in 1936, and his son Hugh succeeded him as chief in 1963.

The Mackays claim to have founded the earliest of clan societies in **Glasgow** in 1806, and it was at this time that the Mackay **tartan** went into production at **Bannockburn**. Strathnaver probably contains a higher concentration of one name than any area of comparable size in Britain, despite the **clearances**, thus earning its name 'The Mackay Country'. Clan associations flourish throughout the world, their activities monitored by the clan journal published in **Edinburgh**.

MACKAY, Donald, 1st Lord Reay (1591–1649) Soldier

After succeeding his father, Hugh Mackay of Farr, as head of the **Clan Mackay** (1614), Donald raised a regiment from amongst his clansmen and took them to fight for Christian IV of Denmark where they became known as 'the invincible regiment'. Collecting more recruits (1628) plus the title of Lord Reay (from **Charles I**), he and the regiment transferred to the service of Gustavus Adolphus of Sweden (1629) and earned further plaudits. Like so many Scottish mercenaries, Reay returned to Scotland in the late 1630s but, ambiguous in his support of the **Covenant**, withdrew to the Continent only to reappear at the head of his troops in 1644, this time on behalf of the King. They took part in the defence of Newcastle against the army of the Covenant led by two other ex-Swedish mercenaries, **David** and **Alexander Leslie**. When forced to yield, Reay was taken prisoner and despatched to **Edinburgh Castle**. He was freed after **Montrose**'s victory at Kilsyth but went into exile in 1649 and died at Bergen. His son and heir, John 2nd Lord Reay, also fought for the Royalist cause.

MACKAY, Hugh, of Scourie (c1640–92) General

A **Sutherland Covenanter**, Mackay (who inherited Scourie when both his elder brothers died resisting raids from **Caithness**) sought employment abroad at the 1660 Restoration. He served under **Monmouth** in regiments supplied by **Charles II** to Louis XIV. In 1674, when Charles repudiated the alliance, he transferred his allegiance to William of Orange. Colonel in 1677, he was recalled (1685) to England to oppose Monmouth's Rising and served briefly on the Scots Privy Council (with **John Graham of Claverhouse**, his former comrade). He returned to the Netherlands until he and the Scots Brigade landed in 1688 with William.

Described as 'a Scotch Gentleman very large in his person', and as 'the piousest man I ever knew, in a military way', by **Bishop Burnet**, he was competent but vain. Made Williamite Commander-in-Chief in Scotland against Claverhouse, he marched from **Edinburgh** to **Inverness** and back to 'put the Lord Dundie from forming a party'; the planned fortnight's sweep lasted three months and covered 650 miles, his '200 Old Foot' sometimes keeping the dragoons at a trot over drovers' trails. A second expedition, to re-establish **Monk**'s fort at **Inverlochy** (**Fort William**), ended at **Killiecrankie**.

Sabotaged by politicians and kept short of funds, he ringed the Highlands with strongpoints until the clans were defeated at **Cromdale**, 1690. He served in Ireland before returning to the Netherlands where he was killed at Steinkirk, 24 July 1692.

His gift to the army was the offset bayonet, replacing wooden-hafted 'plugs' which were awkward to fit, blocked the musket-barrel and were easily sliced off by a broadsword.

MACKAY, John (1865–1909) Gaelic Scholar
Born in **Glasgow** to a family who were victims of the **Sutherland clearances**, Mackay was bred a literate **Gaelic** speaker and pursued his education in night schools. This enabled him to rise to high seniority in the firm of a Glasgow flour merchant. But his passionate concerns were the history, traditions and poetry of the Gaels, particularly of his lost homeland, which he constantly revisited. He became President of the **Clan Mackay** Society, of the Gaelic Society of **Inverness** and of the Glasgow Cowal Shinty Club. By the time **An Comunn Gaidhealach** held its first National **Mod** in **Oban** in 1892, Mackay had already founded The Celtic Monthly in which he was able to promote its activities as well as the cause of **shinty**. A biographical appreciation of Mackay, broadcast in his native language, has been published in Gairm, no 161, 1993.

MACKAY, Robert, see **DONN, Rob**

MACKENZIE, Agnes Muriel (Mure) (1891–1955) Author and Historian
Born in **Stornoway**, **Lewis**, the daughter of a physician, Agnes Mure Mackenzie (the 'Mure' was adopted as a nom de plume) became a successful and popular writer on Scottish literature and history, and an historical novelist, despite being handicapped by bad eyesight and hearing. After graduating from **Aberdeen University** she lectured at **Aberdeen** and London. Her first novel Without Conditions appeared in 1924 along with a study on Women in Shakespeare's Plays. A later product of research, The Process of Literature, gained her a DLitt from Aberdeen (1929). She contributed to a growing interest in older Scottish literature with an Historical Survey of the latter to 1714 (1933). Scottish Pageant, a 4-vol anthology of Scottish writing, appeared in 1946–9.

Mure Mackenzie moved naturally from literature and historical fiction to exposition of Scottish history from a moderate nationalist point of view. She challenged the prevailing **Whig**/Unionist orthodoxy which saw the Anglo-Scottish **Union** of 1707 as the culmination of an inexorable and beneficial process, and tended to gloss over its unpopularity and the economic dislocation it created at the time. As a Highlander, and notably in her Robert the Bruce, King of Scots (1934), she laid greater stress than most earlier historians on the contribution of Gaelic Scotland to national development. Eventually her general overview of Scottish history extended to a series of six volumes, from The Foundations of Scotland (1938) to Scotland in Modern Times, 1770–1939 (1942), as well as several other period studies. **The Saltire Society**, of which she became president, was her vehicle for a more active promotion of Scottish culture. Her surviving correspondence and papers, including some manuscript poetry, are in the **National Library of Scotland**.

MACKENZIE, Sir Alexander (c1755–1820) Explorer
Probably born in **Inverness**, Mackenzie went to Canada in 1779 and by 1784 was employed by the North West Company, a rival of the Hudson's Bay Company in its westward drive to secure fur trading arrangements. While based at Fort Chipewyan (north of Alberta and at that time the furthest outpost of the trading companies), Mackenzie, 'endowed by nature [as he puts it] with an inquisitive mind and an enterprising spirit, possessing also a constitution and power of body equal to the most arduous undertaking', resolved to 'test the practicability of penetrating across the continent of America' to the Pacific Ocean. He set off with two birch-bark canoes manned by eight Indian men and four of their wives in June 1789. During 100 days of travel he crossed the Great Slave Lake and descended a vast river to what was evidently the sea, for it boasted whales and a tide. But it was not the Pacific. The river, Canada's longest, was thereafter named the Mackenzie; the sea was the Arctic Ocean. In 1792–3 he resumed 'the favourite project of my own ambition' and struck out by a more southerly route. He crossed the Rockies and, after a nine-month odyssey of adventure, struck the Pacific coast on Queen Charlotte Sound north of what is now Vancouver. He was thus the first white man to travel coast to coast across North America. He published a narrative of his travels in 1801, was knighted in 1802, and was married (to a Miss Mackenzie who seems to have been half his age) in 1812. He died near **Dunkeld** while travelling with his young family to **Edinburgh** from his newly acquired estate at Avoch (near **Fortrose**) where he is buried.

MACKENZIE, Alexander (1822–92) Canadian Premier
Born at Logierait, **Perthshire**, and brought up in **Dunkeld** (where his house still stands), Mackenzie followed his father into the building profession. In 1842 he emigrated to Ontario, set up a business there, and was soon joined by the rest of his family. His strong liberal opinions were first voiced as editor of the local newspaper, then as Member of the Provincial Assembly, and in 1867 as Member of the first Dominion House of

Commons. He was simultaneously chosen as leader of the young Liberal Party. In 1873 an opposition motion criticising **Sir John MacDonald**'s handling of the Canadian Pacific Railway project brought the government's resignation. Mackenzie took over as Canada's first Liberal Premier. A handsome victory in the 1874 election returned Mackenzie to power but he was defeated in 1878 and resigned the party leadership two years later, though remaining an MP until his death. Public works and national integration featured prominently in his programme; the Pacific Railway was begun in spite of his earlier opposition. He made two return trips to Scotland, was made a Freeman of several Scottish burghs, and was entertained by the Queen but thrice refused a knighthood. He died in Toronto and was buried near his home at Sarnia.

MACKENZIE, Sir Alexander Campbell (1847–1935) Musician and Composer

Principal of the Royal Academy of Music in London from 1888–1924, founder of the Associated Board examinations, distinguished conductor, admired administrator and teacher, ex **music hall** pianist, **Edinburgh** music teacher with well over 100 weekly pupils, professional violinist in the Electoral Orchestra at Sonderhausen at the age of 11 and son of a distinguished Edinburgh violinist – a glance back through Mackenzie's career makes it hard to credit that he was also a very fine and prolific composer.

His first publication, the *Piano Quartet* of 1873, is one of the finest contributions to the repertoire, a beautifully crafted work of depth and character; the *Benedictus* for small orchestra is one of the loveliest pieces of sustained melodic writing of any period; and of his numerous orchestral works, the overtures *Coriolanus* and *Britannica* are on the one hand powerfully dramatic and on the other full of fun, grandeur and warmth. The *Pibroch Suite* for violin and orchestra and the *Scottish Concerto* for piano and orchestra were performed by Sarasate and Paderewski respectively and deserve more than the occasional revival.

Perhaps his finest work is the oratorio *The Rose of Sharon* – a setting of parts of the Song of Solomon which contain passages of ravishing sensual beauty, which partly explain the neglect of the work by choral societies run by conductors who disapproved of that book of the Bible, not to mention Mackenzie's assertion that with the revision of the oratorio 'any trace of a religious basis disappeared'. Not only are the individual solos beautifully made and orchestrated, but the build-up of the major 'scenes' shows a mastery of structure and pace. The full impact of Mackenzie's work as a composer cannot be assessed until more of his music is revived.

MACKENZIE, Alexander Marshall (1848–1933) Architect

Mackenzie is best remembered for his **Marischal College** buildings (1903), one of **Aberdeen**'s distinctive landmarks. A native of **Elgin**, Mackenzie was educated in Aberdeen and **Edinburgh**. Unlike many of his contemporaries, he returned to the north-east and set up practice in Elgin in 1870, where his father had worked as an architect. There he was mainly concerned with

public buildings; he also restored the old Town House. In 1877 he moved to Aberdeen as a partner of James Matthews, a family friend and one of his former teachers. Making good use of the local granite, Mackenzie became a prominent church architect. Craigiebuckler Church, Aberdeen, usually seen as his best, brought him to the attention of the General Trustees of the **Church of Scotland**, who appointed him as their architect. Mackenzie designed **Crathie** Church (1894) for **Queen Victoria** and Prince Albert at **Balmoral**, and Mar Lodge, the autumn residence of their eldest daughter, the Princess Royal. Among other works were the war memorial and Cowdray Hall, Aberdeen (opened by King George V in 1925); he also designed the Waldorf Hotel and Australia House in London, the latter in conjunction with his son, A G R Mackenzie.

MACKENZIE, Charles Frederick (1825–62) Mathematician and Bishop

Born in Portmore, **Peeblesshire**, and partly educated at **Edinburgh Academy**, Mackenzie was the younger brother of William Forbes Mackenzie, later MP for **Peebles** and responsible for the 'Forbes Mackenzie Act' regulating liquor sales. Charles Frederick showed an early aptitude for mathematics and after graduation became a fellow and examiner in maths at Caius College, Cambridge (1852). At about the same time he was ordained in the Anglican Church and determined to become a missionary. His first posting was as archdeacon in Durban where he scandalised the local synod with High Church leanings and a novel suggestion that African Christians were entitled to the same rights as white Christians. A more congenial calling came from the Universities Mission to Central Africa which was keen to co-operate with **David Livingstone**. In 1861 Mackenzie was consecrated in Cape Town as Bishop of Central Africa and then joined Livingstone for his abortive attempt to explore the Rovuma River. In spite of their doctrinal differences, the two got on well, Livingstone describing Mackenzie as 'quite a brick of a bishop'. From the Shiré River they marched, Mackenzie with a crozier in one hand and a gun in the other, into the Blantyre Highlands and there Mackenzie established his mission at Magomero. His noble attempt to set up a model Christian society which would proselytise purely by example was marred by several hostile raids designed to thwart slave-dealing neighbours. These later attracted much criticism. He died within a few months of arrival when he contracted malaria while on an expedition to meet his sister and Dr Livingstone.

MACKENZIE, Clan

Cernunnos, the Horned One, was an antlered god whom pagan **Celts** in Gaul revered as their ancestor. Effigies of this being survive in England, together with the myth of Herne the Hunter. In Gaelic Scotland he emerged as *Coinneach*, the Bright One, complete with antlers. When the English language reached the Children of Coinneach they chose the name Kenneth, although it is not the name of a historical progenitor as in the case of **Clan Donald** or **Clan Leod**, those two rival kinship groups in the **Hebrides** whose antecedents help to explain the MacKenzie hostility to both. With the introduction of **heraldry** into the Gaelic world

Cernunnos was represented by a stag's head in the MacKenzie coat of arms.

The family seem to have originated in the Beauly Firth area, to have been constables of **Eilean Donan Castle, Kintail**, under the **Earls of Ross**, but to have rejected the latter's accommodation with **Robert I** and to have been in eclipse until the death of **David II**, last of the house of Bruce. Thereafter MacKenzie fortunes revived dramatically. Under the motto *Cuidich an Righ*, 'Help the King', they declined to join the **Harlaw** campaign and became energetic supporters of a distant government in destroying the power of the **Lords of the Isles**. For his services Alasdair of Kintail was rewarded with lands confiscated from MacDonald in 1477. He gave the name Kenneth to his son, whose effigy may be seen in **Beauly** Priory where he was buried in 1492. By 1508 Kintail had been erected into a feudal barony, and it was as Lords of Parliament that the MacKenzies were able to expropriate the **MacLeods** of **Lewis**. The disreputable details are related in Donald MacDonald's *Lewis: A History of the Island*, 1990. The conquest was all but complete when Colin, Lord MacKenzie of Kintail, died in 1611. His son was created Earl of Seaforth in 1623, taking his title from the most impressive sea loch in Lewis. It is to the credit of this family that in an island which they administered for the most part as absentees they planted the burgh of **Stornoway**, the only substantial town in the Hebrides and the seat of the Council of the Isles today. By 1718 the greatest number of **tacksmen** in the island were MacKenzies, who were also most prominent among the burgesses, although MacLeod remains the commonest name in Lewis. The **5th Earl of Seaforth** was attainted for his part in the **Jacobite Rising** of 1715; his clansmen acquired distinction in many fields during that century. Kenneth MacKenzie (**Coinneach Odhar**) was outstanding among the **bards**, Colin MacKenzie combined his duties as a soldier with oriental scholarship, and **Alexander MacKenzie** became in 1793 the first white man to cross Canada. So it continued in the 19th century, when MacKenzies were among the few who succeeded in depriving the MacDonalds of the highest offices in the new dominion of Canada. In New Zealand as Minister for Lands, Sir John MacKenzie (1836–1901), a native of Ardross who as a child had seen victims of the Glen Calvie **clearances** sheltering in Croick churchyard [see **Ardgay**], made amends by buying and breaking up large estates and by introducing a Lands for Settlement Act. At home another John MacKenzie published *The Beauties of Gaelic Poetry*, the finest anthology that had yet appeared, while W C and Alexander MacKenzie published valuable works of Highland history. The line of Seaforth is extinct (as forecast by *Coinneach Odhar*), but the chiefship of the children of the Bright One is held by the Earls of Cromartie, still addressed formally as *Cabar Féidh*, Stag Antlers.

MACKENZIE, Colonel Sir Colin
(1755–1821) Surveyor and Orientalist
Born at **Stornoway**, the son of its first postmaster, MacKenzie spent 10 years as a local customs officer before sailing to India; it is said that while collaborating on a life of **John Napier**, the inventor of logarithms, he had become intrigued by the Hindu system of logarithms.

In Madras he was gazetted an Ensign in the East India Company's service and took part in the 3rd Mysore War, the capture of Pondicherry (1793) and Colombo (1796), and the 4th Mysore War. During the siege of Srirangapatnam (1799) he was with Colonel Arthur Wellesley, the future Duke of Wellington, during a night foray in which the latter was accused of cowardice. But this imputation was rejected on the ground that it would also have had to apply to MacKenzie 'whose bravery and sangfroid in action are proverbial'. Heroics apart, MacKenzie had already made his name as a military surveyor. On Wellesley's commendation he now undertook a survey of Mysore's 40,000 square miles, the most ambitious undertaking of its kind. It took 9 years and, in addition to maps, resulted in a 7-vol *Memoir* unique in the scope of its enquiry. For MacKenzie's antiquarian interest in mathematics had now broadened into a fascination with all aspects of Indian antiquity. Ably assisted by a team of devoted Indian scholars he scoured south India for archaeological, sculptural and textual evidence of its history. He has been variously credited with the 'discovery' of the Jains (of whom he published a history), of the largest monolithic sculpture in the world (at Sravana Belgola) and of the most important Buddhist site in south India (at Amaravati). Further discoveries followed in Java, which he surveyed during the British occupation under Raffles, and in Bengal where MacKenzie was posted as India's Surveyor-General.

The MacKenzie Collection (of manuscripts, coins, inscriptions, etc) may be the largest hoard of historical material ever amassed. There are said to be 8000 volumes in the Madras library alone; more found their way to Calcutta and London. Even those with no regard for oriental scholarship found his determination 'quite extraordinary' (Lord William Bentinck). Wellington, regretting his absence at Waterloo, recalled that he had never known 'a more zealous, a more diligent, or a more useful officer'. He died in India.

MACKENZIE, Sir (E M) Compton
(1883–1972) Writer
Born in West Hartlepool, the eldest son of the writers Edward Compton and Virginia Bateman, he resumed the family name of Mackenzie as a way of emphasising his Scottish heritage. He was educated at St Paul's School and Magdalen College, Oxford, where he graduated with a degree in Modern History (1904). He studied briefly for the English Bar, but soon gave it up to become a writer, producing his first work, the play *The Gentleman in Grey*, in 1907. This was followed by *Carnival* (1912) and the hugely successful novel *Sinister Street* (1918), which greatly impressed Ford Madox Ford and influenced F Scott Fitzgerald in his early writing.

During World War I Mackenzie served with the Royal Navy in the Dardanelles, later working for military intelligence in Greece. His experiences in the war were later recounted in *Gallipoli Memories* (1929), *Athenian Memories* (1931) and *Greek Memories* (1932). After the war he lived for a short time on the Mediterranean island of Capri, the result of which was a series of novels set in the area, including *Vestal Fire* (1927) and *Extraordinary Women* (1928).

In 1928 he settled on the Isle of **Barra** in the Outer

Hebrides, and became involved in Scottish politics, joining the **Scottish National Party**. During this period he was the literary critic for the *Daily Mail* (1931–5), edited several journals, made frequent radio broadcasts and wrote prolifically. His most significant and popular works were written in the 1930s and 40s. His most ambitious work, the 6-vol fictional series *The Four Winds of Love*, appeared between 1937–45, and traced the of its Scottish protagonist, John Ogilvie, from the turn of the century to 1945. Following this Mackenzie turned to comedy, producing such popular works as *Whisky Galore* (1947) and *Rockets Galore* (1957), both of which were made into successful films. Between 1963 and 1971 Mackenzie produced 10 volumes of his autobiography *My Life and Times*. He was made an OBE in 1919, knighted in 1952 and received honorary degrees from the **University of Glasgow** and St Francis Xavier University, Nova Scotia. He died in **Edinburgh**.

MACKENZIE, George, 1st Viscount Tarbat and 1st Earl of Cromartie (1630–1714)

A **Ross**-shire landowner and lawyer, born in **Fife** and educated at **St Andrews** and **Aberdeen**, Mackenzie joined his associate **Sir John Middleton** in support of **Charles II** during the Cromwellian period and eventually went into exile. He was rewarded at the Restoration as a Lord of Session (1661–3) but ousted by **John Maitland, Earl of Lauderdale**. He returned to office in 1678 as Justice General and as Clerk Register (1681). Though a loyal servant of **James VII**, he found no difficulty in coming to terms with the Williamite revolution and, 'suave and insinuating' (W Ferguson), played a prominent role in attempts to win over the **Jacobite** Highlands. He was appointed Secretary of State in 1702 and displayed much ingenuity and little principle in the run-up to the **Act of Union**, which he supported. Amongst numerous pamphlets, including one vindicating **Robert III**, 'the worst of kings and the most miserable of men', he wrote 'Several Proposals Conducing to a farther Union of Britain' in 1711. The Viscountcy of **Tarbat** had been conferred on him in 1685 and the Earldom of Cromartie in 1703.

MACKENZIE, Sir George, of Rosehaugh (1636–91) Lawyer

Born in **Dundee**, a grandson of Lord Mackenzie of **Kintail**, George was educated at **King's College**, **Aberdeen**, became advocate in 1659 and 10 years later an MP. He was appointed Lord Advocate (1677) in which office he acquired notoriety as 'Bluidy Mackenzie', the ruthless prosecutor of **Covenanters** and abettor of **John Graham of Claverhouse**. Amongst those he sent to their death were James Mitchell (1678) and the **9th Earl of Argyll** (1685). On a happier note, as Dean of Faculty (1682) he was prominent in establishing the **Advocates' Library** which in 1925 became the **National Library of Scotland**.

Apart from *Aretina or the Serious Romance* (1661) he wrote mainly legal texts, including *Institutions of the Law of Scotland* (1684) which established his reputation as an institutional writer and *Laws and Customs of Scotland in Matters Criminal* (1674). Other works include *Observations on the Acts of Parliament* (1686) and an outstanding text on Heraldic Law, the *Observations on the Laws and Customs of Nations as to Precedency; with the Science of Heraldry as part of the Law of Nations* (1690). His minor works include *Jus Regium* (1684) and a political tract, 'The Vindication of the Government of Scotland during the Reign of **Charles II**'.

MACKENZIE, Henry (1745–1832) Novelist, Essayist and Poet

The label of 'a man of feeling' adhered to Henry Mackenzie ever after the publication of his first novel. It provides a good example of the difference that often exists between the author and his work, a difference particularly striking in the case of Mackenzie, **Edinburgh**-born literary lawyer, Comptroller of Taxes for Scotland (1799), founder member of the **Royal Society of Edinburgh** (1783), Trustee of the **Theatre Royal** (1801–8), one of the directors of the Highland Society of Scotland, and doyen of the Edinburgh literati, whose first venture in literature, *The Man of Feeling*, was published anonymously in 1771. This, the most popular novel of its decade in Britain, tells the story of one Harley, a young man characterised by extraordinary sensibility and idealising sentimentality. The first printing was sold out in a few months, and by 1820 the novel had appeared in nine different editions and was reprinted several times. It was translated into French, German, Italian, Polish and Swedish. The immediate success of *The Man of Feeling* stimulated the author to write a sequel, *The Man of the World* (1773). The hero, who throws himself into selfish pleasures and ends up in misery and ruin, is drawn in contrast to the somewhat lachrymose Harley. *Julia de Roubigné*, an epistolary romance, appeared in 1777, written in imitation of Richardson's *Clarissa*.

Mackenzie's literary reputation was already well established by the time he edited his two periodicals,

Henry Mackenzie as an octogenarian, by Colvin Smith, c1827 (SNPG)

moral weeklies, *The Mirror* (1779–80) and *The Lounger* (1785–7). Many of the essays contributed by himself focus on the subject of life in society as essentially social, very much – referring to **Francis Hutcheson**, **David Hume**, **Adam Smith** and **Adam Ferguson** – a tenet of the **Scottish Enlightenment**. Publishers took Mackenzie's advice on more than one occasion before accepting a manuscript for publication. He supported **Robert Burns** by writing a most favourable and influential review of the **Kilmarnock** poems (*Lounger*, 97), and he gave **Sir Walter Scott** a start on the ladder towards literary fame. When Scott published his *Waverley*, the dedication to 'our Scottish Addison' was directed at Mackenzie.

Even by 18th century standards, Mackenzie may truly be called a prolific letter-writer. His correspondents included writers, publishers, friends in Scotland, England and France, politicians, ministers, diplomats and members of his family. His letters make up a unique collection of contemporary information on the cultural, intellectual, social and political setting of their time. They follow the socio-cultural and literary cross-currents of one of the most significant periods of modern Scotland, extend their view to England and, though not forgetting regional boundaries and identities, include the European dimension. A unifying, if not solitary element in a rapidly changing cultural landscape, Mackenzie was a living connection between the age of Hume and the age of **Hogg**, between Edinburgh old and new. The reputation he enjoyed outlived, to a certain degree, the conditions of his success.

MACKENZIE, Osgood (1842–1922) Gardener

The only child of the second marriage of Sir Francis Mackenzie of **Gairloch** to Mary Hanbury, Osgood Mackenzie was born in France. When his father died in 1843 his mother made Gairloch, on the west coast of **Ross**-shire, her permanent home. She gave Osgood a small gun as a reward for learning to swim when he was nine. He soon became a good shot and as his knowledge of the countryside increased, so did his passion for all things natural, and for the customs and folklore of the district (see his *A Hundred Years in the Highlands*).

In 1862 his mother bought him the two adjoining estates of **Inverewe** and Kernsary. Inverewe had several miles of coastline and the neck of a barren peninsula was chosen as the site for a house. In 1864, having fenced off the peninsula to keep out marauding sheep, he planted a shelter belt round it of Scots and Corsican pine. Some 15 years later he introduced shrubs and specimen trees, and when these survived he began to plant rare and exotic species which also flourished in the mild climate. Horticulturalists from afar came to visit Inverewe, and the garden, now owned by the **National Trust for Scotland**, remains a testimonial to his vision and expertise.

MACKENZIE, William, 5th Earl of Seaforth (d.1740)

Kenneth Mackenzie, 4th Earl, followed **James VII** into exile in France and was there created 1st Marquis. He died in 1701 but his heir, William, remained staunchly **Jacobite** and was in the forefront of the 1715 rising.

As a result his lands and title were forfeited in 1716. He again put himself at the head of the clan when he landed in **Lewis** with other leaders of the abortive 1719 rising. After the **Battle of Glenshiel** he returned to the Continent but in 1726 made his peace with the Hanoverians and was pardoned. His lands, never effectively taken over by the Commission for Forfeited Estates because of their remoteness, were restored. Not so his title, although in 1771 it was recreated for his grandson who raised the **Seaforth Highlanders**. The recreated title lapsed for want of heirs in 1815.

MACKENZIE, William (1791–1868) Optical Surgeon

Born in Queen Street, **Glasgow**, Mackenzie studied medicine at **Glasgow University**, travelling widely before settling again in his native city in 1818, specialising in diseases of the eye. Author of a standard textbook on the subject, Mackenzie was a co-founder of the Glasgow Eye Infirmary in 1824.

MACKENZIE, William Lyon (1795–1861) Canadian Reformer

Mackenzie was born in **Dundee**, the only son of a weaver, originally from **Glenshee**, who died soon after his birth. He attended school in Dundee and was apprenticed in several trades, including a newspaper, before moving with his mother to **Alyth** where they ran a shop and lending library. When this went bankrupt Mackenzie left Scotland and in 1820 sailed to Canada. He settled in Toronto, soon married, and was joined by his mother, a **Free Church Presbyterian**. Mackenzie did not share her religious views but, in the name of reform, for the next 40 years he brought to bear on Canadian politics all the zeal, populism, and combative bigotry of a fanatical 17th century **Covenanter**. Initially he identified with the reformist ideas of **Joseph Hume** and others in London and through the columns of his newspaper *The Colonial Advocate* savaged what he saw as the prodigality, monopolistic corruption and privilege of the ruling Tories. Personal invective won him the nickname of 'William Liar Mackenzie'. He was a formidable presence in Upper Canada's Legislative Assembly, when not barred from entry, and was elected mayor of Toronto in 1834.

At about this time he started looking to the United States for his constitutional model; *The Advocate* lost its 'Colonial' and then became *The Constitution*. In 1837, despairing of political action, he began organising militant cells. Rebellion may be too strong a word for the demonstration in support of his Declaration of Independence which brought his supporters to Toronto in December; it certainly implies greater co-ordination than Mackenzie was capable of. The 'rebels' were easily dispersed and Mackenzie was obliged to seek sanctuary in the US. There he remained for 12 years, one of them spent in gaol and all in considerable financial distress. He returned to Canada under an 1849 amnesty and sat in the united legislature (1850–8) where he continued to aggravate enemies, alienate friends and espouse every reform issue available. No one doubted his patriotism; many acknowledged his contribution to the new and eventually independent Canada; but none found him an easy colleague.

MACKENZIES OF ACHILTY

Poems by two successive chiefs of this Mackenzie sept, situated west of **Dingwall**, survive. Alasdair Mac Mhurchaidh (d.1642) was the fourth chief. He writes of the conflict between spirit and flesh, using metres and language that show classical bardic influence. His son, Murchadh Mor, was Seaforth's factor in **Lewis**, and has left a charming poem about his boat, which he calls *An Làir Dhonn* ('The Brown Mare'), two poems on the exile of **Charles II** and an elegy for Donald of Sleat (1643). For some of these texts, see W J Watson, *Bàrdach Ghàidhlig*, 1918, 1976.

MACKINNON, Sir William (1823–93)
Shipowner and Colonial Developer

MacKinnon, born in **Campbeltown**, was first apprenticed to a local grocer, then moved to **Glasgow** where he worked for a merchant engaged in the India trade. In 1847 he went out to Calcutta to join a friend who was freighting cargoes in the coastal trade of the Bay of Bengal. Together they launched the firm of MacKinnon & Mackenzie and, with a single vessel plying between Bengal and Rangoon, started the Calcutta and Burmah Steam Navigation Company (1856). In 1862 the latter became the British India Steam Navigation Company. Operations were extended to other ports in the east and then Africa and the UK, as the company became one of the largest shipping concerns in the world. In 1873 MacKinnon established a ferry service from Aden to Zanzibar where with the help of **John Kirk** he established good relations with the Sultan. The latter was willing to give him a lease of what are now Tanzania, Malawi and Kenya, but the British government declined to sanction the arrangement. Partly in furtherance of this colonial scheme MacKinnon chaired and largely funded the Emin Pasha relief expedition under H M Stanley (1887). But it was German willingness to exploit East Africa which eventually led to the founding of MacKinnon's British East Africa Company (1888) with a lease of the coastal strip round Mombasa. MacKinnon was created baronet in 1889 and also founded the East African Scottish Mission in 1891.

MACKINTOSH, Anne (1723–87) Jacobite

The daughter of James Farquharson of Invercauld, Anne married Aeneas, or Angus, **Mackintosh**. As chief of his **clan**, Angus accepted a commission in the **Black Watch** and raised a company for the Hanoverian army. His mother strongly disapproved and so did his wife who in 1745 raised a company for **Prince Charles Edward Stewart**. She was henceforth known as 'Colonel Anne', a dashing figure who often adopted 'Highlandman's clothes'. In February 1746, when the Prince was her guest at Moy Hall, it was 'the colonel' who, 'running about like a madwoman in her shift', hid him from a raiding party under Lord Loudoun and then frustrated the attackers in the Rout of **Moy**. She was arrested after **Culloden** but not mistreated and, after six weeks' detention in **Inverness**, was released.

MACKINTOSH, Charles Rennie (1868–1928)
Architect, Designer and Artist

Mackintosh was born in **Glasgow**, the son of a police superintendent. During his apprenticeship (1884–9) to the architect John Hutchinson he attended night classes at the **Glasgow School of Art** where he became a protégé of the visionary director **Francis Newbery**. In 1889 he joined Honeyman & Keppie, Architects, as a draughtsman, being made a partner in 1904. Here and at Glasgow School of Art he worked alongside Herbert Macnair, exchanging design ideas. Newbery observed a similarity between their work and that of two day students, the sisters Frances and Margaret MacDonald, and introduced 'The Four' as they became known. Their collaborative work was central to the evolution of 'Glasgow Style' design. Mackintosh married Margaret MacDonald in 1900.

Reviled at the Arts and Crafts Exhibition Society, London, in 1896, the stylised simplicity of Mackintosh's work was acclaimed when first seen in Vienna at the 8th Secessionist Exhibition in 1900. He exhibited there again and also in Munich, Dresden, Turin, Budapest and Moscow. Disillusioned by his lack of recognition as an architect in Glasgow, Mackintosh moved to Chelsea, London in 1913 and gave his attention to textile design and meticulous flower studies. His last architectural project was 78 Derngate, Northampton, in 1917. From 1920 he lived happily in Port de Vendres, France, where he executed many fine watercolours. These are essentially two-dimensional and demonstrate his persistent interest in pattern. He returned to London on account of his health and died there in 1928.

Although his work was feted on the Continent, it was seen as an anathema in Britain. Accordingly, commissions were few and his success brief. Mackintosh only partially shared the ideology of the Arts and Crafts Movement, being interested in the re-interpretation not the revival of tradition, in design not craft. In its search for a new stylised vocabulary his work can be related to contemporary Art Nouveau. However, his contradictory preference for straight lines and clarity visually prepared the way for the 'brutality' of the Modern Movement.

Externally, Mackintosh's buildings are unquestionably Scottish and modern [see **Glasgow: School of Art**, **Martyr's Public School**, **Queen's Cross Church**, **Scotland Street School**, **Willow Tea Rooms** etc, and **Hill House, Helensburgh**]. While overtly referring to traditional Scottish architecture (he admired the dramatic functionalism of castles) he does not revive it in detail. In his experiments with steel construction and glass he anticipates the Modern Movement.

As a designer, Mackintosh rejected both Victorian ostentation and Arts and Crafts worthiness for an ascetic lyricism. Spaces are by turn airy and light or envelopingly dark. White rooms with grey, beige and touches of pink or lilac are exchanged for those with an extensive use of dark stained wood. Decoration, the contribution of Margaret MacDonald Mackintosh, is precious: panels of beaten metal, enamel, coloured and leaded glass or gesso set with semi-precious stones, and reserved for fittings (brackets, lights, etc). Upholstery is spartan and rough in texture and often stencilled. Furniture is used architecturally to define space. Shapes are simple and clean. Sometimes practicality is subordinated to the architectural idea, for example the vertical emphasis of the notorious ladder-backed chairs.

Mackintosh's 1900 design for 'An Artist's Cottage and Studio' has recently (1992) been completed at

Strathnairn near **Inverness**. His *Haus Eines Kunstfreundes* was likewise realised in Glasgow's **Bellahouston Park** in 1990.

MACKINTOSH, Clan

The earliest ancestry is traced to Shaw MacDuff, son of the 3rd Earl of **Fife**, who was of the royal family. Mac-Duff took the name of Mackintosh, '*Mac-an-toisich*', meaning Son of the Chief. He retained in his coat of arms the Lion Rampant of the **Earls of Fife**. In 1163 he came north with **King Malcolm IV** to suppress a rebellion by the men of **Moray**. As a reward for his services he was made Keeper of the Royal Castle of **Inverness**, and received the lands of Petty (4 miles east of Inverness) with the forest of Strathdearn in the glen of the upper **Findhorn**. Petty became the burial place of the chiefs and was last so used in 1957.

Angus, 6th Chief, married in 1291 Eva, the only daughter of Gilpatric or Dougal Gall, Chief of **Clan Chattan** in **Lochaber**. On the death of Dougal, Angus succeeded to the lands, Glenloy and **Loch Arkaig**, and the Chiefship of Clan Chattan. He lived at Torcastle but later removed to **Rothiemurchus** in **Badenoch** and was followed by all Clan Chattan, leaving derelict his Loch-aber lands. This led the **Camerons** later to claim that Mackintosh had deserted the lands and that they effec-tively had taken possession. A long feud developed which was brought to an end by the sale of Glenloy and Loch Arkaig to Cameron of Lochiel in 1666.

Angus Mackintosh led his men in support of **Bruce** at **Bannockburn** and was succeeded by his son William in 1345. In 1336 the Bishop of Moray had granted him the Barony of **Moy**. This later became the home of the chief and has remained so. The first house of the chief was on the island in Loch Moy along with a small village. A little man-made stone island off the southern end of the main island was used as a prison. It was not until 1700 that the island was abandoned as a habitation and the then chief built a new house on the north-west shore of the loch.   Clan Mackintosh dominated the south-eastern approaches to Inverness, as is evidenced by the roadbuilder **General Wade** in 1729 asking the chief to 'desire his people not to molest my workmen'. Smaller clans of Clan Chattan such as MacBean, MacGill-livray and Shaw seem to have largely integrated with Mackintosh in the heyday of the clan system.

In the 1715 **Jacobite Rising** the chief put himself under the command of his more militarily experienced clansman, Brigadier William Mackintosh of Borlum. In 1745 Angus, 22nd Chief, was already serving as a cap-tain in the **Black Watch**, part of the government army, and remained loyal to his oath. His wife, 'Colonel **Anne**' **Farquharson**, stayed at Moy, raised men for **Prince Charles Edward Stewart** and entertained him.

The clan's crest is the **wildcat** and motto 'Touch Not the Cat Bot a Glove' [see **Clan Macpherson**]. There are two **tartans**, the older traditional 'red' Mackintosh and the more recent hunting Mackintosh. Lachlan, the present and 30th Chief tracing continuous descent, lives on at Moy.

MACKINTOSH, Sir James (1765–1832)
Author and Historian

Born near **Inverness**, the precocious Mackintosh studied arts at **Aberdeen** then medicine at **Edinburgh**, where he joined the highest intellectual circles of the day. He turned to politics after a move to London (1788–1804). *Vindiciae Galliae*, his 1791 reply to Burke's *Reflections on the French Revolution*, made his name and won Burke's respect. Well placed in the society of the 'Friends of the People' he became a successful barrister and lecturer on law. Knighted and given a post in Bombay (1804–12), he studied India but was glad to get back to Britain. A **Whig** MP for **Nairn** (1812–32) working hard for Catholic Emancipation, the Reform Bill and criminal law reform, he was also Professor of Law and Politics, East India Company College 1818–24. *A Dissertation on the Progress of Ethical Philosophy*, a *History of the Reformation and Memoirs* (edited by his son) are distinguished fragmentary pro-ductions. **Macaulay** wrote an essay on this man whose greatness and gifts are well evidenced without, alas, the hoped-for history of England which his variety of work did not allow. James M'Cosh in *The Scottish Philosophy* regrets Mackintosh's refusal to become Moral Philo-sophy Professor at Edinburgh in 1820.

MACLACHLAN, Ewen (Eòghan MacLachlainn) (1773–1822) Gaelic Scholar and Poet

From Nether **Lochaber**, MacLachlan was headmaster of the Grammar School in Old **Aberdeen**, and Librarian at **King's College**. He did valuable work on **Gaelic** manuscripts and on collecting vocabulary for the *High-land Society Dictionary* (published 1828). His *Metrical Effusions* (1807) included verse in Latin, Greek, Gaelic and Eng-lish, and he contributed Gaelic poems to Allan MacDou-gall's *Orain Ghaidhealacha* (1798). Alone among the 18th century Gaelic poets, he has extant poems on the four seasons and he composed the popular song *Gur gile mo leannan* ('Fair is My Love'); but his most sustained Gaelic work was his translation of the first 7 books of the *Iliad* (and part of Book 8). His poems were mostly collected in John MacDonald's edition *Ewen MacLachlan's Gaelic Verse* (1937). A number of his letters, including a Gaelic one dated 1811, were edited by D S Thomson in *Scottish Gaelic Studies* (1968).

MCLAGAN, James (1728–1805) Gaelic Scholar

Born at Ballechin, Strathtay, MacLagan was minister at Amulree and **Blair Atholl**. He collected **Gaelic verse** and song from c1755–1805, his large collection of manuscripts being now in **Glasgow University** Library. He corresponded with **James Macpherson** and sent him some **ballad** versions. For a catalogue of Ossianic ballads in his collection see *Scottish Gaelic Studies*, 8, 1958.

MACLAREN, Duncan (1800–86) Reformer and Nationalist

Probably born and certainly brought up in **Dalmally** (where there is a memorial to him near the head of **Loch Awe**), MacLaren arrived in **Edinburgh** in his early teens and was employed at a drapers' shop where, to make up for his lack of stature and education, he is said to have stood on a dictionary all day and to have studied it all night. In his thirties, following the Municipal Reform Act, he engaged in local politics, becoming successively City Bailie, Treasurer, Lord Provost (1851–4) and Liberal MP (1865–81). As Chairman

Duncan MacLaren, by Edward John Gregory from a portrait of 1882 (SNPG)

(1834) of the Central Board of Scottish Dissenters (demanding disestablishment and complete Church independence from temporal control), and as organiser of the 1842 anti-Corn Law protests, he also 'embodied the dictum that dissent was the soul of Liberalism' (Wm Ferguson). Marriage to Priscilla, sister of John Bright, confirmed his radicalism and it was MacLaren who advised Disraeli on the application of the 1867 Reform Bill to Scotland and, by his support, ensured its passage. By increasing the number of Scottish MPs and widening the franchise, this answered many of the demands once voiced by the National Association for the Vindication of Scottish Rights with which MacLaren had been associated (along with **James Grant** and **William Burns**) in 1853–4. At Westminster MacLaren acquired the sobriquet 'The Member for Scotland' which, like Strasbourg's later characterisation of Winnie Ewing as 'Madame Ecosse', hinted at nationalist fulminations. Further pressure on Conservative and Liberal administrations alike eventually brought the secret ballot (1872), universal suffrage (1884) and the creation of a Scottish Secretary (1885), for all of which MacLaren had fought.

MACLAREN, John (1846–1943)
Horticulturalist
Born on a farm near **Stirling**, MacLaren learnt his gardening at **Bannockburn** House, Blair Drummond, **Manderston** and the **Royal Botanic Garden**. In 1869 he emigrated to San Francisco and there converted a field into what later became the botanic garden of Stanford University. Success in coping with Pacific coast conditions led to his appointment as superintendent of the city's parks (1887). He held the post for over half a century, during which his principal creation was Golden Gate Park; to few gardeners can it have been given to lay out such a magnificent site and live long enough to see it mature. Not that the site was initially promising. A wilderness of windswept dunes, it had first to be reclaimed, a task to which MacLaren brought some experience gained on the Firth of Forth. He planted bent grass and then Monterrey pines and cypresses. The wind tore them up and he replanted. Access to the city's refuse enabled him to plant more demanding species in craters filled with nitrogenous matter. He imported many exotics including his favourite rhododendrons and fought a running battle with the encroachment of sand, gifted by each Pacific gale, and of statuary wished on him by a proud city. His *Gardening in California*, 1909, was a notable success; he gained international recognition when he landscaped the Panama-Pacific Exhibition in San Francisco (1915), and in 1931 he received a doctorate from the University of California. Refusing to retire, he remained in his house in Golden Gate Park and continued to superintend the city's other parks until he died, a legendary figure, at the age of 96.

MACLAURIN, Colin (1698–1746)
Mathematician
Born at Kilmodan, **Bute**, MacLaurin was a child prodigy, entering **Glasgow University** at the age of 11 and being appointed Professor of Mathematics at **Aberdeen** at 19. Later holding a similar post at **Edinburgh**, he distinguished himself in mathematical theory and devised seminal work on tidal flows. Believed to have worked himself into ill-health devising Edinburgh's defences against the **Jacobite** army in 1745, he died shortly after returning from flight to England in 1746.

MACLEAN, Alistair (1922–87) Novelist
Though born in **Glasgow**, MacLean was brought up in **Inverness-shire** where his Gaelic-speaking father served as minister. He is said not to have been allowed to speak English until the age of eight. He attended **Inverness** Royal Academy and, returning to Glasgow, Hillhead High School before serving in the Royal Navy during World War II. He then took a degree at **Glasgow University**, became a Glasgow schoolteacher, and tried writing to boost his teacher's salary. Success in a *Glasgow Herald* short story competition brought encouragement from a **Collins** editor to try a novel. 'I had a go and the go went.' *HMS Ulysses*, 1955, based largely on his own wartime experiences, was poorly reviewed and sold massively. So did his second book, *The Guns of Navarone*, 1957, later a film. He left his job and moved to tax-favoured Switzerland. Apart from a spell (1963–6) as a hotelier in Cornwall, he remained there, producing a book a year (many filmed) and realising total world sales of over 200 million. His books have been faulted on many counts – stiff characterisation, hob-nailed humour, few women, too much violence, not enough sex, etc, etc. But he was the first to disclaim literary pretensions, preferring to be judged simply as a storyteller. Relentless action, abundant suspense, and millions of spellbound readers vouch for his success. He died in Munich.

MACLEAN, Charles (c1712–c1765) Composer
After brief periods of teaching music in **Montrose** and at the **Aberdeen** sang school, MacLean became a

professional violinist for the **Edinburgh** Musical Society. Like **Munro** and **McGibbon**, MacLean made a successful blend of Scottish and Italian styles in his variation-sonatas based on Scottish tunes, though his 12 sonatas published in 1737 blend a variety of Continental idioms.

MACLEAN, Sir Fitzroy, of Dunconnel, Bart (1911–96) Soldier, Traveller, Writer

Fitzroy Maclean was the only son of a regular soldier whose family were cadets of West Highland chieftains, the Macleans of Ardgour. Educated in Florence, at Eton and the universities of Marburg and Cambridge he then joined the Diplomatic Service and spent three years in Paris before requesting a transfer to Moscow. In Russia he was a witness at Stalin's notorious Show Trials and travelled extensively (and illegally) throughout Central Asia and the Caucasus.

At the outbreak of war he enlisted in his father's regiment, the **Cameron Highlanders**, as a Private. A Foreign Office attempt to recall him was frustrated by his standing for and winning a by-election in Lancaster. Still on active service, he was flown to Cairo on an aborted mission and there he joined David Stirling who was recruiting the first volunteers for the Special Air Service (SAS) to operate behind enemy lines. After Alamein Maclean started training a new unit of amphibious SAS in the Lebanon, but was sent to Persia to kidnap General Zaliedi, the pro-Axis Governor of Isfahan, which he did with the help of a handful of **Seaforth Highlanders**.

Sir Fitzroy Maclean. Photo: Glasgow Herald, courtesy of Lady Maclean

In 1943 Churchill recalled him to London and told him he was to be parachuted into German-occupied Yugoslavia to report on the Communist guerrilla leader Tito and his Partisans, about whom little was then known, although decoded enemy intercepts suggested they were holding down more German divisions than Mihailovic and his Chetniks. The ensuing Maclean Report (September 1943) collated the experiences of British Liaison Officers from both forces and confirmed the intercepts, but Maclean also warned Churchill of the inevitable political outcome of a Partisan victory. It created something of a sensation and led to a change of direction in Allied strategy and support and, of course, to endless controversy.

In 1946 Maclean married Veronica, daughter of the 16th Lord Lovat and widow of Lieut Alan Phipps RN. He won three more elections in Lancaster and was made a Junior Minister in Churchill's last government. In 1957 he returned to the Highlands with his family, settling into Strachur House in **Argyll**. From 1959–74 he was Conservative and Unionist MP for Bute & North Ayrshire, but continued to travel widely, particularly in the Soviet Union and the Balkans, becoming an acknowledged expert on Russian and Yugoslav affairs. The Macleans bought a house on the Dalmatian island of Korcula and they continued to see Tito, who remained a lifelong friend.

Maclean was created a Baronet in 1957 and a **Knight of the Thistle** in 1993. His books on Central Asia, Russia and Scotland (including a biography of *Bonnie Prince Charlie* and *A Concise History of Scotland*) won widespread acclaim. So did the cuisine at his Creggans Inn at Strachur, another venture into the unknown. A man of great charm, whose anecdotes, however improbable, were never incredible, he was probably personally acquainted with as many world leaders as anyone in Scotland. The suggestion that Ian Fleming based his fictional James Bond on Maclean has been denied, although it remains too plausible not to be repeated.

MACLEAN, Hector (Eachann Bacach), see LAME HECTOR

MACLEAN, John (1879–1923) Socialist Revolutionary

As activist, educator and martyr, Maclean became the conscience of **Red Clydeside** and is Scotland's best-known revolutionary. Too rigid and too radical to be an effective political force, he was yet revered and trusted by all the leaders of the Clydeside left, most of whom had once been his disciples. His international standing may be gauged from his election as honorary president of the first Congress of Soviets and from his appointment by Lenin in 1917 as Bolshevik consul for Scotland.

Born into poverty at **Pollokshaws (Glasgow)**, Maclean worked his way through school to an MA from **Glasgow University** and a short-lived teaching career. Although true to his Calvinist upbringing (he eschewed alcohol, tobacco and sentiment) and Highland background (he endorsed the idea of primitive **clan** society as the prototype for a workers' republic), intellectual conviction and moral outrage made him a confirmed atheist and a doctrinaire Marxist. He joined the Social

Democratic Federation (later the British Socialist Party), edited *Vanguard*, the BSP's Scottish organ, and from 1903 onwards gave regular public lectures on Marxist theory to mass audiences in Glasgow and **Lanarkshire** which included members of the **Clyde Workers Committee** such as **Willie Gallacher** and ILP leaders such as **James Maxton**.

But whereas some of his disciples used World War I as an opportunity to press social and industrial grievances, Maclean saw the war as a matter of imperialist rivalry which was no concern of the international proletariat and could only undermine its solidarity. He therefore condemned it and in 1915, 1916 and 1918 was arrested for sedition and similar offences under the Defence of the Realm Act. In prison (1916–18) his health suffered. He believed he was being surreptitiously drugged; he refused food and had to be force fed. His plight excited vigorous protests, leading to his release and a tumultuous reception on his return to Glasgow.

Neither the armistice nor his release did anything to dull Maclean's zeal. Correctly he predicted a second world war, mistakenly he identified the USA as the likely adversary, and boldly he prescribed 'revolution in Britain no later than this year' as the only preventative. In 1920 he broke with the BSP and began espousing Irish Home Rule as a stage in the anti-imperialist revolution which would usher in first an Irish and then a Scottish Workers' Republic. He also broke with Gallacher and the new Communist Party of Great Britain over his insistence on a separate Communist or Workers' Republican Party in Scotland.

Though twice arrested for sedition in 1921 and once for breach of the peace in 1923 he continued to champion the unemployed and, though increasingly isolated, to contest elections. Far from well and with no chance of a majority he stood for the **Gorbals** constituency in 1923. Round the clock canvassing in mid-November resulted in pneumonia. He died on 30 November; over 10,000 attended his funeral. **Hugh MacDiarmid** has hailed him as 'the greatest leader the working class of Scotland have yet had'; a West Indian vagrant to whom he gave his only overcoat remembered him as 'the greatest man in Scotland, one great lump of kindness and sincerity'.

MCLEAN, Lex (1908–75) Comedian

Born Alexander McLean Cameron in **Clydebank**, Lex McLean graduated from minstrel-show pianist and musician to become a leading comedian and eventually headed record-breaking summer shows at the **Pavilion Theatre, Glasgow**, in the 1960s. He was popular for his vigorous comedy style and at times suggestive but never offensive jokes.

MACLEAN, Sorley/MACGILL-EAIN, Somhairle (1911–96) Poet and Teacher

The colossus of the 20th century revival of **Gaelic** poetry was the son of a tradition-bearer who combined tailoring with **crofting** in **Raasay**. After attending **Portree** High School he gained First Class Honours English at **Edinburgh University** in 1933 and then taught in **Skye**, **Mull** and Edinburgh and as Head at Plockton, Wester Ross (1956–72). He was severely wounded at El Alamein in World War II. His first verses were written in

English imitative of Pound and Eliot, but he soon heeded strong 'ancestral' voices like **Mary Macpherson**, publishing *17 Poems for 6d*, with **Robert Garioch Sutherland** in 1940. He joined the coterie of **Scottish Renaissance** poets – **MacCaig**, **Goodsir Smith**, **MacDiarmid** – whose early work confirmed his conviction that the lyric was 'the summit of all poetry'. His major work *Dain do Eimhir agus Dain Eile* was published by **Robert MacLellan** in 1943; a love sequence for 'Eimhir', the most beautiful of the Ulster heroes' women, lies at its heart. These poems, inspired by an intense love that was lost, 'sing' to the Gael with their rhythmic music – so much so that MacLean is acclaimed as 'one of the great love poets of the world, like Catullus or Donne or Yeats or Sappho' (Smith, 1996). Woven into their fabric, though, were passionate socio-political concerns over the triumph of fascism in the Spanish Civil War; there he saw the same dark forces which had caused **Highland Clearances**. Hatred of the despotism of the British Empire is evident in his unfinished epic *The Cuillins*, where he refers to the rebels of the past like 'the poor great **John MacLean**'. His finest poem is 'Hallaig', from *Reothairt is Contraigh/Spring Tide and Neap Tide* (1977), concerning a cleared village haunted by the dead; its memorable opening is resonant even in English: 'Time, the deer, is in the wood of Hallaig.'

MACLELLAN'S CASTLE, Kirkcudbright

The 'castle' built by Sir Thomas MacLellan, provost of **Kirkcudbright** in the 1570s, was really a grand but late and little-fortified tower house of L-plan design with excrescences both within and without the angle of the L. Now windowless and roofless, its crow-stepped walls and massive chimney stacks form a distinctive feature of the town's skyline. MacLellan married Dame Grizel Maxwell with whom he shares a funerary monument described as 'of late Gothic work influenced by early Renaissance forms', which is in the adjacent Greyfriars Kirk. The original Greyfriars, a convent demolished at the **Reformation**, provided much of the building material for the 'castle'. Robert MacLellan, Sir Thomas's heir, was created Lord Kirkcudbright by **Charles I**, but extravagant habits continued to dog the family. Of the last Lords Kirkcudbright, one was reduced to running an ale house and another to selling gloves in **Edinburgh**.

MACLEOD, Clan

More than any other great Hebridean clan, the Sons of Leod represent the Norse, or **Viking** element in what became the mixed society of the *Gall Gaidheal* (foreigner Gaels) under the last Norse 'Kings' of Man. Liotr, according to a family chronicle now generally recognised as adequately true, was a son or nephew of Olav, King of Man and the North Isles (that is, the **Hebrides** north of **Ardnamurchan**), who died in 1237. Leod (the Gaelic version of the name) inherited **Lewis** and **Harris** but also, on marriage to an heiress in **Skye**, acquired substantial lands there including 'Began's Dun' (**Dunvegan**), which he fortified as his seat of power. At his death (c1280) this great property was divided, his son Tormod receiving Harris, Skye and (a later acquisition) **Glenelg**, while Torcuil (possibly a grandson) became Chief in Lewis. From then on, the Siol Tormod and the Siol Torcuil became separate, though allied, elements in the story, Tormod ruling from Dunvegan, Torcuil from **Stornoway** Castle in Lewis, though with interests in Skye, **Raasay**, **Gairloch** and **Assynt**. Malcolm, 3rd, of Harris, by then under the patronage not only of the **Lords of the Isles** but (more remotely) of the King of Scots, built the stone keep of Dunvegan around 1360. The influence of the Lordship was benign; that of Scotland less so, since it brought in its train the evil of feudal overlordship. When these two influences clashed, the Lordship went down (1493) and thereafter the Hebrides were in almost perpetual turmoil. Despite long land feuds – with the **Frasers** over Glenelg and **Clan Donald** over parts of Skye and the **Uists** – the trend was towards prosperity, though with the sword never long laid aside.

Alexander MacLeod, 8th, of Harris, colourful and particularly well remembered, gets mention in a legal document of 1527 as he who 'dwelleth in ye isles whear ye officers of ye law dare not pass for hazard of their lives'. Despite the apparently hostile environment, this chief built the beautiful Fairy Tower at Dunvegan, the church of St Clement at Rodel, which houses his own elaborate tomb, and installed the **MacCrimmon** dynasty of pipers at Boreraig in Skye. Over the same period the **Mackenzies** began their fatal vendetta against the MacLeods of Lewis with raids into **Gairloch**. Mackenzie of **Kintail**, taking advantage of family dissensions, succeeded not only in planting a bogus heir on Lewis but, dodging a rival move to implant Lowlanders [see **Gentleman Adventurers of Fife**] on the property, laid low until this project failed and was able to scoop all the Lewis lands with the exception of Raasay. As this drama was unfolding, the Siol Tormod was under the firm guidance of perhaps its greatest chief, Ruairidh Mor, who fought in a campaign in Ireland against the forces of Queen Elizabeth, stood by his discredited kinsmen of Lewis and defied **James VI**, yet was subsequently knighted by that monarch and lived well at Dunvegan with minstrels and feasting. He peopled the Isles, notably **Berneray**, with a tough and surviving breed of sons by his splendid wife, Isabel MacDonald of Glengarry who long outlived him, moving to the old dwelling house at Rodel. With her there was Padruig Mor MacCrimmon as piper (his brother Donald was then piper at Dunvegan) and Màiri Nighean Alasdair Ruaidh (**Mary MacLeod**), the first and greatest of the 'modern' Gaelic poets.

Ian 'Breac' MacLeod (d.1693) was the last patron/chief in a position to maintain a household complete with the traditional retinue of piper, **bard**, harper and fiddler and to offer the copious hospitality so well described by his **blind harper**-poet, Ruairidh Dall Morrison. Thereafter all is change and contraction, a gradual drawing of influences away from the Isles in the direction of London and ultimately to new lands overseas. And yet the Chiefs of MacLeod themselves continued to prosper at Dunvegan, precariously through the **Jacobite** period, then more confidently under **General Norman MacLeod**, a capable young soldier who returned from India with a fortune and a young wife and proceeded to modernise the castle before dying in 1801. His legacy, perhaps fortunately reduced in terms of acres, survived the terrible 19th century emigrations, **clearances** and famines under his grandson, who took

a job in London with the sole purpose of earning enough to keep the roof on Dunvegan and his people from starvation.

Sir Reginald MacLeod, a businessman and politician with a steady mind, saw the castle and the remaining Skye property through the critical early years of the 20th century. His daughter, Dame Flora, is remembered as the pioneer of world clanship, that curious sense of brotherhood compounded of sentimentality, kinship and the **tartan** myth. She was the last in the direct line from Ruairidh Mor, being succeeded by a grandson. The clan motto 'Hold Fast' has been upheld with tenacity through some seven centuries and, uniquely for the western clans, the annals of those years are preserved in historic documents at the castle. The Sons of Leod in their millions throughout the developed world have tangible roots to which to return.

MACLEOD, The Very Rev G F, Baron Fiunary (1895–1991) Churchman

Son of a **Glasgow** accountant and MP, George MacLeod was born in Glasgow and educated at Winchester and Oriel College, Oxford. As a captain with the **Argyll and Sutherland Highlanders** in World War I he won the MC and the Croix de Guerre but, appalled by the carnage in the trenches, the war hero returned a pacifist and dedicated Christian. After post-graduate work at **Edinburgh University**, he served as a missionary in British Columbia and then (1926) as minister at **St Cuthbert's Church, Edinburgh**. The city's finest preacher, he again fled the scene of triumph, this time (1933) to a desperate ministry in **Govan** at the height of the Depression. Breakdowns resulted and while convalescing he visited the Holy Land and attended an Easter Service in Jerusalem's Russian Orthodox Church. Thereafter, the man who once quipped that ' "**Presbyterian**" means "best in prayer" but "Episcopal" is merely an anagram for Pepsi Cola' was more ecumenist than **Calvinist**. In some disfavour with the Kirk, he left Govan (1938) to found the **Iona Community**.

This experiment involved restoring the monastic buildings adjacent to the cathedral church. Redundant craftsmen from Clydeside laboured alongside MacLeod's spiritual disciples. Critics found him too ready to act the laird, too much an eccentric showman to be a Christian radical; the Kirk looked askance at an ecumenical brotherhood that smacked of monasticism. But MacLeod proved indomitable, his community flourished, and eventually the **Church of Scotland** came to terms with it. His rehabilitation was completed with his election as **Moderator** of the **General Assembly** (1957–8), the most distinguished incumbent of the 20th century. Though a noted campaigner for nuclear disarmament, his eloquence, sincerity and stature endeared him to the establishment. He became a Chaplain to the Queen, Rector of Glasgow University, Fellow of Oriel and, as a life peer (1967), was the first Kirk minister to sit in the House of Lords. Surviving the publication of his authorised biography (1990) he died at the age of 96. 'This was a titanic figure straddling this century like no other Scot,' wrote a leader writer in the *Glasgow Herald*. 'He was a man of divine eloquence and numinous vision . . . a great radical, a great pacifist, a great churchman.'

MACLEOD, John James Rickard (1876–1935) Physiologist

Born near **Dunkeld**, MacLeod studied medicine at **Aberdeen** and at Leipzig before moving to London, the USA and finally Toronto in Canada, where he undertook important research on carbohydrate metabolism. He recruited the young Frederick Banting and Charles Best to begin a research programme to investigate the role of pancreatic islets in the body's regulation of sugar levels. Posterity seems unsure how much credit to assign to MacLeod for the resulting discovery of insulin, and there was some criticism of MacLeod's acceptance of the 1923 Nobel Prize for Medicine along with Banting. MacLeod returned to Aberdeen as Professor of Physiology in 1928, dying there in 1935.

MACLEOD, Mary (Màiri Nighean Alasdair Ruaidh) (c1615–c1707) Gaelic Poet

Born at Rodel, **Harris**, Mary MacLeod was closely associated with the **MacLeod** chiefs of Harris and **Dunvegan**. Her poetry is mostly in praise of them and other leading clan personalities, and uses many of the traditional figures and references; but it is set out in stressed metres rather than syllabic ones. She was evidently an important force in popularising these metres, which existed well before her time. Unlike her contemporary **Iain Lom**, she does not involve herself in the more general politics of her time, being content to give the flavour of living in the great MacLeod houses:

Gum biodh faram air thàilisg
Agus fuaim air a' chlàrsaich
Mar a bhuineadh do shàr mhac MhicLeòid.

(There was the staccato thump of chessmen
and the sounding of the harp,
as was fitting for MacLeod's excellent son.)

There are hints of her own distress in being for a time excluded from that society, but for the most part we get a warm, colourful appreciation of her patrons and their life-style, set out in fluent, mellifluous language. For texts see J C Watson, *Gaelic Songs of Mary MacLeod*, 1965.

MACLEOD, Rev Norman (i) (Caraid nan Gaidheal) (1783–1862) Gaelic Writer

Born in **Morvern**, MacLeod held charges in **Campbeltown**, Campsie and **Glasgow** and was **Moderator** of the **General Assembly** in 1836. He founded two **Gaelic** periodicals *An Teachdaire Gaelach* (1829–31) and *Cuairtear nan Gleann* (1840–43), and contributed many dialogues and essays to these and to other publications. He was concerned to extend the range of Gaelic writing, eg to current affairs, history, the sciences, pastimes etc, and to make Gaelic writing more accessible to the new literate public created by the Gaelic Schools movement in the first three-quarters of the 19th century. His writings are partially collected in *Leabhar nan Cnoc* ('Book of the Hills', 1834) and the posthumous collection *Caraid nan Gaidheal* (1867). The title of the latter, and the name by which he was known, means 'Friend of the Gaels'.

MACLEOD, Rev Norman (ii) (1812–72) Divine

This Norman Macleod, the son of (i), was born in **Campbeltown** and also became **Moderator** of the **General Assembly** (1869). After studying at **Glasgow University** he was ordained Minister of Loudoun in **Ayrshire**. A liberal churchman, he stayed with the Church during the **Disruption** and, after serving at **Dalkeith**, returned to Glasgow. As a preacher and as a contributor to the religious press he had few rivals; he also supported and visited the **Church of Scotland**'s missions in India. In 1857 he was appointed Chaplain to **Queen Victoria** and from 1860 he edited the Magazine *Good Works*. Other writings included the delightful *Reminiscences of a Highland Parish*, 1867.

MACMILLAN, Daniel (1813–57) Bookseller and Publisher

Macmillan was born on the Isle of **Arran**, the 10th child of a tenant farmer near **Irvine**, where he was educated. He was then apprenticed to a local bookbinder, moved to **Glasgow** in 1831 and to London in 1833. There bookselling proved more to his taste than production. A man of weak constitution but strong religious views, he came to regard the dissemination of printed works as being close to a vocation. With his brother Alexander he started his own shop in London (1843) and then Cambridge (1844), the latter being an immediate success. The brothers also launched into publishing, notching up two quick successes in Charles Kingsley's *Westward Ho!*, 1855, and Thomas Hughes's *Tom Brown's Schooldays*, 1857. In the same year ill health finally got the better of Daniel, but his two sons eventually joined their uncle in the business; one, Frederick, was chairman, the other Maurice, a partner and incidentally the father of Sir Harold Macmillan, the Prime Minister.

MACMILLAN, Kirkpatrick (1813–78) Inventor of the Bicycle

Fellow-villagers rated an inventive type like Kirkpatrick Macmillan, of Courthill Smithy, at Keir Mill, **Dumfriesshire**, as 'mad' for dreaming up an idea such as the first pedal-driven velocipede. But, although known locally as 'Daft Pate', he became in 1839 the inventor of the pedal-driven bicycle, used by millions today.

He rode his cumbersome machine 68 miles over rough roads from his tiny smithy home (still intact today) to **Glasgow**, visiting his two schoolteacher brothers in the city. In June 1842 the inventor was fined 5 Scots shillings for speeding at 8 mph into the **Gorbals** and knocking down a little girl in the crush that awaited this 'Devil on Wheels'. The magistrate at the Gorbals Public Bar was sufficiently impressed to ask Macmillan for a figure-of-eight demonstration in the courtyard, and is said to have slipped him the money for the fine.

Having raced the stage coach on his return to Dumfriesshire, Macmillan went back to the quiet life, but his invention was copied and an English firm put it on sale at £7. Macmillan's early machine, still seen in reproduction at the **Transport Museum** in Glasgow's **Kelvin Hall**, met popular demand for easier travel. It had wooden wheels and iron-band tyres, and was so heavy (57lb/25.8kg) that he pushed off by striking the ground with his feet, protected by iron-spiked boots.

He was one of the characters of 19th century rural Scotland. His son, John Macmillan of Liverpool who became a policeman in that city, told how his father, a keen churchman, refused to let the family even read on a Sunday. He pulled teeth for both humans and horses and was a popular fiddle-player at weddings. He died on 26 January 1878 aged 65, and the plaque on his smithy home reads 'He builded Better than He Knew'.

MACMILLAN, Roddy (1923–79) Actor and Dramatist

Best remembered for his portrayal of Para Handy in the television dramatisations of **Neil Munro**'s eponymous tales, MacMillan had made his name on stage and also wrote for the theatre. He was born and brought up in **Glasgow** and it was in the **Citizens' Theatre** that his *All in Good Faith*, 1954, was first performed: 'it caused a sensation with its vividly realistic portrayal of Glasgow working class life' (T Royle).

MACNAB, Clan

The name Macnab is a rendering of the Gaelic *Mac an Aba* (or *Abba*) – 'The children of the Abbot'. According to tradition the original ancestor was the Abbot of Glendochart and Strathearn, younger son of **Kenneth mac-Alpin**. The Macnabs are thus members of the Siol-an-Alpine, otherwise called Clan Alpine.

Macnab as a surname was first found in a chartulary of 1124; in 1306 Angus Macnab joined MacDougall of Lorn in his victory over **Robert I** at **Dalry (Dalrigh)**, and in his defeat by him at the **Pass of Brander** (1308); after **Bannockburn** (1314) the Macnab lands were for-

Archibald Macnab of Macnab, the last of his line, by an unknown artist, c1830 (SNPG)

feited; in 1336 however Gilbert of Bovain received a charter from **David II** whereby they were restored, and Gilbert is now regarded as the first authentic chief of Macnab.

The Macnab country stretched from **Tyndrum** in **Perthshire** west as far as **Dalmally** in **Argyll** and east down Glendochart to **Killin**, where the old Macnab Castle of Eilean Ran was originally situated on an island on the north bank of the river Lochay. Alternately indebted to and at loggerheads with their powerful neighbours, the Macnabs incurred the wrath of the **Breadalbane Campbells** when the 13th Chief 'Smooth John' led his clan to fight for **Montrose** at the **Battle of Kilsyth** (1645) and for **Charles II** at Worcester (1651). Smooth John was killed near Killin in 1653 by Cromwell's troops who then destroyed the Castle of Eilean Ran. Restored to their lands by Charles II, the Macnabs moved into Kinnell House at Killin which became the family seat.

Although some of his clansmen supported the **Jacobites**, John (15th Chief) was a major in the Hanoverian army during the '45 **Rising**, was taken prisoner at **Prestonpans** and confined in **Doune Castle**. His son, the colourful Francis (16th Chief), 'a prodigious consumer of whisky', fathered countless natural children but no legitimate heir and died in 1816 leaving crippling debts which his nephew Archibald, 17th Chief and last of his line, fled to Canada to escape. In 1828 the Macnab lands, including Kinnell House, were sold to the 4th Earl of Breadalbane. Of Alexander's eight children, none of whom married, three sons predeceased him and his eldest daughter Sarah Anne was recognised as 18th Chief *de jure*. After her death in 1894 the succession to the chiefship was not decided until 1954 when Archibald Corrie, of the Arthurstone branch of the family, who bought back Kinnell House and some of the Macnab lands from the Campbells in 1949, was recognised as 22nd Chief. Today the only original Macnab land still in clan possession is the clan burial ground on the island of Inchbuie in the river Dochart at Killin. The present (23rd) Chief is James Charles Macnab of Macnab, nephew of Archibald Corrie. The clan motto is *Timor Omnis Abesto* – 'Be All Fear Absent'.

MCNEIL, Dr Charles (1881–1964) Physician

Born in **Stranraer**, Wigtonshire, son of a doctor, Charles McNeil was educated at **George Watson's College** and **Edinburgh University**, graduating in 1901. From 1915–18 he was in charge of the Scottish Hospital in Rouen, France, and was mentioned in despatches. Previously assistant physician in the Royal Edinburgh Hospital for Sick Children and paediatrician to the Royal Maternity Hospital, in 1931 Charles McNeil became the first occupant of Edinburgh's new Chair of Child Life and Health. He was a strong advocate of neo-natal care, and a pioneer of health visitors. One of his house physicians at the Simpson Memorial Maternity Hospital recalled that his chief insisted that a large red 'S' should be placed on the chart when a baby smiled after a severe illness; another describes the professor as a man with a gracious manner, a radiant smile and a delightful sense of humour. He was President of the **Royal College of Physicians** from 1940–3 and on his retirement he was given the honorary degree of LL.D of Edinburgh.

MACNEIL, Clan

Although small, Clan Macneil is one of the proudest of the Scottish clans. Its chiefs claim direct descent from Niall of the Nine Hostages, High King of Ireland in the 5th century, through Neil, who left Ireland for Scotland in the early 11th century. The relationship of the two main branches of the clan, that of **Barra** and that of **Gigha-Knapdale** (sometimes called **Colonsay** Macneils), is somewhat unclear, each claiming to be the senior line. Today both are united under a single chief, the Macneil of Barra.

Starting in the 1400s the Macneils maintained a high profile, being much involved in the politics of the **Lordship of the Isles**, as well as in lawlessness and piracy. Particularly notable was Ruari the Turbulent, who seized an English ship and was hauled before **James VI** for having thus offended Queen Elizabeth. The King spared Ruari who reputedly told his sovereign he supposed he had done him a favour by outraging the woman who had murdered the King's mother. The last of the old lawless and raiding chiefs was Ruari Dhu who carried a huge battle axe at **Killiecrankie**, and later refused to take the oath to King William. He died of a dirk wound, incurred on a supposed cattle raid, which was perhaps really a **Jacobite** spy mission.

The outside world gradually intruded on the life of the clan and its chiefs, as Barra became more integrated into modern British society. The **kelp** industry rose and fell, the **potato** came, with its good and its ill. The people of Barra remained poor in worldly goods, although rich of community and spirit. Emigration took its toll, with a diaspora to the mainland, to the American colonies, and later to the United States, to Cape Breton, Australia and New Zealand. But the Gaelic remained as did the Catholic Church, both in Barra and to some extent in Cape Breton.

The stronghold of the Macneils is **Kisimul Castle**. Known as the Castle in the Sea, it sits on a rock in Castlebay and at high tide is surrounded by water. An underground seam brings fresh water through the underlying rock strata to a well. The people needed only to fortify the island to make the bay secure against marauders. As the power of central government superseded the strength of the clans, the importance of Kisimul declined; in the mid-18th century it was abandoned and in 1795 a fire destroyed the roofs and floors. There followed in the 19th century the loss through bankruptcy of Barra itself and its acquisition by one of the more notorious Highland landlords. In 1863 the last of the old chiefs died.

Kisimul Castle was, however, destined to rise again and become once more the home of the Macneil chiefs and a living symbol for the Clan Macneil. In 1937, Robert Lister Macneil of Barra, 45th Chief, re-acquired the estate of Barra and the ruins of the castle. Restoration began in 1938 and was finally completed in 1972.

MACPHEE, Ewen (c1785–c1850) Outlaw

Arrested as a deserter in about 1805, MacPhee made his escape by jumping over a precipice and went to ground on an island in the middle of **Loch Quoich**. There remained for the rest of his life, living in conditions deemed horribly primitive even by his Highland contemporaries. He built a hut of birch sticks and turf in which to shelter from Quoich's excessive rainfall, kept goats and raised a family after persuading a 14-year-old girl to share his dreary kingdom. A man of vast proportions and wild appearance, he always wore Highland dress and never ventured forth without being armed. He was thus held in awe and kept well supplied with provisions. These were supplemented by donations from all over the kingdom when the *Inverness Chronicle* publicised the plight of his family. When in the 1830s the Loch Quoich estate was acquired by the English millionaire and MP Edward Ellice, MacPhee confronted him with a bowl of goat's milk and an offer to respect the Englishman's rights so long as he was left in undisturbed possession of his own kingdom. Ellice evidently accepted. 'The grizzled aspect, intrepid bearing, and free speech of the bold outlaw struck the Englishman with surprise, and Ewen instantly became a sort of favourite' (*Inverness Chronicle*). MacPhee's island, like the Ellice mansion, disappeared beneath the waters of the loch when the level was raised by a **hydro-electric** dam.

MACPHERSON, Clan

The name Macpherson comes from the Gaelic *Mac a Phearsain* and means literally 'Son of the Parson'. In the case of all families related to the Clan Macpherson of **Badenoch** and the Castlelands of **Inverness**, the name refers to Muriach, the lay prior or parson of **Kingussie** in Badenoch, on the upper waters of the **Spey**. His three grandsons were The Three Brethren, from whom are descended all those Macphersons who belong to the three main lines of the clan lineage known as Macpherson of Cluny, Macpherson of Pitmain and Macpherson of Invereshie.

For many generations the chief of the clan, known always as Cluny Macpherson, lived at Cluny Castle, **Laggan**, in the county of Inverness. In 1940 the Cluny estates were sold, and the present chief, Sir William Macpherson of Cluny, lives at Newton Castle, **Blairgowrie**, **Perthshire**, where his great-great-great grandfather settled in 1788, after many years' service in India.

The Macphersons have always been one of the leading clans in the **Clan Chattan** confederacy, together with **Clan Mackintosh**, Clan Shaw and others. The clan and its septs also forged strong friendship with **Clan Grant**, and played an active and sometimes warlike part in the complex relations of those who lived in northern Scotland, until many members of the clan dispersed world-wide after the 1745 Rising.

During this **Jacobite** adventure Cluny's regiment (of some 350 men) marched to Derby to support the Prince. At **Falkirk** they took part in the last successful engagement before the defeat at **Culloden**, suffering many casualties. The clan was detached before Culloden to contain militia posts in **Atholl** and Badenoch, and thus took no part in the fateful last battle. They formed the rearguard as the Prince's army fell back to **Ruthven** in Badenoch. Thereafter the fugitive Prince was sheltered by Cluny [see **Ewen MacPherson**] and his clansmen in the famous cave on the steep side of Creag Dubh, and in the makeshift 'cage' on the slopes of **Ben Alder**. Ewen, who led his clan in these historic months, followed the Prince to France after spending nine long years 'in the heather' protected by his loyal clansfolk.

Present-day Macphersons cover the world. Strong branches of the Clan Association thrive in the USA, Canada, New Zealand and England. The Clan Macpherson House and Museum at **Newtonmore** is a focal point for all, and there can be seen some of the relics of the clan, and much of its history and heraldry.

Three **tartans** are in regular use: the grey Hunting Tartan, the Dress Tartan and the Red or Badenoch Tartan. Of these the present chief favours the Hunting Tartan, which has been worn for at least 200 years by himself and his predecessors. The chief's crest is the wildcat. His motto is 'Touch Not the Cat But a Glove', meaning (in his favourite interpretation) touch not the cat when it is without a glove. The 'glove' of the wildcat is the soft part of the paw into which the claws are normally retracted. When the cat assumes a hostile posture the paw is spread and the claws are bared or ungloved. The motto is a warning to those who would be imprudent enough to engage the Macpherson wildcat in battle.

MACPHERSON, Ewen, of Cluny (c1700–?1756) Jacobite

Though a pillar of the Hanoverian establishment in the Grampians, MacPherson switched allegiance at the beginning of the 1745 **Jacobite Rising**. He may have heeded some advice from his father-in-law, **Simon Fraser, 11th Lord Lovat**, or he may have been rebuffed by General Cope; he was certainly captured during a **Jacobite** attack on **Ruthven Barracks** though this may have been staged to exonerate him from any subsequent accusation of wilful treason. If so it failed. He joined **Prince Charles Edward Stewart** after **Prestonpans**, fought with distinction in the Lake District and, though he missed **Culloden**, was outlawed. 'Of a low stature, very square, and a dark brown complexion', he then survived for nine years in the hills of **Badenoch** thanks to a robust constitution and the loyalty of his clansmen. With his cousin, **Cameron of Lochiel**, he there secreted the Prince in September 1746 and urged the latter's flight to France. 'Cluny's Cage' on **Ben Alder** was one of their hiding places [see also **Newtonmore**]. He was one of those delegated to look after the **Loch Arkaig** treasure but in 1754 was at last authorised by the Prince to repair to France. The DNB gives the date of his death as 1764.

MACPHERSON, James (1736–96) Poet and Translator

Born near **Kingussie**, the son of a farmer, James Macpherson was a student at **Aberdeen** and **Edinburgh Universities**. In 1756 he was put in charge of the charity school at **Ruthven**. Through his friendship with **John Home**, author of *Douglas*, **Adam Ferguson** and **Hugh Blair**, then Professor of Rhetoric at the University of Edinburgh, he was encouraged to follow up his interest in ancient **Gaelic poetry**. His small book of 'translations', entitled *Fragments of Ancient Poetry, Collected in the Highlands of Scotland* (Edinburgh, 1760), was favourably received. In an unsigned preface, Blair suggested that epic poetry relating to **Fingal** and passed on by his son Ossian might still be extant. A subscription was taken to enable Macpherson to make journeys to various parts of the Highlands in search of further manuscripts, resulting in two publications: *Fingal, an Ancient Epic Poem,*

composed by Ossian the son of Fingal (London, 1762) and *Temora, an Ancient Epic Poem* (London, 1765). A 'carefully corrected, and greatly improved' edition was published in 1773 as *The Poems of Ossian* (London). The success in Scotland and England as well as on the Continent surpassed all expectations. *Ossian* soon ranked as a literary sensation. Translations into German, French, Italian, Danish, Swedish, Polish and Russian appeared, not to mention the literary vogue it created and the impact it had on European literature in general. Readers and critics alike enjoyed the poems for their romantic spirit and pure primitivist sentiment, without reflecting upon their authenticity.

But there were also voices of doubt, first and foremost **Samuel Johnson**, claiming that *Ossian* was a literary fraud. In Scotland, **David Hume** and **James Beattie** suggested that Macpherson should produce the Gaelic originals, though others, **Lord Kames** and **Henry Mackenzie** for instance, adhered to their conviction that the poems were translations originating in a genuine, however fragmentary, 3rd century Gaelic epic. After Macpherson's death, Mackenzie was appointed convener of a committee of the Highland Society of Scotland to investigate the nature and authenticity of the Ossianic poems. In their report (1805) the committee took the view that poems existed which could be called Ossianic, and that Macpherson had liberally added passages of his own to create his epics.

As an episode in Scottish literature, Macpherson's *Ossian* sparked off a continuing literary controversy. Equally it is a striking proof of the fact that literary works neither exist outside national identities and traditions nor arise in isolation from the spirit and intellectual climate of their day. However fascinating and intriguing a piece of Scottish, indeed European, literary and cultural history the Ossianic controversy may be, Macpherson failed to realise the full literary and historical significance of the fragmentary evidence he had initially collected. For his so-called translations he made use of what can be regarded as authentic material, generously filling out the plot and adapting text and structure according to his own imagination. Recent criticism seems to be ready to view the Ossianic publications as a much more serious literary-cum-sociocultural outcome than 20th century scholars have been in the habit of doing.

MACPHERSON, Sir John (1745–1821)
Governor-General of India

As a stop-gap Governor-General (1785–6), MacPherson succeeded Warren Hastings and was replaced by Lord Cornwallis; both were initially taken in by his affable manner but both soon recognised him as 'the most contemptible and contemned governor that ever pretended to govern' (Cornwallis). A genial 6ft 3in (1.9m) and not without ability, he had been born in **Skye**, the son of a minister and the first cousin of **James 'Ossian' Macpherson**. After **Edinburgh University** he went to Madras as a purser in the East India Company and inveigled his way into the confidence of the Nawab of the Carnatic. As the Nawab's agent in London he shared handsomely in his liberality and, securing a writership in the Company, returned to Madras to assist in exploiting the Nawab's indebtedness. Dismissed for corruption, he was reinstated in 1781 and mysteriously chosen as a member of the Supreme Council in Calcutta in 1782. Supporting then deserting Hastings, he succeeded to the governor-generalship by seniority and during his brief tenure of office introduced some much needed financial retrenchment while lining his own and his friends' pockets. On returning to England he was created a baronet (1786), awarded a substantial pension, and elected to Parliament. Although unseated and fined for bribery, he contrived another comeback and became an intimate of the Prince Regent. 'He was, of course, quite without principle' (P Moon).

MACPHERSON, Mary (Màiri Mhòr nan Oran) (1821–98) Gaelic Poet

Born in Skeabost, **Skye**, 'Mary of the Songs' lived mainly in **Inverness** and **Glasgow** but identified closely with the **Highland Land War** and the political campaigns that led to the **crofting** legislation of the 1880s [see **Napier Commission** etc]. Her poetry is often down-to-earth and populist, and also shows great independence. Some of her songs in praise and memory of Skye are still very popular eg. *Nuair bha mi òg* ('When I was young'). For texts see D E Meek, *Màiri Mhòr nan Oran*, 1977.

MACQUARIE, Lachlan (1762–1824) Soldier, Governor of New South Wales

A native of the island of **Ulva**, Macquarie volunteered at the age of 14 and served with Highland regiments in America, Jamaica, India and Egypt. In 1807, as a lieutenant-colonel, he returned from India overland through Persia and Russia and in 1809 successfully engineered his appointment as Governor of New South Wales in succession to the impossible Captain Bligh of *Bounty* notoriety. He held the post until 1821, the longest tenure of any Australian governor, during which he transformed the country from an iniquitous gaol into a thriving colony, and Sydney from a shanty settlement into a jaunty little Georgian city. By kindness towards the convict population, encouragement of the pardoned convicts (emancipists), and liberal attitudes towards the Aboriginal population, he set new standards of paternal government. He controlled alcoholism and prostitution, encouraged education and exploration, and embarked on a massive public works programme including schools, hospitals, churches and what is still the grid lay-out of central Sydney.

But such 'a fine example of that breed of Scottish administrators who kept the engine room of Empire working' (Robert Hughes) eventually incurred the censure of the home government for leniency and extravagance. He was replaced by **Sir Thomas Brisbane** and had scarcely cleared his name at the time of his death. Today he is rightly seen as 'the father of Australia'. Sydney's Macquarie University is named after him; so is much of south-east Australia's topography, a fact widely commented on and recorded by **Rev J D Lang** in a verse which ends:

Macquarie Street, Place, Port, Fort, Town, Lake, River,
'Lachlan Macquarie, Esquire, Governor' for ever!

There are biographies by M H Ellis, 1947 and J Ritchie, 1986.

MACQUEEN, Robert, Lord Braxfield (1722–99) Judge

Born in **Lanarkshire**, educated at **Lanark** Grammar School and **Edinburgh University**, and admitted advocate in 1744, MacQueen became a Lord of Session as Lord Braxfield in 1776 and Lord Justice Clerk in 1788.

Robert MacQueen, Lord Braxfield, by Sir Henry Raeburn, c1798 (SNPG)

An expert on feudal law, he acted for the Crown in cases concerning the forfeiture of **Jacobite** estates. The presiding judge at the trial of **Deacon Brodie**, his most infamous trial was that of **Thomas Muir of Huntershill** when even the jury, hand-picked by Braxfield, was stunned by the flagrant injustice of Muir's sentence. Known as the 'hanging judge' and described as 'beetle-browed, red-faced, with glowering eyes, thick lips, and growling voice, which made his victims in the dock to tremble; a man without heart or pity', Braxfield was the model for **Robert Louis Stevenson**'s *Weir of Hermiston*.

MACRAE, Duncan (1905–67) Entertainer

Born in **Glasgow**, of Highland **crofting** stock, John Duncan Macrae was a schoolteacher before making a successful switch to the theatre. He had a lanky, angular figure and wide mouth, apt for comedy, and was often compared for physique with the comedian **Tommy Lorne**. He appeared frequently at the **Citizens' Theatre** in Glasgow and played notable roles in films such as *Whisky Galore*, *The Kidnappers* and *Tunes of Glory* before making his name as a revue and pantomime comedian. He often said that his favourite role was that of a 'dignified fool'. He appeared at the **Edinburgh Festival** and in plays in Glasgow, Edinburgh and London. His recitation of *The Wee Cock Sparra* has become a near-classic.

MACTAGGART, John (1797–1830) Writer

MacTaggart was the author of *The Scottish Gallovidian Encyclopaedia*, 1824, a rare and original work, the only other encyclopaedia of Scottish subjects known to the compilers of this one, and much admired by them. When **J H MacCulloch** described it as 'a grotesquely imperfect magnum opus' MacTaggart would have agreed happily; for, while containing a wealth of improbable information about **Galloway** plus some enjoyable poems and many vernacular terms, it is essentially the creation of a man of decided views, 'ane quarter wise, three quarters mad', who rejoiced to parade them. For his own details one can do no better than turn to the appropriate entry in the *Encyclopaedia*.

'MACTAGGART. This is no less a personage than myself, born some twenty-five years ago, at Plunton, in the parish of Borgue, quite beside the *auld castle o' Plunton*.' It appears that he was one of 11 children and his father a tenant farmer. They moved to near **Kirkcudbright** where MacTaggart found a schoolmaster to his liking. 'I begat an affection for arithmetic ... going through all the count books which came before me like smoke.' But after transferring to Kirkcudbright Academy he 'took a huff at schools and schoolmasters altogether' and aged 12 decided to educate himself. He learnt Latin and French, gleaned much from the *Encyclopaedia Britannica*, and briefly attended **Edinburgh University**. 'Before this time I had taken a ramble through England, had been often in love, had wrote poetry, and devil knows what.' Unfortunately lack of space prevented him from dealing with his 'subsequent wanderings through Scotland, my trip to London, my rebuffs from fortune and my receiving them kindly', etc. He evidently returned to Galloway about 1815 and, despising books, gathered the material for his work on foot and by enquiry.

Sadly the book had to be withdrawn as soon as it was published. An entry on 'THE STAR OF DUNGYLE', a dazzling beauty who bestowed her favours freely only on 'boxers and bruisers ... and she would lay in barns with them at night', clearly identified the lady as a Miss Herron. Her father threatened MacTaggart with an action unless all copies were immediately destroyed. A few, however, survived and there were small reprints in 1876 and 1981, the latter with an invaluable introduction by L L Ardern. After what must have been a terrible disappointment, MacTaggart returned to London, taught maths, tried to start a newspaper, and became a gas company engineer. In 1826 **John Rennie** recommended him for the job of engineer on the Rideau Canal project in Ontario where he renewed his acquaintance with **John Galt** and whence he returned after three years to write a substantial book on Canada. A long poem, *The Engineer*, was in manuscript and an encyclopaedia of Canada in the offing when he died, still only 32, in his beloved Galloway. A contemporary described him as 6ft 2in (1.9m) and of majestic proportions. 'He was fearless in asserting his opinions, hated duplicity, and his friendships were warm and lasting.' Just so with his *Encyclopaedia*.

MACTAGGART, Sir John (1867–1956)
Builder and Contractor
Born and educated in **Glasgow**, MacTaggart's first industrial experience was with Robert Mickel, timber merchants of **Govan**. At the age of 31 he set up in partnership to build tenements in Springburn. Three years later he founded his own firm and proceeded to

construct over 2000 tenements for middle-class dwellers in the south and the west of the city. During and after World War I he became a vocal advocate of solutions to the prevailing housing crisis and, following the Addison Act of 1919, won important local authority contracts at Riddrie and Mosspark. With a reputation for innovation in the use of materials, industrial organisation and labour relations, during the 1930s he exploited the Western Heritable Investment Company in order to construct over 6000 houses under the terms of the 1924 Housing Act. Arguably the single most influential figure in the Scottish construction industry, 'he built over 20,000 flats and houses in Glasgow, **Edinburgh** and London' (*Who's Who*, 1941).

MCTAGGART, William (1835–1910) Painter
An independent and innovative spirit, McTaggart was a unique product of the Scottish school of landscape painting. Born of humble origins in **Campbeltown** his precocious artistic gifts were soon apparent and in 1852 he moved to **Edinburgh** to study at the **Trustees' Academy**. There, under the inspiring tutelage of **Robert Scott Lauder** and alongside a gifted group of contemporaries, including **Chalmers** and **Orchardson**, he developed a highly refined sense of colour and tone. His early work shows the influence of early Italian Renaissance painters and the English Pre-Raphaelites although lacking the latter's peculiar facilities of draughtsmanship. By the 1860s, however, critics were observing a broader and looser handling of paint in his work and increasingly he paid far greater attention to the effects of light and atmosphere than to figures and composition. At the same time he began increasingly to paint out of doors, especially in the summer, working his oil or watercolour sketches up into larger paintings in his Edinburgh studio in the winter. His most celebrated works depict **Carnoustie** Bay in the east or Machrihanish Bay in the west.

Despite their remarkably free handling of paint, McTaggart's works received considerable acclaim. (He often inserted picturesque figures at a later stage to increase their commercial appeal.) Although he visited Paris there is no evidence McTaggart saw the early Impressionists, and his pictures bear only a passing resemblance to their work, being far more deeply rooted in the tradition of **Thomson of Duddingston** and the English painters Turner and Constable. McTaggart had no direct followers but his work inspired many of the younger generation of artists (not least his own grandson, **Sir William**) with its advocacy of plein air painting and freedom of expression. His popularity also served to make the west coast of Scotland a popular artistic haunt.

MACTAGGART, Sir William (1903–81)
Painter
With **William Crozier**, **William Gillies**, **John Maxwell** and **Anne Redpath**, MacTaggart was a central figure during the formative years of the **Edinburgh** School. Born at Loanhead, south of Edinburgh, grandson of the renowned 19th century landscape painter **William McTaggart**, he began his studies at the **Edinburgh College of Art** in 1918. Ill-health prevented his following Crozier and Gillies to study under André Lhote in

Paris, and though through them (he was to share a studio successively with both) he would have become aware of the formal developments taking place in art there, his own early work remained closer in style to the highly coloured Fauvist-inspired landscapes of the then established **S J Peploe** and the other Scottish Colourists [see **Painting in Scotland**]. His first of many annual visits to France was made in 1923 where at Cannes during his first solo exhibition a year later he met Matthew Smith, the English painter who had studied briefly under Matisse and whose increasingly emotional and intuitive style MacTaggart greatly admired.

From the earliest, MacTaggart's laboured and richly coloured use of oil set his work apart from the more refined statements produced by his Edinburgh School contemporaries working in the French tradition of *belle peinture*. The exhibition of work by Edward Munch at the Society of Scottish Artists in 1931 profoundly influenced his style and though he avoided the moral angst that gave the Norwegian artist's work such impact, the many landscapes he painted subsequently in France, Italy and Scotland grew increasingly expressionistic in tenor in his desire to communicate mood. In 1933 he was elected President of the SSA and began teaching part-time at the ECA.

After the war, the glowing colours of paint, though not the religious symbolism, in the work of Rouault played an important part in his development and he turned increasingly to the subject of still-life, often set to great atmospheric effect against the night view from his studio window overlooking Edinburgh's **New Town**. As a member of the Council for the **Edinburgh International Festival** from 1948 he was responsible for a series of exhibitions that greatly distinguished the Festival's early years. A regular exhibitor at the **Royal Scottish Academy**, he was elected its President in 1959 and in 1963 he was knighted for his services to the arts.

MACHAR, Saint (fl.c600)

St Machar is said to have been one of the 12 monks who accompanied **St Columba** to **Iona**. Thence, like St Drostan [see **Deer**], and supposedly after arousing Columba's jealousy, he was despatched to the east and came eventually to **Aberdeen** where he recognised the shape of a crozier in a bend of the river **Don** and so founded his church. But all this could just be a later attempt to give a respected Columban pedigree to one who was really of the **Pictish** Church. Aberdeen's **Cathedral** is dedicated to him.

MAELRUBHA, Saint (c642-722)

Of part **Pictish** blood, this Irish missionary saint came to Scotland from Bangor monastery in Ulster c671. He founded a monastery at **Applecross** in Wester **Ross** which was second only to **Iona** as a Christian centre. Before 700 he is said to have converted the inhabitants of parts of **Banffshire** to Christianity. He lived for a while as a hermit on the Isle of Maree (ie 'Maelrubha') in **Loch Maree** where he is reputed to be buried, but similar claims are made both for Applecross and for the village of Syre in **Strathnaver**. There local legend insists that he was murdered by **Vikings** (and they have a

stone marking his grave to prove it). He is credited with bringing Christianity to much of the far north of Scotland.

MAES HOWE, Mainland, Orkney

Stuart Piggott wrote of the chambered **cairn** of Maes Howe that 'the assured mastery over building material marks it out as a monument in prehistoric Britain comparable only to Stonehenge in its individual handling of an architectural problem.' The gigantic stones of which the chambers and entrance passage are constructed, and the mound 24ft (7.3m) high and 115ft (35m) in diameter that was raised over them, all involved fantastic labour. Maes Howe is considered to represent the culmination of an already ancient local building tradition and to date from around 2800 BC. The similarity of ground plan to that of Newgrange in County Meath suggests the possibility of contacts between **Orkney** and **Ireland**.

In the 12th century **Viking** Norsemen broke into the tomb and carved on its walls the largest single set of graffiti in runic characters found anywhere in Europe. They are devoted mainly to the subject of loot. Unfortunately the first excavation was undertaken in 1861 by breaking into the chamber through the top of the mound.

MAGNUS III OF NORWAY (r.1093-1103)

This turbulent king, known as 'Barfor' in Norwegian and as 'Barelegs' (which is different and suggests that he may have worn some kind of **kilt**) in English, succeeded his father, founder of Bergen, in 1093. By 1098 he had subdued **Orkney**, where he left his son **Sigurd** as his deputy. After plundering the **Hebrides** he made the Isle of Man his base for an invasion of Wales. Happily he perished in Ireland in 1103. It was he who made the first formal treaty with a King of Scots, recognising the Western Isles and **Kintyre** as the property of Norway, which endured until 1266. Magnus lived on in Gaelic **ballads** as *Manus Righ Lochlainn*, a latter-day Menelaus with whose wife the Ossianic hero eloped.

MAGNUS, Saint (d.1116/7) Earl of Orkney

It is curious that the epithet applied to Charles the Great, or Charlemagne ('Magnus'), should have been adopted with such enthusiasm as a personal name by the descendants of the then pagan Norsemen whom Charlemagne harried with such religious zeal. Magnus, the future saint, a grandson of **Thorfinn the Mighty**, shared the Earldom of **Orkney** with his cousin Haakon until the latter decided that the islands held an earl too many. He arranged an Easter tryst on the isle of **Egilsay**, to which Magnus came unarmed according to their agreement. Haakon arrived with an armed band and Magnus was murdered treacherously in circumstances graphically described in the **Orkneyinga Saga**. At first the Bishop of Orkney declined to credit the miracles alleged to have been performed in Magnus's time, probably reflecting that the Earl had shown few signs of sanctity during his life. But in the end he was convinced, and so the process that led to Magnus's canonisation began. Magnus is commemorated in the cathedral named in his honour in **Kirkwall** and, today, by the book written about him by the Catholic Orcadian writer **George**

Maes Howe chambered cairn; 'design and workmanship not otherwise known in Neolithic Britain' (entry p 703) (HS)

Mackay Brown, which helped to inspire Peter Maxwell Davies' opera on the same theme.

MAINLAND, Shetland

The largest island in **Shetland** is known simply as the Mainland, a name which reflects the independent outlook of the islanders for whom the British mainland is more than 100 miles away. It is a large island of 351 square miles with a population of just under 20,000 of whom 8000 live in **Lerwick**. **Scalloway**, with a population of over 1000, is the second largest settlement. Although 55 miles long and 20 miles wide at its widest point, the island is so dissected by long inlets, known as 'voes', that no part is more than three miles from the sea.

Most of the island is composed of hard, non-porous rocks, including schists, gneiss and granite, covered with boulder clay and topped with a blanket of **peat**. The vegetation consists mainly of **heather** and rough grass which support over 200,000 sheep (including lambs), many of them the pure Shetland breed. **Crofting** townships occupy the best land and some have become small villages, among the best examples being Sandwick in the South Mainland, Aith and Walls in the West and Brae and Voe in the North.

Crofting is mainly a part-time occupation, except at the South Mainland where good soils overlie sandstone rock. Elsewhere most people have to travel a considerable distance to jobs at Lerwick, **Sumburgh** Airport or the **Sullom Voe oil** terminal. **Fishing** and fish processing are major industries at Lerwick and Scalloway and there are smaller fishing communities at Skeld, West Burrafirth and Ronas Voe. Since the 1980s **fish farming** has brought much-needed employment to many rural areas.

The island is hilly – well over 1000ft (305m) in places. The scenery ranges from the beautiful sandy beaches of Dunrossness to the rugged cliffs of the West Mainland. In Northmavine Ronas Hill reaches a height of 1468ft (447m), rising steeply from sea level as a spectacular mass of red granite. Because of the salt-laden winds and heavy grazing, trees are confined to fenced plantations in sheltered spots such as Kergord in Weisdale [see also **Shetland**].

MAIR (or MAJOR), John (1467/8–1550)
Philosopher and Historian

A great scholastic logician, Mair was born at Gleghornie near **Haddington**, **East Lothian**. He studied briefly at Cambridge, but as was more usual for a Scot of his day, Paris was his real centre, first as a student and then as one of the most famous teachers in Europe. Back in Scotland (1518–25) he taught at **Glasgow**, then at **St Andrews** before returning to Paris. In 1533 he was Provost of **St Salvator's College** in St Andrews where **John Knox**, one of his pupils, held him in high regard. Theologian and churchman as well as philosopher and logician (an inevitable combination), Mair did not live to see the **Reformation**. Which side he would have taken is an intriguing question; he was certainly a critic of abuses in the Church, and in Paris Jean Calvin was probably one of his pupils.

Mair also wrote an intriguing *Historia Maioris Britanniae* (1521) favouring a unity of Scotland and England, though political difficulties are underlined by its being dedicated to the by then discredited Cardinal Wolsey. Rabelais satirised him and Erasmus was quite rude about him, for Mair was the exponent of an involved scholastic logic which was fast becoming old hat in a Europe of new Greek learning and access to Aristotle in the original. In a 1983 study of an important Mair pupil (George *Lokert the Logician*) Alexander Broadie begins with an outstanding chapter on the cultural import of Mair and notes that Scotland spawned a disproportionate number of such logicians whose long-scorned work produced studies of reasoning potentially fruitful for modern abstract modelling procedures and for the theory of language. And despite being scorned for a manner unfashionable in his day, Mair not least as historian displays an understanding of scientific method well ahead of it. See: *A History of Great Britain*, ed & trans A J G Mackay, Edinburgh, 1892; *The Scottish Tradition of Philosophy*, Alexander Broadie, 1990, is a rare successful generally-addressed work handling the period; the journal *The Innes Review* carries much historical material by John Durkan et al.

John Maitland, 1st Duke of Lauderdale, by Sir Peter Lely, c1665 (SNPG)

MAITLAND, Sir John, of Thirlestane (1543–95) Secretary of State

Like his elder brother **William Maitland of Lethington**, John (or 'Thirlestane') supported the exiled ex-**Queen Mary** in 1570–3 and was one of those who holed out in **Edinburgh Castle** until it was taken by the English for Regent **Morton** in 1573. Lethington escaped punishment by dying; but Thirlestane, too young perhaps for so shrewd a career move, was taken prisoner and remained so for five years. The end of Morton's regency brought release while the advent of **Esmé Stewart** (soon **Earl of Lennox**) and of James Stewart (soon **Earl of Arran**) meant a new generation of powerful patrons with influence over the boy King **James VI**. Under Lennox, Thirlestane became Lord of Session (1581) and, under Arran, Secretary of State (1584). His politics were those of his brother – support for the reformed Church and close relations with England leading to the eventual succession of the young James to both thrones. He survived Arran's fall (1585) and, as James VI took power into his own hands, was advanced to Keeper of the Seal (1586) and Lord Chancellor (1587), 'the first in the century who was neither prelate nor peer' (G Donaldson). With a brief intermission in 1592–4 Thirlestane remained in power until his death. He was liked neither by the nobility, who resented his rise and influence, nor by the King, who welcomed his death as an opportunity to rule on his own. But his abilities were unquestioned and did much to lay the basis for the 40-year 'King's Peace' which began in 1596.

MAITLAND, John, 2nd Earl and 1st Duke of Lauderdale (1616–82)

The grandson of **John Maitland of Thirlestane** and so great-nephew of **William Maitland of Lethington**, this

Maitland succeeded in 1645 to his father's Earldom of Lauderdale, by which title he is usually known. 'A complete politique, like Lethington' (W Ferguson), he had signed the **Covenant** for career reasons rather than conviction and by 1641 was representing the Scottish Assembly in London and was a Commissioner for the Solemn League and Covenant. But by 1647 he was endeavouring to mediate between **Charles I** and his captors and by the end of that year, now a Royalist, he was one of those who secured the King's assent to the **Engagement**. He took no part in the subsequent campaign which ended with the Scots defeat at **Preston**, but in Holland persuaded **Charles II** to come to Scotland for coronation under Covenanting auspices (1650) and attended the King south to defeat at Worcester (1651). Captured and consigned to the Tower of London, he remained in prison until the Restoration (1660), when his friendship with Charles II at last paid handsome dividends.

As alternately Secretary for Scotland in London (he was the 'L' in Charles's acronymic CABAL) and the King's Commissioner in Scotland, he shuttled back and forth for the next 20 years wielding a power over Scottish affairs that was unprecedented in a subject. In the process he gave Scotland its first taste of ministerial government and set for that unfortunate system the standards of corruption, deceit and unscrupulousness which would become its hallmark. To his possible credit, Lauderdale opposed Clarendon's ideas for an ecclesiastical settlement uniform to both England and Scotland; and he showed little enthusiasm for the restoration of episcopacy. As Commissioner he ushered in the conciliatory **Indulgences** of 1669 and when these failed to make much impression on Covenanting intransigence he offered the more comprehensive 1672 Indulgence. Such efforts at reconciliation could be seen as further evidence of patriotism, had he not then presided over a period of renewed repression which culminated in the Battles of **Drumclog** and **Bothwell Brig** and his eventual disgrace.

In reality principle scarcely impinged on his policies, and consistency only when it was expedient, as in his unwavering loyalty to the King. 'Never was Eastern despot blessed with a minister of his will more obedient, docile and sedulous' (J H Burton). Insisting on the supremacy of the royal prerogative, he endeavoured to make Scotland equally subservient. A scholar whose scholarship was ignored and a libertine whose exploits provoked only revulsion, he quarrelled with aides like Rothes (**John Leslie, 7th Earl and 1st Duke**) and Argyll (**Archibald Campbell, 9th Earl**) as readily as he did with rivals like **Middleton** (**John, 1st Earl**). He was created Duke of Lauderdale in 1672 but the dukedom ceased on his death. **Thirlestane**, a monument to his rapacity, remains the home of the Earls of Lauderdale.

MAITLAND, William, of Lethington
(c1525–73) Secretary of State
'Secretary Maitland' was the eldest son of Sir Richard Maitland of Lethington (1496–1586), a lawyer (Lord of Session 1561; Keeper of the Seal, 1562–7), a collector of poetry and, living to 90 in turbulent times, a notable survivor. Since William predeceased his father, he never inherited the title; and since his young brother, **John Maitland of Thirlestane**, also became Secretary of State he (William) is usually known as 'Lethington' (an estate near **Edinburgh** which was later renamed **Lennoxlove**). Educated at **St Andrews** and abroad, he entered the service of **Mary of Guise** (1554) and was appointed Secretary of State (1558). For the next ten years his policies and career closely followed those of **Lord James Stewart, Earl of Moray**, while his influence was not much less. He too supported Mary of Guise until, on joining the **Lords of the Congregation** in 1559, he supported the English alliance against her in 1560, welcomed **Queen Mary** in 1561, urged her claim to succeed to the English throne, and opposed **Knox**'s extremism. He was more directly involved in negotiations for the Queen's possible marriage to Lord Arran, then Don Carlos of Spain, and more conclusively **Darnley**, so did not join Lord James in the **Chaseabout Raid**. He was also more directly implicated in the **Rizzio** murder and in the Darnley murder.

It has been suggested that Lethington was less principled than Lord James, his attachment to the Protestant cause and the English alliance being dictated by political pragmatism rather than ideology. This certainly seemed to be the case after Mary's defeat at **Carberry**. In 1565 he had married Mary Fleming, one of the 'four Maries' who had spent their childhood in France with the Queen and whose loyalty to her would remain strong. His support for the King's party (ie those like Lord James, now Regent, who following Mary's abdication governed in the name of the baby **James VI**) was at best luke-warm. In 1569 he finally made the break and became a supporter of Mary's restoration. He was arrested by Lord James, ostensibly for Darnley's murder, but in his gaoler, **Sir William Kirkcaldy of Grange**, he found a fellow Marian; together they held **Edinburgh Castle** for the ex-Queen until 1573. Lethington refused

to work with **Lennox**, who had assumed the regency after Lord James's death (1570) and would have nothing to do with the 'Pacification of Perth' in early 1573 when the **Hamiltons** and **Huntly** went over to the King's party. This left Grange and Lethington isolated. They continued to hold out in the castle until it was reduced by English intervention in May 1573. It was ironical that the man who had done most to urge accommodation with England should finally be confounded by England. Grange was executed. Maitland would have been had he not died spontaneously; suicide, though suspected, remains unproved.

MAKAR
The word is old Scots and simply means 'maker'. It acquired a specialised meaning as a 'maker of verses', ie a poet, in the 15th century and was so used by **William Dunbar** in his 'Lament for the Makaris'. Dunbar's use of the term to eulogise the poets of his age led to its being subsequently reserved for the Scots poets of the 15th and 16th centuries [see **Robert Henryson**, **Gavin Douglas**, **Alexander Montgomerie**, **Blind Harry**, etc]. Their virtuosity in the **Scots language** and their colourful diction have found many admirers amongst later advocates of the Scots tongue, eg **James Lewis Spence** and most notably **Hugh MacDiarmid**.

MALCOLM I (d.954) King of Alba
The son of **Donald II** and father of Kings Dubh and **Kenneth II**, Malcolm was called *Bobhdhdearg* (the 'Red Roarer' or 'Red Crow'). Succeeding his father in 943, he ruled Cumbria by treaty with Edmund King of the Saxons (Cumbria later became the appanage of the Scots heir apparent: see **David I**). He died in battle against the men of **Moray**.

MALCOLM II (c954–1034) King
Although he was the son of **Kenneth II**, who died c995, disputed inheritance kept Malcolm from the throne until 1005 when he killed his cousin **Kenneth III** at Monzievaird. Having no son himself, Malcolm arranged strategic marriages for his daughters; one, Bethoc, marrying Crinan Abbot of **Dunkeld** (their son would later become **Duncan I**) and another marrying **Earl Sigurd of Orkney**. On Sigurd's death on the battlefield of Clontarf in Ireland at the hands of Brian Boru in 1014, his son (Malcolm's grandson) **Thorfinn** became Scotland's vassal and his lands of **Sutherland** and **Caithness** came under Malcolm's wing. His designs on Northumbria were foiled by the English in 1006 after Malcolm unsuccessfully laid siege to Durham, but in 1018 he allied himself with **Owen, King of Strathclyde** and together they defeated the forces of the English King Canute at **Carham**, thus expanding his territories as far as the **Tweed**. When Owen died childless in 1018, Malcolm claimed **Strathclyde** for his grandson **Duncan**, and it was this manoeuvre, which defied traditional patterns of inheritance, that led his enemies to conspire to his murder at **Glamis**. The so-called 'Malcolm Stone' in the manse garden at Glamis is said to be his grave-slab.

MALCOLM III 'CANMORE' (c1031–93) King
A child when his father **Duncan I** was killed by **MacBeth** (1040), Malcolm spent his youth in exile in North-

umbria with his uncle Earl Siward, who took him to visit the English court of Edward the Confessor. It was with the support of the English King and the help of Siward that Malcolm defeated and killed MacBeth at **Lumphanan** in **Aberdeenshire** in 1057. **Lulach**, Mac-Beth's stepson, was placed immediately on the throne by his supporters, but in March 1058 he too was defeated and killed by Malcolm, who claimed the throne of Scotland as his own.

Variously described as lusty, aggressive, barbarous, opportunistic and a dedicated soldier, Malcolm married twice. His first wife was Ingibiorg (daughter – or, some-times, widow – of **Thorfinn** of **Orkney**), by whom he had two sons, **Duncan II** and Donald (d.1085). After Ingibiorg's death in c1069 Malcolm married **Margaret**, sister of Edgar Atheling, heir to the English throne of Edward the Confessor but kept from it by William the Conqueror. This second marriage produced six sons – Edward (d.1093), **Edgar** (r.1097–1107), Edmund (who would later support his uncle, **Donald Bane**'s claim to the Scottish throne rather than those of his brothers), Ethelred (Abbot of **Dunkeld**), **Alexander I** (r.1107–24) and **David I** (r.1124–53); and two daugh-ters, Edith (known as Matilda, who married Henry I of England, youngest son of William the Conqueror) and Mary (who married the Count of Boulogne).

Throughout his 35-year reign Malcolm Canmore (Gaelic *ceann* = 'head' or 'chief', *mor* = 'great', thus either 'Great Chief' or 'Big Head') played a cat-and-mouse game with the English. He adored his learned and pious English wife and could refuse her nothing; he made no objection to her introduction to the Scottish court of the language and customs of England (she never learned to speak Gaelic), going so far as to declare English the official court language, and he acquiesced in her plans for ecclesiastical reform. More dangerously, so far as relations with England were concerned, he made welcome those of her compatriots forced, as she and her brother had been, to flee the Norman invasion. King William, who had left Scotland much to its own devices for the first few years of his reign, despite invasions of Northumbria and Cumbria by Malcolm in 1069 and 1070, saw the marriage and the subsequent gathering of English exiles north of the border as a distinct threat. In 1072 he marched north to rattle his sabre; Malcolm submitted, acknowledging William as overlord in the **Treaty of Abernethy**, and agreeing to his son Duncan being taken back to England as a hostage.

Treaties and hostages notwithstanding, in 1079 Mal-colm invaded England for a third time, leading a savage raid into Northumbria. Once again the English fought back with an army headed by William's eldest son Robert, and once again Malcolm was forced to submit; and the whole process was repeated yet again in 1091, the submission this time being given to William II (Rufus). Either of the two Williams could have exacted a harsher penalty from their belligerent northern neigh-bour; but it was a clear case of better the devil you know than the devil you don't. Were Malcolm to be deposed, his successor, quite possibly emerging as the result of a **Celtic** backlash against the Anglicisation of the Scottish court under Malcolm and Margaret, might not be so willing to submit.

In 1092 William Rufus wrested from Scotland all Cumbria south of the Solway, and the following year Malcolm marched into England for the last time. He was cornered and killed (some say by trickery) at Alnwick in Northumberland in November 1093. His eldest son and heir, Edward, died in the same affray, and his wife Margaret, already ill, died four days later.

Malcolm was immediately succeeded by his son Duncan II (for six months only) and then by his younger brother Donald Bane (exactly the Celtic reactionary anticipated by William); but eventually four of his sons, Duncan, Edgar, Alexander and David, would reign in turn as Kings of Scotland, and the dynasty he founded – the House of Canmore – would rule over Scotland for more than two centuries.

MALCOLM IV (1141–65) King

Eldest of the three sons of Earl Henry, the only son of **David I**, Malcolm succeeded his grandfather in 1153 at the age of 12. Immediately after Henry's death in 1152 David had proclaimed Malcolm as his heir and sent him on a tour of the country in the company of the **Earl of Fife** to ensure the acceptance of his succession. A year later David died leaving his grandson a momentarily peaceful kingdom, but the accession of a boy-king allowed old troubles to resurface; native earls who had resented David's Normanising policy flexed their muscles; **Somerled**, sub-king of **Argyll** and ruler of the Isles, set out to extend his kingdom in the west; there were rebellions in **Moray** and **Galloway**; and in 1157 Henry II of England announced to Malcolm that he was reclaiming the English counties of Northumberland, Cumberland and Westmorland which he had ceded by treaty to David I. When Malcolm went to France in 1158 to fight for Henry (and was rewarded with a knighthood) it was taken as a sign of weakness and subordination, but he redeemed himself by routing Somerled's forces who were advancing up the **Clyde**. Exhausted by the exigences of kingship, and not pos-sessed of a robust constitution, Malcolm – nicknamed 'the Maiden' since he never married – died at **Jedburgh** at the age of 23 and was succeeded by his much more forceful brother **William I the Lion**.

MALCOLM, Sir John (1769–1833) Governor of Bombay

Born at Burnfoot near **Langholm**, **Dumfriesshire**, Mal-colm left the local school at the age of 12 and through an uncle's influence was interviewed for a cadetship in the East India Company. When asked by the directors what he would do if he met Hyder Ali of Mysore, the 12-year-old replied 'Cut off his heid' and was immedi-ately commissioned. Known thereafter as 'Boy' Mal-colm, he arrived in Madras (1783) in time to participate in the Third and Fourth Mysore wars and then served with **Thomas Munro** on the commission set up to settle Mysore. A diplomatic career appeared to offer more rapid advancement than a military one and he was singled out by Lord Wellesley, Governor-General, to lead a mission to Persia (1799–1800) designed to check French influence and cow the Afghans. It cost much and achieved little but established Malcolm as Calcutta's expert on Persia. A second mission (1808) intended, like **Mountstuart Elphinstone**'s to Kabul, to pre-empt

Sir John ('Boy') Malcolm, as drawn at Abbotsford in 1824 by William Bewick (SNPG)

Russian influence, failed to win a reception, while a third (1810) was rendered redundant by the presence in Teheran of an envoy from the government in London.

Meanwhile Malcolm's considerable ambition had been rewarded, though never satisfied, with his being made Resident in Mysore, political agent to the future Duke of Wellington during the Second Maratha War, and all-purpose trouble-shooter by a succession of Governors-General. Plagued with dysentery, he returned to Britain (1812–17), was made KCB, and enjoyed some literary distinction. In India (1817–22) he for the first time commanded troops in action during the Pindari and the Third Maratha Wars, negotiated the political settlement of central India, but was chagrined by the appointment of Munro and Elphinstone to the Governorships of Madras and Bombay. Worse came when another succeeded Munro, but in 1827 he was finally appointed Elphinstone's successor in Bombay. His three-year tenure was marked by much activity and an unseemly row with the Supreme Court. Back in England (1831) he sat as MP for Launceston and took a determined stand against reform. He died in London. Malcolm's ambition was more than matched by energy and integrity. If not the most endearing of the Scots triumvirate (Elphinstone, Munro and Malcolm) which laid the foundation of the British Raj, he was both respected by Indians and respectful of India.

MALLAIG, Inverness-shire

Railhead of the West Highland Line and roadhead of the Road to the Isles, Mallaig stands at the north-western extremity of **Morar** facing across the Sound of Sleat to **Skye**. It is the main west coast port between **Oban**

and **Ullapool** with a **fishing** fleet, once dependent on **herring** but now devoted largely to prawns, and ferries to Armadale on Skye and to the small isles of **Rum**, **Eigg**, **Muck** and **Canna**. All are spread enticingly across the seaward panorama as seen from above the port. Access by boat to roadless **Knoydart** is also from Mallaig which, at what is now Mallaigvaig, originally faced Knoydart across Loch Nevis a mile north-east of the port. It was here on 5 July 1746 that **Prince Charles Edward Stewart** landed on his return from Skye and would have been captured had he not hidden under a plaid in the bottom of the boat. The few huts which constituted Mallaig then still did so in 1900. The **railway** (1901), the pier, and the herring changed all that.

MAM RATAGAN (RATTACHAN), Wester Ross/Inverness-shire

This is 'a high hill on which a road is cut but so steep and narrow that it is very difficult' (**Dr Johnson**). The doctor's horse staggered during the descent, occasioning the only moment on his entire perambulation of the Highlands and Islands when 'I felt myself endangered'. The Mam still provides the only road access to the **Glenelg** area. From Shiel Bridge, before the ascent, a side road leads to Totaig at the junction of Lochs Alsh and Duich. Here there are the remains of a **broch**, Caisteal Grugaig, and hence there was once a ferry to **Dornie**. From the Mam, spectacular views inland to the Five Sisters of **Kintail** and seawards to the **Cuillins** have been partly obscured by afforestation.

MANDERSTON HOUSE, Nr Duns, Berwickshire

Originally the seat of a branch of the ubiquitous **Home** family and built in 1790, Manderston was acquired in the 1890s by Sir James Miller, brother-in-law to Lord Curzon and son of Sir William Miller of **Leith** who had made a vast fortune trading with Russia. With money no object, Sir James commissioned John Kinross to rebuild Manderston (1903–5); the result is one of the finest Edwardian country houses in Scotland complete with marble floors, stuccoed ceilings and a silver-railed staircase modelled on that in the Petit Trianon in Paris. Hardly having dented his inherited fortune, Miller went on to create elaborate outbuildings including 'the finest stable block in Europe', a vaulted marble dairy in the form of a Roman cloister, a neo-baronial gardener's cottage and a mock tower-house. The whole extravagant ensemble is open to the public.

MANSON, Sir Patrick (1844–1922) Physician and Parasitologist

Born at **Oldmeldrum**, **Aberdeenshire**, the son of a bank manager who was also a substantial farmer, Manson graduated in medicine from **Aberdeen University** in 1865. His first post was in a lunatic asylum in Durham; in 1866 he became Medical Officer in the Chinese Maritime Customs Service in Formosa (Taiwan), and from 1883–9 he practised medicine in Hong Kong where he founded a school of medicine which became the University and Medical College of Hong Kong. In 1889 he retired to **Kildrummy** on Donside, but by 1892 he was back at work in London as physician to the Seamen's

Hospital. During his travels in the Orient he had studied the transmission of such diseases as elephantiasis and malaria, concluding that these were insect-borne. Despite ridicule from his contemporaries, Manson continued his researches, which contributed much to the ultimate control of these illnesses, and encouraged Ronald Ross in his work which earned a later Nobel Prize, to the surprising exclusion of Manson. Appointed Medical Adviser to the Colonial Office in 1897, he founded the London School of Hygiene and Tropical Medicine in 1899 and was knighted in 1903 for his major contributions to science.

MAR, Aberdeenshire
One of the ancient provinces of **Aberdeenshire**, Mar is bounded north by the **Don** and south by the **Dee**. It comprises **Midmar**, Cromar and **Braemar**, the last embracing a large tract of the **Cairngorms** and Grampians where it abuts **Badenoch** and **Atholl**. Here, west of Braemar Castle, is the large Mar estate and Mar Lodge, a rambling red-roofed mock Tudor shooting lodge built by the 1st **Duke of Fife** and his wife Princess Louise (eldest daughter of Edward VII) in 1898. **Queen Victoria** laid the foundation stone. It replaced an equally inappropriate structure (burnt 1895) and has recently been a hotel.

MAR, Earldoms of
This region of **Aberdeenshire** was ruled by the Celtic **Mormaers**, one of whom died on the field of Clontarf in Ireland in 1014. It emerged as one of the original **seven Celtic earldoms** in a charter founding the abbey of **Scone** in 1114–15. Earl William acted as one of the Regents in 1258, and his successor Earl Gratney married **Robert I**'s sister Christian. The earldom passed through the heiress Countess Margaret to William, Earl of Douglas, and through their daughter Countess Isabel to Alexander Stewart, son of the **'Wolf of Badenoch'**. He was one of the protagonists in the **Battle of Harlaw** in 1411, described as a leader of **caterans**. After his death in 1435 the earldom was awarded to various royal **Stewarts** but claimed by Robert Erskine, to whose descendant **John, Lord Erskine** it was granted by **Queen Mary** in 1565. He became Regent for her son **James VI** in 1571 and is commemorated by the surviving façade of his mansion in **Stirling**, known as **Mar's Work**. Thereafter the Erskines of Mar suffered severely for their loyalty to the Stewarts, although it was the **11th Earl John**'s own incompetence in the **1715 Jacobite Rising** that was largely responsible for his misfortunes. Consoled by a Jacobite dukedom, the family did not recover their earldom from forfeiture for over a century. John Erskine, grandson of the attainted Earl, was restored by Act of Parliament in 1825, and his own grandson subsequently became heir also to the Earldom of **Kellie**. There was a bizarre development after his death in 1866, when the heir male was a cousin, while a Mr Goodeve claimed the late Earl's sister (to whom he was married) as heir general. An Earldom of Mar Restitution Act was required in 1885 to disentangle the rival claims, the eventual outcome of which is that today there are two holders of the title, a 30th Earl of Mar, the descendant of Mr Goodeve, and a 14th Earl of Mar who is also 16th Earl of Kellie.

MARCH, Earldom of
The French rank of *Marquis* and the German equivalents *Markgraf* and *Margrave* derive from the same offices which the English established on the Welsh border and the Scots on the English one. It was Patrick, 8th Earl of **Dunbar**, one of the original Scottish earldoms, who was the first to appear in the records as *comes de Marchia*. Thus the post of Warden of the Marches became a hereditary earldom of the Dunbar family. Its most celebrated practitioner was **Black Agnes, Countess of Dunbar,** who in 1338 defended Dunbar Castle against the English. After the forfeiture of 1434, **James II** created his second son Earl of Dunbar and March, only to involve both titles in a second forfeiture for treason in 1487. Thereafter the Earldom of March passed through the hands of various junior members of the royal **Stewart** house, first that of **Lennox** until it became extinct in 1576, then of **James VI**'s lover **Esmé Stewart**. It was held by the disreputable **Robert Stewart**, who became at the age of 19 Bishop of **Caithness** without ever entering holy orders and ended his life in 1586, squandering the revenues of **St Andrews**. By 1619 it was back in the hands of the 3rd Duke of Lennox. This line became extinct in 1672, when **Charles II** conferred the title, together with the Dukedoms of Richmond and Lennox, on his son Charles, whose mother was the French Duchess of Portsmouth. A new creation of 1697 in favour of a younger son of the Earl of Queensberry resulted in its transfer in 1731 to the Earl of Wemyss, whose own title was extinguished after the '45 **Jacobite Rebellion**. But it was restored in 1826, so that there is an Earl of Wemyss and March today, while *The Douglas Peerage* pronounces concerning the older creation that on the death of the 4th Duke of Queensberry in 1810 'the earldom of March, it is supposed, became extinct'.

MAREE, Loch, Ross & Cromarty
Although as remote as anywhere on the Scottish mainland, Loch Maree's exceptional scenic variety has long ensured its celebrity. Ben Lair and the cliffs and gullies of Ben Slioch (3217ft/908m) rear dramatically from its northern shore, islands proliferate in its midst, and Caledonian pines contrast with the quartz profile of Ben Eighe. Thomas Pennant and **Dr John MacCulloch** were among the first to sing its praises and by 1842 a guide book noted that boats and oarsmen were always available to the visitor at one shilling an hour and 'a bottle of whisky for the whole voyage'. After **Queen Victoria**'s visit in 1877 (she stayed at Talladale and gave her name to the Victoria Falls at Slattadale), a steamer plied the loch's 12 miles. 'Maree' is thought to derive from **St Maelrubha** (of **Applecross**), who settled and died on Isle Maree near Letterewe on the north shore. The island had previously been a place of Druidical sacrifice and, according to Pennant, its well was supposed to cure insanity. Nearby Furnace was the site of an iron smelting operation conducted by settlers from **Fife** in the early 18th century. The loch is famous for its **fishing** and enjoys the distinction of being the largest expanse of fresh water in Scotland which has not been tampered with by a **hydro-electric** project.

Loch Maree with Ben Slioch, from an engraving (entry p 709) (SP)

MARGARET, 'Maid of Norway' (c1283–90)

Daughter of Erik II of Norway and Margaret, daughter of **Alexander III**, the infant 'Maid of Norway' was designated heiress to the Scottish throne in 1284 after the death of all Alexander's children, including her own mother. When Alexander himself died in 1286, the three-year-old Margaret, sole surviving descendant in the direct line of the House of Canmore [see **Malcolm III**], was declared Queen. Betrothed to Edward of Caernarvon, heir to Edward I of England [see **Treaty of Birgham**], the Maid left Norway in 1290, but died in **Orkney** without ever having set foot in mainland Scotland. Her death renewed the bitter disputes over the succession which had been temporarily defused by her inheritance, the main contenders, each claiming distant relationship to the royal house, being **John Balliol** and **Robert Bruce, Earl of Annandale**. After conferences at Norham and **Berwick** in 1291, during which both would-be kings (and the other lesser '**Competitors**') acknowledged Edward I's superiority, the English King pronounced in favour of John Balliol, who was crowned at **Scone** in 1292.

MARGARET, Saint (c1046–93) Queen

Margaret was born in Castle Reka, in southern Hungary, where her father, Edward the Exile, son of Edmund Ironside, had been sent for protection to King Stephen of Hungary. Her mother, the Princess Agatha, was either the daughter of Stephen or a cousin of his Queen Gisela.

In 1054 the English Witan (supreme council) summoned Edward the Exile to replace Edward the Confessor as King. He died almost on arrival but his family remained at the English court. On the death of the Confessor the English government refuted the claim of the Exile's son (Margaret's brother) Edgar Atheling to

the kingship on the grounds that he lacked constitutional rights. Harold, son of Earl Godwine, was elected King and following the Norman Conquest of 1066 Edgar was advised to escape. The ship in which he and his family sailed for the Continent was driven off course by gales and landed in the harbour now called St Margaret's Hope in **Fife**.

Malcolm III 'Canmore' came from **Dunfermline** to meet the refugees. He himself had sought sanctuary at the English court after the murder (1040) of his father **Duncan** by **MacBeth**, and had met Margaret as a child. Now, seeing her as a beautiful woman, traditionally he fell deeply in love. Their marriage took place in 1070 and was one of exceptional happiness.

Through her influence over Malcolm, Margaret introduced the language and many of the customs of England to the Scottish court (she never learned to speak Gaelic); revered for her erudition (the less cultured Malcolm reputedly kissed her books daily in homage), her abstinence and her many acts of piety and charity, she encouraged the Church to be organised on a territorial, or diocesan, basis and the **Culdee** settlements were incorporated in, or replaced by, a Continental system of monasticism. Helped by her chaplain Turgot, sent to Scotland by Lanfranc, then Archbishop of Canterbury, she introduced three Benedictine monks to found **Dunfermline Abbey** in 1072 and also built **St Margaret's Chapel** (the oldest example of Norman architecture in Scotland) in **Edinburgh Castle**. She encouraged pilgrims to visit **St Andrews**, then seat of the Scottish primacy, by giving them free passage across the Forth from North to **South Queensferry**, places which still bear her name.

Of the six sons of Malcolm and Margaret, three became Kings of Scotland – **Edgar** (r.1097–1107), **Alexander I** (r.1107–24) and **David I** (r.1124–53). Of their two daughters Edith, the elder (known in England as Matilda or Maud), married Henry I, King of

England (r.1100–35), younger son of William the Conqueror, thus uniting the Norman and Saxon lines; the younger, Mary, married Eustace, Count of Boulogne and their daughter, also Matilda, married Stephen of Mortain, King of England (r.1135–54).

In 1093 the Queen, mortally ill, heard of the death in battle of both her husband and her eldest son Edward at Alnwick in Northumberland. She herself died four days later. Buried at Dunfermline Abbey, she was canonised in 1250.

MARGARET OF SCOTLAND (1425–45)

Eldest daughter of **James I** and Joan Beaufort, Margaret was betrothed at the age of four to the Dauphin Louis (who would succeed to the French Crown as Louis XI in 1461). They were married at Tours in 1436 when she was 11 and he 13, but Louis hated and neglected Margaret and she died childless at the age of 20.

MARGARET TUDOR (1489–1541)

The elder of Henry VIII's two sisters, Margaret Tudor married **James IV** at **Holyrood** in 1503 when she was only 13 years old ('The Marriage of the Thistle and the

Margaret Tudor, Queen of James IV; one of the Stirling Heads (carved wood medallions from Stirling Castle) (© the Trustees of the National Museums of Scotland 1994)

Rose'), had six children of whom only one (**James V**) survived, and was Regent and Guardian for her son after James IV's death at **Flodden** (1514). Described as a capricious political intriguer, in 1515 she married **Archibald Douglas, 6th Earl of Angus** (by whom she had a daughter, Margaret, later Countess of Lennox and mother of **Henry Stewart, Lord Darnley**) which marriage disqualified her as Regent, the role being assumed by **John Stewart, Duke of Albany**. Driven out of Scotland, but returning in 1517 to ally herself this time with Albany, she divorced Angus in 1526, married Henry Stewart, later Lord Methven, and in 1528 helped her son escape Angus's clutches. She died at **Methven** Castle and was buried in the Church of St John in **Perth**.

MARIES, The Four

Mary Beaton, Mary Seton, Mary Fleming and Mary Livingstone ('sirnamed the lusty' according to **John Knox**) were the ladies-in-waiting who accompanied **Queen Mary** to France for her marriage to the Dauphin in 1548. Of noble birth, these four Maries were either joined or replaced by Mary Carmichael and Mary Hamilton, recruited presumably so that the 'corps' of ladies in waiting should 'continue to consist of young virgins, as when originally raised' (**Sir Walter Scott**, 1802). Mary Hamilton's supposed dalliance with **Darnley** is the subject of the ballad 'The Queen's Marie' collected by Scott: 'Yestreen the Queen had four Maries,/The night she hae but three;/There was Marie Seton and Marie Beaton/And Marie Carmichael, and me.' According to **Robert Lindsay,** Maries, or maids, had attended Queen Madeleine, first wife of **James V**, 'Marie' having its etymological derivation in Icelandic *mær*, 'virgin' or 'maid', 'from where it had come to be used in Scots especially for the maids-of-honour attendant on the queen' (Fraser, 1969).

MARISCHAL, Earldom

Two high offices of state commemorate the essential partnership between man and horse which lasted until the invention of the internal combustion engine. One was that of Constable (*Comes Stabuli*: Companion of the Stables), the other that of the Marischal (pron. 'Marshall' from *Marescalci*: Masters of the Mares under the early Frankish kings). In Scotland this developed into a functional hereditary earldom held exclusively by the **Keith** family. It was confirmed by **Robert I** after the Battle of **Bannockburn**, at which Sir Robert Keith used his small body of Scottish horses with great skill, and the earldom was only extinguished after the 10th Earl Marischal espoused the **Jacobite** cause in 1715. While his great castle of **Dunnottar** was reduced to a ruin, the 10th Earl and his brother, **Field Marshal Keith**, enjoyed the friendship of Frederick the Great, though neither left legitimate descendants. The Field Marshal's portrait still hangs in the college of **Aberdeen University** founded by his ancestor, **George Keith, 5th Earl Marischal**, in 1593.

MARKINCH, Fife

Now contiguous with the new town of **Glenrothes**, Markinch supplies what the former lacks in the way of historical pedigree. North-west at Balbirnie and Balfarg stand 'one of the most important groups of monuments of Neolithic and Bronze Age date in eastern Scotland' (B Walker and G Ritchie). The Balbirnie stone circle was excavated in 1971–2 revealing several phases of use and several cists. Pottery went to **Edinburgh** while the stones themselves were re-erected in nearby Balbirnie Park. The Balfarg henge, one of only three single-entrance henges in Scotland, has two **standing stones** remaining. It was also excavated (but not moved) revealing an interior circle of post holes and more pottery and bones. Balbirnie House, now a hotel and the centre of an ancient estate which became a coalfield, now the park, dates from the 16th century but was much extended and elaborately classicised in the 18th and 19th centuries.

On the other (south-east) side of Markinch Balgonie

Castle was rated by members of the Royal Commission on the Ancient and Historical Monuments as 'one of the most interesting' in **Fife**. The beautifully constructed 15th century tower (partially restored in the 1970s) is adjoined by a courtyard with the ruins of later buildings, in one of which lived **Alexander Leslie**, the **Covenanting** General who became Lord Balgonie and 1st Earl of **Leven**.

Prior to 19th century **coal-mining** Markinch was an important **linen** and papermaking centre utilising the river Leven. The parish church of 1786 incorporates a tall 12th century tower (with 19th century spire) while the Session House (1875, **Rowand Anderson**) incorporates a 13th century 'folicaceous capital and canopy'.

MARSHALL, Bruce (1899–1987) Novelist

Once Scotland's most successful novelist (but little read since), Marshall was born in **Edinburgh** and educated at Edinburgh Academy, Glenalmond and **St Andrews University**. He lost a leg in World War I but qualified as an accountant and worked in Paris from 1926–40. His first collection of short stories appeared in 1919. A succession of novels followed, many addressing religious themes with comic abandon. He struck rich with *All Glorious Within* (1944) about a priest in a deprived Scottish community. It ran through ten reprints and sold over a million copies. After the war he gave up accountancy and moved to the south of France, whence came a stream of just-remembered titles like *The Red Danube* (1947), *The White Rabbit* (1952) and *The Black Oxen* (1972), which last follows several generations though a ribald 20th century Edinburgh. For an octogenarian amputee, *One Foot in the Grave* (1987) proved valedictory. He died at Cap d'Antibes in the same year.

MARSHALL, William 'Billy' (c1672–1792) Tinker

Born in either Kirkmichael, **Ayrshire** or Minnigaff, **Kirkcudbrightshire**, Marshall came of gypsy (or tinker) stock. 'A short, thick-set little fellow with dark quick eyes' (**John MacTaggart**), he gained a formidable reputation as a boxer, bandit and smuggler. He is said to have usurped the chiefship of **Galloway**'s tinker clan to become 'king' and then terrorised much of the southwest for most of the 18th century, his only defeat being at the hands of 'a powerful body of tinkers from **Argyll** and **Dumbarton**'. There is considerable unanimity (**Scott** in *Guy Mannering*, MacTaggart, *Blackwood's*) as to his great longevity but less as to his actual exploits. These supposedly included deserting the army seven times and the navy three, raiding as far afield as **Glasgow**, and a major role in the **Levellers**' revolt of 1724. His amorous conquests were also remarkable, including 17 lawful marriages plus illegitimate children beyond reckoning, four of whom were fathered after his 100th birthday. 'He was kind, yet he was a murderer – an honest soul, yet a thief – at times a generous savage, at others a wild pagan . . . in short he understood much of the world – had no fear – a happy constitution – was seldom sick – could sleep on a moor as soundly as in a feathered bed – took **whisky** to excess – died in **Kirkcudbright** at the age of 120 years' (MacTaggart). His tombstone still stands in the graveyard of St Cuthbert's Church, Kirkcudbright.

MARSHALL, William (1748–1833) Fiddler

Marshall's career was in the household of the **Duke of Gordon**, to whom he eventually became factor. He was never a professional musician and often laid his violin aside for months on end, but his contribution to Scottish **fiddle** music was a major one. He extended the variety of keys, as well as calling for regular use of higher positions for the left hand. In this he shows the beginning of the absorption of Continental violin technique as well as style into the mainstream of the traditional where, previously, it had been concentrated in the hands of professional orchestral violinist/composers. He was a master of the **Strathspey** but also composed a number of classical-style minuets dedicated for the most part to leading Tories. His best-known melody is his setting of **Burns**' 'Of a' the airts the wind can blaw'. Marshall was also an exceptionally talented horologist.

MARTIN, Martin (c1660–1719) Author

From Bealach, **Skye**, Martin obtained an MA at **Glasgow University** and a medical doctorate at Leyden (c1712). In between and after, he seems to have returned to Skye as either factor, tutor or physician (or all three) to the **MacLeods** of **Dunvegan**. He wrote two books, *A Late Voyage to St Kilda* (1697) and, inspired perhaps by **Robert Sibbald**'s example, *A Description of the Western Isles of Scotland* (1703). The latter was the first published account of life in the **Hebrides** and an important contribution to topographical studies in Scotland. Amidst much credulous material on **second sight** and other supernatural and superstitious occurrences, it conveys a vivid picture of island society c1695. According to **James Boswell** it was this book, given him as a child, which inspired **Dr Johnson**'s visit to the Highlands and Islands in 1773. Johnson refers to Martin as 'a man not illiterate', but censures him for some inaccurate observations: 'he has often suffered himself to be deceived'.

MARY, Queen 'of Scots' (1542–87)

The only surviving child of **James V** and **Mary of Guise**, Mary was born at **Linlithgow** on 8 December 1542 and became Queen on her father's death six days later. Under the governorship of **James Hamilton**, second Earl of **Arran** and heir presumptive, a pro-English and reforming party was briefly in the ascendant and in 1543 the infant was betrothed to six-year-old Edward, son and heir of Henry VIII. Before the year was out the pro-French and Roman Catholic faction prevailed and that agreement was repudiated. Henry, in retaliation, launched devastating invasions (1544 and 1545) known as 'the **Rough Wooing**', and in 1547 a Scottish defeat at **Pinkie** led to English occupation of much of south-eastern Scotland. Mary was sent for a short time to the security of the island priory of **Inchmahome**. The Scots asked for French help to expel the invaders, and it was given on condition that Mary was sent to France (1548). In 1554 Arran was superseded as governor by Mary of Guise.

In April 1558 the Queen married Francis, the Dauphin, aged 14, and secretly agreed that, should she die without issue, her kingdom would fall to the French Crown. Her husband succeeded as Francis II in July 1559, but he died on 6 December 1560 and in the minority of his brother Charles IX power fell to his

Queen Mary in white mourning, after a portrait by Francis Clouet (SNPG)

English Crown, and Roman Catholics, who did not acknowledge the legality of Henry VIII's marriage to Elizabeth's mother Anne Boleyn, thought Mary's right to that Crown better than Elizabeth's.

After landing at **Leith** (19 August 1561), Mary, on the advice of her half-brother James, **Earl of Moray**, and **William Maitland** of Lethington, Secretary of State, gave the reformed church official recognition and modest endowment, while retaining Mass in her own chapel and prosecuting priests who said Mass elsewhere. Such a moderate, or perhaps equivocal, policy could do much to commend her to Protestants in Scotland, England and the Continent. While her advisers sought a firm understanding with Elizabeth (who offered her favourite, the Earl of Leicester, as a husband for Mary), there were also negotiations for marriage to the Roman Catholic heir to the Spanish throne and other Continental princes. Finally, out of affection rather than policy, Mary married on 29 July 1565 her first cousin, **Henry Stewart, Lord Darnley**, who stood next to her in the English succession.

The marriage ceremony was a Roman Catholic one, although Darnley was apparently a Protestant; Elizabeth professed indignation, so that Scots who favoured an understanding with her found their policy thwarted; and Darnley's family had many enemies among the nobles. Moray and others raised a rebellion, which Mary energetically suppressed, but she was soon estranged from her worthless husband and she relied much on non-aristocratic familiars, including **David Rizzio**, an Italian musician who had become her French secretary.

mother, Catherine de Medici, who was no friend to Mary. Meanwhile a revolution had taken place in Scotland which involved rejection of the French alliance and Papal supremacy, but Mary decided that her best prospects now lay in her native kingdom. On the accession of Elizabeth to the English throne in November 1558, Mary had become heir presumptive to the

The Return of Mary, Queen of Scots, to Edinburgh, *by James Drummond (NGS)*

Disaffected lords disliked Rizzio's influence, Protestants thought him a Papal agent, and to Darnley he seemed too intimate with Mary. A band of Protestant lords, along with Darnley, murdered Rizzio at **Holyrood** on 9 March 1566, in or near the presence of the Queen, who was six months pregnant. Mary survived the ordeal and Prince James (later **James VI**) was born on 19 June.

In the later months of 1566 Mary's disgust with her husband was accompanied by a growing partiality for **James Hepburn, Earl of Bothwell**. Soon there was talk of a divorce from Darnley or of ending the marriage by more violent means. Mary was certainly aware of schemes for her husband's elimination, but it seems unlikely that she had foreknowledge of the plot which actually led to his murder at **Kirk o' Field**, **Edinburgh** (10 February 1567). The truth about that crime continues to elude historians, and the **Casket Letters**, on which reliance was placed to prove Mary's guilt, are not, in the absence of the originals, sound evidence; what existed were probably concoctions made by doctoring genuine letters. Bothwell, however, was universally believed to have been heavily involved in the murder. Yet he was acquitted after a show trial. He then abducted Mary, possibly with her consent (24 April) and obtained a divorce from his wife (7 May). On 15 May Mary married him, to the scandal of even her warmest supporters. She had already taken the reformed church under her protection, and the marriage was a Protestant one. Faced with a confederacy of nobles at **Carberry**, Mary surrendered (15 June), to be imprisoned in **Loch Leven Castle** and compelled to abdicate in favour of her son (24 July). Escaping on 2 May 1568, Mary obtained much support, but was defeated at **Langside** (13 May). Four days later she crossed the Solway and asked for Elizabeth's protection.

At the end of 1568 commissioners of Elizabeth at York and Westminster heard representatives of Mary and her opponents, with a view to determining whether or not Mary should be restored. No decision was formally announced but Mary was detained in England for the rest of her life. In Scotland her cause was maintained against that of King James until 1573. In England she became a focus for plots by English Roman Catholics and foreign agents, all of them frustrated (though sometimes initially encouraged) by English government agents. Elizabeth was frequently urged to have Mary executed, but always hesitated until public revulsion at Mary's complicity in Babington's plot for her assassination forced her hand. Beheaded at Fotheringay (18 February 1587), Mary was buried at Peterborough, whence her body was removed to Westminster Abbey in 1612.

Gordon Donaldson's *Mary Queen of Scots*, 1974, has a final chapter on 'the continuing debate' which briefly reviews the chief writings on Mary during 400 years. The fullest biography now in print is Antonia Fraser's *Mary Queen of Scots*, 1969, which has an extensive bibliography. *Mary Stewart, Queen in Three Kingdoms*, ed Michael Lynch, 1988, is a collection of essays offering several novelties. The Duke of Hamilton's *Maria R: Mary Queen of Scots, The Crucial Years*, 1991, is strong on personalities and contains brief biographies of many of Mary's contemporaries, while Jenny Wormald's *Mary Queen of Scots, A Study in Failure*, 1988, removes the monarch from the froth of public fantasy and exposes her to ruthless but

not entirely unsympathetic scrutiny. M H Armstrong Davidson's *The Casket Letters*, 1965, examines fully a central problem.

MARY OF GUELDRES (d.1463) Queen of James II

Like Joan Beaufort and **Mary of Guise** (Queens of **James I** and **V**), Mary of Gueldres would play a prominent role in Scottish affairs during the minority which followed her husband's premature death. She was born the daughter of Arnold Duke of Gueldres but raised by Philip the Good of Burgundy. A Burgundian alliance favourable to Scottish trade with the Netherlands was the object of the marriage and it was Philip who conducted the negotiations and provided his niece's dowry. Arriving in Scotland in 1449, she was married to the 19-year-old king in **Edinburgh**'s **Holyrood Abbey**. Her entourage was impressive (possibly including some of the artillery that proved to be both the making and undoing of James) and her dowry was generous; but so were the allowances and accommodations promised her in Scotland. **James II**'s speedy move against **Sir Alexander Livingston** was probably designed to provide rents and castles to meet the Queen's expectations. With these ample means she built **Ravenscraig Castle**, said to have been the first designed to accommodate and resist artillery, and founded **Trinity College** in Edinburgh. When James II was killed at **Roxburgh** (1460), she oversaw the successful prosecution of the siege and was then recognised as keeper of the kingdom and of its future King (**James III**, her eight-year-old son), though not as Regent. She was opposed by **James Kennedy, Bishop of St Andrews** and a member of the Regency Council, their differences centring on the extent of Scottish support for the English Lancastrians plus Mary's apparent weakness for Adam Hepburn, Master of Hailes and the future Earl of **Bothwell**. It has been argued that Mary's foreign policy, at least, was the subtler of the two; but apart from the return of **Berwick**, it remained for Kennedy to exploit when the dowager Queen died in 1463.

MARY OF GUISE (or Lorraine) (1515–60)
Wife of James V and Regent

Mary was the daughter of Claude, the 1st Duke of Lorraine from the powerful Guise family. Her first husband, Louis Duke of Longueville, died in June 1537, a matter of days before the death in Scotland of **James V**'s bride of six months, Madeleine daughter of Francis I. The logic of uniting the widowed pair was lost neither on Francis, anxious to retain the just revived **auld alliance**, nor on James, receptive to the idea of a second French dowry. They were married at **St Andrews** in June 1538. As a stop-gap bride, any illusions Mary might have had about ladies of noble birth being other than convertible assets in Europe's dynastic take-over battles were dispelled. She was prepared for the crisis that ensued. Within four years her two sons by James had died, quickly followed by their father (1542), leaving her with a six-day-old daughter (the future **Queen Mary**) on whose betrothal options rested not only the fate of Scotland but the equilibrium of Europe.

Whilst she may well have enjoyed the political game for its own sake, she 'must have been moved mainly

Mary of Guise, Queen of James V and Regent, attributed to Corneille de Lyon (SNPG)

by a sense of duty to her country [France], her family [Guise], her church [Rome], and her daughter's rights' (G Donaldson). During the 1540s, the period of Henry VIII's '**Rough Wooing**', the Queen Mother skilfully fostered and exploited Scottish resentment against English incursions. The occupation of St Andrews (1546) by the 'Castillian' murderers of its archbishop, **David Beaton**, provided a pretext for welcoming French military assistance; and the defeat at **Pinkie** (1547) provided a pretext for her daughter's removal to **Inchmahome** and then France as the betrothed of the Dauphin. The **Treaty of Haddington** also provided for French assistance in defence of Scottish sovereignty; but, with the English occupying large parts of **Fife**, Lothian and the Borders, even the anti-Catholic nobility began to put national interests before religious conviction. Recognising that personal ambition trumped both, Mary made the transition even easier for them by arranging a French dukedom (Châtelherault) for the governor, **James Hamilton, Earl of Arran**, and substantial bribes for the party of assorted Scots whom she escorted to France in 1550. Arran's authority, based on his conciliatory attitude towards the ecclesiastical reformers, finally collapsed in 1553 when the Catholic Mary I succeeded to the English throne, thus removing any prospect of Protestant support from that quarter. Mary of Guise's assorted pro-French party now looked secure; in 1554 the 12-year-old princess Mary was declared of age while her mother was installed as Regent of Scotland.

With French troops far from popular and French *conseillers* in growing evidence, the new Regent went out of her way to appease Protestant opinion. Reformers went unprosecuted, **Knox** revisited Scotland, **Campbells** and **Hamiltons** were gratified with benefices. Until the completion of negotiations over the terms of young Mary's marriage to the Dauphin, conciliation remained the priority; in **Lord James Stewart** and others, Protestant

opinion was even represented amongst the negotiating commissioners. The final agreement (1558) represented the Regent's greatest achievement; but it had been realised at the price of tolerating a growing religious dissent which now fastened on the French marriage as evidence of Catholic betrayal. To the Protestant nobles, who now banded together as the **Lords of the Congregation**, contrary signals such as the unexplained but provocative martyrdom of **Walter Mylne** coupled with further conciliatory gestures over Church liturgy (1558) proved less decisive than the death of Mary I in England and the accession of Elizabeth. The French held Elizabeth illegitimate; Mary, their and Scotland's Queen, was portrayed as England's also; her mother in Scotland was encouraged to clamp down on religious dissidence prior to a united assault on the Protestant pretender in London. But the Lords of the Congregation and the reformist preachers in Scotland had drawn a very different conclusion from Elizabeth's accession and were now emboldened to treat again with the English and defy any counter-reformation tendencies in Scotland.

Knox returned to Scotland in May 1559 and in June, at a moment of high tension generated by the so-called 'Beggars Summons' for the surrender of friaries, he preached his inflammatory sermon in **St John's**, **Perth**. Hostilities followed; the Regent summoned her forces to **Stirling** while Knox and his followers held Perth. Truces were tried and broken and the Regent fell back on **Dunbar**, then regained **Leith**, while the Congregation twice occupied **Edinburgh** and twice withdrew. French troops arrived for the Regent, English money for the Congregation. In October the rebellion became a revolution when in the name of her daughter the Congregation dismissed Mary of Guise as Regent; in March 1560 it became an Anglo-French war as English troops entered Scotland in accordance with the Congregation's request in the **Treaty of Berwick**. They laid siege to Mary's French troops in Leith while French and English emissaries discussed peace. Mary withdrew to **Edinburgh Castle** and there, in June, facing the prospect of an ignominious settlement, she died of dropsy. Respect if not affection brought even opponents like **Archibald Earl of Argyll** and Lord James Stewart to her deathbed. But not Knox; he exulted 'in terms which make it clear why charity has not been thought a notable feature of Scottish **Calvinism**' (J Wormald).

MASSON, David (1822–1907) Biographer and Historian

Masson's reputation rests largely on his 6-vol *Life of John Milton*. The son of a stonemason, he was born in **Aberdeen** and attended university there and in **Edinburgh**. Moving to London he wrote text books for **W & R Chambers** (1847–56) before becoming Professor of English Literature at University College London (1853–65) and then at **Edinburgh University** (1865–95). He also edited *MacMillans Magazine* and wrote biographies of **Drummond of Hawthornden** (1873), Thomas de Quincey (1881) and **Thomas Carlyle** (1885). Meanwhile the Milton opus (1859–80) was steadily accumulating. Historical writings led to his appointment as HM Historiographer Royal for Scotland in 1896 and a prolific career was rounded off by two volumes of autobiography, *Memories of London in the Forties* and *Memories* of *Two Cities*, published posthumously in 1908 and 1911.

MASSON, Francis (1741–1805) Botanist
Born in **Aberdeen**, Masson's horticultural training included an apprenticeship at the Royal Botanic Gardens at Kew. In 1772 he sailed to the Cape of Good Hope with Captain Cook and then travelled across southern Africa with the Swedish botanist Carl Per Thunberg. Masson's introductions to Britain included mesembry-anthemums, heaths, gladiolus and iris, but his speciality was the succulent genus *Stapelia*. After two expeditions to the Cape he returned to Britain in 1795, but two years later he left on a plant collecting trip to Canada where he died in 1805.

MAUCHLINE, Ayrshire
Eight miles south-east of **Kilmarnock**, the village of Mauchline is hallowed ground to **Burns** lovers, for it was during his nine-year tenancy of Mossgiel farm just to the north that the 'ploughman poet' penned many of his most famous lines. The 'wee, sleekit, cowrin, tim'rous beastie' was turned up by Burns' plough in a field at Mossgiel (1785); that 'merry core o' randie, gangrel bodies', 'The Jolly Beggars', frequented 'Poosie Nansie's' cottage; Mauchline kirkyard was the scene of the 'Holy Fair' lashed so scathingly in his 'demoralising and in some instances too just satire'; the Reverend 'Daddy' Auld publicly rebuked Burns and Mauchline-born Jean Armour for their sins in the 'lumpish, plain, sombre' kirk (predecessor of the present handsome Gothic parish church of 1829); the couple were married in a house next to Mauchline Castle and set up home in Castle Street; and so it goes on. Bearing up under this weight of literary association (although probably wishing it had not also been burdened with the pseudo-baronial Burns' Memorial Tower, 1897), Mauchline had a thriving handloom industry in the early 19th century and was renowned also for the manufacture of snuff-boxes and **curling** stones. The castle, also known as Abbot Hunter's Tower, dates from c1450 and was erected by the monks of **Melrose Abbey** for those of their number in charge of managing the Abbey's extensive **Ayrshire** estates.

MAURICEWOOD PIT DISASTER (1889)
63 miners died following an underground fire at Mauricewood pit, near **Penicuik** (**Midlothian**) on 5 September 1889. The cause of the fire is unknown, but the wooden lining of a ventilation shaft appears to have caught fire, generating tremendous heat and smoke and making either escape or rescue by the 960ft (293m) deep main shaft impossible, and rendering the only alternative escape route unusable.

MAVISBANK, Loanhead, Midlothian
Situated on the north side of the valley of the river North Esk just to the south-east of Loanhead, Mavisbank House was the fruit of a unique collaboration between **Sir John Clerk of Penicuik** (1676–1755) and his protégé **William Adam**. Built between 1723–7, the completed house caused quite a stir: 'a free translation of a Palladian villa, elegant in appearance and compact in plan, it set a new architectural fashion for Scottish country mansions of the middle rank' (J G Dunbar). The main two-storey house is of five bays with rusticated piers rising to a cornice surmounted by a pedi-

Mauchline Church and Castle; the church (1829) replaced that in which Robert Burns was married (GWWA)

ment and balustraded parapet, and single arcaded quadrant links extend to pavilions on either side. Adam wanted an extra storey on the main house; Clerk denied him. Clerk wanted his coat of arms in the centre of the pediment; Adam denied him and put a window there instead. The partnership obviously worked well.

Mavisbank was never intended to be Clerk's main residence; he called it his 'summer pavilion'. It stayed in the Clerk family until 1815 and thereafter changed hands several times until it became an asylum towards the end of the 19th century; its condition deteriorated until the house was severely damaged by fire in 1973. Its final demolition, scheduled for March 1987, was only halted at the last minute when the Lothian Buildings' Preservation Trust successfully persuaded the Secretary of State for Scotland to intervene.

MAVOR, Henry (1858–1915) Electrical Engineer

Born in **Stranraer**, the son of a schoolteacher, Mavor became one of the true pioneers of the electrical **engineering** industry in Scotland, having been attracted to it by the work of **Lord Kelvin**. After attending the College of Science and Arts in **Glasgow** he became the local agent for the English electrical company, Crompton. In 1883 he founded the partnership of Muir & Mavor which undertook a wide range of electrical tasks from public lighting at **Queen Street Station** to the manufacture of dynamos. The managerial strength of the young company was enhanced with the addition of Arthur Coulson and Henry's brother Sam. Soon the firm became Mavor & Coulson and, having moved into new premises at Mile End in Glasgow, became the country's leading maker of motors and dynamos. Sam gradually assumed a dominant role re-orienting production towards **coal** cutting equipment and switchgear. Henry, meanwhile, was involved in applying electrical propulsion to ships. He was the father of **Osborne Henry Mavor**, 'James Bridie'.

MAVOR, Osborne Henry, 'James Bridie' (1888–1951) Playwright

O H Mavor was born in **Glasgow**, the son of **Henry Mavor**. Educated at Glasgow Academy and **Glasgow University**, he graduated with a medical degree in 1913. On the outbreak of World War I he joined the Royal Army Medical Corps and served in Flanders and Mesopotamia. He left the Corps after the war ended, but returned to serve with it again during World War II.

In 1919 Mavor settled in Glasgow to practise medicine, and in 1923 married Rona Bremner. During this time he acted as a consulting physician to the Victoria Infirmary and lectured at the Anderson College of Glasgow. Mavor was to become known, however, for his role in promoting the arts in Scotland, both as a playwright and an administrator.

Mavor's first play, The Sunlight Sonata, written under the pseudonym Mary Henderson, was produced in 1928 by the **Scottish National Players** [see **Theatre in Scotland**]. His succeeding works were written under the pseudonym James Bridie. Sunlight Sonata was followed by The Switchback (1929) and What it is to be Young (1929). His first major success, The Anatomist, was produced in

London in 1930 and based on the lives of the 19th century Edinburgh vivisectionist **Dr Robert Knox** and the body-snatchers **Burke and Hare**. Other West End successes followed in the 1930s, including Tobias and the Angel (1930), Jonah and the Whale (1932), A Sleeping Clergyman (1933) and Susannah and the Elders (1937). Mavor's work during this period reflected his interest in Biblical themes and the confrontation and conflict between good and evil. One of his best-known works, Mr Bolfry (1943), explores the latter theme most dramatically, having as its central character the devil in disguise as a minister.

After his service in World War II, Mavor began exploring Scottish themes in works such as The Forrigan Reel (1944), Dr Angelus (1947), John Knox (1947) and Gog and Magog (1948). His final works, set in the modern post-war period, were highly experimental and symbolist in nature, and included Daphne Laureola (1949), The Queen's Comedy (1950) and The Baikie Charivari (1952).

During the latter years of his life Mavor played a key role in promoting Scottish arts and artists. For several years he was the chairman of what was later to become the Scottish Arts Council and in 1943 he founded the Glasgow **Citizens' Theatre**. He also helped establish the first college of drama in Scotland in 1950, and worked hard to promote such events as the **Edinburgh Festival**. He was awarded an honorary LL.D from Glasgow University in 1939, and a CBE in 1946. He died in Edinburgh, having written over 40 plays.

MAXTON, James (1885–1946) Socialist

Born in **Pollokshaws**, **Glasgow**, Maxton took an MA at **Glasgow University** and in 1905 became a teacher like his father. Acquaintance with the slums from which his pupils came, and exposure to the Marxist economics preached by **John Maclean**, brought about his conver-

James Maxton, by Sir John Lavery, c1933 (SNPG)

sion to revolutionary socialism. He joined the **Independent Labour Party** and in association with **John Wheatley** and **Pat Dollan** became one of its most effective public speakers. With Maclean and other **Red Clydesiders** he condemned World War I as a capitalist power struggle in which the workers should take no part and was duly arrested for sedition and imprisoned (1916–17). He stood for the Bridgeton (Glasgow) seat in the 1918 election and won it in 1922, becoming one of the 10 'Wild Clydesiders' who departed for Westminster.

For the next 24 years Maxton represented Bridgeton in Parliament and presided over the steadily dwindling ILP. He never held office, he had a negligible effect on legislation, and he received no honours. Yet he became a national institution respected by friends and opponents alike, indeed loved by them. He was frequently suspended – most notably in 1923 when, recalling the death of his first wife, he accused Tory Members of murder for voicing approval for a cut in Health Board funds. Yet such episodes only boosted his reputation. No one doubted his sincerity; few could resist his charm. 'Picturesque' is an adjective much used by one of his biographers. Beetle-browed with long lank hair and cadaverous countenance, he looked every inch the revolutionary. But in spite of pronouncements considered outrageous even by Labour colleagues, he remained 'the beloved rebel' and 'the most popular man in the House of Commons'.

Although the ILP's Red Clydesiders were largely responsible for **Ramsay MacDonald** becoming leader of the Labour Party, they quickly became disillusioned with Labour's gradualist approach to social reform. Demanding 'Socialism in our Time', Maxton as ILP Chairman (1926–31) and A J Cook of the Miners' Union issued a manifesto (1928) challenging Labour Party policy on a rapprochement with management after the General Strike. The challenge was justifiable but ill-judged in that Maxton had failed to secure ILP approval for the initiative. Criticised by his own party and reprimanded by the Labour Party, Maxton led a revolutionary rump of the ILP which resisted the Labour whip and eventually disaffiliated from the party (1932).

World War II found Maxton as inflexibly pacifist and internationalist as World War I. Challenging the government on every aspect of mobilisation and conscription, he often walked to the voting lobby alone. Yet a more gregarious and indefatigable campaigner never existed. He is said to have 'addressed more meetings than any other man in British history'; Churchill called him 'the finest gentleman in the House of Commons'; others have hailed him as 'the greatest Scotsman of his century'.

MAXWELL, Gavin (1914–69) Writer

The House of Elrig (1965), one of Maxwell's last and most lasting books, vividly describes his idyllic childhood in a wild part of **Wigtownshire**. His father, an army officer, had died soon after he was born and, having had the run of the family estate, Maxwell was eventually packed off to the sterner world of Stowe College and then Oxford. His 'career' comprised numerous short-lived, ruinous and stylish endeavours. He collected geese in Wigtownshire, studied eider duck in Lapland, joined the **Scots Guards**, was seconded to the Special

Operations Executive (but invalided out in 1944), started a shark fishery on Soay (off **Skye**) and became a portrait painter in London. The shark fishery failed but prompted a book, *Harpoon at a Venture* (1952). Travels in Sicily prompted another, and he returned from accompanying Wilfred Thesiger amongst the Marsh Arabs with the material for *A Reed Shaken by the Wind* (1957); also an otter. He later acquired others, settling with them at Sandaig near **Glenelg**. *Ring of Bright Water* (1960), describing this menage, became a best-seller; it was filmed, inspired a lot of imitative works, and made Maxwell a '60s icon. Fellow-travellers descended on Sandaig; the idyll, like all his others, turned sour. He wrote five more books plus the enduring *House of Elrig* before dying of cancer.

MAXWELL, James Clerk (1831–1879)
Theoretical Physicist

Born in **Edinburgh**'s India Street, James Clerk Maxwell was one of the 19th century's outstanding scientists, and a most important theoretical physicist. At first privately educated on his parents' **Galloway** estate at Glenlair, he proceeded to Edinburgh Academy and then to the city's **University** at the age of 16. He had already displayed his precocious talents by writing a scientific paper on how to draw a perfect ellipse using everyday pins and string; this was read (on his behalf) to the Royal Society of Edinburgh when the author was only 14.

In 1850 he became an undergraduate at Trinity College, Cambridge, later becoming a Fellow there during a prize-winning academic career. In 1856 he was appointed Professor of Natural Philosophy at **Marischal College, Aberdeen**, marrying the Principal's daughter. Despite this he lost his appointment in the pending amalgamation with **King's College** and it was not until 1860 that he obtained a similar post at King's College, London. After five years he retired to a country gentleman's existence at Glenlair, but was brought back into the academic world in 1871 to set up a physics laboratory as the first Cavendish Professor of Experimental Physics at Cambridge.

Clerk Maxwell has been described as a 'physicist's physicist', the general public not perhaps being fully aware of his immense contribution to our knowledge of the physical world. Two of his principal areas of research were in electromagnetism and the kinetic theory of gases. His work was so seminal that Albert Einstein was later to say of his research in electrodynamics: 'It was Maxwell who fully comprehended the significance of the field concept; he made the fundamental discovery that the laws of electrodynamics found their natural expression in the differential equations for the electric and magnetic fields.'

No less important were his researches into such disparate topics as the form and content of Saturn's rings – a subject which won him a prize at Cambridge; his findings have since been confirmed by unmanned spacecraft – and into colour blindness, which led him to demonstrate the world's first colour photograph to a London audience in 1861. He also invented the Zoetrope, a device demonstrating movement in two dimensions. Clerk Maxwell was a strong supporter of the British Association for the Advancement of Science and, being particularly noted for the clear and readable prose style of his scientific writings, acted as one of the scientific editors of the much-acclaimed 9th ('Scholar's') edition of the *Encyclopaedia Britannica*, then still a Scottish publication.

MAXWELL, John (1905–62) Painter

A still underestimated talent, John Maxwell brought a distinctive late Romantic sensibility to 20th century Scottish painting. With his colleagues **W G Gillies** and **William Wilson** and his contemporary **James Cowie**, he offset the brash confidence of the Colourists with a quieter neo-Romantic idealism. Born in **Kirkcudbright** he began studying at the **Edinburgh College of Art** in 1921 alongside Gillies. A travelling scholarship to Paris in 1926 brought him under the tutelage of the Modernists Léger and Ozenfant. But he rejected their influence in favour of the Russian émigré painter Marc Chagall and the French Symbolists, particularly the mysterious and unsettling work of Odilon Redon. This concern with an 'inner vision' of the subject found expression in both his figurative and landscape work. He travelled throughout Scotland with Gillies painting ethereal, meticulously sensitive landscapes, mostly in watercolours, sometimes inhabited by vague, fantastic figures. An extraordinary perfectionist, Maxwell destroyed much of his output and the rarity of his work has served to lessen his reputation rather than increase it. He taught at Edinburgh College of Art from 1929–43, but seems to have been a less influential teacher than many of his contemporaries. His last years were dogged with ill-health, although the physical restrictions this imposed reinforced the introverted and visionary quality of his art.

MAY, Battle of the Isle of (Firth of Forth Collisions) (1918)

Over 100 men men died in a naval incident near the Isle of May at the mouth of the Firth of Forth on 31 January 1918, despite the fact that no enemy ships were involved. A lengthy column of heavy British capital ships with their attendant destroyers were taking part in an exercise with a new class of submarines – the K. These had already shown alarming loss of control, one of them having caused the deaths of 33 men in **Gairloch** two years previously. In the Forth K22 suffered a jammed rudder and rammed a sister craft, both nearly being run down by following surface ships; the chaos was compounded by other K submarines returning to look for them. A need for radio silence condemned the submarines to fend for themselves, the result being that K17 was struck by the cruiser HMS *Fearless*; meanwhile K6 and K4 collided with each other, the latter sinking with all hands. The entire crew of K17 took to the water, but most were killed by destroyers steaming through them. All but two of the final death toll of 105 were crew members of the K submarines. The incident was denied by the Secretary of the Admiralty at the time, and is not mentioned in the official history of British naval operations in World War I.

MAY, Isle of, Firth of Forth

About six miles south-east of **Crail** and **Anstruther** (whence a boat can be arranged), the Isle of May lies in the outermost reaches of the Firth of Forth. It is about a mile long with cliffs rising to 150ft (46m), now a nature reserve and a nesting sanctuary for sea-birds. St Adrian, a missionary to **Fife**, is said to have been killed here c870 by Danes, his coffin subsequently being washed ashore at Anstruther. In the 12th century **David I** founded a priory on the island. The monks moved to **Pittenweem** in the 14th century but the shell of their chapel survives. In 1636 the first lighthouse, and oldest survivor of its kind, was built, a three-storey tower with a brazier that burnt 400 tons of **coal** a year. It was funded by a toll on all shipping using the waters between **St Abbs Head** and **Dunottar**. The drowning in heavy seas of the first lighthouse-keeper resulted in the burning for witchcraft of Effie Lang of Anstruther, she being held responsible for raising the storm. When replacing this lighthouse with a larger baronial tower in 1816, **Robert Stevenson** was prevailed on by **Sir Walter Scott** not to demolish the old tower but to 'ruin it *à la picturesque*'. This he did. The Stevenson building, still in use, was assembled by masons at the **Bell Rock** yard in **Arbroath**.

MAYBOLE, Ayrshire

Historic capital of **Carrick** and created a **burgh of barony** for the Earl of Cassillis in 1516, Maybole grew up as a market town serving the wild hinterland of Carrick. At one time no fewer than 28 baronial mansions jostled within the town, the grandest of which, Maybole Castle (c1620 with 19th century additions), still stands in the High Street. Legend has it that here was imprisoned Lady Jean Hamilton, wife of the 6th Earl of Cassillis, who had eloped with Johnny Faa, King of the Gypsies. When captured, Faa and 15 of his men were

Maybole Castle as drawn by R W Billings c1840 (RWB)

supposedly hanged by the wrathful Earl. History, however, records the 6th Earl and his Countess to have been a devoted couple who enjoyed a long and happy married life. No longer the family home of the **Kennedy** Earls of Cassillis, this four-storey L-plan tower house is still in use as estate offices. The ruins of Maybole's Collegiate Church at the foot of **John Knox** Street date from 1371 and the Provost's House (marked by a plaque) was the setting for the famous three-day debate of 1562 between the Reformer and Quintin Kennedy, last Abbot of **Crossraguel**, on the question of whether the bread and wine offered by Melchizedec to Abraham constituted a Mass. With 40 followers each as witnesses, the disputatious pair wrangled themselves to a standstill, the question unresolved.

Thanks, it is thought, to the salubrity of the town's climate, the citizens of Maybole were renowned for their longevity, the 1799 Statistical Account recording that 'the schoolmaster . . . died at the age of 104, three years ago a woman died here aged 105 and there are at present 10 persons whose ages put together amount to upwards of 900 years'. At that time a handloom weaving centre, Maybole later became known for shoe-making, an industry that employed 1500 at its peak in 1890, but the last tannery closed in 1969.

MEARNS, The, Kincardineshire

With Kincardine, like its castle [see **Fettercairn**] long vanished from the map, the county of **Kincardineshire** is often referred to as The Mearns. Both designations cover the same area and are of great antiquity. 'The Mearns' probably derives from the Gaelic *am mhaoirne* meaning 'the **Stewartry**', or possibly from one of **Kenneth II**'s two supposed brothers who are said to have divided **Strathmore** between them, Aeneas (or Oengus) getting **Angus** and Mearnia getting The Mearns. The Howe (or hollow) of The Mearns is the heartland of the county, an area of about 15 miles by six between **Brechin** and **Stonehaven**, seaward of the Grampians and inland of the low hills along the coast. Crossing it in 1773 **Dr Johnson** wrote, 'the country is still naked, the hedges are of stone and the fields so generally plowed, that it is hard to imagine where grass is found for the horses that till them. The harvest, which was almost ripe, appeared very plentiful.' It is indeed one of the most fertile areas in Scotland, the soil rich, reddish and still intensively farmed. The fringes are a different matter. Bloomfield near **Arbuthnott** was the home of Lewis Grassic Gibbon (**Leslie Mitchell**), whose *Sunset Song* is a vivid evocation of The Mearns and especially of their uplands: 'faith it was coarse land and lonely up there on the brae.'

MEDICINAL PLANTS

In Scotland as elsewhere two classes of healers developed in parallel and with mutual distrust; city-based professionals (almost all men), and country-based folk healers (predominantly women). The former had access to substances from all over the known world, while the latter used whatever they could find locally. What they had in common was that the majority of their remedies were plant-based, and the lists of Scottish plants used by both groups are long and very similar.

There is archaeological evidence that Stone Age people living in **Orkney** and along western coasts collected plants for medicinal use. Early Gaelic writings suggest an awareness both of local healing plants and of the most sophisticated contemporary medical techniques. By medieval times monasteries were cultivating many kinds of medicinal plants, both native and introduced, for herbal remedies to treat themselves, visitors and the local population.

From the 18th century onwards there is detailed information from writings of travelling botanists and folklorists, and from the records of the Physic Garden established in **Edinburgh** in 1670. Altogether about 200 species of native Scottish plants were recorded in medicinal use at that time, remedies for a very wide variety of ailments, with some species being used for several purposes. For example, yarrow (*Achillea millefolium*) was used to stop bleeding, heal wounds, treat headaches, consumption, piles, colds, dysentery and diarrhoea, and to dispel melancholy. It was also used to pray for a safe journey and for magical purposes, such as making young women more desirable and revealing the name of their true love. Indeed in traditional medicine there is a thin dividing line between the physical and magical healing properties of plants.

This was the foundation of both the modern pharmaceutical industry, still largely based on plant compounds whether used directly or synthesised, and of current medicinal herbalism, which has survived in Scotland, despite centuries of persecution and derision, due to its power as a healing aid.

MEGGERNIE CASTLE, Glen Lyon, Perthshire

Begun about 1579 by 'Mad' Colin Campbell of **Glen Lyon**, Meggernie Castle was considerably restored in the 17th century and enlarged in the 19th. It stands, tall and white, at the end of an avenue of lime trees deep in Scotland's longest glen. Beech and conifer woods almost surround it. The castle is noteworthy for its ghost, or rather its half-ghost. Several visitors, while sleeping in one of the castle's tower bedrooms, have admitted to being woken by warm kisses bestowed by a maiden of great beauty but sadly truncated form, she having nothing below the waist. These reports nicely complement others concerning the nearby graveyard where a fine pair of legs has been seen sitting on the tombstones. The not unreasonable explanation was that some previous laird, having murdered his young wife in a fit of jealousy, cut her in two and, though he buried the bottom half, was either surprised or slain before he could bury the top. This remained in an attic cupboard, troubled and troublesome.

MEGGINCH CASTLE, Nr Perth

An inscription at Megginch, in the **Carse of Gowrie**, identifies it as having been built by Peter Hay, related to the Hay **Earls of Errol**, in 1575. George Hay (1572– 1634), son of Peter, became Chancellor in 1622, Viscount Dupplin and Lord Hay of Kinfauns in 1627, and Earl of Kinnoull [see **Perth**] in 1633. Soon after his death Megginch was sold to the Drummonds, with whom it remains. The rectangular tower received an L-plan extension in the 17th century; further additions followed including a complete new front in 1817 'which very much impaired its antique character . . .

and changed it from a 16th to a 19th century building'
(**MacGibbon and Ross**). Only the gardens, with notable
rose garden and some very ancient yew and holly trees,
are open to the public.

MEIGLE, Nr Alyth, Perthshire

The abundance of carved stones and cross-slabs found
in the vicinity of this village suggest that it may have
been an ecclesiastical centre of repute in the Dark Ages.
'None of the stones need be dated earlier than about
800 AD and most are later' (B Walker and G Ritchie).
Pictish symbols and beasts are well represented along
with exotics, such as a camel, and various Christian
subjects. From the carvings several items from the
St Ninian's Treasure found in **Shetland** have been identified. All 30-odd stones are housed in a museum and
represent one of the most important collections in the
country. Meigle churchyard is supposedly the burial
place of Queen Guinevere [see **Alyth**] and more certainly of **Sir Henry Campbell-Bannerman** who owned
Belmont Castle (much extended from an original
tower). The font in the church is pre-Reformation with
scenes from the Passion and Resurrection inscribed on
its eight sides.

MEIKLE, Andrew (1719–1811) Agricultural Engineer

Andrew Meikle was the son of James, the millwright
who introduced winnowing machines and the pot
barley mill to Scotland from Holland. Andrew too
became a millwright, working at Houston Mill on the
Rennie family's **Phantassie** estate. In 1768 he and
Robert Meikle (d.1780) took out a patent for a grain
dressing machine. Andrew patented a spring sail for
windmills in 1772, allowing greater safety in the operation of these mills in high winds.

Andrew Meikle's most famous invention was the
drum threshing machine, which he devised with the
assistance of his son George (d.1811) and patented in
England in 1788. Controversy surrounded the invention, with suggestions that it owed much to the work
of Sir Francis Kinloch and others, and that it was merely
an adaptation of the flax scutcher. Nevertheless, Andrew
is recognised today as the inventor of the first practical
threshing machine, which greatly improved the efficiency and lowered the costs of corn milling. Sadly he
made little money from his invention, and £1500 was
raised by subscription in 1809 to help provide for his
old age.

Robert Meikle, who is believed to have been a brother
or cousin of Andrew, was an equally illustrious figure
in Scotland's early industrial history. In 1751 he was
engaged with Andrew as millwright to the Board of
Trustees for Manufactures, and he built mills all over
Scotland. He was also a respected engineer, and among
his commissions was one shared with **James Watt** to
survey an alternative route to the one finally chosen for
the **Forth–Clyde Canal**.

George Meikle played a major role in his father's
millwright's business, as when he constructed an early
threshing mill at Kilbagie in **Clackmannanshire** in
1786. He is best remembered today as the builder of
the great water raising wheel which was used to help
drain Blairdrummond Moss in 1787.

MEIKLEOUR, Perthshire

South of **Blairgowrie**, Meikleour House, built by **David
Bryce** c1870, is screened by a beech hedge which,
planted in 1746, is now about 85ft (26m) high and a
third of a mile long, an arboreal colossus and a major
clipping problem. It flanks the A93 which, south,
crosses the river Isla near its junction with the **Tay**. The
Tay here loops south and on its right bank stand the
remains of ancient Kinclaven Castle, now overgrown,
lost in forestry and hard to find. It commanded a strategically important crossing of the Tay and was a royal
stronghold in 1264. Edward I stayed here in 1296 and
in the following year it was taken by **William Wallace**
and destroyed, all as described in verse by **Blind Harry**.
Yet Edward III held it in 1335 and there was further
destruction in 1336. It comprises a massive enclosing
wall, 130 feet square and once with angle towers. There
is no trace of internal structures. In Meikleour (pron.
M'Clure) a 17th century mercat cross has unusual decoration, possibly St Andrew's crosses. North of the village
runs the Cleaven Dyke, thought to be a **Roman** boundary connected with **Inchtuthil**.

MELLERSTAIN, Berwickshire

Mellerstain House was started by George Baillie of
Jerviswood and his wife **Grizel** (née Home) in 1725
to designs by **William Adam**. 45 years later their son
George Baillie commissioned William's son **Robert
Adam** to complete it. The resulting castellated mansion
is one of the great Georgian houses of Scotland. The
severity of its dignified but perfectly proportioned
exterior is offset by the glorious Italianate terraced gardens (created 1909 by Sir Reginald Blomfield), while
the interiors are all delicacy and refinement, the library
in particular being considered one of Robert Adam's
masterpieces with the exquisite plasterwork of its ceiling
attracting such comparisons as 'a spider's web on a
frosty morning' (Sacheverell Sitwell) or 'a piece of
Wedgwood porcelain' (M McLaren). In 1717 the Baillie
and Hamilton (Earls of **Haddington**) families were
linked by marriage and Mellerstain continues to be the
family home.

MELROSE, Roxburghshire

The first Melrose monastery was at Old Melrose, three
miles east of today's ruin. It was founded by **St Aidan**
from **Iona** by way of Lindisfarne in the 7th century.
St Boisil (hence **St Boswell**) was its second prior and
St Cuthbert its third. Bede mentions it in 731 and,
though rebuilt after destruction by **Kenneth mac-Alpin**
in 839, it seems to have been deserted in the 11th
century. As at **Jedburgh** a new start was made in the
12th century when **David I** encouraged Cistercian
monks from Rievaulx near York to settle in Melrose.
They chose the new site and founded their abbey, dedicated to the Virgin, in 1136. Well endowed with revenues and lands by the monarchy, Melrose became one
of the richest monasteries in Scotland. Waltheof, its
saintly second abbot, was a son of Queen Matilda of
England; **Alexander II** so revered Melrose that he
ordered his body to be buried there. Like the other
Borders abbeys, Melrose fared less well in the 14th
century and was completely destroyed by Richard II in
1385. Today's soaring ruins of pinkish sandstone,

R W Billings' drawing of the presbytery of Melrose Abbey c1840 (RWB)

though following the general layout of the 12th century monastery, are almost entirely those of the more ornate 15th century Gothic abbey which replaced it.

Inscriptions in the aisle chapels establish Melrose's pre-eminence amongst the landed families of the Borders. Abbots like the much attested Andrew Hunter, who was the King's Treasurer in 1450, evidence its political importance. For elaboration and sculptural detail, Melrose has few rivals. The great traceried window in the south transept is complete as are the more perpendicular windows of the east presbytery. That on its east façade led **Sir Walter Scott** to poetical license in the use of the word 'oriel':

> The moon on the east oriel shone
> Through slender shafts of stately stone,
> By foliaged tracery combined;
> Thou wouldst have thought some fairy's hand
> Twixt poplars straight the osier wand,
> In many a freakish knot had twined;
> Then framed a spell when the work was done
> And changed the willow wreaths to stone.
>
> (Lay of the Last Minstrel)

Scott has been criticised in his romanticisation of the Borders abbeys for completely ignoring the fact that they were principally places of worship. He did, however, along with the Scotts of **Buccleuch** who eventually gifted Melrose to the nation, play a part in their preservation. This was appropriate. Devastated in 1544 and 1545 by the Earl of Hertford, Melrose had fallen a prey to anti-clerical neighbours in search of good building materials, foremost amongst whom had been one Sir Walter Scott of **Branxholme**.

Excavations in the 1920s uncovered what may well have been the coffin and monument of the saintly Wal-

theof as well as 'a mummified heart enclosed in a cone-shaped container of lead'. **Robert I** is known to have ordered that his heart be buried at Melrose and, after an abortive attempt to take it to the Holy Land, this wish appears to have been respected. It is not impossible, therefore, that this is indeed the Bruce's heart.

The small town of Melrose clusters around the ruins of its Abbey, the history of which it early shared and the fabric of which it later plundered for its own development. **Newstead**, an eastern suburb, is the site of a once important **Roman** fort, and in Darnick, a western suburb, the delightful 15th and 16th century Darnick tower was so coveted by Scott that he was nicknamed the 'Duke of Darnick'. The Heiton owners, however, were not tempted to sell and Scott built **Abbotsford** instead.

MELROSE, William (1817–63) Merchant

Melrose was born in **Edinburgh**, the son of a tea merchant who by the 1820s had built a thriving business. After serving an apprenticeship with his father's firm he finished his training as tea taster and buyer with a London company. In 1842 he took a post in Canton as taster for Jamieson How & Co and in 1848 as buying agent for Andrew Melrose & Co, ensuring a reasonable profit for his several financial backers as well as for himself. As trading conditions deteriorated in China he diverted much of his investment towards **railway** stocks. He died eight years after his father leaving an estate of only £16,000 but a family name ever since associated with the consumption of tea.

MELVILLE, Andrew (1545–1622) Theologian

Born at Baldowie, near **Melrose** where he learned Greek at the Grammar School, Melville went on to a distinguished academic career in the classical languages at **St Andrews** and Paris. He was appointed to the Humanity Chair at Geneva by Beza, the successor to Calvin, in 1568. Such was his reputation as a scholar and his involvement with Genevan theology that he became Principal of **Glasgow University** on being invited to return to Scotland in 1574.

After the **Reformation** the universities were in reduced and decayed circumstances. Melville revitalised Glasgow and **James VI** gave it a new charter, the Nova Erectio, in 1577. From there he went on to St Andrews in 1580 as Principal of St Mary's College, teaching Hebrew and the oriental languages of Syriac and Chaldaic, the new foundations for Biblical studies. In theology and Church affairs he opposed episcopacy and preached against absolute authority before the **General Assembly**, of which he was **Moderator** several times. He advocated the separation of Church and state to form 'Two Kingdoms', the monarch not head of the Church, but God over all.

His involvement in the writing of the *Second Book of Discipline* of 1578 set forth a pure **Presbyterian** government for the Church. In this **Knox**, the Father of the Reformation and his *First Book of Discipline*, was so much extended that Melville is clearly seen as the true father of a Presbyterian **Church of Scotland**. The system had to be passed by Parliament and the King, who opposed all subversion of his own authority in ecclesiastical matters. Melville, threatened with imprisonment, fled to

England in 1584 and was only able to teach at St Andrews again in 1586 after a time at Oxford and Cambridge. Parliament, which had been forced to pass the 'Black Acts' reasserting episcopacy, eventually approved Melville's system in 1592. However the disputes continued, including the 1596 deputation headed by Melville to remonstrate with the King.

In 1606 James VI (and now I) summoned Melville, his nephew James and others to London. They attended the Hampton Court Conference at which the proposal for a new **Bible** (the King James Version) was put forward. Reacting to the services of the Church of England with a Latin poem of ridicule, Melville was sent to the Tower of London. He was released in 1611, but went into exile as Professor of the University of Sedan. This exile to France lasted until his death in 1622.

An autocrat in all matters ecclesiastical, as were his monarch and his mentors Calvin and Beza, Melville held a European reputation as educationalist and scholar. In Scotland his true role as instigator of Presbyterian Church government is overshadowed by the character of Knox. Consequently he is chiefly remembered for telling James VI that he was 'God's sillie vassal' during their running fight over authority in the Church: a dogmatic fight that cost Melville his livelihood in Scotland and took James to more conducive thrones in England and Wales.

MELVILLE, Arthur (1855–1904) Painter

A member of the loosely knit **Glasgow** School [see **Painting in Scotland**], Melville is celebrated as the most outstanding British watercolourist of his age. Born in Loanhead of Guthrie, **Angus**, he was raised in **East Linton** and studied at the **Edinburgh School of Art** and from 1875 at the life classes of the **Royal Scottish Academy**. Reminiscent of the Hague School, his early oils – freely worked studies of gentle, rural incident – brought him success and in 1878 he left for Paris where he enrolled at the Académie Julian. Sketches in watercolour executed there and at the artists' colonies of Grez and Greville began to mark out his exceptional ability and in 1880 he embarked on a journey through the Middle East that was to prove rich in both adventure and motive for the development of his highly personal style. Delighting in the drama of the Orient, Melville's ostensibly haphazard technique – in actuality the meticulous building of a complex patchwork in washes and blots of colour – superbly conveyed the arid heat, brilliant light and romantic atmosphere of his exotic journey, and the success of his work on his return to Scotland in 1882 established his reputation. Melville held much in common with the evolving Glasgow School. Independently he had rejected the high finish and sentimental subjects of his academic predecessors and he shared with his west coast compatriots an admiration for the 'honest' motifs and painterly language of the French Realists. In 1883 he met the leading Glasgow Boys **Guthrie** and Walton at **Cockburnspath** and, infected by the younger men's enthusiasm, accompanied them frequently on sketching trips round Scotland and to France. From 1897 he devoted himself exclusively to working in oil. Though he worked boldly and confidently in the medium, the results never matched the superb and arresting qualities of his watercolours. A compulsive traveller throughout his life, he died of typhoid contracted on a sketching expedition to Spain.

MELVILLE, David, 2nd Earl of Melville and 3rd Earl of Leven (1660–1728)

As well as succeeding to the Melville Earldom of his father (**George Melville**), David also made good a claim through his mother to the Earldom of Leven (created for **Alexander Leslie**). In 1683 he accompanied his father into exile in Holland and there raised a regiment from other Scots exiles with which he accompanied William of Orange to England in 1688. Participating in **Hugh Mackay**'s campaign against **John Graham of Claverhouse**, this regiment alone behaved with exemplary discipline at **Killiecrankie**. He was appointed Keeper of **Edinburgh Castle** (1689–1702), fought in Flanders (1692) and, a supporter of the **Union** like his father, was a commissioner for the Union negotiations. Restored to Edinburgh Castle (1704) and created a major-general, he was made Commander-in-Chief in Scotland in 1706. As such he had the job of cowing opposition to the Union in Edinburgh and **Leith**, where **Captain Green** had just been lynched for little more than being English. After the Union he went to the House of Lords as one of Scotland's representative peers.

MELVILLE, George, 1st Earl of Melville (c1634–1707)

The Melvilles of Raith and Monimail (not to be confused with the **Dundas** Viscounts Melville) were **Fife** landowners who had supported the **Reformation** and benefited from it. Staunchly but not fanatically **Presbyterian**, George had fallen foul of the Commonwealth and was in London to welcome **Charles II** in 1660. But in **Monmouth**'s army during his campaign in south-west Scotland (1679) Melville vainly interceded for the **Covenanters** and tried to persuade them to lay down their arms. His loyalty suspect, he was implicated in the 1683 Rye House Plot but managed to escape arrest by taking ship from **Kinghorn** to London. There, failing to gain an audience with the King, he again eluded his pursuers and joined other exiles at the court of Prince William of Orange. He crossed to England with the Prince in 1688 and, vindicated once again, was entrusted with the management of the Scots Parliament (1689). In 1690 he oversaw the restoration of Presbyterian supremacy in the **Church of Scotland** but his moderating influence was undermined by the subsequent **General Assembly** which in effect initiated a witch-hunt of episcopal ministers. Though created Earl of Melville (1690), his influence was soon diluted by the intrigues of the **Dalrymples**. He had no part in the **Glencoe Massacre** and spent his last years building **Melville House**.

MELVILLE CASTLE, Nr Dalkeith, Midlothian

'A three storey toy fort with round, Gothic-windowed corner turrets and two storeyed wings' (McWilliam, 1978), Melville Castle (Hotel) lies on the River North Esk near **Dalkeith**. The house was designed by James Playfair in 1786–91 for **Henry Dundas**, later 1st Viscount Melville, of the nearby **Arniston House** family, who acquired the estate through marriage to Elizabeth

Rennie. His son Robert Dundas was a schoolfriend of **Sir Walter Scott**, a frequent visitor to the big houses of **Midlothian** when sheriff, who wrote '. . . To Auchendinny's hazel shade,/And haunted Woodhouselee,/Who knows not Melville's beechy grove/And **Roslin**'s rocky glen,/Dalkeith which all the virtues love/And classic **Hawthornden**?' Melville derives from an Anglo-Norman baron, Male, who settled the lands in the 12th century; one Galfrid de Melville was commander of **Edinburgh Castle** under **Malcolm IV** and justiciary under **William the Lion**.

MELVILLE HOUSE, Monimail, Fife
North of **Ladybank**, Melville House was built for **George, 4th Lord Melville and 1st Earl of Melville** (to which his son added the Earldom of Leven). As a supporter of William of Orange, George became Secretary of State (1689), Commissioner to the **General Assembly** (1690), and President of Council (1696). The house (1697–1703) designed by **James Smith** or possibly **Sir William Bruce**, was 'Fife's first mansion styled symmetrically in classical detail on a grandiose scale' (G L Pride). The ground plan is H-shaped, the elevation stark and lofty, the skyline a battery of chimneys. It is now a school. Its garden wall incorporates Monimail Tower, all that is left of what was once a country palace belonging to the archbishops of **St Andrews**. The upper part is dated 1578, the lower possibly 14th century. **Archbishop Hamilton** (hanged in 1571) may have been its last occupant. He granted it to Sir James Balfour of Pittendreich who then sold it to the 2nd Lord Melville.

MENSTRIE CASTLE, Clackmannanshire
One of the Hillfoots villages (see **Alva**), Menstrie was granted to the Alexander family (previously Alister) who had followed Colin Campbell, 1st **Earl of Argyll**, to **Castle Campbell** in the 15th century. Here was born (1567) **Sir William Alexander**, later Earl of **Stirling** and promoter of the Nova Scotia colony. The present castle, built during his youth, contains a room devoted to the Nova Scotia baronetcies and managed by the **National Trust for Scotland**. L-plan but more a castellate mansion than a castle, the rest of the building has been restored and converted into apartments. Also born here was the soldier **Sir Ralph Abercromby**, the **Tillicoultry** Abercrombies having acquired the property in 1719.

MENTEITH, Earldom of
The district between the Teith and the Forth was first held as one of the Celtic earldoms by Gilchrist in the reign of **Malcolm IV** (1153–65). It passed to the **Comyns** at the height of their power, and then to the **Stewarts** after their fall. The **Regent Duke of Albany**, son of **Robert II**, was also Earl of Menteith when he built **Doune** Castle there. After his son **Murdoch** had been executed in 1425 and his earldom annexed to the Crown, the castle became a favourite royal residence until it became the possession of the Stewart **Earls of Moray**.

MENTEITH, Sir John Stewart de (d.c1329)
Notorious as the knight who in 1305 finally captured **William Wallace** at Robroyston [see **Glasgow**] and

took him to London for execution, Menteith had originally opposed Edward I. But taken prisoner (1296), he had thrown in his lot with the English and in 1297 been appointed keeper of **Dumbarton Castle** and later **Earl of Lennox**. In 1312, while reportedly plotting to do for **Robert I** as he had done for Wallace, he abruptly changed sides again and thereafter 'proved his loyalty and took high place among the king's adherents' (R Nicholson). His national rehabilitation may be said to have been completed when he became one of the signatories of the **Declaration of Arbroath** (1320).

MENTEITH, Lake of, Perthshire
Near **Aberfoyle**, the Lake of Menteith is the only natural expanse of water in Scotland usually called a 'lake'. Why this is so is not certainly known. It has been suggested that its abundance of coarse fish or its rather English parkland setting may offer an explanation; possibly it was a misappropriation of the Gaelic *lairg* denoting the 'plain' of Menteith. Since it was called the 'loch of Menteith' in the early 19th century, the modern title may be a Victorian affectation. Near Port of Menteith are two islands, Inchtalla with a ruined castle once the home of the Earls of Menteith, and **Inchmahome**, site of the celebrated Augustinian priory. Inchmahome's clerics are said to have perfected a novel method of catching pike which involved using a live perch as a lure and tying the other end of the line to the leg of a swan. When the pike struck, the swan would endeavour to take off and, failing to do so, alert the canons who rowed forth to claim their supper. The lake is now stocked with trout and much favoured for angling competitions. It is also the traditional venue for Scotland's only outdoor **curling** 'bonspiel'. The ice has to be 10in (254mm) thick before the event is announced. Teams converge from all over Scotland for a North v South tournament which, when last held (7 February 1979), involved 2000 ends and attracted some 10,000 players and spectators.

MENZIES, Archibald (1754–1842) Botanist
Born in **Weem** near **Aberfeldy** in **Perthshire**, Archibald Menzies worked as a gardener at the **Royal Botanic Garden, Edinburgh** and, under the influence of **Dr John Hope**, collected plants in the Highlands. He later trained in medicine at Edinburgh and joined the navy as assistant surgeon, serving in the American War of Independence and, following peace in 1782, was posted to Halifax, Nova Scotia. He took part in two round the world voyages; 1786–9 with Captain Corbett and 1790–5 with Captain Vancouver on the *Discovery*. His important botanical introductions included the monkey puzzle tree. He ended his career as a doctor in London.

MENZIES, John Ross (1852–1935) Publisher and Distributor
Born in **Edinburgh**, Menzies joined the business which his father had established on a modest basis in **Princes Street**. In association with his brother he pushed the family firm in a westerly direction, opening a branch in **Glasgow** in 1868 followed by bookstalls in virtually every town of significance. He organised the lucrative network of **railway** station bookstalls leaving the firm second only to England's W H Smith in size. As a leading

organisation in the book, periodical and newspaper retailing and wholesale trades, John Menzies remains a household name in Scotland, although, ironically, the company has been owned by its English rivals W H Smith since 1997.

MERMAIDS

With an exceedingly long coastline well endowed with basking rocks, Scotland was once much favoured by mer-folk. In **Lewis**, **Martin Martin** witnessed the annual offering of a cup of ale to a deity called Shony, thought to be a Gaelic 'maid of the waves'. Elsewhere mermaids habitually passed themselves off as seals, but might, when confident of seclusion, remove their seal-skins to take the air. Such was the condition of the mermaid discovered by Roderick Mackenzie, a boat-builder of **Gairloch**. He grabbed her by the hair and only let go when she pledged that none of his boats would ever founder; and never did they. According to **Hugh Miller**, one of her sisters favoured the Cromarty Firth 'and scarcely a winter passed in which she was not heard singing among the rocks or seen braiding up her long yellow tresses on the shore'. But undoubtedly the greatest concentration of mermaids was in **Orkney** and **Shetland**. 'Sea-trows' proved an irresistible temptation to Shetlanders and a brood of children of mixed parentage resulted. In Orkney, as late as 1893, annual sightings were reported by James M Mackinley. Sadly, conservation had yet to become fashionable. One of the last recorded mermaids was spotted soon after amongst the Deerness (Mainland, Orkney) creels and shot. She had 'a small black head, white body, and long arms'.

MERRY, James (1805–77) Coal and Iron Master

Merry was born in New Monkland into a family who were amongst the earliest **coal**masters of the Monkland fields. After attending **Glasgow** High School and **University** he joined the family business. Made a partner in 1830, he secured control five years later on the retiral of his father. Having formed a partnership with Alexander Cunninghame and Alexander Allison he proceeded to construct an industrial empire comprising, by the mid-1850s, 12 collieries, two **iron** works and many iron mines. His business style was autocratic and led to harsh treatment of the workforce but his wealth and marriage proved a springboard for a political career which saw him elected for **Falkirk** in 1857, unseated the following year and re-elected in 1859. He held the seat until three years before his death.

METHIL, Fife

Between and contiguous with **Buckhaven** and **Leven** on the Firth of Forth, Methil became the busiest **coal** port in Scotland in the early 20th century. The dock facilities retained their importance through two world wars and have since been adapted for **oil** rigs. The town has been a **burgh of barony** since 1662 when the 2nd Earl of Wemyss constructed its first harbour.

METHVEN, Nr Perth, Perthshire

This uninspiring village was once the site of a collegiate church founded (1433) by **Walter Stewart, Earl of Atholl**. Very little remains although there is inscrip-

tional evidence that an aisle was added by **Margaret Tudor** who lived and died at Methven Castle. The present castle, lately restored, is a century later and the creation of the 2nd **Duke of Lennox**. One of the last (mid-17th century) tower houses to be built, it stands tall and square, a single block with round angle towers capped with ogee roofs. Two battles were fought nearby – Methven (1306) in which **Robert I** was defeated by the Earl of Pembroke, and **Tippermuir** (**Tibbermore**) (1644), the first of **Montrose**'s victories. A mausoleum in Methven churchyard by James Playfair (1793) has been described as 'one of the most sophisticated Classical buildings in Tayside and **Fife**' (B Walker, G Ritchie).

MID CALDER, Midlothian

The manor of Calder was granted by **Malcolm IV** to Randulph de Clere and from him it became known as Calder-Clere to distinguish it from Calder-Comitis, the adjacent manor which belonged to the **Earl of Fife**. The barony of Calder-Clere was forfeited during the **Wars of Independence** and in 1306 was granted by **Robert I** to James Douglas, progenitor of the **Earls of Morton**, whose title was taken from the lands of Mortoune in Calder parish. The barony of Calder-Comitis, meanwhile, was granted during the reign of **David II** to Sir James de Sandilands, who married a sister of **William Douglas**, and one of whose descendants was created Lord Torpichen in 1579. Mid Calder was once a coaching stop on the main **Edinburgh-Glasgow** road and later, together with its neighbours East and West Calder, a centre of the shale-oil industry. Its great claim to fame, though, lies in the fact that it was in Lord Torpichen's Calder House in 1556 that **John Knox** first celebrated the reformed communion.

MIDDLETON, John, 1st Earl of (1619–74) Soldier and Commissioner for Scotland

Unusually for a future earl, Middleton's origins were obscure and probably humble. He first appears as a pikeman in the regiment raised in 1632–3 by **Sir John Hepburn** for service in France. Having presumably fought in Lorraine, he returned to Scotland (1639) in the **Covenanting** army under **Alexander** and **David Leslie**. From colonel he rose to lieutenant-general and second-in-command at **Philiphaugh** (1645) after which he negotiated the surrender of **Montrose**. Under the **Engagement** he at last found himself on the Royalist side and during the 1648 invasion of England commanded the cavalry at the Battle of **Preston**. Ater the further defeat of the Engagers at **Dunbar**, Middleton held out in the Highlands (1650) and it was in an attempt to join him that **Charles II** briefly eluded his Covenanting hosts and escaped up **Glen Clova**, an incident known as 'The Start'. Under the 1650 **Resolution** Middleton received an amnesty and fought at Worcester where he was captured and sent to the Tower of London. He escaped to France and in 1653–4 briefly commanded a Royalist rising in the Highlands under the Earl of Glencairn as Charles II's commander-in-chief; it collapsed after a skirmish at Dalnaspidal on the **Drumochter Pass**. He returned to the court-in-exile, was created earl (1656) and, at the Restoration, Royal Commissioner to the Scottish Parliament, 'an appointment which incurred aristocratic jealousy' (G Donaldson).

Middleton fanned this jealousy by falling out with **John Maitland, Earl of Lauderdale**, and by supporting the reimposition of episcopacy. Deprived of office in 1663, he ended his days as Governor of Tangier.

MIDGES

Over 30 varieties of midge (*culicoides*) are found in Scotland of which half are thought to bite humans. But of these just one species, the Highland midge (or *culicoides impunctatus*) is mainly responsible for giving midges a bad name. Wonderfully versatile, it is found throughout Scotland at altitudes from the coast to about 1500ft (450m) but more especially in areas of high rainfall (over 50in/1.27m pa) and particularly in the Highlands and Islands. The female *impunctatus* (the male does not bite) is responsible for 90% of all midge bites and, though little more than one millimetre long with a life-span on the wing of only a few weeks, it comes second only to the climate as a deterrent to **tourism**, a menace to **agriculture**, and an incentive to blasphemy.

Curiously, like **Nessie**, midges evaded attention until comparatively recently. Perhaps clansmen of the past bore their attacks with greater fortitude or perhaps the climate and environment were less favourable to their breeding in such astronomical numbers. **Boswell** records a verminous encounter but it is far from certain that midges were responsible; **Dr Johnson** is silent about them; so are **Martin Martin**, Thomas Pennant and even the **Wordsworths**. But a picnic for **Queen Victoria** in 1872 was ruined by an airborne assault and by the turn of the century they were recognised as being one of the less romantic features of Highland life.

In 1944 **Tom Johnston** as Secretary of State initiated a research programme to find a deterrent against midges, and in 1952 a Midge Control Unit was set up at **Edinburgh University**. Although proprietary brands of midge repellents are now widely available and much is known about the midge's life-cycle and habits, neither the welfare state nor biological science has found an ultimate solution.

Reactions to midge bites vary considerably, some victims developing an apparent immunity to the discomfort while others react violently with painful swellings and other complications. Midges may appear at any time of year between April and October but female *impunctati* only require blood for a shorter period which is governed by climatic conditions. Wind, bright sunlight, heavy rain, and drought discourage them; so do smoke and noisy machinery, although it has long been acknowledged that they show a preference for West Highland **railway** stations. Light appears to be more critical than humidity, with subdued light – as in shade, at sunset and sunrise, or when overcast – providing the greatest stimulus to their insatiable appetites.

MIDLOTHIAN

Before the **local government** reorganisation of 1975, Midlothian comprised 203,354 acres (82,358ha), situated with the Firth of Forth to the north, **West Lothian** to the west, **Lanarkshire**, **Peeblesshire**, **Selkirkshire** and **Roxburghshire** to the south, and **Berwickshire** and **East Lothian** to the south-east and east. The southern part of the county was hilly, with the **Pentland Hills** (highest point Scald Law at 1898ft/578m) and Moorfoot Hills (highest point Blackhope Scar at 2136ft/651m) forming a natural border. The coastal plain was fertile and rich in minerals. **Agriculture**, mining and manufacturing were the main occupations.

Edinburgh was the site of the council headquarters, and was the only large burgh in the county. Indeed, Midlothian was sometimes known as Edinburghshire. Small burghs comprised Bonnyrigg & Lasswade, **Dalkeith**, Loanhead, **Musselburgh** and **Penicuik**. Under the local government reorganisation of 1975 a new Midlothian District was set up within Lothian Region. It was smaller than the former county, having lost Musselburgh and **Inveresk** to East Lothian, while Edinburgh became a separate District, absorbing Currie and Cramond. This had the effect of separating Midlothian from the sea. Heriot and Stow were transferred to Borders Region, and East and West Calder to West Lothian. Since 1995 this smaller version of Midlothian has been retained as a single administrative division.

MIDMAR CASTLE, Aberdeenshire

West of **Echt** and east of Torphins, Midmar ranks with **Craigievar**, **Crathes** and **Castle Fraser** as one

Midmar Castle, Aberdeenshire (RWB)

of the great tower houses of the north-east, but it is not open to the public. A Z-plan design with one wing square and turreted, the other round, crenellated and massive (as at Castle Fraser), it dates from 1565. There are later extensions but the interior apparently 'preserves all of its original features' (M Lindsay). Although short on historical associations, it has had many names (Ballogie, Grantfield) and more owners (Brouns, Ogilvies, Forbeses, Grants, Gordons, etc).

MILITARY ROADS

But for the **Jacobite Risings** there would have been no military roads in the Highlands. The Risings of 1689 and 1715 resulted in the founding of a police force of six Highland Companies (disbanded in 1717), the building and strengthening of forts and barracks, a Disarming Act and the forfeiture of Jacobite estates. However in 1724 **Lord Lovat** sent a memorial to George I warning him of the unrest in the Highlands, which caused the startled King to send **Major-General George Wade** to Scotland 'narrowly to inspect the present situation of the Highlanders'. In his report of 10 December Wade estimated that there were 12,000 men 'ready to rise in favour of the Pretender'. Among the General's suggestions was the pregnant phrase that 'from the want of Roads and Bridges government troops were grossly disadvantaged.'

The King and government took swift action. On 24 December Wade was appointed General Officer Commanding-in-Chief, North Britain, with a comprehensive programme and the money to implement it. In addition to carrying out all his other tasks he reported that 'parties of regular troops had been constantly employed in making the roads of communication between Killichuimen [later **Fort Augustus**] and **Fort William**'. The first military road had been made.

The General's strategic plan was to convert the isolated forts of the central Highlands into an interconnected and integrated military base with its 'centrical part' at the new Fort Augustus, with access to the sea at **Inverness** and Fort William, and with road links to **Stirling** and **Perth**. By 1727 the three forts in the **Great Glen** had been connected by road, and a galley had been built to ply between Fort Augustus and the head of **Loch Ness**. Between 1728–30 he built a road from **Dunkeld**, through **Drumochter**, by **Ruthven Barracks**, which he strengthened, and through the Slochd to Inverness. In 1730 there followed a road from **Crieff**, through the **Sma' Glen** (part of **Glen Almond**), thence by **Aberfeldy** and **Tummel Bridge** to Dalnacardoch on the Dunkeld-Inverness road. In 1731 he completed his plan with the wonderful road across the **Corrieyairack**, linking Ruthven and **Dalwhinnie** with Fort Augustus. In six years he had built 240 miles of road and 40 bridges, including the **Tay** Bridge at Aberfeldy, **Tummel Bridge**, High Bridge over the Spean and Garbha Bridge over the **Spey** – all of which except for the High Bridge are in present use – at a total cost of £34,000.

After Wade's departure in 1740 roadmaking was resumed under the competent direction of **Major Caulfeild**, who had been the General's Inspector of Roads. The civil road from Stirling to Crieff was upgraded, and the road from **Dumbarton** by **Loch Lomond** and Glen Croe to **Inveraray** was started in 1744, interrupted by the '45 and eventually completed in 1750.

After the '45 Scotland had, in September 1746, an army of occupation of 15,000, and even in the mid-1750s it numbered 8000. There were permanent barracks at Ruthven, **Braemar, Corgarff, Bernera, Inversnaid**, Fort Augustus, Fort William and Inverness; every year from June to November a chain of detachments of platoon strength linked the forts, and military roadbuilding was accelerated. The Stirling to Fort William road, including the **Devil's Staircase** and the Lairig Mor, was made during 1748–53; **Coupar Angus** to

the new **Fort George** (completed 1763) by **Glenshee**, Braemar and the **Lecht**, 1748–57; Fort Augustus to Bernera (shortest crossing to Skye) by **Glenshiel** and **Mam Ratagan**, 1755–63; Corgarff to **Aberdeen**, Inveraray to **Tyndrum**, **Fettercairn** to **Fochabers** over Cairn o' Mount, and part, at least, of a road from Contin to **Poolewe**. The total, including many shorter cross roads, was over 800 miles. Of the 1500 soldiers employed on roadmaking in 1752, nearly 1400 deposited their arms in **Stirling Castle**, and in the armed rump each man had only nine rounds of ammunition. But, of course, during the lull in the Continental wars, post-Jacobite Scotland was a first-class base camp and training area for the regular army. Parliament was prepared to authorise expenditure on the building of hundreds of miles of roads no longer necessary for military purposes.

After Caulfeild's death in 1767 about another 100 miles of road were built, the last being 960 yards between Perth and Perth Jail, both gaol and road being built by French prisoners-of-war in 1810. The total cost of the post-Wade military roads was £366,000.

There was little change to Wade's methods during the century. The survey was made by a working party of an officer, an NCO and six soldiers with theodolite and chain, just as was done by Watson and **Roy** during their military survey of 1747. Every 10 miles hutted or tented camps and blacksmiths' forges were set up and provisioned, some of which later became **Kingshouses**. Working parties comprised a captain, two subalterns, two sergeants, two corporals, a drummer and 100 men. Privates got an extra sixpence a day, corporals eightpence, sergeants a shilling and subalterns two and six. This was double pay for privates and NCOs. Wade normally used 500 men on a road, but Caulfeild after the '45 used many more. They appear to have worked a 10-hour day at a work rate of one and a half to two yards per man per day. Bridges, traverses and buttresses were built by contracted civil labour, the Tay Bridge in Aberfeldy being designed by **William Adam**. Local authorities were required to supply horses, carriages and gravel. The tools used were shovels, picks, spades, crowbars, barrows, screw-jacks, sledge-hammers, sways and gunpowder. The earth was excavated to make banks on each side, with drainage trenches and paved cross-drains. The roads were bottomed with big stones, followed by smaller stones and topped with at least 2ft (600mm) of gravel. The standard width was 16ft (4.9m) and marking stones were put up to help travellers in snowy weather. Straight lines were used as far as possible, but on steep hills traverses (zig-zags) were made, buttressed by stone and mortar; there were 18 on the Corrieyairack.

Although the new A9, for instance, from Perth to Inverness has largely reverted to the line of the old military road, it should be remembered that these roads were built exclusively for military purposes. Critics should also recall the old adage:

If you had seen these roads before they were
made,
You would hold up your hands and bless General
Wade.

The only non-Highland military road, the **Dumfries** and **Galloway**, was 105 miles long between **Gretna** and **Portpatrick**, with a later spur from **Stranraer** to **Ballantrae**. It was built in the 1760s by Major Caulfeild to facilitate the passage of troops to and from Ireland by the shortest sea crossing.

MILITIA, The

The requirement for every able-bodied male of military age to bear arms if required to do so at the call of his chief or of the Crown is embedded in history and at various stages in Scotland's story the citizen has been called out to do his duty. From an early date a rudimentary organisation existed by which in each county a cadre of officers was appointed and wapinshaws were held at which some basic inspection of arms and weapon training took place. In the time of **James VI** a prohibition was issued against the playing of **football** as it took up time and energy required for training in archery.

The Militia in various areas were called out on occasions which included the Civil Wars, to form the **Highland Host** against the **Covenanters**, to garrison rebellious **Argyll** in 1685 and to take part in suppressing both the '15 and '45 **Jacobite Risings**.

But it was the Militia Act of 1797 which saw the formation of Militia Regiments which became a recognised part of the British Army. The Act was initially misinterpreted and resulted even in rioting before its full implications were understood and accepted. A number of men was set for each county; normal requirements were for annual training only and a bounty was paid. The Militia was however required to embody in time of threat to the nation and various Corps were embodied on the spot; others were to follow later. Service would be confined to the British Isles. Volunteers were allowed to fill the ranks; gaps requiring to be filled thereafter would be by ballot among those liable for service; substitutes were allowed. In fact the Militia was not unpopular and was highly regarded by the Army as a source of recruits for the Line Regiments; it is said that the British Army at Waterloo presented a sight which was anything but uniform, so many men in the ranks were still wearing the tunics of their former militia regiments.

These initial requirements were very much those in force during the 19th century when various units were called up for Home Service during the periods of the Crimea and the Indian Mutiny. The Cardwell Reforms of 1881 saw the existing regiments of the Militia grouped along with Regulars and Volunteers into the new regiments which now covered their geographical areas. The reorganisation saw the following redesignations:

The Edinburgh or Queen's Light Infantry Militia became the 3rd Battalion **The Royal Scots**. The Royal Regiment of Ayr and Wigtown Militia became the 3rd Bn **The Royal Scots Fusiliers**. The Scottish Borderers Militia, who recruited from **Dumfries, Roxburgh, Selkirk** and **Kirkcudbright**, became the 3rd Bn **The King's Own Scottish Borderers**. The 1st Bn and the 2nd Bn 2nd Royal Lanarkshire Militia became respectively the 3rd and 4th Bns of **The Cameronians** (Scottish Rifles). The Royal Perthshire Rifles became The 3rd Bn **Black Watch**. The 1st Bn Royal Lanarkshire Militia became the 3rd Bn **The Highland Light Infantry**, being split

into the 3rd and 4th Bns in 1883. The Highland Rifle Militia recruiting from **Ross, Sutherland** and **Caithness** became the 3rd Bn **The Seaforth Highlanders**. The Royal Aberdeenshire Highlanders Militia became the 3rd **Gordon Highlanders**. The Highland Light Infantry Militia – nothing to do with the regular regiment – recruiting from **Inverness, Banff, Elgin** and **Nairn**, became the 3rd Bn **The Queen's Own Cameron Highlanders**. The Highland Borderers Light Infantry, recruiting from **Stirling, Dumbarton, Clackmannan** and **Kinross**, became the 3rd Bn **The Argyll and Sutherland Highlanders**. The Royal Renfrew Militia became the 4th Bn The Argyll and Sutherland Highlanders.

In addition to these infantry units, The Forfar and Kincardine Militia, and The Berwickshire Militia were converted into Royal Artillery in 1854 when The Fife Artillery Militia and The Edinburgh Artillery Militia were also raised. The Argyll and Bute Rifle Militia was converted to Artillery in 1881.

During the Boer War, all the Scottish Militia Regiments were embodied and most volunteered for service overseas. In 1908 they became Special Reserve Battalions based on regimental depots and during World War I they served at home as training and reinforcement units. They continued to serve as cadres from which reinforcements could be provided for front-line units right up until World War II, being officially disbanded in the early 1950s although by then they had in fact long ceased to exist.

MILL, James (1773–1836) Journalist, Historian and Philosopher

Son of an **Angus** shoemaker, James Mill relied on his precocious intelligence to secure employment as tutor to the local Stuart family. This was followed by a period at **Edinburgh University**, and great admiration for his philosophy professor, **Dugald Stewart**. Mill seemed bound for the kirk and was licensed as a preacher in 1798, but then took various tutoring posts to support private study before moving to London with Sir John Stuart in 1802. There began his literary career; he founded The Literary Journal (1803–6), described by his biographer as 'a summary view of all the leading departments of human knowledge'; in 1804 he published a pamphlet on the Corn Trade; in 1805–6 he edited the Tory St James's Chronicle; and in 1806 he began his History of British India. This last was a huge undertaking even without the other work needed to support his family, such as writing for journals including Edinburgh Review. He met Jeremy Bentham in 1808, became his disciple and received Bentham's financial and practical help.

Though Mill never visited India, his History of British India (1819) won him a London position with the East India Company administering a country he did not understand for a company he had roundly criticised. Thereafter, besides promotion, came various projects on political economy, ethics and psychology, where he deemed the principles of 'associationism' the key to all. At best this undermined some current errors. His belief that he had discovered therein the proper continuation of the Scottish school of Common Sense [see **Thomas Reid**] was as misguided as his atomistic theory itself. His ability to organise and set out clearly Utilitarian and

Associationist doctrines reveals something of the gross oversimplification from which they suffer.

Mill has a huge notoriety as father of the immensely famous London-born John Stuart Mill (1806–73). On the basis of his psychological theory he imposed on that doubtless gifted boy a better than university education between the ages of three and eight (not stopping there). J S Mill's later troubles and confusions may be less the result of this hothouse start (though he grew up a shade desiccated) than of his inability to shed the dearest convictions of a beloved father. James Mill's closest disciple was his biographer, the Aberdonian radical **Alexander Bain** (1818–1903). Together they helped to inspire a more scientific approach in psychology, which exploded their associationist theory. James Mill as a leading so-called Philosophical Radical also helped to inspire a counter-movement, equally reform minded, but dissatisfied with the Mill psychology.

At odds with many leading Scottish thinkers and educators, Mill's followers could see that some Scottish practices nonetheless worked and, in opposition to the moribund Anglican establishment of the day, were a power for reform. As non-Anglicans their sons went to Scottish universities, until their efforts helped found a university in London. (J S Mill's rectorial address at **St Andrews** makes interesting reading.) Even wholesale dismissal of James Mill as a thinker must be accompanied by recognition of his great contribution as an activist and stimulator, not least of critics: he was a force for good without getting too much right. Alexander Bain's biography *James Mill* (1882),and J S Mill's *Autobiography* (1873) remain classic documents. A Seth, *The Philosophical Radicals* is one of a number of late 19th century Scots essays contra the Mills.

MILLAR, Edward (fl.1630) Composer and Master of Music in the Chapel Royal

Millar's *Psalter* of 1635, the first fruits of his appointment by **Charles I** as Master of Music at the (briefly resuscitated) Chapel Royal [see **Stirling Castle**], represents a last-ditch attempt to restore quality and variety to church music. Millar not only printed psalm settings by his 16th century predecessors Kemp, **Peebles** and Blackhall, but settings of his own of psalms 'in reports' – that is with some imitation allowed in the parts. This was a continuation of the work he began in 1626 in James Pont's *Book of Psalmes*.

MILLAR, John (1735–1801) Lawyer

A son of the manse born at Kirk O'Shotts, Millar became a distinguished lawyer and academic, renowned as the father of modern sociology. He was in the forefront of the **Scottish Enlightenment** as a student of **Adam Smith** and later as a colleague of Gershom Carmichael. Admitted advocate in 1760, in 1761 he was appointed the fourth Regius Professor of Law in the **University of Glasgow**, following Hercules Lindsay, a pupil of **William Forbes**.

His reputation as a sociologist rests on his *Origin of the Distinction of Ranks* (1771). His liberal credentials were enhanced by his favourable attitudes towards the American Revolution and his *Historical View of the English Government* (1787). Renowned as a lecturer, he taught widely

in many areas of Scots **Law**, Roman Law and Jurisprudence. Amongst his students were Desnitsky and Tretiyakov, the first professors of, respectively, Law and Legislative Science at Moscow University.

MILLER, Hugh (1802–56) Writer and Geologist

The subject of numerous critical studies and biographies, Miller still eludes classification yet remains an icon in many disciplines whose opinions, though outmoded, command respect and whose prose style retains its vitality. He was born in **Cromarty** on the **Black Isle**, the son of a sea captain who disappeared with his ship when Hugh was only five. Straitened circumstances and a wilful character kept his formal education to a minimum but he responded to the antiquarian and natural history enthusiasms of two uncles. Aged 17 he was apprenticed to a stonemason and pursued this trade across **Ross**-shire for 15 years while experiencing, and later condemning, the cruelties of the **clearances** and the hardships of bothy life. In 1829 he started writing – verses, articles for the *Inverness Courier*, and local folk traditions. The last appeared as *Scenes and Legends of the North of Scotland* (1835). He married (1831) and, securing a position in an **Edinburgh** bank (1834), became embroiled in theological debate and Church politics. Pamphlets arguing against the 'intrusion' of ministers through lay patronage won him the support of the Evangelical party and the editorship of *The Witness* (1835–56), a twice-weekly newspaper representing what became, after the 1843 **Disruption**, the **Free Church**. But Miller also used the paper to serialise the findings of his longtime interest in **geology** and palaeontology. They later appeared as *The Old Red Sandstone* and were followed by other pioneering works on the fish and plant fossils of Ross-shire and on the correspondence between geological 'ages' and the creation theory embodied in the Bible.

The challenge for Miller's biographers has been that of identifying a personal philosophy which reconciles his various interests and achievements as folklorist, geologist, journalist, social conscience and evangelical. Clues are often sought in the tragic manner of his death – he shot himself on Christmas Eve 1856 after a nightmarish dream or vision. Some reason that, never able to reconcile scientific rationalities with the rigidities and experiential undertones of his faith, he succumbed to inner tension; others that he somehow epitomised the eternal Scottish dilemma between the backward-looking dream world of the Gaelic Highlands and the harsh realities of the grafting Lowlands entering the industrial age. Those who knew him invariably recalled his strange detachment and noted a haunting sadness. Recent biographies are by G Rosie and Charles D Waterston.

MINCH, The

This is the sea channel which separates the Outer **Hebrides** from the Inner Hebrides and the Scottish mainland; the 'North Minch' (varying from 24 to 45 miles wide) divides **Lewis** and North **Harris** from the **Sutherland** and Ross-shire coasts, and the 'Little Minch' (varying in width from 14 to 20 miles) divides South Harris, **North Uist** and **Benbecula** from the island of **Skye**.

MINGARY CASTLE, Nr Kilchoan, Ardnamurchan, Argyll

Choked with rubble, including the odd cannon, and yellowed with lichen, the yet imposing ruins of Mingary stand on a throne of rock close to the south shore of **Ardnamurchan**. Like most west coast castles, Mingary was sited for maritime strategy, being originally a stronghold of the MacIans of Ardnamurchan, a sept of the **MacDonald Lords of the Isles**. The main egress is to the sea whence both Loch Sunart and the Sound of Mull could be commanded. Here in 1495 **James IV** took the submission of the island chiefs. In the 1620s Mingary passed to the **Campbells**, but in 1644 **Alasdair MacDonald ('Colkitto')** captured it for the **Marquis of Montrose**. It was recaptured by **General Leslie**, reverted to the Campbells, and was garrisoned during the **Jacobite Risings**. The enclosing wall probably dates from the 13th century like that at **Castle Tioram** in nearby Loch Moidart. But the oblong keep built into an angle of the walls is an 18th century addition erected to shelter the garrison.

MINGULAY, Isle of

Situated at the southern end of the **Hebrides** between **Berneray** and Pabbay, Mingulay is a small island measuring two by one and a half miles, though misleadingly its name in Norse means 'big isle'. It was owned by the **McNeil of Barra**, a paternal laird who took it upon himself to replace his tenants' lost milking cows and to find spouses for widows. McPhee's Hill is named after a rent collector who, landing on the island, found all the inhabitants dead from plague. His companions rowed away in fright leaving McPhee marooned for a year before McNeil gifted him land and resettled the island. The population peaked at 150 in 1881, but by 1912 Mingulay was deserted except for colonies of seabirds nesting in the crags of dramatic sea cliffs. Biulacraig drops a sheer 700 feet to the sea.

MISSIONARIES

The earliest accounts of a mission to spread the Christian faith are the letters of St Paul in the New Testament. This developed into Western and European Christianity through the **Roman** Empire and eventually to Scotland by the efforts of the saints, notably **Ninian** and **Columba**.

Pre-**Reformation** missionaries, mainly Franciscan or Jesuit, reached out as far as China and India; post-Reformation missions followed exploration and the development of trade colonies, often with national rivalry and unfortunate results for native populations. The main expansion was from the evangelism of the 18th century.

Scottish missionaries extended to Africa, India and Asia, financed by the **Church of Scotland** and missionary societies. Notable examples are **Robert Moffat** and his son-in-law **David Livingstone** in the African interior, and **Mary Slessor** of the **United Presbyterian Church** in Calabar. Combining medical and educational foundations with the mixed blessings of Victorian values, their Westernisation often clashed with tribal practices and cultures.

Christianity became a world religion controlled from Europe and was slow to allow national Churches to form until post-colonial times. The first bishop for the breakaway United States was Samuel Seabury, consecrated in **Aberdeen** in 1784 by the **Episcopal Church of Scotland**, thus forming the Anglican communion of national Churches. Not until 1947 did the combined Church of South India begin to erase sectarian missionary rivalry.

Mission activity came full circle in the late 19th century when American evangelists Moody and Sankey sought to convert our unchurched urban poor, and continued in more recent times with the Billy Graham missions to Scotland.

MITCHELL, Sir Andrew (1708–71) Diplomat

The son of a minister at **St Giles'** in **Edinburgh**, Mitchell attended **Edinburgh University** and, aged 20, married his cousin; she died a year later giving birth to a baby daughter who also died. Heart-broken, Mitchell left Scotland, attended Leyden University and was called to the English Bar. In London he served as an Under-Secretary for Scottish Affairs (1741–7) during the '45 **Jacobite Rising** and from 1755 as MP for **Elgin** Burghs. But he was seldom in Scotland, having been appointed (1756) envoy to Frederick the Great. During the Seven Years' War he was present at most of Frederick's battles and became a trusted friend. His memoirs are an important source for Frederick's reign. After the war he continued to shuttle between London and Prussia and when he died in Berlin, the Prussian King is said to have wept at the sight of his funeral cortège.

MITCHELL, Colin (1925–96) Soldier

Despite an aggressively cultivated Scottish persona, Mitchell was in fact born and raised in the south London suburbs of Norbury and Croydon. In 1943 he joined the **Argyll & Sutherland Highlanders**, serving in Italy and then in Korea, Cyprus and Sarawak. Short and pugnacious, he won his sobriquet of 'Mad Mitch' when in 1967, as lieutenant-colonel, he led the Argylls during their occupation of the Crater district of Aden. The media loved his gung-ho bellicosity. Not so his superiors. Denied the DSO which he thought his due, he resigned his commission but resurfaced to lead the 'Save the Argylls' campaign of 1970–1, during which he was elected MP for West **Aberdeenshire**. He served only one term and then devoted his energies to a variety of causes, most notably the clearance of landmines. Reliably reported in all the world's hotspots (Afghanistan, Cambodia, central America, central Africa), he also frequented London's better clubs and had a home in Norfolk.

MITCHELL, Joseph (1803–83) Civil Engineer

Born in **Forres** and educated in **Inverness** and **Aberdeen**, Mitchell followed precisely in the footsteps of his father John, working on the Caledonian **Canal**, attracting the attention of **Thomas Telford** and being appointed to the post of Inspector of Highland Roads and Bridges (1824). He held the post for 40 years and was responsible for creating the network of **Parliamentary Roads**; his and his father's activities, plus much else about the Highlands and Islands in the mid-19th century, are chronicled in the delightfully frank *Reminiscences of my Life in the Highlands*, 1883. He wrote on other subjects, notably **railways**, and played a major part in the surveying and **engineering** necessary to open up the Highlands for railway construction. As engineer to the Scottish Fisheries Board, he also improved harbours from **Dunbar** to **Wick**; and as all-purpose builder in the remoter parts of the Highlands and **Hebrides** he constructed some 40 churches. Few have made a greater mark on the Highlands and attracted less obloquy in the process.

MITCHELL, Leslie, 'Lewis Grassic Gibbon' (1901–35) Novelist

Mitchell was born on his father's farm near Auchterless, **Aberdeenshire**. When he was eight the family moved to the Howe of **The Mearns**, later the setting of Mitchell's most important work, the *Scots Quair* trilogy. Mitchell was educated at **Arbuthnott** School and briefly at Mackie Academy, **Stonehaven**. In 1917 he left to become a journalist in **Aberdeen**, and in 1919 worked in **Glasgow** on the *Scottish Farmer*. He joined the Royal Army Service Corps later that year, serving in the Middle East, Egypt and Mesopotamia. He was discharged in 1923, but returned to work as a clerk in the RAF between 1923–9.

He began writing shortly before leaving the RAF. Initially writing under his own name, he used his foreign experiences to good effect in the non-fictional *The Calends of Cairo* (1931) and in several novels such as *Stained Radiance* (1930), *The Lost Trumpet* (1932), set in Egypt, and *Spartacus* (1933), a tale of the slave revolt in Rome in 73 BC. His last years were productive. He received encouragement from **Hugh MacDiarmid**, with whom he collaborated on *Scottish Scene or the Intelligent Man's Guide to Albyn* (1934), and under the pen name Lewis Grassic Gibbon produced the trilogy of novels *A Scots Quair* published in 1946. The three works, *Sunset Song* (1932), *Cloud Howe* (1933) and *Grey Granite* (1934) trace the life of the central character, Chris Guthrie, from childhood on her father's farm through three marriages, and moves from rural life to urban squalor in an industrial city, and back again. They also chart the social changes wrought on Scotland by World War I and the Depression, and explore the clashes of culture and language between England and Scotland, centring on the main character's ambivalence towards her ancestral land, an ambivalence Mitchell himself shared. Written in a powerful, stylised prose, and making use of northeast Scottish dialect and Scottish archaisms, the works drew comparisons to the social novels of **John Galt**, and despite objections to the raw and frank nature of their subjects, were to become significant influences on later Scottish writers. Mitchell, who had moved to Welwyn Garden City in 1931, died of a perforated ulcer in 1935. A study of his life by I S Munro was published in 1966.

MITCHELL, Stephen (1789–1874)
Tobacconist and Philanthropist

The founder of **Glasgow**'s **Mitchell Library** was one in a succession of Stephen Mitchells, owners of one of the longest-established **tobacco** companies in Britain. Unconnected with Glasgow's 18th century Tobacco Lords, who were commodity traders rather than processors, the Mitchell business was founded in **Linlith-**gow in 1723 and only moved to Glasgow in 1875 when **Blackness**, Linlithgow's port, was closed to tobacco importation by customs and excise. In Glasgow the business was first established in **Candleriggs**, then in St Andrews Square, then in Alexandra Parade. In the course of a century it grew to be one of the largest tobacco companies in Britain. When Stephen Mitchell (the seventh) died in **Moffat** in 1874 he left a bequest of £66,998 which, once interest had rounded it up to £70,000, was to be used for the founding of a library in Glasgow to be named after him. The Mitchell, with a bust of its benefactor, duly opened in 1877 in a building in Ingram Street with 14,432 volumes. The Mitchell business continued until 1901 when, with 12 other companies, it formed the Imperial Tobacco Company.

MITCHELL, Sir Thomas Livingstone (1792–1855) Australian Explorer

Born at Craigend [see **Lennoxtown**] in **Stirlingshire**, Mitchell joined the army and fought in the Peninsular War, following in the footsteps of his elder brother John (1785–1859). The latter became a major-general and wrote on *The Fall of Napoleon* (1845). Thomas, a major by 1838, emigrated to Australia as Surveyor-General of New South Wales. He held the post until his death and, both as jealous explorer and arrogant orchestrator of exploration, figures large in the opening up of Queensland, New South Wales and Victoria. Incidentally he also spattered the region with Scottish place names. His most important expedition (1836) took him west to discover the junction of the Darling River with the Murray and then south through the 'Grampians' to the 'Glenelg' River, 'Victoria Felix' and the south coast. Attempts to find a way north to the Gulf of Carpentaria were less successful and here he was badly upstaged by the eccentric German, Ludwig Leichhardt. He was knighted in 1839.

MITCHISON, Naomi Margaret (1897–1999) Writer

Daughter of **John Scott Haldane** and sister of the geneticist John Burdon Haldane, Naomi Mitchison was a prolific and versatile writer who published more than 70 books – novels, travelogues and three volumes of autobiography – as well as countless articles, short stories, book reviews, essays and poems. Born in **Edinburgh** and educated at Oxford, she married Gilbert (Dick) Mitchison in 1916 while he was on a week's leave from the trenches; after the war he qualified as a barrister, became a Labour MP and later entered the House of Lords; both joined the Fabian Society and Naomi was an active campaigner for women's rights, family planning and world peace and against discrimination, poverty and injustice. They had six children (one of whom died young of meningitis) and homes in London and Carradale in **Argyll**, in both of which they entertained their wide variety of friends and acquaintances from E M Forster, Aldous Huxley and W H Auden to refugees, displaced persons and asylum seekers. *The Corn King and the Spring Queen* (1931) was her best-selling historical novel; *Bull Calves* (1947) is the story of her 18th century Haldane ancestors; *Mucking Around* (1981) describes her fifty years of travelling, including frequent visits to Botswana where the Bakgatla people adopted her as a kind of tribal mother; her many other interests included philosophy, archaeology, agriculture, horticulture and botany. After the death of her husband in 1970 she made her home chiefly at Carradale, serving on the Argyll County Council and the Highlands and Islands Development Board and being made CBE in 1985. Many of her books are still in print.

MOCHRUM, Wigtownshire

The lands of the parish of Mochrum were given to Thomas Dunbar, second son of Patrick **Earl of March**, in 1368, and his descendants built the impressive Old Place of Mochrum some 6 miles north of the present-day village. Unusual in that it consisted of two unconnected towers (the first dating from c1500 and the second from the late 16th century) standing about 5m apart in a courtyard, the Old Place was derelict at the end of the 18th century. Restoration was started in 1876 by the 2nd Marquis of Bute, completed by the **3rd Marquis** in 1911, and included a building connecting the two towers. Mochrum parish also includes **Port William**, the village of Elrig, made famous by **Gavin Maxwell**, and the ruins of Chapel Finian on the shores of Luce Bay, dating from the 10th century, named for St Finian (d.c580) of Moville (County Down) and probably erected for the use of pilgrims coming from Ireland to **St Ninian**'s shrine at **Whithorn**.

MOD, The National

This is a festival of **music**, literature and drama, run by **An Comunn Gaidhealach** (The Highland Association), the premier **Gaelic organisation** (founded 1891). The first Mod was held in **Oban** in 1892. The original model was the Welsh Eisteddfod, and the Mod remains primarily a competitive musical festival, with a large range of solo and choral competitions, for both children and adults, an oral section and various literary competitions, together with the finals of drama competitions. In recent years a non-competitive fringe has developed. There is also a system of local or provincial mods.

This network has involved large numbers of people throughout Scotland in Gaelic music, and the main musical awards, especially the solo Gold Medals and the top choral awards, have considerable prestige. Over the years the range of Gaelic song has been well explored, in an admirably catholic spirit, and there has been a great deal of publication of these songs. There is room, however, for more varied and innovative work in arrangements and new composition. A bardic crown was awarded for many years.

See also **Gaelic Organisations**.

MODERATOR OF THE GENERAL ASSEMBLY

The title and office of the chairman who presides at the **General Assembly** date from 1563, are French in origin and last for one year only. By custom the Moderator merits the accolade of Right Reverend and, on retirement, Very Reverend. As there is no hierarchy in the **Church of Scotland**, he is first among equals without special powers.

The Moderator is elected by a committee, on behalf of the whole Church, from prominent clergy in parish ministry, theological colleges and bearers of significant committee service and returns to his parish afterwards. Ex-Moderators comprise a select and active band of commentators on Church affairs.

As the General Assembly is a legal court, the Moderator presides but has no judicial power. While in office he tours parishes and visits churches abroad as the Church's representative. On national occasions and where statements are expected the Moderator represents the denomination and its views. At the Coronation in 1953 the Moderator presented the Bible to the Queen in recognition of the different established Church in Scotland.

A peculiarity is the wearing of a distinctive dress, a version of 18th century court dress consisting of black knee-breeches, lace jabot, buckled shoes and tricorn hat, an anachronism yet to be discarded. In precedence the Moderator ranks above Scottish peers on court occasions. There is no Parliamentary role and he is not head of the Church itself. The office could be held by an elder or woman minister.

MOFFAT, Dumfriesshire

In December 1332 from Moffat near the head of Annandale **Sir Archibald Douglas** with Robert the Steward (later **Robert II**) and the young **John Randolph Earl of Moray** set forth to surprise **Edward Balliol** at **Annan**, the engagement resulting in Balliol's ignominious flight to Carlisle. Though a place of constant comings and goings athwart the main road into England (but now bypassed by the M74), Moffat only achieved burgh status in 1648 and waited another century before its sulphur springs (discovered 1633) attracted fashionable renown and patronage. To 'the Cheltenham of Scotland' came the luminaries of the **Scottish Enlightenment**, **David Hume, James Boswell, James Macpherson** and **Robert Burns**. In the **railway** age the spa lost out to others more remote (**Bridge of Allan, Strathpeffer**, etc) but continued as the main **tourist** centre in the 'Southern Highlands' with coaches leaving daily for the **Devil's Beef Tub**, the **Grey Mare's Tail** and St Mary's Loch. Hotels and fine houses reflect the town's reputation for salubrity. The main street was said to be the broadest in Scotland and 'the rough hewn' Colvin's fountain, surmounted by a ram, though thought to lower the tone when erected (1875) is now applauded as a suitable reminder of the local importance of sheep farming. Moffat House (John Adam, c1755) was built for the Earl of Hopetoun and was where James Macpherson stayed when working on his *Poems of Ossian*. **John Loudoun Macadam** died in Moffat and is buried in the churchyard. There is a museum in the old bakehouse.

MOFFAT, James (1870–1944) Theologian

A **Glasgow** theologian ordained into the **United Free Church** in 1896, Moffat was successively professor at Mansfield College, Oxford, the United Free College in Glasgow and Union Theological College in New York. In 1913 he translated the New Testament into modern English, which became popular reading, and in 1924 the Old Testament, which did not.

MOFFAT, Dr Robert (1795–1883) Missionary

Born at **Ormiston**, **East Lothian**, Moffat worked as a gardener before being accepted by the London Mission-

Robert Moffat with John Mokaterie and Sarah Robey, by William Scott, 1842 (SNPG)

ary Society and sent to southern Africa. There he remained almost continuously for 54 years, mainly at Kuruman in Bechuanaland (Bophuthatswana). In 1841 he was joined by **David Livingstone**, who had come to Africa on Moffat's advice and who subsequently married his daughter. Moffat also achieved great influence with the Matabele chief, Mosilikatse, and in 1857 travelled north through Botswana to establish a mission in Matabeleland (Zimbabwe). For a one-time gardener his agricultural and building projects are perhaps less notable than his translations of the Bible and *Pilgrim's Progress* into Sechuana. His son, J S Moffat, wrote a biography of his parents, and his grandson, H U Moffat, became Premier of Southern Rhodesia and unveiled the statue to Livingstone, his uncle, at Victoria Falls.

MOIDART, Inverness-shire

Forming a rough parallelogram between Lochs Moidart, Ailort (both salt), Eilt and **Shiel** (both freshwater), the large and sparsely populated district of Moidart lies between **Ardnamurchan** and **Arisaig** on the west coast. The Road to the Isles and the **Mallaig railway** pass along Loch Eilt on its northern edge and there is a coastal road from Kinlochailort to Acharacle. The latter passes Kinlochmoidart House, once a **MacDonald** home where **Prince Charles Edward Stewart** stayed for a week after landing at Arisaig in July 1745. Seven beech trees planted here represent his loyal companions, the **Seven Men of Moidart**, who landed with him. They are not to be confused with the Seven Men of Moriston [see **Invermoriston**] or the Seven Men of **Knoydart**. Nearby **Castle Tioram**, a much earlier home of the **Clanranald MacDonalds**, had been destroyed in the 1715 **Jacobite Rising**. On 18 August Prince Charles Edward crossed to Dalelea on Loch Shiel and was rowed up the loch to Glenaladale prior to the raising of his standard at **Glenfinnan** on the 19th.

MOLAISE, Saint (fl.6th century)

A well-connected missionary, descendant of Ulster kings and reputed grandson of **Aedan**, King of **Dalriada**, as well as nephew of St Blane, Molaise was centred on **Arran** with a retreat in a cave on **Holy Island**. Sligo also claims him with additional names Molios, Luserian and Malachi.

MOLUAG, Saint (d.592)

Although the annals of St Moluag have not survived, he is widely commemorated in legends and place names and is believed to have been of Pictish descent. Yet he came from Ireland and was a relation and 'soulmate' to St Comgall, whom he persuaded to set up the famous monastic school in Bangor (Antrim) and to provide his training as a missionary.

Records agree that he gave **Lismore** its name, but not on what it means, the most likely translation being 'great fort' or 'enclosure' rather than 'garden'. He landed at Port Moluag east of the broch of Tirefor in 562, and built a chapel (the 'Lismore Church Port' referred to in the **Aberdeen** Breviary) with individual monastic cells of wood and wattle. There is no historical evidence to support the story of his chopping off his finger and throwing it ashore in order to claim the island before **Columba** (Columba did not reach **Iona** till 563, and only visited Lismore during his later travels).

Moluag probably established his church and principal muuintir (settlement or community) on the site of the royal burial ground at Clachan. It was a self-supporting group of about 150 lay and clerical members. He then set off on the characteristic missionary task of creating satellite settlements staffed by people trained on Lismore. It seems unlikely that he can have visited every site with which his name is connected, but there are strong grounds for believing that he travelled to **Mull**, **Skye**, Pabbay and even **Lewis** (from where tradition has him setting sail to Iceland) before establishing two more muuintir at Rosemarkie and Mortlach (**Banffshire**). It is a tribute to his enduring influence that they and Lismore became sites of medieval bishoprics.

He died on 25 June 592 (the only fact about him recorded by the Annals of Tigernach), most probably at **Ardclach** (**Nairn**) and was buried at Rosemarkie. An unsubstantiated story tells how 24 strong men fetched his body back to Lismore. Three Lismore relics survive and are credited with miraculous powers – his chair, by the roadside near Clachan; his bell (mentioned in various records), in **Edinburgh**; and his pastoral staff of polished blackthorn, no longer covered in its original gilt, the 'Bachul Mor', which was brought triumphantly back to Lismore by Alastair Livingstone in 1952 after a period of ambiguous safe-keeping in the hands of the **Dukes of Argyll**. Even without a hagiographer, Moluag, 'the pure, the bright, the pleasant' (according to the martyrology of Oengus) ranks with the most famous saints of the Celtic church, rivalling even Columba in missionary endeavour.

MONACH ISLANDS, Outer Hebrides

Now a **National Nature Reserve** with large populations of **seabirds** and **seals**, the Monach Islands lie six miles west of **North Uist**. The three largest islands in the five-island group, Ceann Ear, Shivinish and Ceann Iar, are linked at low tide by causeways, as indeed was the group to the mainland of North Uist by a sand-bar until the 16th century when the link was washed away by an exceptionally fierce tide. On these islands (previously also known as Heisker) **James Erskine, Lord Grange**, abandoned his wife for two years (1732–4) before having her removed to **St Kilda**. The lighthouse on Shillay, the most westerly island, was built in 1864 and in use until 1942, at which time the last members of a population which had reached over 100 in the early 19th century also departed.

MONADHLIATH, Inverness-shire

Running north-east from **Lochaber**, the Monadhliath (ie 'Grey Mountains') divide Speyside and **Badenoch** from the **Great Glen**. They are part of the southern Grampians though neither as high as the **Cairngorms** beyond the **Spey** nor as attractively broken as the northern Grampians beyond the Great Glen. With a regular profile, few rock outcrops and no dominating peaks, they still contain 'irksome solitudes, vast and dreary wastes, which are abandoned to the grouse and the ptarmigan, the roe and the **red deer**' as well as much **forestry. Wade**'s **military road** made use of the **Corrieyairack Pass** in the south-west while the **railway** and the A9 to **Inverness** use the Slochd Pass in the north-east. The former was used by **Prince Charles Edward Stewart** in 1745 as he advanced from Lochaber; and it was into the Monadhliath that a year later he and his companions fled after defeat at **Culloden**.

MONIAIVE, Dumfriesshire

Once a burgh (1636), this village between **Thornhill** and **St John's Town of Dalry** was the home of **James Renwick** the last **Covenanter** martyr, whose birthplace is marked with a monument. It also has literary associations. In Maxwelton House (1641), to the east, lived the young **Annie Laurie** while Craigdarroch (1729, **William Adam**), to the west, became her home after marriage to Alexander Ferguson. Both were buried in Glencairn parish church, Moniaive (or Minniehive) being the principal village in the parish. The Earldom of Glencairn was granted by **James II** to Alexander Cunningham whose descendant, James 14th Earl, is remembered as the friend and patron of **Robert Burns**.

> The mother may forget the child
> That smiles saw sweetly on her knee:
> But I'll remember thee, Glencairn,
> And a' that thou hast done for me!

MONIFIETH, Nr Dundee

On the mouth of the **Tay** between **Broughty Ferry** and **Carnoustie**, Monifieth is part suburb and part resort (beach and **golf courses**). The site is of considerable antiquity if taken to include the souterrains at Ardestie and Carlungie [see **Tealing**], the vitrified fort on the Law of Monifieth, or the once **Culdee** church of St Rule (Regulus). **Pictish** symbol stones and cross-slabs, now in the **Museum of Scotland**, **Edinburgh**, were also found here. Inland the estate of Grange of Monifieth was one of those at which **Montrose** spent a night en route to Edinburgh and execution in 1650. As at **Pitcaple**,

the lady of the house attempted to facilitate his escape, here by getting his guard drunk and dressing the Marquis as a woman. It failed because at least one soldier remained sober enough to penetrate the disguise.

MONK, General George, 1st Duke of Albemarle (1608–70)

George Monk is one of the enigmas of the Civil War period. Born a Royalist, the second son of a minor aristocratic Devon family and fighting on the King's side till his capture by the Parliamentary party at the Battle of Nantwich, he became one of Oliver Cromwell's most effective generals and his deputy in Scotland. Though courted by the King in exile, he served Cromwell with unwavering loyalty, publicly proclaiming his support for his son Richard on his accession as Protector in 1658. It was only in the face of chaos and extreme influence in the army that he secretly responded to approaches from Royalist leaders. Marching across the border from his camp at **Coldstream** on 1 January 1660, he became the most powerful man in England, securing the return of Parliamentary government and the restoration of the Stewart dynasty. Ironically his regiment, named the Coldstream Guards after this event, had been raised for him by Cromwell to fight **Charles I** in Scotland.

The chief threat to the Commonwealth in 1650 had come not from the purely Royalist rising of **Montrose** (who had been executed by the **Covenanters** in May), but from those who supported some combination of Presbytery and/or King. Monk played only a minor part in the defeat of the Scottish army at **Dunbar** on 3 September 1650, but he led the successful sieges of **Tantallon Castle** and **Blackness** in early 1651. Promoted to commander-in-chief after Cromwell pursued the King across the border in August 1651, he completed the reduction of the Covenanters' political and military authority with the submission of **Stirling** and **St Andrews** and the conquest of **Dundee**, where responsibility for excessive brutality has been inconclusively attributed to him.

Despatched north again in April 1654 to put down the rising led by Glencairn and **Middleton**, Monk was from then until the Restoration the lynchpin of English civil and military authority in Scotland, first as commander-in-chief and, after the Ordinance of Union and the establishment of the Scottish Council in 1655, as its most important member. Monk skilfully masterminded the military campaign in which the Royalists were driven into the Highlands and starved of supplies by ruthless destruction of their crops and pasture and of their natural supporters by a characteristic combination of conciliation and coercion. Securing the active help of **Argyll**, whose son supported the Royalists, was a vital step. Their decisive defeat at Dalnaspidal (Glengarry) was followed by the erection of a cordon of fortresses round the Highlands at **Leith, Perth, Ayr, Inverlochy** and **Inverness**. Solidly built and costing an estimated £100,000 each, they were invested with permanent English garrisons and symbolised the imposition of law and order.

Instrument of Cromwell's policies and inheritor of many of the ideas of his predecessor Robert Lilburne, Monk nonetheless made his individual mark. He believed that the political and economic policies applied to Scotland should take into account the reasons for unrest, and he worked hard to reduce ill-judged instructions from London, particularly the high tax assessments and harsh penalties levied on leading Royalists. Although contemporary personal comments on 'honest general George' are favourable, even from many Scots, and although his numerous orders were given with 'such a grace and rigid gentleness', his government was always resented (despite its undoubted physical benefits).

Created Duke of Albemarle at the Restoration, he continued to offer effective and versatile public service, both on land and sea, in his role of Lieutenant-General of the armed forces, and in his direction of the people of London during the Great Plague of 1665. He is buried in Westminster Abbey.

MONMOUTH AND BUCCLEUCH, James, Duke of (1649–85)

Monmouth was born in Rotterdam, the son of 'browne, beautiful, bold, but insipid' Lucy Walters. Mistress of many including the future **Charles II**, she insisted that her baby James was a **Stewart**. But he looked more like a dashing Sidney while the affable vacuity and extrovert manners which soon appealed to the King were certainly not Stewart traits. Known as James Fitzroy or Crofts (after his guardian), he was created Duke of Monmouth when in 1663, aged 14, Charles acknowledged him as his son; he assumed the name of Scott in the same year when he was married to the rich and eligible Anne, Countess of **Buccleuch** in her own right, the title being now made ducal.

Although Charles stopped short of legitimising him, rumours to that effect abounded as the teenage Duke was advanced to the prejudice of the future **James VII** at court, in the army (where he succeeded **Monk**, now Duke of Albemarle, as Captain-General in 1670), and even in academia where he was elected Cambridge's least probable Chancellor. Between masques, amours, and other hot-headed exploits he gained a modest military reputation and in 1679 was sent to Scotland to pacify the **Covenanting** victors of **Drumclog**. Their defeat at **Bothwell Brig** increased his stature but was less notable than the clemency that he subsequently showed to the vanquished.

Monmouth was now becoming closely identified with the Protestant opposition to the Catholic James Duke of York and was increasingly so used by Shaftesbury and others, including the King. York's rehabilitation in 1680 led to Monmouth's temporary eclipse and though he cultivated popular support, especially in the west of England, he was forced into exile by implication in the Rye House Plot (1683). In Holland he made common cause with the **Test Act** fugitive, **Archibald 9th Earl of Argyll**, and together they launched a two-pronged invasion following the accession of **James VII** and II in 1685. **Argyll's rising** in Scotland quickly petered out while Monmouth's in the west country terminated at the Battle of Sedgemoor, after which he was run to ground in a ditch near Ringwood. Brought to London, he showed abject contrition but was nevertheless executed. His widow survived till the age of 81, outliving their eldest son, James Earl of Dalkeith (1674–

1705), so that it was his son Francis (d.1751) who became 2nd Duke of Buccleuch.

MONRO, Professor Alexander (Primus) (1697–1767) Surgeon

Born in London, the son of John Munro, an established **Edinburgh** surgeon (and to whom he was apprenticed), Alexander was taught anatomy by William Cheselden in London and also studied in Paris and Leyden before returning to Edinburgh in 1719. Admitted into the Incorporation of Surgeons, he was appointed Professor of Anatomy in 1720 and won popularity by lecturing in English rather than Latin. He also produced The Anatomy of Human Bones (1726) which was translated into several languages and ran to several editions.

At about this time he wrote a pamphlet urging the setting up of a hospital in which the city's poor could be given free treatment and which, in turn, would give the University medical school a teaching hospital. In 1729 a house off the **Cowgate** was rented for that purpose. Monro was elected to the Board of Managers and carried out all the surgical treatment there, free of charge. This establishment became the **Royal Infirmary of Edinburgh** in 1736, and two years later work was begun on a new purpose-built hospital. From it grew Edinburgh's reputation as a centre for medical teaching.

In 1756 Monro was awarded an MD by **Edinburgh University** and in the same year he became a Fellow of the **Royal College of Physicians** of Edinburgh. This enabled him to practise as a physician and, as a result, he gave up surgery. In 1758 he handed over the teaching of anatomy and surgery to his son, **Alexander Monro (Secundus)**.

In 1764 he published An Account of the Inoculation of Small-Pox in Scotland, the compilation of which set new standards of scientific and medical research. He died in Edinburgh.

MONRO, Professor Alexander (Secundus) (1733–1817) Physician

Born in **Edinburgh**, son of Professor **Alexander Monro (Primus)**, he studied medicine at **Edinburgh University**, Berlin and then Leyden. He returned to Edinburgh in 1758 and took over his father's teaching of anatomy and surgery, sharing his father's professorship. In the same year he became a Licentiate of the **Royal College of Physicians of Edinburgh** and in 1759 a Fellow. He practised, therefore, as a physician, and although he lectured on surgery, he never operated on a patient himself. The Incorporation of Surgeons of Edinburgh felt this purely theoretical approach to be wholly inadequate, and started another series of lectures on the more practical aspects of surgery in Surgeon's Hall and in the **Royal Infirmary**. This caused a good deal of ill-feeling.

Monro's anatomical research included investigations of the brain and nervous system. He explored the communication networks of the ventricles of the brain and discovered what came later to be known as Monro's foramen. **Sir Charles Bell** was to acknowledge the value of his work. Published works included Observations on the Structure and Functions of the Nervous System (1783), A Description of all the Bursae Mucosae of the Human Body (1787) and A Treatise on the Brain (1797). In the 1790s he was an eager supporter of the introduction of the smallpox vaccine to Edinburgh, as 10% of the population then died from the disease.

In 1760 he became Secretary to the revived Philosophical Society and later, after the departure of **David Hume,** he ran the society on his own. In 1783 it received its royal charter as the **Royal Society of Edinburgh,** and Monro was elected to serve on its council. He was also Secretary to the Royal College of Physicians of Edinburgh from 1772–9 and President from 1779–82. In 1798 he successfully petitioned the Town Council to allow him and his son Alexander Monro (Tertius) to share the Chair in Anatomy at Edinburgh University, as he had done with his own father 40 years before. He is buried in **Greyfriars' Churchyard.**

MONS GRAUPIUS, Battle of (84 or 85 AD)

The only set-piece battle between the **Roman** legions of **Agricola** and the **Caledonii** took place on an upland site which Tacitus calls *Mons Graupius.* There **Galgacus** delivered his supposed oration to 30,000 Caledonii before they were defeated by the superior cohesion, tactics and armour of the Roman cohorts. Additionally the Roman cavalry made short work of the native chariots and a Roman fleet supplied the legions' advance up the east coast. Tacitus gives few further clues to the location of *Graupius,* but the archaeological discovery of substantial marching camps in **Angus** and **Aberdeenshire** bears out the theory that it lay in the north-east. Raedykes near **Stonehaven** is one possibility although current opinion favours sites further north, either near **Huntly** or near **Bennachie.**

Much later it is thought that **Hector Boece** misread *Mons Graupius* as *Mons Grampius* and so introduced the 'Grampian Mountains' to Scottish topography. This designation was once interchangeable with The Mounth, ie the hill country along the south bank of the **Dee.** It has since been used with considerable imprecision to indicate the eastern flank of the central Highlands, or all the hill country of Aberdeenshire, **Kincardineshire,** Angus, **Perthshire** and **Stirlingshire.** Today it is commonly used of the hills, including the **Cairngorms,** east and south of the **Spey.**

MONS MEG

Scotland's biggest gun, now reposing silently in the vaults of the 'French Prison' beneath the **Great Hall** of **Edinburgh Castle,** Mons or 'Muckle' Meg was probably made at Mons in Flanders (where a similar gun exists at Ghent) in 1449 by Jehan Cambier, and gifted by Duke Philip the Good of Burgundy to **James II,** his nephew by marriage, in 1457. A type of siege ordnance known as a 'bombard', it is composed of longitudinal iron bars welded and hammered together into a cylinder around which iron hoops are shrunk; the piece may originally have been breech loading as the breech block appears to be screwed in. The overall length is 13ft 2in (4m) with a calibre of 19½in (50cm) and it weighs over 5 tons. For the siege of Norham Castle in Northumberland in 1497 **James IV** employed a small army of 3 wrights, 2 smiths and about 100 others with horses and oxen to transport the gun, which could hurl shot weighing several hundred pounds for up to two miles. After a long service career, Mons Meg was abandoned

after bursting while firing a salute for the Duke of York in 1681. In 1754 it was removed to the Tower of London (in an ignorant bureaucratic error) where it remained until 1829, **Sir Walter Scott** having persuaded George IV to decree its return to Edinburgh.

MONTGOMERIE, Alexander (c1545–97)
Poet

The laureate ('maister poete') at the **Edinburgh** court of **James VI,** Montgomerie belonged to the cadet branch of the powerful **Ayrshire** Eglinton family. His Catholicism, first employed by James in secret dealings with Philip of Spain, led finally to exile and outlawry. His literary significance is primarily historical. He was leader of the vernacular renaissance announced by James in his poetical treatise *The Reulis and Cautelis* (1585). The erudite, courtly, manneristic verse practised by this Castalian Band (which also included William Fowler, John Stewart of Baldynneis and King James) was much later to produce the Burnsean vernacular revival by way of reaction. Montgomerie's major long poem, *The Cherrie and the Slae,* in its rhetorical brilliance and allegorical tediousness, mirrors the strengths and weaknesses of the group fairly accurately.

MONTGOMERIE (or MONTGOMERY), Hugh, 12th Earl of Eglinton (1739–1819)

The Earldom of Eglinton had been created (1508) for Lord Hugh Montgomerie, later a guardian to **James V.** Another Hugh, 3rd Earl, was one of **Queen Mary's** loyalest supporters while Alexander, 10th Earl (1732–

Hugh Montgomerie, 12th Earl of Eglinton, by John Singleton Copley (SNPG)

69) was a noted agricultural improver and the victim of a *cause célèbre* when shot dead, possibly accidentally, by a poacher near **Ardrossan**. He was succeeded by his brother and the latter by his grandson, Hugh 12th Earl, in 1796. Known therefore until his 50s as Hugh Montgomerie of Skelmorlie, the 12th Earl had fought with distinction in the American War of Independence and then in France before becoming MP for **Ayrshire** (1783). On succeeding to the earldom he devoted himself to music, as a keen composer of popular airs, and to grandiose developments like the construction of the massively castellated Eglinton Castle and of the ambitious Ardrossan harbour. The latter, at a cost of £200,000, was completed by his grandson and successor, Archibald William 13th Earl (1812–61), who yet found the wherewithal to cut a famous figure on the Victorian turf and to stage the 1839 Eglinton Tournament. This was a three-day medieval extravaganza, marred by continuous rain but unequalled for lavish hospitality, which Disraeli described in *Endymion*.

MONTROSE, Angus

Montrose has enjoyed an exceptional press. 'Her generous entertainments in every angle, like radiated beams of the sun that invigorate the earth, so naturally do the inhabitants influence their civilities amongst strangers; which remonstrates Montrose a beauty that lies concealed, as it were, in the bosom of Scotland.' Or so thought Richard Frank, Roundhead, angler and most orotund of wordsmiths. **Dr Johnson** pronounced it 'well built, airy and clean' and **Boswell** merely objected that 'Many of the houses are built with ends [ie gables] to the street, which looks awkward.' Others have found this typically Scottish arrangement, with the pends and wynds which it necessitates, rather attractive. 'The aristocrat of Angus', **Nigel Tranter** called it, 'one of the most unusual medium-sized towns in all Scotland'. With the sea to the east, a large tidal basin to the west, and the South Esk River to the south, Montrose enjoys a peninsular situation with a sheltered and once busy port plus extensive links and dunes to the north.

The High Street is exceptionally wide, almost a square, and here stands the church (1791) with a tall detached steeple (1832) by **Gillespie Graham**. Nearby the Old Town House (1763), much admired by Dr Johnson, projects into the street and has an arcaded piazza. Other buildings of note, all 18th and 19th century, attest the popularity of the town with local landowners. That once owned by the Earls of Montrose may have been the birthplace of **James Graham, 1st Marquis**, although the probability is that he was born in Old Montrose, inland from the tidal basin. There is a museum and art gallery containing some **Pictish** cross-slabs, including that from **Farnell**, some geological exhibits, whaling mementoes and paintings. The Montrose Academy, a classical building (1815) with gold dome, is reputedly where Greek was first taught in Scotland when John Erskine of nearby **Dun** established a school in 1554. There is a statue of Sir Robert Peel; **Joseph Hume** and **Sir Alexander Burnes** were born here.

In spite of the town's motto, *Mare ditat, Rosa decorat*, Montrose is named after neither a rose nor a hill, the word deriving from the Gaelic designation of 'a moor on a peninsula'. There was once a castle, where **John Balliol** 'did render quietly the realm of Scotland' to Edward I after his deposition at Stracathro; but the castle was destroyed by **William Wallace** in 1297 and evi-

Montrose High Street c1890 with statue of Joseph Hume (GWWA)

dently not rebuilt. **Royal burgh** status came with the reign of **David II**; thereafter the town quietly prospered thanks to its harbour and trading links. Recent developments connected with the North Sea **oil and gas** industry, plus the VAT 69 distillery, have scarcely prejudiced the town's style or its reputation as a holiday resort with **golf** courses, bird watching around the Montrose Basin, a nature reserve at St Cyrus to the north and the sands of **Lunan Bay** to the south.

MONTROSE, 5th Earl and 1st Marquis of, see GRAHAM, James

MONYMUSK, Aberdeenshire

On the **Don** between **Inverurie** and **Alford**, Monymusk is a largely 19th century village but with a church and 'big hoose' of much greater antiquity. St Mary's, originally the chapel of a **Culdee** community, was established as an Augustinian priory by Gilchrist, **Earl of Mar**, in 1170, from which period date the square tower (minus 19th century crenellation) and the chancel arch. Some of the stone facings are thought to have come from **Kildrummy Castle**. There are two **Pictish** symbol stones built into the nave and another, the Monymusk Stone, in the entrance. The **Monymusk Reliquary** was long held here before being removed to Monymusk House during the **Reformation**. At that time the Forbes family acquired the Monymusk estate and built the main L-plan tower house, since much altered and substantially remodelled for **Sir Archibald Grant**, the agricultural improver, whose father acquired it from the Forbes in 1712. Nearby Pitfichie Castle was also a Forbes property, having previously belonged to the Urry or Hurry family whose scion, General Sir John Hurry, learnt to be a good loser. After defeat by **Montrose** in 1644, then with him in 1650 (**Carbisdale**), he was executed.

MONYMUSK RELIQUARY, The

So called because it was long held at **Monymusk** Priory, then Monymusk House, the reliquary is a small 8th century Celtic box cut from solid wood in the shape of

The Monymusk Reliquary or Breccbennach (© the Trustees of the National Museums of Scotland 1994)

an oratory (with pitched roof) and clad with bronze and silver plates chased and set with semi-precious stones and enamels; hence its Gaelic name Breccbennach 'the speckled and peaked one'. It was believed to contain a bone relic of **St Columba** and as such was entrusted to the abbot of **Arbroath** by **William the Lion** (1211) so that it might be available for blessing the royal troops in battle – as indeed it was at **Bannockburn**. It is now in the **Museum of Scotland** in **Edinburgh**.

MOORE, Sir John (1761–1809) Soldier

The son of an eminent **Glasgow** physician and writer, also John (another of whose sons, Graham, rose to be an admiral), Moore was born in Glasgow and educated at the High School and abroad. He joined the army aged 15, served throughout the American War of Independence, and was elected MP in 1784. He resumed active service (1792) in the Mediterranean and was prominent in ending the French occupation of Corsica, although incurring Nelson's displeasure in the process. There followed further action in the West Indies (1796–7), Ireland (1797–9) and Holland (1799) during which he attained the rank of major-general; his numerous wounds were put down to misfortune and only endeared him to his men. He returned to the Mediterranean in 1800 and during the Egyptian campaign was again severely wounded. A spell of redundancy then enabled him to develop the principles and arrangements for light infantry deployment.

In 1804 he was made KCB and in 1805 lieutenant-general but not till 1808 did he see further action abroad. This was in Spain and Portugal where he commanded the entire British army of some 30,000 men, half of whom were to land at Corunna. Moore and the rest in Lisbon resolved to march overland to join them. Supply shortages obliged them to turn back; then a request for help to defend Madrid was answered, but with disastrous consequences. For although a rendez-vous was effected with the other troops under **Sir David Baird**, the city had already fallen to Napoleon whose vast army now cut off any retreat to Portugal. In a famous march of 250 miles in midwinter, the British troops headed for Corunna, their Dunkirk, and, arriving three weeks later, were just beginning to embark on transports when the French overtook them. Moore was early hit in the shoulder, died that evening, and was buried at midnight, 'the guns of the enemy paying his funeral honours'. 'His talents and firmness alone saved the British army [which escaped next day] from destruction', according to Napoleon. Moore became a national hero and was the first man to be commemorated by a statue in Glasgow's **George Square**.

MORAR, Inverness-shire

This is one of the many west coast peninsulas defined by deep probing sea lochs, in this case Loch Nevis to the north (beyond which lies **Knoydart**) and Loch Ailort and the Sound of Arisaig to the south (beyond which lies **Moidart**). Unlike its neighbours Morar boasts a **fishing** port of some note in **Mallaig** and an embryonic resort in **Arisaig**. Loch Morar, 12 miles long and fresh-water, bisects the district and very nearly makes it two peninsulas, there being only a few hundred yards (across which pass the road and **railway**) between the

Lieut-General Sir John Moore; fragment from The Death of Abercromby by James Northcote (SNPG)

loch's western extremity and the sea. Although the loch is only 40ft (12m) above sea level and although the sea here shelves very gradually, the loch plummets to a depth of over 1000ft (305m), making it the deepest in Scotland or 'on any part of the European plateau, except the submarine valley which skirts the south part of Scandinavia' (**A Geikie**). It has a monster, known as Morag, whose appearance heralds the death of a **Clanranald MacDonald**, and it was where the octogenarian **Simon Fraser, 11th Lord Lovat**, was eventually found, lying on two feather beds at the water's edge, and captured prior to trial and execution for his dubious part in the '45 **Jacobite Rising**. From **Loch nan Uamh** in the south east to Mallaigvaig [see **Mallaig**] in the north-west the area is rich in Jacobite associations.

MORAY

One of the **seven Celtic earldoms** or provinces of Scotland, Moray (pron. 'Murray' and often interchangeable with that spelling), or in Latin 'Moravia', once comprised a vast area extending round the Moray Firth from **Ross** to **Buchan** and south-west to **Atholl** and **Lochaber**. Its coastal heartland, the Laigh of Moray, was considered both the garden and granary of **Caledonia**, well wooded, well farmed and favoured with a sunny climate. This, plus its enormous strategic importance, accounts for its high historical profile evidenced today in the abundance of ancient sites and fine architecture.

The county of Moray, comprising most of the Laigh, the lower **Spey** valley, and the inland Braes of Moray, includes most of this heartland. To the west is

Nairnshire, the south **Inverness-shire** and the east **Banffshire**. The highest point is Carn a Ghille Chearr in the Cromdale Hills in the extreme south. Encompassing 304,931 acres (123,497ha), the county had a population in 1971 of 52,241, occupied in **agriculture**, **fishing** and distilling.

The county town was **Elgin**, the county sometimes having been known as Elginshire. Moray was in fact united for administrative purposes with Nairn, immediately to the west, under the Local Government (Scotland) Act of 1929, and was commonly known as 'Moray & Nairn'. Small burghs in the county included **Burghead**, **Elgin**, **Forres**, **Grantown-on-Spey**, **Lossiemouth** (including Branderburgh) and **Rothes**. Under **local government** reorganisation in 1975 Moray (without Nairn) was swallowed up by Grampian Region, except for Grantown-on-Spey and Cromdale, allocated to Badenoch & Strathspey Districts of Highland Region. Since 1995, the Moray District has included former parts of Banffshire.

MORAY, Earldom of

The heartland of **MacBeth**'s kingdom was bestowed as an earldom by **Robert I** on his supporter, **Thomas Randolph**, in whose family it remained until the death of the 3rd Earl at **Neville's Cross** in 1346. It was in Gordon hands when **Queen Mary** bestowed it on her bastard brother **Lord James Stewart**. The **Earl of Huntly** fought for it, and thus lost his life at **Corrichie** in 1562. The new Earl left a daughter who married Sir James Stewart, Lord Doune. Their son was created Earl of Moray in 1592, only to be murdered by Huntly in the same year. He is immortalised in the ballad of the Bonnie Earl of Moray. His descendants still possess the title as well as the great **Doune Castle** built by **Regent Albany**. They descend from him, and thus from **Robert II** in the legitimate male line, as well as from **James V** through Regent Moray's daughter.

MORAY, Sir Robert (1608–73) Founder of the Royal Society

Born in **Perthshire**, Moray's early life is not well documented, but his military and diplomatic career took him to London, where he pursued his interests in mineralogy and natural history, associating with many influential savants of the time, and made the friendship of **Charles II**. From these contacts came the formation of the Royal Society of London in 1660. In honour of its Scottish founder, the Society still holds its AGM on **St Andrew**'s Day.

MORE, Jacob (1740–93) Painter

Along with **Alexander Nasmyth**, Jacob More was one of the most successful Scottish landscape painters of the 18th century. His early training was with the Norie family of **Edinburgh** who supplied fashionable interior decoration for wealthy clients, including panels painted with appropriately Italianate neo-classical scenes, often commissioned as pendants to works acquired on the Grand Tour. More worked on a number of commissions for the architect **Robert Adam**. This grounding in the much favoured styles of the Old Masters was tempered by his association with the brothers **Alexander and John Runciman** whose own paintings often favoured more sublime or dramatic themes. In 1770 More painted a subject popular with the early Romantic artists – The Falls of Clyde – as two sets, the first with figures in contemporary costume. The successful reception of these works both in Edinburgh and London encouraged More to follow in the footsteps of his compatriot **Gavin Hamilton** and pursue a career in Rome. There More's work reverted to the more idealised neo-classicism of the much admired Claude and Poussin, and although often considered less interesting than his Scottish pictures, demonstrates a superior sense of tone and colour. It was sufficiently admired to bring him a substantial income and More was thus to remain in Rome until his death.

MORGAN, Tommy (d.1958) Comedian

Born in and proud of his native Bridgeton in **Glasgow**, Tommy Morgan was a tall, cherubic-faced **music hall** comedian who acquired a loyal following of summer show audiences at the **Pavilion Theatre**, Glasgow. He worked with his long-time foil, Tommy Yorke, had an amusing gravel voice and a catchphrase 'Aw, Clairty, clairty!', a corruption of 'I declare to goodness!' On stage he reflected the natural working-class humour of the Glaswegian, and had success in pantomime after early days in music hall and with pierrot shows at **Portobello** and other old-time holiday haunts. He was noted for his generous life-style, befriended many performers down on their luck, and died practically penniless.

MORISON, Sir Alexander (1779–1866) Physician

Born in Bailie Fyfe's Close, **Edinburgh**, son of a lawyer, educated at Edinburgh High School and apprenticed to Dr Alexander Wood at the age of 15, Alexander Morison graduated from **Edinburgh University** in 1799. An attempt to set up a practice in London was unsuccessful, but in 1809 he was appointed Visiting Physician to the Private Lunatic Asylum in Surrey, a post he held for over 50 years, and later Physician to the Royal Hospital of Bethlem and Bridewell.

His plans to establish the first chair of mental diseases failed, but in 1823 he initiated a series of lectures first in Edinburgh and then in London, which continued annually for 30 years. These lectures formed the basis of his book *Physiognomy of Mental Diseases*, published in 1838. He was knighted by **Queen Victoria** on her accession to the throne. He bequeathed his house, Larchgrove, **Balerno**, to the **Royal College of Physicians** (of which he was successively Licentiate (1800), Fellow (1801) and President (1827)), and the sum realised from its sale was used to establish the Morison Lectureship and to purchase prizes for nurses with long and faithful service to the insane.

MORISON, James (1816–93) Minister

A **United Secession** minister born at **Bathgate**, Morison was suspended from his **Kilmarnock** charge in 1841. With other suspended ministers he founded the Evangelical Union and a theological college following modified Independency. The Churches combined in 1896 with those founded by the **Haldane** brothers into the Congregational Union.

MORISON, John (Gobha na Hearadh), 'The Harris Blacksmith' (c1796–1852) Gaelic Hymnist

Born in **Harris**, Morison became an SSPCK catechist, closely involved in the evangelical revival in the northern **Hebrides**. He composed many Gaelic hymns, one of the most notable being *An Nuadh Bhreith* ('The New Birth'), which describes the tussle between the unregenerate and the converted, the old and the new. For texts, see George Henderson, *Dàin Iain Ghobha* (1893).

MORMAER

The nature of this ancient Celtic or **Pictish** office remains a matter of speculation. The early medieval Gaelic entries in the **Book of Deer** mention a Mormaer of **Buchan** and another of **Mar**, distinct from the rank of Toiseach. There were also Mormaers of **Moray**, **Angus** and **Lennox**, while **The Mearns** and **Morvern** are thought to incorporate the term. Perhaps these provincial rulers were by definition sea stewards. There is no evidence that the **seven Celtic earldoms** evolved from the Mormaers, though this has been suggested, and the Latin *comes* was used for both.

MORRIS, 'Young Tom' (1851–75) Golfer

The Morrises of **St Andrews** are part of the folklore of **golf** and 'Young Tom' was undoubtedly the finest golfer of his day. Born at St Andrews, he became the youngest ever Open champion at the age of 17 years and 5 months, recording the first championship hole-in-one at **Prestwick** in the first of an unequalled four consecutive wins. He was only 24 and at the height of his powers when the tragic death of his young wife in childbirth dealt him a blow from which he never recovered. He had been partnering his father 'Old Tom' in a great match at **North Berwick** against the brothers Willie and Mungo Park, when the sad news was brought. Young Tom himself was to die in his sleep on Christmas Day of the same year. He can be regarded as having invented the modern approach shot, hitting down on the ball with an iron club, with an open stance, imparting backspin to check the ball on landing, and flighting it most of the way to the flag – as opposed to the traditional pitch and run.

His father, Old Tom, was born at St Andrews in 1821 and competed in every Open championship up to and including 1896. He also won the Open four times and remains the oldest ever winner, having won in 1867 aged 46. Old Tom died at St Andrews in 1908, and is commemorated, amongst other ways, in the name of the final hole at the Royal and Ancient.

MORRISON, Robert (1782–1834) Missionary

A native of **Roxburghshire**, Robert Morrison was sent to Canton by the London Missionary Society in 1807. By 1814 he had translated the New Testament into Chinese and by 1819 had done the same for the Old Testament. He established the Anglo-Chinese College at Malacca in 1818, and published a great Chinese dictionary in 1823. He died in China.

MORTON, Earldom of

It was not long after the downfall of the **Earls of Douglas** in 1455 that James Douglas of **Dalkeith** was created

Earl of Morton. Another **James Douglas** married Elizabeth, daughter of the 3rd Earl, and succeeded to his father-in-law's titles and estates on his death in 1553. Ten years later he became Lord Chancellor and in 1572 followed the ill-fated **Moray**, **Lennox** and **Mar** as Regent of Scotland. He fought off the intrigues of his rivals with great ability until the arrival from France of the boy King's handsome young cousin **Esmé Stewart**, with whom **James VI** fell in love. Esmé and his associates secured the arrest of Morton on a charge of involvement in the murder of **Darnley**, such as might have been brought against half the nobility of Scotland without solving that mystery. In 1581 Morton was executed by the guillotine called 'The Maiden' which he had introduced into the country. His forfeited earldom showed remarkable powers of revival amongst other branches of the Douglas family. During the **Scottish Enlightenment** the 14th Earl of Morton became a distinguished astronomer and President of the Royal Society in 1764.

MORTON CASTLE, Nr Thornhill, Dumfriesshire

'As remote and imperfectly understood as any castle can be', Morton appears to have been a quadrangular structure incorporating a round corner tower at one end and a main entrance with drawbridge and two 'D' shaped towers at the other. **MacGibbon and Ross** saw it as related to **Tulliallan** and **Rait** Castles in being 'an intermediate form between the square keep and the courtyard plan', 'no doubt ... first half of the 15th century'. Little is known of its history although the lands were granted to **Thomas Randolph** and in 1369 passed to the **Douglases** who presumably built most of what remains. It must have been in existence in 1458 when James Douglas of **Dalkeith** was created **Earl of Morton**. Subsequently passing to the Douglas Dukes of Queensberry and **Buccleuch**, it was abandoned in the 18th century.

MORVERN, Argyll

Cut off from the rest of mainland **Argyll** by the long arm of Loch Linnhe, the districts of Ardgour and Morvern were of more significance in the days when west Highland communication was largely by sea [see **Ardtornish**, **Mingary**, etc]. They are still usually reached either via the Corran ferry (near **Ballachulish**) or the **Mull** ferry from Fishnish to **Lochaline**. Both are little populated, hilly, and shrinking, as Glensanda quarry, one of the country's main sources of hard core, eats into the native rock. Ardgour has been **MacLean** country since the 15th century, Morvern since the 17th, although there is a **MacLeod** connection with Fiunary whence **Lord MacLeod** of the **Iona Community** took his title. In the 1970s both districts, along with **Ardnamurchan** to the west and Ballachulish/**Glencoe** to the east, became part of Highland Region (and not, like the rest of Argyll and Bute, part of Strathclyde).

MOTHERWELL, Lanarkshire

Until the late 19th century Motherwell was a modest village (pop c500) in the parish of Dalziel (Dalzell or Dalyell) between affluent **Hamilton** and already industrialised Wishaw and **Shotts**. **Coal**, **iron and steel** pro-

pelled it to the industrial forefront in the space of a generation. In 1871 **Colville**'s iron works switched to steel production and by 1914 Motherwell was the largest steel producer in Scotland. This position was merely confirmed by the siting of the ill-fated Ravenscraig project in the 1950s. Meanwhile Wishaw had been amalgamated with Motherwell and subsequently Shotts has become part of Motherwell district.

Now, with Ravenscraig closed (1991–2) and demolished (1996), the whole area epitomises the plight of an industrial conurbation without an industry. The blast furnaces are out and no phoenix has arisen; but 'surprising Motherwell', as the promotional pamphlets rather desperately call it, is determined to find a new identity. Billed as 'Scotland's most popular attraction', Strathclyde Country Park between Hamilton and Motherwell offers every conceivable activity that a 200 acre (81ha) artificial loch with fairground and parkland can host (including, in 1997–9, Scotland's National Gardening Show), plus the site and rebuilt bath-house of Bothwellhaugh, a **Roman** fort of the **Antonine** period. It occupies land once part of the grounds of Hamilton Palace, subsequently pitted with coal workings, and always much traversed – by the **Clyde**, a Roman road, the main **rail** line to the south and the M74. Also strung along this axis are Baron's Haugh, a nature reserve owned by the RSPB and yet another country park, Dalziel, where Dalziel House (mid-17th century with an older peel tower and 19th century additions) has been restored and converted into flats.

The name of Motherwell is thought to derive from its being the site of a well with curative properties in early Christian times. Its modern equivalent, a pilgrimage centre dedicated to Our Lady of Lourdes, lies 2 miles north at **Carfin**. Cambusnethan Priory commemorates Wishaw's vanished Celtic foundation only in name, being in fact a **James Gillespie Graham** creation of 1819, now vandalised, overgrown and at last living up to its gloomy Gothic aspect.

MOTOR RALLYING AND RACING

RALLYING Scotland's rugged terrain has made it a favourite location for testing cars in rally conditions since the motoring age began. In 1901 the Automobile Club of Britain held a 500 mile trial, in which a **Glasgow**-built Albion came second. Four years later, the Scottish Automobile Club (formed in 1899, and now the Royal Scottish Automobile Club) began a series of reliability trials which in 1932 became the international Scottish Rally. Nowadays covering 700 miles each June, the rally is Scotland's main event, although the RAC Lombard Rally includes some Scottish stages. World champion Colin McRae headed the Scottish challenge in the 1990s.

RACING Not even the lack of a recognised high-performance race venue has prevented Scotland making a major contribution to the sport, particularly post-war. Ecurie Ecosse was formed in 1952 as a non-profit-making syndicate among Scottish racing enthusiasts, and with three XK120 Jaguars and a Ferrari, won 13 out of its first 18 entries. 1956 and 1957 were even better, the team winning both years at Le Mans. The

1950s also saw the emergence of a **Berwickshire**-based team called the Border Reivers, probably best known for bringing the late **Jim Clark** to prominence. Innes Ireland had already become the first Scot to win a major Grand Prix – in the USA in 1961 – and Clark followed his lead, winning 25 Grand Prix races and becoming world champion twice. Even this was excelled by Jackie Stewart, who won the world championship three times and passed Clark's record in 1973. In the 1990s Stewart launched his own racing stable, while David Coulthard, driving for McLaren, boosted Scottish hopes for another world champion.

MOUNT STUART, Isle of Bute

When the original Mount Stuart (built 1716–19) was partially destroyed by fire in 1877, the **3rd Marquess of Bute** commissioned **Robert Rowand Anderson** to build a new house on the same site. Himself a great patron of architecture, the Marquess was pleased with Anderson's design: '. . . it seems to be a splendid palace; there are only a few things, partly in regard to the picturesque and partly the luxurious, in which I suggested alterations.' Construction began in 1880 – building materials transported to the site on a purpose-built railway included vast quantities of red sandstone for the exterior and shiploads of the finest Italian marble for the interior – and continued until the sudden death of the Marquess in 1900. By then his monumental Victorian Gothic extravaganza was almost complete; the first private house in Scotland to be lit by electricity and boasting the first heated indoor swimming pool, it surrounds a 60'-square marble-columned central hall rising three storeys to a stained glass clerestory and vaulted, star-studded roof, and includes three libraries, an observatory (used as an operating theatre when Mount Stuart was a hospital during the First World War and now a conservatory) and a glacial white marble chapel with octagonal tower and lantern inspired by the cathedral in Saragossa. Crammed with portraits, furniture, tapestries, statues and *objets d'art*, many commissioned specially for the house, Mount Stuart continues to be the home of the Bute family and is open to the public.

MOUNTAIN HARE

Sometimes called the blue or arctic hare, the mountain hare is found on high **heather** moors, with heather being its main food. It is indigenous to the Scottish Highlands and is most numerous on **grouse moors** in north-east Scotland, but there have been many introductions to the Lowlands and to some of the Western and Northern Isles. Mountain hares are agricultural pests in some areas but their presence contributes to the ability of **golden eagles** to raise two young, which is more likely in the east than the west. The mountain hare has three moults in the year; the famous white coat of the winter lasts from October to February when it turns brown until May, then for the summer the hare grows

Mousa broch, still standing to a height of 43ft (HS)

a shorter grey-brown coat with a bluish tinge – hence the name blue hare. In winter, if there is no snow on the hillsides they will sit on scree or near holes or among long heather in which they can hide when a predator appears. They feed mostly at night, tending to move downhill to feed and then back up to rest. Leverets are born between February and August and in good years they may have two or three litters, each with one or two young. The main predator is the fox, but adult hares are also taken by golden eagles and **wild cat**, with small leverets also taken by stoats, hen harriers and buzzards.

MOUSA, Shetland

Now uninhabited, the island of Mousa is renowned for its **broch**. Complete to the wallhead, with a height of 43ft (13m), this is the best-preserved of brochs and one of the largest. As at **Clickimin** the interior of the building has been modified with an inner wall – part of a later dwelling constructed in the 2nd or 3rd century AD.

Mousa broch served as a refuge for runaway lovers at least twice in **Viking** times. Around 900 AD, as related in Egil's Saga, an eloping couple were shipwrecked at **Shetland** on their way to Iceland and took refuge in *Morsayarborg*. A similar episode is related in the **Orkneyinga Saga**. In 1153 a certain Erlend abducted Margaret, the mother of Earl Harald Maddadson, from **Orkney** and with a strong band of supporters defied all attempts to remove them. Eventually a truce was declared and the lovers were allowed to marry.

Today Mousa is a Site of Special Scientific Interest because of the large number of **seals** that frequent the rocks and also for its **seabirds**, including storm petrels which nest in the walls of the broch.

MOY, Nr Inverness

The name derives from *magh*, a plain or field, and is found elsewhere, eg in Lochaber. This Moy, home of the chief of **Clan Mackintosh** and closely associated with the '45 **Jacobite Rising**, is 10 miles south of **Inverness** between the rivers Nairn and Findhorn near the main A9 road. In Loch Moy the larger island once boasted a castle which was the Mackintosh stronghold in the 15th–17th centuries; it now sports an obelisk (1824) commemorating Sir Aeneas Mackintosh (d.1820).

Responding to the more settled conditions of the late 17th century the Mackintoshes removed to a mainland site north of the loch and built Moy Hall. Here stayed **Prince Charles Edward Stewart** on the night of 16 February 1746, a fact of which Lord Loudoun in charge of the government forces in Inverness was apprised and determined to take advantage. With 1500 men he marched forth with surprise on his side and the £30,000 bounty in his sights. But a fleet-footed Mackintosh overtook him and reached Moy first. He alerted the Prince, who made for the lochside wearing his bonnet over his night-cap; he also alerted the lady of the house, formidable **'Colonel Anne'** Mackintosh. She despatched the local blacksmith, one Donald Fraser, and four companions to take up position on a drovers' road to the west. There they duly intercepted Loudoun's army, fired their guns (the only casualty was a **Macrim-**

mon, hereditary piper to the **MacLeods**), and emitted such a variety of war cries that the enemy panicked 'and instantly beat a retreat'. Such was the Rout of Moy. After **Culloden** its instigator, Colonel Anne, was arrested at Moy Hall and briefly imprisoned.

The house burnt down about 1800, was replaced in the 19th century with a much grander affair, but this too was abandoned in the 20th century because of dry rot. Today's Moy Hall, still home of the Mackintosh of Mackintosh, is more modest and was built in the 1950s.

MUCHALLS CASTLE, Nr Stonehaven, Kincardineshire

MacGibbon and Ross called Muchalls a house rather than a castle, which description better fits its profile, setting and doubtful defences. Of three storeys with steeply pitched roof, its basic shape is L-plan with an enclosing wall forming a rectangular courtyard between the arms of the L. Over the gateway in this wall an inscription ascribes the work to the Burnetts of Leys in 1619–27 and there is the date 1624 with the royal arms on the overmantel in the Great Hall. Here the ribbed plaster ceiling with a typical Renaissance selection of patrician heads – **Roman**, Biblical, heroic – has been described as 'the handsomest in Scotland'. A secret passage once led from the house to a smugglers' cove on the coast, which here has some of the wildest rock scenery in Britain.

MUCK, Island of, Inner Hebrides

The smallest of the four Small Isles – the others being **Eigg**, **Rum** and **Canna** – and the most southerly, Muck is a flatly sloping, fertile island whose surrounding seas abound with marine species. From one, the porpoise, Muck is thought to take its name – *Muc Mara*, or sea swine, being common in Gallanach Bay. In 1549 Sir Donald Munro described the island as 'very fertile and fruitful of cornes and grassing for all store and very good **fishing**, inhabit and manurit, a good falcon nest on it'. The MacLeans of **Ardnamurchan** held the island for five generations until the last, who fought in the American War of Independence, married an American and had 'numerous issue', ran into debt while acting as Deputy Lieutenant of the Tower of London. The Clanranalds bailed him out in return for Muck until debts forced them to sell. During the 19th century poverty drove many islanders to emigrate, many to Nova Scotia, and in 1854 Muck was sold to Thomas Swinburne, a sea captain. He built Gallanach House, developed the fishing and introduced sheep. In 1879 Lawrence Thompson MacEwen, who already owned much land including Eigg, acquired Muck. Cows were introduced and cheeses exported. Thompson's nephew and heir, Commander William MacEwen, planted the first trees in 1922 and ran Muck's 100 acres as a model island unit, a policy continued to the present day by his son Lawrence aided by the other 25 residents of the island.

MUCKLE FLUGGA, Shetland

At the north end of **Unst** lie the rocks known as Muckle Flugga, the most northerly inhabited island in the UK so long as the lighthouse, built in 1858, remains manned. A short distance away is the uninhabited Out Stack, the most northerly speck of land in the UK.

MUCKLE ROE, Shetland

Situated in St Magnus Bay on the west side of **Shetland**, Muckle Roe has been linked to the **Mainland** of Shetland by a bridge since 1905. It supports a **crofting** community of around 100. The name means 'the big red island', most of the rock being red granite.

MUGDOCK CASTLE, Stirlingshire

Of the ancient seat of the Grahams, Earls (1503), Marquises (1644) and Dukes (1707) of **Montrose**, there remains only one fairly complete tower and the vaulted basement of another. These and one, or perhaps two, others once formed the corners of the 14th century castle of enceinte, a fraction of whose curtain walling also survives. It stands on a promontory, fortified in the 15th century, in Mugdock Loch, a mile north of Milngavie (itself in **Dunbartonshire**, the castle in **Stirlingshire**, and both now part of greater **Glasgow**). To the surviving tower was added in the 17th century a two-storey building and in the 19th century a baronial mansion. Both have since suffered from dereliction but now form part of Mugdock Country Park. The lands were originally granted to David de Graham in the 13th century, the castle becoming the principal seat of the family from the mid-15th until the early 18th centuries with an intermission following the forfeiture of **James Graham 1st Marquis**.

MUIR, Edwin (1887–1959) Poet

One of the 20th century's major poets, a noted critic, translator and autobiographer, Edwin Muir was born on Mainland, **Orkney** but spent his happiest childhood years on the island of Wyre. At a time of agricultural upheaval his father, a farmer, was often in trouble. After various moves the Muir family finally went to **Glasgow** to seek a livelihood. To an Orcadian exile's recoil from the ugly Edwardian city was added the deep trauma of his father's death, the sufferings of two brothers (one dying of a brain tumour, the other of TB), and the death of his mother. Muir's health also faltered, but he prospered in several clerical jobs and briefly as a chauffeur's aide in **Ayrshire**. Experience of a **Gourock** bone-rending firm proved less congenial; the stinking reek outside and the rampant dishonesty within provided the nightmare of the 'Fairport' chapter of *An Autobiography*. Glasgow was not all bad; he relished its cultural life, friendship with **F G Scott** et al, its literary-political societies and the abundance of popularising journals and books. Yet the trauma endured.

In 1908 he began to write (as 'Edward Moore') for the journal *The New Age*. Edited in London by A R Orage, a self-educated Yorkshireman, *The New Age* was intellectual, modern and multicultural. Muir studied Nietzsche and in 1918 'Edward Moore' published the book *We Moderns*. In the same year Edwin met the forceful Willa Anderson. They married in 1919 and, she resigning her teaching post, moved to London. He assisted Orage and did menial jobs; she earned a crust teaching; both delighted in Orage's stimulating associates. With one, Maurice Nicoll, Edwin had sessions of therapy until Nicoll went to France. An interest in dreams and in the synthesising imagination probably began then. Edwin's articles intrigued the editor of an American journal, *The Freeman*, who commissioned more. With prices cheap on the Continent, the Muirs took advice from another *New Age* man, Paul Selver, and went to Prague.

Edwin had never seen a beautiful city. Prague is just that. He 'indulged in an orgy of looking'; they made friends with Karel Capek, went to the opera and theatre, met people; Edwin found the effects of his Glasgow trauma slipping away. They moved to Hellerau near Dresden, where in friendship with a minor German poet he found new literary interests and began to write poetry. This seemed to complete the great healing process.

Such is the tale told in *The Story and the Fable* (1940), the autobiographical work he wrote from personal crisis in the late 1930s. Forgetting and (re)discovery is a motif of even his earliest poems – the 'other road' (or thing) 'you did not see'. Another theme is wandering, whether from restlessness or homelessness, as nomad or refugee. The Muirs had no settled home until the mid-50s and for most of the 1920s they moved around Europe, earning what they could by his reviewing, their translating and writing. For a time they lived in the then obscure St Tropez. During this period Edwin produced works of criticism (*Transition*, 1926; *The Structure of the Novel*, 1929) and novels (*The Marionette*, 1927; *The Three Brothers*, 1931; *Poor Tom*, 1932; the first and third of these of note). There are a few good poems in *First Poems* (1925) but, apart from a rejected work and the intriguing *Variations on a Time Theme* (1934), there was no substantial book of verse till 1937. *Journeys and Places* collects, often drastically revised, poems of the preceding dozen years. Deeply affected by the **ballads**, the tales and the landscapes of Orkney, Edwin also found in Homeric and Biblical narratives a universal setting which liberated his vision and surfaced in some of the *First Poems*. To it he was to return (a key word) in *The Story and the Fable* (which, with the addition of a sequel, later turned into *An Autobiography*) at the end of the 1930s.

The Muirs' son Gavin was born in 1927. Back in Britain they made outstanding translations of Kafka and Hermann Broch, while at times living on tick from a grocer. They were in Hampstead, then **St Andrews**. On a visit to Orkney Willa and Gavin went ahead, leaving Edwin to drive north while making notes for *A Scottish Journey* (1935). His more general observations in *Scott and Scotland* (1936) became lost in narrower controversy than he intended.

Hitler's rise stymied hopes of translation work and of any return to Europe. Willa had been teaching but became ill and needed surgery. Edwin could only find clerical work, working amid disorientation to write *The Story and the Fable*. Then, he says, with Willa's life in danger, he 'discovered he was a Christian': revelation was how his mind made sense of things. The book's success in 1940 brought encouragement, while writing it gave new sureness and insight.

Then came change. Edwin was engaged as a lecturer to various exile groups; the family moved to **Edinburgh**; he did BBC work. Previously trapped in a 'Wayside Station', he found this rewarding work. It continued after 1945 with a British Council post in Prague. Whereas his poetry before 1940 had meditated various generalised situations, his later poems lived such situations. After the *Narrow Place* (1943) of early wartime ordeal came *The Voyage* (1946). In a Prague just released from Nazi rule he lectured at the Charles University (which awarded him an honorary doctorate). The 1948 Communist takeover ended things. The Muirs came back to Britain, Edwin in nervous collapse. *The Labyrinth* (1949) is a great poetic study of political oppression with, at the end, light from a stay in Rome and a new love of the created world which was carried over into *One Foot in Eden* (1956).

As Warden of **Newbattle Abbey** College (**Midlothian**) from 1950–4, Edwin had to fight for his own imaginative approach to education. He taught, was grateful for J C Hall's editing of *Collected Poems* in 1951, and completed *An Autobiography* (1954). He left Newbattle to give the 1954–5 Charles Eliot Norton lectures at Harvard (*The Estate of Poetry*, 1962). The Muirs then settled in Swaffham Priory near Cambridge. Lectureships followed, as did honours (CBE) and degrees. He planned a book on ballads, but his health failed. He died in hospital at Cambridge, his last years having produced much new poetry. See: *Collected Poems* (Faber); *An Autobiography* (Chatto) much reprinted. *The Marionette* was reprinted in 1987; *Uncollected Scottish Criticism* (ed Noble, 1982) and *The Truth of Imagination* (ed Butter, Aberdeen UP, 1988) add to available criticism. *Selected Letters* (ed Butter, 1982). A biography, P H Butter's *Edwin Muir: Man and Poet* is long out of print.

MUIR, John (1810–82) Orientalist

John and **(Sir) William Muir** were among the four sons of a **Glasgow** merchant and magistrate, also John, whose wife received from Sir James Shaw, a Scots-born London merchant and Lord Mayor, the handsome present of four writerships in the East India Company. All four sons therefore proceeded from **Glasgow University** to the Company's Haileybury College and then to India. John, the eldest, reached Calcutta in 1829 and steadily worked his way up through the administrative service until as a judge (1853) he retired, presumably with his fortune made. He had also achieved distinction as a Sanskrit scholar, writing Sanskrit tracts, some of an evangelical flavour, and becoming Principal of Queen's College, Benares, where he pioneered instruction 'concurrently in Sanskrit and English'. Retiring to **Edinburgh**, he continued his Sanskrit studies and produced the 5-vol series of texts entitled *The History of the Peoples of India*, 1858–70. With his brother, Sir William, he also patronised **Edinburgh University**, founding a chair of Sanskrit named after Shaw, the family's benefactor.

MUIR, John (1838–1914) Pioneering Conservationist

Born at **Dunbar**, John Muir lived in the USA from the age of 11. He studied botany in walks across the country, becoming enthused by the natural beauties of the Yosemite valley in California, which he studied 1868–74. Campaigning for its preservation, he secured Congressional approval for its declaration as a National Park in 1890, later succeeding in adding 148 million acres (60 million hectares) of forest land as parkland. Nowadays there are approximately 3000 national parks worldwide, but none in the land of Muir's birth.

MUIR, Sir Robert (1864–1959) Pathologist

Born at **Balfron**, **Stirlingshire**, Muir studied medicine at **Edinburgh University**. Specialising in pathology, he held two professorships, his **Glasgow** appointment lasting from 1899 to 1936. He wrote the standard textbook on the subject in 1924, later helping to found the science of immunology with his studies on breast cancer.

MUIR, Thomas, of Huntershill (1765–99)
Political Agitator

The son of a **Glasgow** merchant, Thomas Muir graduated MA in Glasgow in 1782 and was sent down for political attacks on the professors. He then studied law in **Edinburgh**, becoming an advocate in 1787. An enthusiastic supporter of the French Revolution and the Declaration of the Rights of Man, Muir helped to establish the first Society of the Friends of the People in Scotland in 1792, corresponding with similar societies in France and Ireland. In 1793 he was arrested as an agitator. Released on bail he went to London and Paris where he talked to the leaders of the Revolution. Because of the outbreak of war he had to return by way of Ireland, where he was made a member of the Society of United Irishmen. He was arrested on his return to Scotland.

The growing success of the French Revolution caused panic in the British government which began to pass repressive legislation. In this climate Thomas Muir, tried before the Lord Justice Clerk, **Lord Braxfield**, had no chance, but even the hand-picked jury was aghast when he was sentenced to 14 years' transportation to Botany Bay. This flagrant injustice aroused interest far beyond Scotland and in 1796, with American assistance, he escaped. After an adventurous return via Mexico and Spain Muir was received with much acclaim in France. He repaid the Directoire by writing anti-English propaganda, and in return was named a member of the Directory in the Scottish Republic which France proposed to set up after the planned invasion. Muir, however, died in 1799 and was buried in France.

In some ways Muir may have been a crank, and may well have contributed to his own misfortune, but the fact remains that he was an undoubted martyr to the repressive measures of the establishment. Not for the first time, nor the last, had the spirit of the law been prostituted in the name of 'national security'.

MUIR, Sir William (1819–1905) Colonial
Administrator and Orientalist

Sir William's career followed closely that of his eldest brother, **John Muir**. He too went to India (1837), joined the administrative service, and spent most of his career assessing revenue in what is now Uttar Pradesh. But their courses diverged in two respects. Sir William, 9 years younger, was still in India during the 1857 Mutiny. Based in Agra he played an important intelligence role during the struggle and thereafter advanced rapidly, becoming secretary to Lord Canning (1858), KCSI and Foreign Secretary under Sir John Lawrence (1867) and Lieutenant-Governor of the North-West Provinces. (1868–74). The other major difference was that whereas John had become a Sanskritist whose intellectual home was Benares, William was an Islamicist based at Allahabad where he founded Muir College and the university.

On retiring from India he was appointed to the India Council and is credited with having coined the slightly unfortunate title, Kaisar-i-Hind, by which **Queen Victoria** was to be known to her Indian subjects after her elevation to Empress (1876). With his brother he founded the chair of Sanskrit at **Edinburgh University** and (1885) was appointed principal, a post he held until his death. His main works were a 4-vol Life of Mohomet (1858–61), Annals of the Early Caliphate (1883) and The Mameluke Dynasty of Egypt (1896). All betray sound scholarship, an excellent knowledge of Arabic and the prejudices of a convinced Christian who believed that the Prophet and the Quran were 'the most stubborn enemies of Civilisation, Liberty, and the Truth, which the world has yet known'.

MUIR OF ORD, Ross & Cromarty

Muirs (or moors) afford the ample space needed for the unfenced assembly and exchange of large numbers of cattle and sheep (eg **Stenhousemuir**). In the 19th century the Muir of Ord, two miles north of **Beauly** at the intersection of important routes from the north-west with those from **Caithness** and **Cromarty**, hosted the largest agricultural tryst in the north of Scotland. Here, too, cattle which had travelled thus far from their native pastures over soft and sodden hill trails were shoed for the harder going that lay ahead on the gravelled roadways to the south. But **droving** went out with the coming of the **railway**, and the tryst soon followed it. The muir is now a **golf** course, the village which once served the drover has grown into a straggling town of little character, and the descendants of the blacksmiths have adapted to light **engineering**. East of here the once parish church of Kilchrist was the scene of a not unique conflagration when in 1603 the **MacDonells of Glengarry** locked their **Mackenzie** enemies inside and fired the place. A piper, always handy on these occasions, paraded round the building drowning out any disquieting exclamations from within. Further east Tarradale was the birthplace of **Sir Roderick Murchison**. The area is rich in prehistoric remains including two **standing stones** 'connected in some way with the prophesied extinction of the clan Mackenzie' [see **Coinneach Odhar**] and several chambered **cairns**.

MUIRHEAD, Roland Eugene (1868–1964)
Nationalist

The proprietor of a **Glasgow** tannery, Muirhead used his wealth to set up a 'Scottish Secretariat' for disseminating nationalist ideas while his socialist and pacifist convictions gave the movement ideological rigour. In 1918, already a member of the **Independent Labour Party**, he revived the **Scottish Home Rule Association**; but ten years later, despairing of its effectiveness, he moved to the **National Party of Scotland**, becoming one of its first Parliamentary candidates (for West **Renfrewshire**) and its President. In the NPS Muirhead became closely associated with **John MacCormick** whose populist manner he conspicuously lacked. Together with **Professor A D Gibb** and others they formed the **Scottish National Party** in 1934, Muirhead becoming its Honorary President. He stayed with the SNP when MacCormick split away to form the broad-based Scottish Convention but in 1952, now 82, himself formed a radical splinter group, the Scottish National Congress, under whose auspices *A Constitution for Scotland* was drafted in 1962.

MULL, Island of, Inner Hebrides
Lying off the coast of **Argyll**, Mull forms the western entrance to the Firth of Lorne and Loch Linnhe. To its north, across the narrow, fjord-like Sound of Mull, lie **Morvern** and the **Ardnamurchan** peninsula. To the south are **Colonsay**, **Islay** and **Jura**, while to the west are **Coll**, **Tiree**, **Iona** and the waters of the North Atlantic. With a land area of 353 square miles, its population of about 2500 is scattered thinly but unevenly across the landscape, with the largest settlements at **Tobermory**, Craignure, Salen, Bunessan, Dervaig and Fionnphort.

A feature of the topography is the deep sea lochs which penetrate into the middle of the island – Loch na Keal, Loch Scridain, Loch Buie and Loch Spelve; all provide sheltered anchorages.

Mull is well served by ferries. The main connection is from the railhead at **Oban** to Craignure at the eastern end of the Sound of Mull; this is a 45-minute crossing. A shorter voyage across the Sound of Mull from Lochaline to Fishnish gives access from Morvern, **Lochaber** and **Fort William**, while a car ferry plies from Kilchoan on Ardnamurchan to Tobermory, which is also connected by ferry to Coll, Tiree and the Outer Isles.

A picturesque and hilly island, Mull is dominated by the central mountain of Ben More (3170ft/966m), from which there is a spectacular view. Its scree slopes are the remains of an ancient volcano which exploded 60 million years ago. All around the central plateau are basaltic lavas, forming gigantic terraced steps. The interesting **geology** attracts many students and field workers during the summer months. Near the headland of the Ardmeanach peninsula is **MacCulloch's Tree**, a remarkable geological **fossil** tree discovered in 1819.

There are many sites of archaeological and historical interest, ranging from chambered **cairns** and **standing stones** to vitrified forts, **duns** and **brochs**, and several important castles. The stone circle at the head of Loch Buie, and the linear settings of standing stones in the forestry plantations, are evidence of ceremonial observances in Mull in the Bronze Age, dating to the 2nd millennium BC. The Iron Age Dun Aisgain, near Burg, is exceptionally well-preserved, dating as it does from around 200 BC.

Duart Castle, near Craignure, was probably built as a **MacDougall** castle in the 13th century. The main feature is the tower house built in the late 14th century, when it became the chief residence of the **MacLeans of Duart**. The MacLeans lost their estates in the 1670s, but in 1911 Duart Castle was purchased and restored by Colonel Sir Fitzroy MacLean, 26th Chief of the clan MacLean. It is now a place of pilgrimage for the MacLean diaspora.

Aros Castle, on the Sound of Mull near Salen, dates from the 14th century and was one of the strongholds of the **Lords of the Isles**. Moy Castle, at the head of Loch Buie, was built in the 15th century by the MacLeans

of Lochbuie. The strangely-named Frank Lockwood's Island, east of the entrance to Loch Buie, recalls the Solicitor-General in Lord Rosebery's administration, 1894–5. He was the brother-in-law of the 21st MacLaine (*sic*) of Lochbuie.

Torosay Castle, to the south of Craignure, was built in 1856 in the Scottish baronial style. There are fine gardens, through which runs a narrow-gauge railway which has become a major tourist attraction. Another modern castle is Glengorm, on the Mishnish promontory west of Tobermory; it was built in 1860.

The long, low peninsula of the Ross of Mull is traversed by an ancient pilgrim track, aiming for the island of Iona lying at its western extremity. The modern road system of Mull amounts to over 120 miles, much of it greatly improved in recent years. Close to the south-west tip of the Ross of Mull is the tidal island of Erraid, immortalised by **Robert Louis Stevenson** in *Kidnapped*. It was here that David Balfour was shipwrecked from the brig *Covenant* and began his adventures. The cottages were built as a shore station by the Commissioners of Northern Lights for keepers serving the lighthouses at Skerryvore and Dubh Artach. The engineer on these projects, and others, was **Alan Stevenson**, uncle of the writer. In the 1990s the island was occupied by members of the **Findhorn** Foundation.

The population of Mull grew dramatically in the 18th century and peaked at 10,600 in 1821, but has been declining ever since. In recent years numbers have stabilised, although the replacement of native islanders by both Scottish and English incomers is more apparent, and thus has aroused more controversy on Mull than on the many other Hebridean islands with which it shares this trend.

The island of **Ulva** (Norse: 'wolf island') lies in Loch Tuath, off the west coast of Mull, now connected by a bridge to the neighbouring island of Gometra. The population of over 500 was completely cleared between 1846 and 1851. Owned by Macquaries for over 800 years, it was the birthplace of the father of **Lachlan Macquarie**, Governor of New South Wales. The grandfather of the missionary and explorer **David Livingstone** was a crofter on Ulva.

In modern times the **Forestry Commission**, small-scale **crofting** and **fishing**, sheep farming, **fish farming** and **tourism** (over 600,000 annual visitors) are the major industries.

MUNESS CASTLE, Unst, Shetland
Built in 1598 by Laurence Bruce of Cultmalindie in **Perthshire**, ruined Muness Castle, the most northerly in Britain, consists of an oblong main block with two round towers at diagonally opposite corners (Z-plan). That it was built as a defended dwelling house is clear from the great variety of decorated shot-holes. A carved panel commemorates Laurence Bruce – 'that worthy man' – who fled to **Shetland**, after involvement in some murderous affray, and established a rule in **Unst** as tyrannous as that of his half-brother **Robert Stewart** on the **Mainland** of Shetland.

MUNGO, Saint (c520–c612)
Also known as Kentigern, St Mungo is chiefly identified with **Glasgow**, its Cathedral and the components of the

city's coat of arms. Few facts can be verified from the life written by a Cumbrian monk six centuries after his death as a promotional document for the medieval Church. He is presumed to be the son of Thenew, or Enoch, a daughter of the King of Lothian, born at **Culross** in **Fife**, where he was taught by St Serf at a monastery. He came to Glasgow to bury a monk at a cemetery dedicated earlier by **St Ninian** on the bank of the **Molendinar** burn, now the site of **Glasgow Cathedral** with St Mungo's shrine in the crypt.

As a missionary priest-bishop, Mungo travelled from the **Clyde** to the Clwyd in north Wales, founding the monastery of Llanelwy, now St Asaph. In Welsh he is known as Cynderyn. Other areas of his mission seem to have been in the old kingdom of **Strathclyde** in Cumbria and around **Hoddam** in Dumfriesshire. About 590 he is reputed to have met **St Columba** in Glasgow and agreed their territorial mission boundaries, but this is not recorded by **Adamnan**. It may indicate the meeting of Irish and British Christianity, since Mungo is associated chiefly with Brythonic and Welsh identity. His death in 612 is recorded in the Welsh annals, one of the few facts actually known about him. Most of his life is myth and tradition keyed to other figures to promote his cult.

MUNRO, Alexander (fl.1732) Composer

Nothing is known of Munro's life save that he published 12 violin sonatas in Paris in 1732, each one based on a different Scottish tune but developing it through Continental forms of minuet, corrente, gavotte, etc. Particularly successful is his sonata on 'Bonnie Jean of Aberdeen'.

MUNRO, Sir Hector (1726–1805) General

The son of Hugh Munro of Novar in **Ross & Cromarty**, Sir Hector had the distinction of directing the most important victory yet won by the British in India as well as their most disastrous defeat. After serving with the Hanoverian forces against the **Jacobites**, Munro commanded the 89th Foot (**Gordon Highlanders**) when it embarked for India in 1760. In 1764 he took command of all the East India Company's forces in Bihar, first suppressing an incipient mutiny at Patna and then defeating the combined might of the Moghul Crown Prince and the Nawabs of Bengal and Oudh. This was the 1765 Battle of Baksar (Buxar) which, unlike Clive's farce at Plassey, established the Company's supremacy in Bengal and the British political presence in India. Munro went back to Scotland immediately and in 1768 was returned MP for **Inverness** Burghs. He held the seat for the next 34 years in spite of a return to India in 1778–82 during which he was Commander-in-Chief, Madras. There his successes included the capture of French Pondicherry (1778) and Dutch Negapatnam (1781, and subsequently commemorated by Munro's erection of the Fyrish Monument near **Alness**); both of these were however overshadowed by the catastrophic – and so usually suppressed – Battle of Polilur (1780). In this engagement a force of 8000 under Colonel Baillie (also a Scot) was wiped out by the Mysore Army within a few miles of the force under Munro, which then retreated with heavy losses to Madras. It was said that the defeat resulted from lack of maps, of intelligence, and of an agreed cipher, Munro and Baillie preferring to correspond in Gaelic, which led to misunderstandings.

MUNRO, Hector Hugh, 'Saki' (1870–1916)
Writer

Hector Munro was born at Akyab, Burma, on 18 December 1870, the youngest of three children of an Inspector-General of the Burma police. Both his parents were of Scottish extraction. When his mother died in 1872, he and his siblings were taken in and brought up by two aunts in north Devon. Educated at home until the age of 12, Munro completed his schooling at Exmouth and the Bedford Grammar School. In 1893 he took up an appointment in the Military Police in Burma, but due to ill-health returned to Britain a year later. In 1896 he moved to London and began writing political satires for The Westminster Gazette. These sketches were later published in book form as The Westminster Alice (1902). This was followed by a similar collection, Not So Stories (1902). Munro's first published work, though, was The Rise of the Russian Empire (1900), which traces the development of Russian history up to the period of Peter the Great.

From 1902–8 Munro served as a foreign correspondent for The Morning Post, travelling to the Balkans, Warsaw and Paris. During this time he published a collection of short stories, Reginald (1904), under the pseudonym 'Saki', taken from the name of the cup-bearer in The Rubaiyat of Omar Khayyam. This collection established his reputation as a writer of unusual note and imagination. Other collections followed, including Reginald in Russia (1910), The Chronicles of Clovis (1912), considered by many to contain his best work, and Beasts and Superbeasts (1914). Two further collections were published posthumously, The Toys of Peace (1919) and The Square Egg (1924). Other work included two novels, The Unbearable Bassington (1912) and When William Came (1914).

In 1908 Munro returned to London and began contributing work to a number of papers, including The Bystander and the Daily Express. In 1914, shortly after the outbreak of World War I, Munro enlisted as a private with the Royal Fusiliers, and in 1915 was sent to the front in France. He was killed in action near Beaumont Hamel on 14 November 1916.

MUNRO, Sir Hugh T (1856–1919) Politician and Climber

The man whose name has become a generic term for Scotland's highest mountains was born and brought up in London. He served briefly in southern Africa but after 1885, when not indulging an insatiable appetite for foreign travel, lived mainly on the family estate of Lindertis near **Kirriemuir**, **Angus**. From there 'he organised the political life of Forfarshire [ie Angus] on the Unionist side', although he was never elected MP. And from there he indulged his other passion, for exploring and climbing the Scottish mountains. A founder member and President of the Scottish Mountaineering Club, he contributed to its journal frequently, and most memorably in September 1891 when he published 'Tables giving all the Scottish mountains exceeding 3,000 feet in height'. The tables were largely compiled from Ordnance Survey maps and his total of 238 peaks with 583 tops has since been revised (to 277 and 517 respectively). But Sir Hugh (he inherited a baronetcy) was more than a statistician, and actually made an early attempt to climb them all. He failed by only three, Carn Cloich-mhuillin, Carn Fhidleir and Inaccessible Peak. His final attempt at this last, in the **Cuillins**, was made in 1915 in his 60th year, soon after which he went to Malta with the Red Cross and then France to minister to the wounded of the Great War. He opened a field canteen in Tarascon and died there of pneumonia. His listed peaks came to be known as '**Munros**' and those who aspire to work their way through his list as 'Munro-baggers'.

MUNRO, Neil, 'Hugh Foulis' (1864–1930)
Novelist

Munro was born in **Inveraray**, **Argyll**, the son of a farmer. He was educated at the local school and worked for five years in a law office before taking up journalism as a career. After working for several newspapers he became editor of the *Glasgow Evening News* in 1918, a position he held until 1927 when he retired to Craigendorran, near **Helensburgh** on the **Clyde**.

Munro's early works, *The Lost Pibroch* (1896), a collection of Celtic tales, and *Gilean the Dreamer* (1899), a story of 19th century Scottish life, made use of Celtic myths and traditions, and were written in a Romantic style. He subsequently produced a number of historical novels in the tradition of **Sir Walter Scott** and **Robert Louis Stevenson**. These last included *John Splendid* (1898), set in 17th century Argyll, *Doom Castle* (1901), set during the **Jacobite Rising** of 1745, and *Children of the Tempest* (1903).

In later years Munro turned to writing novels of contemporary life, which were mostly unsuccessful. Also, as 'Hugh Foulis', he began writing humorous tales of life in the west of Scotland – the first of which was

Neil Munro, creator of Para Handy, by Stansmore Dean (SNPG)

Erchie, My Droll Friend (1904) – and the adventures of 'Para Handy', the skipper of a small Clyde puffer, and his crew. These were published as a series of light sketches in the *Glasgow Evening News*, and were an instant success. It is mainly for the Para Handy tales that Munro is remembered today, yet for many years he refused to reveal his authorship for fear of compromising his reputation as a serious author.

The first collection of Para Handy stories, published by Blackwood & Sons as *The Vital Spark* (1906), was followed by *The Daft Days* (1907), *In Highland Harbours with Para Handy* (1911) and *Jaunty Jock* (1918). They were eventually collected together and reissued as *Para Handy and Other Tales* (1931). Munro also wrote poetry, collected in *Bagpipe Ballads* (1917) and *The Poetry of Neil Munro* (1931), and non-fiction works including the descriptive *The Clyde, River and Firth* (1907). His memoir, *The Brave Days*, was published in 1931. He was awarded an honorary LL.D by the **University of Glasgow** in 1908, and died in Helensburgh.

MUNRO, Robert (1868–1955) Secretary of State

A son of the manse, Robert Munro (Lord Alness from 1934) was Secretary of State for Scotland for six years, yet is comparatively unknown today and must qualify as one of the longest-serving Cabinet Ministers not to appear in the *Dictionary of National Biography*. Born at **Alness** near **Dingwall** and educated at **Aberdeen** Grammar School and **Edinburgh University**, Munro was called to the Scottish Bar in 1893 and was a KC by 1910. He entered politics as a Liberal in the same year, representing **Wick** burghs 1910–18 and then Roxburgh & Selkirk 1918–22. His Parliamentary career blossomed with his being appointed Lord Advocate in 1913 and Scottish Secretary three years later. Probably his most important legislative measure was the Education (Scotland) Act of 1918 which replaced 1000 parish school boards with 33 county and 5 city education authorities. The same measure protected the status of denominational (ie Roman Catholic) schools and raised the leaving age to 15. This Act compared favourably with the English educational legislation of the time. After leaving politics, Munro was Lord President for 11 years from 1922–33.

MUNRO, Sir Thomas (1761–1827) Governor of Madras

Least glamorous but most far-sighted of the four founding fathers of British administration in India (**Elphinstone**, Metcalfe, **Malcolm** and Munro), Munro ranks as 'the most admirable of all the [East India] Company's servants' (Penderel Moon, 1989). Born in **Glasgow** the son of Alexander Munro, a **tobacco** trader, he attended **Glasgow University** before sailing for Madras in 1780 as a cadet in the Company's army. After serving in the 2nd, 3rd and 4th Mysore Wars he switched to civil employ as secretary (with Malcolm) on a commission under the future Duke of Wellington to settle parts of Mysore. Here, and after home leave (1807–14) and service in the 2nd Maratha War, as Governor of Madras (1819–27) he developed the system of land assessment and revenue collection known as ryotwari which became the model for the rest of India. Instead of relying on middlemen, this system involved settlement with the peasant farmers themselves. It entailed meticulous field-by-field surveys but once perfected was probably the fairest ever devised in the colonial world; it survives to this day.

Munro's judicial system based on indigenous institutions and employing mainly Indians was less successful. But it typified his conviction, soon to be ignored, that Indians were as trustworthy and able as their foreign overlords. In prophetic words sadly untypical of later generations he told the home authorities 'Your rule is alien and it can never be popular . . . You are not here to turn India into England or Scotland. Work through, not in spite of, native systems and native ways, with a prejudice in their favour rather than against them; and when in the fulness of time your subjects can frame and maintain a worthy government for themselves, get out.' During a farewell tour of his Madras Presidency Munro died of cholera, mourned and missed as few colonial administrators before or since.

MUNROS

Scottish hills of 3000 feet or more above sea-level are known to climbers and ramblers as 'Munros' after **Sir Hugh Munro** who produced the first *Tables* in 1891. These have since been revised and frequently reissued. In the 1930s John Rooke Corbett from Bristol, only the fourth man to have climbed all the Munros, produced an additional list of peaks between 2500 and 3000ft (762–914m) (now known as 'Corbetts'); a further list of hills in the Lowlands of 2000–2500ft (609–762m) was produced by Percy Donald. All are now included in *Munro's Tables* which thus provide the outdoor fraternity with endless challenges.

Although Munro himself just failed to climb all his 238 summits, they had already been conquered by A E Robertson in 1901. Robertson did so over a period of ten years. He admitted that, except for three peaks in the **Cuillins**, all the summits could be reached by 'a fairly easy route', ie demanding no climbing skills; but he took strong exception to those who likened the exercise to kissing all the lamp-posts in **Edinburgh**'s **Princes Street** just because no one else had done so. Such comparisons, though, are still valid and often raised by serious mountaineers.

Injecting the challenge with greater demands on stamina and ingenuity, Brian and Alan Ripley attempted to bag all the Munros in a single continuous journey in 1967. They failed but in 1974 Hamish Brown completed the challenge, covering 1639 miles and 449,000ft (136,855m) of ascent in 112 days. The most insatiable of Munro-baggers, he knew the routes well, having already completed three previous rounds. Kathy Murgatroyd duplicated the feat for the ladies in 1982 and George Keeping in 1984 was the first to complete the entire round on foot; others had used bicycles. Keeping kept going for another month to add the few English and Welsh Munros to his tally. Although metrification transformed Munros into peaks of over 914.4 metres, a somewhat less magical figure, their challenge continues to exercise a fascination. A mid-winter circuit by Martin Moran in 1984–5 was hailed as a remarkable feat; other marathons involving climbing the Munros plus much walking, running, **skiing**, sailing and swimming, or combinations of these, continue to proliferate.

MURCHISON, Roderick Impey (1792–1871)
Geologist

Born at Tarradale, Easter **Ross**, Murchison's family moved to England when he was young. He joined the army, fought in the Peninsular War and, on returning to Britain, took up **geology**. He travelled all over Europe and Scotland with **Charles Lyell**, his researches leading to the classification of the oldest known fossiliferous rocks; his greatest contribution to the science was the mapping of North Wales, where he identified and named the Silurian system, an achievement for which he won the Copley Medal. In 1830 he joined the committee of the Royal Geographical Society becoming, at the age of 38, its youngest member. The Tsar invited him to carry out a geological survey of the Russian empire (1840–5), during which he named the Permian system. President of the British Association in 1846, he became President of the Royal Geographical Society in 1843–5, and again from 1851–3, 1856–9 and 1862–7. In 1855 he was made Director-General of the Geological Survey (later formally establishing the Scottish branch), a post he held until his death.

MURDOCK, William (1754–1839) Pioneer of Gas Lighting

Born in Bello Mill, Lugar in **Ayrshire**, Murdoch was the son of a millwright. In 1777, fascinated by steam engines, he joined Boulton & **Watt** as an assistant at their Soho manufactory. Two years later he was sent to **Wanlockhead** to install a pumping engine, and then to represent the firm in Cornwall.

Murdock (he altered the spelling of his name to suit the English pronunciation) spent 20 years in Cornwall, acting as an engine erector and repairer. In 1784 he devised and built a model steam carriage, but was dissuaded by his employers from patenting his invention. He returned to Birmingham to become manager of the Soho foundry in 1798, and he became a partner in Boulton, Watt & Sons in 1810.

During his stay in Cornwall, Murdock experimented with the manufacture of **coal** gas, and in 1792 is believed to have successfully lit his house in Redruth using his own gas production plant. On returning to Birmingham he persuaded his employers to begin manufacturing his gas plant on a commercial basis. In 1803 the Soho factory became the first industrial premises to be lit by gas, and in 1808 Murdock was awarded the Rumford Gold Medal by the Royal Society for his paper on the installation of gas lighting at a mill in Manchester.

Many of Murdock's mechanical inventions were patented by Boulton & Watt, obscuring his role as one of the most innovative engineers of his day. It is clear, however, that he was the first to devise commercially-viable gas production plant, and he is remembered today as the founder of the gas light industry.

MURRAY, Agnes, 'Muckle-mou'ed Meg' (fl.1611)

In legend this unwinsome daughter of Sir Gideon Murray of Elibank was wed by Willie Scott of Oakwood Tower in **Ettrick**, the son of auld Wat of Harden, a **Border** reiver, as a means of escaping the gallows. Agnes's mother seized upon this unexpected opportunity to marry her off by offering Scott Hobson's Choice – her or the gallows. To her chagrin he first chose the latter, but reneged on execution morn, 'for a' that a Scott thought it naething to die'. What their law-abiding descendant **Sir Walter Scott** described as 'the strangest marriage in history' was formalised on 14 July 1611. The incident was fodder for **James Hogg**'s 'Fray of Elibank' in 'The Mountain Bard' and Alexander Reid's play *The Lass wi' the Muckle Mou'*.

MURRAY, Alexander (1775–1813) Linguist

Born at Minnigaff, **Newton Stewart**, Murray was the son of a shepherd at Clatteringshaws (where an obelisk commemorates him). In surroundings little conducive to scholarship he somehow managed to teach himself Latin, Greek, Hebrew, French, German, 'and some Abyssinian' before proceeding to **Edinburgh University**. The Abyssinian came in useful when he edited the works of **James Bruce** and wrote a biography of him; also when George III received a letter in 'Ethiopic'. In 1806 he was appointed minister of Urr by which time he had mastered several other Middle Eastern languages as well as the difficult tongue of the Laps. Reward in the shape of the Professorship of Oriental Languages at Edinburgh came in 1812, but he died a year later, aged only 38. **John MacTaggart**, the **Galloway** encyclopaedist, greatly regretted that Murray had never brought his scholarship to bear on his native tongue, 'Gallovidians being as good a tribe as any in the neighbourhood of Gondar'; but in 1823 appeared his *History of European Languages*.

MURRAY (de MORAY), Sir Andrew (d.1297) and Sir Andrew (d.1338)

National resentment against Edward I's demotion of Scotland to the status of an English fief provoked a major revolt in the north under Murray as well as that in the south under **William Wallace**. Like Wallace, Murray was a mere knight although not without resources. His father, also Sir Andrew, was the lord of Petty [see **Castle Stuart**] and Avoch (**Black Isle**) and his uncle of **Bothwell**. In 1297 both were English prisoners and Murray, their heir, had himself only just escaped from English captivity. He assembled his retainers at Avoch and, planning an assault on **Urquhart Castle**, had soon raised Moray and linked up with Wallace at **Abbey Craig**. There he fought at **Stirling Bridge** and died soon after, presumably from wounds incurred.

His posthumous son (*pace* the DNB, not the same person), another Sir Andrew, married Christian, sister of **Robert I**, and served as guardian for his nephew **David II** (1332). He was captured near **Roxburgh** (1332) but, ransomed in 1334, resumed the struggle against Edward III and his adherents. In 1335 he defeated David of Strathbogie at Culblean, thus relieving **Kildrummy** where his wife had been under siege; next year the tables were turned as he withdrew from **Lochindorb**, held by David's wife, when Edward III approached. Reappointed guardian (1336) he successfully reduced **Dunottar**, Kinclaven [see **Meikleour**], **St Andrews** and eventually Bothwell (1337) using an appliance known as the 'Bustour' (ie 'Buster'). The cause of his premature death at Avoch in 1338 is not known.

MURRAY, Charles (1864–1941) Poet

Murray was born in **Alford**, **Aberdeenshire**. After training as an engineer in **Aberdeen**, he emigrated to South Africa in 1888, where he became manager of a goldmining company. During the Boer War he fought as a lieutenant in the Railway Pioneer Regiment, subsequently being appointed Deputy Inspector of Mines for the Transvaal in 1901. He was to serve in various government posts in succeeding years, becoming Secretary of Public Works in 1912 and receiving a CMG in 1922. In 1924 he retired to Scotland.

While in South Africa he began writing poetry. His first collection, *A Handful of Heather*, was privately published in 1893, and subsequent collections included *Hamewith*, published in Aberdeen in 1900, *A Sough o' War* (1917) and *In the Country Places* (1920). His work, mostly written in Scottish East Coast dialect, was noted for its perceptive and evocative portrayal of Aberdeenshire country life at the turn of the century. This is reflected in his best-known poem, 'The Whistle'. Murray's work soon became popular in Scotland, and although criticised for its sometimes mawkish **kailyard** sentimentality, proved a forerunner of the modern **Scottish Renaissance** movement in its use of Scottish language and oral traditions. Murray died in **Banchory**, **Kincardineshire**. A memoir by C Christie was published in 1943, and an edition of his *Complete Poems* in 1979.

MURRAY, Chic (1919–85) Comedian

Famed, even more after his death, for his surrealistic style of comedy, Chic Murray toured the **music halls** of Scotland and England with a solo act of comedy patter, and achieved an originality so distinctive that many impersonators still don a flat bonnet and use his nonchalant, throwaway comedy lines in an attempt to win laughs. Born at **Greenock**, he was planning to be a marine engineer in the **shipbuilding** town when he launched into show-business as half of a musical act The Whinhillbillies. The act was later known as Chic and his Chicks, specialising in songs like 'China Doll'. In 1940 he met and later married Maidie Dickson, an **Edinburgh** accordionist and singer, and they developed a lively comedy-musical act, winning success in London with the billing Chic and Maidie, 'The Tall Droll and the Small Moll'. Chic branched into films with a support role in *Gregory's Girl*. He was one of the small group of Scottish comics to win favour with English audiences.

MURRAY, Clan

As with so many clans, the origins of the Murrays are obscure. However the earliest known ancestor, named Freskin, came to Scotland in the mid-12th century. He received grants of land from **David I** in Linlithgowshire and also, after suppressing an insurrection, in **Moray**; from this his grandson took the name 'de Moravia' and from this line were descended the Murrays of **Bothwell** and, from a younger son, the **Earls of Sutherland**. However this line died out and other branches of the Murrays, Fallahill and Blackbarony, were descended from Archibald de Moravia.

The Murrays of **Tullibardine** descended from Malcolm de Moravia whose son's marriage to Ada, daughter of the Seneschal of Strathearn, brought them the lands round Tullibardine which became the family seat. Their descendants added to the lands, which were confirmed by **David II** in 1362, and built the chapel at Tullibardine in 1446. Andrew, a younger brother of the 9th Laird, became Lord Stormont from whom the Mansfields of **Scone** are descended. In 1604 Sir John Murray was granted the Earldom of Tullibardine and his son married Dorothea, daughter of the 5th Earl of **Atholl**.

The Earldom of Atholl had passed through various families since the end of the Celtic line in the 13th century. In 1457 it was granted by **James II** to his half-brother John Stewart. However the 5th Earl had no male heir and the title passed to his widow's second husband and son before being granted, through the eldest daughter Dorothea, to the 2nd Earl of Atholl. Thus their son became the first Murray Earl of Atholl. The second Earl became first Marquis, and the second Marquis was granted the Dukedom of Atholl by Queen Anne in 1703.

The Murray Dukes of Atholl made many notable contributions both to the life of their country and to their estates, based on **Blair Atholl** and covering over 300,000 acres (121,500ha). The first Duke was one of the firmest opponents of the **Act of Union**, as he feared that Scots opinion would not be given due weight in the united Parliament. One of his younger sons **Lord George Murray** became the famous **Jacobite** general of the '45 and besieged his family home, **Blair Castle**, which was being held for the government. His elder brother, the 2nd Duke, in restoring the castle, was responsible for the interior as it can be seen today. He also laid out the grounds and the policies. His grandson became known as the 'planting Duke' for his efforts in growing millions of larch trees on the estate, both to provide the British navy with much-needed timber and to attempt to make the family's fortune.

The 6th Duke founded the **Atholl Highlanders** when he took a 'tail' of retainers to the Eglinton Tournament in 1839 [see **Hugh Montgomerie**]. His wife Duchess Anne was a close friend of **Queen Victoria**, who stayed at Blair Castle in 1844. She was so pleased with her visit that the following year she granted the Duke's Highlanders the right to bear arms, a unique privilege to an individual in this country. The 8th Duke followed the military tradition when he raised the Scottish Horse during the Boer War and commanded them in World War I. The Duke was the initiator of the **Scottish National War Memorial** to commemorate all those who lost their lives in that conflict. His wife Duchess **Katharine** was the first Scottish woman MP and first Conservative woman Minister.

The 10th Duke was considered head of the Murray clan, but on his death only the title passed to John Murray of South Africa. The chiefship, according to the clan's website in 1999, 'has not yet been officially confirmed'. The clan badge is the **juniper** plant and the motto *Furth Forth and Fill the Fetters* dates from 1475 when James II sent the Earl of Atholl on an expedition against a rebellious **Lord of the Isles**.

MURRAY, Lord George (1694–1760)
Jacobite General
As 'the military genius of the '45 [**Jacobite Rising**]' (**Fitzroy Maclean**), Murray has been compared with **James Graham Marquis of Montrose** and **John Gra-**

Lord George Murray, 'the military genius of the '45'; drawing by Sir Robert Strange (SNPG)

ham of Claverhouse, Viscount Dundee. He was the son of John Murray, 1st Duke of **Atholl** (d.1724) and the brother of William Marquis of Tullibardine (1689–1746) and of James 2nd Duke of Atholl (c1690–1764). After joining the **Earl of Mar**'s 1715 **Rising** and the 1719 landing led by brother William which ended at **Glenshiel**, he went into exile and was engaged in fighting in Sardinia. He returned to Scotland with a pardon in the late 1720s and was on friendly terms with brother James, now a **Whig** supporter and Duke of Atholl following the forfeiture of William's right to succeed. In 1745 he agonised hard before joining **Prince Charles Edward Stewart** at **Perth** and jeopardising 'my life, my future, my expectations [and] the happiness of my wife and children'; but 'a principle of (what seems to me) honour and my duty to King and Country outweighs everything'.

He was appointed Lieutenant-General of the Jacobite forces but even before **Prestonpans**, largely his victory, there was friction with the Prince and his close Irish advisers. This resurfaced at Carlisle and Derby. Proud, outspoken and hot-tempered, Murray was nevertheless indispensable and played a crucial role protecting the rear of the army on its withdrawal to Scotland. **Falkirk** was again his victory but he strongly opposed both a stand against Cumberland and the selection of **Culloden** as an appropriate site for Highland tactics. After the battle his right wing was the only section to withdraw in reasonably good order. He reached **Ruthven Barracks** and there received the order to disband. Retiring to France, then Germany and Holland, he never returned to Scotland.

MURRAY, Sir George (1772–1846) Soldier and Statesman
A better soldier than he was statesman, Murray was

orn near **Crieff**, the son of Sir William Murray, and ducated at **Edinburgh** High School and **University**. Ie was commissioned in 1789 and first saw action in landers, his career closely following that of **Sir John Moore**. After Corunna, as Quarter-Master General, his rrangements proved critical in the future Duke of Wellngton's march through Spain. He was rewarded with KCB and made Major-General. In 1814 he was sent o Canada as Lieutenant-Governor but returned almost mmediately to rejoin Wellington. Although he missed Waterloo he was reckoned the most decorated soldier n the British army save only the Iron Duke himself. A ong liaison with the wife of Sir James Erskine, whom he eventually married in 1825, did his career little harm hanks to the Duke's continued patronage. He became MP for **Perth** in 1823, Lieutenant-General and Comnander-in-Chief in Ireland (1825–8) and, in the Wellngton ministry, Colonial Secretary (1828–30).

MURRAY, Sir James (1837–1915)
Lexicographer

Born at Denholm in **Roxburghshire**, the eldest son of Thomas Murray, tailor, and Margaret Scott, James Murray was fascinated by words and sounds from an early age, and once claimed to be able to read 'in a sort of way' 25 or more languages. He became a teacher at Hawick United School in 1854, and was a founder member and the first Secretary of Hawick Archaeological Society in 1856. In 1864 he moved to London for the sake of his wife's health, becoming a bank clerk in Threadneedle Street, then a teacher at Mill Hill School. Murray was elected to the Philological Society in 1868, and his *Dialect of the Southern Counties of Scotland* (1873) was the first scientific study of a modern (Scots-) English dialect. In addition he edited Older Scots texts, including *The Complaynt of Scotlande* for the Early English Text Society.

Approached to become editor of a new dictionary of English based on quotations collected by the Philological Society, he reluctantly decided to abandon a promising teaching career, concluding that it was 'God's will'. The early years of the *New English Dictionary*, better known as the *Oxford English Dictionary* or OED, were plagued by production problems and spiralling costs, but Part I (A to ANT) was finally published in 1884. In 1885 Murray moved from London to Oxford. By 1887, under increasing pressure from Oxford University Press, he fell ill and contemplated resignation, disappointed by the university's failure to grant him an academic post or an honorary degree. In 1897, however, the OED was hailed in The Times as 'not the least of the glories of the University of Oxford', and shortly afterwards it was dedicated to **Queen Victoria**. Murray was knighted in 1908, and became an Honorary D.Litt of Oxford in 1914.

MURRAY, Sir John, of Broughton (1715–77) Jacobite

From Broughton in **Peebles**, Murray attended **Edinburgh University** and soon after was in contact with the **Jacobite** court in Rome. He acted as an agent in Scotland and during visits to Rome (1742) and Paris (1744) became a confidant of **Prince Charles Edward Stewart**. In 1745 he joined the Prince at Kinlochmoidart and was appointed his secretary. As such he drafted the Prince's proclamations, organised his army's commis-sariat, and was one of his most trusted and able advisers. His illness at the time of **Culloden** may have been crucial. After, he fled west to **Lochiel**'s country and is supposed to have been responsible for burying the **Loch Arkaig** treasure. He then travelled in disguise to Peebles but was there arrested in Polmond, the house of his sister. Interrogated in **Edinburgh** and London, he turned King's Evidence, becoming the 'Jacobite Judas' (**Fitzroy Maclean**), although it does not appear that his revelations were crucial except in the trial of **Simon Fraser, 11th Lord Lovat**. Succeeding to his father's baronetcy and a small government pension, he thereafter lived and died in England. His *Memorials* are an important source for the '45.

MURRAY, John (1737–93) Publisher

John Murray was born in **Edinburgh** and after a short naval career established himself as a publishing bookseller in London (1768) at 32 Fleet Street. He published the works of many of his countrymen, including **William Cullen**, Andrew Duncan, John Millar and **Gilbert Stuart**. When the founder died, his wife Hester ran the business, but after two years she remarried and their son John (1778–1843) entered into a partnership with Samuel Highley, the shop manager. The partnership was dissolved and nine years later Murray moved to premises at 50 Albemarle Street, the present location of the firm. Murray was extremely successful, and his drawing room became a centre of literary activity. **Mungo Park**, **Walter Scott** and **Lord Byron** are most notable among his Scottish authors. Murray founded the *Quarterly Review* in 1809 to which Scott was a principal contributor and **J G Lockhart** the editor from 1825–53. John Murray III (1808–92) originated and wrote a number of the travellers' *Handbooks*, some of which are still in use today. He also published important travel literature including **David Livingstone**'s *Missionary Travels and Researches in South Africa* (1857). The John Murray succession, numbering seven, continues to this day.

MURRAY, Sir John (1841–1914) Marine Scientist

Born in Canada to Scots parents, Murray lived in Scotland from the age of 17. After studying oceanography, he was selected to participate in the *Challenger* expedition of 1872–6, supervising its deep-sea dredging operations, but perhaps more importantly, giving vital support in the publication of the expedition's reports. This took 18 years, at one stage financially supported by Murray himself. With Frederick Pullar, he also conducted the bathymetrical survey of Scotland's lochs.

MURRAY, Thomas B (1871–1929) Automobile Manufacturer

Murray was born in **Biggar** and educated at the local board school and then at **George Watson's College** and **Edinburgh University**. After moving to **Glasgow** he worked with, amongst others, **Henry Mavor** and Coulson, the electrical engineers. He then joined Scotland's first motor car project under George Johnstone but, frustrated at the lack of progress, set up the Albion Motor Company in 1899 with the collaboration of Norman Fulton. In 1902 the factory moved to Scotstoun where quality cars and, later, lorries were produced.

The onset of war and the demand for shells and vehicles boosted the company's fortunes. Murray directed the company's sound development in the post-war years. When he died in Switzerland, Scotland lost its greatest automobile pioneer.

MURRAY, William, 1st Earl of Mansfield (1705–93) Judge

Scone, once the touchstone of Scottish monarchy and later the site of a Scottish 'palace', was in eclipse after the **Reformation**. **James VI** granted the lands to David Murray of Gospertie, a relation of the **Murrays** of **Atholl** and **Tullibardine**, who was created Lord Scone (1605) and Viscount Stormont (1621). William, born at Scone, was the son of the 5th Viscount; but the new renown and his Scone earldom would come courtesy of a career in England. From **Perth** Grammar School he proceeded to Westminster School, Oxford University and the English Bar (1730), rising to KC, Solicitor-General, and MP for Boroughbridge by 1742. Notwithstanding the Tullibardine links with the **Jacobites**, nor repeated jibes about them from his great rival, Pitt the Elder (Chatham), Murray prosecuted many of those involved in the 1745 **Rising**. As Attorney-General (1754) in Newcastle's ministry he alone stood up to Pitt's rhetoric, being possessed, according to the DNB, of 'a remarkable talent for declamation'. Impartial and imperturbable, he commanded enormous respect and influence which removal to the Upper House as Lord Mansfield (1756) in Nottinghamshire did little to diminish. He became Lord Chief Justice and was created Earl in 1776. He was succeeded by his nephew David (1727–96), a distinguished diplomat and Secretary of State.

MUSIC IN SCOTLAND

The history of Scottish music can be broadly characterised by the extraordinary vigour and tenacity of its traditional music, both vocal and instrumental; and by the uneven, but occasionally outstanding contributions made by composers working within Western European classical idioms. However, the interaction of the traditional and classical often makes the division seem artificial.

Within the tradition itself there are at least three interactive cultures. The oldest of these is that of the **Gaelic**-speaking west, some of the roots of which can reasonably be claimed to be pre-Christian. This music shares much with Irish traditional music, and types of music referred to in early Irish manuscripts often survive uniquely in the Scottish Gaelic oral tradition. They include charms, work songs, panegyrics, flytings and music for the Celtic harp – the *clarsach*. The music itself has only been written down from the early 17th century onwards, but on stylistic grounds, particularly in relation to poetic form and content, a very much earlier date is accepted for a small but significant proportion. The emergence of the Highland **bagpipes** in the 16th century, and the arrival of the violin in the 17th century, gave rise to instrumental forms which may owe something to older traditions of clarsach playing. The oral tradition of Gaelic music, like that of Scots, is unbroken and has enjoyed continuous creativity alongside the careful preservation as well as the reworking of older material.

The **ballad** and instrumental traditions primarily associated with the Scots tongue emerge from the 13th century onwards. These include epic romance, ballad fricassee, and a variety of dance forms which share some of their roots with the Gaelic tradition. Written evidence for this material only emerges in any quantity in the late 16th century, but (again on stylistic and textual grounds) some of the music is not only probably medieval in origin, but is still performed in a manner though to be close to medieval practice. **Bothy ballads** and industrial and **fishing** songs reflect more recent social developments.

A small but important body of music is associated with Nordic influences, surviving in the unique **Shetland** style of **fiddle** playing and in simple repetitive melodic structures as well as in fragments of ballad material in **Norn**, though this language is no longer spoken. By far the most widely-spoken language in Scotland for the last 200 years has been English, but it is remarkable how little influence it has had on traditional song. Insofar as an English vernacular musical idiom can be established, its influence is also slight. The influence of American music (itself much beholden to Scottish and Irish styles of melody and dance) has, however, been strongly felt over the last half-century.

Scottish music often asserts a clear identity. The preference for gapped scales (especially pentatonic); the different intervallic values which are distinct from both 'just' and 'equal' temperament; the frequent use of rhythmic devices such as the 'Scotch snap', or the running quavers of the **reel** and vigorous dotted rhythms of the **Strathspey**; the tonal device known as the 'double-tonic' (probably derived from the bagpipe scale); the wide melodic range of many folk songs in both Scots and Gaelic; the virtuosic embellishment of simple melodic outlines in the Gaelic and bagpipe traditions, are all characteristic elements. Several of these have influenced, or are derived from, instrumental styles on bagpipes and violin. In the case of the Highland bagpipes, Scotland has given the world one of its best-known and most widespread musical traditions, be it marching to war, on parade, or a lone piper by a graveside.

HISTORICAL OUTLINE The earliest evidence of music-making in Scotland is an 8th century BC fragment of a cast bronze side-blown horn discovered in **Kirkcudbrightshire**. It is of a type which has survived in playable condition and considerable frequency in Ireland. The Caprington Horn (also cast bronze) is Scotland's only playable early artefact, and probably dates from 200 BC–200 AD, but its nearest parallels are Gaulish. Roughly contemporary with it is the Deskford **carnyx**, a beaten bronze trumpet over 5ft (1.5m) long of which the magnificent **Pictish**-style boar's head is all that survives. This instrument was well known in Western Europe, but the Scottish artefact is the only substantial example.

The earliest known depictions of musical instruments occur on Pictish stone carvings. They include several triangular framed harps of varying type, the earliest of which are the oldest known examples of triangular-framed harps anywhere in the world. Triple-pipes, trumpets and what appears to be a barrel drum also feature on these stones, which date from the 8th–10th century AD. From the same period there survive a number of hand **bells**, of lapped and riveted iron and of cast bronze. Several of the latter can still be rung. They are all associated with the early Irish Christian missions to the west of Scotland.

The first music manuscripts containing Scottish material date from the 13th century, though an earlier fragment was lost some 60 years ago. These include chants for **St Columba** (**Inchcolm** Antiphoner), **St Kentigern** (Sprouston Breviary) and **St Andrews** (St Andrews Music Book [W1]). Some of those for St Columba may date from the 7th–10th century, originating in **Iona**. The St Andrews Music Book, consisting largely of music from the Notre Dame school, is the first clear demonstration of Scotland's long and close musical ties with France. However, a substantial amount of music, unique to the manuscript, was added to an existing corpus and is almost certainly of Scottish provenance. Some of this music is in two or three parts and is the oldest surviving Scottish polyphony. A wedding hymn and a hymn to **St Magnus** appear uniquely in a manuscript now in Uppsala, pointing to early medieval Nordic connections. The late medieval period is represented largely in the oral tradition, though a few ballads, a fricassee and plough song were later committed to paper in the 16th and early 17th centuries. The late medieval period is thought to have brought forth many of the 'muckle sangs' (which include the so-called 'Border-ballads'), characterised in melody and text by their spare drama and truthfulness of observation.

With the exception of **James I** (none of whose music survives), named composers only appear in the Renaissance. The Carver Choirbook is named after its leading contributor, arguably Scotland's greatest composer, **Robert Carver**. It contains music by members of the Eton choir school and by Dufay, but Carver's own compositions form the bulk of the manuscript and exhibit a variety, fluency and imaginativeness which show the hand of a master in motets and masses which make astonishing technical demands. His contemporary, **Robert Johnson**, though less distinguished, produced music of great refinement and beauty while responding more readily to the growing movement towards reform which was accepted reluctantly by such as **David Peebles**, but which gave rise to a fine body of psalm and canticle settings preserved along with other material by **Thomas Wode** in the late 16th century. From what has reached us after the wholesale destructions of **Reformation** zealots, it seems clear that there was a flourishing tradition of religious choral singing, calling for the highest standards and fed by compositions of great quality.

Instrumental and secular vocal music from the Renaissance shows an intriguing mix of Continental (especially French) and native elements. Dance forms and courtly songs (the latter were often danced to) reflect the influence of two French Queens of Scotland as well as that of **Queen Mary**, whose youth was spent in France. But Scottish musicians and Scottish versions of the French dance form, the 'branle', were known in France, as was the Scottish **jig** known to Morley in England. Scottish

lutenists were sent to study in the Low Countries, but the many beautiful lute solos in early 17th century Scottish manuscripts show, more than anything else, the influence of the *clarsach* repertoire and the simple but subtly enchanting character of an established native tradition.

Keyboard music of the late 16th century is represented by the outstanding and varied output of **William Kinloch**, but otherwise by only a few distinguished settings of **Duncan Burnett**'s and one masterpiece by James Lauder. In London, the exiled Scot, **Tobias Hume**, was the first to realise the full potential of the viola-da-gamba, as well as composing a number of fine consort pieces, including the renowned consort song 'Cease Leaden Slumbers'. But Hume's appearance in London marks the move south of the Scottish court at the **Union of the Crowns**, a move which was disastrous for the further development of 'musick fyne' – as elaborate art music was known in Scotland.

The 17th century in Scotland, though a period of civil war and religious strife devoid of any substantial compositions until its very end, did produce a considerable body of fine ballads, and was one of the richest periods in the history of Gaelic music, fostering a last flowering of the **bards** and the period of greatest achievement in composition for the Highland bagpipes, during which the unique form of *piobaireachd* was developed. The absorption of new verse forms and the assertion of Gaelic social values which culminated in the **Jacobite Risings** produced a number of poetic masterpieces, almost all of which were sung and for many of which the melodies survive.

Late in the 17th century two remarkable Scottish musicians made themselves known in Europe. **John Abell**, lutenist, violinist, composer and (above all) male soprano, was attached to the English Chapel Royal under **Charles II** and **James VII** but spent many years on the European mainland. **John Clerk** travelled to Italy and studied with Corelli, producing several very fine cantatas. They are the forerunners of the composers of the **Scottish Enlightenment** – men such as **McGibbon**, **Oswald**, MacLean, and Munro who blended the Italian style with the Scottish idiom; or (later in the 18th century) **Kelly** and Foulis, whose influences were almost wholly Continental. Kelly was Scotland's first symphonist and composer of string quartets.

The increasing influence of Italian music met both with creative absorption and native antagonism, the immense popularity of the violin in Scotland bringing the two cultures into direct contact at all social levels. By the end of the 18th century, resistance to European classical styles had grown substantially. Scotland had not only suffered an identity crisis created by the **Treaty of Union**, but had been through the traumatic experience of the Jacobite Risings, the defeat and attempted dismemberment of Highland culture, and was facing up to the appalling social effects of the **clearances** and the Industrial Revolution. An assertion of the older social values inherent in native song was the natural outcome – though in the case of **Macpherson**'s Ossian (which was parallelled by a similar musical antiquarianism), reality and romanticism became strangely mixed, and exercised an astonishing influence abroad.

The early 19th century is represented in classical music by a few isolated figures such as **John Thomson**, first professor of music in Scotland, and **John Donaldson**, one of his successors. Later in the century the immensely talented **Alexander MacKenzie** took a leading role as composer, conductor and administrator in the re-emergence of British music as a significant force, and he was followed by **MacCunn, Drysdale** and **Wallace**. Traditional music added to its repertoire the songs of exile (many collected in North America and Australasia where Gaelic styles of performance have perhaps undergone less alteration), and the songs of industry and of organised agricultural labour. At the same time, new styles and instruments were accepted into the tradition, notably the accordion family as well as the piano. The growth of **music hall** and of **temperance** and **missionary** songs also acted upon and drew from the tradition at large.

The 20th century has seen the gradual establishment of the main musical institutions, though the first full-time symphony orchestra was that of the BBC and was formed only in 1935 with less than 40 musicians. The Scottish Orchestra (now the RSO) only became a full-time symphony **orchestra** after World War II, and **Scottish Opera, Scottish Ballet** and the Scottish Chamber Orchestra came later still. Composers in the first half of the century who made distinguished contributions include **McEwen, Scott** and **Chisholm** – McEwen especially in chamber music, Scott in song and Chisholm as both composer and promoter. The Gaelic **Mod** (instituted in the late 19th century), the folk-song collecting of Tolmie, **Greig** and Duncan, the arrangements of **Kennedy-Fraser** and the founding of the Clarsach Society, were fore-runners of the folk revival which commenced in the 1950s and 60s and shows no sign of diminishing. Only in the late 20th century have the necessary institutions and balance of social forces made possible the sustaining of a large body of professional musicians, including many distinguished composers. Some musicians are happy to cross the borders between classical, folk, pop and jazz; others prefer to sustain the lines of tradition as they perceive them; but for the first time since the early 16th century, the nation is in a position to support a wide variety of musical styles without necessarily endangering any of them.

MUSIC HALL

Music hall in Scotland goes back to the early years of the 19th century, and in the 1870s to 1900s flourished especially round the **Trongate** and **Cowcaddens** of **Glasgow**, and in **Edinburgh** and Leith. Travelling fit-up companies, known as 'penny-geggies', toured the country, among them one presented by the father of **Will Fyffe**. In the cities the taverns hosted comedy actors and jugglers. The Panopticon music hall in **Argyle Street**, Glasgow, flourished around the turn of the century, and saw the stage debut of such later stars as Jack Buchanan and Stan Laurel. The latter's father, Arthur Jefferson, was licensee and manager of the Metropole Theatre in Stockwell Street, Glasgow, once called The Scotia, where **Harry Lauder** made an early appearance as a kilted laddie.

The popularity of music hall survived World War I, and many entertainers, thrown idle after hostilities,

worked hard in dozens of small variety halls to make minor reputations for themselves as comedians, dancers and speciality performers. The period from 1920 to 1940 saw the emergence of holiday revues at resorts on the Firth of **Clyde** and on the **Fife** coast. Shows such as 'The Rothesay Entertainers', staged at **Rothesay** on the Isle of **Bute** by Fife and Fyfe (no relation to Will Fyffe) and those at **Ardrossan, Saltcoats** and **Largs** by Harry Kemp; and at the Ayr Gaiety Theatre by Ben Popplewell and his sons Leslie and Eric, gathered a loyal following and attained a fame still remembered today.

The tradition was still thriving at the start of World War II, and stars like **Dave Willis, Tommy Morgan**, Jack Anthony, **Harry Gordon** ('The Laird of Inversnecky' from **Aberdeen**), Jack Radcliffe and Alec Finlay had strong followings. The post-war years saw the rise of other comedy actors such as Jimmy Logan, Stanley Baxter, **Lex MacLean**, Andy Stewart, **Chic Murray** and Johnnie Beattie, and by female funsters such as Doris Droy, Gracie Clark (of Clark and Murray) and Una MacLean.

The popularity of music hall in Scotland was reflected in the packed audiences who greeted Hollywood stars Danny Kaye, Laurel and Hardy, Bob Hope, Jack Benny and Dorothy Lamour on week-long appearances in the **Empire Theatre**, Glasgow (amusingly dubbed 'the Graveyard of English Comedians') in the 1950s and early 1960s. British performers were also welcomed at the Empire and at the **Alhambra Theatre**, Glasgow, both alas since razed to make way for office blocks. The 'Five Past Eight Revues' at the Alhambra were lavish and spectacular productions, the like of which it would be too costly to mount today.

Music hall, once a great social tradition in Scotland, now survives only in memories and occasional nostalgic flashbacks. But it was wonderful in its long heyday, and the electronic, hi-tech world of television, local, national and global, can never compensate for the happy hours of fellowship and friendship at theatres like the Glasgow Empire, Pavilion and Alhambra, at the **Aberdeen** Tivoli, the **Dundee** Palace, or the Theatre Royal and **Empire** in Edinburgh.

MUSSELBURGH, Midlothian

Originally named Eskmouth, Musselburgh was renamed after a mussel-bank near the mouth of the river Esk sometime before 1200 when the barons assembled at 'Muschelburgh' to swear fealty to the infant son of **William the Lion**, later **Alexander II**. It is reputed to have gained its sobriquet 'the Honest Toun' when the citizens disclaimed any reward for honouring the body of **Robert I**'s nephew, the **Earl of Moray**, who died here in 1332. As part of the parish of **Inveresk**, it was granted to the abbey of **Dunfermline** by **David I**, was a **burgh of regality** from 1562 and received a charter as a **royal burgh** in 1632, an elevation that was successfully challenged by jealous **Edinburgh**.

Fishing was Musselburgh's main industry, the little harbour at Fisherrow also being used for ships trading to Holland and Norway, but severe silting had closed the harbour to all but small fishing and pleasure boats by the early 19th century. Of the Old Bridge over the Esk **Robert Chambers** remarked in his *History of the Rebellion in Scotland 1745–6* (1828) 'it is a structure over which all

Pinkie House, Musselburgh c1840 (RWB)

of noble or kingly birth that had approached Edinburgh for at least a thousand years must certainly have passed.' Although the bridge only dates from the early 16th century he was right in so far as the route did form part of the main road to Edinburgh. The five-arched New Bridge was built by **John Rennie** in 1806 and widened in 1924. A chapel and hermitage dedicated to Our Lady of Loretto were founded in the late 15th/early 16th century and became a place of pilgrimage for the sick and, in particular, for pregnant women seeking a successful delivery. The chapel and a great part of the town were destroyed by the English in 1544 and, although restored, the chapel was destroyed again after the **Reformation** and its stones used in 1590 to build the Tolbooth. In 1816 Musselburgh Links, close to the site of the chapel, were 'trimmed and furnished with appliances suited to the sport of testing and witnessing the comparative locomotive powers of the fleetest horses'; in other words they became a **racecourse**. The links were also reputedly used as a **golf course** by **James IV** in 1504 and from 1836–91 were the home of the Honourable Company of Edinburgh Golfers who then moved on to Muirfield.

Pinkie House on the east side of the town near the High Street dates from the 16th century when the original tower was built by an Abbot of **Dunfermline**. In 1597 it was acquired by Alexander Seton, the builder of **Fyvie Castle** in **Aberdeenshire** and later Earl of Dunfermline, whose additions and improvements included the decoration in tempera of the 'painted gallery', 'whose roof exhibits, in compartments, pedantic and medley groups of the images of heraldry, mythology and capricious creativeness', no longer, thanks to ill-advised restoration in the 19th century, in good repair. The wounded of the **Battle of Pinkie** (fought nearby in 1547) had been housed in the gallery which was turned into a hospital for the occasion. In 1694 Pinkie

Tower and nave of Muthill church (entry p 758) (HS)

House passed to the Marquis of Tweeddale who made his own alterations including the arched doorway on the east front with his initials IH (**John Hay**). Extended again in the 19th century with the addition of a stable block, Pinkie House became a part of Loretto School in 1951 and now serves as one of the boarding houses.

MUTHILL, Nr Crieff, Perthshire

Burnt by retreating Highlanders after the Battle of **Sheriffmuir** (1715), Muthill (sometimes spelt 'Moothill' but pronounced 'Mew-thil') was rebuilt at the instigation of the Drummond Earls of **Perth** whose Drummond Castle is nearby. The village contains the ruined nave and choir, plus the intact tower, of its pre-**Reformation** church. The tower, 70ft (21m) high, resembles that at **Dunning** and dates from the 12th century although the foundations are earlier. The church likewise, although there is documentary evidence of late medieval rebuilding.

MYLNE, John (i) (d.1621), (ii) (d.1657) and (iii) (1611–67) Architects

This **Dundee** dynasty provided a succession of Master Masons of Scotland and of prominent architects for over 200 years. John (i) worked in Dundee in the 1580s and 90s and was responsible for the city's Mercat Cross and for harbour repairs. He built a **Tay** bridge at **Perth** (1604) and worked on several country houses: Bannatyne House, **Angus** (alterations 1589–90) and The Drum, **Edinburgh**, formerly Somerville House (1584–5).

His son, John (ii), rebuilt **Falkland** Church, **Fife**, in 1620 and the **Aberdeen** Tolbooth steeple in 1622–3, and between 1629–30 worked on Drummond Castle, **Crieff**. In Edinburgh, he succeeded William Wallace as Master Mason to the Crown; his sundial at **Holyrood** is dated 1633. In 1636 he resigned his position in favour of his son, another John (iii).

This John's career demonstrates the rising profile of the architect in the social hierarchy. He was a prominent Edinburgh figure, member of the Town Council, Captain of the Pioneers, and Master Gunner of Scotland. In 1652 he went to London as one of the commissioners to negotiate a Treaty of Union with the English Parliament and he represented Edinburgh at the Convention of **Royal Burghs** from 1654–9. Finally in 1662 he became MP for Edinburgh. His achievements as an architect included the **Tron Kirk**, Edinburgh (begun 1637), where he skilfully fused Dutch and Scottish elements. He was also Master Mason to Heriot's Hospital from 1643–59; he fortified **Leith** in 1649–50 and built Fort Charlotte, **Shetland** (1665–6). He was equally able to design country houses, for example Panmure House, Angus, begun 1666. In his versatility he was a leading master in the last phase of Scottish mannerism.

MYLNE, Robert (1633–1710) Architect

A grandson of **John Mylne** (ii), Robert was apprentice to his uncle **John Mylne** (iii). Much of his early work was in **Fife** (Wood's Hospital, **Largo**, 1665; **Wemyss** Castle and **Leslie House**). From 1671 he was involved in the rebuilding of **Holyrood Palace** under **Sir William Bruce**. He also worked with Bruce on the remodelling of **Thirlestane Castle** in the Borders (c1670–80). Bruce and Mylne repeatedly repaired the fortifications of **Edinburgh Castle** and between 1674–87 they constructed a system of cisterns in **Edinburgh**. Apart from his work under Bruce, Robert Mylne was a successful speculative builder and contractor in Edinburgh, building housing in **Leith** and a number of tenements on the High Street, for example **Mylne's Court** (1690). He was notorious for his disregard of building regulations and spent a few days in prison on this count. But his building business secured him handsome profits with which he bought two estates, Balfargie in Fife and **Inveresk** near Edinburgh. His son William (1662–1728) was also a mason, and his grandson Thomas (d.1763) was City Surveyor in Edinburgh.

MYLNE, Robert (1733–1811), William (1734–90) and William Chadwell (1781–1863) Architects

Great-grandson of **Robert Mylne** (1633–1710), this Robert, like his contemporary **Robert Adam**, worked mostly in England. He studied architecture in Paris and Rome (1754–8) and settled in London in the following year. In 1760 he won the competition for Blackfriars Bridge (now demolished). He was always a civil engineer as much as an architect, bridges, **canals** and waterways occupying much of his time. Failing to be appointed Master of Works for Scotland, he held a number of important and prestigious posts such as surveyor of the New River Company (1767), surveyor of St Paul's Cathedral (1766) and Canterbury Cathedral (1767) as well as Clerk of the Works at Greenwich Hospital (1775). Although never as fashionable as Adam, he designed a number of country houses, mostly neo-classical like The Wick, Richmond (1775) or Bickley Place, Kent (c1780). His largest country house, Tusmore (1766–9, now demolished), was neo-Palladian. During the 1770s he carried out major works on **Inveraray**, **Argyll**.

His brother William succeeded to the family business in Scotland, building a bridge over the **Tweed** and collaborating with Robert on other projects. In 1765 he submitted a design for the **North Bridge**, **Edinburgh**, which was accepted. But nearing completion in 1769 the bridge collapsed. After this disaster, Mylne emigrated to America in 1772. First he tried his luck as a planter in South Carolina, then as an architect in New York. Unsuccessful, he finally went to Ireland where he became an engineer to the Dublin Water Works.

William Chadwell Mylne, Robert's son, succeeded to his father's posts as surveyor to the New River Company and the Stationers' Company. For the former he laid out and designed property at Clerkenwell, London, the Gothic St Mark's Church (1826–8) and the Clerkenwell Charity School (1828). He was a prominent member of the **engineering** profession, a member of the Institute of Civil Engineers and treasurer of the Smeatonian Society of Civil Engineers. Notable works were the Garret Hospital Bridge, Cambridge, a single iron arch with Gothic detailing (1835–7, now demolished) and Flint House, Amwell, Herts (1842–4), which he built for himself.

MYLNE (MILN), Walter (c1476–1558)
Protestant Martyr

Parish priest of **Lunan** in **Angus**, Mylne was accused of having ceased to say Mass, but escaped to Germany (1538). There he married and 'was more perfectly instructed in the true religion'. He returned to the north-east in 1556 – so when he was about 80 – and preached the new faith clandestinely until arrested at **Dysart** (1558). Tried in **St Andrews**, he refused to recant and was condemned to death, **Archbishop Hamilton** evidently wanting to make an object lesson of him. After some difficulty finding anyone willing to assist with the arrangements, and in the face of widespread opposition to the martyrdom of an octogenarian, he was duly burnt at the stake, the last Protestant martyr in Scotland before the **Reformation**.

MYRTLE, Bog

Particularly associated with Scotland because of its abundance in damp places in the Highlands and Islands, Bog Myrtle (*Myrica gale*) had important traditional uses. It is a deciduous shrub, up to 2m tall, with grey-green leaves which have a distinctive resinous smell when rubbed, and were used to flavour beer before hops became available. The leaves have insect repellent qualities and have been used in bedding and stored linen, and also as a remedy for intestinal worms.

All ye tourists who wish to be away
From the crowded city for a brief holiday;
The town of Nairn is worth a visit, I do confess,
And it's only about fifteen miles from Inverness . . .

Before **William McGonagall**, it was put on the map of fashionable Victorian health resorts by Dr John Grigor, an eminent and well-connected physician, who was backed by an 'improving' Provost. Their efforts were aided by the arrival of the **railway** (1855). In 1890 the grateful citizens of the 'Brighton of the North' erected a statue to commemorate their medical benefactor. It was removed some years ago from the High Street to the grounds of Viewfield House, a Georgian mansion which serves as the Nairn Museum and Literary Institute.

Although an **oil** rig construction yard at nearby **Ardersier** provides some employment, the beaches and golf courses retain their popularity. The recently rejuvenated harbour (the original was built in 1820 by **Thomas Telford**) can berth up to a hundred pleasure craft, and an excellent indoor swimming pool was built in 1983 on the same site as its Victorian predecessor. With **Culloden** and **Fort George**, **Brodie**, **Cawdor** and **Kilravock** in the vicinity, Nairn is well placed to cater for today's more mobile **tourists**. Nairn railway station should be a tourist attraction in its own right; its size and splendour are a tribute to its builders and a fitting memorial to the days when the town was very much a fashionable resort.

And in conclusion I will say for good bathing
  Nairn is best
And besides its pleasant scenery is of historical
  interest
And the climate gives health to many visitors while
  there
Therefore I would recommend Nairn for balmy
  pure air.

  (William McGonagall)

NAIRN, Sir Michael (1838–1915) Linoleum Manufacturer

Nairn was born in **Kirkcaldy** and educated at the town's Burgh School. His father, also Michael, had in effect pioneered Scotland's floorcloth industry, but died suddenly leaving the firm under a partnership including his wife Catherine. Michael junior rapidly came to dominate the enterprise after his admission to partnership in 1861. He oversaw a huge expansion in production and much technical innovation. From 1876 he directed the manufacture of linoleum, building an industrial empire with factories in the United States, Germany and France. He withdrew from management in 1909, having been created a baronet in 1904. His personal estate of over one million pounds would have been larger had he not made generous donations to Kirkcaldy's High School and Hospital.

NAIRN, Nairnshire

When **Dr Johnson** passed through Nairn in 1773 he remarked 'At Nairn we may fix the verge of the Highlands; for here I first saw **peat** fires, and first heard the Erse language.' Although Gaelic is not heard on the streets today, the town, which is the administrative centre of Nairn District, was incorporated in Highland Region after **local government** reorganisation in 1975 and from 1995 into the Highland Council Area. As its ancient name of Invernairn suggests, it is located by the mouth of the river Nairn on the south shore of the Moray Firth, 16 miles north-east of **Inverness**. In existence by 1214, it is one of the earliest of the north-east's **royal burghs**. The medieval castle was, however, 'cast doun' in the 16th century. Around 1830 Nairn was described as 'a town of very old-fashioned appearance, consisting chiefly in one long street'. But before the end of the century it had been transformed and, as a result of very extensive rebuilding, what remained of medieval Nairn was largely obliterated. Apart from part of the market cross, only the street outline survived. However, with its narrow streets and jammed-close simple cottages, the once distinct Fishertoun retains its old-world character. Here there is a small museum dealing with the folklore and history of the once sizeable **fishing** community. Unfortunately the collapse of the **herring** industry in the 1920s–30s and the silting of the harbour mouth led to the demise of Nairn as a fishing port.

Famous for its sands and **golf** links, Nairn remains first and foremost a holiday town and residential centre.

NAIRNE, Carolina, Lady (1766–1845) Songwriter

Lady Nairne was born into the **Jacobite** family of Oliphant of Gask, and was descended from the Robertsons of Struan through her mother. She was known throughout her life as a poet of distinction, and she followed the careers of **Burns** and **Hogg** with interest. But nothing of hers was published, except pseudonymously, until after her death. She then emerged as the author of a large number of lyrics, many of them of a Jacobite flavour, including 'The Laird o' Cockpen', 'Caller Herrin'', 'Charlie is my darling', 'Will ye no come back again', and 'The Land o' the Leal', all now an integral part of the culture of Scotland.

NAIRNSHIRE

Before the **local government** reorganisation of 1975, Nairnshire was a small county of 104,251 acres (42,221ha) east of **Inverness**, bordered by **Inverness-shire** to the west and south, **Moray** to the east, and with the Moray Firth to the north. Like neighbouring Moray, it had high ground to the south, the highest point being Cairn Glas at 2162ft (659m). The coastal

Lady Carolina Nairne (née Oliphant) with her son, by Sir John Watson Gordon (SNPG)

plain was more fertile, drained by the principal rivers, the **Findhorn** and the Nairn. **Agriculture** and **fishing** were the principal occupations. The county town and only burgh was **Nairn**, but under the 1929 Local Government Act, the county was united with Moray for administrative purposes, a county clerk's office remaining in Nairn to oversee such district functions as housing. In 1975 the former county was merged into Nairn District of Highland Region and since 1995 has remained part of the Highland Council Area.

NAPIER, Sir Charles (1786–1860) Admiral

Like his equally celebrated cousins (General Sir Charles James of the Sind Campaign and General Sir William Francis of the Peninsular War), Sir Charles seems to have placed little store by his Scottish ancestry; but he at least was born in Scotland – at Merchiston Hall near **Falkirk**. Joining the navy (1799), it was also in Scotland that he boarded his first ship. Thereafter he took every advantage of the many engagements on offer in the Mediterranean, Atlantic and West Indies to rise rapidly through the ranks. In 1833–5, faced with a slack period, he served, for a considerable fee and a local title, as admiral of a Portuguese fleet which restored the Queen, after a succession of remarkable engagements, and which established Napier as a near-mythical hero. Sadly, adulation turned an effective commander into a vain showman who disobeyed orders in Syria and negotiated without authority in Egypt (1840). He retired as admiral, won few friends as an MP, and spent his last years at another 'Merchiston Hall', his renamed house in Sussex. He published accounts of his Portuguese and Syrian campaigns in which his achievements are not understated.

NAPIER, David (1790–1869) Marine Engineer

Napier worked in his father's **engineering** business in **Glasgow**, building the boilers and making the engine castings for **Henry Bell**'s *Comet*. The success of this vessel persuaded him to specialise in marine engineering and invest in steamships. He built the Camlachie Foundry to the north-east of Glasgow in 1814 and the famous Lancefield Foundry on the **Clyde** in 1821. He helped inaugurate steamer services from the Clyde to Belfast, on **Loch Lomond**, and across the English Channel. In 1836 he moved to Millwall on the Thames where he considered prospects for iron **shipbuilding** to be brighter. His business prospered.

NAPIER, John (1550–1617) Inventor

Born in **Edinburgh**, or possibly **Balfron**, Napier studied at **St Andrews University** from the age of 13, becoming the 8th Laird of **Merchiston** five years later. Much involved in agricultural activity, religious controversy and military science – he designed an 'armoured chariot' – Napier also showed a strong interest in mathematics. From around 1590 he began devising a scheme of natural logarithms to the base e. His was the first system to be published, although the German horologist Joost Burgi was also working on a logarithm system. Napier also invented what is believed to be the world's first mechanical computing device, a series of numbered rods called 'Napier's Bones'. His castle at Merchiston is incorporated into the campus of Napier College (University) in Edinburgh.

NAPIER, Robert (1791–1876) Engineer and Shipbuilder

Born in **Dumbarton**, the cousin of **David Napier**, he trained as a smith. In 1821 he leased the Camlachie Foundry from David and began constructing land engines. He built his first marine engine in 1823 for the PS *Leven* which is preserved outside the **Denny** Test Tank in Dumbarton. Other orders soon followed for his improved engines. In 1827 he acquired the Vulcan Foundry not far from the banks of the **Clyde**. He moved to the Lancefield Foundry when his cousin left for London in 1836 and four years later built the engines for the first four **Cunard** liners. He began iron **shipbuilding** in **Govan** in 1843 building a succession of pathbreaking liners and naval vessels. He retired in 1860, widely regarded as the father of the Clyde shipbuilding and marine **engineering** industries.

NAPIER COMMISSION (Royal Commission on the Crofters and Cottars of Scotland)

In response to agitation by the Highland Land Law Reform Association (later the **Highland Land League**) and in the face of open defiance of authority by the **crofting** community [see **Battle of Braes**, **Glendale Martyrs**], in 1883 the Liberal government of Lord Gladstone set up a Royal Commission of inquiry. Chaired by Lord Napier, a distinguished member of the Indian Administrative Service, the commission comprised two landowners who were not unsympathetic to the crofters' plight (Donald Cameron of Lochiel and Sir Kenneth Mackenzie of **Gairloch**), two Gaelic scholars (Professor Donald MacKinnon of **Edinburgh University** and

Sheriff Alexander Nicholson), and one MP who was also a member of the Highland Land Law Reform Association (Charles Fraser-Mackintosh). In effect the Commission was expected to find for the crofters and to recommend legislation similar to Gladstone's Irish Land Act of 1881.

During 1883–4 the Commission toured the Highlands and Islands collecting evidence; in the process its members were shipwrecked off **Stornoway**. The crofters, at first suspicious and anxious about recriminations, quickly overcame their reticence. The resultant report is the most voluminous, authoritative and damning ever compiled on the inequities and hardships experienced by the Gaelic tenantry during the 19th century. Acknowledged by all parties as exceptionally thorough, it has been extensively used by later writers on the **clearances**.

But while the Commission's enquiries lent weight to the crofters' grievances, its recommendations failed to satisfy them. In what has been described as a brave attempt 'to resurrect the traditional Highland township as a kind of peasant commune' (T C Smout) the Commission recommended security of tenure only for the larger more viable crofts, urged collective responsibility for rents and public works, and suggested a right of compulsory purchase over adjacent privately owned lands. This last provision outraged landowning interests, while the suggestion that only larger crofters should have security of tenure alienated crofting opinion in general and **cottars** in particular. The **Crofters' Holdings Act** of 1886, though a direct result of the Napier Commission, ignored most of its suggestions and duly replicated the terms of the Irish Land Act.

NARES, Sir George Strong (1831–1915)
Admiral and Arctic Explorer

A native of **Aberdeen**, George Nares joined the navy at the age of 14. In 1872 he was appointed Captain of the *Challenger* expedition to explore the southern oceans. He stayed with the *Challenger* until January 1875, earning a reputation as a generous and patient commanding officer, before returning to England from Hong Kong to command the *Alert* and the *Discovery* on an Arctic expedition which, it was hoped, might reach the North Pole. It did not but it crossed 82° North after forcing a way between Greenland and Ellesmere Island. It was then driven back by scurvy. His *Voyage to the Polar Seas* (2 vols) was published in 1878. Knighted on his return from the Arctic in 1876, he was made Rear-Admiral in 1887 and Vice-Admiral in 1892.

NASMYTH, Alexander (1758–1840) Painter and Architect

One of the most successful and influential painters of landscape in the history of Scottish painting, Nasmyth, born in **Edinburgh**, studied briefly at the **Trustees' Academy** before being appointed studio assistant to the portraitist **Allan Ramsay** in London. Ramsay instilled in him the principles of good drawing as the basis of all good painting, as well as introducing him to the **Enlightenment** concepts of man's relationship to nature and the landscape. Nasmyth set himself up in 1778 in Edinburgh as a portrait painter but, after a protracted visit to Italy from 1782–4, increasingly turned to landscape as a preferred subject. As it was, his well known

Fox-ite sympathies lost him many potential sitters. During this period Nasmyth formed a close friendship with fellow radical **Robert Burns**, sharing not only politics but a profound love of the landscape. His painting, like Burns's poetry, attempted to qualify the human experience of nature, placing figures and architectural conceits within untamed Scottish scenery. He was much influenced by the popular 'vedute' of Claude and Poussin and his work shares their use of framing devices and carefully contrived recession. Although not adverse to tinkering with the elements of the landscape for compositional effect, Nasmyth often went one better, producing architectural plans for the buildings and classical caprices that appeared in his paintings. **St Bernard's Well** on the **Water of Leith** [see **Edinburgh**] was actually built to his specifications and he always recommended it to his students as an ideal subject.

Nasmyth's art school opened in 1798 and his teaching philosophy emphasised the need to draw from nature rather than from static studio busts. His prolonged sketching trips around Edinburgh influenced many younger artists and formed the basis of the 19th century Scottish landscape tradition. His more celebrated pupils included Hugh 'Grecian' Williams, John Thomson and his own children, a notable artistic brood, particularly Patrick and **James**. A typical polymath of his time, Nasmyth also successfully tried his hand at naval **engineering**, theatrical scene-painting and optical science.

NASMYTH, James (1808–90) Engineer

James Nasmyth was born in **Edinburgh**, the son of the artist **Alexander Nasmyth**. He was educated at Edinburgh High School and the School of Arts, and in 1829

First Attempt; self portrait by James Nasmyth, 1881 (SNPG)

became an assistant to Henry Maudsley at the latter's Lambeth Engine Works in London. In 1831 he set up his own **engineering** workshop in Edinburgh, moving to Manchester the following year and finally, in 1837, opening the Bridgewater Foundry in Patricroft.

Nasmyth specialised in the design and manufacture of machine tools, but he also built hydraulic presses, pumps and over 100 locomotives. His numerous important inventions included a safety ladle for foundries, the steam hammer, and the steam pile-driver. He was an implacable foe of restrictive labour practices in the engineering industry, and an advocate of 'free trade in ability'. To improve the efficiency of his factory in the production of standardised machine tools, and to undermine the influence of the craft unions, he introduced a forerunner of the modern assembly line at Patricroft.

Nasmyth retired from business at the early age of 48 to pursue his hobby, astronomy. He built his own reflective telescopes, was the first astronomer to observe solar flares, and published an important paper on the appearance of the surface of the moon in 1874. His greatest claim to fame, however, is as the inventor and manufacturer of standardised automatic machine tools, reducing the dependence of industrialists on skilled labour and ushering in the age of mass production.

NATIONAL DRAMA, The

The term refers to a 19th century dramatic genre, peculiar to Scotland and dealing with Scottish subjects. Stage adaptations from *Ossian* (*Oscar and Malvina*, 1791) and **Scott**'s poems (*Lady of the Lake*, 1810) showed that the caricature Scotsman (Sir Archy Macsarcasm) and rustic ballets (*Highland Frolics*) of the 18th century no longer sufficed in the Romantic early 19th century. Censorship from London, suppressing nationalist (ie **Jacobite**) sentiment on the Scots stage (Duval's *Prince Charles Stewart*), was swept aside by adaptations of the Waverley novels which played all over Britain. Their popularity and respectability brought many Scots into theatres for the first time, eager to see plays featuring Scots as major characters in familiar settings, speaking in Scots dialect and singing Scots songs. The best of them were presentations of the national history and character (*Gilderoy*, *Cramond Brig*), whilst the worst were melodramas which swathed cliché in **tartan** (*Dark Donald*, *The Idiot of the Cliff* or *The Dog of Loch Lomond*). The National Dramas boosted the security of the patent houses with solid commercial success (*Rob Roy* became known as the 'Managerial sheet-anchor'), and gave the minor theatres and 'geggies' a semi-legitimate repertoire with which to compete. A succession of Scottish vocalists (John Wilson) and character actors ((the real) Mackay) built their careers around the National Drama. In Scotland it was as popular as Shakespeare and the theatres decorated their auditorium walls and curtains (**Theatre Royal**, Dunlop Street, **Glasgow**), public rooms (**Her Majesty's**, **Dundee**) and programmes (**Theatre Royal**, **Edinburgh**) with its heroes and heroines. Mid-century the major theatres reduced their use of the National Drama to one or two lavish productions per year, timed to coincide with the Fair holidays [see **Glasgow Fair**]; however the geggies continued to use the full National repertoire and they and the annual revivals continued into the early 20th century.

NATIONAL GALLERIES OF SCOTLAND

The National Gallery of Scotland opened in **Edinburgh** in 1859 and since that date has expanded to incorporate a **Scottish National Portrait Gallery** and a **Scottish National Gallery of Modern Art**, all housed in buildings of varying architectural interest [see **Edinburgh**], plus an out-station at **Paxton House** in Berwickshire. The original building was proposed as a result of the overcrowding of the neighbouring Royal Institution, home to many organisations, not least the **Royal Scottish Academy** who annually required the entire building for their summer exhibition. The inconvenience this caused was exacerbated by the increasing size of the Institution's own collection of paintings which had no permanent home. It was decided, therefore, that a new building should be constructed, half of which would be given over to the permanent display of a national collection and half to the Royal Scottish Academy for their exhibitions. After extraordinary complications (both financial and architectural) a new building was built to the designs of **Sir William Playfair**, although he was not to live to see its completion. The impressive neo-classical building favoured the elegant Ionic order and formed a pleasing contrast to the Doric of Playfair's earlier Royal Institute. The interior consisted of a sequence of parallel octagonal galleries which were to be decorated by the innovative house-painter and colour-theorist D R Hay. Since 1859 the interior of the building has been considerably modified. The most significant change occurred in 1906 when the Royal Scottish Academy returned to the Royal Institute building, at a stroke doubling the space available to the National Gallery. Later extensions involved the construction of two sequences of upper level galleries and, in 1976, a new subterranean wing, now home to the Scottish collections.

In 1882 a National Portrait Gallery was opened, occupying an exceptional Gothic-Venetian sandstone building in Queen Street, built by **Rowand Anderson**. Its construction gave some overflow for the already extensive national collection as well as satisfying the Victorian desire for a show-case of images of interesting and edifying individuals. The final part of the triumvirate, the Gallery of Modern Art, opened in 1960 in a relatively modest Georgian house in the midst of the **Royal Botanic Gardens**. In 1983 it moved to considerably more grandiose premises – the old John Watson's School, west of central Edinburgh – ironically the oldest building of the three, a rather heavy-handed neo-classical essay by **William Burn**.

The strongest part of the national collection remains the Scottish School. Much of the initial endeavour to create the National Gallery was as a home for great Scottish paintings, and a series of acquisitions and donations (not least by the Royal Association) ensures that it holds the finest collection of Scottish painting in the country. The Gallery of Modern Art perpetuates the original ideals by purchasing outstanding examples of contemporary Scottish art. The collection of English and European works is also remarkably strong, arguably second in quality only to the National Gallery in London. This has been partly due to an increasingly sensitive and inspired policy of acquisition, but mostly thanks to some spectacular donations, legacies and loans. These include the Duke of Sutherland loan (important works by Poussin, Raphael and Rembrandt), the Vaughan Bequest (Turner), the Cowan Smith Bequest (Goya, Chardin) and, more recently, the Maitland Collection (Cézanne, Gauguin, Degas). The investment of legacies has enabled the Gallery to make important acquisitions far beyond the reaches of its normal means. The National Gallery building at **The Mound** has recently undergone extensive interior renovations, restoring it to a state close to that existing in 1859. A heavier hang of pictures has enabled a greater proportion of the permanent collection to go on show, at the same time freeing space for temporary exhibitions which have maintained a consistently oustanding balance of popular appeal and academic merit.

NATIONAL LIBRARY OF SCOTLAND, The

The National Library of Scotland was founded as the library of the **Faculty of Advocates** some time in the 1680s. The exact date is open to question; the first mention of the intention to found a library appears in the Faculty's minutes for July 1680, and a catalogue in manuscript existed by January 1683. However, **Sir George Mackenzie**'s inaugural oration is dated 15 March 1689, and the Library itself chose to celebrate 1989 as the year of its tercentenary.

Sir George Mackenzie of Rosehaugh, King's Advocate, persecutor of the **Covenanters** and one of the least attractive figures of 17th century Scotland, may be said to have redeemed himself by his enthusiastic championship of the Library. He perceived the need for it, and he laid down the rules for its development. Though Mackenzie was in no doubt that the books in the Library should be primarily legal, he realised that there were associated subjects of interest to lawyers. History, criticism and rhetoric, the 'handmaidens of jurisprudence' as he described them, were obviously matters on which the advocates should have books, and while it is clear that Mackenzie himself interpreted these subjects rather narrowly, the loophole was exploited. Before 1700, important literary collections – such as the books of Lord George Douglas – and historical ones – such as the papers of Sir George Balfour of Denmilne – had already been acquired. Apart from the subject matter of the Library, the growth of its stock was remarkable, and when the first published catalogue appeared in 1692, it contained 3140 volumes.

Indeed, from very early, the Library had an active and clearly stated collecting policy. In 1682 a 'Programme' was printed in which the Faculty offered to buy law books from private individuals, and in 1699 a more generally worded 'Memorial' encouraged the gift or sale to the Library of historical manuscripts of all sorts. The quality of the Library was recognised well beyond the confines of the Faculty, and before the beginning of the 18th century it was already being used by outsiders.

It was therefore not surprising that in the provisions of the Copyright Act of 1709, the Advocates' Library was chosen, along with those of the four Scottish universities, to have the privilege of legal deposit, that is, the right to a copy of every book published in the British Isles. This privilege, exercised from that day to this as vigorously as resources have permitted, is the basis of the National Library's pre-eminence today.

The funding of the original Library derived from entrance dues paid by newly qualified advocates. This for obvious reasons was always a fluctuating and uncertain source, but the legal deposit privilege, which ensured a steady flow of British publications, meant that such other funds as were available could be used for antiquarian or foreign purchases as opportunity allowed. But the Library finances remained a source of worry, and it was not put on a proper footing until the Library was taken over by the state in the 20th century.

The Library was first stored in a house off **Parliament Close**. In February 1700 this house was burnt to the ground in the great fire which devastated that part of the town, and the books were only saved by the heroic efforts of the Librarian, James Stevenson. The following year the Library was moved into the Laigh **Parliament Hall**, where it was to remain for the next two and a half centuries. Many efforts were made throughout the 18th and 19th centuries to find more suitable accommodation for it, and it is interesting to remember that the Upper **Signet Library**, one of the most beautiful buildings of classical **Edinburgh**, was originally constructed to house the Advocates' Library, though its occupation was of very short duration.

Throughout the 18th century, the Library flourished under a succession of distinguished librarians. **Thomas Ruddiman** – whose 50 years on the staff from 1702–52, the last 24 as Librarian, included the passing of the Copyright Act, and the publication of the Catalogue of 1742 – set administrative and professional standards which remain a source of admiration today. His successor, **David Hume**, benefited the Library by his international contacts, though his attempts to introduce some contemporary French literature were firmly crushed by the Faculty. In the second half of the century the Library was able to play its own role in Scotland's outstanding contribution to the Age of **Enlightenment**.

The 19th century was a period of increasing difficulty. The great increase in book production made the legal deposit seem something of a burden, a burden not lightened by the fact that the universities gave up the privilege in 1837, leaving the Advocates' Library as the only copyright library in Scotland.

From as early as 1808, the suggestion was made that the Advocates' Library was in practice the National Library of Scotland, and from 1853 there were serious attempts to involve the state in its financing. Nothing, however, happened until after World War I when the influence of **Ramsay MacDonald** as Prime Minister, and the gift of £100,000 by his best friend **Sir Alexander Grant**, the biscuit manufacturer, established a basis for the transfer of the Library to the nation. The National Library came into existence formally on 26 October 1925.

The new Library still had difficulties before it, the greatest of which was space. Though it was now the National Library, it was still in the same premises, and almost from the beginning the search for a new building became a major preoccupation. The site of the former Sheriff Court on **George IV Bridge** was eventually chosen, and after some administrative difficulties, and with a further gift of £100,000 from Sir Alexander, building began in November 1937. Work was interrupted by World War II, and the building was not finally opened until 1956. It was thought that it would meet all requirements until the end of the century, but by 1970 it was already full.

The **Heriot-Watt University** was at that time in process of moving to its campus at Riccarton, and it was hoped that the site of the University's buildings, so conveniently close on the other side of the **Cowgate**, might have been used by the Library for an extension. This was not to be however; suspension of the move to Riccarton in 1975 compelled the Library to look elsewhere. In order to overcome the immediate space problems, the Library had acquired the disused Middlemas's biscuit factory in Causewayside, hoping to move out of it when the Heriot-Watt site became available. When this prospect disappeared, it was decided to use the site of the factory for the Library's new building, and phase I of the Causewayside Building was opened to widespread acclaim in 1989.

The National Library of today is a far cry from its predecessor of the 17th and 18th centuries. The growth of the Library, forced on by the operation of the Copyright Act and by the existence of funds to permit extensive foreign and antiquarian buying, has produced a bookstock which now amounts to some 6 million. More rigorous enforcement of the Act has resulted in the development of important **music** and map collections, the latter of which, with over 1.6 million items including the **Bartholomew** archive, is one of the largest of its kind in the world.

And there have been many other developments, well beyond the imagination of Sir George Mackenzie. There was a long-felt need for a science library in Scotland along the lines of that attached to the British Library in London. The Copyright Act had always brought in the output of British scientific books, but the Library was fundamentally orientated towards the humanities, and tended to develop strengths in that area rather than spread its resources more widely. In 1977, however, a working party recommended the establishment of a science library, and in 1981 a scheme was approved for such a library based on the National Library's collections and on the foreign periodicals acquired by the **Royal Society of Edinburgh**. In spite of setbacks and limited funding the Scottish Science Library opened to the public in the new Causewayside building in the summer of 1989, and was followed in the autumn by the Business Information Service.

Advances in the Library's traditional services have also taken place. The expensive and time-consuming work of cataloguing is now widely shared by the introduction of co-operative cataloguing systems, and not only can the Library now benefit from work done elsewhere, particularly in the British Library, but it is able to make the results of its own work more quickly available through an on-line catalogue for use by readers.

The Library plays an essential role in the library services of the whole country. In 1974 the operations of the Scottish Central Library, inter-library loans and the upkeep of the Scottish Union Catalogue were taken over by the National Library. This led to the formation of the Library and Information Services Committee (Scotland) in 1982 under the auspices of the National Library but to provide a channel of communication between the library community at large and the Secretary of State.

In the year 1988–9, the Library received some 345,100 printed items, or well over 1000 every working day. Manuscript accessions filled some 270m of shelves. The Library served a total of 85,279 readers, dealt with 26,085 inter-library loan requests, and produced 75,408 photocopies and 65,957 frames of microfilm for those who wished to consult the Library's holdings from a distance.

In all this, however, the Library has not forgotten its traditional role as the guardian of the written heritage of the nation. The books of today are made available with all the efficiency of modern technology, but the Library continues to acquire great manuscripts and great literary treasures when they become available. Great libraries such as those of Newhailes, of Blairs College or of the first Earl of **Haddington**; great manuscripts such as the **Iona** Psalter, the Murthly Hours, and the **Scott** manuscripts from the Pforzheimer Collection; and great archives such as those of **Field Marshal Earl Haig**, of the Marquises of Tweeddale, and of the Earls of Minto, continue to arrive. History begins now, and the Library tries to ensure that it acquires the valuable material of today which it will be difficult or impossible to obtain in the future. In the words of the Librarian, 'The Library serves the Scotland of today, but is answerable to the Scotland of tomorrow.'

NATIONAL NATURE RESERVES

The Nature Conservancy Council (under its new guise as part of Scottish Natural Heritage) selects, establishes and manages a series of National Nature Reserves throughout Britain, and they represent a wide range of habitats and species. Some of the most outstanding of these are to be found in Scotland, including the largest in Britain at the **Cairngorms** (25,949ha) and the first NNR to be established in Britain at **Beinn Eighe** in Wester **Ross**, where most of the 4758ha are owned by the NCC.

There are four main functions of such reserves: habitat management, research, access/amenity, and interpretation. Management includes fencing to exclude stock and **deer**, controlled grazing by sheep, and planting of trees. Research may be pure research, as with some of the studies of **red deer** on **Rum**, or more general local research, ie monitoring the success and failure of nesting black-throated **divers**. The NCC is charged with allowing access to all reserves provided this is compatible with the wildlife conservation interests of the area. There is open access to most of the 67 NNRs in Scotland, although this is inevitably restricted by the remoteness of some of those on islands. The most popular reserves, such as **Loch Lomond** north of **Glasgow**, Inverpolly north of **Ullapool** and Sands of Forvie on the north-east coast, have thousands of visitors each year. The pressure of such numbers involves building bridges, making walkways and putting stiles over fences. The Beinn Eighe and Inverpolly Reserves have visitor centres and nature trails and at the latter there is a combined wildlife and **geology** trail.

The machair on the Western Isles and the **seabird** colonies on **St Kilda** are of international renown and importance. Remnants of the once great **Caledonian**

Forest are included in reserves such as Glan Tanar in Grampian Region and Glen Strathfarrar near **Inverness**. These probably represent the closest habitat to the old 'wildwood' of Britain and are the haunt of the **Scottish crossbill**, **capercaillie** and **crested tit**. In contrast the **Monach Isles** in the Outer **Hebrides** have a grey **seal** rookery of 12,000 adults in October producing around 2000 pups a year – possibly the largest rookery of this species in the world.

Such is the importance of the Scottish reserves that some have won international acclaim; St Kilda was awarded a Diploma by UNESCO and its listing as a World Heritage Site was the first for wildlife in Britain and the first one ever in Scotland.

NATIONAL PARTY OF SCOTLAND, The (1928–34)

The creation of the NPS 'marked the emergence of [Scottish] nationalism as an independent political movement, distinct from any British political party' (M J Hanham). Forerunner of the **Scottish National Party** (SNP), the NPS was inaugurated at **Stirling** by die-hards of the Scottish National League, including the Hon **S R Erskine of Mar** and C M Grieve (**Hugh MacDiarmid**). But it quickly attracted disillusioned left-wingers from the **Scottish Home Rule Association**, such as **Roland Muirhead** and **John MacCormick** who became President and Secretary, and with whom Celtic nationalists such as Erskine had little in common. The new party fared badly in the 1929 elections; its only triumphs were a saved deposit at East **Renfrewshire** (1930) and the election of **Compton Mackenzie** as rector of **Glasgow University** (1931). Torn between radical ideology and the need to broaden its appeal, variously branded as Marxist or Catholic, and hopelessly upstaged by the economic crisis of the '30s, the NPS welcomed the break-away from Conservative ranks of a group of moderate home-rulers known as the Scottish Party and, at the price of a purge of its own extremists (including Grieve), merged with it to form the SNP.

NATIONAL TRUST FOR SCOTLAND, The

With over 100 properties and nearly 200,000 members the National Trust claims to be 'the leading conservation body in Scotland'. Its function, implied in the full title of 'The National Trust for Scotland for Places of Historic Interest or Natural Beauty', is more copiously defined as 'promoting the preservation of lands, buildings, places and articles of national architectural, artistic, antiquarian, or historic interest, or lands of natural beauty along with their animal and plant life.' This wide area of concern is matched by wide powers which enable the Trust to purchase and hold properties inalienably, or to manage them solely or jointly, or to regulate their use in the interests of conservation. A concern for the national heritage beyond its trusteeship of such designated properties is also acknowledged.

Borrowing from both American and English precedents, the Trust was founded in 1931 when the Association for the Preservation of Rural Scotland under the chairmanship of Sir Ian Colquhoun of **Luss** acknowledged the necessity of a statutory body with proprietorial rights. Parliamentary sanction came in 1935 with the establishment of the Trust as a non-governmental body enjoying charitable status and empowered to act in concert with other statutory authorities. It is governed by a Council comprising President, Vice-Presidents, and up to 100 members, half elected. An Executive Committee, appointed by the Council, manages the Trust through various sub- and standing committees.

The first property acquired by the Trust was **Crookston Castle** near **Paisley**; it was presented by **Sir John Stirling Maxwell** of **Pollok**, one of the Trust's first Vice-Presidents, in 1931. Castles and tower houses were destined to form the Trust's stock-in-trade and now include such notable examples as **Craigievar**, **Crathes** and **Castle Fraser**. Soon after Crookston, the purchase of **Culross Palace** (**Fife**) absorbed nearly half the Trust's then available funds and led to a growing involvement in the preservation of **Culross** itself as a uniquely unspoilt 17th century burgh. An interest in urban conservation and in restoring humbler properties, designated 'little' and 'lesser' houses, continues.

Similarly the 1932 acquisition of part of the site of **Bannockburn** has been followed by other battle grounds, notably **Culloden** and **Killiecrankie**, while purchases in **Glencoe** in the 1930s have led to an extensive portfolio of wilderness areas, including **Ben Lawers**, **Kintail**, **Torridon**, **Fair Isle** and **Iona**. Some, designated National Parks, are equipped with visitor centres; all, in accordance with the Trust's aims, are open to the public. Perhaps its most ambitious initiative in terms of encouraging awareness of conservation is the Country Park established at **Culzean Castle**.

NATIONALIST COVENANTS, The (1930 and 1949)

In a bid to broaden their appeal and awaken ancient sympathies, 20th century nationalist leaders, and in particular **John MacCormick**, hit on the emotive idea of solemnly signing and circulating a nationalist covenant. The first, drawn up when MacCormick was in the **National Party of Scotland** and launched in **Stirling** in 1930, bound its signatories 'to restore the independent national status of Scotland' and to set up 'an independent parliament in Scotland' as soon as a majority of Scottish citizens had signified support. Following his split with the **Scottish National Party** in 1942, MacCormick's broad-based Scottish Convention adopted a similar ploy in 1949. The Convention was a cross-party organisation of more moderate outlook, like the **Scottish Home Rule Association** of earlier times. The new covenant spoke, therefore, of constitutional 'reform' rather than independence, and of a Scottish Parliament 'within the framework of the United Kingdom'. This wording brought 2 million signatures, but failed to win endorsement for the Convention or its covenant from any of the major political parties.

NEIDPATH CASTLE, Nr Peebles

Roofed, in fair repair, and gloriously sited above a bend in the **Tweed**, Neidpath nevertheless lacks the celebrity attached to other tower houses in the Borders in that its history is short on recorded massacres and raids. Even **Sir Walter Scott** somehow neglected to immortalise it. The worst depredation on record concerns a tree-felling programme undertaken by the 4th Duke of Queensberry which provoked an angry sonnet from **William Words-worth**. ('Degenerate **Douglas**! Oh the unworthy Lord!' etc. who could level 'A brotherhood of venerable trees,/ Leaving an ancient dome, and towers like these,/Beggared and outraged!') There never was an ancient dome, and there is only one tower, although composed, in rather a squashed L, of two angles, one of which was severely damaged by Cromwell's artillery. Built in the late 14th century, remodelled in the 17th and again in the 19th, the castle has passed from the **Frasers of Lovat** to the **Hays**, the Douglases of Queensberry, the Scotts of Buccleuch, and now the Earls of Wemyss whose heirs have the title of Lord Neidpath. The rounded angles of the walls are notable, and the effect of roofing-in the parapet and squaring the turrets is to provide an inviting garret above the otherwise stern façades.

NEILL, James George Smith (1810–57)
Soldier
One of the heroes of the 1857 Indian Mutiny (alternatively one of the worst imperialist oppressors of the National Uprising), Neill was born and educated in **Ayr** before attending **Glasgow University** and obtaining a cadetship in the East India Company. In Madras he was patronised by **Sir Thomas Munro**, a relative by marriage, who would surely have disapproved of his later conduct. He served in the 2nd Burmese War (1852–4) and in Turkey during the Crimean War. Returning from home leave he was overtaken by news of the Mutiny's outbreak and his appointment to command of the Madras Fusiliers. Rapidly despatched up the Ganges to Allahabad, he secured that important point but was superseded in command of the force to relieve Cawnpore (Kanpur) and Lucknow by Brigadier-General Havelock. Neill took this badly and to the heightened feelings of the moment were added a degree of personal bitterness. But nothing can excuse the revolting retribution meted out to those mutineers deemed responsible for the massacre of British women and children in Cawnpore. Neill ordered them to clean the house in which the butchery had taken place by licking up every trace of blood; the lash was freely used to enforce the order; the prisoners were then hanged from an adjacent gibbet. His subsequent bravery at Lucknow, where he fell in action, brought extravagant commendations. His undoubted courage was seen as justifying what was then regarded as necessary severity but now as wanton brutality. A massive statue commemorates him in Ayr.

NEILSON, James (1792–1865) Inventor
Born at Shettleston, then a village near **Glasgow**, Neilson left school at 14. Studying in what spare time he had from his work as a pit mechanic, he obtained a foreman's post at Glasgow Gas Works but, more importantly, devised a system of improving **iron** production by using hot air in the smelting process. This took time to implement, being the opposite of contemporary practice, but Neilson patented the process in 1828, defending his rights in three court trials. He was a keen supporter of **education** for the working man.

NELSON, Thomas (1822–92) Publisher
After leaving **Edinburgh** High School Nelson joined the Edinburgh bookselling business started by his father, also Thomas, and run by his brother William. His main interest was initially in bookbinding, then other aspects of book production; plants were set up in Edinburgh and London and by 1878 the company had a workforce of 600. Nelson also invented a rotary press which was shown at the 1851 Great Exhibition. As an editor he launched *The Children's Paper*, a highly successful monthly, and developed the firm's educational list. Maps and atlases also interested him and he became a director of **Bartholomew's**. As well as building a handsome mansion in Edinburgh's Queen's Park, he acquired the family estate on the south shore of **Loch Etive** in **Argyll**.

NESBIT, Battles of (1355 and 1402)
Nesbit is in Northumbria, south of **Berwick** and east of **Coldstream**. In 1355, during Edward III's absence in France, a Scottish force here defeated an English one (and captured Sir Thomas Gray) prior to sacking Berwick. Edward returned to exact revenge in his 1356 **Burnt Candlemas** campaign. In the 1402 encounter the Scots fared worse when Sir Patrick Hepburn of Hailes and other **Lothian** notables were routed and captured. Neither 'battle' had been much more than an affray but, in attempting to exact revenge for the second, **Archibald 4th Earl of Douglas** ('the Tyneman') and others provoked the real thing at the Battle of Homildon (1402) where they spectacularly 'tyned' (ie 'lost'); the English saw it as revenge for **Otterburn** (1388).

NESS, Loch, Inverness-shire
Second only to **Loch Lomond** in surface area but double its volume, Loch Ness is about 23 miles long, an average of one mile wide, and exceptionally deep (max depths are variously stated as between 750 and 1000ft). The ratio of surface area to depth accounts for its never having frozen over in recent centuries. It is the most obvious feature of the **Great Glen**, hills rising steeply and with somewhat monotonous symmetry on both sides. At the head of the loch **Fort Augustus** lies close to its main feeder from Loch Oich and Glengarry. Indentations on its north shore at **Invermoriston** and **Drumnadrochit** lead into Glenmoriston and Glen Urquhart. Its only egress is via the short river Ness into the Beauly Firth. Before the construction of **Wade**'s road (or the opening of the **Caledonian Canal**) it was an important means of communication with the West Highlands. Both Cromwell and Cumberland maintained sloops to patrol its waters and there were several ferries. Oddly none of this traffic produced any recorded sightings of **Nessie**.

NESSIE (The Loch Ness Monster)
Monsters, **kelpies** and other water beasts feature prominently in Highland folklore and are associated with numerous lochs and rivers. But until comparatively recently there was only one recorded sighting of such a phenomenon on **Loch Ness** or the river Ness. This is in **Adamnan**'s *Life of St Columba* and credits the saint with miraculously cowing an *aquatilis bestia* and so saving some of his followers. Considering that in late Victorian times six steamers a day plied the loch on cruises up the **Caledonian Canal** it is indeed remarkable that nothing untoward was reported. Yet not until 1932 did the spate of recent sightings begin. These beggar credulity no

more than the far-fetched explanations offered to explain them away. There is a rough consensus as to the appearance of the creature – snail-like head, long neck, flexible serpentine body – though not as to its size, a pointer perhaps to there being several of different ages. Imputations of malevolence are unsubstantiated, pace Adamnan. Nessie enjoys the affection of many and deserves the admiration of all. In spite of numerous expeditions and despite the cameras, binoculars and sonar sensors regularly trained on the loch, Nessie resolutely defies science. Irrefutable proof of the existence of one or more monsters remains as elusive as irrefutable proof that such do not exist.

NETHY BRIDGE, Inverness-shire

On a tributary of the **Spey** four miles south-west of **Grantown**, Nethy Bridge nestles on the edge of Abernethy Forest and shares something of **Aviemore**'s piste-and-backpack culture. **Castle Roy** is nearby and across the Spey near Dalnain Bridge is the recently restored Muckerach Castle, the original seat of the **Grants** of **Rothiemurchus**. It was built by Sir Patrick Grant in 1598, a simple L-plan with square keep and round angle tower corbelled out to the square at third-storey level. A walled courtyard, one of whose round towers survives, evidently adjoined it.

NETTLES

It is hard to imagine a more useful Scottish plant than the now despised nettle, so delicious and nutritious to eat that Scots gardeners used to force the frost-sensitive shoots under glass as 'early spring kale', while St Kildans danced merrily after drinking nettle ale made from the roots fermented with barley meal dough. Nettle juice was used as a substitute for rennet when cheese-making in the Highlands and Islands. Medicinal uses were as a spring diuretic, to relieve nosebleeds and headaches, to make cough syrup (**Lewis**) and to induce sleep (**Skye**).

Shetlanders placed nettles gathered at Halloween between the sheets of a loved one for the unlikely purpose of securing his or her affection, while nettles gathered on St John's eve could be used to undo a spell cast on milk production, if the plants were picked on the suspected witch's land and put under the milk pails.

The use of nettle fibres to weave cloth persisted in Scotland until at least the late 18th century and may have begun in prehistoric times. Nettle fabric could be made as fine as linen, and was very strong and durable, but was gradually replaced by flax which produces longer, finer, more easily extracted fibres on poorer soil than nettles. The fabric could even be self-dyed: young nettle tops produced both yellow and grey-green dyes, which have been used in the manufacture of **Harris Tweed**. Perhaps the great variety of uses to which nettles were put reflects the fact that they grew round every dwelling, thriving in the nitrogen-rich soil beside walls of houses with no internal sanitary facilities.

NEVILLE'S CROSS, Battle of (1346)

Responding to a call from his ally Philip VI of France (whose forces had been defeated by Edward III at Crécy and were now besieged at Calais), and perhaps also hoping to emulate his father's success in battle against the English, **David II** led a sizeable force into England in October 1346. Unimpeded until they reached Durham, they were finally halted by an army led by the Archbishop of York at Neville's Cross. In the ensuing battle the **Earls of Moray** and **Strathearn** were killed, the **Earls of Fife**, **Menteith**, **Sutherland** and **Wigtown**, together with the King, were taken prisoner, and the **Earl of March** and **Robert the Steward** quietly withdrew to Scotland. David, who had received a serious arrow-wound to the face in the fighting, spent the next 11 years as a 'prisoner' at the court of Edward III in London, apparently 'greatly preferring the easy life of the English court to the cares and burdens of kingship in Scotland' (**Fitzroy Maclean**).

NEVIS, Ben, Nr Fort William, Inverness-shire

Although the highest mountain (4406ft/1343m) in Scotland and the British Isles, Ben Nevis is not the loveliest. From **Fort William** it is completely hidden by the town's backdrop of Cow Hill. It is not often visible from elsewhere, clouds obscuring its summit to deposit their 157in (3987mm) of annual average precipitation before racing inland on one of the mountain's 261 gales per year. (The name 'Nevis' derives from the Gaelic nèamh, 'heaven' or 'clouds', thus 'the mountain with its head in the clouds'.) When not obliterated it appears, as seen from the **Great Glen**, more hump than peak. The scale is elusive until it is appreciated that the cliff wall which closes the north-west facing corrie between it and Carn Mor Dearg (4012ft/1223m) is in fact 2 miles long and 2000ft (610m) high, a welcome challenge to climbers. Lesser mortals – walkers, runners, visiting celebrities and the sponsored bearers of pianos, beds, etc – generally prefer to address the climb by way of the footpath from Achintee in Glen Nevis. The summit promises extensive views (weather permitting) to the **Cuillins**, **Cairngorms**, Ben Lomond, **Jura**, and, allegedly, Ireland. It is otherwise a wasteland of boulders. The meteorological observatory here was manned night and day from 1883–1904 but then closed. Nor can one expect much of the nearby Temperance Inn which provided its last bed and breakfast (10 shillings in 1898) at about the same time.

East of Carn Mor Dearg the Nevis range continues through Aonach Mor (with Scotland's newest ski centre, opened 1990) and Aonach Beg to the Grey Corries. The Spean river flanks the range to the north and Glen Nevis to the south. Partly accessible by road, the latter is a renowned beauty spot. Beyond the road-end the gorge formed as the river squeezes between Aonach Beg and the serrated Mamore hills is 'one of the great sights of the Highlands . . . with a Himalayan character not seen elsewhere in this country' (W H Murray). The path continues on to Loch Treig and **Corrour**. The lower part of Glen Nevis also forms the end of the West Highland Way which from **Kinlochleven** has followed **Caulfeild**'s military road by Loch Lundavra before cutting across to Glen Nevis and Fort William.

See also **Geology**.

NEW GALLOWAY, Kirkcudbrightshire

A village at the head of Loch Ken, New Galloway was created a **royal burgh** (the smallest in Scotland) by charter of **Charles I** c1630 in favour of Sir John Gordon of Lochinvar. Kenmure Castle, long a **Gordon** strong-

Ben Nevis from Corpach pier, near Fort William (BRC)

hold, occupies an easily defended natural hill over-looking New Galloway and Loch Ken. An earlier castle on the site, one of many said to have given refuge to **Queen Mary** on her flight after the **Battle of Langside** (1568), was largely destroyed by Cromwell's troops. The present roofless ruin dates mainly from the 16th century, was originally E-plan extended in the 19th century to form two sides of a square courtyard, and is now dangerously unsound. On another hillside to the west of the village, Kells churchyard has some delightful tombstone carvings and epitaphs, the upright Adam and Eve stone (1707) in memory of Robert Corson, his wife Agnes Herese, and their nine children having particular charm. New Galloway lies at the centre of the **Galloway Hydro-Electric** scheme, the first large-scale hydro-electric scheme in Scotland (1929–35).

NEW LANARK, Lanarkshire

Coming upon New Lanark over the lip of the steep brae behind it is a startling experience. No amount of preparatory research can give a true idea of the scale and unspoilt integrity of the 18th century industrial 'village' hunkered down on the banks of the **Clyde**. For here are no trim rows of cottages, no pump or green or hostelry. Instead three massive seven-storey sandstone mill blocks are set in a sweeping curve along the riverside, backed and flanked by rows of only slightly smaller subsidiary buildings, the whole apparently trapped between the torrent of water in front and the near-vertical hill behind.

The site, described as 'a mere morass situated in a hollow den and of difficult access', was purchased from local landowner **Lord Braxfield** in 1783 by **Glasgow** banker and entrepreneur **David Dale** and his partner, the English pioneer of **cotton**-spinning Robert Arkwright. What made the 'hollow den' so perfect in their eyes was the proximity of the Clyde, here a fast-flowing river hurtling through a narrow gorge; its power could turn the great waterwheels which would drive the mechanical spindles which, within ten years, would make New Lanark's mills not only the largest cotton mills in Britain but the biggest single industrial enterprise in Scotland.

In 1785 Dale's partnership with Arkwright was dissolved and, as sole proprietor, Dale continued his development. Construction of the mills was followed by construction of workshops and dyeworks, and accommodation, shops and a school for the millworkers. Drawing initially on the surrounding parishes of Lanarkshire and then on the orphanages of **Edinburgh** and Glasgow for his workforce, Dale was also quick to offer accommodation and employment to emigrating Highlanders and their families en route via Glasgow to a new life in America.

The inventions of Arkwright and his contemporaries revolutionised the textile industry and increased production of cotton yarns 300-fold in the space of less than a century. But although the mechanical spinning process was labour intensive, the workforce needed nimble fingers rather than great skill – hence the preponderance of children in Dale's employ. By 1793 there were 1157 people working at New Lanark, nearly 800 of whom were children. Dale, however, was a benevolent industrialist and New Lanark was not destined to become just another sweat-shop born of the Industrial Revolution. When the No 1 Mill burnt to the ground in 1788 he continued to pay full wages to every employee until it was rebuilt and work could restart.

By the turn of the century as many people were visiting New Lanark to observe Dale's experiments in **education** and community living as to witness the miracles of modern mechanisation. The workers were a well-housed, closely-knit community and the orphaned children were well fed, neatly clothed and, most surprising of all, well educated, attending school for two hours of every working day. Unusually for the age, and as a result of Dale's own non-conformist attitudes, organised religion did not figure large in the daily life of New Lanark, and not at all in the school curriculum. Although the village would later boast a small church, it never had a manse.

In 1800 Dale sold New Lanark to his son-in-law Robert Owen, an ambitious young Welshman with even more progressive ideas for social reform. Owen saw in New Lanark an opportunity 'to commence the most important experiment for the happiness of the human race that had yet been instituted at any time and in any part of the world.' Building on Dale's foundations, he extended the school, abolishing the system of punishment and reward in favour of the encouragement of learning for the pleasure of acquiring knowledge. He raised the minimum age for millworkers from six to 12, opened what was surely the industrial world's first on-site crèche so that mothers would be free to work, introduced a system of contributory welfare, stocked the village shop with good quality produce which was sold to his employees at near cost price, and – his crowning glory – opened the New Institute for the Formation of Character where the children and young people of the village were taught music, singing and dancing.

The success of his enterprise at New Lanark, and the impact of his ideas on educationalists and reformers throughout the world, led to an invitation to Robert Owen to start up a similar enterprise in America. In 1824 he sailed for the New World, leaving New Lanark in the hands of one of his partners, whose sons continued to manage it in accordance with Owen's ideas for another 50 years. Even when it was sold to a firm of **Gourock** ropemakers in 1881, little changed. Auxiliary steam power was introduced and diversification led to the production of rope, fishing nets, canvas and sail-cloth; but cotton-spinning remained the mainstay, orders were still being sent all over the world, and the strong community feeling persisted until the end. This came in 1967 when the ropeworks closed down; new buyers could not be found, and New Lanark was faced with demolition. Only timely intervention by a variety of conservation bodies in the early 1970s led to its preservation, gradual restoration and re-opening as an industrial heritage site and living museum. Even the community is returning, with a Housing Association overseeing the restoration of the former workers' accommodation blocks into comfortable and stylish homes. It is now run by the New Lanark Conservation Trust and has become one of Scotland's most visited and most unusual **tourist** attractions.

Newark Castle, Port Glasgow (RWB)

NEWARK CASTLE, Port Glasgow, Renfrewshire

Now stranded amidst the debris of post-industrial dereliction, Newark once graced a smiling Clydeside that was ignorant alike of **shipbuilding** and social deprivation. It may be so again. Below a skyline now of tower blocks there was once just the tower house built by George Maxwell of Finlaystoun which is Newark's 15th century nucleus. **James IV** stayed here in the 1490s, at about which time a separate gatehouse tower was constructed. A century later the two were linked with a mansion block which combines Renaissance features (eg window and door pediments) with traditional turrets and crow-step gables. In 1668 the Maxwells sold part of Newark estate to the burgesses of **Glasgow** who required a harbour facility in deep water. Hence **Port Glasgow** which, despite the 18th century deepening of the upper **Clyde**, prospered and duly edged the Maxwells out of Newark. So derelict as to be suitable only for 'working men's families' in the 19th century and for vagabonds and vandals in the 20th, the castle was eventually taken into state care.

NEWARK CASTLE, Nr Selkirk

Not to be confused with **Newark Castle** on the **Clyde**, nor with Newark Castle in **Fife**, nor even with Newark Castle at **Ayr**, this is **Sir Walter Scott**'s Newark whose 'stately tower looks out from Yarrow's birchen bower' where *The Lay of the Last Minstrel* was relayed to the Duchess of Buccleuch. From their nearby Georgian mansion of Bowhill, the Buccleuchs still have in their care the ruins of Newark. These consist of a rugged but roofless tower house plus the remains of its barmkin. Like **Neidpath**, the castle dates from around 1400 and stands on rising ground above a bend in the river (Yarrow) which thus serves as a partial moat. Once a royal hunting seat in the **Ettrick Forest**, it was a **Douglas** stronghold before passing to the Scotts of Buccleuch. After the **Battle of Philiphaugh** in 1645 a hundred or more defeated Royalists took refuge here and were brutally massacred by the victorious **Covenanters**, their ministers failing to persuade **David Leslie** of the merits of clemency. High above the river in the woods on the other side stands the ruined cottage of Foulshiels in which **Mungo Park** and his 13 siblings were raised. The cottage is about the same size as one of Newark's cap houses.

NEWBATTLE ABBEY, Midlothian

Founded for Cistercian monks by **David I**, colonised from **Melrose**, and patronised by successive Scottish monarchs, Newbattle became one of the wealthiest of the medieval abbeys of the **Lothians**. Marie de Coucy, wife of **Alexander II**, was buried in the abbey choir in 1241. The fruits of this patronage earned the monks of Newbattle a reputation as 'astute and rapacious accumulators of worldly property'. But they seem to have put their wealth to good use, for they have been credited not only with founding the salt panning industry at **Prestonpans** (12th century), but also with operating the first **coal**-mine in Scotland (13th century) and with initiating organised agriculture in **Midlothian** (13th century). Destroyed by the English in 1385, Newbattle was rebuilt by the monks over a period of 40 years only to be destroyed again by Hertford c1545. After

the **Reformation** Mark Ker (or Kerr), who had become a Protestant in 1560, was made the first **commendator** of Newbattle in 1564 and promptly built himself a house incorporating what was left of the abbey ruins (little more than the foundations). His son, also Mark, succeeded to the commendatorship in 1584, three years later was granted the entire abbey estate as a temporal barony by **James VI**, was created Lord Newbattle in 1591 and by 1606 had become Earl of Lothian. The 4th Earl of Lothian was created Marquis in 1701. Newbattle Abbey was extended and modernised in the 18th and 19th centuries and remained the home of the Kerr family until the 1930s when it was given in trust to the nation by Philip Kerr, 11th Marquis of Lothian, for use as an adult education college. **Edwin Muir** was based here 1950–4.

NEWBERY, Francis Henry (1855–1946)
Painter and Art Educationalist

As Director of the **Glasgow School of Art** from 1885–1918, Newbery was responsible for its transformation from a traditionally organised municipal art school into an internationally recognised centre for modern art education. During his regime Glasgow was to develop as one of the most dynamic centres for the production of art and design in Europe, eclipsing **Edinburgh**'s long-standing reputation as the artistic capital of Scotland.

Born in Devon, Newbery studied at the Bridport School of Art and at the National Art Training Schools – now the Royal College of Art – in London where, under the Director Thomas Armstrong, he was introduced to the socialist principles of William Morris upon which he was to base his educational ideals. In Glasgow he embarked upon an adventurous staffing policy, disregarding traditional categories of status between the Fine and Applied Arts and, though he himself was a painter, placing particular emphasis on the teaching of design. In 1889 he married Jessie Rowat, a former student of the school, and from 1894 she taught there, establishing classes in embroidery and enamelling that became equal in importance to drawing and painting in the School's curriculum. Amongst the many individuals who benefited from the hot-house atmosphere created by Newbery were the architects Herbert MacNair and **Charles Rennie Mackintosh** who attended evening classes at the School between 1884–93. Through Newbery they were introduced to the sisters Margaret and Francis MacDonald and in the four's subsequent artistic collaborations – that locally earned them the name the 'Spook School' – they emerged as the leading proponents of the 'Glasgow Style', the most original and imaginative British contribution to the international decorative style known as Art Nouveau.

The success of Newbery's efforts in Glasgow attracted an increasing number of students to the School and he made it his further plan to find a new building that would replace the already cramped premises within the Glasgow Corporation Galleries. The decision to employ the designs of Mackintosh, who at the beginning of its construction was not yet 30, resulted in a building considered at the forefront of the development of the International Style in 20th century European architecture. In 1902 Newbery was responsible for the organisation of the Scottish section at the International

Exhibition in Turin, which did much to promote the Glasgow Style abroad, and through such contacts he was able to attract the best students and teachers to the School. Upon his retirement he returned to Devon where he devoted himself to painting until his death.

NEWBURGH, Nr Ellon, Aberdeenshire
At the mouth of the Ythan, Newburgh was once a port of some consequence. Now it is visited for **Aberdeen University**'s ornithological and botanical research station. Nearby the roofless Knockhall Castle is 16th century and L-plan but with the addition of a projecting square tower. It was built by Sinclair of Newburgh but quickly passed to the Udny family in whose care it was accidentally burnt in 1734. The Udnys were saved from sharing its fate by the family's jester, Jamie Fleeman, otherwise 'The Laird of Udny's Fool'.

NEWBURGH, Fife
This small **royal burgh** owed its privileges and patronage to **Lindores Abbey**. It stands on the Firth of **Tay** facing Mugdrum Island which here splits the firth into the North and South Deeps. Weaving and then linoleum provided employment but by 1898 it had become 'an uninteresting town of one street', and has not changed markedly since. To the west Mugdrum House (18th century) has Mugdrum Cross, an armless shaft too weatherworn and defaced for much of its relief sculpture to be discernible. 'MacDuff's Cross' further west is in fact a cup-marked boulder with no evidence of a cross in spite of a legend awarding its destruction to **Knox**'s zealots. Its role as a place of sanctuary for any MacDuff guilty of murder is also doubtful. Nearby Pitcairlie House belonged to the Leslie **Earls of Rothes** and then to a cadet branch with the title of Lord Lindores. Basically 16th century and Z-plan it has been described as 'a composite building where each addition sought no quarter from what went before' (G L Pride).

NEWCASTLETON, Roxburghshire
The parish and old village (no longer in existence) of Castletown in the southernmost corner of **Roxburghshire** were so called after the profusion of castles and peel-towers, mostly in **Armstrong** or Elliott possession, that thronged this wild and strife-ridden stretch of the Border. Of these **Hermitage Castle**, ever the strongest, is the only notable survivor. A minute inserted in the parish records of January 1649 records how 'the English army of General Cromwell, on their return to England, did lie at the kirk of Castletown several nights, in which time they brake down and burnt the communion-tables and the seats of the kirk; and carried away the minister's books and also the books-of-session – with which they lighted their tobacco pipes – the baptism, marriage, and examination rolls, from October 1612 to September 1648, all which were lost and destroyed.' In 1793 the 3rd Duke of Buccleuch founded the new village, Newcastleton, to house hand-loom weavers. Its neat arrangement of streets on an elongated grid plan is a marked contrast to its wild and isolated surroundings.

NEWHAILES, Nr Musselburgh, East Lothian
The plain exterior of Newhailes conceals a contrasting grandeur within which has survived remarkably

untouched from the 1730s. Originally called Whitehill, the centre block was built by the architect **James Smith** for himself in 1686; it was a simplified version of the compact hip-roofed house introduced by **Sir William Bruce** at **Dunkeld**. After Smith's bankruptcy in 1707, the house was bought by Sir David Dalrymple and renamed after his **East Lothian** estate of Hailes; a partial refit was done by **William Adam** c1720. This was followed by the addition of the flanking blocks and interiors (some possibly designed by John Adam) which were completed by 1757 for James Dalrymple, 'the builder of Newhailes'. The magnificent gilded state apartments are embellished with plasterwork by Thomas Clayton, carved woodwork by William Strachan, marble by the Cheere brothers and landscapes by William Norie. At Newhailes in the 1750s during the **Scottish Enlightenment**, **David Dalrymple, Lord Hailes**, the distinguished judge and historian, penned his *Annals of Scottish History* in the vast library, 'the most learned drawing-room in Europe' (Johnson, 1773). His books are cared for by the **National Library**, the house by the **National Trust for Scotland**.

NEWMILNS, Ayrshire
Created as a **burgh of barony** for Campbell of Loudoun in 1490, Newmilns, with neighbouring Darvel, expanded as a centre of muslin weaving and lace making when power mills were introduced by Alexander Morton in 1876. Newmilns' oldest building is the square four-storey Newmilns Tower (c1530) used successively as residence, prison, court and store; its most attractive is the small church-like Town House, a crow-stepped Tolbooth (1739). Loudoun parish church (1844) has graves and memorials to various **Covenanting** martyrs, a connection of which the town has always been proud.

NEWPORT-ON-TAY and TAYPORT, Fife
Now at the south end of the **Tay** Road Bridge, Newport was established in 1822 as the **Fife** ferry port for **Dundee** and continued so until the construction of the road bridge. It thus supplemented the older ferry from nearby Tayport to **Broughty Ferry**. The latter, a rail ferry from 1846, declined after the construction of the **Tay Rail Bridge** (1887, from Wormit on the west side of Newport); but it was still in operation at the turn of the century. Although the pier is 1822 to designs by **Telford**, Newport is mainly Victorian and was once much patronised by Dundee's **jute** barons. Tayport is older and was once more industrialised. Its old parish church, subsequently a community centre, has a tower that distinctly leans; and its fine Catholic church (Our Lady of the Sea, 1938, **Reginald Fairlie**) has a *Stella Maris* statue by Hew Lorimer which complements that on the other side of Scotland in **South Uist**.

NEWSPAPERS
Scotland's first newspaper was a short-lived reprint of a London publication, the *Diurnal Occurrances touching the Dailie Proceedings in Parliament*, printed in **Edinburgh** in 1641. This communicated English Parliamentary news. Nearly another ten years passed before the first indigenous Scottish newspaper appeared – the *Mercurius Scoticus* which was first published in **Leith** in July 1651 and

SCOTTISH NEWSPAPER CIRCULATIONS (to nearest 1000, 1998 figures)

		Began	Circulation
Press & Journal (Aberdeen) Aberdeen Journals Ltd	Daily	1747	105,000
The Herald (Glasgow) Scottish Media Newspapers Ltd	Daily	1785	101,000
The Scotsman (Edinburgh) Scotsman Publications Ltd	Daily	1817	81,000
Evening News (Edinburgh) Scotsman Publications Ltd	Daily	1873	81,000
Evening Times (Glasgow) Scottish Media Newspapers Ltd	Daily	1876	117,000
Evening Express (Aberdeen) Aberdeen Journals Ltd	Daily	1879	66,000
Daily Record (Glasgow) Scottish Daily Record & Sunday Mail Group	Daily	1895	715,000
Evening Telegraph (Dundee) D C Thomson Ltd	Daily	1905	32,000
Sunday Mail (Glasgow) Scottish Daily Record & Sunday Mail Group	Sundays	1919	810,000
Sunday Post (Dundee) D C Thomson Ltd	Sundays	1920	739,000
Courier & Advertiser (Dundee) D C Thomson Ltd	Daily	1926	96,000
Scotland on Sunday (Edinburgh) Scotsman Publications Ltd	Sundays	1987	114,000

numbered 21 editions, irregularly printed weekly and fortnightly by one Evan Tyler.

From 1712 newspapers were subject to the Stamp Tax and frequently came under government influence or control, so it is not too surprising to find that the nation's oldest newspaper still appearing is one containing official and statutory announcements, the Edinburgh Gazette. Originally printed in Edinburgh by James Watson for publisher James Donaldson in February 1699, it is now published twice weekly by HMSO. The longest-lived 'news'paper in the literal sense is the Aberdeen Press and Journal, which first emerged as Aberdeen's Journal in 1747. The Glasgow Herald was first published in 1783, and The Scotsman in 1817. Two years later the Six Acts further curtailed the freedom of the press, although there was an increase in publishing activity after the 1832 Reform Act.

By the 20th century, the Scots had become such avid newspaper readers that 20 national titles were produced, with a gradual introduction of English-based titles with special Scottish editions. Among the most famous of Scottish newspaper publishers is the **D C Thomson** company in **Dundee**, responsible for such national institutions as the *Weekly News* (1894–) and *Sunday Post* (1920–) as well as two Dundee newspapers and a fleet of comics and magazines [see also **Periodicals**].

In **Glasgow** the *Glasgow Herald* (renamed *The Herald* in 1992) and *Sunday Herald* (launched 1999) are produced by Scottish Media Newspapers Ltd, while the *Daily Record* and *Sunday Mail* are produced by a Scottish outpost of the Mirror Group with considerable local autonomy. A Scottish edition of the *Sun* is also printed in Glasgow, but the Scottish editions of the *Daily Mail* and the *Daily Express* are no longer printed north of the border.

Edinburgh's output includes *The Scotsman* – not the largest quality circulation in Scotland, despite its official-sounding title – as well as *Scotland on Sunday* and *Evening News*, all products of Thomson Regional Newspapers. **Aberdeen** produces the aforementiond 'P & J' and *Evening Express*, published by Aberdeen Journals, while the Dundee output is centred on D C Thomson and includes the *Courier* and *Evening Telegraph*.

Approximately 190 local newspapers are printed in Scotland. This figure includes the recent rash of freesheets which have in some cases replaced more traditional priced papers, but not community newspapers. From Scotland's largest town, **Paisley**, with such local papers as the *Paisley Daily Express* (1874–), to the smallest rural communities, local newspapers are often more keenly read than the national press. The *Dumfries and Galloway Standard* (1843–) and *Southern Reporter* (1855–) are among the best-known in southern Scotland. North of the central belt, the *Oban Times* (1861–) and *Inverness Courier* (1817–) have forged considerable reputations, while such island papers as the *Orcadian* (1854–) and *Shetland Times* (1872–) are intensively circulated in their areas. A comparative newcomer, the **Skye**-based *West Highland Free Press* (1972–), is a lively addition to the newsagents' counters in the north-west and Western Isles.

The volatile nature of newspaper publishing is indicated by the number of failed titles in the not too distant past. Well-known Glasgow titles such as *The Bulletin* (ceased 1960) and *Evening Citizen* (ceased 1974) have been joined in oblivion by the *Scottish Daily News*, printed briefly in 1975–6 by a workers' collective in somewhat controversial circumstances when the *Express* pulled up its Scottish roots. Outram's attempt to set up a quality Sunday paper, the *Sunday Standard*, failed in the 1980s (1981–3) as did the *Sunday Scot* in 1991. Most of the London Sundays now produce Scottish editions or supplements.

NEWSTEAD, Nr Melrose, Roxburghshire

The **Roman** army under **Agricola** is thought to have moved into southern Scotland (c81 AD) in two columns, one in the west advancing through Annandale to the **Clyde** (roughly along the line of the present A(M)74) and one in the east along a road later called Dere Street (now the A68). The fort at Newstead, called Trimontium by the Romans, overlooked the ford where Dere Street crossed the river **Tweed** and was the centre of a network of forts linked by roads and constructed to control the local tribes. Remains of other of these forts include the important site on Eildon Hill North (thought to have been a signalling station) as well as

Oakwood, Woden Law, Pennymuir, Rubers Law and Bonchester Hill. Excavations carried out at Newstead between 1905–10 led to some remarkable finds including carpenters' tools, leather shoes, brooches, bronze wine jars, swords, spear and arrowheads and several cavalry helmets. They also revealed that the fort was dismantled when Agricola withdrew (c86 AD) but was later rebuilt with additional ramparts to serve as one of the furthest outposts of the **Antonine Wall**. No structural remains survive.

NEWTON STEWART, Wigtownshire

This small market town lies on the west bank of the river Cree which marks the boundary between **Kirkcudbrightshire** and **Wigtownshire**. It grew on the site of an ancient ford across this shallow stretch of the river, and was thus originally known as Fordhouse of Cree, but was renamed Newton Stewart by William Stewart, third son of the second Earl of **Galloway** and proprietor of the Castle Stewart estate, who was granted a burgh charter by **Charles II** in 1677. For some reason that the writer does not specify, an 1843 Gazetteer reports that the new burgh was thereafter settled by 'the idle, the giddy, and those who hung loose upon society', and developed a reputation as a haunt of smugglers. Towards the end of the 18th century the estate was purchased by William Douglas (see **Castle Douglas**) and renamed Newtown Douglas, but neither the new name nor the **cotton** mills and carpet factory he built here caught on and all three fell into disuse. The church at Minnigaff, a suburb or 'residential annexe' of Newton Stewart although across the Cree and therefore strictly speaking in Kirkcudbrightshire, was built in 1836 to plans by **William Burn** and has some fine stained glass. In the churchyard beside the ruins of its 16th century predecessor, itself on the site of an older building, are some 11th century sculptured cross-slabs, one of which was discovered in use as the lintel of Minnigaff's old market house and the other serving as the doorstep of the old church.

NEWTONMORE, Inverness-shire

This village in **Badenoch** is the first of the Strathspey resorts encountered by the traveller heading north. Of no antiquity, it owes its existence to its location – on **Wade**'s road over the **Corrieyairack Pass**, on the main **railway** line to **Inverness**, and at the junction of the modern A9 to the north with a road from **Fort William**. Besides pony-trekking and mountain sports, the village is notable for its highly successful **shinty** team and for its **Clan Macpherson** museum. Cluny Castle, towards neighbouring **Laggan**, traditionally housed the clan Chief, **Macpherson of Cluny**, and from there came many of the museum's treasures including the Black Chanter (which supposedly fell from the skies during the **Battle of the Clans**), the remains of James Macpherson's fiddle [see **Banff**], and various relics of the '45 **Jacobite Rising**. The Macpherson of the day proved the staunchest of **Stewart** supporters and after **Culloden** spent nine years in hiding before escaping to France. Throughout this period he was loyally supported by his clansmen but so keen were his pursuers that he spent long periods in an underground hideout, a woodland 'cage', and in a cave on Creag Dhu, a high rockface near the castle (and also the rallying cry of the clan). Cluny Castle was burnt down by his enemies but later rebuilt and, like Ardverickie on **Loch Laggan**, is said to have interested **Queen Victoria** as a possible Highland home. Nearby, by the confluence of the **Spey** with the Truim (whence the main road descends from the **Drumochter Pass**) was fought the 1386 Battle of Invernahaven between the **Camerons** and a confederacy of **Mackintoshes**, Macphersons and Davidsons. The Macphersons fell out with their allies and watched; the Camerons won but then withdrew.

NIDDRY CASTLE, West Lothian
Niddry Castle stands on a hillock hard by the main **Edinburgh-Glasgow railway** line about half a mile south-east of Winchburgh. Anciently known as Niddrie Seaton (or Seton), it was built c1500 by George 3rd Lord Seton (killed at **Flodden** 13 years later) as a robust four-storey L-plan tower house, and was later extended by the addition of a fifth storey. It was to Niddry that **George 5th Lord Seton** welcomed **Queen Mary** after her dramatic escape from **Loch Leven Castle** in 1568. The castle and its lands remained in Seton hands until passing to the Hopes of **Hopetoun** during the reign of **Charles I**.

NIGG, Ross & Cromarty
The anvil-shaped peninsula between the **Dornoch** and **Cromarty Firths** has the parish of Nigg as its southern extension. This terminates to the south-east in the cliffs of the North Sutor guarding the approach to the Cromarty Firth and to the south-west in the yards and ancillary buildings of an **oil** platform fabricators; they lie close to the site of Dunskaith Castle, supposedly built (1179) by **William the Lion** as a defence against **Viking** invasion. Nearby Nigg church, white-harled and rectangular, dates from 1626 but was somewhat altered in the 18th century when an aisle was added. Its most famous possessions are the great **Pictish** cross-slab, richly carved with bosses, interlace and biblical scenes, and a Cholera Stone beneath which in 1832 a church elder buried the cholera 'cloud' having first captured it in a bag, like a swarm of bees. One of the gravestones here is the work of **Hugh Miller**.

Inland and on the other side of Nigg Bay's tidal flats Tarbat House was built (1787) for **Sir George Mackenzie** but sold by the Earl of Cromartie in 1966 and gutted by fire in 1987. Recognised by conservationists as 'one of the most important Georgian country houses in the Highlands', it may yet be saved. Balnagown Castle in the same district has experienced a different fate. Granted to Hugh Ross, half brother of the last **Earl of Ross**, in 1372, it became the home of the chiefs of the Clan Ross and was still in Ross hands in 1900 when a guidebook described it as 'one of the grandest examples of Scottish architecture of the 16th century'. However the extensive 18th century additions must throw doubt on this verdict while recent 'improvements' flatly contradict it.

NINIAN, Saint (c360–c432)
Apparently the son of a converted British chieftain, Ninian by tradition founded a church, and was a **Roman**-trained bishop, at **Whithorn** in **Galloway**. Recent archaeological excavation confirms a settlement of Britons to which he possibly returned c394 after some time in Gaul. He is the first named Christian of Scottish record, known from Bede's *Historia Ecclesiastica* of 731. His church, the Candida Casa, or White Stone Church, has yet to be confirmed. Its influence as a mission station in the 5th century is evident in the spread of Christianity to the east of Scotland and the southern **Picts** before the Irish church influence of **St Columba** in the following century from **Iona**.

The connection with his contemporary St Martin of Tours is unknown except in tradition and in Bede. The association of his name with many churches and place-names throughout Scotland indicates more a cult than personal exploration or mission tours. He seems to have been the catalyst for the remnants of Christianity begun during Roman occupation. His location on the Solway, on the opposite shore to the end of Hadrian's Wall, was opportune. A significant community, in residence continually until **Viking** trading days, is being discovered by ongoing digs. His death, presumably at Whithorn, did not terminate an isolated Christian centre, since Welsh and Irish missions continued to radiate from it.

NISBET, Sir John, Lord Dirleton (1609–87)
Lawyer
Nisbet was a member of that caste of 17th century Scots lawyers who were simultaneously famed for intellectual achievement and barbaric behaviour. Whilst recognised by his peers as accomplished in the law, he was also renowned for his pursuit of **Covenanters**. His political ambitions led him (1664) to combine the offices of Lord Advocate (at that time the most powerful office of state in Scotland) with a senatorship of the College of Justice. He wrote *Some Doubts and Questions in the Law especially of Scotland* (1690), popularly referred to as 'Dirleton's Doubts', and was responsible for collecting the *Decisions of the Lords of Council and Session* between 1665–77.

NISBET, Murdoch (fl.1520)
Possibly one of the **Lollards** of **Kyle**, Nisbet fled his native **Ayrshire** when reformers of religion were subject to persecution. He used Wycliff's translation into English to commence a Scots Bible. His New Testament in a hybrid language of Scots and English was never published as he died in hiding.

NITSHILL COLLIERY DISASTER (1851)
Now a suburb of **Glasgow**, Nitshill was the scene of Scotland's first major colliery disaster, when 61 men and youths died on Saturday 15 March 1851. At 4.40 am an underground explosion occurred at a depth of more than 1000 ft (305m), just as the main shift of workers were assembling at the pithead to descend. Casualties were thus mercifully lighter than they might have been, although many of the dead were accounted for by the failure of improvised – although courageous – rescue attempts to overcome afterdamp. Only two men were brought out alive from the affected area, terribly burned, after being trapped underground for 45 hours.

NON-JURORS
Some clergy from the established Church during the 17th century Episcopacy felt unable to take the oath of

allegiance to King William III while **James VII** lived. They were deprived from the Church as 'non-jurors'. The term applied to their followers (and some English clergy) through the 18th century. They eventually formed the Scottish **Episcopal Church**.

NORIE-MILLER, Sir Francis (1859–1947)
Insurance Company Director
Born in Surrey, Norie-Miller began his business career in fire insurance and in 1887 became the chief officer of the recently formed General Accident and Employers Liability Assurance Association of **Perth**. In an astonishing career he transformed this parochial institution into one of the leading British insurance companies. During the inter-war years motor insurance proved the area of fastest growth and General Accident became the third largest company in the field. Knighted in 1936, Norie-Miller held the post of magistrate in his adopted city for nearly five decades. He was also briefly elected MP for Perth, where his company, despite its UK-wide scale of operations, remained sited.

NORN
The basically Norse (or **Viking**) language once spoken in **Orkney** and **Shetland** was known as Norn. It was still in everyday use in many of the islands in the 18th century while fragments – rhymes, specialised works, a few documents and many peculiarities of pronunciation and accent – survived into the 20th. The impact of the Scots tongue and of English is evident from 1469 but Norse continued to supply a fuller vocabulary for such activities as **fishing**, farming and weather assessment. With the revival of Nordic studies in the present century and with the search for a cultural identity in the Northern Isles, such fragments have been carefully studied by scholars such as Hugh Marwick of Orkney and Jakob Jacobsen from the Faroes. The latter's composition of *An Etymological Dictionary of the Norn Language* had reached 'w' at the time of his death, was published posthumously (1928–32) and reissued by the Shetland Islands Council in 1993.

Modern visitors to especially Shetland may be under the impression that Norn is still being spoken. Sadly, close attention will reveal contemporary Shetlandic as an English dialect albeit larded with peculiarities. Thus the English 'th' becomes 'd' or 't' (so 'da' = 'the') while 'du' enjoys a currency as the second person singular which 'thou' has long since lost.

NORTH, Christopher, see WILSON, John

NORTH BERWICK, East Lothian
Distinguished by its prefix from **Berwick-on-Tweed** (previously sometimes known as South Berwick), North Berwick was a **burgh of barony** held by the **Earls of Fife** from the 12th century, then by the **Douglases** (1371–1455) and granted (1479) to the **Earl of Angus**, occupant of nearby **Tantallon Castle**, whose family retained it until the early 18th century. The remains of a Cistercian nunnery founded c1150 by the Earls of Fife can still be seen in the grounds of an old people's home in the town, while the remains of the 12th century parish church have been excavated by the harbour. In the North Berwick witchcraft trials of 1591 several

witches (some accounts say it was just one, others that there were 96) were accused of conspiring to bring disaster on the King, **James VI**, during his voyage to Norway for his marriage to **Anne of Denmark** (1589). The witches' (unsuccessful) defence was that they had been operating on the instructions of the devil who had appeared to them in the pulpit of the parish church in the form of **Francis Stewart, 5th Earl of Bothwell**. Bothwell was promptly imprisoned but later escaped. The decline of North Berwick's traditional role as a **fishing** and trading port in the 19th century coincided with its increasing popularity as a holiday resort, a role which it successfully maintains today.

NORTH RONALDSAY, Orkney
This northernmost of the **Orkney** islands never exceeds two miles in breadth, and only reaches five in length at its extreme limits. Possessing no **peat**, its inhabitants were for the most part dependent on cow dung (converted into what they called 'scons') and on dried sea ware for their fuel. The most singular peculiarity of the island is the manner in which the islanders pasture their sheep. It is still as described in the *Statistical Account* of 1845: 'with the exception of a very few [sheep] kept on the largest farm for killing, they are all shut out by a high dyke which encompasses the whole island to the mere shores, and a little bit of waste ground left for them here and there. Their sole food, almost, is the sea-weed that happens to be drifted ashore, and as this comes most plentifully during winter, that is their fattening season, especially before the cold weather of the new year sets in.' In 1993 this wall was breached in the same storms that wrecked the oil-tanker *Braer*; it has since been rebuilt.

NORTH UIST, Outer Hebrides
The island of North Uist lies between **Harris** and **Benbecula** and has a land area of 118 square miles and a population of about 1500. The chief village is Lochmaddy, linked by car ferry to Tarbert in Harris and Uig in **Skye**. A causeway links North Uist to Benbecula where there is an airport. The highest hill is Eaval (1138ft/347m) in the south-east corner of the island.

North Uist is a Protestant island, in contrast to its southern neighbours, and as such has more in common with Harris. The intervening Sound of Harris is too deep to be bridged with a causeway, although a passenger ferry links Newtonferry in North Uist with **Leverburgh** in Harris.

The north and west coasts of North Uist have attractive sandy bays backed by wide expanses of machair, ablaze with brilliantly coloured wild flowers in spring and summer. The east coast of the island is rocky, sea-weed-strewn and deeply indented by sea-lochs, Loch Eport in particular almost cutting the island in two, while the sheer number and tortuosity of the inland freshwater lochs makes North Uist an angler's paradise, giving the landscape a luminous shimmer and rendering the cartographer's task nigh impossible.

The island is dotted with interesting archaeological sites of different periods, notably the Neolithic chambered **cairn** of Barpa Langass, between Clachan and Lochmaddy, the only chambered cairn in the Western Isles with an intact burial chamber, and an impressive monu-

'The Giant's Leg', Noss (SP)

Grenitote is the excavated archaeological site of the Udal, a settlement site occupied from the Bronze Age until the 19th century.

During the centuries of Norse occupation, North Uist was farmed by colonists from Norway, who have left their mark on the landscape in the many Norse place-names. The name 'Uist' is from the Norse i-vist, an abode or 'in-dwelling'. There is an important but ruinous medieval church site at Teampull na Trionaid in the south-west of the island, near the township of Carinish, reputedly founded by **Somerled**'s daughter Beathag early in the 13th century. The sons of the chiefs were sent to be educated at the monastery and college here.

The fertility of the island, and the 18th century **kelp** boom, encouraged settlers and by the beginning of the 19th century the population of the island had reached 5000. From about 1823 onwards, though, the spreading horror of evictions and **clearances** reached North Uist and more than 1000 islanders were forced from their homes under the direction of the landowner, Lord MacDonald of Sleat, culminating in violent and bloody confrontation between crofters and police at Sollas. The MacDonalds of Sleat [see **Clan Donald**], descendants of Somerled, held the island from 1495 until 1855. The economy of the island today is based on **crofting** and **fishing** (mainly for lobsters and crabs), **tourism**, scallop farming, knitwear and tweed, and the alginate factory at Sponish on Loch Maddy.

ment, 25m in diameter and 4m high. Another cairn, at Clettraval, has been severely robbed but is of interest because it belongs to the **Clyde** type, and is thus unique in the **Hebrides**. On the western slopes of Blashaval (358ft/109m) in the north-west of the island are three Bronze Age **standing stones** called Na Fir Bhreige, 'the false men', improbably said to be the graves of three spies who were buried alive. The Iron Age dun an t-Siamain, on a small island in a loch on the west side of Eaval, can be reached by a curved causeway. Another site on an island in a loch is the broch of Dun an Sticir not far from Newtonferry, while to the north of

NOSS, Shetland

Separated by a narrow sound from **Bressay**, opposite **Lerwick**, the island of Noss is inhabited only during the lambing season and during the summer when a warden is stationed here. In 1870 the island was leased by the Garth Estate to the Marquis of Londonderry and used for breeding **Shetland ponies** for his **coal**-mines in Durham. The pony pund and farmhouse were restored in 1986. The whole island is now a nature reserve. Its sheer sandstone cliffs, 600ft (183m) high at the Noup, are crammed with nesting **seabirds**.

OATMEAL

As the true staple of the Scottish diet, oatmeal in its many incarnations – as gruel, brose, crowdie, porridge, oatcakes and a variety of scones and puddings – has been described as 'the backbone of many a sturdy Scotsman'.

The simplest brose is speedily made by pouring boiling water onto a handful of oatmeal with a pinch of salt; variations include adding a knob of butter or replacing the water with hot milk or with kail, bone or vegetable stock. A similar mixture of oatmeal with a cold liquid – water, buttermilk, milk, cream, ale or **whisky** – is properly called crowdie (the name given also to a form of milk-cheese) but has a variety of regional and descriptive names: fuarag, milk-brose, cream-crowdie, etc. According to F Marian MacNeill (1885–1973), the doyenne of Scottish food writers, the famous Atholl Brose was originally oatmeal stirred into a glass of whisky; a later version being sweetened with heather honey and now frequently made with equal quantities of whisky and cream.

Although porridge can be made with rolled oats (a process which involves passing the grain through hot rollers which crush and partially cook it), the original and best porridge is made by adding medium-ground oatmeal to boiling water, stirring with a spirtle the while to avoid lumps, and simmering for 30 minutes or less, salt being added halfway through the cooking process. It is then served very hot accompanied by a glass of cold milk or cream, the spoon being dipped first into the hot porridge and then into the cold milk. It can be taken sprinkled with more salt, or with sugar, honey, or toasted oats, and is traditionally eaten standing up or even walking round the table. Opinions vary as to whether this tradition is an expression of respect for one of life's essentials, or merely as an aid to the digestion. In **Orkney** and **Shetland** porridge is often made with bere-(barley-)meal.

Cooked porridge, poured into a special tray or 'porridge-drawer' and left to cool, could then be sliced and carried as a travelling 'piece' as an alternative to oatmeal bannocks (large scones). Oatcakes, being more brittle, did not travel so well.

Oatmeal is also the fundamental ingredient of many another Scottish delicacy including **haggis**, mealie or white pudding (a sausage made with tripe and onions), black pudding (a similar sausage but made with pig's or ox's blood instead of tripe), sowans (oat husks and meal steeped in water, strained and left to ferment and separate, the solid matter at the bottom being the sowans), and cranachan (toasted oatmeal stirred into lightly whipped cream to which can then be added fresh fruit, particularly raspberries).

OBAN, Argyll

The principal town in **Argyll** and the main port for the **Hebrides**, Oban is a Victorian creation and none the worse for it. In 1784 the French geologist B Faujas St Fond found just 'a little hamlet' and a single inn. Efforts at the turn of the century to establish a **fishing** fleet, a **cotton** mill (by **David Dale**), and even a naval base, made little difference. In 1811 it was created a **burgh of barony** by a charter granted to the **Duke of Argyll** but in 1819 it was still described merely as 'a village in Argyllshire'. The population, then estimated at 1000, had risen to only 1742 by 1859. Yet by the end of the century it was over 5000 and there were eight hotels, half of them 'first class and very expensive'. Thanks to the steamship and the **railway**, Oban had become 'the Charing Cross of the Highlands'.

Of an Edwardian summer's evening bands played at either end of the Corran Esplanade and the harbour was jammed with yachts and steamships. **MacBrayne**'s advertised steamers sailing twice daily to **Tobermory** (**Mull**), daily to **Inverness** via the **Caledonian Canal**, to **Glasgow** via the **Crinan Canal**, and to **Iona** and **Staffa**, plus thrice-weekly services to Glasgow by the Mull of **Kintyre**, to **Coll** and **Tiree** via Mull, to **Portree** (**Skye**) and **Gairloch** via Mull and **Glenelg**, to **Stornoway** (**Lewis**) via **Ullapool** and **Lochinver**, to **Lochmaddy** (**North Uist**) via **Rum** and **Dunvegan** (Skye), and to Lochmaddy via **Castlebay** (**Barra**) and **Lochboisdale** (**South Uist**). Today's schedule, pitiful by comparison, offers daily sailings to **Craignure** (Mull), **Lismore**, **Castlebay** and **Lochboisdale**, and approximately thrice weekly sailings to **Colonsay**, Coll and Tiree.

Oban, by Sir James Guthrie (NGS)

Now less fashionable, Oban combines its **tourist** trade with important facilities as the main town of the west Highlands and south Hebrides. Its hospitals and high school have catchment areas extending from Mull to **Appin**, **Lorne** and **Loch Awe**. The first National **Mod** was held here in 1892 and has many times returned; the Gaelic of the islands may be heard in the shops. The Argyllshire Gathering in August is one of the major **Highland Games**.

Population increase has long since seen the town outgrow its narrow site between the bay and the steeply rising hills. Housing developments have crept up Pulpit Hill and sought out any adjacent hollows (Dunbeg and Soroba). Yet the town centre retains its essentially scenic character and the steep roads behind offer spectacular views over the harbour, over the island of **Kerrera** which guards its entrance, and over the hills of Mull in the distance. Inland the skyline is broken by what looks like a replica of the Colosseum and is in fact just that. 'McCaig's Tower' was erected by a local banker, John Stuart McCaig, at a cost of £5000 in 1897. It was projected as a job-creation scheme but doubts as to this worthy motive were raised when it was learnt that the apertures were to be filled with statues of dead McCaigs. It was never completed, happily perhaps.

Oban's other outstanding landmark is best seen from the sea. Standing on a promontory and guarding the north entrance to the harbour, Dunollie Castle is the ancient stronghold of the **MacDougall** Lords of Lorne. It dates from the 12th century but only the square tower and a bit of wall are left. **Dunstaffnage Castle**, also once a MacDougall stronghold, lies four miles north-east of Oban.

O'BRIEN, Charles (1882–1939) Composer

Born into his family's fourth generation of professional musicians, O'Brien studied composition under **Hamish MacCunn** and became conductor of the Edinburgh Royal Choral Union and Director of Music at the Royal Blind School. His works include an attractive *Clarinet Sonata* and a well-wrought and varied *Piano Sonata* as well as a *Symphony in F Minor* and the occasionally revived concert overture *Ellangowan*.

OCHIL HILLS

Chiefly in **Perthshire** but extending into **Kinross-shire**, **Clackmannanshire** and **Stirlingshire**, the Ochils are a prominent range running from the Forth near **Stirling** to the **Tay** near **Perth** and dividing **Fife** from Strathearn and **Strathallan**. The principal pass is that formed by **Gleneagles** and **Glen Devon**; the main summits Ben Cleugh (2363ft/720m), Dumyat (or Dunmyat) and King's Seat.

OCTAVIANS

After the death of **John Maitland of Thirlestane**, **James VI** declared that he would 'no more use chancellor or other great men in those his causes, but such as he might convict and were hangable'. In 1596 he duly dismissed his treasurer and introduced a team of eight men of humbler rank to reorganise his finances. They were well chosen; many subsequently served him in other capacities; none merited hanging. The eight (hence 'Octavians') were David Carnegie of Culluthie,

James Elphinstone, **Thomas Hamilton**, John Lindsay, Alexander Seton, Sir John Skene, Walter Stewart and Peter Young.

OENGUS (or ANGUS) (d.761) Pictish King

Initially achieving hero status for having fought his way past no less than five rival claimants to the **Pictish** kingship, Oengus, son of Fergus, is credited with overthrowing the Scots of **Dalriada** as well as with leading successful campaigns against the Britons and the Angles. As with so many matters Pictish, legends about Oengus abound; one tells of a victory in battle achieved by the intervention of **St Andrew**, whereupon the grateful Pict dedicated a church to the saint around which eventually grew the town that would bear his name; another asserts that the relics of St Andrew arrived in Scotland during Oengus's rule, whereupon he adopted him as his own (and thus ultimately also Scotland's) patron saint. There is some duplication of these legends in relation to a later, 9th century, Oengus.

OGILVIE (OGILVY), James, 1st Earl of Seafield and 4th Earl of Findlater (1644–1730)

An advocate (1685) and MP for **Banffshire** (1681–), Ogilvie opposed the Revolution settlement but in 1696 abandoned his **Jacobite** sympathies, becoming Secretary of State and a Williamite loyalist in the face of the outcry over the **Darien disaster**. His clever and unscrupulous management of Parliament was duly rewarded with the Viscountcy (1698) and Earldom (1701) of Seafield and the Lord Chancellorship (1702). In the same year he was appointed one of the Scottish commissioners for the **Union** and, using similar tactics, became its most successful organiser. When the Scottish Parliament was finally dissolved he dismissed it as 'the end o' an auld sang'. He set off for Westminster, a seat in the English House of Lords and membership of the English Privy Council. Yet by 1713, having succeeded to the Earldom of Findlater (1711), he was reviving the 'auld sang' as he urged the Lords to repeal the Union; it had not worked; he cited old Scottish grievances and he cited new English taxes. The motion failed by just four proxy votes.

OGILVIE, John (1579–1615) Saint

Scotland's only post-**Reformation** saint, Ogilvie was born near **Keith** in **Banffshire**, educated by Jesuits in Germany, joined the order on entering his novitiate in 1599 and was ordained in Paris. Returning to Scotland disguised as a soldier, he was arrested in 1614 in **Glasgow**, then held in **Edinburgh** before being tried and hanged in Glasgow. As a martyr of the counter-Reformation, he was beatified in 1929' and canonised in 1976.

OIL AND GAS

The discovery of any major source of natural energy within a nation's territorial boundaries is liable to be portrayed as fortuitous. No exception was made when in the 1970s it became apparent that vast off-shore oil and gas reserves lay within the Scottish sector of the North Sea. But this discovery, let alone its speedy and successful exploitation, would scarcely have been

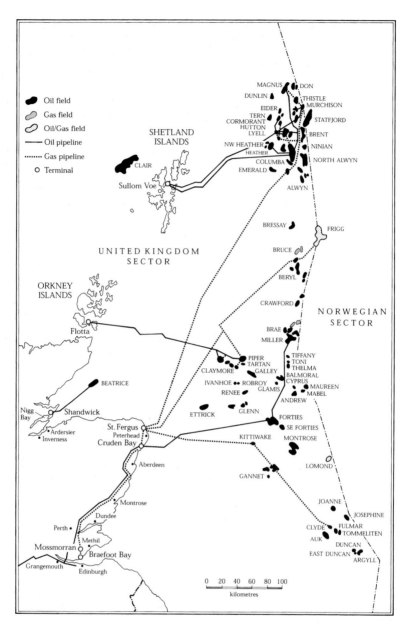

Oil field
Gas field
Oil/Gas field
—— Oil pipeline
.... Gas pipeline
○ Terminal

SHETLAND ISLANDS

MAGNUS   DON
DUNLIN   THISTLE
EIDER   MURCHISON
TERN   STATFJORD
CORMORANT
HUTTON
LYELL   BRENT
NW HEATHER   NINIAN
HEATHER
COLUMBA   NORTH ALWYN
EMERALD
                    ALWYN

CLAIR

Sullom Voe

BRESSAY   FRIGG

UNITED KINGDOM SECTOR

BRUCE

BERYL

ORKNEY ISLANDS

CRAWFORD

NORWEGIAN SECTOR

Flotta

BRAE
MILLER

PIPER   TIFFANY
TARTAN   TONI
CLAYMORE GALLEY THELMA
                        BALMORAL
BEATRICE   IVANHOE ROBROY CYPRUS
                RENEE GLAMIS MAUREEN
                                        MABEL
                            ANDREW

Nigg Bay   Shandwick
Ardersier   ETTRICK   GLENN
Inverness   FORTIES
            St. Fergus   SE FORTIES
            Peterhead   KITTIWAKE MONTROSE
Cruden Bay

Aberdeen   LOMOND
                GANNET

                            JOANNE
Montrose   JOSEPHINE
Dundee   CLYDE FULMAR
Perth   TOMMELITEN
                            AUK
Mossmorran Methil   DUNCAN
        Braefoot Bay   EAST DUNCAN
Grangemouth Edinburgh   ARGYLL

0 20 40 60 80 100
kilometres

possible in most other parts of the world. Unlike **coal**, the location of oil and gas reserves appears the work of a capricious Nature anxious to compensate otherwise unfavoured regions of the globe. Typically the largest reserves are found where there is no industrialised economy in desperate need of them, no indigenous expertise to develop them, and no guarantee of the political stability essential to attract outside investment. The North Sea, although posing a formidable technological challenge, was different. Its energy yield was conveniently placed to meet the vast demands of the UK and European economies, all highly industrialised, reasonably stable, but hitherto dependent on imported oil and gas.

In the UK as a whole the processing and consumption of oil and gas had risen sharply throughout the 20th century. Scotland could claim a particularly distin-

guished 19th century contribution as the birthplace of **William Murdock**, who developed **coal**-gas and gas lighting, and as the home and site (**Bathgate**) of **James Young**'s pioneering extraction of shale-oil to produce paraffin, also mainly for lighting. Oil and gas technology advanced rapidly as the UK played a major role in the development of overseas fields; and during the inter-war years some modest exploration led to the discovery of small gas fields near **Edinburgh** (as well as in England) and prompted a Petroleum (Production) Act in 1934 which vested ownership of on-shore reserves in the Crown. Post-war some awareness of an off-shore potential may have underlain the UK government's **1955** annexation of **Rockall** which vastly increased the UK's claims over the continental shelf prior to the 1958 Geneva Conventions which laid down the criteria for dividing the seabed between adjacent jurisdictions. Although the UK did not ratify this agreement until 1964, the discovery of Holland's vast Groningen on-shore gas field in 1959 had already established the possibility of other major gas reserves in adjacent areas of the continental shelf and had provided the incentive to explore them. The first UK exploration licences were issued in 1964 and the first gas field was found in the English sector of the North Sea in 1965.

Oil discoveries awaited the issue of drilling licences in Scottish waters. The first well was drilled in 1967 and the first major find was the Forties field (240 million tonnes) 100 miles off **Aberdeen** in 1970. It came just six months after the chairman of BP, the company involved, had predicted no major finds in the North Sea. Though quickly followed by the discovery of the Brent field (off **Shetland**, 229m tonnes) in 1971 and of numerous smaller fields, early excitement continued to subside in the face of costs that made North Sea oil little better than an insurance against the stoppage of supplies from elsewhere. But by the time the first oil came ashore (by pipeline from the Forties field to Cruden Bay south of **Peterhead**) in 1975, this insurance was paying off. The OPEC-organised hike in oil prices in 1973–4 had transformed the whole scene. Suddenly North Sea oil became competitive as higher per barrel prices made marginal fields viable, while further exploration became a priority as self-sufficiency was deemed desirable. Exploration peaked in 1975 with 80 wells drilled and 27 'significant oil and gas finds'; discovered reserves rose from 500 million tonnes in 1971 to 1800 million tonnes in 1976 as the extensive fields north-east of Shetland – Cormorant, Dunlin, Murchison, Magnus, Thistle, Ninian, etc – and those east of **Orkney** – Piper, Claymore, etc – were drilled.

Since the mid-1970s the pace of exploration has slowed, partly because the more accessible reserves have already been located and partly as a result of government policy to steady the rate of investment and extraction. The exploration boom years of the mid-1970s led to production peaks in the 1980s (128 million tonnes in 1986) well in excess of domestic demand. Production has since been reined back to around 90 million tonnes per year, a figure in line with domestic production which still places the UK in the top 12 oil producing nations (just behind Nigeria but ahead of Libya).

Current assessments of the recoverable reserves remaining depend on a number of variables, most notably future trends in oil prices and government taxation. These could materially affect the amount of oil recoverable from existing fields (initially only 30% but potentially as high as 70%) as well as the discovery and development of new fields such as those thought to lie in the deeper waters west of Shetland. Crucial here is the development of new technologies for both exploration and extraction. Twenty-five years ago the technology for any off-shore development scarcely existed; 25 years hence reserves now considered irrecoverable could be reclaimed as a matter of course. Suffice it to say that oil reserves on the UK continental shelf probably remain substantial (1981 estimates suggested 200–400 million tonnes of oil and about half the equivalent in gas) although the recoverable percentage is heavily dependent on extraneous factors.

The effect of this bonanza on the national economy has been significant. By 1981 it was estimated that North Sea oil and gas were contributing over 4% to the UK's GDP, nearly £12 billion to the annual balance of payments, and over £6 billion a year to government revenues. More significant for Scotland has been the investment generated locally. Although initially much equipment came from overseas, three-quarters of the value of orders placed by the industry is now thought to have been met from domestic suppliers. Few ports on the east coast have not been affected by the off-shore industry's supply and safety (a priority heightened by the **Piper Alpha disaster**) arrangements. Aberdeen has been transformed into an oil capital with one of the busiest heliports in the world and **Grangemouth** into the North Sea's major refinery. 3500 miles of pipeline conduct oil from the East Shetland basin to the **Sullum Voe** terminal, from the Piper and Claymore fields to Flotta on Orkney, and from the Forties field to Cruden Bay and thence to Grangemouth; gas pipelines from the Frigg field as well as from all the major oil fields (including Brent, 278 miles away, the longest deep-water pipeline in the world) converge on the St Fergus terminal near Peterhead whence gas liquids are piped to Mossmorran in **Fife** for processing.

During the 1970s deep-water facilities for the construction and maintenance of rigs and production platforms also brought some investment to the west coast. Construction yards at **Kishorn** in Wester **Ross** and Ardyne Point in **Argyll** have since been abandoned but Clydeside continues to benefit with its manufacturing industries supplying pumps, compressors, cranes and supply vessels. Platform construction and maintenance, a vulnerable and volatile industry, has become concentrated round the Moray Firth at **Nigg Bay** opposite **Cromarty** and **Ardersier** near **Fort George** as well as at **Methil** in Fife. In 1993 the UK's off-shore supply industry was reckoned the world's second largest with one-third of its orders coming from overseas. The North Sea oil and gas industry as a whole was estimated to employ, directly and indirectly, about 300,000 people. Its development has been described as 'one of the major industrial achievements of the 20th century'.

OLDMELDRUM, Aberdeenshire

This small town (created a burgh in 1672) beside the main road from **Aberdeen** to **Banff** has a square, a town hall with clock tower, a few shops and a distillery. It commands a rich agricultural landscape lavishly endowed with architecture: **Tolquhon**, **Barra**, **Udny**, **Haddo**, **Fyvie**, **Pitmedden** and a host of lesser attractions are all within 10 miles.

OLIPHANT, Margaret (née Wilson)
(1828–97) Novelist

Margaret Wilson was born at Wallyford, near **Edinburgh**, grew up in **Glasgow** and Liverpool, and in 1849 published her first novel, *Passages in the Life of Mrs Margaret Maitland*. The work, with its sharp delineation of Scottish character and setting, proved extremely popular and went through three successive editions. She followed this with *Caleb Field* (1851) and *Merkland* (1851). In 1853 her novel *Katie Stewart* was serialised in **Blackwood's Magazine**, beginning a professional and personal association

Margaret Oliphant, by Janet Mary Oliphant, 1895 (SNPG)

with the Blackwood firm and family that was to last until her death in 1897.

In 1852 she moved to London where she married her cousin, artist Francis William Oliphant. Her work continued unabated, and she produced several novels for serialisation in *Blackwood's*, including *A Quiet Heart* (1854), *Zaidee* (1856) and *The Athelings* (1857). She was soon earning a steady income from her work, which she was to need after her husband died in 1857, leaving her in debt and with three children to provide for. Between 1861–76 she embarked on an ambitious series of novels on English provincial life, which was to include some of her most accomplished work. The 7-novel series, entitled 'The Chronicles of Carlingford', was closely modelled on Anthony Trollope's Barsetshire novels, and bore similarities in concerns and themes to the works of George Eliot. The series included *Salem Chapel* (1863), *The Rector and the Doctor's Family* (1863), *The Perpetual Curate* (1864) and her best-known work, *Miss Marjoribanks* (1866). The final novel in the series, *Phoebe Junior: A Last Chronicle of Carlingford*, was published in 1876.

In 1864 her daughter died, and soon afterwards Margaret Oliphant took charge of three of her widowed brother's four children. This, plus the strain of supporting her two remaining children, took its toll on her writing. After 1866 her work never achieved the critical success of her earlier efforts. By the time of her death in London, Margaret Oliphant had produced over 100 novels, almost 30 works of non-fiction, and over 200 articles for *Blackwood's Magazine*.

OLIPHANT, Sir William (d.1329) Soldier

Oliphant's erratic career may be typical of many during the Anglo-Scottish wars of the early 14th century; if so it is a salutary warning against calling them '**Wars of Independence**'. He first appears fighting for **John Balliol** at the **Battle of Dunbar** (1296) where he was taken prisoner by Edward I's troops. Two years later he was fighting for Edward I in Flanders but by 1304 was again opposing him as, in command of **Stirling Castle**, he alone withstood the English invaders. Forced to surrender after a three-month siege, he was sent to the Tower of London but released (1308) by Edward II and it was for him that in 1313 he held **Perth** with an English garrison against **Robert I**. This time he surrendered after six weeks and escaped back to England. But by 1317 Robert was pleased to be conferring favours on him and by 1320 he was again attending the Scots Parliament, presumably rehabilitated.

ORCHARDSON, Sir William Quiller (1832–1910) Painter

An immensely stylish artist, Orchardson was born in **Edinburgh** and trained under **Lauder** at the **Trustees' Academy**, forming one of a remarkably talented generation of painters, including **Chalmers**, **Pettie** and **McTaggart**. Like them his early work was biased towards the fashion for history painting, but he soon moved from gloomy Scottish Protestant scenes to light airy evocations of 18th and 19th century salon life. His acute observation of the nuances of social convention combined with accurate historical record and a fluid, assured style, ensured his success. He moved to London in 1862 and became a popular and regular exhibitor at the Royal Academy. His works are distinctive – loose brushwork, delicately controlled, floating hues of colour – involving the daring use of open space and elaborate figure composition. One of his late masterpieces, *The Borgia* (1902, **Aberdeen Art Gallery**), restricts the dramatic action to the bottom third of the painting, the upper section being a complex textured design of architecture and vegetation, showing how aware Orchardson was of modern artistic developments, particularly Art Nouveau and the sub-Impressionism of Whistler and his followers. Orchardson was the first Scottish artist since **Wilkie** to enjoy unqualified success in London and although he remained in the south until his death, enjoying the accolades and social standing of a successful Victorian artist, he always retained strong ties with his native land. He is buried in St Paul's Cathedral.

ORCHARDTON TOWER, Nr Dalbeattie, Kircudbrightshire

Tower houses of rectangular groundplan, often extended to form an L-plan or Z-plan, are the norm. Sometimes, as at **Castle Fraser**, they incorporate a round or drum tower. But there is only one extant tower house which is purely 'O-plan'. This is Orchardton, 'a building of such modest demeanour that the Lord of **Borthwick** [**Castle**; a particularly imposing L-plan] might perhaps have been pardoned for mistaking it for a dovecot' (J G Dunbar). A tower house it nevertheless is, complete with barmkin, machicolated parapet, cap house, and once a not-so-great hall measuring 5.2m in diameter. Built by John Cairns in 1456 it passed to the Maxwells like nearby **Threave** and was no doubt gutted like **Caerlaverock** and Threave by **Covenanters** in the mid-17th century.

ORCHESTRAS

Until the Scottish National Orchestra was founded in 1891, orchestral musicians in Scotland tended to be brought from over the border for the special occasion. Even so, the SNO was part-time until 1951 and acquired its first Scottish conductor (Alexander Gibson) in 1959. The BBC Studio Orchestra of 35 professional players was formed in 1935 but achieved symphonic status as the **BBC Scottish Symphony Orchestra** only in 1967. Since then Scotland has been firmly on the orchestral world map.

There have been regular flowerings of interest in classical music: at the court in the 1590s; again, in 1695, it was reported that there were 'eleven professional musicians in **Edinburgh**'; in the mid to late 18th century, with **Oswald** and **Kelly** as indigenous examples, and throughout the 19th century. Edinburgh Musical Society (Britain's first) was founded in 1728 and **St Cecilia's Hall** in 1762. Music festivals flourished between 1815–43, first in Edinburgh, then in **Aberdeen** and in **Glasgow**. The **Reid** Concert at the **University of Edinburgh** was first performed in 1841. Glasgow Choral Union had an orchestra of part-amateur musicians. But the **Edinburgh International Festival** (founded 1947) has probably exerted more influence on the quality of musical life in Scotland than any other event. Through its influence have evolved **Scottish Opera**, **Scottish Ballet** and even (after decades of indecision) the promise of a venue in the capital worthy of music's grandest achievements.

ORD OF CAITHNESS, Sutherland/Caithness

'Ord', Gaelic for 'hammer', gives its name to the precipitous coastal pass north of **Helmsdale** that leads from **Sutherland** into **Caithness**. The **Rev Donald Sage** wrote of it in 1825 'The old road over this promontory – the same identically which William, Earl of Caithness, nearly four centuries ago, had passed with his gallant band, clad in green, to the fatal battle of **Flodden** – was really dangerous. It lay within a foot, and stretched along the very edge, without any protecting buttress, of a precipice 800ft above the sea.' A new road was built in 1804, but even today's A9 remains dramatic enough.

ORKNEY

The Orkney islands (67 in all, one-third inhabited) enjoy the distinction of possessing the highest concentration of prehistoric monuments that have been discovered anywhere in northern Europe. There are various reasons for this. Their rocks of Old Red Sandstone split easily into flags, an ideal building material. The greater part of the land surface is gently rolling and fertile, lapped by the warm waters of the Gulf Stream. They were not covered by the dense forests that once presented such a daunting challenge to settlers using only stone tools.

The first colonists arrived before 3500 BC and on **Papa Westray** they built the stone houses that are the earliest surviving dwellings on record in Britain. Their inhabitants are identified by the Unstan ware they manufactured, pottery bowls of a kind found in the Unstan burial **cairn** a few miles from **Stromness**. But it is on the isle of **Rousay** that their most remarkable monuments have been found; the long chambered cairn of Midhowe with its herringbone stonework and 12 stalls, Blackhammer with its entrance passage at right-

angles to the chamber as at Unstan, and Taversoe Tuick. This last consists of two chambers, one on top of the other on their slope, the lower entered from the opposite side of the mound to the upper one, and containing side compartments cut into the rock.

All this invention culminated, sometime before 2700 BC, in what has been described as 'one of the greatest architectural achievements of the prehistoric peoples of Scotland' (Anna Ritchie): the chambered tomb of **Maes Howe**. There are no henge monuments in Continental Europe, and of the four in Britain, two are in England and two in Orkney. It is thought that while the burial cairns were built for the interment of members of a family group, the stone circles and henges were meeting places for very much larger social units. The henge of Stenness near Maes Howe is of roughly the same date and once contained 12 **standing stones**. Beyond, on its slope above the Harray Loch, stands the Ring of Brogar, which once possessed 60 stones, surrounded by a ditch cut deep into the surrounding rock.

Contemporary with these monuments is the settlement of **Skara Brae**, which was occupied from about 3000 BC until a great storm caused its inhabitants to flee their dwellings around 2200 BC. What part this community of perhaps 50 people at any one time played in erecting the great monuments of Maeshowe, Stenness and Brogar remains a matter of surmise.

From about 2000 BC new concepts reached Orkney, attested by different burial practices, the introduction of Beaker pottery and a knowledge of metals. The bodies of the dead were interred in individual cists under earthen mounds. In the largest of these, the Knowes of Trotty, was found what Gordon Childe described as 'wealth worthy of a Wessex princess – four gold sun disks and an amber necklace. Sun disks are generally considered to be of Irish gold and Irish inspiration, but they were popular at an early date in Denmark too. The amber beads include remains of spacers of the peculiar type found in English Wessex graves, and also in the Shaft Graves of Mycenae and other Mycenaean tombs between 1600 and 1450 BC.' Childe concluded that Orkney was involved at that time in 'the far-flung network of largely maritime trade which linked Denmark, Ireland and Cornwall and of which some vital threads were in the hands of the lords of Wessex, although it was ultimately supported by the reliable market of rich Mycenae.'

A deterioration of the weather after 1500 BC led to land hunger as a blanket of **peat** began to engulf the older sites. During a period of migration and tribal strife the first iron-using folk reached Orkney, speaking an archaic form of the Celtic family of languages. At Quanterness Colin Renfrew has excavated a building occupied between 800 and 200 BC which may be the precursor of the defensive towers known as **brochs**.

On either side of Eynhallow Sound a chain of these structures was built by what appears to have been a new warrior aristocracy. At Gurness on a promontory of the mainland the broch was surrounded by three stone-faced ramparts and ditches, while the broch beside the ancient chambered cairn of Midhowe on the isle of Rousay opposite was fortified by a great wall with a ditch on either side of it. Perhaps the enemy

Standing stones from the great Ring of Brogar near Stenness, Orkney (HS)

Orkney continued

against whom they were designed were such as the legendary Irish hero Labraid Loingseach, who 'smote eight towers in Tiree . . . [and] ventured upon many of the islands of Orkney'.

But it appears that the warlike mainland tribes against whom the **Romans** fought at **Mons Graupius** may have offered the most serious threat. At any rate Orosius recorded that in 43 AD some Orkney chiefs made a formal submission to the Emperor Claudius, seeking the protection of the Pax Romana. By 200 AD the threat seems to have diminished to the extent that the brochs of Gurness and Midhowe were being used as quarries for the dwellings that proliferated in and around them.

In 297 a panegyric poem addressed to the Emperor Constantius referred to the peoples who lived north of the **Antonine Wall** (and who were neither Gaelic Scots nor Welsh Britons) as Picti. Thus begins the historical **Pictish** period which lasted until 850. King Brude (554–84) was overlord of Orkney when **St Columba** recommended his missionaries to this Pictish ruler. In the words of his biographer, **Adamnan**, 'If they, by any chance, should come after a long journey to the islands of Orkney, commend them earnestly to this sub-king, whose hostages are in your power, so that no harm may befall them at his hands.' Just such an island potentate is depicted on a stone found on the Brough of Birsay, with two members of his retinue. It belongs to the period of the 7th and 8th centuries in which other finds here support the impression that this was the residence of one of Orkney's ruling families.

The portrait stone contains four of the mysterious symbols which appear with such remarkable consist-

ency throughout Pictland, some of them accompanied by equally baffling ogam inscriptions. This form of writing, invented in Ireland before 400, was used by the Picts to preserve some lost pre-Celtic language. On the bone handle of a knife found at Gurness such an inscription was incised on its own. Interesting souvenirs of the **Celtic Church** in Orkney are the little iron bells found in Birsay and at the broch of Burrian. It is hard to discover with certainty when the symbols were first used in the islands, but happily there is a site on the isle of **Sanday** where a slab containing two such symbols was placed face downwards as a paving stone in about 550. So it is possible that they ante-date Christianity here.

As for the monastic sites that awaited the onslaught of the **Vikings**, there were those of Birsay and Deerness as well as on other islands whose names and incised crosses are suggestive, such as Papa Stronsay and Papa Westray. Many of them await further investigation. The raids which began in the 790s led to particularly dense settlement in Orkney, transforming its islands into the seat of a powerful Norse earldom.

Its incumbents married into the Celtic royal house. **Earl Sigurd**, who perished in the Battle of Clontarf in 1014, had for his mother the daughter of an Irish King. His son **Thorfinn the Mighty** was the grandson of **Malcolm II** King of Scots through his mother. Before his death in 1064 Thorfinn made his seat in Birsay according to *Orkneyinga Saga*, where he built 'a splendid minster' beside his palace. It used to be assumed that both were located on the Brough of Birsay until Raymond Lamb questioned this in 1972 (vol 105, *Proceedings of the Society of Antiquaries of Scotland*). The little church built on the site of the former Pictish monastery is now considered to be that of an early 12th century Norse monastery. Above it are what Anna and Graham Ritchie have described as 'some of the finest examples of Norse hall houses ever found in Scotland'. Below are other ruins whose identity remains controversial.

During the 12th century a Norwegian tycoon built himself a stone castle on the summit of the little isle of Wyre, which remains the oldest surviving in what is now Scotland. Here his son Bishop Bjarni grew up, doubtless worshipping in the chapel of St Mary in the dell below. It was Bjarni who composed the only significant work of Norse poetry to have survived in these islands, his 'Lay of the Jomsvikings'. He also played an influential part in securing the canonisation of **Earl Rognvald**.

This was an indirect consequence of the quarrel between Thorfinn's two grandsons, **Magnus** and **Haakon**. What evidence survives does not suggest that Haakon was especially wicked, nor Magnus outstandingly good. But Haakon murdered Magnus on the isle of Egilsay, probably in 1117, a not unusual way of disposing of rivals in those days. His nephew Rognvald went on a crusade (though it could have been mistaken for a piratical expedition, in that he kidnapped Christians and sold them in a Muslim slave market) accompanied by his Bishop William. Probably this helped to defray the cost of building the cathedral built in honour of St Magnus. When Rognvald was murdered by his relatives in the conventional way in 1158, he too became eligible for the accolade of martyrdom, which was bestowed on him 30 years later.

Orkneyinga Saga preserves to the last the flavour of that robust age. In about 1200, it relates, the Orkney Earl ordered John Bishop of **Caithness** to be blinded and have his tongue torn out. His successor Adam was murdered in 1222 at his episcopal seat in Halkirk. In a revenge killing, Earl John was murdered in **Thurso** in 1231, without any prospect of canonisation. This honour was bestowed instead on Bishop Adam's successor **Gilbert of Moray**, who had certainly exhibited courage, if not sanctity, in accepting such a hazardous post. Earl John's assassins found a safe refuge in Kolbein Hruga's castle on Wyre.

For want of a male heir this premier Norse earldom passed in the female line to the Scottish house of **Angus**, and in 1379 it became the prize, by similar descent, of **Henry Sinclair**. By this time Norway was beginning her years of subjection to the Danish Crown, and in 1468 a Danish King did what no Norwegian sovereign would have contemplated. Christian I pledged Orkney's crown rents as security for part of the dowry of his daughter Margaret on her marriage to **James III**. When the islands were not redeemed, King James purchased the earldom from William Sinclair, transferred the bishopric from the See of Trondheim to that of **St Andrews**, and annexed Orkney to the Scottish Crown. He even bestowed the Cathedral of St Magnus upon the 'Provost, magistrates and Community of **Kirkwall**' without so much as seeking the Pope's permission.

It was the beginning of a long period of misery for the islanders. The udallers had been explicitly protected, when their islands were pawned, in the enjoyment of the Norse code of law under which the cultivator was the owner of his land. But by force and fraud their Scottish masters soon undermined these titles, and the

Reformation enabled them to embezzle the Church lands as well. For instance, **Bishop Adam Bothwell** endowed his sister Margaret and her husband **Gilbert Balfour** with the emoluments of the isle of Westray. Not only did the islanders find themselves paying Church tithes to this pair, they were also compelled to provide what amounted to slave labour in building the great castle of Noltland [see **Westray**] with its triple tiers of gunloops. Of these William Douglas Simpson has observed: 'no provision for firearm defence upon so lavish a scale . . . exists, so far as I am aware, in any British castle – or indeed, I believe, in any castle on the Continent.'

Against whom could such defence have been required on this remote island? Balfour played a leading part in the murder of **Darnley** and, after his sleazy career obliged him to flee to Sweden, was executed there for his part in a plot against the King. Noltland Castle had been built to no purpose. Likewise the great palace of Birsay which **Robert Stewart** compelled the islanders to build for him soon afterwards, when **Queen Mary** leased Orkney to her bastard half-brother in 1564. His iniquities led the Scottish feudatories (not the natives) to submit complaints against him in **Edinburgh** in 1587, to which **James VI** responded by creating him Earl of Orkney.

In 1592 he was succeeded by his son **Patrick**, whose crimes moved **Bishop James Law** to write to James VI in 1608: 'Alas, dear and dreaded Sovereign, truly it is to be pitied that so many of your Majesty's subjects are so manifoldly and grievously oppressed; some by ejection and banishment from their homes and native soil, others by contorting the laws and extorting their goods, the most part being so impoverished that some of them neither dare nor may complain, but in silent and forced patience groan under their grievance.' Only occasionally did they find the courage to strike back. When Earl Patrick's toady, Harry Colville, was appointed to the Church living of Orphir, his parishioners hunted him to his death in 1596.

Not content with the palace of Birsay, Earl Patrick embarked on the building of another in Kirkwall, where the Bishop's palace embellished by **Bishop Reid** might well have sufficed him. It has been judged the finest achievement of Renaissance architecture in Scotland, but it brought him no more satisfaction than Noltland to Gilbert Balfour. He was summoned to Edinburgh, not to answer for his maltreatment of Orcadians, but on a charge of treason. In 1615 he was executed with his son when it was found that he was so ignorant 'he could scarce rehearse the Lord's prayer'.

The islands were next leased to farmers-general, of whose rapacity a minister wrote in 1627, 'in respect of the great duty paid to His Majesty out of this **udal** land, and the augmentation of it so oft, and of the great number of people sustained upon this land, these mean udal people are not able to live.' When **Charles I**'s subjects rose in rebellion against him, he granted (1643) the northern isles to the **Earl of Morton**, in the hope of binding him and the isles to the Royalist cause. **Montrose** succeeded in extracting £100,000, 2000 men and 300 horses from Orkney, whose raw levies were cut to pieces by mounted dragoons in his final defeat at **Carbisdale** (1650).

When **Charles II** was restored to his throne in 1660 he extracted no less than £182,000 from Orkney before handing the islands back to the Morton family. These fleeced the islanders with a thoroughness reminiscent of the practices of Earl Patrick. A century of **Stewart** rule had reduced them to the very depths of degradation.

Harassed on land, Orcadians found an increasing outlet at sea, to which the development of Stromness as a port made an important contribution. In 1700 it had been 'very inconsiderable, consisting of only half a dozen houses with slated roofs and a few scattered huts'. So the Rev William Clouston testified (1794) in his able contribution to the first *Statistical Account*. But its fine harbour could accommodate vessels of 100 tons burden. Unfortunately these included ships of the Royal Navy with their press gangs, so that an Edinburgh newspaper reported in 1759: 'by a letter from Orkney we are informed that there has been a very hot press there; and that all the farmers' servants without distinction have been taken up that were judged fit for service.'

But there were also opportunities for voluntary service, after the Hudson's Bay Company began recruiting for their Canadian enterprises in 1702, while the danger to shipping in the English Channel caused by Britain's wars greatly augmented the use of Stromness as a safe haven. Whaling ships made regular visits in search of crews and provisions. Captain Cook's ships returned here after his murder in Hawaii in 1779. The 18th century witnessed a shift in activity from the eastern ports of Britain which traded with Europe, in favour of those that lay on the western trade routes, and this was reflected in the relative fortunes of Stromness and Kirkwall.

Kirkwall, Orkney's capital, had enjoyed the privileges of a **royal burgh** since 1486. The Convention of Royal Burghs used to be described as the oldest existing representative body in Europe, and its burgesses constituted the third estate in the Scottish Parliament. After the abolition of this body by the **Treaty of Union** in 1707 their convention remained determined to defend their exclusive rights. The dispute between Stromness and Kirkwall reached the Court of Session in 1742, and continued until Kirkwall lost her appeal in the House of Lords in 1758. But Stromness failed to obtain costs, so that Alexander Graham, the merchant whose persistence had led to this victory, found himself ruined. Nevertheless he had successfully undermined the anachronistic privileges of the royal burghs from distant Stromness. His memorable achievement is told in Ian Macinnes's 'The Alexander Graham Case', *Orkney Heritage*, ed W P L Thomson, 1981.

Distant oceans continued to take their toll. The Rev George Low wrote in his entry on Birsay and Harray in the first *Statistical Account* that 'most of the people of the barony and Marwick are bred fishermen, and multitudes of our young men go to sea, both in merchant and in his Majesty's service; few in proportion of whom ever return to settle here.' Stromness was Sir John Franklin's last landfall before he crossed the Atlantic on his fatal expedition in 1845. It was the Orcadian explorer **John Rae** who won the reward for discovering the fate of his men.

In 1914 nearby **Scapa Flow** became the anchorage of the British fleet, and here the German fleet was scuttled in 1919 before the eyes of a party of schoolchildren on a water-borne picnic from Stromness.

In the 1970s Orkney was faced by the prospect of North Sea **oil**, for which a terminal was constructed on the isle of Flotta in Scapa Flow. The islands attracted a more particular interest soon after Britain entered the European Economic Community in 1974. The discovery that there were deposits of uranium along the coast near Stromness led the South of Scotland Electricity Board to acquire from local landowners the right to extract it for a period of seven years from 1976, when the agreement was signed. This marked the beginning of a battle with the Goliath of central government such as had never before been seen in Orkney's history.

In 1979 there was a silent march in which 1500 people crowded through the narrow streets of Kirkwall with their banners of protest. The Midsummer Festival of the Arts in Kirkwall was enlivened in 1980 by the words of **George Mackay Brown** set to music by Sir Peter Maxwell Davies which will outlive the chicaneries of politicians. A delegation went to London led by the Convener of the Orkney Islands Council, Edwin Eunson, and supported by the Member of Parliament for the Northern Isles, **Jo Grimond**. An attempt was made to introduce an anti-uranium Bill, and although it was frustrated, there has been no further move to prospect for uranium in Orkney (see Marjorie Linklater, 'Uranium: a Questionable Commodity', *Orkney Heritage*, 1981).

Marjorie is the widow of **Eric Linklater**, whose books *The Men of Ness* and *The Ultimate Viking* are among those that have kept the islands in the forefront of European literature despite the loss of their Norse language. George Low found that Orcadians could still recite the Lord's Prayer in Norse in the 1770s, and that in **North Ronaldsay** they had not forgotten the macabre song of the Norns, weaving the web of destiny when Earl Sigurd was killed at Clontarf in 1014. Ernest Marwick gathered the fragments of this heritage in his *Anthology of Orkney Verse*, 1949, in which the 'Lay of the Jomsvikings' and other Norse poetry is published in translation, and in his *The Folklore of Orkney and Shetland*, 1975.

While **Edwin Muir** and George Mackay Brown are outstanding among Orcadian men of letters using the English language, there are also those, such as the Kirkwall draper Robert Rendall, who used a language based partly on his Norse heritage and partly on the speech beyond the Pentland Firth. George Mackay Brown said of his poems that some of them are 'as good as anything that has been published in Scotland this century'. But remarkable as is the eloquence of a people numbering less than 20,000 who have lost their language, it must yield pride of place to what he hailed as 'Orkney's progress in a few years out of serfdom into full economic freedom'.

ORKNEY AND SHETLAND SHEEP

Scotland's native sheep were small-bodied animals with low carcase weights and a primitive form of fleece in which coarse hairs acted as an outer coat and fine wool provided insulation close to the skin. The fleece was shed in a summer moult. Such sheep were the result of the crossing of Scandinavian and, perhaps, **Roman** sheep with **Soay**-type animals.

These native breeds were of no interest to modern farmers and by 1840 had been practically wiped out. In **Shetland** today, most sheep (known as improved Shetlands) are descended from crosses of the native sheep with imported **Cheviots**, though a handful of the native breed (known collectively as moorit Shetlands) survive. In **Orkney** only the remarkable flock on **North Ronaldsay** is of the ancestral stock.

North Ronaldsay and moorit Shetland sheep exist in a very wide range of colours and fleece types; some individuals produce fine white wool, others are dark and hairy and close to the original native type. In both breeds, most males and about 20% of the females are horned.

The North Ronaldsay sheep have a surprising adaptation; they are confined to the seashore by a wall, built probably at about the time the **runrig** system was abolished in 1832. They live on seaweed, except that ewes are put onto grass at lambing time. Seaweed is washed up in abundance in winter, but in summer food is hard to find and the sheep graze growing weed or wait for pieces to be washed ashore.

The Rare Breeds Survival Trust runs a reserve flock of North Ronaldsay Sheep on Linga Holm, off Stronsay. The moorit Shetland is also a rare breed, though becoming very popular with spinners and weavers.

ORKNEYINGA SAGA

Subtitled 'The History of the Earls of Orkney', this Norse or **Viking** saga is thought to have been written in Iceland about 1200 although parts clearly derive from much older oral traditions. It deals with the history of **Orkney** and **Caithness** from the 9th to the 12th centuries and throws considerable light on events and personalities elsewhere in Scotland as well as in Norway. Given the 'laconic and pathetically meagre' Scottish sources of the period, it is of crucial importance. There are, though, problems about its chronology and about identification. Like most sagas it does not shy from repetition; battles and raids provoke divisions of the earldom, and appeals to Norway provoke more battles and raids. The earlier sections deal with fictive and mythic material but by the 12th century the narrative is fuller and more credible with **St Magnus**, **Earl Rognvald** (and his crusade) and Harald Maddadson (son of Maddad, **Earl of Atholl**) receiving detailed treatment. Lesser characters are notable for their imaginative names. History would be none the worse for more like Einar Buttered-Bread, Thorfinn the Skull-Splitter, Arni Pin-Leg, Thorarsin Bag-Nose and Sygtstygg Silk-Beard.

ORMISTON, East Lothian

There is something about the dignified simplicity of Ormiston's mercat cross that makes later, more elaborate 'crosses' look overblown. One of the few surviving truly cruciform pre-**Reformation** crosses, dating from the middle of the 15th century, it stands in a railed enclosure in the middle of the High Street of the planned village of Ormiston. The planner (c1735) was agricultural improver John Cockburn, who also built Ormiston Hall (1745–8, only fragments remaining) on the site of an earlier house in which the reformer and martyr **George Wishart** was hiding (1545) when surprised and abducted by **Bothwell**.

ORONSAY, Island of, Inner Hebrides

Oronsay (Norse *orfiris-ey* – 'ebb-tide island', or possibly derived from St Oran, a disciple of **St Columba**, and therefore sometimes Oransay) lies immediately to the south of **Colonsay**, to which it is linked at low tide by a sandy and potentially hazardous causeway. **Islay** is 5½ miles to the south, while the west coast of **Jura** is nine miles to the east. There are only six permanent inhabitants.

Mesolithic shell mounds dating from before 4000 BC provide one of the earliest records of human settlement in Scotland, while the Iron Age fort of Dun Domhnuill is a fine example of its type, sitting on top of a *roche moutonée*, a glacial feature combining good natural defence with easily defended access.

Oronsay was once the site of a thriving Augustinian priory, of which the impressive ruins of the church and cloisters still survive. Founded under the patronage of the **Lords of the Isles** between 1330–50, it was the location of one of the workshops in the West Highlands which produced intricately carved grave-slabs and stone crosses until 1500. The Oronsay Cross is a fine example.

ORR, John Boyd (1880–1971) Nutritionist and Nobel Laureate

Born at **Kilmaurs** near **Kilmarnock**, John Boyd Orr qualified in medicine and physiological chemistry and was appointed to head a nutritional research unit near **Aberdeen**. War, however, intervened and he saw service in the army, where he won the MC and the DSC at the Somme and Passchendaele respectively, before joining the Royal Navy.

Returning to his interrupted career, Boyd Orr was successful in securing financial help in 1923 in establishing the Rowett Research Institute at Bucksburn, near Aberdeen. Under his leadership this rapidly became a centre for excellence in nutritional science, proving in 1927 the value of milk supplied to school children, a measure quickly implemented in British schools. He then argued for a national food policy taking into account social needs, but this proved a little too revolutionary for the government of the day, although Boyd Orr was made an FRS in 1932 and was knighted in 1935. During World War II Boyd Orr was an adviser to the Minister of Food and it was no surprise that he was chosen to become the Director-General of the Food and Agriculture Organisation of the newly formed United Nations in 1945. He laid firm foundations for the FAO, but failed to persuade the international community to accept a supra-national body to supervise food production, and resigned shortly afterwards in disappointment. Had his plans been implemented possibly the chronic problem of worldwide food shortages might be less acute today. After retiring to take up farming in **Angus**, Boyd Orr received a number of honours for his work. Principal among these was the Nobel Peace Prize in 1961 – only the second to be awarded to a Scot – and a baronetcy in 1949. He died at **Brechin** in 1971.

OSPREY

The success story of the osprey (*pandion haliaetus*) has made it a serious rival to the **golden eagle** as Scotland's most cherished bird. A summer visitor (unlike other raptors it migrates to West Africa for the winter), it breeds nowhere else in Britain and for 40 years failed to do so in Scotland. Prior to 1950 no osprey had been reported as nesting in **Rothiemurchus** (Loch-an-Eilean Castle was the favourite site) since 1902 or on **Loch Arkaig** since 1908; the last reported sighting was on Loch Loyne in 1916. **Fishing** interests accounted for the initial persecution and egg collectors for the final extinction. With warped logic the latter boasted of their exploits (see C St John's *Tour in Sutherland*, 1884), as if by securing an egg or a stuffed bird they had preserved for science and posterity a valuable specimen of a species which nature was determined to remove from the extant list. Thus it is told that in 1851 one Lewis Dunbar, in the course of robbing the Loch-an-Eilean site five years in succession, arrived there at 3 am in a snowstorm after a 20-mile hike. Undeterred, the doughty Dunbar swam to the island, removed two eggs, and returned by swimming on his back with an egg in each hand; he then blew the eggs and rinsed them out with **whisky** before cheerfully hiking back to **Granton** with his valuable prize and an excellent yarn.

Such attitudes no longer prevail, but when to universal delight a pair of ospreys were again seen near **Boat of Garten** in 1952, egg collectors were re-alerted. In 1958 one eluded the 24-hour surveillance, climbed the tree in which the birds were nesting, and made off with both eggs, having replaced them with two suitably blackened farmyard eggs (which did not hatch). The Loch Garten site has since bred successfully and remains Britain's most carefully protected and frequently visited nest (from a safe distance by up to 20,000 bird watchers a year). Intentionally this has somewhat obscured the success of re-colonisation elsewhere. There are now (1999) thought to be about 120 breeding pairs in Scotland.

Subsisting almost entirely on fish, the osprey is sometimes known as the fish-hawk, fishing-eagle and eagle-fisher. Its diet includes, besides trout, pike, carp, roach, bream and even grey mullet caught in saline estuaries. There is no truth in its supposed powers to draw fish to the surface; they swim there voluntarily and, in the fish-farmer's cages, invitingly.

OSWALD, James (1710–69) Composer and Music Publisher

Oswald started his professional career as a dancing master in **Dunfermline** and **Edinburgh**. He was a proficient violinist and an excellent cellist and from as early as 1731 was experimenting with Italian and Scottish styles. His *Sonata on Scots Tunes*, though based on Continental dance forms, uses a different tune for each movement. It was published in 1740 at which time he began the first of a long series of publications of which 15 volumes of Scottish airs appeared under the title *The Caledonian Pocket Companion*.

In 1741 Oswald moved to London, soon setting up business as a publisher on his own, founding the Society of the Temple of Apollo (partly devoted to music by expatriate Scots) and publishing his own *Colin's Kisses* (1742), thoroughly Scottish in character and with a fair claim to be the world's first song-cycle. His *Airs for the Seasons* (1747) consist of 96 sonatas, each inspired by a different plant. The whole conception realises an ideal blend between nature and artifice as symbolised by the quotation from Horace which heads each volume, the

music blending the native (particularly Scottish) air with the Italianate figured-bass, which Oswald handles with variety and skill. Several of the plants' visual, medical and symbolic characteristics are given clear expression in the music.

Among many other publications may be mentioned the charming *Twelve Divertimenti* of 1758 for the English guitar; his two satirical cantatas, *The Dustcart* and *The Wheelbarrow*; a satirical song 'The Dancing Master' (no doubt born of experience); two Masonic anthems of 1740; and *Fifty-Five Marches for the Militia*, composed for the raising of county **militia** in England and Wales. Oswald is a superb miniaturist, writing in the *style galant* but with a freshness and depth of feeling in many works not usual in the style. In gathering these into compendiums of various sorts Oswald does not attempt to manufacture large-scale forms, but makes a powerful aesthetic statement for the rights of melody in the larger scale of things.

OTTERBURN, Battle of (1388), see James DOUGLAS, 2nd Earl of Douglas

OUT SKERRIES, Shetland

The Out Skerries (often abbreviated to 'Skerries') lie to the north-east of the **Shetland** island of **Whalsay**. Here on two square miles of rather poor land live about 90 people, dependent on **fishing** and salmon farming with **crofting** as a minor subsidiary. The island is blessed with excellent harbours and now enjoys a regular roll on/roll off ferry service from **Lerwick**. Mousay and Burray, the main islands, were connected by a road bridge in 1957, replacing an earlier footbridge. The lighthouse on Bound Skerry was built in 1858 by **David** and **Thomas Stevenson**. Before its construction shipwrecks were numerous.

OWEN THE BALD (d.c1018) King of Strathclyde

Owen the Bald, probably the son of Owen Drumnagal, was one of the last Kings of **Strathclyde**, but as it is now thought that Strathclyde became a sub-kingdom of Scotland in the 10th century, he must have ruled as a vassal. His support of **Malcolm II** at **Carham** in 1018 raises a further problem in that Welsh sources give the year of his death as 1015.

OYNE, Aberdeenshire

A village 'at the back o' **Bennachie**', Oyne has three notable castles. Westhall, small, 16th century and L-plan, once belonged to the bishopric of **Aberdeen**. It stands to the north. South and more impressive is Harthill, a Z-plan with one wing round and the other square; it was built by Patrick Leith in the early 17th century, deliberately burnt by one of his debt-ridden descendants who had decided to seek his fortune in London, and faithfully restored in recent years. Although also in Oyne parish, Place of Tillyfour is five miles south. L-plan, of 1508, it was restored in 1884 by, amongst others, **Robert Lorimer**.

OYSTERS

From prehistoric times until the 19th century the European 'native' oyster, *ostrea edulis*, flourished in millions

An Oyster Cellar in Leith, *by John Burnet (NGS)*

around many of Scotland's river estuaries and sea lochs. However, during the past 150 years or so these populations have dwindled to the point of disappearance. Today only a very few beds remain on the west coast.

For hundreds of years the Forth was one of the great centres of oyster fishing in Europe and the oyster 'scalps' appeared inexhaustible. In the late 18th and early 19th centuries 30 million oysters a year were dredged from the Forth alone, mostly destined for the London and Dutch market, but heavy over-fishing and pollution destroyed the industry. At the International Fisheries Exhibition in **Edinburgh** in 1882 there were exhibits in the oyster section from France and England but none from Scotland. There are now no oysters in the Forth.

On the west coast the native oysters were largely cleared out by over-fishing alone rather than pollution. While in 1864 the Sea Fisheries Commission found evidence of large oyster beds stretching from **Portree** in **Skye** to the **Isle of Lewis**, with most sea lochs having a considerable population, by the turn of the century the oysters had all but disappeared. Stern, even cruel methods were employed to protect oyster beds. In 1771

the **Duke of Argyll**'s chamberlain wrote to inform him that in order to protect young oysters on the foreshore at **Inveraray** in Loch Fyne, he had warned the towns-people that they and their children would be 'imprisoned and banished' if caught stealing oysters.

In the 18th century, during Edinburgh's 'Golden Age', the enjoyment of oysters was a central part of social and cultural life. Millions were consumed by all classes. The annals of the Cleikum Club recall that 'the principal taverns of our old city used to be called "oyster taverns". How many celebrated wits and bon vivants have dived into the dark defiles of closes and wynds in pursuit of this delicacy and of the wine, the wit and the song that gave it zest.'

In 'Kay's Portraits' of notable Edinburgh figures an oyster lassie is depicted. This brawny sisterhood sold oysters in Edinburgh's **New Town**. Their street cry 'Wha'll o' caller ou' (who will have fresh oysters) was one of the best-known and best-loved of the time.

Robert Fergusson, the laureate of 'Auld Reekie' and the poet who inspired **Burns**, was a devotee of oysters and wrote at length about them in a poem which starts:

> September's merry month is near
> That brings in Neptune's caller cheer
> New oysters fresh
> The halesome and nicest gear
> of fish or flesh.

Fergusson considered the oyster a cure-all – 'whether you hae the head or heart ache, it aye prevails.' Sadly his confidence was misplaced – he died in 1774 at the age of only 24.

In recent years the introduction from specialist hatcheries of the Pacific oyster, *crassostrea gigas*, into west Highland lochs has created a new oyster industry with tremendous potential [see **Fish Farming**]. Loch Fyne is the main centre of production. The tradition of oyster bars is being revived and several have started up in Edinburgh. The Loch Fyne Oyster Bar at the head of Loch Fyne sells more oysters than any other single outlet in Britain. It now seems possible that the oyster may yet be restored to its former position as Scotland's favourite shellfish.

PAINTING IN SCOTLAND

THE 18TH CENTURY AND BEFORE An indigenous tradition of painting in Scotland did not properly emerge until the mid-17th century. Few important examples of earlier date survive, thanks presumably to the zeal with which the **Reformation** was welcomed and the consequent destruction of idolatrous images. A further setback occurred with the removal of the royal court to London in 1603, which effectively destroyed the patronage base for a nascent portraiture tradition.

It is not until the 1640s that we begin to see the appearance of specifically Scottish artists working within their native land. The Aberdonian **George Jamesone** produced a number of fine portraits in the Netherlandish manner, recalling the work of the Low Countries artists who had found patronage at the court of **James VI**. Jamesone's pupil, **John Michael Wright**, was considerably more successful, travelling widely and finally styling himself 'The King's Painter' on the basis of a portrait of **Charles II**.

By the beginning of the 18th century professional portraitists were well established in Scotland and the increasing prosperity of the Scottish aristocracy provided ample opportunities for **Edinburgh** artists such as Richard Waitt and **William Aikman**. The latter travelled to Italy, signalling the end of Scottish artists' attachment to the Dutch School and the triumph of the fashionable Italian style.

This became apparent with the increasing demand for decorative landscape scenes, usually produced to order for insertion within the neo-classical architectural interiors made popular by the **Adam** family. Throughout the 18th century painters, formerly engaged in the more mundane task of house-painting, worked exclusively on such schemes. In particular the Warrender and Norie families were much in demand, and their work – misty classical landscapes derived from the paintings of Poussin and Claude – reached a comparatively high level of sophistication. It was in this artisan-based practice that many of the great early Scottish landscape painters had their apprenticeship.

By the 1750s Scottish portraiture was entering its finest period. Social, intellectual and commercial life was focused on Edinburgh and with the construction of the **New Town** and its elegant, spacious interiors, demand for portraits soared. In the figure of **Allan Ramsay** Scotland found its first major painter. His style, influenced by a sojourn in Italy and his admiration for the French Rococo, was entirely new.

RAEBURN AND HIS CONTEMPORARIES Ramsay's reputation was soon eclipsed, however, by the young **Henry Raeburn** who trained as a miniaturist and began painting portraits around 1778. His sophisticated style, influenced by visits to Italy and by the highly regarded paintings of Joshua Reynolds, led to innumerable commissions. It is through his eyes that the characters of the 'Golden Age' of the **Scottish Enlightenment** are seen. In his series of larger-than-life portraits of Highland chieftains from the 1810s Raeburn created defining icons of Scottishness, visual realisations of the romanticisation of Scotland which, beginning with **Walter Scott**, was to reach its apotheosis in the Victorian era. No Scottish portrait painter was to equal Raeburn. Indeed his pupil, **John Watson Gordon**, was one of his few successors to devote his career solely to portraiture. Increasingly Scottish painters were to see portraiture as 'bread-and-butter' art and turn their attentions to two sorts of painting singularly suited to the history and temperament of Scotland – landscape and genre.

NASMYTH AND LANDSCAPE PAINTING **Alexander Nasmyth**, almost an exact contemporary of Raeburn, exerted a magisterial influence on 19th century Scottish painting. Called 'the Father of Scottish landscape painting', his paternalistic encouragement extended well beyond his large family (nearly all artists of talent) to include almost a whole generation of middle-class amateur and professional painters who attended his drawing classes and accompanied him on sketching trips from Edinburgh's **Arthur's Seat** to the **Pentlands**. Possessed of great technical mastery and venerating the elaborate compositional schemes of Claude and Poussin, Nasmyth also laid much emphasis on drawing direct from nature. His more celebrated admirers included the **Rev John Thomson** of Duddingston, Hugh 'Grecian' Williams and the Glaswegian **Horatio McCulloch**, although all three favoured more grandiose interpretations of landscape than their more mathematically-minded mentor. In the expressive impasto of Thomson's storm-scenes or the sublime vistas of McCulloch one sees the path that leads to **McTaggart** and the gradual domination of medium over subject-matter.

WILKIE AND GENRE Although Scotland produced more than its fair share of landscape painters in the early and mid-19th century, there were none of such consequence as the English painters Turner and Constable. However, in the field of genre painting, which was to become inimitably Scottish, and in the figure of **David Wilkie**, Scotland produced an artist whose reputation was never equalled. Emerging from a naive, rustic painting tradition, exemplified by Walter Geikie, Alexander Carse and **David Allan**, Wilkie became the undisputed master of 'low-life' – portrayals of the day-to-day existence and occasional celebrations of the rural village communities he had known as a child – which he treated with wit and humour but without being patronising. His debut in London in 1806 with *The Village Politicians* created a sensation.

Scott's novels encouraged the public to admire the picturesque qualities of the Scottish people, and Wilkie's success led to a host of Scottish artists descending on London anxious to meet the demand for sentimental scenes of Highland home and hearth. Wilkie felt strongly that Scots artists ought to establish an independent presence in London and actively encouraged his contemporaries, such as John Burnet, Alexander Fraser and William Simson, to join him. However, fierce competition with indigenous artists often led to disappointment and it was not until later in the century that the Faed brothers and John Phillip reasserted the strength of Scottish genre painting in the south.

Wilkie's influence cannot be overestimated and his later, rather histrionic, royal portraits and history pieces should not detract from the enormous impact of his earlier work on contemporaries in England and abroad. Considered one of the great artists of his time, he single-handedly established the presence and potential of the Scottish School on a national and international stage.

LAUDER AND THE EMERGENCE OF THE SCOTTISH SCHOOL As Wilkie turned to commissioned work and Mediterranean subject matter, much of his popular following waned. The taste he had created for Scottish genre subjects made it difficult for Scottish artists to find buyers or patrons when they turned to so-called 'high art': history and religion. **Robert Scott Lauder**, who had trained in Edinburgh in the 1820s, was to find this his undoing. In Italy he had been part of a circle of Scots (including **David Scott** and **William Dyce**) who espoused the paintings of the Old Masters, notably Michelangelo and, in the case of Lauder, Rubens. The efforts of such artists to establish a truly British School of history painting reached their apotheosis with the 1847 competition for murals to decorate the new Houses of Parliament. However, the controversy and farcical proceedings that surrounded this venture practically undid all their efforts and Lauder's magnificent and seminal painting *Christ Teacheth Humility* was rejected.

Lauder returned to Scotland in 1852 to take up the post of Head of the **Trustees' Academy**. Under his direction the Academy became the pre-eminent teaching institution in Scotland and during his nine-year tenure nurtured some of the great names of 19th century Scottish painting. McTaggart, **Chalmers**, MacWhirter, **Orchardson**, Graham and Pettie, to name but a few, never forgot Lauder's influence, and in their work, with its distinctive concern for colour and atmosphere, we see the emergence of a distinct Scottish 'style' of painting. The 'Scottish School' began to be seen as a coherent entity and the popularity of the **Royal Scottish Academy** exhibitions and the **Royal Association** reflected the increasing appreciation of Scottish art amongst the urban middle classes.

Lauder's pupils, with great verve and originality, reinterpreted the hackneyed themes of Scottish art – rustic interiors, misty landscapes, dramatic historical events – as essays in tone and light, and their work was much sought after. Other notable painters of the period include **Sir William Fettes Douglas**, **James Drummond**, **David Roberts** and **Sir George Harvey**, all extremely prolific artists who enjoyed the well-to-do existence typical of the successful Victorian. But their work is very much of its period, and it was to be Lauder's pupils, notably McTaggart and Orchardson, whose increasing painterly sophistication and denial of

obvious or anecdotal subject matter was to point the direction for Scottish art in the changeable late years of the century.

THE LATE 19TH CENTURY: NEW DIRECTIONS English painting of this period could never escape the influence of the Pre-Raphaelite Brotherhood or Ruskin, their great champion. Although much maligned, their obsession with exact detail and 'truth to nature' became characteristic of much English Victorian painting. In Scotland, however, with the exception of a few peripheral figures (**Joseph Noel Paton**, **William Bell Scott**), this did not occur. Instead painters were far more concerned with tonal values of light and their painterly expression. Even artists such as Orchardson and Pettie, who moved to London, continued to explore the potential of open brushwork and the sublimation of the subject in favour of atmosphere.

In the figure of William McTaggart Scotland produced an artist who took these ideas to such an extreme that it has been suggested his work mirrors that of the French Impressionists. But while the Impressionists sought to reduce a scene to the basic components of light and shade, McTaggart elaborated the subject with fierce brushwork and daring contrasts of empty space and detail. His paintings of the 1890s are worthy successors to the revolutionary landscape sketches of Constable. An isolated and curiously down-to-earth figure, McTaggart had no pupils and it is only echoes of his technique that one sees in the work of admirers such as J L Wingate and W M Fraser.

McTaggart, whose large storm-tossed canvases were quite literally painted at the height of the storm, was one of Scotland's first exponents of *plein-airisme* – painting direct from nature, encouraged by the physicial associations of a specific place – but very soon this approach was to become the norm amongst a rising generation of artists. And for the first but certainly not the last time, the focus of artistic initiative was to move to the west.

THE GLASGOW BOYS Unlike the case of McTaggart, the influence of contemporary French painting on the Glasgow Boys was manifest and never disputed. The popular vogue for the landscape paintings of the Barbizon School and their followers in the 1860s and 70s – Courbet, Millet, Corot and, in particular, Bastien-Lepage – encouraged these young painters to eschew the seemingly reactionary tenets of the Edinburgh establishment and instead travel to France to study. What impressed them was the immediacy and realism of French painting – ordinary life as it really was without any idealising or romanticising gloss. These lessons they applied to Scottish subjects and in paintings like **James Guthrie**'s *A Hind's Daughter* (1883) or E A Walton's *The Herd Boy* (1886) one sees an honest and unaffected response to the subject not seen in Scotland since the naïve precursors of Wilkie.

A more amorphous group than is generally realised, the 'Boys' also included in their number those – notably **Lavery**, Kennedy and Roche – who endeavoured to emulate the facile Impressionism of the international artistic circle based at Grez near Fontainebleu, as well as those – **Hornel** and **Henry** especially – who increasingly turned to the purely decorative aspects of subject matter and paint.

Spurned by the RSA, the 'Boys' exhibited to much acclaim throughout the 1890s in London and Europe, lending a renewed impetus to the Scottish School. Although their work, both stylistically and in its use of deliberately anti-picturesque subject-matter, was in reaction to the stale traditions of the RSA, it is representative of the continuity of Scottish art: the adoption of Continental ideas and their reworking into a distinctively Scottish idiom. And so, as the new century dawned, the pastoral realism of the 'Boys' became the accepted mainstream of Scottish art and the rebels of the 1880s the establishment figures of the 1900s.

ART NOUVEAU AND FIN DE SIÉCLE As the Glasgow Boys in the 1890s asserted the painterly qualities of their art – emphasising the physical nature of paint on canvas – so some of their contemporaries endeavoured to break down the traditions that expected paintings to be framed and hung on a wall. Decorative art, and its extraordinary manifestation as 'Art Nouveau', was as much in vogue in Scotland as elsewhere and in **Charles Rennie Mackintosh** the country produced one of the major figures of the moment. His early paintings, virtually interchangeable with those of his associate and future wife (Margaret MacDonald), are redolent of the age and in their gloomy symbolism and obscure subject matter readily deserve their mocking epithet 'Spook School'. His later paintings, however – bold still-lifes and sun-drenched landscapes, are *tours de force* of decorative watercolour painting, defiantly transforming Art Nouveau motifs into a virtual jazz-age idiom.

Mackintosh's paintings are a unique manifestation of the 'Glasgow Style' and have only recently received the critical attention formerly reserved for his architecture. Edinburgh, however, produced an energetic circle of painters working in a distinctive decorative mode. Centred in the **Old Town**, the pre-eminent figure was **John Duncan**, whose elaborate bejewelled compositions, based on ancient Scottish myth, are the visual embodiments of the romanticised Celtic Renaissance ideals of his literary and artistic colleagues. Although stylistically such art is something of a cul-de-sac in the history of Scottish painting, it did forge links with similar movements in Germany and Austria to a far greater extent than anything happening in England. It has long been acknowledged that at this period (as so often before and since) Scots artists were far more highly regarded in Continental Europe than they were in England, or even in their native land.

THE COLOURISTS The dominating influence of French art in Europe was to continue to affect the development of Scottish painting well into the 20th century. The distraction of Art Nouveau aside, the true heirs of the Glasgow Boys were the four artists who were to become known as the 'Scottish Colourists' – **S J Peploe, J D Fergusson, G L Hunter** and **F C B Cadell**. Like so many of their contemporaries, all except Hunter made the obligatory pilgrimage to the ateliers of Paris in the early years of the century and steeped themselves in the work of the Impressionists and their more daring successors.

In 1906 Peploe and Fergusson saw the paintings of Matisse and his fellow 'Fauves' and the impact of these vibrant, dramatic essays in colour was immediate. Cadell and Hunter arrived at their colourful palettes by more circuitous routes, but certainly by the early 1920s all were painting in a sufficiently similar manner to be viewed as a distinct group. The activities of the **Glasgow** dealer Alexander Reid, who arranged all their early shows, was crucial in bringing their work before the public, although none was to enjoy the popular or commercial success their work has had since their deaths. They were by no means avant-garde painters; indeed their choice of subject matter – New Town interiors, **Iona** landscapes, fashionable models – was mildly conservative. Nonetheless, during a comparatively arid period for Scottish painting their confident and fluid interpretations of the new French-inspired colour theories, if rather timid in comparison, acted as a beacon to a new generation of Scottish painters.

THE ART SCHOOLS It is at this stage that Scotland's four art colleges began to play a central role in the development of Scottish painting. The diminution of the Trustees' Academy after 1858 had left something of a void in Scottish art teaching and the bohemian appeal of the Parisian ateliers had proved a more attractive option to many than the staid RSA life classes that remained. However, by 1885, under the mastership of **Francis Newbery**, **Glasgow School of Art** had come into its own as a forward-looking and unstuffy establishment, an outlook exemplified by its selection of the young Charles Rennie Mackintosh as architect of its new building in 1895.

Edinburgh College of Art opened its doors in 1909 and had soon established a character quite different from its western counterpart. Allowing its individual teachers considerable freedom, much like its predecessor the Trustees' Academy, enabled it to attract distinguished artists onto the staff. Thus painters of the stature of Robert Burns, Henry Lintott, Adam Bruce Thomson and, later, Penelope Beaton and **William Gillies**, oversaw students throughout their schooling.

Glasgow, perhaps because it was the older establishment, retained a rather more academic approach, encouraging draughtsmanship and life studies, and there is an observable trend throughout the first half of the 20th century of those artists taught in Glasgow – **William MacCance, James Cowie, Robert Colquhoun** – exhibiting a greater concern for linear qualities than those from Edinburgh – **John Maxwell, Anne Redpath, William MacTaggart** – for whom 'painterliness' and colour were all-important.

The opening of colleges in **Aberdeen** and **Dundee** (Gray's and Duncan of Jordanstone) prior to World War I and the emergence of **Hospitalfield** as a serious institution gave both artists and students in Scotland unparalleled opportunities to remain in their native land. Close student-teacher relationships – non-existent in Paris and often absent in English schools – became a part of Scottish artistic training and remains one of its most attractive features today.

THE EAST COAST TRADITION By the 1930s, largely thanks to the activities of the College of Art, the focus of development in Scottish painting had returned to Edinburgh. The so-called 'Edinburgh School' of Gillies, Maxwell, **Crozier**, Redpath, **Johnstone**, MacTaggart et al, although self-consciously Modernist (the influence of Matisse, Picasso and Klee – all seen in Edinburgh in the 1920s – is paramount), still chose to paint subjects – modest still-lifes, local landscapes – that would have been familiar to predecessors of any generation. Their concession to Modernism was in their use of bold colouring, flattened forms and vigorous and expressive application of paint; an approach best captured in the French term *belle peinture*.

The easy appeal of their work often belies the effort involved. John Maxwell destroyed much of his work, realising his failure to render the inherent poetry of the simple Scottish landscapes he painted. Such angst reveals an oft-ignored undercurrent in Scottish painting between the wars which links figures from both east and west. Returning to the Scottish landscape for inspiration young painters found themselves weighed down with the baggage of Modernism in its widest sense – its lack of values and its secular lack of faith. Cowie, Gillies, Maxwell, **William Wilson**, **Robert Henderson Blyth** and, later, the English refugee **Joan Eardley**, portrayed the Scottish landscape not with the secure confidence of McCulloch or McTaggart, but as unsettled and haunting. Less well-defined than the sometimes contrived sensibilities of their 'Neo-Romantic' counterparts in England, there is still a feeling of disquiet in the work of many 1930s Scottish painters, an unconscious melancholy that characterised so much British cultural life on the eve of war.

POST-WAR PAINTING Diversity and eclecticism characterise post-war Scottish painting. While the traditions of the 1930s continued in the hands of the art school teachers, their followers and the Royal Scottish Academy, so a number of young painters were to leave Scotland, seeking inspiration from the Abstract Expressionist movement which, having developed in New York, had emerged triumphantly in Paris. Three artists – William Gear, Alan Davie and Eduardo Paolozzi – were to go on to establish international reputations but were to remain essentially London-based. Their reworkings of abstract expressionism, 'Pop' art and gestural painting bear no specifically Scottish hallmarks and, unlike their expatriate predecessor, David Wilkie, their nationality has played no part in their success.

Some painters – notably Robin Philipson – chose to remain in Scotland but established modest reputations in London, although the focus of Modernist innovation has been so New York-based since the late 1950s as to preclude their reputations from extending further. The increasingly conservative approach of the RSA has led to considerable disillusionment among some of Scotland's more avant-garde painters. While other exhibiting institutions – particularly the Society of Scottish Artists – have endeavoured to remedy this situation, there is still a feeling that the Scottish institutions have failed Scotland's best artists. Certainly those who are best known abroad – Gear, Davie, Paolozzi, Ian Hamilton Finlay, John Bellany – rarely exhibit in Scotland and have never shown at the RSA.

THE PRESENT AND THE FUTURE Modern Scottish painting has received a fillip in recent years with the appearance of the so-called 'New Glasgow Boys'. These artists, most of whom trained at Glasgow School of Art, are generally, although by no means exclusively, hallmarked by their concern for social issues and their expression in a hard-edged, figurative style. Their work is certainly new and vigorous and, if nothing else, has given the lie to the suggestion that Scotland has become artistically moribund.

Their success has initiated a wealth of experimentation and fresh thinking from the graduates of art schools and although opportunities for showing in Scotland are still painfully few, there is reason to be optimistic about the future of painting in Scotland.

At the same time the art market and academe have combined to promote Scottish painting to an unprecedented degree. The major Scottish galleries have put on many outstanding exhibitions reassessing nearly all aspects of Scottish art history, and the market has kept pace with this renewed interest. Scottish painting is now more discussed, written about, analysed, collected and looked at than it has ever been before.

PAISLEY, Renfrewshire

Paisley lies seven miles west of **Glasgow**, is contiguous with it and includes Glasgow Airport, yet it somehow retains its distinct character. In the early 19th century it had the third largest population in Scotland (ahead of **Aberdeen** and **Dundee**) and it remains one of the ten largest towns. Size apart, its distinction was neatly encapsulated by John Kent, an ingenious local rhymester:

> Yet Paisley's name is widely spread,
> And history doth show it's
> Been famed alike for shawls and thread,
> For poverty and poets.

The poets included **Robert Tannahill, Alexander Wilson** and **John Wilson**; the poverty, with a fifth of the workforce unemployed in 1841, was self-evident and, for the same reason, still is. But shawls and thread, weaving and spinning, won the town even greater renown. 'Paisley' became better known as the design motif of its silks and **cottons** than as a place, while its production of cotton thread was the largest in the world. As elsewhere [see eg **Calton Weavers**], the skilled crafts involved in pattern-making and weaving spawned a peculiarly pensive and disputatious workforce who embraced sectarian radicalism in both politics and religion, while their capitalist employers became ever more paternal and patronage-conscious. The downtown skyline of **Oakshaw** ridge consists almost entirely of jostling churches and institutions (mostly founded by the **Coats** and Clark families) while the weaving suburb of Charleston was commonly known as 'the republic'.

Prior to the 17th century the town's history is largely that of **Paisley Abbey**, a grant by charter of **James IV** (1488) having conferred **burgh of barony** rights on the abbot. After the **Reformation** these passed to the **Hamiltons** (soon Dukes of Abercorn), to the Cochranes, later Earls of Dundonald, and then to the town's bailies in 1658. The Cochranes retained property here until 1764 when it was repurchased by the Hamiltons of Abercorn.

At the time of the **Union** there already existed a manufacture of muslins and **linens** which were exported by boat down the White Cart river. The first mention of sewing thread occurs in 1730 and by 1760 silk gauze was a major production. Steam power revolutionised the spinning process at the turn of the century. In 1826 James Coats built the first of his great thread mills at Ferguslie (one of which survives), and by mid-century the Coats and Clark families dominated the town's, and the nation's, production.

Meanwhile in 1805 shawl manufacture had been introduced, copying the designs (but cutting the prices) of the much prized Kashmiri shawls made fashionable by the Empress Josephine. The Jacquard loom was first used in Britain in Paisley, one such now forming part of the display of shawl manufacture in the Paisley Art Gallery and Museum. Of the Kashmiri designs, that based on the almond fruit, more commonly known as the 'teardrop', became immensely popular and invariably figured in the town's silk and cotton productions. For obvious reasons, though, the exceptionally fine quality of the Kashmir wool shawl, derived from the undercoat of the Tibetan goat, proved hard to reproduce. Shawls went out of fashion in the 1870s and although thread was still produced in Paisley, the 20th century brought a much greater variety of industries, as typified in the Hillington Industrial Estate (1937), Linwood and Glasgow Airport.

Oakshaw

Although **Paisley Abbey** is on the right bank of the White Cart river, the medieval town developed on the left bank and spread round and up the low ridge of Oakshaw, on which there may once have been a **Roman** fort. In the 18th and 19th centuries the ridge became a prime site for buildings jealous of their civic prestige and/or profile. Churches include the cathedral-size **Thomas Coats** Memorial Baptist Church (Hippolyte Blanc, 1894) with tower and open crown spire, the high-steepled High Church (1750), the no-steepled Middle Church (1779), St John's Church (1862), the Congregational Church (1887), the United Free Church (1826), the Gaelic Church (1793), the once Cameronian Church (1820) – and more. Here too are several schools and the Coats Observatory, also a meteorological and seismological station with some notable astronomical instruments.

Stanely and Gleniffer

South of Paisley the Stanely reservoir was created (1836–8) to meet the water needs of the town's fast-expanding industry. It laps the base of Stanely (Stanley) Castle, a roofless 15th century L-plan fortalice built by the Maxwells of **Newark** and **Haggs** Castles [for Haggs see **Glasgow**]. Paisley suburbs now lap both the reservoir and the neighbouring Braes of Gleniffer, once celebrated by **Robert Tannahill**:

Keen blaws the win' o'er the braes o' Gleniffer,
The auld castle's turrets are covered wi' snaw;
How changed frae the time when I met wi' my lover
Amang the brume bushes by Stanely green shaw;

PAISLEY ABBEY

On the east bank of the White Cart river, the one-time site of a Celtic monastery dedicated to St Mirin (or Mirren, a name now more familiar as that of **Paisley**'s premier **football** club) was chosen about 1163 by Walter fitz Alan, **Stewart** (ie Steward) of Scotland for **David I**, as suitable for the foundation of a priory. Clunian monks from Wenlock in Shropshire, the Stewart's home county, arrived in 1169. The priory became an abbey in 1219 but was destroyed by the English in 1307 for supporting **William Wallace**, a native of nearby Elderslie (where there is a memorial and other supposed associations). Of this Norman foundation the most notable relic is the deeply recessed west door, like that at **Dunblane**. Rebuilding in the 15th century restored the nave but in 1533, anticipating the **Reformation**, the tower collapsed, destroying the choir and north transept. The nave with vaulted aisles including that of St Mirin (1499 and incorporating a frieze of carved panels illustrating scenes from the saint's life) continued in use as the parish church, but the rest of the building lay in ruins until restoration in the 19th and 20th centuries by, amongst others, **R Rowand Anderson** and **Robert Lorimer**.

There is uncertainty about the authenticity of a burial chest supposed to contain the remains of **Marjorie Bruce**, daughter of **Robert I** and wife of another Walter the Steward (**Walter Stewart**, 1293–1326). But the Barochan Cross, large with much-weathered relief carving, is unquestionably an early Christian cross, possibly 8th century. It was removed here from Mill of Barochan while other relics of the **Celtic Church**, including a stone sarcophagus, were removed from Abbot's Inch,

West front of Paisley Abbey c1840 (RWB)

the area now occupied by **Glasgow** Airport, to Inchinnan parish church.

Apart from the church, little remains of the abbey although at the Reformation one wing of the cloister was converted into a residence for the **commendator**. Known as the Place (ie Palace) of Paisley, it was occupied by the Dundonald and Abercorn Earls before being converted into artisans' flats and eventually restored. A further relic of the medieval abbey was discovered in 1990, namely the main drain, a remarkably capacious (1 x 1.5–2m) and well built (arched and paved) conduit of which 100m has been traced. Given the excitement archaeologists now derive from middens and refuse tips, much is expected from a painstaking examination of the drain's silt. In 1991 items identified included 'a complete early 16th century chamber pot, the matrix of an abbot's seal, and fragments of slate covered with graffiti, writing, and the earliest polyphonic music to be discovered in Scotland'.

PAPA STOUR, Shetland

Off the west coast of **Shetland** lies the island of Papa Stour, with a population of about 40. The name, given by Norse settlers of the 9th century, means 'the big island of the priests', referring to priests of the early **Celtic Church** whom the pagan **Vikings** found living here. In Norse times it was part of an important estate owned by Duke Haakon Magnusson, who became King of Norway in 1299. Shetland's oldest document refers to a dispute over land that took place in the Duke's house on Papa Stour.

The island is famous for its coastal scenery, especially its long penetrating sea caves and tunnels and its abundant bird life. It is served by a small cargo boat based at West Burrafirth on the **Mainland**.

PARK, Mungo (1771–1806) Explorer

Born at Foulshiels in the Yarrow Valley, Park was a contemporary and neighbour of the future **Sir Walter Scott** and of **James Hogg**, 'the Ettrick Shepherd'. The ruins of his parents' cottage there seem tiny; yet Mungo was one of 14 children who were raised in reasonable comfort. He was destined by parental choice for the Church; but medicine was his preference and after an apprenticeship in **Selkirk** he went to **Edinburgh University**.

Chance plays its part in many an eventful life. What steered Park's course was his elder sister's marriage to an émigré Borderer whose London seed business gave him an entrée to the world of botanists such as Sir Joseph Banks. On qualifying as a doctor, Mungo Park headed south where, through this connection, he was appointed assistant surgeon on an expedition to Sumatra.

His work went far beyond that of his appointment, and Banks was impressed by the botanical and scientific data he collected. At the time of his return, the newly formed Africa Association was looking for a leader for its expedition to find the source of the Niger; Park volunteered, and Banks's endorsement and his own enthusiasm overcame any qualms the Association may have had about his youth and lack of experience.

At the age of 24, therefore, Park set off from the Gambia with six African companions, into completely unmapped, unexplored – and potentially hostile – territory. 'My baggage was light,' he wrote, 'consisting chiefly of provisions for two days; a small assortment of beads, amber and tobacco, for the purchase of a fresh supply, as I proceeded; a few changes of linen, an umbrella, a pocket sextant, a magnetic compass and a thermometer; together with two fowling pieces, two pairs of pistols, and some other small articles.' It was an expedition of pure discovery; unlike his successors in exploration, Park had no wish either to evangelise or to open up trade routes.

It was 18 months before he reappeared, having undergone horrendous hardship and privation. Some of this was caused by the terrain and the climate; but he was also taken prisoner and ill-treated by Arab tribes. Nevertheless he explored the upper reaches of the Niger (in Mali) and mapped it. During all his trials he kept a journal which, later published as *Travels into the Interior of Africa*, reveals much of his own personality. It was not just the topography of West Africa that he recorded, but the culture and social mores of the people who inhabited it. He can be seen to respect the indigenous cultures; and his own modesty and lack of vainglory shine through.

That unpretentiousness was also evident in the manner of his return. Finding no immediate sailing ship to Britain from the Gambia, he went via America on a slave ship, arriving in London early one morning two and a half years after his departure. He had long been given up for dead. Yet, not wishing to disturb his brother-in-law's sleep, he strolled around the botanic gardens until a suitable waking hour. A few days later, his arrival in his home town of Selkirk was even less ceremonious; his family were disturbed at night by a knocking at the door. 'That'll be our Mungo,' remarked a younger brother who had made no earlier comment, 'I did see him getting out of the coach in the Square.'

Park now embraced the quiet life of a Border doctor. He married the daughter of the Selkirk surgeon to whom he had been apprenticed; his letters to her are full of an unaffected and uninhibited feeling. They settled in **Peebles**, and Park formed a friendship with Walter Scott who was now Sheriff of **Selkirkshire**. But, before long, 'the spell of Africa was upon him – that nameless charm of which no man can purge his blood once he has been inoculated.' When, in 1804, he was invited to head a government expedition to complete his exploration of the Niger, the lure was one which not even his love for his wife and family could counterbalance.

Before his departure, Park visited Scott at his then home at Ashiestiel on the banks of the **Tweed**. They forded the river together on parting, and Park's horse stumbled. 'I'm afraid, Mungo, that's a bad freit,' opined Scott superstitiously, to which came the rejoinder, 'Freits follow those that look for them.'

But the expedition had more freits, or bad omens, than a stumbling horse. On his previous expedition Park had travelled light, with no European companions. In no way could his entourage have spelled aggression to the native population. Now, given the authority of government, his party consisted of 40 Europeans, most of whom were military. A delayed start meant that they travelled in the rainy season, and other trials affected them.

Never was the description of West Africa as 'The White Man's Grave' more appropriate. Destroyed by fever and dysentery, only 11 of the original party reached the Niger; before they were ready to make their way downstream, six of those had perished. Amid this unending disaster, Park displayed all the leadership and courage of a true hero. But the end came in the rapids of Bussa (in Nigeria). Whether their boat was ambushed or whether it struck a rock is unknown. All that is certain is that Park and his remaining companions were drowned.

Mungo Park's statue – a fine one, by the sculptor **Thomas Clapperton** – stands at one end of Selkirk High Street; an inferior one of his friend and neighbour Walter Scott is at the other. The latter is one of many; the former is unique.

PARLIAMENTARY ROADS

The second phase of Highland road building, in the early 19th century (the first being the construction of the **military roads** in the mid-18th), was born of social and economic necessity aided by a possible twinge of governmental conscience; for the main feature of the agrarian revolution in the Highlands had been the supplanting of people by sheep and depopulation had reached crisis level.

In the latter part of the 18th century over 1000 miles of roads in Scotland had been listed as 'military'. But as the army of occupation dwindled to a token force, no troops were available for any real form of road maintenance; and after 1789 soldiers were no longer so employed. So ended 64 years of military road making and maintenance. Highland roads and bridges were thus in a bad state of repair and in many cases impassable for carriages while provision for the stage coach made realignment a necessity. Perhaps the best example of this was the decision to abandon the **Devil's Staircase** and the Lairig Mor and build a new road through **Glencoe**, across **Loch Leven** by the **Ballachulish** ferry, and so by Onich to **Fort William**. In London there were mixed feelings about Highland roads and bridges – including total abandonment. In the end, however, most roads on the Highland edge were handed over to local authorities which had a sufficient population to bear the cost of maintenance, while those in districts which were 'very poor and thinly inhabited' would be maintained by the government. The Contin to **Poolewe** road, which probably never existed as an entity, and the **Fort Augustus** to **Bernera** road were struck off the list.

Backed by his GOC **General Abercrombie**, Colonel Anstruther, Inspector of Roads, had strongly favoured continuing to maintain the military roads, arguing that without them the Highlanders would 'in a few years relapse into their former ignorance or desert their country'. So the government instructed **Thomas Telford** to make a survey of Highland communications in 1801–2, based on social and economic needs. Among those whom he interviewed was the Highland and Agricultural Society, which argued for not only roads but also bridges, **canals** and harbours, first to counteract the disastrous depopulation of the **clearances**, and secondly to stimulate a more diversified economy. The result was the Highland Road and Bridge Act of 1803,

by which the government would meet half the expense of any necessary works, the other half to be met by landowners and others who might benefit, but with the amazing omission of any provision for repairs and maintenance.

Telford, like **Wade** before him, was entrusted with implementation of the ideas he had formulated. Starting in 1804 and going on for a good 20 years parliamentary roads were built: from Fort William to **Arisaig**; Loch Oich to **Kinlochhourn**; Corran Ferry to Loch Moidart; **Spean Bridge** by **Laggan** to Pitmain; **Oban** to Crinan; **Dingwall** to Loch Carron and **Kyle of Lochalsh**, also to **Wick**, **Thurso** and **Tongue**; Loch Fyne to the **Clyde** ports; in **Arran**, **Skye**, **Jura** and **Islay**. Major bridges such as those at **Dunkeld**, **Fochabers**, **Forres**, **Ballater** and **Craigellachie** were constructed. Harbours and jetties for ferries and fishery were made, and the Caledonian Canal was dug. As in the case of the military roads, Telford insisted on the necessity of establishing inns on the new roads, and as he had to cater for stage coaches, no gradient would exceed 1:20. For the second time in a century the Highlands became a hive of communications activity. One of his proposals was to abandon the road by Black Mount and Glencoe in favour of a new road from Spean, by Loch Treig, **Rannoch Moor** and the head of **Glen Lyon** to **Killin** (much of which would be the path taken by the West Highland **Railway** at the end of the century). Although it was 15 miles shorter, the route was rejected. Like Wade, Telford was also interested in a road from **Ruthven** by Glen Feshie to **Braemar**.

In the midst of all this activity the Commissioner for Highland Roads and Bridges, appointed to administer the 1803 and any subsequent Acts, had to report that because there was no provision for the maintenance of parliamentary roads, they 'were falling into decay'. An Act of 1810 empowering counties to assess themselves for road maintenance achieved nothing. After protracted negotiations the Act of 1814 was passed 'for maintaining and keeping in repair certain Roads and Bridges in Scotland for the purpose of maintaining Military Communications'. All roads and bridges would be maintained at public expense for one year. Thereafter the counties would pay three-quarters of the cost, the government would pay the remainder, plus any salaries. The Act was compulsory for parliamentary roads, but only for such military roads as the counties handed over to the Commissioners. **Inverness**, **Moray** and **Argyll** handed over their roads, a total of 283 miles, but **Perth** and **Dumbarton** opted out, with disastrous results for travellers. An Act of 1819 increased the government grant, and in 1820 another Act forced **Perthshire** to maintain the military road to **Drumochter** in as good a state as its continuation northwards to Inverness. A Toll Gate Act of 1823 empowered the northern counties to charge tolls if they desired, and soon stage and mail coaches were plying the Highland roads.

It would be wrong to ignore the contribution of the **Mitchell** family to Highland communications at this time. In 1814 John Mitchell was appointed Senior Inspector, to be succeeded in 1824 by his son, **Joseph**, at the age of 21. While Telford was engaged in his multifarious activities furth of Scotland, it was the Mitchells who saw that all the building and maintenance work was carried out according to specification. Joseph remained Inspector until the disbandment of the Commissioners in 1863, by which time, not surprisingly, he had become a leading figure in promoting the Highland Railway, the line to Strone (later extended to Kyle of Lochalsh) and the line to Wick and Thurso.

Until their disbandment in 1863 the Commissioners for Highland Roads and Bridges still officially used the term 'military roads' even when they were crossed by tollgates and ran alongside the new railways. In their final report they recalled that they had built 930 miles of parliamentary roads at a cost of £540,000 (including £50,000 from the funds of the forfeited estates), and that after the addition of the military roads in 1814, they had 1200 miles under their care.

The roads made by Telford and Wade served the Highlands well in the context within which they were conceived. To criticise Wade for not making provision for the stage coach and Telford for not envisaging the capabilities of the internal combustion engine is grossly unfair to two distinguished transport engineers.

PATERSON, James (1854–1932) Painter

Best remembered for his associations with the 'Glasgow Boys' [see **Painting**], Paterson, like his equally talented colleague **Joseph Crawhall**, was always somewhat on the fringes of the circle, pursuing an independent and individual course. Born into the prosperous **Glasgow** middle classes he persuaded his father to let him give up the family business in favour of a fashionable artistic training in Paris. There, as well as meeting some of the future 'Boys', he was exposed to the work of the Barbizon and Realist painters and was influenced by their uncompromising natural observation, bold use of brushwork and concern with delicate tonal values. Paterson returned to Scotland in 1882 and two years later moved to the small **Dumfriesshire** village of **Moniaive**. His work from this period – landscapes in oils and watercolours charting the subtle changes of light and weather – is his best. Like his Glasgow colleagues he eschewed the picturesque or generic, rebelling against the ascendancy of such themes, prevalent in the conservative east coast **Royal Scottish Academy**. He exhibited at the recently formed avant-garde New English Art Club in London and helped set up the *Scottish Art Review* which propagated many of the ideas of the Glasgow Boys. Like many of the 'Boys', however, notably **Guthrie** and Walton, Paterson's work became increasingly conservative and decorative as he grew older. He moved to **Edinburgh** in 1905 and was soon elected to membership of the maligned RSA, later becoming a popular Librarian and Secretary. His work never lost its edge and his later watercolours, in particular, are as accomplished an expression of the medium as anything painted by a Scottish artist this century.

PATERSON, Robert (1715–1801)
Stonemason

The son of a farmer from near **Hawick**, **Roxburghshire**, Paterson served his apprenticeship as a stonemason at a quarry in Nithsdale, **Dumfriesshire**. A **Cameronian** himself, he devoted 40 years of his life to 'wandering about the country among the kirk-yards, with a little white shelty [pony], cleaning and taking parental charge

of the martyrs' [**Covenanters**'] gravestones. Wherever he found these stones, whether on wild moors or lonely kirkyards, the fogg [lichen] he scoured neatly out of them and renewed their inscriptions with his chisel. He often would weep as he laboured, so overpowering were his feelings' (**John MacTaggart**). The story of his life inspired **Walter Scott**'s *Old Mortality*; the story of his death is recorded by MacTaggart; 'One night, as he wandered through Annandale, he took too much of the "cratur" [whisky] that "doiter'd" him, and made him lose his way; and having wandered on until he and his companion became quite exhausted, he alighted off the back of his faithful comrade for the last time and betook himself to a quarry hole for shelter and there, with the fatigue and the "nappie" he fell asleep – no more to waken in this world – for a stormy night of sleet came on, and the cold froze the warm blood in the heart of Auld Mortality; but his memory shall not perish.' He was buried at **Caerlaverock**.

PATERSON, Sir William (1658–1719)
Financier

Born in Tinwald, **Dumfriesshire**, but raised in England from early childhood, Paterson made his fortune in trade with the West Indies. In 1691 he advocated the establishment of the Bank of England of which, on its foundation in 1694, he became one of the first directors. When the Scottish Parliament passed an act for the establishment of a 'Company of Scotland Trading to Africa and the Indies' (1695), Paterson became one of the scheme's most ardent promoters, and when London's funding for the enterprise failed, took an active part in raising the necessary capital of £400,000 from within Scotland. He was also responsible for suggesting **Darien** on the Panama isthmus as the ideal location for a Scottish colony and, with his wife, sailed with the 'Darien Expedition' in 1698. Of the 1200 Scots who set out from **Leith**, only 900 survived the experience; of them 150 died on the voyage north and fewer still made it back to Scotland the following year. William Paterson, his health broken and his fortune gone, was among the survivors. His wife was not. Two years later he was closely involved with drafting the trade and finance articles of the **Treaty of Union**, of which he had long been a firm supporter, and in 1707 was elected MP for **Dumfries** burghs in the first Union Parliament. In 1715 he was awarded £18,000 compensation for the losses incurred in the Darien Venture.

PATNA, Ayrshire

Connections, if there are any, between this mining village on the little Doon and its Indian namesake, the state capital of Bihar on the mighty Ganges, are not obvious. In a setting 'confined, tumulated and bleak', **Ayrshire**'s Patna aimlessly ambles; its houses, according to Fullarton's *Gazetteer*, 'lie as aspersedly amongst the fields as a handful of corn does amongst the clods'. Mining has long since ceased but bucolic tranquillity has yet to be restored.

PATON, Sir Joseph Noel (1821–1901)
Painter

The nearest Scotland came to a fully-fledged Pre-Raphaelite painter, Joseph Noel Paton combined consummate craftsmanly skills with a deep love of antiquarianism and mythology. Born near **Dumfermline**, he was apprenticed at an early age to his father, a successful damask designer from whom he inherited both artistic skill and an interest in antique armour and Scottish history. He studied at the Royal Academy Schools in London from 1842 and befriended John Everett Millais who later tried to bring Paton into the nascent Pre-Raphaelite Brotherhood. But although he applauded the Brotherhood's concern for meticulous detail and truth to nature, Paton did not share their High Church beliefs or rigorous obsession with early Renaissance technique. Despite winning a prize in the competition for murals for the recently completed Houses of Parliament, he found little to keep him in London and returned to Scotland in 1845. The following year he completed his most ambitious painting to date, *The Quarrel of Oberon and Titania*, a remarkably detailed and intricate fantasy painting. It enjoyed immense success and was purchased by the Royal Association for presentation to the **National Gallery of Scotland** where it now hangs.

Over the next few years Paton's reputation was made with such works as well as with scenes portraying Scottish mythology or popular history, all executed in exquisite detail and later much admired by the critic John Ruskin. In later years Paton turned to more weighty religious subjects, now thought rather ponderous and moralising. The success in London of his Crimean War picture *In Memoriam* brought him commissions from **Queen Victoria** to paint her children, but Paton's bad health prevented their completion. He exerted a considerable influence from his **George Square** studio in **Edinburgh** on the younger generation (including **John Duncan**) and built up a collection of antiquarian armour that was deemed second to none.

PAXTON HOUSE, Berwickshire

West of **Berwick-upon-Tweed** and on the north bank of the river, Paxton House dates from 1758 and is thought to have been the work of the **Adam** brothers, probably John and **Robert**. 'Massive and somewhat superb', it echoes their work at **Dumfries** and **Hopetoun**. The restrained Doric portico gives access to rooms lavishly plastered by Adam and furnished by Chippendale. It was built for Patrick Home in anticipation of his marriage to an illegitimate daughter of Frederick the Great. When the match failed to materialise, Home consoled himself with a Grand Tour during which he bought mainly Italian paintings. To house this collection George Home, Lord Wedderburn, eventually commissioned **Robert Reid** to design an in-house gallery. It was completed in 1811 and is now 'the only remaining room in a Scottish country house built specifically to display pictures and predates all Scottish institutional or public galleries' (*Glasgow Herald*). The collection has since been sold and the house presented to the nation by its owner, the Labour MP John Home Robertson. But the gallery, restored to its sumptuous 1876 decor, is now open to the public as the first permanent outstation of the **National Galleries of Scotland**.

PEAT

'A good quiet fuel' (**F Fraser Darling**), peat was once dug and burnt throughout Scotland although its use is

Digging peat at Ness, Isle of Lewis (NHP)

now limited to the Islands and parts of the Highlands. The word is of **Celtic** origin and the last great accumulation of peat may date from Celtic times. The several feet of peat removed from round the base of the **Callanish** stones in **Lewis** had clearly formed after their erection while **Flanders Moss**, well wooded in **Roman** times, had become a formidable bog by the Middle Ages.

The formation of peat results from organic matter accumulating faster than its rate of decomposition. Typically partially decomposed plants – sedges, rushes, reeds and mosses, especially sphagna – form a soggy blanket which builds up over the years and, compressed by its own growing weight and by moisture, partially carbonises. The rate of accretion is probably not more than 0.5mm per year but may eventually result in peat depths of up to 10m. Favourable conditions for its formation are thought to be essentially climatic, accumulation resulting from increased rainfall and lower temperatures. Similarly a slight increase in temperatures or decrease in rainfall may reverse the process and result in peat reduction. The stratigraphy of peat, like that of glacial ice, has been used to study climatic change.

The composition of peat varies from a highly fibrous turf-like material to a hard brown clay, depending on age, location and constitution. In its natural state it contains over 90% water. Heavy, therefore, and liable to crumble, it demands both physical effort and technical ingenuity before it becomes a burnable substance. Cutting, drying, transport and storage was a major preoccupation for a large part of the population and spawned a variety of local implements and traditions; they may be studied in numerous local museums and archives.

Peat cutting, usually in the late spring, involved the whole community and provided a welcome occasion for outdoor socialising enriched by lore. The scars of peat hags bear testimony to the extent of these endeavours and, particularly in the Outer **Hebrides**, individual peat stacks still dwarf the haystacks and afford to each croft house additional shelter and architecture.

After World War II research was undertaken to extend the exploitation of this indigenous, natural and environmentally acceptable fuel source and to develop peatlands themselves. Proposals to use peat for electricity generation or paper production, or to extract from it ammonia or alcohol, came to nothing in Scotland, but the Ekenberg process for turning peat into carbonised briquettes with calorific values comparable to **coal** extended domestic consumption. More significantly, large areas of peat bog were drained for **agriculture** and especially **forestry**.

Subsequently environmentalists and scientists have decried this depletion of natural wetlands (eg the **Flow Country**). Peat bogs are now seen as valuable carbon 'sinks' or banks, endangered alike by global warming and human exploitation, whose erosion will result in the siltation of reservoirs and hydro lochs and will affect the quality of drinking water. The peat bog, once seen as a sour indictment of the stagnant state of Highland agriculture, is now hailed as a priceless eco-system in need of protection even from those who merely wish to continue using it as 'a good quiet fuel'.

PEDEN, Alexander (c1626–86) Covenanter

Born at Sorn near **Mauchline** in Ayrshire, Alexander Peden was the most charismatic and inspirational of **Covenanting** preachers. The son of a gentleman farmer, close neighbour and friend of the Boswells of **Auchinleck**, (forebears of **James Boswell**), Peden was educated at **Glasgow University**, became schoolteacher at **Tarbolton** and was ordained minister of New Luce in **Galloway** (1660), but held the post for only two years before being deprived. He became 'chief and monarch of those wandering heralds of God' preaching at **Conventicles** throughout the south-west. Given to 'inexplicable premonitions and presentiments', his skill at evading arrest became legendary, but he disclaimed his nickname of 'the Prophet' explaining that it was only because he was 'the friend of God' that he could see through 'the thin veil which hides the future' (A Smellie). For 11 years he quartered the country, sleeping in caves or byres and preaching in the fields, his impassioned sermons touching and sometimes terrifying his listeners. In June 1673, at a Conventicle near **Ballantrae**, his luck ran out. Seized by a party of dragoons, he was taken to **Edinburgh** and sentenced to four years' imprisonment on the **Bass Rock** to be followed by a further year in the **Tolbooth**. Released in 1678 but sentenced with 60 others to banishment, he was put on board a vessel bound for America. When the boat reached London, however, they were all inexplicably released, and Peden made his way back to Scotland.

Frequently urged to join the **Cameronians** but finding their methods too rigid, he resumed his wandering existence, dividing the remaining years of his life between the south-west of Scotland and the north of Ireland. He died at his home at Sorn, still a fugitive, in January 1686, and was buried secretly by his friends the Boswells in their family vault at Auchinleck. But his resting place was discovered, his tomb rifled by dragoons and his body exhumed, to be suspended from a gibbet on **Cumnock** hill. When it was cut down it was reburied, as befitted a common criminal, at the foot of the gallows tree. But the Covenanters had their quiet revenge. Where previously the deceased of Cumnock had been buried in the village churchyard, from that day the bereaved took their dead out to the 'Hill of Reproach' 'that they might sleep the sufficient sleep by the side of Alexander Peden' (Rev J A Wylie).

PEEBLES, David (d.1579) Composer

Remembered in particular for his exquisite and smooth-flowing setting of Si Quis Diliget Me which he presented to **James V** in 1531, Peebles may also be the composer of the anonymous mass in six parts, Felix Namque. After the **Reformation** he was commissioned by James Stewart, prior of **St Andrews**, to harmonise the psalms, leaving out any 'curiosity' in the music. He evidently found the restriction on his style irksome for Wode claims that 'he was not earnest' in the task and would not have completed it without badgering. The settings are, nonetheless, very fine.

PEEBLES, Peeblesshire

Charmingly situated on the north bank of the river **Tweed** and surrounded by gentle rolling hills, Peebles has none of the 'close-knit, slightly wary atmosphere' of many more southerly Borders towns whose 'eyes were always open and ears pricked for the gleam of invader's steel or the beat of reivers' hooves' (**N Tranter**). Yet during its long history it has been touched, and sometimes battered, by many of Scotland's dramas. A **royal burgh** from the reign of **David I**, its castle (long gone) was a favourite hunting lodge of **Alexander III** who founded Cross Kirk in 1261 on the site of the discovery of a 'magnificent and venerable cross' (**John of Fordun**). The nave and west tower of this church remain, as do the remains of St Andrews Church, founded in 1195, a collegiate church in 1543 and damaged when much of the town was reduced to ashes by Hertford's troops in 1545. Amongst Peebles' other antiquities, the slightly mutilated mercat cross dates from the 14th/15th century and the five-arched stone bridge over the Tweed, widened in 1834 and again in 1900, from 1467. Reduced to ashes once more, but this time by accident, in 1607, Peebles was garrisoned (c1650) by Cromwell's artillery while they were trying to reduce nearby **Neidpath Castle**; its inhabitants, living up to their peaceable reputation, were notable for their absence from the insurrections of **Rullion Green** and **Bothwell Brig**, and although a few fought at **Philiphaugh**, none volunteered to join **Prince Charles Edward Stewart** when he passed through in 1745 on his way to **Dumfries**.

The more recent history of Peebles has a strong literary flavour; **William** and **Robert Chambers** were both born in the town's Biggieknowe area, **James Hogg** and Christopher North (**John Wilson**) were frequent visitors to the town; **Robert Louis Stevenson** lived here for a spell in his youth and **S R Crockett** in his declining years, and **John Buchan** spent many youthful holidays at the Peebles home of his grandparents. Not-so-literary associations are with the 4th Duke of Queensberry, **Wordsworth**'s 'Degenerate Douglas' and perfidious feller of trees at Neidpath, who was born in Peebles in 1725, and with the explorer **Mungo Park** who settled as a surgeon in the town in 1801, but lasted only two years before leaving once more for his beloved Africa. Long a centre of woollen manufacture, Peebles has more recently developed as an attractive – yet still peaceable – holiday resort.

PEEBLESSHIRE

Before the **local government** reorganisation of 1975, Peeblesshire was a southern county occupying 222,240 acres (90,007ha), situated with **Midlothian** to the north and north-east, **Selkirkshire** to the east and south-east, **Lanarkshire** to the west and **Dumfriesshire** to the south. With its highest point at Broad Law at 2754ft (839m), Peeblesshire was described in the relevant volume of the *Third Statistical Account* (1964) as 'an upland county with an average height above sea level probably greater than any other county in Britain'. The area was drained by the river **Tweed**, accounting for its other name, Tweeddale. **Agriculture**, mainly sheep-farming, and **forestry** were the main occupations, along with some textile manufacturing. The county town was Peebles, the only other small burgh being **Innerleithen**. In the local government reorganisation of 1975, Peeblesshire was converted intact into Tweeddale District in Borders Region, and after 1995, with the abolition of the Regions and two-tier local government, remained part of the Borders Council Area.

PENCAITLAND, East Lothian

The environs of the village of Pencaitland (six miles south-west of **Haddington**) were described in 1830 as resembling 'fine central England, all cultivated, all luxuriant, all charmingly frilled and flounced with hedge-rows and trees, but without one marked feature – simply an expanse of prettiness' (Fullarton's *Gazetteer*). The village itself is divided into Wester and Easter Pencaitland by the river Tyne, here crossed by a three-arched bridge dating from 1510; the former has the mercat cross (in the form of a sundial and dating from c1695) and the latter the parish church, 'a picturesque pile of various dates and architectural styles' with a side chapel probably dating from the 13th century.

Just south of the village Fountainhall, previously named Penkaet Castle, is a delightful mansion of the late 16th and early 17th century, while to the north Winton House, built c1619 by George, 8th Lord Seton and 3rd Earl of Winton on the site of an older house destroyed by Hertford in 1544, was designed by William Wallace, Master Mason to the King and architect of **Edinburgh**'s **Heriot's Hospital**. Secondary to Seton Palace [see **Seton House**] as the family's residence, it is generally agreed to be one of the finest examples of Renaissance architecture in Scotland, with English-

Winton House near Pencaitland; drawing by R W Billings (RWB)

looking spiral carved chimneys and notable internal plasterwork.

PENICUIK, Midlothian

Like nearby Loanhead and **Lasswade**, Penicuik on the west bank of the river North Esk was renowned for its papermills. The lands of Penicuik along with the house of Newbiggin were acquired by John Clerk in 1646; he was created a baronet in 1679. His son **Sir John Clerk of Penicuik**, Scotland's leading patron of the arts and arbiter of taste in the first half of the 18th century, was the builder of **Mavisbank House** (1723–7), and he in turn was succeeded (1755) by his son James, also an enthusiastic patron of the arts and a competent amateur architect who demolished Newbiggin and designed Penicuik House (1761) to take its place. He also laid out the new planned village of Penicuik (1770). The last papermill closed down in 1975 and Clerk's planned village has long since been submerged in later developments which turned the hamlet into a sizeable town with modern industries including the famous Edinburgh Crystal works. Penicuik House was gutted by fire in 1899 and only the shell remains, the Clerk family finding James Clerk's stable block more than adequate alternative accommodation.

PENNAN, Aberdeenshire

This attractive village squeezed between red sandstone cliffs west of **Fraserburgh** and almost in **Banffshire** was once a smugglers' paradise and then a thriving **fishing** port. To the east Aberdour Bay was where, according to the **Book of Deer**, **St Columba** landed with his disciples Drostan and Fergus. St Drostan's Well commemorates this event and there is a ruined medieval chapel nearby with gravestones dating back to the 16th century. The missionaries were granted by the **mormaer** of Buchan a *cathair* that has been identified with Dundarg, a promontory east of the bay, where there was once a **Pictish** fort. Frequently refortified in medieval times and again in the 16th century, it now boasts a house built only in 1938. West of Pennan, the rocky coastline embraces Troup Head where at Cullykhan archaeologists have traced 2000 years of occupation in another promontory fort, 'a late Bronze Age refuge, an Iron Age citadel and an early Pictish fort' where subsequently were built a medieval castle and an 18th century shore defence.

PENTLAND HILLS, Midlothian/Peeblesshire/Lanarkshire

A broken range of hills stretching some 16 miles in a south-westerly direction from about 3 miles south-west of **Edinburgh** to near **Carnwath** in **Lanarkshire**, the Pentlands afford good pasturage for sheep and healthy recreation for city-dwellers. The highest point is Scald Law (1898ft/579m). Both the **Water of Leith** and North Esk river have their sources here, and reservoirs in the hills store much of Edinburgh's water supply.

PENTLAND RISING, The (1666)

Covenanters' Revolt

So named because it ended in the **Pentland Hills** at **Rullion Green**, the Pentland Rising marked the outbreak of hostilities against the Restoration settlement (including **Charles II**'s re-establishment of episcopacy and of lay patronage over Church appointments). Covenanting ministers who had declined to accept the new order were deprived of their living and replaced by often unpopular 'curates'. But, particularly in the south-west, many congregations remained loyal to the **Covenants** and to their deprived ministers. Their clandestine 'conventicles' were outlawed; to disperse them, to fine adherents and to round up the recalcitrant clergy, troops were billeted on offenders. On 13 November 1666 a scuffle between soldiery and offenders at St John's Town of **Dalry** precipitated reaction. The **Conventiclers**, evidently not unprepared, summoned their forces and entered **Dumfries** where **Sir James Turner**, commander of the troops in the region, was captured. Protesting their loyalty to both King and Covenant, the insurgents then proceeded towards **Edinburgh** where they anticipated general support and a chance to petition the King against prelacy. Reaching **Lanark**, they numbered about 1000 under Colonel James Wallace, but thereafter dissent, indiscipline and heavy rain thinned their ranks. A superior force under **Sir Thomas Dalyell** eventually dispersed them at Rullion Green. Casualties were not especially heavy but exemplary use was made of prisoners and captured fugitives, 36 of whom were executed.

PEPLOE, Samuel John (1871–1935) Painter

With the other Scottish Colourists, **Cadell**, **Fergusson** and **Hunter**, Peploe is considered one of the most significant figures in 20th century Scottish **painting**. Born in **Edinburgh**, he worked for a legal firm before enrolling at the Edinburgh College of Art in 1891, and in 1894, encouraged by the example of the Glasgow Boys, he went to Paris where he attended the Académies Julian and Colarossi. In 1895 he visited Amsterdam where he

Self portrait by Samuel John Peploe (SNPG)

was deeply impressed by the work of Frans Hals, but the fluid brushwork of his early still-lifes demonstrated the importance he attached to modern French art and in particular to the bold lighting effects in the work of Manet. His first exhibition in 1903 established his reputation and the following year he joined Fergusson in France on the first of regular summer visits there. The brilliant light brightened both men's palettes whilst the still-lifes and sensuous figure compositions, influenced by Sargent and Whistler, that Peploe produced in his Edinburgh studio became increasingly impressionistic in their handling. In 1910 he settled in Paris where exposure to the innovations of Matisse and the Fauves encouraged in his work an unprecedented spontaneity and daring use of pure colour. Through Fergusson he met many of the leading avant-garde figures of the day and, in his admiration for Cézanne, his interest developed in the formal and spatial complexities of painting. After his return to Edinburgh in 1912 he turned increasingly to still-life in his quest to paint perfectly balanced and harmonious compositions. From 1920 his summers were spent with Cadell on **Iona** where the intense greens and blues of the landscape and sea stimulated a renewed intuitive response to painting which had been missing in his work since 1910–11. With his fellow Colourists, his admiration for French art and love simply of picture-making was vitally to influence a generation of artists in Scotland after him. Towards the end of his life he taught part-time at the Edinburgh College of Art.

PERIODICALS AND JOURNALS

Scotland's first periodically-produced publication was the *Diurnal Occurrances touching the Dailie Proceedings in Parliament*, reprinted from the London press in 1641. This was short-lived, but by 1750 seven periodicals were regularly appearing and twice as many within another 25 years. By 1900, no fewer than 7319 periodical publications had appeared in Scotland, including those which changed their title and many which were ephemeral.

The first of today's general interest publications to appear was the *Scots Magazine*, originally published by a consortium of booksellers and printers in **Edinburgh** in 1739. Now an attractive high-circulation monthly with wide appeal, it has no direct link with its 1739 predecessor and did not appear between 1826 and 1924. It was taken over by its present publisher, **D C Thomson** of **Dundee**, in 1927.

Scotland's periodical output has reflected the nation's academic status from the latter part of the 18th century onwards. In 1754 the first scientific journal – the *Essays and Observations, Physical and Literary* – was published by an informal learned society in Edinburgh and was succeeded in 1773 by the *Medical and Physical Commentaries* produced by the Edinburgh Philosophical Society. In 1788 the first volume of the *Transactions of the Royal Society of Edinburgh* was published, and continues to appear frequently, the Society being the most prolific publisher of original scientific papers north of Cambridge. Other academic journals produced north of the border include the *Scottish Geographical Magazine*, published by the **Royal Scottish Geographical Society** since 1885, and the *Scottish Medical Journal*, published since 1956 as a combination of the *Glasgow Medical Journal* (begun 1828) and its Edin-

burgh counterpart whose origins went back to 1805. Even encyclopaedias have been published in serial form, particularly in Edinburgh in the late 18th and early 19th centuries, the well-known **Britannica** representing the best example.

In the 19th century Edinburgh became the matrix for two influential magazines, the **Edinburgh Review** and **Blackwood's Magazine**. They represented opposed political viewpoints (the former 'Whig' or Liberal, the latter Conservative), pitting such contributors as Wilberforce, **Macaulay** and **Thomas Carlyle** against **James Hogg**, George Eliot and Thomas de Quincey. The *Edinburgh Review* ceased publication in 1929, *Blackwood's* in 1980.

D C Thomson of Dundee is undoubtedly Scotland's outstanding newspaper and magazine publisher. Its portfolio of periodical titles ranges from *Commando War Stories in Pictures* to *The People's Friend*, while its most famous comic publications include the *Beano* and the *Dandy*, introducing such characters as Dennis the Menace, Desperate Dan and the Bash Street Kids to successive generations of young readers, many of them beyond Scotland's shores. In July 1999 the publication of the 3005th edition of the *Dandy* created a new world record for a children's comic.

The **Glasgow** firm of George Outram published, in addition to the Glasgow *Herald* and *Evening Times*, such diverse periodicals as the *Aberdeen Leopard*, *Climber and Hillwalker*, *Scottish Farmer* and *Scottish Field*. The Edinburgh-based Scottish Academic Press currently produces 12 periodicals, most of them learned, such as the *Scottish Journal of Geology*.

PERTH, Earldom and Dukedom

As chiefs of Clan Drummond the Earls of Perth are styled in Gaelic *An Drumanach Mor* (The Great Man of **Drymen**). They appear to be of noble Celtic origin, though it is not until 1225 that charters preserve the name of Malcolm Beg, their earliest historical ancestor, as Seneschal of the **Lennox**. His son Malcolm of Drymen was twice captured by the English during the **Wars of Independence**, and his grandson fought at **Bannockburn**. In about 1345 the Drummond Chief John married the heiress of **Stobhall**. The title Lord Drummond was bestowed in 1488, and the 4th Baron was created Earl of Perth in 1605. The 4th Earl became a Catholic convert and joined **James VII** in exile, where he was consoled by a dukedom. His family took part in the **Jacobite** uprisings of 1715 and 1745 (the 2nd Duke commanded the cavalry at **Sheriffmuir** and the 3rd a wing of the Jacobite army at **Culloden**), but when the 6th Duke of Perth died in 1760 his title became extinct. The succession to the earldom was the subject of rival claims within the Drummond family and, after the reversal of attainders, became vested in 1853 in the ancestor of the present (17th) Earl of Perth, a Catholic whose family chapel enjoys the rare distinction that it was never desecrated.

PERTH, Five Articles of (1618)

After succeeding to the English throne **James VI** made several attempts to unite his kingdom by standardising English and Scottish practice. In ecclesiastical affairs this meant restoring authority and funding to the bishops and introducing such liturgical reform as would bring the Scottish Church into line with the Anglican. Meeting resistance to the latter from radical **Presbyterians**, the King sought the approval of the **General Assembly** at **St Andrews** in 1617. The Assembly in effect rejected his proposals; but the King responded with threats which he made good at a carefully packed assembly in **Perth** in 1618 which approved five articles restoring (1) the Christian calendar, the sacraments of (2) private communion, (3) baptism and (4) confirmation, and (5) the custom of kneeling to receive communion. The last provoked the bitterest opposition which became widespread even amongst the loyal laity and threatened James's whole ecclesiastical settlement. In practice it and the other articles were largely ignored but not forgotten. **Charles I** inherited Scottish subjects highly suspicious of royal interference in liturgical matters and the next General Assembly, when it finally met in 1638 in **Glasgow**, would sweep out the Five Articles along with the bishops.

PERTH, Perthshire

A **royal burgh** since at least the 13th century, a royal residence in medieval times, and the county town of **Perthshire**, Perth is also known as 'The Fair City' and the 'Ancient Capital of Scotland'. Its fairness is not in dispute. On the level west bank of the **Tay** just above the Firth and between the leafy parks of the **North and South Inches**, its quiet terraces and numerous church towers retain their scale and grace unruffled by intrusive development. From **Kinnoull Hill** or Moncrieff (now crossed by the M90 from the south) the overview described by Tennant as 'the glory of Scotland' is still arresting. Yet, though well endowed with religious establishments, Perth was never an episcopal see in its own right, making its claim to city status doubtful. And with neither the architecture nor the pedigree of **Stirling**, any talk of an ancient capital rests heavily on

associations and endowments incidental to its proximity to **Scone**.

The name probably derives from the site, Aber-tha (the mouth of the Tay), becoming the Bertha of the **Romans** and the Perth of today. References to 'St John's Town at Perth' or 'at the mouth of the Tay' bear this out, **St John's** being the great church of St John the Baptist, still the most important historical and architectural relic. St John's toun, anglicised to St Johnstone, remained an alternative designation and is still that used by Perth's premier **football** club.

The Roman fort of Bertha stood two miles to the north where the Almond joins the Tay. That the medieval town grew with a grid pattern of streets seems to have been a response to the rectangular shape of what was then a promontory between the North and South Inches (islands) rather than evidence of further Roman planning. As with most estuarial settlements the numerous priorities – a safe river crossing by ford, ferry or bridge, a sheltered and navigable basin, and a salubrious and defensible building site – did not precisely coincide. Additionally Perth was (and, hosting the country's premier bull sales, still is) an extremely important agricultural centre which never became quite as dependent on trade, manufacture and industry as, say, **Dundee** or **Aberdeen**. To the consequent indifference and comparative immunity to the volatile fortunes of **fishing**, textiles and **engineering**, Perth may owe its composure and modest air of prosperity.

The earliest records date from the 12th century and reveal a town of considerable ecclesiastical, commercial and administrative importance. Royal favour is indicated by the profusion of monastic privileges and establishments, Blackfriars, Greyfriars, Whitefriars and Carthusians all having their separate houses within the walled

Perth from Kirkton Hill c1880 (GWWA)

city. Parliaments and Church councils occasionally convened here. In 1311 **Robert I** captured the town and in 1437 **James I** was assassinated at Blackfriars, his favourite residence. In between took place the gladiatorial **Battle of the Clans** (1396) on the North Inch, **Robert III** presiding.

The first timber bridge across the Tay is sometimes credited to the Romans. If true, it was probably short-lived. A stone bridge was built in 1329 but thrice partially washed away in the 16th century. Rebuilt with 10 arches in 1616 and described by **James VI** as 'a most precious jewel of our kingdom', it lasted just five years. For the next century and a half, until Smeaton's still-surviving bridge was erected, all traffic was by ferry. The town itself, low-lying on its alluvial promontory, was subject to periodic inundations and probably sustained more damage from these than from its numerous sieges.

No less destructive was the great wave of iconoclasm which followed **John Knox**'s fiery sermon of 11 May 1559. Delivered in St John's, it launched the **Reformation** and nowhere with more ferocity than in the Fair City itself. Ecclesiastical treasures were destroyed or dissipated, churches defaced, funds alienated. But to blame Knox, or even the 'rascall multitude' whom he condemned, for the poverty of Perth's surviving architecture, would be wrong. As elsewhere the real culprits were post-Reformation indifference and 19th century development.

During James VI's reign Perth was reported as suffering from the loss of royal patronage following the **Gowrie Conspiracy** (1600) and then James's accession to the English throne. **Montrose** occupied the town in 1644, **Charles II** enjoyed the **Covenanters'** cold hospitality during his brief Scottish sojourn of 1651, and Cromwell appropriated much of the masonry from Greyfriars to build his citadel on the South Inch. Yet in 1689, when **Graham of Claverhouse** had just seized the city, Thomas Morer reckoned Perth still 'the second city of Scotland' with a booming **linen** trade worth over £40,000 pa. Occupation by the **Jacobites** in 1715 (and again in 1745) proved no more disastrous, according to Defoe. He reckoned the town actually benefited from the military operations and put the value of its linen trade at more than that of the rest of Scotland combined.

Linen and then **cotton** continued as the manufacturing mainstay of both the town and its hinterland into the 19th century. But the port (although still in use) lost out to places like **Newburgh** in **Fife** and Dundee, which could accommodate ships of greater draught. Ancillary industries such as shoemaking, dyeing and haberdashery also achieved prominence. Pullars of Perth, now best known for its dry-cleaning, was said to be the largest dye works in the world at the turn of the century with a labour force of 1700. The Tay salmon fisheries shipped fish direct to London and the river also yielded freshwater pearls, though these were very much more rare.

Thanks to the natural green belt of the river and the two Inches, modern development adjoins the old town only to the north and west, with Kinnoull and Bridgend across the river as villa retreats. Among the principal employers are a large insurance company and several major **whisky** distilleries which have their offices, though not their distilleries, in the town.

Balhousie Castle

West of the **North Inch**, Balhousie Castle dates from the 15th century and became the home of the Earls of **Kinnoull**. Of this structure no externals remain although within the rebuilt and baronialised castle are earlier features. The adjacent area served as barracks and parade ground of the **Black Watch**, a regiment with a **Perthshire** pedigree [see **Aberfeldy**], and the castle now houses a Black Watch museum. There is also a memorial garden to Field Marshal Earl Waverley, Colonel of the Regiment and last-but-one Viceroy of India.

Branklyn Garden

Acquired by the **National Trust for Scotland** in 1967 and described by it as 'the finest two acres of private garden in the country', Branklyn was the creation of John and Dorothy Renton who built a house on **Kinnoull Hill** in 1922 and then laid out their garden of modest dimensions but exceptional and exotic interest. Large and small-leaved rhododenrons, magnolias and conifers are well represented but its glory lies in the detail of alpines, primulas and, above all, mecanopsis.

Fair Maid's House

'Out of immaterial legend a house, in Curfew Row, has been conjured for **Sir Walter Scott**'s *Fair Maid Of Perth*' (M Mclaren). It stands roughly where once stood the medieval timbered castle of Perth and, as the old Glover's Hall, lent itself to accommodating Simon Glover, the father of Scott's Fair Maid. Heavily restored and now a gallery and craft shop, its doubtful authenticity serves to emphasise Perth's paucity of pre-18th century architecture.

Kinnoull Hill

Across the **Tay** from Perth the ground rises to Kinnoull Hill (729ft/222m), which forms the western extremity of the **Sidlaws**. Immediately across the **Perth Bridge**, Bridgend was where Ruskin stayed as a boy. The old church possesses an elaborate memorial to George Hay of **Megginch**, Chancellor of Scotland and 1st Earl of Kinnoull, one of whose descendants was responsible for the twin castellate follies, said to have been suggested by a trip up the Rhine, which command the precipitous heights of Kinnoull and adjacent Binns Hill as they overlook the Tay. Below Binns, Kinfauns Castle, now a hotel, was built for Lord Gray in 1822 but occupies the site of a much earlier house and of lands originally granted by **Robert I** to a supportive French pirate known as The Red Rover. Although ringed with villas to the west and north, the top of Kinnoull has been preserved as a public park with rewarding views over the city and the Firth.

North and South Inches

Originally islands in the **Tay** flanking the promontory on which the city grew, the Inches still impart to central Perth a green and pleasing aspect plus ready recreational space. The larger North Inch was the setting for the **Battle of the Clans** (1396), witnessed by **Robert III** from Blackfriars, a palace as much as a monastery which stood where now runs Charlotte Street. **James I** took up residence in it and was murdered there by **Sir Robert Graham** in spite of the attempt by **Katherine ('Barlass') Douglas** to hold the door by using her arm as the bolt. The North Inch continues as a field of mortal combat with **football** and **cricket** pitches, **golf course** and large indoor sports centre. The South Inch, reserved for more frivolous sports like witch-burning, archery, putting and children's play areas, was once the site of Cromwell's citadel. No trace remains. It is overlooked by the Georgian houses of Marshall Place (**Sir Robert Reid**, 1801), where stands St Leonard's in the Fields (1884) with a crown steeple and, next the river, the **Old Waterworks**.

Old Waterworks (or Roundhouse)

Fine architecture is not always associated with public utilities and certainly a waterworks is not an obvious candidate for treatment as a neo-classical rotunda complete with triumphal column. Such was the case in Perth though; and proud as the Perthensians were of their handsome new pumping station beside the **South Inch**, opinion reckoned its internal arrangements were even more remarkable than its outward appearance. It was built in 1832 to designs by Dr Adam Anderson, rector of Perth Academy and later Professor of Natural Philosophy at **St Andrews**, who was also responsible for the mechanics and plumbing. These comprised a suction pipe embedded in gravel below the water level on Moncrieff island in the **Tay**, a settlement tank in the basement of the rotunda, and a great reservoir above it within the domed and balustraded second storey which, though adorned with much architectural detail and painted to match the stone below, is in fact of cast iron. Power was provided by a steam pump behind the building with the triumphal column, complete with urn, serving as its smokestack. Hence the Latin motto above the door which translates as 'Water I draw by fire and water'. The pumping station was in operation until 1965 but was then stripped and has latterly served as a Tourist Information Centre.

Perth (Old) Bridge

Rising by over 15ft (4.6m) when in spate, the **Tay** at Perth proved more than a match for the low-slung bridges which were periodically thrown across it. When that built in the early 17th century was deemed beyond repair after just five years, no attempt to replace it was made till 1766. The new bridge, of nine arches and 840 feet between the **North Inch** and **Kinnoull**, was designed by John Smeaton, the English architect of the **Deveron** bridge at **Banff** and of the Eddystone Lighthouse. It was completed in 1771, widened in 1869, and is still in use today though now supplemented by the Queen's Bridge (1960) downstream. Smeaton ensured that the height of his arches would allow for the passage of spate water and took elaborate precautions to protect the piers. **Hydro-electric** works upstream in the Tummel basin have since reduced the flood threat. This bridge also had the distinction of being the only Tay bridge to carry trams, horse-drawn from 1859 but electric between 1905–29 when the service ceased.

St John's Church

Often likened to a cathedral, St John's Kirk has been the pride and focus of Perth for nearly 900 years. From it derives the city's alternative name of St John's Toun (St Johnstone) and in it **John Knox** preached the sermon (1559) which began the **Reformation** in Scotland. It is also the city's oldest surviving building. The original dedication was as 'The Kirk of the Holy Cross of St John the Baptist' and the first documentary reference is from 1126 when its revenues were granted to the abbey of **Dunfermline**. **Robert I** ordered its restoration, Edward III of England is supposed to have murdered his brother here, and **James I** to have been buried here as also was the heart of **Alexander III**. Later **Montrose** used it as a prison and Cromwell as a court; **Charles I** and II both worshipped here as did **Prince Charles Edward Stewart**.

The building as it survives is basically 15th century, cruciform, with a tall central tower, battlemented and with a short spire. Parts of the structure may be older; all has been much restored. Rid of its 40 altars by Knox's zealots, in 1598 it was divided into two parish kirks and in 1773 into three, like **Glasgow Cathedral** and **Aberdeen**'s **St Nicholas**. Restoration to a single church was undertaken in the 1920s when the north transept was converted into a war memorial. The work was supervised by **Sir Robert Lorimer**, the stained glass of the eastern window being by Douglas Strachan.

The Salutation Hotel

One of several hotels claimed as the oldest in Scotland, the Salutation has the added distinction of having saluted as guests both **Prince Charles Edward Stewart**, who stayed in room 20, and the Beatles, who stopped for tea. In between it evidently fell on hard times for Victorian guidebooks rate it merely as 'commercial', the lowest grading. A stone in the courtyard bears the motto and arms of the **Earl of Moray** and is dated 1619. The present building is interesting but subsequent. No doubt here once stood one of the many townhouses of the aristocracy, all now vanished.

PERTH, Treaty of (1266)

After the death of Norway's King Haakon IV in **Orkney** in 1263, and **Alexander III**'s subsequent success in taking control of all the Western Islands, Haakon's son Magnus IV was forced to acknowledge that the great **Viking** era in the western isles was over. In the Treaty eventually signed at **Perth** on 2 July 1266 he handed over the **Hebrides** and Man to Scotland in return for a payment of 4000 merks in annual instalments and 100 merks a year 'in perpetuity'.

PERTHSHIRE

Before the **local government** reorganisation of 1975, Perthshire was one of Scotland's biggest counties, comprising an area of 1,586,577 acres (642,563ha). It lay almost exactly in the centre of Scotland, forming the south-east corner of the Highlands, with **Angus** to the east, **Kinross** and **Fife** to the south-east, **Argyll** to the west, and **Inverness-shire** and **Aberdeenshire** to the north-west and north. It included the Grampians in its highland area, with the **Ochil** and **Sidlaw Hills** to its south-east, but with the fertile **Carse of Gowrie** stretching eastwards from the county town of **Perth**. Agriculture was a major occupation, including fruit-growing, but **forestry**, **whisky** distilling and **tourism** were also important.

Perth was the only large burgh, the small burghs comprising **Aberfeldy, Abernethy, Alyth, Auchterarder, Blairgowrie** & Rattray, **Callander, Coupar Angus, Crieff, Doune, Dunblane** and **Pitlochry**. In 1929 Perthshire was joined by **Kinross-shire** for administrative purposes. Under the 1975 local government reorganisation, the majority of Perthshire was absorbed into Perth & Kinross District of Tayside Region, along with one parish from Angus, while the Longforgan area passed to Dundee District within Tayside. Callander, Doune, Dunblane and part of the western area of the county were allocated to Stirling District in Central Region, and Muckhart to Clackmannan District in Central Region. With the abolition of the Regions in 1995, Perth & Kinross District became the autonomous Perthshire & Kinross Council Area.

PETERCULTER, Aberdeen

Peterculter grew on the strength of the papermill established in 1751 on the Culter (pron. Cooter) burn. The 'Peter' derives from the church of St Peter (1779 but preceded by another of the same name) which complements that of Maryculter on the other (south) side of the **Dee**. The old chapel of St Mary was built by the Knights Templar in the 13th century on lands granted by **William the Lion** in 1187. Almost nothing survives, but gravestones and some fine effigies have been removed to the **Church of St Nicholas** in **Aberdeen**. A new St Mary's Chapel (1901) is part of nearby Blairs College, a Roman Catholic seminary. Peterculter is now too accessible to Aberdeen to be other than a desirable suburb. Its only curiosity is a garish statue, said to have been a ship's figurehead but much replaced, of **Rob Roy MacGregor**. It stands above the Leuchar Burn which, as with the river in **Glen Lyon**, he is said to have leapt. The feat is hardly less remarkable than the outlaw's presence here, so far from his **Breadalbane** haunts.

PETERHEAD, Aberdeenshire

Largest town in **Buchan** and second largest in **Aberdeenshire**, Peterhead occupies an exposed promontory ending in what was once an island and is now the most easterly point on the Scottish mainland. Like **Fraserburgh** to the north, Peterhead depends on the sea's bounty; and just as the former owes its existence to the Frasers of Philorth so the latter was the pride and product of the Keiths of Inverugie. In the mid-16th century Robert Keith, Abbot of **Deer**, exchanged some lands for those of Altrie including Keith Insch where in 1593 his nephew, the **5th Earl Marischal**, founded the village of Peter-ugie (later Peterhead). The Keiths eventually forfeited their foundation after supporting the **Jacobite** cause in 1715 (**James Francis Edward**, 'The Old Pretender', landed at Peterhead on 22 December 1715, by which time his cause was already lost). **James Keith** and his brother, the 10th Earl Marischal, sought service with Frederick the Great of Prussia, the former becoming a Field Marshal commemorated by a statue in Potsdam of which a replica, donated by Wilhelm I, was erected in Peterhead 1868. It stands in front of the

Town House, built (1788) by John Baxter, which has a tall steeple, four-faced clock and bell. The parish kirk (1804) in Maiden Street also has a steeple.

The Keiths resumed their Inverugie estates after reinstatement in 1759. Briefly the town's keen breezes, bracing waters and Jacobite associations recommended it as a kill-or-cure health resort for the nobility. But the late 18th century also brought an expansion of its harbour facilities as local crews, renowned for their seamanship, exploited the whale and seal fisheries. By 1820 it was Britain's principal whaling port and by the end of the century it also had Scotland's third largest **herring** fleet. A new Harbour of Refuge was developed at the turn of the century. White fish followed the herring boom and when even cod became scarce, North Sea **oil and gas** obligingly filled the vacuum. Peterhead now services the needs of off-shore rigs and pipelines; St Fergus (5 miles north) is the gas terminal for the Frigg Field and Cruden Bay (8 miles south) the oil terminal for the Forties Field.

Immediately north-west of the town, beside the Ugie, lie the scant remains of Inverugie and Ravenscraig, castles of the Keiths and Cheynes respectively. To the south on a brae facing the harbour are a tall tower erected to commemorate the repeal of the Corn Laws, and the grim Victorian terraces of Peterhead Prison. If prisons commemorated their inmates, there should be a plaque to record the sufferings of **John Maclean**, who was held here during World War I.

PHILIPHAUGH, Battle of (1645)

After their crowning victory at **Kilsyth**, **Montrose**'s forces dispersed, their leader apparently unassailable in Scotland. **Alasdair MacDonald** opened a campaign in **Kintyre**; the **Gordons** and assorted Highlanders headed home. Montrose marched east, aiming to raise the Borders for **Charles I**. But as **David Leslie** crossed into Scotland at the head of his **Covenanting** veterans, the Border families prevaricated, then (probably) betrayed Montrose. On 13 September at Philiphaugh near **Selkirk** his 700 Irish infantry were finally surprised and routed. Their commander arrived when the battle was already lost. It is said that he nevertheless decided to enter the fray – a claim which in the case of Montrose may be believed – but was dissuaded by his companions. Instead he fled north, back to the Highlands. Meanwhile Leslie had granted quarter to his prisoners and then, under pressure from his following of righteous clerics, authorised their slaughter. It took place at **Newark Castle**. Years later it was with the Lordship of Newark that David Leslie was rewarded.

PHILIPSON, Sir Robin (1916–92) Painter

'One of the leading painters of the generation following that of **Gillies**' (Gage, 1977), Philipson was born in Broughton-in-Furness and schooled in **Dumfries** and **Edinburgh** College of Art (1936–40). He served in India and Burma in World War II and joined the Edinburgh College staff in 1947, being Head of the School of Painting (1960–82); a President of the **Royal Scottish Academy**, he was knighted in 1976. One of the Edinburgh circle of William Gillies and **John Maxwell**, his early work owes much to his almost chance discovery of the Austrian Expressionist Oskar Kokoschka; best seen

The Battle of Philiphaugh, from an engraving (SW)

in his large **Edinburgh Castle** set-piece, *The View from My Studio Window* (1954). From 1956, however, he forged his own technically brilliant style, notably in the *Fighting Cock* series exhibited in 1958.

PHILOSOPHY AND PSYCHOLOGY

Metaphysical Scotland
'The Scottish Philosophy' is a term applied in particular to an approach in general derived from **Thomas Reid**, **Francis Hutcheson**, **Adam Smith** and others. But this was only one, albeit notable, phase in a continuity that in some respects reaches back to **Duns Scotus**, the greatest of many Scots whose contribution to medieval scholasticism was made in mainland Europe. In Scotland itself, Gaelic **bards** aside (although their systematic of virtues amounts to a considered ethical system), Scots philosophy begins with the foundation of the first university at **St Andrews** in 1411. Here the conjunction of Laurence of Lindores, Lokert, Ireland and **John Mair** constituted an early 'Scottish Philosophy'. (More complex relationships between their work and that of Reid's generation are argued in Alexander Broadie's *The Scottish Tradition of Philosophy*, 1990.) If somewhat dated in Continental terms, the St Andrews philosophers were hardly indicative of unmitigated backwardness. The new Renaissance study of Greek, and the science and learning of the 17th century were truly revelational; but such subjects were hardly ready for systematisation. They were liable to be grouped together under a false model taken from one of the new studies, like mathematics; or, in broader terms, literary style was liable to be taken

for substance. It is arguable that when Scots philosophy has re-emerged, whether with Hutcheson, Sir William Hamilton or Edward Caird, it is the residual perspective in Scottish university teaching that has mattered. Philosophy in the Middle Ages was the handmaid of theology and law. Hence the study and development of formal argumentation was crucial to serious disputation. Aristotle, studied in the original, turned out not to be the proto-Christian he had been taken for; yet the discipline of orderly thought still profited from him.

An unsound mathematical-deductive approach led the Englishman Hobbes (1588–1679) to argue that all human conduct derives from selfishness. This view was opposed by sundry of his countrymen, including Shaftesbury, but it was the Scots-trained Hutcheson who had the grounding to bring in the evidence systematically. Hutcheson's teacher, Gershom Carmichael (1672–1729), was the first Professor of Moral Philosophy at **Glasgow University**. He had begun as a 'regent' whose job it was to teach most of the curriculum. But the innovation of professorships allowed concentration on one subject and so the opportunity for more than routine teaching. The professor had time for study, writing and the improvement of teaching, which last Hutcheson took to with a will, lecturing in English and not, as hitherto, in Latin. He stands out as a model periodically returned to, the Scots philosophy professor. But earlier Scots had also been famed as teachers, Mair, and also Gilbert Jack (d.1628) at Leyden, among several.

Hutcheson preached sound doctrine which was not lacking in argument. This was a major advance on **James Beattie**'s 1770 *Essays on the Nature and Immutability of Truth*, written against a misunderstood **David Hume**. (But then Beattie, compared to his **Aberdeen** colleagues Reid and **Turnbull**, was as unusual in his shallowness as in the fame it won him.) Like Reid, Hutcheson was no moral agnostic and urged the truth of his beliefs with learned critical argument designed to inspire. The same lofty ideal is found in his much later successor, Edward Caird (1835–1907). With scant regard for the Hutchesonian ideas taught him as an undergraduate, Caird still began his professorship with praise of the high Hutchesonian calling; and this was continued by Caird's pupil-successor Henry Jones (d.1921). Caird and Jones sent philosophy professors in startling numbers as far afield as New Zealand, Australia and USA not to mention Liverpool and Birmingham.

A like idea is exemplified by George Jardine (1774–1827), Professor of Logic and Rhetoric at Glasgow, who in his *Outlines of a Philosophical Education* (2nd edn 1825) devised a study programme of argument and of writing fitted to the early teenage students of his day. Glasgow's first English Literature professor, John Nichol, would have revived Jardine's work for an era when students arrived at university somewhat older had he not been denied the philosophy professorship because of his views on the kirk. Logic teaching needs to be more than routine. Amid many later changes, **John Anderson** in Australia was notable in carrying on Jardine's general ideal, and also in continuing to oppose what Scots philosophers from the 1870s saw as a blind enthusiasm for mathematical forms. The Scots Logic course, sound in theory, was also for those without special philosophical ambitions who nonetheless required to sort substance from style.

In the 19th century, a great age of Scottish scholarship, Sir William Hamilton of **Edinburgh** (1788–1856) was an inspiration. Notable too for essays on the deplorable state of Oxford University published in the *Edinburgh Review* (1831), Hamilton is a 'hollow colossus' to those judging his sometime fame against his published works. Not without pure philosophic insights, he was also concerned to alter perspectives; he advocated wider and deeper learning; writing books as monuments to himself was irrelevant. A great reviver, his day was lucky to have him. His students went far, some preferring (as philosopher) his great friend **J F Ferrier**.

Hamilton's critique of Oxford hints at that explicit attention to questions of change and decay in education which was philosophers' work. Modern philosophy has grown up with all the other special disciplines, some of which broke from it. Theology, social and political studies, psychology, economics, and the study of literature (and in a language not English) were all in *potentia* part of the course in Hutcheson's day; and the philosopher also studied some physical science (Natural Philosophy). Separate studies give information only by first imposing artificial divisions between aspects of knowledge. The Scottish generalist education is recognition of that, and claims as evidences of cross-disciplinary fertilisation **Clerk Maxwell** in Physics (seeing unfounded moral assumptions in the theories of scientists he outstripped) and Jardine's pupil **McLeod Campbell** in Theology (the supposed 'Calvinism' of a black kirk is based on notions Calvin actually refutes). The works of Plato were sorted out with benefit of the same background by Lewis Campbell, biographer of Clerk Max-

well and a great Greek scholar who pays tribute to Hamilton in *The Nationalisation of the Old English Universities* (1902). Scottish philosophers and English radicals together fought for educational reform. In the 20th century Campbell's pupil John Burnet, as well as **A D Lindsay**, wrote against blinkered specialisation and the decay of the university ideal avowed by Hamilton.

After Ferrier, German philosophy established an important bridgehead epitomised by *The Secret of Hegel* (1865) by James Hutchison Stirling, an admirer of **Thomas Carlyle**. R W Emerson attempted to persuade Stirling to move to America and to help advocate German philosophy in a land dominated by 'The Scottish Philosophy'. Edward Caird, who was another Carlyle devotee, along with his contemporaries William Wallace (1844–97) and D G Ritchie (1855–1903), also had an interest in German philosophy which was bound up with liberal, even adoctrinal, Christianity and the pursuit of radical social reform without loss of soul. Practical contact counted for much; the so-called Idealists of Caird's circle and school did not merely pioneer the thinking behind subsequent state interference and social provision but also campaigned for causes such as the extension of education and women's rights. Their theory of citizenship has today been lost to political debate, a real impoverishment. In **R B Haldane** the movement had the first Labour Lord Chancellor.

George Croom Robertson (1842–92), the early recipient of a Ferguson scholarship in the 1860s, studied widely in Europe and set an agenda for the exploration of British philosophical continuity. First editor of the British philosophy journal MIND from 1876, he worked variously to raise British philosophy to a Continental level, and he also considerably advanced psychological study. He, like Robert Adamson and Edward Caird, pioneered work on the philosophy of Kant. In the 20th century Norman Kemp Smith and H J Paton made Scotland the leading world centre of Kantian studies. Adamson was one pioneer of a school called 'critical realism', grounded in his study of the whole huge range of European philosophy. He relates to German contemporaries, as also to **J F Ferrier**, in considering how knowing comes about and how the mind (unconsciously) organises knowledge. His view of the relation of mind to world is important to questions of later psychological theory, as well as to the basis of morality and the tests we have of truth in argument.

Adamson's pupil Norman Kemp Smith (1872–1958) advanced a view which might sum up the medieval legacy. Humanity is capable of entrenchment in the past, also of enthralment by novelty. Confronting modern physiological psychology with Calvin's doctrine of man, he inspired John Anderson while seeing that the really necessary innovation was to be made in the way his teacher John Burnet (1859–1928) had enabled an earlier generation of philosophers to take aboard new scientific material. He did not follow Burnet into *Early Greek Philosophy*, but wrote *The Philosophy of David Hume* (1941) as a culmination of the scholarly movement of his Victorian predecessors. This established the historical context of Hume's writings. Thus the immense difficulties of the greatest Scots philosopher's work, his personal idiosyncrasy, his historically remote formulation and contemporary reference, were overcome. The

Philosophy and Psychology continued

resulting critical account of Hume's philosophy is no less modern a contribution to thought than any other book of the age. If our life is very much an affair of determining mechanisms we are also 'wiser than we know'. Kemp Smith was, among other things, also a great teacher of the study of argument.

To date the last Hutchesonian stylist who also wrote books, John Macmurray (1892–1976) was Professor of Moral Philosophy at **Edinburgh University** until 1958. Delivered magnificently to a large class (colleagues sat in, too), his lectures have been echoed in many books, several written as public lectures and broadcasts. His first book, *Freedom in the Modern World* (1932) was a series of BBC radio talks from the time of another Jones pupil, **John Reith**. Macmurray opposes agnosticism in morals, discusses intentionality or motivation, contrasts cultural traditions and urges a scientific spirit and the rationality of religion – all themes of the 18th, and notably the late 19th, centuries, when the Gifford lectures at the Scottish universities were endowed (1887). Gifford lecturers have included William James, Karl Barth, George Steiner, Schweitzer, Gabriel Marcel and John Macmurray (*The Self as Agent*/*Persons in Relation* 1953–4). Although Macmurray's books are almost all long out of print, they argue for the centrality of Scots philosophy, not its immortality. However, there is now an 'International John F Macmurray Society' in North America.

Psychology

Psychology was part of the philosophy curriculum even before the 1920s, and is obvious in any philosophical approach which takes seriously the formation of beliefs. Thus especially in Thomas Reid's 'Philosophy of Common Sense' the operation of unconscious processes is not the formation of delusions but cognition of reality. Reid's fellow Aberdonian **Alexander Bain** (1818–1903) was a disciple of **James Mill** and held that our view of things is formed by mechanical neural processes which connect separate ideas (whereas mainstream Scots insisted that nurture and experience focus within an initially undifferentiated field). Bain sponsored the journal MIND, which early published G F Stout (1860–1944), a County Durham man who was Philosophy Professor at St Andrews and immensely influential. James Drever of Edinburgh was a lesser figure of note, who dubbed his pupil Kenneth Craik (1910–45) 'a genius'. Craik, like other psychologists, learned from Kemp Smith. His work on mechanical intelligence was applied in World War II RAF bomber guidance systems. Ian D Suttie (1889–1935) was more a psycho-analyst whose *The Origins of Love and Hate* (1935) rejects a 'taboo on tenderness', thus revising Freud; likewise W R D Fairbairn (1889–1962), whose first studies in philosophy at Edinburgh taught him that human conduct cannot all derive from one pleasure-seeking impulse. Late in life Fairbairn achieved international fame because the core notion of Scottish philosophy exposed a deficiency in Freudian teaching (*Psychoanalytic Studies of the Personality*, 1951). The now perhaps bankrupt 'revolution in philosophy' which dominated British work after 1945 (Russell, Ayer, Ryle), and closed off the Scots continuity, may be said both to have founded itself on and to have foundered on psychological assumptions long rooted in Scotland.

See: 'Philosophy in the Scottish Universities', John Veitch, MIND 1877; *The Scottish Tradition of Philosophy*, A Broadie, 1990; *Scottish Philosophy*, James M'Cosh, 1875, *Scottish Philosophy*, A Seth, 1885; *Studies in the Philosophy of the Scottish Enlightenment*, ed M A Stewart, 1990; *Scottish Philosophy in its National Development*, Henry Laurie, 1902; *A History of European Thought in the Nineteenth Century*, III-IV, J T Merz, 1912; *A Hundred Years of British Philosophy*, Rudolph Metz, 1938; *The Democratic Intellect*, 1961 and *The Crisis of the Democratic Intellect*, 1986, G E Davie; *A Hundred Years of Philosophy*, J Passmore, 1966; *The Intellectual Development of Scotland*, Hector MacPherson, 1911; *Lord Gifford and His Lectures*, Stanley L Jaki, 1986; *Philosophy, Politics and Citizenship*, A Vincent and R Plant, 1984; *A School of Thinking*, R R Calder 1991. On thinkers current between 1876–1920, essays and writings of that period are often very readable, and of generally startling quality.

PICTS

As a defined group of people, the Picts enter history in 297 AD, when a **Roman** writer named Eumenius referred to the inhabitants of Northern Britain collectively as *Picti*. This date is purely arbitrary; it just happens to mark the oldest surviving use of the word, which may have been coined some time earlier, and anyway the Picts did not 'arrive' – in a sense they had always been there, for they were the descendants of the first people to inhabit what eventually became Scotland. Their distant origins lay in Celtic central Europe, and their ancestors, having migrated to new territory released from the grip of the ice-sheets, developed during the Bronze and Iron Ages through a tribal system. A dozen such units amalgamated into the major groupings of the **Caledonii** and the Maeatae, eventually becoming the nation-state we know as Pictland. The Picts may therefore be seen as the true aboriginals of the country now called Scotland.

One of the great attractions of the Picts, and equally a source of great frustration, is that they are surrounded by so many unanswered (and in some cases unanswer-

Silver plaques with Pictish symbols found at Norrie's Law, Fife (© the Trustees of the National Museums of Scotland 1994)

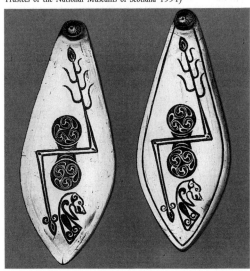

able) questions. Even their real name is a mystery, for we do not know what they called themselves (the name Picti, 'the Painted Ones', may be no more than a nickname employed by Roman garrisons on the frontiers of Empire). The system of symbols which they employed to proclaim a series of stereotyped messages provides one of the great enigmas of early historical studies. They have left no written records apart from very late copies of king-lists in Latin, yet it is known that the Picts possessed the art of writing. The nature of their material culture is almost unknown to us, for the archaeological record is thin, with the exception of some sites in the Northern Isles which must not be regarded as typical. They built their forts in easily defended locations – craggy eminences and promontories – often on the sites of earlier Bronze or Iron Age **duns** so that it is not easy to separate Pictish material from that belonging to earlier and/or later periods.

The physical extent of Pictland, while perhaps not possible to delineate precisely on a map, may be guessed at with reasonable accuracy because of two principal factors. One is the distribution of **standing stones** bearing Pictish symbols; the other is the distribution of place-names beginning with the element 'Pit' (derived from *pett*, 'a parcel of land') which, although a little more constricted on the northern and western periphery, covers much the same area. From this and other evidence, we may deduce that the land of the Picts covered the whole of the northern half of Scotland, including the Northern Isles and the Outer and northern Inner **Hebrides**, extending down the eastern side as far as, or perhaps a little way south of, the Firth of Forth.

The domestic culture of the Picts most probably centred on timber. As place-name evidence suggests, the landscape would have been heavily wooded (apart from the far north); their sculptured stones illustrate items of wooden furniture, such as chairs and benches, and presumably they used smaller wooden items too, though none of these is known to have survived. Surprisingly few metal objects have been recovered, the most important being spectacular items of personal adornment made of gold or silver, notably those from the hoards found at Norrie's Law (near **Largo, Fife**), Gaulcross (near Fordyce, **Banffshire**) and St Ninian's Isle (near Dunrossness, **Shetland**). Other Pictish artefacts are rare; a few bone or antler combs, iron knives with bone handles, and painted pebbles, most coming from the far north. Considering their supposed warlike tendencies, it is disappointing that we have no Pictish weapons, and again we must turn to stone art to see their swords, shields, spears and cross-bows.

Indeed it is the standing stones of the Picts, which they embellished with their unique symbols and other designs, that constitute their principal legacy in material terms. The majority of these stones belong to one of two groups: Class I being rough boulders bearing incised designs consisting of symbols only, cut on the most suitable flattish surface, for example those from Dunnichen (**Angus**), Easterton of Roseisle (**Moray**) and St Peter's (**South Ronaldsay, Orkney**); and Class II being dressed rectangular slabs bearing relief sculpture, consisting of the Christian cross and narrative scenes in addition to symbols, for example those from Eassie (Angus), Chapel of Garioch (**Aberdeenshire**) and

Hilton of Cadboll (**Ross & Cromarty**). Many stones, however, fall somewhere between these two groups. (An additional classification distinguishes as Class III stones those with only Christian images on both sides.) Dozens of these stones still stand as field monuments, one of the best groups being at **Aberlemno** (Angus); many others may be seen in museums, both local and national, and there are fine collections at Rosemarkie (**Ross & Cromarty**), **Meigle** and **St Vigeans**.

There are numerous aspects to the fascination which these stones engender – the rugged simplicity yet perfect harmony of early examples contrasted with the subtle complexity and sophistication of later productions, vehicles both for displaying the talent of craftsmen and for communicating a presumably important variety of pictorial messages, some representational, some imagist, some symbolic. It is their symbols for which the Picts are famous above all else, and theories abound as to the meaning and purpose of symbol stones: memorials (though not necessarily grave-markers) of persons of high status; territorial notice-boards proclaiming the ownership of land or land-rites; records of marriage alliances, or early forms of charter reinforcing social positions of power and prestige.

Whatever their precise meaning, the symbol-stones testify to a hierarchical society which probably contained such elements as royal lineages, a warrior aristocracy, a powerful priesthood (no single category being necessarily exclusive of the others), skilled craftsmen, poets and **bards**, etc. Yet it all came to an abrupt end. If 'Who were the Picts?' is an intriguing question which has only a fragmentary answer, then 'What happened to the Picts?' is even more compelling and more mystifying. It seems that **Viking** pressure on the Scottic colony of **Dalriada** (part of **Argyll**) caused the Scots under **Kenneth mac-Alpin** to expand eastwards, gaining control of Pictland initially by dynastic means and securing their dominance either in battle as possibly depicted on Sueno's Stone [see **Forres**] or by the treacherous, ritualistic slaughter of the Pictish leadership. Quite suddenly, around the middle of the 9th century, the Picts ceased to exist as a national entity with clearly definable and recognisable characteristics, disappearing into history as mysteriously as they had arrived.

PIGS

Pigs have never been as important in Scotland as in England. While small farmers kept a few pigs, there simply did not exist the crop surpluses to support a large population; pigs eat the same kinds of food as people. Further, Scottish woods did not have the same high density of acorn-bearing oak trees as English woods. Industrialised, intensive pig rearing started in the English cities before 1800, when pigs cleared up the wastes of the food and drink industries, eating brewers' grains, whey, slaughterhouse offal, etc. Such industries were less developed in Scotland. Consequently there are no traditional, established Scottish breeds of pig and it is only in this century that pig farming has become important.

PIG AND PORK TABOOS For a country in which the wild boar still rooted until the late 17th century (one of the last was killed in **Cowal** in 1690), it is hard to find an

810

explanation for the taboo against pigs and pork-eating. It is unknown in other Celtic lands and the only obvious answer, explored by many writers, supposes its importation from the Semitic east at some early period. Certainly it proved a lasting prejudice for according to **Sir Walter Scott** no Lowlander would touch pork 'til within the last generation'. This is, of course, no longer the case, **Aberdeenshire** in particular having a good ham, sausage and bacon tradition. But in the Highlands the taboo against pig-keeping lingers and, like **Dr Johnson**, the traveller may still record 'that I never saw a hog in the Hebrides except one at **Dunvegan**'. Fishermen seem to have been especially susceptible to pig-phobia, **Caithness** men fearing even to mention the creature by name. This may have been because the pig was often associated with the devil. Conversely there is evidence of early, probably **Pictish**, swine cults (eg boar stones).

PILKINGTON, Frederick Thomas (1832–98)
Architect

Pilkington is one of the more interesting 19th century Scottish architects, but also one of the least known. Apprenticed to his father, Thomas Pilkington, he is mostly associated with church design (South Church, **Penicuik**, 1862–3; Trinity Church, **Irvine**, 1861–3). A convinced Gothicist, Pilkington was influenced by the English High Victorian Movement. His churches were eclectic in detail, although he favoured Early French Gothic. They were no scholarly reproductions of medieval designs but a fusion of medieval and 19th century design elements and forms. The best example is probably the Barclay Church, Bruntsfield, **Edinburgh** (1862). He was equally at home designing country houses or villas for the middle classes (The Kirna, 1867, and Stoneyhill, 1868, both in Walkerburn, **Peeblesshire**, or Craigend Farm, Edinburgh, 1869), small houses and shops as in Penicuik, and farms and institutional buildings (Children's Home, Larbert, **Stirlingshire**, 1862–3). All his buildings bear his distinctive marks, often using polychrome stonework, elaborate foliage carving and fantastic, almost bizarre, detailing. He also designed a number of buildings in England such as St Michael's Church, Stamford, 1852.

PINE MARTEN

Sometimes called the 'sweet marten' or the 'marten-cat', the pine marten (*Martes martes*) haunts woodland from the remnants of the old Forest of Caledon to fragments of woodland surviving alongside river gorges. A shy, beautiful and very graceful animal, the pine marten climbs trees with the agility of a squirrel, but will also hunt freely on the ground, eating a varied diet of birds' eggs, small mammals, insects and berries. Once found throughout the Highlands, intense persecution brought the population to the edge of extinction towards the end of the 19th century, reducing its territory to the far north-west – and the subsequent massive reduction in woodland cover threatened the species still further. Indeed it owes its survival to its ability to adapt to new environments as the old forests disappeared, forcing it to learn to live among the rocks on treeless hills. But its increase in numbers and its return to many of its former haunts in the last two decades has been spectacu-

lar, thanks to re-afforestation. It is now fully protected by the Wildlife and Countryside Act of 1989, but its liking for poultry and game birds means that it is still regarded by some as an enemy and a pest. Pine martens breed only once a year, mating in July or August, although delayed implantation means that the female does not start to incubate her young until January. The average litter of three young is born in March or April, the female nesting in scree, tree roots or disused birds' nests.

PINE, Scots

In Britain, native Scots pine (*Pinus sylvestris*) forests are confined to the Scottish Highlands, but in Europe and Asia they are widespread, occurring from Spain to Finland and east to the Pacific coast. Formerly natural pine forests covered much of the Highlands below 600m, but now there are less than 40 sites with trees believed to be direct descendants of the ancient Forest of Caledon. The largest of these are in Speyside, Deeside, Glen Affric and the Black Wood of **Rannoch**. Characteristics of Scots pine include reddish bark, needles in pairs, and cones that take two years to mature. Scots pine is commonly grown in **forestry** plantations; the timber (deal) has many uses and straight trees are frequently made into telegraph poles. In the past the resinous wood was a source of varnish, tar 'fir-candles' and a healing ointment.

PINKERTON, Allan (1819–84) Detective

Born in **Glasgow**, Pinkerton was 10 when his father, a police sergeant, was maimed in a riot. Obliged to help support his family, the son trained as a cooper and in 1842, evidently fearing arrest, fled to America. He married the day before sailing. Amateur law enforcement while plying his trade as a cooper in Chicago led to his appointment as deputy-sheriff, then sheriff and Chicago's first detective (1850). In the same year he started a private agency working mainly for the railroad companies. His reputation grew with his case-book as numerous railroad robberies were investigated. In 1861 he frustrated an attempt on President Lincoln's life, and was co-opted into organising a secret service for the Ohio Police Department. He spent the Civil War engaged in counter-espionage under an alias. After the war Pinkerton's agency, now nationally renowned, continued to grow with offices in New York and Philadelphia. In the 1870s and 80s his sons increasingly directed its activities as Pinkerton himself turned to writing, churning out a series of memoirs and semi-autobiographical case histories which proved immensely popular.

PINKERTON, John (1758–1826) Historian

A native of **Edinburgh** who trained as a lawyer, Pinkerton lived in London from 1780 and in Paris from 1802 till his death. He wrote 24 books including two histories of Scotland, the first of which – *An Inquiry into the History of Scotland Preceding the Reign of Malcolm III* (1789) – dismissed the **Celts** as a race vastly inferior to the Scots, a claim which he was to repeat in later works; but his *History of Scotland from the Accession of the House of Stewart to Mary* (1797) was more restrained and is infinitely more valuable. His *Select Scottish Ballads* (1783), published as a collection of traditional poems, included several which he later admitted were forgeries written by himself.

PINKIE, Battle of (1547), Nr Musselburgh, East Lothian

Also known as Falside and Pinkie Cleugh, the battle of Pinkie on 10 September 1547 (henceforth 'Black Saturday') proved counter-productive both for the Scots, who lost it with appalling casualties, and for the English, whose distinctly '**rough wooing**' of the young Princess **Mary** merely precipitated her marriage to the French Dauphin. The English, commanded by the experienced Duke of Somerset (previously Earl of Hertford), numbered about 16,000 disciplined troops including cavalry, artillery and naval support. The Scots, less disciplined, weak in cavalry, and commanded by the uncertain Arran (**James Hamilton, 2nd Earl**), had the advantage of numbers (perhaps 36,000) and position; they were drawn up behind the river Esk, barring the road to **Edinburgh**, while the English lines straggled from Falside to the beach. 'The battle . . . was to be lost chiefly through the needless abandonment of a strong position' (Sir Bernard Fergusson). Mistaking an English tactical manoeuvre for preparations for retreat, Arran ordered a general attack and crossed the Esk, thus surrendering his advantage. English cavalry charges were held but their artillery took effect. When Arran chose to construe the regrouping of Huntly's troops as evidence of treachery, and when his Highlanders showed more appetite for plunder than casualties, a rout ensued. Perhaps 15,000 Scots were slain and a further 1500 captured. English fatalities may have been 500.

PIOBAIREACHD (PIBROCH)

Literally 'pipe music', *piobaireachd* is taken exclusively to mean *cèol mòr*, 'big music' (as opposed to *cèol beag*, the 'small music' of the pipes which comprises individual airs and dance tunes). The term refers to a set of variations for Highland **bagpipes**, based on an *urlar* (literally 'ground', meaning theme). In modern practice these variations increase in decorative complexity without interruption and end with a repeat (usually partial) of the opening *urlar*. Originally the *urlar* was repeated in the middle of the *piobaireachd*, and the complexity of the throws (decorations) was even greater than it is today. The origins of the form are obscure, there being unique characteristics as well as obvious relationships with the **clarsach** and **Gaelic** vocal repertoires.

The piping and compositional skills involved were passed down in families by a combination of hereditary gifts and intensive tuition, usually centred on the family household on traditionally held lands. Chief amongst these families are the **MacCrimmons** of **Skye**, the **Mackays** of **Raasay** and **Gairloch**, the **MacDonalds**, the MacArthurs and the **MacDougalls**. The assignment of titles to tunes and tunes to individual composers in the 17th and early 18th centuries is largely based on tradition, but a number can be reasonably dated and assigned, such as 'I Got a Kiss of the King's Hand', composed in 1651 by a John McGurmen. The earliest source of *piobaireachd* and comment upon it by a piper is Joseph MacDonald's manuscript treatise *A Complete Theory of the Highland Bagpipe* written in 1760 and published in inaccurate form in the early 19th century. Donald

MacDonald's *A Collection of Ancient Martial Music* of 1822 and Angus Mackay's *A Collection of Ancient Piobaireachd* are also seminal, though increasing attention is being given to manuscript sources.

PIPE BANDS

The gradual emergence of the pipe band with its attendant drummers, performing *cèol beag* exclusively, is a direct consequence of the adoption of the instrument by the military, when Highland regiments were raised and the **bagpipes** were reinstated after a period of proscription following the failure of the '45 **Jacobite Rising**. The drumming shows a virtuosic combination of old Scottish techniques and traditional military styles. In good pipe band playing the unanimity of both pipers and drummers in these highly embellished melodies and rhythms calls for a very high degree of technical expertise. Scottish-style pipe bands are found throughout the world and in some cases have now reached standards comparable to those in Scotland.

PIPER ALPHA DISASTER (1988)

Proof that the **oil and gas** industry could equal the worst accidents in **coal-mining** came with the Piper Alpha disaster on 6 July 1988. The oil rig Piper Alpha was owned by a consortium led by the Occidental Oil company and was based in the North Sea 110 miles off **Aberdeen** with 226 men on board.

At about 10pm a support vessel alongside reported an explosion on board the rig, followed immediately by a fire producing an intense fireball and dense black smoke. Emergency systems, including water deluge sprays, failed to operate, while crewmen had to escape as best they could. Within 20 minutes, evacuation by lifeboat or helicopter became impossible when a major explosion took place, its effects felt up to 1000 yards away. Within a further 30 minutes another explosion followed, this one destroying a rescue boat and killing its occupants. The superstructure of the rig now started to collapse in on itself and most of the crew were trapped in the accommodation quarters, from where 81 bodies were later recovered. There were 62 survivors (although one died later in hospital), most of them having managed to reach lower levels of the platform by stairs or rope. Fifteen men jumped from the 133ft (40.5m) high pipe deck and five from the 174ft (53m) high helicopter deck. Two rescue workers perished, giving a death-toll of 167. Thirty bodies were never found.

A Public Inquiry was conducted before Lord Cullen on behalf of the Department of Energy, opening on 13 July 1988 and reporting on 19 October 1990. It concluded that the initial explosion was caused by the combustion of condensate leaking from a pressure valve which had not been properly sealed, and the inquiry made appropriate safety recommendations to prevent any recurrence of such a horrendous disaster.

PITCAIRN, Robert (c1747–70) Sailor

As midshipman on the 'unseaworthy' sloop *Swallow* accompanying an expedition to look for the 'southern continent' in 1767, Robert Pitcairn was the first to spot the island, thereafter named Pitcairn Island, that later became famous as the home of the *Bounty* mutineers. His next voyage, on board the Bengal-bound *Aurora*, ended in mystery when the ship and its entire complement – which included the three Supervisors of the East India Company – vanished without trace somewhere in the Indian Ocean in the early months of 1770.

PITCAIRNE, Archibald (1652–1713)
Physician

Born in **Edinburgh**, Pitcairne took an MA in divinity at the city's university at the age of 19 before qualifying in medicine in France. Appointed to a professorship in Leyden and then in Edinburgh, he became involved in medical controversy, arguing that physicians should abandon the philosophical approach to medical matters. Regarded with horror by the 'pious Presbyterians as a man who mocked at Scripture, flouted at religion, jeered at Ministers of the everlasting Gospel, and entertained his iniquitous friends with profanity', he was renowned for charging 'exorbitant consultation fees from the rich and serving the poor from kindness'. He helped found the **Royal College of Physicians** in Edinburgh in 1681 and, unusually for a physician, was elected to the **College of Surgeons** in 1701.

PITCAPLE HOUSE, Nr Inverurie, Aberdeenshire

Pitcaple is another of **Aberdeenshire**'s numerous Z-plan castles, the arms of the Z being round towers at opposite angles of the main block, as at **Terpersie**. The original was probably built soon after the lands were granted to David Leslie by **James II** (1457), but the present structure is mainly 17th century with 19th century additions including a wing added by **William Burn**. Rich in historical associations, it was visited by both **James IV** and **Queen Mary** who is said to have planted (1562) the thorn tree around which **Charles II** danced, presumably for joy, after landing from Holland en route to his coronation at **Scone**. This showed scant regard for the fate of Montrose, or '**James Graham**, a traitor to his country' as his captors insisted, who three months earlier had been held in Pitcaple en route to **Edinburgh** and execution. The wife of the Leslie laird supposedly pointed out to him a handy garde-robe (lavatory flue) down which he might escape. Montrose took one look at it and opted to take his chances in Edinburgh rather than 'be smothered in that hole'. The castle passed to the Lumsdens in the 18th century and remains in that family.

PITLOCHRY, Perthshire

With more hotels and **tourist** facilities than perhaps any town of comparable size, Pitlochry has been a major centre for visitors to the Highlands for 150 years. Yet in the 1842 edition of Anderson's *Guide to the Highlands* it is not even mentioned. Evidently **Queen Victoria**'s visit to the area two years later was the making of the town. By the end of the century it had 7 hotels, 3 banks, 4 churches and was reckoned 'a favourite summer resort'. So it remains, thanks to its position at Scotland's geographic centre, to its fine setting in the wooded Tummel valley, and to its proximity to numerous scenic attractions (**Blair Atholl**, **Killiecrankie**, Lochs Tummel and **Rannoch**, **Glen Shee** etc). More recently the Tummel Valley **hydro-electric** scheme provided the town with its own loch (whose dam has a salmon ladder), and the Pitlochry Festival Theatre (1951, new premises

The Dunfallandy Stone, a Pictish cross-slab near Pitlochry (HS)

opened 1981) with its own summer season. In the immediate vicinity the old village of Moulin, to the north, has a church dated 1613 and the ruins of Castle Dubh (Black Castle) dating from the 14th century. To the south across the river stands the Dunfallandy Stone (or cross-slab), an exceptionally fine piece of 8th-century **Pictish** carving with a cross of decorative panels surrounded by animals and angels on one side, seated figures beside a cross, a horseman, blacksmith's tools and more symbols on the other.

PITMEDDEN, The Great Garden of,
Oldmeldrum, Aberdeenshire

Laid out by Alexander Seton, Lord Pitmedden, in 1675, the 'Great Garden' is a walled enclosure on two levels with ogee roofed pavilions, sundials and fountains. Pit-medden House was destroyed by fire in the 19th century and the geometry of its formal garden had been ravaged by potato drills when in 1952 it was gifted to the **National Trust for Scotland** along with a generous endowment. The Trust thereupon undertook an ambitious task of restoration which included the re-creation of its four large rectangular parterres. Assuming that the original designs were inspired by **Charles I**'s **Holyroodhouse** garden and were similar to those of other Seton gardens, Dr J S Richardson laid out the intricate patterns of box hedging and bedding plants which typify the formal charm of the period. Only the actual plants are untypical, 17th century varieties being thought too dull for modern tastes. The garden is now open to the public; an exhibition of 19th and early 20th century farm implements can be found in the adjacent Museum of Farming Life.

PITSLIGO, Nr Fraserburgh, Aberdeenshire

Inland and slightly east of **Rosehearty**, ruined Pitsligo Castle stands forlornly in the middle of a cornfield. Pigeons, deserters from the fanciful Mounthooly **Doocot** to the west, roost within; there is no evidence of conservation and the surviving structures, two storeys high, are unsafe. They include a rectangular keep, built in 1424, a drum tower and 16th–17th century exten-sions. The castle belonged to the Forbes family, created Lords of Pitsligo in 1633. The 4th Lord Pitsligo opposed the **Act of Union** and played a distinguished role in both **Jacobite Risings**. Although aged 68, he survived **Culloden** and went into hiding. The district has caves and culverts where 'the most popular man in the county' found refuge. Loyally protected by his neigh-bours, he was still a fugitive when he died in 1762, aged 84. He was buried in the family vault of old Pitsligo Kirk, now a neat ruin in the churchyard of its 19th century replacement.

PITTENWEEM, Fife

To the east of **St Monans** lies Pittenweem, the 'place of the cave', and a **royal burgh** with a charter of 1541. **St Fillan**'s Cave in Cove Wynd is traditionally associated with that 7th century missionary saint, and is now in the care of the local Scottish **Episcopal Church**. The present parish church incorporates the old Tolbooth Tower (1588) and adjoins the much altered Augustinian priory (15th century onwards) which replaced an earlier one on the **Isle of May**. Other historic buildings include the house in Routine Row where the events leading up to the **Porteous Riot** took place (see **Sir Walter Scott**'s *Heart of Midlothian*), Kellie Lodging (c1590), the town house of the Earls of Kellie, and the Gyles, once the home of Captain James Cook, who carried **Charles II** over to France after the Battle of Worcester in 1651. The burgh records advise that over a hundred local seamen died at the **Battle of Kilsyth** in 1645, so that seventeen boats were left to rot at their moorings in Pittenweem harbour. The town also had an unenviable record for witch-hunting, with persecutions continuing as late as 1705. Now Pittenweem is home to the bulk of the East Fife **fishing** fleet, and the venue for a popular annual Arts Festival. Nearby are **Kellie Castle** and **Balcaskie House**.

PLAYFAIR, John (1748–1819) Geologist

Born at Benvie near **Dundee** and educated at **St Andrews University**, graduating in mathematics in 1765, Playfair was minister of Liff and Benvie from 1773–83. Appointed Professor of Mathematics at **Edin-burgh** in 1785, he developed an interest in **geology** through his friendship with **James Hutton** and in 1805 changed his chair for that of Natural Philosophy. One of the original members of the **Royal Society of Edin-burgh**, Playfair championed Hutton's cause and sup-ported his 'Theory of the Earth' with *Illustrations of the Huttonian Theory* published in 1802. John Playfair's younger brother William had to flee Paris for his life after opposing the French Revolution, and his nephew, also **William**, was the Edinburgh architect.

PLAYFAIR, William Henry (1790–1857)
Architect

Together with colleagues such as **William Burn** and **James Gillespie Graham**, Playfair dominated the Scot-tish architectural scene during the first half of the 19th century. The son of the architect James Playfair (1755–94), he trained both in **Edinburgh** under William Stark and in London under Robert Smirke. In 1816 he visited France. When he returned to Edinburgh in 1817 he instantly established himself professionally by winning the commission for the completion of **Adam**'s unfinished **University** building. His exterior follows the original plans, but the interiors are his own. In the following year he designed the plans for the **Calton Hill** estate on the eastern edge of the **New Town**. He went on from there to become the pre-eminent designer of public buildings in Edinburgh; many of the landmarks of the capital are his work, such as the **National Monument** on Calton Hill (1824–9), the **Royal Scottish Academy** (1822, enlarged 1831) and the **National Gallery** on **The Mound** (1850–7). Although he is mainly associated with Greek revival (at its best, maybe, at the Surgeons' Hall, begun 1829), he was also well versed in other styles. His spiky Gothic **New College** (1846–50) at the top of the Mound is aligned with the grid pattern of the first and second phases of the New Town and, together with the classical galleries, provides a spectacular entry into the **Old Town**. Unlike Burn or Gillespie Graham, Playfair was no mass producer. His early country houses were Italianate villas, but after 1830 he mostly preferred the vernacular of the 16th and 17th centuries.

PLOUGHGATE

Mainly used in southern Scotland, the ploughgate was a notional unit of land in the Middle Ages. It denoted the area, rather variable because of different soils, which a team of eight oxen might expect to plough in one year. An oxgang (or bovate) represented one part of such a measurement. Typical equivalents were 104 acres (42ha) to 1 ploughgate and 13 acres (5.2ha) to 1 oxgang. Such terms clearly implied cultivable ground rather than pasture. It is disputed whether or not they indicate that only oxen, and not horses, were used to draw the plough.

PLUSCARDEN ABBEY, Nr Elgin, Moray

Founded by **Alexander II** in 1230 as a priory for the **Valliscaulian** order, Pluscarden was damaged in

Pluscarden Abbey in the 19th century before restoration (RWB)

Edward I's invasion of **Moray** in 1303 and burned by **Alexander Stewart**, the 'Wolf of Badenoch', in 1390. It was taken over by Benedictines in 1454, but after the **Reformation** it fell into disuse and decay. Bought by **John Stuart, 3rd Marquess of Bute** in 1897, it was returned to the Benedictines by his son in 1943; the monks of the Prinknash community in Gloucestershire set about the task of restoring the abbey and established a new community there in 1948. In 1974 Pluscarden regained abbey status; restoration has continued; the grand cruciform church and abbey buildings contain some original frescoes and magnificent modern stained glass; the abbey operates as an active religious community and a centre for spiritual renewal and retreat.

POOLEWE, Ross & Cromarty

Loch Ewe, somewhat bigger than **Gairloch**, its neighbour to the south, has Poolewe as the main village and port at its head. The short river Ewe drains nearby **Loch Maree** where place-names like Kinlochewe and **Inverewe** suggest that the river may once have been just a tidal pool and the two lochs contiguous. A gun emplacement on the west shore of Loch Ewe recalls its importance as a naval base during World War II. The main attraction, apart from the magnificent scenery, is the Inverewe Garden. Hence to **Braemore** and **Corrieshalloch** the coastal route via Dundonnel (deer) Forest is remembered as Destitution Road (1851), one of many job creation schemes designed to provide subsistence for victims of the **Potato Famine**.

POPULATION

The population of Scotland on 21 April 1991, the date of the most recent census, was 4,962,152, a decrease of 168,583 (0.33%) on the previous census 10 years earlier [Source: *1991 Census Report for Scotland*, Part 1, Vol 1, HMSO, 1993]. Provisional figures confirm that **Glasgow** remained the largest city with 654,000 (112,000 down on 1981), **Edinburgh** had 422,000 (15,000 down), **Aberdeen** 201,000 (3000 down) and **Dundee** 166,000 (14,000 down) [Source: *Scottish Abstract of Statistics*, 1993].

Responsibility for monitoring Scotland's population lies with the Registrar General for Scotland at New Register House, Edinburgh, with detailed administration undertaken from Ladywell House, Edinburgh 12. This office organises the census which is taken once a decade, always in a year ending with the digit '1'. For this purpose, Scotland is divided into 20 administrative areas, each under an Area Manager responsible for the issue and subsequent collection of census forms and the recruitment and training of enumerators. The information is then collated at former factory premises in Hillingdon, Glasgow, where some 80% of the UK's forms are processed, creating 1700 short-term jobs. Population information is finally published in such documents as *Census 1991* available through Her Majesty's Stationery Office. The 1991 census was the first to include a question on ethnic origin, emphasising the increasing cosmopolitanism of Scotland's population.

HISTORY OF SCOTTISH POPULATION CENSUSES In 1755 Alexander Webster, an Edinburgh minister, produced *An Account of the Number of People in Scotland*, a survey containing information collated from correspondence with **Church of Scotland** ministers throughout the country. Although many of them responded to Webster's request for enumeration details by listing the number of 'examinables' – people of any age capable of answering questions on the Catechism – this pioneering demographer used an extrapolated formula to allow for the omission of young children and those of different religious persuasions to produce reasonably accurate figures for society as a whole. He calculated Scotland's population at 1,265,380, with that for Edinburgh being only 2000 less than that deduced from the next set of emergent figures which came from the *Statistical Account*.

Sir John Sinclair's private initiative in persuading **Church of Scotland** ministers to gather information about their parishes in the form of the *Statistical Account* (1791–9) was a highly commendable attempt to collate contemporary information about places of habitation, agriculture, occupations and population. While this was based on ministers' estimates and did not involve individual questioning of the kind employed nowadays, it was still an improvement on the English situation, and the *Statistical Account* is an invaluable tool for the historian and social scientist. (*A Second Statistical Account* was compiled in the 1830s and published in 1845, and a *Third* was started after World War II and is still incomplete at the time of writing.)

Most authorities believe that, as far as can be calculated, Scotland's population in 1600 was about 800,000 and had grown to around 1 million by the time of the **Treaty of Union** in 1707. Real growth did not show until around the middle of the 18th century, reaching 1.6 million in 1801.

Early official censuses began in 1801 on both sides

of the border. In Scotland these were the responsibility of local Sheriff Deputes in the counties, and Provosts and Lord Provosts in the towns and cities. The actual enumeration was done by schoolmasters, the census period lasting for about six weeks from mid-March. Not until 1841 was the sample taken on a single day, adding considerable doubt as to the accuracy of earlier results. In addition, registration of births, marriages and deaths was not compulsory in Scotland until 1855.

PARTICULAR CHARACTERISTICS It seems that the Scot is essentially an urban creature. In 1931 two-fifths of the population lived in only five major centres – Glasgow, Edinburgh, Dundee, Aberdeen and **Paisley**. In 1981, 1.89 million inhabited the metropolitan area of **Strathclyde**, 37% of the nation's population in a single conurbation. This centralisation was the result of the Industrial Revolution, when labour-intensive industries such as **coal-mining**, **shipbuilding**, manufacturing and textiles required a large local labour force. Movement to urban areas was facilitated by **railways** from the 1840s onwards, overcoming what were previously primitive transport conditions. In post-war years there has been something of a move away from the cities with the setting up of five New Towns, a deliberate policy of population dispersal, and increased car ownership resulting in more commuting from rural areas.

Agricultural reorganisation and improvements in public health made their own contributions to the 19th century increase in Scotland's population, although the former included enclosures disrupting more traditional farming methods and accelerating the move to cities. At the same time, agricultural innovations improved the quality of life and partly prevented the famine conditions which periodically affected Ireland.

Life expectancy was also enhanced by improvements in medical science and public health, although life expectancy in Scotland has never been as great as south of the border. It is a sad irony that the nation which has made such a substantial contribution to the furtherance of medicine and surgery still shows such vulnerability to heart disease and other mortal illnesses.

Nevertheless, the population increase would have been even greater had emigration not figured in the equation. The Highland **clearances** loom large in this; there were pronounced waves of emigrants in the 1850s, 1880s, early 1900s and 1920s. North America, Australia and New Zealand were the most popular destinations abroad, but many simply took what **Dr Johnson** described as 'the noblest prospect which a Scotchman ever sees; the high road that leads him to England'. In the 10 years between the 1921 and 1931 censuses, a time of depression in trade and employment, the national population fell by 40,000; the decrease between 1971–81 and 1981–91 may owe more to birth control.

In their 1961 book *Scotland's Scientific Heritage*, surveying Scotland's achievements in science and technology, A G Clement and R H S Robertson ascribe the decline in Scotland's intellectual performance in the 20th century to 'the high rate of emigration', particularly among the better-educated. It is certainly true that of eight (up to 1993) Nobel Prize winners born in Scotland, only one was working in Scotland when he won his award;

brainpower is apparently one of the country's greatest exports.

Balanced against this, there have been successive waves of incoming migrants from Ireland, Italy, the Baltic area and the Commonwealth. In 1981 140,943 Scottish residents had been born outside the UK, with 27,018 from Eire and 33,255 from Asia. The biggest group of non-Scots resident north of the border are in fact English-born – 297,784 in 1981, approximately 5.7%.

Further details on Scotland's population can be obtained from the many publications of the Registrar General or, from a historian's perspective, in M Flinn's *Scottish Population History from the 17th century to the 1930s*, CUP, 1977.

PORT GLASGOW, Renfrewshire

Before dredging (1740s onwards), no ship of any draught could proceed up the **Clyde** beyond **Dumbarton**. Severely disadvantaged without a deep-water port, the merchants of **Glasgow** began to seek a downriver frontage in the 1660s. Dumbarton and **Troon** both rejected their advances lest a new port 'raise the price of provisions to their inhabitants'. But Sir Patrick Maxwell of Newark apprehended no such difficulties and New-Port-Glasgow, adjacent to **Newark Castle** and 20 miles west of the city, was duly laid out in the 1690s. By 1710 it was the principal customs house on the Clyde and in 1775 was formed into a municipality which included Newark and was now called simply Port Glasgow. The mainly North American trade spawned sugar refineries, ropeworks (the great mill of **Gourock** Ropeworks still stands) and **shipbuilding**. Here John Wood built **Henry Bell**'s *Comet* (a small replica of which is displayed in a car park) and here Reid & Company designed the floating church used by the congregation of **Strontian** after the 1843 **Disruption**. **William Lithgow**, one of Reid's apprentices, eventually dominated the local industry, much as Scott-Lithgow's large but redundant gantry still dominates the waterfront. On the steep brae above is stacked low-cost housing with compensating views across the river. The classical Town Buildings (1815) are by **David Hamilton** while, to the east, Broadfield Hospital (1870) is by **David Bryce**.

PORT LOGAN, Wigtownshire

On Logan Bay, one of the few sheltered spots on the wild and rocky west coast of the Rhinns of **Galloway**, this village (also sometimes called Port Nessock) was developed as a port between 1818–20 by Colonel Andrew McDouall of Logan in a briefly successful attempt to divert the lucrative Irish trade from **Portpatrick**. The remains of his pier tipped by a lighthouse tower still jut out into the bay. A tidal pool in the rocks, excavated and stocked mainly with cod as a fish-larder by the McDoualls in 1800, could qualify as one of the earliest attempts at **fish farming** in Scotland; the 30 or so fish it contained were fed by hand and became so tame they rose to the surface at the sound of a bell. It still operates as a tourist attraction. The nearby Logan gardens were taken over by the **Royal Botanic Garden Edinburgh** in 1968 as one of their outstations [see **Botanic Gardens**]. On Ardwell Point just north of Logan Bay the remains of the Ardwell Broch, sometimes called

'Doon Castle', are the best-preserved of any in Galloway, although modest by comparison with the mighty **brochs** of **Mousa** or **Glenelg**. Between Port Logan and Sandhead Kirkmadrine Chapel, rebuilt at the end of the 19th century from the ruins of medieval Kirkmadrine Church, houses the oldest Christian monuments in Scotland outside **Whithorn**. The most important are two inscribed pillar stones dating from the 5th and 6th centuries, but there are also several crosses covering the period from the 8th to the 12th centuries, all of which were discovered among the ruins of the earlier church.

PORT WILLIAM, Wigtownshire

Founded by, and named after, Sir William Maxwell of Monreith in c1775, Port William on the east side of Luce Bay was famous as a haunt of smugglers until the establishment of a customs post in 1788. In the grounds of nearby Monreith House (1799, with lovely gardens and the White Loch which, according to legend, only freezes one half at a time) are the Drumtroddan **standing stones** (two still erect, one prostrate, and each measuring about 3m in height) and several groups of cup-and-ring marked stones. Monreith Bay to the south of Port William has developed into a popular tourist spot thanks to its fine sandy beach. The statue of an otter on the headland overlooking the bay is a memorial to **Gavin Maxwell**, author of *The House of Elrig: An Autobiography of Childhood* [see **Mochrum**].

PORTEOUS AFFAIR, The (1736)

In 1736 Andrew Wilson, a smuggler, was sentenced to death and hanged in **Edinburgh**'s **Grassmarket**. His crime, with which the people of Edinburgh were in some sympathy, was to have robbed a customs officer, his defence that repeated seizure of his goods by the said customs officer had reduced him to penury and he had therefore been forced 'to reimburse himself for his losses'. In the tumult of public outrage that followed his execution sticks were brandished and stones thrown, whereupon the Captain of the Town Guard, locally-born John Porteous, ordered his troops to fire on the crowd, killing and wounding up to 30 people.

Porteous, described by **Sir Walter Scott** in *The Heart of Midlothian* as 'a man of profligate habits, an unnatural son and a brutal husband', was tried and sentenced to death for wilful murder, and his execution date set for 8 September. The crowd gathered once again in the Grassmarket to see justice being done. 'The place of execution was crowded almost to suffocation . . . and resembled a huge dark lake or sea of human heads, in the centre of which arose the fatal tree, tall black and ominous, from which dangled the deadly halter.' The crowd, though, was orderly. 'The thirst for vengeance was in some degree allayed by its supposed certainty; and the populace, with deeper feeling than they are wont to entertain . . . prepared to enjoy the scene of retaliation in triumph, silent and decent, though stern and relentless.' As the appointed hour for the execution came and went with no sign of the condemned man being brought to the gallows, rumblings of unrest were heard. Then rumours started to spread that 'the magistracy of the city . . . had defrauded public justice'.

The Porteous Mob, by *James Drummond* (NGS)

Porteous had petitioned for mercy from Queen Caroline (acting as Regent for George II), and word had just reached Edinburgh that his sentence had been postponed for six weeks. When, at last, the magistrates plucked up the courage to make a public announcement to this effect, some sections of the crowd prepared to disperse, but others, enraged by the notion of a powerful man escaping the justice that had been meted out to a common man, decided to take the law into their own hands. With much yelling and shouting and beating of drums, an angry mob stormed the **Tolbooth**, burnt down the doors and dragged John Porteous out. There was no looting or wanton violence; passers-by were respectfully advised to keep out of the way; the crowd 'meditated not the slightest wrong or infraction of the law, excepting so far as Porteous himself was concerned'. They escorted the Captain of the Town Guard back to the Grassmarket and hanged him from a dyer's pole.

The Prime Minister, Robert Walpole, threatened the city of Edinburgh with dire punishment as a result of this unhappy episode, and it was only through the intervention of **John Campbell, 2nd Duke of Argyll**, that the punishment was limited to the disqualification of the Provost and a fine of £2000, which went to Porteous's widow.

PORTKNOCKIE, Banffshire
On the Moray Firth between **Cullen** and **Findochty**, Portknockie has shared their fate as a **fishing** port, its boats now operating (if at all) out of **Buckie** or **MacDuff**. It was founded in 1677 by fishermen from Cullen. The cliff scenery hereabouts is particularly dramatic.

PORTPATRICK, Wigtownshire
Now a small **fishing** and holiday resort, Portpatrick on the west coast of the Rhinns of **Galloway** was the main port for trade with Ireland during the 17th and 18th centuries. A regular postal service operated by packet-boat between the two countries from 1662, the town's first pier was built by the Post Office in 1774, and by 1790 20,000 head of cattle and horses a year were being shipped the 21 miles across the North Channel to Portpatrick from Donaghadee in County Down on their way to Scottish markets. The short crossing also served to turn Portpatrick into the **Gretna Green** for Ireland, records showing that '198 gentlemen, 15 officers of the army or navy, and 13 noblemen' took advantage of the more relaxed Scottish marriage laws before 'the practice was happily annihilated by the interference of the Church Courts' in 1826. However Portpatrick's harbour and post office pier were too small and too exposed to accommodate steamships and, with the advent of the steam age, a grand new harbour was planned to designs by **John Rennie**, construction starting in 1821. Suddenly 'in place of a few fishermen lounging about and wondering why the **herring** have not arrived, you see 800 able-bodied men whose labours are . . . triumphing over the most formidable obstacles of nature' (Fullarton's *Gazetteer*); a population of about 100 in 1730 had grown to nearly 1000 a century later. But before the new facilities were completed **Stranraer** had taken over as the main port for steamships connecting to Larne and the livestock trade

was operating directly to **Glasgow** and Liverpool. Rennie's harbour at Portpatrick silted up, his piers were wrecked by storms and the new lighthouse was dismantled, shipped off and rebuilt in Colombo. The large Portpatrick Hotel was opened in 1905 and the town has since concentrated on the holiday trade.

PORTREE, Skye
The main town and 'capital' of **Skye**, with a sheltered natural harbour facing east over the Sound of **Raasay**, Portree was so named (*port righ* = 'king's harbour') after the visit of **James V** during his 1540 tour of the **Hebrides**. In June 1746 **Prince Charles Edward Stewart**, disguised as 'Betty Burke', arrived at Portree with **Flora MacDonald**; the room where they parted before the Prince's onward flight to Raasay, and where he presented Flora with a gold locket containing his portrait as thanks for her assistance in his escape, is now part of the Royal Hotel. Formerly connected by steamer to **Kyle of Lochalsh**, Portree harbour still has a small **fishing** fleet, although the town's main industry is now **tourism**.

PORTSOY, Banffshire
No longer a **fishing** port, Portsoy remains the 'neat, thriving place' noticed by Robert Southey in 1819. Steep streets descend from the modern town to the harbour, first built by an Ogilvie of **Boyne** in the 16th century but twice rebuilt in the 19th century. Here cluster the restored town houses, fishermen's cottages, inn and warehouses, mostly 18th and 19th century, which figure in the picture postcards. Ogilvies secured a charter for the **burgh of barony** in the late 16th century and later Ogilvies protected the export (1700) of its green and flesh-coloured serpentine known as Portsoy marble. There are said to be Portsoy marble chimney pieces in the palace of Versailles. Latterly the town's prosperity rested on fishing but it is now a resort for the discerning, with **Fordyce**, **Boyne** and Findlater castles all within easy walking distance.

POTATO FAMINE (1846)
Potatoes have been grown in Scotland since the 17th century, but it was only in the late 18th century and especially in the Highlands and Islands that population pressures and shortage of arable land (much of which had been taken out of cultivation during the first phase of the **clearances**) created a nutritional dependence on 'tatties'. As in Ireland, the potato's high yield per acre obliged many communities to grow and eat little else; and as in Ireland the sudden appearance of potato blight (*phytophthora infestans*) in 1845–6 spelt catastrophe. Overnight, and throughout the **Hebrides** and the Highlands, the haulms wilted and the tubers rotted. Blackened fields and a nauseating stench heralded 'a human tragedy unparalleled in modern Scottish history' (James Hunter).

Compared with Ireland, deaths from starvation were few. The government in London responded quickly by sending the admirable Sir Edward Pine Coffin to assess the relief needs plus two naval frigates to act as floating meal depots. Church and private charities also swung into action, forming a well-endowed Fund for the Relief of the Destitute Inhabitants of the Highlands. Even some

Portree, Skye in the 1880s (GWWA)

of the lairds, most notably Norman MacLeod of **Dunvegan** who bankrupted himself in the process, rose to the occasion.

Yet if the death toll was small, disease and hardship were acute. Before the relief arrived whole townships were reduced to scavenging for cockles and seaweed. As surely as malnutrition brought disease, relief brought profiteering by lairds and merchants. Victorian charity was available only to the utterly destitute and in return for hard labour. An already impoverished tenantry parted with their livestock, ate their seed grains, and sank into irredeemable debt. Charity-funded construction projects barely sustained the enfeebled labourers while their creations, the 'destitution roads', benefited mainly the landowners. The effects of the famine, and the need for relief, lasted until the 1850s, only to be partially obviated by what seemed to the sufferers even less desirable expedients – further clearances and mass emigration.

POTTERY

Pottery has been made in Scotland since ancient times, but it was only during the second half of the 18th century, when the Scottish economy revived after a long period of stagnation, that pottery production could be properly included in the list of Scottish industries. It tended to gravitate towards those places which could satisfy its basic needs – clay to make the pots and **coal** to fire them, a pool of labour to man the factories, and a ready-made means of transporting the finished ware, which at that time meant by sea. Two areas were of crucial importance in those early days: **Glasgow** and its hinterland (notably the Delftfield Pottery), and a string of **East Lothian** coastal townships – **Prestonpans**, Cuthill, Morrison's Haven, West Pans, **Musselburgh** and **Portobello**. Skilled English artisans were encouraged to settle in both Glasgow and **East Lothian**, and although their early endeavours had mixed results, their pioneering work provided the necessary toehold for the industry to expand on a sound basis of Scottish expertise. The great boom in production occurred when men of vision realised that there was a potential market for their wares far beyond the bounds of their homeland. Various classes of goods were exported to many countries around the world, ensuring that Scottish pottery had a significant place in the mercantile life of the nation. Factories proliferated, and the industry became a noteworthy employer as production increased through the 19th century.

The range of wares covered the entire ceramic spectrum, from fine porcelains to coarse fireclays, the mainstays being domestic and utilitarian stoneware. Various techniques were employed to decorate the earthenware, most commonly transfer-printing, sponge-printing (a Scottish speciality) and hand painting. A small proportion of the stoneware was saltglazed. Glasgow remained the pre-eminent centre, with some 50 potteries operating in the city at different times, some rivalling

819

Church Street, Portsoy, as photographed by George Washington Wilson (entry p 818) (GWWA)

the largest firms in Staffordshire. Bell's Pottery and Britannia Pottery making earthenware, and Barrowfield Pottery and Port Dundas Pottery making stoneware, were indeed industrial giants in their day. Elsewhere in the west, there were notable potteries at **Pollokshaws**, **Rutherglen** and **Greenock**. In the east, several pottery towns emerged, such as Prestonpans, Portobello, **Bo'ness**, **Alloa** and **Kirkcaldy**. Smaller but very interesting works flourished at Dunmore, **Aberdeen**, **Cumnock** and elsewhere. The Scottish potteries showed a remarkable degree of inventiveness; hundreds of registered designs and patents testify to this. However, the industry suffered greatly with the loss of export markets caused by World War I and changing social conditions, and the Depression of the 1920s saw its virtual demise. Now the factories are little more than workshops, comparatively small in scale and few in number. Only one of the old companies, Buchans of Portobello, still exists, though since 1972 it has operated in new works at **Crieff**. It stands alone as a reminder of the great days of this vanished industry.

DUNMORE WARE Dunmore Pottery was situated near the town of **Airth** in **Stirlingshire**. It started as a quiet country pottery, but changed dramatically in the 1860s under its energetic and imaginative proprietor, Peter Gardner. Its products gained widespread renown for their unconventional shapes and adventurous glazes. Despite this, the Pottery remained a small concern right up to its closure about 1910, but it was supported by the local nobility and patronised by royalty. Dunmore Ware became extremely popular during the last quarter of the 19th century.

SPONGEWARE Sponge-printing was a cheap, unsophisticated but effective means of decorating white earthenware. It involved tying a piece of sponge, or more usually simply cutting the root of a marine sponge, so that it formed a pattern and using it to dab colour onto bisque-fired works. One of the most prolific producers of spongeware was the Links Pottery of David Methven & Sons in Kirkcaldy; it was also made at Bo'ness, Greenock and by several of the Glasgow factories. Popular because of its low cost and its homely charm, it was produced in great quantity between approximately 1850 and 1925. Spongeware is not unique to Scotland, but it was certainly a Scottish speciality, and was widely exported.

WEMYSS WARE This is certainly the most famous brand of ceramics made in Scotland. It was produced at the Fife Pottery of Robert Heron & Son in the Gallatown area of Kirkcaldy from 1882, though it formed only a small proportion of the factory's output. Initially the pots were single-coloured, but this changed when the Pottery's owner, Robert Methven Heron, returned from Bohemia with a team of skilled decorators, led by Karel Nekola. He was a supremely gifted artist, painting natural scenes of flowers, fruit, birds and animals, and also indulging in commemorative items and commissioned pieces. Wemyss Ware continued to be made after his death in 1915, becoming rather jazzy in the 1920s. When the Fife Pottery closed around 1930, Wemyss Ware had a final phase at Bovey Tracey in Devon, production finally ceasing about 1952. Today it is the most avidly collected of all Scottish ceramic products.

CRAFT POTTERY Even before the demise of the Scottish pottery industry, there were signs of an emergent craft movement. The Port Dundas Pottery in Glasgow and

Buchan's Pottery at Portobello, two of the largest stoneware factories, devoted part of their production, albeit a tiny part, to handcrafted artistic wares. Early in the 20th century, Hugh Allan (Allander Pottery, Milngavie) and Henry Wyse (Holyrood Pottery, Edinburgh) provided an exciting foretaste of the craft pottery of the future. Between the wars, however, studios tended to be the domain of artists rather than craftsmen (Bough in Edinburgh, Mak'Merry in East Lothian and others), who used skilled brushwork to decorate factory-made pots. It was really only from the middle of the 20th century that Scotland's four art colleges began turning out trained potters capable of sustaining the business of producing ceramic wares through all the various processes. The former largely-centralised factory groupings were now replaced by a broad and even spread of small potteries throughout the land, with just as many functioning in secluded Highland glens and Atlantic islands as nearer the urban population centres. By the 1970s more than 100 were in operation, the majority being single-person or husband-and-wife concerns. A few of these practitioners have studied historic pottery, and while in no way copying the wares of the past, a certain degree of influence is evident. The majority of modern craft potters, however, have forsaken the older ways for novelty of form, often more sculptural than functional, and spectacular glazing effects, the key word being innovation.

POWER GENERATION

Historians believe that water power technology was introduced to Scotland during the Middle Ages, when the water wheel was adopted as an alternative to muscle power to drive corn milling machinery. By the middle of the 18th century, water power was being used in bone, threshing, paper, saw and textile mills as well as to work draining and lifting engines in mines and the bellows in metal smelting works.

Steam did not begin seriously to challenge the ascendancy of water as the motive power of the Industrial Revolution until the early 19th century, but Scots rapidly acquired a reputation for their willingness to apply and develop steam power in industry. **William Symington** and **Henry Bell** were the pioneers of steam navigation in Britain, and the river **Clyde** became the home of some of the world's greatest ship and marine engine builders. Scottish **engineering** companies came to dominate the market for steam **locomotives**, pumps and other steam driven machines.

After **William Murdock** devised the first commercially viable gas manufacturing plant, Scots were quick to appreciate the potential of **coal** gas for lighting. **James Watt** commented in 1805 on the widespread use of gas for illumination in **Glasgow**, and in 1816 the **Edinburgh** Gas Lighting Co was formed to supply gas commercially. Companies were set up across Scotland to supply gas for street lighting, public buildings and the home, most of those in the cities and large towns subsequently being acquired by the municipal authority. The first gas meters were introduced in the 1840s, and gas stoves became widely available through company and municipal rental and hire purchase schemes during the 1880s. While Scottish industry relied upon steam technology for power, the population of Scotland's industrial communities came to rely on gas to provide light, heat and cooking facilities in their homes.

After the nationalisation of the gas industry in 1948, responsibility for the 197 independent Scottish gas units was entrusted to the Scottish Gas Board, one of the 12 gas boards under the authority of the Gas Council. It was replaced after reorganisation in 1973 by Scottish Gas, under the more centralised control of the British Gas Corporation. In 1965 natural gas was discovered in the North Sea and Scotland was converted to natural gas between 1970–7, with most of the country's supply coming ashore after 1978 at the St Fergus Terminal in Aberdeenshire. British Gas plc was floated in 1986, with British Gas Scotland (now Scottish Gas) as the Scottish arm of the privatised company. [see **Oil and Gas**]

Just as Glasgow led the country in exploiting the potential of gas for lighting, so it also pioneered the commercial development of electricity generation. The first British **railway** station to be lit by electricity was St Enoch's in 1879, and in 1885 the electrical engineers **Mavor** & Coulson opened Scotland's first electricity generating station in Glasgow, with the Royal Exchange and the Post Office among the first customers. Glasgow Corporation acquired the firm's business in 1892, creating a municipal electricity department which began lighting city streets with arc lamps the following year. Municipal monopolies of electricity supply became common but, as in the gas industry, independent companies were able to thrive supplying electrical power to small towns and rural areas, and the Clyde Valley Electrical Co, founded in 1901, became Scotland's largest.

In 1926 the newly created Central Electricity Generating Board (CEGB) was charged with creating a National Grid in the United Kingdom, and the first area grid scheme was inaugurated in central Scotland the following year. Despite rapid progress with the grid, however, and even after the founding of the Grampian Electrical Supply Co in 1922, the central and western Highlands remained largely beyond the reach of electricity supply. Only after the creation of the North of Scotland Hydro Electric Board in 1943, and the inauguration of a series of spectacular **hydro-electric** schemes, was electricity gradually introduced to the more inaccessible and neglected communities of the north.

Britain's municipal and private electricity companies were nationalised in 1947, and placed under the control of the British Electrical Authority. In England, electricity was produced by the CEGB and distributed by 12 area boards, but in Scotland both generation and supply were entrusted to the two regional authorities, the South of Scotland Electricity Board (SSEB) and the North of Scotland Hydro Electric Board (NSHEB). While the SSEB relied heavily on coal-fired power stations, and the NSHEB on hydro schemes for their generating capacity, both took steps to develop oil- and gas-fired stations.

Work began on the construction of the first fast reactor nuclear power station to supply electricity to a commercial grid, at **Dounreay** in Caithness, in 1955. It supplied electricity to the NSHEB from 1960 until the reactor was closed in 1977, by which time Dounreay's Prototype Fast Reactor, opened in 1975, had begun to generate. The construction by the Atomic Energy Authority of a nuclear power station at Chapelcross in

Annan was also started in 1955, and like the SSEB's **Hunterston 'A'** and 'B' power stations in **Ayrshire** (built in 1957–64 and 1967–76 respectively) and Torness in **East Lothian** (built 1978–89), it supplied electricity to the SSEB grid.

In 1990, in preparation for the privatisation of the electricity industry in Scotland, the SSEB was split up into two companies, ScottishPower plc, which was to be privatised, and Scottish Nuclear Ltd, to run and operate the Advanced Gas Cooled Reactor (AGR) power stations at Hunterston 'B' and Torness. As well as being expected to generate the base load requirement for ScottishPower and Scottish Hydro-Electric (the successor of the NSHEB), Scottish Nuclear was also given responsibility for decommissioning the two ageing Magnox reactors at Hunterston 'A' which closed in 1990. In the same year it was announced that the fast breeder reactor programme at Dounreay would terminate in 1994. In 1996 Scottish Nuclear and Nuclear Electric (its English equivalent) became subsidiaries of the holding company, British Energy (whose head office is in Edinburgh), apparently as a prelude to privatisation of the remaining nuclear programme.

In 1998, with the deregulation of the utility markets, ScottishPower, British Gas and Scottish Hydro-Electric (now Scottish and Southern Energy plc) were all free to compete, with other companies, for gas and electricity supply business throughout the United Kingdom. ScottishPower has grown rapidly, acquiring and growing electricity and other utility business in Britain and in the USA, and by 1999 had become Scotland's largest industrial company.

PRESBYTERIANS

Scotland is the only country where the established Church, the **Church of Scotland**, is presbyterian rather than structured episcopally, ie with a hierarchy ruled by bishops (*episkopoi*) as in the Catholic and Anglican Churches. The roots of Presbyterianism are in Judaism, where the synagogue and congregation were directed by elders (*presbuteroi*) according to Old Testament norms. Christians of the early Church followed the same regime until the priesthood evolved.

After the **Reformation** some Protestant Churches sought to recreate a purer Church government, and to avoid abuse of power by returning to early Church patterns. The prototype was Geneva where by 1559 Calvin had devised the essentials of Presbyterian beliefs and democratic order in his *Institutes* and *Ecclesiastical Ordinances*. The Church was to be independent from the state and was to be governed by a sequence of courts from Kirk Session, Presbytery and Synod to **General Assembly** in which all ministers would be equal, including the presiding **Moderator**, and laymen given representation. Both ministers and elders were thus presbyters, according to Calvin's interpretation of scripture, with Christ the sole Head of the Church.

The system, adopted by English-speaking exiles in Geneva, was introduced to Scotland by **John Knox** on his return in 1560, but not implemented. After his death in 1572, **Andrew Melville**, also Geneva trained, dominated theological and ecclesiastical progress. In 1581 the *Second Book of Discipline* spelled out the Scottish form. Parliament approved Presbyterian church courts

in 1592, some of which survived the reintroduction of episcopacy by **Stewart** kings in the 17th century struggles over Church power which saw the rise of the **Covenanters**. The Revolution settlement of 1690 ignored the accommodations suggested by **Archbishop Robert Leighton** for bishops together with presbyteries. From then on Presbyterianism was the established Church and this was later guaranteed by the 1707 **Act of Union**. The main bishops' party became the **Episcopal Church of Scotland**.

In belief the Presbyterians retained **Calvinism** as a base. This was developed in 1647 at the Westminster Assembly of Divines to produce the Westminster Confession and catechisms which, after the Bible, are still the definitive statements of doctrine. Essentially it is a reformed Protestant faith which is Trinitarian, believing God to be the Creator and salvation obtained through Jesus Christ. As such it is part of the universal Church Catholic committed to missionary work at home and abroad.

In worship Presbyterians use no prayer books or set liturgy. Services are structured around Biblical readings, hymns and prayers led by a minister, with special affection for the Old Testament psalms in both the metrical version and paraphrase. The sermon is central to worship with the pulpit a dominant feature of the architecture, often centrally placed and ascended by steps, giving rise to the phrase to 'sit under' a popular preacher. Such an auditorium style of church, reflecting emphasis on The Word, had been anticipated in 16th century European practice. In Scotland older churches lost their altars at the time of the Reformation.

The communion service is held quarterly or monthly as a special occasion. In the past it was annual with preparation for a week beforehand, when no work was done. This still obtains in Highland **Free Presbyterian** observance. The Church year is less observed with the exception of Easter and Christmas.

The Presbyterian elder has a specific role in pastoral care and spiritual concerns in conjunction with the minister. Elders, male or female, are elected members of the congregation who oversee management corporately in the Kirk Session and individually by assigned districts of the parish. Some are elected representatives to Presbyteries and the General Assembly. On election an elder is 'ordained' for life (in a form different from clergy), assists in distribution of the communion and may take services. Age is no criterion as an elder may be elected at 21.

Presbyterians in England were persecuted well into the 17th century. As part of a bargain to support Cromwell in the Civil War, the Scots expected England to accept Presbyterianism as per the 1643 Solemn League and Covenant, but the English Puritans and Independents did not honour the deal. English Presbyterians grew into a substantial dissenting body until, in 1972, they joined with most of the Congregational Church (ironically descended from Cromwell's Independents) to form the United Reformed Church. In Canada a similar merger occurred as early as 1925, but substantial Presbyterian churches remain in the USA, Commonwealth countries (as a result of missionary activity) and the European heartland.

A tendency to disagree over the polity of the Church

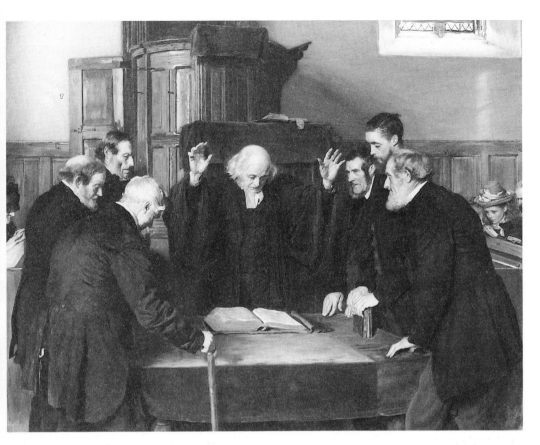

The Ordination of Elders in a Scottish Kirk, by *John Henry Lorimer* (NGS)

made Presbyterians a fissile denomination. Originally Covenanters were independent minded and in conflict with authority. (Some remained at large after 1690 and still are.) The **Secession Church** was a distinct threat in the 18th century, as was the **Free Church** in the 19th, with many others in between. But for Presbyterians today the only significant alternative to the Church of Scotland is the harder line Free Presbyterian Church, vocally Calvinistic and predominantly Gaelic. The parent Church of all English-speaking Presbyterians remains the established Church of Scotland with its Old Testament symbol, the burning bush, and Latin motto *Nec tamen consumebantur*, 'never consumed', which is borrowed from Continental Huguenots of the main Genevan origin. [See chart p. 995]

PRESTON, Battle of (1648)

In July 1648 **James 1st Duke of Hamilton**, leader of the **Engagers**, crossed the border into England at the head of a 20,000-strong army. His intention was to reinforce demands for the liberation of **Charles I** (currently held prisoner on the Isle of Wight) and for the fulfilment of the **Covenant**. But his army was underequipped and badly led and did not receive the anticipated support from English Royalists. Allowed to reach Lancashire before Cromwell moved to halt its progress, the Scottish force was comprehensively defeated at and

around Preston between 17 and 19 August, 2000 men being killed and more than 8000 taken prisoner. Hamilton himself surrendered on 25 August and was beheaded in March of the following year.

PRESTON, East Lothian

Named 'priests' town' after the monks of **Newbattle Abbey** who had lands here, Preston today is 'not so much a town or a village as an interesting incident alongside the road to **North Berwick**' (C McWilliam) and on the edge of Prestonpans. Its yellow sandstone Mercat Cross, frequently described as the finest and most handsome in Scotland, dates from c1617; the 15ft (4.5m) central shaft has a rectangular capital surmounted by a unicorn, the whole being set on top of a pilastered rotunda with scallop-headed niches and a door to a stairway leading up to the shaft platform. In the 12th century the monks founded the salt pans from which Prestonpans takes its name and used locally dug **coal** to heat sea-water in the evaporation process. The Scottish Mining Museum at Prestongrange incorporates the 1874 Beam-Engine house and other mining artefacts.

Old Hamilton House adjoining Preston's main street is a charming two-storey laird's house built in 1628 for Sir John Hamilton, brother of the 1st Earl of Haddington, and now owned by the **National Trust for Scotland**. Northfield House on the opposite side of the road dates from 1611 and has some fine tempera painted ceilings, only discovered under later plaster-

The Mercat Cross at Preston, East Lothian (HS)

work in 1956. The 15th century Preston Tower, enlarged in the 17th century by the addition of a new top floor above the original parapet walk, was burned by the Earl of Hertford in 1544, by Cromwell in 1650 and by accident in 1663, whereupon its owners, the Hamiltons of Preston, built Preston House as a replacement. It is now also a ruin. The site of the **Battle of Prestonpans** lies just to the east of the town.

PRESTON MILL, East Linton, East Lothian
Grain has been milled on this site by the river Tyne since the 12th century; much of the existing fabric of Preston Mill dates from the 17th century, with additions and renovations in 1749 and 1760. With one short interruption when it was inundated to roof level by a flood in 1948, Preston Mill has been working ever since. The great iron wheel, 13ft (3.96m) in diameter and 3ft 2in (1m) wide, dates from the 1760 renovation and was probably cast at the **Carron Company**'s **Falkirk** foundry. The kiln has a conical roof and windvane, the mill building and the outbuildings are built of orange sandstone rubble with red pantile roofs, and the whole is somewhat reminiscent of a Kent oast-house. It was presented to the **National Trust for Scotland** in 1950 and subsequently 'adopted' and now operated by the milling company Rank Hovis MacDougall. The delightfully named Phantassie Farm just south of the mill was the birthplace of the engineer **John Rennie** (1761–1821); the farm's distinctive beehive-shaped Phantassie **Doocot**, with nesting places for 500 birds, dates from the 16th–17th century.

PRESTONPANS, Battle of (1745)
As soon as news of **Prince Charles Edward Stewart**'s landing in Scotland reached **Edinburgh** on 8 August 1745, the Hanoverian commander Sir John Cope set out with a hastily assembled and ill-prepared army, determined to crush the rebellion before it had time to gather strength. Reaching **Dalwhinnie** on 26 August, he was warned by his spies that the **Corrieyairack** Pass was held by a **Jacobite** force of 3000 (in fact it was as yet only half that) poised to pick off anyone trying to cross it. With insufficient provisions to return the way he had come, yet knowing the race back to Edinburgh was now on, Cope withdrew to **Inverness** and thence to **Aberdeen** where he summoned ships to take his army back to **Dunbar**. The Jacobites won the race, Prince Charles Edward entering Edinburgh on 17 September, the day that Cope disembarked at Dunbar.

On the assumption that any Jacobite attack would come from the west, Cope marched towards Edinburgh and then drew up his army at Prestonpans (near **Musselburgh** and close to the battlefield of **Pinkie**, 1547) to await reinforcements from Berwick. But **Lord George Murray**, the Jacobite commander, was a wily tactician. Circling round to the south, he launched his attack instead from the east, taking Cope by surprise and from the rear. According to one historian, the Battle of Prestonpans was all over in a quarter of an hour; another avers that the rout of government forces by the Jacobites took less than 10 minutes. The result was politically important in that, with the exception of **Edinburgh**, **Stirling** and **Dumbarton Castles** and the Highland forts, the whole of Scotland was now under Jacobite control. But even more significant was the psychological boost it gave to the Prince himself and to the Jacobite cause as a whole; even Horace Walpole in London was forced to admit that the Highlanders 'were not such raw ragamuffins as they were represented'.

PRESTWICK, Ayrshire
The charter dated 19 June 1600 confirming and renewing the status of Prestwick expressly states that it was known to have been a free **burgh of barony** since 'beyond the memory of man'. The ruined Church of St Nicholas is thought to date from the 12th century, while the vestigial remains of the Chapel of **St Ninian** mark the site of a leper hospital founded by **Robert I** when he thought himself cured of the disease after drinking from a nearby well. With the arrival of the **railway** in 1841 and of the **golf course** in 1851 (the first Open Championship was played here in 1860), the village of Prestwick grew into a fashionable summer resort for the **Glasgow** middle classes. Prestwick **Airport** dates from the founding in 1935 of Scottish Aviation Ltd by David McIntyre and the Marquis of Clydesdale (later Duke of Hamilton) who, in 1933, had been the first to fly over Everest. During World War II the airfield became the headquarters of RAF Ferry Command and of the USAF Transport Command and later its enviable fair-weather record ensured its development into an international civil airport.

PRIMROSE, Archibald Philip, 5th Earl of Rosebery (1847–1929) Prime Minister
Although Rosebery was not born in Scotland, the family

'The Street, Prestwick' c1880 (GWWA)

and the title were Scottish. Its first holder, Sir Archibald Primrose (1661–1723), son and grandson of **Edinburgh** judges, had opposed **James VII** and, as MP for Edinburgh (1695), supported William and, as a Commissioner, the **Union**; he was rewarded with the Viscountcy and then the Earldom of Rosebery near Edinburgh. His great-great-grandson, Archibald Philip, was educated at Eton and Oxford and on succeeding to the title (1868) sat in the Lords as a Liberal. He eventually succeeded Gladstone as Prime Minister (1894–5). Although not a success, he unlike other 'Scots' Prime Ministers of the period (**Balfour**, **Campbell-Bannerman**, **Bonar Law**, **Ramsay MacDonald**) did at least take more than a purely electoral interest in Scottish affairs. In particular he lobbied for administrative change whereby Westminster would be obliged to take account of Scotland, then, as he put it, 'mumbling the dry bones of political neglect'. As a result he was given an under-secretaryship at the Home Office with specific responsibility for Scottish affairs. This minor concession soon led to the creation of the Scottish Office under its own Secretary (though not for another 40 years its own Secretary of State). Rosebery's other political concerns were largely with the role of the Lords and of the Empire. Outside politics, where he preferred to be, he was a noted racehorse owner (winning the Derby three times) and the author of several biographies.

PRIMROSE, Scottish

Primula scotica is one of the few plants which is endemic to Scotland, ie it has never occurred as a wild plant anywhere else. This perennial herb is confined to the far north, on the coast of **Caithness**, **Sutherland** and **Orkney**. It is a tiny plant, only 10cm tall, bearing beautiful purple flowers with a yellow eye. During recent decades the population of the Scottish Primrose has declined and conservation measures have been declared necessary to ensure its survival.

PRINCESS VICTORIA, SS

The loss of the **railway**-owned car ferry *Princess Victoria* on 31 January 1953 resulted in the heaviest loss of life (133) in a shipping accident in peacetime around the Scottish coast. It was the first accident on the **Stranraer–Larne** route in 82 years.

Equipped with stern doors for loading vehicles, the *Princess Victoria* was a **Clyde**-built steamer plying between Scotland and Northern Ireland until caught up in the storms of early 1953. After leaving Stranraer early in the morning, the ship was in difficulty even before leaving Loch Ryan and appeared to head northwards into the wind to maintain control on mountainous seas. Within two hours she radioed that control had been lost and that she was at the mercy of the weather. 45 minutes later she added that her stern doors had given way, and that she was taking in water. The ferry was thought to be near Corsewall Point off the Rhinns of **Galloway** (where the SS *Rowan* had foundered with 34 casualties on 9 October 1921), but rescue operations were hindered by confused position messages and the lack of powerful tugs. In fact, the *Princess Victoria* foundered in heavy seas much closer to the Irish coast than would-be rescuers had expected. Only 41 were saved out of 174 passengers and crew.

PRINGLE, John Quinton (1864–1925)
Painter

Born in the East End of **Glasgow**, Pringle was apprenticed to an optician at the age of 12 and this was to remain his profession all his life. He began drawing at an early age and in 1883 enrolled in evening classes in art organised by the Glasgow School Board. In 1885 he was awarded a bursary enabling him to study at the **Glasgow School of Art** where his considerable talent was admired and encouraged by the Director **Francis Newbery** and by fellow student **Charles Rennie Mackintosh**, and for the next 10 years he attended morning and evening classes there. His decision to remain an amateur artist belied his deep enthusiasm for the subject. He read avidly the latest art journals and frequented the Glasgow galleries and annual exhibitions of the Glasgow Institute, admiring the work of the Pre-Raphaelites, the Glasgow Boys [see **Painting**] and in particular their muse Jules Bastien-Lepage, whose square, dabbing brushwork he adopted. His early pictures demonstrate delicate and intricate detail which, coupled with their frequently small scale, lends them something of the quality of miniature painting. The time demanded by his exacting method, painstakingly building his compositions from a mosaic of colour, meant his output was low and from 1896, when he established his own business in Glasgow's **Saltmarket**, the time left to him for painting was reduced further.

During the early 1900s the backyards and street-scenes that were his earlier subjects gave way to more poetically treated landscapes often occupied by children at play, and as his palette lightened his technique grew close in style to the pointillism of the French Neo-Impressionists. His only trip to the Continent however was not made until 1910 and he would have known little of their work first hand. In 1911 the death of his sister, who was also his housekeeper, severely affected him and from then until 1920 his output was even more limited and restricted to watercolour. In 1923, his health failing, he sold his business. Devoting himself to painting he travelled widely through Britain. Confined to his home during his last year, the still-lifes and interiors he painted before his death from cancer are amongst his finest works.

PRISONS

In early and medieval times the function of such prisons as existed in Scotland was purely custodial. Justice was summary. The wrongdoer was held until he could be disposed of – by execution, banishment or until compensation was made. Prisons were town prisons (tolbooths), barons' prisons in their castles, and state prisons (King's castles). Banishment was the kernel of penal philosophy and from this developed transportation to American plantations, as in 1678 (**Covenanters**), and after the '15 and the '45 (**Jacobites**).

Not until the 18th and 19th centuries did deterrence and retribution become firmly established at the centre of the penal system. Although long-term prisoners and certain classes of offender – those accused of witchcraft, political offences, religious dissent and financial default – might be held in more secure establishments, the typical small-town prison of the 18th century was a mere hovel or vault and not particularly secure. But with the Penal Servitude Acts of 1855 and 1857 and the ending of transportation to Australia in 1867, larger, safer prisons became necessary. The hulks of convict ships, moored in English estuaries, served briefly, although models for the new institutions were already in existence at **Perth** and Dartmoor.

In many respects the filthy, promiscuous 18th century prisons were less inhuman than the repressive silent ones of the 19th century. Crank and treadmill typified the retribution demanded by the religious climate of the period; the illness, insanity and death of many inmates, some of them mere children (not until 1908 was it forbidden to send children under 14 to prison), served as a deterrent.

While the historical development of the prison systems in England and Scotland were separate, a degree of standardisation was achieved by the Prison Act of 1877 which laid down general principles. But as regards overall control there were to be separate organisations; in England the Home Office and in Scotland the Scottish Home and Health Department. Since the re-establishment of the

Scottish Parliament in 1998 responsibility for the Scottish Prison Service (SPS) has passed to the Scottish Executive, to whom the Chief Executive of the SPS reports.

In 1998–9 Scotland's average daily prison population stood at around 6000. Textiles, engineering, painting and decorating, horticulture and agriculture are among the main forms of employment on offer. Educational opportunities through O and H grades to university level are also afforded.

Scotland's prisons are: ABERDEEN (short-term local prisoners); BARLINNIE (Scotland's largest prison with c1000 long-term male prisoners from the west of Scotland); CASTLE HUNTLY (open prison); CORNTON VALE (Scotland's only all-female prison); DUMFRIES (young offenders' institution); EDINBURGH (SAUGHTON) (short-term prisoners from **Edinburgh**, parts of **Fife**, Lothians and Borders); FRIARTON (small (c90 inmates) short-term medium-security prison, near Perth); GLENOCHIL (long-term male adults with a separate young male offenders facility); GREENOCK (GATESIDE) (for adult male prisoners awaiting trial or sentence); INVERNESS (PORTERFIELD) (remand and short-term adult prisoners from Highlands, Western Isles, Orkneys and **Moray**); KILMARNOCK (Scotland's newest prison (opened March 1999) and first provided under the Private Finance Initiative); LONGRIGGEND (annexe to Barlinnie holding male remand prisoners under the age of 21); LOW MOSS (short-term male prisoners serving up to 12 months); NORANSIDE (open prison near Forfar); PERTH (adult male prisoners serving less than 4 years with separate long-term secure unit); PETERHEAD (secure prison for long-term prisoners with special unit for sex-offenders); POLMONT (Scotland's largest young offenders' institution); SHOTTS (maximum security for long-term adult male prisoners).

PROSCRIPTION, Act of (1747)

Introduced by Lord Hardwicke in the aftermath of the last **Jacobite Rising**, the 1747 Act of Proscription banned the wearing of **tartan** and Highland dress in the Highlands by any but the military. Combined with a subsequent measure to abolish the hereditary jurisdictions of the chiefs, the Act was an endeavour to destroy the troublesome **clan** system and undermine the social cohesion of 'these barbarous and disloyal savages', thus preventing any possibility of another rising. It was not until 1782 that, largely due to the efforts of the Highland Society of London, the Proscription was lifted.

'PROTESTORS'

During the period of Cromwellian rule (1650–60) the Scots clergy were bitterly divided between those, usually described as moderate, who were willing to acknowledge a role for the state in Church affairs, and those who objected to any such erastian compromise. The moderates, or **'Resolutioners'**, had Royalist sympathies and could expect few favours from Cromwell although they were in a majority. Their rivals, previously known as **'Remonstrants'**, became 'Protestors' when they objected to the authority of the General Assemblies of 1651 and 1652 on the grounds that they were dominated by 'corrupt' (ie Resolutioner) elements. By instead insisting on the continuance of the 1650 Assembly (on whose Commission they had enjoyed a majority), the Protestors in fact seceded. Come the restoration of the monarchy and of bishops, this schism would deepen, with many Protestors being further marginalised as the much persecuted **Covenanters** of the 1660s–80s.

PRYDE, James Ferrier (1866–1941) Painter

Born in **Edinburgh**, Pryde inherited from his father – the headmaster of the Queen Street Ladies' College – a romantic devotion to the theatre that would deeply affect both his art and life. He was taught at the **Royal Scottish Academy** Schools where his gift for portraiture won him the admiration of Glasgow Boys **James Guthrie** and E A Walton and with their encouragement he travelled to Paris where he studied under Bouguereau at the fashionable Académie Julien. On his return Pryde settled in London but remained little known – partly a result of his recalcitrant attitude towards exhibiting – until his collaboration from c1894 with his brother-in-law William Nicholson on a remarkable series of graphic designs made under the name 'J & W Beggarstaff'. Receiving commissions from, amongst others, Henry Irving for his latest theatrical productions, their work, characteristically simple but highly effective arrangements of boldly silhouetted forms and profiles, was startlingly novel, and a pioneering contribution towards wider Continental developments in poster design begun by the Frenchman Jules Chéret.

Pryde's paintings, chiefly of architecture and interiors occupied by figures dwarfed by their surroundings, though closer in mood and tone to the work of his English contemporaries, particularly Walter Sickert, are indebted to his romanticised memories of the grandeur of his native city. In 1909 he began his most notable series of paintings, entitled *The Human Comedy*, inspired by **Queen Mary**'s four-poster bed at **Holyroodhouse**, **Edinburgh**. Reminiscent of majestical theatrical settings and rendered in appropriately sombre colours, they are filled with an overriding sense of drama pervasive in all his work. This, coupled with the obscurity of any real incident, leaves his art somewhat lacking and hollow.

PTARMIGAN

The name ptarmigan comes from the Gaelic *tarmachan*, and the 'pt' seems to have been first mentioned in *Scotia Illustrata* by **Sir Robert Sibbald** in 1684. The breeding population is confined to north and west Scotland where for most of the year ptarmigan (*Lagopus Mutus*) live, feed and breed above 2500ft (762m). Rarely disturbed on their lonely hilltops, they were described by one 19th century naturalist as 'seldom shy or wild, but coming out from among the scattered stones, uttering their peculiar croaking cry and running in flocks near the intruder like tame chickens'.

The ptarmigan has developed an elaborate camouflage to compensate for the lack of cover in its chosen habitat; in summer the wings and underparts are white while the rest of the plumage is brown, mottled with black; in autumn the upper parts take on a grey mottling and in the winter the entire bird becomes pure white except for the red wattle over the eye and a black or brown tail; even the legs and feet are white feathered. The ptarmigan is unique amongst British birds in adopting this Arctic trait, and its white winter plumage is responsible for its local names of 'snow grouse', 'white game' and 'white partridge'.

There is evidence of a decline in ptarmigan numbers in many areas, especially on the edge of their range in Scotland – as in **Skye**, **Rum** and the Outer **Hebrides**. Declines on the mainland have in part been associated with the increase in **skiing** facilities; not only have the birds been known to fly into overhead wires, but a corresponding increase in the numbers of crows and gulls scavenging for scraps of the sportsmen's food has led to an increase in predation on ptarmigan eggs and chicks. As ptarmigan often occur in small discrete populations on isolated hills, they can be adversely affected by shooting, and many people believe that they should no longer appear on the quarry list of gamebirds. The present breeding population is estimated at less than 10,000 pairs.

QUAICHS
From the Gaelic *cuach*, a cup or bowl, a quaich (usually pron. 'quake') is a shallow drinking vessel peculiar to Scotland. It invariably has flat projecting handles or lugs, usually two at opposite sides of the rim, and was originally made of wood. Examples fashioned from a single piece of wood exist although a staved construction, as with a barrel, was more common, the separate sections being held together with willow withies or metal hoops. Silver was first used for the mountings in the 17th century and by 1700 was used for the entire quaich. Easily spilled, quaichs lost out to the cup and the glass in the 19th century but continued to be popular as commemorative presents and prizes. Collections like those in the **National Museums of Scotland** include examples in horn, pewter, brass and even marble. The more usual silver quaich may be embossed or engraved; chasing on the bowl sometimes recalls the original staved construction. Distinctively Scottish, and a deceptively capacious receptacle for whisky, the quaich has now become something of a national shibboleth.

QUARRYING AND EXTRACTION
The 19th century was the heyday of **coal** and **iron** extraction; today these industries have been replaced by the development of substantial **oil and gas** reserves around Scotland's coasts. In addition many other traditional industries which were once exploited on an enormous scale have declined, such as slate, granite and sandstone quarrying. Extraction of natural resources is controlled by market forces, cost effectiveness and environmental acceptability.

IRON was one of the earliest metals mined in Scotland, but it was not until the 18th century that Carboniferous ores were used, with the opening of the **Carron** iron-works at **Falkirk**. The ores utilised during the Industrial Revolution were the famous 'blackband' ironstones, a sedimentary deposit of iron called siderite found amongst Coal Measures notably in **Ayrshire** and **Lanarkshire**. A similar ironstone, this time Jurassic in age, was worked extensively on **Raasay** during World War I. No iron ores are presently extracted [see **Iron and Steel**].

LEAD or Galena was extensively mined in Scotland from the Middle Ages, the largest works being at **Leadhills** and **Wanlockhead** in **Dumfriesshire**, which date back to the 13th century. Elsewhere significant lead-mining took place on **Islay**, at **Strontian**, **Tyndrum** and in Galloway, especially during the late 18th and 19th centuries. Most lead mineralisation (together with zinc and copper ores) dates back to Carboniferous times, when hydro-thermal fluids were injected into faults cutting country rocks to form mineral veins up to 6 metres thick. Copper was also mined across the Dalradian outcrop during the last century on Islay, around Loch Fyne and at Sand Lodge on **Shetland**.

SILVER AND GOLD have been found in many places in Scotland, but only in small amounts. Silver occurs at **Alva, Clackmannanshire**, and at Hilderstone, **Linlithgow**, the former mined in the early 18th century, the latter in the 17th. Both produced small quantities of silver for a time from hydrothermal veins cut into Devonian and Carboniferous strata. More significant amounts of gold have been located recently near Tyndrum in **Perthshire**, where it occurs in veins in Dalradian schists, apparently in commercial quantities. The best-known occurrence of gold, however, was the 'gold-rush' at **Kildonan** in the 1860s, when alluvial gold was discovered in the **Helmsdale** River, derived from veins in the granite/schist bed-rock. Gold was also found at Leadhills in the 15th–16th centuries, and is currently being assessed in other parts of the Southern Uplands.

BARYTE In recent times this mineral has taken on renewed economic significance for use in the oil industry. Older mineral workings have been re-assessed, notably at Strontian, and a new large, high-grade baryte source has been discovered near **Aberfeldy** in Dalradian schists. The deposit seems to have formed from seepage of barium brines onto the bottom of the old Dalradian seafloor, which were then later caught up in the formation of the Caledonian mountains. In the past baryte was mined in Glen Sannox, **Arran**, at Muirshiels, **Renfrewshire** and Gass Water, Ayrshire.

GRANITE is not so widely exploited for building stone as it used to be. The largest quarry in Scotland is now Glensanda in **Morvern**, where 7 million tonnes of crushed granite aggregate are extracted annually and exported abroad. Other sites, for example on **Harris**, are threatened with equally gargantuan developments. On a smaller scale, granite is quarried for roadstone at **Bonawe (Loch Etive), Furnace** on Loch Fyne, near **Dalbeattie** and on the Ross of **Mull**, whose quarries provided much red granite for building projects in London in the 19th century, notably the Albert Memorial. The most extensive use of granite in Scotland was in the building of the granite city of **Aberdeen** and towns such as **Peterhead**. Red, pink and grey granites have been exploited from Caledonian intrusions, the rock colour being determined by its feldspar content. The largest excavation was Rubislaw Quarry in Aberdeen, where granite extraction began in the 18th century and continued until the quarry's closure in the 1970s. Other igneous rocks still continue to provide much material for roadstone chippings and **rail** ballast, especially the Carboniferous and Permian dolerites and felsites of Lanarkshire and Ayrshire.

SANDSTONE Traditional Scottish building stones such as old red and new red sandstones are also not as widely quarried as during the 19th century. The red sandstones of the Midland Valley, **Dumfries**, **Caithness** and **Orkney** were extracted on a large scale and transported primarily by Scotland's rail network, Nowadays, quarrying is very much reduced, although the famous Locharbriggs Red Sandstone Quarry still provides an attractive stone for important building projects such as the **Burrell Museum**. Both **Glasgow** and **Edinburgh** utilised local sandstones extensively in the 19th century for housing expansion, with large quarries at Giffnock, **Dalmeny**, Craigleith and **Craigmillar**.

SLATE quarrying has also virtually ceased. During the 19th century large quarries were opened in the Dalradian slate belt, notably at **Ballachulish** and in the 'slate islands' of **Easdale**, **Seil** and **Luing** in **Argyll**. The Ballachulish quarries employed hundreds of men during their heyday; in 1875 25 million slates were extracted. Disaster struck the Seil quarries in 1881 when the sea broke through and flooded the deep pits. Both areas suffered from competition from Welsh slates, which eventually forced their rundown and closure.

LIMESTONE was once extracted and burnt for its lime content across the Midland Valley, where Carboniferous limestones are concentrated. The largest quarry is at **Dunbar**, where the rock is taken for cement production; others are active in the North Ayrshire limestone outcrop. In the Highlands the Dalradian 'Tay' limestone outcrops over an extensive, if narrow, area, and the rock is still exploited, notably in Argyll, Perthshire, **Banffshire** and Shetland.

Marble is formed from limestone affected by heat from igneous intrusions. **Skye** marble, quarried at Torrin, has long been famous for its decorative and architectural uses. Here a Cambrian age limestone was baked into marble by a Tertiary granite intrusion. The celebrated **Iona** marble was quarried from pre-Cambrian veins on the island from the 16th century and is well displayed in the Cathedral. The marble is a pale metamorphosed limestone enhanced by green serpentine.

TALC AND SERPENTINE (metamorphosed igneous rocks) have both been extracted from Dalradian schists in the Highlands. The largest quarries are on Shetland (**Unst** and Cunningsburgh), where talc is taken for roofing felt, paint and the chemical industry. Serpentine has been wrought mainly for decorative purposes at **Portsoy**, on Shetland, and along the Highland Boundary Fault.

GLASS SAND High-grade glass sand has been extracted at **Lochaline**, **Morvern**, for some time; its purity is in the order of 99.8% silica. The rock is a white Cretaceous sandstone, preserved beneath a thick cover of Tertiary basalts. It was once used for optical glass, but is now exported for glassware.

See also **Coal**, **Oil and Gas**.

QUEEN ELIZABETH, SS

When the **Queen Mary** was conceived it was Cunard's intention to build two giant liners to operate a weekly service to the USA. This plan was frustrated by the slump

and Ship No 552 was not commissioned from **John Brown** [see **Shipbuilding**] until 1936. She was launched by the new Queen Elizabeth in September 1938. Fitting out was not complete at the declaration of war and in February 1940, amidst great secrecy, she sailed still half-finished for New York to escape the danger of enemy bombing. Her speed was so great that her convoy escorts could not keep up, nor could U Boats mount a successful attack. Fitted out as a troopship in Singapore, from 1943–5 she and her sister ship carried 320,000 US servicemen to Europe. She entered service as a passenger liner in 1946 and was soon as popular as the *Queen Mary*. She was withdrawn in 1969 and subsequently sold to C Y Tung of Hong Kong as a home for Seawise University. Arriving in Hong Kong early in 1972, she was destroyed by fire.

QUEEN MARY, SS

In the autumn of 1930 Cunard decided to build a giant luxury liner for the North Atlantic run, commissioning Ship No 534 from **John Brown** of **Clydebank** in December [see **Shipbuilding**]. Work started in the new year against a background of deepening world recession. In December Cunard was unable to continue to finance the contract, largely through its own intransigence, and work stopped. The yard was forced to lay off 3000 men and the abandoned hull soon became a national symbol of the slump – as if, in the words of **George Blake**, 'shipbuilding man had done too much'. Work did not resume until February 1934 and the vessel was launched amidst great excitement in September by Queen Mary. She entered service in June 1936, quickly winning the Blue Riband and becoming popular with

The Queen Mary *beginning to take shape at John Brown's Clydebank yard in September 1932 (BRC)*

American passengers. On the outbreak of hostilities in 1939 she was converted into a troopship. When the USA entered the war in 1943 she and her newly built sister, the **Queen Elizabeth**, acted as Atlantic ferries for GIs posted to Europe. With the coming of peace she returned to the Atlantic passenger service, being withdrawn in 1967. She is now berthed at Long Beach, California – as a maritime museum and hotel.

QUEEN'S OWN CAMERON HIGHLANDERS, The

The regiment was raised in 1793 by Colonel Allan Cameron of Erracht as the '79th Cameronian Volunteers'. The title was changed in 1804 to the '79th Cameronian Highlanders' and in 1806 to the '79th Cameron Highlanders'. In 1877 **Queen Victoria** added 'Queen's Own' and the regiment adopted blue facings instead of the original green on becoming a Royal Regiment.

In 1881 the regiment was unique among those not in the senior 25 in avoiding amalgamation, although transformation into the Third Battalion of the **Scots Guards** was threatened. The Highland Light Infantry Militia and the Inverness-shire Volunteers joined the regiment at the time. The 10th (Liverpool Scottish) Battalion, the King's Regiment, was affiliated in 1922 and became a part of the Camerons in 1937.

Early service included the Low Countries and Egypt; this was followed by Copenhagen, Corunna, the Peninsula, Waterloo, the Crimea, the Indian Mutiny and Egypt again. The regiment raised 13 battalions in World War I who served on the Western Front and in Macedonia, winning 58 battle honours. In World War II the regiment served in France in 1940, Abyssinia, North Africa, Sicily, Italy, Burma and in north-west Europe, being awarded a further 55 honours, bringing the regimental total to 134. After the war it saw service in Aden.

The regiment recruited in **Inverness-shire** where its headquarters were at Cameron Barracks, **Inverness**. From its foundation it wore a special regimental **tartan**; in 1945 the pipers were granted the right to wear the Royal Stuart. Since 1841 they had worn eagles' feathers in their glengarries. The regiment was allowed the blue hackle to be worn in the bonnet in 1951, some ten years after a direct approach to the King had resulted in its being approved by him but not by the Army Council. The Camerons marched past to 'Pibroch o' Donuil Dubh' (pipes) and 'Logie o' Buchan' (band).

HRH The Duke of Edinburgh became Colonel-in-Chief of the Camerons in 1953. In 1961 the regiment merged with the Seaforth Highlanders to become **The Queen's Own Highlanders (Seaforth and Cameron)**, and in 1994 was almagamated with the **Gordon Highlanders** to form the Highlanders (Seaforth, Gordon and Cameron).

QUEEN'S OWN HIGHLANDERS, The
(Seaforth and Cameron)

The regiment was formed in 1961 from the amalgamation of **The Queen's Own Cameron Highlanders** with **The Seaforth Highlanders** (**Ross**-shire Buffs, The Duke of Albany's) thus bringing together the old 72nd, 78th and 79th Highlanders.

Shortly after formation the regiment saw active service

in Brunei and it has since served several times in Northern Ireland and in the Gulf. Regimental Headquarters are at Cameron Barracks, **Inverness**, with the Regimental Museum at **Fort George**. The regiment possesses a total of 199 battle honours.

The Queen's Own Highlanders wear **kilts** of the **Mackenzie tartan** and trews of the Cameron of Erracht sett; Pipes and Drums and Military Band reverse this. Pipers wear eagles' feathers in their glengarries and the blue hackle, formerly worn by the Camerons, is worn by all the others.

The regiment marches past in quick and slow time respectively to 'Pibroch o' Donuil Dubh' (pipes) and 'The Regimental March of the Queen's Own Highlanders' (band) and to 'The Garb of Old Gaul' (pipes and band). HRH The Duke of Edinburgh, previously Colonel-in-Chief of the Camerons, continued in the same capacity for The Queen's Own Highlanders. In 1994 the regiment was amalgamated with the **Gordon Highlanders** to form the Highlanders (Seaforth, Gordon and Cameron).

QUEENSBERRY, Dukes etc, see DOUGLAS, James, 2nd Duke of Queensberry

QUEENSFERRY, see SOUTH QUEENSFERRY

QUINTINSHILL (GRETNA) RAIL CRASH (1915)

Britain's worst rail disaster took place on the Caledonian **Railway** at Quintinshill near **Gretna**, Dumfries and Galloway, just a few miles north of the Anglo-Scottish border (and about 20 miles south of **Lockerbie**, later the site of the country's worst air disaster). On 22 May 1915 three trains, two travelling north and one south, collided at Quintinshill with the loss of 227 lives. Many of the bodies proved untraceable as intense fire incinerated the wreckage of the trains.

It all began when a local train heading northwards from Carlisle was halted by signal at Quintinshill. To allow a northbound express to pass, the train was reversed from the down to the up (ie southward) line as the Quintinshill loops were full. The signalling staff appear to have ignored various procedural rules and became preoccupied with falsifying paperwork, while a crewman from the local train omitted to remind the signalman that his train now stood in the way of southbound traffic.

A heavily-laden troop train was then signalled 'all clear' southwards through Quintinshill, and this train, comprising antiquated coaching stock with gas lighting, struck the local at almost full speed, causing the troop train to telescope into half its length. As if this were not enough, the northbound express from London (Euston) ploughed into the wreckage. All but nine of the fatalities were on the troop train.

Most of them were men of the 7th Battalion **Royal Scots** on their way to service overseas after volunteering from the **Leith** and **Musselburgh** areas; a red granite memorial in the form of a Celtic cross stands in Rosebank Cemetery, Pilrig, **Edinburgh**, in memory of the 214 dead soldiers. Two of the signalmen were arrested and later tried at the High Court in Edinburgh. Found guilty of manslaughter, one was sentenced to three

Billiard room with sporting trophies in Glen Quoich Lodge, now submerged (GWWA)

years' imprisonment, the other to 18 months. Surprisingly, one of them was later re-engaged by the Caledonian Railway Company, but not as a signalman.

QUOICH, Glen, Inverness-shire

Included in the ancestral lands of the **MacDonells** of neighbouring **Glengarry**, Glen Quoich was split off and sold in 1838 to defray the MacDonell debts which had been rising ever since the **Jacobite** disasters. The purchaser, who later also acquired Glengarry, was the Rt Hon Edward Ellice MP, sometime Chairman of the Hudson's Bay Company and a distinguished political figure. Ellice spent half of each year at his Glen Quoich residence and entertained lavishly and fashionably. When **Joseph Mitchell** stayed there in 1850 he was the only guest without a title. The visitors' book includes comments from **Sir Roderick Murchison**, **Sir Archibald Geikie**, **Sir Edwin Landseer**, Prosper Mérimée (who complained bitterly about the **midges**), **Lord Dalhousie**, etc.

Ellice and his family cultivated good relations with their tenants (e.g. **Ewen MacPhee**), but conducted a massive assault on the estate's 'vermin' in order to improve its sporting potential. For the period 1837–40 the tally for Glens Quoich and Garry combined included 198 **wildcats**, 67 **badgers**, 48 otters, 27 **white-tailed** eagles, 18 **ospreys**, 15 **golden eagles**, 275 kestrels, 63 goshawks, 285 common buzzards, 371 rough-legged buzzards, 3 honey buzzards, 78 merlins, 63 hen harriers, 5 march harriers, etc. Presuming comparable vendettas elsewhere in the name of sport it is unsurprising that many of these species would be extinct in Scotland by the end of the century. In 1893 Lord Burton shot a stag with 20 points to its antlers.

The Ellice house and its garden were inundated when **Loch Quoich** was dammed for **hydro-electric** generation. All that remains of this once celebrated salon are a few rhododendron bushes above the waterline on the loch's bleak north shore.

QUOICH, Loch, Inverness-shire

This large freshwater loch between **Glen Garry** and Barrisdale (**Knoydart** peninsula) belies its bleak aspect and was once a place of great charm and considerable population. Poverty compelled the population to remove in the 19th century and a **hydro-electric** dam in the 20th inundated all the cultivable land, most of the islands, and the celebrated policies of **Glen Quoich** house. The level of the loch, thus artificially raised by some 100ft (30m), has seldom fallen, Quoich having an excessive rainfall even by West Highland standards. The annual average of 225in (5.71m) cited by **Sir Frank Fraser Darling** (1955) may make it the wettest spot in Europe.

before he paid for his island. The Highlands and Islands Development Board, established in 1965, possessed the powers to rescue Raasay, but it was not until 1979 that it paid Dr Green £135,000 for property he had acquired in the previous decade for less than £8000.

It has opened a hotel there, while Raasay House is run as an adventure school and other young people visit the Youth Hostel. The ageing population is supplemented by summer settlers in such places as Hallaig from which the native inhabitants were evicted during the **clearances**. See R Sharpe, *Raasay, A Study in Island History: Docs & Sources*, 1978, and *A Study in Island History*, 1982.

RAASAY, Island of, Inner Hebrides

The island of Raasay lies between **Skye** and the west mainland, separated from the former's Trotternish Peninsula by the Sound of Raasay and with the mainland district of **Applecross** eight miles to the east. 13 miles long and up to three miles wide, Raasay is a hilly island, rising in the centre to the flat-topped Dun Cann (1456ft/444m) where **Boswell** 'danced a Highland dance' during his visit to the island with **Dr Johnson** in 1773. There is a short ferry connection to Sconser on the Isle of Skye.

For much of its history Raasay was the property of a branch of the **Macleods** of **Lewis**, descendants of Torcuil son of Leod. They survived as Chiefs when Lewis was lost to the **Mackenzies** of **Kintail**, living in the fairytale castle of Brochel until the death by drowning of the Chief Iain Garbh in 1671. He was commemorated by a **MacCrimmon** *piobaireachd* and by three famous Gaelic elegies. Two decades later the Skye physician **Martin Martin** wrote of the islanders' attitude to their Chiefs: 'they have as great a veneration for them as any subjects can have for their king.'

The island suffered severely for its support of the **Jacobite** cause in the '45, but it recovered its prosperity and would have done so more permanently but for the iniquitous salt tax which prevented its inhabitants from marketing the riches of their surrounding seas. As a Minister wrote in the *Statistical Account* in the 1790s, 'The men of Raasay are excellent fishers and excellent seamen . . . they are more expert in fishing and appear to be fonder of a seafaring life than most of their neighbours.'

But the island's exceptionally cultured Chiefs made a most precious contribution to Scotland's heritage before their regime came to an end. John Mackay, born in Raasay in 1767, inherited the MacCrimmon tradition, and as piper to MacLeod transmitted the art to his son. **Angus Mackay** became the first piper to **Queen Victoria** and in 1838 published his great collection of *piobaireachd*, a legacy as precious as that of another great native of the island, the poet **Sorley Maclean**.

In 1843 the last resident chief was driven into bankruptcy, sold his island and sailed away to Tasmania. Thereafter, in the course of a disastrous century, Raasay passed through the hands of a West Indian sugar planter and his son, a Highland speculator of the most unscrupulous kind, a London romantic, a sporting industrialist, a firm of ironmasters, and a government department. By this body it was sold to the egregious Dr Green in Kent, who virtually obtained it for nothing, since he was able to resell small parcels of his property

RACING

William the Lion (1143–1214) organised a horse race on Lanark Moor which may make Scotland the birthplace of British racing. More recently, Scotland boasted 15 official racecourses; today five survive. **Ayr**, **Edinburgh** and **Hamilton Park** hold summer flat race meetings; **Kelso**, **Perth** and Edinburgh have winter jumping meetings.

Racing is funded principally by grants from the Racecourse Betting Levy Board, entry money from spectators and competitors, and commercial sponsorship. Bookmakers, long criticised for their removal of money from the business, are now amongst its most generous sponsors; there is much advertising to be gained. Prizes range from £2500 for midweek minor meetings to £75,000 for the Ayr Gold Cup. Hamilton Park was the instigator of the popular evening meetings and also first to complete all racing barriers in the modern plastic safety rail.

In the spring National Hunt racing, or point-to-point steeplechasing, draws local crowds. These are amateur fund-raising events to keep foxhunting alive, but are attended by people of diverse political allegiances. Hunt racing stipulates a minimum equine age of 5 years, jockey age of 18 years, weight of 11 stone, and a normal distance of three miles. Prize money is negligible. Many good chasers, horse and human alike, are discovered hunt racing, and old campaigners prolong their racing days competing at level weights.

Chasers running 'under rules' carry 10–12½ stone over 2–4 miles and jump about 20 substantial fences built from birchwood with gorse facings. Hurdlers race over wooden panels of birch about 3ft (1m) high, distances are the same. Flat race horses are usually tried as 3-year-olds, the more precocious as 2-year-olds, but carry lower weights over shorter distances than jumpers.

Turf Personalities

The most famous 19th century Scottish trainer was Matt Dawson, who won the Derby in 1860 with Thormanby. Dawson had the legendary Fred Archer as an apprentice at 11 years old. Archer became champion jockey at the age of 17, but tragically committed suicide at 21 after his wife died in childbirth.

Charlie Cunningham rode and trained his own horses at Wooden, Kelso, with staggering success from 1865–91, in spite of having a heavyweight 6ft 3in (1.9m) frame. He was early to develop the style of shorter stirrup leathers and tighter contact with the horse's mouth. Champion amateur in 1852, he had 47 wins from 100 rides. He bought three horses from the same mare that won him 51 races from 68 starts between them. In the three seasons from 1854 he won 52 from 100 starts, 49 from 100 and 47 from 76 respectively. On one day at Rugby he won all six races; another day he took his horse from the shafts of his carriage to win a race at Kelso, reharnessed and took his family home. He was disappointed five times in the Grand National. His famous Why Not was second with him in 1889, fourth after falling and remounting in 1890, but fell so heavily at the second last in 1891 that Cunningham was forced to hang up his saddle for ever.

Stewart Wight's stables were a source of inspiration for the traditional Scots racing farmer. Pupils included Fulke Walwyn, who rode Reynoldstown to win the Grand National for the second time in 1937; Reg Tweedie, owner and trainer of Scotland's favourite steeplechaser Freddie; and Adam Calder whose daughter Doreen rode his home-bred and trained Flying Ace to win over 55 Hunter chases and point-to-points.

George Boyd, training star of the 1950s, sent out 700 flat winners from his east-coast yard. His horses worked on the sands which gave them the advantage of fitness during arctic seasons or droughts. The colourful Ken Oliver, who rode his own mare to win the Scottish Grand National in 1950, sent out 5 winners of this 4-mile marathon from his **Hawick** yard. Rhona Oliver, the trainer, risked her precious Wyndburgh to run second in the Grand National three times. That controversial character Harry Bell had a very close Grand National second with Sebastian V; he also trained him to win the Scottish National in 1977; in 1972 and again in 1981 he won the same race with a 66–1 outsider carrying the lowest weight.

The Dun brothers of Heriot and the Macmillan brothers from **Lockerbie** regularly plundered the rich southern prizes, by combining professionalism with canny Scots horsemanship; like most mentioned before, they ignored the tempting offers for their mounts; theirs were simply 'Not For Sale'.

Scotland's hero of the turf is naturally a horse. A bay gelding who in his 74 jumping races never fell, though the last fence of his last race was his undoing. He grossed £100,000, winning 20 races, and when after a comfortable retirement he died in 1998, a headstone was raised in his honour and an oak tree planted in his memory. His name, Peaty Sandy.

Racecourses

AYR Flat and National Hunt. Scotland's only Group One course and venue for the Scottish Grand National. It moved (1907) to today's site from Belleisle where racing had been enjoyed since 1576. A left-handed flat track of 1 mile 4 furlongs with 4 furlong run-in. Best attendance was nearly 20,000 for Grand National day in 1969. Now averages 15,000; 12,000 watch the September Gold Cup worth £75,000. Draw favours low numbers 7 furlongs and up. Middle draws best in large fields on 5–6 furlong course.

EDINBURGH Founded in 1816 as Musselburgh Race Course, flat only. The frost-free shores of the Firth of Forth allow a winter-long schedule. A chasing course opened in 1978. The average gate is 2000 for a 1 mile 2 furlong right-handed track with 4 furlong run-in. The flat course is 1 mile 2 furlong with a straight 5 furlong course. Draw favours high numbers in 7–8 furlong races. Prize money totals about £20,000 for a day's racing.

HAMILTON PARK Flat racing only in a parkland setting 9 miles from **Glasgow**. Crowds of 7000 support the Saints and Sinners evening meeting (a fundraising event in aid of selected charities which appeals to all strata of Scottish society). A 6 furlong straight course with right-handed loop, 1 mile 5 furlongs. Draw favours middle to high numbers in straight course races.

KELSO National Hunt racing only on left handed 1 mile 2 furlong circuit. Long uphill run in. Uphill and downhill fences help attract hopeful Cheltenham Festival runners. Knowledgeable and friendly racegoers average 3000. The late Arthur Stevenson is still the top trainer with 105 winners.

PERTH National Hunt racing only. Flat parkland setting, right handed 1 mile 2 furlong course. Average crowd 2000. In 1978 Jonjo O'Neill rode five winners in an afternoon, and simultaneously broke the record for number of winners in a season.

RAE, Dr John (1813–93) Arctic Explorer

Of the many Orcadians who reached northern Canada in the employ of the Hudson's Bay Company, Rae was the most outstanding. Born near **Stromness**, he joined the Company as a surgeon after studying medicine in **Edinburgh**. His first journey, of which he published a narrative (1850), was to Repulse Bay, north of Hudson's Bay, in 1846–7. Returning to London he was immediately sent to join **Dr John Richardson**'s 1848–9 expedition searching for the missing John Franklin along the Arctic coast east of the Mackenzie River. In

Dr John Rae, the Arctic explorer, by Stephen Pearce (SNPG)

1850 he commanded a second Franklin expedition which in the course of a 1200-mile voyage extended the search east to Woolaston Land and Victoria Island. For the scientific results of this and his first journey he was awarded the Royal Geographical Society's Founder's Gold Medal (1852). A third journey (1853–4) to complete the survey of Canada's northern coastline finally succeeded, where so many had failed, in resolving the mystery of Franklin's disappearance. While exploring the east coast of the Boothia peninsula he had encountered Eskimos who knew where Franklin's ships had been abandoned and who had items from the expedition in their possession. Hastening home with the news, Rae found himself in line for part of the £10,000 reward; he used the money to build a schooner. Survey work, mostly for the overland telegraph, kept him in Canada until the mid-1860s when he returned to London where he eventually died; he was buried in **St Magnus' Cathedral**, **Kirkwall**. His achievements he ascribed to an ability to learn from, and live like, an Eskimo. He was also possessed of extraordinary stamina, once walking the 40 miles from Hamilton to Toronto in seven hours after which he went out to dinner none the worse for his exertion.

RAEBURN, Sir Henry (1756–1823) Portraitist

Without doubt the pre-eminent Scottish portrait painter of his age, Raeburn's reputation is now deemed on a par with the most celebrated of his English contemporaries, Reynolds, Gainsborough, Romney and Lawrence. Deeply attached to Scotland, Raeburn only lived out of the country on two occasions – a brief visit to Italy in 1784 and an even briefer stay in London in 1810. Born in **Edinburgh** and educated at **George Heriot's Hospital**, he was apprenticed at the age of 16 to a jeweller, James Gilliland. He began to paint miniatures and his exceptional talents soon came to the attention of David Martin, then Edinburgh's leading portraitist. Under his

Sir Henry Raeburn's Rev Robert Walker Skating (NGS)

guidance Raeburn developed an austere, sparse style, best exemplified in his precocious portrait of the geologist **James Hutton** (c1776, **Scottish National Portrait Gallery**). The visit to Italy, and contact with Sir Joshua Reynolds, opened up Raeburn's brushwork and palette. His unique style evolved – broadly worked areas combined with flourishes of detail – creating a whole that is more than merely the sum of the parts, effortlessly imbuing the character of the sitter. His landscape backgrounds, such as the ethereal, misty hills behind *Sir John and Lady Clerk of Penicuik* (1792, National Gallery of Ireland), are a particular delight of his early work, later replaced by more austere dark, studio-based portraits. With the death of Martin in 1798 Raeburn assumed an unrivalled position in Scotland and the York Place studio he moved into that year attracted an increasingly rich and aristocratic clientele. His full-length portraits of two Highland chieftains – *MacDonell of Glengarry* (**National Gallery of Scotland**) and *The McNab* (United Distillers) – were exhibited in London to great acclaim and embody the romantic ideals of Raeburn's contemporary **Sir Walter Scott** better than many later Victorian interpretations. His own portrait of Scott is one of the best-known representations of the writer. Raeburn employed a number of studio assistants who painted copies of portraits as well as completing works unfinished at the artist's death. Problems of attribution are, therefore, common. Raeburn's fundamentally empirical, rather than intellectual, approach to portraiture marks him down as essentially a man of the **Scottish Enlightenment**. It is apt that it is through his eyes the leading figures of that golden age are seen.

RAILWAYS

The railway network in Scotland is run by Railtrack with internal passenger trains operated by Scotrail, once part of the provincial sector of British Rail (nationalised in 1948, denationalised in 1994). Other operators are principally GNER on the east coast line to England and Virgin on the west coast line. The gauge is standard (4ft8½in/1435mm) and the system extends to 1674 route-miles (2678 km), approximately 300 miles of which was electrified with overhead 25kV in 1989. The system is administered from Scotrail House, 58 Port Dundas Road, **Glasgow**. In addition a few lines are preserved privately, while **Glasgow Underground** and suburban lines are run by Strathclyde Passenger Transport Executive.

EARLY ORIGINS The mining of **coal** stimulated the construction of early railways, more properly known as waggonways, in Scotland as in other parts of the UK. The first was laid out between **Tranent** and **Cockenzie** (**East Lothian**) in 1722, but there appear to have been two earlier attempts to construct such waggonways. According to the records of the Scottish Privy Council, a Thomas Tullock applied in 1604 to build 'workis for the commodious and aisie transporting of coillis' at **Inveresk**, near **Musselburgh**. 42 years later a James Allan petitioned the Scottish Parliament for permission to construct a similar waggonway from Stacks, near **Bo'ness**, to the south shore of the Forth. There is no direct evidence that either line was actually constructed, so credit for building the first waggonway north of the

Rock cutting at Bishopton for the Glasgow, Paisley & Greenock Railway c1841, by William Mackenzie (ML)

Railways continued

border must be given to the **York Buildings Company**, an English concern which took over the estate of the Earl of Winton who forfeited his lands at Tranent in Haddingtonshire (now East Lothian) for supporting the **Jacobite Rising** of 1715. Coal-mining was already a fairly intensive industry at Tranent, and its output could be transported more easily to the sea two miles to the north by the construction of a wooden-railed waggonway along which coal trucks could be moved by horse-power. The line enjoyed unusual notoriety by being fought over in the **Battle of Prestonpans** during the '45, and there is a passing mention of it in the famous song 'Hey Johnnie Cope'. The gauge of the line is believed to have been initially about 3ft 3in (1m), but it was relaid with wrought-iron rails, and regauged to standard with cast-iron rails in the 1850s before being superseded by 1886. The course of this, Scotland's first railway, is still perfectly visible in the East Lothian landscape.

Probably the biggest waggonway connecting collieries with a **canal** was the Monklands system northeast of Glasgow. In the early years of the 19th century railways gradually made a transition from transport adjunct connecting a particular industrial site to a harbour or waterway to inter-community link. The **Kilmarnock & Troon** Railway in **Ayrshire** was such a transitional line, opened with 4ft (1.2m) gauge in 1812, using L-shaped wedge rails and carrying passengers. The line experimented with steam power in 1816 or 1817, being the first in Scotland to do so, and was absorbed by the Glasgow Kilmarnock & **Ayr** in 1841 (later the Glasgow & South Western). Influenced by its success, and by that of the Stockton & Darlington in 1825, three Scottish railways were authorised in 1826 and all were working within 5 years. They were the

Edinburgh & **Dalkeith**, and the Garnkirk & Glasgow – both built originally to 'Scotch Gauge' of 4ft 6in (1.37m) – while the Newtyle Railway was gauged at 4ft 6½in (1.385m). The emergence of the steam locomotive (to which **James Watt** had contributed so much) had converted waggonways from localised horse-drawn (or even hand-powered) concerns to public utilities.

It was not until the end of the 1830s, and several years after England, that the railway first began to be viewed by Scots as an inter-city connection. Although canal transport was newly available between Edinburgh and Glasgow, it was natural that the 45-mile distance would seem little of a barrier to rail connections, and much Lancastrian capital was invested in setting up the Edinburgh & Glasgow Railway. Opened in 1842, it was engineered by John Miller on gentle gradients throughout except in Glasgow, where the canal proprietors were powerful enough to force the new line to be taken down a steep (1 in 42) gradient from Cowlairs, through a 1000yd (914m) tunnel, and into **Queen Street Station**. At the eastern end Haymarket was the Edinburgh terminus, until local conservationists (led by **Lord Cockburn**) were overcome and the line continued eastwards to the newly planned Joint Station, later to be known as **Waverley**. From 1846 two other lines operated here: the North British to **Berwick**, and the much-renamed Edinburgh **Leith** and **Granton** to Edinburgh's port and the **Burntisland** ferry at Granton.

The Cowlairs ambulance team of the North British Railway in 1892 (ML)

The early 1840s was the time when 'railway mania' raged and many rail schemes, wild and impractical, were speculated over, most never to be heard of again when economic conditions worsened. So many schemes were postulated for connecting the Scottish central belt with English markets that the government was forced to set up the Smith-Barlow Commission to decide on possible routes. In 1841 this recommended a west coast route to England via Annandale and Carlisle, to connect with the planned Lancaster and Carlisle Railway, and thus reach Crewe, the industrialised Midlands and of course London. However, if construction were not quickly started, an east-coast line through Berwick was to be considered, and this in fact was the first to be built, by the North British Railway, opened between Edinburgh and Berwick in 1846, the first line actually to cross the border. It had then no physical connection with the corresponding railway coming north, the Newcastle and Berwick (soon to be the North Eastern Railway) until Robert Stephenson completed the magnificent Royal Border Bridge, opened by **Queen Victoria** in 1850. (Despite its name, this structure is entirely in England.) The recommended route southwards, to be built by the Caledonian Railway, was slow to organise and construct, giving heart to a rival Glasgow-Carlisle scheme via Kilmarnock and **Dumfries**, later known as the Glasgow & South Western.

In fact all three lines across the border were open by 1850, being joined in 1862 by a North British Edinburgh-Carlisle line (known as the 'Waverley Route'), although its viability would always be undermined by being forced to proceed through the barren hills of Liddesdale rather than Langholm because of inter-company rivalry.

By the end of the 1860s the general outline of the Scottish rail network was virtually complete, except for lines in the West Highlands to **Oban**, **Kyle of Lochalsh**, **Fort William** and **Mallaig**, the great bridges across the Forth and **Tay** estuaries, and suburban lines in the growing cities, particularly Glasgow. From this time on to 1923 (when a reorganisation called the Grouping took place), Scotland's railways were run by five companies – the North British, Caledonian, Glasgow & South Western, Highland and Great North of Scotland.

NORTH BRITISH RAILWAY The largest Scottish railway (1389 route-miles operated by 1107 locomotives in 1922), the NBR originally comprised the Edinburgh–Berwick line opened in 1846 and a branch from the capital to **Hawick**. In 1862 it enlarged its operations northwards by combining with the Edinburgh, **Perth & Dundee** (originally the Edinburgh, Leith & Newhaven), with which it shared a terminal site in Edinburgh, and which pioneered the world's first train ferry in regular service, between Granton (Edinburgh) and Burntisland in **Fife**. This had been devised by Thomas Bouch, an ill-starred engineer knighted for his design of the **Tay Bridge**, and who was working on the original **Forth Bridge** design when the Tay structure collapsed with heavy loss of life in 1879. However, his ferry concept, in the form of the *Leviathan* and several sister ships, was a feature of the Scottish transport scene for more than 40 years.

In 1865 the North British made an even more propitious amalgamation, when it surprisingly merged with the pioneering inter-city link, the Edinburgh & Glasgow. This was a potentially lucrative line whose history was blemished by bad management but which saw off competition from the **Union Canal** (which it purchased in 1849) and the Caledonian. It gave the ambitious NBR entrée into Glasgow, where it was soon to rival the Caledonian in the construction of suburban lines. These included the underground line in a tunnel through Queen Street (Low Level) Station, operated by steam power until 1962. At the other end of the scale the NBR built (through a subsidiary company) the West Highland Railway, conquering **Rannoch Moor** and connecting Fort William and Mallaig with Glasgow via Loch Lomondside and **Crianlarich**.

The Tay Rail Bridge was the company's first major engineering challenge, and its failure in 1879 was its worst ever accident. A replacement bridge with two tracks was not opened until 1887, by which time the Forth Rail Bridge was under construction. This latter was undertaken with assistance from three English companies (the Midland, North Eastern and Great Northern), joining the NBR in a consortium known as the Forth Bridge Railway Company (which outlived all its parent railways by 25 years before nationalisation in 1948).

The Forth Bridge, arguably the greatest 19th century engineering structure in the world, was designed by Sir John Fowler and Benjamin Baker, and based on the cantilever principle with three huge diamond-shaped towers carrying a two-track viaduct no less than 150ft (46m) above high-water with two spans each of 1710ft (518m); its approach viaducts gave a total length of 1½ miles. Opened in 1890 by the Prince of Wales (later Edward VII), it provided a direct route from Edinburgh (and from Glasgow via Winchburgh) to Fife, Perth and the Tay Bridge. It made possible the 1895 railway race to **Aberdeen**.

This was the second of three races from London – to Edinburgh in 1888 and 1901, and to Aberdeen in 1895. Apart from giving much excitement to railway enthusiasts, who saw unprecedented times achieved (Aberdeen in 8hrs 32 minutes), the first two races had the unhappy effect of making the competing companies, worried by hostile public opinion after an accident to an Anglo-Scottish express in 1896, sign an agreement to keep express times between London and Edinburgh deliberately slow, a cartel arrangement which lasted until 1932.

The North British had been involved in the 1895 and 1901 races, but it was never known for its high speeds, for its lines were often constructed in piecemeal fashion with sharp gradients and link tunnelling. Its steam **locomotives**, the most famous being Atlantic 4-4-2s designed by W P Reid in 1906, were painted an unusual gamboge colour – rather like olive-green. From about 1900 to the end of the company's life in 1923 most of its passenger engines were named after characters from the novels and poems of **Sir Walter Scott**. Two locomotives are presently preserved in Scotland; 4-4-0 No 256 *Glen Douglas* at the Glasgow Museum of Transport and 0-6-0 No 673 *Maude* on the Bo'ness & Kinneil Railway.

THE CALEDONIAN RAILWAY With the emphasis on the definite article, The Caledonian Railway regarded itself as the principal Scottish railway, despite a near-disastrous start. Named by the Smith-Barlow Commission as the 'official' and indeed unique railway link between England and Scotland, its initial reliance on English capital, already heavily committed in existing railway projects, meant a slow start in constructing its line northwards from Carlisle through Annandale (ie **Lockerbie**) and over the 1000ft (305m) **Beattock** pass, which surveyors originally believed would be impossible for locomotives to climb. As it was, Beattock bank, 10 miles at a gradient of around 1 in 75, was a serious impediment to northbound trains until the Crewe–Glasgow line was electrified by British Rail in 1974. At **Carstairs**, traffic to Glasgow and Edinburgh split at a Crewe-style station.

The company's first headquarters were in **Princes Street**, Edinburgh, although they soon moved to Glasgow, where the first terminus was at Townhead. Access to the city was originally gained by traversing the early Garnkirk line to Townhead, but larger terminal facilities were soon gained at Bridge Street in 1849, and the **Clyde** was crossed to the site of the present **Central Station** 30 years later. This was greatly enlarged by 1906. Like the North British, the Caledonian had its own underground line running north and south under the city, again steam-powered (and not to be confused with the Glasgow Underground), and opened by 1896. Services to and from Glasgow and the north used Buchanan Street terminus, closed in 1966 and now the site for Scotrail HQ. The resulting lack of a through station for Glasgow has always been a problem – services between England and Perth/Dundee/Aberdeen skirt the city by an avoiding line via Law Junction and **Cumbernauld**.

In Edinburgh, no proper terminus worthy of the capital was constructed by the Caledonian until 1893, some 45 years after a foundation stone had been laid. Unlike Glasgow's Central, Edinburgh's Princes Street Station (its main entrance actually in Rutland Street) closed in 1965, and was demolished, leaving the company's Caledonian Hotel alone on the site. Dundee's West terminus was also Caledonian (closed 1965), while the company shared major stations at Carlisle, Perth and Aberdeen.

The Caledonian had outposts at **Oban**, **Portpatrick** (a joint line) and even Brayton in Cumbria (reached by crossing the **Solway Viaduct** in which the Caledonian heavily invested), but its main characteristic was its operation of fast express trains, including Pullman cars and hauled by a series of 'Dunalastair' 4-4-0 steam locomotives designed by J F McIntosh and regarded throughout Europe as the finest of their kind. With locomotives painted Prussian blue, its passenger trains out of Glasgow (Central) to England, or from Buchanan Street to Aberdeen, were in a class of their own. The company's participation in the three railway races was exemplary and exactly what could be expected from a line with a tradition of high-speed running. Had the Caledonian merged with the Edinburgh & Glasgow before 1865 as was expected – the two companies even published joint revenue results at one time – the North British would not have gained such a firm hold in Glasgow and the joint organisation would have become the giant among railways which the Caledonian's staff always felt it to be. In 1922 it owned approximately 1100 route-miles of track, with 346 passenger stations, and operated 927 locomotives. Three of these are preserved in Scotland – unique 4-2-2 No 123, and 0-6-0 No 828 at Glasgow's Museum of Transport, and 0-4-4 tank engine No 419 on the Bo'ness and Kinneil Railway.

The company's worst accident was the worst in British railway history. In 1915, at **Quintinshill** north of **Gretna Green**, 227 passengers were killed in a multiple pile-up caused entirely by human error and unofficial working practices.

GLASGOW & SOUTH WESTERN RAILWAY Formed by the amalgamation of the Glasgow, Dumfries & Carlisle and the Glasgow Kilmarnock & Ayr Railways, this company monopolised much of its geographical area, becoming better known for its services from Glasgow to the Clyde coast and to **Stranraer** than for its Anglo-Scottish traffic; this passed through Kilmarnock and Dumfries to Carlisle by running southwards from Gretna junction over Caledonian tracks and then to English destinations via the Midland Railway. It enjoyed considerable traffic in the Ayrshire coalfield.

Its Glasgow terminus was St Enoch, closed in 1966, its locomotive works at Kilmarnock. With a livery of dark green, its locomotives totalled 528 in 1922, one of them, tank engine No 9 of 1917, still to be seen at the Glasgow Museum of Transport. Its greatest engineering work was the Ballochmyle viaduct in Ayrshire, whose central arch has a diameter of 181ft (55m), the largest in Britain at the time of construction (1846), while this 7-arch structure is regarded as the highest in Britain at 164ft (50m) above the bed of the river. (The Forth Rail Bridge is approximately 156ft (48m) above sea-level.)

The GSWR was immortalised by an unofficial historian, David L Smith, whose written reminiscences of working life on the 'Sou'West' were as unique as they are absorbing. In 1922 the GSWR owned 493 route-miles and 163 passenger stations.

HIGHLAND RAILWAY Responsible for opening up the Scottish Highlands to the ordinary traveller, the Highland constituted a star-shaped system based on **Inverness**. There was a main line southwards to meet the Caledonian and NBR at Perth, and this was engineered by **Joseph Mitchell** over **Drumochter** (1484ft/452m) and Dava (1052ft/305m). A more direct line between Inverness and **Aviemore** was later opened over Slochd (1315ft/401m). Other 'arms' ran east to **Keith**, giving permitted running into Aberdeen, and northwards to the ultimate northern coast of the British mainland at **Wick** and **Thurso**, and also north-west to Kyle of Lochalsh. The system is still basically complete.

The line had a rugged policy of independence from other companies and a deadly rivalry with the Great North of Scotland Railway. Its locomotive department produced some exceptional engines, including the first 4-6-0 wheel arrangement in Britain. Known as the 'Jones Goods' after its English-born designer David Jones, the first example of the class, numbered 103, is preserved in Glasgow's Museum of Transport. At the Grouping of Britain's railways at the beginning of 1923, the Highland owned 506 route-miles of track and 173 locomotives.

GREAT NORTH OF SCOTLAND RAILWAY Based on Aberdeen, this smallest of Scotland's pre-Grouping companies ran from **Fraserburgh** in the north to the Granite City, with lines westward to Keith and as far west as **Lossiemouth** on the **Banffshire** coast, and to **Ballater** in Royal Deeside. It owned 336 route-miles of track and 122 locomotives by 1922. Sadly, of its 134 stations, only five remained open by 1988. One unusual aspect of its locomotive department was its use of 4-4-0 locomotives equally on passenger and freight trains, one of them, No 49 *Gordon Highlander*, being preserved in Glasgow's Museum of Transport.

In 1923 the North British and Great North of Scotland

were merged into the London & North Eastern Railway, while the other three were swallowed up by the London Midland & Scottish. In 1948 these two major companies were nationalised and Scotland's railways were then run by the British Railways Board. The size of the system was greatly reduced by closures in the early 1950s and 1960s, and the last steam locomotive operated on normal services on BR tracks in 1966. A number of preservation initiatives help keep alive the history of Scotland's railways, and the visitor is recommended to visit the Glasgow Transport Museum in the **Kelvin Hall** and the Scottish Railway Preservation Society headquarters at Bo'ness in Central Region.

RAIT CASTLE, Nr Nairn

A most unusual, if not unique, hall-house south of **Nairn**, Rait is early (late 13th/early 14th centuries) and with its pointed windows and doorway could easily pass for a church. Rectangular with a round tower attached to one of the angles, it could also be described as L-plan yet it is emphatically not a tower-house. The two storeys are missing their roof (pitched with short corbelled parapets at the gable ends) and their only floor (between the ground-level storehouse and the first-floor hall). The hall has fireplace, latrine, and those mullioned Gothic windows plus the only entrance which was reached from outside by a wooden staircase; it also has a slot for a portcullis. The de Rait family, who built it, may have been **Comyns** and had taken the English side during the **Wars of Independence**, though this scarcely explains their very un-Scottish 'castle'. They removed elsewhere after killing the Thane of **Cawdor** in 1404. The 'castle' passed to the **Mackintoshes** and then to the **Campbells** of Cawdor.

RAMSAY, Allan (1684–1758) Poet and Editor

Although he was a native of **Leadhills**, the mining district of **Lanarkshire**, Ramsay is more readily associated with **Edinburgh** and the **Pentland Hill** country of the **Midlothian** and **Peeblesshire** border. It was to Edinburgh that he came in 1700 to be apprenticed as a wigmaker; and it was Edinburgh that remained the centre of his commercial, social and intellectual world. Literature, in one form or another, gradually replaced the skilled craft for which he had been trained as the central motivating force of his life. He became a bookseller, with shops successively in Niddry's Wynd and the **Luckenbooths** in the **High Street**. At the latter premises he established, in 1725, what was probably the earliest circulating library in Britain. In 1736 he became a theatrical impresario, and opened a playhouse in Carruber's Close. This was suppressed by the magistrates of Edinburgh. He also dabbled in auctioneering and in dealing in decorative art objects. But in time he grew weary of commercial activities, and withdrew from public life to a house he had built on the **Castle Hill**. Here, and at the Midlothian seat of his great friends the **Clerks of Penicuik** and the Forbeses of Newhall, where he spent long periods, he lived a life of Horatian retirement and virtuous ease.

After early poetic efforts written for the Easy Club – a nationalist and **Jacobite** literary body – Ramsay published his first quarto collected edition in 1721. This

Allan Ramsay the poet, by his son Allan Ramsay the artist, 1729 (SNPG)

was followed in 1728 by a second collection of verse. The Scots poems in these volumes show Ramsay at his best as a master of vernacular satiric humour, especially in the mock elegy and the verse epistle. His offerings in Augustan English, in which he saw himself as some sort of Scottish Pope, were much less successful. His imitations of Horace are an aspect of his quasi classical lifestyle, and go some way towards endowing the Midlothian uplands with the spirit of the Sabine hills.

As an editor, Ramsay played an important part in preserving and handing on to succeeding generations the heritage of earlier Scottish poetry. In 1724 he published *The Ever Green*, an anthology of Middle Scots verse, notably that of **Dunbar** and **Henryson**, most of which he gathered from the **Bannatyne Manuscript**, recording his indebtedness to this source in a note in one of the volumes of that great treasury of the verse of the **Makars**. The five volumes of his *Tea-Table Miscellany* (1724–37) brought together many of the traditional songs and **ballads** of Scotland, to which he added compositions of his own. Ramsay was not a scholarly or impartial editor; but he was, nevertheless, a vital link in the transmission of the texts of much of Scotland's earlier literary heritage.

By far the most celebrated of Ramsay's works was *The Gentle Shepherd*, a pastoral comedy which received extravagant praise throughout the 18th and earlier 19th centuries for its portrayal of rustic life and manners. Originating in 1725, the drama was subsequently transformed into a ballad opera on the model of John Gay's *Beggar's Opera*. **Boswell** and **Burns** were among those who admired the work unreservedly and excessively as the finest and most realistic pastoral ever written.

Ramsay had always been interested in the visual arts. He encouraged the artistic education of his son **Allan** (1713–84), who attained the greatest distinction as one of the finest of British portrait painters. The younger Ramsay had a subsidiary career as a man of letters; and thus, together, father and son embody something of the ideal of the unity of the sister arts.

RAMSAY, Allan (1713–84) Portraitist and Essayist

Ramsay was the leading British portrait painter before the young Joshua Reynolds made his mark in the 1750s. He was also a philosopher and pamphleteer, a significant figure in the **Scottish Enlightenment**.

He was born in the parish of New Kirk, **Edinburgh**, the eldest of the many children of the poet **Allan Ramsay**. Through his father's celebrity he met eminent literary men in his youth. Ramsay senior had prints as well as books to inspire the boy. Already by the age of 16 Ramsay was capable of drawing the accomplished self-portrait now in the **National Gallery of Scotland**. One of his father's friends was **Sir John Clerk of Penicuik** who allowed him to copy Old Masters in his collection.

On leaving school Ramsay entered the London studio of the Swedish painter Hans Hysing. He returned to Edinburgh in 1733 and set up as a portrait painter in his father's house in the **High Street** and designed him an octagonal house for his retirement, derided by the local folk as a 'Guse-pye'. He began to attract a fashionable clientele. The works of this period have some distinction but they are still 'provincial' in style, the ponderous baroque style of the Sir Godfrey Kneller tradition. In 1736 Ramsay went to Italy, accompanied by Dr Alexander Cunyngham (later known as Sir Alexander Dick). In Rome he studied under Francesco Imperiali, but was more decisively influenced by one of Imperiali's former pupils, the portrait painter Pompeo Batoni.

The effects of these influences were seen in the fine portraits Ramsay painted after he left Italy in 1738, including a sensitive study of his first wife, Anne Bayne. In that year he set up a London practice in Covent Garden, charging 8 guineas a head. He also enrolled himself in the academy in St Martin's Lane which Hogarth had established three years earlier.

Ramsay's European training gave him the edge over contemporary British portraitists. The 'social mask' and stock attitudes were giving way to the rococo taste for the informal, unaffected and natural. The sitter's individuality and humanity, rather than 'nobility', were now to be emphasised. George Vertue, who visited Ramsay's studio in the late 1730s, noted how successful he was becoming. Ramsay was winning such important sitters as Lord Hardwicke and the **2nd Duke of Argyll**. He painted women with grace and subtle colour. 'Mr Reynolds seldom succeeds in women,' wrote Horace Walpole; 'Mr Ramsay is formed to paint them.' Ramsay's portrait of his second wife Margaret Lindsay, one of the best-loved images in Scottish painting, remains his most vivacious and intimate.

Ramsay was not content to be just a painter. He fancied himself as a *philosophe*. The philosophy, like the art, was on the European model. He visited Voltaire and painted Rousseau (who however disliked the resulting image, describing it as '*un Cyclope affreux*'). Diderot got hold of the wrong end of the stick when he retailed the rumour that Ramsay 'paints badly but reasons very well'. In 1752 Ramsay published his first two essays. One, 'On Ridicule', paid tribute to 'the incomparable Hogarth'. The other was on a legal case that divided all Britain in 1753–4; that of Elizabeth Canning, a London serving girl who claimed she had been carried off to a brothel in Enfield, outside London, had refused to become a prostitute and had escaped after a month of bread-and-water imprisonment in an attic. Canning's alleged captors were brought to trial and one of them, a gypsy woman, was sentenced to death for robbing the girl of her stays. Ramsay, masquerading as 'a clergyman', wrote a pamphlet attacking Canning's story; this pamphlet, more than any other, was credited with turning public opinion against the girl, who was later convicted of perjury and transported to America. Voltaire, who also wrote a pamphlet about the Canning case, praised Ramsay's essay. What prompted the artist's interest in the case has never been satisfactorily explained.

In the year of the Canning pamphlet, Ramsay returned to his roots in Edinburgh where he painted many eminent people, including Lord Auchinleck, the father of **James Boswell**. In 1754 he founded the Select Society, a debating club, in association with his friends **David Hume** and **Adam Smith**. From 1754 to 1757 he made a second, protracted visit to Italy, where be became a friend of the architect **Robert Adam**. In 1755 he published a pamphlet on Taste, with the central argument that taste cannot be measured or judged by any absolute standard.

In 1758 he painted one of his most acclaimed portraits, of **John Stuart, 3rd Earl of Bute** – showing to best advantage the legs of which the statesman was so proud. When, on the accession of Bute's pupil King George III (1760), Ramsay was appointed Court Painter, satirists claimed he had the patronage because Lord Bute was a Scot – a Stuart, indeed. Laurence Sterne said 'Mr Ramsay, you paint only the Court Cards, the King, Queen and Knave' (by the Knave he meant Bute). In 1767 Ramsay was appointed Principal Painter in Ordinary to the King.

Ramsay never exhibited at the Royal Academy, perhaps because he did not want to join an institution presided over by his arch-rival Reynolds. This *hauteur* kept him from the public eye. In 1773 he fell and dislocated his right arm so badly that it never recovered. He could still draw by resting the arm on a table or desk, but his genius was never seen at its full power again. He dedicated the rest of his life to literary and archaeological pursuits.

In the 19th and 20th centuries, Ramsay's reputation slid into decline. Two books – Desmond Shawe-Taylor's *The Georgians: Eighteenth Century Portraiture and Society* (1990) and Alastair Smart's *Allan Ramsay: Painter, Essayist and Man of the Enlightenment* (1992) – have restored him to his place as one of the pre-eminent artists of the 18th century, in the company of Reynolds, Gainsborough and Romney.

RAMSAY, Edward Bannerman Burnett
(1793–1872) Dean of Edinburgh

The son of Alexander Burnett, Sheriff of **Kincardineshire** (who changed his surname on inheriting the Yorkshire estates of his uncle Sir Alexander Ramsay), Edward Ramsay spent much of his childhood in Yorkshire and was educated at Durham Cathedral School and St John's College, Cambridge. Ordained in 1816, he served as curate in two English parishes before moving to **Edinburgh** in 1824. Minister of **St John's Episcopal Church** in **Princes Street** from 1830 until his death 42 years later, he was appointed Dean of the Diocese of Edinburgh in 1841. One of the city's best-known and best-loved figures, Dean Ramsay was philanthropist, musician and avid charity fund-raiser as well as a successful author – in addition to numerous religious works, his *Reminiscences of Scottish Life and Character* (1858), a charming collection of anecdotes and vignettes, ran to 22 editions in his lifetime. The Dean Ramsay Memorial, in the shape of a 7.3m high Celtic cross designed by **Robert Rowand Anderson** and paid for by public subscription, was erected outside St John's Church in 1878.

RAMSAY, James Andrew Broun, 10th Earl and 1st Marquis of Dalhousie **(1812–60)**
Governor-General of India

Ramsays have held land at Dalhousie (near **Dalkeith**) since the 12th century; the earldom came courtesy of **Charles I** in 1633. George 9th Earl (1770–1848) had a distinguished career as commander of a division in the Peninsular War, Lieutenant-Governor of Nova Scotia (1816) and then Governor of Canada (1819). James, born at Dalhousie, accompanied his parents to Canada but was sent home for education at Harrow and then Oxford (by which time his father was Commander-in-Chief in India). Elected MP for **Haddington** (1837), he went to the Lords in the following year on the death of his father. In 1845 he succeeded Gladstone as President of the Board of Trade. With an ability exceeded only by his extraordinary industry, in 1848 aged 35 he was appointed the youngest ever Governor-General of India. He held the post for eight years, an unusually long stint, and at the time was rated India's most effective 19th century ruler. Certainly a great deal was achieved. To Dalhousie's acquisitive policies (which added Punjab, Oudh, much of central India, and part of Burma), British India, and later independent India, owed its considerable integrity. To his energy it also owed its integration, as he brought to the East the first fruits of Victorian industry with thousands of miles of roads, railways, canals and telegraph lines. Yet he was not a sympathetic figure. 'He could not see with other men's eyes; or think with other men's brains; or feel with other men's hearts' (J W Kaye). He despised Indians and alienated his colleagues with a dictatorial manner. But when he left (1856), worn out by his endeavours, he was a hero. The deluge came a year later in the form of the Indian Mutiny; Dalhousie's reputation plummeted and he died in 1860. Undoubtedly his insensitivity had in part provoked the rising; on the other hand, his roads and railways facilitated its suppression.

RAMSAY, Sir John, 1st Earl of Holderness
(c1580–1629) Courtier

A close favourite of **James VI**, Ramsay was the man who killed **John Ruthven, 3rd Earl of Gowrie**, in the puzzling scuffle known as the **Gowrie Conspiracy** of 1600. He subsequently accompanied James to England and was created Viscount Haddington and then Earl of Holderness (1621).

RAMSAY, Sir William **(1852–1916)** Chemist

Born in **Glasgow** and educated at the city's **University** and in Germany, Ramsay developed into one of chemistry's most astute experimenters. In academic posts in Bristol and London he carried out brilliant research on the inert gases, identifying argon and helium and discovering neon, krypton, xenon and radon. His work laid the foundation for much of nuclear science, and he deservedly won the Nobel Prize for Chemistry in 1904.

RANDOLPH, Thomas, Earl of Moray **(d.1332)**

The son of Sir Thomas, Chamberlain and executor of **Devorguilla Balliol**, and of Isabella, daughter of Countess Marjorie of Carrick, Thomas Randolph was thus **Robert I**'s step-nephew. After capture at **Methven** (1306) he joined the English side until captured by **James Douglas**. He then rejoined Robert I but scorned guerrilla war as 'ungentlemanly'. He was given the Earldom of **Moray** in 1312. In March 1314 he took **Edinburgh Castle**, climbing the Rock by night, and commanded the vanguard at **Bannockburn**. He then fought in Ireland with **Edward Bruce** (1315–16) and as Lord of Man (1316) regained that island and raided Anglesey (1317). In 1318, with Douglas, he recovered **Berwick** and raided England. He also served as envoy to the Pope (1323), obtaining Papal recognition of Robert I, and as envoy to France (1326, Treaty of Corbeil). Nominated a future Guardian in 1318, he took office in 1329 but died at **Musselburgh** while preparing to counter **Edward Balliol**'s plans. His daughter, **Black Agnes, Countess of Dunbar**, was worthy of him.

RANKINE, William John MacQuorn **(1820–72)** Engineer and Scientist

Macquorn Rankine was born in **Edinburgh**, the son of an engineer. He studied for two years at **Edinburgh University**, and in 1838 became a pupil of the Irish engineer John MacNeill. After completing his pupilage he continued to practise as an engineer, while conducting his own research on **railway** engineering, molecular physics and thermodynamics; in 1853 he was elected FRS. Rankine's work on thermodynamics, with that of Carnot and Clausius, was built upon by **William Thomson** in his formulation of the laws of transformation and equivalence. In 1855 Rankine was appointed Professor of **Engineering** and Mechanics at **Glasgow University**.

Rankine's contribution to the development of a systematic programme of training for engineers was enormous. He campaigned vigorously for the introduction of a Certificate of Proficiency in Engineering Science, and after its introduction at Glasgow in 1863 he pressed for a BSc degree, which was introduced shortly after his death in 1872. He was an excellent teacher, who emphasised the 'mutual dependence and harmony between sound theory and good practice', and he was responsible for establishing the University's famous 'sandwich courses' in co-operation with leading industrialists in Scotland. As well as over 150 scientific papers, he wrote engineering textbooks and manuals which became standard works of reference for students around the world. His stated aim, 'the advancement of science as applied to practice in the mechanical arts', was pursued in all his work as an engineering scientist and teacher.

Rankine has been described as 'the father of engineering science in this country' in recognition of his achievements both as a theoretical scientist and as an educator. He was the first President of the Institution of Engineers in Scotland.

RANNOCH MOOR, Argyll/Perthshire

'A broad, undulating waste of bog, heath-clad hillock and loch' (**F Fraser Darling**), the great moor of Rannoch covers over 50 square miles between Bridge of Orchy, **Glencoe** and Loch Rannoch. Excluding such peripheral villages, it is probably the largest uninhabited wilderness in the British Isles. Its average height is about 1000ft (305m), but the surrounding mountains hint at an Ice Age origin as a vast glacial basin. It was subsequently clothed in **Caledonian forest**, remnants of which still stand at Black Mount and Crannach (both near Bridge of Orchy) and Loch Rannoch; more lie embedded in the **peat**. Cattle rustlers made use of the forest's cover until the 18th century when the burning of oak for charcoal for **iron** smelting and the construction of the **military road** put paid to both trees and outlaws. The military road (1748–53) hugs the western skirt of the moor as do the West Highland Way and, parallel, the present A82; all meet at **Kingshouse**. The **Glasgow–Fort William** railway took a more adventurous line across the south of the moor to Rannoch and then north to **Corrour**, the most desolate station in Britain, having neither electricity nor road. Where the peat is impossibly thick the sleepers were laid on brushwood. Some idea of the extent of lochs and burns may be gained from claims to have swum across the moor (improbable), to have skated across it (credible), and to have fished across it (delightful).

RAVENSCRAIG CASTLE, Kirkcaldy, Fife

A fortification dictated by its site, Ravenscraig was designed to render impregnable, even to cannon, a rocky promontory jutting into and commanding the Firth of Forth between **Kirkcaldy** and Dysart. As at **Tantallon**, therefore, its principal structures face inland across a ditch at the neck of the promontory. They comprise two horseshoe-shaped towers, with walls 14ft (4.25m) thick, connected by a curtain wall incorporating the main entrance, some two-storey buildings and, above them, a massively strong gun-looped parapet. Work began in 1460 when the site was gifted to **Mary of Gueldres**, wife of **James II**. She continued with the construction after his death but after her own death **James III** exchanged the still incomplete Ravenscraig for **Kirkwall Castle**. It therefore passed to the **Sinclair Earls of Orkney** who finished construction to a modi-

fied design in the 16th century and remained in occupation till the 17th. Now a substantial ruin, it is managed by the local council.

REAY, Caithness

This scattered village, not far from the border with **Strathnaver** (now incorporated in **Sutherland**), is embellished by a most distinctive 18th century church. Nearby stands the mansion of Sandside in its woodland and beyond it a **golf course** beside its pleasant bay. This property was sold by Lord Forbes to Donald, Chief of **Mackay**, only a short while before he was created Lord Reay in 1628. It is odd that he took a title from outside the Mackay country, and from a property that he possessed only briefly before it was alienated to the Innes family. The most notable minister to serve the parish of Reay was Alexander Pope, who entered his charge in 1734 and collected Gaelic **ballads** before **James Macpherson** provoked the Ossianic controversy. Pope's Latin tribute to **Rob Donn** Mackay is inscribed on that bard's memorial at **Balnakil**. He also visited a very different kind of poet, his namesake in Twickenham. Beside the cemetery of Reay stand the substantial remains of the Crosskirk, perhaps 12th century, where a finely carved **Pictish** cross-slab is also preserved.

RED CLYDESIDE

During and after World War I the political complexion of **Glasgow** and the **Clyde** underwent a radical change. Formerly a Liberal stronghold, in 1922 Glasgow returned 10 **Independent Labour Party** MPs (out of a total for the city of 15); except for a hiccough in 1931 it has remained staunchly Labour ever since. This transformation was precipitated by a series of confrontations in which a dedicated group of left-wing activists seemed to many outsiders to be threatening a revolution comparable to that already underway in Russia. But although some Red Clydesiders (**John Maclean, William Gallacher**, Arthur McManus) espoused Marxist doctrines and were lionised by Lenin, it is now thought that the ideological content of the upheaval may have been exaggerated. The majority (including **David Kirkwood, James Maxton, Patrick Dollan, John Wheatley** and **Tom Johnston**) were more ambivalent, championing a variety of social, industrial and sectarian causes as well as pacifism, **temperance** and nationalism.

Painting Clydeside red may be seen as a threefold process. The primer was applied in 1915–16 by the **Clyde Workers Committee** which invoked Marxist ideas of proletarian solidarity to frustrate the war effort and exploited wartime demands on labour to foment industrial unrest. After a lull, agitation for a shorter working week and the uncertainty of the postwar economic climate led to the **Bloody Friday Riot** of 1919 – a belated undercoat. The political manoeuvring that ensued, and above all the shift towards Labour of the Irish Catholic vote, ensured the electoral triumph of 1922. The cliché of Red Clydeside had become a glossy political reality.

Pledging to right the world's wrongs, or at least to shatter the complacency of Westminster, 'the wild Clydesiders' were given a tremendous send-off on the night train to London. A psalm was sung and the new MPs were likened to the **Covenanters** of old. But although they played a part in securing the election of **Ramsay MacDonald** as leader of the Labour Party, they made little collective impact on Parliament other than adding character to its proceedings. Concerted action from a group of men with such diverse priorities was bound to be difficult. Individually, though, Johnston and Wheatley were destined to leave their mark on the statute book.

REDDING PIT DISASTER (1923)
40 miners died in Redding pit near Polmont, **Stirlingshire**, on 25 September 1923, when water flooded workings which had been developed on a level lower than older workings which had themselves become flooded. Although a barrier of sandstone 80ft (24m) thick acted as a bulwark between the old and new mines, an undetected shaft existed between them, and when this gave way 40 died. Five survivors were recovered after no less than 10 days underground.

REDPATH, Anne (1895–1965) Painter
Born in **Galashiels**, the daughter of a textile designer, Redpath studied at the **Edinburgh** College of Art and Moray House College of Education between 1913–17. In 1919 she was awarded a travelling scholarship which took her to Brussels, Bruges, Paris, Florence and Sienna, where she was greatly impressed by early Italian painting. After her return she married James Beattie Michie, an architect with the War Graves Commission, and for the next 14 years they lived in France. Though she continued to paint during this period, the majority of her time was devoted to raising her family and it was not until several years after their return to Scotland in 1934 that she was able to fulfil her considerable promise as an artist.

Self portrait by Anne Redpath (SNPG)

Like **Crozier**, **Gillies**, **MacTaggart** and **Maxwell**, her Edinburgh School contemporaries, Redpath was deeply influenced by modern French painting and her especial enjoyment of surface pattern and colour demonstrated her clear affinity with the lively *belle peinture* tradition in French art. Of paramount influence on her own development was the work of Matisse, and in Redpath's informal arrangements of gaily decorated objects, tabletops and interiors, she shared his lyrically composed and sensuous approach to picture making. In contrast to the artistically unproductive years of her earlier career, the peripatetic life she led after the war was continually to influence and alter her style. The controlled patterning and careful colour harmonies that distinguish her early landscapes and still-lifes, such as her masterpiece of c1942, *The Indian Rug* (Scottish National Gallery of Modern Art), gave way to a more expressive use of paint that after visits to Spain (1952), Brittany (1953) and Corsica (1954) became increasingly high-keyed in palette and more boldly and richly worked. In 1955 serious illness, which recurred in 1959, severely affected her output, but in her later years she brought to her subjects a new freedom in her vigorous and textured handling of paint, suggestive of a knowledge of contemporary American and European abstraction.

REEL
This is a Scottish dance form incorporating a setting step and a travelling figure, at various times danced by three, four, six or eight dancers. The oldest patterns may have been circular but the figure of eight is now the norm. The music is characterised by even and rapid quaver motion, with eight quavers and two beats to the bar. The American hoe-down is derived from the reel.

See also **Dancing**.

REFORMATION, The
By the early 16th century the corrupted medieval order of Western Christendom was challenged. The power and malpractice of the Papacy was the principal target of protests by individuals and groups adopting new political thinking, nationalism and humanism that became both the Renaissance and the Reformation.

The German states and Scandinavia overthrew Papal theology and liturgy after Luther published his treatises in 1520. In Geneva Calvin had founded a theocratic state of presbyters by 1541, influencing the Netherlands and France. Henry VIII in England usurped control of the Church in 1534, a change which was political and national, translated the mass from Latin and destroyed monastic orders.

Scotland, remote, underdeveloped, but with European connections, was late to reform. Church dominance and corruption was compounded by a French Regent, **Mary of Guise**, and persecution of dissent by the **Beaton** Archbishops of **St Andrews**. Already by 1494 the **Lollards** of Kyle were influenced by Wycliff; Tyndale's translations enabled the Bible to be read when Luther's works were banned. **Hamilton** in 1528 and **Wishart** in 1546 were among martyrs for the reformed faith learned via the Continent. Factions in the nobility, opposed to the Catholic Queen Regent, adopted Protestant views. In 1557, as the **Lords of the Congre-**

gation, they subscribed a band or Covenant to establish the reformed faith.

After Wishart's death and the assassination of Cardinal Beaton, the focus of reform was **John Knox** who returned in May 1559 after exile and study in Geneva and England. In the middle of virtual civil war he preached at **Perth** and St Andrews. The resulting wanton destruction of ornate church interiors and monastic buildings by local mobs was denounced by Knox.

The Protestant party gained support to oppose the French forces of the Regent. Sieges and skirmishes lasted a year during which some of the hierarchy turned to the reformed side, but too late to change the existing Church. On the death of the Regent in June 1560, during the siege of **Leith**, the Protestant forces triumphed with help from English troops. The **Treaty of Edinburgh** in July concluded civil strife, removing both French and English. It enabled Parliament in August to abolish Papal jurisdiction, ban mass and accept the Confession of Faith written by Knox.

The reformed **Church of Scotland** then had a creed but no structure, financial security or resources. The nobility commandeered Church lands and wealth for themselves, obstructing the completion of reformation. A programme of Church government and social reform, the First Book of Discipline, was written by Knox and five other learned clergy, based on Genevan principles. The return in 1561 of **Queen Mary**, a Catholic, prevented the equivalent of the Church of England of which the monarch was head. The result was the evolution of the **General Assembly** as clerical parallel to the Three Estates in secular powers.

The Catholic bishops, suspended from office, were not persecuted; some reformed, some fled to France, others remained in retirement retaining some revenues. Briefly episcopacy was replaced by superintendents, an office Knox, as minister of **St Giles**, refused for himself. Full **Presbyterian** form was not established until **Melville**'s Second Book of Discipline completed the Reformation a generation later.

REGALIA

Anciently styled 'The Honours of Scotland', the Regalia proper – or 'Honours Three' – embracing the Crown, Sceptre and Sword of State, are among the oldest Crown Jewels in Europe. 'The Crown serves as the distinctive personal symbol of the King; the Sceptre is the emblem of his royal person, and lastly, the Sword signifies at once justice and the right of peace and war' (Collier, 1970). The Crown was remodelled by **James V** in 1540 but the circlet itself, now consisting of a fillet of gold enriched with flat wire mouldings and 23 large precious stones interspersed with 20 pearls (seven of native origin) may have been first formed for **Robert I** in the early 14th century. The gold is partly, if not entirely, of Scottish origin. The 24in (60cm) long silver gilt Sceptre was gifted by Pope Alexander VI to **James IV** in 1494 and refashioned by James V. The 4ft6in (1.37m) Sword of State, along with the woven lace sword-belt and scabbard, was presented to James IV by Pope Julius II in 1507. The last Scots coronation was that of **Charles II** held at **Scone** in 1651. Later that year **William Keith**, the Earl Marischal, removed the Honours from the clutches of Cromwell to **Dunnottar Castle** whence they

were smuggled to **Kinneff** and hidden until the Restoration. Thereafter the Regalia continued to be displayed at the Scots Parliament until 1707 when the terms of the **Treaty of Union** ensured they were not removed to England. Locked in an oak chest in the Crown Room at the **Palace** in **Edinburgh Castle**, they lay undisturbed until 1818 when, largely due to **Sir Walter Scott**, they were 'discovered lying at the bottom covered with linen cloths, exactly as they had been left in the year 1707'. The Honours of Scotland are now on permanent display in the Crown Room of Edinburgh Castle.

REGIMENTS, Expatriate Scottish

Few if any military traditions have been so widely exported or so keenly followed as that of Scotland and in particular that of the Highlands. Earlier examples apart, the movement gained momentum in the later 19th century with the formation of Scottish (or perhaps Highland – for the **kilt** was the preferred garb in almost all cases) Companies around the globe which in due course became full-strength battalions. Now the blood is inevitably becoming thinner and changes in the world situation have cut down the number of units; but there remain today very many more Scottish Regiments outside the British Army than within it.

In North America, General Inglethorpe raised a body of Highland Rangers to aid in the settlement of Georgia as early as 1739. The 84th Royal Highland Emigrants, two battalions strong, were raised in 1775 for service in the American Revolution from soldiers settled in North America and taken on as a Regular Regiment of the British Army. From American Loyalists were raised the North Carolina Highlanders, 600 strong, while the Queen's Rangers included a Highland Company also clad in the kilt. The various Militia Regiments of Glengarry in Ontario of the 1830s were almost exclusively of Highland origin although they had no Scottish feature in their dress. In the American Civil War the 79th Cameron Highlanders of New York served on the Union side; they originally wore the kilt which they changed for **tartan** trews.

Canada remains the chief centre of expatriate Scottish Regiments. Highland Companies were originally formed as early as 1837 and today there are no less than 17 Highland Regiments in the Canadian Army. None is part of the permanent Regular Army, although two regular battalions of Highlanders were raised in the Korean War period, taking on the identity of the 1st and 2nd Battalions of The Black Watch of Canada. During World War I, special battalions were raised for service overseas in the Canadian Expeditionary Force and nearly 30 of these had a Scottish identity, most being clad in the kilt.

Australia followed a similar pattern. At one time there were Scottish Volunteer Units across most of the Dominion. Only the Queensland Scottish Rifles failed to survive. Today the former New South Wales Scottish, the South Australian Scottish, the Victorian Scottish, the Cameron Highlanders of Western Australia and the Byron Scottish are represented by a company apiece forming part of a local battalion with, in several cases, pipes and drums also on the Battalion strength.

The Calcutta Scottish were raised in India as a volunteer battalion in 1914 and served until Partition; the

Bombay Scottish served as a company of the Bombay Volunteer Rifles during World War I. There were Scottish companies in the Rangoon Volunteer Rifles in Burma; in the Shanghai Volunteer Corps; in the Hong Kong Defence Force in China and in the Straits Settlements Volunteer Force in Singapore. All the above units were clad in the kilt; none survived for long after World War II.

New Zealand contains two battalions of New Zealand Scottish affiliated to the Black Watch. Their forerunners include a number of Highland Companies and the Dunedin Highland Rifles.

By an irony of fate, South Africa now has more kilted regiments in being than it appears will Scotland itself; the Cape Town Highlanders, the Transvaal Scottish, the Pretoria Highlanders and the First City Regiment all being kilted, while the Witwatersrand Rifles are dressed, as were the Cameronians, in Douglas tartan trews. All are active components of their country's defence force.

Scotland has even carried her traditions over the border to England; a Scottish Volunteer Unit was raised in London in 1789 to counter the threat of French invasion. In 1859 a similar unit was raised which became **The London Scottish**. Reduced, like **The Liverpool Scottish** (originally raised as a volunteer battalion of the King's Regiment in 1900), to a company in the 1960s, and both forming part of the 51st Highland Volunteers, they have since reverted to companies of a local Territorial Army Battalion in London and Liverpool respectively. No fewer than five Service Battalions of the Northumberland Fusiliers were raised in 1914–15 as the Tyneside Scottish, the regiment serving with distinction in two world wars.

REID, Sir George Houston (1845–1918)
Australian Statesman

Reid's father, minister at **Johnstone** in **Renfrewshire** where George Houston was born, emigrated to Melbourne in 1852 and then joined **J D Lang** in Sydney. George started in the colonial treasury as a clerk (1846), took an early interest in politics and studied law, being admitted to the Bar in 1879. He entered the provincial parliament in the following year and soon won recognition as 'perhaps the best platform speaker in the Empire'. Although a champion of free trade as against imperial protection and of other liberal values, his attitude has been described as 'if never cynical, always pragmatic'. In 1894 he took office as Premier of New South Wales and played a leading role in the discussions about forming an Australian federation. Reservations about the final Bill led to his being caricatured as 'Yes-No Reid' and to an erosion of his support. He resigned in 1899 but served as Premier of the Australian Commonwealth 1904–5. In 1909 he was appointed Australian High Commissioner in London and made KCMG. Notable for his massive girth, drooping moustache, and eye-glass, he made a considerable impression and was even elected to the House of Commons (1911).

REID, John (1721–1807) General and Musician

Reid entered the army in 1745 and saw service in Flanders, the West Indies and North America, becoming a general in 1798. He died in possession of substantial

wealth which he left to the **University of Edinburgh** for the establishment of a chair of **music**, and for the endowment of a concert to be held annually on his birthday. The present Reid School was built with his money. Reid's flute playing was particularly celebrated and his two sets of *Six Sonatas* for flute and continuo were published by **Oswald**. Some are still in the repertoire. The sonatas have an occasional and appealing Scottish flavour, though they are uneven in quality, the second set being much the better. His marches are still played in Britain and North America, 'The Garb of Old Gaul' being famous in many contexts.

REID, Robert (d.1558) Bishop of Orkney
Cistercian abbot of **Kinloss** and secretary to **James V**, Reid went to France, England, Spain and Rome on embassies. Rewarded with the priory of **Beauly**, he was also president of the **Court of Session** as Bishop of **Orkney**. He died, possibly poisoned, when returning from arranging **Mary**'s marriage to the Dauphin. His legacy for a college in **Edinburgh** was applied to the **University** of which he is credited founder.

REID, Robert (1774–1856) Architect
Reid began his long career as a public architect in 1803 when he was commissioned to design the **Law Courts** at Parliament Square in **Edinburgh** (1804–10). From this initial commission he went on to become the principal government architect in Scotland. In 1808 he was awarded the title of King's Architect and Surveyor in Scotland, an office which was merged to Master of Works and Architect in 1824. When a separate Scottish Office of Works was established in Edinburgh, Reid became its head. Unfortunately this office was closed again in 1839 and the Scottish Works directed from London. Reid was the architect of St George Church, **Charlotte Square**, Edinburgh (1811–14, now West Register House) and extended **Adam**'s **Register House** (1822–34). He was also responsible for the neoclassical picture gallery at **Paxton House, Berwickshire** (1811–14). Before he became fully occupied with his public career, Reid, in conjunction with the architect-builder William Sibbald, laid out and planned the northern **New Town** in 1801–2. This scheme was the largest single development in the Edinburgh New Town; it reached from Heriot Row and Abercromby Place to Fettes Row in the north and Bellevue Crescent in the east. Reid was responsible for the elevational designs of most of the principal streets such as Heriot Row, Abercromby Place and Great King Street. Remarkably unified in style, the northern New Town has survived virtually unaltered and has some of the most dramatic and impressive vistas in Edinburgh, for example, down Howe Street to St Stephens Church and over the Forth to **Fife**.

REID, Thomas (1710–96) Philosopher
Father of the 'Scottish Philosophy of Common Sense', Reid was born in Strachan, **Kincardineshire**, one in a succession of sons of the manse. His mother was a **Gregory** of the family of mathematicians. At **Marischal College, Aberdeen** (1722–6) he studied under **George Turnbull**, and after graduation became college librarian, studying much in mathematics. In 1737 he was

presented as minister of New Machar, a procedure resented by his parishioners though in time he became well liked. There he continued in private study and married in 1740. As Professor and Regent at **King's College**, Aberdeen (1752) he taught science and was wary of reforms which made a professor teacher of one subject to all classes, rather than all to one, fearing that the new arrangement might destroy the personal relationship between teacher and taught.

Founder of the Aberdeen Philosophical Society, Reid, in reaction to **Hume**'s *A Treatise of Human Nature*, began what became *An Inquiry into the Human Mind on the Principles of Common Sense*, 1764. In the same year Reid succeeded **Adam Smith** as Moral Philosophy Professor at **Glasgow**. He retired in 1780, and produced *Essays on the Intellectual Powers of Man* (1785) and *Essays on the Active Powers of the Human Mind* (1788), an appropriate title for the output of a still vigorous 78-year-old. His wife died in 1792, by which date eight of their nine children had also died. A prodigious walker even in his eighties, a considerable mathematician and the expounder of interesting utopian political ideas (discussed in his mss), Reid died on 7 October 1796.

His Glasgow pupil **Dugald Stewart** (1753–1828) as professor at Edinburgh enhanced Reid's influence, which had a complex history in the 19th century. In France the enthusiasm of Victor Cousin (1792–1867) as Minister of Public Instruction fostered it on generations of Lycée teachers. James M'Cosh and many another in North America made Reid long a force there. And in Reid's own day a follower worked out his principles further (see *The Common Sense Philosophy of James Oswald* by Gavin Ardley, 1987). Reid's name was also in vogue at Cambridge in the decades before and after 1890, although there a failure to appreciate the holistic orientation of his thought proved fatal.

Reid's *Common Sense* refers to something between 'good sense' and a generally sound and overall view of things in general which people have much of the time and necessarily rely on. He misunderstood Hume, but at the same time criticised what are actual and recurring errors in human thought. Reid comes into his own where abstract theory leads into absurdity and disorientation, and he is currently undergoing revival. Alas Keith Lehrer's 1989 *Thomas Reid* fails to dispute with views Reid is opposed to – the whole point! – and is obscure. Common sense demands a Reid book as yet unwritten. *The Works of Thomas Reid*, ed and annotated by Sir William Hamilton, are now in print in a German edition of the best cheap modern reproduction, but at a frightening price. MIT Press (USA) have published both collections of *Essays*, but no Reid is easy to find. *Philosophers of the Enlightenment* (ed Gilmour, Edinburgh, 1989) has an essay by R F Stalley; *Common Sense* by Lynd Forguson (London, 1989) is a general philosophy book with a chapter on Reid in the most up-to-date context. *The Scottish Philosophy* by James M'Cosh (1895) has been too rare for too long.

REID, Sir William (1791–1858) Military Engineer and Meteorologist

A son of the manse from Kinglassie in **Fife**, Reid attended **Musselburgh** school and **Edinburgh** Academy before going south to the Military Academy at Wool-

wich. In 1809 he joined the Royal Engineers and fought with distinction and conspicuous bravery throughout the Peninsular War (he and a friend called Wright were frequently noticed by Wellington as 'Read and Write'). There followed service in Louisiana (1816) and Algiers (1817), plus a long period on half pay. In 1831 he first visited the West Indies to rebuild government offices in Barbados that had been destroyed by a hurricane. The study of hurricanes and storms, their frequency, paths and behaviour, then became a major preoccupation on which he wrote extensively and for which he was elected to the Royal Society and awarded a CB. From 1839–48 he was Governor of Bermuda and then of Barbados where he was long remembered for a host of agricultural and social improvements. His last appointments were as Chairman of the Executive Committee of the 1851 Great Exhibition and Governor and Commander-in-Chief in Malta. A major-general (1856), he died in England.

REITH, John Charles Walsham, 1st Baron Reith of Stonehaven (1899–1971) Broadcaster

A pioneer of British and world broadcasting and a leading exponent of the view that broadcasting should be institutionalised as a public service, Reith was at the head of the BBC for 16 years, from its earliest days as a commercial company until he resigned in 1938 to run Imperial Airways. During World War II he was three times a Minister of the Crown and also served in the Royal Navy.

After the war he was a vigorous Chairman of the Colonial Development Corporation and held a number of directorships. Yet it was his constant complaint that his energies and talents had never been fully utilised and in spite of his many honours, he believed that his service to the state had not received adequate recognition.

Born in **Stonehaven**, Reith was a son of the manse, a towering figure with a volcanic temperament. His father did not believe he was cut out for university and after schooling in **Glasgow** he served instead a five-year **engineering** apprenticeship. The prominent scar on his left cheek was caused by a sniper's bullet in 1915. He was general manager of **William Beardmore** & Co before going to the BBC (1922).

Deeply emotional, strongly Sabbatarian and a teetotaller for much of his life, Reith was convinced from an early age that he was called to some great task. He set about building up the BBC with immense vigour, and the organisation bore his stamp for many years. He was an arresting public speaker. Some of his staff feared him, others held him in great affection.

His readiness to take on all comers, whether press barons or cabinet ministers, did not win him only friends. He clashed with Winston Churchill over the General Strike and over India, and never forgave Churchill for excluding him from his wartime ministry. He also came to believe that his successors at the BBC had destroyed most of what he had created. Although he could be both charming and generous, Reith's impatience and bitter self-absorption took a heavy toll of his private life, and in later years his relations with his children were not happy.

He wrote two notable volumes of autobiography. The fine portrait of him in old age by Sir Gerald Kelly hangs in Broadcasting House in London. See I MacIntyre, *The Expense of Glory: A Life of John Reith*, 1993.

REMONSTRANCE, The (1650), 'REMONSTRANTS'

Those extreme **Presbyterians**, mostly from south-west Scotland, who had championed the **Act of Classes** in 1649, renewed their commitment to it in a Remonstrance signed at **Dumfries** on 17 October 1650. Defeat earlier in the year at **Dunbar** had reopened a division within clerical ranks. Moderate opinion (**'Resolutioners'**) favoured a relaxation of the disqualifications embodied in the Act of Classes so as to enlist Royalist supporters. But the extremists remonstrated that only a stricter application of the Act could ensure a thoroughly purged and so 'holy army'. Condemned by the Committee of Estates in November and defeated by Cromwellian forces in December, the Remonstrants of 1650 would regroup as the **'Protesters'** of 1651.

RENFREW, Renfrewshire

The town of Renfrew lies close to the south bank of the river **Clyde** three miles north-east of **Paisley** and five miles west of **Glasgow**. The burgh of Renfrew was founded c1124 by **David I**; the lands of Renfrew were the first mentioned of the estates specified in the charter granted by **Malcolm IV** in 1157 in favour of Walter Fitz Alan [see **Stewarts**], the first High Steward of Scotland.

Walter, the sixth High Steward, married **Marjorie**, daughter of **Robert I (the Bruce)**, in 1315. Their son, **Robert II**, became the first monarch in the Stewart line. As the Great Steward of Scotland, the present Prince of Wales is also the Baron of Renfrew, a title originally granted to the heir apparent to the Scottish throne by the burgh of Renfrew in 1404.

Renfrew was made a **royal burgh** in 1396 after having received a charter from Robert III. Subsequent confirmatory charters were granted by **James VI** in 1575 and also in 1614, by which time the monarch had become King James I of the United Kingdoms of Scotland and England.

At the Battle of Renfrew in 1164 the army of **Malcolm IV** defeated the forces of **Somerled**, who had been recognised by Norway as 'King of the Isles', and who died in the battle. The Stewards were granted the Isle of **Bute** as a result of their contribution towards the defeat of Somerled. The **9th Earl of Argyll** was captured while proceeding towards Renfrew in April 1685. He had returned from exile in Holland to lead a rebellion in south-west Scotland. Argyll spent the first night of his captivity in one of the rooms in the Palace of Paisley which was attached to the Abbey, before being taken to **Edinburgh** where he was beheaded at the **Mercat Cross** on 30 June 1685.

In 1614 the burgh of Renfrew was the principal port on the Clyde. The first **shipbuilding** firm, Barr & McNab, was established in 1844. William Simons & Co moved to Renfrew in 1860, and in 1895 reorganisation of Simons & Co led to the formation of Lobnitz & Co. Babcock & Wilcox came to Renfrew in 1895, and Carntyne Steel Castings moved to the town in 1907. Hillingdon Industrial Estate, which was within the burgh boundary, was established in 1938 and was the first industrial estate of its type to be situated in Scotland.

Among the notable buildings of the town are the Town Hall, which was erected during 1871–3, partially destroyed by fire in 1878, but soon renovated. It was designed by the architect James Lamb in mixed French Gothic style with a massive square tower at the east end, rising to 105ft (32m) with corbelled turrets and ornamented cresting. Renfrew Old Parish Church was designed by **J T Rochead** in 1861–2 in the lancet Gothic style.

Renfrew's famous sons include Archibald Campbell, 1st Lord Blytheswood (1837–1908), MP for the Western Division of Renfrewshire 1873–4 and 1885–92. Formerly Vice-Lieutenant and Convener of the Country of Renfrew and Colonel and ADC to **Queen Victoria**, he was also an enthusiastic amateur scientist and carried out experiments on X-rays. The poet Andrew Park (1807–63) was born in Renfrew; twelve volumes of his poems were published in 1854. Professor William Barclay, CBE DD (1907–78) was minister of Trinity Church Renfrew from 1933–47. From 1963–74 he was Professor of Divinity and Biblical Criticism at the **University of Glasgow**, and achieved a worldwide reputation for his theological publications.

RENFREWSHIRE

The name 'Renfrew' is derived from the Brythonic *Rhyn* – a point of land – and *frew* – the flowing of the water. This refers to the confluence of the rivers Gryfe and **Clyde**. Renfrewshire belonged to the ancient Caledonian Damnonii and was later part of the kingdom of **Strathclyde**. The western part of the shire was formerly known as Strathgryfe and by that title was granted to **Walter** 1st High Steward of Scotland. Before 1404 Renfrewshire seems to have been included in the county of **Lanark**, but became a separate county when **Robert III** granted the Barony of Renfrew to his son and heir James (later **James I**).

Prior to 1891 the county was bounded on the north by the river Clyde and **Dunbartonshire**, on the northeast by **Glasgow**, on the east by **Lanarkshire**, south-south-west by the Cunningham district of **Ayrshire** and west by the Firth of Clyde. In 1891 the independent burghs of Crosshills, Pollokshields East, Pollokshields and the district of Mount Florida were brought within the boundaries of Glasgow. The burgh of Kinning Park became part of Glasgow in 1905. In 1912 the burghs of **Pollokshaws**, Cathcart, Scotstoun East, Anniesland and Jordanhill were transferred to Glasgow and in 1926 Scotstoun West and Yoker were similarly transferred.

As a result of **local government** reorganisation in 1975 the former burghs of **Greenock**, **Port Glasgow**, **Gourock**, **Barrhead**, **Renfrew**, **Johnstone** and **Paisley** lost their independent status. Three district councils were formed within Strathclyde Region: Inverclyde District Council, based in Greenock; Renfrew District Council, based in Paisley; and Eastwood District Council, based in Giffnock. In the subsequent 1995 reorganisation which abolished the Regions, these three Districts became respectively Inverclyde, Renfrewshire and East Renfrewshire Council Areas.

RENNIE, John (1761–1821) Engineer

John Rennie was born in Phantassie, **East Lothian**, the son of a prosperous farmer. He spent much of his youth working with the millwright **Andrew Meikle** and in 1780 matriculated to study at **Edinburgh University**. During vacations, Rennie undertook some contracts as a millwright, the first of which is said to have been to install a Meikle threshing machine at Know Mill on his family's estate (1779), and the second to fit out a corn mill at Invergowrie. In 1783 he left university and toured the great **engineering** workshops and some notable civil engineering sites in England, returning to Scotland to build his first bridge, over **Edinburgh**'s **Water of Leith**. The following year he was invited by Boulton & **Watt** to design and install steam-powered machinery in the Albion Flour Mills in London.

Radical innovations in the design of the millwork at the Albion Mills, completed in 1786, established Rennie's reputation as one of Britain's leading mechanical engineers, and he received commissions to design corn mills in Britain and on the Continent, as well as machinery for sugar plantations, breweries, a dyeworks and the Royal Mint. In 1791 he moved his engineering workshops to Blackfriars, occupying part of the Albion Mills site after the destruction of the latter in a fire. By then Rennie was already making a name for himself in other branches of engineering.

Rennie's services were sought by English **canal** companies, and he was appointed the engineer for the Kennet & Avon, the Rochdale, the Lancaster and many other waterways. He was also responsible for the construction of the Crinan Canal in **Argyll**, built between 1793 and 1801. His most important dock and harbour commissions included those for London Docks (1800–5) and the massive Plymouth Breakwater, which he reported on in 1806 and which was commenced six years later. In 1799 and 1807 he advised the Town Council of **Glasgow** on means of widening the river **Clyde**, making a further report in 1807 on improvements to the harbour.

His talents as a bridge builder were rivalled only by those of **Thomas Telford**, and he was praised for dispensing with the traditional hump-backed design, preferring to carry the roadway over the bridge on the level. He was particularly proud of a bridge he built at **Kelso** (1799–1803), but is better known as the engineer for Lambeth, Waterloo, Southwark and London Bridges, the latter completed after his death.

One of the first British engineers to apply scientific theory to the practical tasks of his profession, Rennie's advice was highly valued. He helped ensure the acceptance of Telford's ambitious plans to bridge the Menai Straits, superintended **Robert Stevenson**'s work on the construction of the **Bell Rock Lighthouse**, and persuaded Henry Bessemer to publish the results of his pathfinding research on steelmaking. His other achievements included the drainage of marsh land in Lincolnshire and other English counties. He was elected FRS in 1798, and is buried in Westminster Abbey.

Rennie's business was carried on after his death by his sons George (1791–1866) and John (1794–1874), the former concentrating on the mechanical engineering side of the business, and John, who was knighted after the completion of London Bridge in 1831, on civil work.

RENTON, Dunbartonshire

Renton in the Vale of Leven developed as a result of the bleaching, dyeing and printing industry which began at the Dalquhurn Works in 1715. Dalquhurn was also the birthplace of the 18th century novelist **Tobias Smollett**. A monument on the main street commemorates him, and Renton owes its name to one of his relations, a Miss Renton of Lammerton.

RENWICK, James (1662–88) Covenanter

Born in **Moniaive**, **Dumfriesshire**, Renwick was the son of a devoutly religious weaver who swore he watched his baby son praying in his cradle. A student at **Edinburgh University** when he witnessed the execution of **Donald Cargill** (1681), Renwick was inspired to join the **Cameronians** who sent him to Holland to study for the ministry. Ordained in Rotterdam (1683) he returned to spend four years as a field preacher, evading capture despite being declared an outlaw and a rebel, baptising more than 600 children, and in May 1685 issuing the second **Declaration of Sanquhar**. Never physically strong, he wrote (Dec 1687) in a letter to **Sir Robert Hamilton** that 'excessive travel, night wanderings, unseasonable sleep and diet, and frequent preaching in all seasons of weather, especially in the night, have so debilitated me that I am often incapable for any work.' In this feeble state he was taken to the house of a friend in Edinburgh to recuperate, but was overheard praying and betrayed to the City Guard. The Privy Council condemned him to death on three charges; that he refused to acknowledge the King's authority; that he would not pay cess (tax) to His Majesty; and that he counselled his followers to come armed to their meetings – all of which Renwick freely admitted. Knowing that his death and martyrdom would only

John Rennie, by Sir Henry Raeburn, c1810 (SNPG)

inspire his followers and rebound on themselves, his captors reprieved him for a week, during which they tortured him to try and make him repent so that they could release him. But he was unshakeable. On 17 February 1688 the 26-year-old preacher was executed in the **Grassmarket**, 'the last Scottish martyr to die a public and judicial death in the cause of the **Covenant**'.

REPENTANCE TOWER, Nr Ecclefechan, Dumfriesshire

Built by John Maxwell, Lord Herries, in the mid-16th century, this fortified beacon tower atop Trailtow Hill bears over its lintel the enigmatic one word inscription 'REPENTANCE'. Herries' seat was **Hoddam Castle**, to build which, so the story goes, he demolished a chapel, possibly some part of the chapel and monastery founded nearby by **St Kentigern** in about 575 AD (and excavated in 1991). Overcome with remorse, and perhaps under ecclesiastical pressure, Herries erected the tower by way of public repentance. Another version contained in the **ballad** 'Lord Herries' Lament' traces his remorse to the forcible drowning of some English prisoners in an attempt to lighten his ship after a particularly successful raid in the Solway Firth. The tower served its purpose well, withstanding an English siege in 1570.

'RESOLUTIONERS' (1650)

After Cromwell's defeat of the Scots army at **Dunbar** (1650), moderate **Presbyterians** questioned the wisdom of the army purges which had been sanctioned by the **Act of Classes**. Reacting to the **Remonstrance** of the extremists, they passed (in a commission of the General Assembly) the 'first public resolution' (14 December 1650). This relaxed the Act of Classes to allow Royalists who had supported **Montrose** or the **Engagement** to enlist so long as they were not sworn enemies of the **Covenant** or outrageous libertines. The objecting Remonstrants were duly condemned and in 1651 the Act of Classes was fully rescinded. The coronation of **Charles II** at **Scone** (1 January 1651) further united erstwhile Engagers with the Resolutioners; but their joint defiance of Cromwell proved short-lived, ending disastrously at the Battle of Worcester.

REST AND BE THANKFUL, Argyll

En route from **Arrochar** to **Cairndow** the A82 road crosses an 860ft (262m) pass between Lochs Long and Fyne. It is known as the Rest and Be Thankful after the inscription on a rough stone bench at its summit. Presumably this was executed by **William Caulfeild** who built the first military road over the pass in 1746–8. **Dr Johnson** noted it in 1773, as did **William Wordsworth** in 1803:

> Doubling and doubling with laborious walk,
> Who that has gained at length the wished-for height,
> This brief, this simple wayside call can slight,
> And rest not thankful?

RESTENNETH PRIORY, Nr Forfar, Angus

Although little, if any, of Restenneth's impressive remains is earlier than 1000 AD, the church was undoubtedly a Pictish foundation. In 710 Nechtan MacDerile, King of **Picts**, had asked the Abbot of Wearmouth in Northumbria for 'Roman' missionaries and masons. St Boniface responded and it was he or his disciples who founded the church of St Peter in the

Tower and spire of Restenneth Priory near Forfar (HS)

Pictish heartland at Restenneth. Its most striking feature is a fine octagonal spire (15th century) atop the tall square tower (c1100), of which the bottom 3m are clearly older still, though probably not 8th century. Nave and cloister (it became an Augustinian priory in the 12th century) are visible in outline but the choir (13th century) is complete to roof level with fine lancet windows. **Boece** records that in about 1100 **Alexander I** removed here the annals of **Iona**, possibly in response to Norse domination of the **Hebrides**. The earliest charter is said to have been granted by **David I**; **Malcolm IV** made the priory subordinate to **Jedburgh**; and **Robert I**'s son Prince John was buried here.

RHYNIE, Aberdeenshire

At the head of Strathbogie and commanding the route south to **Lumsden** and Donside, Rhynie proclaims its importance with an abundance of **standing stones** and symbol stones plus one of the highest hill forts in Scotland atop Tap o' Noth (1851ft/564m). Now surrounded by **forestry**, the outer ramparts of this vitrified fort enclose nearly an acre. Rhynie itself has a spacious village square and, to the south, the graveyard and a fragment of the 17th century parish church. Nearby Druminnor Castle, home of the Forbeses until they removed to the 19th century Castle Forbes near **Alford**, dates from the late 16th century but may include older work. In the wing of the L-plan (round but with a massive square and gabled top storey above heavy corbelling) the arch of the doorway is unusually segmented. Above it there are Forbes coats of arms. Within, an inscription in the lower hall pleasantly declares it 'A Happy Room'. The castle has been restored.

RICHARD OF ST VICTOR (d.1173)
Theologian

A great systematiser of mystical theology, this Scot (who is known only from his time in Paris) had a huge impact on subsequent mystical literature and medieval theology and philosophy (eg Eckhart, **Scotus**). Of deep psychological understanding, '[he] became more than man' (Dante, *Paradiso*). According to Richard, *Contemplatio* is the mode of knowing everything from the humblest existence to the being of God. The highest stage of the mystical life leads to the Christ-like life of service. Sub-prior of the abbey of St Victor (1159), he became prior in 1162, when Ernisius was elected Abbot. Ernisius was an intriguer who wasted abbey funds, had favourites and persecuted others. The Pope praised Richard's work, which led to Ernisius's deposition (1172). When he died in 1173 Richard seems to have been in the abbey some 35 years. See: F C Coplestone's *Mediaeval Philosophy* (vol 2, part I); *Selected Writings on Contemplation* (tr & ed C Kirchberger, 1957) has full commentary.

RICHARDSON, Sir John (1787–1865)
Explorer and Naturalist

Born in **Dumfries**, where his father was Provost and a friend of **Burns**, Richardson studied medicine at **Edinburgh University** before joining the navy (1807) as a surgeon. After the Napoleonic Wars he returned to Edinburgh to specialise in botany and mineralogy, interests which recommended him to John Franklin as sur-

geon, naturalist and second-in-command of his first expedition. This overland journey (1819–22) across northern Canada to explore its Arctic coastline was 'one of the most horrible on human record'. Scientific discoveries were overshadowed by appalling deprivation, heavy loss of life and considerable heroics in which Richardson played a prominent role. On one occasion, dragged senseless from an icy river, he was severely burnt and temporarily paralysed by the attempts to revive him; on another he assumed the responsibility of killing one of his men, partly in self-defence, partly on suspicion of the man having murdered, cooked and deceived him into eating another companion. His stature was legendary and in 1825 he again accompanied Franklin to the Canadian Arctic, this time conducting his own explorations east of the Mackenzie River. For the next 20 years he was physician to the Royal Hospital at Haslar but in 1847 made a final Arctic journey with **Dr John Rae** to search for the missing Franklin. He was knighted in 1846. Besides contributions to Franklin's narratives, he wrote the sections on botany, zoology and ichthyology for other Arctic narratives and published a journal (1851) of his search for Franklin.

RINTOUL, Robert Stephen (1787–1858)
Journalist

Born in Tibbermore (**Tippermuir**) near **Perth**, Rintoul was apprenticed to a printer in **Edinburgh** before moving to **Dundee** (1809) as a printer with the *Dundee Advertiser*. By 1811 he was also editor as the paper took a strong line on reform; amongst Rintoul's supporters were **Thomas Chalmers** and **Francis Jeffrey**. A move to Edinburgh in 1825 was a failure but in London, with the help of influential backers, he founded a social and literary weekly (1828). It was named *The Spectator* and was supposed to be non-political; but it soon came out in favour of the Reform Bill, Rintoul insisting on 'the Bill, the whole Bill and nothing but the Bill'. The phrase, like the paper, has had a long currency in various political camps. During his 30 years as editor Rintoul attracted many notable contributors including Jeremy Bentham and John Stuart Mill. He sold out in 1858 and died six weeks later.

RITCHIE, David (c1740–1811) 'The Black Dwarf'

The inspiration behind **Sir Walter Scott**'s 'Elshender the Recluse' and the 'Black Dwarf' of Mucklestane Moor, 'Bowed Davie' was born at **Lyne**, **Peeblesshire**, the son of a Stobo slate-quarrier. **Mungo Park**, his doctor in **Peebles**, described his legs as being like corkscrews; his features were grotesque, he grew only 3'6" tall and had to propel himself about oar-like with a pole. Apprenticed to an **Edinburgh** brushmaker, he later emigrated to Dublin, but unable to tolerate the mockery directed at his deformity he returned, embittered, to the village of Manor in Peeblesshire where he squatted at Woodhouse by the old peel-tower. When not peregrinating the parish singing Shenstone's Pastorals, he gardened and kept bees by the tiny, turfed cottage built from stone of his own quarrying. In 1796 he scared the wits out of Scott by cleiking the door and enquiring 'Man, hae ye ony poo'er [magic]?' Scott was living at Hallyards, where a statue of misanthropical Davie stands today. Despite Davie's wish to be buried on Woodhill, he was interred at Manor Kirkyard. After exhumation in 1821 his skull and leg-bones were removed to **Glasgow** Medical School; the former was replaced but not the latter.

RIZZIO (RICCIO), David (c1533–66)
Musician and Courtier

The son of a Turin musician, Rizzio first played for the Archbishop of Turin, then at the court of Savoy. Accompanying a diplomatic mission from Savoy to Scotland (1561), he won the attention of **Queen Mary** and became her confidant and French secretary (1564). He probably did not become her lover, and he supported her marriage to **Darnley**. But as a low-born foreigner with high pretensions, and a Catholic who doubtless encouraged the Queen in abandoning her conciliatory policy towards her Protestant subjects, he was cordially detested by almost everyone. The Queen's decision to summon for trial those like **James Stewart Earl of Moray**, who had opposed her in the **Chaseabout Raid**, precipitated action against Rizzio. Darnley, jealous of Rizzio's influence with the Queen, signed a bond undertaking to rid the country of those, including 'a stranger Italian called David', who abused the Queen's hospitality; Moray and his supporters, anxious to pre-empt their trial by a measure that would panic the Queen into reconciliation, responded with a bond to support Darnley in his claim to the matrimonial crown. The murder took place in **Holyroodhouse** in the presence, or near presence, of the six-months pregnant Queen. Patrick Lord Ruthven and **James Douglas Earl of Morton** were amongst the butchers; but the dagger they left in Rizzio's body was that of Darnley. The murder served well the purposes of the Protestants, reuniting them and

The Murder of Rizzio, by Sir William Allan (NGS)

restoring Moray; it did little for the hapless Darnley; as for the unfortunate Rizzio, it is hard to see him as other than a convenient scapegoat.

ROB ROY, Steamship

The *Rob Roy* was designed by **David Napier** in 1818 to demonstrate that ocean navigation by a steam boat was safe and practical. Before commissioning William Denny of **Dumbarton** to build the hull, he conducted the first model trials to determine the hull shape in the Camlachie burn. With engines from Napier's own works, the *Rob Roy* inaugurated steamer sailings between the **Clyde** and Belfast. Two years later the vessel was transferred to the south coast to open a cross-Channel service between Dover and Calais. She created such a good impression that the French government purchased her, renaming her *Henri Quatre*.

ROBERT I 'THE BRUCE' (1274–1329) King

Eldest son of Robert (son of **Robert Bruce of Annandale**) and Marjorie, Countess of **Carrick**, the future Robert I was born at **Turnberry** but grew up knowing Antrim and **Kintyre** as well as his father's lands (**Annandale**, **Aberdeen** and England). At 18 he replaced his father as Earl of Carrick; he married Isabel of Mar, who died young leaving a daughter **Marjorie**.

Both Bruces, father and son, refused support to **John Balliol**, 1296, and like most landholders (not **William Wallace**) gave fealty to Edward I of England, Robert senior remaining pro-English until his death in 1304. Robert Junior, declaring 'I must be with my own,' joined Wallace and became a Guardian with **John Comyn (ii)**.

When Edward offered a truce (1302) Robert rejoined him, suspecting Papal and French plans to restore Balliol. He married Elizabeth de Burgh of Ulster (died

1327), gave token support to Edward's 1303 campaign, and joined his 'Scottish Council'. His father's death made him reputedly the richest man in England.

In 1306 he abandoned all this for open rebellion [see John Comyn (ii)]. Enthroned at **Scone** by **Isabella, Countess of Buchan**, with widespread support, he was routed at **Methven** and **Dalry** (**Tyndrum**), and escaped to the Isles via **Loch Lomond** and **Kintyre**; many of his followers were executed, including three of his brothers [and see **Marjorie Bruce**].

Next year he returned to begin a guerrilla war (**Glen Trool, Loudoun Hill**), then marched up the **Great Glen** to **Inverness**, gathering support and destroying castles. By mid-1308 he held all north of the Forth except some garrisons. While his brother **Edward Bruce** overran **Galloway**, Robert was in **Argyll** (**Pass of Brander**). Parliament met at **St Andrews**, March 1309.

Lothian and the Borders were gradually regained (**Berwick** only in 1318); captured castles were destroyed but defenders were given safe passage homeward, in marked contrast to Edward I's practice. Some followers disapproved (**Thomas Randolph**), and Edward Bruce's truce for **Stirling** made **Bannockburn** inevitable.

Cross-border raids (**Sir James Douglas**) deprived English armies of support and caused rising disaffection. A winter campaign in Ireland in support of Edward Bruce narrowly escaped disaster. Robert rejected Papal letters to 'Robert Bruce, Governor of Scotland' and a Papal remonstrance produced the **Declaration of Arbroath**. Edward II led an army to **Edinburgh** (1322) but retreated in the face of famine caused by a scorched-earth defence; in 1327 Edward III's attempt never crossed the border. His advisers negotiated the **Treaty of Edinburgh** (1328) which was signed at Robert's bedside in **Holyrood**; he lay gravely ill 'of a general numbness caused by much cold-lying' (though leprosy was rumoured). In spring he was carried on pilgrimage to **Whithorn**, returning to die in his manor of **Cardross** on 7 July 1329.

Innumerable stories testify to his courage, good humour and humanity; he was greatly loved. His dying wish, to crusade like his grandfather Bruce of Annandale, was fulfilled when James Douglas carried his heart into battle against the Moors in Spain. The heart returned to **Melrose**; the King's body was buried in **Dunfermline**. His son **David II** succeeded him; from his daughter Marjorie came the **House of Stewart**.

ROBERT II (1316–90) King

Son of **Walter**, 6th High Steward of Scotland, and **Marjorie Bruce**, daughter of **Robert I**, Robert II was aged 55 when he succeeded his uncle **David II** in 1371. Eight years older than David, he had inherited the Stewardship from his father and, as heir apparent, had shared in the regency during David's childhood sojourn in France (1333–41) and again during his imprisonment (1346–57) following capture at **Neville's Cross**. Apart from the fact that Robert fought with vigour at **Halidon** (1333) and with very little at Neville's Cross (1346), 'there are few medieval sovereigns about whom so little is known and of whom it is so difficult to form any clear picture' (G Donaldson). In 1347 he married Elizabeth Mure of Rowallan, by whom he already had several children (whose legitimacy would remain in doubt, despite the issue of a Papal dispensation, on the grounds of their parents' too-close consanguinity), including John, Earl of Carrick (later **Robert III**), **Robert Stewart, Earl of Fife** and Menteith (later **Duke of Albany**), and **Alexander**, the 'Wolf of Badenoch'. Known to have fathered some 21 children in all, his only indisputably legitimate offspring were the four born of his second marriage to **Euphemia Ross**. Seemingly with as little flair for ruling as for fighting, and already elderly and infirm when he came to the throne, Robert II allowed power to pass to his eldest son the Earl of Carrick, later **Robert III** (1384) and then, when he also was rendered infirm by a riding accident (1388), to the Earl of Fife. Robert II died at **Dundonald Castle** in **Ayrshire**.

ROBERT III (1337–1406) King

The eldest son of **Robert II** and his first wife, Elizabeth Mure of Rowallan, Robert III was great-grandson of **Robert I (the Bruce)**. Considered illegitimate by the Church on account of the too-close consanguinity of his parents, his birth, and that of his three brothers and six sisters, was legitimised by Papal dispensation in 1347. He married **Annabella Drummond** in 1367 and had seven children, including **David, Duke of Rothesay**, and James (later **James I**). Variously described as 'gentle', 'feeble', 'timid', 'melancholy' and 'unfit to rule', and crippled as the result of a riding accident in 1388, he succeeded his father in 1390. His baptismal name, John, had unfortunate connotations in view of the fates that had overtaken three other Kings John (of England, Scotland and France), so he chose instead to be crowned Robert III. His reputed kindliness and love of justice – strangely illustrated by his attendance as a spectator at the infamous **Battle of the Clans** – ill-qualified him to reign over a lawless and increasingly disordered country; his health (and his faculties) became steadily more precarious, and by 1399 much of his authority had been transferred to his younger brother, the **Duke of Albany**, and his eldest son, the Duke of Rothesay – the former an ambitious schemer and the latter a licentious profligate. In 1402 Rothesay, held prisoner in **Falkland Palace** by his uncle Albany, died apparently of starvation, and Robert sent his younger son James to safety in France in 1406. But the 12-year-old prince was captured by pirates off Flamborough Head and handed over as a prisoner to Henry IV of England. Describing himself as 'the worst of kings and the most miserable of men', Robert III died, some say of grief, in April 1406.

ROBERTON, Sir Hugh (1874–1952)
Conductor and Arranger

Sir Hugh's Orpheus Choir was a legend in its day. Its sentimental, almost swooning style was immensely popular and very carefully manufactured and controlled. Roberton's many arrangements of Scottish and other airs for the choir were entirely appropriate.

ROBERTS, David (1796–1864) Painter

Renowned for his atmospheric paintings and lithographs of the Near and Middle East, Roberts was also

David Roberts in Arab attire, by Robert Scott Lauder (SNPG)

an immensely successful theatrical painter and designer. Born in **Edinburgh**, he trained initially as a house-painter (working on some of the interior decoration for **Scone Palace**) before being invited to paint backdrops at the Theatres Royal in **Glasgow** and Edinburgh. His success in this field and his innate grasp of broad painterly effects and perspectives brought him commissions from the Theatre Royal, Drury Lane, where in 1826 he painted the backdrops for the first British production of Mozart's Die Entführung aus dem Serail which overnight established his reputation. Increasingly, however, he was turning to easel painting and from 1824 onwards travelled extensively on the Continent sketching architectural subjects which he worked up into large projects in his London studio. These he exhibited with success in London and Edinburgh. In emulation of **Wilkie**, Roberts visited Spain in 1832, and the success of the lithographs he produced after this trip enabled him to give up scene-painting and, in 1838, embark on an even more ambitious journey through Egypt and the Holy Land. This resulted in some of his most dramatic paintings, incorporating architecture and landscape into wide panoramas, foreground figures emphasising scale and giddy perspective. John Ruskin later criticised this contrived, theatrical technique but Roberts, who never lost his bluff Scots manner, gave the English critic short shrift. Elected to the Royal Academy in 1841, Roberts was also an honorary member of the RSA. Although he never lived in Scotland again he returned annually, frequently exhibiting there, and the wide dissemination of his Holy Land lithographs and later works brought him equal celebrity on both sides of the border, a rare achievement for a Scottish artist.

ROBERTSON, Angus (Aonghas MacDhonnchaidh) (1873–1948) Gaelic Poet and Novelist

Born in **Skye**, Robertson lived mainly in **Glasgow** and London. Three instalments of his Gaelic novel An t-Ogha Mor ('The Big Grandson') appeared in the periodical An Sgeulaiche (1909–10), and the novel was finally published in 1913. His other main Gaelic publication was Cnoc an Fhradhairc (1940), which included a lengthy philosophical and pastoral title-poem. His language tends to be complicated and arcane, but his poetry has a strong individuality. Many books from his library were donated to the Celtic department at **Glasgow University**.

ROBERTSON, Douglas Argyll (1837–1909) Ophthalmic Surgeon

Born in **Edinburgh**, the son of a surgeon at Edinburgh's **Royal Infirmary** who himself had an interest in ophthalmology, Douglas Argyll Robertson was educated at Edinburgh Institution, Neuwied in Germany, and the **Universities of Edinburgh, St Andrews** and Berlin. In 1867 he was appointed assistant ophthalmic surgeon at the Edinburgh Royal Infirmary and later became full surgeon, a post he held until 1897.

Essentially a practical surgeon, Argyll Robertson had little time or inclination for writing. However, two articles published in the Edinburgh Medical Journal were of such consequence as to stamp his name indelibly in the annals of ophthalmology; his Observations on the Calabar Bean showed that it contained physostigmine, an alkaloid antagonistic to atropine; and in 1869–70 he recorded a series of cases showing that spinal cord diseases may be associated with loss of the light reflex of the pupil, the pupillary movement on accommodation remaining normal. This clinical observation became known universally as the Argyll Robertson pupil.

President of the Edinburgh College of Surgeons, he was surgeon-oculist in Scotland to **Queen Victoria** and King Edward VII, President of the Ophthalmological Society of Great Britain and a member of the **Royal Company of Archers**. He was also an outstanding golfer, being the winner of the gold medal of the Royal and Ancient Golf Club in 1865, 1870, 1871 and 1872. He founded the Royal Colleges' Golf Club and to this day the surgeons and physicians compete annually for the Argyll Robertson Medal.

ROBERTSON, John (1782–1868) Engineer

Born in Neilston on 10 December 1782, Robertson was a practical and innovative engineer who began his career at the age of 14 as an apprentice spinning-wheel wright. He contributed to the development of steam heating, boiler efficiency and steam engine design. But he is chiefly remembered for building the engine of the **Comet**. In his maturity he ran steamships on his own account; but business success eluded him and he was declared bankrupt in July 1828. In later life he was dependent on loyal friends who respected his personality and achievements. He died in **Glasgow**.

ROBERTSON, William (1721–93) Historian

A central figure in the **Scottish Enlightenment**, Robertson is less remembered than friends like **David**

Hume and **Allan Ramsay** or even than his biographer **Dugald Stewart**. Yet his reputation as both historian and churchman was once so awesome that even his sisters 'were careful to address him as ''Sir'' ' (H G Graham). The son of a minister, he was educated at **Dalkeith** and **Edinburgh University** where he studied divinity and read voraciously prior to becoming the minister of Gladsmuir near **Haddington** and then of **Lady Yester's Kirk** and **Greyfriars'** in **Edinburgh**. In an impeccably conducted career ('he seldom made a joke and never made a blunder') he became a founding member of the Select Society (1754), Principal of Edinburgh University (1762) and, suitably for an avowed 'moderate' in ecclesiastical affairs, **Moderator** of the **General Assembly** (1763). His first book, *The History of Scotland During the Reigns of Queen Mary and James VI*, did much to restore historical writing as a respectable subject. Some marvelled at its judicious tone, its painstaking analysis, and its exploration of causality; others at its elegant style 'unmarred by Scotticisms', although **Dr Johnson** demurred, likening its sonority to his own − 'too many words, and those big ones'. Works on the reign of the Emperor Charles V and the history of America followed, earning Robertson more paeans and substantial fees. But, averse to the sometimes grimy scrutiny of records and archives, he has since suffered at the hands of both more assiduous researchers and less fastidious writers.

ROBERTSON, William (c1786−1841)
Architect
Robertson practised mainly in and around **Elgin**. He is probably best known for his measured drawings of **Elgin Cathedral**, one of Scotland's most impressive Gothic ruins. As an architect he was versatile, designing churches (Episcopal church and parsonage, Elgin, 1825; **Buckie** Chapel, 1835, now demolished) and commercial buildings (National Bank, **Dingwall**, 1835), as well as country houses (Aberlour House and church, **Banff**, 1838).

ROBISON, John (1739−1805) Physicist
Born at Boghall, **Stirlingshire**, Robison took his MA at **Glasgow University** at the age of 17 and served in the navy at Quebec in 1759. He studied chemistry under **Joseph Black** at Glasgow, then served in a military capacity in Russia before taking up the chair of Natural Philosophy at **Edinburgh** in 1773. A founder member of the **Royal Society of Edinburgh**, Robison was its first General Secretary. He contributed to the 3rd edition of the *Encyclopaedia Britannica* and published a polemic about an (imagined) international conspiracy against European governments.

ROCHEAD, John Thomas (1814−78)
Architect
Although Rochead was born in **Edinburgh** and eventually retired there, he spent most of his working life in **Glasgow** and most of his buildings can be found there. At the early age of 16 Rochead was apprenticed to **David Bryce** and afterwards worked as a draughtsman for **David Hamilton** and for the firm of Hurst & Moffat in Doncaster. He opened his own practice in Glasgow in 1841, one year after he had won the first premium

in the competition for the Roman Catholic cathedral in Belfast. As a skilful draughtsman and versatile architect, Rochead developed a highly successful practice with a reputation for ecclesiastical work. His Italianate palazzo-style offices for the Bank of Scotland at Vincent Place and **George Square**, Glasgow (1865−9) were as competent as his classical John Street Church (1859−60) or the Gothic Park Church, Lynedoch Place, Glasgow (1858). His domestic designs range from urban terraces in Glasgow (Grosvenor Terrace, 1855; Buckingham Terrace, 1852−8) to country houses in the Borders (Sillerbut Hall, **Hawick**). Rochead was a respected member of the architectural profession, and when **Queen Victoria** visited Glasgow he was chosen to design a temporary arch for the occasion. One of his most famous works is the **Wallace** Monument in **Stirling** (1868), the commission for which he won after two keen competitions.

ROCK DOVE
In the late 1970s there were still thought to be a few colonies of pure rock doves (*Columba livia*) on the mainland of northern Scotland, but by the 1980s the only place you could hope to find them was in the Western and Northern Isles, where they live in colonies on remote sea cliffs. The scarcity of this ancestor of the domestic pigeon stems not from persecution or reduced habitat, but rather from so many years of interbreeding with feral **doocot** pigeons that it is now almost impossible to distinguish the pure-bred from the hybrid. Even 150 years ago naturalists were complaining that 'this hardy little blue pigeon is so intermingled with the house-pigeon, which it so exactly resembles, that it is difficult to decide now if any of the real wild birds still remain' (Charles St John).

ROCKALL
The granite outcrop of Rockall (Gaelic *sgeir rocail*, 'sea rock of roaring'), measuring 100ft by 80ft (30 by 24m), lies in the North Atlantic 184 miles west of **St Kilda**. It was annexed in 1955, then added to the territories of the United Kingdom by Act of Parliament in 1972. Its acquisition will be important in international law if, as suspected, there are **oil** reserves under the adjacent sea bed. In 1904 the Danish steamer *Norge* struck a reef near Rockall; more than 600 Scandinavian emigrants were lost. Most of the 163 survivors were cared for at **Stornoway** in **Lewis**.

ROGNVALD, Saint, Earl of Orkney (d.1158)
Baptised Kali, son of Kol, Rognvald was a nephew of **St Magnus**. Paul, son of Haakon his uncle's murderer, was **Earl of Orkney** when Kali arrived from Norway, having made a pact with God that he would build a great cathedral in the saint's honour if he should win the earldom. In 1137 he did so, changed his name to Rognvald, and moved the bishopric from **Birsay** to **Kirkwall**. Here he founded the cathedral which remains among the wonders of northern Europe, the achievement of a small island community over a period of centuries, and one of only two in Scotland to have survived the piety of the **Reformation**. In 1151 Bishop William, known as 'The Old' because he held his office from 1115 to 1181, and who would promote the canonisation of Rognvald, accompanied the Earl on what

was called a crusade, though it could have been mistaken for a piratical expedition recalling those of the **Vikings**. They even rounded up Christians for sale in a Muslim slave market, which may have helped to raise funds for the building of the cathedral. Rognvald was murdered by his relatives in 1158 and canonised some decades later, largely through the good offices of the poet Bishop Bjarni.

ROMAN CATHOLIC CHURCH IN SCOTLAND

After training in Rome **St Ninian** became the first Scottish bishop c397 although the **Celtic Churches** were then geographically and theologically distant. They only accepted European norms in 664 and, influenced by **St Margaret** and **Alexander I**, Roman organisation in the 11th and 12th centuries. The United Church became a major power in the administration of the kingdom in early medieval times, directed from Rome and under Papal authority. Later, it resisted change too long, was corrupted by power, and persecuted Protestants until overthrown by the **Reformation** of 1560.

Unlike in England, there was no organised Counter-Reformation in Scotland. Some bishops reformed; the archbishop of **St Andrews**, **John Hamilton**, was hanged as a traitor in 1571 and **James Beaton**, Archbishop of **Glasgow**, died in Paris in 1603, ending the hierarchy. Catholics remained mostly in the Highlands and Islands, served by mission priests among whom was the Jesuit martyr **John Ogilvie**, hanged in 1615, canonised in 1976.

An anti-Catholic mob sacked **James VII**'s Catholic chapel in **Holyrood** in 1688 but priests trained in the Scots Colleges in Paris, Valladolid and Rome served the remnant under Vicars-Apostolic from 1694 and persevered in Lowland and Highland Districts until the hierarchy was restored in 1878. **Jacobite** association revived persecution, destroying the turf seminary of the 'heather priests' at Scalan (Aberdeenshire). By 1800 there were 30,000 Catholics mostly in the north-east and the **Hebrides**; chapels were built with respected clergy functioning in society from 1793.

In 1829 the Catholic Directory was first published, the seminary was refounded at Blairs (**Aberdeenshire**), and emancipation removed restrictions. By the mid-19th century Irish immigration had increased congregations in central Scotland dramatically, producing urban and rural Catholic diversity as well as polarising Protestant and Catholic rivalry even to the **football** teams of Glasgow. Catholic education required separate schools, brought into the state system in 1918, and religious orders returned, as at **Fort Augustus** and **Nunraw**.

ROMAN INVASIONS

Unlike England, Scotland cannot be considered as having been part of the Roman Empire. There were, though, a number of Roman incursions from the north of England, following which parts of the country were briefly retained under Roman military rule while tribes in the southern Lowlands were frequently under treaty obligations to the Romans. The evidence for the routes taken by these incursions and for the extent of the subsequent occupations is largely archaeological and so to some extent conjectural. But for the invasions themselves there is also documentary evidence.

AGRICOLA The first incursion was that of **Cnaeus Julius Agricola** on behalf of the Emperor Vespasian in 79 or 80 AD. From Carlisle he reached the Forth-**Clyde** isthmus where he established a string of defences. Roads linked them to major forts at **Inveresk** on the Firth of Forth and at **Newstead** near **Melrose**; scouting parties reached **Perthshire**. In 82 Agricola came north again, this time veering into **Galloway** and **Ayrshire** to subdue the Novantae tribe, and in 83 he pushed up through **Stirlingshire** and Perthshire into **Angus** and **Aberdeenshire**. Camps identified with this advance have been found at **Stracathro**, **Dunblane**, **Ardoch**, Ythan Wells, etc as far north as **Moray**. There seem to have been several prongs to the advance and their precise routes are uncertain. The construction of a major fort at **Inchtuthill** is seen as evidence that Agricola intended to hang on to his conquests, and in 84 they were consolidated with another advance up the east coast, supplied from the sea, which culminated with victory over the **Caledonii** at **Mons Graupius**. But in 87 Inchtuthill's still incomplete fortress was abandoned. Agricola returned to Rome and his Scottish conquests were soon being whittled away. Ardoch and/or the Gask ridge defensive system may have been retained for another decade but in 105 even Newstead was burnt. It is not known whether these withdrawals were for strategic reasons or under pressure from some or all of the Lowland tribes (Selgovae, Votadini, Damnonii, etc).

The reality of this withdrawal was recognised in 118 when the Emperor Hadrian ordered the construction of a wall between the Tyne and the Solway. Hadrian's Wall is south of what is now Scotland's border but a few outposts beyond it were retained, including one at Birrens near **Ecclefechan**.

ANTONINE INVASIONS In 138–9, in spite of the effort involved in Hadrian's Wall, the Emperor Antoninus Pius ordered his governor Q Lollius Urbicus to subdue the Lowlands once again and re-establish the Forth-Clyde defensive system. His **Antonine Wall** between Bridgeness on the Forth and Old Kilpatrick on the Clyde, though turf-built, was fronted by a defensive ditch wider and deeper than that of Hadrian's Wall. Like the latter, it was as much a defensive axis, with forts beyond and behind it, as a barrier. The wall was built in the early 140s but seemingly abandoned in 154–5 in favour of Hadrian's, only to be reoccupied around 160–3 and abandoned once again. A third occupation has been suggested for 185–207.

SEVERAN CAMPAIGNS In response to what was evidently a general uprising by the Scottish tribes, the Emperor Septimius Severus and his sons Caracalla and Geta came in person to Britain and launched a heavy four-year (208–11) offensive against the Caledonii and the Maeatae, the latter possibly a new confederation of tribes north of the Forth; both groups were soon to be lumped together by the Romans as Picti or **Picts**. Operations seem to have been based on Carpow, a new legionary base on the **Tay** estuary, and to have extended into Angus and possibly beyond. Two distinct series of large campsites suggest possible itineraries. The rebellious tribes are said to have been forced to come to terms. But when Severus died (211), his sons returned to Rome and the frontier was again withdrawn to Hadrian's Wall. To the extent that the frontier thereafter remained quiet, this demonstration of imperial might seems to have been effective and may have been bolstered by subsequent forays to collect tribute as far north as the Forth.

LATER CAMPAIGNS A century later in 306 the Emperor Constantius and his son Constantine (later Emperor) are said to have underaken a repeat of the Severan invasion. Pottery finds at **Cramond** and Carpow support the contention. There are further reports of punitive advances under Constantine, his son, and Julian. But by now the Picti were clearly on the offensive. By 367 Picts and (Irish) Scots were over-running Hadrian's Wall which was finally abandoned by the Romans about the year 400.

RORIE, David (1867–1946) Poet and Folklorist

This **Edinburgh**-born country doctor, who practised mainly in the mining villages of **Fife** and lower Deeside, is renowned as a poet, especially for his song 'The Lum Hat Wantin' the Croon', the title also of his collected poems (1933) which have since run to many editions. A shrewd (and often cynical) observer of human nature (especially his patients), he handled **Scots** superbly, and the accuracy and maturity of his first book of poems, The Auld Doctor (1920), brought him fame and recognition. His horrific Great War experiences on the Western Front are handled thoughtfully and with humour in his wry Medico's Luck in the War (1929). An excellent popular writer, story-teller, raconteur and broadcaster, perhaps his greatest importance lies in his lifelong, unique and pioneering folklore studies especially in folk medicine, on which he gained his MD, and which have recently been published, edited by the late David Buchan as Folk Tradition and Folk Medicine in Scotland (1994). See also William Donaldson, David Rorie: Poems and Prose (1983).

ROSEBERY, 5TH EARL OF, see PRIMROSE, Archibald Philip

ROSEHEARTY, Aberdeenshire

Four miles west of **Fraserburgh** on **Aberdeenshire**'s northern coast, Rosehearty was created a **burgh of barony** in the 1680s for Lord Forbes of Pitsligo, the ruins of whose **Pitsligo Castle** lie to the south-east. Once a busy **fishing** port, it was supposedly founded by some shipwrecked Danes in the 14th century. It is now 'essentially a dormitory for Fraserburgh'.

ROSLIN CASTLE and CHAPEL, Midlothian

Between **Penicuik** and **Lasswade**, Roslin (also spelled Rosslyn), a mining village on the bank of the river North Esk, is renowned for its ruined castle and collegiate church of St Michael. The oldest part of the castle – the keep – dates from the end of the 14th century and was built by **Henry Sinclair, Earl of Orkney**, on a rocky promontory jutting into a loop of the river which winds round the castle on three sides. Henry's

Roslin Chapel with the spiral 'Prentice Pillar' (RWB)

son William, the builder of Roslin Chapel, extended the castle in the 15th century and isolated it on its rock by cutting a deep gorge across the access on the fourth side and spanning the chasm with a drawbridge (later replaced by a bridge). Seriously damaged by Hertford in 1544, Roslin Castle was restored c1580 with a domestic range being added in the 16th/17th century.

The chapel, or collegiate church of St Michael, was established by William Sinclair in 1447 a short distance from the castle on the site of a former chapel. Intended as a cruciform collegiate church, it was never finished and consists only of a choir, parts of the east transept walls and a sacristy. Though not large, 68ft by 38ft (21 by 11.5m) and 40ft (12m) from floor to tunnel-vaulted roof, the whole chapel is profusely decorated with sculpture and carvings: 'Every conceivable roof rib, capital, boss, arch and corbel is encrusted – whether human or animal figures, mouldings or foliage' (J R Baldwin). Depictions include the Seven Deadly Sins, the Seven Cardinal Virtues, the Dance of Death and statues of apostles and martyrs. 'The sculpture has a denseness and repetitiousness that resembles cake-icing or topiary more than carving in stone' (C McWilliam). The most famous feature is the 'Prentice Pillar', described in a 19th century pamphlet as having 'on the base several dragons in the strongest kind of basso relievo chained by the heads and twisted into one another. From base to capital and weaving in the spiral way are four wreaths of the most curious sculpture of flower-work and foliage, the workmanship of each being different . . . so exquisitely fine are these wreathings that I can resemble them to nothing else but Brussels lace.' Legend has it that the pillar was carved by an apprentice while the master-mason was away; on his return he was so jealous of its brilliance that he killed the apprentice with a mallet. Damaged by an **Edinburgh** mob in 1688, the chapel was fully restored in 1862 by the Earl of Rosslyn for **Episcopalian** use.

ROSNEATH, Dunbartonshire

Known in ancient times as the 'Virgin's Promontory', Rosneath lies between the Gareloch and the **Clyde** Estuary. The peninsula was visited by **Sir William Wallace**, who supposedly leapt to safety from a cliff near Rosneath Castle to escape his English pursuers. Farming and **herring** fishing have been the main local occupations through the centuries.

ROSS, Alexander (1834–1925) Architect

The Victorian and Edwardian architecture of **Inverness** and the Scottish Highlands is greatly indebted to Alexander Ross. Born in **Brechin**, his family moved to Inverness when he was very young. There he trained as an architect with his father and quickly became one of Inverness's leading architects. He laid out and designed much of the area west of the river Ness and was responsible for the construction of Queensgate. His most famous work was St Andrew's Cathedral (1871). From 1871 onwards he was a member of the town council and became Provost in 1889. A **Freemason**, he was also an active member of the **Gaelic** Society, concerned with the preservation of the historical roots and characteristics of Highland life. The output of his office was immense; he designed over 80 churches, over 30 public and innumerable domestic buildings. Much of his work was for the expanding 'leisure industry' of the Highlands in the late 19th century – hotels (**Aviemore** Hotel, 1899–1900), shooting lodges and mansion houses (Skibo Castle, additions and alterations, 1899). His churches can be found all over the north of Scotland from **Caithness** (St John's Episcopal Church, **Wick**, 1876) to **Skye** (St Columba's Episcopal Church, **Portree**, 1884). His monument to **Flora Macdonald** on Skye illustrates his regard for the history of Scotland.

ROSS, Earldom of

Originally part of **MacBeth**'s kingdom of **Moray**, Ross was detached as a separate earldom in favour of Malcolm MacHeth by **Malcolm IV** (1141–65). After his insurrection had been quelled in 1179 by **William I** (1165–1214), his son **Alexander II** (1214–49) bestowed the earldom on Fearchar Mac an t-Sagairt, who was probably heir to the O'Beolains, hereditary chiefs of **Applecross** of royal descent. Late in the following century it passed through the heiress Euphemia to Sir Walter Leslie. The Clan Ross descends from her uncle Hugh Ross of Balnagowan. When Donald of the Isles married the Leslie heiress, he was compelled to assert his rights *jure uxoris* against rival **Stewart** claimants. This gave rise to the **Battle of Harlaw** in 1411. The **Lords of the Isles** became Lords of Parliament as Earls of Ross until John, last Lord of the Isles, was deprived of the title in 1476, following his treasonable correspondence with England. Even before he had also forfeited his lordship (1493), **James III** had created his second son Duke of Ross (1488). As a dukedom it was held by Alexander, son of **James IV**, then **Henry, Lord Darnley**, and the future **James VI** and **Charles I**.

ROSS, Euphemia (d.1387) Wife of Robert II

Easily confused with her contemporary, Euphemia Countess of Ross (c1343–95, daughter of William **Earl of Ross** and countess in her own right, wife of Sir Walter Leslie and then of **Alexander Stewart**), this Euphemia was the sister of William Earl of Ross and so her namesake's aunt. She too was married twice. Her first husband, John Randolph **Earl of Moray** was killed at **Neville's Cross** (1346). After a Papal dispensation (1355) she was remarried to Robert the Steward, the future **Robert II**. The wedding cemented the so-called 'Highland Party' (including Robert the Steward, Walter Leslie now Earl of Ross, John, first **Lord of the Isles**, and John of **Lorne**) which troubled **David II** after his return from English captivity. Robert had two sons by Euphemia: David Stewart, Earl of Strathearn, and Walter Stewart, Earl of **Caithness**, **Atholl** and Strathearn. Some thought their claim to the throne better than that of Robert's children by his mistress and first wife, Elizabeth Mure; indeed Walter Stewart was promised the crown by **James I**'s murderers; he was executed instead. The youngest of Robert's children by his first wife was Alexander Stewart, the self same 'Wolf of Badenoch' who married Euphemia's niece Euphemia.

ROSS, Admiral John (1777–1856) Arctic Explorer

Born at Inch near **Stranraer** in **Wigtownshire**, fourth of the five sons of Rev Andrew Ross, John Ross entered the Royal Navy as a First-Class Volunteer at the age of nine. He made several voyages to the Baltic during his apprenticeship, and served with distinction in the Napoleonic Wars. His first expedition to the Arctic in a renewed search for a North-West Passage in 1818 failed when Ross was deceived by a mirage into thinking that

Admiral Sir John Ross of the North-West Passage, by Benjamin Rawlinson Faulkner (SNPG)

the channel generally believed to be the gateway to the passage was blocked by a range of mountains. Two years later, Lieutenant Edward Parry (who had been with Ross on his abortive trip) returned from another Admiralty expedition in which he had sailed right through Ross's supposed mountains and further west and north than any previous explorer. Parry's account threatened to destroy Ross's reputation, and Ross resolved to mount another expedition, independent of the sceptical Admiralty, 'as the means of effectively silencing the tongue of slander'. Financed by Felix Booth, who had made a fortune distilling gin, Ross purchased, reinforced, equipped and provisioned the *Victory*, and left London for the Arctic in June 1829.

With his nephew, English-born James Clerk Ross, who had sailed on Parry's expedition as well as his uncle's first, as second-in-command, and a crew of 23 men, Ross followed Parry's route north between Greenland and mainland America to the top of Baffin Bay, through Lancaster Sound (the scene of the mirage) and into a promising inlet, sailing 250 miles past Parry's furthest point and naming the land to the west Boothia Felix for their patron. With supplies for three years, they passed the winter of 1829–30 in reasonable health, carrying out scientific experiments and making forays overland, during one of which James Clerk Ross established that the inlet was a dead end. When spring came they would have to turn back into Lancaster Sound and look for another passage. But spring never came. Not until the following September did the ice loose its grip and the *Victory* once more set sail. It made three miles before being trapped again. The only success of the winter of 1830–31 was James Clerk Ross's discovery of the Magnetic North Pole. Three members of the crew died of scurvy before the ice freed them on 28 August 1831. This time they made four miles. By May 1832 they had been frozen into the ice for all but three days out of more than two and a half years. Ross decided to abandon the *Victory* and head back to Lancaster Sound overland to where Parry had been forced to abandon one of his ships and its stores eight years before. Although there was no sign of the ship, three of its boats and its entire stores were intact, allowing them to survive their fourth Arctic winter, the worst they had known; the lowest temperature recorded was -52°F (-47°C). When they finally set sail in the boats on 14 August 1833 it was to travel 73 miles in one day, and on the 26th they spotted a sail. By a strange quirk of fate, the vessel that rescued them was the *Isabella*, the very same ship in which Ross had made his first Arctic journey in 1818.

On 19 October Ross and his crew arrived back in London after four and a half years in the Arctic, a record that would stand for nearly a century. Their achievements were considerable – surveys and maps had been made of hundreds of miles of previously unknown coast, detailed information had been obtained on all aspects of science and wildlife, and above all stood James Clerk Ross's discovery of the Magnetic North Pole. They had not discovered the North-West Passage. But John Ross returned convinced that he had proved once and for all that no such passage existed. And for all practical purposes he was right. 72 years later Roald Amundsen managed to squeeze his way through the icebergs in

his tiny ship and pass from the Atlantic to the Pacific. But the dreams of a commercial highway from east to west finally died after Ross's ordeal, and the captain of the *Victory* could look back on his journey knowing that his reputation was restored and his name firmly placed amongst those of celebrated Arctic explorers.

John Ross retired to North-West Castle, his home at the head of Loch Ryan, emerging in 1850 at the age of 73 to return to the Arctic in an unsuccessful attempt to find the explorer Sir John Franklin, of whose expedition nothing had been heard for five years. Appointed Rear-Admiral (rtd) on his return in 1851, Ross died in London in his 80th year. His nephew James Clerk Ross is better known for his subsequent Antarctic exploration.

ROSS, William (Uilleam Ros) (1762–c1791)
Gaelic Poet

Born in **Skye**, Ross worked as a schoolteacher in **Gairloch**, Wester Ross. His maternal grandfather was the poet and piper *Am Pìobaire Dall* (The Blind Piper). Only about 30 of William's poems survive, apparently from the oral recitation of friends. An early editor, John Mackenzie, was probably responsible for the myth of his love-lorn, romantic life; the poetry gives just as good evidence of a more earthy and everyday outlook. There are signs of classical schooling in his verse, and of acquaintance with Scottish verse (**Burns** and others) and with **James Macpherson**'s Ossianic writings; but the native **Gaelic** influence is strong, in praise-songs for chiefs, songs in praise of **whisky**, songs of country courting with a touch of ribaldry and satire, and a Song to Summer which falls into the tradition of seasonal poems popularised by Alasdair Mac Mhaighstir Alasdair (**Alexander MacDonald**). His elegy for **Prince Charles Edward Stewart** shows that a sentimental regard for the Prince survived.

> Bha 'n t-àl òg nach fac' thu riamh
> Ag altrum gràidh dhut agus miadh
> (The young generation that never saw you
> nursed love for you, and respect.)

His two most famous poems are *Feasgar Luain* ('Monday Evening'), a carefully structured, rather formal poem which tells how he first met Mòr Ros, the **Stornoway** girl he fell deeply in love with; and the editorially named poem *Oran eile* ('Another Song'), which in much starker terms recounts his rejection by Mòr.

> Tha durrag air ghur ann mo chàil
> A dh' fhiosraich do chàch mo rùn
> (A maggot is breeding within me,
> that has told my secret to all.)

The secret is of hopeless love and of a death-wish. But Mòr had married in 1782; and it was apparently tuberculosis that ended the poet's life. This need not destroy the legend, though it tempers it. Ross's poems still retain a warm appeal for modern readers. The most recent edition of his work is George Calder's *Gaelic Songs by William Ross* (1937).

ROSS & CROMARTY

Before the **local government** reorganisation of 1975, Ross & Cromarty was a northern county which occupied 1,977,254 acres (800,788ha) stretching from coast to coast, with **Sutherland** to the north and **Inverness-shire** to the south, and included the **Isle of Lewis**. The indented western coastline of mainland Ross & Cromarty included such sea-lochs as Broom and Ewe, and **Gruinard** Bay. The county's highest point was Mam Soul (*Sodhail*) at 3862ft (1177m).

The original population was **Pictish**, much harried by **Viking** invaders. In the 11th century **David I** of Scotland extended his influence into the area, creating the **Earldom of Ross**. Ross and Cromarty were created separate counties in the 17th century, being amalgamated under the 1889 Local Government (Scotland) Act. **Harris tweed** production, **whisky** distilling and **agriculture** were the principal occupations, with aluminium smelting carried out at **Invergordon** at one time, while **oil**-related industries have recently become important.

Dingwall was the county town, with **Cromarty**, **Fortrose**, **Invergordon**, **Stornoway** and **Tain** as the other small burghs. In the 1975 local government reorganisation Ross & Cromarty District took over almost all of the mainland county, with the exception of its south-west area (transferred to Skye & Lochalsh), all this in the new Highland Region. Lewis, the island portion of the former county, became part of the new Western Isles authority. Since 1995, with the abolition of the Regions and two-tier local government, Ross & Cromarty has been part of the Highland Council Area.

ROSSEND CASTLE, Burntisland, Fife

Commanding **Burntisland** harbour, the main tower of the castle carries the date 1544, although the lower storeys may be earlier and the upper were altered and heightened when it was incorporated in the adjoining early 17th century extension. Here during a visit by **Queen Mary** in 1563 the poet Pierre Chastelard was discovered hiding in the royal bedchamber. Something similar had just happened in **Holyroodhouse** and, according to **John Knox**, the Queen had given her French admirer ample encouragement. But a second intrusion was evidently deemed excessive; lest, perhaps, it become a habit. Chastelard, though pardoned the first time, was now tried and executed at **St Andrews**. 90 years later a speedy surrender saved the castle from Cromwell's artillery; in 1715 it was briefly in **Jacobite** hands and later purchased by a **Campbell** who gave it the name of Rossend. The present century nearly saw its demise as, sunk to serving as a boarding house, it was condemned by the local council, then saved by the Secretary of State at the behest of conservationists. It has since been restored as the offices of an architectural partnership.

ROSYTH, Fife

On the Firth of Forth, the lands of Rosyth with what remains of Rosyth Castle were acquired by the government in 1903 for the purpose of constructing a naval base and dockyard. A 'garden city' to house the labour force grew with the development of the yard. The castle, an L-plan tower atop a rock and reachable only at low tide by a causeway, is now even less accessible, completely surrounded by the navy's top-security activities. Prior to being attacked and partly destroyed by Cromwell it belonged for over 250 years to descendants of the brother of **Walter the Steward**. Its **Stewart** connections are preserved in the initials MR (*Maria Regina*) and date 1561 above the entrance, probably commemorating **Queen Mary**'s return from France in that year.

West of Rosyth a range of lime kilns (1777–8) survive facing Charlestown Harbour. The harbour was developed in 1770 to export the local limestone which, both as building material and as ground lime for soil application, played an important role in the agricultural improvements of the age. The scheme was the brainchild of Charles Bruce, 5th Earl of **Elgin**, who laid out and named the village of Charlestown. Nearby, the Elgin residence is Broomhall (1796–7), large, neo-classical and well stocked with art treasures, many Greek, collected by the **7th Earl** of Elgin Marbles fame.

ROTHES, Earldom and Dukedom

One of Scotland's most successful dynasts was Bartolf the Fleming, whose family adopted **Leslie** as their surname, being the name of their property in **Aberdeenshire**. They became **Earls of Ross** and in about 1488 George, son of Norman Leslie of **Rothes** in **Moray**, was created Earl of Rothes. The 3rd Earl was killed at **Flodden** in 1513. His son **George Leslie, 4th Earl**, was acquitted in 1546 on a charge of complicity in the murder of **Cardinal Beaton**. The 5th played a leading part in the murder of **Rizzio**, but fought for **Queen Mary** at **Langside** and remained active in public life until his death in 1611. **John Leslie, 7th Earl**, was a courageous Royalist who became Lord Treasurer of Scotland after the restoration of **Charles II**. The estates forfeited during the interregnum were now entailed with his titles on the name of Leslie, and consequently passed through his daughter Margaret at his death. But the dukedom to which he was elevated in 1680 was extinguished. The present Leslie chief, 21st Earl of Rothes, owes his position to a number of subsequent heiresses of the name.

ROTHES, Moray

South of **Elgin**, nearly in **Banffshire**, and deep in the Speyside distilling country, the little burgh of Rothes is notable as the provenance of the **Leslie Earldom of Rothes** and of Glen Grant **whisky**. All that remains of the Leslie castle is part of its curtain wall and traces of foundations. It probably dates from the 15th century, perhaps from George Leslie's elevation to the earldom by **James II**. The town (just) has on occasion been badly affected by the flooding **Spey**, here joined by the Rothes burn from Glen of Rothes (on no account to be confused with the **Fife** New Town of **Glenrothes**).

ROTHESAY, Isle of Bute

A town of considerable antiquity, a **royal burgh** from 1401 and the capital of 'Buteshire', Rothesay gives its name to the oldest dukedom of Scotland, created in 1398 for **David**, son of **Robert III**, and now held by the Prince of Wales. Growing up around the eponymous bay and its **castle**, the town became a popular holiday resort in the early 19th century and reached its peak of celebrity as a destination for trippers going **'doon the watter'** from **Glasgow**. The architecture of Rothesay has since been tactfully described as 'beckoning wedding-cake' and its shops as 'attractively strident'. Brave in the face of declining trade, the town continues to cast out its (mainly **tartan**) lures to the **tourists** who arrive by way of the car ferry from **Wemyss Bay**.

Rothesay Castle from the north-west, by David MacGibbon (MR)

ROTHESAY CASTLE, Isle of Bute

One of the best-preserved medieval castles in Scotland, dating from the late 12th century, Rothesay Castle is an almost circular castle of enclosure surrounded by a moat. 'Set on an area of no immediately obvious defensive potential' (G Ritchie and M Harman), it was dis-

Sundown over Rothesay in the late 1880s with paddle steamers Sultana and Marquis of Bute (BRC)

missed by a 19th century expert on matters military as 'a piece of fortification, even on the ancient principles, wretchedly deficient, and argues very little in favour of the military knowledge that erected it. Even the gate is neither flanked nor machicolated; and it might have been mined or assaulted at almost any point.' Indeed in 1230 it was beseiged and captured by **Vikings** (the defenders resorting to pouring molten lead and pitch from the battlements), and occupied again by King Haakon of Norway before the **Battle of Largs**. The four drum towers (only one still entire) were added around 1300 and the impressive gatehouse was completed in 1541. Restored in the 19th century by the **3rd Marquis of Bute**, the castle was placed in the guardianship of the state in 1951, although the Stuart family remain hereditary keepers. **Mount Stuart**, on the east coast south of Rothesay, is now the family seat.

ROTHIEMURCHUS, Inverness-shire

South of **Aviemore** on the right bank of the **Spey**, the forest and estate of Rothiemurchus fringe the **Cairngorms** and are justly renowned for majestic scenery. Although long exploited for their timber (floated down to **Speymouth**), the woodlands retain fine examples of **Caledonian forest** and are rich in fauna, including the rare **crested tit**. The popularity of such sylvan splendour so near to Aviemore is reflected in numerous developments – visitor, **whisky** and **fishing** centres at Inverdruie, hotel at Coylum Bridge. On picturesque Loch an Eilean in the heart of Rothiemurchus, the ruins of an island castle resembling **Lochindorb** date from the 15th century. With square keep and enclosing walls Loch an

Eilean Castle was also once a stronghold of **Alexander Stewart**, 'Wolf of Badenoch', although probably a **Comyn** property before that. **Ospreys** nested here in the 19th century and, addressed from the shore, the walls are said to give off a triple echo. The island, like the rest of the forest, came into the possession of the **Grants** of Rothiemurchus who, with their cousins at Tullochgorum (near **Boat of Garten**) severely tested the rhyming expertise of Sir Alexander Boswell, son of **James**, **Dr Johnson**'s biographer:

> ...Come the Grants of Tullochgorum,
> Wi' their pipers gaun before 'em.
> Proud the mothers are that bore 'em . . .
>
> Next the Grants of Rothiemurchus,
> Every man his sword and dirk has,
> Every man as proud's a Turk is . . .

ROUGH WOOING, The (1543–7)

After the **Battle of Solway Moss** and the death of **James V**, the Scots Parliament agreed to a proposal (embodied in the **Treaty of Greenwich**, 1543) whereby Henry VIII's heir Edward, aged 6, should be betrothed to James V's heir **Mary**, aged 6 months. But within a year the Scots Parliament and the vacillating Arran (**James Hamilton, 2nd Earl**, now Governor of Scotland) changed their minds. There were fears that English ideas of federation involved too much subjugation and that the French alliance, which Henry had sought to negate, was of more value than an English one. Henry reacted by despatching (1544) forces under the Earl of Hertford which captured **Leith** and ravaged the Borders. This exercise was repeated in 1545 and again in 1547 as Hertford, now Protector (Henry having died in January 1547) and Duke of Somerset, revived plans for a dynastic Protestant union and again tried to impose them by force. His invasion, culminating in the **Battle of Pinkie**, was mightily successful. But, as before, it served only to revive French interest and to antagonise many Scots who, like the Earl of Huntly, 'did not so much mislike the [English] match, as the rough manner of wooing'. Accordingly in July 1548 it was agreed that Mary should marry the French Dauphin. She sailed for France within the month.

ROUSAY, Orkney

The more fertile side of this rather hilly island, facing Eynhallow Sound, is rich in prehistoric monuments. Here on Moa Ness have been found **Pictish** and **Viking** graves in a cemetery used from the 5th to the 9th century. The silver-gilt ringed pin known as the Westness Brooch accompanied a young woman and her newborn child. Nearby there was a Viking boathouse. Further evidence that an early and substantial Norse settlement lay along this shore includes two boat graves in which were buried clinker-built oak vessels, weapons, weaving implements and jewellery.

Less than a mile away a Norse farmstead has been excavated which appears to have been the home of Sigurd of Westness. The **Orkneyinga Saga** relates how Earl Paul Haakonsson perished here, whose father had murdered **St Magnus**. In 1136, when **Rognvald** had already invaded **Orkney**, Earl Paul went otter hunting

on Rousay with Sigurd of Westness. Sweyn of Gairsay (the 'Ultimate Viking' of **Eric Linklater**'s story) sailed up the sound and kidnapped Paul, who was never seen again. Rognvald gained the earldom and fulfilled his vow to build the cathedral of St Magnus.

From the 17th to the 19th century Westness became the property of the Traill family, who probably came to Orkney as servants of the **Stewart** earls. In 1863 Westness House passed to General Traill-Burroughs, who returned from India to carry out the only substantial evictions of native inhabitants that occurred in Orkney, and to commission **David Bryce** to build him Trumland House. His regime was responsible for the removal of **Edwin Muir**'s parents from neighbouring Wyre when the poet was still a child (described in W P L Thomson's *The Little General and the Rousay Crofters*, 1981).

Not far from this baronial pile a co-operative fish factory serves the islanders of Rousay, Wyre and **Egilsay** who fish for crabs, lobsters and scallops.

ROWAN

Rowan trees can still be seen growing beside many **cairns**, stone circles and Scottish houses both old and new, attesting to long belief in the rowan's magic powers. Rowan wood was thought more potent than any other against evil or bad luck – perhaps because it bears bright berries in the magic colour red – and was incorporated into nearly every object that might need protection: house and byre, butter churn and barrel, yoke and plough, cart and boat, spinning wheel and mill wheel, and finally the coffin.

A rowan switch would be used to herd sheep and cattle, while a sprig of rowan over the byre door and tied to the cow's tail (often with red string) protected milk and beast, and on a horse's tail kept the evil eye from travellers. No witch could enter a house past a rowantree by the door, and at Beltain (1 May) the whole house would be decorated with rowan branches and all sheep and lambs made to jump through a rowan hoop.

More practical uses for rowan were in dyeing (black and orange), and the berries were fermented into a cider-like drink as well as making the familiar rowan jelly. The bark made a poultice for adder bites.

ROXBURGH, Roxburghshire

The town of Roxburgh was a royal burgh in the early 12th century and its castle a favourite royal residence. In 1239 the marriage of **Alexander II** to Marie de Coucy took place in Roxburgh Castle, as did the birth two years later of their son (later **Alexander III**), at which time the town was said to be 'fourth in Scotland in point both of population and of general importance' (Fullarton's *Gazetteer*). Over the next century both castle and town were taken by the English, recaptured, and taken again, finally spending 100 years under English control. After the siege of 1460 in which they were finally won back by the Scots and during which **James II** was killed by an exploding cannon, 'that the place might thenceforth cease to be a centre of rapine and violence, or a cause of future strife between the nations, the victors reduced it to a heap of ruins' (Redpath). Nothing remains of either town or castle today save a few grassy mounds. The village of Roxburgh two miles south of the site of the castle, although almost as old, was never of sufficient size or importance to attract much attention, and therefore survived.

ROXBURGH, William (1751–1815) Botanist
Born at Craigie in **Ayrshire**, William Roxburgh trained in medicine at **Edinburgh** under **Dr John Hope** and then became surgeon's mate on board an East India Company vessel. In 1776 he was appointed medical officer and in 1781 was posted to Samulcotta, a hill station north of Madras, and studied the local flora. From 1793–1813 he was Superintendent of Calcutta Botanic Garden, greatly enlarging and ordering the collections. He used local draughtsmen to produce over 2500 coloured drawings which illustrated his important works: *Plants of the East Coast of Coromandel* (1795–1819), *Flora Indica* and *Hortus Bengalensis*. He died in Edinburgh in 1815.

ROXBURGHSHIRE
Before the **local government** reorganisation of 1975, this was a Border county, sharing its southern boundary with the English counties of Cumberland and Northumberland. Spanning 30 miles east to west, where its boundaries were **Berwickshire** and **Dumfriesshire** respectively, it comprised 425,564 acres (172,524ha), with **Selkirkshire** and **Midlothian** to the north. The county was once known as Teviotdale, the Teviot being the principal river, joining the **Tweed** at **Roxburgh**, once an important Border stronghold. The Slitrig, Rule, Kale and Jed are the other major rivers, and the highest point is 1385ft (422m) in the **Eildon Hills**. The county was constituted by **David I** in 1018, but suffered much from English predation, particularly in the 16th century. **Agriculture** and textiles were the main occupations. The county town was **Newtown St Boswells**, although the major burghs were **Hawick**, **Jedburgh**, **Melrose** and **Kelso**. In the 1975 reorganisation, most of the former county passed into Roxburgh District of Borders Region, along with Nenthorn parish from Berwickshire. The burgh of Melrose, however, passed into Ettrick & Lauderdale District. Since the abolition of the Regions and two-tier local government in 1995, however, the whole of Roxburghshire has been part of the Borders Council Area.

ROY, William (1726–90) Surveyor and General
The son of a factor on the Hallcraig estate near **Carluke**, Roy was born at Miltonhead. Little is known of his education although it must have been notable, for in about 1741 he obtained a commission in the army and in 1747 was entrusted with making a survey of the Highlands as part of the post-**Culloden** initiative to open up the area with **military roads**. 'In this way it came about that the first methodical operations for a military survey of Great Britain took place at the distant point of **Fort Augustus**' (*Glasgow Herald*). Eight years later the project was suspended, by which time Roy had extended operations into the Lowlands. In 1764 his *Military Antiquities of the Romans in Britain* was published; in 1767 he was elected FRS; and in 1781 he became a major-general. His great work, the first trigonometrical survey of the British Isles, began at the instigation of the King and the Royal Society with the measuring of the famous Hounslow Baseline in 1784. 5.19 miles long, its accuracy became legendary. From it the triangulation was extended to Kent, Land's End and then north. The survey reached Scotland in 1809, but was not completed till 50 years later. Roy had died suddenly while preparing a paper for the Royal Society which posthumously awarded him its Copley Medal.

ROYAL ASSOCIATION FOR THE PROMOTION OF THE FINE ARTS IN SCOTLAND
Founded in 1834, the RAPFAS exerted a considerable influence on taste and patronage in the Scottish visual arts throughout much of the 19th century. The initial impetus to form the Association came from the photographer **D O Hill** who was concerned at the lack of patronage of Scottish artists, notably the paucity of sales at the annual **Royal Scottish Academy** exhibition. The Association was formed with the intention that a number of pictures should be purchased annually and then distributed to members by means of a lottery. The Association was enthusiastically received and within six years there were over 6000 subscribers, many of whom were probably more attracted by the idea of a legalised lottery than by ideals of artistic beneficence. Soon a large number of imitators sprung up throughout the country but, unlike these, RAPFAS always maintained a strict control of which purchases were made at the RSA. With its enormous spending power it was thus able to purchase not only the finest works, but paintings by promising younger artists.

The extent of its influence can be gauged by its 1842 report which shows 142 purchases at the RSA, almost a quarter of the entire exhibition. Although this purchasing policy attempted to encourage originality it was inevitably biased towards the staples of the Scottish School – landscape subjects and genre. The names of **Horatio McCulloch**, **Sam Bough** and the Faed brothers appeared frequently on the lists.

As early as 1836 RAPFAS decided that in addition to the lottery, special engravings of acclaimed paintings would be commissioned and distributed to all subscribers. At least one engraving was commissioned every year and by the 1860s books of illustrative engravings were being commissioned from leading Scottish artists. As well as providing encouragement to the moribund Scottish engraving industry, these commissions became staples for many artists. In 1849 it was proposed that one of the annual purchases should be donated as the basis of a Scottish national collection. By this system some of the most important Scottish paintings of the period were given to the nation, and it is thanks to the generosity of RAPFAS that such works as **Lauder**'s *Christ Teacheth Humility*, **Drummond**'s *Porteous Mob* and **Noel Paton**'s *Oberon and Titania* now hang in the **National Gallery of Scotland**. By the 1880s the Association's membership was significantly reduced. Its reports blame the recession but it appears rather that attempts to boost membership by offering subscribers greater numbers of reproductions, using inferior machine engraving and new photographic techniques, backfired and lessened its attractions. The RAPFAS faded into obscurity in the 1890s. However, in its 50-year history it had had a greater influence on Scottish art than any other organisation or individual. Membership was remarkably international and thus the Association did much to disseminate widely the idea of a distinctly 'Scottish School' of **painting**, albeit one based largely on the imagery of **Walter Scott** and **Robert Burns**.

ROYAL COLLEGE OF PHYSICIANS, see **EDINBURGH: PHYSICIANS' HALL**

ROYAL COLLEGE OF SURGEONS

On 1 July 1505 the town council of **Edinburgh** granted its Seal of Cause, or Charter of Privileges, to the Barber Surgeons, enabling them to practise surgery within the city boundaries. This seal was formally ratified by **James IV**, and in a letter dated 1567 (which still survives) **Queen Mary** granted the Barber Surgeons a special exemption from carrying arms in battle, so long as they treated the wounded.

In 1694 William and Mary granted the Incorporation a Gift and Patent, giving the surgeons sole control over surgery in south-east Scotland, and making them responsible for the teaching of anatomy. In order to comply with this responsibility they had to have a fully equipped anatomy theatre, and as a result the first purpose-built Surgeon's Hall was opened. The building still remains (much altered) and is now the **University of Edinburgh** Department of Oral Medicine and Oral Pathology.

Until 1770 the College consisted only of Fellows, who were admitted by examination and had to be Burgesses of the City of Edinburgh. In that year, however, a new examination was introduced: the Licentiateship. After the 1858 Medical Act, the examination amalgamated with the Licentiateship of the Royal College of Physicians to form a basic medical qualification, as an alternative to the University MD. In 1884 the Licentiate examination of the Royal College of Physicians and Surgeons of **Glasgow** joined this double qualification, forming the famous Triple Qualification, which still exists. In 1778 King George III granted the Incorporation a Royal Charter, from which time it became known as the Royal College of Surgeons of the City of Edinburgh.

In 1826 the anatomist John Barclay left the College his outstanding collection of anatomical specimens, but only on condition that they were all displayed in one place. Since the internal fabric of the Old Surgeon's Hall was in a very poor state, new premises had to be found to house the collection, and the present building in Nicolson Street, designed by **W H Playfair**, opened in 1832. Extensive alterations were carried out to Playfair's building in 1907–9; the old Barclayan Museum upstairs was completely gutted, re-worked and extended to create the present Main Hall and the College Museum spread into neighbouring tenements in Hill Square.

After World War II the College expanded considerably and now has Fellows in all parts of the world. In 1955 it launched its *Journal of the Royal College of Surgeons*, and in 1989 opened a museum of its history and of the history of medicine in Edinburgh in the Sir Jules Thorne Hall.

ROYAL COMMISSION ON ANCIENT AND HISTORICAL MONUMENTS, see **HISTORIC SCOTLAND**

ROYAL (DICK) SCHOOL OF VETERINARY STUDIES, Edinburgh

Founded in 1823 by **William Dick**, son of a Whitehorse Close blacksmith, the Royal (Dick) Veterinary College occupies undistinguished premises at Summerhall overlooking **Edinburgh**'s **Meadows**. The 'Dick Vet' was the second such British institution established after the London Veterinary School (1791), where Dick enrolled in 1817. In 1823 he opened at his own expense the Edinburgh Veterinary School in Clyde Street, off **St Andrew Square**, where his father now had his forge. A pioneer instructor, Professor Dick attracted many students, for his lectures encompassed other subjects than the horse which was the main focus for study in London. The present college, established in 1906, became part of the **University of Edinburgh** Faculty of Medicine in 1951. A Veterinary Field Station operates as part of the Edinburgh Centre of Rural Economy on the Bush Estate, **Midlothian**, where there is a large animal hospital.

ROYAL GLASGOW INSTITUTE OF THE FINE ARTS

Established in 1861 as the Glasgow Institute of the Fine Arts, its founding objective was to encourage 'among all classes a taste for Art generally, and more especially for contemporary Art'. Granted a Royal Charter in 1896, its annual exhibitions remain today the foremost of their kind for the visual arts in the west of Scotland. Before the Institute's inception, several attempts had been made to further the cause of the arts in **Glasgow**, hitherto secondary in importance to **Edinburgh** as the artistic centre of Scotland. In 1753 the printers **Robert** and **Andrew Foulis** opened an Academy of Fine Arts within **Glasgow University**, the first organised art school in Scotland, pre-dating the Royal Academy in London by 15 years, but after financial difficulties forced its closure in 1775 little impetus remained to encourage or attract artists to the city. Under the auspices successively of the Institution for Promoting and Encouraging the Fine Arts in the West of Scotland, the Glasgow Dilettanti Society and the West of Scotland Academy, exhibitions were held in the city from 1821 until 1853. Though well intentioned and born out of a genuine desire to promote the arts within Glasgow and the needs of artists working in the west (then facing an increasingly partisan **Royal Scottish Academy**), poor organisation and lack of permanent exhibition facilities meant their efforts were intermittent and short-lived.

In the mid-1850s a movement was set afoot to establish a continual series of annual art exhibitions which would provide a showcase for working artists and a fillip to artistic patronage in the west. Exhibitions were held in the city's McLellan Galleries from the year of the Institute's foundation until 1880 when they transferred to their own purpose-built rooms on the opposite side of **Sauchiehall Street**. In 1904 they returned to their original home, vacated by the move of the city's collection of paintings to **Kelvingrove** in 1902, where they continue today. In the early decades of its history the Institute pursued its policy of promoting a wider interest in contemporary art by including in its annual exhibitions representations of work from other national schools. In the 1870s and 1880s loans of work by French and Dutch realist painters, then at the height of their popularity amongst Glasgow collectors, were profoundly to influence the development of the leading figures of the Glasgow School, since recognised as amongst the foremost British painters of the late 19th century.

ROYAL HIGHLAND FUSILIERS (Princess Margaret's Own Glasgow and Ayrshire Regiment)

The Royal Highland Fusiliers came into being in 1959 with the amalgamation of the **Royal Scots Fusiliers** and the **Highland Light Infantry**. This enforced marriage of one of the oldest Lowland regiments with the second senior Highland regiment was not well received at first and there was a strong campaign against it. But the marriage went ahead and, as is the case with many such arranged unions, the outcome has been remarkably successful, with the new regiment part of the Lowland Brigade. Since amalgamation the RHF have seen active service in Northern Ireland and in the Gulf.

The regiment wear trews of the **Mackenzie** (HLI) **tartan** with the pipers and drummers in kilts of Erskine tartan. The Drum-major in No 1 Dress still wears the Fusilier bearskin head-dress and a white hackle is worn in the Tam o' Shanter bonnet. The regiment marches past in quick and slow time to 'Hielan' Laddie' and 'Blue Bonnets over the Border' (pipes), 'British Grenadiers' and 'Whistle o'er the Lave o't' (band) and 'My Home' (pipes) and 'The Garb of Old Gaul' and 'The March of the 21st Regiment' (band) respectively. It recruits in **Glasgow** and **Ayrshire**; Regimental Headquarters is in Glasgow.

HRH Princess Margaret became Colonel-in-Chief on formation, having previously held the same appointment in the HLI.

ROYAL INCORPORATION OF ARCHITECTS IN SCOTLAND

The RIAS was first formed as the Institute of Scottish Architects from a meeting of the **Edinburgh** Architectural Association and the Institute of **Glasgow** Architects chaired by **Robert Rowand Anderson** in 1916. Its antecedents were the 1850 Architectural Institute of Scotland, which had failed in the early 1870s, and its predecessor, the Institute of Architects in Scotland, which collapsed within a few years of its foundation in 1840. Anderson himself bequeathed his Edinburgh town house and library at 15 Rutland Square to the Institute as its headquarters (which it remains to this day), also leaving the residue of his estate on provision that it secured a Royal Charter within two years of his death in 1921. The unifying force in **architecture** in Scotland, the incorporation has recently promoted greater public appreciation of the built environment through its myriad publications, ever mindful of the obligation of its first charter – 'To foster the study of the National Architecture of Scotland and to encourage its development.'

ROYAL SCOTS, The (The Royal Regiment)

Having originally raised a regiment for service under Gustavus Adolphus, **Sir John Hepburn** then raised a second one largely from Scots in France in 1633. Known as Le Régiment d'Hebron, it arrived back finally in the UK from French service in 1678, two battalions strong, having only briefly served in Britain previously in 1662 and 1667. Hepburn himself had been killed in 1636, being succeeded by Lord James Douglas, later Earl of Dumbarton.

Early battles of the regiment include Tangier (1680), Namur (1695), Blenheim, Ramillies, Oudenarde and Malplaquet. It later served at Fontenoy, in North America, the Peninsula, Waterloo, the Crimea, the Indian Mutiny and China. In World War I 35 battalions of Royal Scots fought on the Western Front, in Macedonia, Gallipoli, Egypt, Palestine and, in 1919, in Russia, winning 79 battle honours. In World War II the regiment fought in France in 1940, Italy, Burma, and in north-west Europe. The 2nd Battalion was captured at Hong Kong. The regiment won a further 39 battle honours bringing the overall total to 146. Since 1945 the Royal Scots have seen active service in Cyprus, Suez, Northern Ireland and the Gulf.

Clad in **tartan** trews in 1881, the Royal Scots in 1907 substituted Hunting Stewart for the original Government tartan. Regimental marches for both pipes and band are 'Dumbarton's Drums' (quick) and 'The Garb of Old Gaul' (slow). Regimental Headquarters is in **Edinburgh Castle** and the recruiting area comprises Edinburgh and the Lothians. The Colonel-in-Chief is HRH the Princess Royal.

As senior Infantry Regiment of the Line, the 1st of Foot, hence nicknamed 'Pontius Pilate's Bodyguard', the regiment escaped amalgamation in 1881 – when it absorbed the Edinburgh Light Infantry Militia and the various Volunteer infantry battalions of the Lothians – and again in 1993 when a planned merger with the **King's Own Scottish Borderers** was shelved. In 1996 the Royal Scots moved to Colchester to join 24 Airmobile Brigade, part of the British contribution to NATO's Multi-National Division which has the capability to deploy troops at short notice anywhere in the world.

ROYAL SCOTS DRAGOON GUARDS (Carabiniers and Greys)

The regiment was formed in 1971 through the amalgamation of the 3rd Carabiniers (Prince of Wales's Dragoon Guards) with **The Royal Scots Greys** (2nd Dragoons). Although absorbing traditions from all three regiments (the Carabiniers were themselves a 1922 amalgamation of the 3rd Dragoon Guards (Prince of Wales's) and the Carabiniers (6th Dragoon Guards)), the character of the regiment is overwhelmingly Scottish and it is clearly seen as the successor to the Greys as Scotland's only cavalry regiment.

Recently the regiment has seen service in Northern Ireland and the Gulf. It boasts a total of 90 battle honours.

The regiment marches past in quick and slow time respectively to 'Hielan' Laddie' (pipes), '3DGs' (band) and 'My Home' (pipes) and 'The Garb of Old Gaul' (band). Regimental Headquarters is in **Edinburgh Castle**. Her Majesty the Queen is Colonel-in-Chief as she was of the Greys.

ROYAL SCOTS FUSILIERS, The

Raised by the **Earl of Mar** in 1678 and known by his name, the regiment initially wore a uniform of local grey cloth from which they gained the sobriquet 'Mar's Grey-breeks'. In 1707 they became the Scots Fusiliers and in 1712 the Royal North British Fusiliers. In 1751 they were numbered 21st and in 1877, while keeping the number, 'Scots' was substituted for 'North British' in their title. As one of the senior 25 infantry regiments, they escaped amalgamation in 1881, when the Royal Ayr and Wigtown Militia and the two battalions of Ayrshire Volunteers became part of the regiment.

Initially raised to fight the **Covenanters** for **James VII**, they transferred allegiance to King William. Their early battles included Blenheim, Oudenarde, Ramillies, Malplaquet and Dettingen, after which they served in North America, Burma, the Crimea and on the Frontier. They also fought at **Culloden**.

World War I saw 18 battalions of the regiment serving in Macedonia, Gallipoli, Egypt, Palestine and on the Western Front, winning 65 battle honours. A further 51 honours were added by the regiment in World War II serving in France in 1940, Sicily, Italy, Burma and north-west Europe, bringing the overall total to 132. After the war the regiment saw service in India at partition, in Malaya and in Cyprus.

Clothed in **tartan** trews in 1881, the regiment wore the Government tartan in a special regimental form before adopting Hunting Erskine in 1948. The pipers adopted Dress Erskine in 1928. In full dress all but pipers wore the Fusilier bearskin head-dress. The regiment marched past to 'Hielan' Laddie' (pipes) and 'British Grenadiers' (band) in quick time and to 'The Garb of Old Gaul' in slow time. The Regimental Headquarters was in **Ayr** and the regiment recruited from that county.

In 1959, after a considerable battle to retain its identity, the Regiment was merged with The Highland Light Infantry to form **The Royal Highland Fusiliers**.

ROYAL SCOTS GREYS, The (2nd Dragoons)

This regiment was formed in 1681 from three new Troops of Horse added to three already raised in 1678. The Colonel was **General Thomas Dalyell** of the Binns and the unit title was 'The Royal Regiment of Scots Dragoons'. 'North British' was substituted for 'Scots' in 1707 while in 1751 the title became 'The 2nd or Royal North British Dragoons'. In 1866 '(Scots Greys)' was added until 1877 when the regiment became 'The 2nd Dragoons (Royal Scots Greys)'. Finally, in 1920 the title of 'The Royal Scots Greys (2nd Dragoons)' was adopted.

After early service in Scotland, the regiment fought at Blenheim, Oudenarde, Malplaquet and Dettingen. They were at **Sheriffmuir** in 1715 and a century later at Waterloo. Both here and at Balaclava in the Crimea they distinguished themselves as part of the Union Brigade. They also fought in South Africa. In World War I the Greys won 26 battle honours on the Western Front. They added a further 20 in World War II, fighting in Syria, North Africa, Italy and north-west Europe and making a grand total for the regiment of 59.

Long famous for the grey horses which gave the regiment its title, the Greys were also unique for their bearskin head-dress. The eagle badge commemorated their capture of a French Eagle at Waterloo. Regimental tunes were 'Garb of Old Gaul' (walk), 'Keel Row' (trot), 'Bonnie Dundee' (canter) and 'Hielan' Laddie' (dismounted march past). More recently a pipe band was added to the regiment which, along with the regimental band, achieved the remarkable feat of having a chart-topping hit with their version of 'Amazing Grace'.

Her Majesty the Queen was Colonel-in-Chief of the regiment whose headquarters was in **Edinburgh Castle**. In 1971 the regiment was amalgamated with the 3rd Carabiniers (Prince of Wales's Dragoon Guards) to become **The Royal Scots Dragoon Guards** (Carabiniers and Greys).

ROYAL SCOTTISH ACADEMY

The Royal Scottish Academy is the pre-eminent professional exhibiting institution for artists in Scotland. It has had a relatively turbulent history, however, and has never enjoyed universal support from the Scottish artists it was founded to represent. The Scottish Academy was established in 1826 and received its Royal Charter 12 years later. Based on the example of the Royal Academy in London, its purpose was to hold exhibitions of work by living artists, endeavour to instruct students, provide charitable funds for destitute artists and, on occasion, elect Honorary Members as a mark of esteem. 24 artists supported the establishment of the Academy, including the painter William Simson, the architect **Thomas Hamilton** and the painter, later photographer, **D O Hill**. A number withdrew support, dubious of the institution's intentions, but were all re-admitted three years later.

The Academy's exhibitions were held in rooms in **Edinburgh**'s Waterloo Place until 1835 when they moved westwards to the Royal Institution building at the foot of **The Mound**. At the same time the Academy began its collection of Diploma pictures, works donated by members upon election, which now constitutes a formidable (if incomplete) collection of Scottish art, unfortunately rarely exhibited. At last receiving its Royal Seal in 1838 the RSA entered its most prosperous and successful period under its second President, **Sir William Allan**, and Secretary, D O Hill. With the highly beneficent patronage of the Royal Association, its annual exhibition became a lucrative source of income for both Academy and exhibiting artists, increasingly attracting visitors from England and overseas and deemed second only in influence to the Royal Academy.

Other rivalries were becoming apparent however. The Royal Institute and the Board of Trustees, who had together begun the formation of a national collection, objected to the annual usurpation of their building by the Academy which required them to clear the galleries. Furthermore, a long-standing argument between the RSA and the Trustees' Academy over the responsibility for instruction of students began to simmer. The final resolution, decided after the arrival of an English civil servant to clear up the mess, was the construction of a new building to be shared by the RSA and the nascent **National Gallery**. Completed in 1858 to **Playfair**'s design it solved the Academy's problems of space and gave it the facilities to take over the Trustees' Academy's teaching duties. Membership of the RSA throughout this period reads like a roll-call of great Scottish artists.

By the 1860s, however, the Academy's conservatism and resolutely east-coast bias resulted in the establishment of a rival body, the **(Royal) Glasgow Institute**, which throughout the last decades of the 19th century pursued a comparatively avant-garde policy, inviting numerous renowned foreign artists to exhibit. The vigorous French-influenced talents of the Glasgow Boys and the Colourists [see **Painting**] were largely ignored by the RSA, at least until their artistic reputations were well established.

Through the early years of the 20th century the influence of the RSA decreased as it, like so many Victorian artistic institutions, found itself unable to cope with the dramatic advances of the Modern Movement. In 1906, faced with the increasing overcrowding of the National Gallery, the government advocated the return of the RSA to the Royal Institute building. The RSA were to have free tenancy of the ground floor and the use of the galleries for their annual exhibition and diploma show. The building was to be run, however, by the Board of Trustees of the National Gallery, an arrangement which in recent years has caused some friction between the two institutions. The institute building was re-modelled internally by W T Oldrieve and, despite the RSA being merely tenants, became known as 'The Royal Scottish Academy'.

Throughout this century the influence of the RSA has waxed and waned. It has retained its east-coast bias and on those occasions when the impetus of new Scottish art has been removed from the capital (such as the 1980s revival of figurative art in **Glasgow**) its influence has seemed marginal and parochial. On the other hand, during the 1950s its walls displayed all that was best of the lively *belle peinture* tradition, embodied by **Redpath**, **MacTaggart** and **Gillies**. It has nurtured many of Scotland's finest talents but today is something of a shadow of its former self, although the remarkable loyalty of its members and supporters will doubtless ensure its continuation for the foreseeable future.

ROYAL SCOTTISH GEOGRAPHICAL SOCIETY

The **Edinburgh**-based RSGS was founded in 1884 with branches in **Dundee** and **Glasgow**. Henry Morton Stanley, between claiming the Congo for Belgium and going to the relief of Emin Pasha, gave the inaugural address at all three. A further branch was opened in **Aberdeen** in 1885. Like the London Royal Geographical Society, the Society rode the high tide of empire as it feted explorers and engaged in the scientific advances of the day. Edinburgh, where the *Challenger* expedition to investigate the world's oceans had been conceived and where **Sir John Murray** was now trawling every scientific discipline to produce its 50-volume report, was a recognised centre of oceanographic studies. But the Society also succeeded to a long and distinguished tradition of Scottish geography, typified by James Geikie's 1865 *The Scenery of Scotland*, in which **geology**, meteorology and cartography featured prominently. Founding members of the Society included **J G Bartholomew**, 'the chief architect of its prosperity', whose *Survey Atlas of Scotland* would be the result of collaboration with the Society. It was partly in recognition of the role that geographical data must play in administration and planning that **Lord Rosebery** was chosen as the Society's first President. Its publication, the monthly *Scottish Geographical Magazine*, appeared in February 1865 and, like the Society, is still flourishing.

ROYAL SOCIETY OF EDINBURGH

Scotland's national academy of science, the Royal Society of Edinburgh (RSE) was formed in 1783 during **Edinburgh**'s 'Golden Age' of the **Scottish Enlightenment**, when an authoritative learned society was required to formalise much of the city's intellectual activity. Based on the former Philosophical Society, the RSE's Royal Charter was received on 6 May 1783, although its armorial bearings were not awarded until 1967. The RSE's aim was 'the advancement of (all) learning and useful knowledge', and there was initially an active literary element, with **Sir Walter Scott** as the Society's president from 1820–32. This subject area was reactivated in the late 1970s, but the organisation of scientific meetings and symposia is the RSE's principal function, along with publishing. Begun in 1788, the RSE *Transactions* contained **James Hutton**'s seminal paper *The Theory of the Earth* in its very first volume. Since 1909, when it moved from the Royal Institution on **The Mound**, the RSE has been based at 22–4 George Street, Edinburgh.

RUDDIMAN, Thomas (1674–1757)
Philologist

Born at Boyndie in **Banffshire**, Thomas Ruddiman studied classics at **King's College**, **Aberdeen** (1690–4) and was schoolmaster at **Laurencekirk** (1695–1700). A chance meeting with **Archibald Pitcairne** led to his removal to **Edinburgh** in 1700 where the physician found employment for his protégé as a sub-librarian at the **Advocates' Library**; within two years he was Assistant Librarian and by 1706 he was editing and preparing books for publication for his friend and fellow-**Jacobite**, the printer Robert Freebairn. Freebairn's 1710 reprint of **Gavin Douglas**'s translation of Virgil's *Aeneid* included Ruddiman's 'learned and erroneous' glossary of Scots words, the first of its kind, while his controversial introduction to the 1715 edition of the works of **George Buchanan** caused 'wrangles that lasted for 40 years'.

With his younger brother Walter, Ruddiman started his own printing business in 1712, producing the works of **Allan Ramsay** and James Anderson as well as his own *Rudiments of the Latin Tongue* (1714) and *Grammaticiae Latinae Institutiones* (1725–32), works that became standard texts for the study of Latin and established Ruddiman as one of the foremost classical scholars of his age. 'His time was passed in writing treatises learnedly, printing classic texts accurately, controverting vituperatively, marrying frequently, and becoming more prosperous yearly' (H G Graham). Joint printer to **Edinburgh University** from 1728, Ruddiman was Chief Librarian of the Advocates' Library from 1730–52 – a tenure of unrivalled length and achievement, at the end of which he handed over to **David Hume**.

The 'well-known and eminently respectable old scholar, with his thin wiry form, erect and active walk, his solemn face, with the bushy eyebrows, and those piercing eyes which daunted any who ventured to question his opinion' died in Edinburgh and was buried in **Greyfriars' Churchyard**.

RUGBY

Rugby football in Scotland is invariably of the 15-a-side Union variety, administered by the Scottish Rugby

Union at **Murrayfield** in west **Edinburgh**. This is also the site of the national stadium accommodating approximately 67,500 spectators. From 1973 to 1995 adult rugby was organised into a league of seven (originally six) divisions, with district leagues below, and with a Border league running concurrently. The game is popular with Scotland's private schools and a number of state secondary schools.

HISTORY Although English in its origin, rugby union football has been taken to heart by sporting Scots, particularly in the Borders and central belt, without being able to dislodge **football** (soccer) from its pinnacle as the principal Scottish sporting preoccupation.

History records that the 'football' so disliked by the Scottish kings of the 15th and 16th centuries as a distraction from archery training bore more resemblance to rugby than association football, as well as a striking likeness to all-out warfare, as seen by the casualty list following an England–Scotland match at Bewcastle (Cumbria) in 1599. The Border area seems to have known hand-ball games since the time of the **Romans**,and these still live on in certain street games in **Hawick** and **Jedburgh**.

However it was the spread of the codified game from England in the first half of the 19th century which revolutionised existing handling ballgames in the south of Scotland. H H Almond of Merchiston School in Edinburgh is generally credited with popularising rugby among fee-paying schools, while Borderers of all social origins soon recognised a game close to their hearts. In 1858 the first 'senior' game was played in Scotland between Edinburgh Academicals and a University team. Spread over four successive Saturdays, it involved 50 players. Not surprisingly, in 1868 a number of Scottish clubs formulated a book of rules called the 'Green Book', and this was probably used in the first international, against England, in March 1871.

On 3 March 1873 the Scottish Football Union was formed, comprising eight clubs, soon to be joined by six from the Borders. By 1990 the total was 112 clubs involved in league rugby, with 153 at district level. In 1922 the SFU decided to move from its inadequate Inverleith ground and acquired land at Murrayfield. A national stadium was opened there in 1925, the year after the SFU became the Scottish Rugby Union. Murrayfield housed probably its – and Britain's – biggest rugby crowd (more than 104,000) in 1975, although the construction of new stands has since reduced its capacity to 67,500. The playing area has enjoyed undersoil heating since 1959.

INTERNATIONAL RUGBY The first international rugby match under the new, but still evolving, code of rules was played at Raeburn Park in Edinburgh on 27 March 1871, Scotland winning a 20-a-side contest against England by a goal and a try to a try. It was the beginning of a fixture which was to become a highlight of the sporting calendar, graced by the award of a unique trophy, known as the Calcutta Cup, from 1879. Up to 1990, Scotland had won 40 contests to England's 49, with 17 drawn. The 1990 result at Murrayfield was unprecedentedly important since it would decide which side would win the Grand Slam, Triple Crown and Five

Nations Championship as well as the Calcutta Cup. Scotland achieved this result (by 13 points to 7) under the superb captaincy of David Sole on 17 March 1990, in a match unique in the annals of the game.

Scotland's international record is, however, more one of steadfast effort than perennial achievement. Despite winning the Grand Slam in 1925, 1984 and 1990 and the Triple Crown in 1891, 1895, 1901, 1903, 1907, 1925, 1933, 1938, 1984 and 1990, and narrowly missing another Grand Slam in 1999 with a 21–24 defeat to England which nevertheless took the Five Nations Championship north of the border, Scotland's record is perhaps statistically the least impressive of the Home Nations. Nevertheless, an improvement in playing quality has been discernible in recent times, particularly compared to the lean years between 1938–84.

WORLD CUPS

1987 Scotland participated in the first World Cup, held in Australia and New Zealand, qualifying for the quarter-finals only to crash to New Zealand, the eventual winners.

1991 Scotland lost in the semi-final to England at Murrayfield to a late Rob Andrew drop goal and lost the 3rd/4th play-off match 13–6 to the All Blacks.

1995 In South Africa, Scotland went out in the quarter-finals 51–30 to the All Blacks. It was Gavin Hastings' last international.

1999 After defeating Uruguay 43–12, Samoa 35–20 and Spain 48–0, but losing to South Africa 46–29 in the group stage (all matches at Murrayfield), Scotland went out in the quarter-finals to a 30–18 defeat, yet again by the All Blacks. It was Jim Telfer's last match as coach.

CLUB RUGBY In the 1973–4 season this was organised into six divisions, with the 5th division divided into east and west zones, and the west zone subdivided the following season. From 1975–6 this was standardised as seven divisions, with district divisions beneath.

The advent of professionalism in 1995 led to Premier and national league teams co-existing with professional district teams, creating tension, rivalry and seemingly endless bickering. The original four district teams (Caledonia, Glasgow, Edinburgh and Scottish Borders) were formed to compete in European competitions such as the Heineken Cup and the European Conference. In 1998 the first two and the last two combined to form the 'Superteams', the Edinburgh Reivers and the Glasgow Caledonians. Every player in Scotland with a professional contract from the SRU plays for one or other of these sides, leaving club rugby to pick up the pieces. In season 99/00 these two professional teams played in the 'Celtic League' with teams from Welsh Division 1.

SEVEN-A-SIDE RUGBY is a Scottish variation of the 15-man game, producing a fast-moving handling contest enjoyable to player and spectator alike. It originated at Melrose in 1882, ostensibly to raise money for the local club at the instigation of the neighbourhood butcher, and most clubs now organise Sevens tournaments at the end of the season.

RULLION GREEN, Battle of (1666)

Having reaffirmed the **Covenant** at **Lanark**, the insurgents of the **Pentland Rising** marched on **Edinburgh**. But the support expected there did not materialise; the **Castle**'s cannon were wheeled to the gates and the Covenanters, reduced by desertions and dispirited by the weather, halted at Colinton then withdrew into the **Pentland Hills**. There, on 28 November 1666 on the east slope of Carnethy, **Sir Thomas Dalyell**'s superior force was bravely resisted until dusk and the inevitable defeat. About 50 of the Covenanters fell and about 80 were taken prisoner. Of the latter, 36 were hanged; others were shipped to Barbados.

RUM, Island of, Inner Hebrides

The largest and most spectacular of the Inner Hebridean Islands, Rum (previously Rhum) measures some 16 miles square and its diamond shape is dissected by four precipitous mountain passes. The pinnacles of the Rum Cuillins reach 2000ft (610m) and contain semi-precious stones and rocks similar to those found on the moon. Unfortunately they are also the first hit by Atlantic depression clouds, giving an annual rainfall of 90in (2.29m). Originally the island was thickly forested and inhabited by **red deer**; the 300 or so now remaining are the subject of an intensive study being undertaken by Cambridge University.

Anciently settled, as indicated by the earliest excavations of Mesolithic man in Scotland, the island was held by the Clanranalds until the 15th century when, it is said, they exchanged Rum for MacLean of **Coll**'s 'great galley' but tried to renege on the deal after discovering that the timbers were rotten. In the 19th century the island was leased for sheep farming, and 350 of the 400 inhabitants were miserably shipped to Nova Scotia. The 2nd Marquess of Salisbury bought Rum in 1845 as a sporting estate, but his son, the Conservative Prime Minister, was too busy to pay visits. In 1879 John Bullough, a self-made Lancashire textile machinery manufacturer, acquired the estate. His son George built Kinloch House, a red sandstone edifice of baronial grandeur, and lived accordingly. A slump in **cotton** prices ended this era, the population fell to 20 and, in 1957, the Nature Conservancy Council purchased Rum with the aim of restoring the natural vegetation and wildlife. There are rare alpine plants, an indigenous breed of fieldmouse and pony, feral **goats**, golden and white-tailed **sea eagles**, and a 120,000-strong colony of Manx shearwaters nest in underground burrows in the south of the island. Kinloch House is now run as a hotel. In 1991 the Nature Conservancy Council decided to revert to the original Gaelic spelling of the island's name. Known as 'Rhum' since the turn of the century, it is thought the 'h' was added by George Bullough because he did not want the name of his island to be associated with the alcoholic drink. There is not, however, and never has been an 'Rh' prefix in the **Gaelic language**

RUNCIMAN, Alexander (1736–85) and JOHN (1744–68) Painters

The brothers Runciman, like their near contemporary **Jacob More**, trained initially as decorative house-painters. Born in **Edinburgh**, they both evidenced at an early age an ability to compose decorative neo-classical landscapes, much beloved of **Robert Adam** as components of his interiors.

After his successful apprenticeship with the Norie family in Edinburgh, Alexander set up his own professional practice in 1767 in association with his brother. They received a commission from Sir James Clerk to decorate his new house at **Penicuik** and used the advance from this (with Clerk's blessing) to travel to Rome. There Alexander immersed himself in studying from the antique and emulating the favoured Old Masters, Michelangelo, Poussin and Claude; he became close friends with the English Romantic painter Fuseli.

John, on the other hand, looked to the Northern Schools, seeking inspiration from Teniers and Rubens. His small oils and drawings that survive from this period show a fascination with rich jewelled tones and atmospheric effects, demonstrating great potential. But the combination of a weak constitution, a nervous disposition and a degree of artistic calumny brought on a bout of consumption from which he died in Naples at the age of 24.

Alexander returned to Scotland in 1771 and executed a remarkable series of murals for Penicuik House – classical motifs applied to **St Margaret** and the legend of Ossian – sadly destroyed in the 1899 fire. Appointed to the mastership of the **Trustees' Academy**, he attempted to establish a reputation as a history painter, although his delicate ethereal landscapes found buyers far more readily than his rather overwrought depictions of ancient history. He was also an accomplished etcher and it is in this medium that his fluid, instinctive draughtsmanship is most apparent.

Although a more lively and sociable figure than his brother, Alexander was possessed of a similarly weak constitution and died suddenly in Edinburgh a year short of his fiftieth birthday.

RUNRIG

As a synonym for the pre-18th century (and so pre-**Union**) agrarian system in Scotland, the term runrig has become somewhat freighted with emotion. Possibly to emphasise the indigenous nature of the system, the word (sometimes two words) is said to derive from the **Gaelic** roinn-ruith. But its use in non-Gaelic areas from at least the 15th century argues in favour of a Scots origin, the 'rig' being a strip of land 'ridged' by the plough, and the 'run' its often tortuous configuration.

The distinctive features of the runrig system were that the rigs, the arable strips, were periodically reallocated amongst a township's tenants and were usually worked collectively. Such evidence of communal tenure, of an equitable system of tenure rotation, and of co-operative labour has been favourably contrasted with the rigidity of the tenant–landlord relationship which resulted from 18th century enclosure and improvement. This has led some left-wing writers to portray the system as tantamount to an indigenous workers' collective. Its survival in the Highlands and Islands until abolition as a result of the **clearances** further endowed the system with Arcadian associations cherished in folk memory.

Socially the system had much to recommend it, but whether it was agriculturally efficient is another matter. It certainly made for complications. Such was the post-allocation trading in rigs in **Orkney** that one group of rig holders found themselves part owners, tenants of three lairds, and also all tenants of each other. W P L Thompson, who quotes this example, also supplies a short vocabulary of Orcadian terms for a rig: 'flaa, tie, geyro, skutto, spieldo, reeb, dello, merkister, un-sett, on-sett, out-break and out-tilling'.

RUTHERFORD, Daniel (1749–1819)
Physician, Botanist and Chemist
Son of **John Rutherford**, the first Professor of the Theory and Practice of Medicine at **Edinburgh University**, Daniel Rutherford graduated from Edinburgh in 1772 and then travelled for three years, visiting hospitals in France and Italy. He started practice in **Edinburgh** in 1775 and two years later was elected a Fellow of the **Royal College of Physicians**, serving as Secretary for 11 years, as Censor for six, and President of the Society from 1796–8.

He was also appointed Professor of Medicine and of Botany (1786) and Keeper of the **Royal Botanic Garden** in Edinburgh, positions he held for 34 years. On the death of Dr Cullen he was elected a physician to the Royal Infirmary. According to **Sir Robert Christison**, who attended his lectures, Rutherford never contributed a single investigation to the progress of the science which he taught, and yet 'his lectures were extremely clear and full of condensed information; his style was beautiful and his pronunciation pure and scarcely Scottish'.

Rutherford was an uncle to **Sir Walter Scott**, and in his *Life of Sir Walter Scott* **J G Lockhart** quotes a letter from Sir Walter to his brother in which is recorded the deaths of three of the Rutherford family in one week. They were Scott's mother, his uncle (Daniel Rutherford), and an aunt, Miss C Rutherford. 'It is a most uncommon and afflicting circumstance that a brother and two sisters should be taken ill the same day – that two of them should die without any rational possibility of the survivance of the third – and that no one of the three could be affected by learning the loss of the others.'

Daniel Rutherford's reputation as a chemist was established at the age of 21 when he discovered nitrogen. It was much to his regret that he did not obtain the Chair of Chemistry at Edinburgh.

RUTHERFORD, John (1695–1779) Physician
Born in the manse of Yarrow in **Selkirk**, John Rutherford studied philosophy and mathematics at **Edinburgh University** and served as an apprentice to an **Edinburgh** surgeon. After further studying anatomy, surgery and *materia medica* in London, he travelled to Paris, Leyden and Rheims where he graduated MD in 1719. On his return to Edinburgh he, along with Andrew St Clair, Andrew Plummer and John Innes, successfully petitioned the Town Council to use a house they had purchased as a chemical laboratory and a place of instruction for students. Two years later, in 1726, the council elected Rutherford and St Clair Professors of Medicine and Plummer and Innes Professors of Medicine and Chemistry, all without salary. They also petitioned the Town Council for permission to use a piece of derelict ground adjacent to their house for the purpose of growing plants and herbs to furnish apothe-

caries' shops and for the instruction of medical students. To Rutherford goes the credit of being the first to start clinical teaching in the **Royal Infirmary**, the first session being in the winter of 1746–7. He continued the lectures for 20 years, and from 1752–6 was President of the **Royal College of Physicians**. Through his daughter Ann, John Rutherford was the grandfather of **Sir Walter Scott**. His son **Daniel Rutherford** also later became Professor of Medicine at Edinburgh and President of the Royal College.

RUTHERFORD, Samuel (1600–61)
Covenanter
Born at Crailing near **Jedburgh**, **Roxburghshire**, Samuel Rutherford was first student then Professor of Latin at **Edinburgh University** (1623–5). Ordained minister of Anwoth (1627) but suspended (1636), he was an early and fervent adherent to the **Covenant** (1638). Teacher rather than preacher, he became Professor of Divinity, Principal of New College and eventually Rector at **St Andrews University** (1639). He was a compulsive correspondent and writer, 250 of his *Letters* being published (c1640), followed by *Exercitationes per Divina Gratia* denouncing state interference in Church affairs. After the Restoration a decree was issued against his most controversial work, the 'tediously pedantic' *Lex Rex* advocating the right to depose kings; all copies were to be seized and burned either at the **Mercat Cross** in **Edinburgh** or at the gates of New College, **St Andrews**. Rutherford himself was stripped of all his posts at the University and charged with treason. But the 'doyen of Scottish thinkers and teachers' was already on his death bed; he died before the citation reached St Andrews.

RUTHERGLEN, Declaration of (1679)
On 29 May 1679, the anniversary of **Charles II**'s Restoration, armed **Covenanters** (including some of the murderers of **Archbishop Sharp**) rode into **Rutherglen** where they extinguished the celebratory bonfires, lit their own to burn all Acts of Parliament and Privy Council since 1660, and read a declaration against episcopacy, **Indulgences**, and violations of the **Covenant**. This action was seen as flagrant provocation and brought the recall of **John Graham of Claverhouse** to avenge it. He failed to do so at **Drumclog** three days later; three weeks later **Monmouth** succeeded at **Bothwell Brig**.

RUTHERGLEN, Lanarkshire
A fact not readily conceded by all Glaswegians is that for most of the city's history its main rival has been not **Edinburgh** but Rutherglen. Claimed as the oldest royal burgh in Scotland, it certainly predates **Glasgow**, having received a charter from **David I**. Here **William Wallace** is said to have signed a treaty with the English in 1297 and here **Sir John Menteith** plotted his capture (at **Robroyston**) in 1305. Throughout the Middle Ages, while Glasgow remained the ecclesiastical focus, Rutherglen was the commercial and political centre, occupying the **Clyde**'s south bank at its tidal limit just above **Glasgow Green**. The castle, recaptured from the English by **Robert I** in 1305, was frequently a royal residence until burned by **Regent Moray** after **Queen Mary**'s defeat at **Langside**; no trace now remains. Although by the time of the 1679 **Declaration of**

Rutherglen Station from King Street in 1907 (ML)

Rutherglen the town's trade was in decline 'because Glasgow lyes between it and the sea', in the 18th century it kept abreast of neighbouring **Govan** and Glasgow with a thriving handloom industry and **coal-mining**. Until 1832 it was one of the four Clyde burghs (with Glasgow, **Renfrew** and **Dumbarton**) which returned a single MP and in 1856 it ventured tentatively into **shipbuilding** with the Seath yard producing several **cluthas** and steamers in spite of the river's low-tide depth of only 2ft (60cm). By now, though, its battle with Glasgow for supremacy had become one for survival. Vigorously resisting incorporation within the metropolis, it survived the major encroachments of the later 19th century, successfully petitioned against that of 1912 which ended the brave struggle of Govan and **Partick**, and was still independent in the 1950s. The anachronism (part of Rutherglen is barely two miles from **George Square**) ended with the 1975 reorganisation of **local government**, when Rutherglen officially became part of the City of Glasgow.

RUTHVEN, John, 3rd Earl of Gowrie (c1577–1600)

John succeeded his brother, the 2nd Earl, in 1588 when aged about 11. He became a distinguished student of **Edinburgh University** and Padua; and like his father and grandfather was accused of practising necromancy and witchcraft. Hereditary Sheriff of **Perthshire**, he was elected Provost of **Perth**. He also inherited the debt of £80,000 owed by the King to his father **William**.

James VI was enticed to Gowrie's town house in Perth on 5 August 1600. There, in his own words, he was held prisoner until rescued by his courtiers. During the ensuing struggle both Gowrie and his brother Alexander were killed in what came to be known as the **Gowrie Conspiracy**. Consequently the titles, honours and lands of the family were forfeited and the name of Ruthven proscribed in November 1600.

The surname of Ruthven was restored in 1641 during the lifetime of Thomas (cousin of the 3rd Earl), created 1st Lord Ruthven of Freeland. The Scottish Barony of Ruthven then descended through the male and female line to the Earl of Carlisle who, on the death of his mother in 1982, became the 12th Baron Ruthven of Freeland.

The Earldom of Gowrie was recreated when Alexander Gore-Arkwright (2nd son of the 9th Baron Ruthven), Governor-General of Australia 1936–44 and holder of the Victoria Cross, was created Earl of Gowrie in the peerage of the United Kingdom in 1945. His son died of wounds in 1942 after leading an SAS raid in North Africa, and his grandson, who succeeded him in 1955, was a Minister of the Crown.

RUTHVEN, Patrick, 1st Earl of Forth and of Brentford (c1573–1651) Soldier

Spanning half a century and many countries, Ruthven's military career typified that of many Scots in the religious wars of the 17th century. The younger son in a cadet branch of the Ruthven [see **Huntingtower**] family, he first appeared in the Swedish army (c1606), having no doubt been recruited in Scotland. By 1625 he was Colonel of a regiment in the service of Gustavus Adolphus, who greatly valued his valour and his intelligence-gathering, the result of an ability to 'drink immeasurably and preserve his understanding to the last'. Raised to the Swedish equivalents of major-general and an earldom, he returned to Scotland in 1638 in the service of **Charles I**. Commanding **Edinburgh Castle** (1640–1) he defied the **Covenanting** forces but was eventually forced to surrender. The King rewarded him with the Earldom of Forth and, after evidence of his strategic skills at the Battle of Edgehill, with command of the Royalist army. Though now entering his 60s he captured Brentford, whence his second earldom (the first had been declared forfeit by the Scottish Parliament which branded him a traitor), and was wounded at both Battles of Newbury. In 1644 Prince Rupert replaced him, Ruthven being 'much decayed in his parts and, with the long continued custom of immoderate drinking, dozed in his understanding'. Dozed or not, in 1649 he revisited Sweden to raise support for the King and in 1650 accompanied **Charles II** to Scotland where his titles and estates were restored at the Parliament held at **Perth**. He died in **Dundee** a few weeks later.

RUTHVEN, William, 1st Earl of Gowrie (c1541–84)

The family of Ruthven (pron. 'Riven') is of Northumbrian or Scandinavian descent. Its titles come from the lands and barony of Ruthven near **Perth**, held since the reign of **William the Lion** until 1600. The Barony of Ruthven was created in 1487.

The 3rd Lord Ruthven, ringleader of the murderers of **David Rizzio**, died in 1566. His son, William, succeeded as the 4th Baron. A Privy Councillor, he was High Treasurer of Scotland from 1571, an extraordinary **Lord of Session** from 1578, hereditary Sheriff of **Perthshire** and elected Provost of Perth.

He was suspected of being in sympathy with **Queen Mary** when holding her prisoner in 1567, but fought against her at **Langside** in 1568. In 1571–5 he defeated the Kerrs and perpetuated a feud with Lord Oliphant. He was created Earl of Gowrie on 15 August 1581, the lands of the dissolved **Scone** Abbey being later erected into his earldom.

As leader of the militant Protestants, he apprehended **James VI** in the **Ruthven Raid** in 1582 and held him prisoner in the House of Ruthven [see **Huntingtower**] until the King agreed to his terms.

Gowrie, who now headed the government, remained subservient to Queen Elizabeth when threatened with Queen Mary's release. But James escaped from his imprisonment in June 1583 and then promptly reinstated the **Earl of Arran** to his Privy Council despite Queen Elizabeth's protests. Arran had been spared by Gowrie, but now ordered his arrest and Gowrie, convicted of treason, was beheaded in May 1584.

RUTHVEN BARRACKS, Kingussie, Inverness-shire

Like **Bernera**, Ruthven (pron. 'Riven') Barracks were built following the 1715 **Jacobite Rising** to provide accommodation and security for a Hanoverian garrison. They stand on a motte commanding upper Speyside on which the **Comyns** once had a stronghold. Though roofless, they are more accessible and so better tended

than Bernera. The main block consists of two three-storey houses, facing each other across the parade ground and joined by the enclosing walls. There are gabled towers in two corners which served as guardhouse and bakehouse. An additional guardhouse and stable was added (1734) by **General Wade** for a detachment of dragoons. The garrison's full complement may have been 120 men but in 1745 there were only a dozen under a sergeant to resist the besieging Jacobites. They held out but surrendered in 1746 when attacked with artillery. After **Culloden** it was the Jacobites' turn to seek Ruthven's safety. Here they rallied and then dispersed, unable to offer an effective resistance. The barracks were not re-occupied and therefore fell into disrepair.

RUTHVEN RAID, The (1582)

The Ruthven Raid was a political coup organised by **William Ruthven, 1st Earl of Gowrie** and leader of the militant **Presbyterians** in Scotland. This faction greatly feared the influence of **Esmé Stewart** (created **Duke of Lennox** in 1581) over the young **King James VI**. Lennox supported the Catholic interest and the cause of **Queen Mary**. Suspected of being a Catholic spy, he intrigued with France and Spain. His election to the Privy Council in 1581 seriously alarmed the Presbyterians, who proclaimed him an agent of the Counter-Reformation. Although Lennox did then accept the reformed faith and although James VI signed the Negative Confession (denouncing all connections with the Catholic Church), his government not only refused to accept the proceedings of the **General Assembly** which condemned the office of bishop, but appointed an incumbent to the vacant see of **Glasgow** from which Lennox drew substantial revenues. And when the new bishop was excommunicated by the presbytery of **Edinburgh**, the sentence was annulled by royal proclamation. Further claims against Lennox included that of extravagance; Gowrie, the Treasurer, proved debts amounting to £45,000.

In August 1582 Gowrie managed to waylay, or possibly abduct, the King while he was hunting in Atholl. He then held him prisoner in the House of Ruthven (**Huntingtower**) until, on the following morning, James signed a proclamation declaring himself a free King and ordering the banishment of Lennox. Lennox returned to France where he died the following year. The new government headed by Gowrie established Presbyterian control, but in June 1583 James escaped from his captors and a year later Gowrie was duly beheaded for treason.

RUTHWELL, Nr Annan, Dumfriesshire

In the parish church of this village between **Dumfries** and **Annan** was re-erected (1887) the stone Ruthwell Cross, 'the most important Anglian cross in Scotland'. When it was originally erected and whether in Ruthwell (pron. 'Rivvel') are unknown. 'The symbolism of its carvings, suggestions about its missing pieces, the source of the design and its carvers, and its probable date are all subjects which have given rise to enough scholarly literature to paper the walls of the kirk' (G Stell). Its carving is probably early 8th century and, before being smashed and buried at the time of the

The Ruthwell stone cross of the early 8th century (HS)

Reformation, it certainly stood at Ruthwell, although this seems unlikely to have been its original site. On the main faces of the cross-shaft the carvings, in Hellenistic style, depict biblical scenes with Latin inscriptions while the sides of the shaft are covered with vine-scrolls with margins containing a runic text on the theme of the Creation, 'a precursor of the Anglo-Saxon poem, *The Dream of the Rood*'. This, and the fact that Rheged, the Carlisle area, was acquired by the Northumbrian Angles, provide the vital clue to its Northumbrian provenance. The high standards of the sculpture, the related inscriptions, and the thematic integration of the whole, place the Ruthwell Cross amongst the foremost monuments of Dark Age Christianity.

Prior to re-erection in the church, the cross was exhumed and set up in the manse garden (1823) by the Rev Henry Duncan, minister of Ruthwell 1798–1846 and founder of, amongst numerous other schemes for the betterment of his parishioners, the first Savings Bank (1810). He is commemorated by a pyramid in the Free Church, to which he adhered at the time of the **Disruption**, and a museum in the cottage where he began his **bank**.

the **Mackay** country. He made no attempt to publish these reminiscences, but they were edited by his son, the Rev Donald Fraser Sage, and appeared in 1889 as *Memorabilia Domestica*. Lord **Napier**, whose **Commission** had recently been investigating the events described in such vivid detail in Sage's diary, extolled its virtue. But more recently Rosalind Mitchison has poured scorn on its veracity, on the curious grounds that Sage later joined the **Free Church** in the **Disruption** of 1843; 'the taint of religious prejudice is apparent'.

ST ABB'S HEAD, Berwickshire

A mass of cliffs formed by volcanic action, St Abb's Head is a **nature reserve (National Trust for Scotland)**, having the largest colony of cliff-nesting **seabirds** in south-east Scotland (visitors' centre open April–September). A diving club operates from here and helps to maintain a voluntary Marine Reserve. A lighthouse, erected in 1861 and not open to the public, stands on the headland, and remains of a 7th century nunnery, founded by St Ebba, daughter of Ethelfred, have been found nearby.

ST ANDREWS, Fife

On the way to nowhere, with a north-east exposure to the seldom balmy zephyrs of the North Sea, and without any obvious assets of industrial or commercial relevance, St Andrews nevertheless became a place of great political importance, the country's ecclesiastical capital and its first seat of scholarship. Though undermined by the **Reformation**, it subsequently reclaimed some of this prominence thanks to its **University** and to its other 'royal and ancient' institution, that devoted to the no less demanding requirements of **golf**.

Both its name and its foundation are traced to the apparently fortuitous arrival at what was then the **Pictish** settlement of Kinrymont (Kilrymont) or Cendrigmoniad of the relics of **St Andrew**, the brother of St Peter. One version credits a Pictish King Angus or Oengus with bringing the relics from Northumberland in the mid-8th century, another credits a 4th century St Rule (Regulus) with obtaining them from Patras (where St Andrew had been crucified on a saltire, or diagonal cross) and being charged to deliver them in 'a region towards the west, situated in the utmost part of the world'. This turned out to be Scotland where Regulus came ashore after shipwreck at Kinrymont. Some accounts combine both versions and most also add a visionary element in which St Andrew (or his cross) makes a personal appearance to ensure a Scots or Pictish victory. At Kinrymont there seems to have been an already existing establishment of the **Celtic Church**, possibly founded by the Irish St Kenny; there is also evidence of a pre-Christian swine cult (hence Boarhills to the south-east).

Possession of such VIP relics produced a dramatic upgrading of the site. **Culdee** monks started their own establishment where the foundations of the Church of the Blessed Mary on the Rock are still visible. Kinrymont was rededicated and became St Andrews; the saint became Scotland's patron, and the site a royally patronised place of pilgrimage which in 908 also became the see of the only Scottish bishopric. Contacts with the Northumbrian Church had continued and in

SADDELL ABBEY and CASTLE, Kintyre, Argyll

The ruins of the only Cistercian abbey in **Argyll** lie in woodland at the foot of a glen in east **Kintyre**. Only the chancel and north transept of the church, and fragments of the refectory, stand; the other buildings around the cloister are marked by grassy mounds. There are fine carved stones. The house was founded around 1160 with monks from Mellifont in Ireland by **Somerled**, King of Man and the Isles, believed to be buried here. Never a large establishment, by 1508 three elderly monks remained as pensioners in lodgings. The monastic lands were annexed to the Bishopric of Argyll, and the ruins were eventually robbed for building stone, some of it used in the castle, built 1508–12 by Bishop David Hamilton, burnt by English raiders in 1538, thereafter rebuilt and enlarged. It stands by the bay, a typical tower house rising above additions. It belongs to the Landmark Trust and is not normally open to the public, but can be seen from nearby. Its most remarkable internal feature was a pit-prison, entered only by a trapdoor in the main entrance passage – an effective cure for uninvited callers.

SADLER, Sir Ralph (1507–87) English Diplomat

First in Scotland c1536 to influence **James V** against Rome, Sadler remained in **Edinburgh** as Henry VIII's envoy and in 1542 was able to report back that the baby **Queen Mary** was 'as goodly a child as I have seen'. The following year – by now a seasoned diplomat with a thorough understanding of the Scots – he warned his monarch that his insistence on having custody of Mary on her engagement to Prince Edward would jeopardise the **Treaty of Greenwich**; to no avail. He fought with Hertford at the **Battle of Pinkie**, but returned to Scotland in 1559, now in the employ of Elizabeth I's Secretary of State, Sir William Cecil. His mission this time was to provide covert funds and moral support to the **Lords of the Congregation** in their dealings with **Mary of Guise**, furthering Cecil's aims of driving the French out of Scotland, establishing Protestantism north of the border, and forging an Anglo-Scottish alliance.

SAGE, Donald (1789–1869) Minister

Sage's exceptionally valuable memoir comprehends the life and times of his grandfather Eneas Sage (1694–1774), minister of Loch Carron, of his father Alexander Sage (1753–1824), minister of **Kildonan**, and of his own ministries, including the one in which he witnessed the **clearances** conducted by **Patrick Sellar** in

Off St Andrews, by Sam Bough (NGS)

St Andrews continued

1107, when a prior of Durham became Bishop of St Andrews, perhaps through the influence of **Queen/ Saint Margaret**, the see passed from the influence of the Celtic Church to that of Rome. 20 years later Bishop Robert, previously prior of **Scone**, introduced Augustinian canons, who gradually supplanted the Culdees. The burgh received its first charter (from **David I**) c1140. Bishop Robert also began construction of the priory (which had its first prior in 1144) and of St Rule's Church, of which the tower and choir survive; both priory and diocese must rapidly have outgrown St Rule's for by 1161 Robert's successor, Bishop Arnold, with encouragement from **Malcolm IV**, had begun the adjacent **Cathedral**, indisputably the largest in the country.

The 13th century saw the completion of the Cathedral's nave and the reconstruction of its west front, following storm damage, by **Bishop Wishart** in the 1270s. Wishart also introduced the Dominican Blackfriars. His successor-but-one finally consecrated the new Cathedral in 1318. This was **Bishop Lamberton** whose support of **William Wallace** and crowning of **Robert I** had earned him two years' imprisonment in England and had resulted in Edward I removing the Cathedral's lead. Lamberton also rebuilt the battered Bishop's Palace or **Castle** which had first been erected c1200. It was 'dang doun' by the English and then again by **Andrew**

Murray (Moray) during the **Wars of Independence** but rebuilt by Bishop Walter Traill at the end of the 14th century.

A fire in that century and more storm damage (to the south transept) in 1409 kept the Cathedral's masons busy till the mid-15th century. Meanwhile Traill's successor, **Bishop Wardlaw**, founded (1412) Scotland's first university, and tutored **James I** in the rebuilt Castle. After his English captivity the King took up residence in the Castle; **Bishop Kennedy**, Wardlaw's successor, founded St Salvator's (1450), the University's second college, and governed the realm during **James II**'s minority. **James III** may have been born in the Castle (1451), and with the Cathedral at last restored to its glory the see of St Andrews was upgraded as Scotland's first archbishopric in 1472.

By then the original north-south axis of the town along Castle Street had been altered to an east-west axis along North and South Streets which diverge from the parallel just enough to show a reverential convergence on the Cathedral. Bisecting the acute angle between them, Market Street recalls the market that grew up in its midst while north of North Street and parallel to it, The Scores bounded the cliffs between the Castle and what would become the **golf course**. The West Port marked the landward limits of the town and the Kinness Burn, with the **harbour** at its mouth, the southern boundary.

In the 16th century the town enjoyed some commercial importance thanks to the harbour and, with royal and ecclesiastical patronage waxing strong, looked set for a noble future. The crisis came with the **Reformation**. Not only did St Andrews become associated with the excesses of its two **Beaton** archbishops and with the martyrdom of **Hamilton**, **Wishart** and **Mylne** (among others), but it also lost its whole *raison d'être* as pilgrimages were frowned upon, all religious foundations and seminarist colleges pillaged and downgraded, and episcopacy itself discredited and intermittently abolished. Most notably during the Castle siege (1546–7) of Beaton's murderers and other reformers, including **Knox**, St Andrews appeared to have backed the wrong side. Deprived of its ecclesiastical prominence, it had no commercial alternative to fall back on, unlike **Glasgow** or **Aberdeen**.

Between 1559, when Knox preached in **Holy Trinity Church** about the expulsion of the money changers from the temple, and 1679, when **Archbishop Sharp** was murdered by **Covenanters** on Magus Muir [see **Cupar**], every phase in the protracted religious turmoil emphasised the importance of **Edinburgh** and Glasgow and the growing irrelevance of St Andrews. In 1689 the University again misjudged events and favoured the **Jacobite** cause; so did the whole town in 1715. By then it had become notorious for filthy streets, decaying buildings and corrupt academics; even the air, usually adjudged so healthful, was characterised as 'thin and piercing' and fatal to valetudinarians.

In reversing this decline golf, its national popularity taking off about 1840, is usually credited as the decisive factor [see **Royal and Ancient Golf Club**]. Equally important were a number of other local initiatives, such as the foundation of **Madras College** and later St Leonards School, or Provost Playfair's creation of a **New Town**. The changing social climate of the period and the advent of the **railways** encouraged the development of resorts and spas plus a more inventive use of leisure. St Andrews quickly established itself as the most fashionable of golf resorts; and places at its revitalised University once again became sought after. Instead of the one 'pothouse' of 1829, a guide of 1896 lists six large hotels, all 'good' or 'very good' and 'numerous lodgings, all very full in autumn, especially during golf meetings'. Unindustrialised and so undisturbed by the social traumas of the 20th century, St Andrews remains immersed in its contemplation of antiquities, scholarship and trajectories. **Andrew Lang**'s lines might apply to devotees of any one of them.

> St Andrews by the Northern Sea
> A haunted town it is to me.

Blackfriars', South Street

Founded in 1516 this Dominican establishment proved short-lived when, like its sister house in **Perth**, it fell victim to **Reformation** iconoclasm (1559) and subsequent neglect. All that remains is the north transept of the chapel. It is, though, architecturally notable with vaulted roof and a half-octagonal apse with pointed windows, one of which has been enlarged to accommodate a 19th century re-creation of the original tracery.

Castle

Fragmentary and not especially impressive, the rugged remains of St Andrews Castle sprawl over a prime site between the old town and the encroaching sea-cliffs; they also afford an intimate commentary on the crucial **Reformation** crisis of 1546–7. Parts of the main fore tower are thought to date from 1200 when Bishop Roger here constructed the first episcopal palace. Repeatedly battered and rebuilt (once by **Bishop Lamberton**) during the **Wars of Independence**, it continued as the bishop's palace though increasingly conforming to the role and architecture of a castle. In the 1390s it was rebuilt by Bishop Walter Traill as a castle of enclosure with curtain walls that followed the contours of the cliffs; as at **Ravenscraig**, the main defensive features (tower, ditch, drawbridge, etc) guarded the landward approaches. In the tower and adjacent ranges lived **Bishop Wardlaw**, then his pupil, **James I**, and subsequently **Bishop Kennedy**. **James III** may have been born here and during his reign Cathedral's first archbishop, Patrick Graham, was imprisoned here. Thereafter the Castle's prisoners vied for celebrity with their gaolers. In the aftermath of **Flodden** the archbishopric was disputed between four contenders, one of whom, the poet **Gavin Douglas**, held the Castle and was then briefly incarcerated in it. As archbishop from 1522 **James Beaton** (d.1539) held court on a grand scale and was succeeded by his even grander nephew, **Cardinal David Beaton**.

Patrick Hamilton's martyrdom by Archbishop Beaton ignited the Reformation; Cardinal Beaton kept it blazing with the immolation (1546) of **George Wishart**, who during his trial had been held in the Castle's notorious bottle dungeon (in the Sea Tower). Beaton and other clerics are supposed to have watched the painfully slow torching of Wishart from cushioned comfort atop the Castle's walls. Three months later the tables were turned as the Cardinal's mangled corpse dangled from the same walls. Outraged by his treatment of Wishart, John Leslie, a brother of the **Earl of Rothes**, and other reform-minded sympathisers, had seized the Castle during repair work and murdered the Cardinal: 'and when he was lying over the wall, ane called Guthrie pisched in his mouth'. Joined by more Lutheran sympathisers, including **John Knox**, the rebels held out in the Castle (hence 'Castillians') for nearly a year. They were bombarded from any convenient vantage point including the **Cathedral**, and they were undermined by an extraordinarily capacious shaft, duly negated by a counter-mine from within the Castle (both still open for inspection). Eventually both Castle and Castillians were pounded into surrender by a French fleet summoned by **Mary of Guise**. Knox and the rest were deported; **John Hamilton** succeeded Cardinal Beaton as Archbishop; and most of the remaining Castle was demolished.

Today's ruins are therefore largely those of its replacement built by Hamilton, whose arms are above the main entrance, in 1549–71. Its dilapidation is the result neither of the siege nor of the Reformation's anti-clericalism, but of a neglect which overtook the rest of the town during the 17th century when deprived of its ecclesiastical relevance. During the Cromwellian Commonwealth the town council itself ordered the use of the Castle's masonry for rebuilding the **harbour**. In the 19th century the encroaching sea removed what was left of the east range and its corner tower. There remain sections of the curtain walls, parts of the Sea and Kitchen Towers, and the still intact parapeted fore-tower with west wing and entrance.

Cathedral

In a level enclosure strewn with masonry and lapped by the town on one side and the sea on the other stand the ruins of the Cathedral and its associated buildings. Weather-worked and turret-topped fangs of stone stab at the sky, fulfilling even the most romantic expectations. This is hallowed ground; its 1000-year pedigree as a place of Christian pilgrimage rivals that of **Iona** or **Whithorn**, while it dwarfs both as a centre of ecclesiastical authority and a focus of Scottish history. Tall twin towers linked by a lofty gable wall constitute the Cathedral's nearly complete 12th century east front. Its windows, three round-headed lancets topped by a larger, later (15th century) pointed window, gape seawards, 'those rent skeletons of pierced wall through which our sea winds moan and murmur' (Ruskin). Part of the nave's south wall marches off into the distance in bays which betray both the original rounded Romanesque and the later, reconstructed Gothic. The nave terminates in a slender pinnacle, precariously guyed by a buttress strutt and the outline of a Gothic window; this was the south-west angle tower and beneath its window, once one of three, blind arcading surmounts the small and deeply recessed main entrance. An

Tower and church of St Rule flanked by the ruined extremities of St Andrews Cathedral (RWB)

improbable distance from the west gable, it was once two bays further away when in its original form the Cathedral was 355ft (108m) long and the largest church in Britain save only Norwich Cathedral. Storm damage in the 13th century necessitated the reconstruction (1273–9) and foreshortening. In other respects the outline of nave, choir and transepts must be inferred from foundations, pillar stumps and a section of the south transept.

Sections of the precinct wall also survive, including gateways and towers; so do parts of the chapter house, cloister and warming house, now the **museum**. These pertained to the adjoining priory, the Cathedral serving as the church to both the Augustinian monastic establishment and the bishopric.

Within the precinct and just south-east of the Cathedral, another slender tower of sterner aspect adjoined by a narrow section of choir is all that remains of the Church of St Rule (Latin: Regulus) which preceded the Cathedral and was built, possibly by masons from Yorkshire, c1130. Earlier still, and between the precinct wall and the sea, foundations are still visible of the **Culdee** Church of the Blessed Mary on the Rock. The nave may be as early as 9th–10th century, although transepts and choir came later. This must once have housed the relics of **St Andrew** and have been the earliest focus of pilgrimage. Fragments of several early Christian (8th–10th century) cross-slabs found here are now in the museum and testify to **Celtic**/Culdee links with the Anglian church of Northumberland.

Deans Court, North Street

'The oldest dwelling on the oldest domestic site in St Andrews' (G L Pride), Deans Court stands at the **Cathedral** end of North Street and dates from the early 16th century but was repaired by Sir George Douglas c1585 (his much-worn arms are above the gateway) and considerably remodelled in the 19th century, then restored in the 20th. In 1931 it was converted into a **University** hall of residence but ground-floor vaulting and 18th century panelling are still notable.

Harbour

With St Andrews Bay 'proverbially dangerous to navigators', the harbour developed at the mouth of the Kinness Burn south of the projecting rocks whereon stand the **Cathedral** – and so to some extent sheltered by both. A fair trade grew up with France, Flanders, Holland and the Baltic in the 15th century and 200–300 vessels were reported in attendance for the annual Senzie fair. But the harbour could never become a major port and in the late 17th century declined in significance even more rapidly than the town it served. Pier repairs and extensions, as when masonry from the Castle was used in 1656, served only to improve accommodation for **fishing** boats and to provide the **University**'s inmates with a popular promenade.

Holy Trinity Church

Although the fine tower is a survival of the church founded by Bishop Wardlaw in 1411, the rest of this remarkable building is a 1907–9 recreation of a medieval burgh church by **P MacGregor Chalmers**. Authentic in detail if not true to the original design, it has been likened to 'a dictionary of architectural quotations' (J Gifford) in which the scholar of Scottish ecclesiastical architecture will delight in identifying the provenance of individual features (eg windows from **Seton** chapel, nearby St Leonards chapel, **Aberdeen**'s **St Machar's**, etc). Much of the exceptional stained glass is by Strachan. In the south transept the monument to **Archbishop James Sharp** is in black and white marble, possibly Dutch, and dated to c1679, the year of his assassination.

Madras College, South Street

Founded by **Dr Andrew Bell** in 1832 on principles developed in India as his 'Madras System', Madras College is now St Andrews' main secondary school. In addition to new buildings in Kilrymont, it still occupies the grand Jacobean-style college specially built in South Street by **William Burn** in 1832–4. Set well back from the street, where the remaining transept of **Blackfriars'** is prominent, its two-storey front, with bay windows and shaped gables, and the flanking wings are well served by the intervening acres of lawn.

Museums

In addition to the mainly archaeological and architectural museum in the **Cathedral** precinct, there is a **golf** museum on Pilmuir Links and a museum belonging to the St Andrews Preservation Trust at 12–16 North Street. The latter fills restored 17th century accommodation with items from the town's 19th century social history. Also in North Street, a fine Georgian **Adam**-style house is now the Crawford Centre for the Arts, a **University** venue for exhibitions and performances.

New Town

In imitation of **Edinburgh**, the north-west of St Andrews overlooking the bay and the links was developed as a new town in the 19th century. Amongst the formal squares, crescents and gardens, many now serving **University** purposes, Playfair Terrace (1846–52) recalls Provost Hugh Playfair who was largely responsible for the initiative; it was designed by George Rae who also built Gillespie Terrace at the west end of The Scores. Here, near the bandstand, is the Martyrs' Memorial (1842) commemorating the town's five martyrs to the **Reformation** cause, including **Patrick Hamilton**, whose initials in the cobbles beneath St Salvator's tower mark the site of his burning; **George Wishart**, similarly commemorated outside the **Castle**; and the octogenarian **Walter Mylne** who was burnt outside the **Cathedral**.

Queen Mary's House, South Street

Although it is unclear whether **Queen Mary** ever stayed here, **Charles II** probably did in 1650. It was built (c1525) as a merchant's house and is now the library of St Leonards Girls' School. The plain street elevation is belied by a charming crow-stepped garden frontage with romantic elements such as a prominent oriel window and a splayed stair tower rising to a corbelled cap-house.

Royal And Ancient Golf Club

Golf has been played on St Andrews links since at least the early 17th century; 'The Society of St Andrews Golfers' dates from 1754. But **Boswell** and **Johnson** made no mention of the game when visiting St Andrews in 1773 and neither did Lord Teignmouth when advocating the attractions of the town in 1829. Considering that there was 'only one miserable inn or rather pothouse' it may be assumed that the links were frequented mainly by local residents. In 1834 the 'Society' secured the patronage of William IV (III of Scotland) and changed its name to the 'Royal and Ancient' in a document which also declared St Andrews 'the Alma Mater of golf'.

10 years later the production of golf balls was listed as the town's one and only manufacture and **Lord Cockburn** cited golf as being 'as much a staple of the place as old churches and colleges are . . . and has for ages been so'. The links, like the adjacent **New Town**, came into their own as a result of conscious promotion in the 1830s–50s by such as Provost Playfair. Golf itself was then winning new advocates with the introduction of the cheaper gutta-percha ball; so was St Andrews with the coming of the **railway**. To the same period belongs the R & A Club House, begun by George Rae in 1854 and subsequently extended sideways and upwards. The result, though 'hardly worthy of the club's reputation' (J Gifford) is now so hallowed as to disdain architectural merit.

See also **Golf Courses**.

West Port, South Street

Commissioned as a replica of **Edinburgh**'s now lost **Netherbow** Port, St Andrews' West Port has been described as 'the best extant example in Scotland' of a civic gate. Built in 1589, the arched pend is flanked by half-octagonal towers with gun slits and topped by a corbelled parapet with square cannon holes. The additional arched side buttresses are 19th century, like the relief panel of **David I** on horseback which replaced the royal arms.

ST ANDREWS UNIVERSITY

Although mentioned in 1410, Scotland's first university is usually dated to **Bishop Henry Wardlaw**'s 1412 charter or its 1413 confirmation by the (Avignon) Pope, Benedict XIII. Wardlaw was first Chancellor and Laurence of **Lindores** first Rector and Dean of Arts; the latter had a silver mace, still extant, specially cast as a symbol of authority. The foundation was expanded in 1450 when **Bishop James Kennedy** endowed St Salvator's College, in 1512 when Prior Hepburn founded St Leonards College, and in 1538 when **Archbishop James Beaton** founded St Mary's. Also attached to the university was **Blackfriars'** (1516).

Though teaching subjects other than theology, all were essentially seminaries prior to the **Reformation**. Thereafter Blackfriars' ceased to operate, St Mary's specialised in theology, and the others in arts and philosophy. The library was founded in 1611 and, with lands transferred from the Church, the University enjoyed something of a golden age during the late 16th and early 17th centuries; notable alumni included **George Buchanan, John Napier, James ('the Admirable')**

Gate tower and church of St Salvator's College, part of the University of St Andrews (RWB)

Crichton, **Andrew Melville** and the two martial **Grahams, James (Marquis of Montrose)** and **John (Viscount Dundee)**. But in the later 17th century, as **Edinburgh** usurped its pre-eminence, decline saw the amalgamation of St Salvator's and St Leonards, and a revival of plans to resite the entire establishment in **Perth**. Relief came courtesy of the 19th century enthusiasm for **golf**, which made St Andrews once again fashionable, and of the 19th century reorganisation of the universities.

Now scattered throughout the town, the University's original buildings were concentrated in the area west of the **Cathedral**. In North Street St Salvator's College retains its lofty gate tower (c1460) and spire with the arms of Bishop Kennedy above the entrance. His large but damaged tomb, of French workmanship, is built into the north wall of the adjacent chapel, also of c1460 but embellished in the 19th century and furnished (stalls, screen) in the 20th by **Reginald Fairlie**. On the other side of the gate tower the Hebdomadar's Building, with notable panelling, also dates from the 1460s but an extra storey was added in the 17th century.

Much closer to the Cathedral, St Leonards Chapel predates the college that it once served, having been built c1413 as a parish church. For such an unassuming building it has had a complicated architectural history and a chequered career. It still belongs to the University although all the neighbouring buildings, including ranges (17th century) once part of the St Leonards College, now form St Leonards Girls' School.

St Mary's College along with the 17th century University library plus its 19th century extension form a delightful quadrangle of buildings in South Street. The 16th century west range of the college survives though with its exterior Georgianised and its interior frontage remodelled when the adjacent library was built c1620. The Founders Tower has a prominent corbelled belfry, and the corner stair tower a fine ogee roof. Though much extended and altered, the library retains its two large halls, that on the ground floor having served as a parliament hall in 1645–6.

ST BOSWELLS, Roxburghshire

The village of St Boswell, named after St Boisel or Bossil who was prior of Old **Melrose** immediately before **St Cuthbert**, was famed for the size of its village green (at 40 acres (16ha) said to be the largest in Scotland) and for the importance of the annual cattle and horse fair held thereon. **James Hogg** is said to have refused **Walter Scott**'s offer of a ticket to the coronation of George IV at Westminster Abbey because it clashed with St Boswells Fair. Just to the north-west Newtown St Boswells grew up around the **railway** station in the mid-19th century and later became the county town of **Roxburghshire** and the headquarters of the Borders Regional Council.

ST COLUMBA'S CAVE, Ellary, Argyll

On Loch Coalisport (side road from Achahoish) in **Knapdale** are two caves in a cliff behind a ruined 13th century church. The smaller one was possibly a hermitage; the larger one contains an altar on a rock-shelf beneath carved crosses. Local tradition insists **St Columba** came here en route to **Iona**. The main cave was a fishermen's bothy when a 19th century laird had it cleaned out under antiquarian supervision, resulting in the removal of 2m of accumulated occupation material to form a tip outside. A ladder restored access to the altar, until in 1959 the landowner began replacing this with earth from the tip. The chance find of an antler sewing-needle alerted him and local archaeologists, and riddling produced finds of all periods from prehistoric to recent, including flint, antler and bone tools, pottery, metalworking debris, quantities of shells and food bones, and a folding pocket balance, possibly **Viking**.

ST FILLANS, Perthshire

At the east end of Loch Earn, the village of St Fillans is a 19th century creation of the Drummond family [see **Drummond Castle**]. It is named after either the 8th century Irish **St Fillan** or the 6th century Celtic St Faolean the Leper, one of whom was supposedly based at nearby Dundurn. This craggy eminence commanding upper Strathearn was the site of a 7th century fort, probably **Pictish**, mentioned in the **Iona** annals, and apparently resembling that at **Dunadd**. Parts of the walls are still visible. Excavations in the 1970s revealed artefacts including a decorated leather shoe.

ST KILDA, Outer Hebrides

A part of Britain but a world apart, the Hebridean island of St Kilda existed in almost complete isolation from the mainland for centuries. Its small, indigenous population thrived until, in the 19th century, the island was 'discovered' by missionaries and **tourists** who, bearing the

George Washington Wilson's 1885 photograph of the St Kilda parliament (GWWA)

gifts of civilisation, helped bring about the community's gradual destruction. The population declined and in 1930 the islanders, no longer self-sufficient, were evacuated. Today only a handful of St Kildans are still living, scattered throughout Britain. Except for a military installation on the island, it has remained uninhabited, though as a **National Nature** and **bird reserve**, recently declared a World Heritage Site, it attracts a steady tide of visitors to its wild, hauntingly beautiful shores.

The archipelago of St Kilda, consisting of Hirta (the main island, 1575 acres (640ha) in area, also known as St Kilda) and its satellites, Soay, Boreray and the Dun, lies out on the edge of the continental shelf, 110 miles west of the Scottish mainland. Surrounded by cliffs rising to 1400ft/427m (the highest in Europe) and deep water, the islands are formidably inaccessible. Their isolation and sub-oceanic climate played a decisive part in the lives of the inhabitants. Frequent storms from September to April often prevented anyone getting on or off St Kilda for weeks at a time. Yet, in summer, spells of clear warm weather can make the islands seem, as one St Kildan put it, 'like no paradise on earth'.

The premier **seabird** breeding station in Britain, St Kilda is an ornithologist's dream. To the St Kildans the birds were something more. Theirs is the story of a bird culture, of a people whose survival depended on the enormous colonies of gannets, fulmar and puffins that dominate the ecology and character of the islands. The birds provided them with food, medicine, shoes, a source of revenue and a unique way of life. But in winter the birds fly south; only the St Kilda wren, a

true subspecies and, like the St Kilda mouse, resident since before the last Ice Age, remains year round.

For most of its history St Kilda was a self-supporting commonwealth with an economy geared to its isolation. It was first settled at least 2000 years ago by Neolithic wanderers. In common with most Hebridean islands, St Kilda subsequently saw **Celtic** invaders, early Christian anchorites and **Vikings**, all of whom contributed to the islanders' racial stock and successful adaptation to their remote existence. From the end of the 14th century until 1930 the islands belonged to the **MacLeods** of **Harris** and **Dunvegan** (**Skye**). Once a year a MacLeod steward visited St Kilda to see to the islanders' needs and collect rent, which they paid in the feathers, oil and dried carcases of seabirds. Imports were limited to bare necessities. Paying the rent was the responsibility of the whole community. Arable land, pasture, livestock, fowling cliffs, boats and ropes were all held in common, yet scrupulously divided into plots and portions among the island's families – each contributing towards the rent according to an intricate system of ownership rights.

Decisions on all matters concerning the community were made by the St Kilda parliament. A deliberative assembly of the grown males on the island (the women had their own informal gathering) met every morning except Sunday to decide what work should be done that day, and discuss a wide-ranging agenda. Parliament ensured that no islander was raised above another and that all shared the common wealth or want. In 1697 **Martin Martin**, a literary tutor to the MacLeods, visited St Kilda and found that although life there was simple and severe, its people seemed 'happier than the generality of mankind'.

The St Kildans, 180 strong in Martin's day, lived above Village Bay in a long row of turf-roofed dwellings called the Street – now ruined though later (1860) cottages are progressively being restored by the **National Trust for Scotland**. Some of the older houses were of a prehistoric beehive type, like the stone *cleits* dotted about the island in which the people stored food and **peat**. The remains of one such hut are known as Lady Grange's House – after the unfortunate woman who spent eight years exiled on St Kilda for threatening to reveal her husband's **Jacobite** sympathies in 1734 [see **James Erskine, Lord Grange**].

The islanders lived mainly on a diet of fulmar and gannets, which they ate either fresh in season or cured. Both species were harvested young (before they could fly) from nesting ledges on the cliffs. Puffins were taken fully grown and had to be caught with fowling rods or snares. Fowling was the most important activity on St Kilda. By the time they were 16 boys had to be fully-fledged cragsmen. A young St Kildan could not marry before he had proved himself in the ritual of the Mistress Stone, balancing on one foot over a sheer 250ft (76m) drop to demonstrate by his courage and skill the ability to support a wife. Stories dramatising the dangers of fowling perpetuated the myth of the heroic cragsman. But in later years as the male population declined, fewer risks were taken and fowling lost much of its former prestige.

Fishing was never popular with the islanders, and while farming supplemented their diet, it remained a secondary occupation. Summers were short and the return on the crops poor. The St Kildans owned a small herd of cattle and about 2000 sheep pastured on Hirta and Boreray. The sheep on Soay, which belonged to MacLeod, were a pure primitive breed kept only for their wool. Transferred to Hirta after the evacuation, they have since reverted to the wild [see **Soay Sheep**].

Except for the steward's yearly visit, the islanders'

only means of communicating with the outside world was the 'St Kilda mailboat', a piece of hollowed-out wood containing a letter, instructions for the finder to post it, and a penny for the stamp. Launched when the wind was in the north-west, more often than not it eventually turned up on the west coast of Scotland. In the early 19th century, the remoteness and simplicity of the St Kildans created an interest in Britain's only 'primitive' society that caught the romantic Victorian imagination. Soon enough the world began its bid to bring 'lone St Kilda' into its fold.

The islanders, unfailingly hospitable, even though contact with outsiders carried the risk of infection, had even less immunity against the benefits of civilisation. In 1822 St Kilda was first subjected to dogmatic religion with the arrival of John MacDonald, the 'Apostle of the North'. Until then the St Kildan's close relationship with nature had taken the ritual form of Druidism, while the precepts of early Christianity had shaped his relationship with his fellow man. Because of the islanders' natural devoutness and superstitious character, missionaries gained an easy ascendancy over their hearts and minds. While some ministers worked hard to raise their standard of living and introduce education, others forced a sabbatarianism so extreme that the St Kildans were prevented from doing the vital work of the community.

Tourism had an equally malign effect. The 'steamer season' soon became the most important part of the St Kildan year. The islanders made a little money selling tweed and birds' eggs as souvenirs but, patronised by the visitors and often subjected to ridicule, they gradually lost respect for their own ancient customs and way of life. As contact with the mainland increased, what had always been a strong and healthy people became susceptible to previously unknown diseases. More than any other, *tetanus infantum*, endemic throughout the 19th

Packing St Kilda tweed c1920 (SEA)

century, contributed to the decline of the community, claiming 8 out of 10 children. The population loss was never made up and the emigration of 42 islanders to Australia in the 1850s may have sealed the community's fate.

Unable to adapt to the modern world, St Kilda's economy collapsed. The demand for seabird products had dwindled and the islanders, demoralised and fatalistic, no longer produced enough food for their own needs. They came to rely more and more on the devitalising charity of their MacLeod landlords and other concerned well-wishers. As early as 1875 there was talk of evacuation, but the islanders gained a reprieve with the arrival of World War I, when a navy station was established on Hirta. After the war, the community struggled on another 10 years, while most of the young men left the island. The population fell from 73 in 1920 to 37 in 1928. Successive crop failures and influenza epidemics reduced life to a miserable level. On 29 August 1930, at the request of the islanders, St Kilda was evacuated.

The St Kildans were settled on the mainland and given jobs by the **Forestry Commission**. But they lacked the determination to begin life afresh and the community gradually dispersed. For all the grief it caused, most regarded the evacuation as inevitable. The community had been living on borrowed time since the turn of the century, when its survival became dependent on communications with the mainland, which had improved enough to destroy St Kilda's independence, but not enough to bring the island into the swim of Scottish life.

ST MONANS (MONANCE), Fife
To the east of Elie [see **Earlsferry**] a clifftop walk leads past the ruins of Ardross Castle, stronghold of the Dishington family (relatives of **Robert I**), and Newark Castle (once owned by **General David Leslie**, the victor of **Philiphaugh**, and considered for restoration by **Sir Robert Lorimer** on behalf of **Sir William Burrell**), to St Monans. St Moinenn was a 6th century Bishop of Clonfert in Co Galway, and it is likely that his bones were brought here by Irish missionaries fleeing before the **Viking** invasions. The religious connection has persisted to the present day, for St Monans supports several evangelical sects such as the Open and Close Brethren, more commonly found in the Moray Firth **fishing** communities. This religious fervour, together with unusual fisher surnames like Fyall, Gowans and Hutt, and the 'characteristic drawl or drone' commented on by a recent writer on East **Fife** dialect, combine to make St Monans one of the most distinctive fisher-towns on the east coast. But its great glory is the parish church built by **David II** in 1362–70 and restored by **William Burn** in 1826–8. In the clifftop graveyard skull-and-crossbones-decorated mariners' graves are regularly washed by the salt sea-spray. In death as in life the St Monans people can say, in the words of their burgh motto, *Mare Vivimus* (We Live by the Sea).

ST NINIAN'S ISLE, Shetland
Off the south-west coast of **Shetland**, St Ninian's Isle is joined to **Mainland** by a 600m sand bar – a feature known to geologists as a tombolo. This is reckoned to be the finest example in the world. An early Christian

'The most important single discovery in Scottish archaeology.' Silver and silver gilt items from the St Ninian's Isle treasure (© the Trustees of the National Museums of Scotland)

Church, dedicated to **St Ninian**, was built here in the 6th or 7th century AD. In 1958 excavations at the site revealed a treasure trove of 28 silver objects, which had been hidden hurriedly, possibly during a **Viking** raid. The objects are now preserved in the **Museum of Scotland** in **Edinburgh**.

ST VIGEANS, Arbroath, Angus
On a mound less than two miles from **Arbroath Abbey**, St Vigeans was once the parish church of **Arbroath** and in fact predates the Abbey. The name is supposed to derive from a Celtic St Fechin (d.664); parts of the church date from 1100 and of the tower from the 15th century, though both have been altered and restored. During one such restoration the 32 carved stones which stood within or formed part of the structure were removed to the nearby cottage museum. They constitute one of the most important collections of **Pictish** Christian art and include the Drosten Stone, a cross-slab with Pictish symbols plus one of the very few inscriptions in Roman letters to be found on such stones. The first word is DROSTEN; the rest is much worn, only partly legible, and of doubtful meaning.

SALMOND, James Bell, 'Wayfarer'
(1891–1958) Author and Editor
Born in **Arbroath**, James Salmond attended the **University of St Andrews** before serving in the **Black Watch** during World War I. After the war he became a journalist, and in 1927 was made editor of the **Dundee** based *Scots Magazine*. He later edited the *Northern Review*. As an editor he gave encouragement to, and published works by, such authors as **James Leslie Mitchell**, **Lewis Spence** and **Neil M Gunn**. Salmond also wrote for the *Scots Magazine* under the pseudonym 'Wayfarer'. A collection of his poetry, written for the magazine, was published as *The Old Stalker* in 1936. Other works include *Wade in Scotland* (1934), an edition of works by **Andrew**

'A quaint figure in baggy pleated trousers'. Detail from a Pictish cross-slab in St Vigeans Museum (HS)

Lang, *Andrew Lang and St Andrews* (1944) and *The History of the 51st Highland Division* (1953). Salmond helped found the Scottish branch of the Youth Hostel Association, and played a significant role in promoting theatrical events in connection with **Arbroath Abbey**. He died in **St Andrews**.

SALTCOATS, Ayrshire

Central of the 'Three Towns' formed by **Ardrossan**, Saltcoats and **Stevenston** on the **Ayrshire** coast, Saltcoats – also known until the 18th century as Saltcottis or Saltcottes – began as a late medieval salt-producing and fish-curing village. Nearby **coal** outcrops were used to boil sea water. The town was first granted a charter in 1528.

Local coal was exported to Ireland in the 17th and 18th centuries; and small-scale chemical production, a by-product of salt manufacture, lasted until the mid-19th century. The ruins of an engine house to de-water local mines (only the second in Scotland) can still be seen near the beach between Saltcoats and Stevenston. All mining ended soon after World War I, along with **shipbuilding**. A **canal** which ran for approximately two miles between the harbour and the mines was opened in 1772 – the first commercial waterway in Scotland. Some handloom weaving lasted into the very early 20th century, but from the 1880s until the trade collapsed after World War II Saltcoats became one of the most popular holiday venues for working-class families from **Glasgow** and the rest of industrial central Scotland.

Few particularly famous inhabitants are recorded, although mention must be made of Betsy Miller (d.1864), the female master of the trading brig *Clytus* and reputedly the only woman ever entered as a shipmaster in the British Registry of Tonnage. Relics of the town's nautical past can be viewed at the North Ayrshire Museum in Saltcoats. Like Ardrossan, the town had links with the enterprising Guthrie newspaper family who founded the *Ardrossan and Saltcoats Herald* (1853). A scion of the family, Arthur Guthrie, helped found the Institute of Journalists in Scotland in 1890.

SALTIRE SOCIETY, The

Founded in 1936, the Saltire Society seeks to preserve and promote Scottish culture in an age when its distinctive character and traditions are particularly vulnerable to erosion. The journalist George Malcolm Thomson and Professor **Andrew Dewar Gibb** were amongst its founder membrs, **Eric Linklater**, **Hugh MacDiarmid**, **Edwin** and Willa **Muir** amongst its early recruits. Though the Society campaigns on relevant issues, it disclaims any political or sectarian affiliation and is run by its members through a small staff with offices in **Edinburgh**.

With branches throughout Scotland the Society's activities are diverse. Competitions and awards, some sponsored by industry, highlight Scottish excellence in housing design, civil **engineering** and environmental planning as well as in literature, **music**, **education**, history and arts and crafts. It also contributes to the **Edinburgh Festival** and has a major publication programme. Members (by subscription) are offered a programme of cultural and social events; funding is by sponsorship, government grants, donations, legacies and subscriptions.

SALVESEN, Salve Christian Frederick (1827–1911) Shipowner

The Christian Salvesen Group is a reminder of the ancient trade links between Scotland's east coast ports and Scandinavia. It was largely the creation of S C F Salvesen who, born in Norway, first worked in his uncle's **shipping** agency in **Grangemouth** before returning (1853) to Scotland to manage its **Leith** offshoot, Salvesen-Turnbull. He took British citizenship in 1859; his uncle died in 1865; and Turnbull, the Scottish partner, was removed in 1872. Salvesen rapidly developed the agency business and then began operating his own vessels. As of old, timber and timber products were the main imports, **coal** the main export. By the turn of the century Salvesen had what was possibly the largest shipping agency on the east coast and some 30 vessels. The company also diversified into whaling with stations in Iceland and the Falklands.

SANDAY, Orkney

This island with its dozen or so pendicles enclosing deep sandy bays has proved a magnet to humans, birds and marine animals alike. Even by Orcadian standards it is rich in Neolithic monuments, though many have suffered from coastal erosion. Quoyness chambered tomb, dating from about 2000 BC, and excavated by Gordon Childe in 1952, is especially remarkable, with its tall central chamber surrounded by six cells. Childe pointed out the Irish and Iberian affinities of tombs of this class. For want of **peat**, the earliest inhabitants burnt dung, as the islanders were still doing in the 19th century. One of the most important funerary sites that awaits excavation lies at Tofts Ness in the extreme north of the island, which contains about 500 burial mounds. **Pictish** and **Viking** settlements have likewise fallen prey to the encroaching sea, but weaponry has been recovered from several pagan Norse graves of the age when Sanday became known as **Orkney**'s granary. Today its fertile farmlands support nearly 550 inhabitants, rearing beef cattle and sheep where their ancestors exported grain. The women have formed a knitting co-operative which exports garments containing the intricate star, tree and snowflake patterns, and precious ground has been sacrificed to an airfield and a **golf course**.

SANDY, James (c1766–1819) Inventor

James Sandy lived his whole life in **Alyth**, **Perthshire**, and despite suffering crippling leg injuries in two childhood accidents, which confined him to bed for most of his life, attained great local celebrity because of his extraordinary mechanical genius. His bed was converted into a workbench and fitted out with lathes, vices and cases for all manner of tools. He learned to make a variety of appliances, including musical instruments, clocks, telescopes and electrical devices. His home was regarded as the coffee-house of the town, frequented by his many friends and admirers. His main fame came from his invention of the 'invisibly-hinged snuff box'.

SANQUHAR, Dumfriesshire

A small burgh of great antiquity and a **royal burgh** since 1598, Sanquhar is on the upper Nith in bleak moorland surroundings. The castle ('sanquhar' is from two Gaelic words meaning 'old fort') was once a **Ross** stronghold but passed to the Crichtons in the 14th century (and was birthplace of 'The Admirable' **James Crichton**) and then to the **Douglases of Drumlanrig** in 1630. William Douglas, 1st Duke of Queensberry and the builder of Drumlanrig Castle, is said to have spent only one night in his new home before returning to Sanquhar. His son, however, preferred the new house and Sanquhar Castle was abandoned to 'plunderers who used it as a quarry for their sties and hovels'. It remains a ruin in spite of attempts at restoration in the 1890s. One 'hovel' which benefited from the quarry was **William Adam**'s early Georgian Tolbooth (1735), 'one of the most handsome in the country', which now houses a local museum. It is surmounted by a short clock tower with octagonal cupola and was erected at the expense of the 3rd Duke of Queensberry. When patronised by the signatories of the **Sanquhar Declarations**, the town throve on stocking manufacture but subsequently turned to **coal-mining** and **cotton** milling. The site of the mercat cross to which the Declarations were affixed is marked; part of the cross is built into St Ninian's Free Church. A shop in the High Street is said to be the oldest post office in Britain (1763).

SANQUHAR, Declarations of (1680 and 1685)

On 22 June 1680, first anniversary of **Bothwell Brig**, 20 horsemen with swords and pistols drawn rode into Sanquhar (**Dumfriesshire**), gathered round the mercat cross, sang a psalm, and read a notice. This disowned

Charles II as 'usurper and tyrant' and declared war on him 'under the standard of Our Lord Jesus Christ, Captain of Salvation'. The notice was then fixed to the cross by Michael and **Richard Cameron**. After the débâcle of Bothwell Brig, the **Cameronians** (or Remnant) claimed to be the sole 'representatives of the true Presbyterian Kirk and covenanted nation of Scotland'. Cameron died a month later at **Airds Moss**, but his followers (**Cargill**, **Renwick**) continued to reaffirm the Declarations of **Rutherglen** and Sanquhar as when, in 1685, Renwick posted a second Sanquhar Declaration on behalf of 'the contending and suffering remnant' of a much persecuted but uncompromising **presbyterianism**.

SARK, Battle of (1448)

One of a continuing series of cross-border engagements, the so-called Battle of Sark was fought on the north bank of the tiny river Sark which feeds into the Solway Firth near **Gretna**. On this occasion (23 October 1448) the invading English under the Earl of Northumberland were repulsed by the Scots under Hugh Douglas, Earl of Ormonde.

SAUCHIE TOWER, Nr Alloa, Clackmannanshire

This rectangular four-storey tower was built about 1430 by Sir James Schaw whose family had acquired by marriage the Sauchie lands originally granted to Henri de Annand by **Robert I**. Little altered but now derelict, it is still considered capable of restoration, being complete to the machicolated parapet and with an unusual octagonal cap-house with conical roof. Sir James, as Governor of **Stirling Castle**, was implicated in the murder of **James III**. The Keepership nevertheless remained in the family and to it Sir Alexander Schaw added the hereditary office of Master of the Royal Wine Cellar (1592). Daniel Defoe, in the 18th century, reckoned **Clackmannanshire** to have the largest export of **coal** in Scotland. Nearby, in the disused Devon Colliery, one of the few surviving beam engines (for pumping water from the pit) has been preserved.

SAUCHIEBURN, Battle of (1488)

Having already antagonised many of his nobles by promoting commoners into positions of influence in their stead [see **Archibald Douglas, 5th Earl of Angus**], **James III** succeeded in alienating a whole lot more by forfeiting supporters of his brother **Albany** (1484) and by annexing the revenues of **Coldingham Priory** to the Chapel Royal (1488). This created a powerful alliance of the dispossessed barons: the **Homes** who had previously benefited from the revenues of Coldingham, the Hepburns, the Earl of Angus and the **Earl of Argyll** – an alliance which was strengthened by their managing to secure the person of Prince James, the 15-year-old heir apparent. James III had support of his own, including the **Earls of Crawford, Huntly, Atholl, Marischal** and **Errol** and the Bishops of **Aberdeen** and **St Andrews**. But his attempts at conciliation were insufficient to placate the insurgents who announced their intention of proclaiming Prince James as King. The ensuing battle (on 11 June) at Sauchieburn, three miles south-west of **Stirling**, was an untidy affair. James's horse bolted during the battle and threw him. The rest of the story is not known for sure; legend has it that he was badly wounded and called for a priest, and that it was the cleric answering this summons who drew a dagger and murdered the King. His body was certainly found the following morning at Beaton's Mill near **Bannockburn**. It seems doubtful whether the murder was planned by the insurgents, who had sought to control but not to overthrow the King. His death was officially recorded as an accident, and **James IV** would wear an iron chain round his body for the rest of his life in penance for having been thus involved in the death of his father.

SCALLOWAY, Shetland

The ancient capital of **Shetland**, Scalloway is now an attractive village (plus a less attractive quay area) built around a sheltered bay on the west coast of Shetland's **Mainland**. It is dominated by the ruins of Scalloway Castle, built in 1600 by **Earl Patrick Stewart**, a man detested for his oppressive laws, including the rule that every able-bodied man had to work unpaid at the building site. Following the Earl's arrest in 1609 and his execution in **Edinburgh** in 1615, the castle became ruinous. It is still impressive, however, a four-storey high oblong block with an adjoining stair tower.

In the 19th century Scalloway became the centre of Shetland's distant-water fishery at Iceland, Faroe and **Rockall**, the salted cod being dried on the beaches for export to Spain. This was followed by a **herring** boom in the early part of the 20th century. The village is still the main commercial and **fishing** port on the island's west coast, while the recently completed North Atlantic Fisheries College offers courses in fishing, fish processing and **fish farming**.

The village played an important part in World War II as a secret base from which Norwegians crossed the North Sea in fishing boats carrying weapons and ammunition for the Norwegian Resistance. Many lives were lost in this hazardous operation, which is described in David Howarth's wartime classic *The Shetland Bus*.

SCALPAY, Island of, Outer Hebrides

The island of Scalpay (Norse *skalp-r ay*, the island shaped like a boat) lies in the Outer **Hebrides**, just off the south-east corner of **Harris** at the entrance to East Loch Tarbert and since August 1998 linked to its larger neighbour by a bridge. Although only two square miles in area, the population is about 450, constituting a dense and tightly-knit community with a deserved reputation for innovation and enterprise. Its fishing fleet has been modernised, with the result that during the **fishing industry**'s recent difficulties Scalpachs have maintained their island as a lively and viable community. In 1861 the population was 388, including some families evicted from the island of Pabbay in the Sound of Harris; by 1921 it had peaked at 624.

On the south-east corner of Scalpay is Eilean Glas lighthouse, now automatic. Its predecessor was one of the four original lighthouses built by the Commissioners of Northern Lights in 1789. The keepers' cottages are now holiday houses. In December 1962 six Scalpay men went out in a small open boat in a gale to rescue the crew of the trawler *Boston Heron*; their consummate seamanship and bravery was recognised by the RNLI.

SCAPA FLOW, Orkney

The seaway running between the mainland of **Orkney** and **Hoy** used to be one of the most important anchorages of the Royal Navy. The British Grand Fleet sailed from here to fight the German fleet off Jutland in May

Scalloway Castle and harbour, Shetland (HS)

1916, and here the latter was interned after the German surrender. On 21 June 1919 a party of schoolchildren from **Stromness** were given a rare treat when they were taken by boat amongst the German warships, to see them scuttled and sinking on all sides. In October 1939 HMS *Royal Oak* was torpedoed by a submarine that penetrated the Flow's defences, with tragic loss of life. Its victims were buried in the naval cemetery at Lyness and the **Churchill Barriers** were built beyond.

SCARBA, Isle of, Argyll
This island, rising to 1470ft (448m), resembles a round mountain lifting out of the sea. Described as a barren mass 'of dark slate streaked with pale silvery bands of gleaming quartzite', its wild and inhospitable landscape is now grazed by sheep and deer. In 1764 60 people lived on the island and there were two farms. The last burial at the old ruined chapel at Kilmory took place in 1850; today there are no permanent residents. Off the southern end of the island is the famous whirlpool of **Corrievrechan**.

SCHIEHALLION, Perthshire
The name of this detached and finely shaped quartzite peak (3547ft/1081m) is thought to derive from the Gaelic word for '**fairies**' plus some diminutive form of 'Caledon', making it 'the fairy hill of the Caledonians'. Much lore attaches to it as a result. It is also of scientific note for here in 1774–6 Dr Nevil Maskelyne, Astronomer Royal, conducted experiments with a plumb line to determine the attraction of the mountain mass, from which the mean density of the earth was calculated. Further experiments were made in the 19th century by **Dr John Playfair**, the mathematician, and **Dr John MacCulloch**, the geologist. Located between Lochs **Tay** and Tummel, it is seen to best effect, and most readily climbed, from the **Kinloch Rannoch** area.

SCHOOL OF SCOTTISH STUDIES, The, Edinburgh
Established in 1951 by the **University of Edinburgh**, the School is the only centre for inter-disciplinary research on a wide range of Scottish subjects. Its archives (cassettes, films, photographs and manuscripts) specialise in oral and folk tradition as embodied in songs, **ballads**, **music**, tales and reminiscences. Materials for place-name studies are also available, and the School hosts the Linguistic Survey of Scotland (Gaelic and Scots) and the Institute for Historical Dialectology. The School of Scottish Studies has the only Chair in Scottish Ethnology (essentially folklore) which, since 1987, has been the core subject in its degree courses.

SCONE, Nr Perth, Perthshire
Now practically in **Perth** itself, Scone (pron. 'Scoon') was traditionally the place where Scotland's kings were enthroned (though not necessarily crowned, coronation being a 13th century affectation). It had probably been a **Pictish** capital and a centre of the **Celtic Church** before **Kenneth mac-Alpin** made it his capital (along with **Dunkeld**) c850 and brought hence the Stone of Destiny (or **Stone of Scone**). The Church, like the Stone, lent legitimacy to kingship and in 1120 **Alexander I** superseded the Celtic (probably **Culdee**) establishment

with a priory of Augustinian canons which became an abbey in 1160. Even after Edward I's removal of the Stone (1296) Scone continued as the place of coronation; in 1318 it was a Parliament at Scone which first recognised the claims of **Stewart** succession; and in 1371 **Robert II** was duly crowned there. The last Scone coronation was that of **Charles II** in 1651.

Sadly the importance of the site is not matched by what remains today. The abbey was ransacked in 1559 after **John Knox**'s inflammatory sermon at **St John's Kirk** (Perth) and the lands passed to the **Earl of Gowrie**. Forfeited after the **Gowrie Conspiracy** (1600), they were then granted to Sir David Murray whose descendants as Lords Stormont and Scone and (post 1776) Earls of Mansfield still occupy them.

Parts of the 17th century house (built over the ruins of the abbey) reputedly remain inside Scone Palace. This is a castellated Gothick extravaganza designed by William Atkinson in 1802 and now energetically promoted as 'one of Scotland's finest historic homes'. To provide the obligatory acres of terrace, lawn and pinetum, the old village of Scone was removed. There remain, scattered about the policies, the village cross, gateway, moot hill and a bit of the parish church – follies for the curious as well as perches for the peacocks.

The interior of Scone Palace (open to the public) is more rewarding, with fine collections of porcelain, ivories, oils and furniture, much family memorabilia and a long gallery floored with ancient bog-oak which Prince Albert used as a **curling** rink.

SCONE, STONE OF
Also known as the Stone of Destiny, this block of sandstone has been revered for centuries as a holy relic allegedly from the Middle East, brought to Scotland in the 9th century and used as part of the enthronement ceremony of, successively, Dalriadic, Scottish, English and British monarchs.

It is reputed to have been used as a pillow by Jacob in biblical times and then transported through Egypt, Sicily, Spain and Ireland before being brought to Scotland. (**Sir Compton Mackenzie**, on the other hand, believed the stone had been quarried in the **Oban** area; see also **Dalriada** for an alternative version.) It was used for the installing of Dalriadic monarchs at **Iona**, **Dunadd** and **Dunstaffnage** and finally at **Scone** when that became the capital of the Scottish kingdom around 840 AD. In 1292 **John Balliol** became the last king to be enthroned in Scotland on the stone. It was removed by Edward I of England four years later, taken south and installed in Westminster Abbey. Although the Scots won its return under the Treaty of Northampton in 1328, it remained under the Coronation Throne at Westminster for more than 600 years. On Christmas morning of 1950 it was removed from Westminster by Scottish nationalists, smuggled back to Scotland and symbolically placed in **Arbroath Abbey**, the location of the 1320 **Declaration of Arbroath**; but it was repossessed after an absence of only four months. Not until 1996 was the Stone of Scone finally, and officially, returned to Scotland. Since 30 November, St Andrew's Day, 1996, it has been on public display at **Edinburgh Castle**, despite a vigorous argument in favour of it being returned to its earlier home at Scone. This was overruled on the grounds that it would be impossible to install the necessary security in what is in effect a private home. The stone is 26in long, 16in wide and 11in high (660 x 400 x 280cm) and weighs 336 lbs. Its only decoration is described as a Latin Cross.

SCOTIA

Professor Croft Dickinson defined the use of the term thus: 'Until the 10th century *Scotia* meant Ireland. In the 10th century *Scotia* was being used for the mainland of modern Scotland to the north of the Forth and **Clyde**, and the Forth was sometimes called ''The Scots Water''. From about the middle of the 11th century *Scotia* gradually came to mean the whole of modern Scotland, although even at the beginning of the 14th century we still find modern Scotland divided into the districts of ''**Galloway**'', ''Lothian'' and ''Scotland'' – this last district embracing the land to the north of the Forth and the Clyde'. It appears to have been Ammianus in the 4th century who first mentioned the Scots in Ireland. By the end of the following century they had crossed the sea to establish their Kingdom of **Dalriada** in **Argyll** [see also **Caledonia**, **Alba**, etc].

SCOTS GUARDS, The

Although there are other versions, it appears that the regiment was raised in 1662 as the Scots Regiment of Guards, taking its place after the Grenadier and Coldstream Guards. Subsequent titles included 3rd Foot Guards (1713) Scots Fusilier Guards (1831) and present title (1877).

Early battles included Namur (1695), Dettingen and Fontenoy. Thereafter they fought in the Peninsula, at Waterloo, in the Crimea and in Egypt. Three battalions of the regiment served on the Western Front in World War I, winning 33 battle honours. In World War II the Regiment served in Norway, North Africa, Italy and in north-west Europe, winning a further 41 battle honours. Subsequent active service has included Malaya, Borneo and Northern Ireland. The 2nd Battalion took part in the Falklands campaign where it distinguished itself in the battle for Tumbledown Mountain. Several members of the battalion were decorated and two more battle honours added, bringing the total to 94.

The regiment has always been clothed as other regiments of the Brigade of Guards although suggestions have been made on occasion that they should assume **tartan** trews. The pipers wear Royal Stewart tartan; all ranks' forage caps have a diced band; buttons are worn in threes and there is no plume in the bearskin.

The regiment marches past in quick and slow time to 'Hielan' Laddie' and 'Garb of Old Gaul' played by both pipes and band. The Scots Guards recruit all over Scotland and in north-west England. Regimental headquarters are in Birdcage Walk, London. Her Majesty the Queen is Colonel-in-Chief of all the regiments of the Household Division; HRH the Duke of Kent has been Colonel of the regiment since 1974.

SCOTSTARVIT TOWER, Nr Cupar, Fife

A notable landmark of obvious military potential, Scotstarvit dates only from the late 16th century and was never intended for defence; it merely exhibits the vigour (or conservatism) of the vernacular tower house style.

Far from military, its main association is literary; for here was penned an eccentric polemic against corrupt politicians as memorable for its insights as for its tongue-twisting title – *Scot of Scotstarvit's Staggering State of the Scots Statesman*. The author, Sir John Scot (1595–1670), has been called 'the Scottish Montaigne'. Married to the sister of **William Drummond of Hawthornden**, he was also a poet in his own right, a noted topographer, and a Privy Councillor and Lord of Session until discarded by Cromwell. Scotstarvit did not merit Cromwell's attention and remains one of the best-preserved tower houses. It now belongs to the **National Trust for Scotland** but is in the care of **Historic Scotland**.

SCOTT, Alexander (c1515–c83) Poet

Beyond the existence of a canon of some 35 poems, preserved for us mostly in the **Bannatyne Manuscript**, surprisingly little is known about Alexander Scott. The name is a common one, and there is always some doubt as to the identification of the poet with those of his name who appear in the records. What follows is therefore to some extent conjectural.

Scott, a musician by profession, is probably that one who in 1539 received the revenue from the parsonage of **Ayr** which was attached to the **Chapel Royal** in **Stirling**. In 1548 he was granted a canon's portion in the **Priory of Inchmahome** as musician and organist, and in the same year was called parson of Balmaclellan, a post also attached to the Chapel Royal. It is possible that he went to France with **Queen Mary** in 1548. He seems then to have got into some personal difficulties, partly due to a tendency towards Protestantism, and partly due to his marriage, which seems not to have been a success. His poem 'To luve unluvit' is said to have been written when his wife left him. In the 1560s, however, his fortunes may have improved. He was a canon at Inchaffray, and he was wealthy enough to purchase lands at Madderty in **Perthshire** and Balfour in **Fife**.

Scott's poetry has been compared unfavourably with that of his contemporary **Montgomerie**. It is true that he does not have the extraordinary metrical range of the younger man, and later criticism, such as that of **Allan Cunningham**, that he had 'more sweetness than strength . . . he flows smooth but he seldom flows deep' was long accepted. But in recent times he has been revalued, and the intensity of his emotions, the ease which which his poetry, as befits that of a musician, has so frequently been turned into song, and the eternal appeal of his love poems, though expressed in the courtly language of the period, ensure him a lasting reputation.

SCOTT, David (1806–49) Historical Painter

One of the few Scottish artists to attempt wholeheartedly to paint in the 'Grand Manner' of history **painting**, David Scott's career was marked by failure and critical neglect. Born in **Edinburgh**, the son of a successful engraver, he attended classes at the **Trustees' Academy** from an early age. His first major canvases, painted in the early 1820s, already evidence the melancholy and neurotic tendencies that were to dog his working life. Either of allegorical subjects or drawn from classical myth, they combine sculptural Michelangelesque figures with dramatic perspective and gloomy atmospheric effects. Although largely ignored by the public, these works were much lauded by Scott's fellow artists, admiring, perhaps, his unflinching (and uncommercial) espousal of the highest aesthetic ideals, and Scott was elected Royal Scotttish Academician at the age of 24. Two years later he made the obligatory pilgrimage to Rome where he remained for 18 months. As well as immersing himself in the work of the Ancients and the much-vaunted Michelangelo, he sought inspiration from the less fashionable Baroque painters, Caravaggio and Guido Reni. On his return to Edinburgh he applied these principles to dark expressive subjects – *Philoctetes* (1839, **National Gallery of Scotland**), *The Russians Burying their Dead* (1831, **Hunterian Art Gallery**, **University of Glasgow**), *The Traitor's Gate* (1841, National Gallery of Scotland) – evoking by compositional and painterly effect an extraordinary sense of claustrophobia and psychological despair. His late works were often of an exceptional size (up to 18ft/5.5m wide) and consequently rarely found buyers. Scott's spirit was constantly depressed by his commercial failure, although he never compromised his remarkable and disturbing aesthetic vision. After his early death (aged 43) his reputation was partly restored by his younger brother **William Bell Scott** who wrote an admiring biography. He remains one of the most unusual artistic figures of the period.

SCOTT, Francis George (1880–1958) Composer

'F.G.', as he is often known, came from the Borders, failed to graduate from **Edinburgh University**, qualified as an English teacher and taught, in particular, the young **Hugh MacDiarmid**, with whom he later formed a close artistic relationship, setting many of MacDiarmid's poems as well as assisting MacDiarmid in their composition – in particular with *A Drunk Man Looks at the Thistle*. He took an external Mus Bac at Durham, became a music lecturer at a teacher training college and was awarded an honorary Doctorate in Music by **Glasgow University**.

The major part of his compositional output consists of songs which he published in six volumes of *Scottish Lyrics*, being largely settings of poems by Scots from many different periods. His idiom is varied but always imbued with a sense of melody that is Scottish in essence, even in songs whose harmonies and outlines are strongly influenced by his contact with the Second Viennese School in the 1920s. His feeling for the vocal line was no doubt encouraged by the fact that his wife was a singer and he himself had a pleasant voice. The MacDiarmid settings are among the finest of his distinguished output, songs like 'The Eemis Stane', 'Milkwort and Bog Cotton' and 'Crowdieknowe' evoking not just the atmosphere but the complex inner psychology of poems which to others would have been impossibly challenging.

SCOTT, John (1783–1821) Author and Editor

From **Aberdeen**, Scott there attended school and **Marischal College** before working in the War Office and travelling in Europe; he wrote two books on Paris

(1814, 1816) and edited a couple of literary periodicals before becoming the first editor (1820) of the famous *London Magazine*. This attracted a dazzling array of contributors (Lamb, Hazlitt, de Quincey, Keats, **Carlyle**, etc) and posed a serious challenge to the more opinionated *Blackwood's* whose **J G Lockhart** savaged the *London* men as the low-born 'Cockney School of Poetry'. Forced to retaliate, Scott became embroiled in a bitter slanging match which ended disastrously: in a duel with one of Lockhart's friends Scott was killed.

SCOTT, Lady John (1811–1900) Composer and Songwriter

Born Alicia Anne Spottiswoode at Westruther in **Berwickshire**, and married in 1836 to Lord John Scott, brother of the 5th **Duke of Buccleuch**, Lady Scott was a noted composer of popular Scottish songs, and one of the earliest collectors of folk music. She is best remembered as the composer of the melody for '**Annie Laurie**'.

SCOTT, Michael (d.c1235) Philosopher and 'Wizard'

Although possibly born in Durham, Scott seems to have been of Borders parentage. After doing the rounds of Europe's medieval universities he was appointed official astrologer by the Emperor Frederick II and in Toledo was commissioned to produce two translations of Aristotle from the extant Arabic texts. The little that is known of him derives largely from these and other surviving works on **philosophy** and astrology. He may have returned to Scotland and died at **Melrose**; or he may have remained on the Continent and died in Italy. Although essentially a scholar, astrology cast him as a wizard to later generations and, as such, legends of Scott were taken up by writers from Dante to **James Hogg** and **Sir Walter Scott** (for whom 'he cleft the Eildon hills in three and bridled the **Tweed** with a curb of stone' in *The Lay of the Last Minstrel*).

SCOTT, Michael (1789–1835) Writer and Businessman

Born at Cowlairs, **Glasgow**, on 30 October 1789, Michael Scott was the fifth and youngest son of a Glaswegian merchant. He was educated at Glasgow High School and attended the **University of Glasgow** from 1801–5. On graduating he went to Kingston, Jamaica, where he initially managed estates before setting up in business. On an extended return visit to Scotland in 1817–18 he married Margaret Bogle. They lived in Jamaica until 1822, when they returned to settle in Glasgow. Scott subsequently became a partner in firms trading in Glasgow and Venezuela.

Scott's experiences in the West Indies formed the basis for a vivacious and vivid novel, *Tom Cringle's Log*, which first appeared in serial form in *Blackwood's Magazine* between September 1829 and August 1833. A second novel, *The Cruise of the 'Midge'*, also appeared in *Blackwood's* between March 1834 and June 1835. Both were written anonymously, and were subsequently republished in book form in Paris in 1834 and 1836 respectively.

SCOTT, Sir Walter (1771–1832) Novelist and Poet

Walter Scott was born in **Edinburgh**. His father, also Walter (1729–99), was the son of a Border farmer and became a Writer to the Signet; his mother, Anne Rutherford (1739–1819), was the daughter of **John Rutherford**, the physician. At least six of their children died in infancy; six, Robert, John, Walter, Anne, Thomas and Daniel, survived into adulthood. At 18 months young Walter contracted poliomyelitis and became lame in his right leg. He was sent to recuperate on his grandfather's farm, Sandyknowe, near **Kelso**. He spent much of the next five years at Sandyknowe and imbibed the oral, historical and literary culture of the Borders. He heard **ballads** and traditional songs; he heard stories about Border heroes, about the **Jacobites** defeated in 1746, and about the American War; he lived under a monument from Border history, **Smailholm Tower,** a massy red fortified dwelling which dominated the surrounding landscape. He returned to his father's house in 1777; from 1779–83 he was at the High School of Edinburgh where he received a thorough grounding in Latin literature. He attended **Edinburgh University** from 1783–6, and again from 1789–92. He was apprenticed to his father in 1786, but found the work so tedious that he decided to aim for the Bar; he was admitted to the **Faculty of Advocates** in 1792.

Although Scott had a successful career and performed his duties diligently (he was Sheriff-Depute of **Selkirkshire** 1799–1832 and Principal Clerk to the **Court of Session** 1806–30), the **law** was always secondary to literature. His earliest verses date from 1782; his first publication, a translation from the German of two poems by Burger, appeared in 1796. His reputation was made by his ballad collection Minstrelsy of the Scottish Border (1802–3). Judged by 20th century editorial standards the Minstrelsy is flawed; Scott was not a field collector

Sir Walter Scott, by Sir William Allan (SNPG)

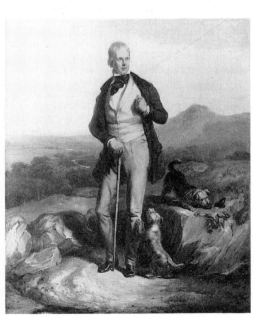

and used texts gleaned by others; he fused versions and borrowed bits from other ballads to create 'better' texts; he did not publish the music. But he himself belonged to the ballad tradition; he only did what any good singer would do with a defective version – improve it by drawing on the common stock of ballad materials; and what he printed persuaded the public that traditional literature could also be great literature. The Minstrelsy is also the first comprehensive display of Scott's artistic and scholarly methods; he reworks inherited materials creatively and explains them with notes that are at once enlightening, curious and learned.

In the years that followed Scott edited literary works such as the medieval romance Sir Tristrem (1804), The Life and Works of John Dryden (18 vols, 1808) and The Life and Works of Jonathan Swift (19 vols, 1814). He also edited collections of historical documents. He wrote long poems in imitation of ballads and medieval romances, and in so doing created a new kind of Romantic poetry. He published 23 works of prose fiction between 1814–31 and within both the long poems and the novels there are some very fine lyrics. He wrote contemporary history, such as his Life of Napoleon Buonaparte (9 vols, 1827); and he wrote two histories of Scotland and one of France. His Lives of the Novelists (1820) was designed to parallel **Johnson**'s Lives of the English Poets. And he reviewed extensively; his pieces on Cromek's Reliques of Robert Burns, on Byron's Childe Harold's Pilgrimage, Canto 4, and on Jane Austen's Emma are among the very best contemporary essays on these authors.

In 1797 Scott married Charlotte Charpentier, a French émigrée and a ward of the Earl of Downshire. Although the marriage was harmonious, there was little intellectual rapport and Charlotte neither shared nor understood her husband's enthusiasms. They had four children; Sophia (1799–1837) who married **John Gibson Lockhart**; Walter (1801–47); Anne (1803–33) and Charles (1805–41). While the Court of Session was sitting they lived in Castle Street in Edinburgh, but out of term they lived in the country, first at **Lasswade**, then from 1804 at Ashestiel near **Galashiels**, and from 1812 at **Abbotsford** near **Melrose**. Much of the profit from Scott's immense productivity was invested in Abbotsford, and a great deal of imaginative effort went into its development; it was initially a four-roomed cottage but he gradually built a new house; he bought land and rechristened its features so that he could locate such Border legends as the meeting of True Thomas with the queen of fairyland in the ballad 'Thomas Rhymer'. He had an active family and a busy social life; he was much involved in political management and patronage; he had an immense correspondence; as his fame grew he suffered from a continuous stream of visitors. Scott was greatly sociable and very active, but amidst all this bustle he was essentially lonely, living an imaginative life which he revealed to others only in and through his writings.

In January 1826, in a period of economic crisis, he became insolvent following the failure of his publishers **Archibald Constable** & Co, and of his printers **James Ballantyne** & Co. He could have chosen to become bankrupt, but instead he pledged his future literary earnings to a trust which gradually repaid his creditors. The total debt was over £120,000. He wrote prodigiously: four works of fiction, the *Life of Napoleon*, works of history, and reviews. But the greatest project was an edition of his own novels, for which Scott revised the text, and wrote introductions and notes. The new edition, known as the Magnum Opus, appeared in 48 volumes at monthly intervals between 1829–33. As a result of all these efforts nearly £50,000 had been paid off by his death. But the heroism of his final years was also tragic. His wife died in May 1826, shortly after the financial collapse. His Edinburgh house was sold to pay debts and during term he lived in lodgings. He worked excessively and obsessively in the interest of creditors. He wore himself out; between 1830–2 he suffered four strokes, and, in spite of a tour to Malta and Italy in 1831–2 in search of health, recovery was not possible. He died at home at Abbotsford on 21 September 1832.

The major facts of Scott's life are beyond dispute; but the interpretation of the man and his achievement is highly controversial. Regarded in his own day as one of the greatest of writers, and rewarded with great wealth and a baronetcy (1820), he was later seen as venal, and his successive novels merely romances, repetitiously reworking established motifs, and perpetuating deluding myths about Scottish history and nationhood. Although there have been many ramifications, the debate has centred on three issues: his business dealings and their implications for his writing, his absorption in history, and his artistry.

In 1805 Scott had become a partner in the printing business of James Ballantyne & Co; Ballantyne managed the business and Scott provided much of the work, for nearly all his books were printed there. Scott had various publishers, but the most important was Archibald Constable & Co of Edinburgh. Constable and his partners realised that Scott was their most important commercial asset, and that they needed to get from him a continuing supply of new works to maintain their cash-flow. But Scott knew his own market value, and drove hard bargains. He lived beyond his means, and Abbotsford was an expensive imaginative and social indulgence. Each of these factors: the demands of the printing business and of the publisher, a costly mode of life, and Abbotsford, constituted permanent pressure towards over-production. Some works, such as *Peveril of the Peak* (1822), written in a state of exhaustion after he had stage-managed George IV's visit to Edinburgh, would have been better not written at all. But at other times the pressure seems to have stimulated creativity, and the many critics of Scott's over-production have not been able to demonstrate that a single work would have been better had he worked less frantically. His work was written quickly, but usually only after a period of six months to a year of maturing plans and ideas. It was corrected and revised; the manuscripts and proofs of the novels show that every work was subjected to at least three stages of authorial improvement, which rather belies the off-hand, self-disparaging way in which he talked of his own art.

Further, the crash of 1826 was caused not by greed or fraud, but by business conditions. Both the printing and publishing businesses were severely undercapitalised and effectively relied on bank borrowings for working capital; and when in the general financial crisis of 1825–6 the banks refused to extend their credit, the businesses folded. There was no limited liability in 1826, and Scott, the only one of those involved with a capacity to generate new wealth, undertook to repay his own private debt, the debts of the printing business, and the debts of the publishers for which he was legally liable. The desire to blame seems misguided. Those who believe that one should live within one's income will disapprove of Scott's life on credit; but artists take risks and Scott's risk-taking had a spectacular outcome.

Secondly, in the mid-20th century Scott's overwhelming interest in history was subject to considerable criticism. His life spanned the six momentous decades of the American Revolution, the French Revolution, the Napoleonic Wars, and in Britain the Industrial and Agrarian Revolutions. Yet, the argument went, he largely wrote about history, and particularly Scottish history, not what was changing around him. The demand for 'relevance' is simple-minded, and denies the metaphoric and metonymic nature of literature. Some of Scott's historical novels may be seen as allegories; they study contemporary issues in a context of the past. Others study contemporary issues by examining their historical origins: *The Tale of Old Mortality* is one of the greatest of this kind. And the majority of his greatest works of fiction are at least in part concerned with the processes of change. But above all, Scott's examination of history is his response to a changing world, as he made clear in his first substantial publication, the *Minstrelsy*: 'By such efforts, feeble as they are, I may contribute somewhat to the history of my native country; the peculiar features of whose manners and character are daily melting and dissolving into those of her sister and ally.' By concentrating on the historical experience of Scotland, by examining its institutions, and by using its language, he created that consciousness of Scotland which has sustained a sense of nationhood in a country without statehood. The objections of professional historians to Scott are testimony to his immense success in generating images of Scotland; it may be argued that the great object of the flowering of Scottish history in recent decades has been the destruction of inherited perceptions of Scotland.

Scott's reputation was at its nadir in the middle decades of the 20th century, and while a rejection of the kind of Scotland he represented was part of the dislike, the major objection was that he was a bad artist. Times change: the criteria used by E M Forster, for example, in his attack on Scott in *Aspects of the Novel* (1927) are themselves historically conditioned. In the mid-20th century there was a predisposition for a very direct narrative (such as Jane Austen's) which could offer precise moral discrimination. Nowadays the openness which characterises Scott's fiction is again valued. Scott tends to dramatise narrators so that the relativity of narratorial view can be perceived; he allows characters to offer their own perception of things without apparent mediation through his use of direct speech; he makes use of many different kinds of poetry and fiction within the one work. Each of these is evidence of a novelist who is fully aware of the contingency of truth. At the end of the 19th century Walter Scott achieved 'classic' status and was considered suitable for school reading. The result was widespread dislike. Scott is not a children's author. He is highly political, and very interested in political ideas. But thinking in Scott is never 'difficult', and in the greatest Scott novels, works such as *Old Mortality*, *Rob Roy*, *The Heart of Midlothian*, *The Bride of Lammermoor* and *Redgauntlet*, artistic inventiveness is allied to intellectual challenge.

The most attractive way of meeting Scott the man is through his own autobiographical writings: 'Memoirs', in *Scott on Himself*, ed David Hewitt (1981) and his *Journal*, ed W E K Anderson (1972). J G Lockhart's *Memoirs of the Life of Sir Walter Scott, Bart* (7 vols, 1837) still gives the best biographical impression of Scott although it is not reliable, while the best one-volume biography is by **John Buchan** (1932).

There is as yet no proper bibliography of Scott's works. The most useful straightforward listing is at the end of Lockhart's *Life*. There is a more extended list of the various editions of Scott's books in *The Cambridge Bibliography of English Literature*.

There is no critical edition of Scott's poetry. His principal long poems are: *The Lay of the Last Minstrel* (1805), *Marmion* (1808), *The Lady of the Lake* (1810), *Rokeby* (1812) and *The Lord of the Isles* (1815).

Nor is there a critical edition of his fiction, but it is expected that the novels will all appear in the Edinburgh Edition of the Waverley Novels between 1993–2000. His novels are: *Waverley* (1814), *Guy Mannering* (1815), *The Antiquary* (1816), *Tales of My Landlord* containing *The Tale of Old Mortality* and *The Black Dwarf* (1816), *Rob Roy* (1818), *The Heart of Midlothian* (1818), *Tales of My Landlord*, third series, containing *The Bride of Lammermoor* and *A Legend of Montrose* (1819), *Ivanhoe* (1819), *The Monastery* (1820), *The Abbot* (1820), *Kenilworth* (1821), *The Pirate* (1822), *The Fortunes of Nigel* (1822), *Peveril of the Peak* (1822), *Quentin Durward* (1823), *St Ronan's Well* (1824), *Redgauntlet* (1824), *Tales of the Crusaders* containing *The Talisman* and *The Betrothed* (1825), *Woodstock* (1826), *Chronicles of the Canongate* (1827), *The Fair Maid of Perth* (1828), *Anne of Geierstein* (1829) and *Tales of My Landlord* containing *Count Robert of Paris* and *Castle Dangerous* (1832).

The only collection of Scott's prose works to approach comprehensiveness is *The Prose Works of Sir Walter Scott, Bart*, ed J G Lockhart (28 vols, 1834–6). His letters were edited by H J C Grierson and others in 12 vols (1932–7).

There is a large secondary literature on Scott. Complete listing will be found in J C Corson, *A Bibliography of Scott, 1797–1940* (1943) and Jill Rubinstein, *Sir Walter Scott: A Reference Guide* (1978). The seminal modern study of Scott is David Daiches' 'Scott's Achievement as a Novelist' in *Literary Essays* (1956); Thomas Crawford's short work *Scott* (1982) is highly stimulating and suggestive.

SCOTT, William Bell (1811–90) Painter

Born in **Edinburgh**, the younger brother of artist **David Scott**, William initially trained as an engraver in his father's successful practice in **Parliament Square**. In 1837 he moved to London to concentrate on historical and figurative paintings but his failure to establish a reputation forced him, in 1844, to take up the post of Master of the Government School of Design at Newcastle. He spent his summers in London, however, and formed a close relationship with the Pre-Raphaelite painter Dante Gabriel Rossetti. His own paintings adopted many Pre-Raphaelite aspects – meticulous detail, high finish, medieval and mythical subject matter – although like fellow Scot **Joseph Noel Paton** he was never closely associated with the Brotherhood. His finest work came relatively late in his career. A series of murals for Wallington Hall, Morpeth, completed in 1861, depicting scenes from Northumbrian history, included a remarkable essay in social realism, *Iron and Coal*, based on Scott's close examination of local industry and design. A later mural commission for Penkill Castle in **Ayrshire** has barely withstood the ravages of the damp west coast climate. From 1865 Scott spent many of his summers at Penkill and formed a deep romantic attachment to its owner, Miss Alice Boyd. She was the model for one of his most charming paintings, *Una and the Lion*, now in the **National Gallery of Scotland**. Also an accomplished poet and writer, Scott gained much acclaim from his memoir of his brother David, always considered by William (and now, largely, by posterity) the greater artist of the two.

SCOTTISH BALLET

Lack of resources and organisation rather than lack of will delayed the foundation of a national ballet company for Scotland until 1969. Several attempts had been made in the years after World War II to create just such a company: Margaret Morris's Celtic Ballet Company and Celtic Ballet Theatre in **Glasgow** and a short-lived Scottish National Ballet which ran out of funds and closed within a year of its 1960 debut; Veronica Bruce's Cygnet Ballet and Intimate Ballet Theatre; Marjory Middleton and the **Edinburgh** Ballet Club founded by Jean Shaw; Catherine Marks's Glasgow Theatre Ballet. With the exception of the Cygnet Ballet, which did receive a one-off grant from the Council for the Encouragement of Music and the Arts, none of these attempts received public subsidy, neither did their directors co-operate in achieving the ambition to which each confessed.

In August 1968 it was finally announced that the Bristol-based Western Theatre Ballet had been invited by the Scottish Arts Council to move to Glasgow as a full-time, permanent company to be known as the Scottish Theatre Ballet. A small company with a reputation for dramatic productions, the WTB had toured Britain and Europe since its foundation in 1957 and made its Scottish debut at the **Edinburgh Festival** in 1961. The first performance under its new name was at the **Perth** Theatre in April 1969, followed by a famous debut at the **King's Theatre** in Glasgow on 3 May 1969 in Berlioz's *The Trojans*, a collaboration with **Scottish Opera** starring Janet Baker and conducted by Alexander Gibson. Renamed Scottish Ballet in 1974, the company has, like its sister organisation Scottish Opera, become known for dramatic, innovative and stylish productions.

SCOTTISH CIVIC TRUST, The

A charitable organisation, the Scottish Civic Trust has as its aims the encouragement of high standards in architecture and planning, the conservation of buildings of artistic distinction and historic interest, and the encouragement of public awareness of its heritage. It was founded in 1967 by Viscount Muirshiel, the Trust's first Chairman, and Dr Maurice Lindsay, its founder Director.

Its achievements have included the co-ordination of the survey of the Georgian **New Town** of **Edinburgh** and the subsequent setting up of the Edinburgh New Town Conservation Committee and Facelift Glasgow, a civic clean-up which played some part in the initial stages of the remarkable physical regeneration of the fabric of **Glasgow**'s heritage. The Trust was responsible for the arrangements leading to the successful conservation of **David Dale** and Robert Owen's model industrial village of **New Lanark**; it reports on listed buildings threatened with demolition or major alteration, as a result of which new uses have been found for more than 500 such buildings; and it issues on behalf of the **Scottish Office** a periodic directory of listed buildings under threat and available for sale or rent, *Historic Buildings at Risk*. Although it receives government and local authority grants, it is conditionally required to secure 51% of its support from industry, business or charitable individuals.

SCOTTISH CONVENTION (1942–50)

The Scottish Convention was an all-party association of moderate Scottish nationalists formed in 1942 by a group of dissident members of the **Scottish National Party** after **Douglas Young** had been elected Chairman over William Power. Young was leader of the SNP majority who regarded conscription of Scots by the British Parliament as unlawful under the **Treaty of Union**. The dissidents, under **John MacCormick**, rejected an anti-war stance. A further ground of disagreement concerned whether Scottish nationalism had to be pursued through conventional party politics, or could better be advanced by all-party and cross-party groupings and activities. Convention, being for the latter view, organised a series of hugely successful and broadly representative Scottish National Assemblies in 1947, 1948 and 1949, and in 1949 launched for signature the second **Nationalist Covenant**, a petition pledging its signatories to do all in their power to establish a Scottish Parliament for Scottish affairs within the framework of the United Kingdom. Approximately two million out of three million electors signed the Covenant, and in due course greater administrative devolution to the Scottish Office was conceded; the eventual establishment of a **Scottish Parliament** was realised in 1998. In 1950 Scottish Convention was subsumed within a new, wider Scottish Covenant Association, which was finally wound up in 1962 after John MacCormick's death.

SCOTTISH DIVISIONS (Military)

The formation of the Territorial Force in 1908 led to a reorganisation of the old Volunteer Units in Scotland, initially grouped in brigades made up of battalions of the same regiment, into two complete Territorial Divisions (51st and 52nd) with their full complement of supporting arms and services. These divisions remained in being in peace and war until 1967 when, on the reduction of the Territorial Army, they were reduced to one infantry battalion each, the 51st and 52nd Lowland Volunteers.

THE 51ST HIGHLAND DIVISION (until 1915 the 1st Highland Division) went to France in early 1915 and was in action at Festubert in May. From then until the end of the war it took part in most of the major actions of that sanguinary conflict, earning itself a matchless reputation as a division which was specially called on for the most important tasks. Its character was recognised by the Germans who christened the kilted warriors 'the ladies from Hell' and who in a captured report were found to have rated the 51st as the most formidable of all the Allied formations.

In 1939 the division again mobilised and formed part of the British Expeditionary Force in France in 1940. Overrun by the advancing German *Blitzkrieg*, after a gallant defence, Divisional HQ and two of its three brigades were forced to surrender at St Valéry-en-Caux in June 1940. The survivors of the Third Brigade joined the second-line Scottish Division which henceforth took over the identity of the division of which it was in fact an offshoot, each Territorial Battalion having split in two just before the outbreak of war.

In 1942 the new 51st sailed to join the 8th Army in the Middle East under its new commander, General Montgomery. From then on it fought across the desert, playing a leading role in all the great actions of Alamein, Mareth and Wadi Akarit. It fought through the short but bloody Sicilian campaign before being brought home to take part in the invasion of Europe. Here for a time its *élan* deserted the by now battle-weary division, but it recovered in time to regain its old reputation with much hard fighting across the Rhine and into Germany.

In recent military history there can be few if any formations which have captured such a reputation from friend and foe alike as did the 51st. Its pride in itself as a division was notably fierce, embodied in the famous 'HD' of the divisional sign which led to the early sobriquet of 'Harper's Duds' from the name of its GOC and in World War II to the nickname 'the Highway Decorators' due to the enthusiasm with which the division used the sign to mark its passage.

Although always primarily a Highland formation, the 51st was a broad church which in its time embraced many units from elsewhere, from the brigade of Lancashire troops which joined it for a time in 1914–15 to the famous battalion of machine-gunners from the Middlesex Regiment which formed an integral part of the World War II 51st. (It was men of the 51st who, incarcerated in the German prisoner-of-war camp at Laufen after the disaster at St Valéry, created the steps for the **reel** initially known as the 'Laufen Reel', later as the 'St Valéry' and since as the famous 'Reel of the 51st Division'.) No matter where they came from, or where they served, all those who have served in its ranks are intensely proud to have belonged to this most elite division.

THE 52ND LOWLAND DIVISION was made up of Lowland Territorial Battalions with, however, its Third Brigade composed of three battalions of **Highland Light Infantry** and one of Argylls. Mobilised in 1914, it proceeded to Gallipoli in mid-1915 where it took part in much hard fighting. Evacuated to Egypt in January 1916 where it fought in defence of the Suez Canal, the division took part in the invasion of Palestine the following year and in April 1918 was moved to the Western Front where it took part in the final battles of the war.

Once more called up in 1939, the division spent the early years of the war at home. Its time came after the Normandy landings in June 1944; during the last months of the war it fought its way across Europe and into Germany for final victory.

THE 9TH (SCOTTISH) DIVISION was one of the first divisions of the New Army formed as a result of the famous call to arms by the newly appointed Secretary of State for War, Lord Kitchener, in August 1914. Initially composed of service battalions of all the Scottish infantry regiments, the division arrived in France in May 1915 and was engaged in the Battle of Loos in September of that year. Its first big engagement was the Battle of the Somme in July 1916 by which time one of its former brigades had been replaced by the South African Brigade whose 4th Battalion were the kilted South African Scottish. Thereafter the division was constantly in action until the end of the war, when it was stood down having sustained over 52,000 casualties.

In 1939 the division was once more called into being, this time based on the duplicated Territorial Battalions of the first line 51st Highland Division whose identity was taken on by the 9th Division after the surrender at St Valéry.

THE 15TH SCOTTISH DIVISION After the raising of 'the First Hundred Thousand', a similar number of men were called on to form the Second New Army in September 1914. Their early training was carried out in civilian clothes since arms and uniforms were not available, but by June 1915 the division was ready and in July it moved to France. In September that year it took part in the Battle of Loos after which it saw much action on the Somme, at Ypres and at Arras. By the end of the war it had suffered over 45,000 casualties. As with the 9th Division, all the Scottish regiments were represented.

The division was again raised in 1939, based on the duplicated battalions of the 52nd Lowland Division, one of its brigades containing battalions of the Highland Light Infantry being designated a Highland Brigade; by the end of the war two out of the three brigades were so designated and at one time or another battalions of every Scottish infantry regiment, both Highland and Lowland, had served in the division. It spent the early years of the war at home, being called on to provide many replacements, but it was eventually restored to the Higher Establishment and landed in France in mid-June 1944. It was hotly engaged in the fighting that preceded the Normandy breakout and then in Holland before leading the assault across the Rhine into Germany along with the Highland Division.

THE SCOTTISH DIVISION Today's Scottish Division is a purely administrative rather than a tactical organisation. It was set up in 1968, when the infantry regiments of the British Army, already grouped in brigades, were further organised into divisions with a common policy on such matters as recruitment and initial training, officer promotion, personnel records and the like.

At the time of writing the division is made up of the Highland and the Lowland Brigades, a total of seven regiments, comprising seven regular and five volunteer battalions, but this number is to be reduced by two regular battalions. It does not include the **Royal Scots Dragoon Guards** or the **Scots Guards**, who form part of the Royal Armoured Corps and the Household Division respectively.

There is an administrative headquarters based on **Edinburgh Castle** under a Divisional Brigadier, while the General Officer Commanding Scotland is *ex-officio* Colonel Commandant of the Division and represents the collective views of its Colonels of Regiments when required.

SCOTTISH ENLIGHTENMENT, The

As a term denoting the whole phenomenon of Scottish intellectual, literary, scientific and artistic achievement in the 18th and early 19th centuries, 'the Scottish Enlightenment' is of recent currency. It first came to be used as a matter of course in the 1960s and 70s; and one problem is that it can suggest too strongly the then popular notion of a backward country fructified solely by importations from the contemporary European Enlightenment. That obscures a longer-term native continuity plus the Scottish Enlightenment's distinct character. Whereas, for instance, the French Enlightenment was a movement of reason against an *ancien régime* of Church and state, the Scottish Enlightenment was shaped by a sense of the *need* for such a regime after the 1707 **Act of Union** and the removal of the Scots Parliament to Westminster.

Even before 1707 Scotland, as the smaller partner in the 1603 **Union of Crowns**, had responded with a growth in trade and in the universities, where the study of **law**, medicine, mathematics and physical science showed new vitality (notwithstanding such darker events as famines in the 1690s, the **Darien** débâcle and the execution for heresy of the **Edinburgh** student Thomas Aikenhead in 1696).

The 17th century perspective thus discounts the idea of a new civilised European Enlightenment spirit and hints at a fundamental reorientation of thinking, one element in which was the resilience of a humanist tradition with reference to Greek and **Roman** models; another was the liberal thought inspired by John Locke in England and developed by **Francis Hutcheson** and **George Turnbull**; and a third, crucially, was a scientific element which accounted for both the distinctive character of the Scottish universities and their students' intellectual cast of mind. Scotland produced major scientists: Robert Simson in mathematics, **William Cullen** and **Robert Whytt** in medicine and physiology, Cullen's pupil **Joseph Black** in chemistry, **James Hutton** in **geology**. More to the point, lessons from such great English scientists as Newton and Boyle were applied to questions of method.

Besides the teaching of science in the curriculum, scientific method became a major element in university teaching. Intellectually-minded students abandoned a moribund theology for science, and whereas poor Aikenhead had died in a rash endeavour to use the new science to reform theology, his shocking death did inspire a new, moderate and liberal thinking which took wider effect in the 19th century. To mention **Robert**

Burns here may seem odd, yet those most over-quoted lines of his which strike a modern ear as needless platitude were novel in his day. They record ideals and perceptions anent man, well allied to the Scottish Enlightenment's new emphasis on experience as opposed to authority and the catechised, legalistic vulgarisations and perversions of **Calvinist** theology.

Typically the Scottish Enlightenment has been associated with the cultural and intellectual life of 18th century Edinburgh and such intellectual clubs as the Poker and the Select; also with the earlier Rankenian Society where George Turnbull and others as students discussed new scientific ideas in the 1720s, with the Anderston Club in **Glasgow** where **Dr Johnson** felt ruffled, and with the **Aberdeen** Philosophical Society which saw, beside **Thomas Reid**, the theology professor George Campbell produce a work of lasting worth (*The Philosophy of Rhetoric*). The spirit which elicited books and contributions to discussions is not the only thing notable, for what these clubs represent besides academic attention to scientific method is a crucial establishment of scientific community, a critical and co-operative spirit.

From a combination of contemporary circumstances and the academic emphasis on method, there also came about a remarkable marriage in the Scots mind between theoretical and practical concern. The universities were held in a certain esteem for their practical value, not merely medicine but chemistry and geology having an applied dimension; with a horticultural spin-off from work in the Physic Garden, all three contributed to agricultural improvement whereby famine might be averted and rents increased. In Glasgow Professor **Adam Smith** socialised with, informed, and probably learned from the Glasgow **Tobacco** Lords who by 1776 were sufficiently familiar with business diversification not to be bankrupted by the closing of North American trade. Wider concerns are suggested by the example of another Scots economist, the '**Jacobite** Chancellor of the Exchequer' Sir James Steuart, whose *The Principles of Political Oeconomy* (1776) essayed valuable theses concerning the problems of a small country with a bigger, better endowed neighbour. In exile Steuart had made use of the most extensive range of observations imaginable.

A further commendation of the universities was that their teaching of Moral **Philosophy** was very much an advocacy of the Good Life, like a Minister's sermon. It also embraced other studies, and was in most cases an education in ordered critical thinking, but this was perhaps incidental so far as some civic bodies were concerned. They cherished teachers such as the mathematician Simson for his prestige and its attraction to students from far and wide. The appointment of gifted men of wide-ranging intelligence had good if unintended consequences.

That the civic authorities were active and ambitious might be seen as an effect of the 1707 Union. Likewise the fact that Edinburgh – not least as the capital, centre for Law and other pre-1707 institutions – had the educated population to sustain the intellectual life which carried over from the Poker and Select Clubs into the later reviews (**Edinburgh Review**, **Blackwood's**, etc). The moral and bookish interests of the moneyed or landed more-or-less gentry were also important. Latterly, when

Naomi Mitchison essayed a literary epic intended to inspire post-war reconstruction in the 1940s, it was to 1747 that she turned (*The Bull Calves*, 1947). There she found in a liberal context an example of moral and practical enterprise, science and co-operation, and a feeling for the Good Life which has intrigued reforming politicians ever since Hutcheson was studied by Thomas Jefferson. The outstanding scholar of the Scottish Enlightenment was indeed the German philosopher Hegel (1770–1832), whose work, despite the failure of his hopes for a liberal Prussia, helped to recover Scottish Enlightenment ideals after the Industrial Revolution (which some scholars see as having overwhelmed them). Subsequently the Russian intelligentsia of the 19th century and the disillusioned ideologues of the later 20th have noted how the Scottish Enlightenment recoiled from the revolutionary ideas of 1789 France and sought elsewhere for the basis of a modern liberal society.

Some historians have nevertheless deplored 18th century Scottish ideas from a perspective sympathetic to the English Utilitarian movement led by Jeremy Bentham; they detect an authoritarian and Calvinist influence dominating the Scottish Enlightenment to retrograde effect. Herein the truth is as ill served as by the Thatcherite misreading of Adam Smith; for what characterises the Scottish Enlightenment and its sometimes Hegelian heirs who criticised Utilitarianism (from Hutcheson Stirling to Edward Caird and A D Lindsay) is an awareness of the basis and the necessary institutions of a society. This relates to the more profound anthropology and sociology of the Enlightenment, which has drawn the attention of Alasdair Macintyre in the 1980s, and which remains (with certain other neglected contributions) a major item of more than merely historical interest.

Had it thrown up an incredible number of men of genius and no more, the Scottish Enlightenment would belong to the *Guinness Book of Records*. But for every dazzling genius such as **David Hume** or Adam Smith, there was a host of lesser luminaries. If **Lord Monboddo**'s ideas about language and man's lost tail seem quaint, one can as well point to **Lord Kames**'s writings on Aesthetics, to the literary studies pioneered by Adam Smith and followed up by **Hugh Blair**, to Smith's star pupil John Millar (who wrote more than *On the Origin of Distinction in Ranks*) and to more scientists than named above. They were somehow inspired, capable of critical orderly thinking, while aspiring to the widest perspective. Macintyre's lecture 'The Ideal of an Educated Society' says a great deal. 18th century Scotland was no paradise, but why did so much go right?

This sociological question echoes the Scottish Enlightenment's contribution to sociology and anthropology, each rooted in an observational and comparative method, and in the natural sciences as practised by Newton and Boyle. Experiment is not possible for the social scientist; he can only ask how things came to be as they are, or were. In an age when life was physically improving and there was some basis of optimism, this question was crucial in directing the attention of Scottish Enlightenment thinkers towards historical study, notable in **William Robertson**, David Hume and **Adam Ferguson**. There is also the historical framework of Adam Smith's economics, and Ferguson's protosociology, in which reference extends beyond Greece and Rome to American Indians and Ferguson's fellow Gaels. Travellers' reports of ancient tribes were an influential contemporary factor. The Ossianic poetry of **James Macpherson** was not a mere literary forgery but, informed by older literary sources, a reconstruction of what according to current science 3rd century AD **Celtic** society must have been like. That it belongs to the sentimental literary genre of **Henry Mackenzie**'s *The Man of Feeling* was less noticeable in an age which needed Burns's emphasis on the experienced (rather than doctrine-bound) life. For Ferguson, who accepted the doctrine of 'stages' of society (cf Adam Smith) and who was in European terms a near counter-Enlightenment thinker, the ideal of a more natural man served as a warning against the atrophy of normal passion which could result from alienation and excessive socialisation.

This was very much in line with the more general awareness that man is a social being, shaped and determined by background, not purely selfish but ruled also by concern for others. Whether this empirical realist insight into human motivation owed something to the proximity of economically disparate groups, or to inter-Scottish and Scots-English contrasts is worth asking. It presumed an awareness of interdependencies in society, perhaps fostered by a folk-memory of famines, vagabondage, and general insecurity. The Scottish Enlightenment provided a working model of a modern society not unaware of its precariousness.

It is perhaps best described neither as a movement nor a period, but rather as a singular and dynamic phenomenon, characterised by historical reference, not reducible to formulae, and resulting from various earlier movements and tendencies which began to interact. It became a dominant force toward the middle of the 18th century but there is room for argument concerning its later days. How far **Scott** belongs to the intellectual movement, and whether his novels reflect a hardening of scientific speculations into questionable doctrine is often in dispute. It certainly had its continuation in the historical, philosophical and anthropological studies of the 19th century; and its influence is detectable as late as **William Robertson Smith** and the 9th edition of *Encyclopaedia Britannica*. The universities were shaped by it, but perhaps most notably the intellectual life of the clubs and reviews continued, whether through the mid-19th century New Speculative Society (whose foundation invoked the Aberdeen Philosophical) or in the informal meetings of an intellectual community of scholars, theologians and educational reformers which included John McLeod Campbell and the Oxford reformer Benjamin Jowett. To the spirit of the Scottish Enlightenment we also owe the paintings of **Raeburn** and the buildings of **Robert Adam**. The advances in 18th century Scottish trade and manufactures should be related to it as also any number of books and characters. There is more to such a phenomenon than history.

See: G E Davie, *The Scottish Enlightenment and Other Essays*, 1991; *Origins and Nature of the Scottish Enlightenment*, ed R H Campbell, A S Skinner, 1982; *The Science of Man and Science and Philosophy in the Scottish Enlightenment*, both ed P H Jones, 1989; *Studies in the Philosophy of the Scottish Enlightenment*, ed M A Stewart, 1990; *Scotland in the Age of Improvement*, ed R Mitchison and N Phillipson, 1970; and Alasdair Macintyre's *Whose Justice? Which Rationality?* and *The Idea of an Educated Public*, 1989.

SCOTTISH HOME RULE ASSOCIATION, The (1886–1929)

With a lapse during World War I, the SHRA provided a forum for devolutionists and nationalists until the emergence of the **National Party of Scotland** in 1928. Although it revived the grievances of **James Begg** and **William Burns**, its name and its political clout came courtesy of Ireland's Home Rulers when Gladstone's espousal of the Irish cause led many Liberals to adopt the concept of Home Rule All Round, ie for Scotland and Wales as well as for Ireland. Besides this Liberal phalanx, typified in the 1880s by **Lord Rosebery** [see **Primrose, Archibald Philip**], the SHRA attracted a rich variety of patriots and pamphleteers including aristocrats such as **John Stuart, 3rd Marquess of Bute** (a Catholic convert who advocated a **Scottish Parliament**), **Jacobite** eccentrics like the Australian-born Theodore Napier (who published *The Fiery Cross* and took to parading in Highland dress at **Culloden**) and middle class romantics like Charles Waddie (who produced *Scotia's Darling Seat: A Home Rule Sermon, and other Poems* (1890) and *How Scotland Lost Her Parliament and What Came of It* (1902)). At the other end of the political spectrum it also enjoyed the support of Highland radicals such as Charles Fraser-Mackintosh of the **Highland Land Law Reform Association**, and of Labour leaders like **Keir Hardie** and **Ramsay MacDonald**. But although numerous Home Rule Bills were discussed in the pre-war years, they were invariably either deferred until the Irish issue was settled or passed over in the pressure of other business. Revived in 1918, the Association assumed a more Socialist posture under the leadership of **William Gallacher**, **Thomas Johnston** and **Roland Muirhead**. With the support of both Labour and **Independent Labour Party** leaders, more motions were discussed, more Bills introduced, without effect. In desperation Muirhead in 1928 opted for more direct political action and opened negotiations with other nationalist groupings which led to the foundation of the National Party of Scotland.

SCOTTISH NATIONAL PARTY, The

The party, committed to restoring Scottish independence, was founded in 1932 from the union of the **National Party of Scotland** (1928–32) and the more moderate but rightist Scottish Party (1930–2). Its origins lay in disenchantment with the failure of regular party politics to secure governmental reform in Scotland. Despite commitments by Liberal, Labour and **Independent Labour Party** to Home Rule, and despite many parliamentary motions and even Bills (the most successful overtaken by war in 1914), no progress had been achieved. The NPS arose in 1928 after the parliamentary defeat of the Rev James Barr's Bill for Scottish Self Government during the second minority Labour government. **Compton Mackenzie** was elected Rector of **Glasgow University** in 1931, but otherwise the early NPS and Scottish National Party period was not marked with great electoral success until the wartime party truce, when good by-election results were achieved in 1940 (**Argyll**), 1943 (**Kirkcaldy**) and 1945 (when

Robert McIntyre won **Motherwell**). Controversy over policy towards the war caused a serious split in 1942, and the hiving-off of the **Scottish Convention** led by **John MacCormick**, leaving **Douglas Young**, Robert McIntyre and others in the leadership of the SNP.

After the war, the Scottish **Nationalist Covenant** was for a while the main vehicle of nationalist advance in Scotland. The SNP fought few seats, enjoyed little electoral success, but consolidated itself as a political party with exclusive membership and strong internal discipline under the chairmanship successively of Robert McIntyre, James Halliday and Arthur Donaldson. In the 1960s a new, dynamic, younger team emerged personified by such as Ian MacDonald and William Wolfe, who recorded spectacular improvements in by-elections in Bridgeton and West Lothian. The general elections of 1964 and 1966 showed considerable if less spectacular improvement, foreshadowing huge advances in Pollock (nearly won by George Leslie in early 1967) and **Hamilton**, captured from Labour by Winnie Ewing in November 1967. Thereafter there was a great leap forward in the local elections of 1968 which led Harold Wilson to establish a Royal Commission on the Constitution and Edward Heath to propose a Scottish Assembly to undertake scrutiny of Scottish legislation in his 'Declaration of **Perth**'. But success found the SNP too inexperienced in the arts of politics and in party discipline; there was a falling back in 1970, Mrs Ewing losing her seat and only Donald Stewart being elected, for the Western Isles.

When the Royal Commission reported in 1973, recommending devolved Scottish and Welsh Assemblies within the UK, the idea was received lightly in Parliament. But all changed in the general election of 1974 when (foreshadowed by Margo MacDonald's by-election victory in **Govan** in late 1973) the SNP won seven and then 11 seats, with a share of the poll rising beyond 30% and threatening the unionist parties (especially Labour) in most of the remaining seats in Scotland. The whole Parliament of 1974–9 was preoccupied, on the domestic front, with attempts to resolve the nationalist demands in Scotland and Wales by the provision of devolved assemblies, finally provided for in 1978 by the Scotland and the Wales Acts. The SNP, notwithstanding internal controversy on the advisability of being drawn into support for schemes less than its final objective of independence, gave support to the proposal for a devolved assembly as a first step on the road to independence. But opposition from within the governing Labour party led to delay, and then to a commitment to advisory referenda in Scotland and Wales, and then to a requirement that the proportion of 'yes' votes had to be at least 40% of the whole electoral roll. Finally, the referendum campaign in the winter months of 1979 coincided with the government's 'winter of discontent'; the final result, though showing a small majority in Scotland for the proposed assembly, fell short of the 40%. The SNP resolved to press the government for implementation nevertheless, and, failing a clear commitment, to seek a general election on this issue. In March 1979 the SNP Parliamentary Group took part in the No Confidence motion which brought down the Callaghan government; but the SNP vote collapsed to 17% in the ensuing

general election, and only Donald Stewart (Western Isles) and Gordon Wilson (**Dundee** East) held their seats. Later that summer Winnie Ewing continued a remarkable career by winning the Highlands and Islands seat in the first European Parliamentary Election.

There followed a period of controversy among those (the '79 Group') who favoured a move to the left in party policy, and more traditionalist-minded groupings which felt that 'independence – nothing less' must be the SNP's line. Meanwhile, the formation of the Social Democratic Party and its alliance with the Liberals put great pressure on the SNP vote in areas where it had been strongest, as well as capturing headlines and 'third party' sentiment. So the 1980s were a period of retrenchment and redefinition. This came to an end in 1988 with a commitment to a policy of 'independence in Europe', stressing Scotland's potential role as a member state in the EC, and underlining the left-of-centre strands in the party's existing policy commitments. The election of Jim Sillars (former Labour MP, former leader of the breakaway Scottish Labour Party) as MP for Govan in a by-election in November 1988, following on a relative improvement in the general election of 1987, with three members (Margaret Ewing, Andrew Welsh and Alex Salmond) taking seats, marked a new beginning. Then in 1989, when Gordon Wilson resigned after 12 years as party leader, Alex Salmond won the national Convenorship in a contest with Margaret Ewing, parliamentary leader, and the new image of the party as a left-of-centre social democratic party with a strong stress on Scotland's place and role in Europe became clearly defined.

In the 1990s the SNP came in from the cold. With Ireland providing an encouraging example of independence within Europe, with the Conservative vote in Scotland disappearing, and with the Labour and Liberal paarties converging over constitutional reform, the Nationalists emerged as a credible opposition. Having boycotted the Scottish Constitutional Conference but endorsed the referendum on a **Scottish Parliament**, the SNP ran Labour a close second in the 1999 Scottish elections and looked forward to the 2003 elections with a pledge to hold another referendum, this time on independence.

SCOTTISH NATURAL HERITAGE, see GOVERNMENT

SCOTTISH OFFICE, see GOVERNMENT

SCOTTISH OPERA

Glasgow-based Scottish Opera started life in 1962 with six performances at the city's **King's Theatre** organised by Alexander Gibson, then Musical Director of the Scottish National Orchestra. The ambitious debut programme, which included Puccini's *Madam Butterfly* and Debussy's *Pelléas et Mélisande*, was both a critical and popular success; a second season the following year included performances in **Edinburgh**, a third in 1964 took Scottish Opera to **Aberdeen** and in 1967 they performed at the **Edinburgh Festival**. Financial problems notwithstanding, the company extended both its repertoire and its touring programme, performing in many Scottish cities and towns as well as in England and overseas. Since 1975 it has found a permanent home in Glasgow's

Theatre Royal and has won an international reputation for dramatic, stylish and adventurous productions. Scottish Opera for Youth was formed in 1971 to introduce schoolchildren to the joys of the form, while Opera-Go-Round is a smaller touring company which performs, with only a few singers and a piano, in village halls throughout the country for the same purpose.

SCOTTISH PARLIAMENT, The

From at least the 16th century until the 1707 **Act of Union**, Scotland had its own parliament. It developed in tandem with the Convention of Estates (they being the nobility, clergy and burghs), from which it was not easily distinguished. Nor, any more than similar institutions elsewhere, did it endorse interests other than these. It was an important body, symbolic of Scotland's independence, but in no sense representative of the Scottish people or accountable to them.

The institution established by the Scotland Act of 1998 was thus the first democratic parliament in Scottish history. Conceived out of the need to make government more responsive to Scottish opinion, obliged to consult widely, and elected in such a way as to ensure the proportional representation of most voter preferences, the new Parliament has strong democratic credentials. If, as the Scottish Constitutional Convention insisted, sovereignty in Scotland lies with the people, Parliament's importance may come to transcend its competence.

The Demand for Devolution

Campaigns for a reform of the constitution which would either restore Scotland's independence or produce a significant devolution of power from the UK government date back more than 100 years to the **Scottish Home Rule Association.** The 1930 **Nationalist Covenant** drawn up by the **National Party of Scotland** demanded 'an independent parliament' and this became standard fare in the manifestos of the **Scottish National Party** (SNP), founded in 1932. The big UK parties paid little heed until the 1960s when the SNP began winning a significant share of the Scottish vote and then captured its first Westminster parliamentary seat in the 1967 **Hamilton** by-election. This and similar nationalist successes in Wales led Harold Wilson's Labour government to set up a Royal Commission in 1969. Its **Kilbrandon Report** recommended directly elected assemblies in Scotland and Wales while Edward Heath's Conservative government adopted a similar resolution in the 'Declaration of Perth'. But neither party included these proposals in its 1974 manifesto and the SNP duly won 7 seats in that year's February election.

In the second election of 1974 the SNP surged to 11 seats despite the Labour government's September White Paper recommending Welsh and Scottish assemblies, the latter to have legislative (but not tax-raising) powers. Dogged by the government's indecision and fragility, this proposal, heavily qualified by the need for advisory referenda and then by an amendment which stipulated that majority approval must represent at least 40% of the total electorate, eventually made it into the statute book as the Scotland and Wales Acts of 1978. The referenda were held in 1979 and, although that for Scotland received majority approval, the majority fell short of the 40% threshold. The Labour government was promptly defeated in a 'no-confidence' motion and Margaret Thatcher's May '79 victory ushered in 18 years of Conservative government. One of her first moves was to repeal the Scotland and Wales Acts.

The hostility of the Thatcher and Major governments to any form of devolution proved decisively counterproductive, most obviously in the dwindling Conservative vote in Scotland. In 1987 the Conservatives won just 10 Scottish seats to Labour's 50. Since the Conservatives nevertheless enjoyed a massive UK majority, the 'Doomsday Scenario' had dawned under which Scotland was governed by an administration which its electorate had manifestly rejected. Even fair-minded unionists perceived the injustice. A cross-party Campaign for a Scottish Assembly, launched in 1980, produced The Claim of Right for Scotland (1988) which advocated a Scottish Constitutional Convention. Set up in 1989, this SCC was supported by most local authorities, trades unions, churches and several parties including Labour and the Liberals, although not the SNP (which was unwilling to compromise on full independence) nor the Tories (who portrayed devolution as separatism). The SCC's publications, especially Scotland's Parliament: Scotland's Right (1996), upped the stakes; a parliament (rather than 'an assembly') with law-making and tax-raising powers was now envisaged, and a composite form of election with an element of proportional representation was endorsed.

These proposals featured in the Labour and Liberal manifestos for the 1997 election. Tony Blair's New Labour duly swept the polls while the still antidevolutionist Conservatives won not a single seat in Scotland. A White Paper, Scotland's Parliament, added further detail and was published within three months. It proposed an immediate referendum, which was held in September '97. The SNP, persuaded now that a parliament was an acceptable step towards eventual independence, joined the other two parties in a campaign to win a 'YES-YES' vote to the two-part question: should there be a Scottish Parliament (74.3% 'yes') and should it have tax-raising powers (63.5% 'yes'). Only the Conservatives had campaigned for 'NO-NO'. The ensuing Scotland Act, a complex piece of legislation beginning invitingly enough with 'There shall be a Scottish Parliament', became law in November 1998.

The Scotland Act 1998

The Act establishing the Scottish Parliament is in six parts with 116 sections and runs to 40,000 words. Much of it seeks to fence off the new parliament's areas of competence so that it neither compromises the sovereignty and obligations of the Westminster Parliament nor prejudices the integrity of the United Kingdom. Scotland's parliament is therefore neither independent nor sovereign and can legislate only in areas devolved to it. The Westminster Parliament can enlarge or reduce these areas of competence; it can legislate to overrule or nullify an act of the Scottish Parliament; it could even legislate to the effect that 'there shall not be a Scottish Parliament'.

However, these prescriptive rights are to some extent offset by the adoption of an apparently generous principle of legislative devolution. Based on 'the retaining model', it devolves all the powers of the central authority (the UK Parliament) in respect of Scotland to the subordinate authority (the Scottish Parliament) save for those specifically 'retained'. (The principle contained in the 1978 Act was the reverse; under its 'transferring model' the central authority would have devolved or 'transferred' only those powers specifically listed.) The onus in the 1998 Act lies on Westminster defining the powers which it wishes to retain. All else is presumed to have been transferred. The Act is thus not about what the Scottish Parliament can do but what it cannot do.

The areas exempted from the Scottish Parliament's legislative competence are specified in detail and include the constitution and Crown, defence and the armed forces, foreign affairs and international trade and development, immigration and nationality, central economic and fiscal management, employment and social security, energy, transport regulation and safety, the regulation of **broadcasting** and various professional bodies, equality of opportunity, abortion, drugs etc. etc. In some instances (eg taxation) the reserved subjects are so broad that exceptions which come within the Scottish Parliament's competence (eg local taxes) have to be listed, thereby apparently turning the 'retaining' principle on its head.

By a process of deduction, the main subjects devolved are therefore health, **education** (including training), **local government**, social work, housing, transport, **tourism**, some economic development (eg Scottish Enterprise, Highland and Islands Enterprise), **law** and various home affairs (**prisons**, police, fire service etc.), environmental and heritage protection, **agriculture**, **forestry** and **fishing**, sport and the arts. The list is not dissimilar to that of the Scottish Office's responsibilities prior to devolution (or that of the new Welsh Assembly), and it is subject to the same financial constraints in its reliance on a bloc grant from the UK government. The big difference is that the Scottish Parliament can now legislate on all these matters. It can also adjust the funds available to it by raising or reducing the rate of UK income tax by 3p in the pound for Scottish taxpayers.

Elections

The 1998 Act also details the frequency and method of election. Elections are to be held every four years on an 'Additional Member System'. This is a hybrid of the Westminster-style 'first past the post' system and a proportional system. Of the total number of 129 Members of the Scottish Parliament (MSPs) 73 are elected on the Westminster system from the same constituencies which elect to Westminster (except that **Orkney** and **Shetland**, though constituting one Westminster constituency, are separated into two constituencies for Scottish elections).

The remaining 56 MSPs are chosen in a separate ballot (but held simultaneously) in which voters signify their preference not for a candidate (unless he is standing as an independent) but for a party. These votes are counted on a regional basis, the regions currently corresponding to the eight existing constituencies used for elections to the European Parliament. The seven successful candidates from each such region are chosen from lists of contenders previously submitted by the political parties (or from amongst the independents).

The calculation involved in awarding these seats takes account of the party allegiance of candidates already elected by the direct Westminster method within each region. This makes it appear more complicated than it is. Basically, the votes cast for each party (and each independent) in the regional election are totalled up. These totals are then divided by the number of MSPs from their respective parties already elected within that region by the direct method; and to these totals one is in each case added. Thus if, say, the Labour vote in the regional ballot totalled 100,000 and 4 Labour MSPs had already been returned from constituencies within that region by the direct method, the 100,000 is to be divided by five. The party (or independent) who emerges from this calculation with the highest number is awarded the first regional seat. Exactly the same calculation is involved in awarding the next seat, with the voting totals being again divided by the number of MSPs in each party already elected (so including the winner of the first calculation) plus, again, that notional one. Thus, had Labour won the first regional seat, its 100,000 would this time be divided by six while the sums for the other parties would remain the same. And so on, seven times, until all seven regional seats have been allocated.

The Scottish Executive

This is the preferred name for what at Westminster is termed 'the government'. Likewise its leader is 'First Minister' rather than 'Prime Minister'. It comprehends all his subordinate ministers and law officers (Lord Advocate and Solicitor General). The procedure for choosing an executive is similar to that at Westminster. Office is held at the sovereign's pleasure but, in practice, depends on the executive retaining the support of parliament. Resignation is a statutory requirement if the executive loses a vote of 'no confidence'. Ministers, but not law officers, must be MSPs and each must be approved by parliament before their names are submitted to the sovereign. They may not be members of the Westminster or European Parliaments (hence the resignation of Donald Dewar as Secretary of State for Scotland before being eligible to become Scotland's first First Minister).

The Presiding Officer

The 1998 Act gives the Scottish Parliament considerable freedom in the choice of its working procedures in the hope, voiced in various consultative documents, that its conduct may prove more responsive, informal and open, and less adversarial, than that of its Westminster counterpart. Considerable responsibility therefore rests with its Presiding Officer who, as well as performing the role of Westminster's Speaker, must oversee this laying down of ground rules, principally in the form of standing orders. The Presiding Officer (and his two deputies) is elected by parliament and is supposed to be non-partisan. Sir David Steel was chosen as the first incumbent.

See also **Government and Administration**, **Local Government**, **The West Lothian Question**, and, for the location and inauguration of the new parliament, the 'Scottish Parliament' sub-entry in the **Edinburgh** entry.

'SCOTTISH RENAISSANCE', The

The movement dubbed 'the Scottish Renaissance' by the Frenchman Professor Denis Saurat arose after World War I out of a desire among writers (and one composer in particular, **Francis George Scott**) to re-establish Scottish artistic values reflecting the 20th century. **Lewis Spence** (*Collected Poems*, 1953) tried to revive a form of medieval Scots. But it was **Hugh MacDiarmid** (C M Grieve), in his two volumes of Scots lyrics *Sangschaw* (1935) and *Pennywheep* (1926), and in the long poem of satirical comment interspersed with lyrics, *A Drunk Man Looks at the Thistle* (1926), who really established the Renaissance movement. He has remained its greatest adornment, in spite of the fallaway of much of his later work, abounding, as it does, in not always fully digested or acknowledged quotations from other writers. In the 1930s his only follower of distinction was **William Soutar** (*Poems of William Soutar*, ed Aiken, 1986). **Edwin Muir**'s philosophical poems in English (*Collected Poems*, 1963) also won wide recognition, although his *Scott and Scotland* (1936), suggesting that Scots was no longer a valid language for modern thought, led to a bitter feud with MacDiarmid, which Muir treated with tolerant sufferance.

The novelist **Sir Compton Mackenzie**, though a Scot by adoption and an ardent Scottish nationalist, at first made a distinguished contribution to English literature with his early novels, though in his old age he produced a series of comic Highland novels, of which *Whisky Galore* (1947) is the best-known. **Eric Linklater** contributed both Rabelaisian comedy and a glimpse of **Orkney** life and history in his novels and a classic book about the islands. Most significant of all, perhaps, was **Neil M Gunn**, whose novels dealt with many of the crisis points in Highland history – *Sun Circle* (1933), *The Silver Darlings* (1941), etc – sensitively reflecting social conditions in the north. George Blake chronicled life in the industrial town of Garvel, his name for **Greenock**, from the beginning of the 19th century to the aftermath of World War II. Though Fred Urquhart's first short stories deal with rural farmworkers' lives, his novel *Time Will Knit* (1938) is concerned with their **Edinburgh** urban counterparts.

It was during World War II that what Linklater called the 'second wind' phase of the Scottish Renaissance emerged. Its poetic focus was to some extent the four issues of *Poetry Scotland* (edited by Maurice Lindsay, with MacDiarmid as co-editor of No 4) and more generally, *Scottish Art and Letters*, edited by R Crombie Saunders, both produced by the Glasgow publisher William Maclellan, who also published the two volumes of **Douglas Young**'s poems, the early work of **Sydney Goodsir Smith** and W S Graham, and books by Ruthven Todd (the only Scottish member of the 'Macspaunday' '30s group) and Maurice Lindsay.

Goodsir Smith's *Under the Eildon Tree* (1948) established his reputation for urbane wit (his *Collected Poems* of 1976 unfortunately belies its title, missing out, for example, 'The Riggins o' Chelsea', one of his finest poems). The more colloquial Edinburgh poet **Robert Garioch**'s wit, though usually couched more formally (*Collected Poems*, 1977), is no less pointed and typically Scottish.

Of English-writing poets, **Norman MacCaig** (*Collected Poems*, 1990) brought his metaphysical imagery and keen perception to bear on scenes (often Highland), people and creatures. **Iain Crichton Smith**, novelist and short-story writer as well as poet (*Selected Poems*, 1982), usually of the problems faced by the contracting **Gaelic** culture and Highland way of life. The novelist, short-story writer and poet **George Mackay Brown** (*Greenvoe*, 1972, *Magnus*, 1973, *Selected Poems*, 1977) captured the 'feel' of Orkney better than any other writer. George Bruce records effectively the hard qualities of the north-east and the way of life of its **fishing** communities (*Collected Poems*, 1971), as did Alexander Scott, mostly in Scots, in relation to **Aberdeen** (*Collected Poems*, 1979). Glasgow has been the inspiration of Maurice Lindsay and of the versatile and hugely inventive Edwin Morgan (*Collected Poems*, 1990) who has also found inspiration in space travel and in devising concrete verse.

The corresponding revival in Scotland's numerically third, but oldest language, Gaelic, produced **Sorley Maclean** (Somhairle Macgill-eain – *Collected Poems*, 1990), whom many regard as the finest poet the language has ever had; **George Campbell Hay** (Deòrsa Caimbeul Hay – *Fuaran Slèibh*, 'Upland Spring' 1947, *O na Ceithir Airden*, 'From the Four Airts', 1952, and *Wind on Loch Fyne*, 1948) who, due to bad health, enjoyed only a short creative period, much of his work concerning itself with his feelings for nationhood; and Derick S Thomson (Ruaraidh MacThomais), teacher and critic as well as poet.

During the late 1970s and throughout the 1980s, social realism replaced the idealistic nationalism of the Scottish Renaissance (often, though, allied to strong international feelings about Scotland's place in Europe). Morgan's poetry perhaps reflects both climates, that of Liz Lochhead, Robert Crawford and others predominantly the latter. In fiction, too, James Kelman and, recently, Janice Galloway, have given voice to the more inarticulate strategy of urban communities, as to some extent does Alasdair Gray, who, however, has never again quite achieved the comic near-genius of his novel *Lanark* (1987). Allan Massie is another novelist ranging widely in subject matter, from Roman history to medieval Scotland and modern Europe, though a more 'establishment' figure politically than some of his contemporaries.

The motivation behind the Scottish Renaissance may have shifted towards what, in Victorian parlance, would have been called a 'working class' culture. MacDiarmid would not have objected; indeed he could never quite reconcile his desire to be the poet of the masses with his realisation that his poetry was intellectually beyond them. Nor does this shift imply that the Renaissance's 'third wind' writers eschew political concern for the survival of Scotland's nationhood. Quite the reverse.

SCOURIE, Sutherland

This township north of Eddrachillis Bay and opposite Handa island is in the northernmost area where the Atlantic palm grows after its journey along the Gulf Stream from the Gulf of Mexico. Here Aodh [see **Aed**], Chief of **Mackay**, planted his son Donald before his death in 1572, whose great-grandson was **Hugh**

Mackay of Scourie, the kingmaker of the Revolution of 1688. As General of the Scots Brigade in the Netherlands he sailed with William of Orange in October of that year and was appointed Commander-in-Chief in Scotland. Before he could be created Earl of Scourie he died in action in 1692.

SCRABSTER, Caithness

In Norse *Skara Bolstadr* (Skara Farm), Scrabster forms a relatively secure anchorage in the lee of Holburn Head on the west side of **Thurso** Bay. It seems likely that there was a **Viking** place of strength here in the 12th century, when Earl Harald crossed from **Orkney** to mutilate Bishop John in Scrabster. Bishop Gilbert built a new castle at Scrabster after his elevation in 1223, which continued to be the local residence of his successors until the abolition of episcopacy. Excavation shows that it was remodelled in the 15th century. Today Scrabster is the mainland port serving Orkney and the Faroe islands.

SEABIRDS

Although few British seabirds nest only in Scotland, the country does host Britain's largest and most spectacular breeding colonies. Gannets, or Solan Geese, breed off both the east coast (eg **Bass Rock**) and the west, where **St Kilda**, with 60,000 breeding pairs, is the largest gannetry in the world; the same remote archipelago also supports 300,000 pairs of puffins.

Breeding populations are, however, subject to considerable fluctuation. In 1877 St Kilda had the only

Scrabster pier c1890 with the St Olaf ferry to Orkney (GWWA)

British breeding colony of fulmars; they were reputed to have been there for about 900 years. But in 1878 breeding fulmars were also found on **Foula** (**Shetland**); and so began their extraordinary and unexplained expansion. They are now widespread round most of the UK coastline and, with numbers still increasing, have adapted to nest sites on the open ground (as opposed to cliffs), in old buildings, and several miles inland as in the north-west Highlands.

Black guillemots, often called tysties, are found mainly in Scotland but only recently have modern methods of census revealed the importance of the local breeding stock. It was thought, for instance, that the **Monach Isles National Nature Reserve** possessed only 80 pairs. Then in 1987 a new count, made between 5 and 6 am when both birds are off the nest, revealed a population of 850 which made this the largest known colony in Europe with over 2% of the total British population.

Rarer seabirds which breed only in Scotland include the Arctic skua and the great skua (or bonxie), although the latter is also spreading, possibly courtesy of the offal increasingly dumped in the sea by trawlers and factory ships. The rarest of all Britain's seabirds, the Leach's petrel, has so far been found in only six remote locations, namely St Kilda, the **Flannan Isles**, North Rona, Sula Sgeir and two new colonies in the Northern Isles. Like the storm petrel [see **Mousa**] and the Manx shearwater, these birds only come to their nesting sites (burrows, stone walls) under cover of darkness, a habit which combined with their eerie calls has won them legendary notice. On **Rum** a hill is named after the Manx shearwaters which here breed unusually in ele-

vated colonies. Hearing the birds calling from their burrows, the **Vikings** immediately realised that they were amongst trolls and promptly named the place Trollival, 'the landmark of the trolls'.

SEAFORTH, Earldom

The founders of the Earldom of Seaforth upstage the **Campbells** of **Argyll** in addressing their Chief as the incarnation of the pagan stag-god, *Caber Feidh*. His ancient designation, *Cernunnos*, the Horned One, dates from pre-Christian times in Europe, and he was perhaps feared or revered in southern Britain as Herne the Hunter before he reappeared in the northern Highlands as the divine ancestor of Clann Mhic Choinnich (**Mackenzie**), 'son of the Bright One'. Like the Campbells, the Seaforths showed extreme hostility towards **clans** of historical origin such as the **MacLeods** of **Lewis**, whom they had succeeded in supplanting by 1623, when Colin Mackenzie was created Earl of Seaforth. The barbaric means by which this was achieved (in collusion with the **Edinburgh** mafia) have been neatly summarised by a member of the family in *Burke's Peerage*: Mackenzie of **Kintail**, one of the most unscrupulous of that age, 'was instrumental in civilising the Western Isles'. The Earldom of Seaforth was extinguished after the 1715 **Jacobite Rising** in circumstances allegedly prophesied by **Coinneach Odhar**, 'the Brahan Seer', recreated in 1771 but lapsed for want of an heir in 1815.

SEAFORTH HIGHLANDERS, The (Ross-Shire Buffs, The Duke of Albany's)

The regiment derives from the 1881 amalgamation of the 72nd (Duke of Albany's Own) Highlanders with the 78th Highlanders (the Ross-shire Buffs). At the same time the Highland Rifle Militia and the Volunteer Battalions of Ross, Sutherland, Caithness and Moray became part of the new regiment.

The 72nd were originally numbered the 78th when raised in 1778 by the **Earl of Seaforth**, being renumbered the 72nd in 1786. Their early services included the Cape, India, South Africa, the Crimea, Indian Mutiny and Afghanistan. In 1809 they were among those regiments who lost their Highland identity, but this was restored to them in 1823 along with the subtitle of 'the Duke of Albany's Own'. The 78th were raised by Francis Humberstone Mackenzie in 1793, shortly afterwards adding the title 'the Ross-shire Buffs'. They served in the Low Countries, in India, Egypt, Java, Persia, the Indian Mutiny and in Afghanistan.

Nineteen battalions of Seaforths served in World War I, in Macedonia, Palestine, Mesopotamia and on the Western Front. They gained 54 battle honours. A further 54 were gained in World War II, when the regiment served in France in 1940, North Africa, Sicily, Italy, Burma, Madagascar and in north-west Europe. Post-war active service included Malaya (twice) and Java.

The 72nd wore the Government **tartan** on raising and the version of Royal Stuart known as Prince Charles Edward when restored to Highland dress in 1823. The 78th wore the government sett with an added white and red line and this became known as the Mackenzie tartan, being adopted by the combined regiment in 1881. The Sutherland Volunteer – later Territorial – Battalion always wore the Government tartan. The regi-

mental marches were 'Pibroch o' Donuil Dubh' (pipes) and 'Blue Bonnets over the Border' (band). The Regimental Headquarters was at **Fort George** and the Seaforths recruited from the counties of **Sutherland** and **Caithness, Ross & Cromarty, Moray** and **Nairn**.

In 1961 the Seaforth Highlanders were amalgamated with **The Queen's Own Cameron Highlanders** to form **The Queen's Own Highlanders**.

SEALS

At many times of the year grey and common (or harbour) seals can be seen in the same areas around Scotland's coast, though common seals tend to occupy more sheltered coastal areas. They use different areas for breeding: common seal females usually give birth to their pups below the high-tide mark on sandbanks or rocky skerries. Pups have moulted into their first 'adult' coat *in utero* and are able to swim with their mother on the next incoming tide. Grey seals, on the other hand, form large breeding aggregations on isolated islands in the **Inner** and **Outer Hebrides**, **Orkney**, the Firth of Forth, and on the remote and inaccessible mainland coasts of Loch Eriboll and east **Sutherland**. Grey seal pups are born with a white coat or lanugo which they moult about the time they wean (at 18 to 23 days). Although they are capable of swimming (and occasionally swim in the sea or in small pools), pups tend to remain on land until they leave at 4–5 weeks of age.

Despite their name, common seals are less abundant in Scotland than grey seals. During aerial surveys carried out in 1996 and 1997 in Scotland, 29,600 common seals were counted out of a northern hemisphere total of approximately 600,000. These numbers represent the minimum size of the population since an unknown number of seals would have been at sea when the surveys were carried out and therefore not counted. Grey seal population estimation is based on annual surveys of pup production at the main British breeding colonies. Pup production figures are obtained from aerial photography and, for a few sites, from ground counts. In 1998 the Scottish grey seal population was estimated to be 104,100, approximately one third of the world total. Grey seals are restricted to the North Atlantic and adjacent waters (Baltic and White Seas). The world's biggest breeding colony is on Sable Island, off Nova Scotia in Canada, with the **Monach Isles**, a collection of five islands off **North Uist**, close behind.

In the latter part of the 20th century the grey seal population increased dramatically and, although they are protected during their breeding season, one important contributory factor to this increase was the depopulation of many offshore islands and the corresponding decrease in persecution and increase in available breeding habitat.

SEAWEED

Seaweed has been an important resource for people living near the coast in Scotland since prehistoric times; indeed it was so highly valued that it was traded far inland and in cities right into the 20th century. Several nutritious kinds were eaten raw or in soups, stews and puddings, and many tons are still collected annually as fodder and green manure for potatoes and other crops. Special rituals were followed to ensure a good 'crop'

Skye crofters manuring with seaweed for a potato crop (GWWA)

of seaweed, such as offering ale to the sea god Shony on **Lewis**, or pouring porridge into the sea around Hebridean islands on Maundy Thursday, while chanting incantations.

Dried seaweeds were smoked or chewed as tobacco substitutes, while medicinal uses included relieving fever, scurvy, burns, headaches, sleeplessness and constipation. In **Caithness** many people went to the 'ebb' at least once a year – the best time being early on a May morning – to eat dulse and other seaweeds, washed down with copious draughts of salt water; this they thought better for their health than any spa.

Filamentous seaweeds were made into rope, **fishing** lines and nets, while ashes from burnt seaweed were a valuable source of salt to preserve food, and the basis of the **kelp** industry. Today, factories in the **Hebrides** and **Orkney** still collect and process seaweed into brown granules of alginic acid to be used in desserts, drinks and other foodstuffs, in paint, pharmaceuticals and textile manufacture.

SECESSION CHURCHES

The first secession from the established **Church of Scotland** in 1690 centred on **Ebenezer Erskine**, minister at **Stirling** in 1731, who opposed patronage, slackening of orthodox beliefs and found the **General Assembly** too compliant.

With three other dissenting clergy he formally seceded from the views of the Church in 1733, created an Associate Presbytery and was deposed from his living

in 1740. Conservative in belief but evangelical, as moderation and toleration arose elsewhere, the Secession Church renewed the **Covenant** in 1743. It split in 1747 over the Burgess Oath (which referred to 'the true religion . . . authorised by the laws') into Burgher and Anti-Burgher Churches. Each divided again into two, Auld Lichts and New Lichts, in 1799 and 1806. The two New Lichts churches came together in 1820 to create the **United Secession Church**. (Most of the Burgher Old Lichts rejoined the Church of Scotland in 1839.)

A second secession formed the Relief Church in 1761, again over patronage of a more liberal and anti-Covenanter persuasion. By 1806 there were at least five Secession Churches, each with their own clergy, buildings and ministry training according to their aspect of dissent and flavour of orthodoxy.

In 1847 the Relief Churches joined with the United Secession to create the **United Presbyterian Church**. Most secession congregations had come into the **Free Church** by 1900 forming the **United Free Church**. Inevitably, remnants held to older constitutions. [See chart p. 1041]

SECOND SIGHT

The faculty of seeing events and people far removed from the see-er's (or seer's) immediate and present situation is so well attested in almost every account of Scotland, and especially of the Highlands and Islands, as to constitute a trait. In the past every **clan** and township seems to have had its recognised seer, although in a sense the power was thought common to all, if latent in most, and capable of arousal by a practising seer or by certain disciplines. 'The sight is not criminal,' wrote **Robert Kirk**, 'since a man can come by it unawares and without consent; but it is certain he sees more fatal and fearful things than he do gladsome.' Death and disaster constituted the commonest visions, and since whatever the seer saw must inevitably come to pass, the sight could be more of a curse than a blessing. Witness the **Killin** seer who, pressed to explain his exit from an ale house when his neighbour entered, revealed that he had just seen the neighbour's death two days hence; 'at which the neighbour stabbed the seer and was himself executed two days after the fact'. In a class of their own are **Thomas of Ercildoune** and **Coinneach Odhar** ('the Brahan Seer') who foresaw national developments and technological advances like the **Caledonian Canal**, **railways** and aeroplanes. More typically the seer saw funeral processions. He also recognised and interpreted the activities of **fairies** and occasionally engaged in divination. Thus the shoulder bone of a sheep might reveal to him 'if whoredom be committed in the owner's house'.

SECURITY, Acts of (1704 and 1707)

In the serve-and-volley exchanges between the English and Scots Parliaments prior to their **Union**, the 1703/4 Act of Security was the Scottish response to the English Act of Settlement (1701) whereby succession to the Crown of England and Scotland was settled (after Queen Anne) on the Hanoverians. Such disregard for Scotland's constitutional sensibilities provoked even office-holders, and it was the Lord Privy Seal, John Murray 1st **Duke of Atholl**, who proposed the Security Act. This reserved to the Scottish Parliament the right to nominate its own successor to the Crown who would not be the same as that of England unless the sovereignty of the kingdom (ie the Scottish Parliament) had first been guaranteed. In other words in Scotland the succession was to be seized as an opportunity to press for reforms which would limit not just the royal prerogative but its use and abuse by English ministries to manage Scottish affairs. Deferring to just such pressures, **James Douglas 2nd Duke of Queensberry**, the Commissioner for Scotland, declined to give the royal assent to the Bill but in 1704 his successor, **John Hay 1st Marquis of Tweeddale**, was obliged to do so in order to get a vital supply Bill passed. The English Parliament's volleyed return was the **Alien Act**.

The 1707 Act of Security guaranteed the continuance of the **Church of Scotland** with its **presbyterian** structure as the established Church in Scotland after Union.

SEIL ISLAND, Argyll

This island is joined to the mainland by the so-called 'bridge over the Atlantic', built to a design of **Thomas Telford** in 1792, that arches high over the sound of Seil. At the far end is 'Tigh na Truish' – 'the House of the Trousers' – where clansmen returning from the mainland would change back into their **kilts** in the days when wearing **tartan** was forbidden. Long known primarily as one of the slate islands – slate was extracted here from the 16th century and the villages of Balvicar and Ellanabeich grew up around the industry – Seil also boasts the ruins of a medieval chapel at Kilbrandon

(named after Brennan, an Irish missionary who preceded **Columba**) and of Ardfad Castle, a **MacDougall** stonghold.

SELKIRK, Alexander (1676–1721) Sailor

Born in **Largo**, **Fife**, the son of a cobbler, Selkirk ran away to sea at the age of 27 after several close calls with the law. He joined the hydrographer, navigator and explorer-turned-buccaneer William Dampier, and became sailing master of the privateer *Cinque Ports*. In 1704, having quarrelled with his captain, he requested to be put ashore on the uninhabited South Pacific island of Juan Fernandez, 800 miles off the coast of Chile, where he lived alone for four years and four months before being rescued in 1709 by another privateer under the command of Woodes Rogers. He returned to Largo in 1712, and the account of his experiences published the following year inspired Daniel Defoe to write *Robinson Crusoe* (1719). Selkirk returned to sea and at his death in 1721 was a lieutenant in the Royal Navy. A suitably Crusoe-like statue of him stands on the site of the cottage where he was born.

SELKIRK, Selkirkshire

On a terrace of hills overlooking the Ettrick Water, Selkirk was a **royal burgh** in the 13th century, though its even older Tironensian Abbey, founded 1113 by Earl David (later **David I**) was moved to **Kelso** in 1128 'on account of inconvenient accommodation'. Despite its proximity to the turbulent border, the town did not loom large in Scottish history until 1513 when 100 men of Selkirk (known as 'souters', shoemakers, from the town's premier manufacture) marched to fight for their king at **Flodden.**

> On red Flodden's dreadful day
> When other pow'rful clans gave way,
> The burly sutors firmly stood
> And dyed the field with Southron blood
> > **Hogg**, 'Russiade'

One solitary 'sutor' is said to have returned from the battle bearing a captured English banner which he cast to the ground in the market place with the news that all his comrades had perished. So enraged were the English at the resistance offered by the Selkirk men that they ransacked and burnt the town, which was later awarded 1000 acres of **Ettrick Forest** by **James V** in appreciation of their valour and in order that they might have timber for rebuilding. The tragedy is commemorated in Selkirk's annual Common Riding Festival. A statue of the lone survivor by **Thomas Clapperton** was raised in the market place on the 400th anniversary of the battle and the banner itself is proudly displayed in the town's museum. This is a great place for statues; **Sir Walter Scott**, Sheriff of Selkirk from 1799–1832, watches over his former domain from a 20ft (6m) pedestal in the market place while **Mungo Park**, the African explorer born four miles away at Foulshiels, stands at the end of the High Street staring at the Municipal Buildings and dreaming of the Niger. Clapperton also sculpted the town's war memorial to a design by **Robert Lorimer**. From his temporary lodgings in Selkirk **James Graham, Marquis of Montrose**, marched the two miles to **Philiphaugh** on 13 September 1645. After his defeat in the unequal battle, Montrose fled north while **David Leslie** and his **Covenanters** embarked on the appalling slaughter of prisoners at nearby **Newark Castle**.

SELKIRKSHIRE

Before the **local government** reorganisation of 1975, Selkirkshire was an inland county situated in the south of Scotland, surrounded by **Peeblesshire** to the west, **Midlothian** to the north, **Roxburghshire** to the east and **Dumfriesshire** to the south. Hilly in outline, with its highest point at Ettrick Pen (2269ft/692m), the county's terrain was broken by two major river valleys – the Ettrick and the Yarrow – while the **Tweed** flows through part of the northern half of the former county, whose area was 121,240 acres (49,065ha). **Agriculture** was the principal occupation in the landward area, with **forestry** increasing in importance, while textiles and electronics were important in the two burghs, **Selkirk** and **Galashiels**. Although the latter was the larger of the two, Selkirk was the county town. **Sir Walter Scott** was its Sheriff from 1799 until his death in 1832. In the local government reorganisation of 1975, Selkirkshire formed a major part of the new Ettrick & Lauderdale District in Borders Region. In the local government reorganisation of 1975, Selkirkshire formed a major part of the Ettrick & Lauderdale District of Borders Region, and since 1995 has remained part of the Borders Council Area.

SELLAR, Patrick (1780–1851) Factor

Sellar studied law in **Edinburgh** before entering the service of **Elizabeth, Countess of Sutherland** in her own right and wife of the Marquess of Stafford. It was this that gave him the opportunity to play his notorious part in the Sutherland **clearances**, as a vitriolic **Gaelic** poem composed at the time describes. But Sellar was defended by his son in a book published in 1883 and then by his grandson in the *Dictionary of National Biography*. As recently as 1981 Rosalind Mitchison has written: 'The picture of Sellar resorting to force is unproved and at odds with his known character.' Philip Gaskell had anticipated her contempt for the Gaelic traditional evidence when, in 1968, he wrote of 'the absurdity of the Sellar folklore which still persists in Scotland'.

Lord Napier [see **Napier Commission**], who could judge the veracity of the purveyors of that folklore when they appeared before him, wrote in 1889: 'The burning of the dwellings was the natural, almost inevitable result of the cruel policy of eviction.' As for Sellar's part, the Countess herself wrote privately: 'The more I see and hear of Sellar the more I am convinced that he is not fit to be trusted further than he is at present. He is so exceedingly greedy and harsh with the people, there are heavy complaints against him from **Strathnaver**.' After Sellar's acquittal her Commissioner, **James Loch**, wrote to her that Sellar 'was really guilty of many very oppressive and cruel acts'. As some are still pleased to point out, there are two sides to this story, one of them purveyed by people whose contempt for the Gaelic evidence is equalled by their ignorance of that language.

SEMPILL, Sir James, of Beltrees (1566–1625) Courtier and Satirist

Sir James's dates coincide exactly with those of **James**

VI, to whom he owed his career. His father was Sir John Sempill of Beltrees near **Lochwinnoch** (**Renfrewshire**), and his mother Mary Livingstone, close friend of **Queen Mary** (indeed, one of her '**Four Maries**'). From this connection the young Sempill was educated with the young **Stewart** under the supervision of **George Buchanan**. He then attended **St Andrews University** and assisted the King with the preparation of his *Basilicon Doron*, 1599. From the same year he served as James VI's agent in London, was knighted in 1600, and headed a mission to France in 1601. He returned to Scotland after the **Union of the Crowns** and wrote, among other things, *A Pick-tooth for the Pope or The Packman's Pater Noster*, satirical verses aimed at the Papacy.

SEMPILL (SEMPLE), Robert (c1530–95)
Ballad Writer

Little is known about this Robert Sempill save that he had no connection with the **Sempills of Beltrees**. He appears to have lived in Paris and to have witnessed the 1572 St Bartholomew's massacre, about which he penned one of his 'ballatis'. But he must also have been resident in **Edinburgh** at about the same time for another deals with the siege of that city by **James Douglas, 4th Earl of Morton** in 1568–73. All reveal strong reformist sympathies, none more so than a scurrilous attack on Patrick Adamson, the Archbishop of **St Andrews**.

SEMPILL (SEMPLE) OF BELTREES, Robert (c1595–1665) and Francis (c1616–82) Poets

The son and grandson of **Sir James Sempill** both achieved literary distinction. Robert was educated at **Glasgow University** and is remembered for 'The Life and Death of the Piper of **Kilbarchan**', otherwise 'The Epitaph of Habbie Simpson', a mock elegy on the death of a piper and on the folk festivities in which he had participated. Its half-humourous, half-nostalgic tone was much copied; so, notably by **Burns**, was its stanza form which **Allan Ramsay** dubbed 'standart Habby'. A sequel, 'Sawney Briggs' could have been the work of Robert or of Francis, a lawyer and wit who has also been linked with 'Maggie Lauder'.

SETON, Alexander, 1st Viscount Kingston (c1620–91)

The third son of George Seton, Earl of Winton, Alexander was educated abroad and again left Scotland so as not to have to sign the **Covenant**. As a result he was excommunicated. His father supported the **Engagement** but Alexander remained in France with the future **Charles II**. He returned with him to Scotland in 1650 and was created Viscount Kingston soon after Charles's coronation at **Scone**.

SETON, George, 5th Lord Seton (c1527–85)

The staunchest of Catholics and so a most unpopular Provost of **Edinburgh** (1557, 1559) under **Mary of Guise**'s regency, Seton became **Queen Mary**'s most loyal supporter. His daughter Mary had been one of the four young **Maries** sent to France with the Queen in 1548. On the Queen's return (1561) Seton became a close adviser and, almost alone, seems never to have deserted her. He was the first to receive her after her escape from **Loch Leven Castle** and was duly captured at **Langside**. Mary Seton also remained exceptionally loyal, never marrying, accompanying the Queen into her English exile, and remaining with her until her execution, after which she retired to a nunnery in France.

SETON, Sir William, of Pitmedden (d.1744)
Politician and Essayist
Seton was the son of Sir Alexander Seton, 1st Baronet of **Pitmedden** who had been a Lord of Justiciary and MP before removal by **James VII** for opposing repeal of the **Test Act**. Like his father, William became MP for **Aberdeen** (1702) and then played an important part in the debate over the **Act of Union**. From a disinterested writer on trade whose sympathies lay with those who opposed the pro-English court and ministry, he was induced by the offer of a £100 pa pension to champion the cause of a full incorporating Union. As parliamentarian, propagandist, and one of the Union commissioners, he did so with cool logic and persuasive effect.

SETON HOUSE, East Lothian
Seton Palace, home of the most loyal of **Queen Mary**'s supporters, **George 5th Lord Seton** (c1527–85), was described as 'much the most magnificently structured and furnished house in Scotland'. With the forfeiture of the Seton estates in 1715 it was allowed to decay until finally demolished in 1789 in preparation for the construction on the site of Seton House (or Castle). Designed by **Robert Adam** for Alexander Mackenzie, who had acquired the land from the **York Buildings Company**, Seton House has in turn been described as 'the most perfectly executed of the castle type which he developed in Scotland . . . marking the high point in Adam's synthesis of neo-classical geometry and picturesque diversity' (C McWilliam). Nearby Seton Collegiate Church dates from the 15th century and includes fragments of its 13th century predecessor. Partly demolished after the **Reformation**, it still displays the splendid vaulted chancel and polygonal apse, traceried windows and Seton funerary monuments.

SEVEN CELTIC EARLDOMS
Uncertainty surrounds the existence, status and composition of the so-called Seven Celtic Earldoms. Legend has the kingdom of **Alba** divided into the seven provinces of **Angus**, **Atholl**, Strathearn, **Fife**, **Mar** (including **Buchan**), **Moray** (including **Ross**) and either **Caithness**, **Argyll**, **Menteith** or **Lennox**. Each was supposedly ruled by a 'sub-king', variously described as the forerunner or successor of the **mormaer**. The latter title was rendered in Latin as *comes*, the word also used for 'earl', which resulted in these provinces being later considered as earldoms. But mormaer is now thought to have been a **Pictish** title and some of the seven (or more) earldoms were clearly more Pictish or Norse than Celtic. In 1290 **Robert Bruce of Annandale** seems to have invoked this long-defunct grouping to contest the **Balliol** claim to the throne. On doubtful grounds he claimed that 'the seven earls of Scotland' had an ancient right to name the king and he accordingly instigated them to protest against the Balliol succession. The protest was in vain,

and according to Ranald Nicholson the precedent may have been drawn from German imperial practice rather than Scottish tradition.

SEVEN MEN OF MOIDART
This is the name given to the group who accompanied **Prince Charles Edward Stewart** on his voyage from France to Scotland in July 1745 and who landed with him on the **Moidart** Peninsula. They were William Lord Tullibardine, the titular Duke of Atholl who had been deprived of his title after taking part in the 1715 **Jacobite Rising**; Sir Thomas Sheridan, the Prince's 70-year-old Irish tutor; Aeneas MacDonald, banker and friend of the Prince; John William O'Sullivan, a soldier of fortune; Sir John MacDonald, a lieutenant-colonel in the Irish Brigade of the French army; Colonel Francis Strickland from Westmorland, whose father had accompanied **James VII** to France in 1688; and the Reverend George Kelly, a **non-juring** clergyman.

SHAIRP, John Campbell (1819–85)
Academic and Poet
In anthologies J C Shairp comes next to W Shakespeare, a cruel proximity. But as Professor of Poetry at Oxford (1877–87) Shairp was a respected literary figure in his day and a perceptive critic. He came from **West Lothian** and was educated at **Edinburgh** Academy, **Glasgow University** and Balliol College, Oxford, where he won the Newdigate (poetry) Prize. He returned to Glasgow (1856) after 10 years of schoolteaching, as Assistant Professor of Greek but soon moved to **St Andrews**, becoming Professor of Latin and Principal of United College (1868) before finally heading for the Poetry Chair at Oxford. In St Andrews he founded the cottage hospital and obliged his students to wear bonnets instead of mortar boards (because 'anglicised Scotchmen are generally poor creatures and an anglicised Scotland will be a contemptible country'). His literary sympathies, however, were with the English Lake Poets and from the safety of Oxford he essayed a damning and not forgotten critique of **Robert Burns** (1879).

SHANKLY, Bill (1913–81) Football Manager
Not the most successful **football** manager in terms of trophies but undoubtedly one of the game's most important in terms of his legacy, Bill Shankly was born at Glenbuck in **Ayrshire**, and seemed destined for a career down the mines. His footballing talents allowed him to escape and he played first for Carlisle and then Preston North End, but after winning five Scotland caps his playing career was cut short by war in 1939. Thereafter management was to prove his calling. He managed Carlisle, Grimsby, Workington and Huddersfield before taking over at Liverpool in 1959, steering the club back into the first division in 1962, winning the First Division Championship in '64, '66, and '73, the FA cup in '65 and '74 and the UEFA cup in 1973 and along the way signing Kevin Keegan from Scunthorpe. His belief in a simple, patient method of play based on passing sowed the seeds for the great, all-conquering Liverpool sides of the next decade. 'The socialism I believe in,' he said, 'is not really politics it's a way of living . . . with everyone helping each other and everyone having a share of the rewards. It's the way I see the game, the way I see

life.' More famously, and only half-joking, he declared that 'Football is not a matter of life and death, it's far more important than that.' Charismatic and quick-witted, Shankly remains a club hero to this day. He retired in 1974 and was awarded the OBE the same year.

SHANKS, John (1825–95) Sanitary Engineer

Born in **Paisley**, the son of a handloom weaver, Shanks was apprenticed as a plumber and practised his trade in Paisley and then **Barrhead**. Experimenting in the design of sanitary appliances, he founded the firm Shanks & Co in Barrhead in 1875 with his brother Andrew. Shanks proved a remarkable inventor, especially of patent water closets. The firm grew, in conditions of social concern for public health, to become the largest employer in the town and the leading sanitary engineering business in Scotland.

SHAPINSAY, Orkney

Shielding **Kirkwall**'s harbour, Shapinsay bears much the same relationship to the **Orkney** capital as does **Bressay** to **Lerwick**, the **Shetland** capital. From Elwick Bay King Haakon sailed south in 1263 to defeat at **Largs** while at a place called Grucula on the west coast one of **Agricola**'s galleys is supposed to have been wrecked when sailing round the north of Scotland in 84 AD. The island is comparatively fertile and produces its own cheese. A Colonel Balfour and his son were responsible for the 19th century agricultural improvement and for the improbable Baronial pile that is Balfour Castle (1848). From Quholm in the opposite (north-east) corner came a family called Irving who emigrated to America in the 1760s, espoused the revolutionary cause, and made money. A son, born in New York in 1783 and loyally christened Washington Irving, became America's first internationally successful writer, the friend of **Sir Walter Scott** and the author of, amongst other works, an essay on Rip van Winkle and a monumental biography of George Washington.

SHARP, James (1613–79) Archbishop of St Andrews

Born in **Banff** and educated in the old Episcopal heartland of **Aberdeen**, Sharp left for England after the 1638 **Covenant**. Returning to Scotland in 1643 as Professor of Philosophy at **St Andrews**, he became minister of **Crail** in **Fife** in 1649. Always a controversial cleric, his **Presbyterian** zeal was tempered by his sympathy for the Royalist cause which resulted in his imprisonment in London in 1651. Cromwell recognised his ability and liberated him to represent Scottish Church grievances to **General Monk** in 1660.

At the Restoration **Charles II** rewarded him with the Archbishopric of St Andrews, though he was attending court to represent moderate Presbyterians, and used him during the persecutions of the **Covenanters**. His acceptance of the harsh government measures of the **Duke of Lauderdale** was in contrast to the mediating role of **Bishop Leighton**. Sharp's was the oppressive style of imposed Episcopacy, in his own interests, and in 1668 he was shot at in **Edinburgh** by an opposing extreme Covenanter.

In 1679, crossing **Magus Moor** near St Andrews, in

James Sharp, Archbishop of St Andrews, after Sir Peter Lely (SNPG)

his ostentatious coach and in the company of his daughter, he was brutally murdered by a marauding band of zealous Fife Covenanters waiting in ambush for another target. This provoked further rebellion in the west and the persecutions of **John Graham of Claverhouse**. It provided the sole excuse for his memorial calling him 'a most holy martyr', which he was not.

SHARP, William 'Fiona MacLeod' (1855–1905) Author and Poet

Born in **Paisley**, the eldest son of a merchant, Sharp was partly brought up in the Highlands until the age of 12 when his family moved to **Glasgow**. He attended Glasgow Academy and the **University of Glasgow**, but in 1874 was taken out of university by his father to work as a lawyer's clerk. He was sent to Australia in 1876, shortly after his father died, in part to recuperate from suspected consumption. Sharp returned to London in 1877 where he worked intermittently in a bank and sought to establish himself as a journalist and writer. He began associating with various Pre-Raphaelite figures, and with the encouragement of Dante Gabriel Rossetti started to write verse, publishing his first collection, The Human Inheritance, in 1882. This was followed by Earth's Voices (1884) and Romantic Ballads and Poems on Phantasy (1888).

In 1890 he left London to travel through North America and Europe. He continued to wander around the world throughout the rest of his life. In 1890–1 he stayed in Rome, where he created his literary *alter ego* the Celtic feminine bard 'Fiona MacLeod'. He invented a biography for her, which he inserted in Who's Who, and went to great lengths to conceal her true identity [see **Celtic Twilight**]. Under this name Sharp produced several mystical works, including novels such as Pharais: A Romance of the Isles (1894), The Mountain Lover (1895) and Green Fire (1896), and a verse collection, From the Hills of Dreams (1901). All were heavily infused with Celtic nostalgia and a worship of nature. Under his own name, William Sharp wrote several collections of short stories and novels, including *The Sport of Chance* (1888), *The Children of Tomorrow* (1889) and, in collaboration with the American author Blanche Willis Howard, *A Fellowe and His Wife* (1892). He died in Sicily.

SHAWFIELD RIOTS, The (1725)

Often bracketed with the **Edinburgh Porteous Riot** (1736), the **Glasgow** Shawfield Riots point up resentment against the **Act of Union** and the power vacuum in Scotland consequent upon it. The protest stemmed from the imposition of a malt tax which added 3 pence to the price of a barrel of beer. The MP for Glasgow, a man not helped by being called Campbell, had supported the measure; his house, Shawfield, was therefore the main target of the June riot; how much damage it sustained is uncertain. Troops from the **Dumbarton** garrison under a Captain Bushel attempted to disperse the mob but only inflamed it by indiscriminate shooting. The Provost and council claimed that nine people were killed, but their evidence was tainted by ill-disguised support for the rioters. Meanwhile there was much official uncertainty as to who should intervene and with what powers. The Scottish Secretary (the Duke of Roxburghe) did nothing, and the Lord Advocate, **Robert Dundas** had just been removed for opposing the tax. Eventually it was his successor, **Duncan Forbes**, who ordered in **General Wade** to restore order. The Provost and magistrates were arrested along with some of the rioters; released, the former returned to a hero's welcome while most of the latter were sentenced to banishment, imprisonment or public flogging. Duncan Campbell, the MP, received generous compensation with which he bought an estate in **Islay**. Captain Bushel, though pursued by the civic authorities, received official protection.

SHEEP, see BLACKFACE, CHEVIOT, SOAY

etc.

SHERIFFMUIR, Battle of (1715)

The 1715 **Jacobite Rising** started in earnest when, on 6 September, **John, 6th Earl of Mar** (known as 'Bobbing John' for his habit of changing sides) raised the standard of **James Francis Edward Stewart**, the Old Pretender, at **Braemar** and set off southwards to join up with Jacobites in England. By the end of the month he had gathered a force of some 12,000 and occupied **Inverness**; by November he occupied the east coast as far south as **Perth**, and was now ready to head for England.

In the interim, however, **John, 2nd Duke of Argyll**, had rallied a pro-Hanoverian force of some 4000 and moved to block Mar's route past the Forth. By the time the two armies met on 13 November 1715, Mar's numerical superiority had been somewhat reduced by his decision to send William Mackintosh of Borlum and 2000 men across the Forth to **Edinburgh** and thence to join the Jacobites of south-west Scotland. But he still had 10,000 men to Argyll's 4000.

Sheriffmuir lies a little to the north-east of **Dunblane** in **Perthshire** on the western slopes of the **Ochils**. Argyll drew up his forces on the rising ground; he himself commanding the right and General Whetham the left. MacDonell of **Glengarry**, Maclean of **Duart** and

MacDonald of Clanranald, who commanded the centre and right wing of the rebel army, commenced the battle with a furious attack on General Whetham. The Highlanders charged sword in hand and 'with such impetuosity' that the left wing of the King's troops immediately gave way, and a 'complete rout and prodigious slaughter' took place. General Whetham fled at full gallop to **Stirling** and there declared the royal army totally defeated. Meanwhile Argyll, at the head of a party of dragoons, had attacked the other flank of his enemy and driven them back about two miles to the edge of the Allan Water. The left flank of each side had thus been defeated, and neither wished to prolong the battle. Mar withdrew to Perth and Argyll to Dunblane.

> There's some say that we wan,
> And some say that they wan,
> And some say that nane wan at a', man;
> But ae thing I'm sure,
> That at Sheriffmuir
> A battle there was that I saw, man
> And we ran and they ran, and they ran and we ran,
> And we ran and they ran awa' man.
>
> *Anon*

Although both sides claimed victory, it was the Jacobite cause that was in fact defeated. Mar's failure to crush Argyll was bad propaganda and the French and the Spanish were thereafter reluctant to support what was apparently a failing cause. The Rising lingered on for a further two and a half months, but even the arrival of James Francis Edward at **Peterhead** three days before Christmas 1715 could do nothing to revive it.

SHERRIFF, George (1898–1967) Plant Hunter

Born in Larbert, **Stirlingshire**, George Sherriff served in the army during World War I and then became Vice-Consul and eventually Consul at Kashgar (Sinkiang). From 1932 he undertook a series of adventurous plant collecting trips in the Eastern Himalaya with botanists Frank Ludlow and, on occasions, Sir George Taylor of Belhaven. They collected over 21,000 specimens (including primula, rhododendron and meconopsis) and Sherriff also took thousands of photographs. He received the Victoria Medal from the Royal Horticultural Society. He retired in 1952 to Ascreavie near **Kirriemuir** and, with his wife, developed a fine garden with many Himalayan plants.

SHETLAND

In the jargon of the European Community Shetland is one of a number of 'Peripheral Maritime Regions', and it is indeed peripheral when viewed, as it usually is, in a British context. But in the context of a Scandinavian-based civilisation which extended from the Baltic to Greenland and from the North Cape to Normandy, Shetland was almost central. Little more than 160 miles separate the easternmost islands of the Shetland group from Utvaer Light off the Norwegian coast, and **Lerwick**, Shetland's capital, is almost equidistant (200 miles) from Bergen in Norway, **Aberdeen** in Scotland and Torshavn in Faroe. These geographical facts have done much to determine the history, economy and culture of the islands.

As soon as the inhabitants of Norway discovered that there was land to the west – perhaps through the chance deposit on their shores of plant-life and artefacts, or even of storm-driven mariners – migration began to lands which offered plunder for the rapacious and agricultural opportunities for the peaceable and industrious. Shetland, though it had limited arable land, was attractive enough to land-hungry Norwegians who sought pasture for sheep and cattle, as well as rich **fishing** and the fowling-cliffs to which they were accustomed at home. Peaceful settlement probably preceded by many generations the **Viking** raids on which attention is usually focused. However, Shetland was often only the first stage in migration to the west and south in an era of astounding Scandinavian expansion.

The islands had been inhabited before such identifiable migrants appeared. There are ample signs of pre-Norse inhabitants dating from Stone Age, Bronze Age and early Iron Age times, and at **Jarlshof** near the southern tip of the **Mainland**, Shetland's largest island, there can be seen remains of a series of cultures extending through those ages and on to the 16th century. Easily the most impressive prehistoric structures are the **brochs**, dating from the beginning of the Christian era. The broch culture was centred on **Orkney**, but Shetland (like **Caithness**) has nearly as many brochs as Orkney, and they include the finest of them all, on **Mousa**.

History begins with Harald the Fairhaired, who united Norway into one kingdom at the end of the 9th century. To consolidate his position he had to conduct a campaign against Vikings (some of them his defeated enemies) who were infesting Shetland, Orkney and the **Hebrides**. He established an Earldom of Orkney which included Shetland, Caithness and **Sutherland** and which was ruled from 911 by men of the same family as the dukes who ruled Normandy.

There had been Christianity in the islands before the time of Harald the Fairhaired, but he was a pagan and the Earls of Orkney were not converted to Christianity until about 990. In the next century the Earl established a bishopric for Orkney and Shetland; it was part of the ecclesiastical province of Trondheim, where the Norwegian bishop had his seat.

Shetland remained under Norwegian sovereignty for six centuries, usually as part of the Orkney Earldom (which was latterly held by Scots), but from 1195 until at least 1379 under a governor appointed directly from Norway, which meant that Shetland escaped some of the Scotticisation which affected Orkney. Yet there was a degree of Scottish penetration, if only through the appointment of Scots to offices in the Church, for the Bishops of Orkney were Scots from about 1400. It was important, too, that from 1380 the Norwegian crown was worn by Danish kings, who took little interest in the empire west-over-sea. The place-names of Shetland are almost 100% Norwegian, and the dialect spoken today, though basically a form of Lowland Scots, contains many Scandinavian words and idioms. The local boats, like those of Norway, Faroe and Iceland, plainly descend from the Viking ships of 1000 years ago.

In 1468, when it was arranged that **James III** of Scotland should marry Margaret, daughter of Christian I of Denmark and Norway, her dowry was put at 60,000 florins of the Rhine. Christian was to pay 10,000 down, and for 50,000 he pledged his lands and rights in Orkney. But he found that he could raise only 2000 and therefore in 1469 pledged his lands and rights in Shetland for the balance of 8000. In a quite distinct transaction in 1470, the Earl of Orkney (and Shetland) made over his own lands to the King of Scots, to whose Crown they were annexed. The royal rights, and sovereignty over the islands, merely pledged in 1468–9, were never formally transferred to Scotland, and when the question was last raised officially, in 1667, it was not denied that the right of redemption still existed.

However, the process of Scotticisation was irreversible. Scotsmen acquired lands as well as offices in the islands. The earldom property was granted by the Scottish kings to their own kinsmen, notably **Robert Stewart** (illegitimate son of **James V** and half-brother of **Queen Mary**), who built a house at Jarlshof, and Robert's son **Patrick**, who built **Scalloway** Castle about 1600. Laurence Bruce of Cultmalindie, who built Scotland's most northerly castle, at **Muness** in **Unst**, in 1598, had the same mother as Robert Stewart. Norwegian law, long preserved in the islands, was abolished in 1611 and the last surviving legal document written in Norse belongs to 1607. **Udal** tenure, by which land was held by individuals in absolute property, without superiors, was largely replaced by the feudal system and the accumulation of large estates on which most farmers were only tenants. Although some native usages long survived, the judicature and the administration gradually became indistinguishable from those of Scotland.

The 16th century saw the **Reformation**, the course of which in Shetland had some parallels to what happened in Scandinavia, whence some Lutheran influence may well have come. The reform of the Church in the diocese of Orkney and Shetland was carried through by the bishop; it took a moderate course, and no Roman Catholicism survived. The **Presbyterian** system did not operate until the 17th century, and later schisms, which split the **Church of Scotland**, left little mark on the islands.

Norway was not the only Continental country which influenced Shetland. Bergen, which had been the main focus of communication with Norway (and whose harbour is still approached from the north by Hjeltefjord, or 'Shetland Fjord'), was itself a member of the Hanseatic League of towns, in which German influence predominated (from headquarters at Lubeck). Therefore Shetland's external trade was for generations largely in the hands of merchants from Hamburg and Bremen who sent ships each year to lie in Shetland voes (inlets) and exchange foodstuffs and artefacts for white fish caught and cured by the natives. The **herring** fishing, on the other hand, was conducted largely by Dutchmen until after 1700. In the 18th century, when the rich fishings around the islands were for the first time controlled from Shetland bases, local landlords (by this time mostly of Scottish descent) doubled as merchants, and their tenants, who by their catches of fish paid their rents and obtained the imported goods in which the merchants dealt, were in a state of something like servitude.

The population, which had probably been about

10,000 in 1600, rose to its maximum of 31,670 in 1861. As additional land had to be taken in for cultivation, areas were peopled which had not been inhabited in 1600 and are not inhabited today, and the number of inhabited islands rose to over 30. Large numbers of cattle were kept and crops of oats, bere (barley) and potatoes were grown for human consumption. Each tenant had a **croft**, comprising a few acres of arable land and grazing rights in the 'scattald' or common pasture. But holdings became so small that there was no possibility of making a living from them. It was not in the interests of the landlords to encourage or even permit emigration, but many men found their way out of the islands, partly through the activities of the press gangs which forced seafaring men into the Royal Navy in the late 18th and early 19th centuries and partly by voluntarily joining ships bound for whaling in the Arctic. The women, besides doing much of the agricultural work when the men were away or were fishing, knitted fine shawls and other articles from the many-coloured **wool** of the local sheep.

After 1886 the **Crofters' Act** removed many of the controls which landlords had exercised. In the same era there were notable changes in fishing. The large six-oared boats in which the 'haaf' or deep-sea fishing for white fish had been pursued and which, despite their wonderful sea-going qualities, had sometimes suffered appalling disasters, were superseded by decked boats; oars and sails were superseded by steam and trawling was introduced. The herring fishing had unparalleled success, culminating in the record year of 1905, when over a million barrels were cured in Shetland for export all over Europe. Now free to sell their labour anywhere, Shetlanders made their careers largely in the merchant navy. Women adapted their work to changing fashions, and between the wars, when hand-spinning almost vanished, they had more time to concentrate on knitting and turned their attention largely to the colourful **Fair Isle** patterns. A number of minor industries made modest contributions to the economy; in the early 19th century the making of **kelp** from **seaweed** was profitable; for some generations copper was worked in the south Mainland and chromate of iron in Unst; in the late 19th century and the early 20th red granite was quarried in the island of Hildasay and there were whaling stations in the north Mainland; ponies were bred for work in the **coal-mines** of the south.

Shetland was from time to time involved in British wars where naval operations were taking place in northern waters. Scalloway Castle was garrisoned during the Dutch War of Cromwell's time (1652–4) and there was a fort at Lerwick during the Dutch Wars of 1665–7 and 1672–4. The still existing Fort Charlotte was named after the Queen of George III during the American War of Independence (1776–83) and is an example of a pattern of fortification which had been common throughout western Europe since the mid-16th century. In World War I a cruiser squadron was based in the great stretch of enclosed water on the west side, entered through 'Swarbacks Minn'; there was a seaplane base at Catfirth, and a number of gun emplacements and similar remains from that conflict are still to be seen, for example at the Knab, Lerwick and the Ander Hill

in **Bressay**. World War II, when there was intense activity by land, sea and air in the whole area from Norway to Iceland, gave Shetland unprecedented importance. Large numbers of servicemen were stationed in the islands, there was a seaplane base in **Sullum Voe** and a number of 'incidents' when bombs were dropped or lighthouses were machine-gunned. After Norway was occupied by the Germans, small vessels operated the 'Shetland Bus' (first from Lunna, later from Scalloway) to maintain links with the Norwegian resistance.

The armed forces had little enduring effect on Shetland's way of life and economy. The years just after World War II were perhaps the most dispiriting in the islands' history. The Crofters' Act, though well intentioned, had disastrous effects. Crofters were no longer under any constraint to work their holdings and – after a brief pause following World War II when there was some reclamation of moorland – something of a flight from cultivation occurred and the once ubiquitous cow seemed almost to vanish. In the century after 1883 the number of cattle dropped from 22,000 to 7000 and that of sheep rose from 80,000 to 260,000. Whole areas were depopulated and the number of inhabited islands dropped to about 15. The population stood in 1961 at little over 17,000, not much more than half of what it had been a century earlier. The great days of the herring fishing had ended with World War I and although there was an occasional good season between the wars, that industry seemed to be heading for extinction – and in one later year reached that point. White fishing was more successful, but instead of being spread through the islands, was concentrated in **Skerries**, **Whalsay**, Lerwick, Scalloway and **Burra** Isle. For a time Shetlanders returned to the Antarctic whaling, but this petered out by the early 1960s. New arrangements for recruitment to Britain's dwindling merchant navy put an end to the old pattern of employment there. Economic depression was reflected in demoralisation: 'This place is dying' was a phrase often heard.

Some revival was on the way by the 1960s, mainly in fishing, and morale improved. Thus the **oil** developments of the 1970s did not enter a community which lacked the vitality to come to terms with them. Oil from fields east of Shetland was first piped to Sullum Voe in 1978. The enormous construction activity had required a workforce of about 7000 men, the great majority of them necessarily imported. It was significant that **Sumburgh** airport, through which most of them came and went, handled up to 700,000 passengers in a year. But wages for Shetland men and women rocketed, and unimagined affluence hit the islands. The population rose sharply to over 25,000, but later fell back to 22,000.

Once the construction phase was over, there was still money to be made – and wisely distributed by the Shetland Islands Council for every kind of good cause. But other changes had helped to shape a new situation: the processing of fish for freezing and exporting, exploitation of shellfish (lobsters, scallops, mussels) and large-scale salmon farming. Nearly a quarter of Shetland's jobs depend on fish. A warning of their vulnerability came in 1993 when the tanker *Braer* was wrecked near Sumburgh. Its 80,000-ton spillage of oil would have been an economic, as well as an environmental, disaster if heavy seas had not largely dispersed it and favourable tides and currents diverted it.

Orkney and Shetland sent an MP to the Scottish Parliament before 1707 and to the British Parliament thereafter – although, owing to the peculiar nature of the franchise, before 1832 only Orcadians had a vote. Since the 1975 reorganisation of **local government** Shetland's local authority has been the Shetland Islands Council, and under the Scotland Act of 1998 Shetland is represented in the **Scottish Parliament** by its own MSP (ie not shared with Orkney).

A significant part in Shetland's life and economy is now played by **tourism**. The attraction of the islands as a place for holidays was slow in coming, mainly because of the sheer ignorance which still largely prevails in the rest of the world, but partly because of difficulty of access. There has long ceased to be any excuse for ignorance. Many books have been written about Shetland from **Sir Walter Scott**'s *The Pirate* (1822) onwards, and in recent years (when the islands have for one reason or another often been in the news) the number of relevant volumes actually in print has been as high as 50. Access from Britain used indeed to be incredibly difficult, partly because Shetland's commerce was so largely with the Continent and partly because the seas separating the place from Scottish ports were notoriously hazardous. But with the development of steam navigation, from 1836 onwards, there were great improvements and by 1891 five steamships weekly in summer and three in winter plied between Aberdeen and Shetland. Air travel arrived just before World War II and expanded rapidly. For a time it seemed that passenger services by sea were heading for extinction, but when (from 1977) larger and stabilised drive-on drive-off ships offered greater reliability and operated overnight services (14 hours) passengers came flocking back – with their cars. Since 1987 there have been crossings between Lerwick and Aberdeen six nights a week. In recent summers a large vehicle and passenger carrier has linked Shetland to Denmark, Norway, Faroe and Iceland.

The area of Shetland is only 547 square miles, but the total length of the archipelago equals the distance from Aberdeen to **Edinburgh**. Internal transport is therefore important. The main roads now far exceed what normal traffic requires, and even the narrower roads are well engineered and surfaced. Car ferries link nearly all the other islands to the Mainland.

In the 19th century many visitors came for the trout fishing but the pre-eminent attractions nowadays are for ornithologists and admirers of cliff scenery, in which the Shetland coast, rising to over 1200ft (366m) at the Kame of **Foula**, over 900ft (274m) at Fitful Head and Saxa Vord and to more than 400ft (120m) at many other points, surpasses all other places in the British Isles save **St Kilda** and the island of **Hoy** in Orkney. The highest hill (Roeness) is less than 1500ft (457m) and the general character of the inland landscape is gently undulating moorland. As the islands are almost treeless, the hills have characteristically clear-cut outlines and the landscape is seen at its best when variety comes from a combination of bright sunlight and light cloud. Although Lerwick is in the same latitude

(60°10') as Cape Farewell in Greenland, Leningrad and the wastes of eastern Asia and Canada which are reckoned Arctic regions, extremes of both heat and cold are checked by the Gulf Stream and by the proximity of the sea, from which no place in Shetland is more than three miles distant. The temperature on most days in the year falls within a range of about 45–55°F (7–13°C). In midsummer, with the sun falling to only 6° below the horizon, there is perpetual daylight. Rainfall is far lower than in western Scotland and western Norway. The feature which some find most disagreeable is the gales, but there may also be calm spells and light winds at any season. The islands have a great appeal to people who seek a measure of solitude, and are a paradise to anyone who has the use of a boat.

SHIANT ISLANDS, Outer Hebrides

Set in the **Minch** some five miles south-east of **Lewis**, the three Shiant Islands, Garbh Eilean, Eilean an Tighe and Eilean Mhuire, boast spectacular cliffs rising to over 400ft (120m) which support large colonies of puffins, guillemots and fulmars. In the 1930s the islands, which had a total population of eight at the turn of the century, were owned by **Sir Compton Mackenzie** who spent some time living and writing on Eilean an Tighe.

SHIEL, Loch, Inverness-shire

Over 20 miles long, very narrow and highly scenic, Loch Shiel lies between Ardgour and **Moidart** due west of **Fort William**. The Road to the Isles and the **Mallaig railway** skirt the head of the loch at **Glenfinnan** where the latter is carried on a many-arched viaduct. This glen is named after the 6th century Celtic St Finnan whose church was some distance down the loch on St Finnan's Isle. Here are buried many MacDonalds of Moidart and from here hailed the great Gaelic poet **Alexander MacDonald** (Alasdair mac Mhaighstir Alastair), the son of the church's last Episcopalian minister. The loch ends at Acharacle, just a mile or so short of the sea.

SHINTY

Its Gaelic name, *camanachd*, identifies shinty as possibly the oldest organised team game of western Europe still played to virtually the same rules. In the pre-Christian epic *Táin Bó Cúalgne* the hero **Cú Chulainn** is depicted taking part in this sport. In 563 **Columba** left Ireland for Scotland in the wake of a quarrel that had supposedly broken out during a game of *camanachd*, so it was brought to Scotland in that year, if not before. Its continuing connection with **Iona** is attested by a 15th century memorial stone which depicts not only the owner's broadsword beneath his name in the old Lombard script, but also his *caman* (stick) with a ball beside it. In Ireland the game developed into hurling, with a larger, softer ball and a shorter, thicker club, and with the establishment of the Irish Hurley Union of 1879, the sport developed a political significance which led to a British government ban in 1917 on carrying a hurling *caman* in public. It was **John Mackay**, the **Glasgow**-born son of a family evicted in the **Sutherland clearances**, who performed a similar service in Scotland for *camanachd* (or shinty – from *sinteag*, 'leap' – as it had come to be called there). As soon as he had founded *The Celtic Monthly* in 1892, he used its pages to present this sport as the embodiment of Highland identity, and to publish portraits and profiles of its leading exponents. His journal ended with his untimely death in 1909 but his influence endured.

Today shinty remains an amateur sport played mainly in the west and central Highlands and **Skye** but also popular in Glasgow, **Aberdeen** and anywhere else with a sizeable Highland community. The rules were standardised in the 19th century and call for a ball of leather outside and cork within, and for hooked sticks with a triangular cross-section which tends to flight the ball; as in ice hockey, both sides of the hook are used to strike the ball, but there are no restrictions on the height to which a stick may be raised. Front teeth often suffer. Pitch, goals and penalty areas follow the arrangement of a football field although the dimensions differ. The sport is now administered by the Camanachd Association and, depending on weather conditions, is played throughout the year with a brief summer break. There are numerous challenge trophies, tournaments, and a league, reorganised in the 1990s into an eight-team premier division plus a first, second and third division north and a first and second division south. Better press and television coverage are attracting more sponsorship and since 1993 a senior-level international between Scotland and Ireland has become a regular fixture. Although the rules of shinty and hurling are standardised for this match, it is probably the only international in the world in which one team is equipped quite differently from the other.

SHIPBUILDING AND MARINE ENGINEERING

ORIGINS In Scotland, with its long indented coastline and numerous inland lochs, boats were the most convenient form of transport from the earliest times. Until the 18th century most vessels [but see *Great Michael*] seem to have been constructed by groups of itinerant shipwrights who made their way round the coast, building and repairing vessels as the need arose. During the early 18th century, permanent shipyards were established on the east coast at **Aberdeen**, **Arbroath**, **Dundee** and **Leith**, and on the Lower **Clyde** by such men as John Scott at **Greenock** in **Renfrewshire**, who formed his company in 1711, and by the Ritchie brothers at **Saltcoats** in **Ayrshire**. At first these yards built small vessels needed for the local and coastal trade, but gradually they began to construct larger ocean-going ships, using timber mostly imported from Wales or North America. Until the American War of Independence (1776–83) most of the ships used on transatlantic voyages by Scotland's **tobacco** and sugar merchants were built in America where there was a plentiful supply of suitable timber. When the war prevented merchants from ordering new tonnage in America, they began to buy from local yards and quite soon a flourishing shipbuilding industry developed in the north-east of Scotland and at the Lower Clyde ports of Greenock, **Port Glasgow** and **Dumbarton**.

STEAM At the same time, **Glasgow** and its surrounding towns became important centres of the fast-developing textile industry, using machinery imported from Eng-

land. After **James Watt**'s development of the separate condenser (in which steam was for the first time condensed outside the cylinder) and, later in the 1780s, the rotary engine, many textile mills were powered by steam. It was not long before local millwrights and engineers began to build steam engines, experimenting with them in the propulsion of ships.

The first commercially viable steamboat, the **Comet**, was built for **Henry Bell** in 1812. With its hull built on the Lower Clyde by an established wooden shipbuilder and its engine and boilers in Glasgow, it set a pattern in steamboat construction which others quickly followed. Between 1812 and 1820, 42 steam ships were built on the river by such established concerns as **William Denny** of Dumbarton, **Scotts of Greenock** and JW Fife of **Fairlie**. The engines were supplied mostly by Glasgow millwrights and engineers, including Duncan McArthur of Camlachie, who trained two celebrated men, **David Napier** and James Cook. Napier and his cousin **Robert** were to become the chief innovators in the development of the marine engine during the 1820s. Robert Napier started his own marine engineering business in 1821, when his cousin opened a large works at Lancefield on the Clyde in the middle of Glasgow. Together they developed a number of improvements to marine engines, culminating in the side lever steeple engine of 1835, so called because of its shape. The following year David Napier leased the now well established Lancefield Foundry to Robert and moved to London. Over the next 20 years the Lancefield Foundry acted as the kindergarten of the Clyde shipbuilding industry. Robert Napier trained men such as William Denny III, the brothers James and George Thomson, John Elder, Charles Randolph and William Pearce, all of whom were prominent shipbuilders later in the century.

IRON Although the Clyde had enjoyed a lead in steam shipbuilding, this was lost in the 1820s and '30s as shipbuilders elsewhere in Britain copied and improved on Henry Bell's example. The Clyde recaptured its dominant position in the next decade by the introduction from England of the new cost-saving technique of **iron** shipbuilding. The first iron shipyard on the Clyde was opened in 1834 by Tod & MacGregor at Meadowside at the mouth of the river Kelvin. It was, however, the entrepreneurial skill of Robert Napier that made the Clyde's reputation for iron shipbuilding. In 1841 Napier opened his own iron shipyard across the river from Lancefield at **Govan**, launching his first ship, the *Vanguard*, in 1843. Despite the misgivings of Lloyd's and the Admiralty, iron ships were an immediate success in the passenger markets; although the initial price was higher, running costs were about 25% less than for wooden hulls. Robert Napier sold his first iron ships to those firms with whom he already had special relationships, either as an engineer or financier, but by the 1860s he had penetrated nearly every passenger market and had built ships for many different owners, including several foreign firms and navies.

BUSINESS METHODS In winning contracts, Napier was often prepared to offer financial inducements or assistance. In 1834 he built the *Dundee* and the *Perth* for the Dundee, Perth & London Shipping Co, deliberately at a loss so as to gain further orders. He justified this in a letter to Patrick Wallace in 1833: 'In getting up the first of these vessels, great care and attention would be necessary to gain the different objects in view and, in doing this, an extra expense may be incurred, but which may be avoided in all the other vessels.' When Samuel Cunard established his British & North American Royal Mail Steam Navigation Co in 1839, Napier took a shareholding in the venture and in return secured orders for the first four vessels. These practices were adopted by many of Napier's pupils when they came to manage their own enterprises. In the 1850s Peter Denny, senior partner in William Denny & Bros, made substantial investments in the ships constructed by his firm.

Perhaps the two most important firms to be established by Napier's employees were J & G Thomson and Randolph, Elder & Co. James and George Thomson set up as marine engineers at the Clyde Bank Foundry in Finnieston in 1847 and John Elder joined the established millwrighting business of Randolph, Elliot & Co in 1852, the name being changed to Randolph, Elder & Co.

COMPOUND ENGINES Both firms quickly gained a reputation for the quality of their products. Randolph, Elder & Co developed the main compound engine, building the first in 1854 for the *Brandon* of the London & Limerick Steamship Co. This engine, in which the steam passed through first a high pressure and next a low pressure cylinder, reduced the rate of **coal** consumed per indicated horsepower from about 4½ to 3¼ lbs. It was ideally suited to the long sea routes to West Africa, Australia, the West Indies and South America, especially down America's coal-less Pacific coast. In the late 1850s Randolph, Elder & Co installed compound engines in most of the Pacific Steam Navigation's fleet with a startling effect on fuel consumption, which was reduced in the case of the *Bogota* from 38 cwts per hour to 19. Both companies depended on family links in establishing their businesses. J & G Thomson opened a shipyard in Govan in 1851 and between then and 1872 built, out of a total production of 110 vessels, 42 ships for companies or individuals connected with **G & J Burns**. Their brother Robert had trained with this firm and was Superintendent Engineer with its sister concern, Cunard & Co. When Randolph, Elder & Co began iron shipbuilding at a small yard in Govan in 1860, they built their first vessel, the *MacGregor Laird*, for the African Royal Mail Co in which John Elder's brother Alexander held a senior position. In 1868, with John Dempster, another employee, he founded Elder, Dempster & Co and the British & African Steam Navigation Co, in which Charles Randolph was one of the principal shareholders. From 1861 to 1874 Randolph, Elder & Co built 16 ships for these concerns.

By the 1860s the contribution of firms like J & G Thomson and Randolph, Elder & Co had given the Clyde an unrivalled position as the most important centre of iron shipbuilding in Britain. Between 1860–70 just over 1 million tons of iron ships were constructed in Britain, of which just under 800,000 tons were built on the Clyde. To accommodate this increase in production, large shipyards were laid out. **Barclay Curle & Co**,

founded in 1845 at Stobcross Pool in the centre of Glasgow, moved down the river to a larger yard in 1855 to allow the firm to compete for bigger vessels. In 1864 Randolph, Elder & Co moved to a new shipyard on a green field site at Fairfield on the south side of the river – 'Having gone lower down the river than any of the other large Glasgow builders, Messrs Randolph, Elder at Fairfield about as complete and convenient a shipbuilding establishment as any in the world.' This investment allowed the firm, which was renamed John Elder & Co at the same time, to dominate Clyde shipbuilding. In 1869, the year of John Elder's death, the firm built 14 steamships and three sailing ships totalling 25,235 tons, nearly double the production of any other Clyde yard. Threatened by this competition, **Alexander Stephen & Sons**, who had moved from Dundee to Kelvinhaugh in 1851, shifted in 1869 to open parkland at Linthouse in Govan, next door to Fairfield. They were followed down the river by J & G Thomson, who moved in 1871 to a remote site at Dalmuir on the north bank of the river, named **Clydebank** after the yard. The **engineering** and boiler works remained in the Thomson's original premises at Finnieston and Kelvinhaugh until 1881–3 when new works were built at Clydebank.

SPECIALISATION By this time individual yards in Scotland had begun to specialise in certain types of vessel, partly as a consequence of the physical limitations of sites and partly as a reflection of the familial and financial relationships between shipbuilders and shipowners. Alexander Hall & Co had established a reputation for fast large sailing vessels with the 'Aberdeen' clipper bow. The Stephen family yards in Dundee were well known as builders of whaling craft with specially strengthened hulls to operate in ice flows. On the Clyde in the 1870s William Simons of **Renfrew**, who had started as general shipbuilders in Greenock in 1818, were producing mainly dredgers and ancillary craft. Russell & Co was established at Port Glasgow in 1874 specifically to build large sailing vessels, the bulk carriers of their day. On the Forth, Ramage & Ferguson, established in 1878, devoted attention to building both sailing and steam yachts. This trend in specialisation continued in the last three decades of the century as vessels became larger and more complex. The yards on the upper reaches of the Clyde, such as Alexander Stephen & Sons, Barclay Curle & Co and Charles Connell & Co, capable of building the largest ships of the 1880s, could not increase their capacity without moving. Such restrictions encouraged firms to reinforce their links with their major customers, offering them greater financial inducements and designing vessels to match the specific requirements of each trade. Barclay Curle & Co formed strong links with the Glasgow-based British India Steam Navigation Co while Cairds of Greenock was linked with British India's competitor, P&O, and Scotts of Greenock to the China Steam Navigation Co.

STEEL With the development of mild steel in the late 1870s, Scottish shipbuilders quickly abandoned wrought iron in favour of this new material which was lighter and could be rolled into much wider plates. This allowed for the construction of even larger vessels. By

Shipbuilding and Marine Engineering continued
1884, 45% of launchings on the Clyde were steel ships and within five years this total had risen to over 97%. The changeover from iron to steel necessitated extensive re-equipment of the yards with bending rollers and cranes capable of handling the larger plates and sections. Mild steel, which was tougher than iron, made it possible to raise boiler pressure safely which, in turn, permitted A C Kirk of Robert Napier & Sons to introduce the triple expansion engine in 1881. This engine which, as its name implies, had three cylinders, was much more economic in service than the existing compound engine and soon became popular with owners, attracting more custom to the Clyde.

RATIONALISATION Although the output from the Clyde shipyards expanded dramatically between 1870 and 1913 to reach a peak of over 3/4 million tons, it would be misleading to suggest that the growth was consistently sustained. The industry was subject to periods of boom and slump. The marked effect of the trade cycle on the industry's output is a reflection of the direct relation of shipbuilding to world trade for, with the onset of a depression, freight rates fell and owners cancelled contracts for new tonnage. The shipbuilders reacted by reducing prices and by offering even more generous financial support. Wages were cut, often triggering industrial unrest in the yards. This combination of circumstances forced weaker firms out of business. In September 1878, in the trough of one of the worst depressions in the 19th century, J E Scott, owner of the Cartsdyke shipyard in Greenock, became

bankrupt. He had begun shipbuilding in 1874 with a capital of £2,500 borrowed from friends. He had good returns in 1874 and 1875, but was in difficulty in 1876 through contracting to build hulls for three steamers, all of which were delayed by strikes and lockouts caused by wage reductions. He made a loss from every vessel from the beginning of 1877 until the time of his failure in 1878. Such an experience was not uncommon; even the large and prestigious firm of J & G Thomson experienced serious financial problems in the late 1880s.

At the turn of the century sail finally gave way to steam for tramp ships as the triple expansion engine proved itself economic and efficient in operation, and as insurance on sailing vessels became more and more expensive. Yards on the Clyde such as Russell & Co, and Connells of Whiteinch, and Alexander Hall in Aberdeen, switched almost overnight to steamship building. This change had important consequences for owners. Many found the expense of re-equipping prohibitive and withdrew, allowing new steamship companies to take their place. Simultaneously, under the threat of competition from the armaments firms of Armstrong Whitworth and Vickers with yards on the Tyne and at Barrow-in-Furness in Cumbria, the structure of the Clyde industry was changing. In 1899 **John Brown & Co**, the Sheffield steelmakers, took over the yard of J & G Thomson at Clydebank to provide an outlet for their heavy forgings. In the same year **William Beardmore**, the owner of the Parkhead Forge in the east of the city,

Preparing hull supports and drag chains for a launch at Alexander Stephen & Sons' Linthouse shipyard (BRC)

purchased the goodwill of Robert Napier & Sons with the intention of moving the yard downstream to new large purpose-built naval shipbuilding and engineering works at Dalmuir. These took five years to complete and cost over £1 million. Early in their construction, William Beardmore ran out of money and was forced to sell a controlling interest in his business to Vickers Sons & Maxim. This combination troubled John Browns and the **Fairfield Shipbuilding & Engineering Co** (previously John Elder & Co), both of which by now depended on warship contracts for a large slice of their order book. During 1906–7 they entered into an agreement with the Sheffield and Birkenhead steelmakers and shipbuilders Cammell Laird to form the Coventry Syndicate to tender jointly for naval work and to build an ordnance factory at Coventry. In 1907 a much more powerful alliance was forged when John Browns acquired a 50% shareholding in the Belfast shipbuilders **Harland & Wolff** to create the largest shipbuilding group in the world. The purpose of this alliance was to give John Browns entry to Harland & Wolff's group of prestigious customers for large passenger liners and Harland & Wolff access to John Brown's turbine technology and cheap forgings. The marine turbine, a rotary engine driven by passing steam under pressure through blades attached to a spindle, had been developed in the north-east of England by Sir Charles Parsons from the turn of the century and perfected for the propulsion of warships and large passenger vessels by John Browns.

INCOMERS These changes in ownership and connections were accompanied by the arrival of a newcomer on the river from London, the specialist warship builders **Yarrow & Co**. This firm had decided to move because space at their Thames-side site was limited and both wages and steel were cheaper in Glasgow. Their new yard, situated at Scotstoun, was constructed in less than 12 months. Six years later Harland & Wolff made a direct investment on the river by purchasing the London & Glasgow Engineering and Iron Shipbuilding Company, owners of the Middleton shipyard in Govan and the Lancefield Engine Works across the river in Finnieston. The Middleton shipyard was to provide the company with additional capacity, while the Lancefield Works were converted for the manufacture of the newly invented internal combustion diesel engine. Lord Pirrie, the Chairman of Harland & Wolff, was enthusiastic about the potential of the marine diesel, which had been developed on the Continent, particularly in Germany and Denmark. He outmanoeuvred Barclay Curle & Co to acquire the United Kingdom licence for the Danish Burmeister & Wain engines and in 1912 began building their diesels at Lancefield for installation in ships built by Harland & Wolff either in Glasgow or Belfast. In 1913 the Tyne shipbuilders Swan Hunter acquired Barclay Curle.

WARTIME BOOM After the outbreak of World War I in August 1914, the Admiralty began to place orders for new naval ships with established warship-builders and to divert supplies of steel away from merchant builders. As the war intensified, so orders were placed with other specialist builders like Dennys and Lobnitz on the Clyde

and Alexander Hall in Aberdeen. Tramp shipbuilders, such as Russell & Co of Port Glasgow, Henry Robb of Leith and the **Caledon** yard of Dundee, that lacked naval or specialist experience, were left at a considerable disadvantage. There were also major labour difficulties due to the large number of skilled men who had volunteered at the beginning of the war. A solution to this problem was found by persuading the unions to agree to semi-skilled men doing skilled jobs and the introduction of women workers. By early 1917, with rapidly escalating losses of merchant ships, a merchant shipbuilding programme became an urgent priority. The young **James Lithgow**, a partner with his brother Henry in Russell & Co, was recalled from the Front to manage a new Department of Merchant Shipbuilding. He pushed through a programme for constructing tramp ships to standard designs and for the extension of shipyards. Under this scheme several Scottish yards increased their capacity by adding new berths and enlarging engine works. To meet the greatly increased demand for steel, new steelworks were constructed. Lithgow's efforts were well rewarded with a huge rise in output. At the end of the war the capacity of the Clyde industry alone had increased by about a third. The owners optimistically assumed that all this additional capacity could be profitably employed in peacetime.

The war had brought further concentration. Russell & Co of Port Glasgow, which changed its name to **Lithgows Ltd** in 1918, continued a policy of acquisition started in 1912, by taking over the neighbouring yards of Robert Duncan & Co and William Hamilton Ltd. Harland & Wolff, either itself or through its association with the Royal Mail Shipping Group, purchased Caird & Co of Greenock, A & J Inglis of Pointhouse, D & W Henderson of Meadowside and Archibald MacMillan of Dumbarton. Directly after the war it also acquired **David Colville** & Sons, the **Lanarkshire** steelmakers. Most of the other larger shipbuilders on the Clyde formed similar links with steelmakers. In 1920 William Beardmore & Co, despite its already substantial investment in steel-making capacity, joined with Swan Hunter, Wigham, Richardson & Co, the owners of Barclay Curle, to acquire the Glasgow Iron & Steel Co, which had a well equipped works at Wishaw. During the year Lithgows acquired the Clydesdale works of James Dunlop & Co, and a syndicate comprising Alexander Stephen & Sons, Yarrow & Co, Scotts Shipbuilding & Engineering Co of Greenock, and the Campbeltown Shipbuilding Co, bought the Steel Company of Scotland.

PEACETIME SLUMP At first it seemed that the shipbuilders' confident predictions about future prospects were justified. Order books were filled as shipowners sought to replace tonnage lost during the war, but by the opening months of 1921 the economy was moving sharply into recession. Shipbuilders found it increasingly difficult to secure contracts for new vessels in a very dull market. Faced with this collapse in demand, the shipbuilders found their integration with steelmakers an embarrassment. Early in 1923 urgent talks were held between all the steelmaking companies in Scotland in an effort to find ground for common agreement to rationalise the industry. These talks came to nothing as it soon became apparent that William Beardmore & Co, one of the principal instigators, was in serious financial difficulties. Beardmore's position worsened steadily throughout the 1920s, culminating in a massive reduction in the company's capital in 1928. By this time many Scottish shipbuilding companies, along with their competitors elsewhere in Britain, were in desperate trouble. Demand for new tonnage had remained at a very low level for all types of vessel since 1921 and the signing of the Washington Treaty in December of that year had reduced naval shipbuilding almost to nothing. Henry Robb Ltd, the Leith shipbuilders, took over two of their competitors on the Forth – the Leith yard of Hawthorn Leslie, the Tyne shipbuilders, in 1924, and Cram & Somerville Ltd in 1926. At the end of April 1929 Sir James Lithgow and other representatives of the industry as a whole met the Governor of the Bank of England, Montagu Norman, to propose the formation of an association to close redundant yards financed by a levy of 1% on all new tonnage launched. Norman was enthusiastic and the company National Shipbuilders Security Ltd (NSS) was established a year later. Its first action was to acquire the shipbuilding rights over the Dalmuir Yard of William Beardmore & Co.

The formation of NSS coincided with the massive slump in the world economy and rumours that the Royal Mail Group, which owned Harland & Wolff and its subsidiaries, was more or less insolvent. This cast a shadow over the efforts to rationalise the Scottish steel industry, which were now about to bear fruit in the restructuring of the industry around David Colville & Sons. As Colvilles was peripheral to the Royal Mail Group, those responsible for the rescue of the group allowed the amalgamation to go ahead. Later NSS was able to acquire from this group the building rights over Caird's yard at Greenock, MacMillan's yard in Dumbarton and D & W Henderson's yard at Meadowside. By 1937 NSS had succeeded in reducing capacity on the Clyde by some 19%; seven yards had been closed, two had been mothballed, and three were working under restricted quotas. These were years of crisis. In December 1931 work on the new giant liner, Ship No 534 (the **Queen Mary**), building at John Brown's Clydebank yard, was suspended because the owners, Cunard, could not agree terms with the government for additional finance. 3000 men were laid off. The enormous, almost completed, hull on the ways soon became a national symbol of the Depression. In his book *The Shipbuilders* which portrays the problems of the Clyde industry in the early 1930s, **George Blake** described the hull as 'looming in its abandonment like a monument to the glory departed, as if shipbuilding man had tried to do too much and had been defeated by the mightiness of his own conception'. Work did not resume until 1934 when Cunard reluctantly agreed to amalgamate with the White Star Line in return for government finance for the ship and a second superliner, the **Queen Elizabeth**.

RECOVERY AND WORLD WAR II By the time the *Queen Mary* was launched in September 1934, the outlook for the Scottish yards was improving following the government's decision to rearm in response to the threat posed by Hitler's Germany. But shipbuilders were not enthusiastic about investing in new plant for the rearmament programme as they feared that when it ended in 1938 they would be left with redundant capacity as in 1919. During the war all the Clyde yards were pressed into national service and some of those which had been closed by NSS were temporarily reopened. In raising output, the Admiralty and the Department of Merchant Shipbuilding, led by Sir James Lithgow, concentrated on increasing productivity using new methods of construction such as welding rather than enlarging yards. Engineers with no experience of shipbuilding, such as P & W MacLellan of Glasgow, were employed in fabricating simple hulls for landing craft and the floating structures used in the Mulberry harbour which was floated across the Channel after the Allied landing.

Launch of SS Belfast at Stephen's yard in 1954 (BRC)

After the war demand for all types of ships was strong. But shipbuilders remained reluctant to invest heavily in new facilities. Steel was in short supply and the government imposed severe restrictions on materials for new buildings. When world demand showed no sign of slackening, yards began to plan new plant to meet strengthening competition from Japan, Germany and Scandinavia; but they seriously misjudged the market in believing that demand for their traditional products would remain buoyant. The staple product of the Clyde – passenger ships of all varieties – prospered briefly because of wartime sinkings and the technical difficulties that delayed the introduction of cheap, reliable air transport. Barclay Curle & Co, Alexander Stephen & Sons and Fairfield extensively re-equipped in the early 1960s, largely to meet markets that were to disappear within a few years. As a result, the firms failed; Barclay Curle closed its shipyard in 1965, Fairfield went into liquidation in the same year, and Alexander Stephen & Sons' yard was dismantled in 1968.

THE CRISIS OF THE '60s The demise of the passenger ship market in the 1960s was accompanied by a change in world shipping practice. Up-river harbours were closed in favour of ports at river mouths, and consequently the demand fell for dredgers, in which four Clyde yards specialised. At the same time new roads and bridges replaced ferries, which had been built by the smaller Scottish yards since the 1840s. In 1958 the dredger-building firms of William Simons & Co and Lobnitz & Co, neighbours in Renfrew, amalgamated and were taken over a year later by G & J Weir, the Glasgow marine pump manufacturers, who in turn sold the goodwill to Alexander Stephen & Sons in 1964 and closed the yards. William Denny & Bros of Dumbarton, specialists in ferries, went into liquidation in 1962 after an abortive attempt to reconstruct as hovercraft builders. The following year, under pressure from the government, Harland & Wolff withdrew from the Clyde to concentrate on their Queen's Island yard at Belfast.

Although closures were inevitable, neither the builders nor the government were prepared for the crisis on the Upper Clyde in the mid-1960s. Desultory attempts had been made by the shipbuilders throughout the 1950s to find a solution by amalgamation. John Brown had made occasional overtures to Fairfield, and Lithgow had tried in turn to sell Fairfield to shipowning companies. By 1962 the situation had become impossible; the majority of the yards on the Upper Clyde were incurring substantial losses through fixed-price contracts, poor productivity, and rising material costs. On the liquidation of Fairfield Shipbuilding & Engineering Co in 1965, Fairfield (Glasgow) Ltd was formed to manage the shipyard, with government backing and under the control of Iain Stewart. He was convinced that the shipbuilding industry was not managerially equipped to remain competitive, principally through bad labour relations, reinforced by lack of communication and a failure to introduce the production techniques being evolved in the engineering industry. In Fairfield (Glasgow) Ltd he tried to correct both these problems. With the first he was partially successful, but the price that had to be paid in wages was high and only aggravated the problems of other yards by pushing up the wages rate generally on the river. The introduction of production engineering was fiercely criticised by other builders in the belief that shipbuilding could not be forced into the straitjacket of work measurement and standard time. Unfortunately Iain Stewart did not have time to prove his case. In 1967 the Geddes Committee, condemning the industry for its short-sighted attitudes, recommended the amalgamation of all the surviving yards on the upper reaches of the Clyde (John Brown, Yarrow & Co, Charles Connell & Co, Alexander Stephen & Sons and Fairfield) into Upper Clyde Shipbuilders Ltd. The amalgamation was pushed through in 1968 by the Labour government, in the belief that Geddes and the government knew best, and without taking the specialities of the individual firms into account. The engine works were split off and remained independent. John Brown and Fairfield, as large passenger shipbuilders, themselves ill-sorted bedfellows, were quite unsuited to amalgamation with Alexander Stephen

& Sons, small passenger shipbuilders, whose yard was anyway not viable, and Charles Connell & Co, traditionally tramp builders. Yarrow & Co, as naval specialists, were always the odd man out. Moreover if Upper Clyde Shipbuilders Ltd was to have effected a long-term reconstruction of the industry on the Clyde it required a fresh start. Unfortunately several loss-making and very specialised contracts, such as the *Queen Elizabeth 2* and HMS *Fife*, were carried forward. As a result the company was unable to implement Geddes' recommendation to build standard cargo ships on a production-line basis to meet certain specific target dates. In the event Yarrow & Co withdrew in 1971 and **Upper Clyde Shipbuilders** was liquidated in 1972. The blaze of publicity surrounding the collapse of the company, and the subsequent work-in, forced Edward Heath's Conservative government to abandon its 'lame duck' policy and provide a rescue package. The Fairfield and Connell yards were reformed as Govan Shipbuilders Ltd and the Clydebank yard sold to Marathon (UK) Ltd for building **oil** exploration rigs, later passing to the French group UIE.

By contrast the yards of the Lithgow group at Port Glasgow, Scotts Shipbuilding & Engineering Co at Greenock, and Yarrow & Co, were able to remain independent. Yarrow, on the formation of Yarrow Admiralty Research Department (YARD) in 1948–9, had effectively tied up the naval market, leaving all the other naval builders at a disadvantage. Lithgow's Kingston yard was reconstructed to build very large crude carriers and laid out to facilitate an efficient materials flow and to keep charges to a minimum. Although the group had acquired the engine works of John Kincaid & Co, Rankin & Blackmore and David Rowan & Co in the inter-war years, these companies had wisely been allowed to retain their autonomy. With the fall in demand the firm was able to close David Rowan and Rankin & Blackmore without damaging the group as a whole. Kincaid's was left as the group's engine builders and maintained its competitiveness by strong management and a continuous programme of re-equipment. Scotts Shipbuilding & Engineering Co was better placed on the Lower Clyde at Greenock than up-river builders and had, anyway, always effectively straddled the naval, passenger and cargo ship markets by specialising in submarines, second- and third-rate liners, and by building oil tankers and general cargo ships. Following the recommendations of the Geddes Committee Lithgow and Scotts were obliged to amalgamate in 1967. Similarly, on the east coast, Caledon Shipbuilding & Engineering Co of Dundee merged with Henry Robb of Leith to form the short-lived Robb Caledon Shipbuilders Ltd.

NATIONALISATION AND OIL RIGS Over the next 10 years the world market for ships of all types deteriorated badly. Even Japan, which had taken Britain's place as the leading shipbuilding country in the 1960s, found it difficult to win custom. Demand for very large tankers, which had become popular after the closure of the Suez Canal, evaporated after the Yom Kippur war of 1974 as inflation bit deep and world oil consumption plummeted. The search for alternative sources of oil on the seabed created demand for totally new types of floating structure, met largely by the creation of new rig-building yards operated by structural and civil engineers rather than traditional shipbuilders. A number of rig building yards were opened around the Scottish coast, notably at Ardyne Point on the Firth of Clyde, **Nigg** Bay in **Ross & Cromarty**, **Methil** and Kinghorn in **Fife**. The Labour government responded by nationalising the shipbuilding industry in 1977, the only conceivable way of retaining any semblance of an industry in the United Kingdom. The existing structure was retained under the umbrella of a holding company, British Shipbuilders Ltd. On the Clyde Scott Lithgow was encouraged to diversify into the construction of large production oil platforms, using the big slip designed to take large tankers. After the election of Mrs Thatcher's Conservative government in 1979, there was a move to privatise the profitable parts of the nationalised industry and reduce the enormous losses that were being clocked up by the other sections. In 1985 Yarrow Shipbuilders Ltd, the specialist warship constructors, was acquired by GEC. The year before, when it became apparent that Scott Lithgow, which had attempted to diversify into oil rig building, was in serious financial and technical difficulties, the business was sold in a rescue package to the Trafalgar House group. Its capacity has since been closed. Ferguson-Ailsa, which specialises in small off-shore vessels and dredgers, has been rationalised into one yard at Port Glasgow and has been amalgamated with the North Devon company Appledore Shipbuilders Ltd.

The outlook for what is left of the Scottish industry remains bleak. Low oil prices mean a shortage of orders for exploration and production rigs while the end of the Cold War has led to a cutback in naval orders. Yarrows, the only surviving builder of warships, is now owned by GEC while Fairfields of Govan, the other remaining upper Clyde shipbuilder, has passed to the Finnish company Kvaerner and then on to GEC. Every change of ownership brings more job losses, and the struggle for orders goes on.

Barclay Curle & Co

John Barclay began shipbuilding at Stobcross Pool, **Glasgow**, in 1818. His son Robert expanded the business and developed a repair yard, largely to careen American-built clippers. In 1845 the partnership between Robert Barclay, Robert Curle and James Hamilton, which gave its name to the company, was formed. The partners took on John Ferguson as yard manager to develop **iron** shipbuilding and in 1848 launched one of the largest vessels then built on the **Clyde**, the City of Glasgow, 500 tons. In 1855 the company moved down-river to Whiteinch, where larger vessels could be built. Two years later an independent engine works was established. The firm specialised from the 1870s in cargo passenger liners largely for services to India and aross the North Atlantic. These included the Jutlandia (1911), the first ocean-going diesel engine ship constructed in Britain. The following year Barclay Curle took over the North British Engine Works and itself became a subsidiary of the Tyne shipbuilders Swan Hunter. Despite extensive modernisation the shipyard was closed in 1965.

William Beardmore & Co

Beardmores traced its origin to the establishment of a forge in the east end of **Glasgow** by the Reoch brothers in 1841. William Beardmore was brought up from London to help run the concern in 1861, particularly to fashion armour plate for an ironclad being built at **Robert Napier**'s yard. Under his direction the forge became the largest in Scotland. When he died in 1877, his son (also **William Beardmore**) took control, expanding the forge, diversifying into steelmaking in the 1880s and later armour plate production. When his larger customers formed alliances with English armour plate makers he bought Napier's yard and built a large new naval construction works at Dalmuir. But he had overstretched himself and was forced to sell out to the Sheffield forgemasters and shipbuilders Vickers. During World War I the business expanded to include munitions manufacture, airship and aircraft construction, the building of tanks, motor vehicles and later **locomotives**. In the Depression that followed, these ventures proved uneconomic and the company had to be rescued by the Bank of England. All the plant, including the Dalmuir yard, was closed except for the Parkhead Forge, which eventually passed to Firth Brown. It closed in the early 1980s and is now the site of Glasgow's **Forge** Shopping Centre.

John Brown Shipbuilding & Engineering Co

This celebrated shipyard had its origins in 1847 when the brothers James and George Thomson established the Clyde Bank Foundry, a marine engineering business, at Finnieston, **Glasgow**. A shipyard was opened four years later. The first vessel, the Cunard paddle steamer Jackal, was launched in 1852. From the outset the firm specialised in high quality passenger craft, building the Cunard record-breaker, Russia, in 1867. The move down-river to **Clydebank** in 1879 and the opening of a large modern engine works from 1884 enabled the firm to become one of the leading British shipbuilders with vessels like the elegant City of Paris and City of New York in 1888. In 1897 the firm was reconstructed as the Clydebank Shipbuilding & Engineering Company, passing out of the hands of the Thomson family. The new company did not prosper and in 1899 it was taken over by the Sheffield steelmakers and forgemasters John Brown & Co, who at once modernised the plant, winning much business (the ill-fated Lusitania for Cunard in 1907 and HMS Hood in 1920). The yard was seriously affected by the Depression and in 1932 lack of finance forced work to be abandoned on the giant Cunarder, Ship No 534, which became a national symbol of the slump. The decision to restart construction in 1934 brought hope to the whole country. Named **Queen Mary**, she was instantly popular with passengers on the North Atlantic. The fortunes of the yard recovered during World War II and in the early 1950s. In 1965 the shipyard became part of the newly constituted Upper Clyde Shipbuilders and completed its last major contract, the QE2, four years later. Shipbuilding ceased in 1972.

Caledon Shipbuilding & Engineering Co

This shipyard was established by W B Thompson in 1874 at Marine Parade, **Dundee**. After training as an engineer, Thompson had worked for several years as manager of the **engineering** department of the Abo shipyard in Finland, returning home in 1866 to establish the Tay Foundry in Dundee. The yard was named after his first contract – a yacht for the Earl of Caledon. Over the next 25 years Thompson developed a successful steam shipbuilding business, specialising in tugs. In 1884 he built the *Indra*, the most powerful tug in the world. Four years later he expanded his business by moving to the Craigie yard (renamed Caledon). The *Californian*, built in 1901, gained notoriety in 1911 by failing to answer the stricken *Titanic*'s call for help. The firm constructed the first motor tanker, the *Sebastian*, in 1913. Towards the end of World War I a completely new yard was laid out. In the inter-war years Caledon pioneered new designs in coastal craft and motor cargo liners. It amalgamated with the shipbuilders Henry Robb of **Leith** in 1968 to form Robb Caledon. The yard closed in the 1980s.

William Denny & Bros, Dumbarton

Although the firm of William Denny & Bros was not established until 1845, the family had long been associated with shipbuilding on the lower **Clyde**. In 1814 William Denny II, the father of the founder, had built the *Marjory*, the first **iron** steamer on the Thames. The company opened an engine works in 1850 and began specialising in river craft. Under the direction of Peter Denny the family took a large shareholding in the Irrawaddy Flotilla Company, immortalised in Rudyard Kipling's 'The Road to Mandalay'. In 1883 William Denny III constructed the first commercial test tank in the world, with advice from R E Froude, the son of its inventor. It still survives in the care of the Scottish Maritime Museum and is open to the public. The firm built the first steel ship, the *Rotomahana*, in 1878 and the first turbine steamer, the *King Edward*, in 1901. Denny's remained wedded to their traditional market until the late 1950s when they made an abortive attempt to diversify into hovercraft. Their business closed in 1962.

Fairfield Shipbuilding & Engineering Co

In 1852 John Elder, the son of David Elder (**Robert Napier**'s works manager), joined the well established millwrighting business of Randolph Elliot & Co. Immediately the firm began making marine engines and boilers. Two years later, in collaboration with **William MacQuorn Rankine**, the partners invented the marine compound engine which reduced **coal** consumption by a quarter and later by more than a half. Orders flowed in from companies operating long-haul routes. In 1864 the Fairfield shipyard was laid out on a greenfield site in **Govan**, one of the largest and most complete of the time. Four years later a vast new engine works was constructed at Fairfield. By that time 111 compound engines had been built. John Elder died in 1869 and the firm was taken over by William Pearce, general manager of Robert Napier's works, who reconstructed the firm as Fairfield Shipbuilding & Engineering. Under his control it became perhaps the most important yard in Western Europe, constructing some of the fastest and most technically advanced ships of the time. Between 1875–85 Pearce designed a series of 'greyhounds of the Atlantic' that held the Blue Riband, including the *Arizona* (1879) and the *Umbria* and *Etruria*. At the same time the firm's development of the even more efficient triple expansion engine opened up new markets for

vessels trading on the very long routes to India and the Antipodes. The size of the berths at Fairfield made it difficult for the business to compete for the largest liners after 1900. To compensate Fairfield successfully entered the naval market. In 1919 it became part of the ill-starred Northumberland Shipbuilding Group, which collapsed in 1927. Badly hit by the Depression and lacking adequate financial resources, the business was acquired by the **Port Glasgow** shipbuilding family of **Lithgows** in 1933. But by 1965 there were serious financial problems and closure was only avoided by the intervention of the government and the formation of Fairfield (**Glasgow**) Ltd, which in turn became part of **Upper Clyde Shipbuilders** in 1968. When UCS in turn collapsed in 1977 under pressure from the shop stewards' work-in, the yard was reconstructed as Govan Shipbuilders. Since then it has achieved a reputation for the quality of its passenger ferries, liquid gas carriers and bulk carriers.

Hall Russell & Co, Aberdeen

Alexander Hall & Co owed its origins to the firm of Gibbon Cochar & Hall founded in 1790 to build sailing ships for the coastal trades. This company was successful in designing the 'Aberdeen' clipper bow for large fast ocean-going sailing vessels, many of which were operated by the **Aberdeen** White Star Line. By the end of the century the company was specialising in trawlers, drifters and other small craft. Subsequently the firm amalgamated with Hall Russell & Co, general engineers, which had been established in 1864. After a chequered history in the 1980s, the yard is now closed.

Harland & Wolff

Lord Pirrie, the Chairman of Harland & Wolff, the Belfast shipbuilders, gave notice in 1911 that he was keen to build ships in mainland Britain. He quickly acquired the London & **Glasgow** Shipbuilding & Engineering Co with a yard on the **Clyde** at **Govan**. This was extensively refitted and its engine works (previously **Robert Napier**'s Lancefield Works) re-equipped to build the newly developed marine diesel engine. More acquisitions followed during World War I: on the Lower Clyde, Cairds of **Greenock** and Archibald MacMillan & Son of **Dumbarton**, and on the Upper Clyde D & W Henderson of Meadowside and A & J Inglis of Pointhouse. In the aftermath of hostilities, Pirrie planned huge investments on the Clyde, including the construction of the giant Clyde Foundry. These projects were abandoned with the worsening economic conditions. MacMillans and Cairds closed, along with the Henderson shipyard and the Clyde Foundry. The Govan and Pointhouse yards and the Lancefield Engine Works remained open until the mid-1960s when on government orders operations were concentrated in Belfast.

Lithgows Ltd, Port Glasgow

This business was established in 1874 by three experienced shipbuilders, Joseph Russell, Anderson Rodger and William T Lithgow, to build large sailing ships – the bulk carriers of their day. They were remarkably successful and purchased the Kingston Yard in 1882 when, instead of building to order, they took the novel decision to begin constructing standard vessels. They were also willing to invest in the ships they built. The partnership was dissolved in 1891 and Lithgow carried on at the Kingston Yard alone. He abandoned sail in favour of steam at the turn of the century, specialising in steam tramps. By the time he died in 1907 he had made over £2 million out of the business. He was succeeded by his sons, **James** and Henry, who during and after World War I expanded the enterprise into a large shipbuilding group, owning the Hamilton Yard in **Greenock**, the Fair-field Yard in **Glasgow** and several other **engineering** concerns. The Lithgow Yard was forced to amalgamate with **Scotts** to form Scott-Lithgow in 1967. It was nationalised and eventually closed in the 1980s.

Robert Napier & Sons

Robert Napier, the father of **Clyde** shipbuilding, began business in 1823 when he leased the Camlachie Engine Works from his cousin **David Napier**. When David moved to London in 1836, Robert took over his Lancefield Engine Works not far from the centre of **Glasgow** on the north side of the river. He built on his cousin's reputation for quality, training many of the men who were to found shipyards and marine engine works on the Clyde and further afield in the later 19th century. He also developed a close relationship with Samuel Cunard, helping to finance his shipping enterprise and supplying engines and later ships. Robert opened an **iron** shipyard in 1841 in **Govan**. The yard and engine works soon enjoyed an international reputation for the quality and reliability of its products. Robert Napier retired in 1860, leaving the firm in the hands of his two sons. On his death the yard was sold to a consortium led by A C Kirk, an able engine designer but an inadequate man of business. In 1899–1900 the firm was taken over by the steelmakers **William Beardmore & Co**, which in the next five years moved it to a new naval shipbuilding works at Dalmuir – adjacent to the **John Brown** Yard. The Dalmuir yard was never a success and closed in 1930.

Scotts Engineering Co, Greenock

The oldest shipyard on the **Clyde** was founded by John Scott in 1711 to build **fishing** and small coastal craft. It was not until the 1790s that the firm began to construct ocean-going vessels for the East and West Indian trades. The Scotts were related to **James Watt** and quickly took advantage of his inventions for steam propulsion, building two steamers by 1816 and between 1819–21 the largest steamships in Britain. An engine works was established in 1825 and Scotts became second only to **Robert Napier** for the quality and reliability of their steamships. In 1865 they constructed for Alfred Holt some of the first long-distance steamers powered by the newly developed compound engines. The family became closely related to the Swires, owners of the China Steam Navigation Company, building nearly all their vessels. Scotts were also naval engineers from 1803, going on to build dreadnoughts and submarines. The firm was forced to merge with **Lithgows** in 1967 to form the Scott-Lithgow Group. This was nationalised and subsequently sold to Trafalgar House who have mothballed the yard and use the erecting shops for heavy fabrication.

Alexander Stephen & Sons

Alexander Stephen began building ships at **Burghead**, eight miles from **Lossiemouth** on the Moray Firth, in 1750. He was succeeded by his nephew William, who moved to Footdee, **Aberdeen** in 1793. William's son, also William, set up a yard at **Arbroath** in 1824. In 1828 both yards went bankrupt and were taken over by the elder William's son, Alexander, who renamed the enterprise Alexander Stephen & Sons. The Aberdeen yard closed in 1830 and in 1843 the centre of production moved to **Dundee**. Eight years later Alexander opened an **iron** shipyard at Kelvinhaugh in **Glasgow** before finally settling at Linthouse in 1861. An engine works was added in 1871. This building has been reconstructed as the Scottish Maritime Museum at **Irvine** in **Ayrshire**. The Dundee yard was closed but the Linthouse yard prospered, specialising in intermediate passenger/cargo vessels until it effectively closed in 1968.

Yarrow & Co

Yarrows, the well known naval shipbuilders, was established at Poplar on the Thames in 1865 by Alfred Yarrow, specialising at first in launches and river steamers. Torpedo boats and destroyers followed. By 1906 the yard on the Thames was too small and Yarrow decided to move to Scotstoun on the **Clyde**, laying out a complete new yard and engine works in 18 months. The business continued to specialise in destroyers and fast craft and diversified into the construction of watertube boilers. After an unhappy association with Upper Clyde Shipbuilders in the late 1960s, the company regained its independence. It was nationalised but is now part of GEC.

SHIPPING

Until the **Act of Union** with England in 1707 it was illegal for Scots to trade with English colonies. Directly this prohibition was removed Scotland's overseas trade grew quickly and with the Industrial Revolution Scots shipping came into its own. Scottish sailors and masters were soon known throughout the world, their reputation eclipsed only in the 19th century by the Scots engineer, who had often trained in one of the **Clyde** shipyards. Many British shipping companies, including Cunard, were founded, or part-founded, by Scots. P&O, founded in 1834, was dominated by the Scots **Arthur Anderson**, Sir Thomas Sutherland and Sir James Mackay, first Earl of Inchcape. Other well known passenger lines based in Scotland included Paddy Henderson, formed in 1840 to trade with Burma, the Anchor Line offering services on the North Atlantic (set up in 1856) and the British India Steam Navigation Co established in **Glasgow** in 1862 to trade via the Cape of Good Hope to India. Scottish-owned ships traded everywhere, carrying tea, **wool**, guano, **coal** and many other commodities. Except for passenger and fast cargo services, sail dominated the oceans of the world until the end of the 19th century. When steam finally replaced it, some lines were wound up while others invested in new tramps. Tramp ship companies were nicknamed with typical Scottish humour – Hogarth's of Glasgow were known for example as Hungry Hogarth's. Badly hit by the inter-war recession, Scottish shipping recovered during and immediately after World War II, but declined steadily

Stephen's fitting-out basin on the Clyde (BRC)

from the late 1960s along with the rest of British shipping.

SHIRTS, Battle of the (1544)

On 3 July 1544, in perhaps the bloodiest battle ever fought in the Highlands, some 400 members of the **Clan Fraser**, returning home by way of the **Great Glen**, were engaged by up to 700 of the Clans Ranald, **Cameron** and **Donald**. A dispute over the chieftainship of the Clan Donald of **Moidart** had originally provoked the feud, but in the ensuing battle nothing short of annihilation appealed to the combatants. On a blistering hot day both armies stripped to just their long shirts – hence *Blar na Leine*, 'the field of the shirts' – and then stood their ground on a spot at the southern end of Loch Oich near **Laggan**. From noon till dusk they hacked and thrust, retreating only as far as the waters of the loch, there to continue the butchery in a cooler element. It is said that out of 1000 fighting men only four Frasers and eight of the confederates survived. Amongst the dead were **Lord Lovat** and the Master of Lovat (chief and heir of the Frasers) and the MacDonald Chief. The confederate clans laid claim to this thoroughly pointless victory and were duly visited by a punitive expedition under the 4th **Earl of Huntly** on behalf of **James V**.

SHORT, James (1710–68) Instrument Maker

Short was born in **Edinburgh** and became a protégé of **Colin McLaurin** who encouraged his facility for producing scientific instruments, in particular reflecting telescopes, using firstly glass and later speculum metal. Settled in London from 1738, Short became an outstanding telescope maker; two of his instruments were used by Captain Cook on his first voyage in 1769 to observe the Transit of Venus. Short also had his own observatory and is believed to have been denied the post of Astronomer Royal only on a patron's whim.

SHORTHORN CATTLE

Shorthorns arose in the 18th century in Yorkshire from crosses of Dutch cattle with local stock. Careful selection and breeding led to fine beef cattle which became the most influential breed in the Western world. Later, their milking qualities were developed and the Shorthorn is the classic British dual purpose (beef and milk) breed.

Amos Cruickshank, tenant of Sittyton near **Aberdeen** from 1837 to his death at the age of 88 in 1895, developed the beef qualities of the breed to a greater extent than anyone else. Cattle of his breeding, at first called the Scotch or Aberdeen Shorthorn, then the Beef Shorthorn, did particularly well on the richer rangelands of South America where they laid the foundations for productive beef industries.

From the 1960s this export trade collapsed and the Beef Shorthorn became a rare breed in Britain, with fewer than 1500 breeding females today. Like the **Aberdeen-Angus** it has been squeezed by the big-bodied Continental breeds and today's breeders are seeking to meet the threat by breeding for faster growth and bigger body size.

SHOTTS, Lanarkshire

On moorland east of **Motherwell**, Shotts was once supposed to have the highest arable land in Scotland, with Hirst Hill being the highest point between the firths of **Clyde** and Forth. It was certainly the highest point and halfway stage on the **Edinburgh-Glasgow** road. Before the opening of the **railway**, 20–30 public coaches a day rattled through the parish. Development of the **Lanarkshire coal**field in the late 18th century and the opening in 1802 of the Shotts **iron** works, a serious rival to **Carron Company**, made it a show town of the Industrial Revolution. A century and a half later the last blast furnace was dismantled and the last pit closed (1961). New industries and a major new **prison** provide some alternative employment.

SIBBALD, Sir Robert (1641–1722) Physician

The son of David Sibbald, Keeper of the Great Seal of Scotland under the Earl of Kinnoul, Robert Sibbald was born in **Edinburgh**, studied medicine at **Edinburgh University** and then spent 18 months at Leyden and a further year in Paris studying anatomy and surgery. A strong interest in medicinal botany led him, together with **Andrew Balfour**, to set up Edinburgh's Physic Garden, first near **Holyrood**, then at **Trinity College Kirk** (the site of the present **Waverley Station**). As well as being the basis of the **Royal Botanic Garden**, this collection greatly enhanced Edinburgh's position as a medical centre.

In 1679 Sibbald received from **Charles II** patents to be his Geographer and Physician for Scotland, together with the King's instructions to publish 'the natural history of the country and the geographical description of the kingdom'. Although he had for some time been researching a gazetteer, this further commission was, as he admitted in his *Autobiography*, 'the cause of great pains to me – buying all the books and manuscripts and procuring information from all parts of the country, even the most remote isles'. Despite his pique when he realised that he was paying his researcher more than he himself was receiving from the King, Sibbald, knighted in 1682, eventually published his *Scotia Illustrata* in 1684.

His brief conversion to Roman Catholicism in 1685 resulted in near assassination when 'an angry mob' (whom he does not identify) broke into his house, forced their way into his room and searched his bed, while he escaped out of a window. 'I repented of my rashness and resolved to return to the church I was born in.' Appointed Professor of Medicine at Edinburgh later that same year, Sibbald was a founder member and early President of the **Royal College of Physicians** of Edinburgh. In addition to his *Scotia Illustrata*, he published four books on the **Roman** antiquities of Scotland (1707), histories of the shires of **Stirling**, **Linlithgow** and **Fife** (1710), and a description of the **Orkney** Islands (1711). After his death many of his books and manuscripts were bought by the **Faculty of Advocates** for their library.

SIDLAW HILLS, Perthshire/Angus

Since a 'law' is a hill, the term should really be just Sidlaws. Forming the southern boundary of **Strathmore**, this low range extends from Kinnoull Hill outside **Perth** almost to **Montrose**. The hills are most prominent where they parallel the Firth of **Tay** above the **Carse of Gowrie**, their southern slopes being here known as the Braes of Gowrie. At 1492ft (455m) Craigowl Hill north of **Dundee** is the highest point.

SIGURD, Earl of Orkney (d.1014)

It was related of Olaf Tryggvason, King of Norway, that he came to **Orkney** in about 995, soon after his conversion to Christianity, and threatened death and destruction unless Sigurd and all his dependants accepted instant baptism. The Earl was convinced by this robust argument, or professed to be. Since Sigurd's mother was the Christian daughter of an Irish king and his wife a daughter of **Malcolm II**, King of Scots, it is likely he was already better instructed in the faith than King Olaf appears to have been. Sigurd accompanied Sitric, the Norse King of Dublin, to do battle with the Irish High King, Brian Boromha, at Clontarf, in 1014. King Brian, the one man who almost succeeded in creating a united Ireland, died there. So did Sigurd, leaving an infant heir, **Thorfinn**, to become the greatest of the Orkney earls.

SIMPSON, Archibald (1790–1847) Architect

Aberdeen's leading architect in the early 19th century, Simpson was responsible for much of the city's public architecture (eg the Royal Infirmary, 1844). After a short apprenticeship with a local builder, he went to London in 1810 to work with Robert Luger. A trip to Italy completed his education and he returned to Aberdeen in 1813. For the next 30 years he shared all the major architectural commissions in the city with the City Architect John Smith. Simpson made good use of the local granite, in particular its monumental qualities. He designed right across the spectrum of 19th century eclecticism from his Greek Revival Music Hall, the County Assembly Rooms (1820–2) to his mainly Gothic churches. In 1843–4 he designed a group of free churches [see **Aberdeen: Triple Kirks**] unusual for their octagonal brick spires. His most successful ecclesiastical building was probably Woodside Church (1846). Simpson never practised outside his native Aberdeen.

SIMPSON, Sir George (1792–1860)
Administrator and Traveller

The son of George Simpson of Loch Broom in Wester **Ross**, George junior was educated in Scotland but then worked in London in a commercial office before emigrating to Montreal (1820) and joining the Hudson's Bay Company. When the Company merged with the North-West Company (1821), Simpson's authoritarian style resulted in a meteoric rise to control of all the Company's Canadian operations. Exploration being essential to the growth of trade, he supported attempts to open the Arctic coast by, among others, **John Rae** and **Thomas Simpson**, his nephew, who had little good to say of him. In 1828 George himself crossed the continent, 3260 miles in under three months, and in 1841–2 performed an 'overland' journey round the world. The sections across Canada, Siberia, Russia and Europe constituted the 'overland'; it took 20 months, rather less than it took to produce the narrative of his journey (1847). He was knighted in 1841, died at Lachine, and was buried in Montreal.

SIMPSON, Sir James Young (1811–70)
Physician
The seventh son of a **Bathgate** banker, Simpson justified his family's expectations when he entered **Edinburgh University** at the age of 14. Two years later he started to study medicine, gained his MD in 1832 and became Professor of Midwifery in 1835. Searching for an anaesthetic to ease the pain of childbirth, he experimented first with sulphuric ether and then with chloroform. He tested the latter on himself and his colleagues; all slid beneath the table unconscious. Chloroform was not his invention but his persistence and advocacy in the face of denunciations of its physical and moral implications eventually resulted in its general adoption. After Simpson's appointment as one of **Queen Victoria**'s Physicians in Scotland (1847) criticism was silenced when her son Prince Leopold was delivered under anaesthetic in 1853. International honours followed and in 1866 Simpson was the first man to be made a baronet for services to medicine. He made other important improvements in obstetric and gynaecological practice and also wrote on literary and archaeological subjects. He is memorialised by a statue in **Princes Street Gardens** and an inscription on his house at 52 **Queen Street**, where he died. His family declined the offer of burial in Westminster Abbey in favour of Warriston cemetery in **Canonmills**.

SIMPSON, Thomas (1808–40) Arctic
Explorer
The son of a **Dingwall** schoolmaster, Simpson attended **King's College**, **Aberdeen** before going to Canada (1829) in the employ of the Hudson's Bay Company of which his uncle **George Simpson** was Governor. Thomas felt himself ill-served by this family connection, but it must have played a part in his selection (1836) as second-in-command to P W Dease (a veteran of Franklin's second expedition) in an ambitious scheme to complete the exploration of Canada's Arctic coastline. This involved linking discoveries made by **Alexander Mackenzie** and Franklin around the Mackenzie and Coppermine Rivers with (1) those made in the north of Alaska from the Pacific and (2) those made from the Atlantic by Captains Back, Parry and **John Ross**. Tackling (1) first, Dease and Simpson wintered on Lake Athabasca, reached the mouth of the Mackenzie in July 1837, and then canoed westwards. Ice prevented the whole expedition from reaching Point Barrow, their Alaskan objective, but Simpson managed to complete the survey on foot. They returned to the Great Bear Lake for the winter of 1837–8 and, after an abortive push east, again in '38–9 the third summer the expedition finally succeeded in following the coastline east to Back's Great Fish River and the Ross Strait east of Boothia. Except for the Boothia Peninsula itself, Dease and Simpson

could claim (and Simpson did) to have established the existence of a north-west passage. This was never conceded mainly because Simpson never returned. After a shoot-out with his French Canadian followers, Simpson himself was shot, possibly by his own hand, more probably by his remaining companions (see *Life and Travels of Thomas Simpson* by Alexander Simpson, his brother, for a not unbiased assessment). It was not the first fracas he had been involved in; he was not an easy man to get along with. 'Fame I will have, but it must be alone,' he wrote.

SINCLAIR, George (d.1696) Mathematician
Born probably in **East Lothian**, Sinclair held professorships in **philosophy** and mathematics at **Glasgow University** over two distinct periods (1654–66 and 1689–96). He also spent a major part of his life in **Leith**, effectively acting as a scientific consultant to **coal**-mine owners on drainage matters, and advising the city of **Edinburgh** on the creation of its water supply in 1673–4.

SINCLAIR Earls of Orkney (1379–1471)
Henry de St Clair, whose family were of Norman origin, was granted lands in Lothian in 1162. To one of his descendants, Henry Sinclair (d.c1400), the Earldom of **Orkney** passed in 1379 after the extinction of the male line of Norse earls and after passing through several heiresses. Henry was succeeded as Norway's premier earl by his son, also Henry (d.1418), who as Admiral of Scotland sailed with **James I** when he was captured by the English. His son William (c1404–80), the last Sinclair Earl of Orkney, was also Admiral and conveyed James's 11-year-old daughter **Margaret of Scotland** to France in 1436 for her marriage to the Dauphin. After the Crown rents of Norway were pledged as dowry for Margaret of Denmark-Norway, the bride of **James III**, the latter induced the Sinclair family to convey to him the earldom (1471), for which they received ample compensation. The family remained **Earls of Caithness** (William having been so created in 1455), a title that has survived to this day.

SINCLAIR, Sir John, of Ulbster (1754–1835)
Agriculturalist and Statistician
From a cadet branch of the **Sinclair Earls of Caithness and Orkney**, John was born in **Thurso** Castle, educated at **Edinburgh** High School and **Edinburgh**, **Glasgow** and Oxford universities, called to both the Scottish and English Bars, and early inherited considerable property in **Caithness**. He was also MP for the county and sat in the Commons almost continually from 1780–1811, becoming baronet in 1786. Few subjects remotely connected with politics, economics, military deployment, medicine or science failed to elicit some contribution from his ever-active pen but it is as an agricultural improver, not the first but certainly one of the most eloquent, that he is primarily remembered. On his Caithness estates he experimented with drainage, crop rotation and new breeds of livestock, notably the **Cheviot sheep**, although no improver was more solicitous that such introductions should not disadvantage his tenantry; had he foreseen that **wool** production or **potato** dependence would be an excuse for the **clear-**

Sir John Sinclair in tartan trews, by Sir Henry Raeburn (NGS)

ances he would have been horrified. In 1793 he proposed the setting up of a Board of **Agriculture** and duly became its first President (1793–8).

Meanwhile another pet project, the result of research into land assessment and his *History of the Public Revenue*, 1784, was taking shape. This was the first *Statistical Account of Scotland*, 1791–8, a 20-volume county by county survey inspired by the work of **Sir Robert Sibbald** which was largely amassed from the reports of local ministers, Sinclair being a lay member of the **General Assembly**. In the 1790s he proposed the introduction of exchequer bills and raised the **Rothesay** and **Caithness Fencibles**; they served in Ireland while Sinclair expounded on military strategy and insisted that **tartan** trews were both more authentic and appropriate than **kilts**. He oversaw publication of **James Macpherson**'s Ossianic compilation in 1807 and was made a Privy Councillor in 1810. By then his energy was flagging; so was his fortune. As with other improvers his schemes, including the building of Thurso, did not immediately pay off.

SINCLAIR, Oliver, of Pitcairns (d.1560)

The last of **James V**'s favourites (although not, as was the rule with many of his predecessors, low-born, being a grandson of Earl William Sinclair of **Orkney**), Oliver Sinclair was made keeper of **Tantallon Castle** after the banishment of the **Douglases**. When the feu of Orkney and **Shetland** was resumed by the Crown during James's visit to the islands in 1540, Oliver Sinclair was appointed Justice, Sheriff, Admiral and Bailie. In 1542 he was put in command of the Scots army at the **Battle of Solway Moss**, during which débâcle he was taken prisoner by the English. His capture contributed to the despair and depression which ended in James's death two weeks after the battle.

SKARA BRAE, Mainland, Orkney

This Stone Age domestic settlement beside the bay of Skaill in **Orkney** Mainland was occupied between 3100 and 2450 BC, when the bay was still an inland freshwater loch. Little remains of the earliest dwellings on the top of which at least six new houses were built. These in turn gave way to the latest sequence of homes, still for the most part intact to their roof levels. Evidently they were abandoned hurriedly as the result of a storm which sealed the site. Another storm uncovered it in 1824. It was Stuart Piggott who, in 1936, first dated its inhabitants to the Neolithic period by identifying their pottery as 'grooved ware'. Six successive excavations have revealed them as farmers, fishermen and hunters, who carved ceremonial objects such as stone balls and a macehead, while they were well supplied with domestic implements, ornaments and even cosmetics. Today 10 of their houses with their connecting passages provide 'one of the most vivid insights into the life of prehistoric man' to be found in Europe (A & G Ritchie).

SKIING

The first recorded sortie on skis in Scotland was in 1890 when W W Naismith, founder of the Scottish Mountaineering Club, ventured into the **Campsie Fells** on heavy wooden Nordic-style planks. As a mountaineer he was interested in skis as a form of cross-country transport; but although he and some of his sturdier mountaineering cronies persevered, Nordic skiing had limited appeal in Scotland. Snow conditions were unpredictable and rarely ideal, possible routes were limited, and it required real dedication to carry weighty and cumbersome equipment up into the hills in order to cover distances on skis that would arguably be easier to cover on foot.

Development of the alternative Alpine (or downhill) style of skiing – much more rewarding and nothing like so strenuous – led to the founding of the Ski Club of Great Britain in 1903 and of the Scottish Ski Club in 1907. But the members of the latter (which included Naismith) were all mountaineers; reluctant to abandon their hard-won cross-country skills and scorning the new-fangled, shorter skis increasingly favoured elsewhere, they continued to pit their stamina against the inaccessible wilds of **Ben Nevis**, **Glencoe**, **Ben Lawers** and the **Cairngorms**. Not until the eve of World War I did Alpine skiing really start to catch on in Scotland, and no sooner had it done so than the war itself put paid to the nascent sport. The Scottish Ski Club did not re-form until 1929, and thereafter improved equipment, easier access to the hills and a succession of cold snowy winters vastly widened the sport's appeal, although skiers still had to carry their skis to the top of each run. The first powered ski-tow operated on Ben Lawers in **Perthshire** in the late 1940s with similar contraptions being rigged up at Glen Clunie and

The Neolithic settlement of Skara Brae, Orkney (entry p 921) (HS)

Glenshee in the Cairngorms, but it was not until 1956 that the first permanent ski-lift was installed at Glencoe. Since then well equipped resorts at Glenshee, the Lecht, Cairngorm and Aonach Mor in the Nevis range have been developed to offer all the facilities of the true Alpine resorts, with national and even international events being staged – weather permitting. For the Scottish climate, which sprinkles ideal skiing days sparsely amongst weeks of thawing warmth or blinding blizzard, still frequently provokes the cry uttered by a frustrated cross-country skier in 1920: 'Snow conditions will always prevent us from becoming really expert at home . . . even on the highest hills conditions are usually bad.' Despite adverse weather conditions, the popularity of the sport has developed almost beyond the capacity of the resorts. Environmentalists, hill-walkers and purist mountaineers are becoming seriously alarmed at the proliferation of chair-lifts, ski-tows, car parks and peripheral facilities that service the resorts. Against these genuine concerns has, as always, to be set the enormous value of the winter **tourist** trade to local economies.

Were the future of skiing in Scotland to depend solely on its popularity and the facilities provided (which include the biggest dry ski slope in Europe at **Edinburgh**'s Hillend Park), then it would be rosy indeed. Yet a succession of mild winters in the late 1980s and early '90s seriously threatened the viability of the companies who run the resorts; success or failure thus lies ultimately in the lap of the (weather) gods.

SKINNER, James Scott (1843–1927) Violinist Born in **Banchory**, Skinner was playing in the local dance bands by the age of seven. In 1855 he joined Dr Mark's touring orchestra of musical orphans, which gave him a sound formal training. He subsequently returned to **Aberdeenshire**, though his life was, to the end, a constant series of tours and concerts all over the United Kingdom and as far afield as the USA. His formal musical education allowed him greater virtuosity both in performance and in composition than was usual amongst fiddlers of his time, and his work marks a departure from the dull and derivative material which appeared after **Marshall** and the **Gows**. His 'Bonnie Lass o' Bon Accord' remains firmly in the repertoire of present-day fiddlers.

James Scott Skinner, by David Waterson, 1912 (SNPG)

SKINNER, John (1721–1807) Priest

For 65 years from 1742 **Episcopalian** priest of Longside in **Aberdeenshire**, Skinner was also a Church historian, poet and song writer, respected by **Burns** particularly for 'Tullochgorum'. Although not a **Jacobite**, he suffered persecution in 1746 and 1753. Both his son and grandson were bishops of the **Scottish Episcopal Church**.

SKIPNESS CASTLE, Kintyre, Argyll

This castle commands Kilbrannan Sound and the **Clyde** estuary. Dugald *ruadh* MacSween [see **Castle Sween**] had a tower, now the north-west corner of the enclosure, and a chapel here. The curtain wall was built in the 1260s by the Earl of **Menteith**, and was later strengthened, leaving the chapel windows sealed in the seaward wall beside the gateway (the northern entrance is recent). The 16th century tower house uses the east gable of Dugald's tower, reversing its windows. Kilbrannan Church replaced the chapel.

Archibald Campbell, 1st of Skipness, married **Janet Douglas, Lady Glamis**; she was burnt for witchcraft and he died attempting to escape from **Edinburgh Castle** (1537). Skipness was besieged in 1646 and its demolition was ordered in 1685, but the **Campbells** kept possession till 1843, though they had moved to a new house and turned the castle into a farm steading in the late 18th century. (In the churchyard by the ruined Kilbrannan, a headstone depicts an 18th century plough team of four horses and two men.)

SKYE, Island of, Inner Hebrides

The island of Skye (Gaelic: *An t-Eilean Sgitheanach*) covers 535 square miles, with a complicated topography featuring fingers of land separated by sea lochs penetrating far inland. The names of Lochs Snizort, Dunvegan, Harport, Eishort, Ainort and Sligachan reveal the mixture of **Viking** and **Gaelic** culture which has influenced the island over many centuries.

Geologically, Skye is renowned for its lava landscapes, especially in the Trotternish area where the Old Man of Storr and the unusual formations of the Quiraing attract many visitors. Also greatly admired, whenever visible through the ubiquitous mist, are the **Cuillins**, jagged mountains of hard gabbro beloved by generations of climbers. The Red Cuillins, made of only slightly less hard granite, have eroded into more rounded shapes and have slopes of scree. The fertility of some parts of the island derives from underlying sandstones and limestones which surface around the volcanic rocks.

A rich variety of archaeological and historical monuments testifies to Skye's long and turbulent history. Of particular interest are the **brochs** of Dun Ardtreck near Carbost and Dun Beag, just west of Bracadale, both very neatly built using square-sided facing stones. Clach Ard, Tote, is a **Pictish** symbol stone, unusual in the **Hebrides**.

Skye is part of the heartland of Gaelic culture, with a large proportion of the population of 8866 (1991) speaking Gaelic in everyday life. Although under threat, particularly from incomers, it is currently enjoying a resurrection of interest, assisted by a Gaelic College (*Sabhal Mor Ostaig*), Gaelic poetry (eg **Sorley Maclean**), plus some economic support from the Highlands and Islands Development Board and spiritual underpinning from the extreme Sabbatarian **Free Church**. Local museums at Luib, Colbost, Glendale and Kilmuir help interpret **crofting** society to visitors.

In the 19th century the traditional way of life was under~~min~~ed, with an estimated emigration of 30,000 betwe~~en~~ 1840–88. In 1882 the **Battle of Braes** saw a

A Skye crofter's home, or 'black house', c1885 (GWWA)

confrontation over grazing rights between local farmers in the Braes district near **Portree** and 50 **Glasgow** policemen imported to keep control. After a pitched battle, gunboats were sent and a force of marines landed at Uig. The ensuing public outcry led to the **Napier Commission**, established by Gladstone, which resulted in the **Crofters' Act** of 1886, providing security of tenure at a fair and controlled rent. This system, which replaced the original communal townships, remains in force today.

The principal residence of the **MacDonalds** of Sleat from 1815 was Armadale Castle, a small surviving portion of which has been renovated and opened to the public as the **Clan Donald** Centre. Previous MacDonald castles included Dun Scaich on the west side of the Sleat peninsula, Knock Castle or Castle Camus, also in Sleat, and Duntulm, a spectacular site at the north end of Trotternish, abandoned about 1730. **Dunvegan Castle**, the ancient seat of the **MacLeods** of **Dunvegan** and **Harris**, occupies a rocky site on the east shore of Loch Dunvegan. The keep dates to the 14th century. In part of the later 18th century buildings is an exhibition covering the history of the Clan MacLeod.

Skye has four ferry terminals and a bridge, opened in 1995. It spans the narrows between **Kyle of Lochalsh**, the railhead on the mainland, and **Kyleakin** on Skye, so named because it was the kyle where King Haakon of Norway moored his longships in 1263 on his voyage to the **Battle of Largs**. A few miles to the south is a seasonal ferry connection from **Glenelg** to Kylerhea – another short crossing through treacherous tidal races. At the southern end of the Sleat (pronounced 'Slate') peninsula a ferry connects Armadale to **Mallaig**, another railhead, with connections through **Fort William** to Glasgow. At the opposite end of Skye, from the harbour of Uig in the Trotternish peninsula, there are ferry connections to the Outer Hebrides (**Tarbert**, Harris and **Lochmaddy**, **North Uist**). Another short crossing connects Sconser on Skye to the island of **Raasay**.

All these ferries, and the island's extensive road system, are stretched beyond capacity in the summer **tourist** season, when over a million visitors sail (but now mostly drive) 'over the sea to Skye'. Although crofting and **fishing** still form the basis of the island's economy, tourism and light industry, including electronics, are now vitally important. A famous **whisky** distillery at Carbost, the Talisker Malt Whisky Distillery, was established in 1833. Most of its production is blended for export. There are guided tours during the tourist season.

Portree is the main town, with hotels, shops, **banks** and all the usual services, including a tourist information centre. Skye Week, an annual festival of culture and leisure events, is one of the major events of the year. From **Broadford**, a large village with craft shops and an annual folk festival, a scenic road leads eventually to **Elgol**, from where there is a fine view of the Cuillin ridge. A track leads from Elgol to the Sligachan Hotel past Loch Coruisk. There are many other thriving crofting townships throughout the island.

Of the many areas in Skye of outstanding natural beauty, none is more spectacular than the Neist peninsula west of Dunvegan. On the western tip is the Neist Point lighthouse, overlooking towering cliffs alive with seabirds. Those nearby are the 967ft (295m) cliffs of Waterstein Head. Far out to the west North and **South Uist** and **Benbecula** are visible. In the Sleat peninsula, the village of Eilean Iarmain (Isleornsay) is situated in a more fertile, sheltered landscape. The small tidal island of Ornsay has a ruined chapel and an unmanned lighthouse.

SLAINS CASTLE, Nr Peterhead, Aberdeenshire

There are two Slains Castles, both located perilously close to sea cliffs north of **Aberdeen**, both built by the Hays, **Earls of Errol**, and both ruins. The earlier comprises a defiant tower of masonry on a headland due east of **Ellon**; it was destroyed, along with **Huntly Castle**, by James VI in 1594. The later, begun in 1597 seven miles to the north, was the 9th Earl's riposte. Originally a tower, it was expanded into a quadrangular structure, remodelled in 1836, but unroofed and abandoned in 1925. It stands on the seaward edge of a field just north of Cruden Bay where Bram Stoker once stayed. Slains, it has been suggested, gave him the idea for Count Dracula's castle. It was also here that **Johnson** and **Boswell** were invited to stay, and whence they visited the nearly **Bullers of Buchan**, at the start of their 1773 tour of the Highlands. Johnson thought well of 'the grandeur and the elegance' of the Errol establishment and pronounced Slains' situation 'the noblest he had ever seen'. Boswell, of course, agreed, noting that 'the King of Denmark is Lord Errol's nearest neighbour to the north-east'.

SLESSOR, Mary (1848–1915) Missionary

Born in **Aberdeen**, Mary Slessor was the daughter of a shoemaker whose profligacy and drunkenness lost him his job in 1857. The family moved to **Dundee** where 11-year-old Mary was sent to work in the **jute** mills. Her two elder brothers died in their teens and when their father died soon after Mary's 14th birthday she was left to provide for her sick mother and two small sisters. In 1875, when the youngest was old enough to work, Mary applied to the Foreign Mission Board of the **United Presbyterian Church** for a posting to West Africa.

Arriving in Calabar, Nigeria, in 1876, she soon came into conflict with the narrow mission attitudes to 'heathens and savages' and requested a transfer to a remote inland region as yet unvisited by missionaries or, indeed, by white men of any description. There she started to study native customs and superstitions; she learned to eat native food, gave up her conventional petticoats in favour of a tentlike garment called a 'Mother Hubbard', stopped wearing shoes and cut her hair short for convenience. Horrified by the local custom of killing twins at birth and abandoning any baby whose mother died in childbirth, Mary adopted as many of these unfortunate infants as she could save and soon had a large family. She was adopted in turn by the local tribe who called her 'Ma', cared for her during her frequent bouts of malaria, and protected her from the pitfalls of life in the jungle. That doughty African traveller Mary Kingsley, who visited Calabar in 1894, found 'this very wonderful lady . . . living entirely alone (as far as white folks go) in a clearing in a forest . . . and ruling as a veritable white chief over the entire Okyon district. Her very great abilities have given her among the savage tribe a unique position and won her a profound esteem. Her knowledge of the native, his language, his ways of thought, his diseases and his difficulties, is extraordinary; the amount of good she has done no man can fully estimate.'

Having, by her unconventionality, distanced herself from white authority both spiritual and temporal, Mary Slessor was finally granted official status as the magistrate for Okyon in 1905. 10 years later she succumbed to dysentery and malaria, and died in Calabar at the age of 67.

SMA' GLEN, The, Perthshire

This four-mile defile through which the river Almond cuts from the hills into lower **Glenalmond** was once a noted access route from **Crieff** and Stratheam to **Aberfeldy** and the Highlands. **Prince Charles Edward Stewart** withdrew through it in 1746 and soon after **General Wade** built a road, now replaced by the A822. It is also of ancient strategic importance as witnessed by the site of a **Roman** fort and nearby watchtower at Fendoch and, a mile north-west, of a large **dun** (Dun Mor) within two ruinous walls high on a hill, all at the southern end of the glen. At the other end a 'rude flat stone', removed to its present position by Wade's road-builders who found ancient bones beneath it, is known as Ossian's Stone. The assumption that the grave had been that of Ossian found favour with **William Wordsworth**:

> In this still place, remote from men,
> Sleeps Ossian in the narrow glen:
>   In this still place, where murmurs on
> But one meek streamlet, only one.

SMAILHOLM TOWER, Nr Kelso, Roxburghshire

Though neither as large as **Newark** nor as elaborate as **Greenknowe**, Smailholm better evokes the military and custodial importance of a Borders tower house. Thrusting four-square upwards from a rocky mound, it commands a vast extent of country and is said to have been used 'as a landmark to direct vessels to **Berwick**' (25 miles away). High up on the gutter-level well walk, a seat for a lookout and a recess for his lantern testify to its role as a watchtower. The date of construction is uncertain and there is evidence of rebuilding. But the general elevation of vaulted ground-floor cellar, first-floor hall, and second- and third-floor bedrooms, all connected by a spiral staircase within the angle of the 2m thick walls, is typical. So is the surrounding but now vestigial barmkin.

Originally belonging to the Pringle family who were much troubled by English raiders during the 16th century, it passed to the Scott family of Harden in the 17th century. By 1774 it was the property of Robert Scott who lived with his wife and daughter in the adjacent farmhouse of Sandyknowe. Into their care was sent the lame toddler called **Walter** who was Robert Scott's grandson. The proximity of Smailholm 'standing stark and upright like a warden' made a great impression on the child. Smailholm would feature in the **ballad** The

Smailholm Tower as drawn by MacGibbon and Ross c1880 (MR)

Eve of St John and in Marmion; and it was to Smailholm that Sir Walter Scott returned with the painter J M W Turner in the last year of his life. The tower, now open to the public, includes a display of costume figures, tapestries, and paintings illustrative of Scott's associations with the place and of the ballads.

SMELLIE, William (1740–95) Editor

Born in **Edinburgh**'s Pleasance and apprenticed into the printing trade from the age of 12, Smellie was largely self-taught, becoming an expert on natural history with his own major botanical collection. He is mainly remembered now for editing the first edition of the **Encyclopaedia Britannica**, published in 1768, with 15 major subject areas written by him. He was also Secretary to the **Society of Antiquaries** and a friend of **Robert Burns**.

SMILES, Samuel (1812–1906) Writer

A native of **Haddington** and childhood friend of **Jane Welsh** (later **Carlyle**), Smiles studied medicine at **Edinburgh University** and practised in Haddington before removing to Leeds as a surgeon and editor of the Leeds Times. There he met George Stephenson and wrote his biography (1857). Lives of the Engineers (1861–2) expanded this theme and was followed by a host of edifying industrial biographies on the likes of Thomas Edward, Cobbler and Naturalist (1876), Robert Dick, Baker and Geologist (1878) and Jasmin, Hairdresser and Poet (1891). His considerable reputation, however, rests on works of more obvious social and moral worth. Self-Help (1859), which contained potted biographies of the really great, urged its readers to 'Do thou likewise' and was a massive success. It inspired a series of books with equally mouth-watering titles: *Character* (1871), *Thrift* (1875) and *Duty* (1880).

SMITH, Adam (1723–90) Economist and Philosopher

Born in **Kirkcaldy** five months after the death of his father, the town's Comptroller of Customs, Adam Smith attended the Burgh School before going on to **Glasgow University** at the age of 14. There he studied mathematics, physics and **philosophy** (this last under the tutelage of **Francis Hutcheson**, then at the height of his career). From 1740–6 Smith was Snell Exhibitioner at Balliol College, Oxford, returning to **Edinburgh** in 1746 where he gave a series of public lectures on rhetoric.

The success of these lectures led to his being appointed Professor of Logic at Glasgow in 1751, where he delivered the *Lectures on Rhetoric and Belles Lettres* which survive today only in the notes made by his students. In 1752 he became Professor of Moral Philosophy at Glasgow, a post that he held for 12 years, and in 1759 he published a further series of his lectures under the title *The Theory of Moral Sentiments*. He resigned in mid-session in 1764, refunding tuition fees despite student protests that he had already given more than value. He had accepted a post as tutor to the 3rd **Duke of Buccleuch** and his brother. Touring the Continent with his pupils was an attraction, as was a subsequent life pension equivalent to his professional salary. In France he made contact with the Physiocrats and with philosophers such as Quesnay, Turgot and Necker. The tour had a tragic outcome; the illness of both his pupils led to the death of the younger boy, and Smith accompanied the Duke home with the coffin.

From 1766 Smith was in Kirkcaldy for 10 years, living with his mother (he never married) and working on *An Inquiry into the Nature and Causes of the Wealth of Nations* (1776). In the same year his faithful account of the death of his friend **David Hume** caused a minor scandal in 'respectable society', which was shocked by the idea of an atheist being able to die in such serenity. In 1788 Smith moved to Edinburgh on his appointment as Commissioner of Customs for the city, taking up residence with his mother in **Panmure House** in the **Canongate**. In his last years he asked his friends **James Hutton** and **Joseph Black** to burn many of his papers, leaving the sanctioned items for posthumous publication as *Essays on Philosophical Subjects* (1795). He died in Edinburgh on 17 July 1790.

Smith's *Essays* include a fascinating 'Essay on the First Formation of Languages' and a 'History of Astronomy' which describes the process of scientific discovery as the resolution of an initial unsettling wonder, and neither the essays nor the *Theory of Moral Sentiment* should be eclipsed by *The Wealth of Nations*. Smith was no less a philosopher for not having written 'pure' philosophy. If 'philosophy' in his day included the modern 'social science', then in pursuing theoretical interest from wonderment and from public concern, Smith often sheds light on general questions by implication.

His moral philosophy is excellent psychology. There is no 'moral sense'; upbringing and experience form moral propensities, sociability and sympathy (Smith's term implying 'empathy'). A key Smithian idea is of

the 'impartial spectator' – as if a judge of one's deeds, created by experience of others' judgements of them, sat in one's own breast, contributing to the formation of moral judgements. Morality comprises various factors – not merely self-interested calculation (which however does occur in *unrestrained* tyrants).

Self-interest is operative in morality. Indeed it is commended – but only as a *restrained* passion. In *The Wealth of Nations* the baker sells bread out of his self-interest, which is not the same as unbridled selfishness. Man is essentially *active*. Central to Smith is not a dogma of market forces, unbridled pursuit of gain, but recoil from the evil of *stagnation*. Society has advanced, through stages of hunting, herding, agrarianism and commercialism. He commends the existence of cities as on the one hand countering tyrants by spreading power, on the other hand creating markets, manufactures and possibilities of exchange, and so stimulating agricultural activity rather than rural stagnation. He has a sense of the movement in things. With specialisation and the 'Division of Labour' a machinist can achieve in one operation what the manual worker would achieve in several. This is a boon. But it is necessary to safeguard the machinist's humanity by the public provision of sympathetic and beneficial working conditions. For Smith, market failure is not merely failure of trade, but failure of social provision. **Education** is a necessity against uninformed revolt, which creates only misery and is doomed by incompetence. If French writers taught him to view society as merely an organism sustained by multiple interactions, his genius was in both observation and the working out of implications. He doubtless discussed trade with merchant friends in Glasgow in the 1750s, but did not simply reflect their practice; he worked features of it into an instructive scheme.

Adam Smith by R H Campbell and A S Skinner is a splendid brief biography, alas with no bibliography. The Glasgow edition of Smith's works includes a biography with a set of very good essays. *The Wealth of Nations* is available in many editions; the Penguin, while it prints only Books I-III (the crucial ones) includes A S Skinner's essay – the best introduction to Smith. *The Individual and Society* by A L Macfie is commended too.

SMITH, Alexander (1830–67) Writer

Although best known in his short lifetime as a poet, Smith is now read for his prose, especially the classic *A Summer in Skye*, 1865. He was born in **Kilmarnock** and like his father began as a pattern designer in the textile trade. His first poems appeared in 1853 and in the following year he secured a post as secretary to **Edinburgh University**. Further collections of verse attracted the attention of **W E Aytoun**, who lampooned him as one of the 'spasmodic poets' in *Blackwood's*. He also wrote two rather unsuccessful novels, interspersed by *Dreamthorp*, a collection of essays, and the **Skye** travelogue. He died, a lesson to all, 'of overwork and trying to support a family on a writer's income'.

SMITH, Donald, Lord Strathcona and Mount Royal (1820–1914) Canadian Entrepreneur

Smith was born in **Forres**, the son of a tradesman. He joined the Hudson's Bay Company as a clerk and had risen to Chief Factor and head of its Montreal department by 1868. An astute financial manager, he allowed neither sentiment nor principle to cloud his judgement or mar his progress. Buying up shares in the Company, he eventually rose to a directorship and (1889) the governorship. He also engaged in politics, representing **John Alexander MacDonald** in negotiations with the Red River rebels in 1870 and securing MacDonald's downfall in the 1873 election. As a director of the Canadian Pacific Railway he was therefore obliged to keep a low profile when under MacDonald's dispensation **George Stephen** (Smith's cousin) and William van Hoorn finally completed the project. Smith nevertheless drove the last spike, was pictured doing so, and was generally credited with the achievement. Knighted in 1886, he served as federal Canada's first High Commissioner in London and was created 1st Baron Strathcona. His wealth, estates (eg **Colonsay**), benefactions (in Scotland as well as Canada), financial wizardry, and dubious methods have prompted comparisons with Cecil Rhodes. But Rhodes was a visionary, Smith merely an opportunist.

SMITH, George (1824–1901) Publisher

Smith's father, also George, founded with Alexander Elder the London publishers and East India agents Smith & Elder. Like his father, the younger George was born at **Elgin** but, joining the firm in 1838, spent most of his life in London. He took sole control in 1846 and quickly acquired an impressive list of authors including John Ruskin, W M Thackeray and Charlotte Brontë; Smith's mother provided the model for Mrs Bretton in *Villette* and he for Dr John. Launching into periodicals, Smith produced *The Cornhill Magazine* (1859) and, into newspapers, *The Pall Mall Gazette* (1865). But today his reputation as a far-sighted publisher must rest with *The Dictionary of National Biography* of which he was the founder (1882) and sole proprietor.

SMITH, Iain Crichton (1928–98) Poet and Novelist

'A bilingual Gaelic schizophrenic' as he called himself, Smith was born in **Glasgow** but, following the early death of his father, was raised in poverty amongst the **Gaelic**-speaking community of Point on the **Isle of Lewis**. His mother gutted **herring** to make ends meet. After attending the Nicolson Institute in **Stornoway** and **Aberdeen University**, Smith taught English in **Clydebank** and from 1955–75 at the High School in **Oban**, where he was rejoined by his mother. Her stern character and unflinching dedication would resurface in his fictional creations and became a paradigm of Gaeldom's rugged tenacity.

His first collection of poems was in English (*The Long River*, 1955), his second in Gaelic under the name Iain Mac a'Ghobhainn (*Burn is Aran*, 1960). A fourth, *Deer on the Hill* (1962), while paying homage to **Duncan Bàn Macintyre**, used the **red deer**'s habitat of a 'halfway kingdom' between earth and sky as a metaphor for the human condition between the mundane and the eternal. 'Just think of it as venison by Tennyson,' he told a radio producer. There followed short stories, more poems, plays, translations from the Gaelic of **Sorley MacLean**, criticism, and several distinguished novels. *Consider the*

Lilies (1968) is set against the background of the **Clearances** and stands out as a justly popular classic, eloquent in its economy of language and immediate in its restrained appeal.

After the death of his mother in 1969, Smith married Donalda Logan of **Taynuilt** and found a softer focus for his verses. He lived in her **Argyll** village for the rest of his life. Anything but parochial in his interests, he delighted generations of pupils with a self-effacing and unpredictable humour yet he was deeply troubled by human injustice and inadequacy. He won innumerable awards, held several doctorates and was attached to half a dozen universities as writer-in-residence or visiting professor. But celebrity no more impressed him than did cant, dogma or affectation. Gentle irreverence, devastating honesty and a passion for language (Gaelic and English) illuminated both his life and his writings.

SMITH, James (c1645–1731) Architect

A prominent figure in Scottish social and political life, Smith was the son of a master mason. He studied architecture in Italy and was closely connected to **Robert Mylne**, whose daughter he eventually married. A burgess of **Edinburgh** and MP for **Forres** 1685–6, he succeeded **Sir William Bruce** as 'Surveyor and Overseer of the King's Works' in 1683. In this capacity his chief responsibility was the maintenance of **Holyrood House**. After the **Union** his contract was renewed but without a salary. This was the beginning of Smith's enduring financial difficulties; even private commissions seem to have ceased after 1710. His surviving drawings show mostly variations on Palladian themes; he had formed an interest in Palladio during his time in Italy. But his executed buildings show little of this influence. His best-known works are the **Canongate Church**, Edinburgh (1688–90), **Drumlanrig Castle**, **Dumfries** (1680–90), Yester House, **East Lothian** (c1700–15) and **Dalkeith** House near Edinburgh (remodelled 1702–10). As an engineer he was responsible for the planning of a water supply for Scottish towns (1696) and he conducted a survey for a possible **Forth-Clyde Canal** during the 1720s.

SMITH, James (1789–1850) Agricultural Engineer

Born in **Glasgow**, Smith studied at the city's **University** before starting work in the family's **cotton** mills at **Doune** in **Perthshire**. When improving the mill's water supply from the nearby river Teith, he built what is believed to be the first salmon ladder to allow passage for spawning fish. However, **agriculture** proved his main area of interest; he built a model of a practical reaping machine when only 22 as well as pioneering deep-ploughing and land drainage techniques.

SMITH, John (Iain Mac a' Ghobhainn) (1848–81) Gaelic Poet

Known as the Bard of Iarsiadar (on Uig, **Lewis**), Smith was a medical student at **Edinburgh** when he contracted tuberculosis, returning to Uig c1774, the year of the **Bernera Riot**. His poems probably largely post-date that year. He tells the story of **Coinneach Odhar**, 'the Brahan Seer', in the style of the Ossianic ballads, and composed witty local verse; but his deservedly most famous poem is *Spiorad a' Charthannais* ('The Spirit of Kindliness'), a mordant indictment of feudal tyranny in the Highlands, contrasted with the ideals of true religion. See, for poems, I N MacLeod, *Bàrdach Leòdhais* (1916) and for comment D Thomson, *Introduction to Gaelic Poetry* (1974, 1990).

SMITH, John (1938–94) Politician and Advocate

Smith's death of a heart attack on 12 May 1994 affected both the Labour Party, of which he was leader, and the British electorate. House of Commons business was suspended and members of the public laid flowers outside Labour headquarters. The loss of a politician of such integrity and genial rectitude was deeply felt.

Born in **Dalmally**, raised in **Ardrishaig** (where his father was head of the primary school) and educated in **Dunoon**, Smith would claim to be 'the first West Highlander to lead the opposition'. At **Glasgow University** he was joint national winner of the *Observer* Mace, a national student debating competition, and was clearly destined for either the **law** or politics. He opted for both, being called to the Bar and twice unsuccessfully contesting East **Fife**. In 1970 he was adopted for the safe Labour seat of North **Lanarkshire** and, as Monklands, held it for the rest of his life. Harold Wilson's 1974 offer of the Solicitor Generalship for Scotland he rejected to avoid being 'parked in a legal by-way'. Instead he held a junior post in Tony Benn's Energy Department where he proved a tough negotiator on North Sea **Oil**. As deputy to Michael Foot in the Privy Council Office in 1976 he pioneered the complexities of devolution and in 1978 entered the Callaghan cabinet as Trade Secretary. At 40, he was the youngest Cabinet Minister in recent times. It was a short-lived distinction. The Thatcher victory in 1979 meant that the rest of his career was spent on the opposition front bench (wryly, perhaps, he would choose Patsy Cline's 'I've Loved and Lost Again' as one of his Desert Island Discs). He was a much respected shadow Chancellor and then, following Neil Kinnock's 1992 defeat (to which Smith's redistributive tax proposals may have contributed) he was decisively elected leader of the Labour Party.

Socialism for Smith was a matter of morality, not ideology. Old Labour found him to its right and New Labour (as it would become) to its left, although it learnt from his pro-European and pro-devolution prompting. He favoured a Bill of Rights and a written constitution. The certainties of the law retained his affection and from the family home in **Edinburgh**'s Morningside he continued to practise during parliamentary recesses. Perhaps his legal grasp and formidable intelligence obscured our vision of the Britain he might so easily have led. The new modernists, his erstwhile disciples Tony Blair, Gordon Brown and Peter Mandelson, were already impatient with his consensual approach to Labour Party reform and critical of his hard-won compromise with the trades unions over 'one man one vote'. But Smith provided the platform for their victory in 1997. He made people feel differently about Labour, lifted the party's depression, and reinstated its governing credentials.

Largely thanks to his wife Elizabeth, he had triumphed over a 1988 heart attack and celebrated by scaling 108 of the 277 Munros – the nearest he ever got to a personal publicity campaign. The second, fatal, heart attack brought him back to the West Highlands; a regular churchgoer, he was buried in a moving ceremony on the island of **Iona**.

SMITH, Joseph (fl.c1750–80) Mob Leader

'A little crooked man of great and upright spirit', Smith (or 'Bowed Joe') acquired such an ascendancy over **Edinburgh**'s less privileged citizenry that he became known as 'General' Smith. A cobbler by trade, he lived 'in some obscure den in the **Cowgate**' (**Robert Chambers**, *Traditions of Edinburgh*, vol 2, 1825). Yet so powerful was his demagoguery, so inspired his protests, and so formidable his support that even the city's magistrates feared and cultivated him. A mob of 10,000 he could apparently raise in less than an hour. They were deployed in a variety of causes, some petty, others momentous, as when in 1768 Smith took the side of Archibald Douglas in the **Douglas Cause**. More popular still was his 1763 attack on John Wilkes who, with a devil on his shoulder, was hanged in effigy as a protest against issue 45 of Wilkes's *North Briton* with its attack on **John Stuart, 3rd Earl of Bute** and Scots in general. Smith had a wife, who was always obliged to walk well behind him, and a powerful whistle with which he summoned her. He died, according to Chambers, 'by a fall from the top of a **Leith** stage-coach, in returning from the Races, while in a state of intoxication, about the year 1780'.

SMITH, Madeleine Hamilton (1835–1928) Supposed Murderess

The granddaughter of **David Hamilton** and the daughter of George Smith, both **Glasgow** architects, Madeleine was the subject of 'the most baffling murder trial of modern times'. An attractive and intelligent girl from a respectable home in Blythswood Square, she had taken a lover, Pierre Emile l'Angelier, a clerk from Jersey, who after a three-year liaison died of arsenic poisoning. At her trial (1857) in **Edinburgh** it was shown that Madeleine had indeed purchased arsenic and, in her imminent marriage to a more respectable suitor, had ample motive for wanting rid of l'Angelier. But there was no evidence of her having met him to administer the dose. Brilliantly defended by **John Inglis**, she was released with a 'not proven' verdict but amidst suspicions of rank-closing amongst the middle class and only after the publication of her letters to her lover. These and their revelation of gaslight amours amongst the bustled bourgeoisie excited sensational comment. She later married (1861) a London publisher and, after emigrating to America, remarried. Hollywood is said to have threatened her with possible deportation for her refusal to star in a film about her life. Offering spirited resistance she died, carrying her secret to the grave.

SMITH, Sydney Goodsir (1915–75) Poet

Sydney Goodsir Smith was born in New Zealand, but his family returned to Scotland when he was two years old. His nature was always rebellious and restless, from an aborted study of medicine at **Edinburgh** to subsequent expulsion from Oriel College, Oxford (he *did* take a degree in history), through to the diverse experi-

Sydney Goodsir Smith, by Denis Peploe (SNPG)

mental tangents of his finest work. Goodsir Smith was turned down for military service in both the Spanish Civil War and World War II due to chronic asthma, perhaps fortunately – for the early 1940s saw the appearance of his first books of poetry. Early work was in English but, encouraged by Hector McIver and the examples of **MacDiarmid**, he began writing in Scots, systematically forging his own distinctive style.

Skail Wind (1941) was shaky but seminal, laying foundations for stronger work to come. This was first apparent in *The Wanderer and Other Poems* (1943), with the book's long title poem in strong Scots indicating significant structural and linguistic innovations and development. *The Wanderer* signalled what became a lifelong engagement with longer poetic forms and functions as a template for his finest achievement, *Under the Eildon Tree* (1948). This poem-sequence is a potent mix of diverse linguistic levels, modes of rhetoric, structural pyrotechnics, elaborate humour and self- (and style-) effacement. Irony and juxtaposition are central in a work rooted equally in modernist and Scottish tradition. Collections of shorter poems abound, notably *Figs and Thistles* (1959); and he produced further important poem-sequences such as *Kynd Kittock's Land* (1965), plays, notably *The Wallace* (1960), and an experimental novel, *Carotid Cornucopius* (1947).

SMITH, Sir William Alexander (1854–1914)
Founder of the Boys' Brigade

A native of **Thurso**, Smith moved to **Glasgow** at the age of 13 on the death of his father, an officer of dragoons turned businessman. He was there brought up by an uncle whose wholesaling business he joined as an apprentice and later, with a brother, started his own firm of Smith & Smith. He also joined both the **Lanarkshire** Rifle Volunteers, the YMCA and the **Free Church**, becoming closely associated with the Rev George Reith, father of the BBC's **Lord Reith** and minister of the College Free Church. Military and religious enthusiasms fused in 1883 when, while endeavouring to handle a rebellious Sunday School in North Woodside, he hit on the idea of subduing his pupils and of relieving the tedium of religious instruction by introducing paramilitary principles. The Boys' Brigade which resulted was dedicated to 'the advancement of God's Kingdom among Boys' and quickly spread throughout Scotland, Britain and the Commonwealth. To generations of 'Boyhood' (always with a capital 'B') he became The Founder (also with capitals), an awesome figure of rigid posture and strict ideas who yet had some insight into the youthful male personality which struck a chord. He married twice and eventually gave up his business

Sir William Alexander Smith, founder of the Boys' Brigade, by Alexander Ignatius Roche (SNPG)

to concentrate on the Brigade as its secretary and organiser. But myth as much as modesty seems to have totally eclipsed his private affairs; he became an embodiment of his movement as others, such as Baden-Powell, essayed variations on the theme. He was knighted in 1909 and died in London the day after presiding over one of the Brigade's mass rallies in the Albert Hall. Both his sons took up the call and one, Stanley, succeeded him as Brigade Secretary.

SMITH, William Robertson (1849–94)
Scholar

Born at Keig near **Alford**, Smith studied at **Aberdeen**, **Edinburgh**, Bonn and Gottingen before being appointed professor of Hebrew and Old Testament Exegesis at Aberdeen's **Free Church** College. An outstanding orientalist and a biblical scholar of progressive views, he was dismissed (1881) after a celebrated trial for heresy when he suggested in an entry for the **Encyclo-**

paedia Britannica that the Pentateuch could have been the work of more than one author. In the same year he became joint editor of the *Encyclopaedia* (classic 9th edition) and in 1887 chief editor. By now he was at Cambridge as Professor of Arabic (1883), University Librarian (1886) and 'one of the founding fathers of modern anthropology' (T C Smout).

SMOLLETT, Tobias (George) (1721–71)
Novelist

Tobias Smollett was born in **Dunbartonshire**, the grandson of a prominent Scottish political figure, Sir James Smollett. He was educated at **Dumbarton** Grammar School and **Glasgow University**, where he graduated with a degree in medicine in 1739. He subsequently moved to London in the hopes of finding a sponsor for his play *The Regicide*. His lack of financial and literary success prompted him to join the navy as a ship's surgeon, and in 1741 he set sail as part of a British expeditionary fleet against Spanish forces in the West Indies. Shortly after participating in the abortive attack on Cartagena, Smollett left the force and settled in Jamaica, where he married the daughter of an English planter. In 1744 he returned to London, where he set up an unsuccessful medical practice, and began publishing his literary work. His first publication, in 1746, was the sentimental patriotic poem 'The Tears of Scotland', which concerned the **Jacobite Rising** of 1745. Further works followed, including two satires on London life, *Advice* (1746) and *Reproof* (1747).

In 1748 Smollett published his first novel, *The Adventures of Roderick Random*. A critical success, its picaresque style and descriptive strengths drew favourable comparisons with the works of Henry Fielding. This was followed by a similar work in 1751, *The Adventures of Peregrine Pickle*, and in 1753 *The Adventures of Ferdinand Count Fathom*, a Gothic horror work which pioneered a style that became extremely popular towards the end of the 18th century.

In 1756 Smollett became the co-founder of *The Critical Review*, a journal he edited until 1763. An article in this publication attacking Admiral Knowles led to Smollett being fined and imprisoned for libel for three months in 1760. Despite its notoriety *The Critical Review* was not a success, and Smollett turned to hackwork and translations to support himself and his family. In 1756 he published a 7-vol travel anthology, *A Compendium of Authentic and Entertaining Voyages*, and between 1757–8 a *History of England*. *The Adventures of Sir Launcelot Greaves*, a clumsy imitation of Cervantes' *Don Quixote*, was published in book form in 1762. Between 1762–3 Smollett edited the Tory journal *The Briton*, which was quickly eclipsed by its rival *The North Briton*.

In 1763 Smollett's health deteriorated, and he began a series of recuperative journeys which were to form the basis of his caustic work *Travels Through France and Italy*, published in 1766. Its corrosive tone and travel descriptions led Laurence Sterne to dub him 'Smelfungus'. Smollett's final work, considered by many to be his finest, was the epistolary novel *The Expedition of Humphrey Clinker*, 1771. Shortly after its publication Smollett died in Livorno, Italy.

SMOO CAVE, Nr Durness, Sutherland

A deep creek some two miles east of **Durness** afforded shelter for small craft that could be beached here. At its head is the entrance to a cave in the limestone, 50ft (15m) high and 100ft (30m) in breadth. It was made famous by **Sir Walter Scott**'s visit in 1814 and by a Daniell print. More recently it has been made accessible to **tourists** by military engineers, who have built a stepped path down the steep descent to its entrance and a railed wooden gangway to the first of the lochs within the cave. This is fed by a stream which tumbles in a waterfall through a hole in the roof. A low arch divides the first stretch of water from the second, each about 30m in length. For the most part the roof varies from 20–60ft (6–18m) in height and stalactites and stalagmites add to the enchantment of the surroundings.

SNOW BUNTING

Although mainly an October-April visitor to coasts and hills around Britain, a very small number of snow bunting (*plectrophenax nivalis*) – rarely more than half a dozen pairs – nest on the high tops in the central Highlands, where they are on the extreme southern edge of their Arctic/sub-Arctic range. In Iceland, where the alpine zone is much lower, both the snow bunting and **ptarmigan** breed down to sea level. Most breeding sites are in the high corries of the **Cairngorms** but occasionally a pair nests elsewhere in the Highlands, as in 1954 when one pair nested and raised a brood on **Ben Nevis**. The large numbers of snow bunting that over-winter in Scotland have now become a regular feature around car parks at ski resorts where, like house sparrows, they take food. The white feathers on their wings, less obvious when they are on the ground, give a flock in flight the semblance of drifting snowflakes.

SOAY SHEEP

These are relics of prehistoric husbandry, little changed since sheep were first farmed in Britain nearly 4000 years ago. Somehow they survived on the island of Soay (in the **St Kilda** group), and there is still a strong population there whose ancestors probably arrived in prehistoric times. In 1930, when the people of St Kilda were evacuated together with their livestock, 107 sheep were brought from Soay and released on Hirta (the main island). Now they live free of human interference, providing biologists with valuable insights into how populations of mammals are regulated in the absence of predation.

Sheep were taken from Soay in Victorian times to form ornamental flocks on estates like Woburn Abbey in Bedfordshire. The mainland Soay breed is in many ways different from that of St Kilda, where only about half the females (and almost all the males) are horned. Mainland breeders have preferred ewes to have horns, and have generally preferred a uniformly brownish colour, while on St Kilda there is quite a variety of colours.

The Soay is a small-bodied sheep, now popular with smallholders and hobby farmers, and supported by the Rare Breeds Survival Trust. Its one great drawback as a domestic breed is the near-impossiblity of rounding up a flock with dogs – a group thus approached will quickly scatter and the only way to catch them is to run individuals into corners or to exhaustion.

'SOBIESKI STEWARTS', The

Two brothers, 'John Sobieski Stolberg Stuart' (c1795–1872) and 'Charles Edward Stuart' (c1799–1880) revived the unsubstantiated claim of their father, a Lieutenant Thomas Allan RN, to be the legitimate son of **Prince Charles Edward Stewart** by Louise of Stolberg. The Prince styled himself 'Count of Albany', and hence the title which the Sobieski Stewarts successively assumed. Both are said to have fought for Napoleon at Waterloo and subsequently to have come to Scotland. Amongst those who listened sympathetically to their tale and indulged their pretension was **Lord Lovat** who installed them at Aigas on an island in the Beauly River. Together they produced several collections of verse and the *Vestiarium Scoticum*, an 'ancient' work on **clan tartans** whose authenticity is as bogus as its authors' descent.

SOLWAY MOSS, Battle of (1542)

Having successfully routed the English army at **Haddon Rig** (August 1542), **James V** mustered another army to invade England. It gathered at **Lochmaben** where James decided to wait, sending 10,000 men under the command of **Oliver Sinclair of Pitcairns** to cross the river Esk and 'harry into England' as far as they could. On 24 November the Scots army was met at Solway Moss by a 3000-strong English force under Sir Thomas Wharton. What should have been an easy Scottish victory was a disaster. Oliver Sinclair, one of James's 'favourites', was regarded by the nobles as an upstart. Not only did they refuse to obey his orders, but they started to fight amongst themselves and some even turned away. The Borderers saw no reason to risk their lives for a king at whose hands they had suffered years of persecution; many others preferred imprisonment at the hands of the English to death for the sake of a king they no longer trusted; and the dark memory of **Flodden** still weighed heavy on many a Scot's fighting spirit. In the ensuing pandemonium few were killed but as many as 1200 Scots were captured, including Oliver Sinclair. James withdrew to **Edinburgh** and thence to **Linlithgow**. His death two weeks after the battle – and a mere six days after the birth of his daughter **Mary** – removed any desire Henry might have had to press home his advantage; the course of history was changing, and it behoved the English King to withdraw his forces and await events.

SOLWAY VIADUCT

From 1869 to 1935 the Solway Firth was spanned by a **railway** viaduct, Europe's longest when first built, between Bowness (Cumbria) and a site approximately 1½ miles south-east of **Annan** in **Dumfriesshire**. Built by the **Kelso**-born engineer James Brunlees (1816–92) for the Solway Junction Railway, the structure was intended to carry trains of haematite ore from west Cumberland to the smelters of **Lanarkshire** without going through Carlisle. It was 1774m long, 11m above low water, and comprised 5000 tons of metal. Closed to traffic in 1921, it offered a dangerous and unofficial walkway between the two countries until demolished by its then owners, the London Midland & Scottish Railway, in 1935. Its stone-faced approach viaducts can still be seen on both sides of the estuary.

SOMERLED (c1126–64)

Somerled was a pivotal figure in west Highland history at a period when a more homogeneous Hebridean society was forming out of its Norse and Celtic parts. Though a flimsy Norse influence was to linger for another century, that culture declined as the language and culture of Gaeldom flourished. According to **Clan Donald** historians, Somerled's mother was Norse while his father, Gillebride, claimed descent from the kings of **Dalriada**. His name, *Sumar-lidi* (Summer Traveller, the season when **Vikings** went looting) is gaelicised as Somhairle and anglicised as Sorley.

Somerled waged war against Norse settlers in the southern **Hebrides** until, in 1156, with a fleet said to number 80 galleys, he won a great victory off **Islay**. He claimed and married Ragnhilde, daughter of Olaf, King of Man, and acquired the title 'Regulus' (sub-king) of **Argyll**, rendered in Gaelic *Ri Innse Gall is Ceann Tir*, Ruler of the Strangers' Isles and **Kintyre**. His main fortress was probably Dunivaig, Islay; Claig Castle off **Jura** may also have associations. Remarkably, considering the lack of detailed information from this time, Somerled is also credited with the invention or introduction of the hinged rudder, which might well have contributed to his success over conventional longships. A grave-slab said to carry his effigy is to be seen at **Saddell Abbey** in Kintyre, founded from Mellifont in Ireland in 1160, no doubt under his patronage.

His eldest son, Ranald (Reginald), succeeded to his Hebridean possessions, but it is from his grandson Donald that the clan takes its patronymic. Not till three generations later did the chiefs of Clan Donald adopt the title *Dominus Insularum*, **Lord of the Isles**, which they then held till its forfeiture to the Crown in 1493. The title is currently held by the Prince of Wales.

Olaf the Red was murdered in 1154; his son, Somerled's brother-in-law Godred, forced to battle in 1156, fled to Norway in 1158 to plead for help against the might of Somerled, but the Regulus had by then turned his attention to the overlord of his mainland possessions. Moving up the **Clyde** with a large force in 1164, he camped at **Renfrew** and began negotiations with representatives of the King of Scots. He was killed by treachery and his force retreated.

SOMERVILLE, Mary (1780–1872)
Mathematician

Mary Fairfax was born in **Jedburgh**, the daughter of Admiral Sir William Fairfax, one of Nelson's captains. She had received only one year's formal education by the age of 20. But, having studied algebra surreptitiously, Mary Somerville (as she became after her second marriage) became a noted mathematician, making her reputation by translating the research of Laplace before going on to publish a number of scientific works, in one of which she predicted the discovery of an unknown planet, Neptune. She was still writing when she died in Italy in 1872. Oxford's Somerville College is named after her.

Mary Somerville (née Fairfax), by Thomas Phillips, c1834 (entry p 931) (SNPG)

SOUTAR, William (1898–1943) Poet

William Soutar was born in **Perth** into a middle-class family; his father, the son of a **Perthshire** farmer, and his mother, the daughter of a Perth Sergeant of Police, were Scots in speech and character and deeply religious, adherents of the Auld Licht, or United Original **Secession Church**. William, their only son, attended the Southern District School in Perth (where he was a rebellious pupil and led a school strike in 1911) and Perth Academy, where he distinguished himself in sports and academic subjects and began to write poetry.

His two years in the Royal Navy (1916–18), serving mainly in the North Atlantic, were to be his only experience of life in the outside world. In 1918 he contracted a mysterious ailment which affected his legs and feet, an illness which never completely left him. He recovered enough to go to **Edinburgh University**, initially studying medicine but switching to English language and literature. His application to the craft of verse made certain aspects of academic studies seem uncongenial, and he came into direct conflict with the University authorities over the compulsory study of Anglo-Saxon. He left university in June 1923 with a third class honours degree and was accepted for teacher training at **Moray House** College of Education. But in October of that year it became obvious that his health was worsening; he returned home to Perth for medical treatment. The condition, later diagnosed as a form of spondylitis, continued to deteriorate until, by 1930, he was completely bedridden.

Soutar's letters from the Navy confirm his literary bent and on his first real day of active service in 1917 he began a diary which he kept up all his life. By 1922 he was in communication with **Hugh MacDiarmid** and saw himself in the forefront of the Scottish literary renaissance. His first book of poems, *Gleanings by an Under-graduate*, was published in 1923, a volume of rather Edwardian-style poems in English, flushed with a youthful, romantic vision of life. Contact with MacDiarmid's experiments with synthetic Scots and his own firm background in spoken Scots led Soutar to follow suit. A further catalyst was his parents' adoption in 1927 of a distant relative, Evelyn, then a child of six. Soutar's second book of poems, *Conflict*, again in English, appeared in 1931, but for some years he had been writing poems to amuse his little sister, lively and inventive poems he called 'bairnryhmes', which appeared in 1933 under the title *Seeds in the Wind*. That book, and *Poems in Scots*, published two years later, established Soutar as a poet of stature and a writer for children to rival **Robert Louis Stevenson** and Walter de la Mare.

A book-length selection from his diaries (but a tiny fragment of the whole) was published in 1954 as *The Diary of a Dying Man*, described by its editor Alexander Scott as 'a self-portrait unrivalled in this age for insight and detail', and by Thomas Mallon, American author of a study of famous diaries, as 'a neglected classic'. It was reprinted in 1988. The diaries reveal the nature of Soutar's life, especially after becoming bedridden in 1930, his innermost thoughts and his responses to the world outside, both literary and political (he was a socialist and a pacifist). Above all they reveal his courage and dry sense of humour. He eventually died of TB.

Soutar published 10 volumes of poetry, including riddles, epigrams and other poetic fragments. A large selection of his poetry, edited by W R Aitken, was published in 1988, but a full *Collected Poems* is yet to appear. His letters remain unpublished.

SOUTERRAINS, see TEALING

SOUTH QUEENSFERRY, West Lothian

An old and highly individual former **royal burgh** (1636) overshot by the **Forth** Road and **Rail Bridges**, Queensferry curves its quaint, long and narrow High Street for about half a mile along a steep, rocky shelf on the shore below **Dalmeny**. The Anglo-Saxon Princess Margaret fetched up on the Binks while fleeing from William the Conqueror and seeking the sanctuary of **Malcolm III 'Canmore'** across the Firth of Forth at **Dunfermline**; after she became **Queen Margaret** in 1071, free passage for pilgrims en route to **St Andrews** was guaranteed by the King via the 'Queen's Ferry'. (Begun by **David I** in 1129, the public service closed on the opening of the Forth Road Bridge in 1964). St Mary's Episcopal Church (restored 1890) was perhaps begun soon after 1441 when James Dundas of **Dundas Castle** granted the White Friars lands 'lying in the town of the ferry . . . for the church of St Mary the Virgin and . . . buildings . . . in the form of a monastery' which operated as a hospice until the **Reformation**. During the 17th century, when 'the Ferry' conducted a vigorous trade with northern Europe, the very distinctive terraced High Street was first developed; the houses on the steep south side are set back from the roadway with their pavements raised above cellars; the Tolbooth, Laburnum House, the Black Castle (1626) and Plewlands House (1641) reflect this period of prosperity. The Hawes Inn (1683) was the scene of the fictional liaison between Captain Hoseason of the brig *Covenant* of Dysart and

Uncle Ebenezer prior to the trepanning of David Balfour in **Robert Louis Stevenson**'s *Kidnapped*. During the Ferry Fair each August, the **'Burry Man'** is supported on his perambulation around the town.

SOUTH RONALDSAY, Orkney

Connected to the **Orkney** mainland by the **Churchill Barrier** causeways, this island also contains the ferry terminal at Burwick, 6½ miles from **John O'Groats** across the Pentland Firth. The service operates only during the summer months, and the plan to introduce a vehicle ferry remains unfulfilled.

A stalled **cairn** dating from about 3000 BC is known as the Tomb of the Eagles, owing to the number of **sea eagles'** claws found in it. In old St Mary's Church there is a memorial with Latin inscription to Sir Hugh Hackro, knighted by **Robert I** in 1314 for his services at **Bannockburn**. There also remains the school built by William Tomison, founder of Edmonton in Alberta, Canada, to provide free education from 1787 until 1884, by which time the state had undertaken this responsibility. Another native who made his mark in Canada was John Norquoy, born near Burwick, first Prime Minister of Manitoba from 1870–9. Those content to remain at home, plus numerous incomers, enjoy an island surrounded by seas exceptionally rich in fish, on land well suited to animal husbandry.

SOUTH UIST, Outer Hebrides

The island of South Uist, the second largest in the Outer **Hebrides**, is linked to **Benbecula** in the north by a causeway. With a land area of 141 square miles, it has a population of just over 2000. The east coast is deeply indented by four sea lochs, at the head of the most southerly of which is the main village and ferry terminal, Lochboisdale, with ferry connections to **Oban** and Castlebay (**Barra**). From the south tip of South Uist there are passenger ferries to **Eriskay** and Barra.

The mountainous spine of the island runs almost the full length of its eastern side, rising to 2034ft (620m) at Beinn Mhor and 1988ft (606m) at Hecla. The west coast has 20 miles of virtually unbroken beach, silvery shell sand backed by dunes and the springy grass of the machair making for excellent coastal walking, usually with an invigorating breeze blowing off the Atlantic. Between the mountains and the machair the peaty moorland is broken by more than 190 freshwater lochs, with excellent trout and sea-trout **fishing**. The Loch Druidibeg **National Nature Reserve** to the north of Drimsdale provides an ideal habitat for many species of waterfowl, including native greylag geese, which breed here.

Sites of archaeological interest include the excavated prehistoric aisled house at Kilphedar and the Reinaval passage grave on the northern shoulder of the hill just south of the township of Mingary. Dun Mor is an Iron Age fortified island in a loch just south of West Gerinish, while Dun Uiselan is a similar site in another loch west of Ollag. Two churches at Howmore, dedicated to St Mary and **St Columba**, may date from early Christian times, perhaps as early as the 7th century. The graveyard at Hallan contains one of the few 16th century carved grave-slabs to be found in the Western Isles.

Just north of Milton a cairn marks the birthplace of **Flora MacDonald**, who helped **Charles Edward Stewart** evade capture and assisted his escape. With the Prince disguised as her maid 'Betty Burke', they sailed to **Skye** from Benbecula in a small boat on 28 June 1746.

The island suffered badly from **clearances** in the 19th century as a result of the policies of Colonel Gordon of Cluny, who bought it, along with the neighbouring islands of Benbecula and Eriskay, from the **MacDonalds** of Clanranald in 1838. Between 1841–61 the population fell from 7300 to 5300 as townships were cleared for sheep. Many islanders emigrated to North America.

South Uist's economy is dominated by the army missile range on the north-west corner of the island from where rockets are fired out over the Atlantic, their progress monitored by a tracking station on **St Kilda**. Other sources of income are **crofting**, fishing (mainly for lobsters and crabs), shellfish farming and **seaweed** processing. The missile range control installation, known locally as 'space city', dominates the skyline of Rueval, and dwarfs the 30ft granite statue of Our Lady of the Isles by Hew Lorimer (1959). The mainly Roman Catholic and Gaelic-speaking islanders have a more relaxed attitude to life than their Protestant neighbours of **North Uist** and Benbecula.

SPEAN BRIDGE, Inverness-shire

Eight miles east of **Fort William** the river Spean from **Loch Laggan** constituted a formidable obstacle to traffic through the **Great Glen**. General **Wade** bridged its gorge at High Bridge (1737, parts still standing), and thereabouts in 1745 some **MacDonalds** of Keppoch (Roy Bridge) ambushed and eventually captured two companies of government troops on their way to reinforce Fort William. The engagement marked the opening of the '45 **Jacobite Rising**. In 1819 **Telford** chose an easier route over the Spean one mile to the east where the village of Spean Bridge subsequently developed round the junction with the A86 to **Badenoch** and Speyside. West of the village on rising ground beside the A82 stands the Commando Memorial (1952), a bronze of three soldiers on a stone plinth commanding magnificent views south to **Ben Nevis** and north across the Great Glen to **Achnacarry**, where the commandos trained and had their headquarters during World War II. South of the village the road passes the numbered steadings of the 'Great Glen Cattle Ranch', a venture set up by Joseph Hobbs in the 1940s–50s. Hobbs, from Hampshire, had made a fortune in Canada, lost it in the Depression and made another in Scotch **whisky** which he then ploughed (and drained) into this unpromising stretch of **Lochaber** moorland.

SPENCE, Sir Basil (1907–76) Architect

Spence was born in India but educated in **Edinburgh** where he also studied architecture. After training he briefly went to London to work in the office of Edwin Lutyens, who was to be a lasting influence. In 1930 he returned to Edinburgh, first to work with William Kininmonth in the practice of **Rowand Anderson** & Paul, then on his own. Before the war most of his work was in Scotland and ranged from housing to commercial buildings and country houses. In 1951 he was involved with the Festival of Britain, designing the Sea and Ships Pavilions. His greatest success came in the same year when he won the competition for Coventry Cathedral. The design, completed in 1962, with its sensitive use of the old bombed cathedral, is seen as his masterpiece. From the mid-50s onwards his firm acted as planning consultants to a number of universities (**Edinburgh**, Sussex, Liverpool and Nottingham). Whether he designed housing or offices, Spence was always boldly modern, translating and developing the concept of monumentality into contemporary design (Knightsbridge Barracks, London, 1970; British Embassy, Rome, 1971). His designs attracted as much praise as controversy and he is regarded by many as one of the leading British 20th century architects.

SPENCE, (James) Lewis (Thomas Chalmers) (1874–1955) Poet and Anthropologist

Born at **Broughty Ferry** near **Dundee**, Spence studied dentistry at the **University of Edinburgh** and in 1889 became a sub-editor of The Scotsman. He subsequently edited various journals, including the British Weekly from 1906–9. On leaving the British Weekly he became interested in anthropology. An expert on the mythologies and customs of ancient Mexico, South America and the Middle East, he wrote several works on the subject, including The Mythologies of Ancient Mexico and Peru (1907), A Dictionary of Mythology (1910), An Encyclopaedia of Occultism (1920) and The Magic Arts in Celtic Britain (1945). For his work in this field, Spence was elected a Fellow of the Royal Anthropological Institute.

He also became known as a poet, producing work based on his studies of the style and language of the **Makars**. His collections of poetry, such as The Phoenix (1924) and Weirds and Vanities (1927) were well received, and praised by **Hugh MacDiarmid** among others. Spence's efforts to experiment with Old Scots dialect played a part in reviving interest in Scottish literature and Scots poetry, and he became associated with the **Scottish Renaissance** movement, along with **Marion Angus**, **Alexander Gray**, **William Soutar**, Hugh MacDiarmid and others. He was also involved in the Scottish nationalist movement, becoming one of the founders of the **National Party of Scotland** in 1928, unsuccessfully contesting a parliamentary seat as a Nationalist candidate, and writing articles on Scottish independence. He died in **Edinburgh**.

SPEY, River, Inverness-shire/Moray/Banffshire

Its length (variously estimated at between 90 and 100 miles) makes the Spey Scotland's second river. But although it passes through Lowland country in its latter stages, its character is Highland throughout, making it unnavigable and of commercial importance only for timber extraction [see **Speymouth**]. Its renown therefore depends entirely on its superlative scenery, its salmon **fishing**s and its **whisky** distilleries. The Spey's source is usually taken to be tiny Loch Spey high in the **Monadhliath** north of **Loch Laggan**. From Melgarve it is accompanied down to Laggan by **Wade**'s road from the **Corrieyairack Pass**. The Truim joins it at **Newtonmore** and the river assumes its north-easterly course as it sweeps into the Highland playground along the A9. The Tromie and Feshie waters from **Badenoch** here join as, with the Monadhliath to the right and the **Cairngorms** to the left, the river meanders grandly into Strath-

spey (roughly from **Aviemore** to **Aberlour**). At **Grantown** begin the best salmon fishings, the Speyside Way (mainly following the disused **railway** line) and the Speyside distilleries. Few of these draw water from the river itself and some are a fair distance from it; **Glenlivet**, for instance, home of some of the choicest malts, feeds into the Avon (pron A'an), itself the largest of the Spey's tributaries. From Aberlour and a brief excursion along the edge of **Banffshire**, the river returns to **Moray** and, veering north through fine woodlands to pass **Rothes** and **Fochabers**, finally enters the Moray Firth between Kingston and Tugnet.

SPEYMOUTH, Moray

Strictly speaking Speymouth parish does not include the mouth of the **Spey**, just its west bank inland. Hereabouts was a ford of great importance used by the troops of Edward I (twice) and by those of Cromwell, **Montrose** and Cumberland. The latter, on his way to **Culloden**, camped by the manse of Red Kirk 'where he slept' under the same roof as, a few nights previously, had most of the **Jacobite** notables. South of here and of Mosstodloch village, William Duff of Dipple, and later Braco lived (1684) before amassing the fortune which launched his family on their meteoric rise to the **Dukedom of Fife**. In the process they acquired, amongst many, Innes House, a 17th century L-plan tower house, now much altered. It was once the home of Jane Innes, a great beauty who married Thomas Pitt, interloper and Governor of Madras (twice) who acquired the Pitt diamond and was the grandfather of Chatham and the great grandfather of Pitt the Younger. Innes is in the parish of Urquhart which also includes the true Speymouth village of Garmouth, where **Charles II** landed in 1650 and was obliged to sign the Solemn League and **Covenant**, and Kingston. The latter was so named by **shipbuilders** from Kingston upon Hull who settled here in the late 18th century to capitalise on timber floated down the Spey and duly produced 300 ships, many of them clippers. On the other side of the river's mouth their achievement is amongst those celebrated in a museum housed in what was once an icehouse. Well named Tugnet, the icehouse vaults were where in the 18th and 19th centuries salmon netted at the mouth of the river were stored and packed prior to despatch. The ice was collected during the winter, the whole operation employing about 150 people.

SPOTTISWOODE, John (1565–1639) Archbishop

Made Archbishop of **Glasgow** by **James VI** in 1603 and of **St Andrews** in 1615, Spottiswoode was a strong advocate of Episcopacy, pushing through the **Five Articles of Perth** in 1618. He crowned **Charles I** at **Holyrood** in 1633 and was appointed Chancellor of Scotland in 1635. His criticism of Charles I's **Prayer Book** resulted in his deposition and excommunication by the **General Assembly** in 1638.

SPYNIE, Nr Elgin, Moray

Though now three miles from the sea and represented only by its ruined palace, Spynie was once a port and township on the Lossie estuary. Perhaps in the 17th century a bar of sand and shingle finally cut it off from

Spynie Palace near Elgin, as drawn by R W Billings in the 1840s (RWB)

the sea and turned its tidal reach into marsh and loch, most of which **Telford** drained in the 19th century by digging a **canal** to **Lossiemouth**. Crops now grow where once was the celebrated sheet of water which fringed Spynie Palace. 'One of the finest 15th century castles', it qualified as a palace by being the residence of the Bishops of **Moray** who, though their cathedral was transferred to **Elgin** in 1224, continued to live in their waterside palace until after the **Reformation**. Of the extensive and romantic ruins, the oldest part is thought to be the gateway in the eastern wall of enclosure. An unusually grand and elaborate affair with portcullis and stairway to the battlements above, it dates from the early 15th century and was probably the work of craftsmen who were rebuilding **Elgin Cathedral** after its destruction by **Alexander Stewart**, the 'Wolf of Badenoch'. The six-storey keep, with walls 70ft (21m) high and 10ft6in (3.2m) thick, dates from about 1470 and was built by Bishop David Stewart in defiant response to the **Earl of Huntly**'s threat 'to pull the bishop out of his pigeon-holes'. The exterior remains complete to the parapet corbels and there was once an adjoining range of buildings. Smaller towers, less well preserved, stood at the other three corners of the enclosing wall.

Queen Mary stayed here in 1562; **James VI** presented it to a son of the Earl of Crawford, then demanded it back; after the Restoration it was returned to the Church, but in 1686 abandoned to neglect and casual vandalism, in which state it remains.

STAFFA, Island of, Nr Mull, Argyll

A small island of great celebrity, Staffa comprises 71 acres (28ha) of columnar basalt topped by soil and grass. The hexagonal columns result from the slow cooling of tertiary basalt lava 60 million years ago and are geologically similar to the Giant's Causeway in Antrim and to the Ardmeanach peninsula on **Mull**, six miles to the south-east.

The island enjoys the distinction, rare in the British Isles, of having been 'discovered' by an explorer. Acting on the advice of a Mr Leach, in 1772 Sir Joseph Banks, one-time companion of Captain Cook, latterly President of the Royal Society and the great impresario of exploration, directed his ship towards the island while returning from a voyage to Iceland. He was impressed. Of the cave that he named, mistakenly, after Fingal [**Finn mac Cumhal**], he felt 'forced to acknowledge that this piece of architecture, formed by nature, far surpasses that of the Louvre, that of St Peter at Rome, all that remains of Palmyra and Paestum, and all that the genius, the taste and the luxury of the Greeks were capable of inventing'. Coinciding with the height of neo-classicism – **Robert Adam** was then working on **Mellerstain House** – this news of indigenous pillared halls in the **Hebrides** occasioned considerable excitement.

To view 'the greatest natural curiosity in Europe if not in the world' visitors converged on Staffa. They included **Sir Walter Scott** (1810), John Keats (1818), Felix Mendelssohn (1829, whose *Hebrides Overture* was inspired by the noise of the sea in Fingal's Cave, otherwise *An Uamh Binn* – the melodious cave), J M W Turner (1830), **William Wordsworth** (1833), **Queen Victoria** and Prince Albert (1836), Jules Verne (1839), **David Livingstone** (1864), **Robert Louis Stevenson** (1870), etc. The boatmen of **Oban** and **Mull** made good money but it does not appear that the island was

Interior of Fingal's Cave, Staffa, from an engraving (SP)

reinhabited. In 1772 Banks had found one family in desperate residence. Crops of oats and potatoes were reported but before the end of the 18th century the island was deserted save for summer graziers. It was said that the last residents moved out when severe winter storms so buffeted the island that their house, 'though situated in the middle', began to vibrate and 'the pot which hung over the fire partook of it'. Deciding that 'nothing but an evil spirit could have rocked it in that way', they took the first opportunity to evacuate. Three **red deer**, reported as resident in 1800, presumably swam back to Mull whence they must have come.

The island, now in the care of the **National Trust for Scotland**, may be reached by boat from Mull, **Iona** and Oban, but landing is still only possible in calm seas.

STANDARD, Battle of the (1138)

On the death (1135) of the English King Henry I, **David I** of Scotland initially espoused the cause of Henry's daughter (and his own niece) Matilda against Stephen (who was married to another of his nieces). Subsequently persuaded by Stephen to change sides, but reverting to the support of Matilda when Stephen failed to make good his promise of the Earldom of Northumberland for his own son Henry, David eventually decided his best interests lay not in becoming embroiled in an English civil war, but in advancing his own borders southwards. Launching a ferocious invasion through Northumberland and Durham in January 1138, he was eventually faced with an English army under Thurstan, Archbishop of York, near Northallerton in the

North Riding of Yorkshire. The ensuing engagement on 22 August, in which David's forces were heavily defeated, became known as the Battle of the Standard after the tall mast hung around with religious relics and carried as a talisman by Thurstan's army.

STANDING STONES

Along with **cairns**, **duns**, **crannogs**, **brochs** and hill forts, standing stones constitute an important and ubiquitous element in Scotland's impressive prehistoric heritage. Any monolith that is erect or otherwise visually arresting, whether isolated or part of some larger layout, may pass as a standing stone (eg on an Ordnance Survey map). But archaeologists need to be more precise. They usually classify separately those stones which form part of a circle, as at **Callanish**, **Clava**, or Loanhead of Daviot (near **Oldmeldrum**). Such arrangements, usually associated with a burial cairn, are classified as stone circles and belong to the Neolithic period. So do the rarer henge monuments, like that at Ballymeanoch near **Lochgilphead**, which are distinguished by concentric earthworks and may include an arrangement of standing stones (although Scotland possesses no actual henges, or 'hanging' lintel stones, as at Stonehenge).

Similarly, though perhaps two millennia later, those stones and slabs engraved with **Pictish** symbols and/or crosses are also separately classified. Known as symbol stones and cross-slabs, they date from the 7th century AD onwards and so belong to history rather than prehistory. And the same goes for the inscribed grave stones and crosses of the early Christian era in the south-west (from the 5th century on) and in **Dalriada** (8th century on).

Having thus excluded stone circles, henge monuments and Pictish and Christian stones and slabs, the term 'standing stone' can be reserved primarily for erect stones or slabs, mostly of the Bronze Age. They occur in many parts of the country, occasionally in pairs or in conjunction with a cairn, and occasionally engraved with cup-and-ring marks. Such marks, which also appear on natural outcrops of rock, remain unexplained. So does the significance of the standing stones. Attempts to read into the marks some devotional or astronomical significance, or into the alignment of the stones with local features some calendrical, directional or territorial significance have yet to win widespread acceptance. On the other hand, the great labour involved in erecting massive stones or in incising cup-and-ring marks bespeaks something more than art or fancy.

STANLEY, Nr Perth, Perthshire

Perth's answer to **New Lanark**, Stanley was purpose-built as a **cotton** mill and dormitory village by George Dempster of Dunnichen with advice from Richard Arkwright in 1785. The original village had been named for Lady Amelia Stanley, daughter of the Earl of Derby and wife of the Marquis of **Atholl**. The mill, a courtyard with a tall chimney and three sides of handsome mill buildings, stands by the **Tay** whose waters originally powered the machinery. In the 19th century it employed up to 1200 people for whom the village provided both terraced and tenement accommodation plus school, shops, church, etc. Much altered in the course of continuous occupation and operation, the whole forms an interesting contrast to self-consciously restored New Lanark.

STEELL, Sir John (1804–91) Sculptor

Born in **Aberdeen**, Steell studied as an artist in **Edinburgh** and Rome but, leaving painting to his brother Gourlay (1819–94) who became curator of the **National Gallery** in Edinburgh, he worked in stone and bronze. Figures of **Sir Walter Scott**, **Robert Burns** (New York), **Queen Victoria**, Prince Albert, **Lord Dalhousie** (Calcutta) and numerous busts testify to his ability to meet the considerable Victorian demand for statuary. He was appointed the Queen's Sculptor in Scotland and knighted. His most famous works are probably the Edinburgh equestrian compositions of the Duke of Wellington in **Princes Street Gardens** and 'Alexander taming Bucephalus' at the **City Chambers**.

STEIN, Jock (1922–85) Football Player and Manager

Born at Burnbank in **Lanarkshire**, Jock Stein, a young man of impressive physique, started work down the local mines before taking up professional **football** with Albion Rovers and then with Llanelli Town in Wales. In 1951 he returned to Scotland to play as centre half for Celtic, captaining them to a League and Cup double three years later. No more than an average professional player, he rapidly came into his own as a manager when he began an illustrious career at Dunfermline Athletic in 1960. Showing a unique talent for motivating players, and an uncanny ability to spot weaknesses in the opposition, Stein's side won the Scottish Cup in 1961 and made a big impression in European ties. In 1964 he moved to Hibernian, whence he abruptly returned to Celtic in March 1965. Within months his team won the Cup and went on to an awesome record of nine successive championships, the European Cup in 1967 – Britain's first – and a second unsuccessful European Cup Final appearance. In 1978 Celtic rather surprisingly allocated Stein a commercial position unacceptable to him. He preferred the management of Leeds United but was soon asked to succeed Ally MacLeod as manager of Scotland, a job he had earlier held on a caretaker basis in 1965. His management reign included the 1982 World Cup competition, but he collapsed tragically on 10 September 1985 when attending a Wales v Scotland match which guaranteed Scotland a fourth successive appearance in the World Cup Finals. Jock Stein had been made a CBE in 1970.

STENHOUSE, John (1809–80) Scientist

Born in **Glasgow**, Stenhouse was educated at the city's **University**, studying chemistry there and at Giessen under Justus Liebig. His academic career was affected by ill-health, but this did not prevent him from discovering the disinfecting properties of wood charcoal applied to air filters, thus making him the inventor of the gasmask. He was a founder member of the Chemical Society and a Fellow of the Royal Society.

STEPHEN, George, Lord Mountstephen (1829–1921) Canadian Financier

The son of a **Dufftown** carpenter, Stephen began his career as a draper with apprenticeships in **Aberdeen**, **Glasgow** and London before emigrating to Canada in 1850. There he joined and soon took control of a relative's drapery business. He also diversified into banking, becoming a Director and then President (1876) of the Bank of Montreal. In 1878 with his cousin **Donald Smith** and other Scots Canadians he bought up a US railway concession to complete the Great Northern line. This venture produced vast profits; the same consortium, encouraged by **J A MacDonald**'s privatisation of the project, then took on the construction of the Canadian Pacific line [see also **Donald Smith**]. As President of Canadian Pacific (1880–8) Stephen more than anyone was responsible for seeing its completion. In 1891 he was created 1st Baron Mountstephen, the title deriving from a peak in the Rockies which had itself been named after him. He returned to Britain in 1893. Aberdeen was amongst those cities which benefited from his numerous donations and bequests.

STEVENSON, Alan (1807–65) Lighthouse Engineer

The eldest son of **Robert Stevenson**, Alan was born in **Edinburgh** and followed his father into the family business of lighthouse engineering. Appointed Engineer to the Northern Lighthouse Board from 1843–53, his greatest achievement was the construction of the 138ft (42m) Skerryvore lighthouse (off **Tiree**) over a five-year period.

STEVENSON, David (1815–86) Lighthouse Engineer

The second son of **Robert Stevenson**, David succeeded his elder brother **Alan** as Engineer to the Northern Lighthouse Board in 1853, becoming responsible for the construction of 30 lighthouses. His invention of an aseismatic arrangement for the protection of lighthouse mechanisms from earthquakes greatly benefited navigation, particularly in Japan.

STEVENSON, Robert (1772–1850) Lighthouse Engineer

Robert Stevenson was born in **Glasgow**, the son of a West Indies merchant who died in 1774. In 1791 he entered the service of Thomas Smith, a lampmaker and the Engineer to the Northern Lighthouse Board, who became his stepfather the following year. Stevenson spent three winters studying at **Glasgow University** (he later studied for three seasons at **Edinburgh University**), and then in 1796 took charge of the lighthouse side of Smith's business. He married Smith's daughter Jane in 1799, one year before completing his apprenticeship and becoming a partner in the firm.

In 1797 Stevenson succeeded Smith as the Engineer to the Board, and went on to design and supervise the construction of 18 lighthouses, the first erected on the **Bell Rock** off **Arbroath** (1806–11). Stevenson was highly praised both for the design of his lighthouse towers and for the advanced lighting equipment he installed, and was recognised as the leading authority on lighthouses of the day.

He was also active in other branches of **engineering**, including **canal** building, harbour improvements, river widening, and drainage schemes such as that for **Edinburgh**'s **Nor' Loch**. The capital's elegant Regent Road is

Robert Stevenson and one of his lighthouses, by John Syme, c1833 (SNPG)

the most famous of the routes he laid out, and Glasgow's Hutcheson Bridge [see **Victoria Bridge**] (1829, but replaced in 1871) the most impressive of several he built. He was also very interested in **railways**, surveying routes such as that for the Stockton and Darlington Railway, later built by Robert Stephenson. He advocated the adoption of the flanged **locomotive** wheel and was credited by Stephenson with suggesting the use of malleable rather than cast-iron rails.

Stevenson's sons **Alan** (1807–65), **David** (1815–86) and **Thomas** (1818–87) became partners in the family firm, with David assuming control of the general management of the business. Between them the brothers were responsible for the construction of over 40 lighthouses, and for many other important engineering projects in Britain and abroad. Overshadowed by the literary fame subsequently attained by Thomas's son **Robert Louis Stevenson**, the Stevenson engineers deserve greater recognition as some of the most accomplished and successful in Scottish history.

STEVENSON, Robert Louis (Lewis Balfour) (1850–94) Author

The best-loved literary figure of his time as much for his attractive personality as for his authorship of *Treasure Island*, *Kidnapped* and *Dr Jekyll and Mr Hyde*, Stevenson was born in **Edinburgh** on 13 November 1850, the only child of **Thomas Stevenson**. He described his childhood in detail in his autobiographical essays and vividly recalled its emotions and pleasures in *A Child's Garden of Verses* (1885). After an irregular schooling, frequently interrupted by illness, he entered **Edinburgh University** to train as an engineer; but his ambition from an early age had been to become a professional writer and in 1871 his father agreed that as a compromise he should study **law**. He was admitted advocate in 1875 but never practised. During these years he rebelled against the

conventions of respectable Edinburgh society and there were bitter quarrels with his father (a devout **Presbyterian**) about religion.

In 1873 Stevenson met the critic Professor Sidney Colvin who became his lifelong friend and literary mentor, and Mrs Frances Sitwell (who later married Colvin); they recognised his genius and gave him much-needed encouragement. To Mrs Sitwell Stevenson poured out long emotional letters about his problems and his literary projects. Slowly, with Colvin's help, he began to achieve a reputation with his essays (later collected in *Virginibus Puerisque*, 1881) and short stories (collected in *New Arabian Nights*, 1882). Another close friendship (broken only by a quarrel in 1888) was formed with the poet and critic W E Henley with whom he later wrote four unsuccessful plays including *Deacon Brodie* (1880).

The closest friend of his youth was his painter cousin R A M (Bob) Stevenson, and he spent much time with him in France. His early travels were undertaken so that he could write books about them. *An Inland Voyage* (1878), describing a canoe journey, was followed by *Travels with a Donkey in the Cevennes* (1879). *Edinburgh: Picturesque Notes* (1878) is the classic account of the city whose climate he hated but which always haunted his imagination.

In the art colony of Grez in 1876 Stevenson fell in love with Fanny Vandegrift Osbourne, an American 10

Robert Louis Stevenson in Samoa two years before his death, by Count Girolamo Nerli, 1892 (SNPG)

years older than himself who was estranged from her husband. She returned to California in 1878 and in August 1879, to the violent disapproval of her father, Stevenson followed her, travelling cheaply by immigrant ship and then by train across America, recording his experiences in *The Amateur Emigrant* (1895) and *Across the Plains* (1892). The hardships of the journey and the poverty endured in Monterey and San Francisco wrecked his health and he suffered the first of the haemorrhages of the lung which plagued the rest of his life. He and Fanny (who had divorced her husband) were married in San Francisco in May 1880 following a telegram from his father assuring them of financial support. After a honeymoon in a deserted mining camp (recounted in *The Silverado Squatters*, 1883) they returned to Edinburgh and to full reconciliation with Stevenson's parents.

Stevenson's illness, diagnosed as tuberculosis, meant that he spent much time in bed, his life undoubtedly prolonged by Fanny's nursing. The next seven years were occupied in a vain search for health; two winters were passed at Davos, Switzerland, two summers in the Scottish Highlands and 18 months in the south of France; they finally settled at Bournemouth for three years. Stevenson's melodramatic short story 'The Pavilion on the Links', (1880) set on the coast near **North Berwick**, was followed by two fine stories written at **Pitlochry** in 1881: 'Thrawn Janet', a supernatural tale in Scots, and 'The Merry Men' – 'a fantastic sonata about the sea and wrecks'. Later that year at **Braemar** he began *Treasure Island* (1882), one of the best children's stories in the language.

Wider recognition came with *The Strange Case of Dr Jekyll and Mr Hyde* (1886), the allegorical thriller on the dual nature of man, and *Kidnapped* (1886), a skilful evocation of 18th century Scotland. Two very different works were the mannered romance *Prince Otto* (1885) and the historical potboiler for children *The Black Arrow* (1888). Stevenson made no claim to be a major poet, but *Underwoods* (1897) showed him to be a graceful and original one in both English and Scots. An exchange of articles on the art of fiction led, while he was at Bournemouth, to a warm and lasting friendship with Henry James.

His father's death left Stevenson free to go to America with his wife, mother and young stepson, Lloyd Osbourne, and they spent the winter of 1887–8 at Saranac Lake in the Adirondacks. Here he wrote a series of essays for *Scribner's Magazine*, began his tragic novel *The Master of Ballantrae* (1889), set in 18th century Scotland and America, and collaborated with his stepson on the humorous novel *The Wrong Box* (1889).

In June 1888 he chartered the yacht *Casco* and with his family sailed from San Francisco for the South Seas. On this and two subsequent voyages in trading vessels he visited the Marquesas Islands, Tahiti, Hawaii, the Gilbert Islands, Samoa and Australia; he described his experiences in *In the South Seas* (1896) and used the background in *The Wrecker* (1892), the long diffuse novel written with his stepson. Finding that the climate suited him, Stevenson settled in Samoa from October 1890 with his family (later joined by his stepdaughter, Isobel, who acted as amanuensis) and lived in a large house on the Vailima Plantation. Here he regained a measure

of better health, exulted in being able to enjoy outdoor life again, and became deeply involved in Samoan life and politics; but there were strains due to Fanny's serious mental illness in 1893 and he overworked himself in order to earn the large sums necessary to maintain the estate. The South Seas provided him with fresh themes: his realistic story 'The Beach of Falesa', included in *Island Nights' Entertainments* (1893), and the grim tale 'The Ebb-Tide' (1894) indicated significant new directions. But he found himself increasingly turning in imagination to Scotland. *Catriona* (1893), the sequel to *Kidnapped*, was followed by work on the unfinished *St Ives* (1897), set largely in Edinburgh during the Napoleonic Wars, and he projected other Scottish novels including one on the **Covenanters** whose writings had fascinated him since boyhood. He was working at the height of his mature powers on his unfinished masterpiece *Weir of Hermiston* (1896), set in early 19th century Edinburgh and the Lammermuirs – its main character based on **Robert MacQueen, Lord Braxfield** – when he died suddenly and unexpectedly of cerebral haemorrhage on 3 December 1894.

The romantic legend created by sentimental admirers has helped obscure the recognition of Stevenson as a serious writer, and academic critics have largely ignored or patronised him; but those readers prepared to explore beyond the popular works that made him famous will find a wealth of good things. See: The Works, Tusitala Edition, 35 vols, 1923–4; *Collected Poems*, ed J A Smith, 1971. Biographies: Life, G Balfour, 1901; *Voyage to Windward*, J C Furnas, 1952; RLS, A Life Study, J Calder, 1980.

STEVENSON, Thomas (1818–87) Civil Engineer

Born in **Edinburgh**, the youngest son of **Robert Stevenson**, Thomas entered the family **engineering** business at the age of 17. His invention of azimuthal condensing lights greatly advanced the progress of lighthouse illumination, and his interest in meteorology was marked by the introduction of the 'Stevenson Screen' for thermometer protection. The father of **Robert Louis Stevenson**, Thomas was elected President of the **Royal Society of Edinburgh**.

STEVENSTON, Ayrshire

First mentioned in a charter c1240, Stevenston is one of **Ayrshire**'s 'Three Towns' (with **Ardrossan** and **Saltcoats**). In the late 19th century nearby Ardeer Sands yielded some important archaeological finds, including prehistoric weapons. It became a **coal**-mining centre until the pits were exhausted at the turn of the century. The Nobel Company (inventors of dynamite – now the Nobel division of ICI) set up a factory at nearby Ardeer in 1873 and, despite contraction, ICI remains the most important local employer. Like its neighbouring towns, Stevenston has suffered from poor housing and unemployment in recent years.

STEWART, Alexander, Earl of Buchan (c1343–c1405) 'Wolf of Badenoch'

Fourth son of **Robert II** by his mistress (later second wife) **Elizabeth Mure**, Alexander was granted land in the Badenoch and Strathspey area in 1371, adding considerably to it by his marriage to the Countess of Ross.

Already in conflict with the clergy due to his appointment as the King's Lieutenant north of the Forth, Stewart appears to have exacerbated this opposition by his unfaithfulness to his wife. Censured by the Bishop of **Moray**, Stewart and his men in reprisal razed the town of **Forres** in May 1390, before going on to burn down the **cathedral** and other buildings in **Elgin** the following month. As a result Stewart, rapidly becoming known as the 'Wolf of Badenoch', was excommunicated. With many details of his life unclear, the 'Wolf' was awarded perhaps an undeserved degree of immortality by being cast as the eponymous hero of a novel by **Sir Thomas Dick Lauder** in 1870.

STEWART, Alexander, 3rd Duke of Albany (c1454–85)

Second son of **James II** and **Mary of Gueldres**, the 3rd Duke of Albany was imprisoned by his brother **James III** in 1479, the King having been warned by a witch of his impending murder by a close relative. Another brother, John **Earl of Mar**, was also captured and 'bleid to dead' in a bath, but Albany contrived a dramatic escape from **Edinburgh Castle** and fled to France. In 1482 he returned to London and made a deal with Edward IV whereby he would acknowledge the superiority of the English King in return for support for his own claim to the throne of Scotland. After laying siege to **Berwick** with an English army under Richard, Duke of Gloucester (later Richard III), and already calling himself 'Alexander IV', Albany headed for Edinburgh to enlist the support of the nobles against James III. But his links with England were too strong for that support to be wholehearted. Although initially appeased by James with the appointment of Lieutenant-General of the Kingdom, Albany's star faded. In 1483 his estates were forfeited and he was once more forced to flee to England. An abortive raid on **Lochmaben** in 1484 resulted in his flight to France where in 1485 he was mortally wounded in a jousting tournament against the Duke of Orléans (later Louis XII). His son **John, 4th Duke of Albany**, became Regent for **James V**.

STEWART, Alexander (1813–83) Physician

Born at **Bolton**, **East Lothian**, Stewart studied Greek and medicine at **Glasgow University** before taking up a medical career based in London from 1839. He was concerned with improving hygiene in hospitals, but his main achievement was to differentiate between typhus and typhoid fever (usually credited to Sir William Jenner), allowing quite different treatments.

STEWART, Andy (1933–93) Entertainer

This popular kilted minstrel was training to be an actor when his gift for mimicry made itself apparent. He became like a Scottish version of the perky Andy Hardy character portrayed in films by Mickey Rooney. His TV performances in *The White Heather Club* featured a swinging kilt topped by a boyish-faced lad singing stirring songs about hills, lochs and islands. He won over a Royal Variety Performance in London mimicking Elvis Presley singing 'Donald, Where's Your Troosers?' (Stewart is said to have written that number in 10 minutes as he sat, minus trousers, in the toilet of a London recording studio.) He wrote the words of 'A

Scottish Soldier', linked them to a pipe tune and sold 3 million records to stay for over a year in the Top 50 in North America. He took his concert unit with great success to the United States, Canada, Australia and New Zealand. Despite many recurring bouts of ill-health he kept returning to **theatre** engagements and was performing at a charity show in the **Usher Hall, Edinburgh**, on the night before he died in October 1993.

STEWART, Prince Charles Edward (1720–88) 'The Young Pretender', 'Bonnie Prince Charlie'

The grandson of **James VII** and son of **James Francis Edward, 'the Old Pretender'**, Prince Charles Edward

Prince Charles Edward Stewart, aged 55 and no longer so bonnie, probably by Hugh Douglas Hamilton (SNPG)

was born in Rome. His mother, Clementina Sobieski, was a granddaughter of John Sobieski, King of Poland, with whom his father's relations were unhappy. Nor had his father acquitted himself with credit in the **Jacobite Rising** of 1715. But his supporters were heartened by his heir, who served with such courage as an adolescent at the siege of Gaeta that his commander wrote 'I wish to God that some of the greatest sticklers in England against this family of Stuarts had been eyewitnesses of this prince's resolution during that siege.' In 1740 he wrote to his father, 'I go, Sire, in search of three crowns, which I doubt not but to have the honour and happiness of laying at your majesty's feet. If I fail in the attempt, your next sight of me shall be in my coffin.' He was commended for his gift for conversation as well as his taste in music and the fine arts.

In 1745 this promising youth determined to raise his standard in Scotland 'if he took only a single footman with him'. He pawned his jewels, borrowed 180,000 livres and although a supporting force commanded by the Maréchal de Saxe was wrecked by a storm, Charles

940

himself landed in **Moidart** with seven men. Four of the **'Seven Men of Moidart'** were Irish, which may have seemed auspicious inasmuch as Irish officers in the French army had played a conspicuous part in the victory over British and Dutch forces at Fontenoy in May 1745, but the objectives of these Irishmen were different; they possessed the ear of the Prince; and they were soon at open enmity with his ablest Scottish general, **Lord George Murray**.

Charles himself would nurse a lifelong resentment that so many Highland chiefs failed to support his cause. But initially it prospered. He raised his standard in **Glenfinnan** on 19 August 1745 and by September he had captured **Edinburgh** and won the overwhelming victory of **Prestonpans**. Against the advice of Murray, Charles invaded England, influenced by his Irish advisers, and after the capture of Carlisle he dismissed Murray. But his Highlanders refused to serve under anyone else, and so it was Murray who, as his general, was able to frustrate the desire of the Prince's Irish favourites to advance on London from Derby. The English Catholics had not risen on behalf of the Jacobites. Three battalions of Guards and seven infantry regiments had been recalled from Flanders, and the Prince's army lay between these and 6000 Dutch troops under the command of **Field Marshal Wade**. The decision to retreat was taken on 5 December and the Jacobites reached Scotland to discover that Lord John Drummond had landed there with a French force. All of its officers were Irishmen in the French service, which increased the tension. As the event was to prove, these men enjoyed the privileges of foreign nationals, and ran no risk of forfeiture or of being disembowelled alive as traitors (the fate of those who garrisoned Carlisle).

The Jacobites enjoyed one last crushing victory at **Falkirk**, against the bestial and incompetent General Hawley. Then Charles wasted time and resources in an attempt to capture **Stirling Castle** before retiring to **Inverness**. His able captain, Lord Elcho, was forced to retreat from the **Spey** when Cumberland arrived at the river with his army. He reached **Culloden** to find Charles evidently out of touch with reality. 'His boastfulness that night was unworthy of a Prince,' Elcho remarked. The following night he ordered the fatal march to **Nairn** to attack the enemy camp. Murray turned back in direct opposition to his command, but could not prevent the massacre the following morning, 16 April.

Charles blamed Murray for the disaster, and left his supporters to shift for themselves while he thought only of returning to France. It is well attested that Elcho's last words as he left were 'There goes a damned Italian coward.'

It was not until September 1746 that the Prince succeeded in sailing from Scotland in a French ship. During the months he spent as a fugitive he lived in increasing fear that the Highlanders would betray him, apparently oblivious of the appalling sufferings they were enduring on his behalf. The romantic legend of his feelings of attachment to his faithful Highlanders has burgeoned from that day to this, but John S Gibson has demonstrated conclusively how far that is from the truth in a chapter in The '45 (1988) edited by Lesley Scott Moncrieff. Typical of this attitude was his resentment that Lady

Margaret MacDonald of Sleat did not come in person to meet him, although her husband was a Hanoverian and she ran a grave risk in aiding him when **Flora MacDonald** brought him to her house at a time when it contained officers of King George. The Gaels had failed him, and he never forgave them.

By 1750 he was secretly in London, where he declared himself a Protestant, which would not have pleased his Irish supporters. He formed an association with a Miss Walkenshaw, whose sister was housekeeper to the Dowager Princess of Wales. When his supporters pointed out the possible danger to their personal safety he refused to discontinue the relationship, declaring that it was not because he loved her, but because he would not take orders from a subject. In the event Miss Walkenshaw fled from his brutality. The Prince's father also endured his share of the ingratitude of the **Stewarts**, against which Lord Sinclair had warned Lord Elcho, and which Charles had inherited in such large measure. After his return from Scotland, he never saw his father again during the remaining 20 years of his life. After the death of James, the Pope declined to recognise the apostate Prince as King.

Clementina Walkenshaw, mistress of Prince Charles Edward Stewart; artist unknown (SNPG)

In 1772 he married Princess Louise of Stolberg. It was an unenviable lot for a girl of under 20 years to be united with a drunkard of over 50, especially when he beat her, and arranged a bedlam of alarm bells lest anyone should gain access to her. She fled from him in 1780 into the arms of the poet Alfieri. As Princess of Stolberg she was later made welcome at the court of George III. Charles next invited Charlotte, his daughter by Clementina Walkenshaw, to share his home, and created her Duchess of Albany. It was in her arms that he died in Rome, the last rites performed by his brother

Henry, Cardinal Duke of York. It is not known whether Charles was aware that he had three grandchildren by Charlotte's liaison with a French Archbishop. His great-grandson Charles Edward (b.1784) lived into the reign of **Queen Victoria** and died in Scotland. By this time the legend of the Bonnie Prince had almost totally effaced the squalid aftermath of a career that had begun with such promise.

STEWART, David, Earl of Carrick and 1st Duke of Rothesay (1378–1402)

Variously described as able and effective or headstrong, dissolute, and 'ill-advisedly ambitious', David Stewart was certainly a contrast to his father **Robert III**. As eldest son and heir apparent, he succeeded to the Earldom of **Carrick** on his father's accession (1390) and was created Duke of **Rothesay** in 1398. The King's weakness in dealing with disturbances in the north-east and with the defiance of his brother, **Robert Stewart**, now created 1st **Duke of Albany** (these were among the first Scottish dukedoms), led to David's appointment (1398) as Lieutenant of the Kingdom and its effective ruler, albeit through a council which included Albany and his supporters. In 1400 he married Marjory, daughter of **Archibald 'the Grim' 3rd Earl of Douglas**. George Dunbar, Earl of March, thinking he had secured the heir apparent's hand for his own daughter, invited Henry IV of England to intervene (1400–1). Rothesay successfully held **Edinburgh Castle** against the invaders and Robert III was thus saved the indignity of paying homage to Henry. But in 1400 Rothesay's position was fatally weakened by the deaths of his three main supporters, his Douglas father-in-law (1400), his mother **Annabella Drummond** (1401) and the Bishop of **St Andrews** (1401). When his three-year lieutenancy ended in 1401, he was arrested and confined in **Falkland Palace** by Albany. There he died, possibly of dysentery, reputedly of starvation. Control of the kingdom passed to Albany but the Dukedom of Rothesay went to David's seven-year-old brother, the future **James I**.

STEWART, David (1772–1829) Soldier and Author

Although Stewart attained the rank of major-general after a distinguished career with the 42nd and 78th Highlanders in the West Indies and Egypt, his fame rests on his *Sketches of the Character, Customs, and Present State of the Highlanders of Scotland . . .* (1822). Prompted by his researches into regimental history and by his family background as the son of Robert Stewart of Garth [see **Castle Menzies**], the *Sketches* 'became the foundation of all subsequent works on the **clans**'. On the strength of them and of his friendship with **Sir Walter Scott**, Stewart played a prominent part in the ceremonial arrangements for the visit to **Edinburgh** of George IV in 1822. Although his book had been criticised for its **Jacobite** sympathies, Stewart loyally adjusted the Hanoverian's plaid and pronounced the King 'a very pretty man'. He succeeded to Garth soon after, and in 1829 served as Governor of St Lucia where he died of fever, 'widely regretted'.

STEWART, Sir Donald Martin (1824–1900)
Soldier

Born in **Forres**, Stewart attended local schools including that at **Dufftown** where he may have coincided with **George Stephen**, later a close friend. After **Aberdeen University** he joined the Bengal Native Infantry (1840), saw action on the North-West Frontier (1854–5) and distinguished himself during the 1857–8 Mutiny by passing through enemy lines to Delhi. A major-general by 1868 he commanded the Bengal Brigade in Abyssinia under **Sir Robert Napier** and was then sent to settle the Andaman Islands. There, during an official visit in 1872, Lord Mayo, the Viceroy, was assassinated. Stewart blamed himself and withdrew on home leave. He returned to India five years later and commanded the Kandahar section during the 2nd Afghan War. An able but modest soldier, he felt that his KCB in Afghanistan had been won 'under false pretences'; no such protest came from Sir Frederick Roberts (later Lord Roberts of Kandahar), who consistently outscored Stewart in the vainglory stakes. In 1881 General Stewart was appointed Commander-in-Chief in India. He held the post till 1885. A field marshal (1894), he was appointed Governor of Chelsea Hospital in 1895. He died in Algeria.

STEWART, Dugald (1753–1828)
Educationalist, Writer and Philosopher

Son of Matthew Stewart (1715–85), **Edinburgh University**'s Professor of Mathematics, Dugald grew up there and at the family's summer home, **Catrine** in **Ayrshire**, where **Burns** visited. While at **Glasgow University** he came under **Thomas Reid**'s influence, but after only a year his ailing father brought him back to Edinburgh to teach in his place; they held the Professorship of Mathematics jointly from 1775. In 1785 Dugald

Professor Dugald Stewart, by Sir Henry Raeburn, c1810 (SNPG)

Stewart succeeded **Adam Ferguson** as Edinburgh's Professor of Moral Philosophy. Always frail, after the death of a son in 1809 he resigned teaching duties to Thomas Brown (1810–20) and retired on Brown's death. From *Elements of the Philosophy of the Human Mind* (3 Vols, 1792–1817), which says well what Reid says toilingly, Stewart's fame as the leading English-speaking philosopher in his day derives. Notable for his *Life and Writings of Adam Smith*, he taught **Scott**, **James Mill** and many others. His account of a 'Scottish School' of **philosophy** linking Reid and **Hutcheson** gave the notion real currency. See James M'Cosh, *The Scottish Philosophy* (1875).

STEWART, Esmé, 1st Duke of Lennox (c1542–83)

Son of John, 3rd son of the 3rd **Earl of Lennox** (and so first cousin to **Henry, Lord Darnley**), Esmé Stewart grew up in France and succeeded his father as the Seigneur D'Aubigny. This 'fascinating Frenchman' arrived in Scotland in 1579, was warmly welcomed by the young and largely friendless **James VI**, and quickly became his closest confidant and, some say, his lover. In 1580 James made him Earl of Lennox (the title having been resigned by the aged Robert Stewart), and in 1581 created him Duke of Lennox. That same year Lennox and his associates secured the arrest of ex-**Regent Morton** on a charge of involvement in Darnley's murder; Morton was executed and Lennox elected to the Privy Council. His influence over the young King and their increasing intimacy raised a 'Popish Scare' among militant **Presbyterians**, who suspected him of being a Catholic spy acting for the French and Spanish governments. Even James's signature of the Negative Confession was not enough to allay their fears. In 1582 **William Ruthven, 1st Earl of Gowrie** and leader of the militant Presbyterians, captured the King [see **Ruthven Raid**] and forced him to sign an order banishing the Duke of Lennox, who returned to France, where he died the following year. His son Ludovic became 2nd Duke of Lennox and his daughter married the 1st **Marquis of Huntly**.

STEWART, Frances Theresa, Duchess of Richmond and Lennox (1647–1702)

Described by Samuel Pepys as 'the greatest beauty' he had ever encountered, Frances Stewart was the granddaughter of Walter Stewart, one of **James VI**'s 'Octavians' who became Lord Blantyre, his father having been a Stewart of Minto and **Commendator** of **Blantyre** Priory. She was educated in France and appointed maid of honour to Catherine of Braganza. As a notable adornment to the Restoration court, 'la belle Stuart' numbered amongst her most ardent admirers **Charles II**. Whether she became his mistress is uncertain, but the King was unamused by her elopement (1667) with Charles Stewart, grandson of **Esmé Stewart** and 6th **Duke of Lennox** as well as 3rd Duke of Richmond. She returned to court and favour after her marriage and is thought to have provided the model for 'Britannia' on the British coinage. In her will she decreed that Lethington, once the **Maitland** home, be henceforth known as **Lennoxlove**.

STEWART, Francis, 5th Earl of Bothwell (c1563–c1612)

Son of John Stewart, illegitimate son of **James V**, and Jean, sister of **James Hepburn, 4th Earl of Bothwell**, Francis Stewart inherited the title and estates of his uncle in 1581. Cultured and mercurial, but unstable to the verge of insanity, it was a thirst for power rather than any strong religious conviction that led him to set himself up as leader of the ultra Protestants objecting to **James VI**'s leniency towards the Catholic earls of the north. His weighty connections – cousin of the King, nephew of **Lord James Stewart, 'Regent Moray'**, brother-in-law of **8th Earl of Angus** – made him a useful ally, but the rising power of **Maitland of Thirlestane**, with whom his family had long been at feud, eventually destroyed his influence both with them and with the King. Disgraced by accusations of conspiring with witches to destroy the King, he was imprisoned in April 1590, escaped in June and was outlawed. In December, still on the run, he attacked **Holyrood** at the head of a band of his Borderers but again escaped; was forfeited by Parliament, only to reappear at **Falkland** in June 1592 in a failed attempt to capture the King. He finally fled Scotland in 1595, much to everyone's relief, and died in poverty in Naples.

STEWART, Henry, Lord Darnley (c1545–67)

Elder son of the 4th **Earl of Lennox**, Lord Darnley became the first Scottish husband of **Queen Mary**, and so briefly Scotland's uncrowned 'King Henry'. Brought up in Protestant England, young Darnley was allowed to travel to Scotland by Queen Elizabeth I in 1565 where Queen Mary took a liking to him (though her cousin), not least because of his height. She made him **Earl of Ross** and Duke of Albany, and married him on 29 July

'King' Henry Stewart, Earl of Darnley and Queen Mary's consort, by an unknown artist (SNPG)

1565. Darnley then began a tempestuous 18-month period in which he alienated many of the Scottish nobles by his arrogant manner, became estranged from his royal wife, and met his death by violent means.

Having conspired to have Mary's secretary, **David Rizzio**, put to death in March 1566, Darnley achieved a temporary reconciliation with his wife, fathering a child – **James VI** – before entering covert negotiations with foreign powers in pursuit of the Crown for himself, being prepared to embrace Roman Catholicism to achieve this end. After he had fallen ill, possibly with syphilis, he was brought to **Edinburgh** by the Queen to convalesce at **Kirk o'Fields**. On 10 February 1567 an explosion blew the house apart; Darnley was later found dead in the garden, probably from strangulation. **James Hepburn, 4th Earl of Bothwell**, Mary's subsequent husband, was almost certainly involved in these dubious proceedings.

STEWART, Lord James, Earl of Moray (1531–70) Regent

Lord James was the illegitimate son of **James V** and Margaret (née Erskine) wife of Robert Douglas of **Loch Leven**. In 1536 the King broached with the Pope the subject of a divorce for Margaret so that he might marry her; had it succeeded, Lord James would have been legitimised and Scotland might have had a more imposing and even abler **James VI**. Instead Lord James grew up in obscurity though well provided for as, aged eight, **Commendator** of **St Andrews** (1538). He was educated at the **University** there and, as a layman enjoying the fruits of a monastic establishment, must have been disposed towards Protestantism. A meeting with **Knox** in 1555 may have confirmed his religious allegiance; he would remain one of the most consistent

James Stewart, Earl of Moray and Regent, from an engraving (SW)

and apparently sincere supporters of the **Reformation**. Yet he first appears as a supporter of **Mary of Guise** and a commissioner sent to France to negotiate the marriage of his half-sister **Mary** with the Dauphin (1558). Not till the confrontation between Mary of Guise and the **Lords of the Congregation** at **Perth** (1559) did he finally desert her. He played a crucial role in the civil struggle that followed and, in the **Treaty of Berwick** (for support from Elizabeth of England), discovered his other conviction: 'To the day of his death Lord James's two fixed principles were the dominance of Protestantism at home and friendship with England abroad' (M Lee).

Designs on the Crown have often been imputed to him but find little support in his conduct. In 1560–1, as one of the governing council, he allowed the Reformers to make the running and, on the death of Francis I, sped to France to prepare Mary for a return to Scotland. Naturally he insisted that she respect the Reformation and defer to moderate Protestant opinion rather than to Catholic earls like **Huntly**; in return he, Lord James, would use his English contacts, such as Robert Cecil, to secure from Elizabeth recognition of Mary's claim as successor to the English throne. The Queen's personal reign thus began on a promising note. With **William Maitland of Lethington**, Lord James became her closest adviser and supporter, fending off radical reformers like Knox (who objected to her mass) and crushing Catholic dissidents like Huntly; the latter's opposition had as much to do with jealousy of Lord James himself whose elevation to the **Earldom of Mar** (1562) and then **Moray** (1563) impinged on the **Gordon** domination of the north.

Meanwhile prospects of the English succession had receded as Elizabeth survived a health scare, temporised, and muddied the issue with preconditions about whom Mary should marry. The Queen's selection (1565) of **Henry Stewart, Lord Darnley** in the face of Elizabeth's disapproval spelt the end of Lord James's negotiations and the eclipse of his influence. He stepped down from the council and, as in 1559, broke into open rebellion. But this time he received little support from the Protestant nobility, and the **Chaseabout Raid** ended with his seeking sanctuary in England. Early in the following year the Queen's disenchantment with Darnley, and her Protestant subjects' with **David Rizzio**, brought about his return. Just before the expected forfeiture of his Moray earldom, Rizzio was murdered. A pardon for Lord James had been promised by Darnley in return for his support, although he had no part in the deed.

In early 1567 Lord James managed an equally equivocal stance over the murder of Darnley. Soon after, he took the sensible decision to go abroad as any residual sympathy for his half-sister evaporated in the face of her scandalous affair with, and marriage to, **Bothwell**. He was still away at the time of **Carberry** and Mary's capture and abdication; but he returned soon after and was the only candidate acceptable to all parties (except the Queen's) for the role of Regent for the infant James VI; the appointment was confirmed by the reluctant and captive Mary but opposed by the Gordons and the **Hamiltons**. They and others rallied to Mary on her escape from **Loch Leven Castle** (1568) and, after defeat by Lord James at **Langside**, still looked to the restoration of Mary, now a refugee in England. Negotiations with Elizabeth over recognition of his regency brought Lord James to York and London (1558). The issue, confused by the English Queen's ambiguous attitude towards Mary which at one moment meant that Lord James was on trial, the next that Mary was, was only resolved when Lord James was prevailed upon to produce the 'Casket Letters'.

He returned to Scotland with grudging English support and endeavoured to prolong this by suppressing border raids and assisting Elizabeth against her northern earls. He also received submission from Huntly but was obliged to imprison **Châtelherault**, the Hamilton chief. Unsurprisingly it was a Hamilton (James of Bothwellhaugh) who in January 1570 took aim at Lord James as he rode through **Linlithgow** and fired a shot from which 'the good regent' died within a matter of hours. Neither his ambition nor his occasional treachery were remarkable for a man born without a natural constituency into an age of exceptional ferment; and his sustained yet moderating support of the Reformation proved crucial to its success in Scotland. (See biography by M Lee, 1953.)

STEWART, James Francis Edward (1688–1766) 'The Old Pretender'

The only surviving son of **James VII** and Mary of Modena, James Francis Edward was born in St James's Palace, London. Accounts to the contrary, namely that the infant was an impostor smuggled into the Queen's bedchamber in a warming pan, were **Whig** inventions designed to discredit **Jacobite** allegiance. The title 'Old Pretender' served a similar purpose although strictly just an anglicisation of the French *pretendant* meaning 'claimant'. Also known as 'the old Chevalier [de Saint

Prince James Francis Edward Stewart aged 13 when, with James VII dying, he became the not-so-old 'Pretender'; by François de Troy (SNPG)

George]', he was brought up in France, 'a reserved and melancholy youth' (M Linklater), created Prince of Wales by his father and, on his father's death in 1701, proclaimed King of England, Scotland and Ireland at St Germain. The title was recognised by France and Spain although contrary to the Act of Succession in England.

In Scotland residual loyalty to the **Stewarts** was rekindled by antipathy to the 1707 **Act of Union**, a fact communicated to James by his agents. A letter asking for French support promised that the whole nation was ready to rise as soon as the 'King' landed. Louis XIV responded by organising a small fleet which sailed, with James aboard, from Dunkirk in 1708. The voyage was rough and the 19-year-old Pretender proved a bad sailor; he was also convalescing from measles. The fleet reached the Firth of Forth and looked set for a warm reception. But the arrival of an English squadron under Admiral Byng aborted plans to disembark at **Burntisland** and make for **Stirling**. The fleet sailed north, James vainly pleading to be put ashore, and then back to France.

In 1708–9 James served with the French forces at Malplaquet and Oudenarde, winning a reputation for bravery which even Marlborough acknowledged. But by the Peace of Utrecht, Louis was obliged to expel him from France. He moved to Lorraine. The Hanoverian succession of 1714 fanned Jacobite sentiment throughout Britain much as the Act of Union had, and still did, in Scotland. When **John 6th Earl of Mar** raised the Jacobite standard in 1715, his doubtful credentials were more than offset by the enthusiastic response on both sides of the border. Word of this was sufficient to bring James again to Dunkirk, this time in disguise, whence he sailed for Scotland for the last time. 'It required real talent for Mar to lose the game, but he proved equal to the challenge' (B Lenman). By the time the much proclaimed 'King' landed at **Peterhead**, **Sheriffmuir** had been fought but not won, and the Jacobites had lost the initiative. James spent six winter weeks in Scotland but got no further south than **Perth** before withdrawing up the east coast and taking ship back to France from **Montrose** (1716).

He returned to Lorraine, then to Italy, whence he was summoned to Spain to head the small armada organised by Cardinal Alberoni to invade England in 1719. Before he reached it at Corunna, the fleet was wrecked; only the diversionary expedition to Scotland actually materialised and was duly suppressed at the **Battle of Glenshiel**. James withdrew from Spain and, finding support from the papacy, settled in Rome. His marriage to the 15-year-old Clementina Sobieski, granddaughter of Poland's King John Sobieski, in 1719 brought joy to neither but resulted in the birth of the bonnie **Prince Charles Edward Stewart** (1720), 'the Young Pretender', and the more scholarly Prince Henry Benedict (1725–1807), later a cardinal, who would assume the title of 'Henry IX' (1788).

Disagreements over the upbringing of these children and alienation from his wife won James few friends in Rome. In Scotland Jacobite sympathies survived in spite of the intrigue-ridden court in exile, not because of it; and in 1744–5 it was again a foreign initiative, this time by France, which launched the last Jacobite rising.

In James's name Prince Charles Edward raised the standard at **Glenfinnan** but the Old Pretender took no part in the endeavour and, after the débâcle, was shunned by his son. Unlike Charles, he remained a staunch Catholic and a dignified, if sad, figure who had endured more than his fair share of the Stewarts' bad luck and had displayed rather less than his share of their notorious failings. He was buried in St Peter's, Rome, where George III would erect a monument by Canova over his tomb.

STEWART, John, Earl of Buchan
(c1380–1424) Chamberlain

Second son of **Robert, Duke of Albany**, John Stewart was created Earl of Buchan by his father in 1406, became Chamberlain in Albany's place (or on his behalf) in 1408 and in 1417 laid unsuccessful claim to the **Earldom of Ross**. He was one of the commanders of the large expeditionary force sent to France in 1418 and shared in the unexpected Franco-Scottish victory over the English at Baugé in Anjou (March, 1421), being made a Constable of France by the Dauphin as a reward; he was killed, along with **Archibald, 4th Earl of Douglas**, in the Franco-Scottish defeat by the English at Verneuil.

STEWART, John, 4th Duke of Albany
(1481–1536) Governor of Scotland

Born in France, son of **Alexander Stewart, 3rd Duke of Albany**, John Stewart was first cousin to **James IV**. James's death at **Flodden** (1513) left Scotland once again with an infant King – the 17-month-old **James V** – and with a Queen Mother, **Margaret Tudor**, as Regent. To those Scottish nobles already planning a renewal of hostilities against England, the sister of Henry VIII was a most unsatisfactory Governor; they looked to France, their old ally, for an alternative. Albany, already heir-presumptive to the Scottish throne, was a natural choice, but Louis XII, with little faith in Scotland's schemes and already planning a truce with England, refused to let Albany leave.

In 1514, however, Margaret Tudor married **Archibald Douglas, 6th Earl of Angus**, thus disqualifying herself as Governor; Albany was again summoned. He arrived in **Edinburgh** in May 1515 with orders from the French King (now Francis I – Louis having died in January) to keep the Scots quiet. Speaking only French and accompanied by a large and extravagant French household, Albany might have proved unpopular. But his steady loyalty to the young King and the resolution with which he banged together the heads of the squabbling nobles (removing that of the 3rd Lord Home for treason) won him many friends.

His regency coincided with a period when Scotland was sidelined by England and France in the face of their more pressing preoccupations elsewhere in Europe; Albany's attempts at international diplomacy were thus allowed to have little effect. When he went to France in 1517 to negotiate the Treaty of Rouen, in which France and Scotland agreed to assist each other in the face of any English aggression against either, Francis I kept him there for four years lest his return to Scotland precipitate action against England. In 1521, however, Henry VIII and the Emperor Charles V agreed jointly to attack France, and Albany was sent back to Scotland to muster support for Francis. But by now Scottish ardour for another war with the English had cooled, and Albany had once more to resign himself to settling domestic rather than international disputes. He surrendered his regency in 1524 when the 12-year-old **James V** was invested as King, and returned to France, where he died, childless, in 1536.

STEWART, Matthew, 4th Earl of Lennox (1516–71)

Matthew, the 4th **Stewart Earl of Lennox**, succeeded his father in 1526. Captured at **Solway Moss** (1542) and sent as a prisoner to England, he was persuaded (or bribed) to support an Anglo-Scottish alliance and returned to Scotland in 1543 to promote Henry VIII's plan to marry **Queen Mary** to his son Edward Prince of Wales [see **Treaty of Greenwich**]. Forfeited for supporting the English through the **Rough Wooing**, he returned to England (1545). In 1544 he had married Margaret Douglas, daughter of Margaret Tudor and the **6th Earl of Angus**; their elder son was **Henry, Lord Darnley** and it was only when the eyes of Queen Mary lighted on this 'slender and exquisite' youth that Lennox was allowed to return to Scotland. After Mary's departure, Lennox followed the **Earl of Moray** as Regent for his grandson, **James VI**, but was stabbed to death at **Stirling** in a fight between supporters of the King and those of his mother. He was succeeded by his younger son, Charles (d.1576).

STEWART, Murdoch, 2nd Duke of Albany (c1362–1425) Regent

Taken prisoner by the English after Homildon (1402) and ransomed in 1415, Murdoch Stewart inherited both the **Dukedom of Albany** and the Regency of Scotland on the death of his father **Robert Stewart** in 1420. But he had inherited none of his sire's intelligence or subtlety, and for the remaining four years of **James I**'s imprisonment in England and France Murdoch's incompetence hastened Scotland's already severe financial and administrative disintegration. When James finally returned home in 1424 'he found the authority of the Crown weakened, the power of the great nobles dangerously inflated, the administration chaotic, and poverty, lawlessness and pestilence abounding' (**Fitzroy Maclean**). Determined to stamp his authority immediately – and no doubt still bearing a grudge for his years of neglect at the hands of the 1st Duke – the King took drastic action against the house of Albany. Within a year Murdoch, his sons Walter and Alexander and his father-in-law the octogenarian Earl of Lennox were seized (a third son James fled into exile in Ireland), tried before an assize, convicted of a variety of crimes including extortion and beheaded in front of **Stirling Castle**. Their titles (which included the **Earldom of Menteith**) were annexed to the Crown.

STEWART, Patrick, Earl of Orkney (d.1615)

Succeeding his father **Robert Stewart** to the Earldom of **Orkney** in 1593, Patrick was summoned before the Council in the following year on an accusation from the Hanseatic port of Danzig that he had seized one of its ships. By 1606, according to **Spottiswoode**, he had 'undone his estate by riot and prodigality'. Brought to justice at last in 1609, he was accused of having forced the islanders 'to work to him all manner of work and labour by sea and land'. Itemising his enormities, the indictment added 'all sorts of servile and painful labour, without either meat, drink or hire'. Thus were built the great castle of **Scalloway** in **Shetland** and the Renaissance palace whose ruins still stand beside the cathedral in **Kirkwall**. An anonymous chronicler recorded that he 'was long in favour with the King' and it was treason, not his treatment of the islanders, that caused his downfall. Removed to **Dumbarton** in 1612 and ordered to surrender his castles in Orkney and Shetland, he commanded his son Robert to hold them for him. Robert was defeated, captured and hanged in **Edinburgh** with his accomplices in 1614. Patrick's final despicable act was to attempt to save himself by blaming his adolescent son. The ministers who visited him on the eve of his execution (1615), as Calderwood reported, 'finding him so ignorant that he could scarce rehearse the Lord's Prayer, entreated the Council to delay the execution some few days till he were better informed'. Earl Patrick was married but left no legitimate children.

STEWART, Robert, 1st Duke of Albany (c1340–1420) Regent and Governor

The younger brother of **Robert III** (whose baptismal name had in fact been John), and older brother of **Alexander**, the 'Wolf of Badenoch', Robert Stewart, **Earl of Fife**, was the most capable of the sons of **Robert II**. As such he had been made Governor two years before the death of his father and retained the office on the succession of his brother in 1390, being created 1st Duke of Albany in 1398. When the King's ill-health forced his virtual abdication in 1399 in favour of his elder son **David, Duke of Rothesay**, much of the power in the land already lay in Albany's hands. In 1406 he almost certainly contrived the murder of his nephew Rothesay, who died 'in mysterious circumstances' at **Falkland**, whereupon Albany once again became Lieutenant and Governor of the Realm. His not unreasonable expectations of one day inheriting the throne were given a boost by the capture by the English of the 12-year-old Prince James in 1406, shortly followed by the death of the King. Albany was appointed Regent by a General Council at **Perth**. Devious, cynical, and politically astute, he ruled Scotland for the next 14 years, preferring to make deals with the more powerful barons, particularly the **Earl of Douglas**, rather than attempt to crush them, thus preserving the peace as well as filling his own coffers. The only serious attempt to usurp his authority foundered (through none of his own doing) when the inconclusive **Battle of Harlaw** (1411) sent **Donald of the Isles** home to lick his wounds. Albany made no attempt to secure the release of his nephew, now **James I** (although when his own son **Murdoch** was captured at Homildon in 1402 he did negotiate a ransom for him in 1415), and when he died in 1420 at the age of over 80, he left Murdoch to inherit both the Dukedom and the Governorship of Scotland.

STEWART, Robert, Earl of Orkney (1533–93)

A son of **James V** and Euphemia Elphinstone, Robert Stewart was one of the bastard step-brothers to whom Queen Mary extended such an unwise indulgence; in this case it was her Orcadian subjects rather than herself who paid the heavy price. In 1539 James V endowed him with the emoluments of the **Abbey of Holyrood** and in 1564 Mary leased **Orkney** and **Shetland** to him. In 1569 he exchanged the temporalities of Holyrood for those of Orkney with its **Bishop Adam Bothwell**, who complained in 1570 that he had 'violently intruded himself on his whole living with bloodshed and hurt of his servants'. Robert Stewart was imprisoned by the Regent **James Douglas, Earl of Morton** in 1575 for his treasonable offer of Orkney to the King of Denmark, and revenged himself by engineering Morton's downfall after his release. His step-brother Lawrence Bruce became the chief instrument of his extortions in Orkney and Shetland, for which the island feudatories indicted him in **Edinburgh** in 1576. But he was not brought to trial and in 1581 **James VI** created him Earl of Orkney. A second complaint against his oppressions merely resulted in a confirmation of his titles. He married a daughter of the **Earl of Cassillis** by whom he sired five sons and four daughters in addition to his illegitimate children. The ruins of his palace at **Birsay** and the so-called **Jarslhof** in Shetland are the conspicuous monuments of his tyranny; it was exceeded only by that of his son **Earl Patrick**, who succeeded him.

STEWART, Sir Thomas Grainger (1837–1900) Physician

Born in **Edinburgh**, educated at the High School and **Edinburgh University**, Grainger Stewart studied in Berlin, Prague and Vienna before being appointed House Physician at Edinburgh's **Royal Infirmry**. Early in his career he was appointed Lecturer on *Materia Medica* in the Extra-mural School. On his appointment as Pathologist to the Royal Infirmary he became Lecturer on Pathology and later took over the lectureship of Practices of Medicine. In 1876 he was elected to the Chair of Medicine at Edinburgh University. Appointed Physician to **Queen Victoria** and knighted for his services to the royal household in Scotland, he made important contributions to medical literature with his *Practical Treatise on Bright's Disease* and *Diseases of the Nervous System*. He was President of the British Medical Association (1898), President of the **Royal College of Physicians** (1889–91), and at the time of his death was President of the Edinburgh Medical Missionary Society.

STEWART, Walter (1293–1326) 6th High Steward of Scotland

The son of James, 5th High Steward (d.1309) [see **Stewarts**], who had been a guardian under **Queen Margaret** and later aligned with **William Wallace** and **Robert I**, Walter was associated with **Sir James Douglas** in the command of a division at **Bannockburn**. He was subsequently knighted and married to **Marjorie**, then the only legitimate child of Robert I. Their son, also Robert (1316–90), was recognised as heir presumptive by a parliament at **Scone** in 1318 but at **Cambuskenneth** in 1326 this claim was adjusted to take account of the prior claim of **David**, Robert I's late-born son. The chances of a Stewart succession then seemed remote although eventually the son of Walter and Marjorie did succeed as **Robert II**, the first of the Stewart kings.

Walter had meanwhile become Governor of Scotland (1316) and had continued to show military promise in the defence of **Berwick**, but died in his prime.

STEWARTON, Ayrshire

Long known as 'The Bonnet Toun', Stewarton has had a bonnet-making industry since the 16th century, specialising in the manufacture of such regimental headgear as the tam o'shanter, the balmoral and the glengarry. In the 19th century the Stewarton manufacturers diversified into knitwear, hosiery and **wool**-spinning. Appropriately, the town was the birthplace of **David Dale** (1739–1806), pioneering founder of the **cotton** mills at **New Lanark** with Richard Arkwright and later of those at **Catrine** with Claud Alexander of Ballochmyle.

STEWARTRY

The term 'stewartry' was applied to any area which was Crown property and therefore administered by a steward rather than a sheriff. In the case of the Stewartry of **Kirkcudbright**, annexed to the Crown in 1455 by **James II** when he finally broke the power of the **Douglas** Lords of **Galloway**, the term became part of the name of the county, and is still extant in the Stewartry district of Dumfries and Galloway.

STEWARTS, The

The Stewarts were originally a feudal Lowland family. Their first traceable ancestor was Flaald, a Breton nobleman living in the 11th century, who was hereditary Seneschal or Steward of Dol. As Brittany had been colonised from Britain, it is likely that the family was of Celtic stock. His son Alan fitz Flaald (fitz = Breton 'son of') followed the Norman dynasty to England, becoming Sheriff of Shropshire, whence his son Walter fitz Alan moved north to Scotland prior to 1164.

David I granted strategically important lands in what are now **Renfrewshire** and **East Lothian** to Walter, and created him hereditary Lord High Steward of Scotland. This was the greatest office in the realm and the duties included keeping the Exchequer and, at times, the assumption of military command in battle. For about 200 years the family held the appointment until the 7th High Steward became King of Scotland. The titles Steward and Stewart are synonymous; Walter 3rd Steward adopted the name of his office as his surname and thus became the first Stewart from whom all of the name are descended. Stewart is the original spelling but the variations 'Stuart' and 'Steuart' have also subsequently been used. Incidentally, the fesse chequay in most Stewart armorial bearings is supposed to represent the chequered board or cloth used in early times for computing the Exchequer accounts.

In 1314 **Walter, 6th High Stewart**, distinguished himself as a commander at **Bannockburn** and was knighted by **Robert the Bruce** on the battlefield and later given the hand of the King's daughter **Marjorie** in marriage. In 1316 Marjorie was thrown from a horse and died. It is said that the monks of **Paisley Abbey** saved the life of her infant son by performing a primitive Caesarian operation.

Fifty years later this son became King **Robert II**, the first of the Royal Stewarts. Thus started the line of 14 sovereigns of Scotland of whom five also reigned in England, from **James VI** of Scotland and I of England in 1603 until Queen Anne died in 1714. Thereafter **James Francis Edward**, the 'Old Pretender', son of **James VII** (II), failed to reclaim the throne in 1715; the hopes of his son **Charles Edward** were extinguished at **Culloden**; and his other son Henry, styled Duke of York, became a cardinal and died, the last male of his line, in Italy in 1807 [see **Jacobites**, etc]. HM Queen Elizabeth II is, however, a direct descendant of the Royal Stewarts through the female line.

During the 200 years that the Stewarts held office as High Stewards, the star of the House of Stewart was in the ascendant. Their power increased, their possessions became more widespread and their influence in affairs of state waxed ever greater. It was only after they ascended the throne that fate seemed to turn against them; there followed a melancholy tale of misfortune which ended 400 years later on the field of Culloden and earned for them the name of 'The Unlucky House of Stewart'. Of the 14 crowned Stewart monarchs, four were beheaded or murdered, two died in battle, one in exile and two of broken hearts.

With the patronage and support of the royal House of Stewart, their relations could hardly fail to prosper and multiply despite the tumultuous and warlike environment of Scotland in those days. It is perhaps significant that the first four Scottish dukes and the first marquis ever to be created were all Stewarts, and at one time or another Stewarts have held 16 earldoms from **Galloway** in the south to **Orkney** in the north.

The main Lowland branches of the Stewarts are those of the Earls of Galloway who, in the absence of a chief, are considered to be senior representatives of the race, and the Shaw-Stewarts, Baronets of Ardgower in Renfrewshire, the original Stewart territory in Scotland. The Stuarts of **Traquair** at **Innerleithen** still occupy (1491–1991) what is believed to be the oldest inhabited house in Scotland.

During the course of the 14th and 15th centuries three branches of the Stewart family settled north of the **Highland line** on the mainland. Probably the best-known historically were the Stewarts of **Appin**. The other two branches were known as the Stewarts of **Atholl** and of **Balquhidder**. All three adopted in large degree the customs and organisations of the Gael; and as surnames gradually began to be used in the Highlands, it is probable that many of the native inhabitants, who had hitherto used only patronymics, took the name of their chiefs and leaders. Thus the Stewart **clans** were founded. Each of these branches must be treated separately for their stories seldom intermingled, although they did sign a Bond of Accord after Lord Kilpont's murder c1646.

The Stewarts of Appin in **Lorn** spring from an allegedly illegitimate son of John Stewart, Lord of Lorn, who was a descendant of the 4th High Stewart's younger brother Sir John Stewart of Bonkyl. The clan has the only chief of the race and two circumstances influenced their organisation and way of life. Firstly their loyalty to their kinsmen of the royal house, as a result of which there were few wars, risings or disputes on their behalf that were not ardently supported by the Stewarts of Appin. Secondly the proximity of their lands to those of the **Earls of Argyll**, chiefs of the **Campbells** who would have liked to make them their vassals, required an effective martial capability. The Appins managed to preserve their lands and freedom but their loyalty eventually led them to the field of Culloden in 1746. Their contingent, numbering some 300 clansmen, suffered casualties of 93 killed and 67 wounded.

The largest grouping of Stewarts in the Highlands was in Atholl and many live there today. They can hardly be described as a clan, having no chief, but were composed of small landowning families who had a loose connection with the early Stewart **Earls of Atholl** at **Blair Castle**. Within Atholl the Stewarts intermingled and co-existed amicably with the Robertsons (*Clan Donnachaidh*) as Athollmen. Most of these Atholl Stewarts sprang from a natural son of the notorious but colourful terror of the north, **Alexander Stewart**, Earl of Buchan, known as the 'Wolf of Badenoch'. He was the third son of Robert II and more of his illegitimate heirs were settled in Stewart lands in **Aberdeenshire**, **Banffshire** and **Moray**.

The Balquhidder Stewarts, starting in 1490, formed a grouping around William Stewart, Royal Baillie of the Crown lands of Balquhidder. The Stewarts of Ardvorlich on Lochearnside became leaders, but not chiefs, of a clan after 1580. This clan enjoyed a reputation for successful cattle raiding against their richer Lowland neighbours. Later they were prominent in many armed forays.

In addition, north of the Highland line, Sir James Stewart, a natural son of Robert II, was appointed Sheriff of **Bute** and was a forebear of the Stuart Marquises of Bute, Keepers of **Rothesay Castle**. The Isle of Bute is clearly Stewart territory.

Today Stewarts are found all over the world. The Gaelic saying *Stiubhartaich, cinne nan righ s'nan ceard* (Stewarts, race of kings and of tinkers), confirms the diversity of the name (though it is said that the tinkers originally took the name for the sake of the respectability it conferred).

The Stewart Society was founded in 1899 in **Edinburgh**, one of its objects being to collect and preserve the history and tradition of the name. In this it has been singularly successful for *The Stewarts*, a magazine published under its auspices, contains a mass of information. The Society owns a library which contains many books connected with Stewart history. More recently a Clan Stewart Society has been established in the USA.

There are two plant badges associated with the Stewarts; the oak which appears to go back to the time of the establishment of the race, and the **thistle** which would seem to have a special association with the royal house of Stewart. The predominantly green Hunting Stewart **tartan** is commonly worn, and the red, so-called 'Royal Stewart' is worn with more formal evening dress and some military uniforms, However the Stewarts of Appin, Atholl, Bute and Galloway have their own variations of tartan.

STIRLING, Stirlingshire

Given its position in the country's geography, the wonder is that Stirling, 'the glory of Scotland' (J A MacCulloch) and often the centre of government, never became the capital. Prior to the 17th century a roadless barrier formed of the **Campsie Fells** and **Flanders Moss** effectively severed the north-east and Highlands from the central Lowlands. For other than marauders and sailors the only obvious way through this barrier was across the meadows that bordered the Forth in its few twisting miles between the Moss and the tide. This was precisely the stretch over which fell the shadow of a massive outcrop of basaltic rock, the natural fortress which became **Stirling Castle**. Commanding a tidal reach for seaborne trade and the only north-south route for internal trade, Stirling held the key to the country's wealth as well as its governance.

Yet no major city grew from this convergence of circumstances. The relative decline of Stirling's strategic and commercial importance coincides with its political decline following the **Union of the Crowns**, thus apparently lending weight to the contention that distortions of Scottish history can be blamed on English influence. Such notions of a site already closely associated with the patriots **Wallace** and **Bruce**, and sandwiched between **Bannockburn** and **Stirling Bridge**, **Sauchieburn** and **Sheriffmuir**, reserve for Stirling a special place in Scottish affections. The launching of the **Nationalist Covenant** here in 1930 was no coincidence.

Roman occupation of Stirling can safely be assumed, although unauthenticated by archaeology. Like **Edinburgh**, the site also has Arthurian associations [see **King's Knot**]; 'Striveling' and 'Snowdon' were alternatives to 'Stirling', their provenance uncertain. Its recorded history begins in the early 12th century when **Alexander I** died in Stirling Castle and when **David I** granted **royal burgh** status (1124). The medieval town spread down the south-east ridge from the Castle and north to Stirlingshore, the port and ferry to **Cambuskenneth**. **Stirling Bridge**, where William Wallace defeated (1297) the English after Edward I's capture of the Castle in 1296, is thought to have been near Kildean, now the site of what may be the largest livestock market in Europe, successor to the trysts of **Crieff** and **Falkirk** and a reminder of Stirling's commercial importance. Besieged in 1304 and again in 1314, Stirling was the last castle of note to hold out against Edward I and then, in English hands again, was disinvested by **Edward Bruce** on the understanding that its Governor would surrender if not relieved. In coming to its rescue Edward II was defeated at nearby **Bannockburn**, the Castle was duly surrendered and, in accordance with Robert I's usual policy, dismantled.

The earliest surviving structures in today's Castle are 15th–17th century when under the patronage of the **Stewarts** Stirling enjoyed its golden age as a royal residence and centre of government. It was also a place of dire judgement, **James I** executing the **Dukes of Albany** and **Lennox** on the Mote or Heading Hill in 1425 and **James II** murdering the **8th Earl of Douglas** then throwing his corpse out of a window in 1452. **James III** was born here (1451) and murdered nearby after the Battle of Sauchieburn. The Castle's Great Hall, begun in his reign, was completed by **James IV** who seems to have preferred it to his **Holyroodhouse** in Edinburgh. **James V**, largely brought up at Stirling after his father's death at **Flodden**, built the Castle's Palace and, absenting himself from it to rove incognito amongst his subjects, adopted the sobriquet of 'the Gudeman o' Ballengeich',

Ballengeich being a **croft** just north-east of the Castle. **Mary**, though preferring Edinburgh, was crowned in the castle chapel in 1543 and may have been responsible for the battery known as the French Spur. **James VI**'s first Parliament met in the Great Hall in 1578, but for sheer magnificence the high point of royal patronage was the celebration to mark the birth in 1594 of **Prince Henry**, first son of James VI who had himself been baptised and crowned in Stirling.

Thereafter Stirling readied itself for visits by **Charles I** in 1633 and **Charles II** in 1650, plus bombardment and capitulation to **General Monk** in 1651. Designated one of four Scottish fortresses which were to be kept in good repair after the **Act of Union**, the Castle underwent extensive refortification and duly withstood both **Jacobite Risings**, the **Earl of Mar** being held back at Sheriffmuir in 1715, and **Prince Charles Edward Stewart**'s artillery failing to make any impression in 1746. In the 19th century the Castle declined into irrelevance and decay as a barracks, while the town at its foot transformed itself into a modest commercial and agricultural centre. In mid-century about 100 vessels a year still loaded at Stirlingshore whence a twice-daily steamboat sailed to **South Queensferry**. But, unsuitable for any craft of over 70 tons, the river port soon lost out to **Bo'ness** and **Grangemouth**. Compensation arrived courtesy of the **railway** and the development of nearby **Bridge of Allan** as a major health resort. Recognition of Stirling's historical importance and **tourist** potential followed, beginning with the erection of the Wallace Monument on nearby **Abbey Craig** in the 1860s. The famous view from the walls of Stirling Castle, embracing so much of Scotland's history, received its final and no less prominent feature with the construction a century later of **Stirling University**.

Argyll Lodging

'The most important surviving town house of its period' and 'Scotland's finest surviving Renaissance mansion' now echoes to the tramp of boots as one of the country's more desirable youth hostels. It stands splendidly atop the **Castle** Rock between the **Church of the Holy Rude** and the Castle esplanade. Little altered and well preserved, the 'Ludging' crowds round three sides of a cobbled courtyard, screened from the street by a wall with a rusticated gateway, and with extensions to the rear. Conically capped corner towers flank the three-storey façade whose pinkish harling is as canvas to the high relief embroidery of the ornately carved stonework over the entrance, windows and dormers. The building was begun as an L-plan tower by **William Alexander, 1st Earl of Stirling**, and continued by his son in the 1630s. When the former died bankrupt in 1640, work stopped. It was resumed after purchase by **Archibald, 9th Earl of Argyll** in 1666, the final (south) wing being completed in 1674. The 4th Duke of Argyll sold it to the state. It served as a military hospital throughout the 19th century; its present use by the Scottish Youth Hostel Association suggests a similar role for other historic but redundant buildings.

Broad Street

Certainly wide but known as Market Street when it was the hub of the burgh, Broad Street climbs gently towards the **Castle** with a stepped skyline of sober four-storey terraces, now more residential than commercial. Dominating the south side, the Town House (1703–5) with projecting square tower topped by a Dutch-style pavilion was designed by **Sir William Bruce** of **Kinross**

Courtyard of Argyll Lodging (Argyll's Ludging), Stirling (RWB)

House but subsequently extended. Outside it stands the Mercat Cross with original unicorn finial (known as 'Puggy'), while opposite is the street-facing gable of Norie's Lodging (1671). James Norie was Town Clerk and, to judge by the Latin inscriptions on his window pediments, a pillar of righteousness. 'A good conscience is as a brazen wall' says one. **Darnley**'s House in Bow Street was supposedly that used by **Queen Mary**'s consort. With a commanding view up Broad Street to the Castle, it would have been ideal for surveillance but was probably not built till the end of the 16th century.

Church of the Holy Rude

This large and conspicuous parish church adjacent to **Stirling Castle** testifies to the importance of the medieval burgh and to the value of royal patronage. The nave and tower at its west end were built in 1456–70, possibly on the site of the church mentioned in the 12th century. Private donations funded additional chantry chapels of which only that of St Andrew (1483) survives. In 1507 a second phase of construction saw the erection of the choir, a loftier continuation of the nave, ending in an apsidal presbytery. Transepts were planned to give the usual, and in this case appropriate ('Rude' = rood, cross) cruciform shape with a lofty central tower. But the tower was never built and the transepts only added in 1936 as part of a major restoration which ended the **Reformation** division of the church into two and removed 19th century accretions. In this church in 1544 **Mary of Guise** was appointed Regent and in 1567 the one-year-old **James VI** was crowned, **Knox** preaching the sermon, the **Earl of Atholl** carrying the crown,

Morton the sceptre, and **Mar** the King. The large cemetery, an extension of the old churchyard, reaches to the Castle car park and contains two notable funerary monuments: a conspicuous pyramid with marble sculptures commemorating the **Covenanters** and an octagonal glass-domed pavilion containing two marble females representing the **Wigtown Martyrs**. Both were commissioned by William Drummond in 1858.

King's Knot

The south-east view from the **Castle** takes in King's Park, once a royal hunting reserve and latterly an extensive and leafy suburb. In the foreground, directly below the Castle Rock, the grassy outline of the formal and geometrical gardens can be clearly seen. Of the two adjoining designs, that consisting of a raised octagonal mound within a square is properly the King's Knot and, prior to its design as a garden, was identified as the round table of King Arthur and his knights. Both gardens are thought to have been laid out in 1628 for **Charles I** and would have been planted with box hedges and perhaps heraldic flower designs as at **Pitmedden**. No doubt there were also architectural features. The weeds had taken over by the end of the 17th century and an attempted restoration in the 19th century probably changed the design of the Knot.

Mar's Work

All that remains of the Renaissance mansion built by **John, 5th Lord Erskine and 1st/6th Earl of Mar** is

Mar's Work (Wark), Stirling, c1840 (RWB)

the weatherworn and mutilated façade. The Erskines had been hereditary keepers of **Stirling Castle** since 1360. Befitting this role, John chose a site hard by the Castle but died in 1572, a year after building had started. If the façade with its grand entrance and flanking octagonal towers was intended as one side of a courtyard, it is clear that the 'wark' was never completed. Heraldic panels above the entrance pend are those of **James VI** and **Mar**. As with the Royal Palace in the Castle, the main apartments would have been on the first floor and the exterior lavishly endowed with sculptures. The building was still in use by 'Bobbing John', **6th/11th Earl of Mar**, but suffered badly during the 1745 **Jacobite Rising**. It was ruinous by 1777 and remains so.

Old Bridge

A rare survival, the late medieval stone bridge across the Forth below **Stirling Castle** is of four semi-circular arches supported on triangular cut-waters above substantial piers. Archways once guarded the approaches and the refuges were roofed. It was built c1500, one arch being demolished in 1745 to hold the **Jacobites** at bay but subsequently rebuilt. The **Battle of Stirling Bridge** (1297) may have been fought on this site but not on this bridge; the 13th century bridge is thought to have been of timber and probably upstream at Kildean. In 1831 a new bridge by **Robert Stevenson** was built downstream to relieve the old.

St John Street

Running parallel to **Broad Street**, also leading down from the **Castle**, and forming the other main street of the medieval town, St John Street is dominated by the **Church of the Holy Rude** at its head. Behind the church in a side street Cowane's Hospital was built by **John Mylne** in 1639 from a bequest by the merchant John Cowane. Intended as an eventide home for 'decayed Guild brothers and burgesses', it was converted for use as the Guildhall in 1852. The central projection of its E-plan design is a four-storey tower with a statue of Cowane above the main entrance. Turning down St John Street, Bruce of Auchebowie's House (possibly 1520 but much altered) faces the Boys' Club, a 20th century reconstruction with suitable exhortations to 'Play the Game', etc. Further down, between the redundant military prison and the Old High School (with green domed observatory donated by **Sir Henry Campbell-Bannerman**), stands Erskine Church (1824), a classical building, sadly now gutted, which replaced the original seceders' church founded here by **Ebenezer Erskine** in the 1740s. A many-pillared monument in front of the church marks the position of Erskine's grave. St John Street becomes Spittal Street, named after Robert Spittal, tailor to **James IV** and a noted philanthropist whose Hospital, or almshouse, adjoins Darrow Lodging, the former 17th century, the latter 16th but both restored in the 1950s.

STIRLING, Raid of (1584)

James VI, restrained by the **Earl of Gowrie** and his associates after the **'Ruthven Raid'** (1582), regained his freedom in June 1583. He then reappointed James Stewart, **Earl of Arran** (also held prisoner during the Gowrie ascendancy) and several of his supporters to the

Privy Council. But Arran's opponents, encouraged by Walsingham (Queen Elizabeth of England's emissary), hatched a new conspiracy and the **Earls of Mar**, **Glamis** and **Angus** and the Lords John and Claude Hamilton seized **Stirling Castle** in April 1584. Aid from England failed to materialise; James raised a large army to besiege the conspirators; they fled ignominiously to England. The execution of Gowrie on 2 May then stabilised the authority of both the King and his government.

STIRLING BRIDGE, Battle of (1297)

The Battle of Stirling Bridge was **William Wallace**'s one great military victory, and established him as the leader of Scottish resistance to the English rather than merely a spirited outlaw. After defeats at **Berwick** and **Dunbar** (1296), **John Balliol** had surrendered to the English and was humiliated, taken prisoner and sent to England. Edward I then made a triumphal tour north as far as **Elgin**, collecting the **Stone of Destiny** from **Scone** on his way back south. Regarding Scotland now as his for the ruling, he established John de Warenne, Earl of Surrey, as Governor and Hugh de Cressingham as Treasurer. The revolt that spread in response to this imposition was led by Wallace in the south-west and **Andrew Murray** (or de Moray) in the north-east, their combined forces comprising an enthusiastic army of volunteers (as opposed to the feudal hosts that had failed at Berwick and Dunbar). The English army led by Surrey and Cressingham which set out from Berwick at the end of August to quash the rebellion was large, well equipped and very confident of its superiority. Wallace and Murray and their troops were massed on the **Abbey Craig** (now the site of the Wallace Monument) when the English arrived on the south bank of the Forth on 10 September 1297. There was a ford some miles downstream, but Treasurer Cressingham, reluctant to waste time and money and impatient to get the battle over, led the English vanguard over the narrow wooden Stirling Bridge early on the following morning. Wallace and Murray waited until about half the English forces were across before launching their attack. Cressingham was one of the first to die in the massacre that followed (his skin was said to have been cut up and made into souvenirs). The bridge was soon choked with bodies, preventing Surrey and the remaining English from crossing to join the affray. English losses were enormous, Scottish losses few (but Andrew Murray was fatally wounded), and Surrey fled back to Berwick. Having written to Hamburg announcing 'the liberation of Scotland', Wallace went on to recapture Berwick and raid other parts of Northumberland. In March 1298 he was made Guardian of the Realm in the name of John Balliol.

STIRLING CASTLE

Defoe compared Stirling Castle to Windsor, finding it 'more than Windsor in strength and somewhat less in greatness', while the editor of Fullarton's 1843 *Gazetteer* was reminded of 'Athens, Golcondah [Hyderabad, India] and the old town of **Edinburgh**'. The last provides the usual comparisons, both Scots castles being not homogeneous fortresses but fortified rock headlands commanding extensive low ground on all sides except along their sloping access ridges (here to the south-

'The Prospect of Their Majesties' Castle of Stirling' in c1690, by John Slezer (TS)

east). If anything Stirling's debt to nature rather than art is even greater than Edinburgh's, with 340ft (104m) of sheer black precipice between it and the level carseland below. This inaccessibility explains the uncastellated and almost domestic profile of chimneys, gables and dormers which crowns the rock when seen from the west and north.

Defensive arrangements were vital only to command the crossing of the Forth to the north-east and, of course, the main access route up the ridge (on which the town developed). Here, at the top of the approach, an open area, subsequently used as a parade ground when the Castle served as an 18th/19th century barracks, provided a field of fire for the flanking battery

Façade of James V's Palace flanked by the Great Hall in the outer courtyard of Stirling Castle (RWB)

The restored Great Hall of Stirling Castle

known as the French Spur and for the central battery (16th century, also spur-shaped but altered and enlarged in 1708–14 to form an outer courtyard within a walled and moated extension, Guardroom Square, reached by a drawbridge). A further drawbridge (both are now gone) and a transe, or underpass, had to be negotiated before reaching the main entrance in the Forework (c1500–10), a wall stretching right across the ridge with round towers flanking the entrance (both since truncated), further towers to left and right (both since removed), and the square corner towers of which the Prince's survives although the Elphinstone was reduced in the 17th century.

From these towers the enclosing walls follow the rock's perimeter to form a quadrangle within which are two courtyards containing the principal, mainly 16th–18th century, buildings. These comprise (1) the Palace built by **James V** in the 1540s with an elaborate Renaissance façade of windows and cusped niches occupied by statues atop spiralled columns, thought to be the work of French masons. The main apartments were on the first floor but have been much altered. Massive fireplaces and the collection of carved wooden medallions (the Stirling Heads), which once decorated the ceiling of the King's apartment, give some idea of its original magnificence.

At an angle to the Palace, and connected to it by a Gothic bridge, the Great Hall (2) presents a gable to the outer courtyard and forms the eastern side of the inner. The oldest extant building in the Castle (excluding perhaps that part of the north gate known as the

Mint) and the finest surviving medieval hall in Scotland, it is attributed to **Robert Thomas Cochrane** but was still under construction by **James IV** in 1500. Defoe echoed John Taylor, the water-poet, in declaring it 'the noblest I ever saw in Europe, both Height, Length and Breadth' (respectively 54ft, 126ft and 37ft/16.5, 38.5 and 11.2m). Having served as a Parliament Hall and been the scene of celebrations marking the birth of **Prince Henry**, first son of **James VI**, it underwent partition and dereliction as a barracks and riding school before its recent restoration was taken in hand. Essentially an enclosed space of noble proportions and now lost detail, its notable features include the great hammerbeam roof (restored), five vast fireplaces, and paired windows including two fine oriels.

At right angles to the Great Hall, the Chapel Royal (3) was the result of James VI's lavish requirements for Prince Henry's baptism in 1594, although it may incorporate an earlier building. A chapel, funded by Alexander I, is mentioned in 1124 and by 1501 James IV had secured approval for a college of priests (16 canons and six boy clerics all trained in song). Plain and rectangular, the main entrance has classical pillars; the remains of tempera paintings by Valentine Jenkin (1628) were discovered during restoration. Completing the inner courtyard, a range of buildings known as the King's Old Building (4) runs between the Chapel and the Palace. Remodelled after a fire in the 19th century and now principally occupied by the museum of the **Argyll and Sutherland Highlanders**, this building defies architectural interpretation but may well include the royal apartments built in 1496 and eventually superseded by the Palace.

Within outer walls hugging the furthest perimeter of the rock and affording dramatic views over the Forth, Stirling Bridge, **Abbey Craig** and the **King's Knot** are numerous small gardens and defensive features. To the commanding location of the castle Stirling owes its existence. Until the 18th century burgh and Castle shared the same history [for which see **Stirling**].

STIRLING UNIVERSITY

Founded in 1967, the University is located in **Bridge of Allan** to the north of the town. Airthrey Castle (partly **Robert Adam**) provides the administrative block and Airthrey Estate the campus with long white blocks ranged round the landscaped loch. Prominent here is the MacRobert Arts Centre (1971), a venue for exhibitions and performances donated by the MacRobert Trust. Considering that, unlike other new universities, Stirling was a new foundation and not simply a renamed College of Higher Education, it has achieved a considerable reputation in several fields without entirely forgoing the notoriety that more established institutions can pass off as evidence of vitality.

STIRLING-MAXWELL, Sir William
(1818–78) Art Historian and Collector

The only son of Archibald Stirling of Keir near **Bridge of Allan**, William added the name Maxwell when he succeeded to the Maxwell baronetcy of **Pollok**, now in **Glasgow**, in 1865. He was born at Kenmure, on the other side of Glasgow, and after graduating from Trinity College, Cambridge, travelled in Spain and the Mediterranean, writing *Songs of the Holy Land*, 1846, and the 3-vol *Annals of the Artists of Spain*, 1848. As critic and collector he pioneered the appreciation of Spanish art, filling both Keir and Pollok (open to the public) with an outstanding display, including works by El Greco, Murillo, Goya and Rubens. In 1852 he was elected MP for **Perthshire** and, with one brief gap, held the seat for the next 26 years. As well as serving on the Universities Commission and the Historical Manuscripts Commission, he was a trustee of the British Museum and the National Gallery, and Rector of **St Andrews** (1862), **Aberdeen** (1870) and **Edinburgh** (1872), completing a full house of Scottish universities (possibly a record) by becoming Chancellor of **Glasgow** (1875). Collecting books, especially **Gaelic** texts, and breeding **shorthorns** and Clydesdales, were wholly in character for this model Victorian laird. He married twice and was twice widowed, his second wife being the celebrated wit and writer the Hon Mrs Caroline Norton, whose affair with Lord Melbourne is supposed to have provided the story for George Meredith's *Diana of the Crossways*. She was 69 by the time she married Stirling-Maxwell and, no longer such a noted beauty, died three months later. He died the following year in Venice.

STIRLINGSHIRE

Before the **local government** reorganisation of 1975, Stirlingshire was an irregularly-shaped county of 288,349 acres in the heart of mainland Scotland, bounded by **Dunbartonshire**, **Lanarkshire** and **West Lothian** to the south and south-west, with **Perthshire** to the north and **Clackmannanshire** to the east. The Forth was the main river along with the Kelvin, Avon,

Carron and Endrick. **Loch Lomond** was partly in the county, Ben Lomond (3192ft/973m) representing its highest point. The main occupations were **agriculture**, **coal-mining**, manufacturing, with **oil** refining and petrochemicals in the **Grangemouth** area.

The county town was **Stirling**, although **Falkirk** was the largest burgh. Small burghs comprised **Bridge of Allan**, Denny & Dunnipace, **Kilsyth** and Grangemouth (although this last was almost as large as Stirling). In the 1975 local government reorganisation, Stirlingshire disappeared into Central Region, split into Falkirk and Stirling Districts. The latter district received three burghs and surrounding areas from Perthshire, while Kilsyth was transferred to Cumbernauld District in Strathclyde. In the subsequent reorganisation of 1995 which abolished the Regions, Stirling District became the autonomous Stirling Council Area.

STOBHALL, Perthshire

Eight miles north of **Perth** on a ridge above the **Tay**, Stobhall (or Stobshaw) was once the main seat of the Drummond family and subsequently their dower house when **Drummond Castle** was built in 1487. Like a smaller version of **Dunnottar**, Stobhall consists of several disconnected buildings, rather than a single tower house, all surrounded by an outer wall. The oldest, dated 1578, is L-plan, one wing being a chapel with notable painted ceiling and stone altar, aumbry and stoup. The Drummonds remained Catholic during the **Reformation**, the other wing, with a stair tower in the angle, being evidently the priest's house. Much later, according to M Lindsay (*Castles of Scotland*, 1986), it was briefly the home of the Pre-Raphaelite threesome John Ruskin, his wife Effie Gray, and her subsequent husband John Everett Millais. The dower house itself is dated 1671, a plain building with some original interior features and an adjoining entrance gateway with fine mouldings.

STOER, Assynt, Sutherland

The point of Stoer, a landmark to seamen as mentioned in a famous poem by **Rob Donn** Mackay, crowns the peninsula of Assynt that extends into the North **Minch**. It is mainly composed of Torridonian sandstone and contains some of the oldest rocks of this kind. Among the wonders of its coastal scenery is the free-standing stack known as the Old Man of Stoer, 220ft (67m) high and not to be confused with Storr, on **Skye**.

STONE OF SCONE, STONE OF DESTINY, see SCONE, STONE OF

STONEHAVEN, Kincardineshire

On the east coast between **Montrose** and **Aberdeen**, Stonehaven stands between two headlands at the mouths of the Carron and Cowie Waters. It consists of an old town ('Old Steenie') south of the Carron, the new town between the Carron and the Cowie, and a once separate village, Cowie, to the north. The old town was largely the creation of **George Keith, 5th Earl Marischal** under whose patronage it became the county town of **Kincardineshire** (1600), a **burgh of barony** (1607) and a port. It fared less well thereafter, being burnt by **Montrose** (1645), occupied by Cromwellian forces (while

steeple (1790), is notable as the venue for a **Hogmanay** celebration in which the young men whirl fireballs round their heads. The custom must be of great antiquity and is presumed to have the effect of warding off evil.

Cowie, with a **golf course** and other attractions, predates both Stonehavens and was once the site of a castle built by **Malcolm III 'Canmore'**. The ruins of a cliff-top church dedicated to St Mary of the Storms remain, part dating from the 13th century. On the other, south-west, side of the town Dunnottar parish church (1593 but much rebuilt) boasts a separate Marischal aisle (1582) to commemorate the 5th Earl. Here too is the famous **Covenanters'** Stone commemorating nine of those who perished in Dunnottar Castle in 1685. **Sir Walter Scott**'s encounter (1793) with **Robert Paterson**, who was cleaning the stone, provided the inspiration for *Old Mortality*. Fetteresso, inland from Stonehaven and near its present bypass, has the remains of yet another ancient parish church plus those of Fetteresso Castle where **James Francis Edward Stewart** was proclaimed King as James VIII on 2 January 1716.

About four miles north-west of Stonehaven an archaeological site of considerable extent and interest sprawls across the area known as Raedykes. It includes at least five separate ring **cairns** (2nd–3rd millennium BC) plus 'the best preserved **Roman** earthwork in Grampian' which is thought to date from **Agricola**'s campaign of AD 84.

STORNOWAY, Isle of Lewis

The Hebridean capital of Stornoway has been the principal settlement of the Outer Isles for many centuries and is the only 'town' in the islands. The medieval castle (it was destroyed by Cromwellian troops in 1654) was the stronghold of the **MacLeods** of **Lewis** from the 13th century. The town benefited from the sale of Lewis to James Matheson in 1844 [see **Jardine Matheson**]; a period of mid-Victorian civic energy improved roads, gas and water supplies, enlarged and modernised the harbour facilities, and led to a period of growth and prosperity. Many new houses were built, and nearly all the architecture of Stornoway is 19th century or later.

Matheson built Lews Castle, an imposing castellated mansion now used as a College of Further Education. Its grounds consist of a square mile of deciduous woodland, unique in the Outer Isles. The core of the town has several fine buildings, including Amity House, the offices of the Pier and Harbour Commission, and the former Town Hall, built in 1905 in Scots Baronial style and now housing a new museum, *Museum nan Eilean, Steornabhagh*, which interprets the **geology**, archaeology and history of the islands and also accommodates special exhibitions.

One of the most important buildings in Stornoway is the Nicholson Institute, from which school generations of scholars have progressed to academic fame and fortune. A suburban area has grown in recent years, beyond which is a hospital and an industrial estate, which includes mills where **wool** for **Harris tweed** is dyed and spun and the completed tweeds are washed and inspected.

Stornoway is one of the principal ferry terminals in the Outer **Hebrides**, connected to **Ullapool** by car ferry,

Stonehaven Harbour, by Sir William Fettes Douglas (NGS)

besieging the Keiths' **Dunnottar Castle**, 1651–2) and by Cumberland's troops (1746, following the town's declared support of the **Jacobite** cause). But in 1759 the Quaker Barclays of Urie bought an adjacent estate and in 1795 **Robert Barclay**, back from Jamaica with a fortune to spend, laid out the new town. 30 years later **Robert Stevenson** cleared the harbour of a major rock obstruction in time for the town to cash in on the late 19th century **herring** boom.

On the quay the 17th century Tolbooth, crow-stepped and of red sandstone, is the oldest building. In 1748, from a cell within, three local ministers of the **Episcopal Church** contrived to perform baptisms by pouring water through their barred windows onto the proffered babes below. The building now houses a local museum in which such events are remembered. Also commemorated, by a plaque in the new town's Market Square, is the inventor **R W Thomson** who was born here in 1822. The old town's High Street, with mercat cross and

Stornoway from the south c1890 (GWWA)

the journey taking 3½ hours, and is also the administrative centre of the Western Isles local authority, Comhairle nan Eilean. It is a bustling, even slightly cosmopolitan community – many foreign vessels, especially from Eastern Europe and the former Soviet Union, make use of the fine harbour for shelter from North Atlantic storms, and Gaelic-speaking Pakistani shopkeepers add to the ambience.

The urban landscape – tenements, red sandstone villas, suburban streets – is reminiscent of many small Scottish towns, and seems strange in the Hebrides.

To the east of Stornoway is the well populated Eye peninsula – the district called Point. At the neck of the peninsula is Stornoway Airport with links to **Barra** and **Glasgow**. The tiny Loganair planes share the facilities with a NATO base – yet another threat to the island way of life.

Stornoway is at the centre of Gaeldom, the last bastion of those pillars of Hebridean society, the **Free Church** and the **Gaelic language**. Books and periodicals in Gaelic bring poetry and prose, both past and present, to the Gaelic-speaking community, and particular stress is placed on education in Gaelic, from pre-school playgroups through to sixth year. Two newspapers interpret the local scene, the somewhat old-fashioned *Stornoway Gazette* and the Skye-based *West Highland Free Press*.

STRACATHRO, Nr Brechin, Angus

It was in the then parish church of Stracathro, north of **Brechin**, in 1296 that Edward I humiliated **John Balliol** by depriving him of the title and trappings of kingship. There were also two Battles of Stracathro, the first in 1130 when **David I** defeated Angus **Earl of Moray**, a grandson of **Lulach**, and the second in 1452 when the 4th **Lindsay Earl of Crawford**, also known as 'Beardie' or the 'Tiger Earl', was defeated but not cowed by the **Earl of Huntly**.

STRACHAN, John (1778–1867) Bishop of Toronto

Born in **Aberdeen** and an MA (1797) of **Aberdeen University**, Strachan went to Canada in 1799 to teach. In 1806 he was ordained in the **Episcopal Church** and soon became identified with the conservative element in Upper Canada. **William Lyon Mackenzie** scorned him as 'a diminutive, paltry, insignificant, Scotch turncoat parish schoolmaster', but by 1823 he was a Director of the Bank of Upper Canada and the first President of the Canadian Board of Education. He founded numerous schools and in 1821 had been involved in upgrading **James MacGill**'s Montreal College into MacGill University. A staunch upholder of ecclesiastical privilege and patronage, he was appointed the first Bishop of Toronto in 1839.

STRAITON, Ayrshire

Seven miles south-east of **Maybole** and situated on rising ground on the banks of the river Girvan, Straiton is one of **Ayrshire**'s most picturesque villages, 'uniform in plan, skirted with wood, and overhung by green declivities'. The uniformity belongs to the two rows of neat cottages built c1760 by Thomas, **Earl of Cassillis** which line the High Street. The church (1758, restored 1901) contains a pre-**Reformation** chantry chapel founded about 1350 and enlarged in the 15th century, and some notable stained glass. Just north of the village the grandiose Tudor-Gothic Blairquhan Castle (**William Burn**, 1820–4) is reminiscent of Crawford Priory near **Cupar** in **Fife**, although in a far better state of repair and seasonally open to the public.

STRANRAER, Wigtownshire

Situated at the head of Loch Ryan, Stranraer took advantage of the natural shelter of its position to build two piers (1820 and 1836–40) to capture the lucrative Irish ferry trade which had previously operated to **Portpatrick**. This trade, still the town's lifeblood, has brought disadvantages in the vast and still increasing volume of heavy traffic on the A75 road which slices through Dumfries & Galloway to its junction with the A(M)74 at **Gretna**. The town itself, a **burgh of barony** since 1596 and a **royal burgh** from 1617, 'straggles in an absent-minded and unbuttoned way around the curve of the coast' (T Lang) and around its one notable antiquity, the Castle of St John, built c1520, used by **John Graham of Claverhouse** as his headquarters in 1682, transferred to **Kennedy** and then **Dalrymple of Stair** ownership, extended (upwards) and later serving as gaol and storehouse. Near Stranraer's East Pier stands North-West Castle, now a hotel but formerly the home of **Captain John Ross** (1777–1856), Arctic explorer and seeker of the eponymous North-West Passage.

STRATH HALLADALE, Sutherland

A document of 1631 defines the border between **Strathnaver** and **Caithness** as the ridge called Drumholstein east of the Halladale river. Its strath, which extends from Melvich on the north coast to the heights of the Ben Griams almost due south, was in dispute between the **Murrays** and **Mackays** until 1597. It was then purchased by William, brother of Uisdean, Chief of Mackay, progenitor of the Mackays of Bighouse. Since it was Uisdean's son who was created Lord Reay, they were not eligible to succeed to the peerage. But they flourished in Strath Halladale until William's descendant sold his patrimony to the house of **Sutherland** in 1830. Their estate documents are preserved in the Scottish Record Office and some of their sculptured stones have been moved for their better protection to the Strathnaver Museum.

STRATHALLAN, Perthshire

Between **Auchterarder** and **Dunblane**, Strathallan is best known for its disused airfield, sometime a museum with exhibits mostly from World War II, and for Strathallan School, a noted establishment but not in Strathallan (founded, 1912, at **Bridge of Allan** but now at Freeland near Forgandenny just south of **Perth**). At Blackford, once the main ford on the Allan Water, **William Wallace** is said by **Blind Harry** to have defeated a detachment of English troops and dumped their bodies in the river. Hard by, Carsebreck Loch was once, like **Lake of Menteith**, the site of **curling** bonspiels. The Drummond Lairds of Strathallan estate included William, 1st Viscount Strathallan, who has the doubtful distinction of introducing the thumbscrew into Scotland. The 7th Viscount, dying at **Culloden**, is said to have taken the last sacrament in **oatmeal** and **whisky**, bread and wine being either unobtainable or less to his taste.

STRATHAVEN, Lanarkshire

An important weaving centre in the 19th century, Strathaven (pron. Straiven) is the only town in the district of Annandale south of **Hamilton**. The castle of Avondale (or Strathaven) was acquired by **James Hamilton of Finnart** c1538 and then passed to the **Dukes of Hamilton** but had previously belonged to the **Earls of Douglas** and then been granted to Andrew Stewart who was created Lord Avondale (1455). The present ruin dates from the 15th century but 'for safety reasons is not open to the public'. The town's John Hastie Museum has a fine collection of **pottery** and porcelain as well as weaving and **Covenanting** exhibits while the Hamiltons' 17th century Town Mill now hosts an arts centre.

STRATHBOGIE CASTLE, see HUNTLY CASTLE

STRATHCLYDE, Kingdom of

Strathclyde (which was probably identical with the Kingdom of Cumbria) was founded during the **Roman** occupation of Britain. The **Antonine Wall**, built c120 AD, formed the kingdom's northern border. At its maximum extent it reached to the **Lothians** and included present-day Cumbria. Its inhabitants were Britons, probably descended from the Novantae in south-west Scotland; the genealogy of its kings reputedly stemmed from Magnus Maximus, who aspired to be Roman Emperor in 383; and their principal stronghold was **Dumbarton Rock**.

The Strathclyde Britons were Christians by the mid-5th century, when St Patrick berated their King Ceretic for crimes including the selling of Christians as slaves to the Scots and **Picts**. **St Mungo** was reputedly established in the see of **Glasgow** c573.

In the mid-7th century, Angles from Northumberland reached the Solway and isolated Strathclyde. The Picts remained hostile and in 756 **Oengus** McFergus, King of the Picts, joined with the Angles to besiege and capture **Dumbarton**. The fortress was taken again in 870 by **Viking** raiders from Ireland. That same year the King of Strathclyde was killed by **Constantine I**, King of Alba/Scotia, and the kings of Strathclyde thereafter were subservient to the Scottish monarch. Norse invasions continued and in 1000 Ethelred II ravaged Strathclyde. But in 1018 **Malcolm II** defeated the English at **Carham**, supported by **Owen the Bald**, reputedly the last King of Strathclyde. The kingdom's independence ended between 960–1018 and by 1034 it was part of the realm of **Duncan I** of Scotland.

STRATHCLYDE UNIVERSITY

The University of Strathclyde, **Glasgow**'s second university, was established in 1964 through the amalgamation of the Royal College of Science and Technology and the Scottish College of Commerce. Both these institutions had long histories. The Royal College dates back to Anderson's University founded under the will of **Professor John Anderson** in 1796, and the College of Commerce back to the Glasgow Educational Association founded in 1845. After a difficult start, Anderson's University flourished in the early 19th century with some distinguished teachers, such as the chemist Andrew Ure and the pioneer of mechanics institutes George

Birkbeck. The University is based around the old Royal College built of red sandstone in 1901. Since its foundation the University has maintained its reputation for scientific and technical education, while at the same time broadening its teaching into the humanities. New buildings have been constructed on the campus: the School of Architecture (1966), and old ones taken over and restored: the **Barony** and **St David's (Ramshorn) Churches**.

STRATHGLASS, Inverness-shire
The river Glass, formed by streams from Glens Affric and Cannich, flows north-east roughly parallel to the **Great Glen** and 10 miles north of it. Joined by the river Farrar at Struy, the Glass becomes the Beauly but the glen remains Strathglass to the Beauly Firth. Above **Beauly**, 'through scenery unrivalled in Great Britain' (*Murray's Guide*, 1898), the river once surged down a gorge known as The Dhruim and over Kilmorack Falls; it is now somewhat tamed by **hydro-electric** containment. On the left bank Farley forest has at least four **duns**, including that of the Fhamhair (or **Formorian**), and there are more near Struy. Between, Aigas is named after the island in the river where the oft-hunted **Simon Lord Lovat** took refuge in his youth and where, to the house subsequently built there, Robert Peel and the **Sobieski Stuarts** in turn retreated. Near the confluence with the Farrar stands Erchless Castle, a 17th century L-plan tower house much altered in the 19th century. It was once the ancestral home of The Chisholm. From Cannich minor roads finger into Glens Affric and Cannich. Along with Strathfarrar, these are prime contenders for the tag of loveliest Highland glen. All three have magnificent native woodlands not entirely smothered by **forestry** planting and large stretches of water (lochs Beneveian, Mullardoch and Monar) which even hydro dams have failed to disfigure.

STRATHMIGLO, Fife
West of **Auchtermuchty**, Strathmiglo is also a 15th century burgh which later became a centre of the weaving industry. Its Town House tower (1734) with parapet and spire is almost identical to Auchtermuchty's. An abundance of **cairns**, tumuli, **standing stones**, etc, recorded in the 19th century, prompted one writer to assume that a major battle, possibly even **Mons Graupius**, had been fought in the vicinity. Towards **Abernethy** stands Balvaird Castle, a ruined L-plan tower house of the late 15th century built by a son of Sir William Murray of **Tullibardine**. The Rev Andrew Murray, a descendant, was created Lord Balvaird by **Charles I**, the title and property eventually passing to the **Scone** Earls of Mansfield.

STRATHMORE, Perthshire/Angus/ Kincardineshire
Strathmore, 'the great strath', designates the fertile lowlands south-east of the Grampians just as Glen More, the **Great Glen**, designates their boundary to the north-west. It is sometimes taken to extend from **Dunbartonshire** to **Stonehaven**, but more commonly from **Perth** to Stonehaven. It thus comprises all the lowlands bordered to the south-east by the **Sidlaws** (principally the **Tay** and Isla basin) plus the Howes of **Angus** and **The**
Mearns to the north. For the Earldom of Strathmore see **Glamis**.

STRATHNAVER, Sutherland
The west coast of this province extends south from **Cape Wrath** to Assynt. Its eastern frontier borders **Caithness** while its underbelly marches with **Sutherland**. So it appears on the map which Gerard Mercator published in Germany in 1595. Timothy Pont's map, which was published by Blaeu in the mid-17th century, is probably earlier than Mercator's and delineates Strathnaver on a larger scale. In the Middle Ages it formed with Sutherland and Caithness the far-flung Diocese of Caithness. **Donald of the Isles** recognised the Chief of **Mackay** as its sole superior in a charter of 1415. So did **James IV** in documents of 1497 and 1506. But soon afterwards the Gordons succeeded in establishing themselves as **Earls of Sutherland**, and by 1588 they had secured the superiority of Strathnaver. In 1642 they acquired the *dominium utile* of the Naver valley from which the province derives its name, and from this time the Gordon earls began to call their eldest sons 'Lord Strathnaver', anticipating Letters Patent from the Crown which alone can create a peerage title. When these failed to materialise, the Sutherland lords of **Dunrobin** attempted to give credence to the bogus title by inscribing it in stone on their buildings. It was never clear whether their pretensions extended to the entire province, to the Naver valley only, or to the little township at its midst. The deception was unmasked when the succession to the Sutherland Earldom itself became the subject of litigation in 1766. No party to the dispute mentioned the existence of any Strathnaver peerage. Nor could the purchase of the remainder of Strathnaver from the Mackay Chief in 1829 and from Mackay of **Strath Halladale** in 1830 create one. The continued assertion of it, so offensive to the Mackays of Strathnaver, must rank as one of Scotland's most hoary hoaxes.

In 1814 Strathnaver witnessed some of the worst **clearances** when **Patrick Sellar**, the new leaseholder on the right bank of the Naver, expelled his tenants and fired their houses to make way for sheep. Five years later the **Countess of Sutherland** subjected her tenants on the left bank to the same horrors.

STRATHPEFFER, Nr Dingwall, Ross & Cromarty
The Victorian spa *par excellence*, Strathpeffer owed its celebrity to Dr Thomas Morrison of **Aberdeenshire** who, in 1819, declared its waters the most efficacious in Britain, and to Dr Thomas Thomson (1773–1852, the father of **Thomas Thomson** the naturalist) who, as Professor of Chemistry at **Glasgow University**, analysed the waters and found their hydrogen content higher than that of Harrogate's. Iron and sulphur springs were also developed. The first pump room opened in 1820; villas, hotels and hospitals followed along with special coach services and eventually a **railway** station (1885). While the pungent waters and 'balsamic airs' wrought wonders for the gouty, the dyspeptic and the scorbutic, their healthier companions tramped up Ben Wyvis and practised their quadrilles. Not till World War I did fashion finally desert Strathpeffer. Its harled and dormered villas still peek from wooded terraces, more

Simla than Leamington. The smaller, or Upper, Pump Room now displays an exhibition of the spa in its hey-day while Spa Cottage houses a museum of Victoriana and dolls, and the railway station has become a craft and visitor centre.

Near the station a **Pictish** symbol stone is also known as the Eagle Stone, an eagle being clearly distinguishable. It has latterly been associated with the clan Munro, whose crest is an eagle, although it stands close to the grounds of the **Mackenzie** Castle Leod, an L-plan tower house with a large gabled block in the angle of the L, which was erected in the early 17th century by Sir Roderick Mackenzie, uncle or brother of the 1st Lord Mackenzie of **Kintail** and long remembered as the 'Tutor of Kintail'. His grandson George Mackenzie was created Viscount Tarbat and 1st Earl of Cromartie, the title still held by the Laird of Leod who is also clan chief. Meanwhile the Kintail Mackenzies, **Earls of Sea-forth**, held sway at nearby Brahan Castle which, like their line, is no more, **Coinneach Odhar** ('the Brahan Seer') having predicted their extinction.

South of the town the 'Cat's Ridge', *Druimm a Chait*, is crowned by the partially excavated and impressive hill fort of Knock Farril, heavily vitrified and with what was once probably a well. Somewhere below it took place a ferocious battle (1429) between the clans **Mac-Donald** and Mackenzie. Kenneth, the 6th Mackenzie Chief, had accepted Margaret, a daughter of the **Lord of the Isles**, as his wife; but finding her to be blind in one eye, he sent her home with a horse, a groom and a dog, all likewise blind in one eye. To this slight the MacDonalds responded with suitably blind fury, invading Mackenzie territory and being worsted in the battle.

STRATHSPEY REEL

This is the name given – from the late 18th century – to that dance form and its accompanying music which epitomises the 'Scottish Snap' (short-long, long-short notation) and which, more than any other, is Scotland's own contribution to **dance**. The 'snap' occurs in *puirt-a-beul* (mouth music) from the Gaelic west, which would clearly pre-date the association with Strathspey. Angus Cumming, a fiddler of the region who published *A Collection of Strathspeys, or Old Highland Reels* in 1780, merely commented that the style of the Strathspey reel was 'preserved in the greatest purity' there. It has certainly been a great favourite in the north-east ever since.

STRATHYRE, Perthshire

Aligned almost north-south, Strathyre provides a direct access route to the Highlands. Its popularity with **tourists** dates from the publication of **Sir Walter Scott**'s *Lady of the Lake*, set hereabouts ('Ben Ledi saw the cross of fire/It glanced like lightning up Strathyre'). Recently the leisure business has been developed by the **Forestry Commission** whose cabins, campsites and evergreen amenity signs bristle beside Loch Lubnaig. At Ardvoch, near the village of Strathyre, was born **Dugald Buchanan**, the Gaelic poet.

STRICHEN, Aberdeenshire

It was to Strichen, 10 miles inland from **Fraserburgh**, that **Johnson** and **Boswell** made a detour to inspect what they called 'a Druidical circle' (ie a stone circle).

Having chosen one of the least impressive in the county, they were duly disappointed. Their host, Captain Fraser, was the son of Lord Strichen who had founded the village in 1764. His descendants were responsible for giving nearby Mormond Hill its white horse, white stag (both turf cut-outs filled with quartz) and its now ruined hunting lodge. Captain Fraser also founded a **linen** spinning settlement which, not to be outdone by **New Lanark**, he called New Leeds. 'Mormond Braes' are the subject of a famous **bothy ballad**, such compositions being a speciality of **Buchan**.

STROMNESS, Mainland, Orkney

This port started to burgeon beside the deep sheltered anchorage of Hamnavoe with the growth of transatlantic commerce. The Hudson's Bay Company began to recruit here at the outset of the 18th century and by 1800 Orcadians supplied three-quarters of its Canadian work-force. By then whaling ships were also recruiting their crews in Stromness. The 21 houses and shops of 1792 had increased to 385 houses by 1821 and to 500 in 1841, with four inns and 34 public houses. Amenities for passing ships included the well (still preserved) opposite Login's Inn, from which vessels of the Hudson's Bay Company, of Captain Cook's expedition and later of the Franklin expedition drew their water supply. The British Navy came with its press gangs.

A natural history museum was founded in 1837, and expanded to include exhibits of the Hudson's Bay Company, whaling and other far-flung maritime enterprises, as well as mementos of the German fleet scuppered in **Scapa Flow**. Boat building flourished, and the first mail boat to make regular crossings of the Pentland Firth was constructed here in 1856.

Today Stromness is linked to **Scrabster** (**Caithness**) by vehicle ferry, while the town still contains two boatyards and **fishing** continues to underpin its economy. But such a burgh was bound to attract an increasing number of **tourists**, drawn here by the writings of long-time resident **George Mackay Brown**, by the Pier Arts Centre housed on a quay in former Hudson's Bay Company premises, and by the fascination of its long narrow street along the shore, from which the stone houses stray in clusters to paddle at the water's edge.

STRONTIAN, Argyll

Near the head of Loch Sunart, Strontian is the principal village in the sparsely populated districts of Ardgour and **Morvern**. The local lead mines were first worked in the early 18th century and assumed importance during the Napoleonic Wars as a source for bullets. Other rare minerals were found here, most notably, in 1764, 'Strontianite' by Sir Humphrey Davy. Strontium salts are used to make fireworks burn red, and Strontium 90 is a particularly nasty radioactive isotope. Miners and others joined the **Free Church** at the **Disruption** (1843) and, refused land for a church, made and moored a floating church in the loch which served them well for nigh on 30 years.

STRUAN, Perthshire

Five miles up the Perthshire Garry from **Blair Atholl** and near the **Falls of Bruar**, Struan churchyard is the ancient burial place of the clan Robertson. A Clan

Stromness c1890 from the north-west looking towards Hoy (GWWA)

Donnachaidh museum celebrates this and other **clans** (MacRobert, Duncan, etc) descended from Stout Duncan (or Donnachy) who fought with **Robert I** and whose grandson Robert was the progenitor of the Robertsons. For sustained and impeccable **Jacobite** credentials none can rival Alexander Robertson of Struan who fought under **John Graham of Claverhouse** in 1689, the **Earl of Mar** in 1715, and **Prince Charles Edward Stuart** in 1745. It is said that 2000 clansmen attended his funeral and carried his body from **Loch Tay** to Struan. Down Glen Errochty a road leads to **Kinloch Rannoch** where more Robertsons are buried.

STUART

The usual Scottish spelling is 'Stewart' or 'Steward', denoting descent from Walter, 3rd High Steward of Scotland. As a surname 'Stewart' is preferred; but 'Stuart', the anglicised version commonly used of the royal house of Stewart after 1603, is here retained for later surnames where it has become an accepted spelling. The change is thought to have been a concession to the French, good friends to many 'Stewarts', whose language has no 'w'.

STUART, Gilbert (1743–86) Historian

Gilbert Stuart was born in **Edinburgh**, where he trained as a lawyer, a profession he abandoned in favour of a literary career. In his first historical work, the *Antiquity of the English Constitution* (1768), and in his most successful work, *A View of Society in Europe* (1778), he boldly challenged the political ideas of **David Hume** and other established figures of the **Scottish Enlightenment**. In 1773 he returned to Scotland after gaining hard-won recognition on London's Grub Street and founded the *Edinburgh Magazine and Review*. This periodical continued for less than three years, but it established an authoritative critical approach which was taken up by 19th century reviewers such as **Francis Jeffrey**. In 1780 Stuart produced his *History of Mary Queen of Scots*, a passionate defence of the Queen at a time when she was held in general disrepute. The tragic tone of Stuart's prose ran contrary to the irony and scepticism of the Enlightenment historical writing but anticipated the romanticism of the next generation. After failing to earn the acclaim he believed was his due, Stuart ended his life a disappointed man, steeped in alcohol yet as a political commentator fighting adversaries such as **William Robertson** and **Henry Dundas** to the end. (See biography by William Zachs, 1991.)

STUART, John, 3rd Earl of Bute (1713–92)
Prime Minister

The Earldom of **Bute** had been created (1703) for Sir James Stewart (Stuart), a Commissioner in the abortive **Union** negotiations of 1703, whose family had been keepers of **Rothesay Castle** and Sheriffs of Bute. The 1st Earl was quickly succeeded by his son and then

(1723) by his Eton-educated grandson. A Scots representative peer from 1738, the 3rd Earl arrived in London in 1745 and, while waiting for the rain to stop at the Egham races, was summoned by Frederick, Prince of Wales to make up a table of whist. Thus began a close association with the frivolous Prince (d.1751), a scandalously intimate connection with his wife Princess Augusta, and a highly influential relationship with their son George III. When the last succeeded to the throne (1760) Bute became a Privy Councillor (1760), Secretary of State (1761) and Prime Minister (1762) as First Lord of the Treasury. He lasted only a year but negotiated the Treaty of Paris which ended the Seven Years' War. Its terms did nothing for his popularity which as an absolutist, a Scot, a **Stewart**, a royal favourite 'and an honest man' was as abysmal as Wilkes could make it. His influence with the King remained unimpaired for a few more years but after 1768 he travelled and devoted himself to botanical studies and other gentlemanly pursuits. Among those who benefited from his literary patronage was **Dr Johnson**.

STUART, John MacDouall (1815–66)
Australian Explorer
Born in Dysart, **Fife**, John MacDouall Stuart was rejected by the army on account of his diminutive stature. He trained as a civil engineer, fell in love, and then discovered his fiancée kissing his best friend. Without waiting for an explanation he took ship for the other side of the world. He arrived in Adelaide, South Australia in 1839 and quickly found work with the government survey which was trying to extend the colony to the north in search of new grazing lands. In 1844 he was employed as a draughtsman by Charles Sturt, 'the father of Australian exploration', and accompanied him on his last expedition to the Murray and Darling rivers.

He made the first of his own expeditions in 1858. His ability to travel fast and light prompted one of his companions to comment that 'as an explorer, Stuart has no equal; he has a hardihood by nature to endure thirst and hunger, a good practical knowledge of botany, of surveying, of astronomy and of medicine; he can shoe his own horse and has the pluck of a giant in his puny frame'.

In 1859 the government of South Australia announced that it was offering a £2000 prize to the discoverer of a route across the centre of the continent for the Overland Telegraph. An extension to the existing line which linked Europe and India had been under discussion for some time, and the colonies of Victoria, South Australia and New South Wales were all determined that the line should be under their control. Intercolonial rivalry was intense. One month after Stuart's departure from Adelaide in March 1860, another expedition, led by Burke and Wills, left Melbourne in Victoria with the same aim.

By the end of April Stuart and his two companions were in sight of the centre of Australia. In the 24 years since the first official white settlers had arrived in South Australia no less than six different exploring parties had set out expressly to reach this point. All had failed. Now Stuart built a cairn to mark the spot, planted a British flag, 'gave three hearty cheers for this symbol of civil and religious liberty' and pressed on northwards. But

by August they were back in Adelaide, forced by thirst, scurvy and unfriendly Aborigines to abandon their efforts to reach the north coast. The South Australian Parliament immediately voted a sum of £2500 for a larger and better-equipped expedition, and on 17 November 1860, with 12 men, 49 horses and undiminished enthusiasm, Stuart left Adelaide again. This time he got within 200 miles of the north coast before being forced back by an impenetrable tangle of scrub. His return to Adelaide was greeted with the news that Burke and Wills, on their Victorian expedition, had succeeded in reaching the north coast on the Gulf of Carpentaria, but that they had both perished on the return journey. Their route, however, had proved unsuitable for the Overland Telegraph.

Stuart was by now 46 years old. Never robust, his health had been gradually eroded by four years of almost constant travel. But on 25 October 1861 he left Adelaide on his fifth great journey. This time he made it, reaching the Indian Ocean at Van Diemen's Gulf on 25 July 1862. The return journey of 2000 miles was a nightmare – a combination of scurvy, arthritis and internal ulcers made it impossible for Stuart to ride and for most of the way he was carried on a stretcher slung between two horses. On 27 November a farm hand at one of South Australia's outlying stations saw 10 gaunt and ragged men – one lying on a stretcher – wearily leading a string of limping, skeletal horses out of the shimmering heat of the north.

The Royal Geographical Society in London awarded Stuart their Patron's Gold Medal and by 1872 the Overland Telegraph line from Darwin to Adelaide following Stuart's route was complete. Stuart himself had returned to England in 1864, lonely, sick and nearly blind, to be cared for by his sister in London. Within a year his eyesight and memory had failed completely and he died at the age of 50. His birthplace in Rectory Lane, Dysart is now the John MacDouall Stuart Museum.

STUART, John Patrick Crichton, 3rd Marquis of Bute (1847–1900)
The elder son of **John Stuart, 3rd Earl of Bute**, was created marquis 1796. His son, also John, married the Crichton heiress to the earldom of **Dumfries** and succeeded to that title, their son (another John) becoming 2nd Marquis of Bute with the surname Crichton Stuart. John Patrick, who was therefore great-great-grandson of the 3rd Earl, was born at **Mount Stuart** in **Bute** and succeeded aged one when his father died. His mother died 10 years later when he was at Harrow. Bute proceeded to Christ Church, Oxford and in 1868 took the still scandalous step of becoming a Roman Catholic, a conversion which is thought to have prompted Disraeli's *Lothair*. Barred from public office and by nature more interested in scholarship, Bute travelled extensively, learnt Hebrew, Coptic and Arabic, and became an authority on Eastern religions, on early Christianity, and on Catholic liturgy (publishing a translation of *The Breviary*, 1879). In Wales, where the family had inherited extensive estates, he built Cardiff docks and experimented with viticulture. But it was in Scotland that he left his most lasting mark as the restorer of **Falkland Palace**, **Rothesay Castle**, **Pluscarden** and **St Andrews** Priories and other buildings. He also rebuilt Mount

Stuart and made generous benefactions to **Glasgow** and **St Andrews Universities**. He wrote and lectured on Scottish history and was one of rather few aristocratic advocates of home rule and a Scottish Parliament.

SUILVEN, Sutherland

The ridge, a mile and a half long, which forms the summit of Suilven, consists of three peaks, although it appears to be one when seen from the east or west. It is perhaps the most spectacular even of the Assynt hills, a buttress of Torridonian sandstone on a bed of granite rising to a height of 2399ft (731m).

SULLUM VOE, Shetland

A deep-water inlet off **Yell** Sound in the north of **Shetland**, Sullum Voe was an important base for seaplanes in World War II. There followed three decades of inactivity until it was chosen as the site for Britain's largest **oil** terminal. Two massive submarine pipelines bring in crude oil from the Brent and Ninian complexes in the East Shetland Basin and, after being stabilised, the oil is shipped out to refineries.

The terminal occupies 1000 acres (400ha) and the total cost of construction was £1.3 billion. Designed to handle 70 million tonnes of oil a year, the terminal is operated by BP Petroleum Development Ltd on behalf of around 30 companies.

SUMBURGH, Shetland

At the south end of the **Mainland** of Shetland, Sumburgh is an area of great variety with spectacular coastal scenery and some of the best farmland in Shetland. Sumburgh Airport, the main air terminal for the islands since 1933, has played a major role in the development of the North Sea's **oil**fields. A short distance away lie

the ruins of **Jarlshof**, one of the most important archaeological sites in Europe.

The cliffs at Sumburgh Head are crowned with a lighthouse, built in 1820, whose rays shine out over Sumburgh Roost, a notorious tidal stream where the North Sea meets the Atlantic. Tucked away in a corner at Grutness is the Mainland terminal for the **Fair Isle** mailboat.

SUMMER ISLES, Wester Ross

Lying close to the mainland just to the north-west of Loch Broom and reached from either **Ullapool** or Achiltibuie in Wester **Ross**, these islands were brought to public attention by the naturalist **Sir Frank Fraser Darling**, who farmed the 804 acres (327ha) of Tanera Mor 1939–44, and wrote about his experiences in his book *Island Farm*. In 1881 there were 118 residents on Tanera Mor, all of whom had left by 1931. In recent years some of the cottages have been renovated for holiday accommodation, and every now and again small groups of incomers have been tempted to settle permanently on the island. Amongst the more than 15 other islands in this group, all now uninhabited, are Priest Island and Isle Martin, owned by the RSPB. There is a good view of the islands from the Ullapool-**Stornoway** ferry.

SUTHERLAND

With a population of just over 13,000 scattered throughout an area of 1,484,846 acres (600,909ha), Sutherland can claim the distinction of being the most sparsely populated county in Scotland. It stretches from the Atlantic on the west and north, with **Caithness** to the north-east and the **Dornoch Firth** and **Ross &**

Inchnadamph and Ben More Assynt in Sutherland (GWWA)

Cromarty to the south, its greatest length being 63 miles and greatest breadth 60. Consisting mainly of moor and mountain, the county's highest point is Ben More Assynt, 3273ft (998m). Previously under Norse rule, Sutherland was claimed for the Scottish Crown by **William the Lion** in the 12th century.

The county offices were in **Golspie** although **Dornoch** was the largest town and often considered the county capital. Under the **local government** reorganisation of 1975, the county of Sutherland became the Sutherland District of Highland Region; since the abolition of the Regions in 1995 it has remained part of the Highland Council Area.

SUTHERLAND, Earldom and Dukedom

The 'southland' of the **Vikings**, in the coastal plain below **Caithness**, was erected into an earldom c1235 in favour of William of **Duffus**, descendant of a Fleming named Freskin. The family adopted Sutherland as their surname and it became that of a Gaelic **clan**. When **James IV** invested the **Earl of Huntly** with vice-regal powers in the north as his Lieutenant, Huntly used them to seize the Sutherland Earldom for his brother Adam Gordon. Thus in 1494 he obtained a 'brieve of idiocy' against the 8th Earl, John, who had maintained himself effectively through troubled times for 40 years. John's heir, Alexander, was declared a bastard although his mother, daughter of Ross of Balnagowan, received widow's terce as Countess until her death. When Alexander tried to gain his inheritance he was murdered in 1518. Adam Gordon, who had married Alexander's sister Elizabeth, issued a charter in that year in which he styled himself Earl of Sutherland. Alexander's son John was murdered by the Gordons in 1550 but also left sons, so that there are legitimate Sutherland chiefs and earls of that name to this day. From **James VI** the Gordons obtained a charter stipulating that the earldom should never part from their surname, lest it be lost to them through an heiress. They were thus barred from the chiefship, which remained with Sutherland of Duffus, the true heir. The 16th Earl who died in 1733 adopted the surname of Sutherland, but on the death of the 18th in 1766 the ancient proviso threatened to prove fatal. The claim of his only daughter **Elizabeth** was not only contested by Sutherland, enquiring how many centuries were required to legalise Gordon crimes, but also by the Gordons of **Gordonstoun**. After a costly lawsuit the baby Countess won, to marry into the fabulously wealthy Leveson-Gower family and to preside over the Sutherland **clearances**. Her English husband incurred unmerited odium. He had been systematically robbed by his wife's greedy Lowland servants before being raised to a dukedom in the last six months of his life. On the death of the 5th Duke in 1963 the earldom passed to his niece and the dukedom to a cousin.

SUTHERLAND, Robert Garioch, 'Robert Garioch' (1909–81) Poet

Born in **Edinburgh** and educated at the city's **High School** and **University**, Robert Sutherland was a schoolteacher in Edinburgh and London and Writer in Residence at Edinburgh University (1927–31). During World War II he served with the Royal Corps of Signals and spent three years as a prisoner of war (1942–5). His poems, written in Scots as a defiant stand against the increasing anglicisation of his native tongue and published under the pseudonym 'Robert Garioch', vividly capture the atmosphere of Edinburgh and display a wry humour often directed against the hypocrisy of the Establishment. His first collection, shared with **Sorley Maclean**, was published as *17 Poems for 6d* in 1940 and was followed by, among others, *Selected Poems* (1966) and *Collected Poems* (1977). His translations from the Latin of **George Buchanan**'s two biblical dramas *Jephthes* and *Baptistes* are much admired.

SWAN, Annie S (1859–1943) Novelist

Annie Swan was born in **Edinburgh**, one of seven children of a farming family. Educated at the Ladies' College in Edinburgh, she began her literary career writing children's stories and contributing to *The Christian Leader*, a religious journal founded by the Revd Howie Wylie. Her first novel, *Ups and Downs* (1878), was unsuccessful. Her second, *Aldersyde* (1883), a romance set on the east coast of Scotland, made her name and established her as a novelist in the tradition of **Margaret Oliphant**. That same year she married James Burnett Smith, a schoolmaster, and moved to **Fife**.

In 1885 they moved to Edinburgh, where Burnett Smith began training in medicine at the **University**. During this time Annie Swan published a series of Scottish-based social realism novels, including *Carlowrie* (1884), a sequel to *Aldersyde*, *The Gates of Eden* (1886) and *Across Her Path* (1889), which was turned into a play in 1890. Encounters with Scottish industrial life are reflected in several subsequent works, including *Who Shall Serve?* (1891) and *A Bitter Debt* (1893).

In 1892, removed to London, Annie's literary career really began to flourish. Her fictional work now consisted chiefly of light romances; she also contributed to women's magazines. She was awarded a CBE in 1930, and died in Gorebridge, having written over 197 novels. Her autobiography was published in 1934, and an edition of her letters in 1945.

SWAN, Joseph (1796–1872) Engraver and Publisher

Swan served his apprenticeship in **Edinburgh** with the engraver John Beugo and set up his own business in **Glasgow** in 1818. One of the first to apply steam to the lithographic printing process, he made his name with illustrations of rare plants for the Royal Botanical Institution of Glasgow and went on to specialise in Scottish town- and landscapes. His first major publication was *Views of Glasgow & Its Environs* (1826), based on pictures by contemporary Scottish artists. This was followed by *Select Views of the River Clyde* (1828) and *Views of the Lakes of Scotland* (1830) as well as works on **Paisley**, **Dundee**, **Fife** and **Perthshire**, culminating, in 1845, with illustrations for Fullarton's *Gazetteer of Scotland* and James Brown's *History of the Highlands and of the Highland Clans*. Treasurer of the Glasgow Mechanics Institution (founded 1823), Swan was responsible for the engravings illustrating their magazine, including portraits of **James Watt** and **John Anderson** and their numerous inventions. He died in Glasgow and was buried in the city's **Necropolis**.

SWEETHEART (NEW) ABBEY,
Kirkcudbrightshire

Five miles south of **Dumfries**, Sweetheart was founded by **Devorguilla Balliol** in 1273. Its appeal is more romantic than architectural, the name deriving from the *dulce cor* ('sweet heart') of John Balliol (d.1268, father of King **John Balliol**) which Devorguilla, his wife, preserved in a casket of ivory banded with silver. She is said to have carried it with her until her own death in 1290 when she was buried at Sweetheart with the casket on her breast. A now headless effigy of her thus clutching the casket still survives. More prosaically her foundation was also known as New Abbey since its Cistercian monks came from the older foundation at **Dundrennan**. The cruciform abbey church of red sandstone dates from the late 13th and 14th centuries and, though roofless, is notably intact. It still dominates the adjacent village with a central tower reminiscent of contemporary fortalices. The conventual buildings have fared less well although the monastery's boundary wall is still an impressive feature. At the **Reformation** Abbot Gilbert Brown declined to surrender his charge and enjoyed support both from the Catholic Maxwells and the local people. Twice evicted and arrested, he twice returned and was not finally forced into exile until 1610. Affection for the place resurfaced in 1779 when a local fund was raised to ensure the Abbey's preservation. It is now in state care.

New Abbey village is remarkably unspoilt. The 18th century Corn Mill still functions, having been preserved by Charles W Stewart who donated it along with his

Sweetheart (or New) Abbey as drawn by R W Billings (RWB)

Shambellie House to the nation in 1978. The house (**David Bryce**, 1856), 'uniquely unfortunate in its building history' since 'almost everything that could go wrong with its construction, did so' (A Rowan), is now an outstation of the **Royal Museum of Scotland** and houses Stewart's collection of European fashionable dress in a Museum of Costume.

SWINTON, Alan (1863–1930) Electrical Engineer

Born in **Edinburgh**, Swinton was apprenticed to a Tyneside **engineering** firm but for 17 years acted as a consultant electrical engineer. He devised lead cabling for marine electric systems, and advised on municipal power generation. He also took the first X-ray photograph in Britain, one month after Röntgen, and is credited with cathode ray oscillograph research in 1908 which anticipated the invention of television.

SYME, David (1827–1908) Newspaper Proprietor

The youngest son of a schoolmaster, Syme was born in **North Berwick** and worked as a proofreader in **Glasgow** before emigrating (1851) to gold-rush California. Failing to get rich there, he moved on to Ballarat near Melbourne, Australia, and made money as a prospector and contractor. His brother Ebenezer (1826–59) had also emigrated to Victoria and together the two bought up the insolvent Melbourne *Age*. David took over the running of the paper when his brother died. He halved its sale price and began crusading on a few specific issues – land reform, protection against imports and

Professor James Syme, by George Richmond, c1857 (SNPG)

self-government. From 2000 copies circulation grew steadily, then sensationally. He slashed the price twice more in the 1860s; the 15,000 copies a day in 1868 had become 120,000 by 1899 and *The Age* was reckoned the most penetrative paper in the Empire. Australia's first press baron failed to live up to the flamboyance of some of his successors or of American counterparts like **James Gordon Bennett**. Something of a recluse with few friends and no charm, he sacrificed personal interests to his paper. It continued to champion working class interests and liberal reforms and wielded enormous political influence, its support of Australian federation being critical. Syme had other interests, notably in **philosophy** and farming. His family life was impeccable and his philanthropy notable.

SYME, James (1799–1870) Surgeon

Born in **Edinburgh** and educated at the High School, Syme was interested in scientific matters from an early age and in 1818 described his discovery that cloth soaked in a solvent made from caoutchouc distilled from coal tar was fully waterproof. Unfortunately for him he did not patent this discovery; five years later **Charles Macintosh** did.

In 1823 Syme became a Fellow of the **Royal College of Surgeons of Edinburgh**, and during 1824–5 founded his own medical school in Brown Square, where he taught anatomy and surgery. Always a controversial figure in the medical world, he was barred from practising at the Edinburgh **Royal Infirmary** and founded his own hospital at Minto House (site of the present **Royal Museum of Scotland**). This surgical hospital closed in 1833.

An outstanding diagnostician, Syme was also a superb teacher, with a very concise, almost terse, style of lectur-

ing. He became the first real teacher of clinical surgery and in 1848 published *Contributions to the Pathology and Practice of Surgery.*

His differences with the authorities resolved, he became Professor of Clinical Surgery at **Edinburgh University** in 1833 with his own wards at the Royal Infirmary. President of the Royal College of Surgeons of Edinburgh from 1849–50, he also proved himself an able medical politician, acquiring a new charter for the College which severed all its previous links with the town council, enabling the College to be known by its current name. In 1854 he wrote to Lord Palmerston suggesting the appointment of a medical board to regulate the teaching and practice of medicine in the UK and Ireland. This board should set the minimum educational requirements for doctors, visit the licensing bodies regularly, publish a national register of medically qualified people, and punish all those who wrongly called themselves 'Doctor'. His suggestions were incorporated into the 1858 Medical Act, which set up the General Medical Council on which Syme represented the Universities of Edinburgh and **Aberdeen**.

SYMINGTON, Ayrshire

Both the **Ayrshire** and the **Lanarkshire** Symingtons take their names from Symon Loccard who held the lands of both under Walter, 1st Steward [see **Stewarts**] and was the progenitor of the Lockharts of Lee and other families of the name. The parish church in the Ayrshire Symington dates from the 12th century and is 'easily the oldest in Ayrshire still in ecclesiastical use' (R Close). 18th century alterations disguised much of the original Norman building, but this was uncovered when the church was sympathetically restored as a World War I memorial in 1919.

SYMINGTON, William (1764–1831)
Engineer

William Symington was born in **Leadhills, Lanarkshire**, the son of a mine superintendent. He became interested in steam engines while working for the Wanlockhead Mining Co, and in 1779 he assisted his brother George, the company's engineer, in the construction of a Boulton & **Watt** pumping engine, which was erected by **William Murdock**. Symington went on to devise improvements to the steam engine which he patented in 1787. He built his first mine engine in 1791, and left his job to become a freelance engine builder and consultant, closely associated with the **Carron Company**.

Symington was eager to explore the wider applications of steam power. In 1786 he built a working model steam carriage, but was unable to raise sufficient capital to develop the invention commercially. He was then approached by the banker and entrepreneur Patrick Miller to provide a steam engine for a paddle boat. The experimental steamboat performed with limited success during trials on Dalswinton Loch in 1788, but a second vessel, fitted with a more powerful engine, steamed on the **Forth–Clyde Canal** the following year. Miller lost his enthusiasm for the project, but Symington was then commissioned to build marine engines for two barges belonging to the canal's Commissioners. In 1801 he patented an engine which provided direct drive to the paddles of a boat, and this engine, fitted on the *Charlotte Dundas II*, proved highly successful in steam trials in 1803. Once again, however, Symington's sponsors decided not to proceed with the development.

He fell on hard times after the last of the steamboat trials; demand for his pumping and lifting engines declined; some of his ventures in mine management were unsuccessful; and he became embroiled in costly litigation. In 1829, his health broken, he went to live in London with his daughter. He died there two years later.

Symington claimed to have been the first Briton 'to effectively apply the power of the steam engine to the propelling of vessels'. Although his reputation as a marine engineer was eclipsed by the subsequent commercial triumphs of Robert Fulton and **Henry Bell**, he is now recognised as a pioneer of steam navigation.

TACKS, TACKSMEN

A tack is a tenancy or lease, usually of land, the tacksman being the leaseholder or tenant. Within **clan** society tacksmen were usually closely related to the clan chief and played an important social and military role. 'Next in dignity to the laird', according to **Dr Johnson**, they acted as middlemen, holding large tracts at modest rent which were then sub-let to less exalted clansmen at a substantial profit. In return for this favourable arrangement, the tacksman's loyalty was secured and, more important, he was obliged to act as recruiting officer and commander of his tenantry whenever the clan mustered. In the 18th century when this military function lapsed, and in the 19th when the **clearances** ended his social and economic functions, the tacksman became an anachronism. Many espoused emigration and with varying success urged their tenants to accompany them, typically to Canada.

TAIN, Ross & Cromarty

Once described as 'so irregular and at the same time so tame and unattractive that any attempt to describe it would be a waste of words' (Fullarton's *Gazetteer*), Tain is a **royal burgh** of great antiquity and character on the south side of the **Dornoch Firth**. Its earliest extant charter is that of 1587 but there is confirmation of its burgh status dating back to 1457 while in 1439 a committee had traced the original charter back to **Malcolm III 'Canmore'**. The claim is less fanciful than most, given that the town's patron, St Duthus or Duthac, is known to have been born here about 1000 and to have died in Ireland in 1065, whence his remains were brought back to Tain. Part of the chapel in which they were first housed still stands near the sea. It became an important place of pilgrimage and sanctuary though the latter availed neither **Robert I**'s wife and daughter, who were here taken prisoners by the **Earl of Ross** and handed over to the English (1306), nor the laird of Freswick who died when the chapel was burnt by his freebooting pursuer in 1427.

Two other medieval churches associated with St Duthac continued the tradition of pilgrimage, **James IV** making annual visits for 20 years. One, built about 1400, survived the **Reformation** though losing most of its internal fixtures and has since been restored. The traceried windows and oak pulpit, supposedly presented by **James Stewart, Earl of Moray** and Regent for **James VI**, are notable. The other, nearby and dating from about 1300, is a vestigial ruin and may have been the

collegiate church of the priests entrusted with the care of the sanctuary.

Of secular buildings the most impressive is the solid-looking tower with five conical turrets which is the Old Tolbooth (1706–33). Attached to it, the baronial-style court house dates from 1848. The old Royal Academy of Tain (1812) is now a resource centre and residential home, but there is an interesting local museum in Castle Brae. With a seaward prospect of dunes Tain was never a port. It is said that at one time the Dornoch Firth could be crossed at low tide by anyone with a plank long enough to bridge the main channels. Near the new A9 bridge a long spit of sand still probes across the firth and was once the site of the important Meikle Ferry. Here in the autumn of 1709 a boat overloaded with fair-goers from **Sutherland** sank with the loss of 99; **Bonar Bridge** eliminated this crossing but at the price of a long detour. Between Tain and the Meikle Ferry the distillery is that of Glenmorangie, famed for its single malt **whisky**.

TAIT, Archibald Campbell (1811–82)
Archbishop of Canterbury

Born in **Edinburgh** and educated at the **Edinburgh Academy**, **Glasgow University** and Balliol College, Oxford, Archibald Tait was ordained as an Anglican priest in 1836. Six years later he succeeded Matthew Arnold as headmaster of Rugby School. During his seven years as Dean of Carlisle (1849–56) five of his daughters died of fever. Appointed Bishop of London in 1856, he was elevated to Archbishop of Canterbury in 1869, with his son-in-law **Randall Davidson** as chaplain.

TAIT, Peter Guthrie (1831–1901)
Mathematician and Physicist

Born at **Dalkeith** and educated at **Edinburgh** and Cambridge, Tait became Professor of Natural Philosophy at **Edinburgh University** in 1860, holding the post for neary 40 years. He specialised in thermoelectrics, materials science and some of the more everyday applications of physics – in 1896, for example, he published a classic paper on the trajectory of a **golf** ball. One of his sons, a champion amateur golfer, died in the Boer War and Tait himself died shortly after.

TAIT, Robert Lawson (1845–99)
Gynaecologist

Born in **Edinburgh**, Tait studied medicine at **Edinburgh University**, but practised most of his life in England, mainly in Birmingham from 1868. Specialising in abdominal surgery, he became a leading gynaecologist and a pioneer of aseptic surgery. He publicly supported Darwinian evolution, and enjoyed a career as a local politician in his adopted city. He died in Llandudno.

TANISTRY

An old Celtic law of succession whereby the heir to the throne was chosen from a group which included anyone whose great-grandfather had been a king, the system of tanistry also applied to lesser inheritances, eg to that of a chiefship or earldom. The monarch (or chief) would nominate as his heir, or 'tanist', he whom he deemed 'by age, strength and character most suited to the hour'. Although it ensured that there was always an adult heir (thus avoiding the fraught royal minorities which would later plague Scotland), the system had disadvantages: any 'tanist' would be sure to have disappointed rivals willing and able to step in should disaster befall the chosen one. 'The result was frequent war and murder; a high wastage rate of the royal kin' (R Mitchison). The system of tanistry lingered until **David I** asserted the hereditary principle by nominating his son Henry as his heir in 1144 (in the event Henry predeceased his father by a year, but Henry's son **Malcolm IV** did inherit in his place), and was still favoured by many in the disputes over the succession on the death in 1290 of **Margaret, Maid of Norway**.

TANNAHILL, Robert (1774–1810)
Songwriter

Born in Castle Street, **Paisley** (where a memorial plaque marks his birthplace), Robert Tannahill was the son of a handloom weaver. His songs, 'gentle, artless lyrics set to traditional music', became widely popular, the best known being 'Braes o' Gleniffer' and 'Jessie the Flower o' Dunblane'. His suicide in Paisley **Canal** at the age of 35 is variously attributed to his dislike of popularity, his dismay at having a collection of songs rejected by a publisher, or, less specifically, to 'a fit of melancholia'.

TANTALLON CASTLE, Nr North Berwick, East Lothian

One of the most evocative ruins in Britain, Tantallon owes its celebrity to its massive scale and spectacularly wild setting. Backing onto the Firth of Forth with only the sugarlump of the **Bass Rock** for company, its long parenthesis of weathered masonry marches with the racing clouds and commands the roughest sea. From flanking towers, each perched above precipitous cliffs, the massive 50ft (15m) walls converge on a central gatehouse-keep, completely screening the small promontory beyond and thus rendering this now grassy platform as impregnable from the land as do the cliffs from the sea. 'Ding doon Tantallon, mak a brig' to the Bass' (Knock down Tantallon, make a bridge to the Bass Rock) went the saying, apparently an unanswerable putdown to anyone proposing that which was clearly impossible. **Sir Walter Scott** (in *Marmion*) further immortalised the towers of Tantallon:

> Broad, massive, high and stretching far,
> And held impregnable in war,
> On a projecting rock they rose,
> And round three sides the ocean flows.
> The fourth did battled walls enclose
> And double mound and fosse . . .

Dating from the mid-14th century, the castle (which is little more than the great wall and its towers plus a moat and outworks) belongs to that class of buildings known as castles of enceinte (or 'enclosure'), rambling constructions very different from the bluff keeps of earlier times or the trim tower houses of a later age. William, 1st Earl of Douglas, may have built it and was certainly in residence by 1374. It passed to his illegitimate son George, 1st Earl of Angus, and thereafter this stronghold of reddish rock shared the turbulent

'Broad, massive, high and stretching far . . .'. Tantallon Castle on the Firth of Forth (RWB)

fortunes of the Red **Douglases**, passing in and out of their hands with tedious regularity. In 1491 and again in 1528 it was besieged and blockaded to little effect. During the 1530s, while in **James V**'s keeping, the castle was greatly strengthened with new parapets and a complete rebuild of the fore, or gatehouse, tower. But by 1651, when **General Monk** laid siege to a body of moss troopers (irregulars who were harassing Cromwell's communications), ordnance improvements had outstripped fortifying expedients. The ruin of today is much as Monk's successful storming left it.

TARBAT NESS, Ross & Cromarty
At the northern extremity of the **Nigg–Fearn** peninsula between the **Cromarty** and **Dornoch Firths**, Tarbat Ness is a promontory pointing north-east and guarding the mouth of the Dornoch Firth; its lighthouse (1830) is reputedly one of the tallest in Britain. Portmahomack, the main village, once a **fishing** port and now a resort, derives its name from St Colmac. It faces across the Firth while on the other side of the narrow peninsula the cliff-top ruins of Ballone Castle face out to sea. Ballone was reputedly occupied by the **Earls of Ross** but the present ruin, Z-plan with some intricate corbelling and ample gunloops, dates from the 16th century. Tarbat Old Church at Portmahomack has an unusual domed belfry; its churchyard has yielded many fragments of **Pictish** cross slabs, now removed to the **Museum of Scotland** in **Edinburgh**.

TARBERT, Argyll
At the north end of the **Kintyre** peninsula (and not to be confused with Tarbet, **Dunbartonshire** or Tarbert, **Harris**), Tarbert (**Argyll**) is situated on the narrow isthmus between West and East Lochs Tarbert. It was across this isthmus that **Magnus Barelegs**, son of King Olaf of Norway, had himself dragged in one of his ships in 1098, claiming thereby that Kintyre was an island, and thus a **Viking** possession. Overlooking the **fishing** and yachting harbour is Tarbert Castle, repaired by **Robert I** in 1325–9; the present tower dates from the 1490s. Once a major centre of ring-net fishing for **herring**, there is still a small fishing fleet and some small-scale industry, including sailmaking and boatbuilding. Tarbert is the setting for *Gillespie* by **John MacDougall Hay** (1881–1919) and for many poems in Gaelic and English by his son, **George Campbell Hay** (1915–84).

TARBERT, Isle of Harris
Tarbert on **Harris**, like its namesake in **Argyll**, is situated on the east loch which forms the isthmus (ie *tarbert*) and has a harbour, the terminus for car ferries from Uig on **Skye**. Though no more than a village, the few shops, the hotel, the terminus, and its central location between north and south Harris make it the 'island's' capital. The isthmus is less than half a mile wide. A road round the north shore of East Loch Tarbert leads to Kyle Scalpay and the ferry to **Scalpay** while a similar road along the north shore of West Loch Tarbert peters out at the sands of Hushinish opposite Scarp. En route it meanders onto the lawns and through the arched gateway of Amhuinnsuiddhe Castle, built by the Earl of Dunmore in 1868 but soon acquired by Sir Samuel Scott from whom **Lord Leverhulme** purchased the estate in

1919. The castle is now run by a sporting syndicate; the **fishing**, if one may judge by the large numbers of sea-trout and salmon to be seen attempting to run up from the bay immediately in front of the castle, is of the finest.

TARBOLTON, Ayrshire
A mining village seven miles north-east of **Ayr**, Tarbolton was destined for celebrity from the moment the 17-year-old **Robert Burns** moved with his father to Lochlea farm some three miles distant in 1777. For the next seven years the poet and his brother Gilbert whiled away their free time in the village, boosting its leisure facilities by founding the Bachelors' Club in 1781. The Club was a debating society admitting to membership any 'cheerful, honest-hearted lad; who, if he has a friend that is true and a mistress that is kind, and as much wealth as genteely make both ends meet – is just as happy as this world can make him'. It met in a two-storey thatched cottage in the Sandgate, the only surviving 17th century building in Tarbolton, acquired and restored by the **National Trust for Scotland** in 1938. It was in this same building that Burns joined the St James Lodge of the **Freemasons** in 1781, quickly becoming Deputy Master. The village would provide many of the scenes and characters for his early works, notably 'Death and Doctor Hornbrook', satirising John Wilson, the local schoolteacher turned apothecary. Other notable Tarbolton buildings are the parish church (1821, Robert Johnston) with 90ft (27m) spire and the aggressive red stone Lorimer Library (1879, Gabriel Andrew).

TARBOLTON AIR CRASH (1948)
A KLM Royal Dutch Airlines Constellation aircraft crashed near Tarbolton, Ayrshire on 21 October 1948 when attempting a night landing in poor visibility at **Prestwick** Airport. Although in contact with ground controllers, and despite being sighted from the ground, the pilot aborted the landing but fouled an electricity cable and crashed in flames. All but one of the 40 on board perished.

TARLAND, Nr Aboyne, Aberdeenshire
The Cromar village of Tarland owes much to the MacRobert Trust which converted Cromar House, acquired from the 1st **Marquis of Aberdeen** by Sir Alexander MacRobert in 1918, into an RAF rest centre. The Trust also runs a large model farming enterprise. South-east of the village, off the road to **Aboyne**, there is a recumbent stone circle at Tomnaverie and long **cairns** on Balnagowan Hill. To the north the Culsh souterrain, a 1st century BC underground and stone-lined store house, may be explored on all fours with a torch. Amongst numerous **Pictish** symbol stones in the area the cross slab in Migvie graveyard is notable.

TARTAN
Like the cut and origins of the **kilt**, the design and provenance of the patterns known as tartan are highly contentious. There is consensus neither as to the etymology of the word, the patterns to which it originally referred, the garments to which it applied, or the purpose, if any, which it served prior to the 19th century.

Tartan *continued*

Two versions, to some extent complementary, to some extent contradictory, follow: the first argues for a Celtic derivation, the second stresses military purpose.

1. It is curious that the Scotti of Ireland, who were not colonised by the **Romans**, should have adopted a costume more suited to a Mediterranean climate. Scottic ancestors had been depicted earlier than 500 BC wearing tight trousers that somewhat resembled modern trews. Their version of the Roman *tunica*, a form of shirt that ended a little above the knee, was marked with stripes which denoted the rank of the wearer. A High King wore seven stripes, one of purple, while an Ollamh, a head of the learned orders, was dignified as next in importance with six stripes. The garment was called a *léine* in **Gaelic** and was generally of **linen**.

As for these stripes, the word *tarsna* in Old Irish means a cross-piece, while Middle Irish preserves the variant *tarstan*. Dineen's dictionary of Modern Irish gives to *tarsna* the meanings 'transverse' or 'crosswise'. In Modern Scottish Gaelic *tarsuinn* means 'across'. Alan Bruford has argued convincingly for this Gaelic derivation of the term 'tartan' (*Gaelic and Scots in Harmony*, ed Derick S Thomson, 1990).

When the Scotti colonised **Argyll**, giving to Scotland its new name and latest language, they also evolved a variant form of the traditional dress. In due course the word 'tartan' is found here, describing a patterned fabric associated with the Gaels, although at the time nothing comparable is to be read in the far ampler Gaelic literature of Ireland. Yet it is not the costume with which tartan is associated today that appears in the Lord High Treasurer's accounts of 1538: 'Heland tartane to be hoiss.' On the other hand, the Frenchman Jean de Beaugué does describe what appears to be the tartan plaid, worn by Highlanders who took part in the siege of **Haddington** in 1549: '*Ils sont nuz fors de leurs chemises taintes et de certaines couvertures légères faites de laine, de plusieurs couleurs.*'

George Buchanan amplified this description in 1581, describing the costume of the Hebrideans in Latin: 'They delight in variegated garments, especially stripes, and their favourite colours are purple and blue. Their ancestors wore plaids of many colours, and numbers still retain this custom.' It is a pity that Buchanan did not render *Veste gaudent varia ac maxime virgata* in his native Gaelic, so that we might know whether he was describing tartan. When Lughaidh O'Clery wrote in Gaelic in 1594 about Highland dress, he used the term *breacbhrait ioldathacha* for their evidently tartan plaids: 'They were recognised among the Irish soldiers by the distinction of their arms and clothing, their habits and language, for their exterior dress was mottled cloaks of many colours.' Not only had their speech diverged from its parent root; another difference distinguishing the Scottish from the Irish Gaels was that the Irish *brat* (mantle) had become a *breacbhrait* (a tartan or chequered mantle).

When John Taylor 'the Water Poet' visited **Braemar** in 1618, he remarked likewise on the Highlanders he saw 'with a plaid about their shoulders, which is a mantle of divers colours'. He reserved the word tartan, like **James V**'s accountant in the previous century, for their stockings, 'which they call short hose, made of a warm stuffe of divers colours, which they call Tartant'. But since Taylor has used the term 'divers colours' also to describe the plaids, the term tartan can presumably be applied to these equally.

The various ways in which the *breacbhrait* might be worn are depicted in the engravings of members of Mackay's Regiment which were drawn from life and published in Stettin in 1631. The pattern appears to be identical in them all, but it cannot be inferred from this that they were wearing a **clan**, or even a regimental, tartan. The first suggestion that any such significance may be found in the particular sett of a tartan occurs at the very end of the 17th century, in the writings of a physician who was a native of **Skye**, writing in English. **Martin Martin** recorded the disappearance of the *léine* in the **Hebrides**: 'The first Habit wore by Persons of Distinction in the Islands was the *Leni-Croich*, from the Irish word *leni* which signifies a Shirt, and *Croch*, Saffron, because their Shirt was dyed with that herb ... but the Islanders have laid it aside about a hundred years ago.'

The tartan plaid had come into its own: 'The *Plad* wore only by the Men, is made of fine Wool, the Thread as fine as can be made of that kind; it consists of divers Colours, and there is a great deal of ingenuity requir'd in sorting the Colours, so as to be agreeable to the nicest Fancy. For this reason the Women are at great pains to give an exact Pattern of the *Plade* upon a piece of Wood, having the number of every thread of the stripe on it ... Every Isle differs from each other in their fancy of making *Plaids*, as to the Stripes in Breadth and Colours. This Humour is as different thro' the main Land of the *Highlands* in so far that they who have seen those Places is able, at the first view of a Man's *Plaid*, to guess the place of his Residence.' Presumably those sett sticks were handed down in families of weavers, preserving the continuity of a particular tartan, which consequently became associated with that area. If it was occupied by a certain clan, it is possible that the provenance of the sett was already being transferrred from the neighbourhood to its inhabitants before the proscription of Highland dress.

But it is significant that Gaelic literature is silent on this subject. In 1703 it was recorded in the **Grant** country that Ludovick Grant of that Ilk, 'and the tennantes and indwellers on these landis, are ordained to have readie tartans short coates and trewes and short hose of red and grein set duce, all broad springed'. But upwards of a dozen family portraits painted in the time of his son provide the evidence that not even his own family had adopted it as their clan tartan.

The patriot bard Alasdair Mac Mhaighstir Alasdair **(Alexander MacDonald)** extolled the *Breacan Uallach* (the Gallant Tartan) at the time of the '45 **Jacobite Rising**, but not any particular sett it displayed. His younger contemporary **Duncan Bàn Macintyre** was perhaps the first in modern times to use tartan as a Gaelic word, so that it should be pronounced 'tarstan', as in Middle Irish. But he was referring only to the kind of fabric.

> Bonaid ghorm a'bhil' shiod ort
> 'S peiteag riomhach de'n tartan.
> (You wear a silk-edged blue bonnet
> and a gorgeous waistcoat of tartan.)

The watershed is the proscription of Highland dress which lasted from 1746–82. During that period the Gallant Tartan could be worn legally only by members of the armed forces. **The Black Watch**, formed in 1739, had been the first Highland Regiment to be dressed in tartan, and the manner in which they wore the *breacbhrait* was depicted in six engravings, published in 1743. Three of its Independent Companies were commanded by **Campbells**, and it was on these grounds that the Black Watch or Government Tartan was claimed by the Campbells and remains their clan tartan to this day. It was likewise adopted by that other Hanoverian clan, the **Sutherlands**, whose tartan was remarked upon in 1819 as being identical to that of the **Argyll and Sutherland Highlanders**.

By this time **John Jamieson** had stated in his *Etymological Dictionary of the Scottish Language*, published in 1808: Tartan 'is not Gaelic or Irish. It seems to have been imported, with the manufacture itself, from France or Germany. Fr. *tiretaine*, signifies linsey-woolsey, or a kind of it worn by the peasants of France.'

Sir Walter Scott opined that enthusiasm for tartan was kindled in the Lowlands by a crisis of identity following the incorporating **union** with England in 1707. He certainly did much to stimulate it when he stage-managed the state visit of George IV to **Edinburgh** in 1822. His son-in-law **Lockhart** grumbled that Scott 'has ridiculously made us appear to be a nation of Highlanders, and the **bagpipe** and the tartan are the order of the day'. There appeared the supposedly ancient manuscript depicting clan tartans called *Vestiarium Scoticum*, about which **Sir Thomas Dick Lauder** wrote to Scott in 1829: 'A book of this kind containing authority so invaluable must become extremely popular. At present a woeful want of knowledge on the subject prevails. Some of the clans are at this moment ignorantly disputing for the right to the same tartan, which, in fact, belong to none of them, but are merely modern inventions for clothing Regimental Highlanders.'

Here is the supposition that there were genuine clan tartans from the period before the proscription, to be found by diligent search. James Logan undertook this task, observing in 1831: 'Fanciful varieties of tartan and badges were passed off as genuine, and the attempt to set the public right on these matters is likely to meet the objections of many'. His attitude was supported by the high authority of the **Encyclopaedia Britannica**, first published in Edinburgh in 1771, and still decreeing in its 1911 edition that 'many new and imaginary "setts" have been invented by manufacturers, with the result of introducing confusion in the heraldry of tartans, and of throwing doubt on the reality of the distinctive "setts" which at one time were more or less recognised as the badge of various clans.'

Even John Jamieson's bogus derivation of the word tartan was still being purveyed in this august compendium 100 years later. 'From *tiretaine*, "linsie-wolsie", Sp. *tiritaña*, a kind of woollen cloth, perhaps from its thinness and lightness, cf *tiritar*, to tremble with cold.' Or more probably with indignation, especially when the same false derivation is to be found in *The Scottish National Dictionary*, 1931–76.

As for the notion that there is a 'heraldry of tartans'

to be safeguarded from defilement, the truth is rather that the Lord Lyon has become involved in recent times in a field in which the Scottish heralds were never to be seen of old, Thus, when the Canadian press tycoon was created Lord Thomson of Fleet, he was granted a coat-of-arms supported by a shepherd 'wearing a kilt of the usual tartan proper to Thomson of that Ilk and his dependers'. Today it is more conventional for the Chief of a particular name to ordain a tartan, as when Sir Iain Moncrieffe of that Ilk did so, not as Albany Herald, but as Chief.

In such ways as this the undiminished demand for clan setts has been met. Donald C Stewart wrote in his definitive *The Setts of the Scottish Tartans* (1950): 'At one time peculiar to the Highlands, tartan has come to be regarded as native to Scotland in general.' It had become fashionable for Lowlanders to claim Highland ancestry: 'However accurate or fanciful these claims, the wearing of tartan and of the Highland dress has steadily increased throughout the country, and shows no sign of receding.'

It only remained for Lowlanders to claim that tartan and Highland dress really originated with themselves and were adopted later by the Gaels. R M D Grange advanced this theory in *A Short History of the Scottish Dress* in 1966. His book contains a very full collection of early references to tartan, from which he draws questionable conclusions. For instance he comments on the Treasurer's reference of 1538: 'From this we might assume that the use of tartan was now spreading to the Highlands.' He permitted himself to conclude: 'It seems that tartan – and the tartan plaid – originated in the Lowland districts and its popularity spread to the Highlands.'

As for the *Vestiarium*, this was essentially a collaboration between Donald C Stewart and J Charles Thompson, and the book was eventually published in 1980, edited by the principal living scholar in this field, James D Scarlett, under the title *Scotland's Forged Tartans*. Since then Scarlett has published *The Tartan Weaver's Guide* (1985), in which he has reproduced 142 tartans with their thread counts and the source of the first recorded sett. He acknowledges Donald C Stewart as his primary authority.

2. In its original form the word 'tartan' – from the French *tartaine* – denoted a type of material, no more or less; the word has subsequently replaced the Gaelic *Breacan* or multi-coloured cloth. This is now taken to mean a pattern repeated both by the warp and the weft of the cloth in the same sequence, colours and proportions; even this was not always the case in some earlier examples which are quite irregular. Last of all, significance has been ascribed to various patterns which have become a means of identification. It is this which gives Scottish tartan its particular mystique.

Quite how old is the use of 'tartan' in this way is still hotly debated, and there are still some who would claim that, right back into the mists of time, each of the clans and families of Scotland was immediately recognisable by the pattern or sett of the tartan that it wore. The idea is attractively romantic, but the evidence for it is extremely slight and it rests on one or two isolated and far from conclusive examples. While there is plenty of evidence to suggest that Highlanders wore tartan, there is very little which fits with the idea that a widespread system of recognition existed before the early 1800s.

Contemporary 18th century portraits, on the other hand, show very clearly that the sitters frequently wore garments of several different tartans, few if any of which have any recognisable connection with the clan tartans of today.

Martin Martin, whose *Description of the Western Isles of Scotland* was published in 1703, does claim that it was possible to tell the place of a man's residence by the pattern of his plaid, but even this much-quoted instance does no more than suggest that certain patterns were particularly popular in certain districts, and were held in stock and sold by the local weavers.

The same author also claimed that these patterns were recorded and preserved by the use of pieces of wood around which were wound threads in the right number and colour to enable reproduction of the various tartans. It is strange that not one example of this practice has survived – if indeed it was ever widespread, or existed at all.

The vast weight of evidence, if not totally conclusive, suggests however that prior to the very end of the 18th century, as far as the population in general was concerned, there was no idea of using a uniform tartan as a means of identification and that choice depended, as when buying, say, a tweed jacket today, on what was available, what took the purchaser's fancy and what his sporran could afford.

But the importance of tartan and Highland dress is shown by the fact that it was banned in the Highlands after the '45 Jacobite Rising as part of the government campaign to reduce this troublesome part of the world to obedience, and it was not until 1782 that, largely due to the efforts of the Highland Society of London, the proscription was lifted.

Both before and during this period, tartan had been used as part of military uniform. The early Highland Regiments of the late 17th century army wore ordinary line uniform, and it would seem to be **The Royal Company of Archers**, founded in 1676 and now The Queen's Body Guard for Scotland, who first appear in tartan; the earliest known portrait showing this is dated around 1700.

Whether the various Independent Highland Companies wore a uniform tartan is doubtful – they probably wore their own clothes – but it appears that the six Independent Companies of 1725 did so, before they were regimented as what is now the Black Watch in 1739. Their tartan, the familiar blue, black and green sett, has been referred to as '42nd', 'Black Watch', 'Government' and 'Universal'. It is worn as a clan tartan – usually in somewhat lighter tones – by the Campbells, three of the original six Black Watch companies having been Campbell ones, and as an alternative clan tartan by the Grants and the Munros, both of which clans played a major part in the original regiment. It is also worn by the Sutherlands, due to their connection with the various 18th century regiments of Sutherland Fencibles and with the 93rd Sutherland Highlanders.

The 18th century saw the raising of over 100 Highland Regiments, most of them short-lived. A consider-able number wore this tartan, while others sought to differentiate it with coloured lines. The resulting patterns were taken up by the clans most closely connected with the regiment concerned and thus were born such 'clan' tartans as Gordon, Mackenzie, (Hunting) Robertson and Campbell of **Breadalbane** (earlier pattern).

It seems certain that the general idea of using tartan as a means of identification owes its origin to the use of uniform tartans by the army.

The whole subject needs to be put in context with the amazing surge of Romance associated with the Highlander. Sparked by the writings of **James 'Ossian' Macpherson**, nurtured by the magnificent military record of the Highland Regiments, fanned by the novels of **Sir Walter Scott**, the trend came to a head with the 1822 Royal Visit to Edinburgh by George IV which resulted in so many of today's traditions. Thereafter a stream of books on the subject, and **Queen Victoria**'s endless enthusiasm, produced the highly coloured view of clans and tartans with which we are so familiar today.

In 1816 the Highland Society of London commenced its tartan collection, having written to the clan chiefs the previous year to invite them to deposit a signed and sealed sample of their clan tartan with the Society. A number did so, although there were others who were unable to comply, and the Society corresponded with those who had no idea as to what their tartan might be.

But by now the idea of 'clan' tartan was well entrenched; its growth may be traced in the correspondence and pattern books of the early tartan manufacturers, notably Wilsons of **Bannockburn**. The firm was producing new patterns each season for its travelling salesmen to sell. Many of these new patterns were at first distinguished by a number before acquiring a name – which could either be a clan name, a geographical name or the name of a famous person in fact or fiction. There is no evidence whatsoever to show that these geographical names were any more than means of identification or that they had anything to do with the local patterns which Martin Martin claimed to have seen. And chiefs who asked for 'their' tartan were duly supplied.

The waters were further muddied by the egregious **Sobieski Stewart** brothers who proclaimed themselves to be the grandsons of **Prince Charles Edward**. Among their many claims was the possession of a remarkable 16th century volume describing clan tartans. For various reasons the original volume was never available for expert scrutiny, and the descriptions it contained are really too vague for any accurate rendition – a fact which did not stop them producing a considerable number of today's setts.

The manufacturers of course were delighted by all this and co-operated enthusiastically with demands for more and yet more clan patterns. In particular the convention by which a myriad different names are held to 'belong' to this or that clan is largely their doing, so that today there is hardly a name in the British Isles, let alone Scotland, that will not be found to confer the 'right' to wear this or that sett. But even this is not enough, and tartans are now available for names that never had any pretension to being clans in their own right, as well as for organisations of every sort – even **football** teams – and the invention of new tartans has even been extended to commemorate certain events.

For there is no body to regulate tartans. Authority for stating what is or is not the tartan of his clan rests with the Chief. Over the rest there is no control. The Lord Lyon's very real powers do not extend to tartans as they do to matters armorial; he may record clan tartans officially when requested, but no more than this. Other bodies, such as the Scottish Tartans Society, may advise and record, but they have no official standing whatever. The result is a great deal of myth, misunderstanding and commercial exploitation.

People talk glibly about their 'right', or being 'entitled' to wear this or that tartan – as often as not through some remote female ancestor. In fact no such right or entitlement exists; anyone can buy and wear any tartan that takes their fancy. Strictly speaking only the holders of the name concerned or one of its recognised septs should wear its tartan. Wives should wear their husband's tartan and more distant relationships do not apply. But these conditions apply more in the breach than in the observance, and no great harm is done thereby. It is the invention of bogus 'reasons' rather than the actual wearing of any particular tartan that is the chief cause of offence.

The manufacturers have caused considerable confusion. Clans with a bright tartan are given a duller 'Hunting' sett; those with a dull sett are given a brighter 'Dress' tartan. This last description is also given to a whole range of relatively recent patterns based on a white ground. These showy, not to say garish, versions, much loved by professional dancers and by tourists, apparently owe their origin to the general design of women's plaid or *arisaid* which, being largely undyed, was cheaper to produce. Apart from that they have no historical provenance. Chiefs and their immediate families were on occasion persuaded that they should have a pattern exclusively of their own, often differentiated by the addition of a white stripe, but this is surely the negation of what a clan tartan stands for.

Further confusion has been given by the use of such terms as 'Modern', 'Ancient', 'Reproduction' and 'Muted', all of which refer to the colours in which the tartan is produced rather than to the pattern of the tartan itself. Indeed the use of 'Ancient' dyes is more recent than that of those described as 'Modern'.

There is no ancient significance in the actual colours employed – 'yellow for the prairies, black for coal, blue for the sea' and so on – as is sometimes claimed. Nor does tartan have any connection with **heraldry**.

The number of tartans continues to proliferate. The Scottish Tartans Society makes valiant efforts to record all known examples. It has attracted a number of collections and artefacts to its keeping and runs an excellent small museum formerly in **Comrie** but recently moved to **Stirling**. Other early collections of note include the Highland Society of London's collection, now in the hands of the Royal Museums of Scotland, and the Cockburn Collection in the **Mitchell Library**, **Glasgow**, both dating from the early 1800s; the **Inverness** Museum houses the noteworthy MacBean Collection. The correspondence and early pattern books of Wilsons of Ban-

nockburn are to be found in profusion both in Stirling and in the **National Library of Scotland**. The published works of Messrs D C Stewart, John Telfer Dunbar and James Scarlett provide most information on the subject of tartans themselves, although the definitive book on the evolution of clan tartan has yet to be written.

TAY, Loch, Perthshire

The sixth largest loch in Scotland, about 14 miles long and averaging a mile in width, Loch Tay lies at the heart of **Breadalbane** with **Ben Lawers** dominating its north shore. At its west end at **Killin** it is entered by the rivers Dochart and Lochay; from **Kenmore** at its east end flows the river **Tay** proper. Here a small island is said to have been the site of a priory or nunnery founded (1122) by **Alexander I** whose wife Sybilla was buried here. Salmon apart, no monsters are recorded of Loch Tay, but a curious phenomenon was twice observed in the late 18th century near the priory island. In calm conditions the water along the shoreline suddenly began to ebb and flow in quick succession, eventually by as much as 100ft (30m), as a 5ft (1.5m) wave swept up the loch. The river Tay at Kenmore was observed to change direction and, as the weed began to trail upstream, to flow into the loch until no water at all was left under Kenmore Bridge. This happened in 1784 and again in 1794, the perturbation lasting several days.

TAY, River, Perthshire

From its remotest source to the open sea the Tay is undoubtedly Scotland's longest river. The claim is, however, disputed. Some maintain that, whatever its source, it is only actually called the Tay after it emerges from **Loch Tay**; others that although the Firth of Tay is undoubtedly its estuary, this extra 25 miles of tidal water should be excluded. In both cases the reduction leaves the **Spey** as the longest river. Yet others argue that the Tummel (including tributaries), which joins the Tay above **Dunkeld** and has the larger volume and remoter source, should be considered the main river and so Scotland's longest.

Howsoever, the received wisdom is that the source of the Tay is that of the dashing Cononish Water on Ben Lui near **Tyndrum**. Thence as the Fillan and then the Dochart it flows steadily north east to reach Loch Tay below the Falls of Dochart at **Killin**. It emerges at **Kenmore** as the Tay proper and continues north-east past **Aberfeldy** until it receives the Tummel. Turning south and now a noble steep-banked flood, it swishes past **Dunkeld Cathedral** and rolls east again before making its sharpest bend round Kinclaven Castle near **Meikleour**. Joined by the Isla it now meanders through the stately pastures of **Strathmore**, its waters ruffled only by the Campsie Linn near **Stanley**. Just north of **Perth** it receives the Almond and then glides past the city and way below the high motorway bridge from Moncrieffe to Kinnoul, before merging with the Firth and its junction with the Earn. The last bridges (good reason to include the Firth in its length) are of course the Tay road and **rail bridges** at **Dundee**.

TAY RAILWAY BRIDGE

The **Tay** Railway Bridge carries the line from London (King's Cross) and **Edinburgh** to **Dundee** and

Aberdeen across the Tay estuary from Wormit in **Fife** into the city of Dundee itself. It is 3429yds (3135m) long and carries two tracks. Sanctioned in 1881, it opened on 11 July 1887 operated by the North British Railway, only a few yards west of the site of the first **rail** bridge across the Tay.

For this is the second rail structure over the estuary; the first was approved by Parliament in 1870, and opened in 1878 to a design by Sir Thomas Bouch. Single-track, it was 55yds short of two miles long and a maximum of 88ft (27m) high to allow maritime access to **Perth** Harbour, and included 13 sections of high girders each over 225ft (68m) in length. Unfortunately, not long after Bouch had been knighted for his work, part of the structure collapsed under a passing train during a storm on the night of 28 December 1879; 75 passengers and crew were killed. At the subsequent inquiry, whose findings were published in a lengthy report in July 1880, it emerged that Bouch had not properly allowed for wind-pressure on the viaduct, and that the contractor, left unsupervised, had used imperfect metal castings. Bouch was roundly blamed for the disaster and dismissed from the **Forth Bridge** project, where he was about to build a huge suspension bridge with parallel rail tracks suspended by chains high above the Forth. He died shortly afterwards, his health affected by the disaster. The stumps of his bridge can still be seen in the waters of the Tay.

TAYLOR, Dr John (1805–42) Chartist Leader

Born into considerable affluence at Newark Castle, **Ayr**, Taylor studied medicine but soon devoted himself to radical issues and the cause of political liberty. Part of his fortune was spent fitting out a ship to help the Greek independence movement. In 1832 and '34 he stood as a Radical candidate for Ayr Burghs and was briefly imprisoned for challenging the victor to a duel. In 1836 he represented **Glasgow** at the London Anti-Corn Law Association and in the same year joined the *Liberator*, a Trades Unionist and Radical publication, as assistant

editor. Restyled the *New Liberator* with Taylor as editor, the paper played an influential role in early **Chartism**, but closed down in 1839. With the encouragement of Feargus O'Connor, Taylor, 'the most abused man in Scotland', continued to advocate even revolution and republicanism in order to introduce reform. This made him the most militant radical in Scotland, yet he also formed D'hurna societies, a form of non-violent protest evidently derived from India (*dharna* being a kind of hunger strike), whose members pledged themselves to boycott heavily taxed items (liquor, tea, etc) with the idea of depriving the government of revenue. In 1839 he represented **Paisley** at the great Chartist Convention in London, but soon proved too radical for his fellow Scots. An inscription which accompanies the statue later erected to his memory in Wallacetown Cemetery, Ayr, records that 'Politically he was the eloquent and unflinching advocate of THE PEOPLE'S CAUSE, freely sacrificing health, means, social status, and even personal liberty, to the advancement of measures then considered extreme, but now acknowledged to be essential to the well-being of the state.'

TAYMOUTH CASTLE, Nr Kenmore, Perthshire

The prodigious growth of Taymouth Castle in the 18th and 19th centuries faithfully mirrored the fortunes of its **Campbell** inmates, the lairds of Glen Orchy, Earls and then Marquises of **Breadalbane**. Initially from **Kilchurn** on Loch Awe, the Campbells moved east to **Loch Tay** as their estates sprawled ever nearer to a continuous belt from the Atlantic to the North Sea. Taymouth, then known as Balloch Castle, was occupied by 'Slippery John', 1st Earl of Breadalbane, who in 1733 commissioned **William Adam** to add two classical wings to Balloch's central keep. The 3rd Earl demolished the keep completely, replacing it with a four-storey neo-Gothic block designed by James and Archibald Elliot and closely resembling **Inveraray Castle** with its round corner towers and massive central tower (1810). Its blueish greystone, more attractive than Inveraray's greenish sandstone, was quarried locally near Bolfracks House (now notable for its delightful if precipitous gardens). In the 1820s the Adam wings were altered and extended beyond either recognition or reason to create more architectural acres. The interior, with public rooms by Francis Bernasconi and **James Gillespie Graham**, included fantastic plasterwork, wood carving and painted ceilings. Pavilions, parterres and follies were dotted about the grounds, the setting being further enhanced by lavish planting and the Breadalbanes' reintroduction of the **capercaillie**. In 1842 **Queen Victoria** graced Taymouth with a visit. Thereafter the castle, like the Breadalbanes, has fallen on hard times. Sold in 1922, it has been variously resurrected as a hotel, a hospital, a Civil Defence establishment and a school.

TAYNUILT, Argyll

Site of the earliest monument to Nelson and Trafalgar (erected by **Bonawe** quarry workers), Taynuilt lies peacefully at the north-west foot of **Cruachan**. Originally composed of a number of **crofting** hamlets along the main **Oban** road, it first took its name from the church at Muckairn. As road traffic increased so too did the importance of coaching inns, and the name later changed to *Tigh an Uilt*, or House by the Burn, the site of the present hotel. The **railway** arrived in 1880 and the village has since spread steadily in five main directions, to Glen Nant, Glen Lonan, up the river Awe and up and down **Loch Etive**.

TEALING, Nr Dundee, Angus

Here, five miles north of **Dundee** (and also at Carlungie and Ardestie, eight miles east of Dundee), has been excavated a souterrain (or, sometimes, 'earth house') dating from the 1st–2nd centuries AD. Souterrains are trenches faced with stone, here about six feet square and 50–100 feet long but seldom straight. They were originally roofed with stone or wood, and some still are (though none of these). The dates argue against any connection with the **Picts**; they were the work of their Iron Age predecessors. And they were not 'houses' or 'passages'. Rather, it seems, they were storage chambers, especially of grain. Excavations elsewhere suggest that they may have been entered from within a timber house which has long since disappeared. In other words they were entered as cellars. It is, however, perfectly credible that Picts and others may subsequently have used them as places of refuge and shelter. Hence they are sometimes called 'weems' from the Gaelic *uaimh*, a cave.

At Tealing there is also a **doocot** of some distinction in that it is dated (1595), carries the arms and initials of its builder (Sir David Maxwell) and is of unusual design, with a pitched roof and crowstep gables.

TELFORD, Thomas (1757–1834) Civil Engineer

The son of a **Dumfriesshire** shepherd and a product of the Scottish parish school system, Thomas Telford plied his trade as a stonemason in the Borders, in **Edinburgh** (where he worked on the construction of the **New Town** and also contributed poetry to the *Edinburgh Magazine*) and in London. He acquired an influential patron in the MP William Pulteney, and superintended a number of large building projects in the south of England before his appointment, in 1788, to the post of Surveyor of Public Works for Salop. In 1793, at the age of 36, he was engaged as the agent, engineer and architect for the construction of the Ellesmere **Canal**, winning acclaim for his design and for the execution of the spectacular aqueducts at Chirk and Pont Cysylltau.

In 1796 he was appointed engineer to the British Fisheries Society, and when in 1801 the government wanted a communications survey of the Highlands, they appointed Telford. His surveys were masterly and, as in the case of **General Wade** in the 18th century, he was the automatic choice to implement his own proposals. In the 20 years after 1804 he constructed over 900 miles of **parliamentary roads** and 120 bridges in the Highlands in addition to harbours and jetties for ferry and fishery use, plus the Caledonian Canal.

He also built roads, bridges, canals and harbours in Wales, England and even in Sweden. As an example of his prodigious work rate, in 1818 he was engaged in the construction of the Menai Bridge, Holyhead Harbour, the London to Holyhead road (A5), the **Glasgow** to Carlisle road, the Caledonian Canal, the Gloucester Canal, Harbours at **Dundee** and Lynn, and did a survey of a road from Glasgow to **Portpatrick**, at which time he was also the first President of the Institute of Civil Engineers.

One of the most versatile and innovative civil engineers of all time, he invariably combined functional durability with aesthetic acceptance in structures such as the Menai Bridge, Froncysillte Aqueduct, the **Dunkeld** and **Craigellachie** Bridges and the Caledonian Canal. He continued to act as consultant and engineer for road, bridge and canal projects until the end of his life, and was associated with improvements to the river **Clyde**, the construction of St Katherine's Dock in London, the **Dean Bridge** in Edinburgh, the Gotha Canal in Sweden and many other works. Like Wade, his military predecessor in Scotland, he is buried in Westminster Abbey.

TEMPERANCE MOVEMENT

At the beginning of the 19th century, drinking customs permeated Scottish society at every level. Eminent judges and clergymen were esteemed for their ability to hold their liquor, and a journeyman's first wages, by long tradition, were expended on **whisky** and ale for his workmates. In 1822 the duty on spirits was lowered from 7 shillings to 2 shillings and sixpence per gallon, and in Scotland, where 'freedom and whisky' were believed to 'gang thegither', this led to a dramatic increase in spirit consumption, from 2,079,000 gallons in 1822 to 5,777,000 gallons in 1829.

The first Scottish temperance societies were in favour of moderation in the use of alcohol, blaming cheap spirits for the appalling condition of the slum dwellers and the destitute. As the societies grew influential, they became less tolerant, and it was not long before spirits, wine and beer were being impartially denounced as 'demon drink'. What had begun as a plea for temperance became a total abstinence movement embracing tens of thousands of men, women and children.

James Dunlop (1789–1868), a **Greenock** lawyer and philanthropist, was recognised in his own lifetime as 'the father of temperance in Great Britain'. In October 1829 he established temperance societies in **Maryhill** and Greenock. Dunlop enlisted the support of **William Collins**, founder of the publishing house, and both men travelled extensively, lecturing on the evils of strong drink, with the result that temperance societies were soon flourishing in other parts of the country. In 1839 *The Temperance Society Record*, written, printed and published by William Collins, made its appearance, and that same year the Collins press produced an estimated half a million temperance tracts.

In August 1842 Father Theobald Mathew, 'the Irish apostle of temperance', visited **Glasgow**. Special trains brought supporters from **Edinburgh**, **Ayrshire**, **Lanarkshire**, **Dunbartonshire** and **Stirling**; a procession of 50,000 people marched to **Glasgow Green** to hear him preach, and in the course of three days an estimated total of 40,000 people signed the pledge to abstain from alcohol. The first juvenile temperance association was founded in **Paisley** in 1830. The Band of Hope, the most successful temperance youth movement, originated in Leeds in 1847, and the first Scottish branches were established a few years later.

The most militant teetotallers were strongly influenced by the American state of Maine, which had forbidden the general sale of intoxicants in 1846. The Forbes Mackenzie Act of 1853, called after its sponsor, the MP for **Peeblesshire**, closed Scotland's pubs on Sundays but allowed hoteliers to supply drink to residents and bona fide travellers; the latter multiplied every Sunday as people from neighbouring towns such as Glasgow and Paisley hastened in opposite directions. As a result of Sunday closing, shebeens – illicit drinking dens – flourished.

The International Order of Good Templars, prohibitionist in its aims, was introduced to Scotland by an exiled Scot who had settled in the United States. The first Scottish lodge was established in Glasgow in August 1869, and by 1876 there were no fewer than 1131 lodges, with a total membership of 83,717. Temperance friendly societies such as the Independent Order of Rechabites and the Order of the Sons of Temperance owed much to the sickness benefit and life insurance schemes which they operated.

In the late 19th century, while radical teetotallers were clamouring for prohibition, other more moderate campaigners were pressing for 'reformed' pubs. They were influenced by the example of the Swedish town of Gothenburg, where the spirit trade was in the hands of a trust company or *bolag*, and the town treasury received the bulk of the profits. The Public House Trust (Glasgow District) Limited, modelled on Earl Grey's Public House Trust Company in Northumberland, came into being in 1901 with a capital of £25,000 in £1 shares. In the same year trusts of a similar nature were launched elsewhere in Scotland. The directors were well-known citizens or country gentlemen, and the return to shareholders was limited to interest on capital.

By the 1890s the temperance movement claimed to have a large majority in Glasgow Corporation; 50 of the 75 members were believed to be favourably disposed to temperance reform; 35 of the 50 were said to be total abstainers, and of the 14 magistrates 11 were teetotallers. In 1899 Samuel Chisholm, an implacable opponent of the licensed trade, became Glasgow's Lord Provost, and his three-year tenure of office was something of a 'McCarthy era' in terms of temperance militancy and intolerance.

At the turn of the century, political support for temperance reform was strong, and the prohibition of the 'liquor traffic' was part of the original programme of the Scottish Labour Party, founded in 1888. The Scottish Prohibition Party, formed in **Dundee** in 1901, was totally uncompromising in its approach to the 'drink question'. The Party's leading personality, Edwin Scrymgeour, was elected to Dundee Town Council in 1905. In 1922 he unseated Winston Churchill from his Dundee constituency and became Britain's first and only Prohibitionist MP.

The object of the Temperance (Scotland) Act of 1913 was to give the electorate of a district the right to decide by majority vote such issues as the limitation of licence and local prohibition. World War I intervened, and it was not until 1920 that the first 'local veto' polls were held. Poll results fell far short of the expectations of ardent temperance campaigners, who had hoped that in time 'local veto' would lead to nationwide prohibition.

At its peak of influence, the Scottish temperance movement was a force to be reckoned with, censuring pervasive and deleterious drinking habits, pressurising public opinion, and paving the way for the major licensing laws of the 19th and early 20th centuries. Unhappily the movement's rejection of the pub as a social institution gave rise to repressive municipal edicts which gradually reduced the majority of Scottish pubs to bleak 'drinking shops' where women were unwelcome and music and games forbidden.

In 1890 Glasgow's Town Council passed a resolution that no more licensed premises would be allowed on Corporation property. The resolution remained in force until the 1960s, with the result that **Easterhouse**, Drumchapel and other huge post-war Corporation housing estates were initially 'dry' and have few licensed premises even today. The 1976 Licensing (Scotland) Act liberalised Scottish licensing laws and swept away most of the consequences of a century of temperance militancy. The Act exorcised 'demon drink', abolishing veto polls and making provision for Sunday opening, all-day licences and family certificates. Sunday closing still applies to licensed grocers, but there is now little prospect of a return to the intolerant attitudes which characterised the heyday of the Scottish temperance movement.

TEMPLE, Midlothian

A deep-set hamlet nestling in the wooded valley of the River South Esk near Gorebridge, Temple takes its holy name from the military order of the Knights Templar, whose Scottish headquarters was established here in 1153; **David I** gave them 'the manor and chapel of Balantravach'. This presence lasted until their suppression in 1312 by Pope Clement V, when the preceptory was given to the Knights Hospitallers or Knights of St John at **Torpichen** who assumed their role in the kingdom. The ruined parish kirk is of later date, although it possibly existed as early as the mid-14th century; the old 'Templar's Cross' adorned the gable but the inscription – 'VAESACMHIM' – below the belfry baffles antiquarians.

TEMPLETON, John (1802–86) Singer

Templeton made his first major success standing in for the part of Don Ottavio in Mozart's *Don Giovanni*. He became leading tenor to the Spanish mezzo-soprano Marie Felecita Malibran, made a powerful impression on Bellini and Auber and was in such demand that he sang different roles at Covent Garden and Drury Lane on the same day. Latterly he toured in North America, specialising in Scottish songs.

TENNANT, Sir Charles (1823–1906)
Chemical Manufacturer

Tennant was born in **Glasgow**, the grandson of his namesake who had founded a business empire based upon the manufacture of chemicals at **St Rollox** in Glasgow. Educated at **Ayr** Academy and trained commercially in Liverpool, he joined the family company in 1850 as a partner. Vigorous expansion into the fields of mining, metallurgy and explosives followed, together with the development of important mines in the south of Spain. In 1872 he led the formation of the Steel Company of Scotland and in 1876 that of Nobel's Explosives Limited. Politically he was a prominent Liberal, serving as MP for Glasgow (1877–80) and **Peebles** and **Selkirk** (1880–6), although in 1903 he switched his allegiance to the Conservatives. Created a baronet in 1885, he relished the life of a country gentleman in **Peeblesshire**, and left an estate worth over £3 million.

TENNANT, William (1784–1848) Poet and Scholar

Born in **Anstruther**, **Fife**, the son of a merchant farmer, Tennant was crippled in early childhood and spent his formative years studying at home, finishing his education at **St Andrews University** (1799–1801). He went on to act as a clerk for his brother, a corn merchant, devoting his leisure time to studying classics, literature, and Hebrew, Arabic and Persian. In 1813 he was appointed parish schoolmaster of **Lasswade**, near **Edinburgh**, and later moved on to become classics master at **Dollar** Academy, before finally being appointed Professor of Oriental Languages at St Andrews University in 1834.

In 1812 he published his first and best-known work, the mock-heroic poem *Anster Fair*. Written in *ottava rima*, or octave stanzaic form, it proved very popular and is said to have inspired **Lord Byron** in the composition of *Don Juan*. Tennant went on to write two historical verse tragedies, *Cardinal Beaton* (1823) and *John Baliol* (1825), and the long poems *The Thane of Fife* and *Papistry Storm'd* (1827). In 1840 he published his *Synopsis of Chaldaic and Syriac Grammar* which remained in use as a standard textbook for many years. He died in Anstruther on 14 October 1848.

TENTSMUIR, Fife

Between **Leuchars** and Tayport [see **Newport-on-Tay**] in the north-east corner of **Fife**, the large expanse of Tentsmuir is the result of a slowly receding tideline. Its scrub and dunes were once the resort of pirates and smugglers but now, partly **Forestry Commission** and partly nature reserves (Tentsmuir Point and Morton Lochs), are more visited for their flora and fauna (particularly wintering **waders**). In 1957 a Stone Age site near Morton Farm yielded evidence of human occupation dating back to 4000 BC. The middens of refuse and shells also included stone implements and suggested about 700 years of seasonal occupation.

TERPERSIE CASTLE, Nr Alford, Aberdeenshire

In the parish of Tullynessle, little Terpersie is possibly the earliest Z-plan castle, consisting of a main block with two round towers at opposing angles. It was built in 1561 for William Gordon, a son of Gordon of Lesmoir, who fought at **Corrichie**. Burnt by Colonel Baillie between the **Montrose** battles of **Auldearn** and **Alford** (1645), it was restored and still in **Gordon** possession at the time of the 1745 **Jacobite Rising** when George Gordon went into hiding in the attic. There he was eventually discovered by Hanoverian troops; but he was so well disguised that release seemed possible. Unfortunately he was brought before his children, whose cries of 'Daddy' soon rendered them both fatherless and homeless; he was executed at Carlisle and the property forfeited. The castle has recently been restored.

TEST ACT, The (1681)

Designed to establish royal supremacy in Church and state and, following **Drumclog** and **Bothwell Brig**, to outlaw **Covenanters**, **Conventiclers** and **Cameronians**, the Test Act obliged all lay and ecclesiastical office holders to swear to uphold the 1560 Confession of Faith [see **Reformation**]. It 'could hardly be taken without qualification by any conscientious man' (G Donaldson), since the Confession, little remembered and long redundant, appeared to conflict with the insistence on royal supremacy. **Archibald 9th Earl of Argyll** identified this inconsistency and was forced to flee the country. As enforced by **James VII**, then Duke of York, and **John Graham of Claverhouse**, the Act merely exacerbated dissent, alienated more ministers, and in the south-west ushered in the **Killing Time**.

THEATRE IN SCOTLAND

Until the 17th century the theatrical tradition of Scotland followed the same pattern as that of England, including mystery plays, pageants and morality plays – the most significant example surviving being *Ane Plesant Satyre of the Thrie Estaites* (**Sir David Lindsay**), first performed in 1522. However the influence of the Kirk, and the removal of the court and its many retainers to England in 1603, combined to halt any theatrical development until the 1750s. Even then, due to the Licensing Act (1737), dramatic activity was severely restricted and few examples of indigenous drama, such as *The Douglas* (**John Home**, 1756), survive.

During the 19th century more theatres opened but were mainly occupied by stock companies or English touring companies producing English and Continental drama. The end of the 19th century saw the largest number of theatres and **music halls** ever to exist in Scotland, but national material was largely restricted to pantomimes and adaptations of the novels of **Sir Walter Scott**. Only during the 20th century have a substantial number of playwrights and theatre companies come to the fore and established a Scottish theatrical tradition.

This tradition has developed in two directions – one towards a distinctly Scottish drama in the sense of work by native playwrights (as in the work of The Scottish National Players, Unity Players, Scottish Theatre Company), and the other towards developing companies based in Scotland but with an undesignated repertoire. These aims are not mutually exclusive and most companies have at some time in their history encompassed both. The debate over a 'national' company continues – whether there should be such a company, what form it should take, etc. Meanwhile the 20th century has seen rapid developments with the founding of seven extant repertory companies (**Perth** 1935, **Dundee** 1939, Byre, **St Andrews** 1939, **Glasgow** Citizens' 1943, **Pitlochry** Festival Theatre 1951, **Edinburgh** Traverse 1963, Edinburgh Royal Lyceum 1965), numerous touring companies, a drama school (established in 1950 alongside the Royal Academy of Music in Glasgow), a Youth Theatre and a strong amateur dramatic movement (Scottish Community Drama Movement, 1926).

Theatre Companies

GLASGOW REPERTORY Founded in 1909 by Alfred Wareing, an associate of Miss Horniman who started the Abbey Theatre in Dublin, Glasgow Repertory was one of the first companies in Britain to dedicate itself to 'art' theatre, and was an important element in the development of the repertory movement. It opened with *You Never Can Tell* (Shaw) in the Royalty Theatre in **Sauchiehall Street** (seating 1400) and continued a precarious existence until 1914, the only year in which it made a profit. The programme over the five years included more than 30 new plays, among which was the first British production of Chekhov's *The Seagull* in November 1909.

SCOTTISH NATIONAL PLAYERS Initiated before the First World War by the St Andrew Society of Glasgow, its first performance was not until January 1921 in the Royal Institute of Glasgow. Inheriting the funds of the Glasgow Repertory, its members, most of whom were amateurs, performed over 100 plays between 1921 and 1936, many written to fulfil the company's aim of producing work dealing with 'Scottish life and characters'. Supported by the Scottish National Theatre Society (formed 1922), they provided the main outlet for Scottish playwrights between the wars and were the first to produce the work of James Bridie (**O H Mavor**). They performed in the Highlands as well as in Glasgow, and paid three visits to London. The Players as a company came to an end in 1934 but the Society continued to exist and produce plays until 1939 when the outbreak of war once again put a stop to their efforts.

UNITY PLAYERS This group sprang directly from the strong amateur dramatic movement that was particularly active in Glasgow between 1918–45. It started in 1941 as an amateur group and although a professional company was formed in 1945, the amateur company continued alongside. Funds came from box-office takings for both companies and occasionally from the newly established Arts Council. Committed to 'proletarian' drama, but not overtly political, the Unity Players performed throughout Scotland and also in England, including London where they had their greatest financial success with *The Gorbals Story* (Robert McLeish). This

naturally encouraged the company to expand, but subsequent productions did not prove such box-office successes and the Players disbanded in 1951 due to lack of funds.

CITIZENS' THEATRE COMPANY, GLASGOW Founded in 1943 by a board including Dr Henry Mavor CBE (James Bridie), the company's main instigator and driving force until his death in 1951, the Citizens' Theatre Company originally occupied the Athenaeum Theatre in Buchanan Street. In September 1945 it moved to its present home at the Royal **Princess's Theatre**, renamed the Citizens' Theatre, in the **Gorbals**. Its first production was *The Holy Isle* by Bridie, but its repertoire covered a wide range of British dramatists and since 1970, under the directorship of Giles Havergal OBE, it has become renowned for its presentation of European drama – including 15 British premiers and 13 world premiers. The company also ran a studio theatre (The Close) in the next-door building from 1965 until it burnt down in 1973.

EDINBURGH GATEWAY COMPANY Founded in 1953 by the playwright **Robert Kemp** with £1000 from subscribers and £1000 from the Arts Council, this company took its name from the premises it occupied in a former cinema on Leith Walk with the unlikely landlord of the **Church of Scotland**. It survived for 12 seasons, producing many Scottish plays and providing a forum for many native actors and directors, notably Tom Fleming, **Roddy MacMillan** and **Duncan Macrae**. Without local authority funding the survival of the company became increasingly precarious and it was with obvious relief that in 1965 the board felt they could transfer their efforts to promote Scottish drama to the Edinburgh Civic Theatre Company [see Royal Lyceum Theatre Company].

TRAVERSE THEATRE COMPANY Scotland's first and best-known studio theatre company, the Traverse began in 1963 in the premises of a former brothel on Edinburgh's **Royal Mile** with a season including the British premier of Jarry's *Ubu Roi*. Founded by an American, Jim Haynes, with the aim of continuing the theatrical experiments of the **Edinburgh Festival** throughout the year, it took its name from the original seating arrangement with the audience on two sides. Until 1988 it maintained club status, enabling it to claim exemption from the censorship imposed by the Theatres Act (abolished 1968) and to raise funds from its membership. Since the second night of its existence, when an actress was accidentally stabbed on stage, it has been beset by financial and physical problems. It moved to the **Grassmarket** in 1969 and then to more comfortable premises beside the Usher Hall in **Lothian Road** in 1992. Despite endless threats to its existence, it has continued to be the most important forum for new work in Scotland and has hosted and produced many outstanding new productions from home and abroad.

ROYAL LYCEUM THEATRE COMPANY It first performed in October 1965 as the Edinburgh Civic Theatre Company, based in the Royal Lyceum Theatre in Grindlay Street, from which it later took its name. The theatre, built in 1883, had been host to many touring companies, but this was its first permanent repertory company. The company is administered by a trust made up of members of the Edinburgh District Council and of the company, several of whom had originally been involved in the running of the Edinburgh Gateway Theatre, including the first artistic director, Tom Fleming, and the playwright Robert Kemp. A studio theatre (The Little Lyceum) was opened in a nearby building in 1975 and operated during the Edinburgh Festival and periodically throughout the year until it was demolished in 1989.

SCOTTISH YOUTH THEATRE Established in 1977 and based in Edinburgh until 1989, the Scottish Youth Theatre then moved to the Old Athenaeum Theatre in Glasgow to establish its own venue and theatrical centre. It runs courses throughout the year, covering the whole of Scotland, in all aspects of theatre. There is also a month-long summer festival during which some 120 young people aged between 12 and 21 act in and stage manage their own productions. Its activities also include a Young Playwrights Festival to encourage new writing talent.

TOURING COMPANIES Theatre companies specifically formed to tour the country did not emerge until the 1970s, the most prominent and longstanding being 7:84 Scotland, formed by John McGrath in 1973 as an offshoot of 7:84 England. The success of its first production, *The Cheviot, the Stag and the Black Black Oil* encouraged it, and a succession of companies since, to exist without being attached to any particular theatre, touring village halls, local theatres and civic centres throughout the country. These companies have ranged from a short-lived Gaelic company based on **Skye** (Fir Chlish) to a thriving rock musical company based in Glasgow (Wildcat). During the 1980s the 'Scottish Theatre Company' attempted to provide a large-scale touring company producing Scottish plays but was unable to survive financially. In recent years several touring companies have attached themselves to theatres to provide a more secure base (eg Communicado/Royal Lyceum Theatre, Borderline/**Ayr** Theatre), and several theatre companies have spawned touring companies (Citizens'/TAG, **Scottish Opera**/Opera-go-Round).

THERMOPYLAE, Sailing Vessel
A clipper built by Hood of **Aberdeen** in 1868 for George Thomson's Aberdeen Line, the *Thermopylae* became the rival for speed and gracefulness of the **Cutty Sark**. The following year she was the first tea ship home, completing the passage from China in just 91 days. She set a remarkable record in 1870 when she sailed 330 nautical miles in a single day. When the tea races were eclipsed by steam, the *Thermopylae* switched to the Australasian wool trade, making a record-breaking passage of 59 days from London to Melbourne. She ended her career with her masts cut down as a Portuguese training ship.

THIRLESTANE CASTLE, Lauder, Berwickshire
Until the end of the 16th century the Maitland residence was at old Thirlestane Castle, an L-plan tower some

two miles east of **Lauder**. In 1590 **John Maitland of Thirlestane** (1543–95), Secretary of State (1584) and Lord Chancellor (1587), built himself a square tower house nearby which was remodelled in 1670–6 for the **Duke of Lauderdale** by **William Bruce**. With **Robert Mylne** as master mason, Bruce created today's Thirlestane Castle, a massive red sandstone edifice comprising a central six-storey block with projecting three-storey wings and an unusual series of semi-circular stair towers, three on each of the long walls, providing direct access to the upstairs bedrooms. Plasterers who had been working on **Holyroodhouse** and Dutch joiners who had been working on the Duke's London house at Ham were responsible for the sumptuous ornamentation of the interior, and were reputed to have spent five years just working on the ceiling of the Long Drawing Room, 'the richness and grandeur of which is unequalled anywhere in Scotland'. Restored in the 19th century, Thirlestane is still the home of the Earls of Lauderdale and contains a fine collection of furniture, china and paintings.

THISTLE
The thistle has been an important symbol in Scottish **heraldry** for over 500 years, but botanists are confused as to which of the several native and introduced thistles this heraldic symbol represents. The spear thistle, musk thistle, melancholy thistle, stemless thistle, Our Lady's thistle and cotton thistle are all contenders.

The first use of the thistle as a royal symbol in Scotland appears to have been on silver coins issued by **James III** in 1470, and the **Order of the Thistle** was founded by **James VII** in 1687. There is no historical evidence for the popular legend of an invading **Viking** treading on a thistle and crying out, thus giving the Scots warning of an attack, but the motto *nemo me impune lacessit* (loosely translated as 'No one attacks me with impunity') is usually associated with the Scottish thistle badge.

THISTLE, Order of the
Scotland's premier Order of Chivalry is correctly entitled The Most Ancient and Most Noble Order of the Thistle and was founded by **James VII** on 29 May 1687. Since c1502 a collar of thistles has surrounded the Royal Arms of Scotland, but there is no evidence for a constituted Order of the Thistle before 1687. For a period during the 18th century there were two Orders of the Thistle, that awarded by monarchs of the United Kingdom, and that issued by the **Jacobite** sovereigns in exile on the Continent.

Award of the Order is by the personal choice of the sovereign and is normally restricted to Scots who have made a contribution to the life of Scotland or in the wider sphere of United Kingdom interests. Prime Ministers, civil and colonial administrators and men of martial prowess have been created Knights of the Thistle. The only foreign Knight was the late King Olav V of Norway who was installed in 1962. The Chapel of the Order, opened in 1911, is within the High Kirk of **St Giles** in **Edinburgh**. Women have been eligible for membership of the order since 1987, the first such creation being that in 1996 of Marion Anne Fraser, HM High Commissioner of the General Assembly of the **Church of**

Scotland 1994–5, who now styles herself Lady Fraser LT (Lady of the Thistle).

Originally the Order consisted of the sovereign and 12 Knights, but this was increased to 16 in 1821. Members wear a dark green velvet mantle, a gold collar composed of thistle and rue links from which hangs a gold and enamel St Andrew pendant. Knights also wear a silver Breast Star which bears a thistle surrounded by the motto of the Order: NEMO ME IMPUNE LACESSIT – 'No one assails me with impunity' – and from a green ribbon a gold medal with St Andrew and the motto. Various officers are attached to the Order, namely a Chancellor, Dean, King of Arms, Secretary, Usher of the Green Rod and three Heralds and three Pursuivants.

THOMAS OF ERCILDOUNE 'THE RHYMER' (c1210–c1290)

A border laird of this name occurs in a charter of the 1260s but the task of disentangling fact from myth in this case is an impossible one. Thomas the Rhymer is important primarily as the mythic *fons et origo* of Scottish vernacular verse. Whether or not there are genuine claims for this status depends on how seriously one takes a reference in a later, northern English redaction of the *Romance of Sir Tristrem*. There, Thomas is credited with authorship of the work, which probably was first written in the mid to late 13th century.

Paradoxically, the factual grounds for the myth are more secure than those for the poet. This Thomas does appear to have followed Geoffrey of Monmouth's practice of composing darkly prophetic sayings. From this grows his reputation as man of magic who spent seven years in elfland. Frequently, in this disguise, he appears in later poems and dramas, perhaps most unexpectedly as a councillor to **Robert I (the Bruce)** in Patrick Gordon's 17th century *Historie*. The flash of light which announces him and the parting through 'schaples air' is a fair image for the place in Scottish literature of one who enlightens through possibility rather than essence.

THOMPSON, Sir James (1835–1906)
Railway Manager

Thompson was born at Kirtlebridge, **Dumfriesshire**, but moved as a boy to Carlisle where he was educated at the Academy. He started work as a junior clerk with the Caledonian Railway Company based in **Glasgow** and proceeded to rise through the ranks. In 1882 he was appointed general manager in conditions of severe competition with the North British and Glasgow & South Western **railway** companies. The projects with which he was associated were numerous: new lines into **Ayrshire** and **Dunbartonshire**, the suburban services in the south of Glasgow, the low level at **Glasgow Central**, etc. He also pioneered cheap third class travel, workmen's fares and dining cars. The first Scottish railway manager to be knighted (1897), he left the Caledonian the leading company in Scotland.

THOMSON, Alexander 'Greek' (1817–75)
Architect

Known as 'Greek' for his supposedly Grecian designs, Thomson, **Glasgow**'s most original Victorian architect, was born at **Balfron**, **Stirlingshire**, the 17th child in a family of 24. Apprenticed to John Baird, he lived and worked in Glasgow all his life. There his buildings contribute greatly to the city's rich legacy of Victorian architecture. He designed every conceivable building type, from warehouses and office buildings to tenements, churches and mansion houses. One of his most successful domestic designs was a monumental terrace at Moray Place, which stands out through its purity of proportion and scarcity of ornament. But his churches were probably his greatest contribution to 19th century neo-classical architecture. The three **United Presbyterian** churches at Caledonian Road (1856), St Vincent Street (1859) and **Queens Park** (1867, now demolished) use not only neo-classical but also Egyptian and even Hindu motifs, in compositions reminiscent of Schinkel's work earlier in the century. His expressive and almost abstract use of Grecian patterns anticipated architectural development in the early 20th century. From the 1860s onwards he began to experiment with the use of new materials, iron-framed constructions and whole façades of cast iron and glass. In this too he pre-empted future developments. His architecture had a strong theoretical base which he communicated through many publications and lectures, often in his capacity as President of the Glasgow Institute of Architects. Of late Thomson's reputation as a master of architectural geometry and a highly individual stylist has soared deservedly. Comparisons with **Charles Rennie Mackintosh** are not misplaced.

THOMSON, Bryden (1928–91) Conductor

'Jack' Thomson was one of the outstanding Scottish conductors of the century. His excellent ear, superb stick technique and ability to let the music speak for itself were matched by a fiery temperament. He was Principal Conductor of the Ulster Orchestra, the RTE Orchestra and the Scottish National Orchestra, but was particularly associated with the Young Musician of the Year Awards which he regularly conducted. He especially championed the music of John Maxwell Geddes, from whom he commissioned a number of works. His support for Scottish contemporary music was honoured by a Scottish Society of Composers–Performing Rights Society Award.

THOMSON, Sir Charles Wyville (1830–82)
Oceanographer

Born at **Linlithgow**, Thomson studied medicine at **Edinburgh**, but showed more interest in natural history, becoming Professor in the subject at **Edinburgh University** in 1870. Two years later he led the civilian team of scientists on the 68,890-mile cruise of HMS *Challenger*, discovering life forms down to unprecedented depths of 3000 fathoms. Knighted for this work, his health failed when attempting to publish the massive array of data collected, and this work was taken over by **John Murray**.

THOMSON, David Couper (1861–1954)
Newspaper Proprietor

Born in **Dundee**, the son of William, a merchant clothier who founded the Thomson steamship line, David was educated at Newport Primary School and Dundee High School. He was briefly employed in his father's **shipping** business before being given responsibility for running three Dundee **newspapers**, including the *Courier* and the *Argos*, which William had purchased. Success came with the appearance of *My Weekly*, a girls' magazine. D C Thomson & Company was formed as a limited company in 1906 and expansion continued rapidly with the launching of the *Sunday Post* in 1915. There can be no doubting the impact of his deeply held conservative views. In the aftermath of the General Strike he forced his employees to sign a document requiring them to surrender trade union membership. The 1930s saw the launch of the *Beano*, the *Dandy* and other comics and women's magazines. Their mélange of morality, couthy humour, respectability, romanticism and sporting endeavour proved commercially successful and impacted on the daily life of millions of Scots. D C died in 1954, two years after another battle to keep his company from the taint of **trade unionism**.

THOMSON, George (1754–1851) Music Collector
Thomson's professional career was as secretary for 50 years to the Board of Trustees for the Encouragement

George Thomson, watercolour by William Nicholson, c1817 (SNPG)

of Arts and Manufactures in Scotland, but his fame rests on his collection and publication of the traditional songs of Scotland, Ireland and Wales. In particular he encouraged **Burns** to complete or alter a number of traditional songs, and then persuaded many of the leading composers of the day, notably Haydn and Beethoven, to write accompaniments for them.

THOMSON, James (1700–48) Poet
Born at Ednam, **Roxburghshire**, the son of a minister, James Thomson was educated at **Jedburgh** School and the **University of Edinburgh**, where he studied Divinity. With the encouragement of his friend the playwright David Malloch, he abandoned his studies in 1725 and went to London where he tutored for a short period

and wrote 'Winter' (1726), the first of four poems in blank verse later collected as *The Seasons* (1730), and originally published between 1726–30. *The Seasons*, one of Thomson's most popular works, is considered a precursor of the Romantic movement in its descriptive emphasis on landscape and nature. Despite Thomson's original views of nature, his over-ornate and artificial language led many Romantics to reject his work.

Thomson also wrote extensively for the stage, producing such tragedies as *Sophonisba* (1730), *Agamemnon* (1738), *Tancred and Sigismunda* (1745) and *Coriolanus* (1748). He collaborated with David Malloch on *The Masque of Alfred* (1740), for which he wrote the song 'Rule Britannia'.

He also wrote *Liberty* (1735–6), a poem inspired by a European tour he undertook as tutor to Lord Chancellor Talbot's son in 1731. It was dedicated to the Prince of Wales, who awarded him a pension and later secured him the sinecure of Surveyor-General of the Leeward Islands. He retired from public life in 1740 and, shortly before his death in Richmond in 1748, published the Spenserian allegory *The Castle of Indolence*, which is considered by many to be his masterpiece. He was buried in Richmond Church.

THOMSON, James 'BV' (1834–82) Poet
Born in **Port Glasgow**, the son of a merchant seaman, but brought up in an orphan asylum in London (both parents having died soon after moving south in 1842), James Thomson has been described as a professional pessimist. Trained as an army schoolmaster but dismissed the service for 'breach of discipline' (a military euphemism for, in his case, alcoholism), he wrote 'sombre and sonorous' poems, many of which were published in the *National Reformer*. After a year in America working for a mining company (1872), he went to Spain as a war correspondent with the Carlists (1873) before returning to London where depression and loneliness inspired his greatest work, the long poem *City of Dreadful Night*, contributed to the *National Reformer* in 1874 and published in 1880. Continued alcohol and narcotics abuse led to his death in London's University College Hospital in June 1882. (His pseudonym 'BV', Bysshe Vanolis, under which he sometimes published, was a combination of Shelley's second name and an anagram of 'Novalis', the pen-name of the German Romantic poet Friedrich von Hardenberg.)

THOMSON, James (d.1927) Architect
Thomson was an apprentice of W M Garvie CE in **Edinburgh**, and became **Dundee** City Architect in 1904 and City Engineer in 1906. His first buildings were Blackness and Coldside Libraries (1909), St Roques Library in Blackscroft (1910) and Ward Road Museum (1911). More notable was his drawing for a new city centre for the site of Earl Grey Dock, a single central structure set in gardens and tree-lined avenues. When (Sir) **James Caird** donated £100,000 for the building of a new City Hall and Concert Hall in 1914, Thomson's plans fell, but he designed the Caird Hall with the colonnade gifted by Mrs Marryat, Caird's sister. Thomson was responsible for the Logie housing estate (1919) with its distinct heating system and four-in-a-block houses, each with a bow-fronted window, and later for the planning of

Craigie Garden Suburb or Craigiebank, also in 1919. His vision in proposing Dundee's outer ring-road, the Kingsway, built in the 1920s, was far ahead of his time.

THOMSON, James (Suemas MacThòmais) (1888–1971) Gaelic Scholar

Born at Tong, **Lewis**, Thomson was the first crowned **Bard** of the National **Mod** (1923) and was involved in the pioneering of Gaelic teaching in secondary schools. He edited an influential short anthology of **Gaelic poems** for such teaching – An Dìleab ('The Legacy', 1932) – and co-edited a collection of Lewis songs Eilean Fraioch (1908). He also edited An Gaidheal from 1958–62. His own Gaelic poems were collected in the volume Fasgnadh ('Winnowing') in 1953. His elegant prose writings are as yet uncollected.

THOMSON, The Rev John, of Duddingston (1778–1840) Painter

Although self-consciously proclaiming his amateur status at all opportunities, Thomson was, in fact, one of the most commercially successful landscape painters in early 19th century Scotland. Born the son of an **Ayrshire** minister, his main choice of career was never in doubt. However while completing his Divinity studies at **Edinburgh** he began taking lessons at **Alexander Nasmyth**'s art classes and was greatly influenced by his teacher's espousal of drawing directly from nature. At the same time he made the acquaintance of **Sir Walter Scott**, and his paintings are far closer to the spirit of Scott than the later illustrative works so much admired by the Victorians. Like Scott he tried to represent the romantic 'associations' evoked by landscape, and his storm-wracked, fluidly painted depictions of dramatic Scottish scenery are intended to excite the emotions of the spectator as well as merely describe the topography. Unlike Nasmyth or his predecessors, Thomson was never directly exposed to the work of Claude and Poussin and so his work, while sometimes guilty of poor draughtsmanship or ungainly composition, is truly Scottish in character: an unconditioned, if romantic, response to the landscape. As such it had a profound impact on the younger generation of Scottish artists, notably **Lauder** and **McCulloch**. Thomson worked briefly with J M W Turner between 1818–22 and travelled with him sketching in Scotland. This may have encouraged him to attempt more histrionic and exaggerated effects in his later works, but he lacked Turner's flair and such paintings are less successful. It is not known to what extent he neglected his parishioners in **Duddingston** during this time. He was certainly not reliant on any stipend and through the sales of his paintings became a very wealthy man.

THOMSON, John (1805–41) Composer

Apart from the splendid Weberesque overture Hermann, little of Thomson's music is known. His two piano trios are fine works, the C major Trio of 1832 boasting a particularly lovely Adagio, and the G minor Trio of 1826, stormy, sometimes fierce, but with passages of Schubertian warmth, is probably the work that impressed his younger contemporary, Mendelssohn, when the latter visited **Edinburgh**. Thomson studied in Germany with a letter of introduction to the Mendelssohn family and probably moved on to meet Schumann. His Drei Lieder of 1838 are among the most beautiful examples of the form. His Rondo for piano, composed in 1828, demonstrated a lively pianistic technique, and his six-part glee When Whispering Winds is a beautiful contribution to a then popular genre. He composed three operas, a flute concerto, a flute quartet and a number of other works, including concert arias and a profound but very simple Bagatelle for solo piano. Thomson became first Reid Professor of Music, but died tragically young shortly after taking up the appointment.

THOMSON, Joseph (1858–95) Explorer

Born at Penpont near **Thornhill** in **Dumfriesshire**, Thomson was the son of a builder. He studied science at **Edinburgh University** and then joined the Royal Geographical Society's 1878–9 expedition in East Africa as botanist and geologist. The expedition under **A K Johnston** was to explore a route from Dar-es-Salaam to Lakes Nyasa (Malawi) and Tanganyika. When Johnston died in the early stages, Thomson, though only 21, found himself in command. 'I felt I must go forward,' he wrote, 'whatever might be my destiny. Was not I the countryman of **Bruce**, **Park**, **Clapperton**, **Grant**, **Livingstone** and [Lovett] Cameron?' He passed Lake Nyasa, explored Lake Tanganyika, and came within a day's march of the Congo before being forced back. A second expedition in 1883–4 took him from Mombasa to Lake Victoria through the dangerous Masai country. In the course of it he visited Mounts Kenya and Kilimanjaro, was the first to divine the importance of the Rift Valley, 'discovered' the Thomson's Falls (Nyapuhura), sighted the gazelle now named after him, and, on his return, received the RGS's Founder's Medal. Further expeditions to Sokoto (Nigeria), the Atlas Mountains (Morocco) and Northern Rhodesia (Zambia) followed. But his health was by now impaired and he died soon after returning to Scotland. A glorious exception amongst 19th century travellers in Africa, Thomson displayed inexhaustible good humour, preferred charm to coercion, and refused either to flog his followers or to shoot at adversaries. 'He who goes slowly, goes safely; he who goes safely, goes far' was his motto. He wrote well (To the African Lakes, 1881, Through the Masai Land, 1885, etc). There is a biography by his brother J B Thomson.

THOMSON, Robert William (1822–73) Engineer

Thomson was born in **Stonehaven**, the son of a factory owner. In 1836 he went to Charleston, South Carolina to work for a merchant, but returned to Scotland two years later and became assistant to a civil engineer. He developed a method of firing explosive charges by electricity while assisting his employer in the demolition of **Dunbar** Castle, and in 1841 went to London to demonstrate his invention to Michael Faraday. He subsequently worked for the contractors Sir William Cubitt and Robert Stephenson and set out in business as a civil engineer on his own account in 1844. He patented an india-rubber pneumatic tyre the following year, and in 1849 an improved fountain pen, but his inventions apparently failed to attract the interest of manufacturers.

Thomson went to Java in 1852 as an agent for a

manufacturer of sugar machinery. He continued to spend his spare time inventing, making improvements to his employers' machines and designing a portable steam crane and a hydraulic dock. He retired from business in 1862 and went to live in **Edinburgh**, devoting the remainder of his life solely to developing other inventions, which included an elliptic rotary engine. In 1867 he patented the first successful mechanical road haulage vehicle, a steam traction engine, which was first produced commercially in 1872. The heavy machine was made suitable for road travel by the adoption of thick rubber pad tyres to distribute the weight over the road surface. 'Thomson Steamers' were exported around the world during the remainder of the 19th century. They proved their worth in transporting heavy loads over long distances where no **railway** network existed, or in docks and other places where cargoes had to be transported rapidly over short distances.

THOMSON, Thomas (1817–78) Botanist

As part of his medical training Thomson studied botany under Sir William Hooker at **Glasgow University** where his father, also Thomas, was Professor of Chemistry. He wrote on the molluscs of the **Clyde** and on the presence of pectin in carrots before entering the East India Company's service as a surgeon (1840). At Ghazni during the disastrous First Afghan War he was captured but managed to bribe his captors. He then served in the Sikh Wars before being appointed to **Alexander Cunningham**'s Tibetan Boundary Commission (1846–9). As its geologist and botanist Thomson explored more of Zanskar and Ladakh than any of his companions. He also produced a book in which the pioneering nature of his travels is well concealed by scientific observations. In 1849 he joined J D Hooker, the son of Sir William and a close friend, on his botanising tour of Sikkim, the Assam hills and the Ganges delta. He returned from India to convalesce and, working at Kew, wrote with Hooker the first volume of *Flora Indica*. This major undertaking received little official encouragement. Thomson went back to India where he became superintendent of the Calcutta Botanical Garden and Professor of Botany (1854–61). His achievement as an explorer was finally recognised by the Royal Geographical Society which in 1866 awarded him one of its two gold medals.

THOMSON, William (fl.1730) Music Publisher

Thomson's *Orpheus Caledonius* of 1725 was the first publication of Scottish songs with the words. Thereafter he and the poet **Allan Ramsay** pirated material from each other's editions.

THOMSON, William, Lord Kelvin (1824–1907) Scientist and Inventor

Thomson was born in Belfast. In 1832 his father was elected Professor of Mathematics at **Glasgow University** and Thomson matriculated to study there at the age of 11. In 1841 he went to pursue his studies at Peterhouse College, Cambridge, returning to **Glasgow** in 1846 to become Professor of Natural Philosophy.

Thomson established his academic reputation in the science of thermodynamics, proposing an absolute scale of temperature – the Kelvin scale – and then formulating

Sir William Thomson, Lord Kelvin, by William Rothenstein, 1904 (SNPG)

during the early 1850s the laws of equivalence and of transformation. Later he enunciated the doctrine of available energy, laying firm foundations for study in this important branch of physics.

While continuing his theoretical research, Thomson was also active as a practical scientist, conducting pioneering work on the development of electric telegraphy. After propounding the theory of electric oscillations in 1853, he carried out a series of experiments to develop an insulated electric telegraph cable, and invented the mirror galvanometer, an ingenious telegraph message receiver. In 1856 he became a director of the Atlantic Telegraph Company, and ten years later he supervised the laying of the cable from Ireland to Newfoundland which revolutionised transatlantic communications. He was knighted in 1866 for his contribution to telegraphy, and in 1874 he was elected President of the Society of Telegraph Engineers.

Thomson believed that 'the life and soul of science is its practical application,' and he was one of the greatest inventors of his age. A keen sailor, he invented an improved naval compass, a navigational sounding machine and a tide predictor, as well as numerous electrical measuring and telegraphic instruments. By 1900 he had patented 56 of his inventions, which were developed and manufactured for him by the Glasgow instrument makers James White & Co. Thomson became a partner in the firm, and also set up another partnership, Jenkin, Varley & Thomson, to control his patents.

Despite his teaching commitments and growing business interests, Thomson did not abandon his work in pure science. He made important contributions to the theories of elasticity and of waves, gyrostatics, magnetism and atmospheric electricity. His most recent biographer has described him as 'an entrepreneur in scientific ideas as much as in technology', recognising his ability to exploit and to build upon the theoretical work of others, as well as his great talents as a mathematical physicist. Possessed of immense intellectual energy, he wrote his first scientific paper at the age of 15 and published another 660 during the following 68 years.

Thomson received many awards and honours in the course of his long academic and business career. He was a Fellow of the Royal Society (1851) and President of the British Association (1871) and the Royal Society (1890–5). In 1892 he was created Baron Kelvin of **Largs**, and he became a member of the Order of Merit and a Privy Councillor (both 1902) and Chancellor of Glasgow University (1904). He is buried in Westminster Abbey.

THORFINN, Earl of Orkney (c1009–65)

Succeeding his father **Earl Sigurd** as an infant in 1014, and possessing a Celtic mother and grandmother, Thorfinn is an example of the mixed race that was evolving in all ranks of society at the end of the **Viking** age. He seems to have spent more of his time at the court of his grandfather **Malcolm II**, King of Scots, than at that of his own sovereign the King of Norway. When Malcolm died in 1034 Thorfinn was his heir by descent, since his mother was the King's elder daughter, while the younger was married to Abbot Crinan of **Dunkeld**. It is something of a mystery why Earl Thorfinn or the **tanist** heir, **MacBeth** of **Moray**, allowed Crinan's son **Duncan** to succeed to the Crown. When King Duncan, after a disastrous invasion of England, attempted to enter the lands of his Norwegian cousin, Thorfinn chased him to his death in 1040. MacBeth then assumed the Crown and lived in amity with the Earl until this King's death in 1057. It appears that they made a pilgrimage to Rome together and certainly both men endowed the Church. Thorfinn, who was remembered after his death as 'Thorfinn the Mighty', established **Orkney**'s first bishopric at **Birsay**, where he built what the *Orkneyinga Saga* described as a splendid minster, near to which he resided in his latter years. His daughter Ingibiorg became the first wife of **Malcolm III 'Canmore'**, though Malcolm also had the temerity to attempt an invasion of Thorfinn's islands.

THORNHILL, Dumfriesshire

'The most tidy, neat, and generally attractive village of its class in Britain' was how an 1844 gazetteer described Thornhill. Then as now it owed its respectability to nearby **Drumlanrig** whose **Queensberry** dukes endowed the village with its market cross equivalent, a column topped by the winged Queensberry horse (1714), and whose **Buccleuch** dukes built the church (1841). If, as seems probable, the Anglian cross shaft at Nith bridge is still in its original position, Thornhill must have been a centre of early Christian settlement in the 8–9th centuries. The great ramparts of Tynron Doon, two miles west, span a long period of occupation from the Iron Age until the 16th century when an L-plan tower house stood on the site. Other castles in the area include **Morton**, Tibbers (repaired by Edward I but destroyed by **Robert I** in 1311), Closeburn (a 14th century tower of the Kirkpatrick family), and of course Drumlanrig. South of Thornhill off the road to **Dumfries** lies Ellisland farm into which moved **Robert Burns** and Jean Armour in 1788. Burns's agricultural endeavours failed as usual, but here he wrote, among much, *Tam O'Shanter*. South-west of Thornhill, Keir was the birthplace of **Kirkpatrick ('Daft Pate') Macmillan**.

THREAVE CASTLE, Kirkcudbrightshire

Built on an island in the river **Dee** by **Archibald 'the Grim', 3rd Earl of Douglas**, between 1369–90, Threave Castle consists of a sombre, grey, four-storey 70ft (21m) high tower with a small courtyard surrounded by a wall (rebuilt c1455 on earlier foundations) with three-storey round towers with loop holes. 'Anciently an infernal place, its thick walls, narrow windows and staircases and the dungeon yet remaining in perfection, make the blood *freeze* – it seems as if it had been built for the sole purpose of conducting savage deeds' (**MacTaggart**, 1824). The name, formerly 'Thrave', 'Trief' or 'Thrieve', is derived from an old Welsh word meaning 'a homestead', but according to MacTaggart it is 'probably connected with *riee* – to rob – being quite a pit of robbers and murderers'. The most notorious of these was **William, 8th Earl of Douglas** (c1425–52) – 'one of the most horrible devils that ever appeared in Scotland'. In 1452 the Earl captured MacLellan of **Kirkcudbright** by bribing one of his servants with the promise of a ladleful of gold. When the servant claimed his reward the Earl 'caused the gold to be melted and poured it down his throat'. He then, in direct contravention of the orders of the King, **James II**, proceeded to hang the unfortunate MacLellan from the gallows knob which still protrudes over the castle's main doorway. In 1455 James laid siege to Threave and forced its surrender with a bombardment, the cannon for which were brought with some difficulty from **Linlithgow**. Repaired after **Flodden**, the castle shared the same fate as **Caerlaverock** when it was seized and vandalised by **Covenanters** in 1640 after a 13-week siege, leaving only the shell to brood over the now peaceful countryside. The **National Trust for Scotland** operates its School of Practical Gardening in the grounds of nearby Threave House.

THURSO, Caithness

The fact that **Earl Rognvald**'s corpse was brought here after his murder in 1158 suggests that there may already have been a chapel on the site of St Peter's Church. It was Bishop Gilbert who built St Peter's after his elevation in 1223, though most of the surviving structure dates from the 16th century or later. A Norse standing cross with a runic inscription incised up its shaft has been removed from here to the Thurso Museum. There was a **Viking** stronghold nearby, stormed by **William the Lion**'s troops late in the 12th century as a reprisal for the mutilation of Bishop John. It stood on the spot occupied by the manse of St Andrew's Church and is commemorated by Castlegreen. The town's commercial enterprises received surprising recognition in 1330 when **David II** decreed that its unit of weight should be observed throughout the country. Yet it was not until 1633 that Thurso was granted the status of a **burgh of barony**, with the right to trade within Scotland. A dispute of 1635 opens a window on these activities. In **Stornoway** 20 barrels of **herring** were consigned to the ship of a **Dundee** merchant which called at Thurso. Here Thomas Gunn added to her freight 10 barrels of beef, 43 oxen and cow hides, 16 stone of goose feathers, 100 lamb skins, 50 calf skins and 36 ells of double white plaiding. Before all these goods could be unloaded at **Leith** they were listed by the parties to the dispute.

Thurso continued to thrive, to a degree that must have been galling to the burgesses of **Wick**. Before the century was out, the new town had been planned by **Sir John Sinclair** of Ulbster, whose statue so justly stands in its central garden. As late as 1945 the town was confined to the west side of the Thurso river, overlooked by the great Victorian Gothic castle on the opposite bank. Sir Archibald Sinclair, 1st Viscount Thurso, was the last to live in it before it was reduced to a ruin. Today Thurso has burgeoned beyond its entrance gate, while to the west it has reached the threshold of Pennyland House, home of **Sir William Smith**, the founder of the **Boys' Brigade**.

TIGHNABRUAICH, Argyll
Pronounced 'Ty-na-broo-aich', this village on the Kyles of **Bute** has been described as 'one of the most beautiful of the **Clyde**' (W H Murray). At the southern end of the **Cowal** peninsula, it was developed in the 19th century as 'a small colony of marine villas' and is now a popular sailing resort.

TILLICOULTRY, Clackmannanshire
Like **Alva** and other Hillfoots villages, Tillicoultry prospered in the 19th century when its fast-flowing burn provided a ready source of power for woollen mills whose product could be easily exported to a **tartan** conscious UK public. Four mills survive with the Clock Mill operating as the centre of the Hillfoots Mill Heritage Trail. The burn joins the river Devon where, at Harviestoun, **Robert Burns** visited **Gavin Hamilton** and much admired young Charlotte, Mrs Hamilton's daughter:

Let Bourbon exult in his gay, gilded lilies,
And England triumphant display her proud Rose;
A fairer than either adorns the green valleys
Where Devon, sweet Devon, meandering flows.

Nearby on a spur of the **Ochils**, Castle Craig is the site of a hill fort with large boulder rampart and smaller well-built circular enclosure, the latter probably later and post-**Roman**.

TIORAM (or TIRRIM) CASTLE, Nr Acharacle, Inverness-shire
Like **Mingary Castle**, Tioram's massive crenellated wall of enclosure dates from the 13th century; its keep and tower house are much later. The whole is now ruined but might prove less of a restorational challenge than Mingary. The site of Tioram is more like that of **Castle Stalker**, being a rocky islet (in Loch Moidart) which can be reached on foot across a spit of land at low tide. If not built by John, 1st **Lord of the Isles** and Chief of the **Clan Donald**, it certainly passed to his wife Amy who was domiciled here when he rejected her to marry Margaret, daughter of **Robert II**; it is from the abandoned Amy that the **Clanranald** branch of the **MacDonalds** are descended. Tioram was besieged by the **Earl of Huntly** in 1554 and a century later by Cromwell's army. In 1715 it was burnt on the orders of Allan

of Clanranald to discourage an attack by the **Campbells** while Clanranald was busy about the **Jacobite** cause.

TIPPERMUIR (or TIBBERMORE), Battle of (1644)
The year-long string of victories in which **James Graham, 1st Marquis of Montrose** resurrected the Royalist cause began with his effecting a rendezvous with **Alasdair MacDonald** and the latter's Irish troops at **Blair Atholl** in August 1644. They immediately marched on **Perth**. On 1 September at the village of Tippermuir, 4 miles west of the city, the **Covenanters** hastily prepared for battle. Their commander, Lord Elcho, had a force both numerically larger and better armed than Montrose, but the Royalists had the more resourceful commander and a slightly better position.

Montrose stationed the Irish infantry, under Alasdair MacDonald, in the centre of the line, while he himself commanded the Highland foot and the cavalry on the wings. The armies were within musket shot of each other when the Covenanters sent out a small force of cavalry to decoy the enemy's fire. This provoked Alasdair MacDonald into immediate attack. The Irish fired one round of shot and then fought with sword, pike and stones. The Covenanters, overcome by the force of the onslaught, broke ranks and fled. Few were killed in the action but an estimated 2000 died in the ensuing rout. By sunset Montrose was master of Perth and his remarkable string of victories had begun.

TIREE, Island of, Inner Hebrides
A flat, windswept island, its level landscape broken only by sand dunes, occasional rocky knolls and the hills of Ben Hynish (462ft/141m) and Beinn Hough (390ft/119m) at its western extremities, Tiree lies to the west of **Mull** and is reached by ferry from **Oban**. A popular destination for surfers, it is busier and much more fertile than its northern neighbour, **Coll**, and has a population of about 800 on a land area of 29 square miles.

The underlying bed-rock is Lewisian gneiss, but windblown sand has allowed fertile, well-drained machair to cover most of the island. Known in Gaelic as the land of corn (Tir-Iodh), Tiree supported 4450 souls in 1831. Following famines and evictions, the population had declined to 2700 by 1881. At the height of the **tourist** season today it approaches the levels of the last century.

There are several interesting archaeological sites, including the excavated **broch** of Dun Mor Vaul; the finds are in the **Hunterian Museum** at **Glasgow University**. On the shore between Vaul and Balephetrish is a glacial erratic, the 'ringing stone', covered with over 50 Bronze-Age cup marks.

The ferry terminal and main township is at Scarinish, but there are several **crofting** townships on the island, many with restored thatched houses. There is an airstrip at The Reef, with connecting daily flights to **Glasgow** and **Barra**, and, on the western skyline, a massive dimpled military communications 'golfball' has become a landmark.

TIT, Crested
This very small species (*Parus cristatus scoticus*) poses a mystery, in that whilst it breeds over most of Europe,

in Britain it is restricted to the central Highlands of Scotland, based mainly on Speyside. Its traditional habitat is the old **Caledonian pine forest**, and before this forest was extensively felled it seems likely that the crested tit was much more widespread. However the Scottish crested tit must have been isolated for a long time, as it has evolved into a different race from its European counterpart. There is some evidence that in the late 1980s there was a slight spread in its range to the north and west. There is also an indication that it can survive in conifer plantations once the conifers are over 20 years old, so there is potential for further expansion in its range and numbers. At the end of the 1980s the number of breeding pairs was estimated to be under 1000, but this varies greatly depending on the severity of winters.

Only two of the British tits actually excavate their own nest holes – the willow tit (*Parus montanus*) and the crested tit. When nest boxes are put up for these two species the boxes are filled with chippings to make the birds believe that they are excavating for themselves.

TOBACCO TRADE, The

Throughout much of the 18th century **Glasgow** was the main entrepôt for the importation into Europe of North American tobacco. The wealth generated by this trade created its Merchant City where many of the street names commemorate 'Tobacco Lords' (Ingram Street, Buchanan Street, Glassford Street, Cochrane Street, not to mention Virginia Street); it also generated the financial institutions and to some extent the capital which funded Glasgow's dramatic rise as an industrial centre.

When the **Act of Union** opened colonial trade to Scottish merchants **Greenock** and **Port Glasgow** were particularly well sited to cash in on the trade with North America and the West Indies because of shorter sailing times and less risk of hostile interference (than in, say, the English Channel). The Caribbean, producing mainly sugar, was less important than Virginia and Maryland, producing mainly tobacco, since the more numerous colonists there also represented an important market for manufactured goods. Meeting this demand, especially for **linens** and **iron** hardware, did much for the west of Scotland's incipient industries.

To purchase tobacco against sales of exported manufactures entailed a system of agencies and warehouses scattered about the producing areas. The main tobacco syndicates thus invested both personnel and capital in the colonies as well as in the necessary shipping. At home they also invested in those industries (including **agriculture**) which supplied the colonies, and in Europe (especially France) they developed the commercial links vital for the re-export trade which accounted for the bulk of tobacco imports. The result was a sophisticated trading cycle involving considerable capital and commensurate risk.

During the boom years of the 1760s and 70s vast fortunes were made and Glasgow rapidly became a city of high fashion and lavish expenditure. There were also spectacular casualties. Control of the trade rested with a small group of syndicates operating through numerous family-based companies. At any one time there were probably no more than two dozen 'Tobacco Lords' amongst whom William Cunninghame, Alexander

Speirs, James Buchanan and John Glassford are notable.

It has been assumed that the American War of Independence ruined both the trade and those engaged in it. There were certainly heavy losses in America and on the high seas (eg to **John Paul Jones**). But T M Devine (in *The Tobacco Lords*, 1975) argues convincingly that Glasgow's merchants reacted vigorously to the crisis, that high prices compensated for declining volume during the war, and that after it the comparatively low level of tobacco imports was the result not of Glasgow merchants withdrawing from the trade, but of shipment being made direct from America to Continental Europe rather than via the **Clyde**.

TOBERMORY, Mull

The chief town of **Mull**, Tobermory (from the Gaelic *Tobar Mhoire*, 'Mary's Well') is one of the smallest Scottish burghs, as well as one of the most colourful. Brightly painted houses line the sheltered natural harbour which, further protected by Calve Island in the Sound of Mull, is one of the safest in the **Hebrides**. The town was built (1787–8) by the British Fisheries Society but has relied heavily on **tourism** since the decline of the **herring** fishing in the 19th century. Now yachts and pleasure boats have replaced the herring fleet, with additional marine interest being provided by the wreck of the *Florida*, a galleon from the Spanish Armada which sank in Tobermory Bay in 1588, reputedly carrying £300,000 worth of gold bullion. Treasure hunters are still drawn to the wreck even though its yield has been minimal and it lies buried under a 30ft (9m) layer of clay in 60ft (18m) of water (W H Murray). Tobermory is connected by car ferry to Kilchoan on **Ardnamurchan** as well as to **Coll**, **Tiree** and the Outer Isles.

TOLQUHON CASTLE, Nr Oldmeldrum, Aberdeenshire

Believing this castle to have been the work of French masons endeavouring to soften the 'rude strength' of Scottish castellar architecture, R W Billings called it a 'grotesque mansion'. Better informed (**MacGibbon and Ross** could find absolutely no evidence of foreign involvement), Billings might have been less dismissive. Tolquhon was indeed designed more for effect than defence, and is the finer for it.

It is, though, unusual, being one of very few castles in Grampian built round a courtyard. Except for the ruinous Preston tower (15th century), the whole was 'begun be William Forbes 15 Aprile 1584 and endit be him 20 October 1589', as an inscription declares. Forbes, the 7th Lord of Tolquhon, succeeded on his father's death at **Pinkie** (1547). Immensely proud of his new castle, its furnishings and books, he was evidently a cultured and gracious laird. His successors fared less well, losing heavily in the **Darien Company** and being forcibly ejected for debt default in 1718. The castle was bought by the **Earl of Aberdeen**, remained habitable until the end of the 19th century, and passed to the state as a ruin in 1929.

Sited on a tree-girt knoll, its principal glory is the north façade, flanked by corner towers (one the Preston) and with an arched portal between two small drum towers with grilled windows. Above the portal are the armorial panels of Forbes and **James VI** and beside it

Gateway of Tolquhon Castle (RWB)

relief effigies, one of which may be Forbes himself. Within, the courtyard is cobbled; service buildings lie on either side with the main house, including a four-storey tower, at the far (south) end. Though roofless, a fair impression of Tolquhon's gracious living arrangements can be formed.

TOMINTOUL, Banffshire

Possibly the highest (1160ft/354m) village in the Highlands, Tomintoul (pron. Tommin-towel) was founded by the 4th **Duke of Gordon** in 1750. The planned creation of an improving laird, it comprises a main street and tree-lined square in bleak surroundings between the upper Avon and Conglass Water. **Queen Victoria** reckoned it 'the most tumbledown, poor-looking place I ever saw' (1860), but today it thrives on **tourism** thanks to the notoriety of the **Lecht** road south to **Cockbridge** (invariably the first to be closed by snow), to the village's **whisky** associations (smuggling as well as distilling) and to its convenience as a centre for walking, **fishing**, skiing, etc on the north side of the **Cairngorms**. Two miles on the Tomintoul side of the Lecht summit, the Well of Lecht is marked by a white stone plaque recording the construction of the **military road** from **Ruthven** on Speyside south to **Blairgowrie** in 1754. An **iron** mine nearby was worked by the **York Buildings Company** at about the same time.

TONGUE, Sutherland

Situated in spectacular surroundings in the heart of the **Mackay** country, this became the seat of the chiefs after their castle Borve (13 miles along the coast to the east) was destroyed by the **Gordons** of **Sutherland** in 1554. The name is Norse, and on a peninsula in the shallow waters of the Kyle stands a ruined fort that may date from **Viking** times. But it is known in Gaelic as Kintail Mackay, to distinguish it from Kintail Mackenzie in the south-west. The home of the Chiefs was destroyed after Donald Mackay, 1st Lord Reay, espoused the cause of **Charles I**, and republican troops came to garrison Tongue. A fine new mansion was built in 1678, which the 3rd Lord Reay (1680–1748) embellished with an additional wing. He also constructed what is thought to have been the first road fit for a horse-drawn carriage in the Mackay country, to carry him to the interesting T-shaped church less than a mile away. This contains an underground vault for the interment of the Chiefs, and boasted until recently the rare amenity of a carved wooden laird's loft. Regrettably, this has been removed to **Edinburgh**. In March 1746 a luckless sloop called the *Hazard* foundered among the shoals of the Kyle with a consignment of gold for the **Jacobites**. The Hanoverian Mackays incarcerated its crew in the boathouse that still stands near Tongue house. Ewen Robertson (1842–95), bard of the **clearances**, represented this neighbourhood eloquently before the **Crofters' Commission** in 1883 and is commemorated by a local monument.

TOOTHILL REPORT

The product of an Inquiry into the Scottish Economy 1960–1, by the Scottish Council (Development and Industry), this report by Sir John Toothill (1908–86) argued for selective concentration on growth industries in Scotland in a bid to increase prosperity and ease unemployment. It also drew attention to the serious effect of emigration on the Scottish labour force. Its recommendations were accepted by the then Secretary of State for Scotland, John Maclay, and led to the creation of the Scottish Development Department within the Scottish Office.

TORHOUSEKIE STANDING STONES, Wigtownshire

These Bronze Age stone settings at Torhouse, four miles west of **Wigtown** on the B733, have remained little known; though not in the class of Stonehenge, Avebury or **Callanish**, they are nevertheless impressive. The principal stone circle is made up of 19 granite boulders on end, with a further three in line across the interior. The diameter of the circle varies from 61 to 66ft (18–20m), the boulders standing 5 to 11ft (1.5–3.3m) apart; those on the west side are smaller and closer than those in the east. A penannular ring of smaller stones, the diameter of the ring 25ft (7.6m) in one direction and 16ft (4.8m) in the other, lies within the large circle. 200 yards north-west of the large stone circle is another circle, and 80ft (24m) south of the large circle is a boulder set on end facing the large circle. About 130 yards due east of the large circle is a third circle; and across the road are three boulders on a curving line which seem, before the agricultural **clearances** of the late 18th century, to have formed part of yet a fourth circle. A round **cairn**, presumably also Bronze Age, lies not far away.

The careful placing of the boulders attests the simple

astronomical and calendrical skills of that time and makes a deep impression to this day. The setting, standing among gently rolling and now richly agricultural hillocks, has always been impressive, so that tradition gives it as the burial place of the mythical Corbredus Galdus (Tacitus' **Galgacus** – 'They made a desert and they call it peace'), who is also reputed to be buried at **Cairnholy**, a great Neolithic courtyard cairn and chambered tomb 10 miles east across Wigtown Bay.

TORMORE, Moray

Said to be the first distillery to be built in the Highlands in the 20th century, Tormore was designed by Sir Albert Richardson and opened in 1960. Together with the adjacent workers' houses, splendidly set amidst lawns, it has been described as 'the most beautiful industrial structure in the Highlands' (M McLaren). The claim is not without substance.

TORPICHEN, West Lothian

Torpichen Preceptory, five miles south of **Linlithgow**, was the only Scottish house of the Knights of St John of Jerusalem, otherwise known as the Knights Hospitaller, established here during the reign of **David I**. Their church – nave, aisle, transepts and central tower – was started c1200, complete by the mid-13th century and held the right of sanctuary. A stone in the churchyard, resembling a milestone with a cross carved on top, marks the centre of the privileged sanctuary ground attached to the preceptory, and a circle of similar stones stood around the edge of the estate, each a mile distant from the centre and some still standing. All the space within the circle formed by these 'extreme' or 'refuge' stones was as much a legal sanctuary as the church itself and offered protection against the law to every criminal or debtor who entered and remained within its precincts. The chancel and the nave, reputed to have been of great length and used as the parish church until replaced by the present church in 1757, have gone; the tower and the transept, substantially heightened in the 15th century, remain and were used after the **Reformation** as the courthouse of the Regality of Torpichen, granted c1560 to the last Preceptor, Sir James Sandilands, later raised to the peerage as Lord Torpichen. An exhibition tells the story of the Knights Hospitaller, not to be confused with the Knights Templar, a rival body 'unfrocked and put under ban' in 1312, their extensive property passing to the Knights of St John.

TORRIDON, Wester Ross

In keeping with the idea of land as a public amenity, and for administrative and promotional convenience, the Highlands are increasingly portrayed as a collection of individual wilderness areas. Several of these – **Glencoe**, **Kintail**, **Cairngorm** – are now designated as parks or reserves, each with its own recreational and scientific facilities. Amongst them the Torridon estate (**National Trust for Scotland**) and neighbouring Ben Eighe (Scottish Natural Heritage) were singled out by the mountain connoisseur W H Murray as exhibiting 'more beauty than any other district of Scotland including **Skye**'.

Situated between Lochs **Maree** and Torridon, the property includes the nine peaks of Ben Eighe itself, the seven peaks of the long Liathach ridge and, to the west and north, Ben Alligin and Ben Dearg. White quartzite caps some of the Liathach peaks and on Ben Eighe has yielded 'fossils of some of the earliest animals on earth'. The reddish Torridonian sandstone is everywhere eroded into corries, crags and pinnacles of sculptural quality.

The Torridon estate passed to the National Trust for Scotland in 1967 after being accepted by the Inland Revenue as part payment of duty on the 4th Earl of Lovelace's estate.

TOURISTS AND TOURISM

Holiday resorts and tourism became growth areas in 19th century Scotland. Seaside holidays led to the rise of popular resorts like **Portobello**, **Broughty Ferry**, **Dunoon** and **Rothesay**. Coincidentally Scotland as a country, with particular emphasis on the Highlands, was gaining favour as a holiday destination for visitors from England and overseas. The mostly well-to-do tourists from outside were drawn not by the attractions and limited facilities of the beach resorts, but by the vogue for spas (**Strathpeffer**, **Bridge of Allan**, **Moffat**), sporting activities and traditional culture and scenery. In the long term these earlier interests have proved to be the more durable, as the traditional seaside resorts, particularly those which grew because of their proximity to the large urban centres, went into decline during the second half of the 20th century.

Scotland's transformation into a tourist centre owed most to its portrayal as a land of romance and picturesque beauty. Although other authors, such as **James Macpherson**, were influential, this new view was largely due to the writings of **Sir Walter Scott**. He more than any other altered people's perceptions (not least the Scots' own) and thus shaped the image of both the country and the people. The 'Bonnie Scotland' image was further boosted when **Queen Victoria** and Prince Albert chose **Balmoral** (1848) for a holiday home. Balmoral was, of course, a sporting estate, and similar properties were purchased by wealthy incomers for the increasingly fashionable pursuits of **deer stalking**, **grouse shooting** and **fishing**. In the 20th century such blood sports have continued in vogue although their cost means a restricted number of participants.

The 1920s and 30s saw the arrival of car- and bus-borne tourists, a phenomenon which contributed to the decline of the long-stay holiday which was the staple source of income for resorts like Bridge of Allan and **Kingussie**. Health spas were out of fashion but the continued growth in popularity of **golf** proved beneficial to such meccas as **North Berwick** and **St Andrews**.

The 1930s, a time of economic depression and of stiff competition from climatically more favoured countries, also brought demands for the more effective promotion and marketing of Scotland's attractions. The creation in 1945 of the Scottish Tourist Board (STB), with **Tom Johnston** as the highly effective first Chairman, marked a new beginning in this respect. The post-war period saw the Tourist Board expand its services, providing accommodation lists, guide books and a variety of enterprising publications which met the needs of those who sought activity holidays or who had other specialised interests.

As initially the STB put a great deal of emphasis into enticing exiles and the descendants of emigrants back to Scotland, it agitated for the restoration of direct sailings from North America to the **Clyde**. While some transatlantic liners were routed to the Clyde, this service, which was crucial for the North American market, was not maintained. When jet aircraft replaced ocean liners, tourist interests similarly agitated for better and more competitive airline services. The case for and against **Prestwick** airport replaced Clyde sailings as a tourist industry *cause célèbre* but has since been silenced by the development of **Glasgow**'s International Airport.

In the immediate post-war years the traditional seaside resorts enjoyed a brief boom, although they faced increasing competition from the larger English resorts. But the rise in the standard of living in the 1950s and 60s greatly increased the number of cars and thus changed patterns of holiday-making. The Scottish working classes had become more mobile and, like middle-class holiday makers in pre-war days, often opted for touring holidays, utilising short-stay bed and breakfast accommodation. Alternatively, if staying for the traditional week or fortnight, they preferred self-catering accommodation in a flat or static caravan. The greatest threat to the prosperity of the older seaside resorts came with the boom in foreign travel which started in the 1960s. The masses abandoned Rothesay for Rimini and Portobello for Palma, where the sunshine was guaranteed.

Remote communities in the Highlands and elsewhere benefited most from the growth in motoring holidays. But here there was an environmental cost with the proliferation of unsightly caravan sites in sensitive areas. Some of the early **skiing** developments, particularly at **Cairngorm** and **Glenshee**, also aroused the ire of conservationists.

On the other hand the transformation of **Aviemore** into an all-year-round holiday resort has been one of the success stories of Scottish tourism. Local interests started the process in the early 1960s with the construction on Cairngorm of an access road and chair lift for skiers. Money from local and central government and business sources was poured into skiing developments at Aviemore and elsewhere. The most recent ski resort at Aonach Mor near **Fort William** was opened in 1989, though the explosion in popularity of this sport threatens – when the weather permits – to overwhelm the facilities.

Joining with the STB in promoting Scotland as a tourist area was the Highlands and Islands Development Board (later Highlands and Islands Enterprise), formed in 1965, which helped to finance new facilities, including the Aviemore Centre, and also had the necessary funds to advertise the scenic and other attractions of the Highlands. In 1969 the STB was restructured and for the first time given adequate funds for research and publicity and to help finance new hotels and projects such as heritage centres (eg **New Lanark**). In many projects there has been close collaboration with local tourist boards and other government agencies such as HIE, Scottish Natural Heritage and the **Forestry Commission**.

Great emphasis has also been given to the promotion of business and urban tourism. The success since 1947 of its International **Festival** has consolidated **Edinburgh**'s position as second only to London in the British tourist league. More recently Glasgow has made spectacular progress, opening the very popular **Burrell** Art Gallery in 1983 and running a highly successful Garden Festival in 1988. Astute marketing and politicking also brought Glasgow the title of European City of Culture in 1990 and of Architecture and Design in 1999. The further development of the cities as tourist centres with an international appeal provides some compensation for the decline of the older seaside resorts and the loss of their traditional markets.

TOWIE BARCLAY CASTLE, Nr Turriff, Aberdeenshire

Privately owned and restored in the 1960s, Towie Barclay consists of a squat two-storey keep with just sufficient of an easterly appendage to merit designation as L-plan. Once taller (two storeys were removed in

Hall of Towie Barclay Castle as drawn by R W Billings c1840 (RWB)

1792), it is so again thanks to a 'penthouse' with pitched roof and gables which rises phoenix-like from the surrounding parapets of the old keep. This latter dates from the 16th century and has exceptionally fine vaulting in the basement, the great hall and the adjoining oratory. From its erstwhile owners, the Barclays of Towie, was descended the Prince Barclay de Toille (Tolley) who commanded the Russian forces against Napoleon and duly featured in Tolstoy's *War and Peace*.

TRADE UNIONISM IN SCOTLAND

Embryonic workers' organisations existed in Scotland from the late 17th century, the most common form of combination being the journeymen's societies which, though constituted largely for friendly society purposes, could easily be converted to provide the necessary organisation in a trade dispute. By the second half of the 18th century permanent organisations of this type were common among tailors, shoemakers, masons and others in all the main cities. Disputes were most commonly the consequence of rising prices.

The coming of the Industrial Revolution intensified conflict between masters and men as social relationships were transformed. The most notable strike and challenge to the authorities was by the **Calton Weavers** of **Glasgow** in 1787 when troops killed six of the 7000 weavers (and their families) out on strike. Ruthless suppression by the authorities became the pattern of the next three decades but, despite the legal restrictions, trade union activity remained high, though sporadic. In 1812 there was a major weavers' strike in Glasgow and the west of Scotland which lasted three months before the union leadership was seized and jailed.

There followed a downturn in activity but a revival came with the emergence of the reform movement, the best-organised being the **cotton** spinners and the miners. A three-month strike and conviction of the leaders of the Glasgow Cotton Spinners' Union was followed by massive protests which ended with their release in 1840. This strike and the depression of 1838–42 dealt a serious blow to Scottish trade unionism.

Local issues and organisations tended to prevail. Although willing to collaborate with management, unions could still be well organised and could successfully engage in action. In the 1860s, for example, demands for the 9-hour day were advanced by building workers, engineers and boilermakers. The 'New Model' unionism made headway amongst skilled workers and the 1850s and 60s saw also the foundation of trades councils consisting of representatives of different unions in the main Scottish urban areas.

As late as 1892 there were only 147,000 trade unionists in Scotland. However both the 'new unionism' and later the 'labour unrest' of 1910–14 brought, in parallel with developments south of the border, an increase in the number of semi-skilled, unskilled and women trade unionists. The Scottish Trades Union Council, which still plays a key role in events, was founded in 1897, at the instigations of the Trades Councils.

Much of the militant reputation of trade unionism in Scotland stems from the events of '**Red Clydeside**' and from the '**Bloody Friday**' riot of 1919 in **George Square**, **Glasgow**. The General Strike of 1926 was solid in Scotland with areas like **Fife** displaying the greatest degree of militancy and organisation.

After World War II the long-term economic boom led to the growth of trade unionism in terms of both numbers and strength. A significant feature was the development of deep-rooted shop stewards' organisations across and within workplaces and industries. The movement was put to the test in the celebrated battle against the closure of the **Upper Clyde Shipbuilders** in 1971 and in the successful miners' strikes of 1972 and 1974.

Scotland has experienced the decline of much of its traditional industrial base in the quarter-century since the mid-seventies. Although the miners (1984–5) and

Caterpillar workers (1987) ultimately lost their battles to prevent the destruction of their jobs and communities, it could be a grave mistake to suppose that the current reversals in Scottish trade unionism are a permanent feature. Revival has always followed retreat as the economy restructures and as new layers of workers become amenable to organisation and activity.

TRAMS AND TRAMWAYS

Scotland's first passenger tram service opened in **Edinburgh** in 1871, the precursor of over 30 built in and between Scottish towns and cities before World War I. The earliest were horse-drawn, but in August 1877 the Vale of **Clyde** Tramway Co inaugurated the UK's first urban steam tram service on its **Glasgow** to **Govan** route, just two days before steam trams began to run in **Dundee**. The Edinburgh & Northern Tramway Co was another innovator, introducing cable-drawn trams in 1888; Edinburgh's cable-car system was the most complex and one of the largest in the world until its electrification in 1923.

The first electric tramway in Scotland was a short private route serving Carstairs House in **Lanarkshire**. It was opened in 1886, two years after an experimental electric tram ran on trials to Haymarket Station in Edinburgh. Glasgow Corporation was the first operator in Scotland to introduce an electric tram service, on its Springburn route in 1898, and completed the electrification of the city's system in 1901. Most of the operators who had not already followed Glasgow's lead began the process of electrification soon afterwards.

The years 1900–14 were the heyday of the tram, and communities from **Rothesay** to Cruden Bay (the hotel tramway in Cruden Bay was the northernmost tramway in the UK) made full use of the cheap and reliable services provided. By 1914 Scottish tramways were carrying over 500 million passengers per year. Competition from trolley and motor buses grew, however, along with complaints that the trams aggravated traffic congestion in urban centres. Most of Scotland's tramways were closed between 1919–39. Edinburgh, Dundee and **Aberdeen** Corporations, three of the biggest operators, dug up their tramlines during the 1950s. Glasgow, which had since the 19th century possessed the most extensive tramway system in the UK

Glasgow's first electric tramcar with its driver, conductor and guard, 1898 (ML)

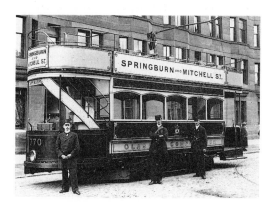

outside London, was the last to banish the 'shooglies' from the city's streets, in 1962.

TRANENT, East Lothian

The mining town of Tranent south of **Prestonpans** was the scene of the worst of several riots that followed the implementation of the Militia Act of 1797 by which **Militia** regiments were raised to supplement the regular army. A quota of recruits was set for each county; volunteers were allowed to fill the ranks and any gaps remaining would be filled by ballot. Substitutes were permitted, a bounty would be paid, and service would be confined to the British Isles. Mishandling of the balloting by the authorities however led to misunderstandings; a group of Tranent miners resisted and then clashed with the troops sent to keep order. In the ensuing riot 11 men were shot dead by the military and many more were wounded in what became known as 'the massacre of Tranent'.

TRANTER, Nigel Godwin (1909–2000)
Writer

Born in **Glasgow**, the son of a minister in the Catholic Apostolic Church, Tranter was educated at **George Heriot's School**, **Edinburgh**. He trained as an accountant but wrote full-time from 1935 – bar war service in the Royal Artillery 1939–45. Influenced by **John Buchan**, he completed an astonishing 130 books, including historical fiction, westerns and thrillers. Although popular in content, his historical works, notably the **Robert Bruce** trilogy (1969–71) and *The Wallace* (1975), were impeccably accurate in their research. He also wrote on topography and his 5-volume *The Fortified House in Scotland* remains an outstanding contribution to castle conservation. He embraced national causes – the Scottish **Covenant**, the **Forth Road Bridge**, the return of the **Stone of Destiny** and the **Scottish Parliament**. Practising *mens sana in corpore sano*, he wrote while he walked. His daily six-hour, 10–12 mile constitutional on the **Forth** near his home at **Aberlady** made him a kenspeckle figure haunting the shoreline. Superstitiously, he never finished the final page of one book until ready to begin the first of the next.

TRAPRAIN LAW, East Lothian

Until the early years of the 20th century Traprain Law just to the south of **East Linton** was merely a conspicuous landmark looking like a 'harpooned whale' in the **East Lothian** countryside which was known, from its old Celtic name of Dunpender, to have been the site of a prehistoric hill fort. Excavations on the site of the fort in 1919 revealed it as something much more when one of the workers brought up a silver bowl on the end of his pick. Further, more careful, excavation uncovered a small pit containing over 100 pieces of **Roman** silver with a total weight of over 54lbs (24kg). They included wine jugs, goblets, bowls and spoons, objects with Christian iconography and depictions of Bible stories, fragments of mirrors and ointment jars, military buckles and four silver coins. Very few of the objects were whole, but some have been reconstructed from the pieces into which they had been cut, possibly preparatory to melting down. The dates on the coins indicate that the treasure, now in the **Royal Museum** in **Edin-**

Roman silver and silver-gilt vessels of c AD 400 from Traprain Law (© the Trustees of the National Museums of Scotland 1994)

burgh, was buried about AD 410–25. Archaeologists are undecided whether it was the loot of a robber band or a 'deposit account' intended for use as a bribe or as payment for military or diplomatic services. This remarkable treasure, together with other less dramatic archaeological discoveries on Traprain Law, indicates that the site was occupied for more than 1000 years from the later Bronze Age to at least the end of the Roman era. The turf ramparts enclosed an area of more than 40 acres (16ha), making the fort the largest, with Eildon Hill, in south-east Scotland. At the time the hoard was buried it was a stronghold or even the capital of the native tribe known to the Romans as the Votadini.

TRAQUAIR, Innerleithen, Peeblesshire

'Here,' said Daniel Defoe as he passed through Tweeddale in the 1720s, 'are two Monuments, all Scotland not affording the like, of the Vanity of Worldly Glory.' One was the **Earl of Morton**'s unfinished Drochil Castle near **Lyne**. The other was 'the Palace of Traquair'. That must be one of the few disparaging remarks ever made about what is surely the most delightful, and certainly one of the oldest inhabited of Scotland's great houses.

In the 12th century the lands of Traquair were part of a royal hunting forest; **David I**, **Malcolm IV**, **William the Lion**, **Alexander II** and **Alexander III** all dated charters from the tall tower that constituted the hunting lodge, and Traquair was visited by Edward I in 1304, Edward II in 1310 and later also by **Queen Mary**, **Darnley** and the baby soon to be **James VI** in 1566. In the 15th century it was gifted by **James III** to his half-brother the Earl of Buchan who in turn passed it to his illegitimate son James Stuart; it is still in (Maxwell-) Stuart ownership. The original tower house forms the north-east corner of the present château-style mansion, most of which was added by Sir John Stuart, created Earl of Traquair in 1633 and Lord High Treasurer of Scotland under **Charles I**. One of his 'improvements' involved diverting the river **Tweed** which ran 'so conveniently near that the laird could fish for salmon

Traquair House from the south-west as drawn by MacGibbon and Ross (MR)

from his bedroom window – and so inconveniently near that his cellar was often flooded' (T Lang) to a new course about 400m away. Even Defoe had to admit that 'the House is noble, the design great, and well finish'd'. But no sooner was it 'finish'd' than the unfortunate 1st Earl, 'sunk by the Adversity of the Times', was evicted by his enemies and died in abject poverty in **Edinburgh**, just a year before the Restoration of **Charles II** would have restored his fortunes and reputation. His son the 2nd Earl added the wings and the formal courtyard (1695–1705), and the house has remained little changed since. At the end of the tree-lined avenue in front of the house are the famous 'steekit yetts' (stuck gates). In **Walter Scott**'s version of the story they were closed after **Prince Charles Edward** passed through in 1745, never to be opened until a **Stewart** monarch should once again sit on the throne. Another version has the 7th Earl closing them on the death of his wife in 1796, insisting they should not be opened until another countess sought entry; there never was another countess, the Earldom dying out (1861) with his son the 8th Earl, who never married. Either way, the gates are still shut.

TRAQUAIR, Phoebe Anna (1852–1936)
Artist
Born in Dublin, Phoebe Anna Moss moved to **Edinburgh** in 1873 on her marriage to Ramsay Traquair, Keeper of the Natural History Department of the Edinburgh Museum of Science and Art. A remarkable artist whose vast and varied output covered such fields as jewellery enamelling and book illuminating and binding, her first loves were embroidery and mural painting. The magnificent murals in the former Catholic and Apostolic Church in Edinburgh's East London Street took her seven years (1893–1900) to complete, while those in **St Mary's Cathedral** Song School and **St Giles'**

Thistle Chapel (also Edinburgh) moved a contemporary critic to 'catch her breath at surroundings so rich; scintillating and glowing like a jewelled crown'. Feted during her lifetime, Phoebe Traquair was the first woman member of the **Royal Scottish Academy** (1920) and a driving force in the Arts and Crafts revival of the time. The sentimental religiosity of much of her work, clearly demonstrating her desire 'to uplift the spirits' of those who viewed it, caused her to fall sadly out of fashion for many years, but she is now attracting renewed interest.

Self portrait by Phoebe Anna Traquair, 1911 (SNPG)

TRONDRA, Shetland
The island of Trondra provides shelter for the harbour at **Scalloway** on the west coast of **Shetland**. The island suffered from depopulation until in 1970 it was linked to the **Mainland** by a bridge. The population now stands at over 100.

TROON, Ayrshire
The natural harbour formed by the promontory that curves into the Firth of **Clyde** at Troon (*trwyn* or 'trone'

from the Cymric meaning 'nose') was developed c1808 by William Henry Bentinck, 4th Duke of Portland, as a port from which to ship **coal** mainly to Ireland. The Duke then laid out the town of Troon around his harbour. Plans to construct a **canal** for transporting the coal the 9 miles from the **Kilmarnock** pits had fallen through, but in 1812 the Kilmarnock and Troon **Railway** was opened for that purpose; by 1840 165,850 tons of coal were passing through the port each year, the Ailsa **Shipbuilding** Company was providing alternative employment for the growing population, while 'not a few of the inhabitants [were drawing] an entire or partial maintenance from letting lodgings to families of sea-bathers' enjoying the bracing air on Troon's long sandy beaches. For the next century Troon led a successful double life as both industrial centre and holiday town, the balance gradually shifting towards the latter with the development of the town's five **golf courses**, of which three are public. More **golf** is probably now played in Troon than in any other town in Scotland. Architecturally unremarkable, Troon nevertheless has some interesting churches, including the bulky sandstone Old Parish Church (Hippolyte Blanc, 1894) and the far more pleasing Our Lady of the Assumption (**Reginald Fairlie**, 1911), as well as the classical copper-domed Marr's College built in the 1920s with a bequest from Troon-born industrialist Charles Kerr Marr.

TROSSACHS, The, Perthshire

Although the term is now loosely used to designate all the scenic country between **Callander** and **Loch Lomond**, The Trossachs is properly only the short defile of about a mile between Lochs Achray and **Katrine**, 10 miles due west of Callander. Flanked by Ben An (1520ft/463m) to the north and Ben Venue (2386ft/727m) to the south, the defile is narrow and choked with rocks and hillocks overgrown with rowan, oak and hazel, the aspect being one 'of roughness and wildness, of tangled inextricable boskiness totally unexampled, it is supposed, in the world' (Fullarton's *Gazetteer*). Hence 'The Trossachs', ie 'The Bristled Country'. In **Scott**'s The *Lady of the Lake* Fitz-James here lost his horse; the lake was of course Loch Katrine, since 1859 the source of much of **Glasgow**'s water, and the lady was Ellen Douglas after whom an island at the east end of the loch is named. The area also features in Scott's *Rob Roy*, this being the **MacGregor** country. **Rob Roy MacGregor** was born in Glengyle, at the west end of the loch, and Bealach na Bo (Cattle Pass) is supposed to have been much used by MacGregors when returning home with other people's stock.

TRUSTEES' ACADEMY

The Trustees' Academy was the most influental art school in Scotland in the 19th century and largely responsible for the remarkable flowering of Scottish artistic talent in the second half of the century. The cumbrously titled 'Board of Trustees for the Encouragement of Manufactures for Scotland' established, in 1760, a Drawing Academy as part of their policy of improving the quality of design in the manufacturing industries. By the turn of the century the curriculum had broadened to include the fine arts, and by 1822 the Academy was considered of sufficient importance

to be offered rooms (albeit attic rooms) in the recently built Royal Institution building in **Edinburgh**. These new premises enabled the Academy to expand its collection of plaster casts from the antique which were used as the main basis for teaching and which had threatened to engulf the Academy's old rooms in Picardy Place. Furthermore, for the first time the facility for drawing from the live model was provided. The absence of this provision had formerly forced such talented artists as **David Wilkie** to depart for London to complete his training.

Nearly all aspiring Scottish artists of note endeavoured to spend some time at the Academy, where they were taught by some of the most respected of their seniors. **Alexander Runciman** had taught there in the early days and by the time of the Academy's removal it was being run by the respected watercolourist Andrew Wilson, soon after replaced by the history painter **Sir William Allan**. During the 1840s the influence of the Academy partially deteriorated (not helped by some extraordinary infighting with their fellow tenants, the **Royal Scottish Academy**, who wished to set up their own school), but in 1852 an old Academy pupil, **Robert Scott Lauder**, was appointed Director and the Academy entered its finest period. Lauder, who had been working in London for a number of years, was a strict disciplinarian, but also introduced some radical innovations. He encouraged pupils to begin **painting** as early as possible (rather than endless drawing) and encouraged discussion and experimentation with colours and pigments, subject of much theorising at the time. His pupils included **McTaggart**, **Chalmers**, MacWhirter, **Orchardson**, **Graham** and Pettie, who never forgot the influence of Lauder and were to go on to become the most successful and influential artists of their generation. In 1858, with the completion of the **National Gallery of Scotland**, the government gave in, obliged the Trustees to run the National Gallery and forced them to hand over the running of life classes to the RSA. Lauder was dismayed. Left only with the antique and design classes, the Trustees' Academy was effectively downgraded to its old role as a School of Drawing and Design. Lauder left after only three years, his unhappiness compounded by seeing the new RSA schools being run along English lines. Robbed of its inspirational role the Trustees' Academy gradually faded, disappearing altogether in the late 1870s.

TULLIALLAN CASTLE, Kincardine on Forth, Fife

Although well equipped for defence with a drawbridge and portcullis, Tulliallan was not designed as a castle but as that 'rare building type, the Scottish hall-house'. Normally in a castle the ground floor would be reserved for storage while the main entrance would be by stairs to the first floor. Here entrance and living quarters (with some fine vaulting) are on the ground floor. The vaulting resembles that in **Glasgow Cathedral** with which Tulliallan is linked in that it was once owned by the **Blackadder** family. Almost nothing else is known of its history or occupants, making any architectural appreciation difficult. **MacGibbon and Ross** thought it 15th century, Walker and Ritchie 13th–14th centuries; the former also detected similarities with **Rait** and **Morton**

Tullibardine Chapel near Auchterarder (HS)

castles. The first floor may have been one vast hall but has clearly been altered at some time.

TULLIBARDINE CHAPEL, Nr Auchterarder, Perthshire

Three miles of minor road west of **Auchterarder**, Tullibardine Chapel stands alone amidst fields, a private collegiate chapel preserved intact since before the **Reformation**. Its cruciform plan includes a small tower and traceried windows. The openwork timber roof and heraldic carving are notable. It was founded by Sir David Murray in 1445. Tullibardine had been held by the **Murray** family from 1320 but marriage to a daughter of the Earl of Atholl in 1629 resulted in the Murrays being created **Earls of Atholl** and their heirs using the Tullibardine title. It is recorded that the length and breadth of **James IV**'s battleship the *Great Michael* was 'planted in hawthorn at Tullibardine by the wright that helped make her'.

TULLIBOLE CASTLE, Kinross-shire

A mile east of Crook of Devon [see **Glen Devon**], Tullibole is described as 'a good example of a laird's house of the early 17th century, built on the "palace" plan' (RCAHMS). It is rectangular in ground plan with a small wing that contains the main entrance and stairwell, while the profile is vertical with the usual corner turrets plus an unusual bartizan above the entrance. Yet internally the arrangements are noticeably more convenient than those of a traditional tower house, with ample stairs and no vaulting. It was built by John Halliday, the son of an **Edinburgh** advocate, whose initials appear on the coat of arms above the doorway along with the date 2 April 1608. Exactly a century later the property passed to the Moncrieff family and is still in use.

TUMMEL BRIDGE, Perthshire

Meteorologically notorious for its minimum temperatures, Tummel Bridge owes its existence first to **Wade** who built (1733) its now superseded bridge, then to the North of Scotland **Hydro-Electric** Board whose various lochs, dams and power stations stretch from **Rannoch** to **Pitlochry**, and finally to the **Forestry Commission** whose Tummel Forest Park is equally extensive. The 'village' is mostly a recent creation comprising timbered chalets, caravans, lawson cypress, and all the facilities deemed necessary for a large holiday development. Scenic splendour is provided by **Schiehallion** to the south, Loch Rannoch to the west and Loch Tummel to the east. All are liberally signposted with 'forest walks', 'visitor centres' and 'viewpoints'. ('Queen's View', for instance, where **Victoria** inspected the vista, is on the road to Pitlochry.)

TURNBERRY, Ayrshire

Little now remains of the ancient fortress of Turnberry Castle on the rocky promontory jutting into the sea between **Culzean** and **Girvan**, but its name has gone down in history as the probable birthplace in 1274 of **Robert I**. It was to this castle that his father **Robert de Bruce** (1242–1304), later Earl of Carrick, was taken by the widowed Marjorie, Countess of Carrick in c1271 and where they were secretly married. The castle was the meeting place of the supporters of the Bruce's claim to the throne of Scotland in 1286 and in 1306 it was garrisoned by the English under Earl Percy before he and his troops were attacked and routed by Robert I in 1307. 'It received such damage in the storming as to be virtually destroyed; and it does not appear to have ever afterwards been inhabited' (Fullarton's *Gazetteer*). A lighthouse was built on the promontory in 1873.

Turnberry's other, and more recent, claim to fame is

that of having been the first purpose-built **golf** resort in Scotland with two **golf courses** among the sand dunes by the shore. The Turnberry club was founded in 1902, the enormous first-class hotel was constructed by the **Glasgow** & South Western **Railway** in 1904 and the complex included railway connections south to **Girvan** and north to **Ayr** and Glasgow. The golf links were used as a military airfield during both world wars but later carefully reconstructed to championship standard.

TURNBULL, Rev George (fl.1720)

'An able man, long forgotten yet somewhat memorable,' George Turnbull laboured as Regent Professor of **Marischal College Aberdeen** during the 1720s. For £40 pa 'he taught the whole range of human knowledge which was requisite for a university curriculum'. Amongst his pupils was **Thomas Reid** whose 'common sense **philosophy**' owed not a little to Turnbull's insistence on common sense in philosophy. Grown tired of this drudgery, Turnbull eventually moved to England and entered the Anglican Church. He also 'laboriously, voluminously and almost annually' churned out books on philosophy and art 'which the world received with provoking indifference'. Yet fame, of a sort, he was not to be denied. H G Graham, who records his story so affectingly, invites the reader to study carefully a Hogarth painting called *Beer Street*. Here 'we see a porter drinking copiously from a mug to refresh his exhausted frame after depositing on the ground a heavy load of five ponderous folios intended for the trunkmaker; and on the back of one of them we read the title, *Turnbull on Ancient Painting*'. The trunkmaker was where unsaleable books were sent for recycling as trunk linings. 'Such was not the sort of immortality poor Turnbull expected.'

TURNER, Sir James (1615–c1686) Soldier

The son of the minister of **Borthwick** and **Dalkeith**, Turner served in a Scottish contingent under Gustavus Adolphus during the Thirty Years' War but 'swallowed without chewing in Germanie a very dangerous maxim, that so [long] as we serve our master honestlie, it is noe matter what master we serve'. While others juggled their religious scruples with their monarchist sympathies, Turner turned coat with an indifference that scandalised his age; it is thought that he may have provided the model for **Sir Walter Scott**'s 'proud, passionate, hasty and furious' Dugald Dalgetty in *The Legend of Montrose*. Turner fought for and against the **Covenanting** army in the 1640s and for the Royalists in 1650–1, after which he went into exile with **Charles II**. The Restoration brought a knighthood and command of operations against the Covenanters in south-west Scotland, to whom he became known as 'Bloody Bite-the-Sheep'. His 1666 oppressions precipitated the **Pentland Rising** during which he was surprised and captured at **Dumfries**. He escaped at **Rullion Green** but during the conciliatory lull ('The Blink') associated with the **Indulgences** he was arraigned for his conduct and exactions and deprived of his commission. He wrote *Pallas Armata*, a collection of military essays, and exculpatory memoirs.

TURRA COO, The

The normally placid **Aberdeenshire** town of **Turriff** was stirred into a riotous frenzy in 1913 by a white milk cow. The cause of the trouble was the National Insurance Act of 1911, introduced by Lloyd George when Chancellor of the Exchequer. Although the legislation marked a major advance in social welfare, it was widely disliked, especially in rural areas, where ill-health and unemployment were not significant problems. This was particularly the case in the north-east, and attention focused on Robert Paterson, an innovative farmer at Lendrum near Turriff. He organised a mass meeting for farmers and farmworkers (both categories being obliged to contribute to the scheme) and set an example by refusing to pay National Insurance stamps for his men. He was duly charged with non-payment, convicted and fined £15 (20 offences at 15 shillings each). Paterson paid the fine, but refused to pay the arrears which were due – a much smaller amount – objecting to several matters of procedure. The Scottish Insurance Commissions responded by ordering the poinding (legal seizure) and sale of his property.

The Sheriff Officer at Turriff went to Lendrum to poind a cow, choosing not one of the valuable beasts from the dairy herd, but the horned white milk cow which served the Paterson household. She was led to Turriff on foot, bearing slogans painted on her hide by Robert Paterson, and presented for sale in the Market Square, as neither of the town's marts would handle the proceedings. The Square was filled with a crowd some 1500 strong, the largest assembly the town had ever witnessed, and when the cow appeared at the appointed hour (noon on Tuesday 9 December 1913) three cheers were called for the 'Fite Coo'. The beast, already unsettled by the noise of the crowd and the barking of dogs, was in great discomfort as efforts had been made to clean off the painted slogans using turpentine. Someone cut the rope and the cow made off, eventually getting back to Lendrum. The crowd meantime turned their attention on the auctioneer, who had been drafted in from **MacDuff**. Fireworks were set off and various missiles were thrown, including sootbags, eggs and, in the dialect of the district, 'an antrin cloddie and a kail runt or twa'. This minor riot caused the auctioneer to flee the scene, and the sale was abandoned.

A few days later the cow was taken by the authorities to **Aberdeen** and sold privately for £7 (more than enough to cover Paterson's arrears). Eight men were subsequently tried for public order offences, including Robert Paterson; the verdict was 'not proven', and they were regarded locally as heroes. A number of farmers clubbed together and bought back the cow, the animal returning to Turriff to a tumultuous welcome; her neck and horns were garlanded, a band heralded her arrival in the Square by playing 'See, the Conquering Hero Comes!' and once more she bore appropriate slogans, including 'Free! Divn't ye wish that ye were me!' Poems were written, a considerable quantity of souvenirs were manufactured, and in 1971 a cairn was erected at Lendrum in commemoration of the Turra Coo.

TURRIFF, Aberdeenshire

The red sandstone burgh (since 1511) of Turriff stands above the junction of the Idoch with the river **Deveron** in rich farming country south of **Banff**. **Agriculture** remains its mainstay if not its currency [see **Turra Coo**].

It is thought to have originally been a **Pictish** settlement where a St Congan (or Cowan) established the first church well ahead of **Malcolm III 'Canmore's** supposed **Celtic** foundation. Ruins of a pre-**Reformation** church on the Celtic site include the partly roofed choir, a belfry with a bell dated 1577 and numerous memorials of the Hay, Forbes and Barclay of Towie families. The town's lay patrons included the **Comyn Earls of Buchan** and later the Hay **Earls of Errol**. Its main claim to a place in the history books is as the site of the first engagement in the Bishops' Wars [see **Charles I**] (and so of the Civil War). In February 1639 the **Gordon Earl of Huntly**, a Royalist of **episcopalian** sentiments, failed to dislodge **James Graham, Marquis of Montrose** (commanding a force of **Covenanters**) in the Raid of Turriff; but in May of the same year the Royalist **Gordons** tried again and this time routed the Covenanters (now under a Forbes) in the 'Trot of Turriff'. The castles of **Delgatty**, **Towie Barclay** and **Craigston** are all nearby.

TWEED, River
Fourth longest of Scotland's rivers (after the **Tay**, the **Spey** and the **Clyde**), the Tweed moves up to second place on the list (behind only the Tay) if measured by the size of its catchment area (the Tweed drains about 1870 square miles to the Tay's 2400), but lays some claim to first place as the most beautiful. Its source at Tweed's Well near the **Peeblesshire/Lanarkshire** border lies only a few miles from the source of both the Annan which drains south into the Solway Firth and of the Clyde which eventually drains westward through **Glasgow**. For their first dozen or so miles Tweed and Clyde run north and more or less parallel until, near **Biggar**, the Clyde comes within seven miles of a tributary of the Tweed, a circumstance that at one time suggested a scheme (never in fact attempted) in which the waters of the Clyde would be diverted eastwards to increase the navigable length of the Tweed from its mouth at **Berwick**. This first stretch of the Tweed is also the steepest and by the time it reaches its first town, **Peebles**, it has already descended 1000 of its total 1500ft fall. From Peebles onwards its gentle meandering flow has rendered it largely unsuitable as a source of power for industry; stately homes (**Traquair, Abbotsford, Floors Castle**) outnumber factories along its banks, and its towns (Peebles, **Melrose**, **Kelso**) are prosperous market towns rather than manufacturing centres. Although tweed cloth is produced in some of the Tweed towns, the name does not derive from the river, but was a misreading in London of the Scots word 'tweel' or 'twill'.

The slow current, with deep pools interspersed with shallow banks of gravel and pebbles, has kept the Tweed free from river traffic and, according to Blaeu's *Atlas Scotiae* (1654), at that time free from bridges the entire 70 miles from Berwick to Peebles. This being border country, bridges were only an invitation to invaders – but this being a shallow river, fords served equally well as crossing places [see **Ladykirk**]. The same pools and shallows have also ensured the Tweed's celebrity as a salmon-**fishing** river. Running as it does through Peeblesshire, **Selkirkshire** and **Roxburghshire**, the Tweed is only a true border river for some 12 miles of its

95-mile length, dividing Scotland from England between a point just west of **Coldstream** to another just east of Paxton, and passing into England for the last two miles before reaching its mouth at Berwick.

TWEEDSMUIR, Peeblesshire
On the banks of the **Tweed** not many miles north of the river's source at Tweed's Well near the **Devil's Beef Tub**, the village of Tweedsmuir found fame when **John Buchan** took the title Lord Tweedsmuir, although the inevitable John Buchan Centre is in fact at **Broughton**. Nearby Talla Loch was constructed by the damming of the 'cold wild mountain stream' of Talla Water in 1905 to form a reservoir supplying **Edinburgh**. In the centre of Tweedsmuir village the Romanesque church was built in 1874–5 on the site of an earlier church of 1648, and the churchyard has a memorial stone to 'John Hunter, martyr, who was cruelly murdered at Corehead by Col. James Douglas and his party for his adherence to the word of God and Scotland's Covenanted work of Reformation, 1685.'

TYNDRUM, Perthshire
With two **railway** stations (Tyndrum Upper and Lower) and two more within five miles (**Crianlarich** and **Bridge of Orchy**), Tyndrum determinedly caters for the motorist. The name means 'the house on the ridge' (ie the east-west watershed), and at 900ft (274m) in bleak surroundings the village is periodically threatened with an **Aviemore**-style development. In 1306 Dail Righ (**Dalry**) near the hotel was the site of a battle in which **Robert I** was defeated by John of Lorne, son of Alexander MacDougall of Argyll, who thereby acquired the brooch of **Lorne**. Lead workings west of the village were spasmodically mined in the 18th and 19th centuries; now, when the price rises high enough to make it worthwhile, gold is laboriously extracted from shale at Cononish. Cononish Water, draining the slopes of Ben Lui, is the uppermost reach of the **Tay**; on its south bank, beside the **Oban** line, a remnant of **Caledonian forest** survives amidst the serried ranks of sitka spruce favoured by the **Forestry Commission**.

TYNNINGHAME, East Lothian
Tynninghame House, a 'plain old Scottish country house' of the 17th century, was transformed by **William Burn** for the Earl of **Haddington** in 1829 into a handsome Scottish Baronial mansion with new façades of local red sandstone and a plethora of turrets and pepperpots; an appropriate centrepiece for the famed Binning Wood. Planted by Thomas, 6th Earl of Haddington, from 1707, this remarkable forest initially covered 300 acres (121ha) and later many more with the trees arranged in avenues diverging from three centres and 'affording extensive and beautiful walks and rides'. Maintained by successive earls, the forest was sacrificed during World War II for its timber, but has since been replanted. The gardens at Tynninghame were even more famous, particularly for the holly hedges which 'aggregately extend to about 9000ft [2700m], with a breadth of 10 or 11ft [3m] at the base and a height of from 15 to 20ft [5–6m]; they are arranged in double rows flanking spacious walks and are clipped twice a year' (Fullarton's *Gazetteer*). In the grounds of

Tynninghame House are the charming but skeletal remains of the 12th century church dedicated to St Baldred, who lived for some time in a cave on the **Bass Rock** in the early 7th century.

TYTLER, James (1745–1804) Chemist, Journalist, etc

Born at Fern in **Angus**, James Tytler was a much underrated polymath who, after service as a whale-boat surgeon, spent most of his life in **Edinburgh** as a chemist and journalist, living often in great poverty after an imprudently early marriage.

Known as 'Balloon Tytler', he was the first man in Great Britain to use a hot-air balloon to rise from the earth's surface, reaching a height of 350ft (107m) on 27 August 1784. He achieved this pioneering flight from the Comely Green Garden in Edinburgh's Abbeyhill district, landing without mishap at **Restalrig** village nearby.

Probably his greatest contribution to posterity, however, was his editorship of the second edition of the *Encyclopaedia Britannica*, which he undertook over the years 1776–84 for a mere 16/- (80p) a week. During this time he expanded the work from 3 to 10 volumes, his biographer Sir James Fergusson remarking (in *Balloon Tytler*, 1972) 'The quality of information digested in the *Encyclopaedia* is astonishing considering that it was almost all sought out, composed or abridged by a single man, and all of it at some stage written out in his own clear hand.' Tytler's contribution, amounting to nearly 9000 double-columned pages, was not credited in the *Encyclopaedia* itself.

After publishing a pamphlet the authorities considered seditious, Tytler fled to the USA, dying at Salem, Massachusetts in the same poverty which had characterised his unusual life.

TYTLER, Patrick Fraser (1791–1849) Historian

With William Tytler, author of a 1759 defence of **Queen Mary**, as his grandfather and with Alexander Fraser Tytler, Professor of Universal History at **Edinburgh**, as his father, it was not incredible that Patrick Fraser Tytler should evince an interest in the past. Born

Patrick Fraser Tytler, by Sir John Watson Gordon (SNPG)

in Edinburgh, he attended the High School and the **University** where he read **law**. He then made the 'grand tour', began writing for **Blackwood's**, and together with **Sir Walter Scott** and Thomas Thomson, a clerk of records, started the Bannatyne Club (1823); it was named after George Bannatyne of the **Bannatyne Manuscripts** and was dedicated to publishing historical and literary texts; Tytler edited **General Hugh Mackay**'s *Memoirs* for the club. He also produced lives of **James Crichton** and **Sir Thomas Craig** before embarking, with Scott's encouragement, on his major work, a 9-vol *History of Scotland* (1828–43). It stops at 1603 but, based on the records and other primary sources, is still valuable. During its preparation he also produced *Lives of the Scottish Worthies* in three volumes and other, mainly biographical, works. He died in England but is buried in Edinburgh's **Greyfriars' Churchyard**.

U

UAMH, Loch nan, Arisaig, Inverness-shire
Were its pronunciation more obvious to English
speakers ('naan Ooa', 'of the cave') this loch south-east
of **Arisaig** would surely have entered everyday parlance.
For here on 25 July 1745 **Prince Charles Edward
Stewart**, accompanied by the **Seven Men of Moidart**,
disembarked from the French vessel *Du Teillay* to launch
the '45 **Jacobite Rising**, and here again on 19 September 1746 the chased and chastened Prince re-
embarked at the end of that tragic affair, this time on
the peculiarly ill-named l'*Heureux*. The spot is marked
with a cairn. On the first occasion he spent a week at
Glen Borrodale house, a guest of Angus MacDonald,
before moving on to **Moidart** and **Glenfinnan**. In April
1746 he returned there as a fugitive after **Culloden**,
and from Loch nan Uamh sailed to **Scalpay** in East Loch
Tarbert (**Harris**). Returning yet again, now in disguise,
in July 1746, he found the house burnt down and
search parties scouring the neighbourhood. For a time
he was hidden in a cave and then smuggled inland to
Loch Quoich before his final rendezvous with l'*Heureux*.

UDAL LAW
The Norwegian system of land tenure, standard in **Orkney** and **Shetland**, permitted any settler to enclose what
land he chose to cultivate and to hold it without obligation of service to a superior. The basis of its valuation
was the merk, a term that denoted its quality. A merk
of the most productive land might comprise one acre,
while poorer land extended to five acres (2ha). The
common grazing beyond was called the scattald, and
the scat, or tax, for its use was based on the number
of merks in the possession of the cultivator. Udal law
also gave unrestricted access to the foreshore. It was
never abolished by Act of Parliament in the Northern
Isles, merely eroded, most recently by the Court of
Session judgement (1958) concerning the ownership
of the **St Ninian's Isle** treasure.

UDNY CASTLE, Nr Oldmeldrum,
Aberdeenshire
Anywhere but Formartine (the castle-rich country
between the Ythan and the **Don**), a 100ft (30m) tower
house like Udny would be renowned and widely documented. Square with rounded angles, corner turrets and
ornamental battlements, it has five storeys linked by a
circular staircase. It probably dates from the 16th century; **MacGibbon and Ross** record a tradition that it
was the work of three successive Udny lairds 'and that
it ruined them all'. A baronial mansion was added in

Udny Castle, by R W Billings (RWB)

the 1870s and demolished in the 1960s. The castle is
now fully restored and in private hands.
   At Udny Green a circular single-storey shed-like structure with a sturdy door is the old Mort House (1832)
where fresh corpses were secured against body-
snatchers. Such was the demand from anatomists that
even burial was no guarantee of eternal rest. But carefully secured behind the four locks of the Mort House,
coffins could be left for up to three months until
decomposition rendered their contents unsaleable.

UDSTON COLLIERY DISASTER (1887)
73 miners died in a colliery disaster at Udston, two
miles from **Hamilton**, on the morning of Saturday 28
May 1887. An underground explosion and fire at the
bottom of the 850ft (260m) deep pit claimed most
of the casualties, although one of the two mineshafts
remained open and rescuers were able to search for
survivors, albeit in highly dangerous conditions. The
incident took place not far from **Blantyre**, the scene of
Scotland's worst mining disaster 10 years previously,
and particularly dangerous working conditions might
reasonably have been anticipated by the mine managers.
As at Blantyre, unauthorised shot-firing was later suspected as having triggered the accident.

UIG CHESSMEN
These **Viking**-age chessmen, found at Uig on the west
coast of the Isle of **Lewis** in 1831 by a crofter whose
cows stumbled on them in the sand dunes, date from the
12th century and are regarded as the oldest authentically
European chess pieces. The originals are now divided
between the **Royal Museum of Scotland** in **Edinburgh**
and the British Museum in London. Reproductions of
complete sets and individual pieces are available. They

Viking bishops, queen, king, pawn and knight; the 12th century Uig (or Lewis) chessmen (© the Trustees of the National Museums of Scotland 1994)

were originally carved in walrus ivory, probably obtained from Scandinavian settlements in Greenland, and arrived in the sands of Ardroil, near Uig, about 1150. At the time the **Hebrides** were still under Norse rule and remained so until the **Treaty of Perth** in 1266.

The king, queen, bishops, knights and rooks depict a medieval monarch and his entourage, while they are defended by Viking warrior pawns. These are particularly fearsome, depicted biting hard on the edge of their shields, eyes popping, in true Viking 'berserk' fashion.

The extent of Viking domination in Lewis is revealed by a study of place-names, many of which, including Uig (vik, a bay) are of Norse origin. Many fine artefacts of the period have been found on Viking-age archaeological sites, including distinctive tortoise-shaped brooches, bone pins and portable weighing scales for itinerant traders in precious metals. But the Uig chess set is the most superb of all finds from Viking Scotland. It represents the final flourishing of Norse settlement in the Western Isles, for shortly afterwards **Somerled**, the son of Gillebride, defeated a Norse fleet and re-established Celtic control of Norse territories.

UISTS, see NORTH UIST and SOUTH UIST

ULLAPOOL, Ross & Cromarty

Loch Broom, like other west-coast sea lochs, once attracted prodigious shoals of **herring**. In the 19th century fisheries were established at the mouth of the loch on Isle Martin and on the Tanera Isles (in the **Summer Isles**). Their success encouraged the British Fisheries Society to begin laying out a new port at Ullapool in 1788. Throughout the early 19th century the town continued to grow although as early as 1830 it was clear that herring stocks were in decline. A dismal failure, 'the large and dreary fishing village' of 1900 never warranted a **railway** connection. Revival came courtesy of improved road links and the well-chosen harbour. East-coast trawlers, moving to the **Minch** in the 1920s, found it a convenient haven and landing place; latterly it has become a favoured rendezvous for the factory ships of Eastern Europe, while **tourism** and the Ullapool–**Stornoway** ferry bring a further influx of visitors.

The port stands on a level spit jutting into the loch on the north-east shore. Many of the whitewashed buildings date from its 18th century foundation and from **Thomas Telford**'s tenure of the post of Surveyor of Buildings. Notable are the Old Bank House, the now Caledonian-**MacBrayne** office, the warehouse known as the Captain's Cabin which houses the one-roomed private Lochbroom Museum, and the Parliamentary Church, designed by **Telford**, opened in 1829 and now renovated and refurbished as the Ullapool Museum and Visitor Centre. Across the loch on its south-west shore the impressive **dun** of Lagaidh or Loggie has been partly excavated by a team from **Glasgow**'s **Hunterian Museum** and found to comprise a 1st millennium BC fort, partly vitrified, an early AD dun or **broch**, and a small 12th century motte and bailey castle. At Rhiroy nearby are the remains of another broch and north of Ullapool Dun Canna on a sea promontory can be reached after a considerable walk from Blaghasary.

ULSTER, Plantation of

'The most successful Scottish colony of all time' (G Donaldson) was that in northern Ireland. It began in the reign of **James VI** when attempts to pacify the **Hebrides** [see **Fife, (Gentlemen) Adventurers of**] and **Kintyre** by settling them with Lowlanders spilled over into Antrim. These pioneers were followed (1606), as part of official policy, by others recruited by Hugh Montgomery, later Viscount of Airds, and James Hamilton, later Viscount Clandeboye, who had purchased titles forfeited by the O'Neills in County Down. Further forfeitures in 1607 and government land sales in 1609 found more takers in the Scottish Lowlands and by mid-century the Scots population in Ulster had risen to 40–50,000. Migration continued throughout the century and the Scottish numbers may have doubled by the end of it.

Donaldson draws a parallel with the contemporaneous settlement of the Anglo-Scots border. There as in Ulster the **Union of the Crowns** ended the custom of miscreants being able to seek refuge, dissidents support, and mercenaries employment, by crossing the border. Traditionally several Scottish families and more recently some Highland mercenaries had managed to defy authority on both sides of the North Channel by keeping one foot in English Ulster and another in Scottish **Galloway** or **Argyll**.

ULVA, Isle of, Mull, Argyll

Volcanic terraces and columnar basalts give the 'wolf isle' a distinctive shape. Best known for its part in **Thomas Campbell**'s poem 'Lord Ullin's Daughter', which tells the sad tale of the eloping Chief of Ulva and his young bride who drowned at Ulva Ferry while fleeing from her parents, the island was briefly visited by **Boswell** and **Johnson** in 1773: 'To Ulva we came in the dark, and left it before noon the next day . . . being informed that there was nothing worthy of observation.' In the early 19th century it had a busy **kelp** manufacturing industry and was also the home of MacArthur's Piping College. In 1837 the population of the island was 604, but after the 1847 **potato famine** the numbers were dramatically reduced. **David Livingstone**'s father was a crofter here, and General **Lachlan Macquarie**, Governor of New South Wales 1809–21, was born on the island.

UNION, Act and Treaty of (1706–7)

Just as, for centuries before the Union, many Englishmen had accepted the necessity of Scotland becoming part of England so, centuries after, many Scots still reject any such notion. **Bannockburn** was won, **Flodden** lost; the **Reformation** triumphed, the **Jacobites** did not; these issues are decided. But the Union is different. It remains in the realm of current affairs, refusing to become history. The most dispassionate analysis of how it came about invites debate, while an assessment of its consequences may yet be premature.

Although **James VI** had vainly urged closer integration, Union was certainly not a necessary outcome of the 1603 **Union of the Crowns**; more often than not dynastic unions proved short-lived and politically inconsequential. Nor was it advanced by the 'shot-gun' union effected by Oliver Cromwell in 1652–60; if anything this unhappy experience should have resulted in the permanent estrangement of Scotland; unsurprisingly suggestions for even an economic union (1668) let alone a parliamentary union (1670) failed to win support. The latter, like a similar move in 1689, was prompted by an absentee sovereign who found the idiosyncrasies of Scotland's religious and political rivalries a tax on both comprehension and patience, while in 1689 royal anxieties about latent Jacobitism amongst the Scottish nobility also played a part. So although amongst those managing Scottish affairs on London's behalf, such as **Lauderdale** and **Tweeddale**, there was a grim awareness that Union must soon force its way to the forefront, the idea was anathema to the mass of the people.

And so it remained. But this did not prevent a variety of exceptional issues becoming so fortuitously linked in the first six years of the new century as to convince a sizeable body of informed Scottish opinion that Union was in its own, and perhaps Scotland's, interests. Foremost were the consequences of the collapse of the **Darien scheme** which became apparent about 1700. This should have stirred Scottish animosity, and did; but to cooler heads, English and Scottish, it betrayed the impossibility of Scotland pursuing a foreign, colonial and economic policy that was not identical with England's; it convinced many Scots that access to colonial markets was only possible through Union, and many Englishmen that affording this access might prove the lesser of two evils given the Scottish capacity for troublemaking and smuggling. Additionally it left a lot of impoverished Scottish stockholders looking to Union as their only chance of compensation.

Almost simultaneously the question of the succession surfaced when in 1700 the only surviving child of Princess (Queen in 1702) Anne died. The English Parliament passed an Act of Settlement (1701) whereby the succession was to pass to Sophia of Hanover and her issue, she being a daughter of **Elizabeth**, daughter of James VI. Scotland's Parliament was not consulted about this, nor about war with France which was now declared (War of the Spanish Succession); nor in 1702 was the Scottish Parliament a representative body (the opposition had walked out complaining of its unconstitutionality) when **James Douglas 2nd Duke of Queensberry**, the Queen's Commissioner in Scotland, pushed through a Bill nominating commissioners to treat for Union. In the event this was a false start since the English commissioners proved unenthusiastic. But in Scotland pique at all these measures surfaced in 1703 when a new Parliament snubbed first the Hanoverian settlement by passing an **Act of Security** which reserved to Scotland the right to make its own choice about the succession, and then the war, by a further Act which reserved to itself the right to decide matters 'Anent Peace and War'. Significantly, both these Acts were phrased in terms of the Scottish kingdom's security, which meant in effect the liberties of its Parliament and Church from royal, ie London's, interference; as well as the Darien collapse, the Hanoverian succession and the French war, constitutional reform was on the agenda.

The Act of Security specifically linked any acceptance of the Hanoverian succession to guarantees of reform and therefore amounted to an ultimatum. The English Parliament, increasingly disposed towards Union by anxieties about French support for the Jacobites, responded in kind with the **Alien Act** (1705). This allowed 10 months for the Scots to repeal the Act of Security and either accept the Hanoverian settlement or enter into serious negotiations about Union; failure to do so would be penalised by ending the Scottish right to English citizenship which had been won by James VI and by ending the duty-free trade in Scottish cattle, **linen** and **coal** entering England. As five years earlier over the Darien affair, Scotland indulged in hysterical anglophobia [see **Thomas Green** incident] but quickly perceived the gravity of the threat, especially to its exports. Three months short of the deadline commissioners were again appointed to treat with their English counterparts over Union.

The negotiations over the treaty seem to have been rather less critical than the prior nomination of the commissioners and the subsequent handling of the Bill in Parliament. Political parties scarcely existed, but there has been much analysis of the motives and manipulative devices employed by the major personalities and 'interests'. Although initially a majority of Scottish MPs (the 'Country party') opposed Union it was a majority with no answer to the pressing economic arguments in favour of the move, and no consensus about other political priorities. In the event it was easily split, first when **James Hamilton, 4th Duke of Hamilton** unexpectedly threw his weight behind allowing the Queen to select the commissioners (who were therefore largely predisposed to accepting the best terms they could get), and subsequently when the so-called *squadrone volante* were detached from the opposition to support the Bill in Parliament. Masterminding this 'management' on behalf of the government were **John Campbell, 2nd Duke of Argyll** and James Douglas, 2nd Duke of Queensberry.

The treaty consisted of 25 articles. Federal and gradualist arrangements favoured by some of the opposition had been ruled out by the English. The Union was to be an 'incorporating' one, with the two kingdoms accepting one parliament, one flag, one sovereign (Hanoverian after Anne), one coinage, one system of taxation and one trading regime. The independence of the Scottish legal system and, by a separate bill, of the Scottish Church were guaranteed. Debate focused largely on the number of seats to be reserved for Scotland in the House of Commons (eventually 42) and Lords (eventually 16), and the size and allocation of the 'Equivalent' (eventually £398,000); this was a sum to be used to offset Scotland's liability for England's national debt, to encourage Scottish industry and, more delicately, to pay for arrears of salaries and compensate Darien losers. Whether these last constituted bribery, and the extent to which other payments and rewards influenced the outcome, is hotly disputed.

The first of these articles was passed in the Scottish Parliament in November and, as popular opposition rent the kingdom, the final vote on the treaty was carried by 110 votes to 67 in January 1707. Dissolution followed in April and the Union became effective on 1 May.

Thereafter, and for at least a generation, resentment grew and even erstwhile supporters expressed regret. But in the short term it is hard to see how a non-Hanoverian succession, as envisaged in the Act of Security, could have done other than invite war or how isolation, as envisaged in the Alien Act, could have proved other than financially disastrous. From **Fletcher of Saltoun** and **John Hamilton of Belhaven** there came powerful and emotive arguments against Union; but they offered no viable alternative and could not gainsay the economic advantages which would eventually prove real enough. The problem for later generations lies in the realisation that the circumstances which conspired to make the Union unavoidable soon ceased to operate. In the context of empire, then of commonwealth, and now of Europe, alternatives *have* emerged. The Scotland Act of 1998 which reinstated the **Scottish Parliament** suggests an eagerness to explore them.

UNION CANAL

Properly entitled the **Edinburgh** and **Glasgow** Union **Canal**, this waterway in fact connected Scotland's capital city with Lock 16 of the **Forth–Clyde** Canal at **Falkirk**, making possible through journeys between Edinburgh and Glasgow.

Excavations for the Union Canal began in 1817, Messrs **Burke and Hare** being two of the navvies employed, and it opened in December 1822. It was 31½ miles long, 5ft (1.5m) deep and 37ft (11m) wide at the surface. Its course includes a 700yd (640m) tunnel south of Falkirk and four aqueducts, all still extant, the longest being the Avon viaduct, 12 arches, 810ft (247m) long and 86ft (26m) high, the best-known probably the **Water of Leith** structure at Slateford, eight arches, 500ft (152m) long and 75ft (23m) high.

The Union Canal began by bringing **coal** to Edinburgh from central Scotland, but six passenger boats were in use daily by 1835, the eastern terminus being at Port Hopetoun, now the site of Lothian House in Lothian Road. Port Hamilton, off Morrison Street, was the coal basin at the Edinburgh end. The canal was cut back to the south side of Fountainbridge in 1921, when it had been in **railway** ownership for 62 years, and it was formally closed in 1965. Despite being culverted in the Kingsknowe area, the canal, which has a new aqueduct straddling the A720, remains a permanent part of the landscape of east central Scotland.

UNION OF THE CROWNS (1603)

James VI's 1603 accession to the English throne as James I stemmed from his great-grandmother being **Margaret Tudor**. Sister of Henry VIII and wife of **James**

IV, she was the mother of **James V** who alone amongst Henry VII's grandchildren (James V, Edward VI, Mary I and Elizabeth I) produced an heir (**Mary** 'Queen of Scots'). Henry VII had been warned that in giving his daughter to a **Stewart** there was a risk of a Stewart one day laying claim to the English throne. Rightly, though, he thought that this might not be such a bad thing. Any Scottish monarch succeeding to the English throne would soon realise that his interests and security lay in the more powerful kingdom, which would be all the more secure for Scottish subordination and the end of the **auld alliance**. He failed, however, to take into account the improbable situation in which a Stewart claimant happened to be French-educated, indeed an ex-Queen of France, with religious views that were anathema south of the border. This was the problem posed by Queen Mary of Scotland when **Lord James Stewart** and **Maitland of Lethington** tried to persuade Cecil and Elizabeth to settle the succession question in her favour. Her son, James, always looked a better bet, and behaved with exemplary restraint when his mother was executed (1587) and during the Spanish Armada (1588). Although Elizabeth still declined to name him her heir outright, closer Anglo-Scottish relations and the absence of any other contender led to a smooth transition when eventually she died.

Henry VII's prophecy was soon realised and James found little difficulty in adjusting to more luxurious surroundings and a less rumbustious nobility. He planned to make triennial visits to Scotland and hoped to unite his kingdoms further. Neither materialised. Whether an absentee sovereign was good or bad for Scotland is debatable. Union of the Crowns did improve links between the kingdoms; James built a new bridge at **Berwick** and set up a better postal service. It also eliminated the longstanding problem of lawlessness in the Borders; they were to be henceforth known as 'the middle shires'; commissions were set up and miscreants hanged; the warlords became **ballad** material. 'As a major problem the Border was finished . . . It was a foretaste of the settlement . . . of the Highlands' (R Mitchison).

UNITARIANISM

Unitarians are a small religious group travelling the by-paths of the Christian tradition rather than the safe central highway. They draw on Judeo-Christian teachings about responding to God's love by loving their neighbours as themselves, drawing wisdom from the world's religions and insights from science, humanism and personal experience. Unitarians have no creeds but traditionally have held that God is one and Jesus human (Unitarianism), God's love is effective for all (Universalism) and human nature is worthy.

The Unitarian Thomas Aikenhead was Britain's last executed heretic (**Edinburgh**, 1697). **Church of Scotland** moderates with Unitarian tendencies were **Glasgow** professors John Simson, **Francis Hutcheson** and William Leechman and **Ayrshire** ministers William McGill and William Dalrymple. The best known Scottish Unitarian was **Robert Burns**. Other significant Scottish Unitarians include **Stephen Mitchell**, founder of the Glasgow Library, Charles Jenner the Edinburgh retailer, Thomas Fyshe Palmer the political martyr, George Hope the agricultural reformer, and **Mary Somerville** the mathematician. James Martineau, the Unitarian theologian, lived at **Rothiemurchus** where he is commemorated, and Elizabeth Blackwell, the first registered woman doctor in Britain and America and a Unitarian, is buried at Kilmun. **Alexander Graham Bell**, Scots-born inventor of the telephone, described himself as 'a Unitarian agnostic'.

Organised Unitarianism in Scotland derives from (1) a response to Calvinism's tyrannous God and (2) the influence of English Unitarians. Each Unitarian congregation is sovereign, calling a minister of either sex. There is a Scottish Unitarian Association, a General Assembly of Unitarian and Free Christian Churches and an International Association for Religious Freedom which links Unitarianism and other liberal religious organisations, Christian and non-Christian.

UNITED ESTABLISHED CHURCH OF SCOTLAND

Final moves to reunification of the **Church of Scotland** were possible after the unification of the **Free Church** and incorporated seceders of the United Presbyterian Church [see **United Secession Churches**] in 1900. Expensive and embarrassing property disputes with their dissident remainders were resolved by Act of Parliament in 1905. The disestablishment lobby accepted the clearer position of the Church of Scotland's independence in all spiritual matters and its recognition by the state in another Act of 1921. Free, Protestant, lawful, and adhering to the principles of the **Reformation**, this Church was compatible with the **United Free Church**. They joined together on 2 October 1929 with a service of thanksgiving in **St Giles Cathedral**, Edinburgh. [See chart p. 1041]

UNITED FREE CHURCH

By 1900, when this Church was formed, many of the divisions of the **Presbyterian** churches were resolving their differences. The United Free Church brought together the main **Secession Church** streams, by then called United Presbyterian, and the **Free Church** into a strong, progressive Church independent still from the establishment, which they both continued to oppose. The original rifts of 1733 and 1843, both over patronage in Church government, had been settled by the repeal in 1874 of the 1712 Patronage Act. Disestablishment became less of a factor, enabling union with the **Church of Scotland** in 1929, though with property squabbles at all stages.

UNITED KINGDOM, SS

Built by Steele of **Greenock** on the lower **Clyde** in 1826, she was the largest steamship afloat – 160ft (49m) long with engines of 200 horsepower constructed by **David Napier**. It was widely predicted that she would sink on her maiden voyage; but instead she made the voyage around the north of Scotland to **Leith** in 65 hours. She then served on the London-Leith route and with regular times of 40 to 50 hours was believed to be the fastest vessel afloat.

UNITED SECESSION CHURCH

Until 1820 the **Presbyterian** Churches in Scotland operated as at least six Churches, each with its own degree of orthodoxy in faith and government. The United Secession Church was formed of 280 congregations when New Lichts Burghers of 1799 and New Lichts Anti-Burghers of 1806 came together. Both were from the **Secession Church** of 1733 which split over the Burgher Oath in 1747. In 1847 the United Secession Church fused with the Relief Church, a liberal and anti-**Covenanting** tradition operated from the **Church of Scotland** in 1761. Together they became the United Presbyterian Church until joining with the **Free Church** in 1900 as the **United Free Church**. [See chart p. 1041]

UNST, Shetland

One of the three North Isles of **Shetland**, Unst, with an area of 45 square miles, supports a population of just under 1000. While **crofting** is the main occupation, salmon farming is of considerable importance and since 1957 the RAF station at Saxavord, the highest hill on the island, has provided a large number of jobs.

The island has several sheltered anchorages, of which Baltasound was once a major **herring** port. It is still the largest village in Unst and its pier is used by **fishing** boats seeking shelter and by cargo vessels loading talc, which is quarried extensively in the island. Another mineral, chromite, was quarried in the 19th century and geologists believe that the island's unique assemblage of rocks may contain further minerals.

Numerous churches, the mansion houses of Belmont and Buness, and the ruins of **Muness Castle** indicate the island's importance over many centuries. Uyeasound and Haroldswick are attractive villages, the latter with the most northerly post office in the UK.

The scenery is superb and wildlife abounds, especially at Hermaness, the noted **bird sanctuary**. Other parts of the island are classed as Sites of Special Scientific Interest because of the rare suite of plants growing on almost barren areas of serpentine rock.

UPPER CLYDE SHIPBUILDERS' WORK-IN (1971–2)

Shipbuilding on the **Clyde** appeared to enter its death throes when Upper Clyde Shipbuilders (UCS) went into liquidation in June 1971. The Conservative government of Edward Heath, committed to reducing public subsidies to ailing industries and no friend to Clydeside or, it was said, to Scotland, had precipitated the crisis by hastening the detachment of **Yarrows**, the profitable naval element in the group, and by undermining the group's fragile credit with statements precluding any further government assistance. Of UCS's remaining four yards, those at **Govan** (the recently reorganised **Fairfields**) and at Linthouse (**Alexander Stephen**) were offered an olive branch but there was to be no reprieve for C Connell at Scotstoun or for **John Brown** at **Clydebank**. Losses and late-delivery penalties incurred by the last in the construction of the *Queen Elizabeth II* had contributed substantially to the financial crisis; but the disaster which now threatened Clydebank was likened to the effect of German bombing there during World War II.

Led by a new generation of highly articulate '**Red Clydesiders**' including the Communists Jimmy Reid and Jimmy Airlie, the John Brown workforce adopted the then novel industrial tactic of a 'work-in' and began mobilising mass support. 'UCS' became 'Unity Creates Strength' as 'the greatest demonstration since the days of the **Chartists**' saw 200,000 march in support on 18 August; one-day sympathy strikes were organised elsewhere and £250,000 was raised to support the action. Meanwhile behind closed gates the threatened workers sought to put their own house in order by overriding ancient rivalries and fostering solidarity between those still at work and those made redundant.

Fears of civil disobedience proved unfounded as police, liquidators and workers showed respect for one another's positions. After more than six months even the government appeared to relent when the Scotstoun yard was added to those at Govan and Linthouse which were to be reprieved and reorganised with a large grant as Govan Shipbuilders; meanwhile out of nowhere an American buyer in the shape of Marathon was found for Clydebank. Demands for 'the Four Yards and all the Labour Force Intact' appeared to have been met. But neither of these solutions proved other than stop-gap, while the government's acclaimed 'U-turn' had less to do with the UCS work-in than with events at Rolls-Royce and in the pits. The 'something very like a victory' claimed by Tony Benn and other supporters proved short-lived and empty. Even the ploy of the work-in, when next invoked by employees of the *Scottish Daily Express* in 1975–6, proved an ineffectual form of industrial action. Whether the UCS protest was really 'a crucial moment in modern British politics' (J Foster and C Woolfson, *The Politics of the UCS Work-In*, 1986) or 'merely a publicity coup' (C Harvie, *No Gods and Precious Few Heroes*, 1981) will long be debated.

URQUHART, David (1805–77) Diplomat and Author

Born in **Cromarty**, Urquhart was educated abroad (except for Oxford) and spent his early career in the eastern Mediterranean. He served in the Greek navy during the Greek War of Independence and at Constantinople as a member of Sir Stratford Canning's mission (1831–2) and as secretary to his embassy. Recalled (1837) because of his antipathy to Russia and his championship of Turkish autonomy, he was elected MP for Stafford (1847–52), edited a diplomatic journal, and wrote books on the Middle East.

URQUHART, Sir Thomas (1611–60) Writer

The Laird of **Cromarty** was, throughout his life, an ardent Royalist. Knighted by **Charles I**, in 1641 he fought for the monarchy at Worcester and was imprisoned by Cromwell. Despite flamboyant attempts to buy his freedom by offering the Lord Protector the first complete Universal Language, he was not finally released until the early 1650s. Even then it seems he was ordered to remain abroad, as he was in Zeeland in 1655 and is found there again three years later. The delightful tale that he died of an uncontrollable fit of laughter when hearing of the Restoration of **Charles II** certainly fits the date and his known character.

Urquhart was too idiosyncratic a man and a writer to found any school or belong to any tradition. His prose is as delightful as his poetry is ponderous. In prose he can transmit the joy of one finding adventure in words themselves. Whether presenting a new trigon-

ometry (*Trissotetras*, 1645), celebrating the heroic feats of the Admirable (**James**) **Crichton** (*The Jewel*, 1652), outlining a Universal Language which reads as well backwards as forwards (*Logopandecteision*, 1653) or outdoing Rabelais (whom he translated) in excess and coarseness (*Gargantua and Pantagruel*, 1653), the true object of his admiration remains the English language.

URQUHART CASTLE, Nr Drumnadrochit, Inverness-shire

On a headland south of Glen Urquhart bay, Urquhart Castle commands extensive views up and down **Loch Ness** and was once the most important fortification in the **Great Glen** between **Inverlochy** (**Fort William**) and **Inverness**. Today only its 17th century tower retains an architectural profile, but archaeologically the whole site, strewn with ruins and surrounded by an enclosing wall rising sheer from the loch, is impressive and interesting. Vitrified remains attest the existence of an Iron Age timber-laced fortress south of the landward access where a Norman motte and bailey had replaced it by the 12th century. In the 13th century the lordship was granted to the Durward family and then passed to the **Comyns** of **Badenoch** before Edward I's troops occupied the castle in 1296 and again in 1303. It was regained by **Robert I** about 1308 and by the end of the century had been designated a royal castle. But the crown's authority was repeatedly usurped in the 15th century by the **MacDonald Lords of the Isles** as they pushed through the Great Glen to challenge royal supremacy in the north. In 1509 **James IV** granted the lordship to John Grant of Freuchie who, along with his successors, was responsible for most of what remains in the way of defences. Further MacDonald raids produced substantial booty and necessitated further repairs, still underway in the 17th century when **Covenanters** (1645) and **Jacobites** (1689) both disputed the castle. It was partially blown up when evacuated by government troops in 1691 and thereafter decayed rapidly.

URR, Motte of, Stewartry of Kirkcudbright

Motte of Urr, the huge earthwork base of a timber tower with attached bailey to house merchants and mercenaries, rises on the west bank of the Urr in a quiet arable valley three miles NNW of **Dalbeattie**, a mile south of Haugh of Urr, and roughly two miles north of another great motte at Buittle, now covered by the ruins of a courtyard castle. A plan of 1831 shows a spur projecting from beneath the earthwork, probably part of an earlier ringwork.

Urr was excavated by Dr Brian Hope-Taylor in 1951 (a quadrant) and 1953 (an octant) with an investigation of the timber bridge from the motte top to the outside; the huge postholes of the central tower were revealed, and the palisade with Ulster-style archers' foxholes containing iron arrowheads. Finds indicated a date in the late 12th century, but on clearing out a robber pit near the end of the second season, an earlier level, six feet lower, was revealed, with an occupation from around 1130 which ended in burning – probably in the anti-Norman revolt of 1174.

The de Berkeley family held the lands and motte, probably planted there by the King to counterbalance the powerful sub-kings of **Galloway** who held Buittle.

Urquhart Castle, by Hugh William Williams (NGS)

A burgh developed outside the motte on the southern slope – it was in existence by 1262 when 'burgenses de Hur' are mentioned – and outlines of roads and buildings can be seen in a low sun.

Two common medieval legends are associated with the motte – that of the dragon which encircled it and was slain by a knight who got himself swallowed with razor blades all over his armour, and that of the old woman who secured a large estate by running round it while **Bruce** supped his porridge in her cottage.

Urr and Bass of **Inverurie** are Scotland's two largest intact mottes.

V

men lost, on 15 October 1915 following a submarine attack. In contrast, the loss of the *Vanguard*, at the same location as *Royal Oak* but in the previous war, was accidental and usually ascribed to unstable ammunition; she was a veteran of the Battle of Jutland and the only British battleship to be lost in World War I.

VAILA, Shetland

The small island of Vaila, off the west coast of **Shetland**, was chosen by **Arthur Anderson** as the base for his Shetland Fishery Company of 1837, which marked the beginning of the end of landlords' control over Shetland's **fishing** industry. Vaila Hall, one of the finest mansions in Shetland, was built in the 1890s by Herbert Anderton, a Yorkshire mill-owner.

VALENTINE, Harben James (1872–1949)
Card Manufacturer

Valentine was born in **Dundee** into a family who had established a printing, photographic and stationery business which he joined at the age of 13. The key decision was made in 1898 when Valentines exploited their mastery of the new photographic processes to grow rapidly in the postcard 'boom' of the turn of the century. Managing director (1900) and chairman (1907), Valentine floated his company, weathered the difficult years following World War I and diversified into the birthday card and calendar trade. By his death the company name was firmly established throughout Britain and much of the English-speaking world.

VALLISCAULIANS

This French order of monks of the 13th century is unknown in Britain except in Scotland. Two priories, at **Ardchattan** and **Beauly**, later became Cistercian. The third at **Pluscarden** became Benedictine on the decline of the original order after two centuries.

VANGUARD, HMS, Loss of (1917)

The sinking of the battleship HMS *Vanguard* is believed to have accounted for the biggest loss of life (804 men and boys) in a single accident in Scotland or within Scottish waters. Moored in the World War I fleet anchorage of **Scapa Flow**, **Orkney**, the 19,250-ton *Vanguard* blew up without warning on 9 July 1917. There were only two survivors. Prince Albert (later King George VI) was serving on a sister ship nearby and was appalled at how such a huge capital ship could vanish so quickly.

The sinking of the battleship HMS *Royal Oak* on 14 October 1939 produced an even higher death-toll (833 lives lost), but that was the direct result of enemy action – by torpedoes from German submarine U-47 which had managed to penetrate the Flow's defences and escaped successfully. Similarly, the cruiser HMS *Hampshire* was lost off Orkney on 5 June 1916 with 643 casualties, including Lord Kitchener, after hitting a mine. Another war victim in Scottish waters was HMS *Hawke*, with more than 400

VATERSAY, Island of, Outer Hebrides

Three square miles in area, with a Gaelic-speaking population of around 70, Vatersay lies to the south of **Barra**, to which it is connected by a causeway opened in 1990 at a cost of £4 million. In 1911 there were 288 people on this tiny island, including many immigrants from Barra and **Mingulay**. The present **crofts**, Post Office, church, school and village are scattered around the island's five miles of road. The highest point is Heishival Mor (625ft/190m); to the south are the Bishop's Isles and Mingulay, all now uninhabited.

VICTORIA, Queen (1819–1901)

The Queen and Prince Albert first visited Scotland in 1842, four years after her coronation. Arriving by sea at **Leith**, they found **Edinburgh** 'quite beautiful'. They explored **Perthshire** and read *The Lay of the Last Minstrel*; the Prince tried out the **deer stalking**. For both it was the beginning of a life-long love affair with the Highlands. As a **Stewart** descendant [see **Elizabeth of Bohemia**], the Queen's adoption of **tartan**, porridge and whatever else met then notions of Highland identity was no sillier than the homage paid to other Scottish totems by many of her subjects. She sensed Scotland's alienation, the result of residual **Jacobite** sentiment and political (mis)management after the **Act of Union**, and perhaps hoped to redress it by creating a Scottish identity for the royal family. But the sincerity of her affection for the people and the country cannot be questioned (which is more than can be said for some of her Stewart predecessors and their Jacobite successors).

The 1842 visit, only the second by a reigning British sovereign since the Union, would become an annual migration. Balmoral was rented (1848) and then purchased (1852) after which the construction of **Balmoral Castle** began. From this base the Queen and Prince Albert undertook frequent and sometimes arduous excursions throughout the Highlands. Her *Leaves from a Journal of our Life in the Highlands*, 1867, and *More Leaves*, 1883, 'achieved a fame and popularity unrivalled by any royal or ruling author since Julius Caesar composed his *Commentaries* on the Gallic War' (**E Linklater**); her sketches and paintings also had a wide currency. Together these royal productions did more to popularise the Highlands than even **Sir Walter Scott**'s novels. Nor was the rest of Scotland neglected. Royal patronage became a new feature of Scottish life; numerous monuments were unveiled and exhibitions opened, and to the Queen's love of tartan, shawl and tweed weavers from **Paisley** to **Brora** owed their livelihoods.

VIKINGS

The invasions and settlement of Vikings from Scandinavia was the most formative influence in Scotland to follow the establishment of **Dalriada** around the year 400. Curiously, it was a Northumbrian scholar who pinpointed this time-span. Alcuin was recording the

The Visit of Queen Victoria and Prince Albert to Hawthornden, 14 September 1842, *by Sir William Allan, 1844 (SNPG)*

Vikings *continued*

destruction of the Celtic monastery of Lindisfarne in 793: 'It is some 350 years that we and our forefathers have inhabited this lovely land, and never before in Britain has such a terror appeared as we have now suffered at the hands of the heathen. Nor was it thought possible that such an inroad from the sea could be made.' The Vikings owed their success to their invention of the keel, mastery of rudder and sail, and skill in navigation. This enabled them to make long sea journeys in their beautifully designed boats with effective forces of fighting men. In 794 they sacked **Iona**, and returned in successive years to loot and murder. The library which had supplied the erudition for **Adamnan**'s life of **Columba** was destroyed, and although a copy of his biography survived on the Continent, the chronicle of Iona was lost. The **Pictish** society of **Shetland** and **Orkney** was totally submerged; the **Hebrides** fell under Norse control, and much of the mainland also. In 839 the Danes inflicted a crushing defeat on the mainland Picts, and this facilitated the takeover of **Kenneth mac-Alpin**, who established himself as the first King of the Picts and Scots in the heartland of old **Alba**.

For the most part it was sea-rovers from Norway who came to Scotland to raid and to colonise. The largest settlement yet discovered here was unearthed at **Jarlshof** in Shetland and another has been excavated on the fertile peninsula of the Udal in **North Uist**. Characteristically, both were planted on the sites of dispossessed Pictish and Scottish inhabitants. On the Brough of **Birsay**, however, the long-houses of the Norse settlers respected the sacred site of a Pictish monastery. Here in Orkney King Olav Trygvasson of Norway is credited with ordering the baptism of **Earl Sigurd** in 955 after his own conversion. It is the burials of those who had not yet adopted Christianity that provide the most illuminating evidence of their lives. A ship burial on the isle of **Colonsay** contained a horse as well as ornaments, weapons and crosses inscribed on two stone slabs as a precaution. Three other ship burials have been discovered on the isle of Sanday, a satellite of **Canna**. It was a custom of the pagan Vikings, who were slave traders, to include women among their grave goods, but the only example of this yet unearthed occurred in a 9th century burial on the Isle of Man. Here a woman was interred face downwards over the body of a Viking chieftain, her skull shattered from behind. In **Caithness**, which became a part of the Orkney earldom, pagan burials along the coast precede the evidence of settlement. In 1117 **Earl Magnus** was murdered by his cousin on the isle of **Egilsay**, providing this region with its first saint. His nephew **Earl Rognvald** became the second, after leading a crusade which had the appearance of a piratical expedition, and founding the magnificent cathedral of **Kirkwall**, dedicated to Saint Magnus. On the island of **Wyre** a Norwegian tycoon called Kolbein Hruga had built what remains the earliest stone castle in Scotland, and his son Bishop Bjarni promoted Rognvald's canonisation after the Earl had been murdered by his relatives in 1158. Bjarni also composed the only surviving Norse poem of this age and area, his *Lay of the Jomsvikings*.

There can be no doubt that all this creative energy spread to Caithness, although the evidence for it, such as that of a cross with a runic inscription discovered at St Peter's Church, **Thurso**, remains disappointingly slight. It is confirmed by the place-name evidence, which extends south through the Norse **Sutherland** to where **Dingwall** commemorates a *Thingvollr* or Norse place of assembly. On the other side of Scotland the Hebrides became known as the Norse Southern Isles, and beyond them the Isle of Man was a favourite base for plundering expeditions before the period of settlement. It is thought that Godred Crovan's home may have been in **Islay** before he became King of Man and the Isles in 1079. It was he who established the Tynwald which still assembles annually at St John's on 5 July. This may have been a sacred site long before the time of the **Celtic Church**. Like the Orkney earls, King Godred and his descendants were subordinate to the paramount sovereignty of the Kings of Norway.

In the period of confusion after the death of King Orry (as Godred is remembered) **Magnus III** of Norway, known as 'Barefoot' or 'Barelegs', began his devastating expedition through Orkney and the Hebrides in 1098. It is believed that many of the island woodlands were destroyed forever before he reached Man. From there he assaulted **Galloway** and Anglesey and made the first formal treaty with a King of Scots which recognised the Norwegian claim to the Hebrides and even to **Kintyre**. This he achieved by having his skiff drawn over the isthmus at **Tarbert** with its rudder set, according to the terms which **King Edgar** had agreed. Fortunately Magnus Barefoot perished in Ireland in 1103, to be immortalised in Gaelic tradition and songs that turn Norwegian victories into defeats.

The victories were real when **Somerled** took the field against Godred II, to whose sister he was married. Despite his Norse bye-name, Somerled was of Gaelic parentage, a descendant of the ancient aristocracy of Dalriada. In 1156 he defeated Godred in a decisive naval engagement off **Colonsay** and added **Mull** and Islay to his mainland kingdom of **Argyll**. Godred retained **Lewis** and **Skye**, where a later King of Man planted a relative named Liotr (Leod) on the rock of **Dunvegan** to administer these islands on his behalf.

King Somerled was killed in 1164, but his son Ranald continued the work he had begun of rebuilding Iona's monastic buildings in stone. His grandson Donald became the progenitor of the great **Clan Donald, Lords of the Isles**, where the ancient **Gaelic language** and culture flowed back, even as far as **Lewis** where to this day four out of five place-names are of Norse origin. Somerled's son Dougal was progenitor of the clan **MacDougall** whose representative Ewen was invested as King by Haakon IV of Norway in 1248 – his response to the attempt of the King of Scots to purchase the Hebrides from him. But in 1266, after the fiasco of the expedition to **Largs**, Norway ceded its islands, with **Kintyre** and Man, by the **Treaty of Perth**. Liotr was still living to witness the demise of the Norse hegemony, which was to transform his own descendants into those patrons of Gaelic culture the **Clan MacLeod**. The Norse influence lasted longest in Shetland. The Shetlanders had fought against King Sverri in the civil war for the crown of Norway that he won in 1184. As a reprisal, Sverri detached Shetland from the Orkney earldom and placed it directly under his rule in Bergen, where it remained for 200 years while the other islands were infiltrated increasingly by Scottish influences. Many Shetlanders would congratulate themselves on that 12th century error of judgement.

W

WADE, George (1673–1748) Soldier and Road-builder

George Wade was Irish. He saw military service in Flanders and Spain between 1692 and 1710, becoming a major-general in 1714 and MP for Bath in 1722. From 1724–40 he was Commander-in-Chief North Britain, during which time he built 240 miles of **military roads** in the Highlands (including the **Dunkeld** to **Inverness** road, the **Fort Augustus** to Inverness road on the south side of **Loch Ness**, the spectacular road over the **Corrieyairack Pass**, and that through the **Great Glen**) and 40 bridges (most famously the **Tay** Bridge at **Aberfeldy**), giving the region its first ever 'made roads'. He was promoted lieutenant-general in 1727 and general in 1739. In 1742 he became a Privy Councillor and in 1743 a field marshal. During the War of the Austrian Succession he was Commander-in-Chief British Forces in Flanders 1744–5 and as Commander-in-Chief Home Forces he presided over the court martial which tried and exonerated **Sir John Cope** for his conduct during the '45 **Jacobite Rising**.

He has the somewhat dubious distinction of being the only commoner to appear in the National Anthem,

Field Marshal George Wade, attributed to Johan van Dienst (SNPG)

in which hope is expressed that General Wade will 'like a torrent rush, rebellious Scots to crush', and that he will 'confound their politics, frustrate their knavish tricks'. An easygoing socialite, Wade lacked the qualities which make a great field commander, and probably regarded his tour of duty in Scotland as his happiest and most successful. He was even a shareholder in the lead and strontium mines at **Strontian**. He died in London at the age of 75, leaving a fortune of £100,000, and was buried in Westminster Abbey.

WADERS

Small numbers of rare waders breeding in Scotland include the wood sandpiper, green sandpiper, red-necked phalarope and Temminck's stint; there are also larger numbers of whimbrel. Two other rare waders, the dotterel (*Charadrius Morinellus*) and the greenshank (*Tringa Nebularia*), have attracted much attention. In the mid-1980s there were thought to be no more than 60 to 100 breeding pairs of dotterel left in Britain, almost all in the **Cairngorms**. However an extensive survey of this apparently threatened species in 1988 revealed an estimated total of 500 pairs. Whether this dramatic find indicated an increase in population or was merely the result of improved survey methods is impossible to say. Dotterels nest mainly on bare high plateaux over 2500ft (762m), and have the reputation of being very tame, the brooding adult sitting so tightly on its nest that it can be approached and even stroked. Their Gaelic name *An Tamadan Mointich* means 'peat-bog fool' because fowlers in the old days would simply lift the bird off its nest and take both it and its eggs. The name 'dotterel' comes from the same root as 'dotty', and even their specific Latin name *Morinellus* means 'little fool'. Less foolish, however, is the dotterel's elaborate distraction display to protect its chicks in which it will lead the intruder – whether fox, crow or man – away from the nest by stumbling along in a crouching run trailing an apparently broken wing, before flying back in a wide circle to join its brood.

The elusive greenshank inhabits desolate expanses of moorland in the Highlands, **Skye** and the Outer **Hebrides**. In all the recent arguments between foresters and conservationists about the planting up of **Sutherland's Flow Country**, the hardest fight of all centred on this species; the less than 1000 pairs that breed mainly in **Caithness** and Sutherland are a significant proportion of the entire European population. The argument on their behalf pointed out that birds nesting in such specialised habitats would not be able to find new breeding grounds in Britain if they were displaced. To many, the sight and sound of the greenshank over open moorland are as evocative of the Scottish Highlands as the **golden eagle**, the **red deer** or the salmon.

WALFORD, Lucy Bethia (née Colquhoun) (1845–1919) Novelist

Lucy Colquhoun was born in **Portobello**, the daughter of a former army officer. Educated at home by various governesses, she read avidly and was strongly influenced by the works of Charlotte Yonge and Jane Austen, influences later reflected in her writing. In 1869 she married Alfred Saunders Walford and moved to London. There, as Lucy Walford, she contributed various sketches and stories to **Blackwood's Magazine**. In 1874

Blackwood & Sons published her first novel, *Mr Smith: A Part of his Life*. It was a great success, and was admired by **Queen Victoria** for its wholesome humour and highly domestic theme. Several novels of a similar nature followed, including *Pauline* (1877), *The Baby's Grandmother* (1884), *Cousins* (1885) and *The History of a Week* (1886). Walford also wrote extensively for various London journals including the *World*, and from 1889–93 was the London correspondent for the New York *Critic*. Her last novel, *David and Jonathan on the Riviera*, was published in 1914. Her autobiography, *Recollections of a Scottish Novelist*, was published in 1910.

WALKER, HELEN (c1710–91) 'Jeanie Deans'

Whilst the identity of other characters in **Sir Walter Scott**'s novels has often provoked speculation, there is no mystery about Jeanie Deans, the heroine of *The Heart of Midlothian*. She was Helen Walker, a farmer's daughter from Dalwhairn in the parish of Irongray (**Kirkcudbrightshire**) north-west of **Dumfries**, whose younger sister, Isabella or Tibby, had indeed been sentenced to death for infanticide at Dumfries court some time prior to 1736. Religious scruple and a lofty sense of propriety prevented Helen from committing a perjury which might have saved her sister; but, with the conviction of the righteous, Helen then walked barefoot to London (it took 14 days) where she gained an audience with **John Campbell**, the mighty **2nd Duke of Argyll**, who duly secured a pardon. Isabella later married the father of the murdered child and lived in Whitehaven. Helen appears to have remained near Dumfries, a proud and prickly spinster of very limited means who in old age darned stockings and kept chickens. She was selling chickens in the vicinity of Lincluden Abbey, 'a little, rather stout-looking woman ... covered in a tartan plaid', when she was discovered by a Mrs Goldie who pieced together her story with little help from the reticent heroine and, 26 years later, sent an account of it to the author of the Waverley Novels. Helen Walker, 'between seventy and eighty years old' at the time of her meeting with Mrs Goldie, died soon after and was buried in Irongray churchyard. Scott showed his gratitude to her memory by erecting a gravestone with a rather sententious inscription of which Helen would have strongly disapproved. She would probably not have thought much of *The Heart of Midlothian* either, especially her transference from Dumfries to **Edinburgh**.

WALKER, Johnnie (1805–59) Whisky Distiller

Born at Todrigg farm near **Kilmarnock**, Johnnie Walker established a grocery and spirit shop in the town in the early 1820s. His blend of **whisky** was an immediate success and as the business grew he brought his son Alexander into the firm. He, more than anyone, transformed the small local business into a world leader and a valuable earner of foreign currency for the Scottish and UK economy. Contrary to popular belief, the company does not have a distillery in Kilmarnock, but both Red and Black Label brand whiskies are blended and bottled in the town.

WALLACE, Sir William (1270–1305) Patriot

Regarded by many as the founder of Scottish nationalism; William Wallace fought hard and suffered terribly for his adherence to the concept of Scotland as a nation independent of its larger and more powerful neighbour to the south. The second son of Sir Malcolm Wallace of Elderslie, **Renfrewshire**, William did not emerge from obscurity until the age of 27, when he became a principal in one of the then frequent uprisings against the occupying English. In May 1297 he killed the English Sheriff of **Lanark**, possibly to avenge the death of his, or a colleague's, lover or wife, and after joining forces with **Andrew Murray**, enjoyed considerable military success over the invaders at the **Battle of Stirling Bridge** on 11 September of that year. Despite being heavily outnumbered, the Scots enjoyed a strategic advantage which was rapidly enriched by English tactical errors in trying to make an opposed crossing of this bridge.

Now proclaimed as the people's champion, Wallace recaptured **Berwick** and raided other parts of Northumberland. In March 1298 he was made Guardian of the Realm in the name of **John Balliol**, and attempted to muster foreign support, particularly from the German cities of the Hanseatic League, while the enemy from the south prepared to reoccupy its troublesome northern neighbour. In the spring of 1298 England's Edward I, the 'Hammer of the Scots', led an army northwards, meeting Wallace's troops at **Falkirk** on 11 July. Wallace had a small cavalry force available to him under the command of **Sir John Comyn (i)**, although it appears to have been ineffective and the Scottish spearsmen had to bear the brunt of the assault. They finally succumbed to the terrible effects of the English longbow, which was sufficient to win the day.

Wallace seems to have then disappeared back into obscurity for a time, resigning as Guardian, and attempting to raise military help and diplomatic recognition on the Continent in 1298–9. With Scotland so divided, and with so many Scots nobles prepared to accept the authority of Edward, Wallace's return was a risky venture and he was betrayed to the invader in 1305. Despatched as a prisoner to London by **Sir John Menteith**, governor of **Dumbarton**, Wallace faced a charge of treason at Westminster Hall – clearly unjust, since he had never acknowledged English authority. Sentenced to the usual punishment, he was hanged, disembowelled and beheaded on 23 August of that year. His limbs were sent to Newcastle, Berwick, **Perth** and **Stirling** to discourage other Scottish patriots.

Sir William has been superseded in the eyes of posterity by the more successful **Bruce**, but there seems little doubt that he was an inspiration to the latter, and undoubtedly suffered more for his nationalism. The *Dictionary of National Biography* acknowledges him as 'the chief champion of the Scottish nation in its struggle for independence'. His contribution to Scotland is commemorated by the Wallace Memorial on **Abbey Craig** dominating the Forth valley north of Stirling, and by smaller memorials at his birthplace of Elderslie and near **St Boswells**. Statues of Wallace and Bruce (the former by Alexander Carrick) appropriately guard the gatehouse at **Edinburgh Castle**.

WALLACE, William (1768–1843) Mathematician

Born at **Dysart**, **Fife**, Wallace was apprenticed to an **Edinburgh** bookbinder before becoming a printing house warehouseman. He taught himself Latin, French and mathematics, went on to **Edinburgh University**, was appointed to **Perth** Academy in 1874 and contributed to the *Transactions of the Royal Academy of Edinburgh* (**Royal Scottish Academy**) and *Encyclopaedia Britannica*. His patron, **John Playfair**, persuaded him to apply for a post at the Royal Military College, Great Marlow in 1803; he was Professor of Mathematics at Edinburgh (1819–38) but forced to retire through ill-health, and helped establish the New, now **City Observatory** on **Calton Hill**. His *Geometrical Theorems and Analytical Formulae* (1838) details the two inventions for which he is best known: the eidograph producing scaled enlargements or reduced copies of maps and plans, and the chorograph enabling any triangle to be drawn given one side and two angles.

WALLACE, William (1860–1940) Composer

Not to be confused with the Irish composer William Vincent Wallace, William Wallace graduated MB and MCh in 1885 at **Glasgow University** and went on to study ophthalmology in Vienna, Paris and Moorfields; but the ear proved stronger than the eye and he finally settled on **music**, studying at the Royal Academy of Music in London, where he continued as a teacher for many years. As a composer his main contribution was as the first British exponent of the symphonic poem, of which he wrote at least six. His suite for Maeterlinck's *Pélleas et Mélisande* is particularly lovely, and he wrote a number of fine songs. Wallace was also a playwright and a somewhat eccentric music theorist.

WANLOCKHEAD, Dumfriesshire

Lead is said to have been discovered near the Mennock Pass by a German in the reign of **James V**. The first mine dates from 1681 but not till the second half of the 18th century was the enterprise rewarded with commercial success. Wanlockhead village, 1380ft (420m) above sea level and claimed as the highest in Scotland, grew up to serve the lead mines and, since the closure of the Glencrieff mine in the 1950s, has been largely sustained by the interest in industrial archaeology. One of the mines, Loch Nell (1710), is open to inspection. Additionally there is a museum housed in miners' cottages, a beam-engine used for pumping out the mines ('the only known water-powered beam engine of its kind in Britain to survive intact'), a miners' library (1850), church, smelt mills, etc. Plans are afoot to reopen the Wanlockhead-**Leadhills** light **railway**, Leadhills offering further mining mementoes across the county border in **Lanarkshire**. The latter lies on land previously owned by the Earls of **Hopetoun**, while Wanlockhead belonged to the **Dukes of Buccleuch**.

WARDLAW, Elizabeth (née Halket) (1677–1727) Poet

Born in **Fife**, Elizabeth Halket was the daughter of Sir Charles Halket of Pitfirrane. In 1696 she married Sir Henry Wardlaw of Pitcruivie and in 1719 she published 'Hardyknute', a work she claimed was a fragment of an ancient **ballad** found in a vault in **Dunfermline**. It was included as an example of the traditional ballad in **Allan Ramsay**'s *Evergreen* published in 1724. Subsequent

investigation has suggested that the work was in fact written by her, and modelled on the ballad 'Gilderoy'. She is also said to have reworked other pieces in a similar fashion, including 'Sir Patrick Spens'.

WARDLAW, Henry (c1378–1440) Bishop

A nephew of Cardinal Wardlaw of **Glasgow**, Henry studied in France and was preferred Bishop of **St Andrews** in 1403. As founder of **St Andrews University** in 1411 he based the concept on the College of Paris. The first **Lollard** heretic, Resby, was burnt in 1402 during his term of office.

WARS OF INDEPENDENCE, The (1297–1304, 1306–28)

After the forced abdication of **King John Balliol**, Edward I of England claimed overlordship of Scotland 'from of old', ignoring **William the Lion**'s Treaty of Canterbury and **Birgham**. On John Balliol's abdication Edward imposed direct rule. Local revolts (eg of **William Wallace**) spread as leaders escaped, like **Andrew Murray**, or were released, like **John Comyn (i)**.

Scotland had two forces: a feudal army of landholders obliged to provide a knight and four or five followers for a month, and the defensive 'Scottish Army', every man between 16 and 60 with whatever weapons he had. Neither had mobilised since the 1263 **Battle of Largs**, whereas Edward had just conquered Wales.

Some accepted Edward's claim, others covertly backed resistance, many changed sides. **Stirling Bridge** excepted, most set battles were Edward's; the resistance developed methods of sabotage, raiding and capturing strongpoints by infiltration. They fought in Balliol's name till 1304, the Community of the Realm electing Guardians and conducting diplomatic relations with the Pope and France; even in the first phase, an underground civil administration survived.

A major invasion (1303–4) compelled **John Comyn (ii)** to negotiate terms, refusing unconditional surrender; these included a 'Scottish Council' to draw up a 'constitution'. Wallace's capture and judicial murder made many think again; in 1306 **Robert I (the Bruce)** renewed the struggle which culminated at **Bannockburn** and ended with the **Treaty of Edinburgh** (much of the final phase was fought in northern England).

WATERSTON, James (1811–83) Physicist

Born in **Edinburgh**, Waterston studied at **Edinburgh University** and taught in India before returning to Scotland to undertake private scientific research. His major achievement was to work out the kinetic theory of gases years before Clausius and **Clerk Maxwell**, but his paper was rejected by the Royal Society of London in 1845 as 'nonsense'. It was later championed by Lord Rayleigh, nine years after the death of this underrated Scottish physicist.

WATERSTON, Jane Elizabeth (1843–1932) Doctor

The daughter of an **Inverness** bank manager, Jane Waterston received a limited education privately and at the Inverness Royal Academy. In 1865 she offered her services to the **Free Church** Foreign Mission Committee and in particular to Dr James Stewart who had accompanied **David Livingstone** in 1861–2 and who now required an assistant to run a girls' school beside his boys' school at Lovedale in the Cape Province of South Africa. From 1867–73 Waterston brought her formidable energy to bear on the education of Lovedale's African pupils, acquiring a good knowledge of Xhosa and a reputation for championing the right of women to active participation in the improvement of society. Her great ambition was to become a medical missionary; to acquire a medical qualification, no easy matter for a woman in the 1870s, she returned to London to study under **Sophia Jex-Blake** and Elizabeth Garrett Anderson. She eventually made the Medical Register by way of the Dublin College of Physicians and in 1879 set out for the Central African Mission established at Livingstonia on Lake Nyasa. The mission was in turmoil and Jane's sojourn short. 'The first woman doctor in Central Africa' lasted only four months. She returned to Lovedale and then to Cape Town (1883) where she set up a Free Dispensary for women and children in the poorest districts of the city. In 1888 she was in **Edinburgh** to qualify as a Licentiate of the **Royal College of Surgeons**, but the rest of her long life was otherwise devoted to bringing medical aid to the poor, the lepers and the convicts of Cape Province. As South Africa's first woman doctor 'and perhaps the oldest woman practitioner in the British Empire', she became an institution, feared by some, loved by many, and revered by all.

WATSON, John 'Ian MacLaren' (1850–1907) Minister and Novelist

Born in Essex to Scottish parents, Watson was brought up in **Perthshire** and educated at **Perth** Academy, the **University of Edinburgh** and New College, Edinburgh, from where he was ordained **Free Church** Minister of Logiealmond, Perthshire, in 1873. In 1880 he took charge of the **Presbyterian** Church in Sefton Park, Liverpool, remaining in the post for 15 years and playing a leading role in civic affairs and in the founding of Liverpool University. His first book, *Beside the Bonnie Brier Bush*, published in 1894 under the pseudonym 'Ian MacLaren', was an instant success and he followed it with several more short story collections detailing life in the fictional Scottish village of 'Drumtochty', probably based on Logiealmond. The saccharine sentimentality of these tales placed Watson firmly in the **Kailyard school** of Scottish writers, but they were immensely popular in both England and America where he made lecture tours in 1896 and 1899. Under his own name he also published many theological works, and his clerical career included a term as Moderator of the Presbyterian Synod (1900) and as President of the National Free Church Council (1907). He died in Iowa in the course of his third American lecture tour and was buried in Liverpool.

WATSON, Sir Patrick (1832–1907) Surgeon

Born in **Edinburgh**, Watson studied medicine at **Edinburgh University** before serving in the Crimean War. On his return to Edinburgh he specialised in surgery, pioneering in ovariotomy and joint excision. Twice elected President of the **Royal College of Surgeons**

in Edinburgh, he was a firm supporter of the medical education of women.

WATSON, William J (1865–1948) Gaelic Scholar

Born in Easter **Ross**, and Rector successively of **Inverness** Royal Academy and the **Royal High School of Edinburgh**, Watson was Professor of **Celtic** at **Edinburgh University** from 1914–38. It was a highly productive tenure, during which he produced his influential texts *Rosg Gàidhlig* ('Gaelic Prose', 1915) and *Bàrdachd Ghàidhlig* ('Gaelic Poetry', 1918), his classic *History of the Celtic Place-names of Scotland* (1926) and *Scottish Verse from the Book of the Dean of Lismore* (1937), thus laying secure foundations for place-name studies and the study of classical **Gaelic verse**. He was also the moving force behind the setting up of the Scottish Gaelic Texts Society in 1934.

WATSON-WATT, Sir Robert (1892–1973) Radar Pioneer

Born at **Brechin**, Watson Watt (as he was then called) studied at **Dundee**, showing particular interest in radio waves. Following government service in World War I, he investigated how an aircraft could be tracked by its distortion of radio signals, leading to his historic recommendation in 1935 that a practical system of radar defences could be set up, as indeed it was under his supervision, and played a major part in winning the Battle of Britain. In 1942, Watson-Watt (who now hyphenated his surname) was knighted for his work. He died in **Inverness**.

WATT, James (1736–1819) Inventor

Born in **Greenock**, James Watt's name became synonymous with the emergence of the steam engine as a source of power for industry and transport in the Industrial Revolution. The young Watt worked as an instrument repairer at **Glasgow University**, where, with his sharp intellect and mathematical abilities, combined with a technical facility of a high order, he rapidly impressed his elders and contemporaries, who included the famous chemist **Joseph Black**. While repairing an elementary Newcomen steam engine, Watt realised that he could build a better one. Contrary to legend he did not in fact first discover the power of steam while watching a domestic kettle boiling. The secret, he realised, was to build an engine with a separate condenser, but unfortunately this came to him while taking a Sunday stroll on **Glasgow Green** and, this being Scotland in 1765, he had to wait until the next day to put his calculations on paper.

For the next nine years Watt's work on steam engines was hindered by technical and financial problems, which led him to undertake surveying work for such **canals** as the Forth & **Clyde**, the Caledonian, the Crinan and the Monkland. The first two were resurveyed and built by others, but Watt himself began constructing the last mentioned. His life changed in 1774 when he was offered a partnership with Matthew Boulton, a progressive and generous entrepreneur who had recently built the impressive Soho ironworks near Birmingham. Watt never looked back, perfecting his production of stationary steam engines for mine-pumping and factory power, while advancing from reciprocating

James Watt, drawing by John Henning, 1809 (SNPG)

to rotative engines. In this he was assisted by the **Ayrshire**-born **William Murdock**, an able accomplice who was ill-advisedly persuaded by Boulton and Watt to give up work on a steam road locomotive but who later pioneered gas lighting.

Watt coined the original formula to define 'horsepower', and his lesser achievements include a pantograph to copy drawings, and the wet contact process of letter copying. Much of his later energy was wasted in patent disputes, but he was elected to the Royal Society of London and the French Academy, and in 1803 was given an honorary law degree by his former employer, Glasgow University. Buried at Handsworth Church in Warwickshire, he is commemorated by a statue in Westminster Abbey as the inventor who made the Industrial Revolution possible.

WAUCHOPE, Andrew Gilbert (1846–99)
Soldier

The descendant of a distinguished **Covenanting** family, Wauchope was born at Niddrie Marischal in **Midlothian**, educated in England, and briefly joined the navy before switching to the army and a commission in **The Black Watch** (1865). He served in the Ashanti War (where he was wounded), Cyprus and Egypt (wounded again) before returning to Scotland to convalesce. In 1882 he stood against William Gladstone for the Midlothian Parliamentary seat; he lost but cut Gladstone's majority from 4631 to 690. Back in the army and a colonel by 1888, he served in Sudan under Kitchener (1898) and in the same year was promoted to major-general. He died in the Boer War leading a night attack on Boer trenches at Magersfontein.

WAULKING SONGS

These are Gaelic songs that were used as a rhythmic accompaniment to the waulking or fulling of cloth/

tweed, a process of beating wet cloth in order to make its texture more closely-knit and durable. This was traditionally carried out by a band of women (usually about 10 or 12) seated around a long trestle table, thumping the web of cloth against the boards and keeping it circulating. The length of the web was measured from time to time, until the desired shrinkage had been achieved. There were some localities where men performed the waulking, and also where the feet rather than the hands were used (this was called *luadh-chas*).

The songs are referred to as *òrain luadhaidh* (songs of waulking). There was more than one type, with variations of rhythm and speed to accord with the different parts of the waulking cycle, eg a type known as a clapping song was used when, at an advanced stage in the process, the tweed was folded and patted into shape.

The team had a leader, who normally sang the verses of the songs, while the whole team joined in the choruses. These were usually extensive, often with both short and long passages which were interjected between lines or half-lines of the songs. There follows an example of this, showing the pattern of line repetition and alternation of chorus segments. These segments are underlined.

<u>Hè mandu</u> *'s truagh nach tigeadh* <u>hè mandu</u> *siud gam iarraidh*
<u>hè mandu</u> *gille 's litir* <u>hao ri oro</u> *each is diallaid*
<u>hè mandu hao o ho to hò ro o hao hò</u>.
<u>Hè mandu</u> *gille 's litir* <u>hè mandu</u> *each is diallaid*
<u>hè mandu</u> *shnamhainn na caoil* <u>hao ri oro</u> *air an tarsaing*
<u>hè mandu hao o ho to hò ro o hao hò</u>.
(If only there would come for me a lad with a
    letter, a horse saddled, I would swim the kyles,
    straight across them.)

This is an example from a waulking song which the writer often heard his mother sing. She had been used to seeing and hearing waulking songs in her parents' house in Keose, **Isle of Lewis**, where she was born in 1887. Such traditional waulkings survived marginally until after World War II, and had already been promoted as a musical 'act' in the course of the 20th century, as the actuality became a treasured memory rather than a necessary activity. Now virtually all processing of tweed is done on machines and in mills.

A fairly small sub-class of waulking songs is specifically connected, in terms of composition, with the work process: eg the clapping songs; there is also a class of match-making songs in which the names of men were linked with specific girls in the waulking party. These were improvised to bring in the personalities involved, and perhaps a touch of humour or satire. There is little reason to suppose that the class of waulking songs as a whole was composed for this specific work process. It is more likely that existing songs meant to accompany other work processes were adapted to the cloth-working one. It is likely that some at least of the songs with elaborate choruses were in origin dance-songs.

Certainly the vast majority of the waulking songs make no reference to the waulking process. Instead they are embedded in the general community fabric, and tell of the experiences of members of the community: love or war, birth or death, companionship or feud. They chronicle private emotions and celebrate victory in battle. There is plenty of evidence to show that the songs travelled from one part of Gaelic Scotland to another, sometimes undergoing serious sea-change in the process; examples of **Perthshire** songs recorded in the mid-18th century show up again in the Western Isles in the mid-20th, but with signal differences. There is some evidence of a kind of communal composition, with stock phrases, lines or more extended passages apparently removable from one song to another, at the singer's whim (or that of local tradition).

A few brief quotations may help to identify the flavour of this song tradition:

(1) (A specific cloth-waulking song)
Iomair o ho, clò nan gillean (repeated thrice)
Bho dhòrn gu dòrn, clò nan gillean . . .
(Walk/move o ho the cloth of the lads,
from fist to fist, the cloth of the lads . . .)

(2) Alasdair òig, mhic 'ic Neacail,
B' fheàrr leam fhìn gum beirinn mac dhut,
Dhà no trì dhiubh, sia no seachd dhiubh . . .
(Young Alasdair, son of Nicholson,
I would love to bear you a son,
Two or three of them, six or seven . . .)

(3) E hò ro ho ro ho Na 'n cuimhne leibh
O hì ri rì hi ri ho ro ho Là na h-Airde?
Na 'n là eile, Mille-gàrraidh? . . .
(Do you remember the Battle of the Aird?
Or the other battle of Mille-gàrraidh? . . .)

(4) (A matchmaking song)

Faighibh dhomhsa leannan trath.
Im èile hog-i-ò
Hòg-o-bhi 's na hò-ro gheallaidh
Im èile hog-i-ò.
Cuiridh mi Donnchadh ann ad dhàil . . .
(Get me a sweetheart soon . . .
I'll send Duncan your way . . .)

A considerable recorded archive of waulking songs is held by the **School of Scottish Studies** at **Edinburgh University**, and there has been quite extensive publication of the songs, sometimes the words only but often words and melodies. Some of these collections are: Frances Tolmie's Collection, in *Journal of the Folk-Song Society*, No 16, 1911; *Eilean Fraoich*, 1938,1982; Margaret Fay Shaw, *Folksongs and Folklore of South Uist*, 1955, 1977; J L Campbell and F Collinson, *Hebridean Folksongs*, Vols I-III, 1969, 1977, 1981.

WAVERLEY, Paddle Steamer

A trip **'doon the watter'** in a **Clyde** paddle steamer was a favourite day out for many Glaswegian families from the mid-19th century until shortly after World War II. There is now only one paddle steamer left on the Clyde, the *Waverley* – the last sea-going paddle steamer in the world. The *Waverley* was built in 1946–7 by A & J Inglis at their Pointhouse yard for the London & North Eastern **Railway** Co to operate on the Clyde. When she was withdrawn from service in the 1970s she was saved by a group of enthusiasts. Although still based on the Clyde

she makes summer sailings from ports around the coast of Britain, maintaining a tradition that dates back to the very beginning of steam propulsion.

WEDDERBURN, Alexander, 1st Earl of Rosslyn (1733–1805) Lord Chancellor

Born in **Edinburgh** and educated at **Dalkeith** School and **Edinburgh University**, Wedderburn was enrolled as advocate in 1854 and quickly proved a formidable debater. He defended **David Hume** against Church censure and was a member of the Select Society; but, having resolved to make his mark in London, he chose to leave Edinburgh in sensational fashion by insulting the Lord President of the **Court of Session** with a theatrical tossing of his gown onto the Bar (1757). In London he was soon called to the English Bar and, primed with elocution lessons to remove his 'provincial' accent, launched into an erratic legal and political career. He appeared for the defence in the **Douglas Cause**, sat in Parliament for at least four different constituencies, and espoused such politics as would enhance his value to opponents anxious to win him over. In 1771, after a particularly dramatic switch of allegiance, he was appointed Solicitor-General in North's government and then (1778) Attorney-General. On being appointed Chief Justice to the Court of Common Pleas he took the title of Baron Loughborough (in Leicestershire), but changed even that to Baron Loughborough (in Surrey). His ultimate goal, the Lord Chancellorship, came courtesy of Pitt in 1793. Never popular, and a judge 'of very modest reputation', he was eventually eased from office (1801) with the Earldom of Rosslyn.

WEEM, Nr Aberfeldy, Perthshire

Just across **Wade**'s **Aberfeldy** bridge, Weem village rests against the steep and densely wooded Weem Rock whereon lie St David's well and cave, both near inaccessible. The old church, long since superseded by its grander neighbour, is used as the Menzies mausoleum (**Castle Menzies** is nearby). Mentioned in 13th century charters, the simple building dates from about 1510. Inside are two stone crosses from Dull (4 miles west), the site of a **Culdee** monastery founded by **Adamnan**. A third is still on site; they are thought to have marked the limits of the monastic enclosure. Parts of Weem Hotel date to the 16th century; Wade stayed here when building his bridge.

WEIGHTS AND MEASURES

The controlled use of weights and measures in Scottish burghs goes back to the earliest phase of burgh history. Dealing in false measures was a crime against both society and the Crown, and at one time was punishable by death or the cutting off of any member of the body. Despite attempts at standardisation, there always seemed to be many areas of confusion, such as whether measures should be heaped or straiked (levelled). The firlot caused particular problems, having different capacities for different commodities, and also varying for the same commodity in different parts of the country. The Scottish system of weights and measures should have come to an end in 1707, as Clause xvii of the **Act of Union** abolished them in favour of their English equivalents. However, the old Scots measures proved very durable, and even some official sets retained units such as the chopin and the mutchkin until the end of the 19th century; it was not until the 20th century that a common standard was established throughout the country.

WEIR, William Douglas, Lord Weir (1877–1959) Engineer
Born in **Glasgow**, educated at **Allan Glen's** and Glasgow High School, Weir was apprenticed as an engineer at the firm his father had established, G & W Weir. He became a director in 1898 and managing director four years later. An interest in cars and buses did not deflect him from the firm's main business of supplying pumps, primarily, for government naval contracts in Britain and worldwide, and he played a central role in the war effort when engaged by the Ministry of Munitions to secure supplies from the west of Scotland. For this contribution he was knighted (1917) and raised to the peerage (1918). A firm believer in advanced production methods and payment by results, he met with labour problems during and after the war. But the greatest danger now came from the downturn in trade, and it is perhaps his major achievement to have ensured the survival of the firm in the inter-war years. Throughout he played a prominent role in moulding official policy and in a range of industrial organisations. Created Viscount in 1938, he was again employed by the government when World War II broke out, becoming a director-general at the Ministry of Supply.

WELL OF THE HEADS, Invergarry, Inverness
Situated on the west shore of **Loch Oich**, this gruesome monument comprises seven severed heads carved in stone plus an inscription in Gaelic, English, French and Latin. It was erected by the last **MacDonell** of **Glengarry** in 1812 to commemorate his ancestor's achievement in exacting summary justice on seven murderers. But the inscription may be misleading. The events in question occurred about 1665, not 'in the 16th century'. The seven murderers' victims had been the sons and heirs of **MacDonell of Keppoch**, but it was the latter's sister who, by persuading the **clan bard** to compose an irresistibly poignant lament, did most to ensure vengeance. MacDonell of Glengarry seems to have prevaricated, in spite of the lament and in spite of orders from the Privy Council. It was probably Sir James MacDonald of Sleat who eventually despatched a force to tackle the seven murderers. After an epic struggle the **Skye** men overpowered the miscreants, severed their heads and washed them in the eponymous well before presenting them to MacDonell of Glengarry. Far from being proof of Glengarry's 'ample and summary vengeance', this procedure may have been intended as a criticism of his supineness.

WELSH, David (1793–1845) Minister
A minister of the Established Church from **Moffat** in **Dumfriesshire**, later Professor of Church History at **Edinburgh University**, Welsh was in the chair at the 1843 **General Assembly**, and led the seceders from the hall to form the **Free Church of Scotland** [see **Disruption**]. He was an energetic fund-raiser for their **New College**.

WEMYSS, EAST, WEST and COALTOWN OF, Fife
The name derives from the sandstone caves (or 'weems' from the Gaelic *uaimh*) which pock the cliffs facing the Firth of Forth east of East Wemyss. Like those at **Covesea** they contain, amongst later graffiti, some incised representations of the **Pictish** symbols and animals more commonly found on symbol stones and cross-slabs. Above stands the ruin of MacDuff's Castle, traditionally associated with the 'Thane of Fife', although the present structures, essentially two towers, are mainly 16th century. In the 14th century the land was held by the Wemyss family, passed to others by marriage, but was regained in 1630 by John 1st Earl of Wemyss. MacDuff's Castle remained habitable till after the Restoration although the 2nd Earl moved to Wemyss Castle near West Wemyss. 'An extensive but composite mansion' (15th century and later), this is said to be where **Queen Mary** first met **Darnley** (1565). In the gardens are the Wemyss burial ground and the ruins of a fine 16th century house. Accessible **coal** seams at Lochgelly and elsewhere accounted for the Wemyss family's wealth as also for the 19th century development of Coaltown of Wemyss as miners' accommodation and of West Wemyss as a major coal port. The harbour is now filled in but a modest 18th century Tolbooth with handsome clock tower survives.

WEMYSS, James (1610–67) Master Gunner
Born into the **Fife** family of Wemyss which specialised in artillery service, James moved to England at a young age, his prowess being sufficient to see him appointed Master Gunner to **Charles I** in 1638. In the ensuing Civil War he appears to have changed sides a number of times (escaping unharmed from the losing side at the **Battle of Dunbar** in 1650), but survived with his reputation intact, serving also as Master Gunner to **Charles II** in 1666–7. He patented an improved version of the leather guns of his uncle Robert Scott.

WEMYSS, Randolph G E (1858–1908) Coalmaster
Born on his father's estate at **Wemyss** in **Fife**, Randolph was only five years old when he inherited. On leaving Eton he travelled in the United States and returned determined to apply new mining techniques on his properties in East Fife. Much of the 1880s was spent in building a transport infrastructure (docks at **Methil** and **railways** through the estates) to ensure the carriage of the **coal** from his developing collieries. In 1894 he founded and became chairman of the Wemyss Coal Company Ltd which proceeded to open up a string of pits; by 1908 the total output amounted to 1.4 million tons. He also enjoyed a brief adventure in South Africa during the Boer War and indulged his passion for fox-hunting. The latter supposedly diverted his attention from business but scarcely detracts from his achievement of creating a local empire based on coal in the East Fife area.

WEMYSS BAY, Renfrewshire
Between **Largs** and **Gourock**, Wemyss Bay was a place of no note until, provided with a pier, it became the **railway** embarkation point for **Rothesay** and the **Isle of Bute**. Hotels and holiday homes made it a resort but

the chief structure of interest is still the station, opened in 1865 by the Wemyss Bay Railway Company but rebuilt on a grand scale in 1903 by the Caledonian Railway Company. Its mock Tudor exterior with a clock tower barely hints at the great web of steel and glass which radiates from the central circular booking office within. The encircling concourse, with bar, tea-room and shops, was designed to handle a mass stampede of holidaymakers as they swarmed off the platforms and wheeled down a spacious covered way, also glass and girders, to the waiting ferry. Only immediate access to **Hampden Park** could possibly justify such generous crowd space and triumphal architecture. Undermanned and ill served, the station was yet extensively restored in 1993–4. To the south, Skelmorlie Castle (1502 and 1638) was the home of the Montgomerie family, Sir Robert Montgomerie being the man responsible for Skelmorlie Aisle in **Largs**. It was later the home of the Earls of Eglinton. Inland at Outerwards and at Larg Moor above **Greenock** two **Roman** forts, outliers of the **Antonine Wall**, are visible. Excavation of the latter suggested a permanent garrison which probably kept a look-out over the Firth of **Clyde** although there was no evidence of a tower.

WEST LINTON, Peeblesshire

The first written record of the village of West Linton dates from the 12th century, when it was known as Lyntoun Roderyck, identified perhaps with a previous ruler of **Strathclyde** whose territory included this area. Later it was known simply as Lyntoun, and acquired the designation 'West' in the 19th century in order to distinguish it from other villages of the same name.

It is situated at the point where the river Lyne emerges from the **Pentland Hills**, and near the crossing of two important highways. The road to the north-west, now a track for most of its length, linked the Borders with the Central Lowlands. When the **droving** trade was at its height many thousands of sheep and cattle passed annually along this road and through the village, where a toll was levied at the toll house still to be seen at the foot of the lower green. At this time, Linton was noted for its sheep fairs, reputed to be the largest in Scotland, and for the distinctive coarse-wooled sheep of the area known as the Linton breed, now extinct.

In 1803 a horseman's mutual aid society was formed, the members of which were known as Whipmen. Traditions associated with the Society have been maintained and developed over the years and continue into the present time, culminating in a week of celebration held in the village every June.

The village is also noted for its tradition of stone carving, several examples of which may be seen in the main street and in the old kirkyard.

WEST LOTHIAN

Before the **local government** reorganisation of 1975, West Lothian – also known as Linlithgowshire – was a central Scottish county, bounded by **Midlothian** to the east, the Firth of Forth to the north, **Stirlingshire** to the west and **Lanarkshire** to the south-west. From the Forth, the terrain of the county rose towards high moorland in the south and west. The Almond and Avon were the principal rivers flowing northwards to the Forth.

Agriculture, **coal-mining** and manufacturing were the main occupations, with shale-oil extraction an important 19th century industry. The county town was **Linlithgow**, the other burghs comprising Armadale, **Bathgate**, **Bo'ness**, **Queensferry**, Whitburn, as well as **Livingston**, a New Town set up by legislation of 1946. In 1975 most of the former county became part of West Lothian District in Lothian Region, gaining East and West Calder from Midlothian, but losing Queensferry and **Kirkliston** to **Edinburgh** District and Bo'ness to **Falkirk** District in Central Region. Since the 1995 abolition of two-tier local government, this new version of West Lothian has become an autonomous Council Area.

'WEST LOTHIAN QUESTION', The

So called because it was repeatedly asked at Westminster by the Labour MP for **West Lothian** (Tam Dalyell), the question highlights an anomaly which arises in a post-devolution United Kingdom. Put simply, it asks why Westminster MPs from English constituencies should be denied any say in Scottish affairs as devolved to the **Scottish Parliament** when Westminster MPs from Scottish constituencies retain the right to speak and vote on similar subjects as they affect England. Where is the logic and what will be the consequences?

One outcome is prefigured in the Scotland Act of 1998. The traditional over-representation of Scotland, as compared to England, in the Westminster Parliament is to be redressed. There will be a reduction in the number (72) of Scottish MPs and it is likely to be achieved by enlarging some Scottish constituencies. But these constituencies are also used in elections to the Scottish Parliament. The change will therefore also reduce the number of directly elected MSPs; and since the ratio of directly elected MSPs to proportionally elected MSPs is protected, it will also mean a reduction in the number of MSPs elected from the regional party lists. Thanks to 'the West Lothian Question', under the terms of the Scotland Act the Scottish Parliament faces early decimation.

WESTLOTHIANA, Fossil

The oldest known **fossil** reptile in the world was unearthed in **West Lothian** in 1989. Hitherto the earliest was an animal called Hylonomus from 300-million-year-old late Carboniferous rocks in Nova Scotia. The new specimen was discovered in early Carboniferous shales near **Bathgate** by the professional collector Stanley Wood.

In early Carboniferous times, 338 million years ago, central Scotland was a swamp of primitive plants. Through the humid greenery scuttled insects, millipedes and spiders, chased by newt-like amphibians that had evolved only a few million years previously. The amphibians were not fully land-living animals as they had to return to the water to breed, and spent the early part of their lives as water-living tadpoles. Not until the reptiles evolved, with their hard-shelled eggs, did truly land-living vertebrates arrive.

The new fossil is of a lizard-like animal, 200mm (8in) long. We cannot tell definitely that it laid eggs, but we can distinguish the skeleton from that of an amphibian by the bones of the foot, and of the skull behind the eye. In honour of the place where it was found, the little reptile was given the generic name *Westlothiana* in 1990. From animals like this evolved the dinosaurs, the birds, the mammals, and ultimately ourselves.

WESTMINSTER-ARDTORNISH, Treaty of (1462)

Improbably linking the palace of Westminster with the remote little **Morvern** keep of **Ardtornish**, this treaty of 1462 between Edward IV of England and John **Lord of the Isles** was Edward's response to Lowland Scottish support for the rival house of Lancaster during the English Wars of the Roses (and **James III**'s minority). In return for becoming Edward's liege (and so renouncing any tenuous links with the Scottish monarchy) the Lord of the Isles received an English pension and the promise of half Scotland north of the Forth if and when Scotland succumbed to English conquest; the other half was to go to England's other Scottish ally, the **9th Earl of Douglas**. Since the Lord of the Isles was then established in **Inverness** and claimed also the **Earldom of Ross**, he already held most of his half. The treaty merely highlighted this and flaunted his defiance. It brought a predictable response when both James III and **James IV** began dismantling the Lordship and reducing its strongholds.

WESTRAY and PAPA WESTRAY, Orkney

It is thought that these islands in the north-west of the **Orkney** archipelago may have been joined when the two earliest habitations to have been discovered in the British Isles were built on the satellite isle. The exceptional fertility of the soil must have attracted the first settlers, as it did the Norsemen later. The two long stone dwellings with curved ends stand beside one another,

Noltland Castle, Westray, by R W Billings (RWB)

connected by a passage. They contained the round-bottomed Unstan ware and have been dated to around 3500 BC. A larger settlement at Noltland on Westray is less well preserved.

An incised cross helps to account for the presence of one of the *Papae* of the **Celtic Church** (from whom the pendicle takes its name), before this became a prestigious family estate during the Saga period.

Noltland also contains the great stronghold which that most evil of **Fife** adventurers, **Gilbert Balfour**, built here. As Master of the Household to **Queen Mary** he probably played the leading part in the murder of **Darnley**, unknown to his mistress. He married Margaret, sister of **Adam Bothwell**, Bishop of Orkney, who endowed him with the episcopal property of Westray at a time when the **Lords of the Congregation** of Jesus Christ were expressing their piety throughout the country in an orgy of looting. At Noltland Balfour employed what amounted to slave labour in erecting this monument to his megalomania. Its circular stone staircase is second only to that of **Fyvie Castle**, while its triple tiers of gunloops are without parallel in Scotland, if not in Europe. Balfour was executed for his part in a conspiracy against the King of Sweden before he could enjoy his place of strength in a remote island, nor did anyone else enjoy it. Noltland Castle continues to disfigure Westray, yet another reminder of **Stewart** rule in these islands.

WHALSAY, Shetland

With an area of only nine square miles, Whalsay is one of the smaller inhabited islands of **Shetland**; yet its 1000 people have turned it into one of the most prosperous in the whole of Scotland. The secret is their attachment to **fishing**, which they have developed into a multi-million pound business. In the 1970s, when most Shetlanders

were abandoning **herring** fishing because of the threat from Norwegian purse seiners, Whalsay men built up their own fleet of nine purse seiners – nearly a quarter of the present UK total. There is also a large fleet of white fish vessels and a processing plant which provides jobs for a large number of women. In recognition of the island's dependence on fishing, Shetland Islands Council, with help from the government and the EEC, spent millions of pounds in the late 1980s in expanding the harbour at Symbister.

WHEATLEY, John (1869–1930) Minister of Health

Born in Ireland, Wheatley was only nine when his family moved to Bargeddie in **Lanarkshire**. There he worked in the **coal**-mines for 13 years before taking up journalism and printing. He was thus nearly 40 when in 1908 he joined the **Independent Labour Party** and became involved in the politics of **Red Clydeside**. Seniority, acumen, and influence amongst the Irish community (he founded the Catholic Socialist Party) recommended him as adviser to **David Kirkwood** and as patron to **Pat Dollan** and **James Maxton**. From 1910–22 he served on **Glasgow** Town Council, supporting the activities of the **Clyde Workers Committee** but avoiding the government purges which consigned its leaders to prison. By highlighting Glasgow's acute housing problems and by organising, with Dollan, the switch of the Catholic vote to Labour, Wheatley masterminded the ILP's triumph in the 1922 election and, as MP for Shettleston (Glasgow), was himself one of the 'wild Clydesiders' who headed for Westminster.

In the Lib-Lab government of 1924 **Ramsay MacDonald**, anxious to placate his ILP left-wingers, gave Wheatley the Health portfolio. Unexpectedly Wheatley proved an outstanding success, notably for his Housing Act. This provided local authorities with government subsidies to offset the borrowing costs entailed in council house building programmes. Drawing on his considerable experience of the subject, Wheatley drafted a Bill and skilfully piloted it through Parliament. Although curtailed in 1926, the Act is reckoned to have given Scotland 75,000 much-needed new homes and to have established the pattern that led to the postwar building programmes. Many regard Wheatley's Housing Act as the greatest achievement of the Red Clydesiders; some as their only achievement.

In 1929 Wheatley was not given office in the new Labour government, largely because of his close association with James Maxton and the extreme left of the ILP. He might have prevented the final break between the ILP and the Labour Party, but he died suddenly in 1930.

WHEATLEY REPORT

The Royal Commission on **Local Government** in Scotland was set up in 1966 under the chairmanship of Lord Wheatley (1908–88). Comprising nine members, three of them MPs, it reported in September 1969 after analysing the existing state of Scottish local authorities. Among the anomalies it uncovered was the fact that **Paisley**, with a 95,000 population, had no responsibility for **education**, while no fewer than 23 counties with smaller populations were so charged. The commission recommended a 'tier' system of local government, consisting of seven regions and 37 districts, all with appropriate responsibilities. Community councils would operate at local level. This proved to be the basis for the local authority reform that followed the 1973 Local Government (Scotland) Act and was put into effect from 1975. The number of authorities differed from those recommended, and the much criticised system was finally abandoned in 1995.

WHIGGAMORE RAID, The (1648)

From 'whig', to spur on, and 'more', ie mare, Whiggamore is said to have been a term of scant respect applied to those mounted **drovers** from **Galloway** and the south-west who annually sold their cattle in central Scotland. Hence it was applied to the armed and radical **Covenanters**, also from the south-west, who rallied after the defeat of the **Engagers** at Preston and swept into **Edinburgh** to end the rule of the ungodly. The Committee of Estates fled and remaining Engagers resigned. To secure their triumph the '**Whigs**' entered into a short-lived [see **Battle of Dunbar**] alliance with Cromwell and passed the detested **Act of Classes**.

WHIGS

The term derives from the **Whiggamore Raid** (1648) and was first used in 1657 (OED) to denote a dissenting **Presbyterian** or **Covenanter**. Both **Graham of Claverhouse** and **Gilbert Burnet** used it as a pejorative for **Conventiclers** who resisted the Restoration settlement. Post-1679 it was applied to those who opposed the succession of **James VII** and thus after 1687 to a supporter of the Williamite Revolution. Hence it entered English political life as a label for the interests and party which opposed **Jacobites** and 'Tories' (also once a pejorative term, but of Irish origin).

WHISKY

Whisky is Scotland's drink, made in Scotland, but now drunk all over the world. Whisky is Scottish, but 'Scotch' is whisky; whiskey with an 'e' is Irish, rye is Canadian and Bourbon American whiskey. No other country has ever been able to manufacture anything like Scotch.

Traditionally it has been suggested that whisky, like Christianity, came to the Highlands from Ireland, perhaps in the 6th or 7th centuries AD. But archaeological excavation on the island of **Rum** in 1986 found spores and pollen suggesting that an 'alcoholic drink' was made about 6000 years ago. The name is derived from the **Gaelic** *uisgebeatha*, meaning the water of life, and shortened to usqua or usky. Whisky had reached the court of **James IV** by 1500. Around this time the Barbers and Surgeons of **Edinburgh** were given the right to make and sell aqua vitae or usqua.

The first tax on whisky was imposed by the Scots Parliament in 1644, at a time when most distilling was carried out in the countryside on a small scale in private stills. Households were permitted to make spirit for their own use, although its sale was illegal. The history of distilling, and the effect of excise on it, is complicated. Illicit stills became commonplace, particularly in the Highlands, and they were not brought under control until the beginning of the 19th century. Whisky at this time was a fiery spirit of inconsistent quality which was

The Glenrothes Distillery c1920 (BRC)

Whisky continued

not generally acceptable to potential drinkers in England. A market was created when the *phylloxera* epidemic severely affected European vineyards with a decrease in the production of brandy as well as wines. Whisky was wanted, but it took a group of enterprising Scotsmen to recognise that a consistent whisky could best be produced by blending different types, notably malt and grain.

Malts

Malt whisky is made from a watery extract of malted barley fermented by yeast and distilled in onion-shaped *pot-stills* from which the alcohol is driven off by heat. The first step is to *steep* the barley in water. It is then *malted*, a process which used to be carried out on the floor of a malting house, but now is done in Saladin boxes or revolving drums. The green malt is spread over the floor of the kiln and dried by heat from a furnace fired by **peat** and coke. The kiln traditionally had a pagoda-like ventilator at its top, and this characteristic structure has been retained by most distilleries, even though they may no longer do their own malting. The process of malting is continued until rootlets have developed. After drying, the malt is ground into *grist* and mixed with water in a metal vat called a *mash tun*. After eight hours or so, the fluid (*wort*) is fermented in large *wash-backs* which used always to be made of wood, but now stainless steel is preferred. Yeast is added and fermentation begins, the process being like brewing and lasting about 40 hours. The resulting *wash* consists of

water, yeast and about 7% alcohol per volume. This is distilled in a pot-still, the alcohol being driven off before the water, and collected first in a low wines receiver and then in a spirit receiver. The relatively crude spirit needs to mature in wooden casks before it becomes recognisable as drinkable whisky. Traditionally, sherry casks were used, but oak Bourbon casks are sometimes preferred and are more readily available. Oak casks may be filled with sherry to stain the wood or a cheaper substitute, paxarette, can be used. The casks each hold between 50 and 100 gallons. The period of *maturation* varies and takes from 8 to 15 years; the longer the time the better (and the more expensive) the whisky. The colourless liquid gradually absorbs colour from the cask and becomes more golden. Unlike wine, whisky does not alter once it is bottled. Most malt whisky now goes for blending, but between 90 and 100 single malts are bottled for drinking, although these form only about 2% of the total volume of whisky marketed.

Grain

Grain whisky is a comparatively recent invention and was not introduced until the 1830s. It was made from maize, and a little malted barley, in a patent still devised by Robert Stein of Kilbagie (**Clackmannanshire**). His patent was quickly superseded by the Coffey still which originated in Dublin. After fermentation, the wash goes through two columns, each about 40ft (12m) high; the first is the rectifier and the second the analyser. Steam is driven through a series of perforated trays over which the wash trickles and the alcohol is condensed by a cold water coil. The whole process is both quicker and cheaper than malt distilling; and the spirit produced is nearer to pure alcohol. Grain whisky is made in large industrial plants, mostly in the neighbourhood of **Glasgow** and Edinburgh. Although it is drinkable, it is rarely bottled on its own, but it has come to form the basis of most whisky on the market.

Blends

It was the demand for whiskies which were consistent in both taste and price which led to the production of blended whisky in the second half of the 19th century. The mixture of the cheaper grain whisky with a number of different, but more delectable, malts led to an acceptable product which became the basis of Scotland's greatest export industry. A standard blend, of which there are more than 200 varieties, may contain as many as 30 or 40 different malts and perhaps six or seven different grain whiskies. The reason for the large number of malts is to safeguard the blender from closure of malt distilleries, as happens from time to time; he can in any circumstances continue to produce his own consistent style of whisky. The choice of constituents is made by highly skilled blenders who rely entirely on their nose, rather than taste.

The proportion of malt to grain is critical, but the precise constituents are a closely guarded secret. A good quality blend may contain an equal quantity of grain and malt, but the proportion may be in the region of 60% grain (or 60% malt). Cheaper whiskies may, it is said, have as much as 80% grain; but a de luxe blend will have more and better quality malts. Blending first began with the vatting (mixing in a vat) of various malts, and there are a number of high class vatted malts on the market today.

The problem of definition had to be faced at the turn of the century when pure grain whisky was being sold in London as 'Scotch Whisky'. Conflict developed between the grain distillers and blenders on the one hand and the malt distillers on the other. This dispute came to a head in 1905 when Islington Borough Council prosecuted publicans for selling as whisky 'articles not of the nature, substance and quality demanded'. Complicated legal arguments followed and it was not until 1909 that a report was produced by a Royal Commission. It was concluded that the name 'whiskey' (sic) should not be restricted to the product of the pot-still and it was defined as 'a spirit obtained from a mash of cereal grains saccharified by diastase'. No special legislation was considered necessary and no minimum period of maturation was laid down. This was a victory for the blenders over the malt distillers, and it was now possible to make and distribute blended whisky on a larger scale and at a cheaper cost to meet the increasing demand.

Malt Distilleries

Malt distilleries are relatively small. Their number has varied over the years depending on the general level of economic prosperity; during the 1970s there were just over 120, but this decreased during the subsequent recession. The prime requirement is an abundant supply of good water, traditionally running off granite through peat.

Most distilleries are in the Highlands and many are grouped along the banks of the river **Spey** or its tributaries. The Glenlivet was the first to be licensed in 1824 under the government's new act. At one time many in the area incorporated the name Glenlivet with their own; for example Dufftown-Glenlivet. But this is no longer permitted. Among the most famous Highland malts are Macallan, Glenfarclas, Glen Grant, Knockandu, Cardhu, Glenfiddich, Strathisla and Tamnavulin; these are all bottled as single malts which are readily available and excellent to drink.

Apart from malts originating in Speyside, there are other distilleries beyond the Highland Line. The best-known of the northern group are Glenmorangie, Dalmore and Pulteney. The first is made in **Tain**, and is unusual because it uses hard water running over red sandstone and the spirit stills are exceptionally tall. Eastern malts include Fettercairn, Glen Garioch and Lochnagar. Those in **Perthshire** are Blair Atholl, Tullibardine, Glenturret and Glengoyne.

The island malts are Highland Park and Scapa on **Orkney** in the north, Talisker on **Skye**, and **Jura**. These are to be distinguished from the **Islay** malts with their characteristic iodine-like taste; the best known are Laphroaig, Bowmore and Bruichladdich.

There used to be 32 distilleries around **Campbeltown** on the **Kintyre** Peninsula, but only one – Springbank – remains. Finally there is a group of Lowland malts; the best-known being Auchentoshan in **Dunbartonshire** and Rosebank near **Falkirk**.

Most of these distilleries can easily be visited and have well run reception centres. They generally have a *silent season* in July or August, but may have arrangements for visitors during this period. There is a well-advertised Whisky Trail on Speyside, organised by the Scottish Tourist Board, on which six or seven of the more famous distilleries can be visited by a circuitous route. Nowadays relatively little labour is needed to run an efficient distillery and a resident exciseman is no longer required, although a revenue assistant known as a watcher will be present in every establishment.

The reason for the unique taste of each single malt lies in a number of factors. The local water is perhaps the most important and it may be that its softness allows various substances, as well as maltose, to be dissolved from the malt mash. The peat too must play a part by its effect on the water and also by its use in the kilns where the smoke transmits flavour to the drying barley. The shape and size of the stills themselves are considered to contribute to the flavour, although it is not clear how this is so. The method of firing may also be relevant; the type of cask is important, and so is the atmosphere in which the casks are stored, the cool damp climate of the Highlands being ideal. Distillers keep the whisky in their own warehouses even after it has been sold to brokers. Finally the chill-filtering (to remove any substances which might cause cloudiness) and the nature of the water added to bring the whisky to the required strength may be factors. But the mystique of malt whisky and the secrecy which surrounds aspects of its production continue to defy scientific analysis and to frustrate would-be competitors.

Whisky Companies

THE DISTILLERS COMPANY LTD (DCL) was formed in 1877 when six Lowland grain distillers came together to protect their interests. Other firms long associated with the popularisation of blended whisky joined it, including:

JOHN HAIG The Haig family became involved in distilling in the 18th century and were connected with the Stein family when the first John Haig married Margaret Stein in 1751. Another John built the distillery at Cameronbridge in 1824 and the headquarters were at **Markinch**. Various amalgamations took place and the company was acquired by DCL in 1919. The blend *John Haig* remains well known and popular; the de luxe *Dimple* comes in a characteristic bubbled bottle.

JOHN DEWAR (b. 1806) became a wine and spirit merchant in **Perth**. By 1923 seven distilleries were owned by the firm and two years later they became part of DCL. Their blend retains its high quality and so does their de luxe *Ancestor*.

JOHN WALKER The first **John Walker** was a grocer in **Kilmarnock** and his son opened a London office in 1880. They also joined with other firms and became part of DCL in 1925. Their two most famous brands, *Red Label* and the de luxe *Black Label* are, in the words of their early advertisement, 'still going strong'.

JAMES BUCHANAN began by working in a **shipping** office in Glasgow, but set up a London office as a whisky merchant in 1884. After developing an active business, Buchanan's amalgamated with Dewars and joined DCL in 1925. Their *Black & White* whisky is sold all over the world, but not in the United Kingdom.

JAMES LOGAN MACKIE was himself a distiller who formed his own company. He was succeeded by his nephew Peter Mackie. He registered the name *White Horse* and amalgamated with DCL in 1927 to form the 'Big Five' with Haig, Dewar, Walker and Buchanan.

WILLIAM SANDERSON lived in **Leith** where he developed what he called 'mixture whisky' in his father's wine and spirit business. This led to *VAT 69* which was introduced in 1882. The House of Sanderson joined DCL in 1937.

By this time DCL controlled a large number of companies, including the Scottish Malt Distillers Ltd and the Scottish Grain Distillers Ltd, and dominated the whisky industry. It was, however, badly affected by the recession in the 1970s and became involved in an acrimonious takeover battle in 1985. Acquisition in 1986 by Guinness plc (who had also acquired Bells the previous year) provoked well founded accusations of commercial malpractice and bitter resentment amongst patriotic Scots.

A further merger in 1997 between Guinness and Grand Metropolitan produced Diageo, while their spirit arms (United Distillers and International Distillers & Vintners) were amalgamated as United Distillers & Vintners (UDV). Although, as part of the merger, Dewars along with four distilleries passed to the Bacardi-Martini Group, UDV produces Johnnie Walker Red Label and J&B Rare, the world's two best-selling whiskies.

Apart from UDV, numerous other companies, some

in Scottish hands and all subject to amalgamation and takeovers, continue to thrive.

WILLIAM GRANT & SONS are a good example of a family firm which has remained independent and has been outstandingly successful. The first William Grant was born in 1839, and after learning shoe-making, built Glenfiddich distillery which opened in 1887. His company decided to concentrate on producing the single malt *Glenfiddich* in 1962. An intensive marketing campaign resulted in rising sales and led to a general increase in the popularity of other single malts as well as their own. The name of Grant is associated with other firms making whisky. J & G Grant, who are not related to the William Grant family, have owned the Glenfarclas distillery since 1865 and continue to bottle a first-class single malt of that name. J & J Grant (*Glen Grant*), on the other hand, amalgamated with G & J G Smith to become The Glenlivet & Glen Grant Distilleries Ltd in 1952 before being acquired by Seagram in 1978.

SEAGRAM is a good example of the successful incursion of an overseas company, in this case Canadian. Samuel Bronfman built a distillery in Montreal in 1924 and two years later purchased Joseph E Seagram & Sons Ltd of Waterloo, Canada. In Scotland the firm bought the Robert Brown Co in 1935, and further acquisitions were Chivas Bros of **Aberdeen** in 1948 and the Milton (renamed Strathisla) distillery in 1950. This set the scene for further expansion which included building a new distillery, Glen Keith, followed by the Braes of Glenlivet in 1975 and Alt à Bhainne in 1975. Their best-known de luxe blend *Chivas Regal* has been a market leader.

North American interests were maintained by Hiram Walker, who acquired George Ballantyne & Son Ltd in 1936 and a number of malt distilleries after World War II. They were, however, absorbed by Allied Lyons (later Allied-Domecq plc) in 1986.

Publiker Industries Inc are represented by Inver House distilleries. European companies have become involved in Scotland in recent years: Pernod Ricard own companies running Aberlour and Edradour distilleries; Cointreau acquired Glenturret in 1981; a subsidiary of Martini & Rossi owns MacDuff distillery, and a Spanish company bought Macnab Distilleries Ltd in 1973. The Japanese, enthusiastic whisky drinkers, acquired Tomatin distillery in 1986, and have also bought substantially into Stanley P Morrison, whose malts, *Bowmore* (from Islay) and *Glengarioch* (in **Aberdeenshire**) are readily available and popular. It should not, though, be assumed that the control of whisky-making is passing out of Scottish hands; some Scottish companies have remained independent and successful.

MACDONALD MARTIN DISTILLERIES is well established under family control. Their single malt, *Glenmorangie*, is skilfully marketed and has sold well. Their most popular blend is *Highland Queen*.

HIGHLAND DISTILLERIES were formed in 1887 and owned Bunnahabhain and Glenrothes distilleries, subsequently acquiring Glenglassaugh, Tamdhu and Highland Park. In 1970 they bought Matthew Gloag & Son,

Corking bottles at Highland Park Distillery, Orkney, c1900 (BRC)

Whisky continued

who produce *The Famous Grouse*, said to be the most popular whisky in Scotland. In 1999 the company was bought by the Edinburgh Group, a large private company with extensive whisky interests, and William Grant & Sons.

Two London wine merchants have special interests in whisky. Berry Bros & Rudd of St James's have produced their *Cutty Sark* blend since the early 1920s. Justerini & Brooks, now part of the International Distillers & Vintners group, are responsible for J & B *Rare*, a blend whose taste and pale colour make it particularly popular in the United States.

ARTHUR BELL & SON, now part of UDV, played an important part in the growth of the industry. Founded by Arthur Bell in 1895, and beginning as blenders for the local people, the company bought Blair Atholl, Dufftown and Inchgower distilleries in the years before 1939. After the war they continued to expand, but became vulnerable and were taken over by Guinness. Their standard blend, *Bell's Extra Special*, has been the leading brand in the United Kingdom.

The Pleasures of Whisky

The different varieties make whisky a drink for all occasions: a blend with soda (and even ice) is excellent for quenching the thirst; a single malt with a modicum of water is a delectable aperitif, and a 15-year-old malt may be savoured like brandy after dinner. Whisky, as might be expected, goes particularly well with **haggis**.

The bottle's label should make it clear whether the whisky is a blend or a malt. If a blend, there may not necessarily be a great deal of other label information,

but the size of the bottle should be stated: nowadays 70cl or 24.6 fl oz is standard in the UK. The alcoholic strength should also be given. In the past, degrees proof was used and the standard strength was 70°. A new numerical system was introduced in 1970 which gives the strength in percentage of alcohol by volume: 70° proof now becomes 40% alcohol per volume; and a stronger whisky labelled in the past as 100° proof should now be 57% alcohol. For the time being both measures are usually given side by side. The label of de luxe blends will sometimes indicate that, for example, all the malts are over, say, 12 years old. There is never any indication of the proportion of grain to malt.

A single malt should, and invariably does, give the age. There is a widely held impression that malts are so precious that they should be drunk neat without water. This is not upheld by most experts who favour anything from a splash of water to a half-and-half mixture. Just as it is not sensible to generalise about which is the best malt, so the amount of water is not something to argue over. The best water comes from a Highland spring. Soda water, acceptable with a blend, tastes terrible with any malt.

Whether or not the average person can distinguish between different whiskies is doubtful. But no one should confuse a malt with a blend, and with practice individual malts have recognisably different tastes. Real experts score very highly in any test.

Whisky Liqueurs

Recent years have seen a proliferation of Scotch whisky liqueurs. Atholl Brose, Johnnie Walker Liqueur, Glayva and Lochan Ora from yesteryear have been joined more recently by liqueurs from Glenfiddich, Glenturret, Old Pulteney, Wallace and the more exotically named Cock o' the North and Stags Breath. However, the best-known and most successful of them all is Drambuie (from the Gaelic, *an dram buidheach* – the drink that satisfies), which is available in over 200 countries worldwide. The recipe at the heart of Drambuie is reputed to have been gifted to Captain John MacKinnon of Strathaird by **Prince Charles Edward Stewart** in 1746 in grateful thanks for helping him escape from the government forces pursuing him after **Culloden**. What is certain is that his descendant Malcolm Mackinnon started producing Drambuie commercially in Edinburgh in 1906 by adding this recipe, and a **heather** honey syrup, to the finest of aged Scotch whiskies, many of which are 15- to 17-year-old malts. Drambuie remains to this day a family-owned company.

See: *Whiskies of Scotland*, R J S McDowall and William Waugh, 1986; the classic *The Whisky Distilleries in the United Kingdom*, A Barnard, 1887; and *The Making of Scotch Whisky*, Michael J Moss and John R Hume, Edinburgh, 1981.

WHITE PARK CATTLE

From medieval times the family of the **Dukes of Hamilton** kept an ornamental herd of cattle at Cadzow in Châtelherault Park, near **Hamilton** in **Lanarkshire**. These animals were white with black ears and feet, and all bore horns. They were hunted on special occasions. Other such park herds were to be found, but they either died out or could only be maintained in numbers by crossing with other breeds. The one herd left untouched was that which continues to thrive at Chillingham Park in Northumberland. A reserve herd of Chillingham cattle is kept near **Fochabers** as a safeguard against extinction. The Cadzow cattle, with the other park herds excepting Chillingham, have been merged into the White Park breed of which there are fewer than 200 breeding females.

WHITEBEAMS, Arran

Two of the world's rarest trees occur in the wild only in a remote glen in the north of the Isle of **Arran**. These are the endemic Arran Whitebeams, *Sorbus arranensis* and *Sorbus pseudofennica*. The former probably arose from hybridisation of the common **rowan** (*Sorbus aucuparia*) with the rare whitebeam *Sorbus rupicola*. Subsequent fertilisation of *Sorbus arranensis* by rowan gave rise to the second endemic species, *Sorbus pseudofennica*. Although these 'species' appear to be intermediate in character between the two parents because they produce genetically identical offspring, they are recognisably different and have been given different names.

WHITEHILLS, Banffshire

In 1839 the Revd Alexander Anderson described Whitehills' society as 'quite unique', and it remains little changed. This is the typical north-east **fishing** community, intensely independent, tight knit, and seemingly more attuned to the keen winds of the North Sea than to the rich rural landscape behind or the busy roads that pass it by. Names like Lovie and Watson, which filled the Rev Anderson's parish register, now fill the telephone directory. Continuity counts, as does resilience. The village that emerged with the 19th century **herring** boom became a town with the 20th century white fish trade, and still depends on the seine net. Unendowed with architecture, its character lies in its isolated setting, its harbour (1900) and its people.

WHITEKIRK, East Lothian

Whitekirk's 15th century church was built by a well and a shrine to Our Lady of **Haddington**, recorded in the 14th century as a great place of healing. **James I**, an enthusiastic patron of pilgrims, built hostels here for their shelter and in 1435 it was visited by Aeneas Silvius Piccolomini, a Papal Legate who became Pope Pius II, to give thanks for his deliverance from a shipwreck. Gutted in 1914 by a fire thought to have been started by suffragettes, the church was restored in 1917 by **Robert Lorimer**. During the punitive and fiery English campaign of 1356 known as **'Burnt Candlemas'** Edward III landed a force of troops at Whitekirk before marching on Haddington.

WHITELAW, William (1868–1946) Railway Chairman

Whitelaw was born in Gartsherrie House, **Coatbridge**, and educated at Harrow and Cambridge. Elected for **Perth** as a Conservative in 1892 he lost the seat three years later and, despite repeated attempts to re-enter Parliament, failed to achieve the political distinction reserved for his grandson and namesake (the Conservative Home Secretary and ally of Margaret Thatcher). Instead he emerged as a **railway** company executive of

distinction, firstly with the Highland Railway Company and later with the North British Railway of which he became Chairman in 1912. In the post-war years he won nearly £10 million compensation for the company for damages incurred through the stresses of war and was a prominent spokesman and lobbyist in the controversy surrounding the future of the railways. After the Railways Act of 1921 he became Chairman of the LNER where he cut costs and instituted a federal structure for the newly merged company.

WHITHORN, Wigtownshire

The cradle of Christianity in Scotland, the hallowed shrine of **St Ninian**, and an important place of pilgrimage for more than four centuries, Whithorn now has little in the way of grandiose ruins to elevate the spirits or summon up its venerable ghosts. In 1186 Fergus, Lord of **Galloway**, restored the bishopric, founded a priory and built a Romanesque cathedral which in the 13th century was incorporated in a priory church serving as the cathedral of the diocese of Galloway. It is vestiges of this priory, with additions dating from succeeding centuries, that form the bulk of the ecclesiastical remains.

According to Bede's *Historia Ecclesiastica* of 731, St Ninian made his headquarters at Whithorn at the beginning of the 5th century and built his *Candida Casa*. Little tangible evidence of his settlement remains. The most important, and least controversial, relic of his era is the inscribed pillar stone known as the *Latinus* stone, the earliest Christian memorial in Scotland (discovered during excavations in the late 19th century and now displayed, along with later stones, in Whithorn Museum). There is still no certainty about the exact location of the *Candida Casa*; claims that it was on the **Isle of Whithorn** have been largely discounted, current thinking placing it at the eastern end of the crypt of the medieval cathedral-priory.

It was the vaulted underground crypt that became the shrine to St Ninian and the great draw for pilgrims. For 400 years from Fergus's foundation until the **Reformation** crowds converged on Whithorn from all parts of the country and included many Scottish monarchs. **Robert I** visited the shrine a few months before his death in 1329; in the 15th and 16th centuries **James I** and the **Regent Albany** ordered safe-conducts to be granted to pilgrims to Whithorn; in 1473 **James III** and his Queen, Margaret of Denmark, made a 'state visit' to Wigtownshire which included a call at the shrine; **James IV**, the most frequent of all royal pilgrims, made his most urgent pilgrimage in 1507 when he travelled on foot from **Edinburgh** to seek the saint's intercession for his wife **Margaret Tudor** who was seriously ill – on her recovery they made another pilgrimage together (on horseback) to give thanks. Visits by **James V** are recorded in 1526 and 1533, and in 1563 **Queen Mary** made the last royal pilgrimage. So popular had Whithorn become as a place of pilgrimage that it even survived the Reformation and an Act of Parliament had to be passed in 1581 to prohibit the practice.

For some time thereafter the buildings at Whithorn were allowed to fall into decay, but the nave of the cathedral was rebuilt by Bishop Gavin Hamilton in 1610 and served as the parish church until the building of

Romanesque doorway and nave of Whithorn Priory (HS)

the present parish church nearby in 1822. Since 1908, when the site was placed in the care of the Ministry of Public Buildings and Works, excavations at Whithorn have produced more important carved stones and a variety of priceless artefacts, including the famous 12th century crozier, now in Edinburgh's **Royal Museum**.

WHITHORN, Isle of, Wigtownshire

Three miles south of **Whithorn**, this small village was built on what was once an island, now linked to the mainland by a causeway. Its sheltered harbour has made it a popular boating and holiday resort. In medieval times it was the port of entry for pilgrims to Whithorn from Ireland and the Isle of Man, and from points on the Scottish and English coasts. On the seaward side of the Isle are the ruins of a small chapel standing in a walled enclosure. Thought to date from the end of the 13th century, and built on the remains of an earlier chapel, this chapel was dedicated to **St Ninian** but contained no trace of early Christian remains.

WHITTINGHAME, East Lothian

James Balfour of Balbirnie bought the Whittinghame estate in 1817, pulled down most of the 'decayed' village and commissioned Sir Robert Smirke to build Whittinghame House. Described (by J G Dunbar) as 'dignified if uninspired' and by the *New Statistical Account* as 'a splendid mansion of Grecian architecture', Whit-tinghame was altered and extended in 1827 by **William Burn** and was the birthplace (1848) of the owner's grandson and future prime minister **A J Balfour**. Whit-tinghame Tower to the south-west of the mansion was built by one of the **Douglas** family, later **Earls of Morton**, in the late 15th century. Here **Regent Morton** (the 4th Earl) is said to have discussed with **Bothwell** and **Lethington** plans to assassinate **Darnley**.

WHYTE, Ian (1901–60) Composer and Conductor

Best remembered nowadays as a conductor who possessed an ear of legendary accuracy and sensitivity, Whyte was in fact a prolific composer. Besides his ballet *Donald of the Burthens*, which was produced with considerable success at Covent Garden, his works include a *Violin Concerto* which was admired by Max Rostal, and a *Symphony* performed at the **Edinburgh Festival** – at which he often conducted the **BBC Scottish Symphony Orchestra** of which he was principal conductor from 1946 until his death. One of his most successful orchestral works was the symphonic tone poem *Edinburgh*, and he produced a vast quantity of arrangements for broadcasts as well as being closely involved in the first attempt at a broadcast history of Scottish **music**.

WHYTT, Robert (1714–66) Physician

Born in **Edinburgh** the son of an advocate, Whytt studied medicine in Edinburgh for four years under **Professor Alexander Monro** Primus with further studies in London, Paris, Leyden, Rheims and **St Andrews**. One of the first doctors in Scotland to undertake medical research, particlarly in physiology, in 1743 he published a paper *On the Virtues of Lime Water in the Cure of Stone*; from 1744–51 he was engaged in the preparation of a work *On the Vital and other Involuntary Motions of Animals* and in 1755 he published *An Inquiry into the Causes which Promote the Circulation of Fluid in the very Small Vessels of Animals*. He was the first to describe dropsy of the brain in children, which he called *hydrocephalus internus*, now recognised as tuberculous meningitis. His paper on the subject was published after his death in his book *The Writings of Robert Whytt* (Edinburgh, 1768). His writings became known throughout Europe, particularly *On Nervous Hypochondriac or Histeric Diseases* published in 1764. In 1747 he was appointed to the Chair of Institutes of Medicine at **Edinburgh University**. He was the first Physician to the King in Scotland and became President of the **Royal College of Physicians** in 1763.

WICK, Caithness

Wick and **Thurso** have experienced the same rivalry as **Kirkwall** and **Stromness** in the **Orkney** islands to their north. In both cases it is the westerly town (Thurso, Stromness) that possesses the better natural harbour, but the one nearer Europe (Wick, Kirkwall) that was invested with the exclusive right to trade abroad as a **royal burgh**. Wick did not obtain its charter until 1589, but as its Norse name *Vik* implies, its past dates from Viking times. Its castle of Oldwick is probably the oldest in **Caithness**. Perched on a peninsula between two narrow precipitous geos, with a ditch protecting it from the mainland, this must have been the resort of **Rognvald**, Earl and Saint, as well as of other Norse notables when they visited the mainland. The rectangular tower stands three storeys high and is almost devoid of architectural features. By 1660 Wick contained only 500 inhabitants and 100 years later it still lacked a harbour, while Thurso had grown to nearly three times its size. Then in 1790 **Thomas Telford** made his survey and in 1803 began work on a harbour, and on a new town south of the river. This he named after his patron, a neighbouring laird in **Dumfriesshire** who had changed his name to that of the Pulteney heiress he married. Pulteneytown had its separate council until it became part of the royal burgh in 1902.

The **herring** boom, for which such timely provision had been made, brought hosts of Gaels from the west in search of seasonal work. This led to the Great Fight of Wick (*Sabaid Mhor Inbhir Uige*) in 1859. It began with two children quarrelling over an apple and expanded into the last conflict between Gaels and 'foreigners' in Scotland. (To this day the Caithness folk answer cheerfully to the Gaelic term *Gallaich*, foreigners, just as Hebrideans refer to their islands as *Innse Gall*, Foreigner Isles, as though they were still inhabited by the Norsemen.)

Wick's Pulteneytown harbour as photographed by George Washington Wilson (GWWA)

The strife in Wick continued for a week; a detachment was landed from the warships *Jackal* and *Princess Royal*; the West York Rifles were despatched from **Edinburgh**. In 1826 a distillery had been opened in Wick but this does not seem to have inflamed the strife; it continues in production. The herring capital of Europe (60,000 barrels in 1817) suffered severely from the decline of the fisheries, but it has found a less fickle source of prosperity in the manufacture of Caithness Glass. A curing yard with kipper kiln and cooperage is preserved as the Wick Heritage Centre.

WIGTOWN, Wigtownshire

Anciently Wigtoun or Wigtoune, later Wigton and now officially Wigtown (the same applying to the shire), this small town unusually sited on a hill looking out over Wigtown Bay was a **royal burgh** from 1292 or possibly even earlier. Its castle (long gone) was captured by Edward I of England in c1296, retaken by **Robert I** and later alienated to the **Douglases**, reverting to the Crown on their fall in 1455. Beside the parish church (1853) are ruins of its predecessor (1730) and some fragments of an older church dedicated to St Machitis (d.554). The churchyard has an inscribed stone in memory of the **Wigtown Martyrs**. They are also commemorated in the 'Martyrs' Stake Car Park' at the foot of the hill and, with other **Covenanting** martyrs, in the Martyrs' Monument. The town's broad main street boasts two mercat crosses, the first 'a structure of great architectural elegance and adorned with tasteful sculpturings' (Fullarton's *Gazetteer*) erected in 1738 and the second 'a ponderously buttressed granite structure' (C H Dick) in 1816 to commemorate the victory of Waterloo. In 1996 a committee was set up by **Strathclyde University** to select a Scottish Book Town to be developed along the lines of Hay-on-Wye in England. The six towns proposed were **Dalmellington, Dunblane, Gatehouse of Fleet, Moffat, Strathaven** and Wigtown – and in 1997 the committee pronounced in favour of Wigtown. Four miles north-west of Wigtown are the **Torhousekie standing stones**.

WIGTOWN MARTYRS, The (1685)

Four women, Margaret MacLachlan (or Lachlison), Margaret and Agnes Wilson, and Margaret Maxwell were tried as **Conventiclers** in **Wigtown** in April 1685, **Grierson of Lag** being one of the justices. All were found guilty, but Maxwell won her freedom by abjuring the **Cameronian** declarations, and Agnes Wilson, aged 13, was granted a reprieve on grounds of her youth. That left Margarets MacLachlan and Wilson, the former over 60 and illiterate, the latter 18 and educated. In accordance with recent instructions from **Edinburgh**, both were condemned to death by drowning. They were duly tied to stakes at the mouth of the river Bladnoch in Wigtown Bay where 'the cruel crawling foam' of the incoming tide slowly overwhelmed them. Their deaths were subsequently embellished by the faithful and queried by the quizzical. Accounts of the incident differ materially; the precise date is doubtful; and there is evidence of a reprieve being granted at least for Margaret MacLachlan. But opinion now favours the view that this incident, the most notorious of the **Killing Time**, did indeed take place. A monument to the martyrs stands above Wigtown and a stake in the estuarine flats may be where, as Margaret Wilson's tombstone relates, 'Within the sea tyd to a stake/She suffered for Christ Jesus sake.' They are also commemorated in white marble in the graveyard of **Holy Rude Church, Stirling**.

WIGTOWNSHIRE

Before the **local government** reorganisation of 1975, Wigtownshire formed the extreme south-west corner of Scotland. 311,984 acres (126,258ha) in area, the county had a coastline of 120 miles, with the Irish Sea to the south and west and with its south-western part, the Rhinns of **Galloway**, forming a double-headed peninsula caused by the indentations of Loch Ryan to the north and Luce Bay to the south. The promontory to the east of this was known as the Machars. Most of the county was made up of stony moorland, rising to no more than 1000ft (300m). Principal rivers were the Cree, Bladnoch, Tarff and Luce. **Agriculture**, particularly dairy-farming, was the principal occupation. Along with neighbouring **Kirkcudbrightshire**, this was one of only two mainland counties in Scotland whose boundaries did not require redesignation under the Local Government (Scotland) Act of 1889.

The county town was **Wigtown**, the county's other burghs being **Newton Stewart, Whithorn** and **Stranraer**. In 1975 the entire county became the Wigtown District of Dumfries & Galloway Region, incorporating also part of the western area of Kirkcudbrightshire, and since 1995 has been part of the Dumfries & Galloway Council Area.

WILD CAT

An elusive, agile and occasionally ferocious creature of the remote woodlands and moorlands of the Highlands, the wild cat (*Felis sylvestris*) is taller and sturdier than the domestic cat, with a shorter, bushier tail, characteristically striped. Its consummate skill as a hunter of small mammals and birds placed it high on the 19th century gamekeeper's 'most wanted' list, and it was trapped or shot as 'vermin' at every opportunity. Its existence was further threatened in the 20th century when the introduction of myxomatosis decimated the population of one of the wild cat's staple foods, the rabbit. In recent years its numbers are thought to have increased somewhat, partly because of legislation over traps and persecution and partly because of increased afforestation throughout northern Scotland. The picture, however, is far from clear as in the last decade or so there has been widespread interbreeding with feral cats, and it seems likely that only a very few pure wild cats remain in Scotland.

Inhabiting the most lonely and inaccessible ranges of rock and mountain, the wild cat is seldom seen during the daytime. Hunting alone or in pairs at dawn or dusk, it will either lie in ambush for its prey or stalk silently till the last pounce. The 19th century naturalist Charles St John described the wild cat's cry as 'wild and unearthly – I do not know a more harsh and unpleasant cry, or one more likely to be the origin of superstitious fears', while the naturalist **Seton Gordon** wrote in 1947 of its strength and agility: 'One was disturbed at a peregrine falcon's eyrie on a rock 60 foot high, lost its footing and fell, bounding and bumping like a football the whole 60 feet, at the end striking a wire fence with great violence, and then running off as if nothing had happened.' The wild cat makes its nest in holes among rocks, hollow trees or burrows in the ground; the kittens are independent at around five months and fully grown by about 10 months.

WILKIE, Sir David (1785–1841) Genre and Historical Painter

The most celebrated Scottish artist of the early 19th century, Wilkie's reputation was made virtually overnight at the 1806 Royal Academy exhibition. Born in **Fife**, he had entered the **Trustees' Academy** in **Edinburgh** in 1799 where he had been taught by the famous painter of Scottish low life, **David Allan**. He moved to London in 1805 and the following year exhibited *Village Politicians* (1806, The Earl of Mansfield) at the Royal Academy. The London audience, assuming they had encountered a naturally-gifted, untrained rustic prodigy, enthusiastically acclaimed the young Scot and his unaffected depictions of daily life.

Over the next few years Wilkie maintained his popular success with Scottish genre scenes, widely distributed and collected as prints. As a document of social history his paintings are exceptional, and their ability to capture and coalesce a wealth of tiny incident was to influence a generation of Scottish and English genre painters. They recall the traditions of Dutch and Flemish painting and Wilkie soon earned the sobriquet 'The Scottish Teniers'. He was elected Royal Academician in 1811.

For the next 15 years Wilkie was at the centre of a colony of expatriate Scots artists in London anxious to emulate his success, although none ever matched his celebrity. This period of Wilkie's career culminated in 1822 with the exhibition of *The Chelsea Pensioners* (1822, Victoria and Albert Museum, Apsley House, London), which required a crush barrier to keep back the crowds. Jaded, perhaps, by the public's insatiable appetite for genre, Wilkie turned to history painting, but his depiction of George IV visiting Edinburgh lacked gravitas or authority.

Overstrained by work he suffered a nervous breakdown and made a recuperative trip to Italy where the works of the Old Masters profoundly affected him. The English painter Haydon later declared 'Italy was Wilkie's ruin.' It is certain that his Italian and Spanish paintings, which combined the sophisticated composition of Michelangelo with the fluid brushwork and high colours of Velazquez, disappointed his London admirers greatly. Wilkie continued his attempts at grand history painting of events recent and past but, despite royal patronage, never regained his early popularity. His immediate and vivid sketches from life, executed on a visit to the Holy Land in 1840, are arguably the best products of his later career. Wilkie took ill and died on the return trip; he was buried at sea near Malta, an event immortalised by his friend and colleague J M W Turner in his painting *Peace: Burial at Sea* (1842, Tate Gallery, London).

WILLIAM I 'the Lion' (1143–1214) King

Grandson of **David I**, William succeeded his brother **Malcolm IV** in 1165. His nickname 'the Lion' (or 'Lyon') seems to have been coined by later historians rather than by his contemporaries, and it is uncertain whether it referred to his physical strength and longevity (which were in marked contrast to Malcolm's)

Sir David Wilkie's Sheepwashing *(NGS)*

or to the heraldic device which he is thought to have adopted on his standard [see **Scottish Lion**].

Determined from the start to win back the northern English counties ceded to his grandfather (1149) but reclaimed from Malcolm by Henry II of England (1157), William invaded Northumberland in 1174 but was captured at Alnwick. Held prisoner for five months, he was forced by the **Treaty of Falaise** to accept English overlordship not only of himself and his kingdom but also of the Scottish Church. The Scottish bishops, however, appealed to the Pope to support their independence under the direct jurisdiction of Rome, which appeal was finally granted in 1192. The other conditions of the Treaty remained in force until the death of Henry II in 1189, when William was able to cancel them in the Treaty (or 'Quitclaim') of Canterbury in return for money needed by Richard I (the Lionheart) for his crusades.

In 1178 William founded the **Abbey of Arbroath** which he dedicated to Thomas à Becket (who had been murdered by Henry II in 1170), partly out of his friendship for 'the troublesome priest' and partly, it is thought, to rub salt in Henry's wounds which had been smarting since Thomas's martyrdom (1173). The rebellions in **Galloway** and **Ross** which had plagued his brother's reign continued sporadically throughout William's although he managed to contain both. In 1186 he married Ermengarde de Beaumont; she bore him one son, who succeeded him as **Alexander II**, and three daughters, all of whom married Englishmen.

WILLIAMSON, Peter (1730–99) Adventurer

The son of an **Aboyne** crofter, Williamson aged 8 was playing on the quay at **Aberdeen** when he was enticed aboard a ship and trapped below decks. There for a month during which the vessel sailed to America he remained, 'the victim of that villainous and execrable practice called kidnapping'. In Philadephia he was sold for 'about £16' to a kindly pioneer, originally from **Perth**, who brought him up. A free man at 17, he worked as a labourer, then married the daughter of a planter whose dowry comprised 200 acres on the Pennsylvania frontier. Fortune, though, never smiled on Williamson for long. Alone one night, he was surprised by Indians on the warpath and led away as his home went up in flames. During this second captivity he witnessed a succession of dreadful raids and scalpings. After a couple of months he managed to escape and reached the safety of his father-in-law's house (1755). Thinking to put his experience to some use, he now volunteered for military service against the Indians. He was promptly captured by the French and underwent further mistreatment as a prisoner of war before being shipped out of Quebec back to England. Discharged at Plymouth, he again sought to make something of his 'life and vicissitudes' by writing an account of them. It was published in York in 1758 and seems to have done well, a third edition appearing in **Glasgow** before the end of the year.

Meanwhile Williamson had regained Aberdeen, 20 years after his disappearance. Instead of a civic reception he was greeted with a libel suit. The early pages of his book had implicated certain Aberdonian merchants in his kidnapping; they were torn out, 'burnt at the mercat cross by the common hangman', and Williamson was fined and banished. He moved to **Edinburgh** and set up a tavern with a signboard that described him as 'Peter Williamson from the Other World'. He also counter-sued the Aberdeen magistrates and, testimony to the basic truth of his improbable tale, won damages of £100.

He remained in Edinburgh for the rest of his life, remarried, divorced, branched out into printing and bookselling, and became something of a city celebrity. From his ever fertile imagination came 'the basket scythe' (a labour-saving harvester), the 'Impenetrable Secrets' (a pack of cards which 'discover the thoughts of one's mind in a very curious and extraordinary manner'), a portable printing press, *The Scots Spy* or *Critical Observer* (a short-lived periodical) and, to considerable acclaim, the first street directory of the city and its first ever penny post. The directory proved a modest bestseller and the postal service won him compensation of £25 a year for life when taken over by the government in 1791.

WILLIS, Dave (1895–1973) Entertainer

One of Scotland's funniest **music hall** comedians, Dave Willis (David Williams) was dubbed 'the Charlie Chaplin of Scotland' – indeed Chaplin himself rated him one of Scotland's foremost clowns. He starred in **Edinburgh**, **Glasgow**, **Ayr** and other revue and variety theatres in the 1930s and 40s, and was a stalwart of the now legendary 'Half-Past Eight' summer shows. His Hitler-style moustache was a trademark, and his impersonation of the German leader once led to German students demonstrating against him from a box at the **King's Theatre**, Edinburgh. He latterly fell on hard times, having lost a £30,000 investment in a Firth of **Clyde** hotel. His son Denny Willis followed his father into variety and pantomime.

WILSON, Alexander (1766–1813)
Ornithologist

Born and slightly educated in **Paisley**, Wilson was apprenticed as a weaver at the age of 13, working in his home town, **Lochwinnoch**, and **South Queensferry**. During a spell as a pedlar he began writing and selling popular verses which in 1793 landed him in Paisley gaol for libel. Released, he emigrated (1794) to North America and after employment in an engraver's shop and then as a school teacher, embarked somewhat casually (1803) on a study of American birds. Ornithological exploration combined with sales tours to collect subscriptions for his proposed work on American birds took him from the St Lawrence to the mouth of the Mississippi and inland to Ohio. He travelled rough and mostly alone but for 'Poll', a Carolina parrot. 'I carried it upwards of a thousand miles in my pocket, where it was exposed all day to the jolting of the horse, but regularly liberated at meal times and in the evening, at which it always expressed great satisfaction.' Poll eventually drowned in the Gulf of Mexico and Wilson himself died after swimming a river in pursuit of a rare bird. Seven volumes of his *American Ornithology* had been published during his decade as a bird-hunter and a further two volumes appeared posthumously. He is buried in Philadelphia and commemorated by a statue within the grounds of **Paisley Abbey**.

WILSON, Charles T R (1869–1959) Physicist
Born at Glencorse, **Midlothian**, into a farming family, Wilson overcame conditions of great poverty to take up a research career at Cambridge, becoming Professor of Natural Philosophy there in 1925. Although fascinated by electrical phenomena in the atmosphere, Wilson's greatest achievement was the construction of a cloud chamber to allow the photographing of extra-terrestrial particles. This won him the 1927 Nobel Prize for Physics. Still active in meteorological research at the age of 90, he died at Carlops, near his birthplace.

WILSON, Sir Daniel (1816–92) Antiquarian and Anthropologist
Amongst the numerous family of an **Edinburgh** wine merchant, originally from **Argyll**, Daniel and George (1818–59) Wilson became notable in scientific and antiquarian circles in the Edinburgh of the mid-19th century. George, a chemist of bird-like demeanour who had had one foot amputated, became founding director of the Industrial Museum of Scotland, later incorporated in the **Royal Museum of Scotland**, and first Professor of 'Technology', a subject he did much to define, at **Edinburgh University**. Daniel, on the other hand, is credited with coining the word 'prehistoric' and was more closely associated with the **Society of Antiquaries**. His first major work, *Memorials of Edinburgh in Olden Times* (1848), had whetted an interest in archaeology which was then fired by his identification of the site of **St Margaret's Chapel** in **Edinburgh Castle**. The preservation of the chapel and of the city's other antiquities became a priority for which he worked through the Society of Antiquaries. He was also instrumental in persuading the government to take over the Society's poorly funded museum. The deal hinged on the Society first organising its contents, a labour which Wilson addressed with energy, adopting the Danish system of classifying the 'prehistoric' material into Stone, Bronze and Iron Age. This pioneering work resulted in *The Archaeology and Prehistoric Annals of Scotland* (1851), 'the starting point for modern Scottish archaeology and a landmark in the history of British archaeology as a whole' (M Ash).

In 1852 Wilson was appointed Professor of History and Literature at University College, Toronto, and began his new career as an educationalist, for which he was knighted, and anthropologist, the latter a development of his interest in prehistory and the common ancestry of man. He published on North American ethnology and organised through **Sir George Simpson** a collection of Athabascan artefacts for his brother's museum. For the Society of Antiquaries Museum he tracked down and sent home the crozier of **St Fillan** which had been taken to Canada in 1818. He is buried in Toronto.

WILSON, George Washington (1823–93) Photographer
The second son of a **Banffshire crofter**, George Washington Wilson was a gifted artist who trained in **Edinburgh**, London and Paris before setting up as a portrait artist in **Aberdeen** in 1849. In c1852 he diversified into offering photographic portraits using the recently perfected wet collodion process, which he went on to apply to capturing outdoor scenes. By 1856 he could offer a series of 44 stereoscopic views taken in Aberdeen and the north-east. Private commissions from **Queen Victoria** and Prince Albert to record the rebuilding of **Balmoral** established his reputation and led to the designation Photographer to the Queen.

By the early 1860s, through submissions to exhibitions and photographic journals, he had won international acclaim for his instantaneous techniques, capturing light and movement, notably in striking cloud and water effects (Loch of Park series, The Breaking Wave) and street scenes (**Princes Street**, 1859); for his artistic composition; and for the first publication of cabinet and albumen prints. At the 1862 International Exhibition in London Wilson gained the only medal awarded to a Scottish photographer. By 1891 he had won 27 prize medals from all parts of the world

Wilson and the company he founded played a key role in the growth of Scottish **tourism**, responding to the demand for picturesque and historic views, and opening up new areas. Notable series produced on travels throughout the length and breadth of the British Isles by Wilson himself and by staff photographers include the Channel Fleet off the south coast of England in 1860 and 1862 (subsequently in the Firth of Forth and Firth of **Clyde**), English cathedrals in the period 1860–3 onwards, St Kilda (1885), **Skye** and the Outer **Hebrides**, **Orkney** and **Shetland**, and the building of the **Tay** and **Forth Rail Bridges**.

One of the first to apply mass production techniques to landscape views, Wilson established with entrepreneurial acumen the largest commercial photographic business in the country. His sons John, Louis and Charles joined him in the firm, assuming control in 1888 (John and Charles left in 1901 to set up a new company, Wilson Brothers, specialising in lantern slides). Charles Wilson and Fred Hardie visited South Africa and Australia in the 1890s. By the time of Wilson's death in 1893 his business was already in decline, and in 1908 G W Wilson & Co was wound up and its assets sold by auction. Fred Hardie acquired for his own use some 40,000 glass negatives, which in 1954 were presented by his successor, Archie Strachan, to **Aberdeen University** Library, where they are now conserved, catalogued, computer-indexed and printed to order.

WILSON, James (d.1789) Poet
A lame (literally) poet who dubbed himself 'Claudero', James Wilson lamented the 'North British' haste in ridding **Edinburgh**'s **Old Town** of much of its medieval antiquity; he also lucratively lampooned douce citizens with skeletons in their closets. A native of **Cumbernauld**, he had been mercilessly beaten as a lad by the local presbyter whom he had peppered with pebbles from a tree; thereafter he limped about on a crutch. True to style, however, he was the first to mock his own affliction: 'Men's works generally resemble themselves; if the poems are lame, so is the author – CLAUDERO!'

In Edinburgh he lived a precarious existence in the **Cowgate** where he ran a small private school of sorts, supplementing his meagre income through performing 'half-merk' marriages at the White Hart Inn in the **Grassmarket**. 'The Laureat of the Mob' was almost the sole remonstrant against the destruction of the Gothic gate of the **Palace of Holyroodhouse** (1753), **Mercat Cross** (1756), **Netherbow** (1764) and the desecration of **Holyrood Abbey** (1768). Nevertheless he also penned panegyrics of civic praise: his 'eulogy on laying the Foundation stone of **St Bernard's Well**', which claims 'It clears the intestines and an appetite gives,/ While morbific matters it quite away drives' continues even more execrably: 'Great [George] Drummond improveth what nature doth send;/To country and city he's always a friend.' Claudero quit Edinburgh for a while in 1765 in protest against the proposal to relocate the venerable equestrian statue of **Charles II** in **Parliament Square**; his *Epistle to Claudero, on his arrival at London, 1765* suggested the fate which would befall the Scots capital in his absence:

> Now vice may rear her Hydra's head,
> And strike defenceless virtue dead;
> Religion's heart may melt and bleed
> With grief and sorrow
> Since satire from your streets is fled
> Poor Edinburrow.

WILSON, James (1805–60) Political Economist

Like **Rintoul** of *The Spectator*, Wilson of *The Economist* came from a modest Lowland background. He was born in **Hawick**, educated in Quaker schools, and then apprenticed to a Hawick hatmaker. Millinery took him to London where he started his own business and began taking an interest in economics. He wrote on the repeal of the Corn Laws and on the currency before founding and editing *The Economist* (1843) which advocated free trade and appeared weekly. It still does and is now one of the world's most influential journals of political economy. In 1847 Wilson entered Parliament as a Liberal, serving in the Treasury, Board of Trade and India Board of Control. He was appointed Privy Councillor in 1859 and the first financial member of the Council of India. There, although he died of dysentery in the following year, he redeemed the economy after the ravages of the Mutiny and introduced income tax and strict accounting controls as part of a radical and lasting reform of the public finances.

WILSON, John 'Christopher North' (1785–1854) Author and Editor

Born in **Paisley**, John Wilson was the eldest son of a wealthy gauze manufacturer, and a descendant through his mother, Margaret Sym, of **James Graham, Marquis of Montrose**. He was educated in Paisley and Mearns, and on the death of his father in 1797 entered **Glasgow University**, where he distinguished himself as a scholar and an athlete. In 1803 he began studies at Magdalen College, Oxford. He won the Newdigate Prize for Poetry in 1806, and in 1807 graduated with the highest honours.

On graduating, Wilson used part of a substantial inheritance from his father to purchase a small estate at Elleray in the Lake District. Here he met and became close friends of **William Wordsworth**, Samuel Coleridge, Robert Southey and Thomas de Quincey, and under their influence began dedicating much of his time to writing. In 1811 he married Jane Penny, daughter

Professor John Wilson ('Christopher North'), by Sir John Watson Gordon, 1829 (SNPG)

of a Liverpool merchant, and in 1812 published two collections of poetry, *The Isle of Palms and other Poems* and *The Magic Mirror*.

In 1815 Wilson lost most of his inheritance due to the mismanagement of his estate by an uncle, and was forced to return to his mother's home in **Edinburgh**, where he took up **law**. He soon gave up legal work to join the editorial staff of the newly established **Blackwood's Magazine**, and became one of its most important and prolific contributors, writing under the pseudonym 'Christopher North'. His work included contributing to the notorious 'Chaldee Manuscript', which launched the magazine, writing over half the series *Noctes Ambrosianae*, which ran from 1822–35, and producing 'Lights and Shadows of Scottish Life', a series of stories on Scottish country life which was published in book form in 1822. Other works include the novels *The Trials of Margaret Lyndsay* (1823) and *The Foresters* (1825).

In 1820 Wilson was appointed for political reasons to the Chair of Moral Philosophy at **Edinburgh University**. Although lacking formal qualifications for the job, and overstretched by his literary and editorial work, he took up the post, and relied on a friend to produce his lecture notes. In 1851 he resigned due to ill health, and was granted a government pension of £300 a year.

WILSON, John (1804–75) Missionary and Orientalist

From **Lauder** in **Berwickshire**, Wilson attended **Edinburgh University** and there determined on a missionary career in India. He was ordained (1828) and reached Bombay under the auspices of the Scottish Missionary Society. He was dissuaded from Poona, his original destination, by **Sir John Malcolm**, who feared the effect of any proselytising on its Brahminical residents. He therefore stayed in Bombay where both he and his wife Margaret founded schools and learned Marathi, Margaret becoming the first white woman to do so, according to her tombstone. Wilson also mastered Gujerati and Sanskrit and, unlike his Calcutta counterpart **Alexander Duff**, was happy to teach in these languages and to concede the existence of merit in India's native cultures. Such indulgence placed him in the ranks of the orientalists, a 'brahminised' breed despised by the majority as represented by **Macaulay**. Unbothered, Wilson continued to radiate wisdom and humour from his Ambroli cottage (still surviving) where he sat 'in an ill-cut coat, reading Milton and enjoying a bottle of cold tea' (G Tindall, City of Gold, 1982). Oriental scholars remember him as the man who first made some headway in deciphering the Ashoka Brahmi script, a labour which greatly assisted James Prinsep in the breakthrough which would reveal India's classical Buddhist past. He also wrote on the Parsis and collaborated with **Sir James Fergusson** on the cataloguing of India's rock-cut temples. Soon after its foundation he was chosen Vice-Chancellor of Bombay University and, during home leave in 1870, **Moderator** of the **Free Church General Assembly**. He died in Bombay where his Wilson College on Back Bay still operates.

WILSON, Robert (1803–82) Engineer
Born at **Dunbar**, Robert Wilson was the son of a fisherman. Despite a rudimentary education, he showed a flair for **engineering**, producing a workable model of a ship's propeller at the age of 24. For this he was honoured by the Highland and Agricultural Society, although his invention failed to interest the Admiralty. He moved to Manchester where he assisted **Nasmyth** with his steam-hammer, and was rewarded by the navy for producing a double-action torpedo propeller in 1880. A much underrated inventor, Wilson died at Matlock in Derbyshire.

WILSON, William (1905–72) Artist
Considered amongst the foremost Scottish printmakers of the 20th century, Wilson is remembered equally as one of the leading stained-glass artists of his generation. Born in **Edinburgh**, he worked for **Bartholomews**, the mapmakers, before entering the Edinburgh College of Art. Studying etching and engraving under E H Lumsden, his work met with early success and in 1932 he was awarded a **Royal Scottish Academy** Travelling Scholarship that took him to France, Germany, Spain and Italy. In 1934 he won further awards that allowed him to study printmaking at the Royal College of Art in London and stained-glass design in Germany. During this period he worked for the Edinburgh stained-glass firm of Ballantynes before opening his own studio in 1937. His crowded, figurative style and bold, lively colouring can clearly be seen in his first important commission, a series of windows enriching the now offices of the Guardian Royal Exchange Assurance Company, **St Andrews Square**, Edinburgh (1938). He rapidly established a wide reputation, designing and executing stained glass for many ecclesiastical and other public and private buildings both in Britain and abroad.

In the 1930s Wilson was also Secretary to the Scottish Society of Artist Printmakers and in this highly active period of his career he made frequent sketching trips around Scotland, often in the company of the similarly acclaimed and gifted artist Ian Fleming. Like Fleming, Wilson's admiration for the art of the Italian *quattrocento* and for the draughtsmanship of Breughel and Dürer is evident in his formidably detailed and highly sensitive approach to landscape, though the stylised treatment of his compositions demonstrates his acquaintance with the innovations of Cubism and its manipulation of pictorial space. Wilson was also a fine painter in watercolour, particularly of architectural subjects, and the boldness and fluidity he developed in this medium helped effect a wider move in his art away from the hard-edged qualities that characterised his early printmaking towards a more human rendering of his subjects, closer in style to the loosely expressed landscapes of **Gillies** and the Edinburgh School. Sadly the loss of his eyesight in 1961 brought his career to a halt.

WINZET, Ninian (c1518–92) Priest
While schoolmaster at **Linlithgow**, this **Renfrew** priest disputed with the Protestants and was deprived at the **Reformation**. His Certane Tractatis written in **Scots** against **Knox** in 1562 forced his exile to Antwerp and then study in Paris. Becoming a Benedictine, he was Abbot of the Scottish monastery of Ratisbon (Regensberg, Germany) from 1575.

WISHART, George (c1513–46) Reformer and Martyr
Born in **Angus** and educated at **Aberdeen University**, Wishart became a schoolmaster in **Montrose**, where he was charged with heresy for teaching the Greek New

George Wishart, by an unknown artist but dated 1543 (SNPG)

Testament. A year later similar charges were laid against him in Bristol and caused his flight to Europe. He studied with the Calvinists in Germany and Switzerland and then spent six years in Cambridge before returning to preach in Scotland in 1543, assisted by **John Knox**. Arrested by **Bothwell**, he was tried and burned for heresy by **Cardinal David Beaton** at **St Andrews**. It is unclear whether he was involved in proposals to murder Beaton, supposedly made by a Scotsman to Henry VIII.

WISHART, Robert (c1240–1316) Bishop of Glasgow

A graduate of Bologna and/or Paris, Wishart was appointed Bishop of **Glasgow** in 1271, attended the Council of Lyons in 1274, and was a Guardian of the Realm after the death of **Alexander III** in 1286. He backed **Robert Bruce of Annandale**'s claim to the throne, sponsored **William Wallace**, and joined the Bruces in 1297. In the same year he was amongst those who capitulated to the English at **Irvine**. As a hostage he was imprisoned at **Roxburgh** till 1300 and then exiled to southern England. Released in 1305 to help the imposed administration, he instead became **Robert I**'s chief adviser (or 'the Bad Bishop' according to English spies) and provided the robes and banner for Robert's coronation. Captured again (1306) he was held in chains at Portchester till 1308, then sent to Avignon for Papal judgement. Blind and frail, he was finally exchanged in 1314 [see **Marjorie Bruce**]. An effigy of him survives in **Glasgow Cathedral**.

WITHERSPOON, John (1723–94) Theologian

From Yester near **Haddington**, John Witherspoon was the scholarly minister of Beith in **Ayrshire** and then **Paisley** before going to America as Principal of Princeton Presbyterian College in New Jersey in 1768. As a representative of New Jersey at the Continental Congress, he was the only clergyman to be a signatory of the Declaration of Independence in 1776.

WODE (WOOD), Thomas (fl.1562–92) Musicologist

A priest from **Lindores Abbey**, Wode's double set of five partbooks (most of which survive) constitute one of the most important sources for 16th century Scottish **music**. They are also known as Wode's *Psalter* because they contain harmonisations of the psalms and canticles, mostly commissioned from **Peebles** by James Stewart, Prior of **St Andrews**. Besides these, Wode recorded secular music ranging from fricassees in the late 15th century style to Renaissance partsongs for the Scottish court. The partbooks are also valuable for their marginalia which include comments on musical life at the time, biographical details of composers and illustrations of musical instruments. Wode wrote despairingly after the **Reformation** that 'I cannot understand bot musicke sall pereische in this land alutterlye', and he was right to claim that his five books 'wer worthy thair wayght of gould'. Indeed they are worth a good deal more.

WODROW, Robert (1679–1734) Minister

Educated in his native **Glasgow**, while minister of Eastwood Wodrow collected a vast amount of information on the **Covenanters** of the Restoration period. A valued historian, though biased against **Episcopacy**, his works and unpublished manuscripts are still a major source of Church and state affairs in the 17th century.

WOLFSON, Sir Isaac (1897–1991) Businessman and Philanthropist

Described by *The Times* as 'the biggest private benefactor since [Lord] Nuffield', Wolfson was made a freeman of the City of **Glasgow** and was also the first Scots-born founder of an Oxford college since **Devorguilla Balliol**. He was born in Glasgow, the son of a Russian Jewish cabinet-maker who had emigrated to the city. Aged 15 he left **Queens Park** school to work for his father but was soon recruited as a salesman by Universal Stores, then a small mail order company. Rising rapidly to control of what became Great Universal Stores in 1930, Wolfson engaged in a series of takeovers from which GUS emerged as a major high street retailer. At the time of his death the group was still the UK's largest mail order company and the fifth largest retail conglomerate, behind Marks & Spencer and three food chains. The Wolfson Foundation, financed by its abstemious benefactor, supported a host of worthy schemes in health education and youth activities as well as co-founding postgraduate Wolfson Colleges in both Oxford and Cambridge. Israel also benefited from his generosity and it was there that he died.

WOOD, Alexander (1817–84) Physician

Born in **Cupar**, **Fife**, Alexander Wood was one of the first pupils of Edinburgh Academy and graduated MD from **Edinburgh University** in 1839. He conducted a general practice in the **New Town** of **Edinburgh** and lectured on the Practice of Physic in the Extra-Mural School. An antagonist of homeopathy, he published two books, *Homeopathy Unmasked* and, a year later, *Sequel to Homeopathy Unmasked*. His greatest claim to fame was as the first doctor in Britain to give pain-relieving drugs by injection. When injecting a birthmark with an acid solution of chloride of iron 'using the elegant little syringe made by Mr Ferguson of Giltspur Street, London', it occurred to him that the syringe might be used to inject a narcotic in cases of neuralgia. In an article in the *Edinburgh Medical and Surgical Journal* of 1855 he described how he 'visited a patient suffering from cervico-brachial neuralgia at 10 pm on 28 November 1853 and injected 20 drops of a solution of muriate of morphia of a strength about double that of the official preparation. When seen at 11 am the next day, the patient was still asleep and was aroused with difficulty.' The doctor realised that the benefit to his patient from the injection was 'probably from absorption of morphine and not a local effect'. Wood took an active interest in medical politics and philanthropic work and was successful in improving the sanitary state of Edinburgh.

WOOD, Andrew (c1455–1515) Naval Commander

Sometimes called 'the Scottish Nelson', Wood may have been a native of **Largo** and was certainly granted the **tack** of lands there about 1477. By then he seems to have been a merchant and sea-captain based at **Leith**. By 1484 the tack had become a feu in recognition of Wood's maritime services in the Firth of Forth. As one

Packing wool by compressing it in a wool sack, 1892 (entry p 1034) (SEA)

of **James III**'s most trusted supporters he played a prominent role in the events leading up to the **Battle of Sauchieburn** (1488), making his vessels available to ferry the King between Leith and **Fife** and supplying the King's army via **Blackness Castle**. After James's murder he quickly adjusted to supporting **James IV** and in 1489–90 undertook to defend the Firth of Forth against English interlopers. His exploits in command of the *Yellow Carvel* and the *Flower* resulted in the capture of three ships under the command of Stephen Bull and represented a major achievement for Scotland's incipient naval power. Wood was rewarded with a knighthood, and various privileges including custody of **Dunbar** and the right to build a fortalice and erect a **burgh of barony** at Largo. In 1498 he was again engaged in naval operations, this time in the Firth of Clyde and Western Isles. He may later have been commander of the *Great Michael*. 'Many of the exploits with which his name has been connected are probably fictitious' (DNB); it depends on how much credence is given to **Robert Lindsay of Pitscottie**.

WOOD, John (c1810–71) Explorer

Improbably it fell to Wood, a naval officer, to explore the landlocked heart of Asia and discover the source of the Oxus river (Amu darya). From his account (pub 1841) it appears that he hailed from either **Perthshire** or **Loch Aweside**. 'Of an extremely retiring disposition', nothing is known of him until in 1835–6, when as a lieutenant in the Indian navy charged with assessing the navigational possibilites of the Indus river, he accompanied **Alexander Burnes** to Punjab and Afghanistan. Thence, in mid-winter, he set off alone but for native guides through the Hindu Kush and into the Pamirs to discover the source of the Oxus. Blizzards delayed him; the temperature fell to minus Fahrenheit. But on 19 February 1838, at 16,500ft (5029m) on the 'Roof of the World', he discovered a frozen lake, Sir-i-Kol, whence flowed the Oxus (although Lord Curzon later quibbled over whether it was the main stream). The Royal Geographical Society awarded Wood its Patron's Gold Medal, but he never collected it, emigrating first to New Zealand, then Australia, before finally returning to India, where ('preferring rather to wear out than to rust out') he spent his final days back on the Indus in charge of a steam flotilla.

WOOD, Thomas P McKinnon (1855–1927)
Secretary for Scotland

Born at Stepney in London, the son of a Scottish businessman, Wood had literary ambitions and worked for a time in **Edinburgh** on the staff of the *Encyclopaedia Britannica* before entering the family business and then local politics in London. Stepping up to the House of Commons as Liberal MP for **Glasgow** (**St Rollox**) in 1906, he was promoted through junior ministerial ranks to become Secretary for Scotland in 1912. He held the post until 1916 through a period of unequalled legislative activity and into an age of unprecedented warfare. Historians have criticised him for his indecisive stance during the Glasgow rent strikes in the early part of the war, and he lost his seat in 1918. Unsuccessful in finding a London seat, Wood returned to business and was chairman of three companies at the time of his death.

WOOL

Commercial wool farming was introduced to Lowland Scotland by the Cistercians and other monastic orders in the Middle Ages. By the end of the 13th century substantial quantities of wool were being exported to the Continent although it remained predominantly a household industry, serving local demand for plaids, hosiery, etc. The poor quality of Scottish wool, and craft restrictions in the burghs, hampered development and, although government encouragement during the 17th century led to the establishment of several factories (eg the Woollen Manufactory of **Glasgow**, 1699), these enterprises met with limited success in producing quality woollen goods.

With the introduction of large sheep farms in the Highlands from the mid-18th century, some landlords encouraged woollen manufacture, and **Inverness** became one of the country's major wool markets. It was in the Borders, however, where the superior wool-bearing **Cheviot** largely replaced the **Blackface sheep** during the late 18th century, that the manufacturing industry made its greatest progress. The fashion for **tar-**tans and tweeds which arose during the 1820s created further demand. The Borders manufacturers also led the way in introducing power frames to make knitted hosiery and underwear. The industry revived in traditional manufacturing centres in **Aberdeenshire**, the **Alloa** area and the west of Scotland, and was successfully transplanted to the **Hebrides**. By 1878 there were 246 woollen factories in Scotland employing over 10,000 men and over 12,500 women. In addition the Scottish carpet industry, with its twin capitals in Glasgow and **Kilmarnock**, prospered with the growth in domestic demand for home furnishings.

From the mid-19th century, finer foreign wools were preferred to, or mixed with, home-grown as manufacturers continued to concentrate on the premium market for woollen yarns, knitwear and tweed, both in Britain and abroad. After World War I knitwear companies diversified into sweaters and cardigans, and a reputation for quality garments was fostered by firms such as Robert Pringle & Son of Alloa. The industry contracted significantly after 1945 in the face of foreign competition and changing fashion. Since 1960 it has been dominated by Coats Paton Ltd (which became Coats Viyella plc in 1986). Small independent firms have survived, however, on the strength of flair and innovation in the design and marketing of luxury knitwear.

'Wool washing, South Harris'; photograph by George Washington Wilson (GWWA)

WORDSWORTH, Dorothy (1771–1855) and William (1770–1850)

The Wordsworths visited Scotland in August and September 1803 with Samuel Taylor Coleridge. Dorothy put together 'not a Journal, for we took no notes, but recollections of our tour in the form of a Journal' (first published 1877). In an open Irish jaunting car drawn by 'an aged but stout and spirited horse', they first visited **Burns**'s widow and tomb. From **Glasgow** and **Loch Lomond** they reached the **Trossachs**, when Coleridge went off on his own (to **Glencoe**, **Fort Augustus**, where he was arrested as a spy, **Edinburgh** and home). The Wordsworths in the next three weeks found their way by **Inveraray**, **Loch Awe**, **Appin** and Glencoe to **Crieff**, **Callendar** and Edinburgh. 'Scotland is the country above all others that I have seen in which a man of imagination may carve out his own pleasures,' wrote Dorothy; the delight of her book is the revelation of ordinary life at the time through the genius of her sympathy. At **Lasswade** en route for home they called for breakfast – unintroduced – on **Sir Walter Scott**. Her account of a less adventurous visit in 1822 is also of interest. William's relevant poems are 'To Burns's Sons', 'The Highland Girl', 'The Narrow Glen', 'Stepping Westward', 'Rob Roy's Grave', 'The Solitary Reaper', 'Kilchurn Castle', 'Neidpath Castle', 'Yarrow Unvisited', 'Sonnet on Killiecranky', 'The Matron of Jedburgh'.

WRESTLING

The earliest physical record of wrestling in Scotland dates from the 6th–7th century and consists of three carved stones, two **Pictish** and one from **Dalriada**. Each depicts a wrestling position which is instantly familiar to the modern wrestler. A stone from Tullibole in **Clackmannan** which is now in the **Museum of Scotland** in **Edinburgh**, though weathered, shows an incident in a bout where the attacker is using a throw known today as an 'Inner Hook'. There is no closed hold and the men appear to be engaged in a form of 'Loose Hold' wrestling.

Loose Hold, that is when no fixed starting position is adopted, developed in the 19th and early 20th centuries, through Lancashire Catch-as-catch-can, into Olympic Free Style. Modern Free Style is a fast, arduous, highly technical and vastly popular international sport. Its similarities to the traditional wrestling styles of central Asia and the Indian sub-continent aided its technical development and international progress.

In Scotland and the north of England another style is also practised. Backhold is its oldest name, but it is often wrongly referred to in Scotland as Cumberland style; Scots rules have always been different from those used in the north of England. This style of wrestling is depicted on two sculptured stones; Eilean Mor off **Knapdale** and The Prince's Stone in the grounds of Glenfurness House near **Nairn**. It is still widespread throughout Scotland, and the Scottish Amateur Wrestling Association is currently trying to organise and register wrestlers; but it is a very informal sport, practised mostly at a variety of **Highland Games** and other local events from **Sutherland** down to the Borders and into northern England.

There was another style which, although still in the rule book of the Scottish Amateur Wrestling Association as 'Scots Style', is never practised. Some writers refer to it as the 'Dinnie Style'. Their story is that it was invented out of frustration by Donald Dinnie when he and other 'Heavies' could not cope with the more skilled 'Cumberland' wrestlers from England. It is more likely to have been one of the local versions of the rules which Dinnie seized upon in the period before wrestling had an organised governing body and standardised rules.

In Backhold the wrestlers take hold round each other's waist, right hand under the left arm. When both men close their hands the referee shouts 'Hold' and the bout begins – should any part of a wrestler's body except the soles of his feet touch the ground then the bout is lost. Wrestlers are not allowed to break their grip until an opponent hits the ground. Usually bouts are best of three falls; semi-finals and finals are best of five. The simple rules of Backhold wrestling allow the bouts to be easily understood by non-wrestlers and make it suitable for large outdoor venues.

Wrestling in the Western Isles owes much to its popularity among officers and men of the **Lovat Scouts**. Two variations were practised by the Highlanders in the regiment. One used the same rules as the rest of Scotland, the other did not allow tripping and is consistent with a sport played by boisterous young men in rural Scandinavia. This restricted form of wrestling, which is really just a trial of strength, developed in Europe into Greco-Roman, often called 'Classical' wrestling, one of the three Olympic styles (the others are Freestyle and Judo).

It is an interesting thought that the primitive style of wrestling, called by the Norsemen *Hryggspenna* (back-spanning), is still practised in the **Hebrides** and has a similar custom of always calling out the rules prior to a bout, though here naturally the referee calls out in Gaelic '*Lamh an iochdair – lamh an uachdair*' ('One hand down, one hand up'); the signal to start, '*Ceart*', is given by the referee when he is sure that a fair hold has been taken by both men.

There are many historical references to wrestling in Scotland. Unfortunately, due to the universality of the sport, no one thought to write down the rules, but 'first down to lose' seems to have been widespread. Sports historians have not yet been able to clarify when or where in Scotland the idea of pinning an opponent's shoulders to the mat to gain victory either developed or was first introduced.

WRIGHT, John Michael (1617–1700)
Portraitist

The son of a Scottish tailor resident in London, Wright was in **Edinburgh** by 1636, the sole pupil of the celebrated portraitist **George Jameson(e)**. After an apprenticeship of five years he travelled to Rome and in 1648 was accepted into the Academy of St Luke. Then at its most prestigious, its membership encompassed all the leading Italian and many foreign artists, most notably Poussin and Velazquez. In 1656 Wright returned via Flanders to England. In contrast to Lely, whose portraiture dominated the market during the years of the Restoration, Wright's sitters are rendered with an insight which is sensitive to character and individual. Typical is his portrait of the architect **Sir William Bruce** (1664, **Scottish National Portrait Gallery**), a refreshingly unmannered and appropriately composed tribute to a fellow artist, painted with a clarity that looks forward to the **Scottish Enlightenment**. Although he was frequently patronised by the Scottish nobility and married a Scottish wife, it is not known whether he ever returned to Scotland; he eventually settled in Ireland.

WYND, Oswald (1913–98) Novelist

The son of Scots **missionaries** from **Perthshire,** Oswald Wynd was born in Tokyo and educated at the American School there. In 1932 he returned to Scotland, where his studies at **Edinburgh University** were interrupted by World War II. Enlisting in the **Scots Guards**, he was commissioned in the Intelligence Corps because of his fluent Japanese and sent to Malaya. On the Japanese invasion in 1941 he was captured in the jungle at Johore while his Indian Army brigade covered the retreat to Singapore. He spent three years as a prisoner of war in personally trying circumstance – he had formerly had high regard for the Japanese – and received mention in despatches as interpreter on others' behalf. While in the mines at Hokkaido he began to write a novel, *Black Fountains*, which won the Doubleday Prize in 1947. Concerning a young man caught up in the war against the Japanese, this launched him on a long literary career which produced over a dozen novels in his own name as well as a crop of thrillers, written by 'Gavin Black', around the adventures of a British businessman working in the Far East. After the war he lived in the USA where he completed *When Ape is King* (1949), also based on his wartime experiences. In 1953 he returned to Scotland, but his early years in Japan continued to pull him to the East; in 1977 he produced his most successful novel, *The Ginger Tree*, which explores the strict societal codes operating between the British and Japanese at the beginning of the century. He died at **Crail**, **Fife**.

unbroken career into the 20th century. It sent a contingent to the Imperial Yeomanry during the South African War, and fought in World War I in Gallipoli, Egypt and then in Palestine, forming together with men of the Lanarkshire Yeomanry a battalion of the **Royal Scots Fusiliers** in the 'Broken Spur Division' which ended the war on the Western Front. Converted to Royal Artillery, in World War II it provided 151st and 152nd (Ayrshire Yeomanry) Field Regiments, RA, fighting in North Africa, Italy and north-west Europe. The regiment was restored to a cavalry role after the war as a regiment in the Royal Armoured Corps.

THE LANARKSHIRE YEOMANRY Descended from the Upper Ward Yeomanry raised in Lanarkshire in 1819, the regiment sent a contingent to the Scottish Battalion of Imperial Yeomanry in South Africa. It fought in Gallipoli and Egypt in World War I before joining the Ayrshire Yeomanry to form a joint battalion of Royal Scots Fusiliers for service in Palestine and then on the Western Front. The regiment was converted to a gunner role and provided 155th and 156th Regiments, Royal Artillery, in World War II. The 155th was captured in Singapore while the 156th served in north Africa, Italy and north-west Europe. After the war the Lanarkshire Yeomanry were reformed as an armoured unit of the Territorial Army.

THE LOTHIANS AND BORDER HORSE YEOMANRY The regiment derives from Yeomanry regiments raised in 1797 in **Berwickshire**, **Midlothian** and **East Lothian** which later incorporated **Sir Walter Scott**'s corps, the Royal **Edinburgh** Volunteer Light Dragoons. In 1888 the successor unit was the Lothians and Berwickshire Yeomanry Cavalry which in due course sent a contingent to serve in the war in South Africa. During World War I it served as three squadrons; one serving on the Western Front until absorbed by the 17th Royal Scots; the other two also on the Western Front before going to Macedonia. In 1922 the regiment became an armoured car company of the Royal Tank Corps until 1936 when it became an armoured regiment which was duplicated in 1939 on the expansion of the Territorial Army (TA).

The 1st Regiment went to war as the Divisional Armoured regiment of the 51st Highland Division and most of its personnel were captured at St Valéry. The reconstituted regiment served in north-west Europe from 1944 while the 2nd Regiment served as a tank unit in North Africa and Italy. On the re-raising of the TA in 1947 the regiment became a regiment of the Royal Armoured Corps.

THE QUEEN'S OWN ROYAL GLASGOW YEOMANRY The **Glasgow** and Lower Ward of Lanarkshire Yeomanry came into being in 1848. (There had been an earlier unit, the Glasgow Light Horse, from 1796–1822.) The regiment received the accolade of 'The Queen's Own Royal' from **Queen Victoria** in 1849. It sent a contingent to the South African War which served in the Imperial Yeomanry. In World War I the three squadrons of the regiment served independently of each other; 'A' and 'B' on the Western Front, while 'C' fought in Gallipoli and in Palestine.

YELL, Shetland

The second largest island in **Shetland**, with an area of 83 square miles, Yell has a relatively small population of just under 1000. Most live in and around Mid Yell at the island's narrow waist, where there are shops, the island's junior high school, a leisure centre and a shell-fish processing plant. The land is largely covered with **peat**, traditionally dug by **crofters** for fuel and now worked commercially. This combination of bleak monotonous aspect and declining population led **Eric Linklater** in 1965 to call Yell 'the problem child of the [Shetland] archipelago'. Its population has since declined still further in spite of valiant attempts to provide employment and recreation facilities.

At the north end Cullivoe has retained its dependence on **fishing** and a new deep-water harbour (opened in 1991) could pave the way for further developments. Burravoe, the largest settlement in South Yell, has several fine buildings, including St Colmac's Episcopal Church and the Old Haa of Brough, once a merchant's house and now an important museum and visitors' centre. 15 Norse chapel sites have been identified and 12 **broch** sites; none, however, can rival those of **Mainland** and **Mousa**.

YEOMANRY

'Yeomanry' is the title given to units of volunteer part-time cavalry. They were first raised in Scotland during the Napoleonic period, mostly in the Lowlands, although in due course there was to be one remarkable unit of Highland Yeomanry.

Like their comrades, the Volunteer Infantry, the Yeomanry held themselves in readiness for Home Defence throughout the period. They continued to serve after the Volunteer Infantry were disbanded and it was only in 1838 that most Yeomanry units were stood down. The **Ayrshire** and **Lanarkshire** units, however, remained in being until 1859 when the renewed threat of French invasion once more summoned patriotic citizens to arms.

From the revived Yeomanry of 1850 stem a number of regiments which sent strong contingents to the South African War and which saw much service in the two world wars. Not included here are the **Lovat Scouts** who were technically Scouts, not Yeomanry, when first raised.

THE AYRSHIRE YEOMANRY (EARL OF CARRICK'S OWN) Scotland's senior Yeomanry Regiment, raised in 1793 as the Ayrshire Yeomanry Cavalry, has enjoyed an

The regiment transferred to the Royal Artillery after the war, firstly as a field regiment but then becoming 54th Anti-Tank Regiment, RA, in 1938. The following year it also formed the duplicate 64th Anti-Tank Regiment. The regiments saw active service in France in 1940, Singapore, North Africa, Sicily, Italy and in north-west Europe. The regiment was re-raised in 1947 as the Queen's Own Royal Glasgow Yeomanry, Royal Armoured Corps (TA).

THE FIFE AND FORFAR YEOMANRY Although earlier units of Yeomanry had been raised in both **Fife** and **Forfar**, the regiment traces a continuous descent from the Fifeshire Mounted Volunteer Rifles (later the Fifeshire Light Horse Volunteer Corps) of 1860 and the Forfar Light Horse Volunteer Corps of 1876 which united in 1901 to become the Fife and Forfar Imperial Yeomanry. ('Imperial' was dropped from the title in 1908 on the formation of the Territorial Army.) No less than 500 Fife and Forfar Yeomen volunteered and fought in South Africa. The regiment served in Gallipoli in World War I before converting to infantry as 14th Bn the Black Watch and fighting in Egypt and Palestine. It recovered its cavalry role after the war and was converted into an armoured regiment which was duplicated prior to the outbreak of World War II. Both regiments of Fife and Forfar Yeomanry served in north-west Europe in 1944–5, one having already been in France in 1940. The regiment was re-raised after the war as a regiment of the Royal Armoured Corps.

THE SCOTTISH HORSE In 1900 an offer to raise a regiment of Scots in South Africa was received from the Caledonian Society of Johannesburg. This was accepted and the Marquis of Tullibardine, son and heir of the **Duke of Atholl**, was given command of the Scottish Horse. A second regiment was then raised with the active support in Australia of the Caledonian Society of Melbourne and of the Highland Society of London in the UK. Both served with much distinction in the South African War. Following the war and disbandment, a further regiment of Scottish Horse was raised in 1902 in South Africa which served as a unit of the Transvaal Volunteer Force until disbanded as part of overall reductions in 1907. Meanwhile, back in Scotland, Lord Tullibardine had been asked in 1903 to raise yet another regiment of Scottish Horse from the counties of **Argyll**, **Perth**, **Aberdeen**, **Banff** and **Moray**. This became two regiments strong with a third being added on the outbreak of war in 1914.

The 1st and 2nd Scottish Horse fought in Gallipoli and Egypt. They were then merged to form the 13th (Scottish Horse) Bn, **The Black Watch**, and as such fought on in Macedonia and then on the Western Front. Converted to the role of gunners, in 1939 the regiment produced the 79th and 80th Medium Regiments, Royal Artillery. Both regiments made a great name for themselves, the 79th serving in north-east Europe and the 80th in Sicily and Italy. In 1947 the regiment was once again brought into being as a unit of the Royal Armoured Corps.

POST-WAR TO THE PRESENT Initially restored to the established role of modern cavalry as armoured regi-

ments in the post-war Territorial Army, the Yeomanry suffered the full impact of the various reorganisations of that force. In 1956 the regiments were reduced to three in number. The Ayrshire Yeomanry were left untouched but the Lanarkshire Yeomanry, the Queen's Own Royal Glasgow Yeomanry and the Lothian and Border Horse Yeomanry were merged to form the Queen's Own Lowland Yeomanry. At the same time the Fife and Forfar Yeomanry merged with the Scottish Horse to become the Fife and Forfar Yeomanry/Scottish Horse (FFY/SH). On the formation of Volunteers and Territorials in the new TAVR of 1968, when the Volunteers were given an increased role, all three regiments were tasked as lower grade Territorials. By 1970 all three were reduced again to cadre strength and continued to train largely at their own expense. At this time the FFY/SH were renamed the Highland Yeomanry. In 1972 the Ayrshire Yeomanry were reformed as a squadron in the Queen's Own Yeomanry, part of the highly equipped and trained Volunteers, but in 1975 the cadres of the Queen's Own Lowland Yeomanry and the Highland Yeomanry ceased to exist, their identity being taken on by two Volunteer squadrons of the Royal Corps of Transport.

'Options for Change' has however brought new life to the Scottish yeomanry with a new regiment to be raised in Scotland on the base provided by the surviving Ayrshire Yeomanry squadron.

YETHOLM, Roxburghshire

The twin villages of Town Yetholm and Kirk Yetholm lie on either side of the Bowmont Water very close to the border. In the early 19th century Kirk Yetholm was described as being 'remarkable for the moral peculiarities of its population for whom no employment offers in the vicinity, and who swell the ranks of pauperism, smuggling and equivocity of pursuit'. Yetholm was also home for a long time to the Faa family, the 'royal house' of Scottish gypsies, the last of whom, 'Queen' Esther Faa Blythe, was buried here in 1883. **Sir Walter Scott** based his character Meg Merrilies in *Guy Mannering* on Jean Gordon, a native of Yetholm and wife of Patrick Faa. Having seen her husband transported for fire-raising and three of her four sons hanged for sheep-stealing, Jean herself died of exhaustion and exposure after being stoned by a mob and thrown into the river Eden for shouting support for the **Jacobites** in the main street of Carlisle (c1746).

YORK, Treaty of (1237)

In the prolonged and tortuous exchanges by which the Kings of England and Scotland gradually disentangled their precedence and territories, the Treaty of York represents something of a turning point. The Scottish Kings' claims to the Earldom of Northumbria dated back well over a century and subsumed claims to other lands in England; the English Kings' claims to suzerainty over the Scottish Kings dated back to the 11th century and, since the 1174 **Treaty of Falaise**, had included some claim to suzerainty over the Scottish realm. Attempts to deny the Scottish claim to Northumbria brought King John of England north and resulted in the 1209 Treaty of Norham by which the earldom was promised not to the Scots King, **William**, but to his heir, Alexander.

This promise was never honoured and in 1235, in spite of the now **Alexander II**'s marriage to Joan, sister of Henry III of England, the Scots King was again warned to observe his subordinate status as per the Falaise treaty. The warning came from the Papacy but at Henry III's instigation. Alexander II rejected the warning and with the agreement of both sovereigns the Papal legate, Otto, was asked to arbitrate. By the compromise hammered out at York, Alexander finally surrendered his claims to the Northumbrian earldom in return for actual lands in Cumberland. 'In the simplest terms, Alexander II was bought off.' The Scots 'settled for what they could get, but what they were given scarcely represented the paper value of what they gave up' (A A M Duncan). Demands for, and promises of, the Northumbrian earldom now ceased to be a factor in Anglo-Scottish relations; but the English claim to suzerainty remained and would be exploited, notably by Edward I.

YORK BUILDINGS CO, The

In 1675 **Charles II** granted letters patent to allow a waterworks to be built in the grounds of York House on the south side of the Strand in London. The water, pumped from the Thames, supplied St James's and Piccadilly. In 1691 the waterworks were incorporated by Act of Parliament.

In 1715, following the **Jacobite** Rebellion, a number of forfeited estates were exposed for sale. Legislation in 1719 allowed purchasers to grant annuities on the value of their shares and the York Buildings Company was bought by a consortium to exploit this opportunity. The issue was at once oversubscribed. The capital reached £1,259,575 and £10 shares cost £305 within weeks. Buying land worth £122,749, the company quickly became the biggest landowner in Scotland, with **Sir Archibald Grant of Monymusk** as one of its leading beneficiaries and manipulators. But in spite of 'furious energy, progressive ideas and inspired dishonesty' (Bruce Lenman) it failed to prosper. In 1720, after the collapse of the 'South Sea Bubble', York Buildings stock fell rapidly and was soon unsaleable. In 1728 the company purchased forests in **Abernethy** from Sir James Grant for £7000. A plan to make masts for the Royal Navy failed and in four years the charge of the timber trade had exceeded its returns by nearly £28,000. **Coal** works and a glass factory at **Port Seton** were also unsuccessful. Lead mines at **Strontian**, leased in 1730, were abandoned in 1737.

In 1829 an Act of Parliament dissolved the corporation and provided for the sale of the waterworks and remaining property. Evidence of the company's activities survive in such unlikely additions to the map as a hamlet on the shores of **Loch Awe** called New York.

YOUNG, Douglas (1913–73) Poet

Born at Tayport, Douglas Young was educated at Merchiston Castle School, **Edinburgh** and the **University of St Andrews**, where he was a classical scholar, becoming a lecturer in Greek at **Aberdeen University**. In 1941 he joined the **Scottish National Party** and, although he would probably have been rejected on medical grounds because of his bad eyesight, resisted conscription and was imprisoned in Edinburgh. From 1947–68 he taught at University College, **Dundee**, and at his *alma mater*, then was appointed Professor of Classics at McMaster University, Canada and in 1973 Professor of Greek at the University of North Carolina, USA.

Young wrote a clear classical Scots, as his three collections, *Auntran Blads* (1943), *A Braird o' Thristles* (1947) and *Selected Poems* (1950) testify. He also made some excellent translations into Scots of the Gaelic poets **George Campbell Hay** and **Sorley Maclean**. He wrote two Scots versions of classical plays, *The Burdies* and *The Puddocks* from the Greek of Aristophanes, and two highly readable city profiles, *Edinburgh in the Age of Reason*, 1967, and *St Andrews: Town and Gown*, 1969. For his scholarly textual achievements, the reader is referred to *A Clear Voice: Douglas Young, Poet and Polymath*, (ed C Young and D Morrison).

YOUNG, James (1811–83) Chemist

Born in **Glasgow**, Young studied chemistry at night-school and then at Glasgow's Anderson College, where he was a friend and fellow-student of **David Livingstone**. A student of **Thomas Graham**, Young then became his assistant at University College, London. Realising the potential for extracting paraffin from **oil**-rich shales and **coals**, Young moved to the **Lothians** (1850) where he set up a successful industry, to the continuing disfigurement of the landscape, and earned himself the nickname 'Paraffin Young'. He sold his business in 1866, undertaking research in pure science and endowing a chair at Anderson College (now **Strathclyde University**).

YOUNGER, George, Viscount Younger of Leckie (1851–1929) Brewer and Politician

George Younger was born in **Alloa** and educated at **Edinburgh Academy** and **University**. On the death of his father and at the age of 17 he took control of the family **brewing** concern which under his direction expanded rapidly in boom conditions. In 1897 he became chairman of the limited company as the industrial belt of central Scotland, the north of England and the colonial markets all proved profitable. He was elected Unionist MP for **Ayr** (1906–22) and held prominent positions in the Conservative Party (Chairman in 1917). He was raised to the peerage in 1918.

His brother William (1857–1925) also played an important role in the firm and assumed control (1886) of the Edinburgh brewery of **William McEwan**, his uncle, when the latter entered Parliament. George Younger retired in 1924.

Z

ZETLAND

The Norse *Hjaltland* ('High Land') for Scotland's most northerly islands has been variously rendered in Scots and English as 'Hetland', 'Yetland', 'Zetland' and '**Shetland**'. Although the last is now usual, 'Zetland' survived until 1975 in the title of the Zetland County Council. It still survives in the title of the earldom, created in 1838 for Laurence Dundas (of **Port Dundas, Glasgow** fame) and superseded in 1892 by the marquisate awarded to his grandson. Its inclusion, for want of other words beginning with a 'Z', in alphabetical listings of Scottish subject matter could prolong its currency, as herein.

APPENDIX I

Presbyterian Churches of Scotland Post-1700

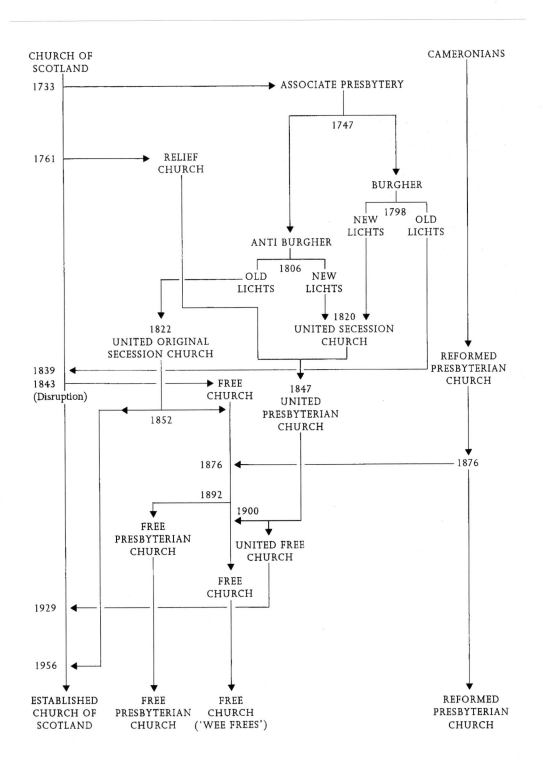

APPENDIX II

The House of Canmore to the House of Stewart

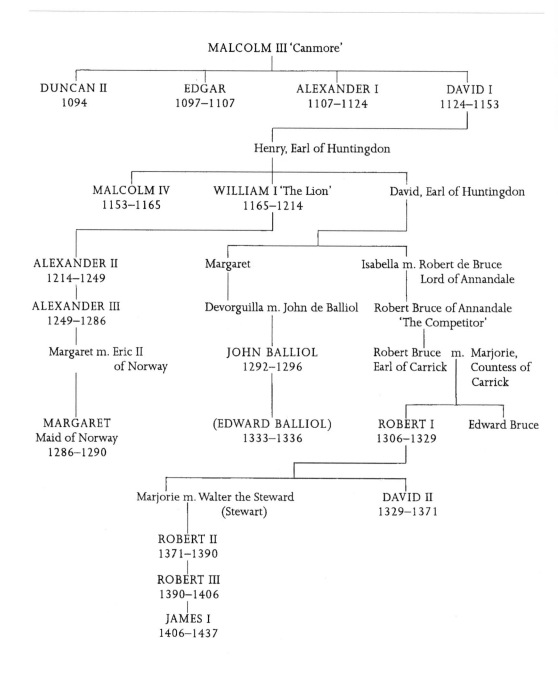

MALCOLM III 'Canmore'

DUNCAN II 1094   EDGAR 1097–1107   ALEXANDER I 1107–1124   DAVID I 1124–1153

Henry, Earl of Huntingdon

MALCOLM IV 1153–1165   WILLIAM I 'The Lion' 1165–1214   David, Earl of Huntingdon

ALEXANDER II 1214–1249   Margaret   Isabella m. Robert de Bruce Lord of Annandale

ALEXANDER III 1249–1286   Devorguilla m. John de Balliol   Robert Bruce of Annandale 'The Competitor'

Margaret m. Eric II of Norway   JOHN BALLIOL 1292–1296   Robert Bruce m. Marjorie, Earl of Carrick Countess of Carrick

MARGARET Maid of Norway 1286–1290   (EDWARD BALLIOL) 1333–1336   ROBERT I 1306–1329   Edward Bruce

Marjorie m. Walter the Steward (Stewart)   DAVID II 1329–1371

ROBERT II 1371–1390

ROBERT III 1390–1406

JAMES I 1406–1437

APPENDIX III

The House of Stewart to the House of Hanover

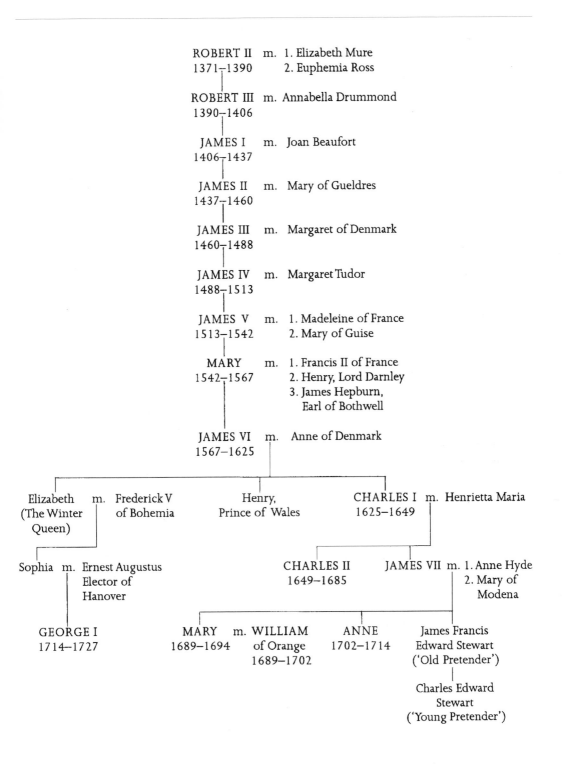

ROBERT II   m. 1. Elizabeth Mure
1371–1390   2. Euphemia Ross

ROBERT III   m. Annabella Drummond
1390–1406

JAMES I   m. Joan Beaufort
1406–1437

JAMES II   m. Mary of Gueldres
1437–1460

JAMES III   m. Margaret of Denmark
1460–1488

JAMES IV   m. Margaret Tudor
1488–1513

JAMES V   m. 1. Madeleine of France
1513–1542   2. Mary of Guise

MARY   m. 1. Francis II of France
1542–1567   2. Henry, Lord Darnley
                 3. James Hepburn,
                    Earl of Bothwell

JAMES VI   m. Anne of Denmark
1567–1625

Elizabeth   m. Frederick V   Henry,   CHARLES I m. Henrietta Maria
(The Winter   of Bohemia   Prince of Wales   1625–1649
 Queen)

Sophia m. Ernest Augustus   CHARLES II   JAMES VII m. 1. Anne Hyde
            Elector of   1649–1685   2. Mary of
            Hanover   Modena

GEORGE I   MARY   m. WILLIAM   ANNE   James Francis
1714–1727   1689–1694   of Orange   1702–1714   Edward Stewart
                                1689–1702   ('Old Pretender')

                                                              Charles Edward
                                                                  Stewart
                                                             ('Young Pretender')

APPENDIX IV

Kings of France, Scotland and England

FRANCE	SCOTLAND	ENGLAND
	Kenneth mac-Alpin 843–58	
	Donald I 858–62	
	Constantine I 862–77	
	Aed 877–78	
	Giric & Eochaid 878–89	
	Donald II 889–900	
	Constantine II 900–43	
	Malcolm I 943–54	
	Indulf 954–62	
	Dubh 962–66	
	Culen 966–71	
	Kenneth II 971–95	
	Constantine III 995–97	
	Kenneth III (+ Giric?) ?997–1005	
	Malcolm II 1005–34	
Henry I 1031–60	Duncan 1034–40	
	Macbeth 1040–57	
	Lulach 1057–58	
Philip I 1060–1108	Malcolm III 1058–93	William I 1066–87
	Donald III 1093–94	William II 1087–1100
	Duncan II 1094	
	Donald III (rest'd) 1094–97	
	Edgar 1097–1107	
Louis VI 1108–37	Alexander I 1107–24	Henry I 1100–35
Louis VII 1137–80	David I 1124–53	Stephen 1135–54
	Malcolm IV 1153–65	Henry II 1154–89
Philip II 1180–1223	William I 1165–1214	Richard I 1189–99
Louis VIII 1223–26		John 1199–1216
	Alexander II 1214–49	Henry III 1216–72
Louis IX 1226–70	Alexander III 1249–86	
Philip III 1270–85		Edward I 1272–1307
Philip IV 1285–1314	Margaret 1286–90	
	Interregnum 1290–92	
	John 1292–96	
	Interregnum 1296–1306	
Louis X 1314–16	Robert I 1306–29	Edward II 1307–27
Philip V 1316–22		
Charles IV 1322–28		

FRANCE	SCOTLAND	ENGLAND
Philip VI 1328–50	David II 1329–71	Edward III 1327–77
Jean II 1350–64		
Charles V 1364–80	Robert II 1371–90	Richard II 1377–99
Charles VI 1380–1422	Robert III 1390–1406	Henry IV 1399–1413
	James I 1406–37	Henry V 1413–22
Charles VII 1422–61	James II 1437–60	Henry VI 1422–61
Louis XI 1461–83	James III 1460–88	Edward IV 1461–83
Charles VIII 1483–98		Edward V 1483
		Richard III 1483–85
Louis XII 1498–1515	James IV 1488–1513	Henry VII 1485–1509
Francis I 1515–47	James V 1513–42	Henry VIII 1509–47
Henry II 1547–59	Mary I 1542–67	Edward VI 1547–53
Francis II 1559–60		Mary I 1553–58
Charles IX 1560–74		Elizabeth I 1558–1603
Henry III 1574–89		
Henry IV 1589–1610	James VI 1567–1625	James I 1603–25
Louis XIII 1610–43	Charles I 1625–49	Charles I 1625–49
Louis XIV 1643–1715	Charles II 1649–85	Interregnum 1649–60
	(exiled 1651–60)	
		Charles II 1660–85
	James VII 1685–89	James II 1685–89
	William & Mary 1689–1702	William & Mary 1689–1702
	Anne 1702–07	Anne 1702–07
	Anne 1707–14	
Louis XV 1715–74	George I 1714–27	
	George II 1727–60	
Louis XVI 1774–93	George III 1760–1820	
Louis XVII 1793–95		
–		
Louis XVIII 1814–24		
Charles X 1824–30	George IV 1820–30	
	William IV 1830–37	
	Victoria 1837–1901	
	Edward VII 1901–10	
	George V 1910–36	
	Edward VIII 1936	
	George VI 1936–52	
	Elizabeth II 1952–	

ILLUSTRATION ACKNOWLEDGEMENTS

The editors are most grateful to various archives, galleries, libraries and museums who have given permission for the reproduction of illustrations. These are acknowledged in the captions as follows:

BRC: The Business Record Centre, Glasgow University
GWWA: The George Washington Wilson Archive at Aberdeen University
HS: Historic Scotland
ML: The Mitchell Library, Glasgow
MS: Museum of Scotland
NGS: The National Gallery of Scotland
NHP: Ness Historical Project
NMS: The National Museums of Scotland
SAU: St Andrews University Library
SBA: The Scottish Brewing Archive
SEA: The Scottish Ethnological Archive
SNPG: The Scottish National Portrait Gallery

Other sources of non-copyright illustrations, kindly photographed by Frank Walton of Oban, are acknowledged in the captions as follows:

MR: *The Castellated and Domestic Architecture of Scotland*, by David MacGibbon and Thomas Ross, Edinburgh, 1887
RWB: *Baronial and Ecclesiastical Antiquities of Scotland*, by Robert William Billings, London and Edinburgh, 1845–52
SP: *Scottish Pictures*, by S C Green, London, nd (c1885)
SW: *The Scots Worthies*, by J A Wylie, London, nd
TS: *Theatrum Scotiae*, by John Slezer, London, 1693

The photographs of the Clyde Auditorium and of SV *Glenlee* are reproduced courtesy of Nell Keay, and that of the Great Hall of Stirling Castle by courtesy of Christina Noble.

INDEX

Carmichael, William 64
Carnasserie Castle **145**
Carnbane Castle 486
Carnegie, Andrew **145–6**
  160 247 279 280
  309 471 567
Carnegie, David of
  Culluthie, Octavian
  380 779
Carnegie, David of
  Stronvar 60
Carnegie Trust 229 327
Carnoustie **146** 495 702
Carnwath **146** 661
Carnyx **146** 754
Carpow 16 855
Carr, Robert of
  Ferniehurst, later
  Duke of Somerset 579
Carrbridge **146**
Carrick, Ayrshire 50 111
  146 593 719
Carrick Castle **146–7**
Carron Company 19 91
  147 181 314 378
  505 568 824 966
Carse, Alexander 790
Carse of Gowrie **147–8**
  151 387 558 720 919
Carsethorn 608
Carsluith Castle 202
Carsphairn **148**
Carstairs **148** 436
Carstares, William 53 **148**
  164 372 433
Carswell, John, Bishop
  145 **148** 425
Carver, Robert **148–9**
  755
Casket Letters **149** 642
  714 945
Cassillis (Cassellis),
  Earldom **149** 214 593
  720
Cassillis House **149** 593
Castillians 715 874
Castle Campbell **149–50**
  240 613
Castle Douglas **150** 429
  774
Castle Fraser **150**
Castle Gloom *see* Castle
  Campbell
Castle Grant **150–1** 206
  229 408 506
Castle Huntly,
  Longforgan, nr
  Dundee 147 **151** 412
Castle Kennedy **151**
Castle Leod 960
Castle Levan 499
Castle Law 16
Castle Menzies 37 **151**
  1014

Castle O'er (Over,
  Overbie) 375
Castle of Clunie 88
Castle of Mey **151**
Castle of Park **151–2** 490
Castle Roy **152** 768
Castle Sinclair 443
Castle Stalker **152** 986
Castle Stuart **152**
Castle Sween 36 **152** 169
  601
Castle Tioram (or Tirrim)
  243 730 733 **986**
Castle Toward 283
Castlebay, Barra 68 612
Castlecary 32 **152**
Castlecary Rail Collision
  (1937) **152–3**
Castlecraig 206
Castledykes Roman Fort
  148
Castlemilk Moorit Sheep
  153 661
Castleton **153**
Caterans **153** 589
Caterthuns, The **153**
Cathcart, Gen Charles
  Murray, 2nd Earl of
  Cathcart **153**
Cathcart, Sir George
  (1794–1854) General
  153
Cathcart, Ihone [John] of
  Carltoun 221
Cathcart, Gen William
  Schaw, 1st Earl of
  Cathcart
  (1755–1843) **153**
Cathcart Castle 153 475
Catrine **153** 221 948
Catterline 289 605
Cattle, Beef 14 20 25 26
  33 124 132 255 379
  429 537 652 667
  672; Dairy 50–1 150
  328 442 571 652
  667 *see also* droving,
  livestock farming etc.
Caulfeild, William **154**
  237 727 848
Caw, Sir James Lewis **154**
Cawdor Castle 133 135
  154 601 838
Ceilidhs 66 **154**
Cellardyke 31
Celtic Art **154–5** 189
  206 551 595
Celtic Church 18 20 33
  140 **155** 164 189
  192 211 232 233
  282 464 530 557
  567–8 591 595–6
  650 784 794 853
  872 884 1017

Celtic Earldoms 30 45
  113 595–6 650 739
  903
Celtic FC 397–8 467 557
  937
Celtic Language 128
  155–6 529 620
Celtic Mythology **156–7**
  209 235 269 377
  387–8 546
Celtic Plainchant 76 **157**
Celtic Twilight **157** 904
Celts and Gaels 128 155
  157
Central Electricity
  Generating Board
  (CEGB) 821–2
Ceres, Fife **157**
Ceretic, King of
  Strathclyde 958
Challenger Expedition 753
  762 865 981
Chalmers, George Paul
  157–8 791
Chalmers, James **158**
Chalmers, Peter
  Macgregor **158** 875
Chalmers, Thomas 31 73
  140 **158** 188 238
  261 416–7 460 476
  478 570 849
Chamberlain, Office of
  626
Chambers, Robert 142
  158–9 326 589 756
  799
Chambers, Sir William
  (1723–96) Architect
  159 317
Chambers, William
  (1800–83) Publisher
  158 **159** 309 317
  322 326 799
Chancellor, Office of 626
Chantrey, Francis Legatt
  216 329 509
Chapel of Garioch **159**
  160 810
Chapelcross 822
Chariots of Fire 647
Charles I 24 31 91 139
  159–61 186 196 226
  244 259 280 296
  323 324 357 369
  371 444 496 502
  522 532 579 643
  729 734 823 934
  950
Charles II 91 112 118
  133–4 148 **161–2**
  185 186 197 225
  226 283 295 324
  338 339 371 382
  485 562 579 580

  624 642 643 664
  705 725 735 739
  803 813 843 870
  876 884 902 904
  919 943 950
Charles Connell & Co,
  Shipbuilders 910 914
  1003
Charleson, Ian 647
Charlotte of Mecklenburg
  Strelitz, Queen of
  George III 309 340
  551 907
Charpentier, Charlotte
  887
Chartism 145 **162** 184
  193 670 975
Chaseabout Raid (1565)
  162 496 522 609
  944
Chastelard, Pierre 858
Châtelherault Country
  Park **520–1** 1023
Chattan, Clan 52 130
  152 **162–3** 169 692
  699
Chavasse, Capt Noel,
  RAMC 652
Checkland, S G 62–4
Chepman, Walter **163**
  304 369
Cheviot Sheep 86 **163**
  173 376 920 1034
Cheyne, Bishop Henry 4
  5
Chiesley (or Chieslie),
  John of Dalry 315
  318 661
Chiesley (or Chieslie),
  Rachel, Lady Grange
  315 373 734 879
Childe, Gordon 292 783
  881
China 111 136 408 411
  507 584–5 647 661
  708 722
China Steam Navigation
  Co 910 917
Chirnside **163** 170
Chisholm, Erik **163** 756
Chisholm, Samuel 977
Chopin, Frederick 586
Christian I of Denmark
  and Norway 785 906
Christison, Sir Robert **163**
  868
Church of Scotland 91–2
  136 148 161 **163–4**
  196 237–8 324 371
  373 416 433 568
  696 722 73 731 732
  776 815 822–3 843
  901 1002 1003 *see*
  also General Assembly

1057

Colquhoun, Patrick, Lord Provost of Glasgow 458 469
Colquhoun, Robert **189** 198 547 792
Columba, Saint 4 18 20 40 155 157 164 **189** 190 244 260 421 471 557 564 566–7 591 594 604 646 650 748 755 784 801 877 908
Colville, David **189–90** 198 224 568 *see also* David Colville & Sons
Colville, Rev Harry (d 1596) 95
Colville, John 616
Colvin, Professor Sidney 938
Comet, The 74 **190** 191 245 530 761 816 852 909
Comiston *see* Edinburgh
Comlongan Castle **190** 191
Commando Memorial 17 933
Commendators 151 **190–1** 214 260 373 490 523 605
Commissary Court 56 627 629
Commissioners for Forfeited Estates 128 203 1039
Communist Party of Great Britain 428–9 674 681
Company of Scotland Trading to Africa and the Indies *see* Darien Venture
Competitors, The 59 111 **191** 192 230 710
Comrie **191** 270
Comrie Castle 151
Comunn Gaidhealach, An 65 **191–2** 426 564 732
Comyn, Alastair of Dunphail 229
Comyn, Alexander, 2nd Earl of Buchan 192 566
Comyn, John (i) (d 1303) Guardian and 'competitor' 191 **192** 563 1010 1011
Comyn, John (ii) (d 1306) **192** 224 264 431 850 1011
Comyn, John 'the Red' of Badenoch (fl 1267) 87 192

Comyn, John, 3rd Earl of Buchan 566
Comyn, Walter, Earl of Menteith (c1190–1258) **192** 557
Comyn, William, Earl of Buchan (fl 1219) 113 192 233
Conan, Saint **192** 222
Conchobar, King of Ulster 235
Congregation, Lords of *see* Lords of the Congregation
Conn of the Hundred Battles, High King of Ireland 242
Connel, Argyll 39 **192** 375 436
Connery, Sean 353
Connolly, Billy 461
Conon Bridge 85 237
Conon Hydro Electric Scheme 555
Constable, Office of 372 626 711
Constable, Archibald, Publisher 1 58 **192** 193 312 331 358 369 887–8
Constable, Thomas 58 369
Constantine, Emperor 855
Constantine, Saint 464
Constantine I **193** 242 594 958
Constantine II **193**
Constantine III **193** 594
Constantius, Emperor 855
Conventiclers 142 162 **193** 197 257 449 503 512 598 607 643 799 801 978
Convention of Estates 165 626 627
Convention of Scottish Local Authorities (COSLA) 658
Cook, Capt James (fl 1651) 814
Cook, Thomas 568
Cope, Gen Sir John 154 226 331 574 824 1009
Corbeil, Treaty of (1326) 46
Corbett, John Rooke 750
Corbett, Thomas Godfrey Polson, 2nd Baron Rowallan 601
Corgarff Castle **194** 242 634 727
Corncrake 81 **194**

Cornhill *Magazine* 927
Corpach 139 **194** 409
Corran ferry 741
Corrichie, Battle of (1562) 62 **195** 496 739
Corriechoille 132
Corries, The 395–6
Corrieshalloch Gorge **195**
Corrievrechan **195** 587 884
Corrieyairack Pass 123 **195** 226 727 734 774 824
Corrimony Cairn 255
Corrour **195** 841
Corstorphine *see* Edinburgh
Cortachy Castle 612
Cospatric, Earl of Dunbar 223 291 543
Cottars **195–6** 206 539 762
Cotton 21 57 69 88 129 153 182 **196** 222 253 286 388 432 451–2 473 595 769–70 793 803 936 991
Coucy, Marie de 23 771 860
Coulthard, David 742
Coupar Angus **196** 727
Court of Barony 626
Court of Session 19 **196** 225 295 337 338 341 543 583 627 628 629 634 635 636 637 1014
Cousin, David 308 315 325 334 359
Coutts, John and Thomas **196**
Covenant, National (1638) 53 142 161 162 **196–7** 256–7 259 310 322 346 350 351–2 449 496 502 531 584 598 627 643 705
Covenant, Solemn League and (1643) 142 161 **197** 449 501 522 529 531 705 822–3
Covenanters 21 25 56 70 80 85 95 114 125 132 136 142 161–2 174 193 **196–7** 224 265 266 296 311 321 322 369 429 441 512 515 517 520 528 531 559 584 643 734 775 797 799 801 806

822 827 847 867 868 902 904 951 978 985 996 1013 1018 1026
Covenants, Nationalist (1930 and 1949) 441 673 766 890 893 949
Covesea 8 499 545 1015
Cowal 146 **197** 283 542 986
Cowdenbeath **197**
Cowie, James 90 **197–8** 289 547 792
Cox, James **198**
Coxton Tower **198**
Crab (or Craib), John 5
Craig, Adam 385
Craig, James 75 **198** 297 311 333 346
Craig, Sir John **198–9** 569
Craig, Sir Thomas **199** 629 998
Craig Castle, Lumsden 668
Craigcrook Castle *see* Edinburgh
Craigellachie 48 **199** 506 976
Craigentinny *see* Edinburgh
Craigie, Sir William **199** 646
Craigievar Castle 36 **199** 420
Craigleith *see* Edinburgh
Craiglockhart *see* Edinburgh
Craigmillar Castle *see* Edinburgh
Craigmillar Conference 313
Craignair 213
Craigneil Castle 188
Craignethan Castle **199–200** 523 618
Craignish **200**
Craignure 747
Craigroyston, Stirling 683
Craigston Castle **200** 603
Craik, William of Arbigland 608
Crail, Fife 37 **200**
Cramond *see* Edinburgh
Crannogs 49 88 148 **200** 237 317 619
Cranston, Catherine 483
Crarae **200** 418
Crathes Castle 61 118 **200–1**
Crathie **201** 687
Crawford, Earldom of 33 85 **201** 363 496 957

hydrographer **224–5**
Dalrymple, Sir David,
Lord Advocate 225
519
Dalrymple, Sir David,
Lord Hailes
(1726–92) Historian
and judge 224 **225**
346 584 772
Dalrymple, Sir David of
Hailes (1692–1751)
225 772
Dalrymple, James, 1st
Viscount Stair
(1619–95) Jurist 74
87 **225** 305 629
Dalrymple, Janet 87 225
Dalrymple, John, 1st Earl
of Stair (1648–1707)
Judge 136 151 162
219 **225** 315 326
629
Dalrymple, John, 2nd Earl
of Stair (1673–1747)
Soldier and diplomat
151 **225–6** 305 334
488
Dalrymple, William, 4th
Earl of Dumfries &
3rd of Stair 265
Dalswinton 19 215
Dalswinton Loch 966
Dalwhinnie **226** 604 727
824
Dalyell, Sir John Graham
(1775–1851)
Antiquarian and
musicologist **226**
Dalyell, Robert, Earl of
Carnwath (fl 1639)
146
Dalyell, Gen Sir Thomas
'Tam' (c1599–1685)
2 21 80 143 **226** 315
801 864 867
Dalzell Iron Works 188
198
Damian, John (fl 1577)
48 267
Damnonii 660
Dancing **226–7** 538 546
584 842 960
Dandie Dinmont **240**
Daphne, SS, Disaster
(1883) **227**
Darien Venture 62 186
227–8 449 507 524
529 574 640 797
891 987
Darling, Sir Frank Fraser
228–9 289 544 798
831 841 963
Darnaway Castle **229**
Darnick Tower 722

Darvel, Ayrshire 393
667
Darwin, Charles 439
440
Dauney, William **229**
Davach **229**
David Colville & Sons,
Steelmakers 198–9
568 569 672 741
912
David I (1084–1153)
King 3 23 36 51 101
111 112 130 185
229 246 263 278
279–80 293 305 307
316 323 355 360
407 448 473 520
565 582 620 625–6
641 721 936 950
957 969
David II (1324–71) King
31 78 112 121 165
185 208 **229–30** 247
252 286 353 355
357 520 597 751
768 851 880 985
David, Duke of Rothesay
see Stewart
David of Huntingdon
(?1144–1219) 58 85
111 **230** 277 566
647
David of Strathbogie, Earl
of Atholl 45 237 751
Davidson, John
(1857–1909) Poet
230
Davidson, Randall
Thomas
(1848–1930)
Archbishop of
Canterbury **230** 968
Davidson, Provost Robert
4
Davie, Alan 793
Davie, Cedric Thorpe **230**
Davies, Sir Peter Maxwell
393 547 704 786
Daviot 163
Davy, Sir Humphrey (fl
1764) 960
Dawson, Matt 832
Dawyck Botanic Garden,
Stobo 94 257
Dean Castle, Kilmarnock
230 598
Dean of Lismore, Book of
the **230–1** 235 387
410 422 423–4 651
Dean Village *see*
Edinburgh
Deanston Cotton Mill 253
Death **231–2**
Dee, River 3 7 11 13 15

16 58 62 99 127 156
176 201 **232** 390
Deer, Book of 155 **232**
422 625
Deer, Red 128 229
232–3 234 376 587
867
Deer, Roe **233**
Deer, Sika **233**
Deer Abbey,
Aberdeenshire 232
233
Deer Forests **234**
Deer Stalking **234–5**
Deerhound 239 **240** 348
Defoe, Daniel 26 49 59
92 111 112 161 257
263 296 331 343
353 450 524 564
570 606 608 609
669 901 952 992
Deirdre of the Sorrows
210 **235** 375 424
Delgatty (Delgatie) Castle
235–6
Dempster, George of
Dunnichen 936
Denmylne Castle 2
Denness, Mike 204
Deskford, Banffshire
236
Deskford Carnyx 754
Destitution Roads 815
818–9
Destiny, Stone of *see*
Scone, Stone of
Deveron, River 2 14 62
113 125 **236** 996
Devil's Beef Tub **236** 439
732 997
Devil's Elbow **236** 490
634
Devil's Staircase, **236** 487
727
Devolution 57 253 360
501 595 895–6
Dewar, Donald 349 896
Dewar, James
(1842–1923)
Industrial chemist
236
Dewar, John (d 1872)
Gaelic folklorist **236**
425
Dewar, John (b 1806)
Wine and spirit
merchant 14 1021
Dewar, John Alexander
(Lord Forteviot)
(1856–1929) Distiller
236
Dewar Manuscripts 137
Diarmad, Fingalian hero
387 490

Dick, Sir Alexander 339
840
Dick, James 599
Dick, Lord Provost Sir
James 299 319 339
Dick, Robert of Thurso
411
Dick, Sir William of Braid
236 299 305 339
862
Dickens, Charles 453 454
584
Dickinson, Professor Croft
885
Dickson, Maggie (fl
1728) **237**
*Dictionary of National
Biography* 927
*Dictionary of the Older Scottish
Tongue* 199
Dingwall **237** 539 572
677 1008
Dinnet 232 **237**
Dirleton Castle **237** 238
334 431
Disarming Acts (1716,
1725, 1747) **237**
Discovery, RRS *see* Dundee
Disruption, The (1843) 2
9 11 47 73 121 140
158 164 **237–8** 239
297 308 344 384
416 496 540 567
683 619 729 1015
Distilleries 36 58 62 86
97 107 116 122 138
201 226 263 315
320 489 562 571
587 590 738 781
804 924 934 989
1018–22
Distillers Company
Limited (DCL) 236
1020–1
Divers, Black-Throated,
Red-Throated, Great
Northern 81 82 83
238–9
Dixon, William 568
Dobson, H J 525
Dobson, William 502
Dochart, Falls of 598
Dr Jekyll and Mr Hyde 106
Dogs **239–40**
Dollan, Sir Patrick Joseph
180 **240–1** 559 718
841 1018
Dollar 149 **241**
Dolly the Sheep **241** 299
Don, George
(1764–1814)
Botanist **241**
Don, River 3 10 194 **242**
391 486

Glengoyne Malt Distillery
597 1020
Glenlee, SV 479 481
Glenlivet **489** 1020
Glenlivet, Battle of (1594)
133 372 **489** 496
Glenluce Abbey 151 158
278 **490**
Glenmorangie 1021
Glenmoriston 506 563
Glenrothes **490**
Glensanda quarry 741
828
Glenshee 236 **490–1** 727
922
Glenshiel, Battle of
(1719) **491** 574 590
606 752 945
Glentrool **491**
Glentrool, Battle of
(1307) **491** 851
Gloag, Mrs Anne 414
Glomach, Falls of 246
491 606
Goatfell 44 438
Goats, Wild **491–2** 511
Gododdin (Votadini) 293
Godred Crovan, King of
Man and the Isles
(1079) 530 1008
Gogar House *see*
Edinburgh
Golborne, James 179
Golden Retriever **240**
Goldsmith, Samuel 91
Golf 99–100 146 290
292 320 463 **492–3**
494–5 740 757 760
824 852 873 874
876 968 994 996
Golf Courses 8 11 49 62
90 99 103 116 142
146 204 211 247
262 276 303 305
315 317 325 329
376 410 463 489
492–3 **493–5** 507
514 621 640 659
666 680 738 841
876 956 994 996
Golspie 82 283 **495**
Gordon, Aberdeenshire
14
Gordon, Adam 194 324
495 498 552 964
Gordon, Alexander, 3rd
Earl of Huntly (d
1524) **495** 552
Gordon, Alexander, 4th
Duke of Gordon
(c1745–1827) 240
495 498 988
Gordon, Alexander of
Auchintoul 2

Gordon, Charles, 1st Earl
of Aboyne 16
Gordon, Charles of
Buthlaw 126
Gordon, Charles of Cluny
(fl 1785) 305
Gordon, Dr Cuthbert 210
Gordon, Elizabeth,
Countess of
Sutherland
(1766–1839) 79 168
173 **495** 596 658
902 959 964
Gordon, George, 4th Earl
of Huntly (1514–62)
195 **496** 498 517
564 739 918 944
Gordon, George, 5th Earl
of Huntly (d 1576)
496 944
Gordon, George, 6th Earl
& 1st Marquis of
Huntly (1562–1636)
324 489 **496** 552–3
613
Gordon, George, 2nd
Marquis & 7th Earl of
Huntly (1592–1649)
489 **496** 498 522
553 997
Gordon, George, 1st Earl
of Aberdeen
Gordon, George 'the
Wicked', 3rd Earl of
Aberdeen 368
Gordon, George, 1st
Duke of Gordon
(1643–1716) 304
356 503
Gordon, George, 5th
Duke of Gordon 7 28
365
Gordon, George of Gight
124
Gordon, George
Hamilton, 4th Earl of
Aberdeen 12 406
496–7 498 518
Gordon, Georgiana,
Duchess of Bedford
28 235 603
Gordon, Harry
(1893–1954) **497**
Gordon, James of
Rothiemay (fl 1661)
4
Gordon, Jane, Duchess of
Gordon (d 1812) 28
226 331 498 603
Gordon, Jane, Countess of
Sutherland 107
Gordon, John
(c1618–86)
Cartographer 498

Gordon, Sir John 195
Gordon, Sir John, Son of
4th Duke of Huntly 9
195 495
Gordon, John, Earl of
Sutherland 107
Gordon, John of
Abergeldie 15
Gordon, Col John of
Cluny 68 76 111 173
933
Gordon, Sir John of
Haddo (fl 1644) 12
496 498
Gordon, Sir John of
Lochinvar 768
Gordon, John Campbell,
7th Earl & 1st
Marquis of Aberdeen
12 **497** 518
Gordon, Sir John Watson
(1788–1864) Painter
350 **497** 761 790
998
Gordon, Patrick
(1635–99) Soldier
497–8
Gordon, Robert 10 498
Gordon, Sir Robert 59
Gordon, Sir Robert, 'Tutor
of Sutherland' 443
Gordon, Sir Robert of
Gordonstoun 222 499
Gordon, Robert of
Straloch
(1580–1661)
Cartographer **498** 540
Gordon, Seton **498** 1026
Gordon, William, Bishop
(d1577) 3
Gordon, William, 2nd
Earl of Aberdeen
517–8
Gordon, Sir William of
Embo 562
Gordon Castle 119 396
498
Gordon Family 25 486
498 552–3 641
Gordon Highlanders 28
498 652 665 676
728 748
Gordon Setter **240**
Gordon-Cumming,
Constance **499**
Gordon-Cumming,
Roualeyn 499
Gordonstoun 16 66 245
499
Gore-Arkwright,
Alexander, Earl of
Gowrie 869
Gorebridge 43 92
Gorgie *see* Edinburgh

Gosford House, Aberlady
15
Gospatrick *see* Cospatrick
Gourdon 561
Gourock 179 245 442
499
Gourock Ropework
Company 83 499 770
816
Govan Shipbuilders Ltd
914 1003
Government and
Administration,
National 360
499–501 895–6
Government, Local 360
654–8 896 1018
Gow, John 292
Gow, Nathaniel 385 **501**
Gow, Niel 119 226 280
385–6 **501**
Gowrie Conspiracy
(1600) 237 257 342
501–2 551 578 803
840 869 884
Graham, Alexander 786
Graham, Cuthbert 10 592
Graham, Euphemia 248
Graham, H G 87 852
Graham, Harry 4
Graham, James, 5th Earl &
1st Marquis of
Montrose (1612–50)
2 4 5 12 25 40 48 61
87 114 133 142 161
171 236 261 277 283
291 329 409 449 496
502 541 560 563 601
675 735 737 744 806
813 901 986 997
Graham, James
(1745–94) Medical
practitioner **502**
Graham, James Gillespie
(1776–1855)
Architect 17 27 51
106 157 165 217
266 324 327 334
347 477 **502–3** 562
586 737 741 976
Graham, Sir John de 388
Graham, John of
Claverhouse, Viscount
Dundee (1648–89) 2
87 96 99 165 172
197 251 256–7 263
276 296 304 354
356 462 **503** 573–4
597 598 685 689
868 958 961 978
1018
Graham, Lilias (fl 1829)
470
Graham, Murray Andrew,